Fachwörterbuch

Fertigungstechnik

von
Prof. Dr. Klaus Lochmann
Dipl.-Inf. Katrin Hädrich

Ernst Klett Sprachen

Barcelona · Belgrad · Budapest
Ljubljana · London · Posen · Prag
Sofia · Stuttgart · Zagreb

PONS Fachwörterbuch
Fertigungstechnik

Von: Prof. Dr. Klaus Lochmann, Dipl.-Ing. Katrin Hädrich

Bearbeitet von: Ian Dawson

Warenzeichen
Wörter, die unseres Wissens eingetragene Warenzeichen darstellen, sind als solche gekennzeichnet. Es ist jedoch zu beachten, dass weder das Vorhandensein noch das Fehlen derartiger Kennzeichnungen die Rechtslage hinsichtlich eingetragener Warenzeichen berührt.

Dieses Werk folgt der amtlichen Regelung der deutschen Rechtschreibung in der Fassung von 2006.

1. Auflage 2007 (1,01)

© Ernst Klett Sprachen GmbH, Stuttgart 2007

Alle Rechte vorbehalten

Internet: www.pons.de
E-Mail: info@pons.de

Projektleitung: Astrid Proctor

Einbandgestaltung: Schmidt & Dupont, Stuttgart
Logoentwurf: Erwin Poell, Heidelberg
Logoüberarbeitung: Sabine Redlin, Ludwigsburg
Satz: Dörr + Schiller GmbH, Stuttgart
Produktion: Isabella Helm, Medienproduktion, Herrenberg
Printed in Germany

ISBN 978-3-12-517844-1

Vorwort

Etwa seit Ende der 60er-, Anfang der 70er-Jahre des 20. Jahrhunderts wurde Deutsch als bis dahin wesentliche Sprache in Wissenschaft und Technik durch das Englische abgelöst.

Vor allem mit der etwa ab 1990 in verstärktem Maß einsetzenden Globalisierung industrieller und wissenschaftlicher Verflechtungen wurde Englisch als Mittel zur Verständigung zwischen Managern, Ingenieuren oder Wirtschaftlern in signifikant zunehmendem Maß von Bedeutung z. B. bei

- Errichtung oder Verlagerungen von Fertigungsbereichen in wirtschaftlich interessanten Regionen der Erde,
- Abstimmungen zwischen Fertigungsabläufen in unterschiedlichen Staaten oder Regionen sowie
- Kooperationen innerhalb der weltweiten Vergabe von Entwicklungsarbeiten.

Mit dem vorliegenden PONS Fachwörterbuch Fertigungstechnik Englisch/Deutsch soll ein praktisch orientiertes Hilfsmittel zur sachlich korrekten Übertragung von Begriffen zu einem Wissensgebiet vorgelegt werden, welches innerhalb von Globalisierungsaktivitäten von besonderer Bedeutung ist. Enthalten sind etwa 35.000 Stichwörter und Wendungen in jeder Sprachrichtung aus üblichen Verfahrenshauptgruppen im Maschinenbau, wobei auf Fachbegriffe aus dem Gebiet der Fügetechnik (Schweißen, Löten, Kleben) weitestgehend verzichtet wurde, da hier umfassende Übertragungshilfen bereits vorliegen und es sich außerdem um ein in inhaltlicher Hinsicht deutlich abgrenzbares Gebiet der Fertigungstechnik (eigene Verfahrenshauptgruppe) handelt.

Vorgesehen ist die Nutzung des vorliegenden Wörterbuches dabei vor allem durch Fachkräfte im betriebspraktischen Einsatz sowie Studierende und Lehrende technischer/fertigungstechnischer Fachrichtungen.

Selbstverständlich werden Anregungen zur weiteren Entwicklung des Wörterbuches, zu Ergänzungen oder Erweiterungen jederzeit gerne entgegengenommen.

Prof. Dr.- Ing. habil. Klaus Lochmann (Hrsg.)
Dipl.- Ing. (FH) Katrin Hädrich

Abkürzungsliste – List of abbreviations

Abk.	Abkürzung	abbreviation
allg.	allgemein	general(ly)
chem.	Chemie	chemistry
el.	Elektrotechnik, Elektronik	electrical engineering, electronics
f	Femininum	feminine
m	Maskulinum	masculine
math.	Mathematik	mathematics
mech.	mechanisch	mechanical
nt	Neutrum	neuter
obs.	veraltet	obsolete
phys.	Physik	physics
pl	Plural	plural
techn.	technisch	technical
UK	britisches Englisch	British English
US	amerikanisches Englisch	American English

A a

a.c. Wechselstrom *m*
a.c. power Netzanschluss *m*
a.c. voltage Wechselspannung *f*
A/D converter A/D Wandler *m*
aback rückwärts
abandon a project ein Projekt fallen lassen
abate nachlassen
Abbé principle Abbéscher Grundsatz *m*
abbreviated designation Kurzbezeichnung *f*
abbreviation Abkürzung *f*, Kurzzeichen *nt*
ABC analysis ABC-Analyse *f*
ABC classification ABC-Klassifizierung *f*
ABC distribution ABC-Verteilung *f*
ability Vermögen *nt*, Fähigkeit *f*
ability to dissipate Ableitfähigkeit *f*
ability to estimate Schätzfähigkeit *f*
ability to hold the cutting power Schnitthaltigkeit *f*
ability to maintain cutting power Schneidhaltigkeit *f*
ability to retrain cutting edge Schneidhaltigkeit *f*
ability to separate Separierfähigkeit *f*
ability to withstand exposure Beanspruchbarkeit *f*
ablated material abgetragenes Material *nt*
ablation Ablation *f*
able fähig
ABM (asynchronous balanced mode) gleichberechtigter Spontanbetrieb *m*
abnormal steel Sonderberuhigter Stahl *m*
abolish aufheben
abolishment Aufhebung *f*
abort abbrechen
abortion Abbruch *m*
above oben, über, oberhalb, darüber- (liegend)
above ground level über dem Erdboden

above-ground high pressure gasholder oberirdischer Hochdruckgasbehälter *m*
above-ground storage oberirdische Lagerung *f*
abrade erodieren, angreifen, abscheuern, reiben, schleifen, abschleifen, verschleißen
abraded material Abrieb *m*, abgeriebenes Material *nt*
abraded particle Verschleißteilchen *nt*, Abschliff *m*
abrading Abtragen *nt*
abrading instalment Abtragrate *f*
abrading technique Abtrageverfahren *nt*
abrasion Abrieb *m*, Verschleiß *m*, Abtragung *f*, Reibung *f*, Abnutzung *f*
abrasion characteristic Verschleißcharakteristik *f*
abrasion field Verschleißgebiet *nt*
abrasion resistance Abriebfestigkeit *f*, Scheuerfestigkeit *f*, Verschleißwiderstand *m*
abrasion stress Schleifbeanspruchung *f*
abrasion test Abnutzungsversuch *m*, Scheuerprüfung *f*
abrasion wear Abrieb *m*
abrasion-proof abriebfest, verschleißfest
abrasive reibend, Schleifmaterial *nt*
abrasive action Verschleißwirkung *f*
abrasive belt Schleifband *nt*
abrasive belt grinding Bandschleifen *nt*
abrasive body Schleifkörper *m*
abrasive body dimension Schleifkörperabmessung *f*
abrasive body operation mixture Schleifkörperbetriebsgemisch *nt*
abrasive body overrunning Schleifkörperüberlauf *m*
abrasive body shape Schleifkörperform *f*
abrasive body wear Schleifkörperverschleiß *m*

abrasive coating beschichtetes Blech *nt*, Abriebbeschichtung *f*
abrasive cut-off machine Trennschleifmaschine *f*
abrasive cutting Durchschleifen *nt*
abrasive cutting machine Trennschleifmaschine *f*
abrasive cutting point Schneidspitze *f*
abrasive dressing wheel Abrichtscheibe *f*
abrasive dust Schleifstaub *m*
abrasive effect Schleifwirkung *f*
abrasive grain Schleifkorn *nt*
abrasive grains ausgebrochene Schleifkörner *ntpl*, Schmirgelkörner *ntpl*
abrasive grit Abrieb *m*, Schleifkorn *nt*, Schleifstaub *m*
abrasive lapping wheel Läppschleifscheibe *f*
abrasive mark Bearbeitungsspur *f*
abrasive member Schleifkörper *m*
abrasive powder Schleifpulver *nt*
abrasive power Angriffsschärfe *f*
abrasive stick Schleifkörper *m*
abrasive-stick dresser Abrichtstift *m*
abrasive tool Schleifwerkzeug *nt*
abrasive wheel (grobkörniger) Schleifkörper *m*, Trennscheibe *f*
abrasive wheel cutting-off machine Trennschleifmaschine *f*
abrasives Schleifmittel *nt*
abscissa Abszisse *f*, X-Achse *f*
absence of lag Verzögerungsfreiheit *f*
absent fehlend
absolute absolut
absolute acceleration Absolutbeschleunigung *f*
absolute dimension Absolutmaß *nt*, Bezugsmaß *nt*
absolute dimension programming Absolutmaßprogrammierung *f*
absolute encoder Absolutwertgeber *m*
absolute measurement Absolutmesssystem *nt*, Absolutmessung *f*
absolute measuring system Absolutes Messsystem *nt*
absolute positioning Absolutpositionierung *f*
absolute value Absolutwert *m*
absolute value transmitter Absolutwertgeber *m*
absolute velocity Absolutgeschwindigkeit *f*
absorb absorbieren, dämpfen, neutralisieren, saugen, aufsaugen, auffangen
absorbable absorbierbar
absorbed impact energy verbrauchte Schlagarbeit *f*
absorbent Absorptionsmittel *nt*
absorbent filter Absorptionsfilter *m*
absorber Absorber *m*, Absorptionsmittel *nt*, Dämpfer *m*
absorber index Absorptionsindex *m*
absorber material Absorbermaterial *nt*
absorber pattern Absorbermuster *nt*, Absorbermodell *nt*
absorbing energy Energie *f* aufnehmend
absorption behaviour Absorptionsverhalten *nt*
absorption Absorption *f*, Aufnahme *f*, Einleitung *f*, Neutralisierung *f*
absorption of quanta Quantenabsorption *f*
absorption of stray current Streustromabsaugung *f*
absorption through the wall Wandabsorption *f*
abstract (from) abstrahieren (von)
abut stoßen, anstoßen
abut against each other aneinanderstoßen
abut against one another gegeneinanderstoßen
abut one against the other aneinanderstoßen
abutment Widerlager *nt*
abutment of raised edge Bördelstoßkante *f*
abutting end Stoßfläche *f*
AC Wechselstrom *m*
AC generator Wechselstromgenerator *m*
AC machine Wechselstrommaschine *f*
AC mains Wechselstromnetz *nt*
AC mains power supply Wechselstromversorgung *f*
AC network Wechselstromnetz *nt*
AC output Wechselspannungsausgang *m*

AC power port Wechselspannungsversorgungsanschluss *m*
AC system Wechselstromnetz *nt*
AC voltage Wechselspannung *f*
accelerant corrosion test Schnell-Korrosionsuntersuchung *f*
accelerate hochlaufen, beschleunigen
accelerated ageing künstliche Alterung *f*
accelerated test procedure Schnellprüfverfahren *nt*
accelerated weathering Schnellbewitterung *f*
acceleration 1. Hochlauf *m*, Hochfahren *nt*, Beschleunigung *f* 2. *(Zeit)* Zeitraffung *f*
acceleration conveyor Beschleunigungsförderer *m*
acceleration due to free fall Fallbeschleunigung *f*
acceleration due to gravity Erdbeschleunigung *f*
acceleration factor Zeitraffungsfaktor *m*
acceleration load Beschleunigungsbeanspruchung *f*
acceleration period Beschleunigungsperiode *f*
acceleration torque Hochlaufmoment *m*
accelerator control lever Stellteil *nt* für Beschleunigung
accept abnehmen, annehmen, übernehmen
accept an order einen Auftrag *m* annehmen
acceptable annehmbar
acceptance Annahme *f*, Abnahme *f*, Übernahme *f*
acceptance backlash Abnahmeflankenspiel *nt*
acceptance certificate Abnahmeprotokoll *nt*
acceptance confirmation Akzeptanzquittung *f*
acceptance drawing Abnahmezeichnung *f*
acceptance inspection Annahmeprüfung *f*
acceptance of goods Warenannahme *f*, Wareneingang *m*
acceptance of orders Auftragsannahme *f*
acceptance position Übernahmeposition *f*
acceptance probability Annahmewahrscheinlichkeit *f*
acceptance report Abnahmeprotokoll *nt*
acceptance sampling Qualitätskontrolle *f*
acceptance sampling inspection Annahmestichprobenprüfung *f*
acceptance testing Abnahmeprüfung *f*
accepted good Gutteil *nt*
accepted part Gutteil *nt*
acceptor aufnehmendes Medium *nt*
access anfahren, ansteuern, betreten, aufsteigen (auf), ansprechen, zugreifen (auf); Betreten *nt*, Aufsteigen *nt*, Zustieg *m*, Zutritt *m*, Zugang *m*, Zugangsmöglichkeit *f*, Zugriff *m*
access area Vorzone *f*, Lagervorfeld *nt*, Regalvorfeld *nt*, Vorfeld *nt*
access authority Zugriffsrecht *nt*
access authorization Zugangsberechtigung *f*, Zugriffsberechtigung *f*
access cover Abdeckung *f*
access direction Zugriffsrichtung *f*
access door Zugangstür *f*
access entitlement Zugriffsrecht *nt*
access frequency Zugriffshäufigkeit *f*
access from above übergreifen; Übergreifen *nt*
access from behind Umgreifen *nt*; umgreifen
access from beneath untergreifen; Untergreifen *nt*
access height Zugriffshöhe *f*
access level Zugangsebene *f*
access opening Zugriffsöffnung *f*
access path Zugriffspfad *m*
access platform Zugangsplattform *f*
access point Entnahmezone *f*
access prohibition Zutrittsverbot *nt*
access supervision Zugangskontrolle *f*
access time Zugriffszeit *f*
access to danger zone Zugang *m* zum Gefahrenbereich
access ways Zugänge *mpl*

accessibility Zugänglichkeit *f*
accessible begehbar, zugänglich
accessories Ausstattung *f*, Ausrüstung *f*, Zurüstung *f*, Zubehörteile *ntpl*, Zubehör *nt*
accessories interlocked with fasteners mitverspannte Zubehörteile *f*
accessory Zusatzausrüstung *f*, Zusatzgerät *nt*, Zusatzeinrichtung *f*, Zubehör *nt*
accessory drive Hilfsantrieb *m*
accessory part Zubehörteil *nt*
accessory product Zubehör *nt*
accident Störfall *m*, Unfall *m*, Zufall *m*
accident hazard Unfallgefährdung *f*
accident management Störfallmagnet *nt*
accident prevention Unfallverhütung *f*
accident prevention regulations Unfallverhütungsvorschriften *fpl*
accident protection Unfallschutz *m*
accident research Unfallforschung *f*
accidental versehentlich, zufällig
accommodate unterbringen, aufnehmen, anpassen
accommodating hole Aufnahmebohrung *f*
accommodation Unterbringung *f*
accompany begleiten
accompanying begleitend
accompanying document Begleitpapier *nt*, Warenbegleitschein *m*
accompanying the goods warenbegleitend
accomplish bewerkstelligen, durchführen, ausführen, machen
accomplishment Leistung *f*
accord übereinstimmen (mit)
accordance Übereinstimmung *f*
according entsprechend
account plan Kontenplan *m*
accountancy Verwaltung *f*
accounting of departmental participation in covering costs Deckungsbeitragskostenrechnung *f*
accounts payable interface Kreditorenschnittstelle *f*
accretion Zunahme *f*
accrue zunehmen
accumulate akkumulieren, zunehmen, sammeln, ansammeln, stauen, summieren
accumulated tooth spacing error Summenteilfehler *m*
accumulating chain conveyor Staukettenförderer *m*
accumulating roller conveyor Staurollenförderer *m*
accumulation Ansammlung *f*, Häufung *f*, Akkumulation *f*
accumulation of chips (or chip fragments) Spanhäufung *f*
accumulation of gases Gasbildung *f*
accumulation point Sammelstelle *f*
accumulative modulus Speichermodul *nt*
accuracy Genauigkeit *f*, Richtigkeit *f*
accuracy group Genauigkeitsgruppe *f*
accuracy of dimension Maßgenauigkeit *f*
accuracy of estimating Schätzungenauigkeit *f*
accuracy of flatness Plangenauigkeit *f*
accuracy of load Steigungsgenauigkeit *f*
accuracy of measurement Messgenauigkeit *f*
accuracy of position Lagerichtigkeit *f*
accuracy of positioning Zentriergenauigkeit *f*, Einstellgenauigkeit *f*
accuracy of reading Ablesegenauigkeit *f*
accuracy of reproduction Nachformgenauigkeit *f*
accuracy of spacing Teilungsgenauigkeit *f*
accuracy of the mean Richtigkeit *f*
accuracy of tripping Anschlaggenauigkeit *f*
accuracy of work Arbeitsgenauigkeit *f*
accuracy to shape Formtreue *f*, Formgenauigkeit *f*
accuracy to size Maßgenauigkeit *f*, Maßhaltigkeit *f*
accurate genau, präzise
accurate to dimension maßgerecht
accurate to shape formtreu
accurate to size maßgerecht
acetone-resisting acetonbeständig
acetylene Azetylen *nt*
Acetylene Code Acetylenverordnung *f*

acetylene cylinder Azetylenflasche *f*
acetylene generator unit Acetylenentwickleranlage *f*
acetylene inlet pressure Acetylenzustromstück *nt*
acetylene manifold Acetylenverteilungsleitung *f*
acetylene pressure regulator Acetylendruckminderer *m*
acetylene torch Acetylenfackel *f*
acetylene welding Azetylenschweißen *nt*
achieve erreichen, bewirken
achievement Leistung *f*
achievement of objectives Zielerreichung *f*
acid Säure *f*
acid Bessemer steel Bessemerstahl *m*
acid covered electrode sauerumhüllte Elektrode *f*
acid insoluble säureunlöslich
acid traces Säurespuren *fpl*
acknowledge bestätigen, quittieren, rückmelden
acknowledgement Quittung *f*, Rückmeldung *f*, Bestätigung *f*, Quittierung *f*, Quittieren *nt*
acknowledgement message Rückmeldung *f*
acknowledgement obligation Quittierpflicht *f*
acknowledgment time Quittierzeitpunkt *m*
Acme thread Trapezgewinde *nt*
Acme trapezoidal thread Acme-Trapezgewinde *nt*
AC-operated wechselstrombetätigt
acorn nut Hutmutter *f*
acoustic signal akustisches Signal *nt*
acoustical akustisch
acquire erwerben, beschaffen
acquisition Erfassung *f*, Beschaffung *f*
acquisition cost(s) Beschaffungskosten *pl*
acquisition market Beschaffungsmarkt *m*
acquisition order Beschaffungsauftrag *m*
acquisition program Beschaffungsprogramm *nt*

across quer, durch, über
acrylate compound Acrylverbindung *f*
acrylethylene oxide plastics Acrylethylenoxidplast *nt*
acrylic acid ethyl ester Acrylsäureethylenester
acrylonitrile content Acrylnitritgehalt *m*
act (as/upon) wirken (als/auf), einwirken
act against gegenwirken
acting wirksam
acting groove Wirkfuge *f*
action Eingriff *m*, Handlung *f*, Tätigkeit *f*, Wirkung *f*, Einwirkung *f*, Maßnahme *f*, Vorgang *m*, Arbeitsgang *m*
action block Aktionsblock *m*
action instruction Handlungsanweisung *f*
action length Tätigkeitsdauer *f*
action of forces Zwangskräfte *fpl*
action of heat Wärmeeinwirkung *f*
action of industrial atmosphere Industrielufteinwirkung *f*
action of water Wassereinwirkung *f*
action period Belegzeit *f*
action place Wirkstelle *f*
action plan Maßnahmenplanung *f*
action point Eingriffstelle *f*
action time Tätigkeitszeit *f*
action type Tätigkeitsart *f*
action-related behaviour wirkungsmäßiges Verhalten *nt*
action-related connection Wirkungszusammenhang *m*
action-related consideration wirkungsmäßige Betrachtung *f*
action-related dependence of signals wirkungsmäßige Abhängigkeit *f* von Signalen
activate aktivieren, auslösen, betätigen, anstoßen
activated carbon method Aktivkohleverfahren *nt*
activating a key durch Tastendruck *m*
activating addition Aktivierungszusatz *m*
activation Aktivierung *f*
activation overvoltage Aktivierungsüberspannung *f*

**activator residues *pl* Aktivatorrückstände *mpl*
active aktiv, wirksam
active corrosion aktive Korrosion
active cutting edge aktive Schneide *f*, Hauptschneide *f*
active cutting motion Wirkbewegung *f*
active cutting profile aktives Schneidenprofil *nt*
active element aktives Element *nt*
active element aktives Glied *nt*, Steller *m*
active flank aktive Flanke *f*
active force generates the cutting power Aktivkraft *f* erzeugt die Spanungsleistung
active grain count aktive Kornzahl *f*
active grinding wheel surface aktive Schleifscheibenoberfläche *f*
active major cutting edge aktive Hauptschneide *f*
active material aktive Masse *f*, aktives Material *nt*
active medium Wirkmedium *nt*
active minor cutting edge aktive Nebenschneide *f*
active portion of a broach Schneidenteil *m* des Räumwerkzeuges
active pulse Wirkimpuls *m*
active resistance ohmscher Widerstand *m*
active surface Nutzfläche *f*
active wedge measured plane Wirkkeilmessebene *f*
active-gas-metal-arc welding Metall-Aktivgas-Schweißen *nt*
activities endangering the line leitungsgefährdende Einwirkung *f*
activities plan Aktivitätenplan *m*
activity measuring instrument Aktivitätsmessgerät *nt*
activity plan Aktivitätenplan *m*
activity-driven aktivitätsgetrieben
activity-oriented aktivitätsorientiert
actual tatsächlich, wirklich, Ist *nt*
actual angular position Ist-Drehstellung *f*
actual angular size Winkel-Istmaß *nt*
actual bookkeeping Ist-Verbuchung *f*

actual breaking load Ist-Bruchkraft *f*
actual capacity wirkliche Tragfläche *f*
actual centre distance Achsabstands-Istmaß *nt*
actual centre variation Ist-Mittenabweichung *f*
actual characteristic Ist-Kennlinie *f*
actual cone angle Ist-Kegelwert *m*
actual cone generator Ist-Kegelmantellinie *f*
actual cone section Ist-Kegelquerschnitt *m*
actual crowning Ist-Breitenballigkeit *f*
actual data Ist-Daten *pl*
actual date of exit Ist-Abgang *m*
actual deviation Ist-Abmaß *nt*
actual dimension Istmaß *nt*, Istgröße *f*
actual direction of cut tatsächliche Schnittrichtung *f*
actual figure Ist-Wert *m*, Ist-Zahl *f*
actual figures Ist-Daten *pl*
actual generator Ist-Erzeugende *f*
actual lead Ist-Steigungshöhe *f*
actual line Ist-Linie *f*
actual output Ist-Abgang *m*
actual position Weg-Istwert *m*, Istwert *m*, aktuelle Position *f*, Ist-Position *f*
actual pressure angle Ist-Eingriffswinkel *m*
actual profile Ist-Profil *nt*
actual receipt Ist-Zugang *m*
actual resistance Wirkwiderstand *m*
actual size Ist-Größe *f*, Ist-Maß *nt*
actual status Ist-Zustand *m*
actual temperature (indicating) scale Ist-Wertanzeigeskala *f* eines Thermometers
actual time Ist-Zeit *f*
actual tooth surface Ist-Flankenform *f*
actual tooth trace Ist-Flankenlinie *f*
actual value Ist-Wert *m*, tatsächlicher Wert *m*
actual value input signal Ist-Wert-Eingangssignal
actual value transmitter Ist-Wert-Geber *m*
actual variation Ist-Abweichung *f*
actualization Aktualisierung *f*
actuate starten, betätigen
actuated by adhesion kraftschlüssig

actuating Betätigung *f*
actuating drive Stellantrieb *m*
actuating element Betätigungsorgan *nt*
actuating force Betätigungskraft *f*
actuating lever Betätigungshebel *m*
actuating tag Schaltfahne *f*
actuating type Betätigungsart *f*
actuation Betätigung *f*, Schaltung *f*
actuator Bedienelement *nt*, Stellglied *nt*, Betätigungseinrichtung *f*, Aktor *m*, Antrieb *m*
actuator component Stellteil *nt*
actuator control Thyristorstellung *f*
actuator level Aktorebene *f*
actuator transmission Stellgetriebe *nt*
actuators Aktorik *f*
acute spitz
acute angle spitzer Winkel *m*
acute-angle bulging Knickbauchen *nt*
adapt (to) einrichten, umstellen (auf), anpassen
adaptability Anpassungsfähigkeit *f*
adaptation Anpassung *f*
adapted for geeignet für
adapter Zwischenstück *nt*, Führungsbüchse *f*, Übergangshülse *f*, Hülse *f*, Einsatz *m*
adapter end of a union Einschraubzapfen *m* einer Verschraubung
adapter fitting Anschlussstück
adapting program logic logische Programmanpassung *f*
adaptation Angleichung *f*, Umstellung *f*
adaptation time Umstellzeit *f*
adaptive anpassend
adaptive control Adaptive Steuerung (AC) *f*
adaptive optics adaptive Optiken *fpl*
adaptor (adapter) Verbindungsteil *nt*, Passstück *nt*, Einsatz *m*
adaptor end *(Verschraubung)* Zapfen *m*
adaptor flange Aufnahmeflansch *m*
add addieren, hinzufügen, ergänzen, zugeben, aufschlagen, einsetzen
add carry Übertrag *m*
add instruction Additionsbefehl *m*
add on anbauen, Zusatzgerät *nt*
added filler material Zusatzwerkstoff *m*

added safety erweiterte Sicherheit *f*
addendum Zahnkopf *m*, Zahnkopfhöhe *f*, Kopfhöhe *f*
addendum alteration Kopfhöhenänderung *f*
addendum angle Kopfwinkel *m*
addendum flank Zahnflanke *f*, Kopfflanke *f*
addendum modification coefficient Profilverschiebungsfaktor *m*
addendum modification factor Profilverschiebungsfaktor *m*
addendum modification guidelines *pl* Profilverschiebungsrichtlinien *fpl*
addendum-modified internal gear pair profilverschobenes Innenradpaar *nt*
adder Addierer *m*
adding stopwatch Additionsstoppuhr *f*
addition Zusatz *m*, Ausbau *m*, Aufschlag *m*, Zuschlag *m*, Ergänzung *f*, Erweiterung *f*
addition polymerization Polyaddition *f*
addition time Zusatzzeit *f*
addition to materials Materialzugang *m*
addition to stocks Lagerzugang *m*
addition unit Addierer *m*
additional ergänzend, zusätzlich
additional charge Zuschlag *m*
additional claim Nachforderung *f*
additional delivery Nachlieferung *f*
additional draw Weiterschlag *m*
additional equipment Zusatzeinrichtung *f*
additional factor Zuschlagsfaktor *m*
additional function Zusatzfunktion *f*
additional lift Zusatzhub *m*
additional loading Zusatzbelastung *f*, Zusatzlast *f*
additional outlay Mehraufwand *m*
additional stress Zusatzbeanspruchung *f*
additional supply Nachlieferung *f*
additional symbol Zusatzsymbol *nt*
additional test Zusatzprüfung *f*
additional tolerance Zusatztoleranz *f*
additional treatment Nachbehandlung *f*

additional ventilation Zusatzbelüftung *f*
additions Zugaben *fpl*
additive Zusatzmittel *nt*, Zusatz *m*
add-on block Aufbaufeld *nt*
add-on part Anbauteil *nt*
address Adresse *f*, adressieren, ansprechen
address array Adressfeld *nt*
address field Adressfeld *nt*
address memory Schreib-Lese-Speicher *m*, RAM
addressable adressierbar
addressing Adressierung *f*, Ansprechen *nt*
addressing input Adresseneingang *m*
adequate angepasst, angemessen
adequate protection hinreichender Schutz *m*
adhere kleben, verkleben, aufkleben, befestigen, binden, haften (an), zusammenhängen
adherence Haftung *f*
adherent zusammenhängend
adherent surface layer Reaktionsschicht *f*
adhesion Klebfestigkeit *f*, Haftung *f*, Verklebung *f*, Kraftschluss *m*
adhesion coefficient Kraftschlussbeiwert *m*
adhesion fracture Adhäsionsbruch *m*
adhesion gripper Adhäsionsgreifer *m*
adhesion strength Trennkraft *f*
adhesion wear Adhäsionsverschleiß *m*
adhesive adhäsiv, klebend; Klebstoff *m*
adhesive agent Haftmittel *nt*, Kleber *m*
adhesive bonding Aufkleben *nt*
adhesive compound Klebkitt *m*
adhesive constituent Klebstoffbestandteil *m*
adhesive dissolver Kleblöser *m*
adhesive film Klebstofffilm *nt*, Haftfolie *f*, Klebefolie *f*
adhesive for metal Kleber *m* für Metall, Metallklebstoff *m*
adhesive for paper Papierkleber *m*
adhesive for vulcanised rubber Kleber *m* für Gummi
adhesive force Haftkraft *f*, Haftung *f*
adhesive formulation Klebstoff-Ansatz *m*
adhesive label Haftetikett *nt*
adhesive layer Klebschicht *f*, Klebstoffschicht *f*
adhesive liquid Klebflüssigkeit *f*
adhesive nameplate Klebschild *nt*
adhesive paper Haftpapier *nt*
adhesive processing Klebstoffverarbeitung *f*
adhesive property Klebeigenschaft *f*
adhesive putty Klebkitt *m*
adhesive putty mixture Klebkittmischung *f*
adhesive retaining layer haftmittelhaltige Schicht *f*
adhesive shear strength Haft-Scherfestigkeit *f*
adhesive suspension Klebsuspension *f*
adhesive tape Klebeband *nt*
adhesive tensile strength Haftzugfestigkeit *f*
adhesive wax Klebwachs *nt*
adhesive with rapid solvent action stark lösender Klebstoff *m*
adhesives *pl* Klebstoffe *mpl*
adamantine diamanthart
adjacent nebeneinander liegend, angrenzend, übereinander liegend, benachbart
adjacent aisle Nachbargasse *f*
adjacent compartment Nachbarfach *nt*
adjacent to the aisle gangseitig
adjacent parallel flanks benachbarte gleichgerichtete Flanken *fpl*
adjoining benachbart
adjoining face angrenzende Fläche *f*
adjoining room Nachbarraum *m*
adjoining sectioned areas aneinandergrenzende Schnittflächen *fpl*
adjust anstellen, einstellen (auf), verstellen, nachstellen, stellen, richten (auf), einrichten, ausrichten, justieren, berichtigen, regeln, anpassen, abgleichen
adjust longitudinally längsverstellen
adjust to ductile consistency ziehbar einstellen
adjust to spraying consistency spritzbar einstellen
adjustability Einstellbarkeit *f*, Regulier-

barkeit f, Nachstellbarkeit f
adjustable justierbar, einstellbar, regelbar, verstellbar, nachstellbar
adjustable beam pallet racking (APR) Palettenregal nt mit verstellbaren Balken
adjustable block Gleitschieber m, Klemmplatte f, Klemmstück nt
adjustable chain gear Kettenverstellgetriebe nt
adjustable crossbeam Verstelltraverse f
adjustable dog verstellbarer Anschlag m
adjustable dogs pl einstellbare Knaggen fpl
adjustable feed trip dog einstellbarer Anschlag m zur Vorschubausrückung f
adjustable gage einstellbare Lehre f
adjustable head horizontal milling machine Planfräsmaschine f mit verstellbarem Spindelkopf
adjustable hydraulic flow control valve for infinitely variable feed rate einstellbares Drosselventil nt für stufenlos veränderliche Vorschubgrößen
adjustable index sector verstellbares Zeigerpaar nt für Teilscheibe
adjustable overarm braces verstellbare Gegenhalterscheren f
adjustable racking Regal nt mit verstellbaren Fachböden
adjustable range Verstellbereich m
adjustable speed motor Motor m mit regelbarer Drehzahl
adjustable spindle machine Maschine f mit verstellbarer Spindel
adjustable square verschiebbarer Anschlagwinkel m
adjustable to an angular position schrägverstellbar
adjustable-rail planer-type milling machine Langfräsmaschine f mit verstellbarem Querbalken
adjusting Einstellen nt
adjusting butterfly valve Stellklappe f
adjusting dog Stellklaue f
adjusting gate valve Stellschieber m
adjusting gib Nachstellleiste f
adjusting key Stellkeil m

adjusting lever Verstellhebel m
adjusting member Stellteil nt
adjusting part Stellteil nt
adjusting ring Stellring m
adjusting screw Stellspindel f, Einstellschraube f
adjusting time Einstellzeit f
adjustment Einstellen nt, Einstellung f, Zustellung f, Justierung f, Berichtigung f, Nachstellen nt, Nachstellung f, Verstellen nt, Verstellung f, Regulierung f, Anpassung f
adjustment bush Nachstellhülse f
adjustment characteristic Stellverhalten nt
adjustment for position of stroke Hublagenverstellung f
adjustment for wear Verschleißausgleich m
adjustment gib Stellleiste f
adjustment of the operator's seat Sitzverstellung f
adjustment of the spindle head Spindelkopfsenkrechtverstellung f
adjustment travel Stellweg m
adjustment washer Passscheibe f
admeasuring apparatus Ausmessgerät nt
administer verwalten
administration Verwaltung f
administration area Verwaltungsfläche f
administration building Verwaltungsgebäude nt
administration costs Verwaltungskosten pl
administration level Administrationsebene f
administration of data flow Datenflussverwaltung f
administration of storage locations Lagerplatzverwaltung f
administration system Verwaltungssystem nt
administrative regulation Verwaltungsvorschrift f
administrator (ADMIN) Systemadministrator m
admissible zulässig
admission Zugang m, Eintritt m

admission (impact) Beaufschlagung *f*
admission supervision Zugangskontrolle *f*
admit durchlassen, zulassen, beaufschlagen
address part Adressenteil *m*
address range Adressbereich *m*
advance zustellen, verschieben, vorschieben, heranführen, vorrücken (lassen), vorbringen, Vorschieben *nt*, Voreilung *f*, voreilend, Fortschritt *m*
advance cam Anlaufkurve *f*
advance chamber bushing Vorkammerbuchse *f*
advance speed Vorschubgeschwindigkeit *f*
advancement Vorrücken *nt*
advantage Vorteil *m*
advantageous vorteilhaft
advertent aufmerksam
advise beraten
Advisory Committee Tolerances AA-Toleranzen *fpl*
aerate belüften, lüften
aeration Durchlüftung *f*
aerial Antenne *f*
aerial field Antennenfeld *nt*
aerobic corrosion aerobe Korrosion *f*
aerostatic guidance aerostatische Führung *f*
affect einwirken auf, wirken auf, beeinflussen
affect adversely beeinträchtigen
affiliation Zugehörigkeit *f*
affix aufkleben
aft adjustment Rückwärtsverstellung *f*
after costs Folgekosten *pl*
after injection Nachspritzen *nt*
afterage nachaltern
afteraging Nachalterung *f*
afterglow Nachglimmen *nt*
after-heating Nachbeheizung *f*
after-lubrication injection metering device Nachschmiereinleitungsverteiler *m*
after-polymerisation Nachpolymerisation *f*
after-running *(Maschinen)* Nachlauf *m*
after-shrinkage in volume Volumennachschwindung *f*

against gegen
agate mortar Achatreibschale *f*
agate pestle Achatpistill
age altern
age-harden altern
age-hardening Altern *nt*
age-hardening crack Aufhärtungsriss *m*
ageing Alterung *f*, Altern *nt*
ageing accelerator Alterungsbeschleuniger *m*
ageing chamber Alterungskammer *f*
ageing induced crack Alterungsriss *m*
ageing inhibiter Alterungsschutzmittel *nt*
ageing under exposure to light Lichtalterung *f*
agent chemisches Mittel *nt*
age-resistant alterungsbeständig
agglutinate ankleben
aggregate Aggregat *nt*
aggregate defective area gesamte Fehlerfläche *f*
aggregate tolerance Summentoleranz *f*
aggregation Aggregation *f*, Aggregat *nt*
aggressive medium Angriffsmittel *nt*
aggressive substances angreifende Stoffe *mpl*
aging Alterung *f*
aging factor Alterungszustand *m*
agitate bewegen
agree upon abstimmen, übereinstimmen (mit), vereinbaren
agreed load Lastannahme *f*
agreement Vereinbarung *f*, Abstimmung *f*, Übereinstimmung *f*, Abklärung *f*
ahead vorn, voraus, vorwärts
adhesive grease Haftschmiere *f*
aid Mittel *nt*, Hilfsmittel *nt*
aim Ziel *nt*; richten (auf), zielen (auf)
aims Zielsetzung *f*
air Luft *f*, lüften, belüften
air afterheater Luftnacherhitzer *m*
air bleed Entlüftungsstelle *f*
air cargo Luftfracht *f*
air change Luftwechsel *m*
air chuck Pressfutter *nt*
air circulation Luftführung *f*

air circulation type central heating installation Luftheizungsanlage *f*
air cleaning machine Ausblasmaschine *f*
air cleanness Luftreinheit *f*
air combination Luftzusammensetzung *f*
air conditioner Klimaanlage *f*, Lüftung *f*
air conditioning Klimatisierung *f*, Klimaanlage *f*, Lüftung *f*
air conditioning appliance Lüftungsgerät *nt*
air conditioning technology Klimatechnik *f*, Raumlufttechnik *f*
air core Luftkern *m*
air damper control Luftklappensteuerung *f*
air deficiency safety device Luftmangelsicherung *f*
air discharge opening Abluftöffnung *f*
air emulsification Luftemulgierung *f*
air escape Luftabzug *m*
air exhauster Entlüfter *m*
air extraction rate Abluftleistung *f*
air flow control Luftstromregelung *f*
air flow controller Luftstromregler *m*
air flow device Luftleiteinrichtung *f*
air freight Luftfracht *f*
air gap Luftspalt *m*
air gauging pneumatische Längenmessung *f*
air heating stove Feuerluftheizofen *m*
air humidity Luftfeuchte *f*
air impulse process Luftimpulsverfahren *nt*
air infiltration heat requirement Lüftungswärme *f*
air inlet Lufteinlass *m*
air input filter Zuluftfilter *m*
air intake Lufteinlass *m*
air level Libelle *f*
air motion Luftbewegung *f*
air passage Luftdurchtritt *m*, Luftdurchlass *m*
air permeability Luftdurchlässigkeit *f*
air permeable luftdurchlässig
air preheating device Luftvorwärmanlage *f*
air preparation facility Luftaufbereitungsanlage *f*
air pressure Luftdruck *m*
air renewal Lufterneuerung *f*
air route Luftstrecke *f*
air shut-off damper Luftabsperrklappe *f*
air stream Luftstrom *m*
air stream forming process Luftstromformverfahren *nt*
air stria Luftschliere *f*
air throughput Luftdurchsatz *m*
air turbulance device Luftwirbeleinrichtung *f*
air vent Luftabzug *m*
air vice pneumatisch betätigter Schraubstock *m*
air void content Luftgehalt *m*
air/dust mixture Staub-Luft-Gemisch *nt*
air-actuated druckluftbetätigt
air-actuated luftbetätigt
airborne noise emission Luftschallemission *f*
airborne noise measurement Luftschallmessung *f*
airborne sound emission Luftschallemission *f*
airborne sound insulation Luftschalldämmung *f*
air-cooled luftgekühlt
air-cooled condenser Kondensator *m* mit Luftkühlung
air-core coil Luftkernspule *f*
air-core winding Luftkernspule *f*
aircraft Luftfahrzeuge *ntpl*
aircraft construction Flugzeugbau *m*
air drain petcock Entlüftungshahn *m*
airflow noise Luftströmungsgeräusch *nt*
airflow of the ventilating system Strömungsfeld *nt* der Lüftungsanlage
airflow pattern Luftströmungsfeld *nt*
air-hardening Lufthärtung *f*
air-hardening steel lufthärtender Stahl *m*
airhouse Traglufthalle *f*
air-inflated structure Traglufthalle *f*
air-inflated tent Traglufthalle *f*
airing Lüftung *f*
air-inleakage Falschlufteinbruch *m*
air-load ratio setter Luft-Last-Verhält-

nissteller *m*
airmail paper with diazo coating Luftpostpapier *nt* mit Lichtpausschicht
air-operated luftbetätigt, druckluftbetätigt
air-operated chuck Pressluftfutter *nt*
air-power drill Druckluft-Kleinbohrmaschine *f*
air-pre-heater Luftvorerhitzer *m*
air-relieve valve Entlüftungsventil *nt*
air-sealed luftundurchlässig
air-tight luftundurchlässig
air-tightness Luftundurchlässigkeit *f*
aisle Gang *m*, Gasse *f*, Regalgang *m*, Bedienungsgang *m*
aisle axis Gassenachse *f*
aisle clearance Gangfreimaß *nt*
aisle detection Gangerkennung *f*
aisle emergency lighting Gangnotbeleuchtung *f*
aisle equipment Gassenausrüstung *f*
aisle lateral direction Gangquerrichtung *f*
aisle length direction Ganglängsrichtung *f*
aisle side gangseitig, gassenseitig
aisle-to-aisle transfer Umsetzen *nt*
aisle vertical direction Ganghochrichtung *f*
aisle width Gangbreite *f*, Gassenbreite *f*
akin to daylight tageslichtähnlich
alarm Alarm *m*, Warnsignal *nt*, Meldung *f*
alarm device Meldeeinrichtung *f*
alarm limit Alarmgrenze *f*
alarm message Alarmmeldung *f*
alarm threshold Alarmschwelle *f*
acrylated alkyd resin acryliertes Alkydharz *nt*
aldehyde condensation product Aldehyd-Kondensationsprodukt *nt*
alert Warnsignal *nt*
alert box Warnbox *f*
algorithm Algorithmus *m*
align einstellen, ausrichten, justieren, ausfluchten, fluchten, abgleichen, orientieren, richten (auf)
aligning Ausrichten *nt*, Fluchten *nt*
alignment Ausrichtung *f*, Justierung *f*, Anordnung *f*, Abfluchtung *f*, Ausfluchtung *f*, Axialität *f*, Einstellen *nt*, Flucht *f*, Fluchten *nt*, Reihe *f*, Abgleich *m*, Orientierung *f*
alignment accuracy Fluchtgenauigkeit *f*, Seitengenauigkeit *f*
alignment pin Passstift *m*
alignment section Führungsstück *nt*
alignment station Ausrichtstation *f*
aluminium pigment Aluminiumpigment *nt*
alkali resistance Alkaliresistenz *f*
alkali solubility Alkalilöslichkeit *f*
alkaline battery alkalische Batterie *f*
all-angle milling head auf jeden Winkel verstellbarer Fräskopf *m*
all-electric vollelektrisch
Allen set screw Gewindestift *m* mit Innensechskant
allied zugehörig
alligator shear Hebelschere *f*
all-layer sample Allschichtprobe *f*
all-levels sample Allschichtprobe *f*
all-metal nut Glanzmetallmutter *f*
allocate zuteilen, verteilen, anordnen, zuweisen, zuordnen, vergeben, umlegen
allocation Zuteilung *f*, Zuordnung *f*, Zuweisung *f*, Verteilung *f*, Anordnung *f*, Vergabe *f*, Umlage *f*, Umlegung *f*
allocation list Zuordnungsliste *f*
allocation of accounts Kontierung *f*
allocation of samples Aufteilung *f*
allocation of storage locations Lagerplatzvergabe *f*
allocation table Zuordnungstabelle *f*, Zuordnungsliste *f*
all-over vollflächig
allow ermöglichen, zulassen, freigeben
allow to drain austropfen lassen
allowable zulässig
allowable maximum pull höchstzulässiger Zug *m*
allowance Kleinstspiel *nt*, Maßabweichung *f*, Zugabe *f*, Zulassung *f*, Toleranz *f*, Übermaß *nt*, Spiel *nt*
allowance Abmaß *nt*
allowance for external dimensions Abmaß *nt* für Außenmaße
allowance for internal dimensions Abmaß *nt* für Innenmaße

allowed gestatten
allowed time Vorgabezeit *f*
allowed time establishment Vorgabezeitermittlung *f*
alloy Legierung *f*
alloy for cutting tools Schneidlegierung *f*
alloy steel legierter Stahl *m*, Sonderstahl *m*
alloying Auflegieren *nt*
alloying coating Auflegierungsschicht *f*
all-purpose universal
allround visibility Rundumsicht *f*
almost zero fast „Null"
along the aisle gangseitig
alongside längsseits, längs
alongside each other nebeneinander
alphanumeric notation Alphanumerische Schreibweise *f*
alphanumerical alphanumerisch
alter verändern, abändern
alter instruction Änderungsbefehl *m*
alter statement Schaltbefehl *m*
alterable veränderbar
alteration Änderung *f*, Veränderung *f*
alteration in magnetic fields Magnetfeldänderung *f*
alteration in material characteristic Stoffeigenschaftsänderung *f*
alteration of a contract Vertragsänderung *f*
alteration service Änderungsdienst *m*
alternate wechseln, wechselseitig
alternate angle side and face cutter Kreuzzahnscheibenfräser *m*
alternate angle staggered tooth type tee-slot cutter kreuzverzahnter T-Nutenfräser *m*
alternate communication Wechselbetrieb *m*
alternate gash plain mill kreuzverzahnter Walzenfräser *m*
alternate helical tooth cutter kreuzverzahnter Fräser *m*
alternate nicking auf Lücke stehende Spanbrechernuten *fpl*, gegeneinander versetzte Kerbung *f*
alternate operation Wechselbetrieb *m*
alternate tool Schwesterwerkzeug *nt*
alternate tooth milling cutter kreuzverzahnter Fräser *m*, Fräser *m* mit versetzten Zähnen
alternating bending testing machine Wechselbiegemaschine *f*
alternating climate of the hot humid type Wechselklima *nt* mit feuchter Wärme
alternating current Wechselstrom *m*
alternating damp heat atmosphere Schwitzwasserwechselklima *nt*
alternating electric field elektrisches Wechselfeld *nt*
alternating field Wechselfeld *nt*
alternating flexural loading schwingende Biegebeanspruchung *f*
alternating hypothesis Alternativhypothese *f*
alternating light operation Wechsellichtbetrieb *m*
alternating shock load stoßartige Wechselbeanspruchung *f*
alternating storage Wechsellagerung *f*
alternating strain Verformungswechsel *m*
alternating temperature test Temperaturwechselprüfung *f*
alternation Wechseln *nt*, Wechsel *m*, Umstellung *f*
alternation switch Umschalter *m*
alternative Wahl *f*, Möglichkeiten *fpl*, Variante *f*
alternative of load Lastspiel *nt*
alternative path alternativer Zweig *m*
alternator Wechselstrommaschine *f*
aluminium cast iron Aluminiumguss *m*
aluminium deposition Aluminiumauftragung *f*
aluminium extruded section Aluminiumstangenpressprofil *nt*
aluminium filter equivalent Aluminiumgleichwert *m*
aluminium-killed steel Sonderberuhigter Stahl *m*
aluminium-oxide tool tip Aluminiumoxidschneide *f*
aluminous abrasive Kunstkorund *nt*, Elektrokorund *nt*
aluminous oxide wheel Aluminiumoxidscheibe *f*
ambiance Umgebung *f*

ambient atmosphere – analyse

ambient atmosphere Umgebungsklima *nt*
ambient conditions Umgebungsbedingungen *fpl*
ambient temperature Umgebungstemperatur *f*, Raumtemperatur *f*
ambiguous vieldeutig
amelioration liming Meliorationskalkung *f*
amend berichtigen, ändern
amendment Änderung *f*
amendment of drawing Zeichnungsänderung *f*
American petroleum thread amerikanisches Petroleumgewinde *nt*
aminoplast Harnstoffmasse *f*
aminoplast adhesive Aminoplastkleber *m*
aminoplast/phenolic compression moulding material Aminoplast-/Phenoplastpressmasse *f*
aminoplastic synthetic resin aminoplastisches Kunstharz *nt*
amorphous amorph
amount Menge *f*, Betrag *m*, Größe *f*, Summe *f*
amount carried Übertrag *m*
amount of abrasion Verschleißbetrag *m*
amount of angularity Schrägstellung *f*, Größe *f* des Winkels
amount of back-off Größe *f* des Freiwinkels
amount of chip space Größe *f* des Spanraumes
amount of deposited metal Schweißgutmasse *f*
amount of eccentricity Exzentrizität *f*
amount of feed Vorschubgröße *f*, Vorschub *m*
amount of filler Lotmenge *f*
amount of goods handled Umschlag *m*
amount of material removed abgenommenes Werkstoffvolumen *nt*
amount of metal removed Spanmenge *f*, Spanabnahme *f*
amount of stock left for Übermaß *nt* als Bearbeitungszugabe für, Zugabe *f* für
amount of stock removed abgenommenes Spanvolumen *nt*
amount of storage Speichermenge *f*
amount of wear Verschleißbetrag *m*, Verschleißgröße *f*
amount to betragen
ampere hour Amperestunde *f*
ampere turns Durchflutung *f*
ampere windings Durchflutung *f*
ampere-hour meter Amperestundenzähler *m*
ample umfangreich
amplification Verstärkung *f*
amplification factor Kv-Faktor *m*
amplified verstärkt
amplifier Verstärker *m*
amplifier chain Verstärkermesskette *f*
amplifier with negation indicator negierender Verstärker *m*
amplify verstärken
amplitude Ausschlag *m*
amplitude of movement Bewegungsamplitude *f*
amplitude of oscillation Schwingungsausschlag *m*
amplitude oscillation Amplitudenschwingung *f*
amplitude response Amplitudengang *m*
amplitude-modulated amplitudenmoduliert
anaerobic corrosion anaerobe Korrosion
analogue input analoger Eingang *m*
analogue input unit Analogeingabeeinheit *f*
analogue output analoger Ausgang *m*
analogue output unit Analogausgabeeinheit *f*
analogue reading scale indication Skalenanzeige *f*
analogue-to-digital converter (ADC) Analog/Digital-Wandler *m*
analogue value processing Analogwertverarbeitung *f*
analogue-digital-converter Analog-Digital-Umsetzer *m*
analogue position feedback transmitter Ist-Wert-Geber *m*
analogue analog
analyse analysieren, bestimmen, unter-

suchen, zergliedern
analysis Analyse *f*, Betrachtung *f*, Zergliederung *f*
analysis designation Analysenbezeichnung *f*
analysis method Analysenverfahren *nt*
analysis of forces Kraftzerlegung *f*
analysis process Analyseprozess *m*
analysis sample Analysenprobe *f*
analytical analytisch
analytical moisture Analysefeuchtigkeit *f*
analytically moist state analysefeuchter Zustand *m*
analyze analysieren, bestimmen, untersuchen, zergliedern
unambiguous eindeutig
anchor Anker *m*
anchor Verankerung *f*, verankern
anchor bolt Ankerbolzen *m*, Fundamentschraube *f*
anchor reinforcing bars Bewehrungsstäbe *mpl* verbinden
anchorage Befestigung *f*, Verankerung *f*, verankern
anchoring Verankerung *f*
anchoring element Aufspannelement *nt*
anchoring method Verankerungsmethode *f*
anchoring sleeve Aufspannhülse *f*
anchoring surface Aufspannfläche *f*
ancillary conditions Randbedingung *f*
ancillary device Zusatzeinrichtung *f*
ancillary equipment Zusatzausrüstung *f*, Zusatzgeräte *ntpl*
ancillary personnel costs Personalnebenkosten *pl*
AND UND
AND circuit UND-Schaltkreis *m*
and crater cavity Endkraterlunker *m*
AND dependency UND-Abhängigkeit *f*
AND element UND-Schaltung *f*
AND element with one dynamic input UND-Glied *nt* mit einem dynamischen Eingang
AND gating UND-Verknüpfung *f*
AND relation UND-Verknüpfung *f*
AND with negated output UND-Glied *nt* mit negiertem Ausgang, NAND-Glied *nt*
AND with one input negated UND-Glied *nt* mit Negation eines Eingangs
AND/OR operation UND/ODER Schaltfunktion *f*
AND-gate UND-Gatter *nt*, UND-Schaltung *f*
angle Winkel *m*, Schenkel *m*, Knie *nt*
angle block Winkelendmaß *nt*
angle cut Schrägschnitt *m*
angle cutting Schrägschneiden *nt*
angle data *pl* Winkelangaben *fpl*
angle encoder Winkelcodierer *m*
angle end mill Winkelfräser *m* mit Zylinderschaft
angle error Winkelfehler *m*
angle gauge Winkelendmaß *nt*
angle light scanner Winkellichttaster *m*
angle measure Winkelmaß *nt*
angle measurement Winkelmessung *f*
angle measuring device Winkelmessgerät *nt*
angle measuring instrument Winkelmessgerät *nt*
angle milling attachment Winkelfräseinrichtung *f*
angle milling cutter Winkelfräser *m*, Winkelstirnfräser *m*
angle milling fixture Winkelfräseinrichtung *f*
angle milling spindle Winkelfrässpindel *f*
angle non-return valve Rückschlageckventil *nt*
angle of application of force Kraftangriffswinkel *m*
angle of approach Eingriffswinkel *m*, Spanumfangswinkel *m*
angle of beam spread Öffnungswinkel *m*
angle of blasting Strahlwinkel *m*
angle of chamfer Anschnittwinkel *m*
angle of contact Umschlingungswinkel *m*
angle of cut flank Schnittflankenwinkel *m*
angle of deflection at failure Biegewinkel *m* beim Bruch
angle of deformation Verformungs-

angle of drift – angular indexing

winkel *m*
angle of drift Abtriftwinkel *m*
angle of drop Anhubwinkel *m*, Fallwinkel *m*
angle of fall Fallwinkel *m*
angle of impact Aufprallwinkel *m*
angle of incidence Einfallswinkel *m*
angle of inclination Neigungswinkel *m*
angle of intersection Kreuzungswinkel *m*
angle of keenness Keilwinkel *m*
angle of point Querschneidenwinkel *m*, Spitzenwinkel *m*
angle of refraction Brechungswinkel *m*
angle of relief Freiwinkel *m* an der Fase, hinter der Schneide
angle of rise Steigwinkel *m*
angle of rotation of weld Nahtdrehwinkel *m*
angle of slope Ablenkwinkel *m*
angle of support Auflagewinkel *m*
angle of the tool helix Drallwinkel *m*
angle of thread Flankenwinkel *m* eines Gewindes
angle of tilt Drehwinkel *m*, Kippwinkel *m*
angle of twist Drallwinkel *m*, Verdrehwinkel *m*
angle of vision Sehwinkel *m*
angle of wrap Umschlingungswinkel *m*
angle on the cutting part Winkel *m* am Schneidteil
angle pattern valve Eckbauventil *nt*
angle plate Aufspannwinkel *m*, Winkeleisen *nt*
angle pressure reducing valve Druckmindereckventil *nt*
angle probe Winkelprüfkopf *m*
angle safety valve Sicherheitseckventil *nt*
angle screen Ecksieb *nt*
angle standard Winkelnormale *f*
angle support Auflagewinkel *m*
angle tool Prismenmeißel *m*
angle transducer Winkelmesswandler *m*
angle transmitter Winkelgeber *m*
angle transmitter-receiver probe SE-Winkelprüfkopf *m*
angle vertical to the cutter axis Stirnfreiwinkel *m*
angle weld Eckschweißung *f*, Abkantnaht *f*
angled schräg
angled base cylinder-envelop abgewickelte Grundzylindermantelfläche *f*
angled position of the burner schräg stehender Brenner *m*
angled specimen Winkelprobe *f*
angled specimen with incision Winkelprobe *f* mit Einschnitt
angled test specimen Winkelprobe *f*
angled type double-ended ring spanner abgewinkelter Doppelringschlüssel *m*
angular eckig, winklig, kantig
angular acceleration Winkelbeschleunigung *f*
angular adjustable schrägverstellbar
angular adjustment Schrägverstellung *f*, Schrägstellung *f*
angular cut schräger Schnitt *m*
angular cutter Winkelfräser *m*
angular deformation Winkelverformung *f*
angular deviation Winkelabweichung *f*
angular dimension Winkelmaß *nt*
angular displacement Winkelverschiebung *f*
angular division of workpiece Teilung *f* des Werkstücks nach Winkelmaß
angular downfeed schräger Tiefenvorschub *m*, schräger Senkrechtvorschub *m*
angular drive Winkelantrieb *m*
angular edged vollkantig
angular encoder Winkelschrittgeber *m*
angular end milling schräges Fräsen *nt* in axialer Richtung des Schaftfräsers
angular error Winkelfehler *m*
angular feed Winkelvorschub *m*
angular frequency Winkelfrequenz *f*
angular gashing Fräsen *nt* geneigter Schlitze
angular grinding Schrägschleifen *nt*
angular gripper Winkelgreifer *m*
angular guide Winkelführung *f*
angular half side mill Winkelstirnfräser *m*
angular indexing Teilen *nt* nach Win-

kelmaß
angular limit of size Winkelgrenzmaß *nt*
angular magnification Konvergenzverhältnis *nt*
angular milling Winkelfräsen *nt*, Schrägfräsen *nt*
angular milling attachment Winkelfräskopf *m*
angular milling head Winkelfräskopf *m*
angular milling operation Fräsarbeit *f* an schrägen Flächen
angular misalignment Abwinkelung *f*, Winkelversatz *m*
angular movement Winkelbewegung *f*
angular parallels Keilpaar *nt*, Keilstück *nt*
angular pitch Teilungswinkel *m*
angular planing Schräghobeln *nt*
angular plunge grinding Schrägeinstechschleifen *nt*
angular position Drehstellung *f*
angular position measurement Winkelmessung *f*
angular position variation *(z. B. der Welle des Getriebezuges)* Drehstellungsabweichung *f*
angular positioning Schrägstellung *f*
angular range Winkelbereich *m*
angular setting Schrägeinstellung *f*, Winkeleinstellung *f*
angular size Winkelmaß *nt*
angular spacing Gradteilung *f*, Winkelteilung *f*
angular strain Winkelverformung *f*
angular table setting Tischschrägverstellung *f*
angular teeth *pl* Schrägverzahnung *f*
angular tensile test Schrägzugversuch *m*
angular tilt Schrägstellung *f*, Schrägkippen *nt*
angular tolerance Winkeltoleranz *f*
angular turning Winkeligdrehen *nt*, Kegeldrehen *nt*
angular unit Winkeleinheit *f*
angularity Winkeligkeit *f*
angularity tolerance Neigungstoleranz *f*

anion exchanger Anionenaustauscher *m*
anisochronous zeittaktungsgleich
anneal ausglühen, glühen, tempern
annealing Tempern *nt*, Glühen *nt*
annealing cathode Glühkathode *f*
annealing colours *pl* Anlassfarben *fpl*
annealing for removal of work-hardening Entfestigungsglühen *nt*
annealing for spherical carbides Glühen *nt* auf kugelige Karbide
annealing from hot working heat Glühen *nt* aus der Warmformhitze
annealing heat colours *pl* Glühfarben *fpl*
annealing pot Tempertopf *m*
annealing process Temperverfahren *nt*
annealing skin Glühhaut *f*
annular ringförmig
annular clearance Ringspalt *m*
annular groove ringförmige Auskehlung *f*
annular magnet Ringmagnet *m*
annular plate Ringplatte *f*
annular ring Ringscheibe *f*
annular segment Kreisringstück *nt*
annular spring Ringfeder *f*
annulus Ring *m*
annunciation Melden *nt*
anode Anode *f*
anode inclination angle Anodenneigungswinkel *m*
anodic attack on the metal anodischer Metallabtrag *m*
anodic oxidisability Anodisierbarkeit *f*
anodic oxidising grade Eloxalqualität *f*
anodic partial current anodischer Teilstrom *m*
anodic partial current density anodische Teilstromdichte *f*
anodic polarisation *(el. chem.)* anodische Polarisation *f*
anodise eloxieren
antecedent Bedingung *f*
antenna Antenne *f*
antenna mast Antennenträger *m*
anterior diaphragm Vorderblende *f*
anti-backlash device Spielausgleicheinrichtung *f*, Gleichlauffräseinrich-

tung *f*
anti-backlash longitudinal table feed nut Mutter *f* der Tischlängsvorschubspindel mit Spielausgleich
anticipate antizipieren, vorhersehen
anticipating voreilend
anticipatory vorausschauend
anti-clockwise gegen den Uhrzeigersinn, im Gegenuhrzeigersinn, linksdrehend
anti-clockwise rotation Linkslauf *m*, Linksdrehung *f*
anti-collision device Anfahrschutzeinrichtung *f*
anti-collision protection Zusammenstoßsicherung *f*
anti-corrosion coating Korrosionsschutzbeschichtung *f*
anti-corrosion lining Korrosionsschutzauskleidung *f*
anti-corrosion oil Rostschutzöl *nt*
anti-dazzle filter Blendschutzfilter *m*
anti-derailment device Sicherung *f* gegen Umkippen/Umstürzen, Sicherung *f* gegen Entgleisen
anti-drumming compound Entdröhnungsmasse *f*
anti-fall device Antifalleinrichtung *f*
anti-falling device Sicherung *f* gegen Abstürzen
anti-fatigue sleeve Dehnhülse *f*
antifriction bearing Wälzlager *nt*
antifoam Entschäumer *m*
anti-foaming agent Entschäumer *m*
antifriction material Gleitwerkstoff *m*
antimicrobic antimikrobiell
antimony-containing soft solder antimonhaltiges Weichlot *nt*
antimony-free solder antimonfreies Lot *nt*
anti-oxidant oil oxydationsbeständiges Öl *nt*
antiozonant Antiozonans
anti-parallax reading parallaxfreie Ablesung *f*
anti-radiation stabilizer Strahlenschutzmittel *nt*
anti-rust test Korrosionsschutzprüfung *f*
anti-skid rutschhemmend
anti-slip gleitsicher
anti-slip plate Gleitschutzblech *nt*
antistatic antistatisch
anti-vibration levelling mount Antivibrationsgestell *nt*
anti-vibration mounting Antivibrationsgestell *nt*
anti-wear properties Verschleißfestigkeit *f*, Verschleißbeständigkeit *f*
anvil Amboss *m*, Widerlager *nt*, Messzapfen *m*
apart from neben, außer
apart from execution time Nebendurchführungszeit *f*
apart from utilization period Nebennutzungszeit *f*
aperiodic fluctuating stress unperiodische Schwingbeanspruchung *f*
aperture Einrastung *f*, Zugriffsöffnung *f*, Spalt *m*, Loch *nt*, Öffnung *f*, Mündung *f*, Einfahröffnung *f*, Lochung *f*
aperture occupied sensor Fachbelegtsensor *m*
aperture of the test sieve Prüfsieböffnung *f*
aperture plate Lochblende *f*
apex Scheitel *m*, Spitze *f*
apex to back distance Einbaumaß *nt*
apice Scheitelpunkt *m*
apparatus Apparatur *f*
apparatus Gerät *nt*, Apparat *m*
apparatus check Gerätekontrolle *f*
apparatus for sensory analysis sensorisches Untersuchungsgerät *nt*
apparatus plug Gerätestecker *m*
apparent elastic appliance Nachgiebigkeit *f*
apparent modulus Kriechmodul *nt*
apparent power Scheinleistung *f*
apparent power input Scheinleistungsaufnahme *f*
appearance Aussehen *nt*
appearance of the fracture Bruchbild *nt*
append anhängen
appendix Zusatz *m*, Anhang *m*
appliance Gerät *nt*, Apparat *m*, Apparatur *f*, Vorrichtung *f*, Einrichtung *f*
appliance inlet valve Geräteanschlussschieber *m*
appliance pressure governor Geräte-

druckregler *m*
appliance rating plate Geräteschild *nt*
applicable brauchbar
application 1. Einsatz *m*, Anwendung *f*, Gebrauch *m*, Verwendung *f*, Anwendungsfall *m* **2.** *(Schmierung auf einen Reibungspunkt)* Aufbringung *f*, Applikation *f*
application factor Betriebsfaktor *m*
application group Anwendungsgruppe *f*
application layer Anwendungsschicht *f*
application of adhesive Klebstoffauftrag *m*
application of filler metal Lot *nt* zuführen
application of glue Leimauftrag *m*
application of heat Wärmeeinwirkung *f*, Hitzeeinwirkung *f*
application option Einsatzmöglichkeit *f*
application possibility Anwendungsmöglichkeit *f*
application program Anwendungsprogramm *nt*, Anwenderprogramm *nt*
application time Einsatzzeit *f*
application-specific anwendungsspezifisch
applicator opening farthest from the focal point brennfleckfernste Tubusöffnung *f*
applied angelegt
apply einbringen, einlegen, aufbringen (auf), beaufschlagen, anlegen, befestigen, angreifen, anbringen, einfallen, anwenden
apply a little solvent anlösen
apply a vacuum ein Vakuum erzeugen
apply adhesive Klebstoff auftragen
apply coatings kaschieren
apply for anmelden, gelten für
apply glue Leim auftragen
apply in plated form aufplattieren
apply with pressure mit Druck beaufschlagen
applying heat Hitzeeinwirkung *f*
appointment Termin *m*
apportion umlegen, aufteilen, zuteilen, verteilen
apportionment Verteilung *f*, Aufteilung *f*, Zuteilung *f*, Umlegung *f*
apportionment of costs Umlage *f*
appraisal Abschätzung *f*
appraisal drawing Gutachtenzeichnung *f*
appraise begutachten
apprentice trainer Ausbilder *m*
apprentice training school Berufsschule *f*
apprentice workshop Lehrwerkstatt *f*
approach Anfahren *nt*, Annäherung *f*, Aufsuchen *nt*, Heranführung *f*; nähern, annähern, heranfahren, heranführen, zuführen
approach angle Annäherungswinkel *m*, Einstellergänzungswinkel *m*
approach contact Eintrittseingriff *m*
approach inaccuracy Anfahrungenauigkeit *f*
approach motion Anstellbewegung *f*, Einlauf *m*
approach of cutter Anlaufweg *m* des Fräsers, Anschnittweg *m* des Fräsers
approach section Anlaufstrecke *f*
approach side *(Fräser)* Anschnittseite *f*
approach to problem solving Lösungsansatz *m*
approach to solution Lösungsweg *m*
appropriate sinnvoll, geeignet, angemessen, sachgerecht, passend
approval Genehmigung *f*, Gutbefund *m*, Zulassung *f*, Abnahme *f*
approval criterion Abnahmekriterium *nt*
approval date Abnahmetermin *m*
approval measure Abnahmeschritt *m*
approval procedure Genehmigungsverfahren *nt*
approval record Abnahmeprotokoll *nt*
approve genehmigen, zulassen
approved nicht beanstandet, zugelassen
approved welder geprüfter Schweißer *m*
approximate nähern
approximate dimension Ungefährmaß *nt*
approximate size Ungefährmaß *nt*
approximate solution Näherungslösung *f*
approximately näherungsweise, annä-

hernd
approximation Annäherung *f*, Näherung *f*
appurtenance(s) Zubehör *nt*
apron Bettschürze *f*, Einfassung *f*, Supportschlossplatte *f*, Stahlhalterklappe *f*, Schlosskasten *m*, Schürze *f*, Querschlitten *m* des Tisches
apron box Schlosskastengehäuse *nt*
apron clamping bolt Klemmschraube *f* des Klappenträgers
apron for saddle-type turret Schlosskasten *m* für Revolverkopf
apron front Schlossplatte *f*
apron housing Räderplatte *f*, Schlosskasten *m*, Schlosskastengehäuse *nt*, Schürze *f*
apron slide Querschlitten *m* des Tisches
apron wall Schlossplatte *f*
aqueous chlorine solution wässerige Chlorlösung *f*
aqueous solution wässrige Lösung *f*
arable area Ackerfläche *f*
arbitration test Schiedsversuch *m*
arbitrary willkürlich
arbitrary point beliebiger Punkt *m*
arbitrary units willkürliche Einheiten *fpl*
arbitration Zuteilung *f*
arbitration case Schiedsfall *m*
arbitration cross-section Zuteilungsquerschnitt *m*
arbitration test specimen Schiedsprobe *f*
arbor brace Gegenhalterschere *f*
arbor bracket Dorntraglager *nt*
arbor cutter Aufsteckfräser *m*
arbor nut Dornmutter *f*
arbor press Dornpresse *f*
arbor support Traglager *nt*, Stützarm *m*
arbor supporting bracket Dornstützlager *nt*
arbor type mill Aufsteckfräser *m*
arbor yoke Führungslager *nt*, Traglager *nt*
arbor Spanndorn *m*, Aufspannbolzen *m*, Dorn *m*, Aufsteckdorn *m*
arbor hole Bohrloch *nt*
arc Bogen *m*, Kreissegment *nt*, Lichtbogen *m*, Petrinetzpfeil *m*, Pfeil *m*
arc burn Zündstelle *f*
arc erosion Lichtbogenerosion *f*
arc grinding Strahlenschliff *m*
arc length Bogenlänge *f*
arc measure Bogenmaß *nt*
arc of circle Kreisbogen *m*
arc of contact Berührungsbogen *m*
arc pressure welding using a magnetically moved arc Lichtbogenpressschweißen *nt* mit magnetisch bewegtem Lichtbogen
arc shaped kreisbogenförmig, bogenförmig
arc shrinkage Bogeneinlauf *m*
arc spraying Lichtbogenspritzen *nt*
arc spraying wire Lichtbogenspritzdraht *m*
arc strike Zündstelle *f*
arc strike point Nahtansatz *m*
arc stud welding with initiation by means of a collar Lichtbogenbolzenschweißen *nt* mit Ringzündung
arc welding Lichtbogenschweißen *nt*
arc welding using a magnetically moved arc Schmelzschweißen *nt* mit magnetisch bewegten Lichtbogen
arc welding with electrode fed by spring pressure Federkraftlichtbogenschweißen *nt*
arch wölben, Wölbung *f*
archives Archiv *nt*
arcing marks Brandspuren *fpl*
arcing spot Schmorstelle *f*
area Fläche *f*, Bereich *m*, Zone *f*, Stelle *f*
area distribution flächenmäßige Verteilung *f*
area drainage Flächenentwässerung *f*
area for small parts storage Handlager *nt*
area near grain boundaries korngrenzennaher Bereich *m*
area of contact Berührungsfläche *f*
area of cut Schnittfläche *f*
area of exposure Aufnahmefeld *nt*
area of fill Flächenaufschüttung *f*
area of hazard Gefahrbereich *m*
area of incidence Auftreffbereich *m*
area of measurement surface Messflächeninhalt *m*

area planning Flächenplanung *f*
area to be left clear *(Metallspritzen)* Freiraum *m*
area-dose product Flächendosierprodukt *nt*
area-measured moulding material flächige Formmasse *f*
area-measured plastic product flächiges Kunststoff-Erzeugnis *nt*
area-measured product flächenhaftes Erzeugnis *nt*
area-measured support flächenhafter Träger *m*
area-related mass flächenbezogene Masse *f*
areas *pl* **of application** Anwendungsgebiete *ntpl*, Einsatzbereiche *mpl*
aerometer Aräometer *nt*
arithmetic closing tolerance Toleranz *f* des Schließmaßes einer Maßkette, arithmetische Schließtoleranz *f*
arithmetic mean arithmetischer Mittelwert *m*
arm Arm *m*, Ausleger *m*, Kragarm *m*, Schenkel *m*, Steg *m*
ARM (asynchronous response mode) Spontanbetrieb *m*
arm brace Gegenhalterschere *f*
arm bracket Auslegerschelle *f*
arm head slide Hobelkopfschlitten *m*
arm of a Wheatstone half-bridge Wheatston'scher Brückenzweig *m*
arm ways Auslegerführungsbahn *f*
armature Armatur *f*, Rotor *m*, Läufer *m*, Anker *m*
armature coil Läuferspule *f*
armature slot Läufernut *f*
armature winding Läuferwicklung *f*
armour plate Panzerplatte *f*
armour plate planer Panzerplattenhobelmaschine *f*
armour plate planing Panzerplattenhobeln *nt*
armoured hose Panzerschlauch *m*
armrest Lehne *f*
aperture Blende *f*
arrange einrichten, platzieren, ausrichten (an), anordnen, ordnen, organisieren
arranged angeordnet

arrangement Ausrichtung *f*, Disposition *f*, Anordnung *f*, Ordnung *f*, Vorkehrung *f*, Aufbau *m*, Vorrichtung *f*, Montage *f*
arrangement drawing Anordnungszeichnung *f*
arrangement in layers lagenweise Anordnung *f*
arrangement of means of production Produktionsmittelgestaltung *f*
arrangement of measuring points Messpunktanordnung *f*
arrangement of the bays Facheinteilung *f*
arrangement of wheels Radanordnung *f*
arrangement option Anordnungsmöglichkeit *f*
arranging Ausrichten *nt*
array Anordnung *f*, ordnen
arrest hemmen, arretieren, sperren, festhalten, stoppen, einklinken, stillsetzen, zurückhalten; Arretierung *f*
arresting Blockierung *f*
arrestor Fangeinrichtung *f*
arrestor stay Fangklinke *f*
arrival Eintreffen *nt*, Ankunft *f*
arrival note Ankunftsanzeige *f*
arrivals 1. Zugang *m* 2. *(Waren)* Wareneingänge *mpl*
arrive ankommen, eintreffen, einlaufen
arriving Ankunft *f*, einlaufend
arrow Pfeil *m*
arrow key Richtungstaste *f*
arrow line Pfeillinie *f*
arrowhead Pfeil *m*
article Artikel *m*
article characteristic Sachmerkmal *nt*
article identity Artikelidentität *f*
article structure Artikelstruktur *f*
articulation Gelenkverbindung *f*
articulation of the axle Pendelung *f*
articulated wheels Gelenkräder *ntpl*
articulated schwenkbar, pendelnd
articulated axle Pendelachse *f*
articulated fork truck Schwenkgabelstapler *m*
articulated lifting platform Scherenhubtisch *m*
articulated pipe Gelenkrohr *nt*

articulated retractable device Schwenkschubeinrichtung *f*
articulated retractable fork Schwenkschubgabel *f*
articulated steering Knicklenkung *f*
articulated tiller handle schwenkbare Deichsel *f*
articulating arm Gelenkarm *m*
articulation Pendelung *f*, Gelenk *nt*, Knick *m*
articulation joint Gelenkpunkt *m*, Gelenk *nt*
articulation point Aufhängung *f*, Anlenkpunkt *m*
articulation zone Knickbereich *m*
artificial künstlich
artificial intelligence (AI) künstliche Intelligenz *f*
artificial leather on a bonded fabric basis Vlieskunstleder *nt*
artificial leather sheeting Folienkunstleder *nt*
artificial ventilation technische Belüftung *f*
as a function of in Abhängigkeit *f* von
as a percentage prozentual, in Prozent
as delivered form Lieferform *f*
as quenched hardness Abschreckhärte *f*
asbestos Asbest *nt*
ascend auffahren, steigen, ansteigen, Aufstieg *m*
ascending gradient Steigung *f*
ascending numerical value aufsteigender Zahlenwert *m*
ascertain ermitteln, abklären, feststellen, ermitteln
ascertainable erfassbar
ascertained systematic deviation festgestellte systematische Abweichung *f*
ascertainment Feststellung *f*, Ermittlung *f*, Prüfergebnisse *ntpl*
ASCII (American Standard Code for Information Interchange) ASCII (amerikanischer Standardcode für den Informationsaustausch)
ASCII keyboard ASCII-Tastatur *f*
A-scope presentation A-Bild *nt*
ash Asche *f*

ash residue Veraschungsrückstand *m*
ashing crucible Veraschungstiegel *m*
ashlar Quader *m*
ashpan Aschenkasten *m*
ashpit Aschenraum *m*
aside zur Seite *f*
ask for anfordern
aslope schief
aspect relation Aspektverhältnis *nt*
asphalt raw powder Asphaltrohmehl *nt*
assemblage Montage *f*, Zusammenbau *m*
assemble einbauen, aufbauen, anbauen, montieren, zusammenstellen, zusammenfügen, zusammenbauen, zusammensetzen, sammeln, paaren
assembled condition Einbauzustand *m*
assembler Monteur *m*, Mechaniker *m*, Installateur *m*
assembling Fügen *nt*, Montage *f*
assembling drawing Zusammenbauzeichnung *f*
assembly Aufbau *m*, Einbau *m*, Fügen *nt*, Paaren *nt*, Montage *f*, Aufstellung *f*, Anordnung *f*, Zusammenbau *m*, Zusammenstellung *f*, Zusammenfügung *f*, Anlage *f*, Aggregat *nt*, Baugruppe *f*, Bauteil *nt*, Verband *m*
assembly bevel Einpressfase *f*
assembly by force fitting Fügen *nt* durch Einpressen
assembly by shrinkage Fügen *nt* durch Schrumpfen
assembly clearance Einbauspiel *nt*
assembly component Fügeteil *nt*
assembly computer Montagerechner *m*
assembly control Montagesteuerung *f*
assembly course Montageablauf *m*
assembly course planning Montageablaufplanung *f*
assembly dimension Einbaumaß *nt*
assembly drawing Zusammenstellungszeichnung *f*
assembly fixture Montagevorrichtung *f*
assembly force Einpresskraft *f*
assembly in layers Lagenbildung *f*
assembly in rows Reihenbildung *f*

assembly instruction Montageanweisung *f*, Montageanleitung *f*, Einbauvorschrift *f*
assembly line Montageband *nt*
assembly manager Montageleitung *f*
assembly master computer Montageleitrechner *m*
assembly order Montageauftrag *m*
assembly part Fügeteil *nt*
assembly parts list Montagestückliste *f*
assembly plant Fertigungsstätte *f*
assembly precaution Anbauvorschrift *f*
assembly process Fügevorgang *m*
assembly program Montageprogramm *nt*
assembly room Versammlungsraum *m*
assembly scaffold Montagegerüst *nt*
assembly shop Montagewerkstatt *f*
assembly stage Montagestufe *f*
assembly temperature Fügetemperatur *f*
assembly tools for screws and nuts Schraubwerkzeug *nt*
assembly warehouse Baugruppenlager *nt*
assembly work Montagearbeiten *fpl*
assess erfassen, bewerten, beurteilen
assessable beurteilbar
assessment Beurteilung *f*, Bewertung *f*, Erfassung *f*
assessment criteria Bewertungsmerkmale *ntpl*
assessment group Bewertungsgruppe *f*
assessment of actual inputs/outputs Ist-Aufnahme *f*
assessment of efficiency Gütebeurteilung *f*
assessment of fractured surface Bruchflächenbeurteilung *f*
assessment scheme Bewertungssystem *nt*
assets Vermögen *nt*
assign zuteilen, zuweisen, anweisen, zuordnen
assign a higher priority höhere Priorität verleihen, Priorität erhöhen
assignment Zuteilung *f*, Zuweisung *f*, Zuordnung *f*, Belegung *f*, Adressenzuordnung *f*, Aufgabe *f*, Auftrag *m*
assignment list Adresszuordnungsliste *f*
assist unterstützen
assistance Unterstützung *f*
assistant Helfer *m*
assisting processes Nebenprozesse *mpl*
associated dazugehörig, zugehörig, zugeordnet, zusammenhängend
associated number zugehörige Zahl *f*
association 1. Zuordnung *f* **2.** *(Waren)* Sortiment *nt*, Warensortiment *nt*
assume annehmen, voraussetzen
assumed direction of cut angenommene Schnittrichtung *f*
assumed load conditions Lastannahme *f*
assumed working plane angenommene Arbeitsebene *f*
assumption Annahme *f*, Vermutung *f*, Voraussetzung *f*
assurance of system reliability Anlagensicherung *f*
assurance program Sicherungsprogramm *nt*
assure sicherstellen
asymmetric contour milling asymmetrisches Konturfräsen *nt*
asymmetric edge preparation unsymmetrische Nahtvorbereitung *f*
asymptotic asymptotisch
asynchronous asynchron, zeitversetzt
asynchronous axis asynchrone Achsen *fpl*
asynchronous balanced mode (ABM) gleichberechtigter Spontanbetrieb *m*
asynchronous mode Asynchronbetrieb *m*
asynchronous motor Asynchronmotor *m*
asynchronous response mode (ARM) Spontanbetrieb *m*
at bei
at excessive speed beschleunigt
at ground level auf dem Erdboden
at high levels hoch gelagert
at inclined T-joint HY-Naht *f* mit Kehlnäten am Schrägstoß
at least mindestens

at one setting in einer Aufspannung *f*
at rest ruhend
at right angles to rechtwinklig zu
at the bottom *(Gefäße)* unten
at the consignee's beim Empfänger *m*
at the customer's premises beim Empfänger *m*
at the direction of the user nach Wahl des Verwenders
at the ends stirnseitig
at the front stirnseitig
at the same time zeitgleich
at the sides längsseitig
at the similar time gleichzeitig
at the top oben
atmosphere Atmosphäre *f*
atmosphere pressure Umgebungsdruck *m*
atmospheric atmosphärisch
atmospheric attack atmosphärische Beanspruchung *f*
atmospheric change Klimawechsel *m*
atmospheric humidity Luftfeuchte *f*
automatic controlled stop Zwangabschaltung *f*
atomic absorption spectroscopy Atomabsorbtionsspektroskopie *f*
atomic laser atomarer Gaslaser *m*
atomic number Ordnungszahl *f*
atomised salt spray Salzsprühnebel *m*
atomize zerstäuben
atomized spray Sprühnebel *m*
atomizing Zerstäuben *nt*
atomizing nozzle Zerstäubungsdüse *f*
atomizing oil burner Ölzerstäubungsbrenner *m*, Ölgebläsebrenner *m*
attach montieren, anbringen, befestigen, aufstecken, anbauen, anschlagen
attach by bolts festschrauben
attach by screws festschrauben
attach by welding festschweißen, anschweißen, aufschweißen
attached piece Ansatzstück *nt*
attached to built-on angebaut
attaching by welding Aufschweißen *nt*
attachment 1. *(Zusatz)* Zubehör *nt*, Zurüstung *f*, Zusatzeinrichtung *f*, Zusatzgerät *nt*, Aufbaugerät *nt* **2.** *(Geräte)* Vorrichtung *f*, Arbeitsvorrichtung *f*, Ausrüstung *f*, Ausstattung *f*, Einrichtung *f* **3.** *(Installation)* Montage *f*, Anbau *m*, Einbau *m*, Anbringung *f*, Befestigung *f*
attachment arm Aufsteckarm *m*
attachment camshaft Hilfssteuerwelle *f*
attachment drawing Anbau-Zeichnung *f*
attachment for planing inclined flat surfaces Schräghobeleinrichtung *f*
attachment for shaping cylindrical work Rundhobeleinrichtung *f*, Rundhobelapparat *m*
attachment for taper milling Kegelfräseinrichtung *f*
attachment position Montagelage *f*
attachment range Anbringungsbereich *m*
attachments Anbauten *mpl*
attack Abtrag *m*, Angriff *m*
attack conditions *pl* Angriffsbedingungen *fpl*
attack-blocking glazing angriffhemmende Verglasung *f*
attain erreichen, erzielen
attainable results of working erreichbares Arbeitsergebnis *nt*
attempt Versuch *m*, versuchen
attend bedienen, pflegen, warten, beaufsichtigen
attendance Wartung *f*, Bedienung *f*, Pflege *f*
attendance time Wartezeit *f*
attendant Bediener *m*
attendant phenomenon Nebenerscheinung *f*
attended beaufsichtigt
attention Aufmerksamkeit *f*, Achtung *f*
attentive aufmerksam
attentiveness Aufmerksamkeit *f*
attenuate dämpfen
attenuate herabsetzen, schwächen, verkleinern
attenuation Dämpfung *f*
attenuation of light Lichtschwächung *f*
attenuation equivalent value Schwächungsgleichwert *m*
attestation Bescheinigung *f*

attestor Prüfperson *f*
attract anziehen
attraction Anziehung *f*
attribute zuordnen
attribute characteristics Attributmerkmale *ntpl*
attribution Zuordnung *f*
audible akustisch
audible signal akustisches Signal *nt*
audible signal device Hörmelder *m*
audible warning akustische Warnung *f*
audio akustisch
audio test Hörtest *m*
audit Audit *nt*; auditieren
auditive akustisch
auditor Auditor *m*
auger Schnecke *f*
auger filling machine Scheckenfüllmaschine *f*
augment vergrößern
augmentation Zunahme *f*
augmented reality erweiterte Realität *f*
austempering region Bainitstufe *f*
austenitizing temperature Austenisierungstemperatur *f*
austenitizing time Austenitisierungsdauer *f*
authority Behörde *f*
authority contact Behördenkontakt *m*
authorization Zulassung *f*, Berechtigung *f*
authorization level Berechtigungsstufe *f*
authorization token Sendeberechtigung *f*
authorize bevollmächtigen, berechtigen, zulassen
authorized zuständig
authorized person Berechtigter *m*, Bevollmächtigter *m*
authorized presentative Bevollmächtigter *m*
automatic screw machine Schraubenautomat *m*
auto-centring Selbstzentrierung *f*, selbstzentrierend
autoclave press Kesselpresse *f*
autocollimating light scanner Autokollimationslichttaster *m*
auto-cycle ... mit automatischem Arbeitsablauf
auto-cycle milling machine Fräsmaschine *f* mit selbsttätigem Arbeitsablauf
auto-excitation Selbsterregung *f*
autogenous technology Autogentechnik *f*
auto-lathe Kleinautomat *m*
automat Automat *m*
automate automatisieren
automated automatisiert, automatisch
automated equipment automatisiertes Gerät *nt*
automated guided vehicle system (AGVS) fahrerloses Transportsystem (FTS) *nt*
automated steering acquisition vorgewählte automatische Lenkung *f*
automatic selbsttätig, automatisch, vollautomatisch, zwangsläufig
automatic actuator Selbststellglied *nt*
automatic advance Vorschubeinrichtung *f*
automatic atomizing oil burner automatischer Ölzerstäubungsbrenner *m*
automatic backlash elimination automatischer *m* Ausgleich des Totganges
automatic bar machine Stangenautomat *m*
automatic boring machine Bohrautomat *m*, Bohranbauautomat *m*
automatic chucking machine Magazinautomat *m*, Futterautomat *m*
automatic circuit-breaker Selbstausschalter *m*
automatic circular saw sharpener Kreissägenschärfautomat *m*
automatic circular-sawing machine Kreissägenautomat *m*
automatic control Regelungstechnik *f*, selbsttätige Regelung *f*, selbsttätige Schaltung *f*
automatic control mechanism Steuerung *f*
automatic control of cutting speeds Schnittgeschwindigkeitsregelung *f*
automatic control regulation Regeln *nt*
automatic control technology Regelungs- und Steuerungstechnik *f*

automatic controller Regler *m*
automatic copier Kopierautomat *m*
automatic copying lathe Kopierdrehautomat *m*, Kopierdrehmaschine *f*
automatic crankshaft lathe Kurbelwellendrehautomat *m*
automatic cycle automatischer (oder selbsttätiger) Arbeitsablauf *m*
automatic cycle control Programmsteuerung *f*
automatic cycle milling machine Pendelfräsmaschine *f*
automatic cycle table control Sprungvorschub *m*
automatic destacking Ausstapelautomatik *f*
automatic disconnection Zwangstrennung *f*
automatic double spindle rotary type miller Zweispindelrundtischfräsautomat *m*
automatic double-head milling machine Doppelspindelautomat *m*
automatic drilling machine Bohrautomat *m*
automatic drum-type turret lathe Trommeldrehautomat *m*
automatic firing device Feuerungsautomat *m*
automatic forming lathe Fassondrehmaschine *f*
automatic forming machine Fassonautomat *m*
automatic gas burner automatischer Gasbrenner *m*
automatic gas firing unit Gasfeuerungsautomat *m*
automatic gear cutting machine Räderfräsautomat *m*
automatic gear hobbing machine Zahnradwälzfräsautomat *m*
automatic gear milling machine Räderfräsautomat *m*
automatic guided vehicle (AGV) Gleis- und fahrerloses Flurförderfahrzeug *nt*
automatic hobber Wälzautomat *m*
automatic keyway and slot milling machine Nutenfräsautomat *m*
automatic lathe Drehautomat *m*

automatic lathe operator Automatendreher *m*
automatic lathe setter Automateneinrichter *m*
automatic lock Selbsthemmung *f*
automatic milling machine Fräsautomat *m*
automatic mode Automatikbetrieb *m*
automatic monitoring automatische Bildübertragung *f*, selbsttätige Überwachung *f*
automatic multicut lathe Vielschnittautomat *m*, Vielstahlautomat *m*
automatic multi-tool lathe Vielstahlautomat *m*
automatic oil firing unit Ölfeuerungsautomat *m*
automatic operation Automatikbetrieb *m*
automatic packaging machine Verpackungsautomat *m*
automatic placement machine Bestückungsautomat *m*
automatic plating unit Galvanisierautomat *m*
automatic positioning Zwangspositionierung *f*
automatic punch machine Lochstreifenschreibmaschine *f*
automatic release Selbstauslösung *f*
automatic request for repetition Wiederholungsanforderung *f*
automatic roughing lathe Schruppautomat *m*
automatic screw machine Schraubenautomat *m*, Formautomat *m*
automatic screw steel Automatenstahl *m*
automatic sequence control Folgeschaltung *f*
automatic shielded-arc welding maschinelles Schutzgasschweißen *nt*
automatic soldering automatisches Löten *nt*
automatic SRM Automatik-RBG *nt*
automatic stacking Einstapelautomatik *f*
automatic stacking system Stapelautomatik *f*
automatic system Automat *m*

automatic thread cutting device Gewindeschneidautomatik *f*
automatic tracer-controlled miller selbsttätige Nachformfräsmaschine *f*
automatic tracer-controlled toolroom machine Nachformfräsautomat *m*
automatic traverse Selbstgang *m*
automatic turret lathe Automatendrehmaschine *f*, Revolverautomat *m*, selbsttätige Revolverdrehmaschine *f*, Automat *m*
automatic turret lathe with auxiliary cam control Automat *m* mit Hilfskurvensteuerung
automatic turret screw machine Revolverautomat *m*
automatic two-spindle rotary type miller Zweispindelrundtischfräsautomat *m*
automatic worm hobbing machine Schneckenfräsautomat *m*
automatic-acting shut-off feature selbsttätig absperrende Sicherung *f*
automatically acting selbsttätig wirkend
automatically acting brake selbsttätig wirkende Bremse *f*
automatically controlled automatisch gesteuert
automatically monitored selbstüberwachend
automatically opening zwangsöffnend
Automatically Programmed Tools APT
automatic closed loop control selbsttätige Regelung *f*
automatic-cycle knee-type milling machine Konsolfräsmaschine *f* mit Sprungtischbewegung
automation Automatisierung *f*, Automation *f*
automation of inventory processes Lagerautomatisierung *f*
automation stage Automatisierungsstufe *f*
automatic chip disposal unit Einrichtung *f* zur automatischen Späneabfuhr
automatize automatisieren

automatic lathe for taper turning Kegeldrehautomat *m*
autonomous selbststeuernd, selbstständig
authorized befugt
autosupervision Selbstüberwachung *f*
auto-test Selbstprüfung *f*, Selbsttest *m*
auto-transformer Spartransformator *m*
auxiliary means Hilfsmittel *nt*
auxiliary zusätzlich, hilfs ...
auxiliary arc Hilfskreisbogen *m*
auxiliary area Hilfsfläche *f*
auxiliary ballast weight Zusatzballastgewicht *nt*
auxiliary body Hilfskörper *m*
auxiliary column Hilfsständer *m*
auxiliary contact point Hilfskontakt *m*
auxiliary device Hilfsgerät *nt*
auxiliary dimension Hilfsmaß *nt*
auxiliary division Hilfsteilung *f*
auxiliary drive Nebenantrieb *m*
auxiliary duty switch Hilfsbetriebsschalter *m*
auxiliary equipment Hilfseinrichtung *f*, Sonderausführung *f*
auxiliary feed Zusatzvorschub *m*
auxiliary functions Hilfsfunktionen *fpl*
auxiliary hoist unit Hilfshubeinrichtung *f*
auxiliary hoist valve Hilfshubventil *nt*
auxiliary level Hilfsebene *f*
auxiliary material Hilfsstoff *m*
auxiliary measuring device Hilfsmittel *nt*
auxiliary operating switch Hilfsbetriebsschalter *m*
auxiliary plane Hilfsebene *f*
auxiliary plane distance Hilfsebenenabstand *m*
auxiliary power Hilfsstrom *m*
auxiliary power port Hilfsversorgungsanschluss *m*
auxiliary power supply Hilfsstromversorgung *f*
auxiliary power switch Hilfsstromschalter *m*
auxiliary production device Fertigungshilfsmittel *f*
auxiliary quantity Hilfsgröße *f*
auxiliary rolling table Rollenbahn *f*

auxiliary seat Hilfssitz *m*
auxiliary sentence Nebensatz *m*
auxiliary standard Hilfsständer *m*
auxiliary upright Hilfsständer *m*
auxiliary wheel Hilfsrad *nt*
auxiliary winding Hilfsstrang *m*
auxiliary actuation Hilfsantrieb *m*
auxiliary drive Hilfsantrieb *m*
auxiliary equipment Zusatzausrüstung *f*
auxiliary rolling table Hilfslaufbahn *f*
availability Verfügbarkeit *f*, Vorhandensein *nt*
availability calculation Verfügbarkeitsermittlung *f*
availability characteristic Verfügbarkeitskenngröße *f*
availability of materials Materialverfügbarkeit *f*
availability of stock for delivery Lieferbereitschaft *f*
availability ratio Verfügbarkeitsgrad *m*
availability test Verfügbarkeitstest *m*
availability verification Verfügbarkeitsnachweis *m*
available vorrätig, verfügbar, vorhanden, lieferbar
available inventory Dispobestand *m*
available process for each unit Betriebsmittelzeit *f* je Einheit
avaluative nicht auswertbar
average mitteln; durchschnittlich; Durchschnitt *m*, Mittelwert *m*
average rate per week Wochendurchschnitt *m*
average sample Durchschnittsprobe *f*
average speed mittlere Geschwindigkeit *f*
average value Durchschnittswert *m*, Mittel *nt*, Mittelwert *m*
averaged level Mittelungspegel *m*
average-value curve Mittelwertskurve *f*
averaging Mittelwertbildung *f*, Mittelung *f*
averaging device Mittelungseinrichtung *f*
averaging tooth traces *pl* ausmittelnde Flankenlinien *fpl*
avoid umgehen, ausweichen, vermeiden, vorbeugen
avoidance Vermeidung *f*
avothane Avothan *nt*
award a contact vergeben
award of contract Vergabe *f*
A-weighted sound power level A-Schallleistungspegel *m*
awkward shaped sperrig
awl Ahle *f*
axes Achsen *fpl*
axes assignment Achszuordnung *f*
axial axial
axial alignment Achsenfluchtung *f*
axial angle axialer Spanwinkel *m*
axial angular impulse Flächenträgheitsmoment *nt*
axial backlash Axialspiel *nt*
axial displacement Achsverschiebung *f*, Axialverschiebung *f*
axial eccentricity Planlaufabweichung *f*
axial engagement axialer Eingriff *m*
axial feed method Axialverfahren *nt*
axial flow fan Axialventilator *m*
axial flow turbo compressor Turboaxialverdichter *m*
axial force Axialkraft *f*
axial grinding axiales Schleifen *nt*
axial inclination Achsenneigung *f*, Achsneigung *f*
axial load fatigue testing Dauerschwingversuch *m* mit axialer Beanspruchung
axial module Axialmodul *nt*
axial pitch Axialteilung *f*
axial pitch variation Axialteilungsabweichung *f*
axial plane Achsenebene *f*, Axialschnitt *m*
axial play Längsspiel *nt*
axial position Geradeaus-Stellung *f*
axial profile Axialprofil *nt*
axial rake axialer Spanwinkel *m*
axial rake angle Rückenwinkel *m*
axial running Planlauf *m*
axial running error Planlauffehler *m*
axial runout Axialschlag *m*
axial section Achsenschnitt *m*
axial skew Achsschränkung *f*, Achsenschränkung *f*
axial slip Planschlag *m*

axial speed Axialgeschwindigkeit f
axial table feed motion axiale Tischbewegung f
axial table feed per stroke axialer Tischvorschub m pro Hub
axial table feed speed axiale Tischvorschubgeschwindigkeit f
axial thrust Längsdruck m
axial vacuum pump Axialvakuumpumpe f
axially aligned achsfluchtend
axially movable achsbeweglich
axially symmetrical rotationssymmetrisch
axially true hole achsengerechte Bohrung f
axis Achse f
axis calibration Messfehlerkompensation f
axis change Achsentauschen nt
axis intersection angle Achsenkreuzungswinkel m
axis lag Nachlauf m
axis motion Achsbewegung f
axis of constraint Führungsachse f
axis of constraint of the gear Radführungsachse f
axis of coordinates Koordinatenachse f
axis of gyration Drehachse f
axis of inclination Neigungsachse f
axis of rotation Rotationsachse f, Drehachse f
axis of symmetry Symmetrieachse f
axis of translation Schubachse f
axis of unit Kipplinie f
axis of work Werkstückachse f
axle Radachse f, Laufachse f
axle collar Achsbund m
axle position Achslage f
axonometric projection axonometrische Projektion f

B b

back hinterlegen, stützen, tragen, unterstützen
back and forth wechselsinnig, vor und zurück
back clearance angle Rückfreiwinkel *m*
back cone Rückenkegel *m*
back cone angle Rückenkegelwinkel *m*
back echo Bodenecho *nt*, Rückwandecho *nt*
back end piloting Führung *f* am Endstück/Räumwerkzeug
back engagement Schnitttiefe *f* einer Schneide
back force Passivkraft *f*
back gearing Zahnradvorgelege *nt*
back gears Rädervorgelege *nt*, Zahnradvorgelege *nt*
back of the rack Regalrücken *m*
back off hinterarbeiten, abschrägen
back out herausziehen, herausfahren
back panel Rückwand *f*
back pin rückwärtiger Raststift *m*
back plane Rückebene *f*
back pressure space Gegendruckraum *m*
back rake Rückspanwinkel *m*, Rückwinkel *m*
back rake angle Spitzenspanwinkel *m*, Rückwinkel *m*
back rest Gegenhalter *m*, Rückenstütze *f*
back slope Spitzenspanwinkel *m*
back stop 1. Durchschubsicherung *f* 2. *(in Tiefenrichtung)* Tiefenanschlag *m*
back stroke Leerhub *m*
back titration Rücktitration *f*
back-to-back Rücken- an- Rücken
back up 1. zurückstoßen, zurücksetzen, gegenhalten, puffern, Puffer *m* 2. Reserve *f* 3. Unterlage *f*
back wall Rückwand *f*
back wall echo train Rückwandechofolge *f*
back wedge angle Rückkeilwinkel *m*
backed off mit Freiwinkel *m*, hinterschliffen
backface rückseitiges Plandrehen *nt*
back-fill material Verfüllmaterial *nt*
back-filled soil angeschütteter Boden *m*
backfiring Rückschlag *m*
backfitting Nachrüstung *f*
backflow Rückfluss *m*
background Hintergrund *m*, Kulisse *f*, Nulleffekt *m*
background data Hintergrunddaten *pl*
background noise Fremdgeräusch *nt*
background pulse count Nulleffektimpulszahl *f*
backing Rückseite *f*, Rücken *m*, zurück, rückwärtig, nach hinten
backing Unterlage *f*, Verstärkung *f*, Unterschicht *f*, Unterstützung *f*
backing block Stützbloch *m*
backing card Trägerpappe *f*
backing film Trägerfolie *f*
backing material Stützkörperwerkstoff *m*, Unterlegstoff *m*
backing off Hinterschliff *m*, Hinterschleifen *nt*, Hinterdrehen *nt*
backing plate Unterlegblech *nt*
backing strip Unterlegstreifen *m*
backing-off attachment Hinterdreheinrichtung *f*
backlash 1. Spiel *nt*, Umkehrspiel *nt*, Nachlauf *m*, Spielraum *m*, Rückwirkung *f* 2. *(Gewinde)* toter Gang *m*
backlash compensation Spielausgleich *m*
backlash determination Spielbestimmung *f*
backlash eliminator Rückschlagsicherung *f*, Spielausgleich *m*
backlash fluctuation Flankenspielschwankung *f*
backlash increase Spielvergrößerung *f*
backlash modification *(bei Zahnflanken)* Spieländerung *f*
backlash system of fits Flankenspielpasssystem *nt*
backlash-free spielfrei, ohne toten Gang *m*

backlash-modifying effect spielverändernder Einfluss *m*
backlash-reducing factors *pl* spielverkleinernde Einflüsse *mpl*
backlocking Sicherheitssperre *f*
backlog Rückstand *m*
backoff Zeitverzögerung *f*
back-off angle Freiwinkel *m*, Hinterschliffwinkel *m*
back-off clearance Freiwinkel *m*, Hinterschliff *m*
backplane Rückwandplatine *f*
backplane bus Rückwandbus *m*
back-radiated heat rückstrahlende Wärme *f*
banking angle Neigungswinkel *m*
backrest Lehne *f*
back-run Rücklauf *m*
back-run safety device Rücklaufsperre *f*
backstreaming of oil Ölrückstrom *m*
backstroke Rückgang *m*, Rückhub *m*
back-up copy Sicherungskopie *f*
back-up duration Pufferdauer *f*
back-up line Halteseil *nt*
back-up ring Stützring *m*
back-up time Pufferzeit *f*
back-up washer Stützscheibe *f*, Stützring *m*
backward rückwärts
backward channel Rückweg *m*
backward drive Rückwärtsfahren *nt*
backward driving direction Fahrtrichtung *f* rückwärts
backward movement Rücklauf *m*
backward path Rückweg *m*
backward rolling motion Rückwälzung *f*
backward schedule Rückwärtsterminplanung *f*
backward tilt Rückwärtsneigung *f*
backwards zurück, rückwärtig, nach hinten
bad schlecht
baffle Prallblech *nt*, Ablenkplatte *f*
baffle core Prallkern *m*
baffle plate Stauscheibe *f*, Zwischenplatte *f*, Trennungsblech *nt*, Prallblech *nt*, Umlenkblech *nt*
bag Sack *m*, Klotzbodenbeutel *m*

bag fill and seal machine Beutelfüll- und -verschließmaschine *f*
bag presenting machine Beutelzuführmaschine *f*
bag sealing machine Beutelverschließmaschine *f*
bainite range Bainitstufe *f*
baking enamel Einbrennlack *m*
baking residue Einbrennrückstand *m*
balance auswuchten, ausrichten, wuchten, abgleichen, kompensieren; Waage *f*, Auswuchtwaage *f*; im Gleichgewicht halten; Gleichgewicht *nt*, Abgleich *m*
balance approved by the Official Department for Weights and Measures Eichamtswaage *f*
balance ledger Saldenliste *f*
balance quality Wuchtgüte *f*
balance screw *(für Uhren)* Körnerschraube *f*
balance type density meter Dichtwaage *f*
balance weight Ausgleichsgewicht *nt*, Gegengewicht *nt*
balanced ausgeglichen
balanced disc stop valve Absperrklappe *f*
balanced station Hybridstation *f*
balanced steel halbberuhigter Stahl *m*
balancing Wuchten *nt*
balancing device Auswuchteinrichtung *f*
balancing fixture Wuchtvorrichtung *f*
bale Ballen *m*
bale clamp Ballenklammer *f*
baled pulp Zellstoffballen *m*
ball Kugel *f*
ball and nipple connection Kugelbuchsenverschraubung *f*
ball and rod bearing lineares Rollenkugellager *nt*
ball bearing Kugellager *nt*
ball bearing table Kugeltisch *m*
ball bearings Kugellagerung *f*
ball catch Kugelverschluss *m*
ball compression test Kugeldruckversuch *m*
ball cup Kugelpfanne *f*
ball drop test Kugelfallversuch *m*

ball end milling – barrel plating

ball end milling Formfräsen *nt*
ball fastener Kugelverschluss *m*
ball handle Ballengriff *m*
ball indentation Kalotte *f*
ball joint Kugelgelenk *nt*
ball oversize Kugelübermaß *nt*
ball screw Kugelumlaufspindel *f*
ball slide Schlitten *m* mit Kugelführung
ball stopper Kugelverschluss *m*
ball transfer table Kugeltisch *m*
ball turning Kugeldrehen *nt*
ball turning lathe Kugeldrehmaschine *f*
ball type lubricating nipple Kugelschmiernippel *m*
ballast Ballast *m*, Zusatzgewicht *nt*
ballast container Ballastbehälter *m*
ball-draw viscosimeter Kugelziehviskosimeter *nt*
ball-end cutter Fräser *m* mit runder Stirn
ball-end mill Schaftfräser *m* mit runder Stirn
ballistic power Perkussionskraft *f*
ball-nose end mill Schaftfräser *m* mit runder Stirn
ball-shaped kugelförmig
band banderolieren, Band *nt*, Banderole *f*
band deviation Streifenauslenkung *m*
band gate Bandausschnitt *m*
band of thermoplastic film Stretchfolienband *nt*
band single-way light barrier Bandeinweglichtschranke *f*
band weld sealing Heizelementrollbandschweißen *nt*, Rollbandschweißen *nt*
banding Binden *nt*
banding machine Banderoliermaschine *f*
bandsaw Bandsäge *f*
bandsaw blade Bandsägeblatt *nt*
bandsaw blade welder Bandsägenschweißgerät *nt*
bandsawing Bandsägen *nt*
bandsawing brazing device Bandsägenhartlötgerät *nt*
bandwidth Bandbreite *f*
bar Strich *m*, Balken *m*, Schiene *f*, Riegel *m*, Stange *f*, Griffstange *f*, Bügel *m*, Stab *m*; verriegeln, absperren
bar armature Stabläufer *m*
bar automatic Stangenautomat *m*
bar axis Stabachse *f*
bar chart Balkendiagramm *nt*
bar chucking Stangenspannung *f*
bar code Barcode *m*, Balken- oder Strichcode *m*
bar code area Barcodefeld *nt*
bar code pin Barcodestift *m*
bar code scanner Strichcodelesestift *m*
bar code stripe Barcodestrich *m*
bar code system Strichcodesystem *nt*
bar code wand Barcodestift *m*
bar coding Strichcodierung *f*
bar diagram Stabdiagramm *nt*
bar drawing Stabziehen *nt*
bar feeding attachment Stangenvorschubeinrichtung *f*
bar guide Werkstoffführung *f*
bar magnet Stabmagnet *nt*
bar material Stangenwerkstoff *m*, Stangenmaterial *nt*
bar rotor Stab *m*
bar stock Rohstange *f*, Stangenmaterial *nt*, Werkstoffstange *f*
bar stock guide Werkstoffführung *f*
bar stock lathe Drehmaschine *f* für Stangenarbeit
bar stop Stangenanschlag *m*
bar wave Stabwelle *f*
bar with wider gripping ends Schulterstab *m*
bar work stangenarbeit *f*
barcode Barcode *m*, Balken- oder Strichcode *m*
bare resistance-type instantaneous heater Blankwiderstands-Durchlauferhitzer *m*
barrel Fass *nt*, Trommel *f*, Skalenhülse *f*, Teilungshülse *f*
barrel body Trommelkörper *m*
barrel cam Trommelkurve *f*
barrel clamp Fassklammer *f*
barrel dryer Trommeltrockner *m*
barrel finishing Poliertrommeln *nt*
barrel nut Zylindermutter *f*
barrel plating Trommelgalvanisierapparat *m*

barrel shape Tonnenform *f*
barrel slide grinding Trommelgleitschleifen *nt*
barrel tuMbling process Trommelpolierverfahren *nt*
barrel with screw cap Spundfass *nt*
barrel-type roll piercing Schrägwalzen *nt* zum Lochen mit tonnenförmigen Walzen
barrier Schranke *f*, Sperre *f*
barrier layer Sperrschichtmantel *m*
bar-shaped stabförmig
base Basis *f*, Auflage *f*, Auflageebene *f*, Fuß *m*, Sockel *m*, Ständer *m*, Stützpunkt *m*, Grundfläche *f*, Grundplatte *f*, Boden *m*, Unterteil *nt*, Unterlage *f*, Fundament *nt*, Gestell *nt*
base band Basisband *nt*
base band emitter Basisband *nt*
base board Fußleiste *f*
base casting Bodenguss *m*
base circle arc Grundkreisbogen *m*
base circle diameter Grundkreisdurchmesser *m*
base circle pitch Grundkreisteilung *f*
base circle rubbing Streifen des Grundkreises
base circle variation Grundkreisabweichung *f*
base clearance angle Basisfreiwinkel *m*
base cylinder director Grundzylindermantellinie *f*
base cylinder envelope Grundzylindermantel *m*
base cylinder normal pitch Grundzylindernormalteilung *f*
base diameter Grundkreisdurchmesser *m*
base frame Unterbau *m*
base helix Kehlschraubenlinie *f*, Grundflankenlinie *f*, Grundzylinderflankenlinie *f*
base helix angle Grundschrägungswinkel *m*
base jaw Grundbacke *f*
base material Trägerwerkstoff *m*, Grundwerkstoff *m*
base metal Grundmetall *nt*
base monitoring Bodenüberwachung *f*
base of a rim Felgenbett *nt*
base of gear tooth Zahnfuß *m*
base of slot Schlitzgrund *m*
base of the neck *(eines Glaskolbens)* Halsansatz *m*
base pitch measurement Eingriffsteilungsmessung *f*
base plate Sockelplatte *f*, Grundplatte *f*, Fundamentplatte *f*, Fußplatte *f*
base slide Unterschlitten *m*
base space width Grundlückenweite *f*
base spiral angle Erzeugungswinkel *m*
base surface Grundfläche *f*
base surface value Grundflächenzahl *f*
base tangent length Zahnweite *f*
base tangent length callipers Zahnweitenmessschraube *f*
base tangent length deviation Zahnweitenabmaß *nt*
base tangent length fluctuation Zahnweitenschwankung *f*
base tangent length micrometer Zahnweitenschieblehre *f*
base tangent length tolerance Zahnweitentoleranz *f*
base tooth thickness Grundzahndicke *f*
base tooth trace Grundflankenlinie *f*
base-circle error Grundkreisfehler *m*
base plate Grundplatte *f*
basic characteristic value Grundkennzahl *f*
basic climate Grundklima *nt*
basic concept Grundgedanke *m*
basic condition Grundzustand *m*
basic cone angle Nennkegelwinkel *m*
basic cone length Nennkegellänge *f*
basic construction unit Baueinheit *f*
basic covered electrode basisumhüllte Elektrode *f*
basic crown gear Bezugsplanrad *nt*
basic cycle Grundzyklus *m*
basic data Ausgangsdaten *pl*
basic depth of thread Höhe *f* des Profildreiecks
basic design Grundgestaltung *f*, Grundaufbau *m*, Grundform *f*, typische Ausführung *f*
basic drive module Basisantriebsmodul *nt*

basic edge shape Grundfugenform *f*
basic equipment Grundausrüstung *f*
basic firebed Grundglut *f*
basic function Grundfunktion *f*
basic gears Grundgetriebe *nt*
basic grid Raster *nt*
basic height of thread Höhe *f* des Profildreiecks
basic insulation Basisisolation *f*
basic load Nennbelastung *f*
basic logistics concept logistisches Grundkonzept *nt*
basic machining time Bearbeitungsgrundzeit *f*
basic mixture Grundmischung *f*
basic nut Einheitsmutter *f*
basic nut system System *nt* der Einheitsmutter
basic part drawing Rohteilzeichnung *f*
basic PC Grund-SPS *f*
basic PC-system SPS-Grundsystem *nt*
basic PLC Grund-SPS *f*
basic population Grundgesamtheit *f*
basic position Grundposition *f*, Grundstellung *f*
basic positioning Grobpositionierung *f*
basic process Grundprozess *m*
basic profile Grundprofil *nt*
basic rack 1. Bezugsprofil *nt* 2. *(Verzahnung)* Bezugszahnstange *f*
basic range Grundreihe *f*
basic rate of taper Nennverjüngung *f*
basic rating Spanvolumen *nt*
basic sheet Rohblatt *nt*
basic single V-butt weld V-Grundfugennorm *f*
basic size Grundmaß *nt*, Nennmaß *nt*
basic specification factor Grundbestimmungsgröße *f*
basic speed Grunddrehzahl *f*
basic status Grundzustand *m*
basic strength Grundfestigkeit *f*
basic system Basissystem *nt*
basic temperature Bezugstemperatur *f*
basic test Grundprüfung *f*
basic title block Grundschriftfeld *nt*
basic tolerance Grundtoleranz *f*
basic truncation *(e. Gewinde)* Grundabflachung *f*
basic unit Grundeinheit *f*

basic-hole Einheitsbohrung *f*
basic-shaft system Einheitswelle *f*
basin form Tümpelform *f*
basis Untergrund *m*, Grundfläche *f*, Basis *f*, Grundlage *f*,
basis for decision Entscheidungsgrundlage *f*
basis for the invitation for tender Ausschreibungsgrundlage *f*
basis material Grundwerkstoff *m*
basis shape Grundform *f*
basket band screening machine Korbbandsiebmaschine *f*
batch Menge *f*
batch Menge *f*, Stückzahl *f*, Charge *f*, Fertigungslos *nt*, Fertigungsauftrag *m*, Los *nt*, Serie *f*, Reihe *f*, Stapel *m*; stapelweise verarbeiten, dosieren
batch allocation Chargenzuordnung *f*
batch casting process Seriengießverfahren *nt*
batch milling Fräsen *nt* in Reihenfertigung
batch number Chargennummer *f*
batch processing Stapelverarbeitung *f*
batch production Chargenproduktion *f*, Serienfertigung *f*, Losgrößenfertigung *f*, Reihenfertigung *f*, reihenmäßige Herstellung *f*
batch production machine Massenfertigungsmaschine *f*, Reihenfertigungsmaschine *f*
batch process Chargenprozess *m*
batch size Losgröße *f*
batch stock control Chargenbestandsführung *f*
batch terminal Stapelverarbeitungsmaterial *nt*
batch variation Losstreuung *f*
batching Stapelung *f*
batching equipment Dosiereinrichtung *f*
bath size Chargengröße *f*
battery Batterie *f*, Akkumulator *m*
battery charge Ladezustand *m*
battery charger Batterieladegerät *nt*
battery charging Batterieladung *f*
battery charging connection Batterieladeanschluss *m*
battery charging system Batterielade-

system *nt*
battery compartment Batterieeinbauraum *m*
battery container Batteriekasten *m*, Batterietrog *m*
battery discharge Batterieentladung *f*
battery drive Batterieantrieb *m*
battery exchange Batteriewechsel *m*
battery level Akkustand *m*
battery lid Batteriedeckel *m*
battery life Batteriestandzeit *f*
battery mass Batteriegewicht *nt*
battery powered batterieelektrisch betrieben
battery powered calculator netzunabhängige Rechenmaschine *f*
battery rated voltage Batterienennspannung *f*
battery space Batterieeinbauraum *m*
battery terminal Batterieklemme *f*
battery type storage tank Batteriebehälter *m*
battery unit Batterieeinheit *f*
battery-charge monitoring Ladezustandskontrolle *f*
battery-charging trip Batterieladefahrt *f*
battery-powered truck Elektroflurförderzeug *nt*
baud Baud
bay Abteilung *f*, Fach *nt*
bay cross bracing vertikale Diagonalaussteifung *f*, Rückenverstrebung *f*
bay divider *(Vorrichtung)* Kanaltrennung *f*
bay division Kanaltrennung *f*, Stellplatzteilung *f*
bay grid Fachraster *nt*
bay ground Lagerfachgruppe *f*
bay position Fachposition *f*
BCD-code (Binary Coded Decimal Code) BCD-Code *m*
be absorbed einleiten
be adapted for eignen
be displaced herausspringen
be in compliance with entsprechen
be invalidated ungültig werden
be lacking fehlen
be liable for *(finanziell)* haften
be made to coincide *(Flächen)* zur Deckung bringen
be missing fehlen
be not order-tied auftragsgebunden sein
be out of action stillstehen
be permanent bleiben
be slow nachlaufen
be tangent tangieren
be within tolerances toleranzhaltig
backed-off hinterdreht
bead Umbördelung *f*; umbördeln, bördeln
bead of varnish Lackwulst *f*
bead seal Stoßnaht *f*
beading Umbördeln *nt*, Sicken *nt*
beak Horn *nt*
beam 1. *(Bauteil)* Supportträger *m*, Ausleger *m*, Träger *m*, Balken *m*, Schiene *f*, Schenkel *m*, Riegel *m*, Ständer *m* 2. *(Licht)* strahlen, Strahl *m*, Lichtstrahl *m*
beam direction change Strahlumlenkung *f*
beam impact test Kerbschlagbiegeversuch *m*
beam interruption Strahlungsunterbrechung *f*
beam method Balkenmethode *f*
beam of light Lichtstrahl *m*
beam processes Strahlverfahren *ntpl*
beam quality performance number Strahlqualitätszahl (K) *f*
beam reversing Strahlumlenkung *f*
beam shaping Strahlgestaltung *f*, Strahlformung *f*, Strahlbildung *f*
beam trammels Stangenzirkel *m*
beam welding Strahlschweißen *nt*
beam-like sample balkenförmige Probe *f*
beams of coherent light gebündelte Lichtstrahlen *f*
bear tragen
bearer Klotz *m*
bearer checking Kufenkontrolle *f*
bearer of characteristics Merkmalsträger *m*
bearer sensing device Klotztaster *m*
bearing 1. Kugellager *nt*, Peilung *f*, Auflager *nt*, Lager *nt*, Lagerung *f* 2. *(Größe, Ausdehnung)* Stützweite *f*

bearing area Auflageebene *f*
bearing bush Lagerbüchse *f*, Lagerschale *f*
bearing capacity Tragfähigkeit *f*
bearing capacity of the ground Bodentragfähigkeit *f*
bearing cone Tragkegel *m*
bearing face Auflageseite *f*, Auflageebene *f*, Auflagefläche *f*
bearing friction value Lagerreibwert *m*
bearing journal Lagerzapfen *m*
bearing journal diameter Lagerzapfendurchmesser *m*
bearing plate Trageplatte *f*
bearing pressure Anpressdruck *m*
bearing seat Lagersitz *m*
bearing seat dimensions Lagersitzabmessungen *fpl*
bearing shell Lagerschale *f*
bearing side Auflageseite *f*
bearing spigot *(Gestängerohre)* Lagerzapfen *m*
bearing spigot diameter Lagerzapfendurchmesser *m*
bearing support Traglager *nt*
bearing surface Auflage *f*, Lagefläche *f*, Anlagefläche *f*, Auflageebene *f*
beat klopfen, schlagen
beater box Mahlbüchse *f*
beater element Mahlkörper *m*
beating stage Mahlstufe *f*
becoming visible Sichtbarwerden *nt*
bed Bett *nt*, Maschinentisch *m*, Unterlage *f*
bed gap Bettkröpfung *f*
bed shear Bettwange *f*
bed slides Bettführungsbahnen *f*
bed turret Bettrevolver *m*
bed ways Bettführungsbahnen *f*
bedding Auflager *nt*, Auflagerbett *nt*, Auflagerung *f*
bedding layer Unterlage *f*
bedewing Betauung *f*
bedplate Grundplatte *f*
bed-type milling machine Fräsmaschine *f* mit feststehendem Bett, Fräsmaschine *f* mit beweglichem Spindelstock, Planfräsmaschine *f*
bedway Bettbahn *f*, Bettführungsbahn *f*
before vor

begin anfangen
beginning Anfang *m*
beginning routine Vorlauf *m*
behaviour Verhalten *nt*
behaviour of the molten pool Schmelzbadverhalten *nt*
Behind Tape Reader Input (btr-input) BRT-Eingang *m*
bell Muffe *f*
bell type pressure gauge Glockenmanometer *nt*
bell-crank drive Winkeltrieb *m*
bellmouthing Vorweite *f*
bell-mouthed mit trichterförmiger Öffnung *f*
bellows type cover harmonikaähnlicher Schutz *m*
bell-type spindle housing Bohrglocke *f*
belonging zugehörig
below darunter, darunterliegend, unter, unten, unterhalb, bis einschließlich
below-table fluoroscopy Untertischdurchleuchtung *f*
belt Trumm *nt*, Band *nt*, Riemen *m*, Gurt *m*
belt band Gurt *m*
belt conveyor Förderband *nt*, Bandförderer *m*, Gurtbandförderer *m*, Transportband *nt*
belt gear Riemengetriebe *nt*
belt grinder Bandschleifmaschine *f*
belt pull Riemenzug *m*
belt pulley Riemenscheibe *f*, Riemenrad *nt*
belt pusher unit Bandvorschubgerät *nt*
belt sander *(für Entrostung)* Bandschleifer *m*
belt sprayer Bandsprühanlage *f*
belt system Gurtsystem *nt*
belt wrap Umschlingungswinkel *m*
bench Werkbank *f*, Maschinenbett *nt* mit Füßen, Gerüst *nt*
bench drilling machine Tiefbohrmaschine *f*, Tischbohrmaschine *f*
bench lathe Tischdrehmaschine *f*, Drehmaschine *f* in Tischausführung, Mechanikerdrehmaschine *f*
bench micrometer Standschraublehre *f*
bench milling machine Planfräsma-

schine *f*, Fräsmaschine *f* mit beweglichem Spindelstock, Werkbankfräsmaschine *f*
bench oiler Ölkanne *f*
bench plate Anreißplatte *f*
bench turret lathe Tischrevolverdrehmaschine *f*
benchmark Vergleichspunkt *m*
benchmark figures Eckdaten *pl*
benchmarking Bewertung *f*
bend Bogen *m*, Krümmung *f*, Knick *m*, Kurve *f*; wölben, beugen, bücken, krümmen, biegen
bend about the line of the notch schwenkbiegen
bend cold in kaltem Zustand biegen
bend off abbiegen
bend out ausbiegen
bend specimen Faltprobe *f*
bend test jig Biegevorrichtung *f*
bend test jig with mandrel Biegeversuch *m* mit Biegestempel
bend test press Biegeprüfpresse *f*
bend test with lateral bend specimens Biegeversuch *m* mit Seitenbiegeproben
bend test with longitudinal bend specimens Biegeversuch *m* mit Längsbiegeproben
bend test with notched transverse bend specimens Biegeversuch *m* mit gekerbten Querbiegeproben
bendable biegsam
bending Biegen *nt*, Biegung *f*, Ausbiegen *nt*, Durchbiegung *f*, Wölbung *f*
bending and straightening machine Biege- und Richtmaschine *f*
bending angle to onset of cracking Biegewinkel *m* bis zum Anriss
bending load Biegebeanspruchung *f*
bending moment Biegemoment *nt*, Wölbmoment *nt*
bending oscillation Biegeschwingung *f*
bending press Biegepresse *f*
bending radius Biegeradius *m*
bending roller Biegerolle *f*
bending strength Biegesteifigkeit *f*, Biegefestigkeit *f*
bending stress Biegespannung *f*, Wölbspannung *f*

bending stress on the tension side Randbiegespannung *f*
bending test apparatus Biegeprüfgerät *nt*
bending tool Biegewerkzeug *nt*
bending without radial force querkraftfreies Biegen *nt*
bend-over test Faltversuch *m*, technologischer Biegeversuch *m*
bent krumm
bent cutting tool for corner work gebogener Eckdrehmeißel *m*
bent finishing tool gebogener Schlichtmeißel *m*, Eckenmeißel *m*
bent locator pin Winkelstecker *m*
bent-over test specimen Winkelprobe *f*
beryllium filter equivalent Berylliumgleichwert *m*
beside neben
bespoke nach Kundenwunsch
best before haltbar bis
best possible value höchstmöglicher Wert *m*
beta distribution Betaverteilung *f*
between zwischen
between-centres turning operation Spitzendreharbeit *f*
between-grind broach life Standzeit *f* des Räumwerkzeuges zwischen zwei Nachschliffen
between-grind life Standzeit *f*
bevel Schräge *f*, Fase *f*, Kantenabschrägung *f*, kegeliger Anschnitt *m*; abschrägen, abkanten, fasen, anfasen, abfasen, schräg
bevel angle Fasenwinkel *m*, Ablenkwinkel *m*
bevel cutting Schrägschnitt *m*
bevel gear Kegelrad *nt*, Kegelradgetriebe *nt*
bevel gear blank Werkstückkegelrad *nt*
bevel gear cutter Kegelradfräser *m*, Kegelradhobelmeißel *m*
bevel gear cutting machine Kegelradverzahnmaschine *f*
bevel gear formed cutter Kegelrad-Formfräser *m*
bevel gear generator Kegelradhobler *m*, Kegelradhobelmaschine *f*, Wälz-

kegelradhobelmaschine *f*
bevel gear hob Kegelradwälzfräser *m*
bevel gear machining Kegelradbearbeitung *f*
bevel gear milling machine Kegelradfräsmaschine *f*
bevel gear pair Kegelradpaar *nt*
bevel gear planer Kegelradhobler *m*
bevel gear planing machine Kegelradhobelmaschine *f*
bevel gear roughing machine Kegelradvorfräsmaschine *f*
bevel gear shaper Kegelradhobelmaschine *f*
bevel gear tooth system Kegelradverzahnung *f*
bevel gear transmission Kegelradgetriebe *nt*
bevel protractor Anlegewinkelmesser *m*
bevelled abgeschrägt, abgefast, kegelig, schief
bevelled edge Schrägkante *f*
bevelled steel straight-edge Messlineal *nt*, Haarlineal *nt*, Kantenlineal *nt*, Messerlineal *nt*
bevelling Fasen *nt*, Abfasen *nt*, Abkanten *nt*, Abfasung *f*
bevelling of the edges Kantenabschrägen *nt*
beware of fernhalten
beyond hinaus, über, jenseits
B-horizon Unterbodenmelioration *f*
bias vorspannen
bias of result systematische Ergebnisabweichung *f*
bias voltage Vorspannung *f*
biaxial biaxial, zweiachsig
biaxial stress condition zweiachsiger Spannungszustand *m*
bicycle screw thread Fahrradgewinde *nt*
bid Angebot *nt*
bidding Angebotsabgabe *f*
bi-directional wechselseitig, in zwei Richtungen, bidirektional
bidirectional shift register Vorwärts-Rückwärts-Schieberegister *nt*
bifurcate gabelförmig verzweigen
bifurcation gabelförmige Verzweigung *f*

big groß, umfangreich
bilateral doppelseitig, zweiseitig
bilet Knüppel *m*
bilk goods Massengut *nt*, Schnittgut *nt*
bill of delivery Lieferschein *m*
bill of materials (BOM) Teileliste *f*, Stückliste *f*
bill of materials explosion Stücklistenauflösung *f*
bimodal distribution zweigipflige Verteilung *f*
bin Kasten *m*, Behälter *m*, Vorratsbehälter *m*
bin card Lagerfachkarte *f*
bin front Lagerfachöffnung *f*, Regalanschlag *m*
bin group Lagerfachgruppe *f*
binary binär
binary character Binärzeichen *nt*
binary circuit element Binärschaltung *f*
binary code Binärcode *m*
binary coded natural BCN
binary combinational element binäres Verknüpfungsglied *nt*
binary de-energizing circuit binärer Abschaltkreis *m*
binary digit Binärziffer *f*
binary digital element Binärschaltung *f*
binary divider Binärteiler *m*
binary image evaluation Binärbildauswertung *f*
binary number Binärzahl *f*
binary signal Binärsignal *nt*
binary stage Binärstufe *f*
binary storage element binäres Speicherglied *nt*
binary switching chain binäre Schaltkette *f*
binary switching-element binäres Schaltglied *nt*
binary-coded binärcodiert
binary-coded decimal (BCD) binärcodierte Dezimaldarstellung *f*
binary-coded decimal code binär codierter Dezimalcode (BCD) *m*
binary-decimal code Binär-Dezimal-Code *m*
bind binden

bind in boards kartonieren
binder Binder *m*, Klemme *f*
binder coating Bindemittelüberzug *m*
binder in adhesive Klebstoff-Grundstoff *m*
binder screw Klemmschraube *f*
binding Binden *nt*
binding agent Bindemittel *nt*
binding bolt Klemmbolzen *m*, Feststellschraube *f*
binding in boards Kartonieren *nt*, kartonierend
binding margin Heftrand *m*
binding nut Gegenmutter *f*
binding resin Bindeharz *m*
binding srength Bindefestigkeit *f*
binding threads *pl* Bindfaden *m*
binding-wet soil haftnasser Boden *m*
binomial binomial
binominal Binom *m*
biodegradation biologischer Abbaugrad *m*
bioler construction Kesselbau *m*
biometric data Biometriedaten *pl*
bipolar zweipolig
bisector of area Flächenschwerpunkt *m*
bismuth Wismut *nt*
bisphenol Bisphenol *nt*
bistable element of the master-slave type IK-Kippglied mit Zweiflankensteuerung *f*
bit 1. Bit *nt* **2.** Bohrschneide *f*, Schneide *f* **3.** *(Nummer)* Binärziffer *f*
bit error rate Bitfehlerrate *f*
bit insert Einsatzwerkzeug *nt*
bit memory Merker *m*
bit rate Bitrate *f*
bit tool Einsatzmeißel *m*
brittle spröde
bit-type insert Einsatzmeißel *m*
bitumen binder Asphaltbinder *m*
bitumen roof sheeting Bitumendachbahn *f*
bitumen tar concrete Asphaltteerbeton *m*
bitumen-resistant sheeting of non-rigid PVC bitumbeständige PVC-weich-Bahn
bituminous surfacing bituminöse Befestigung *f*
bituminous waterproof sheeting for fuse welding Bitumenschweißbahn *f*
build-up of load Auflastentwicklung *f*
bivariate bivariat, zweidimensional
bivariate normal distribution zweidimensionale Normalverteilung *f*
black-and-white schwarz-weiß
black-ground method Schwarzgrundverfahren *nt*
blackheart malleable cast iron schwarzer Temperguss *m*
black-heart malleabilizing process amerikanisches Temperverfahren *nt*
blackout Stromausfall *m*
blade 1. *(Werkzeug)* Messer *nt*, Blatt *nt*, Klinge *f*, Schaufel *f* **2.** *(Messtechnik)* Messschiene *f*
blade clearance Schneidspalt *m*
blade grinding Messernachschliff *m*
blade inserted cutter Fräser *m* mit eingesetzten Messern
blade life Lebensdauer *f* des Messers, Standzeit *f* eines Messers
blade renewable Messerauswechslung *f*
blade taper untere und obere Anschrägung *f*
blank Attrappe *f*, Formular *nt*, Vordruck *m*, Zuschnitt *m*, Rohling *m*, Rohteil *nt*; leer, roh, unbeschaltet,
blank and pierce die Folgeschnitte *mpl*
blank area Leerfläche *f*
blank combustion Blindverbrennung *f*
blank component drawing Rohteilzeichnung *f*
blank determination Blindbestimmung *f*
blank-draw ratio Ziehverhältnis *nt*
blank flange with female face Blindflansch *m* mit Rücksprung
blank flange with male face Blindflansch *m* mit Vorsprung
blank flange with raised face Blindflansch *m* mit Dichtleiste
blank holder Niederhalter *m*
blank measurement Leermessung *f*
blank part Blindteil *nt*
blank solution Blindlösung *f*
blank thickness *(Fließdrücken)* Rohteil-

dicke *f*
blank value Blindwert *m*
blank value determination Blindwertbestimmung *f*
blanking Ausschneiden *nt*, Schneiden *nt*, Stanzteil *nt*
blanking and cutting die Schnittwerkzeug *nt*
blanking machine Stanze *f*
blanks Zuschnitte *mpl*
blast *(Gebläseluft)* Wind *m*
blast furnace Hochofen *m*
blasting Strahlen *nt*
blasting abrasive Strahlmittel *nt*
blasting agent Strahlmittel *nt*
blasting cubicle Strahlkabine *f*
blasting hall Strahlhalle *f*
blasting technology Strahlverfahrenstechnik *f*
bleaching solution Bleichlauge *f*
bleed 1. *(Flüssigkeiten)* anzapfen **2.** *(Gase)* abblasen
bleed hole Abblasöffnung *f*
bleeding of steam Dampfentnahme *f*
blemish Fehler *m*, Makel *m*
blend mischen; Mischung *f*; vermengen, verschmelzen
blend into übergehen in
blind hole Blindloch *nt*, Sackloch *nt*, Grundloch *nt*
blind hole extension Grundlochüberhang *m*
blind process Blindprozess *m*
blind rivet Blindniet *m*
blind spade Blindscheibe *f*
blind tapped hole Gewindegrundloch *nt*
blind-end hole geschlossene Bohrung *f*
blind-hole plate Blindlochscheibe *f*
blink blinken
blinking Blinken *nt*
blinking frequency Blinkfrequenz *f*
blinking stroke Blinkhub *m*
blinking-off condition Blink-Aus-Zustand *m*
blinking-on condition Blink-Ein-Zustand *m*
blister Blister *m*
blister fill and seal machine Blisterfüll- und -verschließmaschine *f*

blister packaging machine Blisterpackmaschine *f*
blister sealing machine Blisterverschließmaschine *f*
blistering Ausblühung *f*
block 1. hemmen, arretieren, sperren, blockieren, verriegeln, absperren, Klemmstück *nt*, Unterlegeklotz *m*, Baustein *m*, Block *m*, Vorlegekeil *m*, Vorlegeleiste *f* **2.** *(Messtechnik)* Maßbild *nt*, Maßblock *m*, Maßklötzchen *nt*, Parallelendmaß *nt* **3.** Feld *nt*, Bereich *m*
block and tackle Flaschenzug *m*
block brake Backenbremse *f*
block control Blocksteuerung *f*
block cycle time Blockzykluszeit *f*, Satz- Zykluszeit *f*
block delete Satzüberlesen *nt*
block diagram Blockschaltbild *nt*, Blockbild *nt*
block drawing Druckstockzeichnung *f*, Klischeezeichnung *f*
block gauge Maßbild *nt*, Maßblock *m*, Maßklötzchen *nt*, Parallelendmaß *nt*
block indexing Schrittteilung *f*, Sprungteilung *f*
block layout Blocklayout *nt*
block method of spacing Schrittteilmethode *f*
block nozzle Blockdüse *f*
block number Satznummer *f*
block of memory Speicherblock *m*
block rest Blocksupport *m*
block section control Blockstreckensteuerung *f*
block soldering Blocklöten *nt*
block storage Blocklagerung *f*, Blocklager *nt*
block subdivision Feldeinteilung *f*
block time Blockzeit *f*
block warehouse Blocklager *nt*
block/sequence search Satzsuchen *nt*
blockage Stauung *f*
blockboard Blockspan *m*
blocked gesperrt
blocked storage Sperrlager *nt*
blocked telltale pipe verstopftes Abzugsrohr *nt*
blocking Arretierung *f*, Sperrung *f*, Sperren *nt*

blocking action Sperrung *f*
blocking position Sperrstellung *f*
block-shear specimen Blockscherprobekörper *m*
blotch *(Öl)* Fleck *m*
blow 1. schlagen, Schlag *m* **2.** *(Luft)* ausblasen
blow gun Ausblasvorrichtung *f*
blow torch Gebläse *nt*
blowback flap Verpuffungsklappe *f*
blow-back flap Explosionsklappe *f*
blow-cut fuse Durchschlagsicherung *f*
blower Lüfter *m*, Gebläse *nt*, Ventilator *m*
blowing fan Gebläse *nt*
blow-off abheben (vi/vt); Abreißen *nt*
blow-off capacity Abblaseleistung *f*
blow-off rate Abblaseleistung *f*, Abblasrate *f*
blow-off valve Sicherheitsventil *nt*
blow-out facility Ausblaseeinrichtung *f*
blowout panel ausblasbare Wand *f*
blowpipe guidance Brennerführung *f*
blowpipe head port Brennerkopfbohrung *f*
blowpipe setting Brennereinstellung *f*
blow-pipe support Brennerstütze *f*
blowtorch for soldering Lötlampe *f*
blue brünieren
blue gel Blaugel *nt*
blue stain Bläuepilz *m*
blueprint Plan *m*
bluish blaustichig
blunt stumpf, unscharf
blunting Abstumpfung *f*
blur (optisch) Unschärfe *f*, unscharf
board 1. aufsteigen (auf), Brett *nt*, Platine *f* **2.** *(Schiene)* Kufe *f*
board checking Kufenkontrolle *f*
bodily injury Körperverletzung *f*
bodily protection Körperschutz *m*
body Körper *m*, Gehäuse *nt*, Rahmen *m*
body contract Masseschluss *m*
body of an oil *(Zähigkeit)* innere Struktur *f* eines Öls
body of rules and regulations Regelwerk *nt*
body part Schachtelkörper *m*
body slot Fräskörperschlitz *m*
body turn Körperdrehung *f*

body-centred raumzentriert
body-fit passgerecht
body-fit bolt Passschraube *f*
bodying *(Öl)* Eindickung *f*
bodywork Aufbau *m*, Aufbauten *mpl*
bogie Drehgestell *nt*
bogie wheels Drehschemelräder *ntpl*
boiled linseed oil Leinölfirnis *m*
boiler Kessel *m*
boiler attendant Kesselwärter *m*
boiler base Kesselsohle *f*
boiler flow temperature Kesselvorlauftemperatur *f*
boiler flue outlet Kesselabgasstutzen *m*
boiler for central heating Heizkessel *m*
boiler framing Kesselgerüst *nt*
boiler output Kesselleistung *f*
boiler output just capable of being maintained aufrechterhaltbare Kesselleistung *f*
boiler return Kesselrücklauf *m*
boiler room Heizraum *m*, Kesselhaus *nt*
boiling fractions *pl* siedende Anteile *mpl*
bolster unterbauen, unterlegen
bolt Schraube *f*, Bolzen *m*, Durchgangsschraube *f*, Riegel *m*; verschrauben, verbinden, anschrauben, befestigen, sperren
bolt bar Bolzenstange *f*
bolt clamping Bolzenspannung *f*
bolt cutter Bolzenschere *f*
bolt down festschrauben, aufspannen
bolt finished to size Fertigschraube *f*
bolt for looms Webmaschinenschraube *f*
bolt force Schraubenkraft *f*
bolt hole spacing Lochabstand *m*
bolt joint Schraubenverbindung *f*
bolt milling machine Bolzenschaftfräsmaschine *f*
bolt on aufschrauben
bolt retaining device Schraubensicherung *f*
bolt thread Außengewinde *nt*
bolt thread cutting machine Bolzengewindeschneidmaschine *f*
bolt threaded pin Bolzen *m*, Gewindebolzen *m*

bolt washer Unterlegscheibe *f*, Bolzenscheibe *f*
bolt with plain shaft length Schraube *f* mit gewindefreier Schaftlänge
bolt with reduced shank Schraube *f* mit dünnem Schaft
bolt with waisted shank Schraube *f* mit Dehnschaft
bolt/nut fastening Schrauben-Muttern-Verbindung *f*
bolted bolzenbefestigt
bolted fastening Verbindung *f* mittels Schrauben, Schraubverbindung *f*
bolted fastening with waisted shank Schraubenverbindung *f* mit Dehnschaft
bolted joint Schraubverbindung *f*
bolting Verschraubung *f*, Befestigung *f*
bomb method Bombenverfahren *nt*
bond Verbund *m*, Bindung *f*, Verband *m*; verkleben, verbinden, binden
bond area Klebfläche *f*
bond defect Bindungsfehler *m*
bond energy Bindungsenergie *f*
bond structure Bindungsaufbau *m*
bond type appropriate to the type of duty beanspruchungsgerechte Bindung *f*
bonded abrasive grain gebundenes Schleiferkorn *nt*
bonded joint Klebung *f*
bonded metal joint Metallklebung *f*
bonded nozzle Klebstutzen *m*
bonded single lap joint einschnittig überlappte Klebung *f*
bonded socket joint Klebmuffe *f*
bonded specimen Verbundprobe *f*
bonded tyre wheel Vollgummirad *nt*, festverbundene Bereifung *f*
bonding Verklebung *f*, Verbindung *f*, Bekleben *nt*
bonding agent Haftmittel *nt*
bonding characteristic Verankerungsmöglichkeit *f*
bonding condition Klebbedingung *f*
bonding force Bindungskraft *f*
bonding impedance Anschlussimpedanz *f*, Verbindungsimpedanz *f*
bonding instruction Klebanleitung *f*
bonding material Bindemittel *nt*
bonding of bodies by means of

bonding foil Kleben *nt* von Körpern mittels Klebfolie
bonding surface Klebstelle *f*, Bindefläche *f*, Haftfläche *f*
bonnet Kappe *f*
book buchen
book in einbuchen
book incoming goods Wareneingang buchen
booking Buchung *f*
booking date Buchungsdatum *nt*
booking number Buchungsnummer *f*
Boolean aussagenlogisch
Boolean algebra Aussagenlogik *f*
Boolean data Boolesche Daten *pl*
Boolean term boolesche Verknüpfung *f*
Boolean variable Boolesche Variable *f*
boom Ausleger *m*, Tragdorn *m*
boost verstärken
booster Kompressor *m*, Gebläse *nt*, Zusatztriebwerk *nt*, Zusatzverstärker *m*
booster pump Hilfspumpe *f*, Vorpumpe *f*
borax Borax *nt*
boraxed geboraxt
border Grenze *f*, Rand *m*; umbördeln, bördeln, einfassen, begrenzen
border of system Systemgrenze *f*
border off application Anwendungsgrenze *f*
bordering Bördeln *nt*
bordering closure Bördelverschluss *m*
bordering machine Bördelmaschine *f*
bordering tool Bördeleisen *nt*
bore Bohrung *f*, Bohrloch *nt*, aufbohren, ausdrehen, innenausdrehen, bohren, innendrehen
bore correction Kalibrierkorrektur *f*
bore diameter Bohrungsdurchmesser *m*, Achslochdurchmesser *m*
bore envelope Bohrungsmantelfläche *f*
bore hole Bohrung *f*, Bohrloch
bore of pipe lichte Weite *f* eines Rohres
bore size Bohrungsdurchmesser *m*, lichte Weite *f*
borehole Bohrung *f*, Bohrloch *nt*, Aussparung *f*, Ausdrehung *f*
boring Bohren *nt*, Vollbohrung *f*, Innenausdrehen *nt*, Innendrehen *nt*, Aufbohren *nt*, Ausbohren *nt*, Ausdre-

hen *nt*
boring and cutting-off machine Dreh-Bohr-Abstechbank *f*
boring and facing lathe Bohr- und Plandrehmaschine *f*
boring and facing mill Ausbohr- und Stirndrehmaschine *f*
boring attachment *(Innenausdrehen)* Bohreinrichtung *f*
boring bar Bohrstange *f*, Ausbohrstange *f*
boring bit Innenausdrehzahn *m*
boring centre Bohrzentrum *nt*
boring chip Innenausdrehspan *m*, Vollbohrspan *m*
boring chuck Innendrehfutter *nt*
boring fixture Bohrvorrichtung *f*
boring head Bohrkopf *m*, Aufbohrkopf *m*, Bohrsupport *m*, Bohreinrichtung *f*
boring machine Bohrmaschine *f*
boring machine operator Bohrer *m*, Bohrmaschinenbediener *m*
boring machine table Aufspanntisch *m*
boring machines *pl* Bohrmaschinen *fpl*
boring mill Bohrwerk *nt*
boring out Ausbohren *nt*
boring practice Bohrtechnik *f*
boring quill Bohrpinole *f*
boring sleeve Bohrpinole *f*
boring spindle Bohrspindel *f*
boring spindle head Bohrspindelkopf *m*
boring tool Bohrwerkzeug *nt*, Bohrmeißel *m*, Bohrstange *f*, Aufbohrmeißel *m*, Ausdrehmeißel *m*, Bohrstahl *m*, Bohrschlichtstahl *m*, Innendrehmeißel *m*, Innenausdrehmeißel *m*, Innendrehwerkzeug *nt*
boring tool for corner work Eckbohrmeißel *m*, Innenseitenmeißel *m*
boring tool for corner work abgesetzter Bohrmeißel *m*
boring tool holder Bohrmeißelhalter *m*, Bohrstangenhalter *m*, Innendrehmeißelhalter *m*
boring unit Bohreinheit *f*
borings Span *m*, Bohrspäne *f*

boron Bor *nt*
boron carbide Borkarbid *nt*
boron fibre Borfaser *f*, Borfasergelege *nt*
boron fibre reinforced moulding material borfaserverstärkter Formstoff *m*
boron treatment Borieren *nt*
boss Nabe *f*, hervorstehendes Stück *nt*
boss axis Nabenachse *f*
boss of a hub Nabenstirnfläche *f*
boss spacing Nabenabstand *m*
both beide
both-way beidseitig
bottle Flasche *f*
bottleneck Engpass *m*, Verkehrsstau *m*
bottleneck analysis Engpassanalyse *f*
bottling Halsen *nt*, Einhalsen *nt*
bottling device Ablöscheinrichtung *f*
bottom Sohle *f*, Fuß *m*, Boden *m*, unteres Ende, Unter ...
bottom carriage Bodentraverse *f*
bottom clearance reduction Kopfspielverkleinerung *f*
bottom die Untergesenk *nt*
bottom edge Unterkante *f*
bottom flange Unterflansch *m*
bottom force Unterteil *nt*
bottom hole Blindloch *nt*, Sackloch *nt*, Grundloch *nt*
bottom hook unterer Gabelhaken *m*
bottom limit untere Endstellung *f*
bottom of the groove Rillengrund *m*, Seilgrund *m*
bottom of the pipe trench Rohrgrabensohle *f*
bottom of the tooth space Zahngrund *m*, Zahnlückengrund *m*
bottom pan Bodenteller *m*
bottom part Unterteil *nt*
bottom plate Bodenblech *nt*, Fundamentplatte *f*, Bodenplatte *f*, Grundplatte *f*
bottom rail Fahrschiene *f*
bottom side Unterseite *f*
bottom slide Unterschieber *m*, Untersupport *m*, Planschlitten *m*
bottom surface Unterkante *f*
bottom wrap Fußwicklung *f*
bottom-pour Stopfenpfanne *f*

bought parts Zukaufteile *ntpl*
bounce Sprung *m*; springen
bounce against prallen gegen
bounce on aufprallen
bouncing Aufprall *m*, Rückprall *m*
bound 1. begrenzen, abgrenzen, gebunden 2. Sprung *m*; springen
boundary Grenze *f*, Umgrenzung *f*, Begrenzung *f*, Rand *m*
boundary case Grenzfall *m*
boundary conditions Randbedingung *f*
boundary line Begrenzungslinie *f*
boundary of the weld Nahtbegrenzung *f*
boundary profile Hüllprofil *nt*
boundary ring Begrenzungsring *m*
boundary stress Randspannung *f*
boundary surface Grenzfläche *f*, Mantel *m*
boundary surfaces of the space Raumumschließungsflächen *fpl*
boundary value Randbedingung *f*
bow Bogen *m*, Krümmung *f*, Bügelgriff *m*, Bügel *m*; beugen
bow nut Korbmutter *f*
bowl Becken *nt*, Schale *f*, Napf *m*
bow-type drawing pen Zweizungenziehfeder *f*
box Schachtel *f*, Gehäuse *nt*, Kiste *f*, Kasten *m*, Zelle *f*, Kabine *f*, Behälter *m*, Verpackung *f*
box column Kastenständer *m*
box column drilling machine Kastenständerbohrmaschine *f*, Ständerbohrmaschine *f*
box nut Überwurfmutter *f*
box of shape Formkasten *m*
box pallet Boxpalette *f*
box section rechteckige Form *f*
box section overarm Gehäuse *nt*
box section process Kastenformverfahren *nt*
box spanner Steckschlüssel *m*
box table Kastentisch *m*
box-column design Kastenständerbauart *f*
box-column-type radial drilling machine Kastenständerradialbohrmaschine *f*
box-section bed Kastenbett *nt*

box-section slab Platte *f* aus Hohlkasten
box-section type floor slab Aufspannart *f* in Kastenbauart
box-type column Kastenständer *m*
brace verspannen, verankern, abspannen, absteifen, aussteifen, versteifen, verstreben, verklemmen, klammern, unterbauen; Verstrebung *f*, Verband *m*, Klammer *f*, Aussteifung *f*, Brücke *f*, Stütze *f*, Strebe *f*
brace pin Spannstift *m*
bracing Verstrebung *f*, Verband *m*, Verankerung *f*, Verspannung *f*, Abspannung *f*, Versteifung *f*, Strebe *f*
bracing member Versteifungselement *nt*
bracing rip Rippe *f* zum Versteifen
bracket Schelle *f*, Haken *m*, Klammer *f*, Träger *m*, Stütze *f*, Arm *m*
bracket plate Befestigungsplatte *f*
bracket table Konsolführung *f*
braided hose umflochtener Schlauch *m*
brake verzögern, abbremsen, bremsen; Bremse *f*
brake application delay Bremsenansprechverzögerung *f*, Einfallzeit *f* der Bremse
brake component Bremsteil *nt*
brake drum Bremstrommel *f*
brake life Bremsenstandzeit *f*
brake lining Bremsbelag *m*
brake mark Bremsspur *f*
brake motor Bremsmotor *m*
brake pad Bremsbacke *f*
brake reaction time Einfallzeit *f* der Bremse
brake service life Bremsenstandzeit *f*
brake shoe Bremsschuh *m*
brake type catching device Bremsenfangvorrichtung *f*
braking Abbremsung *f*, Verzögerung *f*
braking and locking device Feststellvorrichtung *f*
braking characteristics Bremsverhalten *nt*
braking control Bremssteuerung *f*
braking deceleration Bremsverzögerung *f*
braking device Bremseinrichtung *f*,

Abbremseinrichtung *f*, Feststellvorrichtung *f*
braking distance Bremsweg *m*
braking force Bremskraft *f*
braking method Bremsverfahren *nt*
braking path Bremsweg *m*
braking procedure Bremsvorgang *m*
braking shoe Bremsbacke *f*
braking system Bremsanlage *f*, Bremssystem *nt*
braking time Bremszeit *f*
braking to stop Haltebremsung *f*, Stoppbremsung *f*
braking torque Bremsmoment *m*
braking work Bremsarbeit *f*
branch Zulauf *m*, Abzweig *m*, Abzweigung *f*, Zweig *m*; verzweigen, abzweigen
branch address Verzweigungsadresse *f*
branch if verzweigen wenn
branch instruction Verzweigungsbefehl *m*
branching Verzweigung *f*
branching crack verästelter Riss *m*
branching factor Verzweigungsgrad *m*
branching point Verzweigungsstelle *f*
branch-off units Verzweigungselemente *ntpl*
brand Marke *f*, Sorte *f*
brass Messing *nt*
brass finisher's lathe Leitspindeldrehmaschine *f*
brass-coloured messingfarben
braze hartlöten
braze welding Lotschweißen *nt*
brazed conical nipple Lötkegelbuchse *f*
brazed or soldered seam weld gelötete Liniennaht *f*
brazed union Lötverschraubung *f*
brazed-on tip hart aufgelötetes Plättchen *nt*
brazed-tip carbide tool Werkzeug *nt* mit hart aufgelöteten Hartmetallplättchen
brazed-tip tool Werkzeug *nt* mit hart aufgelöteter Schneide
brazing Hartlöten *nt*, Schweißlöten *nt*
brazing alloy *(über 450 °C)* Lot *nt*, Hartlot *nt*

brazing seam shrinking eingefallene Lötnaht *f*
brazing spelter Messinghartlot *nt*
brazing under an inert protective gas Löten *nt* unter inertem Schutzgas
brazing with preshaped filler Hartlöten *nt* mit Lotformteilen
breadth Weite *f*
break 1. Bruch *m*, Riss *m*, Sprung *m*; zerreißen, abreißen, reißen, zerbrechen, unterbrechen, abkanten, brechen, abscheren 2. Pause, Unterbrechung *f* 3. *(Werkzeug)* Abkantpresse *f*
break away losbrechen, ausbrechen
break contact Öffner *m*
break contact element Öffner *m*
break down 1. ablängen, zerlegen, gliedern 2. *(Fehler)* zertrümmern, durchschlagen, zusammenstürzen, versagen, ausfallen
break duration Pausendauer *f*
break line Bruchlinie *f*
break out ausbrechen, herausreißen
break the circuit ausschalten
break the corners anfasen
break through durchbrechen
break time Ausschaltzeit *f*
break up *(Späne)* aufreißen
break up into a fine mist zerstäuben
break up into segments reißen von Spänen
breakage Bruch *m*
breakage cut-out Bruchsicherung *f*
breakage point Bruchstelle *f*
breakdown Ausfall *m*, Versagen *nt*, Betriebsstörung *f*, Störung *f*, Störfall *m*, Abbruch *m*, Durchschlag *m*, Gliederung *f*, Zusammenbrechen *nt*; zusammenbrechen
breakdown diode Zenerdiode *f*
breakdown in electrolyte Elektrolytdurchschlag *m*
breakdown in parts of the system Teilsystemausfall *m*
breakdown of the system Anlagenstillstand *m*
breakdown potential Durchbruchspotential *nt*
breakdown torque Kippmoment *nt*
breakdown voltage Durchschlagspan-

nung *f*
breaking 1. Bruch *m*, Bruchstelle *f*, Brechen *nt*, Zerreißen *nt* **2.** Zerlegen *nt* **3.** *(Bleche)* Abkanten *nt*
breaking by bending Biegebrechen *nt*
breaking by twisting Drehbrechen *nt*
breaking current Ausschaltstrom *m*
breaking elongation Bruchdehnung *f*
breaking force Bruchkraft *f*
breaking length Reißlänge *f*
breaking load Bruchlast *f*, Reißkraft *f*
breaking of the corners Kantenbrechen *nt*
breaking off Abbrechen *nt*
breaking resistance Bruchwiderstand *m*
breaking the corners Anfasen *nt*
breaking voltage Abschaltspannung *f*
breaking-down Zusammensturz *m*
break-make before brake contact Öffnerwechsel *m*
break-make-brake contact Öffnerwechsel *m*
break-proof bruchsicher
breast drill Bohrgewinde *nt*, Brustbohrmaschine *f*
breast planer Blechkantenhobelmaschine *f*, Grubenhobelmaschine *f*
breather Atmungsventil *nt*, Entlüftungsventil *nt*, Luftventil *nt*, Schnüffelventil *nt*
breather line Entlüftungsleitung *f*
breech cover Verschlusskappe *f*
Brewster window Brewsterfenster *m*
brick clamp Steinklammer *f*
brick setting Einmauerung *f*
bridge Brücke *f*, Portal *nt*, überbrücken
bridge carousel Brückenpaternoster *nt*
bridge crane Brückenkran *m*
bridge plate Überladebrücke *f*
bridge rectifier Brückengleichrichter *m*
bridge type vertical carousel Brückenpaternoster *nt*
bridgeover Überbrückung *f*
brief kurz
brief description Kurzbeschreibung *f*
bright hell, leuchtend
bright drawn tube zugblankes Rohr *nt*
bright nickel coat Glanznickelschicht *f*
bright nickel plating Glanzvernickelung *f*
bright switching Hellschaltung *f*
brightness Helligkeit *f*
bright glänzend
Brinell hardness Brinellhärte *f*
bring a standstill zum Stillstand bringen
bring about verursachen
bring into line angleichen
bring point Bringplatz
bring to rest anhalten, stillsetzen
bristle brush Borstenpinsel *m*
brittle brüchig
brittle chip Kurzspan *m*, spritziger Span *m*
brittle crack Sprödriss *m*
brittle-rigid cellular plastics sprödharter Schaumstoff *m*
broach Räumwerkzeug *nt*, Räummaschine *f*, Räumnadel *f*, räumen, Kaliberdorn *m*
broach and centre machine Räum- und Zentriermaschine *f*
broach assembly zusammengesetztes Räumwerkzeug *nt*
broach carrier Räumwerkzeugträger *m*
broach cutting section Schneidenteil *m* des Räumwerkzeuges
broach front pilot Führungsstück *nt* an der Aufnahme des Räumwerkzeuges
broach handling Zubringung *f* des Räumwerkzeuges
broach handling unit Zubringeinrichtung *f* an der Räummaschine
broach holder Räumnadelhalter *m*
broach insert Schneideinsatz *m* für das Räumwerkzeug
broach lifter cylinder Räumnadelanhebezylinder *m*
broach pull down machine Ziehräummaschine *f* mit nach unten gehenden Arbeitsgang
broach pull head Werkzeughalter *m* des Zugorgans der Räummaschine
broach puller Ziehwerk *nt* an der Räummaschine
broach ram Räumschlitten *m*, Räumstößel *m*
broach slide Räumschlitten *m*
broach tool Räumwerkzeug *nt*

broached surface geräumte Fläche *f*, Arbeitsfläche *f* beim Räumen
broacher Räummaschine *f*
broach-handling slide Anhebeschlitten *m*, Räumwerkzeugzubringerschlitten *m*
broaching Räumen *nt*
broaching fixture Räumvorrichtung *f*
broaching job Räumarbeit *f*
broaching machine Räummaschine *f*
broaching operation Räumarbeit *f*
broaching pass Räumdurchgang *m*
broaching rate Stückzahl *f* beim Räumen
broaching roam Räumstößel *m*
broaching setup Räumaufspannung *f*
broaching tool Räumwerkzeug *nt*
broaching tools Räumwerkzeuge
broaching work Räumarbeit *f*
broachings *pl* Räumspäne *mpl*
broad weit
broad band Breitband *nt*
broad band noise breitbandiges Geräusch *nt*
broad cut finishing Breitschlichten *nt*
broad cutting tool Breitmeißel *m*
broad finish cutting Breitschlichtschneiden *nt*
broad finish milling Breitschlichtfräsen *nt*
broad finishing tool Breitschlichtmeißel *m*
broad nose finish tool Breitschlichtmeißel *m*
broad nose tool Breitmeißel *m*
broadband breitbandig
broadband transmission Breitbandübertragung *f*
brokes *pl* Ausschuss *m*, Abfälle *mpl* bei der Verarbeitung
bronze brünieren, Bronze *f*
bronze plated by immersion tauchverbronzt
bronze-plate verbronzen
broomy divergierend
brown coal Braunkohle *f*
brown coal range Grudeherd *m*
brownout Unterspannung *f*, Spannungsabfall *m*
browsing Blättern *nt*

brush Bürste *f*, bürsten
brush rocker Bürstenbrücke *f*
brush support Bürstenbrücke *f*
brushing Abpinseln *nt*, Anstreichen *nt*
brushless bürstenlos
brush-like fracture besenförmiger Bruch *m*
gross demand Bruttobedarf *m*
B-scope presentation B-Bild *nt*
bubble through hindurchperlen
bubbles Luftblasen *fpl*
bucket Eimer *m*
buckle Spange *f*, Schnalle *f*; verziehen, aufbeulen, verbiegen, krümmen, knicken, werfen
buckling Knick *m*, Knickung *f*, Ausknicken *nt*, Beulen *nt*
buckling arm Knickarm *m*
buckling arm robot Knickarmroboter *m*
buckling coefficient Knickzahl *f*
buckling length Knicklänge *f*
buckling length coefficient Knicklängenbeiwert *m*
buckling mechanism Knickmechanismus *m*
buckling point Knickpunkt *m*
buckling resistance Beulfestigkeit *f*
buckling strength Knickfestigkeit *f*
buckling stress Knickbelastung *f*
buckling test Knickversuch *m*
bucky floor stand Rasterbodengerät *nt*
bucky table Rasteraufnahmetisch *m*
bucky wall stand Rasterwandgerät *nt*
budget Kostenrahmen *m*
budgeting Budgetierung *f*
buff polierläppen
buffer puffern, zwischenspeichern, Puffer *m*
buffer area onhand quantity Vorzonenbestand *m*
buffer bottle Pufferflasche *f*
buffer characteristic Pufferkennlinie *f*
buffer collision Pufferfahrt *f*
buffer end forces Pufferendkräfte *fpl*
buffer forces Pufferkräfte *fpl*
buffer function Pufferfunktion *f*
buffer impact Pufferstoß *m*
buffer inventory Pufferlager *nt*
buffer layer Pufferschicht *f*

buffer medium Puffermedium *nt*
buffer memory Zwischenspeicher *m*
buffer path Pufferweg *m*
buffer plate Pufferplatte *f*
buffer size Puffergröße *f*
buffer stock Pufferbestand *m*
buffer storage Zwischenspeicher *m*
buffer time Pufferzeit *f*
buffer zone Pufferzone *f*
buffered gepuffert
buffered mode Pufferbetrieb *m*
buffering Puffern *nt*, Pufferung *f*
bufferless pufferlos
buffing Polierläppen *nt*
bug Fehler *m*
build 1. bauen, einbauen, aufbauen, errichten, ausführen 2. *(schwingen)* aufschaukeln
building Gebäude *nt*
building block Baukasten *m*
building block system Baukastensystem *nt*
building brick machine tool Werkzeugmaschine *f* nach Baukastenweise
building deformation Gebäudeverformung *f*
building designer Bauplaner *m*
building form Gebäudeform *f*
building inspectorate approval bauaufsichtliche Zulassung *f*
building installations Haustechnik *f*
building level Gebäudeebene *f*
building part Gebäudeteil *nt*
building site production Baustellenfertigung *f*
building structure Hallenkonstruktion *f*
building up flame spraying Auftragspritzen *nt*
building up of the cutting edge Schneidenaufbau *m*
build-up cycle Einschwingspiel *nt*
built in eingebaut
built up in layers schichtweise aufgebaut
built-in burner Einbaubrenner *m*
built-in micrometer Einbaumessschraube *f*
built-in spot light Platzleuchte *f*
built-on aufgebaut

built-up cutting edge Aufbauschneide *f*, Schneidenansatz *m*
built-up teeth *pl (Räummaschine)* Zahnungseinsätze *mpl*
built-up type cutter Fräser *m* mit eingesetzten Zähnen
bulb condenser Birnenkühler *m*
building mass factor Baumassenzahl *f*
bulge Aufwölbung *f*; aufweiten, aufbeulen
bulge height Wölbhöhle *f*
bulging Knickbiegen *nt*, Ausbauchen *nt*
bulk Schüttgut *nt*, geschüttet
bulk emptying Schüttentleerung *f*
bulk goods Schüttgut *nt*
bulk material Massengut *nt*, Schüttgut *nt*
bulk modulus of elasticity Kompressionsmodul *nt*
bulk polymer Massepolymerisat *nt*
bulk production Fertigung *f* größerer Mengen
bulk sample Sammelprobe *f*
bulk sampling Sammelprobenentnahme *f*
bulk transport Schüttguttransport *m*
bulk volume Schüttvolumen *nt*
bulk-head union elbow Winkelschrottverschraubung *f*
bulkhead union with riveting flange Annietschottstutzen *f*
bulky sperrig
bulky goods Sperrgut *nt*
bumper Prallwand *f*, Bumper *m*
bunch Pulk *m*; einem Pulk bilden aus
bunching Pulkbildung *f*
bundle Bündel *nt*, Verbund *m*, Bund *m*, Stapel *m*, Verbundstapel *m*; bündeln
bundle of laminations Blechpaket *nt*
bundle of stator laminations Ständerblechpaket *nt*
bundle of stator plates Ständerblechpaket *nt*
bundle storage Bundlagerung *f*
bundled coil *(von Rohren)* Ringbund *m*
bundled layer gebundene Schicht *f*
bundling Verbundstapelung *f*, Bündeln *nt*
bung Spund *m*
bungle Pfusch *m*

buoyancy units schwimmende Geräte *ntpl*
buoyancy-flotation method Auftriebmethode *f*
buoying upwards Aufschwimmen *nt*
burden Traglast *f*
burette stopcock with angular bore Bürettenhahn *m* mit Winkelbohrung
burglar resistance Einbruchhemmung *f*
buried sewer Grundleitung *f*
burificate abzweigen
burification Abzweigung *f*
burn Brandfleck *m*, Verbrennung *f*; brennen, verbrennen
burn constricted eingeschnürt brennen
burn in einbrennen
burn out durchbrennen, durchbrechen; Durchbrennen *nt*
burn without leaving any residue rückstandslos verbrennen
burner Brenner *m*
burner crosspiece Brennergeschränk *nt*
burner cup wall Brennertopfwand *f*
burner heat load Brennerwärmebelastung *f*
burner nozzle Brennerermüdung *f*
burner rating Brennerleistung *f*
burner start-up Brennerstart *m*
burner thermal output Brennerwärmeleistung *f*
burner valve Brennerarmatur *f*
burning Verbrennung *f*, Brand *m*
burning behaviour Brandverhalten *nt*
burning cabinet Brennkasten *m*
burning down time Planbrennzeit *f*
burning sequence Brennablauf *m*
burning speed Brenngeschwindigkeit *f*
burnish glätten, polieren, polierdrücken, bräunen, brünieren
burnisher Glättzahn *m*
burnishing Polierdrücken *nt*, Polierrollen *nt*
burnishing broach glättende Räumnadel *f*
burnishing effect Glättwirkung *f*
burnt gas temperature Rauchgastemperatur *f*

burnt-through weld spot durchgebrannter Schweißpunkt *m*
burn-up Abbrand *m*
burr Grat *m*, Schnittgrat *m*, Schleifgrat *m*; putzen, abgraten, entgraten
burred gratig
burring Entgraten *nt*, Abgraten *nt*
burring chisel Abgratmeißel *m*
burr-removing device Entratungseinrichtung *f*
burr-removing machine Abgratmaschine *f*
burst zersprengen, platzen, bersten, springen, zerreißen, reißen, Zerreißen *nt*
bursting Bersten *nt*
bursting diaphragm Berstmembran *f*
bursting disc Reißscheibe *f*, Berstscheibe *f*
bursting pressure test Berstdruckprüfung *f*, Berstdruckversuch *m*
bursting resistance Berstwiderstand *m*
burying Einerdung *f*
bus Bus *m*
bus bar Stromschiene *f*
bus system Bussystem *nt*
bus-capable busfähig
bush Muffe *f*, Buchse *f*, ausfüttern
bush on aufbüchsen
bushing Ausfüttern *nt*, Buchse *f*
bushing plate Buchsenplatte *f*
business line Bus *m*
butadiene-acrylonitrile rubber Butadien-Acrylnitril-Vulkanisat *nt*
butane Butangas *nt*
butt aneinanderstoßen, anstoßen, stumpf aneinanderfügen
butt joint Stoßfuge *f*, Stoßnaht *f*
butt joint with double-V weld Stumpfstoß *m* mit X-Naht
butt joint with flash Stumpfstoß *m* mit Gratnaht
butt press welding Pressstumpfschweißen *nt*
butt seam Stoßnaht *f*
butt weld Stoßnaht *f*, stumpfschweißen
butterfly nut Flügelmutter *f*
butterfly valve stem Klappenwelle *f*
butterfly valve with progressive adjustment characteristic Klappe *f*

mit stetigem Stellverhalten
bottom chisel Abschrot *m*
bottom clearance Kopfspiel *nt*
bottom-up von unten nach oben
button Knopf *m*, Druckknopf *m*, Schaltfläche *f*
buttress Sägegewinde *nt*
buttress thread Sägengewinde *nt*
buy kaufen, einkaufen
buy externally zukaufen
buyer Käufer *m*
by ... degrees um ... Grad
by batch stapelweise
by blocks blockweise
by bytes byteweise
by form and friction grip form- und kraftschlüssig
by hand von Hand *f*, manuell
by hydraulic device druckabhängig
by layers lagenweise
by machine maschinell
by motorized device motorisch
by page seitenweise
by parts teilweise
by stack stapelweise
by the factor um den Faktor
by the nature of the process verfahrensbedingt
bypass überbrücken, Überbrückung *f*, Umgehung *f*
bypass Beipass *m*, Umgehung *f*; vorbeiströmen, umgehen, umleiten, kurzschließen
bypass line Umgehungsleitung *f*
bypass pipe Umlaufleitung *f*
bypass sample Nebenstromprobe *f*
byproduct Abfallprodukt *nt*
byte Byte *nt*
byte timing Zeichentakt *m*

C c

cab Führerstand *m*, Fahrerkabine *f*, Kabine *f*
cabin Führerstand *m*, Fahrerkabine *f*, Kabine *f*, Zelle *f*
cabinet Schrank *m*
cabinet end leg Kastenfuß *m*
cabinet floor stand Kastenständer *m*
cabinet leg Kastenfuß *m*
cable Strang *m*, Seil *nt*, Leitung *f*, Kabelleitung *f*, Kabel *nt*; verkabeln
cable brake Seilzugbremse *f*
cable connection Kabelanschluss *m*
cable conveyor Seilförderer *m*
cable drum Trommel *f*, Kabeltrommel *f*
cable entry Kabeleinführung *f*
cable layout Verkabelungsplan *m*
cable pull Seilzug *m*
cable reel Leitungstrommel *f*
cable sheath soldering Kabelmantellötung *f*
cable sheathing Leitungsschlauch *m*
cable shield Kabelschirm *m*
cable stranding machine Kabelverseilmaschine *f*
cable winch Seilwinde *f*
cable-connected mit Kabel *nt*
cableless ohne Kabel *nt*
cabling Verkabelung *f*
cadmium Cadmium *nt*
cadmium oxide vapours *pl* Kadmiumoxiddämpfe *mpl*
cadmium solder Kadmiumlot *nt*
cadmium-containing solder kadmiumhaltiges Lot *nt*
cage Käfig *m*, Klappbox *f*
cage armature Käfigläufer *m*
cage motor Kurzschlussmotor *m*, Kurzschlussläufermotor *m*
cage ring Kurzschlussläuferring *m*
cage rotor Stabläufer *m*, Käfigläufer *m*
cake sintern
calcine brennen
calculate rechnen, berechnen, ermitteln, beziffern, dimensionieren
calculated rechnerisch
calculated price kalkulierter Preis *m*
calculated useful life rechnerische Nutzungsdauer *f*
calculation Kalkulation *f*, Rechnen *nt*, Berechnung *f*, Ermittlung *f*
calculation check Kontrollrechnung *f*
calculation error Rechenfehler *m*
calculation example Berechnungsbeispiel *nt*
calculation factor Rechengröße *f*
calculation formula Berechnungsformel *f*
calculation method Berechnungsverfahren *nt*
calculation of errors Fehlerrechnung *f*
calculation of load-carrying capacity Tragfähigkeitsberechnung *f*
calculation pattern Kalkulationsschema *nt*
calculation program Rechenprogramm *nt*
calculation quantity Rechengröße *f*
calculation rule Berechnungsvorschrift *f*
calculation table Berechnungstabelle *f*
calculator Rechner *m*
calculator coarse draft Rechnergrobkonzept *nt*
calculator for extensive use Rechenmaschine *f* für Dauereinsatz
calculator for occasional use Rechenmaschine *f* für gelegentlichen Gebrauch
calculator powered by disposable battery Rechenmaschine *f* mit Einwegbatterie
calculator powered by rechargeable battery Rechenmaschine *f* mit aufladbarer Batterie
calculator with keyboard-controlled addressable storage Rechenmaschine *f* mit tastengesteuertem Speicher zum Akkumulieren
calculator with programmability programmierbare Rechenmaschine *f*
calculator with programme-controlled addressable storage Rechenmaschine *f* mit programmgesteuertem

Speicher zum Akkumulieren
calculator without addressable storage Rechenmaschine *f* ohne Speicher zum Akkumulieren
calculator without programmability nichtprogrammierbare Rechenmaschine *f*
calculatory kalkulatorisch
calender Kalander *m*
calender drive Kalanderantrieb *m*
calender file Kalenderdatei *f*
calibratable eichfähig
calibrate kalibrieren, eichen
calibrated straightedge graviertes Lineal *nt*
calibrating Kalibrieren *nt*
calibrating solution Eichflüssigkeit *f*
calibration Kalibrierung *f*, Kalibrieren *nt*, Prüfen *nt*, Messung *f*, Eichprüfung *f*
calibration block Vergleichskörper *m*, Eichblock *m*, Eichung *f*, Justierkörper *m*
calibration certificate Kalibrierschein *m*
calibration constant Kalibrierkonstante *f*
calibration curve Eichkurve *f*
calibration gas Kalibriergas *nt*
calibration reflector Justierreflektor *m*
calibration reflector echo Justierreflektorecho *nt*
calibration regulations Eichordnung *f*
calibration stamp Eichstempel *m*
calibration unit Kalibriereinheit *f*
calibre Kaliber *nt*
calliper messen, ablehren, abgreifen, ausmessen; Taster *m*
calliper rule Schublehre *f*
call Abruf *m*; aufrufen
call for bids ausschreiben; Ausschreibung *f*
call for tender Ausschreibung *f*, Angebotsanforderung *f*; ausschreiben
call of program module Bausteinaufruf *m*
call on auffordern
call procedure Anmeldeverfahren *nt*
call progress signal Dienstsignal *nt*
call request abgehender Ruf *m*
call up abfragen, abrufen, anwählen; Anwahl *f*
called line identification Anschlusskennung *f* der gerufenen Station
caller for tenders Ausschreibender *m*
call-in Aufruf *m*
calling for tenders Angebotsanforderung *f*
calling line identification Anschlusskennung *f* der rufenden Station
calling procedure Abrufverfahren *nt*
calling up Abfragen *nt*
calliper messen, ablehren, abgreifen, ausmessen; Taster *m*
calliper gauge Messschieber *m*
calliper square Tiefenlehre *f*
callipering Messung *f*, Prüfung *f*, Prüfen *nt*
callipers *pl* Taster *m*
calorific value Heizwert *m*
calorifier Wassererwärmer *m*
calorifier tube nest Heizrohrbündel *nt*
calorimeter vessel Kalorimetergefäß *nt*
cam Anschlagnocken *m*, Steuerkurve *f*, Arbeitskurve *f*, Kurve *f*, Kurvenscheibe *f*, Nocke *f*, Daumen *m*, Knagge *f*
cam and profile miller Kurven- und Profilfräsmaschine *f*
cam contour Kurvenzug *m*
cam contour grinder Nockenschleifmaschine *f*
cam coupler Koppelkurve *f*
cam coupler mechanism Koppelkurvengetriebe *nt*
cam disk Kurvenscheibe *f*
cam drum Kurventrommel *f*
cam follower roll Kurvenrolle *f*
cam front lathe Nockenfrontdrehmaschine *f*
cam lever Kurvenhebel *m*
cam mechanism Kurvengetriebe *nt*
cam milling Nockenfräsen *nt*
cam milling attachment Kurvenfräseinrichtung *f*
cam plate Nockenplatte *f*
cam roller Kurvenroller *m*, Kurvenrolle *f*
cam stick Nockenstange *f*
cam switch Nockenschalter *m*
cam trail Kurvengetriebe *nt*

camber Säbeln *nt*
camber grinding machine Balligschleifmaschine *f*
cam-controlled kurvengesteuert
cam-controlled automatic Kurvenautomat *m*
cam-crank mechanism Kurvenkurbelgetriebe *nt*
came message Kam-Meldung *f*
camel hair brush Kamelhaarpinsel *m*
camera Kamera *f*
camera system Kamerasystem *nt*
camgrinding attachment Kurvenschleifeinrichtung *f*
cam-lock spindle nose Camlockspindelkopf *m*
camlock type mounting Camlockschnellspannung *f*
cam-lock type mounting Camlockschnellspannung *f*
camp-on Warten *nt*
camshaft Kurvenwelle *f*, Nockenwelle *f*, Steuerwelle *f*
camshaft drive gear Nockenwellenantriebsrad *nt*
can Kanister *m*, Kapsel *f*, Dose *f*; kapseln
can miller Kurvenfräsmaschine *f*
can milling Kurvenfräsen *nt*
can sealing machine Bördelverschließmaschine *f*
cancel stornieren, aufheben, annullieren, zurücknehmen, löschen
cancel button Stornierfeld *nt*
cancel out ausgleichen, vereinfachen
cancellation Aufhebung *f*, Stornierung *f*
cancelling Rücknahme *f*
canister Kanister *m*
canning Kapselung *f*
cant abschrägen, schräg legen, abfasen, umkippen, kippen, umkanten, kanten
canted schräg
cantilever Supportträger *m*, Träger *m*, Ausleger *m*, Querbalken *m*, Kragarm *m*; überhängend, überstehend, vorkragend, freiliegend
cantilever racking Kragarmregal *nt*
cantilever racking storage Lagerung *f* von Langmaterial, Langmateriallager *nt*
cantilever racking with fixed arms nicht höhenverstellbares Kragarmregal *nt*
cantilever racking with removable arms höhenverstellbares Kragarmregal *nt*
cantilever wheels fliegend gelagerte Räder *ntpl*
cantilevered freitragend, fliegend gelagert
canting Abfasung *f*, Abfasen *nt*
cap Deckel *m*, Kappe *f*, Kalotte *f*
cap bolt Hutschraube *f*
cap nut Überwurfmutter *f*
cap screw Kopfschraube *f*
capability Fähigkeit *f*
capability of being duplicated Reproduzierbarkeit *f*
capability of deformation Formänderungsvermögen *nt*
capable fähig
capable of bearing tragfähig
capable of being bypassed umgehbar
capable of being cold-headed kaltstauchbar
capable of being cured in the hot condition warm härtbar
capable of being rubbed off abreibbar, ausreibbar
capable of being shut off absperrbar
capable of flow fließfähig
capable of lifting *(Hub)* tragfähig
capable of operation funktionsfähig
capable of plastic shaping plastisch verformbar
capable of supporting multi-user operation mehrplatzfähig
capacitance *(el.)* Kapazität *f*
capacitive load kapazitive Last *f*
capacitive operation kapazitiver Betrieb *m*
capacitor *(el.)* Kondensator *m*
capacitor motor Kondensatormotor *m*
capacity Kapazität *f*, Fassungsvermögen *nt*, Aufnahmefähigkeit *f*, Leistung *f*, Arbeitsleistung *f*, Arbeitsbereich *m*, Umfang *m*, Messweite *f*, Weite *f*, Geräumigkeit *f*
capacity adjustment Kapazitätsabgleich *m*, Kapazitätsanpassung *f*
capacity estimate Kapazitätsabschät-

capacity extrapolation – carbon affinity

zung *f*
capacity extrapolation Kapazitätshochrechnung *f*
capacity for expansion Erweiterbarkeit *f*
capacity modification Kapazitätsänderung *f*
capacity of vice jaws Spannweite *f* der Schraubstockbacken
capacity requirement Kapazitätsanforderung *f*
capacity reserve Kapazitätsreserve *f*
capacity schedule Kapazitätsterminplanung *f*
capacity smoothing Kapazitätsausgleich *m*
capacity utilization Kapazitätsauslastung *f*
cape chisel Kreuzmeißel *m*
capillary filling pressure kapillarer Fülldruck *m*
capillary joint Lötstelle *f*
capillary rise Saughöhe *f*
capillary socket Lötmuffe *f*
capillary solder fitting Kapillarlötverbindung *f*, Fittings für Lötverbindungen, Lötfittings
capillary solder joint Kapillarlötverbindung *f*
capillary soldering Kapillarlötung *f*
capillary T-bore stopcock Kapillardreiwegkegelhahn *m*
capillary tubes of the thermometer Thermometerkapillare *f*
capillary viscosimeter Kapillarviskosimeter *nt*, Kapillarviskosimetrie *f*
capital demand Kapitalbedarf *m*
capital demand plan Kapitalbedarfsplan *m*
capital investment Kapitaleinsatz *m*
capital lock-up Kapitalbindung *f*
capital spending Investitionsvolumen *nt*
capital tie-up Kapitalbindung *f*
capital tie-up costs Kapitalbindungskosten *pl*
capstan *(Rad)* Drehkreuz *nt*
capstan lathe Sattelrevolverdrehmaschine *f*, Drehmaschine *f* mit Sattelrevolver

capstan washer *(für Muttern)* Bördelscheibe *f*
capstan wheel Handkreuz *nt*
capsule Kapsel *f*
captive C washer Schwenkscheibe *f*
captive screw unverlierbare Schraube *f*
captive washer unverlierbare Scheibe *f*
captive washer component unverlierbares Unterlegteil *nt*
captivity Unverlierbarkeit *f*
carbide Karbid *nt*
carbide cutter Hartmetallfräser *m*
carbide cutting edge Hartmetallschneide *f*
carbide cutting section Hartmetallschneidenteil *nt*
carbide cutting tool Hartmetallmeißel *m*
carbide drill Hartmetallbohrer *m*
carbide edge Hartmetallschneide *f*
carbide facing Hartmetallauflage *f*, Hartmetallbestückung *f*
carbide insert Hartmetalleinsatz *m*
carbide metal Hartmetall *nt*
carbide milling Fräsen *nt* mit Hartmetallwerkzeug
carbide planing Hobeln *nt* mit Hartmetallmeißel
carbide shaping Kurzhobeln *nt* mit Hartmetallmeißel
carbide tip Hartmetallschneide *f*, Hartmetallplättchen *nt*, Schneidplättchen *nt*, Schneidplatte *f*
carbide tipping Hartmetallbestückung *f*
carbide tool Hartmetallwerkzeug *nt*
carbide turning tool Hartmetalldrehwerkzeug *nt*
carbide-tipped hartmetallbestückt, HM-bestückt
carbide-tipped cutter hartmetallbestückter Fräser *m*
carbide-tipped tool hartmetallbestücktes Werkzeug *nt*, hartmetallbestückter Meißel *m*
carbide-tooled mit Hartmetallwerkzeugen ausgerüstet
carbonic acid ester Kohlensäureester
carbon Kohlenstoff *m*
carbon affinity Kohlenstoffaffinität *f*

carbon brush Kohlebürste *f*
carbon characteristic Kohlenstoffverlauf *m*
carbon content Kohlenstoffgehalt *m*
carbon copy (cc) Kohlepapierdurchschlag *m*
carbon disulfide Schwefelkohlenstoff *m*
carbon fibres Kohlenstofffasergelege *nt*
carbon mould block Formkohle *f*
carbon oxide Kohlendioxid *nt*
carbon steel Kohlenstoffstahl *m*
carbon steel C-Stahl *m*
carbonate rock Carbonatgestein *nt*
carboy Ballon *m*
carburettor Vergaser *m*
carburettor fuel Vergaserkraftstoff *m*
carburise karburieren
carburization Aufkohlung *f*
carburization compound Aufkohlungsmittel *nt*
carburization depth Aufkohlungstiefe *f*
carburizing behaviour Aufkohlungsverhalten *nt*
carburizing steel Einsatzstahl *m*
card file Kartei *f*
card holder Beschriftungsfeld *nt*
card index Kartei *f*
card perforating Kartenlochen *nt*
card perforator Kartenlocher *m*
card punch Kartenlocher *m*
card punching Kartenlochen *nt*
card reader Kartenleser *m*
cardan joint Kardangelenk *nt*
cardan shaft Kardanwelle *f*
cardboard Vollpappe *f*, Pappe *f*, Karton *m*
cardboard box Kartonbox *f*, Pappschachtel *f*
cardboard grip arm Kartongreifer *m*
care 1. *(Wartung)* Pflege *f* **2.** *(Achtung)* Vorsicht *f*
care for pflegen
carefully trued edge fein justierte Kante *f*
cargo Fracht *f*, Ladung *f*
cargo winch Ladewinde *f*
carousel Drehregal *nt*, Karussell *nt*
carousel segment Karussellsegment *nt*

carousel storage system Karussellager *nt*
carriage Bettschlitten *m*, Werkzeugschlitten *m*, Schlitten *m*, Support *m*, Wagenvorschub *m*, Wagen *m*, Fahrwerk *nt*
carriage way Supportführung *f*
carriage guideways Bettschlittenführung *f*, Schlittenführung *f*
carriage track Bettschlittenbahn *f*, Supportführung *f*
carriage type drafting machine Laufwagenzeichenmaschine *f*
carriage wing Bettschlittenwange *f*
carrier Träger *m*, Mitnehmer *m*
carrier air flow controller Tragluftflussregler *m*
carrier assembly Tragsatz *m*
carrier frequency method Trägerfrequenzverfahren *nt*
carrier gas Fördergas *nt*, Trägergas *nt*
carrier plate Mitnehmerscheibe *f*
carrier platform Trägerplattform *f*
carrier preparation Trägermittel *nt*
Carrier Sense Multiple Access with Collision Detection CSMA/CD
carrier wave Trägerwelle *f*
carry aufnehmen, befördern, mitnehmen, tragen, führen, halten, unterstützen
carry along mitführen
carry away abführen
carry bit Übertragsbit *nt*
carry forward übertragen
carry input Übertragseingang *m*
carry off ableiten, wegleiten
carry out durchführen, ausführen, realisieren
carry output Übertragungsausgang *m*
carry over Übertrag *m*; übertragen
carrying away Abführung *f*
carrying capacity Tragfähigkeit *f*
carrying chain Tragkette *f*
carrying chain conveyor Tragkettenförderer *m*
carrying force Tragkraft *f*
carrying power Tragkraft *f*
carrying ram Tragdorn *m*
carrying roller Tragrolle *f*
cart Wagen *m*, Transportbehälter *m*

Cartesian coordinates Kartesische Koordinaten *fpl*
Cartesian robot kartesischer Roboter *m*
cartridge Patrone *f*, Kassette *f*
cartridge frame Kassettengestell *nt*
cartridge layer Kassettenlage *f*
cartridge magazine Kassettenmagazin *nt*
cartridge storage system Kassettenlager *nt*
cartridge tunnel Kassettentunnel *m*
carton Karton *m*, Schachtel *f*, Faltkiste *f*, Faltschachtel *f*, Kollo *nt*; kartonieren
carton blank Faltschachtelzuschnitt *m*, Schachtelzuschnitt *m*, Kartonzuschnitt *m*
carton blank erecting machine Faltschachtelzuschnittaufrichtmaschine *f*
carton body Schachtelkörper *m*
carton clamp Kartonklammer *f*
carton closing machine Faltschachtelverschließmaschine *f*
carton erecting machine Faltschachtelaufrichtmaschine *f*
carton fill form and seal machine Faltschachtelform-, -füll- und -verschließmaschine *f*
carton flow rack Kollidurchlaufregal *nt*
carton tray Kartontray *nt*
cartonboard Karton *m*, Kartonage *f*, Pappe *f*
cartonboard blank Kartonzuschnitt *m*, Pappezuschnitt *m*
cartonboard skillet Kartontray *nt*
cartonboard sleeve Pappschachtel *f*
cartoner Kartoniermaschine *f*
cartoning Kartonieren *nt*; kartonierend
cartoning machine Faltschachtelmaschine *f*, Kartoniermaschine *f*
case 1. Schachtel *f*, Gehäuse *nt*, Kiste *f*, Faltkiste *f*, Faltschachtel *f*, Kasten *m*, Kassette *f*, Behälter *m*, Verpackung *f*, Verkleidung *f*, Ummantelung *f*, Umhüllung *f*; verkleiden **2.** *(Möbel)* Schrank *m* **3.** Fall *m*
case blank Faltschachtelzuschnitt *m*
case by case fallweise
case erecting machine Faltschachtelaufrichtmaschine *f*
case gluing machine Klebstoffauftragverschließmaschine *f*
case of emergency Notfall *m*
case of loss Schadensfall *m*
case of malfunction Störfall *m*
case stapling machine Heftklammerverschließmaschine *f*
case study Arbeitsbeispiel *nt*
case taper Klebebandverschließmaschine *f*
case-harden einsatzhärten
casing Hülle *f*, Gehäuse *nt*, Verkleidung *f*, Kapsel *f*, Kapselung *f*
casing wall Gehäusewand *f*
cask Fass *nt*
cask fill and seal machine Fassfüll- und -verschließmaschine *f*
cask or keg fill and seal machine Fass- oder Kegfüll- und -verschließmaschine *f*
cassette Kassette *f*
cast gießen
cast components Gussteile *ntpl*
cast integrally with angegossen
cast iron Grauguss *m*, Gusseisen *nt*
cast iron machining Gussbearbeitung *f*
cast iron material Gusseisenwerkstoff *m*
cast iron mould Kokille *f*
cast iron shot *(als Strahlmittel)* Gussschrott *m*
cast iron spigot Gussrohrspitzende *nt*
cast member Gussteil *nt*
cast on angießen
cast part design Gussteilgestaltung *f*
cast part error Gussteilfehler *m*
cast parts Gussteile *ntpl*
cast solder filaments *pl* gegossene Lotfäden *mpl*
cast steel Stahlguss *m*
cast steel flange Stahlgussflansch *m*
cast-alloy cutter Fräser *m* aus Gusslegierung
castle nut Kronenmutter *f*
castellated portion *(e. Kronenmutter)* Krone *f*
castellating Schlitzen *nt* von Kronenmuttern
casting Guss *m*, Gussstück *nt*,
casting alloy Gusslegierung *f*
casting basin Gießbecken *nt*

casting case Gussgehäuse *nt*
casting characteristic Gießeigenschaft *f*
casting cleaning Gussputzerei *f*
casting resin moulding material Gießharzmasse *f*
casting flaw Gussfehler *m*
casting general tolerance Gussallgemeintoleranz *f*
casting material Gusswerkstoff *m*
casting part Gussteil *nt*
casting proceedings Gießvorgang *m*
casting process Gießverfahren *nt*
casting resin containing filler gefülltes Gießharz *nt*
casting resin moulded material Gießharzformstoff *m*
casting resin moulded material with plastic flow Gießharzformstoff *m* mit plastischem Fließen
casting stress Gussspannung *f*
casting stuff Gussteilmasse *f*
casting technology Urformtechnik *f*
casting temperature Gießtemperatur *f*
casting tolerance series Gusstoleranzreihe *f*
casting tolerance Gusstoleranz *f*
casting tolerance group Gusstoleranzgruppe *f*
casting tool Urformwerkzeug *nt*
castings Gussteile *ntpl*
castle nut Kronenmutter *f*
castor Gleitrolle *f*, Laufrolle *f*
catalogue Liste *f*
catalogue of machines Maschinenkartei *f*
catalogued device listenmäßiges Gerät *nt*
catalyser Katalysator *m*
catapult schleudern
catch schnappen, einschnappen, einhaken, einklinken, einrasten, abfangen, auffangen, fangen, rasten; Fang *m*, Knagge *f*, Sperre *f*, Sperrhaken *m*, Sperrklinke *f*, Schaltklinke *f*, Raste *f*, Selbsthaltung *f*
catch fire zünden
catch in einrasten
catch load Fanglast *f*
catch pin Fangstift *m*

catch plate Mitnehmerscheibe *f*
catch point Fangstelle *f*
catching Fang *m*, Fangen *nt*
catching block Fangraum *m*
catching device Sperrfangvorrichtung *f*, Fangvorrichtung *f*
catching mechanism Fangmechanismus *m*
catching operation Fangvorgang *m*
catching path Fangweg *m*
catching pulley Fangrolle *f*
catching rail Fangschiene *f*
catching roller Fangrolle *f*
catchment area Auffangraum *m*
catchment tank Auffangbehälter *m*
category Grad *m*
cathead Katzenkopf *m*
cat-head Schraubenfutter *f*
cathode Kathode *f*
cathode ray system Kathodenstrahlsystem *nt*
cathode ray tube (CRT) Kathodenstrahlröhre *f*
cathode surface Kathodenfläche *f*
cathode-ray-tube-module Bildteil
cathodic corrosion protection kathodischer Korrosionsschutz *m*
cathodic partial stage kathodischer Teilschnitt *m*
cantilever shelving Kragarmregal *nt*
cattle feed boiler Futterkessel *m*
cause Ursache *f*; hervorrufen, bedingen, bewirken, verursachen
cause of the fault Störungsursache *f*
caused by bedingt durch
causer Verursacher *m*
causing skidding conditions Glätte bildend
caustic ätzend
caustic curve Kaustik *f*
caustic lye Ätzlauge *f*
caustic potash solution Lauge *f*
caustic potash solution Kalilauge *f*
caustics Kaustik *f*
cauterise zerfressen
caution Achtung *f*, Vorsicht *f*, Warnung *f*
cavity Lunker *m, mpl*, Hohlraum *m*, Raum *m*
cavity block Gesenk *nt*

cavity milling Raumformfräsen *nt*
CCD-camera CCD-Kamera *f*, ladungsgekoppeltes Bildwanderelement *nt*
CCD-element CCD-Element *nt*
cease aufhören
ceiling Geschossdecke *f*, Decke *f*
ceiling fan Deckenfächer *m*, Ventilator *m*
ceiling stand Deckenstativ *nt*
cell Zelle *f*, Klasse *f*
cell box Zellengefäß *nt*
cell computer Zellenrechner *m*
cell container Zellengefäß *nt*
cell control Zellensteuerung *f*
cell controller Zellenrechner *m*
cell mounting Zelleneinbau *m*
cell oven Zellenofen *m*
cellar Keller *m*
cell-type oven Zellenofen *m*
cellular foam structure Schaumstoffgefüge *nt*
cellular glass Schaumglas *nt*
cellular material Schaumstoff *m*
cellular material formed in situ formgeschäumter Kunststoff *m*
cellular materials *pl* Schaumstoffe *mpl*
cellular plastics Schaumstoff *m*, Schaumkunststoff *m*
cellular plastics structure Schaumstoffgefüge *nt*
cellular rubber Schaumgummi *m*
cellular storage heater Zellenspeicher *m*
cellular structure Zellgefüge *nt*
cellular test specimen Schaumstoffprobe *f*
cellulose acetate injection moulding material Celluloseacetatspritzgussmasse *f*
cellulose aceto butyrate injection moulding material (or compound) Celluloseacetobutyratspritzgussmasse *f*
cellulose covered electrode zelluloseumhüllte Elektrode *f*
cellulose sheeting Cellulosebahn *f*
CE-marking CE-Zeichen *nt*
cement 1. binden, sintern 2. *(Baustoff)* Zement *m*
cement sand forming process Zementsandformverfahren *nt*

cement sand process Zementsandverfahren *nt*
cement-carbide boring tool Hartmetallaufbohrwerkzeuge *ntpl*
cement-carbide insert Hartmetalleinsatz *m*
cemented carbide Hartmetall *nt*, Sintermetall *nt*, Sinterkarbid *nt*
cemented carbide tool Hartmetallwerkzeug *nt*
cemented insert Hartmetalleinsatz *m*
cemented nozzle Klebstutzen *m*
cemented socket joint Klebmuffe *f*, Aufklebemuffe *f*
cemented tungsten carbide gesintertes Wolframkarbid *nt*
cemented-carbide tip Hartmetallplättchen *nt*
cementing Aufkohlung *f*, Sintern *nt*
cementing clip Klebschelle *f*
cementing several layers on top of each other Aufeinanderkleben *nt* mehrerer Lagen
centre Drehspitze *f*, Körnerspitze *f*, Spitze *f*, Mittelpunkt *m*, Zentrum *nt*; zentrieren, ankörnen
centre distance Achsabstand *m*
centre drilling Zentrierbohren *nt*
centre grinding Schleifen *nt* zwischen Spitzen
centre lathe Spitzendrehmaschine *f*
centre line Drehachse *f*, Mittenachse *f*
centre offset Außermittigkeit *f*, Mittenversetzung *f*
centre point Zentrum *nt*
centre punch Körner *m*, ankörnen
centre punching Körnen *nt*
centre sleeve Reitnagel *m*
centre sleeve guide Pinolenführung *f*
centre-drive axle lathe Achsenfertigdrehmaschine *f*
centred zentrisch
centring Zentrierung *f*, Zentrieren *nt*
centring accessory Zentrierhilfe *f*
centring collar Zentrierring *m*
centring device Zentriervorrichtung *f*
centring edge Zentrierkante *f*
centring error Zentrierfehler *m*
centring lathe Anbohrmaschine *f*
centring location Bereitstellplatz *m*,

Zentrierplatz *m*
centring point Zentrierpunkt *m*
centring sleeve Zentrierhülse *f*
centring station Zentrierstation *f*
centring tool Zentriermeißel *m*
centreless spitzenlos
centreless cylindrical grinder spitzenlose Schleifmaschine *f*
centreless cylindrical grinding spitzenloses Rundschleifen *nt*
centreless grinder Rundschleifmaschine *f*
centreless grinding spitzenloses Schleifen *nt*
centreless grinding method spitzenloses Schleifverfahren *nt*
centreless plunge grinding Ansatzschleifen *nt*
centreless-type internal grinding machine spitzenlose Innenschleifmaschine *f*
centreline Mittellinie *f*
centre-type grinding Rundschliefen *nt* zwischen Spitzen
central mittel, zentral
central braking and/or locking device Zentralfeststeller *m*
central control Zentralsteuerung *f*
central control lever Zentralsteuerhebel *m*
central control panel Bedienungszentrale *f*, Hauptschalttafel *f*
central control room Leitstand *m*
central heating room Heizraum *m*
central length Mittenmaß *nt*
central line Mittenlinie *f*
central moment zentrales Moment *nt*
central office Zentrale *f*
central part mittlerer Teil *m*
central pinion Sonnenrad *nt*
central pintle Mittelzapfen *m*
central pivot Drehzahlverhältnis *nt*
central plane Mittenebene *f*
central point Mittelpunkt *m*
central position Mittigkeit *f*, Mittellage *f*
central processing unit (CPU) Zentraleinheit *f*
central ray Zentralstrahl *m*
central switch desk Hauptschaltpunkt *m*
central ventilating station Lüftungszentrale *f*
centralized air conditioning plant Klimazentrale *f*
centralized hot water installation zentrale Warmwasserbereitungsanlage *f*
centralized supply zentrale Versorgung *f*
centralized ventilation and air conditioning installation Lüftungs- und Klimazentrale *f*
centre 1. Mitte *f*, Zentrum *nt*, Kern *m*, Kernstück *nt*; zentrieren, richten (auf) 2. ankörnen
centre angle Zentriwinkel *m (e. Rades)*
centre bore Zentrierbohrung *f*
centre contact Mittentragen
centre distance Achsenabstand *m*, Mittenabstand *m*
centre distance allowance Achsabstandsmaß *nt*
centre distance alteration Achsabstandsänderung *f*
centre distance basis Einheitsachsenabstand *m*
centre distance deviation Achsabstandsabweichung *f*
centre distance fluctuation Achsabstandsschwankung *f*
centre distance line Achsabstandslinie *f*
centre distance modification Teilkreisabstand *m*
centre distance modification coefficient Teilkreisabstandsfaktor *m*
centre distance tester Stichmaßprüfer *m*
centre gauge Mittigkeitslehre *f*
centre hole Zentrierbohrung *f*
centre lathe Spitzendrehmaschine *f*
centre line Mittellinie *f*, Mittelpunktlinie *f*, Längsachse *f*
centre line between cutting edges Querschneide *f*
centre line cross Mittellinienkreuz *nt*
centre mark Ankörnung *f*
centre of area Flächenschwerpunkt *m*
centre of gravity Schwerpunkt *m*
centre of mass Schwerpunkt *m*

centre-of-mass motion Schwerpunktbewegung *f*
centre of push/pull bar Bügelmitte *f*
centre of rotation Drehpol *m*
centre of the circle Kreismittelpunkt *m*
centre of the journal Zapfenmitte *f*
centre of the tolerance zone Toleranzfeldmitte *f*
centre plane Mittelebene *f*
centre portion Mittelteil *nt*
centre-to-centre distance Mittenabstand *m*, Abstand *m* von Mitte zu Mitte
centre track Mittelregal *nt*
centred random quantity zentrigierte Zufallsgröße *f*
centreline Achse *f*
centreline of the notch Kerbmitte *f*
centreline to top height Bauhöhe *f*
centrepiece Mittelteil *nt*
centrical zentrisch
centrifugal zentrifugal
centrifugal blasting Schleuderstrahlen *nt*
centrifugal force Zentrifugalkraft *f*
centrifugal force plant Fliehkraftanlage *f*
centrifugal force sizer fliehkraftsicher
centrifugal turbo-compressor Turboradialverdichter *m*
centrifugal wheel principle Schleuderradprinzip *nt*
centrifuge beaker Zentrifugenbecher *m*
centring Zentrierung *f*
centroid Schwerpunkt *m*
centripetal zentripetal
centroid Schwerpunktmitte *f*
ceramic bit keramischer Einsatzmeißel *m*
ceramic cutting material keramischer Schneidstoff *m*
ceramic cutting tool Keramikschneidwerkzeug *nt*
ceramic pyrometer Schmelzkörper *m*
ceramic slow combustion stove keramischer Dauerbrandofen *m*
ceramics Keramik *f*
certificate Bescheinigung *f*, Nachweis *m*
cessation Aufhören *nt*

CFK prepeg Kohlenstofffasergelege *nt*
C-fork C-Gabel *f*
chafe scheuern
chain verketten, verknüpfen; Kette *f*
chain adjuster Kettenspanner *m*
chain barrier Kettensperre *f*
chain conveyor Kettenförderer *m*, Transportkette *f*
chain dimensioning aneinandergereihte Maße *f*, Maßkette *f*
chain discharge Kettenauslauf *m*
chain drive Kettengetriebe *nt*, Kettentrieb *m*, Kettenantrieb *m*
chain driven roller conveyor Rollenkettenförderer *m*
chain guard Kettenschutz *m*
chain hoist Kettenzug *m*
chain lift Kettenhub *m*
chain line Strichpunktlinie *f*
chain link Kettenglied *nt*
chain magazine Kettenmagazin *nt*
chain of transportation means *(Serie)* Transportkette *f*
chain-pulled conveyor Schleppkettenförderer *m*
chain pulley Kettenrolle *f*
chain reaction Kettenreaktion *f*
chain sampling inspection Kettenstichprobenprüfung *f*
chain storeroom Kettenmagazin *nt*
chain stretcher Kettenspanner *m*
chain string Kettenstrang *m*
chain structure Kettenstruktur *f*
chain system Kettensystem *nt*
chain tension Kettenspannung *f*, Kettenzug *m*
chain termination Kettenendbefestigung *f*, Kettenendverbindung *f*
chain tightener Kettenspanner *m*
chain wheel Kettenrad *nt*, Zahnkranz *m*
chaining Verkettung *f*, Verknüpfung *f*
chain-line circle strichpunktierter Kreis *m*
chair castor test Stuhlrollenversuch *m*
chalk Kreide *f*
chalking scale Abkreidungsskala *f*
chamber Zelle *f*, Kammer *f*
chamber diameter Kammerdurchmesser *m*
chamfer abschrägen

chamfer Schräge *f*, Fase *f*, Anfasung *f*, kegeliger Anschnitt *m*, gebrochene Kante *f*, Kantenabschrägung *f*, Kerbe *f*; abkanten, abschrägen, abfasen, anfasen, fasen
chamfer angle Fasenspanwinkel *m*
chamfer relief angle Seitenfreiwinkel *m*
chamfer to permit insertion *(bei Spannstiften)* Einführfase *f*
chamfered corner Eckenfase *f*
chamfered corner length Breite *f* der Eckenfase
chamfered cutting edge gefaste Schneide *f*
chamfered nut Mutter *f* mit Fase *f*
chamfering Fasen *nt*, Anfasen *nt*, Abfasen *nt*, Abkanten *nt*, Kantenbrechen *nt*
chamfering from the rear rückseitiges Anfasen *nt*
chamfering hob Abrundwälzfräser *m*, Abkantwälzfräser *m*
chamfering slide Abschrägsupport *m*
chamfering tool Fasenmeißel *m*, Abfasmeißel *m*, Anfasmeißel *m*, Anschrägmeißel *m*
chance Zufall *m*
chance failure Zufallsausfall *m*
change verändern, abändern, schalten, wechseln, auswechseln, wandeln; Änderung *f*, Veränderung *f*, Wechsel *m*
change between aisles Gassenwechsel *m*
change gear Wechselrad *nt*, Aufsteckrad *nt*
change gear box Wechselrädergetriebekasten *m*, Wechselräderkasten *m*
change gear calculation Wechselräderberechnung *f*
change gear drive Wechselrädergetriebe *nt*
change gear mechanism Wechselrädergetriebe *nt*
change gears umschalten, schalten
change gradually into übergehen
change in centre of gravity position Schwerpunktveränderung *f*
change in direction of rotation Drehsinnwechsel *m*
change in shape Verformung *f*
change management Änderungsmanagement *nt*
change of aisle Gassenwechsel *m*, Gangwechsel *m*
change of attachment Umrüstung *f*
change of fixed rail Festanschlagwechsel *m*
change of object Objektveränderung *f*
change of place Ortsveränderung *f*
change of position Lageveränderung *f*
change of state Zustandsänderung *f*
change of temperature Temperaturwechsel *m*
change over umstellen (auf), umrüsten, umschalten; Wechseln *nt*, Wechsel *m*, Umstellung *f*, Rüstvorgang *m*
change-pole polumschaltbar
change poles umpolen
changeable veränderbar
change-gear transmission Räderwechselgetriebe *nt*
changeover Umstellung *f*, Umrüstung *f*, Übergang *m*
change-over and resetting Umrüstung *f*
change-over contact Wechsler *m*
change-over gate Signalweiche *f*, Umschalttor *nt*
change-over switch Umschalter *m*
changeover time Umstellzeit *f*, Umrüstzeit *f*
change-over time Umschlagzeit *f*
change-over valve Umsteuerventil *nt*
changes in demand Nachfrageschwankung *f*
changing Wechseln *nt*; veränderlich
changing of wheels Radwechsel *m*
changing the setup Umspannen *nt*
changing volume Umschaltvolumen *nt*
channel einschleusen, einkehlen, auskehlen, riefen; Nut *f*, Kanal *m*, Tunnel *m*, Rinne *f*, Riefe *f*, Ausgaberinne *f*, Spur *f*
channel structure Kanalstruktur *f*
chaplet Kernstütze *f*
character Zeichen *nt*, Schriftzeichen *nt*
character area Zeichenfeld *nt*
character by character zeichenweise *f*
character centreline spacing Zeichenmittelabstand *m*

character encoder Klarschriftcodierer *m*
character mode zeichenweiser Betrieb *m*
character set Zeichenvorrat *m*
character string Zeichenkette *f*, Zeichenfolge *f*
characteristic Merkmal *nt*, Verlauf *m*, Kennlinie *f*, Kennmerkmal *nt*
characteristic acoustic impedance Schallkernimpedanz *f*
characteristic curve Kennlinie *f*
characteristic data Kenndaten *pl*
characteristic factor Kenngröße *f*
characteristic feature Kennmerkmal *nt*
characteristic impedance Schallwellenwiderstand *m*
characteristic line Kennlinie *f*
characteristic mark Kennzeichen *nt*
characteristic value Kennzahl *f*, Kennwert *m*
characteristic value for the operation Betriebskennwert *m*
characteristic value method Kennzahlenmethode *f*
characteristic values Kennwerte *mpl*
characteristic X-radiation charakteristische Röntgenstrahlung *f*
characteristic data *pl* Kenngrößen *fpl*
charge Umlage *f*, Los *nt*, Fertigungslos *nt*, Ladung *f*, laden, aufladen, füllen, einfüllen, beschicken
charge coefficient Ladefaktor *m*
charge exchange Ladungsaustausch *m*
charge off abbuchen
charge reversal Umladung *f*
charge to capacity auslasten
charge transfer *(el. chem.)* Ladungsdurchtritt *m*
charge-coupled device ladungsgekoppeltes Bildwandlerelement *nt*, ladungsgekoppeltes Speicherelement *nt*
charged couple device (CCD) ladungsgekoppeltes Bildwandlerelement *nt*, ladungsgekoppeltes Speicherelement *nt*
charger Ladegerät *nt*
charging Beschickung *f*, Ladung *f*, Laden *nt*
charging aisle Beschickungsgang *m*

charging buffer Beschickungspuffer *m*
charging characteristic Ladekennlinie *f*
charging chute Füllschacht *m*
charging current Ladestrom *m*
charging cycle Ladezyklus *m*
charging device Chargiergerät *nt*
charging equipment Ladeausrüstung *f*
charging level Batterieladezustand *m*
charging line Zulaufleitung *f*
charging memory Beschickungsspeicher *m*
charging platform Ladebühne *f*
charging point Beschickungsstelle *f*, Ladestelle *f*
charging robot Beschickungsroboter *m*
charging roller Zulaufrollengang *m*
charging space Füllraum *m*
charging station Ladeort *m*
charging status Batterieladezustand *m*
charging technology Ladetechnik *f*
charging test Ladegerät *nt*
charging time Beschickungszeit *f*, Ladezeit *f*, Füllzeit *f*
Charpy impact flexural test Schlagbiegeversuch *m* nach Charpy
Charpy impact test Kerbschlagbiegeversuch *m* nach Charpy
chart Tabelle *f*
chase strehlen
chase parting line Backentrennfläche *f*
chaser Strehler *m*
chasing Strehlen *nt*
chasing attachment Strehleinrichtung *f*
chasing die Strehlerbacken *m*
chasing stroke Strehlgang *m*
chassis Fahrgestell *nt*, Karosserie *f*, Fahrzeugrahmen *m*, Rahmen *m*
chassis frame Fahrzeugrahmen *m*
chassis profile Rahmenkontur *f*
chatter Schlag *m*, Rattern *nt*; rattern
chatter mark Rattermarke *f*, Ratternarbe *f*
chatter vibration Ratterschwingung *f*
chatter-free ratterfrei
chattering Rattern *nt*
chatter-proof stable ratterfrei
check kontrollieren, überprüfen, prüfen, nachprüfen, testen, vergleichen, abfra-

gen; Überprüfung f, Anriss m, Nachprüfung f, Versuch m, Kontrollversuch m
check digit Prüfziffer f
check flange Anlaufflansch m
check gauge Prüflehre f
check handler Prüfroutine f
check in einbuchen
check list Checkliste f
check marks Netzrisse mpl, Schleifrisse mpl
check note Prüfvermerk m
check nut Gegenmutter f
check out Austragen nt; austragen
check plug Passdorn m
check program Testprogramm nt
check routine Prüfroutine f, Testprogramm nt, Prüfprogramm nt
check test Kontrollprüfung f
check the calculation nachrechnen
check valve Rückschlagventil nt, Absperrventil nt
check valve with shut-off feature absperrbares Rückschlagventil nt
checked by drawing scrutiny zeichnungsgeprüft
checker Prüfer m
checking Kontrolle f, Prüfung f, Messen nt, Nachprüfen nt
checking aid Kontrollhilfsmittel nt
checking dimensions Nachmessen nt
checking in goods into the warehouse Ware ins Lager einbuchen
checking marks Netzrisse mpl, Schleifrisse mpl
checking operation Kontrollvorgang m
checking point Kontrollpunkt m
checking size Nachmessen nt
checking the load whilst moving Durchlaufmessung f
checkweigher Kontrollwaage f
cheek Wange f, Seitenwange f
cheese head thread cutting screw Zylinderschneidschraube f
cheese-head screw Rundkopfschraube f
chemical chemisch
chemical abrading chemisches Abtragen nt
chemical binding agent chemische Bindemittel $ntpl$

chemical coating chemische Beschichtung f
chemical dissolving process chemisches Ablöseverfahren nt
chemical etching chemisches Ätzen nt
chemical milling Formätzen nt
chemical preservation chemischer Schutz m
chemical pulp Chemiezellstoff m
chemical store Chemikalienlager nt
chemically immune chemisch beständig
chemical-mechanical planish processing CMP (chemisch-mechanisches Planieren) -Bearbeitung f
chemical-thermal burring chemisch-thermisches Entgraten nt
cherry Kugelfräser m, Gesenkfäser m; Gesenke ausfräsen
cherrying Kugelfräsen nt
chest Kiste f, Kasten m
chick-change device Schnellwechseleinrichtung f
child resistant package kindergesicherte Packung f
chill erkalten, abschrecken
chill casting Kokillengießen nt, Kokilenguss m
chill casting process Kokillengießverfahren nt
chilled cast blasting agent Handgussstrahlmittel nt
chilled mould Kokille f
chilling Abschrecken nt
chilling process Abkühlvorgang m
chimney flank Schornsteinwange f
chimney installation Schornsteinanlage f
chimney outlet Schornsteinmündung f
chimney performance Schornsteinleistung f
chip ausbrechen, meißeln; Schnitt m, Span m
chip board Spanplatte f
chip breaker Spanbrecher m, Spanbrechernut f, Spanformer m, Spanstufe f
chip breaker angle Keilwinkel m des Spanbrechers
chip breaker distance Abstand m der Spanleitstufe, Spanbrecherabstand m

chip breaker groove eingeformte Spanleitstufe *f*, Spanleitstufe *f*
chip breaker groove depth Tiefe *f* der Spanbrechernut
chip breaker groove radius Radius *m* der eingeformten Spanleitstufe, Radius *m* der Spanbrechernut
chip breaker height Spanbrecherhöhe *f*
chip breaker land width Fase *f* der Spanleitstufe *f*, Spanflächenbreite *f* an der Spanbrechernut
chip breaker nick Spanleitstufe *f*
chip breaker orientation angle Lagewinkel *m* des Spanbrechers
chip breaker wedge angle Spanbrecher-Keilwinkel *m*
chip broken up into small fragments kurzgebrochener Span *m*
chip categories Spanarten
chip chute Spanleitblech *nt*, Spänerutsche *f*, Spänefang *m*
chip clearance Spandurchgang *m*, Spanraum *m*, Späneraum *m*
chip clogging Späneverstopfung *f*, Spänestau *m*
chip collector Spanfänger *m*, Spänefang *m*, Spanfangschale *f*, Spanplatte *f*
chip compartment Späneauffangraum *m*, Spänefangraum *m*, Späneraum *m*
chip congestion Spänestau *m*
chip control Spanlenkung *f*
chip conveyor Spanförderer *m*
chip cross-section upsetting Spanquerschnittsstauchung *f*
chip cross-sectional area Spanquerschnitt *m*
chip curl Spanlocke *f*
chip disposal Spänebeseitigung *f*
chip entanglement Spanverstopfung *f*
chip flattening Spanbreitung *f*
chip flow Spanablauf *m*, Spanfluss *m*, Spänefluss *m*, Spanabfluss *m*
chip flow angle Spanablaufwinkel *m*
chip flow direction Spanflussrichtung *f*
chip formation Spanbildung *f*, Spanentstehung *f*, Spanformung *f*
chip forms Spanformen *fpl*
chip forming machining spanende Bearbeitung *f*
chip fragment Späneteilchen *nt*, Kurzspan *m*
chip groove Spannut *f*, Spanflächenfase *f*
chip load per tooth (*Fräsen*) Spantiefe *f* je Zahn
chip pan Spänefangschale *f*, Späneschale *f*, Spänewanne *f*
chip particle Späneteilchen *nt*
chip pocket Spannut *f*
chip removal Spänebeseitigung *f*, Spanabnahme *f*, Späneabfuhr *f*
chip removing process Zerspanvorgang *f*
chip shortening Spankürzung *f*
chip speed Spangeschwindigkeit *f*
chip tangle Wirrspan *m*
chip test Spanprüfung *f*
chip thickness compression ratio Spandickenstauchung *f*
chip thicknessing Spandickung *f*
chip tray Spanfangschale *f*, Späneschale *f*
chip trough Späneauffangrinne *f*, Spänerinne *f*
chip variable Spangröße *f*
chip-bearing surface Spanfläche *f*
chip-breaking groove Spanbrechernut *f*
chipless process spanloses Verfahren *nt*
chipper Splittstreuer *m*
chipping Ausbruch *m*, Ausbrechen *nt*
chipping of the cutting edge Schneidenausbruch *m*
chips *pl* Schneidspäne *mpl*
chipset Chipsatz *m*
chisel Meißel *m*, meißeln
chisel disposal Spanabfuhr *f*
chisel off abstemmen
chisel planing Wälzhobeln *nt*
chiselled kantig
chi-squared distribution Chiquadratverteilung *f*
chlorated VC homopolymer chloriertes VC-Homopolymerisat *nt*
chloric acid Chlorsäure *f*
chlorinated diphenyl chloriertes Diphenyl *nt*
chlorinated rubber adhesive Chlor-

kautschuk-Kleber *m*
chlorinator Chlorgasdosieranlage *f*
chlorine gas mass flow Chlorgasmassenstrom *m*
chloroprene rubber Chloroprenkautschuk *m*
chock Vorlegekeil *m*, Vorlegeleiste *f*
choice Wahl *f*, Auswahl *f*, Möglichkeiten *fpl*
choice of location Standortwahl *f*
choke drosseln, stauen, verstopfen, Drossel *f*
choose auswählen, wählen
chop stempeln, Stempel *m*
chop off abhacken, abschneiden
chopped moulding material geschnitzelte Pressmasse *f*
chord Sehne *f*
chord deflection Sehnenbiegung *f*
chord inflection Sehnenbiegung *f*
chordal dimension Sehnenmaß *nt*
chordal height Höhe *f* über der Sehne
chordal measurement Zahndickenmessung *f*, Sehnenmessung *f*
chordal pitch Zahnteilung *f*
chromate protective coat Chromatschutz *m*
chromating Chromatierung *f*
chromating chemical Chromatierchemikalie *f*
chromating solution Chromatierlösung *f*
chrome diffusion Chromatierung *f*
chromize chromieren
chromium Chrom *nt*
chromium mask Chrommaske *f*
chromize chromatieren
chromotopic method Chromotopsäuremethode *f*
chronology Chronologie *f*
chuck Spannfutter *nt*, Spannvorrichtung *f*, Futter *nt*; klemmen, einspannen, aufspannen, spannen
chuck backplate Futterplatte *f*
chuck jaw Einspannbacke *f*
chuck jaws *pl* Futterbacken *fpl*
chuck mounting Futterbefestigung *f*
chuck register Futteranlage *f*
chuck spring collet Federspannfutter *nt*

chuck work Futterarbeit *f*
chucking Einspannen *nt*, Einspannung *f*, Aufspannen *nt*
chucking cam Spannkurve *f*
chucking capacity Spannweite *f*
chucking device Spannvorrichtung *f*
chucking fixture Spannwerkzeug *nt*, Spannzeug *nt*, Spanneinrichtung *f*, Spanner *m*
chucking lathe Drehmaschine *f* für Futterarbeiten, Revolverdrehmaschine *f* für Futterarbeiten
chucking machine Revolverdrehmaschine *f* für Futterarbeiten
chucking spindle Spannspindel *f*
chute Rinne *f*, Ausgaberinne *f*, Leitblech *nt*, Rutsche *f*, Riefe *f*; gleiten, rutschen
chute feed Zuführung *f* von Werkstücken über Leitblech
CIM (Computer Integrated Manufacturing) CIM (Computer-integrierte Fertigung)
cinders Asche *f*
continuous joint geschlossene Fuge *f*
cipher Zahl *f*, Ziffer *f*
circle Kreis *m*
circle diagram Kreisdiagramm *nt*
circle method Kreismethode *f*
circle of curvature Krümmungskreis *m*
circle of holes Lochkreis *m*
circles Ronden *fpl*
circular aperture Kreisblende *f*
circuit Schaltung *f*, Kreislauf *m*, Glied *nt*
circuit algebra Schaltalgebra *f*
circuit board Platine *f*
circuit boards Platinen *fpl*
circuit breaker Leistungsschalter *m*, Überlastschalter *m*, Trennschalter *m*
circuit card Leiterplatte *f*
circuit diagram Schaltplan *m*
circuit element Schaltelement *nt*
circuit of conveyance Transportkreislauf *m*
circuit of transportation Transportkreislauf *m*
circuit protector Schutzschalter *m*
circuit value Stromkreiswert *m*
circuit breaker *(el.)* AUS-Schalter *m*
circuitry Schaltung *f*

circular kreisförmig, kreisrund, rund, rund laufend
circular arc Kreisbogen *m*
circular arc base line kreisbogenförmige Teilungsgrundlinie *f*
circular arc gear teeth Kreisbogenverzahnung *f*
circular bending Rundbiegen *nt*
circular blank diameter Rondendurchmesser *m*
circular blanks Ronden *fpl*
circular broach Räumwerkzeug *nt* mit kreisförmigen Querschnitt
circular chaser Rundstrehler *m*
circular cone Kreiskegel *m*
circular conveyor Karussell *nt*, Kreisförderer *m*
circular conveyor with hangers Kreisförderer *m* mit Gehängen
circular copying attachment Rundkopiereinrichtung *f*
circular cut Kreisschnitt *m*
circular disc-shaped reflector Kreisscheibenreflektor *m*
circular diving table Rundtisch *m* mit Teileinrichtung
circular division of work Rundteilen *nt* des Werkstücks
circular drilling machine Säulenbohrmaschine *f*
circular electrode Kreiselektrode *f*
circular feed Rundvorschub *m*
circular form Kreisform *f*
circular form bending Runden *nt*
circular form toolpost Rundformmeißelhalter *m*
circular forming tool Formscheibenstahl *m*, Rundformmeißel *m*
circular graduation Kreisskala *f*
circular interpolation Kreisinterpolation *f*, Zirkularinterpolation *f*
circular level Dosenlibelle *f*
circular milling Rundffräsen *nt*, Zirkularfräsen *nt*
circular milling attachment Rundkopierfräsapparat *m*, Rundfräseinrichtung *f*
circular milling operation Rundfräsarbeit *f*
circular milling table Rundfrästisch *m*

circular path Kreisbahn *f*
circular pitch Zahnteilung *f*
circular pitch measurement Kreisteilungsmessung *f*
circular pitch variation Kreisteilungsabweichung *f*
circular planing attachment Rundhobeleinrichtung *f*, Rundhobelapparat *m*
circular point guidance Kreispunktführung *f*
circular polarization Zirkularpolarisation *f*
circular profiling Rundkopieren *nt*
circular recessing Fräsen *nt* keilförmiger Ausschnitte, Fräsen *nt* kreisförmiger Auskehlungen
circular revolving table Rundtisch *m*
circular saw Kreissäge *f*
circular saw grinder (grinding machine) Kreissägeblattschärfschleifmaschine *f*
circular saw-blade Kreissägeblatt *nt*
circular sawing Kreissägen *nt*
circular slot milling Rundnutenfräsen *nt*
circular slotting Rundstoßen *nt*
circular spacing Rundteilen *nt*
circular table Rundtisch *m*
circular turning tool Rundformmeißel *m*
circular work Bearbeitung *f* mit Rundvorschub, rundes Werkstück *nt*
circular-cylindrical form Kreuzzylinderform *f*
circularity Rundheit *f*
circularity tolerance Rundheitstoleranz *f*
circular milling operation Rundfräsen *nt*, Rundfräsverfahren *nt*
circular-sawing machine Kreissägemaschine *f*
circulate zirkulieren, kreisen, umlaufen, umwälzen
circulating umlaufend
circulating conveyor Umlaufförderer *m*
circulating lubricating system Umlaufschmieranlage *f*
circulating type water heater Umlaufwasserheizer *m*

circulation Zirkulation *f*
circulation index Umwälzzahl *f*
circulation pump Umwälzpumpe *f*
circulation speed Umlaufgeschwindigkeit *f*
circulation storage system Umlauflager *nt*
circulation thermostat Umlaufthermostat *nt*
circulation water Kreislaufwasser *nt*
circulatory umlaufend
circulatory type gas water heater Umlaufgaswasserheizer *m*
circumference Umfang *m*, Kreisumfang *m*, Peripherie *f*
circumferential angle Umschlingungswinkel *m*
circumferential backlash Drehflankenspiel *nt*, Verdrehspiel *nt*
circumferential backlash fluctuation Drehflankenspielschwankung *f*
circumferential direction Umfangsrichtung *f*
circumferential fillet joint umlaufende Kehlnaht *f*
circumferential grinding Umfangschleifen *nt*
circumferential indexing Teilen *nt* eines Kreisumfanges
circumferential joint ringsum verlaufende Naht *f*
circumferential joint weld Verbindungsrundnaht *f*
circumferential line Umfangslinie *f*
circumferential speed Umfangsgeschwindigkeit *f*
circumferential surface Mantelfläche *m*, Umfangsfläche *f*, Zylinderfläche *f*
circumscribe umgrenzen
cistern manometer Gefäßmanometer *nt*
civil engineer Bauingenieur *m*
civil engineering reasons bautechnische Gründe *mpl*
clack chain protection Schlaffkettenschalter *m*
clack chain switch Schlaffkettenschalter *m*
clad plattieren

cladding Verkleidung *f*, Plattierung *f*
cladding by welding Schweißplattierung *f*
claim beanspruchen, nachfordern, anfordern; Beanstandung *f*
claim for indemnity Schadensersatzanspruch *m*
claim management Nachforderungsmanagement *nt*
clamping time Aufspannzeit *f*
clamp klemmen, befestigen, spannen, einspannen, aufspannen, feststellen, klammern; Spannschraube *f*, Spanneisen *nt*, Klemmung *f*, Klemmschraube *f*, Klemme *f*, Klammer *f*, Schelle *f*
clamp arm Klammerarm *m*
clamp bed Rundführung *f*
clamp bolt Spannbolzen *m*
clamp connection Klammerverbindung *f*
clamp coupling Schalenkupplung *f*
clamp dog Spannkolben *m*
clamp in place festklemmen
clamp in position festklemmen
clamp pressure Klammerdruck *m*
clamp taut straff einspannen
clamp turning device Klammerwender *m*
clamping klammernd, klammern *nt*, Befestigung *f*, Festklemmung *f*, Klemmen *nt*, Aufspannen *nt*, Klemmvorgang *m*, Feststellung *f*, Aufspannung *f*, Einspannung *f*, Festhalten *nt*
clamping area Aufspannfläche *f*
clamping bell Spannglocke *f*
clamping bolt Spannbolzen *m*, Befestigungsschraube *f*
clamping claw Spannklaue *f*
clamping claw gripper Spannklauengreifer *m*
clamping device Spannwerkzeug *nt*, Spannzeug *nt*, Spannvorrichtung *f*, Aufspannvorrichtung *f*, Klemmeinrichtung *f*, Klemmvorrichtung *f*
clamping element Spannelement *nt*
clamping fixture Spannvorrichtung *f*, Spannmittel *nt*, Spannzeug *nt*, Einspannvorrichtung *f*, Spannwerkzeug *nt*, Spanner *m*
clamping force Spannkraft *f*

clamping gib – clear width 74

clamping gib Spannleiste *f*
clamping into position Festspannen *nt*
clamping jaw Klemmbacke *f*, Spannbrücke *f*, Spannbacke *f*, Spannpratze *f*
clamping member Spannelement *nt*
clamping pivot Einspannzapfen *m*
clamping position Spannlage *f*
clamping position setting Spannlagebestimmung *f*
clamping roller Klemmrolle *f*
clamping roller catching device Klemmrollensperrfangvorrichtung *f*
clamping screw Feststellschraube *f*
clamping slot Spannschlitz *m*
clamping table Aufspanntisch *m*
clamping tool Aufspannwerkzeug *nt*, Spannzeug *nt*
clamp-type toolholder Klemmhalter *m*
clapper Meißelklappe *f*, Stahlhalterklappe *f*, Klappe *f*
clapper block Meißelklappe *f*, Stahlhalterklappe *f*
clapper box Meißelklappe *f*, Stahlhalterklappe *f*
clapper clamping unit Klemmschraube *f* für den Klappenträger
claret red discoloration weinrote Verfärbung *f*
clarification Abschlämmung *f*
clarify abklären
clashing Anstoßen *nt*
clasp Spange *f*, Schnalle *f*; umklammern
class Klasse *f*, Stufe *f*
class identification Gütegradkennzeichen *nt*
class limit Klassengrenze *f*
class midpoint Klassenmitte *f*
class of insulation Isolationsklasse *f*
class of operating time Laufzeitklasse *f*
class of products Warengruppe *f*
class one equipment Betriebsmittel *ntpl* der Schutzklasse 1
classification Klassifizierung *f*, Einordnung *f*, Gliederung *f*, Untergliederung *f*, Unterteilung *f*, Einstufung *f*, Aufteilung *f*, Klassenbildung *f*
classification of areas Zoneneinteilung *f*

classification of zones Zoneneinteilung *f*
classification possibility Klassifizierungsmöglichkeit *f*
classify einordnen, klassifizieren, einstufen, gliedern, sortieren, unterteilen
claw Pratze *f*, Klaue *f*
claw clamping Krallenspannung *f*, Hakenspannung *f*, Klauenspannung *f*
claw coupling Klauenkupplung *f*
clay Ton *m*
clean rein, sauber, reinigen, putzen
clean before hand vorreinigen
clean cut sauberer Schliff *m*
clean gas gereinigtes Gas *nt*
clean zone reiner Bereich *m*
cleanability Reinigungsmöglichkeit *f*
cleaner Reinigungsmaschine *f*
cleaning Reinigung *f*, Reinigen *nt*
cleaning machine Reinigungsmaschine *f*
cleaning pipe Reinigungsrohr *nt*
cleaning stage Reinigungsschritt *m*
clean-just putzgerecht
cleanliness Reinheit *f*, Sauberkeit *f*
cleanroom Reinraum *m*
cleanroom conditions Reinraumbedingungen *fpl*
cleanroom manufacture Reinraumproduktion *f*
cleanroom system Reinraumsystem *nt*
cleanroom technology Reinraumtechnik *f*
cleanse spülen
clear 1. abheben, löschen, entfernen, räumen, freikommen, freiarbeiten
2. übersichtlich, licht, durchsichtig
3. scharf
clear confirmation Auslösebestätigung *f*
clear cutter Freischneidwerkzeug *nt*
clear entry freier Abstand *m*
clear faults entstören
clear inscription eindeutige Aufschrift *f*
clear of entfernt von, mit Abstand von, ohne Berührung mit
clear span freie Stützweite *f*
clear text Klartext *m*, Klarschrift *f*
clear transparent klardurchsichtig
clear width nutzbare Breite *f*

clearance Spielraum *m*, Abstand *m*, Zwischenraum *m*, Freimaß *nt*, Spiel *nt*, Kopfspiel *nt*, Spurspiel *nt*, Spalt *m*, Abstand *m*, Aussparung *f*, Hinterdrehung *f*
clearance angle Hinterschliffwinkel *m*, Freiwinkel *m*
clearance angle of chamfer Anschnitthinterschliffwinkel *m*
clearance angle of the circular skiving cutter Schälradfreiwinkel *m*
clearance at the joint Fügespiel *nt*
clearance between spigot and socket Muffenspaltweite *f*
clearance dimension lichte Abmessung *f*
clearance fit Spielpassung *f*, Laufpassung *f*
clearance flank Spielflanke *f*
clearance gauge Umgrenzung *f* des lichten Raumes
clearance groove Einstich *m*
clearance hole Durchgangsloch *nt*
clearance in air Luftstrecke *f*
clearance of stocks Lagerräumung *f*
clearance space 1. Toleranzfeld *nt* 2. Spalt *m*
clearcut indication eindeutige Anzeige *f*
clearing Löschen *nt*, Entfernung *f*, Räumen *nt*
clearing documents Zollpapiere *ntpl*
clearly eindeutig
clearly arranged übersichtlich
cleave spalten
cleft Spalte *f*
clevis Schäkel *m*
clevis pin Bolzen *m*
clevis-type connector Einhängeverbindung *f*
click-and-dog arrangement Sperrklinkeneinrichtung *f*
click-and-pawl Sperrklinkeneinrichtung *f*
click in einrasten
client Kunde *m*, Auftraggeber *m*
client data Kundendaten *pl*
client order Kundenauftrag *m*
climate Klima *nt*, Klimazone *f*
climate associated with the landscape landschaftsgebundenes Klima *nt*
climatic klimatisch
climatic conditions Klimaverhältnisse *ntpl*
climatic effects Klimaeinflüsse *mpl*
climatic stability Klimakonstanz *f*
climb steigen, klettern; Aufstieg *m*, Steigen *nt*
climb cutting Gleichlauffräsen *nt*
climb milling gleichläufiges Fräsen *nt*
climb-cut glattlauffräsen
climb-cut milling gleichläufiges Fräsen *nt*, Gleichlauffräsen *nt*
climb-cut milling machine Gleichlauffräsmaschine *f*
climb feed method Gleichlauffräsverfahren *nt*
climbing drum peel test Trommelschälversuch *m*
climbing flame Kletterflamme *f*
clinch bördeln
clinch nut Einnietmutter *f*
clinching machine Bördelmaschine *f*
cling haften (an)
clip Klemme *f*, Schelle *f*; klemmen, klammern, umklammern, scheren
clip closing machine Clipverschließmaschine *f*
clip on aufstecken
clipping Abgratschneiden *nt* von Gussteilen oder Formwerkstücken, Beschneiden *nt* zum Entfernen eines Grates von Gussteilen oder Formwerkstücken
clock Uhr *f*; takten
clock generator Taktgeber *m*
clock memory Taktmerker *m*
clock pulse Zeittakt *m*, Takt *m*
clock unit Taktgeber *m*, Zeiteinheit *f*
clockwise im Uhrzeigersinn, rechtsdrehend
clockwise direction Uhrzeigersinn *m*
clockwise rotation Rechtslauf *m*, Rechtsdrehung *f*
clog stauen
clogging Stauung *f*, Verstopfung *f*
clogging of chips Spanstauung *f*
close eng, dicht, nah, nahe, lückenlos; schließen, verschließen
close down schließen
close joint Fuge *f* ohne Stegstand

close limit enge Auswahl *f*
close limit production Fertigung *f* unter Einhaltung enger Toleranzen
close limits Maßgrenzen *f*
close soldering joint Lötspalt *m*, Spaltlötverbindung *f*
close soldering joint width Lötfugenbreite *f*, Lötspaltbreite *f*
close to real life business praxisnah
close tolerance grooved pin Passkerbstift *m*
close tolerance grooved pin with gorge Passkerbstift *m* mit Hals
closed geschlossen, zu, eingefahren
closed chain dimensioning geschlossene Maßkette *f*
closed cracks *pl* geschlossene Risse *mpl*
closed insert nut Gewindebuchse *f*
closed loop Regelkreis *m*, Regelstrecke *f*; geschlossen prozessgekoppelt
closed loop control plant Regelung *f*
closed loop controlled system Regelstrecke *f*
closed loop controlling Regeln *nt*
closed loop controlling system Regeleinrichtung *f*
closed loop process Regelungsvorgang *f*
closed loop structure Kreisstruktur *f*
closed loop system Geschlossener Regelkreis *m*
closed pores *pl* geschlossene Poren *fpl*
closed position Geschlossenstellung *f*
closed shelf Regal *nt* mit Rück- und Seitenwänden
closed shelving Regal *nt* mit Rück- und Seitenwänden
closed square pressure gas welding geschlossenes Gaspressschweißen *nt*
closed-cell expanded material geschlossenzelliger Schaumstoff *m*
closed-die coining Massivprägen *nt*, Vollprägen *nt*
closed-die forming Gesenkformen *nt* mit ganz umschlossenem Werkstück
closed-die press forming with flash Formpressen *nt* mit Grat
closed-die press forming without flash Formpressen *nt* ohne Grat
closed-die upsetting Formstauchen *nt*
closed-loop control Regelung *f* mit geschlossenem Ein- und Ausgang, Regelkreis *m*
closed-type heating system geschlossene Heizungsanlage *f*
close-flattened specimen dicht gefaltete Probe *f*
close-grained feinkörnig
closely lückenlos
closely measured genau bemessen
closely spaced eng
close-meshed engmaschig
closeness Nähe *f*
close-pitch fluting feine Profilierung *f*
closer Schließer *m*, Aufsatz *m*
close-spaced characters Engschrift *f*
close-spaced lettering Engschrift *f*
close-toleranced engtoleriert
closing Verschließen *nt*
closing date Stichtag *m*
closing date inventory Stichtagsinventur *f*
closing dimension Schließmaß *nt*
closing element Sperrteil *nt*
closing ends of hollow items in dies Schließen *nt* der Enden hohler Werkstücke im Gesenk
closing force Schließkraft *f*
closing machine Verschließmaschine *f*
closing material Verschließhilfsmittel *nt*, Verschließmittel *nt*
closing motion Schließbewegung *f*
closing time Sicherheitszeit *f* „Betriebszustand"
closing time adjustment Schließzeiteinstellung *f*
closing tolerance Schließtoleranz *f*
closing unit Schließeinheit *f*
closure Verschluss *m*, Verschließmittel *nt*
closure demand Schließkommando *nt*
closure element Sperrteil *nt*
closure for blow-down Ausblasverschluss *m*
closure signal Schließsignal *nt*
closures on branches Abzweigverschlüsse *mpl*
cloth with diazo coating Gewebe *nt* mit Lichtpausschicht *f*

clothing material Bekleidungsmaterial *nt*
cloud point Trübungspunkt *m*
cloudy verschleiert
clout nail Breitkopfstift *m*
cluster Pulk *m*
cluster gear Stufenrad *nt*
cluster sample Klumpenstichprobe *f*
cluster sampling Klumpenprobenahme *f*
clustered porosity Porennest *nt*
clustering Pulkbildung *f*
clutch Kupplung *f*, Schaltkupplung *f*; kuppeln, einrücken, schalten, umklammern
clutch band plate Kupplungsscheibe *f*
clutch drive Kupplungsgetriebe *nt*
clutch enclosure Kupplungsgehäuse *nt*
clutch gear Kuppelrad *nt*
clutch operating device Kupplungsschaltorgan *nt*
clutching Kuppeln *nt*
CNC (Computerized Numerical Control) CNC
coach bolt Flachrundschraube *f*
coagulum content Koagulatgehalt *m*
coal dust Kohlenstaub *m*, Kohleabriebstaub *m*
coal-fired water heater with storage cylinder Speicher-Kohle-Wasserheizer *m*
coarse grob, rau, roh
coarse adjustment Grobeinstellung *f*
coarse cellular foam grobporiger Schaumstoff *m*
coarse dust filter Grobstaubfilter *m*
coarse form error Grobpassfehler *m*
coarse grade generator Grobkornentwickler *m*
coarse pitch grobe Steigung *f*
coarse pitch trapezoidal screw thread steilgängiges Trapezgewinde *nt*
coarse ripples *pl* Querkerben *fpl* in der Decklage
coarse thread Grobgewinde *nt*
coarse-feed series Grobvorschubreihe *f*
coarse-grained grobkörnig
coarse-pitch cutter Fräser *m* mit grober Zahnteilung
coarse-pitch thread Regelgewinde *nt*
coarse-tooth heavy-duty plain milling cutter Hochleistungswalzenfräser *m* mit großem Drall
coat überziehen, umhüllen, kaschieren, beschichten, anstreichen, ummanteln; Überzug *m*, Mantel *m*
coat of metal phosphate Metallphosphatschicht
coat soldering Auftraglöten *nt*
coated beschichtet, oberflächenbehandelt, überzogen, umhüllt
coating Schicht, Beschichtung *f*, Belag *m*, Umhüllung *f*, Auftragung *f*, Auftrag *m*, Überzug *m*, Anstreichen *nt*
coating by spraying Überzugsspritzen *nt*
coating material Überzugswerkstoff *m*
coating method Beschichtungsverfahren *nt*
coating of conductive silver Leitsilberschicht *f*
coating spread with a float Spachtelbelag *m*
coating thickness Überzugsschichtdicke *f*
coating time Belegungszeit *f*
coating weight per unit area Flächengewicht *nt*
coaxial koaxial
coaxial cable Koaxialkabel *nt*
coaxial cylinder gleichachsiger Zylinder *m*
coaxiality tolerance Koaxialitätstoleranz
cobalt steel Kobaltstahl *m*
cobweb-like surface cracks *pl* spinnennetzartige Oberflächenrisse *mpl*
cock Hahn *m*, Ventil *nt*
code Code *m*, Codierung *f*; codieren, verschlüsseln
code checking Codeprüfung *f*
code length Codelänge *f*
code letter Kennbuchstabe *m*
code number Zählnummer *f*
code of programming Programmierungscode *m*
code pattern Codemuster *nt*
code specification Codespezifikation *f*
code system Kodierungssystem *nt*
coder Codierer *m*

coder converter Codeumsetzer *m*
codeword Codewort *nt*
coding Codierung *f*, Verschlüsselung *f*
coding machine Codiermaschine *f*
coding strip Codierleiste *f*
coefficient Faktor *m*, Beiwert *m*
coefficient of compressibility Kompressibilitätskoeffizient *m*
coefficient of correlation Korrelationskoeffizient *m*
coefficient of friction Reibwert *m*
coefficient of holding power Haftbeiwert *m*
coefficient of impregnation Tränkungswert *m*
coefficient of linear thermal expansion thermischer Längenausdehnungskoeffizient *m*
coefficient of refraction Brechungskoeffizient *m*
coefficient of variation Variationskoeffizient *m*
coefficient of wear Abnutzungsfaktor *m*
coefficient of pressure increase Druckanstiegskoeffizient *m*
coefficient of thermal conductivity Temperaturleitzahl *f*
cog Zapfen *m*
cognate linkage Ersatzgetriebe *nt*
cohere zusammenhängen
coherent zusammenhängend, kohärent
cohesion Kohäsion *f*, Zusammenhang *m*
cohesion fracture Kohäsionsbruch *m*
cohesive kohäsiv
cohesive metal coat zusammenhängender Metallüberzug *m*
coil Ring *m*, Spule *f*, Wendel *m*, Bund *m*, Rolle *f*, Spirale *f*; spulen (um, auf), aufwickeln, wickeln
coil chip Wendelspan *m*, Spiralspan *m*, Schraubenbruchspan *m*
coil excitation Spulenerregung *f*
coil passing a heavy current hochstrombelastete Spule *f*
coil resistance Wicklungswiderstand *m*
coil spring Schraubenfeder *f*
coil up aufrollen
coiled bundle Ringbund *m*
coiled tube Trompetenrohr *nt*

coiled-up chip Wendelspan *m*
coiler Wickler *m*, Wickeleinrichtung *f*
coiling Aufwickeln *nt*
coincide übereinstimmen (mit), zusammenfallen
coincidence Zusammenfallen *nt*, Zufall *m*
coincidental zufällig
cold kalt, Kälte *f*
cold adhesive Kaltklebstoff *m*
cold air control damper Kaltluftregelklappe *f*
cold bonding Kaltkleben *nt*
cold breaking temperature Kältebruchtemperatur *f*
cold brittleness Kaltsprödigkeit *f*
cold chamber machine Kaltkammermaschine *f*
cold chisel Kaltmeißel *m*
cold circular saw Kaltkreissäge *f*
cold crack Kaltriss *m*
cold crushing strength Druckfestigkeit *f* bei Raumtemperatur
cold extrusion Kaltfließpressen *nt*
cold flow property Kältefließfähigkeit *f*
cold flowability Kaltfließfähigkeit *f*
cold form fill and seal machine Kaltform-, -füll- und -verschließmaschine *f*
cold formability Kaltformbarkeit *f*
cold forming Kaltformen *nt*, Kaltumformen *nt*
cold forming by spinning Abschreckdrücken *nt*, Drückwalzen *nt*
cold head capability Kaltstauchbarkeit *f*
cold headed kaltgestaucht
cold header Kaltstauchmaschine *f*
cold heating Kaltstauchen *nt*
cold junction Kaltlötstelle *f*
cold lap Mattschweißstelle *f*
cold moulding material Kaltformmasse *f*
cold plasticity Kaltformbarkeit *f*
cold pressure extrusion welding Fließpressschweißen *nt*
cold pressure upset welding Anstauchschweißen *nt*
cold processable sealant kalt verarbeiteter Dichtstoff *m*
cold reforming Kaltumformen *nt*

cold resisting kältefest
cold restart Kaltstart *m*
cold rolled section Kaltprofil *nt*
cold rolled strip Kaltband *nt*
cold rolling Kaltwalzen *nt*
cold saw Kaltsäge *f*
cold set casting moulded material kaltgehärteter Gießharzformstoff *m*
cold set grease kalt versteiftes Schmierfett *nt*
cold setting resin moulding material kaltgehärtete Gießharzmasse *f*
cold shortness Kaltbruch *m*
cold start Kaltstart *m*
cold storage room Kühlraum *m*
cold store Kühlhaus *nt*
cold straighten kaltrichten
cold upsetting Kaltstauchen *nt*
cold water inlet pipe Kaltwasserzuleitung *f*
cold water pressure Kaltwasserdruck *m*
cold welding by the arc method elektrisches Kaltschweißen *nt*
cold work kaltbearbeiten
cold working Kaltformen *nt*
cold-bend kaltbiegen
cold-chamber pressure casting Kaltkammerdruckguss *m*
cold-chamber pressure die-casting machine Kaltkammerdruckgießmaschine *f*
cold-chamber process Kaltkammerverfahren *nt*
cold-extrusion die Kaltfließpresswerkzeug *nt*
cold-extrusion process Kaltfließpressverfahren *nt*
cold-flowable kaltfließfähig
cold-forge kaltschmieden
cold-forgeable kaltstauchbar
cold-form kaltbearbeiten, kaltformen
cold-formable kaltformbar, kaltverformbar
cold-heading machine Kaltstauchmaschine *f*
cold-heating die Kaltstauchmatrize *f*
cold-process kaltverarbeiten
cold-roll kaltwalzen
cold-workable kaltverformbar

collapse zusammenlegen, zusammenklappen, zusammenbrechen, zusammenfallen, zusammenstürzen; Zusammensturz *m*, Zusammenbrechen *nt*
collapse in profits Gewinneinbruch *m*
collapsible klappbar, zusammenklappbar, zusammenlegbar
collapsible tube Quetschtube *f*
collapsing test Knickversuch *m*, Ausknickversuch *m*
collar Hülse *f*, Buchse *f*, Abstandsring *m*, Zwischenring *m*, Bund *m*, Manschette *f*, Skalentrommel *f*, Skalenring *m*
collar diameter Bunddurchmesser *m*
collar nut Mutter *f* mit Bund
collaring holes by drawing Kragenziehen *nt*
collect ansammeln, sammeln, erfassen, auffangen, erheben, einziehen
collecting magnet Sammelmagnet *nt*
collecting tray Fangschale *f*
collection Erfassung *f*, Erhebung *f*, Einzug *m*
collection drawing Sammelzeichnung *f*
collection of data Datenerhebung *f*
collection of rows Reihensammlung *f*
collection point Sammelstelle *f*
collective heating system Sammelheizung *f*
collector Kollektor *m*, Kommutator *m*
collector brush Stromabnehmer *m*
collector line Schleifleitung *f*
collector motor Kollektormotor *m*
collet Reduziereinsatz *m*, Spannzange *f*
collet chuck Spannfutter *m*, Zangenspannfutter *nt*
collet chucking Zangenspannung *f*
collet gripping Zangenaufnahme *f*
collet gripping mechanism Zangenspannung *f*
collet mounting Zangenaufnahme *f*
collide kollidieren, aufprallen, zusammenprallen, zusammenstoßen
collide with rammen
collimate einblenden
collimated ray beam ausgeblendetes Strahlenbündel *nt*
collision Kollision *f*, Aufprall *m*, Zusam-

menprall *m*, Zusammenstoß *m*
collision guard Rammschutz *m*, Kollisionsschutz *m*
collision prevention Kollisionsschutz *m*, Kollisionsverhinderung *f*
collision prevention sensor Kollisionsschutzsensor *m*
collision prevention sensors Kollisionsschutzsensorik *f*
collision protection Kollisionsschutz *m*, Aufprallschutz *m*
collision stopping power Stoßbremsvermögen *nt*
collisions occur zusammenprallen
collaborate mitwirken
collaboration Mitwirkung *f*
colorimetric method farbmetrisches Verfahren *nt*
colour Farbe *f*
colour arrangement Farbgestaltung *f*
colour impression Farbaufdruck *m*
colouration Tönung *f*
coloured pigment Buntpigment *nt*
coloured stain Farbfleck *m*
colour-indicator titration Farbindikatortitration *f*
colouring matter farbgebender Stoff *m*
colouring substance farbgebender Stoff *m*
colourless chromating Farbloschromatierung *f*
column 1. Ständer *m*, Säule *f*, Stütze *f*, Mast *m* **2.** *(Tisch)* Spalte *f*
column and knee type machine Konsolmaschine *f*
column-and-knee type vertical-spindle milling machine Senkrechtkonsolfräsmaschine *f*
column-and-knee-type miller Konsolenfräsmaschine *f*
column attachment Kolonnenaufsatz *m*
column base Ständerfuß *m*
column clamp mechanism Ständerklemmung *f*
column depalletizer Säulendepalletierer *m*
column face Ständerwange *f*
column heading panel Kopfleiste *f*
column instrument Säulengerät *nt*
column movement Ständerverstellung *f*
column of flue gas Rauchgassäule *f*
column palletizer Säulenpalettierer *m*
column piloting cutter Säulenführungsschneidwerkzeug *nt*
column profile Stützenprofil *nt*
column splice Stützenstoß *m*
column stacking Säulenstapelung *f*
column travel Ständerverstellung *f*
column traverse Ständerverstellung *f*
column traversing feed Ständervorschub *m*
column Vees Ständerprisma *nt*
column way Ständerausführung *f*
column ways Führungsbahnen *fpl* am Ständer, Ständerführung *f*
column with V-ways Ständer *m* mit Prismenführung
column-type machine Ständermaschine *f*
combination Kombination *f*, Kombinierbarkeit *f*, Verbund *m*, Zusammenfügung *f*
combination blanking and piercing Gesamtschneiden *nt*
combination broach-burnisher tool Räum- und Glättwerkzeug *nt*
combination cutter Gesamtschneidwerkzeug *nt*
combination gauge block Maßbild *nt*, Maßblock *m*, Maßklötzchen *nt*, Parallelendmaß *nt*
combination of systems Anlagenverbund *m*
combination of tolerance zones Paarung *f* von Toleranzfeldern
combination pliers Kombinationszange *f*
combination plunge traverse grinding Verbundschleifen *nt*
combination socket Kombinationsmuffe *f*
combination tool block Mehrfachmeißelhalter *m*, Blockmeißelhalter *m*
combination toolholder Mehrfachmeißelhalter *m*
combination turning Dreh- und Bohrmaschine *f*
combination turret lathe Schlittenre-

volverdrehmaschine *f*, Bettschlittenrevolverdrehmaschine *f*, Revolverdrehmaschine *f* mit Querschlitten auf dem Bettschlitten
combination wrench Ringmaulschlüssel *m*
combinatory switching kombinatorische Schaltung *f*
combine kombinieren, zusammenfügen, vereinen, verbinden
combined cycle kombiniertes Spiel *nt*
combined douche kombinierte Spülung *f*
combined drawing gemeinsames Ziehen *nt*
combined drill and milling cutter Bohrfräswerkzeug *nt*
combined fuel burner Kombinationsbrenner *m*
combined inputs *pl* verknüpfte Eingänge *mpl*
combined planing and milling machine Hobel- und Fräsmaschine *f*
combined pressboard Verbundspan *m*
combined pressboard sheet Verbundspantafel *f*
combined square Vee-guide Flachbahn- und Prismaführung *f*
combined station Hybridstation *f*
combined vertical and horizontal milling machine Lang- und Senkrechtfräsmaschine *f*
combined warehouse Kombinationslager *nt*
combined-operation work Verbundarbeit *f*
combing position kämmende Stellung *f*
comb staple method Kammstapelverfahren *nt*
combust verbrennen
combustible brennbar
combustible gases brennbare Gase *ntpl*
combustible waste matter *pl* brennbare Abfälle *mpl*
combustion Verbrennung *f*, Abbrand *m*
combustion air Verbrennungsluft *f*
combustion air limiter Verbrennungsluftbegrenzer *m*

combustion air throttle valve Verbrennungsluftklappe *f*
combustion crucible Verbrennungstiegel *m*
combustion cup Verbrennungstiegel *m*
combustion dish Verbrennungsschale *f*
combustion factor Abbrandfaktor *m*
combustion performance testing verbrennungstechnische Prüfung *f*
combustion period Abbrandperiode *f*
combustion process Verbrennungsablauf *m*
combustion space pressure Feuerraumdruck *m*
combustion-engined verbrennungsmotorisch
comby narbig
come clear of freikommen
come in einlaufen
come loose sich lockern
come to a standstill zum Stillstand *m* kommen
come-along clamp Greifzug *m* (zum Verlegen)
comfort Bequemlichkeit *f*
coming loose Lockern *nt*
command befehlen; Auftrag *m*, Befehl *m*, Bedienanweisung *f*, Kommando *nt*
command position Sollposition *f*, Sollwert *m*
command processing (EDV) Auftragsverarbeitung *f*
command signal Führungssignal *nt*
command variable action Führungsverhalten *nt*
command variable control Führungssteuerung *f*
comma-shape kommaförmig
commence anfangen
commencement Anfang *m*
commencement chip thickness Spanstärke *f* am Anfang des Schnittes
commencement of crack Rissbeginn *m*
comment Kommentar *m*; kommentieren
commerce Handel *m*
commercial district Gewerbegebiet *nt*
commercial sample Warenmuster *nt*

commercially available handelsgängig
commissioning test Anlaufprobe *f*
commission kommissionieren
commission work station Kommissionierarbeitsplatz *f*
commissioner Kommissionierer *m*
commissioning 1. Kommissionierung *f*, Kommissionieren *nt* **2.** Inbetriebnahme *f*
commissioning area Kommissionierungszone *f*
commissioning cart Kommissionierwagen *m*
commissioning certificate Inbetriebnahmeprotokoll *nt*
commissioning conveyor Kommissionierfahrzeug *nt*
commissioning description Inbetriebnahmebeschreibung *f*
commissioning sequence Inbetriebnahmeprozedur *f*
commissioning stacker Kommissionierstapler *m*
commissioning station Kommissionierplatz *m*
commodities Verbrauchsartikel *f*
commodity goods Verbrauchsartikel *f*
common üblich
common calliper rule Werkstatt-Schieblehre *f*
common calliper square Werkstatt-Schieblehre *f*
common mode Gleichtakt *m*
common mode coupling Gleichtakteinkopplung *f*
common zone allgemeiner Verkehrsbereich *m*
commonly used gebräuchlich
common-mode voltage Gleichtaktspannung *f*
communicate kommunizieren, mitteilen
communication 1. Kommunikation *f*, Kommunizieren *nt*, Übermittlung *f*, Informationsaustausch *m* **2.** *(IT)* Verbindung *f*
communication area Kommunikationsbereich *m*
communication characteristics Kommunikationseigenschaften *fpl*

communication distance Kommunikationsabstand *m*
communication duration Kommunikationsdauer *f*
communication error Fehler *m* in der Verbindung
communication module Kommunikationsbaugruppe *f*
communication partner Kommunikationspartner *m*
communication port Kommunikationsschluss *m*
communication process Kommunikationsprozess *m*
communication range Kommunikationsbereich *m*
communication time Kommunikationszeit *f*
commutate wenden, kommutieren, umpolen
commutating frequency Umschaltfrequenz *f*
commutating pole Wendepol *m*
commutation Kommutierung *f*
commutator Kommutator *m*, Umschalter *m*, Stromwender *m*
commutator sparking Bürstenfeuer *nt*
commute umwandeln, kommutieren
compact 1. dicht, kompakt, festigen, verdichten **2.** verpressen, pressformen, Pressling *m*
compact condition gestopfter Zustand *m*
compact design Kompaktbauweise *f*
compactable soil verdichtungsfähiger Boden *m*
compacted apparent bulk density Stampfdichte *f*
compacting in the space between pipe and trench wall Zwickelverdichtung *f*
compaction Verpressen *nt*
compaction on either side of the bottom half of the pipe Zwickelverdichtung *f*
compactness Festigkeit *f*
compactness of the packing Lagerungsdichte *f*
companion part Gegenstück *nt*
company Unternehmen *nt*

company organization Aufbauorganisation *f*
company policy Unternehmenspolitik *f*; unternehmenspolitisch
company standard Werknorm *f*
company-specific unternehmensspezifisch
comparability Vergleichbarkeit *f*
comparable vergleichbar
comparative vergleichend
comparative characteristic value Vergleichskennzahl *f*
comparative index Vergleichszahl *f*
comparative scattering body Vergleich-Streukörper *m*
comparative test Vergleichsuntersuchung *f*
comparative tracking index (CTI) Vergleichszahl *f* der Kriechwegbildung *f*
comparator Vergleicher *m*
compare gegenüberstellen, vergleichen
comparing element Summierglied *nt*
comparing operation Vergleichsoperation *f*
comparing point Vergleichsstelle *f*
comparison section Vergleichsstrecke *f*
comparison Vergleich *m*
comparison of the offers Angebotsvergleich *m*
comparison stress Vergleichsspannung *f*
comparison test Vergleichsversuch *m*
comparison-tolerance Vergleichstreubereich *m*
compartment Gehäuse *nt*, Innenraum *m*
compartment end stop Durchschubsicherung *f*
compasses *pl* Zirkel *m*
compatibility Kompatibilität *f*, Verträglichkeit *f*
compatibility level Verträglichkeitspegel *m*
compatible kompatibel, vertraglich, übereinstimmend
compatible with the system systemkompatibel
compel zwingen
compensate ausgleichen, kompensieren

compensate for wear Verschleiß ausgleichen
compensate pressure Druck ausgleichen
compensating coupling Ausgleichskupplung *f*
compensating device Ausgleichsvorrichtung *f*
compensating mutual inductance Kompensationsgegeninduktivität
compensation Kompensation *f*, Ausgleich *m*
compensation memory Ausgleichsspeicher *m*
compensation motion Nachstellbewegung *f*
compensation stress Druckbeanspruchung *f*
compensation time Ausgleichszeit *f*
compensation value Ausgleichswert *m*
compensation washer Ausgleichsscheibe *f*
compensator Wippe *f*
compensatory coil Kompensationswicklung *f*
compensatory time off Zeitausgleich *m*
compensatory winding Kompensationswicklung *f*
compete konkurrieren
competence Befugnis *f*, Kompetenz *f*, Zuständigkeit *f*
competent fachkundig, sachkundig, qualifiziert, zuständig, befugt
competition Wettbewerb *m*
competitive advantage Wettbewerbsvorteil *m*
competitive pressures Wettbewerbsdruck *m*
competitor Konkurrent *m*
compilation Erstellung *f*, Zusammenstellung *f*, Übersetzung *f*
compilation run Übersetzungslauf *m*
compilation time Übersetzungszeit *f*
compile zusammenstellen, kommissionieren, erstellen, übersetzen
compile and go übersetzen und starten
compile inspection documents Prüfbeleg erstellen
compile time Übersetzungszeit *f*

compiler Compiler *m*, Kompilierer *m*, Übersetzer *m*
complain about reklamieren, beanstanden
complaint Reklamation, Beanstandung *f*
complaints processing Reklamationsbearbeitung *f*
complementary cone Ergänzungskegel *m*
complement Gegenstück *nt*
complement angle Komplementwinkel *m*
complementary cone angle Ergänzungskegelwinkel *m*
complementary cone apex Ergänzungskegelspitze *f*
complementary output komplementärer Ausgang *m*
complementary purchase Zukauf *m*
complete fertig stellen, komplettieren, vollenden, ergänzen, abwickeln, abschließen; komplett, vollständig, voll, lückenlos, gesamt, ganz
complete acceptance Gesamtabnahme *f*
complete demineralization Vollentsalzung *f*
complete failure Totalausfall *m*
complete floor area demand Gesamtgeschossflächenbedarf *m*
complete gear body geschlossener Radkörper *m*
complete processing Komplettbearbeitung *f*
complete shrink wrap Vollschrumpffolienumhüllung *f*
complete traverse grinding Pendelschleifen *nt*
complete traverse thread Längsgewinde *nt*
complete traverse thread grinding Gewindelängsschleifen *nt*, Längsgewindeschleifen *nt*, Gewindedurchgangsschleifen *nt*
complete vertical integration vollständige vertikale Integration *f*
complete volume Komplettmenge *f*
completed fertig gestellt
completely rotatable umlauffähig
complement ergänzen

completeness Vollständigkeit *f*
completion Fertigstellung *f*, Abwicklung *f*
complex control factor komplexer Regelfaktor *m*
complex grease Komplexfett *nt*
complex loop gain komplexe Kreisverstärkung *f*
complex modulus komplexer Modul *m*
complex shape Vielgestaltigkeit *f*
compliance Übereinstimmung *f*, Entsprechung *f*
compliance with delivery deadlines Liefertermineinhaltung *f*
compliance with delivery quantities Liefermengeneinhaltung *f*
comply übereinstimmen (mit), entsprechen
compole Wendepol *m*
component Bestandteil *nt*, Komponente *f*, Einzelteil *nt*, Bauelement *nt*, Maschinenelement *nt*, Bauteil *nt*, Stückteil *nt*, Stück *nt*, Werkstück *nt*
component assembly Bauteilgruppe *f*
component burner Teilbrenner *m*
component current Teilstrom *m*
component drawing Stückzeichnung *f*, Teilzeichnung *f*
component failure Fügeteilbruch *m*
component flame Teilflamme *f*
component of force in cutting Schnittkraftkomponente *f*
component of stable shape formstabiles Teil *nt*
component of the cutting force Zerspankraftkomponente *f*
component of unstable shape nicht formstabiles Teil *nt*
component part Einzelteil *nt*
component shown with break lines unterbrochen gezeichnetes Teil *nt*
component supplying industry Zulieferindustrie *f*
component supplier Zulieferer *m*
component testing Teilprüfung *f*
component testing installation Bauteilprüfanlage *f*
component unscrambler Ausrichtmaschine *f* für Packhilfsmittel
component-based automation kom-

ponentenbasierende Automatisierung *f*
components force sensor Komponentenkraftsensor *m*
compose zusammensetzen
composite gemischt
composite assembly drawing Verbundgruppenzeichnung *f*
composite can Kombidose *f*
composite design Verbundausführung *f*
composite error Gesamtfehler *m*, Sammelfehler *m*
composite error testing Sammelfehlerprüfung *f*
composite film Verbundfolie *f*
composite fracture Mischbruch *m*
composite hypothesis zusammengesetzte Hypothese *f*
composite metal nut kombinierte Metallmutter *f*
composite pattern Verbundausführung *f*
composite plant gemischter Betrieb *m*
composite sample Sammelprobe *f*
composite specimen Verbundsystem *nt*
composite tool zusammengesetztes Werkzeug *nt*
composite type Verbundausführung *f*
composite wheel Rad *nt* aus mehrerer Materialien
composite wheel centre Radkörper *m* aus mehreren Bestandteilen
composition Aufbau *m*, Aktivierung *f*, Beschaffenheit *f*, Zusammensetzung *f*, Zusammenstellung *f*
compound mischen; Verbindung *f*
compound excitation Compounderregung *f*, Doppelschlusserregung *f*
compound foil Verbundfolie *f*
compound forming the coating layer Deckschichtverbindung *f*
compound indexing Verbundteilen *nt*
compound joints *pl* zusammengesetzte Nähte *fpl*
compound layer thickness Verbindungsschichtdicke *f*
compound lifting jack Teleskophubzylinder *m*
compound motor Doppelschlusserregung *f*
compound quantity Compoundmenge *f*
compound slide rest Kreuzsupport *m*, Kreuzschlitten *m*
compound spring type straight pin Verbundspannstift *m*
compound tool Verbundwerkzeug *nt*
compound type Compoundtyp *m*
compound vertical milling attachment Senkrechtfräsvorrichtung *f* mit Kreuzschlitten
compound vertical-spindle attachment Senkrechtfräsvorrichtung *f* mit Kreuzschlitten
compound-rest slide Kreuzschlitten *m*
comprehend umfassen
compress drücken, komprimieren, pressen, verpressen, verdichten, quetschen, zusammendrücken, zusammenpressen, stauchen
compress under heat verpressen
compress work Staucharbeit *f*
compressed air Druckluft *f*, Pressluft *f*
compressed air ageing Luftdruckalterung *f*
compressed air blasting Druckluftstrahlen *nt*
compressed air cylinder Pneumatikzylinder *m*
compressed air principle Druckluftprinzip *nt*
compressed air regulator Druckluftdruckminderer *m*
compressed air system plan Druckluftschaltplan *m*
compressed flat rod for laminated plastics Flachleiste *f* bei Schichtpressstoffen
compressed sheet Flachpressplatte *f*
compressed-air line Druckluftleitung *f*
compressibility Kompressibilität *f*
compressibility factor Kompressibilitätsfaktor *m*
compressible kompressibel
compressing Verpressen *nt*
compression Druck *m*, Kompressionsdruck *m*, Kompression *f*, Komprimierung *f*, Zusammendrückung *f*, Zusammendrücken *nt*, Stauchung *f*

compression at fracture Bruchstauchung f
compression coil Kompressionsspule f
compression coupling Klemmkupplung f, Schalenkupplung f
compression error Stauchfehler m
compression flexometer Kompensationsflexometer nt
compression force Druckkraft f
compression mould pressen, formpressen; Pressung f, Pressform f
compression mould attachment Presswerkzeugaufsatz m
compression mould block Presswerkzeugblock m
compression moulded material Pressstoff m
compression of sand Sandverdichtung f
compression offset yield stress Stauchspannung f
compression phase Kompressionsphase f
compression proving element Druckmesskörper m
compression proving ring Druckbügel m
compression relationship Stauchverhältnis nt
compression resistance Stauchwiderstand m
compression resistance test Stauchwiderstandsprüfung f
compression shear test Druckscherversuch m
compression stress Druckspannung f
compression stress value Stauchhärte f
compression stress-strain characteristics Federkennlinie f
compression surface finishing Glattprägen nt
compression test Stauchprüfung f
compression time Presszeit f
compression travel Stauchweg m
compression yield Stauchspannung f
compression zone bent outwards Druckkzone aufgebogen
compression-loaded druckbelastet
compression-proof druckfest

compressive clamp Federspanneisen nt
compressive deformation Längenänderung f
compressive failure Druckspannungsbruch m
compressive loading Dehnbeanspruchung f
compressive preloading Druckvorbeanspruchung f
compressive reforming Druckumformen nt
compressive set Druckverformungsrest m
compressive stress-strain curve Druckspannung-Stauchungs-Kurve f
compressive wave Kompressionswelle f
compressive yield stress Quetschspannung f
compressor Verdichter m
comprisal Einschluss m
comprise umfassen, einschließen, enthalten
composition of the filler metal Lotzusammensetzung f
compulsory zwangsweise, zwangsläufig
computation Berechnung f
computational mistake Rechenfehler m
compute ausrechnen, berechnen, rechnen
Computer Aided Design (CAD) CAD (Computer unterstütze Konstruktion) f
Computer Aided Engineering (CAE) CAE (Computer unterstützes Ingenieurwesen) nt
Computer Aided Manufacturing (CAM) CAM (Computer unterstütze Fertigung) f
Computer Aided Planning (CAP) CAP (Computer unterstütze Planung, Fertigungsvorbereitung) f
Computer Aided Programming maschinelle Programmierung f
Computer Aided Quality Assurance (CAQ) CAQ (Computer unterstützte Qualitätssicherung) f
Computer Aided Testing (CAT) CAT

(Computer unterstütztes Prüfen) *nt*
Computer Aided Three-Dimensional Interactive Applications CATIA
computer control unit Computersteuergerät *nt*
computer load Rechnerlast *f*
computer processing system DV-System *nt*
computer processor Rechnerwerk *nt*
computer program Rechenprogramm *nt*
computer simulation Rechnersimulation *f*
computer system Rechnersystem *nt*
computer-aided rechnergestützt
computer-assisted measurement rechnergestütztes Messen *nt*
computer-controlled rechnergesteuert
computer-controlled machine datengesteuerte Maschine *f*
computer-drawn rechnergezeichnet
computerization concept informationstechnisches Konzept *nt*
computer-supported computergestützt
computing element Rechenglied *nt*
computing time Rechenzeit *f*
concatenate verketten
concatenation Verkettung *f*
concave hohl
concave cutter Konkavfräser *m*
concave fillet joint Kehlnaht *f* mit hoher Oberfläche
concave gear Kehlrad *nt*
concave grinding Hohlschliff *m*
concave grinding attachment Hohlschleifvorrichtung *f*
concave milling cutter Fräser *m* für Halbkreisprofil
concave rack hobbing machine Hohlzahnstangenwälzfräsmaschine *f*
concave weld Kehlnaht *f*
concavity on root side Wurzelrückfall *m*
concentrate bündeln, anreichern
concentration 1. Aufmerksamkeit *f*, Konzentration *f* **2.** *(Werkstoff)* Anreicherung *f*
concentration of plasticiser vapour Weichmacherdampfkonzentration *f*
concentration overvoltage Konzentrationsüberspannung *f*
concentration resistance Konzentrationswiderstand *m*
concentric chuck Universalfutter *nt*
concentric datum surface zentrische Bezugsfläche *f*
concentric jet burner Flammenstrahlbrenner *m*
concentric konzentrisch
concentricity Mittigkeit *f*, Rundlauf *m*, Rundlaufgenauigkeit *f*
concentricity deviation Rundheitsabweichung *f*
concentricity error Rundlauffehler *m*
concentricity test Rundheitsprüfung *f*
concentricity tolerance Rundlauftoleranz *f*
concentricity tolerancing Rundlauftolerierung *f*
concentricity variation Rundlaufabweichung *f*
concept Konzept *nt*, Plan *m*, Begriff *m*
concept phase Vorplanungsphase *f*
concept planning Vorplanung *f*
conceptually projected vorprojektiert
concern own betriebseigen
concerning über *(ein Thema)*
conclude abschließen, folgern
conclude a sale einen Verkauf *m* abschließen
concluding planning report Planungsabschlussbericht *m*
conclusion Folgerung *f*, Konklusion *f*
conclusion of a contract Vertragsabschluss *m*
conclusion of planning Planungsabschluss *m*
concordant übereinstimmend
concrete Beton *m*
concrete bedding Betonauflager *nt*
concrete floor Betonfußboden *m*
concrete for a surround Ummantelungsbeton *m*
concrete joint sealing compound Beton-Vergussmasse *f*
concrete pipe Betonrohr *nt*
concrete pipe with adapter fittings Betonrohr *nt* mit Anschlussstücken
concrete pipe with base Betonrohr *nt*

mit Fuß
concrete pipe with bottom slab Betonrohr *nt* mit Bodenplatte
concrete pipe with branch Betonrohr *nt* mit Zulauf
concrete pipe with channel Betonrohr *nt* mit Gerinne
concrete pipe with concentric cross-section Betonrohr *nt* mit Kreisquerschnitt
concrete pipe with egg-shaped cross-section Betonrohr *nt* mit Eiquerschnitt
concrete pipe with extra wall thickness Betonrohr *nt* mit verstärkter Wanddicke
concrete pipe with offset extensions Betonrohr *nt* mit seitlichen Ansätzen
concrete pipe with rebate Betonrohr *nt* mit Falz
concrete pipe with side branch Betonrohr *nt* mit Seitenzulauf
concrete pipe with socket Betonrohr *nt* mit Muffe
concrete pipe with spigot end Betonrohr *nt* mit Spitzende
concrete pipe with top branch Betonrohr *nt* mit Scheitelzulauf
concrete roof Betondach *nt*
concrete structure Betonkonstruktion *f*
concrete surface Betonoberfläche *f*
concrete surround Betonummantelung *f*
concrete wall Betonwand *f*
condensate collector Kondensatsammler *m*
condensate cooler Kondensatkühler *m*
condensate drain Kondensatabfluss *m*, Kondensatableiter *m*
condensate piping Niederschlagwasserleitung *f*
condensate return Kondensatrückführung *f*
condensate trap Kondensatabscheider *m*, Kondensatableiter *m*, Wassertopf *m*
condensation Kondensatfeuchte *f*, Kondenswasserbildung *f*, Betauung *f*
condensation atmosphere Kondenswasserklima *nt*

condensation climate Schwitzwasserklima *nt*
condensation effect Schwitzeffekt *m*
condensation water alternating atmosphere Kondenswasserwechselklima *nt*
condense verdichten
condenser Kondensator *m*, Verdichter *m*, Verflüssiger *m*
condenser discharge arc stud welding Lichtbogenschmelzschweißen *nt* mit Spitzenzündung
condenser lens Monogenisierungslinse *f*
condenser with water re-cooling Kondensator *m* mit Wasserrückkühlung
consignment size Sendungsgröße *f*
condition Bedingung *f*, Voraussetzung *f*, Auflage *f*, Beschaffenheit *f*, Zustand *m*; bedingen, aufbereiten
condition as delivered Anlieferzustand *m*
condition at a give temperature temperieren
condition for use Verarbeitungszustand *m*
condition of test specimen Probenzustand *m*
conditional bedingt
conditional distribution bedingte Verteilung *f*
conditional expectation bedingter Erwartungswert *m*
conditional jump bedingter Sprung *m*
conditioned atmosphere Prüfklima *nt*
conditioned by the manufacturing process herstellungsbedingt
conditioned by the material werkstoffbedingt
conditioned by the plant anlagebedingt
conditioning Vorbehaltung *f*, Aufbereitung *f*, Behandlung *f*, Angleichen *nt*
conditioning atmosphere Vorbehaltungsklima *nt*
conditioning cell Klimazelle *f*
conditioning chamber Klimaraum *m*
conditioning of samples Probenbehandlung *f*
conditioning time Angleichzeit *f*

conditions *pl* **applicable to individual family of machines** maschinenspezifische Bedingungen *fpl*
conduct ausführen, durchführen, leiten, fortleiten, führen; Durchführung *f*
conduct away abführen
conduct of test Versuchsdurchführung *f*
conductance Durchführung *f*
conducted leitungsgebunden, leitungsgeführt
conducted emission leitungsgebundene Aussendung *f*
conducting leitfähig
conducting away Abführung *f*
conduction *(Wärme)* Leitung *f*
conduction resistance welding konduktives Widerstandspressschweißen *nt*
conductive leitfähig
conductive resistance Ableitwiderstand *m*
conductive wheel elektrisch leitfähiges Rad *nt*
conductivity Leitfähigkeit *f*, Ableitung *f*
conductivity measurement Leitfähigkeitsmessung *f*
conductor Leiter *m*
conductor cross section Leitungsquerschnitt *m*, Leiterquerschnitt *m*
conduit Rohr *nt*, Kanal *m*, Leitkanal *m*, Leitung *f*, Rohrleitung *f*
conduit box Klemmenkasten *m*
cone Kegel *m*, Konus *m*
cone angle tolerance Kegelwinkeltoleranz *f*
cone bearing Konuskugellager *nt*
cone brake Kegelbremse *f*
cone diameter tolerance Kegeldurchmessertoleranz *f*
cone distance Teilkegellänge *f*
cone drive Stufenscheibenantrieb *m*
cone form tolerance Kegelformtoleranz *f*
cone generating angle Kegelerzeugungswinkel *m*
cone generator Kegelmantellinie *f*
cone penetration Konuspenetration *f*
cone point Spitze *f*
cone pulley Stufenscheibe *f*
cone pulley drive Stufenscheibengetriebe *nt*
cone tolerance field Kegeltoleranzfeld *nt*
cone tolerance space Kegeltoleranzraum *m*
cone tolerance system Kegeltoleranzsystem *nt*
coned half-dog point Ansatzspitze *f*
cone-roll piercing Schrägwalzen *nt* zum Lochen mit kegelförmigen Walzen
cone-shaped kegelförmig
cone turning Kegeldrehen *nt*
cone-type face milling cutter with inserted blades Fräskopf *m* mit eingesetzten Messern
confidence coefficient Sicherheit *f*
confidence interval Vertrauensbereich *m*, Schätzbereich *m*
confidence level statistische Sicherheit *f*, Vertrauensniveau *nt*
confidence limit Vertrauensgrenze *f*
configuration Konfiguration *f*, Form *f*
configuration management Konfigurationsmanagement *nt*
configuration of the surface Oberflächengestalt *f*
configurations Umriss *m*
configure konfigurieren, gruppieren, zusammenstellen
confine beschränken
confined geschlossen, umschlossen
confined space geschlossener Bereich *m*
confined spaces *pl* geschlossene Räume *mpl*
confines geschützter Bereich *m*
confirm bestätigen, quittieren
confirm key Quittiertaste *f*
confirmation Bestätigung *f*, Quittierung *f*, Quittieren *nt*
confirmed deadline bestätigter Termin *m*
conformable surface Quadermessfläche *f* mit abgerundeten Ecken und Kanten
conformance Übereinstimmung *f*
conformity Übereinstimmung *f*
conformity category Gerätekategorie *f*
confuse verwechseln
confusion Verwechslung *f*

congestion – connector

congestion Stau *m*, Verkehrsstau *m*
conglutinate verkleben
conglutination Verklebung *f*
congruence Übereinstimmung *f*
congruent übereinstimmend
conical konisch, kegelig, kegelförmig
conical base Kegelbett *nt*
conical body Kegelkörper *m*
conical capped end Kegelkopf *m*
conical clutch Kegelkupplung *f*, Konuskupplung *f*
conical end surface kegelige Stirnfläche *f*
conical joint surface kegelige Fügefläche *f*
conical spring washer Spannscheibe *f*
conical spring washer for screw assemblies Spannscheibe *f* für Kombi-Schrauben
conical surface Kegelfläche *f*
conical weld Kegelmantelnaht *f*
coniferous pulp Nadelholzzellstoff *m*
coning *(Radscheiben)* Kümpeln *nt*
conjoin with one another aneinanderfügen
conjunction Konjunktion *f*, Zusammentreffen *nt*
conjunction element Konjunktionsglied *nt*
conjunction measurement Anschlussmessung *f*
conjunctive combination konjunktive Verknüpfung *f*
connect anschließen, anbinden (an), verbinden, ankuppeln, kuppeln, koppeln, verknüpfen, zusammenfügen, zusammenhängen, Verbindung *f* herstellen
connect in series in Reihe schalten, vorschalten, zwischenschalten
connect serially in Reihe schalten
connect together non-demountably unlösbar verbinden
connect upstream vorschalten
connected angeschlossen, zusammenhängend, nachgeschaltet
connected in parallel parallel geschaltet
connected in series in Reihe geschaltet
connected rest Doppelsupport *m*
connected slide rest Doppelsupport *m*
connecting Ankuppeln *nt*
connecting bend Anschlussbogen *m*, Verbindungsbogen *m*
connecting block Schaltleiste *f*
connecting cable Anschlusskabel *nt*, Verbindungslasche *f*, Verbindungskabel *nt*
connecting conduit Verbindungsleitung *f*
connecting element Verbindungsteil *nt*
connecting line Verbindungslinie *f*, Verbindungsleitung *f*
connecting link Zwischenglied *nt*
connecting module Anschaltbaugruppe *f*
connecting pin Verbindungsstift *m*
connecting pipeline Anschlussleitung *f*
connecting piping Verbindungsleitung *f*
connecting rod Kurbelstange *f*, Verbindungsstange *f*, Pleuelstange *f*, Koppel *f*
connecting sewer Anschlusskanal *m*
connecting sleeve Rohrmuffe *f*
connection Zusammenfügung *f*, Verbindung *f*, Anbindung *f*, Verknüpfung *f*, Kontakt *m*, Anschluss *m*, Ankuppeln *nt*
connection facility Anschlussmittel *nt*
connection line Anschlussleitung *f*
connection means Anschlussmittel *nt*
connection nozzle Anschlussstutzen *m*
connection of appliances Armaturenanschluss *m*
connection point Anschlussstelle *f*
connection pressure Anschlussdruck *m*
connection sleeve Verbindungsmuffe *f*
connection tongue Anschlusszunge *f*
connectionless verbindungslos
connections Zusammenhänge *mpl*, Verbindungen *fpl*
connective Verknüpfung *f*
connective network Verknüpfungsnetzwerk *nt*
connectivity Vernetzung *f*
connector Verteiler *m*, Zwischenverbindung *f*, Steckverbindung *f*, Verbinder *m*, Verbindungsteil *nt*, Klemme *f*,

Schalter *m*
connector cable Verbindungskabel *nt*
connector shell Steckergehäuse *nt*
connexion Verbindung *f*
contour segment programming Konturzugprogrammierung *f*
consecutive nachfolgend
consequent Konklusion *f*
consideration Berücksichtigung *f*
considered in strength terms festigkeitsmäßig
consign übergeben
consignation warehouse Konsignationslager *nt*
consignee Empfänger *m*
consignment Kommission *f*, Sendung *f*
consignment of goods Warensendung *f*
consist of bestehen aus
consistency Übereinstimmung *f*, Widerspruchsfreiheit *f*
consistent übereinstimmend, widerspruchsfrei
consistent data konsistente Daten *pl*
console Pult *nt*
conspicuous auffällig
conspicuousness Auffälligkeit *f*
constancy in size Maßkonstanz *f*
constant dauernd, stetig, beständig
constant chord konstante Sehne *f*
constant climate Konstantklima *nt*
constant current Konstantstrom *m*
constant length of threaded end konstante Zapfenlänge *f* von Kegelstiften
constant light Gleichlicht *nt*
constant light operation Gleichlichtbetrieb *m*
constant load Dauerbelastung *f*
constant of the filler Lotkonstante *f*
constant tensile stress ruhende Zugbeanspruchung *f*
constant voltage Konstantspannung *f*
constituent of the formula Formelbestandteil *m*
constituent part Bestandteil *m*
constituent Bestandteil *m*
constrain zwingen
constrained eingespannt
constrained contact Zwanglaufsicherung *f*
constrained motion Zwanglauf *m*
constraint Zwang *m*
constricted arc welding Plasmaschweißen *nt*
constriction Einschnürung *f*, Verjüngung *f*, Verengung *f*
construct ausführen, aufbauen, bauen
constructing owner Bauherr *m*
construction Konstruktion *f*, Gestaltung *f*, Ausführung *f*, Aufbau *m*, Bauweise *f*, Bauausführung *f*, Bau *m*, Bauart *f*, Montage *f*
construction element Bauglied *nt*
construction member Bauteil *nt*, Bauglied *nt*
construction of tools Werkzeuggestaltung *f*
construction of water heating installations Wassererwärmungsanlagenbau *m*
construction outlay Bauaufwand *m*
construction site Baustelle *f*
construction steel Baustahl *m*
constructional baulich
construction-conditioned welding feasibility konstruktionsbedingte Schweißmöglichkeit *f*
construction-related welding security konstruktionsbezogene Schweißsicherheit *f*
consult beraten
consultancy Beratung *f*
consultant Berater *m*
consulting Beratung *f*
consumable Schweißzusatz *m*
consumable welding material Schweißzusatzwerkstoff *m*
consumables Verbrauchsmaterial *nt*
consume verbrauchen
consumer Verbraucher *m*
consumer goods Verbrauchsgüter *ntpl*
consumer site Verbraucherort *m*
consumer's risk Abnahmerisiko *nt*
consumption Verbrauch *m*
consumption data Verbrauchsdaten *pl*
consumption rate Verbrauchsmenge *f*
consumption-controlled stock verbrauchsbesteuertes Material *nt*
contact Kontakt *m*, Berührung *f*, Bezie-

contact angle – contingency table

hung *f*, Auftreffen *nt*, Eingriff *m*; auftreffen, berühren, antasten
contact angle Umfassungswinkel *m*
contact area Auflagebereich *m*, Berührungsfläche *f*
contact brush Schleifbürste *f*
contact closure Kontaktgabe *f*
contact corrosion Kontaktkorrosion *f*
contact distance Taststrecke *f*
contact face Anlaufstirnfläche *f*
contact flow *(Logistik)* Kontaktsstrom *m*
contact intensity Kontaktstärke *f*
contact length Kontaktlänge *f*
contact line Berührlinie *f*, Schleifleitung *f*
contact pattern test Tragbildprüfung *f*
contact person Ansprechpartner *m*
contact plan Kontaktplan *m*
contact point Auftreffpunkt *m*, Messamboss *m*, Messeinsatz *m*
contact pressure Anpressdruck *m*, Andruck *m*, Messdruck *m*
contact pressure *(Glattwalzen)* Anpressdruck *m*
contact pressure indicator Messdruckanzeiger *m*
contact ratio 1. Überdeckung *f* 2. Eingriffsteilung *f* der Flanken
contact roll Anpressrolle *f*, Andruckpolster *nt*
contact roller Führungsrolle *f*
contact rule Anlagelineal *nt*
contact scheme Kontaktplan *m*
contact stiffness Kontaktsteifigkeit *f*
contact stylus Messbolzen *m*
contact stylus instrument Tastschnittgerät *nt*
contact surface Anschlagfläche *f*, Berührungsfläche *f*, Kontaktfläche *f*, Aufstandsfläche *f*
contact system Tastsystem *nt*
contact thermometer Berührungsthermometer *nt*, Kontaktthermometer *nt*
contact tip angle Tastspitzenwinkel *m*
contact to friction Reibberührung *f*
contact to impact Schlagberührung *f*
contact uncertainty Schallunsicherheit *f*

contact voltage Berührungsspannung *f*
contact zone Kontaktzone *f*, Berührungszone *f*
contactable part berührbares Teil *nt*
contact-free kontaktlos, berührungsfrei
contact-free measuring berührungslos Messen *nt*
contacting Antastung *f*, berührend
contactless kontaktlos, berührungslos, berührungsfrei
contactless measuring berührungslos Messen *nt*
contactor Schalter *m*
contain enthalten
container Container *m*, Behälter *m*, Tank *m*, Kollo *nt*
container bottom Behälterboden *m*
container construction Behälterbau *m*
container dimensions *pl* Behältergröße *f*
container fork pocket Containergabeltasche *f*
container handler Containerstapler *m*
container inlet Behältereinlauf *m*
container outlet Behälterauslauf *m*
container rack Behälterregal *nt*
container size Behältergröße *f*
container spreader Containerspreader *m*
container tippler Behälterkippgerät *nt*
containing filler füllstoffhaltig
contaminant verschmutzte Substanz *f*
contaminate verschmutzen, verunreinigen
contamination Verunreinigung *f*, Verschmutzung *f*
contamination agent Kontaminationsmittel *nt*
contamination of air Luftverunreinigung *f*
contamination of water Wasserverunreinigung *f*
contamination solution Kontaminationslösung *f*
contamination spot Kontaminationsfleck *m*
content Inhalt *m*, Gehalt *m*
contents Inhalt *m*
context Zusammenhang *m*
contingency table Kontingenztafel *f*

continuation sheet Folgeblatt *nt*
continue to glow weiterglimmen
continuity durchgängige Verbindung *f*
continuous laufend, fortlaufend, umlaufend, endlos, dauernd, durchgehend, stufenlos, kontinuierlich, beständig, stetig
continuous acting element stetig wirkendes Glied
continuous alternating current Dauerwechselstrom *m*
continuous broaching ununterbrochenes Räumen *nt*
continuous casting Stranggießen *nt*, Strangguss *m*
continuous casting process Stranggießverfahren *nt*
continuous chip Scherspan *m*, Fließspan *m*
continuous chip without built-up edge Abscherspan *m*
continuous controlling system stetig wirkende Regeleinrichtung *f*, stetige Regeleinrichtung *f*
continuous conveyor Steigförderer *m*
continuous curly chip Wendelspan *m*, Lockenspan *m*
continuous dew test Dauerbetauungsversuch *m*
continuous dimension line durchzogene Maßlinie *f*
continuous direct current Dauergleichstrom *m*
continuous double helical teeth Pfeilverzahnung *f*
continuous duty Dauerbetrieb *m*
continuous feed blasting plant Durchlaufstrahlanlage *f*
continuous function chart kontinuierlicher Funktionsplan *m*
continuous handling equipment Steigförderer *m*
continuous hauling plant Stetigförderanlage *f*
continuous length with repeating pattern Bahn *f* mit Rapport
continuous line Volllinie *f*
continuous milling machine Durchlauffräsmaschine *f*
continuous observation Dauerbeobachtung *f*
continuous operation Dauerbetrieb *m*, Durchlauf *m*
continuous path (CP) durchgehende Bahn *f*
continuous path control Bahnsteuerung *f*
continuous random variable stetige Zufallsvariable *f*, kontinuierliche Zufallsvariable *f*
continuous random variate kontinuierliche Zufallsvariable *f*, stetige Zufallsvariable *f*
continuous rating Dauerleistung *f*
continuous replenishment laufende Aufstockung *f*
continuous rotary miller Rundtischfräsautomat *m*, Senkrechtfräsmaschine *f* mit Rundtisch
continuous rotary milling machine Rundtischfräsautomat *m*, Senkrechtfräsmaschine *f* mit Rundtisch
continuous secondary current Sekundärdauerstrom *m*
continuous spiral chip Wendel *m*, Abfließspan *m*
continuous steam output Dampfdauerleistung *f*
continuous stream ink jet coder kontinuierlicher Tintenstrahlcodierer *m*
continuous transition stetiger Übergang *m*
continuous travel Abrollen *nt*
continuous wave Dauerschall *m*
continuous weld nicht unterbrochene Naht *f*
continuously adjustable stufenlos regelbar
continuously controlled stufenlos geregelt
continuously controlled burner stetig geregelter Brenner *m*
continuous-type method Durchlaufverfahren *nt*
continuous-type preheater Durchlaufvorwärmer *m*
contortion Überrollen *nt*, Verdrehen *nt*
contort überrollen, verdrehen, verformen
contortion Verformung *f*, Verdrehen *nt*

contour kopieren, nachformen, profilieren, nachfräsen, nachformfräsen, formen, Konturen bearbeiten, zweidimensional nachformen; Form *f*, Umfang *m*, Kontur *f*, Umriss *m*, Gestalt *f*, Profil *nt*, Außenlinie *f*
contour boring Umrissbohren *nt*, Konturformbohren *nt*
contour copying profiling Umrisskopieren *nt*
contour face plankopieren
contour grinding Profilschleifen *nt*, Formschleifen *nt*, Nachformschleifen *nt*
contour mill kopierfräsen, formfräsen, umrissfräsen
contour miller Nachformfräsmaschine *f*, Formfräsmaschine *f*
contour milling Umrissfräsen *nt*, Formfräsen *nt*, Nachfräsen *nt*, Planfräsarbeit *f*, Umrissfräsarbeit *f*
contour milling machine Kopierfräsmaschine *f*, Umrissfräsmaschine *f*, Umrissnachformfräsmaschine *f*
contour milling method Umrissfräsverfahren *nt*
contour of wheel face Schleifscheibenprofil *nt*
contour planning Umrisshobeln *nt*, Umrissnachformhobeln *nt*
contour planning Nachformhobeln *nt*
contour shaper Formhobler *m*, Umrissnachformhobelmaschine *f*
contour shaping machine Kehlhobelmaschine *f*
contour turning Umrissdrehen *nt*, Kopierdrehen *nt*, Formdrehen *nt*
contour-grind formschleifen
contouring formgebende Bearbeitung *f*, Formgebung *f*, Formung *f*, Umrisskopieren *nt*, Nachformen *nt*, Nachfräsen *nt*
contouring control Bahnsteuerung *f*, Fühlersteuerung *f*
contouring lathe Formdrehmaschine *f*
contouring machine Kopiermaschine *f*
contouring profile milling Umrissfräsen *nt*
contouring tool Formmeißel *m*
contouring tracer control Umrissfühlersteuerung *f*

contouring work Planfräsarbeit *f*, Umrissfräsarbeit *f*
contour-plane nachformen, nachformhobeln
contour-planer Kopierhobelmaschine *f*, Nachformhobelmaschine *f*
contour-turn formdrehen
contract 1. verengen, kontrahieren, zusammenziehen 2. Vertrag *m*, Auftrag *m*, Abmachung *f*, Abkommen *nt*
contract examination Vertragsprüfung *f*
contract heat treatment workshop Lohnhärterei *f*
contract party Vertragspartei *f*
contracting by spinning Einhalsen *nt* durch Drücken, Engen *nt* durch Drücken
contracting party Vertragspartei *f*
contraction Schwund *m*
contraction in area Querschnittsschwächung *f*
contraction narrowing Einengung *f*
contractor Auftragnehmer *m*, Lieferant *m*, Unternehmer *m*, Kontraktor *m*
contractual joint venture Projektkooperation *f*
contractually stipulated vertraglich festgelegt
contradiction Widerspruch *m*
contradictory widersprechend
contrary widersprechend, entgegengesetzt, umgekehrt
contrast Kontrast *m*
contrast character to background Zeichenkontrast *m*
contrast reduction Kontrastminderung *f*
contrast with gegenüberstellen
contrate gear pair Stirnplanradpaar *nt*
contribution Umlage *f*
contrivance Gerät *nt*, Apparat *m*
control steuern, ansteuern, stellen, schalten, überwachen, lenken, prüfen, nachprüfen, überprüfen, regeln, kontrollieren, bedienen; Schaltung *f*, Führung *f*, Steuerung *f*, Regelung *f*, Ansteuerung *f*, Steuereinrichtung *f*, Stellteil *nt*, Bedienung *f*, Bedienelement *nt*, Überwachung *f*, Überprü-

fung *f*, Lenkung *f*, Kontrolle *f*
control slide valve Steuerschieber *m*
control air Steuerluft *f*
control and information protocol Steuerungs- und Informationsprotokoll *nt*
control and protective switching device Steuer- und Schutzschaltgerät *nt*
control area Steuerungsbereich *m*
control barrel Steuertrommel *f*
control block Ventilkörper *m*
control board Hauptschalttafel *f*, Schaltschrank *m*
control booking Kontrollbuchung *f*
control box Steuerkopf *m*, Steuerschrank *m*
control butterfly valve Regelklappe *f*
control cab Steuerkabine *f*
control cabinet Schaltschrank *m*
control cam Schaltnocke *f*
control card technique Kontrollkartentechnik *f*
control centre Steuerzentrale *f*, Leitstand *m*
control centre personnel Leitstandpersonal *nt*
control character Steuerzeichen *nt*
control characteristic Regelkennlinie *f*
control circuit Schaltkreis *m*, Steuerkreis *m*, Steuerstromkreis *m*, Steuerleitung *f*, Regelkreis *m*
control circuit device Steuerregelgerät *nt*
control command Steuerkommando *nt*
control concept Steuerungskonzept *nt*
control console Schaltpult *nt*, Steuerpult *nt*, Steuerstand *m*
control cubicle Schaltschrank *m*
control current Steuerstrom *m*
control data Steuerdaten *pl*
control dependency Steuerabhängigkeit *f*
control desk Schaltpult *nt*, Steuerpult *nt*, Bedienfeld *nt*
control device Schaltvorrichtung *f*, Steuereinrichtung *f*, Regeleinrichtung *f*, Stellteil *nt*
control devices Steuerungen *fpl*
control disc Steuerscheibe *f*
control element Regelglied *nt*, Steuerelement *nt*, Steuerungselement *nt*, Steuerungskomponente *f*, Bedienungselement *nt*, Schaltorgan *nt*, Schaltung *f*, Stellglied *nt*
control equipment Steuereinrichtung *f*, Steuerungseinrichtung *f*, Regelwerk *nt*
control flux density Aussteuerungsinduktion *f*
control from the floor Flursteuerung *f*
control gate valve Regelschieber *m*
control gear Schaltwerk *nt*, Regeleinrichtung *f*
control guard Kontrollschutzeinrichtung *f*
control hierarchy Steuerungshierarchie *f*
control impulse Steuerimpuls *m*
control independently wechselweise schalten
control input Steuereingang *m*
control instruction Steueranweisung *f*
control jack Arbeitszylinder *m*
control lamp Signallampe *f*
control level Steuerungsebene *f*, Steuergriff *m*, Steuerhebel *m*, Bedienungshebel *m*, Schalthebel *m*, Schalter *m*, Stellteil *nt*
control light Kontrollampe *f*
control line Steuerleitung *f*
control logic Steuerlogik *f*
control means Steuerungsmittel *nt*
control measurement Kontrollmessung *f*
control mechanism Stellteil *nt*, Schaltsteuerung *f*
control member Bedienungselement *nt*, Schaltorgan *nt*
control memory circuit Steuerprogrammspeicher *m*
control mode Systemzustand *m*, Steuerungsart *f*
control of access Zugangssicherung *f*
control of discharge Ablaufregelung *f*
control operation Steuervorgang *m*
control overpressure Steuerüberdruck *m*
control panel Bedieneinheit *f*, Bedientafel *f*, Bedienungsplatte *f*, Gerätetafel *f*, Schalttafel *f*, Schaltfeld *nt*, Schaltkas-

ten *m*, Steuertafel *f*, Steuerpult *nt*
control part Regelteil *nt*
control pendant Steuerpendal *nt*
control period Kontrollzeit *f*
control point Schaltstelle *f*, Steuerstelle *f*
control position Steuerstand *m*, Fahrerstand *m*
control process Kontrollvorgang *m*
control program Steuerungsprogramm *nt*, Steuerungssoftware *f*, Steuerprogramm *nt*
control range Regelspanne *f*
control response date Einsteuerungstermin *m*
control response stage Einsteuerungsvorgang *m*
control room Schaltwarte *f*, Warte *f*
control rule Steuerungsregel *f*
control sample Kontrollprobe *f*
control software Steuerungssoftware *f*
control stand Steuerstand *m*
control station Kontrollstation *f*, Leitgerät *nt*, Leitstand *m*, Bedienungsstand *m*, Steuerstelle *f*, Schaltpult *nt*, Schalttafel *f*
control stick Steuerknüppel *m*
control strategy Steuerungsstrategie *f*
control switch Steuerschalter *m*
control system Leittechnik *f*, Steueranlage *f*, Steuersystem *nt*, Steuereinrichtung *f*, Steuerung *f*, Überwachungssystem *nt*, Regler *m*, Zielsteuerung *f*, Regeleinrichtung *f*
control system message Leittechnikmeldung *f*
control technique Steuerungsverfahren *nt*
control technology Regelungstechnik *f*, Regelungsobjekt *nt*
control test Kontrollprüfung *f*
control time Schaltzeit *f*
control unit Regelvorrichtung *f*, Steuereinheit *f*, Steuergerät *nt*, Regler *m*
control valve Regelventil *nt*, Steuerventil *nt*
control voltage Steuerspannung *f*
control wheel Vorschubreihe *f*, Regelscheibe *f*
control worm Schaltschnecke *f*

controllability Regulierbarkeit *f*, Steuer- und Regelbarkeit *f*
controllable regelbar, verstellbar, steuerbar
controlled acceleration kontrollierender Anlauf *m*
controlled atmosphere chamber Klimaraum *m*
controlled by an operator walking with the truck mitgängergeführt
controlled cooling geregeltes Abkühlen *nt*
controlled system Strecke *f*, Steuerstrecke *f*, Regelstrecke *f*
controlled variable Regelgröße *f*
controlled-volume pump Dosierpumpe *f*
controller Regler *m*, Regelgerät *nt*, Steuerung *f*, Steuerorgan *nt*, Steuergerät *nt*, Steuerprogramm *nt*
controller device Steuergerät *nt*
Controller Rea Network CAN-Bus
controlling *(mit Rückmeldung)* Regeln *nt*
controlling equipment Stelleinrichtung *f*
controlling means Regler *m*
controlling output steuernder Ausgang *m*
controls *pl* Schaltelemente *ntpl*
convection Konvektion *f*
convection type heater with fan Konvektionsheizgerät *nt* mit erzwungener Konvektion
convection type heater without fan Konvektionsheizgerät *nt* mit natürlicher Konvektion
convection type heating Konvektionsheizung *f*
convection type heating appliance Konvektionsheizgerät *nt*
convective dissipation of heat konvektive Wärmeabgabe *f*
convention Vereinbarung *f*
conventional herkömmlich
conventional cut Gegenlauffrässchnitt *m*
conventional hexagon turret Sternrevolver *m*
conventional hexagon turret stor-

age Sternrevolverspeicher *m*
conventional milling Gegenlauffräsen *nt*, Fräsen *nt* im Gegenlauf
conventional true value richtiger Wert *m*
converge zusammenlaufen
convergence Konvergenz *f*
convergence ratio Konvergenzverhältnis *nt*
convergent konvergent *f*
converging konvergent *f*
converging section Zusammenführung *f*
conversion Umrechnung *f*, Umwandlung *f*, Umformen *nt*, Umformung *f*, Umsetzung *f*, Umbau *m*, Umrüstung *f*, Umstellung *f*, Übergang *m*
conversion formula Umrechnungsformel *f*
conversion kit Umrüstsatz *m*
conversion of the firing system Feuerungsumbau *m*
conversion program Umsetzprogramm *nt*
conversion relationship Umwertungsbeziehung *f*
conversion scatter band Umwertungstreuband *nt*
conversion set Umrüstsatz *m*
conversion work Umbauarbeiten *pl*
convert umsetzen, umwandeln, wandeln, umbauen, umrüsten, umformen, umstellen
converter Codeumsetzer *m*, Umsetzer *m*, Umwandler *m*, Wandler *m*
converter, frequency ~ *(el.)* Umrichter *m*
convertible open side planer-miller Langfräsmaschine *f* in Einständerkonstruktion mit ausfahrbarem Seitenständer
convertible-fuel boiler Umstellbrandkessel *m*
convex ballig
convex cutter Konvexfräser *m*
convex double-V butt joint Doppel-V-Naht *f* mit gewölbten Oberflächen
convex grinding attachment Balligeinrichtung *f*
convex milling attachment Balligfräseinrichtung *f*
convex milling cutter Fräser *m* für Halbkreisprofil
convex profile gauge Konvexlehre *f*
convex square butt joint I-Naht *f* mit beidseitig gewölbten Oberflächen
convex surface of the bend Biegerücken *m*
convex tooth cutting Balligverzahnen *nt*
convex turning attachment Balligdreheinrichtung *f*
convexity Balligkeit *f*
convey übermitteln, fördern, befördern, leisten
conveyance Transport *m*, Beförderung *f*, Förderung *f*, Zufuhr *f*, Abfuhr *f*
conveyance capacity Förderkapazität *f*
conveying Beförderung *f*
conveying belt Transportband *nt*, Förderband *nt*
conveying capacity Transportleistung *f*
conveying characteristic Förderverhalten *nt*
conveying distance Transportweg *m*
conveying route Förderstrecke *f*
conveying system Transportsystem *nt*
conveying technology Fördertechnik *f*
conveying unit Fördereinheit *f*, Fördereinrichtung *f*
conveyor Förderer *m*, Förderelement *nt*, Fördereinrichtung *f*, Förderanlage *f*, Zulaufrollengang *m*
conveyor battery Fahrzeugbatterie *f*
conveyor belt Förderband *nt*, Mitnahmeband *nt*
conveyor belt housing Fördererüberdachung *f*
conveyor chain Transportkette *f*
conveyor control Förderanlagensteuerung *f*
conveyor line Förderstrecke *f*
conveyor line mode Fließlinienbetrieb *m*
conveyor roller Transportrolle *f*
conveyor system Fördertechnik *f*, Förderanlage *f*
conveyor technology Fördertechnik *f*
conveyor worm Förderschnecke *f*

convolution Welle *f*
convulse erschüttern
cooking range Kochherd *m*
cool kühlen
cool down abkühlen, erkalten; Abkühlung *f*
coolant Kühlmittel *nt*, Kühlflüssigkeit *f*
coolant circuit Kühlmittelkreislauf *m*
coolant flow Kühlmittelfluss *m*
coolant removing Kühlmittelabführung *f*
coolant supply Kühlmittelzuführung *f*
coolant-lubricant-detergent Kühl-Spül-Schmiermittel (KSSM) *nt*
cool-down curve Abkühlungskurve *f*
cooled to extremely low temperatures unterkühlt
coolers Kühlraum *m*
cooling Abkühlung *f*, Kühlung *f*
cooling agent Kühlmittel *nt*
cooling capacity Kühlleistung *f*
cooling characteristic Abkühlungsverlauf *m*
cooling condition Abkühlbedingung *f*
cooling equipment Kühleinrichtung *f*
cooling fluid Kühlmittel *nt*
cooling liquid Kühlflüssigkeit *f*, Kühlmittel *nt*
cooling load Kühllast *f*
cooling lubricant Kühlschmierstoff *m*
cooling lubricant emulsion Kühlschmier-Emulsion *f*
cooling lubrication Kühlschmierung *f*
cooling period Kühlzeit *f*, Abkühlungsdauer *f*
cooling proceedings Kühlvorgang *m*
cooling process Abkühlvorgang *m*
cooling section Kühlstrecke *f*
cooling slot Kühlungsnut *f*
cooling system Kühlung *f*
cooling tension Abkühlspannung *f*
cooling time Abkühlungsdauer *f*
cooling trap Kühlfalle *f*
cooperate zusammenarbeiten, zusammenwirken, mitwirken
cooperation Mitwirkung *f*, Zusammenwirken *nt*, Zusammenarbeit *f*, Zusammenspiel *nt*
cooperative test Ringversuch *m*
co-operative test Rundversuch *m*

coordinate Koordinate *f*; koordinieren, abstimmen, zuordnen
coordinate boring Koordinationsbohren *nt*
coordinate boring and drilling machine Koordinatenbohrmaschine *f*
co-ordinate dimensioning Koordinatenbemaßung *f*
coordinate guidance Koordinatenführung *f*
coordinate jig boring machine Koordinatenbohrmaschine *f*
coordinate metrology Koordinatenmesstechnik *f*
coordinate positioning Koordinatenpositionierung *f*
coordinate setting Koordinateneinstellung *f*
coordinate system Koordinatensystem *nt*
coordinate table Koordinatentisch *m*, Messtisch *m*
coordinate transformation Koordinatentransformation *f*
coordinates Koordinatenwerte *mpl*
co-ordinates measuring apparatus Koordinatenmessgerät *nt*
coordination Abstimmung *f*, Koordination *f*
coordination deadline Abstimmungstermin *m*
copal solution adhesive Kopalkleber *m*
copier unit Kopierwerk *nt*
coping Ausklinken *nt*
coplanar planparallel
copolymerizable copolymerisierbar
copolymerize copolymerisieren
copper Kupfer *nt*, verkupfern
copper bit for soldering Lötkolben *m*
copper cast iron Kupferguss *m*
copper filter equivalent Kupfergleichwert *m*
copper loss Kupferverlust *m*
copper plated by immersion tauchverkupfert
copper smelting slag Kupferhüttenschlacke *f*
copper strip test Kupferstreifenprüfung *f*

copper vapour laser *(CVL)* Kupferdampflaser *m*
copper zinc Kupferzink *nt*
copper-containing solder gekupfertes Lot *nt*
copper-laminated plastics kupferkaschierter Schichtpressstoff *m*
copy kopieren, nachformen, kopierdrehen, pausen, nachbilden; Nachbildung *f*
copy and die milling cutter Kopier- und Gesenkfräser *m*
copy card Kopierkarte *f*
copy grinding Kopierschleifen *nt*, Nachformschleifen *nt*
copy machining Nachformarbeit *f*
copy milling Kopierfräsen *nt*, Nachformfräsen *nt*
copy milling machine Nachformfräsmaschine *f*, Kopierfräsmaschine *f*
copy milling operation Nachformfräsarbeit *f*
copy planing Nachformhobeln *nt*
copy turning Nachformdrehen *nt*, Kopierdrehen *nt*
copy-face plankopieren
copying 1. Kopieren *nt*, Nachformen *nt*, Reproduzieren *nt* 2. *(Drehen)* Nachformdrehen *nt*
copying accuracy Nachformgenauigkeit *f*
copying attachment 1. Kopiervorrichtung *f*, Kopiereinrichtung *f*, Nachformeinrichtung *f*, Kopierwerk *nt* 2. *(Drehen)* Nachformdrehvorrichtung *f*
copying attachment with tangential tracer control Tangentenfühlersteuerung *f*
copying device Kopiervorrichtung *f*
copying equipment Kopiervorrichtung *f*
copying feed motion Kopiervorschubbewegung *f*
copying lathe Nachformdrehmaschine *f*, Kopierdrehmaschine *f*
copying mill Kopiermaschine *f*
copying miller Nachformfräsmaschine *f*, Nachformfräsautomat *m*
copying operation Nachformarbeit *f*
copying shaper Nachformstößelhobelmaschine *f*, Nachformwaagerechtstoßmaschine *f*, Kopierwaagerechtstoßmaschine *f*
copying slide Kopierschlitten *m*
copying system Nachformverfahren *nt*, Nachformsteuerung *f*
copying tool Kopiermeißel *m*
copying tracer Kopierfühler *m*, Kopiertaster *m*
copying turret lathe Revolverkopierdrehmaschine *f*, Revolverkopiermaschine *f*
copy-mill nachformen, nachformfräsen, kopierfräsen, nachfräsen
copy-plane kopierhobeln, nachformhobeln, nachformen
copy-planer Kopierhobelmaschine *f*, Nachformhobelmaschine *f*
copy-planing attachment *(Langhobelmaschine)* Nachformhobeleinrichtung *f*
copy-shaping Nachformhobeln *nt*
copy-shaping attachment *(Waagerecht-Stoßmaschine)* Nachformhobeleinrichtung *f*
copy-turn kopieren, nachformen, nachformdrehen, nachdrehen, kopierdrehen
copy-turning attachment Kopierdreheinrichtung *f*, Nachformdreheinrichtung *f*
copy-turning lathe Nachformdrehmaschine *f*, Kopierdrehmaschine *f*
cord Kordel *f*, Schnur *f*
cords *pl* Schlieren *fpl*
core Kern *m*, Kernhülse *f*, Kernstück *nt*
core baking drying Kerntrocknung *f*
core cross-section Kernquerschnitt *m*
core diameter Kerndurchmesser *m*
core fire process Kernschießverfahren *nt*
core hardness Kernhärte *f*
core loss Eisenverlust *m*
core mark Kernmarke *f*
core plug Kernstopfen *m*
core process Kernprozess *m*
core production Kernherstellung *f*
core region Kerngebiet *nt*
core shift Kernverlagerung *f*, Kernverschiebung *f*
core spun yarn Umwindungsgarn *nt*
core stove Kerntrockenkammer *f*

core stove oven Kerntrockenofen *m*
cored hole vorgegossenes Loch *nt*
core-extrusion machine Kernstopfmaschine *f*
core hole Kernloch *nt*
corner Ecke *f*, Schneidenecke *f*; eine Kurve fahren
corner chamfer Eckenfase *f*
corner drilling machine Eckenbohrmaschine *f*
corner fitting Eckverbindung *f*
corner joint Eckstoß *m*
corner plate Knotenblech *nt*
corner point Eckpunkt *m*, Kopfeckpunkt *m*
corner radius Eckenrundung *f*, Eckenradius *m*
corner radiusing Eckenrundung *f*, Eckenrunden *nt*
corner removed from longitudinal edge of face gebrochene Längskante *f*
corner removed from longitudinal edge of root face gebrochene Steglängskante *f*
corner rounding Eckenrunden *nt*
corner roundness Eckenrundung *f*
corner weld test piece Ecknahtprüfstück *nt*
corner-deceleration Eckenbremsen *nt*
cornered eckig
cornering Kurvenfahrt *f*
corner-rounding cutter Radiusfräser *m*
corporate organization Unternehmensorganisation *f*
correct sachgerecht, fachgerecht, einwandfrei, richtig, genau; beheben, korrigieren, berichtigen, verbessern, ausgleichen
correct connection ordnungsgemäßer Anschluss *m*
correct design for corrosion protection korrosionsschutzgerechte Gestaltung *f*
corrected measured value berichtigter Messwert *m*
correction Korrektur *f*, Verbesserung *f*, Behebung *f*, Ausgleich *m*, Berichtigung *f*
correction factor Korrekturfaktor *m*
correction message Korrekturmeldung *f*
correction of the alignment Verlegekorrektur *f*
correction value Korrrekturwert *m*
correction values Korrekturwerte *mpl*
corrective stretching Beihalten *nt*
correctly shaped formrichtig
correctness Richtigkeit *f*
correlation Korrelation *f*, Zusammenhang *m*, Abstimmung *f*
correlation system Zuordnungssystem *nt*
correspond übereinstimmen (mit), entsprechen
correspondence Übereinstimmung *f*, Entsprechung *f*
corresponding flanks *pl* gleichnamige Zahnflanken *fpl*
corresponding to the standard normgerecht
corridor Korridor *m*
corrode korrodieren, zerfressen, anfressen
corroding ätzend
corrosion Korrosion *f*
corrosion category Korrosionsgrad *m*
corrosion coating Korrosionsschutzumhüllung *f*
corrosion due to differential aeration Korrosion *f* durch unterschiedliche Belüftung
corrosion fatigue Korrosionsermüdung *f*
corrosion hazard Korrosionsgefährdung *f*
corrosion immunity Korrosionsunempfindlichkeit *f*
corrosion inhibiting oil Korrosionsschutzöl *nt*
corrosion inhibiting wax Korrosionsschutzwachs *nt*
corrosion pit Rostnarbe *f*
corrosion preventing property Korrosionsschutzeigenschaft *f*, korrosionsverhindernde Eigenschaft *f*
corrosion preventive oil Korrossionschutzöl *nt*
corrosion promoting korrosionsfördernd
corrosion protecting action Korrosi-

onsschutzwirkung *f*
corrosion protection measure Korrosionsschutzmaßnahme *f*
corrosion protection preparation Korrosionsschutzmittel *nt*
corrosion protection system Korrosionsschutzsystem *nt*
corrosion protection work Korrosionsschutzarbeit *f*
corrosion protective system Korrosionsschutzanlage *f*
corrosion resistant korrosionsbeständig, korrosionsfest
corrosion test Korrosionsprüfung *f*, Korrosionsuntersuchung *f*
corrosion under deposits Berührungskorrosion *f*, Korrosion *f* unter Ablagerungen
corrosion-preventing additive Korrosionsschutzzusatz *m*
corrosion-preventing behaviour Korrosionsschutzverhalten *nt*
corrosion-preventive korrosionshindernd
corrosive action Korrosionseinfluss *m*
corrosive medium korrosives Mittel *nt*, angreifendes Mittel *nt*
corrosive substance ätzender Stoff *m*
corrosive wear Korrosionsverschleiß *m*
corrosivity Korrosivität *f*
corresponding entsprechend
corrugated wellig, gewellt, gerieft
corrugated board Wellpappe *f*
corrugated board blank Wellpappezuschnitt *m*
corrugated board case Wellpappefaltschachtel *f*
corrugated cardboard Wellpappe *f*
corrugated perforation Riffellochung *f*
corrugated spring washer gewellte Federscheibe *f*
corrugated tool Stufenhobelmeißel *m*
corrugating Wellbiegen *nt*
corundum Korund *m*
cosiness Behaglichkeit *f*
cosiness factor Behaglichkeitsfaktor *m*
cosiness feeling Behaglichkeitsempfinden *nt*
cost accounting Kostenrechnung *f*

cost by delayed performance Terminverzugskosten *pl*
cost centre Kostenstelle *f*
cost centre delivery Kostenstellenbelieferung *f*
cost estimate Kostenschätzung *f*
cost framework Kostenrahmen *m*
cost indicator Kostenkennzahl *f*
cost management Kostenmanagement *nt*
cost of change-over Rüstkosten *pl*
cost of conveyance Transportkosten *pl*
cost of manufacture Fertigungskosten *pl*
cost optimization Kostenoptimierung *f*
cost planning Kostenplanung *f*
cost pressure Kostendruck *m*
cost reduction Kostensenkung *f*
cost scheduling Vorkalkulation *f*
cost-benefit analysis Kosten-Nutzen-Analyse *f*
cost-benefit ratio Kosten-Nutzen-Verhältnis *nt*
cost-determined sample kostenbestimmte Stichprobe *f*
cost-effective wirtschaftlich
co-stressed retaining element with spring action mitverspanntes federndes Sicherungselement *nt*
costs Kosten *pl*
costs sort Kostenart *f*
costs type Kostenart *f*
cosy behaglich
cotter Sicherungsstift *m*
cotton fabric shreds Baumwollgewebeschnitzel *nt*
cotton fabric strip Baumwollgewebebahn *f*
cotton wool wad Wattetupfer *m*
couch Grundierung *f*
coulping system Kopplungssystem *nt*
count Stückzahl *f*, Zählerstand *m*, zählen
count down Rückwärtszählen *nt*
count filling machine Zählfüllmaschine *f*
count of the counter Zählerstand *m*
count up Vorwärtszählen *nt*
countable zählbar
counter Zähler *m*

counter gear teeth Gegenverzahnung *f*
counter module Zählerbaugruppe *f*
counter position Zählerstellung *f*
counter reading Zählerstand *m*
counter torque Gegenmoment *nt*
counter tracer Umrissfühler *m*
counter tube Zählröhre *f*
counteract entgegenwirken
counteractive measure Gegenmaßnahme *f*, Gegensteuerung *f*
counterbalance mit Gegengewicht *nt* versehen, ausgleichen; Ausgleich *m*
counterbalanced mit Gegengewicht
counterbalanced lift truck Gegengewichtstapler *m*
counterbalanced truck Gegengewichtstapler *m*
counterbore aufbohren, ausbohren, ausdrehen, ansenken, versenken, zylindrisch senken; Senker *m*, Halssenker *m*, Senkung *f*
counterbore for cheese head screws Senkung *f* für Zylinderschrauben
counterbore with guide Zapfensenker *m*
counterboring zylindrische Einsenkung *f*, Senkung *f*, zylindrisch Senken *nt*
counterboring tool Senkwerkzeug *nt*
counter-clockwise (ccw) Linkslauf *m*, gegen den Uhrzeigersinn, im entgegengesetzten Uhrzeigersinn
counter-compounding Gegenkompoundierung *f*
counterflow exchanger Gegenstromapparat *m*
counterforce Gegenkraft *f*
countering Kopieren *nt*
cauterize abbeizen
cauterizing Abbeizen *nt*
countermeasure Gegenmaßnahme *f*
counterpart rack Erzeugungszahnstange *f*
countershaft Vorlegewelle *f*, Vorgelegewelle *f*, Vorgelege *nt*, Riemenvorgelege *nt*
countersink ansenken, aussenken, senken, versenken, zylindrisch senken, kegelig senken; Spitzsenker *m*
countersink bolt Senkschraube *f*

countersinking kegelige Einsenkung *f*, Senken *nt*, Spitzsenken *nt*, Versenken *nt*, Kegeligsenken *nt*, Senkung *f*
counter-sinking Reiben *nt*
countersinking cutter Senker *m*
countersinking tool Senkwerkzeug *nt*
counterstay Gegenstütze *f*
countersteering Gegensteuerung *f*
countersunk bolt Senkbolzen *m*
countersunk double-nib bolt Senkschraube *f* mit zwei Nasen
countersunk flat head tapping screw Senkblechschraube *f*
countersunk head fitting screw with torque-set recess Senkpassschraube *f* mit Flügelkreuzschlitz
countersunk head screw threaded to head Senkschraube *f* mit Gewinde und Kopf
countersunk head thread cutting screw Senkschneidschraube *f*
countersunk rivet joint Senknietverbindung *f*
countersunk square neck bolt for woodwork Senkholzschraube *f* mit Vierkantansatz
countervail kompensieren
counterweight Gegengewicht *nt*, Gewichtsausgleich *m*
counterweight profile Gegengewichtskontur *f*
counting Zählung *f*
counting code Zählcode *m*
counting input Zähleingang *m*
counting measuring instrument zählendes Messgerät *nt*
counting stage Zählstufe *f*
country of origin Ursprungsland *nt*
count-statistical error zählstatistischer Fehler *m*
couple einkoppeln, koppeln, kuppeln, rückkoppeln, anlenken
couple with anhängen
coupler Koppel *f*
coupler connector Steckvorrichtung *f*
coupler curve Koppelkurve *f*
coupler mechanism Koppelgetriebe *nt*
coupler point Koppelpunkt *m*
coupling Kupplung *f*, Kopplung *f*, Einkopplung *f*, Kuppeln *nt*

coupling for interference Einkopplung *f* von Störsignalen
coupling height Kupplungshöhe *f*
coupling hole Anschlussbohrung *f*
coupling means Kupplungen *fpl*
course Ablauf *m*, Verlauf *m*, Fahrkurs *m*
course of a project Projektablauf *m*
course of calculation Berechnungsgang *m*
course succession Ablauffolge *f*
course tooth milling cutter Fräser *m* mit Grobverzahnungen
covariance Kovarianz *f*
cover belegen, überziehen, umhüllen, ummanteln, überschütten, verkleiden, abdecken, kaschieren, beschichten überdachen; Schutz *m*, Verkleidung *f*, Belag *m*, Umhüllung *f*, Überdachung *f*, Abdeckung *f*, Kappe *f*, Deckel *m*
cover mask Anbdeckmaske *f*
cover material Überschüttung *f*
cover plate Deckplatte *f*, Abdeckblech *nt*
cover run concavity Decklagenüberwölbung *f*
cover run reinforcement Decklagenüberhöhung *f*
cover sheet Deckblatt *nt*
cover sheet dispenser Deckblattaufleger *m*
cover strip Deckstreifen *m*
cover thickness Belagstärke *f*
coverage Arbeitsradius *m*
coverage limit Anteilsgrenze *f*
covered überdacht
covered cast-core electrode umhüllte Stabelektrode *f*
covered radiator verkleideter Heizkörper *m*
covered rod electrode umhüllte Stabelektrode *f*
covering Gehäuseabdeckung *f*, Überschüttung *f*, Belag *m*
covering coat deckende Schicht *f*
covering compound Umhüllungsmasse *f*
covering contribution above own costs Deckungsbeitrag *m*
covering material Umhüllungsmasse *f*
covering residues Unhüllungsrückstände *mpl*
cow-catcher Schienenräumer *m*
c-point K-Punkt *m*
CPU (Central Processing Unit) CPU
C-push frame Schubrahmen *m*
crack springen, reißen, brechen, zerbrechen, platzen; Sprung *m*, Spalt *m*, Riss *m*, Durchriss *m*, Bruch *m*
crack configuration Rissverlauf *m*
crack emerging at the surface Anriss *m*
crack formation Rissbildung *f*
crack growth Risswachstum *nt*
crack initiation limit Rissbildungsgrenze *f*
crack initiation-peel resistance Anrissschälwiderstand *m*
crack resistance on exposure Lichtrissbeständigkeit *f*
cracking Rissbildung *f*, Reißen *nt*
cracking force Anrisskraft *f*
cradle Wälzkörper *m*
cradle ladle Krangießpfanne *f*
cradle link Wälzhebel *m*
craft paper Kraftsackpapier *nt*
craftsman Facharbeiter *m*
C-rail C-Schiene *f*
cramp Spange *f*, Haken *m*
crane Kran *m*, Hebezeug *nt*
crane bridge Kranbrücke *f*
crane driving Kranfahren *nt*
crane jib Kranarm *m*, Kranausleger *m*
crane racking RFZ-Regal *nt*
crane trolley Krankatze *f*
crane way Kranbahn *f*
crank Kurbel *f*, Handkurbel *f*, Kulisse *f*; biegen, beugen, kröpfen
crank arm Kurbelschwinge *f*
crank cheek Kurbelwange *f*
crank drive Schwingantrieb *m*
crank mechanism Kurbelbetrieb *m*, Kurbelgetriebe *nt*
crank pin Kurbelzapfen *m*
crank planer Hobelmaschine *f* mit Kurbelantrieb
crank press Kurbelpresse *f*
crank shaper Waagerechtstoßmaschine *f* mit Kurbelscheibenantrieb
crank slotter Senkrechtstoßmaschine *f* mit Kurbelscheibenantrieb

crank slotting machine Senkrechtstoßmaschine *f* mit Kurbelscheibenantrieb
cranked gekröpft
cranked hexagon wrench key abgewinkelter Sechskantschraubendreher *m*
cranked planing tool gebogener Hobelmeißel *m*
cranked wrench key Winkelschraubendreher *m*
cranking Kröpfen *nt*
crankshaft Kurbelwelle *f*
crankshaft grinding machine Kurbelwellenschleifmaschine *f*
crankshaft lapping machine Kurbelwellenläppmaschine *f*
crankshaft turning lathe Kurbelwellendrehmaschine *f*
crash zusammenstoßen; Zusammenstoß *m*, Aufprall *m*
crash into aufprallen
crash protection Aufprallschutz *m*
crate Kiste *f*, Kasten *m*
crate stacking/unstacking machine Kasten-Stapel-Entstapelungsmaschine *f*
crate turnover device Kastenwendegreifer *m*
crater auskolken; Kolk *m*, Auskolkung *f*, Verschleißmulde *f*
crater crack Erstarrungsriss *m*
crater overhang Kraterüberstand *m*
crater-free finish kraterfreie Ausführung *f*
cratering Kolkbildung *f*, Auskolkung *f*, Kolkung *f*
crater-like coating kraterartiger Belag *m*
crater-shaped pit kraterförmige Vertiefung *f*
crawl kriechen, schleichen
crazing Glasurrisse *mpl*
crease Knitterstelle *f*, Sicke *f*
crease angle Knitterwinkel *m*
crease recovery angle Knittererholungswinkel *m*
creasing Sicken *nt*
creasing tendency Knitterneigung *f*
create erzeugen
creation Erzeugung *f*
creative forming Urformen *nt*

credit terms Kreditkonditionen *fpl*
creep bending test Zeitstandbiegeversuch *m*
creep schleichen, kriechen, wandern
creep behaviour in bending Zeitstandbiegeverhalten *nt*
creep behaviour in tension Zeitstandzugverhalten *nt*
creep compressive test Zeitstanddruckversuch *m*
creep diagram Zeitstandschaubild *nt*
creep feed Kriechgang *m*, Schleichgang *m*
creep feed grinding Tiefschleifen *nt*
creep limit 0,2%-Dehngrenze *f*
creep limit of the bond Dauerstandbindefestigkeit *f*
creep rupture strength of the bond Zeitstandbindfestigkeit *f*
creep rupture strength Zeitbruchfestigkeit *f*
creep speed Schleichgang *m*, Schleichfahrt *f*, Kriechgeschwindigkeit *f*
creep speed running time Schleichfahrzeit *f*
creep strength Dauerstandfestigkeit *f*, Zeitdehnspannung *f*
creep test Kriechversuch *m*, Dauerversuch *m*
creep yield Kriechnachgiebigkeit *f*
creepage Kriechen *nt*
creepage distance Kriechstrecke *f*, Kriechweg *m*
creeping Kriechen *nt*
creep-shear test Zeitstandscherversuch *m*
crest 1. Spitze *f*, Kopffläche *f* 2. *(Gewinde)* Gewindespitze *f*
crest clearance Kopfspiel *nt*, Spitzenspiel *nt*
crest of the bend Biegescheitel *m*
crest radius Außenabrundung *f*
crimping Walzrunden *nt* zu kegeligen Werkstücken
crimp umbördeln, falzen, falten, quetschen, plissieren, raffen; Falz *m*, Falte *f*
crimp closing machine Falzverschließmaschine *f*
crimping Umbördeln *nt*, Falzen *nt*
crimping unit Reffeinrichtung *f*

crinkled spring washer gewellter Federring *m*
crushing point Quetschstelle *f*
crisp scharf *(abgegrenzt)*
crisp set scharfe Menge *f*
criterion *(Kennzeichen)* Merkmal *nt*
criterion of damage Schädigungsmerkmal *nt*
critical kritisch
critical buckling stress Stabilitätsgrenze *f*
critical path method Netzplantechnik *f*
critical point Schwachstelle *f*
critical region kritischer Bereich *m*
critical value kritischer Wert *m*
croning process Croningverfahren *nt*
crooked gekrümmt, krumm, verzogen
crop Schnitt *m*
crop up auftreten
cropping Abschneiden *nt*, Schneiden *nt*
cropping with web discard Abschneiden *nt* mit Stegabfall
cross quer, durchqueren, durchlaufen, überfahren, überschreiten, quer verlaufend; Kreuz *nt*
cross adapter Kreuzverbindungsstutzen *m*
cross adjustment Querverstellung *f*
cross arm Ausleger *m*, Querbalken *m*
cross bar 1. *(quer)* Querbalken *m*, Querträger *m* **2.** *(in Tiefenrichtung)* Tiefenbalken *m*
cross beam Supportquerbalken *m*, Traverse *f*, Querbalken *m*, Querhaupt *nt*
cross bed Querbett *nt*
cross brace Tiefenverband *m*
cross carriage Querverschieber *m*, Quertraverse *f*
cross classification zweifache Aufteilung *f*, zweifache Varianzanalyse *f*
cross construction Kreuzverbindung *f*
cross corner Eckumsetzer *m*
cross drive Querantrieb *m*
cross drive for rotating assembly Querantrieb *m* der Drehgabelvorrichtung
cross feed Querverschiebung *f*, Quervorschub *m*, Planzug *m*
cross feed motion Planvorschub *m*, Planbewegung *f*
cross feed screw Querschubspindel *f*, Planspindel *f*
cross feed stop Queranschlag *m*
cross fitting Kreuzverbindungsstutzen *m*
cross girder Querträger *m*
cross girth Traverse *f*, Querhaupt *nt*
cross hatch Kreuzschliff *m*
cross hatch angle Kreuzschliffwinkel *m*
cross hole drilling Querlochbohren *nt*
cross member Querträger *m*
cross milling Fräsen *nt* in Querrichtung, Querfräsen *nt*
cross motion Querverschiebung *f*
cross rail Supportquerbalken *m*, Querbalken *m*, Querführung *f*, Ausleger *m*
cross rail planing head Querhobelsupport *m*
cross rib Querrippe *f*
cross roller bearing Kreuzrollenlager *nt*
cross roller positioning table Kreuzrollentisch *m*
cross roller table Kreuzrollentisch *m*
cross roller way Kreuzrollenlager *nt*
cross rolling Querwalzen *nt*
cross rolling of shapes Profilquerwalzen *nt*
cross scraping Querschaben *nt*
cross section Querschnitt *m*
cross section under investigation Betrachtungsquerschnitt *m*
cross section upsetting Querschnittsstauchung *f*
cross sectional area of cut Spanungsquerschnitt *m*
cross sectional region Querschnittsbereich *m*
cross selection Queranwahl *f*
cross slide Plansupport *m*, Planschieber *m*, Querbalken *m*, Querschlitten *m*, Quersupport *m*, Unterschlitten *m*, Querschieber *m*
cross slide motion Planbewegung *f*
cross slide rest Querschlitten *m*, Planschlitten *m*
cross slot Quernut *f*
cross stop Queranschlag *m*, Plananschlag *m*

cross travel Querbewegung *f*, Planzug *m*
cross traverse Quergang *m*
cross traverse slide Querschlitten *m*
cross wire Fadenkreuz *nt*
cross wire micrometer Fadenkreuzmikrometer *nt*
crossbar Querstange *f*, Querriegel *m*
crossbeam Querträger *m*, Quertraverse *f*
crossbeam accommodating gear mechanism Traverse *f* mit eingebautem Getriebe
cross-bore querbohren
cross-cut test Gitterschnittprüfung *f*
cross-drill querbohren
crossed gekreuzt
crossed helical gear Schraubrad *nt*
crossed helical gear pair Zylinderschraubradpaar *nt*, Schraubradpaar *nt*, Zylinderrad *nt* mit Doppelschrägverzahnung
crossed helical worm gear Schneckenschraubrad *nt*
crossed-axes angle Achskreuzwinkel *m*
crossed-axes point Achskreuzpunkt *m*
crossfire irradiation Kreuzfeuerbestrahlung *f*
cross-hatched finish Kreuzspur *f*
cross-hatched pattern Kreuzarbeitsspur *f*
crosshead Traverse *f*, Quertraverse *f*, Querhaupt *nt*
crossing Kreuzung *f*, Überfahren *nt*
crossing angle *(von zwei Radachsen)* Kreuzungswinkel *m*
crossing line *(e. Radpaares)* Kreuzungslinie *f*
crossing mode Kreuzbetrieb *m*
crossing point Kreuzungsstelle *f*, Kreuzungspunkt *m*
cross-layering kreuzweise Schichtung *f*
cross-level Kreuzlibelle *f*
cross-linking reaction Vernetzungsreaktion *f*
cross member Querbalken *m*
crossover Übergang *m*
cross-over joint Kreuznaht *f*
cross-plane querhobeln

cross-project projektübergreifend
crossrail Supportträger *m*, Querbalken *m*, Supportquerbalken *m*, Balken *m*, Träger *m*
crossrail clamping Querbalkenklemmung *f*
crossrail clamping device Querbalkenklemmung *f*
crossrail elevating motor Querbalkenhöhenverstellmotor *m*
crossrail feed screw Supportspindel *f*
crossrail guide Querbalkenführung *f*
crossrail head Horizontalsupport *m*, Ständerschieber *m*
cross-rail head Querbalkensupport *m*, Support *m*, Höhensupport *m*
crossrail locking mechanism Querbalkenklemmung *f*
crossrail motor Querbalkenmotor *m*
crossrail slide Querbalkenschieber *m*
crossrail slide Supportschieber *m*, Senkrechtschlitten *m*
crossrail with cross feed gearbox Querbalken *m* mit Quervorschubgetriebekasten
crossrail-lock clamp Querbalkenklemmung *f*
cross-reference Querverweis *m*
cross-reference list Querverweisliste *f*
cross-section with channel Querschnitt *m* mit Rinne
cross-sectional area Querschnittsfläche *f*, Querschnitt *m*
cross-sectional area of chip Spanquerschnitt *m*
cross-sectional area of the pass Querschnitt *m* der Spannungsschicht
cross-sectional area of the test specimen Probenquerschnitt *m*
cross-sectional reduction by inching the workpiece forward Absetzen *nt* durch Recken
cross-sectional velocity Querschnittsgeschwindigkeit *f*
cross-slide toolbox Horizontalsupport *m*, Support *m*
cross-sliding quer verfahrbar
cross-sliding column Kreuzbett *nt*
cross-sliding hexagon turret lathe Revolverdrehmaschine *f* mit Quer-

schlitten auf dem Bettschlitten
cross-sliding turret lathe Planrevolverdrehmaschine *f*
cross-sliding-column type of construction Kreuzbettbauweise *f*
cross-struts Verstrebung *f*
cross-system systemübergreifend
crosstalk Überlagern *nt* von Signalen
cross-tie Querverband *m*
crossways quer
crosswise quer
crosswise direction Querrichtung *f*
crowbar Brecheisen *nt*
crowd vorquetschen
crowding Stauchung *f*
crowning attachment Balligeinrichtung *f*
crown gear Planrad *nt*, Tellerrad *nt*
crown gear angular pitch Planradteilungswinkel *m*
crown gear pitch Planradteilung *f*
crown gear reference circle Planradteilkreis *m*
crown gear reference plane Planradteilebene *f*
crown gear system Planradverzahnung *f*
crown gear teeth Planradzahn *m*
crown line Scheitellinie *f*
crown of the pipe Rohrscheitel *m*
crown turret Kronrevolver *m*
crown wheel Kronenrad *nt*
crowned ballig
crowned gear teeth breitenballige Verzahnung *f*
crowned tooth cutting Balligverzahnung *f*
crowning Breitenballigkeit *f*, Längsballigkeit *f*, Balligverzahnen *nt*, Balligverzahnung *f*
CRT (Cathode Ray Tube) CRT
CRT-module Bildteil
crucible Gießtiegel *m*, Tiegel *m*
crucible furnace Tiegelofen *m*
crucible tippler Tiegelkippgerät *nt*
crucible-lime process Tiegelkalkverfahren *nt*
cruciform weld Kreuznaht *f*
crude roh
crumble bröckeln, zersetzen, zerbröckeln, abbröckeln, ausbröckeln
crumbling Zersetzung *f*, Zerbröckeln *nt*
crumbling chip Bröckelspäne *f*
crumbling of the cutting edge Abbröckeln *nt* der Schneide
crumbling temperature Ausbröckelungstemperatur *f*
crumbly bröckelig
crush quetschen, mahlen, brechen, zusammendrücken
crush dressing Einrollprofilieren *nt*, Einrollen *nt*
crush resistance Stauchwiderstand *m*
crush-dress einrollprofilieren
crush-dressing attachment Einrollvorrichtung *f*
crush-dressing device Einrollvorrichtung *f*
crusher Mühle *f*
crusher roll Profilrolle *f*, Pressrolle *f*
crusher roll pressure Einrolldruck *m*
crusher roll spindle Profilrollenspindel *f*
crusher wheel Pressrolle *f*
crushing Zusammendrücken *nt*, Einrollprofilieren *nt*, Profilieren *nt*, Quetschen *nt*
crushing load Scheiteldruckkraft *f*
crushing zone Quetschbereich *m*
crystal mosaic Mosaikschwinger *m*
crystalline solid body laser kristalliner Festkörperlaser *m*
C-scope presentation Drei-C-Bild
C-shaped profile C-Profil *nt*
C-type spot welding head Schweißbügel *m*
cube Kubus *m*, Würfel *m*
cube glue Würfelleim *m*
cube test Würfeldruckprüfung *f*
cube utilization Raumausnutzung *f*
cubic kubisch, räumlich
cubical würfelförmig
cuboid Quader *m*
cuff Stulpe *f*
commutator Kollektor *m*
cumulative error Summenfehler *m*, Sammelfehler *m*, Gesamtfehler *m*
cumulative frequency Häufigkeitssumme *f*
cumulative frequency curve Häufig-

keitssummenkurve *f*
cumulative frequency polygon Summenlinie *f*
cumulative pitch test Summenteilungsprüfung *f*
cumulative pitch-span variation Teilungssummenabweichung *f*
cumulative probability function Verteilungsfunktion *f*
cumulative relative frequency relative Häufigkeitssumme *f*
cumulative sum Häufigkeitssumme *f*
cumulative variation Summenabweichung *f*
cumulative working pitch variation Wälzsummenteilungsabweichung *f*
cup Becher *m*, Schale *f*, Napf *m*
cup fill and seal machine Becherfüll- und -verschließmaschine *f*
cup head lubricating nipple Trichterschmiernippel *m*
cup wheel Topfscheibe *f*
cupboard Schrank *m*
cupola blower Kupolofengebläse *nt*
cupola furnace Kopolofen *m*
cupola lining Kupolofenausfütterung *f*
cupola melting Kupolofenschmelzen *nt*
cupped socket Kugelmuffe *f*
cupping Tiefen *nt*
cupping behaviour Tiefungsverhalten *nt*
cupping by detonation with an explosive Tiefen *nt* durch Detonation eines Sprengstoffes
cupping by explosion of a gas mixture Tiefen *nt* durch Explosion eines Gasgemisches
cupping by spark discharge Tiefen *nt* durch Funkenentladung
cupping by temporary expansion of highly compressed gases Tiefen *nt* durch kurzzeitige Entspannung hochkomprimierter Gase
cupping test tool Tiefungsprüfwerkzeug *nt*
cupping with action media *pl* Tiefen *nt* mit Wirkmedien *ntpl*
cupping with action media with effect associated with energy Tiefen *nt* mit Wirkmedien mit energiegebundener Wirkung
cupping with action media with effected associated with force Tiefen *nt* mit Wirkmedien mit kraftgebundener Wirkung
cupping with active energy Tiefen *nt* mit Wirkenergie
cupping with amorphous solid materials having an effect associated with energy Tiefen *nt* mit formlos festen Stoffen mit energiegebundener Wirkung
cupping with amorphous solid materials having an effect associated with force Tiefen *nt* mit formlos festen Stoffen mit kraftgebundener Wirkung
cupping with compliant tool Tiefen *nt* mit nachgiebigem Werkzeug
cupping with compressed air Tiefen *nt* mit Druckluft
cupping with fluids having an effect associated with energy Tiefen *nt* mit Flüssigkeiten mit energiegebundener Wirkung
cupping with fluids having an effect associated with force Tiefen *nt* mit Flüssigkeiten mit kraftgebundener Wirkung
cupping with gases having an effect associated with energy Tiefen *nt* mit Gasen mit energiegebundener Wirkung
cupping with gases having an effect associated with force Tiefen *nt* mit Gasen kraftgebundener Wirkung
cupping with magnetic fields Tiefen *nt* mit Magnetfeldern
cupping with rigid tool Tiefen *nt* mit starrem Werkzeug
cupping with tools *pl* Tiefen *nt* mit Werkzeugen
cup-shaped cutter Topffräser *m*
cure ausvulkanisieren
curemetry Vulkametrie *f*
curing condition Härtebedingung *f*
curl rollen
curling Einkräuselung *f*, Lockenbildung *f*, Rollbiegen *nt*, Einrollen *nt*
curling by spinning Randeinrollen *nt* durch Drücken

curling cut *(auf Span bezogen)* Schälschnitt *m*
curly chip Wendelspan *m*, Spiralspan *m*
current 1. aktuell, laufend 2. *(el.)* Strom *m*
current absorption Stromaufnahme *f*
current adjustment Stromangleichung *f*
current carrying part stromführendes Teil *nt*
current conduction Stromleitung *f*
current consumption Stromentnahme *f*
current contact tube Stromkontaktrohr *nt*
current control Stromregelung *f*
current control programme Stromprogramm *nt*
current converter Stromrichter *m*
current delivery Stromlieferung *f*
current density-potential curve Stromdichte-Potential-Kurve *f*
current direction Stromrichtung *f*
current displacement Stromverdrängungseigenschaft *f*
current drain Stromentnahme *f*
current generation Spannungserzeugung *f*
current leakage Isolationsfehler *m*
current limitation Strombegrenzung *f*
current limiter Strombegrenzer *m*
current line Stromleitung *f*
current meter Messflügel *m*
current network Stromnetz *nt*
current on contact Schaltstrom *m*
current operation laufender Betrieb *m*
current path Strombahn *f*
current production Spannungserzeugung *f*
current sinking Strom ziehend
current source inverter *(netzseitig)* Stromrichter *m*
current sourcing Strom liefern
current stage gegenwärtiger Stand *m*
current status Ist-Zustand *m*
current supply Stromzufuhr *f*
current transformer Stromwandler *m*
current-carrying energized Strom führend
current-loop interface Linienstromschnittstelle *f*
cursor Cursor *m*
curtain Vorhang *m*
curtain hook Vorhanghaken *m*
curtain of warm air Warmluftschleier *m*
curtosis Kurtosis *f*
curvature Bogen *m*, Wölbung *f*, Krümmung *f*
curvature through Durchwölbung *f*
curve Bogen *m*, Kurve *f*; wölben, krümmen
curve display Kurvenbild *nt*
curve of deformation versus time Zeit-Verformungs-Linie *f*
curve of stress versus number of cycles Spannungslaufkurve *f*
curve parameter Kurvenparameter *m*
curved gekrümmt, krumm
curved cut Kurvenschnitt *m*
curved cutting edge kurvenförmige Schneide *f*
curved guide mechanism Kurvenführungsgetriebe *nt*
curved path electrode travel bogenförmig bewegte Elektrode
curved scale gekrümmte Skala *f*
curved spring washer gewölbter Federring *m*, Federscheibe *f*, Hochspannfederring *m*
curved stroke Bogenstrich *m*
curved surface gekrümmte Fläche *f*
curved three-dimensionally räumlich gekrümmt
curved tooth bevel gear bogenverzahntes Kegelrad *nt*
curved washer Scheibenfeder *f*
curve-going kurvengängig
curve-of deformation against time Zeit-Verformungs-Linie *f*
curvexity Wölbung *f*
curving tear propagation bogiges Weiterreißen *nt*
cushion dämpfen, puffern, abfedern; Dämpfer *m*
cushion catching device Gleitfangvorrichtung *f*
cushion cylinder Zylinder *m* mit dämpfendem Endanschlag
cushion of air Luftkissen *nt*

cushioning Dämpfung *f*, Abfederung *f*
cushioning action Dämpfungsvorgang *m*
cushioning cylinder Stoßdämpfer *m*
custom made nach Kundenwunsch
customer Kunde *m*, Auftraggeber *m*, Empfänger *m*, Käufer *m*
customer expectation Kundenerwartung *f*
customer orientation Kundenorientierung *f*
customer relationship management (CRM) Kundenbeziehungsmanagement *nt*
customer satisfaction Kundenzufriedenheit *f*
customer schedule control Kundenterminsteuerung *f*
customer service Kundenservice *m*
customer specific kundenspezifisch
customer supply Kundenbelieferung *f*
customer-oriented kundenorientiert
customer's need Kundenwunsch *m*
customer's order placement Kundenauftrag *m*
customer's requirements Kundenwunsch *m*
customized nach Kundenwunsch
customs *(Verwaltung)* Zoll *m*
customs documents Zollpapiere *ntpl*
customs duty Zoll *m*
customs tariff Zolltarif *m*
customs tariff number (CTN) Zolltarifnummer *f*
cut zerspanend bearbeiten, trennen, zerspanen, spanen, abspanen, fertigen, durchstechen, scheren, schneiden, überschneiden; Schnitt *m*, Span *m*
cut away abschneiden
cut badly verschneiden
cut clear freischneiden
cut dimension plane Spanungsmessebene *f*
cut edge Schnittkante *f*
cut expenses Kosten senken, Einsparungen machen
cut front Schnittfront *f*
cut front inclination Schnittfrontneigung *f*
cut gears verzahnen

cut gears by the generating method wälzzahnen
cut in einstechen
cut into sections ablängen
cut joint Schnittfuge *f*
cut joint width Schnittfugenbreite
cut length Zuschnittlänge *f*
cut made on pipe ends Rohrendschnitt *m*
cut of equal depth gleichdicker Span *m*
cut off schneiden, abschneiden, abtrennen, abhacken, abfräsen, abstechen, abschalten, schließen, unterbrechen
cut off by abrasive cutting durchschleifen
cut off the engine Gas wegnehmen
cut off to length ablängen
cut out ausschneiden, abschalten; Sicherung *f*
cut part Schnittteil *nt*
cut per tooth Schnitttiefe *f* je Zahn
cut performance Schneidleistung *f*
cut process Abhebeverfahren *nt*
cut surface Schnittflanke *f*
cut teeth zahnen, verzahnen
cut to size zuschneiden
cut width Schnittbreite *f*
cuttability Spanbarkeit *f*
cutable spanbar
cut-back bitumen chippings Verschnittbitumensplitt *m*
cut-in potential Einschaltpotential *nt*
cut-off circuit Abschaltkreis *m*
cut-off grinding Trennschleifen *nt*, Trennen *nt*
cutoff operation Abstecharbeit *f*
cut-off operation Trennschnitt *m*
cut-off saw Trennsäge *f*
cut-off tool Stechmeißel *m*, Abstechmeißel *m*
cutout Sicherheitsausschalter *m*, AUS-Schalter *m*
cut-out milling Ausschneidfräsen *nt*
cutout potential Ausschaltpotential *nt*
cuts Zuschnitte *mpl*
cuttability Zerspanbarkeit *f*, Schneidfähigkeit *f*, Schneidhaltigkeit *f*, Schnittfähigkeit *f*, Schnitthaltigkeit *f*
cutter 1. Schneidwerkzeug *nt*, Meißel *m* **2.** *(Fräsen)* Fräser *m*, Fräswerk-

zeug *nt*
cutter arbor 1. Spanndorn *m* **2.** *(Fräsen)* Fräsdorn *m*, Aufsteckfräsdorn *m*
cutter arbor nut *(Fräsen)* Fräsdornmutter *f*
cutter bit Einsatzmeißel *m*
cutter blade 1. Messer *nt* **2.** *(Fräsen)* Fräserzahn *m*
cutter chuck 1. Spannfutter *nt* **2.** *(Fräsen)* Fräsfutter *nt*
cutter clamp Messerklemme *f*
cutter compensation Radiuskorrektur *f*
cutter diametral pitch Diametral-Pitch eines Werkzeuges
cutter edge Fräserschneide *f*
cutter for milling half circles Halbkreisfräser *m*
cutter for stub-arbor mounting Fräser *m* zum Aufstecken auf fliegend angeordnetem Dorn
cutter head 1. Messerkopf *m* **2.** *(Fräsen)* Fräskopf *m*, Frässpindelkopf *m*
cutter holder Messerblock *m*
cutter interference Unterschnitt *m*
cutter life Fräserstandzeit *f*
cutter lift Fräserabhebung *f*
cutter location data (CLDATA) Schnittverlaufs- und Werkzeugbahndaten *pl*
cutter mill Langlochfräser *m*
cutter milling machine Werkzeugfräsmaschine *f*
cutter misalignment Fräserversatz *m*
cutter module Werkzeugmodul *nt*
cutter pitch Fräserzahnteilung *f*
cutter radius compensation Fräserradiuskorrektur *f*
cutter relief Fräserabhebung
cutter retraction Fräserabhebung
cutter speed Fräserdrehzahl *f*
cutter spindle 1. Arbeitsspindel *f* **2.** *(Fräsen)* Frässpindel *f*
cutter standard basic rack tooth profile Werkzeugbezugsprofil *nt*
cutter tooth Fräserzahn *m*
cutter wear Fräserverschleiß *m*
Cutter-Line Data (CLDATA) CL-Data (Schnittverlaufswerkzeugbahndaten)
cutting 1. zerspanende Bearbeitung *f*, spanabhebende Bearbeitung *f*, Zerspanung *f*, Schnitt *m*, Zuschnitt *m*, Spanen *nt*, Zerspanen *nt*, Schneiden *nt* **2.** Überschneidung *f* **3.** *(feilen)* Hauen *nt*
cutting ability Schneidhaltigkeit *f*
cutting action Schneidarbeit *f*, Spanung *f*, Zerspanung *f*, Angriff *m* eines Schneidwerkzeuges
cutting additions Beschneidezugaben *f*
cutting agent Schleifmittel *nt*
cutting agent grain Schleifmittelkörnung *f*
cutting agent type Schleifmittelart *f*
cutting alloy Schneidmetall *nt*
cutting angle Schnittwinkel *m*, Schneidwinkel *m*, Schneidenwinkel *m*
cutting blade Messer *nt*
cutting blade life Messerstandzeit *f*
cutting blowpipe Brenner *m*
cutting by the whirling method Wirbelspanung *f*
cutting by whirling process Wirbelzerspanung *f*
cutting capacity Abspanleistung *f*, Schnittleistung *f*, Spanleistung *f*, Zerspanungsleistung *f*, Schneidfähigkeit *f*, Durchzugkraft *f*
cutting ceramics Schneidkeramik *f*
cutting cycle Zerspanungsvorgang *m*, Bearbeitungsablauf *m*
cutting cylindrical gears Verzahnen *nt* von Stirnrädern
cutting depth Spantiefe *f*, Schnitttiefe *f*
cutting diamond Schneiddiamant *m*
cutting die Schnittmatrize *f*, Schneidbacke *f*
cutting distance Schneidweg *m*, Schnittweg *m*
cutting down Gleichlauffräsen *nt*
cutting edge Schneide *f*, Schneidkante *f*, Schneidlippe *f*, Meißelschneide *f*
cutting edge angle Einstellwinkel *m* der Stirnschneide, Schneidenwinkel *m*, Komplementwinkel *m* des Einstellwinkels *m*
cutting edge back rake Spanwinkel *m*
cutting edge design Schneidkantengestaltung *f*

cutting edge geometry Schneidengeometrie *f*
cutting edge misalignment Schneidkantenversatz *m*
cutting edge normal plane Werkzeugschneidennormalebene *f*, Wirk-Schneidennormalebene *f*
cutting edge of the tool Werkzeugschneide *f*
cutting edge plane Schneidenebene *f*
cutting edge principal point Schneidenbezugspunkt *m*
cutting edge profile Schneidenprofil *nt*
cutting edge roundness Schneidkantenrundung
cutting edge side rake Spanwinkel *m*
cutting edge support Schneidenträger *m*
cutting efficiency 1. Zerspanungsleistung *f*, Wirkungsgrad *m* bei der Zerspanung **2.** *(Fräsen)* Fräsleistung *f*
cutting edge Schneide *f*
cutting energy Schnittenergie *f*
cutting expenses Kostensenkung *f*, Einsparung *f*
cutting face Schneidfläche *f*, Spanfläche *f*, Zahnbrust *f* einer Spanfläche
cutting feed Arbeitsvorschub *m*, Schnittvorschub *m*
cutting force rising Schnittkraftanstieg *m*
cutting fluid Schneidflüssigkeit *f*
cutting force Schnittkraft *f*, Schneidkraft *f*, Zerspankraft *f*, Spanungskraft *f*, Durchzugkraft *f*
cutting force components Komponenten *f* der Schnittkraft
cutting force relationship Schnittkraftbeziehung *f*
cutting from the solid Schneiden *nt* aus dem Vollen
cutting gap Schneidspalt *m*
cutting grain Schleifkorn *nt*
cutting insert Schneidplatte *f*
cutting instalment Schneidrate *f*
cutting life Standzeit *f* der Schneide
cutting line Schnittlinie *f*
cutting lip Hauptschneide *f*
cutting load Schnittkraft *f*, Schnittlast *f*
cutting machinability Schneidbearbeitbarkeit *f*
cutting machine life Lebensdauer *f* der Schneidmaschine
cutting machining spanende Bearbeitung *f*
cutting main group Spanungshauptgruppe *f*
cutting manufacturing spanende Fertigung *f*
cutting material Schneidstoff *m*
cutting material composition Schneidstoffzusammensetzung *f*
cutting material selection Schneidstoffauswahl *f*
cutting materials Schneidstoffe *mpl*
cutting medium Schneidwerkstoff *m*, Zerspanungsmittel *nt*
cutting method Schneidverfahren *nt*
cutting motion Schnittbewegung *f*, Schneidbewegung *f*
cutting movement Schnittbewegung *f*, Zerspanbewegung *f*
cutting nozzle part Schneiddüsenbohrung *f*
cutting of teeth Verzahnung *f*
cutting off Abtrennen *nt*, Abstechen *nt*, Abschneiden *nt*, Abtrennung *f*
cutting off to length Ablängen *nt*
cutting oil Schleiföl *nt*
cutting operation Zerspanungsarbeit *f*, Zerspanarbeit *f*, Schneidarbeit *f*, Zerspanungsvorgang *m*, Zerspanvorgang *f*, Zerspanung *f*, Spanung *f*, spangebende Bearbeitung *f*, spanabhebende Bearbeitung *f*
cutting order Zuschnittauftrag *m*
cutting orifice Schneidbohrung *f*
cutting part Schneidteil *nt*
cutting path Fräsweg *m*, Schnittbahn *f*, Schnittweg *m*
cutting performance Spanungsleistung *f*, Schnittkraft *f*
cutting perpendicular force Schnittnormalkraft *f*
cutting plane Schneidebene *f*, Werkzeugschneidenebene *f*
cutting point Schneidenpunkt *m*, Schnittstelle *f*
cutting position Arbeitsstellung *f*
cutting power Spanungsleistung *f*,

Schnittleistung *f*, Schnittfähigkeit *f*, Schnittkraft *f*
cutting pressure Schnittkraft *f*
cutting process Schneidvorgang *m*, Schneidverfahren *nt*, Spanung *f*, Zerspanung *f*
cutting property Zerspanungseigenschaft *f*, Schneidfähigkeit *f*, Zerspanbarkeit *f*
cutting quality Schneidfähigkeit *f*
cutting rake Spanwinkel *m*
cutting rate Schnittgeschwindigkeit *f*
cutting relation Spanungsverhältnis *nt*
cutting ring Schneidring *m*
cutting section Schneidenteil *m*
cutting sequence Schnittfolge *f*
cutting sizes Schnittgrößen *fpl*
cutting solution Kühlmittel *nt*
cutting speed Schnittgeschwindigkeit *f*
cutting speed during the forward stroke Vorlaufschnittgeschwindigkeit *f*
cutting spindle Frässpindel *f*
cutting spindle quill Frässpindelhülse *f*
cutting stroke Hobelgang *m*, Schnitthub *m*, Arbeitshub *m*
cutting stroke of the ram Stößelverlauf *m*
cutting technique Zerspanmethode *f*, spanabhebendes Verfahren *nt*
cutting technology Trenntechnik *f*
cutting teeth *pl (Räumwerkzeug)* Schneidenzähne *mpl*
cutting template Schneideschablone *f*
cutting thickness Spanungsdicke *f*
cutting time Schnittzeit *f*
cutting tip 1. Schneidplatte *f* **2.** *(Bohrer)* Bohrerspitze *f*
cutting to size Zuschneiden *nt*
cutting tool Arbeitsmeißel *m*, Bearbeitungswerkzeug *nt*, Schneidwerkzeug *nt*, Schneidmeißel *nt*, Schneidstahl *m*, Meißel *m*, spanabhebendes Werkzeug *nt*, spanendes Werkzeug *nt*, zerspanendes Werkzeug *nt*, Spanungswerkzeuge *ntpl*
cutting tool angle Schnittwinkel *m*, Schneidenwinkel *m*
cutting tool edge Werkzeugschneide *f*, Meißelschneide *f*
cutting tool for lathe work Drehmeißel *m*, Drehstahl *m*
cutting tool geometry Schneidengeometrie *f*
cutting tool nose Meißelspitze *f*
cutting tool shank Drehmeißelschaft *m*
cutting tool tip Werkzeugschneide *f*, Schneidplatte *f*, Schneidwerkzeugplättchen *nt*
cutting tooth Schneidzahn *m*, Werkzeugzahn *m*
cutting torch Schneidbrenner *m*
cutting torque Schnittmoment *m*
cutting up 1. Zerschneiden *nt* **2.** *(Fräsen)* Gegenlauffräsen *nt*
cutting variable Zerspangröße *f*, Zerspanungsgröße *f*, Schnittgröße *f*
cutting volume Spanungsvolumen *nt*, Schnittvolumen *nt*
cutting wedge Schneidkeil *m*
cutting wedge angle Keilwinkel *m*
cutting wheel efficiency Scheibenleistung *f*
cutting width Spanungsbreite *f*, Schneidbreite *f*
cutting work Schnittarbeit *f*
cutting-off machine Trennmaschine *f*
cutting-off slide Abstechschlitten *m*
cutting-off spindle Abstechspindel *f*
cutting-off tool Abstechwerkzeug *nt*, Stechmeißel *m*
cutting-off toolholder Abstechmeißelhalter *m*
cuttings Span *m*, Schneidspäne *f*, Verschnitt *m*, Schnitzel *ntpl*
cuttings for analysis purposes Analysespäne *f*
cutting thrust Schnittkraft *f*
CVL *(copper vapour laser)* Kupferdampflaser *m*
cyanotype method Cyanotype
cycle 1. Zyklus *m*, Spiel *nt*, Arbeitsspiel *nt*, Takt *m*, Kreislauf *m*, Umlauf *m*, Ablauf *m*, Arbeitsablauf *m*, Arbeitsvorgang *m*, Periode *f*, Rhythmus *m* **2.** *(Vibration, Oszillation)* Schwingspiel *nt*
cycle frequency Schwingspielfrequenz *f*, Schalthäufigkeit *f*
cycle hardening Pendelhärten *nt*
cycle milling Pendelverkehrfräsen *nt*, Pendelfräsen *nt*

cycle of motion Bewegungsablauf *m*
cycle of movement Bewegungsablauf *m*
cycle requirement Spielzahlanforderung *f*
cycle setting Einstellung *f* des Arbeitsablaufes
cycle stroke Schwinghub *m*
cycle thread Fahrradgewinde *nt*
cycle time Zykluszeit *f*, Spielzeit *f*, Taktzeit *f*, Umlaufzeit *f*
cycle time verification Spielzeitüberprüfung *f*
cycled operation Taktbetrieb *m*
cycle-driven taktgetrieben
cyclic zyklisch
cyclic loading schwingende Beanspruchung *f*
cyclic motion Bewegungsablauf *m*
cyclic motor Drehfeldmotor *m*
cyclic redundancy check (CRC) zyklische Blockprüfung *f*
cyclic stress Wechselbeanspruchung *f*, Schwingungsbeanspruchung *f*
cyclical periodisch
cyclical accelerator Kreisbeschleuniger *m*
cycloidal gear pair Zykloidenradpaar *nt*
cylindrical surface Zylinderfläche *f*
cycloid Zykloide *f*, Zykloidenabschnitt *m*
cyclised natural rubber Zyklokautschuk *m*
cyclised natural rubber adhesive Zyklokautschukkleber *m*
cyclohexanone solution Cyclohexanonlösung *f*
cycloid Radkurve *f*, Radlaufkurve *f*, Zykloide
cycloidal gear Zykloidengetriebe *nt*, Zykloidenzahnrad *nt*, Zykloidenverzahnung *f*
cycloidal gear pair Zykloidenradpaar *nt*
cycloidal gear teeth Zykloidenverzahnung *f*
cycloidal tooth system Zykloidverzahnung *f*, Zykloidenverzahnung *f*
cylinder Zylinder *m*, Walze *f*
cylinder bit Kanonenbohrer *m*
cylinder boring and milling machine Zylinderbohr- und -fräswerk *nt*
cylinder boring machine Zylinderbohrmaschine *f*
cylinder cam Trommelkurve *f*
cylinder method Zylinderverfahren *nt*
cylinder temperature Zylindertemperatur *f*
cylindrical zylindrisch, rund
cylindrical bending block Biegezylinder *m*
cylindrical cam groove Zylindernutkurve *f*
cylindrical cam milling attachment Mantelkurvenfräseinrichtung *f*
cylindrical coil Zylinderspule *f*
cylindrical contouring Rundkopieren *nt*
cylindrical crossed helical gear Stirnschraubrad *nt*
cylindrical crossed helical gear pair Stirnschraubradpaar *nt*
cylindrical fit Rundpassung *f*
cylindrical former Biegezylinder *m*
cylindrical gear Stirnrad *nt*, Zylinderrad *nt*
cylindrical gear pair Zylinderradpaar *nt*, Stirnradpaar *nt*
cylindrical gear production Stirnradherstellung *f*
cylindrical gear teeth Stirnradverzahnung *f*
cylindrical gear tooth system Stirnradverzahnung *f*
cylindrical gear transmission Stirnradgetriebe *nt*
cylindrical gear with involute teeth Stirnrad *nt* mit Evolventenverzahnung
cylindrical grinder Rundschleifmaschine *f*
cylindrical grinding Flachschleifen *nt*, Rundschleifen *nt*
cylindrical grinding operation Rundschleifarbeit *f*
cylindrical interference fit zylindrische Presspassung *f*
cylindrical joint Drehschubgelenk *nt*
cylindrical lantern gear Triebstockrad *nt*
cylindrical lantern pinion and wheel Triebstockradpaar *nt*

cylindrical lantern tooth system Triebstockverzahnung *f*
cylindrical lapping Rundläppen *nt*
cylindrical limit plug gauge Grenzlehrdorn *m*
cylindrical milling cutter Walzenfräser *m*
cylindrical milling machine Walzenfräser *m*
cylindrical plug gauge Zylinderlehrdorn *m*
cylindrical plunge grinder Einstechrundschleifmaschine *f*
cylindrical precision grinder Präzisionsrundschleifmaschine *f*
cylindrical roller bearing Rollenkugellager *nt*, Zylinderrollenlager *nt*
cylindrical rotary valve Drehkolbenventil *nt*
cylindrical slab miller Walzenfräser *m*
cylindrical spirit level vial Röhrenlibelle *f*
cylindrical surface Mantelfläche *f*
cylindrical surface grinding Rundschleifen *nt*
cylindrical tooth system Zylinderradverzahnung *f*
cylindrical turning Runddrehen *nt*, Zylindrischdrehen *nt*
cylindrical worm Zylinderschnecke *f*
cylindrical worm gear set Zylinderschneckenradsatz *m*
cylindricity Zylindrizität *f*
cylindricity tolerance Zylinderformtoleranz *f*
cycloid Orthozykloide *f*
Cyrillic letters kyrillische Zeichen *ntpl*

Dd

D bistable element D-Kippglied *nt*
d.c. contactor Gleichstromschütz *nt*
d.c. generator Gleichstromgenerator *m*, Gleichstrommaschine *f*
d.c. motor Gleichstrommotor *m*
d.c. operated gleichstrombetätigt
d.c. output Gleichspannungsausgang *m*
d.c. power port Gleichspannungsversorgungsanschluss *m*
d.c. relay Gleichstromschütz *nt*
d.c. shunt motor Gleichstromnebenschlussmotor *m*
d.c. signal Gleichstromimpuls *m*
d.c. test Gleichspannungsprüfung *f*
d.c. voltage Gleichspannung *f*
d.c. voltage changer Umrichter *m*, Gleichumrichter *m*
d.c.motor Elektronikmotor *m*
d.c-a.c. converter Wechselrichter *m*
daily täglich
dam stauen
dam up dämmen
damage Schaden *m*, Beschädigung *f*; schaden, beschädigen
damage level Schädigungspunkt *m*
damage resembling a pit muldenähnliche Beschädigung *f*
damage sustained during transport (or in transit) Transportschaden *m*
damage to health Gesundheitsschädigung *f*
damaged schadhaft
damaging Beschädigung *f*
damaging deformation Schädigungsverformung *f*
damaging effect schädigende Wirkung *f*
damaging energy Schädigungsarbeit *f*
damaging force Schädigungskraft *f*
dammar solution adhesive Dammarkleber *m*
damp nass, feucht; Feuchtigkeit *f*, Schwade *f*; dämpfen
damp alternating atmosphere Feuchtwechselklima *nt*
damp heat apparatus Schwitzwassergerät *nt*
damp heat atmosphere Schwitzwasserklima *nt*
damp proofing of buildings Bautenabdichtung *f*
damped laminated system schwingungsgedämpftes geschichtetes System *nt*
dampen befeuchten
dampening Befeuchtung *f*
damper Dämpfer *m*
damping Dämpfung *f*
damping behaviour Dämpfungsverhalten *nt*
damping capacity Dämpfungsfähigkeit *f*
damping power Dämpfungsfähigkeit *f*
damping property Dämpfungsfähigkeit *f*
damping value Dämpfungsgröße *f*
danger Gefahr *f*
danger inhibiting gefahrverhindert
danger message Gefahrmeldung *f*
danger of scaling Versteinungsgefahr *f*
danger of shear failure Grundbruchgefahr *f*
danger of slipping Rutschgefahr *f*
danger of stumbling Stolpergefahr *f*
danger of tipping over Kippgefahr *f*
danger period Gefährdungszeit *f*
danger point Gefahrstelle *f*
danger preventing gefahrverhindert
danger sign Warnschild *nt*
danger signal Warnsignal *nt*
danger zone Gefahrbereich *m*
dangerous gefährlich
dangerous effect gefahrbringende Wirkung *f*
dangerous spot Gefahrenstelle *f*
dark dunkel
dark field Dunkelfläche *f*
dark switching Dunkelschaltung *f*
darkening of colour Dunkelfärbung *f*
dash *(Querstrich)* Strich *m*
dash line Strichlinie *f*
dashpot Stoßdämpfer *m*, Puffer *m*

dashpot (brake) Bremszylinder *m*
data Daten *pl*, Werte *pl*, Kennwerte *mpl*, Angaben *fpl*
data access method Datenzugriffsmethode *f*
data acquisition Datenlesen *nt*, Datenerfassung *f*, Datenerhebung *f*
data archiving Datenarchivierung *f*
data bank Datenbank *f*
data bank security Datenbanksicherung *f*
data base Datenbank *f*, Datenbanken *fpl*
data carrier Datenträger *m*, Informationsträger *m*
data carrier speed Datenträgergeschwindigkeit *f*
data circuit-terminating equipment (DCE) Datenübertragungseinrichtung *f*
data collection Datenerfassung *f*
data communication Datenkommunikation *f*
data communication equipment Datenübertragungseinrichtung *f*
data comparison Datenvergleich *m*
data concentrator Datenkonzentrator *m*
data coupling Datenkopplung *f*
data documentation Datendokumentation *f*
data exchange Informationsaustausch *m*, Datenaustausch *m*
Data Exchange Format DXF (Datenaustauschformat *nt*)
data field Datenfeld *nt*
data file access module Datenzugriffsmodul *nt*
data flow Datenfluss *m*
data input Dateneingang *m*
data interchange Datenaustausch *m*
data interchange format Datenaustauschformat *nt*
data interface Datenschnittstelle *f*
data inventory Datenbestand *m*
data link layer Verbindungsschicht *f*
data logging system Datenerfassungs- und Aufzeichnungssystem *nt*
data memory Datenspeicher *m*, Informationsspeicher *m*
data of the master parts record Teilestammdaten *pl*
data output Datenausgang *m*, Datenausgabe *f*
data pair Datenpaar *nt*
data point Messpunkt *m*
data position Datenstelle *f*
data preparation Informationsaufbereitung *f*
data processing Datenverarbeitung *f*, Informationsverarbeitung *f*
data processing centre DV-Zentrale *f*
data processing level Datenverarbeitungsebene *f*
data processing system EDV-System *nt*
data protection measure Datensicherungsmaßnahme *f*
data radio Datenfunk *m*
data recording Datenaufzeichnung *f*
data security Datensicherheit *f*
data sheet Datenblatt *nt*
data source Datenquelle *f*
data storage Datenspeicher *m*, Datenhaltung *f*
data storage media/medium Datenträger *m*
data storage unit Datenspeicher *m*
data structure Datenstruktur *f*
data structure concept Datenstrukturierung *f*
data system adjusted application EDV-technische Anpassung *f*
data systems technology Datentechnik *f*
data table Wertetabelle *f*
data terminal equipment (DTE) Datenendeinrichtung *f*
data transfer Datenübertragung *f*
data transfer device Datenübertragungseinrichtung *f*
data transfer procedure Datenübertragungsverfahren *nt*
data transfer rate Datenübertragungsrate *f*
data transfer speed Datenübertragungsgeschwindigkeit *f*
data transmission Datenübertragung *f*
data transmission volume Datenübertragungsmenge *f*
data word Datenwort *nt*

date−deceleration 118

date datieren; Datum *nt*, Termin *m*, Zeitpunkt *m*
date of delivery Liefertermin *m*
date of receipt Wareneingangsdatum *nt*
date stamp Zeitstempel *m*
date verification Datumsprüfung *f*
datum Systemebene *f*
datum axis Bezugsachse *f*, Systemachse *f*
datum line Profilmittellinie *f*, Profilbezugslinie *f*, Bezugslinie *f*
datum median plane Bezugsmittelebene *f*
datum plane Systemebene *f*, Profilbezugsebene *f*, Bezugsebene *f*
datum point Nullpunkt *m*, Bezugszahl *f*
datum tooth trace Bezugsflankenlinie *f*
day Tag *m*
day to day täglich
daylight proportion Tageslichtquote *f*
daylight quota Tageslichtquote *f*
dayroom Tagesraum *m*
DCE clear indication Auslösemeldung *f*
DCE common return DÜE Rückleiter *m*
DCE not ready *(Datenkommunikation)* DÜE nicht bereit
DCE provided information *(Datenkommunikation)* DÜE-Information *f*
deactivate ausschalten
deactivated abgeschaltet
dead centre tote Spitze *f*, feststehende Spitze *f*, Totpunkt *m*, Gegenspitze *f*
dead earth Erdschluss *m*
dead load 1. Eigenlast *f* **2.** *(Belastung)* ruhende Beanspruchung *f*
dead lock Zuhaltungsschloss *nt*
dead man device Totmanneinrichtung *f*
dead man's button Totmanneinrichtung *f*
dead man's control Totmannschaltung *f*
dead man's device Sicherheitsfahrschaltung *f*
dead man's handle Totmanneinrichtung *f*
dead motor Motorausfall *m*
dead stop gripping device Sperrfangvorrichtung *f*
dead stop method Endpunktverfahren *nt*
dead stop titration apparatus Endpunkttitrationsgerät *nt*
dead tailstock centre Reitnagel *m*
dead time Nebenzeit *f*, Verlustzeit *f*, Wartezeit *f*, Totzeit *f*
dead travel toter Gang *m*
dead weight Totgewicht *nt*, Masse *f*
dead zone tote Zone *f*, Unempfindlichkeitsbereich *m*
dead-end station Kopfstation *f*
deadline Termin *m*, Frist *f*
deadlock Stillstand *m*, Verklemmung *f*
deadtime Pause *f*
deadweight Eigenlast *f*
deadweight coefficient Eigenlastbeiwert *m*
deaerate lüften, entlüften
deaerator Entlüfter *m*
dealuminification Entaluminierung *f*
de-ash *(Asche)* abschüren
de-ashing Aschenaustrag *m*
de-ashing system Entschlackungseinrichtung *f*
debit abbuchen
debit entry Abbuchung *f*
deboard aussteigen
deboss tiefprägen
debossing Tiefprägen *nt*
debugging Fehlerbeseitigung *f*
deburr entgraten, abgraten
deburring-machine Abgratmaschine *f*
decade Dekade *f*
decade counter tube dekadische Zählröhre *f*
decarburization depth Entkohlungstiefe *f*
decarburize abkohlen
decarburized-annealed with heart malleable cast iron entkohlend geglühter Temperguss *m*
decelerate langsam werden, verzögern, abbremsen, verlangsamen, Geschwindigkeit abnehmen, auslaufen
deceleration Verzögerung *f*, Verlangsamung *f*, Abbremsung *f*, Geschwindigkeitsabnahme *f*, Auslauf *m*, Auslaufen *nt*

deceleration and stopping cam Verzögerungs- und Anhaltenocke *f*
deceleration by pole-changing Umschaltverzögerung *f*
deceleration cam Verzögerungsnocke *f*
deceleration due to braking Bremsverzögerung *f*
deceleration during the catching operation Fangverzögerung *f*
deceleration period Verzögerungsperiode *f*
decentralized dezentral
dechuck ausspannen
decide entscheiden
deciduous pulp Laubholzzellstoff *m*
decimal Dezimalzahl *f*
decimal point programming Dezimalpunktprogrammierung *f*
decimal system Dezimalsystem *nt*
decimal-geometrical progression based on decimals dezimalgeometrische Reihe *f*
branch point Verzweigungsstelle *f*
decision Entscheidung *f*
decision making Entscheidungsfindung *f*
decision point Entscheidungsstelle *f*
decision rule Entscheidungsregel *f*
decision support Entscheidungshilfe *f*
decision support system (DSS) Entscheidungsunterstützungssystem (EUS) *nt*
decision table Entscheidungstabelle *f*
decision to place the order Vergabeentscheidung *f*
decision tree Entscheidungsbaum *nt*
declaration *(IT)* Vereinbarung *f*
declaration part Vereinbarungsteil *nt*
declarative character Vereinbarungszeichen *nt*
declarative statement Vereinbarungsanweisung *f*
declaratives Vereinbarungsteil *nt*
declarator Vereinbarungszeichen *nt*
declare *(IT)* vereinbaren
declination Schräglage *f*
decline stage Degenerierungsphase *f*
de-clinkering facility Schlackenaustrag *m*
declutch ausdrücken, auskuppeln, entkuppeln
decode decodieren
decoder Decoder *m*
decommission außer Betrieb setzen, stilllegen
decommissioning Ausmusterung *f*, Stilllegung *f*, Außerbetriebnahme *f*, Außerbetriebsetzung *f*
decomposable *(in einzelne Elemente)* zerlegbar, zersetzbar
decompose zersetzen, zerlegen
decomposing agent Aufschlussmittel *nt*
decomposing flask Zersetzungskolben *m*
decomposition Abbau *m*, Zerlegung *f*, Zersetzung *f*
decomposition characteristics Entspannungsverhalten *nt*
decomposition method Aufschlussverfahren *nt*
decomposition phenomenon Zersetzungserscheinung *f*
decomposition product Zersetzungsprodukt *nt*
decomposition temperature Zersetzungstemperatur *f*
decompress entspannen
decompression Dekompression *f*, Entspannen *nt*
decontaminate dekontaminieren
decorative laminated sheet dekorative Schichtpressstoffplatte *f*
decorative layer Dekorschicht *f*
decouple auskoppeln, entkoppeln
decoupling Auskoppeln *nt*, Entkopplung *f*
decrease vermindern, abnehmen, herabsetzen, reduzieren, verringern, mindern, fallen, abfallen, absinken, sinken; Abnahme *f*, Rückgang *m*, Reduzierung *f*, Verringerung *f*, Verminderung *f*, Herabsetzung *f*, Nachlassen *nt*, Absinken *nt*
decrease key Weniger-Taste *f*
decrease of performance Leistungsabnahme *f*, Leistungsminderung *f*
decrease of volume Volumenabnahme *f*
decrease the load entlasten

decreasing nachlassend
dedenda Zahnfüße *mpl*
dedendum Fußhöhe *f*, Zahnfußhöhe *f*
dedendum angle Fußwinkel *m*
dedendum circle Fußkreis *m*
dedendum flank Fußflanke *f*
deduce herleiten
deem to be good als gut befinden
deenergize ausschalten
de-energize aberregen, entregen, entspannen
de-energized entregt, stromlos
de-energizing Entspannen *nt*, Entregung *f*
deenergizing action Ausschaltvorgang *m*
de-energizing circuit Abschaltkreis *m*
deep tief
deep discharge Tiefentladung *f*
deep draw form-fill and seal machine Tiefziehform-, -füll- und -verschließmaschine *f*
deep draw work Tiefzieharbeit *f*
deep drawing by detonation of an explosive Tiefziehen *nt* durch Sprengstoffdetonation
deep drawing by electric discharge Tiefziehen *nt* durch elektrische Entladung
deep drawing by the effect of a magnetic field Tiefziehen *nt* durch Einwirkung eines Magnetfeldes
deep drawing in first draw Tiefziehen *nt* im Erstzug
deep drawing with action media Tiefziehen *nt* mit Wirkmedien
deep drawing with action media with effect associated with energy Tiefziehen *nt* mit Wirkmedien mit energiegebundener Wirkung
deep drawing with action media with effect associated with force Tiefziehen *nt* mit Wirkmedien mit kraftgebundener Wirkung
deep drawing with active energy Tiefziehen *nt* mit Wirkenergie
deep drawing with amorphous solids with effect associated with energy Tiefziehen *nt* mit formlos festen Stoffen mit energiegebundener Wirkung
deep drawing with amorphous solids with effect associated with force Tiefziehen *nt* mit formlos festen Stoffen mit kraftgebundener Wirkung
deep drawing with compliant pad Tiefziehen *nt* mit nachgiebigen Kissen
deep drawing with compliant punch Tiefziehen *nt* mit nachgiebigen Stempel
deep drawing with compliant tool Tiefziehen *nt* mit nachgiebigen Werkzeug
deep drawing with fluid pressure on both sides Tiefziehen *nt* mit zweiseitigem Flüssigkeitsdruck
deep drawing with fluid pressure on one side Tiefziehen *nt* mit einseitigem Flüssigkeitsdruck
deep drawing with fluids with effect associated with energy Tiefziehen *nt* mit Flüssigkeiten mit energiegebundener Wirkung
deep drawing with fluids with effect associated with force Tiefziehen *nt* mit Flüssigkeiten mit kraftgebundener Wirkung
deep drawing with gas pressure with evacuation of the matrix Tiefziehen *nt* mit Gasdruck durch einseitigen Überdruck
deep drawing with gas pressure with positive pressure on one side Tiefziehen *nt* mit Gasdruck durch einseitigen Überdruck
deep drawing with gases with effect associated with energy Tiefziehen *nt* mit Gasen mit energiegebundener Wirkung
deep drawing with gases with effect associated with force Tiefziehen *nt* mit Gasen mit kraftgebundener Wirkung
deep drawing with membrane Tiefziehen *nt* mit Membran
deep drawing with rigid tool Tiefziehen *nt* mit starrem Werkzeug
deep drawing with rubber pad Tiefziehen *nt* mit Gummikissen
deep drawing with rubber punch

Tiefziehen *nt* mit Gummistempel
deep drawing with sand/steel balls Tiefziehen *nt* mit Sand/Stahlkugeln
deep drawing with tools Tiefziehen *nt* mit Werkzeugen
deep drawing with water bag Tiefziehen *nt* mit Wasserbeutel
deep drawn pack Tiefziehpackung *f*
deep hole boring Aufbohren *nt*, Tieflochbohren *nt*
deep offset double-end box wrench tief gekröpfter Doppelringschlüssel *m*
deep offset double-ended ring spanner tief gekröpfter Doppelringschlüssel *m*
deep tilling Tieflockern *nt*
deep welding Tiefschweißen *nt*
deep-draw tiefziehen
deep-freeze tiefkühlen
deep-hole boring machine Tieflochbohrmaschine *f*
deep-hole boring tool Tieflochbohrer *m*
deep-hole drilling Tieflochbohren *nt*
deep-hole drilling machine Tieflochbohrmaschine *f*
deep-hole milling Tieflochfräsen *nt*
deep-hole tool Tieflochbohrbohrwerkzeug *nt*
deep-level borehole tiefliegende Bohrung *f*
deep-wall tray Flachtray *m*
default Standardeinstellung *f*, Vorbelegung *f*
default value *(IT)* Standardwert *m*, Voreinstellung *f*
defect Defekt *m*, Fehler *m*, Mangel *m*, Beschädigung *f*, Fehlstelle *f*; defekt
defect discernability Fehlerkennbarkeit *f*
defective Fehlstück *nt*; defekt, mangelhaft, fehlerhaft, schadhaft, mängelbehaftet, gestört
defective part fehlerhaftes Teil *nt*
defer zurückstellen
deficiency Fehler *m*, Mangel *m*, Nachteil *m*, Ausfall *m*
deficient mangelhaft, ungenügend, unzulänglich
deficit in Mangel *m* an

define 1. bestimmen, umgrenzen **2.** *(IT)* vereinbaren
defined boundary surface definierte Grenzfläche *f*
defined plane vorgegebene Ebene *f*
defined point Bezugspunkt *m*
defined point on the chip breaker Spanbrecherbezugspunkt *m*
defining material Bestimmungsmaterial *nt*
definitely edged kantig
definition Definition
definition of the image Bildschärfe *f*
definition sheet Definitionsblatt *nt*
definitive eindeutig
deflect auslenken, ablenken, ausschlagen, sich biegen, durchbiegen, verformen, wölben, abweichen, ausweichen, umlenken, verladen, abweisen
deflect sideways seitlich ausweichen
deflecting bar Abweisschiene *f*
deflecting blade Abweisschiene *f*
deflecting curve Abweiskurve *f*
deflecting magnetic field ablenkendes Magnetfeld *nt*
deflecting surface abweisende Fläche *f*
deflection 1. Abdrängung *f*, Auslenkung *f*, Ablenkung *f*, elastische Durchbiegung *f*, Verbiegung *f*, Verformung *f*, Wölbung *f*, Verlagerung *f*, Schiefstellung *f*, Abweichung *f*, Abweichen *nt*, Ausweichen *nt*, Durchbiegen *nt* **2.** Durchgang *m* **3.** *(Federelemente)* Durchfederung *f*
deflection angle Anschlagwinkel *m*, Federwinkel *m*
deflection coil Ablenkspule *f*
deflection current Ablenkstrom *m*
deflection mechanism Umlenkungsmechanismus *m*
deflection mirror Ablenkspiegel *m*, Umlenkspiegel *m*
deflection of mast Mastdurchbiegung *f*
deflection of the pointer Zeigerausschlag *m*
deflection of trade Umlenkung *f* der Handelsströme
deflection pulley Umlenkrad *nt*
deflection range Federwegbereich *m*
deflection sheave Umlenkrad *nt*

deflection system Ablenksystem *nt*
deflection-resistant biegesteif
deflector 1. Umlenkblech *nt*, Abweiser *m*, Fußabweiser *m* **2.** *(Rad)* Radschutz *m*
deflector blade Umlenkzunge *f*
deflector plate Ablenkplatte *f*
deform verformen, deformieren, verzerren
deformable verformbar, deformierbar
deformation Beschädigung *f*, Verformung *f*, Deformation *f*, Verzerrung *f*, Formverzerrung *f*, Durchbiegung *f*
deformation angle Verformungswinkel *m*
deformation behaviour Formänderungsverhalten *nt*, Verformungsverhalten *nt*
deformation characteristic Verformungskenngröße *f*
deformation cycle Verformungsspiel *nt*
deformation data Stauchungswerte *pl*
deformation difference Verformungsdifferenz *f*
deformation due to alternating load effects Lastwechselverformung *f*
deformation element Verformungskörper *m*
deformation impediment Verformungsbehinderung *f*
deformation limit Verformungsgrenze *f*
deformation measuring device Längenmessgerät *nt*
deformation modulus Deformationsmodul *m*
deformation of the pipe Rohrverformung *f*
deformation process Verformungsvorgang *m*
deformation speed Formänderungsgeschwindigkeit *f*
deformation stability Formänderungsfestigkeit *f*
deformation state Formänderungszustände *mpl*
deformation value Federwert *m*
deformation zone Verformungszone *f*
deformed verformt
defrost enteisen

defuzzification Defuzzifizierung *f*
degasification Entgasung *f*
degassing time Entgasungszeit *f*
degating unit Angussentfernungsvorrichtung *f*
degradation Abbau *m*, Verschlechterung *f*
degrade verschlechtern
degreasant Entfettungsmittel *nt*, Fettlösemittel *nt*
degrease entfetten
degreasing Entfettung *f*
degreasing by solvent vapour Lösungsmitteldampfentfettung *f*
degreasing by wet chemical methods nasschemisches Entfetten *nt*
degree of action Tätigkeitsgrad *m*
degree of accuracy Genauigkeitsgrad *m*, Toleranzstufe *f*
degree of automation Automatisierungsgrad *m*
degree of blistering Blasengrad *m*
degree of chalking Kreidungsgrad *m*
degree of changing Umbauungsgrad *m*
degree of cleanliness Reinheitsgrad *m*
degree of coherence Kohärenzgrad *m*
degree of concentration Konzentrationsgrad *m*
degree of deformation Formänderungsgrad *m*
degree of delignification Aufschlussgrad *m*, Delignifizierungsgrad *m*
degree of discharging Entladetiefe *f*
degree of elongation Längungsgrad *m*
degree of flattening Breitungsgrad *m*
degree of freedom Freiheitsgrad *m*
degree of fusion Aufschmelzgrad *m*
degree of goal accomplishment Zielerreichnungsgrad *m*
degree of imaging Abbildegrad *m*
degree of lengthening Längungsgrad *m*
degree of membership Zugehörigkeitsgrad *m*
degree of oscillation Schwingungsausschlag *m*
degree of pollution Verschmutzungsgrad *m*
degree of protection *(Maschinen)*

Schutzart *f*
degree of purity Reinheitsgrad *m*
degree of rebuilding Umbauungsgrad *m*
degree of reflection Reflexionsgrad *m*
degree of resolution of detail Detailerkennbarkeit *f*
degree of rubber hardness Gummihärtegrad *m*
degree of service Servicegrad *m*
degree of stretching Reckgrad *m*
degree of swelling Quellungsgrad *m*
degree of taper Verjüngungsgrad *m*
degree of taper (broach) Vorschub *m* je Zahn
degree of thermal transparency Wärmedurchlassgrad *m*
degree of time using Zeitnutzungsgrad *m*
degree of upsetting Stauchungsgrad *m*
degroup entgruppieren
dehumidifier Enfeuchter *m*
dehumidify entfeuchten
designate bestimmen
delamination force of the node-to-node bond Knotenanrisskraft *f*
delamination load Spaltkraft *f*
delay verzögern; Verzögerung *f*
delay circuit Verzögerungsschaltung *f*
delay line storage unit Laufzeitspeicher *m*
delay period Verzögerungszeit *f*
delay time Verzögerungszeit *f*, Laufzeit *f*, Totzeit *f*
delay time lag Verzögerung *f*
delayed zeitversetzt, verzögert
delayed crack Wasserstoffriss *m*
delayed monostable element monostabiles Kippglied *nt* mit Verzögerung
delayed single shot monostabiles Kippglied *nt* mit Verzögerung
delete löschen
deletion Löschvorgang *m*
deliver abgeben
delignification Delignifizierung *f*
delimitations *pl* Begrenzungen *fpl*
deliver ausliefern, liefern, anliefern, übergeben
deliver current Strom *m*
deliver in addition nachliefern

deliverable lieferbar
delivering lorry Anliefer-LKW *m*
delivery Lieferung *f*, Belieferung *f*, Anlieferung *f*, Auslieferung *f*, Übergabe *f*
delivery control Lieferüberwachung *f*
delivery control member Regelorgan *nt* für Fördermenge
delivery date Liefertermin *m*
delivery date deviation Lieferterminabweichung *f*
delivery date reliability Liefertermintreue *f*
delivery deadline Liefertermin *m*
delivery documents Lieferunterlagen *pl*
delivery drawing Lieferzeichnung *f*
delivery efficiency Liefergrad *m*
delivery end of the cooling tube Kühlrohrablauf *m*
delivery flow Zuflussstrom *m*
delivery forecast Lieferabruf *m*
delivery head Förderhöhe *f*
delivery note Lieferschein *m*
delivery on call Lieferabruf *m*
delivery order Auslieferungsauftrag *m*
delivery performance Lieferleistung *f*
delivery plan Anlieferplan *m*
delivery pump Förderpumpe *f*
delivery quality Lieferqualität *f*
delivery quantity Liefermenge *f*
delivery quantity deviation Liefermengenabweichung *f*
delivery quantity reliability Liefermengentreue *f*
delivery rate Fördermenge *f*
delivery receipt Wareneingangsbescheinigung *f*
delivery reliability Liefertreue *f*
delivery schedule Lieferabruf *m*
delivery specification Lieferspezifikation *f*
delivery status Lieferstatus *m*
delivery time Lieferzeit *f*
delivery volume Fördervolumen *nt*
delta connection Dreieckschaltung *f*
delta-connected in Dreieckschaltung *f*
demand Nachfrage *f*, Bedürfnis *nt*; nachfragen, anfordern
demand amplification Bedarfsverstärkung *f*

demand assessment Bedarfsermittlung *f*
demand data Nachfragedaten *pl*
demand disposal Bedarfsdisposition *f*
demand for accuracy Genauigkeitsanspruch *m*
demand forecast Nachfrageprognose *f*
demand of heat quantity Wärmemengenbedarf *m*
demand planning Bedarfsplanung *f*
demand resolving Bedarfsauflösung *f*
demand-activated manufacturing nachfragegesteuerte Produktion *f*
demarcation Abgrenzung *f*
demesh ausdrücken
demineralized water vollentsalztes Wasser *nt*
demist entfeuchten, entnebeln
demister Enfeuchter *m*
de-mixing tendency Entmischungsneigung *f*
demolish zerstören
demolition Zerstörung *f*
demonstrate zeigen, demonstrieren
demoulding Ausformen *nt*
demoulding depth Ausformtiefe *f*
demoulding draft Ausformschräge *f*
demount demontieren, abbauen, abnehmen
demountable tyre wheels demontierbare Bereifung *f*
demounting Demontage *f*, Abnahme *f*, Abbau *m*
damped gedämpft
demulsibility Wasserabscheidevermögen *nt*
demulsion characteristic Demulgierungsgrad *m*
denest entstapeln
denester Entstapelungsmaschine *f*, Entstapler *m*
denesting Entstapeln *nt*
denesting machine Entstapelungsmaschine *f*
denickelification Entnickelung *f*
denominator Nennergröße *f*
denominate benennen
denomination Benennung *f*
denote bezeichnen
dense dicht, kompakt

density Schwärzung *f*
density condition Schwärzungsbedingung *f*
density hydrometer Dichte-Aräometer *nt*
density of pits Lochzahldichte *f*
density of radiograph Filmschwärzung *f*
density range Schwärzungsbereich *m*
dent Vertiefung *f*, Delle *f*, Kerbe *f*, Unebenheit *f*
denumerable abzählbar
depacketize zerlegen, entpaketieren
depacketizing Zerlegen *nt*
depalletize depalettieren, umstapeln
depalletizer Depalettierer *m*
depalletizing Umstapeln *nt*
depalletizing process Umstapelvorgang *m*
depart abfahren
department Abteilung *f*
departure Abfahrt *f*
departure angle Abfahrtwinkel *m*
depend on abhängen von
dependable sicher
dependable in service betriebssicher
dependency Abhängigkeit *f*
dependency notation Abhängigkeitsnotation *f*
dependent abhängig
depending on each case fallbezogen
depending on tolerance toleranzabhängig
dephlegmator Dephlegmierkolonne *f*
deposit Ablagerung *f*, Niederschlag *m*, Übergabe *f*; ablagern, absetzen, ablegen, abscheiden, aufsetzen, abgeben, hinterlegen
deposit point Übergabeplatz *m*
deposit station Absetzstation *f*
deposited run Auftragraupe *f*
deposited welding Auftragschweißen *nt*
depositing Ablegen *nt*, Abgeben *nt*
depositing of dust Verstaubung *f*
deposition Auftragung *f*
deposition rate Einbringleistung *f*, Auftragleistung *f*
deposition ratio Ausziehverhältnis *nt*
deposition welding of buffer layers

Auftragschweißen *nt* von Pufferschichten
deposition welding of claddings Auftragschweißen *nt* von Plattierungen
deposition welding of hard surfacing layers Auftragschweißen *nt* von Panzerungen
deposit-weld auftragschweißen
deposition weld Auftragschweißung *f*
depot Lager *nt*
depreciate abschreiben
depreciation Abschreibung *f*
depress niederdrücken, drücken
depression Druckminderung *f*, Unterdruck *m*, Niederdrücken *nt*, Vertiefung *f*, Mulde *f*, Unebenheit *f*
depression in the terrain Geländemulde *f*
depressurizing Druckentlastung *f*
depth Tiefe *f*, Tiefenrichtung *f*
depth cutting type of broach senkrecht zur Werkstückoberfläche schneidendes Räumwerkzeug *nt*
depth factor Tiefenfaktor *m*
depth feed Tiefenvorschub *m*, Senkrechtvorschub *m*
depth feed adjustment Tiefenzustellung *f*
depth gauge Tiefenmessschieber *m*
depth measurement Tiefenmessung *f*
depth measuring blade Tiefenmessstange *f*
depth measuring device Eindringtiefenmesseinrichtung *f*
depth micrometer Tiefenmikrometer *nt*
depth milling Tiefenfräsen *nt*
depth of attack Angriffstiefe *f*
depth of cover Überdeckungshöhe *f*, Überschüttungshöhe *f*
depth of cover material over the crown of the pipe Scheitelüberdeckung *f*
depth of cut Spantiefe *f*, Schnitttiefe *f*, Spanstärke *f*
depth of cut preselector Spantiefenvorwähler *m*
depth of engagement Tragtiefe *f*
depth of focus Schärfentiefe *f*
depth of fundamental triangle Profilhöhe *f*
depth of gap Ausladung *f*
depth of grain cut Schnitttiefe *f* der Schleifscheibe
depth of insertion Einstecktiefe *f* bei Muffen
depth of penetration Eindringtiefe *f*
depth of recess Einstechtiefe *f*
depth of shade standard Farbtiefstandard *m*
depth of shelving Fachtiefe *f*
depth of surface smoothness Glättungstiefe *f*
depth of thread Gewindetiefe *f*
depth of throat Ausladung *f* des Maschinenständers
depth of tooth Zahnhöhe *f*, Lückentiefe *f*
depth of water penetration Wassereindringtiefe *f*
depth of waviness Wellentiefe *f*
depth resolving power Tiefenauflösungsvermögen *nt*
depth stop Tiefenanschlag *m*
depth-setting standard Tiefeneinstellnormal *nt*
dequeue aus einer Warteschlange entnehmen
derail entgleisen
derailment Entgleisung *f*
derating Herabsetzung *f*
degressive pitting degressive Grübchenbildung *f*
derivation *(math.)* Ableitung *f*
derivation of stray current Streustromableitung *f*
derivative action differenzierendes Verhalten *nt*
derivative action controlling system D-Regeleinrichtung *f*
derivative action factor D-Beiwert *m*, Differenzierbeiwert *m*
derivative element D-Glied *nt*, Differenzierglied *nt*
derive herleiten, ableiten
derive from ableiten von
derived quantity abgeleitete Größe *f*
derrick crane Wippkran *m*
derust entrosten
derusting process Entrostungsverfah-

ren *nt*
descaling Entzundern *nt*
descend abwärts bewegen, absinken, sinken, senken, niedergehen, abseilen
descender device Abseileinrichtung *f*
descending numerical value absteigender Zahlenwert *m*
descent Senkvorgang *m*, Sinkbewegung *f*, Senkbewegung *f*, Absinken *nt*, Senken *nt*
descent rate Absinkgeschwindigkeit *f*
describe beschreiben
description Beschreibung *f*, Charakteristik *f*, Machart *f*
description media Beschreibungsmittel *nt*
description of procedures Verfahrensbeschreibung *f*
descriptioning statistics beschreibende Statistik *f*
descriptive beschreibend
deselect demarkieren
desigate bezeichnen
design Aufbau *m*, Gestalt *f*, Gestaltung *f*, Konstruktion *f*, Entwurf *m*, Entwicklung *f*, Konzept *nt*, Bauform *f*, Ausbildung *f*, Ausführung *f*, Typ *m*, Auslegung *f*, Bauart *f*, Montage *f*, Skizze *f*, Plan *m*, Zeichnung *f*; auslegen, gestalten, konzipieren, planen, entwickeln, konstruieren, entwerfen, projektieren
design base cylinder Sollgrundzylinder *m*
design bureau Konstruktionsbüro *nt*
design check Vorprüfung *f*
design control Designlenkung *f*
design costs Konstruktionskosten *pl*
design criterion Auslegungskriterium *nt*
design data Konstruktionsvorgaben *pl*
design department Konstruktionsabteilung *f*
design direction Sollrichtung *f*
design documents Konstruktionsunterlagen *pl*
design engineer Konstrukteur *m*
design feature Baumerkmal *nt*, konstruktives Merkmal *nt*, Konstruktionsmerkmal *nt*

design for assembly montagegerechtes Gestalten
design for testability prüfgerechtes Gestalten *nt*
design level Gestaltungsebene *f*
design measure konstruktive Maßnahme *f*
design of bevel gear planing machines Kegelradhobelmaschinenbau *m*
design of jigs and fixtures Vorrichtungsbau *m*
design office Konstruktionsbüro *nt*
design parts list Konstruktionsstückliste *f*
design point Auslegungspunkt *m*
design drawing Konstruktionszeichnung *f*
design shaping Formgestalten *nt*
design specifications Konstruktionsunterlagen *pl*
design stress rechnerische Beanspruchung *f*
design surface Solloberfläche *f*
design trench width Berechnungsgrabenbreite *f*
design value Rechenwert *m*
design verification Konstruktionsprüfung *f*, Vorprüfung *f*
designate kennzeichnen, markieren, benennen
designation Kennzeichnung *f*, Bezeichnung *f*, Benennung *f*
designation system Bezeichnungssystematik *f*
design-basis accident Kritikalitätsunfall *m*
designed for transport transportgerecht
designer Konstrukteur *m*, Gestalter *m*, Zeichner *m*, Entwerfer *m*
designing Konstruktion *f*, Projektieren *nt*
designing conform to safety principles sicherheitsgerechtes Gestalten *nt*
desired gewünscht
desired angular size Winkelsollmaß *nt*
desired indication Soll-Anzeige *f*
desired status Soll-Zustand *m*
desired temperature set point scale Sollwert-Einstell-Skale *f*

desired value Sollwert *m*
desired value/actual value comparator Soll-Istwert-Vergleicher *m*
desired variable Aufgabengröße *f*
desk Pult *nt*, Tisch *m*
desk-top calculator Tischrechner *m*
deskill *(Arbeit)* vereinfachen
deslagging Abschlackung *f*
despatch drawing Versandzeichnung *f*
destack ausstapeln
destacking operation Ausstapelvorgang *m*
destination Ziel *nt*, Zielort *m*, Bestimmung *f*, Haltepunkt *m*
destination address Zieladresse *f*
destination mark Zielkennzeichen *nt*
destination of travel Fahrtziel *nt*
destine bestimmen
district heating scheme Fernheizanschluss *m*
destroy zerstören
destruct zerstören
destructible zerstörbar
destruction Zerstörung *f*
destructive pitting fortschreitende Grübchen *nt*
destructive testing of welds zerstörende Schweißnahtprüfung *f*
desuperheater Enthitzer *m*
detach abtrennen, ablösen, aushängen, abmontieren, abbauen, abnehmen, entfernen, zerlegen, auseinander nehmen, lösen
detachable lösbar, abnehmbar, ausbaubar
detachable connection lösbare Verbindung *f*
detachable hose connection lösbarer Schlauchanschluss *m*
detachable member lösbares Teil *nt*
detachable part lösbares Teil *nt*
detail Einzelheit *f*
detail drawing Stückzeichnung *f*, Teilzeichnung *f*
detail of the racking compartment Fachdetail *nt*, Facheinfahrbreite *f*
detailed drawing Detailzeichnung *f*
detailed representation ausführliche Darstellung *f*
detailed statement Begleitschein *m*

details Angaben *fpl*
details of space requirements Raumbedarfsmaße *ntpl*
detect auffinden, feststellen, erkennen, ermitteln
detection Detektion *f*, Erkennung *f*, Feststellen *nt*, Ermittlung *f*
detection field Detektionsbereich *m*
detection probability Nachweiswahrscheinlichkeit *f*
detection sensitivity Nachweisempfindlichkeit *f*
detector Wächter *m*
detector of position Positionsschalter *m*, Positionsdetektor *m*
detent Klinke *f*
detent Raste *f*, Sperrklinke *f*, Arretierung *f*, Auslöser *m*
detent pawl Sperrklinke *f*, Schaltklinke *f*
detergent ablösendes Mittel *nt*, Detergent *nt*
detergent additive Reinigerzusatz *m*
detergent solution Waschmittellösung *f*
deteriorate beschädigen, verschlechtern
deterioration Alterung *f*, Verschlechterung *f*, Zerstörung *f*
determinable bestimmbar, messbar
determinant Bestimmungsgröße *f*
determination Festlegung *f*, Prüfung *f*, Bestimmung *f*, Ermittlung *f*, Messung *f*
determination of bearing Standortbestimmung *f*
determination of errors Fehlerbestimmung *f*
determination of properties Eigenschaftsprüfung *f*
determination of the centre gravity Schwerpunktbestimmung *f*
determine bestimmen, prüfen, festlegen, feststellen, ermitteln, messen, dimensionieren
determined by utilization betriebsbedingt
determining Messen *nt*
detin entzinnen
detonation Detonation *f*
detonation effect Detonationswirk-

detonation guard – diagnostics

ung *f*
detonation guard Detonationssicherung *f*
detonation spraying Flammstockspritzen *nt*
detract from the clarity undeutlich machen
detrition Abrieb *m*
develop entwickeln, ausbilden
develop into abwickeln
developed base circle arc abgewickelter Grundkreisbogen *m*
developed line gestreckte Länge *f*
development planning Bebauungsplanung *f*
developer Entwickler *m*
developing fire fortentwickelter Brand *m*
development Entwicklung *f*
development costs Entwicklungskosten *pl*
development of smoke Qualmentwicklung *f*
development order Entwicklungsauftrag *m*
development scheme Bebauungsplan *m*
development tendency Entwicklungstendenz *f*
deviate umlenken, ablenken, abweichen
deviating abweichend
deviation 1. Ablenkung *f*, Abweichung *f*, Bahnabweichung *f*, Abmaß *nt*, Abweichen *nt* **2.** *(Messtechnik)* Maßabweichung *f*
deviation angle Ablenkwinkel *m*
deviation diagram Abmaßschaubild *nt*
deviation factor Abmaßfaktor *m*
deviation for external sizes Abmaß *nt* für Außenmaße
deviation for internal sizes Abmaß *nt* für Innenmaße
deviation from the desired value Sollwertabweichung *f*
deviation from the helical form Abweichung *f* von der Schraubenlinienform
deviation from the specified values *pl* Maßabweichung *f* von den Sollma-

ßen
deviation in delivery quantities Liefermengenabweichung *f*
deviation in form and position Form- und Lageabweichung *f*
deviation of dual cone width Zweikegelweitenabmaß *nt*
deviation of dual flank roll test centre distance Zweiflankenwälzabstandsabmaß *nt*
deviation of structure Gefügeabweichung *f*
deviation of the angles Winkelabweichung *f*
deviation of the diametral two-ball measurement Abmaß *nt* des diametralen Zweikugelmaßes
deviation of the generator Abweichung *f* der Erzeugenden
deviation of the normal chordal tooth thickness Abmaß *nt* der Zahndickensehnen
deviation of tip circle Kopfkreisabmaß *nt*
deviation on roundness Rundheitsabweichung *f*
deviation range Abweichungsspanne *f*
deviation series Abmaßreihe *f*
device Gerät *nt*, Apparat *m*, Vorrichtung *f*, Einrichtung *f*, Instrument *nt*, Arbeitsmittel *nt*
device affording protection against scattered radiation Störstrahlenschutzvorrichtung *f*
device for measuring the moment Momentmesseinrichtung *f*
device for signal input Gerät *nt* zur Signaleingabe
device verification Gerätestatus *m*
device write fault Schreibfehler *m*
device-related gerätetechnisch
devoid of form error formfehlerfrei
dew point corrosion Taupunktkorrosion *f*
dewetting Entnetzen *nt*
diacritical sign diakritisches Zeichen *nt*
diagnosis Diagnose *f*
diagnosis tool Diagnosegerät *nt*
diagnostic diagnostisch
diagnostics Diagnosemöglichkeit *f*,

Diagnoseverfahren *nt*
diagonal diagonal; Diagonale *f*
diagonal brace Diagonale *f*, Diagonalrippe *f*, Diagonalverband *m*
diagonal cross Diagonalkreuz *nt*, liegendes Kreuz *nt*, aufliegendes Kreuz *nt*
diagonal cross scraping Diagonalquerschaben *nt*
diagonal cut Gehrungsschnitt *m*
diagonal cutting Schrägschnitt *m*
diagonal hobbing Diagonalfräsen *nt*
diagonal hobbing attachment Diagonalwalzfräseinrichtung *f*
diagonal hole Schrägbohrung *f*
diagonal members Verstrebung *f*
diagonal motion Diagonalfahrt *f*
diagonal movement Diagonalfahrt *f*
diagonal shaving Diagonalschaben *nt*
diagonal technique Diagonalverfahren *nt*
diagonal to quer zu, diagonal
diagonal travel Diagonalfahrt *f*
diagonally braced diagonalverrippt
diagram Plan *m*, Diagramm *nt*, Schaubild *nt*
diagram method Diagrammverfahren *nt*
diagrammatic representation schematische Darstellung *f*
dial Zahlenscheibe *f*, Scheibe *f*, Zifferblatt *nt*, Wahlscheibe *f*, Einstellscheibe *f*, Skalenring *m*, Skalenscheibe *f*, Skala *f*; wählen
dial calliper Messschieber *m* mit Rundskala
dial depth gauge Messuhrentiefenlehre *f*
dial division Rundskala *f*
dial gauge Messuhr *f*
dial gauge calliper Tastermessuhr *f*
dial gauge indexing attachment Messuhrenteilvorrichtung *f*
dial indicator Anzeigeskala *f*, Zeigerlehre *f*, Feinzeiger *m*, Messuhr *f*
dial indicator stylus Messuhrtaster *m*
dial thickness indicator Messuhrdickenmesser *m*
dial-type milling machine wählergesteuerte Fräsmaschine *f*
dialog Dialog *m*, Wechselwirkung *f*

dialog mode Dialogbetrieb *m*
dialogue Dialog *m*
dialogue instruction Dialogbefehl *m*
dialogue program generator Dialogprogrammgenerator *m*
diameter Durchmesser *m*
diameter dimension Durchmessermaß *nt*
diameter of the cylinder Zylinderdurchmesser *m*
diameter of turns Winkeldurchmesser *m*
diameter over groove edges *(bei Kerbstiften)* Aufkerbdurchmesser *m*
diameter series Durchmesserreihe *f*
diameter symbol Durchmesserzeichen *nt*
diameter/pitch combination Durchmessersteigungskombination *f*
diameter-dependent durchmesserabhängig
diameter-related tolerance durchmesserbezogene Toleranz *f*
diametral dimension Durchmessermaß *nt*
diametrically opposed diametral gegenüberliegend
diamond Diamant *m*; diamantläppen
diamond boring Diamantbohren *nt*, Feinbohren *nt*
diamond concentration Diamantkonzentration *f*
diamond cubic Diamantgitter *nt*
diamond dresser *(Schleifscheibe)* Abdrehdiamant *m*
diamond dressing device Diamantabrichtgerät *nt*, Diamantabzieheinrichtung *f*
diamond drill bit Diamantbohrkrone *f*
diamond drilling Diamantbohren *nt*
diamond drilling machine Diamantbohrmaschine *f*
diamond edge Diamantschneide *f*
diamond grain Diamantkorn *nt*, Diamantkristall *nt*
diamond grain concentration Diamantkornkonzentration *f*
diamond grain size Diamantkorngröße *f*
diamond grit Diamantkörnung *f*

diamond knurling Kordeln *nt*
diamond life Diamantstandzeit *f*
diamond particle Diamantsplitter *m*
diamond pattern rautenförmig angeordnet
diamond point Diamantspitze *f*
diamond powder Diamantstaub *m*
diamond roller truer Diamantabrichtrolle *f*
diamond section Diamantbelag *m*
diamond shaped rautenförmig
diamond stylus Diamanttastnadel *f*
diamond tip Diamantspitze *f*
diamond tipping Diamantbestückung *f*
diamond tool Diamantwerkzeug *nt*
diamond truing Diamantabrichten *nt*
diamond truing device Diamantabdrehvorrichtung *f*
diamond wheel dresser Diamantabrichter *m*
diamond-impregnated grinding face Diamantbelag *m*
diamond-impregnated wheel Diamantscheibe *f*
diamond-knurled kordiert
diamond-shaped knurling Kordeln *nt*
diamond-tipped diamantbestückt
diaphragm Membrane *f*, Blende *f*
diaphragm control Membransteuerung *f*
diaphragm type expansion tank Membranausdehnungsgefäß *nt*
diaphragm valve Membranarmatur *f*
diaphragm-actuated shut-off valve Absperrarmatur *f* mit Membranantrieb
diathermic unit Diathermiegerät *nt*
diazo coating Lichtpausschicht *f*
diazo compound Diazoverbindung *f*
diazocopy Lichtpause *f*
diazocopy film Lichtpausfilm *m*
diazocopy material Lichtpausmaterial *nt*
diazotype method Lichtpausverfahren *nt*
diazotype paper Lichtpauspapier *nt*
dictated by functional factors funktionsbedingt
die Form *f*, Gesenk *nt*, Aufnehmer *m*, Druckstempel *m*, Matrize *f*, Schneidbacke *f*, Schneideisen *nt*

die and mould copy miller Gesenk- und Formennachformfräser *m*
die beading Gesenksicken *nt*
die bending Gesenkbiegen *nt*, Biegen *nt* im Gesenk
die bending providing initial curling Ankippen *nt*
die bending providing initial rounding Anbiegen *nt*
die block Pressform *f*
die block shaper Form- und Stempelhobler *m*, Kehlhobelmaschine *f*
die broaching Gesenkherstellung *f* durch Meisterform
die cast Druckguss *m*
die cast form Druckgussform *f*
die casting Druckguss *m*
die casting alloy Druckgusslegierung *f*
die collaring Bundanstauchen *nt* im Gesenk
die down abklingen, ausschwingen
die flanging Gesenkbördeln *nt*
die forging Gesenkschmieden *nt*, Schmieden *nt* im Gesenk
die forming Gesenkformen *nt*
die forming by drawing Formstanzen *nt*, Formziehen *nt* im Gesenk, Gesenkziehen *nt*
die forming with partly enclosed work Gesenkformen *nt* mit teilweisem Werkstück
die hand Schneidkopf *m*
die heading Kopfanstauchen *nt* im Gesenk
die hobbing Einsenken *nt*
die making Herstellung *f* von Gesenken, Gesenkherstellung *f*
die mill Gesenkfäser *m*
die sinker Nachformfräsmaschine *f*, Gesenkfräsmaschine *f*, selbsttätige Nachformfräsmaschine *f*, Nachformfräsmaschine *f* mit dreidimensionaler Steuerung, Waagerechtprofilfräsmaschine *f*
die sinking machine Gesenkfräsmaschine *f*, Matrizenfräsmaschine *f*, Nachformfräsmaschine *f*, Nachformfräsmaschine *f* mit dreidimensionaler Steuerung
die slotter Senkrechtstoßmaschine *f* zur

Bearbeitung von Matrizen, Kehlhobelmaschine *f*
die squeezing Gesenkdrücken *nt*
die stamping press Gesenkpresse *f*
die straightening by press forming without flash Gesenkrichten *nt*
die typing Gesenkherstellung *f* durch Meisterform
die upsetting Gesenkstauchen *nt*, Anstauchen *nt* im Gesenk
die-forge gesenkschmieden
die-forging component Gesenkschmiedeteil *nt*
die-forging part Gesenkschmiedeteil *nt*
dielectric Dielektrikum *nt*; dielektrischer Nichtleiter *m*
dielectric breakdown strength Durchschlagfestigkeit *f*
dielectric constant Dielektrizitätskonstante *f*
dielectric drier Hochfrequenztrockner *m*
dielectric layer dielektrische Schicht *f*
dielectric strength Isolationsfestigkeit *f*, Durchschlagfeldstärke *f*, Spannungsfestigkeit *f*
dielectric strength breakdown voltage Durchbruchspannung *f*
dielectric withstand test Isolationsprüfung *f*
dielectric withstand voltage Isolationsspannung *f*
die-milling machine Gesenkfräsmaschine *f*
diesel Dieselmotor *m*
diesel engine Dieselmotor *m*
diesel truck Flürförderzeug *nt* mit Dieselmotor
diesel-driven generating set Dieselaggregat *nt*
die-sink nachformen, nachfräsen, nachformfräsen, Gesenke ausfräsen
die-sinking Gesenkfräsen *nt*
die-sinking Nachfräsen *nt*, Gesenkarbeit *f*
die-sinking cutter Gesenkfräser *m*
die-slotting attachment Kehlhobeleinrichtung *f*
die-stock Kluppe *f*

die-work Gesenkarbeit *f*
differ from abweichen von, unterscheiden von
difference Differenz *f*, Unterschied *m*
difference in density Schwärzungsdifferenz *f*
difference in height Höhendifferenz *f*
difference in measuring force Messkraftunterschied *m*
difference in position Lageunterschied *m*
different ungleich
differential compounding Gegenkompoundierung *f*
differential excitation Selbsterregung *f*
differential gear unit Differentialgetriebe *nt*
differential indexing head Differentialteilgerät *nt*
differential locking Differenzialsperre *f*
differential measurement Unterschiedsmessung *f*
differential mode Gegentakt *m*
differential mode coupling Gegentakteinkopplung *f*
differential pressure Differenzdruck *m*
differential pressure gauge Differenzdruckmesser *m*
differential pressure manometer Differenzdruckmanometer *nt*
differential pressure measuring device Druckdifferenzmesseinrichtung *f*
differential pressure pipe Wirkleitung *f*
differential pressure principle Differenzdruckprinzip *nt*
differential pressure switch Differenzdruckschalter *m*
differential pressure switching point Differenzdruckschaltpunkt *m*
differential voltage Differenzspannung *f*
differentiate unterscheiden
difficult schwierig, schwer
difficult to ignite schwer entflammbar
difficult to machine schwer bearbeitbar
difficulty flammable floor covering schwer entzündlicher Fußbodenbelag *m*

difficulty in bonding Verklebungsschwierigkeit f
diffract beugen
diffraction Beugung f
diffraction figure Beugungsbild nt
diffraction fringe Interferenzstreifen m
diffraction grating Beugungsgitter nt
diffraction property Beugungseigenschaft f
diffraction spectrum Beugungsspektrum nt
diffuse in eindiffundieren
diffuse out ausdiffundieren
diffusible hydrogen diffusibler Wasserstoff m
diffusion Diffusion f
diffusion layer Diffusionsschicht f
diffusion overvoltage Diffusionsüberspannung f
diffusion wear Diffusionsverschleiß m
dig in *(Meißel in Werkstück)* einhaken
digit Ziffer f, *(einstellige)* Zahl f, Zahlenstelle f
digital digital
digital computer Digitalrechner m
digital control numerische Steuerung f, digitale Steuerung f
digital data processing digitale Informationsverarbeitung f
digital data storage Digitaldatenspeicherung
digital division Ziffernschritt m
digital increment Ziffernschritt m
digital input digitaler Eingang m
digital input signal digitales Eingangssignal nt
digital input unit Digitaleingabeeinheit f
digital interval Ziffernschrittwert m
digital measuring step digitaler Messschritt m
digital measuring system digitales Messsystem nt
digital motion control digitale Bewegungssteuerung f
digital output digitaler Ausgang f
digital output unit Digitalausgabeeinheit f
digital pulse digitaler Impuls m
digital reading Ziffernanzeige f

digital readout digitale Anzeige f
digital scale Ziffernskala f
digital sequence Ziffernfolge f
digital signal processor digitaler Signalprozessor m
digital state digitaler Zustand m
digital-to-analogue converter (DAC) Digital/Analog-Umsetzer m
digital-analogue converter Digital-Analog-Umsetzer m
digitally operating installation digital arbeitende Anlage f
digitizer pulse transmitter Impulsgeber m
digitizing digitalisieren
dilatation Wärmedehnung f
dilate *(durch Wärme)* ausdehnen
dilutability Verdünnbarkeit f
dimension Abmessung f, Maß nt, Größe f, Umfang m, Ausmaß nt; bemessen, dimensionieren, bemaßen, vermaßen
dimension arrowhead Maßpfeil m
dimension chain Maßkette f
dimension chain theory Maßkettentheorie f
dimension data pl Maßangaben fpl
dimension designation Größenbezeichnung f
dimension figure Maßzahl f
dimension for auslegen
dimension gap Maßlücke f
dimension letter Maßbuchstabe m
dimension line arc Maßlinienbogen m
dimension line draw to towards the object from outside von außen herangezogene Maßlinie f
dimension line termination Maßlinienbegrenzung f
dimension lines spaced one above the other übereinanderliegende Maßlinien fpl
dimension modification Abmessungsänderungen fpl
dimension quality Maßqualität f
dimension reading Maßablesung f
dimension relation Abmessungsverhältnis nt
dimension sheet Maßblatt nt
dimension standard Abmessungsnorm f, Maßnorm f

dimension unit Maßeinheit *f*
dimensional maßlich
dimensional accuracy Maßgenauigkeit *f*, Maßhaltigkeit *f*
dimensional constraints Maßeingang *m*
dimensional drawing Maßzeichnung *f*
dimensional gauge Maßlehre *f*
dimensional metrology Messtechnik *f*
dimensional stability Maßbeständigkeit *f*, Maßhaltigkeit *f*, Dimensionskonstanz *f*
dimensional tolerance Maßtoleranz *f*
dimensional tolerance zone Maßtoleranzfeld *nt*
dimensional variation Maßschwankung *f*, Maßabweichung *f*
dimensionalized representation dimensionsbehaftete Darstellung *f*
dimensionally stable moulded part formbeständiges Formteil *nt*
dimensioned vermaßt
dimensioned point Maßstelle *f*
dimension-fitting passgerecht
dimension-fitting tolerance passgerechte Toleranz *f*
dimensioning Dimensionierung *f*, Bemaßung *f*, Bemessung *f*, Vermaßung *f*, Maßeintragung *f*
dimensioning of a sphere Kugelbemaßung *f*
dimensioning principle Bemaßungsgrundsatz *m*
dimensioning rule Bemaßungsregel *f*
dimensionless quantity dimensionslose Größe *f*
dimensionless representation dimensionslose Darstellung *f*
dimensionless variable dimensionslose Größe *f*
dimensions Abmessungen *fpl*
dimensions at different locations auseinander liegende Maße *ntpl*
dimensions of the warehouse Lagerabmessung *f*
dimensions *pl* **at cast parts** *pl* Abmessungen *fpl* an Gussteilen
dimensions *pl* **without tolerance indication** Maße *ntpl* ohne Toleranzangaben

dimetric projection dimetrische Projektion *f*
diminish nachlassen
diminished cross section Querschnittsschwächung *f*
diminution Verminderung *f*
diminish vermindern
dimple Grübchen *nt*
dimpled gewalzt
DIN-based drawing DIN-gerechte Zeichnung *f*
diode Diode *f*
diagonal schräg
dionate Dionat
dip Durchhang *m*, Eintauchen *nt*; eintauchen, tauchen, durchhängen
dip enamelling Tauchemaillieren *nt*
dip tank Schrumpftank *m*
dip tinning Tauchverzinnen *nt*
dip washing and preservation equipment Tauchwasch- und Konservieranlage *f*
dipolar character Dipolcharakter *m*
dipping and weighing method Tauchwägeverfahren *nt*
dipping bath Lötbad *nt*
dip-wettability Tauchnetzvermögen *nt*
dip-wetting ability Tauchnetzvermögen *nt*
direct 1. lenken, führen, leiten, steuern, richten *(auf)* **2.** gerade, direkt
direct address direkte Adresse *f*
direct addressing direkte Adressierung *f*
direct along vorbeiführen
direct call *(Kommunikationstechnik)* Direktruf *m*
direct contact heated tool welding direktes Heizelementschweißen *nt*
direct control Direktschaltung *f*
direct current Gleichstrom *m*
direct dispatch Direktversand *m*
direct effect unmittelbare Wirkung *f*
direct extrusion of rods Vollvorwärtsstrangpressen *nt*
direct extrusion of rods and tubes Vorwärtsstrangpressen *nt*
direct impact extrusion Vorwärtsfließpressen *nt*
direct impact extrusion of cup-

shaped sections Napfvorwärtsfließpressen *nt*
direct impact extrusion of rods Vollvorwärtsfließpressen *nt*
direct indexing direktes Teilen *nt*
direct indexing head einfacher Teilkopf *m*
direct marking Direktbeschriften *nt*
direct measurement direkte Wegmessung *f*
direct motor drive Einzelantrieb *m*
direct-on-line starting Direkteinschaltung *f*
direct order Direktbestellung *f*
direct ordering Direktbestellung *f*
direct output direkte Ausgabe *f*
direct projection welding zweiseitiges Buckelschweißen *nt*
direct representation direkte Darstellung *f*
direct starting Direktanlauf *m*
direct storage Direktlagerung *f*
direct switching Direkteinschaltung *f*
direct switching starter Direkteinschalter *m*
direct torque control direkte Drehmomentregelung *f*
direct tubular impact extrusion Hohlvorwärtsfließpressen *nt*
direct voltage Gleichspannung *f*
direction Richtung *f*
direction change Umlenkung *f*
direction change mechanism Fahrtrichtungsumkehrmechanik *f*
direction control lever Fahrtrichtungshebel *m*
direction control valve Wegeventil *nt*
direction faced by the operator Blickrichtung *f* des Fahrers
direction of acceleration Beschleunigungsrichtung *f*
direction of action Wirkungsrichtung *f*
direction of closing Zu-Richtung *f*
direction of cutting Schnittrichtung *f*
direction of flow Durchflussrichtung *f*
direction of hand Steigungsrichtung *f*
direction of incidence Einstrahlrichtung *f*, Einstrahlungsrichtung *f*
direction of motion Bewegungsrichtung *f*, Fahrtrichtung *f*

direction of movement Bewegungsrichtung *f*
direction of opening Auf-Richtung *f*
direction of plunging Durchziehrichtung *f*
direction of primary motion Schnittrichtung *f*
direction of propeller rotation Laufraddrehsinn *m*
direction of rotation Drehrichtung *f*
direction of sound incidence Schalleinfallsrichtung *f*
direction of the cut Schnittrichtung *f*
direction of the feed motion Vorschubrichtung *f*
direction of transport Förderrichtung *f*, Wanderungssinn *m*
direction of travel Transportrichtung *f*, Bewegungsrichtung *f*, Fahrtrichtung *f*
direction of writing Schreibrichtung *f*
direction ot tearing Reißrichtung *f*
directional in Bewegungsrichtung, richtungsabhängig, richtungs ...
directional characteristic Richtcharakteristik *f*
directional comparator richtungsabhängiger Vergleicher *m*
directional efficiency Richtwirkung *f*
directional element gerichtetes Glied *nt*
directional locking device Richtungsfeststeller *m*
directional thermal response gerichteter Temperaturgang *m*
directionally dependent richtungsabhängig
directionally independent richtungsunabhängig
directive Richtlinie *f*
directivity Richtcharakteristik *f*
directivity index Richtwirkungsmaß *nt*
directly proportional to direkt proportional
directly-fired storage heater direkt befeuerter Speicher *m*
director Umsetzer *m*
director line Mantellinie *f*
directory Verzeichnis *nt*
directrix Leitlinie *f*
dirt Verschmutzung *f*, Schmutz *m*

dirt groove Schmutznute *fpl*
dirty verschmutzen; schmutzig
disabled manövrierunfähig
disadvantage Schaden *m*, Fehler *m*, Nachteil *m*
disadvantageous nachteilig
disassemble zerlegen, auseinander nehmen, demontieren, ausbauen
disassembling Demontage *f*
disassembly Zerlegung *f*, Ausbau *m*, Abbau *m*, Demontage *f*
disaster control Katastrophenschutz *m*
disc Scheibe *f*
disc cam Scheibenkurve *f*, Flachkurve *f*
disc crank Kubelscheibe *f*
disc feeder Tellerbeschicker *m*
disc flatness Scheibenebenheit *f*
disc magazine Tellermagazin *nt*
disc miller Scheibenfräser *m*
disc spring Tellerfeder *f*
disc storeroom Tellermagazin *nt*
disc turret Scheibenrevolver *m*
disc wear Scheibenverschleiß *m*
discard Abfall *m*
discharge ausschleusen, auslassen, abschieben, abladen, entsorgen, entladen, entschicken, ablassen, abblasen, ableiten, löschen; Auslass *m*, Auslauf *m*, Abfluss *m*, Entladung *f*, Entsorgung *f*, Abfuhr *f*
discharge air outlet Abluftdurchlass *m*
discharge branch Entleerungsstutzen *m*
discharge capacity Ablassleistung *f*
discharge channel Entladungskanal *m*
discharge current Ableitstrom *m*
discharge duration Entladungsdauer *f*
discharge measuring cross section Durchflussmessquerschnitt *m*, Abflussmessquerschnitt *m*
discharge nozzle Ablaufstutzen *m*
discharge of chips Späneabfuhr *f*
discharge of condensate Tauwasserableitung *f*
discharge outlet Ablaufstutzen *m*
discharge point Übergabeplatz *m*
discharge safety device Ablaufsicherung *f*
discharge side Abblasseite *f*
discharge valve Druckventil *nt*, Abflussventil *nt*
discharger Behälterentleerungsgerät *nt*
discharging Entladung *f*, Entschickung *f*, Entladen *nt*, Löschen *nt* von Ladungen *fpl*
discharging behaviour Entladeverhalten *nt*
discharging current Entladestrom *m*
discharging cycle Entladezyklus *m*
discharging duration Entladedauer *f*
discharging gap Entladungsspalt *m*
discharging phase Entladephase *f*
discharging process Entladungsvorgang *m*
discharging relation Entladeverhältnis *nt*
discharging time Entladezeit *f*
discharging voltage Entladespannung *f*
disclose offen legen
disclosure Offenlegung *f*
discoloration method Verfärbungsverfahren *nt*
discolouration range Verfärbungsbereich *m*
disconnect entkoppeln
disconnect abtrennen
disconnect ausschalten, abklemmen, Verbindung *f* trennen, unterbrechen, abtrennen, trennen, lösen, auslösen, abschalten, ausschalten, ausrücken, abkuppeln, entkoppeln
disconnect terminal Trennklemme *f*
disconnecting switch Trennschalter *m*
disconnection Abkuppeln *nt*, Abrennen *nt*, Entkopplung *f*
discontinue aussetzen, unterbrechen
discontinuous diskontinuierlich, unstetig
discontinuous acting element unstetig wirkendes Glied *nt*
discontinuous chip Span *m*, Bruchspan *m*, Reißspan *m*, Abreißspan *m*
discontinuous joint unterbrochene Fuge *f*
discontinuous transition unstetiger Übergang *m*
discount unberücksichtigt lassen
discover entdecken
discrepancy Abweichung *f*, Abwei-

chen *nt*
discrete diskret
discrete random variable diskrete Zufallsvariable *f*
discrete tone Einzelton *m*
discriminate unterscheiden
discrimination threshold Ansprechschwelle *f*
discrimination value Anlaufwert *m*, Ansprechwert *m*
discriminator Vergleicher *m*
disc-type shaper cutter Scheibenschneidrad *nt*
discuss abklären
disengage ausrücken, ausschalten, ausdrücken, auslösen, ausklinken, trennen, lösen, aushängen, absetzen, herausfahren
disengage the clutch auskuppeln
disengagement Ausschalten *nt*, Abschaltung *f*, Ausschaltung *f*, Trennung *f*, Auslösung *f*, Aushängen *nt*, Ausklinken *nt*, Herabgleiten *nt*, Auslösung *f*
disengaging Absetzen *nt*
disentangle entflechten, entwirren
disentanglement Entflechtung *f*
dished head Klöpperboden *m*
dishing Kümpeln *nt*
disiccant Trockenmittel *nt*
disimprove verschlechtern
disimprovement Verschlechterung *f*
disintegrate aufschlagen, zersetzen, auflösen
disintegration Zersetzung *f*, Auflösung *f*
disintegrator Aufschlaggerät *nt*
disjoining trennend
disjunction ODER-Verknüpfung *f*, Disjunktion *f*, Inklusives ODER *nt*
disjunctive disjunktiv
disjunctive combination disjunktive Verknüpfung *f*
disjunctively combined inputs *pl* disjunktiv verknüpfte Eingänge *mpl*
disk Scheibe *f*
disk brace Scheibenbremse *f*
disk cam Nocke *f*
disk drive Laufwerk *nt*
disk operating system Rechnerbetriebssystem *nt*
disk wheel Rillenscheibe *f*
dislocation Verschiebung *f*
dislocation ticket Ausfassbeleg *m*
dislodged fragments of coatings *pl* abgestrahlte Beschichtungsteile *ntpl*
dislodging Absplittern *nt*
dismantlement Auflösung *f*
dismantlable zerlegbar
dismantle auflösen, ausbauen, abbauen, zerlegen, demontieren, auseinander nehmen
dismantle pallets Paletten auflösen
dismantling Ausbau *m*, Lösen *nt*, Abbau *m*, Demontage *f*, Auflösung *f*, Zerlegung *f*
dismantling tool Abzieheinrichtung *f*
dismember zerlegen, zergliedern
dismount 1. ausbauen, abbauen, zerlegen, demontieren 2. absteigen (von)
dismountable zerlegbar
dismounting Demontage *f*, Abnahme *f*, Abbau *m*
disorder Fehler *m*, Störung *f*
dispatch WA (Warenausgang) *m*, Auftragseinlastung *f*, Kommissionierung *f*, Versand *m*, versenden
dispatch advice Lieferschein *m*
dispatch an order einen Auftrag einlasten
dispatch order Versandauftrag *m*
dispatch warehouse Versandlager *nt*, Kommissionierungslager *nt*
dispense verteilen, aufteilen, abgeben, freigeben
dispensing Abgeben *nt*, Abgabe *f*
dispensing machine Verteilmaschine *f*
dispersion Verteilung *f*, Aufteilung *f*
disperse aufschlämmen, dispergieren
dispersion Dispersion *f*, Streuung *f*
dispersion coefficient Streukoeffizient *m*
dispersion element Zerteilerelement *nt*
displace verdrängen, verlagern, versetzen, verschieben, verrutschen, fördern
displaced verrutscht
displacement Verlagerung *f*, Verschiebung *f*, Versetzung *f*, Verschieben *nt*, Lageveränderung *f*, Versatz *m*, Verstel-

displacement body *(Pumpe)* Verdränger *m*
displacement cylinder Verdrängungstiegel *m*
displacement device Verdränger *m*
displacement filling machine Verdrängerfüllmaschine *f*
displacement of bonded test piece Fugeteilverbindung *f*
displacement of the axes Achsversatz *m*
displacement of the buffer Pufferhub *m*
displacement phase Verdrängerphase *f*
displacement type armature Schiebeanker *m*
displacing Herausspringen *nt*
display anzeigen, zeigen; Anzeige *f*, Bildschirm *m*
display an X-ray pattern ein Röntgenbild sichtbar machen
display and printing calculator anzeigende und druckende Rechenmaschine *f*
display area Anzeigebereich *m*
display box Anzeigefeld *nt*
display device Anzeigegerät *nt*
display diaphragm Bildschirmblende *f*
display duration Anzeigedauer *f*
display exchange Bildwechsel *m*
display selection Bildanwahl *f*
display unit Anzeigegerät *nt*
display update Bildaktualisierung *f*
display work station Bildschirmarbeitsplatz *m*
displayed information ausgebende Information *f*
disposable pallet Einwegpalette *f*
disposal Entsorgung *f*, Beseitigung *f*, Abfuhr *f*, Verschrottung *f*
disposal costs Entsorgungskosten *pl*
disposal of chips Späneabfuhr *f*
disposal unit Entsorgungsanlage *f*
dispose entsorgen, beseitigen, verschrotten, abgeben, abführen
disposing Abführen *nt*
disposition Lage *f*, Anordnung *f*, Disposition *f*
disposition centre Dispositionstelle *f*

disposition data Dispositionsdaten *pl*
disproportion Missverhältnis *nt*
disproportionate unverhältnismäßig
disrupt zerreißen, reißen
disruption Ausbruch *m*, Zerreißen *nt*
disruption rip Riss *m*
disturbance message Störungsmeldung *f*
dissect zerlegen, zergliedern
dissection Zergliederung *f*, Zerlegung *f*
dissection-sheet drawing Zerschneideblattzeichnung *f*
dissipate abführen, ableiten, verlieren, verstreuen, verbrauchen, verteilen, neutralisieren
dissipating Abführen *nt*, Abfuhr *f*, Abbau *m*, Verbrauch *m*
dissipating energy Energie *f* aufnehmend
dissipation Ableitung *f*, Verlust *m*, Neutralisierung *f*
dissipation of noise Lärmausbreitung *f*
dissipative braking Verlustbremsung *f*
dissociation of steam Wasserdampfspaltung *f*
dissolution Ablösen *nt*, Ablösung *f*, Zerlegung *f*
dissolution of material Materialauflösung *f*
dissolvable löslich
dissolve zersetzen, auflösen, lösen, herauslösen
dissolving process Ablösevorgang *m*
distance Abstand *m*, Entfernung *f*, Distanz *f*, Strecke *f*, Weglänge *f*, Wegstrecke *f*, Zwischenraum *m*
distance across corners Eckenmaß *nt*
distance between abutting faces Stirnflächenabstand *m*
distance between edges Kantenabstand *m*
distance between end faces Stirnseitenabstand *m*
distance between fusion faces Stirnflächenabstand *m*
distance between rows Reihenabstand *m*
distance between serrations Rastenabstand *m*
distance between supports Stüt-

zweite *f*
distance between the axles Radachsenabstand *m*, Achsabstand *m*
distance control system Abstandsregelsystem *nt*
distance controlling Abstandsregelung *f*
distance measurement Abstandsmessung *f*
distance of fall Fallhöhe *f*
distance of fixture Befestigungsabstand *m*
distance of reach Sicherheitsabstand *m*
distance perpendicular to the axis achsensenkrechter Abstand *m*
distance piece Distanzstück *nt*
distance travelled during speed change Umschaltweg *m*
distillation drop Destillattropfen *m*
distillation flask Destillationskolben *m*
distinct scharf
distinguish unterscheiden
distort verzerren, verdrehen
distorted verzogen
distortion Verziehen *nt*, Verzerrung *f*, Verzug *m*, Verformung *f*, Verdrehung *f*, Verwindung *f*, Verdrehen *nt*
distortionless verzerrungsfrei
distribution groove Verteilernut *f*
distribute verteilen, zuteilen, umlegen
distributed AND connection Phantom-UND-Verknüpfung *f*
distributed connection Phantomverknüpfung *f*
distributed load of the mast Säulenstreckenlast *f*
distributed OR connection Phantom-ODER-Verknüpfung *f*
distributor Verteiler *m*
distributing conveyor *(Förderer)* Verteilanlage *f*
distributing station Verteilstation *f*
distribution Zuteilung *f*, Verteilung *f*, Umlegung *f*, Distribution *f*, Vertrieb *m*
distribution centre Absatzzentrum *nt*
distribution echelon Absatzstufe *f*, Distributionsstufe *f*
distribution function Verteilungsfunktion *f*
distribution installation Verteilungsanlage *f*
distribution market Absatzmarkt *m*
distribution of actual sizes *(im Toleranzfeld)* Ist-Maßverteilung *f*
distribution of forces Kraftfluss *m*
distribution of molecular weight Molekulargewichtsverteilung *f*
distribution rake Verteilrechen *m*
distribution rule Verteilregel *f*
distribution system Verteilanlage *f*, Vertriebsprogramm *nt*, Vertriebssystem *nt*
distribution time Verteilzeit *f*
distribution trolley Verteilwagen *m*
distribution warehouse Verteillager *nt*
distribution-free test verteilungsfreier Test *m*
district heating line Fernheizleitung *f*
district heating plant Fernwärmeanlage *f*
disturb stören
disturbance Störung *f*
disturbance radiation Störstrahlung *f*
disturbance variable Störgröße *f*
disturbance variable feedforward Störgrößenaufschaltung *f*
disturbed gestört
disturbing vibrations Störschwingungen *pl*
diverge zerstreuen, sich erweitern
divergence Abzweigung *f*, Divergenz *f*
divergent divergierend
diversification Diversifikation *f*
diversify diversifizieren, variieren
diversion Umleitung *f*
diversity factor Gleichzeitigkeitsfaktor *m*
divert umleiten, ablenken
dividable unterteilbar
divide abteilen, gliedern, einteilen, aufteilen, teilen
divide into sections unterteilen in Teile (oder Abschnitte oder Sektionen)
divide up zerlegen
divided Gewinnanteil *m*
divided sample Teilprobe *f*
divided table geteilter Tisch *m*
divided-table planer Hobelmaschine *f* mit zwei Arbeitstischen für kontinuierliches Arbeiten

divider Nachlaufsperre *f*, Fachteiler *m*, Fachteilung *f*
dividers *pl* Zirkel *m*
dividing Zerteilen *nt*
dividing apparatus Teilapparat *m*
dividing attachment Teileinrichtung *f*
dividing error Teilungsfehler *m*
dividing head Teilkopf *m*
dividing line Teilungslinie *f*
dividing method Teilverfahren *nt*
dividing wall Trennwand *f*
dividing-head plate Teilscheibe *f*
diving key transmission Ziehkeilgetriebe *nt*
division Abteilung *f*, Teilung *f*, Fachteilung *f*, Gliederung *f*, Einteilung *f*, Teilungssteg *m*, Steg *m*
division inserting machine Stegeinsetzmaschine *f*
division point Teilungspunkt *m*
division sign Divisionszeichen *nt*
division unit Teilungseinheit *f*
divisor Teiler *m*
DNC (Direct Numerical Control) DNC (Direkte Numerische Kontrolle *f*)
dock andocken
dockboard Überfahrplatte *f*
docking Andocken *nt*
docking station Andockstation *f*
document Beleg *m*, Dokument *nt*, Dokumentation *f*, Unterlage *f*
document accompanying goods Warenbegleitschein *m*
document encoder Belegcodierer *m*
document flow Belegfluss *m*
documentation Konstruktionsunterlagen *pl*
documents Unterlagen *fpl*
doesn't equal ungleich
dog 1. Mitnehmer *m*, Klaue *f*, Knagge *f*, Nocken *m*, Anschlagnocken *m*, Anschlag *m* **2.** *(Drehen)* Drehherz *nt*
dog actuated nockenbetätigt, anschlagbetätigt
dog clutch milling Klauenfräsen *nt*
dog stop Knagge *f*
dog-controlled anschlaggesteuert
dolly Hebel *m*
dolly gegenhalten
domed nut Hutmutter *f*
domed type hohe Hutmutterform *f*
domestic equipment Heimgeräte *ntpl*
domestic heating oil Haushaltsheizöl *nt*
domestic slow combustion range Dauerbrandherd *m*
domestic storage tank Haushaltsbehälter *m*
dome tipped electrode ballig aufsetzende Elektrode *f*
donor abgegebenes Medium *nt*
door Tür *f*, Tor *nt*
door closer Türschließer *m*
door closer with hydraulic damping Türschließer *m* mit hydraulischer Dämpfung
door closing means Türschließmittel *ntpl*
door hook Türhaken *m*
door key Türschlüssel *m*
door motion Türbewegung *f*
door panel Türfüllung *f*
door-fall hook for trap doors Fallhaken *m* für Drehflügeltüren
dope dotieren, chemische Zusätze beifügen
Doppel-HV-Fuge K-Fuge *f*
DOS (Disc Operating System) DOS (mit Disketten operierendes System)
dosage monitoring device Dosisüberwachungsgerät *nt*
dose zuteilen, dosieren
dose accumulation effect Dosieraufbaueffekt *m*
dose rate reduction coefficient Dosisschwächungskoeffizient *m*
dosimetry Dosimetrie *f*, Dosismessverfahren *nt*
dosing Dosierung *f*
dosing device Dosiervorrichtung *f*
dosing machine Dosiermaschine *f*
dosing piston Dosierkolben *m*
dot Punkt *m*
dot AND Phantom-UND-Verknüpfung *f*
dot diagram Punktediagramm *nt*
dot-lit lamp Punktleuchte *f*
dot OR Phantom-ODER-Verknüpfung *f*
dot printer Nadeldrucker *m*
dot-scanning method Punktrasterverfahren *nt*

dotting Punktierung *f*
double cam principle Doppelkurvenprinzip *nt*
double-sided shelving Doppelregal *nt*
double doppelt, zweifach; das Zweifache *nt*; doppeln, verdoppeln
double acting doppelt wirkend
double articulated connection Doppelgelenkanschluss *m*
double column planer-miller Portalfräsmaschine *f*, Doppelspindelfräsmaschine *f*, Doppelständerfräsmaschine *f*, Zweiständerplanfräsmaschine *f*
double cropping doppeltes Abschneiden *nt*
double current collector doppelter Stromabnehmer *m*
double cycle Doppelspiel *nt*
double depth doppeltief
double engagement *(bei Planetengetrieben)* Doppeleingriff *m*
double enveloping worm gear set Globoidschneckenradsatz *m*
double enveloping worm wheel globoidisches Schneckenrad *nt*
double fixed-bed miller Doppelplanfräsmaschine *f*
double flip Doppelflip *m*
double gripper Doppelgreifer *m*
double head Doppelsupport *m*
double head milling machine Doppelfräsmaschine *f*
double helical gear Stirnrad *nt* mit Doppelschrägverzahnung
double helical gear pair Stirnradpaar *nt* mit Doppelschrägverzahnung *f*, Zylinderradpaar *nt* mit Doppelschrägverzahnung
double helical teeth Doppelschrägverzahnung *f*
double hexagon bolt Zwölfkantschraube *f*
double hexagon head bolt with waisted shank Zwölfkantdehnschraube *f*
double hexagon head fitting bolt Zwölfkantpassschraube *f*
double hexagon head nut Zwölfkantmutter *f*
double hexagon head nut with col-
lar Zwölfkantmutter *m* mit Bund
double horizontal milling machine Doppelwaagerechtfräsmaschine *f*
double housing milling machine Doppelspindelfräsmaschine *f*, Doppelständerfräsmaschine *f*, Zweiständerplanfräsmaschine *f*
double housing plano-miller Langfräsmaschine *f*
double indexing Doppelschaltung *f*
double layer Zweischicht *f*
double line Doppelzeile *f*
double link Zweischlag *m*
double male connector Doppelgewindestutzen *m*
double mast Zweifachhubgerüst *nt*
double multiple disc clutch Doppellamellenkupplung *f*
double pan balance zweischalige Waage *f*
double pedal drive control Doppelpedalsteuerung *f*
double plano-milling machine Doppellangfräsmaschine *f*
double projection welding Doppelbuckelschweißen *nt*
double rocker Doppelschwinge *f*
double round corner Doppelhohlkehle *f*
double row spaced spot weld zweireihige Punktnaht *f*
double rule Doppellinie *f*
double sided run Doppelregal *nt*
double socket transition piece Doppelmuffenübergangsstück *nt*
double standard planer Doppelständerhobelmaschine *f*
double station vertical-spindle rotary continuous milling machine with four double-unit milling heads Senkrechtrundtischfräsautomat *m* mit zwei Spannstellen und vier Doppelfräsköpfen
double stroke Doppeltakt *m*
double taper seal Doppelkegelring *m*
double taper sleeve Doppelkegelring *m*
double tapered grinding wheel Doppelkegelschleifscheibe *f*
double thread zweigängiges Gewin-

de *nt*
double tracked zweispurig
double Vee-guide Doppelprismaführung *f*
double wash bottle Doppelwaschflasche *f*
double word Doppelwort *nt*
double yoke Doppeljoch *nt*
double-angle cutter Winkelfräser *m* für Werkzeuge mit gefrästen Zähnen für Spannuten mit Drall
double-armed zweiarmig
double-bend kröpfen
double-bevel butt joint Doppel-HV-Naht *f*
double-bevel butt joint with broad root face Doppel-HY-Naht *f*
double-bevel groove Doppel-HV-Fuge *f*
double-bevel weld with broad root face DHY-Fuge *f*
double-bevel weld with root face welded with double fillet weld Doppel-HY-Naht mit Doppelkehlnaht
double-bevel weld with root face welded with double fillet weld K-Stegnaht *f* mit Doppelkehlnaht
double-column horizontal milling machine (or miller) Doppelständerwaagerechtfräsmaschine *f*
double-column milling machine Zweiständerfräsmaschine *f*, Zweiständerplanfräsmaschine *f*, Doppelständerfräsmaschine *f*
double-column planer Doppelständerhobelmaschine *f*, Zweiständerhobelmaschine *f*
double-column press Doppelständerpresse *f*
double-column vertical turning and boring mill doppelständiges Drehwerk *nt*, Zweiständerkarusselldrehmaschine *f*, Großkarusselldrehmaschine *f*
double-column planing and milling machine Zweiständerhobel- und -fräsmaschine *f*
double-cut broach zweiseitig schneidendes Räumwerkzeug *nt*
double-cut planing Hobeln *nt* mit Spanabnahme in beiden Richtungen

double-cutting tool Meißel *m* mit zwei Schneiden
double-cutting tool assembly Zweiwegehobelvorrichtung *f*
doubled glass filament gefachtes Glasseidengarn *nt*
double-deep doppeltief
double-edged zweischneidig
double-end mill doppelseitiger Langlochfräser *m*, zweiseitiger Schaftfräser *m*
double-end miller Zweispindelfräsmaschine *f* mit einander gegenüberliegenden Spindeln zur Bearbeitung von Werkstücken
double-end milling machine Zweispindelabflächmaschine *f* zum gleichzeitigen Fräsen der Stirnflächen von Wellen, Zweispindelfräsmaschine *f* mit einander gegenüberliegenden Spindeln zur Bearbeitung von Werkstücken
double-ended doppelseitig
double-ended flex head socket wrench Doppelgelenksteckschlüssel *m*
double-ended precision boring machine doppelseitiges Feinstbohrwerk *nt*
double-ended socket spanner Doppelsteckschlüssel *m*
double-ended union Doppelstutzen *m*, Einschraubstutzen *m*
double-ended union used as an adaptor for butt joints T-Einschraubstutzen *m* in Stoßausführung für Rohrverschraubungen
double-glazed window Doppelscheibenfenster *nt*
double-housing planer Zweiständermaschine *f*, Zweiständerhobelmaschine *f*
double-housing planing machine Zweiständerhobelmaschine *f*
double-I butt joint Doppel-HU-Naht *f*
double-I butt weld Doppel-HU-Naht *f*
double-leaf door zweiflügelige Tür *f*
double-necked distilling flask Doppelhalssiedekolben *m*
double-pole zweipolig
doubler Verdoppler *m*
double-rowed zweireihig

double-sided tooth system doppelseitige Zykloidenverzahnung *f*
double-spindle machine Doppelspindelmaschine *f*
double-spindle-vertical milling attachment Doppelspindelsenkrechtfräsmaschine *f*
double-start bolt thread zweigängiges Bolzengewinde *nt*
double-start thread doppelgängiges Gewinde *nt*
double-start trapezoidal screw thread with clearance zweigängiges Trapezgewinde *nt* mit Spiel
double-stroke planing Zweiweghobeln *nt*
double-U butt weld DU-Fuge *f*
double-V butt joint Doppel-V-Naht *f*
double-V butt weld with broad root face DY-Naht *f*
double-V groove Doppel-V-Fuge *f*, X-Fuge *f*
double-V-butt weld Doppel-V-Naht *f*, DV-Naht *f*
double-Vee Doppelprisma *nt*
double-wall radiography Doppelwanddurchstrahlung *f*
double-wheel tool grinder Doppelscheibenwerkzeugschleifmaschine *f*
double-word addressing Doppelwortzugriff *m*
doubling Verdopplung *f*
doubling circuit Verdoppler *m*
double head miller Fräsmaschine *f* mit Doppelfrässpindel
double head milling machine Fräsmaschine *f* mit Doppelfrässpindel
dovetail Schwalbenschwanz *m*, Schwalbenschwanzführung *f*; verzinken, verschwalben, Schwalbenschwanznuten ausarbeiten
dowel Passstift *m*, Dübel *m*; dübeln
dowel pin plate Säulenplatte *f*
down hinunter, nach unten, ab, bergab, herab
down time Nebenzeit *f*, Verlustzeit *f*
downcomer Fallleitung *f*
down-cut grinding Gleichlaufschleifen *nt*
down-cut milling machine Gleichlauffräsmaschine *f*
downfeed Tiefenvorschub *m*, Abbewegung *f*, Senkrechtvorschub *m*
down-feed milling gleichläufiges Fräsen *nt*
down-feed milling machine Gleichlauffräsmaschine *f*
down-feed screw Tiefenzustellspindel *f*
down-gate Gießtrichter *m*
down-grinding Gleichlaufschleifen *nt*
downhill Sturzzug *m*
downhill motion Talfahrt *f*
downhill travel Talfahrt *f*
download *(EDV)* laden
down-load Laden *nt*
down-mill cutting Gleichlauffräsen *nt*
downpipe Fallleitung *f*, Regenfallrohr *nt*
downpipe offset Fallleitungsverziehung *f*
downstairs nach unten, unten
downstream unterhalb, nachgeschaltet, stromabwärts
downstream operations Weiterverarbeitung *f*
downstroke Abwärtshub *m*
down-swept flue Sturzzug *m*
downtime Ausfallzeit *f*, Stillstandszeit *f*, Störungsdauer *f*, Wartezeit *f*, Totzeit *f*
downtime costs Ausfallkosten *pl*
downward motion Senkbewegung *f*
downward run Talfahrt *f*
downward traverse Abbewegung *f*
downwards herab, abwärts, hinunter, nach unten
dozing mode Schlummerbetrieb *m*
draft 1. Skizze *f*, Entwurf *m*; skizzieren, zeichnen 2. *(Gussstück entformen)* Ausformschräge *f*
draft drawing Entwurfszeichnung *f*
drafting machine Zeichenmaschine *f*
draftsman Zeichner *m*
draftsperson Zeichner(in) *m,f*
draftswoman Zeichnerin *f*
drag 1. schleifen, drücken, quetschen, schleppen, mitreißen, reißen 2. *(Schneide)* Zwischenschneide *f*
drag angle Riefenwinkel *m*
drag bar Tragkette *f*
drag bar feeder Tragkettenförderer *m*

drag chain Schleppkette *f*
drag chain conveyor Schleppkettenförderer *m*, Schleppförderer *m*
drag link Doppelkurbel *f*
drag mark Druckstelle *f*, Drehriefe *f*
drag table Schlepptisch *m*
drag-indicator tester Schleppzeigergerät *nt*
drain channel Ablaufrinne *f*
drain cock Ablasshahn *m*
drain device Ablasseinrichtung *f*
drain filter Dränfilter *m*
drain gutter Ablaufrinne *f*
drain Abfluss *m*, Ableiter *m*, Rückfluss *m*, Senke *f*; ablassen, abfließen, leerlaufen, entleeren, zurückfließen lassen
drain out fließen aus
drain plug Ablassschraube *f*
drain shaft Dränschacht *m*
drain valve Ablassventil *nt*
drain valves Auslaufarmaturen *f*
drainage *(Flüssigkeit)* Ablauf *m*
drainage area Dränfläche *f*
drainage network Drännetz *nt*
drainage pit Entwässerungsgrube *f*
drainage plough Dränpflug *m*
drainage system for premises Grundstücksentwässerungsanlage *f*
draining tube Ableitungsrohr *nt*
draught limiter Zugbegrenzer *m*
draught regulating device Zugregeleinrichtung *f*
draught requirement Zugbedarf *m*
draught-free ventilation zugfreie Lüftung *f*
draughtsman Ersteller *m* einer Zeichnung
draughtsman Zeichner *m*
draughtsperson Zeichner(in) *m,f*
draughtswoman Zeichnerin *f*
draw 1. *(malen)* skizzieren, zeichnen 2. *(ziehen)* Zug *m*; ziehen, saugen, ansaugen
draw along vorbeiziehen
draw as continuous line eine Linie durchziehen
draw conditions Ziehverhältnisse *pl*
draw current from Strom entnehmen von
draw grooves Nuten ziehen
draw head Ziehkopf *m*
draw home hineinziehen
draw in einziehen, hereinziehen, Anzug *m*
draw in shortened form gekürzt zeichnen
draw in the mated condition ineinander zeichnen
draw off wegziehen von, abziehen von
draw out herausziehen, recken
draw ring Ziehring *m*
draw rod Zugstange *f*
draw separately herauszeichnen
draw staggered versetzt zeichnen
draw the tolerances into a design tolerieren, Toleranzen angeben in einer Zeichnung
draw to a larger scale vergrößert zeichnen
draw to scale maßstäblich zeichnen
draw up erstellen
draw wire Seilzug *m*
draw with a fanning action fächelnd führen
drawback Nachteil *m*
drawbar Deichsel *f*, Zugstange *f*
drawbar drag Abbremsung *f*
drawbar pull Zugkraft *f*
drawbolt Spannschraube *f*
drawcut Rücklaufspan *m*
draw-cut shaper Waagerechtstoßmaschine *f* mit ziehenden Schnitt
draw-cut type keyseater Keilnutenziehmaschine *f*
drawer Schublade *f*
drawer divider Schubladenunterteilung *f*
draw-in arbour Spanndorn *m*, Anzugdorn *m*
draw-in bolt Anzugsschraube *f*, Zugschraube *f*
draw-in collet Spannpatrone *f*
draw-in collet chuck Spannzange *f*
draw-in spindle Anzugspindel *f*
drawing 1. *(malen)* Skizze *f*, Plan *m*, Zeichnung *f*; zeichnerisch 2. *(Zug)* Ziehen *nt*
drawing amendment service Zeichnungsänderungsdienst *m*

drawing area Zeichenfläche f, Zeichnungsfeld nt
drawing board Zeichenbrett nt, Zeichnungsträger m
drawing board with free margin Zeichenbrett nt mit Zusatzfläche
drawing by a sliding action Gleitziehen nt
drawing containing preprinted representations Zeichnungen fpl mit vorgedruckten Darstellungen
drawing dealing with oversize parts Übermaßzeichnung f
drawing dealing with wearing parts Verschleißteilzeichnung f
drawing ink Tusche f
drawing instrument Reißzeug nt, Zeichenmittel nt
drawing of current Stromentnahme f
drawing of tubular bodies Hohlgleitziehen nt
drawing office work Zeichenarbeit f
drawing over fixed mandrel by a sliding-action draw Gleitziehen nt über festen Stopfen (oder Dorn)
drawing over floating mandrel by a sliding-action draw Gleitziehen nt über losen Stopfen (oder Dorn)
drawing over travelling mandrel Gleitziehen nt über mitlaufende Stange
drawing panel Zeichnungsfeld nt
drawing practice Zeichnungswesen nt
drawing practice standard Zeichnungsnorm f
drawing producer Zeichnungsersteller m
drawing scrutiny Zeichnungsprüfung f
drawing sheet Zeichnungsblatt nt
drawing staggerings Zugabestufungen
drawing under combined tension and compression (Metallumformung) Durchziehen nt
drawing-in Einziehen nt, Ansaugen nt
drawn-arc welding Langlichtbogenschweißen nt
draw-through sample Durchzugprobe f
dress nachschärfen, aufbereiten, abrichten, abdrehen
dress off putzen, abarbeiten
dressing Abrichten nt, Abziehen nt, Endbearbeitung f, Nachbearbeitung f
dressing device Abziehvorrichtung f
dressing mechanism Abrichtgerät nt
dressing pass traverse Abrichtzyklus m
dressing speed Abrichtgeschwindigkeit f
dressing time Abrichtzeit f
dressing tool Abrichtwerkzeug nt
drew bevels pl Aushebeschrägen fpl
drier Entfeuchter m
drift hole Austreibloch nt
drift slot Austreibschlitz m
drift test specimen Aufweitprobe f
drifting Aufweiten nt an Enden
drifting optics Aufweitungsoptik f
drill bohren aus dem Vollen, vollbohren, bohren; Bohrer m, Spiralbohrer m, Bohrwerkzeug nt
drill and tap grinder Bohrer- und Gewindebohrerschärfmaschine f
drill centre Bohrmitte f
drill chuck Bohrfutter nt
drill flute Bohrernut f
drill grind Bohreranschliff m
drill head Bohrkopf m
drill hole Bohrloch nt
drill jig Bohrlehre f
drill life Bohrerstandzeit f
drill out ausbohren
drill pipe thread for well drilling Gestängerohrgewinde nt für Tiefbohrtechnik
drill pipe thread for well sinking Gestängerohrgewinde nt für Brunnenbau
drill pointing Bohrerausspitzen nt
drill press Bohrmaschine f
drill socket Bohrfutterkegel m
drill spindle Bohrspindel f
drilled hole Bohrung f, Bohrloch nt
drillhead Bohrkopf m
drillhole Bohrung f, Bohrloch nt
drilling Bohren nt aus dem Vollen, Lochbohren nt, Vollbohren nt, Vollbohrung f
drilling and boring lathe Dreh- und Bohrmaschine f

drilling and milling machine Bohr- und Fräsmaschine *f*
drilling attachment *(Vollbohren)* Bohreinrichtung *f*
drilling capacity Bohrleistung *f*
drilling chip Innenausdrehspan *m*, Vollbohrspan *m*
drilling cycle Bohrzyklus *m*
drilling cycles *(G80-G89)* Bohrzyklen *mpl*
drilling fixture Bohrvorrichtung *f*
drilling head Bohrkopf *m*
drilling machine Bohrmaschine *f*
drilling machine table Bohrtisch *m*
drilling machines *pl* Bohrmaschinen *fpl*
drilling motor Bohrmotor *m*
drilling operation Vollbohrarbeit *f*
drilling out Ausbohren *nt*
drilling practice Bohrtechnik *f*
drilling slide Bohrschlitten *m*
drilling spindle Bohrspindel *f*
drilling spindle head Bohrspindelkopf *m*
drilling spindle sleeve Bohrspindelhülse *f*
drilling unit Bohreinheit *f*
drillings *pl* Bohrspäne *mpl*
drinking utensils Trinkgeschirr *nt*
drip tropfen
drip collector Abtropfbehälter *m*
drip loss Tropfverlust *m*
drip mould Unterschneidung *f*
drip nose Unterschneidung *f*
dripping down *(von Kondensat)* Herabtropfen *nt*
dripping water Abtropfwasser *nt*
drive Laufwerk *nt*, Antrieb *m*, Trieb *m*, Mitnahme *f*; antreiben, treiben, mitnehmen, fahren
drive acceleration Fahrbeschleunigung *f*
drive against auffahren
drive at zielen auf
drive axle Antriebsachse *f*
drive backwards rückwärts fahren
drive belt Antriebsriemen *m*, Treibriemen *m*
drive box Antriebsgehäuse *nt*
drive braking Fahrverzögerung *f*
drive concept Antriebskonzept *nt*
drive controller Fahrregler *m*
drive element Antriebselement *nt*
drive forwards vorwärts fahren
drive in hineinfahren, einfahren; Einfahren *nt*
drive instruction Fahrauftrag *m*, Fahrbefehl *m*
drive mechanism Fahrwerk *nt*, Antrieb *m*
drive module Antriebsmodul *nt*
drive motor Antriebsmotor *m*, Fahrmotor *m*
drive power Antriebsleistung *f*
drive powers *pl* Antriebsleistungen *fpl*
drive program Treiberprogramm *nt*
drive shaft Antriebswelle *f*
drive speed Fahrgeschwindigkeit *f*
drive together ineinanderschieben
drive type fastening Mitnehmerverbindung *f*
drive under unterfahren; lastunterfahrend
drive unit Fahrantrieb *m*, Antrieb *m*
drive vibrator Antriebsschwinge *f*
drive wheel Antriebsrad *nt*, Laufrad *nt*
drive wheel bore Laufradbohrung *f*
drive wheel diameter Laufraddurchmesser *m*
drive wheels angetriebene Räder *pl*
drive-in pallet racking Einfahrregal *nt*
drive-in racking Einfahrregal *nt*
driven angetrieben
driven gear getriebenes Rad *nt*
driven side Abtrieb *m*, Antriebseite *f*
driver 1. Drehherz *nt*, Mitnehmer *m*, Mitnehmerbolzen *m*, Treiber *m*
2. *(Fahrzeug)* Fahrer *m*
driver plate Mitnehmerscheibe *f*
driver position Fahrerplatz *m*
driver-controlled fork truck Sitzgabelstapler *m*
driverless fahrerlos
driverless transport system fahrerloses Transportsystem (FTS) *nt*
driverless truck fahrerloses Flurförderzeug *nt*
driver-operated mit Fahrer
driver's seat Fahrersitz *m*
drive-steer axle angetriebene Lenk-

achse *f*
drive-steer wheel angetriebenes Lenkrad *nt*
drive-through pallet racking Durchfahrregal *nt*
drive-under truck Unterfahrwagen *m*
driving Fahren *nt*
driving above oben fahrend
driving along the side seitenfahrend
driving below unten fahrend
driving carrier Mitnehmer *m*
driving chain Antriebskette *f*
driving command Fahrauftrag *m*, Fahrbefehl *m*
driving command echo Fahrauftragsrückmeldung *f*
driving controls *pl* Fahrsteuerelemente *ntpl*
driving coordinator Koordination „Fahren" *f*
driving disk Treibscheibe *f*
driving dog Mitnehmer *m*, Drehherz *nt*
driving element Antriebsglied *nt*
driving function Fahrfunktion *f*
driving gear treibendes Rad *nt*
driving hole Mitnehmerloch *nt*
driving light Fahrbeleuchtung *f*
driving mechanism Triebwerk *nt*
driving mechanism class Triebwerksgruppe *f*
driving member Antriebselement *nt*
driving noise Fahrgeräusche *pl*
driving pin Mitnahmestift *m*, Triebstock *m*
driving pinion Antriebsritzel *nt*
driving plate Mitnehmerscheibe *f*
driving position Fahrerstand *m*, Fahrerplatz *m*
driving spindle Antriebsspindel *f*
driving square *(Werkzeug)* Verbindungsvierkant *m*
driving square for pocket socket wrenches Verbindungsvierkant *m* für Maschinenschrauberwerkzeuge
driving wheel Treibscheibe *f*
drop Abnahme *f*, Abfall *m*, Druckabfall *m*, Tropfen *nt*; fallen lassen, abfallen, abnehmen, absenken, herabfallen, tropfen, sinken
drop bottom container Behälter *m* mit Bodenentleerung, Fallbodenbehälter *m*
drop casting fallendes Gießen *nt*
drop energy Fallenergie *f*
drop forge gesenkschmieden; Gesenkschmiede *f*
drop forging Gesenkschmieden *nt*, Schmieden *nt* im Gesenk
drop forging die Schmiedegesenk *nt*
drop forging shop Gesenkschmiede *f*
drop hammer Fallhammer *m*
drop height at fracture Fallhöhe *f* beim Bruch
drop in atmospheric humidity Luftfeuchtegefälle *nt*
drop in force Kraftabfall *m*
drop in tool life Standzeitabfall *m*
drop off absetzen
drop on demand ink jet coder Drop-on-demand-Tintenstrahlcodierer *m*
drop out of engagement ausschwenken
drop packing machine Fallpackmaschine *f*
drop sequence Fallfolge *f*
drop speed Absenkgeschwindigkeit *f*
drop table Falltisch *m*
drop test Tüpfelprüfung *f*
drop test machine Fallprüfmaschine *f*
drop through durchfallen
drop with trailing thread langziehender Tropfen *m*
drop worm Fallschnecke *f*
dropin Störsignal *nt*
drop-on lid Stapelbügel *m*
dropping point apparatus Tropfpunktgerät *nt*
drum Walze *f*, Trommel *f*, Fass *nt*, Kanister *m*
drum brake Trommelbremse *f*
drum cam Trommelkurve *f*
drum chock Fassauflage *f*
drum clamp Fassklammer *f*
drum clamp arm Fassklammerarm *m*
drum gripper Fassgreifer *m*, Trommelgreifer *m*
drum indexing Trommelschalten *nt*
drum magazine Trommelmagazin *nt*
drum miller Trommelfräsmaschine *f*
drum motor Trommelmotor *m*

drum pan Trommelpfanne *f*
drum racking Trommelregal *nt*
drum storage stack Fasslager *nt*
drum treatment Trommelbehandlung *f*
drumming noise Dröhnen *nt*
drum-type continuous milling machine Trommelfräsmaschine *f* für durchlaufendes Fräsen
drum-type indexing miller Fräsmaschine *f* mit Schalttrommel, Trommelfräsmaschine *f* mit Indexschaltung
drum-type indexing milling machine Trommelfräsmaschine *f* mit Indexschaltung
drum-type machine Fräsmaschine *f* mit Aufspanntrommel
drum-type miller Fräsmaschine *f* mit Drehtrommel, Trommelfräsmaschine *f*
drum-type milling machine Trommelfräsmaschine *f*
drum-type turret Trommelrevolver *m*
drum-type turret lathe Trommelrevolverdrehmaschine *f*
dry trocknen; trocken
dry bending strength Trockenbiegefestigkeit *f*
dry bright *(von Draht)* trockenblank
dry cleaning chemisch reinigen
dry cutting Trockenschliff *m*, Trockenschleifen *nt*
dry deposit method of fluorescence inspection Fluoreszenzverfahren *nt* mit trockenem Niederschlag
dry gas meter Trockengaszähler *m*
dry grinding Trockenschleifen *nt*
dry ink Trockentinte *f*
dry milling Trockenfräsen *nt*
dry natural rubber substance Kautschuktrockensubstanz *f*
dry pressing Trockenpressen *nt*
dry truing Trockenabrichten *nt*
dry weight Trockenmasse *f*
dry zone Trockenzone *f*
drying channel Trockenkanal *m*
drying machine Trocknungsmaschine *f*
design feature Gestaltungsmerkmal *nt*
DTE clear request Auslöseaufforderung *f*
DTE common return *(Kommunikationstechnik)* DEE Rückleiter *m*

DTE uncontrolled not ready *(Kommunikationstechnik)* DEE ungesteuert nicht bereit
dual cone width Zweikegelweite *f*
dual copying lathe Doppelkopierdrehmaschine *f*
dual flank composite error Zweiflankenwälzfehler *m*
dual flank lead Zweiflankensteigung *f*
dual flank measurement Zweiflankenmessung *f*
dual flank pitch Zweiflankenteilung *f*
dual flank roll tester Zweiflankenwälzprüfgerät *nt*
dual fuel boiler Wechselbrandkessel *m*
dual operating system Doppelbetätigung *f*
dual purpose Doppelzweck *m*
dual ram broaching machine Doppelstößel-Räummaschine *f*, Zwillingsräummaschine *f*
dual system Dualsystem *nt*
dual table planer type miller Langfräsmaschine *f* mit zwei Tischen
dual wheel Doppelrad *nt*
dual-based division Zweiterteilung *f*
dual-channel triggering redundante Ansteuerung *f*
dual cone width measurement Zweikegelweitenabmessung *f*
dual-fuel engine Mehrstoffmotor *m*
dual spacing Mittenabstand *m*
duct Kanal *m*, Rohr *nt*, Röhre *f*
duct deposit Staubablagerung *f*
duct humidity regulator Kanalfeuchteregler *m*
duct length Kanalstrecke *f*
duct system Kanalnetz *nt*
ducted warm air system Warmluftheizung *f*
ductile verformbar, dehnbar, geschmeidig
ductile fracture Zähbruch *m*
ductile yield Bruchdehnung *f*
ductility Dehnbarkeit *f*
ductility-dip crack Sprödriss *m*
ducting Kanalnetz *nt*
due fällig
due to *(wegen)* aus
dull abstumpfen, stumpf machen,

stumpf werden, mattieren, unscharf, stumpf
dull appearance stumpfes Aussehen *nt*
dulling Abstumpfung *f*, Mattierung *f*, Mattieren *nt*, Mattwerden *nt*, Eckenabstumpfung *f*
duly ordnungsgemäß
dumb-bell test piece Stabprobe *f*
dummy cover Blinddeckel *m*
dummy test Leerversuch *m*
dump abkippen
dun mahnen
dunning letter Mahnung *f*
duo mill Duowalzwerk *nt*
duplex Doppel ...
duplex head Doppelsupport *m*
duplex head miller Fräsmaschine *f* mit Doppelfrässpindel
duplex machine Doppelspindelmaschine *f*
duplex milling gleichzeitiges Fräsen *nt* mit zwei Fräsköpfen
duplex milling machine Doppelfräsmaschine *f*
duplex mode Duplexbetrieb *m*
duplex planer Doppelhobelmaschine *f*
duplex plano-miller Doppellangfräsmaschine *f*
duplex radial planing attachment Doppelrundhobeleinrichtung *f*
duplex tool rest Doppelsupport *m*
duplex toolholder Doppelmeißelhalter *m*, Aufbaumeißelhalter *m*
duplex version Duplexausführung *f*
duplex-head milling machine Doppelspindel-Planfräsmaschine *f*
duplex-type milling machine Zweispindelplanfräsmaschine *f*
duplicate dreidimensional nachfräsen, dreidimensional nachformfräsen, kopieren, dreidimensional nachformen, doppeln, nachbauen, reproduzieren
duplicate Nachformen *nt*
duplicate in three dimensions dreidimensional nachformen, raumnachformen
duplicate machining Nachformarbeit *f*, Nachformen *nt*
duplicate part Serienteil *nt*
duplicate production Großserienfertigung *f*, Serienfertigung *f*, reihenmäßige Herstellung *f*, Massenherstellung *f*
duplicate turning Nachformdrehen *nt*
duplicating 1. *(Fräsen)* Formfräsen *nt*, Nachfräsen *nt*, Kopieren *nt*, Reproduzieren *nt* **2.** *(Drehen)* Nachformdrehen *nt*
duplicating accuracy Nachformgenauigkeit *f*
duplicating attachment 1. Nachformeinrichtung *f*, Kopiereinrichtung *f* **2.** *(Drehen)* Nachformdrehvorrichtung *f*
duplicating lathe Nachformdrehmaschine *f*, Kopierdrehmaschine *f*
duplicating machine 1. Kopiermaschine *f* **2.** *(Fräsen)* Nachformfräsmaschine *f* mit dreidimensionaler Steuerung
duplicating trial *(bei Schriften)* Vervielfältigungsversuch *m*
duplication Nachformarbeit *f*, Verdopplung *f*
duplicator 1. Nachformeinrichtung *f*, Kopiereinrichtung *f* **2.** *(Fräsen)* Nachformfräsmaschine *f* mit dreidimensionaler Steuerung, Gesenkfräsmaschine *f*, selbsttätige Nachformfräsmaschine *f*
durability Haltbarkeit *f*, Lebensdauer *f*
durable haltbar
durable form process Dauerformverfahren *nt*
durable model Dauermodell *nt*
durable resistant beständig
durable shape dauerhafte Form *f*
duration Dauer *f*, Zeitspanne *f*
duration of ageing Alterungsdauer *f*
duration of loading Beanspruchungsdauer *f*
duration of transaction Transaktionsdauer *f*
duration per charge Brenndauer *f*
during während
duromer Duromer *nt*
dust Staub *m*
dust carbide generator Staubentwickler *m*
dust emission control Staubauswurfbegrenzung *f*
dust guards *pl* Staubschutz *m*
dust particle Staubpartikel *nt*

dust research institute Staubforschungsinstitut *nt*
dust-free blasting staubfreies Strahlen *nt*
dust-proof staubdicht
dust-proof protection Staubschutz *m*
dust-protected staubgeschützt
dust-tight staubdicht
dusty staubig, staubbelastet
duty Aufgabe *f*, Beanspruchung *f*
duty cycle Arbeitszyklus *m*
duty cycle factor relative Einschaltdauer *f*
duty cycle time Arbeitszyklusdauer *f*, Einschaltdauer *f*
duty type Betriebsart *f*
DVM shallow notch specimen DVM-Kleinkerbprobe *f*
DVM wide notch specimen DVM-Flachkerbprobe *f*
dwell Stillstand *m*, Stillstandsdauer *f*, Verweilzeit *f*, Ruhe *f*, Halt *m*; verweilen, rasten
dwell phase Rastphase *f*
dwell teeth *pl* Führungszähne *mpl*
dwell time Haltezeit *f*, Verweildauer *f*, Bewegungspause *f*
dwelling Halten *nt*, Anhalten *nt*
dwelling place Haltemöglichkeit *f*
dwelling position Haltepunkt *m*
dye ink Farbstofftinte *f*
dye penetrant inspection Farbeindringprüfung *f*
dye staining test Anfärbeversuch *m*
dye yield Farbausbeute *f*
dye bath Färbebad *nt*
dyestuff laser Farbstofflaser *m*
dying down of oscillations Ausschwingen *nt*
dynamic behaviour dynamisches Verhalten *nt*
dynamic brake Bremse *f*

dynamic cell Mehrfachzelle *f*
dynamic cell positioning Mehrfachzellenschutzeinrichtung *f*
dynamic effect Kraftwirkung *f*
dynamic factor Stoßfaktor *m*
dynamic fatigue loading Dauerschwingbeanspruchung *f*
dynamic fatigue test Dauerschwingversuch *m*
dynamic fatigue test by axial loading Dauerschwingversuch *m* mit axialer Beanspruchung
dynamic fatigue test by constant load pounding Dauerschwingversuch *m* mit Eindruck-Schwellbereich
dynamic fatigue test on single lap joints Dauerschwingversuch *m* an einschnittig überlappten Klebungen
dynamic friction Bewegungsreibung *f*
dynamic input dynamischer Eingang *m*
dynamic loading dynamische (oder schwingende) Belastung *f*
dynamic modulus dynamischer Modul *nt*, Speichermodul *nt*
dynamic modulus of elasticity dynamischer Dehnmodul *nt*
dynamic modulus of shear dynamisches Schubmodul *nt*
dynamic rack storage Durchlaufregallager *nt*
dynamic racking Durchlaufregal *nt*
dynamic seal Abdichtung *f* beweglicher Teile gegeneinander, dynamische Dichtung *f*
dynamic shelving Durchlaufregal *nt*
dynamic stiffness dynamische Steifheit *f*
dynamic storage Durchlauflager *nt*, Durchlauflagerung *f*, Laufzeitspeicher *m*
dynamics Dynamik *f*
dynamometer dynamischer Kraftmesser *m*

E e

ear Öse *f*
ear width Schenkelweite *f*
earing test Zipfelprüfung *f*
early failure Frühausfall *m*
early warning Frühwarnung *f*
early warning indicator Frühwarnindikator *m*
earth Masseschluss *m*, Masse *f*, erden
earth Erde *f*
earth conductor Schutzleiter *m*
earth connection Erdschluss *m*
earth fault Erdschluss *m*
earth leakage resistance Erdableitungswiderstand *m*
earth loading Erdbelastung *f*
earth-covered pipeline erdbedeckte Rohrleitung *f*
earthed geerdet
earthed-natural connection Nullung *f*
earthing Ableitung *f*, Nullung *f*, Erdung *f*
earthing strap Erdungsband *nt*, Schleifband *nt*
ease in operation Bedienungserleichterung *f*
ease of cutting Zerspanbarkeit *f*
ease of cutting property Zerspanbarkeit *f*
ease of decontamination Dekontaminierbarkeit *f*
ease of machining Zerspanbarkeit *f*
ease of maintenance Wartbarkeit *f*
ease of servicing Wartbarkeit *f*
easily inflammable leicht entflammbar
easing Lockern *nt*
easy leicht
easy machining leicht bearbeitbar, gut zerspanbar
easy to mount leicht montierbar
easy-to-reach griffbereit
eccentric 1. außerachsig, außermittig, exzentrisch; Exzenter *m* 2. *(nicht korrekt)* verrutscht
eccentric cam Exzenter *m*
eccentric gear exzentrisches Rad *nt*

eccentric press Exzenterpresse *f*
eccentric quill *(außermittige)* Spindelhülse *f*
eccentric shaft Exzenterwelle *f*
eccentric turning außermittiges Drehen *nt*
eccentric worm pump Exzenterschneckenpumpe *f*
eccentricity Exzentrizität *f*, Außermittigkeit *f*, Mittenabweichung *f*
exchange Auswechseln *nt*
echo rückmelden, Rückmeldung *f*
echo cluster Echogebirge *nt*
echo height Echohöhe *f*
echo height ratio Echohöhenverhältnis *nt*
echo indication Echoanzeige *f*
echo side Echoseite *f*
ecological ökologisch
economic betriebswirtschaftlich
economic efficiency Wirtschaftlichkeit *f*
economic efficiency checking Wirtschaftlichkeitsprüfung *f*
economic feasibility study Wirtschaftlichkeitsanalyse *f*
economic output Regelleistung *f*
economical sparsam, wirtschaftlich
economize sparen
economy Wirtschaftlichkeit *f*, Sparsamkeit *f*
economy calculation Wirtschaftlichkeitsrechnung *f*
economy measure Sparmaßnahme *f*
eddy Turbulenz *f*, Wirbel *m*; wirbeln
eddy current Wirbelstrom *m*
eddy current loss Eisenverlust *m*
eddy current method Wirbelstromverfahren *nt*
eddy current motor Stromverdrängungsmotor *m*
edge Schneide *f*, Kante *f*, Rand *m*, Seite *f*; kanten, besäumen
edge angle Eckenwinkel *m*
edge band Kantenabdeckung *f*
edge chipping Schneidenausbruch *m*,

Kantenausbruch *m*
edge covering Kantenabdeckung *f*
edge cracking Kantenaussprünge *f*
edge crush resistance Kantenstauchwiderstand *m*
edge flaming Kantenbeflammung *f*
edge form Fugenform *f*
edge loading Kantenbelastung *f*
edge misalignment versetzte Schweißkante *f*
edge of the object Körperkante *f*
edge planer Blechkantenhobelmaschine *f*
edge protection Kantenschutz *m*
edge rack Randregal *nt*
edge radiusing Kantenrundung *f*
edge raising Randhochstellen *nt*
edge raising by spinning Randhochstellen *nt* durch Drücken
edge retraction Kanteneinzug *m*
edge sealing machine Seitenverschließmaschine *f*
edge sharpness Scharfkantigkeit *f*
edge stability Kantenfestigkeit *f*
edge stress Kantenbeanspruchung *f*
edge stress on the side subject to tensile stress in bending biegezugseitige Randspannung *f*
edge swelling Kantenquellung *f*
edge tear load Kanteneinreißkraft *f*
edge wear Kantenverschleiß *m*, Verschleiß *m* an der Werkzeugschneide
edged kantig
edge-holding property (or quality) Schneidhaltigkeit *f*
edgeless unscharf, stumpf
edge-machine Kanten bearbeiten
edge-planing Kantenhobeln *nt*
Edison thread Elektrogewinde *nt*
edit aufbereiten
editing Aufbereitung *f*
effect wirken, bewirken, leisten; Wirkung *f*, Einwirkung *f*, Wirkungsgrad *m*, Auswirkung *f*, Leistung *f*
effect a sale einen Verkauf abschließen
effect of faults Störungsauswirkung *f*
effect of forces Krafteinfluss *m*
effect of moisture Feuchtigkeitseinwirkung *f*
effect of wind Windeinwirkung *f*

effect reference system Wirkbezugssystem *nt*
effective effektiv, wirklich, wirksam
effective area Wirkfläche *f*
effective braking Nutzbremsung *f*
effective clearance angle wirksamer Freiwinkel *m*
effective diameter Flankendurchmesser *m*
effective direction of cut tatsächliche Schnittrichtung *f*
effective feed Wirkvorschub *m*
effective flank nutzbare Flanke *f*
effective interference Haftmaß *nt*, wirksames Übermaß *nt*
effective output Effektivausbringung *f*
effective pile thickness Polschichtdicke *f*
effective power Wirkungsleistung *f*
effective profile Ist-Profil *nt*
effective radius Wirkradius *m*
effective rake Arbeitsspanwinkel *m*
effective range Wirkbereich *m*
effective resistance Wirkwiderstand *m*
effective root diameter Fußnutzkreisdurchmesser *m*
effective throughput effektiver Durchsatz *m*
effective time Wirkzeit *f*
effective travel Wirkweg *m*
effectiveness Wirksamkeit *f*
effector Roboterwirkglied *nt*
efficacious wirksam
efficacy Wirksamkeit *f*
efficiency Aufnahmefähigkeit *f*, Wirkungsgrad *m*, Leistung *f*, Kapazität *f*, Tragfähigkeit *f*
efficiency calculation Wirtschaftlichkeitsrechnung *f*
efficient leistungsfähig, wirksam
effort Anstrengung *f*, Aufwand *m*
egg-shaped cross-section Eiquerschnitt *m*
egress 1. verlassen, aussteigen; Verlassen *nt* **2.** Abstieg *m* von
eight words-n bit memory Achtmal-n-Bit-Schreib-Lese-Speicher *m*
eject auswerfen, herausschleudern, wegfliegen, herausspritzen, ausstoßen
ejection Auswerfen *nt*, Herausschleu-

dern *nt*, Wegfliegen *nt*
ejection bush Ausdrückbuchse *f*
ejection plate spring Ausdrückplattenfeder *f*
ejector Auswerfer *m*, Auswurf *m*
ejector bush Ausdrückbuchse *f*
ejector bushing plate Ausdrückbuchsenplatte *f*
ejector plate Ausdrückplatte *f*
ejector system Auswerfersystem *nt*
elapse verstreichen, ablaufen
elapsed abgelaufen
elastic elastisch, dehnbar
elastic bending limit Federbiegegrenze *f*
elastic limit Streckengrenze *f*
elasticity Dehnbarkeit *f*
elasticity property Elastizitätseigenschaft *f*
elastoelectric elastoelektrisch
elastomechanical elastomechanisch
elastomer film Elastomerfolie *f*
elastomer floor covering Elastomerbodenbelag *m*
elastomer metal bond Elastomermetallbindung *f*
elastomer component Elastomerkörper *m*
elastomeric flexible polyvinylchloride dehnbares weiches Polyvinylchlorid *nt*
elastomers *pl* Elastomere *ntpl*
elbow Winkel *m*, Kniestück *nt*, Knie *nt*
elbow bulkhead fitting for butt joints Winkelschottstutzen *nt* in Stoßausführung
elbowtooth bogenverzahnt
electroplate galvanisieren
electric batterieelektrisch
electric air heater Elektrolufterhitzer *m*
electric arc furnace Lichtbogenofen *m*
electric charge elektrische Ladung *f*
electric circuit Stromkreis *m*
electric compressing Elektrostauchen *nt*
electric conductive substrate elektrisch leitendes Substrat *nt*
electric control system elektrische Steuerung *f*
electric current Strom *m*

electric device Stromverbraucher *m*
electric fencing Elektrozaun *m*
electric field elektrisches Feld *nt*
electric forklift truck Elektrostapler *m*
electric heating appliance Elektrowärmegerät *nt*
electric mains Netzanschluss *m*
electric monorail conveyor Elektrohängebahn *f*
electric monorail system (EMS) Elektrohängebahn *f*
electric motor Elektromotor *m*
electric power Anschlussleistung *f*, elektrische Energie *f*, Strom *m*
electric roughening elektrisches Aufrauen *nt*
electric shock elektrischer Schlag *m*
electric spraying Elektrospritzen *nt*
electric strength Spannungsfestigkeit *f*
electric stylus instrument elektrisches Tastschnittgerät *nt*
electric switch cabinet Elektroschaltschrank *m*
electric thread Elektrogewinde *nt*
electric truck Elektroflurförderzeug *nt*
electrical elektrisch
electrical contact elektrischer Kontakt *m*, Stromkontakt *m*
electrical contact face elektrische Kontaktfläche *f*
electrical engineering installation elektrotechnische Anlage *f*
electrical engineering product elektrotechnisches Erzeugnis *nt*
electrical equipment elektrische Ausrüstung *f*
electrical hazard elektrische Gefährdung *f*
electrical industrial facilities elektrische Betriebsmittel *f*
electrical installation elektrische Anlage *f*
electrical interlocking elektrische Verriegelung
electrical junctions elektrische Verbindungen *fpl*
electrical linear measurement elektrische Längenmessung *f*
electrical output signal elektrisches Ausgangssignal *nt*

electrical overloading elektrische Überlastung *f*
electrical pressboard Elektropressspan *m*
electrical processes elektrische Verfahren *ntpl*
electrical storage heater Elektrospeicher *m*
electrical system elektrische Anlage *f*
electrically driven elektrisch angetrieben
electrically erasable programmable read-only memory (EEPROM) elektrisch löschbarer programmierbarer Nur-Lese-Speicher *m*
electrically interlocked door Tür *f* mit elektrischer Sicherheitssperre
electrics Elektrik *f*
electro discharge machining Funkenerodieren *nt*
electro-magnetic compatibility (EMC) elektromagnetische Verträglichkeit (EMV) *f*
electro-acoustic measurement elektroakustische Messung *f*
electro-acoustic transducer elektroakustischer Wandler *m*
electro-chemical elektrochemisch
electro-chemical abrading elektrochemisches Abtragen *nt*
electrochemical coating elektrochemische Beschichtung *f*
electro-chemical corrosion elektrochemische Korrosion *f*
electrochemical corrosion protection elektrochemischer Korrosionsschutz *m*
electro-conducting material elektronenleitender Werkstoff *m*
electrode bracket assembly Elektrodenhalterung *f*
electrode indentation defect Elektrodeneindruckfehler *m*
electrode Elektrode *f*
electrode actuating mechanism Elektrodenantrieb *m*
electrode arc strike Elektrodenzündstelle *f*
electrode cap Elektrodenkappe *f*
electrode feed roller Elektrodenvorschubrolle *f*
electrode guide Elektrodenführung *f*
electrode holder and adapter Elektrodenhalterung *f*
electrode positing Galvanisation *f*
electrode reaction Elektrodenreaktion *f*
electrode surface area Elektrodenoberfläche *f*
electrode wheel bearing assembly Rollenlagerung *f*
electrode with alloyed core rod kernstablegierte Elektrode *f*
electrodeposit galvanisieren
electroerosion Elektroerosion *f*
electroform Galvanoplastik *f*
electroformed nickel galvanogeformter Nickel *m*
electroforming Galvanoformung *f*
electroforming plant Galvanoformungsanlage *f*
electro-luminescence screen Elektrolumineszenzschirm *m*
electrolyte Elektrolyt *nt*
electrolyte circulation Elektrolytumwälzung *f*
electrolyte container Elektrolytbehälter *m*
electrolyte density Elektrolytdichte *f*
electrolyte resistance Elektrolytwiderstand *m*
electrolytic abrading elektrolytisches Abtragen *nt*
electrolytic attack on the metal elektrolytischer Metallabtrag *m*
electrolytic corrosion elektrolytische Korrosion *f*
electrolytic grinding Elysierschleifen *nt*
electrolytic machining Elysieren *nt*
electrolytic milling Elysierfräsen *nt*
electrolytic mud Elektrolytschlamm *nt*
electrolytic oxidation reaction elektrolytische Oxidationsreaktion *f*
electrolytic plating bath Galvanisierbad *nt*
electrolytic reaction elektrolytische Reaktion *f*
electrolytic reduction reaction elektrolytische Reduktionsreaktion *f*

electrolytic turning Elysierdrehen *nt*
electrolytically tinned tinplate elektrolytisch verzinntes Weißblech *nt*
electromagnet Elektromagnet *m*
electromagnet filter Elektromagnetfilter *m*
electro-magnet head Elektromagnetkopf *m*
electro-magnetic elektromagnetisch
electro-magnetic brake Elektromagnetbremse *f*, elektromagnetische Lamellenbremse *f*
electromagnetic clutch Magnetkupplung *f*
electromagnetic dead stop method elektromagnetische Endpunktbestimmung *f*
electro-magnetic interference elektromagnetische Beeinflussung *f*
electro-mechanical elektromechanisch
electron acceptor Elektronennehmer *m*
electron beam Elektronenstrahl *m*
electron beam lithography Elektronenstrahllithographie *f*
electron beam machining Elektronenstrahlbearbeitung *f*
electron beam plant Elektronenstrahlanlage *f*
electron beam weld Elektrodenstrahlschweißnaht *f*
electron radiator Elektronenstrahler *m*
electron-conducting solid elektronenleitender Festkörper *m*
electronic control box Schaltschrank *m*
electronic copying system Nachformsystem *nt*
electronic current transducer elektronsicher Stromwandler *m*
electronic handwheel elektronisches Handrad *nt*
electronic measuring equipment Messelektronik *f*
electronic motor Elektronikmotor *m*
electrochemical manufacture (ECM) elektrochemische Fertigung *f*
electroplating of plastics Kunststoffgalvanisierung *f*

electroplating Galvanisieren *nt*, Galvanisation *f*
electroplating bath Galvanisierbad *nt*
electroplating drum Galvanisiertrommel *f*
electroplating process Galvanisierverfahren *nt*
electroplating shop Galvanisierwerkstatt *f*
electroplating tank Galvanisierwanne *f*
electro-sensitive elektrosensitiv
electrosensitive protection device trennende Schutzeinrichtung *f*
electrostatic elektrostatisch
electrostatic air filter Elektroluftfilter *m*
electrostatic charge elektrostatische Aufladung *f*
electrostatic charges Ableitfähigkeit *f*
electrostatic discharge Entladung *f* statischer Elektrizität
electrostatic precipitator elektrostatischer Abscheider *m*
electrostatic sensitive devices elektrostatisch gefährdete Bauteile *ntpl*
electrotyping Galvanoplastik *f*
element Element *nt*, Glied *nt*, Teil *nt*, Bauteil *nt*, Bestimmungsstück *nt*, Bestimmungsgröße *f*
element dimension Teileabmessung *f*
element form Teileform *f*
element of the mast structure Hubgerüstelement *nt*
element of the workpiece geometry Formelement *nt* des Werkstückes
element with equal interval timing Glied *nt* mit Zeitrasterung
element with two-level action Glied *nt* mit Zweipunktverhalten
elementary function Grundfunktion *f*
elementary particle reaction Elementarteilchenreaktion *f*
elephant machine tool Schwerstwerkzeugmaschine *f*
elevatable anhebbar
elevate erhöhen, heben, hochheben, anheben
elevated angehoben
elevated operator position angehobe-

ner Fahrerplatz *m*
elevated temperature age hardening Warmauslagern *nt*
elevating anhebbar, hebbar; Heben *nt*
elevating driver position hebbarer Fahrerplatz *m*
elevating mechanism Höhenverstellung *f*
elevating operator's position hebbarer Fahrerplatz *m*, angehobener Fahrerplatz *m*
elevating pier Hubsäule *f*
elevating platform Hubtisch *m*
elevating slide Anhebeschlitten *m*
elevation Anheben *nt*, Erhöhung *f*, Überhöhung *f*
elevation of the building Gebäudeschnitt *m*
elevator Hebezeug *nt*, Senkrechtförderer *m*, Aufzug *m*
eleven-disc pack Elfplattenstapel *m*
eliminate aufheben, beseitigen, wegnehmen, entfernen
elimination Eliminierung *f*, Beseitigung *f*, Ausschaltung *f*
elimination of damages Schadensabwendung *f*
elimination of fault Entstörung *f*
elliptic elliptisch
elliptical image Ellipsenaufnahme *f*
elongate dehnen, längen, ausdehnen, verlängern, strecken, recken
elongated projection Langbuckel *m*
elongated weld gestreckte Naht *f*
elongating Dehnen *nt*, Dehnung *f*, Längendehnung *f*, Vordehnung *f*
elongation Verlängerung *f*
elongation after fracture Bruchdehnung *f*
elongation at break Reißdehnung *f*
elongation at failure Bruchdehnung *f*, Reißdehnung *f*
elongation at fracture of reduced-section specimen Kerbbruchdehnung *f*
elongation at maximum load Dehnung *f* bei Höchstkraft
elongation at yield stress Dehnung *f* bei Streckspannung
elongation due to bending Biegedehnung *f*
elongation due to tearing Reißdehnung *f*
elongation piece Verlängerungsstück *nt*
eluate Eluat *nt*, Elutionsmittel *nt*
elute eluieren
embankment pipeline Dammleitung *f*
embed einbetten, integrieren
embed in concrete einbetonieren
embedded integriert, eingebaut, eingebettet
embedding coating Einbettungsüberzug *m*
embody verkörpern
emboss hochprägen, hohlprägen, prägen
emboss coder Prägecodierer *m*
embossing Prägung *f*, Hochprägen *nt*
embossing with lead/moulding cement Hohlprägen *nt* mit Blei/Treibkitt
embossing with rubber pad Hohlprägen *nt* mit Gummikissen, Prägen *nt* mit Gummikissen
embrace umfassen, umklammern
emerge austreten
emerging piece Ausfallteil *nt*
emergency brake Notbremse *f*, Sicherheitsbremse *f*
emergency braking Notbremsung *f*
emergency braking system Notbremssystem *nt*
emergency braking to stop Not-Aus-Stoppbremsung *f*
emergency chimney Notschornstein *m*
emergency circuit Notschaltung *f*
emergency control position Notsteuerstand *m*
emergency control stand Notsteuerstand *m*
emergency cutout Notausschalter *m*
emergency device Notfalleinrichtung *f*
emergency disconnection Notabschaltung *f*
emergency egress Notabstieg *m*
emergency exit Notausgang *m*, Notausstieg *m*
emergency knockout *(bei Gefahr)* Ausschalttaste *f*

emergency lighting Notbeleuchtung *f*
emergency lowering Notabsenkung *f*
emergency lowering control Notabsenkung *f*
emergency maintenance fehlerlos
emergency operating system Notbetriebseinrichtung *f*
emergency operation Notbetrieb *m*
emergency operation strategy Notbetriebsstrategie *f*
emergency power generation set Notstromaggregat *nt*
emergency running property Notlaufeigenschaft *f*
emergency shutdown Notabschaltung *f*
emergency shutdown system Notabschaltsystem *nt*
emergency situation Notfall *m*
emergency stop Notstoppeinrichtung *f*, Nothalteinrichtung *f*, Not-Aus *nt*, Nothalt *m*
emergency stop button Notschalter *m*
emergency stop circuit Not-Aus-Kreis *m*
emergency stop command Not-Aus-Befehl *m*
emergency stop device Not-Aus-Einrichtung *f*
emergency stop equipment Not-Aus-Einrichtung *f*
emergency stop order Not-Aus-Befehl *m*
emergency stopping device Notstoppeinrichtung *f*, Nothalteinrichtung *f*
emergency strategy Notfallstrategie *f*, Notstrategie *f*
emergency switch Gefahrenschalter *m*, Notschalter *m*
emergency switch off Notbefehlseinrichtung *f*
emery Schmirgel *m*
emission Emission *f*, Störaussendung *f*
emission limit Emissionsgrenzwert *m*
emission loss Leistungseinbuße *f*
emission of quanta Quantenemission *f*
emission sound pressure level Emissionsschalldruckpegel *m*
emissions Abgase *ntpl*
emissive power Strahlungsleistung *f*

emit aussenden, austreten, ausstrahlen, abstrahlen, senden
emit rays Strahlen aussenden
emit sparks Funken sprühen
emitted interference Störaussendung *f*
emitter Sender *m*, Strahler *m*
emitter receiver light scanner Sender-Empfänger-Lichttaster *m*
empirical standard deviation empirische Standardabweichung *f*
empirical distribution function empirische Verteilungsfunktion *f*
employ verwenden, benutzen, beschäftigen, anwenden
employ cutting speeds Schnittgeschwindigkeiten verwenden
employee Mitarbeiter *m*
employee hour Mitarbeiterstunde *f*
employment Einsatz *m*, Anwendung *f*, Verwendung *f*
empties Leergut *nt*
empty entleeren, schütten, entladen, leeren, unbeladen, leer
empty compartment Leerfach *nt*
empty container Leerbehälter *m*, Leergebinde *nt*
empty container handler Leercontainerstapler *m*
empty containers Leergut *nt*
empty drum Leergebinde *nt*
empty pallet Leerpalette *f*
empty pallet magazine Leerpalettenmagazin *nt*
empty pallets delivery Leerpalettenanlieferung *f*
empty running Leerfahrt *f*
empty trip Leerfahrt *f*
emptying under suction Leersaugen *nt*
emulsifiable emulgierbar
emulsifier Emulgierzusatz *m* zu Öl
emulsifying apparatus Emulgiergerät *nt*
emulsifying cylinder Emulgierzylinder *m*
enable ermöglichen, berechtigen, befähigen, freigeben
enabling Freigabe *f*
enabling input vorbereitender Eingang *m*

engagement *(Gang)* Einlegen *nt*
encapsulate kapseln
encapsulated vergussgekapselt, gekapselt
encapsulation Kapselung *f*, Vergusskapselung *f*
encase ummanteln, kapseln
encasement Ummantelung *f*
encasing Ummantelung *f*
enhance erweitern
enhancement Erweiterung *f*
encircle umfassen, umgeben, einschließen
enclose umschließen, umzäunen, umwehren, überdachen
enclosed geschlossen, umschlossen, überdacht
enclosed cab geschlossene Kabine *f*
enclosed conductor system geschützte Schleifleitung *f*
enclosed scale thermometer Einschlussthermometer *nt*
enclosed structure geschlossene Bauweise *f*
enclosing guard Verkleidung *f*
enclosing in a tent Einzelten *nt*
enclosure Gehäuse *nt*, Kapselung *f*, Überdachung *f*
enclosure port Gehäuseanschluss *m*
encode codieren, verschlüsseln
encoder Encoder *m*, Codierer *m*, Geber *m*, Messgeber *m*
encoding Verschlüsselung *f*, Codierung *f*, Codieren *nt*
encoding prescription Bildungsvorschrift *f*
encompass umgreifen
encroach übergreifen
end Ende *nt*, Spitze *f*, Seite *f*, Stirn *f*, Stumpf *m*; enden, beenden
end block Maßbild *nt*, Maßblock *m*, Maßklötzchen *nt*, Parallelendmaß *nt*
end block gage Endmaß *nt*
end clearance Axialspiel *nt*
end clearance angle Freiwinkel *m*, Stirnfreiwinkel *m*
end connections Wickelkopf *m*
end customer Endkunde *m*
end cutting edge Stirnschneide *f*, Nebenschneide *f*

end distance Stirnabstand *m*, Vormaß *nt*
end effector Greiforgan *nt*
end face Stirnfläche *f*; abflächen
end face mill Walzenstirnfräser *m*
end flank Freifläche *f*
end flap Endlasche *f*
end flap carton closing machine Endlaschenfaltschachtelverschließmaschine *f*
end groove weld Stirnfugennaht *f*
end journal Stirnzapfen *m*
end load case packing machine Faltschachtelverpackungsmaschine *f* mit horizontaler Zuführung
end measure Maßbild *nt*, Maßblock *m*, Maßklötzchen *nt*, Endmaß *nt*, Parallelendmaß *nt*
end mill Schaftfräser *m*, Fingerfräser *m*, Stirnfräser *m*
end mill adapter Zwischenstück *nt* für Schaftfräser
end mill cutter Schaftfräser *m*
end milling Schaftfräsen *nt*, Stirnfräsen *nt*
end milling attachment Fingerfräseinrichtung *f*
end milling machine Endfräsmaschine *f*
end of aisle equipment Endhalteeinrichtung *f*
end of arm tooling *(allg. Bezeichnung für Industrieroboter-Werkzeuge)* Werkzeug am Ende des Roboter-Armes
end of block character Satzendezeichen *nt*
end of cutting Schneidenende *nt*
end of data (EOD) Datenende *nt*
end of program (EOP) Programmende *nt*
end of program module Bausteinende *nt*
end of rope Seiltrumm *nt*, Trumm *nt*
end of transmission Übertragungsende *nt*
end of work Arbeitsende *nt*
end point distillation Siedeendpunkt *m*
end position Endlage *f*
end position disconnection Endla-

genabschaltung *f*
end relief Freiflächenfase *f*
end relief angle Fasenfreiwinkel *m*, Stirnhinterschliffwinkel *m*
end ring Kurzschlussläuferring *m*
end stop Endhaltestelle *f*, Endanschlag *m*, Endbegrenzung *f*, Längsanschlag *m*
end stop device Endhalteeinrichtung *f*
end stroke device Endbegrenzungssystem *nt*
end support column Gegenständer *m*
end thrust axialer Druck *m*
end tooth Stirnzahn *m*
end value Endwert *m*
end windings Wickelkopf *m*
endanger gefährden
endangered point gefährdete Stelle *f*
endangering Gefährdung *f*
end-brazed carbide tool an der Stirn gelötetes Hartmetallwerkzeug *nt*
end-controlled von einem Ende aus gesteuert
end-cut single point tool Kopfmeißel *m*
end-cut tool Breitschlichtmeißel *m*, Kopfmeißel *m*
end-cutting in axialer Richtung schneidend, mit der Stirnseite schneidend
end-cutting finishing tool Schlichthobelmeißel *m*
end-distance hardness curve Stirnabstand-Härte-Kurve *f*
ending Beendigung *f*
ending tool Kuppendrehwerkzeug *nt*
endless conveyor Kreisförderer *m*
endless screw Schnecke *f*
end-lip angle Stirnkeilwinkel *m*
end-of transmission label Übertragungsendezeichen *nt*
end-of-range sensitivity Endempfindlichkeit *f*
endorsement Sichtvermerk *m*
end-position sensor Endlagenfühler *m*
endurance Standvermögen *nt*, Standzeit *f*
endurance limit Dauerfestigkeit *f*
endurance stress Dauerbeanspruchung *f*
endurance test Dauerversuch *m*, Dauerprüfung *f*
endwise in Achsrichtung *f*, axial
endwise horizontal container hochkant liegender Behälter *m*
endwise horizontal tank hochkant liegender Behälter *m*
endwise vertical container hochkant stehender Behälter *m*
endwise vertical tank hochkant stehender Behälter *m*
end-working tool slide Hauptwerkzeugschlitten *m*, Hauptschlitten *m*
enema Einlauf *m*
energetic energetisch
energize betätigen, erregen
energizing Betätigung *f*
energizing action Einschaltvorgang *m*
energizing current Erregerstrom *m*
energy Energie *f*
energy attenuation coefficient Energieschwächungskoeffizient *m*
energy averaging energetische Mitteilung *f*
energy carrier Energieträger *m*
energy consumption Energieverbrauch *m*
energy conversion coefficient Energieumwandlungskoeffizient *m*
energy converting Energie wandelnd
energy effect Energieeinwirkung *f*
energy flow Massenstrom *m*, Energiefluss *m*
energy flow diagram Sankey-Diagramm *nt*
energy incoupling Energieeinkopplung *f*
energy influence Energieeinwirkung *f*
energy input Energie einbringen
energy input per unit length Streckenenergie *f*
energy level Energieniveau *nt*
energy lock-out Energiesperre *f*
energy power Leistung *f*
energy produced by catching Fangenergie *f*
energy radiated Strahlungsleistung *f*
energy requirement Energiebedarf *m*
energy saving Energie sparend
energy source Energiequelle *f*
energy storage mechanism Energie-

speicher *m*
energy supply Energieversorgung *f*
energy supply chain Energieführungskette *f*
energy surge Stoßspannung *f*
energy switch Energieschalter *m*, Kraftschalter *m*
energy system electronics engineer Energieanlagenelektroniker *m*
energy transfer medium Energieträger *m*
energy transformation coefficient Energieabsorptionskoeffizient *m*
energy expended aufgewandte Arbeit *f*
enfold umschlingen
engage eingreifen, rasten, einrasten, einrücken, einfahren, kuppeln, einlegen, einschalten, schalten, ineinander greifen, fassen, aufnehmen
engage in einstecken
engage the brake Bremse anlegen
engage the clutch einkuppeln
engage the transmission Gang einlegen
engaged eingelegt, eingerastet, eingeschaltet, im Eingriff
engagement Eingriff *m*, Einrückung *f*, Schaltung *f*, Ineinandergreifen *nt*, Wirksamwerden *nt*
engagement factor Überdeckungsgrad *m*
engagement index Eingriffsgröße *f*
engagement region Eingriffsgebiet *nt*
engaging Einrasten *nt*, Aufnehmen *nt*, Festhalten *nt*, Einrücken *nt*, Fassen *nt*
engaging and disengaging schaltbar
engaging and disengaging clutch schaltbare Kupplung *f*
engaging dog Mitnehmerklaue *f*
engine Verbrennungsmaschine *f*, Verbrennungsmotor *m*, Motor *m*, Kraftmaschine *f*
engine compartment Motorraum *m*
engine cylinder Motorzylinder *m*
engine lathe Zug- und Leitspindeldrehmaschine *f*, Leit- und Zugspindeldrehmaschine *f*, Spitzendrehmaschine *f* mit Leitspindel
engine lubricating oil Motorenschmieröl *nt*

engine-powered mit Verbrennungsmotor
engine torque Motordrehmoment *nt*
engineering Maschinenwesen *nt*, Technik *f*
engineering data Dokumentation *f*
engineering department Konstruktionsabteilung *f*
engineering drawing Konstruktionszeichnung *f*, technische Zeichnung *f*
engineering drawings *pl* technische Zeichnungen *fpl*
engineering precision measurement Feinmesswesen *nt*
engineering science Technik *f*
engineering service *m* technischer Dienst *m*
engineering specialist Fachingenieur *m*
engineer's square *(Werkzeug)* Winkel *m*
angle of slope Neigungswinkel *m*
English thread Zollgewinde *nt*
engrave gravieren
engraved eingeprägt
engraved text Walzaufschrift *f*
engraving cutter Gravierfräser *m*
engraving machine Graviermaschine *f*
engraving miller Gravierfräsmaschine *f*
enlace umschlingen
enlacement Umschlingung *f*
enlarge ausbauen, erweitern, aufbeulen, aufweiten
enlargement Ausbau *m*, Erweiterung *f*
enlargement of the original Originalvergrößerung *f*
enquire abfragen, anfragen
enquiry Abfrage *f*, Anfrage *f*
enrich anreichern
enrichment Anreicherung *f*
ensure sicherstellen, gewährleisten, garantieren
ensure constancy Konstanthalten *nt*
entanglement Erfassung *f*
entangle verwickeln, erfassen, umschlingen
entangle with *(Kabel)* überfahren
entangled chip Wirrspan *m*
entanglement Überfahren *nt*, Verwicklung *f*

entangling Verwickeln *nt*
enter eintragen, eingeben, einlaufen, einfahren, einführen, betreten, eindringen
enter key Eingabetaste *f*
enter the cut anschneiden
entering Betreten *nt*, Einfahren *nt*
entering and leaving Ein- und Ausfahren *nt*
entering angle Einstellwinkel *m*
entering end Anschnittseite *f*
enterprise Unternehmen *nt*
entire vollständig, gesamt, ganz
entire system Gesamtanlage *f*
entireness Vollständigkeit *f*
entity Einheit *f*, Entität *f*
entrain mitnehmen, mitführen
entrainment Mitführen *nt*, Mitnahme *f*
entrance Zustieg *m*, Zutritt *m*, Zugang *m*, Eintritt *m*, Eingang *m*
entry Einbuchung *f*, Buchung *f*, Eintragung *f*, Einlauf *m*, Einfahrt *f*, Eingabe *f*, Zugang *m*, Einschleusstelle *f*, Einfahren *nt*
entry and exit Ein- und Auslauf *m*
entry and exit point Ein- und Auslaufstelle *f*
entry angle Einfahrwinkel *m*
entry clearance Eintrittsspiel *nt*, Einfahrmaß *nt*
entry conveyor Einlaufband *nt*
entry data Eingabedaten *pl*
entry dimension Einfahrmaß *nt*
entry distance Einfahrweg *m*
entry event Buchungsvorgang *m*
entry field Eingabefeld *nt*
entry guidance Einführungszentrierung *f*
entry in a drawing Zeichnungseintragung *f*
entry opening Einsteigöffnung *f*
entry permit Passierschein *m*
entry pilot Einführeinsatz *m*, Einführzapfen *m*
entry point Einlaufstelle *f*, Einlauföffnung *f*, Einlauf *m*
entry taper *(bei Muffen)* Einführkonus *m*
entry unit Eingabegerät *nt*
envelop umhüllen, einwickeln

envelope Mantel *m*
envelope line Mantellinie *f*
envelope resistance Umhüllungswiderstand *m*
envelope surface Mantelfläche *f*
enveloping body diameter Toleranz *f* des größten Durchmessers
enveloping cut Hüllschnitt *m*
enveloping line Hülllinie *f*
enveloping machine Einwickelmaschine *f*
enveloping surface Hüllfläche *f*
enveloping surface method Hüllflächenverfahren *nt*
enveloping worm wheel Globoidschneckenrad *nt*
environ umgeben
environment Umfeld *nt*, Umgebung *f*, Umwelt *f*
environmental circumstances Umweltbedingungen *fpl*
environmental condition Umgebungsbedingung *f*
environmental conditions Umfeldbedingungen *pl*, Umweltbedingungen *fpl*
environmental correction Umgebungskorrektur *f*
environmental hazard gefahrbringende Umgebung *f*
environmental influence Umgebungseinfluss *m*
environmental influences Umgebungseinflüsse *mpl*, Umwelteinflüsse *f*
environmental parameter Umwelteinflussgröße *f*
environmental protection Umweltschutz *m*
environmental stresses *pl* Umweltbelastung *f*
environmental test procedure Umweltprüfverfahren *nt*
envisage erwarten
envisaged weld vorgesehene Schweißung *f*
epicyclic gear Umlaufrad *nt*
epicyclic transmission Planetengetriebe *nt*
epicycloid Epizykloid *m*, Radlinie *f*
epicycloidal gear train Umlaufgetriebezug *m*, Planetengetriebezug *m*

epoxy compound Epoxidverbindung f
epoxy epoxidisch
epoxy group Epoxygruppe f
epoxy resin moulding material Epoxidharzformmasse f, Epoxidharzpressmasse f
e-procurement elektronische Beschaffung f
Epstein square Epstein-Rahmen m
depth crowning Höhenballigkeit f
equipment engineering Gerätetechnik f
equal gleichmäßig, gleich
equal angle cutter Prismenfräser m
equal distribution Gleichverteilung f
equal-handed flanks pl gleichnamige Zahnflanken fpl
equal-interval timing Zeitrasterung f
equality Gleichheit f
equalize ausgleichen, angleichen
equalizing attachment Aufteileinrichtung f
equalizing charging Ausgleichsladen nt
equalizing lapping Passläppen nt
equally spaced gleichmäßiger Abstand m, abstandsgleich
equate gleichsetzen
equation Gleichung f, Ausdruck m, Formel f
equation between quantities Größengleichung f
equidistant äquidistant, gleich weit entfernt
equidistant lines pl Linien fpl im gleichen Abstand, gleichabständige Linien fpl
equidistant path äquidistante Bahn f
equidistant section Äquidistanzschnitt m
equilibration Gewichtausgleich m
equip einrichten, ausrüsten, ausstatten, versehen, anbringen
equipment Ausrüstung f, Ausstattung f, Anlage f, Einrichtung f, Zurüstung f, Betriebsmittel nt, Gerät nt, Apparatur f, Vorrichtung f
equipment class Betriebsmittelklasse f
equipment data Betriebsmitteldaten pl

equipment for leisure Freizeitgeräte $ntpl$
equipment model Betriebsmittelmodell nt
Equipment Safety Law Gerätesicherheitsgesetz nt
equipment switch Geräteschalter m
equipment under control Steuerungsobjekt nt, Regelungsobjekt nt
equipment under test (EUT) Prüfling m
equipotential bonding Potentialausgleich m
equipotential bonding bus bar Potentialausgleichsschiene f
equipotential bonding system Potentialausgleichsanlage f
equipotential factor Potentialfaktor m
equivalence Äquivalenz f
equivalent Entsprechung f
equivalent cylindrical gear teeth Ersatzstirnradverzahnung f
equivalent grinding wheel radius äquivalenter Schleifscheibenradius m
equivalent load Ersatzlast f
equivalent mass Ersatzmasse f
equivalent reference circle diameter Ersatzteilkreisdurchmesser m
equivalent spur gear teeth Ersatzgeradverzahnung f
equivalent spur gear tooth system Ersatzgeradverzahnung f
equivalent system Ersatzsystem nt
equivalent tooth system Ersatzverzahnung f
equivalent tooth thickness half angle Ersatzzahndickenhalbwinkel m
equivalent value Gleichwert m
erasable löschbar
erasable programmable read only memory (EPROM) löschbarer programmierbarer Nur-Lese-Speicher m
erase löschen
erect zusammenbauen, aufrichten, errichten, montieren, aufstellen
erecting machine Aufrichtmaschine f
erection Aufbau m, Aufstellung f, Montage f, Zusammenbau m, Aufrichten nt
erection accuracy Montagegenauigkeit f

erection crane Montagekran *m*
erection scaffold Montagegerüst *nt*
erection tolerance Montagetoleranz *f*
erection work Montagearbeiten *fpl*
ergonomic ergonomisch
ergonomics Ergonomie *f*
ergonomic design ergonomische Gestaltung *f*
erode abtragen, erodieren, anfressen, zerfressen
eroding Erodieren *nt*, Abtragen *nt*; erodierend
eroding machine Erodieranlage *f*
eroding process Erodierverfahren *nt*
eroding speed Erodiergeschwindigkeit *f*
eroding tool Erodierwerkzeug *nt*
erosion Abtragung *f*, Erosion *f*
erosion front Erosionsfront *f*
erosion test Erosionsprüfung *f*
erosive erodierend
error Fehler *m*, Abweichung *f*
error checking number *(EDV)* Prüfziffer *f*
error compensation Fehlerkompensation *f*
error detecting code prüfbarer Code *m*
error due to inertia forces trägheitsbedingter Fehler *m*
error-free störungsfrei, fehlerfrei
error-free component abweichungsfreies Bauteil *nt*
error-free gear fehlerfreies Zahnrad *nt*
error identification Fehlererkennung *f*
error in concentricity Rundlauffehler *m*
error in focusing Einstellfehler *m*
error in operation Bedienungsfehler *m*
error in service Bedienungsfehler *m*
error limit propagation Fehlergrenzenfortpflanzung *f*
error limits in error limit propagation Fehlergrenzenfortpflanzung *f*
error of coaxiality Koaxialitätsabweichung *f*
error of measurement Messabweichung *f*
error of result Ergebnisabweichung *f*
error of the division Teilungsfehler *m*
error of the first kind Fehler *m* erster Art
error on straightness Geradheitsabweichung *f*
error pattern Fehlerverlauf *m*
error process Fehlprozess *m*
error propagation law Fehlerfortpflanzungsgesetz *nt*
error rate Fehlerrate *f*
error signal Fehlersignal *nt*
error tolerance Fehlertoleranz *f*
error trace Fehlerbild *nt*, Fehlerlinie *f*
error treatment Fehlerbehandlung *f*
escape Flucht *f*, Entkommen *nt*, Fluchtweg *m*, Undichtheit *f*; entweichen
escape of chips Spanabfluss *m*
escape passage Fluchtweg *m*
escape provision Fluchtmöglichkeit *f*
escape route Rettungsweg *m*, Fluchtweg *m*
essential sachlich
establish aufstellen
ester oil Esteröl *nt*
ester-like esterartig
aesthetics Ästhetik *f*
estimate überschlägige Berechnung *f*, Schätzfunktion *f*, Schätzung *f*, Annahme *f*; schätzen
estimate of operating economy Wirtschaftlichkeitsrechnung *f*
estimate value Schätzwert *m*
estimating ability Schätzvermögen *nt*
estimation Schätzung *f*, Abschätzung *f*, Kostenvoranschlag *m*
estimation error Schätzfehler *m*
estimation interval Schätzungsintervall *m*, Schätzbereich *m*
estimator Schätzfunktion *f*
etch ätzen, abätzen
etching Ätzen *nt*
etching off Abätzen *nt*
Euclidian euklidisch
Euro flat pallet Euroflachpalette *f*
Euro pallet Europalette *f*
evacuate evakuieren, ein Vakuum erzeugen
evacuated luftleer
evacuation Evakuierung *f*
evacuation channel Evakuierkanal *m*
evaluate bewerten, auswerten, ermitteln

evaluation Auswertung *f*, Beurteilung *f*, Bewertung *f*, Ermittlung *f*, Abschätzung *f*
evaluation diagram Auswertdiagramm *nt*
evaluation form Auswertungsbogen *m*
evaluation formula Auswertformel *f*
evaluation logic Auswertelogik *f*
evaluation method Auswerteverfahren *nt*, Auswertungsverfahren *nt*
evaluation of bids Angebotsbewertung *f*
evaluation procedure Auswertungsverfahren *nt*
evaluation software Auswertungssoftware *f*
evaluation unit Auswerteeinheit *f*
evaporate verdunsten, verdunsten lassen
evaporate ageing procedure Verdunstungsbeanspruchung *f*
evaporating material Verdampfungsgut *nt*
evaporation Verdampfung *f*, Verdunstung *f*
evaporation crucible Verdampfungstiegel *m*
evaporation meter Verdunstungsmesser *m*
evaporation of oil Ölverdampfung *f*
even gerade, glatt, eben, flach, gleichmäßig
even element Geradeglied *nt*
even number gerade Zahl *f*
even numbers of teeth geradzahlige Zähnezahlen
evenly spaced abstandsgleich
evenness Ebenheit *f*
event Ereignis *nt*
event causing damage schädigendes Ereignis *nt*
event management Ereignisverwaltung *f*
event of a fire Brandfall *m*
event of catching Fangfall *m*
event of damage Schadensfall *m*
event of fault Störfall *m*, Fehlerfall *m*
event of loss Schadensfall *m*
event-driven ereignisgesteuert
evenly distributed gleichmäßig verteilt

event-oriented ereignisorientiert
events log Meldeprotokoll *nt*
evidence Nachweis *m*
ex stock ab Lager
exact genau, präzise
exactness 1. *(Fehler)* Genauigkeit *f*, Richtigkeit *f* **2.** *(Zeit)* Pünktlichkeit *f*
examination Überprüfung *f*, Prüfung *f*, Untersuchung *f*
examination centre Untersuchungsstelle *f*
examination of sludge Schlammuntersuchung *f*
examination of weakest points Schwachstellenanalyse *f*
examination report Untersuchungsbericht *m*
examine überprüfen, prüfen, untersuchen
examining authorities Prüfamt *nt*
excavate ausheben
excavation Aushub *m*
excavation of trench Grabenaushub *m*
exceed überschreiten, übersteigen
exceedance Überschreitung *f*
exceeding Überschreitung *f*
excess Überschuss *m*, Auswuchs *m*; überschüssig, übermäßig
excess air adjuster Luftüberschusseinsteller *m*
excess consumption Mehrverbrauch *m*
excess current Überlaststrom *m*
excess feed Übervorschub *m*
excess load Überlast *f*
excess of demand Nachfrageüberhang *m*
excess pressure Überdruck *m*
excess quantity Übermenge *f*
excess temperature Übertemperatur *f*
excess voltage Überspannung *f*
excess weight Überlast *f*
excess-current switch Überlastschalter *m*
excessive übermäßig
excessive force Überlastung *f*
excessive length Überlänge *f*
excessive roll-over Schweißgutüberlauf *m*
excessive strain Überbeanspruchung *f*

excessive stress Überbeanspruchung *f*
exceptional case Ausnahmefall *m*
exchange austauschen, tauschen, vertauschen, ersetzen, wechseln, auswechseln; Austausch *m*, Tausch *m*, Wechsel *m*
exchange battery Wechselbatterie *f*
exchange of drawings Zeichnungsaustausch *m*
exchange pallet Tauschpalette *f*
exchangeability Tauschfähigkeit *f*, Austauschbarkeit *f*
exchangeable austauschbar, auswechselbar
exchangeable container Wechselbehälter *m*
excitation Erregung *f*
excitation amplitude Erregungsamplitude *f*
excitation of vibrations Schwingungserregung *f*
excite erregen
exciting current Erregerstrom *m*
exciting winding Erregerwicklung *f*
exclude ausschließen
exclusion air Luftabschluss *m*
exclusive NOR Exklusiv-NOR *nt*
exclusive OR Exklusiv-ODER *nt*
executable ablauffähig
execute durchführen, ausführen, ausüben
execution Ausführung *f*, Durchführung *f*
execution button Ausführungstaste *f*
execution deadline Durchführungstermin *m*
execution of the inspection Abnahmedurchführung *f*
execution of the weld Schweißausführung *f*
execution planning Ausführungsplanung *f*
execution programming Ablaufprogrammierung *f*
execution time Ausführungszeit *f*, Durchführungszeit *f*
executive control program Steuerprogramm *nt*
executive program Betriebsprogramm *nt*, Steuerungssoftware *f*

exercise ausführen
exert an influence upon Einfluss ausüben
exert effect auswirken auf
exert upon ausüben
exfoliation Aufblätterung *f*, Delaminierung *f*
exhaust entleeren
exhaust *(Fahrzeug, Maschine)* Auspuff *m*
exhaust emission Abgasemission *f*
exhaust gas Abgas *nt*
exhaust gas cooler Abgaskühlvorrichtung *f*
exhaust gas flue Abgaskanal *m*
exhaust gas hood Abgasabzug *m*
exhaust gas offtake Abgasabzug *m*
exhaust gas purifier Abgasreiniger *m*
exhaust line Rückflussleitung *f*
exhaust system Abgassystem *nt*, Absauganlage *f*
exigence Notwendigkeit *f*
Eximer angeregtes Molekül *nt*
existence Vorhandensein *nt*
existing vorhanden
exit 1. Ausgang *m*, Abgang *m*, Ende *nt*, Ausfahrt *f*, Auslauf *m*, Abflussöffnung *m*, Ausstieg *m*; aussteigen
exit point Auslaufstelle *f*
exited dimer *(Eximer)* angeregtes Molekül *nt*
EX-OR Exklusiv-ODER *nt*
expand ausbauen, erweitern, aufweiten, weiten, aufbeulen, spreizen, dehnen, ausdehnen
expand by means of a mandrel aufdornen
expandable ausbaubar
expanded metal Streckmetall *nt*
expanded range gespreizter Bereich *m*
expanded synthetic resin Kunstharzschaum *m*
expanded T-piece Einwalz-T-Stück *nt*
expanding Aufweitrecken, Aufweiten *nt*, Weiten *nt*
expanding adhesive film Expansionsklebfolie *f*
expanding by detonation of explosives Weiten *nt* durch Sprengstoffdetonation

expanding by effect of a magnetic field Weiten *nt* durch Einwirkung eines Magnetfeldes
expanding by electric discharge Weiten *nt* durch elektrische Entladung
expanding by spark discharge Weiten *nt* durch Funkenentladung
expanding by spinning Aufweiten *nt* durch Drücken, Weiten *nt* durch Drücken
expanding by temporary expansion of highly compressed gases Weiten *nt* durch kurzzeitige Entspannung hoch komprimierter Gase
expanding coil Expansionsspule *f*
expanding with action media Weiten *nt* mit Wirkmedien
expanding with action media with effect associated with energy Weiten *nt* mit Wirkmedien mit energiegebundener Wirkung
expanding with action media with effect associated with force Weiten *nt* mit Wirkmedien mit kraftgebundener Wirkung
expanding with active energy Weiten *nt* mit Wirkenergie
expanding with amorphous solids with effect associated with energy Weiten *nt* mit formlos festen Stoffen mit energiegebundener Wirkung
expanding with amorphous solids with effect associated with force Weiten *nt* mit formlos festen Stoffen mit kraftgebundener Wirkung
expanding with compliant tool Weiten *nt* mit nachgiebigem Werkzeug
expanding with gas pressure Weiten *nt* mit Gasdruck
expanding with gases Weiten *nt* mit Gasen
expanding with gases with effect associated with force Weiten *nt* mit Gasen mit kraftgebundener Wirkung
expanding with liquids with effect associated with energy Weiten *nt* mit Flüssigkeiten mit energiegebundener Wirkung
expanding with liquids with effect associated with force Weiten *nt* mit Flüssigkeiten mit kraftgebundener Wirkung
expanding with mandrel Weiten *nt* mit Dorn
expanding with rigid tool Weiten *nt* mit starrem Werkzeug
expanding with rubber punch Weiten *nt* mit Gummistempel
expanding with sand/steel balls Weiten *nt* mit Sand/Stahlkugeln
expanding with spreading tool Weiten *nt* mit Spreizwerkzeug
expanding with tools Weiten *nt* mit Werkzeugen
expanding with water bag Weiten *nt* mit Wasserbeutel
expanding with gases with effect associated with energy Weiten *nt* mit Gasen mit energiegebundener Wirkung
expansion Ausdehnung *f*, Dehnung *f*, Dehnen *nt*, Nachrüstung *f*, Erweiterung *f*, Ausbau *m*, Ausbreitung *f*
expansion apparatus Ausgleicher *m*
expansion arbor Spreizdorn *m*
expansion at fracture Bruchaufweitung *f*
expansion behaviour Ausdehnungsverhalten *nt*
expansion bellows joint Expansionsbalg *m*
expansion bend Dehnungsbogen *m*
expansion connector for valves Armaturenanschlussstück *nt*
expansion fitting Dehner *m*
expansion joint Ausdehnungsfuge *f*, Dehnungsfuge *f*, Längenausgleicher *m*
expansion kit Nachrüstsatz *m*
expansion pipe Ausdehnungsleistung *f*
expansion screw Stellschraube *f*
expansion tank with shut-off facility absperrbares Ausdehnungsgefäß *nt*
expansion tank without shut-off facility unabsperrbares Ausdehnungsgefäß *nt*
expansion trap Entspannungstopf *m*
expansion water Ausdehnungswasser *nt*
expectation value Erwartungswert *m*
expected erwartet

expected value Erwartungswert *m*
expediter Disponent *m*
expel ausstoßen
expend aufwenden
expendable part Verschleißteil *nt*, Wegwerfteil *nt*
expenditure Aufwand *m*
expenditure of work Arbeitsaufwand *m*
expenditure on inspection equipment Prüfaufwand *m*
expense Kostenaufwand *m*, Aufwand *m*
experience Praxis *f*, Erfahrung *f*
experience background Erfahrungshintergrund *m*
experienced fachgerecht
experiment Versuch *m*, Experiment *nt*, versuchen, experimentieren
experimental stage Versuchsstadium *nt*
expert Sachverständiger *m*, Sachkundiger *m*, sachkundig
expert knowledge Expertenwissen *nt*
expert pressure on Druck ausüben auf
expert system Expertensystem *nt*
expire auslaufen, ablaufen
expiry Ablauf *m*, Auslaufen *nt*
explanatory caption Hinweisüberschrift *f*
explode explodieren
profiler Nachformfräser *m*
explore abtasten, abstufen
explosion chamber Sprengkammer *f*
explosion hazard Explosionsgefahr *f*
explosion prevention and protection Explosionsschutz *m*
explosion protection Explosionsschutz *m*, Zündschutz *m*
explosion suppression Explosionsunterdrückung *f*
explosion train Explosionskette *f*
explosion-forming Explosionsumformung *f*
explosion-proof area Explosionsschutzbereich *m*
explosion-proof equipment Explosionsschutzausrüstung *f*
explosion-roof explosionsgeschützt
explosive explosiv, explosionsfähig; Sprengstoff *m*

explosive charge Sprengladung *f*
explosive gas atmosphere gasexplosionsgefährdeter Bereich *m*
explosive hazard Explosionsgefährlichkeit *f*
explosive risk Explosionsgefährlichkeit *f*
explosive stud Sprengbolzen *m*
explosive substance Explosivstoff *m*
exponent Exponent *m*
exponential distribution Exponentialverteilung *f*
exponential smoothing exponentielle Glättung *f*
expose aussetzen, freilegen
exposed herausstehend, ungeschützt, freiliegend
exposed radiator unverkleideter Heizkörper *m* (oder Radiator *m*)
exposed to radiation strahlenexponiert
exposure Aufnahme *f*, Aussetzung *f*, Einwirkung *f*
exposure conditions *pl* Belichtungsbedingungen *fpl*
exposure counter Aufnahmezähler *m*
exposure rate Belichtungsgröße *f*
exposure screen Aufnahmefolie *f*
exposure time Einschaltzeit *f*
exposure to corrosion Korrosionsbeanspruchung *f*
exposure to hazards Gefahrenaussetzung *f*
express delivery Expressdienst *m*
express order Eilauftrag *m*
expression Ausdruck *m*
expressive representation einprägsame Darstellung *f*
extend vorschieben, ausfahren, ausschieben, verlängern, längen, dehnen, ausdehnen (auf), strecke, herausragen, reichen, ausbauen, erweitern
extend into hineinreichen
extend over hinausragen über
extendable einschiebbar
extended ausgefahren
extended boss-type cutter Glockenschneidrad *nt*
extended coverage test Erweiterungsprüfung *f*
extended enterprise erweitertes Un-

ternehmen *nt*
extended NAND erweitertes NAND-Glied *nt*
extended of APT (Automatically Programmed Tools) EXAPT (Erweiterung automatischer Programmwerkzeuge *f*)
extender element Erweiterungsglied *nt*
extender function Erweiterungsfunktion *f*
extender resin Extenderharz *nt*
extending Dehnen *nt*, Strecken *nt*, herausragend
extending by stretching Längen *nt*
extending speed Ausfahrgeschwindigkeit *f*
extensible ausziehbar
extension Ausschub *m*, Dehnung *f*, Längendehnung *f*, Längenausdehnung *f*, Verlängerung *f*, Erweiterung *f*, Verbindungsteil *nt*, Hinausragen *nt*, Ausschieben *nt*, Ausbau *m*, Ausfahrt *f*, Ausfahren *nt*
extension and compression cycle Dehn-Stauchzyklus *m*
extension and retraction Ein- und Ausfahren *nt*
extension at break Dehnung *f* beim Reißen
extension block Erweiterungsfeld *nt*
extension input Erweiterungseingang *m*
extension insert bit Verbindungsteil *nt*
extension mast Teleskopmast *m*
extension piece Verlängerungsstück *nt*
extension pipe Erweiterungsleitung *f*
extension sensor Dehnungssensor *m*
extension sleeves Gabelverlängerung *f*
extension stage Ausbaustufe *f*
extension travel Ausfahrweg *m*
extension work Ausbauarbeiten *pl*
extensometer gauge length Gerätemesslänge *f*
extensometer Dehnungstaster *m*, Verlängerungsmessgerät *nt*, Längenmesseinrichtung *f*, Längenänderungsmessgerät *nt*
extent Ausmaß *nt*, Größe *f*, Maß *nt*, Umfang *m*, Grad *m*
extent of blistering Blasengrad *m*
extent of inspection Prüfumfang *m*
exterior rear-view mirror äußerer Rückspiegel *m*
external extern, äußere/r/s
external broach Außenräumwerkzeug *nt*
external broaching Außenräumen *nt*
external broaching machine Außenräummaschine *f*
external conductor Außenleiter *f*
external control Fremdüberwachung *f*
external cooling Fremdkühlung *f*
external current consumption Fremdstromanlage *f*
external cylindrical grinding Außenrundschleifen *nt*
external cylindrical lapping Außenrundläppen *nt*
external cylindrical lapping machine Außenrundläppmaschine *f*
external effect äußere Einwirkung *f*
external face grinding Außenplanschleifen *nt*
external facing Außenplandrehen *nt*
external fitting member Außenpassteil *nt*
external gear außen verzahntes Rad *nt*, Außenrad *nt*, Zahnrad *nt* mit Außenverzahnung
external gear pair Außenradpaar *nt*
external gear wheel Außenrad *nt*
external grinding Außenschleifen *nt*
external helical cylindrical gear außenverzahntes Schrägstirnrad *nt*
external helical gear teeth Außenschrägverzahnung *f*
external ignition Fremdzündung *f*
external key Fremdschlüssel *m*
external light Fremdlicht *nt*
external measurement Außenmessung *f*
external memory externer Speicher *m*
external micrometer Bügelmessschraube *f*
external part of the transmission Außengetriebeteil *nt*
external pressure Außendruck *m*
external pressure roll Außendruckrolle *f*
external source truck Flurförder-

zeug *nt* mit Fremdstromantrieb
external spraying Außenspritzung *f*
external straight cylindrical gear außenverzahntes Geradstirnrad *nt*
external straight spur gears *pl* außenverzahnte Geradstirnräder *ntpl*
external taper Außenkegel *m*
external thread Außengewinde *nt*
external thread grinder Außengewindeschleifmaschine *f*
external thread whirling Außenwirbeln *nt*
external tooth system Außenverzahnung *f*
external transmission Außengetriebe *nt*
external turning Außendrehen *nt*
externalize offen legen
externally cooled fremdgekühlt
externally soldered end Außenlötende *nt*
externally sourced fremdbezogen
externally toothed außenverzahnt
externally toothed bevel gear außenverzahntes Kegelrad *nt*
externally toothed central gear *(e. Umlauf-Getriebezuges)* außenverzahntes Zentralrad *nt*
externally toothed gear Außenzahnrad *nt*
externally toothed intermediate gear außenverzahntes Zwischenrad *nt*
externally toothed planet gear außenverzahntes Umlaufrad *nt*
externally toothed spur gear außenverzahntes Stirnrad *nt*
extinguish löschen
extra Sonderwunsch *m*
extra attachment Zusatzeinrichtung *f*
extra change Aufschlag *m*
extra equipment Sonderzubehör *nt*, Zusatzeinrichtung *f*, Zusatzausrüstung *f*, Sonderausstattung *f*
extra expenditure Mehraufwand *m*
extra price Mehrpreis *m*
extra space Zusatzfläche *f*
extract abrufen, ausziehen, ziehen, herausziehen, abführen
extract a root Wurzel ziehen aus
extractable ausziehbar, extrahierbar

extractable constituents extrahierbare Bestandteile *f*
extracted air Abluft *f*
extracted air cross-section Abluftquerschnitt *m*
extraction Ausziehen *nt*, Ziehen *nt*
extraction line Entnahmeleitung *f*
extraction of plasticiser Weichmacherextraktion *f*
extraction of steam Dampfentnahme *f*
extractor Ausziehwerkzeug *nt*, Abzieheinrichtung *f*
extractor air cut Abluftdurchlass *m*
extra-fine particle filter Feinststaubfilter *m*
extraneous ignition Fremdzündung *f*
extrapolation Hochrechnung *f*
extreme Extremsituation *f*
extreme of adjustment Endstellung *f*
extreme point of stroke Hubendlage *f*
extreme position Endstellung *f*, Endlage *f*
extreme table position Tischendstellung *f*
extreme value Extremwert *m*
extreme value distribution Extremwertverteilung *f*
extremely dirty schmutzintensiv
extremely dusty staubintensiv
extremity of fork arm Gabelzinkenspitze *f*
external thread turning Außengewindedrehen *nt*
extrudate Extrudat *nt*
extrude extrudieren, fließpressen, strangpressen
extruded aluminium section Aluminiumstrangpressprofil *nt*
extruder Extruder *m*
extruder barrel Extruderzylinder *m*
extruder screw Extruderschnecke *f*
extruder-screw channel Extruderschneckengang *m*
extruding Durchdrücken *nt*, Extrudieren *nt*
extrusion Extrusion *f*, Strangpressen *nt*, Fließdrücken *nt*, Fließpressen *nt*
extrusion cylinder Extrusionszylinder *m*
extrusion die Pressmatrize *f*

extrusion mixture Pressmasse f
extrusion moulding Extrudieren nt
extrusion of rods and tubes Strangpressen nt
extrusion ram Extrusionskolben m
extrusion-mould extrudieren
eye Öse f

eye level Augenhöhe f
eye protector Augenschutzgerät nt
eyelet Öse f
eyepiece micrometer Okularschraubenmikrometer m
eyepiece screw Okularschraube f

Ff

fabric based tape Gewebeband *nt*
fabric finish Gewebefinish *nt*
fabric finished with synthetic resin kunstharzausgerüstetes Gewebe *nt*
fabric layer Gewebeschicht *f*
fabric thread Gewebefaden *m*
fabric weave Gewebebindung *f*
fabricate fertigen, herstellen, erzeugen
fabrication Fertigung *f*, Herstellung *f*, Erzeugung *f*
fabrication by welding schweißtechnische Fertigung *f*
fabrication quality control Fertigungskontrolle *f*
fabrication time Auftragszeit *f*
fabric-filled moulding material Textilschnitzelpressmasse *f*
face 1. *(Fertigungsschritt)* abplanen, planarbeiten, planbearbeiten, planen, Stirnfläche *f* herstellen **2.** Planfläche *f*, Front *f*, Stirn *f*, Seite *f*, Fläche *f*, Frontseite *f*, Vorderseite *f*, Vorderfläche *f*, Stirnfläche *f*, Stirnseite *f*, Spanfläche *f*, Fassade *f* **3.** *(Beschichtung)* beschichten, Deckschichtebene *f*, Deckschicht *f* **4.** *(Verzahnungstechnik)* Zahnbrust *f* **5.** *(Drehen)* plandrehen, abdrehen
face angle Schneidenwinkel *m*, Komplementwinkel *m* des Einstellwinkels, Brustwinkel *m*, Radialwinkel *m*
face being built up Auftragfläche *f*
face bond Deckschichtklebung *f*
face cam Nutkurve *f*, Plankurve *f*
face copying Plannachformen *nt*
face cutter edge Stirnschneide *f*
face cutting edge Stirnschneide *f*
face gear Tellerrad *nt*
face grinder Planflachschleifmaschine *f*, Planschleifmaschine *f*, Schleifmaschine *f* zum Schleifen planer Flächen
face grinding Stirnschliff *m*, Planschleifen *nt*, Flachschleifen *nt*
face grinding attachment Planschleifeinrichtung *f*
face grinding machine Planschleifmaschine *f*, Flachschleifmaschine *f*

face grinding wheel Stirnschleifkörper *m*
face-ground formed milling cutter an der Spanfläche nachgeschliffener Formfräser *m*
face land Spanflächenfase *f*, Fase *f* an Stirnschneiden
face lapping Planläppen *nt*
face material Deckschichtwerkstoff *m*
face mill Stirnfräser *m*, Planfräser *m*
face milling Planfräsen *nt*, Flächenfräsen *nt*, Stirnfräsen *nt*, Stirnen *nt*, Walzstirnfräsen *nt*
face milling cutter Flächenfräser *m*, Stirnfräskopf *m*, Stirnfräser *m*, Planfräser *m*
face milling head Planfräskopf *m*
face milling operation Walzenstirnfräsen *nt*, Planfräsarbeit *f*
face milling work Planfräsarbeit *f*
face of a column Wange *f* eines Maschinenständers
face of butt weld Stoßflanke *f*
face of cutter tooth Fräserbrust *f*, Spanfläche *f* eines Fräserzahnes
face of the cut Schnittflanke *f*
face of the rack Regalseite *f*
face of the tooth Zahnflanke *f*
face plate Planscheibe *f*
face play Zahnflankenspiel *nt*
face profiling Plannachformen *nt*
face ride fasenartiger Anschliff *m* auf der Spanfläche
face slide Schieber *m*
face spanner Einsteckschlüssel *m*
face turning Plandrehen *nt*
face-centred flächenzentriert
face-grind anschleifen, planschleifen
face-milling and centring machine Abfläch- und Zentriermaschine *f*
face-plate lathe Drehwerk *nt*
faceplate pit Planscheibengrube *f*
face-turn plandrehen
facilitate erleichtern
facilitation Erleichterung *f*
facilities *pl* Einrichtungen *fpl*

facility Gebäude *nt*, Vorrichtung *f*, Einrichtung *f*
facility for prestressing Vorspannmöglichkeit *f*
facility management Haustechnik *f*
facility request Leistungsmerkmalanforderung *f*
facing 1. *(Fertigungsverfahren)* Plandreharbeit *f*, Planarbeit *f*, Planbearbeitung *f*, Planbearbeiten *nt* **2.** Beschichtung *f*, Belag *m*, Verkleidung *f* **3.** Blickrichtung *f* **4.** *(Fräsen)* Flächenfräsen *nt* **5.** *(Drehen)* Plandrehen *nt*
facing away form the mast mastabgewandt
facing away from the load Blickrichtung *f* entgegengesetzt zur Last
facing chip Plandrehspan *m*
facing cutter Stirnfräser *m*
facing dog Queranschlag *m*
facing finishing turning Planfeindrehen *nt*
facing lathe Kopfdrehmaschine *f*, Plandrehmaschine *f*
facing machine Plandrehmaschine *f*
facing material Schlichte *f*
facing operation 1. *(allg.)* Bearbeitung *f* einer Fläche, Planarbeit *f* **2.** *(Drehen)* Plandreharbeiten *fpl*
facing precision turning Planfeindrehen *nt*
facing slide Querschlitten *m*, Planschieber *m*
facing the aisle gangseitig
facing the mast mastzugewandt
facing tool Plandrehmeißel *m*
facing toolholder Plandrehmeißelhalter *m*
facing work Plandreharbeit *f*
facings Span *m*
facing-type milling cutter Stirnfräser *m*
factor Faktor *m*, Größe *f*
factor of evaluation Bewertungsgröße *f*
factor of influence Einflussgröße *f*
factor of location Standortfaktor *m*
factor table Faktortabelle *f*
factory Betrieb *m*, Fabrik *f*, Werk *nt*
factory accident Betriebsunfall *m*

factory comparison Betriebsvergleich *m*
factory computer Fabrikrechner *m*
factory data acquisition Betriebsdatenerfassung *f*
factory model Fabrikmodell *nt*
factory organization Betriebsorganisation *f*
factory own betriebseigen
factory planning Fabrikplanung *f*
factory premises Werksgelände *nt*
factory-made werkseitig hergestellt
fading stage Ausbleichungsstufe *f*
fail ausfallen, versagen, aussetzen
fail to observe give-way right Vorfahrt missachten
failing Ausknicken *nt*
fail-safe ausfallsicher, fehlersicher, versagenssicher
fail-safe principle Prinzip *nt* des sicheren Fehlverhaltens
fail-safe shutdown fehlersichere Abschaltung *f*
failure Fehler *m*, Versagen *nt*, Ausbleiben *nt*, Betriebsstörung *f*, Störung *f*, Störfall *m*, Ausfall *m*, Panne *f*, Bruch *m*, Zusammenbrechen *nt*, zusammenbrechen
failure analysis Schadensanalyse *f*
failure cause Ausfallursache *f*
failure caused by wear Verschleißausfall *m*
failure logging Störungsprotokollierung *f*
failure memory Störungsspeicher *m*
failure mode Schadensart *f*
failure of a flame Abreißen *nt* einer Brennerflamme
failure of power Energieausfall *m*
failure of the gear Getriebebruch *m*
failure of the hydraulic system Ölverlust *m*
failure of the mains voltage Netzspannungsausfall *m*
failure of the specimen Probenbruch *m*
failure quota Ausfallrate *f*
failure rate Ausfallrate *f*
failure-safe betriebssicher
faithfulness to deadlines Terminein-

haltung *f*
fall fallen, abstürzen, stürzen, sinken, herabfallen, herunterfallen (auf), abnehmen; Fall *m*, Absturz *m*, Sturz *m*, Abnahme *f*
fall arrestor *(Sicherheitstechnik)* Seilkürzer *m*
fall below unterschreiten
fall braking device Falldämpfer *m*
fall of voltage Spannungs(ab)fall *m*
fall-arrester gear Fallstopp *m*
falling Absturz *m*, herabfallend
falling ball test Kugelfallversuch *m*
falling dart test Pfeilfallversuch *m*
falling delay Ausschaltverzögerung *f*
falling hazard Absturzgefahr *f*
falling weight test Fallbolzenversuch *m*
false falsch
false jaw Aufsatzklaue *f*
false jaws *pl* Einsatzbacken *fpl*
falsify verfälschen
family of grooves Rillenschar *f*
family of numbers Nummerkreis *m*
family parameter Scharparameter *m*
fan Lüfter *m*, Gebläse *nt*, Ventilator *m*
fan belt Keilriemen *m*
fan impeller Ventilatorenlaufrad *nt*
fan out Ausgangslastfaktor *m*, Ausgangsbelastbarkeit *f*
fan power Lüfterleistung *f*
fan room Lüfterraum *m*
fan-assisted air heater Warmlufterzeuger *m*
fan-assisted burner Gebläsebrenner *m*
fan-cooled gebläsegekühlt
far field resolution Fernauflösungsvermögen *nt*
family of characteristics Kennlinienfeld *nt*
fast schnell
fast clutch nicht schaltbare Kupplung *f*
fast drive Schnelltrieb *nt*
fast motion Zeitraffer *m*
fast traverse Eilgang *m*
fast/slow speed switching time Umschaltzeit *f* von schneller zu langsamer Geschwindigkeit
fasten festhalten, befestigen, montieren, festmachen, anziehen

fasten by wedges verkeilen
fasten secure sichern, befestigen
fastener Befestigungselement *nt*, Befestigungsmittel *nt*, mechanisches Verbindungselement *nt*
fastening Befestigung *f*
fastening bolt Befestigungsschraube *f*
fastening dimensions *pl* Anschlagmaße *ntpl*
fastening element Verbindungselement *nt*, Verbindungsteil *nt*
fastening method Befestigungsart *f*
fastening pin Befestigungsstift *m*
fastening screw thread Befestigungsgewinde *nt*
fast-moving item Schnellläufer *m*
fast-moving items A-Sortiment *nt*
fastness of the finish to ironing Bügelechtheit *f*
fastness to acid spotting Säureechtheit *f*
fastness to bleaching with hypochloride Hypochloritbleichechtheit *f*
fastness to bleaching with peroxide Peroxidbleichechtheit *f*
fastness to bleaching with sodium chlorite Chloritbleichechtheit *f*
fastness to brightening *(Textilien)* Avivierechtheit *f*
fastness to bucking *(Textilien)* Beuchechtheit *f*
fastness to carbonizing Karbonisierechtheit *f*
fastness to cold vulcanizing Kaltvulkanisierechtheit *f*
fastness to cross-dyeing Überfärbungsechtheit *f*
fastness to degumming Entbastungsechtheit *f*
fastness to dry cleaning Trockenreinigungsechtheit *f*
fastness to dry-heat pleating Trockenhitzeplissierechtheit *f*
fastness to dry-heat setting Trockenhitzefixierechtheit *f*
fastness to fulling Walkechtheit *f*
fastness to hot water Heißwasserechtheit *f*
fastness to mercerizing Mercerisierechtheit *f*

fastness to nitrogen oxides Stickoxidechtheit *f*
fastness to organic solvents Lösungsmittelechtheit *f*
fastness to potting Pottingechtheit *f*
fastness to rubbing Reibechtheit *f*
fastness to soda boiling Sodakochechtheit *f*
fastness to steaming Dämpfechtheit *f*
fastness to vulcanizing in open steam Heißdampfvulkanisierechtheit *f*
fastness to vulcanizing with hot air Heißluftvulkanisierechtheit *f*
fastness to weathering Wetterechtheit *f*
fat-liquoring substance fettende Substanz *f*
fat liquors and greases for leather Lederfettungsmittel *nt*
fatigue crack Ermüdungsriss *m*
fatigue cracking Ermüdungsrissbildung *f*
fatigue failure Dauerbruch *m*
fatigue strength Dauerfestigkeit *f*
fatigue stress under fluctuating stress Zeitschwellfestigkeit *f*
fatigue test Dauerfestigkeitsversuch *m*
fatigue testing machine Schwingprüfmaschine *f*
fatigue Ermüdung *f*, ermüden
fatigue behaviour Dauerschwingverhalten *nt*
fatigue cycle Schwingspiel *nt*
fatigue limit strength value Dauerfestigkeitswert *m*
fatigue strength Ermüdungsgrenze *f*
fatigue strength for infinite time Dauerstandfestigkeit *f*
fatigue testing machine Dauerschwingprüfmaschine *f*
fastness to decatizing Dekaturechtheit *f*
fault Fehler *m*, Störung *f*, Fehlstelle *f*
fault access tree Fehlersuchbaum *m*
fault analysis Fehleranalyse *f*
fault bypassing Fehlerumgehung *f*
fault condition Fehlerbedingung *f*
fault current Fehlerstrom *m*
fault current breaker FI-Schutz *m*
fault detection Fehlererkennung *f*

fault diagnosis Fehlerdiagnose *f*
fault duration Störungsdauer *f*
fault elimination Fehlerbeseitigung *f*, Störungsbeseitigung *f*
fault exclusion Fehlerausschluss *m*
fault finding Fehlersuche *f*
fault in the fabric Gewebefehler *m*
fault indication Fehlermeldung *f*
fault indicator Fehlerzählgerät *nt*, Störungsmelder *m*
fault liability Störanfälligkeit *f*
fault localization Schadenlokalisierung *f*
fault log Störungsbuch *nt*
fault message Störungsmeldung *f*, Fehlermeldung *f*
fault monitoring Fehlerverfolgung *f*
fault plan Störplan *m*
fault probability Fehlerwahrscheinlichkeit *f*
fault recording Störungsprotokollierung *f*
fault repair Fehlerbeseitigung *f*
fault report Störungsmeldung *f*
fault shut-down Störabschaltung *f*
fault status Störungszustand *m*
fault tree Fehlerbaum *m*, Schadensbaum *m*
fault-free fehlerlos
fault-free faultless fehlerfrei
fault-prone fehleranfällig, störanfällig
faulty schadhaft, mangelhaft, fehlerhaft, störungsbehaftet, gestört
faulty contour gestörte Kontur *f*
faulty control Fehlsteuerung *f*
faulty design Fehlkonstruktion *f*, Konstruktionsfehler *m*
faulty engagement Fehlschaltung *f*, versehentliche Einschaltung *f*
faulty manipulation Fehlgriff *m*
faulty operation gestörter Betrieb *m*, Fehlschaltung *f*
faulty switching Fehlschaltung *f*
favourable günstig
FBD language Funktionsbausteinsprache (FBS) *f*
feasibility Realisierbarkeit *f*, Durchführbarkeit *f*
feasibility study 1. (Vorhaben) Projektstudie *f* **2.** *(BWL Kosten)* Wirtschaftlich-

keitsrechnung *f*
feasible realisierbar, durchführbar
feather Feder *f*, Passfeder *f*
feather edge zugeschärfte Kante *f*, Schleifgrat *m*
feather key Federkeil *m*, Schiebekeil *m*
feathered aufgekeilt
feature darstellen; Kennmerkmal *nt*, Merkmal *nt*, Kennzeichen *nt*, Eigenheit *f*
feature extraction Merkmalsextraktion *f*
feature line Lichtkante *f*
feature presentation Merkmalsausprägung *f*
feature transformation Merkmalstransformation *f*
Federal Health Office Bundesgesundheitsamt *nt*
Federal Institute for Materials Testing Bundesanstalt *f* für Materialprüfung
feed Vorschub *m*, Zustellung *f*, Zuführung *f*, Zuschub *m*, Zuförderung *f*, Zufuhr *f*, Zulauf *m*; zubringen, zuleiten, zuführen, einfüllen, beschicken, vorschieben
feed back rückkoppeln
feed box with rapid traverse motor for traversing the railhead Schaltkasten *m* mit Schnellverstellung für die Supportbewegung
feed by hand von Hand beistellen
feed chain Vorschubkette *f*
feed change gear Wechselräder *ntpl* für den Vorschub
feed control Vorschubregelung *f*, Vorschubsteuerung *f*
feed control lever Vorschubschalthebel *m*
feed device Vorschubgerät *nt*
feed dial Vorschubeinstellscheibe *f*
feed direction Zulaufrichtung *f*
feed dog Vorschubknagge *f*
feed driving disc Nutenscheibe *f* der Querschubeinrichtung
feed drum Vorschubtrommel *f*
feed end of the cooling tube Kühlrohreinlauf *m*
feed energy Vorschubenergie *f*

feed engagement Vorschubeingriff *m*
feed force Vorschubkraft *f*
feed forward Vorsteuerung *f*; vorschieben
feed forward process optimization gesteuerte Prozessoptimierung *f*
feed gear mechanism Vorschubantrieb *m*, Vorschubgetriebe *nt*
feed gear train Vorschubgetriebe *nt*
feed gearbox Vorschubräderkasten *m*, Vorschubgetriebe *nt*
feed hopper Aufgabetrichter *m*, trichterförmige Zuführungseinrichtung *f*
feed in current Strom einspeisen
feed in(to) einspeisen, zufördern, einführen, einschleusen
feed line Zuleitung *f*, Zulaufleitung *f*, Zuführstrecke *f*, Speiseleistung *f*
feed lines Schleifzüge *mpl*
feed mark Vorschubmarke *f*
feed motion 1. *(Werkzeugmaschinen)* Vorschub *m*, Vorschubbewegung *f* **2.** *(Schaltung)* Schaltbewegung *f*
feed motion angle Vorschubrichtungswinkel *m*
feed oil Vorlauföl *nt*
feed out ausschleusen, ausgeben
feed perpendicular force Vorschubnormalkraft *f*
feed power Vorschubleistung *f*
feed pre-selector Vorschubvorwähler *m*
feed pressure Speisedruck *m*
feed ratchet wheel Schaltrad *nt*, Vorschubklinkenrad *nt*
feed rate Vorschub *m*, Vorschubwert *m*, Vorschubgröße *f*, Vorschubgeschwindigkeit *f*
feed regulator Vorschubregler *m*
feed reverse Vorschubumsteuerung *f*
feed reverse control Umsteuern *nt* der Vorschubrichtung
feed rod Zugwelle *f*, Zugspindel *f*, Vorschubwelle *f*
feed roll Transportrolle *f*
feed rows Vorschubreihen *fpl*
feed screw Förderschnecke *f*, Vorschubgewindespindel *f*
feed screw for traversing railheads Spindel *f* für Supportbewegung

feed selection switch Vorschubwahlschalter *m*
feed selector Vorschubwähler *m*, Vorschubwahlschalter *m*
feed setting Vorschubeinstellung *f*, Zustellung *f*
feed setting depth Zustelltiefe *f*
feed shaft Vorschubwelle *f*, Zugspindel *f*
feed speed Vorschubgeschwindigkeit *f*
feed sprocket wheel Vorschubrad *nt*
feed steppings Vorschubstufungen *fpl*
feed switch Vorschubschalter *m*
feed system Zuführsystem *nt*, Speisesystem *nt*
feed thrust Vorschubkraft *f*
feed transmission agent Vorschuborgan *nt*
feed travel Vorschubweg *m*
feed trip Vorschubausrückung *f*
feed water control Speisewasserregelung *f*
feed water de-aerator Speisewasserentgaser *m*
feed water preheater Speisewasservorerwärmer *m*
feed wheel Transportband *nt*
feedback Rückmeldung *f*, Rückkopplung *f*, Steuerungssystem *nt* mit Rückmeldung, Rückführung *f*
feedback control Regelung *f*
feedback decision Rückmeldeentscheidung *f*
feedback device Messwertgeber *m*
feedback loop Rückkopplungsschleife *f*
feedback quantity Regelgröße *f*
feedback signal Istwert *m*
feedbox Vorschubräderkasten *m*, Vorschubgetriebe *nt*, Schlosskastengetriebe *nt*, Vorschub-Schaltkasten *m*
feed-control knob Vorschubkopf *m*
feeder Speiser *m*, Zubringerband *nt*, Zuführungsleitung *f*, Zubringer *m*, Zuführeinrichtung *f*, Zuleitung *f*, Vorschubapparat *m*
feeder attachment Beschickungseinrichtung *f*
feeder equipment Zuführeinrichtung *f*
feeder loader Zubringer *m*
feeding Einspeisen *nt*, Vorschieben *nt*, Zuführung *f*, Beschickung *f*, Bereitstellung *f*, Nachschub *m*, Eingabe *f*
feeding attachment Beschickungseinrichtung *f*
feeding device Zubringer *m*
feeding frequency Beschickungsfrequenz *f*
feeding mechanism Einrichtung *f* für den Vorschub, Vorschubgetriebe *nt*
feeding path *(als Bewegung)* Vorschub *m*
feeding point Beschickungsstelle *f*
feeding pressure Zuführdruck *m*
feeding screw Zuführschnecke *f*
feeding type Beschickungsart *f*
feedstock Vorratsmenge *f*
feel fühlen, tasten
feeler Fühler *m*, Taster *m*, Fühlstift *m*, Taststift *m*
feeler gauge Fühlerlehre *f*, Fühler *m*
feeler head Tastkopf *m*
feeler pin Taststift *m*, Messstift *m*, Taster *m*
feed reversal Vorschubumsteuerung *f*
felt packing Filzdichtung *f*
felt shrinkage Filzschrumpfung *f*
felting behaviour Filzverhalten *nt*
felting material Verfilzungsstoff *m*
female hohl
female connector Steckerbuchse *f*
female gauge Kaliberring *m*
female part of ground joint Hülsenschliff *m*
female piece Matrize *f*
female thread Innengewinde *nt*
female-faced flange Rücksprungflansch *m*
fence Gitter *nt*, Leiste *f*, Umzäunung *f*, Zaun *m*
fence (in) umzäunen
fencing Umzäunung *f*, Zaun *m*
fender 1. *(Automatisierung, Materialfluss)* Schienenräumer *m* **2.** *(Sicherheitstechnik)* Anfahrschutz *m*
ferrite Ferrit
ferrite core Ferritkern *m*
ferrosalt method of reproduction Eisensalzlichtpausverfahren *nt*
ferrous material Eisenwerkstoff *m*
ferrous scrap Alteisen *nt*, Eisen-

schrott *m*
ferrule Zwinge *f*, Pressklemme *f*, Ring *m*
fetch holen
fetch point Holplatz *m*
fibre Faser *f*
fibre bundle Faserbündel *nt*
fibre cable Faserkabel *nt*
fibre clots *pl* Stippen *fpl*
fibre glass Glasfaser *f*
fibre glass fabric Glasgewebe *nt*
fibre mat Fasermatte *f*
fibre material Fasergut *nt*
fibre rope Faserseil *nt*
fibre stock suspension Faserstoffsuspension *f*
fibre strand Faserstrang *m*
fibre testing machine Faserprüfmaschine *f*
fibreboard Wellpappe *f*
fibre-reinforced reaction resin moulding material glasfaserverstärkter Reaktionsharzformstoff *m*
fibrous faserig
fibrous cellulose Cellulosefaser *f*
fibrous structure electrode Faserstrukturelektrode *f*
fibrous structure-plate battery Faserstrukturplattenbatterie *f*
fiction grip Kraftschluss *m*
fiducial line Bezugslinie *f*
field Feld *nt*, Bereich *m*, Fach *nt*
field area network Feldbussystem *nt*
field attenuation Felddämpfung *f*
field bus Feldbus *m*
field coil Erregerwicklung *f*
field data Einsatzdaten *pl*
field definition Feldanweisung *f*
field index Feldindex *m*
field lens Sammellinse *f*
field measuring device Feldmessorgan *nt*
field of activity Arbeitsgebiet *nt*
field of application Anwendungsbereich *m*
field of duties Aufgabenbereich *m*
field of observation Betrachtungsbereich *m*
field of sight *(Bildschirm)* Gesichtsfeld *nt*
field of use Verwendungsbereich *m*

field of view Sichtfeld *nt*
field of vision Blickfeld *nt*
field profile Einsatzprofil *nt*
field regulator Feldsteller *m*
field test Feldversuch *m*, praktischer Versuch *m*
field winding Erregerwicklung *f*
field wiring Feldverdrahtung *f*
field wiring terminal Feldanschlussklemme *f*
figure Ziffer *f*, Zahl *f*, Bild *nt*, Abbildung *f*; beziffern, berechnen, zahlen
figures Zahlenangaben *f, fpl*, Zahlenmaterial *nt*
filaments Fäden *mpl*
file 1. *(Fertigungstechnik)* feilen
  2. *(Werkzeug in Fertigung)* Feile *f*
  3. *(IT)* ablegen, archivieren; Datei *f*, Ordner *m*
file handle Feilenheft *nt*
file name Dateiname *m*
file transfer protocol (FTP) Dateitransferprotokoll *nt*
filiform corrosion Fadenkorrosion *f*
filiform corrosion attack fadenförmiger Angriff *m*
filing 1. *(IT)* Ablage *f*, Ablegen *nt* 2. *(mit dem Werkzeug)* Feilen *nt*
filing and sawing machine Feil- und Sägemaschine *f*
filing of textual material Schriftgutverfilmung *f*
filings Feilspäne *mpl*
fill (in) befüllen, einfüllen, füllen, belegen
fill and close machine Füll- und Verschließmaschine *f*
fill goods Füllgut *nt*
fill height inspection machine Füllhöheninspektionsmaschine *f*
fill level set point setter Füllstandsollwertsteller *m*
fill nozzle Füllstutzen *m*
fill pipe Füllleitung *f*
fill up to the brim randvoll füllen
filled befüllt
filled package Packstück *nt*
filler Lot *nt*
filler cap Eingussverschluss *m*
filler filament Schweißschnur *f*

filler material Schweißzusatzwerkstoff *m*, Schweißzusatz *m*
filler material of different composition artfremder Zusatzwerkstoff *m*
filler material of the same composition artgleicher Zusatzwerkstoff *m*
filler metal Lot *nt*
filler metal erosion Anlösung *f*
filler metal in grain form Kornlot *nt*
filler metal of like kind artgleicher Zusatzwerkstoff *m*
filler metal of unlike kind artfremder Zusatzwerkstoff *m*
filler metal overflow Lotüberlauf *m*
filler point Füllstelle *f*
filler rod Einsatzstab *m*, Füllstab *m*
filler shape Lotform *f*
filler strip Schweißstreifen *m*
filler wire consumed with carrying current stromführend abgeschmolzener Schweißdraht *m*
filler-run welder Fülllagenschweißer *m*, Füllschweißer *m*
fillet Ausrundung *f*, Abrundung *f*, Hohlkehle *f*, Zahnfußausrundung *f*
fillet groove auskehlen
fillet surface Fußrundungsfläche *f*
fillet weld Kehlnaht *f*, Halsnaht *f*
fillet weld with no fusion at root Kehlnaht *f* mit nicht erfasster Wurzel
fillet weld with undercut Kehlnaht *f* mit Einbrandkerbe
filleting tool Hohlkegelmeißel *m*
filling Befüllung *f*, Füllung *f*
filling and dosing machine Füll- und Dosiermaschine *f*
filling and sealing machine Füll- und Verschließmaschine *f*
filling arrangement Fülleinrichtung *f*
filling degree Füllungsgrad *m*
filling for the first time Erstbefüllung *f*
filling height Füllhöhe *f*
filling level Füllgrad *m*, Füllhöhe *f*, Füllstand *m*, Füllstandshöhe *f*
filling machine Füllmaschine *f*
filling of vacancies Stellenbesetzung *f*
filling operation Füllvorgang *m*
filling point Befüllungsstelle *f*
filling pressure Fülldruck *m*
filling station Füllstation *f*
filling valve Füllventil *nt*
filling-in Eingabe *f*
fillister head runder Schraubenkopf *m*
fill-up hour Einfüllstunde *f*
fill-up quantity Füllmenge *f*
film Bildschicht *f*, Folie *f*, Schicht *f*
film adhesively bonded between the sheets eingeklebte Folie *f*
film and band wrapping machine Folien- und Bandeinschlagmaschine *f*
film base Filmträger *m*
film carriage Folienschlitten *m*
film cassette Filmkassette *f*
film casting Foliengießen *nt*
film cord device Folienkordeleinrichtung *f*
film cutting appliance Folienschneidgerät *nt*
film edge Folienende *nt*
film evaluation Filmauswertung *f*
film negative material Negativlichtpausfilm *m*
film of silicone grease Silikonfettfilm *m*
film processing Filmverarbeitung *f*
film reel Folienrolle *f*
film releasing plasticiser weichmacherabgebende Folie *f*
film rust formation Flugrostbildung *f*
film specimen Folienprobe *f*
film stretching Foliendehnung *f*
film stretching device Foliendehnsystem *nt*
film strip Folienstreifen *m*, Folienbahn *f*
film transport Folientransport *m*
film web Folienbahn *f*
film with diazo coating Film *m* mit Lichtpausschicht
filming of drawings *pl* Zeichnungsverfilmung *f*
film-making equipment Filmgeräte *ntpl*
filter Filter *m*, filtern
filter cartridge Filterhülse *f*
filter crucible Filtertiegel *m*
filter element Filtereinsatz *m*
filter for suspended matter Schwebstofffilter *m*
filter method Filtermethode *f*
filtration device Filterapparat *m*

filtering earth Filtererde *f*
filtratable abfiltrierbar (a.)
filtration performance Filterleistung *f*
fin Grat *m*, Rippe *f*, Naht *f*; rippen
fin seal Faltnaht *f*
final approval Endabnahme *f*
final assembly Endmontage *f*
final condition Endzustand *m*
final control element Stellglied *nt*, Steuerorgan *nt*, Stellgerät *nt*
final controlling element Stellglied *nt*
final degreasing Fertigentfettung *f*
final destination Zielort *m*
final discharging voltage Entladeschlusspannung *f*
final flanging Fertigbördeln *nt*
final gauge length Messlänge *f* nach dem Bruch
final inspection Endkontrolle *f*
final position Endeinstellung *f*
final pressure Enddruck *m*
final product Endprodukt *nt*
final reduction apparatus Endzerkleinerungsgerät *nt*
final reduction in size Endzerkleinerung *f*
final return motion Rückkehr *f*
final run reinforcement Decklagenüberhöhung *f*
final sample Endstufenprobe *f*
final shape Endform *f*
final sizing Fertigkalibrieren *nt*
final speed Endgeschwindigkeit *f*
final state Endzustand *m*
final trimming Nachschneiden *nt*
final value distribution Endwert *m*
final weighing Endwägung *f*
finally electrolytically galvanized galvanisch schlussverzinkt
finally galvanized schlussverzinkt
final-run welder Decklagenschweißer *m*
finance flow Geldfluss *m*
financial economy Finanzwirtschaft *f*
financial market Finanzmarkt *m*
financial policy Finanzpolitik *f*
financial resources Finanzmittel *ntpl*
find finden
find out ermitteln
finding Feststellung *f*, Prüfergebnisse *ntpl*
finding the tolerances by calculation rechnerische Toleranzfindung *f*
findings *pl* Befund *m*
fine fein
fine adjustment Feineinstellung *f*, Feinnachstellung *f*, Feinzustellung *f*
fine adjustment valve Feineinstellventil *nt*
fine boring Feinbohren *nt*, Feinstbohren *nt*
fine boring machine Feinbohrwerk *nt*, Feinbohrmaschine *f*
fine cotton fabric Baumwollfeingewebe *nt*
fine feed Feinvorschub *m*
fine feed handwheel Handrad *nt* für Feinvorschub
fine feed setting Vorschubfeinzustellung *f*
fine finishing Feinbearbeitung *f*
fine finishing technique Feinbearbeitungsverfahren *nt*
fine grinding Feinschleifen *nt*
fine honing Fertighonen *nt*
fine machining Feinbearbeitungsprozess *m*
fine mechanics Feinwerktechnik *f*
fine mesh gauge engmaschig
fine pitch thread Feingewinde *nt*
fine pitched cutter Fräser *m* mit feiner Zahnteilung
fine planning Feinplanung *f*
fine positioning Feinpositionierung *f*
fine setting Feineinstellung *f*
fine thread Feingewinde *nt*
fine time schedule Terminfeinplanung *f*
fine turning Feindrehen *nt*
fine turning tool Feindrehmeißel *m*
fine-boring tool Feinbohrwerkzeug *nt*
fine-edge blanking Feinschneiden *nt*
fine-grained feinkörnig
fine-hole boring Feinbohren *nt*
fine-lace chip Bandspan *m*
fine-layered resin-bonded densified laminated wood feinschichtiges Kunstharz-Pressholz *nt*
finely broken chip Kurzspan *m*
fine-particle filter Feinstaubfilter *m*

fine-step feinstufig
fine-tooth cutter Fräser *m* mit Feinverzahnung
finger Zapfen *m*
finger clamp Spanneisen *nt* mit Stift
finger tip Fingerspitze *f*
finger tip control Tippschaltung *f*, feinfühlige Schaltung *f*
finish Ausführung *f*, Beschaffenheit *f*, Oberflächengüte *f*, Endbearbeitung *f*; endbearbeiten, schlichten, veredeln, enden, beenden
finish with broad cut breitschlichten
finish broach fertig räumen, schlichträumen
finish by grinding überschleifen
finish cut fertig bearbeiten, nachschneiden
finish cutting blade Schlichtmesser *nt*
finish draw Fertigschlag *m*
finish eroding Schlichterodieren *nt*
finish facing Planschlichten *nt*
finish grind Schlichtschliff *m*, Fertigschliff *m*; feinschleifen
finish grinding Feinschliff *m*, Fertigschliff *m*, Fertigschleifen *nt*
finish honing Feinziehschleifen *nt*
finish lapping Fertifläppen *nt*
finish machining Endbearbeitung *f*, Nacharbeit *f*, Schlichten *nt*, spanende Feinbearbeitung *f*
finish milling Schlichtfräsen *nt*, Fertigfräsen *nt*, Feinfräsen *nt*, Nachfräsen *nt*
finish rolling by the infeed method Glattwalzen *nt* im Einstechverfahren
finish rolling of bar stock by the through-feed method Glattwalzen *nt* von Stäben im Durchlaufverfahren
finish shaving Nachschneiden *nt*
finish size Fertigmaß *nt*
finish to size auf das Fertigmaß bringen
finish turning Feindrehen *nt*, Schlichtdrehen *nt*
finish-bright hochglanzpolieren
finish-cutting Schlichten *nt*
finished fertig
finished and unfinished products warehouse Erzeugnislager *nt*
finished elastomer item Elastomerfertigteil *nt*
finished good store Fertigwarenlager *nt*
finished goods Fertigerzeugnisse *ntpl*, Fertigwaren *fpl*
finished goods inventory (FGI) Fertigwarenlager *nt*
finished goods stockpile Fertigwarenlager *nt*
finished goods warehouse Fertigwarenlager *nt*, Warenausganglager *nt*
finished part fertig bearbeitetes Teil
finished part drawing Fertigteilzeichnung *f*
finished part length Fertigteillänge *f*
finished parts Fertigteile *f*
finished parts warehouse Fertigteillager *nt*
finished product Fertigprodukt *nt*
finished products Fertigwaren *fpl*
finished size Fertigmaß *nt*
finish-face planschlichten
finishing Schlichten *nt*, Endbearbeitung *f*, Nachbearbeitung *f*, Feinbearbeitung *f*, Weiterverarbeitung *f*, Beendigung *f*
finishing broach Schlichträumwerkzeug *nt*
finishing cut Schlichtschnitt *m*
finishing cutter 1. *(allg. Werkzeug)* Schlichtmeißel *m*, Schlichtstahl *m*, Kopfmeißel *m* **2.** *(Werkzeug beim Fräsen)* Nachfräser *m*, Schlichtfräser *m*
finishing dimension Fertigmaß *nt*
finishing form Endform *f*
finishing grinding Feinschleifen *nt*
finishing hob Schlichtfräser *m* (Wälzfräser)
finishing particle Schlichtteilchen *nt*
finishing plant Weiterverarbeitungsbetrieb *m*
finishing platform Nachlaufbühne *f*
finishing point Endpunkt *m*
finishing table Ablagetisch *m*
finishing tool Schlichtmeißel *m*, Schlichtstahl *m*, Kopfmeißel *m*
finishing-milling spindle Schlichtfrässpindel *f*
finish-machinability Schlichtbearbeitbarkeit *f*
finish-machine fertig bearbeiten,

schlichten, feinstbearbeiten, nachbearbeiten
finish-machining operation Schlichtarbeit *f*
finish-mill fertig fräsen, schlichtfräsen, feinstfräsen, schlichten, nachfräsen
finish-planing Schlichthobeln *nt*
finish-turn schlichtdrehen, schlichten, fertig drehen, nachdrehen
finite value endlicher Wert *m*
finless gratlos
finning Verrippung *f*
finish grinding Schlichtschleifen *nt*
fir tree profile Tannenbaumprofil *nt*
furan basis Furanbasis *f*
fire Feuer *nt*, Brand *m*
fire behaviour Brandverhalten *nt*
fire box Feuerstätte *f*
fire duration Branddauer *f*
fire extinguisher Feuerlöscher *m*
fire extinguishers Löschgeräte *ntpl*
fire fighting equipment Feuerwerksausrüstung *f*
fire hazard Brandgefährlichkeit *f*
fire load Brandlast *f*
fire outbreak point Brandausbruchstelle *f*
fire patch Brandstelle *f*
fire performance Brandverhalten *nt*
fire point Brennpunkt *m*
fire prevention vorbeugender Brandschutz *m*
fire protection Brandschutz *m*
fire protection door Feuerschutztür *f*
fire safety in building baulicher Brandschutz *m*
fire shaft method Brandschachtverfahren *nt*
fire stage Brandstadium *nt*
firebed Feuerbett *nt*
fire-fighting Brandbekämpfung *f*
fire-fighting operations *(Brandschutz)* Löscharbeiten *fpl*
fire-place Feuerstätte *f*
fire-proof feuerfest, feuersicher
fire-resistant feuerfest, schwer entflammbar
firing Feuerung *f*, Befeuerung *f*, Schießen *nt*
firing controller Feuerungsregler *m*

firing equipment Beheizungseinrichtung *f*
firing installation Feuerungsanlage *f*
firing method Feuerungsart *f*
firing plant Feuerungsanlage *f*
firing system Feuerungsanlage *f*
firing wire Zünddraht *m*
fork cycle time Gabelspielzeit *f*
fork truck Gabelstapler *m*
firm fest, straff
firm order Festauftrag *m*
firmly adherent fest haftend
firmly bonded deposits festsitzende Ablagerungen *fpl*
firmness Festigkeit *f*
firmware Firmware *f*
first cycle machining Bearbeitung *f* im ersten Arbeitsgang
first aid erste Hilfe *f*
first break Schwellwert *m*
first customer shipment Erstauslieferung *f*
first cut of arc Bogenanschnitt *m*
first cut of circular arc Bogenanschnitt *m*
first cut of curve Bogenanschnitt *m*
first cut of horn Hornanschnitt *m*
first cut system Anschnittsystem *nt*
first face erste Spanfläche *f*, erste Spanflächenfase *f*
first filling Erstbefüllung *f*
first flank erste Freifläche *f*
first grind Anschleifen *nt*
first message Erstmeldung *f*
first order Erstbestellung *f*
first pass Anstich *m*
first-run lubrication oil Schmierölvorlauf *m*
fish joint Überlaschung *f*
fissure Spalte *f*, Riss *m*, Haarriss *m*, Sprung *m*
fit Passung *f*, Passungssitz *m*, Sitz *m*; justieren, einpassen, anpassen, passen, einfügen, einbauen, zusammensetzen, anbringen, montieren, aufstecken, ausrüsten, ausstatten
fit size Passmaß *nt*
fit to one another einander anpassen
fit together ineinander passen, aneinander fügen, zusammenbauen

fit tolerance Passtoleranz *f*, Passungstoleranz *f*
fit tolerance zone Passtoleranzfeld *nt*
fit with versehen mit
fit with blind flanges blindflanschen
fitted washer aufgesteckte Scheibe *f*
fitted with versehen mit, ausgerüstet mit
fitter Monteur *m*, Mechaniker *m*, Installateur *m*
fitting 1. *(Installation)* Einbau *m*, Montage *f*, Befestigung *f*, Anbringung *f*, Justierung *f*, Einpassen *nt*; passend **2.** *(Bauteil)* Armatur *f*, Anschluss *m*, Verbindungselement *nt*
fitting accuracy Passgenauigkeit *f*
fitting and assembly tool Montagewerkzeug *nt*
fitting at assembly Einpassarbeit *f*
fitting bolt Passschraube *f*
fitting clearance Passungsspiel *nt*
fitting dimension Einbaumaß *nt*
fitting for soldered capillary solder fitting Fitting *nt* für Kapillarlötverbindung
fitting instruction Montageanweisung *f*
fitting joint Passfuge *f*
fitting key Passfeder *f*
fitting length Passlänge *f*
fitting member Passteil *nt*
fitting part Passteil *nt*
fitting pin Passstift *m*
fitting position Einbaulage *f*
fitting screws Passschraube *f*
fitting surface Passfläche *f*
fitting surfaces *pl* **of cylindrical form** kreiszylindrische Passflächen *fpl*
fitting together ineinander Passen *nt*; aneinander passend
fitting with socket Formstück *nt* mit Muffe
fitting work Passarbeit *f*
fitting-in Einpassung *f*
fitting-on Aufstecken *nt*
fittings Zubehörteile *ntpl*, Zubehör *nt*, Beschläge *mpl*, Armaturen *fpl*
fit-up aid Montagehilfe *f*
fit-up fixture Hilfsvorrichtung *f*
five times fünffach

five-based division *(e. Skala)* Fünferteilung *f*
five-spindle automatic lathe Fünfspindelautomat *m*
five-station turret Fünfkantrevolverkopf *m*
fix festmachen, spannen, festspannen, aufspannen, einspannen, anbringen, befestigen, verankern, feststellen, festlegen, peilen; Peilung *f*
fixed fest, feststehend, fest montiert, ortsfest, stationär, starr, nicht tragbar
fixed bed filter Festbettfilter *m*
fixed bed miller Langfräsmaschine *f*, Planfräsmaschine *f*
fixed bed type milling machine with double horizontal spindle Zweispindelplanfräsmaschine *f*
fixed castor Bockrolle *f*
fixed command control Festwertregelung *f*
fixed data carrier (FDC) festkodierter Datenträger (FDT) *m*
fixed end stop Prellbock *m*
fixed forks starre Gabeln *fpl*
fixed gauge Festmaßlehre *f*
fixed guard feststehende Schutzeinrichtung *f*, Absperrung *f*
fixed height load carrying truck Wagen *m* mit fester Plattform
fixed height platform truck Wagen *m* mit fester Plattform
fixed link Gestell *nt*
fixed location storage Festplatzlagerung *f*
fixed nozzle Festdüse *f*
fixed pallet stretch wrapper Umlaufpalettenstretchwickler *m*
fixed platform truck Plattformwagen *m*, Plattformhubwagen *m*
fixed point Festpunkt *m*
fixed pulley Festscheibe *f*
fixed square fester Anschlagwinkel *m*
fixed stairway eingebaute Treppe *f*
fixed stop Festanschlag *m*
fixed tray conveyor Umlaufförderer *m*
fixed wire-wound resistor Drahtfestwiderstand *m*
fixed zero dimension Bezugsmaß *nt*
fixed-axle gear transmission Standge-

triebe *nt*
fixed-bed milling machine Planfräsmaschine *f*
fixed-bed milling machine with horizontal spindle Waagerechtproduktionsfräsmaschine *f*
fixed-bed type miller Planfräsmaschine *f*
fixed-bed type milling machine with three spindle heads Planfräsmaschine *f* mit drei Frässpindelköpfen
fixed-centre turret lathe Planrevolverdrehmaschine *f*
fixed-centre turret machine Sattelrevolverdrehmaschine *f* mit waagerecht angeordnetem Revolver
fixing Befestigung *f*, Einspannung *f*, Fixierung *f*, Verankerung *f*, Aufspannen *nt*
fixing bolt Befestigungsbolzen *m*
fixing device Befestigungsteil *nt*, Befestigungsvorrichtung *f*
fixing hole Befestigungsbohrung *f*
fixing materials Befestigungsmaterial *nt*
fixing of the location Standortbestimmung *f*
fixing point Befestigungspunkt *m*
fixing position Befestigungspunkt *m*
fixing sensors Peilsensorik *f*
fixture Aufnahme *f*, Einrichtung *f*, Vorrichtung *f*, Halterung *f*, Aufspannvorrichtung *f*, Spannzeug *nt*
fixture drawing Spannzeugzeichnung *f*
fixtured honing tool Honahle *f*
fixtures Vorrichtungen *fpl*
flanged connection Flanschverbindung *f*
Flade potential Fladepotential *nt*
flag Merker *m*
flake Schuppe *f*
flake board Spanplatte *f*
flake glue Plättchenleim *m*
flake off abblättern
flakes *pl* Schuppen *mpl*
flaking Ausbruch *m*
flame Flamme *f*
flame atomic absorption flammenatomabsorptions-spektroskopisches Verfahren *nt*
flame boring Brennbohren *nt*
flame brazing Flammhartlöten *nt*
flame cleaning device Abbrenngerät *nt*
flame configuration Flammenform *f*
flame control Flammenüberwachung *f*
flame cutter Schneidbrenner *m*
flame cutting Brennschneiden *nt*
flame cutting gas cutting autogenes Brennschneiden *nt*
flame cutting slag Brennschlacke *f*
flame cutting torch Brennschneider *m*
flame deseaming Brennflämmen *nt*
flame detector Flammenwächter *m*
flame detector relay Flammenwächterrelais *nt*
flame fault shutdown Störabschalter *m*
flame gouging Brennhobeln *nt*, Brennfugen *nt*
flame grooving Brennfugen *nt*
flame hardening Gasflammenhärtung *f*
flame heating Flammwärmen *nt*
flame heating process Flammwärmverfahren *nt*
flame lift-off Flammenabheben *nt*
flame monitor wiring Flammenfühlerleitung *f*
flame monitoring Flammenüberwachung *f*
flame monitoring device Flammenüberwachungseinrichtung *f*
flame performance Flammenleistung *f*
flame phosphating Flammphosphatieren *nt*
flame priming Flammgrundieren *nt*
flame retardant schwer entflammbar
flame retardation flammwidrig
flame scarfing Brennflämmen *nt*
flame sensor Flammenfühler *m*
flame soldering Flammweichlöten *nt*
flame soldering and brazing Flammlöten *nt*
flame spray flammspritzen
flame spread Brandausbreitung *f*
flame spread rate Flammenausbreitungsgeschwindigkeit *f*
flame stress relieving Flammentspannen *nt*
flame transmission Zünddurch-

schlag *m*
flame trap Flammendurchschlagsicherung *f*
flame-cut brennschneiden, schneidbrennen
flame-on response time Anmeldezeit *f*
flame-out response time Abmeldezeit *f*
flameproof flammenfest, druckfest
flame-proof flammensicher
flameproof clothing Flammenschutzkleidung *f*
flameproof enclosure druckfeste Kapselung *f*
flame-resistant epoxy resin flammwidriges Epoxidharz *nt*
flame-retarding additive flammhemmender Zusatz *m*
flame-swept parts feuerberührte Teile *ntpl*
flammability test Brennbarkeitsprüfung *f*
flammable brennbar, zündfähig
flange bördeln, umbördeln, flanschen; Falz *m*, Bund *m*, Flansch *m*
flange facing Flanschfläche *f*
flange modulus Flanschwiderstand *m*
flange plate joint Gurtplattenstoß *m*
flange wheel Flanschrad *nt*
flange with butt welded collar Flansch *m* mit Anschweißbund
flanged angeflanscht
flanged connection Flanschanschluss *m*
flanged pipe gebördeltes Rohr *nt*
flanged rim Bördelrand *m*
flange-mounted motor Flanschmotor *m*
flanging Bördeln *nt*, Bördelung *f*
flanging machine Bördelmaschine *f*
flanging tool Bördelwerkzeug *nt*
flank Flanke *f*, Gabelseite *f*, Wange *f*, Freifläche *f*
flank angle Flankenwinkel *m*, Teilflankenwinkel *m*
flank angle of workpiece Werkstückflankenwinkel *m*
flank bearing Zahnflankentragfähigkeit *f*
flank control Flankensteuerung *f*

flank correction Flankenkorrektur *f*
flank direction Flankenrichtung *f*
flank face of the thread Gewindeflankenfläche *f*
flank lead Steigung *f*
flank loading Flankenbeanspruchung *f*
flank measure Flankenmaß *nt*
flank micrometer Flankenmikrometer *m*
flank modification Zahnflankenveränderung *f*
flank of tooth Zahnflanke *f*
flank pitch Teilung *f*
flank play Zahnflankenspiel *nt*
flank profile Freiflächenprofil *nt*
flank section Flankenschnitt *m*
flank spacing Zahnflankenabstand *m*
flank test diagram Flankenprüfbild *nt*, Flankenlinienprüfbild *nt*
flank testing machine Flankenprüfgerät *nt*
flank variation Flankenabweichung *f*
flank wear Freiflächenverschleiß *m*
flap Stecklasche *f*, Lasche *f*, Klappe *f*, Schenkel *m*, klappen
flap and folding box Klapp- und Faltbox *f*
flap box Klappbox *f*
flap operated foot valve Fußklappe *f*
flap tear propagation Schenkelweiterreißversuch *m*
flare ausdehnen, weiten
flash 1. *(Erscheinung bei Fertigung, Nachbearbeitung)* Schneidegrat *m*, Grat *m*; abgraten, abschmelzen
2. *(Licht)* blinken, verblitzen
flash butt weld abbrennstumpfschweißen
flash ignition Fremdzündung *f*
flash lamp Blitzlampe *f*
flash memory Flashspeicher *m*
flash trap Entspanner *m*
flash trimming Abgraten *nt*, Abgratschneiden *nt* von Schmiedestücken, Beschneiden *nt* zum Entfernen eines Schmiedegrates
flash welding Abbrennschweißen *nt*
flash welding from cold Abbrennstumpfschweißen *nt* aus dem Kalten
flashback Rückschlag *m*

flash-back Flammendurchschlag *m*
flashback arrester Flammendurchschlagsicherung *f*
flash-butt welding Abbrennstumpfschweißen *nt*
flash-butt welding machine Abbrennstumpfschweißmaschine *f*
flashed verblitzt
flashing 1. *(Platte)* Abdeckblech *nt* **2.** *(Licht)* Blinken *nt* **3.** *(Schutz)* Verwahrung *f*
flashing beacon Blinkleuchte *f*
flashing light Blinklicht *nt*
flashing-light indication Blinken *nt*
flash-off Abbrennlängenverlust *m*
flashover Flammstrahlzündung *f*
flash-over Feuerüberspannung *f*
flash-weld abbrennschweißen
flask Flasche *f*
flask thermometer Sumpfthermometer *nt*
flask with standard ground socket Kolben *m* mit Normschliff
flat glatt, eben, flach, plan, flachliegend
flat bar tension specimen Flachzugprobe *f*
flat bending fatigue test Flachbiegeschwingversuch *m*
flat bottom shelving Fachbodenregal *nt*
flat countersunk head rivet Flachsenkniet *m*, Riemenniet *m*
flat crush resistance Flachstauchfestigkeit *f*, Flachstauchwiderstand *m*
flat crush test Flachstauchversuch *m*
flat double head box wrench gerader Doppelringschlüssel *m*
flat double-ended ring spanner gerader Doppelringschlüssel *m*
flat drawing Flachziehen *nt*
flat ended key for deck screw caps Flachkanteinsteckschlüssel *m* für Deckverschlüsse
flat fit Flachpassung *f*
flat gauging member Flachlehrenkörper *m*
flat glass plate Planglasplatte *f*
flat goods Flachgut *nt*
flat goods storage system Flachgutlagersystem *nt*

flat goods warehouse Flachgutlagersystem *nt*, Flachgutlager *nt*
flat knurled nut flache Rändelmutter *f*
flat laminated moulded section Flachumpressung *f*
flat lapping Flachläppen *nt*
flat lapping machine Flachläppmaschine *f*
flat limit plug gauge Grenzflachlehre *f*
flat longitudinal rolling Flachlängswalzen *nt*
flat longitudinal rolling of hollow items Flachlängswalzen *nt* von Hohlkörpern
flat longitudinal rolling of solid bodies Flachlängswalzen *nt* von Vollkörpern
flat nose pliers Justierzange *f*
flat pallet Flachpalette *f*
flat point Kegelkuppe *f*
flat ramways Stößelflachbahnführung *f*
flat rod Flachvollstab *m*
flat sealing flachdichtend
flat sealing ring Flachdichtring *m*
flat single-V butt joint V-Naht *f* mit ebener Oberfläche
flat single-V butt joint with flat backing run V-Naht *f* mit Gegenlage und ebener Oberfläche
flat skew rolling Flachschrägwalzen *nt*
flat slideway Flachführung *f*
flat surface ebene Fläche *f*
flat tang Austreiblappen *m*
flat thread Flachgewinde *nt*
flat transverse rolling Flachquerwalzen *nt*
flat tray Flachtray *m*
flat turret head Flachrevolverkopf *m*
flat turret lathe Drehmaschine *f* mit flachem Revolvertisch, Flachrevolverdrehmaschine *f*
flat type lubricating nipple Flachschmiernippel *m*
flat type plug gauge Flachlehrdorn *m*
flat way Flachführung *f*, Flachbahn *f*
flat-die thread rolling Gewinderollen *nt*
flatness Ebenheit *f*, Flachlage *f*
flatness deviation Ebenheitsabweichung *f*

flatness tolerance Ebenheitstoleranz *f*
flat-ring turning Planringdrehen *nt*
flat-surface shaping Flächenhobeln *nt*, Kurzhobeln *nt* ebener Flächen
flatted vollkantig
flatten abflachen, glätten, ebnen
flattened plug gauge abgeflachter Lehrdorn *m*
flattened specimen zusammengefaltete Probe *f*
flattening Abflachung *f*, Abplattung *f*
flattening test Flachdrückversuch *m*
flattening test specimen Ringfaltprobe *f*
flatten abplatten
flatting distance Faltbetrag *m*, Plattenabstand *m*
flat-tipped spot welding electrode Punktschweißelektrode *f* mit flach aufsetzender Elektrodenspitze
flaw Fehler *m*, Fehlstelle *f*, Blase *f*, Oberflächenbeschädigung *f*
flaw location scale Ortungsstab *m*
flawless fehlerlos, fehlerfrei, einwandfrei
flawless cut surface fehlerfreie Schnittfläche *f*
flawless thread fehlerfreies Gewinde *nt*
fleecy flauschig
flex beugen, sich biegen
flex cracking test Dauerknickversuch *m*
flex head nut spanner Gelenkgriff *m* mit Außenvierkant
flex head socket wrench Gelenksteckschlüssel *m*
flexibility Biegsamkeit *f*, Dehnbarkeit *f*, Flexibilität *f*, Federungsvermögen *nt*, Nachgiebigkeit *f*, Anpassungsfähigkeit *f*
flexibility Nachgiebigkeit *f*
flexible anpassungsfähig, flexibel, biegsam, dehnbar, elastisch, beweglich, vielseitig
flexible cellular material weich-elastischer Schaumstoff *m*
flexible manufacturing cell flexible Fertigungszelle *f*
flexible manufacturing island flexible Fertigungsinsel *f*
flexible manufacturing system

(FMS) flexibles Fertigungssystem (FFS) *nt*
flexible mass gefederte Masse *f*
flexible packaging film flexibler Packstoff *m*
flexible pipe biegeweiches Rohr *nt*, bewegliche Leitung *f*
flexible polyvinyl chloride weiches Polyvinylchlorid *nt*
flexible production flexible Fertigung *f*
flexible shaft biegsame Welle *f*
flexible tool bewegliches Werkzeug *nt*
flexing test Biegeprüfung *f*
flexion wave Biegewelle *f*
flexographic ink Flexodruckfarbe *f*
flexographic printing Flexodruck *m*
flexometer test Flexometerprüfung *f*
flexural fatigue test Dauerschwingversuch *m*
flexural force Biegekraft *f*
flexural loading Biegebeanspruchung *f*
flexural oscillation Biegeschwingung *f*
flexural stiffness Biegesteifigkeit *f*
flexural strength at rupture Biegefestigkeit *f*
flexural stress Biegespannung *f*
flexural stress at 3.5% strain of the outer fibre Biegespannung *f* bei 3,5% Randfaserdrehung
flexural stress at given deflection Grenzbiegespannung *f*
flexural test Biegeversuch *m*
flexural vibration *(konstante Frequenz)* Biegeschwingung *f*
flexural vibration test Biegeschwingungsversuch *m*
flexural wave length Biegewellenlänge *f*
flexural wave velocity Biegewellengeschwindigkeit *f*
flexurally resistant biegesteif
flexure Biegung *f*, Aufbiegung *f*
flickering *(Bildschirm)* Flimmern *nt*
flimsy schwach
flip wenden, umwenden, umdrehen
flip plate method Wendeplattenverfahren *nt*
flip switch Kippschalter *m*
flipping mechanism Wendemechanik *f*

float 1. *(gleiten)* rutschen **2.** *(schaukeln)* pendeln **3.** *(techn.)* Schwimmer *m*
float layer formation Schwimmhautbildung *f*
float pressure gauge Schwimmermanometer *nt*
float switch Schwimmerschalter *m*
float time Pufferzeit *f*
floating bell gasholder schwimmende Gasglocke *f*
floating body Schwebekörper *m*
floating operation Pufferbetrieb *m*
floating plant schwimmende Geräte *ntpl*
floating ring freibweglicher Führungsring *m*
floating roller peel test Rollenschälversuch *m*
floating tool Pendelwerkzeug *nt*
floating toolholder Pendelfutter *nt*, beweglicher Meißelhalter *m*
flocculator Flokkulator *m*
flock beflocken *nt*
floe meter Volumenstrommessgerät *nt*
flood fluten, überfluten, überströmen
flood method *(Phosphatierung)* Flutverfahren *nt*
flood on anschwemmen
flood soldering Anschwemmlöten *nt*, Schwalllöten *nt*
flooding Berieselung *f*, Fluten *nt*
floor Fahrboden *m*, Fußboden *m*, Boden *m*, Flur *m*, Stockwerk *nt*, Geschoss *nt*
floor anchorage Bodenverankerung *f*
floor area Grundfläche *f*, Geschossfläche *f*
floor area factor Geschossflächenzahl *f*
floor capping Bodenabdeckung *f*
floor conditions Bodenbeschaffenheit *f*
floor covering Fußbodenbelag *m*, Oberbelag *m*
floor friction Bodenreibung *f*
floor height Bodenhöhe *f*, Geschosshöhe *f*
floor level Geschossebene *f*, Bodenebene *f*
floor marking Bodenmarkierung *f*
floor mounted rail Fahrschiene *f*
floor outlet Fußbodendurchlass *m*

floor plate Grundplatte *f*
floor rail Bodenschiene *f*
floor rail head Fahrschienenkopf *m*
floor running unten laufend
floor running rail Fahrschiene *f*
floor slab Bodenplatte *f*, Aufspannfeld *nt*
floor space Aufstellungsfläche *f* einer Maschine, Standfläche *f*, Bodenfläche *f*
floor stand Bodenstativ *nt*, Ständer *m*
floor switch Fußschalter *m*
floor-to-floor-time Boden- zu- Boden-Zeit *f*
floor travelling bodenverfahrbar
floor-bound bodenfahrend, flurgebunden
floor-guided bodengeführt
floor-mounted Unterflur ...
floor-mounted conveying system Unterflurförderanlage *f*
floor-mounted truck conveyor Unterflurförderer *m*
floppy disk Diskette *f*
flotation liquid Auftriebsflüssigkeit *f*
flotation measurement Auftriebsmessung *f*
fluorescence-stimulating fluoreszenzanregend
fluorescence-stimulation Fluoreszenzanregung *f*
fluorescent X-radiation Röntgenfluoreszensstrahlung *f*
fluorine-containing compound fluorhaltige Verbindung *f*
fluoroscopic screen Leuchtschirm *m*
fluoroscopist's working position Durchleuchtungsarbeitsplatz *m*
fluoroscopy equipment Durchleuchtungseinrichtung *f*
fluoroscopy time Durchleuchtungsdauer *f*
flow 1. *(allg.)* Durchfluss *m*, Fluss *m*, Strom *m*, Strömung *f*; fließen, strömen **2.** *(Rohrleitungsbau)* Vorlauf *m*
flow behaviour Fließverhalten *nt*
flow chart Ablaufplan *m*, Flussdiagramm *nt*, Ablaufdiagramm *nt*
flow chip Fließspan *m*, Abfließspan *m*
flow connection Vorlaufanschluss *m*
flow contraction Strahlkontraktion *f*

flow control Ablaufsteuerung *f*, Ablaufkontrolle *f*
flow control valve Messventil *nt*, Stromventil *nt*
flow curves Fließkurven *fpl*
flow diagram Flussdiagramm *nt*, Ablaufdiagramm *nt*
flow limiter Durchflussbegrenzer *m*
flow line Fließband *nt*
flow line production Fließarbeit *f*
flow measuring device Durchflussmessgerät *nt*
flow measuring rule Durchflussmessregel *f*
flow measurement Durchflussmessung *f*
flow medium Durchflussstoff *m*
flow medium marking Durchflussstoffkennzeichnung *f*
flow meter filling machine Volumenstromfüllmaschine *f*
flow of chip Spanabfluss *m*, Spanfluss *m*
flow of chips Spänefall *m*
flow of goods Warenfluss *m*
flow of shear chips Scherspanablauf *m*
flow off entweichen
flow path Fließweg *m*
flow pressure Fließdruck *m*
flow pressure range Fließdruckbereich *m* (Gas)
flow principle Fließprinzip *nt*
flow production Fließfertigung *f*
flow quantity Durchflussmenge *f*
flow rack Durchlaufregal *nt*
flow rack storage Durchlaufregallager *nt*
flow regulation Verkehrsregelung *f*
flow restrictor Durchflusswiderstand *m*
flow safety device Strömungssicherung *f*
flow sheet Ablaufdiagramm *nt*
flow shelf Kollidurchlaufregal *nt*
flow storage Durchlauflager *nt*
flow straightener Gleichrichter *m*
flow switch Strömungsschalter *m*
flow temperature Vorlauftemperatur *f*
flow through durchlaufen, durchfließen
flow time Durchflusszeit *f*
flow turning Fließdrücken *nt*
flow value Fleißwert *m*
flow volume Durchflussvolumen *nt*
flow-control valve with orifice Blendenventil *nt*
flow-operated safety device nachgeschaltete Stromsicherung *f*
flow wrapping machine Oberfolienform-, -füll- und -verschließmaschine *f*
fluctuate schwanken
fluctuating schwankend
fluctuating stress Schwingbeanspruchung *f*
fluctuation Schwankung *f*
fluctuation in demand Nachfrageschwankung *f*
fluctuation in intensity Intensitätsschwankung *f*
fluctuation in operating voltage Betriebsspannungsschwankung *f*
fluctuation of temperature Temperaturschwankung *f*
fluctuation range Schwankungsbreite *f*
fluctuation stress Schwingbeanspruchung *f*
flue damper Drosselorgan *nt*
flue gas Rauchgas *nt*
flue gas by-pass Rauchgasumgehung *f*
flue gas chimney Abgasschornstein *m*
flue gas connection Abgasanschluss *m*
flue gas control flap Rauchgasregelklappe *f*
flue gas cut-off device Abgassperreinrichtung *f*
flue gas damper Abgasklappe *f*
flue gas dew point Abgastaupunkt *m*
flue gas evacuation Abgasabführung *f*
flue gas flue Abgasfang *m*
flue gas pipe Abgasrohr *nt*
flue gas recorder Abgasschreiber *m*
flue gas scrubber Abgaswäscher *m*
flue gas side Abgasseite *f*
flue gas system Abgasanlage *f*
flue gas test section Abgasmessstrecke *f*
flue gas throttling device Abgasdrosseleinrichtung *f*
flue gas tract Abgasweg *m*
flue gas-heated rauchgasbeheizt
flue outlet Abgasstutzen *m*
flue spigot Abgasstutzen *m*

flue wall Zunge *f*
flue-gas pyrometer Rauchgaspyrometer *nt*
fluffless cloth faserfreies Tuch *nt*
fluid flüssig; Fluid *nt*, Flüssigkeit *f*, flüssiges Medium *nt*
fluid cavitation Flüssigkeitskavitation *f*
fluid coupling Strömungskupplung *f*
fluid entrainment vacuum pump Treibmittelvakuumpumpe *f*
fluid filter Fluidfilter *m*
fluid flow Strömung *f*
fluid friction Fluidreibung *f*
fluid friction loss Fluidreibungsverlust *m*
fluid jet Flüssigkeitsstrahl *m*
fluid laser Flüssigkeitslaser *m*
fluid pressing Flüssigpressen *nt*
fluid transmission Strömungsgetriebe *nt*
fluid turbo coupling Turbokupplung *f*
fluid-actuated shut-off valve Absperrarmatur *f* mit Antrieb durch Fluide
fluidal fluidal
fluid-feed milling machine Fräsmaschine *f* mit hydraulischem Vorschub
fluidity behaviour Fließverhalten *nt*
fluorine Fluor *nt*
fluorescent inspection Fluoreszenzprüfung *f*
fluorescent penetrant Fluoreszenzlösung *f*
fluorescent penetrant inspection method Fluoreszenzverfahren *nt*
fluorescence Fluoreszenz *f*
flush 1. (Maße) abgeglichen, bündig; einfluchten, bündig machen **2.** *(mit Flüssigkeit)* spülen, durchspülen
flush away wegspülen
flush-fitting bündig
flushing *(von Rohrleitungen)* Nachspülung *f*
flushing funnel Spültrichter *m*
flushing liquid Spülflüssigkeit *f*
flute Nut *f*, Spannut *f*, Spanraum *m*, Riefe *f*; nuten, wellen, riefen
flute cutting Spiralnuten *nt*
flute into eindrehen
flute miller Nutenfräsmaschine *f*
flute milling Nutenfräsen *nt*, Spannutenfräsen *nt*
fluted gewellt
fluted filter Faltenfilter *m*
fluted radiator profilierter Heizkörper *m*
fluter Wellenbildner *m*
fluting Fräsen *nt* von Nuten, Nutenfräsarbeit *f*, Profilierung *f*, Nutenfräsen *nt*, Nuten *nt*
fluting roll Riffelscheibe *f*
flux *(el.)* Fluss *m*
flux coating Flussmittelumhüllung *f*
flux cored metal-arc welding Metalllichtbogenschweißen *nt* mit Fülldrahtelektrode
flux density Flussdichte *f*
flux density measuring equipment Induktionsmesseinrichtung *f*
flux filling Flussmittelfüllung *f*
flux spatter Flussmittelspitzer *m*
flux trough Pulverkissen *nt*
flux-conducting component Flussleitstück *nt*
flux-filled soldering bar flussmittelgefüllter Lotstab *m*
fly ash deposit Flugstaubablagerung *f*
fly cutter Schlagfräser *m*, Schlagzahn *m*
fly-cutting Schlagfräsen *nt*, Schlagzahnfräsen *nt*
fly nut Flügelmutter *f*
fly-cutter arbour Schlagfräserdorn *m*
fly-cutting operation Schlagzahnfräsarbeit *f*
flying spot Lichtpunkt *m*
flyspun wire electrode Netzmanteldrahtelektrode *f*
flywheel Schwungrad *nt*
flywheel fan schwerer Lüfter *m*
flywheel ring gear Schwungzahnkranz *m*
foam Schaum *m*; aufschäumen, schäumen
foam lining material Unterlagschaumstoff *m*
foam plastics Schaumkunststoff *m*
foam plastics layer Schaumkunststoffschicht *f*
foam tyre geschäumte Bereifung *f*
foam tyre wheel Rad *nt* mit geschäumter Bereifung

foamed-in cellular material eingeschäumter Kunststoff *m*
foaming characteristic Schäumungseigenschaft *f*
foaming power Schäumvermögen *nt*
foaming test Schäumprüfung *f*
focal length Brennweite *f*
focal point Brennpunkt *m*, Brennfleck *m*
focal point diameter Brennfleckdurchmesser *m*
focal point position Brennpunktlage *f*
focal spot of tube Röhrenbrennfleck *m*
focus Fokus *m*, Brennpunkt *m*, Mittelpunkt *m*, Schärfe *f*; fokussieren, bündeln
focus diameter Fokusdurchmesser *m*
focus position Fokuslage *f*
focus radius Fokusradius *m*
focus-film distance Film-Fokus-Abstand *m*
focusing Scharfeinstellung *f*
focusing lens Einstelllupe *f*
focusing of the image Bildeinstellung *f*
focusing scale Einstellskala *f*
focusing screen Mattscheibe *f*
focusing screw Okularschraube *f*
focussing Fokussierung *f*
focussing equipment Fokussiereinheit *f*
focussing lens Fokussierungslinse *f*
focussing optics Fokussieroptik *f*
fog density Schleierschwärzung *f*
fogging Erblindung *f*, Irisation *f*
foil Folie *f*, Blättchen *nt*
foil laminate Verbundfolie *f*
foil laminate lid Verbundfoliendeckel *m*
foil lap joint welding Folienüberlappnahtschweißen *nt*
foil or sheeting Kunststofffolie *f*
foil packaging Folienverpackung *f*
foil releasing plasticiser weichmacherabgebene Folie *f*
foil sealing machine Folienverschließmaschine *f*
fold Abkantung *f*, Falz *m*, Knick *m*, Falte *f*, Einknickung *f*; knicken, falten, falzen, abkanten, zusammenlegen, zusammenklappen, klappen
fold away type klappbar

fold closing machine Faltverschließmaschine *f*
fold on the edge abkanten
fold over abkanten
fold over wrapping machine Oberfolieneinschlagmaschine *f*
fold up hochklappen
fold wrapping machine Falteinschlagmaschine *f*
folded bend Faltbogen *m*
folded spiral-seam pipe Wickelfalzrohr *nt*
folding 1. Falzen *nt*, Abbiegen *nt*; klappbar, zusammenklappbar, zusammenlegbar 2. *(an einer Kante)* Abkanten *nt*
folding apparatus Falzgerät *nt*
folding box Faltbox *f*
folding fork Klappgabel *f*
folding machine Abkantmaschine *f*
folding press Abkantpresse *f*
folding rule Gliedermaßstab *m*
folding up hochklappbar
folding-over Abkanten *nt*
follow 1. mitgehen, folgen, verfolgen 2. *(kopieren)* abtasten
follow rest mitgehender Setzstock *m*
follow the outline abfahren
follow-die cutter Folgeschneidwerkzeug *nt*, Folgeschneiden *nt*
follower drive Schiebertrieb *m*
follower piston Folgekolben *m*
follower rest mitgehender Setzstock *m*
follower roll Tastrolle *f*
following nachfolgend, folgend
following error Nachlauffehler *m*
following process Folgeprozess *m*
follow-up Nachführung *f*, Nachlauf *m*; nachsteuern, nachlaufen
follow-up accuracy Nachfahrgenauigkeit *f*
follow-up control Ablaufsteuerung *f*
follow-up distance Nachlaufweg *m*
follow-up servo Folgeeinrichtung *f*
Food Act Lebensmittelgesetz *nt*
foolproof missgriffsicher
foot Fuß *m*
foot guard Fußschutz *m*
foot lever Fußhebel *m*
foot plate Kufe *f*

foot protection Fußschutz *m*
foot switch Fußschalter *m*
foot-actuated fußbetätigt
foot-controlled fußbetätigt
footing Fußgestell *nt*
foot-mounted in Fußbauform
foot-mounted motor Fußmotor *m*
foot-operated fußbetätigt
foot-operated grease gun Fußpresse *f*
foot-operated lever Pedal *nt*
footplate Aufstandsfläche *f*
footstep Tritt *m*
footstep sound Trittschall *m*
footstock Reitstock *m*
footstock sleeve Reitstockspindel *f*
for bei
for domestic use für den Hausgebrauch
for persons walking on bei Begehen
for the long term langfristig
for the short-term kurzfristig
for travel on the rack structure regalverfahrend
forbid untersagen, verbieten
forbidden untersagt, verboten
force due to rolling friction Verzögerungskraft *f*
force Kraft *f*, Zwang *m*; zwingen, zwängen, drücken
force against andrücken
force arrow Kraftpfeil *m*
force away abdrücken
force calculation Kraftberechnung *f*
force component Kraftkomponente *f*, Kraftwirkung *f*
force component acting perpendicular to shear plane Querkraft *f* senkrecht auf die Scherebene wirkend
force component in the direction of cutting Schnittkraft *f*
force diagram Kräfteplan *m*
force distribution Krafteinteilung *f*
force down herabdrücken, niederdrücken
force due to running askew Schräglaufkraft *f*
force exerted by the tool Zerspankraft *f*
force fit Presspassung *f*
force fitting Einpressen *nt*
force generating equipment Krafterzeugungseinrichtung *f*
force intensification Kraftverstärkung *f*
force limiter Belastungsbegrenzer *m*
force measurement Kraftmessung *f*
force of acceleration Beschleunigungskraft *f*
force of gravity casting Schwerkraftgießen *nt*
force of inertia Massenkraft *f*
force of mortality Ausfallrate *f*
force of the cut Schnittkraft *f*
force of the stylus Fühlerdruck *m*
force off-time Kraftruhezeit *f*
force out (*z. B. Formmasse aus einer Druckkammer*) pressen
force per volume Wichte *f*
force value Kraftgröße *f*
force-closed kraftschlüssig
forced air circulation Zwangsbelüftung *f*
forced circulation heat generator Zwanglaufwärmeerzeuger *m*
forced circulation high temperature water heating appliance Zwanglaufheißwassererzeuger *m*
forced circulation principle Zwanglaufprinzip *nt*
forced draft fan Druckgebläse *nt*
forced external cooling Zwangsbelüftung *f*
forced flexural vibrations erzwungene Biegeschwingung *f*
forced gas test Gaswarnkalibriersystem *nt*
forced ventilation Zwangslüftung *f*
forced vibrations *pl* erzwungene Schwingungen *fpl*, fremderregte Schwingungen *fpl*, fremderzeugte Schwingungen *fpl*
forced-feed circulatory lubrication Druckumlaufschmierung *f*
force-feed lubrication Druckschmierung *f*
forceless interval kraftlose Zeitspanne *f*
force-locked connecting element kraftschlüssiges Verbindungselement *nt*
force-locked fastener kraftschlüssiges Verbindungselement *nt*
force-locked retaining element kraftschlüssiges Sicherungselement *nt*

force-lubricate druckschmieren
force-off abdrücken
forcing screw Abdrückschraube *f*
forbidden unzulässig
fore adjustment Vorwärtsverstellung *f*
forecast Prognose *f*, Vorschau *f*; prognostizieren, vorhersehen
forecast accuracy Prognosegenauigkeit *f*
forecast method Prognoseverfahren *nt*
forecast order Vorschauauftrag *m*
forecourt Vorzone *f*
foreign body Fremdkörper *m*, Fremdstoff *m*
foreign body detecting machine Fremdkörperdetektionsmaschine *f*
foreign matter Fremdkörper *m*, Fremdstoff *m*
foreign metallic inclusions *pl* Fremdmetalleinschlüsse *mpl*
foreign part drawing Fremdteilzeichnung *f*
foreign thread ausländisches Gewinde *nt*
foreman Meister *m*
foreman area Meisterbereich *m*
foresee vorhersehen
foreseeable voraussehbar, vorhersehbar
forward vorwärts
forewarn vorwarnen
forewarning Vorwarnung *f*
forge schmieden
forge force Nachpresskraft *f*
forge rolling Reckwalzen *nt*, Schmiedewalzen *nt*
forge time Nachpresszeit *f*
forge to/on anschmieden
forged tool einteiliges Werkzeug *nt*, Vollmeißel *m*
forging Schmiedestück *nt*, Schmieden *nt*
forging burst Kernzerschmiedung *f*
forging die Schmiedegesenk *nt*
forging drawing Schmiedestückzeichnung *f*
forging plant Schmiedebetrieb *m*
forging shop Schmiedebetrieb *m*
fork Lastgabel *f*, Gabel *f*, Zinken *m*
fork adjusting device Zinkenverstellgerät *nt*

fork aperture Gabeltasche *f*
fork arm Gabelzinken *m*
fork arm blade Gabelblatt *nt*
fork arm carriage Gabelträger *m*, Lastträger *m*
fork arm moment Gabelzinkenmoment *nt*
fork arm shank Gabelrücken *m*
fork backwards Gabelrückfahrt *f*
fork blade Gabelblatt *nt*
fork carriage Gabelträger *m*, Gabelwagen *m*
fork carrier Gabelträger *m*
fork clamp Klammergabel *f*
fork clearance Lichtraumprofil *nt*
fork cycle Gabelspiel *nt*
fork dimensions Abmessung *f* der Gabelzinken
fork down Gabelsenken *nt*
fork entry Einfahrmaß *nt*
fork entry aperture Gabeleinfahrtasche *f*, Staplertasche *f*, Einfahrtasche *f*
fork entry clearance Einfahrtasche *f*
fork extender Schubgabel *f*
fork extension Gabelverlängerung *f*
fork forwards Gabelausfahrt *f*
fork height Gabelhöhe *f*
fork height adjustable relative to cab in der Höhe verschiebbare Gabeln
fork lift Gabelstapler *m*
fork lift truck Gabelstapler *m*, Gabelhubwagen *m*, Gabelhubfahrzeug *nt*
fork lifting Gabelheben *nt*
fork lowering Gabelsenken *nt*
fork mounting Einbau *m* in einer Gabel
fork outwards Gabelausfahrt *f*
fork positioner Zinkenverstellgerät *nt*
fork retraction Gabelrückfahrt *f*
fork rotation speed Drehgeschwindigkeit *f*
fork sag Gabeldurchhang *m*
fork shank Gabelrücken *m*, Gabelschaft *m*
fork spacing Gabelabstand *m*, Abstand *m* der Gabeln
fork spacing adjustment Achsabstandsveränderung *f*
fork spacing adjustment drive *(Achsabstandsveränderung der Gabeln)* Antrieb *m*

fork surfaces Flächen *fpl* der Gabelzinke
fork tension Gabelausfahrt *f*
fork test Gabelversuch *m*
fork tip Gabelspitze *f*
fork tip sensor Sensor *m* in der Gabelspitze
fork tippler Gabelneiger *m*
fork truck Gabelwagen *m*
fork truck with seated driver Sitzgabelstapler *m*
fork truck with standing driver Standgabelstapler *m*
fork up Gabelheben *nt* (Anweisung)
fork wheels Gabelräder *ntpl*
fork width Schenkelweite *f* (Gabeln)
fork withdrawal Gabelrückfahrt *f*
form 1. *(Fertigen)* herstellen, erstellen, umformen, formen, bearbeiten, bilden, ausbilden; Form *f* **2.** *(Papier, Formular)* Formblatt *nt*, Vordruck *m*
form accuracy Formgenauigkeit *f*
form-and casting processes Form- und Gießverfahren *nt*
form and cutter machine Profil- und Fräserschleifmaschine *f*
form and punch shaping machine Form- und Stempelhobelmaschine *f*
form base material Formgrundstoff *m*
form bending Formbiegen *nt*
form bending by a sliding-action draw Gleitziehbiegen *nt*
form broach Formräumwerkzeug *nt*, Räumwerkzeug *nt* für Sonderformen
form broaching Formräumen *nt*
form closure Formschluss *m*
form constraint Formschluss *m*
form copying and profile miller Formkopier- und Profilfräsmaschine *f*, Nachform- und Profilfräsmaschine *f*
form copying and profile milling machine Nachform- und Profilfräsmaschine *f*, Formkopier- und Profilfräsmaschine *f*
form counterbore Formsenker *m*
form cutter Formfräser *m*, Profilfräser *m*
form cutting tool Formmeißel *m*
form deviation Formabweichung *f*, Gestaltabweichung *f*
form dialog Formulardialog *m*
form echo Formecho *nt*
form element Formelement *nt*
form error Formfehler *m*, Passfehler *m*, Formabweichungen *f*
form factor Formfaktor *m*
form fault Formfehler *m*
form fill and seal machine Formfüll- und -verschließmaschine *f*
form fit formschlüssig; Formschluss *m*
form front Formfront *f*
form geometry Gestalt *f*
form grinder Formschleifmaschine *f*
form grinding Profilschleifen *nt*, Formschleifen *nt*
form grinding operation Formschleifoperation *f*
form grip Formschluss *m*
form into a bunch einen Pulk bilden aus
form milling Formfräsen *nt*, Profilfräsen *nt*
form milling machine Kopierfräsmaschine *f*, Formfräsmaschine *f*
form milling method Formfräsverfahren *nt*
form of chip Spanform *f*
form of welding joint Schweißstoßart *f*
form pallets Paletten herstellen
form planes Formhobeln *nt*
form planing Hobeln *nt* nach Schablone, Schablonenformhobeln *nt*
form planing machine Schablonenhobelmaschine *f*
form plate Kopierlineal *nt*, Kopierschiene *f*
form plate holder Kopierschienenhalter *m*
form pressing Formdrängen *nt*
form profile cutter profilgeschliffener Formfräser *m*
form relieved cutter Formfräser *m*, hinterdrehter Formfräser *m*, Fräser *m* mit hinterdrehten Zähnen
form sand Formsand *m*
form shaper Formhobler *m*
form tool gauge Formlehre *f*
form tracer Nachformfühler *m*, Taster *m*
form truing Profilabrichten *nt*
form turn formdrehen, formabrichten

form turning Formdrehen *nt*, Fassondrehen *nt*
form turning attachment Formdreheinrichtung *f*
form turning jobs Formdreharbeiten *fpl*
form turning lathe Formdrehmaschine *f*
form turning tool Formdrehmeißel *m*
formaldehyde condensation product Formaldehydkondensationsprodukt *nt*
forming of burrs Gratbildung *f*
formation Bildung *f*
formation of a protective layer Schutzschichtbildung *f*
formation of creases Knitterfaltenbildung *f*
formation of dust Staubbildung *f*
formation of ice Eisbildung *f*
formation of the ignition flame Zündflammenbildung *f*
formation of the structure Gefügeausbildung *f*
form-copy planing Schablonenverfahren *nt*
form-copying planer Hobelmaschine *f* nach dem Schablonenverfahren
form-cutting method Formverfahren *nt*
form design drawing Formgebungszeichnung *f*
form-duplicating machine Nachformmaschine *f*
formed milling cutter Formfräser *m*
formed tool Formmeißel *m*
formed wheel Formscheibe *f*, Profilscheibe *f*
former Schablone *f*
former pin Führungsstift *m*
former plate Formlineal *nt*, Leitlineal *nt*
former slide Kegelschlitten *m*
form-grind formschleifen
forming Umformen *nt*, Verformen *nt*, Verformung *f*, Abformung *f*, Formgebung *f*, Formung *f*, Bearbeitung *f*
forming cut Formschnitt *m*
forming forces *pl* Umformkräfte *mpl*
forming lapping Maßläppen *nt*
forming machine Umformmaschine *f*, Formmaschine *f*
forming power Umformleistung *f*
forming process Umformvorgang *m*
forming production Formenherstellung *f*
forming resistance Umformwiderstand *m*
forming speed Umformgeschwindigkeit *f*
forming technology Umformtechnik *f*
forming tool Formmeißel *m*
forming tools *pl* Formwerkzeuge *ntpl*
forming wax Formwachs *nt*
forming work Umformarbeit *f*
form-locked connecting fastener formschlüssiges Verbindungselement *nt*
form-locked connecting element formschlüssiges Verbindungselement *nt*
form-relieved cutter hinterdrehter Fräser *m*
form-tooth grinding Formzahnradschleifen *nt*
form-true profilabrichten
formula Formel *f*
formula constituent Formelbestandteil *m*
front and rear drive unit Vorder- und Hinterradantrieb *m*
forth nach vorn
forthwith unverzüglich
forward Übertrag *m*; weiterleiten
forward direction Flussrichtung *f*, Vorwärtsrichtung *f*
forward driving direction Fahrtrichtung *f* vorwärts
forward edge adjustment Vorderkanteneinstellung *f*
forward force Schließkraft *f*
forward gear Vorwärtsgang *m*
forward inching *(Maschinen)* Reckung *f*
forward motion Vorlauf *m*
forward motion of the upsetting slide Stauchschlittenvorwärtsbewegung *f*
forward movement Vorwärtsbewegung *f*
forward pressure-off time Offenhaltezeit *f*
forward rotation Vorlauf *m*

forward schedule Vorwärtsterminplanung *f*
forward speed Vorwärtsgang *m*
forward stroke Schnitthub *m*
forward stroke of the ram Stößelverlauf *m*
forward tilt Vorwärtsneigung *f*
forward time Schließzeit *f*
forward travel direction Vorwärtsfahrtrichtung *f*
forwarding Weiterleitung *f*
forwarding agent Spedition *f*, Spediteur *m*
forwarding charges Speditionskosten *pl*
forwarding company Spedition *f*
forwarding expenses Speditionskosten *pl*
forwarding trade Spedition *f*
forwards nach vorn
foul (with) aneinander stoßen
fouling (with) Anstoßen *nt*
foundation Fundament *nt*
foundation bolt Ankerbolzen *m*, Fundamentschraube *f*
foundation drawing Fundamentzeichnung *f*
foundations Baugrundsetzungen *fpl*
founding Guss *m*
foundry Gießerei *f*
foundry core Gießereikern *m*
foundry crucible Gießereitiegel *m*
foundry form Gießereiform *f*
foundry pattern Gießereimodell *nt*
foundry process Gießereiprozess *m*
foundry technology Gießereitechnologie *f*, Gießtechnologie *f*
foundry-just gießgerecht
four spindle automatic lathe Vierspindler *m*, Vierspindelautomat *m*
four way mixer valve Vierwegemischer *m*
four wheel brake Vierradbremse *f*
four wheel drive Vierradantrieb *m*
four wheel steering Vierradlenkung *f*
four wheel truck Vierradstapler *m*
four ball tester Vierkugel-Apparat *m*
four-directional lift truck Vierwegestapler *m*
four-edged vierkantig

fourfold vierfach
four-head planer Hobelmaschine *f* mit vier Supporten
four-jaw chuck Vierbackenfutter *nt*
four-point loading Vierpunktbelastung *f*
four-sided area vierseitige Fläche *f*
four-speed gear mechanism with clutch selection Ruppergetriebe *nt*
four-spindle automatic bar machine Vierspindelstangenautomat *m*
four-spindle automatic chucking machine Vierspindelfutterautomat *m*
four-spindle chucking automatic Vierspindelfutterautomat *m*
four-spindle drilling machine vierspindlige Bohrmaschine *f*
four-spindle profiler with two-dimensional control Vierspindelnachformfräsmaschine *f* für zweidimensionales Fräsen
four-spindle tracer milling machine vierspindelige fühlergesteuerte Fräsmaschine *f*, Vierspindelnachformfräsmaschine *f* mit Fühlersteuerung
four-station turret Blockrevolver *m*
four-way flat pallet Vierwegeflachpalette *f*
four-way pallet Vierwegepalette *f*
four-way socket wrench Kreuzsteckschlüssel *m*
four-way tool block Vierfachmeißelhalter *m*, Blockmeißelhalter *m*
fourway-boring machine Vierwegebohrmaschine *f*
fourway-drilling machine Vierwegebohrmaschine *f*
four-wheeled zweiachsig
fractile Quantil *nt*
fraction Teil *m*, Bruchteil *m*, Bruch *m*, Riss *m*
fraction of a millimetre Millimeterbruchteil *m*
fractionating column Dephlegmierkolonne *f*
fractioning column Destillationsaufsatz *m*
fractions *pl* Anteile *mpl*
fracture Bruch *m*; zerbrechen, brechen, reißen

fracture behaviour Bruchverhalten *nt*
fracture drop height Bruchfallhöhe *f*
fracture in the adhesive layer Klebschichtbruch *m*
fracture marking Bruchauffälligkeit *f*
fracture of the specimen Probenbruch *m*
fracture versus time curve Zeit-Bruch-Linie *f*
fracture zone Bruchzone *f*
fractured chip Reißspan *m*
fractured part Bruchstück *nt*
fracturing Reißen *nt*
fragile zerbrechlich, brüchig
fragile goods *pl* empfindliche Güter *ntpl*
fragility Zerbrechlichkeit *f*
fragment Teilchen *nt*
fragmental chip Span *m*, Abreißspan *m*, Reißspan *m*, Kurzspan *m*, Bruchspan *m*
frail zerbrechlich
frame Ständer *m*, Gestell *nt*, Rahmen *m*, Gehäuse *nt*, Bügel *m*; einrahmen
frame burner Rahmenbrenner *m*
frame cross bracing Seitenverstrebung *f*
frame depth Rahmentiefe *f*
frame edge Rahmenkante *f*
frame of the door Türzarge *f*
frame structure Rahmen *m*
frame width Rahmenbreite *f*
framework Rahmen *m*, Gerüst *nt*
framework contract Rahmenvertrag *m*
framing Gerüst *nt*, Rahmen *m*, Einrahmen *nt*
free frei, licht, lose
free area Freifläche *f*
free bending freies Biegen *nt*
free corrosion potential freies Korrosionspotential *nt*
free cutting gut zerspanbar
free cutting property Zerspanbarkeit *f*, Schnittbearbeitbarkeit *f*
free dimension Freimaß *nt*
free fall freier Fall *m*
free field *(Schall)* Hallfreifeld *nt*, Freifeld *nt*
free from bending stresses biegespannungsfrei

free from distortion verzerrungsfrei
free from vibrations schwingungsfrei
free from wear verschleißfrei
free lift Freihub *m*
free lift height Freihubhöhe *f*
free machining property Zerspanbarkeit *f*, Bearbeitbarkeit *f*
free machining quality Schnittbearbeitbarkeit *f*
free margin Zusatzfläche *f*
free of harmonics überschwingungsfrei
free of play spielfrei
free of smoke rauchfrei
free of soot rußfrei
free of undercut unterschnittfrei
free passage ungehinderter Durchtritt *m*
free ranging nicht geführt, frei fahrend
free size Freimaß *nt*
free size tolerance Allgemeintoleranz *f*, Freimaßtoleranz *f*
free size tolerance for castings Gussfreimaßtoleranz
free size tolerance space Freimaßtoleranzraum *m*
free space for feet Fußfreiraum *m*
free standing frei stehend
free swinging frei pendelnd
free width lichte Breite *f*
free-cutting steel Automatenstahl *m*
freedom Freiheit *f*
freedom from chatter Ratterfreiheit *f*
freedom from cracks Rissfreiheit *f*
freedom from interference Störfreiheit *f*
freedom from sediment Satzfreiheit *f*
freedom of movement Bewegungsmöglichkeit *f*
free-enterprise marktwirtschaftlich
free-fall stop test Freifallfangprobe *f*
free-fall test Freifallprobe *f*
free-flow chain conveyor Staukettenförderer *m*
free-flow roller conveyor Staurollenförderer *m*
free-foamed cellular material freigeschäumter Schaumstoff *m*
freehand freihändig
freehand line Freihandlinie *f*
free-lift mast Teleskopmast *m*

freely programmable frei programmierbar
freely supported frei pendelnd aufgehängt
free-machining or quality Bearbeitbarkeit *f*
free-machining steel Automatenstahl *m*
free-mounted radiator frei aufgestellter Radiator *m*
freeness value brought about by beating Mahlgrad *m*, Mahlzustand *m*
free-standing chimney freistehender Schornstein *m*
freeze kühlen
freezer Kühlraum *m*, Kühlhaus *nt*
freezing Befrostung *f*, Vereisung *f*
freight Fracht *f*, Ladung *f*
freight container Frachtcontainer *m*, Container *m*
freight forwarder Spediteur *m*
frequency analyser Frequenzanalysator *m*
frequency Frequenz *f*, Rhythmus *m*, Häufigkeit *f*
frequency amplifier Gleichspannungsfrequenzmessverstärker *m*
frequency band Frequenzband *nt*
frequency converter Frequenzumrichter *m*, Umrichter *m*
frequency counter Frequenzzähler *m*
frequency density Häufigkeitsdichte *f*
frequency density function Häufigkeitsdichtefunktion *f*
frequency distribution Häufigkeitsverteilung *f*
frequency generator Frequenzgenerator *m*
frequency meter Frequenzmesser *m*
frequency of occurrence Eintrittshäufigkeit *f*
frequency of testing Prüfhäufigkeit *f*
frequency of use Nutzungshäufigkeit *f*
frequency range Frequenzbereich *m*
frequency study Häufigkeitsstudie *f*
frequency weighting Frequenzbewertung *f*
frequency-controlled frequenzgeregelt
frequency-regulated frequenzgeregelt

frequent häufig
fresh air inlet Frischlufteinlass *m*
fresh air operation Frischluftbetrieb *m*
fresh emulsion Neuemulsion *f*
fresh rust Neurost *m*
freshly mixed concrete Frischbetonmischung *f*
fret *(Korrosion)* fressen
fretting rust Passungsrost *m*
friable bröckelig
friction Reibung *f*
friction and winding losses Reibungsverlust *m*
friction area Reibfläche *f*
friction bearing Gleitlager *nt*
friction brake Reibbremse *f*
friction braking device Bremsenfangvorrichtung *f*
friction clutch Reibkupplung *f*, Reibungskupplung *f*, Rutschkupplung *f*
friction coefficient Reibkoeffizient *m*
friction element Reibelement *nt*
friction energy Reibungsarbeit *f*
friction force coefficient Kraftschlussbeiwert *m*
friction free Kraftschluss *m*
friction gear Reibradgetriebe *nt*
friction gearing Reinradgetriebe *nt*
friction grip Reibungsschluss *m*
friction grip coefficient Kraftschlussbeiwert *m*
friction lining Reibbelag *m*
friction locking Reibungsschluss *m*
friction loss Eigenverbrauch *m*
friction of flanges Spurkranzreibung *f*
friction part of the brake Bremsreibpartner *m*
friction part of the clutch Kupplungsreibpartner *m*
friction partner Reibpartner *m*
friction process Reibungsgeschehen *nt*
friction property Reibeigenschaft *f*
friction roller Reibrolle *f*
friction safety clutch Sicherheitsrutschkupplung *f*
friction saw Reibsäge *f*
friction stud welding Reibbolzenschweißen *nt*
friction surface Reibfläche *f*, Reiboberfläche *f*

friction transmission Reibradgetriebe *nt*
friction welding Reibschweißen *nt*
frictional durch Reibung, reibend
frictional connection Kraftschluss *m*
frictional force Reibungskraft *f*
frictional heat Reibungswärme *f*
frictional loss Reibungsverlust *m*
frictional motion Reibbewegung *f*
frictional pairing Reibpaarung *f*
frictional resistance Reibungswiderstand *m*
frictional rubbing forces kraftschlüssige Kräfte *fpl*
frictional wheel Reibrad *nt*
frictional wheel gear Reibradgetriebe *nt*
friction-disc clutch Lamellenkupplung *f*
friction-driven live roller conveyor Rollenbahn *f* mit Reibantrieb
frictionless reibungsfrei
friction-locked connecting element kraftschlüssiges Verbindungselement *nt*
friction-locked retaining element kraftschlüssiges Sicherungselement *nt*
friction-locking joint actuated by longitudinal forces längskraftschlüssige Verbindung *f*
fringe pattern Streifenbild *nt*
fritted base Frittenboden *m*
fritted wash bottle Frittenwaschflasche *f*
forced lubrication Druckschmierung *f*
frog and switch planer Weichenzungenhobelmaschine *f*
from *(Platz)* von, aus
from ... to ... von ... bis ...
from a safety point of view sicherheitstechnisch
from above von oben
from below von unten
from either direction wechselseitig
from one direction einseitig
from standstill aus dem Stand
from the bottom up von unten nach oben
front vorder/e/er/es, fassadenseitig, frontseitig; Front *f*, Vorderseite *f*, Stirn *f*, Kopf *m*, Fassade *f*

front angle Einstellwinkel *m* der Nebenschneide
front area Vorzone *f*, Lagervorfeld *nt*, Regalvorfeld *nt*, Vorfeld *nt*
front axle Vorderachse *f*
front brace Gegenhalterschere *f*
front cutting edge Nebenschneide *f*, Stirnschneide *f*
front edge Nebenschneide *f*, Stirnschneide *f*, Vorderkante *f*
front edge of the support Auflagenvorderkante *f*, Stützenvorderkante *f*
front elevation Vorderansicht *f*
front end vorderes Ende *nt*, Vorderseite *f*, Stirnfläche *f*, Stirnseite *f*, Frontseite *f*
front end wear Stirnflächenverschleiß *m*
front extension chuck Vorderendfutter *nt*
front face Vorderseite *f*, Vorderfläche *f*, Stirnseite *f*, Lastanlagefläche *f*
front face of the shank Lastanlage *f*
front flap Vorderwandklappe *f*
front intensifying screen Vorderfolie *f*
front panel Frontplatte *f*
front part Vorbau *m*
front plate Frontplatte *f*
front rake Neigungswinkel *m*
front rake angle Spitzenspanwinkel *m*, Radialwinkel *m*
front ramp Kopframpe *f*
front side Stirnseite *f*
front slide Vorderschlitten *m*
front spindle end vorderes Spindelende *nt*
front stacking frontseitiges Stapeln *nt*
front standard vorderer Ständer *m*
front top rake angle Spitzenspanwinkel *m*
front upright Vorderständer *m*
front view Aufriss *m*
front wall Stirnseite *f*, Vorderwand *f*
front wall of the machine base Wange *f* eines Maschinenständers
front wheel Vorderrad *nt*
front wheel drive Frontantrieb *m*
front wheel driven frontgetrieben
front window Windschutzscheibe *f*
front windshield Windschutzscheibe *f*

frontal section Frontabschnitt *m*
front-seated Fahrersitz *m* in Fahrtrichtung
frost Frost *m*; mattieren
frost alternating test Frostwechselversuch *m*
frost resistance Frostwiderstandsfähigkeit *f*
frosting Mattieren *nt*, Mattierung *f*
frozen-in tension eingefrorene Spannung *f*
fuel Brennstoff *m*, Kraftstoff *m*, Treibstoff *m*
fuel charge Brennstofffüllung *f*
fuel charging Brennstoffbeschickung *f*
fuel container Kraftstoffbehälter *m*
fuel cut-off *(e. Feuerung)* Absperreinrichtung *f*
fuel degasifier Brennstoffentgaser *m*
fuel feed interlock Brennstoffverriegelung *f*
fuel feeding device Brennstoffnachförderung *f*
fuel gas line Brenngasleitung *f*
fuel gas throughput Brenngasdurchfluss *m*
fuel gasifier Brennstoffvergaser *m*
fuel hopper Brennstoffmagazin *nt*, Füllraum *m* eines Kessels
fuel leakage Kraftstoffleckage *f*
fuel oil Heizöl *nt*
fuel oil extraction line Heizölentnahmeleitung *f*
fuel oil filter Heizölfilter *m*
fuel oil hose Heizölschlauch *m*
fuel oil level Heizölstand *m*
fuel oil line Heizölleitung *f*
fuel oil piping Heizölleitung *f*
fuel oil preheater Heizölvorwärmer *m*
fuel oil preheating Heizölvorwärmung *f*
fuel oil preheating system Heizölvorwärmung *f*
fuel oil return line Heizölrücklaufleitung *f*
fuel oil storage tank code Heizölbehälterrichtlinien *fpl*
fuel oil supply Heizölversorgung *f*
fuel quantity Brennstoffmenge *f*
fuel sample Brennstoffprobe *f*

fuel selector Brennstoffwähler *m*
fuel source Kraftstoffzuleitung *f*
fuel storage room Brennstofflagerraum *m*
fuel supply system Kraftstoffanlage *f*
fuel system Kraftstoffsystem *nt*
fuel take-off Flüssiggasauslass *m*
fuel tank Tank *m*, Kraftstoffbehälter *m*, Treibstofftank *m*
fulcrum Stützpunkt *m*, Drehpunkt *m*, Drehachse *f*
fulcrum pin *(Bauelement)* Drehachse *f*
fulfil erfüllen, einhalten
fulfilled erfüllt
fulfilled correctly in terms of quantity mengengerecht erfüllt
fulfilled correctly in terms of type artgerecht erfüllt
fulfilled correctly in terms of volume mengengerecht erfüllt
fulfilled correctly in terms of deadlines termingerecht erfüllt
fulfilment Erfüllung *f*, Einhaltung *f*
fulfilment of orders Auftragserfüllung *f*
full voll, vollständig
full bearing satte Auflage *f*
full charging Vollladung *f*
full circle Vollkreis *m*
full dog point *(Schraube)* Zapfen *m*
full flank volle Flanke *f*
full form „Go" gauge Vollformgutlehre *f*
full form casting process Vollformgießverfahren *nt*
full length parallel grooved pin Zylinderstift *m*
full length parallel grooved pin with pilot Zylinderstift *m* mit Einführende
full length taper grooved pin Kegelkerbstift *m*
full load Volllast *f*
full load torque volles Drehmoment *nt*
full of scale maßstäblich
full pallet roller conveyor Vollpalettenrollenbahn *f*
full power volle Leistung *f*; vollkraftbetrieben
full scale maßstäblich
full scale proof of competence großer Befähigungsnachweis *m*

full screen ganzer Bildschirm *m*
full section Vollschnitt *m*
full squared vollkantig
full swing Durchschwingen *nt*
full test Vollprüfung *f*
full wave rectification Vollwellengleichrichtung *f*
full-charge cycle Vollladezyklus *m*
full-circle profiler Nachformfräsmaschine *f* mit Vollumrisskreisform, Vollumrissnachformfräsmaschine *f*
full-circle profiling machine Vollumrissnachformfräsmaschine *f*
full-edged vollkantig
full-length engagement of the screw (or bolt) thread Verschlussschraube *f* über gesamte Gewindelänge
full-load speed Volllastdrehzahl *f*
full-load start Volllastanlauf *m*, Schweranlauf *m*
full-scale marking off drawing Fertigungsriss *m*
full-scale representation Naturgröße *f*
full-shank bolt Vollschaftschraube *f*
fully voll
fully austenitic weld metal vollaustenitisches Schweißgut *nt*
fully automatic lathe Drehvollautomat *m*, Vollautomat *nt*, Drehbank *f*
fully automatic machine Vollautomat *m*, vollselbsttätige Maschine *f*
fully cylindrical plug gauge vollzylindrischer Lehrdorn *m*
fully flat vollflächig
fully graphic vollgraphisch
fully illuminated ausgeleuchtet
fully mechanized plasma welding vollmechanisches Plasmaschweißen *nt*
fully mechanized soldering vollmechanisiertes Löten *nt*
fully plastic condition vollplastischer Zustand *m*
fume Dampf *m*
fumes Rauch *m*, Rauchgase *ntpl*
function Funktion *f*, Verwendung *f*; funktionieren, ansprechen, wirken (als)
function block diagram (FBD) Funktionsbausteinsprache (FBS) *f*
function description Funktionsbeschreibung *f*
function diagram Funktionsschema *nt*
function indicator Funktionsanzeiger *m*
function keyboard Funktionstastatur *f*
function key Funktionstaste *f*
function module Funktionsmodul *nt*
function reference Funktionsaufruf *m*
function table Funktionstabelle *f*
function test Funktionsprüfung *f*
functional funktional, funktionsfähig, operativ
functional capability Funktionsfähigkeit *f*
functional change Funktionsveränderung *f*
functional control Bedienbarkeit *f*
functional disorder Fehlfunktion *f*
functional earth Funktionserde *f*
functional earthing point Funktionserdanschluss *m*
functional efficiency Funktionstüchtigkeit *f*
functional element Funktionselement *nt*
functional extra-low voltage Funktionskleinspannung *f*
functional ground Funktionserde *f*
functional grouping Funktionsgruppierung *f*
functional impairment funktionsstörender Fehler *nt*
functional level Funktionsebene *f*
functional operation Steuerung *f*
functional parameter Funktionalparameter *m*
functional plan Funktionsplan *m*
functional program Funktionsprogramm *nt*
functional prototype Funktionsprototyp *m*
functional reason funktionstechnischer Grund *m*
functional reliability Funktionstüchtigkeit *f*
functional specification Pflichtenheft *nt*
functional target Zielfunktion *f*
functional test Funktionsprüfung *f*
functional unit Funktionseinheit *f*
functional verification Funktionsprü-

fung *f*
functionality Funktionsfähigkeit *f*
functionally important datum plane funktionswichtige Bezugsebene *f*
functionally significant dimension funktionsbedingtes Maß *nt*
functioning Funktion *f*
function-related dimensioning funktionsbezogene Maßeintragung *f*
fundamental deviation Grundabmaß *nt*
fundamental deviation of screw thread Gewindegrundabmaß *nt*
fundamental frequency method Grundschwingungsmessverfahren *nt*
fundamental heat circuit diagram Wärmegrundschaltplan *m*
fundamental standard Grundnorm *f*
fundamental tolerance group Grundtoleranzreihe *f*
fundamental triangle Grunddreieck *nt*
fungal decay Pilzbefall *m*
funnel Trichter *m*
funnel model Trichtermodell *nt*
furnace Brandraum *m*, Ofen *m*
furnace base Ofensockel *m*
furnace engineering Feuerungstechnik *f*
furnace pressure controller Feuerraumdruckregler *m*
furnace-type air heater Feuerlufterhitzer *m*
furnish fördern, liefern
further processing Weiterverarbeitung *f*
fusability of fuel ash Ascheschmelzverhalten *nt*
fuse 1. *(schmelzen, auftauen)* abschmelzen, ausschmelzen, schmelzen **2.** *(sichern)* Sicherung *f*; absichern
fuse element Sicherungselement *nt*
fused alumina Kunstkorund *nt*, Elektrokorund *nt*
fused area Ausschmelzung *f*
Fused Deposition Modeling FDM (Schmelzmodellherstellung *f*)
fused lead bath Bleischmelze *f*
fused material Schmelze *f*
fused salt bath Salzschmelze *f*
fused soldering Einbrennlötung *f*
fused-on spatter angeschmolzener Schweißspritzer *m*
fusion surface Bindefläche *f*
fusible abschmelzbar
fusible alloy Schmelzlegierung *f*
fusing 1. *(Schmelze)* Schmelzen *nt* **2.** *(Sicherheitstechnik)* Absicherung *f*
fusing contact Schmorkontakt *m*
fusion Schmelzen *nt*, Schmelzung *f*
fusion build-up welding Schmelzauftragschweißen *nt*
fusion brazing depending on capillary action kapillaraktives Spaltlöten *nt*
fusion depth Aufschmelztiefe *f*
fusion edge Schmelzkante *f*
fusion face Stirnfläche *f*
fusion flow test Ablaufversuch *m*
fusion frequency Verschmelzungsfrequenz *f*
fusion joint welding Schmelzverbindungsschweißen *nt*
fusion method Aufschlussverfahren *nt*
fusion sealing machine Schmelzschweißverschließmaschine *f*
fusion soldering Schmelzlöten *nt*
fusion welding Schmelzschweißen *nt*
fusion welding by thermo-chemical energy Gießschmelzschweißen *nt*
fusion zone Anschmelzzone *f*
fusion-welded spaced spot weld schmelzgeschweißte Punktnaht *f*
future zukünftig
fuzzification Fuzzifizierung *f*
fuzziness Unschärfe *f*
fuzzy unscharf
fuzzy control Fuzzy-Control *f*
fuzzy logic Fuzzy-Logik *f*
fuzzy logic operator Fuzzy-Operator *m*
fuzzy set unscharfe Menge *f*
fuzzy-control language Fuzzy-Control-Sprache *f*

G g

G type reference centre distance tooth system GV-Null-Verzahnung *f*
gauge messen, vermessen, ausmessen, kalibrieren, eichen, prüfen; Maß *nt*, Eichmaß *nt*, Lehre *f*, Maßstab *m*, Messgerät *nt*, Spur(weite) *f*
gauge block Endmaß *nt*, Messscheibe *f*
gauge block measuring Messen *nt* mit Parallelendmaßen
gauge body Lehrenkörper *m*
gauge design Lehrenaufbau *m*
gauge deviation Lehrenabmaß *nt*
gauge dimension Lehrenmaß *nt*
gauge dimensional tolerance Lehrenmaßtoleranz *f*
gauge handle Lehrengriff *m*
gauge length Messstrecke *f*, Messlänge *f*
gauge length at fracture Messlänge *f* beim Bruch
gauge mark Messmarke *f*
gauge member Lehrenkörper *m*
gauge segment Lehrensegment *nt*
gauge with spherical inspection faces Lehre *f* mit kugelförmigen Prüfflächen
gauged length Messstrecke *f*
gauging Messen *nt*, Prüfen *nt*, Abtasten *nt*, Messung *f*, Prüfung *f*, Abgleich *m*
gauging device Abtastvorrichtung *f*
gauging head Messkopf *m*
gauging holes Bohrungslehrung *f*
gauging internal threads Muttergewindelehrung *f*
gauging member Messkörper *m*, Messstück *nt*
gauging member with plug-in gauge handle Messkörper *m* mit Einsteckgriff *m*
gauging method Messverfahren *nt*
gauging of bolt threads Bolzengewinde-Lehrung *f*
gauging operation Messvorgang *m*
gauging practice Lehrenmesstechnik *f*
gauging surface Prüffläche *f*

gauging system Lehrensystem *nt*
gain erwerben
gain in tool life Standzeitgewinn *m*
gall reiben, scheuern, sich festfressen
galvanic galvanisch
galvanic anode galvanische Anode *f*
galvanic current source galvanische Stromquelle *f*
galvanic isolation galvanische Trennung *f*
galvanically isolated galvanisch getrennt, potentialgetrennt
galvanizing start layer Galvanikstartschicht *f*
galvanize verzinken
galvanized verzinkt
galvanized by flame-spraying flammspritzverzinkt
galvanizing Galvanik *f*, Verzinken *nt*
galvanometer Galvanometer *nt*
gamma emitter Gammastrahler *m*
gamma radiation plant Gammabestrahlungsanlage *f*
gamma-emitting system Gammabestrahlungsanlage *f*
gamma-ray radiograph Gammafilmaufnahme *f*
gamma distributed gammaverteilt
gang channel nut Annietmutternleiste *f*
gang drilling machine Reihenbohrmaschine *f*
gang mill bearbeiten mit Doppelspindelstock oder Satzfräser; Satzfräser *m*
gang milling Fräsen *nt* mit Satzfräsern, Fräsen *nt* mit Werkzeugsatz, Satzfräsen *nt*, Sattelfräsen *nt*
gang milling cutter Satzfräser *m*
gang planing Hobeln *nt* mit mehreren Meißeln gleichzeitig
gang tool Meißelsatz *m*, Werkzeugsatz *m*
gang tool block Mehrfachmeißelhalter *m*
gang toolholder Mehrfachmeißelhalter *m*

gang up aufspannen
gang-cutter Satzfräser *m*
ganged cutters Satzfräser *mpl*, Fräser *m* zu einem Satz zusammengestellt
ganging Sattelfräsen *nt*
gang-type toolholder Mehrmeißelaufspannung *f*, Mehrstahlhalter *m*
gangway Fahrweg *m*, Laufsteg *m*
gantry Brücke *f*, Gerüst *nt*, Portal *nt*, Kranportal *nt*, Fasslager *nt*
gantry crane Laufkran *m*, Portalkran *m*, Brückenkran *m*, Bockkran *m*
gantry machine Gantrymaschine *f*
gantry robot Portalroboter *m*
gantry robot system Überfahrlager *nt*
gap Spalt *m*, Spalte *f*, Zwischenraum *m*, Lücke *f*, Aussparung *f*, Abstand *m*
gap bridge Einsatzbrücke *f*
gap conditions Spaltbedingungen *fpl*
gap dimension *(bei Gesenkschmiedestücken)* Lückenmaß *nt*
gap formed by a mould eingeformte Fuge *f*
gap gauge Rachenlehre *f*
gap in a letter *(e. Schablonenschrift)* Buchstabensteg *m*
gap lathe Drehmaschine *f* mit gekröpftem Bett
gap oscillation Spaltoszillation *f*
gap width Lückenbreite *f*, Spaltbreite *f*
gaping Klaffen *nt*
gap-type filter Spaltfilter *m*
gas 1. Gas *nt* 2. *(Arbeit)* Gasaufnahme *f*
gas appliance Gasgerät *nt*
gas brazing Gaslöten *nt*
gas burner for use without fan Gasbrenner *m* ohne Gebläse
gas concentration measurement Gaskonzentrationsmessung *f*
gas consumer installation Gasverbrauchseinrichtung *f*
gas control valve Gaseinstellventil *nt*
gas cushion Gaspolster *nt*
gas cutting Brennschneiden *nt*
gas cutting practice Brennschneidtechnik *f*
gas cylinder valve Gasflaschenventil *nt*
gas detection Gaserfassung *f*, Gaskonzentrationsmessung *f*
gas detection system Gaserfassungssystem *nt*, Gaswarnsystem *nt*
gas discharge Gasdurchgang *m*
gas discharge safety valve gasablassendes Sicherheitsventil *nt*
gas distribution system Gasnetz *nt*
gas draw-off valve Gasentnahmehahn *m*
gas equipment gastechnische Ausrüstung *f*
gas exhausting Gasabsaugung *f*
gas explosion process Gasexplosionsverfahren *nt*
gas failure safety device Gasmangelsicherung *f*
gas fire-place Gasfeuerstätte *f*
gas firing component Gasfeuerungsteil *nt*
gas firing installation with induced draught fan Gasfeuerungsanlage *f* mit Saugzugventilator
gas flaw Gasblase *f*
gas flow Gasdurchgang *m*, Gasstrom *m*
gas flow pressure Gasfließdruck *m*
gas formation Gasentwicklung *f*
gas fraction Gasfraktion *f*
gas generating plant Gaserzeugungsanlage *f*
gas group(ing) Gasgruppe *f*
gas ignition burner Gaszündbrenner *m*
gas ignition system Gaszündanlage *f*
gas injection Gaseinspeisung *f*
gas injector pipe Gaseinspeisungsrohr *nt*
gas inlet pipe Gaszuleitung *f*
gas issue Gasabzug *m*
gas laser Gaslaser *m*
gas leak tester Gasspürmessgerät *nt*
gas off-take Gasabzug *m*
gas penetration Gaseindringung *f*
gas penetration test Gaseindringprüfung *f*
gas permeability Gasdurchlässigkeitsprüfung *f*
gas porosity Gasporosität *f*
gas powder welding Gaspulverschweißen *nt*
gas pressure monitor Gasdruckwächter *m*
gas regression Gasrücktritt *m*

gas release Gasfreigabe *f*
gas safety tubing Sicherheitsgasschlauch *m*
gas sensor Gassensor *m*, Gasfühler *m*, Gasmesskopf *m*
gas sensor head Gasfühlerkopf *m*
gas storage water heater Vorratsgaswasserheizer *m*
gas suction Gasabsaugung *f*
gas take-off point Gasentnahmestelle *f*
gas test chamber Gasprüfzelle *f*
gas torch Gasbrenner *m*
gas welding filler rod Gasschweißstab *m*
gas-aerated concrete block Gasbetonblockstein *m*
gas-aerated concrete building plate Gasbetonbauplatte *f*
gas-conveying portion gasführendes Teil *nt*
gas-cushioned system Gaspolsteranlage *f*
gas-cut brennschneiden
gas-cut part Brennschneidteil *nt*, brenngeschnittenes Teil *nt*
gaseous gasförmig
gaseous state gasförmiger Aggregatzustand *m*
gas-fired boiler Gaskessel *m*
gas-fired circulatory type water heater Gasumlaufwasserheizer *m*
gas-fired heater gasbefeuerter Warmlufterzeuger *m*
gas-flow integrator Gasdurchflussintegrator *m*
gash Spanlücke *f*, Spannut *f*, Stoßfuge *f*
gash *(Verzahnung)* Zahnlücke *f*; Zahnlücken einstechen, Zahnlücken ausfräsen, Zahnlücken vorfräsen
gash angle Lückenwinkel *m*
gash lead Nutensteigung *f*
gash lead error Nutensteigungsfehler *m*
gash milling cutter Vorfräser *m* für Zahnräder
gashing Einstechverfahren *nt*, Vorfräsen *nt*, Fräsen *nt* von Schlitzen, Zahnlückenfräsen *nt*, Vorfräsen *nt* von Zahnlücken
gashing angle Lückenwinkel *m*
gashing cutter Zahnformvorfräser *m* für Fräszahnlücken
gashing method Einstechverfahren *nt*
gasification engineering Vergasungstechnik *f*
gasification space Vergasungsraum *m*
gasket Dichtung *f* zwischen runden Flächen
gasket strip Dichtband *nt*
gasket surface Dichtfläche *f*
gasoline Benzin *nt*, Vergaserkraftstoff *m*
gasoline engine Benzinmotor *m*
gasoline truck Flurförderzeug *nt* mit Vergaserkraftstoffmotor
gassing Gasentwicklung *f*, Gasung *f*
gas-tight gasdicht
gas-weld gasschweißen
gate Angusssteg *m*, Gießtrichter *m*, Gatter *nt*, Tor *nt*, Klappe *f*, Durchlass *m*, Durchgang *m*
gate Schaltelement *nt*
gate input Schalteingang *m*
gate pattern Angussspinne *f*, Angussverteiler *m*
gate valve Schieber *m*, Absperrschieber *m*, Absperrventil *nt*
gate valve stem Schieberspindel *f*
gate valve with progressive adjustment characteristic Schieber *m* mit stetigem Stellverhalten
gate width Stegbreiten
gated verknüpft
gateway Übergang *m*
gather sammeln, raffen
gathering Reckstauchen *nt*, Anstauchen *nt*, Rollen *nt*, Sammeln *nt*
gathering by die stretching Reckstauchen *nt*
gauge messen, vermessen, ausmessen, kalibrieren, eichen, prüfen; Maß *nt*, Eichmaß *nt*, Lehre *f*, Maßstab *m*, Messgerät *nt*, Spur(weite) *f*
gauge block Endmaß *nt*, Messscheibe *f*
gauge block measuring Messen *nt* mit Parallelendmaßen
gauge body Lehrenkörper *m*
gauge design Lehrenaufbau *m*
gauge deviation Lehrenabmaß *nt*
gauge dimension Lehrenmaß *nt*
gauge dimensional tolerance Lehrenmaßtoleranz *f*

gauge handle – gear hub 204

gauge handle Lehrengriff *m*
gauge length Messstrecke *f*, Messlänge *f*
gauge length at fracture Messlänge *f* beim Bruch
gauge mark Messmarke *f*
gauge member Lehrenkörper *m*
gauge segment Lehrensegment *nt*
gauge with spherical inspection faces Lehre *f* mit kugelförmigen Prüfflächen
gauged length Messstrecke *f*
gauging ablehren; Messen *nt*, Prüfen *nt*, Abtasten *nt*, Messung *f*, Prüfung *f*, Abgleich *m*
gauging device Abtastvorrichtung *f*
gauging head Messkopf *m*
gauging holes Bohrungslehrung *f*
gauging internal threads Muttergewindelehrung *f*
gauging member Messkörper *m*, Messstück *nt*
gauging member with plug-in gauge handle Messkörper *m* mit Einsteckgriff
gauging method Messverfahren *nt*
gauging of bolt threads Bolzengewindelehrung *f*
gauging operation Messvorgang *m*
gauging practice Lehrenmesstechnik *f*
gauging surface Prüffläche *f*
gauging system Lehrensystem *nt*
gear 1. *(Verzahnung)* Zahnrad *nt*; verzahnen, verbinden durch Zahnräder, übersetzen, eingreifen, ineinander greifen 2. *(Getriebe)* Gang *m*, Übersetzung *f*
gear axes occupying non-varying positions lagenunveränderlich gelagerte Radachsen *fpl*
gear blank unbearbeiteter Radkörper *m*, Zahnradkörper *m*, Zahnradrohling *m*
gear body Radkörper *m*
gear centre Radmitte *f*
gear cluster Räderblock *m*
gear cone Stufenräderblock *m*
gear cutter Verzahnungswerkzeug *nt*, Zahnradfräser *m*
gear cutting Verzahnung *f*, Zahnradfräsen *nt*

gear cutting attachment Zahnradfräseinrichtung *f*
gear cutting error Verzahnungsfehler *m*
gear cutting formate method (or process) Formateverfahren *nt*
gear cutting in clusters Verzahnen *nt* in Paketen
gear cutting machine Verzahnungsmaschine *f*, Verzahnmaschine *f*, Zahnradfräsmaschine *f*
gear cutting rolling cone Wälzkegel *m*
gear cutting technique Verzahnungstechnik *f*
gear cutting tool Verzahnungswerkzeug *nt*, Schneidrad *nt*
gear design Verzahnung *f*
gear drive Zahngetriebe *nt*, Zahnradgetriebe *nt*, Getriebe *nt*
gear element Verzahnungsteil *nt*, Bestimmungsstück *nt* von Zahnrädern
gear engineering Verzahnungstechnik *f*
gear fit Getriebepassung *f*
gear fit selection Getriebepassungsauswahl *f*
gear generation machine Verzahnmaschine *f*, Zahnradwälzfräsmaschine *f*
gear generator Wälzhobelmaschine *f*, Verzahnmaschine *f*, Zahnradhobelmaschine *f*, Zahnradstoßmaschine *f*, Zahnradwälzstoßmaschine *f*
gear grinder Zahnflankenschleifmaschine *f*
gear grinding Zahnradschleifen *nt*
gear hob Verzahnungsabwälzfräser *m*, Verzahnungswälzfräser *m*, Zahnradwälzfräser *m*
gear hobber Zahnradwälzfräsmaschine *f*, Räderfräsmaschine *f*
gear hobbing Zahnradfräsen *nt*, Verzahnung *f* mittels Wälzverfahren, Räderwalzfräsen *nt*
gear hobbing machine Zahnradwälzfräsmaschine *f*, Wälzfräsmaschine *f*, Verzahnmaschine *f*, Räderfräsmaschine *f*
gear hobbing technique Zahnrad-Wälzfräsverfahren *nt*
gear hub Zahnradnabe *f*

gear lapping machine Zahnradläppmaschine *f*
gear lever Schaltstange *f*
gear lubrication Getriebeschmierung *f*
gear mechanism Rädergetriebe *nt*
gear milling Zahnradfräsen *nt*, Zahnformfräsen *nt*
gear milling cutter Verzahnungsfräser *m*
gear milling machine Zahnradfräsmaschine *f*, Räderfräsmaschine *f*
gear motor Getriebemotor *m*
gear of the single helical type schräg verzahntes Rad *nt*
gear of the spur type Rad *nt* mit Geradverzahnung
gear output speed Getriebeabtriebsdrehzahl *f*
gear pair Zahnradpaar *nt*, Radpaar *nt*
gear pair at extended centres V-Plus-Radpaar *nt*
gear pair at reduced centres V-Minus-Radpaar *nt*
gear pair with intersecting axes Radpaar *nt* mit sich schneidenden Achsen, Kegelradpaar *nt*
gear pair with modified centre distance V-Radpaar *nt*
gear pair with non-parallel nonintersecting axes Schraubradpaar *nt*, Hypoidradpaar *nt*, Radpaar *nt* mit gekreuzten Radachsen
gear pair with parallel axes Radpaar *nt* mit parallelen Achsen, Stirnradpaar *nt*, Zahnradpaar *nt* mit parallelen Achsen
gear pair with reference centre distance V-Null-Radpaar *nt*
gear pairing Zahnradpaarung *f*, Radpaarung *f*
gear planer Zahnradhobelmaschine *f*
gear planing machine Zahnradhobelmaschine *f*
gear production Verzahnung *f*
gear rack Zahnstange *f*
gear ratio Zähnezahlverhältnis *nt*, Zahnradübersetzung *f*, Getriebeübersetzung *f*
gear reduction Räderumsetzung *f*, Zahnraduntersetzung *f*

gear ring Zahnkranz *m*, Radbandage *f*
gear roughing cutter Zahnformvorfräser *m*
gear shaft Getriebewelle *f*, Zahnwelle *f*
gear shaper Zahnradstoßmaschine *f*, Wälzstoßmaschine *f*, Wälzhobelmaschine *f*, Zahnradhobelmaschine *f*
gear shaping cutter Schneidrad *nt*
gear shaving Zahnradschaben *nt*
gear size Getriebegröße *f*
gear slotting machine Zahnradstoßmaschine *f*
gear standard basic rack tooth profile Zahnradbezugsprofil *nt*
gear stocking cutter Zahnformvorfräser *m*
gear teeth Radverzahnung *f*
gear teeth axis Verzahnungsachse *f*
gear teeth grinding Zahnflankenschleifen *nt*
gear teeth on the workpiece Werkstückverzahnung *f*
gear tester Zahnradprüfgerät *nt*
gear together miteinander kämmen
gear tooth Zahn *m*
gear tooth cutter Verzahnungsfräser *m*
gear tooth face cutter Zahnflankenfräser *m*
gear tooth fit Verzahnungspassung *f*
gear tooth grinder Zahnflankenschleifmaschine *f*
gear tooth individual variation Verzahnungseinzelabweichung *f*
gear tooth pitch error Zahnradteilungsfehler *m*
gear tooth profile Verzahnungsprofil *nt*, Zahnprofil *nt*
gear tooth quality Verzahnungsqualität *f*
gear tooth spacing error Zahnlückenfehler *m*
gear tooth system Radverzahnung *f*, Verzahnung *f*
gear tooth tolerance Verzahntoleranz *f*
gear tooth tolerance system Verzahnungstoleranzsystem *nt*
gear train Rädergetriebe *nt*, mehrfache Radpaarung *f*, Zahnradübersetzung *f*
gear transmission Getriebe *nt*
gear transmission control Getriebe-

schaltung *f*
gear type pumping set Zahnradpumpenaggregat *nt*
gear unit Getriebe *nt*
gear wheel Großrad *nt*
gear wheel manufacturing Zahnradfertigung *f*
gear wheels Zahnräder *ntpl*
gear width Zahnradbreite *f*
gear with pointed teeth Punktverzahnung *f*
gearbox Getriebe *nt*, Antriebskasten *m*, Getriebekasten *m*, Rädergetriebe *nt*, Räderkasten *m*
gearbox for table drive Tischantriebskasten *m*
gear-crank mechanism Räderkurbelgetriebe *nt*
gear-cutting axis Verzahnungsachse *f*
gear-cutting process Verzahnungsverfahren *nt*
geared verzahnt
geared drive Rädertrieb *m*
geared head lathe Drehmaschine *f* mit Getriebespindelkasten, Drehmaschine *f* mit Räderspindelkasten
geared headstock Räderspindelstock
geared lathe Drehmaschine *f* mit Rädervorgelege
geared scroll chuck Kranzspannfutter *nt*
geared shaper Waagerechtstoßmaschine *f* mit Stößelantrieb durch Zahnstange
geared slotting machine Senkrechtstoßmaschine *f* mit Zahnräderantrieb
geared to über Zahnräder verbunden mit
gear-generating grinder Zahnradwälzschleifmaschine *f*
gearing Verzahnung *f*, Verbindung *f* durch Zahnräder
gearing layout Getriebeplan *m*
gearing ratio Räderverhältnis *nt*, Zahnradübersetzung *f*
gear-tooth calliper Zahnmessschieblehre *f*
gear-tooth number Zähnezahl *f* des Zahnrades
gear-tooth number factor Zähnezahlfaktor *m*
gearwheel Getrieberad *nt*
geat heißlaufen
general generell, allgemein
general construction steel allgemeiner Baustahl *m*
general arrangement drawing Gesamtzeichnung *f*, Übersichtszeichnung *f* (deprecated)
general bookkeeping department Sachbuchhaltung *f*
general conditions Rahmenbedingungen *fpl*
general contractor Generalunternehmer *m*
general development scheme Generalbebauungsplan *m*
general drawing Gesamtzeichnung *f*, Übersichtszeichnung *f*
general drawing general plan Übersichtszeichnung *f*
general overhaul Generalüberholung *f*
general plan *(Zeichnung)* Übersicht *f*
general purpose pallet unterfahrbare Palette *f*
general purpose portable generator Montageentwickler *m*
general purpose register Generalregister *nt*
general purpose screw thread Gewinde *nt* für allgemeine Anwendung
general purpose trapezoidal screw thread Trapezgewinde *nt* allgemeiner Anwendung
general storage area Freilager *nt*
general symbol Grundschaltzeichen *nt*
general tolerance Allgemeintoleranz *f*, Freimaßtoleranz *f*
general utility tool Universalwerkzeug *nt*
generalize verallgemeinern
generally accepted üblich
general-purpose lathe Universaldrehmaschine *f*, Mehrzweckdrehmaschine *f*
general-purpose machine Universalmaschine *f*
generate 1. erzeugen, hervorrufen, verursachen, bewirken 2. *(Zerspanung)* wälzen, walzfräsen
generate gears wälzzahnen

generate teeth verzahnen
generated gear Wälzzahnrad *nt*
generating Durchwälzen *nt*, Generieren *nt*, Generierung *f*, Hobeln *nt*, Wälzen *nt*, Wälzfräsen *nt*
generating action Wälzvorgang *m*
generating addendum modification coefficient Erzeugungsprofilverschiebungsfaktor *m*
generating centre distance Erzeugungsachsabstand *m*
generating circle Erzeugungskreis *m*
generating circle of contact Erzeugungswälzkreis *m*
generating conditions Erzeugungsbedingungen *fpl*
generating cradle Wälzkörper *m*
generating cutter Wälzwerkzeug *nt*
generating gear Erzeugungsrad *nt*, erzeugendes Rad *nt*
generating gear pair Erzeugungsradpaar *nt*
generating gear planing machine Wälzhobelmaschine *f*
generating grinder Wälzschleifmaschine *f*
generating grinding Wälzschleifen *nt*
generating infeed Einwälzen *nt*
generating machine Verzahnungsmaschine *f*, Wälzmaschine *f*
generating mating area Erzeugungspaarungsfeld *nt*
generating method Wälzverfahren *nt*, Wälzfräsverfahren *nt*
generating motion Abwälzung *f*, Wälzbewegung *f*, Wälzung *f*
generating operation Wälzarbeit *f*
generating path of contact Erzeugungswälzbahn *f*
generating pitch surface Erzeugungswälzfläche *f*
generating planing method Wälzhobeln *nt*
generating process Wälzverfahren *nt*, Abwälzverfahren *nt*
generating rolling Wälzrollen *nt*
generating shaping Wälzhobeln *nt*, Wälzstoßen *nt*
generating shaping tool Wälzstoßwerkzeug *nt*
generating skiving Wälzschälen *nt*
generating straight line erzeugende Gerade *f*
generating tool Wälzwerkzeug *nt*
generating train Erzeugungsgetriebe *nt*
generation Erzeugung *f*
generation by planing with rack shaped cutter Wälzstoßen *nt* mit Kammmeißel
generation by shaping of straight spur gears Wälzstoßen *nt* geradverzahnter Stirnräder
generation of teeth Verzahnung *f* mittels Wälzverfahren
generation of underpressure Unterdruckerzeugung *f*
generation planning Wälzhobeln *nt*
generation shaping Wälzstoßen *nt*
generation of heat Erwärmung *f*
generator 1. *(Zerspanung)* Verzahnungsmaschine *f*, Wälzmaschine *f* **2.** *(el.)* Stromerzeuger *m* **3.** *(Fläche)* Erzeugende *f* e. Evolventenfläche
generator angle variation Erzeugendenwinkelabweichung *f*
generator for soldering duty Lötentwickler *m*
generator form variation Erzeugendenformabweichung *f*
generator rated power Generatornennleistung *f*
generator rated speed Generatornenndrehzahl *f*
generator rated voltage Generatornennspannung *f*
generator test range Erzeugendenprüfbereich *m*
generator unit Entwicklungsanlage *f*
Geneva cross Malteserkreuz *nt*
Geneva stop Malteserkreuz *nt*
gentle gedämpft, sanft
geometric progression Stufensprung *m* von Drehzahlen, geometrische Reihe *f*
geometric quantity geometrische Größe *f*
geometrical räumlich
geometrical component of metal-cutting Zerspangröße *f*

geometrical deviation Formabweichung f
geometrical error Formabweichung f
geometrical precision Formgenauigkeit f
geometrical resolution geometrische Zerlegung f
geometrical unit of area geometrische Flächeneinheit f
geometrical variation Formabweichung f
geometrically correct levelling *(z. B. einer Rohrsohle)* Nivellement *nt*
geometrically true formrichtig
geometry Geometrie f, Gestaltung f
geometry of metal cutting Zerspanungsgeometrie f
geometry of radiation Einstrahlungsgeometrie f
geometry of the cutting edge Geometrie f der Schneide f
germ poverty Keimarmut f
germ-free ventilation keimarme Belüftung f
get (into) aufsteigen (auf)
get entangled (in/with) verwickeln
get hot heißlaufen
get jammed verklemmen
get off aussteigen
get on zusteigen
get stuck stecken bleiben
get up aufstehen
G-functions G-Funktionen *fpl*
ghost echo Phantomecho *nt*
gib Leiste f
gib head Keilnase f
gibbed mit einer Liste f versehen
gibbed surface broach assembly mit Keilleisten nachstellbares Räumzeug *nt*
gibbet Kragarm *m*
gib-head key Nasenkeil *m*
gill Rohrrippe f
gilled tube Rippenrohr *nt*
girder Tragbalken *m*
girder subject to bending Biegeträger *m*
girder with rigid and movable bearings Stabwerk *nt*
guide vane in an elbow Lenkfläche f in e. Krümmer

guide vane pitch adjustment device Leitschaufelverstelleinrichtung f
give a receipt Quittung ausstellen
give a higher priority Priorität erhöhen
give a sharp bend scharfkantig biegen
give a slurry type seal coating Betonrohre schlämmen
give away ausweichen
give feedback rückmelden
give off abgeben
give over übergeben
give priority Priorität geben
given vorgegeben
given value vorgegebener Wert *m*
give-way right Vorfahrtsregel f
gland Brille f der Stopfbuchse
gland type socket Stopfbuchsenmuffe f
glass Glas *nt*, Scheibe f
glass bead Glaskugel f
glass electrode single-rod measuring cell Glaselektrodeneinstabmesszelle f
glass fibre reinforced laminate glasfaserverstärktes Laminat *nt*
glass fibre reinforced plastics glasfaserverstärkter Kunststoff *m*
glass fibre roving Glasseidenroving
glass fibre roving fabric Glasseidenrovingewebe *nt*
glass filament mat Glasfilamentmatte f
glass filament yarn Textilglasgarn *nt*
glass filter crucible Glasfiltertiegel *m*
glass grit value Glasgrieswert *m*
glass pane Glasscheibe f
glass-to-glass sealing Verschmelzung f
glass-to-metal belt sealing Glasmetallbandverschmelzung f
glass-enclosed verglast
glass-mat-base laminate Hartmatte f
glass-metal soldering Glas-Metall-Lötung f
glassware *(Laborinstrumente wie Kolben, Pipetten, usw.)* Gerät *nt*
glassy band glasiger Streifen *m*
glassy state Glaszustand *m*
glaze verglasen
glazed verglast
glazed ceramic tile glasierte Fliese f

glazed finish lasierender Anstrich *m*
glazing Glänzen *nt*, Verglasung *f*
glide rutschen, gleiten
glide-in racking Einschubregal *nt*
gliding mean value gleitender Mittelwert *m*
glitch Störimpuls *m*
global data Globaldaten *pl*
globe valve Kugelventil *nt*
globoid Globoid *m*
globular kugelförmig
globule Kugel *f*
gloss test Glanzprüfung *f*
glossy glänzend
glove Handschuh *m*
glow leuchten, glühen
glow time Glimmzeit *f*
glowing Glühen *nt*
glue kleben, aufkleben, leimen, beleimen, Klebstoff auftragen, Leim auftragen; Leim *m*
glue deck Leimstation *f*
glue in small particles Kleinstückleim *m*
glue on ankleben
glue reservoir Leimgerät *nt*
glue sealing machine Klebstoffauftragverschließmaschine *f*
glue spreading roll Leimauftragwalze *f*
glue strip Leimspur *f*
glue system Beleimung *f*
glue together verkleben
gluing Leimen *nt*, Leimauftrag *m*, Beleimung *f*, Verklebung *f*, Klebstoffauftrag *m*
gluing ability Verleimbarkeit *f*
gluing operation Klebevorgang *m*
glueless nahtlos
go verlaufen
GO shop gauge Gutarbeitslehre *f*
GO and NOT GO screw limit gauge Gewindegrenzlehre *f*
GO and NOT GO screw plug gauge Gewindegrenzlehrendorn *m*
go away entfernen
GO calliper gauge Gutrachenlehre *f*
GO dimension Gutmaß *nt*
GO gauge Gutlehre *f*
GO gauge block Gutmessscheibe *f*
GO gauge member Gutlehrenkörper *m*
go into reverse in Rückwärtsgang schalten, umschlagen, in Gegenbewegung übergehen
GO limiting size Gutgrenzmaß *nt*
GO mating screw thread gauge Gewindegutgegenlehrdorn *m*
GO measuring plug Gutmesszapfen *m*
go on dauern
GO ring screw gauge Gutgewindelehrring *m*
GO screw calliper gauge Gewindegutrachenlehre *f*
GO screw gauge member Gewindegutlehrenkörper *m*
GO screw ring gauge Gewindegutlehrring *m*
GO screw thread plug gauge Gewindegutlehrdorn *m*
go to verzweigen
go up steigen, klettern
go with mitfahren
goal Ziel *nt*, Zielsetzung *f*
goal accomplishment Zielerreichung *f*
goal-driven zielgesteuert
geometric grinding arc geometrischer Schleifwinkel *m*
goggles Sicherheitsbrille *f*, Schutzbrille *f*
gold colouration Goldfärbung *f*
gondola Gondel *f*
good Gut *nt*
good bearing tragfähig
good range Gutbereich *m*
good/bad sorting Gut-Schlecht-Sortierung *f*
good/bad sorting Gut-Schlecht-Sortierung *f*
goods Waren *fpl*
goods arrival Wareneingang *m*
goods delivery Warenanlieferung *f*
goods distribution system Warenverteilsystem *nt*
goods identification Warenidentifikation *f*
goods in process in Arbeit
goods in stock Lagerbestand *m*
goods issue Warenausgang *m*
goods labelling Warenkennzeichnung *f*

goods marking Warenkennzeichnung *f*
goods on hand Lagerbestand *m*, Vorrat *m*
goods received date Wareneingangsdatum *nt*
goods receiving department Warenannahme *f*
goods-to-man Ware *f* zum Mann
goods transfer Warenübergabe *f*
goods-in Wareneingang *m*
goods-out Warenausgang (WA) *m*
goose neck finishing tool gekröpfter Schlichtmeißel *m*
goose-neck tool gekröpfter Meißel *m*
goose-necked gekröpft
goose-necked finisher gekröpfter Schlichtmeißel *m*
goose-necked finishing tool gekröpfter Schlichtmeißel *m*
go-side Gutseite *f*
gouging process Hobelverfahren *nt*
governing Regeln *nt*
govern regeln
governed by functional requirements funktionsbedingt
governor Regelgerät *nt*, Regulator *m*
GO-workpiece Gutwerkstück *nt*
grab Greifer *m*; greifen
grabbing device Greifvorrichtung *f*, Greiftechnik *f*, Greifeinrichtung *f*, Greifer *m*
grabbing mechanism Greifvorrichtung *f*, Greiftechnik *f*
grabrail Geländer *nt*
gradation Stufensprung *m*
grade 1. Klasse *f*, Sorte *f*, Rang *m*; sortieren, einstufen, abstufen, einteilen 2. *(Werkstoffprüfung)* Härtegrad *m*, Härte *f* 3. *(~ in)* übergehen 4. *(QS)* Gütegrad *m*, Qualität *f*
grade of accuracy Genauigkeitsgrad *m*
grade of calibration Kalibriergrad *m*
graded in size in Größe verschieden, abgestuft nach der Größe
graded micro structure abgestufte Mikrostruktur *f*
gradient Gefälle *nt*, Bahnneigung *f*, Neigung *f*, Gefällstrecke *f*, Ganghöhe *f*
grading Stufung *f*, Abstufung *f*, Einstufung *f*, Einteilung *f*

grading plant Sortieranlage *f*
grading proportion Körnungsanteil *m*
grading test Beurteilungsprüfung *f*
gradual allmählich
graduate einteilen, stufen, abstufen, mit Teilstrichen versehen
graduated abgestuft
graduated circle Teilkreis *m*
graduated collar Buchse *f* mit Gradeinteilung, Skalenring *m*, Skalentrommel *f*
graduated cylinder Messzylinder *m*
graduated dial scale Rundskala *f*
graduated disk Skalenscheibe *f*
graduated flask Messkolben *m*
graduated indexing dial Teiltrommel *f*
graduated wash bottle Messwaschflasche *f*
graduating Anbringen *nt*, Graduieren *nt*
graduation Gradeinteilung *f*, Maßstab *m*, Messeinteilung *f*, Teilung *f*, Teilstrich *m*, Stufung *f*, Abstufung *f*
graduation in degrees Gradeinstellung *f*
grain Korn *nt*; granulieren
grain count Kornzahl *f*
grain eruption Kornausbruch *m*
grain marks Riefen *fpl*
grain method Grießverfahren *nt*
grain proportion Kornanteil *m*
grain size Körnung *f*
grain structure Korngefüge *nt*
graining Granulierung *f*
grainy surface character narbiger Oberflächencharakter *m*
gram-molecule Mol *nt*
granular glue Körnerleim *m*
granular materials Granulat *nt*
granular solder Kornlot *nt*
granular sub-grade course *(in der Grabensohle)* Sauberkeitsschicht *f*
granularity Auflösungsvermögen *nt*, Körnigkeit *f*
granulate granulieren
granulating Granulierung *f*
granule mixture Korngemenge *nt*
granules Granulat *nt*
granulometric composition Kornzu-

sammensetzung *f*
graph Schaubild *nt*, Kurve *f*, Diagramm *nt*, graphische Darstellung *f*
graphic Grafik *f*
graphical zeichnerisch, grafisch
graphical documents Zeichnungsunterlagen *fpl*
graphical language grafische Sprache *f*
graphical method zeichnerisches Verfahren *nt*
graphical representation graphische Darstellung *f*
graphical symbol Schaltzeichen *nt*
graphical user interface grafische Benutzeroberfläche *f*
graphite corrosion Graphitierung *f*
graphite black graphitschwarz
graphite brush Kohlebürste *f*
graphite lubricant Graphitschmiermittel *nt*
graphite skeleton Graphitskelett *nt*
grapping mechanism Greifeinrichtung *f*
grappler Greiferzange *f*, Greifzange *f*
grasp with tongs mit Zangen *fpl* arbeiten
grass Aufrauung *f*
grated flooring 1. Lochblech *nt*, Rost *m* **2.** *(Durchleuchtung)* Lichtgitterrost *m*
graticule Fadenkreuz *nt*
grating Gitter *nt*, Gitterrost *m*
grating floor Lichtgitterrost *m*
grating interval Gitterkonstante *f*
gravel bed filter Mischbettfilter *m*
gravel-sand bedding Kiessandauflager *nt*
gravimetric filling machine Wägefüllmaschine *f*
gravitation-counterflow sizer Schwerkraftgegenstromsichter *m*
gravitational force Schwerkraft *f*
gravity Schwerkraft *f*
gravity accumulator Gefällespeicher *m*
gravity arc welding with covered electrode Schwerkraftlichtbogenschweißen *nt*
gravity axis of the weld area Schweißnahtflächenschwerachse *f*
gravity chill casting Schwerkraftkokillenguss *m*
gravity die-casting Schwerkraftkokillenguss *m*, Kokillenguss *m*
gravity discharge Schwerkraftauslauf *m*
gravity filling machine Schwerkraftfüllmaschine *f*
gravity force casting Schwerkraftgießen *nt*
gravity pipeline Freispiegelleitung *f*
gravity principle Schwerkraftprinzip *nt*
gravity roller conveyor Schwerkraftrollenbahn *f*, Rollenbahn *f*
gravity roller lane Rollenbahnstrecke *f*
gravity roller system Schwerkraftrollenbahn *f*
gravity type air heating system Schwerkraftluftheizungsanlage *f*
gravity-circulated heating system Schwerkraftheizung *f*
gravity-driven schwerkraftbetrieben
gravity-feed hopper type boiler Füllschachtkessel *m*
gravity-powered schwerkraftbetrieben
gray code Graycode *m*
grease Fett *nt*, Schmierfett *nt*; fetten, schmieren
grease contaminants Fettverunreinigungen *fpl*
grease cup Fettbüchse *f*
grease film Fettschicht *f*
grease gun Druckschmierpresse *f*
grease lubrication Fettschmierung *f*
grease penetration Fettdurchgang *m*
grease permeability Fettdurchlässigkeit *f*
grease reservoir Fettbehälter *m*
grease spot Fettfleck *m*
grease test rig Fettprüfmaschine *f*
greaser Fettbüchse *f*
grease-soluble fettlöslich
grease-worker Schmierfettkneter *m*
greasing Schmierung *f*
greasing nipple Schmiernippel *m*
greasy fettig, ölig
greasy mass schmalzartige Masse *f*
greater than größer als
greater than or equal to größer gleich
green colouration Grundfärbung *f*
green space Grünanlage *f*

grey bright graublank
grey paste method Graupastenverfahren *nt*
grabbing device Greifeinrichtung *f*
grid Gitter *nt*, Gitterrost *m*, Netz *nt*, Rost *m*
grid constitution Gitteraufbau *m*
grid element spacing Rasterabstand *m*
grid line Rasterlinie *f*
grid point Gitterpunkt *m*, Rasterpunkt *m*
grid reflection light barrier Gitterreflexionslichtschranke *f*
grid square Planquadrat *nt*
grid system Rastersystem *nt*
grid type single-way light barrier Gittereinweglichtschranke *f*
girder Träger *m*
grid-plate electrode Gitterpalettenelektrode *f*
grille 1. Gitterrost *m* **2.** *(Gas)* Luftdurchlass *m*
grind schleifen, abschleifen, beischleifen, mahlen; Schliff *m*
grind cylindrical rundschleifen
grind flat abschleifen
grind profiles profilschleifen
grind wet nassschleifen
grinder Schleifmaschine *f*
grinders Schleifmaschinen *fpl*
grinding Schleifen *nt*, Anschliff *m*
grinding tool Schleifwerkzeug *nt*
grinding abrasive Schleifkorn *nt*
grinding accuracy Schliffgenauigkeit *f*
grinding allowance Schleifzugabe *f*
grinding arc Schleifwinkel *m*
grinding attachment Schleifvorrichtung *f*
grinding cam Schleifkurve *f*
grinding checks Schleifrisse *m*
grinding contact surface Schleifkontaktfläche *f*
grinding crack Schleifriss *m*
grinding cut Schliff *m*
grinding cutter Schleifwerkzeug *nt*
grinding efficiency Schleifleistung *f*
grinding face Schleiffläche *f*, Schliff *m*
grinding finish Schliffgüte *f*
grinding force Schleifkraft *f*
grinding from the solid Schleifen *nt* ins Volle
grinding head Schleifsupport *m*
grinding life Standzeit *f* zwischen zwei Anschliffen
grinding machine Schleifmaschine *f*
grinding machine operator Schleifer *m*
grinding machines Schleifmaschinen *fpl*
grinding marks Schleifspuren *fpl*
grinding operation *(Schleifarbeit)* Schliff *m*
grinding performance Schleifleistung *f*
grinding position Schleifstellung *f*
grinding pressure Schleifdruck *m*
grinding pressure angle Schleifeingriffswinkel *m*
grinding principal point Schleifbezugspunkt *m*
grinding ratio Abtragsquotient *m*
grinding relation Schleifverhältnis (G) *nt*
grinding relief Fußfreischnitt *m*
grinding robot Schleifroboter *m*
grinding table Schleiftisch *m*
grinding time Schleifzeit *f*
grinding to size Maßschleifen *nt*
grinding wheel Schleifscheibe *f*
grinding wheel diameter Schleifscheibendurchmesser *m*
grinding wheel dresser Schleifscheibenabrichter *m*
grinding wheel dressing diamond Schleifscheibeabrichtdiamant *m*
grinding wheel peripheral speed Schleifscheibenumfangsgeschwindigkeit *f*
grinding wheel profile Schleifscheibenprofil *nt*
grinding wheel radius Schleifscheibenradius *m*
grinding wheel rotational frequency Schleifscheibendrehzahl *f*
grinding wheel surface Schleifscheibenfläche *f*
grinding wheel width Schleifscheibenbreite *f*
grindstone Schleifstein *m*
grip 1. fassen, greifen, erfassen, ergrei-

fen; Griff *m* **2.** *(Einspannung)* spannen, einspannen, klemmen; Spannbacke *f*, Spannzange *f*, Klemme *f*
grip arm Greifer *m*
grip lining Klemm-Belag *m*
gripper Greifer *m*, Greiforgan *nt*
gripper finger Zangengreifer *m*
gripper head Greifkopf *m*
gripper jaws Backengreifer *m*
gripper mass Greifermasse *f*
gripper motion Greiferbewegung *f*
gripper path Greifweg *m*
gripper tongs Greiferzange *f*, Greifzange *f*
gripper's central axis Greifermittelachse *f*
gripping Einspannung *f*, Festhalten *nt*, Fassen *nt*, Ergreifen *nt*
gripping appliance Spannvorrichtung *f*
gripping device Greifer *m*, Greiforgan *nt*
gripping exactness Greifgenauigkeit *f*
gripping fixture Spannwerkzeug *nt*, Spannzeug *nt*, Spanner *m*
gripping force Greifkraft *f*
gripping force safety Greifkraftsicherung *f*
gripping jaw Spannbacke *f*
gripping locknut klemmende Sicherungsmutter *f*
gripping mechanism Spanneinrichtung *f*, Greifeinrichtung *f*
gripping method Greiftechnik *f*, Greifmethode *f*
gripping pliers (pl) Greiferzange *f*, Greifzange *f*
gripping speed Greifgeschwindigkeit *f*
grit Schleifstoff *m*
grit mark Schleifmarke *f*
grit size Korngröße *f*
gritty spröde, körnig
grommet Unterlegscheibe *f*
groove nuten, einstechen, riefen, rillen, schlitzen, ausfugen; Aussparung *f*, Schlitz *m*, Langschlitz *m*, Nut *f*, Rille *f*, Rillennute *f*, Kehle *f*, Riefe *f*, Kerbe *f*, Rinne *f*, Seilrille *f*
groove angle Öffnungswinkel *m*
groove chaser Rillenstrehler *m*
groove complex Rillenschar *f*
groove cutting attachment Nutenstoßvorrichtung *f*
groove direction Rillenrichtung *f*
groove milling Nutenfräsen *nt*, Nutenschrittfräsen *nt*, Nutentauchfräsen *nt*
groove profile Rillenprofil *nt*
groove recessing tool Nutenstechmeißel *m*
groove track Rillenverlauf *m*
groove welding Nutschweißen *nt*
grooved genutet, mit Nut
grooved ball bearing Rillenkugellager *nt*
grooved pin with slot for retaining rings Passkerbstift *m* mit Nut und Sicherungsringen
grooved pin with slot for retaining washers Passkerbstift *m* mit Nut für Sicherungsscheiben
grooved union nut Nutüberwurfmutter *f*
grooved wheel Seilrad *nt*
groove-drawing machine Nutenziehmaschine *f*
groove-faced flange Nutflansch *m*
groove-like depression rillenartige Vertiefung *f*
groove-ring collar Nutringmanschette *f*
groove-shaped nutförmig
grooving Einstich *m*, Einstecharbeit *f*, Einkerbung *f*, Nuten *nt*, Rillen *nt*, Nutendrehen *nt*, Rillendrehen *nt*, Ausfugen *nt*, Kerben *nt*
grooving method Einstechverfahren *nt*
grooving tool *(Nuten)* Einstechmeißel *m*
gross calorific value Brennwert *m*, oberer Heizwert *m*
gross sample Sammelprobe *f*
gross weighing machine Bruttowägefüllmaschine *f*
gross weight Bruttogewicht *nt*
ground 1. Flur *m*, Untergrund *m*, Boden *m*, Erde *f*; grundieren **2.** *(el.)* erden; Erde *f*, Masse *f*, Masseschluss *m*
ground and slightly roughened geschurt
ground clearance Bodenabstand *m*,

Bodenfreiheit *f*
ground colour Untergrundfarbe *f*
ground fault Erdschluss *m*
ground fit eingeschliffen
ground flask Schliffflasche *f*
ground glass Mattscheibe *f*
ground level Bodenhöhe *f*
ground loading Bodenbelastung *f*
ground setting Bodensetzung *f*
ground socket Schliffhülse *f*
ground stopper Schliffkern *m*
ground surface Schleiffläche *f*
ground surface pattern Schliffbild *nt*
ground taper socket Kegelschliffhülse *f*
ground thermometer Schliffthermometer *nt*
ground to give clearance mit angeschliffenen Freiwinkel, hinterschliffen
ground tolerance Bodentoleranz *f*
ground water bed Grundwassersohle *f*
ground water interchange zone Grundwasserwechselzone *f*
grounded geerdet
ground-in chip breaker eingeschliffener Spanbrecher *m*, Spanleitstufe *f*
ground-in step type chip breaker Spanleitstufe *f*
grounding *(el.)* Masse *f*, Erdung *f*
grounding strap Erdungsband *nt*
groundwood fibre Holzschlifffaser *f*
group Gruppe *f*, Pulk *m*; einen Pulk bilden aus, gruppieren, klassieren, zusammenstellen, anordnen, sammeln
group container Sammelpackbehälter *m*
group container erecting machine Sammelpackbehälteraufrichtmaschine *f*
group container loading and unloading machine Sammelpackbehälterbe- und -entlademaschine *f*
group container sealing machine Sammelpackbehälterverschließmaschine *f*
group drawing Gruppenzeichnung *f*
group drive Gruppenantrieb *m*
group fusing Gruppensicherung *f*
group message Sammelmeldung *f*
group package Sammelpackung *f*, Sammelpack *nt*
group packaging machine Sammelpackmaschine *f*
group part drawing Gruppenteilzeichnung *f*
group production Gruppenfertigung *f*
group status indication Sammelzustandsanzeige *f*
group technology Gruppentechnologie *f*, Teilefamilien *fpl*
group together zusammenfassen, gruppieren
groupable pulkfähig
grouping Gruppierung *f*, Gruppe *f*, Klassierung *f*, Zusammenfassung *f*, Zusammenstellung *f*, Pulkbildung *f*
grout ausgießen, Vergussmasse *f*
grouted joint vergossene Fuge *f*
grouting compound Vergussmasse *f*
grow zunehmen, wachsen
growing zunehmend
growth Zunahme *f*, Wachstum *nt*
growth of bacteria Bakterienwachstum *nt*
growth stage Wachstumsphase *f*
grub screw Gewindestift *m*
guarantee Garantie *f*; garantieren, gewährleisten
guaranty Garantie *f*
guard Sicherheit *f*, Schutz *m*, Schutzeinrichtung *f*, Umhüllung *f*, Verkleidung *f*, Abdeckung *f*; schützen, sichern, sperren, abdecken, umzäunen, umwehren
guard ensure sichern
guard locking Zuhaltung *f*
guard plate Schutzblech *nt*, Abstreifplatte *f*
guard rail Handlauf *m*, Geländer *nt*, Schutzgeländer *nt*
guarding Schutzeinrichtung *f*, Umwehrung *f*, Verdeckung *f*
guarding of ladder access Steigschutz *m*
guards at the outside edge Vorderschutz *m*
guards at the sides Seitenschutz *m*
guide rail Leitschiene *f*
guidance Spurführung *f*, Führung *f*, Richtlinien *fpl*
guidance computer Leitrechner *m*

guidance control system Leitsteuerung *f*
guidance into the aperture Einführungszentrierung *f*
guidance means Führungseinrichtung *f*
guidance mechanism Führungsgetriebe *nt*
guidance motion Führungsbewegung *f*
guidance on conic sections Kegelschnittführung *f*
guidance path Führungsbahn *f*
guidance signal Führungssignal *nt*
guidance system Leitlinienführung *f*
guidances Führungen *fpl*
guide leisten, leiten, führen
guide bar Führungsstange *f*, Leitschiene *f*, Leitlineal *nt*, Aufnahmedorn *m*
guide block Stufenblock *m*
guide bracket Kopierschienenhalter *m*
guide bush Führungsbüchse *f*
guide column Führungssäule *f*
guide function Führungsfunktion *f*
guide line Leitlinie *f*, Leitfaden *m*
guide line control system Leitlinienführung *f*
guide line controlled leitliniengeführt
guide path Fahrkurs *m*, Fahrweg *m* mit Führung
guide pin Führungsstift *m*, Kopierstift *m*
guide plate Kopierlineal *nt*, Kopierschiene *f*, Umlenkblech *nt*
guide play Führungsspiel *nt*
guide rail Fahrschiene *f*, Führungsschiene *f*, Wegelineal *nt*
guide rod Führungsgestänge *nt*
guide roll Spurrolle *f*
guide roller Führungsrolle *f*, Kopierrolle *f*
guide rules Leitsätze *mpl*
guide screw Leitspindel *f*
guide system Führungssystem *nt*
guide variable Führungsgröße *f*
guide wheel Führungsrad *nt*
guide wire Leitdraht *m*
guide(s) Führung *f*
guided leitliniengeführt, geführt
guideline Richtlinie *f*, Anhaltspunkt *m*
guidelines Richtlinien *fpl*, Regelwerk *nt*
guideway Bettbahn *f*, Bettführungsbahn *f*, Führung *f*, Führungsfläche *f*, Führungsbahn *f*
guiding member Führungsmittel *nt*
guiding members Führungskonstruktion *f*
guiding pulley Führungsrolle *f*, Spannrolle *f*
guiding rule Führungslineal *nt*
gullet Rundung *f* am Zahnfuß, Zahngrund *m*, Zahnlücke *f*
gum gummieren, verkleben
gummed tape gummiertes Klebeband *nt*
gummed tape sealing machine Nassklebebandverschließmaschine *f*
gummed with old oil mit Ölrückständen behaftet
gun drill Kanonenbohrer *m*
gusset Seitenfalte *f*
gusseted mit Seitenfalte *f*
gutter Regenrinne *f*
guy verankern; Verankerung *f*
gyrate sich drehen, umlaufen
gyrating mass Schwungmasse *f*
gyration Umlauf *m*, Drehung *f*, Kreisbewegung *f*
gyratory motion kreisende Bewegung *f*

H h

hack-saw Bügelsäge f
hack-saw machine Bügelsäge f
hack-sawing Bügelsägen nt
hair crack Haarriss m
hairline crack Haarriss m
hairline gauge Strichendmaß nt
half angle of thread Teilflankenwinkel m, halber Flankenwinkel m
half cell Halbzelle f
half duplex transmission Wechselbetrieb m
half length reverse grooved pin Steckkerbstift m
half length taper grooved pin Passkerbstift m
half of film Folienhälfte f
half of the wheel Radhälfte f
half section Halbschnitt m
half sine wave Sinushalbwelle f
half-dog point Gewindestiftzapfen m
half-duplex simplex
half-nut Schloss nt, Schlossmutter f, Mutternschloss nt, geteilte Leitspindelmutter f
half-section drawing Halbschnittzeichnung f
half-side milling cutter Scheibenfräser m mit einseitiger Verzahnung
half-temperature extrusion Halbwarmfließpressen nt
half-tone original Halbtonvorlage f
hall Halle f
hall building Hallenbau m
hall geometry Hallengeometrie f
hall layout Hallenlayout nt
hall-effect probe Hallsonde f
hall-effect sensor Hall-Sensor m
hallway Hausflur m
halo Lichthof m, Lichtschleier m
halogenated product halogenhaltiges Erzeugnis nt
halt stoppen; Stillstand m, Haltestelle f
halve halbieren
hammer Hammer m; hämmern
hammer arrangement Schlageinrichtung f

hammer cladding Hammerplattieren nt
hammer forging Freiformschmieden nt
hammer pipe Kernzerschmiedung f
hamming distance Hammingabstand m
hand 1. Richtung f, Seite f 2. (Körper) Hand f
hand adjustment Handverteilung f, Handeinstellung f
hand brake Feststellbremse f, Handbremse f
hand carriage Handfahrzeuge f
hand cart Handwagen m
hand control Steuerung f von Hand
hand crank Handkurbel f
hand crumpling test Handknautschversuch m
hand die stock Schneidkluppe f
hand fed solder angesetztes Lot nt
hand feed Handvorschub m
hand forklift truck Hubwagen m
hand grip Handgriff m
hand grip area Greifbereich m
hand guard Handschutz m
hand impact screw driver Schlagschraubendreher m
hand lapping Handläppen nt
hand lapping tool Handläppwerkzeug nt
hand lathe Kleindrehbank f
hand lever Handhebel m
hand lever-operated milling machine Handhebelfräsmaschine f, Handfräsmaschine f
hand moulding shop Handformerei f
hand of cut Schneidrichtung f
hand of helix Drallrichtung f
hand of rotation Drehrichtung f
hand of the cut Schnittrichtung f
hand operated handbedient, handbetätigt, von Hand betätigt
hand over übergeben
hand pallet truck Handhubwagen m, Handgabelhubwagen m
hand perspiration Handschweiß m

hand positioning Handverteilung *f*, Handeinstellung *f*
hand power forces Handkräfte *fpl*
hand pump Handpumpe *f*
hand rail Handlauf *m*
hand reach Greifbereich *m*, Greifraum *m*
hand reamer Handreibahle *f*
hand release Handlösung *f*
hand scanner Handscanner *m*
hand scraped handgeschabt
hand setting Handeinstellung *f*
hand soldering manuelles Löten *nt*, Handlöten *nt*
hand tool Handwerkzeug *nt*, Meißel *m*
hand truck Handwagen *m*
hand unit Handgerät *nt*
hand-actuated handbetätigt
hand-guided truck Mitgängerflurförderzeug *nt*
hand-held handgehalten
hand-held calculator Taschenrechner *m*
hand-held hot air blower Hand-Heißluftgebläse *nt*
hand-held machine handbetätigte Maschine *f*
hand-held portable handgehalten tragbar
hand-held welding torch Handschweißgerät *nt*
hand-hold Haltegriff *m*
handhold(s) Haltemöglichkeit *f*, Handgriff *m*
handle Handgriff *m*, Bügelgriff *m*, Hebel *m*, Griff *m*, Zangengriff *m*; hantieren, bedienen, handhaben, bearbeiten, abwickeln, umschlagen (vi/vt), befördern, zubringen, behandeln
handle axis Griff *m*
handle bar Griffstange *f*
handle complaints Reklamation bearbeiten
handle into storage einlagern
handle out of storage auslagern
handle over goods Ware abgeben
handling Handhabung *f*, Förderung *f*, Beförderung *f*, Transport *m*, Zubringung *f*, Abwicklung *f*, Bedienung *f*, Behandlung *f*
handling attachment Aufnahmevorrichtung *f*
handling costs Transportkosten *pl*
handling device Handhabungseinrichtung *f*, Handhabungsgerät *nt*, Förderzeug *nt*
handling equipment Handhabungseinrichtung *f*, Transporteinrichtung *f*, Fördereinrichtung *f*, Förderzeuge *ntpl*
handling key for valves Betätigungsschlüssel *m* für Armaturen
handling machine Handhabungsmaschine *f*
handling means Transportmittel *nt*
handling object Handhabungsgegenstand *m*, Greifobjekt *nt*
handling of complaints Reklamationsabwicklung *f*
handling of goods Warenumschlag *m*
handling operation Transportvorgang *m*
handling over Übergabe *f*
handling over goods Ware *f* abgeben, Warenabgabe *f*
handling parameters *pl* Bearbeitungsparameter *mpl*
handling rate Umschlagsleistung *f*
handling speed Fördergeschwindigkeit *f*
handling time Griffzeit *f*
handling unit Fördereinheit *f*, Fördereinrichtung *f*, Handhabungsgerät *nt*
hand-operated mechanism Handzug *m*
hand-operated milling attachment Handfräsvorrichtung *f*
handrail Geländer *nt*, Geländerrohr *nt*
handrail post Geländerstütze *f*
handshake Quittungsaustausch *m*
handshake message Quittungsaustauschmitteilung *f*
handstamp Handstampfen *nt*
handwheel Handrad *nt*
hand-written handschriftlich
handy praktisch
hang hängen, anhängen
hang over überhängen
hanger strap Hängeanker *m*
hanging label Warenanhänger *m*
harbour clamp Hafenklammer *f*

hard asbestos plate Hartasbestplatte *f*
hard copy Ausdruck *m*
hard disk Festplatte *f*
hard facing Auftragschweißen *nt*, Bestücken *nt* mit Hartmetall
hard hat Helm *m*
hard jointing material Hartdichtungsstoff *m*
hard metal tipped milling cutter hartmetallbestückter Fräser *m*
hard mix from rubber Hartgummimischung *f*
hard soldering Hartlöten *nt*, Schweißlöten *nt*
hard surfacing layer Panzerung *f*
hard-aggregates Hartstoffe *mpl*
hard-aggregates floor screeds Hartstoffestrich *m*
harden härten
hardenability requirement Härtbarkeitsforderung *f*
hardenability response Härtbarkeitsstreuband *nt*
hardened and tempered steel vergüteter Stahl *m*
hardened state Härtung *f*
hardened steel gehärteter Stahl *m*
hardening Härten *nt*, Härtung *nt*
hardening equivalent value Härtungsgleichwert *m*
hardening filter Härtungsfilter *m*
hardening shop Härterei *f*
hardening twice over zweimaliges Härten *nt*
hardfacing Schweißpanzern *nt*
hard-facing electrode Auftragsschweißelektrode *f*
hard-iron star Hartgussstern *m*
hardness Härte *f*
hardness and strength values Härte- und Festigkeitswerte *mpl*
hardness conversion Härteumwertung *f*
hardness distribution Härteverlauf *m*
hardness penetrability Einhärtbarkeit *f*
hardness penetration Einhärtung *f*
hardness penetration effect einhärtende Wirkung *f*
hard-solder hartlöten; Hartlot *nt*

hardware configuration Gerätekonfiguration *f*
hardware monitor Hardwareüberwacher *m*
hardwired festverdrahtet
harm schaden
harmful schädlich
harmful constituents schädliche Bestandteile *mpl*
harmful effect schädigende Wirkung *f*
harmful substance Schadstoff *m*
harmfulness Schädlichkeit *f*
harmless ungefährlich
harmonic Oberschwingung *f*
harmonic wave Oberteil *nt*
harmonization Vereinheitlichung *f*
harmonize vereinheitlichen
HARMST (high aspect ratio micro system technology) HARMST (Hochaspektverhältnis-Mikrosystem-Technologie) *f*
harsh rau
hatch schraffieren; Schraffur *f*
hatched area schraffierter Bereich *m*
hatching Schraffur *f*
haul ziehen, schleppen
haulage Ziehen *nt*, Schleppen *nt*
haulage car Transportwagen *m*
hauling capacity Transportleistung *f*
have a bearing on Einfluss haben auf
having form-fit formschlüssig
having friction grip kraftschlüssig
hazard Gefahr *f*, Gefahrenstelle *f*, Gefährdung *f*
hazard bonus Gefahrenzulage *f*
hazard category Gefahrenklasse *f*
hazard due to the function involved funktionsbedingte Gefahr *f*
hazard flasher Warnblinker *m*
hazard from stray currents Streustromgefährdung *f*
hazard group Gefahrklasse *f*
hazard pictorial Gefahrensymbol *nt*
hazard point Gefahrstelle *f*
hazard source Gefahrenquelle *f*
hazard zone Gefahrbereich *m*
hazardous gefährlich, gefahrbringend, gefährdet, sicherheitsgefährdend
hazardous element gefährliches Bauteil *nt*

hazardous goods Gefahrgut *nt*, gefährliche Güter *ntpl*
hazardous location explosionsgefährdeter Raum *m*
hazardous materials gefährliche Güter *ntpl*
hazardous movement gefährliche Bewegung *f*
hazardous situation Gefährdung *f*, Gefahrenfall *m*
hazardous voltage gefährliche Spannung *f*
Hazen colour index Hazen-Farbzahl *f*
H-beam Doppel-T-Träger *m*
head Kopf *m*, Querbalkensupport *m*, Horizontalsupport *m*, Support *m*
head access hole Kopfloch *nt*
head back den Rückweg einschlagen
head box Oberkasten *m*
head cast Oberkasten *m*
head casting Kopfguss *m*
head form test Phantomfallversuch *m*
head impact toughness Kopfschlagzähigkeit *f*
head mounting Kopfhalterung *f*, Koppelung *f*
head of the rack Regalkopf *m*
head of the rail Schienenkopf *m*
head room Kopffreiheit *f*
head slide Schieber *m*, Meißelschlitten *m*, Senkrechtschlitten *m*
head soundness Kopfschlagzähigkeit *f*
head swivel Drehteil *nt*
head turn Kopfdrehung *f*
header Sammelrohr *nt*
header record Führungssatz *m*
heading Überschrift *f*
headless screw Gewindestift *m*
headline Überschrift *f*
head-mounted display Helmdisplay *nt*
headquarters Zentrale *f*
headroom Bauhöhe *f*
headstock Spindelkasten *m*, Spindelstock *m*
headstock rise-and-fall motion Spindelkastensenkrechtbewegung *f*
headstock side Antriebsseite *f*
headstock spindle Drehspindel *f*, Drehmaschinenspindel *f*, Arbeitsspindel *f*
headstock-motor Spindelstockmotor *m*
headway Durchgangshöhe *f*
health Befinden *nt*
heap of mix Mischguthaufen *m*
hearing loss Gehörschädigung *f*, Hörschädigung *f*
heat heizen, beheizen, erhitzen, erwärmen; Hitze *f*, Wärme *f*, Stahlschmelze *f*
heat balance Wärmebilanz *f*
heat carrier Wärmeträger *m*
heat checking Wärmerissigkeit *f*
heat cold kaltstauchen
heat completely through durchgreifend erwärmen
heat conducting wärmeleitend
heat conservation work Wärmeschutzarbeit *f*
heat consumer Wärmeverbraucher *m*
heat consuming appliance Wärmeverbraucher *m*
heat consumption Wärmeverbrauch *m*
heat control Wärmeführung *f*, Wärmeregelung *f*
heat dissipation Wärmeleitung *f*, Wärmeabfuhr *f*
heat dissipation welding Wärmeleitungsschweißen *nt*
heat distribution system Heizungsnetz *nt*
heat emission Wärmeleistung *f*
heat emission per section Gliedleistung *f*
heat engineering equipment brennstofftechnische Ausrüstung *f*
heat-engineering requirement heiztechnische Anforderung *f*
heat equalization time Wärmausgleichszeit *f*
heat exchange Wärmeaustausch *m*
heat extraction Wärmeentzug *m*
heat flow Wärmefluss *m*
heat flow density Wärmestromdichte *f*
heat generator burning fuel oil Wärmeerzeuger *m* mit Feuerung für Heizöl
heat guide nozzle Wärmeleitdüse *f*
heat insulation Wärmeschutzisolierung *f*, Wärmeisolation *f*
heat of fusion Schmelzwärme *f*
heat of sublimation Sublimationswärme *f*

heat removal Wärmeabfuhr *f*
heat requirement Wärmebedarf *m*
heat requirement calculation Wärmebedarfsrechnung *f*
heat resistant wärmebeständig, hitzebeständig, warmfest
heat seal heißsiegeln
heat seal labelling machine Heißsiegeletikettiermaschine *f*
heat sealable heißsiegelfähig
heat sealing Heizelementwärmekontaktschweißen *nt*, Heißsiegeln *nt*
heat sealing machine Heißsiegelverschließmaschine *f*
heat shrink heißschrumpfen
heat shrinking Heißschrumpfen *nt*, Wärmeschrumpfung *f*
heat sink Wärmeschild *nt*
heat source Wärmequelle *f*
heat storage Warmlagerung *f*
heat storage effect Wärmespeicherwirkung *f*
heat storage energy Warmlagerungsversuch *m*
heat-storage temperature Warmlagerungstemperatur *f*
heat supply Wärmelieferung *f*, Wärmezufuhr *f*
heat through durchwärmen
heat transfer Wärmeübertragung *f*
heat transfer liquid Wärmeübertragungsflüssigkeit *f*
heat transfer medium Wärmeüberträger *m*, Wärmeübertragungsmittel *nt*
heat transfer oil Wärmeträgeröl *nt*
heat transfer surface Wärmeübertragungsfläche *f*
heat transition Wärmeübergang *m*
heat treat wärmebehandeln
heat treatable steel Vergütungsstahl *m*
heat treatment Wärmebehandlung *f*
heat treatment schedule Wärmebehandlungsplan *m*
heat treatment technology Wärmebehandlungstechnik *f*
heat treatment instruction Wärmebehandlungsanweisung *f*
heat up erhitzen
heat vent Wärmeabzug *m*
heat yield Wärmeleistung *f*

heat-affected zone wärmebeeinflusste Zone *f*
heat-bonding Warmkleben *nt*
heated beheizt
heated blade Heizschiene *f*
heated by flue gas abgasbeheizt
heated by waste heat abhitzebeheizt
heated tool groove welding Heizelementnutschweißen *nt*
heated tool welding Heizelementschweißen *nt*
heated tool welding with cutting edge Heizelementtrennnahtschweißen *nt*, Trennnahtschweißen *nt*
heated wedge pressure welding Heizkeilschweißen *nt*
heated wedge-shaped tool Heizkeil *m*
heater Heizung *f*, Heizgerät *nt*
heater outlet Luftauslass *m*
heating Heizung *f*, Befeuerung *f*
heating back pressure turbo-generating set Heizgegendruckturbosatz *m*
heating boiler Heizkessel *m*
heating circuit water Heizungswasser *nt*
heating coil Heizwendel
heating curve Wärmekurve *f*
heating days Heiztage *f*
heating demand Heizungsbedarf *m*
heating electrode Anwärmelektrode *f*
heating element Heizglied *nt*
heating from one side einseitiges Erwärmen *nt*
heating gas chamber Heizgaskasten *m*
heating gas flues *pl* Heizgaszüge *mpl*
heating gas resistance Heizgaswiderstand *m*
heating medium Heizmedium *nt*, Heizmittel *nt*
heating period Heizperiode *f*
heating pipe Heizungsrohr *nt*
heating plant Heizanlage *f*
heating plant for intermittent operation Heizungsanlage *f* mit periodischem Betrieb
heating practice Heiztechnik *f*
heating spiral Heizwendel
heating stove Heizungsherd *m*
heating surface area loading Heizflä-

chenbelastung *f*
heating system Heizsystem *nt*, heiztechnische Anlage *f*, Heizungsanlage *f*
heating system steam valve Heizdampfventil *nt*
heating technology Heiztechnik *f*
heating treatment time Erwärmdauer *f*
heating up Erwärmung *f*, Erhitzung *f*
heat-insulated wärmeisoliert
heat-proof quality Wärmebeständigkeit *f*
heat-resisting hitzebeständig
heat-setting adhesive Warmkleber *m*
heat-treated steel Vergütungsstahl *m*
heat-up pressure Anwärmdruck *m*
heavy schwer, massiv
heavy duty cylindrical milling cutter Hochleistungswalzenfräser *m*
heavy duty milling cutter Hochleistungsfräser *m*
heavy duty slotting machine Hochleistungsstoßmaschine *f*
heavy load conveyor Schwerlastförderer *m*
heavy load lifting beam Schwerlasttraverse *f*
heavy load rack Schwerlastregal *nt*
heavy load roller Schwerlastrolle *f*
heavy load shelving Schwerlastregal *nt*
heavy load spreader Schwerlasttraverse *f*
heavy parts Schwergut *nt*
heavy parts storage Schwergutlagerung *f*
heavy start Schweranlauf *m*
heavy type hohe Form *f*
heavy walled dickwandig
heavy-duty ~ Hochleistungs ~
heavy-duty lathe Hochleistungsdrehmaschine *f*, Großdrehbank *f*
heavy-duty miller Hochleistungsfräsmaschine *f*
heavy-duty plain milling cutter Hochleistungswalzenfräser *m*
heavy-duty production lathe hochleistungsfähige Produktionsdrehmaschine *f*
heavy-duty shell end mill Hochleistungswalzenstirnfräser *m*

hexagon head Außensechskant *m*
heel 1. *(Fertigungstechnik)* Rückseite *f*
2. *(Fördertechnik)* Gabelknick *m*
heel of the tooth Schneidenrücken *m*
height Höhe *f*
height limitation Höhenbegrenzung *f*
height adjustment Höhenverstellung *f*
height for diagonal travel Diagonalfahrthöhe *f*
height gauge Höhenlehre *f*, Höhenmaßstab *m*, Höhenreißer *m* mit Teilung *f*
height level Höhenniveau *nt*
height monitoring Höhenüberwachung *f*
height of centre Spitzenhöhe *f*
height of fall Absturzhöhe *f*
height of flight Treppenlaufhöhe *f*
height of installation Aufstellungshöhe *f*
height of lift Hubhöhe *f*
height of rebound Rückprallhöhe *f*
height position Höhenlage *f*
height positioning Höhenpositionierung *f*
height positioning marker Höhenpositioniermarke *f*
height pre-election Höhenvorwahl *f*
height reference point Höhenpunkt *m*
height tolerance Höhentoleranz *f*
height dimension Höhenmaß *nt*
height of the tooth tip chamfer *(Verzahnungstechnik)* Fasenhöhe *f* des Kopfkantenbruches
helical drallförmig, schraubenförmig, spiralförmig, schraubenlinig
helical arc Schraubenlinienbogen *m*
helical bevel gear Kegelschraubenrad *nt*, Schrägzahnkegelrad *nt*
helical bevel gear pair Schrägzahnkegelradpaar *nt*, Kegelschraubenradpaar *nt*
helical broach Räumwerkzeug *nt* für drallförmige Nuten
helical broaching Drallnutenräumen *nt*, Räumen *nt* von Drallnuten
helical carbide-tipped end mill hartmetallbestückter Schaftfräser *m* mit spiralförmiger Verzahnung
helical compression spring Schrau-

bendruckfeder *f*
helical curve Schraubenkurve *f*, Schraubenlinie *f*
helical drive Tischantrieb *m* über Schrägzahnräder
helical flute Drallnut *f*
helical form Schraubenlinienform *f*
helical form milling Formfräsen *nt* von Schraubennuten
helical gear Schrägzylinderrad *nt*, Schraubenrad *nt*, Stirnrad *nt*, Stirnradgetriebe *nt*, schräg verzahntes Rad *nt*
helical gear pair Schrägzylinderradpaar *nt*, Schrägstirnradpaar *nt*
helical gear shaper Schrägzahnradstoßmaschine *f*
helical gearing Schrägverzahnung *f*
helical groove Drallnut *f*, schraubenförmige Nut *f*
helical guidance lead Schraubenführungssteigungshöhe *f*
helical heating element Heizwendel
helical line Schraubenlinie *f*
helical master gear schräg verzahntes Lehrzahnrad *nt*
helical mill Fräser *m* mit spiralförmiger Verzahnung, Walzenfräser *m* mit Steigungswinkel über 45°
helical mill with pilot spiralverzahnter Fräser *m* mit Führungszapfen
helical milling Fräsen *nt* einer schraubenförmigen Nut, Spiralnutenfräsen *nt*, Spiralfräsen *nt*
helical milling cutter spiralgenuteter Fräser *m*
helical pinion cutter Schrägschneidrad *nt*
helical pitch surface Schraubwälzfläche *f*
helical plain milling cutter Hochleistungswalzenfräser *m*
helical rack schräg verzahnte Zahnstange *f*
helical roll grinding Schraubwälzschleifen *nt*
helical rolling type gear transmission Schraubwälzgetriebe *nt*
helical slab mill Hochleistungswalzenfräser *m*
helical spline broach Räumwerkzeug *nt* für drallförmige Nuten
helical spring Schraubenfeder *f*
helical spur gear schräg verzahntes Stirnrad *nt*, Schrägstirnrad *nt*
helical teeth Schrägverzahnung *f*, Spiralverzahnung *f*
helical tooth cutter Fräser *m* mit Spiralverzahnung
helical tooth spur gear Schrägzahnstirnrad *nt*
helical tooth system Schrägverzahnung *f*
helical tooth trace schraubige Flankenlinie *f*
helical type gear transmission Schraubgetriebe *nt*
helically toothed schräg verzahnt
helices *pl* Spiralen *fpl*, Schraubenlinien *fpl*
helix Flankenlinie *f*, Schraubengang *m*, Schraubenlinie *f*, Drall *m*
helix angle Schrägungswinkel *m*, Drallwinkel *m*, Zahnschrägewinkel *m*
helix angle of threads Steigungswinkel *m* von Gewinden
helix angle range Schrägungswinkelbereich *m*
helix angle variation Schrägungswinkelabweichung *f*
helix arc Schraubenlinienbogen *m*
helix axis Schraubachse *f*
helix interpolation Schraubenlinieninterpolation *f*
helix point Schraubpunkt *m*
helix surface Schraubfläche *f*
helix tooth cutter spiralverzahnter Fräser *m*
helmet Helm *m*
hemisphere Halbkugel *f*
hemming Schwenkbiegen *nt*
hand feed mechanism Handvorschub *m*
hermaphrodite calliper Tastzirkel *m*
herringbone gear Pfeilrad *nt*
herringbone gear shaper Pfeilzahnhobelmaschine *f*
heterogeneous mixed electrode heterogene Mischelektrode *f*
heuristic heuristisch
hexadecimal hexadezimal

hexadecimal code Hexadezimalcode *m*
hexagon Sechskant *m*, Sechseck *nt*
hexagon bolt Sechskantbolzen *m*, Sechskantschraube *f*
hexagon bolt for aircraft workshop facilities Sechskantschraube *f* für Fertigungsmittel in der Luftfahrt
hexagon bolt with large width across flats for high strength friction grip fastenings Sechskantschraube *f* mit großer Schlüsselweite für HV-Verbindungen
hexagon bottom Sechskantgrund *m*
hexagon cap nut Sechskanthutmutter *f*
hexagon drive extension *(für Maschinenschrauber)* Verbindungssechskant
hexagon flat *(e. Mutter)* Sechskantfläche *f*
hexagon head bolt with waisted shank Sechskantdehnschraube *f*
hexagon head screw Sechskantschraube *f*
hexagon head screw with full dog point Sechskantschraube *f* mit Zapfen
hexagon head sheet metal tapping screw Sechskantblechschraube *f*
hexagon head thread cutting screw Sechskantschneidschraube *f*
hexagon head wood screw Sechskantholzschraube *f*
hexagon nut with large width across flats Sechskantmutter *f* mit großer Schlüsselweite
hexagon rod Sechskantvollstab *m*
hexagon screwdriver Sechskantschraubendreher *m*
hexagon set screw with coned half dog point Sechskantschraube *f* mit Ansatzspitze
hexagon set screw with full dog point Sechskantschraube *f* mit kleinem Sechskant und Zapfen, Sechskantschraube *f* mit kleinem Sechskant und Ansatzspitze
hexagon socket countersunk (flat) head screw Senkschraube *f* mit Innensechskant
hexagon socket depth Sechskanttiefe *f*
hexagon socket head cap screws Zylinderschraube *f* mit Innensechskant
hexagon socket screw key with pilot Winkelschraubendreher *m* mit Zapfen für Innensechskantschrauben
hexagon socket screw sealing plug Verschlussschraube *f* mit Innensechskant
hexagon socket set screw Gewindestift *m* mit Innensechskant
hexagon socket set screw with cup point Gewindestift *m* mit Innensechskant und Ringschneide *f*
hexagon socket set screw with flat point Gewindestift *m* mit Innensechskant und Kegelkuppe *f*
hexagon socket set screw with half-dog point Gewindestift *m* mit Innensechskant und Zapfen *m*
hexagon socket wrench *(für Sechskantschrauben)* Steckschlüsseleinsatz *m*
hexagon tube Sechskantrhr *nt*
hexagon turret Sechskantrevolverkopf *m*
hexagon turret lathe Revolverbank *f*, Sternrevolverdrehmaschine *f*
hexagon weld nut Sechskantschweißmutter *f*
hexagon wrench key Sechskantschraubendreher *m*
hexagon wrench key insert Sechskantschraubendrehereinsatz *m*
hexagon wrench key with pilot Sechskantstiftschlüssel *m* mit Zapfen
hexagonal sechseckig, sechskantig, hexagonal
hexagonal bundle Sechskantbund *m*
hexagonal laminated moulded section Sechskantumpressung *f*
hexagonal nut Sechskantmutter *f*
hexagonal wrench Sechskantschlüssel *m*
hexapod Hexapode
hex *(Sechskant)* fräsen
hidden edge unsichtbare Kante *f*
hide substance Hautsubstanz *f*
hierarchical nachgeordnet
hierarchical classification Schachtelmodell *nt*
hierarchical process computing system hierarchisches Prozessrechensys-

tem *nt*
hierarchy Hierarchie *f*
hierarchy of goals Zielhierarchie *f*
hierarchy of objectives Zielhierarchie *f*
high hoch, groß
high aspect ratio micro system technology (HARMST) HARMST (Hochaspektverhältnis-Mikrosystem-Technologie) *f*
high bay racking Hochregal *nt*
high bay storage Hochregallagerung *f*
high bay warehouse Hochregalanlage *f*, Hochregallager *nt*, Kanallager *nt*
high compression load spring washer gewölbter Federring *m*, Hochspannfederring *m*
high contrast reproduction *(e. Lichtpausschicht)* kontrastreiche Wiedergabe *f*
high density polyethylene Niederdruckpolyethylen *nt*
high density warehouse Kompaktlager *nt*
high energy energiereich
high energy forming Hochenergieumformen *nt*
high energy radiation energiereiche Strahlung *f*
high impact strength plastics hochschlagzäher Kunststoff *m*
high infeed palletizer Obenpalettierer *m*
high level depalletizer Kopfentladedepalettierer *m*
high level lift-off depalletizer Kopfentladeabhebedepalettierer *m*
high level lift-off palletizer Kopfladeabhebepalettierer *m*
high level palletizer Kopfladepalettierer *m*, Obenpalettierer *m*
high lift Hochhub *m*
high modulus fibre fabric Hochmodulfasergewebe *nt*
high power switchgear Hochleistungsschaltanlagen *fpl*
high precision Hochpräzision *f*
high precision lathe Feinstdrehmaschine *f*
high precision turning Feinstdreharbeit *f*, Genauigkeitsdrehen *nt*

high pressure Hochdruck *m*
high pressure nozzle Hochdruckdüse *f*
high pressure pressing Hochdruckpressen *nt*
high rupture fuse Überspannungsableiter *m*
high setting Großstellung *f*
high speed flux Schnellschweißpulver *nt*
high speed steam raising unit Schnelldampferzeuger *m*
high speed steel Schnellstahl *m*, Schnellarbeitsstahl *m*, Schnelldrehstahl *m*
high speed steel tip Schnellstahlplättchen *nt*
high speed welding equipment Schnellschweißgerät *nt*
high strength friction grip fastening HV-Verbindung *f*, hochfest vorgespannte Verbindung *f*
high tech Hochtechnologie *f*
high technology Hochtechnologie *f*
high temperature wärmefest
high temperature brazed joint Hochtemperaturlötverbindung *f*
high temperature oxidation Verzunderung *f*, Zunderung *f*
high temperature soldering Hochtemperaturlöten *nt*
high temperature stability Wärmefestigkeit *f*
high temperature water Heißwasser *nt*
high temperature water conveying pipe heißwasserführende Leitung *f*
high temperature water flow temperature Heißwasservorlauftemperatur *f*
high temperature water heating appliance Heißwassererzeuger *m*
high temperature water heating system Heißwasserheizungsanlage *f*
high temperature water pipe Heißwasserleitung *f*
high temperature water return pipe Heißwasserrücklaufleitung *f*
high viscosity grease zähflüssiges Fett *nt*
high voltage Hochspannung *f*

high voltage cable plug and socket Hochspannungssteckverbindung *f*
high-alloy hochlegiert
high-alloy steel hochlegierter Stahl *m*
high-carbon steel hochgekohlter Stahl *m*
high-division index plate Teilscheibe *f* für weiten Teilbereich
high-duty ~ Hochleistungs ~
high-duty automatic Hochleistungsautomat *m*
high-duty hobber Hochleistungswälzfräsmaschine *f*
high-duty metal cutting Hochleistungszerspanung *f*
high-duty milling machine Hochleistungsfräsmaschine *f*
high-duty production machine Hochleistungsproduktionsmaschine *f*
high-efficiency turning Leistungsdrehen *nt*
higher harmonics Schwingungen *fpl* höherer Ordnung
higher limit Größtmaß *nt*
higher order übergeordnet
highest-valued stage höchstwertige Stufe *f*
high-feed milling Fräsen *nt* mit großem Vorschub
high-frequency Hochfrequenz *f*
high-frequency conduction welding konduktives Hochfrequenzschweißen *nt*
high-frequency induction welding induktives Hochfrequenzschweißen *nt*
high-frequency power supply Hochfrequenzstromquelle *f*
high-frequency technology Hochfrequenztechnik *f*
high-frequency welding Hochfrequenzschweißen *nt*, Schweißen *nt* mit Hochfrequenz
high-grade *(z. B. Werkstoffe)* hochwertig
high-level language Hochsprache *f*
high-level stacker Regalstapler *m*
high-lift platform truck Plattformwagen *m*, Plattformhubwagen *m*, Gabelhochhubwagen *m*, Hochhubwagen *m*
high-lift straddle carrier Portalhubwagen *m*
high-lift truck Gabelhochhubwagen *m*, Hochregalstapler *m*
highly stressed hochbeansprucht
high-performance cutting (HPC) Hochleistungsschneiden *nt*
high-performance grinding Hochleistungsschleifen *nt*
high-polymer plastics hochpolymerer Kunststoff *m*
high-power ... *(z. B. Strom)* stark
high-precision machine tool Hochgenauigkeitsmaschine *f*
high-production lathe Hochleistungsdrehmaschine *f*
high-production milling machine Hochleistungsfräsmaschine *f*
high-production rigid gear hobbing machine Hochleistungsstarrfräsmaschine *f*
high-quality hochwertig
high-quality corundum Edelkorund *m*
high-quality laminated fibre material Edelpressspan *m*
high-quality material Qualitätswerkstoff *m*
high-quality steel Edelstahl *m*
high-quality work Qualitätsarbeit *f*
high-rake cutter Fräser *m* mit großem Spanwinkel
high-rake milling Fräsen *nt* mit großem Spanwinkel
high-speed ~ schnell~, Hochleistungs ~, Hochgeschwindigkeits ~
high-speed automatic Schnellautomat *m*
high-speed carbide tool machining Schnellzerspanung *f* mit Hartmetallwerkzeugen
high-speed cutting (HSC) Hochgeschwindigkeitsschneiden *nt*
high-speed drilling attachment Schnellbohrvorrichtung *f*
high-speed forming Hochgeschwindigkeitsumformen *nt*
high-speed fusion method Schnellaufschlussverfahren *nt*
high-speed gear change Schnellschaltung *f*
high-speed grinding Hochgeschwin-

digkeitsschleifen *nt*
high-speed heavy-duty lathe Hochleistungsschnelldrehbank *f*
high-speed lathe Schnelldrehmaschine *f*, Schnellschnittdrehmaschine *f*
high-speed machining Hochgeschwindigkeitsbearbeitung *f*
high-speed milling attachment Schnellfräseinrichtung *f*, Schnellfräsvorrichtung *f*
high-speed milling machine Schnellfräsmaschine *f*
high-speed multi-tool lathe Vielstahlschnelldrehbank *f*
high-speed precision lathe Präzisionsschnelldrehmaschine *f*
high-speed printer Schnelldrucker *m*
high-speed production lathe Produktionsschnelldrehbank *f*
high-speed screw slotter Schnellschraubenschlitzmaschine *f*
high-speed shaper Schnellhobler *m*
high-speed spindle Schnelllaufspindel *f*
high-speed stock removal Schnellzerspanung *f*
high-speed thread milling (roll) Gewindeschlagfräsen *nt*, Wirbeln *nt*
high-speed universal milling attachment Universalschnellfräsapparat *m*
high-speed weigher Schnellwaage *f*
high-speed-cutting-machine HSC-Maschine *f*, Hochgeschwindigkeitsmaschine *f*
high-strength friction-grip bolt with waisted shank Dehnschraube *f*
high-temperature strength Warmfestigkeit *f*
high-temperature alternating stress resistance Wärmewechselfestigkeit *f*
high-temperature resistant construction steel warmfester Baustahl *m*
high-tensile steel hochzugfester Stahl *m*
high-velocity turning Schnelldrehen *nt*
high-voltage current Starkstrom *m*
high-voltage motor Hochspannungsmotor *m*
high-voltage transmission line Hochspannungsleitung *f*
hinder hindern
hindrance Behinderung *f*
hinge Gelenk *nt*, Scharnier *nt*, Angel *f*; gelenkig befestigen, schwenken, klappen
hinged klappbar, aufklappbar, schwenkbar, gelenkig befestigt
hinged cantilever Drehausleger *m*
hinged door Schwenktor *nt*
hinged knee Kniegelenk *nt*
hinged lid Klappdeckel *m*
hinged pin Scharnierstift *m*
hinged plate Wippe *f*
hinged slide rails Wippe *f*
hinged-lid lubricator Klappöler *m*
hip Hüfte *f*
hip height Hüfthöhe *f*
hire mieten
histogram Balkendiagramm *nt*, Histogramm *nt*
history Bearbeitungsablauf *m*
hit prallen gegen, schlagen, treffen
hit a nail into nageln
hit the ground aufsetzen
hitch Ruck *m*
hoar-frost line Sublimationskurve *f*
hob wälzen, wälzfräsen; Wälzfräser *m*
hob slide Ständerschieber *m*
hob teeth verzahnen
hobber Wälzfräsmaschine *f*
hobbing Wälzfräsen *nt*, Wälzen *nt*
hobbing attachment Wälzfräseinrichtung *f*
hobbing cutter Wälzfräser *m*, Abwälzfräser *m*
hobbing head Fräskopf *m*, Frässpindelkopf *m*
hobbing machine Verzahnungsmaschine *f*
hobbing method Wälzverfahren *nt*, Wälzfräsverfahren *nt*
hobbing operation Wälzarbeit *f*
hobbing out attachment Auswälzfräseinrichtung *f*
hobbing process Wälzfräsverfahren *nt*, Wälzfräsen *nt*
hobbing slide Wälzsupport *m*
hobbing tool Wälzwerkzeug *nt*
hobbing unit Wälzsupport *m*, Abwälz-

support *m*
hobbing machine Wälzfräsmaschine *f*
hobcutting Abwälzfräsen *nt*
hog festhaken
hoist anheben, hochheben, heben, winden, aufwinden; Hub *m*, Aufzug *m*, Winde *f*
hoist acceleration Hubbeschleunigung *f*
hoist and brake unit Hubwerkbremse *f*
hoist drive unit Hubwerk *nt*
hoist mechanism Hubwerk *nt*
hoist path Hubstrecke *f*, Hubweg *m*
hoist path limit Hubbegrenzung *f*
hoist path limiter Hubwegbegrenzer *m*
hoist travel limit Endstellung *f*
hoist unit Hubwerk *nt*
hoisting Heben *nt*
hoisting capacity Hubkraft *f*, Hubleistung *f*
hoisting class Hubklasse *f*
hoisting gear drum Hubwerkstrommel *f*
hoisting gears Hubwerk *nt*
hoisting movement Hubbewegung *f*
hoisting platform Hubplattform *f*
hoisting power Hubkraft *f*
hoisting speed Hubgeschwindigkeit *f*
hoisting unit Hebezeug *nt*
hoisting winch Seilwinde *f*
hold Halt *m*, Handgriff *m*; sperren, spannen, halten
hold a tolerance einhalten
hold at an oblique angle schräg halten
hold in place festhalten
hold on hinhalten
hold tag Sperrvermerk *m*
hold-to-run ohne Selbsthalt
hold-to-run control Totmannschaltung *f*
hold to run control for one hand Einhandsteuerung *f*
hold-to-run control for two hands Zweihandsteuerung *f*
hold-to-run handle Totmanneinrichtung *f*
hold-to-run principle Totmannprinzip *nt*
hold together zusammenhalten

hold up gegenhalten (vi/vt)
hold-down Niederhalter *m*; niederhalten
holder Halt *m*, Handgriff *m*, Halterung *f*
holder *(Werkzeug)* Schneidenhalter *m*
holding selbsthaltend; Halten *nt*, Festhalten *nt*, Tragen *nt*
holding device Spannwerkzeug *nt*, Spannzeug *nt*, Spanner *m*
holding disc Haltescheibe *f*
holding element control Haltegliedsteuerung *f*
holding force Haftkraft *f*
holding input Halteeingang *m*
holding of inventories Bestandshaltung *f*
holding of size Maßhaltigkeit *f*
holding power Spannkraft *f*
holding rope *(Greifer)* Halteseil *nt*
holding strap Spanneisen *nt*
holding wheel Haltescheibe *f*
hole Bohrung *f*, Loch *nt*, Lochung *f*; durchstechen
hole basis fit Passung *f* für Einheitsbohrung
hole centre distance Lochabstand *m*
hole centre Lochmitte *f*
hole circle Lochkreis *m*
hole cutter Lochschnittwerkzeug *nt*
hole edge distance Lochrandabstand *m*
hole gauge Bohrungslehre *f*
hole lapping Innenrundläppen *nt*, Bohrungsläppen *nt*
hole mismatch Lochversatz *m*
hole opening Öffnung *f*
hole operation Bearbeitung *f* einer Bohrung
hole pattern Lochbild *nt*
hole penetrameter Bohrlochsteg *m*
hole centre distance Lochmittenabstand
hole size Lochmaß *nt*
hole through the gear Radbohrung *f*
hole type cutter Aufsteckfräser *m*
hollow hohl; Hohlraum *m*
hollow boring Hohlbohren *nt*
hollow chisel Hohlmeißel *m*
hollow cylinder Hohlzylinder *m*
hollow forging Hohlschmieden *nt*, Re-

hollow grinding – horizontal boring, drilling and milling machine

cken *nt* von Hohlkörpern
hollow grinding Hohlschliff *m*
hollow milling cutter Hohlfräser *m*
hollow part Hohlkörper *m*
hollow punch Locheisen *nt*
hollow shaft Hohlwelle *f*
hollow shaft gear Hohlwellenausführung *f*
hollow sphere Hohlkugel *f*
hollow wear Hohlverschleiß *m*
hollow-bore hohlbohren
hollow-core drill Kernbohrkopf *m*, Hohlbohrer *m*
hollow-drill hohlbohren
hollow-punch piercing Hohldornen *nt*
hollow-tipped electrode ausgespart aufsetzende Elektrode *f*
home position Ruhestellung *f*, Grundstellung *f*
homogeneity Homogenität *f*
homogeneous homogen
homogeneous mixed electrode homogene Mischelektrode *f*
homogeneous samples *pl* homogene Proben *fpl*
homogenization Homogenisierung *f*
homogenize homogenisieren
homogenizer Homogenisator *m*
homogenizing Homogenisieren *nt*
hone ziehschleifen, honen
honeycomb Wabe *f*, wabenartiges Gitter *nt*
honey-comb core Wabenkern *m*
honeycomb racking Wabenregal *nt*
honeycomb racking system Wabenregalanlage *f*
honeycomb sandwich Wabenkernverbund *m*
honeycomb shelving Wabenregal *nt*
honeycomb shelving row Wabenregalzeile *f*
honeycomb shelving system Wabenregalanlage *f*
honeycomb storage Wabenlagerung *f*
honeycomb warehouse Wabenlager *nt*
honing Langhubhonen *nt*, Ziehschleifen *nt*, Honen *nt*
honing elements Honelemente *f*
honing machine Honmaschine *f*, Ziehschleifmaschine *f*
honing operation Feinstziehschleifen *nt*
honing stick Schleifkörper *m*
honing tool Honwerkzeug *nt*, Honahle *f*, Schleifahle *f*
hood Verdeckung *f*, Haube *f*, Kappe *f*
hooded apparatus Haubengerät *nt*
hook Spange *f*, Haken *m*, Gabelhaken *m*
hook angle Brustwinkel *m*, Radialwinkel *m*
hook in einhängen
hook retaining face Hakenanlage *f*
hook suspension face Hakenauflage *f*
hook tool Hakenmeißel *m*
hook up 1. Zuschalten *nt*; zuschalten 2. *(Rohrleitungsbau)* Rohranschluss *m*
Hooke's joint Kardangelenk *nt*
hook-in pin Einhängestift *m*
hook-in type beam Einhängeriegel *m*
hook-in type fitting Einhängeverbindung *f*
hook-mounted hakenbefestigt
hook-on type hakenförmig
hook-up plan Rohrleitungsplan *m*
hoop umreifen, umschnüren; Umreifungsband *nt*
hoop-casing Umreifung *f*
hoop-casing machine Umreifungs- und Verschließmaschine *f*
hooping Umschnürung *f*, Umreifen *nt*
hopper Teilzuführungseinrichtung *f*, Beschickungstrichter *m*, Fülltrichter *m*, Füllkasten *m*
horizontal horizontal, waagerecht
horizontal boring Waagerechtbohren *nt*
horizontal boring and milling machine Fräswerk *nt*, Bohr- und Fräswerk *nt*, Waagerechtbohr- und -fräswerk *f*
horizontal boring machine Waagerechtbohrmaschine *f*
horizontal boring mill Fräswerk *nt*, Waagerechtbohr- und -fräswerk *f*, Waagerechtbohrwerk *nt*
horizontal boring, drilling and milling machine Fräswerk *nt*, Waagerechtbohr- und -fräswerk *f*
horizontal boring, drilling and mill-

ing machine with compound table Waagerechtbohr- und -fräsmaschine *f* mit kreuzbeweglichem Aufspanntisch
horizontal boring, drilling and milling machine with non-traversing column and traversing rotary worktable and boring stay Waagerechtbohr- und -fräsmaschine *f* mit feststehenden Ständer und längs sowie quer und rund verstellbarem Tisch und Lünette
horizontal boring, drilling and milling machine with rotary worktable Waagerechtbohr- und -fräsmaschine *f* mit drehbarem Aufspanntisch
horizontal boring, milling drilling and tapping machine Waagerechtbohr-, -fräs- und -gewindebohrmaschine *f*
horizontal brace Horizontalverband *m*
horizontal carousel Umlaufregal *nt*, Horizontalkarussell *nt*
horizontal carousel store Umlaufregallager *nt*
horizontal design Horizontalausführung *f*
horizontal divider Querteiler *m*
horizontal drilling Waagerechtbohren *nt*
horizontal drilling boring and milling machine Waagerechtbohr- und Fräsmaschine *f*
horizontal duplicator Waagerechtprofilfräsmaschine *f*
horizontal dynamic racking Horizontalumlauflager *nt*
horizontal edgewise scale Querskala *f*
horizontal end load cartoner Horizontal-Kartoniermaschine *f*
horizontal fixed-bed milling machine (or miller) Waagerechtproduktionsfräsmaschine *f*
horizontal front clearance Einstellwinkel *m* der Nebenschneide
horizontal gear hobber Waagerechtstoßmaschine *f*, Waagerechtzahnradfräsmaschine *f*
horizontal head Seitensupport *m*
horizontal hobbing Horizontalumschnürung *f*

horizontal internal broaching machine Waagerechtinnenräummaschine *f*
horizontal knee-and-column type miller (or milling machine) Waagerechtkonsolfräsmaschine *f*
horizontal line Waagerechte *f*, Horizontale *f*
horizontal load Horizontalbeanspruchung *f*
horizontal manufacturing-type milling machine Waagerechtproduktionsfräsmaschine *f*
horizontal miller Waagerechtfräsmaschine *f*
horizontal milling and boring machine Waagerechtfräs- und -bohrmaschine *f*
horizontal milling machine Horizontalfräsmaschine *f*, Waagerechtfräsmaschine *f*
horizontal milling spindle head Waagerechtfrässpindelkopf *m*
horizontal motion Horizontalbewegung *f*
horizontal packing machine Horizontalpackmaschine *f*
horizontal pallet strapping machine Horizontalpalettenumreifungsmaschine *f*
horizontal pipeline liegende Leitung *f*
horizontal plane Waagerechte *f*
horizontal planing Waagerechthobeln *nt*
horizontal positioning Horizontalpositionierung *f*
horizontal precision boring machine Waagerechtfeinstbohrwerk *nt*
horizontal precision handlever milling machine Waagerechthandhebelfeinstfräsmaschine *f*
horizontal profiler with two dimensional control Waagerechtnachformfräsmaschine *f* für zweidimensionales Fräsen
horizontal push cut shaper waagerechte Stoßmaschine *f*
horizontal rail *(Hobelmaschine)* Querbalken *m*
horizontal railhead Horizontal-Hobel-

support *m*
horizontal rigid milling machine Waagerechtstarrfräsmaschine *f*
horizontal scanning Zeilenabtastung *f*
horizontal shaper Waagerechtstoßmaschine *f* mit waagerecht verlaufendem Stößel
horizontal spindle milling machine Fräsmaschine *f* mit waagerechter Frässpindel
horizontal strapping Horizontalumreifung *f*
horizontal stress Horizontalbeanspruchung *f*
horizontal surface grinder Waagerechtflächenschleifmaschine *f*
horizontal tie Balken *m*
horizontal time Liegezeit *f*
horizontal travel Fahren *nt*
horizontal travel speed Fahrgeschwindigkeit *f*
horizontal twisting Verdrehung *f*
horizontal tying Horizontalumschnürung *f*
horizontal-spindle knee-and column miller Konsolfräsmaschine *f* mit waagerechter Spindel
horizontal-spindle rotary-table surface grinder waagerechte Rundtischflächenschleifmaschine *f*
horizontal-spindle surface grinder waagerechte Flächenschleifmaschine *f*
horizontal-type shaper Shaper *m*, Waagerechtstoßmaschine *f*, Shapingmaschine *f*
horn 1. *(Akkustik)* Hupe *f*, Signalhupe *f* 2. *(Werkzeug)* Aufnahmedorn *m*
horn shrinkage Horneinlauf *m*
horse Gestell *nt*, Gerüst *nt*
horsehair bristle Rosshaarbürste *f*
horse-power Pferdestärke *f*
horsepower rating Leistung *f*
horseshoe expansion joint Lyra-Ausgleicher *m*
horticultural glass Gartenbau-Glas *nt*
hose Schlauch *m*
hose bursting Schlauchbruch *m*
hose failure Schlauchbruch *m*
host computer Zentralrechner *m*, Leitrechner *m*

host system Zentralrechner *m*
hot heiß, warm
hot air Heißluft *f*
hot channel distribution plate Heißkanalverteilerplatte *f*
hot coining Heißprägen *nt*
hot compression mould warmpressen
hot compression test Warmdruckversuch *m*
hot crack Warmriss *m*
hot crack tendency Warmrissneigung *f*
hot cupboard Wärmeröhre *f*
hot dip coating Schmelztauchüberzug *m*
hot dip method Schmelztauchverfahren *nt*
hot dip tinning Schmelztauchverzinnung *f*
hot draw warmziehen
hot foil coder Heißfoliencodierer
hot form warmformen
hot forming Warmformen *nt*, Warmformgebung *f*
hot galvanizing Feuerverzinkung *f*
hot gas inlet Heizgaszufuhr *f*
hot gas overlap welding Warmgasüberlappschweißen *nt*
hot gas string bead welding Warmgasziehschweißen *nt*
hot gas welding by extrusion of filler material Warmgasextrusionsschweißen *nt*
hot gas welding process Warmgasschnellschweißverfahren *nt*
hot gas welding with torch separate from filler rod Warmgasfächelschweißen *nt*
hot humid climate warmfeuchtes Klima *nt*
hot indentation Warmeindrücken *nt*
hot key Funktionstaste *f*
hot melt Heißschmelzen *nt*
hot melt adhesive system Heißleimsystem *nt*
hot melt glue labelling machine Heißschmelzklebeetikettiermaschine *f*
hot melting Heißschmelzen *nt*; heißschmelzen
hot phosphating Warmphosphatieren *nt*

hot restart Heißstart *m*
hot roll(ing) Warmwalzen *nt*; warmwalzen
hot standby einsatzbereite Reserve *f*
hot water Heißwasser *nt*
hot water blasting Heißwasserstrahlen *nt*
hot water boiler Heizkessel *m*, Warmwasserkessel *m*
hot water central heating system Warmwasserheizung *f*
hot water heating system with flow temperature Warmwasserheizung *f* mit Vorlauftemperatur
hot water rinse bath Heißwasserspülbad *nt*
hot water service pipe Warmwassergebrauchsleitung *f*
hot water supply installation Warmwasserversorgungsanlage *f*
hot water-heated heißwasserbeheizt
hot welding by the arc method elektrisches Warmschweißen *nt*
hot working Warmbearbeiten *nt*
hot wrap heißes Wechseln
hot/cold work hardening Warm-Kaltverfestigen *nt*
hot-/cold-box-process Hot-/Cold-Box-Verfahren *nt*
hot-chamber process Warmkammerverfahren *nt*
hot-dip aluminium coated surface feueraluminierte Oberfläche *f*
hot-drawn warmgezogen
hot-dry climate trockenwarmes Klima *nt*
hot-mould warmpressen
hot-rolled warmgewalzt
hour stamp *(Stunden)* Zeitstempel *m*
house lagern, unterbringen, aufnehmen
house installation Hausanlage *f*
house pressure governor Hausdruckregler *m*
household cleaning agent Haushaltsreinigungsmittel *nt*
household cleaning detergent Haushaltsreinigungsmittel *nt*
housekeeping Reinhaltung *f*
housing Gehäuse *nt*, Rahmenständer *m*, Ständer *m*, Ummantelung *f*, Verkleidung *f*
housing centre distance Gehäuseachsabstand *m*
housing mounting face Gehäuseauflagefläche *f*
housing parting face Gehäuseteilfläche *f*
housing temperature Gehäusetemperatur *f*
H-shaped H-förmig
H-shaped profile H-Profil *nt*, Doppel-T-Profil *nt*
hub Mittelpunkt *m*, Nabe *f*
hub cap Radkappe *f*
hub diameter Nabendurchmesser *m*
hub width Nabenlänge *f*
hub-type gear shaper cutter Halsschneidrad *nt*
hue Farbstich *m*, Farbton *m*
hull Hülse *f*
human error(s) menschliches Fehlverhalten *nt*
human-machine interface (HMI) Mensch-Maschine-Schnittstelle *f*
humid feucht
humid alternative atmosphere Feuchtwechselklima *nt*
humid atmosphere Feuchtklima *nt*
humid stria Feuchtigkeitsschliere *f*
humidification Befeuchtung *f*
humidify befeuchten
humidifying equipment Befeuchtungseinrichtung *f*
humidistat Hydrostat
humidity Feuchtigkeit *f*, Feuchte *f*, Luftfeuchte *f*
humidity balance Feuchtebilanz *f*
humidity cabinet Feuchtigkeitskammer *f*
humidity measurement Feuchtemessung *f*
hundred and eighty degree peel test Winkelschälversuch *m*
hurry ahead vorauseilen
hurt verletzen, Verletzung *f*
hurry on ahead Voreilung *f*; vorauseilen
hybrid Mischform *f*, hybrid
hydraulic impeller hydraulisches Laufrad *nt*

hydraulic ram hydraulischer Kolben *m*
hydrated lime container Kalthydratbehälter *m*
hydraulic hydraulisch
hydraulic accumulator Druckspeicher *m*
hydraulic bevel gear generator hydraulische Kegelradhobelmaschine *f*
hydraulic blasting Druckwasserstrahlen *nt*
hydraulic circuit Hydraulikkreis *m*, Ölkreislauf *m*
hydraulic control centre hydraulische Steuerzentrale *f*
hydraulic control mechanism hydraulische Steuermechanik *f*
hydraulic coupling Hydraulikkupplung *f*
hydraulic damping hydraulische Dämpfung *f*
hydraulic equipment hydraulische Anlage *f*, hydraulische Ausrüstung *f*
hydraulic feed milling machine Fräsmaschine *f* mit hydraulischem Vorschub
hydraulic fluid Hydraulikflüssigkeit *f*
hydraulic leakage test Test *m* zum Halten der Last
hydraulic lifting Hydraulikfluid *m*
hydraulic lowering control valve Rückschlagventil *nt* bei Hydraulikantrieben
hydraulic medium Druckflüssigkeit *f*
hydraulic motor Hydraulikmotor *m*
hydraulic oil Hydrauliköl *nt*, Hydraulikflüssigkeit *f*
hydraulic piston Hydraulikkolben *m*, hydraulischer Kolben *m*
hydraulic planer-miller kombinierte ölhydraulische Doppelständerhobel- und -fräsmaschine
hydraulic press hydraulische Presse *f*
hydraulic pump Flüssigkeitspumpe *f*, hydraulische Pumpe *f*
hydraulic system Hydraulik *f*, Hydrauliksystem *nt*, Hydraulikanlage *f*
hydraulic test Flüssigkeitsdruckprüfung *f*
hydraulic tracer control Kolbensteuerung *f*

hydraulic transmission Strömungsgetriebe *nt*
hydraulic transmission drive Flüssigkeitsgetriebe *nt*
hydraulically operated hydraulisch betätigt
hydraulics Hydraulik *f*
hydraulic jack Hydraulikmotor *m* mit geradliniger Bewegung
hydraulic power pack Hydraulikaggregat *nt*
hydrodynamic hydrodynamisch
hydrogen Wasserstoff *m*
hydrogen induced crack Wasserstoffriss *m*
hydrogen regulator Wasserstoffdruckminderer *m*
hydrometer for technical applications Betriebsspindel *f*
hydrostatic direct impact extrusion hydrostatisches Vorwärtsfließpressen *nt*
hydrostatic direct impact extrusion of rods hydrostatisches Vollvorwärtsfließpressen *nt*
hydrostatic direct rod extrusion hydrostatisches Vorwärtsstrangpressen *nt*
hydrostatic direct tubular impact extrusion hydrostatisches Hohlvorwärtsfließpressen *nt*
hydrostatic guidance hydrostatische Führung *f*
hydrostatic transmission hydrostatic
hydroxidic hydroxidisch
hyperboloid Hyperboloid *m*
hyperboloid bevel gear hyperbolisches Kegelrad *nt*
hyperboloid cylindrical gear hyperbolisches Stirnrad *nt*
hyperboloid functional surface hyperboloidische Funktionsfläche *f*
hyperboloid gear pair Hyperboloidradpaar *nt*
hypergeometric distribution hypergeometrische Verteilung *f*
hypersynchronous übersynchron
hypersynchronous braking übersynchrone Bremsung *f*
hypoid gear Kegelschraubenrad *nt*, Hypoidrad *nt*

hypoid gear pair Kegelschraubenradpaar *nt*, Hypoidradpaar *nt*
hypothesis Hypothese *f*
hypothetical factor for analysis analytischer Ansatz *m*
hypocycloid Hypozykloide

hysteresis Hysterese *f*, Umkehrspanne *f*
hysteresis loop Hystereseschleife *f*
hysteresis loss Magnetisierungsverlust *m*, Eisenverlust *m*
hysteresis of the measuring force Messkraftumkehrspanne *f*

Ii

I/O channel E/A-Kanal m
I/O port E/A-Anschluss m
I/O power port E/A-Versorgungsanschluss m
I/O station E/A-Station f
I-beam Doppel-T-Träger m, I-Träger m
IC engine Verbrennungsmotor m
I-channel E-Kanal m
ID card Ausweiskarte f
ideal layout Ideallayout nt
ideal planning Idealplanung f
ideal variant Idealvariante f
idea phase Ideenphase f
identical gleich, identisch
identification Identifikation f, Identifizierung f, Erkennbarkeit f, Kennung f, Erkennung f, Kennzeichnung f, Kennzeichen nt
identification carrier Identträger m
identification figure Kennziffer f
identification marking of dimensions Maßkennzeichnung f
identification number Identifikationsnummer f, Identnummer f, Kennzahl f
identification of goods Warenidentifikation f
identification of grades Sortenkennzeichnung f
identification of position (I/P) Standortidentifizierung f
identification plate Fabrikschild nt
identification point Identifikationspunkt m
identification signal Kennung f
identification system ID-System nt, Identifikationssystem nt
identification task Identifikationsaufgabe f
identifier Kennung f
identify erkennen, identifizieren, kennzeichnen, ansprechen
identify goods Ware identifizieren
identifying goods (EDV) Ware identifizieren
identity Identität f, Gleichheit f
identity number Identnummer f

idle 1. (z. B. Rohre) leerlaufen 2. (el.) nicht Strom m führend, spannungslos
idle backstroke toter Rücklauf m
idle condition Ruhezustand m
idle length Leerweg m
idle mode Leerlauf m
idle path Totweg m
idle period Nebenzeit f, Verlustzeit f
idle return leerer Rücklauf m
idle return stroke Leerhub m, toter Rücklauf m
idle running Leerlauf m
idle running speed Leerlaufdrehzahl f
idle stroke Leerhub m
idle time Leerlaufzeit f, Leerlauf m, Totzeit f, Stillstandsdauer f, Brachzeit f
idle time during the approach traverse of the cutter Einwälzzeit f
idle wheels nicht angetriebene Räder ntpl
idler Tragrolle f
idler assembly Tragrollensatz m
idler pulley Riemenspannrolle f
idling Leerlauf m
idling point Leerlaufpunkt m
idling speed Leerlaufdrehzahl f
idling speed torque Leerlaufdrehzahl f
ignite entzünden, zünden
ignite completely without any time-lag verzögerungsfrei durchzünden
ignition Entzündung f, Zündung f
ignition aid Zündhilfsmittel nt
ignition cabinet method Brennkastenverfahren nt
ignition circuit Zündstromkreis m
ignition delay Zündverzögerung f
ignition device Zündeinrichtung f
ignition flame burner Zündflammenbrenner m
ignition gas filter Zündgasfilter m
ignition gas valve Zündgasventil nt
ignition lamp Zündlampe f
ignition lead Zündstromleitung f
ignition phase Zündphase f
ignition point Zündpunkt m
ignition ring Zündring m

ignition safety device Zündsicherung *f*
ignition source Zündquelle *f*
ignition stage-discharge Zündungsentladung *f*
ignition switch Zündschalter *m*
ignition system Zündung *f*
ignition temperature Zündtemperatur *f*
ignition time Zündungszeit *f*
ignition transformer Zündtransformator *m*
ignition voltage Zündspannung *f*
ignition wire Zünddraht *m*
ignore übersehen, vernachlässigen, unberücksichtigt lassen
ignored unberücksichtigt
ignoring Vernachlässigung *f*
illuminate beleuchten
illuminating power Leuchtdichte *f*
illumination Beleuchtung *f*
illumination beam path Beleuchtungsstrahlengang *m*
illumination device Beleuchtungseinrichtung *f*
illuminator Filmbetrachtungsgerät *nt*
illustrate *(Bilder)* darstellen
image abbilden; Bild *nt*, Abbild *nt*
image converter Bildwandler *m*
image data Bilddaten *pl*
image evaluation Bildauswertung *f*
image measuring apparatus Bildmessgerät *nt*
image processing computer Bildverarbeitungsrechner *m*
image proof analysis Bildgütenachweis *m*
image quality Bildgüte *f*
image quality indication Bildgütenachweis *m*
image quality indicator Bildgüteprüfkörper *m*
image recording system bildregistrierendes System *nt*
image register Abbildregister *nt*
image sensor Bildsensor *m*
image storage device Bildspeicher *m*
image-forming radiation bilderzeugende Strahlung *f*
imaginary cylinder imaginärer Zylinder *m*

imaginary flawless thread gedachtes fehlerfreies Gewinde *nt*
imaginary pitch point Wälzpunkt *m*
imaging Abbildung *f*
imaging accuracy Abbildungsgenauigkeit *f*
imbalance Unwucht *f*
imbalance motor Unwuchtmotor *m*
incoming transport Antransport *m*
implement Arbeitsgerät *nt*
immediate unverzüglich, sofortig, momentan
immediate access Schnellzugriff *m*
immediate measure Sofortmaßnahme *f*
immediately sofort
immerse tauchen, eintauchen
immersion Lagerung *f*
immersion bath Tauchbad *nt*
immersion heater Siedestab *m*
immersion measuring cell Tauchmesszelle *f*
immersion practice Immersionstechnik *f*, Tauchtechnik *f*
immersion prism Eintauchprisma *nt*
immersion scraping Eintauchschaben *nt*
imminent hazard drohende Gefahr *f*
immobilize abschalten, feststellen
immobilizing Abschalten *nt*
immobilizing brake Feststellbremse *f*
immovable unbeweglich
immune beständig, unempfindlich
immune from sustained backfire rückzündsicher
immunity Beständigkeit *f*, Unempfindlichkeit *f*, Störfestigkeit *f*
immunity level Störfestigkeitsgrad *m*
immunity test Unempfindlichkeitsprüfung *f*
immunity zone Störfestigkeitszone *f*
impact Anprall *m*, Aufprall *m*, Aufprallstoß *m*, Aufschlag *m*, Stoß *m*, Schlag *m*, Beaufschlagung *f*, Auswirkung *f*
impact absorbing stoßdämpfend
impact against Auftreffen *nt*; auftreffen, anstoßen, anschlagen (gegen/auf)
impact behaviour Schlagverhalten *nt*
impact bending load Schlagbiegebeanspruchung *f*

impact bending test Schlagbiegeversuch *m*
impact coefficient Stoßfaktor *m*, Stoßbeiwert *m*
impact drop test Fallversuch *m*
impact energy Stoßenergie *f*
impact extrusion Fließpressen *nt*
impact extrusion with action media Fließpressen *nt* mit Wirkmedien
impact extrusion with rigid tool Fließpressen *nt* mit starrem Werkzeug
impact face Aufprallfläche *f*
impact factor Stoßgrad *m*
impact flexural test Schlagbiegeversuch *m*
impact floor Aufprallboden *m*
impact load Stoßbelastung *f*
impact loading stoßartige Beanspruchung *f*
impact loading of components schlagartige Beanspruchung *f* von Bauteilen
impact piston device *(zum Entrosten)* Schlagkolbengerät *nt*
impact point Auftreffpunkt *m*
impact protection Aufprallschutz *m*
impact resistant schlagfest
impact sensitivity Schlagempfindlichkeit *f*
impact strength Kerbschlagarbeit *f*, Schlagfestigkeit *f*; schlagzäh
impact test Stoßversuch *m*, Schlagprüfung *f*
impact testing apparatus Schlagprüfgerät *nt*
impact velocity Auftreffgeschwindigkeit *f*
impact withstand test Schlagprüfung *f*
impair beschädigen, beeinträchtigen
impairment Beeinträchtigung *f*, Nachteil *m*
impairment of function Funktionsbeeinträchtigung *f*
impart weitergeben, übertragen
impart movement to bewegen
impart pressure unter Druck setzen, Druck ausüben
impartial sampling unparteiische Probenahme *f*
impedance Impedanz *f*, Scheinwiderstand *m*
impedance limit Impedanzgrenzwert *m*
impede hemmen, arretieren, festhalten, bremsen, hindern, behindern, verhindern, beeinträchtigen
impediment Hindernis *nt*
impeller Laufrad *nt*, Antriebsrad *nt*, Gebläserad *nt*
impeller blade Laufradschaufel *f*
impeller blade edge Laufradschaufelkante *f*
impeller vane pitch adjustment device Laufschaufelverstelleinrichtung *f*
imperfect mangelhaft
imperfect shape Formfehler *m*
imperfection Fehler *m*, Unvollkommenheit *f*
impermissible unzulässig
impervious to smoke rauchdicht
impingement of the flame Beflammung *f*
impinge aufprallen
impingement Aufprall *m*
implement Anbaugerät *nt*, Vorsatzgerät *nt*, Gerät *nt*, Instrument *nt*, Werkzeug *nt*; implementieren, realisieren, abwickeln
implement a project ein Projekt durchführen
implementation Implementierung *f*, Durchführung *f*, Realisierung *f*, Abwicklung *f*
implementation description Inbetriebnahmebeschreibung *f*
implementation stage Realisierungsphase *f*
implements Gerätschaft *m*
implosion Implosion *f*
importance Wichtigkeit *f*
important wichtig
impracticable unzweckmäßig
impracticable undurchführbar
impregnated paper getränktes Papier *nt*
impregnating resin material Tränkharzmasse *f*
impregnating resin moulded material Tränkharzformstoff *m*

impregnation Durchtränkung *f*
impressing Eindrücken *nt*, Tiefen *nt*, Delle *f*
impression method Abdruckverfahren *nt*
impression under heat Warmeindrücken *nt*
imprint Aufdruck *m*; bedrucken
improper falsch
improper ungeeignet
improve verbessern, nachbessern, sanieren
improvement Verbesserung *f*, Nachbesserung *f*
improvement of quality Qualitätsverbesserung *f*
impulse Impuls *m*, Puls *m*, Stoß *m*, Anstoß *m*
impulse a.c. power frequency Impulswechselspannungsfrequenz *f*
impulse force Drangkraft *f*
impulse generator device Impulsgeber *m*
impulse peak Impulsspitze *f*
impulse pipe Impulsleitung *f*
impulse response Impulsantwort *f*
impulse sealing Wärmeimpulsschweißen *nt*, Heizelementwärmeimpulsschweißen *nt*
impulse shaping Impulswandlung *f*
impulse sound pressure level Impulsschalldruckpegel *m*
impulse voltage Stoßspannung *f*
impulsive schlagartig, stoßartig
impulsive noise Impulshaltiges Geräusch *nt*
impulsive noise content Impulshaltigkeit *f*
impurity Fremdstoffe *f*, Fremdkörper *m*, *mpl*, Verunreinigung *f*
in hinein
in a cantilever position freitragend
in a counterbalanced position außerhalb der Radbasis
in a laying position liegend
in a medium term mittelfristig
in a series of turns mehrfach
in a spiral pattern spiralförmig
in a upright position stehend
in a vertical downward direction von oben nach unten
in a vertical upward direction von unten nach oben
in batches portionsweise
in bulk unverpackt
in case of emergency im Notfall *m*
in clean and tidy condition besenrein
in correct positional arrangement lagerichtig
in depth in Tiefenrichtung
in fine steps feinstufig
in front vorn, vor
in front side position stirnseitig
in good working order betriebsfähig
in horizontal position liegend
in layers lagenweise
in line with the centre mittig
in many cases vielfach
in motion bewegt
in multiple rows mehrreihig
in normal operation betriebsmäßig
in one layer einlagig
in pairs paarweise
in per cent prozentual
in relation to relativ zu
in series in Reihe, serienmäßig
in situ cellular plastics Ortschaum *m*
in step (with) im Takt
in stock vorrätig
in terms of amount mengenmäßig
in terms of calculation rechentechnisch
in terms of quantity mengenmäßig
in the case of bei
in the long term langfristig
in the manner of a nailhead nadelkopfartig
in the opposite direction in entgegengesetzter Richtung
in the rear rückseitig
in the right projected position projektionsgerechte Lage *f*
in the unladen state unter Eigenlast
in turn im Wechsel
in vertical position stehend
in working order betriebsbereit
inaccessible unzugänglich
inaccuracy Fehler *m*, Ungenauigkeit *f*
inaccuracy of mounting Montageungenauigkeit *f*

inaccurate ungenau
inactive träge
inactive inventory item Lagerhüter *m*
inadequate unangepasst, ungeeignet
inadmissible unzulässig
inadvertent unbeabsichtigt
inapplicable unzutreffend
inappropriate unzweckmäßig, ungeeignet
inattentive nachlässig
inch *1. (Messtechnik)* Zoll *nt* **2.** *(Schalter bei Werkzeugmaschinen)* vorrücken, tippen, tippschalten
inch forward recken
inching Kriechgang *m*, Kriechgeschwindigkeit *f*, Feineinstellung *f*, Langsameinstellung *f*
inching button Tippschalter *m*
inching control Schrittschaltung *f*, Tippschaltung *f*
inching switch Tippschalter *m*
incidence of extraneous light Fremdlichteinfall *m*
incident Störfall *m*
incident management Störfallmagnet *nt*
incident places Einfallstellen *f*
incidental zufällig
incineration crucible Veraschungstiegel *m*
incipient crack Anriss *m*, Anbruch *m*, Beschädigung *f*
incipient explosion Explosionsquelle *f*
incising Beißschneiden *nt*
incision Schnitt *m*
inclinable schrägstellbar, schrägverstellbar, neigbar
inclinable table schrägverstellbarer Tisch *m*, neigbarer Tisch *m*
inclination Schrägstellung *f*, Neigung *f*
inclination angle Neigungswinkel *m*
inclination from the vertical Schiefstellung *f*
inclination measuring system Neigungsmesseinrichtung *f*
inclination transverse to the direction of motion Querneigung *f*
incline schräg stellen, neigen
inclined schräg, schief, geneigt, windschief

inclined axle castor Kugellenkrolle *f*
inclined contact Schrägtragen *nt*
inclined pendulum Neigungspendel *nt*
inclined plane schräg liegende Ebene *f*
inclined roller bearing Schräglager *nt*
inclined run Schrägführung *f*
inclined seat valve Schrägsitzventil *nt*
inclined surface schräge Fläche *f*
inclined tee joint Schrägstoß *m*
inclined track with rollers Rollenbahn *f*
inclined track with skate wheels Röllchenbahn *f*
inclined tube manometer Schrägrohrmanometer *nt*
include umfassen, enthalten
included angle *1.* Öffnungswinkel *m*, eingeschlossener Winkel *m* **2.** *(Gewinde)* Flankenwinkel *m* eines Gewindes
included angle deviation Flankenwinkelabweichung *f*
included cutting angle Eckenwinkel *m*
included plan angle Eckenwinkel *m*, Spitzenwinkel *m*
including einschließlich
inclusion Einschluss *m*
inclusive einschließlich
inclusive OR Inklusives ODER *nt*, Disjunktion *f*
incoming einlaufend
incoming air Zuluft *f*
incoming call ankommender Ruf *m*
incoming date Zugangstermin *m*
incoming goods Wareneingang (WE) *m*
incoming goods booking Wareneingangsbuchung *f*
incoming goods department Wareneingang *m*, Warenannahme *f*
incoming goods entry Wareneingang *m*
incoming goods function Wareneingangsfunktion *f*
incoming goods inspection Wareneingangskontrolle *f*, Eingangsprüfung *f*
incoming goods item Wareneingangsposition *f*
incoming goods list Wareneingangsliste *f*

incoming goods note Wareneingangsschein *m*
incoming goods number Wareneingangsnummer *f*
incoming goods point Wareneingang *m*
incoming goods warehouse Eingangslager *nt*, Wareneingangslager *nt*
incoming line Zuführstrecke *f*
incoming merchandise Wareneingang (WE) *m*
incoming orders Bestelleingang *m*
incoming power supply Netzeinspeisung *f*
incoming supply Zuleitung *f*
incoming supply line Zuleitungsstrang *m*
incompatibility Unverträglichkeit *f*
incompatible with unverträglich mit
incomplete mangelhaft, unvollständig
incomplete interpass fusion Lagenbindefehler *m*
incomplete penetration nicht durchgeschweißte Wurzel *f*
incompletely filled groove Decklagenunterwölbung *f*
incompletely formed thread unvollständig geformtes Gewinde *nt*
inconsistency Ungleichmäßigkeit *f*
inconsistent widersprechend
incorporate einbauen
incorporating eingebaut
incorporation Einbau *m*
incorrect nicht sachgerecht, unrichtig
incorrect behaviour unsachgemäßes Verhalten *nt*
uncover öffnen
increase wachsen, anwachsen, vergrößern, steigern, ansteigen, steigen, zunehmen, erhöhen, verstärken; Steigerung *f*, Erhöhung *f*, Zunahme *f*, Zuwachs *m*, Wachstum *nt*, Verstärkung *f*, Vergrößerung *f*, Anstieg *m*
increase in force Kraftanstieg *m*
increase in volume Volumenzunahme *f*
increase key Mehr-Taste *f*
increase of inventories Bestandsbildung *f*
increase of output Leistungserhöhung *f*
increase of performance Leistungserhöhung *f*
increase the hardness aufhärten
increase the load of belasten
increased erhöht, verstärkt
increasing zunehmend
increasingly gesteigert
increment Inkrement *nt*, Schrittweite *f*, Sprung *m*, Stufe *f*, Stufung *f*, Schritt *m*, Abstufung *f*, Zunahme *f*, Zuwachs *m*
increment cut ungleiche Teilung *f*
incremental inkremental, inkrementell, schrittweise
incremental dimensioning Kettenmaße *ntpl*
incremental infeed unterbrochene Zustellung *f*
incremental jog Schrittvorschub *m*
incremental measuring system inkrementale Wegmessung *f*
incremental radial infeed unterbrochener radialer Tischvorschub *m*
incremental transmitter Inkrementalgeber *m*
incremental transmitter system Inkrementalgebersystem *nt*
incur ereignen, entstehen
in-cut method Verfahren *nt* des Gleichlauffräsens
inadequate unzulänglich
indelible unverwischbar
indemnity Schadenersatz *m*
indent dornen, einkerben, verzahnen
indentation Beulung *f*, Eindrückung *f*, Einschnitt *m*, Einkerbung *f*, Verzahnung *f*
indentation area Eindruckfläche *f*
indentation depth Beultiefe *f*
indentation depth measuring device Eindruckmesseinrichtung *f*
indentation hardness characteristic Eindrückhärtecharakteristik *f*
indentation hardness test Eindrückversuch *m*
indentation tester Eindruckprüfgerät *nt*
indentation under heat Warmeindrücken *nt*
indentation/pulsation range Eindruck-Schwellbereich *m*

indenting Eindrücken *nt*, Verzahnung *f*
independent selbstständig, unabhängig
independent cam control for each operation Mehrkurvensteuerung *f*
independent excitation Fremderregung *f*
independent four-jaw chuck Planscheibe *f*
independent of unabhängig von
independent of location ortsunabhängig
independent of position positionsunabhängig, lageunabhängig
independent of the potential potentialunabhängig
indestructible zerstörungsfrei
index 1. Anzeiger *m*, Marke *f*, Index *m*, Register *nt*, Beiwert *m*; indizieren, anzeigen **2.** *(Alphabet)* alphabetisches Verzeichnis *nt*; alphabetisch ordnen **3.** *(Schaltung)* schalten, umschalten, weiterschalten
index around herumschalten
index base *(Fertigungstechnik)* Teileinrichtung *f*, Rundtisch *m*
index base milling pausenlos Fräsen *nt* mit Rundschalttisch, Fräsen *nt* mit Rundtischteileinrichtung
index centre Teilkopfgerät *nt*, Teilgerät *nt*, einfaches Teilgerät *nt* mit einer Teilspindel
index circle Lochkreis *m*
index crank Teilkurbel *f*
index device unit Teilapparat *m*
index disc Teilscheibe *f*
index disk Teilscheibe *f*
index error Indexfehler *m*
index figure Kennziffer *f*
index gear Teilzahnrad *nt*
index gear hob Schaltradwälzfräser *m*
index head operation Teilarbeit *f*, Arbeit *f*
index milling Schalttischfräsen *nt*
index milling machine Schalttischfräsmaschine *f*
index of refraction Brechzahl *f*
index pin Indexstift *m*
index plate Teilscheibe *f*
index plate with holes Lochteilscheibe *f*
index plunger Raststift *m*
indexed mask Mehrfachmaske *f*
indexing Umschalten *nt*, Teilen *nt*, Teilung *f*, Schaltung *f*, Weiterschaltung *f*, Umschalten *nt*, Schalten *nt*
indexing accuracy Drehgenauigkeit *f*, Umschaltgenauigkeit *f*
indexing attachment Teileinrichtung *f*, Teilapparat *m*
indexing attachment device Teilapparat *m*
indexing attachment fixture Teilapparat *m*
indexing bolt Sperrzapfen *m*
indexing device Teilgerät *nt*
indexing error Fehler *m* beim Teilen, Teilfehler *m*
indexing gearbox Teilungsräderkasten *m*
indexing head Teilkopf *m*
indexing head spindle Teilkopfspindel *f*
indexing latch Indexklinke *f*, Indexraststift *m*
indexing mechanism Schaltwerk *nt*
indexing method Teilverfahren *nt*
indexing motion Drehbewegung *f*
indexing movement Teilbewegung *f*
indexing of inserts Wenden *nt* von Schneidplatten
indexing pin Sperrzapfen *m*
indexing rotary table Rundtisch *m* mit Teileinrichtung, Rundschalttisch *m*
indexing stop roll Anschlagwalze *f* für Revolverkopf
indexing table Indexteiltisch *m*, Schalttisch *m*
indexing table automatic Schalttischautomat *m*
indexing work Teilarbeiten *fpl*
indicate indizieren, zeigen, anzeigen, melden, angeben, bezeichnen
indicated value Messwert *m*
indicating device Anzeigeeinrichtung *f*
indicating gauge Messzeigergerät *nt*
indicating lamp Meldeleuchte *f*
indicating light Anzeigelampe *f*, Leuchtmelder *m*, Kontrollampe *f*
indicating measuring instrument anzeigendes Messgerät *nt*

indicating micrometer Fühlhebelschraublehre *f*
indicating snap gauge Passimeter *nt*
indication Anzeige *f*, Angabe *f*, Aussage *f*, Ablesung *f*, direkte Ausgabe *f*
indication of sections Schnittkennzeichnung *f*
indicator 1. Melder *m*, Messuhr *f*, Anzeige *f*, Zeiger *m*, Anzeigegerät *nt* **2.** *(Nummer)* Kennzahl *f*
indicator calliper Messuhr *f*
indicator reading Zeigerablesung *f*
indifferent unempfindlich
indirect extrusion of rods Vollrückwärtsstrangpressen *nt*
indirect extrusion of rods and tubes Rückwärtsstrangpressen *nt*
indirect force measurement indirekte Kraftmessung *f*
indirect impact extrusion Rückwärtsfließpressen *nt*
indirect impact extrusion of cup-shaped sections Napfrückwärtsfließpressen *nt*
indirect impact extrusion of hollow items Massivlochen *nt*
indirect measurement indirekte Wegmessung *f*
indirect projection welding einseitiges Buckelschweißen *nt*
indirect rod impact extrusion Vollrückwärtsfließpressen *nt*
indirect tubular impact extrusion Hohlrückwärtsfließpressen *nt*
indirect tubular rod extrusion Hohlrückwärtsstrangpressen *nt*
indistinct unscharf
individual einzeln, einzel ...
individual actual size Einzel-Istmaß *nt*
individual availability Einzelverfügbarkeit *f*
individual centre of gravity Einzelschwerpunkt *m*
individual character Einzelzeichen *nt*
individual component Einzelteil *nt*, Einzelkomponente *f*
individual defective area Einzelfehlerfläche *f*
individual drive Einzelantrieb *m*
individual error test Einzelfehlerprüfung *f*
individual groove Einzelrille *f*
individual inspection Einzelkontrolle *f*
individual investigation Einzeluntersuchung *f*
individual joint Einzelnaht *f*
individual layer Einzellage *f*
individual load Einzellast *f*
individual measured value Einzelmesswert *m*
individual measurement Einzelmessung *f*
individual measurement value Einzelmesswert *m*
individual message Einzelmeldung *f*
individual movement Einzelbewegung *f*
individual offtake Einzelabsaugung *f*
individual pack Einzelpackung *f*
individual part Einzelteil *nt*
individual parts warehouse Einzelteillager *nt*
individual piece Einzelstück *nt*
individual pitch test Einzelteilungsprüfung *f*
individual pitch variation Teilungseinzelabweichung *f*
individual reflector Einzelreflektor *m*
individual rod Einzelstab *m*
individual size Einzelmaß *nt*
individual stipulation Einzelfestlegung *f*
individual storage Einzellagerung *f*
individual target Einzelziel *nt*
individual test Einzeluntersuchung *f*
individual tolerance Einzeltoleranz *f*
individual tooth system Einzelverzahnung *f*
individual unit Einzelgerät *nt*
individual value einzelner Wert *m*
individual variation Einzelabweichung *f*
individual weight Einzelgewicht *nt*
individual weld Einzelnaht *f*
individual working variation Wälzeinzelabweichung *f*
indivisible unteilbar
indoor in Räumen
induce induzieren
induced by radiation strahleninduc-

ziert
induced current Induktionsstrom *m*
induced draft fan Saugzuggebläse *nt*
induced draught burner Saugzugbrenner *m*
induced draught fan Saugzuggebläse *nt*
induced voltage Induktionsspannung *f*
in-duct method Kanalverfahren *nt*
inductance Induktivität *f*
inductance-heated annealing equipment Induktionsglüheinrichtung *f*
induction Induktion *f*
induction current Induktionsstrom *m*
induction current of the rotor Läuferinduktionsstrom *m*
induction furnace Induktionsofen *m*
induction hardening Induktionshärten *nt*
induction hardening machine Induktionshärtemaschine *f*
induction heating Induktionserwärmung *f*
induction machine Drehfeldmaschine *f*
induction motor Asynchronmotor *m*, Drehfeldmotor *m*, Induktionsmotor *m*
induction pressure welding induktives Widerstandspressschweißen *nt*
induction resistance welding induktives Widerstandspressschweißen *nt*
induction sealing machine Induktionsschweißverschließmaschine *f*
induction voltage Induktionsspannung *f*
induction welding Induktionsschweißen *nt*
inductive induktiv
inductive actuating tag induktive Schaltfahne *f*
inductive reactance induktiver Blindwiderstand *m*
inductive switching flag induktive Schaltfahne *f*
inductive system Induktivsystem *nt*
inductive technology Induktivtechnik *f*
inductive transmitter induktiver Sender *m*

inductively guided induktiv geführt
inductor Induktor *m*
industrial area Industriegebiet *nt*
industrial atmosphere Industrieatmosphäre *f*
industrial building construction Industriebau *m*
industrial engineer Betriebsingenieur *m*
industrial facilities Betriebsmittel *ntpl*
industrial frequency Industriefrequenz *f*
industrial inspection Fertigungskontrolle *f*
industrial mains Industrienetz *nt*
industrial plant Industrieanlage *f*, Betriebseinrichtungen *fpl*
industrial robot Industrieroboter *m*, Roboter *m*
industrial tool Maschinenmeißel *m*, Maschinenwerkzeug *nt*
industrial tractor Industrieschlepper *m*, Zugmaschine *f*
industrial training fachliche Ausbildung *f*
industrial truck Flurförderzeug (FFZ) *nt*
industrial valve Industriearmatur *f*
industrial water heater Brauchwassererwärmer *m*
ineffective unwirksam
unequal uneben
inequality 1. Abweichung *f*, Ungleichheit *f* **2.** *(Ebene, gleiche Höhe)* Unebenheit *f*, Abweichung *f* von der Ebene
inert träge, inaktiv
inert arc welding Inertgasschweißung *f*
inert gas inertes Gas *nt*
inert gas cylinder Formiergasflasche *f*
inert gas regulator Formiergasdruckminderer *m*
inert-gas arc welding Edelgaslichtbogenschweißen *nt*
inertia Beharrungsvermögen *nt*, Trägheit *f*
inertia force Trägheitskraft *f*
inevitable danger unvermeidbare Gefahr *f*
inexpert unfachgemäß
infeed Tiefenvorschub *m*, Zuförderung *f*, Beistellung *f*

in-feed Vorschub *m*
infeed and outfeed location Ein- und Auslaufstelle *f*
infeed belt Einlaufband *nt*
infeed conveyor Einlauff̈orderer *m*
infeed cycle Einschleustakt *m*, Zustellzyklus *m*
infeed grinding Einstechschleifen *nt*, Tiefschleifen *nt*
infeed handwheel Zustellhandrad *nt*
infeed location Einlaufstelle *f*
infeed method Einstechverfahren *nt*
infeed motion Zuschubbewegung *f*, Zustellbewegung *f*
infeed point Einlagerpunkt *m*
infeed rate Einlagerdurchsatz *m*
infeed slot Einlauföffnung *f*
infeed star Einlaufstern *m*
infeed star wheel Einlaufstern *m*
infeed transfer device Einschubeinrichtung *f*, Einlaufeinrichtung *f*
infeeding Zustellen *nt*
infiltrate einschleusen, einfädeln
infiltration Einfädelung *f*
infinite endlos
infinite value unendlicher Wert *m*
infinitely variable stufenlos, stufenlos regelbar, stufenlos geregelt
infinitely variable adjustment stufenlose Drehzahlregelung *f*
infinitely variable change-speed gear stufenloses Getriebe *nt*
infinitely variable feeds *pl* stufenlos regelbare Vorschübe *mpl*
infinitely variable speed change stufenlose Drehzahländerung *f*
infinitely variable speed control stufenlose Drehzahlregelung *f*
infinitely variable speed drive stufenlose Verstellung *f*
infinitely variable speed gear drive stufenlos regelbares Getriebe *nt*
infinitely variable speed gear transmission stufenlos verstellbares Getriebe *nt*
infinitely variable speed regulation stufenlose Drehzahlregelung *f*
infinitely variable speed transmission stufenloser Antrieb *m*
inflammable zündfähig, brennbar

inflatable tyre Luftreifen *m*
inflation pressure *(Reifen)* Luftdruck *m*
inflow Einfließen *nt*, Einströmen *nt*
inflow side bend zulaufseitiger Boden *m*
influence Beeinflussung *f*, Einfluss *m*, Einfluss *m*; ausüben, einwirken, beeinflussen
influence factor Einflussfaktor *m*
influence quantity Einflussgröße *f*
influenceable beeinflussbar
influencing Beeinflussung *f*
inform *(jemanden über etwas)* mitteilen
information Auskunft *f*, Information *f*, Hinweis *m*, Angabe *f*
information base Datenbank *f*
information demand Informationsbedarf *m*
information density Informationsdichte *f*
information exchange Informationsaustausch *m*
information flow Informationsfluss *m*, Signalfluss *m*
information for use Benutzerinformation *f*
information link Informationsverknüpfung *f*
information path Informationsweg *m*
information plate 1. Hinweisschild *nt*, Informationsschild *nt* **2.** *(Fabrik, Werk)* Fabrikschild *nt*
information point Informationsstelle *f*
information process Informationsablauf *m*
information processing Informationsverarbeitung *f*, Informationstechnik *f*
information processing device informationsverarbeitendes Gerät *nt*
information store Informationsspeicher *m*
information system Auskunftsystem *nt*
information Daten *pl*
informative aussagefähig
infrared hood Infrarotkappe *f*
infrared (IR) Infrarot *nt*
infrared controlled infrarotgesteuert
infrared data transfer Infrarotdatenübertragung *f*
infrared detector Infrarotdetektor *m*

infrared image processing system Infrarotbildverarbeitungssystem *nt*
infrared LED Infrarotlicht-LED *f*
infrared light Infrarotlicht *nt*
infrared radiator Infrarotstrahler *m*
infrared reader Infrarotleser *m*
infrared relay Infrarotrelais *nt*
infrared seeker Infrarotsuchknopf *m*
infrared system Infrarotsystem *nt*
infrared transfer Infrarotübertragung *f*
ingate Gießtrichter *m*
ingate systems *pl* Eingusssysteme *ntpl*
ingoing einzulagernd
ingot mould Kokille *f*
ingot planer Blockhobelmaschine *f*
ingot slicing lathe Blockabstechdrehmaschine *f*
ingot steel Flussstahl *m*
ingot turning lathe Blockdrehbank *f*
ingredient *(chem.)* Beständigkeit *f*
ingress einströmen, eindringen
inhalation Einatmen *nt*
inherent delay Eigenzeit *f*
inherent reflectance factor Eigenreflexionsfaktor *m*
inherent stress Eigenspannung *f*
inherent stress condition Eigenspannungszustand *m*
inherently limited konstruktiv begrenzt
inhibit beeinträchtigen
inhibited charge transfer gehemmter Ladungsdurchtritt *m*
inhibition of the reaction Reaktionshemmung *f*
inhomogeneity Inhomogenität *f*
in-house innerbetrieblich
in-house standard Werknorm *f*
initiating Ingangsetzen *nt*
inimical to mould pilzwidrig
initial ursprünglich, anfänglich, Anfangs...
initial boiling point Siedebeginn *m*
initial breakaway torque Losbrechmoment *m*
initial condition Grundzustand *m*, Anfangsbedingung *f*, Anfangszustand *m*
initial cutting radius Anschmelzradius *m*
initial drainage Vorentwässerung *f*

initial engine torque Anfangsdrehmoment *m*
initial fused area Anschmelzung *f*
initial fusing Anschmelzung *f*
initial generation Einwälzen *nt*, Durchwälzen *nt* über alle Werkzeuge
Initial Graphics Exchange Specification (IGES) IGES
initial lift Initialhub *m*
initial linkage Ausgangsgetriebe *nt*
initial mean stress Anfangsmittelspannung *f*
initial order Erstbestellung *f*
initial pass Anstich *m*
initial phase Einlaufphase *f*
initial piercing Einstechen *nt*
initial pitting Einlaufgrübchen *nt*
initial position Ausgangsstellung *f*
initial pulse rate Ausgangsimpulsrate *f*
initial quantity of material Ausgangsmaterialmenge *f*
initial radionuclide solution Ausgangsradionuklidlösung *f*
initial rationalization stage Rationalisierungsansatz *m*
initial setting Ersteinstellung *f*
initial situation Ausgangssituation *f*
initial state Anfangszustand *m*
initial stress Vorspannung *f*
initial stress amplitude Anfangsspannungsausschlag *m*
initial supplier Erstlieferant *m*
initial tearing Einriss *m*
initial test Erstprüfung *f*
initial transient effect Einschwingerscheinung *f*
initial value Ausgangswert *m*, Anfangswert *m*
initial viscosity Ausgangsviskosität *f*
initial weight Einwaage *f*
initialization Erstbelegung *f*, Initialisierung *f*
initialize erstbelegen, initialisieren, vorbelegen
initiate initialisieren, einleiten, anstoßen, in Gang setzen
initiate emergency safety measures Sicherheitsmaßnahmen einleiten
initiating step Initialschritt *m*
initiation Befehlsgabe *f*, Einleitung *f*,

Anstoß *m*, Anfang *m*
initiator Initiator *m*
inject einspritzen, einspeisen, einschleusen, verpressen
injection Verpressen *nt*, Einspritzen *nt*, Einblasung *f*
injection mixture Spritzgussmasse *f*
injection mouldability Spritzgießbarkeit *f*
injection moulded gear spritzgegossenes Zahnrad *nt*
injection moulding Spritzgießen *nt*
injection moulding material Spritzgießmasse *f*
injection moulding operation Spritzgießvorgang *m*
injection moulding unit Spritzgießeinheit *f*
injection phase Einspritzphase *f*
injection point Einspritzstelle *f*
injection pump Einspritzpumpe *f*
injection speed Einspritzgeschwindigkeit *f*
injection spherical hole Spritzkugelgrube *f*
injection unit Spritzeinheit *f*
injection-mixing chamber burner Injektor-Kammbrenner *m*
injection-mouldable spritzgießbar
injection-moulded adhesive fitting Spritzguss-Klebfitting *m*
injection-moulded fitting Spritzgussformstück *nt*
injection-moulded part dimension Spritzteilabmessung *f*
injection nozzle Einspritzdüse *f*
injector merge Einschleuser *m*
injure verletzen
injurious schädlich
injurious to health gesundheitsschädlich
injury Verletzung *f*
ink Tinte *f*
ink drawing instrument Tuschezeichengerät *nt*
ink jet coder Tintenstrahlcodierer *m*
ink jet printer Tintenstrahldrucker *m*
ink sketch Tuscheskizze *f*
ink writing instrument Tuscheschreibgerät *nt*
ink writing instrument with stencil pen Tuscheschreibgerät *nt* mit Röhrchenfeder
inlay Einlegen *nt*
inlet Eintritt *m*, Zulauf *m*
inlet cross-section Zuluftquerschnitt *m*
inlet instalment Zuluftrate *f*
inlet opening Zuluftöffnung *f*
inlet path Einlaufstrecke *f*
inlet port Eintrittskanal *m*
inlet pressure Zuströmdruck *m*, Einlaufdruck *m*, Vordruck *m*
inlet temperature Zulufttemperatur *f*
inlets Zuläufe *mpl*
in-line transfer machining zerspanende Bearbeitung *f* auf Taktstraße
incorrect fehlerhaft
inner contact Innentragen
inner diameter Innendurchmesser *m*
inner quill Innenpinole *f*
inner surface Innenseite *f*
inordinate ungeordnet
impact energy Auftreffenergie *f*
impact surface Prallwand *f*
imperfect nugget dimension Linsenmaßfehler *m*
in-plant point of coupling anlageninterner Anschlusspunkt *m*
imprint area Berührungsfläche *f*
in-process gauging of a workpiece Messen *nt* des Werkstücks zwischen den Bearbeitungsgängen
in-process inspection Zwischenabnahme *f*
in-process inventory Zwischenlager *nt*
in-process message Zwischenbescheid *m*
in-process stock Zwischenlager *nt*
in-process storage Zwischenlagerung *f*
input 1. einlagern, eingeben; Eingabe *f*, Einlagern *nt* 2. *(Tür)* Eingang *m* 3. *(Leistung, Kraft)* Antrieb *m*, zugeführte Leistung *f*, aufgenommene Leistung *f*, Leistungsaufnahme *f*
input and output Ein- und Auslagern *nt*
input and output variable Ein- und Ausgangsgröße *f*
input angle Antriebswinkel *m*
input circuit with enabling function

Eingangsschaltung *f* mit Vorbereitung
input connection Eingangsverbindung *f*
input conveyor Einlaufförderer *m*
input current Eingangsstrom *m*
input data Eingabedaten *pl*
input element Eingabeglied *nt*
input facility Eingabemöglichkeit *f*
input information Eingangsinformation *f*
input interface Eingabeschnittstelle *f*
input link Antriebsglied *nt*
input memory Eingabespeicher *m*
input module Eingabebaugruppe *f*
input of fuel Brennstoffaufgabe *f*
input order Einlagerauftrag *m*
input part-flow Einlagerteilstrom *m*
input point Einlagerpunkt *m*
input position Einschleusposition *f*
input power *(e. Maschine)* Antriebsleistung *f*
input primary status (IPS) Eingabe Primärstatus *m*
input quantity Eingangsgröße *f*
input rate Einlagerdurchsatz *m*
input rating *(e. Motors)* Antriebsleistung *f*
input reference system Einlagerreferenzsystem *nt*
input secondary status (ISS) Eingabesekundärstatus *m*
input shaft Antriebswelle *f*
input side Aufnahmeseite *f*
input signal Eingangssignal *nt*
input stage Eingangsstufe *f*
input station Einlagerstation *f*
input storage Eingabespeicher *m*
input terminal Eingangsklemme *f*
input time interval Eingabezeit *f*
input value Eingabewert *m*, Eingangswert *m*
input voltage Eingangsspannung *f*
input with polarity indicator Eingang *m* mit Polaritätsindikator *m*
input/output (I/O) Eingang/Ausgang (E/A) *m*
inquiry Abfrage *f*, Anfrage *f*
inrush current Einschaltstrom *m*
inrush current limiter Einschaltstrombegrenzer *m*

inscribe einbeschreiben
inscribed value Aufschriftwert *m*
inscription Aufdruck *m*, Aufschrift *f*
insect attack Insektenbefall *m*
insensitive to vibrations schwingungsunempfindlich
insensitive unempfindlich
insensitivity Unempfindlichkeit *f*
insert einfahren, einlegen, einschieben, einfügen, einführen, einpassen, einbauen, einsetzen, einstecken, zwischenschalten; Einsatz *m*, Verbindungsteil *nt*, Einlage *f*
insert *(Werkzeuge)* Schneideinsatz *m*, Schneidplatte *f*
insert the pin den Stift einrasten
insert bit Schraubendrehereinsatz *m*
insert card Einsteckkarte *f*
insert easily frei einführen
insert technology mittels Kunststoff umspritzte Metallteile
insert tool Einsatzmeißel *m*, Drehling *m*
insertable steckbar
insertable bin Einsatzkasten *m*
insertable tool Einsatzwerkzeug *nt*
inserted blade Einsatzmesser *nt*
inserted blade face milling cutters Fräswerkzeuge *ntpl* mit auswechselbaren Messern
inserted teeth broach Räumwerkzeug *nt* mit eingesetzten Zähnen
inserted tooth fly mill Schlagfräser *m* mit eingesetztem Meißel
inserting platform Einschubstation *f*
insertion Einfügung *f*, Einfahren *nt*, Stecken *nt*
insertion loss Einfügungsdämpfung *f*
insertion opening Einfahröffnung *f*
insertion pocket Einfahrtasche *f*
insertion/extraction Zug-/Schubvorrichtung *f*
in-service behaviour Betriebsverhalten *nt*
in-service limit of error Verkehrsfehlergrenze *f*
inside innen, innerhalb, hinein
inside air humidity value Raumluftfeuchtewert *m*
inside and outside calliper Doppeltaster *m*

inside callipers Innentaster *m*
inside calliper Innentaster *m*
inside diameter Innendurchmesser *m*
inside diameter matching Innenanpassung *f*
inside diameter turning Innendreharbeit *f*
inside finish turning Innenfeindrehen *nt*
inside gripping Innenspannen *nt*
inside heel Innenseite *f* des Gabelknickes
inside height lichte Höhe *f*
inside measurement Innenmessung *f*
inside micrometer Stichmaß *nt*
inside of a fork Vorderseite *f* der Gabel
inside or outside of handrails Geländerholm *m*
inside spring calliper Federlochtaster *m*
inside temperature Innentemperatur *f*
inside thread calliper Flankentaster *m* für Innengewinde
inside thread micrometer Gewindestichmaß *nt*
inside turning tool Inneneinstechmeißel *m*, Innenausdrehmeißel *m*
inside wall Innenwandung *f*
incident dosis rate Einfalldosierung *f*
insider diameter lichte Weite *f*
incident radiation Einfallstrahlung *f*
in-situ soil anstehender Boden *m*
inclination measuring instrument Neigungsmessgerät *nt*
inspect inspizieren, kontrollieren, untersuchen, überwachen, überprüfen, prüfen, nachprüfen, abnehmen
inspect the quality Qualität prüfen
inspection Inspektion *f*, Abnahme *f*, Kontrolle *f*, Überprüfung *f*, Nachprüfung *f*, Prüfung *f*, Revision *f*, Untersuchung *f*, Überwachung *f*
inspection Revision *f*, Untersuchung *f*
inspection by variables Variablenprüfung *f*
inspection condition Abnahmebedingung *f*
inspection control Prüfsteuerung *f*
inspection department Prüfstelle *f*, Abnahme *f*, Revision *f*

inspection documents Prüfbeleg *m*
inspection equipment Prüfmittel *nt*
inspection execution Prüfausführung *f*
inspection facility Kontrollmittel *nt*, Prüfeinrichtung *f*
inspection gauge Abnahmelehre *f*
inspection hole Besichtigungsöffnung *f*
inspection lot Prüflos *nt*
inspection of incoming goods Eingangsrevision *f*, Wareneingangsprüfung *f*
inspection of incoming shipments Wareneingangskontrolle *f*
inspection of outgoing goods WA-Prüfung *f*
inspection plan Prüfplan *m*
inspection planning Prüfplanung *f*
inspection record Prüfprotokoll *nt*
inspection report Prüfbefund *m*, Prüfblatt *nt*
inspection resource Prüfmittel *nt*
inspection result Prüfungsergebnis *nt*
inspection sheet Prüfprotokoll *nt*
inspection status Prüfstatus *m*
inspection test Werksprüfung *f*, Werkstattprüfung *f*, Abnahmekontrolle *f*, Abnahmeversuch *m*, Abnahmeprüfung *f*
inspection time Inspektionsdauer *f*
inspection-oriented dimensioning prüfgerechte Maßeintragung *f*
inspector Prüfer *m*
inspector's stamp Prüfstempel *m*
inspection by attributes Attributprüfung *f*
instrument Gerät *nt*
instability Instabilität *f*, Unstarrheit *f*
instable labil
install anbringen, einbauen, einsetzen, einrichten, aufstellen, verlegen, auflegen, montieren, installieren
install cable Kabel verlegen
install with positive locking in the longitudinal direction längskraftschlüssiges einbauen
installation Installation *f*, Montage *f*, Aufbau *m*, Befestigung *f*, Einrichtung *f*, Errichtung *f*, Einbau *m*, Verlegen *nt*, Aufstellung *f*, Anbringung *f*
installation accuracy Montagegenau-

igkeit *f*
installation drawing Aufstellungszeichnung *f*
installation for shrinkage Schrumpfanlage *f*
installation instruction Einbauanweisung *f*, Einbauhinweis *m*, Montageanweisung *f*, Montageanleitung *f*
installation plant Ablage *f*
installation position Einbauanlage *f*
installation switch Lichtschalter *m*
installation tolerance Montagetoleranz *f*
instalment plan Zahlungsplan *m*
instant Moment *nt*
instant mixer Blitzmischer *m*
instantaneous momentan
instantaneous axis *(e. Wälzgetriebes)* Momentanachse *f*
instantaneous gas water heater Durchlaufgaswassererhitzer *m*
instantaneous gas-fired heater Gadurchlauferhitzer *m*, Gasdurchflusswassererwärmer *m*
instantaneous rotation *(e. Rades)* Momentandrehung *f*
instantaneous transmission ratio momentane Übersetzung *f*
instantaneous type service water heater Durchflussbrauchwassererwärmer *m*
instantaneous water heater Durchlauferhitzer *m*, Durchflusswassererwärmer *m*, Durchlaufwassererhitzer *m*
instep clearance Stufenhöhe *f*
instruct ausbilden, unterrichten, unterweisen, anweisen, einweisen, anleiten
instruction Anleitung *f*, Anweisung *f*, Befehl *m*, Unterweisung *f*, Vorschrift *f*, Einweisung *f*
instruction for installation Installationsvorschrift *f*
instruction for use Gebrauchsanleitung *f*, Gebrauchsanweisung *f*
instruction handbook Betriebshandbuch *nt*, Betriebsanleitung *f*
instruction input Befehlseingang *m*
instruction manual Betriebshandbuch *nt*, Betriebsanleitung *f*, Handbuch *nt*
instruction manual covering operating and regular servicing Betriebs- und Wartungsanleitung *f*
instruction name Befehlsname *m*
instruction output Befehlsausgabe *f*, Befehlsausgang *m*
instruction plate Bedienungsschild *nt*, Maschinenschild *nt*
instruction type Befehlsart *f*
instruction-oriented anweisungsorientiert
instructor Ausbilder *m*
instrument Instrument *nt*, Armatur *f*, Gerät *nt*
instrument adjustment Geräteeinstellung *f*
instrument constant Gerätekonstante *f*
insufficient mangelhaft, ungenügend
insufficient charging Mangelladung *f*
insufficient thickness Nahtdickenunterscheidung *f*
insufflate ausblasen
insufflation Ausblasen *nt*
insulate dämmen, isolieren
insulated isoliert
insulating Isolation *f*; nicht leitend
insulating bush Isolierbuchse *f*
insulating layer Schutzschicht *f*
insulating material Isolierstoff *m*, Dämmstoff *m*
insulating oil sample Isolierölprobe *f*
insulating pliers Isolierzange *f*
insulating slab closure Dämmplattenverschluss *m*
insulating solid wood Isoliervollholz *nt*
insulating spacer Isolierstück *nt*
insulating tape Isolierband *nt*
insulation Isolierung *f*, Isolation *f*
insulation against vibrations Schwingisolierung *f*
insulation class Isolierstoffklasse *f*, Wärmeklasse *f*
insulation failure Isolationsschaden *m*, Isolierungsfehler *m*
insulation layer Isolierschicht *f*
insulation monitoring Isolationsüberwachung *f*
insulation monitoring device Isolati-

onsüberwachungssystem *nt*
insulation plate Isolierplatte *f*
insulation resistance Isolationswiderstand *m*
insulation strength Isolationswiderstand *m*
insulator Nichtleiter *m*, Isolator *m*
insurance Versicherung *f*
insure versichern
insusceptibility Beständigkeit *f*
in-system transfer time Laufzeit *f*, Durchgangszeit *f*
intact ganz
intaglio printing Tiefdruck *m*
intake Eintritt *m*, Zulauf *m*
intake cross-section Zulaufquerschnitt *m*
intake filter Zuluftfilter *m*
intake line Zulaufleitung *f*
intake port Eintrittsöffnung *f*
intake tap Ansaughahn *m*
intakes *pl* Einläufe *mpl*
integer ganze Zahl *f*; ganzzahlig; ganzzahliger Wert *m*
integral Integral *nt*; integriert, ganz
integral action integrierendes Verhalten *nt*
integral action controlling system I-Regeleinrichtung *f*
integral action factor I-Beiwert *m*, Integrierbeiwert *m*
integral element I-Glied *nt*, integrierendes Glied *nt*, Integralglied *nt*
integral multiple ganzzahliges Vielfaches *nt*
integral power ganzzahlige Potenz *f*
integral with ein Ganzes mit
integrate einbeziehen, einbetten, integrieren
integrated eingebaut, eingebettet
integrated circuit (IC) integrierte Schaltung *f*, integrierter Schaltkreis *m*
integrated gauge block eingebautes Endmaß *nt*
integrated structure Regalkonstruktion *f*
integrated system Gesamtkonzeption *f*
integrating measuring instrument integrierendes Messgerät *nt*
integrating meter Zähler *m*

integration Anbindung *f*, Einbindung *f*, Einbettung *f*
integration constant Integrationskonstante *f*
integration measurement Integrationsmessung *f*
integrator Zählwerk *nt*
ingredient Bestandteil *m*
integrity Unversehrtheit *f*
intelligent intelligent
intelligent power module intelligentes Leistungsmodul *nt*
intended bestimmungsgemäß
intended use vorgesehener Verwendungszweck *m*
intended variation gewollte Abweichung *f*
intense stark
intensify intensivieren
intensifying screen Aufnahmefolie *f*
intensity Intensität *f*, Stromstärke *f*
intensity allocation Intensitätsverteilung *f*
intensity distribution Intensitätsverteilung *f*
intensity matrix Intensitätsmatrix *f*
intensity of contact Beziehungsstärke *f*
intensity of transmitted pulse Sendimpulsstärke *f*
intensity-equalized radiation field intensitätsausgeglichenes Strahlenfeld *nt*
intensive grinding Intensivschleifen *nt*
intensive to light lichtunempfindlich
intensively acting quenchant schroff wirkendes Abschreckmittel *nt*
intentional absichtlich, beabsichtigt
intentional damage beabsichtigte Schädigung *f*
interact zusammenwirken, interagieren
interaction Zusammenwirken *nt*, Zusammenspiel *nt*, Zusammenhang *m*, Wechselwirkung *f*, Interaktion *f*
interaction procedure Bedienverhalten *nt*
interaction term Wechselwirkungsglied *nt*
interactive interaktiv
interarrival time Zwischenankunftszeit *f*

intercalate interpolieren
intercept abfangen
intercepting tank Auffangbehälter *m*
interceptor 1. Fang *m*, Abscheider *m* 2. *(Messmittel)* Wasserwaage *f*
interchange austauschen, vertauschen, auswechseln; Austausch *m*
interchange circuit (DIN 66020 T.2) Datennetz *nt*
interchangeability Austauschbarkeit *f*
interchangeable austauschbar
interchangeable European pallet Poolpalette *f*
interchangeable manufacture Austauschbau *m*
interconnect zuschalten, zwischenschalten
interconnected zwischengeschaltet
interconnection Zwischenglied *nt*, Zuschalten *nt*, Verbindung *f*
intercrystalline crack Korngrenzenriss *m*
interdict verbieten
interdiction Verbot *nt*
interest Zins *m*
interest rate Zinssatz *m*
interface Nahtstelle *f*, Trennfläche *f*, Schnittstelle *f*, eine Schnittstelle *f* bilden, Grenzfläche *f*
interface definition Schnittstellendefinition *f*
interface diameter Fugendurchmesser *m*
interface functions Schnittstellenfunktionalität *f*
interface of the weld nugget Schweißfläche *f*
interface partner Schnittstellenpartner *m*
interfere überlagern
interfere with stören, behindern
interference Interferenz *f*, Beeinträchtigung *f*, Beeinflussung *f*, Störung *f*, Störsignal *nt*, Überlagern *nt* von Signalen
interference ability Interferenzfähigkeit *f*
interference apparatus Interferenzgerät *nt*
interference at the joint Fugenpressung *f*

interference band Interferenzstreifen *m*
interference capability Interferenzfähigkeit *f*
interference colours Interferenzfarben *fpl*
interference field Störfeld *nt*
interference filter Interferenzfilter *m*
interference fit Presspassung *f*, Presssitz *m*
interference fit assembly Pressverband *m*
interference fit assembly by force fitting Pressverband *m* durch Einpressen
interference fit assembly by shrinkage Pressverband *m* durch Schrumpfen
interference guide value Übermaßrichtwert *m*
interference immunity Unempfindlichkeit *f* gegen Störungen
interference interface Pressfuge *f*
interference level Störpegel *m*
interference liability Störanfälligkeit *f*
interference maxima Interferenzmaxima *ntpl*
interference method Interferenzmethode *f*
interference pattern Interferenzmuster *nt*, Interferenzbild *nt*
interference pulse Störimpuls *m*
interference pulse suppression Störimpulsunterdrückung *f*
interference spot Interferenzfleck *m*
interference susceptibility Störempfindlichkeit *f*
interference thread Festsitzgewinde *nt*
interference-free interferenzfrei
interference-prone *(el.)* störanfällig
interfering factor Störeinfluss *m*
interferometer Interferometer *nt*
interferometry Lichtinterferenz *f*, optische Messtechnik *f*
interferric gap Luftspalt *m*
interferric space Luftspalt *m*
interior Innere *nt*
interior air condition Raumluftzustand *m*
interior fittings Inneneinrichtung *f*

interior spraying Innenspritzung f
inter-laboratory test Ringversuch m
interlacing Verknäuelung f
interlacing isotherm Vernetzungsisotherm nt
interlaminar failure Schubspannungsbruch m
interlaminar shear failure interlaminarer Schubbruch m
interlaminar tensile strength interlaminare Zugfestigkeit f
interlayer adhesive Zwischenlagenkleber m
interlining Einlagestoff m
interlink verketten, Zwischenglied nt
interlinkage Verkettung f
interlinkage system Verkettungssystem nt
interlinking Verkettung f
interlinking system Verkettungssystem nt
interlock blockieren, verriegeln, gegeneinander verriegeln, sperren, verblocken; Arretierung f, Verblockung f, Verriegelung f, gegenseitige Verriegelung f
interlocked gesperrt, zusammengeschlossen, verzahnt
interlocked control synchronisiertes Steuern nt
interlocked cutter set gekuppelter Fräsersatz m
interlocked layer gekreuzte Schicht f
interlocked with each other miteinander verriegelt
interlocking Blockierung f, Verriegelung f
interlocking arrangement Verriegelung f
interlocking device Verriegelung f
interlocking element Verriegelungselement nt
interlocking plain milling cutter geteilter Walzenfräser m
interlocking safety control Sicherheitsblockierung f
intermating pair of gear wheels kämmendes Räderpaar nt
intermediate zwischengeschaltet
intermediate arbor support Zwischentraglager nt für den Dorn

intermediate assessment Zwischenbeurteilung f
intermediate bearing Zwischenlager nt
intermediate buffer Zwischenpuffer m
intermediate charge Zwischenladung f
intermediate charge cycle Teilladezyklus m
intermediate charge/charging Teilladung f, Zwischenladung f
intermediate coating Zwischenschicht f
intermediate copying paper Zwischenkopierpapier nt
intermediate drive Zwischenantrieb m
intermediate feed mechanism Rückschaltwerk nt
intermediate fraction Zwischenfraktion f
intermediate gear Zwischenrad nt
intermediate half-steps Zwischenwerte mpl
intermediate inspection Zwischenprüfung f, Zwischenabnahme f
intermediate layer Zwischenlage f
intermediate mask Zwischenmaske f
intermediate memory Zwischenspeicher m
intermediate message Zwischenbescheid m
intermediate movement Zwischenbewegung f
intermediate ply (Schichten) Mittellage f
intermediate point Zwischenwert m
intermediate position Zwischenstellung f
intermediate product Zwischenprodukt nt
intermediate rail Zwischenstab m, Knieleiste f
intermediate range Zwischenbereich m
intermediate result Zwischenresultat nt, Zwischenergebnis nt
intermediate screening Zwischensiebung f
intermediate size Zwischengröße f
intermediate slide Zwischenschieber m

intermediate stage Zwischenstufe *f*
intermediate storage Zwischenspeicher *m*, Zwischenpuffern *nt*
intermediate storage facility Zwischenlager *nt*
intermediate storage facility area Zwischenlagerfläche *f*
intermediate storage location Zwischenpuffer *m*
intermediate target Zwischenziel *nt*
intermediate testing of welds Schweißnahtzwischenprüfung *f*
inter-meshing gears *pl* miteinander kämmende Räder *ntpl*
intermit unterbrechen, aussetzen
intermitted cut unterbrochener Schnitt *m*
intermitted feed Ruckvorschub *m*, Sprungvorschub *m*, Sprungschaltung *f*
intermitted feed milling Sprungtischfräsen *nt*
intermitted speed control Impulsbremsung *f*
intermitted table feed Sprungtischschaltung *f*
intermittent stoßartig
intermittent fillet joint with end distance unterbrochene Kehlnaht *f* mit Vormaß
intermittent operation aussetzender Betrieb *m*
intermittent service Aussetzbetrieb *m*
intermolecular force Kohäsionskraft *f*
internal intern
internal boring tool Ausdrehmeißel *m*
internal broach Innenräumwerkzeug *nt*, Räumnadel *f*
internal broaching Innenräumen *nt*
internal broaching machine Innenräummaschine *f*
internal calliper gauge Innentaster *m*, Stichmarke *f*
internal chuck Innenspannfutter *nt*
internal combustion (IC) engine Verbrennungsmotor *m*
internal combustion electric truck elektromotorisch betriebenes Flurförderzeug *nt* mit Verbrennungsmotor
internal combustion truck Flurförderzeug *nt* mit Verbrennungsmotor

internal contours Innenkonturen *f*
internal copying attachment Innenkopiereinrichtung *f*, Innennachformeinrichtung *f*
internal crack Innenriss *m*
internal cutting tool Bohrschlichtstahl *m*, Innenausdrehmeißel *m*
internal cylindrical lapping Innenrundläppen *nt*, Bohrungsläppen *nt*
internal cylindrical lapping machine Innenrundläppmaschine *f*
internal dial gauge Innenmessuhr *f*
internal diameter Innendurchmesser *m*
internal dimension Innenabmessung *f*
internal facing attachment *(Plandrehen)* Innendrehvorrichtung *f*
internal failure interner Fehler *m*
internal fitting member Innenpassteil *nt*
internal force variable Schnittgröße *f*
internal gauge Bohrungslehre *f*
internal gear Hohlrad *nt*, Innenrad *nt*, innenverzahntes Rad *nt*
internal gear addendum Hohlradkopfhöhe *f*, Hohlradzahnkopfhöhe *f*
internal gear addendum modification Hohlradprofilverschiebung *f*
internal gear angular pitch Hohlradteilungswinkel *m*
internal gear corner point Hohlradkopfeckpunkt *m*
internal gear cutting Hohlradverzahnen *nt*
internal gear diameter Hohlraddurchmesser *m*
internal gear milling Innenradfräsen *nt*
internal gear pair Innenradpaar *nt*
internal gear pair at reference centre distance V-Null-Innenradpaar *nt*
internal gear radius Hohlradradius *m*
internal gear root Hohlradfuß *m*
internal gear root diameter Hohlradfußkreisdurchmesser *m*
internal gear root space width limit Hohlradzahnfußlückenweitengrenze *f*
internal gear tip Hohlradkopf *m*
internal gear tip diameter Hohlradkopfkreisdurchmesser *m*

internal gear tip involute Hohlradkopfevolvente *f*
internal gear tooth profile Hohlradzahnprofil *nt*
internal gear tooth root Hohlradzahnfuß *m*
internal gear tooth tip Hohlradkopfkante *f*, Hohlradzahnkopf *m*
internal grind Innenschliff *m*
internal grinder Innenschleifmaschine *f*
internal grinding Innenschleifen *nt*, Innenschliff *m*
internal grinding attachment Innenschleifeinrichtung *f*
internal grinding method Innenschleifverfahren *nt*
internal grinding operation Innenschleifoperation *f*
internal grinding work Innenschleifarbeit *f*
internal honing Innenziehschleifen *nt*
internal ignition Ausbrennen *nt*
internal indicating gauge Passimeter *nt*
internal key seater Innenkeilnutfräsmaschine *f*
internal measurement Innenabmessung *f*
internal measuring instrument Innenmessgerät *nt*
internal micrometer Innenmessschraube *f*
internal milling Innenflächenfräsen *nt*, Innenfräsen *nt*
internal milling attachment Innenfräsapparat *m*
internal performance Eigenleistung *f*
internal polygon slotting attachment Innenmehrkantstoßeinrichtung *f*
internal pressure Innendruck *m*
internal pressure at failure Innendruck *m* beim Versagen
internal pressure bursting test Innendruckberstversuch *m*
internal pressure creep rupture test Zeitstandinnendruckversuch *m*
internal pressure creep test Innendruckzeitstandversuch *m*
internal pressure endurance test Innendruckzeitstandversuch *m*, Zeitstandinnendruckversuch *m*
internal pressure loading Innendruckbeanspruchung *f*
internal pressure roll Innendruckrolle *f*
internal pressure test Innendruckversuch *m*
internal protection Innenschutz *m*
internal quality control Eigenüberwachung *f*, werksinterne Kontrolle *f*
internal resistance Innenwiderstand *m*
internal roughing tool Innenschruppmeißel *m*
internal shaping Innenhobeln *nt*
internal shrinkage Innenlunker *m*
internal side cutting tool Inneneckdrehmeißel *m*
internal side tool abgesetzter Bohrmeißel *m*
internal spline broach Keilnabenräumwerkzeug *nt*
internal spraying Innenspritzung *f*
internal straight cylindrical gear innenverzahntes Geradstirnrad *nt*
internal tab washer Sicherungsblech *nt* mit Innenmasse
internal taper Innenkegel *m*
internal tapping Innengewindeschneiden *nt*
internal thread Innengewinde *nt*, Muttergewinde *nt*
internal thread connection Innengewindestutzen *m*
internal thread cutting Innengewindeschneiden *nt*
internal thread milling Innengewindefräsen *nt*
internal thread milling unit Innengewindefrässupport *m*
internal thread turning Innengewindedrehen *nt*
internal thread whirling Innenwirbeln *nt*
internal toothing Innenverzahnung *f*
internal turning Innenausdrehen *nt*, Ausdrehen *nt*
internal turning attachment Innendrehvorrichtung *f*
internal turning tool Innendrehmei-

ßel *m*
internal work Bearbeitung *f* von Innenflächen, Innenarbeit *f*
internally ribbed mit Innenverrippung *f*
internally soldered end Innenlötende *nt*
internally toothed innenverzahnt
internally toothed bevel gear innenverzahntes Kegelrad *nt*
internally toothed gear Innenrad *nt*
international systems of units Internationales Einheitensystem *nt*
international thread grooving Gewindefurchen *nt* von Innengewinden
interocular distance Augenabstand *m*
interior zone innerer Bereich *m*
interpass temperature Zwischenlagentemperatur *f*
interpass undercut Längshub *m* zwischen den Schweißraupen
inter-penetrating feature Durchdringung *f*
interplant überbetrieblich
inter-plant unternehmensübergreifend
interpolate interpolieren
interpolation Interpolation *f*
interpole Wendepol *m*
interpret übersetzen, interpretieren
interpretation Übersetzung *f*, Interpretation *f*
interpreter Interpretierer *m*, Übersetzer *m*
interpreter unit Auswerteeinheit *f*
interrelation Zusammenspiel *nt*
interrogation Abfrage *f*
interrogation signal Abfragesignal *nt*
inter-run undercut Längshub *m* zwischen den Schweißraupen
interrupted cutting edge unterbrochene Schneide *f*
interrupt Unterbrechung *f*; unterbrechen, abbrechen, aussetzen
interrupt input Alarmeingang *m*
interrupt response time Alarmreaktionszeit *f*
interrupt triggering alarmauslösend
interrupted cut unterbrochener Schnitt *m*

interrupted cutting edge unterbrochene Schneide *f*
interrupted fillet weld unterbrochene Kehlnaht *f*
interrupted hardening unterbrochenes Härten *nt*
interruption Abbruch *m*, Störung *f*, Unterbrechung *f*
interruptor Schalter *m*
intersect überschneiden, schneiden
intersecting aisle Winkelgang *m*
intersection Schnitt *m*, Durchschnitt *m*, Überschneidung *f*, Schnittpunkt *m*, Kreuzung *f*, Stoßstelle *f*
intersection line Schnittlinie *f*
intersection of axes Achsenkreuzung *f*
intersection of welds Nahtkreuzung *f*
intersection point of the gear axes Achsenschnittpunkt *m* von Zahnrädern
intercept abscheiden
interstice Spalte *f*
interval Abstand *m*, Spanne *f*, Intervall *nt*
interval duration Pausendauer *f*
interval estimation Bereichsschätzung *f*
interval motion douche Intervallbewegungsspülung *f*
intervene eingreifen
intervening space Zwischenraum *m*
intervention Eingriff *m*
into hinein
intrasystem systemintern
intermediate storage Zwischenlagerung *f*
intricate verwickelt, kompliziert, schwierig
intrinsic piece Eigenteil *nt*
intrinsic safety Eigensicherheit *f*
intrinsic stability Eigenstabilität *f*
intrinsically safe eigensicher
intrinsically safe circuit eigensicherer Stromkreis *m*
intrinsically safe plant eigensichere Anlage *f*
introduce einführen
introduction Einführung *f*
introductory einführend
intromission angle Einschallwinkel *m*
intromission of sound Einschallung *f*

instable unstabil
instruction list (IL) Anweisungsliste (AWL) *f*
invalid ungültig
invalidity Ungültigkeit *f*
invariable unveränderlich, unveränderbar
inventory level as function of time Zeitmengenabstand *m*
invent erfinden
inventory Bestand *m*, Inventar *nt*, Vorrat *m*
inventory accounting Lagerbuchführung *f*, Lagerbestandsführung *f*
inventory accounts interface Sachkontenschnittstelle *f*
inventory buffer Bestandspuffer *m*, Warenpuffer *m*
inventory build-up Vorratsaufstockung *f*, Lagerauffüllung *f*, Zunahme *f* der Lagerbestände
inventory control Lagerbestandsführung *f*
inventory cost(s) Bestandskosten *pl*
inventory data Lagerdaten *pl*
inventory enquiry Bestandsabfrage *f*
inventory fluctuations Lagerhaltungsschwankungen *fpl*
inventory function Inventurfunktion *f*
inventory holding costs Lagerhaltungskosten *pl*, Bestandshaltungskosten *pl*
inventory item Lagerposition *f*
inventory level Lagerbestand *m*
inventory management Lagerwirtschaft *f*, Bestandsführung *f*
inventory management coupling Bestandsführungskopplung *f*
inventory message Inventurmeldung *f*
inventory movements Lagerbewegungen *pl*
inventory on-hand quantity Inventurbestand *m*
inventory planning Lagerplanung *f*
inventory range Bestandsreichweite *f*
inventory receipt Lagerzugang *m*
inventory reduction Bestandsverringerung *f*
inventory replenishment Lagerauffüllung *f*
inventory report Inventurbericht *m*, Inventurmeldung *f*
inventory sales ratio Lagerumschlag *m*, Umschlagshäufigkeit *f*
inventory scheduling Lagerhaltungsplanung *f*
inventory status report Lagerbestandsaufstellung *f*
inventory stickout as function of time Zeitmengendefizit *nt*
inventory stock Inventurbestand *m*
inventory turnover ratios Lagerkennzahlen *fpl*
inventory value Bestandswert *m*
inventory-making Inventur *f*
inventory-making procedure Inventurverfahren *nt*
inverse umgekehrt
inverse rectifier Wechselrichter *m*
inverse speed-motor Reihenschlussmotor *m*
inversely proportional umgekehrt proportional
inversion Inversion *f*
inversion of direction of rotation Drehrichtungsumkehr *f*
inversion of the direction Richtungsumkehr *f*
invert wenden, umkehren, invertieren
inverted cup seal Hutmanschette *f*
inverted plan Untersicht *f*
inverted Vee-guide Prismenführung *f*
inverted Vees Dachprisma *nt*
inverted Vee-way umgekehrtes V-Prisma *nt*
inverted V-guide Dachprismenführung *f*
inverted V-way Dachprisma *nt*
inverter Inverter *m*, Wechselrichter *m*
investigate untersuchen, prüfen
investigation Prüfung *f*, Untersuchung *f*, Ermittlung *f*
investment Investition *f*
investment budget Investitionsvolumen *nt*, Investitionsbudget *nt*
investment calculation Investitionsrechnung *f*
investment casting Feingießen *nt*
investment casting process Feingießverfahren *nt*

investment compound Formstoff *m* für Modellausschmelzverfahren
investment cost plan Investitionskostenplan *m*
investment costs Investitionskosten *pl*
investment demand Einsatzbedarf *m*
investment estimate Investitionskostenschätzung *f*
investment frame Investitionsvorhaben (*pl*)
investment in new plant and equipment Neuinvestition *f*
investment moulding process Modellausschmelzverfahren *nt*
investment pattern Ausschmelzmodell *nt*
investment planning Investitionsplanung *f*
invitation for tender Ausschreibung *f*
invite for tenders ausschreiben
invocation Aufruf *m*
invoice fakturieren, Rechnung *f*
invoicing Fakturierung *f*
invoke aufrufen
involute curve Evolvente *f*
involute cylindrical gear Evolventenstirnrad *nt*
involute flank Evolventenflanke *f*, evolventische Flanke *f*
involute form Evolventenform *f*
involute function Evolventenfunktion *f*
involute gear Evolvente *f*, Evolventenrad *nt*
involute gear tooth system Evolventenverzahnung *f*
involute helical gear teeth Evolventenschrägverzahnung *f*
involute helicoid Evolventenschraubfläche *f*
involute hob Evolventenwälzfräser *m*
involute length EvIolventenlänge *f*
involute origin Evolventenursprungspunkt *m*
involute profile Evolventenprofil *nt*
involute spur gear pair Evolventengeradstirnpaar
involute to a circle Kreisevolvente *f*
involute tooth flank Evolventenzahnflanke *f*
involve einbeziehen, beteiligen

involvement Beteiligung *f*
inward positioned arrowhead innenstehender Pfeil *m*
iodometric method jodometrische Methode *f*
ion beam Ionenstrahl *m*
ion beam machining Ionenstrahlbearbeitung *f*
ion bond Ionenbindung *f*
ion-conducting medium *(el. chem.)* ionenleitendes Medium *nt*
ion exchange filter Ionenaustauschfilter *m*
ion laser Ionenlaser *m*
ionisation dosimetry Ionisationsdosimetrie *f*
ionization Ionisierung *f*
ionize ionisieren
ionized radiation ionisierte Strahlung *f*
ionizing manometer Ionisationsmanometer *m*
ionizing radiation energy ionisierende Strahlungsenergie *f*
IPC (in-process control) IPK (In-Prozess-Kontrolle)
IPO (internal purchase order) EVA (Einkaufs-/Verkaufs-Auftrag) *m*
IPO form EVA-Formular *nt*
I-point I-Punkt *m*
IR-relay IR-Relais *nt*
iron Eisen *nt*
iron core Eisenkern *m*
iron loss Eisenverlust *m*
iron scrap Alteisen *nt*, Eisenschrott *m*
ironing Abschreckgleitziehen *nt*, Abstreckziehen *nt*
irradiated area Bestrahlungsfeld *nt*
irradiation Bestrahlung *f*, Kurzzeit-Nahbestrahlung *f*
irradiation record Bestrahlungsprotokoll *nt*
irradiation sieve Bestrahlungssieb *nt*
irradiation timer Bestrahlungsuhr *f*
irreducible number nichtteilbare Zahl *f*
irregular irregulär, ungleichmäßig
irregular spacing ungleiche Teilung *f*
irregularity Unregelmäßigkeit *f*, Formfehler *m*, Abweichung *f*, Ungleichheit *f*
irregularity coefficient Ungleichmä-

ßigkeitskoeffizient *m*
irregularity of form Formabweichung *f*
irregularity of surface configuration Gestaltabweichung *f*
irrespective of unabhängig von
irritant gas reizerzeugendes Gas *nt*
irritation stage of a fire Entstehungsbrand *m*
ISA basic-hole system ISA-Einheitsbohrungssystem *nt*
ISA basic-shaft system ISA-Einheitswellensystem *nt*
ISA system of tolerances ISA-Toleranzsystem *nt*
I-shaped profile Doppel-T-Profil *nt*, I-Profil *nt*
ISO fastening screw thread ISO-Befestigungsgewinde *nt*
ISO keyhole notch specimen ISO-Rundkerbprobe *f*
ISO metric fine thread metrisches ISO-Feingewinde *nt*
ISO metric trapezoidal screw thread metrisches ISO-Trapezgewinde *nt*
ISO symbol ISO-Kurzzeichen *nt*
ISO system of fits and tolerances ISO-Toleranz- und Passsystem *nt*
ISO V-notch specimen ISO-Spitzkerbprobe *f*
isochronous zeittaktgleich, zeitgleich
isolate entkoppeln, isolieren
isolated isoliert, getrennt
isolated inclusions vereinzelte Einschlüsse *mpl*
isolated lot einzelnes Los *nt*
isolating device *(Ventilation)* Absperreinrichtung *f*
isolation Isolation *f*, Trennung *f*
isolation device Abschalteinrichtung *f*
isolator Trennschalter *m*
isometric projection isometrische Projektion *f*, isometrische Darstellung *f*
isosceles weld triangle gleichschenkliges Nahtdreieck *nt*
isostatic compressing isostatisches Pressen *nt*
issue ableiten, Ausfluss *m*
issue from ausströmen aus
item Position *f*, Einheit *f*
item number Disponummer *f*
item source certificate Materialherkunftsnachweis *m*
itemize zerlegen
items moving at a medium pace B-Sortiment *nt*
iteration process Iterationsverfahren *nt*

J j

jack Palettenheber *m*, Hubwagen *m*, Hebezeug *nt*, Stützblock *m*, Zylinder *m*; heben, unterbauen
jack screw Hubspindel *f*, Verstellspindel *f*
jack up aufbocken
jacket ummanteln, umhüllen, verkleiden; Mantel *m*, Ummantelung *f*
jacket type gas water heater Außenwandgaswasserheizer *m*
jacketed type fire-place Außenwandfeuerstätte *f*
jacking Heben *nt*
jacking beam Hubtraverse *f*
Jakro beating method Jakro- Mahlverfahren *nt*
jam klemmen, festklemmen, verklemmen, blockieren, festfressen, stauen, ecken; Stau *m*
jam nut Gegenmutter *f*, Kontermutter *f*
jammed festgefahren
jamming Verklemmen *nt*, Festfressen *nt*, Verklemmung *f*, Blockierung *f*
jar 1. erschüttern, rütteln 2. Glasgefäß *nt*
jarring Erschütterung *f*
jaw Backe *f*, Spannbacke *f*, Klaue *f*, Spannklaue *f*, Maul *nt*
jaw opening Backenöffnung *f*
jaw-type pull head Ziehkopf *m* mit Backenspannung
jaw wrench Maulschlüssel *nt*
jenny Tastzirkel *m*
jerk rucken, ruckweise bewegen, rütteln, reißen; Ruck *m*
jerking ruckend
jerky ruckartig, ruckweise, schlagartig
jet Strahl *m*, Düse *f*
jet compressor Strahlverdichter *m*
jet evaporation method Aufblasverfahren *nt*
jet method Strahlverfahren *nt*
jet parameter Stahlparameter *m*
jet quality on performance Strahlqualität *f*
jet velocity Strahlaustrittsgeschwindigkeit *f*

jib Kragarm *m*, Ausleger *m*
jib crane Auslegerkran *m*
jib type crane Kranarm *m*
jig Lehre *f*, Bohrschablone *f*, werkzeugsteuernde Vorrichtung *f*
jig-bore Lehren bohren
jig borer Koordinatenbohrmaschine *f*, Feinbohrmaschine *f*
jig boring Lehrenbohren *nt*
jig boring and milling machine Lehrenbohr- und Fräsmaschine *f*
jig boring machine Lehrenbohrmaschine *f*, Lehrenbohrwerk *nt*
jig boring mill Koordinatenbohr- und -fräswerk *nt*
jig boring work Lehrenbohrarbeit *f*
jig grinder Lehrenschleifmaschine *f*
jig mill Lehrenfräsmaschine *f*
jiggle rücken
jigless production machine Produktionskoordinatenbohrmaschine *f*
jigs Vorrichtungen *fpl*
jim crow Brechstange *f*
jimmy Brechstange *f*
job Personalstelle *f*, Arbeit *f*, Aufgabe *f*, Auftrag *m*
job change over Übergang *m* zu neuer Serie
job index Stellenplanung *f*
job instruction Arbeitsanweisung *f*
job-mixed concrete Ortbeton *m*
job planning Disposition *f*, Arbeitsplanung *f*
job production Einzelfertigung *f*
job routing Fertigungssteuerung *f*
job step Bearbeitungsschritt *m*, Teilaufgabe *f*
jog 1. tippen, tippschalten, langsam bewegen, vorrücken (lassen), auf Einstellung bringen 2. *(Form bearbeiten)* stoßen, senkrechthobeln
jog key Taster *m*, Druckschalter *m*
jogging Rucken *nt*, Feineinstellung *f*, Langsameinstellung *f*, Kriechgang *m*
jogging control Tippschaltung *f*, Schrittschaltung *f*

jogging switch Tippschalter *m*
join fügen, verbinden, zusammenführen, zusammenlaufen, zusammenfügen, zusammentreffen, aneinander befestigen, aneinander fügen
joining Zusammenfügung *f*, Fügen *nt*
joining by creative forming Fügen *nt* durch Urformen
joining by flanging Fügen *nt* durch Bördeln
joining group Fügegruppe *f*
joining pipe Anschlussrohr *nt*
joint 1. (allg.) Fuge *f*, Naht *f*, Stoß *m*, Gelenk *nt*, Verbindung *f*, Verbindungsstelle *f* **2.** *(Materialflusstechnik)* Schlauchanschluss *m*, Schlauchkupplung *f*
joint area Stoßbereich *m*
joint bolt Gelenkbolzen *m*
joint bottom Fugengrund *m*
joint compound Fugenmasse *f*
joint depth Fugentiefe *f*
joint diameter Fugendurchmesser *m*
joint efficiency Stoßfestigkeit *f*
joint face Dichtfläche *f*, Dichtkante *f*
joint flank Fugenflanke *f*
joint gap Dichtungsspalt *m*
joint lapping Stoßläppen *nt*
joint lapping machine Stößläppmaschine *f*
joint moment of several orders Moment *m* mehrerer Ordnungen
joint pressure Fugendruck *m*
joint ring Dichtungsring *m* für den Flansch
joint safety Fugensicherung *f*
joint shear Fugenscherung *f*
joint soldering Verbindungslöten *nt*
joint surface Fügefläche *f*, Fugenfläche *f*, Teilungsfläche *f*
joint test Gemeinschaftsversuch *m*

joint washer Dichtring *m*
joint weld at the boundaries Anschlussnaht *f*
joint with elongated plug weld Langlochnaht *f*
jointed gegliedert
jointed arm robot Drehgelenkroboter *m*
jointed flush vollfugig
jointing Fugenschluss *m*
jointing gap Dichtspalt *m*
jointing medium Dichtmittel *nt*
jointing time Fügezeit *f*
jolt Ruck *m*, Schock *m*, Stoß *m*, rütteln
journal 1. *(Bauteile)* Wellenzapfen *m*, Endzapfen *m*, Achshals *m*, Traglager *nt*, Führungszapfen *m*, Zapfen *m* **2.** *(Bericht)* Protokoll *nt*
journal bearing Wellenlager *nt*, Zapfenlager *nt*, Halslager *nt*, Radlager *nt*
journal envelope Zapfenmantelfläche *f*
journal friction Zapfenreibung *f*
journey there Hinfahrt *f*
journey time Wegezeit *f*
joystick Steuerknüppel *m*
joystick control Steuerung *f* mit Verbundschalter
judge beurteilen
jump springen; Sprung *m*
jump feed Sprungschaltung *f*, Sprungtischvorschub *m*
jump the rails entgleisen
jumper Schaltklinke *f*, Jumper *m*
junction Zusammenführung *f*, Zusammenfügung *f*, Verbindung *f*, Anschluss *m*, Einfädelung *f*
junction line Verbindungsleitung *f*
junk Störsignal *nt*
just in time produktionssynchron
just in time delivery (JIT) produktionssynchrone Anlieferung *f*

K k

kanban processing Kanbanabwicklung *f*
kanban system Kanbansystem *nt*
kappa number K-Zahl *f*
kata factor Katawert *m*
keen scharf
keep führen, verwahren, halten
keep back zurückhalten
keep down niederhalten
keep free of oil ölfrei halten
Keep off! Zutritt verboten!
keep together zusammenhalten
keep under lock unter Verschluss halten
keeper Sicherheitssperrklinke *f*
keeping Verwahrung *f*
keg Fass *nt*, Keg *nt*
keg fill and seal machine Kegfüll- und -verschließmaschine *f*
kerb Bordstein *m*, Bordschwelle *f*
kerf Kerbe *f*
kerf wall Schnittflanke *f*
kerosene Petroleum *nt*
kerosene ignition Leuchtpetroleumzündung *f*
key 1. *(in einer Kerbe)* Feder *f* **2.** *(Druckknopf)* Taste *f* **3.** *(Türschlüssel)* Schlüssel **4.** Keil *m*; aufkeilen, festkeilen, verkeilen
key and slot Feder *f* und Nut *f*
key bar Keilstab *m*
key button Taster *m*, Druckschalter *m*
key data Eckdaten *pl*
key dependence Schlüsselabhängigkeit *f*
key dependence system Schlüsselabhängigkeitssystem *nt*
key drive Mitnahme *f* durch Keil
key field Tastenfeld *nt*
key for access Zugriffsschlüssel *m*
key for hexagon socket screws Winkelschraubendreher *m* für Innensechskantschrauben
key for spline socket screws Winkelschraubendreher *m* für Innenkeilprofilschrauben

key groove Keilnut *f*
key inter-locking device Schlüsseltransfersystem *nt*
key panel Tastenfeld *nt*
key process Schlüsselprozess *m*
key row Tastenleiste *f*
key seat Keilsitz *m*
key switch Schlüsselschalter *m*
keyboard Tastatur *f*
keyboard entry Tastatureingabe *f*
keyboard input Tastatureingabe *f*
keyboard layout Tastenordnung *f*
keyboard section Tastenfeld *nt*
keyed end Einspannteil *nt*
key groove Keilnuten ziehen
keyhole Schlüsselloch *nt*
key-operated switch Schaltschlüssel *m*, Schlüsselschalter *m*
key press Tastendruck *m*
key seat Nut *f*, Keilnut *f*, Längsnut *f*; nuten, Keilnuten einarbeiten, Keilnuten stoßen
key seat slotting attachment Nutenstoßvorrichtung *f*
key seater Keilnutenstoßmaschine *f*, Keilnutmaschine *f*
key seating Keilnutenstoßen *nt*
key seating and slot milling machine Keilnuten- und Langlochfräsmaschine *f*, Nutenfräsmaschine *f*
key seating chisel Nutenmeißel *m*
key-seating tool Keilnutenstoßwerkzeug *nt*, Hobelmeißel *m* zum Keilnutenstoßen
keystroke Tastendruck *m*
keyway Nut *f*, Keilnut *f*, Längsnut *f*, Keilnuten *fpl*; stoßen, nuten
keyway and slot milling automatic Nutenfräsautomat *m*
keyway broach Räumwerkzeug *nt* für Keilnuten
keyway cutter Keilnutenstoßmaschine *f*, Schlitzfräser *m* für Keilnuten, Nutenfräser *m*
keyway cutting Keilnutenstoßen *nt*, Nutenhobeln *nt*, Keilnutenfräsen *nt*,

Keilnutenfräsarbeit *f*
keyway cutting operation Keilbahnfräsarbeit *f*
keyway cutting tool Nutenhobelmeißel *m*
keyway milling Keilnutenfräsen *nt*, Keilnutenfräsarbeit *f*
keyway milling cutter Keilnutenfräser *m*
keyway slotting tool Keilnabenstoßmeißel *m*
keyway tool Keilnutenstoßmeißel *m*
keywaying Keilnutenfräsen *nt*, Keilnutenstoßen *nt*
keywaying attachment Nutenstoßvorrichtung *f*
keywaying operation Keilnutenfräsarbeit *f*
kick-back Rückschlag *m*
kickbar Fußleiste *f*
kicking plate Trittleiste *f*
kickout Auslöseeinrichtung *f*, Auslösung *f*
kill Abbruch *m*; abbrechen
killed steel beruhigt vergossener Stahl *m*
kiln Brennofen *m*
kind (of) Sorte *f*
kind of costs Kostenart *f*
kind of fit Passungscharakter *m*
kind of laser Laserart *f*
kind of warehouse Lagerart *f*
kindling temperature Zündpunkt *m*
kinematic chain kinematische Kette *f*
kinematic grain count kinematische Kornzahl *f*
kinematic grinding arc kinematischer Schleifwinkel *m*
kinematic grinding length kinematische Schleiflänge *f*
kinematic quantity kinematische Größe *f*
kinematic ratio kinematisches Verhältnis *nt*
kinematics Kinematik *f*
kinematics of metal cutting Zerspanungskinematik *f*
kinetic kinetisch
kinetic energy kinetische Energie *f*, Bewegungsenergie *f*
kink Knick *m*, Knitterstelle *f*

kinked line geknickter Linienzug *m*
kinked portion Abknickung *f*
kinked welding rod abgeknickter Schweißstab *m*
kit Kasten *m*
knapsack Tornister *m*
knead kneten
knee Konsole *f*, Sockel *m*, Knie *nt*
knee- and column milling machine Konsolenfräsmaschine *f*
knee- and column type milling machine Ständerfräsmaschine *f*
knee- and column type milling machine with universal table Konsolfräsmaschine *f* mit Universaltisch
knee clamping Konsolklemmung *f*
knee elevating screw Konsolhubspindel *f*
knee rail Knieleiste *f*
knee table Konsolführung *f*, Konsole *f*, Winkeltisch *m*
knee turning toolholder gekröpfter Meißelhalter *m*
kneebrace Aussteifung *f*
kneeless type milling machine Fräsmaschine *f* mit beweglichem Spindelstock, Planfräsmaschine *f*
kneeless-type vertical milling machine Senkrechtplanfräsmaschine *f*
knee-slides Ständerführungsbahn *f*, Konsolführungen *fpl*
kindling temperature Zündpunkt *m*
knee-type hydraulic copying machine Konsolenfräsmaschine *f* mit Hydrokopiereinrichtung
knee-ways Ständerführungsbahn *f*
knife cutting Messerschneiden *nt*
knife edge Haarmesskante *f*, Messlineal *nt*
knife edge type pointer Schneidenanzeiger *m*
knife test Aufsteckversuch *m*
knife-edge straight edge Haarlineal *nt*, Kantenlineal *nt*, Messerlineal *nt*
knife-shaped heating element messerförmiges Heizelement *nt*
knitted fabric Gewerk *nt*
knob Knopf *m*, Drehknopf *m*
knock 1. *(pochen)* klopfen 2. *(Form bearbeiten)* stoßen, senkrechthobeln

knock against prallen gegen
knock down überfahren
knock off abklopfen
knotted (wire) tensile specimen Knotenzugprobe *f*
knotted specimen geknotete Probe *f*
knotted tensile ratio Knotenzugverhältnis *nt*
knotted tensile strength Knotenzugfestigkeit *f*
know-how Erfahrung *f*
knowledge Wissen *nt*
knowledge basis Wissensbasis *f*
knowledge management Wissensmanagement *nt*
knowledge-based wissenbasierend
knowledge-based system Expertensystem *nt*
knuckle thread Rundgewinde *nt* als Fertigungsmittel
knuckle thread for breathing apparatus Rundgewinde *ntpl* für Atemschutzgeräte
knuckle thread for casing tubes Futterrohrrundgewinde *nt*
knuckle thread for sheet metal components Rundgewinde *nt* für Teile aus Blech
knurl kordeln, rändeln
knurl milling head Rändelfräskopf *m*
knurl shaper Rändelstoßmaschine *f*
knurled head screw Rändelschraube *f*
knurled nut Kordelmutter *f*, Rändelmutter *f*
knurling Rändeln *nt*
knurling tool Rändelwerkzeug *nt*
Kusa control Kusaschaltung *f*

L

label beschriften, auszeichnen, etikettieren, markieren; Etikett *nt*, Schild *nt*
label applicator Etikettiermaschine *f*
label inspection machine Etiketteninspektionsmaschine *f*
label printer Etikettendrucker *m*
label printing Etikettendruck *m*
labelling Auszeichnung *f*, Beschriftung *f*
labelling machine Etikettiermaschine *f*
laboratory Labor *nt*
laboratory apparatus Laborgerät *nt*
laboratory building Laborgebäude *nt*
laboratory equipment Laboratoriumseinrichtung *f*
laboratory examination Laborprüfung *f*
laboratory glass Geräteglas *nt*
laboratory glassware Laboratoriumsgeräte *ntpl* aus Glas, Laborgeräte *nt* aus Glas
laboratory hygrometer Laboratoriumsspindel *f*
laboratory metrology Laboratoriumsmesstechnik *f*
laboratory mixing mill Labormischwalzwerk *nt*
laboratory outfit Laborgerät *nt*, Laboratoriumsgeräte *ntpl*
laboratory sample Laboratoriumsprobe *f*
laboratory stand Laborstativ *nt*
laboratory test Laborversuch *m*, Laboratoriumsversuch *m*, Laborprüfung *f*
labour Arbeit *f*, Werkereinsatz *m*
labour inspectorate Gewerbeaufsicht *f*
labour saving arbeitssparend
labour shortage Arbeitskräftemangel *m*
labourer Arbeiter *m*
lace umschnüren, Schnur *f*
lacing Umschnürung *f*
lack (of) mangeln, nicht besitzen, Fehlen *nt*, Mangel *m* (an)
lack of definition Unschärfe *f*
lack of focus Unschärfe *f*
lack of fusion Klebung *f*
lack of inter-run fusion Lagenbindefehler *m*
lack of roundness Unrundheit *f*
lack of space Platzmangel *m*
L-adaptor L-Stutzen *m*
ladder Leiter *f*
ladder arrangement Ladder-Anordnung *f*
ladder diagram (LD) Kontaktplan (KOP) *m*
ladle Gießpfanne *f*
lead screw drive Spindelantrieb *m*
lag verzögern, verlangsamen; Verzögerung *f*, Nachlauf *m*
lag element T-Glied *nt*, Totzeitglied *nt*
lag time Zeitverzögerung *f*
lagging angular position zurückbleibende Drehstellungsabweichung *f*
lamellar lamellar
lamellar chip Lamellenspan *m*
lamellar tearing Lamellenriss *m*
lamina Schicht *f*, Blättchen *nt*, Lamelle *f*
laminate laminieren, lamellieren; Laminat *nt*, Verbund *m*, Schichtstoffverbund *m*, Schichtstoff *m*, Schichtpressstoff *m*, Verbundfolie *f*
laminate under heat verpressen
laminated lamellenförmig, laminiert
laminated core Blechkern *m*
laminated glass Verbundsicherheitsglas (VSG)
laminated graphite Lamellengraphit *m*
laminated leaf spring geschichtete Blattfeder *f*
laminated leather cloth geschichtetes Gewebekunstleder *nt*
Laminated Object Manufacturing LOM (Schichtobjektherstellung) *f*
laminated pane Mehrschichtscheibe *f*
laminated paper panel Hartpapiertafel *f*
laminated paper strip Hartpapierstreifen *m*
laminated plastics Schichtstoff *m*, Schichtpressstoff *m*
laminated plastics panel Schichtpress-

stofftafel *f*
laminated plastics product Schichtpressstofferzeugnis *nt*
laminated safety glass laminiertes Glas *nt*, Zweischichtensicherheitsglas *nt*
laminated system geschichtetes System *nt*, Mehrschichtsystem *nt*
lamination Laminierung *f*, Schicht *f*
lamp Lampe *f*
lamp switching Lampenschalter *m*
LAN (Local Area Network) lokales Netzwerk (LAN) *nt*
lance stechen
lancing Einschneiden *nt*
lancing process Bohrverfahren *nt*
land Fase *f*, Schneidrücken *m*, Zahnrücken *m*
land and groove type of chip breaker Spanleitrille *f* mit Fase
land clearance project Flurbereinigung *f*
land community Bodenverband *m*
land of the face Spanflächenfase *f*
land rake angle Faserspanwinkel *m*
land relief Freiwinkel *m*, Hinterschliff *m* der Fase
land surveying Feldmessung *f*
land wear Verschleißmarkenbreite *f*
land width of the face Breite *f* der Spanflächenfase
land width of the flank Breite *f* der Freiflächenfase
landing Stockwerksflur *m*
landing staying Podest *nt*
lane Gang *m*, Gasse *f*, Spur *f*, Fahrbahn *f*
lane-independent nicht spurgebunden
lane-specific gasspezifisch
language Sprache *f*
language extent Sprachumfang *m*
lantern pin rack Triebstockzahnstange *f*
lap läppen, überlappen
lap carrier Läppscheibenträger *m*
lap joint Übergreifungsstoß *m*, Flächennaht *f*
lap joint with compression weld Überlappstoß *m* mit Quetschnaht
lap joint with lap weld Überlappstoß *m* mit Überlappnaht
lap over Übergreifen *nt*; übergreifen
lap plate holder Läppscheibenträger *m*

lap seam Überlappschweißung *f*
lap test piece Überlappprüfstück *nt*
lap weld Überlappschweißung *f*; überlappt schweißen
lap width Überlappbreite *f*
lap-grinding Läppschleifen *nt*
lapped area Überlappfläche *f*
lapper Läpparbeiter *m*
lapping Läppen *nt*
lapping abrasive Läppkorn *nt*, Läppmittel *nt*
lapping arbor Läppdorn *m*
lapping block Läppplatte *f*
lapping cage Läppkäfig *m*
lapping compound Läppmittel *nt*
lapping compound feed Läppmittelzuführung *f*
lapping duration Läppdauer *f*
lapping mandrel Läppdorn *m*
lapping mixture Läppgemisch *nt*
lapping mixture film Läppgemischfilm *m*
lapping mixture transport Läppgemischförderung *f*
lapping plate Läppplatte *f*
lapping pressure Läppdruck *m*
lapping sleeve Läpphülse *f*
lapping speed Läppgeschwindigkeit *f*
lapping spindle Läppdorn *m*, Läppspindel *f*
lapping technique Läppverfahren *nt*
lapping tool Läppwerkzeug *nt*
lapping velocity Läppgeschwindigkeit *f*
lapping wheel Läppscheibe *f*
large groß, weit, geräumig
large batch production serienmäßige Herstellung *f*
large hole boring Großlochbohrung *f*
large lathe Großdrehmaschine *f*
large lift großer Hub *m*
large load carrier Großladungsträger *m*
large size Großformat *nt*
large sized großformatig
large valves *pl* Großarmaturen *fpl*
large-area forced wetting großflächige Zwangsbenetzung *f*
large-area proportional counter Großflächenproportionalzählrohr *nt*
largeness *(Geräumigkeit)* Weite *f*
large-patch production Großserien-

fertigung *f*
large-scaled weld surface grobschuppige Nahtoberfläche *f*
large-surface flächig
laser lasern; Laserstrahl *m*
laser application Laseranwendung *f*
laser beam Laserstrahl *m*
laser beam alloy Laserstrahllegieren *nt*
laser beam cutting Laserstrahlschneiden *nt*
laser beam guide Laserstrahlführung *f*
laser beam polarization welding Laserstrahlpolarisationsschweißen *nt*
laser beam welding Laserstrahlschweißen *nt*
laser beaming Laserstrahlung *f*
laser bore Laserbohrung *f*
laser camera Kameralaser *m*
laser coder Lasercodierer *m*
laser cutting equipment Laserschneidanlage *f*
laser cutting plant Laserschneidanlage *f*
laser eroding Laserabtragen *nt*
laser focus Laserfokus *m*
laser graving Lasergravur *f*
laser hardening Laserhärten *nt*
laser hole Laserbohrung *f*
laser manufacturing Laserbearbeitung *f*
laser material Lasermaterial *nt*
laser material machining system Lasermaterialbearbeitungsanlage *f*
laser melting up Laserumschmelzen *nt*
laser principle Laserprinzip *nt*
laser printer Laserdrucker *m*
laser scanner Laserscanner *m*
laser soldering Laserlöten *nt*
laser species Laserart *f*
laser support Laserunterstützung *f*
laser surface coating Laseroberflächenbehandlung *f*
laser surface finishing Laseroberflächenbehandlung *f*
laser system Lasersystem *nt*
laser use Laseranwendung *f*
laser welder Laserschweißgerät *nt*
laser welding Laserschweißen *nt*
laser welding extrusion of filler material Lichtstrahlextrusionsschweißen *nt*
laser welding plant Laserschweißanlage *f*
lash zurren
lashing ring Zurrring *m*
lashing strap Zurrgurt *m*
lashings Haltekette *f*, Zurrmittel *nt*
last halten, bestehen bleiben, dauern
last stage of annealing Schlussglühen *nt*
lasting haltbar
latch Riegel *m*, Raste *f*, Klinke *f*, Schnapper *m*; rasten, einrasten
latch Raste *f*; rasten, einrasten
latch-and-fire mechanism federgespannter Auslösemechanismus *m*
latch pin Raststift *m*, Indexstift *m*
lateral seitlich, quer, in Querrichtung *f*
lateral adjustment Seiteneinstellung *f*, Seitenverstellung *f*
lateral and front attachment Dreiseitenstapelanbaugerät *nt*
lateral and front stacking truck Dreiseitenstapler *m*
lateral attachment Seitenstapelanbaugerät *nt*
lateral bearing zone *(von Rohrleitungen)* Ausladung *f*
lateral bend specimen Seitenbiegeprobe *f*
lateral clearance Seitenausladung *f*
lateral feed seitlicher Vorschub *m*, Quervorschub *m*
lateral fitting Ansatzstück *nt*
lateral force Seitenkraft *f*, Querkraft *f*
lateral grinding Seitenschleifen *nt*
lateral guide Seitenführung *f*
lateral handling Seitenschub *m*
lateral handling device Seitenschieber *m*, seitlich ausfahrendes LAM
lateral handling facilities Seitenschub *m*
lateral position Seitenlage *f*
lateral slide Seitenschieber *m*
lateral stability Seitenstabilität *f*
lateral stacking Quereinstapelung *f*
lateral stacking truck Seitenstapler *m*, Zweiseitenstapler *m*
lateral static stability statische Seitenstabilität *f*

lateral support Querauflage *f*
lateral truck Seitenstapler *m*
lateral undercut Randkerbe *f*
lath Leiste *f*, Stab *m*
lathe Drehbank *f*, Drehmaschine *f*
lathe apron Drehmaschinenschlossplatte *f*, Schlossplatte *f*
lathe arbour Drehdorn *m*
lathe bed Drehmaschinenbett *nt*
lathe carriage Drehmaschinensupport *m*
lathe carrier Drehherz *nt*
lathe centre Drehspitze *f*, Körnerspitze *f*, Spitze *f* einer Drehmaschinenspindel
lathe chuck Drehfutter *nt*
lathe cutting tool Drehmeißel *m*, Drehstahl *m*
lathe dog Drehherz *nt*, Spannklaue *f*
lathe for chucking and bar work Drehmaschine *f* für Futter- und Stangenarbeit
lathe for chucking work Drehmaschine *f* für Futterarbeiten
lathe lead-screw Drehmaschinenleitspindel *f*
lathe mandrel Drehdorn *m*
lathe operator Dreher *m*
lathe rest Drehmaschinensupport *m*
lathe room Dreherei *f*
lathe shop Dreherei *f*
lathe spindle Drehspindel *f*, Hauptspindel *f* der Drehmaschine, Arbeitsspindel *f* der Drehmaschine
lathe spindle axis Drehspindelachse *f*
lathe steady Drehmaschinensupport *m*
lathe tailstock Drehmaschinenreitstock *m*
lathe tool Drehwerkzeug *nt*, Drehmeißel *m*, Drehstahl *m*, Abdrehwerkzeug *nt*
lathe tool holder Drehmeißelhalter *m*
lathe with double track bed Drehmaschine *f* mit Zweibahnbett
lathe with lead screw and feed rod Leit- und Zugspindeldrehmaschine *f*
lathe work Dreharbeit *f*
latitudinal quer
latitudinal movement Querfahren *nt*
latitudinal truck Querfahrwagen *nt*

lattice Gitterrost *m*
lattice constant Gitterkonstante *f*
lattice design Fachwerkbauweise *f*
lattice vacancy defect Gitterfehlstelle *f*
launch 1. einführen **2.** *(Vorhaben)* Projektstart *m*
launch customer Erstbesteller *m*
launch order Erstbestellung *f*
level control Füllstandsmessung *f*
lavender-blue lavendelblau
law Gesetz *nt*
law of friction forces Kraftschlussgesetz *nt*
law of generation Erzeugungsgesetz *nt*
law of gravitation Schwerkraftprinzip *nt*
law of propagation of errors Fehlerfortpflanzungsgesetz *nt*
lay 1. anordnen, verlegen, legen, setzen **2.** (ein Seil) Schlagart *f*; schlagen
lay cable Kabel verlegen
lay even glattlegen
lay on auflegen
lay out auslegen, anreißen
lay underneath unterlegen
layer Lage *f*, Schicht *f*, Überzug *m*
layer by layer lagenweise
layer collecting station Lagensammelstation *f*
layer deposit station Lagenabgabestation *f*
layer glue system Lagenbeleimung *f*
layer layout Schichtanordnung *f*
layer of alloy Legierungsschicht *f*
layer of joint sealing compound Vergussmassenschicht *f*
layer of moulding material Formmasseschicht *f*
layer of resin powder Harzpulverschicht *f*
layer pad Zwischenlage *f*, Zwischenbogen *m*
layer pad inserter/remover Zwischenlagenaufleger/-abheber *m*
layer pad insertion Zwischenbogeneinlage *f*
layer pattern Schichtanordnung *f*
layer picking Lagenentnahme *f*
layer preparation table Schichtenbildungstisch *m*

layer process Absenkverfahren *nt*
layer related to the metal arteigene Schicht *f*
layer sheet Zwischenlage *f*, Zwischenbogen *m*
layer sheet dispenser Zwischenlageneinleger *m*
layer sheet spacer Zwischenlage *f*
layer strength Schichtfestigkeit *f*
layer structure Lagenstruktur *f*
layer transfer Lagenumladung *f*
layer transfer lift platform Zwischenlagenhubplattform *f*
layering Schichtung *f*
layering pattern Lagenmuster *nt*, Lagenschema *nt*
layer-wise corrosion schichtförmige Korrosion *f*
lay-flat flachliegend
laying Verlegen *nt*
laying accuracy Verlegegenauigkeit *f*
laying compatibility Verlegbarkeit *f*
laying in made ground Verlegen *nt* in Anschüttmasse
laying out Anreißen *nt*
laying out work Anreißarbeit *f*
laying-out plate Anreißplatte *f*
laying-out tool Richtmittel *nt*
layout Plan *m*, Grundriss *m*, Auslegung *f*, Anordnung *f*, Anriss *m*, Schaltung *f*, Anreißen *nt*
layout man Anreißer *m*
layout method Anordnungsverfahren *nt*
layout planning Layoutplanung *f*
layout plate Anreißplatte *f*
layout point Anordnungspunkt *m*
layout program Layoutprogramm *nt*
layout step Anordnungsschritt *m*
layout tool Anreißwerkzeug *nt*
layout variation Anordnungsvariante *f*
leach Lauge *f*
lead 1. *(steuern, lenken)* leiten, führen **2.** *(Werkstoff, Material)* Blei *nt* **3.** *(Senkblei)* Lot *nt* **4.** *(Gewinde)* Gang *m*, Ganghöhe *f*, Gewindesteigung *f*, Steigung *f*, Steigungshöhe *f*
lead across führen über
lead angle Anschnittwinkel *m*, Schrägungswinkel *m*, Einstellergänzungswinkel *m*
lead bar Leitlineal *nt*
lead bronze Bleibronze *f*
lead equivalent value Bleigleichwert *m*
lead error compensation Steigungsfehlerkorrektur *f*
lead glass panel Bleiglasplatte *f*
lead into einleiten
lead lined grid Bleiraster *nt*
lead moment Gegenmoment *nt*
lead of feed screw Steigung *f* der Tischvorschubspindel
lead of helix Steigung *f* der Schraubenlinie, Drallsteigerung *f*
lead off/away abführen
lead rubber curtain Bleigummivorhang *m*
lead screw Spindel *f*, Leitspindel *f*, Verstellspindel *f*, Spannspindel *f*
lead seal Plombe *f*, Plombenverschluss *m*
lead sealing Verplombung *f*
lead through herausführen
lead time Vorlaufzeit *f*, Beschaffungszeit *f*, Durchlaufzeit *f*
lead variation Steigungshöhenabweichung *f*
lead-acid battery Bleisäurebatterie *f*, Bleiakkumulator *m*
leaded verplombt
leader 1. *(Person)* Leiter *m* **2.** *(Anhaltspunkt)* Bezug *m*, Bezugslinie *f* **3.** *(Zeit)* Vorlauf *m*
leading vorauseilend, voreilend
leading angular position variation voreilende Drehstellungsabweichung *f*
leading cutting edge Hauptschneide *f*
leading edge Vorderkante *f*
leading flame vorlaufende Flamme *f*
leading off Abführen *nt*
leading out ausgehend
leading pinion cutter flank vorlaufende Schneidradflanke *f*
leading tool edge abfallende Schneide *f*, negative Überhöhung *f* der Schneide *m*
leadless flach
lead-pipe nozzle Bleirohrtülle *f*
lead-screw machine Leitspindelma-

schine *f*
lead screw mechanism Spindelantrieb *m*
lead screw nut Mutterschloss *nt*, Schlossmutter *f*
lead-up Vorbereitungsphase *f*
leaf Lasche *f*, Blatt *nt*, Türflügel *m*
leaf chain Laschenkette *f*, Flyerkette *f*
leaf mechanical chain Laschenkette *f*, Flyerkette *f*
leaf type chain Flyerkette *f*
leaflet feeder Beipackzettelzuführmaschine *f*
leak undicht sein, lecken, auslaufen; Leck *nt*
leak preventing device Lecksicherungsgerät *nt*
leak testing apparatus Dichtprüfgerät *nt*
leak tightness Dichtheit *f*
leakage Leck *nt*, Leckage *f*Leck *nt* Undichtheit *f*, Lecken *nt*, Auslaufen *nt*
leakage current Leckstrom *m*
leakage path Kriechstrecke *f*
leakage radiation Durchlassstrahlung *f*
leakiness Undichtheit *f*
leaking undicht; Undichtwerden *nt*
leak-off line Leckgasleitung *f*
leak-proof dicht, abgedichtet, leckdicht
leaky undicht
leap springen; Sprung *m*
learning aids Lernmittel *ntpl*
learning mode Lernmodus *m*
lease vermieten
leasing Vermietung *f*
leasing instalment Leasingrate *f*
least favourable ungünstigst
least significant bit niederwertigste Binärstelle *f*
leather cup Ledermanschettendichtung *f*
leather extract Lederauszug *m*
leave auslaufen, verlassen, abgehen, absteigen (von), hinausfahren, abfahren, ausfahren
leaving Auslaufen *nt*, Verlassen *nt*
leakage *(Flüssigkeit)* Durchschlag *m*
left links
left bracket Klammer *f* auf
left flank Linksflanke *f*

left hand links, linksseitig
left hand motion Linkslauf *m*
left most maximum linkes Maximum *nt*
left side linke Seite *f*
left-bent tool gebogener linker Meißel *m*
left-cut tool linker Meißel *m*
left-hand column linker Ständer *m*
left-hand cutting linksschneidend
left-hand cutting tool linker Meißel *m*
left-hand flank profile Linksflankenprofil *nt*
left-hand helical linkssteigend
left-hand helical cutting edge Schneide *f* mit Linksdrall
left-hand helical tooth system Linksschrägverzahnung *f*
left-hand helix Linksschraube *f*
left-hand involute Linksevolvente *f*
left-hand nut Mutter *f* mit Linksgewinde
left-hand parting tool linker Stechmeißel *m*
left-hand path of contact Linksflankeneingriffslinie *f*
left-hand pitch *(e. Verzahnung)* Linksteilung *f*
left-hand planing tool linker Hobelmeißel *m*
left-hand rail head linker Quersupport *m*
left-hand rotation Drehrichtung *f* nach links
left-hand rotation Linksdrehung *f*
left-hand roughing tool linker Schruppmeißel *m*
left-hand side linke Seite *f*
left-hand spiral Linksdrall *m*
left-hand spiral tooth milling cutter Fräser *m* mit linksgängiger Spiralverzahnung
left-hand teeth linkssteigende Verzahnung *f*
left-hand thread Linksgewinde *nt*
left-hand tooth surface Linksflanke *f*
left-hand twist Linksdrall *m*
left-hand version Linksausführung *f*
left-handed helical motion Linksschraubbewegung *f*

left-handed rotating linksläufig
left-offset cutting tool abgesetzter linker Seitenmeißel *m*
leftward nach links
leg Schenkel *m*, Zweig *m*
leg length Schenkellänge *f*
legend Legende *f*
legibility Lesbarkeit *f*, Leserlichkeit *f*, Lesesicherheit *f*
legible lesbar
leisure facilities Freizeitgeräte *ntpl*
length of solder wire Lotdrahtabschnitt *m*
length Länge *f*, Abschnitt *m*, Teilstrecke *f*
length checking practice Längenprüftechnik *f*
length feed stop Längsanschlag *m*
length measurement Längenmessung *f*
length measuring instrument Längenmessgerät *nt*
length monitoring Längenüberwachung *f*
length of approach path Eintritteingriffsstrecke *f*
length of bay Kanallänge *f*
length of burning time Abbrandzeit *f*
length of cut Schnittlänge *f*
length of engagement tragende Gewindelänge *f*
length of fit Passlänge *f*
length of lay Schlaglänge *f*
length of level reach Haltungslänge *f*
length of natural frequency method Resonanzlängenverfahren *nt*
length of overhang Auskraglänge *f*
length of path of contact Eingriffsfläche *f*, Eingriffsstrecke *f*
length of pipe Rohrstrecke *f*
length of projection of thread (or bolt) end Schraubenüberstand *m*
length of recess path Austrittseingriffsstrecke *f*
length of stroke Hublänge *f*
length of thread dimension Gewindelängenmaß *nt*
length of time Dauer *f*
length of traverse Verschiebeweg *m*
length ratio Längenverhältnis *nt*
length stop Längsanschlag *m*, Längenanschlag *m*
length verification practice Längenprüftechnik *f*
length wear Längenverschleiß *m*
lengthen verlängern, längen, strecken, recken, ausdehnen in Längsrichtung
lengthen of feed Vorschubweglängen *fpl*
lengthening Dehnen *nt*, Längen *nt*, Verlängerung *f*
lengthening of pressing Längenstauchung *f*
lengthening piece Verlängerungsstück *nt*
lengths of fibre arranged in superimposed layers *pl* aufeinandergeschichtete Faserstoffbahnen *fpl*
lengthwise längs, längsseitig, in Längsrichtung *f*
lengthwise direction Längsrichtung *f*
lengthy lang
lens Objektiv *nt*, Linse *f*
lens carrier Objektivträger *m*
lens combination Linsensystem *nt*
lens current Linsenstrom *m*
lens system Linsensystem *nt*
lenticular linsenförmig
lenticular expansion joint Linsenausgleicher *m*
Lenz's law Lenzsche Regel *f*
less or equal to kleiner gleich, kleiner oder gleich
less than kleiner als, unter
less than or equal to kleiner gleich
lessen nachlassen, vermindern
let vermieten
let down absetzen
let in einführen
letter Buchstabe *m*; bezeichnen mit Buchstaben, beschriften
letter symbol reference Buchstabenkennung *f*
lettering Beschriftung *f*
lettering stencil Schriftschablone *f*
level Niveau *nt*, Pegel *m*, Grad *m*, Stand *m*, Stufe *f*, Höhe *f*, Waagerechte *f*, Horizontale *f*; nivellieren, justieren, richten (auf), abgleichen, in Waage *f* bringen; waagerecht, horizontal,

eben
level distribution Pegelverteilung *f*
level filling machine Höhenfüllmaschine *f*
level gauge Fühlhebelmessgerät *nt*
level luffing crane Wippkran *m*
level measurement Niveaumessung *f*
level of abstraction Abstraktionsgrad *m*
level of cleanliness Reinheitsgrad *m*
level of loading Beanspruchungsniveau *nt*
level of manufacturing Fertigungstiefe *f*
level of safety Sicherheitsniveau *nt*
level out ausgleichen, ausrichten
level recorder Pegelschreiber *m*
level sensor Niveausensor *m*
level tolerance Ebenheitstoleranz *f*, Niveautoleranz *f*
levelling Justierung *f*, Einebnung *f*
levelling agent Egalisiermittel *nt*
levelling disc Einstellscheibe *f*
levelling screw Justierschraube *f*
levelness Ebenheit *f*
lever Bedienelement *nt*, Bedienhebel *m*, Hebel *m*, Arm *m*
lever action Hebelwirkung *f*
lever arm Hebelarm *m*
lever brake Handbremse *f*
lever control Hebelschaltung *f*
lever gauging Füllstandsmessung *f*
lever manipulation Hebelbetätigung *f*
lever shear Hebelschere *f*
lever spring balance Hebelfederwaage *f*
leverage Gestänge *nt*, Hebelsystem *nt*, Übersetzung *f* eines Hebels
lever-controlled hebelgeschaltet
lever-controlled lathe Drehmaschine *f* mit Hebelschaltung
lever-operated hebelbetätigt
L-fitting L-Stutzen *m*
LHD (load handling device) LAM (Lastaufnahmemittel) *nt*
L-head fork Schwenkschubgabel *f*
liability finanzielle Haftung *f*, Pflicht *f*
liability insurance association Berufsgenossenschaft *f*
liable to identification identifizierbar
liable to rust rostgefährdet

liberate freisetzen
lid Deckel *m*, Klappe *f*
lidded oval pipe gestürztes eiförmiges Rohr *nt*
lie liegen
lie at right angles to each other rechtwinklig zueinander liegen
lie crossing over each other kreuzend übereinander liegen
lie on/against aufliegen, liegen auf
lie with surfaces one above the other flächig aufeinanderliegen
liability to brittle fracture Sprödbruchneigung *f*
life Haltbarkeit *f*, Lebensdauer *f*, Standzeit *f*
life capacity of a tool Stückzahl *f*, die das Werkzeug während seiner Lebensdauer fertigen kann
life cycle Lebenszyklus *m*
life expectancy Nutzungsdauer *f*
life of rust protection Rostschutzdauer *f*
life of the cutting edge Standzeit *f* der Schneide
life under full load Volllastlebensdauer *f*
lifetime Lebensdauer *f*
lift 1. *(Lasten heben)* Lift *m*, Hub *m*, Aufzug *m*, Vertikalhub *m*, Höhe *f*; anheben, hochheben **2.** *(Luft)* lüften
lift acceleration Hubbeschleunigung *f*
lift and tilt cylinder Hub- und Neigezylinder *m*
lift assembly Hubgerüst *nt*
lift chain Hubkette *f*
lift circuit Hubkreis *m*
lift cylinder Hubzylinder *m*
lift cylinder trunnion Hubzylinderdrehzapfen *m*
lift height Hubhöhe *f*
lift of loading device Vertikalhub *m* der Ladeeinrichtung
lift out ausheben, herausheben
lift out pallets Paletten ausheben
lift rotate movement Dreh-Hub-Bewegung *f*
lift rotate station Dreh-Hub-Station *f*
lift rotate unit Dreh-Hub-Station *f*
lift system Liftsystem *nt*

lift table Palettenladungstisch *m*
lift truck Hubwagen *m*, Flurförderzeug *nt* mit Hubeinrichtung
lift unit Hubeinrichtung *f*
liftable hebbar
liftable driver's seat hebbarer Fahrersitz *m*
lifted angehoben
lifted load Hublast *f*
lifted load coefficient Hublastbeiwert *m*
lifting Abhebung *f*, Hub *m*, Abhub *m*, Abhubbewegung *f*
lifting accessories Hubeinrichtung *f*
lifting and lowering movement Hub- und Senkbewegung *f*
lifting and tilting system Hub- und Neigungssystem *nt*
lifting apparatus Hubeinrichtung *f*
lifting appliance Hebezeug *nt*
lifting assembly Hubeinrichtung *f*, Hubgerüst *nt*
lifting beam Hubtraverse *f*
lifting cable Hubseil *nt*
lifting capacity Hubleistung *f*, Tragfähigkeit *f*
lifting carriage Hubwagen *m*
lifting category Hubklasse *f*
lifting chain Hubkette *f*
lifting class Hubklasse *f*
lifting cog *(Maschine, Nocken)* Zahn *m*
lifting component Hubbauteil *nt*, Palettenladungstisch *m*
lifting cylinder Hubzylinder *m*
lifting device Hebezeug *nt*, Hubvorrichtung *f*
lifting distance Hubstrecke *f*
lifting element Tragmittel *nt*
lifting equipment Hebeeinrichtung *f*
lifting gear Hebezeug *nt*, Hubwerk *nt*
lifting gear drum Hubwerkstrommel *f*
lifting hook Lasthaken *m*
lifting hook nut Lasthakenmutter *f*
lifting hook shank Lasthakenschaft *m*, Hakenschaft *m*
lifting jack Hubzylinder *m*, Hebebock *m*
lifting load Hublast *f*
lifting location Anschlagpunkt *m*
lifting magnet Hebemagnet *m*, Hubmagnet *m*, Lastmagnet *m*
lifting means Hubeinrichtung *f*
lifting mechanism Abhebeeinrichtung *f*, Hebevorrichtung *f*, Hubeinrichtung *f*, Hebetechnik *f*
lifting movement Hubbewegung *f*
lifting nut Bügelmutter *f*
lifting operation Hebevorgang *m*
lifting out Aushub *m*
lifting path Hubweg *m*
lifting platform Hubplattform *f*, Hubtisch *m*
lifting point Anschlagpunkt *m*
lifting power Hubkraft *f*
lifting ram Hubzylinder *m*
lifting speed Hubgeschwindigkeit *f*
lifting station Hubstation *f*
lifting system Hubeinrichtung *f*, Hubsystem *nt*
lifting table Hubtisch *m*
lifting technology Hebetechnik *f*
lifting truck Hubwagen *m*
lifting unit Lastaufnahmemittel (LAM) *nt*
lifting work platform Hubbühne *f*
lifting/traction unit Trag-/Zugmittel *nt*
lift-off abheben, Abreißen *nt*
lift-out device Aushubeinrichtung *f*
lift-up lid Klappdeckel *m*
ligament Steg *m*, Band *nt*
light 1. Licht *nt*, Lampe *f*, Beleuchtung *f*; zum Leuchten bringen; hell 2. *(Gewicht, Masse)* leicht
Light Amplification by Simulated Emission of Modification (LASER) LASER *m* (Licht angeregte Strahlung emittierender Resonator, Lichtverstärkung durch angeregte Strahlungsaussendung)
light amplifier Lichtverstärker *m*
light attenuation factor Lichtschwächungsfaktor *m*
light barrier Lichtschranke *f*
light beam Lichtbündel *nt*
light beam cross-section Lichtfleck *m*
light beam path Lichtbündelung *f*
light beam welding by extrusion of filler material Lichtstrahlextrusionsschweißen *nt*
light booster Lichtverstärker *m*

light colour Lichtfarbe *f*
light cone Lichtvisierblende *f*
light curtain Lichtvorhang *m*
light cut Schnitt *m* mit geringer Spantiefe, leichter Schnitt *m*
light diaphragm Lichtvisierblende *f*
light direction Lichtrichtung *f*
light emitting diode LED
light emitter Lichtsender *m*
light emitter-receiver Lichtsendeempfänger *m*
light emitting diode (LED) Leuchtdiode *f*, Lumineszenzdiode *f*, LED-Anzeige *f*
light equipment Beleuchtungseinrichtung *f*
light flash Lichtblitz *m*
light flux Lichtstrom *m*
light gap Lichtspalt *m*
light gap method Lichtspaltverfahren *nt*
light grid Lichtgitter *nt*
light impulse Lichtimpuls *m*
light in weight leicht
light insensitivity Lichtunempfindlichkeit *f*
light metal Leichtmetall *nt*
light metal alloy Leichtmetalllegierung *f*
light passage Lichtdurchlass *m*
light pen Lichtgriffel *m*
light point Bildpunkt *m*
light precision engineering Feinwerktechnik *f*
light proportion Lichtverhältnis *nt*
light quantum Lichtquant *nt*
light receiver Lichtempfänger *m*
light reproduction Lichtwiedergabe *f*
light roller blind Lichtvorhang *m*, Vorhangeinweglichtschranke *f*
light scanner Lichttaster *m*
light scattering coefficient Lichtstreukoeffizient *m*
light sensitivity Lichtempfindlichkeit *f*
light sensor Lichttaster *m*
light signal Lichtsignal *nt*
light source Lichtquelle *f*, Beleuchtungseinrichtung *f*
light stabilizer Lichtstabilisator *m*
light transmittance spektraler Transmissionsgrad *m*
light veil Lichtschleier *m*
light wave Lichtwelle *f*
light-duty plain milling cutter Walzenfräser *m*
lightfast lichtfest
light-gauge steel construction Stahlleichtbau *m*
lighting Beleuchtung *f*, Leuchten *nt*, Lampen *fpl*
lighting equipment Beleuchtungseinrichtung *f*
lighting intensity Beleuchtungsstärke *f*
lighting mains Lichtnetz *nt*
lightly adhering rust locker sitzender Post *m*
lightly coloured leicht gefärbt
lightning Blitzschlag *m*
lights Lampen *fpl*, Leuchten *nt*
light-sensitive coating lichtempfindliche Schicht *f*
light-slit method Lichtschnittverfahren *nt*
lightweight pipe leichtes Rohr *nt*
lightweight roof structure Leichtdachkonstruktion *f*
light-weight type leichte Ausführung *f*
lignite Braunkohle *f*
like material artgleicher Werkstoff *m*
like soft rubber weichgummiartig
limit Toleranz *f*, Grenze *f*, Grenzwert *m*, Endstellung *f*, Ende *nt*; begrenzen, umgrenzen, beschränken, einschränken
limit cone angle Grenzkegelwinkel *m*
limit distance Grenzabstand *m*
limit exceeded Grenze überschritten
limit for preventing injuries Verletzungsgrenze *f*
limit gauge Grenzlehre *f*
limit gauge system Grenzlehrensystem *nt*
limit gauging Grenzlehrung *f*
limit of detection Erkenntnisgrenze *f*
limit of elasticity Streckengrenze *f*
limit of elasticity in bending Biegeelastizitätsgrenze *f*
limit of error Fehlergrenze *f*
limit of landmarks Gemarkungsgrenze *f*
limit of performance Leistungsgrenze *f*

limit of recrystallization Rekristallisationsgrenze *f*
limit of temperature Grenztemperatur *f*
limit of tolerance Abmaß *nt*
limit of travel Fahrbegrenzung *f*, Fahrtendbegrenzung *f*
limit of variation Streugrenze *f*
limit plug gage Grenzlehrdorn *m*
limit plug gauge with spherical lock Grenzlehrdorn *m* mit Kugelbefestigung
limit plug gauge with trilock Grenzlehrdorn *m* mit Sternnutbefestigung
limit pulse Grenzimpuls *m*
limit risk Grenzrisiko *nt*
limit snap gauge Grenzgewinderachenlehre *f*, Grenzrachenlehre *f*
limit stop Anschlagbolzen *m*, Endanschlag *m*, Anschlag *m* zur Begrenzung der Bewegung
limit stop roller switch Rollenendschalter *m*
limit switch Endschalter *m*, Endtaster *m*, Grenzschalter *m*, Grenztaster *m*, Begrenzungsschalter *m*, Endausschalter *m*
limit value Grenzwert *m*
limit value transmitter Grenzwertgeber *m*
limit violation Grenzwertverletzung *f*
limitation Begrenzung *f*, Beschränkung *f*
limitation of forces Kraftbegrenzung *f*
limitation of stroke Hubbegrenzung *f*
limitation of tolerance zones Einschränkung *f* von Toleranzfeldern
limitation of travel Endbegrenzung *f*, Hubbegrenzung *f*
limited duration zeitlich begrenzt
limited in time zeitlich begrenzt
limited quantity production Kleinreihenfertigung *f*
limiting Beschränken *nt*
limiting conditions Randbedingung *f*
limiting conditions for generating Erzeugungsgrenzbedingungen *fpl*
limiting curve Grenzkurve *f*
limiting deflection Grenzdurchbiegung *f*
limiting deviation Grenzabmaß *nt*
limiting device Endabschaltung *f*
limiting diameter Grenzmaß *nt*, Grenzdurchmesser *m*
limiting dimension Grenzmaß *nt*
limiting energy Grenzenergie *f*
limiting number of load cycles Grenzlastspielzahl *f*
limiting number of pieces Grenzstückzahl *f*
limiting signal Grenzsignal *nt*
limiting signal transmission Grenzsignalgabe *f*
limiting size Grenzmaß *nt*
limiting size of workpiece Werkstückgrenzmaß *nt*
limiting switch Begrenzungsschalter *m*
limiting value Grenzwert *m*
limits of travel paths Fahrspurbegrenzung *f*
linage Verkettung *f*
line 1. *(Schrift)* Schriftzeile *f*, Zeile *f*, 2. *(Konstruktion)* Linie *f*, Strich *m* 3. *(Hohlkörper)* auskleiden, ausgießen, ausfüttern 4. *(Rohre)* Leitung *f*, Rohrleitung *f*, Strang *m*
line assembly work Fließmontage *f*
line boring bar Führungsbohrstange *f*
line by line zeilenweise
line contact Linienberührung *f*
line copy milling Zeilennachformfräsen *nt*
line destination Strangadresse *f*
line display Zeilenanzeige *f*
line drop Spannungsabfall *m*
line equipment Leitungszubehör *nt*
line gauge block Strichendmaß *nt*
line graduation Strichskala *f*
line group Liniengruppe *f*
line input zeilenweise Eingabe *f*
line joint Liniennaht *f*
line marking Furchen *nt*, Anreißen *nt*
line of action Wirkungslinie *f*
line of centres Mittenlinie *f*
line of contact Berührungslinie *f*, Eingriffslinie *f*
line of drain pipes Dränstrang *m*
line of electric flux Feldlinie *f*
line of engagement of left-hand tooth surfaces Linksflankeneingriffslinie *f*

line of engagement of right-hand tooth surfaces Rechtsflankeneingriffslinie *f*
line of intersection Schnittlinie *f*
line of tangential section Tangentialschnittlinie *f*
line of the order Auftragszeile *f*
line operation Leitungsbetrieb *m*
line out anreißen
line scale Strichskala *f*
line scanning Zeilenabtastung *f*
line setup Reihenaufspannung *f*
line spacing Linienabstand *m*, Zeilensprung *m*
line trace for profiling operations Fühler *m* für Nachformarbeit nach Zeichnung
line transient Wischer *m*
line up ausrichten
line vibrations Leitungsschwingungen *fpl*
line weld Liniennaht *f*
line weld on lap joint Liniennaht *f* mit Überlappstoß
linear linear, linearisiert, linienhaft
linear collision stopping power lineares Stoßbremsvermögen *nt*
linear contact Linienberührung
linear corrosion zeilenförmige Korrosion *f*
linear dimension unit Längenmaßeinheit *f*
linear drive Linearantrieb *m*
linear expansion Linearausdehnung *f*
linear indexing geradlinige Längsteilung *f*, Längenteilung *f*
linear interpolation Linearinterpolation *f*
linear mean value linearer Mittelwert *m*
linear measuring instrument Längenmessgerät *nt*
linear misalignment of the edges Kantenversatz *m*
linear motor Linearmotor *m*
linear pitch Teilung *f* einer Planverzahnung
linear porosity Porenkette *f*
linear radiation stopping power lineares Strahlungsbremsvermögen *nt*

linear resistance ohmscher Widerstand *m*
linear scale lineare Skala *f*
linear scale division lineare Skalenteilung *f*
linear size Längenmaß *nt*
linear storage Linienlagerung *f*
linear transmission of force to the assembly linienförmige Krafteinleitung *f*
linear weight Längengewicht *nt*
linear weight force Längengewichtskraft *f*
linearity deviation Linearitätsabweichung *f*
linearity error Linearitätsabweichung *f*
linearization Linearisierung *f*
line-by-line milling Zeilenfräsen *nt*
line-by-line milling method Zeilenfräsverfahren *nt*
line-by-line milling operation Zeilenfräsarbeit *f*
lined pipe Auskleidungsrohr *nt*
line-emission radiation Linienemissionsstrahlung *f*
liner Unterlegstreifen *m*
liner out Anreißer *m*
lines of gravity method Schwerelinienverfahren *nt*
line-scanning light scanner Zeilenlichttaster *m*
line-scanning method Strichrasterverfahren *nt*
line shaft Transmissionswelle *f*
line shaft transmission Transmissionsantrieb *m*
line starter Motorschalter *m*
linguistic sprachlich
linguistic rule linguistische Regel *f*
linguistic term linguistischer Term *m*
linguistic variable linguistische Variable *f*
lining Auskleiden *nt*, Ausfütterung *f*, Verkleidung *f*, Belag *m*, Futter *nt*
lining material Auskleidung *f*
lining out Anreißen *nt*
lining-up Fluchten *nt*
limit cone Grenzkegel *m*
link Bindeglied *nt*, Verbindungsglied *m*, Verbindungsteil *nt*, Verknüpfung *f*, Ge-

lenk *nt*, Glied *nt*; verketten, verbinden, aneinander befestigen, koppeln, verknüpfen
link address Verknüpfungsadresse *f*
link circuit *(Schaltung)* Verbindungsleitung *f*
link drive Kulissenantrieb *m*
link fault Kopplungsstörung *f*
link function Verknüpfungsfunktion *f*
link rod Kulissenstange *f*
linkage 1. Koppelgetriebe *nt*, Kopplung *f* 2. *(Antrieb)* Getriebezug *m* 3. *(IT)* Verknüpfung *f*, Verbindung *f*
linkage of bars Gestänge *nt*
linkage rods *pl* Gestänge *nt*
linkage system Gestängesystem *nt*
linkage wiring Verknüpfung *f*
linked zugehörig, zugeordnet
linking Kopplung *f*
lintel Sturz *m*
lintfree cloth faserfreies Tuch *nt*
lip Schneide *f*, Lippe *f*
lip angle Schnittwinkel *m*, Schneidenwinkel *m*, Meißelwinkel *m*, Keilwinkel *m*
lip clearance Hinterschliff *m*
lip-type of packing Manschette *f*
liquate ausschmelzen
liquation crack Aufschmelzungsriss *m*
liquation process Seigerung *f*
liquefied gas Flüssiggas *nt*
liquefied petroleum gas (LPG) Flüssiggas *nt*
liquefied petroleum gas (LPG) engine Flüssiggasmotor *m*
liquefied petroleum gas (LPG) truck Flürförderzeug *nt* mit Flüssiggasmotor
liquefy schmelzen
liquid flüssig; Flüssigkeit *f*
liquid adhesive putty flüssiger Klebkitt *m*
liquid bag-in-box fill and seal machine Bag-in-Box-Füll- und -Verschließmaschine *f* für Flüssigkeiten
liquid column Flüssigkeitssäule *f*
liquid filler flüssiges Lot *nt*
liquid filling capacity Fließfüllungsvermögen *nt*
liquid filter Flüssigkeitsfilter *m*
liquid glass Wasserglas *nt*
liquid heat transfer medium flüssiger Energieträger *m*
liquid honing Druckstrahlläppen *nt*, Strahlläppen *nt*, Flüssigkeitshonen *nt*
liquid honing equipment Strahlläppanlage *f*
liquid jet pump Strahlflüssigkeitspumpe *f*
liquid level indicator Füllstandsanzeiger *m*
liquid level switch Füllstandschalter *m*, Niveauschalter *m*, Schwimmschalter *f*
liquid metal-heated flüssigmetallbeheizt
liquid phase flüssige Phase *f*
liquid pollutants in the air flüssige Verunreinigung *f* der Luft
liquid receiver Flüssigkeitsauffangtopf *m*
liquid resin Tallharz *nt*
liquid ring compressor Flüssigkeitsringverdichter *m*
liquid ring vacuum pump Flüssigkeitsringvakuumpumpe *f*
liquid state flüssiger Aggregatzustand *m*
liquid thermometer Flüssigkeitsthermometer *nt*
liquid vehicle Tragflüssigkeit *f*
liquid-heated heat exchanger flüssigkeitsbeheizter Wärmetauscher *m*
liquifiable verflüssigbar
list auflisten, aufzählen, zusammenstellen; Liste *f*, Aufzählung *f*, Aufstellung *f*, Tabelle *f*
list generator Listengenerator *m*
list of contents Inhaltsverzeichnis *nt*
list of parts Stückliste *f*
list of spare parts Ersatzteilliste *f*
lithographic lithographisch
lithographic-electroforming-forming-technology LiGA (Lithographie, Galvanoformung, Abformung)-Verfahren *ntpl*
lithography Lithographie *f*
lithopone Farbenzinkoxid *nt*
little klein, gering
live spannungsführend, Strom führend
live centre umlaufende Körnerspitze *f*, umlaufende Spitze *f*
live load Verkehrslast *f*

live part aktives Teil *nt*
live roller conveyor angetriebene Rollenbahn *f*
locking device Verriegelungseinrichtung *f*
load 1. *(Kraft)* Belastung *f*, Druck *m*, Last *f*, Traglast *f*, Lastdruck *m*, Pfostendruck *m*; belasten, auflegen, belegen, beanspruchen auf Last **2.** *(Waren, Güter ~)* Ladung *f*, Ladegut *nt*; beladen, aufladen, einlagern, verladen, laden **3.** *(Werkzeuge, Werkstücke ~)* bestücken, zubringen, zuführen, beschicken **4.** *(Werkstücke befestigen)* spannen, einspannen, aufspannen **5.** *(el.)* Verbraucher *m*
load width Ladungsbreite *f*
load accessory Ladehilfsmittel *nt*
load application line Kraftangriffslinie *f*
load applied midway mittig aufgebrachte Kraft *f*
load axle Lastachse *f*
load backrest Schutzgitter *nt*, Lastenschutzgitter *nt*, Lastschutzgitter *m*
load bearing Tragen *nt* von Last *f*, Aufnehmen *nt* von Last *f*; tragend
load bearing element Lastaufnahmemittel (LAM) *nt*
load bearing flank tragende Gewindeflanke *f*
load bearing implement Lastträger *m*
load bearing nut Tragmutter *f*, Kraftmutter *f*
load bearing roller Tragrolle *f*
load bearing surface Auflageebene *f*
load bearing vehicle Trägerfahrzeug *nt*
load capacity *(der Achse)* Tragkraft *f*
load capacity plate Tragfähigkeitsschild *nt*
load carriage Gabelträger *m*
load carrier Lastträger *m*, Ladehilfsmittel *nt*, Ladungsträger *m*
load carrying Last tragend
load carrying deck Lastplattform *f*
load carrying means Lastaufnahmemittel (LAM) *nt*, Tragmittel *nt*
load carrying rope Tragseil *nt*
load caught Fanglast *f*
load cell Kraftmessdose *f*, Kraftmesszelle *f*, Lastsensor *m*
load centre Lastschwerpunkt *m*
load centre distance Lastschwerpunktabstand *m*
load centre of gravity Lastschwerpunkt *m*
load centre of gravity distance Lastschwerpunktabstand *m*
load change Lastwechsel *m*
load class Lastklasse *f*
load condition Belastung *f*
load control Laststeuerung *f*, Lastkontrolle *f*, Lastsensor *m*
load control system Lastkontrollsystem *nt*
load current Laststrom *m*
load cycle Belastungsverlauf *m*, Belastungsdauer *f*
load dependent belastungsabhängig
load diagram Belastungsbild *nt*, Lastdiagramm *nt*
load dimension Lastabmessung *f*
load distributed over an area Flächenbelastung *f*
load distribution Lastaufteilung *f*, Lastverteilung *f*
load due to wind pressure Windlast *f*
load effect Lasteinwirkung *f*
load end Lastende *nt*
load entering storage Wareneingangslager *nt*
load entry Einschleusstelle *f*
load extender Vorschubgabelträger *m*
load flank tragende Gewindeflanke *f*
load force Lastkraft *f*
load fork Lastgabel *f*
load guiding structure Lastführung *f*
load half-wave Lasthalbperiode *f*
load handling Lasthandhabung *f*, Lastbehandlung *f*
load handling accessory Lastaufnahmemittel (LAM) *nt*
load handling attachment Lastaufnahmemittel (LAM) *nt*
load handling control Lasthandhabungssteuerung *f*
load handling device (LHD) Lastaufnahmemittel (LAM) *nt*
load handling interlock Lastaufnahmemittelverriegelung *f*

load height Ladungshöhe *f*
load holding device Lasthalteeinrichtung *f*
load impedance Bürdenwiderstand *m*
load in compression auf Dehnung beanspruchen
load in shear auf Scherung beanspruchen
load in tension *(Zug)* auf Dehnung beanspruchen
load in the lowered position abgesenkte Last *f*
load indication Kraftanzeige *f*
load indication range Kraftanzeigebereich *m*
load indicator Lastanzeiger *m*
load input Ladeeingang *m*
load leaving storage Warenausgangslager *nt*
load length Ladungslänge *f*
load life Volllastlebensdauer *f*
load lifting facility Lasthubeinrichtung *f*
load lifting force Hubkraft *f*
load lifting means Tragmittel *nt*
load make-up accessory Ladehilfsmittel *nt*
load manipulation Lastbehandlung *f*, Lastmanipulation *f*
load matrix Belastungsmatrix *f*
load measurement Kraftmessung *f*
load measurement error Kraftmessfehler *m*
load measuring equipment Kraftmesseinrichtung *f*
load measuring range Kraftmessbereich *m*
load memory Ladespeicher *m*
load moment Lastmoment *nt*
load moment control Momentsensor *m*
load movement Lastbewegung *f*
load offset Außermittigkeit *f*
load peak Spitzenlast *f*
load per area unit Flächenbelastung *f*
load per axle Achslast *f*
load per square meter Flächenbelastung *f*
load per surface Flächenbelastung *f*
load per upright Pfostendruck *m*
load per wheel Radlast *f*
load pick-up Lastaufnahme *f*
load pick-up and deposit station Lastübergabestelle *f*
load pick-up device Lastaufnahmemittel (LAM) *nt*
load platform Lastplattform *f*
load position monitoring Lastpositionsüberwachung *f*
load position sensing Lastlageerfassung *f*
load profile Lastprofil *nt*
load projecting behind the vehicle hinten überhängende Ladung *f*
load pull Lastzug *m*
load push Lastschub *m*, Abschieber *m*
load ramp Laderampe *f*
load range Traglastbereich *m*
load relieving Entlastung *nt*
load restrainer Lastenschutzgitter *nt*, Lastschutzgitter *m*
load rotational speed Lastdrehzahlen *fpl*
load safeguarding Ladungssicherung *f*
load safeguarding material Ladungssicherung *f*
load safety sensor Lastsicherheitssensor *m*
load sensing system Lastsensor *m*
load sensor Lastsensor *m*, Kraftaufnehmer *m*
load sharing Lastverteilung *f*
load situation Belastungssituation *f*
load spectrum Belastungsspektrum *nt*, Lastkollektiv *nt*
load stabilization Laststabilisierung *f*
load stabilizer Kraftkonstanthalter *m*, Lasthalter *m*
load stopping aids Lastanschlagmittel *nt*
load support Lastauflage *f*, Lastaufnahmemittel (LAM) *nt*
load support profile member Auflageprofil *nt*
load support surface Auflageprofiloberfläche *f*
load supporting means Tragmittel *nt*
load suspension device Lastaufnahmeeinrichtung *f*, Lastaufnahmemittel (LAM) *nt*

load take-up Lastaufnahmemittel (LAM) *nt*
load torque Lastmoment *nt*
load transfer Lastübergabe *f*, Lastwechsel *m*
load transfer area Lastübergabebereich *m*
load transfer deformation Lastwechselverformung *f*
load unit Ladeeinheit *f*
load unit shifter Ladeeinheitenumsetzer *m*
load weighing scales Lastwaage *f*
load wheel Lastrad *nt*
loadability Belastbarkeit *f*
loadable belastbar
load-bearing assembly tragende Verbindung *f*
load-bearing connection Kraftverbindung *f*
load-bearing depth *(e. Gewindes)* Tragtiefe *f*
load-bearing screw thread tragfähiges Gewinde *nt*
load-bearing structural member tragendes Konstruktionsteil *nt*
load-bearing thread length tragende Gewindelänge *f*
load-bearing valve part tragendes Armaturenteil *nt*
load-bearing welded joint tragende Schweißverbindung *f*
load-carrying attachment Lastaufnahmemittel (LAM) *nt*
load-carrying capacity Tragfähigkeit *f*
load-carrying capacity Belastbarkeit *f*
load-carrying capacity involving heavy scoring Fresstragfähigkeit *f*
load-carrying portion Traganteil *m*
load-carrying truck Flurförderzeug (FFZ) *nt*
load-carrying unit Lastaufnahmemittel (LAM) *nt*
load-deflection curve Kraft-Durchbiegungs-Kurve *f*
load-deformation curve Kraft-Verformungs-Kurve *f*
load-deformation diagram Kraft-Verformungs-Diagramm *nt*
load-displacement diagram Kraft-Weg-Diagramm *nt*
loaded belastet, belegt, voll
load-effective thread length tragende Gewindelänge *f*
load-elongation curve Kraft-Längenänderungs-Kurve *f*
loading 1. *(Bauteile durch Kräfte, Druck)* Beanspruchung *f*, Belastung *f*, Last *f*, Beaufschlagung *f*, Belegung *f*, Auflage *f* **2.** *(Waren, Güter)* Ladung *f*, Verladung *f*, Beladen *nt*, Laden *nt* **3.** *(Werzeuge, Werkzeugmaschinen)* Bestückung *f*, Beschickung *f*, Zuführung *f* **4.** *(Werkstücke befestigen)* Einspannung *f*, Aufspannung *f*, Aufspannen *nt*
loading aid Ladehilfsmittel *nt*
loading aisle Beschickungsgang *m*
loading and unloading device Be- und Entladeeinrichtung *f*
loading and unloading station Be- und Entladeeinrichtung *f*
loading attachment Ladeeinrichtung *f*
loading belt Verladeband *nt*
loading bridge Überladebrücke *f*
loading bush Zylinderraum *m*
loading capacity *(Ladeleistung)* Tragkraft *f*
loading chamber Zylinderraum *m*
loading characteristic Belastungskennwert *m*
loading conditions Lastfall *m*
loading control Belastungskontrolle *f*, Lastkontrolle *f*
loading crane Ladekran *m*
loading device Ladeeinrichtung *f*, Beladeeinrichtung *f*
loading device extending speed Ausfahrgeschwindigkeit *f* der Ladeeinrichtung
loading face Bedienungsseite *f*
loading factor Belastungsfaktor *m*
loading gauge Umgrenzungsprofil *nt*
loading lift Ladelift *m*
loading net Ladenetz *nt*
loading of the test specimens Probenbeanspruchung *f*
loading of the test piece Prüfstückbeanspruchung *f*
loading plant Verladeanlage *f*

loading platform Laderampe *f*, Verladerampe *f*
loading point Beschickungsstelle *f*
loading procedure Belastungsvorgang *m*
loading station Beladestation *f*, Ladestelle *f*
loading surface Ladeebene *f*
loading system Beanspruchungseinrichtung *f*
loading time Aufspannzeit *f*
loading time interval 1. *(Kraft, Druck)* Belastungszeitspanne *f* **2.** *(Licht)* Beleuchtungszeitspanne *f*
loading tray Aufgabefläche *f*
loading unit Ladeeinheit *f*, Ladungseinheit *f*
loads concentrated on a point Punktlast *f*
loads concentrated ona point lumped load Punktbelastung *f*
loads imposed by road traffic Straßenverkehrsbelastung *f*
load-time diagram Kraft-Zeit-Diagramm *nt*
lost heat Verlustwärme *f*
local lokal, örtlich
Local Area Network (LAN) lokales Netzwerk (LAN) *nt*
local dosage rate Ortsdosierung *f*
local embrittlement Lokalversprödung *f*
local extension rack lokales Erweiterungsgerät *nt*
local measuring span Teilmessspanne *f*
local pointer Stationsdrucker *m*
local span of error Abweichungsspanne *f* in der Teilmessspanne
local thickness of cut at a selected point on the cutting edge örtliche Spanungsdicke *f* am ausgewählten Schneidenpunkt
local wear Lokalverschleiß *m*
localization of faults Fehlerbestimmung *f*
localizing equipment Lokalisationsgerät *nt*
localize suchen
localized porosity Einzelpore *f*

locally defined ortsabhängig
locally manufactured tank assembled together on site standortgefertigter Behälter *m*
locate 1. bestimmen, einstellen, positionieren, justieren, eine Lage *f* einstellen, eine Lage *f* bestimmen, anordnen, platzieren, anbringen an einer Stelle, lagerichtig anbringen, orten **2.** *(befestigen)* einspannen **3.** *(nachsehen)* suchen
locating Einspannung *f*, Aufspannung *f*
locating bearing Zentrierlager *nt*
locating cone Führungskegel *m*
locating device Fixiereinrichtung *f*
locating in position Lagesicherung *f*
locating plan Lageplan *m*
locating plunger Raststift *m* der Teilscheibe
location Standort *m*, Stand *m*, Lage *f*, Ort *m*, Stelle *f*, Platz *m*, Einstellung *f*, Lage Einstellen *nt*, Anordnung *f*, Lagebestimmung *f*, Ortung *f*
location check Platzkontrolle *f*
location engaged feeler arm Fachbesetzfühler *m*
location fine positioning Fachfeinpositionierung *f*
location for slinging Anschlagstelle *f*
location of installation Aufstellplatz *m*
location of tack weld Heftstelle *f*
location of the joints Stoßstelle *f*
location of utilization Verwendungsart *f*
location parameter Lageparameter *m*
location point Aufnahmepunkt *m*
location position Fachposition *f*
location positioning Fachpositionierung *f*
location tolerance Ortstoleranz *f*
location variant Standortvariante *f*
locational decision Standortentscheidung *f*
locator pin Fixierzapfen *m*
lock befestigen, blockieren, arretieren, sperren, absperren, feststellen, rasten, einrasten, klemmen, abschließen, verschließen, verriegeln; Verriegelung *f*, Absperrung *f*, Arretierung *f*, Verschluss *m*, Sperre *f*, Klemmung *f*, Selbsthaltung *f*

lock bar Riegel *m*
lock bolt Sicherungsschraube *f*
lock flag Sperrvermerk *m*
lock forming by bending Biegeverlappen *nt*
lock forming by twisting Drehverlappen *nt*
lock in position festspannen
lock in position festklemmen
lock latch Schlossfalle *f*
lock nut Gegenmutter *f*, Kontermutter *f*
lock secure sichern
lock together verbinden, verriegeln
lock washer Sicherungsblech *nt*
lockability Feststellbarkeit *f*
lockable abschließbar, blockierbar
locking Festklemmung *f*, Feststellung *f*, Blockierung *f*, Befestigung *f*, Verriegelung *f*, Riegel *m*, Sperren *nt*, Verschließen *nt*, Feststellen *nt*, Einrasten *nt*
locking pin Verschlussstift *m*
locking bar Schnappriegel *m*
locking bolt Sperrriegel *m*
locking brake Haltebremse *f*
locking device 1. Feststelleinrichtung *f*, Sicherung *f*, Arretierung *f*, Arretiereinrichtung *f* **2.** *(Seil)* Seilzugsicherung *f*
locking disk Rastscheibe *f*
locking effect Sicherungswirkung *f*
locking element Sicherungsteil *nt*, Sicherungselement *nt*
locking feature Sicherung *f*
locking handle Knebel *m*
locking pin Verriegelungsstift *m*
locking position Sperrstellung *f*
locking pressure Zuhaltekraft *f*
locking relay Haftrelais *nt*
locking ring Sicherungsring *m*
locking torque Haltemoment *m*
locknut Sicherungsmutter *f*, Spannmutter *f*
locknut with electrolytically deposited surface protection galvanisch oberflächengeschützte Sicherungsmutter
lockout Verriegelung *f*
lock-out Sperre *f*
lock-out release Entriegelung *f*
lockwasher Sicherungsring *m*
lodgement of dirt particles Haftenbleiben *nt* von Schmutzteilen
log Protokoll *nt*
log grapple Holzgreifer *m*
log gripper Blockgreifer *m*
log in anmelden, einwählen, einloggen; Einloggen *nt*, Anmeldung *f*
log paper logarithmisches Papier *nt*
logarithmic decay logarithmisches Dekrement *nt*
logarithmic decrement of mechanical damping Dekrement *nt* der mechanischen Dämpfung
logarithmic plotting logarithmische Aufzeichnung *f*
logbook Störungsbuch *nt*, Prüfbuch *nt*
log-file Logdatei *f*
logger Schreibgerät *nt*
logging in Anmeldung *f*
logging printer Protokolldrucker *m*
logging tongs Holzgreifer *m*
logic circuitry Logikschaltung *f*
logic connection funktionelle Verbindung *f*
logic control system Verknüpfungssteuerung *f*
logic element digitales Verknüpfungsglied *nt*, Logikelement *nt*, Schaltelement *nt*
logic linkage logische Verknüpfung *f*, logische Verknüpfungsschaltung *f*
logic operation logische Verknüpfung *f*, logische Verknüpfungsschaltung *f*, Verknüpfungsergebnis *nt*, Verknüpfung *f*
logic threshold Schnellwertglied *nt*
logical connective logische Grundverknüpfung *f*, Grundverknüpfung *f*
log-in procedure Anmeldeverfahren *nt*
logistic logistisch
logistic costs Logistikkosten *pl*
logistic efficiency Logistikeffizienz *f*
logistic partner Logistikpartner *m*
logistic performance Logistikleistung *f*
logistics Logistik *f*
logistics planning Logistikplanung *f*
logistics service provider Logistikdienstleister *m*
log-normal distribution Lognormalverteilung *f*
follow-up path Nachlaufweg *m*
long lang

long copying Langnachformen *nt*
long goods Langgut *nt*
long goods vertical carousel Langgutpaternoster *m*
long goods carriage Langgutkassette *f*
long goods storage Lagerung *f* von Langmaterial
long goods storage system Langgutlagersystem *nt*
long goods vertical rotary rack Langgutpaternoster *m*
long lace chip Langspan *m*
long necked round bottomed flask Langhalsrundkolben *m*
long profiling Langnachformen *nt*
long run production Serienfertigung *f*, Großserienfertigung *f*, Massenfertigung *f*
long run production machine Massenfertigungsmaschine *f*, Reihenfertigungsmaschine *f*
long socket Langmuffe *f*
long square hoher Vierkantansatz *m*
long taper Langkegel *m*, schlanker Kegel *m*
long term performance test Dauerfunktionsprüfung *f*
long-chip material langspanender Werkstoff *m*
long cutting langspanend
longest edge of the drawing Zeichnungshauptlage *f*
longitudinal longitudinal
longitudinal axis Längsachse *f*
longitudinal bend specimen Längsbiegeprobe *f*
longitudinal bending tensile strength Längsbiegezugfestigkeit *f*
longitudinal bracing Längsverband *m*
longitudinal carriage *(Verschieber)* Längstraverse *f*
longitudinal carrying cable Längstragseil *nt*
longitudinal centre line Längsmittellinie *f*
longitudinal centre plane Längsmittelebene *f*
longitudinal copying Längskopieren *nt*
longitudinal copying attachment Längskopiereinrichtung *f*, Längskopiervorrichtung *f*
longitudinal crack Längsriss *m*
longitudinal displacement Längsverschiebung *f*
longitudinal dynamic stability dynamische Längsstabilität *f*
longitudinal edge of groove Fugenlängskante *f*
longitudinal feed *(Bewegung)* Längsvorschub *m*
longitudinal feed gear mechanism Langzug *m*
longitudinal finish turning Langfeindrehen *nt*
longitudinal force Vorschubkraft *f*
longitudinal form turning Formlängsdrehen *nt*
longitudinal grinding Längsschleifen *nt*
longitudinal joint Längsfuge *f*, Längsfalz *m*
longitudinal joint of web plate Stegblechlängsstoß *m*
longitudinal lifting beam Längstraverse *f*
longitudinal member Längsverband *m*
longitudinal motion Längsbewegung *f*
longitudinal movement Längsfahren *nt*, Längsverschiebung *f*
longitudinal plane of symmetry Längsmittelebene *f*
longitudinal planing Längshobeln *nt*
longitudinal releasing force Längslösekraft *f*
longitudinal rolling Längswalzen *nt*
longitudinal rolling of shapes Profillängswalzen *nt*
longitudinal roughness Längsrauheit *f*
longitudinal scraping Längsschaben *nt*
longitudinal seal Längsnaht *f*
longitudinal shift Längsverschiebung *f*
longitudinal shrink rule Längenschwindmaß *nt*
longitudinal slide Längsschlitten *m*
longitudinal slip Längsschlupf *m*
longitudinal squeezer Längsquetscher *m*
longitudinal stability Längsstabilität *f*

longitudinal static stability statische Längsstabilität *f*
longitudinal stiffness Längssteifigkeit *f*
longitudinal stop Längenanschlag *m*
longitudinal support Längsträger *m*
longitudinal table traverse Tischlängsbewegung *f*
longitudinal thermal expansion coefficient Längenausdehnungskoeffizient *m*
longitudinal traverse Längsbewegung *f*, Langzug *m*, Längsgang *m*
longitudinal trip dog Längsanschlag *m*
longitudinal truck Längsfahrwagen *m*
longitudinal turning Längsdrehen *nt*
longitudinal turning attachment Langdrehvorrichtung *f*
longitudinal turning work Langdreharbeit *f*
longitudinal wave Longitudinalwelle *f*, Dichtewelle *f*
longitudinal weld on a pipe Rohrlängsnaht *f*
longitudinally längs
longitudinally force locked längskraftschlüssig
longitudinally moveable längsbeweglich
longitudinally seamed längs gesiegelt
long-lasting lang andauernd
long-necked flat-bottomed flask Langhalsstehkolben *m*
long-run job große Serie *f*
long-run repetition work große Serie *f*
long-stroke broaching machine Langhubräummaschine *f*
long-stroke machine Langhubmaschine *f*
long-term langzeitig, langfristig
long-term ageing test Langzeitalterung *f*
long-term immersion test Dauertauchversuch *m*
long-term load capacity Langzeitbelastbarkeit *f*
long-term loading Dauerbelastung *f*
long-term performance Dauerbeanspruchbarkeit *f*
long-term protection Dauerschutz *m*
long-term rated current Langzeitnennstrom *m*
long-time ageing test Langzeitalterung *f*
long-time internal pressure loading Langzeitinnendruckbeanspruchung *f*
long-undulation components langwellige Anteile *mpl*
look ahead function Vorausschauende Bahnbetrachtung *f*
look for suchen nach
look over überprüfen
loop Schleife *f*, Kreis *m*, Kreislauf *m*, Regelschleife *f*, Bügel *m*, Öse *f*; umschlingen
loop display Kreisbild *nt*
loop signal Fernsteuerbefehl *m*
loop type clamp (or clip) Schelle *f* in Schlaufenform
loose wandern; locker, schlaff, ungespannt, lose, unverpackt, abnehmbar, spielbehaftet
loose change gear Umsteckrad *nt*
loose coupling schaltbare Kupplung *f*
loose gear Wechselrad *nt*
loose splits lose Backen
loosen aufschrauben, abschrauben, lockern, lösen, nachlassen
looseness Spiel *nt*, Schlaffheit *f*
loosening Lockern *nt*, Lockerung *f*
loosening torque Abschraubmoment *nt*
lorry Lastkraftwagen *m*, Lkw *m*
lose 1. verlieren, nachlaufen; Ausfall *m*, Abfall *m*, Verlust *m* 2. *(Druck)* Druckabfall *m*
loss due to slippage Schlupfverlust *m*
loss in performance Leistungsverlust *m*
loss in substance Substanzverlust *m*
loss lubrication Verlustschmierung *f*
loss modulus Verlustmodul *nt*
loss of braking Bremsverlust *m*
loss of control Kontrollverlust *m*
loss of head 1. Verlusthöhe *f* 2. *(Druck)* Druckverlust *m*
loss of heat quantity Wärmemengenverlust *m*
loss of oil Ölverlust *m*
loss of power Stromausfall *m*
loss of tool hardness Erweichen *nt* der

Schneide
loss of weight by washing out Auswaschverlust *m*
losses *pl* Verluste *mpl*
lost load centre Vorbaumaß *nt*
lost motion play toter Gang *m*
lost shape verlorene Form *f*
lot Posten *m*, Serie *f*, Los *nt*
lot formation Losbildung *f*
lot size Losgröße *f*
loupe Lupe *f*
low klein, tief, gering
low building Flachbau *m*
low capacity machine leistungsschwache Maschine *f*
low carbon steel kohlenstoffarmer Stahl *m*, Flussstahl *m*
low flammability Schwerentflammbarkeit *f*
low flammability plastics schwerentflammbarer Kunststoff *m*
low frequency Niederfrequenz *f*
low infeed palletizer Untenpalettierer *m*
low medium Durchflussmedium *nt*
low noise level Geräuscharmut *f*
low oxide surface oxidarme Oberfläche *f*
low precision Niedrigpräzision *f*
low precision measuring instrument Grobmessgerät *nt*
low pressure Unterdruck *m*
low pressure chill casting Niederdruckkokillenguss *m*
low pressure chill casting process Niederdruckkokillengießverfahren *nt*
low pressure gas supply line Niederdruckgasversorgungsleitung *f*
low pressure gas system Niederdruckgasanlage *f*
low pressure high temperature water generator Niederdruckheißwassererzeuger *m*
low pressure steam raising installation Niederdruckdampfkesselanlage *f*
low scale annealing Zunderarmglühen *nt*
low setting Kleinstellung *f*
low solvent synthetic resin lösungsmittelarmer Kunststoff *m*
low temperature behaviour Verhalten *nt* bei tiefen Temperaturen
low temperature brittleness point Kältesprödigkeitstemperatur *f*
low temperature storage behaviour Kältelagerungsverahlten *nt*
low volatile liquid schwerflüchtige Flüssigkeit *f*
low voltage Niederspannung *f*
low-antimony soft solder antimonarmes Weichlot *nt*
low-density polyethylene Polyethylen *nt* weich
lower untere/r/s, senken, absenken, abbewegen, herablassen, herunterfahren, herabsetzen
lower bed *(Bau)* Unterlager *nt*
lower carriage Fahrrahmen *m*
lower case letter Kleinbuchstabe *m*
lower edge Unterkante *f*
lower end of effective flank Fußende *nt* der nutzbaren Flanke
lower eroding Senkerodieren *nt*
lower eroding machine Senkerodiermaschine *f*
lower explosion limit (LEL) untere Explosionsgrenze (UEG)
lower face of the blade Gabelunterseite *f*
lower face Auflagefläche *f (e. Mutter)*
lower flange of rail Schienenfuß *m*
lower layer sample Unterschichtprobe *f*
lower limit Kleinstmaß *nt*
lower part unterer Teil *m*, Unterteil *nt*
lower reel flow wrapping machine Unterfolienform-, -füll- und -verschließmaschine *f*
lower side Unterseite *f*
lower side band unterer Seitenbereich *m*
lower slewing crane Montagebaukran *m*
lower surface Unterkante *f*
lowering Absenken *nt*, Absinken *nt*, Herablassen *nt*, Senken *nt*, Senkbewegung *f*, Abwärtsfahrt *f*
lowering distance Hubstrecke *f*
lowering motion Senkbewegung *f*
lowering movement Senkbewegung *f*

lowering speed Absenkgeschwindigkeit *f*, Senkgeschwindigkeit *f*
lowest priority geringste Priorität *f*
lowest-valued stage niedrigstwertige Stufe *f*
low-lag plant verzögerungsarme Regelstrecke *f*
low-level depalletizer Bodenladedepalettierer *m*
low-level lift-off depalletizer Bodenladeabhebedepalettierer *m*
low-level palletizer Bodenladepalettierer *m*
low-level-lift-off palletizer Bodenladeabhebepalettierer *m*
low-lift height niedrige Hubhöhe *f*
low-lift order picker truck Niedrigkommissionierer *m*
low-lift straddle carrier Portalwagen *m*
low-lift truck Niederhubflurförderzeug *nt*, Niedrigkommissionierer *m*, nicht stapelnder Hubwagen *m*
low-load start Sanftanlauf *m*
low-maintenance wartungsarm
low-molecular substance niedermolekularer Stoff *m*
low-pass filtering Tiefpassfilterung *f*
low-temperature gas Schwelgas *nt*
low-temperature warehouse Tiefkühllager *nt*
low-vibration running schwingungsarmer Lauf *m*
low-voltage contactor Niederspannungsschaltgerät *nt*
low-voltage control unit Niederspannungsschaltgerät *nt*
low-voltage switching device Niederspannungsschaltgerät *nt*
low-water safety device Wassermangelsicherung *f*
lozenge Raute *f*
lozenged rautenförmig
L-sealing machine Einschlagmaschine *f* mit Winkelschweißung
L-shaped L-förmig
L-shaped profile L-Profil *nt*
lubricant Schmiermittel *nt*, Schmierstoff *m*
lubricant filter point Schmierstofffüllstelle *f*
lubricant metering device Schmierstoffverteiler *m*
lubricant reconditioning Schmierstoffaufbereitung *f*
lubricant reservoir Schmierstoffbehälter *m*
lubricant residues *pl* Schmierstoffrückstände *mpl*
lubricant return Schmiermittelrückführung *f*
lubricant spattering nozzle Spritzdüse *f*
lubricant spray valve Sprühdüse *f*
lubricant spraying Sprühschmierung *f*
lubricants Schmierstoffe *mpl*
lubricate schmieren, fetten
lubricating cycle counter Schmiertaktzähler *m*
lubricating equipment Schmiergerät *nt*
lubricating nipple Schmiernippel *m*
lubricating oil Schmieröl *nt*
lubricating point Schmierstelle *f*
lubrication Schmierung *f*
lubrication cycle Schmiertakt *m*
lubrication cycle time Schmiertaktzeit *f*
lubrication engineering Schmiertechnik *f*
lubrication fluid Schmierflüssigkeit *f*
lubrication oil Schmieröl *nt*
lubricating Schmierung *f*
lubricator Öler *m*
luffing Wippen *nt*
lug Ansatz *m*, Nase *f*, Lappen *m*
luminance Leuchtdichte *f*
luminance distribution Leuchtdichteverteilung *f*
luminescent leuchtend
luminous distribution Helligkeitsverteilung *f*
luminescent pigment Leuchtpigment *nt*
luminosity Helligkeit *f*
luminous digit Leuchtziffer *f*
luminous flux Lichtstrom *m*
luminous spot Lichtzeiger *m*
luminous transmission index Lichttransmissionsgrad *m*

luminous radiation measurement
  Lichtstrahlungsmessung f
lumped load Punktlast f
lunge-cut mill tauchfräsen
luminescent effect Leuchtwirkung f
lute *(dichten)* verkleben
luting agent Dichtungskitt m
lye Lauge f
lying upon another übereinander liegend

M m

Maag generator Maag-Zahnradhobelmaschine *f*
machinability Zerspanbarkeit *f*, Schnittbearbeitbarkeit *f*, Schnittfähigkeit *f*
machinability rating Spanungsgröße *f*, Zerspanbarkeitsgröße *f*
machinability variable Zerspanbarkeitsgröße *f*
machinable zerspanbar, spanbar, bearbeitbar
machine spanen
machine 1. Maschine *f*, Gerät *nt*, Arbeitsmaschine *f*; fertigen, verarbeiten, bearbeiten 2. *(Zerspanung)* zerspanend bearbeiten, zerspanen, abspanen, spanen
machine accessories Maschinenzubehör *nt*
machine all over allseitig bearbeiten
machine area Maschinenfläche *f*
machine attendant Maschinenwärter *m*
machine axis Maschinenachse *f*
machine base Maschinenständer *m*, Ständer *m*
machine bed Maschinenbett *nt*
machine breakdown Maschinenausfall *m*
machine builder Maschinenbauer *m*
machine building Maschinenbau *m*
machine building industry Maschinenbau *m*
machine capacity Maschinenleistung *f*
machine code Maschinencode *m*
machine column Maschinenständer *m*
machine component Maschinenteil *nt*
machine construction Maschinenbau *m*
machine control unit Steuerung *f*
machine cycle Bearbeitungszyklus *m*, Folge *f* der Arbeitsgänge, Maschinenarbeitsablauf *m*, Maschinenzyklus *m*
machine cycle-controlled maschinentaktgesteuert
machine cycle-dependent maschinentaktabhängig
machine data Maschinendaten *pl*
machine design Maschinenentwurf *m*
machine direction Längsrichtung *f*
machine down time Brachzeit *f*
machine efficiency Maschinenleistung *f*
machine element Maschinenelement *nt*
machine family Maschinenlos *nt*
machine for processing materials Verarbeitungsmaschine *f*
machine for three-dimensional milling Nachformfräsmaschine *f* mit dreidimensionaler Steuerung
machine form Maschinenform *f*
machine hourly rate Maschinenstundensatz *m*
machine intensity Maschinenintensität *f*
machine lapping Maschinenläppen *nt*
machine link Maschinenanbindung *f*
machine master data Maschinenstammdaten *pl*
machine master file Maschinenstamm *m*
machine moulding shop Maschinenformerei *f*
machine operation costs Maschinenbetriebskosten *pl*
machine operator Maschinenarbeiter *m*
machine outfit Maschinenpark *m*
machine part Maschinenteil *nt*
machine plate Maschinenschild *nt*
machine pocket Fangraum *m*
machine production times *pl* Maschinenhauptzeiten *fpl*
machine rack Maschinengestell *nt*
machine reamer Maschinenreibahle *f*
machine recovery Wiederherstellung *f* der Betriebsbereitschaft
machine recovery procedure Wiederherstellung *f* der Betriebsbereitschaft
machine reference axis Maschinenbezugsachse *f*

machine relieved hinterdreht
machine room Maschinenraum *m*
machine running time Bearbeitungshauptzeit *f*
machine selection Maschinenauswahl *f*
machine setter Einrichter *m*
machine shaking frequency Maschinenschüttelfrequenz *f*
machine shape Maschinenform *f*
machine shop Maschinenhalle *f*, Maschinenwerkhalle *f*, Werkstatt *f*
machine spindle Hauptspindel *f*
machine stop Maschinenwerkstatt *f*
machine table Maschinentisch *m*
machine taper *(Werkzeug)* Kegel *m*
machine time Maschinenhauptzeit *f*, Maschinenlaufzeit *f*
machine tool Werkzeugmaschine (WZM) *f*, Arbeitsmaschine *f*
machine tool building Werkzeugmaschinenbau *m*
machine tool center Drehspitze *f*, Körnerspitze *f*
machine tool control Steuerung *f* von Werkzeugmaschinen
machine tool control system Werkzeugmaschinensteuerung *f*
machine tool division Werkzeugmaschinenabteilung *f*
machine tool expert Werkzeugmaschinenfachmann *m*
machine tool industry Werkzeugmaschinenbau *m*
machine tool manufacture Werkzeugmaschinenbau *m*
machine tool plant Werkzeugmaschinenfabrik *f*
machine tools *pl* Werkzeugmaschinen *fpl*
machine type Geräteart *f*
machine upright Maschinenständer *m*
machine utilization Maschinenbelegung *f*
machine utilization time Maschinenbelegungszeit *f*
machine vice Maschinenschraubstock *m*
machine zero point Maschinennullpunkt *m*

machine-control interface Anpasssteuerung *f*
machined from the solid aus dem Vollen herausgearbeitet
machined part Formteil *nt*
machined surface bearbeitete Fläche *f*, gefertigte Fläche *f*, Arbeitsfläche *f*
machined surface cut Schnitt *m* an der Arbeitsfläche
machine-dependent deviation maschinenbedingte Abweichung *f*
machine-handling time Nebenzeit *f*, Verlustzeit *f*, Bedienungszeit *f*, Griffzeit *f*
machinery Maschinen *f*, Maschinenpark *m*
machinery breakdown Maschinendefekt *m*
machinery plant Maschinenanlage *f*
machinery safety Maschinensicherheit *f*
machines extent of utilization Maschinenauslastung *f*
machineshop tool Maschinenwerkzeug *nt*
machining zerspanende Bearbeitung *f*, spangebende Bearbeitung *f*, spanabhebende Bearbeitung *f*, spanabhebendes Bearbeiten *nt*, Zerspanung *f*, Verarbeitung *f*, Bearbeitung *f*, Spanen *nt*
machining accuracy Arbeitsgenauigkeit *f (e. Maschine)*
machining allowance Bearbeitungszugabe *f*, Bearbeitungsaufmaß *nt*, Arbeitszugabe *f*
machining centre (MC) Bearbeitungszentrum (BAZ)
machining cycle Arbeitsablauf *m*, Bearbeitungsablauf *m*, Arbeitstakt *m*
machining cycle planning Arbeitsablaufplanung *f*
machining job Zerspanungsarbeit *f*
machining method producing continuous chips Fließspanverfahren *nt*
machining of metals Metallbearbeitung *f*
machining operation Bearbeitungsverfahren *nt*, Bearbeitungsvorgang *m*, Arbeitsvorgang *m*, Zerspanungsarbeit *f*, Zerspanvorgang *f*, spangebende Bear-

beitung *f*, Spanung *f*
machining operation Arbeitsvorgang *m*
machining optimization Spanungsoptimierung *f*
machining output Zerspanungsleistung *f*
machining parameters *pl* Bearbeitungsparameter *mpl*
machining phase Bearbeitungsstufe *f*
machining property Zerspanungseigenschaft *f*, Zerspanbarkeit *f*
machining quality Zerspanungseigenschaft *f*
machining rate Bearbeitungsgeschwindigkeit *f*
machining sequence Bearbeitungsfolge *f*
machining shop Bearbeitungswerkstatt *f*
machining surface Bearbeitungsfläche *f*
machining system Bearbeitungssystem *nt*
machining time Durchlaufzeit *f*, Arbeitszeit *f*, Bearbeitungszeit *f*
machining time per piece Stückzeit *f*
machining times *pl* Bearbeitungszeiten *fpl*
machining variable Zerspangröße *f*, Zerspanungsgröße *f*, Zerspanbarkeitsgröße *f*, Spanungsgröße *f*, Schnittgröße *f*
macro Unterprogramm *nt*, Makro *nt*
macro box Makrofenster *nt*
macro button Makroschaltfläche *f*
macro form Makrogestalt *f*
macro function Makrofunktion *f*
macrocell Makroelement *nt*
macro-climate Makroklima *nt*
macro-crack Makroriss *m*
macro-examination specimen Makroschliff *m*
macrogeometrical surface pattern makrogeometrische Oberfläche *f*
macrosection Makroschliff *m*
MACS (micro adjusting collect system) Mikroeinstellspannsystem *nt*
made hergestellt
made to specification nach Kundenwunsch
magazine Magazin *nt*, Ladevorrichtung *f*
magazine automatic Magazinautomat *m*
magazine feed Magazinzuführung *f*
magazine feeding attachment Magazineinrichtung *f*, Magazin *nt*, Ladevorrichtung *f*
magazine loading attachment Magazinzuführeinrichtung *f*, Magazineinrichtung *f*
magnet Magnet *m*
magnet form process Magnetformverfahren *nt*
magnet stirrer Magnetrührwerk *nt*
magnetic magnetisch
magnetic adhesion magnetische Haftfestigkeit *f*
magnetic board Magnettafel *f*
magnetic card Magnetkarte *f*
magnetic chuck Magnetspannfutter *nt*, Magnetfutter *nt*
magnetic crack detection appliance Durchflutungsgerät *nt*
magnetic crack test Magnetrissprobe *f*
magnetic drum Magnettrommel *f*
magnetic field Magnetfeld *nt*, magnetisches Feld *nt*
magnetic field sensor Magnetfeldsensor *m*
magnetic flux Magnetfluss *m*, magnetischer Fluss *m*
magnetic flux line magnetische Feldlinie *f*
magnetic foil Magnetfolie *f*
magnetic gripper Magnetgreifer *m*
magnetic leakage flux test magnetisches Streuflussverfahren *nt*
magnetic load carrying device Lasthebemagnet *m*
magnetic loss Magnetisierungsverlust *m*, Eisenverlust *m*
magnetic material Magnetwerkstoff *m*
magnetic penetration method magnetische Durchflutung *f*
magnetic pulse welding Magnetimpulsschweißen *nt*
magnetic strip Magnetstreifen *m*
magnetic switch Magnetschalter *m*

magnetic tape Magnetband *nt*
magnetic tape readout device Magnetbandausgeber *m*
magnetic tape-controlled machine tool magnetbandgesteuerte Werkzeugmaschine *f*
magnetizable magnetisierbar
magnetize magnetisieren
magnetizing equipment Magnetisierungsgerät *nt*
magnification Vergrößerung *f*
magnify vergrößern
magnifying glass Lupe *f*
magnifying lens Messlupe *f*
magnitude Größe *f*
main Haupt ...
main time Grundzeit *f*
main basis Hauptbasis *f*
main beam Längsträger *m*
main circuit Hauptstromleitung *f*
main clearance Freiwinkel *m*, Hinterschliff *m* der Fase
main column Hauptständer *m*
main contact point Hauptkontaktpunkt *m*
main contactor Hauptschütz *m*
main control position Hauptsteuerstelle *f*
main control station Hauptsteuerstand *m*
main control switch Steuerschalter *m*
main current Hauptstrom *m*
main cutter spindle Hauptfrässpindel *f*
main cutting edge Hauptschneide *f*
main cutting force Hauptschnittkraft *f*
main cutting pressure Hauptschnittkraft *f*
main dimension(s) Hauptmaß *nt*, Hauptabmessung *f*
main direction of flow Hauptflussrichtung *f*
main direction of travel Hauptfahrrichtung *f*
main drive Hauptantrieb *m*
main drive cylinder Antriebszylinder *m*
main engagement lever Haupteinschalthebel *m*
main formation direction Hauptformrichtung *f*
main frame (IT) Zentrale *f*
main frame structure Hauptrahmen *m*
main header Hauptsammler *m*
main host Haupthub *m*
main isolator Hauptschalter *m*, Netzanschlussschalter *m*
main lift Haupthub *m*
main lifting speed Haupthubgeschwindigkeit *f*
main load Hauptlast *f*
main parting line Haupttrennfläche *f*
main pole Hauptpol *m*
main pole core Hauptpolkern *m*
main process Hauptprozess *m*
main processing unit (MPU) Hauptverarbeitungseinheit *f*
main relay Hauptschütz *m*
main sentence Hauptsatz *m*
main sewer Sammelleitung *f*
main shaft Hauptantriebswelle *f*, Motorwelle *f*
main spindle 1. Hauptspindel *f*, Arbeitsspindel *f*, Spindelstock *m* 2. *(Drehmaschine)* Drehmaschinenspindel *f*
main spindle gear Bodenrad *nt*
main stress axis Hauptspannungsrichtung *f*
main supply Hauptversorgung *f*
main switch Hauptschalter *m*
main time of processes Hauptdurchführungszeit *f*
main tool slide Hauptwerkzeugschlitten *m*, Hauptschlitten *m*
main tool thrust Hauptschnittdruck *m*
main using time Hauptnutzungszeit *f*
main/battery powered calculator Rechenmaschine *f* für netzabhängigen und netzunabhängigen Betrieb
main beam Balken *m*
mainframe computer Zentralrechner *m*, Großrechner *m*
mains 1. Linie *f*, Netz *nt*, Leitung *f*, Hauptleitung *f*, Leitungsnetz *nt* 2. *(Leitungsbau)* Rohrleitung *f*
mains power Netzstrom *m*
mains power supply Netzeinspeisung *f*, Netzstromversorgung *f*
mains powered calculator netzabhängige Rechenmaschine *f*
mains regeneration Netzrückspei-

sung *f*
mains transformer Netztransformator *m*
mains voltage Netzspannung *f*
mains-operated circulating pump Netzumwälzpumpe *f*
maintain aufrechterhalten, warten, behalten, in Stand halten, erhalten, einhalten, beibehalten, pflegen
maintain in condition instand halten, in Stand halten
maintain the path Fahrtrichtung beibehalten
maintainability Wartbarkeit *f*, Instandhaltbarkeit *f*
maintenance Wartung *f*, Instandhaltung *f*, Pflege *f*, Warten *nt*
maintenance area Wartungsbereich *m*
maintenance contract Wartungsvertrag *m*
maintenance costs Instandhaltungskosten *pl*, Unterhaltungskosten *pl*, Wartungsaufwand *m*
maintenance free wartungsfrei
maintenance instruction Wartungsanleitung *f*
maintenance interval Wartungsabstand *m*
maintenance log Wartungsheft *nt*
maintenance logistics Instandhaltungslogik *f*
maintenance man Monteur *m*
maintenance manual Wartungsanleitung *f*, Wartungshandbuch *nt*
maintenance of quality Sicherung *f* der Güte
maintenance personnel Instandhaltungspersonal *nt*
maintenance platform Wartungsbühne *f*
maintenance position Wartungsposition *f*, Wartungsstand *m*
maintenance rate Wartungsintervall *nt*
maintenance requirements Instandhaltungsaufwand *m*
maintenance schedule Wartungsplan *m*
maintenance staff Instandhaltungspersonal *nt*
maintenance unit Wartungseinheit *f*

maintenance work Wartungsarbeit *f*, Instandhaltungsarbeiten *pl*
major diameter Außendurchmesser *m*
major diameter of nut thread Muttergewindeaußendurchmesser *m*
major flank Hauptfreifläche *f*
major priority höchste Priorität *f*
make erzeugen, herstellen, anfertigen, machen; Erzeugnis *nt*, Fabrikat *nt*
make a complaint reklamieren
make a profit Gewinn abwerfen
make a U-turn umdrehen, wenden
make-and-take order Abrufauftrag *m*
make arrangements disponieren, Vorkehrungen treffen
make available bereitstellen
make before change-over Wechslerschließer *m*
make contact 1. ergreifen 2. Schließer *m*
make contact with in Berührung kommen
make difficult erschweren
make efforts Anstrengungen unternehmen
make homogeneous homogenisieren
make-or-buy decision Make-or-buy-Entscheidung *f*
make progress fortschreiten
make provisions Vorkehrungen treffen
make ready for use bereitstellen
make safe absichern
make sure sicherstellen
make tight dichten, abdichten
make up aufbauen
make-break-make contact Wechslerschließer *m*
make-make-break contact Schließerwechsel *m*
maker Hersteller *m*
makeshift Behelfs…
makeshift design Behelfskonstruktion *f*
making Anfertigung *f*
making contact Ergreifen *nt*
making device Anreißvorrichtung *f*
making fixture Anreißvorrichtung *f*
making-off Anreißen *nt*, Anreißarbeit *f*
maladjusted unangepasst
maladjustment Justierfehler *m*
male connector Stecker *m*

male die Stempel *m*
male thread Außengewinde *nt*
male-faced flange Vorsprungflansch *m*
malfunction versagen; Versagen *nt*, Störung *f*, Fehlfunktion *f*, Laufhemmung *f*
malleability Flexibilität *f*
malleable cast iron Temperguss *m*
malleable pig Temperroheisen *nt*
malleabilize tempern
malleabilizing furnace Temperofen *m*
malleabilizing process Temperverfahren *nt*
Maltese cross Malteserkreuz *nt*
man besetzen
man-to-part Mann-zu-Ware-
manage betreiben, verwalten, handhaben
management Verwaltung *f*, Handhabung *f*
management level Unternehmensleitebene *f*
management of resources Ressourcenmanagement
management organization *(BWL)* Führungsstruktur *f*
manager *(Organisator)* Leiter *m*
managing clerk Disponent *m*
management level Leitebene *f*
man-down truck Mann-unten-Stapler *m*
mandrel Dorn *m*, Drehdorn *m*, Dornrad *nt*, Kaliberdorn *m*, Spanndorn *m*, Aufspannbolzen *m*
mandrel bag-in-box machine Dornrad-Bag-in-Box-Kartoniermaschine *f*
mandrel carton form fill and seal machine Dornradfaltschachtelform-, -füll- und -verschließmaschine *f*
mandrel flexible package form fill and seal machine Dornradform-, -füll- und -verschließmaschine *f* für flexible Packungen
mandrel form fill and seal machine Dornradform-, -füll- und -verschließmaschine *f*
mandrel press Dornpresse *f*
mandrel-bending test Dornbiegeversuch *m*
mandrel-mounting reel Dornspule *f*

manoeuvre Manöver *nt*
manoeuvre manövrieren
manoeuvrable manövrierfähig
manoeuvring Manövrieren *nt*
manganese phosphate coating Manganphosphatschicht *f*
mangling Walzrichten *nt* mit mehreren Walzen
manhole bottom section Schachtunterteil *nt*
manhole pit Domschacht *m*
manifold 1. *(Düse)* Verteilerdüse *f* **2.** *(Rohrleitung)* Verteilungsleitung *f*
manifold valve Mehrwegeventil *nt*
manipulate manipulieren, betätigen, hantieren, handhaben, schalten
manipulating speed Stellgeschwindigkeit *f*
manipulating unit Stellgerät *nt*
manipulation Manipulation *f*, Bedienung *f*, Schaltung *f*, Handhabung *f*, Betätigung *f*
manipulator Manipulator *m*, Steller *m*, Arbeitsorgan *nt*, Wendeeinrichtung *f*
man-machine interface (MMI) Mensch-Maschine-Schnittstelle *f*
manning Besetzung *f*
manoeuvrable manövrierfähig
manoeuvring Manövrieren *nt*
manoeuvrability Wendigkeit *f*
manoeuvre manövrieren, wenden, Manöver *nt*
manouevring Wenden *nt*
manpack Tornister *m*
manpower Arbeitskräfte *f*
manpower assignment Personaleinsatz *m*
manpower demand Arbeitskräftebedarf *m*
manpower resources Arbeitskräftereserven *fpl*
manual 1. manuell, handgesteuert, handbetrieben **2.** *(Buch, Anleitung)* QS-Handbuch *nt*
manual brake Handbremse *f*
manual brake release lever Handbremslüfteinrichtung *f*
manual control Handbedienung *f*, Handregelung *f*, nichtselbsttätige Regelung *f*, Handschaltung *f*, Handsteue-

rung *f*, Steuerung *f* von Hand
manual control device Handbediengerät *nt*
manual control doors manuell gesteuerte Tore *ntpl*
manual controller Handbediengerät *nt*
manual data input control Handeingabesteuerung *f*
manual drive manueller Antrieb *m*
manual form Handformen *nt*
manual hot gas welding Warmgashandschweißen *nt*
manual lifting manuelle Lastenanhebung *f*
manual manufacture Handfertigung *f*
manual mode of operation Handbetrieb *m*
manual operation Handbetätigung *f*, Handbetrieb *m*, Handsteuerung *f*
manual preselection Handvorwahl *f*
manual production Handfertigung *f*
manual programming manuelle Programmierung *f*
manual recording Protokollierung *f* von Hand
manual restart of protected output manueller Wiederanlauf *m* bei geschützten Ausgängen
manual shaking rate Handschüttelfrequenz *f*
manual shape Handformen *nt*
manual skill dexterity Handfertigkeit *f*
manual steering system Handsteuersystem *nt*
manual table drive Tischhandantrieb *m*
manual work station Handarbeitsplatz *m*
manual/automatic control switch Hand-Automatik-Schalter *m*, Hand-Regel-Schalter *m*
manually von Hand
manually actuated handbetätigt
manually applied force Handkraft *f*
manually controlled manuell gesteuert, handgesteuert
manually operated handbedient, handbetätigt, von Hand betätigt
manually operated releasing signal Handauslösesignal *nt*
manually tightened angezogen
manufacture weiterverarbeiten, produzieren, erzeugen, fertigen, anfertigen, herstellen, fabrizieren, machen; Erzeugung *f*, Produktion *f*, Anfertigung *f*, Fertigung *f*, Herstellung *f*
manufacture of bevel gear planing machines Kegelradhobelmaschinenbau *m*
manufacture of chill Kokillenbau *m*
manufacture of heavy-duty machines Großmaschinenbau *m*
manufacture of tools Formenbau *m*
manufactured hergestellt
manufacturer Hersteller *m*
manufacturer of casting resin Gießharzhersteller *m*
manufacturer of phenolic plastics Phenoplasthersteller *m*
manufacturer's information Herstellerangaben *fpl*
manufacturer's instructions Herstellerangaben *fpl*
manufacturer's original packaging Herstelleroriginalverpackung *f*
manufacturing Fertigung *f*, Weiterverarbeitung *f*
manufacturing accuracy Herstellgenauigkeit *f*
Manufacturing Automation Protocol MAP
manufacturing cell Zelle *f*
manufacturing comparison Betriebsvergleich *m*
manufacturing costs Herstellkosten *f*, Herstellungskosten *pl*
manufacturing data collection BDE (Betriebsdatenerfassung) *f*
manufacturing documentation Fertigungsunterlagen *fpl*
manufacturing drawing Herstellungszeichnung *f*
manufacturing engineer Betriebsingenieur *m*
manufacturing failure fertigungsbedingter Ausfall *m*
manufacturing machine Bearbeitungsmaschine *f*
manufacturing method Fertigungsmethode *f*, Arbeitsweise *f*

manufacturing operation Weiterverarbeitung *f*
manufacturing plant Fertigungsstätte *f*
manufacturing practice Betriebspraxis *f*
manufacturing process Arbeitsverfahren *nt*, Fertigungsverfahren *nt*
manufacturing programme Fertigungsprogramm *nt*
manufacturing quality Herstellungsqualität *f*
manufacturing security Fertigungssicherheit *f*
manufacturing shop Betrieb *m*, Fertigungsbetrieb *m*
manufacturing specifications Fertigungsunterlagen *fpl*
manufacturing stage Fertigungsstufe *f*
manufacturing supervision Betriebsüberwachung *f*
manufacturing tolerance Herstelltoleranz *f*
manufacturing type miller Planfräsmaschine *f*
manufacturing-type milling machine Langfräsmaschine *f*, Planfräsmaschine *f*
manufacturing-type milling machine with vertical spindle Senkrechtproduktionsfräsmaschine *f*
man-up truck Mann-oben-Stapler *m*
man-way Zugang *m*
many times vielfach
map abbilden
mapping Abbildung *f*
mar beschädigen, kratzen; Kratzer *m*
margin 1. Rand *m* 2. (Bohrwerkzeug) Fase *f* 3. (Preis) Spanne *f*
marginal area Randgebiet *nt*
marginal definition Randschärfe *f*
marginal distribution Randverteilung *f*
marginal expectation Randerwartungswert *m*
marginal variance Randvarianz *f*
mark 1. markieren, kennzeichnen, anzeichnen, bezeichnen, anreißen, ankörnen, beschriften; Zeichen *nt*, Marke *f*, Markierung *f*, Stempelung *f* 2. *(Messtechnik)* Messmarke *f* 3. *(Regelungstechnik)* Signalzustand „Eins" *m*
marker Marke *f*, Zeichen *nt*, Kennzeichen *nt*, Anreißer *m*
marker out Anreißer *m*
marker's name plate Leistungsschild *nt*
market Markt *m*
market analysis Marktanalyse *f*
market economy Marktwirtschaft *f*
market introduction phase Markteinführungsphase *f*
market leader Marktführer *m*
market leadership Marktführerschaft *f*
market maturity Marktreife *f*
market overall view Marktübersicht *f*
market reconnaissance Markterkundung *f*
market research Marktforschung *f*
market saturation Marktsättigung *f*
market segment Marktsegment *nt*
market value Marktwert *m*
marketing Vertrieb *m*, Marketing *nt*
marketing budget accounting Absatzbudgetierung *f*
marketing costs Vertriebskosten *pl*
marketing department Vertrieb *m*
marketing logistics Distributionslogistik *f*
market-oriented marktorientiert
marking Markierung *f*, Kennzeichnung *f*, Bezeichnung *f*, Beschilderung *f*, Beschriftung *f*, Anreißen *nt*
marking gauge Parallelreißer *m*, Reißstock *m*
marking out plate Anreißplatte *f*
marking stencil Anreißschablone *f*
marking tool Anreißzeug *nt*
marking-off table Anreißplatte *f*
marking-off tool Anreißwerkzeug *nt*
marring Beschädigung *f*, Schadensausübung *f*
marshal into singles vereinzeln
martens mirror Spiegelfeinmessgerät *nt*
martensite region Martensitstufe *f*
mash einschalten
mask 1. ausblenden, abdecken; Maske *f* 2. *(Arbeitsschutz)* Mundschutz *m*
mask bit Maskenbit *nt*
mask dragging bewegte Maske *f*
mask file Maskendatei *f*

mask form process Maskenformverfahren *nt*
mask generator Maskengenerator *m*
mask layout Maskenanordnung *f*
mask material Maskenmaterial *nt*
mask membrane Maskenmembran *f*
mask membrane material Maskenmembranwerkstoff *m*
mask method Maskenverfahren *nt*
mask parameter Maskenparameter *m*
mask pores geschlossene Poren *fpl*
mask process Maskenverfahren *nt*
mask scan Maskenscannen *nt*
mask word Maskenwort *nt*
mask-controlled maskengesteuert
masonry Mauerwerk *nt*
mass Masse *f*
mass centre of gravity Massenschwerpunkt *m*
mass constancy Massenkonstanz *f*
mass decrease Masseverringerung *f*
mass flow rate Massenstrom *m*
mass increase Massenzunahme *f*, Gewichtszunahme *f*
mass inertia Massenträgheit *f*
mass loss Massenverlust *m*, Gewichtsverlust *m*
mass loss per unit area flächenbezogener Massenverlust *m*
mass of additional weight Fallmasse *f*
mass-pair production coefficient Masse-Paarbildungskoeffizient *m*
mass part list Mengenstückliste *f*
mass per unit area Flächengewicht *nt*
mass-photo-electric absorption coefficient Massenphotoabsorptionskoeffizient *m*
mass production Massenfertigung *f*
mass radiograph Reihenaufnahme *f*
mass reduction Masseverringerung *f*
mass soldering Komplettlösung *f*
mass temperature Massetemperatur *f*
mass-duplicate in Massen anfertigen
massive vollwandig, massiv
mast Mast *m*
mast base Mastfuß *m*
mast base fastening Mastfußbefestigung *f*
mast base mounting Mastfußbefestigung *f*

mast deflection Mastauslenkung *f*, Mastdurchbiegung *f*
mast guide rail Mastführung *f*
mast guide rail tolerance Mastführungstoleranz *f*
mast oscillation Mastschwingung *f*
mast structure Hubgerüst *nt*, Mastaufbau *m*
mast tilting Mastneigung *f*
mast upright Hubgerüstprofil *nt*, Hubgerüstrahmen *m*, Hubgerüstschiene *f*
masted mit Hubgerüst
master Bezugsstück *nt*, Muster *nt*, Musterstück *nt*, Modell *nt*
master agreement Rahmenvertrag *m*
master clock Taktgeber *m*
master component Muster *nt*
master computer Leitrechner *m*
master control system übergeordnete Steuerung *f*
master controller Steuerschalter *m*
master controller (chisel) Meißelschalter *m*
master data Stammdaten *pl*
master data adjustment Stammdatenabgleich *m*
master data administration Stammdatenverwaltung *f*
master data collection Stammdatenerfassung *f*
master data set Stammdatensatz *m*
master drawing Stammzeichnung *f*, Druckvorlage *f*
master file incorporation Stammdatenübernahme *f*
master ga(u)ge Prüflehre *f*
master gear blank Lehrzahnkörper *m*
master illustration Bildvorlage *f*
master parts record Teilestamm *m*, Teilestammdatei *f*
master parts record unit Teilestammsatz *m*
master plate Kopierlineal *nt*, Schablone *f*
master switch Steuerschalter *m*, Hauptschalter *m*
master system Leitsystem *nt*
master template Urschablone *f*, Kopierschablone *f*
master tracing Mutterpause *f*

master workpiece Muster *nt*
mastication Mastikation *f*
mat Matte *f*
mat black glanzlos schwarz
mat finishing Mattierung *f*
metal braid Metallgeflecht *nt*
match anpassen, übereinstimmen (mit), abstimmen, abgleichen, paaren; Übereinstimmung *f*
match grinding Einpassschleifen *nt*
match-grinding machine Rundschleifmaschine *f* mit Messsteuerung
matching Paarung *f*
matching diameter Anpassdurchmesser *m*
mate *(Zahnräder)* ineinander passen, paaren, kämmen
material Stoff *m*, Material *nt*, Werkstoff *m*, Waren *pl*
material adhesion Stoffhaftung *f*
material and equipment Sachmittel *ntpl*
material and equipment costs Sachmittelkosten *pl*
material arrangements Materialdisposition *f*
material behaviour Werkstoffverhalten *nt*
material booking Materialbuchung *f*
material carrier Materialträger *m*
material characteristic Stoffeigenschaft *f*
material circulation Stoffkreislauf *m*
material colour code Materialfarbcode *m*
material comparative table Werkstoffvergleichstabelle
material costs Materialaufwand *m*, Materialkosten *pl*
material defect Materialfehler *m*, Werkstofffehler *m*
material demand Materialbedarf *m*
material demand assessment Materialbedarfsermittlung *f*
material description Materialbeschreibung *f*
material designation Materialbezeichnung *f*, Materialkennzeichen *nt*
material deviation Werkstoffabweichung *f*

material document Materialbegleitschein *m*
material erosion Werkstoffabtrag *m*
material exposed to heating Erwärmungsgut *nt*
material expulsion Werkstoffauspressung *f*
material flow Materialfluss *m*, Materialstrom *m*, Stofffluss *m*, Mengenstrom *m*
material flow chain Materialflusskette *f*
material flow concept Materialflusskonzept *nt*
material flow diagram Materialflussschema *nt*
material flow form Materialflussform *f*
material flow matrix Materialflussmatrix *f*
material flow part Materialflussbereich *m*
material flow process Materialflussvorgang *m*
material flow study Materialflussuntersuchung *f*
material for protective clothing Schutzanzugstoff *m*
material general costs Materialgemeinkosten *pl*
material group Isolierstoffgruppe *f*
material handling control Materialflusssteuerung *f*
material handling controller Materialflusssteuerung *f*
material loss Materialverlust *m*
material marking Materialkennzeichen *nt*
material master data Materialstammdaten *pl*
material master file Materialstamm *m*
material measure Maßverkörperung *f*
material needs Materialbedarf *m*
material number Werkstoffnummer *f*
material path Materialbahn *f*
material planning Materialplanung *f*, Warendisposition *f*
material prone to cracking rissempfindlicher Werkstoff *m*
material property Materialeigenschaft *f*, Werkstoffeigenschaft *f*

material reduction Werkstoffreduzierung
material related werkstoffbedingt
material removal Zerspanungsvolumen *nt*
material removal rate Zeitspanungsvolumen *nt*
material requirements Materialbedarf *m*
material sample Werkstoffprobe *f*
material selection Materialwahl *f*, Werkstoffauswahl *f*
material stiffness Materialsteifigkeit *f*
material supply process Materialversorgungsprozess *m*
material temperature Massetemperatur *f*
material testing Werkstoffprüfung *f*
material testing machine Werkstoffprüfmaschine *f*
material thickness Materialdicke *f*
material to be conveyed Fördergut *nt*
material to be reduced in size Zerkleinerungsgut *nt*
material to be sandblasted Strahlgut *nt*
material utilization Werkstoffausnutzung *f*
material volume Werkstoffvolumen *nt*
material warehouse Materiallager *nt*
material with-draw Materialentnahme *f*
material-conditioned werkstoffbedingt
material-dependent corrosion materialbedingte Korrosion
material-dependent loss materialbedingter Verlust *m*
materials handling engineering Materialflusstechnik *f*, Fördertechnik *f*
materials handling equipment Transporteinrichtung *f*
materials handling system Teilelogistik *f*
materials handling technology Fördertechnik *f*
materials management Materialwirtschaft *f*, Materialmanagement *nt*
materials procurement Materialbeschaffung *f*
materials provision Materialzugang *m*
materials receipt Materialzugang *m*
materials requirements planning Lagerplanung *f*
materials requisition Materialanforderung *f*
materials supply Materialbereitstellung *f*, Materialversorgung *f*
Materials Testing Institute Materialprüfanstalt *f*
mathematical mathematisch
mathematical statistics mathematische Statistik *f*
mating aneinander passend; Paarung *f*
mating allowance Paarungsabmaß *nt*
mating area Paarungsfeld *nt*
mating assembly Paarung *f*
mating component Anschlussteil *nt*
mating conditions *pl* Paarungsbedingungen *fpl*
mating crown gear Gegenplanrad *nt*
mating dimension Anschlussmaß *nt*, Paarungsmaß *nt*, Passmaß *nt*
mating faces *pl* aneinander passende Flächen *fpl*
mating flank Gegenflanke *f*
mating gear Ineinandergreifen *nt*, Gegenrad *nt*
mating gear circumference Gegenradumfang *m*
mating gears Radpaarung *f*
mating members Passstücke *ntpl*
mating part Passteil *nt*
mating parts *pl* Passstücke *ntpl*, gepaarte Teile *ntpl*
mating pinion zugehöriges Ritzel *nt*
mating plane tooth system Gegenplanverzahnung *f*
mating size Anschlussmaß *nt*, Paarungsmaß *nt*
mating tooth Gegenzahn *m*
mating tooth surface Gegenflanke *f*
matrix Matrix *f*
matrix camera Matrixkamera *f*
matrix code Matrixcode *m*
matrix printer Matrixdrucker *m*
matter Materie *f*, Stoff *m*
mature reifen
maturity Reife *f*
maturity stage Reifenphase *f*

maximization Maximierung *f*
maximize maximieren
maximum Maximum *nt*, voll
maximum backlash größtes Flankenspiel *nt*
maximum check gauging member Maximumprüfkörper *m*
maximum diameter Größtmaß *nt*
maximum dimension Größtmaß *nt*
maximum interference Größtübermaß *nt*
maximum level indicating device Füllstandsanzeige *f*
maximum limit Größtmaß *nt*
maximum liquid level device Füllstandsanzeige *f*
maximum load Höchstbelastung *f*, Höchstbeanspruchung *f*, Höchstlast *f*
maximum master plug gauge Maximumprüfdorn *m*
maximum material profile Maximummaterialprofil *nt*
maximum operator Maximumoperator *m*
maximum permissible höchst zulässig
maximum permissible speed höchst zulässige Drehzahl *f*
maximum quantity Maximalmenge *f*
maximum rake Wirkwinkel *m*
maximum rated lifting speed Nennhubgeschwindigkeit *f*
maximum scale value Skalenendwert *m*
maximum short circuit power Höchst-Kurzschlussleistung *f*
maximum size Größtmaß *nt*
maximum speed Höchstgeschwindigkeit *f*, Höchstdrehzahl *f*, volle Drehzahl *f*
maximum stress 1. *(Belastung)* Höchstbeanspruchung *f* **2.** *(el.)* Oberspannung *f*
maximum surface temperature Oberflächenbegrenzungstemperatur *f*
maximum tensile load Höchstzugkraft *f*
maximum value Höchstwert *m*, Größtmaß *nt*
maximum value limiter Größtwertbegrenzer *m*

maximum voltage Höchstspannung *f*
maximum working pressure maximaler Arbeitsdruck *m*
maximum... größt ...
maximum throughput Grenzdurchsatz *m*
mean Mittelwert *m*, Mittel *nt*, Durchschnitt *m*; durchschnittlich
mean band Mittelwertbereich *m*
mean clearance Mittenspiel *nt*
mean compressive stress Druckmittelspannung *f*
mean cycle time mittlere Spielzeit *f*
mean deviation mittlere Abweichungsbetrag *m*
mean failure detection time mittlere Fehlererkennungszeit *f*
mean interference Mittenübermaß *nt*
mean population Mitteninhalt *m*
mean position Mittellage *f*
mean range Mittenbereich *m*
mean reference line mittlere Bezugslinie *f*
mean shear stress Schubmittelbeanspruchung *f*, Schubmittelspannung *f*
mean square sound pressure mittleres Schalldruckquadrant *nt*
mean strain Mittelverformung *f*
mean stress Vorspannung *f*
mean tensile stress Zugmittelspannung *f*
mean time between failures (MTFB) mittlerer Ausfallabstand *m*
mean time to repair (MTTR) mittlere Dauer *f* bis zur Instandsetzung
mean value Mittelwert *m*
meander cuts Mäanderanschnitt *m*
meander shrinkage Mäandereinlauf *m*
meaningful aussagefähig
means Einrichtung *f*, Mittel *nt*
means of production Produktionsmittel *nt*
means of structuring Strukturierungsmittel *nt*
means of support Tragmittel *nt*
means of suspension Tragmittel *nt*
means of transportation Transportmittel *nt*
meantime Zwischenzeit
measurable messbar

measurand Anzeige *f*, angezeigter Wert *m*, Messgröße *f*
measurand quantity Messgröße *f*, Messwert *m*
measurand value Messgröße *f*
measure Maß *nt*, Maßstab *m*; eichen, messen
measure deviation Maßabweichung *f*
measure feeling Messgefühl *nt*
measure of precaution Vorbeugemaßnahme *f*, Vorsichtsmaßnahme *f*
measure of variability Streuungsmaß *nt*
measure out dosieren
measure systematic deviation maßsystematische Abweichung *f*
measure time Zeit ermitteln, Zeit messen
measure without exerting pressure drucklos messen
measured data 1. Messdaten *pl* 2. *(Zeitpunkt)* Messdatum *nt*
measured length Messlänge *f*
measured number of teeth Messzähnezahl *f*
measured quantity Messgröße *f*
measured size Prüfgröße *f*, Testgröße *f*
measured value Messwert *m*
measured value hysteresis Messwertumkehrspanne *f*
measured value indicator Messwertanzeiger *m*
measured value reversal range Messwertumkehrspanne *f*
measured value sensor Messwertaufnehmer *m*
measured variable Messwert *m*
measured-value indication Messwertanzeige *f*
measurement Maß *nt*, Messung *f*, Abmessung *f*
measurement and control devices *pl* Mess- und Regeleinrichtungen *fpl*
measurement error Messabweichung *f*, Messwertabweichung *f*
measurement expenditure Messaufwand *m*
measurement object Messobjekt *nt*
measurement of characteristic value Kennwertmessung *f*
measurement of maximum precision Feinstmessung *f*
measurement of plasticity Vulkametrie *f*
measurement of temperature Temperaturmessung *f*
measurement of turbidity Trübungsmessung *f*
measurement point Messpunkt *m*
measurement point name Messstellenname *m*
measurement position Messposition *f*
measurement probe Messsonde *f*
measurement reading Messwert *m*
measurement record Messprotokoll *nt*
measurement report Messprotokoll *nt*
measurement signal Messsignal *nt*
measurement surface Messfläche *f*
measurement surface ratio Messflächenmaß *nt*
measurement transfer Maßübertragung *f*
measurement uncertainty Messunsicherheit *f*
measurement vibrator Messschwinge *f*
measuring Messung *f*, Vermessung *f*, Messen *nt*
measuring amplifier Messendverstärker *m*, Messverstärker *m*
measuring and control technology MSR-Technik *f*
measuring anvil Messamboss *m*
measuring apparatus Messgerät *nt*
measuring appliance Messeinrichtung *f*, Messgerät *nt*, Messzeug *nt*
measuring arrangement Messanordnung *f*
measuring ball Messkugel *f*, Messglocke *f*
measuring bench Messbank *f*
measuring capillary Messkapillare *f*
measuring chain Messkette *f*
measuring chamber pressure Druckmessverfahren *nt*
measuring circle Messkreis *m*
measuring cone Messkegel *m*
measuring control Messsteuerung *f*
measuring converter Messumsetzer *m*
measuring device Messvorrichtung *f*,

Messeinrichtung *f*, Messgerät *nt*, Messzeug *nt*, Messsteuerung *f*
measuring element Messstück *nt*, Messelement *nt*, Messorgan *nt*
measuring equipment Messeinrichtung *f*
measuring error Messfehler *m*
measuring face Messfläche *f*
measuring force Messkraft *f*
measuring force reversal range Messkraftumkehrspanne *f*
measuring gear Messgetriebe *nt*
measuring head Messkopf *m*
measuring installation Messanlage *f*
measuring instrument Messinstrument *nt*, Messgerät *nt*, Maß *nt*, Messmittel *nt*, Messwerkzeug *nt*, Messzeug *nt*
measuring instrument manufacturer Messgerätehersteller *m*
measuring instrument with analogue indication Messgerät *nt* mit Skalenanzeige
measuring instrument with digital indication Messgerät *nt* mit Ziffernanzeige
measuring instrument with indirect output Messgerät *nt* mit indirekter Ausgabe
measuring instrumentation Messausrüstung *f*
measuring jet Messdüse *f*
measuring length for the waviness Welligkeitsmessstrecke *f*
measuring line Messteilung *f*
measuring machine Messmaschine *f*
measuring mark Messmarke *f*
measuring means Messmittel *nt*
measuring mechanism Messwerk *nt*
measuring method Messverfahren *nt*
measuring method by interferometry Interferenzmessverfahren *nt*
measuring object Messgegenstand *m*
measuring outfit Messgerät *nt*, Messeinrichtung *f*
measuring pick-up Messwertaufnahme *f*
measuring plunger Messbolzen *m*
measuring point Messspitze *f*, Messstelle *f*, Messpunkt *m*

measuring practice *(betrieblich)* Messtechnik *f*
measuring precision Messgenauigkeit *f*
measuring principle Messprinzip *nt*
measuring program Messprogramm *nt*
measuring range Messbereich *m*
measuring rod Maßstab *m*
measuring roller Messrolle *f*
measuring scatter band Messstreubreite *f*
measuring sensor Messwertgeber *m*
measuring span Messspanne *f*
measuring spindle Messspindel *f*
measuring station Messstelle *f*
measuring system Messsystem *nt*, Messkette *f*, Messeinrichtung *f*, Messanlage *f*
measuring system for counting alpha-particles Messeinrichtung *f* zum Zählen von alpha-Teilchen
measuring tape Messband *nt*
measuring tool Messwerkzeug *nt*, Messzeug *nt*, Messgerät *nt*
measuring touch Messgefühl *nt*
measuring transducer Messumformer *m*
measuring tube Messröhre *f*, Messschenkel *m*
measuring tube with floating body Messrohr *nt* mit Schwebekörper
measuring value Messwert *m*
measuring without contact berührungslos Messen *nt*
measuring zone Messzone *f*
mechanical mechanisch
mechanical clutch schaltbare und formschlüssige Kupplung *f*
mechanical engineer Maschinenbauingenieur *m*, Maschinenbauer *m*
mechanical engineering Maschinenwesen *nt*, Maschinenbau *m*
mechanical engineering calculation maschinentechnische Berechnung *f*
mechanical equipment Maschineneinrichtung *f*, Maschinenanlage *f*
mechanical fastener mechanisches Verbindungselement *nt*
mechanical fasteners mechanische

Verbindungselemente *ntpl*
mechanical gear-shift system mechanisches Schaltgetriebe *nt*
mechanical gripper mechanischer Greifer *m*
mechanical installation maschinelle Einrichtung *f*
mechanical interlock mechanische Verriegelung *f*
mechanical loading mechanisches Beschicken *nt (e. Werkstückes)*
mechanical property Fertigkeitseigenschaft *f*
mechanical stability mechanische Stabilität *f*
mechanical workshop Bearbeitungswerkstatt *f*
mechanically operated mechanisch betrieben
mechanics Mechanik *f*
mechanics of fits Passungsmechanik *f*
mechanics of plasticity Plastizitätsmechanik *f*
mechanism Vorrichtung *f*, Einrichtung *f*
mechanism brake motor Getriebebremsmotor *m*
mechanism element Getriebeglied *nt*
mechanism position Getriebestellung *f*
mechanism selection Vorrichtungsauswahl *f*
mechatronics Mechatronik *f*
median Median *m*, Zentralwert *m*
median band Zentralwertbereich *m*
median plane Mittelebene *f*
medical equipment medizinische Einrichtung *f*
medium Mittel *nt*, Medium *nt*
medium frequency current mittelfrequenter Strom *m*
medium frequency welding Schweißen *nt* mit Mittelfrequenz
medium lift mittlerer Hub *m*; mit mittlerem Hub
medium yielding nitrogen Stickstoff abgebendes Mittel *nt*
medium-frequency conduction welding konduktives Mittelfrequenzschweißen *nt*
medium-frequency induction welding induktives Mittelfrequenzschweißen *nt*
medium-scaled mittelschuppig
medium-sized mittelständisch, mittelgroß
medium-sized companies Mittelstand *m*
medium-spaced lettering Mittelschrift *f*
medium-term mittelfristig
meet 1. treffen, zusammentreffen, auftreffen **2.** *(eine Aufgabe oder Vorgabe ~)* erfüllen, einhalten
meet each other at right angles rechtwinklig aufeinanderstoßen
meet the demand decken
meet the other at an angle schräg gegeneinander stoßen
meeting Gespräch *nt*
meeting functional requirements funktionsgerecht
maintenance interval Wartungsintervall *nt*
melamine formaldehyde condensation resin Melaminformaldehydkondensationsharz *nt*
melamine phenolic resin Melaminphenolharz *nt*
melamine resin compression moulding material Melaminharzpressmasse *f*
melamine resin glue Melaminharzleim *m*
melt schmelzen, ausschmelzen; Schmelze *f*
melt casting Schmelzgießen *nt*
melt cutting Schmelzschneiden *nt*
melt flow index Schmelzindex *m*
melt off abschmelzen
melt up umschmelzen
melting Schmelzen *nt*, Schmelzung *f*
melting basin Schmelztiegel *m*
melting crucible Schmelztiegel *m*
melting furnace Schmelzofen *m*
melting fuse Schmelzsicherung *f*
melting heat Schmelzwärme *f*
melting interval Schmelzintervall *nt*
melting loss Schmelzverlust *m*
melting loss by oxidation Abbrand *m*
melting point Schmelzpunkt *m*
melting temperature Schmelztempe-

ratur *f*
melting zone Schmelzzone *f*
member Teil *nt*, Bauelement *nt*, Glied *nt*
membership Zugehörigkeit *f*
membership function Zugehörigkeitsfunktion *f*
momentary kurzzeitig
memorize speichern
memory Speicher *m*, Magnetspeicher *m*
memory area Speicherbereich *m*
memory back-up Speicherpufferung *f*
memory behaviour Speichereigenschaft *f*, Haftverhalten *nt*
memory card Speicherkarte *f*
memory cell Speicherzelle *f*
memory content Speicherinhalt *m*
memory device Speicherglied *nt*
memory function Speicherfunktion *f*
memory location Speicherzelle *f*
memory selection control Speicherauswahlsteuerung *f*
memory unit Speicherzelle *f*
memory utilization Speicherausnutzung *f*
mend nachbessern
mending Nachbesserung *f*
mending work Nachbesserungsarbeiten *pl*
meniscus Meniskus *m*, Wulstrand *m*
mental overload geistige Überbeanspruchung *f*
mental underload geistige Unterbeanspruchung *f*
menu Menü *nt*
menu dialog Menüdialog *m*
merchandise Waren *pl*
merchandise flow Warenfluss *m*
merchandise flow registration Warenflussverfolgung *f*
merchandise information system (MIS) Warenwirtschaftssystem (WWS) n)
merchandise inventory Warenlager *nt*
mercury Quecksilber *nt*
mercury in-glass thermometer Quecksilberglasthermometer *nt*
mercury nitrate test Quecksilbernitratversuch *m*
merge 1. ausschleusen; Ausschleuser *m*, Einschleuser *m* **2.** *(zusammen ~)* mischen, zusammenführen, zusammenlaufen, zusammentreffen
merge cycle Ausschleustakt *m*
merge element Ausschleuselement *nt*
merge into übergehen in
merge point 1. Ausschleusstelle *f* **2.** *(z. B. Waren zusammenfassen)* Sammelstelle *f*
mergence Zusammenführung *f*
merging 1. Ausschleusvorgang *m* 2. (zusammen) Zusammenstellung *f*, Zusammentreffen *nt*
merging unit Zusammenführungselement *nt*
merry-go-round Karussell *nt*
mesh 1. Gitter *nt*, Masche *f* **2.** *(Zahnräder)* Eingriff *m*; verzahnen, greifen, ineinander greifen, eingreifen, kämmen
mesh box Gitterbox *f*
mesh box pallet Gitterboxpalette *f*
mesh material Maschenware *f*
mesh size Maschenweite *f*
mesh with *(Maschinenteile)* eingreifen
mesh with zero backlash *(Zahnräder)* spielfrei abwälzen
meshed zusammengeschlossen, verzahnt
meshing Eingriff *m*
meshing difficulty Eingriffsschwierigkeit *f*
meshing interference Eingriffsstörung *f*
meshing of the teeth Zahneingriff *m*
meshing point Eingriffsstelle *f*
meshwork Geflecht *nt*
message Nachricht *f*, Meldung *f*; melden
message chronicle Meldeelektronik *f*
message display Meldeanzeige *f*, Meldebild *nt*
message page Meldeseite *f*
message priority Meldungspriorität *f*
message received Nachricht empfangen
message report Meldeprotokoll *nt*
message sequence Meldefolge *f*
message statistics Meldestatistik *f*
message surge Meldeschwall *m*
message text Meldetext *m*

metacentre Metazentrum *nt*
metacentric metazentrisch
metal Metall *nt*
metal band Metallband *nt*
metal bath Metallschmelze *f*
metal bellows Metallbalg *m*
metal blade electrode Metallschneidenelektrode *f*
metal block Metallstempel *f*
metal braiding Metallumspinnung *f*
metal clip Clip *m*
metal coat Metallschicht *f*
metal container Metallbehälter *m*
metal cutting Spanen *nt*, Spanung *f*, Zerspanung *f*, spanende Formgebung *f*, spanende Bearbeitung *f*, Metallzerspanung *f*
metal cutting at elevated temperatures Warmzerspanung *f*
metal cutting element Zerspangröße *f*
metal cutting practice Zerspantechnik *f*, Zerspanungstechnik *f*
metal cutting quantity Zerspangröße *f*, Spanungsgröße *f*
metal cutting work Zerspanungsarbeit *f*
metal detecting machine Metalldetektionsmaschine *f*
metal electrode potential Metallelektrodenpotential *nt*
metal finishing Feinbearbeitung *f*
metal foil Metallfolie *f*
metal forming spanlose Formgebung *f*, Umformung *f*
metal gauze Metallgaze *f*
metal gluing Metallkleben *nt*
metal hose Metallschlauch *m*
metal lattice Metallgitter
metal oxide varistor Metalloxidvaristor *m*
metal part Metallteil *nt*
metal planing machine Metallhobelmaschine *f*
metal plate Metallplatte *f*
metal powder Pulvermetall *nt*
metal removal Spanabnahme *f*
metal removal rate Spanmenge *f*, Abtragsquotient *m*, spezifisches Spanvolumen *nt*
metal removing capacity Zerspanbarkeit *f*, Zerspanleistung *f*
metal rim Metallfelge *f*
metal sheet Feinblech *nt*, Blech *nt*
metal sheeting Blech *nt*
metal spatula Metallspatel *m*
metal spinning Metalldrücken *nt*
metal spraying firm Metallspritzbetrieb *m*
metal spraying technology Metallspritztechnik *f*
metal spraying work Metallspritzarbeit *f*
metal staple Metallklammer *f*
metal strap Metallband *nt*
metal template Metallschablone *f*
metal-to-metal joint metallische Verbindung *f*
metal turner Dreher *m*
metal/metal-ion reaction Metall-Metallionen-Reaktion *f*
metal-clad *(el.)* vollgekapselt
metal cutting Spanen *nt*
metal-cutting capacity Zerspanungsleistung *f*
metal-cutting process Zerspanungsverfahren *nt*
metal-cutting production procedure spanendes Fertigungsverfahren *nt*
metal-cutting research Zerspanungsforschung *f*
metal-cutting technique Zerspantechnik *f*, Zerspanungstechnik *f*
metal-cutting technology Zerspantechnik *f*, Zerspanungstechnik *f*
metal-cutting tool Maschinenwerkzeug *nt* für Metall
metal-cutting tool Zerspanungswerkzeug *nt*, Zerspanwerkzeug *nt*
metal-ion reaction Metallionenreaktion *f*
metal-cutting spanende Bearbeitung *f*, Metallzerspanung *f*
metallic metallisch
metallic coating metallischer Überzug *m*
metallic continuity Stoffschluss *m*
metallic drive screw Metallschneidschraube *f*
metallic effect pigment Metalleffektpigment *nt*

metallic structure Metallstruktur *f*
metallizing material Metallisierungsstoff *m*
metallographic micrograph metallographisches Gefügebild *nt*
metallophysical process metallphysikalischer Vorgang *m*
metallurgy Metallurgie *f*
metal-powder flame cutting Metallpulverbrennschneiden *nt*
metal-powder fusion cutting Metallpulverschmelzschneiden *nt*
metal-resilient jointing Metallweichstoffdichtung *f*
metalworking Metallbearbeitung *f*
metastable metastabil
meter messen, zählen; Messgerät *nt*, Maß *nt*, Zähler *m*
meter man Zählerableser *m*
meter out dosieren
meter reading Zählerstand *m*, Zählerablesung *f*
meter rule Metermaß *nt*, Maß *nt*
metered addition Zudosierung *f*
metered value Messwert *m*
metered volume Dosiervolumen *nt*
metering Zählung *f*, Messung *f*
metering device with injectors Einleitungsverteiler *m*
metering device with restrictors Drosselverteiler *m*
metering piston Dosierkolben *m*
metering pump Messpumpe *f*
methacrylate resin Methacrylatharz *nt*
method Methode *f*, Art *f*, Verfahren *nt*, Verfahrensablauf *m*, Verfahrensgang *m*
method of fixing Verankerungsmethode *f*
method of locking Klemmung *f*
method of measurement Messverfahren *nt*
method of merge Ausschleusvorgang *m*
method of moving the probe Prüfkopfführung *f*
method of operation Betriebsart *f*
method of representation Darstellungsweise *f*
method statement Montageanleitung *f*
methods-time measurement MTM (Methods-Time-Measurement)
methodological error Verfahrensfehler *m*
methylene blue Methylenblau
metric external thread metrisches Außengewinde *nt*
metric fine thread metrisches Feingewinde *nt*
metric ISO thread metrisches ISO-Gewinde *nt*
metric screw thread metrisches Gewinde *nt*
metric tapered external screw thread metrisches kegeliges Außengewinde *nt*
metric thread metrisches Gewinde *nt*
metric thread for force fit metrisches Gewinde *nt* für Festsitz
metrological messtechnisch
metrologist Messtechniker *m*
metrology Messtechnik *f*, Messwesen *nt*
Meyer's tube Zehnkugelrohr *nt*
mezzanine deck Regalbühne *f*
mezzanine floor Zwischengeschoss *nt*, Zwischenbühne *f*, Zwischenpodest *nt*, Lagerbühne *f*
M-functions M-Funktion *f*
mica powder Glimmerpulver *nt*
Micro Adjusting Collect System (MACS) Mikroeinstellspannsystem *nt*
micro adjustment Feineinstellung *f*
micro contour Mikrokontur *f*
micro cracks mikroskopische Risse *mpl*
micro cutting Mikrospanen *nt*
micro eroding Mikroerodieren *nt*
micro flaw Haarriss *m*
micro link Mikrowellensensor *m*
micro milling Mikrofräsen *nt*
micro processing Mikrobearbeitung *f*
micro riffling Mikrofurchung *f*
micro structure Mikrostruktur *f*
micro up-forming Mikroabformung *f*
microbiological mikrobiologisch
microbiological corrosion mikrobiologische Korrosion
microclimate Mikroklima *nt*
microcomputer Mikrocomputer *m*
microcontroller Mikroprozessor *m*
micro-crack Mikroriss *m*

micro-cracked mikrorissig
micro-environment Mikroumgebung f
microfilm mikroverfilmen
microfilming technique Mikrofilmtechnik f
micro-finishing method Feinstbearbeitungsmethode f
micro-honing Fertighonen nt
micrometer Bügelmessschraube f, Feinmessschraublehre f, Feinmessschraube f, Messschraube f, Mikrometer nt
micrometer adjusting screw Feinstellschraube f
micrometer adjustment Feineinstellung f, Feinsteinstellung f
micrometer calliper Bügelmessschraube f
micrometer calliper gauge Feinmessschraublehre f, Feinmessschraube f
micrometer calliper with ratchet stop Feinmessschraublehre f mit Ratsche
micrometer depth gauge Feinmesstiefenlehre f
micrometer eyepiece Mikrometerokular nt, Mikrommeterokular nt
micrometer gauge Werkstattschraublehre f, Mikrometer nt
micrometer lead screw Mikrometerspindel f mit Skalentrommel
micrometer screw Feinmessschraublehre f, Feinmessschraube f, Mikrometerschraube f, Messschraube f, Mikrometer nt
micrometer setting Feineinstellung f
micron Mikrometer nt
microphone path Mikrophonpfad m
micro-pores mikroskopische Poren fpl
micro-porous mikroporig
microprocessor Mikroprozessor m
microradiant Mikroradiant m
microscope tube Mikroskoptubus m
microscopic cracks mikroskopische Risse mpl
microscopic pores mikroskopische Poren fpl
micro-set fein einstellen
microscopic eye-piece Okular nt
micro-switch Mikroschalter m

microwave Mikrowelle f
microwave system Mikrowellensystem nt
microwave technology Mikrowellentechnik f
microwave transmitter Mikrowellensensor m
mid point Mittelstellung f
mid position Mittelstellung f
middle Mitte f
middle band Mittenbereich m
middle run Mittellage f
middle slide Mittelschlitten m
mid-height of the character Mitte f Schrifthöhe
mid-plane Kreuzungsebene f
mid-range Spannenmitte f
migrant echo Wanderecho nt
migrate einwandern
migration Migration f
migration of binder Bindemittelabwanderung f
mild low carbon steel kohlenstoffarmer Stahl m
mild steel Flussstahl m
milestone Meilenstein m
mill 1. fräsen; Fräsmaschine f **2.** *(durch Schleifen)* Mühle f
mill at an angle schrägfräsen
mill into einfräsen
mill off abfräsen
milled surface pattern Fräsbild nt
milled tooth cutter gefräste Fräser m
milling Fräsen nt
milling arbor Fräserdorn m
cutter arbor Fräserdorn m
milling arbour Fräsdorn m
milling attachment Fräseinrichtung f, Fräsapparat m
milling automatic Fräsautomat m
milling capacity Fräsleistung f
milling centre Fräszentrum nt
milling cut Frässchnitt m
milling cutter Fräsmaschine f, Fräser m
milling cutter life Fräserstandzeit f
milling cutter with parallel rows of teeth Stollenfräser m
milling cycle Fräsgang m
milling feed Fräsvorschub m
milling feed of table Tischfräsvor-

schub *m*
milling head Fräsapparat *m*, Frässpindelstock *m*, Frässupport *m*, Fräskopf *m*, Frässpindelkopf *m*
milling head slide Frässupport *m*
milling headstock Frässpindelkasten *m*
milling job Fräsarbeit *f*
milling machine Fräsmaschine *f*, Rotorfräswerk *nt*
milling machine column Fräsmaschinenhersteller *m*
milling machine spindle nose Frässpindelkopf *m*
milling machines *pl* Fräsmaschinen *fpl*
milling of frame contours Rahmenfräsen *nt*
milling operation Fräsarbeit *f*, Fräsarbeitsgang *m*, Fräsgang *m*
milling planer Langhobelfräsmaschine *f*
milling quill Fräspinole *f*
milling sleeve Fräspinole *f*
milling spindle Frässpindel *f*, Arbeitsspindel *f*
milling spindle head Frässpindelkasten *m*, Frässpindelkopf *m*
milling spindle quill Frässpindelhülse *f*
milling surface Walkfläche *f*
milling table Frästisch *m*
milling tool Fräswerkzeug *nt*
milling unit Fräsaggregat *nt*
milling with automatic cycle table control Pendelverkehrfräsen *nt*, Pendelfräsen *nt*
milling with dual setups Schwenktischfräsen *nt*
milling work Fräsarbeit *f*
millings Frässpäne *f*
milliradiant Milliradiant *m*
millwright steel square Flachwinkel *m*
mimic Fließbild *nt*
mineral Mineral *nt*, Mineralstoff *m*, mineralisch
mineral aggregate Mineralstoffgemisch *nt*
mineral fibrous insulating material Mineralfaserdämmstoff *m*
mineral substance constituents Mineralstoffanteile *mpl*
mineral-bound wood wool mineralisch gebundene Holzwolle *f*
mineral-dry-friction-abrasion Mineraltrockengleitverschleiß *m*
mineral-powder flame cutting Mineralpulverbrennschneiden *nt*
miniature photofluorographic equipment Schirmbildaufnahmegerät *nt*
miniature processing Miniaturbearbeitung *f*
miniature screw thread Gewinde *nt* für kleine Durchmesser
minicomputer Minicomputer *m*
miniload storage and retrieval machine Kleinregalbediengerät *nt*
miniload storage system Tablarlager *nt*
miniload system Tablarlager *nt*
minimeter indicator gauge Minimeter *m*
minimization Minimierung *f*
minimize minimieren, verringern, herabsetzen
minimizing of inventories Bestandsminimierung *f*
minimum Minimum *nt*; kleinst, minimal, geringst ...
minimum backlash Kleinstflankenspiel *nt*
minimum chip thickness Mindestspandicke *f*
minimum clearance in air Mindestluftstrecke *f*
minimum cross-sectional area after fracture kleinster Probenquerschnitt *m* nach dem Bruch
minimum dimension Kleinstmaß *nt*
minimum distance Mindestabstand *m*
minimum hardness Mindesthärte *f*
minimum height Mindesthöhe *f*
minimum ignition temperature Mindestzündtemperatur *f*
minimum interference Kleinstübermaß *nt*
minimum limit Kleinstmaß *nt*
minimum marking Mindestkennzeichnung *f*
minimum master plug gauge Minimumprüfdorn *m*
minimum operator Minimumoperator *m*

minimum overpressure Mindestüberdruck *m*
minimum pressure Mindestdruck *m*
minimum quantity Mindestmenge *f*, Kleinstmenge *f*, Minimalmenge *f*
minimum quantity counting Minimalmengenzählung *f*
minimum room dimension Mindestraumgröße *f*
minimum support width Mindestauflagebreite *f*
minimum surface pressure Mindestflächenpressung *f*
minimum turning radius Mindestwenderadius *m*
minimum value Mindestwert *m*, Tiefstwert *m*, Anfangswert *m*
minimum value limiter Kleinstwertbegrenzer *m*
minimum working pressure Mindestarbeitsdruck *m*
minor geringfügig
minor cutting edge Nebenschneide *f*
minor cutting edge angle Einstellwinkel *m* der Nebenschneide
minor diameter Kerndurchmesser *m*, Innendurchmesser *m*
minor diameter of the thread Mutterkerndurchmesser *m*
minor diameter tolerance Kerndurchmessertoleranz *f*
minor flank Nebenfreifläche *f*
minor thread diameter plug gauge Kerndurchmesserlehrdorn *m*
minimum size Kleinstmaß *nt*
minimum breaking load Mindestbruchkraft *f*
minus size variation Minusabweichung *f*
minute klein, sehr gering, fein
minute value Spannungsfestigkeit *f*
minute value of electric strength Ein-Minuten-Stehspannung *f*
minutes Protokoll *nt*
mirror Spiegel *m*; spiegeln
mirror image operation Achsenspiegeln *nt*, Spiegelbildbearbeitung *f*
mirror images of each other spiegelbildlich
mirror revolutions per minute Spiegeldrehzahl *f*
mirror speed Spiegeldrehzahl *f*
mirror wheel Spiegelrad *nt*
mirror-copying spiegelbildliches Kopieren *nt*
mirrored side verspiegelte Seite *f*
mirror-finish hochglanzpolieren
mirror-imaged identical involute tooth flanks *pl* spiegelbildlich gleiche Evolventenzahnflanken *fpl*
misalignment Verschiebung *f*, Fluchtungsfehler *m*, Versetzung *f*, Versatz *m*
miscalculation Rechenfehler *m*
miscellaneous functions Hilfsfunktionen *fpl*
mishandling unsachgemäße Behandlung *f*
mismatch Versatz *m*
misoperation Fehlschaltung *f*
missile shielding concrete Splitterschutzbeton *m*
missing part Fehlteil *nt*
mission Sendung *f*
mist Nebel *m*
mist coolant Kühlmittel *nt* für Ölnebelkühlung
mist cooling Sprühkühlung *f*, Ölnebelkühlung *f*
mistake versehentlicher Fehler *m*; verwechseln
mist-lubrication Ölnebelschmierung *f*
misuse Missbrauch *m*, unsachgemäßer Gebrauch *m*
mitre cut Gehrungsschnitt *m*
mitt Fausthandschuh *m*
mix 1. mischen, verbinden **2.** *(Fehler)* verwechseln
mix back zurückmischen
mix chamber Mischkammer *f*
mix sample Mischgutprobe *f*
mixed gemischt
mixed aniline point Mischanilinpunkt *m*
mixed electrode Mischelektrode *f*
mixed logic gemischte Logik *f*
mixed mode Mischbetrieb *m*
mixed region Mischgebiet *nt*
mixed solution Mischlösung *f*
mixed-cell foam gemischtzelliger Schaumstoff *m*

mixer jet Mischdüse f
mixer unit Mischeinrichtung f
mixing Mischung f, Mischen nt
mixing mill Mischwalzwerk nt
mixing pre-heater Mischvorwärmer m
mixing pre-heater deaerator Mischvorwärmerentgaser m
mixing section Mischstrecke f
mixture Mischung f, Gemisch nt
mixture relation Mischungsverhältnis nt
mobile mobil, beweglich, fahrbar, verfahrbar
mobile carriage Verfahrschlitten m, Verfahrwagen m
mobile data memory mobiler Datenspeicher m
mobile line bewegliche Leitung f
mobile protective seat Schutzkanzel f
mobile rack system Gleitregal nt
mobile racking verfahrbares Regal nt
mobile scaffolding Fahrgerüst nt
mobile shelving Verschieberegal nt, verfahrbares Regal nt
mobile shelving rack store Verschieberegallager nt
mobile storage system Gleitregal nt
mobile X-ray protective seat Röntgenschutzkanzel f
modal function modale Funktion f
mode häufigster Wert m, Modalwert m, Betriebsart f
mode number Modenzahl f
mode of action Benutzungsart f, Wirkweise f
mode of operation Bedienungsart f, Fahrweise f, Arbeitsweise f, Betriebsart f
mode structure Modenstruktur f
mode switch Wahlschalter m
model modellieren; Modell nt, Vorlage f, Typ m, Ausführung f, Bauart f
model building Modellbildung f
model check Modellüberprüfung f
model configuration Modellkonfiguration f
model element Modellelement nt
model equation Modellgleichung f
model forming Modellbildung f
model material Modellwerkstoff m

model parameter Modellparameter m
model structure Modellaufbau m
model verification Modellüberprüfung f
modelling Modellbildung f, Modellierung f
modelling level Modellierungsstufe f
modelling stage Modellierungsstufe f
model size Modellmaße ntpl
modification Änderung f, Variante f, Veränderung f, Umbau m
modification note Änderungsvermerk m
modification of a contract Vertragsänderung f
modification of the flank shape Flankenkorrektur f
modification status Änderungszustand m
modified to impact strength schlagzäh modifiziert
modify modifizieren, verändern, ändern, abändern, abwandeln, umgestalten, umbauen, umarbeiten
modifying Modifizieren nt
modular modular
modular battery Modulbatterie f
modular design Modulbauweise f
modular fixture Baukastenvorrichtung f
modular part list Baukastenstückliste f
modular principle Baukastenprinzip nt
modular robot Baukastenroboter m
modular system Baukastensystem nt
modular tool system modulares Werkzeugsystem nt
modulation Modulation f
modulation rate Schrittgeschwindigkeit f
modulator Modulator m
module Modul nt, Baustein m, Block m
module hob Modulwälzfräser m
module refreshing Bausteinerneuerung f
module renewal Bausteinerneuerung f
module station Einschubstation f
module width Modulbreite f
module-dependent bottom clearance modulabhängiges Kopfspiel nt
module-oriented blockorientiert

module-related bausteinbezogen
modulus of elasticity from the compression test Elastizitätsmodul *nt* aus dem Druckversuch
modulus of cubic compressibility Kompressionsmodul *nt*
modulus of elasticity Dehnmodul *nt*
modulus of elasticity from the bending test Elastizitätsmodul *nt* aus dem Biegeversuch
modulus of elasticity from the tensile test Elastizitätsmodul *nt* aus dem Zugversuch
modulus of loss Verlustmodul *nt*
moist nass, feucht
moist mass Feuchtmasse *f*
moist zone Feuchtzone *f*
moisten anfeuchten, feuchten, benetzen
moisture Feuchte *f*, Feuchtigkeit *f*
moisture expansion Feuchtigkeitsdehnung *f*
moisture measurement Feuchtemessung *f*
moisture repellent feuchtigkeitsabweisend
moisture-sensitive flüssigkeitsempfindlich
mol Mol *nt*
mol mass Molmasse *f*
mould and die duplicator Formen- und Gesenkfräsmaschine *f*, Formen- und Gesenknachformfräsmaschine *f*
moulding die Kokille *f*
mole cross-section Maulquerschnitt *m*
molecular cohesive force Kohäsionskraft *f*
molecular main chain component Molekühlhauptkettenstück *nt*
molecule Molekül *nt*
molecule laser Moleküllaser *m*
molt schmelzen
molten material Schmelze *f*
molten solder Lotschmelze *f*
molten geschmolzen
molybdenum Molybdän *nt*
molybdenum high speed steel Molybdänschnellstahl *m*
moment Moment *m*, Augenblick *m*, Zeitpunkt *m*

moment arm Hebelarm *m*
moment of event Ereigniszeitpunkt *m*
moment of inertia Trägheitsmoment *nt*
moment of mass inertia Massenträgheitsmoment *m*
moment of order Moment *m* der Ordnung
moment of resistance Widerstandsmoment *nt*
moment of torsion Verdrehmoment *nt*
momentary interruption Kurzzeitunterbrechung *f*
momentary switch Tastschalter *m*
momentum Moment *nt*, Impuls *m*
momentum of sales Lagerumschlag *m*
monitor Bildschirm *m*, Monitor *m*, Wächter *m*; überwachen, kontrollieren
monitoring Kontrolle *f*, Überwachung *f*
monitoring area Kontrollbereich *m*
monitoring device Überwachungsgerät *nt*
monitoring equipment Überwachungseinrichtung *f*
monitoring function Überwachungsfunktion *f*
monitoring of the component flame Teilflammenüberwachung *f*
monitoring of the ignition flame Zündflammenüberwachung *f*
monitoring of the starting flame Startflammenüberwachung *f*
monitoring of the steam pressure Dampfdrucküberwachung *f*
monitoring of the water level Wasserstandsüberwachung *f*
monkey wrench *(Werkzeug)* Franzose *m*
monobloc aus einem Stück *nt*
monobloc battery Blockbatterie *f*
monoboard computer Einplatinenrechner *m*
monochromatic monochromatisch
monoclinic moniklin
mono-grade sortenrein
mono-lever control Einhebelsteuerung *f*
monomeric monomer
monomeric plasticizer monomerer Weichmacher *m*
monomeric styrene monomeres Sty-

rol *nt*
mono-product sortenrein
month's program Monatsprogramm *nt*
mordant ätzend
more mehr
more than one shift per day Mehrschichtbetrieb *m*
morphy calliper Tastzirkel *m*
mortise verzapfen
mortising tool Hohlmeißelbohrer *m*
most commonly used measure gebräuchlichstes Maß *nt*
most severely stressed area höchstbeanspruchte Stelle *f*
most significant bit höchstwertige Binärstelle *f*
mother pallet Mutterpalette *f*
motherboard Hauptplatine *f*, Mutterplatine *f*, Trägerleitplatte *f*
motion Verstellung *f*, Bewegung *f*, Gang *m*
motion component Bewegungskomponente *f*
motion control Bewegungssteuerung *f*
motion douche Bewegungsspülung *f*
motion element Bewegungselement *nt*
motion guidance Bewegungsführung *f*
motion law Bewegungsfunktion *f*
motion link Zwischenglied *nt*
motion lock-out Bewegungssperre *f*
motion phase Bewegungsphase *f*
motion process Bewegungsvorgang *m*
motion space Bewegungsraum *m*
motion type Bewegungsart *f*
motionless tensile stress ruhende Zugbeanspruchung *f*
motive power Treibkraft *f*, Triebkraft *f*
motor Motor *m*, Maschine *f*, Verbrennungsmaschine *f*
motor armature Motorläufer *m*
motor capacity Motorleistung *f*
motor control Motorsteuerung *f*
motor driven chain Kettenantrieb *m*, Antriebskette *f*
motor moment of inertia Massenträgheitsmoment *nt* des Motors
motor protecting switch Motorschutzschalter *m*
motor rating Motorleistung *f*
motor shaft Motorachse *f*, Motorwelle *f*
motor speed Motordrehzahl *f*
motor torque Motormoment *nt*
motor vehicle tube Fahrzeugschlauch *m*
motor vehicle tyre Fahrzeugreifen *m*
motor-actuated shut-off valve Absperrarmatur *f* mit Antrieb durch Elektromotor
motor-circuit switch Motorschutzschalter *m*
motor-driven kraftbetrieben
motorized motorisch
mould entformen, formen, gießen, pressen, profilieren; Form *f*, Gießform *f*
mould by extrusion extrudieren
mould driving side Werkzeugantriebsseite *f*
mould growth Schimmelwachstum *nt*
mould in a cold state kalt formen
mould insert Form *f* einsetzen
mould insert nut Einpressmutter *f*
mould misalignment Formversatz *m*
mould parting surface Formteilungsfläche *f*
mould related size *(bei Gussstücken)* formgebundenes Maß *nt*
mould technology Formtechnik *f*
mould under heat warm formen
mould unrelated size nichtformgebundenes Maß *nt*
mould with multiple gate Werkzeug *nt* mit Mehrfachanschnitt
mould with single gate Werkzeug *nt* mit Einfachanschnitt
mouldability Formbarkeit *f*
mouldable timing solder modellierbares Reiblot *nt*
mouldable under heat warm formbar
mould-dependent dimension formgebundenes Maß *nt*, werkzeuggebundenes Maß *nt*
moulded profiliert
moulded fibre building panel Holzfaserplatte *f*
moulded laminated circular tube formgepresstes Rundrohr *nt*
moulded material Pressstoff *m*
moulded part Formstück *nt*
moulded thermosetting material

Pressstoff *m* aus warm härtbarer Formmasse
mould-independent dimension nichtformgebundenes Maß *nt*
moulding Pressteil *nt*, Entformen *nt*
moulding burr Gießansatz *m*
moulding deposit Gießansatz *m*
moulding frame Pressrahmen *m*
moulding machine Formmaschine *f*
moulding material Formstoff *m*
moulding shrinkage Verarbeitungsschwindung *f*
moulding skin Außenhaut *f*
moulding solder Modellierlot *nt*
mount 1. anbauen, einbauen, zusammenbauen, installieren, anbringen, aufstecken, montieren, befestigen, spannen, einspannen, aufspannen **2.** *(klettern)* steigen, aufsteigen (auf), zusteigen
mount of rake Größe *f* des Spanwinkels
mount on aufsetzen
mounted diazo paper Lichtpauspapier *nt* auf Gewebe
mounting Aufbringen *nt*, Anbringen *nt*, Montieren *nt*, Montage *f*, Befestigung *f*, Anordnung *f*, Zusammenbau *m*, Einspannung *f*, Aufspannung *f*, Einbau *m*
mounting and location of the cutting tool Aufnahme *f* und Orientierung *f* des Zerspanwerkzeuges
mounting arbour Spanndorn *m*, Aufspanndorn *m*
mounting axis Aufnahmeachse *f*
mounting bracket Befestigungsschelle *f*
mounting distance Einbaumaß *nt*
mounting face Befestigungsfläche *f*
mounting fixture Aufnahmevorrichtung *f*
mounting flange Spannflansch *m*
mounting gear unit Aufsteckgetriebe *nt*
mounting instruction Einbauvorschrift *f*, Montagehinweis *m*
mounting instructions Montageanleitung *f*
mounting link Lasche *f*
mounting location Einbauort *m*
mounting mandrel Aufspanndorn *m*
mounting of wheels Radbefestigung *f*
mounting plane Anlagefläche *f* der Befestigung
mounting plate Befestigungsplatte *f*
mounting rail Rasterschiene *f*
mounting restriction Montagebeschränkung *f*
mounting surface Befestigungsfläche *f*
mountings *pl* Beschläge *mpl*
mouse button Maustaste *f*
mouth Öffnung *f*, Maul *nt*
mouthpiece Mündung *f*
movable verstellbar, beweglich, fahrbar, verschiebbar, transportabel
movable crossrail beweglicher Querbalken *m*
movable guard bewegliche Absperrung *f*
movable mask bewegte Maske *f*
movable micro structure bewegliche Mikrostruktur *f*
movable platen bewegliche Aufnahme *f*, beweglicher Träger *m*
movable scale verschieblicher Maßstab *m*
move verstellen, einstellen, verschieben, ausschieben, bewegen, befördern, fahren, verfahren, versetzen, verlegen, übertragen, schalten
move away fortbewegen
move back and forth hin- und herfahren
move diagonally diagonal fahren
move down herunterfahren
move downward abbewegen, niedergehen
move forward vorschieben, vorrücken
move latitudinally quer fahren
move longitudinally längs fahren
move on fortbewegen
move out ausziehen
move relative to each other gegeneinander verschieben
move to and fro hin- und herbewegen
move transversally quer fahren, quer verfahren
move when empty Leerfahrt durchführen
movement Bewegung *f*, Verkehr *m*, Verfahren *nt*

movement analysis Bewegungsanalyse *f*
movement by friction surface Reibungsvorschub *m*
movement condition Bewegungsverhältnis *nt*
movement example Bewegungsmuster *nt*
movement of probe Prüfkopfführung *f*
movement of the load Lastbewegung *f*
movement of translation Translationsbewegung *f*
movement path Bewegungsbahn *f*
movement pattern Bewegungsmuster *nt*
moving Einstellen *nt*, Verstellen *nt*, Verfahren *nt*; beweglich
moving guidance Verstellführung *f*
moving grid Laufraster *nt*
moving load bewegte Last *f*
moving mandrel machine Dornschlittenmaschine *f*
moving parts bewegliche Teile *ntpl*, bewegte Teile *ntpl*
moving seal Abdichtung *f* beweglicher Teile
moving stress bewegte Masse *f*
moving workbench fahrende Werkbank *f*
MPC (multi point control) Vielpunktsteuerung *f*
servicing operation Wartungsarbeit *f*
muff Muffe *f*
muffle dämpfen
muffler Dämpfer *m*
multiple disk brake Lamellenbremse *f*
multi point control (MPC) Vielpunktsteuerung *f*
multi row camera Zeilenkamera *f*
multi-angle cut Folgeschnitt *m*
multi-bank panel radiator mehrreihiger Plattenheizkörper *m*
multi-bank panel type radiator mehrreihiger Plattenheizkörper *m*
multi-blade mehrschneidig
multiboard computer Mehrplatinenrechner *m*
multi-capillary Multikapillare *f*
multi-cell Mehrfachzelle *f*
multi-cell dynamic functioning Mehrfachzellenfunktion *f*
multi-cell positioning Mehrfachzellenschutzeinrichtung *f*
multi-channel module Mehrkanalmodul *nt*
multi-circuit module Mehrstromkreismodul *nt*
multi-clock system Mehruhrensystem *nt*
multi-colour light print paper Mehrfarbenlichtpauspapier *nt*
multi-coloured vielfarbig
multi-coloured representation mehrfarbige Darstellung *f*
multi-computer system Mehrrechnersystem *nt*
multi-conductor line Mehrfachleitung *f*
multi-core mehradrig
multi-core stranded filler wire mehradrig verdrillter Schweißdraht *m*
multi-cut copying lathe Vielschnittkopierdrehmaschine *f*
multi-cut lathe Mehrschnittdrehmaschine *f*, Vielstahldrehmaschine *f*, Vielmeißelautomat *m*, Vielschnittdrehmaschine *f*
multicut turret lathe Vielschnittrevolverdrehmaschine *f*
multi-digit mehrstellig
multidimensional mehrdimensional
multi-directional reach truck Mehrwegestapler *m* mit Schubmast
multi-directional truck Mehrwegestapler *m*
multi-disc brake Mehrscheibenbremse *f*
multidisk brake Lamellenbremse *f*
multi-disk clutch Mehrscheibenkupplung *f*
multi-echelon mehrstufig
multi-edge cutting tool mehrschneidiges Werkzeug *nt*
multi-edged vielschneidig
multi-flank cut Mehrflankenschnitt *m*
multi-floor warehouse Stockwerklager *nt*
multi-fuel application Anwendung *f* mehrerer Kraftstoffe
multifuel boiler Wechselbrandkessel *m*

multi-gear pumping set Mehrkreiszahnradpumpenaggregat *nt*
multihead milling machine Mehrspindelfräsmaschine *f*
multi-head milling machine Mehrspindelfräsmaschine *f*
multi-ident capability Multiidentfähigkeit *f*
multi-ident system Multiidentsystem *nt*
multi-lane mehrgassig
multilayer glass Verbundsicherheitsglas (VSG)
multi-layer slab Mehrschichtleichtbauplatte *f*
multi-layer welding mehrlagige Schweißung *f*
multi-level mehrstufig
multi-level action *(von Gliedern)* Mehrpunktverhalten *nt*
multi-level action controlling system Mehrpunktregeleinrichtung *f*
multi-level action element Mehrpunktglied *nt*
multi-level panel type radiator mehrlagiger Plattenheizkörper *m*
multi-line mehrzeilig
multi-line principle operation Mehrleitungssystem *nt*
multiline system Mehrlinienzuführung *f*
multi-line system Mehrleitungsanlage *f*
multi-location storage Mehrplatzlagerung *f*
multi-location system Mehrplatzsystem *nt*, Mehrplatztechnik *f*
multi-mast machine Mehrsäulengerät *nt*
multimodal distribution multimodale Verteilung *f*
multimoment study Multimomentstudie *f*
multi-moment time measurement MMZ (Multi-Moment-Zeitmessverfahren) *nt*
multi-moment-frequency MMH (Multi-Moment-Häufigkeit) *f*
multinomial distribution mehrdimensionale Verteilung *f*
multinomial distribution Multinomialverteilung *f*
multidirectional mehrseitig gerichtet
multipack Mehrfachpackung *f*
multi-pallet clamp Mehrpalettengabel *f*
multi-parameter vielparametrisch, mehrparametrisch
multipart mehrteilig
multiple-disc brake Mehrscheibenbremse *f*
multiple-point truer Mehrkornabrichter *m*
multi-pin mehrpolig
multi-place digital scale mehrstellige Ziffernskala *f*
multi-plant unternehmensübergreifend
multiple vielfach
multiple arc strikes Zündspur *f*
multiple bending in opposite directions mehrfaches Hin- und Herbiegen *nt*
multiple bolted joint Mehrschraubenverbindung *f*
multiple classification *(von Probeneinheiten)* mehrfache Aufteilung *f*
multiple cropping Mehrfachabschneiden *nt*
multiple cutting tool Vielschnittwerkzeug *nt*
multiple cycle Mehrfachspiel *nt*
multiple deep mehrfachtief
multiple deep storage mehrfachtiefe Lagerung *f*
multiple depth mehrfachtief
multiple depth storage mehrfachtiefe Lagerung *f*
multiple diameter turning Absatzdrehen *nt*
multiple edged tool mehrschneidiges Werkzeug *nt*
multiple electrode wheel machine Mehrfachrollenmaschine *f*
multiple equipment Mehrfachvorsatzgeräte *ntpl*
multiple error Mehrfachfehler *m*
multiple exposure Mehrfachbelichtung *f*
multiple folding Mehrfachabbiegen *nt*
multiple gate Mehrfachanschnitt *m*
multiple head milling machine Fräs-

maschine *f* mit mehreren Fräsköpfen
multiple implements Mehrfachvorsatzgeräte *ntpl*
multiple interference fit mehrfacher Pressverband *m*
multiple interrogation Mehrfachabfrage *f*
multiple lapping attachment Vielfachläppvorrichtung *f*
multiple LHD Mehrfach-LAM *nt*
multiple line feed system Mehrlinienzuführung *f*
multiple load capacity Mehrfachzugriff *m*, Mehrfachlastaufnahme *f*
multiple machine allocation Mehrmaschinenbelegung *f*
multiple manning devices Mehrfachbedienung *f*
multiple mask Mehrfachmaske *f*
multiple milling machine Mehrspindelfräsmaschine *f*
multiple nozzle Mehrfachdüse *f*
multiple planing Mehrfachhobeln *nt*
multiple plunger pumping set Mehrkolbenpumpenaggregat *nt*
multiple product feed Mehrsortenzuführung *f*
multiple projection welding Vielbuckelschweißen *nt*
multiple screw connection Mehrschraubenverbindung *f*
multiple spindle milling Mehrspindelfräsen *nt*
multiple splining Vielkeilverzahnung *f*
multiple stack Mehrfachstapel *m*
multiple stack transfer Mehrfachstapelumladung *f*
multiple thread mehrgängiges Gewinde *nt*
multiple tool block Blockmeißelhalter *m*, Vielstahlhalter *m*
multiple tool lathe Vielschnittdrehmaschine *f*
multiple toolholder Vielmeißelhalter *m*, Vielstahlhalter *m*
multiple V-form bending Mehrfachkeilbiegen *nt*
multiple wheels Mehrfachräder *pl*
multiple wound glass filament yarn gefachtes Textilglasgarn *nt*

multiple-aisle mehrgassig
multiple-cam operated automatic turret lathe Mehrkurvenautomat *m*
multiple-cam system Mehrkurvensystem *nt*
multiple-edge tracing Mehrkantensteuerung *f*
multiple-hole drilling attachment Mehrlochbohreinrichtung *f*
multiple-load carrying device Mehrfachlastaufnahme *f*
multiple-point cutting tool mehrschneidiges Werkzeug *nt*
multiple-point truing Mehrkornabrichten *nt*
multiple-product system Mehrsortenzuführung *f*
multiple-purpose machine Mehrzweckmaschine *f*
multiple-range measuring instrument Mehrbereichmessgerät *nt*
multiple-spindle automatic lathe Mehrspindler *m*, Mehrspindelautomat *m*
multiple-spindle boring machine Mehrspindelbohrmaschine *f*
multiple-spindle design Mehrspindelausführung *f*, Mehrspindelbauart *f*
multiple-spindle drilling Mehrspindelbohren *nt*
multiple-spindle drilling head Mehrspindelbohrkopf *m*, Mehrspindelkopf *m*
multiple-spindle drilling machine Vielspindelbohrmaschine *f*
multiple-spindle drilling machine with universally adjustable spindle Gelenkspindelbohrmaschine *f*
multiple-spindle fixed-bed type milling machine Mehrspindelplanfräsmaschine *f*
multiple-spindle honing machine Mehrspindelhonmaschine *f*
multiple-spindle machine Mehrspindelmaschine *f*
multiple-spindle manufacturing-type milling machine Mehrspindelplanfräsmaschine *f*
multiple-start thread n-gängiges Gewinde *nt*
multiple-step push button Mehrstu-

fenkopf *m*
multiple-track bed Dreibahnenbett *nt*, Mehrbahnenbett *nt*
multiple-way boring machine Mehrwegbohrmaschine *f*, Vielwegbohrmaschine *f*
multiple-way machine Mehrwegemaschine *f*
multiple-way switch Mehrwegeschalter *m*
multiple-width code Mehrbreitencode *m*
multiplying gear drive Vervielfachungsgetriebe *nt*, Multipliziergetriebe *nt*
multiplying gear mechanism Multipliziergetriebe *nt*
multi-point mehrpunktfähig
multi-point interface (MPI) Mehrpunktschnittstelle *f*
multi-point milling cutter Mehrzahnfräser *m*
multipoint tool mehrschneidiges Werkzeug *nt*
multiposition Multiposition *f*
multiposition depalletizer Mehrfachlagendepallettierer *m*, Multidepalettierer *m*
multiposition palletizer Mehrfachlagenpalettierer, Multipalettierer *m*, Multipositionspalettierer *m*
multiprocessing Mehrprozessorbetrieb *m*
multi-processing Mehrrechnerbetrieb *m*
multi-processor system Mehrrechnersystem *nt*
multi-product feed system Mehrsortenzuführung *f*
multipurpose vielfach einstellbar
multi-purpose container Mehrwegbehälter *m*
multi-purpose key with inner square Mehrzweckschlüssel *m* mit Innenvierkant
multi-purpose milling machine Mehrzweckfräsmaschine *f*
multipurpose turret lathe Vielzweckrevolverdrehmaschine *f*
multi-rib wheel mehrprofilige Schleifscheibe *f*
multi-room heating stove Mehrzimmerofen *m*
multi-row mehrreihig
multi-run fillet weld mehrlagige Kehlnaht *f*
multi-section pattern Sichtbild *nt*
multi-section radiator mehrgliedriger Radiator *m*
multi-shift operation Mehrschichtbetrieb *m*
multi-speed planer Hobelmaschine *f* mit Vielschnittgeschwindigkeit
multi-spindle bar automatic Mehrspindelstangenautomat *m*
multi-spindle bench-type milling machine Mehrspindelplanfräsmaschine *f*
multi-spline screw Innenkeilkopfschraube *f*
multi-stage mehrstufig
multi-stage gear mating mehrstufige Räderpaarung *f*
multi-stage gear pairing mehrstufige Räderpaarung *f*
multi-stage gear transmission mehrstufiges Getriebe *nt*
multistage sampling mehrstufige Probennahme *f*
multi-start left-hand thread mehrgängiges Linksgewinde *nt*
multi-start right-hand thread mehrgängiges Rechtsgewinde *nt*
multi-start stub metric trapezoidal screw thread mehrgängiges und flaches metrisches Trapezgewinde *nt*
multistation mehrplatzfähig
multi-station boring and milling machine Vielstationenbohr- und -fräsmaschine *f*
multistep mehrstufig
multi-step Mehrstufen ...
multi-storey mehrgeschossig
multi-storey warehouse Stockwerklager *nt*
multi-tier *(Regal)* mehrgeschossig
multi-tier installation Mehrgeschossanlage *f*
multi-tool lathe Vielstahldrehmaschine *f*, Vielmeißelautomat *m*

multi-tool production lathe Vielschnittdrehmaschine *f*
multi-toothed mehrzahnig
multi-toothed cutter mehrzahniger Fräser *nt*
multi-turn coiling Wickeln *nt*
multi-user system Mehrplatzrechner *m*, Mehrplatzsystem *nt*
multivariate mehrdimensional
multiway valve Mehrwegeventil *nt*
multiwheel drive Mehrradantrieb *m*
multi-wheel seam welding machine Mehrfachrollennahtschweißmaschine *f*
multi-wire mehradrig
mushroom head rivet Linsenniet *m*, Flachrundniet *m*
mushroom type condenser Pilzkühler *m*
mute überbrücken, stummschalten
mute signal Überbrückungssignal *nt*
muting Überbrücken *nt*
muting beam Überbrückungsstrahl *m*
muting configure *(stummschalten)* Überbrückung *f*
muting function Überbrückungsfunktion *f*
mutual wechselseitig, gegenseitig
mutual inductance Wechselinduktion *f*

N n

nail Nagel *m*, nageln
nail closing machine Nagelverschließmaschine *f*
nail-head welding Nagelkopfschweißen *nt*
naked eye bloßes Auge *nt*
naked flame offene Flamme *f*
name benennen
naming Benennen *nt*
NAND NICHT-UND *nt*, NAND-Glied *nt*
NAND buffer Leistungs-NAND-Glied *nt*
NAND logic NAND-Verknüpfung *f*
NAND-circuit NAND-Schaltung *f*
NAND-element NAND-Schaltung *f*
NAND-gate NAND-Schaltung *f*
nanotechnology Nanotechnologie *f*
knapsack weld Rucksacknaht *f*
narrow verengen, einengen, schmal, eng
narrow aisle Schmalgang *m*
narrow aisle truck Schmalgangstapler *m*
narrow band spectral analysis Schmalbandspekralanalyse *f*
narrow continuous line schmale Volllinie *f*
narrow-gap gas-shielded welding Schutzgasengspaltschweißen *nt*
narrow-necked volumetric flask Enghalsmesskolben *m*
native systemeigen
native code systemeigener Code *m*
natural natürlich
natural binding agent natürliche Bindemittel *ntpl*
natural characteristic Eigenmerkmal *nt*
natural circulation high temperature water heating appliance Naturumlaufheißwassererzeuger *m*
natural compression yield point natürliche Quetschzone *f*
natural frequency Eigenfrequenz *f*, Eigenschwingung *f*
natural gas Erdgas *nt*
natural gas-fired erdgasgefeuert

natural oscillating period Eigenschwingzeit *f*
natural rubber adhesive Kautschukkleber *m*
natural rubber latex Naturkautschuklatex *nt*
natural rubber vulcanizate Kautschukvulkanisat *nt*
natural strains *pl* Umformgrade *mpl*
natural torsional frequency Dreheigenfrequenz *f*
natural unit natürliche Einheit *f*
n-bar n-gliedrig
NC axis NC-Achse *f*
NC machine tool NC-Werkzeugmaschine *f*
NC program NC-Programm *nt*
NC programming NC-Programmierung *f*
NC-procedural chain NC-Verfahrenskette *f*
near bei, nah, nahe
near floor level Fußbodennähe *f*
near zero inventory Nahe-Null-Inventur *f*
near-net-shape-technology konturnahe Bearbeitung *f*
neat sauber
neatness Sauberkeit *f*
necessary notwendig, erforderlich
necessary machine utilization time erforderliche Maschinenbelegungszeit *f*
necessity Notwendigkeit *f*
neck einstechen, aushalsen, verengen; Ansatz *m*, Kehle *f*, Eindrehung *f*
neck down einengen
neck groove Einstich *m*
necking Aushalsen *nt*, Einstich *m*
necking down Einengung *f*
necking operation Aushalsung *f*
necking tool Einstechmeißel *m* zum Aushalsen
need of force Kraftbedarf *m*
need of power and work Kraft- und Arbeitsbedarf *m*
need of work Arbeitsbedarf *m*

needle Nadel *f*
needle bearing Nadellager *nt*
needle gripper Nadelgreifer *m*
needle penetration Nadelpenetration *f*
needle printer Nadeldrucker *m*
needle pulse Nadelimpuls *m*
needle regulating valve Regelnadelventil *nt*
needle scaler Nadelpistole *f*
needle tear force Nadelausreißkraft *f*
needle tear resistance Nadelausreißwiderstand *m*
needle tear-off resistance Nadelausreißwiderstand *m*
negate negieren
negating input Eingang *m* mit Negation
negating output Ausgang *m* mit Negation
negation Negierung *f*
negation circuit NICHT-Schaltelement *nt*
negative booking Stornobuchung *f*
negative cut Negativschnitt *m*
negative deviation (of the variable) Regeldifferenz *f*
negative extension negative Dehnung *f*
negative method Negativverfahren *nt*
negative pressure Unterdruck *m*
negative pressure attachment Unterdruckanlage *f*
negative pressure drop Unterdruckabfall *m*
negative pressure region Unterdruckbereich *m*
negative-only variation Nur-Minus-Abweichung *f*
negative-rake cutter Fräser *m* mit negativen Spanwinkel
negator Negator *m*, NICHT-Schaltelement *nt*
neglect unberücksichtigt lassen, übersehen, vernachlässigen; Vernachlässigung *f*
negligent nachlässig
negligible vernachlässigbar
negligible error zu vernachlässigende Abweichung *f*
negotiable gradient Steigfähigkeit *f*

negotiate a curve eine Kurve fahren
neighbourhood Umgebung *f*
neighbouring benachbart
neighbouring aisle Nachbargasse *f*
neighbouring compartment Nachbarfach *nt*
neighbouring work area benachbarter Betriebsbereich *m*
neutral neutral
nest (into each other) ineinander schachteln, ineinander stecken
nesting Schachtelung *f*
nesting container Stapelbehälter *m*
nesting depth Schachtelungstiefe *f*
nesting pallet Stapelpalette *f*
net netto
net cross-section Nettoquerschnitt *m*
net data Nettodaten *pl*
net demand Nettobedarf *m*
net demand assessment Nettobedarfsermittlung *f*
net investment Neuinvestition *f*
net weighing machine Nettowägefüllmaschine *f*
net weight Nettogewicht *nt*
netting Netztuch *nt*
network Verbund *m*, Netz *nt*, Netzwerk *nt*, Netzplan *m*; vernetzen
network configuration Netzkonfiguration *f*
network layer Netzwerkschicht *f*
network of suppliers Lieferantennetzwerk *nt*
network plan Netzplan *m*
network plan works Netzplanwerk *nt*
network system Mehrplatzsystem *nt*
network termination *(IT)* Netzanschluss *m*
network termination point Netzanschlusspunkt *m*
networked vernetzt
networked system Mehrplatzrechner *m*
networking Vernetzung *f*
neutral 1. neutral **2.** *(Schalterstellung)* Neutralstellung *f* **3.** *(Schaltungsart)* Sternpunkt *m*
neutral point Sternpunkt *m*
neutral position Neutralstellung *f*, Nullstellung *f*, Ruhestellung *f*

neutralise kompensieren
neutralization Neutralisierung *f*
neutralize neutralisieren
neutron dosimetry Neutronendosimetrie *f*
new condition Neuzustand *m*
new list Neuliste *f*
new plant and equipment expenditure Neuinvestition *f*
new system Neuanlage *f*
newel post Geländerstütze *f*
Newtonian fluid newtonsche Flüssigkeit *f*
next to neben
n-hour n-stündig
nib Nase *f* einer Senkschraube
nibble nibbeln
nibbling Knabberschneiden *nt*
nibbling machine Nibbelmaschine *f*
nick Nut *f*, Kerbe *f*, Riefe *f*, Rille *f*, Schlitz *m*, Spanbrechernut *f*; einstechen, einkerben
nickel Nickel *m*
nickel steel Nickelstahl *m*
night shift Nachtschicht *f*
nil Null *f*
nip off abkneifen
nipper Kneifzange *f*
nipple Nippel *m*
nitride ceramic cutting tool Nitridkeramikwerkzeug *nt*
nitrided case nitriergehärtete Randschicht *f*
nitrided steel Nitrierstahl *m*
nitriding hardness depth Nitrierhärtetiefe *f*
nitrocellulose solution adhesive Nitrocellulosekleber *m*
nitrogenizing depth Aufstickungstiefe *f*
nitrogen Stickstoff *m*
nitrogen cylinder Stickstoffflasche *f*
nitrogen regulator Stickstoffdruckminderer *m*
n-link n-gliedrig
No admittance! Zutritt verboten!
no-backlash spielfrei
noble corundum Edelkorund *m*
noble metal Edelmetall *nt*
node Knoten *m*, Endpunkt *m*, Schwerpunkt *m*
node coordinate Schwerpunktkoordinate *f*
node method Schwerpunktverfahren *nt*
node plane Knotenebene *f*
node point Knotenpunkt *m*
no-go end Ausschussseite *f*
noise Geräusch *nt*, Lärm *m*, Schall *m*, Rauschen *nt*
noise emission Geräuschemission *f*
noise emission parameter Geräuschemissionskenngröße *f*
noise formation Geräuschbildung *f*
noise indication Rauschanzeige *f*
noise intensity Geräuschlautstärke *f*
noise level Geräuschpegel *m*, Geräuschverhalten *nt*, Lärmpegel *m*, Schallpegel *m*, Störpegel *m*
noise limit Geräuschgrenzwert *m*, Lärmgrenze *f*
noise measurement Geräuschmessung *f*
noise measurement method Geräuschmessverfahren *nt*
noise source Schallquelle *f*
noise spectrum Schallspektrum *nt*
noise suppression Rauschunterdrückung *f*
noise trace Rauschanzeige *f*
noise transmitter Geräuschgeber *m*
noiseless geräuschlos, lärmfrei
noise-sensitive lärmsensibel
noisy geräuschvoll
no-load condition unbelasteter Zustand *m*
no-load half wave Leerhalbperiode *f*
no-load loss Leerlaufverlust *m*
no-load operation Leerlauf *m*
no-load running Leerlauf *m*
no-load speed Leerlaufdrehzahl *f*
no-load starting frequency Leerschalthäufigkeit *f*
no-load voltage Leerlaufspannung *f*
nomenclature Nomenklatur *f*
nominal Nenn ...
nominal addendum modification Nennprofilverschiebung *f*
nominal allowance Nennabmaß *nt*
nominal angle Nennwinkel *m*

nominal angular frequency Nennwinkelgeschwindigkeit f
nominal angular size Winkelnennmaß nt
nominal base circle Nenngrundkreis m
nominal base circle diameter Nenngrundkreisdurchmesser m
nominal bore progression Nennweitenstufung f
nominal brightness Nennbeleuchtungsstärke f
nominal capacity Nennleistung f
nominal centre distance Nennachsenabstand m
nominal composition Sollzusammensetzung f
nominal compressive stress Nenndruckspannung f
nominal crowning Nennbreitenballigkeit f
nominal current Nennstrom m
nominal data Nenndaten $ntpl$
nominal diameter of the core Kernstabnenndurchmesser m
nominal dimension Nennmaß nt, Sollmaß nt
nominal disconnected mode (NDM) abhängiger Wartezustand m
nominal efficiency Nennwirkungsgrad m
nominal flank lead Nennsteigerung f
nominal flank pitch Nennteilung f
nominal form *(e. Flankenlinie)* Nennform f
nominal gauge size Lehrensollmaß nt
nominal generator Nennerzeugende f
nominal helix Nennschraubenlinie f
nominal helix angle Nennschrägungswinkel m
nominal illuminance Nennbeleuchtungsstärke f
nominal involute Nennevolvente f
nominal lead Nennsteigungshöhe f
nominal length Nennlänge f
nominal load Nennbelastung f
nominal location Solllage f
nominal moment Nennmoment m
nominal operation Nennbetrieb m
nominal operational current Nennbetriebsstrom m

nominal output Nennleistung f
nominal pitch of the cutter Werkzeugteilung f
nominal power Nennleistung f
nominal pressure angle Nenneingriffswinkel m, Werkzeugeingriffswinkel m
nominal profile Nennprofil nt
nominal rake angle Werkzeugwinkel m
nominal rating Nennleistung f
nominal size Nennmaß nt
nominal size range Nennmaßbereich m
nominal speed Nenndrehzahl f
nominal stress Nennbelastung f
nominal taper Nennkegel m
nominal temperature Nenntemperatur f
nominal thickness of cut Nennspanungsdicke f
nominal thread diameter Gewindenenndurchmesser m
nominal thread size Gewindenenngröße f
nominal time Sollzeit f
nominal tooth trace Nennflankenlinie f
nominal torque Nennmoment m
nominal unit of area of cut Nennspanungsquerschnitt m
nominal value nominaler Wert m, Nennwert m, Sollwert m
nomogram Rechenschaubild nt
non-activated inaktiv
non-active energiefrei
non-adjustable fest
non-adjustable in height nicht höhenverstellbar
non-adjustable racking Regal nt mit festen Fachböden
non-ageing alterungsbeständig
non-alkali soap alkalifreie Seife f
non-appearance Ausbleiben nt
nonapplicability Nichtanwendbarkeit f
non-articulated nicht pendelnd
non-buckling knickfest
non-burned unverbrannt
non-central außermittig
non-circularity Unrundheit f

non-closed offen
non-cohesive mass kurzabreißende Masse *f*
non-coincidence Nichtzusammenfallen *nt*
non-combustibility Nichtbrennbarkeit *f*
non-combustible nicht brennbar, nicht entzündbar
non-combustible gas nichtbrennbares Gas *nt*
non-combustible heating gas nichtbrennbares Heizgas *nt*
non-compliance Nichteinhalten *nt*
non-conforming items fehlerhafte Einheiten *fpl*
non-consumable electrode nichtabschmelzende Elektrode *f*
non-contacting berührungslos
non-continuous unstetig
non-continuous conveyor Unstetigförderer
non-core process Nichtkernprozess *m*
non-crowned gear nichtballiges Rad *nt*
non-cutting stroke Rücklauf *m*
non-decarburized annealed malleable cast iron nicht entkohlend geglühter Temperguss *m*
non-decimal nichtdezimal
nondestructive zerstörungsfrei
nondestructive testing zerstörungsfreie Werkstoffprüfung *f*
non-detachable nicht lösbar
non-directional ungerichtet
nondisjunction ODER-NICHT *nt*
none keine/r/s
non-elevatable nicht hebbar
non-elevating nicht hebbar, nicht hebend
non-equilibrium state Nichtgleichgewichtszustand *m*
non-establishment Nichtzustandekommen
non-ferrous Nichteisen...
non-ferrous casting Nichteisenguss *m*
non-ferrous metal Buntmetall *nt*
non-flammable gas nichtbrennbares Gas *nt*
non-floating rivet nut unbewegliche Annietmutter *f*

non-functioning funktionsuntüchtig
non-generating cutting method spangebendes Formverfahren *nt*
non-geometrical quantity nichtgeometrische Größe *f*
non-guided nicht geführt
non-ignition Nichtzünden *nt*
non-indicating measuring instrument nichtanzeigendes Messgerät *nt*
non-initiation Ausbleiben *nt*
non-integer nicht ganzzahlig
non-interacting rückwirkungsfrei
non-isolated nicht isoliert, unisoliert, potentialgebunden
non-lifting nicht hebend
nonlinear nichtlinear
non-linear scale nichtlineare Skala *f*
non-load bearing fill goods nicht mittragendes Füllgut *nt*
non-load bearing thread flank nichttragende Gewindeflanke *f*
non-load-bearing assembly nichttragende Verbindung *f*
non-load-bearing joint Heftverbindung *f*, nichttragende Schweißverbindung *f*
non-load-bearing reinforcing bar nichttragender Bewehrungsstab *m*
non-machinable unzerspanbar
non-machining time Nebenzeit *f*, Verlustzeit *f*
non-magnetic unmagnetisch
non-metallic locking element nichtmetallisches Sicherungselement *nt*
non-metallic retaining element nichtmetallisches Sicherungselement *nt*
non-metallic nicht metallisch
non-metallic compound Nichtmetallverbindung *f*
non-metallic prevailing torque element Sicherungsteil *nt* aus Nichtmetall bei kombinierten Metallmuttern
non-metallic strapping Kunststoffband *nt*
non-negated connection nicht negierter Anschluss *m*
non-observance Nichtbeachtung *f*
non-operated condition Ruhezustand *m*
non-overcut tooth tip nichtüber-

schnittener Zahnkopf *m*
non-parallelism Unparallelität *f*
non-parallelity Unparallelität *f*, Nichtparallelität *f*
non-periodic nicht periodisch
non-permanent nicht fest
non-polarized unpolarisiert
non-porous blasenfrei
non-portable nicht tragbar
non-positive nicht zwangsgesteuert
non-positive drive kraftschlüssiger Antrieb *m*
non-positively steered nicht zwangsgesteuert
non-productive time Bearbeitungsnebenzeit *f*
non-rackbound regalunabhängig
non-random quantity nichtzufällige Größe *f*
non-reactive steering rückschlagfreie Lenkung *f*
non-reduced section flat specimen ungekerbte Flachprobe *f*
non-relieved tooth tips *pl* ungekürzte Zahnköpfe *mpl*
non-return function Rückschlagfunktion *f*
non-return valve Absperrventil *nt*, Rückschlagventil *nt*, Rückschlagarmatur *f*
non-reversible irreversibel, selbsthemmend
non-round gear unrundes Rad *nt*
non-sag property Standvermögen *nt*
non-sealing connection nichtdichtende Verbindung *f*
non-self-loading trailer Anhänger *m* ohne Ladeeinrichtung
non-self-supporting nicht selbsttragend
non-short-circuiting kurzschlussfrei
non-slip rutschhemmend, schlupffrei
nonsparkling funkenfrei
non-sprung ungefedert
non-stacking nicht stapelnd
non-stacking low-lift straddle carrier Portalwagen *m*
non-stacking straddle carrier Portalwagen *m*
non-stacking truck nicht stapelnder Hubwagen *m*
nonsteady region Unstetigkeitsgebiet *nt*
non-storage type heating appliance Direktheizgerät *nt*
non-symmetrical quantity Unsymmetriegröße *f*
non-systematically grooved surface character ungeordnet rilliger Oberflächencharakter *m*
non-tacky constituent nichtklebender Bestandteil *m*
non-telescopic nicht ineinander schiebbar
non-threaded portion gewindefreier Teil *m*
non-through-welded double square butt joint nicht durchgeschweißte Doppel-I-Naht *f*
non-transferred arc nicht übertragender Lichtbogen *m*
non-transgression Nichtüberschreitung *f*
non-uniformity of crystalline structure Gefügeinhomogenität *f*
non-uniformity of the material Werkstoffinhomogenität *f*
non-uniformity of wall thickness Ungleichwandigkeit *f*
non-vibrating schwingungsfrei
non-warping verzugsfrei
non-wearing verschleißfrei
non-working flank Rückflanke *f*
non-woven interlining Einlagevliesstoff *m*
NOR NICHT-ODER *nt*, NOR-Glied *nt*
NOR with one negated input NOR-Glied *nt* mit einem negierten Eingang
NOR-gate NOR-Schaltung *f*, NICHT-ODER-Schaltung *f*
norm Regel *f*
normal 1. normal 2. *(geometrische Linie)* Normale *f*
normal acceleration of free fall Normfallbeschleunigung *f*
normal back Spanwinkel *m*
normal backlash Normalflankenspiel *nt*
normal base pitch Normaleingriffsteilung *f*, Eingriffsteilung *f* der Flanken, Grundzylindernormalteilung *f*

normal base pitch variation Eingriffsteilungsabweichung f
normal base thickness Grundzahndicke f im Normalschnitt, Zahndicke f auf dem Grundzylinder im Normalschnitt
normal chordal tooth thickness Zahndickensehne f
normal chordal tooth thickness fluctuation Zahndickensehnenschwankung f
normal clearance Normalfreiwinkel m
normal diametral pitch Diametral-Pitch im Normalschnitt
normal distribution Normalverteilung f, Gauß-Verteilung f
normal distribution Normalklima nt
normal incidence Senkrechteinfall m
normal line Senkrechte f
normal load occurring in operation betriebsgemäße Belastung f
normal milling Normalfräsen nt
normal module Normalmodul nt
normal operating conditions Regelbetriebsbedingungen fpl
normal operating position normale Fahrerposition f
normal operation Regelbetrieb m, Normalbetrieb m, bestimmungsgemäßer Betrieb m, Regelbetriebsbedingungen fpl, Echtbetrieb m
normal pitch Normalteilung f
normal plane Normalebene f
normal pressure Normalprofil nt
normal pressure angle Normaleingriffswinkel m, Normalprofilwinkel m
normal profile angle at a point Profilwinkel m im Normalschnitt
normal radiation Normalstrahlung f
normal rake Normalspanwinkel m, Spanwinkel m senkrecht zur Schneide
normal response mode (NRM) Aufforderungsbetrieb m
normal section Normalquerschnitt m, Normalschnitt m, Senkrechtschnitt m
normal shut down Regelabschaltung f, Regelschaltung f
normal space-width Normallückenweite f, Lückenweite f im Normalschnitt
normal to the line of contact Berührungsnormale f
normal to the surface flächennormal
normal to the test face Prüfflächennormale f
normal tooth thickness Normalzahndicke f, Zahndicke f im Normalschnitt
normal wedge angle Normalkeilwinkel m, Wirknormalkeilwinkel m
normalized angular velocity relative Winkelgeschwindigkeit f
normally inflammable normalentflammbar
normally-closed gate Ausschalttor nt
normally-open gate Einschalttor nt
north pole Nordpol m
nose 1. *(an der Spindel)* Spindelnase f, Spindelkegel m **2.** *(am Werkzeug)* Werkzeugspitze f, Spitze f eines Meißels
nose angle Spitzenwinkel m
nosing depth Unterscheidung f
NOT NICHT
NOT AND NICHT-UND nt
not applicable ungültig, entfällt
not equal ungleich
NOT GO screw gauge member Gewindeausschusslehrenkörper m
NOT GO calliper gauge Ausschussrachenlehre f
NOT GO dimension Ausschussmaß nt
NOT GO effective diameter snap gauge Ausschussflankenrachenlehre f
NOT GO gap gauge Ausschussrachenlehre f
NOT GO gauging member Ausschusslehrenkörper m
NOT GO identification Ausschusskennzeichnung f
NOT GO limit Ausschussgrenze f
NOT GO limiting size Ausschussgrenzmaß nt
NOT GO mating screw gauge Gewindeausschussgegenlehrdorn m
NOT GO ring gauge Ausschusslehrring m
NOT GO screw plug gauge Gewindeausschusslehrdorn m
NOT GO screw ring gauge Gewindeausschusslehrring m
not requiring acknowledgement

nicht quittierpflichtig
not stored nicht gespeichert
not straight ungerade
not susceptible to shocks stoßunempfindlich
not suscreptible to vibrations schwingungsunempfindlich
not under load unbelastet
notation Druckvermerk *m*
notch Raste *f*, Kerbe *f*, Aussparung *f*, Rastenklinke *f*; einkerben, abflanschen
notch angle Kerbwinkel *m*
notch in the specimen Probenkorb *m*
notch wear Kerbverschleiß *m*
notched bar impact bending test Kerbschlagbiegeversuch *m*
notched bar impact energy Kerbschlagarbeit *f*
notched bar impact test Kerbschlagversuch *m*
notched tensile test specimen Kerbzugprobe *f*
notched transverse bend specimen gekerbte Querbiegeprobe *f*
notched wheel Rastenrad *nt*
notch-free transition kerbfreier Übergang *m*
notching Ausklinken *nt*, Abflanschen *nt*
NOT-circuit NICHT-Schaltelement *nt*
note Hinweis *m*; beachten, zur Kenntnis nehmen
note box Hinweisbox *f*
notes on installation Montagehinweise *mpl*
NOT-gate NICHT-Baugruppe *f*, NICHT-Gatter *nt*, NICHT-Schaltelement *nt*
NOT-GO end Ausschussseite *f*
NOT-GO gage Ausschusslehre *f*
NOT-GO gauge Ausschusslehre *f*
notice of non-negotiability Sperrvermerk *m*
notification Einmeldung *f*
notional surface gedachte Fläche *f*
NOT-OR NICHT-ODER *nt*
NOT-step NICHT-Stufe *f*
nought Null *f*
novel design Neukonstruktion *f*
Novolak moulding material Novolak-Pressmasse *f*
no-work magnet Haltemagnet *m*

nozzle Düse *f*, Mundstück *nt*
nozzle connection dimension Stutzenanschlussmaß *nt*
nozzle diameter Düsendurchmesser *m*
nozzle distance Düsenabstand *m*
nozzle setting angle Düsenanstellwinkel *m*
n-start thread n-gängiges Gewinde *nt*
nuclear plant kerntechnische Anlage *f*
nuclear radiation detector Kernstrahlungsdetektor *m*
nucleus Kern *m*
nugget overlap Linsenüberschneidung *f*
nuisance Belästigung *f*
null hypothesis Nullhypothese *f*
null indication Nullanzeige *f*
null transmission Nullgetriebe *nt*
nullify aufheben
number beziffern, nummerieren, zählen, bezeichnen mit Zahlen; Zahl *f*, Nummer *f*, Anzahl *f*
number of articles Artikelanzahl *f*
number of consignments Sendungsanzahl *f*
number of crown gear teeth Planradzähnezahl *f*
number of cycles Periodenzahl *f*, Taktzahl *f*, Schwingspieldrehzahl *f*, Spielzahl *f*, Schaltzahl *f*
number of cycles to failure Bruchschwingspielzahl *f*
number of data places Datenstellenzahl *f*
number of dips *(Galvanisation)* Tauchzahl *f*
number of drops Fallzahl *f*
number of drops to fracture Fallzahl *f* beim Bruch
number of electrodes Elektrodenanzahl *f*
number of fatigue cycles Schwingspielzahl *f*
number of flexures Knickzahl *f*
number of internal gear teeth *pl* Hohlradzähnezahl *f/mpl*
number of leads Ganganzahl *f*
number of machine Maschinenanzahl *f*
number of operators Bedieneranzahl *f*

number of pairs of poles Polpaarzahl *f*
number of pallets Palettenanzahl *f*
number of periods Periodenanzahl *f*
number of poles Polzahl *f*
number of quenches Abschreckzahl *f*
number of revolutions Umdrehungszahl *f*, Drehzahl *f*
number of revolutions per minute (r.p.m.) Umdrehungszahl *f*
number of screw threads Gewindeanzahl *f*
number of switching actuations Schalthäufigkeit *f*
number of teeth Zähnezahl *f*
number of teeth of the pinion type cutter Schneidrad-Zähnezahl *f*
number of twists Verwindezahl *f*
number of units Stückzahl *f*
number of wheels Radzahl *f*
number plane Zahlenebene *f*
number printer Nummerndrucker *m*
numbering Bezifferung *f*, Nummerung *f*
numbering practice Nummerungstechnik *f*
numbering systematization Nummerungssystematik *f*
number-place Nummernstelle *f*
numeral Zahl *f*
numeral carrier Zifferntrager *m*
numerator Zähler *m*
numeric digital
numeric control (NC) numerische Steuerung *f*
numeric display digitale Anzeige *f*
numeric key Zifferntastatur *f*
numeric keypad Ziffernfeld *nt*
numerical numerisch
numerical calculation numerische Berechnung *f*
numerical code Zahlencode *m*
numerical control (NC) Datensteuerung *f*, numerische Steuerung *f*, digitale Steuerung *f*
numerical data Zahlenabgabe *nt f/fpl*
numerical equation Zahlenwertgleichung *f*
numerical factor Zahlenfaktor *m*
numerical indication Ziffernanzeige *f*
numerical machining Bearbeitung *f* mit numerischer Steuerung
numerical number numerische Nummer *f*
numerical representation zahlenmäßige Darstellung *f*
numerical value Zahlenwert *m*
numerically controlled function numerisch gesteuerte Funktion *f*
numerically controlled machine datengesteuerte Maschine *f*
numerically-controlled milling machine Numerikfräsmaschine *f*
nut Mutter *f*
nut and tube threading machine Schrauben-, Mutter-, Rohrgewindeschneidmaschine *f*
nut automatic Mutternautomat *m*
nut bearing face Mutterauflagefläche *f*
nut for T-slots Mutter *f* für T-Nuten
nut locking feature Mutternsicherung *f*
nut runner Schraubenanziehmaschine *f*
nut tap Muttergewindebohrer *m*
nut tapping Muttergewindebohren *nt*
nut tapping automatic Muttergewindeschneidautomat *m*
nut thread Innengewinde *nt*, Muttergewinde *nt*
nut with screw clamp retention Mutter *f* mit Bügelsicherung
nutate taumeln
nut-basis system System *nt* der Einheitsmutter
nut-bevelling machine Mutterabkantmaschine *f*

O o

object 1. Gegenstand *m*, Objekt *nt* **2.** *(ablehnen)* beanstanden
object carrier Objektträger *m*
object under test Messgegenstand *m*
objection Beanstandung *f*
objective Ziel *nt*, Objektiv *nt*, Okular *nt*, Zielsetzung *f*
objective criterion sachlicher Gesichtspunkt *m*
objective function Zielfunktion *f*
objects *pl* **assembled to one another** zusammengehörende Teile *ntpl*
objects *pl* **assembled together** zusammengesetzte Gegenstände *mpl*
object-specific objektspezifisch
oblateness Abplattung *f*
obligation to acknowledgement Quittierpflicht *f*
oblique schräg, schief
oblique bore one-way stopcock Einwegschräghahn *m*
oblique grinding Schrägschleifen *nt*
oblique incidence Schrägeinfall *m*
oblique intromission Schrägeinschallung *f*
oblique rake schräger Spanwinkel *m*
oblique section Schrägschnitt *m*
oblique slotted clamp Schrägschlitzklemme *f*
oblique stroke Schrägstrich *m*
oblique transmission Schrägdurchschallung *f*
obliquity Schräge *f*
oblong hole Langloch *nt*
observance Einhaltung *f*, prüfende Beobachtung *f*
observation prüfende Beobachtung *f*
observe beobachten, beachten, überwachen, einhalten
observed value Beobachtungswert *m*
observer Beobachter *m*
obstacle Erschwernis *f*, Hindernis *nt*
obstacle detection Hinderniserkennung *f*
obstacle detection means Hinderniserkennungssystem *nt*
obstruct behindern, verstellen, hindern, drosseln
obstructing edge Störkante *f*
obstruction Hindernis *nt*, Hinderung *f*, Verstellen *nt*
obtain erwerben, erzielen, bekommen, erreichen
obtuse-angled stumpfwinklig
obviate vorbeugen
occupancy of passenger spaces Besetzung *f*
occupation inversion Besetzungsinversion *f*
occupation number Besetzungszahl *f*
occupational accident Arbeitsunfall *m*
occupy belegen, einnehmen, besetzen, beschäftigen
occur auftreten, eintreten
occurrence Eintreten *nt*, Auftreten *nt*, Ereignis *nt*
O-channel A-Kanal *m*
octagon Achteck *nt*, Achtkant *m*
octagon ram head Achtkantmeißelschieber *m*
octagonal achteckig
octoid Oktoide *f*
octoid tooth system Oktoidenverzahnung *f*
odd Ungeradeglied *nt*; ungerade
odd angle cutter Winkelfräser *m* für Werzeuge mit gefrästen Zähnen für Spannuten mit Drall
odd leg Tastzirkel *m*
odd number ungerade Zahl *f*
odd-even check Paritätsprüfung *f*
odd-fluted end mill Schaftfräser *m* mit ungerader Nutenzahl
odourless geruchlos
odourless shielding gas geruchloses Schutzgas *nt*
of brushing consistency streichbar
off aus
off-centre position Außermittigkeit *f*
off-centre verrutscht, exzentrisch, außermittig
offcut Materialabschnitt *m*, Reststück *nt*

offcut factor Reststückzuschlag *m*
off-delay timer Ausschaltverzögerungsglied *nt*
offer anbieten; Angebot *nt*
offer resistance widerstehen
off-grade Abweichung *f* von der Qualität
off-hand curving by stretching Schweifen *nt*
off-hand forming under compression conditions Freiformen *nt*
off-hand grinder Freihandschleifmaschine *f*
offhand grinding Handschliff *m*
off-hand piercing Dornen *nt*
offhand release Spontanfreigabe *f*
off-hand rounding freies Runden *nt*
off-hand sample Stichprobe *f*
official amtlich
official calibration Eichen *nt*
off-load unbelastet
OFF-Position AUS-Stellung *f*
offset absetzen, versetzen, kröpfen; Verziehung *f*, Achsversetzung *f*, Versetzung *f*, Versatz *m*, Ausladung *f*
off-set Regelabweichung *f*
offset axes Achsversatz *m*
offset bend Etagenbogen *m*
offset clamp verstellbares Spanneisen *nt*
offset combination wrench gekröpfter Ringmaulschlüssel *m*
offset compensation Offset
offset compressive yield stress Zwei-Prozent- (2%-) Stauchspannung *f*
offset cutting tool abgesetzter Meißel *m*
offset deviation Achsenversetzungsabmaß *nt*
offset double end box wrench gekröpfter Doppelringschlüssel *m*
offset double head box wrench abgewinkelter Doppelringschlüssel *m*
off-set double-ended spanner gekröpfter Doppelringschlüssel *m*
offset downcomer pipe verzogene Fallleitung *f*
offset handle Winkelgriff *m*
offset in parallel Parallelversatz *m*
offset load außermittige Last *f*

offset milling machine Fräsmaschine *f* mit außermittig schwingender Spindel, Fräsmaschine *f* mit oszillierender Spindel
offset of the cutting edges Schneidkantenversetzung *f*
offset of the edges Kantenversatz *m*
offset path äquidistante Bahn *f*
offset portion Abknickung *f*
offset printing Offsetdruck *m*
offset screwdriver Winkelschraubendreher *m*
offset side tool gebogener Seitenmeißel *m*
offset side-cutting tool abgesetzter Seitenmeißel *m*
offset single-point threading tool gekröpfter Gewindemeißel *m*
offset socket wrench abgewinkelter Steckschlüssel *m*
offset tool gekröpfter Meißel *m*
offset tool face geknickte Spanfläche *f*
offset tool flank geknickte Freifläche *f*
offset variation Achsversetzungsabweichung *f*
offset yield strength 0,1%-Dehngrenze *f*
offset yield stress Dehngrenze *f*
offsetting Kröpfen *nt*
offsetting of the tailstock Reitstockverstellung *f*
offsize Maßabweichung *f*, Abweichung *f* von Maßen
off-size Abmaß *nt*
ohmic resistor ohmscher Widerstand *m*
oil Öl *nt*, ölen, schmieren
oil absorption value Ölzahl *f*
oil bath Ölbad *nt*
oil burner motor Ölbrennermotor *m*
oil burner pump Ölbrennerpumpe *f*
oil burner with stepless control Ölbrenner *m* mit stufenloser Regelung
oil burner with two-step action control Ölbrenner *m* mit Zweipunktregelung
oil burning central heating system ölbefeuerte Zentralheizungsanlage *f*
oil can Ölkanne *f*
oil catcher Ölauffangeinrichtung *f*
oil circuit Ölkreislauf *m*

oil circulation Ölumlauf *m*
oil-cooled ölgekühlt
oil cooling Ölkühlung *f*
oil cup Ölbüchse *f*, Schmierbüchse *f*, Öler *m*
oil derivative Ölderivat
oil film Ölfilm *m*
oil filter Ölfilter *m*
oil firing plant Ölfeuerungsanlage *f*
oil flow meter Ölmengenzähler *m*
oil groove Ölnut *f*, Schmiernut *f*
oil immersion Ölkapselung *f*
oil immersion apparatus Ölkapselung *f*
oil-in-water emulsion Emulsion *f* von Öl in Wasser
oil mist Ölnebel *m*
oil residue Ölrückstand *m*
oil resistant ölfest
oil seal Öldichtung *f*
oil separator Ölabscheider *m*
oil spot Ölfleck *m*
oil storage water heater Ölspeicherwasserheizer *m*
oil vapour loss Öldampfverlust *m*
oil vaporizing burner Ölverdampfungsbrenner *m*
oil-conveying line ölführende Leitung *f*
oil-drain cock Ölablasshahn *m*
oiler Öler *m*
oil-fired furnace Ölofen *m*
oil-hardened ölgehärtet
oil-hardening steel ölhärtender Stahl *m*
oiling point Schmierstelle *f*
oil-protected ölgekapselt
oilstone mit Ölstein *m* abziehen
oil-temper ölanlassen
oily steam ölhaltiger Dampf *m*
old list Altliste *f*
olive Schneidring *m*
omit übergehen, auslassen
omnidirectional ungerichtet, omnidirektional
on *(Schaltung)* ein
on a larger scale in vergrößertem Maßstab *m*
on a non-contact basis berührungslos, berührungsfrei, kontaktlos
on a pro rata basis anteilig
on a spot check basis stichprobenweise
on an internal works basis *(von Vorschriften)* werksintern
on average im Mittel
on board mitgeführt, bordeigen
on both sides beidseitig
on demand auf Anforderung
on line direkt prozessgekoppelt
on no-load unbelastet
on schedule termingerecht, zeitnah
on site vor Ort
on the cathode side katodenseitig
on the drinking water side trinkwasserseitig
on the flue gas side abgasseitig
on the left links
on the left hand side linksseitig
on the right rechts
on the right-hand side rechtsseitig
on the service water side betriebswasserseitig
on time termingerecht, pünktlich
on top of each other übereinander
on/off circuit Abschaltkreis *m*
on/off command Schaltbefehl *m*, Schaltfunktion *f*
on-carriage Transportvorlauf *m*
once a year einmal jährlich
once through abrasive Einwegstrahlmittel *nt*
once-only test einmalige Prüfung *f*
once-through lubrication Durchlaufschmierung *f*
on-delay timer Einschaltverzögerungsglied *nt*
one abrasive body weight Schleifkörpereinzelgewicht *nt*
one after the other nacheinander
one minute residual strain Ein-Minuten-Restdehnung *f*
one minute strain Ein-Minuten-Dehnung *f*
one percent permanent limit of elongation Einprozent-Dehngrenze *f*
one percent proof stress Einprozent-Dehngrenze *f*
one-coil transformer Spartransformator *m*
one-component synthetic resin seal-

ant Einkomponentenkunstharzlack *m*
one-dimensional eindimensional
one-edge control Einkantensteuerung *f*
one-edge tracing Einkantensteuerung *f*
one-man control Einmannbedienung
one-minute test voltage Ein-Minuten-Prüfspannung *f*
one-off part Einzelteil *nt*
one-off print Einzeldruck *m*
one-off production Einzelstückfertigung *f*, Fertigung *f* von Einzelstücken
one-pass cutting Schneiden *nt* in einem Durchgang
one-piece pipe clip einteilige Rohrschelle *f*
one-piece aus einem Stück, einteilig, massiv
one-piece metal nut einteilige Metallmutter *f*
one-piece tubular rivet einteiliger Hohlniet *m*
one-quarter cone Viertelkonus *m*
one-start metric buttress thread eingängiges metrisches Sägengewinde *nt*
one-sided einseitig
one-sided cycloidal tooth system einseitige Zykloidenverzahnung *f*
one-sided lap weld einseitige Flankennaht *f*
one-start right-hand screw thread eingängiges Rechtsgewinde *nt*
one-start screw thread eingängiges Gewinde *nt*
one-start stub metric trapezoidal screw thread eingängiges flaches metrisches Trapezgewinde *nt*
one-start trapezoidal screw thread with clearance eingängiges Trapezgewinde *nt* mit Spiel
one-track mast device Einspurmastgerät *nt*
one-way einseitig
one-way boring machine Einwegbohrmaschine *f*
one-way classification einfache Aufteilung *f* von Probeeinheiten
one-way flow Strömung *f* in einer Richtung

one-way machine Einwegmaschine *f*
one-way taper stopcock Einwegkegelhahn *m*
on-hand quantity Bestand *m*
on-hand stock incorporation Bestandsübernahme *f*
on-hand-status check Verfügbarkeitskontrolle *f*
on-line enquiry Dialogauskunft *f*
on-line master file maintenance program generator Dialogstammdatenverwaltungsprogrammgenerator *m*
on-line open loop offen prozessgekoppelt
on-line pluggable on-line anschließbar
on-line processing Echtzeitverarbeitung *f*, Dialogverarbeitung *f*
on-line program Bildschirmprogramm *nt*
on-load unter Last *f*
on-load data Lastdaten *pl*
on-load speed Lastdrehzahl *f*
On-Off push button switch Ein-Aus-Druckknopfschalter *m*
on-order materials bestelltes Material *nt*
on-piece aus einem Stück *nt*
on-position Einschaltstellung *f*
on-position of the brake Bremsstellung *f*
onset potential Eintrittspotential *nt*
on-site buffer Vor-Ort-Puffer *m*
on-site service guarantee Serviceeinsatzgrenze *f*
onward transmission Weiterführung *f*, Weitergabe *f*, Weiterübertragung *f*
opaque lichtundurchlässig, milchig, trüb
open auf, frei, offen; öffnen
open access freier Zugang *m*
open air climate Freiluftklima *nt*
open and non through going pore offene und nicht durchgehende Pore *f*, Grübchen *nt*
open circuit test Leerlauftest *m*
open circuit water cooling Frischwasserkühlung *f*
open control system offenes Steuerungssystem *nt*
open depot Freilager *nt*

open die forging Freiformen *nt*
open ditch rohrloser Drän *m*
open douche offene Spülung *f*
open flap detector Stecklascheninspektionsmaschine *f*
open joint Fuge *f* mit Stegabstand
open joint brazing Fugenlöten *nt*
open joint soldering Fugenlöten *nt*
open loop offener Regelkreis *m*, offener Wirkungsweg *m*; offen prozessgekoppelt
open loop control Steuerung *f*, Steuerkette *f*, Steuerungstechnik *f*
open loop controlled system Steuerstrecke *f*
open loop controlling system Steuereinrichtung *f*
open order file Auftragsdatei *f*
open pointing Verjüngen *nt* von Hohlkörpern
open position offene Stellung *f*
open riser Steiger *m*
open sided plano-miller Einfachlangfräsmaschine *f*
open square pressure gas welding offenes Gaspressschweißen *nt*
open systems interconnection (OSI) systemfreie Kommunikation *f*
open the circuit ausschalten
open topped oben offen
open type heating system offene Heizungsanlage *f*
open-anneal blauglühen
open-annealing Blauglühung *f*
open-cell foam offenzelliger Schaumstoff *m*
open-centre reel Haspelspule *f*
open-circuit flux Leerfluss *m*
open-circuit potential Ruhepotential *nt*
open-ditch drainage rohrlose Dränung *f*
open-end wrench Maulschlüssel *nt*
open-ended control offene CNC
open-ended slugging spanner Schlagmaulschlüssel *m*
open-ended slugging wrench Schlagmaulschlüssel *m*
opener Öffner *m*
open-flame burner Düsenbrenner *m*
open-front design Einständerkonstruktion *f*, nach vorn offene Konstruktion *f*
opening Anfang *m*, Öffnung *f*, Entriegelung *f*
opening barrier sich öffnende Schranke *f*
opening between the housing Durchgang *m*
opening between uprights Ständerdurchgang *m*
opening capacity Spannweite *f* der Schraubstockbacken
opening time Öffnungszeit *f*, Sicherheitszeit *f* für „Anlauf"
open-outlet water heater Kochendwassergerät *nt*
open-side planer Einständerhobelmaschine *f*
open-side planer-miller Auslegerfräsmaschine *f*
open-side planer-miller with removable housing Langfräsmaschine *f* in Einständerkonstruktion mit ausfahrbarem Seitenständer
open-side plano-miller Langfräsmaschine *f* in Einständerkonstruktion
open-side plate planer Einständerblechkantenhobelmaschine *f*
open-sided planer Einständerhobelmaschine *f*
open-structure wheel grobporige Schleifscheibe *f*
operand Rechengröße *f*
operate betätigen, betreiben, bedienen, arbeiten, wirken, schalten
operating Betätigung *f*
operating ambient air temperature Betriebsumgebungstemperatur *f*
operating area Betriebsfläche *f*, Einsatzumgebung *f*
operating capacity Betriebskapazität *f*
operating classification Triebwerksgruppe *f*
operating component Bedienteil *nt*, Funktionsbestandteil *m*
operating condition(s) Betriebszustand *m*, Betriebsbedingungen *fpl*
operating control Stellteil *nt*
operating current Arbeitsstrom *m*

operating cycle Arbeitsgang *m*, Arbeitsablauf *m*, Arbeitsspiel *nt*
operating day Einsatztag *m*
operating desk Bedienungspult *nt*
operating device Bedienungseinrichtung *f*
operating efficiency Arbeitsleistung *f*
operating element Bedienteil *nt*, Betätigungsorgan *nt*
operating end stop position Betriebsendhalteposition *f*
operating engineer Betriebsingenieur *m*
operating equipment Betriebseinrichtung *f*
operating error Bedienungsfehler *m*
operating fault Betriebstörung *f*, Funktionsstörung *f*
operating frequency Schalthäufigkeit *f*, Betriebsfrequenz *f*
operating guide Bedienungsanleitung *f*
operating handle Bedienungsgriff *m*
operating head Nutzförderhöhe *f*
operating hours Betriebsstunden *fpl*
operating instruction Betriebsanleitung *f*, Bedienungsanleitung *f*, Bedienanleitung *f*, Betriebsanweisung *f*, Betriebsvorschrift *f*, Bedienungsvorschrift *f*
operating insulation Betriebsisolierung *f*
operating level Betriebsebene *f*
operating lever Bedienungsgriff *m*, Bedienungshebel *m*, Schalthebel *m*
operating log Bedienprotokoll *nt*
operating maintenance manual Bedienungs- und Wartungshandbuch *nt*
operating manual Handbuch *nt*, Bedienerhandbuch *nt*, Bedienungsanleitung *f*
operating member Bedienteil *nt*
operating message Betriebsmeldung *f*
operating method Arbeitsverfahren *nt*, Arbeitsweise *f*
operating mode Betriebsweise *f*, Betriebsart *f*
operating panel Bedientafel *f*, Bedienungstafel *f*
operating parameter Betriebswert *m*
operating performance Betriebsverhalten *nt*
operating period Betriebsdauer *f*, Laufzeit *f*
operating plan Arbeitsplan *m*
operating planning Arbeitsplanung *f*
operating platform Bedienungsbühne *f*
operating position Arbeitsstellung *f*, Steuerstand *m*, Fahrerposition *f*
operating precision Arbeitsgenauigkeit *f*
operating pressure Arbeitsdruck *m*, Betriebsdruck *m*
operating pressure of the pneumatic switch Schaltbetriebsdruck *m*
operating principle Arbeitsweise *f*, Arbeitsprinzip *nt*
operating procedure Fertigungsverfahren *nt*
operating range Wirkbereich *m*, Arbeitsbereich *m*
operating requirement Betriebsanforderung *f*
operating safety time Sicherheitszeit *f* „Betriebszustand"
operating sequence Ablauf *m* eines Arbeitsvorganges
operating sphere Funktionsbereich *m*
operating stand Steuerstand *m*
operating state Betriebszustand *m*
operating station Bedienstation *f*
operating status Betriebszustand *m*
operating system Bediensystem *nt*, Betriebssystem *nt*
operating temperature Betriebstemperatur *f*
operating time 1. Arbeitszeit *f*, Bearbeitungszeit *f*, Betriebszeit *f*, Laufzeit *f*, Nutzungszeit *f* **2.** *(anschalten)* Einschaltdauer *f*
operating time class Laufzeitklasse *f*
operating trouble Betriebstörung *f*
operating voltage Betriebsspannung *f*
operation Bedienung *f*, Arbeit *f*, Arbeitsweise *f*, Arbeitsablauf *m*, Arbeitsvorgang *m*, Vorgang *m*, Betrieb *m*, Prozess *m*, Funktion *f*, Einsatz *m*, Betätigung *f*
operation at normal rating Nennbetrieb *m*

operation condition Betriebszustand *m*
operation control Betriebsüberwachung *f*
operation cost per piece Stückkosten *pl*
operation cost(s) Betriebskosten *pl*
operation cycle Arbeitstakt *m*, Operationszyklus *m*
operation drawing Bearbeitungszeichnung *f*
operation feedback Bedienrückmeldung *f*
operation induced alteration betriebsbedingte Änderung *f*
operation instructions Gebrauchsanweisung *f*
operation manual Funktionsbeschreibung *f*
operation number Schaltzahl *f*
operation panel Bedienungsplatte *f*
operation personnel Bedienungspersonal *nt*
operation sequence Bearbeitungsreihenfolge *f*, Arbeitsablauf *m*
operation status Betriebszustand *m*
operation table Wahrheitstabelle *f*
operation time Einsatzzeit *f*
operation window Bedienfenster *nt*
operation(al) control key (OCK) Funktionstaste *f*
operability Funktionsfähigkeit *f*
operational betriebsbereit, funktionsfähig, operativ
operational amplifier Operationsverstärker *m*
operational application betriebliche Nutzung *f*
operational control Bedienbarkeit *f*
operational data Betriebsdaten *pl*
operational efficiency Wirtschaftlichkeit *f*
operational fault Störung *f*
operational order Operationsreihenfolge *f*
operational reliability Betriebstüchtigkeit *f*, Betriebssicherheit *f*
operational resource Betriebsmittel *nt*
operational safety Arbeitssicherheit *f*, Betriebssicherheit *f*, Funktionssicherheit *f*
operational sequence(s) Verfahrensabläufe *f*, Arbeitsfolge *f*
operation-related betriebsbedingt
operations management Ablaufmanagement *nt*
operations planning Disposition *f*, Arbeitsplanung *f*
operations scheduling Fertigungssteuerung *f*
operative funktionstüchtig
operative system Verfahrensschema *nt*
operator 1. Bediener *m*, Bedienperson *f*, Arbeiter *m*, Maschinenarbeiter *m* 2. *(Fahrzeug)* Fahrer *m*
operator accessibility Bedienerberührbarkeit *f*
operator command Bedienanweisung *f*
operator compartment Kabine *f*
operator convenience Bedienerfreundlichkeit *f*
operator facing this way Blickrichtung *f* des Fahrers
operator feedback Bedienrückmeldung *f*
operator interface Bedienerschnittstelle *f*
operator intervention Eingriff *m*
operator panel Bediengerät *nt*
operator prompting Bedienerführung *f*
operator restraining device Rückhaltesicherung *f*
operator restraint system Rückhaltesicherung *f*
operator stand Bedienstand *m*
operators Bedienungspersonal *nt*
operator's cab Fahrerkabine *f*, Kabine *f*
operator's compartment Fahrerplatz *m*
operator's manual Bedienungsanweisung *nt*
operator's overhead guard Fahrerschutzdach *nt*
operator's platform 1. Bedienerplattform *f* 2. *(Fahrzeug)* Fahrerplatz *m*
operators position 1. Führerstand *m*, Arbeitsstandort *m*, Bedienstand *m*, Bedienungsstand *m* 2. *(Fahrzeug)* Fah-

rerplatz *m*
operator's seat Fahrersitz *m*
operator's stand Bedienungsstand
operator's stand-on platform Fahrerstandplattform *f*
operator's weight Fahrergewicht *nt*
opposed direction of rotation gegenläufige Drehbewegung *f*
opposed graduated scale gegenläufige Skalierung *f*
opposed whirling Gegenlaufwirbeln *nt*
opposite gegenüber
opposite cam Gegenkurve *f*
opposite direction Gegenrichtung *f*
opposite direction of rotation entgegengesetzte Drehrichtung *f*
opposite flanks *pl* ungleichnamige Zahnflanken *fpl*
opposite lane Gegenfahrbahn *f*
opposite sign umgekehrtes Vorzeichen *nt*
obtain erhalten
optic Optik *f*
optical optisch, visuell
optical comparator Optimeter *m*, optisches Fühlhebelgerät *nt*
optical dividing head optischer Teilkopf *m*
optical electronic coupling element optoelektronisches Koppelelement *nt*
optical filter optischer Filter *m*
optical instrumentation optische Messeinrichtung *f*
optical measuring equipment Messoptik *f*
optical measuring system Messoptik *f*
optical projection system Projektionsoptik *f*
optical sighting equipment optische Visiereinrichtung *f*
optical signal Leuchtsignal *nt*, optisches Signal *nt*
optical system with projection screen Projektionsablesung *f*
optical warning device Warnlicht *nt*
optically readable optisch lesbar
optimeter Optimeter *m*
optimization Verbesserung *f*, Optimierung *f*
optimize verbessern, optimieren

optimum optimal, Optimum *nt*
option Wahl *f*, Möglichkeit *f*, Variante *f*
optional wahlweise, auf Sonderwunsch
optoelectric optoelektrisch
optoelectronics Optoelektronik *f*
optoreceiver Lichtempfänger *m*
OR ODER *nt*
Or dependency ODER-Abhängigkeit *f*
OR element with one input negated ODER-Glied *nt* mit Negation eines Einganges
or manufacturing-bed type milling machine with three spindle heads Planfräsmaschine *f* mit drei Frässpindelköpfen
OR with inhibiting input ODER-Glied *nt* mit Sperreingang
OR with negated inhibiting input ODER-Glied *nt* mit negiertem Sperreingang
OR with negated output ODER-Glied *nt* mit negiertem Ausgang *m*, NOR-Glied *nt*
order 1. (Einkauf) Bestellung *f*, Auftrag *m*; bestellen, anfordern 2. Kommando *nt*, Befehl *m*, Anordnung *f*; anweisen, anordnen 3. (Serie) Reihenfolge *f*, Folge *f*
order administration Auftragsverwaltung *f*
order backlog Auftragsreserve *f*
order characteristic value Auftragskennzahl *f*
order clearing Auftragsabwicklung *f*
order compilation Kommissionieren *nt*, Kommissionierung *f*
order compilation area Kommissionierungszone *f*, Kommissionierplatz *m*
order compilation factor Kommissionierfaktor *m*
order compilation head Kommissionierkopf *m*
order compilation process Kommissioniervorgang *m*
order compilation robot Kommissionierroboter *m*
order compilation unit Kommissioniereinheit *f*
order completion Auftragserstellung *f*
order completion Auftragsabwick-

lung *f*
order coordinate Auftragskoordinaten *fpl*
order data Auftragsdaten *pl*, Bestelldatum *nt*
order designation Bestellbezeichnung *f*
order drawing Bestellzeichnung *f*
order feedback Auftragsrückmeldung *f*
order fill rate Auftragserfüllung *f*
order flow Auftragsfluss *m*
order forecast Auftragsprognose *f*, Bestellprognose *f*
order function Ordnungsfunktion *f*
order handling Auftragsabwicklung *f*
order indicator Auftragskennzahl *f*
order item Auftragsposition *f*, Bestellposition *f*
order lead time Auftragsdurchlaufzeit *f*
order list Auftragsliste *f*
order loading Auftragseinlastung *f*
order modification Auftragsänderung *f*
order number Auftragsnummer *f*, Bestellnummer *f*, Kommissionsnummer *f*
order of priority Prioritätenfolge *f*
order of processing Bearbeitungsreihenfolge *f*
order picker Kommissionierer *m*, Kommissioniergerät *nt*
order picker truck Sammelhubwagen *m*, Kommissionierfahrzeug *nt*, Kommissioniergerät *nt*
order picking Sortieren *nt*, Kommissionieren *nt*, Kommissionierung *f*
order priority Auftragspriorität *f*
order process chain Auftragsabwicklungsprozess *m*
order processing Auftragsdisposition *f*, Auftragsabwicklung *f*, Bestellbearbeitung *f*
order quantity Bestellmenge *f*
order quantity planning Bestellmengenplanung *f*
order reference Bestellbezug *m*
order scheduling Auftragsterminierung *f*
order size computation Auftragsgrößenrechnung *f*
order statistic Ranggröße *f*
order status Ordnungszustand *m*

order structure Auftragsstruktur *f*
ordered geordnet
ordered value Rangwert *m*
orderer Auftraggeber *m*
ordering process Bestellprozess *m*
orderly ordnungsgemäß
order-picking cart Kommissionierwagen *m*
order-picking platform Kommissionierplattform *f*
order-picking position Kommissionierposition *f*
order-picking station Kommissionierarbeitsplatz *f*, Kommissionierplatz *m*, Kommissionierstation *f*
order-picking table Kommissioniertisch *m*
order-picking truck Kommissionierstapler *m*, Kommissionierflurförderzeug *nt*
order-picking warehouse Kommissionierlager *nt*
order-picking zone Kommissionierungszone *f*
orders Auftragseinlastung *f*
orders data Auftragsdaten *pl*
orders on hand Auftragsbestand *m*
ordinal characteristic Ordinalmerkmal *nt*
ordinal number Ordnungszahl *f*
ordinance Verordnung *f*
ordinance on weights and measures Eichordnung *f*
ordinarily üblicherweise
ordinary üblich
ordinary milling Fräsen *nt* im Gegenlauf, Gegenlauffräsen *nt*
ordinary-type engine lathe Zugspindeldrehmaschine *f*
ordinate Y-Achse *f*, Ordinate *f*
ore Erz *nt*
precision boring work Feinstbohrarbeit *f*
organic and inorganic coating Beschichtung *f*
organic and inorganic coating material Beschichtungsstoff *m*
organization Organisation *f*
organization data Organisationsdaten *pl*

organization means Organisationsmittel *ntpl*
organization of data Ergebnisaufbereitung *f*
organization of the production process Fertigungsablauf-Organisation *f*
organizational dispositiv, organisatorisch
organizational structure Aufbaustruktur *f*, Organisationsstruktur *f*
organize organisieren
OR-gate ODER-Glied *nt*
orientate orientieren
orientation Orientierung *f*, Drehlage *f*
orientation angle Lagewinkel *m*
orientation device Orientierungseinrichtung *f*
orientation of cutting edge Lage *f* der Schneide
orientation of face Lage *f* der Spanfläche
orientation of flank Lage *f* der Freifläche
orientation tension Orientierungsspannung *f*
orientation tolerance Richtungstoleranz *f*
orienter Orientierungsmaschine *f*
orifice Öffnung *f*, Düse *f*, Mündung *f*
orifice plate Drosselblende *f*
orifice welding Düsenschweißen *nt*
origin Herkunft *f*, Ursprung *m*
origin of orders Auftragsquelle *f*
original 1. ursprünglich 2. Vorlage *f* 3. *(Zeichnung, Konstruktion)* Urzeichnung *f*
original condition Ursprungszustand *m*
original cross-section area Anfangsquerschnitt *m*
original documents *pl* Originalvorlagen *fpl*
original drawing Ursprungszeichnung *f*, Zeichnungsoriginal *nt*
original extensometer gauge length Anfangsgerätemesslänge *f*
original gauge length Anfangsmesslänge *f*
original inspection Erstprüfung *f*
original package Originalverpackung *f*
original packing Originalverpackung *f*
original system Originalsystem *nt*
original written documents *pl* Schriftgutvorlagen *fpl*
originate verursachen, entstehen
originator Verursacher *m*
O-ring gasket Rollringdichtung *f*
OR-linked ODER-verknüpft
orthocycloid Orthozykloide *f*
orthogonal rechtwinklig
orthogonal clearance Orthogonalfreiwinkel *m*
orthogonal cut Orthogonalschnitt *m*
orthogonal cutting orthogonale Zerspanung *f*, Zerspanen *nt* ohne Überhöhung der Schneide
orthogonal plane Orthogonalebene *f*
orthogonal wedge angle Orthogonalkeilwinkel *m*
oscillate oszillieren, schwanken, vibrieren, schwingen, pendeln
oscillating oszillierend, pendelnd, reversierend
oscillating arm Kurbelschwinge *f*, Schwingarm *m*
oscillating circuit Schwingkreis *m*
oscillating crank Schwinge *f*
oscillating frequency Schwingfrequenz *f*
oscillating mirror Schwingspiegel *m*
oscillating mirror add-on Schwingspiegelvorsatz *m*
oscillating mirror system Schwingspiegelsystem *nt*
oscillating movement Oszillationsbewegung *f*, Pendelbewegung *f*
oscillating platform *(Fußlenkung)* Wippe *f*
oscillating rotation Schwenkbewegung *f*
oscillating-type abrasive cutting machine Pendeltrennschleifmaschine *f*
oscillation Oszillation *f*, *(freie)* Schwingung *f*, Schwankung *f*
oscillation amplitude Schwingungsamplitude *f*, Schwingungsausschlag *m*
oscillation coefficient Schwingbeiwert *m*
oscillation dynamics Schwingungsdynamik *f*

oscillation generator Schwingungserreger *m*
oscillation level Schwingungsebene *f*
oscillation movement Auf- und Abbewegung *f*
oscillator Schwinger *m*
oscillatory oszillierend
oscillatory mirror Schwingspiegel *m*
oscillatory wave Schwingung *f* (Wellen)
osculating plane Schmiegungsebene *f*
output link Drehschubglied *nt*
output plate Leistungsschild *nt*
out hinaus
out of aus
out of mesh außer Eingriff
out of operation außer Betrieb
out of round unrund
out of true unrund
outage losses Ausfallkosten *pl*
outboard brace Gegenhalterschere *f*
outbound logistics Distributionslogistik *f*, Beschaffungslogistik *f*
outbreak point Ausbruchstelle *f*
outcome Ergebnis *nt*, Resultat *nt*
out-cut milling Gegenlauffräsen *nt*
outdoor im Freien
outdoor climate Freiluftklima *nt*
outdoor exposure Freilandbewitterung *f*
outdoor exposure test Freibewitterungsversuch *m*
outdoor test Freilandversuch *m*
outdoor weathering Bewitterung *f* im Freien, Freibewitterung *f*, Freilandbewitterung *f*
outdoor weathering test Freibewitterungsversuch *m*
outer äußere/r/s
outer casing Mantel *m*
outer conductor Außenleiter *f*
outer diameter Außendurchmesser *m*
outer edge Störkante *f*
outer fibre Randfaser *f*
outer fibre strain Randfaserdehnung *f*
outer veneer Außenfurnier *nt*
outermost äußerste/r/s
outfeed belt Auslaufband *nt*
outfeed conveyor Auslaufförderer *m*
outfeed location Auslaufstelle *f*

outfeed point Auslagerpunkt *m*
outfeed rate Auslagerdurchsatz *m*
outfeed star Auslaufstern *m*
outfit Apparatur *f*, Apparat *m*, Gerät *nt*, Ausrüstung *f*, Einrichtung *f*
outfitter Ausrüster *m*
outflow bend ablaufseitiger Bogen *m*
outgate Steiger *m*, Steigtrichter *m*
outgoing 1. ausgehend 2. *(Lagerung)* auszulagernd
outgoing goods department WA (Warenausgang) *m*
outgoing goods point Warenausgang (WA) *m*
outgoing line Abführstrecke *f*
outgoing merchandise Warenausgang (WA) *m*
outgoing merchandise inventory Warenausganglager *nt*
outgoing merge Ausschleuser *m*
outgoing transport Abtransport *m*
out-house außerbetrieblich
outlay Aufwand *m*
outlay calculation Aufwandsermittlung *f*
outlay estimate Aufwandabschätzung *f*
outlay-benefits analysis Aufwandnutzenbetrachtung *f*
outlet Auslauf *m*, Auslass *m*, Ablauf *m*, Abflussöffnung *m*
outlet nozzle Lüftungsdüse *f*
outlet pressure Hinterdruck *m*, Auslassdruck *m*
outlet pressure of a valve Auslassdruck *m* eines Ventils
outlet report Austrittskanal *m*
outlet section Ausmündungsstück *nt*
outlet stabilizer Austrittsstabilisator *m*
outlet temperature Ablauftemperatur *f*
outlets *pl* Ausläufe *mpl*
outlier Ausreißer *m*
outline Umfang *m*, Kontur *f*, Umriss *m*, Profil *nt*
outline agreement Rahmenvertrag *m*
outlook Ausblick *m*
out-of balance Unwucht *f*
out-off roundness Kreisabweichung *f*
out-of-flatness Unebenheit *f*
out-of-parallelism Unparallelität *f*
out-of-roundness Unrundheit *f*

output 1. Ausgabe *f*, Abgabe *f*, Ausgang *m*, Ausstoß *m*, Ausbringung *f*; ausbringen, ausgeben, auslagern, abfördernd **2.** *(Display)* Anzeige *f* **3.** *(Leistung)* ausbringen; abgegebene Leistung *f*, ausgebrachte Leistung *f*, Arbeitsleistung *f*, Produktion *f*, Fertigungsleistung *f*, Arbeitsleistung *f*, Mengenleistung *f*
output compactness Leistungsdichte *f*
output current Ausgangsstrom *m*
output image Ausgangsbild *nt*
output inspection Ausgangsprüfung *f*
output link Abtriebsglied *nt*
output maximum Leistungsgrenze *f*
output module Ausgangsmodul *nt*, Ausgabebaugruppe *f*
output motion Abtriebsbewegung *f*
output of radiant heat Strahlungswärmeabgabe *f*
output part flow Auslagerteilstrom *m*
output per annum Jahresproduktion *f*
output per section Gliedleistung *f*
output point Auslagerpunkt *m*
output potential Austrittspotential *nt*
output pressure Ausgangsdruck *m*
output pulse Ausgangsimpuls *m*
output quantity Ausgangsgröße *f*
output raising Produktionssteigerung *f*; produktionssteigernd
output range Ausgabebereich *m*, Ausgangsbereich *m*
output rate Auslagerdurchsatz *m*
output reference system Auslagerreferenzsystem *nt*
output relay Ausgangsrelais *nt*
output shaft Abtriebswelle *f*
output signal Ausgangssignal *nt*
output speed Abtriebsdrehzahl *f*, Abtriebszahl *f*
output stage Ausgangsstufe *f*, Endstufe *f*
output station 1. Ausgangspunkt *m* **2.** *(Daten)* Ausgabeeinheit *f* **3.** *(Lager, z. B. Material)* Auslagerstation *f*
output terminal Ausgangsklemme *f*
output unit Ausgabeeinheit *f*
output value Ausgangswert *m*
output valve Ausgangswert *m*
output variable Ausgangsgröße *f*

output voltage Ausgangsspannung *f*
output with polarity indicator Ausgang *m* mit Polaritätsindikator
outrigger Radarm *m*
outsert technology Anspritzen von Kunststoffteilen auf einer Metallplatine
outside äußere/r/s, außen, außerhalb
outside calliper Außentaster *m*, Greiftaster *m*
outside company Fremdfirma *f*
outside diameter Außendurchmesser *m*
outside gripping Außenspannen *nt*
outside spread Außenabstand *m*
outside spring calliper Federaußentaster *m*, Federgreifzirkel *m*
outside supplier Zulieferer *m*
outside surface Mantelfläche *f*
outside temperature Außentemperatur *f*
outside temperature measurement Außentemperaturmessung *f*
outside turning Außendrehen *nt*
outside turning radius Radius *m*, Wendradius *m*
outsource extern beschaffen, durch Fremdbezug beschaffen
outsourcing Fremdbezug *m*, Fremdvergabe *f*
outsourcing control Fremdbezugssteuerung *f*
outsourcing planning Fremdbezugsplanung *f*
outstanding herausragend
outward journey *(z. B. Schienen)* Hinfahrt *f*
outward-positioned arrowhead außenstehender Pfeil *m*
outwards nach außen
oval grinder Ovalschleifmaschine *f*
oval laminated rod Ovalleiste *f*
oval point Linsenkuppe *f*
oven Ofen *m*
oven ageing Ofenalterung *f*
oven dry pulp Otrozellstoff *m*
oven furnace Herdofen *m*
oven furnace shape process Herdformverfahren *nt*
oven furnace shapes Herdformen *nt*
over über

over mounted fliegend gelagert
overall 1. gesamt 2. allgemein, generell
overall assessment Gebrauchsfähigkeitsnachweis *m*, Gesamturteil *nt*
overall design Gesamtlösung *f*
overall dimension Baulänge *f*
overall dimensions Baumaße *ntpl*, Gesamtabmessungen *fpl*
overall effectiveness Gesamtwirkung *f*
overall efficiency Gesamtwirkungsgrad *m*
overall heat requirement Gesamtwärmebedarf *m*
overall height Bauhöhe *f*, Gesamthöhe *f*
overall length Gesamtlänge *f*, Baulänge *f*
overall lift height Gesamthubhöhe *f*
overall mean value Gesamtmittelwert *m*
overall system Gesamtsystem *nt*
overall throughput Gesamtdurchsatz *m*
overall time Gesamtzeit *f*
overall tolerance Gesamttoleranzen *pl*
overall twisting angle Gesamtverdrehwinkel *m*
overall volume Gesamtmenge *f*
overarm Gegenhalter *m*, Oberarm *m*, Balken *m*
overarm brace Stütztraverse *f*, Gegenhalterstütze *f*
overarm power Gegenhaltekraft *f*
overarm support Gegenhalterstütze *f*
overburden überlasten
overcharge überladen, überlasten; Überladung *f*, Überlast *f*
overcharging Überlastung *f*, Überladen *nt*
overcontrol übersteuern; Übersteuerung *f*
overcurrent Überstrom *m*
overcurrent protection Überstromschutz *m*
overcurrent protective device Überstromschutzeinrichtung *f*
overcurrent release Überlastschalter *m*
overcut überschneiden
overcut gear überschnittenes Zahnrad *nt*

overcutting Überschneidung *f*
overdimension überdimensionieren
overdrive Übersteuerung *f*, übersteuern
over-expanding Überdehnen *nt*
overflow funnel Überlauftrichter *m*
overflow storage heater Überlaufspeicher *m*
overflow water Überlaufwasser *nt*
over-gassing Übergasen *nt*
overhang Auskragung *f*, Überkragung *f*, Ausladung *f*, Überhang *m*, Überbau *m*; überstehen, überhängen, auskragen, hinausragen über
overhang angle Überhangwinkel *m*
overhang of the cutting tool Meißelausladung *f*
overhanging überstehend, überhängend
overhaul Reparatur *f*, Nachbesserung *f*; reparieren, überholen, nachbessern
overhaul work Nachbesserungsarbeiten *pl*
overhauling Überholung *f*, Überholen *nt*
overhead darüber angebracht, obenliegend, Ober ...
overhead conveyor Kreisförderer *m*, Hängeförderer *m*
overhead cost Gemeinkosten *pl*
overhead countershaft Deckenvorgelege *nt*
overhead crane Hängekran *m*
overhead door closer Obertürschließer *m*
overhead electric line Freileitung *f*
overhead guard Kabinendach *nt*, Schutzdach *nt*, Fahrerschutzdach *nt*
overhead protection Schutzdach *nt*
overhead track conveyor Schienenhängebahn *f*
over-heating Überwärmung *f*
overhung freitragend
over-igniting Überzünden *nt*
overinflation Überdruck *m*
overlap Überdeckung *f*, Überlappung *f*; überlappen, überschneiden
overlap arc Sprungüberdeckungswälzkreisbogen *m*
overlap degree Überdeckungsgrad *m*
overlap indicator Überdeckungsan-

zeiger *m*
over-lap length *(e. Schrägstirnrades)* Sprung *m*
overlap ratio Sprungüberdeckung *f*
overlap seal Überlappnaht *f*
overlapping Überschneidung *f*, Überlappung *f*; überlappend
overlapping layer überlappende Schicht *f*
overlay Überlagern *nt* von Signalen; überlagern
overlength Überlänge *f*
overload Überbeanspruchung *f*, Überlast *f*; überbelasten, überbeanspruchen
overload capacity Überlastbarkeit *f*
overload clutch Überlastkupplung *f*, Überlastungskupplung *f*
overload current Überlaststrom *m*
overload cutoff Überlastabschaltung *f*
overload cutout device Überlastabschaltvorrichtung *f*
overload indicator Überlastanzeige *f*
overload protection Überlastschutz *m*, Überlastungsschutz *m*, Überlastsicherung *f*
overload release Überlastschalter *m*, Überlastauslösung *f*
overload safety device Überlastsicherung *f*
overload scram Überlastschnellabschaltung *f*
overload sensing device Überladungserkennungssystem *nt*
overload signal lamp Überladungswarnleuchte *f*
overload speed Überlastdrehzahl *f*
overload surge current Überlastungsstromstoß *m*
overload switch Überlastschalter *m*
overload telltale lamp Überladungswarnleuchte *f*
overload test Überlastprüfung *f*, Überlastversuch *m*
overload trip Überlastschnellabschaltung *f*
overloaded run Überlastfahrt *f*
overloaded travel Überlastfahrt *f*
overloading Überlastung *f*, Überladen *nt*; überladen, überlasten
overloading Überladung *f*

overload-proof überlastfest
overlook übersehen, vernachlässigen
overmeasure Teileaufmaße *ntpl*
overmodulate übersteuern
overmodulation Übersteuerung *f*
over-point method Überpunktmethode *f*
overpressure Überdruck *m*
overpressure test Überdruckprüfung *f*
override springen, überspringen, weiterschalten, übersteuern, umgehen, auslassen, überfahren
override switch Umgehungsschalter *m*
overriding Weiterschaltung *f*
overriding reset vorrangiges Rücksetzen *nt*
overrun überfahren
overrun limit Überlaufanschlag *m*
overrun path Überlaufweg *m*
over-running clutch Freilauf- und Überholkupplung *f*
overrunning distance Überlaufweg *m*
overshoot überfahren, hinausschießen, hinausgehen über, hinausgeraten über, überschwingen, überschreiten
overshoot angle Durchschlagwinkel *m*
overshoot distance Überschwingweite *f*
overshooting Überschwingen *nt*
overshot überschritten
oversize Übergröße *f*, Überlauf *m*, Übermaß *nt*, Teileaufmaße *ntpl*; überdimensionieren
oversize format Überformat *nt*
overspeed Überdrehzahl *f*, Übergeschwindigkeit *f*, Schleuderdrehzahl *f*
overspeed governor Geschwindigkeitsbegrenzer *m*
overspeed governor rope Reglerseil *nt*
overspread überspreizen
overspreading Überspreizen *nt*
oversteer Übersteuerung *f*; übersteuern
overstepping Überschreitung *f* von Richtwerten
overstorage Überlagern *nt*
overstore überlagern
overstrain überbeanspruchen, überspannen
overstraining beyond the elastic limit Überschreiten *nt* der Strecke

overstress überlasten, überbeanspruchen; Überlastung *f*, Überbeanspruchung *f*
overstretch überspannen
oversynchronous übersynchron
overtake überholen, vorbeifahren
overtaking Überholung *f*
overtaking principle Überholung *f*
overtemperature Übertemperatur *f*
overtemperature protection Übertemperaturschutz *m*
over-temperature safety device Übertemperatursicherung *f*
overtighten zu fest anziehen
overtiming Überzeit *f*
overtravel Überfahren *nt*; überfahren, hinausfahren über
overturn umstürzen, stürzen, umkippen, kippen
overturning Sturz *m*, Umkippen *nt*, Umstürzen *nt*
overturning degree Überdrehungsgrad *m*
overturning moment Kippmoment *nt*
overturning movement Kippbewegung *f*
overview Übersicht *f*; übersehen
overview display Übersichtsbild *nt*
overview field Übersichtsfeld *nt*
overvoltage Überspannung *f*
over-voltage Überschlagspannung *f*
overvoltage category Überspannungskategorie *f*
overvoltage limiter Überspannungsbegrenzer *m*
overvoltage protection Überspannungsschutz *m*
overvoltage protective device Überspannungsschutzeinrichtung *f*
overvoltage suppressor Überspannungsableiter *m*
overweight Überlast *f*
overwrapping machine Falteinschlagmaschine *f*
own dimension Eigenmaß *nt*
owner Betreiber *m*
owner protection plan booklet Wartungsheft *nt*
oxidation period Alterungsdauer *f*
oxidation reaction Oxidationsreaktion *f*
oxidation stability Oxidationsstabilität *f*
oxidative degradation oxidativer Abbau *m*
oxidative wear Oxidationsverschleiß *m*
oxide ash Oxidasche *f*
oxide ceramic Oxidkeramik *f*
oxide ceramics Oxidkeramik *f*
oxide coating Oxidbelag *m*
oxide film Oxydhaut *f*
oxide layer Oxydschicht *f*
oxide ceramic cutting material oxidkeramischer Schneidstoff *m*
oxide-ceramic cutting tool oxidkeramisches Schneidwerkzeug *nt*
oxide-dissolving capacity Oxidlösevermögen *nt*
oxidize oxidieren
oxyacetylene ring-type burner Acetylensauerstoffringbrenner
oxyacetylene welding and cutting blowpipe Sauerstoffacetylenschweiß- und -schneidbrenner *m*
oxygen Sauerstoff *m*
oxygen pressure ageing Sauerstoffdruckalterung *f*
oxygen pressure chamber Sauerstoffdruckkammer *f*
oxygen pressure regulator Sauerstoffdruckminderer *m*
oxygen shut-off valve Sauerstoffabsperrventil *nt*
oxygen throughput Sauerstoffdurchfluss *m*
ozone cracking Ozonrissbildung *f*

P p

P und D station Übergabestelle *f*
pack verpacken, packen, einpacken, unterbauen, unterlegen, abdichten; Packung *f*
pack lubrication Vorratsschmierung *f*
pack of rod electrodes Stabelektrodenpaket *nt*
pack seal Verpackungsverschluss *m*
package packen, verpacken, abpacken; Packung *f*, Paket *nt*, Gebinde *nt*, Kollo *nt*, Packmittel *nt*, Packstück *nt*
package sorting system Paketsortieranlage *f*
packaged good Packgut *nt*
packaged quantity Packungsmenge *f*
packaged timber gebündelte Holzpakete *ntpl*
packaging practice Verpackungswesen *nt*
packaging Konfektionierung *f*, Verpackung *f*, Verpacken *nt*, Abpacken *nt*
packaging aid Packhilfsmittel *nt*
packaging component Packhilfsmittel *nt*
packaging concept Verpackungskonzept *nt*
packaging container Packmittel *nt*
packaging control Konfektionierungssteuerung *f*
packaging cycle Verpackungszyklus *m*
packaging machine Verpackungsmaschine *f*
packaging material Verpackung *f*, Verpackungsmaterial *nt*, Packstoff *m*
packaging material transport mechanism Packstofftransportvorrichtung *f*
packaging ordinance Verpackungsverordnung *f*
packaging planning Konfektionierungsplanung *f*
packaging strap Verpackungsband *nt*
packaging surface Verpackungsoberfläche *f*
packaging test Verpackungsprüfung *f*
packaging unit Verpackungseinheit *f*, Packungseinheit *f*
packed goods Packgut *nt*
packetize zusammenfügen
packing 1. Packung *f*, Verpackung *f*, Verpacken *nt*, Unterbauung *f* **2.** *(Dichtung)* Beilegering *m*, Abdichtung *f*
packing and unpacking machine Einpack- und Auspackmaschine *f*
packing area Packerei *f*
packing beneath Unterstopfung *f*
packing block Unterlegeblock *m*
packing cord Dichtungsschnur *f*
packing drawing Verpackungszeichnung *f*
packing list Packliste *f*
packing machine Einpackmaschine *f*
packing material Verpackungsmittel *nt*
packing pattern Packmuster *nt*
packing plate Platte *f* zur Unterfutterung
packing ring Dichtring *m*, Dichtungsring *m*
packing shim Packungsscheibe *f*, Unterlegscheibe *f*
packing table Packtisch *m*
packing under Unterstopfung *f*
packing unit Packstück *nt*
packing work station Kommissionierarbeitsplatz *f*
pad Kissen *nt*, Polster *nt*, Puffer *m*, Unterlage *f*; polstern, ausfüttern
pad-weld auftragschweißen
pad-welding Auftragsschweißung *f*
padded gepolstert
padding Ausfütterung *f*
padlock Vorhängeschloss *nt*
page *(Text)* Seite *f*
page acknowledgement Seitenquittierung *f*
page down bildabwärts
page up bildaufwärts
paging Blättern *nt*
pail Eimer *m*
paint Lack *m*, Farbe *f*; lackieren, anstreichen
paint clearance groove Lackkratz-

kerbe *f*
paint-coat anstreichen
painted lackiert
painted surface Farbanstrich *m*
painting Anstreichen *nt*
paints *pl* Anstrichstoffe *mpl*
paintshop Lackiererei
pair Paar *nt*; paaren
pair formation effect Paarbildungseffekt *m*
pair of messages Meldepaar *nt*
pair of suspension elements Tragmittelpaar *nt*
pair of uprights Ständerpaar *nt*
pair production effect Paarbildungseffekt *m*
paired tooth system Paarverzahnung *f*
pairing Paarung *f*
pallet Palette *f*
pallet back stop Palettendurchschubsicherung *f*
pallet band Palettenband *nt*
pallet-band locking Palettenbandverriegelung *f*
pallet bearer Palettenkufe *f*, Kufe *f*
pallet box Palettenbox *f*
pallet carrier Beschickungswagen *m*
pallet chain Palettenkette *f*
pallet chain roller Palettenkettenrolle *f*
pallet changer Palettenwechsler *m*
pallet check Palettenkontrolle *f*
pallet collar Paletten Aufsetzrahmen *m*
pallet compression strapping machine Palettenumreifungspresse *f*
pallet converter Palettenaufsetzgestell *nt*
pallet cross beam Palettentraverse *f*
pallet deck spacer Palettenträger *m*
pallet detection Palettenerkennung *f*
pallet dismantling Palettenauflösung *f*
pallet dismantling machine Palettenauflösungsmaschine *f*
pallet entry Paletteneinlauf *m*
pallet entry point Paletteneinlaufstelle *f*
pallet exchanger Palettentauscher *m*
pallet exit Palettenauslauf *m*
pallet exit point Palettenauslaufstelle *f*
pallet flow racking Palettendurchlaufregal *nt*

pallet foot Palettenkufe *f*, Kufe *f*
pallet forming Palettenherstellung *f*
pallet frame Aufsetzrahmen *m*
pallet-free palettenlos
pallet gripper Palettengreifer *m*
pallet high-bay warehouse Palettenhochregallager *nt*
pallet input Paletteneinlauf *m*
pallet inverter Palettenwendeklammer *f*
pallet lift Palettenheber *m*
pallet lift-out Palettenaushub *m*
pallet lift-out device Palettenaushubvorrichtung *f*
pallet-lift truck Palettenhubwagen *m*
pallet load Palettenladung *f*
pallet lowering Palettenabsenkung *f*
pallet lowering protection Palettenabsenküberwachung *f*
pallet monitoring Palettenkontrolle *f*
pallet monitoring system Palettenkontrollsystem *nt*
pallet output Palettenauslauf *m*
pallet position Palettenposition *f*
pallet racking Palettenregal *nt*
pallet securing Sichern *nt* von Palettenladungen
pallet securing machine Palettenladungssicherungsmaschine *f*
pallet shelving Palettenregal *nt*
pallet shelving store Palettenregallager *nt*
pallet shrink frame Palettenschrumpfrahmen *m*
pallet shrink oven Palettenschrumpfofen *m*
pallet shrink tunnel Palettenschrumpftunnel *m*
pallet shrink wrapper Palettenschrumpffolienmaschine *f*
pallet spacing Palettenabstand *m*
pallet stabilizing accessory Palettensicherungshilfsmittel *nt*
pallet stacker Palettenstapler *m*, Hochhubwagen *m*, Gabelhochhubwagen *m*
pallet stacker/unstacker Paletten-Stapler-Entstapler *m*
pallet-stacking truck Gabelhochhubwagen *m*
pallet store Palettenlager *nt*

pallet strapping machine Palettenumgreifungsmaschine *f*
pallet stretch wrapper Palettenstretchfolienmaschine *f*
pallet truck Gabelhubwagen *m*, Gabelhubfahrzeug *nt*, Palettenhubwagen *m*, Niederhubwagen *m*
pallet turnover clamp Palettenwendeklammer *f*
pallet turnover device Palettenwender *m*
palletize palettieren
palletizer Palettierer *m*
palletizer-depalletizer Palettierer-Depalettierer *m*
palletizer robot Palettierroboter *m*
palletizing palettierend
palletizing capacity Palettierkapazität *f*
palletizing layout Palettieranordnung *f*
palletizing machine Palettierer *m*
palletizing program Palettierprogramm *nt*
palloid spiral bevel gear Palloidspiralkegelräder *ntpl*
palloid tooth system Palloidverzahnung *f*
palm of gloves Handschuhinnenfläche *f*
pan Wanne *f*, Trog *m*, Schale *f*
pan base Schalenfuß *m*
pan vibrator Trogvibrator *m*
pancaking of the sheared slug for extrusion Setzen *nt* von Rohteilen für das Fließpressen
pane Scheibe *f*
panel Feld *nt*, Tafel *f*, Konsole *f*, Schaltpult *nt*, Bedienfeld *nt*
panel provided for scale particulars Feld *nt* für Maßstabangaben
panel provided for the purpose vorgesehenes Feld *nt*
panel radiator Flachheizkörper *nt*
panel type radiator Plattenheizkörper *m*
panelling Verkleidung *f*
panoramic tube Rundstrahlröhre *f*
pantographic engraving machine Pantographengraviermaschine *f*
pantograph-controlled miller pantographengesteuerte Fräsmaschine *f*
pantograph die-sinking and engraving machine Pantographengesenkfräs- und -graviermaschine *f*
pantograph die sinking machine Pantographengesenkfräsmaschine *f*, Nachformfräsmaschine *f* mit Pantographensteuerung für Formen- und Gesenkfräsen
pantograph engraver Nachformfräsmaschine *f* mit Pantographensteuerung
pantograph engraving machine Nachformfräsmaschine *f* mit Pantographensteuerung
pantograph miller Pantographennachformfräsmaschine *f*
pantograph milling machine Pantographennachformfräsmaschine *f*, Nachformfräsmaschine *f* mit Pantographensteuerung
pantograph mold and duplicator Nachformfräsmaschine *f* mit Pantographensteuerung
pantographing Nachformfräsen *nt*
pantograver Nachformfräsmaschine *f* mit Pantographensteuerung
paper Papier *nt*
paper carrier Papierträger *m*
paper film Papierfolie *f*
paper filter method Filterpapiermethode *f*
paper laminate Verbundpapier *nt*
paper roll Papierrolle *f*
paper sample Papierprobe *f*
paperboard Pappe *f*
paperless beleglos
parabola Parabel *f*
parabola interpolation Parabelinterpolation *f*
parachute hardness Auffanggurt *m*
paraffin Paraffin *nt*
paraffin wax Paraffin *nt*
parallax Parallaxe *f*
parallel-axes shaving Parallelschaben *nt*
parallel axis Parallelachsen *fpl*
parallel branch Parallelabzweig *m*
parallel bunch Parallelbündel *nt*
parallel clamp Parallelschraubzwinge *f*
parallel connection Parallelschaltung *f*
parallel crank mechanism Parallelkurbelgetriebe *nt*

parallel data transmission parallele Datenübertragung f
parallel displacement Parallelverschiebung f
parallel external screw thread zylindrisches Außengewinde nt
parallel face lapping Planparallelläppen nt
parallel flanks gleichgerichtete Flanken fpl
parallel flat workpiece parallelflächiges Werkstückelement nt
parallel Go/Not Go screw ring gauge zylindrischer Gewinde-Grenzlehrring m
parallel gripper Parallelgreifer m
parallel input mode Parallelprogrammierung f
parallel interface Parallelschnittstelle f
parallel internal screw thread zylindrisches Innengewinde nt
parallel joint Parallelstoß m
parallel joint with parallel weld Parallelstoß m mit Parallelnaht
parallel key Passfeder f
parallel offset paralleler Versatz m
parallel path Parallelbahn f
parallel pin Zylinderstift m
parallel pin with flat end Zylinderstift m ohne Kuppe
parallel pin without head Bolzen m ohne Kopf
parallel-plane guidance Ebenenparallelführung f
parallel planing machine Langhobelmaschine f
parallel position Parallelstellung f
parallel positioning Parallelstellung f
parallel reaction Parallelreaktion f
parallel register Parallelregister nt
parallel roller journal bearing Zylinderrollenlager nt
parallel shift helical gear Flachgetriebe nt
parallel stroke milling Zeilenfräsen nt
parallel stroke milling method Zeilenfräsverfahren nt
parallel stroke milling operation Zeilenfräsarbeit f
parallel structure Parallelstruktur f

parallel-to-parallel coder Parallel-zu-parallel-Codierer m
parallel-to-serial coder Parallel-zu-seriell-Codierer m
parallel translation Parallelverschiebung f
parallel helical gear pair Schrägstirnradpaar nt
parallelism Parallelität f
parallelism of the axes Achsparallelität f
parallelism tolerance Parallelitätstoleranz f
parallelity Zylindrizität f
parallely connected parallel geschaltet
parameter Parameter m, Kennwert m, Wirkungsgröße f, Einflussgröße f
parameter error Parameterfehler m
parameter input Parametereingabe f
parameter of shape Formparameter m
parameter setting Parametereinstellung f
parameterize parametrieren
parameterizing Parametrierung f
parameters Abmessungen fpl
parametric parametrisch
parametric control Parameterschreiben nt
parametric programming parametrische Programmierung f
parametric test verteilungsgebundener Test m
paramEtErize parametrieren
parchmentizing agent Pergamentierungsmittel nt
parent material Grundwerkstoff m
parent metal Ausgangsmetall nt, Grundmetall nt
parish bound Flurstücksgrenze f
parity Parität f
parity bit Paritätsbit nt
parity character Paritätszeichen nt
parity check Paritätsprüfung f
park stillsetzen, parken
parking Stillsetzen nt
parking brake Feststellbremse f, Handbremse f, Parkbremse f
parking lot Parkfläche f
parking space Parkfläche f
parking station Bahnhof m

parquet adhesive Parkettklebstoff *m*
parrot beak Hakengreifer *m*
parry vorbeugen
part Stück *nt*, Teil *nt*, Werkstück *nt*; trennen
part delivery Teillieferung *f*
part development scheme Teilbebauungsplan *m*
part dimension Teileabmessung *f*
part-ejection device Werkstückauswerfeinrichtung *f*
part feeding Werkstückzubringung *f*
part filling teilweise Füllung *f*
part-mechanized metal active gas welding teilmechanisches Metall-Aktivgas-Schweißen *nt*
part-mechanized soldering teilmechanisiertes Löten *nt*
part moving backwards and forwards translatorisch bewegtes Teil *nt*
part of discontinuous chip Spanbruchstück *nt*
part of inside origin Eigenteil *nt*
part of loss Verlustanteil *m*
part of outside origin Fremdteil *nt*
part of stable shape formstabiles Teil *nt*
part of the pipeline Rohrleitungsteil *nt*
part of unstable shape nicht formstabiles Teil *nt*
part off abtrennen, abhauen, abstechen, scheiden
part order Teilauftrag *m*
part program Teilprogramm *nt*
part program zero Werkstücknullpunkt *m*
part quality Teilequalität *f*
part section Teilschnitt *m*
part sectional drawing Teilschnittzeichnung *f*
part shown with break lines unterbrochen gezeichnetes Teil *nt*
part shrink wrap Teilschrumpffolienumhüllung *f*
part subjected to internal pressure innendruckbeanspruchtes Teil *nt*
part surface formation Teileformgebung *f*
part surface layer Teilerandschicht *f*
part throughput Teildurchsatz *m*

part to be fitted Passteil *nt*
part to be turned *(Werkstück)* Drehteil *nt*
part to be welded eingeformte Schweißstelle *f*
part transfer Teilübergabe *f*
part volume Teilmenge *f*
partial partiell, teilweise
partial acceptance Teilabnahme *f*
partial air stream Teilluftstrom *m*
partial charge Zwischenladung *f*
partial charge/charging Teilladung *f*, Zwischenladung *f*
partial current Teilstrom *m*
partial current density-potential curve Teilstromdichte-Potential-Kurve *f*
partial cut-out Teilausschnitt *m*
partial displacement of the stock relative to adjacent parts *(Metallumformung)* Durchsetzen *nt*
partial distance Teilstrecke *f*
partial failure Teilausfall *m*
partial generate grinding Teilwälzschleifen *nt*
partial heating Teilerwärmung *f*
partial inspection Teilabnahme *f*
partial journey Teilstrecke *f*
partial load Teilgewicht *nt*, Teillast *f*
partial mass Teilgewicht *nt*
partial parting by chiselling Einschroten *nt*
partial plan Ausschnitt *m*
partial section Teilstrecke *f*
partial shipment Teillieferung *f*
partial shrink wrap Teilschrumpffolienumhüllung *f*
partial surround Teilummantelung *f*
partial sound power level Teilschallleistungspegel *m*
partial spreading Einspreizen *nt*
partial stage Teilschritt *m*
partial surface Teilfläche *f*
partial vacuum Unterdruck *m*
partially automatic teilautomatisch
partially fractured angebrochen
participant Teilnehmer *m*
participate beteiligen, teilnehmen (an)
participation Beteiligung *f*
particle Teilchen *nt*, Partikel *nt*
particle category Kornklasse *f*

particle displacement Teilchenverschiebung *f*
particle distribution Kornverteilung *f*
particle energy Teilchenenergie *f*
particle flow density Teilchenflussdichte *f*
particle fluence Teilchenfluenz *f*
particle of moulding material Formmasseteilchen *nt*
particle radiation Teilchenstrahlung *f*
particle scheme Teilchenschema *nt*
particle size Teilchengröße *f*, Korngröße *f*
particle size analysis Korngrößenanalyse *f*
particle size distribution Korngrößenverteilung *f*
particle size group Korngruppe *f*
particulate Partikel *nt*; partikulär
particulate cleanliness Partikeleinheit *f*
partial displacement (of the stock) relative to the surface *(Metallumformung)* Abschieben *nt*
parting Trennen *nt*, Formteilung *f*, Abtrennung *f*
parting by chiselling Abschroten *nt*
parting off Abstechen *nt*, Abtrennung *f*
parting-off lathe Abstechdrehmaschine *f*
parting-off slide Abstechschlitten *m*
parting-off tool Stechmeißel *m*, Abstechmeißel *m*
parting-off toolholder Abstechmeißelhalter *m*
parting off turning Abstechdrehen *nt*
parting plane Teilungsebene *f*
parting surface Teilungsfläche *f*
parting tool Trennwerkzeug *nt*, Stechmeißel *m*, Stechdrehmeißel *m*
parting under heat Warmtrennen *nt*
partition Untergliederung *f*, Unterteilung *f*; unterteilen, untergliedern
partition panel Trennwand *f*
partition wall Zwischenwand *f*, Trennwand *f*, Steg *m*
partitioning Aufteilung *f*
partitioning of the sample Probeteilung *f*
partly formed teilgeformt

partner Partner *m*
partner in the system Systempartner *m*
parts Teile *ntpl*
parts *pl* **drawn in the assembled condition** zusammengebaut gezeichnete Teile *ntpl*
parts carrying voltage unter Spannung stehende Teile
parts commissioning Teilekommissionierung *f*
parts explosion Stücklistenauflösung *f*
parts history Teilestamm *m*
parts list Teileliste *f*, Stückliste *f*
parts list processing Stücklistenverarbeitung *f*
parts master data Teilestamm *m*
parts of the installation supplied by the employer bauseits gestellte Anlageteile *f*
parts of the travel mechanism Fahrwerksteile *ntpl*
parts production Teilefertigung *f*
parts production program Teilefertigungsprogramm *nt*
parts storage Teilelagerung *f*
parts-to-man Ware *f* zum Mann
parts warehouse Teilelager *nt*
parts working surface Teilefunktionsfläche *f*
party information Partnerinformation *f*
party involved Partner *m*
party involved in a project Projektbeteiligter *m*
pass 1. Spanungsschicht *f* 2. *(Schleifen)* Schleifgang *m* 3. Arbeitsgang *m*, Arbeitsvorgang *m*, Gang *m* 4. Passierschein *m*
pass across führen über
pass by vorbeiführen
pass off 1. abführen 2. *(Flüssigkeiten)* ableiten
pass on weiterleiten, weitergeben, übergeben, abgeben
pass over überschreiten übergehen
pass through Durchlauf *m*, Durchgang *m*; Durchgang haben, strömen, fließen, durchfließen, durchlaufen, passieren, durchgehen, durchlassen, durchfallen, hindurchfallen, schleusen
pass-through mode Durchlaufbe-

trieb *m*
passage Durchgang *m*, Durchlassen *nt*, Durchfahrt *f*, Durchtritt *m*, Abfluss *m*, Übergang *m*, Passage *f*, Passieren *nt*
passage below the dew point Unterschreiten *nt* des Taupunktes
passage of a tool Werkzeugdurchgang *m*
passage of electrons Elektronendurchtritt *m*
passage underground *(Unterführung)* Tunnel *m*
passageway Verkehrsweg *m*
passenger Mitfahrer *m*, Passagier *m*
passimeter Passimeter *nt*
passing Durchlassen *nt*, Übergang *m*, Ausweichen *nt*
passing direction Durchlassrichtung *f*
passive passiv
passivate passivieren
passive corrosion passive Korrosion *f*
passive element passives Glied *nt*
passive force Passivkraft *f*
password Kennwort *nt*, Passwort *nt*
password authentication Passwortauthentifizierung *f*
password authentication protocol Passwortauthentifizierungsprotokoll *nt*
password protection Passwortschutz *m*, Passwortsicherung *f*
paste 1. Paste *f* 2. aufkleben
paste dilution resin Pastenverschnittharz *m*
paste filling Pasteneinlage *f*
paste-like consistent salbenartig konsistent
paste on ankleben
paste together verkleben
paste viscosity Pastenviskosität *f*
patch ausbessern
patent application Patentanmeldung *f*
patent drawing Patentzeichnung *f*
paternoster rack Paternosterregal *nt*
path 1. Spur *f*, Weg *m*, Wegstrecke *f*, Bahn *f* 2. *(IT)* Zweig *m*
path bound weggebunden, flurgebunden
path control Bahnsteuerung *f*
path correction Bahnkorrektur *f*
path-dependent spurgebunden

path inclination Bahnneigung *f*
path independent nicht spurgebunden
path length Weglänge *f*
path marker Wegmarke *f*
path of acceleration Beschleunigungsweg *m*
path of action Wirkungsweg *m*
path of contact Eingriffslinie *f*, Wälzbahn *f*
path of the current Strompfad *m*
path of the heating gas Heizgasweg *m*
path pulse generator Wegimpulsgeber *m*
path section Teilstrecke *f*, Bahnabschnitt *m*
path section Bahnabschnitt *m*
path time Wegezeit *f*
path trace Bahnspur *f*
pattern Modell *nt*, Muster *nt*, Vorlage *f*, Schablone *f*, Bild *nt*, Ausführung *f*, Bauart *f*, Bauausführung *f*
pattern drawing Modellzeichnung *f*
pattern making Modellbau *m*
pattern milling attachment Modellfräseinrichtung *f*
pattern timber Modellholz *nt*
pause time Pausenzeit *f*
pawl Klinke *f*, Sperrklinke *f*
pawl- and ratchet mechanism Sperrgetriebe *nt*, Sperrwerk *nt*
pawl arm Schwingungsarm *m*
pay bezahlen (vt/vi), zahlen
pay interest Verzinsung *f*
pay-off package Mehrwegbehälter *m*
paying Zahlen *nt*
payload handling Nutzlastaufnahme *f*
payload pick-up Nutzlastaufnahme *f*
payment Zahlen *nt*, Bezahlung *f*, Zählung *f*
payment plan Zahlungsplan *m*
payment schedule Zahlungsplan *m*
payout Nutzlast *f*
PC-program SPS-Programm *nt*
PC system speicherprogrammierbares Steuersystem *nt*, SPS-System *nt*
peak Spitze *f*
peak and trough höchster und tiefster Punkt *m*
peak frequency Gipfelfrequenz *f*
peak load Lastspitze *f*, Spitzenlast *f*

peak load allowance Überlastbarkeit *f*
peak-to-valley height Rautiefe *f*, Profilrautiefe *f*
peak torque Spitzenmoment *nt*
peak value Extremwert *m*
peak value deviation Scheitelwertabweichung *f*
peak voltage Spannungsspitze *f*, Spitzenspannung *f*
peaked spitz
pearl glue Perlleim *m*
pearlite Perlit *m*
pearlitic perlitisch
specification Bezeichnung *f*
pedal treten; Pedal *nt*
pedal operated fußhebelbetätigt
pedestal Fuß *m*, Fußgestell *nt*, Konsole *f*, Sockel *m*, Ständer *m*
pedestal footing Fußausleger *m*
pedestrian Fußgänger *m*, Mitgänger *m*
pedestrian control Steuerung *f* durch gehende Person
pedestrian-controlled durch mitgehende Person gesteuert, mit Steuerung durch gehende Person, mitgängergeführt
pedestrian-controlled industrial truck Mitgängerflurförderzeug *nt*
pedestrian-controlled truck Flurförderzeug *nt* mit Steuerung durch gehende Personen
pedestrian operation Mitgängerbetrieb *m*
pedestrian propelled handbetrieben, handverfahrbar
pedestrian propelled industrial platform truck handverfahrbarer Plattformwagen *m*
pedestrian truck Mitgängerflurförderzeug *nt*
predetermined festgelegt
peel diagram Schäldiagramm *nt*
peel off abblättern, abschälen
peel resistance Schälwiderstand *m*
peel strength Abzugkraft *f*
peel test Schälversuch *m*
peeling strength *(Beschichtungen)* Abzugskraft *f*
peen *(Hammer)* abhämmern; Finne *f*
peening Abhämmern *nt*

peer gleichberechtigt
peg anstiften, anspitzen, verdübeln, dübeln; Dübel *m*, Zapfen *m*,Stift *m*
pegging Anspitzen *nt*, Anspitzkneten *nt*
pellet 1. Kugel *f*, Granulat *nt* **2.** tablettieren
pellet hardness Einzelperlhärte *f*
pelleter Tablettiermaschine *f*
pelleting Tablettieren *nt*, Tablettierung *f*
pelletize granulieren
pelletized carbon black geperlter Ruß *m*
pelletizing Granulierung *f*
pen stroke method Federstrichverfahren *nt*
pen tip deflection Schreibspitzenauslenkung *f*
penalty for breach of contact Konventionalstrafe *f*
pencil drawing Blei-Zeichnung *f*
pencil sketch Bleiskizze *f*
pendant herabhängend, schwebend; Hängedruckknopftafel *f*, Hängeschalter *m*
pendant control panel Bedienungszentrale *f*, Pendeldruckknopftafel *f*
pendant control planer Hängeschalttafel *f*
pendant control station Kommandotafel *f*
pendant push button station Pendeldruckknopftafel *f*
pendant push button panel Pendelstation *f*
pendant push button station Pendelstation *f*
pendant switchboard schwenkbare Schalttafel *f*
pendulum fall-back Pendelrückfall *m*
pendulum load measurement Pendelkraftmessung *f*
pendulum milling Pendelfräsen *nt*
pendulum pivot Pendeldrehpunkt *m*
pendulum rod Pendelstange *f*
penetrant Eindringmittel *nt*
penetrate hindurchgehen, eindringen, durchdringen, durchstoßen
penetrating agent Penetriermittel *nt*
penetration Penetration *f*, Durchdrin-

gung f, Durchstoß m
penetration intensity Durchdringungsintensität f
penetration of foreign matter Eindringen nt von Fremdkörpern
penetration of foreign particles Eindringen nt von Fremdkörpern
penetration overvoltage Durchtrittsüberspannung f
penetration path Durchstoßweg m
penetration plan Durchbruchsplan m
penetration resistance Durchtrittswiderstand m
penetration test Durchstoßversuch m
penetrator Eindringkörper m, Durchstoßkörper m
pentosan content Pentosangehalt m
penumbra region Halbschattenbereich m
per pro
per cent Prozent nt
per unit time je Zeiteinheit f
perceivable erkennbar
percent by weight Massenanteil m in Prozent
percentage Prozentanteil m, Prozentsatz m; prozentual
percentage elastic elongation prozentuale elastische Dehnung f
percentage elongation at fracture Bruchdehnung f
percentage elongation before reduction Gleichmaßdehnung f
percentage non-proportional elongation nichtproportionale Dehnung f
percentage of methanol-soluble matter methanollöslicher Anteil m
percentage permanent elongation bleibende Dehnung f
percentage ratio of contact area Traganteil m
percentage reduction of area relative Querschnittsänderung f
percentage reduction of area after fracture Brucheinschnürung f, Einschnürung f nach dem Bruch
percentage total elongation gesamte Dehnung f
perceptible wahrnehmbar
perception Wahrnehmung f

perchloric acid tiltration Perchlorsäuretitration f
percussion Perkussion f, Erschütterung f, Schlag m, Stoß m
percussion boring Perkussionsbohren nt
percussion drilling Schlagbohren nt, Perkussionsbohren nt
percussion primer Perkussionszünder m
percussion priming Perkussionszündung f
percussion welding Funkenschweißen nt
percussive force Perkussionskraft f
permanent magnet Permanentmagnet nt
perfect ideal
perfect planning Idealplanung f
perforate lochen, perforieren
perforated card Lochkarte f
perforated plate with round holes Rundlochblech nt
perforated tape Lochstreifen m
perforation Lochung f
perforation test Stempeldurchdrückversuch m
perforator Locher m, Lochschnittwerkzeug nt
perform durchführen, ausführen, leisten
performance 1. Arbeitsweise f, Arbeitsleistung f, funktionelle Gesamtleistung f, Gesamtarbeitsleistung f, Gesamtleistung f, Leistungsfähigkeit f, Leistungsvermögen nt, Leistung f 2. Betriebsdaten pl
performance approval Leistungsabnahme f, Prüfung f
performance calculation Leistungsberechnung f
performance criterion Leistungskriterium nt
performance data Leistungsangaben fpl, Leistungsdaten pl, Leistungsnachweis m
performance in service Betriebsverhalten nt
performance indicator Leistungsindikator m, Leistungskennzahl f

performance processing Ergebnisaufbereitung *f*
performance readiness Leistungsbereitschaft *f*
performance specification Lastenheft *nt*, Pflichtenheft *nt*
performance test Leistungsprüfung *f*, Leistungstest *m*
perforated metal plate Lochblech *nt*
perforated screen insert Lochsiebeinsatz *m*
perimeter Umfang *m*, Umkreis *m*, Kreisumfang *m*
perimeter enclosure Umzäunung *f*, Umwehrung *f*
perimeter guards Umzäunung *f*
period Periode *f*, Dauer *f*, Zeitraum *m*, Zeitabschnitt *m*
period of analysis Betrachtungszeitraum *m*
period of deceleration Verzögerungsdauer *f*
period of delivery Lieferzeit *f*
period of dwell Bewegungspause *f*
period of protection Schutzdauer *f*
period of storage Lagerdauer *f*
period of time Zeitspanne *f*, Zeitdauer *f*
period of utilization Nutzungsdauer *f*
periodic wiederkehrend
periodic duration Periodendauer *f*
periodic system Periodensystem *nt*
periodic time Periodenzeit *f*
periodical periodisch
periodicity Periodenzahl *f*
peripheral grinding Radialschiff *m*
peripheral speed Umfangsgeschwindigkeit *f*
peripheral velocity Umfangsgeschwindigkeit *f*
peripheral peripher; Peripheriegerät *nt*
peripheral cutting edge Stirnschneide *f*, Mantelschneide *f*, Umfangschneide *f*
peripheral cutting edge angle Umfangschneidenwinkel *m*
peripheral cutting edges Umfangsschneiden *nt*
peripheral devices Peripherie *f*
peripheral equipment Peripherie *f*
peripheral force Umfangskraft *f*

peripheral grinding Umfangsschliff *m*, Umfangschleifen *nt*
peripheral length Umfangslänge *f*
peripheral length of grinding wheel Schleifscheibenumfangslänge *f*
peripheral milling Umfangsfräsen *nt*, Umfangswälzfräsen *nt*, Wälzfräsen *nt*
peripheral plunge grinding Umfangeinstechschleifen *nt*
peripheral units Peripheriegeräte *ntpl*
periphery Umfang *m*, Peripherie *f*
periphery of a circle Kreisumfang *m*
permanent fest
permanence of size Maßbeständigkeit *f*
permanent permanent, bleibend, dauernd, ununterbrochen, fix, nicht lösbar, fest installiert
permanent backing strip Beilage *f*
permanent barrier Dauerschranke *f*
permanent elongation bleibende Längenänderung *f*
permanent elongation at fracture bleibende Bruchdehnung *f*
permanent elongation limit bleibende Dehngrenze *f*
permanent extension shortly before failure bleibende Dehnung *f* kurz vor dem Reißen
permanent folding behaviour Dauerfaltversuch *m*
permanent installation feste Installation *f*
permanent joint unlösbare Verbindung *f*
permanent linear change bleibende Längenänderung *f*
permanent magnet Dauermagnet *nt*
permanent magnet synchronous motor permanentmagneterregter Synchronmotor *m*
permanent magnetic chuck Spannfutter *nt* mit Dauermagnet
permanent mould Dauerform *f*
permanent set Verformungsrest *m*
permanent set stress Spannung *f* mit bestimmter bleibender Verlängerung
permanent to dimension maßbeständig
permanent to size maßbeständig

permanent work station ständiger Arbeitsplatz *m*
permanently elastic dauerelastisch
permanently fixed fest angebracht
permanently installed fest installiert, fest eingebaut
permanently plastic dauerplastisch
permanently tyred wheel nicht demontierbare Bereifung *f*
permeability coefficient Permeabilitätskoeffizient *m*, Permeationskoeffizient *m*
permeable durchlässig
permeate durchdringen
permissible zulässig
permissible bending stress zulässige Biegebeanspruchung *f*
permissible dimensional variation zulässige Maßabweichung *f*
permissible geometrical variation zulässige Formabweichung *f*
permissible running error zulässige Laufabweichung *f*
permissible temperature stress Temperaturbeanspruchbarkeit *f*
permissible variation zulässige Toleranz *f*
permissible variation for sizes without tolerance indication Allgemeintoleranz *f*, Freimaßtoleranz *f*, zulässige Abweichung *f* für Maße ohne Toleranzangaben
permissible variation in size Maßtoleranz *f*
permissible wobble Planlauftoleranz *f*
permissible working pressure zulässiger Betriebsdruck *m*
permission to transmit Sendeberechtigung *f*
permit zulassen, erlauben; Zulassung *f*
permittivity Dielektrizitätskonstante *f*
perpendicular rechtwinklig, senkrecht, lotrecht; Senkrechte *f*, Vertikale *f*
perpendicular direction Längsrichtung *f*
perpendicular to rechtwinklig zu, quer zu
perpendicular to path Bahnnormale *f*
perpendicular to the working plane senkrecht zur Arbeitsebene *f*

perpendicularity tolerance Rechtwinkligkeitstoleranz *f*
persist beharren
persistence Nachleuchtdauer *f*
person in charge Bearbeiter *m*
person involved Beteiligter *m*
person responsible for correction Korrekturverantwortlicher *m*
person responsible for systems Systemverantwortliche/r *f/m*
person responsible for the construction Bauverantwortlicher *m*
person responsible for transportation Transportbeauftragter *m*
personal persönlich
personal digital assistant (PDA) persönlicher digitaler Assistent *m*
personnel Personal *nt*
personnel costs Personalkosten *pl*
personnel costs block Personalkostenblock *m*
personnel detection Personenerkennung *f*
personnel detection means Personenerkennungssystem *nt*
personnel detection system Personenerkennungssystem *nt*
personnel placement Personaleinsatz *m*
personnel planning Personalplanung *f*
personnel recruiting Personalbeschaffung *f*
personnel savings Personaleinsparung *f*
pressure measurement nozzle Druckmessstutzen *m*
Petri net Petri-Netz *nt*
Petri network Petri-Netz *nt*
petrol Benzin *nt*, Vergaserkraftstoff *m*
petrol engine Benzinmotor *m*
petrol truck Flurförderzeug *nt* mit Vergaserkraftstoffmotor
petroleum Mineralölerzeugnis *nt*
petroleum wax Paraffin *nt*
pewter *(hochzinnlegiertes)* Lot *nt*
pH-value pH-Wert *m*
phase Phase *f*
phase approach Stufung *f*
phase boundary Phasengrenze *f*
phase displacement Phasenverschie-

bung *f*
phase failure Phasenausfall *m*
phase front Phasenfront *f*
phase lag Phasenlaufzeit *f*
phase-locked loop Phasenregelkreis *m*
phase-modulated phasenmoduliert
phase modulation Phasenmodulation *f*
phase of operation Arbeitsgang *m*
phase position Phasenlage *f*
phase response Phasengang *m*
phase sequence Drehrichtung *f*, Phasenfolge *f*
phase sequence change-over Drehrichtungsumkehr *f*
phase sequence reversal Drehrichtungsumkehr *f*
phase shift Phasenverschiebung *f*
phase voltage Sternspannung *f*, Strangspannung *f*
phase winding Wicklungsstrang *m*
phenoplast thermal fusion adhesive Phenoplastschmelzklebstoff
phenol basis Phenolbasis *f*
phenolic moulding material Phenolharzfolie *f*
phenol plastic material phenolplastisches Harz *nt*
phenol lplastic resin Phenolplastharz *nt*, phenolplastisches Harz *nt*
phenoplastic glue Phenoplastleim *m*
phenoplastic putty Phenoplastkitt *m*
phosphate coat Phosphatschicht *f*
phosphate protective coat Phosphatschutzschicht *f*
phosphating process Phosphatierungsprozess *m*
phosphate anion Phosphatanion
phosphating bath Phosphatierungsbad *nt*
phosphating by stoving processes Einbrennphosphatierverfahren *nt*
photo-chemical photochemisch
photo-electric photoelektrisch
photo electron Photoelektron *nt*
photo fluorescence Photofluoreszenz *f*
photo line Fotozeile *f*
photo lithography Photolithographie *f*
photo polymer Photopolymer *nt*
photocell photoelektrischer Sensor *m*, Fotozelle *f*, Lichtschranke *f*

photochromism of dyeings Photochromie *f*
photocopying paper Ablichtungspapier *nt*, Photokopierpapier *nt*
photocopying paper for direct electrophotographic processes Ablichtungspapier *nt* für direktes elektrophotographisches Kopierverfahren
photocopying paper without silver salt coating Lichtpauspapier *nt*
photoelectric guard Lichtschranke *f*
photoelectric cell (PEC) Fotozelle *f*
photoelectric line tracer Nachführsteuerung *f*
photofluorographic camera Schirmbildkamera *f*
photogrammetry Bildmessung *f*
photograph *(als Bild)* Aufnahme *f*
photographic fotografisch
photographic equipment Aufnahmegerät *nt*
photomaster Druckvorlage *f*
photon Photon *nt*, Lichtquant *nt*
photon beam Photonenstrahl *m*
photon energy Photonenenergie *f*
photon flow density Photonenflussdichte *f*
photon radiation Photonenstrahlung *f*
photoreceiver Lichtempfänger *m*, Photoempfänger *m*
phototransistor Phototransistor *m*
physical körperlich, physisch
physical effort Körperanstrengung *f*
physical entity Größe *f*
physical layer physikalische Schicht *f*
physical-metallurgical physikalisch-metallurgisch
physical properties Festigkeitseigenschaften *f*
physical property Festigkeitseigenschaft *f*
physical resources Sachmittel *ntpl*
physical-technical physikalisch-technisch
piece-handling time Aufspannzeit *f*
pick kommissionieren, entnehmen, auslagern
pick aisle Kommissioniergang *m*
pick-and-place machine Bestückungsautomat *m*

pick-off attachment Auffangvorrichtung *f*, Greifeinrichtung *f*
pick-off gear Aufsteckrad *nt*
pick time Kommissionierzeit *f*
pick up übernehmen, aufnehmen, mitnehmen, auffangen, aufladen; Aufnahme *f*, Aufnehmer *m*
pick-up and delivery station Übergabestelle *f*
pick-up and deposit station Übergabestelle *f*
pick-up location Übernahmeposition *f*, Bereitstellplatz *m*
pick-up position Bereitstellplatz *m*
pick-up station Eingangspunkt *m*, Aufnahmestation *f*
picking Entnahme *f*, Kommissioniervorgang *m*
picker device Entnahmeeinrichtung *f*
picker tube Entnahmerohr *nt*
picket fence Gartenzaun *m*
picket-fence arrangement Picket-Fence-Anordnung *f*
picking Kommissionieren *nt*
picking capacity Pickleistung *f*
picking face Entnahmeseite *f*, Kommissionierposition *f*
picking plant *(Sichtanlage)* Sortieranlage *f*
picking sequence Kommissioniervorgang *m*, Kommissionierweg *m*
picking station Entnahmestation *f*
picking table Kommissioniertisch *m*
picking trays Auslaufrutsche *f*
picking up Aufnehmen *nt*
pickle abbeizen
pickling agent Abbeizmittel *nt*
pickoff gear Umsteckrad *nt*
pictorial symbol Bildzeichen *nt*
picture wiedergeben; Bild *nt*
picture element Rasterpunkt *m*, Bildpunkt *m*, Pixel *nt*
picture measuring apparatus Bildmessgerät *nt*
pie chart Kreisdiagramm *nt*
piece Teil *nt*, Stück *nt*, Werkstück *nt*
piece counter Stückzähler *m*
piece design Teileformgebung *f*
piece of cartonboard Pappezuschnitt *m*

piece of work Werkstück *nt*
piece-production cost Stückkosten *pl*
piece production machining Stückbearbeitung *f*
piece program Teileprogramm *nt*
piece-rate setting Akkordfestsetzung *f*
piece to be soldered Lötgruppe *f*, Lötteil *m*
pieces per hour Stückzahl *f* je Stunde, Stundenleistung *f*
piecework zinc coating Stückverzinken *nt*
pied area Lochfraßstelle *f*
pier Stütze *f*
pierce lochen, durchbohren, durchlochen, durchstoßen
pierced gelocht, gestanzt
pierced hole gelochte Bohrung *f*
piercer Pilgerdorn *m*
piercing holes Lochen *nt*
piercing point Stichstelle *f*
piercing through-holes Durchlochen *nt*
piezo-actuator Piezoaktor *m*
piezo-electric piezoelektrisch
piezo-electric force transducer piezoelektrischer Kraftaufnehmer *m*
piezo-electric load cell Piezokraftmesszelle *f*
piezo-electricity Piezoelektrizität *f*
piezo-ignition Piezozündung *f*
pig iron Roheisen *nt*
pigeon-hole racking Wabenregal *nt*
pigeon-hole racking system Wabenregalanlage *f*
pigeon-hole storage Wabenlagerung *f*
pigeon-hole warehouse Wabenlager *nt*
pigment extract Pigment-Extrakt *nt*
pile Stapel *m*, Säule *f*, Pfahl *m*, stapeln
pile up Stau *m*, stauen, aufschichten, aufstapeln
pilger mandrel Pilgerdorn *m*
pilger-mill roll Pilgerschrittwalzen *nt*
pillar Pfeiler *m*, Pfosten *m*
pilot 1. führen, ansteuern; Führung *f* 2. Erprobung *f*
pilot circuit Steuerstromkreis *m*
pilot current Steuerstrom *m*
pilot flame Sparflamme *f*, Zündflam-

me *f*, Wachflamme *f*
pilot-flame ignition Zündflammenzündung *f*
pilot flame line Wachflammenleitung *f*
pilot gas flame Zündgasflamme *f*
pilot gas pipe Steuergasleitung *f*
pilot gear Führungszahnrad *nt*
pilot hole Führungsbohrung *f*, Vorbohrung *f*
pilot jet Vordüse *f*
pilot lamp Signallampe *f*
pilot lot Vorserie *f*
pilot on tap Vorführzapfen *m* eines Gewindebohrers
pilot plant Versuchsanlage *f*
pilot pressure Steuerdruck *m*
pilot production Vorserie *f*
pilot production phase Vorserienphase *f*
pilot project Vorplanung *f*
pilot recess Schlüsselführung *f*
pilot segment Führungsstück *nt*
pilot taper Kegelzapfen *m*
piloted counterbore Zapfensenker *m*
piloting Führen *nt*, Führung *f*
piloting boring bar Führungsbohrstange *f*
PIM (Power Injection Moulding) Kraftspritzgießen *nt (Mikro-Pulver-Spritzgießen)*
pin befestigen, anheften; Pol *m*, Stift *m*, Zapfen *m*
pin chain Haltekette *f*
pin dimension measurement Bolzenmaßmessung *f*
pin hole Pore *f*
pin lifter Stiftheber *m*
pin of the driving plate Mitnehmerbolzen *m*
pin tooth gearing Triebstockverzahnung *f*
pin type face wrench Zweilochmutterndreher *m*
pin type socket wrench Steckschlüssel *m* mit Griff
pin-type wrench Stiftschlüssel *m*
pin wrench Hakenschlüssel *m* mit Zapfen, Zapfenschlüssel *m*
pincers *pl* Zange *f*, Kneifzange *f*
pinch off abkneifen, abquetschen

pinhead projection Kuppe *f*
pinhole Durchstich *m*
pinion Zahnradgetriebe *nt*, Zahnritzel *nt*, Ritzel *nt*, Trieb *m*
pinion addendum Ritzelkopfhöhe *f*
pinion addendum modification coefficient Ritzelprofilverschiebungsfaktor *m*
pinion and wheel Ritzel *nt* und Rad *nt*
pinion base circle Ritzelgrundkreis *m*
pinion cage Planetenträger *m*
pinion chain Triebstockkette *f*
pinion corner point Ritzelkopfeckpunkt *m*
pinion cutter addendum modification Schneidradprofilverschiebung *f*
pinion cutter addendum modification coefficient Schneidradprofilverschiebungsfaktor *m*
pinion cutter flank Schneidradflanke *f*
pinion cutter lift Schneidradabhebung *f*
pinion cutter tooth root Schneidradzahnfuß *m*
pinion cutter zone Schneidradfeld *nt*
pinion drive Ritzelantrieb *m*
pinion flank Ritzelflanke *f*
pinion gear Zahntrieb *m*
pinion root Ritzelfuß *m*
pinion shaft Ritzelwelle *f*, Planetenradwelle *f*
pinion stud Triebstockbolzen *m*
pinion tip diameter Ritzelkopfkreisdurchmesser *m*
pinion tooth Ritzelzahn *m*
pinion tooth root Ritzelzahnfuß *m*
pinion tooth system Ritzelverzahnung *f*
pinion tooth tip Ritzelzahnkopf *m*
pinion tooth tip thickness Ritzelzahnkopfdicke *f*
pinion type cutter Schneidrad *nt*
pinion-type cutter radförmiges Schneidemesser *nt*, Schneidrad *nt*
pinion which operates the catching device Sicherheitsfangritzel *nt*
pinion which operates the safety gear Sicherheitsfangritzel *nt*
pintle Achse *f*, Stift *m*, Zapfen *m*
pioneering stage Einführungsphase *f*
pipe Rohr *nt*, Rohrleitung *f*

pipe assembly Schlaucharmatur *f*
pipe bedding Rohrauflagerung *f*
pipe bell Rohrmuffe *f*
pipe bend Rohrbogen *m*
pipe bending machine Rohrbiegemaschine *f*
pipe bottom Rohrsohle *f*
pipe break Rohrbruch *m*
pipe clamp Rohrschelle *f*
pipe coating Rohrumhüllung *f*
pipe connection Rohranschluss *m*, Leistungsanschluss *m*
pipe construction work Rohrleitungsbauarbeit *f*
pipe coupling Rohrkupplung *f*
pipe covering Rohrumhüllung *f*
pipe crest Rohrscheitel *m*
pipe drainage without trenches grabenlose Rohrdränung *f*
pipe end closure cap Rohrendverschluss *m*
pipe end plug Rohrverschluss *m*
pipe failure Leitungsbruch *m*, Rohrbruch *m*
pipe fitter Klempner *m*
pipe fitting Rohranschluss *m*
pipe flange Leitungsflansch *m*
pipe fracture Rohrbruch *m*
pipe fracturing Rohrbruch *m*
pipe hanging Rohrleitungsaufhängung *f*
pipe hook Verlegehaken *m*
pipe installation Rohreinbau *m*
pipe installation for drinking water Trinkwasserleitungsanlage *f*
pipe intersection Rohrüberschneidung *f*
pipe joint Rohranschluss *m*
pipe jointing component Rohrverbindungsteil *nt*
pipe-laying contractors Rohrleitungsbauunternehmen *nt*
pipe-laying instruction Verlegeanleitung *f*
pipe-laying operation Rohrlegearbeit *f*
pipe stench trap Rohrgeruchverschluss *m*
pipe support Rohrauflager *nt*
pipe surface Rohrfläche *f*
pipe system diagram Rohrnetzplan *m*

pipe thread Rohrgewinde *nt*
pipe thread for non-pressure tight screw joints Rohrgewinde *nt* für nicht selbstdichtende Gewindeverbindungen
pipe thread where pressure-tight joints are not made on the threads nicht dichtende Rohrgewindeverbindung *f*
pipe union elbow Winkelverbindungsstutzen *m* für Rohrverschraubungen
pipe union with flat seat Rohrverschraubung *f* mit Bunddichtung
pipe union with taper seat Rohrverschraubung *f* mit Kegeldichtung
pipe with über ein Rohr verbinden
pipe with integrally cast flanges Rohr *nt* mit angegossenen Flanschen
pipe with jacket Leitung *f* mit Mantelrohr
pipe with screwed-on flanges Rohr *nt* mit aufgeschraubten Flanschen
pipe with sliding joint at one end Rohr *nt* mit einseitiger Steckmuffe
pipe with sliding socket at both ends Rohr *nt* mit beidseitiger Steckmuffe
pipe with smooth ends Rohr *nt* mit glatten Enden
pipe with welding bevel Rohr *nt* mit Schweißfase
pipe-work drawing Rohrleitungsplan *m*
pipe wrench Rohrschlüssel *m*, Rohrzange *f*
pipe zone Leitungszone *f*
pipelaying Leitungsverlegung *f*
pipeless lunkerfrei
pipeline Rohrleitung *f*
pipeline capable of bearing load tragfähige Rohrleitung *f*
pipeline component Rohrleitungsteil *nt*
pipeline connection Rohrleitungsanschluss *m*
pipeline construction Rohrleitungsbau *m*
pipeline end Leitungsende *nt*
pipeline fitting Rohrleitungsteil *nt*
pipeline gate valve Pipelineschieber *m*
pipeline of glass fibre reinforced

plastics Rohrleitungen *fpl* aus glasfaserverstärktem Kunststoff
pipeline section Leitungsabschnitt *m*, Rohrleitungsabschnitt *m*
pipeline system Rohrleitungsanlage *f*
pipes Lunker *m, mpl*
pipette into einpipettieren
pipette viscosimeter Pipettenviskometer *nt*
pipette with disposable tip Pipette *f* mit Einwegspitze
pipework Rohrleitungen *fpl*, Rohrsystem *nt*
pipework diagram Rohrschema *nt*
piping Rohrleitung *f*
piping anchorage Rohrbefestigung *f*
piping component with parallel thread Rohrteil *nt* mit zylindrischem Gewinde
piping components Rohrteil *nt*
piping diagram Leitungsschema *f*
piping layout Rohranordnung *f*
piping plan Rohrleitungsplan *m*
piping system Rohrsystem *nt*
piping system in shipbuilding Schiffsrohrleitungsbau *m*
piplaying rules Rohrverlegungsrichtlinien *fpl*
piston Kolben *m*
piston-actuated shut-off valve Absperrarmatur *f* mit Kolbenantrieb
piston actuation Kolbenantrieb *m*
piston compressor Kolbenverdichter *m*
piston gasmeter Kolbengaszähler *m*
piston gasmeter with integrating movement Kolbengaszähler *m* mit zählendem Messwerk
piston ring Kolbenring *m*
piston rod Kolbenstange *f*, Pleuelstange *f*
piston rod bearing Kolbenstangenführung *f*
pit zerfressen, anfressen, auskolken, Grübchen bilden; Unebenheit *f*, Grube *f*, Pickel *m*, Mulde *f*, Narbe *f*
pit furnace Schachtofen *m*
pit planer Grubenhobelmaschine *f*
pitch 1. Gang *m*, Ganghöhe *f*, Steigung *f*, Steigungswinkel *m*, Teilung *f*, Schritt *m*, Schrägstellung *f*; schräg stellen **2.** *(Kreis)* Teilkreisteilung *f* **3.** *(Gewinde)* Gewindesteigung *f* **4.** *(Verzahnung)* Zahnteilung *f*
pitch accuracy Teilungsgenauigkeit *f*
pitch angle Kegelwinkel *m*, Teilkegelwinkel *m*
pitch circle Teilkreis *m*
pitch circle arc Teilkreisbogen *m*, Wälzkreisbogen *m*
pitch clearance angle Flankenfreiwinkel *m*
pitch cone Wälzkegel *m*
pitch cone surface Teilkegelmantelfläche *f*
pitch cylinder director Teilzylindermantellinie *f*
pitch diameter Flankendurchmesser *m*, Wälzkreisdurchmesser *m*
pitch diameter tolerance Flankendurchmessertoleranz *f*
pitch error Teilungsfehler *m*, Teilungssprung *m*, Wälzfehler *m*
pitch fluctuation Teilungsschwankung *f*
pitch helix Wälzzylinderflankenlinie *f*
pitch-hole Schlagloch *nt*
pitch line Flankendurchmesserlinie *f*
pitch measurement Teilungsmessung *f*
pitch of the chains Kettenteilung *f*
pitch of the rollers Rollenteilung *f*
pitch plane Wälzebene *f*
pitch span Teilungssumme *f*
pitch-span curve Teilungsspannenkurve *f*
pitch-span tolerance Teilungsspanntoleranz *f*
pitch-span variation Teilungsspannenabweichung *f*
pitch surface Wälzfläche *f*
pitch test Teilungsprüfung *f*
pitch variation Steigungsabweichung *f*, Teilungsabweichung *f*
pitchcone angle Teilkegelwinkel *m*
pits resembling pin pricks Nadelstichartige Vertiefung *f*
pitted uneben, löchrig
pitted coating kraterartiger Belag *m*
pitting Grübchenbildung *f*, Lochfraß *m*, Narbigkeit *f*
pivot Zapfen *m*

pivot Drehbolzen *m*, Schwenkachse *f*, Einstechbolzen *m*, Drehzapfen *m*, Mittelzapfen *m*, Drehgelenk *nt*, Zapfen *m*, Drehpunkt *m*; drehen, schwenken, pendeln, kippen, gelenkig aufhängen
pivot bearing Zapfenlager *nt*
pivot on gelenkig verbinden mit
pivot point Gelenkpunkt *m*
pivoted lever Schwenkhebel *m*
pivoting schwenkbar, kippbar, pendelnd; Drehen *nt*, Schwenken *nt*
pivoting axis Drehachse *f*
pivoting beam-type steer axle Pendelachse *f*
pivoting driver compartment kippbare Kabine *f*
pivoting point Drehpunkt *m*
pivoting shuttle fork Drehschubgabel *f*
pivoting support peg system Schnappriegelschaltradanlage *f*
pixel Pixel *nt*, Bildpunkt *m*
pixel by pixel pixelweise
pixel pattern Bildpunktmuster *nt*
place platzieren, anordnen, legen, vorlegen, verlegen, unterbringen, setzen, stellen, einstapeln; Platz *m*, Ort *m*, Stelle *f*
place an order vergeben
place into einsetzen, einbauen
place liable to cause stumbling Stolperstelle *f*
place of deposit Ablage *f*
place of transshipment Umschlagplatz *m*
place on aufsetzen, bestücken
place orders disponieren
place over stülpen (über)
place packing/unpacking machine Setz-Einpack-Auspackmaschine *f*
place ready to hand bereitstellen
placed angeordnet
placement Bestückung *f*
placing Anordnung *f*
plain flach, glatt
plain bearing Gleitlager *nt*
plain carbon steel unlegierter Kohlenstoffstahl *m*
plain clamp-type toolpost Herzklaue *f*, Spannpratze *f*
plain cutter Walzenfräser *m*

plain cutting zone Glattschnittzone *f*
plain dividing head einfacher Teilkopf *m*
plain grinder Rundschleifmaschine *f*
plain grinding Rundschleifen *nt*
plain grinding machine Rundschleifmaschine *f*
plain horizontal milling machine Einfachwaagerechtfräsmaschine *f*
plain horizontal plano-miller Einfachlangfräsmaschine *f*
plain horizontal-type knee-and-column milling machine einfache Horizontalfräsmaschine *f*, Einfachhorizontalfräsmaschine *f*
plain index centre einfaches Teilgerät *nt*, einfacher Teilapparat, einfaches Teilgerät *nt* mit einer Teilspindel
plain indexing Einfachteilen *nt*
plain knee-and-column type milling machine Einfachständerfräsmaschine *f*
plain milling Walzenstirnfräsen *nt*, Planfräsen *nt*, Planfräsarbeit *f*
plain milling cutter Walzenfräser *m*
plain milling machine einfache Fräsmaschine *f*, einfache Rundfräsmaschine *f*, Walzenfräser *m*
plain milling machine with horizontal spindle Einfachfräsmaschine *f*
plain-parallel bearing Plananlage *f*
plain pattern type spring washer glatter Federring *m*
plain portion glatter Teil *m*
plain slide valve Flachschieber *m*
plain steadyrest feststehender Setzstock *m*
plain text Klartext *m*, Klarschrift *f*
plain tool post einfacher Meißelhalter *m*
plain tool steel unlegierter Werkzeugstahl *m*
plain toolholder Einfachmeißelhalter *m*
plain toolpost Stichelhaus *nt*, Stichelklaue *f*, Spannklaue *f*
plain turning Längsdrehen *nt*
plain-type knee-and-column milling machine einfache Konsolfräsmaschine *f*
plain washer Scheibe *f*, Unterlegschei-

be *f*
plain writing Klarschrift *f*
plan planen, projektieren, entwerfen; Entwurf *m*
plan angle Einstellwinkel *m*, Schneidenwinkel *m*
plan approach angle Hauptschneidenwinkel *m*
plan chart Plantafel *f*
plan in advance vorplanen
plan outline Außenkontur *f*
plan relief angle Einstellwinkel *m* der Nebenschneide
plan view Grundriss *m*, Draufsicht *f*
plan view outline Kontur *f*
planar eben
plane 1. plan, eben; Ebene *f* 2. *(Fertigungsverfahren)* hobeln, abrichten
plane angle ebener Winkel *m*
plane at an angle Schräghobeln *nt*
plane bevel gear Kegelplanrad *nt*
plane bevel gear pair Kegelplanradpaar *nt*
plane by the generating method wälzhobeln
plane gear Planrad *nt*
plane gear transmission ebenes Getriebe *nt*
plane guidance Ebenenführung *f*
plane guidance mechanism Ebenenführungsgetriebe *nt*
plane marks Hobelschläge *mpl*
plane-mill walzfräsen
plane milling Wälzen *nt*
plane of action Eingriffsebene *f*, Eingriffsfläche *f*, Eingriffsfeld *nt*
plane of bending Biegeebene *f*
plane of centre Mittenebene *f*
plane of contact Eingriffsfläche *f*
plane of cutting edge Schneidenebene *f*
plane of division Teilungsebene *f*
plane of impact Aufprallebene *f*, Schlagebene *f*
plane of lamination Schichtebene *f*
plane of measurement Messebene *f*
plane of section Schnittebene *f*
plane of separation Trennungsebene *f*
plane of swing Schwingebene *f*
plane of the drawing Zeichenebene *f*

plane of transverse section Stirnschnittebene *f*
plane off abhobeln
plane-parallel planparallel
plane position Ebenenlage *f*
plane scale ebene Skale *f*
plane surface ebene Fläche *f*
plane tangent Flächentangente *f*
plane tangential to the base cylinder Grundzylindertangentialebene *f*
plane tooth system Planverzahnung *f*, Planradverzahnung *f*
planed surface pattern Hobelbild *nt*
planeless Ebenheit *f*
planer Hobelmaschine *f*, Abrichthobel *m*, Langhobelmaschine *f*, Langtischhobelmaschine *f*, Tischhobelmaschine *f*
planer beam Querbalken *m*
planer bed Hobelbett *nt*
planer drive Hobelantrieb *m*
planer head Querbalkensupport *m*, Horizontalsupport *m*, Hobelmaschinensupport *m*, Support *m*, Werkzeugträger *m*
planer head toolhead Hobelsupport *m*
planer jack Aufspannblock *m*
planer miller Langhobelfräsmaschine *f*, Hobel- und Fräsmaschine *f*, Zweiständerfräsmaschine *f*, Doppelspindelfräsmaschine *f*, Doppelständerfräsmaschine *f*, Langtischfräs- und Hobelmaschine *f*, Zweiständerhobel- und -fräsmaschine *f*, Zweiständerplanfräsmaschine *f*
planer-miller with removable housing Langfräsmaschine *f* mit ausfahrbaren Seitenständern
planer-milling Langhobeln *nt*
planer platen Hobelmaschinentisch *m*
planer poppet Spannbock *m*, Gegenhalter *m*
planer table Hobeltisch *m*, Hobelmaschinentisch *m*
planer tool Hobelmeißel *m*, Hobelmesser *nt*
planer toolhead Hobelmaschinensupport *m*
planer toolholder Hobelmeißelhalter *m*
planer-type horizontal boring and

milling machine Waagerechtbohr- und -fräsmaschine *f* mit axialverschiebbarem Tisch
planer-type milling machine Langfräsmaschine *f*, Portalfräsmaschine *f*
planer-vice Hobelmaschinenschraubstock *m*
planer vise Hobelmaschinenschraubstock *m*
planer work Hobelarbeit *f*
planes *pl* **in the tool-in-hand system** Ebenen *fpl* im Werkzeug-Bezugssystem
planes *pl* **in the tool-in-use system** Ebenen *fpl* im Wirk-Bezugssystem
planet carrier Planetenradträger *m*, Planetenträger *m*
planet gear Umlaufrad *nt*
planet gear carrier Planetenträger *m*
planet wheel Planetenrad *nt*
planetary gear train Planetengetriebezug *m*, Umlaufgetriebezug *m*
planetary gear transmission Planetengetriebe *nt*
planetary gearing Planetengetriebe *nt*
planetary grinder Planetenschleifmaschine *f*
planetary grinding Umschleifen *nt*
planetary miller Planetenspindelfräsmaschine *f*
planetary milling Fräsen *nt* mit Planetenspindelfräsmaschine
planetary milling machine Planetenspindelfräsmaschine *f*
planetary milling quill Rundfräspinole *f*
planetary motion Planetärbewegung *f*
planetary movement Planetenbewegung *f*
planetary plunge-cut thread milling machine Planetenkurzgewindefräsmaschine *f*
planetary rolling Planetenwalzen *nt*
planetary spindle Planetenspindel *f*
planetary-type miller Planetenspindelfräsmaschine *f*
planetary-type thread milling machine Planetenspindelgewindefräsmaschine *f*
planimetry Flächenmessung *f*

planing Hobeln *nt*
planing attachment Hobeleinrichtung *f*, Hobelvorrichtung *f*
planing attachment for machining radius and contours Schräg- und Kurvenhobeleinrichtung *f*
planing by generating template planes Schablonenhobeln
planing crosswise Querhobeln *nt*
planing fixture Hobelvorrichtung *f*
planing head Querbalkensupport *m*, Horizontalsupport *m*, Support *m*
planing head toolhead Hobelsupport *m*
planing inclined (flat) surfaces Schräghobeln *nt*
planing length Hobellänge *f*
planing machine Hobelmaschine *f*, Langhobelmaschine *f*, Langtischhobelmaschine *f*, Tischhobelmaschine *f*
planing method Hobelverfahren *nt*
planing operation Hobelarbeit *f*
planing setup Aufspannung *nt* auf den Hobelmaschinentisch
planing tool Hobelmeißel *m*, Hobelmesser *nt*
planing width Hobelbreite *f*
planish ebnen, glätten, ausbeulen
planishing Schlichten *nt*, Glattdrücken *nt*
planishing tubular bodies outside Außenglattwalzen *nt* von Hohlkörpern
planned replacement time Planwiederbeschaffungszeit *f*
planned time Planzeit *f*
planned value method Planwertmethode *f*
planner Planer *m*
planning Projektierung *f*, Planung *f*
planning aid Planungshilfsmittel *f*
planning basis Planungsgrundlage *f*
planning condition Planungsstand *m*
planning course Planungsablauf *m*
planning data Planungsdaten *pl*
planning deadline Planungstermin *m*
planning drawing Planungszeichnung *f*
planning foundation Planungsgrundlage *f*
planning horizon Planungshorizont *m*

planning method Planungsmethode *f*
planning model Planungsmodell *nt*
planning phase Projektierung *f*, Planungsphase *f*
planning preparation Planungsvorbereitung *f*
planning project Planungsvorhaben *nt*
planning rule Planungsregel *f*
planning stage Planungsphase *f*, Planungsstadium *nt*
planning task Planungsaufgabe *f*
planning team Planungsteam *nt*
plano-miller Langtischfräs- und -hobelmaschine *f*, Langfräsmaschine *f*, Portalfräsmaschine *f*, Hobel- und Fräsmaschine *f*
plano-milling machine Langfräsmaschine *f*, Portalfräsmaschine *f*
plant Betrieb *m*, Fabrik *f*, Werk *nt*, Anlage *f*, Betriebsanlage *f*, technische Anlage *f*, Fertigungsstätte *f*
plant accounting Anlagenbuchhaltung *f*
plant area Anlagenbereich *m*
plant cost accounting Betriebsabrechnung *f*
plant layout Anlagenauslegung *f*, Aufstellung *f* der Maschinen
plant manager Betriebsleiter *m*
plant manager level Betriebsleiterebene *f*
plant model Fabrikmodell *nt*
plant noise level Anlagenlautstärke *f*
plant own betriebseigen
plant planning Fabrikplanung *f*
plant procurement Anlagenbeschaffung *f*
plant records Betriebsaufzeichnungen *fpl*
plant resource Betriebsmittel *nt*
plant segment display Teilanlagenbild *nt*
plant spray oil Pflanzensprühöl *nt*
plant subject to a requirement of acceptance abnahmebedürftige Anlage *f*
plant user Anlagenbetreiber *m*
plant utilization Kapazitätsauslastung *f*
plant with a hot atmosphere Warmbetrieb *m*

plasma arc welding Plasmastrahlschweißen *nt*, Plasmalichtbogenschweißen *nt*, Wolframplasmaschweißen *nt*
plasma beam machining Plasmastrahlbearbeitung *f*
plasma channel Plasmakanal *m*
plasma deposition Plasmabeschichtung *f*
plasma deposition welding Plasmaauftragschweißen *nt*
plasma gas nozzle Plasmagasdüse *f*
plasma jet plasma arc welding Plasmastrahl-Plasmalichtbogenschweißen *nt*
plasma laser Plasmalaser *m*
plasma machining Plasmabearbeitung *f*
plasma-MIG-welding Plasma-Metall-Schutzgasschweißen *nt*
plasma nozzle Plasmadüse *f*
plasma radiating Plasmastrahlen *nt*
plasma torch Plasmabrenner *m*
plaster Gips *m*
plaster base Putzträger *m*
plastic verformbar
plastic backing film Kunststoffträgerfolie *f*
plastic banding Kunststoffbandage *f*
plastic blister Kunststoffblister *m*
plastic box Kunststoffkasten *m*
plastic coating Deckschicht *f*
plastic container Kunststoffbehälter *m*
plastic cover Kunststoffhaube *f*
plastic deformation Formänderung *f*
plastic-elastic behaviour plastisch-elastisches Verhalten *nt*
plastic film Plastikfolie *f*, Kunststofffolie *f*
plastic glider Kunststoffgleiter *m*
plastic mouldability plastische Formbarkeit *f*
plastic of good dimensional stability formfester Kunststoff *m*
plastic packing Kunststoffpackband *nt*
plastic pallet Kunststoffpalette *f*
plastic ring Kunststoffring *m*
plastic ringing machine Kunststoffringsammelpackmaschine *f*
plastic shape Kunststoffschale *f*
plastic shaping plastische Formge-

bung *f*
plastic sheet Kunststofftafel *f*
plastic spreading bildsames Einspreizen *nt*
plastic strap Kunststoffband *nt*
plastic strip Kunststoffstreifen *m*
plastic tape Kunststoffband *nt*
plastic tray Kunststoffwanne *f*
plastic tub Kunststoffwanne *f*
plastic tube Kunststoffrohr *nt*
plastic tubing Kunststoffrohr *nt*
plastics Kunststoff *m*, Plastik *f*
plasticised film weichmacherhaltige Folie *f*
plasticised foil weichmacherhaltige Folie *f*
plasticised moulding material weichmacherhaltige Formmasse *f*
plasticised plastics weichmacherhaltiger Kunststoff *m*
plasticised plastics film weichmacherhaltige Kunststofffolie *f*
plasticised sheeting weichmacherhaltige Folie *f*
plasticizer-absorbing film weichmacheraufnehmende Folie *f*
plasticizer-absorbing foil weichmacheraufnehmende Folie *f*
plasticizer-absorbing plastics weichmacheraufnehmender Kunststoff *m*
plasticizer-absorbing sheeting weichmacheraufnehmende Folie *f*
plasticizer absorption Weichmacheraufnahme *f*
plastics auxiliary Kunststoffhilfsstoff *m*
plastics coated kunststoffbeschichtet
plastics dispersion Kunststoffdispersion *f*
plastics dispersion paint Kunststoffdispersionsfarbe *f*, Dispersionsfarbe *f*
plastics drain pipe Kunststoffdränrohr *nt*
plastics elastomer film Kunststoffelastomerfolie *f*
plastics engineering Kunststofftechnik *f*
plastics faced kunststoffbeschichtet
plastics field Kunststoffgebiet *nt*
plastics gear Kunststoffrad *nt*
plastics insulating tape Kunststoffisolierband *nt*
plastics laminate Kunststofffolienverbund *m*
plastics machine Kunststoffmaschine *f*
plastics moulded material Kunststoffformstoff *m*
plastics moulding Kunststoffformteil *nt*
plastics moulding material Kunststoffformmasse *f*
plastics pipe Kunststoffleitung *f*
plastics pipeline Kunststoffrohrleitung *f*
plastics pressurized tubing Kunststoffdruckrohrleitung *f*
plastics product Kunststofferzeugnis *nt*
plastics releasing plasticiser weichmacherabgebender Kunststoff *m*
plastics surfacing film Beschichtungsfolie *f*
plate Scheibe *f*, Unterlage *f*, Tafel *f*, Platte *f*, Blech *nt*
plate bar Platine *f*, Platte *f*
plate-bending machine Blechbiegemaschine *f*
plate cam Scheibenkurve *f*, Flachkurve *f*
plate-edge planing Blechkantenhobeln *nt*
plate-edge planing machine Blechkantenhobelmaschine *f*
plate locking pin Haltestift *m* der Teilscheibe
plate or sheet materials Platten *fpl*
plate piloting cutter Plattenführungsscheidwerkzeug *nt*
plate planer Blechkantenhobelmaschine *f*
platen 1. Kreis *m* **2.** Tisch *m*, Hobeltisch *m*
plates Platinen *fpl*
platform 1. Plattform *f*, Rampe *f*, Ladefläche *f*, Standfläche *f*, Podest *nt*, Bühne *f* **2.** Tisch *m*
platform and stillage truck Plattformhubwagen *m*
platform stacker Plattformstapler *m*
platform truck Hochhubwagen *m*
plating Belag *m*
platinize platinieren
platinum Platin *nt*

platinum gauze Platinnetz *nt*
platinum resistance thermometer Platinwiderstandsthermometer *nt*
plausibility Plausibilität *f*
plausibility check Plausibilitätskontrolle *f*, Plausibilitätstest *m*
plausible plausibel
play Spiel *nt*, Spielraum *m*
play back wiedergeben
playback Wiedergabe *f*
playing spielbehaftet
pleat Plisseefalte *f*, plissieren
pleat wrapping machine Plissiereinschlagmaschine *f*
pliers *pl* Zange *f*, Kneifzange *f*
pliers feed device Zangenvorschubapparat *m*
plummet Lot *nt*
plinth Fußleiste *f*, Sockel *m*
plot einzeichnen, zeichnen, darstellen, aufreißen; Diagramm *nt*
plotter Plotter *m*
plug 1. Stift *m*, Stecker *m*, Stopfen *m*, Dübel *m*, Spund *m*; dübeln, stecken **2.** *(Messtechnik)* Kaliberdorn *m*
plug and socket device Steckverbindung *f*
plug connection Steckverbindung *f*
plug cover Steckergehäuse *nt*
plug device Steckvorrichtung *f*
plug gauge with taper lock Lehrdorn *m* mit Kegelbefestigung
plug in einstecken, einhängen
plug-in socket Steckmuffe *f*
plug mill Stopfenwalzwerk *nt*
plug of cotton wool Wattestopfen *m*
plug panel Steckerfeld *nt*
plug rolling of tubes Stopfenwalzen *nt* von Rohren
plug socket Steckdose *f*
plug switch Geräteschalter *m*
plug welded joint Lochnaht *f*
pluggable steckbar
plugging Stecken *nt*
plumb Lot *nt*
plumb line Senkrechte *f*
plumber Installateur *m*, Klempner *m*
plumbing trade Installationstechnik *f*
plump line Lotrechte *f*
plunge durchziehen, eintauchen, einstechen
plunge cut Einstich *m*; einstechen
plunge-cut grinder Einstechschleifmaschine *f*
plunge-cut grinding Einstich *m*, Einstechschleifen *nt*, Einstechverfahren *nt* auf Rundschleifmaschinen
plunge-cut method Einstechverfahren *nt*
plunge-cut thread grinder Kurzgewindeschleifmaschine *f*
plunge-cut thread grinding Gewindeeinstechschleifen *nt*, Kurzgewindeschleifen *nt*
plunge-cut thread milling Kurzgewindefräsen *nt*
plunge cutting Einstecharbeit *f*
plunge feed and rolling method Einstechwälzverfahren *nt*
plunge-feed generating method Einstechabwälzverfahren *nt*
plunge-feed hobbing Tauchlängsfräsen *nt*
plunge-feed method Tauchverfahren *nt*
plunge-feed milling Pendeltauchfräsen *nt*
plunge-feed movement Zustellbewegung *f*
plunge-grinding Einstechschleifen *nt*
plunge grinding method Einstechverfahren *nt* auf Rundschleifmaschinen
plunge-mill tauchfräsen
plunge milling Tauchfräsen *nt*
plunge milling machine Tauchfräsmaschine *f*
plunger Kolben *m*, Plungerkolben *m*, Tauchkolben *m*, Stempel *m*, Raststift *m*
plunger mould transferpressen
plunger moulding Spritzpressen *nt*
plunger moulding operation Spritzpressvorgang *m*
plunger pin Raststift *m*
plus variation Plusabweichung *f*
pneumatic motor Pneumatikmotor *m*
microbore tool Feinbohrmeißel *m*
pneumatic pneumatisch
pneumatic chucking Druckluftspannung *f*
pneumatic conveying Druckluftförde-

rung *f*
pneumatic cylinder Pneumatikzylinder *m*
pneumatic-electronic switch pneumatisch-elektronischer Schalter *m*
pneumatic equipment Pressluftanlage *f*, Druckluftanlage *f*, pneumatische Ausrüstung *f*
pneumatic hose Pneumatikschlauch *m*
pneumatic length measurement pneumatische Längenmessung *f*
pneumatic system Druckluftanlage *f*
pneumatic tyre Luftreifen *m*
pneumatic tyre rim Luftreifenfelge *f*
pneumatic tyres Luftbereifung *f*
pneumatic tyred wheel Rad *nt* mit Bereifung mit veränderbarem Lufteinschluss
pneumatic valve Pneumatikventil *nt*
pneumatically actuated druckluftbetätigt
pneumatically driven injection moulding machine Druckluftspritzgießmaschine *f*
pneumatically operated druckluftbetätigt
pneumatics Pneumatik *f*
pocket 1. Tasche *f* **2.** *(Öffnung)* Ausfallöffnung *f* **3.** *(Verzahnung)* Zahnlücke *f*
pocket dial calliper Taschenmessschieber *m* mit Rundskala
pocket milling Taschenfräsen *nt*
pocket-type plate battery Taschenplattenbatterie *f*
pocketing dreidimensionales Fräsen *nt*, Gesenkfräsen *nt*
polished glatt poliert
point 1. Spitze *f*, Stelle *f*, Punkt *m*; spitzen, anspitzen, richten (auf) **2.** *(Werkzeug)* Meißelspitze *f*
point angle Spitzenwinkel *m*
point-by-point exploration punktweises Abtasten *nt*
point contact Punktberührung *f*
point estimation Punktschätzung *f*
point example transformation Punktmustertransformation *f*
point guidance mechanism Punkführungsgetriebe *nt*
point in the grid Rasterpunkt *m*

point in time Zeitpunkt *m*
point in time sampling Probenahmezeitpunkt *m*
point of application of the filler Lotansatzstelle *f*
point of application of the force Kraftangriffspunkt *m*
point of collection Probenahmestelle *f*
point of connection Anschlusspunkt *m*, Anschlussstelle *f*
point of contact Berührungspunkt *m*, Wälzpunkt *m*, Eingriffspunkt *m*
point of control Stellort *m*
point of coordinates Koordinatenpunkt *m*
point of cut Schnittstelle *f*
point of cutting action Eingriff *m* eines Meißels, Schneideneingriff *m*
point of disturbance Störort *m*
point of engagement Eingriffsstelle *f*, Eingriffspunkt *m*
point of gear intermesh Eingriffsstelle *f*
point of gravity Schwerpunktlage *f*
point of impact Auftreffstelle *f*
point of intersection Knotenpunkt *m*, Schnittpunkt *m*, Kreuzungspunkt *m*
point of light Lichtfleck *m*
point of load incidence Kraftangriffspunkt *m*
point of origin Ursprungspunkt *m*
point of presence (POP) Einwahlpunkt *m*
point of resistance Widerstandspunkt *m*
point of rupture Bruchstelle *f*
point of the test needle Prüfnadelspitze *f*
point of truncation Abbruchstelle *f*
point on the tooth surface Flankenpunkt *m*
point position Punktlage *f*
point to zeigen auf
point-to-point (PTP) motion Punkt-zu-Punkt-Bewegung *f*
point-to-point connection Punkt-zu-Punkt-Verbindung *f*
point-to-point control Punktsteuerung *f*
point-to-point positioning control

system Punktsteuerung *f*
point tooth system Punktverzahnung *f*
point transmission of force punktförmige Krafteinleitung *f*
pointed spitz
pointed finishing tool Außendrehmeißel *m*
pointed flame Spitzflamme *f*
pointer Zeiger *m*
pointer deflection Zeigerausschlag *m*, Zeigeranschlag *m*
pointer reading Zeigerablesung *f*
pointer tip Zeigerspitze *f*
pointer variable Zeigervariable *f*
pointing Anspitzen *nt*, Anspitzkneten *nt*
pointing by forging Anspitzen *nt*, Anspitzkneten *nt*
pointing device Koordinatengeber *m*
pointing in roll units Anspitzen *nt* durch Walzen
pointing tool Spitzwinkel *m*
points Schienenweiche *f*
poisonous giftig
polar axis Polarachse *f*
polar coordinate Polarkoordinate *f*
polarity Polarität *f*
polarity indicator Polaritätsindikator *m*
polarity reversal Polumkehrung *f*, Polaritätsumkehr *f*, Verpolung *f*
polarity reversal protection Verpolschutz *m*
polarizability Polarisierbarkeit *f*
polarizable polarisierbar
polarization Polarisation *f*
polarization interference filter Polarisationsinterferenzfilter *m*
polarization resistance Polarisationswiderstand *m*
polarize polarisieren
polarographic method polarographisches Verfahren *nt*
polder Polder *m*
pole Pol *m*
pole changeable polumschaltbar
pole-changing Umpolung *f*
pole reversal Umpolung *f*
pole terminal Polklemme *f*
policy formulation Zielformulierung *f*
polish polieren

polishability Polierbarkeit *f*
polished specimen Schliffprobe *f*
polishing Polieren *nt*
polishing agents Poliermittel *nt*
polishing alumina Poliertonerde *f*
polishing effect Glättwirkung *f*
polishing machine Poliermaschine *f*
poll abrufen
polling Abruf *m*
polling technique Abrufverfahren *nt*
pollutant Schadstoff *m*, verschmutzte Substanz *f*
pollutant atmosphere Schadstoffatmosphäre *f*
pollute verunreinigen, verschmutzen, verseuchen
polluted air unreine Luft *f*
polluted atmosphere verunreinigte Atmosphäre *f*
polluter Verursacher *m* von Umweltverschmutzung
pollution Verunreinigung *f*, Verschmutzung *f*
polyacetaldehyde adhesive Polyacetaldehydkleber *m*
polyacrylethylene oxide adhesive Polyacrylethylenoxidkleber *m*
polyaddition Polyaddition *f*
polycarbonate injection moulding material Polycarbonatspritzgussmasse *f*
polychlorbutadiene adhesive Polychlorbutadiankleber *m*
polycondensation Polykondensation *f*
polycrystal Vielkristall *m*
polyisobutylene sheet Polyisobuthylenbahn *f*
polyester compression moulding material containing glass fibre filler glasfasergefüllte Polyesterpressmasse *f*
polyester fibre Polyesterfaser *f*
polyester reaction resin Polyesterreaktionsharz *nt*
polyester resin Polyesterharz *nt*
polyester resin adhesive Polyesterharzkleber *m*
polyester resin compression moulding material Polyesterharzpressmasse *f*
polyester resin mat Polyesterharz-

matte *f*
polyester thread Polyesterzwirn *m*
polyethylene moulding material Polyethylenformmasse *f*
polyethylene sheathing Polyethylenumhüllung *f*
polygon Polygon *nt*, Vielkant *m*, Mehrkantprofil *nt*
polygon drilling Mehrkantbohren *nt*
polygon edge formation Polygonkantenbildung *f*
polygon length Polygonlänge *f*
polygon line Polygonzug *m*
polygon profile Mehrkantprofil *nt*
polygon turning Mehrkantdrehen *nt*
polygonal kantig, vieleckig
polygonal mirror Polygonspiegel *m*
polygonal mirror wheel Polygonspiegelrad *nt*
polygonal turning jobs Mehrkantdreharbeiten *fpl*
polygonal wheel Polygonrad *nt*
polyimide Polyimid *nt*
polyisoprene Polyisopren *nt*
polymer Polymer *nt*
polymer in emulsion Emulsionspolymerisat *nt*
polymer in microsuspension Mikrosuspensionspolymerisat *nt*
polymer in suspension Suspensionspolymerisat *nt*
polymer latex Kunststofflatex *nt*
polymer optical fibre optische Polymerfaser *f*
polymer plasticizer Polymerweichmacher *m*
polymerizable mixture polymerisierbares Gemisch *nt*
polymerization Polymerisation *f*
polymethane cellular plastics Polymethanschaumstoff *m*
polymethane cold foam PUR-Kaltschaum *m*
polymethyl-methacrylate injection moulding material (or compound) Polymethylmethacrylatspritzgussmasse *f*
polystyrene cellular plastics Polystyrolschaumstoff *m*
polystyrene flakes Polystyrolflocken *fpl*
polystyrene injection moulding material (or compound) Polystyrolspritzgussmasse *f*
polystyrene moulding material Polystyrolformmasse *f*, PS-Formmasse *f*
polystyrene not containing emulsifiers emulgatorfreies Polysterol *nt*
polytropic exponent Polytropenexponent *m*
polyurethane basis Polyurethanbasis *f*
polyurethane elastomer Polyurethanelastomer *nt*
polyurethane solution adhesive Polyurethankleber *m*
polyvinyl acetate adhesive Polyvinylacetatkleber *m*
polyvinyl alcohol glue Polyvinylalkoholleim *m*
polyvinyl chloride coating PVC-Beschichtung *f*
polyvinyl ether adhesive Polyvinylätherkleber *m*
polyvinyl methyl ether Polyvinylmethyläther *m*
pony motor Anwurfmotor *m*
pool tauschen
pool of molten metal Schmelzfluss *m*
pool of solder Lötbad *nt*
pool pallet Tauschpalette *f*, Poolpalette *f*
pooling Tausch *m*
poor schlecht
poor finish geringe Oberflächengüte *f*
poor grinding cut unsauberer Schliff *m*
poor in alignment Kantenversatz *m*
poorly clamped schlecht gespannt
pop from abziehen von
pop-up menu Balkenmenü *nt*
poppet 1. Spannbock *m*, Gegenhalter *m* **2.** *(Schraube)* Spannschraube *f*
popping Puffen *nt*
population Gesamtheit *f*, Grundgesamtheit *f*
population classified into groups Gruppeneinteilung *f* einer Gesamtheit
porcelain Porzellan *nt*
porcelain heater Porzellanheizkörper *m*
pore Pore *f*

pore aperture Porenweite *f*
pore-free enclosed electrode porenfrei umhüllte Elektrode *f*
porosities Porositäten *fpl*
porosity Porigkeit *f*, Porosität *f*
porosity test Porenprüfung *f*
porous porös
porous envelope porenhaltige Umhüllung *f*
porousness Porosität *f*
port 1. Schnittstelle *f*, Anschluss *m*, Öffnung *f*, Kanal *m* **2.** *(Flüssigkeiten)* führen
port cover Staubdeckel *m*
portable mitnehmbar, tragbar, transportabel, ortsbeweglich, fahrbar
portable control unit tragbare Schalteinrichtung *f*
portable equipment ortsveränderliche Einrichtung *f*
portable gas analyzer Handgasspürgerät *nt*
portable measuring device tragbares Messgerät *nt*
portal Portal *nt*
portal automatic Portalautomat *m*
portal device Portalgerät *nt*
portal tie beam obere Querverbindung *f*
portal-type in Portalbauweise
portal-type robot Portalroboter
portal warehouse Portallager *nt*
portative tragfähig
ported mit Kanälen
portion Teil *m*
portion of piping Leitungsteil *nt*
portion of screw thread devoid of material werkstofffreier Teil *m* eines Gewindes
portion of screw thread filled with material werkstofferfüllter Teil *m* eines Gewindes
portion of the surface Flächenteil *nt*
position 1. anstellen, einstellen, in Stellung *f* bringen, anordnen, positionieren, justieren, einrichten, lagerichtig anbringen, orten; Stand *m*, Standort *m*, Lage *f*, Stelle *f*, Stellung *f*, Position *f*, Platz *m* **2.** zentrieren **3.** Personalstelle *f*
position automatically zwangspositionieren
position control Lageregler *m*
position coordinates Stellplatzkoordinaten *fpl*
position coupling Lagekopplung *f*
position dependent positionsabhängig, lageabhängig
position deviations Lageabweichung *f*
position display Positionsanzeige *f*
position encoder Weggeber *m*
position feedback control Lageregelung *f*
position in the joint rolling motion Wälzstellung *f*
position independent positionsunabhängig, lageunabhängig
position measuring equipment Wegmesseinrichtung *f*
position measuring system Wegmesssysteme *ntpl*
position monitoring Positionsüberwachung *f*
position of manufacture Fertigungslage *f*
position of rest Ruhelage *f*, Ruhestellung *f*
position of specimen Probenlage *f*
position of use Gebrauchslage *f*
position positively zwangspositionieren
position reference Lagehinweis *m*
position scheduled control Wegplansteuerung *f*
position sensing Positionsüberwachung *f*, Lageerfassung *f*
position-sensitive device bewegungsempfindliche Einrichtung *f*, Bewegungsmelder *m*
position sensor Bewegungsmelder *m*, Wegfühler *m*
position switch Positionsschalter *m*
positional control Lageregelung *f*
positional accuracy Lagegenauigkeit *f*, Positionsgenauigkeit *f*
positional control Lageregler *m*
positional coordinates Positionskoordinaten *fpl*
positional error Lagefehler *m*
positional error in the front rake Spanflächenlagefehler *m*

positional indication Stellungsanzeige *f*
positional sensor Positionsüberwachungseinrichtung *f*
positional tolerance Positionstoleranz *f*
positional tolerance of a flat surface Positionstoleranz *f* einer ebenen Fläche
positionally controlled lagegeregelt
positioned angeordnet
positioning Einstellen *nt*, Einstellung *f*, Justierung *f*, Anordnung *f*, Platzierung *f*, Positionierung *f*, Ortung *f*
positioning accessory Einfahrhilfe *f*, Positionierhilfe *f*, Positionierungshilfe *f*
positioning accuracy Positioniergenauigkeit *f*, Bereitstellgenauigkeit *f*
positioning aid Positionierhilfe *f*, Positionierungshilfe *f*
positioning automatic control Positionsregelung *f*
positioning control Positioniersteuerung *f*
positioning control system Positionsüberwachung *f*, Positionsregler *m*
positioning controller Positionsregler *m*
positioning device Positioniereinrichtung *f*
positioning display Positionieranzeige *f*
positioning element Stellglied *nt*, Steuerorgan *nt*, Stellgerät *nt*
positioning fixing Lagepeilung *f*
positioning lock Arretiereinrichtung *f*
positioning mark Positioniermarke *f*, Positionsmarke *f*
positioning marker Positioniermarke *f*, Positionsmarke *f*
positioning pin Haltestift *m*
positioning procedure Positioniervorgang *m*
positioning process Positionierverfahren *nt*, Positioniervorgang *m*
positioning scatter band Positionsstreubreite *f*
positioning sensor Positioniersensor *m*
positioning speed Positioniergeschwindigkeit *f*
positioning system Positioniersystem *nt*, Positionierverfahren *nt*
positioning tolerance Positioniertoleranz *f*, Verlegetoleranz *f*
positioning unit Positioniereinrichtung *f*
positive zwangsläufig, zwangsweise, kraftschlüssig
positive connection Kraftschluss *m*
positive displacement design Verdrängerbauart *f*
positive displacement hydraulic pump hydraulische Verdrängerpumpe *f*
positive displacement pump Verdrängerpumpe *f*
positive drive zwangsläufiger Antrieb *m*, zwangsläufige Mitnahme *f*, zwangsläufiger Trieb *m*
positive guidance Zwangsführung *f*
positive location Selbsthaltung *f*
positive locking Formschluss *m*
positive method Positivverfahren *nt*
positive movement Zwanglauf *m*
positive-only variation Nur-Plus-Abweichung *f*
positive operating pressure Betriebsüberdruck *m*
positive pattern-type spring washer aufgebogener Federring *m*
positive positioning Zwangspositionierung *f*
positive pressure Überdruck *m*
positive pressure attachment Überdruckanlage *f*
positive pressure burner Überdruckbrenner *m*
positive pressure region Überdruckbereich *m*
positive rake milling Fräsen *nt* mit positiven Spanwinkel, Fräsen *nt* mit Positivschnitt des Werkzeugs
positive steering Zwangslenkung *f*
positive stop fester Anschlag *m*
positive substance jointing stoffschlüssiges Fügen *nt*
positive variation Plusabweichung *f*
positively acting zwangsläufig wirkend
positively controlled device zwangsgesteuerte Einrichtung *f*
positively controlled shut-off device zwangsgesteuerte Absperrung *f*

positively guided zwangsgeführt
positively mechanized zwangsangetrieben
positively opening zwangsöffnend
positively prevented from zwangsweise gesichert gegen
positively steered zwangsgelenkt
possibility Möglichkeit f
possibility of access Zugangsmöglichkeit f
possibility of interaction Interaktionsmöglichkeit f
possibility of transaction Interaktionsmöglichkeit f
possibility to expansion Erweiterungsmöglichkeit f
possibility to identification Identifizierungsmöglichkeit f
possible möglich
possible materials verarbeitbare Werkstoffe f
possible of application Anwendungsmöglichkeit f
possible to identify identifizierbar
post 1. Pfosten m, Ständer m, Stiel m, Pfahl m 2. *(Arbeitsplatz)* Personalstelle f
post-carriage Nachlauf m
post-ignition time Nachzündungszeit f
post of a pallet Runge f
post pallet Stapelpalette f, Rungenpalette f
post pressure Nachdruck m
post pressure amount Nachdruckhöhe f
post pressure period Nachdruckzeit f
post pressure phase Nachdruckphase f
post-process gauging Messen nt nach Beendigung des Arbeitsganges
post-processing Nachverarbeitung f
post-purge period Nachspülzeit f
post-test Nachversuch m
post-weld time Schmiedezeit f
post weld upsetting length loss Nachstauchlängenverlust m
post weld upsetting time Nachstauchzeit f
postheat nachwärmen
postpone zurückstellen
postponed output retardierter Ausgang m

postprocessor Postprozessor (PP) m
posture Haltung f, Körperhaltung f
postweld heating Nachwärmen nt
pot vergießen
pot galvanizing Feuerverzinkung f
potential Potenzial nt; potenziell
potential equalization Potentialausgleich m
potential for rationalization Rationalisierungspotential nt
potential hardness increase Aufhärtbarkeit f
potential measurement Potentialmessung f
potentially explosive explosionsgefährdet, explosionsfähig
potentiometer Potentiometer nt
potentiometer recorder Kompensationsschreiber m
pothole Schlagloch nt
potting equipment Vergießeinrichtung f
potential separation Potentialtrennung f
pour schütten, gießen
pour in einfüllen
pour point Stockpunkt m
powder Pulver nt
powder-coated pulverbeschichtet
powder coating Pulverbeschichtung f
powder density Stopfdichte f
powder filling Sandkapselung f
powder metal Pulvermetall nt
powder-metallurgical pulvermetallurgisch
powder metallurgy Pulvermetallurgie f
powder processing Pulververarbeitung f
powder production Pulverherstellung f
powder spraying Pulveraufspritzen nt
powdered filler metal pulverförmiger Schweißzusatz m
powdered iron containing covering eisenpulverhaltige Umhüllung f
power 1. Leistung f, Stärke f, Kraft f, Potenz f, Energie f, Vermögen nt 2. *(Antrieb)* Antriebsleistung f; antreiben

power-driven kraftbetrieben
power absorption Leistungsaufnahme *f*
power amplification Leistungsverstärkung *f*
power-assisted kraftunterstützt
power assisted steering Hilfskraftlenkung *f*
power balance Leistungsbilanz *f*
power circuit Stromkreis *m*, Betriebsstromkreis *m*
power consumption Energieverbrauch *m*, Kraftverbrauch *m*, Leistungsaufnahme *f*
power content Energieinhalt *m*
power converter Stromrichter *m*
power current Starkstrom *m*
power demand Leistungsaufwand *m*, Leistungsbedarf *m*
power device Leistungsglied *nt*
power dissipation Verlustleistung *f*
power distribution Kraftverteilung *f*
power divider Leistungssteller *m*
power down feed automatischer Tiefenvorschub *m*, maschineller Tiefenvorschub *m*
power drain Leistungsverlust *m*
power drive Antrieb *m*
power drive system Leistungsantrieb *m*
power electronics Leistungselektronik *f*
power engineering plant energietechnische Anlage *f*
power factor Leistungsfaktor *m*
power factor correction Leistungsfaktorkorrektur *f*
power failure *(el.)* Stromausfall *m*, Netzunterbrechung *f*
power feed selbsttätiger Vorschub *m*
power flow Energiefluss *m*
power for acting levers Verstellkraft *f*
power forward traverse Eilvorlauf *m*, Eilgangvorlauf *m*
power function Gütefunktion *f*
power generator Stromgenerator *m*
power hacksaw Bügelsägemaschine *f*
power injection moulding *(PIM)* Kraftspritzgießen *nt (Mikro-Pulver-Spritzgießen)*
power input Leistungsaufnahme *f*

power installation Starkstromanlage *f*
power interface Versorgungsanschluss *m*
power loss Verlustleistung *f*, Leistungsverlust *m*
power manipulator Kraftmanipulator *m*
power of a machine Leistung *f* einer Maschine
power-operated kraftbetrieben, kraftbetätigt
power operated chuck Kraftspannfutter *nt*
power output abgegebene Leistung *f*
power pack Hydraulikaggregat *nt*
power plant Starkstromanlage *f*
power port Versorgungsanschluss *m*
power profile Energieprofil *nt*
power quality Elektroenergiequalität *f*
power rail Stromschiene *f* (SPS)
power range Leistungsbereich *m*
power rapid travel Eilgang *m*
power rapid traverse Eilgang *m*, Schnellgang *m*
power requirement Leistungsbedarf *m*
power reversal Bremsenenergierückgewinnung *f*
power saw Motorsäge *f*
power screw press mechanische Spindelpresse *f*
power socket wrench Maschinenschrauberwerkzeug *nt*
power source *1.* Antriebsart *f 2. (el.)* Stromquelle *f*
power spring Aufzugsfeder *f*
power station Kraftwerk *nt*
power supply Stromlieferung *f*, Stromeinspeisung *f*, Energieeinspeisung *f*, Energiezufuhr *f*, Energieversorgung *f*
power supply line *(el.)* Energieversorgungsnetz *nt*
power supply system Energiesystem *nt*, Energieversorgungseinrichtung *f*
power system Antriebssystem *nt*
power throughput Leistungsdurchsatz *m*
power tightness Leistungsdichte *f*
power transmission Leistungsgetriebe *nt*

power transmission member Übertragungselement *nt*
power traverse maschinelle Verstellung *f*
power unit Antriebseinheit *f*
power-assisted steering Servolenkung *f*
powered angetrieben, kraftbetrieben, kraftunterstützt
powered pallet truck Hubwagen *m*
powered part kraftbewegtes Teil *nt*
powered roll bed Rollenteppich *m*
powered roller conveyor angetriebene Rollenbahn *f*
powerful stark
practicability Durchführbarkeit *f*
practicability of testing Prüfmöglichkeit *f*
practicable durchführbar
practical praktisch
practical operation Echtbetrieb *m*
practical service test Betriebserprobung *f*
practical usefulness Gebrauchstauglichkeit *f*
practice durchführen, ausführen, verfahren, praktizieren; Praxis *f*, Arbeitsweise *f*, Technik *f*, Betrieb *m*
pre-adjust vorauseinstellen
pre-angle vorwinkeln
pre-anneal for bending biegbar vorglühen
pre-anneal for deep drawing tiefziehbar vorglühen
pre-assigned moulding material vortypisierte Formmasse *f*
pre-assigned type Vortyp *m*
pre-basis Vorbasis *f*
pre-bend vorkrümmen
pre-bending Vorkrümmung *f*
pre-carriage Transportvorlauf *m*
pre-counterbore vorsenken
pre-desiccation Vortrocknung *f*
pre-development phase Vorentwicklungsphase *f*
pre-disintegration Vorzerkleinerung *f*
pre-elongate vordehnen
pre-filtration Vorfilterung *f*
pre-flanging Vorbördeln *nt*
pre-foamed particles vorgeschäumte Teilchen *ntpl*
pre-formed foam plastics Formstück *nt* aus Schaumkunststoff
pre-forming mould Vorpresswerkzeug *nt*
pre-glue vorkleben
pre-glued label Haftetikett *nt*
pre-gummed label applicator Etikettiermaschine *f* für vorgummierte Etiketten
pre-gummed tape sealing machine Nassklebebandverschließmaschine *f*
pre-heating burner Anwärmgerät *nt*
pre-ignition time Vorzündungszeit *f*
pre-image intensification Bildvorverstärkung *f*
pre-inspection Vorabnahme *f*
pre-intensification Vorverstärkung *f*
pre-load Vorkraft *f*
pre-machine vorarbeiten, vorbearbeiten, vorfertigen
pre-machining Vorbearbeitung *f*
pre-made vorgefertigt
pre-mill vorfräsen
pre-product Halbzeug *nt*
pre-purging Luftvorspülung *f*
pre-reduction apparatus Vorzerkleinerungsgerät *nt*
pre-reservation Vorreservierung *f*
pre-scavenging time Vorspülzeit *f*
pre-set voreinstellen, vorgeben
pre-set position vorgegebene Stellung *f*
pre-shear plane Vorscherebene *f*
pre-stagnation zone Vorstauzone *f*
pre-sterilization Vordesinfektion *f*
pre-stressing Vorbeanspruchung *f*
pre-turn vordrehen
pre-turning Schälen *nt*
pre-ventilation Luftvorspülung *f*
pre-washing *(Entrosten)* Vorwaschen *nt*
preadjust voreinstellen
preadjusted vorher eingestellt
preadjusting Voreinstellung *f*
preadjustment Voreinstellung *f*
preallocate vorbelegen, vorbesetzen
preallocation Vorbelegung *f*
preassemble vormontieren
preassembly Vormontage *f*
precaution Schutzmaßnahme *f*, Vor-

sichtsmaßregel *f*, Vorkehrung *f*
precede vorauseilen, vorausgehen
preceding vorhergehend, vorausgehend, vorauseilend, voreilend
preceding operation Vorarbeit *f*
precious metal Edelmetall *nt*
precipitate abscheiden
precipitation Abscheidung *f*
precipitation flask Fällungskolben *m*
precipitation gauge Niederschlagsmesser *m*
precipitation heat treatment Aushärten *nt* mit anschließendem Auslagern
precipitation induced crack Ausscheidungsriss *m*
precipitation recorder Niederschlagsschreiber *m*
precise genau, fein, präzise
precise call Feinabruf *m*
precision turning Feindrehen *nt*
precision Genauigkeit *f*, Präzision *f*
precision bolt Passschraube *f*
precision boring Feinbohren *nt*, Feinstbohren *nt*
precision boring machine Feinstbohrwerk *nt*, Feinbohrmaschine *f*
precision cast iron model melting process Feingussmodellanschmelzverfahren *nt*
precision-casting process Ausschmelzverahren *nt*
precision cutter Feinschnittwerkzeug *nt*, Feinbohrmeißel *m*
precision cutting Genauschneiden *nt*, Feinschneiden *nt*
precision dial indicator Präzisionsmessuhr *f*
precision engineering Feinwerktechnik *f*
precision finish eroding Feinschlichterodieren *nt*
precision finishing Präzisionsbearbeitung *f*
precision form Feingestalt *f*
precision gauge block Maßbild *nt*, Maßblock *m*, Maßklötzchen *nt*, Parallelendmaß *nt*
precision grinding Feinschleifen *nt*
precision grinding method Feinschleifverfahren *nt*, Präzisionsschleifverfahren *nt*
precision hoisting Feinhub *m*
precision hoisting gear Feinhub *m*
precision hoisting speed Feinhubgeschwindigkeit *f*
precision honing Feinziehschleifen *nt*
precision index centres Genauigkeitsteilgeräte *ntpl*
precision indicating gauge Feinzeiger *m*
precision jig borer Feinbohrwerk *nt*
precision job Präzisionsarbeit *f*
precision lathe Feindrehmaschine *f*, Werkzeugmacherdrehmaschine *f*
precision machining Feinbearbeitung *f*, Präzisionsbearbeitung *f*, Genaubearbeitung *f*
precision master gear Lehrzahnrad *nt*
precision measurement Feinmessung *f*
precision measuring device Genauigkeitsmesseinrichtung *f*
precision measuring tool Feinmesswerkzeug *nt*, Feinmesszeug *nt*
precision mechanics Feinmechanik *f*
precision mill feinstfräsen, präzisionsfräsen
precision mutual inductance Präzisionsgegenindukitivtät *f*
precision planing Feinsthobeln *nt*
precision planing machine Feinhobelmaschine *f*
precision refractometer Präzisionsrefraktometer *nt*
precision scale Präzisionsmaßstab *m*
precision screw spindle Genauigkeitsspindel *f*
precision shaping machine Feinhobelmaschine *f*
precision soldering Feinlötung *f*
precision sound level meter Präzisionsschallpegelmesser *m*
precision spirit level Präzisionswasserwaage *f*
precision turning Feindrehen *nt*
precision turning attachment Feindreheinrichtung *f*
precision turning machine Genauigkeitsdrehmaschine *f*, Präzisionsdrehmaschine *f*

precision work Präzisionsarbeit *f*
precoat vorbeschichten, Vorbeschichtung *f*
precolumn Vorspalte *f*
preconditioning Vorbehandlung *f*
preconfigured vorprojektiert
prescription Verordnung *f*
precuring Vorhärtung *f*
precut vorstanzen, vorgestanzt
predetermined vorgegeben, vorbestimmt
predetermined desired value vorgegebener Sollwert *m*
predetermined plane vorgegebene Ebene *f*
predrill vorbohren
predrilled hole vorgebohrtes Loch *nt*
preempt vorbelegen
preempting Vorbelegung *f*
prefabricate vorfertigen
prefabricated component engineering drawing Fertigteilzeichnung *f*
prefabricated materials Materialvorfertigung *f*
prefabrication Vorfertigung *f*
preferential direction Vorzugsrichtung *f*
preferred colour Vorzugsfarbe *f*
preferred dimension Vorzugsmaß *nt*
preferred lead Vorzugssteigung *f*
preferred number series Normalzahlenreihe *f*
preferred tolerance field Vorzugstoleranz *f*
preformat vorformatieren
preformatted vorformatiert, vorgestaltet
preformed moulding material vorgeformte Masse *f*
preforming Vorformung *f*
pregum vorgummieren
preheating Vorwärmung *f*
preheating and cutting nozzle Heiz- und Schneiddüse *f*
preimplementation stage Projektreife *f*
preinvestment study Projektstudie *f*
preliminary acceptance Vorabnahme *f*
preliminary air scavenging Luftvorspülung *f*

preliminary derusting Vorentrosten *nt*
preliminary draft drawing Vorentwurfszeichnung *f*
preliminary examination Voruntersuchung *f*
preliminary inspection Vorabnahme *f*
preliminary investigation Voruntersuchung *f*
preliminary load Vorbelastung *f*
preliminary machine Vorbearbeitung *f*
preliminary mixing process Untermischverfahren *nt*
preliminary planning Vorplanung *f*, Vorausplanung *f*
preliminary project Vorprojekt *nt*
preliminary projection Vorprojektierung *f*
preliminary result Zwischenergebnis *nt*
preliminary scavenging Vorspülung *f*
preliminary scrutiny Vorprüfung *f*
preliminary switch Vorendschalter *m*
preliminary testing Vorprüfung *f*
preliminary treatment of test specimens Probenvorbehandlung *f*
preload vorspannen; Vorspannkraft *f*, Vorspannung *f*
preload deflection Vorspannfederweg *m*
preloading Vorspannen *nt*, Vorspannung *f*
preloading bolt Vorspannbolzen *m*
prelubrication injector metering device Vorschmiereinleitungsverteiler *m*
premature frühzeitig, vorzeitig
premise voraussetzen; Voraussetzung *f*
preoperation drawing Vorbearbeitungszeichnung *f*
preoptive mit Vorwahl
preparation Vorbereitung *f*, Aufbereitung *f*, Anfertigung *f*, Vorbehandlung *f*
preparation allowance time Rüstverteilzeit
preparation effort Aufbereitungsaufwand *m*
preparation in a form suitable for reproduction vervielfältigungsgerechte Ausführung *f*
preparation of drawings Zeichnungs-

erstellung *f*
preparation of stacks Stapelbildung *f*
preparation time Rüstzeit *f*
preparation time base Rüstgrundzeit
preparatory treatment Vorbehandlung *f*
preparatory work Vorbereitungsarbeit *f*
prepare aufbereiten, vorbereiten, herrichten
prepare-recovering time Rüsterholungszeit
prepared flächenfertig
prepegs impregnated with polyester resin Polyesterharzmatte *f*
preplace *(Lot)* einlegen
preponderant proportion überwiegender Anteil *m*
preprint for the photo-reproduction of drawings *pl* Transparentvordruck *m* für Zeichnungen
preprinted drawing Vordruckzeichnung *f*
preprinted drawing sheet Zeichnungsvordruck *m*
preprocess aufbereiten, vorbehandeln, vorverarbeiten
preprocessing Vorverarbeitung *f*, Vorbehandlung *f*
preproduction Vorfertigung *f*
preproduction cost Rüstkosten *pl*
preproduction logistics Vorserienlogistik *f*
prepunched hole diameter *(bei Blechdurchzügen)* Vorlochdurchmesser *m*
prepurge period Vorspülzeit *f*
prerequisite Voraussetzung *f*
preresistor Vorwiderstand *m*
prescribe bestimmen, verordnen, vorschreiben
prescribed deviation vorgegebenes Maß *nt*
prescribed size vorgegebenes Maß *nt*
prescribed surface area Messflächeninhalt *m*
prescribed surface index Messflächenmaß *nt*
prescription Vorschrift *f*
preselect vorwählen
preselectable vorwählbar
preselection Vorwählen *nt*, Vorwahl *f*
preselection control Vorwählschaltung *f*
preselection mechanism Vorwähleinrichtung *f*
preselective vorwählbar
preselector Vorwähler *m*, Vorwählschaltung *f*
preselector dial Vorwählscheibe *f*
preselector mechanism Vorwählschaltung *f*
presence Anwesenheit *f*
presentation layer Darstellungsschicht *f*
presentation of items Bereitstellung *f*
preservation Schutz *m*
preservation of wood Holzschutz *m*
preset voreingestellt, vorbestimmt, vorgegeben, vorher einstellen, vorwählen, voreinstellen; Voreinstellung *f*
preset input Voreinstelleingang *m*
presettable vorwählbar, voreinstellbar
presetting Voreinstellung *f*
presetting element Voreinstellglied *nt*
preshaped filler Lotformteil *m*
presort vorsortieren
press pressen, drücken, zusammendrücken; Presse *f*
press brake Abkantpresse *f*
press building Pressenbau *m*
press button Drucktaste *f*
press button control Druckknopfsteuerung *f*
press down herabdrücken, niederdrücken
press fit Längspresspassung *f*, Pressung *f*
press joint Pressfuge *f*
press key Drucktaste *f*
press manufacture Pressenbau *m*
press nut Einpressmutter *f*
press on andrücken, anpressen, aufpressen
press-on lidding machine Anpressverschließmaschine *f*
press-on tyre wheels aufgepresste Bereifung *f*
press together zusammenpressen
press type broaching machine Stoßräummaschine *f*
pressboard panel Pressspantafel *f*

pressed blank Pressling *m*
pressed bolt fastening Presslochverschraubung *f*
pressed fibre mat Faserkuchen *m*
pressed hole screw Presslochverschraubung *f*
pressed-on aufgezogen
pressing 1. Zusammendrücken *nt* **2.** *(Werkstück)* Pressling *m*
pressing a key durch Tastendruck
pressing force Andruckkraft *f*
pressing on Anpressen *nt*
pressing power Pressdruck *m*
pressing rate Zusammendrückung *f*
pressing-related technical reasons presstechnische Gründe *mpl*
pressure Druck *m*
pressure acceleration impulse Druckbeschleunigungsgrad *m*
pressure adjusting device Druckeinstellvorrichtung *f*
pressure adjusting screw Druckeinstellschraube *f*
pressure angle Eingriffswinkel *m*
pressure-balanced mit Druckausgleich
pressure bearing valve part drucktragendes Armaturenteil *nt*
pressure build-up welding Pressauftragsschweißen *nt*
pressure built-up Druckaufbau *m*
pressure cam Anlaufkurve *f*
pressure casting process Druckgießen *nt*
pressure chamber Druckkammer *f*
pressure chamber ageing Druckkammeralterung *f*
pressure-compensated flow-control valve Stromregelventil *nt*
pressure compensation Druckausgleich *m*
pressure compensation operation Druckausgleichsvorgang *m*
pressure control Druckbegrenzung *f*, Drucksteuerung *f*, Absicherung *f* gegen Überdruck
pressure control valve Druckregelventil *nt*, Überdruckventil *nt*
pressure-controlled druckgesteuert
pressure detector Druckwächter *m*
pressure die cast druckgießen

pressure die casting process Druckgießverfahren *nt*
pressure difference Druckdifferenz *f*
pressure douche Druckspülung *f*
pressure drop Druckabfall *m*, Druckabsenkung *f*
pressure drop test Druckabfallprüfung *f*
pressure drop time Druckabfallzeit *f*
pressure filling machine Überdruckfüllmaschine *f*
pressure flank tragende Gewindeflanke *f*
pressure flexible hose Schlauch *m*
pressure gauge for the outlet pressure Hinterdruckmanometer *nt*
pressure head Druckhöhe *f*
pressure impulse Druckstoß *m*
pressure indication Druckanzeige *f*
pressure jet Druckdüse *f*
pressure joint welding Pressverbindungsschweißen *nt*
pressure limiter *(Druck)* Belastungsbegrenzer *m*
pressure limiting device Druckbegrenzungseinrichtung *f*, Druckbegrenzungsventil *nt*
pressure limiting valve Druckbegrenzungsventil *nt*
pressure loss Druckausfall *m*
pressure lubricant device Druckschmiergerät *nt*
pressure-lubricated druckgeschmiert
pressure maintaining pump Druckhaltepumpe *f*
pressure measuring device Druckmessgerät *nt*
pressure of explosion Explosionsdruck *m*
pressure operated druckbetätigt
pressure proof druckfest
pressure range Druckbereich *m*
pressure reading Druckanzeige *f*
pressure reducer Druckreduzierer *m*, Druckminderer *m*
pressure reducing valve Druckminderer *m*, Druckminderventil *nt*
pressure regulator Druckregler *m*
pressure regulator connection Druckmindereranschluss *m*

pressure relief valve Druckbegrenzungsventil *nt*, Druckbegrenzer *m*
pressure-responsive druckgesteuert
pressure rise time Druckanstiegszeit *f*
pressure roll Anpressrolle *f*
pressure roller Andrückrolle *f*
pressure-sensitive 1. druckempfindlich **2.** *(Klebstoff)* selbstklebend
pressure-sensitive adhesive insulating tape selbstklebendes Isolierband *nt*
pressure sensitive adhesive tape Haftklebeband *nt*
pressure-sensitive film Klebefolie *f*
pressure sensitive labelling machine Haftklebeetikettiermaschine *f*
pressure sensitive mat druckempfindliche Matte *f*
pressure-sensitive tape Selbstklebeband *nt*
pressure sensitive tape sealing machine Haftklebebandverschließmaschine *f*
pressure set point setter Drucksollwertsteller *m*
pressure setting Druckeinstellung *f*, Einstelldruck *m*
pressure shock *(kurzfristig)* Überdruck *m*
pressure signal Drucksignal *nt*
pressure spring Druckfeder *f*
pressure strip Druckleiste *f*
pressure switch Druckschalter *m*, Druckwellenschalter *m*
pressure tank Druckbehälter *m*
pressure threshold Druckschwelle *f*
pressure-tight druckdicht
pressure-tight joint Gewindedichtung *f*
pressure-tight screw fastening selbstdichtende Gewindeverbindung *f*
pressure-tight screw joint selbstdichtende Gewindeverbindung *f*
pressure-tight sealing thread Dichtungsgewinde *nt*
pressure tightness Dichtheit *f*
pressure transfer medium Druckübertragungsmittel *nt*
pressure union Rohrkupplung *f*
pressure vessel Druckbehälter *m*,
Druckluftbehälter *m*
pressure wave Druckwelle *f*
pressure-welded assembly Pressschweißverbindung *f*
pressurized gas cylinder Druckgasflasche *f*
pressureless circulatory lubrication drucklose Umlaufschmierung *f*
pressureless drainage system drucklose Abwasserleitung *f*
pressureless interval drucklose Zeitspanne *f*
pressurization Druckbeaufschlagung *f*, Unterdrucksetzung *f*
pressurize unter Druck setzen
pressurized unter Druck, überdruckgekapselt
pressurized apparatus Überdruckkapselung *f*
pressurized expansion tank Druckausdehnungsgefäß *nt*
pressurized oil assembly Druckölverband *m*
pressurized operation Überdruckbetrieb *m*
pressurized pipeline druckführende Leitung *f*
pressurized preheater Druckvorwärmer *m*
pressurized preheating Druckvorwärmung *f*
pressurized water container Druckwasserbehälter *m*
pressurizing Überdruckkapselung *f*
pressurizing device Überdruckvorrichtung *f*
pressurizing medium Druckmittel *nt*
pressworking Stanzen *nt*
pressworking shop Stanzerei *f*
prestress vorspannen
prestressing Vorspannung *f*
prestretch vordehnen; Vordehnung *f*
prestretching Vordehnung *f*
presuppose voraussetzen
pretension vorspannen
pretensioning Vorspannung *f*
pretreat vorbehandeln
pretreatment Vorbehandlung *f*
perturbation Störung *f*
prevailing torque element Siche-

rungsteil *nt* einer Mutter
prevailing torque part of the nut selbstsichernder Gewindeteil *m* einer Mutter
prevailing torque type element Sicherung *f*, Sicherungselement *nt*
prevailing torque type hexagon locknut selbstsichernde Sechskantmutter *f*
prevailing torque type locknut Sicherungsmutter *f*, selbstsichernde Mutter *f*
prevent vermeiden, vorbeugen, verhindern, verhüten
prevent damage schonen
prevent from hindern an
prevention Prävention *f*, Vermeidung *f*, Verhütung *f*, Verhinderung(smaßnahme) *f*, Schadensabwendung *f*
prevention of accidents Unfallverhütung *f*
prevention of hazards Gefahrensicherung *f*
prevention of slipping Gleithemmung *f*
preventive präventiv, vorbeugend, vorausschauend
preventive measure Vorbeugemaßnahme *f*
preview Vorschau *f*
previous vorausgehend
previous application method Vorstreichverfahren *nt*
prewarn vorwarnen
prewarning Vorwarnung *f*
prewarning limit Vorwarngrenze *f*
prewarning message Vorwarnmeldung *f*
price Preis *m*
price fluctuation Preisfluktuation *f*
price labelling Preisauszeichnung *f*
price list Preisliste *f*
price structure Preisgliederung *f*
pricing Preisgestaltung *f*
prick stechen; Stechen *nt*
prick punch Anreißkörner *m*
pricking grinding Stechschleifen
primary primär, übergeordnet
primary air side Brennerluftseite *f*
primary clearance 1. *(Fläche)* Freiflächenfase *f*, Hinterschliff *m* der Fase **2.** *(Winkel)* Fasenfreiwinkel *m*, Freiwinkel *m* an der Freiflächenfase
primary command Primärbefehl *m*
primary cone of the beam Primärstrahlenkegel *m*
primary cut surface Hauptschnittfläche *f*
primary cutting edge Hauptschneide *f*
primary danger zone Hauptgefahrenbereich *m*
primary demand Primärbedarf *m*
primary key Primärschlüssel *m*
primary land fasenartiger Anschliff *m* an der Schneide
primary material Vormaterial *nt*, Vorwerkstoff *m*
primary mechanism Vorschaltgetriebe *nt*
primary motion 1. Hauptbewegung *f* **2.** (spanende Fertigung) Schnittbewegung *f*
primary no-load current Primärleerlaufstrom *nt*
primary no-load voltage Primärleerlaufspannung *f*
primary pressure Vordruck *m*
primary rake Spanflächenfase *f* mit negativem Spanwinkel
primary rake relief Spanflächenfase *f*
primary sample Erstmuster *nt*, Erststufenprobe *f*
primary side rake angle Seitenspanwinkel *m*
primary sitting up Primärverschlemmung *f*
primary solder Erstlot *nt*
primary status Primarstatus *m*
prime grundieren
prime costs Selbstkosten *pl*, Gestehungskosten *pl*
prime mover Antriebsmotor *m*, Antriebselement *nt*, Kraftmaschine *f*
primed grundiert
primer Grundbeschichtung *f*, Voranstrichmittel *nt*, Grundierung *f*
priming Ansaugen *nt*
priming coat Grundierung *f*
principal Haupt ...
principal component Hauptbestand-

teil *m*
principal cutting edge Hauptschneide *f*
principal feed motion Hauptvorschubbewegung *f*
principal scale Hauptmaßstab *m*
principal part Hauptteil *nt*
principle Prinzip *nt*
principle for design Gestaltungsgrundsatz *m*
principles for the preparation of drawings Zeichnungsrichtlinien *fpl*
print drucken, aufdrucken, bedrucken, pausen
print and apply labelling machine Etikettendruck- und -appliziermaschine *f*
print format Druckbild *nt*
print out ausdrucken; Druckausgabe *f*
printed circuit board (PCB) Leiterplatte *f*, Platine *f*
printed form Formular *nt*
printed wiring board Leiterplatte *f*
printer Drucker *m*
printing Bedrucken *nt*
printing apparatus Drucker *m*
printing calculator druckende Rechenmaschine *f*
printing technique Druckverfahren *nt*
printout Ausdruck *m*
prior machining operations *pl* Vorbearbeitung *f*
prior state Vorzustand *m*
prior to vor
prioritization Prioritätensetzung *f*
prioritize Prioritäten setzen
priority vorrangig; Vorrang *m*, Priorität *f*, Prioritätsstufe *f*
priority control Vorrangschaltung *f*
priority travel Hauptfahrrichtung *f*
prism Prisma *nt*
prism-shaped dachförmig
prismatic bearing surface Prismenführung *f*, prismatische Führung *f*
prismatic bedway Bettprisma *nt*
prismatic bedways Bettführungsprismen *ntpl*
prismatic guideway Bettprisma *nt*
prismatic guideways prismatische Führung *f*, Prismenführungsbahn *f*, Bettführungsprismen *ntpl*
prismatic pair Schubgelenk *nt*
prismatic slideway Prismenführung *f*
prismatic Vees Dachprisma *nt*
prize Gewinn *m*
probability density Wahrscheinlichkeitsdichte *f*
probability distribution Wahrscheinlichkeitsverteilung *f*
probability of dangerous failure gefährliche Ausfallwahrscheinlichkeit *f*
probability of interaction Wechselwirkungswahrscheinlichkeit *f*
probability statement Wahrscheinlichkeitsaussage *f*
probability function Wahrscheinlichkeitsfunktion *f*
probe 1. versuchen 2. *(techn. Gerät)* Sonde *f*, Prüfkopf *m*
probe-to-specimen contact Ankopplung *f*
probing cycles Messzyklen *mpl*
procedure Durchführung *f*, Vorgehensweise *f*, Arbeitsweise *f*, Arbeitsverfahren *nt*, Verfahren *nt*, Verfahrensablauf *m*, Verfahrensgang *m*, Vorgang *m*
procedure-conditioned welding security fertigungsbedingte Schweißsicherheit *f*
procedure for conducting tests Versuchsdurchführung *f*
procedure-related welding security fertigungsbezogene Schweißsicherheit *f*
procedure special features Verfahrensbesonderheiten *f*
proceed 1. verfahren, vorgehen 2. ausgehen (von)
proceeding Maßnahme *f*
proceeding from ausgehend von
process abwickeln, behandeln, bearbeiten, verarbeiten, weiterverarbeiten; Verfahren *nt*, Prozess *m*, Vorgang *m*, Verlauf *m*, Arbeitsablauf *m*
process allocation Vorgangszuordnung *f*
Process and Equipment Automation Real Time Language (PEARL) PEARL (Abk. für Programmiersprache zur Lösung von Aufgaben im Realzeitbetrieb)

process arrangement Prozessgestaltung *f*
process automation Prozessautomatisierung *f*
process-bound prozessabhängig, prozessgekoppelt
process catenation Prozessverkettung *f*
process chain Prozesskette *f*, Verfahrenskette *f*
process chain-linking Prozessverkettung *f*
process chaining Prozessverkettung *f*
process colours Farbskala *f*
process communication Prozesskommunikation *f*
process complaints Reklamation bearbeiten
process computer Prozessrechner *m*
process control Prozessführung *f*, Prozesslenkung *f*, Prozesssteuerung *f*, rechnergestützte Prozessleitung *f*
process control level Prozesssteuerungsebene *f*
process control system Prozessleitsystem *nt*, Prozesskontrollsystem *nt*
process control workstation Prozessführungsplatz *m*
process cost accounting Prozesskostenrechnung *f*
process data Prozessdaten *pl*
process-duration Prozessdauer *f*
process energy source Prozessenergiequelle *f*
process engineering equipment verfahrenstechnische Einrichtungen *fpl*
process field bus (PROFIBUS) Prozessfeldbus *m*
process flow Arbeitsablauf *m*
process identification Prozessidentifikation *f*
process image Prozessabbild *nt*
process inspection Fertigungsprüfung *f*
process instruction Verfahrensanweisung *f*
process interrupt Prozessalarm *m*
process kinematics Verfahrenskinematik *f*
process level Prozessebene *f*
process logic Ablauflogik *f*

process message Prozessmeldung *f*
process model Prozessmodell *nt*
process monitoring rechnergestützte Prozess- und Anlagenüberwachung *f*, Überwachung *f*
process of approval Genehmigungsprozess *m*
process of chip formation Spanausbildung *f*
process of coordination Abstimmungsprozess *m*
process of improvement Verbesserungsprozess *m*
process optimization Prozessoptimierung *f*
process organization Ablauforganisation *f*
process-orientation Prozessorientierung *f*
process-oriented prozessorientiert
process owner Prozesseigner *m*
process plan Prozessplan *m*
process plan production Prozessplanerstellung *f*
process planning Arbeitsablaufplanung *f*, Prozessplanung *f*
process plant verfahrenstechnische Anlage *f*
process principal Verfahrenshauptgruppe *f*
process principle Verfahrensgrundsatz *m*
process quality control Prozessqualitätskontrolle *f*, Qualitätslenkung *f*
process-related prozessbedingt
process reliability Prozesssicherheit *f*
process reliable prozesssicher
process rule Ablaufregel *f*
process specific to diffusion diffusionsbestimmter Prozess *nt*
process specific to reaction reaktionsbestimmter Prozess *m*
process stability Prozesssicherheit *f*
process stabilization Prozessstabilisierung *f*
process stage Prozessstufe *f*
process step Arbeitsgang *m*
process structure Ablaufstruktur *f*
process succession Prozessfolge *f*
process succession assessment Pro-

zessfolgermittlung *f*
process variable Prozessvariable *f*, Prozessgröße *f*
process variables Prozessdaten *pl*
process variant Prozessvariante *f*
process variants Verfahrensvarianten *f*
processable verarbeitbar
processes characterization Verfahrenskennzeichnung *f*
processes of casting Gieß- und Formverfahren *nt*
processing Bearbeitung *f*, Verarbeitung *f*, Behandlung *f*, Aufbereitung *f*, Abwicklung *f*
processing aid Verarbeitungshilfsmittel *nt*
processing auxiliaries Verarbeitungshilfsmittel *ntpl*
processing condition Verarbeitungsbedingung *f*
processing duration Bearbeitungsdauer *f*
processing feature Verarbeitungsmerkmal *nt*
processing guidelines Verarbeitungsrichtlinien *fpl*
processing logic Auswerteelektronik *f*
processing machine Verarbeitungsmaschine *f*, Bearbeitungsmaschine *f*
processing module Bearbeitungsbaustein *m*, Verarbeitungsmodul *nt*
processing of films Folienverarbeitung *f*
processing property Verarbeitungseigenschaft *f*
processing sequence Bearbeitungsreihenfolge *f*
processing stabilizer Verarbeitungsstabilisator *m*
processing station Bearbeitungsstation *f*
processing step Bearbeitungsschritt *m*
processing technique Verarbeitungstechnik *f*
processing the list of parts Stücklistenverarbeitung *f*
processing time Bearbeitungszeit *f*
processing unit CPU-Baugruppe *f*, Verarbeitungseinheit *f*
processor Prozessor *m*

procurement Beschaffung *f*
procurement lead time Beschaffungsvorlaufzeit *f*
procurement logistics Beschaffungslogistik *f*
produce produzieren, fertigen, anfertigen, herstellen, erzeugen, fabrizieren, hervorrufen, verursachen, machen
produce drawings Zeichnungen anfertigen
produce friction reiben
produce mirror-image parts spiegelbildkopieren
produced hergestellt
producer Hersteller *m*
producer's risk Herstellrisiko *nt*
product Erzeugnis *nt*, Produkt *nt*
product arrangement Produktgestaltung *f*
product assortment depth Sortimentstiefe *f*
product buffer Warenpuffer *m*
product cost accounting Produktabrechnung *f*
product comparison Produktvergleich *m*
product costs Produktkosten *pl*
product data Produktdaten *pl*
product data management (PDM) Produktmanagement *nt*
product data model Produktdatenmodell *nt*
product description Produktbeschreibung *f*
product designation Produktbezeichnung *f*
product development Produktentwicklung *f*
product distribution system Warenverteilsystem *nt*
product entry Produkteinlauf *m*
product exit Produktauslauf *m*
product facility group Produktmittelgruppe *f*
product flow Warenfluss *m*, Produktfluss *m*
product flow monitoring Warenflussverfolgung *f*
product for packing Packgut *nt*
product group Erzeugnisgruppe *f*

product identification Warenidentifikation *f*
product liability Produkthaftung *f*
product life Produktlebensdauer *f*
product life cycle Produktlebenszyklus *m*
product line Sortiment *nt*
product-neutral produktneutral
product operator Produktoperator *m*
product or process Kommissioniervorgang *m*
product plan Produktplan *m*
product planning Produktplanung *f*
product quantity (PQ) evaluation PQ (Produktquantitäts-Bewertung *f*)
product range Warensortiment *nt*, Sortiment *nt*, Produktpalette *f*, Produktspektrum *nt*
product-related produktbezogen
product spectrum Erzeugnisspektrum *nt*
product stack Produktstapel *m*
product structuring Produktstrukturierung *f*
product warehouse Erzeugnislager *nt*
production Fertigung *f*, Herstellung *f*, Produktion *f*, Erzeugung *f*, Bildung *f*
production acknowledgement Fertigungsrückmeldung *f*
production area Produktionsfläche *f*
production assortment Fertigungssortiment *nt*
production capacity Fertigungskapazität *f*
production cell Fertigungszelle *f*
production control Produktionssteuerung *f*, Fertigungssteuerung *f*, Betriebsleitung *f*, rechnergestützte Betriebsleitung *f*
production costs Fertigungskosten *pl*, Herstellkosten *pl*, Herstellungskosten *pl*
production cycle Fertigungsablauf *m*
production data Produktionsdaten *pl*, Betriebsdaten *pl*
production data acquisition *(rechnergestützte)* Betriebsdatenerfassung *f*
production demand planning Produktionsbedarfsplanung *f*
production department Betriebsabteilung *f*
production drawing Fertigungszeichnung *f*
production ejection Produktionsausstoß *m*
production engineer Fertigungsingenieur *m*, Fertigungstechniker *m*, Fertigungsplaner *m*, Betriebsingenieur *m*
production engineering Fertigungstechnik *f*
production facility Produktionsstätte *f*
production facility drawing Betriebsmittelzeichnung *f*, Fertigungsmittelzeichnung *f*
production facility group Betriebsmittelgruppe *f*
production failure Produktionsausfall *m*
production feedback Fertigungsrückmeldung *f*
production flow Fertigungsfluss *m*, Produktionsfluss *m*
production general costs Fertigungsgemeinkosten *pl*
production increase Produktionssteigerung *f*
production island Fertigungsinsel *f*
production job Fertigungsaufgabe *f*
production lathe Produktionsdrehmaschine *f*
production logistics Produktionslogistik *f*; produktionslogistisch
production lot Charge *f*, Fertigungslos *nt*
production machine Arbeitsmaschine *f*
production measuring technology Fertigungsmesstechnik *f*
production method Fertigungsverfahren *nt*
production order Betriebsauftrag *m*, Fertigungsauftrag *m*
production-oriented fertigungsorientiert
production-oriented dimensioning fertigungsgerechte Maßeintragung *f*
production part Werkstück *nt*
production parts list Fertigungsstückliste *f*
production payroll accounting Ferti-

gungslohnabrechnung *f*
production plan Fertigungsplan *m*, Arbeitsplan *m*
production planning Fertigungsplanung *f*, Produktionsplanung *f*, Arbeitsplanung *f*
production planning system Produktionsplanungs- und Lenkungssystem *nt*
production plant Werk *nt*
production principle Fertigungsprinzip *nt*
production process Herstellprozess *m*, Fertigungsablauf *m*
production program Produktionsprogramm *nt*
production program planning Produktionsprogrammplanung *f*
production range Fertigungssortiment *nt*
production run 1. Fertigungsablauf *m* **2.** Fertigungsserie *f*
production security Fertigungssicherheit *f*
production sequence Fertigungsablauf *m*
production start Produktionsbeginn *m*
production system Fertigungssystem *nt*
production technique Fertigungsmethode *f*
production technology technologist Fertigungsmesstechniker *m*
production time Hauptzeiten *f*, Arbeitszeit *f*
production trend Entwicklungstendenz *f*
production weld Fertigungsschweißung *f*
productive leistungsfähig
productive capacity Leistung *f*
productive welding time Schweißhauptzeit *f*, reine Schweißzeit *f*
productivity Produktivität *f*
productivity goals Produktivitätszielstellung *f*
productivity reserve Produktivitätsreserve *f*
products Waren *fpl*
profile 1. Profil *nt*, Gestalt *f*, Umriss *m*, Kontur *f*, Außenkontur *f*; profilieren, kopieren, nachformen, formen, zweidimensional nachformen, Konturen bearbeiten **2.** *(fräsen)* nachfräsen, nachformfräsen **3.** *(drehen)* formdrehen
profile accuracy Formgenauigkeit *f*
profile angle Profilwinkel *m*
profile angle variation Profil-Winkelabweichung *f*
profile belt Zahnriemen *m*
profile broaching Profilräumen *nt*
profile centre-line Profilmitte *f*
profile check of loads in movement Durchlaufmessung *f*
profile checking Konturkontrolle *f*, Profilkontrolle *f*
profile configuration Profillinienverlauf *m*
profile constant Profilhaltigkeit *f*
profile corrections Profilkorrekturen *f*
profile cutter Formfräser *m*, Profilfräser *m*
profile cutting tool Profilmeißel *m*
profile datum line Profilmittellinie *f*, Profilbezugslinie *f*
profile deviation Konturfehler *m*
profile displaced tooth system profilverschobene Verzahnung *f*
profile displacement factor Profilverschiebungsfaktor *m*
profile distortion Formverzerrung *f*, Profilverzerrung *f*
profile error Profilfehler *m*
profile finish turning Nachformfeindrehen *nt*
profile form variation Profil-Formabweichung *f*
profile gauge Konturkontrolle *f*, Profilkontrolle *f*, Formlehre *f*
profile grinding Nachformschleifen *nt*, Präzisionsschleifen *nt*
profile ground cutter profilhinterschliffener Fräser *m*
profile lapping Profilläppen *nt*
profile letters erhabene Schrift *f*
profile mill kopierfräsen
profile miller Formfräsmaschine *f*, Umrissnachformfräsmaschine *f*, *(selbsttätige)* Nachformfräsmaschine *f*, Nachformfräsmaschine *f* für zweidimensionales Fräsen

profile milling Profilfräsen *nt*, Umlauffräsen *nt*, Nachfräsen *nt*, Nachformfräsen *nt*, Formfräsen *nt*
profile milling attachment Form- und Fräseinrichtung *f*
profile milling cutter Profilfräser *m*
profile milling machine Kopierfräsmaschine *f*, Profilfräsmaschine *f*, Umrissnachformfräsmaschine *f*, Schablonenfräsmaschine *f*
profile modification Profilmodifikation *f*
profile of the cut surface Schnittflächenprofil *nt*
profile of the face Profil *nt* der Spanfläche
profile of the flank Profil *nt* der Freifläche, Freiflächenprofil *nt*
profile of waviness Welligkeitsprofil *nt*
profile pattern Profilverlauf *m*
profile-plane nachformen, nachformhobeln
profile-planer Nachformhobelmaschine *f*
profile position Profillage *f*
profile recorder Pegelschreiber *m*
profile recording Profilaufzeichnung *f*
profile reference line Profilmittellinie *f*, Profilbezugslinie *f*
profile related profilbezogen
profile relief Profilrücknahme *f*
profile-relieved cutter profilhinterschliffener Fräser *m*
profile rolling Profilwalzen *nt*
profile section Profilschnitt *m*
profile shape of the tooth Zahnform *f*, Zahnprofil *nt*
profile surface grinding machine Profilflächenschleifmaschine *f*
profile test Profilprüfung *f*
profile test range Profilprüfbereich *m*
profile tolerance Linienformtoleranz *f*, Profiltoleranz *f*
profile tracer attachment Umrisskopiervorrichtung *f*
profile tracing Profilabtastung *f*
profile turning Formdrehen *nt*
profile turning attachment Formdreheinrichtung *f*
profile turning tool Formdrehmeißel *m*
profile variation Profilabweichung *f*
profile waviness Profil-Welligkeit *f*
profiler selbsttätige Nachformfräsmaschine *f*, Nachformfräsmaschine *f* für zweidimensionales Fräsen, Kopierfräsmaschine *f*, Formfräsmaschine *f*, Schablonenfräsmaschine *f*, Umrissnachformfräsmaschine *f*
profiling 1. formgebende Bearbeitung *f*, Formgebung *f*, Formung *f* 2. *(Fräsen)* Umlauffräsen *nt*, Nachfräsen *nt*, Profilfräsen *nt*
profiling cut Hüllschnitt *m*
profiling machine Nachformfräsmaschine *f*
profiling operation Planfräsarbeit *f*, Umrissfräsarbeit *f*
profit Gewinn *m*
profitability Wirtschaftlichkeit *f*, Rentabilität *f*
profitable gewinnbringend, nutzbringend, wirtschaftlich
profitableness Rentabilität *f*
program Programm *nt*; programmieren
program-checking Programmprüfung *f*
program control Programmsteuerung *f*
program-controlled programmgesteuert
program-controlled machine programmgesteuerte Maschine *f*
program controlled timing device zeitabhängiges Programmsteuergerät *nt*
program-controlled turret-type drilling machine programmgesteuerte Revolverbohrmaschine *f*
program drum Programmwalze *f*
program duration Programmlaufzeit *f*
program edit Editing *nt*
program flow Programmablauf *m*
program format Programmformat *nt*
program horizon Programmhorizont *m*
program input Programmeingabe *f*
program interrupt Programmunterbrechung *f*
program macro Programmmakro *nt*
program milling Programmfräsen *nt*
program output Programmausgabe *f*
program planning Programmplanung *f*
program production Programmerstel-

lung *f*
program rhythm Programmrhythmus *m*
program structure Programmaufbau *m*
program structure chart Struktogramm *nt*
program verification Programmverifikation *f*
program word Wort *nt*
programmable programmierbar, speicherprogrammiert
programmable controller (PC) speicherprogrammierbare Steuerung (SPS) *f*
programmable controller system SPS-System *nt*
programmable control system speicherprogrammierbares Steuersystem *nt*
programmable logic controller (PLC) speicherprogrammierbare Steuerung (SPS) *f*
programmable read only memory programmierbarer Nur-Lese-Speicher *m*
program Programm *nt*; programmieren
program library Programmbibliothek *f*
programmed control device Programmsteuergerät *nt*
programmed control device dependent on machine cycle maschinentaktabhängiges Programmsteuergerät *nt*
programming Programmieren *nt*, Programmierung *f*, Programmsteuerung *f*
programming and debugging tool (PADT) Programmiergerät (PG) *nt*, Programmier- und Diagnosewerkzeug *nt*
programming costs Programmierkosten *pl*
programming device Programmierhilfsmittel *nt*
programming error Programmierfehler *m*
programming flowchart Programmablaufplan *m*
programming language Programmiersprache *f*
programming operation Programmierbetrieb *m*
programming system Programmiersystem *nt*
programming task Programmieraufgabe *f*
progress Fortschritt *m*; Fortschritte machen, fortschreiten
progress report Fortschrittsbericht *m*, Zwischenbericht *m*, Erfahrungsbericht *m*
progress supervision Fortschrittsüberwachung *f*
progress time measuring Fortschrittszeitmessung *f*
progression Stufenschritt *m*, Stufensprung *m*, Stufung *f*, Abstufung *f*, Folge *f*
progression factor Stufensprung *m* von Drehzahlen
progressive fortlaufend, schrittweise
progressive die Folgeschnitte *mpl*
progressive dimensioning Zuwachsbemaßung *f*
progressive grading of speeds Stufensprung *m* von Drehzahlen
progressive plug gauge Stufendorn *m*
progressive plunger metering device Progressivverteiler *m*
progressive plunger principle of operation Progressivsystem *nt*
progressive plunger system Progressivanlage *f*
progressive ratio Stufensprung *m*
progressively adjustable stufenlos verstellbar
prohibit untersagen, verbieten, untersagt, verboten
prohibited nicht bestimmungsgemäß
prohibiting sign Verbotszeichen *nt*
prohibition Verbot *nt*
project 1. vorkragen, überstehen, auskragen, hervorstehen, herausragen überhängen **2.** richten (auf), projizieren **3.** Projekt *nt*, Vorhaben *nt*, projektieren, planen
project conceptually vorprojektieren
project control Projektüberwachung *f*
project description Projektbeschreibung *f*
project drawing Projektzeichnung *f*
project execution Projektabwicklung *f*
project history Projekthistorie *f*
project implementation Projektabwicklung *f*

project into hineinragen
project is taking shape ein Projekt macht Fortschritte
project management Projektleitung f
project manager Projektleiter m, Auftragsleitung f
project monitoring Projektüberwachung f
project network techniques Netzplantechnik f
project outside hinausstehen über
project planning Projektierung f
project progress Projektfortschritt m
project progress report Projektfortschrittsbericht m
project-related projektbezogen
project scheduling Projektplanung f
project status report Projektlagebericht m
project team Projektgruppe f
projected arrival Planzugang m
projecting Projektierung f
projecting überstehend, überhängend
projection Hinausstehen nt, Hineinragen nt, Projektion f, Verlängerung f, Ausladung f, Überhang m
projection joint by resistant welding Widerstandsbuckelschweißverbindung f
projection length Buckellänge f
projection lens Projektionslinse f
projection line Maßhilfslinie f
projection method Projektionsmethode f
projection of tread *(Stufe)* Unterschneidung f
projection reading Projektionsablesung f
projection screen Projectionsschirm m
projection size Abbildungsgröße f
projection surface Projektionsfläche f
projection welded test piece buckelgeschweißtes Probestück nt
projection welding Buckelschweißen nt
projection welding dies and fixtures Buckelschweißvorrichtung f
projector Bildwerfer m
projection-weld buckelschweißen
proliferation *(z. B. auf dem Gebiet der Rundgewinde)* Verwilderung f

prolongate verlängern
prolongation Verlängerung f
prolonged storage lange Lagerung f
promote fördern
prompt zeitnah, pünktlich
proneness to disorders Fehleranfälligkeit f, Störanfälligkeit f
proneness to fault Fehleranfälligkeit f
prong of a fork Zinken m
proof dicht, beständig
proof against acetone acetonbeständig
proof against burnout ausbrennsicher
proof load test Prüflastversuch m
proof of throughput Durchsatznachweis m
proof stress Dehngrenze f
proof stress at elevated temperature Warmdehngrenze f
proof test Abdrückversuch m, Überlastversuch m
proof-test torque Prüfdrehmoment m
proof tested welder eignungsgeprüfter Schweißer m
prop Gebäudestütze f
propability Wahrscheinlichkeit f
propability calculus Wahrscheinlichkeitsrechnung f
propability theory Wahrscheinlichkeitsrechnung f, Wahrscheinlichkeitstheorie f
propable wahrscheinlich
propagate the tear weiterreißen
propagating brush discharge Gleitstielbüschelentladung f
propagation Ausbreitung f
propagation of radiation Strahlenausbreitung f
propagation resistance Ausbreitungswiderstand m
propane Propan nt
propane consumption Propanverbrauch m
propane gas cylinder Propangasflasche f
propane-heated soldering appliance Propanlötgerät nt
propel antreiben, fahren
propellant Treibmittel nt
propellant energy Treibmittelenergie f

propelling Fahren *nt*, Verfahren *nt*
proper sachgerecht, richtig, ordnungsgemäß
proper functioning Funktionsfähigkeit *f*
proper functioning verification procedure Funktionsnachweisverfahren *nt*
proper protection hinreichender Schutz *m*
proper sequence of operations ordnungsgemäßer Arbeitsablauf *m*
proper use bestimmungsgemäße Verwendung *f*
proper workmanship ordnungsgemäße Fertigung *f*
property Eigenschaft *f*, Beschaffenheit *f*
property land Grundstück *nt*
property demand Grundstücksbedarf *m*
property protection Sachschutz *m*
property threshold value Eigenschaftsgrenzwert *m*
proportion verteilen, aufteilen, abmessen, dimensionieren; Anteil *m*, Verhältnis *nt*
proportional action controlling system P-Regeleinrichtung *f*
proportional action factor Proportionalbeiwert *m*
proportional action value P-Beiwert *m*
proportional band p-Bereich *m*
proportional by weight Gewichtsanteil *m*
proportional degree *(Regelung)* P-Grad *m*
proportional element P-Glied *nt*, Proportionalglied *nt*
proportional plus derivative action controlling system PD-Regeleinrichtung *f*
proportional plus integral action controlling system PI-Regeleinrichtung *f*
proportional plus integral plus derivative action controlling system PID-Regeleinrichtung *f*
proportional test piece Proportionalprobe *f*
proportionate anteilig

proportionate costs Umlage *f*
proportionate share Anteil *m*
proportionately anteilig
proportioning Dosierung *f*
proposal Vorhaben *nt*
propulsion circuit Antriebskreis *m*
propulsion *(Funktion)* Antrieb *m*
propulsion control Antriebsregler *m*
protect sichern, absichern, schützen, umwehren, verwahren
protected against reverse polarity verpolungssicher
protection Schutz *m*, Verwahrung *f*, Absicherung *f*
protection against accidental contact Berührungsschutz *m*
protection against air-borne noise Luftschallschutz *m*
protection against bottlenecks Ausfallsicherung *f*
protection against explosion Zündschutz *m*
protection against failure Ausfallsicherung *f*
protection against scaling Zunderschutz *m*
protection against scattered radiation Streustrahlenschutz *m*
protection against structure-borne noise Körperschallschutz *m*
protection current device Schutzstromgerät *nt*
protection device Schutzvorrichtung *f*, Umwehrung *f*
protection element Schutzelement *nt*
protection from conductible dust Staubschutz *m*
protection from smoke Rauchschutz *m*
protection potential Schutzpotential *nt*
protection provided by metallic coatings Korrosionsschutzüberzüge *mpl*
protection provided by organic or inorganic coatings Korrosionsschutzbeschichtungen *fpl*
protection roof Schutzdach *nt*
protection system Schutzsystem *nt*
protection target Schutzziel *nt*

protective apron Schutzschürze *f*
protective arrangement Schutzmaßnahme *f*
protective atmosphere Schutzgas *nt*
protective band Schutzbinde *f*
protective cabin Schutzkabine *f*
protective cage Schutzkorb *m*
protective cap Schutzkappe *f*
protective casing Schutzgehäuse *nt*
protective chamfer Schutzfase *f*
protective circuit breaker Motorschutzschalter *m*
protective class Schutzklasse *f*
protective clothing Schutzkleidung *f*
protective coating Schutzbeschichtung *f*, Schutzüberzug *m*, Schutzauftragung *f*
protective conductor system Schutzleitungssystem *nt*
protective cowl on grinders Schleifkörperschutzhaube *f*
protective current Schutzstrom *m*
protective device Schutzeinrichtung *f*
protective earth Schutzerde *f*
protective earthing Schutzerdung *f*
protective earthing conductor Schutzleiter *m*
protective earthing port Schutzleiteranschluss *m*
protective effect Schutzwirkung *f*
protective equipment Schutzeinrichtung *f*, Schutzausrüstung *f*
protective equipotential bonding system Schutzpotenzialausgleichsanlage *f*
protective extra-low voltage (PELV) Schutzkleinspannung *f*
protective film Schutzfolie *f*
protective gas Schutzgas *nt*, Zündschutzgas *nt*
protective gloves Schutzgitter *nt*
protective goggles Schutzbrille *f*
protective grating Schutzgitter *nt*
protective ground Schutzerde *f*
protective grounding Schutzerdung *f*
protective hood Schutzhaube *f*
protective impedance Schutzimpedanz *f*
protective insulation Schutzisolierung *f*

protective layer Schutzschicht *f*
protective measure Schutzmaßnahme *f*
protective motor switch Motorschutzschalter *m*
protective packaging Schutzverpackung *f*
protective screen Schutzschirm *m*
protective sinking Schutzsenkung *f*
protective stratum Schutzlage *f*
protective switch Schutzschalter *m*
protective system Schutzart *f*
protective tube housing Röhrenschutzgehäuse *nt*
protective vessel Schutzgefäß *nt*
protective window Schutzfenster *nt*
protector Umwehrung *f*
protocol Protokoll *nt*
protoctor density Protoctordichte *f*
prototype Muster *nt*, Prototyp *m*
prototype development system Prototypentwicklungssystem *nt*
prototype die mould Prototypwerkzeug *nt*
prototype manufacturing Prototypenfertigung *f*
prototype material Prototypenmaterial *nt*
prototype phase Funktionsmusterphase *f*, Prototypenphase *f*
prototype production Prototypenfertigung *f*
protractor Transporteur *m*, Winkelmesser *m*
protrude auskragen
protruding herausstehend
protruding head überstehender Kopf *m*
protruding units Vorbauten *mpl*
protuberance Protuberanz *f*, Kuppe *f*
protrude vorkragen, herausragen, überstehen, heraussstehen, hervorstehen, überhängen
protruding herausragend, überhängend
prove beweisen, nachweisen, sich erweisen
provide 1. beschaffen, bereitstellen, liefern, versorgen 2. abgeben 3. vorsehen, versehen mit
provider Anbieter *m*

providing Bereitstellen *nt*
provision Festlegung *f*, Disposition *f*, Bereitstellung *f*, Vorkehrung *f*, Maßnahme *f*
provision area Bereitstellungsfläche *f*
provision costs Bereitstellungskosten *pl*
provision of goods Warendisposition *f*, Warenbereitstellung *f*
provision system Bereitstellsystem *nt*
provision volume Bereitstellmenge *f*
provisional behelfsmäßig
proximal nah
proximity switch Initiator *m*
proximity Annäherung *f*, Nähe *f*
proximity device Näherungsschalter *m*
proximity indicator Näherungsindikator *m*
proximity sensor Näherungssensor *m*
proximity switch Näherungsschalter *m*, Annäherungsschalter *m*, Magnetschalter *m*
pry Hebezeug *nt*
pry Brecheisen *nt*
pseudo-absolute measuring pseudo-absolute Wegmessung *f*
PTC (positive temperature coefficient) resistor Kaltleiter *m*
PTC thermistor detector Kaltleiterfühler *m*
PTFE-strip PTFE-Band *nt*
put out of operation außer Betrieb setzen
public data network (DIN 66021 T.5) Datennetz *nt*
public supply Netzanschluss *m*
publication Offenlegung *f*
publish offen legen
pull ziehen, Zugkraft *f*, Zug *m*
pull away wegziehen
pull bar Zugstange *f*
pull broach Räumnadel *f*
pull broaching Ziehräumen *nt*
pull chain Zugkette *f*
pull chain conveyor Zugkettenförderer *m*
pull-down menu Balkenmenü *nt*
pull head Ziehkopf *m*
pull in einziehen
pull-in contour Einzugkontur *f*
pull-in point Einzugstelle *f*
pull-in reader Einzugleser *m*, Einbauleser *m*
pull in the chain Kettenzug *m*
pull mechanism Zugeinrichtung *f*
pull of trailing cable Schleppkabelzug *m*
pull off wegziehen, losreißen
pull-off test Abreißversuch *m*
pull out ausziehen
pull-out slip Kippschlupf *m*
pull-out speed Kippdrehzahl *f*
pull-out torque Kippmoment *nt*
pull-type broaching machine Räumnadelziehmaschine *f*
pull-type key seating machine Nutenziehmaschine *f*
pull up durchschalten
pull-up torque Sattelmoment *nt*
puller Ziehkopf *m*, Spannkopf *m*
puller and pusher mechanism Klemmschieber *m*
pulley Rolle *f*, Seilrolle *f*, Laufrolle *f*, Riemenscheibe *f*, Rillenscheibe *f*, Kettenrad *nt*
pulley block Flaschenzug *m*
pulley crown Wölbung *f* an der Riemenscheibe
pulley mechanism Zugmittelgetriebe *nt*
pulling Zug *m*, Ziehvorgang *m*
pulling device Zugvorrichtung *f*, Ziehvorrichtung *f*
pulling force Zugkraft *f*
pulling load Zugbelastung *f*
pulling mechanism Zugvorrichtung *f*, Ziehvorrichtung *f*, Ziehtechnik *f*
pulling off Wegziehen *nt*
pulling power Durchzugskraft *f*, Saugfähigkeit *f*
pulling technique Ziehtechnik *f*
pulp bale Zellstoffballen *m*
pulp chlorination Zellstoffchlorierung *f*
pulp sample Zellstoffprobe *f*
pulse shaping Pulsformung *f*
pulsate schwanken, pulsieren
pulsating pulsierend
pulsating flexural fatigue test Biegeschwellversuch *m*
pulsating flexural load Biegeschwellbeanspruchung *f*

pulsating tensile stress Zugschwellbeanspruchung f
pulsation Pulsieren nt, Schwankung f
pulsation-free pulsationsfrei, gleichmäßig, stoßfrei, schwingungsfrei
pulsation range Schwellbereich m
pulsation welding Schweißen nt mit Stromabfall
pulsatory pulsierend
pulsatory fatigue test Dauerschwellversuch m
pulse Impuls m, Puls m; pulsen
pulse amplitude Impulsdauer f
pulse amplitude modulation Pulsamplitudenmodulation f
pulse bit memory Impulsmerker m
pulse characteristic Pulskennlinie f
pulse code modulation Pulscodemodulation f
pulse contact control Impulssteuerung f
pulse diagram Impulsdiagramm nt
pulse duration Pulsdauer f
pulse duty factor Impulstastverhältnis nt, Tastverhältnis nt
pulse echo equipment Impulsechogerät nt
pulse echo technique Impulsechoverfahren nt
pulse emitting valve Steuerventil nt
pulse emitting valve Impulsventil nt
pulse energy Impulsenergie f
pulse envelope Impulsform f
pulse former Impulsformer m
pulse forming Pulsformung f
pulse frequency modulation Pulsfrequenzmodulation f
pulse generator Impulsgeber m
pulse group Impulsgruppe f, Impulszug m
pulse magnetic field Impulsmagnetfeld nt
pulse-modulated pulsmoduliert, mit Pulsmodulation
pulse modulation Pulsmodulation f
pulse operation Pulsbetrieb m
pulse position Pulsphase f
pulse position modulation Pulsphasenmodulation f
pulse rain Impulszug m

pulse repetition frequency Pulsfrequenz f
pulse shaper Impulsformer m
pulse string Impulszug m
pulse train Pulsfolge f
pulse transit time Impulslaufzeit f
pulse width modulation Pulsweitenmodulation f
pulverise zerstäuben, mahlen
pulveriser Mühle f
pulverization Zerstäuben nt
pulverized coal-fired kohlenstaubgefeuert
plumber's solder Klempnerlot nt
pump Pumpe f; pumpen, fördern
pump-assisted heating system Pumpenheizung f
pump light Pumplicht nt
pump off abpumpen
pump principle Pumpenprinzip nt
pump seating face Pumpenanlagenfläche f
pumpability Pumpbarkeit f
pumped circulation heating system Pumpenheizung f
pumping Pumpen nt, Pumpvorgang m
pumping action Pumpvorgang m
pumping cycle Pumpzyklus m
pumping effort Pumpwiderstand m
pumping of grease Fettförderung f
pumping out Evakuierung f
pumping set Pumpenaggregat nt
pun stampfen
punch Schneidstempel m, Stempel m, Locher m; durchlochen, lochen, perforieren, ankörnen, stempeln, stanzen, durchschlagen, durchstoßen
punch and die clearance Ziehspalt m
punch and die making Schnittbau m
punch and form shaper Form- und Stempelhobelmaschine f
punch form Stempelform f
punch mark 1. Körnermarke f, Körnungspunkt m **2.** (Werkzeug) Körner m
punch marking Körnen nt
punch milling Stempelfräsen nt
punch milling attachments Stempelfräseinrichtung f
punch-scribed angekörnt
punch shaper Stempelhobler m

punchability Lochbarkeit *f*
punched card Lochkarte *f*
punched card control Steuerung *f* mit Lochkartenleser
punched card programming Programmsteuerung *f* mit Lochkarte
punched card readout device Lochkartenausgeber *m*
punched card store Lochkartenspeicher *m*
punched card technique Lochkartentechnik *f*
punched paper type Papierlochband *nt*
punched tape Lochstreifen *m*, Lochband *nt*
punched tape control Lochbandsteuerung *f*
punched tape controlled lochbandgesteuert, lochstreifengesteuert
punched-tape input Lochstreifeneingabe *f*
puncheon Stempel *m*
punching Stanzteil *nt*
punching machine Stanze *f*
punching property Stanzbarkeit *f*
punctiform point contact punktförmige Auflagerstelle *f*
punctiform radiator punktförmiger Strahler *m*
punctual pünktlich
punctuality Pünktlichkeit *f*
puncture Durchstoßen *nt*, Einstich *m*, Stich *m*, Durchschlag *m*; einstechen, durchschlagen
puncture test Durchstoßversuch *m*
puncturing energy Durchstoßarbeit *f*
plunge cutting Tauchfräsen *nt*
punner Stampfer *m*
punning Stampfen *nt*
public highway sewer Straßenkanal *m*
public safety öffentliche Sicherheit *f*
purchase kaufen, einkaufen, beschaffen; Kauf *m*
purchase externally zukaufen
purchase order Bestellung *f*
purchase scheduling Einkaufsdisposition *f*
purchased parts Zukaufteile *ntpl*
purchaser Einkäufer *m*, Käufer *m*, Betreiber *m*
purchasing Beschaffung *f*, Einkauf *m*
purchasing contract Einkaufsvertrag *m*
purchasing decision Kaufentscheidung *f*
purchasing department Einkaufsabteilung *f*
purchasing lead time Lieferzeit *f*
purchasing order Einkaufsauftrag *m*
pure rein, fein
purgation Reinigung *f*
purge reinigen, spülen
purge period Spülzeit *f*
purging Spülung *f*
purging effect Spüleffekt *m*
purging test Reinigungsprüfung *f*
purification Reinigung *f*, Reinhaltung *f*
purify aufbereiten, reinigen
purifying Reinigen *nt*
purity Reinheit *f*
purity grade Reinheitsgrad *m*
purlin Pfette *f*
purlin roof Pfettendach *nt*
purlin spacing Pfettenabstand *m*
purpose of the measurement Messzweck *m*
push Druck *m*, Schub *m*, Stoß *m*, Betätigungsdruck *m*; drücken, stoßen, schieben
push back zurückschieben
push-back cart Einschub *m*
push back into storage zurücklagern
push-back lane Einschubbahn *f*
push-back pallet racking Einschubregal *nt*, Paletteneinschubregal *nt*
push-back racking Einschubregal *nt*
pushbutton panel Druckknopftafel *f*
push broach Räumdorn *m*; stoßräumen
push-button Druckknopf *m*, Druckschalter *m*, Drucktaste *f*, Tastschalter *m*, Taster *m*, Taste *f*
push-button-actuated druckknopfbetätigt
push-button control Druckknopfschaltung *f*, Druckknopfsteuerung *f*, Tastensteuerung *f*
push-button-operated druckknopfbetätigt
push-button station Druckknopftaster *m*

push-button switch Druckknopfschalter *m*
push crack Schubriss *m*
push-cut shaper Waagerechtstoßmaschine *f* mit schiebendem Schnitt
push in einschleusen, einschieben; Einschub *m*
push mechanism Schubeinrichtung *f*
push off abschieben, abdrehen, abstoßen
push on aufsetzen
push onto überschieben
push out herausschieben
push-pull Gegentakt *m*
push-pull device Wendezugeinrichtung *f*
push-pull mechanism Zugschubvorrichtung *f*, Klemmschieber *m*
push-pull output stage Gegentaktendstufe *f*
push-pull test Zug-Druck-Versuch *m*
push rod Schubstange *f*
push-rod conveyor Schubstangenförderer *m*
push through durchstoßen, durchziehen
push-through button Durchdrückknopf *m*
push-through reader Durchzugleser *m*
push/pull handle Bügel *m*
pushed back zurückgeschoben
pusher Abschieber *m*, Andrücker *m*
pushing Schiebevorgang *m*
pushing device Schiebeeinrichtung *f*, Schubvorrichtung *f*

pushing mechanism Schiebeeinrichtung *f*
pushing tractor Schubschlepper *m*
pushup storage Warteschlangenspeicher *m*
put stellen
put aside zurücklegen, zurückstellen
put at risk riskieren
put back zurücklegen, zurückstellen
put down legen
put into operation in Gang setzen, einschalten
put off zurückstellen
put on einschalten, aufsetzen, auflegen
put out for tenders ausschreiben
put out of operation ausschalten, abschalten, stillsetzen, außer Betrieb setzen; Abschaltung *f*
put out of service abschalten, stillsetzen, außer Betrieb setzen
put over stülpen über, überschieben
put together zusammensetzen
put under unterlegen
put upright aufrichten
putting into operation Inbetriebnahme *f*
putting into service Inbetriebnahme *f*, Übergabe *f*, Inverkehrbringen *nt*
putty liquid Kittflüssigkeit *f*
putty powder Kittpulver *nt*
PVC plasticizer fastness PVC-Weichmacherechtheit *f*
PVC rigid pipe PVC-hart-Rohr *nt*
pyramid Pyramide *f*
pyramidal pyramidenförmig

Q q

Q-and-A dialogue Frage-Antwort-Dialog *m*
quietness Ruhe *f*
quotient Quotient *m*
quadrant Quadrant *m*, Kulisse *f*
quadrant turning tool Stelleisen *nt*
quadrant change gear Wechselräderschere *f*
quadrant scale Quadrantskala *f*
quadratic rechtwinklig, quadratisch
quadratic closing tolerance quadratische Schließtoleranz *f*
quadratic tolerance calculation quadratische Toleranzrechnung *f*
quadruple vierfach, Quadrupel *nt*
quadruple mast Vierfachhubgerüst *nt*
quadruple thread viergängiges Gewinde *nt*
quadruplex *(el.)* vierfach
qualification Qualifikation *f*, Eignung *f*
qualification of personnel Personalqualifikation *f*
qualification test Qualifikationsprüfung *f*, Eignungsprüfung *f*
qualifications Fachkompetenz *f*
qualifications profile Eignungsprofil *nt*
qualified qualifiziert
qualified technician Fachmonteur *m*
qualify qualifizieren
qualifying symbol for the function Funktionskennzeichen *nt*
qualitative qualitativ
quality Qualität *f*, Güte *f*, Beschaffenheit *f*, qualitative Beschaffenheit *f*
quality assessment Qualitätsbewertung *f*
quality assurance (QA) Qualitätssicherung (QS) *f*, Gütesicherung *f*
quality assurance requirement Qualitätssicherungsanforderung *f*
quality audit Qualitätsaudit *nt*
quality characteristic Qualitätsmerkmal *nt*, Qualitätskennzahl *f*
quality check Qualitätskontrolle *f*, Qualitätsprüfung *f*
quality circle Qualitätszirkel *m*

quality code Qualitätskennung *f*
quality conformance inspection Wareneingangsprüfung *f*
quality connection (thread) Qualitätsverbindung *f*
quality control Gütekontrolle *f*, Güteüberwachung *f*, Qualitätskontrolle *f*, Qualitätssicherung (QS) *f*, Qualitätsprüfung *f*, Qualitätssteuerung *f*, Qualitätslenkung *f*, Qualitätsüberwachung *f*
quality control card Qualitätsregelkarte *f*
quality control organization Güteschutzgemeinschaft *f*
quality control plan Qualitätskontrollplan *m*
quality demand Qualitätsforderung *f*
quality designation Qualitätskennzeichen *nt*
quality deviation Qualitätsabweichung *f*
quality documentation Qualitätsdokumentation *f*
quality engineering Qualitätstechnik *f*
quality factor Resonanzschärfe *f*
quality grade Gütegrad *m*
quality index Wertigkeitsverhältnis *nt*
quality inspection Qualitätskontrolle *f*, Qualitätsprüfung *f*
quality level Qualitätslage *f*, Qualitätsgrenzlage *f*
quality level value AQL-Wert *m*
quality limit Qualitätsgrenzlage *f*
quality management Qualitätsmanagement *nt*
quality management audit Qualitätsmanagementaudit *nt*
quality management system Qualitätsmanagementsystem *nt*
quality of fit Passungsgüte *f*
quality of service Dienstgüte *f*
quality of workpieces Werkstückqualität *f*
quality planning Qualitätsplanung *f*
quality politics Qualitätspolitik *f*
quality rating Wertigkeit *f*

quality record(ing) Qualitätsaufzeichnung f
quality requirement Güteanforderung f, Qualitätsanforderung f
quality sample of cut surfaces Schnittflächengütemuster nt
quality specification Qualitätsvorschrift f, Gütevorschrift f
quality surveillance Qualitätsüberwachung f
quality system Qualitätssystem nt
quality target Qualitätsziel nt
quality testing Güteprüfung f
quality verification Gütenachweis m
quaternary brazing filler alloy Vierstoffhartlot nt
quantifiable quantifizierbar
quantification Quantifizierung f
quantified system parameter Mengengerüst nt
quantify quantifizieren, messen
quantifying unit Quantifizierungseinheit f
quantile Quantil nt
quantitative quantitativ
quantitative characteristic quantitatives Merkmal nt
quantitative magnitude quantitative Größe f
quantitative behaviour Mengenverhalten nt
quantitative characteristic Größe f
quantitative value Größenwert m
quantity Quantität f, Menge f, Stückzahl f, Größe f, Maß nt, Masse f
quantity for assessment Bewertungsgröße f
quantity framework Mengengerüst nt
quantity list of parts Mengenstückliste f
quantity of data Datenmenge f
quantity of heat Wärmemenge f
quantity production Massenfertigung f, Großserienfertigung f
quantity to be measured Messgröße f
quantization Quantelung f
quantum Quant nt
quantum energy Quantenenergie f
quantum jump Quantensprung m
quantum mechanics Quantenmechanik f
quantum number Quantenzahl f
quantum theory Quantentheorie f
quantum-mechanical quantenmechanisch
guarantee limit of error Garantiefehlergrenze f
quarter bend Rohrbogen m von 90°
quarter-scale cone penetration Viertelkonuspenetration f
quarter-turn screw Blattschraube f
quartz Quarz nt
quartz crystal Quarzkristall m
quasi quasi
quasi range Quasispanne f
quasi-continuous quasikontinuierlich
quasi-rigid quasisteif
quasi-static quasistatisch
quench abschrecken
quenchant Abschreckmittel nt
quench-harden abschreckhärten
quench-hardened abschreckgehärtet
quenching Abschrecken nt
quenching oil Härteöl nt
quenching once only einmaliges Abschrecken nt
query Abfrage f
query (complaint) reklamieren
query read-head Abfragelesekopf m
question-and-answer dialog Frage-Antwort-Dialog m
queue Warteschlange f; eine Warteschlange f bilden, in eine Warteschlange f einreihen
queuing Warteschlangenbildung f
quick schnell
quick change Schnellwechsel m
quick change mounting Schnellwechselhalterung f
quick change swing lathe Drehmaschine f mit veränderlicher Spitzenhöhe
quick change system Schnellwechselsystem nt
quick closing actuator Schnellschlussantrieb m
quick freeze tiefkühlen
quick motion Zeitraffer m
quick motion effect Zeitraffung f
quick power rotation Eilgangumlauf m
quick power traverse movement

Schnellgang *m*
quick return Eilrücklauf *m*
quick reverse Eilrücklauf *m*
quick rotation Schnellgang *m*, schnelle Rotation *f*
quick travel Eilbewegung *f*
quick traverse Eilgang *m*, Schnellgang *m*, Eillauf *m*
quick withdrawal Schnellrückzug *m*
quick-action chuck Schnellspannfutter *nt*
quick-action clutch Schnellschaltkupplung *f*
quick-change chuck Schnellwechselfutter *nt*
quick-change cutter arbor Schnellwechselfräsdorn *m*
quick-change gearbox Nortongetriebe *nt*
quick-change mechanism Schnellwechselgetriebe *nt*, Schwenkrädergetriebe *nt*
quick-change toolholder Schnellwechselkopf *m*, Schnellwechselmeißelhalter *m*
quick-motion apparatus Zeitraffer *m*
quiescent current Ruhestrom *m*
quiet geräuscharm, ruhig
quiet running Laufruhe *f*
quietness in operation Laufruhe *f*
quill Hülse *f*, Pinole *f*, Spindelhülse *f*, Frässpindelhülse *f*
quill adjustment Pinolenverstellung *f*
quill guide Pinolenführung *f*
quota Quote *f*
quotation Angebot *nt*
quotation drawing Angebotszeichnung *f*
quote anbieten

R r

r.f. generator HF-Generator *m*
r.f. welder HF-Schweißgerät *nt*
race Laufring *m*
reachable without any danger gefahrlos erreichbar
rack 1. Gestell *nt*, Regal *nt* **2.** *(für Werkzeuge)* Speicher *m*
rack aisle Regalgang *m*, Regalgasse *f*
rack and pinion drive Zahnstangenantrieb *m*
rack and pinion jack Zahnstangenheber *m*
rack and pinion lifting system Hubeinrichtung *f* mit Zahnstangen
rack and pinion pair Zahnstangenradpaar *nt*
rack aperture Regalfach *nt*
rack area Regalbereich *m*
rack bay Regalreihe *f*
rack brace design Aussteifungskonstruktion *f*
rack bracing Regalverband *m*
rack compartment Regalfach *nt*
rack compartment clearance Fachfreimaß *nt*
rack compartment coordinates Fachkoordinaten *fpl*
rack crack Kammriss *m*
rack datum plane Zahnstangenbezugsebene *f*
rack deflection Regalauslenkung *f*
rack depth Regaltiefe *f*
rack entry width Facheinfahrbreite *f*
rack fine positioning Fachfeinpositionierung *f*
rack flank Zahnstangenflanke *f*
rack for vertical storage of sheet materials Rungenregal *nt*
rack head Regalkopf *m*
rack head carriage Regalkopftraverse *f*
rack height Regalhöhe *f*
rack jobbing Regalpflege *f*
rack length Regallänge *f*
rack location Regalstandort *m*
rack milling Fräsen *nt* von Zahnstangen
rack module Regalmodul *nt*

rack pitch line Wälzgerade *f*
rack run Regalzeile *f*
rack servicing Regalbedienung *f*
rack spine Regalrücken *m*
rack stacker Regalstapler *m*
rack storage Regallagerung *f*
rack store Regallager *nt*
rack structure Regalkonstruktion *f*
rack strut Regalstütze *f*
rack support Regalstütze *f*, Regalständer *m*
rack system Regalanlage *f*, Regalsystem *nt*
rack system level Regalsystemebene *f*
rack system plane Regalsystemebene *f*
rack tooth system Planverzahnung *f*, Planradverzahnung *f*
rack type Regaltyp *m*
rack type generating cutter zahnstangenförmiges Wälzwerkzeug *nt*
rack upright Regalstütze *f*, Regalständer *m*, Regalsteher *m*
rack vibration Regalschwingung *f*
rack width Regalbreite *f*
rackbound regalabhängig
racked geschichtet
racking Regalanlage *f*, Regal *nt*
racking address Fachadresse *f*
racking installation Lageranlage *f*
racking steelwork Regalstahlbau *m*
rack-milling attachment Zahnstangenfräsvorrichtung *f*
rack-operated tailstock for hand lever control Handhebelreitstock *m* über Zahnstange
rack-shaped zahnstangenförmig
rack-shaped cutter Kammmeißel *m*
rack-supported mezzanine Regalbühne *f*
rack-type cutter Kammmeißel *m*, Hobelkamm *m*, Maag-Hobelkamm *m*
radial radial, sternförmig
radial arm Auslegerarm *m*
radial backlash Radialspiel *nt*
radial chisel Radialmeißel *m*
radial die forming Gesenkrunden *nt*

radial dimension Halbmessermaß *nt*
radial drill Radialbohrwerk *nt*, Schwenkbohrmaschine *f*, Auslegerbohrmaschine *f*
radial drill arm Bohrausleger *m*
radial drilling machine Radialbohrmaschine *f*, Schwenkbohrmaschine *f*, Auslegerbohrmaschine *f*
radial engagement radialer Eingriff *m*
radial feed Radialvorschub *m*
radial force Radialkraft *f*, Querkraft *f*
radial grinding radiales Schleifen *nt*
radial hobbing Radialfräsen *nt*
radial inclination angle radialer Neigungswinkel *m*
radial interference fit Querpressung *f*
radial line Mittelpunktstrahl *m*
radial milling *(Methode)* Radialfräsen *nt*
radial mode number radiale Modenzahl *f*
radial packing ring Wellendichtring *m*
radial planing attachment Rundhobeleinrichtung *f*, Rundhobelapparat *m*
radial planing operation Rundhobeln *nt*
radial rake radialer Spanwinkel *m*
radial rake angle Seitenwinkel *m*, Radialwinkel *m*
radial run-out Seitenschlag *m*, Radialschlag *m*, Rundlauffehler *m*
radial shaft Radialwelle *f*
radial shaft sealing ring Radialwellendichtring *m*
radial shrinkage Radialeinlauf *m*
radial single-ball measurement radiales Einkugelmaß *nt*
radial single-roll measurement radiales Einrollenmaß *nt*
radial strain coefficient Querdehnzahl *f*
radial stress Querkraft *f*
radial table feed radialer Tischvorschub *m*
radial table feed motion radiale Tischvorschubbewegung *f*
radial testing Radialprüfung *f*
radial tool Radialmeißel *m*
radial toolholder Radialmeißelhalter *m*
radial tooth Stirnzahn *m*

radial vacuum pump Radialvakuumpumpe *f*
radial-axial feed method Radial-Axial-Verfahren *nt*
radial-feed method Radialverfahren *nt*
radially expanding clutch Spreizringkupplung *f*
radiant 1. Radiant *m* **2.** *(heizen)* strahlend
radiant energy Strahlungsenergie *f*
radiant heat Strahlungshitze *f*
radiant heater Heizstrahler *m*, Wärmestrahler *m*
radiant heating Strahlungsheizung *f*
radiant heating element Strahlungsheizelement *nt*
radiant intensity Strahlungsleistung *f*
radiate strahlen, abstrahlen, ausstrahlen
radiated heat Hitzestrahlung *f*
radiating strahlend
radiating cut Strahlenschliff *m*
radiation Ausstrahlung *f*, Strahlung *f*
radiation attenuation Strahlenschwächung *f*
radiation cross-linking Strahlenvernetzung *f*
radiation detector Strahlungsdetektor *m*
radiation energy Strahlenergie *f*, Strahlungsenergie *f*
radiation exposure Strahlenbelastung *f*
radiation field Strahlungsfeld *nt*
radiation field quantity Strahlungsfeldgröße *f*
radiation field variable Strahlungsfeldgröße *f*
radiation impulse Strahlungsimpuls *m*
radiation intensity Strahlungsintensität *f*
radiation meter Strahlungsmessgerät *nt*
radiation of heat Wärmeabstrahlung *f*
radiation protection Strahlungsschutz *m*
radiation protection accessories Strahlenschutzzubehör *nt*
radiation protection dosimeter Strahlenschutzdosimeter *nt*
radiation protection rule Strahlenschutzregel *f*
radiation protection test Strahlen-

schutzprüfung *f*
radiation pyrometer Strahlungspyrometer *nt*
radiation reversal Strahlenumkehr *f*
radiation sending out Strahlungsaussendung *f*
radiation shielding concrete Strahlenschutzbeton *m*
radiation shielding material Strahlenschutzstoff *m*
radiation source Strahlungsquelle *f*, Strahlenquelle *f*
radiation spectrum Strahlungsspektrum *nt*
radiation stopping power Strahlungsbremsvermögen *nt*
radiation technology Strahlungstechnik *f*
radiation type heating appliance Strahlungsheizgerät *nt*
radiation-sensitive paper strahlungsempfindliches Papier *nt*
radiator Strahler *m*
radiator inlet Heizkörpereintritt *m*
radiator mounting Heizkörpereinbau *m*
radiator outlet Heizkörperaustritt *m*
radiator section Radiatorglied *nt*
radical former Radikalbildner *m*
reading wand Lesestift *m*
radio funken; Funk *m*, Rundfunk *m*
radio frequency hochfrequent; Hochfrequenz *f*
radio frequency generator HF-Generator *m*
radio frequency identification system Hochfrequenzidentifikationssystem *nt*
radio frequency welder HF-Schweißgerät *nt*
radio interference suppression Funkentstörung *f*
radio wave system Rundfunkwellensystem *nt*
radio-controlled funkferngesteuert
radiograph Durchstrahlungsaufnahme *f*
radiographic performance Durchstrahlungsleistung *f*
radiographic table Aufnahmetisch *m*
radiographic test Durchstrahlungsprüfung *f*
radiographing Durchstrahlung *f*
radiography Durchstrahlung *f*
radiography equipment Aufnahmeeinrichtung *f*
radiography position Aufnahmestellung *f*
radiography rate Aufnahmefrequenz *f*
radius Radius *m*, Radien *mpl*, Abrundung *f*; runden
radius at bottom of tooth Zahngrundabrundung *f*
radius at the thread root Radius *m* am Gewindegrund
radius gauge Radienschablone *f*
radius milling Fräsen *nt* von Rundungen
radius milling head Radienfräskopf *m*
radius of circle Kreisradius *m*
radius of curvature Bogenradius *m*, Krümmungsradius *m*, Krümmungshalbmesser *m*
radius of gyration Trägheitsradius *m*
radius of inertia Trägheitsradius *m*
radius of the root rounding Fußrundungsradius *m*
radius planing attachment Rundhobeleinrichtung *f*, Rundhobelapparat *m*, Kurvenhobeleinrichtung *f*
radius planing attachment for machining external curves Rundhobeleinrichtung *f* für konkave Flächen
radius tool Rundmeißel *m*
radiused gerundet, mit Radius
radiusing Abrundung *f*
radiused corner Eckenrundung *f*
radiused half-dog point Ansatzkuppe *f*
ragged eingerissen, schartig, zackig
ragged wheel edge schartige Scheibenkante *f*
rail Supportträger *m*, Ausleger *m*, Bügel *m*, Querführung *f*, Rungenverbindung *f*, Geländer *nt*, Schiene *f*
rail anchor Schienenklemme *f*
rail anchoring device Schienenklemme *f*
rail base Schienenfuß *m*, Fuß *m*
rail clamp Schienenklemme *f*
rail deflection Schienendurchbiegung *f*

rail deformation Schienendurchbiegung *f*
rail elevating motor Querbalkenmotor *m*
rail foot Schienenfuß *m*, Fuß *m*
rail guard Schienenräumer *m*
rail guide Querbalkenführung *f*
rail head width Schienenkopfbreite *f*
rail joint Schienenstoß *m*
rail joint sealing compound Schienenvergussmasse *f*
rail junction *(obere Schiene)* Schienenweiche *f*
rail laid on the floor Bodenschiene *f*
rail milling head Querfrässupport *m*
rail sleeper Geländerholm *m*
rail spike Schienenklammer *f*, Nagel *m*
rail sweep Schienenräumer *m*
rail track Schienenstrang *m*
railborne schienengebunden
rail-dependent schienengebunden
rail-guided schienengeführt
railhead Horizontalsupport *m*
rail-head 1. Querbalkensupport *m*, Support *m*, Quersupport *m* **2.** *(Führung)* Schienenkopf *m* **3.** *(Werkzeug)* Werkzeugträger *m*
railing Geländer *nt*
railing fittings Geländerfittings *mpl*
rail-mounted schienengeführt, schienengebunden
rails and sleepers Bahngestänge *nt*
rail-traverse motor Querbalkenmotor *m*
railway track Schiene *f*
rain water pipe Regenrohr *nt*
rain yield factor Regenspende *f*
raise erhöhen, steigern, heben, hochheben, anheben, abheben, aufwinden, hochsetzen; Erhöhung *f*, Zunahme *f*
raised erhöht, angehoben
raised cheese head screw with point Linsenschraube *f* mit Kuppe
raised countersunk head self-tapping screw Linsensenkblechschraube *f*
raised countersunk head tapping screw Linsensenkblechschraube *f*
raised countersunk head tread cutting screw Linsensenkschneidschraube *f*

raised countersunk head wood screw Linsensenkholzschraube *f*
raised countersunk recessed head tapping screw Linsensenkblechschraube *f* mit Kreuzschlitz
raised edge Bördel *nt*
raised face Dichtleiste *f*
raised rim hole Durchzug *m* erhöht
raised storage area Bühne *f*
raised storage platform Zwischenpodest *nt*, Zwischenbühne *f*, Lagerbühne *f*
raised welding bead überhöhte Schweißraupe *f*
raising Anheben *nt*, Heben *nt*, Hochfahren *nt*
raising and lowering Auf- und Abbewegung *f*
raising delay Einschaltverzögerung *f*
rake Rechen *m*, Spanbrust *f*, Spanfläche *f*
rake angle Spanwinkel *m*, Hinterschleifwinkel *m*
rake face Spanfläche *f*
rake position error Spanflächenlagefehler *m*
release mechanism Ausklinkvorrichtung *f*
ram Kolben *m*, Maschinenstößel *m*, Stempel *m*, Ramme *f*, Stößel *m*; rammen, stampfen
ram attachment Dorn *m*
ram bearing Stößelführung *f*
ram force Stempelkraft *f*
ram guide Stößelführung *f*
ram guideway Stößelführungsbahn *f*
ram head Stößelsupport *m*, Stößelkopf *m*
ram head slide Stößelkopfschlitten *m*
ram pressure Stempeldruck *m*
ram stroke Schlittenhub *m*, Stößelhub *m*, Stößelweg *m*
ram support Stößelabstützung *f*
ram tool Stößel *m*
ram travel Stößelweg *m*
ram type turret lathe Sattelrevolverdrehmaschine *f*, Drehmaschine *f* mit Sattelrevolver *m*
ramification Verzweigung *f*
ramify verzweigen
rammability Stampfbarkeit *f*

rammable stampfbar
rammed clay Stampflehm *m*
rammer Stampfer *m*
ramming Verstampfung *f*, Stampfen *nt*
ramming mixture Stampfmasse *f*
ramming tool Stampfwerkzeug *nt*
ramp Rampe *f*
ramp angle Rampenwinkel *m*
ramp function Anstiegsfunktion *f*
ramp function response Anstiegsantwort *f*
ramp lift Rampenhub *m*
ramp travel Rampenfahrt *f*
ramp-lift function Rampenhub *m*
ram-type milling machine Fräsmaschine *f* mit verschiebbarem Gegenhaltearm
ram-type press Kolbenpresse *m*
ramways 1. Stößelführungsbahn *f* 2. Schlittenführung *f*
random wahllos, zufällig, zufallsbedingt, ungeordnet
random access Zufallszugriff *m*
random cause Zufallsursache *f*
random component Zufallskomponente *f*
random error zufälliger Fehler *m*, Zufallsfehler *m*
random error of result zufällige Ergebnisabweichung *f*
random event Zufall *m*
random failure Zufallsausfall *m*
random influence Zufallseinfluss *m*
random malfunction Zufallsausfall *m*
random procedure Zufallsverfahren *nt*
random process Zufallsverfahren *nt*
random sample Zufallsauswahl *f*, Zufallsstichprobe *f*, Stichprobe *f*
random sampling Zufallsprobenahme *f*, Stichprobenkontrolle *f*
random storage chaotische Lagerordnung *f*, chaotische Einlagerung *f*
random test Stichprobe *f*
random testing Stichprobenkontrolle *f*
random tool access variable Platzcodierung *f*
random variability Zufallsstreuung *f*
random variable Zufallsgröße *f*, Zufallsvariable *f*
random vector Zufallsvektor *m*

randomization zufällige Zuordnung *f*
range Bereich *m*, Stufe *f*, Größe *f*, Reichweite *f*, Spanne *f*, Spannweite *f*, Flucht *f*, Reihe *f*
range between schwanken zwischen
range changing Gangwechsel *m*
range finder Entfernungsmesser *m*
range of adjustment Verstellbereich *m*, Einstellbereich *m*
range of application Arbeitsbereich *m*, Anwendungsbereich *m*, Verwendungsbereich *m*
range of control Regelbereich *m*
range of effectiveness Wirkungsbereich *m*
range of feeds Vorschubbereich *m*
range of inventory Bestandsreichweite *f*
range of sensitivity Ansprechbereich *m*
range of speeds Drehzahlstellbereich *m*
range of spring Federweg *m*
range of the command variable Führungsbereich *m*
range of the desired variable Aufgabenbereich *m*
range of the disturbance variable Störbereich *m*
range of tolerance Toleranzbereich *m*
range of values Wertebereich *m*
rank Rang *m*, Rangzahl *f*
ranking Rang *m*
transport assignment Transportauftrag *m*
repair weld Ausbesserungsschweißnaht *f*
rapid schnell
rapid advance Eilvorlauf *m*, Eilgangvorlauf *m*
rapid approach Eilvorlauf *m*, beschleunigter Vorlauf *m*, Eilgangvorlauf *m*
rapid cleaning tank Schnellreinigungsbehälter *m*
rapid idle movement Eilrücklauf *m*
Rapid Micro Product Developmemt RMPD (Schnellmikroproduktentwicklung *f*)
rapid pallet transfer Palettenschnellwechsel *m*
rapid power traverse Eilgang *m*,

Schnellgang *m*, Schnellverstellung *f*, selbsttätiger Schnellgang *m*
rapid power traverse shaft Eilgangwelle *f*
Rapid Product Development RPD (Schnellproduktentwicklung *f*)
Rapid Prototyping RPD (Schnellproduktentwicklung *f*)
rapid return traverse Schnellrücklauf *m*, Eilrückgang *m*
rapid return Eilrücklauf *m*, beschleunigte Rückführung *f*
rapid return motion Schnellrücklauf *m*
rapid reverse Umsteuerung *f* im Eilrücklauf
rapid rotary motion Eilwälzung *f*
rapid series exposure Schnellserienaufnahme *f*
rapid table traverse Tischeilgang *m*
rapid transfer Schnellwechsel *m*
rapid transfer station Schnellwechselstation *f*
rapid travel Schnellfahrt *f*, Eilgang *m*
rapid traverse Eilgang *m*, Eilbewegung *f*, Schnellgang *m*; durchfahren im Eilgang
rapid traverse control Eilgangsteuerung *f*
rapid traverse drive Eilgangantrieb *m*
rapid traverse jump Eilgangsprung *m*
rapid traverse of milling table Tischfräseilgang *m*
rapid traverse rate of feed Eilvorschub *m*
rare selten
rare gas valve Edelgasventil *nt*
raster Raster *nt*, Rasterung *f*
raster fly cutting Rastereinzahnumlauffräsen *nt*
raster locking Rasterarretierung *f*
raster scanner Rasterscanner *m*
rotational moulding Rotationsformen *fpl*
ratchet and pawl mechanism Sperrgetriebe *nt*, Sperrwerk *nt*
ratchet stop Ratschenantrieb *m*
ratchet Schaltklinke *f*, Klinkenrad *nt*, Knarre *f*, Sperrrad *nt*, Sperrzahn *m*
ratchet and pawl Sperrzahnrad *nt* mit Sperrklinke

ratchet brace Bohrknarre *f*
rate 1. Betrag *m*, Wert *m*, Menge *f*, Größe *f*, Quote *f*; schätzen, messen, bemessen, abmessen, veranschlagen, beurteilen, bewerten **2.** Geschwindigkeit *f*
rate for dimensionieren
rate of airflow Luftleistung *f*
rate of cut Spantiefe *f*
rate of cutting Schnittgeschwindigkeit *f*
rate of cutting speed Vorlaufgeschwindigkeit *f*
rate of data transfer Datenübertragungsrate *f*
rate of delivery of the blasting abrasive Strahlmitteldurchsatz *m*
rate of descent Senkgeschwindigkeit *f*
rate of equity turnover Umschlagshäufigkeit *f*
rate of feed Vorschubwert *m*, Vorschubgröße *f*, Vorschubgeschwindigkeit *f*
rate of filtration Filtriergeschwindigkeit *f*
rate of flame propagation Flammenausbreitungsgeschwindigkeit *f*
rate of flow Strömungsgeschwindigkeit *f*, Strömungsmenge *f*
rate of flow of the test gas Prüfgasdurchfluss *m*
rate of fresh air supply Außenluftrate *f*
rate of increase in the load Kraftzunahmegeschwindigkeit *f*
rate of inventory turnover Umschlagshäufigkeit *f*
rate of movement Bewegungsgröße *f*
rate of outside air supply Außenluftrate *f*
rate of penetration Eindringrate *f*
rate of rapid motion Eilganggeschwindigkeit *f*
rate of reciprocation motion Hubgeschwindigkeit *f*
rate of recrystallization Rekristallisationsgeschwindigkeit *f*
rate of removal Abtragungsgeschwindigkeit *f*
rate of rise Anstiegsgeschwindigkeit *f*
rate of roughing feed Schruppgeschwindigkeit *f*
rate of sewage discharge Abwasserab-

fluss *m*
rate of strain Reckgeschwindigkeit *f*
rate of strain increase Dehnzunahmegeschwindigkeit *f*
rate of strain of the outer fibre Randfaserdehngeschwindigkeit *f*
rate of stress increase Spannungszunahmegeschwindigkeit *f*
rate of taper Kegelverjüngung *f*
rate of travel of workpiece Werkstückgeschwindigkeit *f*
rate of turnover Umschlagshäufigkeit *f*
rate tool of wear Verschleißfortschritt *m* beim Werkzeug
rated Nenn ...
rated availability Verfügbarkeitsgrad *m*
rated capacity Nennleistung *f*, Nenntragfähigkeit *f*
rated current Bemessungsstrom *m*, Nennstrom *m*
rated data Nenndaten *ntpl*
rated frequency Nennfrequenz *f*
rated heat output Nennheizleistung *f*
rated load Nennlast *f*, Nutzlast *f*
rated motor torque Motornennmoment *nt*
rated output Nennleistung *f*
rated power Bemessungsleistung *f*
rated speed Nenngeschwindigkeit *f*, Nenndrehzahl *f*
rated torque Nennmoment *nt*
rated value Nennwert *m*, Bemessungswert *m*
rated value required value Sollwert *m*
rated voltage Nennspannung *f*
rated voltage for fluoroscopy Durchleuchtungsnennspannung *f*
rated voltage for radiography Aufnahmenennspannung *f*
rating 1. Leistungsbemessung *f*, Bemessung *f*, Leistung *f*, Nennleistung *f*, Beurteilung *f*, Bewertung *f*, Auslegung *f*, Einstufung *f* **2.** Kennzahl *f*
rating crack sternförmiger Riss *m*
rating number Kennzahl *f*
rating plate Leistungsschild *nt*
ratings Nenndaten *f*
ratio Verhältnis *nt*, Verhältniszahl *f*
ratio of mesh Eingriffsverhältnisse *ntpl*
ratio of the angle of contact Profilüberdeckungswinkel *m*
rationalization Rationalisierung *f*
rationalize rationalisieren
reverse thread milling machine Längsgewindeschleifmaschine *f*
raw roh, unverarbeitet
raw material Rohstoff *m*, Rohmaterial *nt*
raw material recycling Rohstoffrecycling *nt*
raw materials warehouse Rohmateriallager *nt*
raw piece Rohstoff *m*
raw product Roherzeugnis *nt*, Rohprodukt *nt*
raw products inventory (RPI) Rohproduktelager *nt*
raw rubber Rohkautschuk *m*
raw rubber bale Rohkautschukballen *m*
ray Strahl *m*, strahlen
ray effect Strahleinwirkung *f*
ray bunch Strahlbündel *nt*
ray conductor Stahlleiter *m*
ray cross section Strahlquerschnitt *m*
ray directing Strahlführung *f*
ray emitter Strahler *m*
ray entry side Strahleneintrittsseite *f*
ray exit window Strahlenaustrittsfenster *nt*
ray formation Strahlformung *f*
ray forming Strahlformung *f*
ray ground finish Strahlenschliff *m*
ray index Strahlkennzahl *f*
ray integral Strahlintegral *m*
ray manipulation Strahlführung *f*
Rayleigh-length Rayleigh-Länge
RC-procedural chain RC-Verfahrenskette *f*
RC-smoothing RC-Glättung *f*
reach Ausschubweite *f*, Reichweite *f*, Ausladung *f*, Ausfahrweg *m*, Ausschieben *nt*
reach around umgreifen
reach for reichen
reach fork carrier Schubgabelträger *m*
reach mast Schubmast *m*
reach mast truck Schubmaststapler *m*
reach mechanism Ausschubmechanismus *m*, Schubmast *m*

reach over übergreifen
reach system Schubsystem *nt*
reach truck Schubgabelstapler *m*, Schubstapler *m*
reach under untergreifen
reaching over Übergreifen *nt*
reaching under Untergreifen *nt*
react reagieren, ansprechen, entgegenwirken, gegenwirken
reactance coil Drossel *f*
reacting resin hardener Reaktionsharzhärter *m*
reaction Ansprechen *nt*, Reaktion *f*, Rückwirkung *f*, Rückkopplung *f*, Rückschlag *m*
reaction accelerator Reaktionsbeschleuniger *m*
reaction force Reaktionskraft *f*
reaction measurement Reaktionsmessung *f*
reaction overvoltage Reaktionsüberspannung *f*
reaction partner Reaktionspartner *m*
reaction pressure roller Gegendruckrolle *f*
reaction product Reaktionsprodukt *nt*
reaction resin Reaktionsharz *nt*
reaction resin concrete Reaktionsharzbeton *m*
reaction resin moulded material Reaktionsharzformstoff *m*, Reaktionsharzmasse *f*
reaction resistance Reaktionswiderstand *m*
reaction time Ansprechzeit *f*, Reaktionszeit *f*, Anlaufzeit *f*
reaction to repeated flexure Dauerknickverhalten *nt*
reaction value Anlaufwert *m*
reactive adhesive Reaktivkleber *m*
reactive forces Zwangskräfte *fpl*
reactor Drossel *f*
reactor weld Reaktorschweißung *f*
read lesen, anzeigen
read head Lesekopf *m*
read off ablesen
read only memory (ROM) Nur-Lese-Speicher *m*, 3 ¥ 4-Bit-Lesespeicher
read out device Ausgabegerät *nt*, Ausgeber *m*

read principle Leseprinzip *nt*
read the counter Zähler ablesen
read the meter Zähler ablesen
read/write behaviour Schreib-Leseverhalten *nt*
read/write device Schreib-Lesegerät *nt*
read/write distance Schreib-Leseabstand *m*
read/write head Schreib-Lesekopf *m*
readability Ablesbarkeit *f*
readable lesbar
reader Lesegerät *nt*
readily flammable material leicht entflammbarer Stoff *m*
read-in Übernahme *f*
read-in of information Informationsübernahme *f*
readiness Bereitschaft *f*
readiness for action Startbereitschaft *f*
readiness for delivery Lieferbereitschaft *f*
readiness for operation Betriebsbereitschaft *f*
readiness time Bereitschaftszeit *f*
reading Stand *m*, Anzeige *f*, Messung *f*, Ablesung *f*
reading area Leseebene *f*
reading cycle Lesezyklus *m*
reading device Lesegerät *nt*, Leseeinrichtung *f*, Ablesevorrichtung *f*
reading distance Leseabstand *m*
reading equipment Lesegerät *nt*
reading error Ablesefehler *m*
reading facility Ablesevorrichtung *f*
reading field Lesefeld *nt*
reading free from parallax parallelachsenfreie Ablesung *f*
reading head Lesegerät *nt*
reading in the reverse direction gegenläufige Anzeige *f*
reading magnifier Ableselupe *f*
reading operation Lesevorgang *m*
reading option Lesemöglichkeit *f*
reading pistol Lesepistole *f*
reading point Leseort *m*
reading range Lesebereich *m*
reading run Lesepistole *f*
reading station Lesestation *f*
reading technology Lesetechnik *f*
readjust nachjustieren, nachstellen, ver-

stellen
re-adjustability Nachstellbarkeit f
readjustable nachstellbar
readjustment Nachstellen nt, Nachstellung f, Neueinstellung f
readjustment switch Rückstellungsschalter m
read-only data carrier festkodierter Datenträger (FDT) m
readout Ablesung f, Anzeige f, Sichtanzeige f
ready bereit
ready for market marktreif
ready for operation betriebsbereit, betriebsfähig, einsatzbereit
ready for ordering bestellreif
ready for production betriebsfertig
ready for service betriebsbereit
ready for use einsatzbereit, betriebsbereit, betriebsfertig, bereitgestellt, verwendungsfertig
ready-for-use adhesive Klebstoff m im Verarbeitungszustand
ready-for-use condition verarbeitungsfertiger Zustand m
ready-for use prepared mixture verarbeitungsfertig angesetzte Mischung f
ready-for-use state Verarbeitungszustand m
ready machinability Bearbeitbarkeit f
ready mix fertiges Mischgut nt
ready to assemble montagefertig
ready-to-fit montagefertig
ready to market marktreif
ready-to-mount montagefertig
ready to operate betriebsbereit
ready to use flächenfertig
readymade products konfektionierte Erzeugnisse f
ready-mixed concrete Transportbeton m
real wirklich
real layout Reallayout nt
real life praxisnah
real net output Wertschöpfung f
real number reelle Zahl f
real operation Echtbetrieb m
real planning Realplanung f
real surface Schnitt m, Schnittfläche f
real time Echtzeit f; zeitnah

real time language Realzeitsprache f (PEARL)
real time processing Realzeitbetrieb m, Echtzeitverarbeitung f
real value tatsächlicher Wert m
real variant Realvariante f
realign nachrichten
realignment Nachrichten nt
realizable realisierbar
realization Realisierung f
realize realisieren, in die Praxis umsetzen
real-time clock Echtzeituhr f
real-time data base Echtzeitdatenbasis f
real-time operating system Echtzeitbetriebssystem nt
real-time program Realzeitprogramm nt
real-time system Echtzeitsystem nt
ream reiben, aufreiben, ausreiben
reamed bolt Passschraube f
reamer Ahle f, Reibahle f, Reibwerkzeug nt
reamer fluting cutter Reibahlennutfräser m
reaming Reiben nt
reaming operation Reibarbeit f
rear Heck nt; hinten, hinter, rückseitig, rückwärtig
rear axle Hinterachse f
rear drive Heckantrieb m
rear drive unit Hinterradantrieb m
rear edge Hinterkante f
rear end rückwärtiges Ende nt
rear intensifier screen Verstärkerhinterfolie f
rear intensifying screen Hinterfolie f
rear panel Rückwand f
rear pilot 1. Führungsstück nt
  2. Endstück nt
rear side Rückseite f
rear touch device Rücktasteinrichtung f
rear up aufrichten
rear wheel Hinterrad nt
rear window Heckscheibe f
rearrange umordnen
rearrangement Umordnen nt
rear-view mirror Rückspiegel m

rear-view mirror adjustment Rückspiegelverstellung *f*
reason Ursache *f*
reasonableness check Plausibilitätskontrolle *f*, Plausibilitätstest *m*
reasonably angemessen
reassemble wieder zusammensetzen
rebated joint Falz *m*, Falzverbindung *f*
rebend test Rückbiegeversuch *m*
rebore nachbohren
rebound Rückprall *m*, Abprall *m*; abprallen
rebound impact Prellstoß *m*
rebound resilience Rückprallelastizität *f*
rebounding hammer Fallhammer *m*
rebuild umbauen, modernisieren
rebuilding Umbau *m*, Modernisierung *f*
rebuilt generalüberholt
recalculate nachrechnen
recalculation Nachrechnung *f*
recalibration Nacheichung *f*
recalibrate nacheichen
recall Abruf *m*; abrufen
recarburizer Aufkohlungsmittel *nt*
recarburizing agent Aufkohlungsmittel *nt*
receipt 1. Quittung *f* 2. *(Waren)* Zugang *m*
receipt of goods Wareneingang (WE) *m*, Warenannahme *f*, Annahme *f*, Warenvereinnahmung *f*
receipt of order Auftragseingang *m*, Auftragsannahme *f*
receive empfangen, aufnehmen, annehmen, erhalten, bekommen
receive an order einen Auftrag annehmen
receive goods Waren vereinnahmen
receive packet Empfangspaket *nt*
received quantity Zugangsmenge *f*
receiver 1. Empfänger *m* 2. Tank *m*, Behälter *m*
receiver adaptor Destilliervorstoß *m*
receiver coil Empfangsspule *f*
receiver side Empfängerseite *f*
receiving Aufnahme *f*
receiving advice Empfangsbestätigung *f*
receiving slip Wareneingangsschein *m*
receiving table Aufnahmetisch *m*

receiving ticket Wareneingangsschein *m*
receptacle Steckerbuchse *f*, Buchsenteil *nt*
reception Aufnahme *f*, Annahme *f*, Empfang *m*
reception antenna Empfangsantenne *f*
reception inspection Eingangskontrolle *f*
receptor Rezeptor *m*
reservoir Behälter *m*
recess aussparen, einstechen, schlitzen; Aussparung *f*, Einstich *m*, Einschnitt *m*, Vertiefung *f*, Eindrehung *f*, Ausnehmung *f*
recess by turning ausdrehen
recess contract Austrittseingriff *m*
recess dimension Kreuzschlitzmaß *nt*
recess gauge Kreuzschlitzlehre *f*
recess milling attachment Einstechfräsgerät *nt*
recess turning Einstechdrehen *nt*
recessed ausgespart
recessed countersunk (flat) head screw Senkschraube *f* mit Kreuzschlitz
recessed countersunk (flat) head wood screw Senkblechschraube *f* mit Kreuzschlitz
recessed head screw Kreuzschlitzschraube *f*, Schraube *f* mit Kreuzschlitz
recessed raised cheese head screw Linsenschraube *f* mit Kreuzschlitz
recessed raised countersunk head wood screw Linsensenkholzschraube *f* mit Kreuzschlitz
recessed raised fillister head screw Linsenschraube *f* mit Kreuzschlitz
recessed rim hole Durchzug *m* vertieft
recessed round head wood screw Halbrundholzschraube *f* mit Kreuzschlitz
recessing 1. Aussparung *f*, Ausdrehung *f*, Einstich *m*, Einstecharbeit *f*, Einstechen *nt* 2. Nutendrehen *nt*
recessing feed Einstechvorschub *m*
recessing method Einstechverfahren *nt*
recessing slide Einstechsupportschieber *m*
recessing tool Einstechmeißel *m*, Ein-

stichmeißel *m*, Stechmeißel *m*, Hakenmeißel *m*
recharge nachladen; Nachladung *f*; wieder aufladen
rechargeable wieder aufladbar
recharging Wiederaufladen *nt*
recheck nachprüfen
rechuck umspannen
rechucking Umspannung *f*, Umspannen *nt*
rechucking appliance Umspannvorrichtung *f*
recipe Rezeptur *f*
recipient aufnehmendes Medium *nt*
reciprocal 1. wechselseitig **2.** *(math.)* Kehrwert *m*
reciprocal action Wechselwirkung *f*
reciprocal effect Wechselwirkung *f*
reciprocal milling Pendelverkehrfräsen *nt*, Pendelfräsen *nt*
reciprocal milling operation Pendelfräsarbeit *f*
reciprocate hin- und hergehen, hin- und herbewegen, pendeln
reciprocating oszillierend
reciprocating diaphragm compressor Hubkolbenmembranverdichter *m*
reciprocating engine Kolbendampfmaschine *f*
reciprocating grinding Pendelschleifen *nt*
reciprocating grinding mill feed setting per stroke Pendelschleifen *nt* mit Zustellung pro Hub
reciprocating machinery Maschinen *f* mit hin- und hergehender Hauptbewegung
reciprocating motion hin- und hergehende Bewegung *f*
reciprocating movement Hin- und Herbewegung *f*
reciprocating planing tool hin- und hergehender Hobelmeißel *m*
reciprocating pole Wendepol *m*
reciprocating pump Hubkolbenpumpe *f*
reciprocating stroke hin- und hergehender Hub *m*
reciprocating system Pendelsystem *nt*
reciprocating traverse hin- und hergehende Längsbewegung *f*
reciprocating vacuum pump Hubkolbenvakuumpumpe *f*
reciprocating-cutter generating method Wälzhobelverfahren *nt*
reciprocating-table machine Langtischmaschine *f*
reciprocation Hin- und Hergang *m*, Hin- und Herbewegung *f*
recirculate wieder zuführen, rückführen in den Umlauf
recirculating air operation Umluftbetrieb *m*
recirculation Rückführung *f*
recirculation of blasting abrasives Strahlmittelumlauf *m*
recirculation ventilation Umlüftung *f*
reclaim aufbereiten
reclaimed material Rücklaufmaterial *nt*
reclamation index Rückgewinnungsgrad *m*
reclamp nachspannen
reclamping Umspannen *nt*, nochmaliges Aufspannen *nt*, Nachspannen *nt*, Umspannung *f*, Neuaufspannung *f*
reclosable wiederverschließbar
recluse wieder einschalten, wieder schließen
reclosing Wiedereinschalten *nt*
reclosure Wiedereinschalten *nt*
reclosure preventing device Wiedereinschaltsperre *f*
recognition Erkennung *f*
recognition class Erkennungsklasse *f*
recognition possibility Erkennungsmöglichkeit *f*
recognizable erkennbar
recognize erkennen
recoil Rückprall *m*, Rückschlag *m*
recommended value Richtwert *m*
recommended values Richtwerte *mpl*
recommissioning Weiterbetrieb *m*
recondition erneuern, auffrischen, reparieren, instandsetzen, ausbessern, überholen
reconditioned gebraucht
reconditioning Erneuerung *f*, Instandsetzung *f*, Überholung *f*, Überholen *nt*
reconsign umleiten

reconsignment Umleitung *f*
reconstitute wiederherstellen
reconstruct umbauen
reconstruction Neukonstruktion *f*, Umbau *m*
record aufzeichnen, aufnehmen, dokumentieren, erfassen, protokollieren, registrieren, speichern, schreiben; Aufzeichnung *f*, Register *nt*, Protokoll *nt*
record effect Schallplatteneffekt *m*
recorded value Messwert *m*
recorder Aufzeichnungsgerät *nt*, Schreiber *m*
recording Aufnahme *f*, Aufzeichnung *f*, Registrierung *f*, Erfassung *f*, Protokollierung *f*, Speicherung *f*
recording apparatus Schreiber *m*
recording implement Schreibgerät *nt*
recording measuring instrument registrierendes Messgerät *nt*
recording range Aufnahmebereich *m*
recording sensitivity Registrierempfindlichkeit *f*
resources management Einsatzmittelmanagement *nt*
recover wiedergewinnen, erholen, wiederhergestellt werden, bergen
recovery Wiederherstellung *f*
recovery behaviour Erholungsverhalten *nt*
recovery facility Bergungsmöglichkeit *f*
recovery index Wiedergewinnungsgrad *m*
recovery of damages Schadenersatz *m*
recovery period Erholungszeit *f*
recovery time Erholungszeit *f*
recovery time interval Erholungszeitspanne *f*
recovery time range Erholungszeitbereich *m*
recruit personnel Personal beschaffen
recruitment Personalbeschaffung *f*
recrystallization Rekristallisation *f*
recrystallization annealing Rekristallisationsglühen *nt*
recrystallization temperature Rekristallisationstemperatur *f*
recrystallization texture Rekristallisationstextur *f*
recrystallize rekristallisieren

rectangle Rechteck *nt*
rectangle of area equal to the square flächengleiches Rechteck *nt*
rectangular rechtwinklig, rechteckig
rectangular block specimen quaderförmiger Probekörper *m*
rectangular coil Rechteckspule *f*
rectangular duct Rechteckkanal *m*
rectangular parallel-piped measurement surface Quadermessfläche *f*
rectangularity Rechtwinkligkeit *f*
rectification Nachbesserung *f*, Berichtigung *f*, Behebung *f*
rectification of defects Fehlerausbesserung *f*
rectified gerichtet
rectifier Gleichrichter *m*
rectifier diode Gleichrichterdiode *f*
rectify 1. berichtigen, nachbessern, beheben 2. *(el.)* gleichrichten
rectilinear geradlinig
rectilinear scanning Streifenabtastung *f*
rectilinear table feed motion Tischlängsbewegung *f*
rectilinearity Geradlinigkeit *f*
recuperating spring Rückholfeder *f*
recuperative annealing Erholungsglühen *nt*
recuperator Rückholfeder *f*
recur wiederkehren, wiederholen, wiederholt auftreten
recurrence Wiederholung *f*
recurrent wiederkehrend
recurring periodisch, wiederkehrend, wiederholbar
recurring peak voltage periodische Spitzenspannung *f*
recursive wiederholbar
recut nachgeschnitten
recycle rückführen
recycling Rückführung *f*, Recycling *nt*
recycling material Rückgut *nt*
red hardness Warmhärte *f*
red light LED Rotlicht-LED *f*
reddish colouration Rotfärbung *f*
redeposit umlagern
redepositing Umlagerung *f*
redeposition umlagern
redepositioning Umlagerung *f*

redesign Neukonstruktion *f*, Neuordnung *f*, Umbau *m*, Umgestaltung *f*; umkonstruieren
redirect umleiten
re-direct *(Signalflusswege)* umschalten
redox potential Redoxpotential *nt*
redox reaction Redoxreaktion *f*
redraw umzeichnen
redress aufbereiten, abrichten, nachrichten
redressing Nachrichten *nt*
reduce verringern, herabsetzen, abnehmen, mindern, vermindern, reduzieren, senken, abbauen, verkürzen, nachlassen, einschränken
reduce costs Kosten senken
reduce steplessly to zero stufenlos auf Null herab regeln
reduced eingeschränkt, nachlassend
reduced face reduzierte Spanfläche *f*
reduced income Gewinneinbußen *fpl*
reduced instruction set eingeschränkter Befehlssatz *m*
reduced random quantity reduzierte Zufallsgröße *f*
reduced scale verkleinerter Maßstab *m*
reduced value of a dimension Faktor *m* einer Abmessung
reducer Abschwächer *m*, Reduzierstück *nt*
reducing 1. Reduzieren *nt* **2.** *(Durchmesser)* Verjüngen *nt*, Einstoßen *nt*
reducing by roll stretching Streckreduzierwalzen *nt*
reducing gear Untersetzungsgetriebe *nt*
reducing protective gas reduzierendes Schutzgas *nt*
reducing ratio Verkleinerungsfaktor *m*
reducing socket Reduziermuffe *f*
reducing the ends of solid bodies Verjüngen *nt* von Vollkörpern
reducing union Reduzierstutzen *m*
reduction Verringerung *f*, Herabsetzung *f*, Abnahme *f*, Rückgang *m*, Nachlassen *nt*, Reduktion *f*, Reduzierung, Verkleinerung *f*, Verminderung *f*, Verkürzung *f*, Schwindung *f*, Senkung *f*, Abbau *m*
reduction in cross-sectional area Querschnittsverkleinerung *f*
reduction in machining time per piece Stückzeitverkürzung *f*
reduction in tension Spannungsabbau *m*
reduction in the tensile shearing load Scherzugkraftabfall *m*
reduction measure Schwindmaß *nt*
reduction of area Querschnittsschwächung *f*
reduction of backlash Spielverminderung *f*
reduction of costs Einsparung *f*
reduction of lustre Glanzminderung *f*
reduction reaction Reduktionsreaktion *f*
redundancy Redundanz *f*
redundant redundant
redundant control system redundante Steuerung *f*
redundant dimension Maßüberbestimmung *f*
redundant dimensioning maßliche Überbestimmung *f*
reed contact Reedkontakt *m*
reed switch Blattfederschalter *m*
reef Reff *nt*; reffen
reefing device Reffeinrichtung *f*
reefing unit Reffeinrichtung *f*
reel 1. Rolle *f*, Spule *f*, Trommel *f*, Spulenkörper *m*; winden **2.** *(el.)* Kabeltrommel *f*
reel fed bag fill and seal machine Beutelfüll- und -verschließmaschine *f* mit Beutelzuführung von der Rolle
reel method Weifverfahren *nt*
reel of film Folienrolle *f*
reel up aufspulen
reel without cheeks seitenwandloser Spulenkörper *m*
reeled filler wire gespulter Schweißdraht *m*
reel-fed von der Rolle zugeführt
reeling of tubes by the through-feed method Glattwalzen *nt* von Rohren im Durchlaufverfahren
reemploy wieder verwenden
reemployment Wiederverwendung *f*
re-enlargement Rückvergrößerung *f*
re-enlarging process Rückvergröße-

rungsverfahren *nt*
re-entry Eingriff *m*
re-entry cycle Wiedereintrittszyklus *m*
reface nachspanen, nachplanen
re-face nachdrehen
reference Zuordnung *f*, Bezug *m*; referenzieren
reference analysis Richtanalyse *f*
reference atmosphere Normalklima *nt*
reference axis Bezugsachse *f*
reference bar Prüfmaßstab *m*
reference basis Bezugsbasis *f*, Bezugskreis *m*
reference block Vergleichskörper *m*
reference box Bezugsquader *m*
reference centre distance Nullachsabstand *m*
reference circle Teilkreis *m*, Bezugskreis *m*
reference circle arc Teilkreisbogen *m*
reference circle pitch Stirnteilung *f*, Teilkreisteilung *f*
reference circle plane Teilkreisebene *f*
reference coating Vergleichsanstrich *m*
reference combustion quantity Vergleichsbrandmenge *f*
reference cone Teilkegel *m*
reference cone angle Teilkegelwinkel *m*
reference cone apex Teilkegelspitze *f*
reference cone envelope Teilkegelmantel *m*
reference cone envelope line Teilkegelmantellinie *f*
reference cylinder Teilzylinder *m*
reference cylinder envelope line Teilzylindermantellinie *f*
reference cylinder tooth trace Teilzylinderflankenlinie *f*
reference data *pl* Richtwerte *mpl*
reference datum Referenzgerade *f*
reference diameter Teilkreisdurchmesser *m*
reference dimension Bezugsmaß *nt*
reference dimensioning Bezugsbemaßung *f*
reference earth Bezugserde *f*
reference element Vergleichselement *nt*, Bezugselement *nt*
reference face Bezugsstirnfläche *f*

reference gauge Vergleichsmaß *nt*
reference gauge block Prüfendmaß *nt*
reference gear unit Vergleichsgetriebe *nt*
reference helix Teilzylinderflankenlinie *f*
reference input location Referenzeinlagerplatz *m*
reference length Bezugsstrecke *f*
reference line Hinweislinie *f*, Nulllinie *f*
reference list Zuordnungsliste *f*
reference magnitude Bezugsgröße *f*
reference marker Referenzmarke *f*
reference material 1. Vergleichsstoff *m* 2. Dokumentationsmaterial *nt*, Dokumentation *f*
reference measuring system Vergleichsmesseinrichtung *f*
reference output location Referenzauslagerplatz *m*
reference plane Bezugsebene *f*, Referenzebene *f*, Teilebene *f*
reference plug gauge Prüfmessscheibe *f*, Prüfdorn *m*
reference point Bezugszahl *f*, Bezugspunkt *m*, Referenzpunkt *m*
reference position Solllage *f*
reference profile Bezugsprofil *nt*
reference reflector Vergleichsreflektor *m*
reference sample Vergleichsmuster *nt*
reference scale Vergleichsskala *f*
reference size Bezugsmaß *nt*
reference solution Vergleichslösung *f*
reference sound pressure Bezugsschalldruck *m*
reference sound source Vergleichsschaltquelle *f*
reference storage location Referenzlagerplatz *m*
reference strip Vergleichsstreifen *m*
reference surface Bezugsfläche *f*, Teilfläche *f*, Teilkegelfläche *f*
reference surface contact system Bezugsflächentastsystem *nt*
reference surface of the helical teeth Schrägverzahnungsbezugsfläche *f*
reference system Bezugssystem *nt*
reference system of planes *pl* Bezugsebenen *fpl*

reference tooth trace Teilflankenlinie f, Teilflankenwinkel m, Bezugsflankenlinie f
reference unit Bezugseinheit f
reference value Bezugswert m, Sollwert m, Richtwert m
reference value transmitter Sollwertgeber m
reference visual range Bezugssehweite f
reference centre distance tooth system V-Null-Verzahnung f
referenced ramp function response bezogene Anstiegsantwort f
referencing Referenzierung f
refill auftanken, auffüllen, wieder befüllen, wieder auffüllen, nachfüllen
refill command Nachfüllauftrag m
refill job Nachfüllauftrag m
refill order Nachfüllauftrag m
refill system Nachfüllsystem nt
refilling Wiederauffüllen nt, Auffüllen nt, Wiederbefüllen nt
refine veredeln
refined linseed oil Lackleinöl nt
refined soya bean oil Lacksoyaöl nt
refitting Nachrüstung f
reflect spiegeln, reflektieren
reflecting reflektierend
reflecting foil Reflexfolie f
reflecting mirror Reflexionsspiegel m
reflecting side verspiegelte Seite f
reflection Reflexion f
reflection filter Reflexionsfilter m
reflection light barrier Reflexionslichtschranke f
reflection light scanner Reflexionslichttaster m
reflection line-scanning light scanner Reflexionszeilenlichttaster m
reflection optics Reflexionsoptik f
reflection photometer Reflexionsphotometer nt
reflection tag Reflexionsmarke f
reflective reflektierend
reflective characteristic Reflexionseigenschaft f
reflective tape Reflexfolie f
reflectogram Reflektogramm nt
reflector Reflektor m
reflectorize reflektierend machen
reflux Rückfluss m
reformability Nachformbarkeit f
re-formatting Umformatierung f
reforming Umformen nt, Verformen nt
reforming by bending Biegeumformen nt
reforming by shear Schubumformen nt
refraction Brechung f
refraction intercept Refraktionsinterzept nt
refractive index Brechungsverhältnis nt, Brechzahl f, Brechungsindex m, Brechwert m
refractory feuerfest
refractory lining feuerfeste Ausmauerung f
reference block Kontrollkörper m
reference grid Raster nt
refresh rate Bildelementfolgefrequenz f
refrigerant stability Kältemittelbeständigkeit f
refrigerate kühlen, tiefkühlen
refrigerated warehouse Kühlhaus nt
refrigerating storage house Kühlhaus nt
refrigeration Kühlung f
refrigeration plant Tiefkühlanlage f
refrigeration unit Kühleinheit f
refrigerator Kühlhaus nt, Kälteschrank m
refrigerator oil Kältemaschinenöl nt
refuel auftanken
refurbish sanieren
refurbishment Sanierung f
refuse Verschnitt m, Abfall m
refuse incinerator furnace Abfallverbrennungsofen m, Müllverbrennungsofen m
refuse-fired müllgefeuert
regenerating tank Regenerierbehälter m
region Bereich m
region of the notch Kerbbereich m
regional stock Regionallager nt
register registrieren, anzeigen, zulassen; Register nt, Speicherzelle f
registered zugelassen
registration Registrierung f

registration of data flow Datenflussverfolgung f
regrade abstufen
regress zurücktreten
regression Regression f, Zurücktreten nt
regression calculation Regressionsrechnung f
regression curve Regressionskurve f
regression equation Regressionsfunktion f
regression line Regressionsgerade f
regression surface Regressionsfläche f
regrind nachschleifen, schärfen, anschärfen; Nachschliff m
re-grind nachschleifen, nachschärfen
reground nachgeschnitten
regular gleichmäßig, regelmäßig, normal
regular engine lathe Leit- und Zugspindeldrehmaschine f
regular service Normalbetrieb m
regular test Regelprüfung f
regular type screw thread Regelgewinde nt
regulate stellen, regeln, regulieren, verstellen
regulating action Stellwirkung f
regulating device Steuereinrichtung f, Steuergerät nt
regulating point Stellort m
regulating range Verstellbereich m, Stellbereich m
regulating roll Regelrolle f
regulating wheel *(Vorschubscheibe)* Regelscheibe f
regulation 1. Verstellen nt, Verstellung f, Regulierung f 2. Vorschrift f, Verordnung f, Richtlinie f
regulation wheel Vorschubreihe f, Regelscheibe f
regulations Richtlinien fpl
regulations for the prevention of industrial accidents Unfallverhütungsvorschriften fpl
regulator Regelwerk nt
rehandle umschlagen
rehandling and forwarding Umschlag und Spedition
rehandling and storage Umschlag und Lagerung
rehandling grab Umschlaggreifer m
reharden aufhärten
rehardening Aushärtung f
re-ignition attempt Wiederzündversuch m
reinforce versteifen, verstärken
reinforced concrete Stahlbeton m
reinforced concrete pressure pipeline Stahlbetondruckrohrleitung f
reinforced concrete with untensioned reinforcement schlaff armierter Stahlbeton m
reinforcing member Versteifungselement nt
reinforcement Versteifung f, Verstärkung f
reinforcement of single-Vee groove V-Nahtüberhöhung f
reinforcing fin Stabilisierungsrippe f
reinforcing rib Stabilisierungsrippe f
reinforcing sleeve Verstärkerhülse f
reinspect nachprüfen
reiterate wiederholen
reiteration Wiederholung f
reject verwerfen, abweisen, zurückweisen, beanstanden
reject costs Ausschusskosten pl
reject rate Ausschussquote f
rejection Beanstandung f, Rückweisung f
rejector Abweiser m
rejects Ausschuss m
relate zusammenhängen
related zusammenhängend
related to operator's position arbeitsplatzbezogen
relation Verhältnis nt, Relation f
relation operator Vergleichsoperator m
relation to bezogen auf
relationship Zusammenhang m, Beziehung f, Abhängigkeit f, Relation f
relationship between variables Größenzusammenhang m
relative relativ
relative angular velocity relative Winkelgeschwindigkeit f
relative dimension Relativmaß nt
relative dimension programming Relativmaßprogrammierung f

relative humidity relative Luftfeuchtigkeit *f*
relative motion Relativbewegung *f*
relative movement Relativbewegung *f*
relative notched impact strength relative Kerbschlagzähigkeit *f*
relative resistance to environmental stress cracking relative Spannungsrissbeständigkeit *f*
relative rotation Relativdrehung *f*
relaxation behaviour Relaxationsverhalten *nt*
relaxation modulus Entspannungsmodul *m*, Relaxationsmodul *m*
relaxation oscillation Kippschwingung *f*
relaxation spectrum Relaxationsspektrum *nt*
relaxation test Entspannungsversuch *m*
relay 1. weitergeben **2.** *(el.)* Relais *nt*
relay box Relaiskasten *m*
relay connection Relaisschaltung *f*
relay control system Relaissystem *nt*
relay ladder diagram Kontaktplan (KOP) *m*, Relaiskontaktplan *m*
relay rack Relaisschrank *m*
relay rail Relaisschiene *f*
relay-actuated switch Relaisschalter *m*
relaying Weitergabe *f*
release ausschalten, ausklinken, entriegeln, ausspannen, lösen, auslösen, auflösen, freigeben, loslassen, öffnen; Freigabe *f*, Loslassen *nt*, Auflösung *f*, Auslösung *f*
release bit memory Freigabemerker *m*
release catch Ausklinknase *f*
release device Entriegelungseinrichtung *f*
release film Ablösefolie *f*
release handle Öffnungsgriff *m*
release of fuel gas Brennergasfreigabe *f*
release paper Ablösepapier *nt*
release signal Freigabesignal *nt*
release spring Rückzugfeder *f*
release switch Freigabeschalter *m*
release the brake lüften
release the spring entspannen der Feder
release the tension entspannen
release yield abgeben

releasing Freigabe *f*, Auflösung *f*, Auslösung *f*, Entriegelung *f*, Lüften *nt*, Lösen *nt*, Ausklinken *nt*, Lockern *nt*
releasing force Löschkraft *f*
releasing mechanism Auslösemechanismus *m*
releasing signal Auslösesignal *nt*
relegate to a lesser priority geringe Priorität verleihen
relevant einschlägig
relevant to costs kostenrelevant
relevant to decision making entscheidungsrelevant
reliability Zuverlässigkeit *f*
reliability analysis Zuverlässigkeitsanalyse *f*
reliability assurance Zuverlässigkeitssicherung *f*
reliability attribute Zuverlässigkeitskenngröße *f*
reliability characteristic Zuverlässigkeitskenngröße *f*
reliability growth Zuverlässigkeitswachstum *nt*
reliability in service betriebssicherer Einsatz *m*
reliability level Zuverlässigkeitsrate *f*
reliable zuverlässig, sicher
reliable in service betriebssicher
relieable in operation betriebssicher
relieable in service betriebssicher
relief 1. Abhilfe *f* **2.** Entspannen *nt*, Entlastung *nt* **3.** Hinterdrehung *f*, Hinterschliff *m* der Fase
relief angle Freiwinkel *m*, Hinterschliffwinkel *m*
relief capacity Abblaseleistung *f*
relief grinding Hinterschliff *m*, Hinterschleifen *nt*
relief motion Abhebebewegung *f*
relief of the rooth flank Fußfreischnitt *m*
relief surface Freifläche *f*
relief time Entlastungszeit *f*
relief valve Abblasventil *nt*, Sicherheitsventil *nt*
relief-grind freischleifen, hinterschleifen
relief-ground hinterschliffen
relief-mill hinterfräsen

relief-turn hinterdrehen
relief-turning Hinterdrehen *nt*
relieve abheben, freiarbeiten, hinterarbeiten, abbauen
relieve by turning hinterdrehen
relieve of the load entlasten
relieve the stress entspannen
relieving Abhebung *f*
relieving attachment Hinterdrehvorrichtung *f*, Hinterdreheinrichtung *f*
relieving by grinding Hinterschliff *m*, Hinterschleifen *nt*
relieving lathe Hinterdrehmaschine *f*
relieving toolholder Meißelhalter *m* mit Abhebung
relieving work Hinterdreharbeit *f*
relighting attempt Wiederzündversuch *m*
reload umladen; Umladung *f*
re-loading Umspannung *f*
relocate 1. verlagern, umstellen (auf) **2.** umspannen
relocating Umspannen *nt*
relocating work Werkstückumspannung *f*
relocation Umstellung *f*, Veränderung *f* der Stellung *f*, Verlagerung *f*, Umspannung *f*
relock wieder verschließen
reluctance motor Reluktanzmotor *m*
remachine nacharbeiten
remachine nachbearbeiten
remachining Nacharbeit *f*
remachining Nacharbeit *f*
remain Rest *m*; bleiben, verbleiben, in Einstellung *f* bleiben
remainder Rückstand *m*, Rest *m*, Teilungsrest *m*
remaining restlich
remaining quantity Restmenge *f*
remaining range Restfahrstrecke *f*
remaining ripple Restwelligkeit *f*
remaining travel Restfahrstrecke *f*
remains *pl* **of the weld** Schweißnahtreste *mpl*
remanence Remanenz *f*
remanent remanent
remedy beheben
remedy deficiencies Mängel beseitigen

remedying of defects Mängelbeseitigung *f*
re-mill nachfräsen
remilling Nachfräsen *nt*
remind mahnen
reminder Mahnung *f*
remit zahlen
remittance Zählung *f*, Zahlen *nt*
remittance advice Zahlungsfreigabe *f*
remote entfernt
remote access system Fernzugriffsystem *nt*
remote control Fernbedienung *f*, Fernschaltung *f*, Fernsteuerung *f*
remote-controlled ferngesteuert
remote data transmission Datenfernübertragung *f*
remote diagnosis Ferndiagnose *f*
remote handling device Fernbedienungsgerät *nt*
remote I/O station (RIOS) dezentrale Ein-Ausgabeeinheit (-station) *f*
remote operated fernbetätigt, indirekt bestätigt
remote printer Remotedrucker *m*
remote protective action Fernschutzwirkung *f*
remouldability Nachformbarkeit *f*
remouldable nachformbar
removable ausbaubar, abnehmbar, entfernbar, lösbar
removable resist entfernbare Resistenzschicht *f*
removable tool bit Einsatzmeißel *m*, abnehmbarer Meißeleinsatz *m*
removal Abnahme *f*, Abhebung *f*, Abtrennung *f*, Abtrag *m*, Abtragung *f*, Entfernung *f*, Entnahme *f*, Entzug *m*, Abtransport *m*, Entsorgung *f*, Beseitigung *f*, Abfuhr *f*, Ausbau *m*, Abnehmen *nt*, Entfernen *nt*, Herausnehmen *nt*, Wegziehen *nt*, Ausfahren *nt*, Abräumen *nt*
removal from the mould Entformung *f*
removal of chips Spanabnahme *f*
removal of scale Entzundern *nt*
removal of the load Entlastung *nt*
removal rate Abtragrate *f*
removal volume Abtragvolumen *nt*
removal zone Entnahmezone *f*

remove abtransportieren, entfernen, abheben, abnehmen, entnehmen, abmontieren, ausbauen, beseitigen, entsorgen, abführen, herausheben, wegnehmen, ableiten, ausscheiden
remove by etching abätzen; Abätzen *nt*
remove chips spanen
remove contact with loslassen
remove metal by cutting zerspanen
remove metal by facing abplanen
remove oil contaminations *pl* Ölverunreinigungen entfernen
remove the rust from entrosten
remove the slag abschlacken
sever abtrennen
removing Abführen *nt*, Entnahme *f*
render wiedergeben
render difficult erschweren
render harmless unschädlich machen
render impure verunreinigen
render safe sichern, ungefährlich machen
rendering of accounts Rechnungslegung *f*
renew erneuern, sanieren
renewal Erneuerung *f*, Sanierung *f*, Wiederherstellung *f*
renewed erneut
renewed formation Neubildung *f*
renewing Erneuerung *f*
renovate erneuern
renovation Erneuerung *f*
rent mieten, vermieten; Miete *f*
rental Vermietung *f*, Miete *f*
renting Vermietung *f*
renumber umnummerieren
reorder 1. umordnen **2.** nachbestellen
repack umpacken
repacking Umpacken *nt*
repair nachbessern, ausbessern, reparieren, instandsetzen, in Stand halten; Nachbesserung *f*, Instandhaltung *f*, Instandsetzung *f*, Reparatur *f*
repair of fault fehlerlos
repair socket Reparaturmuffe *f*
repair time Reparaturdauer *f*
repair work Nachbesserungsarbeiten *fpl*, Ausbesserungsarbeiten *fpl*
repair workstation Reparaturarbeitsplatz *m*
repair workstation computer Reparaturarbeitsplatz-Rechner *m*
repair work Reparatur *f*
repalletize umpalettieren
repeat wiederholen, reproduzieren
repeatability Nachformfähigkeit *f*, Reproduzierbarkeit *f*, Wiederholbarkeit *f*, Wiederholgenauigkeit *f*, Reproduzierbarkeit *f*, Möglichkeit *f* der Wiederholung eines Arbeitsganges
repeatability conditions Wiederholungsbedingungen *fpl*
repeatability critical difference kritischer Wiederholdifferenzbetrag *m*
repeatability limit Wiederholgrenze *f*
repeatability measurement series Wiederholmessreihe *f*
repeatability repetitive accuracy Widerholgenauigkeit *f*
repeatability standard deviation Wiederholstandardabweichung *f*
repeatable wiederholbar
repeatable accuracy Wiederholgenauigkeit *f*
repeated wiederkehrend, wiederholt, erneut
repeated flexural stress Dauerknickbeanspruchung *f*
repeated flexural test Dauerbiegeversuch *m*
repeater Übertrager *m*
repeater antenna Umlenkantenne *f*
repeating Reproduzieren *nt*
repeating accuracy Wiederholgenauigkeit *f*
repeating label Wiederholungszeichen *nt*
repel abweisen, abstoßen
repetition Repetition *f*, Reproduktion *f*, Wiederholung *f*, Wiederanlauf *m*
repetition conditions Wiederholbedingungen *fpl*
repetition frequency Folgefrequenz *f*
repetition instruction Wiederholungsbefehl *m*
repetition job Serienarbeit *f*
repetition milling Serienfräsen *nt*
repetition part Wiederholteil *nt*
repetition tolerance Wiederholstreu-

bereich *m*
repetition work Serienfertigung *f*
repetitive accuracy Reproduktionsgenauigkeit *f*
repetitive parts Serienstücke *ntpl*
replace austauschen, ersetzen, wechseln, auswechseln
replaceability Austauschbarkeit *f*
replaceable austauschbar, auswechselbar
replaceable insert Wendeschneidplatte *f*
replacement 1. Auswechseln *nt*, Wechseln *nt*, Austausch *m*, Ersatz *m* **2.** *(QM)* Rückstellung *f*
replacement blade Ersatzmesser *nt*
replacement part Ersatzteil *nt*
replacement period Umschlagzeit *f*
replacement stock Ersatzteillager *nt*
replacement time Wiederbeschaffungszeit *f*
replenish auftanken, auffüllen, wieder befüllen, nachfüllen, ergänzen
replenishment Auffüllen *nt*, Wiederbefüllen *nt*, Wiederauffüllen *nt*, Nachschub *m*
replenishment of stocks Lageraufffüllung *f*
replenishment order Nachfüllauftrag *m*, Auffüllauftrag *m*
replica Ebenbild *nt*, Kopie *f*, Nachbildung *f*, Reproduktion *f*
replicate Parallelbestimmung *f*
replication Wiederholung *f*
report Protokoll *nt*, Meldung *f*, Bericht *m*; berichten, melden
reporting Berichterstattung *f*
reporting system Berichtswesen *nt*
repositioning of members Gliederverstellung *f*
reposition verstellen
repositioning of elements Gliederverstellung *f*
represent darstellen
represent graphically graphisch darstellen
represent broken abgebrochen darstellen
represent in section im Schnitt darstellen

representation Darstellung *f*
representation of a thread Gewindedarstellung *f*
representation of material flow Materialflussdarstellung *f*
representation of results Ergebnisdarstellung *f*
representation to scale maßstäbliche Darstellung *f*
reproduceability Vergleichspräzision *f*
reproduceability limit Vergleichgrenze *f*
reproduceability of th results Reproduzierbarkeit *f* der Ergebnisse
reproduceability standard deviation Vergleichsstandardabweichung *f*
reproduce reproduzieren, nachformen, kopieren, nachbauen, nachbilden, wiederholen
reproducibility Vergleichbarkeit *f*, Reproduzierbarkeit *f*, Wiederholbarkeit *f*
reproducibility condition Vergleichsbedingung *f*
reproducibility standard deviation Vergleichstandardabweichung *f*
reproducible wiederholbar, reproduzierbar, pausfähig
reproducible drawing pausbare Zeichnung *f*
reproducing Reproduzieren *nt*, Nachformen *nt*, Kopieren *nt*
reproduction Reproduktion *f*, Vervielfältigung *f*, Kopierarbeit *f*, Nachformung *f*, Nachbildung *f*, Wiedergabe *f*
reproduction process Reproduktionsverfahren *nt*
reproductive accuracy Nachfahrgenauigkeit *f*
reprogram umprogrammieren
reprogrammable mehrfach programmierbar, umprogrammierbar, wieder programmieren
reprogrammable read-only memory (REPROM) wieder programmierbarer Festspeicher *m*
reprogramming Umprogrammierung *f*
repulse abstoßen
repulsive abstoßend
repurchase Rücknahme *f*
request Anforderung *f*, Aufforderung *f*,

auf Anfrage *f*, Abfrage *f*; anfragen, anfordern, auffordern, abrufen, abfragen
require benötigen, erfordern, beanspruchen, verlangen
required erforderlich
required building space erforderlicher Grundflächenbedarf *m*
required geometrical design form geometrische Sollform *f*
required machine utilization time benötigte Maschinenbelegungszeit *f*
required status Sollzustand *m*
requirement Anforderung *f*, Erfordernis *f*
requirement Bedarf *m*, Vorgabe *f*
requirement extrapolation Bedarfshochrechnung *f*
requirement profile Anforderungsprofil *nt*
requirements specification Pflichtenheft *nt*
requiring acknowledgement quittierpflichtig
requisition Abforderung *f*
reroute umleiten
rerun Wiederholungslauf *m*; wiederholen
RES (reset) Rücksetzen *nt*
resale Wiederverkauf *m*
resale price Widerverkaufspreis *m*
re-schedule umplanen
rescue Rettung *f*
rescue passage Rettungsweg *m*
research Forschung *f*
research and development division Forschungs- und Entwicklungsabteilung *f*
reseat den Sitz neu einschleifen
resell wieder verkaufen
reseller Wiederverkäufer *m*
reservation Belegung *f*, Reservierung *f*
reservation quantity Reservierungsmenge *f*
reserve belegen, reservieren; Reserve *f*
reserve area Reservefläche *f*
reserve demand Reservebedarf *m*
reserve pallet Reservepalette *f*
reservice instandsetzen
reservicing Instandsetzung *f*
reserving Wiederinstandsetzung *f*, Reparatur *f*
reservoir Vorratsbehälter *m*, Sammelbehälter *m*, Tank *m*, Speicher *m*
reset 1. Rückstellung *f*, Nachstellung *f*, Rücksetzen *nt*, Rückstellen *nt*, Nachstellen *nt*; zurückstellen, zurücksetzen, nachstellen, verstellen, rücksetzen, rückstellen, neu einrichten **2.** umrüsten, umspannen **3.** (Schalter) wieder einschalten
re-set *(z. B. Werkzeuge)* umspannen
reset condition Rücksetzzustand *m*
reset contractor Wiedereinschaltschutz *m*
reset device Rückstellung *f*
reset input Rücksetzeingang *m*
reset position Ruhestellung *f*
reset push button Entstördruckknopf *m*
reset switch Rückstellungsschalter *m*
reset time Umrüstzeit *f*
resettable rücksetzbar
resetting 1. Nachstellung *f*, Neueinstellung *f*, Neuaufspannung *f* **2.** Umspannung *f*, Umrüstung *f* **3.** *(Schalter)* Wiedereinschalten *nt*
resetting device Entsperreinrichtung *f*
resetting point Entriegelungsort *m*
resetting time Umrichtezeit *f*
reshape umformen
resharpen nachschärfen, anschärfen, nachschleifen
re-sharpen Nachschliff *m*
resharpening Nachschliff *m*, Nachschleifen *nt*
reshelf zurücklagern, wieder einlagern
reshelving Wiedereinlagerung *f*
residual bleibend, restlich; Rest *m*
residual capacity Restkapazität *f*
residual cross-section Restquerschnitt *m*
residual current Fehlerstrom *m*, Differenzstrom *m*, Reststrom *m*
residual current protective device Fehlerstromschutzschalter *m*, FI-Schutzschalter *m*
residual deformation on compression Druckverformungsrest *m*
residual gas partial pressure Restgaspartialdruck *m*

residual hazard Restgefahr *f*
residual indentation Resteindruck *m*
residual induction Remanenzflussdichte *f*
residual load capacity Resttragfähigkeit *f*
residual magnetic flux density remanente Induktion *f*
residual matter Rückstand *m*
residual oscillation amplitude Restschwingungsamplitude *f*
residual pressure Restdruck *m*
residual pulse rate Restimpulsrate *f*
residual ripple Restwelligkeit *f*
residual risk Restrisiko *nt*
residual strain Restdehnung *f*
residual strength Bruchfestigkeit *f*, Restfestigkeit *f*
residual tool cutting life Reststandzeit *f*
residual value indication Restwertanzeige *f*
residual variance Restvarianz *f*
residuary restlich, übrig
residue Rest *m*, Rückstand *m*, Abfall *m*
residue formation Rückstandsbildung *f*
residue lead time Restdurchlaufzeit *f*
residue of pyrolysis Pyrolyserückstand *m*
residue on evaporation Trockenrückstand *m*
residue-free rückstandsfrei
resilience Elastizität *f*, Nachgiebigkeit *f*, Federung *f*, Federungsvermögen *nt*
resilience characteristic Federcharakteristik *f*
resiliency Stoßaufnahme *f*
resilient nachgiebig, federnd, elastisch
resilient bend Federbogen *m*
resilient jointing Weichdichtung *f*
resin Harz *m*
resin base Harzbasis *f*
resin basis Harzbasis *f*
resin bond Kunstharzbindung *f*
resin powder Harzpulver *nt*
resin solution Harzlösung *f*
resin suspension Harzsuspension *f*
resin varnish Harzfirnis *m*
resin-bonded asbestos floor covering Kunstharz-Asbest-Bodenbelag *m*

resin-bonded densified wood lamination Kunstharz-Pressholz-Erzeugnis *nt*
resist standhalten, aushalten, widerstehen
resist layer Resistenzschicht *f*
resistance Resistenz *f*, Widerstand *m*, Beständigkeit *f*
resistance against penetration by bullets durchschusshemmende Eigenschaft *f*
resistance butt welding Pressstumpfschweißen *nt*
resistance heat Widerstandswärme *f*
resistance lap seam welding Überlappnahtwiderstandsschweißung *f*
resistance membrane Widerstandsmembran *f*
resistance polarisation Widerstandspolarisation *f*
resistance projection welding Widerstandsbuckelschweißung *f*
resistance roller seam welding Widerstandsrollnahtschweißung *f*
resistance soldering machine Zangenlötmaschine *f*
resistance spot Widerstandspunkt *m*
resistance temperature detector Widerstandstemperaturfühler *m*
resistance to abrasion Schabefestigkeit *f*
resistance to caking Blockfestigkeit *f*
resistance to deflection Biegesteifigkeit *f*
resistance to deformation Formänderungswiderstand *m*
resistance to dynamic stresses Schwingungssteifigkeit *f*
resistance to environmental stress cracking Spannungsrissbeständigkeit *f*
resistance to erasure Radierfestigkeit *f*
resistance to fats Speisefettechtheit *f*
resistance to fire Brandsicherheit *f*
resistance to fuel Kraftstoffbeständigkeit *f*
resistance to heat Wärmefestigkeit *f*
resistance to impact Schlagbeständigkeit *f*
resistance to indentation Eindrückwiderstand *m*

resistance to internal ignition Ausbrennsicherheit f
resistance to loading Belastbarkeit f
resistance to motion Bewegungswiderstand m, Fahrwiderstand m
resistance to overturning Umkippfestigkeit f
resistance to paraffin Paraffinechtheit f
resistance to peeling Schälwiderstand m
resistance to rotting verrottungsbeständig
resistance to rusting Rostträgheit f
resistance to spittle Speichelechtheit f
resistance to staining Fleckenunempfindlichkeit f
resistance to stress crazing Spannungsrissbeständigkeit f
resistance to stripping Schälwiderstand m
resistance to stripping of the thread Abstreiffestigkeit f einer Schraube
resistance to sweat Schweißechtheit f
resistance to vibration Schwingungsfestigkeit f
resistance to warping Wölbwiderstand m
resistance to washing Abwaschfestigkeit f
resistance to wax Wachsechtheit f
resistance to wear Verschleißfestigkeit f, Abnutzungsfestigkeit f
resistance welding using rotating transformer Rolltransformatorschweißen nt
resistance welding using sliding contacts Schleifkontaktschweißen nt
resistance-welded seam weld widerstandsgeschweißte Liniennaht f
resistance-welded spaced spot weld widerstandsgeschweißte Punktnaht f
resistant resistent, widerstandsfähig, beständig
resistant heating Widerstandserwärmung f
resistant to abrasion abriebbeständig
resistant to bending biegesteif
resistant to deflection biegestarr
resistant to deformation formbeständig
resistant to glowing cigarettes zigarettenglutbeständig
resistant to leakage currents kriechstromsicher
resistant to warping verwindungssteif
resistant to wear verschleißfest
resisting force Widerstandskraft f
resistive load ohmsche Last f
resistor Widerstand m
resistor characteristic Widerstandskennlinie f
resistor motor Einphasenmotor m
resistance to fracture Bruchwiderstand m
resistance to twisting Verdrehungssteifigkeit f
resizing Nachprägen nt
resolution 1. Auflösung f, Zerlegung f, Auflösungsvermögen nt, Trennvermögen nt **2.** Granularität f
resolutions Vorsätze mpl
resolvable lösbar
resolve zerlegen, auflösen
resolver Funktionsgeber m
resonant cavity Resonator m
resonant circuit Schwingkreis m
resonator Resonator m
resource beschaffen, Betriebsmittel nt
resource data Betriebsmitteldaten pl
resource means base time Betriebsmittelgrundzeit f
resource means setting base time Betriebsmittelrüstgrundzeit f
resource means setting distribution time Betriebsmittelrüstverteilzeit f
resource means setting time Betriebsmittelrüstzeit f
resource run time Betriebsmittelausführungszeit f
resources demand Einsatzmittelbedarf m
resourcing Beschaffung f
respective entsprechend
respirator Mundschutz m
respiratory protection Atemschutz m
respond reagieren, antworten, ansprechen auf
response Ansprechen nt, Reaktion f, Verhalten nt, Antwort f

response delay Ansprechverzögerung *f*
response number Antwortnummer *f*
response pressure Ansprechdruck *m*
response probability Ansprechwahrscheinlichkeit *f*
response time Antwortzeit *f*, Reaktionszeit *f*, Ansprechzeit *f*
response unit Antwortgerät *nt*
responsibility Zuständigkeit *f*, Verantwortung *f*
responsible zuständig, verantwortlich
responsible person Verantwortlicher *m*
responsibleness Verantwortlichkeit *f*
responsivity Ansprechvermögen *nt*
resqueezing Nachdrücken *nt*
rest 1. Rest *m* 2. Auflage *f*, Aufsatz m 3. Ruhepause *f*, Ruhe *f*; rasten 4. Stillstand *m*
rest zone Ruhezone *f*
rest energy Ruheenergie *f*
rest on aufliegen, liegen auf
rest period Stillstandszeit *f*
rest position Endstellung *f*, Ruhelage *f*, Ruhestellung *f*
rest potential Ruhespannung *f*
restack umstapeln
restacking move Umstapelvorgang *m*
restacking time Umstapelzeit *f*
restamp umstempeln
restamping Umstempelung *f*
restart erneut beginnen, wieder anlaufen, wieder einschalten, Wiederanlauf *m*
re-start wiedereinschalten, Wiederanlauf *m*
restarting Wiederanlauf *m*, Wiederinbetriebnahme *f*, Wiedereinschalten *nt*
restorage Wiedereinlagerung *f*
restoration Wiederherstellung *f*
restore zurückstellen, wiederherstellen
restore power wieder einschalten
restoring force Rückstellkraft *f*
restoring spring Rückholfeder *f*
restraighten nachrichten
restraightening Nachrichten *nt*
restrain zurückhalten, sichern
restrain restrict einschränken
restraining rail Führungsschiene *f*
restraint Zwang *m*
restraint system Rückhaltesicherung *f*

restretch nachspannen
restretching Nachspannung *f*
restrict einengen, verengen, drosseln, begrenzen, beschränken
restricted eingeschränkt
restricted area Schutzzone *f*
restricted breathing schadensicher
restricted gate Punktausschnitt *m*
restricted guidance Zwangsführung *f*
restricted linear stopping power beschränktes lineares Bremsvermögen *nt*
restricted proof of competence kleiner Befähigungsnachweis *m*
restricted steering Zwangslenkung *f*; zwangsgelenkt
restricted to the rails schienengebunden
restricted tolerance eingeengte Toleranz *f*
restricted zone abgeschlossener Bereich *m*
restriction Einschränkung *f*, Beschränkung *f*, Verengung *f*, Einengung *f*, Drosselung *f*
restrictor Verdichterdüse *f*
restrictor principle of operation Drosselsystem *nt*
restrictor system Drosselanlage *f*
restrictor valve Drosselventil *nt*
restriking Nachschlagen *nt*
rest-time Pause *f*
rest-time regulation Pausenregelung *f*
result verursachen, sich auswirken, resultieren, führen zu; Resultat *nt*, Ergebnis *nt*
result aggregation Akkumulation *f*
result from resultieren aus
result of measurement Messergebnis *nt*
result side Ergebnisseite *f*
resultant Resultierende *f*; resultierend
resultant cutting direction Wirkrichtung *f*
resultant cutting force Gesamtspanungskraft *f*, resultierende Spanungskraft *f*
resultant cutting speed Wirkgeschwindigkeit *f*
resultant cutting speed angle Wirk-

richtungswinkel *m*
resultant force gesamtresultierende Schnittkraft *f*
results *pl* **of working** Arbeitsergebnisse *ntpl*
resume zusammenfassen; Zusammenfassung *f*
resurface wiederauftragen
retail 1. wieder verkaufen, weiterverkaufen 2. Einzelhandel *m*
retail forecast Verkaufsprognose *f*
retail price Widerverkaufspreis *m*
retail trade Handel *m*
retail warehouse Sortimentslager *nt*
retailer Einzelhändler *m*, Wiederverkäufer *m*
retailer's price Widerverkaufspreis *m*
retailer's stock Handelslager *nt*
retain sperren, halten, behalten, beibehalten, festhalten, zurückhalten, stauen
retainer Raste *f*
retaining effect Sicherungswirkung *f*
retaining element Sicherung *f*, Sicherungselement *nt*
retaining element with spring action federndes Sicherungselement *nt*
retaining nut Sicherungsmutter *f*
retaining pin Sicherungsnadel *f*
retaining ring Sicherungsring *m*
retaining ring with lug Sicherungsring *m* mit Lappen
retaining washer Sicherungsblech *nt*
retard verzögern, verlangsamen
retardation Verzögerung *f*, Drosselung *f*
retardation process Retardationsprozess *m*
retarding device Verzögerungsbremse *f*
retarding devices mechanische Bremsung *f*
retention lip Anschlagkante *f*
retention of position Halten *nt* der Position
retention period Verweildauer *f*
retentive remanent, nicht löschend, aufnahmefähig
retentive-type relay Haftrelais *nt*
retentivity Remanenz *f*
retest Nachprüfung *f*
retighten nachziehen
retool umstellen (auf), umrüsten, einspannen, neu rüsten
retooling Werkzeugumstellung *f*, Einspannen *nt*, Umrüsten *nt*
retract einfahren, einziehen, zurückziehen, zurücknehmen, rücklaufen
retractable einziehbar, zurückziehbar, einschiebbar
retractable C-fork C-Schubgabel *f*
retractable fork Schubgabel *f*
retractable mast Schubmast *m*
retracted eingefahren
retracting Einziehen *nt*
retraction Einfahren *nt*, Rücknahme *f*, Einzug *m*, Zurückziehen *nt*, Einziehen *nt*
retraction of milling head Fräserabhebung
retraction of the tool Meißelabhebung *f*
retractor Seilkürzer *m*
retraining spring Rückholfeder *f*
retreatment Nachbehandlung *f*
retrench Einsparungen machen
retrieval Abfrage *f*, Abförderung *f*, Auslagerung *f*, Entnahme *f*, Bergung *f*, Wiedergabe *f*, Auslagern *nt*, Ausfahren *nt*
retrieval cycle Auslagerspiel *nt*
retrieval frequency Entnahmehäufigkeit *f*
retrieval line Abführstrecke *f*
retrieval of layers Lagenentnahme *f*
retrieval order Auslagerauftrag *m*
retrieval point Auslagerstelle *f*
retrieval process Auslagervorgang *m*
retrieval station Auslagerstation *f*
retrieval time Ausfahrzeit *f*
retrieval unit Entnahmeeinheit *f*
retrieve abfördern, wiedergeben, abrufen, abfragen, auslagern, entnehmen, aufnehmen, abführen, ausfahren
retrieved quantity Abgangsmenge *f*
retriever head Zubringerkopf *m*
retrieving Aufnehmen *nt*
retrofit umrüsten
retrofitting Nachrüstung *f*
retrogress zurückschlagen
retrogress explosively knallend zurückschlagen
return Rückkehr *f*, Rückführung *f*,

Rücklieferung *f*, Rückstellung *f*, Umkehr *f*; umkehren, rücklaufen, zurücksenden
re-turn nachdrehen
return belt Untertrumm *nt*
return channel Ruckstromkanal *m*
return connection Rücklaufanschluss *m*
return flow inhibitor Rückflussverhinderer *m*
return journey Rückfahrt *f*
return line Rückflussleitung *f*
return material Rücklaufmaterial *nt*
return motion Rückwärtsbewegung *f*, Rückgang *m*, Rückstellung *f*
return motion device Rückholvorrichtung *f*
return path Rückweg *m*
return rolling action Rückwälzung *f*
return sheave Umlenkrad *nt*
return speed Rücklaufgeschwindigkeit *f*
return speed limitation Rücklaufbegrenzung *f*
return spring Rückfederung
return spring angle Rückfederungswinkel *m*
return stop Rücklaufsperre *f*
return stroke Rücklauf *m*, Rücklaufweg *m*, Rückhub *m*, Rückgang *m*, Leerhub *m*
return temperature Rücklauftemperatur *f*
return transport Rücktransport *m*
return travel Rücklauf *m*, Rückgang *m*, Rückhub *m*
return traverse Rückgang *m*
return trip Hin- und Rückfahrt *f*
return variable Rückführgröße *f*
returnable mehrweg
returnable pallet Dauerpalette *f*
return-circuit water Rücklaufwasser *nt*
returned zurückgesandt
returning Rückführung *f*
return-stroke interference Rückhubstörung *f*
reusability Tauschfähigkeit *f*
reusable wieder verwendbar, mehrweg
reusable container Mehrwegbehälter *m*
reuse wieder verwenden; Wiederverwendung *f*
reutilization Wiederverwendung *f*
reutilize wieder verwenden
reverberant sound field Hallfeld *nt*
reverberate reflektiert werden
reverberation room Hallraum *m*
reverberation room method Hallraumverfahren *nt*
reverberation time measurement Nachhallzeitmessung *f*
reversal Stornobuchung *f*
reversal Stornierung *f*, Stornobuchung *f*, Umsteuerung *f*, Umkehrung *f*, Wende *f*, Umsteuern *nt*, Wenden *nt*, Umwenden *nt*
reversal of direction Fahrtrichtungsumkehr *f*, Fahrtumkehrung *f*
reversal of forward direction Flussänderung *f*
reversal of polarity Polaritätsumkehr *f*
reversal of poles Polumkehrung *f*
reversal of the direction Richtungsumkehr *f*
reverse rückwärtig, rückwärts, umgekehrt; reversieren, umkehren, umsteuern, umkehren, wenden, umwenden, umdrehen, umschalten, rücklaufen, rückwärts bewegen, wechseln; Umkehr *f*, Rückwärtsgang *m*
reverse bend number Hin- und Herbiegezahl *f*
reverse bending Rückbiegen *nt*
reverse direction Rückwärtsfahren *nt*
reverse dog Umsteuerknagge *f*, Anschlag *m* zum Umsteuern
reverse gear Wendegetriebe *nt*
reverse image attachment Spiegelbildkopiereinrichtung *f*
reverse mirror Rückspiegel *m*
reverse mirror duplicating spiegelbildliches Nachformen *nt*
reverse motion Rückkehr *f*, Rücklauf *m*
reverse movement Rücklauf *m*
reverse polarity Verpolung *f*
reverse redrawing Stülpziehen *nt*
reverse roll coat method Walzenauftragsverfahren *nt*
reverse roll motion Rückwälzung *f*
reverse the polarity of umpolen
reverse torsion test Hin- und Rückver-

windeversuch *m*
reverse voltage Sperrspannung *f*
reversed bending testing machine Wechselbiegemaschine *f*
reversible reversibel, reversierbar, umkehrbar, umsteuerbar
reversible motor Reversiermotor *m*
reversible thermal expansion reversible Wärmedehnung *f*
reversing reversibel, reversierbar, reversierend; Reversieren *nt*, Umschalten *nt*, Umsteuern *nt*, Umkehrung *f*
reversing continuous conveyer Reversierstetigförderer *m*
reversing device Wender *m*
reversing entry Stornobuchung *f*
reversing lever Umschalthebel *m*, Umsteuerhebel *m*
reversing light Rückfahrscheinwerfer *m*
reversing mechanism Wendeherzgetriebe *nt*
reversing mill Reversierwalzwerk *nt*
reversing mill stand Reversierwalzgerüst *nt*, Umkehrwalzgerüst *nt*
reversing mode Reversierbetrieb *m*
reversing motor Reversiermotor *m*
reversing point of motion Bewegungsumkehrpunkt *m*
reversing station Umsetzstation *f*
reversing switch Umschalter *m*, Wender *m*, Stromwender *m*
reversing traverse Umsteuerung *f*
reversing wheel Umlenkrad *nt*
reversion Umkehrung *f*
reversion process Reversierverfahren *nt*
revision of the offer Angebotsüberarbeitung *f*
revolute pair Drehgelenk *nt*
revolution Umdrehung *f*, Drehung *f*
revolution counter Umdrehungszähler *m*
revolution of the wheel Radumdrehung *f*
revolution, number of ~ Drehzahl *f*
revolutions per minute (rpm) Umdrehung *f* pro Minute *f*, Drehzahl *f*
revolve sich drehen, umschalten, rotieren, umlaufen
revolve around kurbeln

revolving umlaufend, mitlaufend, rotierend
revolving table Drehtisch *m*
reweighing rückwägen
re-welding on the root side wurzelseitiges Nachscheißen *nt*
rework nacharbeiten; Nacharbeit *f*, Umarbeiten *nt*
rheogram Fließkurve *f*
rheological condition rheologischer Zustand *m*
rheostat Regelwiderstand *m*
rhoboidal rautenförmig
rhomb Raute *f*
rhomb shaped rautenförmig
rhombic rautenförmig
rhombus Raute *f*
rhythm Rhythmus *m*
rhythmical force variations rhythmisch unterschiedliche Krafteinwirkung *f*
rhythmically varying force rhythmisch unterschiedliche Krafteinwirkung *f*
rib Rippe *f*
ribbed profiliert, verrippt
ribbed base verrippter Boden *m*
ribbed mat profilierte Matte *f*
ribbing Verrippung *f*
ribbon chip Bandspan *m*
ricochet abprallen, Abprall *m*
riddle schüren
riddling arrangement Schüreinrichtung *f*
ride fahren
rider Fahrer *m*, Mitfahrer *m*
rider control Mitfahrersteuerung *f*
rider-controlled mit Mitfahrer
rider-controlled truck Flurförderzeug *nt* mit Fahrersitz, Flurförderzeug *nt* mit Fahrerstand
ridge Grat *m*, Furche *f*, Rille *f*, Riefe *f*, fasenartiger Anschliff *m*; riefen
ridge left by the tool Bearbeitungsriefe *f*
ridged thread gefurchtes Gewinde *nt*
ridgeless riefenlos
riffle furchen, riffeln
rifle drill Gewehrlaufbohrer *m*
rift Spalte *f*

rig Brennstrecke *f*
rig pin Absteckstift *m*
right 1. rechts 2. richtig
right- and left-hand helix cutter Fräser *m* mit Pfeilverzahnung
right angle rechter Winkel *m*
right angle parting-off tool Innenstechdrehmeißel *m*
right angles to quer zu
right angularity Rechtwinkligkeit *f*
right bracket Klammer *f* zu
right flank Rechtsflanke *f*
right hand rechtsseitig, rechtssteigend
right hand path of contact Rechtsflankeneingriffslinie *f*
right most maximum rechtes Maximum *nt*
right of access Zugangsberechtigung *f*
right of way Vorfahrt *f*
right side rechte Seite *f*
right to access Zugriffsrecht *nt*
right to admission Zugangsberechtigung *f*
right-angle head Querhobelsupport *m*
right-angled rechtwinklig
right-bent tool gebogener rechter Meißel *m*
right-cut rechtsschneidend
right-cut milling cutter rechtsschneidender Fräser *m*
right-cut tool rechter Meißel *m*, Rechtsmeißel *m*
right-hand column rechter Ständer *m*
right-hand cutoff tool rechter Stechmeißel *m*
right-hand cutting rechtsschneidend
right-hand cutting tool rechter Meißel *m*, Rechtsmeißel *m*, rechter Drehmeißel *m*
right-hand flank profile Rechtsflankenprofil *nt*
right-hand helical cutting edge Schneide *f* mir Rechtsdrall
right-hand helical tooth system Rechtsschrägverzahnung *f*
right-hand helix screw Rechtsschraube *f*, Rechtsdrall *m*
right-hand involute Rechtsevolvente *f*
right-hand milling cutter rechtsschneidender Fräser *m*

right-hand motion Rechtslauf *m*
right-hand parting tool rechter Stechmeißel *m*
right-hand pitch Rechtsteilung *f*
right-hand rotation Rechtsdrehung *f*
right-hand roughing tool rechter Schruppmeißel *m*
right-hand side rechte Seite *f*
right-hand side tool rechter Seitenmeißel *m*
right-hand side-cutting tool rechter Seitenmeißel *m*
right-hand spiral Rechtsdrall *m*
right-hand spiral-tooth milling cutter Fräser *m* mit rechtsgängiger Spiralverzahnung
right-hand teeth rechtssteigende Verzahnung *f*
right-hand thread Rechtsgewinde *nt*
right-hand tool rechter Meißel *m*, Rechtsmeißel *m*
right-hand tooth surface Rechtsflanke *f*
right-hand turning tool rechter Drehmeißel *m*, rechtsschneidender Drehmeißel *m*
right-hand version Rechtsausführung *f*
right-handed rechtssteigend
right-handed helical motion Rechtsschraubbewegung *f*
right-handed rotating rechtsläufig
right-offset cutting tool abgesetzter rechter Seitenmeißel *m*
right-offset tool abgesetzter rechter Seitenmeißel *m*
rightwards nach rechts
rigid fest, steif, starr, stabil, formstabil
rigid cellular product harter Schaumstoff *m*
rigid container formstabiles Packmittel *nt*
rigid container denester Entstapelungsmaschine *f* für formstabile Packmittel
rigid container orienter Orientierungsmaschine *f* für formstabile Packmittel
rigid container sealing machine Verschließmaschine *f* für formstabile Packmittel

rigid container single liner Vereinzelungsmaschine *f* für formstabile Packmittel
rigid container unscrambler Ausrichtmaschine *f* für formstabile Packmittel
rigid double-column planing machine Zweiständerstarrhobelmaschine *f*
rigid gear hobbing machine Starrwälzfräsmaschine *f*
rigid line Rohrleitung *f*
rigid milling machine Starrfräsmaschine *f*
rigid polyvinyl chloride hartes Polyvinylchlorid *nt*
rigid PVC hartes Polyvinylchlorid *nt*, PVC *nt* hart
rigid restraint starre Einspannung *f*
rigidity Festigkeit *f*, Starrheit *f*, Steifigkeit *f*, Eigensteife *f*, Eigensteifigkeit *f*, Formsteifigkeit *f*, Stabilität *f*
rigidity design Aussteifungskonstruktion *f*
rim Felge *f*, Rand *m*, Radkranz *m*
rim hole Durchzug *m*
rim hole height Durchzughöhe *f*
rim hole height ratio Durchzugverhältnis *nt*
rinsing liquid Spülflüssigkeit *f*
ring 1. Ring *m* 2. überschwingen
ring analysis Ringanalyse *f*
ring bending tensile strength Ringbiegezugfestigkeit *f*
ring conveyance Ringverkehr *m*
ring crush resistance Ringstauchwiderstand *m*
ring eye method Ringösenverfahren *nt*
ring gasket Dichtungsring *m*
ring gate Ringanschnitt *m*
ring gauge Lehrring *m*
ring gear Hohlrad *nt*, Zahnkranz *m*
ring guidance Ringführung *f*
ring guide Ringführung *f*
ring lapping Außenrundläppen *nt*
ring locked union Einschraubstutzen *m* mit Ringsicherung
ring rolling Ringwalzen *nt*
ring spanner Ringmaulschlüssel *m*
ring tensile test Ringzugversuch *m*

ring tensile test specimen Ringzugprobe *f*
ring test piece Ringprobe *f*
ring traffic Ringverkehr *m*
ring wheel Schleifring *m*
ringing Überschwingen *nt*
ringing frequency Überschwingerfrequenz *f*
ring-shaped ringförmig
rinse spülen, abspülen
rinsing Spülung *f*
rinsing medium Spülmittel *nt*
rip reißen, zerreißen
ripen reifen
ripping Zerreißen *nt*
ripple Welligkeit *f*
rise zunehmen, erhöhen, ansteigen, steigen; Anstieg *m*, Erhöhung *f*, Steigung *f*, Steigen *nt*
rise and fall Auf- und Abbewegung *f*
rise-and-fall fixed-bed milling machine Senkrechtfräsmaschine *f* mit senkrecht beweglicher Frässpindel
rise-and-fall miller Senkrechtfräsmaschine *f* mit senkrecht beweglicher Frässpindel, Planfräsmaschine *f* mit Hebe- und Senkeinrichtung für die Spindel
rise-and-fall milling attachment Senkrechtfräseinrichtung *f*
rise in pressure Druckanstieg *m*, Drucksteigerung *f*
rise per tooth Überhöhung *f* von Zahn zu Zahn
riser Setzstufe *f*, Steiger *m*
riser pattern Steigermodell *nt*
riser stick Steigerholz *nt*
rising casting steigendes Gießen *nt*
rising dimensioning sequence steigende Bemaßung *f*
rising gate Steiger *m*
rising hole vent Steiger *m*
rising table Wipptisch *m*
risk Risiko *nt*; riskieren
risk assessment Risikobewertung *f*
risk estimation Risikoabschätzung *f*, Risikoeinschätzung *f*
risk management Risikomanagement *nt*
risk of accident Unfallgefahr *f*

risk of fracture Bruchgefahr *f*
risk of injury Verletzungsgefahr *f*
risk of scoring Fressgefährdung *f*
risk of silting up Verschlammungsgefahr *f*
risk of stumbling Stolpergefahr *f*
risk reduction Risikoverringerung *f*
rive spalten
rivet Niet *m*; nieten, vernieten
rivet closing machine Nietverschließmaschine *f*
rivet header Nietkopfmacher *m*
rivet pin Nietstift *m*
rivet set for flush head rivets Flachdöpper *m* für Senknicte
riveted assembly drawing Nietgruppenzeichnung *f*
riveted joint Vernietung *f*
riveter Nietmaschine *f*, Nieter *m*
riveting machine Nietmaschine *f*
riveting press Nietpresse *f*
riveting scale Nietzunder *m*
road Strecke *f*, Fahrbahn *f*
road debris Fahrbahnteile *ntpl*
road drain Straßenablauf *m*
road tar discharge apparatus Straßenteerausflussgerät *nt*
road traffic Straßenverkehr *m*
road wheels Fahrzeugräder *ntpl*
roadway Förderstrecke *f*
roasting oven Räucheranlage *f*
Roberts' theorem Robertsscher Satz *m*
robin test Ringversuch *m*
robot Roboter *m*
robot control Robotersteuerung *f*
robot depalletizer Depalettierroboter *m*
robot operation Roboterbedienung *f*
robot pallet stretch wrapper Robotpalettenstretchwickler *m*
robot palletizer Palettierroboter *m*
robotics Robotertechnik *f*, Robotereinsatz *m*
robust robust, stabil
robustness Robustheit *f*
rock rütteln, erschüttern, schwingen, schwanken, wippen
rocker Wippe *f*, Schwinge *f*
rocker arm Kurbelschwinge *f*, Schwingarm *m*

rocking Schwingung *f*
rocking arm Schwingungsarm *m*
rocky sub-base felsiger Untergrund *m*
rod Stange *f*, Strang *m*, Stab *m*
rod assembly Gestänge *nt*
rod electrode arc strike Stabelektrodenzündstelle *f*
rod electrode core wire Stabelektroden-Kerndraht *m*
rod electrode with alloy core rod Stabelektrode *f* mit legiertem Kernstab
rod extrusion Strangpressen *nt* von Strängen mit vollem Querschnitt
rod extrusion with action media Strangpressen *nt* mit Wirkmedien
rod extrusion with rigid tool Strangpressen *nt* mit starrem Werkzeug
rod material Stabmaterial *nt*
rod-shaped stabförmig
rod-shaped product stabförmiges Erzeugnis *nt*
roll 1. rollen, abrollen, wälzen, umbördeln; Rolle *f*, Wirbeln *nt* 2. *(Gewinde)* drücken
roll bar Überrollbügel *m*
roll beading Walzsicken *nt*
roll bed Rollenteppich *m*
roll bed conveyor Rollenteppich *m*
roll bending Walzbiegen *nt*
roll body Wälzkörper *m*
roll cart Rollenwagen *m*
roll clamp Rollenklammer *f*
roll down abrollen
roll down zone Abrollzone *f*
roll draw bending to shape in a multiple-roll unit Walzziehbiegen *nt*
roll drawing Walzziehen *nt*
roll drawing of bars Walzziehen *nt* von Stäben
roll drawing of hollow items Walzziehen *nt* von Hohlkörpern
roll drawing of solid items Walzziehen *nt* von Vollkörpern
roll drawing of strip/sheet Walzziehen *nt* von Bändern/Blechen
roll drawing of wire Walzziehen *nt* von Draht
roll drawing over floating mandrel *(Dorn)* Walzziehen *nt* über losen Stopfen

roll drawing over stationary mandrel *(Dorn)* Walzziehen *nt* über festen Stopfen
roll drawing over travelling (live) rod Walzziehen *nt* über mitlaufende Stange
roll feed device Walzenvorschubapparat *m*
roll flanging Walzbördeln *nt*
roll forming to shape Walzprofilieren *nt*
roll grinding Walzenschleifen *nt*
roll lifting cart Rollenhubwagen *m*
roll main time Walzhauptzeit
roll motion Wälzung *f*, Wälzvorgang *m*
roll neck milling machine Walzenzapfenfräsmaschine *f*
roll off abrollen
roll on anrollen, überrollen
roll opening Kaliber *nt*
roll out herausrollen
roll over überrollen
roll over protective structure Überrollschutz *m*
roll pallet Rollpalette *f*
roll pass Kaliber *nt*
roll pressure Walzdruck *m*
roll principle Walzprinzip *nt*
roll relatively to one another gegeneinander abwälzen
roll rounding Walzrunden *nt* zu zylindrischen Werkstücken
roll seam welding Rollennahtschweißen *nt*
roll straightening Walzrichten *nt*
roll torque Walzdrehmoment
roll turning lathe Walzendrehmaschine *f*
roll up aufrollen
roll upender Rollenkippklammer *f*
roll work Wälzarbeit *f*
roll wrapping machine Rolleneinschlagmaschine *f*
roll-drawing of hollow items without central tool Hohlwalzziehen *nt*
rolled gewalzt
rolled thread gerolltes Gewinde *nt*
rolled-in groove eingewalzte Rille *f*
roll-end machine Abflächmaschine *f* für Walzenstirnseiten

roller Walze *f*, Rolle *f*
roller bearing Rollenlager *nt*, Walzenlager *nt*, Wälzlager *nt*
roller bearing friction Wälzlagerreibung *f*
roller blind single-way light barrier Vorhangeinweglichtschranke *f*
roller blind type flap valve Rollladenklappe *f*
roller bracket Rollenschelle *f*
roller chain Rollenkette *f*
roller chain conveyor Rollenkettenförderer *m*
roller channel Rollenleiste *f*
roller circulating guidance Rollenumlaufführung *f*
roller clearance Rollenspiel *nt*
roller conveyor Rollenförderer *m*, Rollengang *m*
roller conveyor frame Rollengestell *nt*
roller counter Rollenzählwerk *nt*
roller crushing attachment Rollprofileinrichtung *f*, Rollprofiliereinrichtung *f*
roller discharge Rollenauslauf *m*
roller follower Fühlerwalze *f*
roller friction Rollreibung *f*
roller limit switch Rollenendschalter *m*
roller marking Wälzprägen *nt*
roller mechanical chain Rollenkette *f*
roller rail Laufschiene *f*, Rollenschiene *f*
roller ring Rollenkranz *m*
roller ring bearing Rollenkranzlagerung *f*
roller slide Schlitten *m* mit Rollenführung
roller spinning Drückwalzen *nt*, Reckdrücken *nt*
roller spinning over conical mandrel Drückwalzen *nt* über kegeligen Dorn
roller spinning over cylindrical mandrel Drückwalzen *nt* über zylindrischen Dorn
roller table Rollentisch *m*
roller toothed gear system Rollenverzahnung *f*
roller track Rollenschiene *f*
roller truer Abrichtrolle *f*
roller type chain Rollenkette *f*
roller vane pumping set Rollenzellenpumpenaggregat *nt*

roller drive Rollenantrieb *m*
roller-flight conveyor Rollenkettenförderer *m*
roller-stamp prägewalzen
rolling Rollen *nt*, Wälzen *nt*, Umstürzen *nt*, Umbördeln *nt*
rolling action Wälzung *f*, Wälzen *nt*
rolling apart Auseinanderrollen *nt* von Rohrstangen
rolling axis Wälzachse *f*
rolling bearing Wälzlager *nt*
rolling bearing grease test rig Wälzlagerfettprüfmaschine *f*
rolling capacity Wälzmöglichkeit *f*
rolling circle Rollkreis *m*
rolling circular shapes Scheibenwalzen *nt*
rolling contact bearing Wälzlager *nt*
rolling drag Rollwiderstand *m*
rolling element Wälzkörper *m*
rolling force Walzkraft, Rollkraft *f*
rolling friction Rollreibung *f*
rolling gear transmission Wälzgetriebe *nt*
rolling hole Walzloch *nt*
rolling inscription Walzaufschrift *f*
rolling mark Walzzeichen *nt*
rolling member Rollenkörper *m*
rolling mill table Rollengang *m*
rolling motion Abwälzung *f*, Wälzbewegung *f*, Wälzung *f*, Abrollen *nt*
rolling of bars/wire Walzen *nt* von Stäben/Draht
rolling of multiple-spline shafts Walzen *nt* von Vielnutwellen
rolling of sectional bars Walzen *nt* von Profilstäben
rolling of strip/sheet Walzen *nt* von Band/Blech
rolling of tubes without internal tool Walzen *nt* von Rohren ohne Innenwerkzeug
rolling on Anrollen *nt*
rolling of square tubes Walzen *nt* von Vierkantrollen
rolling over Überrollen *nt*
rolling resistance Rollwiderstand *m*, Fahrwiderstand *m*
rolling ring drive Rollringgetriebe *nt*
rolling ring mechanism Rollringgetriebe *nt*
rolling speed Walzgeschwindigkeit
rolling type gear pair Wälzgetrieberadpaar *nt*
rolling up Aufrollen *nt*
rolling worm Walzschnecke *f*
roll-motion guidance Wälzführung *f*
roll-motion transmission Wälzgetriebe *nt*
roll-on capping machine Anrollverschließmaschine *f*
rollover board process Wendeplattenverfahren *nt*
roll-over fixture Wendevorrichtung *f*
roll-over station Wendestation *f*
roll-shaped rundstangenförmig
roof Dach *nt*
roof cover Dachabdeckung *f*
roof fan Dachventilator *m*
roof in überdachen
roof of the hall Hallendach *nt*
roof over überdachen
roof sealing strip Dachdichtungsbahn *f*
roof stress Dachlast *f*
roofed überdacht
roofing Überdachung *f*
room Freiraum *m*, Raum *m*
room volume Raumvolumen *nt*
room air conditioner Raumklimagerät *nt*
room air temperature Raumlufttemperatur *f*
room heating appliance Raumheizgerät *nt*
room height Raumhöhe *f*
room humidity regulator Rauchfeuchteregler *m*
room lighting Raumbeleuchtung *f*
room plan Raumplan *m*
room saving Raumersparnis *f*
room-saving platzsparend
root 1. Wurzel *f* **2.** Zahnfuß *m*
root angle Fußkegelwinkel *m*
root bearing Zahnfußtragfähigkeit *f*
root circle Fußkreis *m*
root clearance 1. Spitzenspiel *nt* **2.** *(Verzahnung)* Spiel *nt* an der Zahnwurzel
root clearance diameter Einstichdurchmesser *m*

root concavity Wurzelrückfall *m*, Wurzelkerbe *f*
root cone Fußkegel *m*
root cone apex Fußkegelspitze *f*
root diameter Fußkreisdurchmesser *m*, Kerndurchmesser *m* von Zahngrund zu Zahngrund
root fusion Erfassung *f* der Wurzel
root gap Stegabstand *m*
root mean square ripple factor effektiver Welligkeitsgehalt *m*
root mean square value Effektivwert *m*
root of a gear tooth Zahnfuß *m*
root of a thread Gewindegrund *m*
root of the tooth Zahnfuß *m*, Zahngrund *m*
root overlap Schweißgutüberlauf *m*
root point Fußpunkt *m*, Wurzelpunkt *m*
root radius 1. *(Gewinde)* Radius *m* am Gewindegrund **2.** *(Verzahnung)* Zahngrundabrundung *f*
root radiusing surface Fußrundungsfläche *f*
root radiusing Fußrundung *f*
root relief Fußrücknahme *f*
root rounding Fußrundung *f*
root space width Zahnfußlückenweite *f*
root surface Fußfläche *f*, Fußmantelfläche *f*
root tooth trace Fußflankenlinie *f*
root toroid Fußkehlfläche *f*
root-mean square average (rms) Wurzel *f* aus dem Mittelwert der Quadrate
root-mean-square quadratischer Mittelwert *m*
root-rejecting substance wurzelabweisender Stoff *m*
root-run welder Wurzelschweißer *m*
roots vacuum booster Wälzkolbenvakuumpumpe *f*
rope Strick *m*, Seil *nt*, Strang *m*
rope down abseilen
rope drive Seilantrieb *m*, Seiltrieb *m*
rope drum Seiltrommel *f*
rope ladder Strickleiter *f*
rope lift Seilhub *m*
rope lock Seilzugsicherung *f*
rope locking device Seilzugsicherung *f*
rope pulley Seilrolle *f*
rope termination Seilendbefestigung *f*
rope winch Seilwinde *f*
rope-down device Abseileinrichtung *f*
rose Brauseauslauf *m*
rose bearing Schwenkkugellager *nt*
rotameter principle Schwebekörperprinzip *nt*
rotary umlaufend, drehend, drehbar, rotierend
rotary abrasion test Rundscheuerversuch *m*
rotary boring tool Drehbohrmeißel *m*
rotary broaching Rundräumen *nt*
rotary button Drehknopf *m*
rotary cam and profile milling machine Rundtischkurven- und -profilfräsmaschine *f*
rotary cam miller Rundtischkurvenfräsmaschine *f*
rotary cam milling machine Rundtischkurvenfräsmaschine *f*
rotary continuous miller Rundtischfräsautomat *m*
rotary current Drehstromanschluss *m*
rotary cutter Schneidmühle *f*
rotary cutting dynamometer (RCD) rotierendes Spanungsdynamometer *nt* (oder Spanungskraftmesser *m*)
rotary cutting motion kreisende Schnittbewegung *f*, rotierende Schnittbewegung *f*
rotary distributor Drehverteiler *m*
rotary drilling Drehbohren *nt*
rotary drum miller Fräsmaschine *f* mit Drehtrommel
rotary drum milling machine Trommelfräsmaschine *f*
rotary encoder codierte Drehgeber *mpl*
rotary evaporator Rotationsverdampfer *m*
rotary feed Rundvorschub *m*
rotary feed motion Drehbewegung *f*
rotary field Drehfeld *nt*
rotary file Elektrofeile *f*
rotary indexing machine Rundschaltmaschine *f*
rotary lapping wheel rotierende Läpp-

scheibe *f*
rotary miller Rundlauffräsmaschine *f*, Rundfräsmaschine *f*
rotary milling Rundfräsen *nt*, Rundlauffräsen *nt*
rotary milling attachment Rundfräseinrichtung *f*
rotary milling machine Drehtischfräsmaschine *f*, Rundtischprofilfräsmaschine *f*, Rundlauffräsmaschine *f*, Rundfräsmaschine *f*, Senkrechtfräsmaschine *f* mit Rundtisch
rotary milling operation Rundfräsen *nt*, Rundfräsverfahren *nt*
rotary motion Drehbewegung *f*
rotary movement Umlaufbewegung *f*, Rotationsbewegung *f*
rotary piercing of tubes over a plug Walzen *nt* von Rohren über Stange
rotary piston Kreiskolben *m*
rotary piston drill Rundlaufbohrmaschine *f*
rotary piston pump Kreiskolbenpumpe *f*
rotary piston vacuum pump Drehkolbenvakuumpumpe *f*
rotary planer Endfräsmaschine *f*
rotary plate Drehteller *m*
rotary pointing Verjüngen *nt* von Vollkörpern
rotary profile miller Rundtischfräsmaschine *f*, Rundtischprofilfräsmaschine *f*
rotary profile milling machine Rundtischfräsmaschine *f*, Rundtischprofilfräsmaschine *f*
rotary shaft seal Wellendichtring *m*
rotary shave cutter Schabrad *nt*
rotary slitting press Streifenschere *f*
rotary station Drehstation *f*, Umlaufstation *f*
rotary straightening Umlaufbiegen *nt*
rotary surface broaching Außenrundräumen *nt*
rotary swaging Formrundkneten *nt*, Rundkneten *nt*
rotary swaging by the high-feed method Rundkneten *nt* im Vorschubverfahren
rotary swaging by the infeed method Rundkneten *nt* von Einstechverfahren
rotary swaging of external shapes Formrundkneten *nt* von Außenformen
rotary swaging of internal shapes Formrundkneten *nt* von Innenformen
rotary switch Drehschalter *m*
rotary table Rundtisch *m*, Drehtisch *m*, Drehteller *m*, Rundsupport *m*
rotary table feed Tischrundbewegung *f*
rotary table machine Rundtischmaschine *f*
rotary table miller Rundfräsmaschine *f*, Rundlauffräsmaschine *f*, Rundtischfräsmaschine *f*
rotary table milling machine Rundfräsmaschine *f*, Rundlauffräsmaschine *f*, Rundtischfräsmaschine *f*, Fräsmaschine *f* mit Rundtisch
rotary unit Drehregal *nt*
rotary worktable Rundtisch *m*
rotary-formed milling cutter Kreismesserkopf *m*
rotary-table miller with vertical spindle Rundlaufsenkrechtfräsmaschine *f*, Rundtischfräsmaschine *f*
rotary-table milling Rundfräsen *nt*, Rundlauffräsen *nt*
rotary-table milling machine Rundtischprofilfräsmaschine *f*
rotary-type miller Rundtischprofilfräsmaschine *f*
rotatable drehbar
rotatable restraint drehbare Einspannung *f*
rotatably mounted worm wheel drehbar gehaltenes Schneckenrad
rotate rotieren, umlaufen, drehen
rotate on the spot drehen auf der Stelle, wenden auf der Stelle
rotating umlaufend, mitlaufend, schwenkbar, rotierend, drehbar; Drehen *nt*
rotating anode X-ray tube Drehanodenröntgenröhre *f*
rotating arm Wickelarm *m*
rotating cage Drehkorb *m*
rotating chamber Rotationskammer *f*
rotating chamber filling machine Rotationskammerfüllmaschine *f*
rotating clamp rotierende Klammer *f*

rotating device (RBG) Drehantrieb *m*
rotating diaphragm Lochblende *f*
rotating element Drehteil *nt*
rotating field Drehfeld *nt*
rotating flasher Rundumleuchte *f*
rotating fork Drehgabel *f*
rotating fork assembly Drehgabeleinrichtung *f*
rotating fork device Drehantrieb *m* der Gabeln
rotating handle Kurbel *f*
rotating handle hydraulic pump kurbelbetriebene Hydraulikpumpe *f*
rotating head Drehknopf *m*, Drehgerät *nt*
rotating joint Wellendurchführung *f*, Wellenspalte *f*
rotating link Kurbel *f*
rotating mast Schwenkmast *m*
rotating mast lateral and front stacking truck Schwenkmastdreiseitenstapler *m*
rotating mast side loading lift truck Schwenkmastdreiseitenstapler *m*
rotating mechanism Schwenkeinrichtung *f*
rotating mirror Drehspiegel *m*
rotating mode Wendebetrieb *m*
rotating motion *(Kran)* Schwenkbewegung *f*
rotating operator seat schwenkbarer Fahrerplatz *m*
rotating pallet stretch wrapper Drehtellerpalettenstretchwickler *m*
rotating pick-off device Greifeinrichtung *f*
rotating separator Rotationsabscheider *m*
rotating table Rundtisch *m*
rotation Rotation *f*, Rundlauf *m*, Drehbewegung *f*, Umlaufbewegung *f*, Umdrehung *f*, Drehung *f*, Drehen *nt*
rotation axis Drehachse *f*
rotation flexometer Rotationsflexometer *nt*
rotation forks drehbare Gabeln *fpl*
rotation gear Drehwerk *nt*
rotation picker Rotationsabnehmer *m*
rotation speed Rotationsgeschwindigkeit *f*

rotational rotatorisch
rotational and translational movement Dreh-Hub-Bewegung *f*
rotational copy milling Rotationsnachformfräsen *nt*
rotational motion Drehbewegung *f*, Rotationsbewegung *f*
rotational speed Umlaufgeschwindigkeit *f*, Drehzahl *f*
rotational variable differential transformer rotatorisch variabler Differenzialtransformator *m*
rotationally symmetrical rotationssymmetrisch
rotator Drehgerät *nt*
rotogravure paper Detailzeichenpapier *nt*, Transparentzeichenpapier *nt*
rotor Läufer *m*, Anker *m*, Rotor *m*
rotor circuit Läuferkreis *m*
rotor coil Läuferspule *f*
rotor current Läuferstrom *m*
rotor field Läuferfeld *nt*
rotor groove Läufernut *f*
rotor inductance Läuferinduktivität *f*
rotor iron Läufereisen *nt*
rotor resistance Läuferwiderstand *m*
rotor shaft Läuferwelle *f*
rotor shaft winding Läuferwellenwicklung *f*
rotor slot milling machine Rotornutenfräsmaschine *f*
rotor voltage Läuferspannung *f*
rotor winding Läuferwicklung *f*
rotor-integrated gear rotorintegriertes Getriebe *nt*
rot-proof verrottungsbeständig
rough vorschruppen, schruppen, aufrauen, rau machen; uneben, höckrig, wellig, grob, rau, roh
rough adjustment Grobeinstellung *f*
rough casting dimension Rohgussmaß *nt*
rough cutter Vorschneider *m*, Vorfräser *m*
rough diameter Ausgangsdurchmesser *m*
rough diamond Formdiamant *m*
rough dimension Rohmaß *nt*
rough drilling diameter Vorbohrdurchmesser *m*

rough eroding Schrupperodieren *nt*
rough finish vorarbeiten
rough form Grobgestalt *f*
rough grind grobschleifen
rough grinding Schruppschleifen *nt*
rough grinding machine Grobschleifmaschine *f*
rough honing Vorhonen *nt*
rough lapping Vorläppen *nt*
rough layout Groblayout *nt*
rough machinability Schruppbearbeitbarkeit *f*
rough machining Vorbearbeitung *f*, Schruppbearbeitung *f*, Grobzerspanung *f*
rough measurement Grobmessen *nt*
rough milling Vorfräsen *nt*, Schruppfräsen *nt*
rough milling attachment Vorfräseinrichtung *f*
rough milling spindle Schruppfrässpindel *f*, Vorfrässpindel *f*
rough planing Schrupphobeln *nt*, Vorhobeln *nt*
rough planning Grobplanung *f*
rough positioning Grobeinstellung *f*
rough thread with fissured flanks Rauhgewinde *nt* mit gerissenen Flanken
rough turning Schruppdrehen *nt*, Schruppen *nt*, Raudrehen *nt*
rough work unbearbeitetes Werkstück *nt*
rough-bore vorbohren
rough-boring Schruppbohren *nt*
rough-cut vorfräsen
roughen aufrauen
rougher Schruppräumwerkzeug *nt*
roughing Vorbearbeitung *f*, Schrupparbeit *f*, Schruppen *nt*
roughing broach Schruppräumwerkzeug *nt*
roughing by generation Vorschruppen *nt*
roughing cherrying operation Vorfräsen *nt* runder Gesenkformen
roughing cut Schruppspan *m*, Schruppschnitt *m*
roughing cutter 1. Schruppmeißel *m*, Schruppstahl *m* **2.** *(fräsen)* Vorfräser *m*,
Schruppfräser *m* **3.** *(Verzahnung)* Vorverzahnwerkzeug *nt*
roughing grind Schruppschliff *m*
roughing hob Schruppfräser *m*, Schruppwälzfräser *m*, Vorwälzfräser *m*
roughing operation Schrupparbeit *f*, Schruppschnitt *m*, spanende Vorbearbeitung *f*
roughing pass Schruppdurchgang *m*
roughing speed Schruppgeschwindigkeit *f*
roughing tool Schruppwerkzeug *nt*, Vorschneidmeißel *m*, Schruppmeißel *m*, Schruppstahl *m*
roughing tooth Schruppzahn *m*, Vorschneidzahn *m*
roughing work Schrupparbeit *f*, schruppen
roughly wound annular coil wildgewickelte Ringspule *f*
roughly wound coil wildgewickelte Spule *f*
rough-machine vorbearbeiten, schruppen
rough-mill vorfräsen
roughness Rauheit *f*, Rauhigkeit *f*
roughness height Rautiefe *f*
roughness height rating Rautiefenbemessung *f*
roughness parameter Rauheitsmessgröße *f*
roughness peak Rauheitsspitze *f*
roughness standard Raunormal *nt*
roughness width Rillenabstand *m*
roughnesses Rauheiten *fpl*
rough-plane vorhobeln
rough-routing Schruppfräsen *nt*
rough-service stoßfest
rough-terrain geländegängig
rough-terrain truck geländegängiger Stapler *m*
rough-turn vordrehen
round rund; abrunden
round bar Rundeisen *nt*, Rundstab *m*, Rundstange *f*
round bar vice Schraubstock *m* für rundes Stangenmaterial
round bars Rundmaterial *nt*
round boring tool Rundmeißel *m*
round broach pull type Ziehräumna-

del *f* mit kreisförmigen Querschnitt
round column Rundsäule *f*
round column design Kastenständerbauart *f*
round column drill Rundsäulenbohrmaschine *f*, Säulenbohrmaschine *f*
round column drilling machine Rundsäulenbohrmaschine *f*, Radialbohrmaschine *f* mit runder Säule, Auslegerbohrmaschine *f* mit runder Säule
round column mast Säule *f*
round column radial drill Radialbohrmaschine *f* mit runder Säule, Schwenkbohrmaschine *f* mit runder Säule, Auslegerbohrmaschine *f* mit runder Säule
round component Rundkörper *m*
round corner Hohlkehle *f*
round dryer Rundtrockner *m*
round grip arm Rundgreifer *m*
round head grooved pin Halbrundkerbnagel *m*
round head self-piercing screw Halbrundnagelschraube *f*
round head thread cutting screw Halbrundschneidschraube *f*
round head with oval neck Halbrundkopf *m* mit Ovalansatz
round hole Rundloch *nt*
round hole perforation Rundlochperforation *f*
round laminated moulded section Rundumpressung *f*
round magnet Rundmagnet *m*
round nose turning tool Runddrehmeißel *m*
round nut with set pin hole inside Kreuzlochmutter *f*
round off *(math.)* runden
round pole rotor Rundstabläufer *m*
round rod Rundstab *m*, Rundstange *f*
round roll Rundwalzen
round sealing ring Runddichtring *m*
round stock Rundmaterial *nt*
round table Rundtisch *m*
round table indexing automatic Rundtischschaltautomat *m*
round thread Rundgewinde *nt*
round thread with clearance Rundgewinde *nt* mit Spiel
round thread with flat flank Rundgewinde *nt* mit flacher Flanke
round thread with increased bearing depth Rundgewinde *nt* mit großer Tragtiefe
round thread with steep flank Rundgewinde *nt* mit steiler Flanke
round turret head Trommel *f*
round up aufrunden
round welding rod Rundschweißstab *m*
round worktable Rundtisch *m*
roundabout Karussell *nt*
roundabout store Karusselllager *nt*
round-column-type radial Rundsäulenbohrmaschine *f*
round-die thread rolling Gewindewalzen *nt*
rounded Eckenrundung *f*
rounded cutting edge gerundete Schneide *f*
rounded cutting edge radius Radius *m* der gerundeten Schneide
rounded transition kreisbogenförmiger Überhang *m*
rounded trapezoidal screw thread gerundetes Trapezgewinde *nt*
round-end cutter Fräser *m* mit runder Stirn
round-ended feather key rundstirnige Passfeder
round-hole broaching Räumen *nt* runder Durchbrüche
rounding Rundung *f*, Abrunden *nt*, Abrundung *f*
rounding down Abrundung *f*
rounding increase brought about rounding rundungsbedingte Erhöhung *f*
rounding radius Rundungsradius *m*
rounding rule Rundungsregel *f*
rounding tool Abrundmeißel *m*
rounding value Rundungswert *m*
rounding vibrator Rundvibrator *m*
rounding-up Aufrunden *nt*
roundness Rundheit *f*, Abrundung *f*
round-nose tool Rundmeißel *m*
round-pilot at a square broach runde Aufnahme *f* an quadratischem Räumwerkzeug
round-point tapering die-sinking

cutter kegeliger Gesenkfräser *m* mit runder Stirn
round-robin test Ringversuch *m*
rounds Rundmaterial *nt*
round-shaped shear specimen Rundscherprobekörper *m*
route Strecke *f*, Bahn *f*, Weg *m*, Fahrweg *m*, Fahrkurs *m*
route condition Wegbedingung *f*
route information Weginformation *f*
route marker Wegmarke *f*
route marking Fahrwegmarkierung *f*
route segment Bahnsegment *nt*
router Fräsmaschine *f* zum Ausschneiden von Umrissen aus Blechen mit Handvorschub, Nachformfräsmaschine *f* mit Handvorschub
routine regelmäßig
routine inspection Routineprüfung *f*
routine testing Stückprüfung *f*
routine tests *pl* laufende Prüfungen *fpl*
routing 1. Nachformfräsen *nt* 2. Entflechtung *f*
routing card Arbeitskarte *f*, Laufkarte *f* für das Werkstück *nt*, Arbeitsvorbereitung *f*
routing cutter Gesenkfräser *m*, Langlochvorfräser *m*
routing of airflow Luftführung *f*
routing of the heating gas Heizgasführung *f*
roving fabric Rovinggewebe *nt*
row Flucht *f*, Reihe *f*, Zeile *f*
row of keys Tastenleiste *f*
row of shelves Regalzeile *f*
row preparation table Reihenbildungstisch *m*
row pusher Reihenschieber *m*
row stacking Zeilenlagerung *f*
row storage Zeilenlagerung *f*
row-wise zeilenweise
RS bistable element RS- Kippglied *nt*
RS master-slave bistable element RS-Kippglied *nt* mit Zweizustandssteuerung
rub schleifen auf, reiben
rubber Gummi *m*
rubber belt conveyor Gurtbandförderer *m*
rubber bond Gummibindung *f*

rubber compound Kautschukmischung *f*
rubber fingerstall Gummifingerling *m*
rubber gasket Gummidichtung *f*
rubber test specimen Gummiprobe *f*
rubber-coated textiles gummierte Textilien *fpl*
rubber-elastic gummi-elastisch
rubber-gasketed joint gummiverdichtete Verbindung *f*
rubberized textiles gummierte Textilien *fpl*
rubber-like material hochelastischer Stoff *m*
rubbery elasticity Gummielastizität *f*
rubbing wear Reibverschleiß *m*
rugged robust, stabil
ruggedness Robustheit *f*, Stabilität *f*
ruin zerstören
rule 1. Maß *nt*, Maßstab *m*, Strichmaß *nt*, Messlineal *nt* 2. Regel *f*
rule depth gauge Tiefenschieblehre *f*
rule of thumb Faustregel *f*
ruled area Netzgebiet *nt*
ruled line Netzlinie *f*
ruler Maßstab *m*, Lineal *nt*
rules Regeln *fpl*
rules *pl* **of measurement** Messvorschriften *fpl*
ruling Netz *nt*
run laufen, ablaufen, durchlaufen, verlaufen, durchführen, fahren, antreiben; Durchlauf *m*, Lauf *m*, Verlauf *m*, Kurs *m*, Reihe *f*
run in a straight line geradlinig verlaufen
run analysis Laufbetrachtung *f*
run continuously zügig ziehen
run deceleration Durchlaufverzögerung *f*
run down überfahren
run formation Raupenzeichnung *f*
run idle leerlaufen
run of the crack Rissverlauf *m*
run out ausgehen
run short ausgehen
run spacer Distanzstück *nt*
run time Laufzeit *f*, Durchlaufzeit *f*
run true rund laufen, zentrisch laufen
run untrue verlaufen

run up anfahren, hochlaufen; Hochlauf *m*, Anlauf *m*
run-down cycle Ausschwingspiel *nt*
rung Strompfad *m*
rung ladder Trittleiter *f*
runner 1. Anguss *m*, Angusskanal *m* 2. Kufe *f*
runner gate Gießtrichter *m*
runner plate Angussverteilerplatte *f*
runner system Angusssystem *nt*
runnerless angusslos
running Gang *m*, Lauf *m*
running area Laufbereich *m*
running askew Schräglauf *m*
running one above another übereinander laufend
running rail Laufschiene *f*
running schedule Durchlaufterminplanung *f*
running side by side nebeneinander laufend
running smoothness Laufruhe *f*
running surface Lauffläche *f*
running test Probelauf *m*
running time Laufzeit *f*
running-in period Einlaufbetrieb *m*
run-on point Auflaufstelle *f*
runout Unrundlauf *m*, Schlag *m*
run-out error Laufabweichung *f*
run-out sample Auslaufprobe *f*
run-out tolerance Lauftoleranz *f*
runway Fahrbahn *f*
rupture Bruch *m*, Durchschlag *m*; zerreißen, reißen
rupture disc Berstscheibe *f*
rupture temperature Bruchtemperatur *f*
rupture-proof trennbruchsicher
rupturing Reißen *nt*
rural atmosphere Landatmosphäre *f*
rush job eilige Arbeit *f*
rush order Eilauftrag *m*, Schnellauftrag *m*
rust rosten, Rost *m*
rust away wegrosten
rust conversion process Rostumwandlungsverfahren *nt*
rust converter Rostumwandler *m*
rust formation Rostbildung *f*
rust prevention Rostschutz *m*
rust preventive Rostschutzmittel *nt*
rust protection method Rostschutzverfahren *nt*
rust protection regulations *pl* Rostschutzvorschriften *fpl*
rust removal Entrosten *nt*
rust removal by hand Handentrostung *f*
rust removal tool Entrostungswerkzeug *nt*
rust remover Entroster *m*, Rostentfetter *m*, Rostlöser *m*
rust removing impact hammer Rostklopfhammer *m*
rust stabilizer Roststabilisator *m*
rustiness Rostgrad *m*
rusting Rostbildung *f*
rustless rostbeständig
rustproof rostbeständig
rust-proof priming Rostschutzgrundierung *f*
rust-proofing Rostschutz *m*
rustproofing coating Rostschutzüberzug *m*
rust-resisting rostbeständig
rusty rostig
rutile acid covered electrode rutilsauerumhüllte Elektrode *f*
rutile basic covered rod electrode rutilbasischumhüllte Stabelektrode *f*
rutile cellulose covered electrode rutilzelluloseumhüllte Elektrode *f*
rutile covered electrode rutilumhüllte Elektrode *f*

S s

sachet Siegelrandbeutel *m*
sachet form fill and seal machine Siegelrandbeutelform-, -füll- und -verschließmaschine *f*
sack Sack *m*
sack presenting machine Sackzuführmaschine *f*
sack sealing machine Sackverschließmaschine *f*
sacrificial anode Opferanode *f*
sacrificial layer Verlustschicht *f*
saddle Sattel *m*, Tischsattel *m*, Schlitten *m*, Werkzeugschlitten *m*, Unterschlitten *m*, Querbalkenschlitten *m*, Meißelschieber *m*, Kreuzschieber *m*, Querschieber *m*, Querbalkenschieber *m*, Schieber *m*
saddle clamp Schlittenklemmung *f*
saddle clamping Schlittenklemmung *f*
saddle fitting Sattelstück *nt*
saddle guideway Bettschlittenführung *f*
saddle slideways Schlittenführung *f*
saddle-type turret Schlittenrevolver *m*
saddle-type turret lathe Bettschlittenrevolverdrehmaschine *f*, Schlittenrevolverdrehmaschine *f*
safe gefahrlos
safe dimensions dimensionieren
safe functioning Funktionssicherheit *f*
safe in operation betriebssicher
safe load zulässige Belastung *f*, zulässige Last *f*
safe load indicator Überlastanzeige *f*
safe operating area sicherer Arbeitsbereich *m*
safe to operate betriebssicher
safe work period (SWP) sichere Betriebsperiode *f*
safe working load Tragfähigkeit *f*
safeguard Sicherheit *f*, Sicherungsvorrichtung *f*, Sicherheitsvorrichtung *f*, Sicherung *f*, Schutz *m*, Schutzeinrichtung *f*; sichern, absichern, sicherstellen
safeguard against extraneous light Fremdlichtsicherheit *f*
safeguard against spurious response Fremdlichtsicherheit *f*
safeguarding Absicherung *f*
safekeeping Verwahrung *f*
safety Sicherheit *f*
safety against buckling Beulsicherheit *f*
safety area Sicherheitsfläche *f*
safety assurance Sicherstellung *f*
safety at work Arbeitsschutz *m*
safety bar Sicherungselement *nt*
safety belt Sicherheitsgurt *m*, Gurt *m* zur Absicherung *f*
safety block Sicherungsblock *m*
safety blow-off device Sicherheitsabblaseeinrichtung *f*
safety cable Sicherungsseil *nt*
safety catch Fang *m*, Sperre *f*
safety catching device Fangvorrichtung *f*
safety chain Sicherungskette *f*, Haltekette *f*
safety change-over valve Sicherheitswechselventil *nt*
safety circuit Sicherheitsstromkreis *m*
safety claw Sicherheitshaken *m*, Fanghaken *m*, Schienenklammer *f*
safety clearance Sicherheitsabstand *m*
safety clutch Sicherheitskupplung *f*
safety coefficient Sicherheitsbeiwert *m*
safety coil Schutzspule *f*
safety colour Sicherheitsfarbe *f*
safety considerations Sicherheitsgründe *mpl*
safety contact Sicherheitskontakt *m*
safety cup Sicherungsnapf *m*
safety datasheet Sicherheitsdatenblatt *nt*
safety device Sicherheitsvorrichtung *f*, Sicherheitseinrichtung *f*, Sicherung *f*, Sicherheitsschalter *m*
safety device against accidental contact Beruhigungsschutzeinrichtung *f*
safety distance Sicherheitsabstand *m*
safety drain valve Ablaufsicherung *f*

safety equipment Sicherheitseinrichtung *f*
safety expansion pipe Sicherheitsausdehnungsleitung *f*
safety extra-low voltage (SELV) Sicherheitskleinspannung *f*
safety factor Sicherheitsfaktor *m*, Sicherheitszuschlag *m*
safety feature Schutzeinrichtung *f*, Sicherheitsmerkmal *nt*, Sicherung *f*
safety flow pipe Sicherheitsvorlaufleitung *f*
safety footwear Schutzschuhe *mpl*
safety gear Sicherheitseinrichtung *f*, Fangvorrichtung *f*
safety gear tripping Fangvorgang *m*
safety glass Sicherheitsglas *nt*
safety glasses Sicherheitsbrille *f*, Schutzbrille *f*
safety gloves Sicherheitshandschuhe *f*
safety guard Anfahrschutz *m*, Schutzhaube *f*, Schutzvorrichtung *f*
safety helmet Schutzhelm *m*
safety instruction Sicherheitsbefehl *m*
safety latch Sicherheitsklinke *f*
safety limit switch Sicherheitsgrenztaster *m*
safety load zulässige Beanspruchung *f*
safety lock Sicherheitsschloss *nt*
safety means Schutzmaßnahme *f*
safety measure Vorsichtsmaßnahme *f*, Sicherheitsmaßnahme *f*
safety nut Sicherheitsmutter *f*
safety of operation Betriebssicherheit *f*
safety pawl Sicherheitssperrklinke *f*
safety pin Sicherheitsstift *m*
safety practice through intermediate means mittelbare Sicherheitstechnik *f*
safety practice Sicherheitstechnik *f*
safety practice aid sicherheitstechnisches Mittel *nt*
safety practice measures sicherheitstechnische Maßnahmen *fpl*
safety practice stipulations sicherheitstechnische Festlegung *f*
safety practice through intrinsic design unmittelbare Sicherheitstechnik *f*
safety pressure relief valve Überdruckventil *nt*, Sicherheitsventil *nt*
safety principles Sicherheitsgrundsätze *mpl*
safety problem Sicherheitsproblem *nt*
safety provision Sicherheitsvorkehrung *f*
safety rail Sicherheitsschiene *f*
safety regulation Sicherheitsauflage *f*, Sicherheitsbestimmung *f*
safety related sicherheitsbezogen
safety requirement Sicherheitsanforderung *f*, sicherheitstechnische Anforderung *f*, Sicherheitsbestimmung *f*
safety return pipe Sicherheitsrücklaufleitung *f*
safety reverser Sicherheitsumkehrschalter *m*
safety risk Sicherheitsrisiko *nt*
safety rule Sicherheitsregel *f*
safety shoes Sicherheitsschuhe *mpl*
safety shut-off device Sicherheitsabsperrvorrichtung *f*
safety shutdown Sicherheitsabschaltung *f*
safety shutdown mat Schaltmatte *f*
safety sign Sicherheitszeichen *f*
safety standard Sicherheitsnorm *f*
safety stock Risikobestand *m*, Sicherheitsbestand *m*
safety stop dog Sicherheitsanschlagnocke *f*
safety stress zulässige Beanspruchung *f*
safety support Sicherungsstütze *f*
safety switch Sicherheitsschalter *m*
safety system Sicherheitsanlage *f*
safety technology Sicherheitstechnik *f*
safety temperature limiter Sicherheitstemperaturbegrenzer *m*
safety valve Sicherheitsventil *nt*
safety viewing glass Sicherheitssichtebene *f*
safety when standing Stehsicherheit *f*
safety when walking Trittsicherheit *f*
safety-related parts Sicherheitsbauteile *ntpl*
sag Durchbiegung *f*, Durchhang *m*; durchhängen, nachgeben, durchbiegen
sagging Durchgang *m*
salary Gehalt *m*
sale of withdrawal of goods Waren-

ausgang *m*
sales Vertrieb *m*, Absatz *m*
sales catalogue Preisliste *f*
sales data Verkaufsdaten *pl*
sales data report Verkaufsbericht *m*
sales department Vertrieb *m*
sales depot Vertriebslager *nt*
sales figures Verkaufszahlen *pl*
sales forecast Verkaufsprognose *f*
sales forecast report Verkaufsplanung *f*
sales planning Ansatzplanung *f*, Verkaufsplanung *f*
sales volume Umsatz *m*
sales warehouse Verkaufslager *nt*
salvage rückgewinnen, ausschlachten, reparieren
sample Musterstück *nt*, Muster *nt*, Probe *f*, Probestück *nt*, Warenprobe *f*, Bezugsstück *nt*, Abfrage *f*; probieren, abfragen, abtasten
sample carrier Probenträger *m*
sample composition Stichprobenaufbau *m*
sample conditioning Probenvorbehandlung *f*
sample cut Probeschnitt *m*
sample cut from surfacings Ausbaustück *nt*
sample error Stichprobenabweichung *f*
sample holding device Probenhaltevorrichtung *f*
sample of mineral substances Mineralstoffprobe *f*
sample preparation Probeaufbereitung *f*, Probenvorbereitung *f*
sample sheet Probebogen *m*
sample splitter Probenteiler *m*
sample splitting method Probeteilungsverfahren *nt*
sample stack Probenstapel *m*
sample suspension Probensuspension *f*
sample unit Stichprobeneinheit
sample vibration Probenschwingung *f*
sample workpiece Musterstück *nt*
sampler Probenehmer *m*
sample storage container Probenvorratsgefäß *nt*
sampling Probenahme *f*
sampling action Abtastung *f*
sampling apparatus Probenahmegerät *nt*
sampling at fixed time intervals Probenahme *f* in festen Abständen
sampling container Probebehälter *m*
sampling control Abtastregelung *f*
sampling device Probenahmegerät *nt*
sampling direction Entnahmerichtung *f*
sampling fraction Auswahlsatz *m*
sampling inspection Stichprobenprüfung *f*
sampling plan Stichprobenprüfplan *m*
sampling pump Probenahmepumpe *f*
sampling site Probenahmeort *m*
sampling size Stichprobenumfang *m*
sampling unit Auswahleinheit *f*
sand Sand *m*
sand bunker Sandbunker *m*
sand casting Sandguss *m*
sand dressing Sandaufbereitung *f*
sand founding Sandguss *m*
sand inclusion Sandeinschluss *m*
sand particle Sandteil *nt*
sand remains Sandanbackung *f*
sand trickling method Sandrieselverfahren *nt*
sand washer Sandscheibe *f*
sand-blast sandstrahlen
sandblasting Abstrahlen *nt* mit Sand
sandblasting carried out in the open Strahlen *nt* im Freien
sanding Schmirgeln *nt*
sandwich Verbund *m*, Kernverbund *m*
sandwich brazed hart eingelötet
sandwich foil Verbundfolie *f*
sandwiched übereinander liegend, geschichtet
sanitation facilities Sanitäranlage *f*
Sankey diagram Sankey-Diagramm *nt*
sapphire Saphir *m*
satchel Tornister *m*
satchel bag Seitenfaltbeutel *m*
satellite storage Kanallager *nt*
satellite system Satellitensystem *nt*
satellite vehicle Kanalfahrwagen *m*, Satellitenfahrwagen *m*
satisfy erfüllen, befriedigen
saturate sättigen
saturated steam cylinder oil Sattdampfzylinderöl *nt*

saturated with liquid gas flüssiggasgesättigt
saturation Sättigung *f*
saturation behaviour Sättigungsverhalten *nt*
saturation point Sättigungspunkt *m*
saturation stage Sättigungsphase *f*
saturation water vapour pressure Wasserdampfsättigungsdruck *m*
saucer-head screw Flachrundschraube *f*
save 1. speichern, bergen **2.** *(Kosten)* einsparen, sparen
saving Schonung *f*, Einsparung *f*
saving in material Werkstoffeinsparung *f*
saving of time Zeitersparnis *f*
savings possibility Einsparungsmöglichkeit *f*
saw Säge *f*; sägen
saw band Bandsägeblatt *nt*
saw blade Sägeblatt *nt*
saw tooth Sägezahn *m*
saw waste Sägespäne *mpl*
sawing Sägen
saw-setting machine Schränkmaschine *f*
saw-tooth cutter spitzgezahnter Fräser *m*
saw-tooth thread Sägegewinde *nt*
scab Schülpe *f*
scab formation Schülpenbildung *f*
scaffold Gerüst *nt*
scaffold-like staging gerüstartiges Arbeitspodest *nt*
scald verbrühen, Verbrühung *f*
scale 1. Maßstab *m*, Skala *f*; skalieren, kalibrieren **2.** Sinter *m*, Zunder *m*; abschuppen, abklopfen **3.** *(Gewicht)* wägen, wiegen; Waage *f*
scale angle Skalenwinkel *m*
scale carrier Skalenträger *m*
scale constant Skalenkonstante *f*
scale deposit Steinablagerung *f*
scale division Skalenteil *nt*
scale division with digital increment Skalenteil *nt* mit Ziffernschritt
scale factor Skalenkonstante *f*
scale formation Zunderbildung *f*
scale indication yardstick Maßabstrich *m*
scale interval Teilungswert *m*, Skalenteilungswert *m*, Skalenteilungswert *m*, Skalenwert *m*
scale mark Teilstrich *m*, Teilungszeichen *nt*
scale model testing Modellversuch *m*
scale numbering Skalenbezifferung *f*
scale of the drawing Zeichnungsmaßstab *m*
scale of the survey Aufnahmemaßstab *m*
scale off ablösen, abblättern, abzundern
scale range Anzeigebereich *m*
scale screw Skalenschraube *f*
scale spacing Teilstrichabstand *m*
scale with circular line Skale *f* mit kreisbogenförmiger Teilungsgrundlinie
scale with straight base line Skale *f* mit gerader Teilungsgrundlinie
scaled drawing maßstabgerechte Darstellung *f*
scaling Skalieren *nt*, Maßstabänderung *f*, Größenstufung *f*
scaling-off Entzundern *nt*, Abzunderung *f*
scan 1. abfragen, scannen, lesen, tasten, abtasten, abfühlen, überstreichen; Abfrage *f*, Abtastung *f* **2.** *(mit Ton)* durchschallen
scan frequency Scanfrequenz *f*
scan line Scanlinie *f*
scan method Scanverfahren *nt*
scan process Scanverfahren *nt*
scan time Abtastzeit *f*
scanner Taster *m*, Scanner *m*
scanner system Scannersystem *nt*
scanning Abtastung *f*, Abtasten *nt*
scanning area Tastfläche *f*
scanning command Abtastbefehl *m*
scanning element Rasterpunkt *m*
scanning frequency Zeilenabtastfrequenz *f*
scanning line Abtastlinie *f*
scanning plane Tastebene *f*
scanning range Abtastbereich *m*, Tastweite *f*
scanning rate Abtastrate *f*
scanning result Leseergebnis *nt*
scanning tip Tastspitze *f*

scar Mulde *f*, Narbe *f*
SCARA-robot *(Selective Compliance Assembly Robot Arm)* Schwenkarmroboter *m*
scarce knapp, selten, spärlich
scarf schärfen, anschärfen, abschrägen
scarcity Mangel *m*
scarred surface narbige Oberfläche *f*
scatter streuen
scatter band Streuband *nt*
scatter field Streufeld *nt*
scattered radiation nicht bildzeichnende Strahlung *f*
scattered radiation grid Streustrahlenraster *nt*
scattering Streuung *f*
scattering filter Streufilter *m*
scattering limit Streugrenze *f*
scavenge spülen
scavenging time Spülzeit *f*
scew in easily *(Gewinde)* sich frei aufschrauben lassen
schedule disponieren, terminieren, planen; Terminplanung *f*, Terminplan *m*, Zeitplan *m*
schedule course planning Terminablaufplanung *f*
schedule delay Terminverzug *m*
schedule disposal Termindisposition *f*
schedule effectiveness Termineinhaltung *f*
schedule logic Terminlogik *f*
schedule urgency Termindringlichkeit *f*
schedule variance Terminabweichung *f*
scheduled quantity Ansatzgröße *f*
scheduling delay Terminverzug *m*
schematic arrangement Anordnungsschema *nt*
schematic drawing Schemazeichnung *f*
Schmitt-trigger Schmitt-Trigger *m*
scissor design Scherenkonstruktion *f*
scissor grab Scherengreifer *m*
scissor gripper Scherengreifer *m*
scissor lift Scherenhebebühne *f*
scissor lift pallet truck Scherengabelhubwagen *m*
scissor lifting Scherenhub *m*

scissors Schere *f*
S-conveyor S-Förderer *m*
scoop Greifer *m*, Schaufel *f*, Schüttgutschaufel *f*; laden, schaufeln
scooping Laden *nt*
scope 1. Bereich *m* 2. *(Ausdehnung)* Umfang *m* 3. *(bzgl. Toleranzen)* Geltungsbereich *m*
scope of delivery Lieferumfang *m*
scope of performance Leistungsumfang *m*
scope of responsibilities Aufgabenbereich *m*
scope of testing Prüfumfang *m*
scope of work Arbeitsbereich *m*, Anwendungsbereich *m*
scorching behaviour Anvulkanisationsverhalten *nt*
score 1. anritzen, ritzen, einkerben, beschädigen; Ritzlinie *f*, Riefe *f* 2. zählen
score mark Riefe *f*
scoring Oberflächenbeschädigung *f*, Riefenbildung *f*, Einkerben *nt*
scoring due to polishing Polierriefen *fpl*
scoring effect Fressverhalten *nt*
scotch-yoke mechanism Kreuzschubkurbel *f*
scourable lubricating oil abwaschbares Schmieröl *nt*
scouring Auswaschung *f*
scour-proof scherbeständig
scrap verschrotten; Schrott *m*, Ausschuss *m*, Abfall *m*
scrap component Ausschussteil *nt*
scrap grapple Schrottgreifer *m*
scrap heap Schrotthaufen *m*
scrap metals Abfall *m*, Schrott *m*
scrap percentage Ausschussquote *f*
scrap pile Schrotthaufen *m*
scrap rate Ausschussquote *f*
scrap work Ausschuss *m*
scrape 1. kratzen, schaben 2. drücken
scrape off abkratzen
scrape smooth glattstreichen
scraper Schaber *m*, Abstreifer *m*
scraper for removing swarf Spanabstreifer *m*
scraping tool Schaber *m*
scrapping Verschrottung *f*

scratch kratzen, ritzen; Kratzer *m*, Rille *f*
scratch depth Rillentiefe *f*
screen 1. Monitor *m*, Bildschirm *m*, Schirm *m*, Abschirmung *f* **2.** Ladeplattform *f* **3.** rastern, sieben; Sieb *nt*, Raster *nt*
screen diaphragm Bildschirmblende *f*
screen gauge Sieblehre *f*
screen insert Siebeinsatz *m*
screen mask file Bildschirmmaskendatei *f*
screen off abschirmen
screen printing ink Siebdruckfarbe *f*
screen segment Teilbildschirm *m*
screening Abschirmung *f*, Verdeckung *f*, Umwehrung *f*
screening layer abschirmende Schicht *f*
screw Schraube *f*, Bolzen *m*, Spindel *f*; schrauben, verschrauben
screw and nut table feeding Tischvorschub *m* durch Spindel und Mutter
screw and washer assembly Kombischraube *f*
screw capping machine Schraubverschließmaschine *f*
screw chip Schraubenspan *m*
screw chuck Schraubenfutter *f*
screw clamp retention Bügelsicherung *f* einer Mutter
screw conveyor Förderschnecke *f*, Transportschnecke *f*
screw cutting Gewindeschneiden *nt*
screw cutting plate Gewindeschneidplatte *f*
screw dog Anschlagschraube *f*
screw down verschrauben, zuschrauben
screw driver Schraubenzieher *m*
screw fastening Gewindeverbindung *f*
screw head counterbore Schraubenkopfsenkung *f*
screw into einschrauben in
screw jack Spindel *f*
screw joint Schraubenverbindung *f*
screw lifting system Spindelhubsystem *nt*
screw limit gauge Gewindegrenzlehre *f*
screw limit plug gauge Gewindegrenzlehrendorn *m*
screw milling Spiralfräsarbeit *f*
screw nail Schraubnagel *m*
screw on aufschrauben
screw out herausschrauben
screw pitch gauge Gewindeganglehre *f*
screw plug Schraubverschluss *m*, Verschlussschraube *f*
screw plug gauge Gewindelehrdorn *m*
screw plug hole Einschraubloch *nt*
screw point Gewindeverbindung *f*
screw press Spindelpresse *f*
screw pumping aggregate Schraubenspindelpumpenaggregat *nt*
screw rail anchor Schraubklemme *f*
screw retaining device Schraubensicherung *f*
screw slotter Schraubenschlitzmaschine *f*
screw slotting Schraubenschlitzen *nt*
screw slotting saw Schraubenschlitzsäge *f*
screw spindle Gewindespindel *f*
screw thread Gewinde *nt*, Schraubengewinde *nt*
screw thread calliper Feinmessschraublehre *f* für Gewindemessung
screw thread designation Gewindebezeichnung *f*
screw thread fit Gewindepassung *f*
screw thread for external freezing pipes *pl* Gewinde *nt* für Gefrieraußenrohre
screw thread for general engineering Gewinde *nt* für allgemeine Anwendung *f*
screw thread for glass guards Glasgewinde *nt* für Schutzgläser
screw thread gage Gewindelehre *f*
screw thread measuring method Gewindemessverfahren *nt*
screw thread micrometer Feinmessschraublehre *f* für Gewindemessung
screw thread micrometer calliper Gewindeachsenlehre *f*
screw thread selection Gewindeauswahl *f*
screw thread with flank clearance Gewinde *nt* mit Flankenspiel

screw thread without flaws in flank pitch teilungsfehlerfreies Gewinde *nt*
screw threading die Gewindeschneideisen *nt*
screw threading machine Gewindeschneidmaschine *f*
screw type valve Schraubventil *nt*
screw with captive washer Schraube *f* mit unverlierbarem Unterlegteil
screw with flat-sealing head Schraube *f* mit eben aufliegendem Kopf
screw with internal serrations Innenvielzahnschraube *f*
screw with reduced shank Schraube *f* mit dünnem Schaft
screw with undercut Rillenschraube *f*
screw with waisted shank Schraube *f* mit Dehnschaft
screw within a telescopic cover Teleskopspindel *f*
screw-cutting gearbox Gewinderäderkasten *m*
screw-cutting indicator Gewindeschneidanzeiger *m*
screw-cutting lathe Gewindedrehmaschine *f*
screw-down bonnet type shut-off check valve absperrbares Kopfstückrückschlagventil *nt*
screw-down non-return valve feststellbares Rückschlageckventil *nt*
screw-down straight-way non-return valve feststellbares Rückschlagdurchgangsventil *nt*
screwdriver bit for multispline screws Schraubendrehereinsatz *m* für Innenkeilprofilschrauben
screwdriver bit for screws with internal serrations Schraubendreher *m* für Innenvielzahnschrauben
screwdriver for recessed head screws Schraubendreher *m* für Kreuzschlitzschrauben
screwdriver for slotted grub screws Schraubendreher *m* für Gewindestifte mit Schlitz
screwdriver for slotted head screws Schraubendreher *m* für Schlitzschrauben, Schraubendreher *m* für Kopfschrauben mit Schlitz

screwed and socketed joint Schraubmuffenverbindung *f*
screwed ball end Einschraubkugelkopf *m*
screwed connection Anschlussverschraubung *f*, Schraubverbindung *f*, Schraubenverbindung *f*
screwed drain plug Verschlussschraube *f* für Ölablass
screwed end Einschraubzapfen *m*, Gewindeende *nt*
screwed fastening Verbindung *f* mittels Schrauben, Schraubverbindung *f*
screwed fitting Schraubfitting *m*
screwed flange with socket Gewindeflansch *m* mit Ansatz
screwed flanged joint Flanschverschraubung *f*
screwed insert Einschraubmutter *f*, Schraubdübel *m*
screwed joint Schraubverbindung *f*
screwed pipe connection Gewinderohrverbindung *f*, Gewindefitting *m*, Rohrverschraubungsabschluss *m*
screwed pipe joint for bonding with flat sealing ring Rohrverschraubung *f* mit Klebung mit Flachdichtung
screwed plug Einschraubstutzen *m*
screwed sealing plug Verschlussschraube *f*
screwed union on casks Fassverschraubung *f*
screw-generating grinding Schraubwälzschleifen
screw-head slotting attachment Schraubenschlitzvorrichtung *f*
screw-in gauge ring for D-fuses D-Schraub-Passeinsatz *m*
screw-in group Einschraubgruppe *f*
screw-in heating element Einschraubheizpatrone *f*
screw-in sleeve socket for D-fuses D-Hülsen-Passeinsatz *m*
screw-in tap hole Einschraubgewindeloch *nt*
screwing Verschraubung *f*
screwing hook Einschraubhaken *m*
screwing with the aid of a power wrench Kraftverschraubung *f*
screw-locking thread insert schrau-

bensichernder Gewindeeinsatz *m*
screw-motion transmission Schraubgetriebe *nt*
screw-on cutter Aufschraubfräser *m*
screw-on hole Anschraubloch *nt*
screw-retaining thread insert schraubensichernder Gewindeeinsatz *m*
screw-slotting cutter Schraubenschlitzfräser *m*
scribe anreißen, anzeichnen
scribed line Anrisslinie *f*
scriber Anreißnadel *f*, Reißnadel *f*
scribing Furchen *nt*, Anreißen *nt*
scribing block Parallelreißer *m*, Reißstock *m*
script Schriftart *f*
scroll 1. blättern, scrollen 2. Spindel *f* mit Schraubenpumpe
scroll gear Triebkranz *m*
scrolling Blättern *nt*, Scrollen *nt*
scrupulously clean test apparatus peinlich sauberes Prüfgerät *nt*
sculptured surface Freiformfläche *f*
sea water immersion test Meerwassertauchprüfung *f*
seal 1. Dichtung *f*, Abdichtung *f*, Verschluss *m*, Naht *f*; verschließen, versiegeln, siegeln, abdichten, dichten, verschweißen, plombieren, verplomben, abschließen 2. stempeln; Stempel *m*
seal face Dichtungsfläche *f*
seal housing Vorlagenbehälter *m*
sealant Abdichtmittel *nt*, Dichtstoff *m*
sealed cell verschlossene Zelle *f*
sealing Dichtung *f*, Versiegelung *f*, Sperrung *f*, Verschließen *nt*
sealing agent Dichtmittel *nt*
sealing bar Siegelwerkzeug *nt*
sealing compound Dichtstoff *m*, Abdichtung *f*, Vergussmasse *f*
sealing element Dichtelement *nt*
sealing function Dichtfunktion *f*
sealing liquid Sperrflüssigkeit *f*
sealing machine Verschließmaschine *f*
sealing material Vergussmittel *nt*
sealing of bearings Lagerabdichtung *f*
sealing packing Abdichtung *f*
sealing plug Verschlussschraube *f*, Verschlussstopfen *m*
sealing push-in cap Verschlussdeckel *m* zum Eindrücken
sealing steam Sperrdampf *m*
sealing surface Dichtfläche *f*
sealing washer Dichtungsring *m*, Verschlussscheibe *f*
sealing water Sperrwasser *nt*
seam Überwalzung *f*, Falz *m*, Naht *f*; nähen
seam number Überwalzzahl *f*
seam weld Liniennaht *f*, Rollennahtschweißung *f*, nahtschweißen
seam welding with strip Foliennahtschweißen *nt*
seaming by spinning Falzen *nt* durch Drücken
seamless nahtlos
search (for) Suche *f*; suchen
search system Suchsystem *nt*
season altern
seasonal saisonal
seasoning Entspannung *f*, Alterung *f*
seat Sitzfläche *f*, Sitz *m*, Platz *m*; auflegen, einsetzen, einpassen, hinsetzen, lagern
seat area Auflageebene *f*
seat dresser Ventilsitzfräseinrichtung *f*
seat engaging surface Auflageebene *f*
seat for key Keilsitz *m*
seat index point Sitzindexpunkt *m*
seat mounting Sitzhalterung *f*
seat on aufliegen
seat perpendicular to the direction of motion Quersitz *m*
seat solidly satt aufliegen
seat surface Auflagefläche *f*
seated sitzend
seating Sitzfläche *f*, Sitz *m*, Sitzposition *f*
seating surface Aufnahmefläche *f*
sectional area of chip Spanungsquerschnitte *mpl*
second cycle operation zweiter Arbeitsgang *m*
second draw Weiterschlag *m*
second face zweite Spanflächenfase *f*, zweite Spanfläche *f*
second feed Nachstellarbeit *f*
second flank zweite Freifläche *f*
second power *(math.)* Quadrat *nt*
secondary sekundär, nachgeschaltet

secondary aisle Nebengang *m*
secondary area Nebenfläche *f*
secondary clearance sekundärer Freiwinkel *m*
secondary clearance angle Fasenfreiwinkel *m*
secondary command (SC) Sekundärbefehl *m*
secondary cut surface Nebenschnittfläche *f*
secondary defect Nebenfehler *m*
secondary diaphragm Hinterblende *f*
secondary feed line Nebenleitung *f*
secondary friction Nebenreibung *f*
secondary front cutting edge clearance angle Freiwinkel *m*
secondary impedance Sekundärimpedanz *f*
secondary lane Nebengang *m*
secondary no-load voltage Sekundärleerlaufspannung *f*
secondary pressure Hinterdruck *m*
secondary rake Radialwinkel *m*, Seitenwinkel *m*
secondary short circuit current Sekundärkurzschlussstrom *m*
secondary side rake angle Seitenspanwinkel *m*
secondary silting up Sekundärverschlämmung *f*
secondary solder Zweilot *nt*
secondary spindle Innenspindel *f*
secondary ventilation Nebenlüftung *f*
secondary voltage range Sekundärspannungsbereich *m*
secondary-cutting edge Nebenschneide *f*
second-hand gebraucht
section Abschnitt *m*, Schnitt *m*, Bereich *m*, Abteilung *f*, Profil *nt*, Glied *nt*, Teil *m*, Strecke *f*, Profil *nt*
section boundary Schnittlinie *f*
section computer Bereichsrechner *m*
section diagram method Schnittbildverfahren *nt*
section dimension Teileabmessung *f*
section in the axial plane Achsschnittebene *f*
section lines Schraffur *f*
section lining Schraffur *f*
section modulus Widerstandsmoment *nt*
section of route Bahnsegment *nt*
section outline Profil *nt*
section patrol Streckenbegehung *f*
sectional area Schnittfläche *f*
sectional broach mehrteiliges Räumwerkzeug *nt*
sectional drawing Zeichnung *f* im Querschnitt, Schnitt *m* der Zeichnung, Zeichnungsabriss *m*
sectional drawing of the building Gebäudeschnitt *m*
sectional radiator Gliederheizkörper *m*
sectional representation Schnittdarstellung *f*
sectional type Gliederbauart *f*
sectioning Schnitt *m*
sector scale Sektorskala *f*
setover of the swivel head of the shaper Verstellen *nt* des Drehteils der Waagrechtstoßmaschine
secure fest, sichern, absichern, sicherstellen, befestigen, festhalten, verzurren, spannen, festspannen, verriegeln, blockieren
secure in position einspannen, in Position spannen
secure locking sichere Feststellung *f*
secure safe sicher
securely fixed formschlüssig
securing Befestigung *f*, Absicherung *f*, Sichern *nt*
securing device Transportsicherung *f*
securing machine Sicherungsmaschine *f*
securing pin Befestigungsstift *m*
security of supply Versorgungssicherheit *f*
security tagging Verplombung *f*
sediment Bodenkörper *m*
sedimentary strata Sedimentationsschichten *fpl*
sedimentation analysis Sedimentationsanalyse *f*
sedimentation of iron ochre Verockerung *f*
sedimentation tank Absetzbehälter *m*
seepage Durchströmung *f*, Versickerung *f*

seepage water drain packing Sickerpacking f
seepage water drain pipe Sickerleitung f
seesaw wippen
segment Teil m, Segment nt
segment copying Teilumrissnachformen nt, Nachformen nt im Teilumriss
segment gear Zahnsegment nt
segmental chip Span m, Abreißspan m, Reißspan m, Kurzspan m, Bruchspan m
segmented wheel Segmentscheibe f
segregate absondern
segregated lot aussortiertes Los nt
segregation Seigerung f
segregation behaviour Seigerungsverhalten nt
segregation tendency Entmischungsneigung f
seize 1. festfressen, verklemmen, hängen bleiben 2. *(reservieren)* belegen
seizing Bemessung f
seizure Festfressen nt
select 1. markieren 2. auswählen, anwählen, wählen, aussortieren
select „raise" position auf „Heben" stellen
selected point on the cutting edge ausgewählter Schneidenpunkt m
selected site of thread Gewindeauswahl f
selection Wahl f, Anwahl f, Auswahl f
selection field Anwahlfeld nt
selection of fits Passungsauswahl f
selection operation Anwahlbedienung f
selection signals Wählzeichenfolge f
selective assembly Austauschbau m
selective attack selektiver Angriff m
selective combination weighing machine Auswahlkombinationswägefüllmaschine f
selective compliance assembly robot arm (SCARA) Schwenkarm m
selective grating Selektionsgitter nt
Selective Laser Sintering (SLS) SLS (Pulverlasersintern nt)
selective sampling gezielte Probenahme f
selectivity 1. Auflösungsvermögen nt, Trennschärfe f 2. Granularität f
selector Schalter m
selector fork Schaltgabel f
selector fork friction moment Schaltgabelreibmoment nt
selector switch Wahlschalter m
self monitoring Selbstüberwachung f
self order Eigenauftrag m
self production Eigenfertigung f
self production control Eigenfertigungssteuerung f
self production planning Eigenfertigungsplanung f
self regulating selbstüberwachend
self-acting selbsttätig
self-acting rotary indexing motion of the table selbsttätige Tischrundbewegung f
self-adhesive selbstklebend
self-adhesive emery paper selbstklebendes Schmirgelpapier nt
self-adhesive layer selbsthaftende Schicht f
self-adhesive tape Selbstklebeband nt
self-aligning ball bearing Pendelkugellager nt
self-aligning self-locking collar Schließring m für Neigungsausgleich
self-aligning washer Scheibe f für Neigungsausgleich
self-alignment bearing Pendellager nt
self-braking Selbstbremsung f
self-centring Selbstzentrierung f, selbstzentrierend
self-centring chuck Universalfutter nt, Zentrierfutter nt
self-checking Eigenkontrolle f
self-cleaning property Selbstreinigungsvermögen nt
self-clearing groove Schabennut f
self-closing selbstschließend
self-compensation Selbstausgleich m
self-construction Selbstbau m
self-contained unabhängig, freitragend, selbsttragend
self-curing two-component material selbsthärtender Zweikomponentenstoff m
self-cutting electrode selbstschneidende Elektrode f

self-etch primer Washprimer *m*
self-excitation Selbsterregung *f*
self-excited vibrations selbsterregte Schwingungen *fpl*
self-extinguishing arc absterbender Lichtbogen *m*
self-filter Eigenfilter *m*
self-holding selbsthemmend
self-indexing selbstschaltend
self-induced vibrations selbsterregte Schwingung *f*, selbstinduzierte Schwingung *f*, Eigenschwingung *f*
self-loading trailer Anhänger *m* mit Ladeeinrichtung
self-locking selbsthemmend, Selbsthemmung *f*
self-locking building element selbstsicherndes Bauteil *nt*
self-locking collar Schließring *m*
self-locking device Selbsthemmung *f*
self-locking nut selbstsichernde Mutter *f*
self-locking safety anchorage Steigschutzeinrichtung *f*
self-loosening selbsttätiges Lösen *nt*
self-monitoring check Eigenüberwachungsprüfung *f*
self-priming selbstansaugend
self-propelled motorisch, kraftbetrieben, mit Eigenantrieb, selbstfahrend
self-propelled driving part motorischer Antrieb *m*
self-propelled lifting power motorische Lastenanhebung *f*
self-restricting selbsthemmend
self-retaining selbsthemmend
self-setting natural rubber adhesive selbstabbindender Kautschukkleber *m*
self-sharpening selbstschärfend; Selbstschärfung *f*
self-similarity Selbstähnlichkeit *f*
self-smoothing behaviour Selbstglättungsverhalten *nt*
self-starting selbsterregt
self-supporting freitragend, selbsttragend
self-supporting micro structure selbsttragende Mikrostruktur *f*
self-tapping screw Blechschraube *f*
self-tapping screw thread Gewinde *nt* für Blechschrauben, Blechschraubengewinde *nt*
self-tapping screw with captive washer Blechscheibe *f* mit unverlierbarer Scheibe
self-test Selbstprüfung *f*, Selbsttest *m*
self-vulcanizing natural rubber adhesive selbstvulkanisierender Kautschukkleber *m*
sell verkaufen, umsetzen, absetzen
sell by and best before haltbar bis
seller Verkäufer *m*
selling Absatz *m*
semantics Semantik *f*
semi-automatic halbautomatisch, teilautomatisch
semi-automatic butt welding machine teilselbsttätige Stumpfschweißmaschine *f*
semi-automatic chucking machine Futterhalbautomat *m*
semi-automatic contour milling halbautomatisches Umrissfräsen *nt*
semi-automatic gas burner teilautomatischer Gasbrenner *m*
semi-automatic horizontal milling machine halbautomatische Waagerechtfräsmaschine *f*
semi-automatic lathe Drehhalbautomat *m*, halbautomatische Drehmaschine *f*, Halbautomat *m*
semi-automatic machine Halbautomat *m*
semi-automatic oil burner teilautomatischer Ölbrenner *m*
semi-automatic turret lathe halbautomatische Revolverdrehmaschine *f*, Halbautomat *m*
semicircle Halbkreis *m*
semi-circle test method Bogenprüfverfahren *nt*
semicircular halbkreisförmig
semicircular groove halbkreisförmiger Kerb *m*
semiconductor Halbleiter *m*
semiconductor component Halbleiterbaustein *m*, Halbleiterbauelement *nt*
semiconductor laser Halbleiterlaser *m*
semicrystalline teilkristallin
semi-dry development Feuchtent-

wicklung *f*
semi-dry method Feuchtverfahren *nt*
semi-finished goods Halbwaren *pl*
semi-finished products Halbwaren *pl*
semimicro balance Halbmikrowaage *f*
semi-micro burette Halbmikrobürette *f*
semipermeable teildurchlässig
semi-pneumatic tyre Bereifung *f* mit Lufteinschluss
semi-pneumatic tyred wheel Rad *nt* mit Bereifung mit Lufteinschluss
semi-pointed centre halbe Körnerspitze *f*
semi-rigid halbstabil
semi-silo construction Halbsilobauweise *f*
semi-skilled angelernt
semi-skilled worker angelernter Arbeiter *m*
semi-topping Abrunden *nt*
semi-topping hob Abrundwälzfräser *m*, Abkantwälzfräser *m*
semitransparent teildurchlässig
semi-tubular countersunk head rivet Halbhohlsenkniet *m*
semi-tubular mushroom head rivet Halbhohlflachrundniet *m*
semi-tubular rivet Halbhohlniet *m*
send senden
send back zurücksenden
send packet Sendepaket *nt*
send up weiterleiten
send/receive device Sende-/Empfangseinrichtung *f*
send/receive unit Sende-/Empfangseinheit *f*
sender Sender *m*
sending Sendung *f*
Sendzimir galvanizing *(Beschichtung)* Sendzimirverzinkung *f*
sense 1. fühlen, abfühlen, tasten, erfassen, erkennen 2. Richtung *f*
sense of rotation Drehrichtung *f*
sensing Messwertaufnahme *f*
sensing device Taster *m*, Schutzeinrichtung *f* mit Annäherungsreaktion
sensing probe Messtaster *m*, Messfühler *m*
sensitive empfindlich, gefühlvoll, feinstufig

sensitive adjustment Feinzustellung *f*
sensitive control feinstufige Regelung *f*, feinstufige Schaltung *f*
sensitive drill press Handhebelbohrmaschine *f*
sensitive instruments empfindliche Geräte *f*
sensitive pressure gauge Feinmaßmanometer *nt*
sensitive to heating erhitzungsempfindlich
sensitive to light lichtempfindlich
sensitive tracer Feintaster *m*
sensitivity Empfindlichkeit *f*, feinstufige Schaltbarkeit *f*, Übersetzung *f*
sensitivity analysis Sensitivitätsbetrachtung *f*
sensitivity setting Empfindlichkeitseinstellung *f*
sensitivity to draught Zugluftempfindlichkeit *f*
sensor Aufnehmer *m*, Fühler *m*, Sensor *m*, Taster *m*, Messfühler *m*
sensor beam Taststrahl *m*
sensor data Sensordaten *pl*
sensor data conditioning Sensordatenaufbereitung *f*
sensor element Signalgeber *m*
sensor engineering Sensortechnik *f*
sensor head Fühlerkopf *m*
sensor lead Fühlerleitung *f*
sensor level Sensorebene *f*
sensor mat Schaltmatte *f*, druckempfindliche Matte *f*
sensor selection Sensorenauswahl *f*
sensor technology Sensortechnik *f*
sensorless sensorlos
sensors Sensorik *f*
sensory perception Sinneswahrnehmung *f*
separable zerlegbar
separate separieren, vereinzeln, sortieren, aufteilen, ausscheiden, abscheiden, absondern, teilen, trennen, abtrennen, zerlegen, ablösen, absondern, separat
separate drawing of details *(pl)* Herauszeichnen *nt* von Einzelheiten
separate excitation Fremderregung *f*
separated getrennt, gesondert
separately excited fremderregt

separating arm Fachteiler *m*
separating bar Rungenteilung *f*
separating contactor Trennschalter *m*
separating film Trennfolie *f*
separating filter *(el.)* Weiche *f*
separating force Lösekraft *f*
separating installation Abscheideanlage *f*
separating process Trennvorgang *m*
separating technology Trenntechnik *f*
separation Abheben *nt*, Abtrennung *f*, Trennung *f*, Ablösung *f*, Vereinzelung *f*, Teilung *f*, Zerlegung *f*
separation magnet Spreizmagnet *m*
separation zone Separierzone *f*
separative trennend
separator Separator *m*
sequence Aufeinanderfolge *f*, Rangfolge *f*, Reihe *f*, Reihenfolge *f*, Folge *f*, Ablauf *m*, Sequenz *f*
sequence automatic control Folgeregelung *f*
sequence cascade Ablaufkette *f*
sequence control Programmsteuerung *f*, Folgesteuerung *f*, Ablaufsteuerung *f*
sequence diagram Ablaufdiagramm *nt*
sequence of action Wirkungsablauf *m*
sequence of arrivals Ankunftsreihenfolge *f*
sequence of characters Zeichenfolge *f*
sequence of digits Ziffernfolge *f*
sequence of electrical impulses elektrische Impulsfolge *f*
sequence of figures Ziffernfolge *f*
sequence of movements Bewegungsablauf *m*
sequence of operations Bearbeitungsfolge *f*, Folge *f* der Arbeitsvorgänge, Arbeitsablauf *m*
sequence of orders Auftragsreihenfolge *f*
sequence of pulses Impulsfolge *f*
sequence plan Ablaufplan *m*
sequence programme Ablaufprogramm *nt*
sequence search Satzsuchen *nt*
sequencing Einstellung *f* der Arbeitsfolge, Folgesteuerung *f*
sequential sequentiell

sequential control language Ablaufsteuersprache *f*
sequential control system Ablaufsteuerung *f*
sequential event Folgeereignis *nt*
sequential function chart (SFC) Darstellung *f* nach Ablaufsprache, Ablaufsprache *f*, sequentieller Funktionsplan *m*
sequential inspection Folgeprüfung *f*
sequential program sequentielles Programm *nt*
serial serienmäßig, seriell
serial by bit bitseriell
serial connection Reihenschaltung *f*
serial data transmission serielle Datenübertragung *f*
serial hoist unit Serienhubwerk *nt*
serial number Fertigungsnummer *f*, Fabriknummer *f*, laufende Nummer *f*, Seriennummer *f*
serial scribing ständiges (nicht unterbrochenes) Schreiben *nt*
serial transmission Serienübergabe *f*
serially connected zwischengeschaltet, in Reihe *f* geschaltet
seriation Reihenfolge *f*
serial-to-parallel coder Seriell-zu-Parallel-Codierer
series Serie *f*, Folge *f*, Reihe *f*
series of standards Normenreihe *f*
series characteristic motor Reihenschlussmotor *m*
series connection Reihenschaltung *f*, Hauptschluss *m*
series excitation Reihenschlusserregung *f*
series motor Universalmotor *m*, Hauptschlussmotor *m*
series of measurement Messreihe *f*
series of tests Prüfserie *f*, Versuchsreihe *f*
series production serienmäßige Herstellung *f*, Serienfertigung *f*
series radiogram Röntgenserienaufnahme *f*
series wound dynamo Reihenschlussmaschine *f*
series-manufactured burner Serienbrenner *m*

serrate riffeln, zahnen, kerbverzahnen
serrated blade cutter Messerkopf *m* mit auswechselbaren und geriffelten Messern
serrated lock washer Fächerscheibe *f*
serrated lock washer for screw assemblies Zahnscheibe *f* für Kombischrauben
serration Raste *f*, Kerbverzahnung *f*
serration for screws *pl* Innenvielzähne *mpl* für Schrauben
serration hob Keilverzahnungswälzfräser *m*
service manual Wartungsanleitung *f*, Wartungshandbuch *nt*
serve dienen
service in Stand halten, warten, pflegen; Wartung *f*, Instandhaltung *f*, Pflege *f*, Einsatz *m*, Betrieb *m*, Dienst *m*, Dienstleistung *f*
service a rack Regal bedienen
service bolt force Betriebsschraubenkraft *f*
service brake Betriebsbremse *f*
service circle of contact Betriebswälzkreis *m*
service circuit Betriebsstromkreis *m*
service condition betriebsmäßige Bedienung *f*
service conditions Betriebsbedingungen *fpl*
service cone of contact Betriebswälzkegel *m*
service cylinder of contact Betriebswälzzylinder *m*
service instruction Bedienungsvorschrift *f*
service level Servicegrad *m*
service life Standzeit *f*, Betriebsdauer *f*, Gebrauchsdauer *f*, Nutzungszeit *f*, Nutzungsdauer *f*, Lebensdauer *f*
service life cutting velocities Standzeitschnittgeschwindigkeiten
service load Gebrauchsbelastung *f*
service mass Betriebsmasse *f*
service mass of battery Batteriegewicht *nt*
service performance Gebrauchstüchtigkeit *f*
service personnel Instandhaltungspersonal *nt*
service pressure angle Betriebseingriffswinkel *m*
service program Dienstprogramm *nt*
service property Betriebseigenschaft *f*
service provider Dienstleiter *m*
service quality Verfügbarkeit *f*
service ratio Servicegrad *m*
service requirement Betriebsanforderung *f*
service routine Dienstprogramm *nt*
service strength Betriebsfestigkeit *f*
service stress Betriebsbeanspruchung *f*
service temperature Gebrauchstemperatur *f*
service test *(Erprobung)* Prüfung *f*
service unit Wartungseinheit *f*
service water temperature Gebrauchswassertemperatur *f*
serviceability Brauchbarkeit *f*, Gebrauchstauglichkeit *f*
serviceable brauchbar
servicing Pflege *f*, Wartung *f*, Instandhaltung *f*
servo control Servosteuerung *f*
servo cycle time Servoabtastrate *f*
servo drive Servomotor *m*
servo loop Regelschleife *f*
servo motor Stellmotor *m*, Servomotor *m*
servo-controlled mit Hilfssteuerung *f*, mit Vorsteuerung *f*
servomechanism Folgeregler *m*
servo-mechanism Hilfssteuerelement *nt*, Vorsteuerelement *nt*
session layer Verbindungsschicht *f*, Kommunikationsschicht *f*
set 1. justieren, einstellen, einrichten, verstellen, anstellen, zustellen, setzen, stellen 2. *(Haufen, Stoß, Stapel)* Satz *m*
set to the full-depth position auf volle Schnitttiefe einstellen
set a goal Ziel setzen
set a target Ziel setzen
set an objective Ziel setzen
set at an angle schrägstellen, quer verstellen
set down ablegen, hinsetzen
set drawing Satzzeichnung *f*
set free freisetzen

set input Setzeingang *m*
set of change gears Wechselrädersatz *m*
set of drawings Zeichnungssatz *m*
set of keys Schlüsselsatz *m*
set of pulleys Flaschenzug *m*
set of spanners Schlüsselsatz *m*
set of wrenches Schlüsselsatz *m*
set-over of the compound rest Supportverstellung *f*
set point Sollwert *m*
set right berichtigen
set square Zeichendreieck *nt*
set up aufbauen, errichten, montieren, spannen, rüsten; Rüstvorgang *m*
set value Sollwert *m*, Einstellwert *m*
set-actual comparison Soll-Ist-Vergleich *m*
setback Reduzierung *f*, Rückstellung *f*
set-point transmitter Sollwertgeber *m*
setscrew Einstellschraube *f*, Stellschraube *f*, Klemmschraube *f*
setting Setzen *nt*, Einstellen *nt*, Einspannen *nt*, Einstellung *f*, Einspannung *f*, Anstellung *f*, Aufspannung *f*, Zustellung *f*
setting accuracy Einstellgenauigkeit *f*
setting angle Anstellwinkel *m*
setting data Einstelldaten *pl*
setting deeper Tiefersetzen *nt*
setting disc *(über 18 mm)* Einstellmeßscheibe *f*
setting gauge Einstellmaß *nt*, Einstellehre *f*, einstellbare Lehre *f*
setting of goals Zieldefinition *f*, Zielsetzung *f*
setting of objectives Zielsetzung *f*
setting of the front cutting edge Vorderkanteneinstellung *f*
setting out Anreißen *nt*
setting parameter Einstellparameter *m*
setting plug gauge Einstellmeßscheibe *f*, Einstelldorn *m*
setting ring gauge Einstellring *m*
setting screw Einstellschraube *f*, Stellschraube *f*, Klemmschraube *f*
setting standard Einstellnormal *nt*
setting temperature Erstarrungstemperatur *f*
setting time Rüstzeit *f*, Umrüstezeit *f*

setting to work Inbetriebnahme *f*
setting to zero point Nullpunkteinstellung *f*
setting tolerance Einstelltoleranz *f*
setting tooth Einstellzahn *m*
setting up Rüsten *nt*, Einrichten *nt*, Zurüsten *nt*, Montage *f*, Rüstvorgang *m*, Aufstellung *f*
setting-down point Ablagepunkt *m*
settings information Einstellinformationen *pl*
setting-up time Aufspannzeit *f*, Rüstzeit *f*
settle 1. in Ordnung bringen 2. einpendeln, einschwingen 3. sich senken, sich setzen, abscheiden, ausfällen
settle complaints Reklamation bearbeiten
settled load Beharrungsbeanspruchung *f*
settlement *(Automatisierung, Fundament)* Setzung *f*, Setzungsmulde *f*
settling *(Automatisierung, Fundament)* Setzung *f*, Setzungsmulde *f*
settling of complaints Reklamationsbearbeitung *f*
settling period Beruhigungszeit *f*
settling time Einschwingzeit *f*
setup Einrichten *nt*, Einstellen *nt*, Einrichtung *f*, Einstellung *f*, Aufspannung *f*
set-up and shut-down gesamter Rüstvorgang *m*
set-up and shut-down time gesamte Rüstzeit *f*
set-up costs Rüstkosten *pl*
setup fixture Aufspannvorrichtung *f*
setup time Einrichtezeit *f*
set-up time Umrüstezeit *f*, Rüstzeit *f*
sever abschneiden, trennen, reißen
several mehrere
several machines of the same family Maschinenlos *nt*
several times mehrfach
severance Abtrennung *f*
severe erschwert, schwer, schwerwiegend
severing Abschneiden *nt*, Zerteilen *nt*, Trennen *nt*
severity Schwere *f*
sew nähen

sewage delivery law Abwasserabgabegesetz *nt*
sewage system Abwassernetz *nt*
sewing machine Nähverschließmaschine *f*
shackle insulator Abspannisolator *m*
shade Farbton *m*, Schatten *m*
shade effect Schattenwirkung *f*
shaded line schraffierte Linie *f*
shade-pole motor Spaltmotor *m*
shaft Schacht *m*, Welle *f*, Schaft *m*, Rundschaft *m*
shaft angle deviation Achsenwinkelabmaß *nt*
shaft angle variation Achsenwinkelabweichung *f*
shaft basis fit Passung *f* für Einheitswelle
shaft commissioning system Schachtkommissionierer *m*
shaft connection Wellenverbindung *f*
shaft coupling Wellenkupplung *f*
shaft dislocation Wellenverlagerung *f*
shaft dispensing system Schachtautomat *m*
shaft encoder Winkelcodierer *m*, codierte Drehgeber *mpl*
shaft end Wellenende *nt*, Wellenstumpf *m*
shaft gauge Wellenlehre *f*
shaft hub joint Wellennabenverbindung *f*
shaft lining Schachtfutter *nt*
shaft order compilation system Schachtkommissionierer *m*
shaft position Phasenlage *f*, Achslage *f*
shaft position tolerance Achslagetoleranz *f*
shaft system Schachtsystem *nt*
shaft turning lathe Wellendrehmaschine *f*
shaft-mounted rundschaftbefestigt
shaft-mounted gear Aufsteckgetriebe *nt*
shake schütteln, rütteln, erschüttern; Spiel *nt*
shaking cylinder Schüttelzylinder *m*
shaking flask Schüttelkolben *m*
shaking rate Schüttelfrequenz *f*
shallow flach
shallow coil Flachspule *f*
shallow pattern niedrige Form *f*
shallow pit Mulde *f*
shallow pit corrosion Muldenkorrosion *f*
shallow pit formation Muldenbildung *f*
shelving for archives Archivregal *nt*
shank Schaft *m*, Griff *m*, Stiel *m*, Gabelrücken *m*
shank back rake Spitzenspanwinkel *m*
shank cross-section Schaftquerschnitt *m*
shank cutter Schaftfräser *m*
shank side rake Seitenwinkel *m*, Seitenspanwinkel *m*
shank tool holder Schaftmeißelhalter *m*
shank top Stirnfläche *f* des Gabelrückens
shank type gear shaper cutter Schaftschneidrad *nt*
shank-type cutting tool Schaftmeißel *m*
shank-type keyway cutter Nutenfräser *m*
shank-type milling cutter Schaftfräser *m*
shank-type worm gear hob Schneckenradschaftfräser *m*
shape 1. formen, bearbeiten, bilden, gestalten; Form *f*, Bauform *f*, Umriss *m*, Gestalt *f* 2. *(Planbearbeitung)* hobeln, stoßen, kurzhobeln, senkrechthobeln, profilieren
shape box Formkasten *m*
shape by the generating method wälzhobeln, wälzstoßen, stoßen
shape coefficient Formbeiwert *m*
shape curved surfaces Kehlhobeln
shape cutting Spanung *f*, Zerspanung *f*, spangebende Formung *f*, formgebende Bearbeitung *f*, Formgebung *f*, Formung *f*
shape deviation Formabweichung *f*
shape embodiment Formverkörperung *f*
shape filling Formfüllung *f*
shape filling capacity Formfüllungsvermögen *nt*

shape for test specimens Probenform *f*
shape grinding Formschleifen *nt*
shape mask casting process Formmaskengießverfahren *nt*
shape method Formmethode *f*
shape of cutting edge Schneidenausbildung *f*
shape of spot Punktform *f*
shape on the backstroke rückwärts hobeln
shape on the return stroke rückwärts hobeln
shape parameter Gestaltsparameter *f*
shape process Formprozess *m*
shape stability Formhaltigkeit *f*, Gestaltfestigkeit *f*
shape stopping Formfüllung *f*
shape with formed tool formstoßen
shaped element Formelement *nt*
shaped part Formteil *nt*
shaped profile cutter profilhinterschliffener Formfräser *m*, spitzengezahnter Formfräser *m*
shaper Hobelmaschine *f*, Kurzhobler *m*, Stößelhobelmaschine *f*, Waagerechtstoßmaschine *f*, Hobler *m*, Shaper *m*, Shapingmaschine *f*
shaper cutter Schneidrad *nt*, Stoßmesser *nt*, Stoßwerkzeug *nt*
shaper drive Hobelantrieb *m*
shaper tool Hobelmeißel *m*, Hobelmesser *nt*
shaper toolholder Hobelmeißelhalter *m*
shapes Formteile *ntpl*
shaping 1. Bearbeitung *f*, Bearbeitung *f* zur Formgebung, Formgebung *f*, Formung *f*, formgebend **2.** *(Planbearbeitung)* Stoßen *nt*, Hobeln *nt*, Kurzhobeln *nt*
shaping by design Formgestalten *nt*
shaping by the generating method Wälzstoßen *nt*
shaping machine Hobelmaschine *f*, Waagerechthobler *m*, Kurzhobelmaschine *f*, Stößelhobelmaschine *f*, Waagerechtstoßmaschine *f*, Hobler *m*, Shaper *m*, Shapingmaschine *f*
shaping of pulses Pulsformung *f*

shaping operation *(Stößelhobelmaschine)* Hobelarbeit *f*
shaping temperature Formungstemperatur *f*
shaping tool *(Waagerechthobeln)* Hobelmeißel *m*
shaping width Hobelbreite *f*
shaping with formed tool Formstoßen *nt*
sharp scharf
sharp-cornered cutting edge scharfkantige Schneide *f*
sharp-cornered cutting tool nose scharfkantige Schneide *f*
sharp-edged scharfkantig, scharf
sharp-edged orifice scharfkantige Öffnung *f*
sharpen abrichten, spitzen, schärfen, anschärfen, nachschärfen, nachschleifen
sharpening Schleifen *nt*, Schärfen *nt*, Scharfschleifen *nt*
sharpness Schärfe *f*
sharp-pointed mit scharfer Spitze, mit scharfer Schneide, spitz
shatter crack Innenriss *m*
shave schaben
shaving cut Schabeschnitt *m*
shaving method Schabeverfahren *nt*
shaving tool Schabewerkzeug *nt*, Schabfräser *m*
shavings Späne *mpl*
shear 1. schneiden, scheren; Schere *f* **2.** *(Backe)* Wange *f*, Bettschlittenwange *f*
shear angle Scherwinkel *m*, Abscherwinkel *m*
shear chip Scherspan *m*
shear connector Kopfbolzen *m*
shear cross-section Scherquerschnitt *m*
shear cut scherender Schnitt *m*
shear cutting Zerspanen *nt* mit scherendem Schnitt, Abscheren *nt*
shear deformation Schubverformung *f*
shear failure Scherbruch *m*, Schubbruch *m*, Schubspannungsbruch *m*, Grundbruch *m*
shear fracture Schiebungsbruch *m*
shear load Scherbeanspruchung *f*
shear loading Schubbeanspruchung *f*,

Scherbeanspruchung *f*
shear off abscheren
shear pan Scherenpfanne *f*
shear pin Abscherbolzen *m*
shear plane Scherebene *f*
shear plane angle Scherwinkel *m*
shear plane angle proportion Scherwinkelverhältnis *nt*
shear plane angle relationship Scherwinkelbeziehung *f*
shear plane perpendicular force Schernormalkraft *f*
shear plane tangential force Scherkraft *f*
shear process Schervorgang *m*
shear reach Scherenreach *m*
shear rigidity Schubsteifigkeit *f*
shear specimen Scherprobe *f*
shear speed Schergeschwindigkeit *f*
shear stability Scherstabilität *f*
shear stiffness Schubsteifigkeit *f*
shear strength Scherfestigkeit *f*
shear stress Schubspannung
shear test by tensile loading Zugscherversuch *m*
shear test in flatwise plane Schubversuch *m*
shear test jig Nietschergerät *nt*
shear tool Schermeißel *m*
shear viscosity Scherviskosität *f*
shear wave Scherwelle *f*
shear zone Scherzone *f*
shear-action cutting Scherschneiden *nt*
shear-action cutting tool Scherschneidenwerkzeug *nt*
sheared oil geschertes Öl *nt*
shearing Abschneiden *nt*, Scherschneiden *nt*, Scheren *nt*, Abscheren *nt*, Schneiden *nt*
shearing against elastic pad Schneiden *nt* gegen elastische Kissen
shearing area Scherfläche *f*
shearing disc viscosimeter Scherscheibenviskosimeter *nt*
shearing force Scherkraft *f*, Querkraft *f*, Schubkraft *f*
shearing machine Schere *f*
shearing off Abscheren *nt*, Abscherung *f*

shearing off tool Abscherwerkzeug *nt*
shearing point Scherstelle *f*
shearing resistance Abscherfestigkeit *f*
shearing strength Abscherfestigkeit *f*
shears Schere *f*
sheath-alloyed high performance electrode hüllenlegierte Hochleistungselektrode *f*
sheathed ummantelt
sheathed hose ummantelter Schlauch *m*
sheath ummanteln, umhüllen, verkleiden; Schirm *m*
sheathing Umhüllung *f*, Verkleidung *f*, Ummantelung *f*
sheave Antriebsscheibe *f*, Blockscheibe *f*, Rillenscheibe *f*
sheer draught Längsriss *m*
sheet Folienbahn *f*, Folie *f*, Platte *f*
sheet bar Platine *f*
sheet dissection system Zerschneideblattsystem *nt*
sheet forming Blechumformung *f*
sheet material Flächengebilde *nt*
sheet metal Blech *nt*
sheet metal casing Blechgehäuse *nt*
sheet metal gauge Blechlehre *f*
sheet metal sheathing Blechverkleidung *f*
sheet metal stencil Blechschablone *f*
sheet-metal strip Blechstreifen *m*
sheet metal template Blechschablone *f*
sheet metal working Blechbearbeitung *f*
sheet of emery paper Schmirgelbogen *m*
sheet of fibrous material Faserstoffbahn *f*
sheet of metal Blechtafel *f*
sheet of paper Papierlage *f*
sheet offering maximum dimensional stability Brettaufriss *m*, maßbeständige Tafel *f*
sheet spring nut Federmutter *f*
sheet steel Blech *nt*
sheet storage Blechlager *nt*
sheet thickness Blechdicke *f*
sheet with trapezoidal corrugations Trapezblech *nt*
sheeting Folie *f*, Folienbahn *f*

sheeting releasing plasticiser weichmacherabgebene Folie *f*
shelf Gestell *nt*, Regal *nt*, Fachboden *m*, Tablar *nt*
shelf divider Fachteiler *m*, Fachteilung *f*
shelf grid Regalraster *nt*
shelf life Haltbarkeit *f*, Lagerfähigkeit *f*, Lagereignungsdauer *f*
shelf operating system Regalbediensystem *nt*
shelf reinforcement Bodenverstärkung *f*
shelf space Regalfläche *f*
shell Schale *f*, Hülle *f*, Umhüllung *f*, Verkleidung *f*
shell end mill Walzenstirnfräser *m*
shell nozzle Mantelstutzen *m*
shell tap Aufsteckgewindebohrer *m*
shell tool Aufsteckwerkzeug *nt*
shellac Schellack *m*
shellac adhesive Schellackkleber *m*
shell-type tool Aufsteckwerkzeug *nt*
shelter Unterstand *m*
shelve zurückstellen
shelve a project ein Projekt zurückstellen
shelving Regallagerung *f*, Regal *nt*
shelving aisle Regalgang *m*
shelving bottom Fachboden *m*
shelving capacity Fachfassungsvermögen *nt*
shelving depth Regaltiefe *f*
shelving system Regalsystem *nt*
spherical kugelig
spherical surface kugelige Fläche *f*
spherical triangle error *(bei Wellen)* Gleichdickfehler *m*
shield 1. Blende *f*, Schild *nt*, Schutz *m*, Schutzschild *nt*, Schutzschirm *m*, Schutzeinrichtung *f*; schützen, abschirmen **2.** *(gegen Licht)* Störlichtblende *f*
shielded system Blendensystem *nt*
shielded-arc filler wire Schutzgasschweißdraht *m*
shielding Schirm *m*, Abschirmung *f*, Strahlungsschutz *m*
shielding effectiveness Schirmdämpfung *f*, Schirmdämpfungsfaktor *m*
shielding gas Formiergas *nt*
shielding gas regulator Edelgasdruckminderer *m*
shielding wall Schutzwand *f*
shift 1. einstellen, verstellen, schalten, umschalten, schieben, verschieben, einrücken, schwenken, verrutschen, versetzen, umsetzen, bewegen **2.** verlagern; Verlagerung *f* **3.** *(Arbeitszeit)* Schicht *f*
shift drilling Umschlagbohren *nt*
shift frequency Schalthäufigkeit *f*
shift gear schalten, Gang wechseln
shift input Schiebeeingang *m*
shift leader Schichtführer *m*
shift milling method Umschlagverfahren *nt*
shift operation Schichtbetrieb *m*, Schiebevorgang *m*
shift register Scheiberegister *nt*
shift schedule Schichtplan *m*
shift supervisor Schichtleiter *m*
shiftable verschiebbar
shifter Steuerschieber *m*, Verschieber *m*, Umsetzer *m*
shifting 1. Verschiebung *f*, Versetzung *f*, Verschieben *nt*, Verstellung *f*, Umsetzung *f*, Ortsveränderung *f*, Verstellen *nt*, Umschalten *nt*, Einstellen *nt* **2.** *(einen Hebel)* Bedienung *f*
shifting device Schubvorrichtung *f*
shifting force Schaltkraft *f*
shifting gear Schieberad *nt*
shifting input Schiebeeingang *m*
shifting movement Verschiebebewegung *f*
shifting process Umsetzvorgang *m*
shim Zwischenlegblech *nt*, Unterlegstück *nt*, Unterlegplatte *f*, Beilage *f*; unterlegen, unterbauen
shim for rivet nuts Beilegeblech *nt* für Annietmuttern
shim ring Passscheibe *f*
shine leuchten
shrinkage Lunker *m, mpl*
ship liefern, versenden, verladen
shipment Versand *m*, Lieferung *f*, Verladung *f*
shipping bay Packerei *f*
shipping documents Lieferpapiere *pl*
shipping mass Verlademasse *f*
shipping order Versandauftrag *m*

shock-proof stoßfest
shock Erschütterung *f*, Stoß *m*, Schock *m*; schocken
shock absorber Stoßdämpfer *m*
shock absorbing stoßdämpfend
shock absorption Stoßdämpfung *f*
shock coefficient Stoßfaktor *m*
shock load Stoßbelastung *f*, Belastungsstoß *m*
shock loading Stoßbeanspruchung *f*
shock resistance Erschütterungsfestigkeit *f*, Stoßfestigkeit *f*
shock wave Druckwächter *m*
shock wave effect Druckstoß *m*
shock welding Schockschweißen *nt*
shock-absorber buffer Puffer *m* mit eingebautem Stoßdämpfer
shock-absorbing castor gefederte Rolle *f*
shock-free stoßfrei
shockless stoßfrei
shocklike stoßartig
shoddy work Pfuscharbeit *f*
shoe Setzstockbacke *f*
shoe brake Backenbremse *f*
shoe soling material Schuhbesohlungsmaterial *nt*
shoes *pl* **used of form the weld** nahtformende Backen *mpl*
shooting Schießen *nt*
shop Betrieb *m*, Werkstatt *f*, Werkhalle *f*, Betriebshalle *f*
shop accident Betriebsunfall *m*
shop calendar day (SCD) Betriebskalendertag (BKT) *m*
shop floor programming werkstattorientierte Programmierung (WOP) *f*
shop gauge Arbeitslehre *f*
shop own betriebseigen
shop term Werkstattausdruck *m*
shop test Versuch *m*
short kurz, knapp
short brittleness Kurzbrüchigkeit *f*
short chip Kurzspan *m*
short chip material kurzspanender Werkstoff *m*
short circuit Kurzschluss *m*; kurzschließen
short code Kurzcode *m*
short message Kurzmitteilung *f*
short message service Kurzmitteilungsdienst *m*
short square niedriger Vierkantsatz *m*
short strake ram kurzhubiger Stößel *m*
short taper Steilkegel *m*, steiler Kegel *m*, Kurzkegel *m*
short term kurzzeitig
short type Kurzausführung *f*
short wave Kurzwelle *f*
shortage Mangel *m*, Knappheit *f*
shortage of skilled workers Facharbeitermangel *m*
short-brittle chip kurzgebrochener Span *m*
short-circuit current Kurzschlussstrom *m*
short-circuit proof kurzschlussfest, kurzschlusssicher
short-circuit ring Kurzschlussläuferring *m*
short-circuit rotor Kurzschlussläufer *m*
shortcutting kurzspanend
shorten kürzen, verkürzen
shortening Verkürzung *f*
short run Kleinserie *f*
short-run knapp
short-run job kleine Stückzahl *f*, kleine Serienarbeit *f*
short-stem funnel Trichter *m* mit kurzem Stiel
short-stroke kurzhubig
short-stroke movement kurzhubige Bewegung *f*
short-taper spindle nose Kurzkegelspindelkopf *m*
short-term corrosion test Kurzzeitkorrosionsuntersuchung *f*
short-term internal pressure test Kurzzeitinnendruckversuch *m*
short-term loading Kurzbelastung *f*
short-term storage Kurzzeitlagerung *f*
short-time internal pressure loading Kurzzeitinnendruckbeanspruchung *f*
short-time operation Kurzzeitbetrieb *m*
short-time thermal resistance Kurzzeitwarmfestigkeit *f*
short-undulation components *pl* kurzwellige Anteile *mpl*
short-waviness Kurzwelligkeit *f*

shot granulieren
shot-blasting Abstrahlen *nt* mit Kies, Strahlen *nt* mit Stahlkies
shotpeened disc spring kugelgestrahlte Tellerfeder *f*
shotting Granulierung *f*
shoulder 1. Absatz *m*, Abstufung *f*, Bund *m*, Stufe *f*; absetzen 2. *(Körper)* Schulter *f*
shoulder dimension Absatzmaß *nt*
shoulder grinding Anschlagschleifen *nt*
shoulder milling Ansatzfräsen *nt*, Stufenfräsen *nt*, Strahlspanen *nt*
shoulder of the cut Hauptschnittfläche *f*, Hauptabschnittfläche *f*, Schnittfläche *f*
shoulder tool Seitenmeißel *m*
shoulder turn absatzdrehen
shoulder turning Absatzdrehen *nt*, Ansatzdrehen *nt*
shouldered castellation abgesetzte Krone *f*
shouldered hole abgesetzte Bohrung *f*
shouldered nut Ansatzmutter *f*
shouldered round specimen geschulterte Rundprobe *f*
shouldered test bar Schulterstab *m*
shouldering Absetzen *nt*
shovel schaufeln
show nachweisen, zeigen
show in black geschwärzt darstellen
shower test Beregnungsversuch *m*
shrink zusammenschrumpfen, schrumpfen
shrink force Schrumpfkraft *f*
shrink frame Schrumpfrahmen *m*
shrink hood Schrumpfhaube *f*
shrink hood applicator Schrumpfhaubenüberziehmaschine *f*, Palettenschrumpfhaubenüberziehmaschine *f*
shrink on aufschrumpfen
shrink oven Schrumpfofen *m*
shrink sleeve Schrumpfhülse *f*
shrink sleeving machine Schrumpfhülsenüberziehmaschine *f*
shrink tunnel Schrumpftunnel *m*
shrink wrap Schrumpfverpackung *f*, Schrumpffolienumhüllung *f*; schrumpfverpacken

shrink wrapping *(Schrumpffolie)* Umschlingen *nt*
shrink wrapping machine Schrumpffolieneinschlagmaschine *f*
shrinkable tubing Schrumpfschlauch *m*
shrinkage Schwund *m*, Schwindung *f*, Schrumpfung *f*
shrinkage assembly Schrumpfverband *m*
shrinkage behaviour Schrumpfverhalten *nt*
shrinkage block Schwindvorrichtung *f*
shrinkage cavity Lunkerstelle *f*
shrinkage during drying Trockenschwindung *f*
shrinkage forming Lunkerbildung *f*
shrinkage groove Wurzelkerbe *f*
shrinkage in volume Volumenschwindung *f*
shrinkage measurement Schrumpfungsmessung *f*
shrinkage property Schrumpfungseigenschaft *f*, Schwindungseigenschaft *f*
shrinking Schrumpfen *nt*, Schrumpfung *f*
shrinking equipment Schrumpfeinrichtung *f*
shrinking film Schrumpffolie *f*
shrinking furnace Schrumpfofen *m*
shrinking gun Schrumpfpistole *f*, Handschrumpfgerät *nt*
shrinking on Aufschrumpfen *nt*
shrinking pistol Schrumpfpistole *f*
shrinking unit Schrumpfeinrichtung *f*
shrinkwrap Schrumpffolienumhüllung *f*; schrumpfverpacken
shrinkwrap pack Schrumpfpackung *f*
shrinkwrapping Schrumpfeinschlagen *nt*
shrinkwrapping machine Schrumpffolieneinschlagmaschine *f*
shrinkage dimension Schwindmaß
shrunk-on sleeve Überschiebmuffe *f*
shunt Weiche *f*, Schienenweiche *f*, Nebenschluss *m*; rangieren, verschieben
shunt excitation Nebenschlusserregung *f*
shunt generator Nebenschlussma-

schine *f*
shunt motor Nebenschlussmotor *m*
shunt protection Auffahrschutz *m*
shunt switch Umgehungsschalter *m*
shunting Verschieben *nt*, Rangieren *nt*
shunt-wound drive Nebenschlussantrieb *m*
shut sperren
shut down 1. abschalten, stilllegen, stillsetzen, außer Betrieb setzen 2. Rüstvorgang *m*
shut down behaviour Abschaltverhalten *nt*
shut down time Rüstzeit *f*
shut off abschalten, abstellen, abdrehen, absperren
shut position Geschlossenstellung *f*
shutdown Abschalten *nt*, Abschaltung *f*, Außerbetriebnahme *f*, Stillsetzung *f*, Betriebsstörung *f*, Stilllegung *f*; stillsetzen
shutdown of the burner Brennerabschaltung *f*
shut-down signal Abschaltsignal *nt*
shut-down system Abschaltsystem *nt*
shut-off device Absperreinrichtung *f*, Verschlussorgan *nt*
shut-off flap Absperrklappe *f*
shut-off member Verschlussorgan *nt*
shutoff valve Absperrschieber *m*
shut-off valve Absperrorgan *nt*, Absperrventil *nt*
shut-off zone Absperrbereich *m*
shuttle hin- und herfahren, pendeln
shuttle back and forth hin- und herbewegen
shuttle balt conveyor reversierbarer Gurtbandförderer *m*
shuttle service Pendelantrieb *m*, Wendebetrieb *m*
shuttle valve Wechselventil *nt*
shuttle-type movement reversierbare Bewegung *f*
shuttle-type table hin- und hergehender Tisch *m*
SID (start input data) Startdateneingabe *f*
side Schenkel *m*, Seite *f*, Flanke *f*; seitlich
side accuracy Seitengenauigkeit *f*

side and face milling cutter Scheibenfräser *m*
side angle Komplementwinkel *m* des Einstellwinkels *m*
side band Seitenbereich *m*
side bearing Seitenlager *nt*
side box Seitensupport *m*
side branch Seitenzulauf *m*
side by side nebeneinander
side casting Seitenguss *m*
side clamp Seitenklemme *f*
side clearance Hohlschliff *m*, Seitenfreiwinkel *m*, seitlicher Freiwinkel *m*
side clearance angle *(Seitenmeißel)* Freiwinkel *m*
side column Seitenständer *m*
side content Seiteninhalt *m*
side cutting tool Seitenmeißel *m*
side edge of workpiece Werkstückseitenkante *f*
side elevation Seitenansicht *f*
side face Seitenfläche *f*
side fillet weld Flankenkehlnaht *f*
side flap Seitenklappe *f*
side guards Seitenschutz *m*
side guide Seitenführung *f*
side guide roller Seitenführungsrolle *f*
side gusset Seitenfalte *f*
side head Seitensupport *m*
side housing Ständer *m*
side lift spreader Seitenhubspreader *m*
side loader Seitenschieber *m*
side member Seitenteil *nt*
side mill Scheibenfräser *m*
side milling Seitenfräsen *nt*, Scheibenfräsen *nt*, Walzenstirnfräsen *nt*
side milling cutter Scheibenfräser *m*
side of fusion face Stirnseitenkante *f*
side of gap face Stirnlängskante *f*
side of the thread Gewindeflanke *f*
side protection Seitenschutz *m*
side rake Seitenspanwinkel *m*
side rake angle Seitenspanwinkel *m*, Werkzeugwinkel *m* senkrecht zur Hauptschneide
side ramp Seitenrampe *f*
side relieve Freiflächenfase *f* der Hauptschneide
side rougher Seitenschruppmeißel *m*
side seam glued seitlich verklebt

side seam seal Seitennaht *f*
side shift Seitenschieber *m*
side stressed in tension zugbeanspruchte Seite *f*
side thrust Seitenkraft *f*, Seitenschub *m*
side tippler Seitenkippgerät *nt*
side tool Seitenmeißel *m*
side toolbox Seitensupport *m*, seitlicher Support *m*
side tool-head Seitensupport *m*
side top rake angle Seitenspanwinkel *m*
side travel Translation *f*
side view Seitenansicht *f*
side wall Längsseite *f*
side wear Seitenverschleiß *m*
side wedge angle Seitenkeilwinkel *m*
side-cutting edge angle Schneidenwinkel *m*
side-facing seating Quersitz *m*
side-facing standing Querstand *m*
side handling Seitenschieber *m*, Seitenschub *m*
sidehead Werkzeugträger *m*, Seitensupport *m*, Support *m*
side head screw Spindel *f* zur Verstellung des Ständerschlittens
side load handling Seitenschieber *m*, Seitenschub *m*
side load handling device Seitenschieber *m*
side loader Querstapler *m*
side-loading fork truck Seitenstapler *m*
side-loading truck Querstapler *m*
side-relieved hohlgeschliffen, seitlich hinterschliffen
side-seamed seitenverschlossen
side-seated seitlich sitzend, mit Fahrersitz quer zur Fahrtrichtung
side sheet Seitenwand *f*
side-turning tool Seitendrehmeißel *m*
sidewall Seitenwand *f*
sidewards zur Seite *f*
sideways seitlich
sideways moving shuttle Seitenshuttle *nt*
sidewise seitlich, in seitlicher Richtung *f*
siding *(Bau)* Verkleidung *f*
sieve sieben, Sieb *nt*

sieve frame Siebrahmen *m*
sieve holder Siebhalterung *f*
sifter temperature controller Sichtertemperaturregler *m*
sighting device Visiereinrichtung *f*
sighting device Visiereinrichtung *f*
sign Schild *nt*, Zeichen *nt*, Vorzeichen *nt*, Formelzeichen *nt*; anzeichnen, markieren
sign bit Vorzeichenbit *nt*
sign inversion Vorzeichenumkehr *f*
sign of wear Verschleißerscheinung *f*
sign rule Vorzeichenregel *f*
signal Signal *nt*, Zeichen *nt*; signalisieren, anzeigen, angeben, melden
signal adjuster Signaleinsteller *m*
signal alteration Signalveränderung *f*
signal amplifier Signalverstärker *m*
signal cable Signalleitung *f*
signal converter Signalumformer *m*, Signalwandler *m*, Signalumsetzer *m*
signal current Steuerstrom *m*
signal delay Signalverzögerung *f*
signal diagram Signallaufbahn *f*
signal edge Signalflanke *f*, Flanke *f*
signal edge evaluation Flankenauswertung *f*
signal emission Signalabgabe *f*
signal encoder Signalgeber *m*
signal exploitation Signalverwertung *f*
signal flow Signalfluss *m*
signal flow path Wirkungsweg *m*, Signalflussweg *m*
signal input Signaleingang *m*
signal interface Signalanschluss *m*
signal lamp Signallampe *f*, Leuchtmelder *m*
signal level converter Signalpegelumsetzer *m*
signal light Signalleuchte *f*
signal loss Signalverlust *m*
signal modification Signalveränderung *f*
signal polarity Signalpolarität *f*
signal port Signalanschluss *m*
signal potential Signalspannung *f*
signal processing Signalaufbereitung *f*, Signalverarbeitung *f*
signal prolongation Signalverlängerung *f*

signal sequence Signalfolge *f*
signal structure Signalstruktur *f*
signal switching Signalschaltung *f*
signal to-noise ratio Signal-Rausch-Abstand *m*
signal transducer Signalumsetzer *m*
signal transmitter Signalgeber *m*
signal tuning circuit Abstimmkreis *m*
signalled gemeldet
signalize angeben
signalling Anzeige *f*
signalling device Meldeeinrichtung *f*
signalling point Meldeort *m*
signalling speed Schrittgeschwindigkeit *f*
signalling system Meldesystem *nt*
significance Bedeutung *f*
significance level Signifikanzniveau *nt*
significance test statistischer Test *m*
significant test result signifikantes Testergebnis *nt*
signpost Schilderpfahl *m*
silence Ruhe *f*
silencing Schallminderung *f*, Geräuschdämpfung *f*
silent geräuscharm, ruhig
silent chain Zahnkette *f*
silent running geräuscharmer Lauf *m*, ruhiger Lauf *m*, Laufruhe *f*
silica glass bowl Kieselglasschale *f*
silicate bond Silikatbildung *f*
silicate plastics material Silikatplastikmasse *f*
silicon Silizium *nt*
silicon carbide Siliziumkarbid *nt*
silicon controlled rectifier (SCR) Thyristor *m*, steuerbarer Halbleitergleichrichter *m*
silicone Silikon *nt*
silicone resin Silikonharz *nt*
silicone rubber casting compound Silikonkautschuk-Gießmasse *f*
silicone rubber compound Silikonkautschukmasse *f*
silicone rubber mastic Silikonkautschukknetmasse *f*
silicone blasting agent silikone Strahlmittel *mpl*
silicosis Silikosegefahr *f*
silification *(e. Untergrundes)* Verkieselung *f*
silo Silo *nt*
silo design Silobauweise *f*
silo rack construction Silobauweise *f*
silo rack type Silobauweise *f*
silo theory Silotheorie *f*
silver colouration Silberfärbung *f*
silver content amenable to punching punzierungsfähiger Silbergehalt *m*
silver halide Silberhalogenid *m*
silver plating Silberauflage *f*
silver sensitized paper Silbersalzpapier *nt*
silver sensitized photocopying paper Ablichtungspapier *nt* mit Silbersalzschicht
silver solder Silberlot *nt*
silver stria Silberschliere *f*
silver strip test Silberstreifenprüfung *f*
silver-bearing brazing filler alloy silberhaltiges Hartlot *nt*
silverware solder Silberwarenlot *nt*
similar gleichzeitig
simple einfach
simple gear train Rädergetriebe *nt* mit einfacher Übersetzung
simple hypothesis einfache Hypothese *f*
simple indexing Einfachteilen *nt*, einfaches Teilen *nt*
simple layer einfache Schicht *f*
simple pitch diameter einfacher Flankendurchmesser *m*
simple random sampling ungeschichtete Probenahme *f*
simple station Einfachstation *f*
simple transfer station Einfachwechselstation *f*
simplex simplex
simplex brake Simplexbremse *f*
simplex manufacturing type milling machine Einspindelplanfräsmaschine *f*
simplex operation Simplexbetrieb *m*
simplex transmission Simplexübertragung *f*
simplification Vereinfachung *f*
simplified vereinfacht
simplified view vereinfachte Ansicht *f*
simplify vereinfachen

simulate simulieren, nachbilden
simulation Simulation *f*, Vortäuschen *nt*, Vortäuschung *f*, Nachbildung *f*
simulation experiment Simulationsexperiment *nt*
simulation feedback Simulationsrückmeldung *f*
simulation language Simulationssprache *f*
simulation model Simulationsmodell *nt*
simulation operation Simulationsbetrieb *m*
simulation process coupling Simulationsprozessverknüpfung *f*
simulation program Simulierer *m*
simulation run Simulationslauf *m*
simulation study Simulationsstudie *f*, Simulationsuntersuchung *f*
simulation trial Simulationsexperiment *nt*
simulation-based simulationsgestützt
simulator Simulator *m*
simulator core Simulatorkern *m*
simulator programming Simulatorprogrammierung *f*
simultaneous simultan, gleichzeitig, zeitgleich
simultaneous tomograph Simultanschichtaufnahme *f*
simultaneous twin spindle milling gleichzeitiges Fräsen *nt* mit zwei Spindeln
sine bar Sinuslineal *nt*
sine curve Sinuskurve *f*
sine function Sinusfunktion *f*
sine wave Sinuswelle *f*
sine wave generator Sinusgenerator *m*
single 1. einfach, einzeln, vereinzeln 2. *(Automatisierungstechnik)* Einzel-FTF *nt*
single angle cutter Winkelstirnfräser *m*, Lückenfräser *m*
single bank radiator einreihiger Heizkörper *m*
single bending Einfachbiegen *nt*
single bevel groove plus root face HV-Stegnaht *f*
single block mode Einzelsatzbetrieb *m*

single bolt fixing Rückenlochbefestigung *f*
single bolt hole Rückenloch *nt*
single branch Einfachabzweig *m*
single bulb condenser Ein-Birnenkühler *m*
single chisel technique Einmeißelverfahren *nt*
single clock system Einzeluhrensystem *nt*
single column design Einständerbauart *f*
single column vertical turret lathe Einständerkarusselldrehmaschine *f*
single crystal Einkristall *m*
single cycle Einfachspiel *nt*, Einzelspiel *nt*
single deep einfachtief
single depth einfachtief
single disc cartridge Einzelpalettenkassette *f*
single edged tool einseitiges Werkzeug *nt*
single end offset box wrench gekröpfter Einringschlüssel *m*
single error Einzelfehler *m*
single exposure Einfachbelichtung *f*
single family house with self-contained flat Einfamilienhaus *nt* mit Einliegerwohnung
single fault Einfachfehler *m*
single flange piece Einflanschstück *nt*
single flanged rail wheel Spurkranzrad *nt*
single flank engagement Einflankeneingriff *m*
single gate Einfachanschnitt *m*
single impulse boring Einzelimpulsbohren *nt*
single lap jointed test specimen einschnittig überlappter Probekörper *m*
single latch bolt lock Einfallenschloss *nt*
single layer einlagig; Einzelschicht *f*, einfache Schicht *f*
single level test Einstufenversuch *m*
single liner Vereinzelungsmaschine *f*
single live load wandernde Einzellast *f*
single load Einzelbelastung *f*
single load capacity Einfachlastauf-

nahme f, Einfachzugriff m
single load-carrying device Einfachlastaufnahme f
single measured value Einzelmesswert m
single motor drive Einzelantrieb m
single on-hand quantity *(im Lager)* Einzelbestand m
single opening gap gauge einmäulige Rachenlehre f
single pallet position Einzelpalettenposition f
single pan balance einschalige Waage f
single peak-to-valley height Einzelrautiefe f
single pitch Einzelteilung f
single point thread turning Gewindedrehen nt
single position Monoposition f
single position palletizing Einzelpalettierung f
single probe technique Einkopftechnik f
single production Einmalproduktion f
single pulse operation Einpulsbetrieb m
single quenching einmaliges Abschrecken nt
single rod Einzelstab m
single room heating Einraumheizung f
single round corner Einfachhohlkehle f
single sample einmalige Entnahme f
single side loading truck Quergabelstapler m
single sound event Einzelschallereignis nt
single speed control einstufige Fahrsteuerung f
single spindle automatic lathe Vielmeißelautomat m
single thread eingängiges Gewinde nt
single thread milling cutter Langgewindefräser m
single time measuring Einzelzeitmessung f
single toolholder Einfachmeißelhalter m
single tooth broad finish milling Einzahnbreitschlichtfräsen nt

single wheel Einzelrad nt
single wire Einzeldraht m
single-acting einfach wirkend
single-AGV Einzel-FTF nt
single-axle einachsig
single-bevel butt weld with root face HY-Naht f mit Kehlnähten am Schrägstoß
single-bevel weld with broad root face HY-Naht f
single-cam operated automatic turret lathe Einkurvenautomat m
single-cam system Einkurvensystem nt
single-chisel planes Einmeißelhobeln nt
single-column construction Einständerbauart f
single-column machine Einständermaschine f
single-cone pulley Einscheibe f
single-cropping Einfachabschneiden nt
single-cycle gear cutting Einzelverzahnung f
single-cycle method Einzelverzahnung f
single-digit einstellig
single-edge grinding wheel Einprofilschleifscheibe f
single-edged einschneidig
single-edged cutting tool einschneidiges Werkzeug nt
single-end box wrench Einringschlüssel m
single-ended einseitig
single-ended offset ring spanner gekröpfter Einringschlüssel m
single-ended open-jaw spanner Einmaulschlüssel m
single-ended ring spanner Einringschlüssel m
single-event sound pressure level Einzelereignis-Schalldruckpegel m
single-face four-way entry pallet Vierwegepalette f
single-flank working error Einflankenwälzsprung m
single-flank working test Einflankenwälzprüfung f
single-flank working variation Einflankenwälzabweichung f

single-floor boiler Stockwerkkessel *m*
single-grade sortenrein
single-head engineers wrench Einmaulschlüssel *m*
single-I butt weld HU-Naht *f*
single-J butt weld J-Naht *f*
single-lane eingassig
single-lane conveyance Einbahnverkehr *m*
single-lane traffic Einbahnverkehr *m*
single-lever control Einhebelbedienung *f*, Einhebelsteuerung *f*
single-lever operation Einhebelbedienung *f*
single-line feed system Einlinienzuführung *f*
single-line principle of operation Einleitungssystem *nt*
single-line system Einleitungsanlage *f*
single-line token Zugstab *m*
single-lipped deep-hole drill Einlippentieflochbohrer *m*
single-location storage Einplatzlagerung *f*
single-location system Einplatzsystem *nt*
single-man S/R machine Singleman-RBG *nt*
single-mast Einmast ...
single-mast machine Ein-Säulen-Gerät *nt*
single-parameter digital signal einparametrisches digitales Signal *nt*
single-part production Einzelfertigung *f*
single-phase asynchronous motor Einphasenasynchronmotor *m*
single-phase induction motor Einphaseninduktionsmotor *m*
single-piece aus einem Stück
single-piece production Einzelteilfertigung *f*
single-pin einpolig
single-place digital scale einstellige Ziffernskale *f*
single-point einschneidig
single-point cutting tool Einmeißelwerkzeug *nt*, einschneidiger Meißel *m*, Einzeldrehmeißel *m*
single-point diamond tool Diamanteinzelwerkzeug *nt*
single-point measurement Einpunktmessung *f*
single-point method Einpunktverfahren *nt*
single-point tool Einzelwerkzeug *nt*
single-point wheel truer Einkornabrichter *m*
single-point wheel truing Einkornabrichten *nt*
single-position depalletizer Monopositionsdepalettierer *m*
single-position hob Einstellwälzfräser *m*
single-position palletizer Monopositionspalettierer *m*
single-process tool Einverfahrenwerkzeug *nt*
single-product sortenrein
single-product feed system Einsortenzuführung *f*
single-projection welding Einzelbuckelschweißen *nt*
single-purpose machine Einzweckmaschine *f*, Einfachmaschine *f*
single-purpose welder Einzweckschweißer *m*
single-rib grinding wheel Einprofilschleifscheibe *f*
single-rib wheel einprofilige Schleifscheibe *f*, Einprofilschleifscheibe *f*
single-rod measuring cell Einstabmesskette *f*
single-rod storage Einzelstablagerung *f*
single-rowed einreihig
single-run weld einlagige Schweißung *f*
single-shell hyperboloid einschaliger Hyperboloid
single-shift operation Einschichtbetrieb *m*
single-sided run Einfachregal *nt*
single-skid contact system Einkufentastsystem *nt*
single-spindle automatic multi-tool lathe Einspindelvielstahlautomat *m*
single-spindle automatic screw machine Einspindelform- und -schraubenautomat *m*
single-spindle automatic turret lathe Einspindelautomat *m*

single-spindle automatic turret screw machine Einspindelrevolverautomat *m*
single-spindle index centre Teilgerät *nt* mit einer Teilspindel
single-spindle machine Einspindelmaschine *f*
single-spot welded joint Einzelpunktschweißverbindung *f*
single-stage einstufig
single-stage gear transmission einstufiges Getriebe *nt*
single-start screw thread eingängiges Gewinde *nt*
single-start trapezoidal screw thread with clearance eingängiges Trapezgewinde *nt* mit Spiel
single-step einstufig
single-strand floor-mounted truck conveyor Unterflurschleppkettenförderer *m*
single-T joint T-Stoß *m*
single-tier eingeschossig
single-tip cutter Frässtichel *m*
single tone Singleton *nt*, Einzelton *m*
single-tooth cutting Einzahnschruppen *nt*
single-U joint U-Fuge *f*
single-V butt joint with backing run V-Naht *f* mit Gegenlage
single-V butt joint with different abutting cross-sections V-Naht *f* mit verschiedenen Anschlussquerschnitten
single-Vee groove for corner joint V-Naht *f* am Eckstoß
single-Vee groove with sealing run V-Naht *f* mit Gegenlage
single-walled water heater einwandiger Wassererwärmer *m*
single-wavelength monochromatisch
single-way light barrier Einweglichtschraube *f*
single-well radiography einwandige Durchstrahlung *f*
single-wheel lapping machine Einscheibenläppmaschine *f*
singling Vereinzelung *f*
singling process Vereinzelungsprozess *m*
singling unit Vereinzelungsgerät *nt*

sink 1. ausdrehen, einfräsen, fräsen, spitzsenken, senken, versinken; Senke *f* **2.** (schweißen) Einfallschweißstelle *f*
sink mode output Strom *m* ziehender Ausgang
sinking 1. Senkung *f*, Einsenkung *f* **2.** *(Umformung)* Hohlgleitziehen *nt*
sinking of tubular products Gleitziehen *nt* von Hohlkörpern
sinusoidal sinusförmig
sinter sintern
sinter shaped parts Sinterformteile
sintered carbide Hartmetall *nt*, Sinterkarbid *nt*
sintered carbide metal Sintermetall *nt*
sintered glass filter Glasfritte *f*
sintered metal Sintermetall *nt*
sintered powder metal Metalloxyd *nt*
sintered tool Hartmetallwerkzeug *nt*
sintering Sintern *nt*
sintering material Sinterwerkstoff *m*
sintering point Sinterpunkt *m*
sintering process Sintervorgang *m*
sintering substance Sinterstoff *m*
sinusoidal alternating stress sinusförmige Schwingspannung
sinusoidal characteristics sinusförmiger Verlauf *m*
sinusoidal curve Sinuskurve *f*
siphon Trompetenrohr *nt*
siphon bend Siphonbogen *m*
siphon effect Heberwirkung *f*
siphon line Heberleitung *f*
siphoning system Heberleitungssystem *nt*
siren Sirene *f*
sit sitzen
sit down hinsetzen *nt*
sit down rider-controlled mit Fahrersitz *m*
site Standort *m*
site mixed concrete Ortbeton *m*
site of work Arbeitsplatz *m*
siting Standortbestimmung *f*
sit-on mit Fahrersitz
sit-on truck Sitzflurförderzeug *nt*, Flurförderzeug *nt* mit Fahrersitz
situation Lage *f*, Sachlage *f*
suitable for anodising anodisierbar
suitable for thermal cutting autogen

schneidbar
six speed gearbox sechsstufiger Räderkasten *m*
six spindle drilling machine sechsspindelige Bohrmaschine *f*
six-fold compression mould Sechsfachpresswerkzeug *nt*
six-spindle automatic bar machine Sechsspindelautomat *m*
six-spindle automatic lathe Sechsspindler *m*
six-spindle automatic screw machine Sechsspindelhalbautomat *m*
six-way tool block Sechsfachmeißelhalter *m*
size 1. Maß *nt*, Abmessung *f*, Größe *f*, Baugröße *f*, Format *nt*, Umfang *m*, Ausmaß *nt*, Stärke *f*, Dicke *f*; bemessen **2.** kalibrieren
size alteration Maßänderung *f*
size check Maßprüfung *f*
size grinding Maßschleifen *nt*
size loss Verringerung *f* der Größe, Verlust *m* der Maßgenauigkeit
size of drawing Zeichnungsformat *nt*
size of land Fasenbreite *f*, Zahnrückendicke *f*
size of lettering Schriftgröße *f*
size of standard lettering Normschriftgröße *f*
size of the hall Hallengröße *f*
size of the warehouse Lagergröße *f*
size rolling Maßwalzen *nt*
size specific größenspezifisch
size to width auf Breite bringen
sized kalibriert
sized tool Formmeißel *m*
size-grade sortieren
sizes *pl* **without tolerance indication** Maße *ntpl* ohne Toleranzangaben
sizing 1. Dimensionierung *f* **2.** Maßprägen *nt*
sizing broach Kalibrierräumwerkzeug *nt*
sizing cut Maßspan *m*
sizing press Kaliberpresse *f*
sizing roll Kalibrierwalze *f*
sizing section Kalibrierabschnitt *m* *(~zähne beim Gewindebohren)*
sizing teeth *(pl)* Kalibrierzähne *mpl*

sizing work Kalibrierarbeit *f*
skate wheel Röllchen *nt*
skate wheel conveyor Röllchenbahn *f*
skate wheel conveyor bed Röllchenteppich *m*
skeleton Gerüst *nt*
skeleton container Gitterbox *f*
sketch Skizze *f*; skizzieren
skew geneigt, windschief; schräg laufen; Schräglauf *m*
skew roller Schrägrolle *f*
skew roller conveyor Schrägrollenbahn *f*
skew rolling Schrägwalzen *nt*
skew rolling for expanding over a piercer rod using disc-shaped rolls Schrägwalzen *nt* zum Aufweiten über Stopfen mit scheibenförmigen Walzen
skew rolling for piercing holes Schrägwalzen *nt* zum Lochen
skew rolling of shapes Profilschrägwalzen *nt*, Schrägwalzen *nt* von Formteilen
skew rolling of tubular products Schrägwalzen *nt* von Hohlkörpern
skew rolling of tubular products over a piercer rod using stepped rolls Schrägwalzen *nt* von Hohlkörpern über eine Stange mit Schulterwalzen
skew rolling of tubular shapes Profilschrägwalzen *nt* von Hohlkörpern
skewness Schiefe *f*
skid 1. rutschen; Kufe *f*, Gleitkufe *f*, Gleitschuh *m*, Palettenkufe *f* **2.** *(Fahrzeug)* schleudern
skid channel support Tiefenauflage *f*
skid checking Kufenkontrolle *f*
skid conveyor Skidförderer *m*
skid conveyor system Skidförderanlage *f*
skid down herabgleiten
skid mounting Kufenunterbau *m*
skidding conditions Glätte *f*
skidding down Herabgleiten *nt*
skid-proof gleitsicher
skill Geschicklichkeit *f*
skill test praktische Lehrlingsprüfung *f*
skilled fachgerecht, sachkundig, qualifiziert
skilled labour Fachkräfte *fpl*, gelernte

Arbeitskräfte *f*, Facharbeiter *m*
skilled people Fachkräfte *fpl*
skilled worker gelernter Arbeiter *m*, Facharbeiter *m*
skillet Tray *nt*
skillet erecting machine Trayaufrichtmaschine *f*
skillet-free hülsenlos
skilful fachgerecht
skills Qualifikation *f*
skin Gusshaut *f*
skin crack Hautriss *m*
skin effect Stromverdrändungseigenschaft *f*
skin package Skinverpackung *f*
skin packing machine Skineinschlagmaschine *f*, Skinverpackungsmaschine *f*
skin turning cut *(drehen)* Schälschnitt *m*
skin-miller Flächenformfräsmaschine *f*
skinning Hautbildung *f*
skin-turning Schälen *nt*
skip überspringen
skip distance Sprungabstand *m*
skip lot sampling Sprungstichprobenprüfung *f*
skip-feeding Sprungvorschub *m*
skip-feeding for rapid traverse between gaps Sprungvorschub *m* für Leerwege im Eilgang
skip-milling Fräsen *nt* unterbrochener Flächen
skiving Wälzschälen *nt*
skiving wheel Schälrad *nt*
slab Platte *f*; platinieren
slab drawing Strangziehen *nt*
slab milling Fräsen *nt* mit Walzenfräsern, Planfräsen *nt* mit breitem Schnitt, Planfräsen *nt*, Schälfräsen *nt*, Wälzen *nt*
slab milling cutter Schälfräser *m*, Abwälzfräser *m*, Wälzfräser *m*
slab milling machine Schälfräsmaschine *f*
slab with web Platte *f* mit Steg
slabbing cut Schälschnitt *m*, schälender Schnitt *m*
slabbing cutter Walzenfräser *m*, der breiter als sein Durchmesser ist
slabbing machine Langfräsmaschine *f* zum Flächenfräsen

slab-mill breiter Walzenfräser *m*; Flächen fräsen, fräsen mit breitem Walzenfräser, planfräsen, walzfräsen
slack locker, schlaff, ungespannt, lose; Spiel *nt*, Schlupf *m*
slack chain Schlaffkette *f*
slack chain detection device Schlaffkettensicherung *f*
slack rope Schlaffseil *nt*
slack rope detection device Schlaffseilsicherung *f*
slack rope protection Schlaffseilschalter *m*
slack rope switch Schlaffseilschalter *m*
slack side of a belt ungespanntes Trumm *nt*
slack span ungespanntes Trumm *nt*
slack wire rope Schlaffseil *nt*
slacken lösen, lockern, nachlassen, entspannen
slacken the locking screw one turn Klemmschraube um eine Umdrehung lösen
slacking off Lockern *nt*
slackness Schlaffheit *f*, Spiel *nt*
slag Schlacke *f*
slag basting Schlackenstrahlmittel *nt*
slag inclusion Schlackeneinschluss *m*
slag marksman Schlackenschütze *m*
slag off abschlacken
slag protection Schlackenschutz *m*
slag removal Abschlackung *f*
slag sieve Schlackensieb *nt*
slag strainer Schlackensieb *nt*
slag tap fired boiler Schmelzkammerkessel *m*
slant Neigung *f*
sleeve Hülse *f*, Buchse *f*, Muffe *f*, Zwischenstück *nt*, Manschette *f*, Umhüllung *f*, Banderole *f*, Pinole *f*, Kabelmuffe *f*, Teilungshülse *f*; umhüllen
sleeve fitting Muffenfitting *m*
sleeve joint Manschettenverbindung *f*, Muffenverbindung *f*
sleeve machine Sleevemaschine *f*
sleeve welding with incorporated electric heating element Heizwendelschweißen *nt*
sleeve wrapping machine Schrumpffolieneinwickelmaschine *f*

sleeve-lock Pinolenfestklemmung *f*
sleeving machine Umhüllungsmaschine *f*
slender schlank
slender taper schlanker Kegel *m*
slenderness Schlankheit *f*
slenderness ratio Schlankheitsgrad *m*
slew schwenken
slew rolling of solid sections Profilschrägwalzen *nt* von Vollkörpern
slewable schwenkbar
slewing Schwenken *nt*
slewing mast Schwenkmast *m*
slewing mast structure Schwenkkonstruktion *f*
slewing mechanism Schwenkeinrichtung *f*
slewing motion Schwenkbewegung *f*
slewing ring Drehkranz *m*
slice in Streifen schneiden
slid back zurückgerutscht
slid head Schlitten *m* Räummaschine
slide 1. Schlitten *m*, Schlittenschieber *m* **2.** Gleitschiene *f*, Führung *f*, Rutsche *f*; schieben, abschieben, rutschen, wegrutschen, gleiten **3.** langdrehen
slide back zurückrutschen
slide bar Gleitschiene *f*
slide calliper rule Tiefenlehre *f*, Schieblehre *f*, Schublehre *f*
slide for helical cutting Schrägzahnschieber *m*
slide head 1. Querbalkensupport *m*, Horizontalsupport *m*, Support *m* **2.** *(Planbearbeitung)* Hobelsupport *m*
slide in 1. einschieben **2.** *(Weg)* Einschubbahn *f*
slide into einrücken
slide lock Schieberraste *f*
slide member Schlittenschieber *m*
slide mould with split parting line Schieberwerkzeug *nt* mit Backentrennfläche
slide rail Laufschiene *f*
slide rail Laufschiene *f*
slide resisting bolted joint gleitfeste Schraubenverbindung *f*
slide resisting screwed fastening gleitfeste Schraubenverbindung *f*
slide resisting screwed joint gleitfeste Schraubenverbindung *f*
slide rest Support *m*, Schlittenschieber *m*
slide rule Rechenschieber *m*
slide truck Verschiebewagen *m*
slide type racking Durchrutschregal *nt*
slide with friction reiben
slide-in cart Einschub *m*
slide-in racking Einschubregal *nt*
slider Schieber *m*
slider-and-rocker Schubschwinge *f*
slider crank Schubkurbel *f*
slider straight Schubgerade *f*
slider-crank mechanism Kurbelschleife *f*
slide-resisting bolted fastening gleitfeste Schraubenverbindung *f*
slideway Führung *f*, Führungsbahn *f*, Gleitbahn *f*, Gleitfläche *f*
slideway oil Gleitbahnöl *nt*
sliding 1. Gleiten *nt*; gleitend, verschiebbar **2.** Langdrehen *nt*
sliding bearing Gleitlager *nt*
sliding block 1. Kulissenstein *m* **2.** Gleitschuh *m*
sliding bracket Gleitschelle *f*
sliding calliper Tiefenlehre *f*
sliding cam plate Kurvenschieber *m*
sliding clamp Schieber *m*
sliding clutch Reibungskupplung *f*
sliding component Gleitkomponente *f*
sliding contact Schleifkontakt *m*
sliding direction Gleitrichtung *f*
sliding expansion joint Stopfbuchsausgleichslager *nt*
sliding feed Langvorschub *m*
sliding fit Gleitsitz *m*
sliding friction Gleitreibung *f*
sliding gear Schieberad *nt*
sliding gear drive Schieberadgetriebe *nt*
sliding gear mechanism Verschieberädergetriebe *nt*
sliding gears *pl* Schiebezahnräder *ntpl*
sliding head type single-spindle automatic machine Langdrehautomat *m*
sliding hexagon turret lathe Sattelrevolverdrehmaschine *f* mit waagerecht angeordnetem Revolver

sliding hub Rutschnabe f
sliding indicator Gleitindikator m
sliding jaw Messschenkel m, Gleitbacke f
sliding lane Einschubbahn f, Gleitauflage f
sliding layer Gleitauflage f
sliding member Schieber m
sliding pipe support Rohrgleitlager nt
sliding process Gleitvorgang m
sliding rail Gleitschiene f
sliding spindle quill ausziehbare Spindelhülse f
sliding surface Gleitfläche f
sliding table Schiebetisch m
sliding tee bar with reduced diameters Stufendrehstift m
sliding type fitting Schiebestutzen m
sliding type socket Überschiebmuffe f
sliding block Führungsstein m
slight klein, gering, schwach
slight damage to the surface Oberflächenverletzung f
slight gradient geringe Neigung f
slight lift kleiner Hub m
slight taper schlanker Kegel m
slightly blended gearbox oil mildlegiertes Getriebeöl nt
sling schleudern, anschlagen, befestigen
sling casting Schleudergießen nt, Schleuderguss m
sling casting process Schleudergießverfahren nt
sling net Ladenetz nt
sling rope Anschlagseil nt
slinger process Slingerverfahren nt
slinging Anschlagen nt
slinging point Anschlagpunkt m, Anschlagstelle f
slip rutschen, verrutschen, gleiten, ausgleiten, aufstecken; Schlupf m
slip casting Schlickergießen nt
slip clutch Rutschkupplung f
slip gauge Messblock m, Blockmaß nt, Maßblock m, Maßklötzchen nt, Parallelendmaß nt, Endmaß nt, Maßbild nt
slip grinding Gleitschleifen nt
slip hazard Rutschgefahr f
slip loss Schlupfverlust m
slip off abrutschen

slip resistant rutschhemmend
slip ring Kontaktring m
slip ring motor Schleifringläufermotor m
slip ring rotor Schleifringläufer m
slip sheet Einschussbogen m
slip time Rutschzeit f
slip-in socket Einschiebmuffe f, Einsteckmuffe f
slip-in weld socket joint Einsteckschweißmuffenverbindung f
slip-on flange glatter Flansch m
slip-on flange with brazing collar loser Flansch m mit Lötbund
slip-on flange with butt welded collar loser Flansch m mit Anschweißpunkt
slip-on handle *(für Grenzlehrdorne)* Einsteckgriff m
slip-on welding flange glatter Schweißflansch m
slippage Schlupf m
slippery material gleitfördernder Stoff m
slipping Abrutschen nt, Ausgleiten nt, Rutschen nt, Schlupf m
slipping moment Rutschmoment nt
slipping out Herausrutschen nt
slipping over Aufstecken nt
slipping resistance Schlupfwiderstand m
slipshod work Pfusch m, Pfuscharbeit f
slit Blende f
slitting press Streifenpresse f
slog schwere Arbeit f
slogging Abnahme f
slope abschrägen, neigen; Abschrägung f, Neigung f
slope drainage fitting Böschungsstück nt
slope of the operating characteristic Steilheit f
slope of the tooth Zahnschräge f
slope of weld Nahtneigungswinkel m
slope value Kippwert m
sloped schräg, schief, abgeschrägt
sloping Schrägstellung f
sloping line geneigte Linie f
sloping style standard lettering schräge Normschrift f

sloping surface Fangschräge *f*
slot 1. Nut *f*, Langnut *f*, Längsnut *f*, Langloch *nt*, Schlitz *m*, Rille *f*, Kerbe *f*, Einstich *m*, Aussparung *f*; nuten, langlochen, schlitzen, einstechen **2.** hobeln **3.** Fach *nt*, Öffnung *f*
slot and keyway milling machine Langloch- und Keilnutenfräsmaschine *f*
slot drill Langlochfräser *m*, Fingerfräser *m*, Nutenfräser *m*
slot internally innenstoßen
slot milling Nutenfräsen *nt*, Schlitzfräsen *nt*, Schlitzen *nt*
slot milling attachment *(Langnuten)* Nutenfräseinrichtung *f*
slot milling cutter Nutenfräser *m*
slot milling gashing Schlitzfräsen *nt*
slot milling machine Langlochfräsmaschine *f*
slot milling operation Schlitzfräsarbeit *f*
slot type nozzle Schlitzdüse *f*
slot-in guard rail Steckgeländer *nt*
slot-mill schlitzen
slotted arm Kurbelschwinge *f*, Kulisse *f*
slotted bolt Schlitzbolzen *m*
slotted cheese head screw Zylinderschraube *f* mit Schlitz
slotted countersunk head screw Senkschraube *f* mit Schlitz
slotted countersunk head tapping screw Senk-Blechschraube *f* mit Schlitz
slotted disc water pressure test Schlitzdruckprüfung *f*
slotted head screw Schraube *f* mit Schlitz
slotted headless screw Gewindestift *m* mit Schlitz
slotted hole Langloch *nt*
slotted microwave guide Schlitzhohlleiter *m*
slotted pan head screw Flachkopfschraube *f* mit Schlitz
slotted pan head tapping screw Zylinderblechschraube *f*
slotted raised countersunk head tapping screw Linsensenkblechschraube *f* mit Schlitz
slotted round head wood screw Halbrundholzschraube *f* mit Schlitz
slotted round nut *(für Hakenschlüssel)* Nutmutter *f*
slotted screw driver Schlitzmutterndreher *m*
slotted screw with full dog point Zapfenschraube *f* mit Schlitz
slotted screwed sealing plug Schlitzstopfen *m*
slotted section Selbstbauprofil *nt*
slotted set screw with cup point Gewindestift *m* mit Schlitz und Ringschneide
slotted set screw with flat point Gewindestift *m* mit Schlitz und Kegelkuppe
slotted set screw with half-dog point Gewindestift *m* mit Schlitz und Zapfen
slotter Senkrechthobelmaschine *f*, Senkrechtstoßmaschine *f*, Nutenstoßmaschine *f*, Stoßmeißel *m*
slotter ram Stoßmaschinenstößel *m*
slotting Langlochfräsen *nt*, Nutstoßen *nt*, Senkrechtstoßen *nt*, Hobeln *nt*, Schlitzen *nt*
slotting attachment Senkrechtstoßeinrichtung *f*, Stoßeinrichtung *f*
slotting bar Stoßstange *f*
slotting cutter Langlochfräser *m*, Fingerfräser *m*
slotting device Schlitzeinrichtung *f*
slotting machine Senkrechthobelmaschine *f*, Senkrechtstoßmaschine *f*
slotting saw Schraubenschlitzfräser *m*, Schlitzfräser *m*
slotting setup Aufspannung *nt* für Senkrechtstoßarbeit
slotting tool Nutenstoßmeißel *m*, Hobelmeißel *m*, Stoßmeißel *m*, Stoßwerkzeug *nt*
slow langsam
slow combustion capability Dauerbrandfähigkeit *f*
slow down verzögern, bremsen, verlangsamen, langsamer werden, Geschwindigkeit *f* abnehmen, auslaufen
slow motion screw Feinbewegungsschraube *f*
slow-combustion inset Dauerbrandeinsatz *m*

slowdown Drosselung *f*
slowing-down Verlangsamung *f*, Auslaufen *nt*
slowing-down path Nachlaufweg *m*
slow-moving item Langsamdreher *m*
slow-moving items C-Sortiment *nt*
sludge Bodensatz *m*
sludge content Schlammgehalt *m*
slue schwenken
slugging box wrench Schlagringschlüssel *m*
slugging ring spanner Schlagringschlüssel *m*
sluggish zäh
sluggish-elastic extension träge elastische Dehnung *f*
slumber mode Schlummerbetrieb *m*
slur Schlichte *f*
slush casting Sturzguss *m*
small klein
small batch Kleinserie *f*
small batch production Kleinreihenfertigung *f*, Kleinserienfertigung *f*
small container Kleinbehälter *m*, Kleingebinde *nt*
small heating boiler Kleinheizkessel *m*
small lot Kleinserie *f*
small lot milling Kleinreihenfräsen *nt*
small package Kleingebinde *nt*
small parts Kleinteile *ntpl*
small parts container Kleinladungsträger (KLT) *m*, Kleinteilebehälter *m*
small parts container gripper KLT-Greifer *m*
small parts store Kleinteilelager *nt*
small parts warehouse Kleinteilelager *nt*
small punched card Kleinlochkarte *f*
small run kleine Stückzahl *f*, kleine Serienarbeit *f*
small standard bar Normkleinstab *m*
small water heater Kleinwasserheizer *m*
small welding attachment Kleinschweißeinsatz *m*
smallest possible kleinstmöglich
smallest value Mindestwert *m*
small-scale business Mittelstand *m*
small-scale representation Kleindarstellung *f*

smart intelligent
smelt schmelzen
smelter Schmelzofen *m*
smelter charging Schmelzofenbeschickung *f*
smelting Schmelzen *nt*, Schmelzung *f*
smelting facility Schmelzerei *f*
smelting factory Schmelzbetrieb *m*
smelting loss Abbrand *m*
smith's bellows Blasebalg *m*
smoke Rauch *m*
smoke alarm system Rauchmeldeanlage *f*
smoke chimney Rauchschornstein *m*
smoke control installation Rauchabzugsanlage *f*
smoke detector Brandmelder *m*
smoke duct Rauchkanal *m*
smoke emission limit Rauchauswurfbegrenzung *f*
smoke flue Rauchfang *m*
smoke outlet Rauchabzug *m*
smoke pipe Rauchrohr *nt*
smoke protection door Rauchschutztür *f*
smoke spot number Rußzahl *f*
smoke vent Rauchabzug *m*
smokestack installation Schornsteinanlage *f*
smooth glätten, ebnen; Glätte *f*; erschütterungsfrei, ruckfrei, stoßfrei, reibungsfrei, glatt, eben, stufenlos, nahtlos, sanft, ruhig
smooth as from moulding pressblank
smooth planer Abrichtmaschine *f*
smooth rolling of tubular shapes Profilglattwalzen *nt* von Hohlkörpern
smooth running Laufruhe *f*
smooth surface glatte Oberfläche *f*
smooth surfaced radiator glatter Heizkörper *m*
smooth surfaced sheet glattes Walzfell *nt*
smoothing Glättung *f*, Glätten *nt*
smoothing capacitor Glättungskondensator *m*
smoothing factor Glättungsfaktor *m*
smoothly running ignition weiche Zündung *f*
smoothness Glätte *f*, Glattheit *f*, Eben-

heit *f*
smooth rolling Glattwalzen *nt*
snag abgraten, grobschleifen
snag grinding Grobschleifen *nt*, Vorschleifen *nt*
snagging Abgraten *nt*, Grobschleifen *nt*, Vorschleifen *nt*
snagging grinder Grobschleifmaschine *f*
snake shrinkage Schlangeneinlauf *m*
snap gage lapping machine Rachenlehrläppmaschine *f*
snap gauge Rachenlehre *f*
snap head rivet Flachrundniet *m*
snap hook Karabinerhaken *m*
snap ring groove Sprengringnute
snarling chip Wirrspan *m*
snarly chip Wirrspan *m*
snug anziehen
soak durchweichen, aufsaugen
soaking temperature Durchwärmtemperatur *f*
soaking time Durchwärmzeit *f*
SOC (start output control) Ausgabe Sekundärbefehl *m*
socket Fassung *f*, Stutzen *m*, Halterung *f*, Hülse *f*, Buchse *f*, Muffe *f*
socket base Muffenboden *m*
socket clearance Muffenspiel *nt*
socket connection Halsstutzen *m*
socket design Muffenkonstruktion *f*
socket end cover Muffendeckel *m*
socket entry Muffeneingang *m*
socket gap Muffenspiel *nt*
socket head slot Tauchschlitz *m*
socket pipe Muffenrohr *nt*
socket plug Muffenstopfen *m*
socket ring Taumelscheibe *f*
socket screw thread Muffengewinde *nt*
socket spanner Steckschlüssel *m*
socket union Überwurfschraube *f*
socket welding Muffenschweißen *nt*
socket wrench Steckschlüssel *m*
SOD (start output data) Startdatenausgabe *f*
sodium-cooled natriumgekühlt
soft sanft, nachgiebig
soft jointing material Weichdichtungsstoff *m*
soft mix from rubber Weichgummimischung *f*
soft packing Weichdichtung *f*, Weichpackung *f*
soft skin entkohlte Randzone *f*
soft solder (unter 450°C) Lot *nt*
soft solder alloy Weichlotlegierung *f*
soft solder bath Weichlotbad *nt*
soft soldered joint Weichlötstelle *f*
soft soldering temperature Weichlöttemperatur *f*
soft start Sanftanlauf *m*
soft-elastic state weichelastischer Zustand *m*
soften plastically plastisch erweichen
softening Erweichen *nt*
softening behaviour Erweichungsverhalten *nt*
softening characteristic Erweichungsverhalten *nt*
softening interval Erweichungsintervall *m*
soft keys Softwaretaster *m*
software Software *f*
software adaptation Softwareanpassung *f*
software agent Softwareagent *m*
software development Softwareerstellung *f*
software documentation Programmdokumentation *f*
software element Softwarebaustein *m*
software fault Softwarefehler *m*
software limit switch Softwareendschalter *m*
software structure Softwarestruktur *f*
software-controlled softwaregesteuert
soil verschmutzen
soil slip Bodenrutschung *f*
soilability Verschmutzbarkeit *f*
soil-covered pipework erdbedeckte Rohrleitung *f*
spinning of external flanges Drücken *nt* von Außenborden
solar heating plant Sonnenheizungsanlage *f*
solar radiation Sonnenwärmeeinstrahlung *f*, Sonneneinstrahlung *f*
solder löten; Lot *nt*, Lötmittel *nt*
solder bath Lötbad *nt*

solder coating Lotüberzug *m*
solder filaments *pl* Lotfäden *mpl*
solder lug Lötöse *f*
solder lug for slot-in fixing Lötöse *f* für Einsteckbefestigung
solder lug with no device to prevent turning Lötöse *f* mit Drehsicherung
solder lug with push-through fixing Lötöse *f* mit Durchsteckbefestigung
solder pin Lötstift *m*
solder pin with flange Lötstift *m* mit Flansch
solder pin with flange Lötstift *m* mit Flansch
solder pin with shoulder Lötstift *m* mit Bund
solder point Lotpunkt *m*
solder sealing machine Lötverschließmaschine *f*
solder shape Lotformteil *m*
solder to anlöten
solder wire Lötdraht *m*
solderability test Lötbarkeitsprüfung *f*
soldered component Lötgruppe *f*, Lötteil *m*
soldered joint Lötverbindung *f*
soldered joint endangered by corrosion korrosionsgefährdete Lötstelle *f*
solder-forming flux lotbildendes Flussmittel *nt*, Reaktionslot *nt*
solder-forming flux lotbildendes Flussmittel *nt*, Reaktionslot *nt*
soldering Löten *nt*
soldering behaviour Lötverhalten *nt*
soldering bit Lötkolben *m*
soldering blowlamp Lötlampe *f*
soldering depot Lötdepot *nt*
soldering flux Lötmittel *nt*
soldering iron Lötkolben *m*
soldering joint Lötstoß *m*
soldering point Lotpunkt *m*
soldering process Lötprozess *m*
soldering seam volume Lötnahtvolumen *nt*
soldering stopping medium Lötstoppmittel *nt*
soldering tag Lötfahne *f*
soldering under protective atmospheres Schutzgaslöten *nt*
soldering with components coated with filler metal Löten *nt* mit lotbeschichteten Teilen
soldering with hand fed filler metal Löten *nt* mit angesetztem Lot
soldering with inserted filler metal Löten *nt* mit eingelegtem Lot
soldering with preplaced filler metal Löten *nt* mit angelegtem Lot
soldering with soldering depot Löten *nt* mit Lötdepot
soldering without a flux flussmittelfreies Löten *nt*
solderless joint lötlose Verbindung *f*
solderless olive type tube fitting lötlose Schneidringrohrverschraubung *f*
solderless tube fitting lötlose Rohrverschraubung *f*
solder lug with rivet shank Lötöse *f* mit Nietzapfen
solder poison Lotgift *nt*
solenoid Magnet *m*, Magnetspule *f*, Elektromagnet *m*
solenoid head Elektromagnetkopf *m*
solenoid operation magnetische Betätigung *f*
solenoid switch Magnetschalter *m*
solenoid valve Magnetventil *nt*
solenoid-actuated shut-off valve Absperrarmatur *f* mit Antrieb durch Elektromagnet
solid 1. fest, voll, massiv 2. einteilig
solid adhesive fester Klebstoff *m*
solid bed type milling machine Planfräsmaschine *f*
solid black arrow vollschwarzer Pfeil *m*
solid body laser Festkörperlaser *m*
solid broach einteiliges Räumwerkzeug *nt*
solid cutter einteiliger Fräser *m*, massiver Fräser *m*
solid cutting tool Vollmeißel *m*
solid epoxy resin festes Epoxidharz *nt*
solid forming Massivumformen *nt*
solid fuel boiler Kessel *m* für feste Brennstoffe
Solid Ground Curing SGC (Körperaushärteverfahren *nt*)
solid hob Vollwälzfräser *m*
solid inclusion Feststoffeinschluss *m*
solid ink coder Festtintecodierer *m*

solid metal gasket Metalldichtung *f*
solid milling cutter Vollfräser *m*
solid nickel Hartnickel *nt*
solid plastic wheel Kunststoffrad *nt*
solid plug gauge Volllehrdorn *m*
solid rolling Festwalzen *nt*
solid section voller Querschnitt *m*
solid shaft Vollwelle *f*
solid state fester Aggregatzustand *m*
solid structure Massivbau *m*
solid thimble Vollkausche *f*
solid thread festes Gewinde *nt*
solid tool einteiliges Werkzeug *nt*, Vollmeißel *m*
solid tyre Bereifung *f* aus Vollmaterial, Vollgummireifen *m*
solid tyred wheel Rad *nt* mit Bereifung aus Vollmaterial
solid vee Prisma *nt*
solid wall Vollwand *f*
solid wheel Rad *nt* aus einem Material, Scheibenrad *nt*
solid wheel centre massiver Radkörper *m* aus einem Werkstoff
solid wire electrode Massivdrahtelektrode *f*
solid-carbide finishing shell Schlichtschneideinsatz *m* aus Hartmetall zum Aufstecken auf Räumwerkzeugtragkörper
solid-die cold header Kaltstauchmaschine *f* mit ungeteilter Matrize
solidification Verfestigung *f*
solidification course Erstarrungsverlauf *m*
solidification crack Erstarrungsriss *m*
solidification front Erstarrungsfront *f*
solidification procedure Erstarrungsvorgang *m*
solidify erstarren
solids content Trockensubstanz *f*
solids interceptor Steinschleuse *f*
solids trap Steinfang *m*
solid-type end mill Schaftfräser *m*
solidus temperature Solidustemperatur *f*
solid-walled vollwandig
solubility temperature Lösetemperatur *f*
stator starter Ständeranlasser *m*

stator starting method Ständeranlassverfahren *nt*
stator starting technique Ständeranlassverfahren *nt*
stator winding Ständerwicklung *f*
status Zustand *m*, Status *m*
status criteria Standkriterien
status data Zustandsdaten *pl*
status enquiry Zustandsabfrage *f*
status identification Zustandskennung *f*
status indication Zustandsanzeige *f*
status indicator Zustandsanzeige *f*
status information Zustandsinformation *f*
status message Statusmeldung *f*, Zustandsmeldung *f*
status of delivery Lieferstatus *m*
status scheme Zustandsschaubild *nt*
status sizes Standgrößen
status variable Zustandsgröße *f*
statutory order Rechtsverordnung *f*
statutory order on pressure vessels Druckbehälterverordnung *f*
statutory technical order technische Verordnung *f*
stave Daube *f*
stay 1. Pfosten *m*, Stiel *m*, Gebäudestütze *f* **2.** bleiben, verbleiben, beharren, warten; Verweildauer *f*
stay put in Stellung bleiben
stay rope Halteseil *nt*, Rückhalteseil *nt*
staybolt Stehbolzen *m*
staybolt drilling machine Stehbolzenbohrmaschine *f*
steadily increasing loads zügig wirkende Kräfte *f*
steadiness Kippsicherheit *f*
steady 1. stetig, gleichmäßig, stationär **2.** Gegenhalter *m*, Setzblock *m*
steady flow stationäre Strömung *f*
steady running zügiger Lauf *m*
steady state Dauerzustand *m*
steady state flexural vibration stationäre Biegeschwingung *f*
steady stress ruhende Beanspruchung *f*
steadyrest Festlünette *f*, Lünette *f*, Setzstock *m*
steady-state deviation from the desired value bleibende Sollwertab-

weichung *f*
steady-state transfer factor Übertragungsbeiwert *m*
steam Dampf *m*
steam admission Dampfeinführung *f*
steam blasting Dampfstrahlen *nt*
steam boiler code Dampfkesselverordnung *f*
steam boiler engineering Dampfkesselbau *m*
steam boiler regulation Dampfkesselvorschrift *f*
steam boiler with water injection Dampfkühler *m* mit Wassereinspritzung
steam capping machine Dampfschraubverschließmaschine *f*
steam converter Wasserdampfumformer *m*
steam converting ejector valve Dampfumformejektorventil *nt*
steam cooler Dampfkühler *m*
steam cushion Dampfpolster *nt*
steam energy Dampfenergie *f*
steam generating flask Dampfentwicklungskolben *m*
steam generating plant Dampferzeugeranlage *f*
steam heated dampfbeheizt (a.)
steam inlet branch Dampfeinführungsstutzen *m*
steam main Dampfnetz *nt*
steam offtake Dampfentnahme *f*
steam pleating Dampfplissieren *nt*
steam pressure control Dampfdruckregelung *f*
steam pressure limiter Dampfdruckbegrenzer *m*
steam setting Dampffixieren *nt*
steam soot blower Dampfrußbläser *m*
steam temperature control Dampftemperaturregelung *f*
steam temperature controller Dampftemperaturregler *m*
vaporous dampfförmig
steel rail Stahlschiene *f*
steel Stahl *m*
steel ball impression method Kugeleindrückverfahren *nt*
steel band Stahlband *nt*
steel base Stahluntergrund *m*

steel cable Stahlseil *nt*
steel coil Stahlrolle *f*
steel conduit thread Panzerrohrgewinde *nt*
steel construction Stahlbau *m*
steel cutter blank Stahlfräserrohling *m*
steel facing Anstählen *nt*
steel grit Stahlkorn *nt*
steel measuring tape Stahlmessband *nt*
steel pipe ready for laying verlegefertiges Stahlrohr *nt*
steel plate Stahlblech *nt*, Stahlplatte *f*
steel reinforcement welder Betonstahlschweißer *m*
steel rim travel wheel Stahllaufrad *nt*
steel scrap Stahlschrott *m*
steel sheet Stahlblech *nt*, Blech *nt*
steel shelf Stahlfachboden *m*
steel shot Stahlsand *m*
steel spraying wire Stahlspritzdraht *m*
steel strapping Stahlband *nt*
steel strip Stahlband *nt*
steel tube nozzle Stahlrohrtülle *f*
steel with only low hardness gain gering einhärtender Stahl *m*
steel wool Stahlwolle *f*
steel-on-steel pairs Stahl-Stahl-Paarung *f*
steel-stamp number Kommissionsnummer *f*
steel-toed shoe Schuh *m* mit Stahlkappen
steelworks slag Stahlwerksschlacke *f*
steep steil
steep angle taper Steilkegel *m*
steep fall-off Steilabfall *m*
steep front Steilabfall *m*
steep gradient starke Neigung *f*
steep taper Steilkegel *m*, steiler Kegel *m*, Kurzkegel *m*
steep-flanked single-bevel butt joint Halbsteilflankennaht *f*
steep-flanked single-V butt joint Steilflankennaht *f*
steeply sloping section Steilstrecke *f*
steer steuern, lenken
steer angle Lenkwinkel *m*
steer angle sensor Lenkwinkelgeber *m*
steer axle Lenkachse *f*

steer axle pivotal point Pendeldrehpunkt *m*
steer wheel Lenkrad *nt*
steerable steuerbar
steering Lenkung *f*
steering attachment Lenkvorrichtung *f*
steering control Lenksteuerung *f*, Lenkungssteuerung *f*, Lenkregler *m*
steering direction Lenkrichtung *f*
steering force Lenkkraft *f*
steering gear Lenkgetriebe *nt*
steering motor Lenkantrieb *m*, Lenkmotor *m*
steering on lock eingeschlagene Lenkung *f*
steering operating control Lenkstellteil *nt*
steering shock Rückschlag *m* der Lenkung, Lenkungsrückschlag *m*
steering system Lenksystem *nt*, Lenkungssystem *nt*
steering turnplate Lenkkranz *m*
steering unit Lenkeinheit *f*
steering wheel kick-back Lenkungsrückschlag *m*
stem Einspannschaft *m*, Schaft *m*, Zapfen *m*, Stift *m*; hemmen
stem diameter Stiftdurchmesser *m*, Zapfendurchmesser *m*
stem length Stiftlänge *f*, Zapfenlänge *f*
stem pull-out force Stiftauszugskraft *f*
stem radiation Stielstrahlung *f*
stem retention force Stiftauszugskraft *f*
stencil Schablone *f*
stencil pen Röhrchenfeder *f*
step Stufe *f*, Tritt *m*, Trittstufe *f*, Schritt *m*; absetzen, abstufen, treten
step-and-repeat-technology Schritt- und Wiederholverfahren *nt*
step by step stufenweise, schrittweise
step-by-step switch Schrittschaltwerk *nt*
step chuck Stufenfutter *nt*
step curve of cumulative frequencies Häufigkeitssummentreppe *f*
step depth Stufenbreite *f*
step enabling condition Weiterschaltbedingung *f*
step height Sprunghöhe *f*

step milling Stufenfräsen *nt*
step motor Schrittmotor *m*
step soldering Stufenlötung *f*
step width Stufenweite *f*
stepback reversal error Pilgerschrittumkehrspanne *f*
step-controlled stufig gesteuert
step-down gear Untersetzungsgetriebe *nt*
stepless stufenlos
stepless speed changing stufenlose Drehzahländerung *f*
steplessly variable stufenlos regelbar, stufenlos veränderlich
steplessly variable speed stufenlos veränderliche Drehzahl *f*
stepped gestuft, abgesetzt, abgestuft, überhöht
stepped break Stufenbruch *m*
stepped dimension Absatzmaß *nt*
stepped planing Stufenhobeln *nt*
stepped pulley Stufenscheibe *f*
stepped trench Stufengraben *m*
stepped wedge Stufenkeil *m*
stepping Abstufung *f*, Überhöhung *f*
stepping mechanism Schrittschaltgetriebe *nt*
stepping motor Schrittmotor *m*
stepwise stufig
step-wise change sprungartige Änderung *f*
step-wise change of the manipulated variable Stellgrößensprung *m*
stepwise starting stufiger Anlauf *m*
stereo lithography Stereolithographie (SL) *f*
stretch wrapping Stretchwickeln *nt*
stick 1. klemmen, haften (an), stecken, stecken bleiben, festfahren, festsitzen 2. kleben, aufkleben, anhaften, zusammenhängen
stick electrode Stabelektrode *f*
stick fixed Steuerknüppel *m* fixiert
stick free Steuerknüppel *m* frei
stick into einkleben
sticker Haftmittel *nt*, Kleber *m*
sticking Steckenbleiben *nt*, Klebung *f*
sticking material Anhaftungen *fpl*
stickiness Klebeverhalten *nt*
stick-slip stottern, ruckweise gleiten

stiff steif
stiffen aussteifen, versteifen, verstärken
stiffening Versteifung *f*
stiffening member Versteifungselement *nt*
stiffening tower Aussteifungsturm *m*
stiffness Festigkeit *f*, Steifigkeit *f*, Steife *f*, Formsteifigkeit *f*
stiffness in torsion Torsionssteifigkeit *f*, Torsionssteifheit *f*
stiffness of the pipe Rohrsteifigkeit *f*
stiffness of the soil Bodensteifigkeit *f*
stiffness testing apparatus Steifigkeitsprüfgerät *nt*
stiffening plate Aussteifungsblech *nt*
still air ruhende Luft *f*
stillage Palette *f*, Stapelplatte *f*, Plattform *f*
stillage truck Plattformwagen *m*
stillstand Stillstand *m*
step Stufe *f*
stir rühren, bewegen
stitch heften, nähen; Stich *m*
stitch tear resistance Stichausreißkraft *f*
stitch together zusammenheften
stitched geheftet
stitching Heften *nt*
stochastic relation stochastischer Zusammenhang *m*
stock 1. Vorrat *m*, Lager *nt*, Bestand *m*, Lagerbestand *m*, Inventar *nt*, Material *nt*, Werkstoff *m*; lagern, einlagern **2.** *(Verzahnung)* Zahnlücken vorfräsen **3.** bestücken
stock adjustment Bestandabgleich *m*
stock allowance Materialzugabe *f*, Werkstoffzugabe *f*
stock and die Schneidkluppe *f*
stock cake Stoffkuchen *m*
stock chucking turning machine Stangenfutterdrehmaschine *f*
stock clerk Lagerist *m*, Magaziner *m*
stock concentration Stoffdichte *f*
stock control Bestandskontrolle *f*
stock feed Werkstoffzufuhr *f*, Stangenvorschub *m*
stock feed slide Vorschubschlitten *m*
stock in trade Warenbestand *m*
stock keeping Lagerhaltung *f*, Bestandsführung *f*
stock kept at the workbench Handlager *nt*
stock left Werkstoffzugabe *f*, Materialzugabe *f*
stock management Materialwirtschaft *f*
stock movements Lagerbewegungen *fpl*
stock on hand Warenbestand *m*
stock plan Materialplan *m*
stock planning Materialplanung *f*
stock reel Stangenführung *f*
stock release Materialfreigabe *f*
stock removal 1. Zerspanung *f*, Werkstoffabnahme *f*, Werkstoffabtragung *f*, Spanabnahme *f*, Spanleistung *f*, Spantiefe *f* **2.** *(Schleifen)* Abschliff *m*
stock requirements Materialbedarf *m*
stock sample Stoffprobe *f*
stock shortage Lagerfehlbestand *m*
stock solution Stammlösung *f*
stock system Vorratssystem *nt*
stock to be used Einsatzmaterial *nt*
stock transfer Materialbewegung *f*
stock up bevorraten
stock withdrawal Lagerentnahme *f*
stock-control oriented materialflussorientiert
stocking 1. Lagerhaltung *f*, Lagerung *f* **2.** Bestückung *f* **3.** *(Fräsen)* Vorfräsen *nt*
stocking cutter 1. Vorfräser *m*, Schruppfräser *m* **2.** *(Verzahnung)* Zahnformvorfräser *m*
stocking density Lagerungsdichte *f*
stocking gear milling cutter Zahnformvorfräser *m*
stocking level Bestandsniveau *nt*
stocking policy Bestandspolitik *f*
stock-in-trade Vorrat *m*
stockless lagerlos
stockless production lagerlose Fertigung *f*
stock-on-hand-quantity Materialbestand *m*
stock-out Fehlbestand *m*, Lagerfehlbestand *m*
stockpile Vorrat *m*; bevorraten
stockpiling Bevorratung *f*
stockpiling of spare parts Ersatzteil-

bevorratung *f*
stocks falling short of the minimum Mindestbestandsunterschreitung *f*
stock-sub-location Unterlager *nt*
stock-up order Bevorratungsbestellung *f*
stone abziehen mit Ölstein
stone sub-base steiniger Untergrund *m*
stoneware pipe socket Steinzeugrohrmuffe *f*
stonework Mauerwerk *nt*
stop stoppen, abschalten, aufhören, halten, anhalten, abstellen, hemmen, arretieren, sperren, stillsetzen, stillstehen, stehen bleiben, zum Stillstand bringen; Stopp *m*, Halt *m*, Anschlag *m*, Sperre *f*, Polder *m*, Abschaltung *f*, Stillsetzung *f*
stop bar Anschlagleiste *f*
stop button Ausschaltknopf *m*
stop control AUS-Schalter *m*
stop damper Stoßdämpferanschlag *m*
stop dog Anschlag *m*, Anschlagknagge *f*
stop function Stoppfunktion *f*
stop lever Ausschalthebel *m*
stop mode Stoppmodus *m*
stop period Stillstandszeit *f*
stop pin Anschlagbolzen *m*
stop position Endlage *f*
stop position limitation Endlagenbegrenzung *f*
stop roll Anschlagwalze *f*
stop station Sperre *f*
stop valve Absperrventil *nt*
stop valve with diaphragm control Absperrorgan *nt* mit Membransteuerung
stop valve with float control Schwimmersteuerung *f* eines Absperrorgans
stop valve with piston operation Absperrorgan *nt* mit Kolbenantrieb
stop valve with power operation Absperrorgan *nt* mit Kraftantrieb
stop valve with solenoid operation Absperrorgan *nt* mit Magnetantrieb
stopcock Verschlusshahn *m*
stopcock grease Hahnfett *nt*
stoppage Betriebsstörung *f*, Stillstand *m*, Ausfall *m*
stoppage time Stillstandszeit *f*
stopped position Ruhelage *f*

stopper Stopper *m*
stopping accuracy Anhaltegenauigkeit *f*
stopping attachment Stillsetzeinrichtung *f*
stopping cam Anhaltenocke *f*
stopping distance Anhalteweg *m*, Bremsweg *m*, Stillsetzweg *m*
stopping friction Auslaufreibung *f*
stopping place Haltestelle *f*
stops Anschläge *mpl*
storage Lagerung *f*, Lagerhaltung *f*, Einlagerung *f*, Speicherung *f*, Unterbringung *f*, Verwahrung *f*, Einlagern *nt*, Speichern *nt*
storage aid means Lagerhilfsmittel *nt*
storage alteration Lageränderung *f*
storage and retrieval Ein- und Auslagern *nt*
storage and retrieval (S/R) machine RGB (Regelbediengerät) *nt*
storage and retrieval machine (SRM) Regalbediengerät (RGB) *nt*, Regalförderzeug (RFZ) *nt*
storage and retrieval unit Stapler *m*
storage area Lagefläche *f*, Lagerbereich *m*
storage arrangement Lageranordnung *f*
storage battery batteriebetrieben, mit Fremdantrieb
storage bay Lagerfach *nt*
storage bin Lagerfach *nt*, Lagerbehälter *m*, Regalfach *nt*
storage block Lagerblock *m*
storage booking Lagerbuchung *f*
storage box Lagerkasten *m*
storage building Halle *f*, Lagerhalle *f*, Lagergebäude *nt*
storage capacity Einlagerkapazität *f*, Speicherkapazität *f*
storage cart Einschub *m*
storage characteristic values Lagerkennzahlen *fpl*
storage climate Lagerungsklima *nt*
storage compartment Lagerfach *nt*
storage conditions Lagerungsbedingungen *fpl*
storage container Vorratsbehälter *m*, Lagerbehälter *m*

storage cycle Einlagerspiel *nt*
storage density Lagerverdichtung *f*, Speicherdichte *f*, Lagerungsdichte *f*
storage duration Lagerungsdauer *f*
storage function Lagerfunktion *f*
storage in free bundles Lagerung *f* im freien Bund
storage installations Lagereinbauten *mpl*
storage level Lagerstufe *f*, Speicherebene *f*
storage lift Lagerfähigkeit *f*
storage location Einlagerungsplatz *m*, Regalfach *nt*, Lagerort *m*, Lagerplatz *m*, Stellplatz *m*
storage location administration Lagerplatzverwaltung *f*
storage location assignment Lagerplatzvergabe *f*
storage management system Lagerverwaltungssystem *nt*
storage means Lagermittel *ntpl*
storage medium Speichermedium *nt*
storage modulus Speichermodul *nt*
storage of plate or sheet materials Plattenlagerung *f*
storage order Einlagerauftrag *m*
storage period Ablagerungszeit *f*, Lagerperiode *f*, Verweildauer *f*
storage place Speicherplatz *m*
storage point Einlagerpunkt *m*
storage position Stellplatz *m*
storage process Einlagervorgang *m*
storage property Speicherverhalten *nt*
storage quota Einlagerungsquote *f*
storage rate Einlagerdurchsatz *m*
storage side Einlagerungsseite *f*
storage slot Lagerfach *nt*, Lagerfachöffnung *f*
storage space Lagerraum *m*
storage stability Haltbarkeit *f*, Lagerfähigkeit *f*
storage strategy Lagerstrategie *f*
storage surface Lagergrundfläche *f*
storage system Lagersystem *nt*
storage tank Speicherbehälter *m*
storage technology Lagertechnik *f*
storage temperature Lagertemperatur *f*
storage time Einfahrzeit *f*

storage tower Lagerturm *m*
storage tray Lagerwanne *f*
storage type Lagerungsart *f*, Lagerart *f*
storage type service water heater Speicherbrauchwassererwärmer *m*
storage under heat Warmlagerung *f*
storage unit Lagereinheit *f*
storage water heater Speicherwassererwärmer *m*, Vorratswasserheizer *m*
storage-free lagerlos
store Lager *nt*, Bestand *m*, Speicher *m*; lagern, einlagern, speichern, unterbringen, verwahren
store- and forward network Teilstreckennetz *nt*
store goods Ware einlagern
store height Lagerhöhe *f*
store intermediately zwischenlagern, zwischenpuffern
store of materials and supplies Materiallager *nt*
store tank Vorratsbehälter *m*, Tank *m*
store temporarily zwischenspeichern
storeability Lagerbarkeit *f*
stored articles Lagergut *nt*
stored components speichernde Elemente *ntpl*
stored content Speicherinhalt *m*
stored data gespeicherte Information *f*
stored energy Energie speichernd, potentielle Energie *f*
stored to the back zurückstehend
stored-energy components Energie speichernde Bauteile *ntpl*
stored-energy spring actuation Federspeicherantrieb *m*
storehouse Lagergebäude *nt*
storeman Lagerist *m*, Magaziner *m*
storeroom Magazin *nt*
store-room Lager *nt*, Lagerraum *m*, Speicher *m*
storey Stockwerk *nt*, Geschoss *nt*
storey building Geschossbau *m*
storey height Geschosshöhe *f*
storey level Geschossebene *f*
storing Speichern *nt*
storing goods Ware einlagern
storm water discharge yield factor Regenwasserabflussspende *f*
story Stockwerk *nt*

stove Ofen *m*
stoving Brennen *nt*
straddle umgehen, spreizen, überspreizen, überspannen, überfahren
straddle broaching gleichzeitiges Räumen *nt* paralleler gegenüberliegender Flächen
straddle fork lift truck Schubrahmenstapler *m*
straddle mill Scheibenfräser *m*
straddle milling Fräsen *nt* zweier paralleler Flächen mit zwei Scheibenfräsern
straddle reach truck Schubrahmenstapler *m*
straddle truck Spreizenstapler *m*
straddling Überfahren *nt*, Spreizen *nt*
straight gerade
straight turning Längsdrehen *nt*
straight ahead geradeaus
straight ahead position Geradeausstellung *f*
straight bevel gear Geradzahnkegelrad *nt*
straight bevel gear pair Kegelstirnradgetriebe *nt*, Geradzahnkegelradpaar *nt*
straight bevel gear teeth Geradzahnkegelradverzahnung *f*
straight bore zylindrische Bohrung *f*
straight broaching Räumen *nt* ebener Flächen
straight check valve with shut-off feature absperrbares Durchgangsrückschlagventil *nt*
straight cut Geradschnitt *m*
straight cut control Streckensteuerung *f*
straight edge Maßstab *m*, Lineal *nt*
straight feed Zeilenvorschub *m*
straight flank tool geradflankiges Werkzeug *nt*
straight flute milling Fräsen *nt* gerader Nuten
straight forward geradeaus
straight gear cutting Geradverzahnung *f*
straight grinding Längsschliff *m*
straight grinding wheel Umfangsschleifrad *nt*
straight idler gerade Tragrolle *f*

straight knurling tool Rändelmeißel *m*
straight land Schneidkantenfase *f*, Zahnrückenfase *f*, Fase *f* am Fräserzahn
straight length gerades Rohrstück *nt*
straight line Gerade *f*
straight line control Streckensteuerung *f*
straight line interpolation Geradeninterpolation *f*
straight line parallel gripper Geradenparallelgreifer *m*
straight line position Geradeausstellung *f*
straight lined geradlinig
straight milling Zeilenfräsen *nt*, Längsfräsen *nt*
straight oil Öl *nt* ohne chemische Zusätze
straight pinion cutter Geradschneidrad *nt*
straight rough turning Längsschruppen *nt*
straight safety valve Sicherheitsdurchgangsventil *nt*
straight screw tread connection zylindrische Gewindeverbindung *f*
straight screw tread fastening zylindrische Gewindeverbindung *f*
straight shank Zylinderschaft *m*
straight side tool gerader Seitenmeißel *m*
straight tooth side and face cutter gerade verzahnter Scheibenfräser *m*
straight tooth system Geradverzahnung *f*
straight toothed gerade verzahnt
straight tubular extrusion Strangpressen *nt* von Strängen mit hohlem Querschnitt
straight tubular rod extrusion Hohlvorwärtsstrangpressen *nt*
straight turning Geraddrehen *nt*
straight turning work Längsdreharbeit *f*, Längsdrehen *nt*
straight union with parallel adapter end gerade Verschraubung *f* mit zylindrischem Einschraubzapfen
straight-cut tool gerader Meißel *m*
straighten richten (auf), ausrichten, gerade ausrichten

straightening by offhand bending
Biegerichten *nt*
straightening flat bars by stretching
Recken *nt* von Flachstäben in der Halbzeugfertigung
straightening in patterned dies Prägerichten *nt*
straight-flanked geradflankig
straightforward surfacing einfaches Auftragen *nt*
straight-knurl rändeln
straight-knurling Rändeln *nt*
straight-line linear
straight-line guidance Geradführung *f*
straightness Zylindrizität *f*, Geradheit *f*
straightness deviation Geradheitsabweichung *f*
straightness tolerance Geradheitstoleranz *f*
straight-path electrode travel geradlinig bewegte Elektrode *f*
straight-shank end mill Schaftfräser *m* mit Zylinderschaft
straight-sided geradflankig
straight-tooth cutting Geradverzahnung *f*
straight-tooth master gear geradverzahntes Lehrzahnrad *nt*
straight-way adjusting valve Stelldurchgangsventil *nt*
straight-way control valve Regeldurchgangsventil *nt*
straight-way non-return valve Rückschlagdurchgangsventil *nt*
straight-way pressure reducing valve Druckminderdurchgangsventil *nt*
straight-way throttling valve Drosseldurchgangsventil *nt*
straightway valve Durchgangsarmatur *f*
straight flank gerade Flanke *f*
straight toothed gerade verzahnt
straightening flat bars by stretching Streckrichten *nt* von Flachstäben
strain 1. verformen, dehnen, beanspruchen, belasten, recken; Beanspruchung *f*, Belastung *f*, Formänderung *f*, Verformung *f*, Spannung *f*, Dehnung *f* 2. durchsieben, filtern
strain ageing Reckalterung *f*

strain dependent resistor dehnungsabhängiger Widerstand *m*, Dehnmessstreifen *m*
strain force measurement Dehnungsmessung *f*
strain gauge Dehnungsmessstreifen *m*, Dehnmessstreifen *m* (DMS)
strain hardenability Kalthärtbarkeit *f*
strain hardening Kaltverfestigung *f*
strain measurement Dehnungsmessung *f*
strain of the outer fibre Randfaserdehnung *f*
strain of the outer fibre at fracture Randfaserdehnung *f* beim Bruch
strain of the outer fibre at maximum load Randfaserdehnung *f* bei Höchstkraft
strain rolling Reckwalzen
strain-age cracking Spannungsanlassrissigkeit *f*
strainer Siebeinsatz *m*, Sieb *nt*, Filtersieb *nt*, Saugfilter *m*
straining verformende Beanspruchung *f*
strain-rate Dehngeschwindigkeit *f*
strain-time-curve Verformungs-Zeit-Diagramm *nt*
strand Strang *m*
stranded filler wire verdrillter Schweißdraht *m*
stranded rod Drillstab *m*
stranded wire electrode Drilldrahtelektrode *f*
strange atom Fremdatom *nt*
strengthen festigen
strap 1. Spanneisen *nt*, Pratze *f* 2. umreifen, wickeln 3. Streifen *m*
strap vertically vertikal umreifen
strapping 1. Umreifen *nt*, Umreifung *f* 2. Verpackungsband *nt*
strapping head Umreifungskopf *m*, Wickelkopf *m*
strapping machine Umreifungsverschließmaschine *f*
strapping plant Umreifungsanlage *f*
strategic strategisch
strategy Strategie *f*
strawpulp Strohzellstoff *m*
stray streuen
stray current circuit Streustromkreis *m*

stray electric current Streustrom *m*
stray field Streufeld *nt*
stray radiation Störstrahlung *f*
stray results Ausreißer *mpl*
streaking Streifigkeit *f*
stream Strahl *m*, Strömung *f*, Strom *m*
stream axis Strahlachse *f*
stream in einströmen
stream of lubricant Schmierstoffstrom *m*
stream of scattered light Streulichtstrom *m*
streamline Stromlinie *f*, Strömungslinie *f*
stench trap pipe Geruchsverschlussrohr *nt*
street cap Straßenkappe *f*
strength Stärke *f*, Festigkeit *f*
strength and hardness values Festigkeits- und Härtewerte *f*
strength and requires Kraft- und Arbeitsbedarf *m*
strength at the root Zahnfußfestigkeit *f*
strength category Festigkeitsklasse *f*
strength of materials Werkstofffestigkeit *f*
strength of the weld metal Schweißgutfestigkeit *f*
strength test Festigkeitsprüfung *f*
strength theory Festigkeitslehre *f*
strengthen verfestigen, versteifen, verstärken
strengthening Verstärkung *f*
stress beanspruchen, belasten, dehnen; Beanspruchung *f*, Belastung *f*, elastische Dehnung *f*, Spannung *f*
stress amplitude Spannungsamplitude *f*
stress area Spannungsquerschnitt *m*
stress at 0.2% permanent strain 0,2%-Dehngrenze *f*
stress coefficient Spannungsbeiwert *m*
stress corrosion cracking potential Spannungsrisspotential *nt*
stress cycle Lastspiel *nt*
stress cycles endured Lastspielzahl *f*
stress deformation behaviour Spannungsformänderungsverhalten *nt*
stress due to oscillation Schwingungsbeanspruchung *f*

stress equalization Spannungsausgleich *m*
stress group Beanspruchungsgruppe *f*
stress pattern Beanspruchungsablauf *m*
stress peak Spannungsspitze *f*
stress range for fatigue limit Dauerhubfestigkeit *f*
stress ratio Spannungsverhältnis *nt*
stress relaxation Spannungserholung *f*
stress relief Spannungsabbau *m*
stress resultant Schnittgröße *f*
stress reversals Lastspielzahl *f*
stress spectrum Spannungskollektiv *nt*
stress stage Beanspruchungsstufe *f*
stress value Spannungswert *m*
stressed-type fastening with taper action Spannungsverbindung *f* mit Anzug
stressing Belastung *f*
stressing in tension Zerreißbeanspruchung *f*
stressing leading to scoring Fressbeanspruchung *f*
stress-relieved entspannt
stress-rupture test Zerreißversuch *m*
stress-rupture test specimen Zeitstandprobe *f*
stress-strain diagram Spannungs-Verformungs-Diagramm *nt*
stress-time curve Spannungs-Zeit-Diagramm *nt*
stress-time factor Beanspruchungszeit *f*
stretch dehnen, ausdehnen, ziehen, spannen, strecken, recken; elastische Dehnung *f*
stretch angle Rechtwinkel *m*
stretch at breaking Dehnung *f* bei Bruch
stretch banding machine Stretchfolieneinwickelmaschine *f*
stretch bending tool Ziehbiegewerkzeug *nt*
stretch drawing to shape Streckziehen *nt*
stretch film Stretchfolie *f*
stretch film bundling machine Stretchfolienspiraleinwickelmaschine *f*
stretch film roll Stretchfolienrolle *f*
stretch film roll carrier Stretchfolien-

rollenträger *m*
stretch film wrapping machine Stretcheinschlagmaschine *f*, Stretchfolieneinschlagmaschine *f*
stretch forming Formrecken *nt*, Recken *nt*, Strecken *nt*, Reckung *f*
stretch hood Stretchhaube *f*
stretch hood applicator Stretchhaubenüberziehmaschine *f*
stretch over überziehen
stretch pallet Spannpalette *f*
stretch reducing by roll drawing Nachziehen *nt*, Abschreckwalzziehen *nt*
stretch sleeve Stretchhülse *f*
stretch sleeving machine Stertchhülsenüberziehmaschine *f*
stretch wrap Stretchwicklung *f*, Wickelstretch *m*; stretchwickeln
stretch wrap packing Stretchverpackung *f*, Wickelstretchverpackung *f*
stretch wrapper Stretchwickler *m*
stretch wrapping Umwickeln *nt*
stretch wrapping machine Stretchwickler *m*, Stretchwickelmaschine *f*, Stretchfolieneinschlagmaschine *f*
stretchable plastics material verstreckbarer Kunststoff *m*
stretching Ziehen *nt*, Dehnen *nt*, Reckung *f*
stretching process Streckprozess *m*
stretching unit Reckeinrichtung *f*
stretchwrap stretchwickeln, mit Stretchfolie umwickeln
stretchwrapper Stretchwickler *m*
strewing method Aufstreuverfahren *nt*
striated streifig
strickle tackle Drehschablone *f*
strict control scharfe Kontrolle *f*
strike stoßen, auftreffen, schlagen, senkrechthobeln
strike against anstoßen
striking edge Schneide *f*, Hammerschneide *f*
striking out Herausschlagen *nt*
striking point Zündstelle *f*
striking aid Zündhilfe *f*
string Schnur *f*, Strang *m*
string, character ~ Zeichenfolge *f*
stringer Längsverband *m*
stringy chip Langspan *m*
stringy mass fadenziehende Masse *f*
strip 1. ablösen, entfernen **2.** Band *nt*, Leiste *f*, Streifen *m*, Strich *m*, Streifenmarkierung *f*
strip chart Streifendiagramm *nt*
strip door Streifentor *nt*
strip heater Heizband *nt*
strip off abstreifen
strip packaging machine Streifenformfüll- und -verschließmaschine *f*
strip sabre Säbel *m*
strip sheet Streifenblech *nt*
strip size Streifenformat *nt*
strip specimen Streifenprobe *f*
strip stock Streifenmaterial *nt*
strip type test diagram streifenförmiges Prüfbild *nt*
strip width Strichbreite *f*
strip-chart recorder Streifenschreiber *m*
stripe Strich *m*, Streifen *m*, Streifenmarkierung *f*
stripe width Streifenbreite *f*
strip-heater carrier Heizbandträger *m*
strippable varnish Abziehlack *m*
stripper Abstreifer *m*
stripper force Niederhaltekraft *f*
stripper plate Abstreifplatte *f*
stripper pressure Niederhaltedruck *m*
stripping Ablösung *f*, Entfernung *f*
strobe 1. abtasten **2.** Abtasteingang *m* **3.** *(Motor)* Takt *m* **4.** Strich *m* **5.** *(Strecke)* Weg *m*, Hub *m* **6.** Stoß *m*, Schlag *m*
stroke crank drive Hubkurbeltrieb *m*
stroke frequency Hubfrequenz *f*
stroke frequency range Hubfrequenzbereich *m*
stroke gear Hubrad *nt*
stroke indicator Hubanzeiger *m*
stroke limitation Hubwegbegrenzer *m*
stroke of quill Pinolenhub *m*
stroke of the ram Stößelhub *m*
stroke position mechanics Hubverstelleinrichtung *f*
stroke thickness Strichdicke *f*
stroke width Strichbreite *f*
strong fest, stark, stabil
strong acid number Neutralisations-

zahl *f*
strong base number Neutralisationszahl *f*
structogram Struktogramm *nt*
structural baulich, statisch, strukturell
structural analysis statischer Nachweis *m*, Statik *f*
structural bill of materials Strukturstückliste *f*
structural components statische Bauteile *ntpl*
structural constitution Gefügeaufbau *m*
structural element next in line nachgeschaltetes Bauglied *nt*
structural examination Bauprüfung *f*
structural fire protection baulicher Brandschutz *m*
structural indicator Strukturkennzahl *f*
structural installations bauliche Anlagen *fpl*
structural member Bauglied *nt*, Bauteil *nt*
structural organization Aufbauorganisation *f*
structural shape Gefügeausbildung *f*
structural size Baumaß *nt*
structural stability statische Stabilität *f*
structural steel engineering Stahlbau *m*
structural steel work Stahlbau *m*
structural substance Gerüstsubstanz *f*
structural support statische Stabilität *f*
structural test statische Verifizierung *f*
structural tube Konstruktionsrohr *nt*
structural verification 1. statische Verifizierung *f* **2.** Prüfung *f* der Struktur
structure Struktur *f*, Gefüge *nt*, Gestalt *f*, Aufbau *m*, Zusammensetzung *f*, Konstruktion *f*; strukturieren, gestalten
structure chart symbol Struktogrammsinnbild *nt*
structure devoid of pearlite boundaries perlitrandfreies Gefüge *nt*
structure plan Strukturplan *m*
structure tree Strukturbaum *m*
structure-borne sound Körperschall *m*
structure-borne sound level Trittschallpegel *m*
structure-borne sound testing Körperschallmessung *f*
structured strukturiert
structured control language strukturierte Steuerungssprache *f*
structured query language Datenbankabfragesprache *f*, strukturierte Abfragesprache *f*
structured text (ST) strukturierter Text *m*
strut verstreben, versteifen, aussteifen; Aussteifung *f*, Versteifung *f*, Strebe *f*, Druckstab *m*
strutting Versteifung *f*
stub Stumpf *m*
stub Acme thread Stub-Acme-Gewinde *nt*
stub aisle Stichgang *m*
stub aisle strategy Stichgangstrategie *f*
stub angular cutter Aufsteckwinkelfräser *m*
stub arbour Aufsteckdorn *m*, kurzer Dorn *m*
stub axle Achstunnel *m*
stub axle mounting Einbau *m* auf Achsstummel
stub expansion arbor fliegend aufgespannter Spreizdorn *m*
stub metric trapezoidal screw thread flaches metrisches Trapezgewinde *nt*
stub shaft Wellenstumpf *m*
stub track Stichgleis *nt*
stub weld Stutzennaht *f*
stubby gedrungen
stub-end station Kopfstation *f*
stuck festgefahren
stuck broach festgefahrenes Räumwerkzeug *nt*
stud Ansatzbolzen *m*, Bolzen *m*, Stift *m*, Stiftbolzen *m*, Stiftschraube *f*, Zapfen *m*
stud for drawn-arc stud welding Bolzen *m* für Bolzenschweißen mit Hubzündung
stud for tongues for T-slots Stiftschraube *f* für T-Nutensteine
stud tip Bolzenspitze *f*
stud welding Bolzenaufschweißen *nt*, Bolzenschweißen *nt*
stud welding gun Bolzenaufschweißpistole *f*

stud with serrated ring lock Stiftschraube f mit Ringsicherung
stud-bolt Schraubenbolzen m
stud-bolt with waisted shank Schraubenbolzen m mit Dehnschaft
study Untersuchung f; untersuchen
study drawing Untersuchungszeichnung f
study objective Untersuchungsziel nt
stuff abdichten, ausstopfen
stuff into einstopfen
stuffing box Stopfbuchse f
stuffing box packing Stopfbuchsendichtung f
stuffing box gland Brille f der Stopfbuchse
stump Stumpf m
stumble stolpern
sturdy stark, stabil
style Bauart f, Bauausführung f
styling Formgebung f
stylus Fühlerstift f, Fühler m, Abtaststift m, Taster m, Tastspitze f, Tastfinger m
stylus deflection Tastspitzenauslenkung f
styrene butadiene rubber Styrol-Butadien-Kautschuk m
styrene copolymer Styrolcopolymer nt, Styrolcopolymerisat nt
styrene homopolymer Styrolhomopolymerisat nt
subassemble vormontieren
sub-assemblies Montageteile $ntpl$
subassembly Untergruppe f, Vormontage f
sub-assembly Baugruppe f, Teilmontage f
subcondition Teilbedingung f
subcontact Subunternehmervertrag m, Zuliefervertrag m
subcontractor Subunternehmer m
sub-contractor Lieferant m, Subunternehmer m
subdivide unterteilen, einteilen
subdivision Aufteilung f, Einteilung f, Untergliederung f
subdomain Teilbereich m
subelement Unterelement nt
subfunction Teilfunktion f
subgoal Teilziel nt
subgrade Untergrund m
subgroup Untergruppe f
subject 1. unterliegen, unterwerfen 2. Fach nt, Fachgebiet nt
subject field Fachgebiet nt
subject to aussetzen
subject to a bending load auf Biegung beanspruchen
subject to alternating loads schwingende Beanspruchung f
subject to influence beeinflussbar
subject to testing prüfpflichtig
subject to the risk of corrosion korrosionsgefährdet
subject to the risk of dust staubgefährdet
subject to the risk of explosion explosionsgefährdet
subject to the risk of fire feuergefährdet
subland twist drill for counterbores for slotted cheese head screws Mehrfasenstufenbohrer m für Senkungen für Zylinderschrauben mit Schlitz
sublimation Sublimation f
sublimation curve Sublimationskurve f
sublimation point temperature Sublimationspunkt m
sub-mechanism Teilgetriebe nt
submerge eintauchen
submerged arc joint welding Unterpulververbindungsschweißen nt
submicrometre range Submikrometerbereich m
submit vorlegen
submitter Einsender m
submultiple Teiler m
subobjective Teilziel nt
subordinate group Untergruppe f
subpopulation Teilgesamtheit f
subprocess Teilprozess m
subprogram Unterprogramm nt
subrange Teilbereich m, Teilanzeigebereich m
subroutine Unterprogramm nt
subscriber Teilnehmer m
subscriber line Teilnehmeranschlussleitung f
subscript Index m

subscript pair Indexpaar *nt*
subsection Teilbereich *m*
subsequent nachträglich, nachfolgend, anschließend
subsequent cleaning Nachreinigung *f*
subsequent costs Folgekosten *pl*
subsequent delivery Nachlieferung *f*
subsequent derusting Nachentrosten *nt*
subsequent flushing Nachspülen *nt*
subsequent machining Nachbearbeitung *f*, Nacharbeit *f*
subsequent slipping Nachrutschen *nt*
subsequent treatment Nachbehandlung *f*
subsequent trying Nachtrocknen *nt*
subsequently nacheinander
subset Teilmenge *f*, Untermenge *f*
subsidiary *(Regeln)* unterlagert
subsidiary bulb of Ubbelohde suspended-level viscosimeter Vorlaufkugel *f* eines Ubbelohde- Viskosimeter
subsidiary echo Nebenecho *nt*
subsoil Untergrund *m*
subspecimen Teilprobe *f*, Probeteil *nt*
substance Flächengewicht *nt*
substance capable of migration wanderungsfähiger Stoff *m*
substance favouring corrosion Korrosionsstimulator *m*
sub-standard grade Mindergüte *f*
substitute austauschen, auswechseln, ersetzen; Ersatz *m*
substitute power generator Ersatzstromerzeuger *m*
substitute test specimen Ersatzprobe *f*
substitution Ersatz *m*
substrate Substrat *nt*, Grundwerkstoff *m*, Träger *m*, Trägermaterial *nt*
substrate material Trägermaterial *nt*, Trägerwerkstoff *m*, Untergrund *m*
substructure Unterbau *m*, Unterkonstruktion *f*
sub-surface migration Unterwanderung *f*
subsystem Subsystem *nt*, Teilsystem *nt*
subtask Teilaufgabe *f*
subtending angle Zentriwinkel *m*
subtotal Zwischensumme *f*
subtractor Subtrahierer *m*

subtraction unit Subtrahierer *m*
sub-train of a gear transmission Teilgetriebe *nt*
succeed folgen
succeeding folgend
success Erfolg *m*
successful erfolgreich
succession Folge *f*, Reihe *f*
successive nacheinander, aufeinander folgend
successive cut Folgeschnitt *m*
suck saugen, ansaugen
suck away absaugen
suck up heraussaugen
sucker Sauger *m*
sucking douche Saugspülung *f*
sucking gripper Sauggreifer *m*
suction Saugen *nt*, Ansaugen *nt*, Sog *m*, Ansaugung *f*, Saugwirkung *f*, Unterdruck *m*
suction adaptor Saugvorstoß *m*
suction aid Ansaughilfe *f*
suction boost Verstärkung *f* der Ansaugmenge
suction bulb Saugball *m*
suction cleaning *(Verunreinigungen)* Absaugen *nt*
suction cup Saugkopf *m*, Vakuumsauger *m*, Saugschale *f*
suction device Saugeinrichtung *f*
suction dust remover Staubabsauger *m*
suction filter Saugfilter *m*
suction frame Saugrahmen *m*
suction hood Ansaughaube *f*
suction lift Saughöhe *f*
suction line Absaugleitung *f*
suction pad Vakuumsauger *m*
suction phase Ansaugphase *f*
suction port Ansaugkanal *m*, Saugkammer *f*
suction relief valve Unterdruckventil *nt*
suction side Saugseite *f*
suction strainer Saugkorb *m*
suction-head blasting Saugkopfstrahlen *nt*
sudden plötzlich
sudden failure plötzlicher Ausfall *m*, Sprungausfall *m*
sufficient ausreichend

suggestion Vorschlag *m*
suggestion award Prämie *f* für einen Verbesserungsvorschlag
suggestion for improvement Verbesserungsvorschlag *m*
suit sich eignen, passen, übereinstimmen
suitability Eignung *f*
suitability for impregnation Tränkbarkeit *f*
suitability for use Gebrauchsfähigkeit *f*
suitability for writing Beschreibbarkeit *f*
suitability test Eignungsprüfung *f*
suitable brauchbar, geeignet, passend
suitable for anodising anodisierbar
suitable for automation automatisierungsgerecht
suitable for grouping pulkfähig
suitable for microfilming mikrofilmgerecht
suitable for thermal cutting autogen schneidbar
suitable for thermal cutting brennschneidgeeignet
suitable to only a limited extent bedingt geeignet
suited for geeignet für
sulphite pulp Sulfitzellstoff *m*
sulphur Schwefel *m*
sulphur thermal fusion adhesive Schwefelschmelzklebstoff *m*
sum Summe *f*; summieren
sum of squares of the individual values quadrierte Einzelwerte *f*
sum of the addendum modification Profilverschiebungssumme *f*
sum of the diametral equivalent Durchmesserausgleichsbetrag *m*
summand Summand *m*
summarize zusammenfassen; Zusammenfassung *f*
summary Zusammenfassung *f*
summary indices of action summarische Wirkungsgrößen *fpl*
summary of processes Verfahrensübersicht *f*
summation Summierung *f*
summer hot water service Sommerwarmwasserbereitung *f*

summing element Summierglied *nt*
summing mechanism Summiergetriebe *nt*
summing point Additionsstelle *f*
sun gear zentrales Ritzel *nt*, Sonnenrad *nt*
sun wheel Planetenträger *m*, Sonnenrad *nt*
superficial distribution flächenmäßige Verteilung *f*
superficial hardening Randhärten *nt*
superficial hardness Oberflächenhärte *f*
superficial heating time Anwärmen *nt*
superficial oxidation Randoxidation *f*
superfine grinding Feinstschleifen *nt*, Feinstschliff *m*
superfinish feinstbearbeiten
superfinish grinding Schwingschleifen *nt*
superfinish turning Feinstdreharbeit *f*
superfinisher Feinstdrehmaschine *f*
superfinishing Kurzhubhonen *nt*, Schwingschleifen *nt*, Feinziehschleifen *nt*, Feinbearbeitung *f*, Feinstbearbeitung *f*
super-finishing operation Feinstbearbeitungsvorgang *m*
superheated steam HD-Heißdampf *m*, HD-Sattdampf *m*
superimpose überlagern, übereinander lagern
superimposed übereinander liegend
superimposed hopper Füllschachtaufbau *m*
superimposed motion Überlagerungsbewegung *f*
superimposition Überlagerung *f*
superior überlegen; Vorgesetzter *m*
superordinate übergeordnet
superposition Überlagern *nt*
superstructure Aufbau *m*, Überbau *m*
supersynchronous übersynchron
supervise überwachen, beaufsichtigen; Überwachung *f*
supervision Aufsicht *f*
supervision contract Überwachungsvertrag *m*
supervisor Steuerprogramm *nt*
supervisor state Prozessstabilisierung *f*

supervisory activity Aufsichtstätigkeit *f*
supplies Zubehör *nt*
supple biegsam
supplement Ergänzung *f*, Zusatz *m*; ergänzen
supplementary ergänzend, zusätzlich
supplementary bed with hardened runways Hilfsbett *nt* mit gehärteten Führungen
supplementary data *pl* ergänzende Angaben *fpl*
supplementary drawing Ergänzungszeichnung *f*
supplementary lift Zusatzhub *m*
supplementary measurement Ergänzungsmessung *f*
supplementary programme Zusatzprogramm *nt*
supplementary pump Zusatzpumpe *f*
supplementary symbol Ergänzungssymbol *nt*
supplementary testing Ergänzungsprüfung *f*
supplied parts Zulieferteile *ntpl*
supplier Auftragnehmer *m*, Lieferant *m*, Anbieter *m*
supplier audit Lieferantenaudit *nt*
supplier certificate Lieferantenzeugnis *nt*
supplier data Lieferantendaten *pl*
supplier portfolio Lieferantenportfolio *nt*
supplies Zulieferungen *fpl*, Zuläufe *mpl*
supply beschaffen, liefern, anliefern, beliefern, zuliefern, zuleiten, zuführen, versorgen, einspeisen; Lieferung *f*, Belieferung *f*, Versorgung *f*, Zufuhr *f*, Zulauf *m*, Nachschub *m*, Einspeisung *f*
supply activation Nachschubauslösung *f*
supply bottleneck Versorgungsengpass *m*
supply chain Lieferkette *f*, Belieferungskette *f*, Logistikkette *f*, Versorgungskette *f*
supply chain management Versorgungskettenmanagement *nt*
supply circle Versorgungskreis *m*
supply commissioning Nachschubkommissionierung *f*
supply condition Anschlussbedingung *f*
supply control Nachschubsteuerung *f*
supply current Stromzufuhr *f*
supply feed Zufuhr *f*
supply guarantee Versorgungssicherheit *f*
supply item Zubehörteil *nt*
supply lead Leitung *f*
supply line Zuleitung *f*, Versorgungsleitung *f*, Speiseleitung *f*, Nachschubstrecke *f*
supply network Versorgungsnetz *nt*, Stromversorgungsnetz *nt*
supply of Zuführung *f* von
supply of energy Energiezufuhr *f*
supply part Zubehörteil *nt*
supply path Nachschubstrecke *f*
supply pipeline Verbrauchsleitung *f*
supply pressure Versorgungsdruck *m*
supply resistor Zuleitungsanlasswiderstand *m*
supply system Netz *nt*
supply unit Versorgungsanlage *f*
supply voltage Versorgungsspannung *f*, Netzspannung *f*, Speisespannung *f*
supply with current Strom einspeisen, Strom liefern
support Träger *m*, Stütze *f*, Pfosten *m*, Stiel *m*, Halt *m*, Halterung *f*, Unterstützung *f*, Abstützeinrichtung *f*, Widerlager *nt*, Auflage *f*, Lager *nt*, Arm *m*; halten, tragen, stützen, abstützen, unterstützen, lagern
support angle Auflagewinkel *m*
support beam Auflageträger *m*
support bracket Auflagewinkel *m*
support clamp Halteklemme *f*
support displacement Stützenversatz *m*
support foot Stützenfuß *m*
support knife-edge Auflagerschneide *f*
support leg Schnappriegel *m*
support level Auflageebene *f*
support peg system Schnappriegelanlage *f*
support pressure Auflagedruck *m*
support profile Auflageprofil *nt*
support roll Stützrolle *f*
support roller Tragrolle *f*

support spacing Stützenabstand *m*
support subject to bending Biegeträger *m*
supported unterlagert, unterstützt
supported damped slab gedämpft aufliegende Platte *f*
supported spring-mounted slab gefedert aufliegende Platte *f*
supporting Halten *nt*, Tragen *nt*; tragend
supporting bar Auflageriegel *m*
supporting beam Auflageprofil *nt*, Auflageriegel *m*
supporting block Stützbloch *m*
supporting bracket Tischstütze *f*
supporting fabric Trägergewebe *nt*
supporting force Stützkraft *f*, Stützlast *f*
supporting framework Tragkonstruktion *f*
supporting member Tragelement *nt*
supporting point Stützpunkt *m*
supporting process Stützprozess *m*
supporting profile Auflageprofil *nt*
supporting roller Auflagerrolle *f*
supporting structure Tragkonstruktion *f*
supporting works Tragwerk *nt*
suppose annehmen
supposition Annahme *f*
suppress unterdrücken
suppressed range Unterdrückungsbereich *m*
suppression 1. Unterdrücken *nt*, Unterdrückung *f* 2. Schwingungsdämpfung *f*
supra-plant überbetrieblich, unternehmensübergreifend
surcharge 1. Überlast *f*, zusätzliche Belastung *f* 2. *(Kosten)* Zuschlag *m*, Mehrpreis *m*
surface Fläche *f*, Oberfläche *f*, Untergrund *m*; planarbeiten, planbearbeiten, planen
surface appearance Oberflächenbild *nt*
surface assessment Oberflächenbeurteilung *f*
surface at the bottom of the tooth space Zahnlückengrundfläche *f*

surface attack Flächenabtrag *m*
surface behaviour Oberflächenverhalten *nt*
surface below the cutting edge Freifläche *f*
surface blemish Oberflächenfehler *m*
surface blowhole Außenlunker *m*
surface broach Außenräumwerkzeug *nt*
surface broach bar Schneideneinsatz *m* für das Räumwerkzeug
surface broaching Außenflächenräumen *nt*
surface broaching machine Außenräummaschine *f*, Außenflächenräummaschine *f*
surface by welding Auftragsschweißung *f*
surface carbon content Randkohlenstoffgehalt *m*
surface character Oberflächencharakter *m*
surface cleanliness Oberflächensauberkeit *f*
surface coating Beschichtung *f*
surface condition Schliff *m*, Oberflächenzustand *m*, Oberflächenbeschaffenheit *f*
surface configuration Oberflächengestaltung *f*, Oberflächengestalt *f*, Gestalt *f*
surface contour Oberflächenprofil *nt*
surface cratering *(Spanfläche)* Auskolkung *f*
surface decarburization Randabkohlung *f*
surface decomposition Oberflächenzersetzung *f*
surface decrease Temperaturabnahme *f*
surface defect Oberflächenfehler *m*, Fehlstelle *f*
surface deterioration Oberflächenzerstörung *f*
surface deviations Oberflächenabweichung *f*
surface discontinuity Oberflächenfehler *m*
surface enclosing the space Raumumschließungsflächen *fpl*

surface examination Oberflächenprüfung f
surface finish 1. Oberflächengüte f, Oberflächenzustand m, Oberflächenbeschaffenheit f **2.** *(Bearbeitungsvorgang)* Oberflächenbehandlung f
surface finish turning Außenfeindrehen nt
surface flaw Oberflächenfehler m, Außenfehler m
surface for adhesion Haftfläche f
surface for pedestrian usage begehbare Fläche f
surface foundations Baugrund m
surface fuzz Unsauberkeit f der Oberfläche
surface gauge Parallelreißer m, Reißstock m, Höhenreißer m mit Teilung
surface gauge scriber Parallelreißernadel f
surface grinder Feinflächenschleifmaschine f, Flächenschleifmaschine f
surface grinding Planschleifen nt, Flächenschleifen nt, Flachschleifen nt, Außenschleifen nt
surface grinding machine Flächenschleifmaschine f
surface hardening Oberflächenhärten nt
surface hardness Oberflächenhärte f
surface hardness value Oberflächenhärtewert m
surface heat exchanger Oberflächenwärmeaustauscher m
surface imperfection Oberflächenfehler m
surface impingement of flame Flächenbeflammung f
surface indication Oberflächenkennzeichnung f
surface insulation resistance Oberflächendurchgangswiderstand m, Oberflächenisolationswiderstand m
surface integrity Oberflächenzustand m
surface interruption Flächenunterbrechung f
surface joint Flächennaht f
surface lamination Überschichtung f
surface layer formation Deckschichtausbildung f
surface layer processing Randschichtbehandlung f
surface layer resistance Deckschichtwiderstand m
surface layer treatment Randschichtbehandlung f
surface machining Oberflächenbearbeitung f
surface measurement Oberflächenmessung f
surface measurement method Oberflächenmessverfahren nt
surface metrology Oberflächenmesstechnik f
surface milling Flächenfräsen nt
surface milling operation Flächenfräsarbeit f, Planfräsarbeit f
surface milling work Planfräsarbeit f
surface modification Flächenänderung f
surface moisture Oberflächenfeuchtigkeit f
surface of engagement Eingriffsfläche f
surface of intersection Schnittfläche f
surface of the cladding Plattierungsauflage f
surface of the coating Überzugsoberfläche f
surface of the normal section Normalschnittfläche f
surface of the pitch cylinder Kreiszylinderfläche f
surface outer layer Randschicht f, Randzone f
surface outer layer influence Randzonenbeeinflussung f
surface pattern Oberflächenbild nt, Oberflächengestalt f
surface pipeline oberirdische Rohrleitung f
surface planing machine Abrichthobelmaschine f
surface plate Anreißplatte f, Tuschierplatte f, Prüfplatte f
surface preparation Oberflächenvorbereitung f
surface pressure Anpressdruck m
surface processing Oberflächenbear-

beitung *f*
surface profile Oberflächenprofil *nt*
surface profile tracer Oberflächentastgerät *nt*
surface protecting coating Oberflächenschutzüberzug *m*
surface protuberance Oberflächenausstülpung *f*
surface quality Oberflächenqualität *f*, Oberflächengüte *f*, Oberflächenbeschaffenheit *f*
surface quality measurement Oberflächenmessung *f*
surface requirements Oberflächenansprüche *mpl*
surface resistance Oberflächenwiderstand *m*
surface roughness Oberflächenrauheit *f*
surface roughness value Rauheitsmessgröße *f*
surface sample Oberflächenprobe *f*
surface section Oberflächenschnitt *m*
surface sound pressure level Messflächenschalldruckpegel *m*
surface speed Schnittgeschwindigkeit *f*
surface structure Oberflächenstruktur *f*
surface swelling Anquellen *nt*
surface symbol Oberflächenkennzeichen *nt*
surface temperature Oberflächentemperatur *f*
surface temperature limitation Oberflächenbegrenzungstemperatur *f*
surface texture Oberflächengestalt *f*, Oberflächenfeingestalt *f*
surface texture Oberflächenbeschaffenheit *f*
surface touch Flächenberührung *f*
surface treatment Oberflächenbehandlung *f*
surface undulation Oberflächenwelle *f*
surface unit Flächeneinheit *f*
surface varnishing Oberflächenlackierung *f*
surface wave Oberflächenwelle *f*
surface wear Abrieb *m*
surface work-hardening Oberflächenverfestigung *f*
surface-grind planschleifen, außenschleifen
surface-ground adherent plangeschliffene Klebefläche *f*
surface-mountable oberflächenmontierbar
surface-mountable device (SMD) oberflächenmontierbarer Baustein *m*
surface broaching Außenräumen *nt*
surface-treated oberflächenbehandelt
surfacing 1. Planbearbeitung *f*, Flachprägen *nt* 2. Plattierung *f* 3. Flachprägen *nt* 4. Plandrehen *nt*
surfacing and screw-cutting lathe Leit- und Zugspindeldrehmaschine *f*
surfacing lathe Plandrehmaschine *f*
surfacing layer Befestigungsschicht *f*
surfacing machine Plandrehmaschine *f*
surfacing work Planarbeit *f*
surge Ruck *m*, Stoß *m*
surge immunity Zerstörfestigkeit *f*
surge protective device Überspannungsschutzeinrichtung *f*
surge voltage Überspannung *f*, Stoßspannung *f*
surge voltage protector Überspannungsableiter *m*, Überspannungsschutzeinrichtung *f*
surplus Überschuss *m*
surplus demand Nachfrageüberhang *m*
surplus feed Übervorschub *m*
surplus metal überschüssiges Metall *nt*
surround umgrenzen, umgeben; Einbettung *f*, Ummantelung *f*
surround material Einbettung *f*
surrounded by a mould eingeformte Schweißstelle *f*
surrounding Umgebung *f*, Einbetten *nt*; umgrenzend
surrounding air Umgebungsluft *f*
surrounding area Randfeld *nt*
surrounding medium Umgebungsmedium *nt*
survey of the production plan Produktionsplanungsübersicht *f*
survey plan Vermessungsriss *m*
surveying Vermessung *f*
surveying apparatus Aufnahmegerät *nt*
surveying practice Vermessungstechnik *f*

survival probability Überlebenswahrscheinlichkeit f
susceptibility to cracking Rissanfälligkeit f
susceptibility to failure Störanfälligkeit f
susceptibility to faults Störanfälligkeit f
susceptible to abrasion abriebempfindlich
susceptible to ageing alterungsempfindlich
susceptible to cracking rissanfällig
susceptible to disorders störanfällig
susceptible to moisture feuchteempfindlich
susceptible to oxidation oxidationsempfindlich
susceptibility to failure Störanfälligkeit f
suspend unterstützen, aufhängen (an), freitragen, hängen
suspend command Wartebefehl m
suspended angehoben
suspended (from) hängen
suspended ceiling Zwischengeschoss nt
suspended level bulb Niveaugefäß nt
suspended type hängende Ausführung f
suspension Suspension f, Aufhängung f
suspension anchor with welded bolt end Hängeanker m mit Anschweißende
suspension catch Hakenklemme f
suspension clamp Aufhängeklaue f
suspension element Tragmittel nt
suspension equipment Tragmittel nt
suspension method Schwebeverfahren nt
sustain halten, ertragen
sustained dauernd, andauernd
sustained backfire Rückzündung f
sustained continuous operation ununterbrochener Dauerbetrieb m
sustained short-circuit Dauerkurzschluss m
sustainer Träger m
swage gesenkdrücken
swaging Sickung f

swallowing capacity Schluckvolumen nt
swan-necked gekröpft
swan-necked finisher gekröpfter Schlichtmeißel m
swan-necked finishing tool gekröpfter Schlichtmeißel m
swan-necked rougher gekröpfter Schlichtmeißel m
swap Wechsel m, Austausch m; wechseln, vertauschen
swap body Wechselbehälter m
swapping Vertauschen nt
swarf Schleifspäne mpl, Späneabfall m, ölige Späne f
swarf chute Spänerutsche f
swarf pan Spänewanne f
swarf removal Späneabfuhr f
swarf scraper Spanabstreifer m
swarf tray Spanfangschale f, Spänemulde f
swash-plate Taumelscheibe f
sway Schwankung f, schwanken
swaying schwankend
sweep wobbeln
sweep element Kippglied nt
sweeper Schienenräumer m
swell test Quellversuch m
swelling Quellung f
swelling behaviour Quellverhalten nt
swelling hysteresis Quellungshysterese f
swelling product Quellungsprodukt nt
swept radius Schwenkradius m
swept volume Schwenkbereich m
switch panel Schalttafel f
switched off abgeschaltet
swing 1. schwingen, schwenken, schwanken, wippen, pendeln; freie Schwingung f 2. drehen 3. Drehdurchmesser m, Schwingdurchmesser m, Umlaufdurchmesser m
swing burner Schwenkbrenner m
swing check valve Rückschlagklappe f
swing cutting tool Schwenkmeißel m
swing frame grinder Pendelschleifmaschine f
swing lapping Schwingläppen nt
swing latch Spannriegel m
swing mirror Schwingspiegel m

swing out of the way (upward, down ward, sideways, round) schwenken (weg-, aufwärts, abwärts, seitwärts, rundschwenken)
swing over bed Drehdurchmesser *m* über Bett
swing pull grinding Schwingziehschleifen
swing rest Schwenksupport *m*
swing to an angular position schwenken
swing-folding Schwenkbiegen *nt*
swinging Schwankung *f*, Wippen *nt*; pendelnd, schwankend
swinging arm schwingende Kurbelschleife *f*
swinging stop Wippanschlag *m*
Swiss automatic Langdrehautomat *m*, Einspindelautomat *m* ohne Revolverkopf
Swiss bush-type automatic Langdrehautomat *m*, Drehautomat *m* ohne Revolverkopf
Swiss bush-type automatic lathe Einspindellangdrehautomat *m*
Swiss type screw machine Einspindellangdrehautomat *m*
Swiss-type automatic screw machine Einspindelautomat *m* *(ohne Revolverkopf)*
switch 1. schalten, umschalten, umstellen (auf), wechseln (zu), weiterschalten; Schalter *m*, Tastschalter *m* **2.** Weiche *f*, Schienenweiche *f*
switch back difference Rückschaltdifferenz *f*
switch cabinet Schaltschrank *m*
switch cupboard Schaltschrank *m*
switch difference Schaltdifferenz *f*
switch in *(Schaltgeräte)* einschalten
switch into position *(Hebel)* einschalten
switch lever Schalthebel *m*
switch of pallet Palettenwechsel *m*
switch off ausschalten, abschalten, abstellen
switch on einschalten, anschalten
switch over umschalten, übergehen
switch piece Schaltstück *nt*
switch position Schalterstellung *f*

switch rail planer Weichenzungenhobelmaschine *f*
switch room Schaltraum *m*
switch stage Schaltstufe *f*
switchable schaltbar
switchboard Schalttafel *f*, Schaltbrett *nt*
switchbox Sicherungskasten *m*
switched mode Schaltbetrieb *m*
switched mode power supply Schaltnetzteil *nt*
switched reluctance motor geschalteter Reluktanzmotor *m*
switched thyristor Basisband *nt*
switchgear Schaltgerät *nt*
switchgear box Schaltkasten *m*
switchgear cabinet Schaltschrank *m*
switchgroup Umschalter *m*
switching Schaltung *f*, Weiterschaltung *f*
switching accuracy Schaltgenauigkeit *f*
switching actuation Schalten *nt*, Schaltvorgang *m*
switching algebra Schaltalgebra *f*
switching cam Schaltnocke *f*
switching carriage Verschiebewagen *m*
switching chain Schaltkette *f*
switching circuitry Schaltsystem *nt*
switching device Schalter *m*
switching frequency Schalthäufigkeit *f*, Umschaltfrequenz *f*
switching gate Schalttor *nt*
switching hysteresis Schalthysterese *f*
switching information Schaltinformation *f*
switching installation Schaltanlage *f*
switching movement Schaltbewegung *f*
switching off Abschaltung *f*, Ausschaltung *f*, Abschalten *nt*
switching operation Verknüpfung *f*, Schaltvorgang *m*, Schalten *nt*
switching overpressure Schaltüberdruck *m*
switching point Schaltpunkt *m*
switching pressure Schaltdruck *m*
switching process Schaltvorgang *m*
switching pulse Schaltimpuls *m*
switching rate Umschaltfrequenz *f*
switching sequence Schaltfolge *f*

switching signal Schaltsignal *nt*
switching signal output Schaltsignalausgabe *f*
switching step Schaltschritt *m*
switching system Schaltsystem *nt*
switching time from fast to slow speed Schaltung *f* von höher zu niedriger Geschwindigkeit *f* (oder Drehzahl *f*)
switching-in module Anschaltbaugruppe *f*
switch-on inhibition Einschaltsperre *f*
swivel schwenken, drehen; Schwenkbewegung *f*, Drehscheibe *f*, Drehteil *nt*
swivel axis Schwenkachse *f*
swivel base Drehteiluntersatz *m*, Drehteil *nt*
swivel bearing Schwenklager *nt*
swivel castor Lenkrolle *f*
swivel element Schwenkelement *nt*
swivel head Drehsupport *m*, Kippsupport *m*, schwenkbarer Spindelkopf *m*, Schwenkkopf *m*
swivel head miller Fräsmaschine *f* mit drehbarem Spindelkopf
swivel knee Schwenktisch *m*
swivel pin Drehzahlverhältnis *nt*
swivel pipe coupling Gelenkrohrverbindung *f*
swivel plate Drehplatte *f*
swivel spindle carrier Schwinggehäuse *nt*
swivel table drehbarer Tisch *m*, Schwenktisch *m*
swivel vice drehbarer Schraubstock *m*
swivelling Ausschwenken *nt*
swivelled position Schwenkposition *f*
swivelling drehbar, schwenkbar; Schwenken *nt*
swivelling angle plate table Schwenktisch *m*
swivelling arm Schwenkarm *m*
swivelling attachment Universalspindelkopf *m*
swivelling burner method Schwenkbrennerverfahren *nt*
swivelling control pendant schwenkbare Bedienungstafel *f*
swivelling feature Schwenkbarkeit *f*
swivelling holder schwenkbare Halterung *f*

swivelling knee Schwenktisch *m*
swivelling knee milling Schwenktischfräsen *nt*
swivelling mechanism Schwenkeinrichtung *f*
swivelling movement Schwenkbewegung *f*
swivelling slide rest Schwenksupport *m*
swivelling structure Schwenkkonstruktion *f*
swivelling table ausschwenkbarer Tisch *m*
swivelling template Schwenkschablone *f*
swivelling templet Schwenkschablone *f*
swivelling tool rest Schwenksupport *m*
swivelling work platform Schwenkarbeitsbühne *f*
swivelling worktable Schwenktisch *m*
swivel-mounted schwenkbar
swung-out position ausgeschwenkte Stellung *f*
symbol Symbol *nt*, Zeichen *nt*
symbolization Symbolisierung *f*
symmetrical angle cutter Prismenfräser *m*
symmetrical cross construction kreuzsymmetrischer Aufbau *m*
symmetrical thread symmetrisch geschnittenes Gewinde *nt*
symmetry Symmetrie *f*
symmetry tolerance Symmetrietoleranz *f*
synchro motor Drehfeldmotor *m*
synchronization Synchronisation *f*, Synchronisierung *f*
synchronization unit Synchronisierung *f*
synchronize synchronisieren, takten
synchronized mask synchronisierte Maske *f*
synchronized mask scanning synchronisiertes Maskenscannen *nt*
synchronizer ring Synchronring *m*
synchronizing torque Synchronisationsmoment *nt*
synchro mechanism Synchrongetriebe *nt*

synchronous synchron
synchronous belt Zahnriemen *m*
synchronous belt drive Zahnriementrieb *m*
synchronous data link control synchrone Datenübertragungsprozedur *f*
synchronous data transmission synchrone Datenübertragung *f*
synchronous drive Synchronantrieb *m*
synchronous motion Synchronbewegung *f*
synchronous motor Synchronmotor *m*
synchronous operation Synchronfahrweise *f*, Synchronlauf *m*
synchronous radiation synchrone Strahlung *f*
synchronous range Synchronbereich *m*
synchronous speed Synchrondrehzahl *f*
synchronous time division multiplexing synchrones Zeitmultiplexverfahren *nt*
synchronous vertical carousel Synchronpaternoster *nt*
syntax Syntax *m*
syntax and service report Fehlerprotokoll *nt*
syntax structogram Syntaxstruktogramm *nt*
synthetic synthetisch
synthetic latex paint Lunststofflatexfarbe *f*
synthetic resin Kunstharz *nt*
synthetic resin-asbestos laminated wood Kunstharz-Asbest-Platte *f*
synthetic rubber pipe Kunstgummileitung *f*
synthetic rubber putty Kunstkautschukkitt *m*
synthetic rubber solution Kunstkautschuklösung *f*
sysem model Anlagenmodell *nt*
system System *nt*, Anlage *f*
system self-test Systemeigentest *m*
system analysis Systemanalyse *f*
system architecture Systemarchitektur *f*
system attendant Systembetreuer *m*
system axis Systemachse *f*

system behaviour Systemverhalten *nt*
system border Systemgrenze *f*
system boundary Systemgrenze *f*
system breakdown Systemausfall *m*
system capacity utilization Anlagenauslastung *f*
system check Systemprüfung *f*
system clock Systemuhr *f*
system command Systembedienungsbefehl *m*
system component Systemkomponente *f*
system comprising piping components Rohrsystem *nt*
system control Systemsteuerung *f*, Anlagensteuerung *f*
system control language Systemsteuerungssprache *f*
system control unit (SCU) Systemkontrolleinheit *f*
system conversion Anlagenumbau *m*
system core module Systemkernmodul *m*
system core program Systemkernprogramm *nt*
system crash Systemausfall *m*, Systemabsturz *m*
system dependent systembedingt
system description Anlagenbeschreibung *f*
system design Systembauweise *f*
system designer Anlagenprojekteur *m*
system directory Systemverzeichnis *nt*
system earth reference point Systemerdebezugspunkt *m*
system environment Systemumwelt *f*
system equipment Anlagenausstattung *f*
system error Systemfehler *m*
system expansion Systemerweiterung *f*, Anlagenerweiterung *f*
system failure Systemstörung *f*
system fault spark Systemfehler *m*
system folder Systemverzeichnis *nt*
system frequency welding Netzfrequenzschweißen *nt*, Schweißen *nt* mit Netzfrequenz
system implementation Systemeinführung *f*
system input Systemeingang *m*

system input variable Systemeingangsgröße *f*
system integrator Systemintegrator *m*
system internal data *pl* Systeminterndaten *pl*
system language Systemsprache *f*
system level Systemebene *f*
system life cycle Anlagenlebenszyklus *m*
system limit Systemgrenze *f*
system load Netzbelastung *f*, Systemlast *f*
system load data Systemlastdaten *pl*
system log Systemprotokoll *nt*
system maintenance Anlagenbetreuung *f*
system measurement Netzmessung *f*
system memory Systemspeicher *m*
system monitoring Systemüberwachung *f*
system of coordinates Achsenkreuz *nt*
system of fits Passsystem *nt*
system of fits for gear transmissions Getriebepasssystem *nt*
system of measurement Maßsystem *nt*
system of objectives Zielsystem *nt*
system operator (SYSOP) Systembediener *m*
system output Systemausgang *m*
system output variable Systemausgangsgröße *f*
system performance Systemausführung *f*
system perturbation Netzrückwirkung *f*
system planner Systemplaner *m*
system point Knotenpunkt *m*
system procedurement Anlagenbeschaffung *f*
system proposal Systemvorschlag *m*
system pulse Systemtakt *m*
system recovery Systemfehlerbehebung *f*
system related module systemnaher Modul *m*
system reliability Systemzuverlässigkeit *f*
system request key Systemabfragetaste *f*
system setting Systemeinstellung *f*
system software Systemsoftware *f*
system solution systemtechnische Lösung *f*
system state Systemzustand *m*
system status Systemzustand *m*
system supplier Anlagenlieferant *m*, Systemlieferant *m*
system support Systembetreuung *f*
system technology Systemtechnik *f*
system throughput Systemdurchsatz *m*
system time Systemzeit *f*
system timer Systemzeituhr *f*
system training Systemschulung *f*
system utilization Systemauslastung *f*
system variable Systemvariable *f*
system voltage Netzspannung *f*
systematic arrangement of drawings *pl* Zeichnungssystematik *f*
systematic error systematische Abweichung *f*, systematischer Fehler *m*
systematic sampling systematische Probennahme *f*
systematically grooved surface character geordnet rilliger Oberflächencharakter *m*
system-compatible systemkompatibel
system-independent systemunabhängig
system-internal systemintern
systems analyst Planer *m*, Systemanalytiker *m*
systems of preset times Systeme *f* vorbestimmter Zeiten
system-specific systemspezifisch

T t

tab Nase f, Lappen m
table 1. Tisch m, Planscheibe f **2.** (grafische Darstellung) Tabelle f
table bearing surface Tischauflagefläche f
table clamping Tischfeststellung f
table dog Tischknagge f
table drive Tischantrieb m
table engagement Tischeinschaltung f
table fan Tischventilator m
table feed (axialer) Tischvorschub m
table feed motion Tischvorschubbewegung f
table feed screw Tischspindel f, Tischvorschubspindel f
table feedbox Tischvorschubgetriebe nt
table forward stroke Tischvorlauf m
table guide-way Tischführung f
table hand crank Tischverstellkurbel f
table infeed radialer Tischvorschub m
table lock Tischverriegelung f, Tischklemmung f
table locking Tischklemmung f, Tischfeststellung f
table locking mechanism Tischklemmung f
table lowering Tischabsenkung f
table motion Tischweg m
table of contents Inhaltsverzeichnis nt
table power traverse Tischselbstgang m
table pull Durchzugskraft f, Schnittkraft f
table relief Tischentlastung f
table return Tischrücklauf m
table reversal Tischumkehr f, Tischumsteuerung f
table setting Tischeinstellung f
table skip-feed stop Tischanschlag m
table start Tischeinschaltung f
table stop dog Tischanschlag m
table stroke Tischhub m, Tischweg m
table travel Tischweg m
table traverse Tischhub m, Tischweg m
table trip dog Tischanschlag m
table trip switch Tischauslöseschalter m
table-screw nut Tischspindelmutter f
tablet tablettieren
tabletting Tablettieren nt, Tablettierung f
tabletting machine Tablettiermaschine f
table-type boring drilling and milling machine Tisch-Bohr- und Fräswerk nt
tabular dimension Tabellenmaß nt
tabular drawing Tabellenzeichnung f
tachometer Drehzahlanzeiger m
tack weld Montagehilfsschweißnaht f
tackiness Klebrigkeit f
tacking sequence plan Heftplan m
tackle Seilzug m, Winde f
tackle line Seilzug m
tackle locking device Seilzugsicherung f
tack-welded condition gehefteter Zustand m
tacky constituent klebender Bestandteil m
tactile comparison Tastvergleich m
T-adaptor T-Stutzen m
tag Anhängeetikett nt, Marke f; verplomben
tag labelling machine Anhängeetikettappliziermaschine f
tagging Anspitzen nt durch Walzen
tagline Greifer m
tail board lift Hub(lade)bühne f
tail centre Gegenspitze f, Reitstockspitze f
tail end length Nachlaufstrecke f
tailgate auffahren
tailored to demand bedarfsgerecht
tailored to suit the needs of the market bedarfsgerecht
tailstock Reitstock m
tailstock barrel Reitstockoberteil nt
tailstock base Reitstockunterteil nt
tailstock centre Reitstockkörner m, Reitstockspitze f, Körnerspitze f
tailstock face-plate Reitstockplan-

scheibe *f*
tailstock for drilling and boring Bohrreitstock *m*
tailstock set-over Reitstockverstellung *f*
tailstock sleeve Reitstockpinole *f*, Pinole *f*
tailstock spindle sleeve Reitstockspindel *f*
take 1. *(Stelle)* annehmen **2.** *(aus oder von)* entnehmen
take a cut Span abnehmen
take a light cut einen feinen Span nehmen
take a root Wurzel ziehen aus
take a roughing cut schruppen
take a sample eine Probe nehmen
take action Maßnahmen ergreifen
take along mitnehmen
take away wegnehmen
take back zurücknehmen
take cuts zerspanen
take down 1. *(Arbeit)* abarbeiten **2.** *(Arbeitsschritt)* Rüstvorgang *m*
take in tow abschleppen, bergen
take into consideration beachten
take measurements messen, abgreifen
take measures Maßnahmen ergreifen
take off 1. *(math., Preis)* abziehen (von) **2.** *(Telefon, Deckel)* abnehmen **3.** *(aus Lager)* entnehmen **4.** *(Arbeitsfläche)* abräumen; Abräumen *nt*
take over übernehmen; Übernahme *f*
take part beteiligen
take readings ablesen
take shape fortschreiten, Fortschritte machen
take up 1. *(Rolle)* aufwickeln **2.** *(Werkzeug)* aufnehmen; Aufnahme *f* **3.** *(benutzen)* verbrauchen
take-off pipe Entnahmeleitung *f*
take-off rod Abziehstange *f*
takeover Betriebsübernahme *f*
take-up of hydrogen Wasserstoffaufnahme *f*
take-up strip Nachstellleiste *f*
taking back Rücknahme *f*
taking cuts Spanabnahme *f*
taking down a cut Spanabnahme *f*
taking in Ansaugen *nt*
taking over Übernahme *f*
taking rough cuts grobe Spanabnahme *f*
taking the first cut Anschneiden *nt*
tamp stampfen
tamped apparent density Stampfdichte *f*
tamped clay Stampfmasse *f*
tamped volume Stampfvolumen *nt*
tamper Stampfer *m*
tamping compound Stampfmasse *f*
tandem wheels Tandemräder *ntpl*
tang Zapfen *m*, Aufnahmezapfen *m*, Mitnehmerzapfen *m*
tangency Berührung *f*
tangent Tangente *f*
tangent contact point Tangentenberührungspunkt *m*
tangent portion Tangentenabschnitt *m*
tangential attachment Tangentialeinrichtung *f*
tangential cutter Tangentialmeißel *m*
tangential feed method Tangentialverfahren *nt*
tangential hobbing Tangentialfräsen *nt*, Tangentialwälzfräsen *nt*, Tangentialwälzverfahren *nt*
tangential keying Tangentkeilbefestigung *f*
tangential plane Tabgentialebene *f*, Tangentenebene *f*
tangential profile Tangentialprofil *nt*
tangential section Tangentialschnitt *m*
tangential shrinkage Tangentialeinlauf *m*
tangential speed Tangentialgeschwindigkeit *f*
tangential spindle head Tangentialspindelstock *m*
tangential starting cut Tangentialanschnitt *m*
tangential stretch drawing to shape Tangentialstreckziehen *nt*
tangential table feed motion tangentiale Tischvorschubbewegung *f*
tangential table feed speed tangentiale Tischvorschubgeschwindigkeit *f*
tangential turning tool Tangentialdrehmeißel *m*
tangential-feed headstock Tangentialspindelstock *m*

tank Behälter *m*, Tank *m*
tank and pipeline construction Behälter- und Rohrleitungsbau *m*
tank bottom Behälterboden *m*, Behältersohle *f*
tank crown Behälterscheitel *m*, Tankoberboden *m*
tank inlet Behältereinlauf *m*
tank outlet Behälterauslauf *m*
tanker vehicle coupling Tankwagenkupplung *f*
tanker vehicle pump Tankwagenpumpe *f*
tap 1. *(Gewinde, Bohrung)* Gewinde bohren, anzapfen; Gewindebohrer *m*, Schneidbohrer *m*, Bohrer *m* **2.** *(pochen)* abklopfen
tap drilling Gewindekernbolzen *m*
tap holder Gewindebohrerhalter *m*
tape Streifen *m*, Band *nt*
tape error Streifenfehler *m*
tape feed Streifenvorschub *m*
tape punch Streifenlocher *m*
tape puncher Lochgerät *nt*, Streifenlocher *m*
tape punching Streifenlochung *f*
tape reader Lochstreifenleser *m*, Streifenleser *m*, Streifenlesekopf *m*
tape rule Bandmaß *nt*
tape sealing machine Haftklebebandverschließmaschine *f*
tape with a thermosetting layer of adhesive Band *nt* mit wärmehärtender Klebeschicht
tape-controlled streifengesteuert
taper 1. Kegel *m*, Konus *m*; spitz zulaufen **2.** *(Gewinde)* Ganghöhe *f*, Steigung *f* **3.** *(konstruktive Form)* Abschrägung *f*, Verjüngung *f*
taper action Anzug *m* einer Mitnehmerverbindung
taper adapter Kegeleinsatz *m*, Konuseinsatz *m*
taper adapter end *(e. Rohrverschraubung)* kegeliger Einschraubzapfen *m*
taper angle Kegelwinkel *m*
taper angle tolerance Kegelwinkeltoleranz *f*
taper bar Leitlineal *nt*, Kegellineal *nt*
taper bore Hohlkegel *m*

taper boring Kegelbohren *nt*
taper bushing Kegelbuchse *f*
taper check gauge kegeliger Gewindeprüfdorn *m*
taper drift Aufweitdorn *m*
taper fit Kegelpassung *f*
taper gauge Kegellehre *f*
taper gib Nachstelleiste *f*, Führungsleiste *f*
taper grinding Kegelschleifen *nt*
taper hole Innenkegel *m*
taper lock Kegelbefestigung *f*
taper lock fixing Kegelbefestigung *f*
taper milling Kegelfräsen *nt*
taper milling attachment Kegelfräseinrichtung *f*
taper parallels *pl* Keilstück *nt*
taper pin Kegelstift *m*
taper plug Hahnküken *nt*
taper ratio Kegelverhältnis *nt*
taper reamer Kegelreibahle *f*
taper shank Kegelschaft *m*, Schaftkegel *m*, Vollkegel *m*, Außenkegel *m*
taper shank end mill Schaftfräser *m* mit kegeligem Schaft
taper spindle Kegelspindel *f*
taper toothing Kegelverzahnung *f*
taper turning Kegeldrehen *nt*
taper turning attachment Kegeldreheinrichtung *f*
tape-reading speed Streifenlesegeschwindigkeit *f*
tapered abgeschrägt, kegelig, kegelförmig, konisch, abgeschrägt, spitz zulaufend
tapered external thread kegeliges Außengewinde *nt*
tapered gib Keilleiste *f*
tapered pipe thread kegeliges Rohrgewinde *nt*
tapered roller Kegelrolle *f*
tapered roller bearing Kegelrollenlager *nt*
tapered Whitworth pipe thread kegeliges Withworth-Rohrgewinde *nt*
tapped mit Innengewinde *nt*
tapped delay element Verzögerungsglied *nt* mit Abgriffen
tapped fitting Anbohrarmatur *f*
tapper Gewindebohrmaschine *f*

tappet Anschlag *m*, Stößel *m*
tapping 1. *(Gewinde)* Innengewindeschneiden *nt*, Gewindebohren *nt* 2. *(Hochofen)* Abstich *m*
tapping cutter Gewindefräser *m*
tapping device Klopfeinrichtung *f*
tapping machine Bohrmaschine *f*, Gewindebohrmaschine *f*
tapping motor Gewindebohrmotor *m*
tapping screw Blechschraube *f*
tapping screw assembly Kombiblechschraube *f*
tapping screw thread Gewinde *nt* für Blechschrauben
tapping unit Gewindebohreinheit *f*
tar binder Teerbinder *m*
tar bitumen concrete Teerasphaltbeton *m*
tar impregnated teergetränkt
tar roof sheeting Teerdachbahn *f*
tar stabilization Teerverfestigung *f*
tar-bitumen roof sheeting Teerbitumendachbahn *f*
tare beaker Leerglas *nt*
target Zielsetzung *f*, Soll *nt*, Ziel *nt*
target at zielen auf
target consumption Sollverbrauch *m*
target date Termin *m*, Terminziel *nt*
target figure Planzahl *f*
target figures Zielgrößen *fpl*
target inventory Zielbestand *m*
target quantity Sollmenge *f*
target time Sollzeit *f*
target value Sollwert *m*, Zielgröße *f*
target-performance comparison Soll-Ist-Vergleich *m*
target-skin distance Fokus-Haut-Abstand *m*
tariff Zoll *m*
tariff rate Zollsatz *m*
tarnish Anlauffarbe *f*
tarnish film Anlaufschicht *f*
task Aufgabe *f*, Aufgabenstellung *f*, Auftrag *m*, Arbeit *f*
task area Aufgabenbereich *m*
task description Aufgabenbeschreibung *f*
task force Projektgruppe *f*
task-related aufgabenbezogen
tasteless shielding gas geschmackloses Schutzgas *nt*
taut fest, straff
taut rope fest gespanntes Seil *nt*
taut span gezogenes Trumm *nt*
tax Zoll *m*
tax control Zolldatenkontrolle *f*
taxi mode Taxibetrieb *m*
Taylor principle Taylorscher Grundsatz *m*
T-bulkhead union T-Schottstutzen *m*
teach-in mode Teach-in-Verfahren *nt*
teach-in process Teach-in-Verfahren *nt*
teach-in surface Teach-in-Oberfläche *f*
teaching aids Lehrmittel *ntpl*
teach-in-programming Teach-in-Programmierung *f*
team work Zusammenspiel *nt*
tear 1. zerreißen, reißen, aufreißen; Abriss *m* 2. *(Abrieb)* Verschleiß *m*
tear chip Reißspan *m*, Bruchspan *m*
tear factor Durchreißfaktor *m*
tear growth rate Weiterreißgeschwindigkeit *f*
tear growth resistance Weiterreißwiderstand *m*
tear growth test Weiterreißprüfung *f*
tear growth tester Weiterreißprüfgerät *nt*
tear growth work Weiterreißbarkeit *f*
tear length Reißstrecke *f*
tear loose ausbrechen
tear off abreißen, losreißen
tear open aufreißen
tear out herausreißen
tear propagation Weiterreißen *nt*
tear propagation along a thread fadengerades Weiterreißen
tear resistance Durchreißarbeit *f*
tear tape Aufreißverschlussstreifen *m*
tear tape applicator Aufreißverschlussstreifenappliziermaschine *f*
tearing Riss *m*, Reißen *nt*, Weiterreißen *nt*
tearing force Durchreißkraft *f*
tearing in Einreißen *nt*
tearing off Abreißen *nt*
tearing resistance Durchreißwiderstand *m*
tearing resistance test Durchreißversuch *m*

tearing test Einreißversuch *m*
tearing through Durchreißen *nt*
tear-off package Abreißverpackung *f*
tear-open package Aufreißverpackung *f*
tease auflockern
technical proof stress (0.01%) technische Elastizitätsgrenze *f*
technical aids Hilfsmittel *nt*
Technical and Office Protocol TOP (technisches und kaufmännisches Protokoll)
technical code of practice technische Regeln *fpl*
technical control board technischer Überwachungsverein *m*
technical data technische Daten *pl*
technical department Fachabteilung *f*
technical drawing technische Zeichnung *f*
technical elastic limit technische Elastizitätsgrenze *f*
technical inadequacies *pl* **in the testing** prüftechnische Mängel *mpl*
technical laying disposition verlegetechnische Maßnahme *f*
technical measurement reasons messtechnische Gründe *mpl*
technical product technisches Erzeugnis *nt*
technical specifications technische Daten *pl*
technique Technik *f*, Verfahren *nt*, Arbeitsweise *f*
technique for joining parts Verbindungstechnik *f*
technique main group Verfahrenshauptgruppe *f*
technological bend test Faltversuch *m*, technologischer Biegeversuch *m*
technological data technologische Daten *pl*
technology Technologie *f*, angewandte Technik *f*
technology assessment Technikbewertung *f*
technology engineering Technik *f*
technology of blasting Strahlverfahrenstechnik *f*

tee square Zeichenschiene *f*
teed circuit Arbeitskreislauf *m*
teem gießen, vergießen
tee-piece T-Stück *nt*
teeth characteristics Verzahnungscharakteristik *f*
teeth on the end Stirnzähne *mpl*
teeth on the periphery Umfangszähne *f*
teflon container Teflongefäß *nt*
telecommunication Datenfernübertragung *f*, Fernmeldetechnik *f*
telecommunications processing Nachrichtentechnik *f*
telemetering Fernmessung *f*
telemetry Streckenmessung *f*
telescope Teleskop *nt*; teleskopieren, herausfahren
telescopic teleskopierbar, ausziehbar, ausfahrbar, ineinander schiebbar, einschiebbar, ineinander stapelnd
telescopic arm Teleskoparm *m*
telescopic conveyor Teleskopförderer *m*
telescopic coolant return ausziehbare Kühlmittelrückflussleitung *f*
telescopic fork Teleskopgabel *f*
telescopic fork arm Teleskopgabelzinken *m*
telescopic load fork Teleskopgabel *f*
telescopic system Teleskopsystem *nt*
telescopic table Teleskoptisch *m*
telescoping Teleskopieren *nt*
telescoping mast Teleskopmast *m*
telescopic mast Teleskophubgerüst *nt*
telltale lamp Leuchtmelder *m*
telltale lamp for visual signals Lampe *f* für optische Meldungen
telltale light Kontrolllampe *f*, Anzeigelampe *f*
tell-tale light Warnlampe *f*
telltale pipe Riechrohr *nt*
telpher line Elektrohängebahn *f*
telpherage Elektrohängebahn *f*
temper temperieren, anlassen
temper carbon Temperkohle *f*
temper embrittlement (between 350° C and 550 ° C) Anlassversprödung *f*
temperature Temperatur *f*

temperature class Temperaturklasse *f*
temperature conditioning Temperieren *nt*
temperature conditioning device Temperiereinrichtung *f*
temperature conditioning medium Temperiermittel *nt*
temperature control Temperaturführung *f*, Temperaturkontrolle *f*, Temperaturregler *m*, Temperierung *f*
temperature control cycle Temperaturegelspiegel *m*
temperature control plan Temperierplan *m*
temperature difference Temperaturdifferenz *f*
temperature during erection Aufstellungstemperatur *f*
temperature gradient Wärmegefälle *nt*
temperature indicating crayon Temperaturfarbstift *m*
temperature level Temperaturstufe *f*
temperature limit Temperaturgrenze *f*
temperature limiter Temperaturbegrenzer *m*
temperature management Temperaturführung *f*
temperature measurement Erwärmungsprüfung *f*
temperature measuring value Temperaturmesswert *m*
temperature monitor Temperaturwächter *m*
temperature of recrystallization Rekristallisationstemperatur *f*
temperature of the liquid in distillation flask Sumpftemperatur *f*
temperature on removal from mould Entformungstemperatur *f*
temperature probe Temperaturfühler *m*
temperature range Temperaturbereich *m*
temperature resistance Temperaturbeständigkeit *f*
temperature resistant temperaturbeständig
temperature rise Erwärmung *f*, Temperaturanstieg *m*

temperature sensitive resistor temperaturabhängiger Widerstand *m*
temperature sensor Temperaturfühler *m*
temperature set point setter Temperatursollwertsteller *m*
temperature spread Temperaturspreizung *f*
temperature stability Temperaturbeständigkeit *f*
temperature step Temperaturschritt *m*
temperature system Temperiersystem *nt*
temperature tolerance Temperaturverträglichkeit *f*
temperature versus number of cycles Temperaturlaufkurve *f*
temperature-control liquid Temperierflüssigkeit *f*
temperature-dependent temperaturabhängig
temperature-regulating appliance Temperaturregeleinrichtung *f*
temperature-time sequence Temperatur-Zeit-Folge *f*
temperature-time-limit Temperatur-Zeit-Grenze *f*
temper-brittle anlassversprödet
tempering behaviour Anlassverhalten *nt*
tempering diagram Anlassschaubild *nt*
tempering furnace Anlassofen *m*
tempering medium Anlassmittel *nt*
tempering treatment Anlassbehandlung *f*
template Kopierlineal *nt*, Kopierschiene *f*, Kopierschablone *f*, Schablone *f*, Vorlage *f*, Lehre *f*
template based on drawings Risslehre *f*
template carrier Schablonenträger *m*
template master Urschablone *f*
template swivelling device Schablonenschwenkeinrichtung *f*
templet Schablone *f*, Kopierschablone *f*
temporal zeitlich
temporal limitation zeitliche Begrenzung *f*
temporary zeitweilig, zeitlich begrenzt, vorübergehend

temporary storage Zwischenspeicherung *f*
temporary weld Hilfsschweißung *f*
temporary welding Anschweißen *nt*
ten key block-keyboard Zehnerblocktastatur *f*
tenacity Zähfestigkeit *f*
tenacity behaviour Zähigkeitsverhalten *nt*
ternary brazing alloy Dreistoffhartlot *nt*
tend pflegen zu, neigen zu
tendency Neidung *f*, Tendenz *f*
tendency to ageing Alterungsneigung *f*
tendency to hot cracking Wärmerissneigung *f*
tendency to porosity Porenneigung *f*
tendency to take on useful hardness Neigung *f* zum Einhärten
tendency to transformation Umwandlungsneigung *f*
tender Kostenvoranschlag *m*, Ausschreibung *f*, Angebot *nt*; ein Angebot *nt* unterbreiten
tender documents Vergabeunterlagen *fpl*
tender specification Lastenheft *nt*
tense spannen
tenside solution Tensidlösung *f*
tensile creep rupture strength Zeitstandzugfestigkeit *f*
tensile creep test Zeitstandzugverhalten *nt*
tensile failure Zugspannungsbruch *m*
tensile force Zugkraft *f*
tensile impact behaviour Schlagzugverhalten *nt*
tensile impact strength Schlagzugfestigkeit *f*, Schlagzugzähigkeit *f*
tensile impact test Schlagzugversuch *m*, Schlagversuch *m*
tensile load Zugangsbeanspruchung *f*
tensile loading Dehnbeanspruchung *f*
tensile-loaded zugbelastet
tensile pre-loading Zugvorspannung *f*
tensile proving ring Zugbügel *m*
tensile reforming Zugumformen *nt*
tensile shear test Scherzugversuch *m*, Zugscherversuch *m*

tensile shearing load Scherzugkraft *f*
tensile strength Zugfestigkeit *f*
tensile test Zerreißversuch *m*, Zugversuch *m*
tensile test bar Zugstab *m*
tensile test piece Zugprobe *f*
tensile test specimen Zugprobe *f*, Prüfstück *nt* für Zugfestigkeitsprüfung
tensile test using knotted specimens Knotenzugversuch *m*
tensile testing machine Zerreißmaschine *f*
tensile testing machine with pendulum weighing mechanism Zugprüfmaschine *f* mit Neigungspendel
tensile transverse resistance Zugscherfestigkeit *f*
tension spannen; Spannung *f*, Zug *m*, Ziehen *nt*
tension chain *(zugübertragend)* Zugkette *f*
tension gauge Spannungsmessung *f*
tension in the cable Seilzug *m*
tension set Zugverformungsrest *m*
tension spring Zugfeder *f*, Zugfederung *f*
tension spring balance Zugfederwaage *f*
tension test Zugversuch *m*
tension width Spannweite *f*
tension zone Zugzone *f*
tension zone bent outwards aufgebogene Zugzone *f*
tensional bar Zugstab *m*
tensional member Zugstab *m*
tensional strapping Umreifungsband *nt*
tensionally locked kraftschlüssig
tension-compression testing cylinder Zug-Druck-Prüfzylinder *m*
tensioned straff
tensioning point Spannstelle *f*
tensioning station Spannstation *f*
tensionless state spannungsfreier Zustand *m*
tenso-compressive reforming Zugdruckumformen *nt*
tenso-elastic zugelastisch
tent Zelt *nt*
term 1. benennen; Begriff *m* 2. mathe-

matischer Ausdruck *m*
term of the axes Achsbezeichnung *f*
terminal 1. *(Gerät, Vorrichtung)* Endgerät *nt* **2.** Terminal *nt* **3.** *(el.)* Anschluss *m*, Klemme *f*, Lotpunkt *m*
terminal assignment Anschlussbelegung *f*
terminal block Reihenklemme *f*
terminal board Klemmenbrett *nt*
terminal box Klemmenkasten *m*
terminal connecting plan Anschlussplan *m*
terminal end Seilende *nt*
terminal line Abschlusslinie *f*, Abschlussstrich *m*
terminal pressure Speisespannung *f*
terminal station Endgerät *nt*
terminal unit Endgerät *nt*
terminal voltage Klemmenspannung *f*
terminate enden, beenden, begrenzen
alternating strain Dehnschwingung *f*
terrain liable to slips rutschgefährtetes Gelände *nt*
test 1. *(Kontrolle)* prüfen, überprüfen, abnehmen, untersuchen, testen, erproben, probieren, versuchen; Prüfung *f*, Untersuchung *f*, Erprobung *f*, Versuch *m*, Überprüfung *f*, Test *m*, Abnahmetest *m* **2.** *(Gerät)* Testvorrichtung *f*
test analysis Prüfdatenauswertung *f*
test angle Prüfwinkel *m*
test arrangement Prüfanordnung *f*, Versuchsanordnung *f*
test atmosphere Prüfklima *nt*
test bar Messdorn *m*
test bay Prüffeld *nt*, Prüfstand *m*
test bearing housing Prüflagergehäuse *nt*
test bench Prüfstand *m*
test block Prüfblock *m*
test body Prüfkörper *m*
test byte Prüfbyte *nt*
test category Prüfklasse *f*
test certificate Prüferzeugnis *nt*, Prüfschein *m*, Prüfprotokoll *nt*, Prüfungsbescheinigung *f*
test certification Abnahmeprotokoll *nt*
test chamber Prüfzelle *f*
test characteristic Prüfmerkmal *nt*
test chart Messprotokoll *nt*, Prüfblatt *nt*

test circle Messkreis *m*
Test Code Association technischer Überwachungsverein *m*
test cone Prüfkonus *m*
test costs Prüfkosten *pl*
test criterion Prüfkriterium *nt*
test cutting Zerspanungsprobe *f*
test cycle Testspiel *nt*
test data Prüfdaten *pl*
test data recording Prüfdatenerfassung *f*
test diagram Prüfbild *nt*
test diagram chart Prüfbildblatt *nt*
test diagram curve Prüfbildkurve *f*
test dimension Prüfmaß *nt*
test dimension deviation Prüfabmaß *nt*
test distribution Prüfverteilung *f*
test documents Prüfunterlagen *fpl*
test dome Messdom *m*
test drawing Prüfzeichnung *f*
test duration Testzeit *f*
test emery Prüfschmirgel *m*
test emery paper Prüfschmirgelbogen *m*
test engineering reasons prüftechnische Gründe *mpl*
test equipment Prüfmittel *nt*, Testeinrichtung *f*
test error Prüffehler *m*
test face Prüffläche *f*
test finger Prüffinger *m*
test flame Prüfflamme *f*
test flange Prüfbund *m*
test floor Prüfstand *m*
test for cracks Rissprüfung *f*
test for study purposes Studienversuch *m*
test force Prüfkraft *f*
test force indication Prüfkraftanzeige *f*
test frequency Prüfhäufigkeit *f*, Prüffrequenz *f*
test fuel Prüfkraftstoff *m*
test gas Prüfgas *nt*
test gas bottle Prüfgasflasche *f*
test gear Prüfling *m*
test grease Prüffett *nt*
test heating element Prüfheizkörper *m*
test indentor Prüfstempel *m*
test ink Prüftinte *f*

test installation Versuchsanlage *f*
test institute Prüfinstitut *nt*
test instruction Prüfanweisung *f*
test instrument Prüfgerät *nt*
test item Versuchsteil *m*
test laboratory Prüflaboratorium *nt*
test laminate Prüflaminat *nt*
test liquid Prüfflüssigkeit *f*
test load Prüfkraft *f*, Prüflast *f*
test load indication Prüfkraftanzeige *f*
test load range Prüfkraftbereich *m*
test location Prüfplatz *m*
test lot Prüflos *nt*
test lot size Prüflosgröße *f*
test material Prüfgut *nt*
test medium Prüfmittel *nt*
test method Prüfmethode *f*, Prüfverfahren *nt*, Testverfahren *nt*
test methodology prüftechnische Gesichtspunkte *mpl*
test moment Prüfmoment *m*
test object Prüfgegenstand *m*
test on textiles Textilprüfung *f*
test order Prüfauftrag *m*
test order processing Prüfauftragsbearbeitung *f*
test outcome Prüfergebnis *nt*
test parameter Prüfparameter *m*
test particle Probeteilchen *nt*
test particle size Prüfkorngröße *f*
test path Prüfstrecke *f*, Prüfbahn *f*
test pattern Prüfbild *nt*
test piece Probe *f*, Probestück *nt*, Probekörper *m*, Teststück *nt*, Prüfkörper *m*, Prüfstück *nt*
test piece stored in liquids flüssigkeitsgelagerter Probekörper *m*
test pin Messstift *m*, Prüfstift *m*
test plan Prüfzeichnung *f*
test platform Prüfplattform *f*
test point Prüfpunkt *m*, Testpunkt *m*
test polynomial Prüfpolynom *nt*
test portion *(bei Werkstoffen)* Probe *f*
test preparation Versuchsvorbereitung *f*
test pressure Prüfdruck *m*
test procedure Versuchsdurchführung *f*
test program Prüfprogramm *nt*, Testprogramm *nt*
test rate Prüfgeschwindigkeit *f*

test record Prüfprotokoll *nt*, Abnahmeprotokoll *nt*
test report Prüfbericht *m*, Prüfblatt *nt*
test report book Abnahmeprotokoll *nt*
test report on results Messbericht *m*
test result Prüfbefund *m*, Prüfergebnis *nt*
test rig Prüfgerüst *nt*
test room climate Messraumklima *nt*
test run Testlauf *m*, Probebetrieb *m*, Probelauf *m*
test sample Messprobe *f*, Probe *f*, Prüfmuster *nt*
test sensitivity Prüfempfindlichkeit *f*
test sequence Testablauf *m*
test series Versuchsreihe *f*
test setup Prüfanordnung *f*, Versuchsanordnung *f*, Messanordnung *f*
test sheet Prüfblatt *nt*
test sieving Siebrückstandsbestimmung *f*
test specification Prüfvorschrift *f*
test specimen Prüfstück *nt*, Probe *f*, Probekörper *m*, Probestück *nt*, Versuchsprobe *f*
test specimen in sheet form flächiges Probestück *nt*
test statistic Prüfgröße *f*, Testgröße *f*
test strip Probestreifen *m*
test surface Prüfoberfläche *f*
test symbol Prüfzeichen *nt*
test trace Prüfbildlinie *f*
test tube Probegefäß *nt*
test using small drawn cups Näpfchenziehversuch *m*
test value Prüfwert *m*, Testwert *m*
test vessel Prüfgefäß *nt*
test zone Prüfzone *f*
testability Testbarkeit *f*
tester Prüfer *m*
testing Prüfung *f*, Untersuchung *f*, Erprobung *f*, Versuch *m*, Testen *nt*, Prüfen *nt*, Probieren *nt*
testing aid Prüfmittel *nt*
testing certificate Prüfbescheinigung *f*
testing cup Prüfgefäß *nt*
testing device Prüfvorrichtung *f*
testing equipment Prüfgeräte *ntpl*, Prüfeinrichtung *f*
testing installation Prüfanlage *f*

testing machine Prüfmaschine *f*
testing machinery Prüfmaschinen *fpl*
testing of elastomers Elastomerprüfung *f*
testing of filled packages Packstückprüfung *f*
testing of materials Werkstoffprüfung *f*, Stoffuntersuchung *f*
testing of plastics Kunststoffprüfung *f*
testing outfit Prüfeinrichtung *f*
testing practice Prüfpraxis *f*, Prüftechnik *f*, Untersuchungspraxis *f*
testing staff Prüfpersonal *nt*
testing standard Prüfnorm *f*
testing technique Prüftechnik *f*
testing under load Belastungsprüfung *f*
tether Halteseil *nt*
text Text *m*, Schrift *f*
text communication Textkommunikation *f*
text file data *pl* Textdateidaten *pl*
textile braiding Textilumflechtung *f*
textile fabric area-measured material textiles Flächengebilde *nt*
textile glass roving Textilglasgarn *nt*, Textilglasroving
textual information Textangaben *fpl*
textual language Textsprache *f*
textural strukturell
texture Struktur *f*, Textur *f*
textured surface strukturierte Oberfläche *f*
T-fitting T-Stutzen *m*
T-handle Knebel *m*
the rack's longitudinal bar Regallängsriegel *m*
the side zur Seite *f*
T-head bolt with nib Hammerschraube *f* mit Nase
T-head bolt with square neck Hammerschraube *f* mit Vierkant
thread characteristics Gewindekenngröße *f*
thread end Gewindeende *nt*
thread end with flat point Gewindeende *nt* mit Kegelkuppe
threaded pin Gewindebolzen *m*
thermoset moulded material warmgehärteter Pressstoff *m*
theoretical size Sollmaß *nt*

theoretical figure Sollwert *m*
theoretical angular position Solldrehstellung *f*
theoretical lubricant demand Schmierstoffsollbedarf *m*
theoretical mechanics Festigkeitslehre *f*
theoretical position Solllage *f*
theory of probability Wahrscheinlichkeitstheorie *f*
theory of sampling Stichprobentheorie *f*
theory of the strength of materials Festigkeitslehre *f*
thermal thermisch
thermal acoustical thermoakustisch
thermal ageing Wärmealterung *f*
thermal behaviour Wärmeverhalten *nt*
thermal characteristic wärmetechnischer Kennwert *m*
thermal class Wärmeklasse *f*
thermal conductivity Wärmeleitfähigkeit *f*
thermal contact welding Wärmekontaktschweißen *nt*
thermal crack Warmriss *m*
thermal cut Brennschnitt *m*
thermal cutting thermisches Schweißen *nt*
thermal cutting practice Brennschneidtechnik *f*, thermische Schneidtechnik *f*
thermal cutting process thermisches Schneidverfahren *nt*
thermal cycling effect Temperaturschwankung *f*
thermal cycling test Temperaturwechselprüfung *f*
thermal decomposition thermische Zersetzung *f*
thermal effect Wärmewirkung *f*
thermal efficiency of the arc thermischer Wirkungsgrad *m* des Lichtbogens
thermal expansion Wärmeausdehnung *f*, Wärmedehnung *f*
thermal forces Wärmekräfte *fpl*
thermal fusion adhesive Schmelzklebstoff *m*
thermal gouging thermisches Abtragen *nt*

thermal insulating layer Wärmedämmschicht *f*
thermal insulation thermische Isolierung *f*, Wärmedämmung *f*, Wärmeisolation *f*
thermal insulation jacket Wärmeschutzmantel *m*
thermal limit Temperaturgrenze *f*
thermal loading Wärmebelastung *f*
thermal power plant Wärmekraftanlage *f*
thermal printer Thermodrucker *m*
thermal process thermisches Verfahren *nt*
thermal radiation Wärmestrahlung *f*
thermal rust removal thermische Entrostung *f*
thermal shock plötzlicher Temperaturwechsel *m*
thermal shock stability Temperaturwechselfestigkeit *f*
thermal spraying thermisches Spitzen *nt*
thermal stabilizer Wärme-Stabilisator *m*
thermal storage floor heating Fußbodenspeicherheizung *f*
thermal storage heater Speicherheizgerät *nt*
thermal storage water heater Heißwasserbereiter *m*
thermal stress Wärmebeanspruchung *f*
thermal stress relief thermisches Entspannen *nt*
thermal transmittance Wärmedurchgangszahl *f*
thermal transmittance factor Wärmedurchgangfaktor *m*
thermal transmittance value Wärmedurchgangswert *m*
thermal upthrust Wärmeauftrieb *m*
thermal-affected zone thermische Einflusszone *f*
thermal-cut part brenngeschnittenes Teil *nt*
thermally cut part Brennschneidteil *nt*
thermally cut surface Brennschnittfläche *f*
thermally insulated wall wärmegedämmte Wand *f*

thermo-compression welding Heizelementschweißen *nt*
thermo-copying process Thermokopierverfahren *nt*
thermocouple Thermoelement *nt*
thermocouple anemometer Thermoelementanemometer *nt*
thermo-drying wärmetrocknend
thermoform warmformen
thermoform fill and seal machine Warmformfüll- und -verschließmaschine *f*
thermoformable warmverformbar, thermoplastisch
thermoformed warmgeformt
thermoforming Warmformen *nt*, Warmformgebung *f*, Warmverformung *f*
thermoforming compression moulding material warm formbare Pressmasse *f*
thermo-hydrometer Thermoaräometer *nt*
thermoluminescence dosimetry Thermolumineszensdosimetrie *f*
thermometer holder Thermometerhalterung *f*
thermometer plug Thermometerstopfen *m*
thermometer socket Thermometerstutzen *m*
thermometer vessel Thermometergefäß *nt*
thermometry Temperaturmessung *f*
thermoplast thermoplastischer Kunststoff *m*
thermoplastic film Schrumpffolie *f*
thermoplastic injection moulding compound thermoplastische Spritzgussmasse *f*
thermoplastic injection moulding material thermoplastische Spritzgussmasse *f*
thermoplastic material Schrumpffolie *f*
thermoplastic moulding compound thermoplastische Pressmasse *f*, nicht härtbare Formmasse *f*
thermoplastic moulding material thermoplastische Pressmasse *f*, nicht härtbare Formmasse *f*

thermoplastic polymer Thermoplastpolymer *nt*
thermoplasticity Warmbildsamkeit *f*
thermo-plastics nicht härtbarer Kunststoff *m*
thermoprinter Thermodrucker *m*
thermosensor Temperaturfühler *m*
thermoset casting resin moulding material warmgehärteter Gießharzformstoff *m*
thermosetting moulding material Duroplastformmasse *f*
thermo-setting adhesive warmabbindender Klebstoff *m*
thermosetting adhesive layer wärmehärtende Klebschicht *f*
thermosetting casting resin moulding material warmhärtende Gießharzmasse *f*
thermo-setting compression moulding material warm formbare Pressmasse *f*, warmhärtbare Pressmasse *f*
thermosetting formaldehyde condensation product härtbares Formaldehydkondensationsprodukt *nt*
thermosetting moulding compound härtbare Formmasse *f*, härtbare Pressmasse *f*
thermosetting moulding material härtbare Formmasse *f*, härtbare Pressmasse *f*
thermo-setting moulding material warmhärtbare Formmasse *f*
thermosetting synthetic resin härtbares Kunstharz *nt*
thermoplastic thermoplastisch
thermostat Temperaturwächter *m*, Raumtemperaturregler *m*
thermostatic safety device thermostatische Absicherung *f*
thermotransfer printer Thermotransferdrucker *m*
thick dick
thick oil Dicköl *nt*
thick walled dickwandig
thicken dickflüssiger machen
thickening agent Dickungsmittel *nt*
thickening dipping Dickenstauchung *f*
thickness Dicke *f*, Stärke *f*
thickness calliper Dickentaster *m*

thickness dimension Dickenmaß *nt*
thickness of cut Spanungsdicke *f*
thickness of layer Schichtdicke *f*
thickness of stripes Strichbreite *f*
thimble Skalentrommel *f*, Messtrommel *f*
thin dünn
thin castle nut flache Kronenmutter *f*
thin metal sheet Feinstblech *nt*
thin parallel key niedrige Passfeder *f*
thin sheet metal Dünnblech *nt*
thin taper key with gib head Nasenflachkeil *m*
thin type niedrige Form *f*
thin walled dünnwandig
thimble with clevis Gabelkausche *f*
thin-film friction Dünnfilmreibung *f*
thin-film technology Dünnfilmtechnologie *f*
thin-layer chromatographic method dünnschichtchromatographisches Verfahren *nt*
thinning Dengeln *nt*
thinning variant Ausbreitungsform *f*
third length centre grooved pin Knebelkerbstift *m*
third party Dritter/Dritte *m*
third party device Fremdgerät *nt*
third party performance Fremdleistung *f*
third power dritte Potenz *f*
theory of fits Passungslehre *f*
thorin indicator solution Thorinindikatorlösung *f*
thread Gewinde *nt*, Gewindegang *m*; Gewinde *nt* schneiden
thread profile Gewindeform *f*
thread abbreviation symbol Gewindekurzzeichen *nt*
thread and form grinding wheel Profilschleifscheibe *f*
thread and form-grinding wheel Profilscheibe *f*
thread and worm grinding machine Gewinde- und Schneckenschleifmaschine *f*
thread angle Flankenwinkel *m*, Flankenwinkel *m* eines Gewindes, Gewindewinkel *m*
thread calliper Flankentaster *m*

thread calliper with ball points Kugeltaster *m*
thread chaser Gewindemeißel *m*, Strehler *m*
thread chasing Gewindestrehlen *nt*
thread cutting Gewindeschneiden *nt*
thread cutting attachment Gewindeschneideinrichtung *f*
thread cutting screw Schneidschraube *f*
thread cutting screw with recessed head Gewindeschneidschraube *f* mit Kreuzschlitz
thread cutting tool Gewindeschneidwerkzeug *nt*
thread damage Gewindebeschädigung *f*
thread deviation Gewindeabmaß *nt*
thread dimensioning Gewindebemaßung *f*
thread element Bestimmungsstück *nt* eines Gewindes
thread end Gewindezapfen *m*
thread end with oval point Gewindeende *nt* mit Linsenkuppe
thread fit Gewindepassung *f*
thread flank Gewindeflanke *f*
thread for electric lamp holders *pl* Gewinde *nt* für elektrische Glühlampenfassungen
thread forming Gewindefurchen *nt*
thread forming self tapping screw Blechschraube *f*
thread grinder Gewindeschleifmaschine *f*
thread grinding Gewindeschleifen *nt*
thread grinding method Gewindeschleifverfahren *nt*
thread grinding wheel Gewindeschleifscheibe *f*
thread groove Gewindelücke *f*, Gewinderille *f*
thread grooving Gewindefurchen *nt*
thread hobbing Gewindewalzen *nt*
thread insert Gewindeeinsatz *m*
thread insert for serrated ring locking Gewindeeinsatz *m* mit Ringsicherung
thread lead Gewindesteigerung *f*
thread length Gewindelänge *f*

thread length of the nut Muttergewindelänge *f*
thread measuring wire Messdraht *m*
thread miller Gewindefräsmaschine *f*
thread milling Gewindefräsen *nt*
thread milling cutter Gewindefräser *m*
thread milling hob Gewindewälzfräser *m*
thread peeling machine Gewindeschälmaschine *f*
thread profile Gewindeprofil *nt*
thread ridge Gewindezahn *m*
thread ridging Gewindefurchen *nt*
thread rolling Gewindewalzen *nt*
thread rolling by the plunge-cut method Gewindewalzen *nt* im Einstechverfahren
thread rolling by the through-feed method Gewindewalzen *nt* im Durchlaufverfahren
thread run-out Gewindeauslauf *m*
thread spinning Gewindedrücken *nt*
thread tooth Gewindezahn *m*
thread turning Gewindedrehen *nt*
thread type Gewindeart *f*
thread used in the oil industry Gewinde *nt* für Erdölindustrie
thread used in the petroleum industry Gewinde *nt* für Erdölindustrie
thread whirling Gewindewirbeln *nt*
thread with large clearance Gewinde *nt* mit großem Spiel
thread-bore Gewindebohren *nt*
threaded mit Gewinde *nt*
threaded bore Gewindebohrung *f*
threaded connector end Gewindestutzen *m*
threaded end Gewindeende *nt*
threaded hole Bohrung *f* mit Gewinde
threaded insert Gewindeeinsatz *m*, Einschraubmutter *f*, Schraubdübel *m*
threaded measuring insert Gewindemesseinsatz *m*
threaded pin Gewindezapfen *m*
threaded portion Gewindezapfen *m*
threaded self-locking collar Schließring *m* mit Gewinde
threaded shank Gewindezapfen *m*
threaded spindle nose Gewindespindelnase *f*

threaded stud Gewindebolzen *m*
threaded to head Gewinde *nt* annähernd bis Kopf
threaded fastener Verbindungselement *nt* mit Gewinde
thread-grinding machine Gewindeschleifmaschine *f*
thread guard Fadenschutz *m*
threading Gewindeherstellung *f*, Gewindebohren *nt*
threading bit Gewindemeißel *m*
threading die Gewindeschneideisen *nt*
threading tool Gewindedrehmeißel *m*, Gewindemeißel *m*
thread-milling machine Gewindefräsmaschine *f*
threat Gefährdung *f*
three dimensional defects volumenhafte Fehler *m*
Three Dimensional Printing Dreidimensionaldrucken (TPD) *nt*
three flap carton closing machine Dreilaschenfaltschachtelverschließmaschine *f*
three hundred-degree-embrittlement Dreihundert-Grad-Versprödung
three-spindle manufacturing-type milling machine Planfräsmaschine *f* mit drei Frässpindelköpfen
three times ... das Dreifache
three wire measurement Dreidrahtmessmethode *f*
three-bulb condenser Dreibirnenkühler *m*
three-cornered file Dreikantfeile *f*
three-dimensional räumlich
three-dimensional heat dissipation dreidimensionale Wärmeableitung *f*
three-dimensional milling operation Raumformfräsung *f*
three-dimensional tracer milling Raumformfräsen *nt*
three-jaw chuck Dreibackenfutter *nt*
three-layer slab Dreischichtplatte *f*
three-level signal Dreipunktsignal *nt*
three-o'clock position Drei-Uhr-Lage *f*
three-phase A. C. motor Drehstrommotor *m*
three-phase a.c. Drehstrom *m*
three-phase a.c. operated drehstrombetätigt
three-phase asynchronuous motor with squirrel cage motor Drehstromasynchronmotor *m* mit Kurzschlussläufer
three-phase current feed Drehstromspeisung *f*
three-phase current supply Drehstromanschluss *m*
three-phase operation Drehstrombetrieb *m*
three-phase squirrel cage motor Drehstromkurzschlussläufermotor *m*, Drehstromkurzschlussläufer *m*
three-phase system Drehstromnetz *nt*
three-point loading Dreipunktbeanspruchung *f*
three-row dreireihig
three-shift operation Dreischichtbetrieb *m*
three-shift working Dreischichtbetrieb *m*
three-speed gears Dreiganggetriebe *nt*
three-speed sliding gear drive Dreigangschieberadgetriebe *nt*
three-spindle bench type milling machine Dreispindelplanfräsmaschine *f*, Planfräsmaschine *f* mit drei Frässpindelköpfen
three-spindle drum-type milling machine Dreispindeltrommelfräsmaschine *f*
three-spindle fixed-bed type milling machine Dreispindelplanfräsmaschine *f*
three-spindle milling machine Dreispindelfräsmaschine *f*
three-spindle vertical milling unit dreispindlige Vertikalfräseinheit *f*
three-stage dreistufig
three-stage gear transmission dreistufiges Getriebe *nt*
three-step dreistufig
three-way cock Dreiwegehahn *m*
three-way plug Dreiwegeküken *nt*
three-way pressure reducing valve Dreiwegedruckminderventil *nt*
three-way stacking dreiseitiges Stapeln *nt*
three-way steam converting valve

Dreiwegedampfumformventil *nt*
three-wheel truck Dreiradstapler *m*
three-wheeled Dreirad *nt*
threshold Schwelle *f*
threshold detector Schmitt-Trigger *m*
threshold of indication Anzeigenschwelle *f*
threshold value Schwellenwert *m*
throat Rachen *m*, Hals *m*, Kehle *f*, Durchgang *m*
throat depth Tiefenausladung *f*
throat edge Kehl-Fuge *f*
throat thickness Nahtdicke *f*
throttle drosseln
throttle valve Drosselklappe *f*
throttling valve Drosselventil *nt*
through heat treatability Durchvergütbarkeit *f*
through heating appliance Durchlaufwärmeerzeuger *m*
through ignition Durchzünden *nt*
through piston rod durchgehende Kolbenstange *f*
through roller muldenförmige Tragrolle *f*
through-burning stove Druckbrandofen *m*
through-crack Durchstoß *m*
through-drill durchbohren
through-feed grinding Durchgangsschleifen *nt*, Durchlaufschleifen *nt*
through-going crack durchgehender Riss *m*
through-going mains durchgehende Hauptleitung *f*
through-going pore durchgehende Pore *f*
through-hole Durchgangsbohrung *f*, durchgehende Bohrung *f*, Durchgangsloch *nt*
through-hole durchgehende Bohrung *f*
throughput Durchsatz *m*, Umschlagsleistung *f*
throughput analysis Durchsatzbetrachtung *f*
throughput calculation Durchsatzermittlung *f*
throughput time Durchlaufzeit *f*
throughput verification Durchsatznachweis *m*
through-welded butt joint durchgeschweißter Stumpfstoß *m*
through-welded single-V butt joint durchgeschweißte V-Naht *f*
through-welded single-V butt joint with backing run durchgeschweißte V-Naht *f* mit Gegenlage
throw werfen, schütten, schleudern
throw in einrücken, einkuppeln
throw into engagement einschalten
throw out ausdrücken
throw out of gear ausschalten, ausrücken
throw up hoch schleudern
throw-away carbide insert blade Hartmetallwegwerfmesser *nt*
throw-aways *pl* Wegwerfwerkzeuge *ntpl*
throw-over-limit temperature Grenzübertemperatur *f*
thrust schieben; Druck *m*, Schubkraft *f*, Schub *m*
thrust bearing Drucklager *nt*, Axiallager *nt*
thrust face Anschlag *m*
thrust flank Schubflanke *f*
thrust force Druckkraft *f*, Abdrängkraft *f*, Rückkraft *f*
thrust member Druckstück *nt*
thrust point *(e. Gewindestiftes)* Druckzapfen *m*
thrusting point Stoßstelle *f*
thryristor Thyristor *m*
thumb nut Flügelmutter *f*
thumb screw Flügelschraube *f*
thyristor regulator Thyristorstellung *f*
thyristor-controlled reactor thyristorgesteuerte Drossel *f*
tick Bezugshaken *m*
tidiness Sauberkeit *f*
tidy sauber
tie 1. *(befestigen)* binden, abbinden, festbinden, verbinden, festspannen
 2. Tiegel, Schmelztiegel
tie down zurren
tie positively kraftschlüssig verbinden
tie up umschnüren
tie-in section Anschlussstrecke *f*
tier Reihe *f*, Schicht *f*, Geschoss *nt*; stapeln, schichten, einlagern, abladen

tiering Einlagern *nt*
tight fest, kraftschlüssig, straff, dicht
tighten 1. *(befestigen)* anziehen, spannen, festspannen **2.** *(eine Schraube)* festdrehen, schrauben
tightened inspection verschärfte Prüfung *f*
tightening *(Schraube)* Anzug *m*
tightening strap Umreifungsband *nt*
tightening tool Anziehgerät *nt*
tightening torque Aufschraubmoment *m*
tightness Festigkeit *f*
tightening test Anziehversuch *m*
tiled base stove Kachelgrundofen *m*
tiller Deichsel *f*, Lenkdeichsel *f*, Steuerdeichsel *f*, Handgriff *m*, Knüppel *m*
tiller articulation point Deichselgesenk *nt*
tiller control Deichselsteuerung *f*
tiller handle Deichsel *f*, Deichselgriff *m*
tiller plane Deichselebene *f*
tiller steered truck Deichselwagen *m*
tiller steering Deichsellenkung *f*
tiller-steered mit Deichsellenkung
tilt Kippung *f*, Neigung *f*, Schräglage *f*; kanten, schrägstellen, umkippen, schwenken, kippen, neigen
tilt axis Neigeachse *f*
tilt backwards rückwärts neigen
tilt correction Schräglagenkorrektur *f*
tilt cylinder Neigezylinder *m*
tilt cylinder pin Neigezylinderbolzen *m*
tilt forwards vorneigen
tilt movement Kippbewegung *f*
tilt upwards hochklappen
tiltable verstellbar, schwenkbar, neigbar, kippbar, klappbar
tiltable table schrägverstellbarer Tisch *m*
tilted schief
tilted forwards vorgeneigt
tilted mirror Umlenkspiegel *m*
tilted turret lathe Drehmaschine *f* mit Schrägrevolverkopf
tilting Schrägstellung *f*, Kippen *nt*, Umkippen *nt*, Neigen *nt*
tilting axis Neigeachse *f*, Kippachse *f*
tilting cart Selbstentlader *m*
tilting chute *(Schüttgut)* Wippe *f*
tilting cross beam Kipptraverse *f*
tilting gear Kippantrieb *m*
tilting mirror Kippspiegel *m*
tilting platform Neigeplattform *f*
tilting speed Neigegeschwindigkeit *f*
tilting system Neigeeinrichtung *f*, Neigesystem *nt*
tilting table Kipptisch *m*, Wipptisch *m*, neigbarer Tisch *m*, schrägverstellbarer Tisch *m*
timber Holz *nt*
timber machine Holzbearbeitungsmaschine *f*
time mit Stoppuhr messen, Schaltzeiten bestimmen, Zeit einrichten, Zeit messen; Zeit *f*, Zeitpunkt *m*, Uhrzeit *f*
time axis Zeitachse *f*
time base Grundzeit *f*
time between two consecutive adjustments Nachstellreife *f*
time calculation Zeitberechnung *f*, Zeitkalkulation *f*
time compression Zeitraffung *f*
time constant Zeitkonstante *f*
time controlled zeitabhängig
time delay Zeitverzögerung *f*
time dependent zeitgebunden, zeitabhängig
time derivative zeitliche Ableitung *f*
time each unit Zeit *f* je Einheit
time estimate Zeitschätzung *f*
time for ancillary work Schweißnebenzeit *f*
time frame Zeitfenster *nt*
time function Zeitfunktion *f*
time integral Zeitfläche *f*, Zeitintegral *nt*
time lagged zeitverzögert
time limit zeitliche Begrenzung *f*, Frist *f*
time limitation zeitliche Begrenzung *f*
time measurement Zeitermittlung *f*, Zeitmessung *f*
time of day Uhrzeit *f*
time of dwell Bewegungspause *f*, Verzögerungsdauer *f*, Stillstandszeit *f*
time of movement Bewegungszeit *f*
time of operation Nutzungszeit *f*
time of outflow Ausflusszeit *f*
time of recovery Erholungsdauer *f*
time offset Zeitausgleich *m*

time out Zeitüberwachung *f*
time per cut Maschinenzeit *f*
time planning Terminwirtschaft *f*
time recorder Zeitschreiber *m*
time recording Zeitaufnahme *f*
time register Zeitgeberregister *nt*
time relay Zeitrelais *nt*, Zeitglied *nt*
time saving Zeit sparend
time schedule Terminplan *m*, Zeitplan *m*
time schedule closed loop control Zeitplanregelung *f*
time schedule open loop control Zeitplansteuerung *f*
time scheduling Zeitplanung *f*
time segment Zeitabschnitt *m*
time sharing time sharing
time shifting Terminverschiebung *f*
time slot Zeitabschnitt *m*
time smoothing Zeitausgleich *m*
time span Zeitspanne *f*
time stamp Zeitstempel *m*
time switch Zeitschalter *m*
time target Termin *m*, Frist *f*
time to market Zeit *f* bis zur Marktreife
time to readjustment Nachstellreife *f*
time travel diagram Zeit-Weg-Diagramm *nt*
time unit Zeiteinheit *f*
time using Zeitnutzung *f*
time weighting Zeitbewertung *f*
time window Zeitfenster *nt*
time yield Dauerstandfestigkeit *f*
time-controlled system Zeitprogrammsteuerung *f*
time-cycle controlled zeittaktgesteuert
timed flow filling machine Zeitfüllmaschine *f*
time-deformation limit Zeitverformungsgrenze *f*
time-delayed zeitverzögert
time-dependency diagram Zeitdiagramm *nt*
time-dependent creep compression test Zeitstanddruckversuch *m*
time-dependent sampling zeitproportionale Probenahme *f*
time-dependent stress zeitabhängige Spannung *f*
time-displaced zeitversetzt

time-division multiplex (TDM) Zeitmultiplex *nt*
time-division multiplexing (TDM) Zeitmultiplexbetrieb *m*
time-edge effect Randveränderung *f*
time-independent elastic modulus zeitunabhängiger Elastizitätsmodul *m*
time-limited zeitlich begrenzt
timer Zeitglied *nt*, Zeitschalter *m*, Zeitgeber m, Zeitzählwerk *nt*, Verzögerungsglied *nt*
timer supervision Zeitüberwachung *f*
time-referenced temperature increase zeitbezogene Temperaturzunahme *f*
time-related zeitbezogen
times Zeiten *fpl*
time-stress-strain Zeitspanndehnung *f*
timing Terminierung *f*, Zeitmessung *f*, Zeitgebung *f*
timing circuit Zeitgeberschaltung *f*
timing gear Taktschaltwerk *nt*
timing gear mechanism Zeitschaltwerk *nt*
timing unit Zeitgeber *m*
tin *(Behälter)* Kanister *m*
tin coating Zinküberzug *m*
tine Zinken *m*
tine fork Dorngabel *f*
tinning solder Reibelot *nt*
tinplate Weißblech *nt*
tinting strength Farbstärke *f*
tip 1. Düse *f*, Mundstück *nt*, Spitze *f* **2.** Gabelspitze *f* **3.** *(Werkzeug)* bestücken, mit einer Schneide versehen; Auflageplättchen *nt*, Spitze *f* eines Meißels **4.** kippen, abkippen, wippen, tippen, stürzen **5.** *(Verzahnung)* Zahnkopf *m*
tip angle Kopfkegelwinkel *m*
tip circle Kopfkreis *m*
tip circle diameter Kopfkreisdurchmesser *m*
tip circle radius Kopfkreisradius *m*
tip cone Kopfkegel *m*
tip cone apex Kopfkegelspitze *f*
tip contact Kopftragen
tip diameter Kopfkreisdurchmesser *m*
tip diameter deviation Kopfkreisdurchmesserabmaß *nt*
tip distance Spitzenabstand *m*

tip easing Kopfkürzung *f*
tip ignition Spitzenzündung *f*
tip involute Kopfevolvente *f*
tip limit line Spitzengrenzlinie *f*
tip line Kopflinie *f*
tip of the cutter tooth Werkzeugzahnkopf *m*
tip of the flame Flammenspitze *f*
tip of the pointer Zeigerspitze *f*
tip over umstürzen, umkippen; Umkippen *nt*
tip relief Zahnkopfkürzung *f*, Zahnkopfabrundung *f*, Kopfrücknahme *f*
tip surface Kopfmantelfläche *f*, Kopffläche *f*
tip tooth trace Kopfflankenlinie *f*
tipped solid cutter massiver Fräser *m* mit bestückter Schneide
tipped with sintered carbide mit Sintermetallschneide bestückt
tipper 1. Kippvorrichtung *f*, Wipper *m* 2. *(Entladung)* Selbstentlader *m*
tipping Kippen *nt*, Umkippen *nt*, Umstürzen *nt*; kippbar
tipping axis Kippkante *f*
tippler Wipper *m*
tippling clamp Kippklammer *f*
tippling drum clamp arm Fasskippklammerarm *m*
tippling fork arm carriage Kippgabelträger *m*
tire 1. ermüden 2. *(US)* Reifen *m*
tissue Gewebe *nt*
titanium Titan *nt*
titanium alloy Titanlegierung *f*
title Überschrift *f*, Textkopf *m*
title block Schriftfeld *nt*, Zeichnungsschriftfeld *nt*
title line Kopfzeile *f*
titrating burette Titrierbürette *f*
titrating liquid Titrierflüssigkeit *f*
titration end point Titrationsendpunkt *m*
titration solvent Titrierlösungsmittel *nt*
titration vessel Titriergefäß *nt*
to bis
to and fro hin und her
to-and-fro movement Hin- und Herbewegung *f*
to be betragen

to come to an end ausgehen
to depressurize auf Außendruck bringen
to the left nach links
to the right nach rechts
tobacco smoke Tabakrauch *m*
topping hob Wälzfräser *m* zum Abrunden
to-be model Sollmodell *nt*
toe board Fußleiste *f*
toe clearance Stufentiefe *f*
toe dog Niederhalter *m*, Spannfinger *m*
toe-crack Kerbriss *m*
together with zusammen mit
toggle Kniegelenk *nt*
toggle drawing press Kniehebelziehpresse *f*
toggle lever Kniehebel *m*
toggle press Kniehebelpresse *f*
token Token *m*, Petri-Netz-Knoten *m*, Sendeberechtigung *f*, Sendeberechtigungsmarke *f*, Marke *f*, Zeichen *nt*
token loop Tokenring *m*
token passing Sendeberechtigung *f* „Weiterreichen", Tokenverfahren *nt*
token ring Tokenring *m*
tolerance 1. Spielraum *m*, Toleranz *f* 2. *(Messtechnik)* (zulässige) Maßabweichung *f*
tolerance band Toleranzband *nt*
tolerance calculation Toleranzberechnung *f*, Toleranzrechnung *f*
tolerance centre Toleranzmitte *f*
tolerance chain Toleranzkette *f*
tolerance class Toleranzklasse *f*
tolerance conception Toleranzauffassung *f*
tolerance coupling Toleranzkopplung *f*
tolerance data Toleranzangaben *fpl*
tolerance difference Toleranzunterschied *m*
tolerance end measuring rod Grenzkugelendmaß *nt*
tolerance equation Toleranzgleichung *f*
tolerance family Toleranzfamilie *f*
tolerance field Toleranzfeld *nt*
tolerance gauge Passungslehre *f*, Grenzlehre *f*
tolerance gauge system Grenzlehren-

system *nt*
tolerance grade Toleranzqualität *f*
tolerance group Toleranzgruppe *f*, Toleranzreihe *f*
tolerance in size Maßtoleranz *f*
tolerance indication Toleranzangabe *f*
tolerance investigation Toleranzuntersuchung *f*
tolerance limit Toleranzgrenze *f*
tolerance modification Toleranzveränderung *f*
tolerance of surface profile Flächenformtoleranz *f*
tolerance problem Toleranzproblem *nt*
tolerance provision Toleranzbestimmung *f*, Toleranzfestlegung *f*
tolerance quality Toleranzqualität *f*
tolerance relationship Toleranzrelation *f*
tolerance size Toleranzgröße *f*
tolerance specification Toleranzfestlegung *f*
tolerance standard Toleranznorm *f*
tolerance step Toleranzstufe *f*
tolerance symbol Toleranzkurzzeichen *nt*
tolerance value Toleranzwert *m*
tolerance zone Toleranzfeld *nt*, Toleranzzone *f*
tolerance zone for the roundness of the section Toleranzzone *f* für die Rundheit des Querschnittes
tolerance zone for the straightness of the generator Toleranzzone *f* für die Geradheit der Mantelfläche
tolerance zone selection Toleranzfeldauswahl *f*
toleranced dimension toleriertes Maß *nt*, Passmaß *nt*
tolerance-free toleranzfrei
tolerances *pl* **and fits** *pl* Toleranzen und Passungen *pl*
tolerancing Tolerierung *f*
tolerancing measure Tolerierungsmaßnahme *f*
tolerancing problem Tolerierungsproblem *nt*
tolerate tolerieren
tomographic equipment Schichtaufnahmegerät *nt*

tonal contact Tonhaltigkeit *f*
toner Toner
tong Zangengriff *m*; mit Zangen arbeiten
tong gripper Zangengreifer *m*
tongs Zange *f*, Greifzange *f*
tongue tear growth test Zungenweiterreißversuch *m*
tongue-faced flange Federflansch *m*
tongue-tear resistance Weiterreißwiderstand *m*
tongue-tearing Weiterreißen *nt*
tonnage Menge *f*
tool Arbeitsorgan *nt*, Werkzeug *nt*; bestücken
tool addendum Werkzeugkopfhöhe *f*
tool addendum factor Werkzeugzahnkopfhöhe *f*
tool and cutter grinder Frässchärfmaschine *f*, Werkzeugschleifmaschine *f*
tool and cutting grinder Fräserschleifmaschine *f*
tool and die miller Werkzeug- und Gesenkfräsmaschine *f*
tool and fixture construction Betriebsmittelbau *m*
tool and jig and fixture designer Betriebsmittelkonstrukteur *m*
tool angle Werkzeugwinkel *m*
tool angle convection Festlegung *f* der Werkzeugwinkel
tool apron Meißelklappe *f*, Stahlhalterklappe *f*, Meißelhalterklappe *f*
tool arbour Spanndorn *m*, Aufspanndorn *m*, Werkzeugaufspanndorn *m*
tool back clearance Werkzeugrückenfreiwinkel *m*
tool back rake Werkzeugrückspanwinkel *m*
tool back wedge angle Werkzeugrückkeilwinkel *m*
tool bit Drehzahn *m*, Meißeleinsatz *m*, Schneidplatte *f*
tool bit holder Meißeleinsatzhalter *m*
tool block Stahlhalterkopf *m*
tool box Werkzeugsupport *m*, Support *m*
tool box on cross slide Quersupport *m*
tool carrier Werkzeugträger *m*
tool carrier slide Stößelschlitten *m*
tool changeover Umrüsten *nt*

tool changer Werkzeugwechsler *m*
tool chip Meißelschneide *f*
tool clamping Meißeleinspannung *f*
tool coding Werkzeugcodierung *f*
tool compensation Werkzeugkorrektur *f*
tool coordinate Werkzeugkoordinaten *fpl*
tool coordinate system Werkzeugkoordinatensystem *nt*
tool costs Werkzeugkosten *pl*
tool cutting edge plane Werkzeugschneidenebene *f*
tool cutting life Standzeit *f*
tool cutting life relationship Standzeitbeziehung *f*
tool data Werkzeugdaten *pl*
tool design Werkzeuggestaltung *f*
tool drawing Werkzeugzeichnung *f*
tool drilling and milling machine Werkzeugbohr- und -fräsmaschine *f*
tool edge normal plane Schneidennormalebene *f*
tool ejector Werkzeugauswerfer *m*
tool element Werkzeugteil *nt*
tool engagement point of cutting action Schneideneingriff *m*
tool face Werkzeugspanfläche *f*, Spanfläche *f*
tool face orthogonal plane Lagewinkel *m* der Spanflächenorthogonalebene, Spanflächenorthogonalebene *f*
tool face relief Spanflächenfase *f*
tool face tangential force Spanflächentangentialkraft *f*
tool failure Unbrauchbarwerden *nt* des Werkzeugs
tool feed Meißelvorschub *m*
tool flank Freifläche *f*
tool flank chamfer Freiflächenfase *f*
tool flank orthogonal plane Freiflächenorthogonalebene *f*
tool flank orthogonal plane orientation angle Lagewinkel *m* der Freiflächenorthogonalebene
tool force tangential force Spanflächennormalkraft *f*
tool function Werkzeugaufruf *m*
tool geometrical rake geometrischer Werkzeugspanwinkel *m*

tool geometry Geometrie *f* der Schneide
tool grind Nachschliff *m* des Werkzeugs
tool grinding Werkzeugschleifen *nt*
tool head Stößelkopf *m*
tool head slide Hobelkopfschlitten *m*
tool holder Werkzeughalter *m*
tool holder bit Drehling *m*
tool hole bush Spannhülse *f*
tool interchange Werkzeugwechsel *m*
tool layout Meißelanordnung *f*, Werkzeugeinstellung *f*
tool length Werkzeuglänge *f*
tool length compensation Längenkorrektur *f*
tool life Lebensdauer *f* des Werkzeuges, Standzeit *f*
tool life between resharpening Verschleißstandzeit *f*
tool life characteristics Standzeitverhalten *nt*
tool life criterion Standzeitkriterium *nt*
tool life cutting speed Standzeitschnittgeschwindigkeit *f*
tool life diagram Standzeitschaubild *nt*
tool life index figure Standzahl *f*
tool lift Werkzeugabhebung *f*, Meißelabhebung *f*, Meißellüftung *f*
tool lift control Meißelabhubsteuerung *f*
tool lifter Meißelhebeeinrichtung *f*, Meißelabheber *m*
tool load Schnittdruck *m*
tool machine Werkzeugmaschine (WZM) *f*
tool management Werkzeugverwaltung *f*
tool management system Werkzeugmanagementsystem *nt*
tool mandrel Werkzeugaufspanndorn *m*
tool mark Bearbeitungsspur *f*, Drehriefe *f*
tool material Schneidwerkstoff *m*
tool milling and boring machine Werkzeugfräs- und -bohrmaschine *f*
tool milling machine Werkzeugfräsmaschine *f*
tool monitoring Standzeitüberwa-

chung *f*
tool mounting Meißeleinspannung *f*
tool nose Schneidenecke *f*
tool nose compensation Schneidenradiuskorrektur *f*
tool overhang Meißelausladung *f*, Werkzeugausladung *f*
tool overlap *(Decklage)* Schweißgutüberlauf *m*
tool path Werkzeugbahn *f*
tool point Schneidenkopf *m*, Schneidenspitze *f*, Schneidenecke *f*
tool presetting Werkzeugvoreinstellung *f*
tool pressure Anpressdruck *m*
tool rake Werkzeugspanwinkel *m*
tool rake angle Spanwinkel *m*
tool reference plane Werkzeugbezugsebene *f*
tool reference system Werkzeugbezugssystem
tool releasing Ausspannen *nt* des Werkzeuges
tool relief Meißelabhebung *f*, Meißellüftung *f*
tool relief mechanism Meißelrückzug *m*
tool rest Werkzeugauflage *f*
tool room Betriebsmittelbau *m*
tool section Meißelquerschnitt *m*
tool selection Werkzeugauswahl *f*
tool setter Einrichter *m*
tool setting Meißelanstellung *f*
tool set-up time Aufspannzeit *f* der Werkzeuge
tool shank Werkzeugschaft *m*
tool side clearance Werkzeugseitenfreiwinkel *m*
tool side rake Werkzeugseitenspanwinkel *m*
tool side wedge angle Werkzeugseitenkeilwinkel *m*
tool slide Schlittenschieber *m*, Support *m*
tool steel Werkzeugstahl *m*
tool storage Werkzeugspeicher *m*, Werkzeughaltung *f*
tool system Werkzeugsystem *nt*
tool thrust Schneidenbelastung *f*, senkrechte Schnittkraft *f*, Schnittdruck *m*

tool up Werkzeuge einrichten
tool wear Werkzeugverschleiß *m*
tool wedge measure plane Werkzeugkeilmessebene *f*
toolbox Meißelhalter *m*, Werkzeugträger *m*, Werkzeugsupport *m*
tool-fitting dimension Einbaumaß *nt*
toolhead Querbalkensupport *m*, Horizontalsupport *m*, Meißelhalter *m*, Werkzeugträger *m*, Werkzeugsupport *m*, Support *m*, Stößelkopf *m*
toolhead saddle Supportsattel *m*
toolhead slide Meißelschlitten *m*, Senkrechtschlitten *m*, Supportschieber *m*, Stößelkopfschlitten *m*
toolholder Werkzeughalter *m*, Werkzeugspanner *m*, Werkzeugträger *m*, Meißelhalter *m*
toolholder carrier Meißelhalterträger *m*
toolholder clapper Stahlhalterklappe *f*, Meißelhalterklappe *f*
toolholder flap Meißelhalterklappe *f*
tooling Einrichten *nt*, Einrichtung *f*, Werkzeugausrüstung *f*, Auswahl *f* der Werkzeuge
tooling allowance Bearbeitungszugabe *f*
tooling arrangement Werkzeuganordnung *f*
tooling diagram Werkzeugeinstellung *f*, Werkzeuganordnung *f*
tooling layout Werkzeugbestückung *f*, Werkzeuganordnung *f*
tooling method Arbeitsverfahren *nt*
tooling setup Werkzeuganordnung *f*
tooling time Rüstzeit *f*
tool-in-use-system Wirkbezugssystem *nt*
tool-lift mechanism Meißelhebeeinrichtung *f*
toolmaking Werkzeugmacherei *f*
toolmaker's calliper Zirkel *m*
toolmaker's dividers Spitzzirkel *m*
toolmaker's flat Messscheibe *f*
toolmaker's knife-edge straightedge Haarlineal *nt*, Kantenlineal *nt*, Messlineal *nt*, Messerlineal *nt*
toolpost Meißelhalter *m*
toolroom Werkzeugmacherei *f*

toolroom lathe Werkzeugmacherdrehmaschine *f*
toolroom milling machine Nachformfräsmaschine *f*, Präzisionsfräsmaschine *f*, Werkzeugfräsmaschine *f*, Werkzeugmacherfräsmaschine *f*
tool-room milling machine Präzisionsfräsmaschine *f*
toolside Arbeitsschlitten *m*
toolside movement Supportbewegung *f*
toolslide Werkzeugschlitten *m*
tooth Zahn *m*; verzahnen, zahnen
tooth alignment error Flankenrichtungsfehler *m*
tooth back Zahnrücken *m*
tooth centre Zahnmitte *f*
tooth centre line Zahnmittenlinie *f*
tooth chamfering cutter Zahnkantenabrundfräser *m*
tooth chamfering hob Abrundwälzfräser *m*
tooth chamfering machine Radzahnabrundfräsmaschine *f*
tooth clearance angle Zahnfreiwinkel *m*
tooth clearance tester Zahnluftmessgerät *nt*
tooth crest Zahnkopf *m*
tooth dedendum Zahnfuß *m*
tooth deformation Zahnverformung *f*
tooth depth Zahnhöhe *f*
tooth depth variation Zahnhöhenänderung *f*
tooth design Zahnprofil *nt*
tooth edge Zahnkante *f*
tooth engagement Zahneingriff *m*
tooth engagement Zahneingriff *m*
tooth exit Zahnauslauf *m*
tooth face Zahnbrust *f*, Kopfflanke *f*
tooth face angle Zahnbrustwinkel *m*
tooth face at the tip Zahnkopfkante *f*
tooth face tip Zahnkopfecke *f*
tooth flank Zahnflanke *f*, Fußflanke *f*
tooth flank scraping Zahnflankenschaben *nt*
tooth forming Verzahnung *f*
tooth gap Zahnlücke *f*
tooth generation Erzeugung *f* der Verzahnung

tooth generation by twin reciprocating tools Zweimeißelwälzhobeln *nt*
tooth generation grinding Zahnflankenschleifen *nt*
tooth geometry Verzahnungsgeometrie *f*
tooth gullet Zahngrund *m*, Zahnlücke *f*
tooth height Zahnhöhe *f*, Lückentiefe *f*
tooth honing Verzahnungshonen *nt*
tooth milling cutter Verzahnungsfräser *m*
tooth pitch Zahnteilung *f*
tooth production Verzahnung *f*
tooth profile Zahnflanke *f*, Verzahnungsprofil *nt*
tooth profile error Zahnformfehler *m*
tooth root stress Zahnfußspannung *f*
tooth root surface Zahnfußfläche *f*
tooth set Schränkung *f*
tooth setting Zahnverstellung *f*, Schränken *nt*, Verwinden *nt*
tooth shape Zahnprofil *nt*
tooth space Zahnlücke *f*
tooth space half angle Zahnlückenhalbwinkel *m*
tooth spacing Zahnteilung *f*
tooth surface allowance Flankenabmaß *nt*
tooth surface direction Flankenrichtung *f*
tooth surface form Flankenform *f*
tooth surface profile Flankenprofil *nt*
tooth surface test range Flankenprüfbereich *m*
tooth system Verzahnung *f*, Verzahnungsart *f*
tooth system deviation Verzahnungsabweichung *f*
tooth thickness alteration factor Zahndickenänderungsfaktor *m*
tooth thickness basis Einheitszahndicke *f*
tooth thickness deviation Zahndickenabmaß *nt*
tooth thickness error Zahndickenfehler *m*
tooth thickness fluctuation Zahndickenschwankung *f*
tooth thickness half angle Zahndickenhalbwinkel *m*

tooth thickness limit Kopfdickengrenze *f*
tooth thickness limiting size Zahndickengrenzmaß *nt*
tooth thickness quantity Zahndickengröße *f*
tooth thickness alteration Zahndickenänderung *f*
tooth thickness system of fits Zahndickenpasssystem *nt*
tooth tip Zahnspitze *f*, Kopfkante *f*
tooth tip chamfer Kopfkantenbruch *m*
tooth trace Flankenlinie *f*
tooth trace angle variation Flankenlinienwinkelabweichung *f*
tooth trace configuration Flankenlinienverlauf *m*
tooth trace form variation Flankenlinienformabweichung *f*
tooth trace relief Flankenlinienrücknahme *f*
tooth trace test range Flankenlinienprüfbereich *m*
tooth trace thought of as fully bearing volltragend gedachte Flankenlinie *f*
tooth trace tooth variation Flankenliniengesamtabweichung *f*
tooth trace variation Flankenlinienabweichung *f*
tooth trace waviness Flankenlinienwelligkeit *f*
tooth width Zahnbreite *f*
toothed gezahnt, verzahnt, zusammengeschlossen
toothed belt Zahnriemen *m*
toothed chain Zahnkette *f*
toothed cylindrical gear verzahntes Zylinderrad *nt*
toothed gear Zahnrad *nt*
toothed gearing Zahnradgetriebe *nt*
toothed rack Zahnstange *f*
toothed ring Zahnkranz *m*
toothed shaft Zahnwelle *f*
tooth-end rounding machine Zahnkantenfräsmaschine *f*
toothing Verzahnung *f*
tooth-meshing frequency Eingriffsfrequenz *f*
top Spitze *f*, Oberteil *nt*, Oberfläche *f*, Oberseite *f*; überschneiden
top beam Traverse *f*
top branch Scheitelzulauf *m*
top coat Deckanstrich *m*
top coming cutter rechtsdrehender Fräser *m*
top cover Abdeckboden *m*
top down von oben nach unten
top edge Schmelzkante *f*, Oberkante *f*
top end Tankoberboden *m*
top face Spanfläche *f* eines Drehmeißels
top film Deckfolie *f*
top force Oberteil *nt*
top going cutter linksdrehender Fräser *m*
top guide rail obere Führungsschiene *f*
top hook oberer Gabelhaken *m*
top jaw Aufsatzbacke *f*, Aufsatzklaue *f*
top land Fase *f* an Umfangsschneide
top layer Kopf *m*
top lift spreader Obenhubspreader *m*
top lifting Aufnahme *f* (von oben)
top limit obere Endstellung *f*
top load carton Faltschachtel *f* für Beladung von oben
top load carton erect form fill and seal machine Faltschachtelaufrichtfüll- und -verschließmaschine *f* mit Füllung von oben
top of rack Stapelspitze *f*
top of the rack upright Steherkopf *m*
top plate Deckplatte *f*, Befestigungsplatte *f*
top position oberste Stellung *f*
top priority höchste Priorität *f*
top radius Zahnkopfabrundung *f*
top rail Traverse *f*, Handlauf *m*, Querhaupt *nt*
top rake angle Wirkwinkel *m*
top running oben laufend
top sample Obenprobe *f*
top sheet Deckblatt *nt*
top sheet dispenser Deckblattaufleger *m*
top slide Oberschieber *m*
top speed Höchstdrehzahl *f*
top surface of the weld Nahtoberfläche *f*
top up auffüllen, nachfüllen
top up to the measuring mark auffül-

len bis zur Messmarke
top view Draufsicht *f*
top wrap Kopfwicklung *f*
top/bottom load case packing machine Faltschachtelverpackungsmaschine *f* mit Zuführung von oben/unten
top-controlled oben geführt
topically Aktualität *f*
topmost oberste/r/s
topographical representation lagerichtige Darstellung *f*
topped spur gear überschnittenes Stirnrad *nt*
topping Abkanten *nt*, Abrunden *nt*
topping cutter Gewindefräser *m* für Außendurchmesser
top-plate outer dimensions Befestigungsplattenaußenmaße *ntpl*
topple umkippen
toppling over Umkippen *nt*
top-up quantity Nachfüllmenge *f*
top-up water Nachfüllwasser *nt*
torch Brenner *m*
torch-cut brennschneiden
torispherical head Klöpperboden *m*
torn loose ausgebrochen
torn surface Ausbrechung *f*
toroid Toroide *f*, Ringspule *f*, Toroidspule *f*
toroidal ringförmig
toroidal coil Ringspule *f*, Toroidspule *f*
toroidal drive Toroidgetriebe *nt*
torque Moment *nt*, Drehmoment *m*, Verdrehungsmoment *nt*
torque arm Drehmomentenstütze *f*
torque characteristic Drehmomentenverlauf *m*, Drehmomentenkurve *f*
torque converter Drehmomentenwandler *m*
torque generation Drehmomentenerzeugung *f*
torque limitation Drehmomentbegrenzung *f*
torque measuring device Drehmomentmessgerät *nt*
torque motor Drehmotor *m*
torque sensor Drehmomentensensor *m*
torque spanner Drehmomentenschlüssel *m*

torque testing Drehmomentprüfung *f*
torque-set recess Flügelkreuzschlitz *m*
torsion Torsion *f*, Verwindung *f*, Verdrehung *f*
torsion angle Verdrehungswinkel *m*
torsion axis Verwindachse *f*
torsion bar Drehstab *m*
torsion support Torsionsstütze *f*
torsion test Verwindeversuch *m*
torsion testing Verwindeversuch *m*
torsion testing appliance Verwindeprüfgerät *nt*
torsional fracture Verwindebruch *m*
torsional oscillation Torsionsschwingung *f*
torsional play Verdrehspiel *nt*
torsional shear fracture Verdrehschiebungsbruch *m*
torsional strain Torsionsbeanspruchung *f*, Verdrehungsbeanspruchung *f*
torsional strength Verdrehungsfestigkeit *f*
torsional vibration Drehschwingung *f*
torsional vibration test Torsionsschwingungsversuch *m*
torsional-flexural buckling Biegedrillknicken *nt*
torsionally elastic drehelastisch
torsion-proof drehstarr
torsion-resistant verwindungssteif
torsion-stiff verwindungssteif
total gesamt; summieren; Summe *f*
total head Gesamthöhe *f*
total acid number *(sauer)* Neutralisationszahl *f*
total angle of contact Gesamtüberdeckungswinkel *m*
total angle of transmission Gesamtüberdeckungswinkel *m*
total application factor Gesamtbetriebsfaktor *m*
total arc of transmission Gesamtüberdeckungswälzkreisbogen *m*
total area Gesamtfläche *f*
total breakdown Gesamtausfall *m*, Totalausfall *m*
total breaking and/or locking device Totalfeststeller *m*
total capital spending Gesamtinvestitionsvolumen *nt*

total compressive strain Gesamtstauchung f
total connected load Gesamtanschlusswert m
total contact ratio Gesamtüberdeckung f
total cost Gesamtkosten pl
total cost of ownership Gesamteinsatzkosten pl
total cross-sectional area of the cut Gesamtnennspannungsquerschnitt m
total current Gesamtstrom m, Polarisationsstrom m, Summenstrom m
total current density-potential curve Summenstromdichte-Potential-Kurve f
total error range Wälzfehler m
total estimation error Gesamtschätzabweichung f
total floor space Gesamtgeschossfläche f
total force 1. Gesamtkraft f 2. *(spanend)* Zerspankraft f
total force exerted by the tool Gesamtzerspankraft f des Werkzeuges
total generator variation Erzeugendengesamtabweichung f
total harmonic distortion harmonische Gesamtverzerrung f
total heat requirement Gesamtheizbedarf m
total heating period Erdwärmdauer f
total input system transfer time gesamte Systemeingangsübertragungszeit f
total length of feed Gesamtvorschubweg m
total line Summenzeile f
total loss lubrication system Verbrauchsschmieranlage f
total machining time Gesamtfertigungszeit f, Auftragszeit f
total mass Gesamtgewicht nt
total number of teeth pl Zähnezahlsumme f
total operating time Gesamtlaufzeit f
total operation Gesamtbetrieb m
total output current Gesamtausgangsstrom m
total output system transfer time gesamte Systemausgangsübertragungszeit f
total penetration Gesamteinbrand m
total penetration energy Druckstoßarbeiten fpl
total pitch error Gesamtteilungsfehler m
total pitch variation Teilungsgesamtabweichung f
total profile variation Profilgesamtabweichung f
total pulse count Gesamtimpulszahl f
total quality management ganzheitliches Qualitätsmanagement nt
total sensitivity Gesamtempfindlichkeit f
total service life Gesamtlebensdauer f
total shrinkage in volume Gesamtvolumenschwindung f
total span of error Gesamtabweichungsspanne f
total speed increasing ratio Gesamtübersetzung f
total system response time (TRT) Gesamtantwortzeit f des Systems
total table travel gesamter Fräsweg m
total time Gesamtzeit f
total tolerance Gesamttoleranz f
total torque Gesamtmoment m
total torque exerted by the tool Gesamtmoment m des Werkzeuges
total variation Gesamtabweichung f
totality Gesamtheit f
totally enclosed vollgekapselt
totally enclosed cab geschlossene Kabine f
tote tragen, transportieren
tote bag Tragetasche f
tote box Förderkasten m, Transportkasten m, Transportkommissionierkasten m
totter wackeln
touch tangieren, berühren, tasten; Berührung f, Tastgefühl nt
touch and enclose within berührend einschließen
touch reader Touchreader m
touch screen Berührschirm m
touch up Nachbesserung f
touching guidances Streifenführun-

gen
touching lever Taster *m*, Tasthebel *m*
touchless measurement berührungslose Messung *f*
touch-sensitive berührungsempfindlich
touch-sensitive device berührungsempfindliche Einrichtung *f*
touch-sensitive display berührungsempfindlicher Bildschirm *m*
touch-sensitive screen berührungsempfindlicher Bildschirm *m*
touch-sensitive switch Kontaktschalter *m*
tough zäh
toughened glass Einschichtsicherheitsglas *nt*, temperiertes Glas *nt*
toughness Zähigkeit *f*
toughness behaviour Zähigkeitsverhalten *nt*
toughness property Zähigkeitseigenschaft *f*
tow ziehen, schleppen, abschleppen
tow bar Abschleppstange *f*
tow hook Zughaken *m*
tow tractor Schlepper *m*
towards hin *(zu)*, in Richtung
towards the left nach links
towards the right nach rechts
towed gezogen
towel hook Handtuchhaken *m*
towing Ziehen *nt*, Schleppen *nt*, Abschleppen *nt*
towing bar Zugstange *f*
towing device Abschleppeinrichtung *f*, Anhängevorrichtung *f*
towing tractor Schlepper *m*
towing vehicle Zugmaschine *f*
towrope Abschleppseil *nt*
toxic toxisch
toxic value Giftwert *m*
TP monitor Dialogmonitor *m*
T-peel test Winkelschälversuch *m*
trace 1. *(eine Oberläche)* kopieren, pausen, abfühlen, abtasten, tasten, antasten, entlangfahren an, abfahren, verfolgen **2.** *(Linie, Geometrie)* Linienzug *m*, Spur *f* **3.** *(Monitor)* Anzeige *f*
trace back zurückverfolgen, rückverfolgen
trace program Überwacherprogramm *nt*
traceability Rückverfolgbarkeit *f*
traceable rückverfolgbar
trace abstufen
tracer Fühler *m*, Taster *m*, Fühlstift *m*, Tastfinger *m*
tracer contact pressure Tastendruck *m*
tracer control Kopiersteuerung *f*, Tastersteuerung *f*, Fühlersteuerung *f*
tracer controlled profiler with rotary table Rundtischkopierfräsmaschine *f* mit Fühlersteuerung
tracer device Tastgerät *nt*
tracer disc Tastscheibe *f*
tracer duplicator control Fühlernachformsteuerung *f*
tracer feed Tastvorschub *m*
tracer finger Taststift *m*
tracer head Fühlerkopf *m*
tracer line Begleitlinie *f*
tracer mill fräsen (oder kopierfräsen) mit Fühlersteuerung
tracer pin Taststift *m*, Kopierstift *m*, Abtaststift *m*
tracer point Kopierstift *m*, Tastspitze *f*
tracer roll Fühlerwalze *f*
tracer slide Tastschlitten *m*
tracer tip Tasterschneide *f*
tracer-controlled fühlergesteuert
tracer-controlled copying attachment fühlergesteuerte Nachformeinrichtung *f*, fühlergesteuerte Kopiereinrichtung *f*
tracer-controlled machine tool fühlergesteuerte Werkzeugmaschine *f*
tracer-controlled miller Fräsmaschine *f* mit Fühlersteuerung
tracer-controlled milling machine Fräsmaschine *f* mit Fühlersteuerung
tracer-controlled profile milling machine with two-dimensional control Umrissnachformfräsmaschine *f* mit Fühlersteuerung und zweidimensionaler Steuerung
tracer-controlled profiler Umrissnachformfräsmaschine *f* mit Fühlersteuerung
traces of corrosion Korrosionsspuren *fpl*
traces of fingerprints *pl* Fingerab-

druckspuren *fpl*
tracing attachment Fühlernachformeinrichtung *f*
tracing back Rückverfolgung *f*, Zurückverfolgen *nt*
tracing control Fühlersteuerung *f*
tracing device Tastgerät *nt*
tracing fixture Tasteinrichtung *f*
tracing paper Transparentpapier *nt*
track Bahn *f*, Schienen *fpl*, Gleis *nt*, Strecke *f*, Spur *f*, Fahrspur *f*, Führungsbahn *f*, Laufbahn *f*; verfolgen, abfahren
track guidance Bahnführung *f*
track rail Fahrschiene *f*
track ring Laufring *m*
track roller Spurrolle *f*
track wheel Laufrad *nt*
track width Spurweite *f*
trackage Schienenstrang *m*, Streckenlänge *f*
trackball Rollkugel *f*
track-bound crane schienengebundener Kran *m*
tracking Spurführung *f*, Verfolgung *f*, Spurhalten *nt*, Nachlauf *m*
tracking distance Nachlaufweg *m*
tracking path Nachlaufweg *m*
traction Ziehen *nt*, Zug *m*, Zugkraft *f*
traction battery Antriebsbatterie *f*, Fahrzeugbatterie *f*
traction current Fahrstrom *m*
traction cut Fahrstromunterbrechung *f*
traction flank Zugflanke *f*
traction force Zugkraft *f*
traction mechanism Zugmittel *nt*
traction motor Fahrmotor *m*
traction transmission element Zugmittel *nt*
tractive effort Zugkraft *f*
tractive force Zugkraft *f*
tractive resistance Fahrwiderstand *m*
tractor Schlepper *m*, Trägerfahrzeug *nt*
trade Handel *m*, Gewerk *nt*
trade area Gewerbefläche *f*
trade board Gewerbeaufsichtsamt *nt*
trade goods Handelsware *n fpl*
trade mark ™ Handelsmarke ® *f*
trade school Berufsschule *f*
trademark Marke *f*
traffic Verkehr *m*

traffic area Verkehrsbereich *m*, Verkehrsfläche *f*
traffic jam Verkehrsstau *m*
traffic management Verkehrsregelung *f*
traffic regulation Verkehrsregelung *f*
traffic route Verkehrsweg *m*
traffic way Verkehrsweg *m*
trail schleifen, schleppen
trail edge Nebenschneide *f*
trailer Anhänger *m*
trailer load Anhängelast *f*
trailing angle Einstellwinkel *m* der Nebenschneide
trailing cable Schleppkabel *nt*
trailing cable supply Schleppkabelzustromführung *f*
trailing pinion cutter flank nachlaufende Schneidkantenflanke *f*
train anleiten, einweisen, schulen, ausbilden
train of fused beads Schmelzperlenkette *f*
trained operator Facharbeiter *m*
trainee machine toll operator Auszubildender *m* für Werkzeugmaschinenbedienung
training Schulung *f*, Ausbildung *f*, Einweisung *f*
training activity Schulungsmaßnahme *f*
training aids Ausbildungsmittel *ntpl*
training workshop Lehrwerkstatt *f*
trajectory Bahnkurve *f*, Trajektorie *f*
trajectory calculation Bahnkurvenberechnung *f*
trajectory generator Trajektoriengenerierung *f*
trammel point Stangenzirkel *m*
transact umschlagen
transaction Vorgang *m*, Interaktion *f*, Transaktion *f*
transaction-driven transaktionsgetrieben
transceiver Sender/Empfänger *m*
translucent contrast Transparentkontrast *m*
transduce *(el.)* übertragen
transducer Signalgeber *m*, Wandler *m*, Messwandler *m*, Messwertwandler *m*, Messwertgeber *m*, Messwertumfor-

mer *m*, Umwandler *m*, Übertrager *m*
transfer Transport *m*, Umladung *f*, Umsetzung *f*, Übergang *m*, Transfer *m*, Verlegung *f*, Verlagerung *f*, Versetzung *f*, Übertragung *f*, Übernahme *f*, Übergabe *f*, Weitergabe *f*, Weiterleitung *f*, Weiterschaltung *f*; transferieren, übertragen, umsetzen, versetzen, verlagern, verlegen, übergeben, überladen, umladen, weiterleiten, weitergeben, weiterschalten
transfer aisle Umsetzgang *m*
transfer belt Versetzband *nt*
transfer bridge Überladebrücke *f*
transfer car Transportwagen *m*, Verschiebewagen *m*, Umsetzbrücke *f*
transfer car interlock Umsetzbrückenverriegelung *f*
transfer carriage Verschiebewagen *m*
transfer case Vorschaltgetriebe *nt*
transfer condition Übertragungsbedingung *f*
transfer conveyor Übergabeförderer *m*
transfer device Übergabevorrichtung *f*, Umsetzeinrichtung *f*
transfer distance Übergangsabstand *m*, Übertragungsabstand *m*
transfer drive Transferantrieb *m*
transfer element Übertragungsglied *nt*, Umladeelement *nt*
transfer facility Umsetzeinrichtung *f*
transfer gear box Verteilergetriebe *nt*
transfer instruction Transportbefehl *m*
transfer element Umsetzer *m*
transfer line Fertigungsstraße *f*, Transferstraße *f*
transfer location Übergabeposition *f*
transfer mould Spritzpresswerkzeug *nt*; transferpressen
transfer moulding operation Spritzpressvorgang *m*, Transferpressvorgang *m*
transfer move Umsetzvorgang *m*
transfer of bending moment Biegemomentübertragung *f*
transfer of the load Lastwechsel *m*
transfer pipette Vollpipette *f*
transfer point Übergabeposition *f*, Übergabeplatz *m*
transfer position Übergabeposition *f*

transfer principle Übertragungsprinzip *nt*
transfer statement Übertragungsbefehl *m*
transfer station Übergabestation *f*, Umladestelle *f*, Umsetzstation *f*, Übergabeposition *f*
transfer system Umsetzregal *nt*
transfer ticket Transferticket *nt*
transfer time Umsetzzeit *f*, Übertragungszeit *f*
transfer to reserve Rückstellung *f*
transfer unit Umsetzeinrichtung *f*, Umladungseinheit *f*
transferable übertragbar
transferral Übergabe *f*
transferred arc welding Plasmalichtbogenschweißen *nt*
transform wandeln, umspannen, umformen, umwandeln
transformation Umformen *nt*, Umformung *f*
transformation behaviour Umwandlungsverhalten *nt*
transformed random quantity transformierte Zufallsgröße *f*
transformer Transformator *m*, Umformer *m*, Wandler *m*, Stromwandler *m*, Übertrager *m*
transformer principle Transformatorprinzip *nt*
transformer setting Trafoeinstellung *f*
transforming in the austempering region Umwandeln *nt* in der Bainitstufe
transgress überschreiten
transgression Überschreitung *f*
transgression probability Überschreitungswahrscheinlichkeit *f*
transient 1. kurzzeitig, vorübergehend, transient 2. (el.) Überspannung *f*
transient absorption Z-diode Diode *f* zur Ableitung transienter Überspannung
transient behaviour Übergangsverhalten *nt*
transient deviation from the desired value vorübergehende Sollwertabweichung *f*
transient effect Einschwingvorgang *m*

transient pulse Überspannungsimpuls *m*
transient stage Einschwingphase *f*
transient suppression device Störschutzbeschaltung *f*
transient suppression means Überspannungsbegrenzungseinrichtung *f*
transient voltage suppression Überspannungsschutz *m*
transient voltage suppression diode Überspannungsschutzdiode *f*
transition piece Übergangsstück *nt*
transirradiated material durchstrahlter Stoff *m*
transistor Transistor *m*
transit Transport *m*, Überführung *f*
transit packaging machine Sammelpackmaschine *f*
transit time Umschaltzeit *f*, Umschlagzeit *f*
transition Übergang *m*
transition angle Übergangswinkel *m*
transition fit Übergangspassung *f*
transition radius Übergangsradius *m*
transition time Anlaufzeit *f*
transition value Anlaufwert *m*
transitional period Übergangsfrist *f*, Übergangszeit *f*
translate übersetzen
translating gears Umwandlungsgetriebe *nt*
translating part Schieber *m*
translation Translation *f*, Übersetzung *f*
translational translatorisch
translational motion Translationsbewegung *f*, Schiebung *f*
translatory motion Schubbewegung *f*
translucent contrast copy Transparentkontrastpause *f*
translucent discolouration lasierende Verfärbung *f*
translucent paper Transparentpapier *nt*
translucent paper with diazo coating Transparentpapier *nt* mit Lichtpausschicht
transmissible übertragbar
transmissible film durchlässige Folie *f*
transmissible moment übertragbares Moment *nt*

transmission 1. Trieb *m*, Antrieb *m*, Gang *m*, Transmission *f*, Übermittlung *f*, Übertragung *f*, Weiterleitung *f* **2.** *(Antrieb)* Getriebeübersetzung *f*
transmission agent Übertragungsmittel *nt*
transmission channel Übertragungskanal *m*
transmission characteristic Übertragungskennlinie *f*
transmission circuit Übertragungsstrecke *f*
transmission coil Sendespule *f*
transmission constancy Übersetzungskonstanz *f*
transmission deviation Übersetzungsabweichung *f*, Übertragungsabweichung *f*
transmission distance Übertragungsstrecke *f*
transmission element Getriebeglied *nt*, Trag-/Zugmittel *nt*
transmission error Übertragungsfehler *m*
transmission for instrumentation purposes Messgetriebe *nt*
transmission function Transmissionsfunktion *f*, Übertragungsfunktion *f*
transmission light scanner Transmissionslichttaster *m*
transmission line Übertragungsleitung *f*
transmission line-scanning light scanner Transmissionszeilenlichttaster *m*
transmission link Übertragungsstrecke *f*, Übertragungsabschnitt *m*
transmission member Übertragungsglied *nt*
transmission method Übertragungsverfahren *nt*
transmission of air-borne noise Luftschallübertragung *f*
transmission of force Krafteinleitung *f*
transmission of moment to the assembly Momenteinleitung *f*
transmission of motion Bewegungsübertragung *f*
transmission of rotary motion Drehbewegungsübertragung *f*

transmission of transverse forces Querkraftübertragung *f*
transmission optics Transmissionsoptik *f*
transmission path Übertragungsstrecke *f*, Getriebestrang *m*
transmission protocol Übertragungsprotokoll *nt*
transmission range Sendebereich *m*
transmission rate Übertragungsmenge *f*
transmission ratio Übersetzung *f*, Übersetzungsverhältnis *nt*
transmission shaft Transmissionswelle *f*
transmission speed Übertragungsgeschwindigkeit *f*, Schrittgeschwindigkeit *f*
transmission system Übertragungssystem *nt*
transmission time Übertragungszeit *f*
transmission tolerance Getriebetoleranz *f*
transmission unit Übertragungseinrichtung *f*
transmission variation Übertragungsabweichung *f*
transmission with back gears Getriebe *nt* mit Vorgelege
transmit 1. senden, übertragen, durchlassen, weiterleiten, übermitteln 2. *(Kraft)* ableiten, übersetzen
transmit by wireless funken
transmittable force übertragbare Kraft *f*
transmittance factor Durchlässigkeitsgrad *m*
transmitted light Durchlicht *nt*
transmitted sound pulse Schallsendeimpuls *m*
transmitted torque Übertragungsmoment *nt*
transmitter 1. Geber *m*, Sender *m*, Übertrager *m* 2. *(Messwerte)* Messwertgeber *m*
transmitter frequency Sendefrequenz *f*
transmitter/receiver Sender/Empfänger
transmitter-receiver technique SE-Technik *f*
transmitting measuring instrument übertragendes Messgerät *nt*
transparence Transparenz *f*
transparency Transparenz *f*, Folie *f*
transparent durchsichtig, transparent
transparent film Transparentfolie *f*
transparent foil Transparentfolie *f*
transpassive condition transpassiver Zustand *m*
transpassive corrosion transpassive Korrosion *f*
transport Abfuhr *f*, Zufuhr *f*, Beförderung *f*, Transport *m*, Fördervorgang *m*; befördern
transport area Transportfläche *f*
transport capacity Transportleistung *f*
transport cart Rollenhubwagen *m*, Transportwagen *m*
transport coefficient Transportleistungsziffer *f*
transport command Transportauftrag *m*
transport command administration Transportauftragsverwaltung *f*
transport command processor Transportauftragsverwaltung *f*
transport container Transportbehälter *m*
transport container type Transportbehälterart *f*
transport costs Transportkosten *pl*
transport goods Transportgüter, Ware transportieren
transport instruction Transportanweisung *f*
transport intensity Transportintensität *f*
transport intensity matrix Transportintensitätsmatrix *f*
transport layer Transportschicht *f*
transport load Transportbelastung *f*
transport matrix Transportmatrix *f*
transport organization Transportorganisation *f*
transport package Versandpackung *f*
transport planning Transportplanung *f*
transport range Transportbereich *m*
transport receptacle Transportbehälter *m*

transport request Transportanforderung *f*
transport roller Transportrolle *f*
transport route Transportweg *m*
transport service Transportschicht *f*
transport speed Fördergeschwindigkeit *f*, Transportgeschwindigkeit *f*
transport task Transportaufgabe *f*
transport time Transportzeit *f*
transport trolley Transportwagen *m*
transport unit Transporteinheit *f*
transport value Transportgröße *f*
transportable transportabel
transportation lock Transportsicherung *f*
transportation route Verkehrsweg *m*
transporting goods *(EDV)* Ware transportieren
transporting plant Förderanlage *f*
transporting position Transportstellung *f*
transport-traffic volume-storage TUL (Transport, Umschlag, Lagerung)
transpose übertragen
transposition Übertragung *f*
transposition of lines Verdrillung *f*
transship umladen, umschlagen, überladen
transshipment Umladung *f*, Umschlag *m*
transshipment logistics Umschlagslogistik *f*
transshipment note Warenbegleitschein *m*
transshipment point Umschlagpunkt *m*
transshipment traffic Umschlagverkehr *m*
transshipment warehouse Umschlaglager *nt*
transshipping device Umladevorrichtung *f*
transversal operation Planarbeit *f*
transverse quer, transversal, in Querrichtung; durchlaufen
transverse action Querkraft *f*
transverse angle of transmission Profilüberdeckungswinkel *m*
transverse arc of transmission Profilüberdeckungswälzkreisbogen *m*

transverse axis Querachse *f*
transverse base pitch Grundkreisteilung *f*, Grundzylinderstirnteilung *f*
transverse base thickness Zahndicke *f* auf dem Grundzylinder im Stirnschnitt, Grundzahndicke *f* im Stirnschnitt
transverse bed Querbett *nt*
transverse bend specimen Querbiegeversuch *m*, Querbiegeprobe *f*
transverse carriage Querschlitten *m*, Querverschieber *m*
transverse carrier Querauflage *f*
transverse contact ratio Profilüberdeckung *f*
transverse conveyor Querförderer *m*
transverse copying bracket Plankopierböckchen *nt*
transverse diametral pitch Diametral-Pitch im Stirnschnitt
transverse direction Querrichtung *f*
transverse dog Anschlagnocke *f* zum Ausschalten des Quervorschubs
transverse edge Querkante *f*
transverse extrusion of rods and tubes Querstrangpressen *nt*
transverse feed Quervorschub *m*
transverse force Querkraft *f*
transverse impact extrusion Querfließpressen *nt*
transverse interference fit Querpresspassung *f*
transverse joint Querfuge *f*
transverse joint of web plate Stegblechquerstoß *m*
transverse line of action Profilnormale *f* im Berührpunkt
transverse load Querkraft *f*
transverse milling Querfräsen *nt*
transverse mode voltage Differenzspannung *f*
transverse module Stirnmodul *nt*
transverse moment quer verlaufendes Moment *nt*
transverse normal base pitch Stirneingriffsteilung *f*
transverse operation Planarbeit *f*
transverse path of contact Eingriffslinie *f*
transverse pitch Stirnteilung *f*, Teilkreisteilung *f*

transverse pitch angle Stirnteilungswinkel *m*
transverse plane of the bevel gear Kegelradstirnebene *f*
transverse planing Querhobeln *nt*
transverse pressure angle Stirneingriffswinkel *m*, Eingriffswinkel *m*, Stirnprofilwinkel *m*
transverse pressure angle at a point Stirnprofilwinkel *m*
transverse pressure angle variation Eingriffswinkelabweichung *f*
transverse rigidity Quersteifigkeit *f*
transverse rod extrusion Vollquerstrangpressen *nt*
transverse rod impact extrusion Vollquerfließpressen *nt*
transverse rolling Querwalzen *nt*
transverse roughness Querrauheit *f*
transverse rupture strength Bruchdurchbiegung *f*
transverse seal Quernaht *f*
transverse section Stirnschnitt *m*
transverse slide Querschieber *m*
transverse slip Querschlupf *m*
transverse space width Lückenweite *f* im Stirnschnitt
transverse squeezer Querquetscher *m*
transverse table feed Tischquervorschub *m*
transverse tensile strength Querzugsfestigkeit *f*
transverse tensile test specimen Querzerreißprobe *f*
transverse testing Querprüfung *f*
transverse to quer zu
transverse tooth thickness Stirnzahndicke *f*, Zahndicke *f* im Stirnschnitt
transverse traverse Planzug *m*
transverse tubular extrusion Hohlquerstrangpressen *nt*
transverse tubular impact extrusion Hohlquerfließpressen *nt*
transverse wave Transversalwelle *f*
trap fangen, auffangen, erfassen, ergreifen, einziehen, einschließen, verriegeln
trap door *1.* Klappe *f*, Durchgang *m* *2. (Sicherheitstechnik)* Notausstieg *m*
trapezoid block spring Trapezblockfedern *f*

trapezoid shrinkage Trapezeinlauf *m*
trapezoidal trapezförmig
trapezoidal sheeting Trapezblech *nt*
trapezium Trapez *nt*
trapezium starting cut Trapezanschnitt *m*
trapezoid Trapez *nt*
trapped eingeschlossen
trapping Fangen *nt*, Einziehen *nt*, Erfassung *f*, Einzug *m*
trapping point Einzugstelle *f*
transform umsetzen
travel Bewegung *f*, Verschiebung *f*, Verschiebbarkeit *f*, Hub *m*, Weg *m*, Fahrt *f*; zurücklegen, bewegen, wandern, fahren
travel around herumfahren
travel characteristics Laufeigenschaften *fpl*
travel component Fahrkomponente *f*
travel control Betätigungseinrichtung *f* für Fahrtrichtung
travel control switch Fahrschalter *m*
travel cycle Bewegungsablauf *m*
travel diagonally diagonal fahren
travel diagram Fahrdiagramm *nt*
travel distance Fahrweg *m*
travel drive unit Fahrwerk *nt*, Fahrantrieb *m*
travel forwards vorwärts fahren
travel laterally quer fahren, quer verfahren
travel lengthwise längs fahren
travel light Fahrbahnleuchte *f*
travel limitation Fahrwegbegrenzung *f*
travel mechanism Fahrwerk *nt*
travel motion Fahrbewegung *f*
travel of the ram Stößelweg *m*
travel of the spring system Federweg *m*
travel over überfahren
travel path Fahrweg *m*, Fahrspur *f*, Fahrkurs *m*, Wegstrecke *f*, Verfahrweg *m*
travel period Wegezeit *f*, Fahrzeit *f*
travel rail Fahrschiene *f*
travel roller Laufrolle *f*
travel speed Transportgeschwindigkeit *f*, Fahrgeschwindigkeit *f*
travel state Fahrzustand *m*

travel through durchlaufen
travel time Wegezeit *f*
travel unit Fahrwerk *nt*
travel way Fahrkurs *m*
travel wheel Laufrad *nt*
travel wheel perimeter Laufradumfang *m*
travel wheel periphery Laufradumfang *m*
travel when empty Leerfahrt durchführen
travelling Fahren *nt*, Verfahren *nt*, Fahrbetrieb *m*; verfahrbar
travelling armour plate planer Panzerplattenhobelmaschine *f* mit beweglichen Querbalken
travelling bridge miller Fräsmaschine *f* mit beweglicher Doppelständerbrücke
travelling characteristics Fahrverhalten *nt*
travelling control Fahrsteuerung *f*
travelling head beweglicher Spindelstock *m*
travelling head planer Hobelmaschine *f* mit beweglichem Werkzeug
travelling head shaper traversierende Stößelhobelmaschine *f*
travelling laterally quer verfahrbar
travelling mode Fahrbetrieb *m*
travelling movement Fahrbewegung *f*
travelling on the rack structure regalverfahrend
travelling position Fahrstellung *f*
travelling roller steady mitgehender Rollensetzstock *m*
travelling speed Fahrgeschwindigkeit *f*
travelling spindle head beweglicher Spindelkopf *m*
traverse Querriegel *m*, Querträger *m*, Quertraverse *f*, Bewegung *f*, Weg *m*, Verschiebung *f*; bewegen, verschieben, verfahren, überschreiten, traversieren, hindurchfahren, quer verfahren
traverse bracing Querverband *m*
traverse carriage Quertraverse *f*
traverse distance Verschiebeweg *m*
traverse grinding Längsschleifen *nt*
traverse grinding method Vorschubschleifverfahren *nt*, Längsschleifverfahren *nt*
traverse lifting beam Quertraverse *f*
traverse of the slide Schlittenweg *m*
traverse path Verfahrweg *m*
traverse shaper traversierende Waagerechtstoßmaschine *f*, traversierende Stößelhobelmaschine *f*
traverse thread milling Langgewindefräsen *nt*
traverse thread milling machine Langgewindefräsmaschine *f*
traverse truck Querverfahrwagen *m*
traverse truing Längsabrichten *nt*
traverse-bed shaper Waagerechtstoßmaschine *f* mit traversierendem Stößel
traversing Abtastung *f*, Verschiebung *f*, Verschieben *nt*, Traversieren *nt*; hindurchfahrend, quer verfahrbar
traversing feed Längsvorschub *m*
traversing feed motion Längsvorschubbewegung *f*
traversing grinding method Längsschleifverfahren *nt*
traversing head miller Fräsmaschine *f* mit verstellbarer Spindel
traversing length for a waviness Welligkeitstaststrecke *f*
traversing speed Abtastgeschwindigkeit *f*
traversing table beweglicher Tisch *m*
traversing-head bar machine Langdrehautomat *m*
tray Schale *f*, Gefäß *nt*, Wanne *f*, Trog *m*, Tablett *nt*, Tablar *nt*, Tray *nt*
tray blank Trayzuschnitt *m*
tray denesting machine Trayentstapelungsmaschine *f*
tray erect load and seal machine Trayaufrichtfüll- und -verschließmaschine *f*
tray erecting Trayaufrichtmaschine *f*
tray handling system Tablarfördertechnik *f*
tray handling technology Tablarfördertechnik *f*
tray stacker Traystapler *m*
tray storage system Tablarlager *nt*
tread Stufe *f*, Tritt *m*, Lauffläche *f*; treten
tread width Laufflächenbreite *f*

treadle Fußhebel *m*, Pedal *nt*, Tritt *m*
treat bearbeiten, behandeln, verarbeiten, aufbereiten
treatment Verarbeitung *f*, Behandlung *f*, Pflege *f*
treatment of base material Untergrundbehandlung *f*
treatment of samples Probenbehandlung *f*
trench wall Baugrubenwand *f*
trench with sloping walls Graben mit geböschten Wänden
trend of the function Funktionsverlauf *m*
trend to increase hardness Aufhärtungsneigung *f*
trepan hohlbohren, kernbohren
trepanning and reboring lathe Hohlbohr- und Ausbohrbank *f*
trepanning lathe Hohlbohrbank *f*, Hohlbohrmaschine *f*
trepanning tool Ausdrehmeißel *m*, Hohlbohrer *m*
triad Wertetripel *nt*
trial Probe *f*, Prüfung *f*, Versuch *m*, Erprobung *f*
trial and error Probieren *nt*
trial and error method Probierverfahren *nt*
trial erection Vormontage *f*, Probemontage *f*
trial operation Probebetrieb *m*, Arbeitsversuch *m*
trial period Probezeit *f*
trial run Probebetrieb *m*, Probelauf *m*
triangle Dreieck *nt*
triangle connection Dreieckschaltung *f*
triangle method Dreieckverfahren *nt*
triangular dreieckig
triangular file Dreikantfeile *f*
triangular grid Dreieckraster *nt*
triangular nut Dreikantmutter *f*
triangular scraper Dreikantschaber *m*
triangular screw Dreikantschraube *f*
triangular socket key Dreikant-Steckschlüssel *m*
triangulation Dreiecksmessung *f*, Triangulation *f*
trickle charging Erhaltungsladen *m*
trickling deaerator Rieselentglasung *f*
trigger anfahren, ansteuern, auslösen, einleiten; Ansteuerung *f*, Auslöser *m*
triggering Auslösung *f*
triggering event Fangvorgang *m*, Fangfall *m*
trilateral dreiseitig
trilateral head Seitenschwenkgabel *f*
trilateral retractable fork Seitenschwenkgabel *f*
trilock Sternnutbefestigung *f*
trilock fixing Sternnutbefestigung *f*
trim abgleichen, abgraten, entgraten, beranden, besäumen, beschneiden, putzen
trimmed drawing sheet beschnittene Zeichnung *f*
trimmed photo print sheet beschnittene Lichtpause *f*
trimmed size Endformat *nt*, Fertigformat *nt*
trimming Schneiden *nt*, Beschneiden *nt*, Abgraten *nt*
trimming die Abgratmatrize *f*
trimming margin Beschnittrand *m*
trimming to value Abgleich *m*
trimming tool Abgratwerkzeug *nt*
trip 1. Anschlag *m*, Knagge *f* **2.** Fahrt *f* **3.** abschalten, stillsetzen, loslassen, ausklinken, ausrücken, auslösen, herausspringen; Abschaltung *f*, Auslösung *f*
trip dog Anschlag *m*, Anschlagstift *m*, Anschlagbolzen *m*, Auslösenocken *m*, Anschlagnocken *m*, Anschlagknagge *f*, Schaltstift *m*, Betätigungsnocken *m*, Anschlag *m* für die Auslösung
trip dog carrier Nockenscheibe *f*
trip dog carrier for accelerator mechanism Eilgangnockenscheibe *f*
trip line Steuerleitung *f*
trip pin Anschlag *m*
trip rod Anschlagstange *f*
trip stop Betätigungsnocken *m*
trip worm Fallschnecke *f*
triple dreifach
triple index centre Teilgerät *nt* mit drei Arbeitsspindeln
triple index centres dreifaches Teilgerät *nt*
triple mast Dreifachhubgerüst *nt*

triple thread dreigängiges Gewinde *nt*
triple-row dreireihig
triplex fixed-bed miller Planfräsmaschine *f* mit drei Frässpindelköpfen
triplex manufacturing-type miller Dreispindelplanfräsmaschine *f*
triplex manufacturing-type milling machine Dreispindelplanfräsmaschine *f*
triplex miller Planfräsmaschine *f* mit drei Frässpindelköpfen
triplex milling machine Dreispindelfräsmaschine *f*
triplex-type milling machine Planfräsmaschine *f* mit drei Frässpindelköpfen
tripod Dreibein *nt*, Stativ *nt*
tripod sleeve Stativmuffe *f*
tripping Auslösung *f*, Schaltung *f*, Ausschaltung *f*, Abschaltung *f*, Stillsetzung *f*, Ansprechen *nt*
tripping device (a cut-off system of an oil burning system) *(Abschaltung einer Ölfeuerungsanlage)* Verblockung *f*
tripping mechanism Ausklinkeinrichtung *f*, Auslösemechanik *f*, Auslösemechanismus *m*
tripping point Stolperstelle *f*
tripping speed Auslösegeschwindigkeit *f*
tripping to a line Anschlagdrehen *nt*
tristate Dreizustandsausgang *m*
tristate output Dreizustandsausgang *m*
tristimulus method Dreibereichsverfahren *nt*
trolley 1. *(Transport)* Katze *f*, Laufkatze *f*, Wagen *m*, Karren *m*, Transportbehälter *m* **2.** *(Kanal, Satellit)* Kanalfahrwagen *m*, Satellitenfahrwagen *m*
trolley travel Katzfahrt *f*
trolley travelling gears Katzfahrwerk *nt*
tooth trace testing Flankenlinienprüfung *f*
trouble Störung *f*
trouble shooting Fehlerbestimmung *f*
troublefree reibungsfrei
trouble-free störungsfrei
troubleshooting fehlerlos
trough 1. Trog *m*, Schale *f* **2.** *(für*

Späne) Spänetrog *m*
trough-crack Durchriss *m*
through-hole Durchgangsloch *nt*
trough-shaped idler muldenförmige Tragrolle *f*
truck Flurförderzeug (FFZ) *nt*, Lastkraftwagen *m*, Lkw *m*, Karren *m*, Wagen *m*, Fahrzeug *nt*
truck configurations Staplerumrisse *pl*
truck profile Fahrzeugaußenkontur *f*
truck with a tiller Deichselwagen *m*
truck with elevatable operating position Flurförderzeug *nt* mit hebbarem Fahrerplatz
true 1. rund laufend; zentrieren **2.** richtig **3.** *(in der Größe)* maßgerecht **4.** *(anpassen, justieren)* ausrichten, abrichten
true angle ratio winkelgetreue Übersetzung *f*
true angle Spanwinkel *m*
true cutting angle Schnittwinkel *m*, Schneidenwinkel *m*
true density Reindichte *f*
true porosity Gesamtporosität *f*
true rake Wirkwinkel *m*
true rake angle Spanflächenwinkel *m*, wirksamer Spanwinkel *m*, Wirkspanwinkel *m*, Wirkwinkel *m*
true running Rundlauf *m*, Laufgenauigkeit *f*
true running of end faces Stirnlaufgenauigkeit *f*
true scale Hauptteilung *f*
true size Genaumaß *nt*
true to scale maßstäblich, maßstabsgetreu
true to shape formgerecht
true value wahrer Wert *m*
true within genau auf eine Toleranz, innerhalb einer Toleranz
true zo size maßgenau
true-angle transmission winkelgetreue Übertragung *f*
trueness Richtigkeit *f*
truer mandrel Abrichtdorn *m*
true-running accuracy Rundlaufgenauigkeit *f*
true-running error Rundlauffehler *m*
true-to-scale representation maßstabgetreue Darstellung *f*

truing Abdrehen *nt*
truing attachment Abdrehvorrichtung *f*
truing device Abdrehwerkzeug *nt*
truing plane Abdrehebene *f*
truing templet Abdrehschablone *f*
truncation Abbruch *m*
truncation Abflachung *f*
trunnion 1. Lagerzapfen *m*, Zapfen *m* 2. *(Antriebe)* Drehzahlverhältnis *nt*
trunnion bearing Zapfenlager *nt*
truss Strebe *f*, Träger *m*
truss-head screw Flachrundschraube *f*
truth table Wahrheitstabelle *f*, Wertetabelle *f*, Wahrheitstafel *f*
try prüfen, probieren, testen, erproben, versuchen
try square Anschlagwinkel *m*
T-shaped locator pin Knebelstecker *m*
T-slot T-Nut *f*, Nut *f*, Spannnut *f*, Aufnahmenut *f*
T-slot bolt T-Nutenschraube *f*
T-slot cutter Schaftfräser *m* für T-Nuten
T-square Kreuzwinkel *m*
T-stud T-Stift *m*
tub Fass *nt*, Kübel *m*
tub fill and seal machine Fassfüll- und -verschließmaschine *f*
tube Rohr *nt*, Röhre *f*, Schlauch *m*
tube bundle Rohrbündel *nt*
tube casing Röhrengehäuse *nt*
tube clip Schlaucholive *f*
tube current intensity Röhrenstromstärke *f*
tube drawing Rohrziehen *nt*, Gleitziehen *nt* von Rohren
tube for plumbing Installationsrohr *nt*
tube housing Röhrengehäuse *nt*
tube of plastic material Stretchfolienhülse *f*
tube of thermoplastic film Stretchfolienhülse *f*
tube of thermoplastic material Folienschlauch *m*
tube pitch Rohrleitung *f*
tube segment Rohrabschnitt *m*
tube shield casing Röhrenschutzgehäuse *nt*
tube straightened against a straight edge linealgerichtetes Rohr *nt*
tube strip test specimen Rohrstreifenprobe *f*
tube system Rohranordnung *f*
tube voltage Röhrenspannung *f*
tubing Rohrleitung *f*, Rohre *ntpl*
tubular hohl, rohrförmig
tubular arm Rohrkragarm *m*
tubular bag form fill and seal machine Folienschlauchbeutelform-, -füll- und -verschließmaschine *f*
tubular cantilever Rohrkragarm *m*
tubular film Folienschlauch *m*
tubular part Hohlkörper *m*
tubular plate Panzerplatte *f*
tubular probe Rohrsonde *f*
tubular radiator Rohrheizkörper *m*
tubular solder with flux core Röhrenlot *nt* mit Flussmittelseele
tubular-plate electrode Panzerplattenelektrode *f*
tubular bag Folienschlauch-Beutel *m*
tuck einstecken, klammern
tuck closing machine Einsteck-Verschließmaschine *f*
tucking klammernd, klammern *nt*
tumbler gear Schwenkrad *nt*
tumbler switch Kippschalter *m*
tumbler yoke Schwenkkörper *m*
tumbling 1. Schwenken *nt* 2. *(Fertigungsverfahren)* Trommelpolieren *nt*
tundish 1. Auffangtrichter *m* 2. Abflussbeiwert *m*
tune abstimmen
tungsten carbide Wolframkarbid *nt*
tungsten high-speed steel Wolframschnellstahl *m*
tungsten spatter Wolframspritzer *m*
tungsten-carbide face milling cutter Wolframkarbidmesserkopf *m*
tungsten-carbide insert Wolframkarbideinsatz *m*
tungsten-carbide tipped blade Wolframkarbid bestücktes Messer *nt*
T-union T-Stutzen *m*
tunnel Tunnel *m*
tunnel sprue with restricted gate Tunnelanguss *m* mit Punktanschnitt
tup Fallhammer *m*, Stoßkörper *m*
turbidimetric titration Trübungstitration *f*

turbidity number Trübungszahl f
turbidity titration number Trübungstitrationszahl f
turbine Turbine f
turbo-vacuum pump Turbovakuumpumpe f
turbulator Turbulator m
turbulent air circulation Luftdurchwirbelung f
turn Drehbewegung f
turn 1. schwenken, einschlagen, kurbeln; Wende f, Kurve f, Umdrehung f, Windung f **2.** *(zurück)* Wendung f; wenden **3.** *(herum)* rotieren, umlaufen, drehen **4.** Seilwindung f
turn a neck into eindrehen
turn a shoulder ansatzdrehen
turn away abweisen, abweichen
turn counter-clockwise linksdrehen
turn cylinder surfaces langdrehen
turn down a project ein Projekt ablehnen
turn inside diameters ausdrehen
turn longitudinal langdrehen
turn-milling Drehfräsen nt
turn off 1. *(Schalter)* ausschalten, abschalten **2.** *(drehen)* abdrehen
turn off centre außermittig drehen
turn off rate Abschmelzgeschwindigkeit f
turn on 1. fertigen **2.** *(Schalter)* einschalten, anschalten
turn on the spot drehen auf der Stelle, wenden auf der Stelle
turn out ausweichen, ausstoßen
turn outside diameter außenüberdrehen
turn over wenden, umwenden, umdrehen, umstürzen, umkippen
turn to übergehen
turn to a shoulder absatzdrehen
turn true zentrisch drehen
turn with single-point tool ausdrehen
turnable Drehteller m
turnable lathe Drehmaschine f mit Drehscheibe
turnabout screw Kehrgewindespindel f
turnaround time Umlaufzeit f, Durchlaufzeit f
turn-around time Durchlaufzeit f

turnbuckle Kettenspanner m
turned part Drehteil nt
turned pattern Drehbild nt
turned through versetzt um
turning 1. Drehung f, Drehen nt **2.** Kurvenfahrt f **3.** *(Material; Fertigungstechnik)* Abdrehung f, Abdrehen nt
turning and boring lathe Dreh- und Bohrmaschine f
turning and milling centre Dreh- und Fräszentrum nt
turning attachment Dreheinrichtung f, Drehvorrichtung f
turning between centres Drehen nt zwischen Spitzen
turning capacity Drehleistung f
turning centre Drehspitze f, Drehzentrum nt, Körnerspitze f
turning diameter Drehdurchmesser m, Schwingdurchmesser m
turning drive Drehantrieb m
turning height over table Drehhöhe f über Planscheibe
turning inside diameter Ausdrehung f, Innendrehen nt
turning internal surfaces Innendrehen nt
turning joint Scharnier nt
turning machine Drehbank f, Drehmaschine f
turning necks Nutendrehen nt
turning operation Dreharbeit f
turning pair Scharnier nt
turning passage Wendedurchlass m
turning procedure Wendevorgang m
turning radius Lenkwinkel m, Wendekreis m
turning to a shoulder Absatzdrehen nt
turning tool Drehwerkzeug nt, Abdrehwerkzeug nt, Drehmeißel m, Drehstahl m
turning tool holder Drehmeißelhalter m
turning tool life Drehmeißelstandzeit f
turning tool mark Drehtiefe f
turning tool shank Drehmeißelschaft m
turning toolholder Drehmeißelhalter m

turning tools *pl* Drehwerkzeuge *ntpl*
turning travel Drehweg *m*
turning with drip stop control Anschlagdrehen *nt*
turning work Dreharbeit *f*
turning-in turret lathe Revolverdrehen *nt*
turnings Span *m*, Drehspäne *mpl*
turn-off delay Ausschaltverzögerung *f*
turnover 1. Wendevorgang *m*, Wenden *nt*, Umwenden *nt* 2. (Marketing) Umschlag *m*, Umsatz *m*
turnover capacity Umschlagsleistung *f*
turnover device Wender *m*, Wendevorrichtung *f*
turnover performance Umschlagsleistung *f*
turnover ratios Umschlagskennzahlen *fpl*
turnover unit Wendemaschine *f*
turn-slide crank Drehschubkurbel *f*
turnstile Drehkreuz *nt*
turntable Drehtisch *m*, Drehschemel *m*
turntable axle Drehschemelachse *f*
turntable truck Wagen *m* mit Drehschemel
turret 1. *(Werkzeug)* Revolver *m*, Revolverkopf *m* 2. Dachaufbau *m*
turret automatic Revolverautomat *m*
turret bushing Spannhülse *f*
turret cam Revolverkurve *f*
turret control Revolverkopfsteuerung *f*
turret head Revolverkopf *m*
turret indexing Revolverkopfschalten *m*
turret lathe Revolverdrehmaschine *f*, Drehmaschine *f* mit Sattelrevolver
turret lathe for bar work Revolverdrehmaschine *f* für Stangenarbeiten
turret lathe for facing operations Planrevolverdrehmaschine *f*, Trommelrevolverdrehmaschine *f*
turret lathe work Revolverdreharbeit *f*
turret position Revolverkopfstellung *f*
turret screw machine Revolverdrehmaschine *f*
turret segment lever Revolversegmenthebel *m*
turret slide Revolverschlitten *m*
turret spindle Revolverachse *f*

turret storage Revolverspeicher *m*
turret tailstock Trommelreitstock *m*
turret truck Hochregalstapler *m*
turret turning Revolverdrehen *nt*
turret-type chucking automatic Futterrevolverautomat *m*
twelve disk pack Zwölfplattenstapel *m*
twelve o'clock position Zwölf-Uhr-Lage *f*
twelve-point bolt Zwölfkantschraube *f*
twelve-point bolt with waisted shank Zwölfkantdehnschraube *f*
twelve-point nut Zwölfkantmutter *f*
twelve-point nut with collar Zwölfkantmutter *m* mit Bund
twice zweifach
twin zweifach, Zwillings ..., Doppel ...,
twin cutter bevel gear generator Zweimeißelkegelradhobelmaschine *f*
twin depth doppeltief
twin electrode wheel machine Doppelrollenmaschine *f*
twin tool generating bevel gear planer Zweimeißelkegelradhobelmaschine *f*
twin tyres Zwillingsreifen *mpl*
twin wheel castor Doppelrolle *f*
twin wheel *pl* Doppelrad *nt*, Zwillingsrad *nt*
twin wheel stub axle mounting Doppelradeinbau *m* auf Achsstummel
twine umschlingen
twin-head gear cutting machine Zwillingszahnradfräsmaschine *f*
twin-mast machine Zweisäulengerät *nt*
twin-screw knee-and-column type milling machine Konsolfräsmaschine *f* mit zwei Verstellspindeln
twin-tool planer Zweimeißelhobelmaschine *f*
twin-wheel castor with a pivoting axle Rolle *f* mit Pendelachse
twist verdrillen, drillen, umschlingen, verdrehen, verflechten, verwinden, verspannen; Drehung *f*, Verwindung *f*, Drall *m*
twist drill Spiralbohrer *m*, Bohrer *m*
twist lock Bolzen *m*, Riegelbolzen *m*, Verriegelung *f*

twist together verspleißen
twist warp verdrehen
twistable verwindungsfähig
twist-die closing machine Drillverschließmaschine *f*
twisted verdrillt
twisted cap Schraubverschluss *m*
twisted pair verdrillte Doppelleitung *f*, Zweidrahtleitung *f*
twisting 1. Verwindung *f*, Verdrehung *f*, Verdrillung *f*, Verspannung *f* 2. *(mit rotierender Werkzeugbewegung)* Verdrehen *nt*
twisting angle Verdrehungswinkel *m*
twisting force Verdrehungskraft *f*
twisting moment Verdrehmoment *nt*
twisting play Verdrehspiel *nt*
twisting strain Verdrehungsbeanspruchung *f*
two chisel roll plane Zweimeißelwälzhobeln
two chisel technique Zweimeißelverfahren *nt*
two-axle zweiachsig
two-ball measurement Zweikugelmaß *nt*
two-bank radiator zweireihiger Heizkörper *m*
two-beam compensation method Zweistrahlkompensationsverfahren *nt*
two-bin principle Zweibehälterprinzip *nt*
two-column vertical broaching machine Zweiständersenkrechträummaschine *f*
two-component coating Zweikomponentenbeschichtung *f*
two-component synthetic resin sealant Zweikomponentenkunstharzlack *m*
two-core zweiadrig
two-dimensional zweidimensional, flächig
two-dimensional defects flächige Fehler *m*
two-dimensional heat dissipation zweidimensionale Wärmeableitung *f*
two-dimensional normal distribution zweidimensionale Normalverteilung *f*

two-flank engagement Zweiflankeneingriff *m*
two-flank total composite error test Zweiflankenwälzprüfung *f*
two-flank working distance Zweiflankenwälzabstand *m*
two-flank working error Zweiflankenwälzsprung *m*
two-flank working test Zweiflankenwälzprüfung *f*
two-flank working variation Zweiflankenwälzabweichung *f*
twofold zweifach
two-hand control Zweihandbedienung *f*, Zweihandschaltung *f*
two-hand control device Zweihandschaltung *f*, Zweihandsteuergerät *nt*
two-hand control unit *(als Vorrichtung)* Zweihandschaltung *f*
two-hand operation Zweihandbedienung *f*
two-hand release Zweihandauslösung *f*
two-hand safety control Zweihandsteuerung *f*
two-high mill Duowalzwerk *nt*
two-high reversing mill Duoreversierwalzwer *nt*
two-high stand Duogerüst *nt*, Duowalzgerüst *nt*
two-jaw chuck Zweibackenfutter *nt*
two-lane zweigassig
two-layer Zweischicht *f*
two-layer slab Zweischichtplatte *f*
two-level action Zweipunktverhalten *nt*
two-level action control Zweipunktregelung *f*
two-level action controlling system Zweipunktregeleinrichtung *f*
two-level action element Zeitpunktglied *nt*
two-level radiator zweilagiger Heizkörper *m*
two-level signal Zweipunktsignal *nt*
two-line principle of operation Zweileitungssystem *nt*
two-mast machine Zweisäulengerät *nt*
two-operation calculator Zweispeziesrechenmaschine *f*

two-phase zweiphasig
two-pin *(el. Stecker)* zweipolig
two-point „Not Go" gauge Zweipunktausschusslehre *f*
two-point contact Zweipunktberührung *f*
two-point measurement Zweipunktmessung *f*
two-point suspension Zweipunktaufhängung *f*
two-pole zweipolig; Zweipol *m*
two-reel pallet stretch wrapper Doppelrollenpalettenstretchwickler *m*
two-roller measurement Zweirollenmaß *nt*
two-row zweireihig
two-start bolt thread zweigängiges Bolzengewinde *nt*
two-shift operation Zweischichtbetrieb *m*
two-sided zweiseitig
two-skid contact system Pendeltastsystem *nt*
two-speed gear drive Zweiganggetriebe *nt*
two-speed sliding gear drive Zweigangschieberadgetriebe *nt*
two-spindle attachment Zweispindelkopf *m*
two-spindle bench-type milling machine Zweispindelplanfräsmaschine *f*
two-spindle die sinking machine Doppelspindelgesenkfräsmaschine *f*
two-spindle drum milling machine zweispindelige Trommelfräsmaschine *f*
two-spindle fixed-bed type milling machine Zweispindelplanfräsmaschine *f*
two-spindle keyway copying miller Zweispindellangnutenkopierfräsmaschine *f*
two-spindle miller Doppelfräsmaschine *f*, Fräsmaschine *f* mit Doppelfrässpindel
two-spindle milling machine Zweispindelfräsmaschine *f*
two-spindle profile milling machine Zweispindelprofilfräsmaschine *f*
two-spindle rotary drum miller Zweispindeltrommelfräsmaschine *f*
two-stage gear transmission zweistufiges Getriebe *nt*
two-start thread doppelgängiges Gewinde *nt*
two-start trapezoidal screw thread with clearance zweigängiges Trapezgewinde *nt* mit Spiel
two-state zweiphasig
two-state interlocking Zweiphasenverriegelung *f*, zweiphasenverriegelt
two-step action controller Zweipunkt-Regler *m*
two-tool planer Zweimeißelhobelmaschine *f*
two-track zweispurig
two-track bridge device Zweispurbrückengerät *nt*
two-way boring machine Zweiwegebohrmaschine *f*
two-way drilling machine Zweiwegebohrmaschine *f*
two-way fork clamper Drehgabelklammer *f*
two-way machine Zweiwegemaschine *f*
two-way pallet Zweiwegepalette *f*
two-way planing Vor- und Rücklaufhobeln *nt*
two-way radio Funk *m*
two-way table Zweiwegtafel *f*
two-way traffic Gegenverkehr *m*
two-way valve dependent on lubrication cycle Taktschaltventil *nt*
two-week zweiwöchig
two-wheel lapping machine Zweischeibenläppmaschine *f*
two-width code Zweibreitencode *m*
tying Umschnürung *f*, Binden *nt*
type Art *f*, Ausführung *f*, Ausführungsart *f*, Baumuster *nt*, Bauart *f*, Bauausführung *f*, Typ *m*, Modell *nt*, Sorte *f*
type data sheet Typenblatt *nt*
type of chip Spanart *f*
type of code Codierungsart *f*
type of control Lenkungsart *f*
type of failure Versagensart *f*
type of fixture Befestigungsart *f*
type of function Funktionsart *f*
type of grain Korntyp *m*

type of load Lastart *f*
type of memory Speichertyp *m*
type of order Auftragsart *f*
type of packaging Verpackungsart *f*
type of protection Schutzart *f*
type of stopping Anschlagart *f*
type of stressing Beanspruchungsart *f*
type of system Anlagentyp *m*
type of treatment Behandlungsart *f*
type of wear Verschleißform *f*
type re-testing Typnachprüfung *f*
type rolling Scheibenwalzen *nt*
type series Baureihe *f*
type test Typprüfung *f*
type-assigned moulding material typisierte Formmasse *f*
typeface Schriftart *f*
types of cutting material Schneidstoffarten *fpl*
type-tested boiler baumusterungsgeprüfter Kessel *m*
type-tested model typgeprüfte Ausführung *f*
type-tested pattern typgeprüfte Ausführung *f*
typewriter spacing Schreibmaschinenzeilenhöhe *f*
typical application Arbeitsbeispiel *nt*
tyre bereifen; Bereifung *f*, Reifen *m*
tyre ballast Reifenballast *m*
tyre inflation pressure Reifendruck *m*
tyre racking Reifenregal *nt*
tyre width Reifenbreite *f*

U u

U-bend expansion joint U-Bogen-Ausgleicher *m*
U-bolt grip Schraubklemmung *f*
U-bolt pipe hanger Rundstahlbügel *m*
ultimate elongation Bruchdehnung *f*
ultimate limit switch Notendschalter *m*
ultimate load Traglast *f*, Grenzlast *f*
ultrasonic Ultraschall *m*
ultrasonic drill Ultraschallbohrer *m*
ultrasonic drilling Ultraschallbohren *nt*
ultrasonic drilling machine Ultraschallbohrmaschine *f*
ultra-sonic hot welding Ultraschallwarmschweißen *nt*
ultrasonic indication Ultraschallanzeige *f*
ultrasonic joint lapping Ultraschallstoßläppen *nt*
ultrasonic machining Ultraschallzerspanung *f*
ultrasonic pulse Ultraschallimpuls *m*
ultrasonic pulse-echo instrument Ultraschallimpulsechogerät *nt*
ultrasonic swing lapping USM (Ultraschallschwingläppen) *nt*
ultrasonic testing Überschallprüfung *f*
ultrasonic testing instrument Ultraschallprüfgerät *nt*
ultra-violet radiation UV-Strahlung *f*
ultra-violet radiation source Ultraviolettstrahler *m*
ultra-violet scattered light Ultraviolettstreulicht *nt*
UNA Entadressierung *f*
unacceptable unzulässig
unacknowledged unquittiert
unaddress Entadressierung *f*
unadjusted unangepasst
unaged ungealtert
unaged test specimen ungealterte Probe *f*
unaided eye bloßes Auge *nt*
unalloyed (plain) steel unlegierter Stahl *m*
unaltered unverändert
unanimous übereinstimmend
unarranged fibres *pl* ungeordnete Fasern *fpl*
unassisted nicht unterstützt
unattended unbeaufsichtigt
unattenuated radiation ungeschwächte Strahlung *f*
unauthorized use unbefugtes Benutzen *nt*
unauthorized nicht genehmigt, unbefugt
unauthorized access unbefugtes Betreten *nt*
unavoidable danger unvermeidbare Gefahr *f*
unbalance Unwucht *f*
unbalanced nicht ausgewuchtet, unausgeglichen
unbeaten raw material ungemahlener Rohstoff *m*
unbiased estimator erwartungstreue Schätzfunktion *f*
unbolt abschrauben, losschrauben
unbuffered ungepuffert
unburied pipeline frei verlegte Rohrleitung *f*
unburned unverbrannt
unburnt gas unverbranntes Gas *nt*
uncertain unsicher
uncertainty Unsicherheit *f*
uncertainty factor Unsicherheitsfaktor *m*
uncertainty margin Unsicherheitsspanne *f*
uncertainty of measurement Messunsicherheit *f*, Ergebnisunsicherheit *f*
unchangeable unveränderbar
unchanged unverändert
unclamp lösen, entriegeln, ausspannen, entspannen, abspannen
unclamping Ausspannen *nt*
unclutch entkuppeln, auskuppeln, ausrücken
unclutching Auskuppeln *nt*
uncoated unbeschichtet
uncoated bituminous sheeting

nackte Bitumenbahn *f*
uncoated surface unbeschichtete Oberfläche *f*
uncoil (open) *(öffnen)* abrollen, aufrollen
uncoil violently aufspringen
uncompacted soil unverdichteter Boden *m*
unconditional unbedingt
unconditional jump unbedingter Sprung *m*
unconnected nicht zusammenhängend
unconsidered unberücksichtigt
uncontrolled unkontrolliert, ungeregelt
uncorrected tooth system Nullverzahnung *f*
uncorrugated spring washer ungewellte Federscheibe *f*
uncouple auskuppeln, abkuppeln, entkoppeln
uncoupling Auskuppeln *nt*
uncover aufdecken
uncovered offen
uncritical unkritisch
undenaturated unvergällt
under unter
under box Unterkasten *m*
under cast Unterkasten *m*
under dynamic conditions im dynamischen Zustand
under load unter Last
under normal service conditions betriebsmäßig
under roof überdacht
under-burning stove Unterbrandofen *m*
underclearance Unterfahrhöhe *f*
underclearance method Unterfahrtechnik *f*
undercut freiarbeiten, hinterstechen, unterschneiden; Unterschneidung *f*, gewollter Unterschnitt *m*, Untergriff *m*
undercut angle Spanwinkel *m*
undercutting Unterschneiden *nt*
under-cutting Unterspülung *f*
underdress roh
underfill Nahtunterschreitung *f*
under-fill ungenügende Fugenfüllung *f*
underfloor Unterflur ...
underfloor chain conveyor Unterflurkettenförderer *m*
underfloor chain-pulled conveyor Unterflurschleppkettenförderer *m*
underfloor conveying system Unterflurförderanlage *f*
underfloor drag conveyor Unterflurschleppförderer *m*
underfloor service Unterbodeneinrichtung *f*
undergrinding Unterschleifung *f*
underground Untergrund *m*
underground tubular gasholder unterirdischer Röhrengasbehälter *m*
underlay unterlegen, Untergrund *m*
underload Teillast *f*
underload range Teillastbereich *m*
underneath unten, unterhalb
underpin unterfahren
underpressure Unterdruck *m*
underpressure indicator Unterdruckanzeige *f*
underrate zu niedrig auslegen
under-run unterschreiten
under-rusting Unterrostung *f*
undershoot Eckenrunden *nt*
underside Unterseite *f*, Sohle *f*
undersize Untermaß *nt*
undertighten zu locker anziehen
undervoltage Unterspannung *f*
undesirable unerwünscht
undesired wetting of base metal by filler metal Lotausbreitungsfehler *m*
undimensioned unbemaßt
undirected ungerichtet
undished spring washer ungewölbte Federscheibe *f*
undissolved material ungelöstes Material *nt*
undo lösen, losschrauben, aufmachen
undue unzulässig, unangemessen
undulate schwanken
undulation Schwankung *f*
undulatory rillig
unequal ungleich
unequal angularity Ungleichwinkligkeit *f*, Abweichung *f* von der Gleichwinkligkeit
unequal leg length Ungleichschenkligkeit *f*
unequal period ungleiche Zeit *f*

unequal spacing ungleiches Teilen *nt*
unequivocal eindeutig
unequivocality Eindeutigkeit *f*
uneven ungerade, uneben, ungleichmäßig, rau
unevenness Unebenheit *f*, Rauhigkeit *f*, Abweichung *f* von der Ebene
unexpected unerwartet
unexposed unbelichtet
unextended urea resin ungestrecktes Harnstoffharz *nt*
unfavourable nachteilig, ungünstig
unfeasible undurchführbar
unfinished unbearbeitet, nicht fertig bearbeitet, nicht geschlichtet
unfinished part Rohteil *nt*
unfinished part design Rohteilformgebung *f*
unfinished part length Rohteillänge *f*
unfinished part selection Rohteilauswahl *f*
unfinished part serial number Rohteilsachnummer *f*
unfit ungeeignet
unfortified unbefestigt
ungalvanized unverzinkt
unglazed ceramic tile unglasierte Fliese *f*
ungrease entfetten
unguarded ungeschützt
unguided nicht geführt
unhampered ungehindert
unharmful unschädlich
unhealthy ungesund
uniaxial compression load einachsige Druckbeanspruchung *f*
uniaxial stress condition einachsiger Spannungszustand *m*
uniaxial tensile loading einachsige Beanspruchung *f* auf Zug
uniaxial-fibre-reinforced einachsig faserverstärkt
uniaxial-fibre-reinforced plastics einachsig faserverstärkter Kunststoff *m*
unidirectional unidirektional
unidirectional in einer Richtung
unification Vereinheitlichung *f*
unified vereinheitlicht
unified screw thread UST-Gewinde *nt*
uniform gleichmäßig, gleichförmig, einheitlich
uniform corrosion Flächenkorrosion *f*
uniform distribution Gleichverteilung *f*
uniform indexing Durchführung *f* gleicher Teilungen
uniform surface corrosion gleichmäßige Flächenkorrosion *f*
unify vereinheitlichen
unilateral einseitig
unimodal unimodal
unimodal distribution unimodale Verteilung *f*
unimpeded ungehindert
unimproved unbefestigt
unimproved natural terrain unbefestigter Boden
unintended unbeabsichtigt
unintentional unbeabsichtigt
unintentional switching versehentliches Schalten *nt*
uninterrupted ununterbrochen
uninterruptible unterbrechungsfrei, ununterbrechbar
uninterruptible lower supply unterbrechungsfreie Stromversorgung *f*
union Anschlussstück *nt*
union nut Überwurfmutter *f*
union nut with compression ring and olive Überwurfmutter *f* mit Druckring und Schneidring
union socket Verbindungsmuffe *f*
unit 1. Stück *nt*, Einheit *f* **2.** *(Gerät, Bauteil)* Apparat *m*, Aggregat *nt*
unit assembly system Baukastensystem *nt*
unit construction system Baukastensystem *nt*
unit cost per piece Stückkosten *pl*
unit costs *pl* Standardkosten *fpl*
unit for counting Zähleinheit *f*
unit load Stückgut *nt*, Ladeeinheit *f*
unit load flow Stückgutstrom *m*
unit load merge point Stückgutsammelstation *f*
unit load press Stückgutandrücker *m*
unit load process Stückgutprozess *m*
unit load pusher Stückgutandrücker *m*
unit load safe-guarding Ladeeinheitensicherung *f*

unit narrow aisle storage and retrieval unit for high bay warehouse Elektroschmalganghochregalstapler *m*
unit of bulk material Massenguteinheit *f*
unit of continuous material Aufmachungseinheit *f*, Endlosguteinheit *f*
unit of length Längeneinheit *f*
unit of organization Organisationseinheit *f*
unit of time Zeiteinheit *f*
unit of volume Mengeneinheit *f*
unit price Stückpreis *m*
unit production Einzelfertigung *f*
unit time Zeiteinheit *f*
unite verbinden, vereinigen
unitize vereinheitlichen
unity Eins *f*
unity-based division Einerteilung *f*
univariate eindimensional
universal universal
universal angular milling attachment Universalwinkelfräskopf
universal asynchronous receiver/transmitter (UART) universeller asynchroner Sende-/Empfangsbaustein *m*
universal boring and milling machine Universalbohr- und Fräsmaschine *f*
universal boring drilling and milling machine with swivelling spindle head and rotary column Universalbohr- und Fräsmaschine *f* mit schwenkbarem Spindelkasten und drehbarem Ständer
universal boring tool Universalbohrmeißel *m*
universal centre lathe Universalspitzendrehmaschine *f*
universal chuck Universalfutter *nt*
universal curve guidance allgemeine Kurvenführung *f*
universal cutter and tool grinding machine Universalwerkzeugschleifmaschine *f*
universal cutter head Universalfräskopf *m*
universal cylindrical grinder Universalrundschleifmaschine *f*
universal dividing head Universalteilkopf *m*
universal double duplex milling machine Universalfräsmaschine *f* mit zwei Paaren einander gegenüberstehender Frässpindelköpfe
universal engraving and duplicating machine Universalgravier- und Nachformfräsmaschine *f*
universal gear scroll chuck Universalfutter *nt*
universal generator Alleskornentwickler *m*
universal gripper Allzweckgreifer *m*
universal head milling machine Fräsmaschine *f* mit schwenkbarem Spindelkopf, Fräsmaschine *f* mit Universalspindelkopf
universal head-milling attachment Universalfräsvorrichtung *f*
universal high speed milling machine Universalschnellfräsmaschine *f*
universal hobbing head Universalfräskopf *m*
universal index centre Universalteilgerät *nt*
universal joint Kardangelenk *nt*
universal knee-and-column type milling machine Universalfräsmaschine *f*, Universalkonsolfräsmaschine *f*, Universalständerfräsmaschine *f*
universal lapping machine Universalläppmaschine *f*
universal lathe Universaldrehmaschine *f*, Mehrzweckdrehmaschine *f*
universal letter engraving machine Universalschriftengravierfräsmaschine *f*
universal machine Universalmaschine *f*
universal miller Universalfräsmaschine *f*, Universalkonsolfräsmaschine *f*
universal milling attachment Universalfrässupport *m*
universal milling head Universalfräskopf *m*
universal milling machine Universalfräsmaschine *f*, Universalkonsolfräsmaschine *f*
universal motor Universalmotor *m*
universal pantograph die-sinker Uni-

versalpantographgesenkfräsmaschine *f*
universal pantograph die-sinking machine Universalnachformfräsmaschine *f*, Universalpantographgesenkfräsmaschine *f*
universal pantograph machine Universalpantographgesenkfräsmaschine *f*
universal planer for two-way cutting Universalhobelmaschine *f*
universal precision boring machine Universalfeinbohrwerk *nt*
universal ram-type turret lathe Universalsattelrevolverdrehmaschine *f*
universal resource locator (URL) einheitlicher Ressourcenfinder *m*
universal rivet joint Universalnietverbindung *f*
universal serial bus (USB) universeller serieller Bus *m*
universal shaft Gelenkwelle *f*
universal spiral indexing attachment *(für Spiralfräsarbeiten)* Universalfräsvorrichtung *f*
universal thread milling attachment Universalgewindefräsmaschine *f*
universal tool milling and boring machine Universalwerkzeugfräs- und -bohrmaschine *f*
universal tool milling machine Universalwerkzeugfräsmaschine *f*
universal tool milling machine and die-sinker Universalwerkzeug- und -gesenkfräsmaschine *f*
universally tilting table Tisch *m*
universal-type knee-and-column milling machine Universalkonsolfräsmaschine *f*
universal-type spindle head Universalfrässupport *m*
unjam lüften
unjam time Lüftzeit *f*
unkilled steel unberuhigter Stahl *m*
unknotted specimen ungeknotete Probe *f*
unladen unbeladen, leer
unladen mass Leergewicht *nt*
unladen trip Leerfahrt *f*
unladen trip command Leerfahrauftrag *m*
unladen weight Eigengewicht *nt*

unlaminated plastics foil unkaschierte Kunststofffolie *f*
unlatch lösen, ausklinken
unlevel uneben, ungerade
unlike material nicht artgleicher Werkstoff *m*
unlimited unbegrenzt
unload 1. *(Werkstück aus Futter)* abspannen, ausspannen, **2.** abführen, abnehmen entlasten, entschicken, abladen, entladen, abgeben
unload and reload umladen
unload goods Ware entladen
unloaded unbelastet
unloaded gear transmission unbelastetes Getriebe *nt*
unloaded state unbelasteter Zustand *m*
unloading Abheben *f*, Ausspannen *f*, Entlastung *nt*, Entladung *f*, Entschickung *f*, Entnahme *f*, Abspannen *nt*, Entladen *nt*, Abgeben *nt*
unloading Abnehmen *nt* des Werkstücks
unloading box Entladebehälter *m*
unloading by gravity Schwerkraftentleerung *f*
unloading chute Abführrinne *f*
unloading container Entladebehälter *m*
unloading device Entladeeinrichtung *f*
unloading energy Entladeenergie *f*
unloading goods Ware entladen (EDV)
unloading of layers Lagenentnahme *f*
unloading passage Ausgaberinne *f*
unloading robot Entnahmeroboter *m*
unloading time Entlastungsdauer *f*
unlock entsperren, entriegeln, öffnen, ausklinken, ausspannen
unlocking Entriegelung *f*, Entsperren *nt*, Ausklinken *nt*
unlocking device Entriegelungseinrichtung *f*
unmachinable unzerspanbar
unmachined unbearbeitet
unmachined part calliper Rohteildicke
unmachined work unbearbeitetes Werkstück *nt*
unmoulded plastics ungeformter Kunststoff *m*

unnecessary unnötig
unobstructed 1. *(versperren, behindern)* licht, ungehindert **2.** *(Abrieb, Reibung)* reibungsfrei
unobstructed chip disposal glatter Spanabfluss *m*
unobstructed section profile Lichtraumprofil *nt*
unobtrusive defect unauffälliger Fehler *m*
unobtrusive scratch unauffälliger Kratzer *m*
unordered ungeordnet
unpack auspacken, entpaketieren
unpacked ungepackt, unverpackt
unpacking Entpaketieren *nt*
unpacking machine Auspackmaschine *f*
unpacking station Auspackstation *f*
unpaired ungepaart
unplasticized film weichmacherfreie Folie *f*
unplasticized moulding material weichmacherfreie Formmasse *f*
unplasticized plastics nicht weichgemachter Kunststoff *m*, weichmacherfreier Kunststoff *m*
unplasticized polyvinyl chloride weichmacherfreies Polyvinylchlorid *nt*, PVC *nt* hart
unplasticized PVC moulding material weichmacherfreie PVC-Formmasse *f*
unplug 1. *(allg.)* ziehen **2.** *(el.)* Stecker ziehen
unpressurized storage drucklose Lagerung *f*
unpressurized tank druckloser Behälter *m*
unprocessed starting material unverarbeitetes Ausgangsmaterial *nt*
unproductive time Nebenzeit *f*, Verlustzeit *f*
unprotected ungeschützt
unquote aufheben
unreasonable unverhältnismäßig
unreel abrollen
unregulated ungeregelt
unrelieved nicht hinterschliffen, ohne Freiwinkel
unrelieved tooth tips *pl* ungekürzte Zahnköpfe *mpl*
unrendered unverputzt
unrequested unaufgefordert
unrestrained heat ungebändigte Wärme *f*
unrestricted uneingeschränkt
unrestricted steering nicht zwangsgesteuert
unrestricted travelling freies Fahren *nt*
unroll (öffnen) abrollen, aufrollen
unrust entrosten
unsaponifiable matter nicht verseifbarer Stoff *m*
unsaturated ungesättigte Verbindung *f*
unsaturated polyester resin ungesättigtes Polyesterharz *nt*
unscramble ausrichten (an)
unscrambler Ausrichtmaschine *f*
unscreened pulp unsortierte Zellstoffe *f*
unscrew lösen, abschrauben, losschrauben
unscrewable lösbar
unscrewing torque Abschraubmoment *nt*
unsealed radioactive material offener radioaktiver Stoff *m*
unsecured unbefestigt, ungesichert
unsecured butt joint ungesicherte Stoßfuge *f*
unserviceability Betriebsunbrauchbarkeit *f*
unsheared oil ungeschertes Öl *nt*
unshielded flame offene Flamme *f*
unsized cellulose fibres ungeleimte Cellulosefasern *fpl*
unskilled ungelernt
unskilled people Laien *mpl*
unskilled person Laie *m*
unsolicited unaufgefordert
unsplintered edge nicht gesplitterte Kante *f*
unsprung ungefedert
unsprung weight ungefederte Massen *pl*
unstable instabil, unstabil, unbeständig, unsicher, labil
unstable metal cutting instabile Zerspanung *f*

unstack entstapeln
unstacker Entstapler *m*, Entstapelungsmaschine *f*
unstacking Entstapeln *nt*
unsteady schwankend
unstressed unbelastet, entspannt
unstretched condition ungedehnter Zustand *m*
unsuitable unzweckmäßig, ungeeignet
unsulphonated unsulfonierbar
unsupported freitragend, trägerlos
unsupported length of column freie Knicklänge *f*
unthreaded portion gewindefreier Teil *m*
unthreaded ohne Gewinde *nt*
unthreaded stud Zylinderstift *m*
untie lösen, losbinden
untier (batch) 1. *(Stoß)* entstapeln 2. *(außerhalb lagern)* auslagern 3. *(Teile aufheben)* aufnehmen
untiering Auslagern *nt*
untight undicht
until bis
until breaking starts bis Bremsbeginn
until stocks are exhausted solange Vorrat reicht
untin entzinnen
untoleranced dimension Freimaß *nt*, untoleriertes Maß *nt*
untoleranced dimensions *pl* Maße *ntpl* ohne Toleranzangaben
untoleranced size untoleriertes Maß *nt*
untrained ungeschult
untreated unbehandelt
untreated sheet of resin-bonded densified laminated wood unbearbeitete Tafel *f* aus Kunstharzpressholz
untrimmed sheet unbeschnittenes Blatt *nt*
untrue unrund, ungenau
untrue running Unrundlauf *m*; unrund laufend
unturned welding flange Vorschweißbördel
untwist entwirren
untwisting method Aufdrehverfahren *nt*
unused unverbraucht
unused oil Neuöl *nt*

unvaried unverändert
unwearable unverschleißbar
unweighted unbewertet
unwieldy sperrig
unwind abrollen
unwired unbeschaltet
unwrap auspacken
unwrapping machine Auspackmaschine *f*
up auf, nach oben, hinauf, bergauf
up-and-down method Eingabelungsverfahren *nt*
up-and-down movement Auf- und Abbewegung *f*
up grinding Gegenlaufschleifen *nt*
up to bis zu
up to and including bis einschließlich
up-to-date aktuell
up-to-dateness Aktualität *f*
up-cut grinding Gegenlaufschleifen *nt*
upcut milling Gegenlauffräsen *nt*
up-cut milling gleichläufiges Fräsen *nt*
upcutting Gegenlauffräsen *nt*
update aktualisieren, pflegen
updating Aktualisierung *f*, Pflege *f*
updraft Aufstrom *m*
upending Anstauchen *nt* ohne Gesenk
upending by the electric heating method Elektroanstauchen *nt*
up-feed method of milling Gegenlauffräsverfahren *nt*
upgradable nachrüstbar
upgrade 1. *(Erweiterung)* aufrüsten, erweitern; Aufrüstung *f*, Nachrüstung *f* 2. *(im Gelände)* Steigung *f*
upgrading of the potential Potentialveredlung *f*
uphill bergauf; Steigung *f*
uphill motion Steigungsfahrt *f*
uphill travel Steigungsfahrt *f*
upholding Einhaltung *f*
upkeep Instandhaltung *f*
upkeep-servicing Wartung *f*
up-milling Gegenlauffräsen *nt*
upon bei
upon closing of the contract bei Vertragsabschluss
upon request auf Anforderung, auf Anfrage
upper oberer/oberes

upper edge Oberkante *f*
upper end Kopf *m*
upper face Oberseite *f*, Lastauflagefläche *f*
upper face of the blade Lastauflagefläche *f*
upper guide rail obere Führungsschiene *f*
upper harmonic wave Oberteil *nt*
upper layer sample Oberschichtprobe *f*
upper light Oberlicht *nt*
upper limit Obergrenze *f*, obere Grenze *f*, Größtmaß *nt*
upper part oberer Teil *m*, Oberteil *nt*
upper position obere Endstellung *f*
upper rest obere Endstellung *f*
upper side band oberer Seitenbereich *m*
upper slide Oberschieber *m*, Oberschlitten *m*
upper storey floor Geschossdecke *f*
upper surface Oberseite *f*, Lastauflagefläche *f*
upper web of film Oberfolie *f*
uppermost oberste/r/s
supplier Versorger *m*
upright aufrecht; Ständer *m*, Säule *f*, Stütze *f*, Runge *f*, Pfosten *m*, Portalständer *m*, Gerüstteil *nt*
upright axis Ständerachse *f*, Steherachse *f*
upright conveyor Hochkantförderer *m*
upright drilling machine Ständerbohrmaschine *f*, Senkrechtbohrmaschine *f*
upright foot Steherfuß *m*
upright frame Ständerrahmen *m*
upright housing Ständer *m*
upright position Stand *m* (Stehen)
upright rack Ständerregal *nt*
upset 1. Störfall *m* 2. *(Pläne)* umstürzen, umkippen 3. *(techn. Verfahren)*
upset cold kaltstauchen
upset length loss Stauchlängenverlust *m*
upset ridge *(bei Rohren)* Stauchwulst *f*
upset weld Wulstnaht *f*
upset-forge anstauchen
upsetting Umkippen *nt*, Umstürzen *nt*, Anstauchen *nt*, Stauchen *nt*, Stauchung *f*
upsetting deformation Stauchung *f*
upsetting force Stauchkraft *f*
upsetting slide stroke Stauchschlittenhub *m*
upsetting without die Anstauchen *nt* ohne Gesenk
upsettings Stauchungen *fpl*
upshaping gripper Abformgreifer *m*
upside oberhalb
upstream 1. oberhalb, stromaufwärts 2. *(Baugruppen, z. B. Kupplungen)* vorgelagert, vorgeschaltet
upstroke Rückhub *m*
upturn umdrehen
upward buckling Abwinkeln *nt*
upward pressure on costs Kostendruck *m*
upward tilting hochklappbar
upwards hinauf, nach oben
urban atmosphere Stadtatmosphäre *f*
urea resin base Harnstoffbasis *f*
urea resin glue Harnstoffharzleim *m*
urethane rubber Urethankautschuk *m*
urgency Dringlichkeit *f*
urgent measure Sofortmaßnahme *f*
urgent order Eilbestellung *f*
urgent requirement Eilbedarf *m*
usable nutzbar, verwendbar
usable depth Nutztiefe *f*
usable flank nutzbare Flanke *f*
usable flank profile nutzbares Flankenprofil *nt*
usable floor area nutzbare Geschossfläche *f*
usable moment Nutzmoment *m*
usable pinion tip diameter Ritzelkopfnutzkreisdurchmesser *m*
usable root circle Fußnutzkreis *m*
usable root diameter Fußnutzkreisdurchmesser *m*, Nutzkreisdurchmesser *m*
usable tip circle Kopfnutzkreis *m*
usable tip diameter on pinion Kopfnutzkreisdurchmesser *m* am Ritzel
usage Verwendung *f*
use gebrauchen, verwenden, anwenden, benutzen, nutzen, einsetzen; Benutzung *f*, Nutzung *f*, Verwendung *f*, Einsatz *m*, Anwendung *f*, Gebrauch *m*

use criterion Einsatzkriterium *nt*
use of robots Robotereinsatz *m*
use up verbrauchen, aufbrauchen
used gebraucht
used emulsion Altemulsion *f*
used grease Altfett *nt*
used oil Altöl *nt*
useful nutzbringend, nutzbar, praktisch
useful area Nutzungsfläche *f*
useful heat output Nutzwärmeleistung *f*
useful information Nutzinformation *f*
useful life Nutzungszeit *f*, Nutzungsdauer *f*, Brauchbarkeitsdauer *f*, Standzeit *f*
useful load Gebrauchsbelastung *f*, Nutzlast *f*
useful process Nutzprozess *m*
useful radiation Nutzstrahlung *f*
useful radiation field on entering Nutzstrahleneintrittsfeld *nt*
useful radiation zone Nutzstrahlenbereich *m*
useful ray beam Nutzstrahlenbündel *nt*
useful thread length nutzbare Gewindelänge *f*
useful value analysis Nutzwertanalyse *f*
useful life Lebensdauer *f*
user Anwender *m*, Benutzer *m*, Nutzer *m*, Verwender *m*, Betreiber *m*
user data Anwenderdaten *pl*, Nutzdaten *pl*
user data capacity Nutzdatenkapazität *f*
user environment Benutzerumfeld *nt*

user facility Leistungsmerkmal *nt*
user interface Anwenderschnittstelle *f*, Benutzeroberfläche *f*
user memory Anwenderspeicher *m*
user program Anwenderprogramm *nt*
user program memory Anwenderprogrammspeicher *m*
user program procedure Kommandoprogramm *nt*
user programmer Anwendungsprogrammierer *m*
user prompting Benutzerführung *f*
user surface Anwenderoberfläche *f*
user system Anwendersystem *nt*
user task execution time Benutzertaskausführungszeit *f*
user's logbook Wartungsheft *nt*
user's manual Anwenderhandbuch *nt*
U-shaped U-förmig
U-shaped profile U-Profil *nt*
usual gebräuchlich, üblich
usually üblicherweise
utensil plug Gerätestecker *m*
utensils Gerätschaft *m*
utilisation Gebrauch *m*
utilise benutzen, ausnutzen
utility program Dienstprogramm *nt*
utilizable nutzbar
utilizable reservoir capacity nutzbarer Behälterinhalt *m*
utilization Nutzung *f*, Auslastung *f*
utilization of storage capacity Lagerauslastung *f*
utilize nutzen, verwenden, auslasten
U-tube Haarnadelrohr *nt*
U-turn Wenden *nt*, Wende *f*

V v

vacancy Stelle *f*, freie Stelle *f*
vacuum ansaugen, Vakuum *nt*
vacuum chamber Vakuumkammer *f*
vacuum chuck Saugluftspannfutter *nt*
vacuum conveyor Unterdruckförderer *m*
vacuum cup Vakuumsauger *m*, Saugschale *f*
vacuum filling machine Unterdruckfüllmaschine *f*
vacuum lifter Vakuumheber *m*
vacuum lifting beam Vakuumtraverse *f*
vacuum lifting frame Vakuumtraverse *f*
vacuum load carrying device Vakuumheber *m*
vacuum pad Vakuumsauger *m*
vacuum pre-compressing Vakuumvorverdichten *nt*
vacuum pressure gauge Unterdruckmesser *m*
vacuum pump Vakuumpumpe *f*
vacuum form process Vakuumformverfahren *nt*
valence band Valenzband *nt*
valence-electron Valenzelektron *nt*
valence-electron concentration Valenzelektronenkonzentration *f*
valid gültig
validate validieren
validation Validierung *f*
validity Gültigkeit *f*
validity check Plausibilitätskontrolle *f*, Plausibilitätstest *m*
value 1. *(Messtechnik)* dimensionsloses Maß *nt*, Größe *f* **2.** *(math.)* Wert abgleichen
value added Wertschöpfung *f*
value added tax (VAT) Mehrwertsteuer *f*
value band Werteverlauf *m*
value of a characteristic Merkmalswert *m*
value of a statistic Schätzwert *m*, Kennwert *m*
value pattern Werteverlauf *m*
value-added activities Wertschöpfungsaktivitäten *fpl*
value-added chain Wertschöpfungskette *f*
value-change Werteänderung *f*
values Werte *pl*
valve Ventil *nt*, Schieber *m*
valve base electronics Elektronik *f* der Ventilbasis
valve body Armaturengehäuse *nt*
valve collar Schieberanschlussstück *nt*
valve control Ventilsteuerung *f*
valve seat grinder Ventilschleifmaschine *f*
valve thread Ventilgewinde *nt*
advance length Vorlaufstrecke *f*
vane Flügel *m*
vane pump Flügelpumpe *f*, Flügelzellenpumpe *f*
vane cell pump Flügelzellenpumpe *f*
vane-type anemometer Flügelradanemometer *nt*
vapour Dampf *m*
vaporize verdunsten, verdunsten lassen
vaporizing burner Verdampfungsbrenner *m*
vapour Schwade *f*, Dampfschwaden *m*
vapour blast liquid honing Strahlläppen *nt*
vapour deposition Bedampfen *nt*
vapour space Gasraum *m*
vapour withdrawal gasförmige Entnahme *f*
variability Variabilität *f*, Veränderlichkeit *f*, Schwankung *f*, Streuung *f*
variable 1. variabel, verstellbar, veränderlich, **2.** *(math. phys.)* Variable *f*, Größe *f*
variable block format variable Satzlänge *f*
variable delivery pump Pumpe *f* mit veränderlicher Fördermenge
variable fixed stop Festanschlagwechsel *m*
variable quantity veränderliche Grö-

ße *f*
variable reach truck Stapler *m* mit veränderlicher Reichweite
variable resistor variabler Widerstand *m*, spannungsabhängiger Widerstand *m*
variable sensitivity veränderliche Empfindlichkeit *f*
variable speed control Stufenschaltung *f*, variable Fahrsteuerung *f*
variable speed drive Stufengetriebe *nt*, drehzahlveränderbarer Antrieb *m*
variable speed gear drive Stufenrädergetriebe *nt*
variable speeds gestufte Drehzahlen *fpl*
variable-load drive Regellastgetriebe *nt*
variableness Schwankung *f*, Variabilität *f*
variables *pl* Bestimmungsgrößen *fpl*
variables test Variablenprüfung *f*
variance Varianz *f*
variance-determined sample varianzbestimmte Stichprobe *f*
variant Variante *f*; variabel, veränderlich
variant comparison Variantenvergleich *m*
variant drawing Sortenzeichnung *f*
variate Zufallsgröße *f*, Zufallsvariable *f*
variation 1. Änderung *f*, Veränderung *f*, Abänderung *f*, Variante *f*, Abweichung *f* **2.** *(Größe)* Abweichungsspanne *f* **3.** *(Messtechnik)* Maßabweichung *f* **4.** *(Finanzwesen)* Schwankung *f*, Streuung *f* **5.** *(kundenspezifisch)* Sonderwunsch *m*
variation (of speed ranges) Abstufung *f* (von Drehzahlen)
variation coefficient Variationskoeffizient *m*, relative Standardabweichung *f*
variation in dimension Abweichung *f* vom Maß
variation in the angle of rotation Drehwinkelabweichung *f*
variation of specification factors Abweichung *f* von Bestimmungsgrößen
variation of speed range Drehzahltreppe *f*
variation of the transverse profile Abweichung *f* des Stirnprofils

variation of tooth traces Abweichung *f* von Flankenlinien
variation within the usual scale of workshop practice werkstattübliche Abweichung *f*
variation from equiangularity Ungleichwinkligkeit *f*, Abweichung *f* von der Gleichwinkligkeit
variety Abart *f*
variety of parts Teilevielfalt *f*
variety of variant Variantenvielfalt *f*
varistor variabler Widerstand *m*, spannungsabhängiger Widerstand *m*, Varistor *m*
varnished fabric type Lackgewebeband *nt*
varnished glass fabric Lackglasgewebe *nt*
varnished glass fabric tape Lackglasgewebeband *nt*
varnishes and similar products *pl* Anstrichstoffe *mpl*
vary 1. variieren, verändern, ändern, abweichen **2.** unterscheiden, **3.** verstellen, wechseln **4.** *(el., Regelungen)* regeln
vary from schwanken zwischen
vary infinitely stufenlos verstellen
varying schwankend, unterschiedlich
vat dyeing Küpenfärbung *f*
vaulting test Wölbversuch *m*
V-belt Keilriemen *m*
V-belt drive Keilriemenantrieb *m*
VC monomer VC-Monomer *nt*
VC polymer VC-Polymerisat *nt*
V-die bending Knickbiegen *nt*
VDU access BSA-Zugriff
VDU line Bildschirmzeile *f*
vector Vektor *m*
vector control Vektorregelung *f*
vector feed rate Vektorvorschub *m*
vector graphic Vektorgrafik *f*
Vee V-Prisma *nt*
vee block Prismenstück *nt*
Vee-belt Keilriemen *m*, Flachkeilriemen *m*
Vee-guide Bettprisma *nt*, prismatisch geführte Gleitbahn *f*, prismatische Bahn *f*, Prismenführungsbahn *f*
Vee-guide of (the) crossrail Querbalkenprisma *nt*

Vee-guide-ways Bettführungsprismen *npl*
Vees *pl* prismatische Bahnen *fpl*, V-Bahnen *fpl*
Vee-way Bettprisma *nt*
Vee-way of (the) crossrail Querbalkenprisma *nt*
vehicle Wagen *m*, Fahrzeug *nt*
vehicle calling station Fahrzeugrufstation *f*
vehicle class Fahrzeugklasse *f*
vehicle clearance Wendekreis *m*
vehicle concept Fahrzeugkonzept *nt*
vehicle control system Fahrzeugsteuerung *f*
vehicle controller Fahrzeugsteuerung *f*
vehicle identification Fahrzeugidentifizierung *f*
vehicle registration Fahrzeugzulassung *f*
vehicle transmission Fahrzeuggetriebe *nt*
vehicle ventilation system Fahrzeuglüftungsanlage *f*
velocity Geschwindigkeit *f*
velocity area Geschwindigkeitsfläche *f*
velocity equation Geschwindigkeitsgleichung *f*
velocity head Geschwindigkeitsdruckhöhe *f*
velocity vector Geschwindigkeitsvektor *m*
vendor Verkäufer *m*, Lieferant *m*
vendor portfolio Lieferantenportfolio *nt*
veneer layer Furnierschicht *f*
vent lüften, entlüften, Gas ablassen; Luftdurchlass *m*
vent hole Entlüftungsbohrung *f*
vent pipe Entlastungsrohr *nt*
vent to abblasen
vent valve Entlüftungsventil *nt*, Belüftungsventil *nt*
vented cell geschlossene Zelle *f*
ventilate entlüften
ventilated belüftet
ventilating equipment Lüftungseinrichtung *f*
ventilating plant with humidifying action Lüftungsanlage *f* mit Befeuchtung
ventilation Be-/Entlüftung *f*, Belüftung *f*, Lüftung *f*, Durchlüftung *f*
ventilation appliance Lüftungsgerät *nt*
ventilation engineer Lüftungsingenieur *m*
ventilation flap Lüftungsklappe *f*
ventilation line Lüftungsleitung *f*
ventilation practice Lüftungstechnik *f*
ventilation requirement lufttechnische Anforderung *f*
ventilation system lufttechnische Anlage *f*
ventilation technology Lüftungstechnik *f*, Lufttechnik *f*
ventilator Lüfter *m*, Gebläse *nt*, Ventilator *m*
venting Lüftung *f*, Entlüftung *f*, Be-/Entlüftung *f*
venting facility Entlüftungseinrichtung *f*
venting plug Entlüftungsschraube *f*
venting screw Entlüftungsschraube *f*
verbal notes Wortangaben *fpl*
vehicular traffic Fahrverkehr *m*
verifiable nachweisbar
verification Prüfung *f*, Überprüfung *f*, Nachprüfung *f*, Kontrolle *f*, Nachweis *m*, Verifizierung *f*
verification certificate Prüfbescheinigung *f*
verification limit of error Eichfehlergrenze *f*
verification mark Eichstempel *m*
verification of conformity Bauprüfung *f*
verification of functionality Gebrauchsfähigkeitsnachweis *m*
verification of quality Qualitätsnachweis *m*
verification on commissioning Nachprüfung *f*
verification stage Nachweisstufe *f*
verifier Prüfer *m*
verify überprüfen, prüfen, nachprüfen, vergleichen, nachweisen, verifizieren
verifying Nachprüfen *nt*
verifying calculation Kontrollrechnung *f*
vernier Nonius *m*

vernier calliper Präzisionsschieblehre *f*, Feinmessschiebleher *f*, Messschieber *m* mit Nonius
vernier calliper gauge Feinmessschiebleher *f*
vernier dial Noniustrommel *f*
vernier division Noniusteilstrich *m*, Noniusteilung *f*
vernier mark Noniusstrich *m*
vernier reading Noniusablesung *f*, Skalenanzeige *f* einer Messschraube
vernier scale Nonienteilung *f*, Maßstab *m* mit Nonius
versatile vielseitig
versatility Vielgestaltigkeit *f*, Vielseitigkeit *f*
version Ausführung *f*, Variante *f*
version to be realized Realisierungsvariante *f*
vertical adjustment Höheneinstellung *f*
vertical milling attachment Vertikalfräsapparat *m*
vertex angle of cone Kegelwinkel *m*
vertical vertikal, senkrecht, lotrecht; Senkrechte *f*
vertical adjustment Höhenverstellung *f*, Senkrechtverstellung *f*
vertical adjustment of table Tischhöhenverstellung *f*
vertical automatic production lathe Senkrechtdrehautomat *m*
vertical bar rack Ständerregal *nt*
vertical boring and turning mill Bohr- und Drehwerk *nt*
vertical boring machine Senkrechtbohrmaschine *f*
vertical boring mill Senkrechtbohrwerk *nt*
vertical carousel Vertikalpaternoster *nt*, Paternosterregal *nt*
vertical carousel in serpentine form Schlangenpaternoster *nt*
vertical cartoner Vertikalkartoniermaschine *f*
vertical chain string Vertikalkettenstrang *m*
vertical circulation storage system Vertikalumlauflager *nt*
vertical continuous rotary miller Rundtischfräsmaschine *f*, Rundtischfräsautomat *m*, Rundlaufsenkrechtfräsmaschine *f*, Senkrechtfräsmaschine *f* mit Rundtisch
vertical continuous rotary milling machine Senkrechtfräsmaschine *f* mit Rundtisch
vertical conveyor Senkrechtförderer *m*, Vertikalförderer *m*
vertical copy-milling machine Senkrechtkopierfräsmaschine *f*
vertical cutter head Senkrechtfräskopf *m*
vertical cutting head Senkrechtfräskopf *m*
vertical datum Vertikale *f*
vertical deformation Vertikalverformung *f*
vertical die-sinker Senkrechtnachformfräsmaschine *f*
vertical downfeed Senkrechtvorschub *m*
vertical-downward position Fallposition *f*
vertical drilling machine Ständerbohrmaschine *f*, Senkrechtbohrmaschine *f*
vertical duplicator Senkrechtnachformfräsmaschine *f*
vertical edgewise scale Hochskala *f*
vertical extrusion Vertikalprofil *nt*
vertical feed motion Senkrechtbewegung *f*
vertical fixed-bed miller with longitudinally and cross traversing headstock Senkrechtfräsmaschine *f* mit längs- und querbeweglichem Spindelkasten
vertical form fill and seal machine Vertikalformfüll- und Verschließmaschine *f*
vertical gear generator Senkrechtzahnradstoßmaschine *f*
vertical horizontal carousel store vertikales Umlaufregallager *nt*
vertical intromission Senkrechteinschallung *f*
vertical keyway milling machine Vertikalnutenlangfräsmaschine *f*
vertical knee- and column-type milling machine Senkrechtkonsolfräs-

maschine *f*
vertical lacing Vertikalumreifung *f*
vertical lift Senkrechtabhebung *f*
vertical line Vertikale *f*
vertical line for measurement Messlotrechte *f*
vertical lowering Vertikalsenkung *f*
vertical magnification Vertikalvergrößerung *f*
vertical miller and jig borer Senkrechtfräs- und -lehrenbohrmaschine *f*
vertical milling Senkrechtfräsen *nt*, Vertikalfräsen *nt*
vertical milling attachment Senkrechtfräsvorrichtung *f*
vertical milling head Senkrechtfräsapparat *m*, Senkrechtfräskopf *m*, Vertikalfrässchlitten *m*, Vertikalfräskopf *m*
vertical milling job Senkrechtfräsarbeit *f*
vertical milling machine Senkrechtfräsmaschine *f*, Vertikalfräsmaschine *f*
vertical milling machine with automatic table traverse and-fall miller Senkrechtfräsmaschine *f* mit Selbstgang
vertical milling operation Vertikalfräsarbeit *f*
vertical milling spindle head Senkrechtfrässpindelkopf *m*, Senkrechtfrässpindelstock *m*
vertical milling unit Vertikalfräseinheit *f*
vertical motion Hubbewegung *f*
vertical multiple-spindle drilling and tapping unit Senkrechtvielspindel- und -gewindebohreinheit *f*
vertical order picker Vertikalkommissionierer *m*
vertical pallet strapping machine Vertikalpalettenumreifungsmaschine *f*
vertical path Vertikalweg *m*
vertical planer-miller Senkrechtlangfräsmaschine *f*
vertical plano-milling machine Senkrechtlangfräsmaschine *f*
vertical position Höhenlage *f*
vertical positioning Höhenpositionierung *f*
vertical probe Senkrechtprüfkopf *m*
vertical profiler with two-dimensional control Senkrechtnachformfräsmaschine *f* für zweidimensionales Fräsen
vertical profiling machine Senkrechtkopierfräsmaschine *f*
vertical push-cut shaper Stoßmaschine *f* mit schwenkbarem Stößelkopf
vertical push-cut shaping machine Stoßmaschine *f* mit schwenkbarem Stößelkopf
vertical push-down broaching machine Senkrechtstoßräummaschine *f*
vertical reciprocating motion Auf- und Abbewegung *f*
vertical rotary warehouse Paternosterlager *nt*
vertical section Höhenschnitt *m*
vertical shaper Stoßmaschine *f*, Senkrechtstoßmaschine *f*, Senkrechtstößelhobelmaschine *f*
vertical shaper with adjustable inclination of the ram Senkrechtstößelhobelmaschine *f* mit schräg stellbarer Stößelführung
vertical shaper with swivel toolhead Senkrechtstößelhobelmaschine *f* mit schräg stellbarer Stößelführung
vertical shaping machine Senkrechtstoßmaschine *f*, Senkrechtstößelhobelmaschine *f*
vertical side loader/order picker Vertikalkombikommissionierer *m*
vertical slot milling machine Senkrechtnutenfräsmaschine *f*, Vertikalnutenfräsmaschine *f*
vertical slotting and shaping machine Senkrechtstoßmaschine *f*
vertical spindle head Senkrechtfräskopf *m*
vertical spindle rotary-table miller Rundtischfräsmaschine *f*, Rundtischfräsautomat *m*, Rundlaufsenkrechtfräsmaschine *f*, Karussellfräsmaschine *f*
vertical strapping Vertikalumreifung *f*
vertical strapping machine Vertikalumreifungsmaschine *f*
vertical style standard lettering senkrechte Normschrift *f*
vertical table movement Tischsenkrechtbewegung *f*

vertical to senkrecht zu
vertical tool thrust Senkrechtschnittkraft f
vertical transmission Senkrechtdurchschallung f
vertical transmitter-receiver probe SE-Senkrechtprüfkopf m
vertical travel Hub- und Senkbewegung f
vertical turning and boring mill Karusselldrehmaschine f, Dreh- und Bohrwerk nt, Drehwerk nt mit doppeltem Ständer
vertical turret lathe Karussellrevolverdrehmaschine f, Karusselldrehmaschine f, Drehwerk nt mit einfachem Ständer
vertical turret machine for boring drilling facing and tapping Revolverbohrmaschine f
vertical type rotary rack Paternosterregal nt, Paternoster m
vertically adjustable höhenverstellbar
vertical-spindle attachment Senkrechtfräsvorrichtung f
vertical-spindle column-and-knee miller Senkrechtkonsolfräsmaschine f
vertical-spindle continuous milling machine Senkrechtfräsautomat m
vertical-spindle continuous rotary miller Rundtischfräsmaschine f, Rundtischfräsautomat m
vertical-spindle fixed-bed type milling machine Senkrechtproduktionsfräsmaschine f, Senkrechtplanfräsmaschine f
vertical-spindle manufacturing-type milling machine Senkrechtplanfräsmaschine f
vertical-spindle miller Senkrechtfräsmaschine f
vertical-spindle miller with rotary table Senkrechtrundtischfräsmaschine f
vertical-spindle milling machine Vertikalfräsmaschine f, Senkrechtfräsmaschine f
vertical-spindle reciprocating-table surface grinder Langtischflächenschleifmaschine f
vertical-spindle rotary continuous miller Rundtischfräsautomat m, Rundlaufsenkrechtfräsmaschine f
vertical-spindle rotary continuous milling machine Senkrechtfräsautomat m mit Rundtisch
vertical-spindle rotary-table milling machine Rundlaufsenkrechtfräsmaschine f, Rundtischfräsmaschine f, Senkrechtfräsmaschine f mit Rundtisch
vertical-spindle surface grinder Flächenschleifmaschine f
vertical-type knee-and-column miller Senkrechtkonsolfräsmaschine f
verification of suitability Eignungsnachweis m
vitrified bond keramische Bindung f
vitrified wheel keramisch gebundene Schleifscheibe f
very fine cotton fabric Baumwollfeinstgewebe nt
vessel Hohlkörper m, Behälter m
vessel with dished ends Behälter m mit gewölbten Boden
vessel with jacket Behälter m mit Mantel
V-form bending Keilbiegen nt
V-head Messkeil m
via über
via a sensor über ein Sensor
vibrate rütteln, schütteln, vibrieren, schwingen
vibrated condition geschütteter Zustand m
vibrating reed schwingende Zunge f
vibrating tool schwingendes Werkzeug nt
vibration Vibration f, Erschütterung f, Schwingung f, Schwingung f mit konstanter Frequenz
vibration antinode Schwingungsband nt
vibration behaviour Schwingungsverfahren nt
vibration clamp Schwingklemme f
vibration coefficient Schwingbeiwert m
vibration conveyor Vibrationsförderer m
vibration damping schwingungs-

dämpfend; Schwingungsdämpfung f
vibration generator Schwingungserreger m, Vibrator m
vibration insulation Schwingungsisolierung f
vibration loading Schwingungsbeanspruchung f
vibration method Schwingungsverfahren nt
vibration pick-up Schwingungsaufnehmer m
vibration property Schwingungseigenschaft f
vibration resistant vibrationsfest
vibrational characteristics Schwingungsverhalten nt
vibrational loading Schwingbeanspruchung f
vibration-free schwingungsfrei, erschütterungfrei
vibrationless erschütterungsfrei, schwingungsfrei
vibrator Vibrator m, Rüttelgerät nt
vibrator current Schwingstrom m
vibratory feeder Rüttelschiene f
vibratory in-line Rüttelschiene f
vibratory motion Schwingbewegung f
vibratory rail Rüttelschiene f
vibratory track Rüttelschiene f
Vicat indenting tip Vicatstift m
vice Schraubstock m
vice clamping Schraubstockspannung f, Backenspannung f, Zwingenspannung f
vice jaws pl Schraubstockbacken fpl
vice versa umgekehrt
vicinity Umgebung f, Nähe f
vicinity of the pitch circle Teilkreisnähe f
video display terminal Datensichtgerät nt
video display unit (VDU) Bildschirmanzeigeeinheit f
video screen Bildschirm m
video signal Bildsignal nt
view Ansicht f, Sichtverbindung f
viewing Beobachtung f
viewing angle Beobachtungswinkel m
viewing device Beobachtungsgerät nt
viewing distance Beobachtungsabstand m

viewing slot Sichtschlitz m
vinyl chloride copolymer Vinylchloridcopolymerisat nt, Vinylchloridmischpolymerisat nt
vinyl chloride homopolymer Vinylchloridhomopolymerisat nt
vinyl chloride pure polymer Vinylchloridpolymerisat nt, Vinylchloridreinpolymerisat nt
vinyl-asbestos tile Vinyl-Asbest-Platte f
violate verletzen
violation Verletzung f
virtual virtuell
virtual input virtueller Eingang m
virtual number of teeth Ersatzzähnzahl f
virtual pitch diameter Paarungsflankendurchmesser m
virtually nahezu
visco-elastic behaviour viskoelastisches Verhalten nt
visco-elastic material viskoelastischer Stoff m
viscose Viskose f
viscosity Viskosität f
viscosity build-up Viskositätsaufbau m
viscosity loss Viskositätsabfall m
viscosity-density constant Viskositätsdichtekonstante f
viscosity-density ratio Viskositätsdichteverhältnis m
viscous viskos, zähflüssig, dickflüssig
viscous friction Viskosereibung f
viscous-hard cellular plastics zähharter Schaumstoff m
visibility Durchsicht f, Sicht f
visibility test Sichtmessung f
visual visuell, optisch
visual acuity Sehschärfe f
visual contact Sichtverbindung f
visual control Sichtkontrolle f
visual display Sichtanzeige f
visual examination Sichtprüfung f, Inaugenscheinnahme f
visual indication Sichtanzeige f
visual inspection Sichtprüfung f, Inaugenscheinnahme f
visual observation Betrachtung f
visual read out device Sichtausgeber m
visual signal device Sichtmelder m

visualization Visualisierung *f*
visualize visualisieren
vitrified bonded grinding wheel keramisch gebundene Schleifscheibe *f*
V-notch Nut *f*, Kerbnut *f*
V-notch specimen V-Probe *f*
V-null transmission V-Null-Getriebe *nt*
vocational training Berufsausbildung *f*
voice Sprache *f*, Sprachverbindung *f*
voice entry Spracheingabe *f*
void leer, Lunker *m, mpl*
voids content Hohlraumgehalt *m*
volatile memory flüchtiger Speicher *m*
volatilize verdunsten, verdunsten lassen
voltage Spannung *f*
voltage adjustment Spannungsangleichung *f*
voltage being present anstehende Spannung *f*
voltage calibration Spannungskalibrator *m*
voltage common mode Gleichtaktspannung *f*
voltage detector Spannungsprüfer *m*
voltage divider Spannungsteiler *m*
voltage drop Spannungs(ab)fall *m*
voltage fluctuation Spannungsschwankung *f*
voltage level Spannungspegel *m*
voltage metering Spannungsmessung *f*
voltage peak Spannungsspitze *f*
voltage regulative diode Suppressordiode *f*
voltage ripple Spannungswelligkeit *f*
voltage shaper Spannungformer *m*
voltage surge Spannungsspitze *f*
voltage surge protection Überspannungsschutz *m*
voltage-to-frequency converter Spannungs-Frequenz-Umsetzer *m*
voltage to neutral Strangspannung *f*, Sternspannung *f*
voltage transformer Spannungswandler *m*
voltage transverse mode Differenzspannung *f*
voltage variation Spannungsabweichung *f*
voltage window Spannungsfenster *nt*
volt-ampere reactive (VAR) Blindleistung *f*
volume Volumen *nt*, Umfang *m*, Menge *f*
volume constancy Volumenkonstanz *f*
volume flow Volumenstrom *m*, Mengenstrom *m*
volume flow control Volumenstromsteuerung *f*
volume fluctuation Mengenschwankung *f*
volume limiter Signalbegrenzer *m*
volume measurement Volumenmessung *f*
volume measuring instrument Volumenmessgerät *nt*
volume of distillate Destillatvolumen *nt*
volume of investment Investitionsvolumen *nt*
volume of lubricant Schmierstoffvolumen *nt*
volume of metal removed zerspantes Volumen *nt*, Zerspanungsmenge *f*
volume of metal worn away Verschleißvolumen *nt*
volume of non-volatile matter Festkörpervolumen *nt*
volume of the metal removed by cutting Zerspanungsvolumen *nt*
volume of wheel grain wear Schleifscheibenverschleißvolumen *nt*
volume removed per min minütlich abgenommenes Spanvolumen *nt*
volume removed per regrind je Nachschliff abgenommenes Werkstoffvolumen *nt*
volume resistivity spezifischer Durchgangswiderstand *m*
volume turbidity Volumentrübung *f*
volumes Mengenangaben *fpl*
volumes expressed in Mengenangaben *fpl* ausgedrückt in
volumeter Volumenmessgerät *nt*
volumetric calculation Volumenberechnung *f*
volumetric cup Messbecher *m*
volumetric cup filling machine Messbecherfüllmaschine *f*
volumetric deficiency Volumenfehlbetrag *m*

volumetric efficiency volumetrischer Wirkungsgrad *m*
volumetric flash Messkolben *m*
volumetric flow Volumendurchfluss *m*
volumetric grinding wheel wear Schleifscheibenverschleißvolumen *nt*
volumetric piston filling machine Kolbenfüllmaschine *f*
voluminous umfangreich
vortical kreisend, wirbelig
voucher Quittung *f*
covered filler wire umhüllter Schweißdraht *m*
V-root V-Wurzel *f*
V-thread Spitzgewinde *nt*
V-U butt joint V-U-Naht *f*
V-way prismatische Führung *f*, V-Bahn *f*, V-Prisma *nt*
V-zero transmission V-Null-Getriebe *nt*

Ww

wobbling disc Taumelscheibe *f*
wafer carrier Chipaufnahme *f*, Chipträger *m*
wage Lohn *m*
wage costs Lohnkosten *pl*
wages Lohnsummen *fpl*
wagon Waggon *m*
wagon construction Waggonbau *m*
waisted shank Dehnschaft *m*
wait warten
wait command Wartebefehl *m*
wait instruction Wartebefehl *m*
wait state Wartezustand *m*
waiting Warten *nt*
waiting line Warteschlange *f*
waiting list Warteschlange *f*
waiting loop Warteschleife *f*
waiting period delay Wartezeit *f*
waiting time Wartezeit *f*
wake Sog *m*
walk gehen
walk on begehen
walk test Begehversuch *m*
walking line Auflinie *f*
walking speed Schrittgeschwindigkeit *f*
walkway Gehweg *m*, Fußgängerweg *m*, Weg *m*, begehbare Fläche *f*, Laufsteg *m*
wall Gebäudewand *f*, Wand *f*
wall covering Wandverkleidung *f*, Wandbelag *m*
wall fastening Wandbefestigung *f*
wall mounted pipe clip Rohrschelle *f* für Wandbefestigungen
wall mounted two-piece pipe clip zweiteilige Rohrschelle *f* für Wandbefestigung
wall mounting Wandbefestigung *f*
wall of pipe Rohrwand *f*
wall socket Steckdose *f*
wall thickness Wanddicke *f*
wall thickness discrepancy Wanddickensprung *m*
wall thicknesses Wanddicken *fpl*
wallet-making material Täschnermaterial *nt*
wall-mounted wandbefestigt

wall-mounted fan Wandventilator *m*
want Bedarf *m*, Bedürfnis *nt*; beanspruchen, verlangen
warehouse Lager *nt*, Lagerraum *m*
warehouse administration Lagerverwaltung *f*
warehouse administration computer Lagerverwaltungsrechner *m*
warehouse administration level Lagerverwaltungsebene *f*
warehouse administration system Lagerverwaltungssystem *nt*
warehouse area Lagerbereich *m*
warehouse body Lagerkörper *m*
warehouse check-in Lagereinbuchung *f*
warehouse check-out Lagerausbuchung *f*
warehouse column Lagerspalte *f*
warehouse component Lagerkomponente *f*
warehouse computer Lagerrechner *m*
warehouse configuration Lagerkonfiguration *f*
warehouse control Lagerwesen *nt*
warehouse coordinate Lagerkoordinate *f*
warehouse entry Lagerzugang *m*
warehouse equipment Lagereinrichtung *f*
warehouse exit Lagerabgang *m*
warehouse host computer Lagerrechner *m*
warehouse inventory Lagerbestand *m*
warehouse lane Lagergasse *f*
warehouse layout Lagerkonfiguration *f*
warehouse level Lagerebene *f*
warehouse locations master file Lagerplatzstamm *m*
warehouse management level Lagerleitebene *f*
warehouse master file Lagerortsstamm *m*
warehouse on-hand quantity Lagerbestand *m*
warehouse outgoing Lagerabgang *m*

warehouse premises Lagerbereich *m*
warehouse specification Lagerspezifikation *f*
warehouse station Lagerstation *f*
warehouse stock Warenlager *nt*
warehouse system Lageranlage *f*
warm restart Warmstart *m*
warm up erwärmen
warming up time Aufwärmzeit *f*
warmth of the hand Handwärme *f*
warn warnen
warning Warnung *f*
warning beacon Rundumleuchte *f*, Warnblinklampe *f*
warning device Warneinrichtung *f*, Warnanlage *f*
warning label Warnschild *nt*
warning lamp Signallampe *f*
warning light Warnlampe *f*
warning limit Warngrenze *f*
warning means Warneinrichtung *f*
warning message Warnmeldung *f*
warning prescription Warnungsvorschrift *f*
warning sign Warnzeichen *nt*
warning symbol Warnsymbol *nt*
warning system Warnsystem *nt*, Warneinrichtung *f*, Warnanlage *f*
warp verwerfen, wölben, sich verziehen, krümmen, verkrümmen, verspannen, verwinden
warpage Verkrümmung *f*, Wölbung *f*, Verzug *m*
warped verzogen, windschief
warping Verspannung *f*, Verwindung *f*, Verwinden *nt*
warping moment *(Flächen)* Wölbmoment *nt*
warping resistance Wölbwiderstand *m*
warping stress Wölbspannung *f*
warrant gewährleisten, garantieren
warranty Garantie *f*, Gewährleistung *f*
wash spülen, abspülen, waschen
wash away wegspülen
wash moulding Schlichte *f*
wash primer Haftgrundmittel *nt*, Washprimer *m*
washer Ring *m*, Scheibe *f*, Unterlegscheibe *f*
washer component Unterlegteil *nt*

washer for high strength friction grip fastenings Scheibe *f* für HV-Verbindungen
washer for tapping screw assemblies Scheibe *f* für Kombiblechschrauben
washer of laminated shim material Scheibe *f* aus Sichtblech
washing Spülung *f*
washing liquid Spülflüssigkeit *f*
washing nozzle Spüldüse *f*
washing test Waschprüfung *f*
washing-up liquid lubricate means Kühl-, Spül-, Schmiermittel (KSSM) *nt*
waste Ausschuss *m*, Abfall *m*, Verschnitt *m*, Schrott *m*; verschwenden; Verschwendung *f*
waste bin Abfallbehälter *m*
waste disposal Abfallbeseitigung *f*
waste disposal law Abfallbeseitigungsgesetz *nt*
waste form Taillenform *f*
waste gas Abgas *nt*
waste heat Abhitze *f*
waste oil Altöl *nt*
waste product Abfallprodukt *nt*
waste quantity per unit time Verlustmenge *f* je Zeiteinheit
watch and instrument maker's lathe Uhrmacherdrehmaschine *f*
watch glass dish Uhrglasschale *f*
watch the right of way Vorfahrt beachten
watchdog timer Zeitüberwachungseinrichtung *f*
water Wasser *nt*
water balance coefficient Wasserhaushaltswert *m*
water balance law Wasserhaushaltsgesetz *nt*
water circulation Wasserumwälzung *f*
water conditioning Wasseraufbereitung *f*
water content by mass Massengehalt *m* an Wasser
water cutting plant Wasserschneidanlage *f*
water drain valve wasserablassendes Ventil *nt*
water fill temperature Wassereinfüll-

temperatur *f*
water flow Wasserdurchfluss *m*
water flow monitor Wasserströmungswächter *m*
water glass process Wasserglasverfahren *nt*
water hammer Wasserschlag *m*
water heater Wassererwärmer *m*
water heating boiler Wasserheizungskessel *m*
water heating installation Wassererwärmungsanlage *f*
water injection valve Wassereinspritzventil *nt*
water inlet valve Wasserzuflussventil *nt*
water jet Wasserstrahl *m*
water jet machining Wasserstrahlbearbeitung
water level indicator Wasserstandshöhenanzeiger *m*
water level limiter Wasserstandbegrenzer *m*
water level mark Wasserstandsmarke *f*
water loop Wasserschleife *f*
water mains system Wasserrohrnetz *nt*
water meter with measuring chambers Wasserzähler *m* mit Messkammern
water penetration test Wassereindringversuch *m*
water protection law regulation wasserschutzrechtliche Verordnung *f*
water quenching method Wasserabschreckverfahren *nt*
water radiator Wasserheizkörper *m*
water recirculation cooling plant Wasserrückkühlanlage *f*
water re-cooling Wasserrückkühlung *f*
water repellent wasserabweisend, wasserabstoßend
water resistant wasserbeständig
water sample Wasserprobe *f*
water stain Wasserfleck *m*
water storage tank Wasserspeicher *m*
water supply mains Wasserversorgungsnetz *nt*
water throughput Wasserdurchfluss *m*
water trap Wasserwaage *f*
water treatment Wasseraufbereitung *f*
water vapour volatile wasserdampfflüchtig
water volume Wassermenge *f*
water volume controller Wassermengenregler *m*
water glass Wasserglas *nt*
water-hardening steel wasserhärtender Stahl *m*
water-heating system Wasserheizung *f*
watering resin Gießharz *nt*
water-in-oil emulsion Emulsion *f* von Wasser in Öl, WO- Emulsion *f*
waterproofing foil Abdichtungsfolie *f*
waterproofing sheet Abdichtungsfolie *f*
waterside flow resistance wasserseitiger Widerstand *m*
water-swept parts *pl* wasserberührte Teile *ntpl*
watertight wasserdicht
wattage aufgenommene Leistung *f*
wattmeter method Leistungsmesserverhalten *nt*
Watt's chain Wattsche Kette *f*
wave Welle *f*
wave form Schwingungsverlauf *m*
wave peak Wellenkamm *m*
wave theory Wellentheorie *f*
waveform Wellenform *f*
wavelength Wellenlänge *f*
wavelength of the sound Schallwellenlänge *f*
wavelength stabilized laser wellenlängenstabilisiertes Laser *nt*
wavelength standard Wellenlängennormal *nt*
waviness Welligkeit *f*
waviness width Wellenabstand *m*
wavy wellig
wavy traverse lines Schleifzüge *mpl*
wax coating Wachsauftrag *m*
wax-backed packaging material wachskaschierter Packstoff *m*
way Richtung *f*, Strecke *f*, Weg *m*
way back Rückweg *m*
way-up Steigen *nt*
way-boring machine Wegebohrmaschine *f*
ways Führungen *fpl*, Wege *mpl*
ways and times Wege und Zeiten *pl*
ways for supporting and guiding

the knee Ständerführungsbahn *f*
weak schwach
weak point Schwachstelle *f*
weak spot Schwachstelle *f*
weaken nachlassen, schwächen
weakening Schwächung *f*
weak-point analysis Schwachstellenanalyse *f*
wear (on/out/off) abnutzen, verschleißen; Abnutzung *f*, Verschleiß *m*, Abrieb *m*, Abnutzungserscheinung *f*
wear allowance Abnutzungszugabe *f*
wear behaviour Verschleißverhalten *nt*
wear by cratering Kolkverschleiß *m*
wear compensation Abnutzungsausgleich *m*
wear dimension Abnutzungsmaß *nt*
wear distance Verschleißstrecke *f*
wear due to scoring Fressverschleiß *m*
wear due to sliding action Gleitverschleiß *m*
wear factor Verschleißgröße *f*, Verschleißfaktor *f*
wear forms Verschleißformen *f*
wear instalment Verschleißrate *f*
wear land Verschleißfase *f*
wear land value Verschleißmarkenbreite *f*
wear life Abnutzungsdauer *f*, Standzeit *f*
wear lifespan Verschleißlebensdauer *f*
wear limit Abnutzungsgrenze *f*
wear mark Verschleißmarke *f*
wear measurement Verschleißmessung *f*
wear of cutting face Spanflächenverschleiß *m*
wear part Verschleißteil *nt*
wear point Reibstelle *f*
wear proof verschleißfest
wear range Abnutzungsbereich *m*
wear rate check plug member Abnutzungsprüfkörper *m*
wear reason Verschleißursache *f*
wear resistance Verschleißfestigkeit *f*, Verschleißwiderstand *m*
wear resistant verschleißfest
wear take-up Ausgleich *m* für Verschleiß
wear throughput quantity Verschleißdurchsatzmenge *f*

wear tolerance Abnutzungstoleranz *f*
wear types Verschleißarten *f*
wearable abnutzbar
wear-free verschleißfrei
wearing action Verschleißwirkung *f*
wearing part Verschleißteil *nt*
wearless verschleißfrei
wear-out failure Verschleißausfall *m*
wear-resisting layer Schutzschicht *f* (Bau)
weather Witterung *f*
weather board Deckbrett *nt*
weathering Abwittern *nt*
weathering resistance Verwitterungsbeständigkeit *f*
weatherproof wetterfest, wettergeschützt, witterungsunempfindlich
weaving amplitude Pendelausschlag *m*
weaving arc pendelnder Lichtbogen *m*
web 1. *(Rad)* Scheibe *f* **2.** *(Profil)* Steg *m*, Rippe *f*
web disk wheel Scheibenrad *nt*
web of film Folienbahn *f*
web plate Stegblech *nt*
web section Kernquerschnitt *m*
web taper Kernsteigerung *f*
web-based data exchange Web-basierter Datenaustausch *m*
wedge blockieren, verkeilen, Keil *m*
wedge angle Schnittwinkel *m*, Schneidenwinkel *m*, Meißelwinkel *m*, Keilwinkel *m*
wedge loading Schrägbelastung *f*
wedge measurement plane Keilmessebene *f*
wedge tensile test Schrägzugversuch *m*
wedge-action cutting Keilschneiden *nt*
wedge-shaped kegelförmig, keilförmig, kommaförmig
week Woche *f*
weekly wöchentlich
week's programme Wochenprogramm *nt*
wedge gate valve Keilschieber *m*
weigh wägen, wiegen, beschweren
weighed-out quantity Auswaage *f*
weigher Waage *f*
weighing Wägen *nt*, Wägung *f*

weighing device Wiegeeinrichtung *f*
weighing factor Wichtungsfaktor *m*
weighing glass Wägeglas *nt*
weighing machine Waage *f*
weighing pipette Wägepipette *f*
weighing scales Waage *f*
weighing unit Wägeeinrichtung *f*
weight Gewicht *nt*, Gewichtsstück *nt*, Masse *f*, Last *f*, Lastdruck *m*; bewerten
weight adjustment Gewichtseinstellung *f*
weight alteration Gewichtsveränderung *f*
weight classifying machine Gewichtsklassifizierungsmaschine *f*
weight constancy Gewichtskonstanz *f*
weight counterbalance Gewichtausgleich *m*
weight details Gewichtsangaben *fpl*
weight distribution Gewichtsverteilung *f*
weight force Gewichtskraft *f*
weight grading machine Sortierwaage *f*
weight loading Gewichtsbelastung *f*
weight loss per unit area Flächengewichtsverlust *m*
weight of electrode deposited in unit time Einbringleistung *f*
weight of metal deposited in unit time Auftragleistung *f*
weight of the load Lastgewicht *nt*
weight per unit area flächenbezogene Masse *f*
weight price labelling machine Gewichtspreisauszeichnungsetikettiermaschine *f*
weight specification Gewichtsangabe *f*
weighted average gewichteter Mittelwert *m*, gewogener Mittelwert *m*
weight-in mix Mischguteinwaage *f*
weight-in quantity Einwaage *f*
weighting Gewichtung *f*, Wichtung *f*
weighting factor Gewichtungsfaktor *m*
weight-loaded gewichtsbelastet
weld schweißen; Schweißung *f*, Schweißnaht *f*
weld bend test Schweißfaltversuch *m*
weld composition Nahtaufbau *m*
weld compression force Schweißpresskraft *f*
weld compression time Schweißpresszeit *f*
weld concentration Nahtanhäufung *f*
weld depth Schweißtiefe *f*
weld design Nahtausführung *f*
weld efficiency rating Schweißnahtwertigkeit *f*
weld face Schweißstoßfläche *f*; auftragschweißen
weld flank Nahtflanke *f*
weld for fabricating purposes Fertigungsschweißung *f*
weld image Nahtabbildung *f*
weld inspection Schweißnahtprüfung *f*
weld junction Nahtübergang *m*
weld length Schweißnahtlänge *f*
weld model Nahtausführung *f*
weld nugget diameter Linsendurchmesser *m*
weld on anschweißen, aufschweißen
weld pitch Nahtabstand *m*
weld quality Nahtausführung *f*
weld reliability Schweißsicherheit *f*
weld sealing machine Schweißverschließmaschine *f*
weld seam Naht *f*
weld shape Schweißnahtform *f*
weld speed Schweißgeschwindigkeit *f*
weld spot burnt-through from one side einseitig durchgebrannter Schweißpunkt *m*
weld spotwise punktförmig schweißen
weld subject to long-term stressing dauerbeanspruchte Schweißung *f*
weld symbol Schweißsinnbild *nt*
weld together verschweißen
weld transition Nahtübergang *m*
weld triangle Nahtdreieck *nt*
weld zone Schweißbereich *m*, Schweißnahtbereich *m*
weldable steel wire Schweißstrahlnaht *f*
welded verschweißt
welded assembly Schweißverbindung *f*
welded assembly drawing Schweißgruppenzeichnung *f*
welded brazed and soldered joints Schweiß- und Lötnähte *fpl*
welded conical nipple Schweißkegel-

buchse *f*
welded diaphragm joint Membranschweißdichtung *f*
welded from one side I-Naht *f*; einseitig schweißen
welded joint Schweißverbindung *f*
welded reinforcement joint geschweißter Bewehrungsstoß *m*
welded with two fillets HY-Naht *f* mit Kehlnähten am Schrägstoß
welded-on cross bar aufgeschweißter Querstab *m*
welded-on part Anschweißteil *nt*
welder Schweißer *m*
welder for welding steel Stahlschweißer *m*
weld-facing Auftragsschweißung *f*
welding Schweißen *nt*, Stoffverbinden *nt*, Schweißnaht *f*, Schweißung *f*
welding addition Schweißzusatz *m*
welding auxiliary material Schweißhilfsstoff *m*
welding by bending using a heated tool Heizelementschwenkbiegeschweißen *nt*, Schwenkbiegeschweißen *nt*
welding current range Schweißstromstärkebereich *m*
welding design schweißtechnische Gestaltung *f*
welding equipment schweißtechnische Einrichtung *f*
welding feasibility Schweißmöglichkeit *f*
welding filler Schweißzusatzwerkstoff *m*, Schweißzusatz *m*
welding fixture schweißtechnische Vorrichtung *f*
welding force Schweißkraft *f*
welding from both sides in one pass Schweißen *nt* in Lage und Gegenlage
welding joint face Schweißfugenfläche *f*
welding load Schweißkraft *f*
welding machine control Schweißmaschinensteuerung *f*
welding neck flange Vorschweißflansch *m*
welding of a generally preheat piece of cast iron Gusseisenwarmschweißen *nt*
welding of cast iron without preheat Gusseisenkaltschweißen *nt*
welding of locally preheated piece Halbwarmschweißen *nt*
welding of locally preheated piece of cast iron Gusseisenhalbwarmschweißen *nt*
welding on Aufschweißen *nt*
welding on both sides simultaneously gleichzeitig beidseitiges Schweißen *nt*
welding operator Schweißer *m*
welding personnel schweißtechnisches Personal *nt*
welding power supply Schweißenergiequelle *f*
welding procedure Schweißverfahren *nt*
welding station Schweißplatz *m*
welding steel components to other components Anschweißen *nt* von Stahlteilen an andere Komponenten
welding tensile test Schweißzugversuch *m*
welding using a surrounding inductor Schweißen *nt* mit umschließendem Induktor
welding using alternating current and phase shift Schweißen *nt* mit Wechselstrom und Phasenanschnitt
welding using continuous alternating current Schweißen *nt* mit Dauerwechselstrom
welding using continuous current Schweißen *nt* mit Dauerstrom
welding using continuous direct current Schweißen *nt* mit Dauergleichstrom
welding using multi-current cycle and/or multiforce cycle Schweißen *nt* mit Strom- und/oder Kraftprogramm
welding using pulsed direct current Schweißen *nt* mit impulsförmigem Gleichstrom
welding using rod inductors Schweißen *nt* mit stabförmigen Induktoren
welding with cored-wire electrode Fülldrahtelektrodenschweißen *nt*
welding with drawn arc Schweißen *nt*

mit Hubzündung
welding with elongated weld Schweißen *nt* mit gestreckter Naht
welding with intermittent alternating current Schweißen *nt* mit unterbrochenem Wechselstrom
welding with intermittent direct current Schweißen *nt* mit unterbrochenem Gleichstrom
welding with programme pressure control Schweißen *nt* mit Druckprogramm
welding with slope control Schweißen *nt* mit Stromanstieg
welding with torch directed towards the finished part of the weld schleppendes Schweißen *nt*
welding with torch directed towards the part of the weld still to be made stechendes Schweißen *nt*
welding with weaving pendelndes Schweißen *nt*
welding without preheat Kaltschweißen *nt*
welding yielded a helical seam Schraubenliniennahtschweißung *f*
weldless nahtlos
weldment Schweißung *f*
weldment joint Schweißnaht *f*
weld-on end Anschweißende *nt*, Schweißende *nt*
weld-surface auftragschweißen
well-designed durchkonstruiert
well-fitting passend
welt Falz *m*
went message Ging-Meldung *f*
wet netzen, benetzen, befeuchten; Nässe *f*; nass
wet blasting Nassstrahlen *nt*
wet breaking resistance Nassbruchwiderstand *m*
wet bright nassblank
wet bursting strength Nassberstfestigkeit *f*
wet compressed air blasting Nassdruckluftstrahlen *nt*
wet cooling tower Nasskühlturm *m*
wet cooling tower with forced draught fan Nasskühlturm *m* mit drückendem Lüfter
wet cooling tower with induced draught fan Nasskühlturm *m* mit saugendem Lüfter
wet cutting Nassschliff *m*
wet glue labelling machine Nassklebeetikettiermaschine *f*
wet grinder Nassschleifmaschine *f*
wet incineration Nassveraschung *f*
wet ink coder Nasstintecodierer *m*
wet milling attachment Nassfräseinrichtung *f*
wet pressing Nasspressen *nt*
wet separator Nassabscheider *m*
wet solution method of fluorescence inspection Fluoreszenzverfahren *nt* mit wässriger Lösung
wet tensile test Nasszugversuch *m*
wet turning attachment Nassdreheinrichtung *f*
wet-dry cooling tower with natural draught Nasstrockenkühlturm *m* mit natürlichem Zug
wetness Nässe *f*
wetting Berieselung *f*
wetting angle defect Randwinkelfehler *m*
wetting water Benetzungswasser *nt*
wheel Rad *nt*, Scheibe *f*
wheel abrasive cutting Nassschleifen *nt*
wheel and disk drive Reibradantrieb *m*
wheel base Radstand *m*
wheel bearing Radlager *nt*
wheel body Radkörper *m*
wheel bond Schleifscheibenbindung *f*
wheel boss Radnabe *f*
wheel boss cap Radkappe *f*
wheel braking and/or locking device Radfeststeller *m*
wheel centre Radkörper *m*, Radscheibe *f*
wheel channel Röllchenleiste *f*
wheel crushing attachment Rollprofileinrichtung *f*, Rollprofiliereinrichtung *f*
wheel diagram Kreisdiagramm *nt*
wheel disk Radscheibe *f*
wheel dresser Scheibenabrichter *m*
wheel face Scheibenstirnfläche *f*, Schleiffläche *f*

wheel failure Radbruch *m*
wheel flange Spurkranz *m*
wheel forming Profilabrichten *nt*
wheel friction Rollreibung *f*
wheel grade Schleifscheibenhärte *f*
wheel guard Schutzhaube *f*, Radschutz *m*
wheel hood Radabdeckung *f*
wheel housing Radschutz *m*
wheel hub Radnabe *f*
wheel hub gear Radnabengetriebe *nt*
wheel load Raddruck *m*
wheel loading Radlast *f*
wheel marks Riefen *fpl*, Schleifspuren *fpl*
wheel position indicator Radstellungsanzeiger *m*
wheel pressure 1. Raddruck *m* **2.** *(Schleifen)* Schleifdruck *m*
wheel pressure angle Schleifscheibeneingriffswinkel *m*
wheel rim Radkranz *m*
wheel running surface Lauffläche *f* der Laufräder
wheel segment Schleifsegment *nt*
wheel slide Schleifschlitten *m*
wheel spindle Schleifspindel *f*
wheel suspension Radaufhängung *f*
wheel track Röllchenschiene *f*
wheel tread Lauffläche *f* der Laufräder
wheel wear Radabnutzung *f*
wheel width Radbreite *f*
wheelhead Schleifbock *m*, Schleifkopf *m*
wheelhead slide Schleifschlitten *m*
wheels with metal rims Räder *ntpl* mit Metallfelgen
wheels with pneumatic tyres Räder *ntpl* mit Luftbereifung
wheels with solid tyres Räder *ntpl* mit Vollgummibereifung
wheels with solid tyres for pneumatic rims Räder *ntpl* mit Vollgummireifen für Luftreifenfelgen
wheel-supported radunterstützt
when braking starts bei Bremsbeginn
whilst maintaining unter Beibehaltung von
whim Winde *f*
whirling Wirbeln *nt*
whirling tool Wirbelmeißel *m*
white cast iron Hartguss *m*
white oil Weißöl *nt*
white rust formation Weißrostbildung *f*
white yarn Weißstrick *m*
whiteheart malleable cast iron weißer Temperguss *m*
white-heart malleabilizing process deutsches Temperverfahren *nt*
white-hot weißglühend
white-iron casting Hartgussstück *nt*
Whitworth fine pitch thread Whitworth-Feingewinde *nt*
whole gesamt, ganz
whole body vibration Ganzkörperschwingung *f*
whole depth factor Zahnkopfhöhenfaktor *m*
whole depth of tooth space Zahnhöhe *f*
whole interval Gesamtbereich *m*
wholesale price Wiederverkäuferpreis *m*
wholesaler(s) Großhandel *m*
wick Docht *m*
wick-feed lubrication Dochtschmierung *f*
wicking action Dochtwirkung *f*
wide breit, weit
wide aisle Breitgang *m*
wide area network (WAN) Weiterverkehrsnetz *nt*
wide face square nose tool breiter Drehmeißel *m*
wide finishing Breitschlichten *nt*
wide gantry Flächenportal *nt*
wide load seitlich überhängende Ladung *f*
wide wheel grinding Breitschliff *m*
widen aufbeulen, aufweiten, erweitern, weiten
wide-necked flask Weithalsflasche *f*
wide-necked glass flask with a ground neck Weithalsschliffflasche *f*
wide-necked graduated flask Weithalsmesskolben *m*
widening Erweiterung *f*
wide-pitch fluting grobe Profilierung *f*
wide-pitched mit großer Teilung

wide-range divider Teilkopf *m* für weite Bereiche
wide-spaced lettering Breitschrift *f*
width Breite *f*, Weite *f*, Spannweite *f*
width across corners Eckenmaß *nt*
width across forks Zinkenabstand *m*
width crowing Breitenballigkeit *f*
width dimension Breitenmaß *nt*
width monitoring Seitenüberwachung *f*
width of chip Spanbreite *f*
width of cut Spanungsbreite *f*, Schnittbreite *f*
width of fork arm carriage Gabelträgerbreite *f*
width of intersecting aisle Winkelgangbreite *f*
width of land Fasenbreite *f*
width of line Linienbreite *f*
width of prong Zinkenbreite *f*
width of reduced face Breite *f* der reduzierten Spanfläche
width of tooth face Zahnbreite *f*
width of wear mark Verschleißmarkenbreite *f*
width of wheel face Schleifscheibenbreite *f*, Scheibenbreite *f*
width ratio Breitenverhältnis *nt*
width variation Breitenschwankung *f*
width-modulated pulse signal breitmoduliertes Impulssignal *nt*
winch Seilzug *m*, Seilwinde *f*, Winde *f*, Handkurbel *f*
winch lifting system Windhubsystem *nt*
wind 1. Wind *m* **2.** *(um~, auf~)* wickeln, winden, kurbeln, spulen (um, auf), aufspulen, aufwickeln
wind force Windkraft *f*, Windstärke *f*
wind gauge Windmesser *m*
wind intensity Windstärke *f*
wind load Windlast *f*
wind pressure Winddruck *m*
wind speed Windgeschwindigkeit *f*
wind stress Windlast *f*
wind velocity Windgeschwindigkeit *f*
wind velocity indicator Windmesser *m*
winding Winden *nt*, Wicklung *f*, Windung *f*
winding resistance Wicklungswiderstand *m*
winding rope load Förderseillast *f*
winding up Aufwickeln *nt*
window Fenster *nt*, Schauloch *nt*
window aperture Fensterscheibe *f*
window frame Fensterrahmen *m*
window pane Fensterscheibe *f*
window radiator Fensterheizkörper *m*
window ventilation Fensterlüftung *f*
windscreen Windschutzscheibe *f*
windscreen wiper Scheibenwischer *m*, Wischer *m*
windshield Windschutzscheibe *f*
windshield wiper Wischer *m*
wing Flügel *m*
wing nut Flügelmutter *f*
wing of a door/of a gate Torflügel *m*
wing type union nut Knebelüberwurfmutter *f*
winter space heating Winterheizung *f*
WIP inventory Umlaufbestand *m*
wipe abstreifen, abputzen, wischen
wipe resistance Wischbeständigkeit *f*
wiper Abstreifer *m*
wiping contact Wischkontakt *m*
wire 1. Kabel *nt*, Draht *m*; verkabeln, verdrahten, Kabel verlegen **2.** *(el. schalten)* beschalten
wire a building Leitungen im Gebäude verlegen
wire cable Drahtseil *nt*
wire cage Drahtgitter *nt*
wire drawing Drahtziehen *nt*
wire drawing machine Drahtziehmaschine *f*
wire drop grip Drahtseilklemme *f*
wire electrode Drahtelektrode *f*
wire eroding Drahterodieren *nt*
wire eroding machine Drahterodiermaschine *f*
wire fed forward by a pushing action schiebende Drahtförderung *f*
wire feed speed Schweißzusatzvorschubgeschwindigkeit *f*
wire gauze Metallgaze *f*
wire galvanized after drawing schlussverzinkter Draht *m*
wire mesh Drahtgeflecht *nt*
wire mill Drahtstraße *f*
wire netting Maschendraht *m*

wire pellets Drahtkorn *nt*
wire penetrameter Drahtsteg *m*
wire rope Seil *nt*, Drahtseil *nt*, Seilzug *m*
wire rope guide pulley Seilrolle *f*
wire spiral Drahtwendel *f*
wire tinned after drawing schlussverzinnter Draht *m*
wire wave Drahtwelle *f*
wirebound über Draht
wired AND Phantom-UND-Verknüpfung *f*
wired OR Phantom-ODER-Verknüpfung *f*
wireless drahtlos; Rundfunk *m*
wiring Leitung *f*, Verdrahtung *f*, Verkabelung *f*, Schaltung *f*, Beschaltung *f*, Leitungsverlegung *f*
wiring diagram Schaltplan *m*
wiring error Verdrahtungsfehler *m*
with a low level of heat radiation wärmestrahlungsarm
with casing gekapselt
with complete rotatability umlauffähig
with double-helical teeth pfeilverzahnt
with good grip griffig
with herringbone gear teeth pfeilverzahnt
with operated facing at right angles to the normal line of travel mit Quersitz
with operator standing at right angles to the normal line of travel mit Querstand
with reversal of poles polumschaltbar
with the operator seated forward mit Frontsitz
withdraw ziehen, zurückziehen, zurücknehmen, herausziehen, außer Betrieb setzen
withdraw the plug Stecker ziehen
withdrawable rückziehbar
withdrawal Zurückziehen *nt*, Ziehen *nt*
withdrawal by robots Roboterentnahme *f*
withdrawal from stock Lagerentnahme *f*
withdrawal of gas Gasentnahme *f*
withdrawn position ausgefahrene Stellung *f*
within innerhalb
within reach in Reichweite, in Griffnähe
without ohne
without a diamond diamantfrei
without battery batterielos
without blisters blasenfrei
without casing ungekapselt
without contact berührungsfrei
without error fehlerfrei
without flaws blasenfrei
without interruption lückenlos
without joints stoßfrei
without jolt(ing) ruckfrei
without load in unbelastetem Zustand
without operator attention wartungsfrei
without remachining nacharbeitsfrei
without restrictions uneingeschränkt
without reworking nacharbeitsfrei
without tooling marks riefenfrei
withstand widerstehen, aufnehmen, standhalten, aushalten
withstand test Beständigkeitsprüfung *f*
wobble wobbeln, taumeln; Wobbeln *nt*, Taumeln *nt*, Taumel *m*
wobble frequency Wobbelfrequenz *f*
wobble plate Taumelscheibe *f*
wobble tolerance Planlauftoleranz *f*
wobbling Wobbeln *nt*
wood Holz *nt*
wood dust firing equipment Holzstaubfeuerung *f*
wood wool layer Holzwolleschicht *f*
wood working machine Holzbearbeitungsmaschine *f*
wooden hölzern
wooden board Holzplatte *f*
wooden box Holzkiste *f*
wooden case Holzkiste *f*
wooden pallet Holzpalette *f*
wooden pellet Holzpellets *ntpl*
wooden plate Holzplatte *f*
wooden slab Holzplatte *f*
Woodruff key Scheibenfeder *f*
word Wort *nt*
word processing Wortverarbeitung *f*; wortverarbeitend

work arbeiten, verarbeiten, bearbeiten, funktionieren, wirken, laufen; Arbeit *f*
work area Arbeitsbereich *m*
work bench Werktisch *m*
work blank Rohling *m*
work carrier Werkstückhalter *m*
work centre Körnerspitze *f*
work chucking Werkstückspannung *f*
work cold kaltformen
work controlling Arbeitssteuerung *f*
work cycle Arbeitskreislauf *m*, Arbeitstakt *m*, Arbeitsablauf *m*, Ablauf *m* der Arbeitsgänge
work cycle time Arbeitsspielzeit *f*
work driver Mitnehmer *m*
work ejector Werkstückauswerfer *m*
work feed Werkstoffzufuhr *f*, Werkstückvorschub *m*
work feeding Werkstückzubringung *f*
work fixture Werkstückspanneinrichtung *f*, Werkstückaufspannvorrichtung *f*, Werkstückspanner *m*
work flow Arbeitsablauf *m*
work flow management Ablaufmanagement *nt*, Ablauforganisation *f*
work gap Arbeitsspalt *m*
work gripping Werkstoffspannung *f*
work handle Arbeitsgriff *m*
work handling Transport *m* des Werkstücks
work hardening Kaltverfestigung *f*
work holder Aufnahme *f*
work holding device Haltevorrichtung *f*
work horn Aufnahmedorn *m*
work in hand 1. *(z.Z.)* Werkstück *nt* in Bearbeitung, **2.** *(zukünftig)* vorzunehmende Arbeit *f*
work in process Ware *f* in Arbeit
work layout Anreißen *nt*
work locating fixture Werkstückspanneinrichtung *f*, Werkstückaufspannvorrichtung *f*, Werkstückspanner *m*
work out gestalten
work part Arbeitsstück *nt*
work part coordinate system Werkstückbasiskoordinatensystem *nt*
work parts flow Werkstückfluss *m*
work parts flow system Werkstückflusssystem *nt*
work period Arbeitsperiode *f*
work planning Arbeitsvorbereitung *f*
work platen Arbeitstisch *m*
work process Arbeitsvorgang *m*
work protection Arbeitsschutz *m*
work rest Werkstückauflage *f*
work setting Werkstückaufspannung *f*
work site Arbeitsplatz *m*
work spindle Hauptspindel *f*, Arbeitsspindel *f*, Werkstückspindel *f*, Spindelstock *m*
work stage Arbeitsstufe *f*, Arbeitsstation *f*
work step Arbeitsgang *m*
work steps Arbeitsfolge *f*
work study Arbeitsstudie *f*
work surface Werkstückschnittfläche *f*, Hauptschnittfläche *f*, Schnittfläche *f*
work system Arbeitssystem *nt*
work system planning Arbeitssystemplanung *f*
work test report Werkszeugnis *nt*
work to be done Arbeitsanfall *m*
work together zusammenarbeiten, zusammenwirken
work tolerance Werkstücktoleranz *f*
work tray Werkstück-Kasten *m*
workability Bearbeitbarkeit *f*
workable verformbar
workbench Werkbank *f*
workday Arbeitstag *m*
worked penetration Walkpenetration *f*
worker Arbeiter *m*
worker self testing Werkerselbstprüfung *f*
work-factory-system Work-Factory-System *nt*
work-harden kaltverfestigen, härten bei der Bearbeitung
workholder Aufspannvorrichtung *f*, Aufnahmevorrichtung *f* für Werkstücke
workholding bushing Spannbüchse *f*
workholding device Spanneinrichtung *f*, Spannvorrichtung *f*
workholding fixture Spannzeug *f*, Werkstückspanneinrichtung *f*, Spannvorrichtung *f*, Werkstückaufspannvorrichtung *f*, Werkstückspanner *m*, Aufnahmevorrichtung *f* für Werkstücke
workholding table Arbeitstisch *m*

work-in-progress-inventory Umlaufbestand *m*, Halbwarenbestand *m*
working Machart *f*, Bearbeitung *f*, Lauf *m*
working action Wälzvorgang *m*
working aisle Arbeitsgang *m*
working aisle width Arbeitsgangbreite *f*
working allocation working distribution Arbeitsverteilung *f*
working angle Werkzeugwinkel *m*, Wirkwinkel *m*, Arbeitswinkel *m* des Werkzeuges, Spanwinkel *m*
working angle convention Festlegung *f* der Wirkwinkel
working appliance Arbeitsmittel *nt*
working approach angle Wirkeinstellergänzungswinkel *m*
working area Arbeitsfläche *f*
working area limit Arbeitsfeldbegrenzung *f*
working back clearance Wirkrückfreiwinkel *m*
working back plane Wirkrückebene *f*
working back rake Wirkrückspanwinkel *m*
working back wedge angle Wirkrückkeilwinkel *m*
working background Arbeitsumgebung *f*
working backlash Betriebsflankenspiel *nt*
working capacity Arbeitsleistung *f*
working clearance Wirkfreiwinkel *m*
working concentricity variation Wälzrundlaufabweichung *f*
working condition Betriebszustand *m*
working conditions Arbeitsbedingungen *fpl*
working control Arbeitskontrolle *f*
working cutting edge angle Wirkeinstellwinkel *m*
working cutting edge inclination Wirkneigungswinkel *m*
working cutting edge plane Wirkschneidenebene *f*
working cycle Arbeitstakt *m*, Arbeitsspiel *nt*
working cylinder Arbeitszylinder *m*
working day Arbeitstag *m*
working diagram Arbeitsdiagramm *nt*
working dimension Arbeitsmaß *nt*
working distance Arbeitsabstand *m*
working edge Hauptschneide *f*
working energy Wirkenergie *f*
working engagement Arbeitseingriff *m*
working feed Arbeitsvorschub *m*, Arbeitsgang *m*
working fit Passsitz *m*
working flank Arbeitsflanke *f*
working force Wirkkraft *f*
working gage Arbeitslehre *f*
working joint Arbeitsfuge *f*
working lead angle Wirkeinstellergänzungswinkel *m*
working length Wälzlänge *f*
working light Arbeitsleuchte *f*, Arbeitsscheinwerfer *m*
working load Gebrauchslast *f*
working machine Arbeitsmaschine *f*
working major cutting edge Wirkhauptschneide *f*
working medium Arbeitsmedium *nt*
working memory Arbeitsspeicher *m*
working method Arbeitsverfahren *nt*, Arbeitsweise *f*
working minor cutting edge Wirknebenschneide *f*
working minor cutting edge angle Wirkeinstellwinkel *m* der Nebenschneide
working motion Arbeitsbewegung *f*
working normal clearance Wirknormalfreiwinkel *m*
working normal rake Wirknormalspanwinkel *m*
working object Arbeitsgegenstand *m*
working of the root run Ausarbeiten *nt* der Wurzellage
working oil level Arbeitsölspiegel *m*
working operation Arbeitsvorgang *m*
working orientation angle Wirklagewinkel *m*
working orthogonal clearance Wirkorthogonalfreiwinkel *m*
working orthogonal plane Wirkorthogonalebene *f*
working orthogonal rake Wirkorthogonalspanwinkel *m*

working orthogonal wedge angle Wirkorthogonalkeilwinkel *m*
working overpressure Betriebsüberdruck *m*
working pair Wirkpaar *nt*
working party Arbeitsgruppe *f*
working perpendicular force Wirknormalkraft *f*
working personnel Arbeitspersonal *nt*
working pitch circle Betriebswälzkreis *m*
working plane Arbeitsebene *f*
working platform Arbeitsbühne *f*, Arbeitsplattform *f*
working pleasure Arbeitsfreude *f*
working point Arbeitsstelle *f*
working position Arbeitsposition *f*, Arbeitsstellung *f*
working power Wirkleistung *f*
working pressure level Betriebsdruckstufe *f*
working principle Wirkungsweise *f*, Arbeitsweise *f*
working productivity Arbeitsproduktivität *f*
working provision Arbeitsbereitstellung *f*
working rake Wirkspanwinkel *m*
working reference plane Wirkbezugsebene *f*
working roughness Betriebsrauheit *f*, Betriebsrauhigkeit *f*
working schedule Arbeitsplan *m*
working side clearance Wirkseitenfreiwinkel *m*
working side rake Wirkseitenspanwinkel *m*
working side wedge angle Wirkseitenkeilwinkel *m*
working stroke Arbeitshub *m*
working substance Arbeitsmittel *nt*
working surface Arbeitsfläche *f*, Funktionsfläche *f*
working test Wälzprüfung *f*
working time Arbeitszeit *f*, Nutzungszeit *f*, Einschaltdauer *f*
working traverse Arbeitsgang *m*, Arbeitsbewegung *f*
working variation Wälzabweichung *f*
working voltage Arbeitsspannung *f*

working wedge angle Wirkkeilwinkel *m*
working zone Arbeitsbereich *m*
work-in-progress (WIP) Halbwaren *pl*, unfertige Erzeugnisse *ntpl*, Umlaufbestand *m*
workman Arbeiter *m*
workmanlike fachgerecht
workmanship handwerkliches Können *nt*, handwerkliche Ausführung *f*, werkgerechte Ausführung *f*
work-moving attachment Werkstückbewegungseinrichtung *f*
workpart Arbeitsteil *nt*, Werkstück *nt*
workpiece Werkstück *nt*, Arbeitsteil *nt*, Arbeitsstück *nt*, Bezugsstück *nt*
workpiece bolt thread Werkstück-Bolzengewinde *nt*
workpiece carrier Werkstückträger *m*
workpiece changer Werkstückwechsel *m*
workpiece costs Werkstückkosten *pl*
workpiece cutting Werkstückbearbeitung *f*
workpiece data Werkstückdaten *pl*
workpiece dragging *(Verfahren)* bewegtes Werkstück *nt*
workpiece element Werkstückelement *nt*
workpiece fabrication Teileformgebung *f*
workpiece feed Werkstückzuführung *f*
workpiece gauging Werkstücklehrung *f*
workpiece geometry Werkstückgeometrie *f*
workpiece handling Werkstückbearbeitung *f*
workpiece machining Werkstückbearbeitung *f*
workpiece maximum dimension Werkstückgrößtmaß *nt*
workpiece minimum dimension Werkstückkleinstmaß *nt*
workpiece mount Werkstückhalterung *f*
workpiece nut thread Werkstückmuttergewinde *nt*
workpiece processing Werkstückbearbeitung *f*

workpiece property Werkstückeigenschaft *f*
workpiece quality Werkstückqualität *f*
workpiece reverse side Werkstückgegenfläche *f*
workpiece screw thread Werkstückgewinde *nt*
workpiece tangential velocity Werkstücktangentialgeschwindigkeit *f*
workpiece tolerance Werkstücktoleranz *f*
workplace area Arbeitsplatzfläche *f*
workplace concentration Arbeitsplatzkonzentration *f*
workplace design Arbeitsplatzgestaltung *f*
workplace equipment Arbeitseinrichtung *f*
workplace lighting Arbeitsplatzbeleuchtung *f*
workplace organization Arbeitsplatzgestaltung *f*
work-rest blade Auflageschiene *f*
works Betrieb *m*, Werk *nt*
works certificate Werkszeugnis *nt*
works engineer Betriebsingenieur *m*
works of destination Empfängerwerk *nt*
works standard Werknorm *f*, Hausnorm *f*
works standard specification Betriebsnorm *f*
works test pressure Werkprüfdruck *m*
worksheet Tabelle *f*
workmanship manual Wartungsanleitung *f*
workshop Betrieb *m*, Betriebsstätte *f*, Werkstatt *f*, Betriebshalle *f*
workshop drawing Werkstattzeichnung *f*
workshop facilities Fertigungsmittel *ntpl*, Arbeitsgeräte *ntpl*
workshop facilities planning Fertigungsmittelplanung *f*
workshop facilities selection Fertigungsmittelauswahl *f*
workshop gauge Arbeitsmaß *nt*
workshop generator Werkstattentwickler *m*
workshop order Werkstattauftrag *m*
workshop practice Werkstatttechnik *f*
workshop production Werkstattfertigung *f*
workshop T-square Werkstattwinkel *m*
workshop-orientate programming werkstattorientierte Programmierung *f*
work-spindle drum Werkstückspindeltrommel *f*
workstation Arbeitsplatz *m*
worktable Arbeitstisch *m*, Aufspanntisch *m*, Tisch *m*, Aufspannfläche *f*
worktable of the drilling machine Bohrtisch *m*
work-table-cross feed motion Arbeitstischquerbewegung *f*
work handle element Arbeitsgriffelement *nt*
work planning costs Arbeitsvorbereitungskosten *pl*
world coordinate system Weltkoordinatensystem *nt*
workplace Arbeitsplatz *m*
worm Schnecke *f*
worm cutting Schneckenfräsen *nt*
worm cutting machine Schneckenfräsmaschine *f*
worm gear Schneckenrad *nt*
worm gear cutting Schneckenradfräsen *nt*
worm gear drive Schneckengetriebe *nt*
worm gear finishing hob Schneckenradschlichtfräser *m*
worm gear hob Schneckenradfräser *m*
worm gear milling cutter Schneckenradfräser *m*
worm gear pair Schneckenradsatz *m*, Schneckengetriebe *nt*
worm gear set Schneckenradsatz *m*
worm gears Schneckentriebe *nt*
worm hobbing machine Schneckenwälzfräsmaschine *f*
worm miller Schneckenfräsmaschine *f*
worm milling Schneckenfräsen *nt*
worm milling attachment Schneckenfräsvorrichtung *f*
worm milling machine Schneckenfräsmaschine *f*
worm rotational speed Schneckendrehzahl *f*
worm shaft Schneckenwelle *f*

worm thread milling Schneckengewindefräsen *nt*
worm thread milling machine Schneckengewindefräsmaschine *f*
worm wheel Schneckenrad *nt*
worm wheel cutting Schneckenradfräsen *nt*
worm wheel finishing hob Schneckenradschlichtfräser *m*
worm wheel generating machine Schneckenräderwälzfräsmaschine *f*
worm wheel hob Schneckenradfräser *m*, Schneckenradwälzfräser *m*
worm wheel hobbing Schneckenradfräsen *nt*
wormhole Schlauchprobe *f*
worn abgegriffen
worn out abgenutzt
worsen verschlechtern
worsening Verschlechterung *f*
worst possible value geringstmöglicher Wert *m*
woven fabric inlay Gewebeeinlage *f*
woven material Gewebe *nt*
woven wire screen bottom Drahtsiebboden *m*
wrap 1. Überzug *m*, Verpackung *f*, Wicklung *f*, Windung *f*, Umhüllung *f* **2.** *(um~, ein~)* wickeln, umwickeln, einwickeln, herumlegen, umhüllen, umschlingen, einschlagen, einpacken
wrap allowance Wickelzuschlag *m*
wraparound cartoner Wraparoundkartoniermaschine *f*
wraparound case packing machine Wraparoundfaltschachtelverpackungsmaschine *f*
wraparound lidding machine Wraparoundverdeckelungsmaschine *f*
wraparound sleeving machine Wraparoundumhüllungsmaschine *f*
wraparound tray packing machine Wraparoundtrayverpackungsmaschine *f*
wrapping compound Wickelmasse *f*
wrapped umhüllt
wrapped coating Wickelschicht *f*
wrapping Umhüllung *f*, Umschlingen *nt*
wrapping film Umhüllungsfolie *f*
wrapping foil Umhüllungsfolie *f*
wrapping head Wickelkopf *m*
wrapping machine Einschlagmaschine *f*, Umwickelmaschine *f*, Wickler *m*, Verpackungsmaschine *f*, Umhüllungsmaschine *f*
wrapping machine for shrink films Schrumpffolieneinschlagmaschine *f*
wrapping machine forming a complete wrap Volleinschlagmaschine *f*
wrapping machine which partially wraps products Teileinschlagmaschine *f*
wrapping number Wickelzahl *f*
wrapping pattern Umhüllungsvariante *f*
wrapping program Wickelprogramm *nt*
wrapping ring Wickelring *m*
wrapping tape Wickelband *nt*
wrench Schlüssel *m*, Schraubenschlüssel *m*
wrench cutter Schlüsselfräser *m*
wrench opening Maulweite *f*
wrench opening width across fits Schlüsselweite *f*
wrenchless check schlüsselloses Futter *nt*
wring anschieben
wring together aneinander schieben, aneinander sprengen
wring upon each other aneinander schieben
wringing Anschub *m*
wringing property Anschiebbarkeit *f*
wringing surface Anschubfläche *f*
wringing together Ansprengen *nt*
wrinkle Falte *f*
wrinkle washer federnde und gewellte Unterlegscheibe *f*
wrist Kurbelzapfen *m*
wrist glove Fünffingerhandschuh *m*
write schreiben
write cycle Schreibzyklus *m*
write head Schreibkopf *m*
write off abschreiben
write once-read many einmal schreiben oftmals lesen
writing Schrift *f*
writing cycle Schreibzyklus *m*
writing implement Schreibgerät *nt*

writing property Beschreibbarkeit *f*
written report Niederschrift *f*
wrong falsch
wrong delivery Falschlieferung *f*

wrought copper alloy Kupferknetlegierung *f*
wrought on angesprengt

X$_x$

X-axis X-Achse *f*
X-butt joint Doppel-V-Naht *f*
X-circle V-Kreis *m*
X-circle arc V-Kreis-Bogen *m*
X-circle diameter V-Kreis-Durchmesser *m*
X-circle pitch V-Kreis-Teilung *f*
X-coordinate X-Koordinate *f*
X-cut crystal X-Quarz *nt*
X-cylinder V-Zylinder *m*
X-cylinder normal pitch V-Zylinder-Normalteilung *f*
xenon arc radiation Xenonbogenstrahlung *f*
X-gear V-Rad *nt*
X-gear pair V-Radpaar *nt*, Radpaar *nt* mit Profilverschiebung
x-mm compression resistance x-mm Stauchwiderstand *m*
x-per cent compressive offset yield x-% Stauchspannung *f*
x-per cent compression yield x-% Stauchspannung *f*
X-radiation Röntgenstrahlung *f*
X-radiator Röntgenstrahler *m*
X-ray röntgen, Röntgenstrahl *m*
X-ray current intensity Röntgenröhrenstromstärke *f*
X-ray depth lithography Röntgentiefenlithographie *f*
X-ray equipment Röntgengerät *nt*, Röntgeneinrichtung *f*
X-ray equipment for radiography Röntgenaufnahmegerät *nt*

X-ray examination Röntgenprüfung *f*
X-ray fluoroscopic equipment Röntgendurchleuchtungsgerät *nt*
X-ray generator with mains current correction Röntgengenerator *m* mit Netzangleich
X-ray image Röntgenbild *nt*
X-ray inspection Röntgenprüfung *f*
X-ray pattern Röntgenschattenbild *nt*
X-ray protective clothing Röntgenschutzkleidung *f*
X-ray radiograph Röntgenfilmaufnahme *f*
X-ray radioscopic equipment Röntgendurchleuchtungsgerät *nt*
X-ray sensitive röntgenstrahlenempfindlich
X-ray stereo equipment Röntgenraumbildungsgerät *nt*
X-ray technique Röntgenverfahren *nt*
X-ray test method Röntgenprüfverfahren *nt*
X-ray tube Röntgenröhre *f*
X-ray tube voltage Röntgenröhrenspannung *f*
X-ray warning device Strahlenwarngerät *nt*
X-tooth system V-Verzahnung *f*
xylene method Xylolverfahren *nt*
X-zero gear Nullrad *nt*
X-zero gear pair Nullradpaar *nt*
X-zero tooth system Satzräderverzahnung *f*

Y y

yardstick Maßstab *m*
yarning Verstricken *nt*
Y-axis Y-Achse *f*
Y-branch Schrägabzweig *m*
Y-circle pitch Y-Kreis-Teilung *f*
Y-connected in Sternschaltung *f*
Y-connection Sternschaltung *f*
Y-cylinder normal pitch Y-Zylinder-Normteilung *f*
year of construction Baujahr *nt*
year of manufacture Baujahr *nt*
yellowing Vergilbung *f*
yellowishness Gelbstichigkeit *f*
yield Ausstoß *m*, Produktion *f*, Ausbeute *f*; ausbringen
yield point Streckgrenze *f*, Streckengrenze *f*, Fließgrenze *f*
yield range Fließbereich *m*
yield stress Fließspannung *f*
yielding phenomenon Fließvorgang *m*
yieldingness Nachgiebigkeit *f*
yoke Gabel *f*, Bügel *m*, Balken *m*, Joch *nt*, Traglager *nt*
yoke ear Schenkel *m*
yoke test specimen Bügelprobe *f*
Young's modulus of elasticity statischer Elastizitätsmodul *m*
Y-starting resistor Sternpunktanlasswiderstand *m*
Y-valve Schrägsitzventil *nt*

Z z

Zener diode Zenerdiode *f*
zero Null *f*; auf Null stellen
zero addendum modification Profilverschiebung *f* Null
zero adjustment Nulleinstellung *f*
zero allowance Abmaß *nt* Null
zero conductor Sternpunkt *m*
zero current interval stromlose Zeitspanne *f*
zero damping Nulldämpfung *f*
zero indication Nullpunktanzeige *f*, Nullanzeige *f*
zero inventory Nullbestand *m*
zero lag Nachlaufnull *f*
zero offset Nullpunktverschiebung *f*
zero point Ursprungspunkt *m*
zero point correction Nullpunktkorrektur *f*
zero point drift Nullpunktdrift *m*
zero potential Nullspannung *f*
zero state Nullzustand *m*
zero voltage Nullspannung *f*
zero-backlash centre distance spielfreier Achsabstand *m*
zero-backlash engagement spielfreier Eingriff *m*
zero-backlash mating spielfreie Paarung *f*
zero-current period stromloser Zeitabschnitt *m*
zero-deviation cylindrical gear abweichungsfreies Stirnrad *nt*
zero-play condition spielfreier Zustand *m*
zero-play tooth engagement spiegelfreier Zahneingriff *m*
zero-point-two per cent proof stress Null-Komma-Zwei-Prozent-Grenze *f*
zero-position Nulllage *f*
zero-variation angular position abweichungsfreie Drehwinkelstellung *f*
zero-variation circular pitch abweichungsfreie Kreisstellung *f*
zero-variation cylindrical gear abweichungsfreies Stirnrad *nt*
zigzag bracing Petersverrippung *f*
zigzag configuration of the pipeline zickzackförmige Leitungsführung *f*

zinc Zink *nt*; verzinken
zinc adhesion Zinkhaftung *f*
zinc coating Verzinken *nt*, Zinküberzug *m*
zinc dust coating Zinkstaubbeschichtung *f*
zinc sprayed coating Zinkspritzschicht *f*
zircon Zirkon *nt*
zirconium Zirkonium *nt*
zone Bereich *m*, Zone *f*
zone diameter tolerance field Kegeldurchmessertoleranzfeld *nt*
zone indicator Zonenanzeige *f*
zone of action Eingriffsfeld *nt*
zone of attack Angriffsbereich *m*
zone of fluctuating water level Wasserwechselzone *f*
zone of fusion Schmelzzone *f*
zone type furnace Stufenofen *m*
zoning Zoneneinteilung *f*, Zonung *f*
zoom zoomen
zooming Zoomen *nt*, Zoomfunktion *f*
Z-shaped profile Z-Profil *nt*

A a

A/D-Wandler *m* A/D converter
AA-Toleranzen *fpl* Advisory Committee tolerances
ab *(Richtung)* down
ab Lager ex stock
abändern alter, change, modify
abarbeiten take down, dress off
Abart *f* variety
abätzen etch, remove by etching
Abbau *m* **1.** *(allgemein)* reduction, demounting, dismantling **2.** *(biologisch)* degradation **3.** *(chemisch)* decomposition **4.** *(Demontage)* dismantling, disassembly **5.** *(e. Energie)* dissipation
abbauen reduce; demount; dismantle; relieve
abbeizen cauterize; pickle
Abbeizmittel *nt* pickling agent
Abbéscher Grundsatz *m* Abbé principle
abbewegen lower, move downward
Abbewegung *f* downward traverse; downfeed
abbiegen bend off; fold
Abbild *nt* image
Abbildegrad *m* degree of imaging
abbilden image, map
Abbildregister *nt* image register
Abbildung *f* imaging, mapping; figure
Abbildungsgenauigkeit *f* imaging accuracy
Abbildungsgröße *f* projection size
abbinden tie
Abblaseleistung *f* **1.** *(e. Kessels)* blow-off rate **2.** *(e. Ventils)* blow-off capacity **3.** *(e. Wassererwärmers)* relief capacity
abblasen bleed; discharge; vent
Abblasöffnung *f* bleed hole
Abblasseite *f* discharge side
Abblasventil *nt* relief valve
abblättern flake off, peel off, scale off
Abbrand *m* melting loss by oxidation, smelting loss, combustion
Abbrand *m* *(e. Ofens)* burn-up
Abbrandfaktor *m* combustion factor
Abbrandperiode *f* combustion period

Abbrandzeit *f* length of burning time
abbrechen interrupt, abort, kill, break off
Abbremseinrichtung *f* braking device
abbremsen brake, decelerate
Abbremsung *f* braking, deceleration; drawbar drag
Abbrenngerät *nt* flame cleaning device
Abbrennlängenverlust *m* flash-off
abbrennschweißen flash-weld
abbrennstumpfschweißen flash butt weld
Abbrennstumpfschweißen *nt* **aus dem Kalten** flash welding from cold
Abbrennstumpfschweißmaschine *f* flash-butt welding machine
abbröckeln crumble, spall
Abbröckeln *nt* **der Schneide** crumbling of the cutting edge
Abbruch *m* breakdown; interruption; abortion; kill; truncation
Abbruchstelle *f* point of truncation
abbuchen debit; charge off
Abbuchung *f* debit entry
ABC-Analyse *f* ABC analysis
ABC-Klassifizierung *f* ABC classification
ABC-Verteilung *f* ABC distribution
Abdeckblech *nt* cover plate, flashing
Abdeckboden *m* top cover
abdecken cover, mask, screen, guard
Abdeckung *f* access cover, cover, guard
abdichten make tight, pack, seal (off), stuff
Abdichtmittel *n* sealant
Abdichtung *f* sealing, sealing packing, seal, packing
Abdichtung *f* **beweglicher Teile** moving seal
Abdichtung *f* **beweglicher Teile gegeneinander** dynamic seal
Abdichtungsfolie *f* waterproofing sheet (or foil)
Abdrängkraft *f* thrust force
Abdrängung *f* deflection
Abdrehdiamant *m* *(Schleifscheibe)*

diamond dresser
Abdrehebene *f* truing plane
abdrehen 1. *(allgemein)* shut off, turn off, push off **2.** *(Schleifscheibe)* dress **3.** *(Schleifsteine)* true **4.** *(Planzug)* face
Abdrehschablone *f* truing template
Abdrehung *f* turning; grinding; truing
Abdrehvorrichtung *f* truing attachment
Abdrehwerkzeug *nt* turning (or lathe) tool; truing device
abdrücken force away, force off
Abdrückschraube *f* forcing screw
Abdruckverfahren *nt* impression method
Abdrückversuch *m* proof test
aberregen de-energize
abfahren follow the outline; track, trace; depart, leave; start
Abfahrt *f* departure
Abfahrtwinkel *m* departure angle
Abfall *m* **1.** *(allgemein)* discard, refuse, residue, loss, waste, spillage **2.** *(Druck)* drop, loss **3.** *(Metall)* scrap, scrap metals **4.** *(Spannung)* drop
Abfallbehälter *m* waste bin
Abfallbeseitigung *f* waste disposal
Abfallbeseitigungsgesetz *nt* waste disposal law
Abfälle *mpl* **bei der Verarbeitung** brokes *pl*
abfallen drop, decrease
abfallende Schneide *f* leading tool edge
Abfallprodukt *n* byproduct, waste product
Abfallverbrennungsofen *m* refuse incinerator furnace
abfangen 1. *(allgemein)* intercept, catch **2.** *(Prüflast)* catch
Abfanggeschwindigkeit *f* speed for tripping the catching device
abfasen cant, bevel, chamfer
Abfasmeißel *m* chamfering tool
Abfasung *f* chamfer, canting, bevel, beveling
abfedern cushion, spring
Abfederung *f* cushioning, springing, spring suspension
abfiltrierbar filtratable

Abfläch- und Zentriermaschine *f* face-milling and centering machine
abflachen flatten
abflächen end-face, spot-face
Abflächmaschine *f* **für Walzenstirnseiten** roll-end machine
Abflächmesser *nt* spot-face cutter
Abflachung *f* flattening, flat, truncation
abflanschen notch
abfließen drain (into)
Abfließspan *m* flow chip, continuous spiral chip
Abfluchtung *f* alignment
Abfluss *m* **1.** *(allgemein)* drain **2.** *(Öffnung)* outlet, exit **3.** *(von Spänen)* passage **4.** *(Vorgang)* discharge
Abflussbeiwert *m* discharge coefficient
Abflussmessquerschnitt *m* discharge measuring cross section
Abflussrinne *f* spout
Abflussventil *nt* discharge valve
abfördern retrieve
abfördernd output
Abforderung *f* *(von Lagerbeständen)* requisition
Abförderung *f* retrieval
Abformgreifer *m* up-shaping gripper
Abformung *f* forming
Abfrage *f* inquiry, enquiry, interrogation, query, request, sample, scan, retrieval
Abfragelesekopf *m* query read-head
abfragen call up, check, enquire, request, sample, scan, retrieve
Abfragesignal *nt* interrogation signal
abfräsen cut off, mill off
abfühlen sense, scan, trace
Abfuhr *f* **1.** *(allgemein)* conveyance, transport **2.** *(Späne)* disposal, removal, discharge **3.** *(Wärme)* dissipation
abführen 1. *(allgemein)* carry away, conduct away, dispose off, lead off/away, remove, retrieve, pass off, extract (from) **2.** *(Werkstück)* unload **3.** *(Späne)* remove **4.** *(Wärme)* dissipate
Abführinne *f* unloading chute
Abführstrecke *f* retrieval line, outgoing line
Abführung *f* carrying away, conducting away

Abgabe *f* dispensing, output, release, releasing
Abgabeleistung *f* power output
Abgang *m* exit
Abgangsmenge *f* retrieved quantity
Abgas *nt* 1. *(allg.)* exhaust gas, waste gas 2. *(Rauchgase)* stack gas
Abgasabführung *f* flue gas evacuation
Abgasabzug *m* exhaust gas hood (or offtake)
Abgasanlage *f* flue gas system
Abgasanschluss *m* flue gas connection
abgasbeheizt heated by flue gas
Abgasdrosseleinrichtung *f* flue gas throttling device
Abgase *ntpl* emissions
Abgasemission *f* exhaust emission
Abgasfang *m* flue gas flue
Abgaskanal *m* exhaust gas flue
Abgasklappe *f* flue gas damper
Abgaskühlvorrichtung *f* exhaust gas cooler
Abgasmessstrecke *f* flue gas test section
Abgasreiniger *m* exhaust gas purifier
Abgasrohr *nt* flue gas pipe
Abgasschornstein *m* flue gas chimney
Abgasschreiber *m* flue gas recorder
Abgasseite *f (e. Saugbrenners)* flue gas side
abgasseitig on the flue gas side
Abgassperreinrichtung *f (e. Ölfeuerungsanlage)* flue gas cut-off (or shut-off) device
Abgasstutzen *m* 1. *(e. Heizofens)* flue spigot 2. *(e. Wärmeerzeugers)* flue outlet
Abgassystem *nt* exhaust system
Abgastaupunkt *m* flue gas dew point
Abgaswäscher *m* flue gas scrubber
Abgasweg *m (e. Heizofens)* flue gas tract
abgeben 1. *(allgemein)* deliver, dispose, give off, release, yield 2. *(Informationen)* pass on (to) 3. *(Strom)* provide (to) 4. *(Waren)* dispense, deposit, unload
abgebrochen darstellen represent broken
abgedichtet leak-proof
abgefast bevel
abgeflachter Lehrdorn *m* flattened plug gauge
abgegebene Leistung *f* output, power output
abgeglichen flush
abgegriffen worn
abgehen leave
abgehender Ruf *m (Informatik)* call request
abgeknickter Schweißstab *m* kinked welding rod
abgelaufen *(Zeit)* elapsed, run
abgeleitete Größe *f (e. Berechnung)* derived quantity
abgenommenes Spanvolumen *nt* amount of stock removed
abgenutzt worn out
abgeschaltet deactivated, switched off
abgeschirmt shielded
abgeschlossener Bereich *m* restricted zone
abgeschrägt tapered, sloped, bevelled
abgesenkte Last *f* load in the lowered position
abgesetzt 1. *(Bohrer)* stepped 2. *(Drehmeißel)* shouldered, offset
abgesetzte Krone *f (e. Hutmutter)* shouldered castellation
abgesetzter Bohrmeißel *m* internal side tool, boring tool for corner work
abgesetzter Meißel *m* offset (cutting) tool
abgesetzter rechter Seitenmeißel *m* right-offset tool
abgestrahlte Beschichtungsteile *ntpl* dislodged fragments of coatings
abgestuft 1. *(allg.)* graduated, stepped 2. *(der Größe nach)* graded in size
abgetragener Werkstoff *m* abraded material
abgewickelte Grundzylindermantelfläche *f* angled base cylinder envelope
abgewickelter Grundkreisbogen *m* developed base circle arc
abgewinkelter Doppelringschlüssel *m* angled type double-ended ring spanner, offset double head box wrench
abgewinkelter Sechskantschraubendreher *m* cranked hexagon

wrench key
abgewinkelter Steckschlüssel *m* offset socket wrench
Abgleich *m* alignment, balance, trimming to value, *(US)* gaging, *(UK)* gauging
abgleichen align, balance, trim, *(US)* gage, *(UK)* gauge, adjust, level, match, value
abgraten burr, deburr, flash, snag, trim
Abgratmaschine *f* deburring machine, burr-removing machine
Abgratmatrize *f* trimming die
Abgratmeißel *m* burring chisel
Abgratschneiden *nt* **von Gußteilen oder Formwerkstücken** clipping
Abgratschneiden *nt* **von Schmiedestücken** flash trimming
Abgratwerkzeug *nt* trimming tool
abgreifen 1. *(Maße)* take measurements **2.** *(mittels Taster)* calliper
abgrenzen bound
Abgrenzung *f* demarcation
abhacken cut off, chop off
abhämmern peen
abhängen (von) depend on
abhängig dependent
abhängiger Wartezustand *m* nominal disconnected mode, NDM
Abhängigkeit *f* **1.** *(allg.)* dependency, relationship **2.** *(in ~ von)* as a function of
Abhängigkeitsnotation *f* dependency notation
abhauen part off
Abhebebewegung *f* relief motion
Abhebeeinrichtung *f* lifting mechanism
abheben 1. *(Bewegung nach oben)* lift off, raise **2.** *(Meißel)* clear **3.** *(Späne)* remove **4.** *(Werkzeug)* relieve **5.** *(vereinzeln)* separate
Abheben *nt* **(Werkstück)** unloading
Abhebeverfahren *nt* cut process
Abhebung *f* **1.** *(Bewegung nach oben)* lifting **2.** *(Späne)* removal **3.** *(Werkzeug)* relieving
Abhilfe *f* remedy, relief
Abhitze *f* waste heat
abhitzebeheizt heated by waste heat

abhobeln plane off
Abhub *m* lifting, retraction
Abhubbewegung *f* lifting
A-Bild *nt* A-scope presentation
abkanten 1. *(allg.)* bevel, fold (on the edge), fold over **2.** *(abschrägen)* chamfer, bevel **3.** *(Blech)* break, fold
Abkantmaschine *f* folding machine
Abkantnaht *f* angle weld
Abkantpresse *f* break, folding press, press brake
Abkantung *f* fold
Abkantwälzfräser *m* semi-topping hob, chamfering hob
abkippen dump, tip
abklären ascertain, discuss, clarify
Abklärung *f* agreement
abklemmen disconnect
abklingen die down
abklopfen 1. *(allg.)* knock off, scale, tap **2.** *(Schleifscheibe)* sound out
abkneifen nip off, pinch off
Abknickung *f* *(e. Maßlinie)* offset (or kinked) portion
abkohlen decarburize
abkratzen scrape off
Abkreidungsskala *f* chalking scale
Abkühlbedingung *f* cooling condition
abkühlen cool (down)
Abkühlspannung *f* cooling tension
Abkühlung *f* cool down, cooling
Abkühlungsdauer *f* cooling time (or period)
Abkühlungskurve *f* cool-down curve
Abkühlungsverlauf *m* cooling characteristic
Abkühlvorgang *m* cooling process, chilling process
abkuppeln disconnect, uncouple
Abkürzung *f* abbreviation
abladen discharge, tier, unload
Ablage *f* **1.** *(allg.)* place of deposit **2.** *(Dokumente)* filing **3.** *(Einrichtung)* equipment, installation plant
Ablagepunkt *m* setting-down point
ablagern deposit
Ablagerung *f* **1.** *(allg.)* deposit **2.** *(festsitzende ~)* firmly bonded deposit
Ablagerungszeit *f* storage period
Ablagetisch *m* finishing table

ablängen cut off to length, break down, cut (into sections)
Ablasseinrichtung *f* drain device
ablassen 1. *(Flüssigkeit)* drain **2.** *(Gas)* vent, discharge
Ablasshahn *m* drain cock
Ablassleistung *f* discharge capacity
Ablassschraube *f* drain plug
Ablassventil *nt* drain valve
Ablation *f* ablation
Ablauf *m* **1.** (Bauteil) outlet **2.** *(Arbeit)* process, operation, operation sequence **3.** *(e. Arbeitsvorganges)* operating sequence, work cycle **4.** *(Flüssigkeit)* drainage **5.** *(Geschehen)* course **6.** *(von Vorgängen)* cycle, sequence **7.** *(Zeitgrenze)* expiry
Ablauf *m* **der Arbeitsgänge** work cycle
Ablaufdiagramm *nt* flow diagram, flow sheet, flow chart, sequence diagram
ablaufen run, elapse, expire
ablauffähig executable, loadable
Ablauffolge *f* course succession
Ablaufkette *f* sequence cascade
Ablaufkontrolle *f* flow control
Ablauflogik *f* process logic
Ablaufmanagement *nt* operations management, work flow management
Ablauforganisation *f* process organization, work flow management
Ablaufplan *m* flow chart, sequence plan
Ablaufprogramm *nt* sequence programme
Ablaufprogrammierung *f* execution programming
Ablaufregel *f* process rule
Ablaufregelung *f* control of discharge
Ablaufrinne *f* drain channel (or gutter)
ablaufseitiger Bogen *m* outflow bend
Ablaufsicherung *f* safety drain valve, discharge safety device
Ablaufsprache *f* sequential function chart
Ablaufsteuersprache *f* sequential control language
Ablaufsteuerung *f* sequential control system, flow control, follow-up control, sequence control
Ablaufstruktur *f* process structure
Ablaufstutzen *m* discharge nozzle (or outlet)
Ablauftemperatur *f* outlet temperature
Ablaufversuch *m* fusion flow test
ablegen 1. *(hinlegen)* deposit, set down **2.** *(Dokumente)* file
ablehren 1. *(durch Festmaßlehren) (US)* gaging, *(UK)* gauging **2.** *(durch Strichmaße) (US)* caliper, *(UK)* calliper
ableiten 1. *(beseitigen)* dispose, carry off **2.** *(Flüssigkeiten)* pass off, discharge **3.** *(Gase)* issue **4.** *(Kräfte)* transmit (to) **5.** *(mathematisch)* derive (from) **6.** *(Wärme)* dissipate
Ableiter *m* drain
Ableitfähigkeit *f* ability to dissipate, electrostatic charges
Ableitstrom *m* discharge current
Ableitung *f* **1.** *(el.)* conductivity; earthing **2.** *(Wärme)* dissipation **3.** *(math.)* derivation
Ableitungsrohr *nt* draining tube
Ableitwiderstand *m* conductive resistance
ablenken divert, deflect, deviate
ablenkendes Magnetfeld *nt* deflecting magnetic field
Ablenkplatte *f* baffle, deflector plate
Ablenkspiegel *m* deflection mirror
Ablenkspule *f* deflection coil
Ablenkstrom *m* deflection current
Ablenksystem *nt* deflection system
Ablenkung *f* deflection, deviation
Ablenkwinkel *m* **1.** *(allg.)* deviation angle **2.** *(Schräge)* angle of slope, bevel angle
Ablesbarkeit *f* readability
Ablesefehler *m* reading error
Ablesegenauigkeit *f* accuracy of reading
Ableselupe *f* reading magnifier
ablesen read off, take readings
Ablesevorrichtung *f* reading facility (or device)
Ablesung *f* readout, reading
Ablichtungspapier *nt* photocopying paper

Ablichtungspapier *nt* für direktes elektrophotographisches Kopierverfahren photocopying paper for direct electrophotographic processes
Ablichtungspapier *nt* mit Silbersalzschicht silver sensitized photocopying paper
Ablöscheinrichtung *f* bottling device
Ablösefolie *f* release film
ablösen detach, scale off, separate, strip, release (from), dissolve
ablösendes Mittel *nt* detergent
Ablösepapier *nt* release paper
Ablösevorgang *m (bei Überzügen)* dissolving process
Ablösung *f* 1. *(Strömungslehre)* separation 2. *(chem.)* dissolution 3. *(mech.)* stripping
Abluft *f* extracted air
Abluftdurchlass *m* extractor air cut, discharge air outlet
Abluftleistung *f* air extraction rate
Abluftöffnung *f* air discharge opening
Abluftquerschnitt *m* extracted air cross section
Abmaß *nt* deviation, limit of tolerance, allowance, off-size
Abmaß *nt* **der Zahndickensehnen** deviation of the normal chordal tooth thickness
Abmaß *nt* **des diametralen Zweikugelmaßes** deviation of the diametral two-ball measurement
Abmaß *nt* **für Außenmaße** allowance for external dimensions, deviation for external sizes
Abmaß *nt* **für Innenmaße** allowance for internal dimensions, deviation for internal sizes
Abmaß *nt* **Null** zero allowance
Abmaßfaktor *m* deviation factor
Abmaßreihe *f* deviation series
Abmaßschaubild *nt* deviation diagram
Abmeldezeit *f* flame-out response time
abmessen rate, proportion
Abmessung *f* 1. *(Größe)* size 2. *(Maß)* dimension 3. *(Messergebnis)* measurement
Abmessung *f* **der Gabelzinken** fork dimensions

Abmessungen *fpl* dimensions, parameters, size
Abmessungen *fpl* **an Gussteilen** dimensions at cast parts
Abmessungsänderungen *fpl (Umformen)* dimension modification (forming)
Abmessungsnorm *f* dimension standard
Abmessungsverhältnis *nt* dimension relation
abmontieren detach, remove
Abnahme *f* 1. *(quantitativ)* decrease 2. *(Abbau)* demounting, dismounting 3. *(Betriebsabteilung)* inspection department 4. *(Druck)* drop 5. *(e. Maschine)* acceptance 6. *(e. großen Spans)* slogging 7. *(Geschwindigkeit)* deceleration 8. *(Kontrolle)* inspection 9. *(nach Prüfung)* acceptance, approval 10. *(Rückgang)* decrease, reduction 11. *(Späne)* removal 12. *(techn. Erzeugnisse)* acceptance 13. *(Drehzahlen)* reduction 14. *(Werkzeuge aus Vorrichtung)* removal 15. *(reduzieren)* reduction 16. *(Temperatur, Preise)* fall
Abnahmebedingung *f* inspection condition
abnahmebedürftige Anlage *f* plant subject to a requirement of acceptance
Abnahmedurchführung *f* execution of the inspection
Abnahmeflankenspiel *nt* acceptance backlash
Abnahmekontrolle *f* inspection test
Abnahmekriterium *nt* approval criterion
Abnahmelehre *f* inspection gage (or gauge)
Abnahmeprotokoll *nt* test certification, test record, test report book, acceptance certificate, acceptance report, approval record
Abnahmeprüfung *f* acceptance test (or testing), inspection test
Abnahmerisiko *nt* consumer's risk
Abnahmeschritt *m* approval measure
Abnahmetermin *m* approval date

Abnahmetest *m* test
Abnahmezeichnung *f* acceptance drawing
abnehmbar detachable, removable, loose
abnehmbarer Meißeleinsatz *m* removable tool bit
abnehmen 1. *(abbauen)* demount, detach **2.** *(Geschwindigkeit)* decelerate, slow down **3.** *(prüfen)* accept **4.** *(Späne)* remove, take off **5.** *(Werkstück)* unload **6.** *(entfernen)* detach, remove **7.** *(Kontrolle)* inspect, test **8.** *(nach Prüfung)* accept **9.** *(reduzieren)* reduce **10.** *(Rückgang)* decrease **11.** *(Temperatur, Preise)* fall **12.** *(Druck)* drop
abnutzbar wearable
abnutzen wear (off)
Abnutzung *f* abrasion, wear
Abnutzungsausgleich *m* wear compensation
Abnutzungsbereich *m* wear range
Abnutzungsdauer *f* wear life
Abnutzungserscheinung *f* wear
Abnutzungsfaktor *m* coefficient of wear
Abnutzungsfestigkeit *f* resistance to wear
Abnutzungsgrenze *f* wear limit
Abnutzungsmaß *nt* wear dimension
Abnutzungsprüfkörper *m* wear rate check plug member
Abnutzungstoleranz *f* wear tolerance
Abnutzungsversuch *m* abrasion test
Abnutzungszugabe *f* wear allowance
Abpinseln *nt (Dichtheitsprüfung e. Rohrleitung)* brushing
abplanen face, remove metal by facing
abplatten flattern
Abplattung *f* flattening, oblateness
abplatzen spall off
Abprall *m* ricochet, rebound
abprallen rebound, ricochet
abpumpen pump off
abputzen clean, wipe
abquetschen pinch off, squeeze off
abräumen take off, remove
abreibbar *(von Belägen)* capable of being rubbed off
Abreißen *nt* **1.** *(mech.)* tearing off, breaking **2.** *(e. Brennerflamme)* lift-off, blow-off, failure (of a flame)
Abreißspan *m* fragmental (or discontinuous) chip
Abreißverpackung *f* tear-off package
Abreißversuch *m* pull-off test
Abrichtdorn *m* truer mandrel
abrichten dress, redress, true (up), plane, level, sharpen
Abrichtgerät *nt* dressing mechanism
Abrichtgeschwindigkeit *f* dressing (truing) speed
Abrichthobel *m* planer
Abrichthobelmaschine *f* surface planing machine
Abrichtmaschine *f* smooth planer
Abrichträdchen *nt* star wheel
Abrichtrolle *f* roller truer
Abrichtscheibe *f* abrasive dressing wheel
Abrichtstift *m* abrasive-stick dresser
Abrichtwerkzeug *nt* dressing (truing) tool
Abrichtzeit *f* dressing time
Abrichtzyklus *m* dressing (truing) pass (traverse)
Abrieb *m* **1.** *(allg.)* abrasion, abrasion wear, abrasive grit, surface wear, detrition **2.** *(Ergebnis)* abraded material
Abriebbeschichtung *f* abrasive coating
abriebbeständig resistant to abrasion
abriebempfindlich susceptible to abrasion
abriebfest abrasion-proof
Abriebfestigkeit *f* abrasion resistance
Abriss *m* tear
abrollen uncoil, unreel, unwind, roll (down/off)
Abrollzone *f* roll down zone
Abruf *m* call, polling, recall
Abrufauftrag *m* make and take order
abrufen 1. *(allg.)* call up, poll, recall, retrieve, request **2.** *(Daten)* extract
Abrufverfahren *nt* calling procedure, polling technique
abrunden round (down or off) (to)
Abrundmeißel *m* rounding tool
Abrundung *f* **1.** *(allg.)* rounding off, rounding (up or down) **2.** *(Kante)* radius,

radiusing, roundness **3.** *(Verzahnung, Arbeitsergebnis)* radius, roundness
Abrundwälzfräser *m* chamfering hob, *(US)* semi-topping hob, *(UK)* tooth chamfering hob
abrutschen slip off
Absatz *m* **1.** *(Waren)* sales, selling **2.** *(Körper)* shoulder
Absatzbudgetierung *f* marketing budget accounting
Absatzdrehen *nt* multiple diameter turning, shoulder turning, turning to a shoulder
Absatzmarkt *m* distribution market
Absatzmaß *nt* **1.** *(allg.)* stepped dimension **2.** *(bei Gesenkschmiedestücken)* shoulder dimension
Absatzstufe *f* distribution echelon
Absatzzentrum *nt* distribution centre
Absauganlage *f* exhaust system
absaugen suck away
Absaugen *nt* *(Verunreinigungen)* suction cleaning
Absaugleitung *f* suction line
abschälen peel off
Abschalteinrichtung *f* isolation device
abschalten 1. *(allg.)* turn off, immobilize **2.** *(Arbeitsvorgang)* stop **3.** *(e. Brennerstufe)* cut out **4.** *(e. Ölbrenner)* cut off, shut down **5.** *(el.)* switch off, disconnect **6.** *(Leitungen)* shut off/down, cut off **7.** *(maschinelle Bewegungen)* trip **8.** *(Maschinen)* put out of operation (or service)
Abschaltkreis *m* de-energizing circuit, cut-off circuit, on/off control
Abschaltsignal *nt* shut-down signal
Abschaltspannung *f* breaking voltage
Abschaltsystem *nt* shut-down system
Abschaltung *f* **1.** *(allg.)* shutdown **2.** *(e. Motors)* disengagement **3.** *(el.)* switching off **4.** *(Hebel)* disengagement **5.** *(Maschine)* stopping, stop, put out of operation, tripping **6.** *(Vorschubbewegung)* trip
Abschaltverhalten *nt* shut down behaviour
Abschätzung *f* appraisal, estimation, evaluation
Abscheideanlage *f* separating installation
abscheiden settle, deposit, precipitate, separate, intercept
Abscheider *m* *(elektrostatischer ~)* electrostatic precipitator
Abscheidung *f* precipitation
Abscherbolzen *m* shear pin
Abscheren *nt* shearing, shearing off, shear cutting, breaking
Abscherfestigkeit *f* shearing resistance, shearing strength
Abscherspan *m* continuous chip without built-up edge
Abscherung *f* shearing off
Abscherwerkzeug *nt* shearing off tool
Abscherwinkel *m* shear angle
abscheuern abrade
abschieben discharge, push off, slide
Abschieben *nt* *(Umformtechnik)* partial displacement (of the stock) relative to the surface
Abschieber *m* load push, pusher
abschirmen screen off, shield
abschirmende Schicht *f* screening layer
Abschirmung *f* screening off, shielding, screen
abschlacken remove the slag, slag off
Abschlackung *f* deslagging, slag removal
Abschlämmung *f* clarification
abschleifen grind flat
Abschleppeinrichtung *f* towing device
abschleppen take in tow, tow
Abschleppseil *nt* towrope
Abschleppstange *f* tow bar
abschließbar lockable
abschließen 1. *(Brief, versiegeln)* seal (off) **2.** *(vervollständigen)* complete **3.** *(Räume)* lock **4.** *(Verträge)* conclude
Abschliff *m* abraded particle, stock removal
Abschlusslinie *f* terminal line
Abschlussstrich *m* terminal line
abschmelzbar fusible
abschmelzen 1. *(allg.)* flash, fuse, melt off **2.** *(Elektrode)* consume
Abschmelzgeschwindigkeit *f* turn off rate

abschneiden 1. cut away, cut off **2.** *(rechtwinklig)* square **3.** *(trennen)* sever **4.** *(Halbzeug)* crop off **5.** *(Scherschneiden)* shear **6.** *(abtrennen)* sever
Abschneiden *nt* **mit Stegabfall** cropping with web discard
Abschnitt *m* **1.** *(räuml.)* section **2.** *(e. Linie)* length **3.** *(Material)* offcut
abschrägen 1. *(allg.)* bevel, cant, slope, chamfer, scarf **2.** *(Gewindebohrer)* back off
Abschrägsupport *m* chamfering slide
Abschrägung *f* chamfer, bevel, taper, slope
abschrauben screw off, unbolt, unscrew, loosen
Abschraubmoment *nt (bei Muttern)* loosening (or unscrewing) torque
Abschreckdrücken *nt (Drückwalzen)* cold forming by spinning
abschrecken chill, quench
abschreckgehärtet quench-hardened
Abschreckgleitziehen *nt* ironing
Abschreckhärte *f* as quenched hardness
abschreckhärten quench-harden
Abschreckmittel *nt* quenchant
Abschreckwalzziehen *nt* stretch-reducing by roll-drawing
Abschreckzahl *f* number of quenches
Abschreckziehen *nt (Abschreckgleitziehen)* ironing
abschreiben depreciate, write off
Abschreibung *f* depreciation
Abschrot *m* anvil chisel
abschroten part off (by means of a chisel)
abschuppen scale
abschüren *(Asche)* de-ash
Abschwächer *m* reducer
Abseileinrichtung *f* descender device, rope-down device
abseilen descend, rope down
absenken lower, drop
Absenkgeschwindigkeit *f* drop speed, lowering speed
Absenkverfahren *nt* layer process
Absetzbehälter *m* sedimentation tank
absetzen 1. *(Verkauf)* deposit, disengage, let down, drop off, sell (off) **2.** *(Material)* shoulder, step **3.** *(e. Welle)* shoulder **4.** *(e. Schneidmeißel)* offset
Absetzen *nt* **durch Recken** cross-sectional reduction by inching the workpiece forward
Absetzstation *f* deposit station
absichern 1. *(allg.)* protect, safeguard, make safe, secure **2.** *(el.)* fuse **3.** *(Ladungen)* secure
Absicherung *f* protection, safeguarding, fusing, securing
Absicherung *f* **gegen Überdruck** pressure control
absichtlich intentional
Absinken *nt* descend, lowering, decrease
Absinkgeschwindigkeit *f* descent rate
absolut absolute
Absolutbeschleunigung *f* absolute acceleration
absolutes Messsystem *nt* absolute measuring system
Absolutgeschwindigkeit *f* absolute velocity
Absolutmaß *nt* absolute dimension
Absolutmaßprogrammierung *f* absolute dimension programming
Absolutmesssystem *nt* absolute measurement
Absolutmessung *f* absolute measurement
Absolutpositionierung *f* absolute positioning
Absolutwert *m* absolute value
Absolutwertgeber *m* absolute encoder, absolute value transmitter
absondern separate, segregate
Absorber *m* absorber
Absorbermaterial *nt* absorber material
Absorbermodell *nt* absorber pattern
Absorbermuster *nt* absorber pattern
absorbieren absorb
Absorption *f* absorption
Absorptionsfilter *m* absorbent filter
Absorptionsindex *m* absorber index
Absorptionsmittel *nt* absorbent, absorber
Absorptionsverhalten *nt* absorption behaviour

abspanen cut, machine
Abspanleistung *f* cutting capacity
abspannen unload, unclamp
Abspannisolator *m* shackle insulator
Absperrarmatur *f* **mit Antrieb durch Elektromagnet** solenoid-actuated shut-off valve
Absperrarmatur *f* **mit Antrieb durch Elektromotor** motor-actuated shut-off valve
Absperrarmatur *f* **mit Antrieb durch Fluide** fluid-actuated shut-off valve
Absperrarmatur *f* **mit Kolbenantrieb** piston-actuated shut-off valve
Absperrarmatur *f* **mit Membranantrieb** diaphragm-actuated shut-off valve
absperrbar capable of being shut off
absperrbares Ausdehnungsgefäß *nt* expansion tank with shut-off facility
absperrbares Durchgangsrückschlagventil *nt* straight check valve with shut-off feature
absperrbares Kopfstückrückschlagventil *nt* screw-down bonnet type shut-off check valve
absperrbares Rückschlagventil *nt* check valve with shut-off feature
Absperrbereich *m* shut-off zone
Absperreinrichtung *f* 1. *(bei Brennern)* shut-off device 2. *(e. Feuerung)* fuel cut-off 3. *(Ventilation)* isolating device
absperren 1. *(allg.)* lock, block, bar 2. *(Leitungen)* shut off
Absperrklappe *f* balanced disc stop valve, shut-off flap
Absperrorgan *nt* shut-off valve
Absperrorgan *nt* **mit Kolbenantrieb** stop valve with piston operation
Absperrorgan *nt* **mit Kraftantrieb** stop valve with power operation
Absperrorgan *nt* **mit Magnetantrieb** stop valve with solenoid operation
Absperrorgan *nt* **mit Membransteuerung** stop valve with diaphragm control
Absperrschieber *m* gate valve, shutoff valve
Absperrung *f* fixed guard, lock

Absperrventil *nt* shut-off valve, stop valve, gate valve, check valve, non-return valve
Absplittern *nt* dislodging
abspülen rinse, wash
Abstand *m* 1. *(Entfernung)* distance 2. *(Zeit)* interval 3. *(zwischen Linien)* spacing 4. *(Zwischenraum)* clearance, space, spacing 5. *(Lücke)* gap
Abstand *m* **der Gabeln** fork spacing
Abstand *m* **der Spanleitstufe** chip breaker distance
Abstand *m* **von Mitte zu Mitte** centre-to-centre distance
Abstandbolzen *m* spacer bolt
abstandsgleich equally spaced, evenly spaced
Abstandsmessung *f* distance measurement
Abstandsregelsystem *nt* distance control system
Abstandsregelung *f* distance controlling
Abstandsring *m* collar, spacer, spacing collar
Abstecharbeit *f* cutoff operation
Abstechdrehen *nt* parting off turning
Abstechdrehmaschine *f* parting-off lathe
abstechen cut-off, part-off
Abstechmeißel *m* cut-off tool, parting-off tool
Abstechmeißelhalter *m* parting-off toolholder, cutting-off toolholder
Abstechschlitten *m* cutting-off slide, parting-off slide
Abstechspindel *f* cutting-off spindle
Abstechwerkzeug *nt* cutting-off tool
Absteckstift *m* rig pin
absteifen brace
absteigen (von) dismount (from), leave
absteigender Zahlenwert *m* descending numerical value
abstellen shut off, switch off, stop
abstemmen chisel off
absterbender Lichtbogen *m* self-extinguishing arc
Abstich *m* *(Hochofen)* tapping
Abstieg *m* **von** egress (from)

abstimmen 1. *(allg.)* coordinate, match, tune **2.** *(zwischen Personen)* agree
Abstimmkreis *m* signal tuning circuit
Abstimmung *f* **1.** *(allg.)* coordination **2.** *(von Einflußgrößen)* correlation **3.** *(zwischen Personen)* agreement
Abstimmungsprozess *m* process of coordination
Abstimmungstermin *m* coordination deadline
abstoßen repulse, repel, push off
abstoßend repulsive
abstrahieren (von) abstract (from)
abstrahlen emit, radiate
Abstrahlen *nt* **mit Kies** shot-blasting
Abstrahlen *nt* **mit Sand** sandblasting
Abstraktionsgrad *m* level of abstraction
Abstreckziehen *nt* ironing
abstreifen strip off, wipe
Abstreifer *m* stripper, wiper, drag bar, scraper
Abstreiffestigkeit *f* *(e. Schraube)* resistance (of the thread) to stripping
Abstreifplatte *f* guard plate, stripper plate
abstufen 1. *(allg.)* step, grade, regrade **2.** *(Oberflächen)* explore, trace **3.** *(Skalenziffern)* graduate (in steps)
Abstufung *f* **1.** *(allg.)* stepping, graduation, progression, grading **2.** *(e. Vorschubes)* increment **3.** *(e. Welle)* shoulder **4.** *(von Drehzahlen)* variation (of speed ranges)
abstumpfen dull
Abstumpfung *f* dulling, blunting
Absturz *m* fall, falling
abstürzen fall
Absturzgefahr *f* falling hazard
Absturzhöhe *f* height of fall
Abstützeinrichtung *f* support
abstützen support
Abszisse *f* abscissa
Abtastbefehl *m* scanning command
Abtastbereich *m* scanning range
Abtasteingang *m* strobe (input)
abtasten 1. *(allg.)* follow (copying), scan, trace, sample, strobe, gauge **2.** *(e. Tastsystem)* traverse **3.** *(mit e. Messtaster)* explore **4.** *(Oberflächen)* explore, trace **5.** *(Skalenziffern)* graduate (in steps)
Abtastgeschwindigkeit *f* traversing speed
Abtastlinie *f* scanning line
Abtastrate *f* scanning rate
Abtastregelung *f* sampling control
Abtaststift *m* stylus, tracer (pin)
Abtastung *f* **1.** *(allg.)* sampling action, tracing, scanning, scan **2.** *(e. Tastsystems)* traversing **3.** *(Oberflächen)* tracing
Abtastvorrichtung *f* gauging device
Abtastzeit *f* scan time
abteilen divide
Abteilung *f* **1.** *(Firmensparten)* department, division, section **2.** *(in einer Halle)* bay
Abtrag *m* **1.** *(allg.)* removal **2.** *(Angriff)* attack
Abtragen *nt* **1.** *(allg.)* abrading, erode **2.** *(elektrochemisches ~)* electrochemical abrading **3.** *(elektrolytisches ~)* electrolytic abrading
Abtrageverfahren *nt* abrading technique
Abtragrate *f* removal rate, abrading instalment
Abtragsquotient *m* grinding ratio, metal removal rate
Abtragung *f* **1.** *(allg.)* abrasion, erosion **2.** *(e. Werkstoffes)* removal
Abtragungsgeschwindigkeit *f* rate of removal
Abtragvolumen *nt* removal volume
Abtransport *m* removal, outgoing transport
abtransportieren remove
abtrennen detach, part off, remove, separate, sever, cut off, disconnect
Abtrennung *f* separation, cutting-off, parting-off, parting, removal, severance
Abtrieb *m* driven side, output
Abtriebsbewegung *f* output motion
Abtriebsdrehzahl *f* output speed
Abtriebsglied *nt* output link
Abtriebswelle *f* output shaft
Abtriebszahl *f* output speed
Abtriftwinkel *m* angle of drift

Abtropfbehälter *m* drip collector
Abtropfwasser *nt* dripping water
Abwälzfräsen *nt* hobcutting
Abwälzfräser *m* slab milling cutter, hobbing cutter
Abwälzung *f* generating motion, rolling motion
Abwälzverfahren *nt* generating process
abwandeln modify
abwärts downward, downwards
abwärts bewegen descend
Abwärtsfahrt *f* lowering
Abwärtshub *m* downstroke
abwaschbares Schmieröl *nt* scourable lubricating oil
Abwaschfestigkeit *f* resistance to washing
Abwasserabfluss *m* rate of sewage discharge
Abwasserabgabegesetz *nt* sewage delivery law
Abwassernetz *nt* sewage system
abweichen deflect, turn away, deviate, differ (from), vary
Abweichen *nt* deflection, deviation, discrepancy
abweichend deviating
Abweichung *f* 1. *(e. Oberfläche)* irregularity 2. *(metrologisch)* variation 3. *(qualitätsmäßige)* off-grade 4. *(systematische ~ bei Messfehlern)* error 5. *(vom Kreis)* out-off roundness 6. *(vom Maß)* variation in dimension, offsize 7. *(von Bestimmungsgrößen)* variation, deviation 8. *(von Qualität)* off-grade, deviation 9. *(von Schätzung)* error 10. *(zu vernachlässigende ~)* negligible error 11. *(Ablenkung)* deflection 12. *(Diskrepanz)* discrepancy 13. *(math. Ungleichheit)* inequality
Abweichung *f* **der Erzeugenden** deviation of the generator
Abweichung *f* **des Stirnprofils** variation of the transverse profile
Abweichung *f* **von Bestimmungsgrößen** variation of specification factors
Abweichung *f* **von der Ebene** unevenness, inequality
Abweichung *f* **von der Gleichwinkligkeit** deviation from equiangularity, unequal angularity
Abweichung *f* **von der Schraubenlinienform** deviation from the helical form
Abweichung *f* **von Flankenlinien** variation of tooth traces
abweichungsfreie Drehwinkelstellung *f (Einflankenwälzprüfung)* zero-variation angular position
abweichungsfreie Kreisstellung *f* zero-variation circular pitch
abweichungsfreies Bauteil *nt* error-free component
abweichungsfreies Stirnrad *nt* zero-deviation (or zero-variation) cylindrical gear
Abweichungsspanne *f* 1. *(Anzeige von Messinstrumenten)* span of error 2. *(e. Messelementes)* deviation range 3. *(von Endmaßen)* variation
Abweichungsspanne *f* **in der Teilmessspanne** local span of error
abweisen deflect, repel, reject, turn away
abweisende Fläche *f* deflecting surface
Abweiser *m* deflector, rejector
Abweiskurve *f* deflecting curve
Abweisschiene *f* deflecting bar, deflecting blade
Abwendung *f (e. Schadens)* prevention, elimination
abwickeln complete, handle, implement, process, develop into
Abwicklung *f* completion, handling, implementation, processing
Abwinkeln *nt (Rohrleitungen)* upward buckling
Abwinkelung *f* angular misalignment
Abwittern *nt* weathering
abwürgen *(Motor)* stall
abzählbar denumerable
Abzieheinrichtung *f* extractor, dismantling tool
abziehen (von) 1. *(allg.)* draw off, remove, take off, pop (from) 2. *(von Schleifscheiben)* dress 3. (mit Ölstein) stone
Abziehlack *m* strippable varnish

Abziehstange *f* take-off rod
Abziehvorrichtung *f* dressing device
Abzugkraft *f* peel strength
Abzugskraft *f* *(Beschichtungen)* peeling strength
abzundern scale off
Abzunderung *f* scaling-off
abzweigen burificate, branch
Abzweigung *f* burification, branch, divergence
Abzweigverschlüsse *mpl* closures on branches
acetonbeständig proof against acetone, acetone-resisting
Acetylendruckminderer *m* acetylene pressure regulator
Acetylenentwickleranlage *f* acetylene generator unit
Acetylenfackel *f* acetylene torch
Acetylen-Sauerstoff-Ringbrenner oxy-acetylene ring-type burner
Acetylenverordnung *f* Acetylene Code
Acetylenverteilungsleitung *f* acetylene manifold
Acetylen-Zustromstück *nt* acetylene inlet pressure
Achatpistill agate pestle
Achatreibschale *f* agate mortar
Achsabstand *m* distance between the axles, centre distance
Achsabstandsabweichung *f* centre distance deviation
Achsabstandsänderung *f* centre distance alteration
Achsabstands-Istmaß *nt* actual centre distance
Achsabstandslinie *f* *(e. Radpaares)* centre distance line
Achsabstandsmaß *nt* centre distance allowance
Achsabstandsschwankung *f* centre distance fluctuation
Achsabstandsveränderung *f* fork spacing adjustment
achsbeweglich axially movable
Achsbewegung *f* axis motion
Achsbezeichnung *f* term of the axes
Achsbund *m* axle collar
Achse *f* axis (axes *pl*), centreline, pintle

Achsenabstand *m* centre distance
Achsenebene *f* axial plane
Achsenfertigdrehmaschine *f* *(Bettenmittenantrieb)* centre-drive axle lathe
Achsenfluchtung *f* axial alignment
achsengerechte Bohrung *f* axially true hole
Achsenkreuz *nt* system of coordinates
Achsenkreuzung *f* intersection of axes
Achsenkreuzungswinkel *m* axis intersection angle
Achsenneigung *f* axial inclination
Achsenschnitt *m* axial section
Achsenschnittpunkt *m* *(bei Zahnrädern)* intersection point of the gear axes
Achsenschränkung *f* *(bei Radachsen)* axial skew
achsensenkrechter Abstand *m* distance perpendicular to the axis
Achsenspiegeln *nt* mirror image operation
Achsentauschen *nt* axis change
Achsenversetzungsabmaß *nt* offset deviation
Achsenwinkelabmaß *nt* shaft angle deviation
Achsenwinkelabweichung *f* shaft angle variation
achsfluchtend axially aligned
Achshals *m* journal
Achskeuzpunkt *m* crossed-axes point
Achskreuzwinkel *m* crossed-axes angle
Achslage *f* *(e. Stirnradpaares)* shaft position, axial position
Achslagetoleranz *f* *(bei Stirnradgetrieben)* shaft position tolerance
Achslast *f* load per axle
Achslochdurchmesser *m* bore diameter
Achsneigung *f* axial inclination
Achsparallelität *f* parallelism of the axes
Achsschnittebene *f* section in the axial plane
Achsschränkung *f* axial skew
Achstunnel *m* stub axle
Achsversatz *m* displacement of the axes, offset axes
Achsverschiebung *f* *(bei Leitungsbauteilen)* axial displacement

Achsversetzung *f* offset
Achsversetzungsabweichung *f* offset variation
Achszuordnung *f* axes assignment
Achtmal-n-Bit-Schreib-Lese-Speicher *m* eight words-n bit memory
Achteck *nt* octagon
achteckig octagonal
Achtkant *m* octagon
Achtkantmeißelschieber *m* octagon ram head
Achtung *f* attention, caution
Ackerfläche *f* arable area
Acme-Trapezgewinde *nt* Acme trapezoidal thread
Acrylethylenoxidplast *nt* acrylethylene oxide plastics
acryliertes Alkydharz *nt* alcrylated alkyd resin
Acrylnitritgehalt *m* acrylonitrile content
Acrylsäureethylenester acrylic acid ethyl ester
Acrylverbindung *f* acrylate compound
Adaptive Steuerung (AC) *f* adaptive control
Adaptivsteuerung *f* adaptive control
addieren add
Addierer *m* adder, addition unit
Additionsbefehl *m* add instruction
Additionsstelle *f* summing point
Additionsstoppuhr *f* adding stopwatch
Adhäsionsbruch *m* adhesion fracture
Adhäsionsgreifer *m* adhesion gripper
Adhäsionsverschleiß *m* adhesion wear
adhäsiv adhesive
Administrationsebene *f* administration level
Adressbereich *m* address range
Adresse *f* address
Adresseneingang *m* addressing input
Adressenteil *m* address part
Adressenzuordnung *f* assignment
Adressfeld *nt* address array, address field
adressierbar addressable
adressieren address
Adressierung *f* addressing
Adresszuordnungsliste *f* assignment list
aerobe Korrosion *f* aerobic corrosion
Aggregat *nt* unit, aggregate, aggregation, assembly, package
Aggregation *f* aggregation
Aggregatzustand *m* **1.** *(allg.)* state of aggregation **2.** *(fester ~)* solid state **3.** *(flüssiger ~)* liquid state **4.** *(gasförmiger ~)* gaseous state
Ahle *f* awl, reamer
A-Kanal *m* O-channel
Akkkustand *m* battery level
Akkordfestsetzung *f* piece-rate setting
Akkumulation *f* accumulation, result aggregation
Akkumulator *m* battery
akkumulieren accumulate
Aktionsblock *m* action block
aktiv active, actively
Aktivatorrückstände *mpl* activator residues
aktive Flanke *f* active flank
aktive Hauptschneide *f* active major cutting edge
aktive Kornzahl *f* active grain count
aktive Korrosion active corrosion
aktive Masse *f* active material
aktive Nebenschneide *f* active minor cutting edge
aktive Schleifscheibenoberfläche *f* active grinding wheel surface
aktive Schneide *f* active cutting edge
aktives Glied *nt* *(auch Steller genannt)* active element (also termed manipulator)
aktives Schneidenprofil *nt* active cutting profile
aktives Teil *nt* live part
aktivieren activate
Aktivierung *f* activation, composition
Aktivierungsüberspannung *f* *(el. chem.)* activation overvoltage
Aktivierungszusatz *m* activating addition
Aktivierungszustand *m* *(e. Oberfläche)* state of activation
Aktivitätenplan *m* activity (or activities) plan
aktivitätsgetrieben activity-driven
Aktivitätsmessgerät *nt* activity meas-

uring instrument
aktivitätsorientiert activity-oriented
Aktivkohle-Verfahren *nt* activated carbon method
Aktivkraft *f (erzeugt die Spanungsleistung)* active force (generates the cutting power)
Aktor *m* actuator
Aktorebene *f* actuator level
Aktorik *f* actuators
aktualisieren update
Aktualisierung *f* actualization, updating
Aktualität *f* topically, up-to-dateness
aktuell current, up-to-date
akustisch acoustical, audible, audio, auditive
akustische Warnung *f* audible warning
akustisches Brechungsverhältnis *nt* refractive index
akustisches Signal *nt* acoustic signal, audible signal
Akzeptanzquittung *f* acceptance confirmation
Alarm *m* alarm, interrupt
alarmauslösend interrupt triggering
Alarmeingang *m* interrupt input
Alarmgrenze *f* alarm limit
Alarmmeldung *f* alarm message
Alarmreaktionszeit *f* interrupt response time
Alarmschwelle *f* alarm threshold
Aldehydkondensationsprodukt *nt* aldehyde condensation product
Algorithmus *m* algorithm
alkalifreie Seife *f* non-alkali soap
Alkalilöslichkeit *f* alkali solubility
Alkaliresistenz *f* alkali resistance
alkalische Batterie *f* alkaline battery
Alleskornentwickler *m* universal generator
allgemein general, overall
allgemeine Kurvenführung *f* universal curve guidance
allgemeiner Verkehrsbereich *m* common zone
Allgemeintoleranz *f (auch Freimaßtoleranz)* general tolerance, free size tolerance, permissible variation for sizes without tolerance indication
allmählich gradual
Allschichtprobe *f* all-layer (or all-levels) sample
allseitig bearbeiten machine all over
Allzweckgreifer *m* universal gripper
alphabetisch ordnen index
alphabetisches Verzeichnis *nt* index
alphanumerisch alphanumerical
Alphanumerische Schreibweise *f* alphanumeric notation
Alteisen *nt* iron scrap, ferrous scrap
Altemulsion *f* used emulsion
altern 1. *(allg.)* age, season **2.** *(Leichtmetall)* age-harden
alternativer Zweig *m* alternative path
Alternativhypothese *f* alternating hypothesis
Alterung *f (UK)* ageing, *(US)* aging, seasoning, deterioration
Alterungsbeschleuniger *m* ageing accelerator
alterungsbeständig non-ageing, age-resistant
Alterungsdauer *f* duration of ageing, oxidation period
alterungsempfindlich susceptible to ageing
Alterungskammer *f* ageing chamber
Alterungsneigung *f* tendency to ageing
Alterungsriss *m* ageing induced crack
Alterungsschutzmittel *nt* ageing inhibitor
Alterungszustand *m* aging factor
Altfett *nt* used grease
Altliste *f* old list
Altöl *nt* used oil, waste oil
Aluminiumauftragung *f* aluminium deposition
Aluminiumgleichwert *m* aluminium filter equivalent
Aluminiumguss *m* aluminium cast iron
Aluminiumoxidschneide *f* aluminium-oxide tool tip
Aluminiumoxydscheibe *f* aluminous oxide wheel
Aluminiumpegment *nt* aliminium pegment
Aluminiumstangenpressprofil *nt*

aluminium extruded section
Aluminium-Strangpressprofil *nt* extruded aluminium section
Amboss *m* anvil
amerikanisches Petroleumgewinde *nt* American petroleum thread
Aminoplast/Phenoplast-Pressmasse *f* aminoplast/phenolic compression moulding material
aminoplastisches Kunstharz *nt* aminoplastic synthetic resin
Aminoplastkleber *m* aminoplast adhesive
amorph amorphous
Amperestunde *f* ampere hour
Amperestundenzähler *m* ampere-hour meter
Amplitudengang *m* amplitude response
amplitudenmoduliert amplitude-modulated
Amplitudenschwingung *f* amplitude oscillation
amtlich official
anaerobe Korrosion anaerobic corrosion
analog analogue, analog
Analog/Digital-Wandler *m* analogue-to-digital converter (ADC)
Analogausgabeeinheit *f* analogue output unit
Analog-Digital-Umsetzer *m* analogue-digital converter
Analogeingabeeinheit *f* analogue input unit
analoger Ausgang *m* analogue output
analoger Eingang *m* analogue input
Analogwertverarbeitung *f* analogue value processing
Analyse *f* analysis
analysefeuchter Zustand *m* analytically moist state
Analysefeuchtigkeit *f* analytical moisture
Analysenbezeichnung *f* analysis designation
Analysenprobe *f* analysis sample
Analysenverfahren *nt* analysis method
Analyseprozess *m* analysis process
Analysespäne *f* cuttings for analysis purposes
analysieren analyse
analytisch analytical
analytischer Ansatz *m* hypothetical factor for analysis
analysieren analyse
anbauen attach, mount, add on, assemble
Anbaugerät *nt* attachment, implement
Anbauteil *nt* add-on part
Anbauten *mpl* attachments
Anbauvorschrift *f* assembly precaution
Anbauzeichnung *f* attachment drawing
Anbdeckmaske *f* cover mask
Anbiegen *nt* die bending providing initial rounding
anbieten offer, quote
Anbieter *m* provider, supplier
anbinden (an) connect (to)
Anbindung *f* connection, integration
Anbohrarmatur *f* tapped fitting
anbohren spot-drill, start a hole
Anbohrer *m* start drill, spotting drill
Anbohrmaschine *f* centring lathe
anbringen 1. *(allg.)* apply, attach, fix, mount, equip, install **2.** *(el. Anschlüsse)* fit **3.** *(von Maßeinteilung)* graduate **4.** *(an einer Stelle)* locate
Anbringung *f* attachment, fitting, installation
Anbringungsbereich *m* attachment range
Anbruch *m* incipient crack
andauernd sustained
ändern 1. *(allg.)* alter, change **2.** *(abändern)* modify **3.** *(sich ~)* vary **4.** *(vertraglich)* amend
Änderung *f* **1.** *(allg.)* alteration, change, modification, variation **2.** *(vertraglich)* amendment **3.** *(leichte ~)* modification
Änderungsbefehl *m* alter instruction
Änderungsdienst *m* alteration service
Änderungsmanagement *nt* change management
Änderungsvermerk *m* modification note
Änderungszustand *m* modification status
andocken *vi* dock

Andockstation f docking station
Andruck m contact pressure
Andrückeinrichtung f spring pressure guide attachment
andrücken force against, press on
Andrücker m pusher, press
Andruckkraft f pressing force
Andruckpolster nt contact roll
Andrückrolle f pressure roller
aneinander fügen fit together, join together
aneinander passend fitting together, mating
aneinander passende Flächen fpl mating faces
aneinander stoßen *(Zahnkopfkanten)* foul (with)
aneinander fügen conjoin with one another
aneinandergereihte Maße f chain dimensioning
aneinandergrenzende Schnittflächen fpl adjoining sectioned areas
aneinander schieben wring together, wring upon each other
aneinander sprengen wring together
aneinander stoßen abut one against the other, abut against each other
anfahren 1. *(allg.)* access, address, approach, trigger, run up, start up **2.** *(Kollision)* hit **3.** *(Motor)* start
Anfahrkraft f starting force
Anfahrschutz m fender, safety guard
Anfahrschutzeinrichtung f anti-collision device
Anfahrungenauigkeit f approach inaccuracy
Anfang m beginning, commencement, initiation, opening, start
anfangen begin, commence, start
anfänglich initial
Anfangs... initial
Anfangsbedingung f initial condition
Anfangsdrehmoment m initial (engine) torque
Anfangsempfindlichkeit f start-of-range sensitivity
Anfangsgerätemesslänge f original extensometer gauge length
Anfangsmesslänge f original gauge length
Anfangsmittelspannung f initial mean stress
Anfangsparameter mpl source parameters
Anfangspunkt m starting point
Anfangsquerschnitt m original cross-section area
Anfangsspannungsausschlag m initial stress amplitude
Anfangswert m minimum value, initial value
Anfangszustand m initial condition, initial state
Anfärbeversuch m dye staining test
anfasen break the corners, chamfer, bevel
Anfasmeißel m chamfering tool
Anfasung f chamfer
anfertigen make, manufacture, produce
Anfertigung f **1.** *(allg.)* making, manufacture, production **2.** *(von Zeichnungen)* preparation
anfeuchten moisten
Anflächung f *(als Arbeitsvorgang)* spot facing
anfordern ask for, claim, demand, order, request
Anforderung f request, requirement
Anforderungsprofil nt requirement profile
Anfrage f inquiry (into), enquire, request
anfragen enquire (into), inquire, request
anfressen erode, corrode, pit
Angabe f indication, information, specification
Angaben fpl details, data
angebaut attached (to) built-on
angebbar specifiable
angeben indicate, signal, signalize, specify
Angebot nt offer, quotation, bid, tender
Angebotsabgabe f bidding
Angebotsanforderung f call for tender, calling for tenders
Angebotsbewertung f evaluation of

bids
Angebotsvergleich *m* comparison of the offers
Angebotsüberarbeitung *f* revision of the offer
Angebotszeichnung *f* quotation drawing
angebrochen partially fractured
angeflanscht flanged
angegossen cast integrally with
angehoben lifted, elevated, raised, suspended
angehobener Fahrerplatz *m* elevated operator position, elevating operator's position
angekörnt punch-scribed
Angel *f* hinge
angelegt *(Spannung)* applied
angelernt semi-skilled
angelernter Arbeiter *m* semi-skilled worker
angemessen adequate, reasonably, appropriate
angenommene Arbeitsebene *f* assumed working plane
angenommene Schnittrichtung *f* assumed direction of cut
angeordnet arranged, located, placed, positioned
angepasst adequate
angeregtes Molekül *nt* excited dimer (Excimer)
angeschlossen connected
angeschmolzener Schweißspritzer *m* fusedon spatter
angeschütteter Boden *m* back-filled soil
angesetztes Lot *nt* hand fed solder
angesprengt wrought on
angetrieben driven, powered
angetriebene Lenkachse *f* drive-steer axle
angetriebene Räder *ntpl* drive wheels
angetriebene Rollenbahn *f* live roller conveyor, powered roller conveyor
angetriebenes Lenkrad *nt* drive-steer wheel
angetriebenes Teil *nt* member
angezogen *(von Hand)* manually tightened

angießen cast on
angleichen 1. *(allg.)* equalize, condition **2.** *(Werte)* bring into line
Angleichung *f* *(z. B. von Regelgrößen)* adaptation
Angleichzeit *f* conditioning time
angreifen 1. *(allg.)* apply to, be applied to **2.** *(Schleifkörner)* abrade
angreifende Stoffe *mpl* aggressive substances
angreifendes Mittel *nt* corrosive medium
angrenzend adjacent
angrenzende Fläche *f* adjoining face
Angriff *m* *(e. Schneidwerkzeuges)* cutting action
angriffhemmende Verglasung *f* attack-blocking glazing
Angriffsbedingungen *fpl* attack conditions
Angriffsbereich *m* zone of attack
Angriffsmittel *nt* aggressive medium
Angriffsschärfe *f* abrasive power
Angriffstiefe *f* depth of attack
Anguss *m* runner
Angussentfernungsvorrichtung *f* degating unit
Angusskanal *m* runner
Angusskegel *m* sprue
angusslos runnerless
Angussspinne *f* gate pattern
Angusssteg *m* gate
Angusssystem *nt* runner system
Angussverteiler *m* gate pattern
Angussverteilerplatte *f* runner plate
anhaften adhere, stick
Anhaftungen *fpl* sticking material
Anhaltegenauigkeit *f* stopping accuracy
anhalten stop, bring to rest
Anhaltenocke *f* stopping cam
Anhalteweg *m* stopping distance
Anhaltspunkt *m* guideline
Anhang *m* appendix
Anhängeetikett *nt* tag
Anhängeetikettappliziermaschine *f* tag labelling machine
Anhängelast *f* trailer load
anhängen append, hang, couple with
Anhänger *m* **1.** *(allg.)* trailer **2.** *(mit*

Ladeeinrichtung) self-loading trailer **3.** *(ohne Ladeeinrichtung)* non-self-loading trailer
Anhängevorrichtung *f* towing device
anhebbar elevatable, elevating
anheben elevate, lift, raise, hoist
Anhebeschlitten *m* **1.** *(allg.)* broach-handling slide **2.** *(Räummaschine)* elevating slide
anheften pin (to)
Anheizklappe *f* start-up flap
Anheizschieber *m* start-up slide
Anhubwinkel *m* angle of drop
Anionenaustauscher *m* anion exchanger
Anker *m* armature, rotor, anchor
Ankerbolzen *m* anchor bolt, foundation bolt
Ankippen *nt* die bending providing initial curling
ankleben glue on, paste on, agglutinate
ankommen arrive
ankommender Ruf *m* incoming call
Ankopplung *f* probe-to-specimen contact
ankörnen *(US)* center, *(UK)* centre, centre-punch, mark, punch
Ankörnung *f* centre mark
Ankunft *f* arrival, arriving
Ankunftsanzeige *f* arrival note
Ankunftsreihenfolge *f* sequence of arrivals
ankuppeln connect
Ankuppeln *nt* connection, connecting
Anlage *f* assembly, equipment, plant, system, installation, contact, bearing
anlagebedingt conditioned by the plant
Anlagefläche *f* bearing surface
Anlagefläche *f* **der Befestigung** mounting plane
Anlagelineal *nt* contact rule
Anlagenauslastung *f* system capacity utilization
Anlagenauslegung *f* plant layout
Anlagenausstattung *f* system equipment
Anlagenbereich *m* plant area
Anlagenbeschreibung *f* system description

Anlagenbetreiber *m* plant user
Anlagenbetreuung *f* system maintenance
Anlagenbuchhaltung *f* plant accounting
Anlagenerweiterung *f* system extension
anlageninterner Anschlusspunkt *m* in-plant point of coupling
Anlagenlautstärke *f* plant noise level
Anlagenlebenszyklus *m* system life cycle
Anlagenlieferant *m* system supplier
Anlagenmodell *nt* system model
Anlagenprojekteur *m* system designer
Anlagensicherung *f* assurance of system reliability
Anlagensteuerung *f* system control
Anlagenstillstand *m* breakdown of the system
Anlagentyp *m* type of system
Anlagenumbau *m* system conversion
Anlagenverbund *m* combination of systems
Anlassbehandlung *f* tempering treatment
anlassen 1. *(starten)* start **2.** *(Stahl, Wärmebehandlung)* temper
Anlasser *m* starter, starter motor
Anlassfarben *fpl* annealing colours
Anlassknopf *m* start button
Anlassmittel *nt* tempering medium
Anlassofen *m* tempering furnace
Anlass-Schaubild *nt* tempering diagram
Anlasstransformator *m* starting transformer
Anlassverfahren *nt* starting method
Anlassverhalten *nt* tempering behaviour
Anlassversprödung *f (zwischen 350 und 550 °C)* temper embrittlement
anlassversprödet temper-brittle
Anlauf *m* **1.** *(allg.)* start, start-up, run-up **2.** *(stufiger ~)* stepwise starting
Anlaufbeschleunigung *f* start-up acceleration
Anlaufdrehmoment *m* starting torque
anlaufen start
Anlauffarbe *f* tarnish

Anlaufflansch *m* check flange
Anlaufkupplung *f* starting coupling
Anlaufkurve *f* pressure cam, advance cam
Anlaufphase *f* start-up phase
Anlaufprobe *f* start-up test, commissioning test
Anlaufprogramm *nt* start-up programme
Anlaufschicht *f* tarnish film
Anlaufstirnfläche *f* contact face
Anlaufstrecke *f* approach section
Anlaufstrom *m* starting current
Anlaufstrombegrenzer *m* starting current limiter, starting current limiting
Anlaufverhalten *nt* starting characteristics
Anlaufweg *m* start-up distance
Anlaufweg *m* **des Fräsers** approach of cutter
Anlaufwert *m* **1.** *(allg.)* starting value, discrimination value **2.** *(e. Strecke)* transition value, reaction value
Anlaufzeit *f* transition time, reaction time, starting time, start-up time
anlegen apply to
Anlegewinkelmesser *m* bevel protractor
anleiten instruct, train
Anleitung *f* instruction
anlenken couple, link
Anlenkpunkt *m* articulation point
Anliefer-LKW *m* delivering lorry
anliefern deliver, supply
Anlieferplan *m* delivery plan
Anlieferung *f* delivery
Anlieferzustand *m* condition as delivered
anlösen apply a little solvent
Anlösung *f* filler metal erosion
anlöten solder to
anmelden 1. *(z. B. Internet)* log in **2.** *(Patent)* apply for
Anmeldeverfahren *nt* call procedure, log-in procedure
Anmeldezeit *f* flame-on response time
Anmeldung *f* login, logging in
annähern approach
annähernd approximately
Annäherung *f* **1.** *(von Zahlenwerten)* approximation **2.** *(räumliche)* approach
Annäherungsschalter *m* proximity switch
Annäherungswinkel *m* approach angle
Annahme *f* **1.** *(techn. Erzeugnisse)* acceptance **2.** *(Vermutung)* assumption, estimate, supposition **3.** *(Waren)* reception, receipt
Annahmeprüfung *f* acceptance inspection
Annahme-Stichprobenprüfung *f* acceptance sampling inspection
Annahmewahrscheinlichkeit *f* acceptance probability
annehmbar acceptable
annehmen 1. *(abnehmen)* accept **2.** *(voraussetzen)* assume, suppose **3.** *(erhalten)* receive
Anniet-Mutternleiste *f* gang channel nut
Anniet-Schottstutzen *f* *(für Rohrverschraubungen)* bulkhead union with riveting flange
annullieren cancel
Anode *f* anode
Anodenneigungswinkel *m* anode inclination angle
anodische Polarisation *f* *(el. chem.)* anodic polarisation
anodische Teilstromdichte *f* anodic partial current density
anodischer Metallabtrag *m* anodic attack on the metal
anodischer Teilstrom *m* *(el. chem.)* anodic partial current
anodisierbar suitable for anodising
Anodisierbarkeit *f* anodic oxidizability
anordnen allocate, arrange, locate, position, group, place, lay
Anordnung *f* mounting, array, arrangement, assembly, disposition, placing, layout, alignment, allocation, location, positioning, order
Anordnungsmöglichkeit *f* arrangement option
Anordnungspunkt *m* layout point
Anordnungsschema *nt* schematic arrangement
Anordnungsschritt *m* layout step

Anordnungsvariante *f* layout variation
Anordnungsverfahren *nt* layout method
Anordnungszeichnung *f* arrangement drawing
Anpassdurchmesser *m* matching diameter
anpassen match, adapt (to), accommodate, adjust, fit
anpassend adaptive
Anpasssteuerung *f* machine-control interface
Anpassung *f* adaptation, adjustment
anpassungsfähig flexible
Anpassungsfähigkeit *f* adaptability, flexibility
Anprall *m* impact
Anpressdruck *m* **1.** *(allg.)* contact pressure **2.** *(e. Werkzeuges)* tool pressure, surface pressure, bearing pressure **3.** *(Glattwalzen)* contact pressure (smooth rolling)
anpressen press on
Anpressrolle *f* pressure roll, contact roll
Anpressverschließmaschine *f* press-on lidding machine
anpunkten spot-weld
Anquellen *nt* surface swelling
anquetschen crimp to
anreichern concentrate, enrich
Anreicherung *f* concentration, enrichment
Anreißarbeit *f* making-off, laying-out
Anreißen *nt* **1.** *(allg. Fertigungsschritt)* layout, laying out, lining out, marking, setting out, work layout **2.** *(Längenmaße)* tracing **3.** *(Reißnadel)* scribing, making (off)
Anreißer *m* layout man, liner out, marker, marker out
Anreißkörner *m* prick punch
Anreißnadel *f* scriber
Anreißplatte *f* bench plate, laying-out plate, layout plate, marking-off table, marking out plate, surface plate
Anreißschablone *f* marking stencil
Anreißvorrichtung *f* making device (or fixture)
Anreißwerkzeug *nt* layout tool, marking-off tool
Anreißzeug *nt* marking tool
Anriss *m* **1.** *(allg. Fertigungsschritt)* check, incipient crack, layout **2.** *(Schädigungsmerkmal)* crack emerging at the surface, incipient crack
Anriss-Kraft *f* cracking force
Anrisslinie *f* scribed line
Anrissschälwiderstand *m* crack initiation-peel resistance
anritzen *(e. Oberfläche)* score
anrollen roll on
Anrollverschließmaschine *f* roll-on capping machine
ansammeln accumulate, collect
Ansammlung *f* accumulation
Ansatz *m* **1.** *(e. Schraube)* neck, shoulder **2.** *(als Kurzwort für Ansatzspitze)* coned half-dog point
Ansatzbolzen *m* stud
ansatzdrehen turn a shoulder
Ansatzfräsen *nt* shoulder milling
Ansatzgröße *f* scheduled quantity
Ansatzkuppe *f* radiused half-dog point
Ansatzmutter *f* shouldered nut
Ansatzplanung *f* sales planning
Ansatzschleifen *nt* centreless plunge grinding
Ansatzspitze *f (e. Schraube)* coned half-dog point
Ansatzstück *nt* attached piece, lateral fitting
ansaugen 1. *(allg.)* suck, vacuum, draw **2.** *(Pumpe)* prime
Ansaughahn *m* intake tap
Ansaughaube *f* suction hood
Ansaughilfe *f* suction aid
Ansaugkanal *m* suction port
Ansaugphase *f* suction phase
Ansaugung *f* suction
Anschaltbaugruppe *f* connecting module, switching-in module
anschalten switch on, turn on
anschärfen scarf, sharpen, resharpen
Anschiebbarkeit *f* wringing property
anschieben wring
Anschlag *m* **1.** *(allg.)* stop, trip, tappet, thrust face **2.** *(Regal)* bin front **3.** *(Vorschubbegrenzung)* stop dog, trip dog, trip pin **4.** *(für die Auslösung)* trip dog **5.** *(zum Umsteuern)* reverse dog

6. *(zur Begrenzung der Bewegung)* limit stop
Anschlagart *f* type of stopping
anschlagbetätigt dog-actuated
Anschlagbolzen *m* **1.** *(allg.)* stop pin **2.** *(Schlitten)* limit Stopp **3.** *(Tisch)* trip dog, stop dog
Anschlagdrehen *nt* turning with drip stop control, tripping to a line
Anschläge *mpl (Schneiden)* stops (cutting)
anschlagen 1. *(befestigen)* attach, sling **2.** *(~ gegen)* impact against
Anschlagfläche *f* contact surface
Anschlaggenauigkeit *f* accuracy of tripping
anschlaggesteuert dog-controlled
Anschlagkante *f* retention lip
Anschlagknagge *f* trip dog, stop dog
Anschlagleiste *f* stop bar
Anschlagmaße *ntpl* fastening dimensions
Anschlagnocke *f* **zum Ausschalten des Quervorschubs** transverse dog
Anschlagnocken *m* cam
Anschlagpunkt *m* lifting location, lifting point, slinging point
Anschlagschleifen *nt* shoulder grinding
Anschlagschraube *f* screw dog
Anschlagseil *nt* sling rope
Anschlagstange *f* trip rod
Anschlagstelle *f* location for slinging, slinging
Anschlagstift *m* trip dog
Anschlagwalze *f* stop roll
Anschlagwalze *f* **für Revolverkopf** indexing stop roll
Anschlagwinkel *m* **1.** *(allg.)* deflection angle **2.** *(Messzeug)* try square
anschleifen face-grind
anschließen connect (to/with)
anschließend subsequent, subsequently
Anschliff *m* grinding
Anschluss *m* connection, port, fitting, terminal, junction
Anschlussbedingung *f* supply condition
Anschlussbelegung *f* terminal assignment
Anschlussbogen *m* connecting bend
Anschlussbohrung *f* coupling hole
Anschlussdruck *m* connection pressure
Anschlussimpedanz *f* bonding impedance
Anschlusskabel *nt* connecting cable
Anschlusskanal *m* connecting sewer
Anschlusskennung *f* **1.** *(gerufene Station)* called line identification **2.** *(rufende Station)* calling line identification
Anschlussleistung *f* electric power
Anschlussleitung *f* connecting (pipe)line
Anschlussmaß *nt* mating dimension
Anschlussmessung *f* conjunction measurement
Anschlussmittel *nt* connection means, connection facility
Anschlussnaht *f* joint weld at the boundaries
Anschlussplan *m* terminal connecting plan
Anschlusspunkt *m* point of connection
Anschlussrohr *nt* joining pipe
Anschlussstelle *f* point of connection, connection point
Anschlussstrecke *f* tie-in section
Anschlussstück *(e. Rohres)* adapter fitting, union
Anschlussstutzen *m* connection nozzle
Anschlussteil *nt* mating component
Anschlussverschraubung *f* screwed connection
Anschlusszunge *f* connection tongue
Anschmelzradius *m* initial cutting radius
Anschmelzung *f* initial fused area, initial fusing
Anschmelzzone *f* fusion zone
anschmieden forge to/on
Anschneiden *nt* taking the first cut
Anschneidsenker *m* spot facing cutter
Anschnitt *m* start of the cut, starting cut
Anschnitthinterschliffwinkel *m* clearance angle of chamfer
Anschnittseite *f* **1.** *(allg.)* entering end, starting end **2.** *(Fräser)* approach side

Anschnittsystem *nt* first cut system
Anschnittweg *m* **des Fräsers** approach of cutter
Anschnittwinkel *m* angle of chamfer, lead angle
anschrägen chamfer, bevel
Anschrägmeißel *m* chamfering tool
anschrauben bolt to
Anschraubloch *nt* screw-on hole
Anschub *m* wringing
Anschubfläche *f* wringing surface
anschweißen attach by welding, weld on
Anschweißen *nt* 1. *(Stahlteile an andere)* welding (steel components to other components) 2. *(von Massenanschlüssen)* temporary welding
Anschweißende *nt* weld-on end
Anschweißteil *nt* welded-on part
anschwemmen flood on (filler metal in the molten state)
Anschwemmlöten *nt* flood soldering
ansenken counterbore, countersink, spotface
Ansicht *f* view
Anspitzen *nt* pegging, pointing, pointing by forging
Anspitzen *nt* **durch Walzen** tagging, pointing in roll units
Anspitzkneten *nt* pegging, pointing, pointing by forging
Ansprechbereich *m* range of sensitivity
Ansprechdruck *m* response pressure
ansprechen 1. *(allg.)* function, access, address, identify 2. *(Reaktion)* react, respond (to) 3. *(auslösen)* trip
Ansprechpartner *m* contact person
Ansprechschwelle *f* discrimination threshold
Ansprechvermögen *nt* responsivity
Ansprechverzögerung *f* response delay
Ansprechwahrscheinlichkeit *f* response probability
Ansprechwert *m* starting value, discrimination value
Ansprechzeit *f* reaction time, response time
Ansprengen *nt* wringing together
Anstählen *nt* steel facing

Anstand *m* spacing
Anstauchen *nt* 1. *(allg.)* upset-forging, upsetting, gathering 2. *(im Gesenk)* upset forging, die upsetting 3. *(ohne Gesenk)* upsetting without die, upending
Anstauchschweißen *nt* cold pressure upset welding
anstehende Spannung *f* voltage being present
anstehender Boden *m* in-situ soil
ansteigen ascend, rise, increase
Anstellbewegung *f* approach motion
anstellen 1. *(positionieren)* position 2. *(einstellen)* adjust 3. *(Meißel)* set
Anstellung *f* setting, positioning, adjustment
Anstellwinkel *m* setting angle
ansteuern access, control, pilot, trigger
Ansteuerung *f* control, trigger
Anstich *m* first pass, initial pass
Anstieg *m* increase, rise
Anstiegsantwort *f* ramp function response
Anstiegsfunktion *f* ramp function
Anstiegsgeschwindigkeit *f* rate of rise (of the input signal)
anstiften *(mit Stift)* peg
anstirnen spotface, spot face
Anstoß *m* impulse, initiation
anstoßen activate, initiate, impact against, strike against, butt, abut
Anstoßen *nt* *(von Zahnkopfkanten)* fouling (with), clashing
Anstreichen *nt* brushing, paint-coating, painting, coating
Anstrengung *f* effort
Anstrengungen unternehmen make efforts
Anstrichstoffe *mpl* paints, varnishes and similar products
Anwendersystem *nt* user system
antasten 1. *(allg.)* contact 2. *(Zahnflanken)* trace
Antastung *f* contacting
Anteil *m* proportion, proportionate share
Anteile *mpl* fractions
anteilig proportionate, proportionately, on a pro rata basis
Anteilsgrenze *f* coverage limit

Antenne *f* aerial, antenna
Antennenfeld *nt* aerial field
Antennenträger *m* antenna mast
Anti-Falleinrichtung *f* anti-fall device
antimikrobiell antimicrobic
antimonarmes Weichlot *nt* low-antimony soft solder
antimonfreies Lot *nt* antimony-free solder
antimonhaltiges Weichlot *nt* antimony-containing soft solder
Antiozonans antiozonant
antistatisch antistatic
Antivibrationsgestell *nt* anti-vibration mounting, anti-vibration levelling mount
antizipieren anticipate
Antransport *m* incoming transport
antreiben drive, power, run, propel
Antrieb *m* 1. *(allg.)* drive, driven side, actuator, drive mechanism, power drive, drive unit 2. *(Achsabstandsveränderung der Gabeln)* fork spacing adjustment drive 3. *(Funktion)* propulsion 4. *(mech.)* input
Antriebsachse *f* drive axle
Antriebsart *f* power source
Antriebsbatterie *f* traction battery
Antriebseinheit *f* power unit
Antriebselement *nt* drive element, driving member, prime mover
Antriebsgehäuse *nt* drive box
Antriebsglied *nt* driving element, input link
Antriebskasten *m* gearbox
Antriebskette *f* driving chain, motor-driven chain
Antriebskonzept *nt* drive concept
Antriebskreis *m* propulsion circuit
Antriebsleistung *f* 1. *(allg.)* drive power, power 2. *(e. Maschine)* input power 3. *(e. Motors)* input rating
Antriebsmodul *nt* drive module
Antriebsmotor *m* prime mover, drive motor
Antriebsrad *nt* driver, impeller, drive wheel
Antriebsregler *m* propulsion control
Antriebsriemen *m* drive belt
Antriebsritzel *nt* driving pinion
Antriebsscheibe *f* sheave
Antriebsschwinge *f* drive vibrator
Antriebsseite *f* headstock side
Antriebsspindel *f* driving spindle
Antriebssystem *nt* power system
Antriebswelle *f* input shaft, drive shaft
Antriebswinkel *m* input angle
Antriebszylinder *m* main drive cylinder
Antwort *f* response
antworten respond
Antwortgerät *nt* response unit
Antwortnummer *f* response number
Antwortzeit *f* response time
Anvulkanisationsverhalten *nt* scorching behaviour
anwachsen increase
Anwahl *f* call-up, selection
Anwahlbedienung *f* selection operation
anwählen call up, select
Anwahlfeld *nt* selection field
Anwärmdruck *m* heat-up pressure
Anwärmelektrode *f* heating electrode
Anwärmen *nt* superficial heating time
Anwärmgerät *nt* pre-heating burner
anweisen 1. *(allg.)* instruct, order 2. *(Aufgaben zuordnen)* assign
Anweisung *f* instruction, statement
Anweisungsliste (AWL) *f* intsruction list (IL), statement list
anweisungsorientiert instruction-oriented
anwenden apply, employ, use
Anwender *m* user
Anwenderdaten *pl* user data
Anwenderhandbuch *nt* user's manual
Anwenderoberfläche *f* user surface
Anwenderprogramm *nt* application program, user program
Anwenderprogrammspeicher *m* user program memory
Anwenderschnittstelle *f* user interface
Anwenderspeicher *m* user memory
Anwendung *f* application, employment, use
Anwendung *f* **mehrerer Kraftstoffe** multi-fuel application
Anwendungsbereich *m* scope of work, range (field) of application

Anwendungsfall *m* application
Anwendungsgebiete *ntpl* areas of application
Anwendungsgrenze *f* border off application
Anwendungsgruppe *f* application group
Anwendungsmöglichkeit *f* possible of application, application possibility
Anwendungsprogramm *nt* application program
Anwendungsprogrammierer *m* user programmer
Anwendungsschicht *f* application layer
anwendungsspezifisch application-specific
Anwesenheit *f* presence
Anwurfmotor *m* pony motor
Anzahl *f* number (of)
anzapfen tap, bleed (fluid)
anzeichnen scribe, sign, mark
Anzeige *f* 1. *(allg.)* display, indicator, signalling, trace, readout 2. *(Ablesung)* reading, indication 3. *(angezeigter Wert)* measurand 4. *(Aussage)* output 5. *(LED)* light emitting diode
Anzeigebereich *m* display area
Anzeigedauer *f* display duration
Anzeigeeinrichtung *f* indicating device
Anzeigefeld *nt* display box
Anzeigegerät *nt* display (unit), display device, indicator
Anzeigelampe *f* indicating light, tell-tale light
anzeigen display, read, indicate, index, register, record, signal
anzeigende und druckende Rechenmaschine *f* display and printing calculator
anzeigendes Messgerät *nt* indicating measuring instrument
Anzeigenschwelle *f* threshold of indication
Anzeiger *m* index
Anzeigeskala *f* dial indicator
Anzeigebereich *m* scale range
anziehen 1. *(allg.)* start, fasten, tighten 2. *(physisch)* attract 3. *(Schraube)* snug, tighten
Anziehgerät *nt* tightening tool
Anziehung *f* attraction
Anziehversuch *m (bei Muttern)* tightening test
Anzug *m* 1. *(e. Mitnehmerverbindung)* taper action 2. *(Schraube)* tightening 3. *(Spanndorn)* draw-in
Anzugdorn *m* draw-in arbour
Anzugsmoment *nt* starting torque
Anzugspindel *f* draw-in spindle
Anzugspunkt *m* starting-up point
Anzugsschraube *f* draw-in bolt
Apparat *m* appliance, apparatus, device, unit, set, contrivance
Apparatur *f* apparatus, outfit, equipment, appliance
APT Automatically Programmed Tools
AQL-Wert *m* quality level value
äquidistant equidistant
äquidistante Bahn *f* offset path
Äquidistanzschnitt *m* equidistant section
äquivalenter Schleifscheibenradius *m* equivalent grinding wheel radius
Äquivalenz *f* equivalence
Aräometer *nt* areometer
Arbeistablauf *m (selbsttätiger ~)* automatic cycle
Arbeit *f* 1. *(allg.)* work, operation, labour, task 2. *(Aufgabe)* job 3. *(mit Teilkopf)* index head operation
arbeiten work, operate
Arbeiter *m* labourer, worker, workman, operator, hand
Arbeitsablauf *m* 1. *(allg.)* cycle, sequence of operations, production (operating or machining or work) cycle, process (or work) flow 2. *(automatischer ~)* automatic cycle 3. *(im selbsttätigem ~)* automatic cycle, with automatic cycle
Arbeitsablaufplanung *f* (machining) cycle planning, process planning
Arbeitsabstand *m* working distance
Arbeitsanfall *m* work to be done
Arbeitsanweisung *f* job instruction
Arbeitsaufwand *m* expenditure of work

Arbeitsbedarf *m* need of work
Arbeitsbedingungen *fpl* working conditions
Arbeitsbeispiel *nt* case study, typical application
Arbeitsbereich *m* range (or scope) of work, range of application, capacity, work area, working zone, operating range
Arbeitsbereitstellung *f* working provision
Arbeitsbewegung *f* working motion
Arbeitsbühne *f* working platform
Arbeitsdiagramm *nt* working diagram
Arbeitsdruck *m* operating pressure
Arbeitsebene *f* 1. *(allg.)* working plane 2. *(angenommene ~)* assumed working plane
Arbeitseingriff *m* working engagement
Arbeitseinrichtung *f* workplace equipment
Arbeitsende *nt* end of work
Arbeitsergebnis *nt (erreichbares ~)* attainable results of working
Arbeitsergebnisse *ntpl* results of working
Arbeitsfeldbegrenzung *f* working area limit
Arbeitsfläche *f* 1. *(allg.)* working surface, working area, machined surface 2. *(beim Räumen)* broached surface 3. *(e. Maschinentisches)* working surface (or area)
Arbeitsflanke *f* working flank
Arbeitsfolge *f* operational sequence, work steps
Arbeitsfreude *f* working pleasure
Arbeitsfuge *f* working joint
Arbeitsgang *m* 1. *(allg.)* action, phase of operation, work (or process) step, working aisle, cycle, operation, pass, cutting (or operating) cycle 2. *(Tischbewegung)* working traverse 3. *(Vorschub)* working feed
Arbeitsgangbreite *f* working aisle width
Arbeitsgebiet *nt* field of activity
Arbeitsgegenstand *m* working object
Arbeitsgenauigkeit *f* 1. *(allg.)* operating precision 2. *(e. Maschine)* machining accuracy 3. *(e. Werkstückes)* accuracy of work
Arbeitsgerät *nt* implement
Arbeitsgeräte *ntpl* workshop facilities
Arbeitsgriff *m* work handle
Arbeitsgriffelement *nt* work handle element
Arbeitsgruppe *f* working party
Arbeitshub *m* cutting stroke, working stroke
Arbeitskarte *f* routing card
Arbeitskontrolle *f* working control
Arbeitskräfte *f* manpower
Arbeitskräftebedarf *m* manpower demand
Arbeitskräftemangel *m* labour shortage
Arbeitskräftereserven *fpl* manpower resources
Arbeitskreislauf *m* work cycle, teed circuit
Arbeitskurve *f* cam
Arbeitslehre *f* working gage, shop gage/gauge
Arbeitsleistung *f* 1. *(allg.)* working capacity, operating efficiency, output, performance 2. *(e. Maschine)* output, capacity
Arbeitsleuchte *f* work(ing) light
Arbeitsmaschine *f* machine, working (or production) machine, machine tool
Arbeitsmaß *nt* 1. *(allg.)* workshop gauge 2. *(e. Rachenlehre)* working dimension
Arbeitsmedium *nt* working medium
Arbeitsmeißel *m* cutting tool
Arbeitsmittel *nt* working appliance, device, working substance
Arbeitsölspiegel *m* working oil level
Arbeitsorgan *nt* manipulator, tool
Arbeitsperiode *f* work period
Arbeitspersonal *nt* working personnel
Arbeitsplan *m* operating plan, production plan, working schedule
Arbeitsplanung *f* operating planning, production planning
Arbeitsplattform *f* working platform
Arbeitsplatz *m* site of work, workplace, work site, workstation
Arbeitsplatzbeleuchtung *f* workplace

lighting
arbeitsplatzbezogen related to operator's position
Arbeitsplatzfläche *f* workplace area
Arbeitsplatzgestaltung *f* workplace design, workplace organization
Arbeitsplatzkonzentration *f* workplace concentration
Arbeitsposition *f* working position
Arbeitsprinzip *nt* operating principle
Arbeitsproduktivität *f* working productivity
Arbeitsradius *m* coverage
Arbeitsscheinwerfer *m* working light
Arbeitsschlitten *m* toolside
Arbeitsschutz *m* work protection, safety at work
Arbeitssicherheit *f* operational safety
Arbeitsspalt *m* work gap
Arbeitsspannung *f* working voltage
Arbeitsspanwinkel *m* effective rake
arbeitssparend labour saving
Arbeitsspeicher *m* working memory
Arbeitsspiel *nt* work(ing) cycle, operating cycle
Arbeitsspielzeit *f* work cycle time
Arbeitsspindel *f* main (or work or lathe) spindle, headstock spindle, milling (or cutter) spindle
Arbeitsstandort *m* operator's position
Arbeitsstation *f* work stage
Arbeitsstelle *f* working point, station
Arbeitsstellung *f* operating (or working) position, cutting position
Arbeitssteuerung *f* work controlling
Arbeitsstrom *m* operating current
Arbeitsstück *nt* work part, workpiece
Arbeitsstudie *f* work study
Arbeitsstufe *f* work stage
Arbeitssystem *nt* work system
Arbeitssystemplanung *f* work system planning
Arbeitstag *m* working day, workday
Arbeitstakt *m* work (or operation or machining) cycle
Arbeitsteil *nt* workpiece, work part
Arbeitstfläche *f* working area
Arbeitstisch *m* worktable, work platen, work (-holding) table
Arbeitstischquerbewegung *f* work-table-cross feed motion
Arbeitsumgebung *f* working background
Arbeitsunfall *m* occupational accident
Arbeitsverfahren *nt* manufacturing process, working (operating or tooling) method, procedure
Arbeitsversuch *m* trial operation
Arbeitsverteilung *f* working allocation working distribution
Arbeitsvorbereitung *f* routing card, work planning
Arbeitsvorbereitungskosten *pl* worl planning costs
Arbeitsvorgang *m* operation, pass, cycle, working operation, work process, machining operation
Arbeitsvorrichtung *f* attachment
Arbeitsvorschub *m* working (or cutting) feed
Arbeitsweise *f* technique, procedure, performance, operation, operating principle, working principle, practice, manufacturing (or operating) method, mode of operation, working method
Arbeitswinkel *m* (e. Meißels) working angle
Arbeitszeit *f* 1. (allg.) production time 2. (e. Betriebes) working time 3. (Fertigungsvorgang) operating time 4. (maschinelle) machining time
Arbeitszugabe *f* machining allowance
Arbeitszyklus *m* duty cycle, cycle
Arbeitszyklusdauer *f* duty cycle time (lubrication cycle)
Arbeitszylinder *m* control jack, working cylinder
Archiv *nt* archieve(s)
archivieren file
Archivregal *nt* shalving for archieves
arithmetische Schließtoleranz *f* arithmetic closing tolerance
arithmetischer Mittelwert *m* arithmetic mean
Arm *m* arm, bracket, lever, support
Armatur *f* fitting, armature, instrument
Armaturen *fpl* fittings
Armaturenanschluss *m* connection of appliances
Armaturenanschlussstück *nt* expan-

sion connector for valves
Armaturengehäuse *nt* valve body
Arretiereinrichtung *f* positioning lock, locking device
arretieren arrest, block, impede, lock, stop
Arretierung *f* interlock, location, lock, locking device, arrest, detent, blocking
Art *f* **1.** *(e. Befestigung)* method **2.** *(e. Maschine)* type
arteigene Schicht *f* *(z. B. Zunder oder Rost bei Überzügen)* layer related to the metal
artfremder Zusatzwerkstoff *m* filler metal of unlike kind
artgerecht erfüllt fulfilled correctly in terms of type
artgleicher Werkstoff *m* like material
artgleicher Zusatzwerkstoff *m* filler metal of like kind
Artikel *m* article
Artikelanzahl *f* number of articles
Artikelidentität *f* article identity
Artikelstruktur *f* article structure
Asbest *nt* asbestos
A-Schallleistungspegel *m* A-weighted sound power level
Asche *f* ash, cinders
Aschenaustrag *m* de-ashing
Aschenkasten *m* ashpan
Aschenraum *m* ashpit
Ascheschmelzverhalten *nt* fusability of fuel ash
ASCII ASCII (American Standard Code for Information Interchange)
ASCII-Tastatur *f* ASCII keyboard
A-Sortiment *nt* fast-moving items
Aspektverhältnis *nt* aspect relation
Asphaltbinder *m* bitumen binder
Asphaltrohmehl *nt* asphalt raw powder
Asphaltteerbeton *m* bitumen tar concrete
Ästhetik *f* aesthetics
asymptotisch asymptotic
asynchron asynchronous
Asynchronbetrieb *m* asynchronous mode
asynchrone Achsen *fpl* asynchronous axis

Asynchronmotor *m* asynchronous motor, induction motor
Atemschutz *m* respiratory protection
Atmosphäre *f* atmosphere
atmosphärisch atmospheric
atmosphärische Beanspruchung *f* atmospheric attack
Atmungsventil *nt* breather
Atomabsorbtionsspektroskopie *f* atomic absorption spectroscopy
Attrappe *f* blank
Attributmerkmale *ntpl* attribute characteristics
Attributprüfung *f* inspetion by attributes
ätzen etch
ätzend caustic, corroding, mordant
ätzender Stoff *m* corrosive substance
Ätzlauge *f* caustic lye
Audit *nt* audit
auditieren audit
Auditor *m* auditor
auf 1. *(offen)* open **2.** *(nach oben)* up
auf "Heben" stellen select "raise" position
auf Abstand bringen space
auf Anforderung *f* on demand, upon request
auf Anfrage *f* request, upon request
auf Außendruck *m* **bringen** to depressurize
auf Breite *f* **bringen** size to width
auf das Fertigmaß *nt* **bringen** finish to size
auf dem Erdboden at ground level
auf Einstellung *f* **bringen** jog
auf jeden Winkel verstellbarer Fräskopf *m* all-angle milling head
auf Lücke stehen stagger
auf Lücke stehende Spanbrechernuten *fpl* alternate nicking
auf Null stellen zero
auf rechtem Winkel vorbearbeiten square up
Auf- und Abbewegung *f* raising and lowering, rise and fall, vertical reciprocating motion, oscillating (or up-and-down) movement
auf volle Schnitttiefe einstellen set to the full-depth position

Aufbau *m* **1.** *(allg.)* bodywork, superstructure, structure **2.** *(Aufstellung)* erection **3.** *(Bauweise)* construction **4.** *(Gestaltung)* design **5.** *(Montage)* erection, design, construction, arrangement, installation **6.** *(von Proben)* composition **7.** *(Zusammenbau)* assembly
aufbauen assemble, built up, construct, set up, make up
Aufbaufeld *nt* add-on block
Aufbaugerät *nt* attachment
Aufbaumeißelhalter *m* duplex toolholder
Aufbauorganisation *f* company organization (structure), structural organization
Aufbauschneide *f* built-up cutting edge
Aufbaustruktur *f* organizational structure
Aufbauten *mpl* bodywork
aufbereiten 1. *(allg.)* dress, redress, purify, reclaim, treat, prepare, (pre)process, condition **2.** *(EDV)* edit
Aufbereitung *f* **1.** *(allg.)* preparation, conditioning, processing **2.** *(EDV)* editing
Aufbereitungsaufwand *m* preparation effort
aufbeulen buckle, bulge, expand, enlarge, widen
Aufbiegung *f* flexure
Aufblasverfahren *nt* jet evaporation method
Aufblätterung *f* exfoliation
aufbocken jack up
Aufbohren *nt* **1.** *(allg.)* boring, counterboring **2.** *(tiefe Bohrung)* deep-hole boring
Aufbohrkopf *m* boring head
Aufbohrmeißel *m* boring tool
aufbringen (auf) apply (to)
Aufbringen *nt* mounting
Aufbringung *f* application (of a lubricant upon a wear point)
aufbüchsen bush on
aufdecken uncover
aufdornen expand by means of a mandrel
aufdrehen srew open

Aufdrehverfahren *nt* untwisting method
Aufdruck *m* imprint, inscription
aufdrucken imprint, print (on/to)
aufeinander folgend successive
aufeinander stapeln stack on top of
Aufeinanderfolge *f* sequence
aufeinandergeschichtete Faserstoffbahnen *fpl* lengths of fibre arranged in superimposed layers
Aufeinanderkleben *nt* **mehrerer Lagen** cementing several layers on top of each other
auffächern fan out
auffahren ascend (to), drive against, tailgate
Auffahrschutz *m* shunt protection
auffällig conspicuous
Auffälligkeit *f* conspicuousness
Auffangbehälter *m* catchment tank, intercepting tank
auffangen 1. *(allg.)* catch, pick up, collect, absorb **2.** *(fallende Teile)* trap
Auffanggurt *m* parachute hardness
Auffangraum *m* catchment area
Auffangtrichter *m* tundish
Auffangvorrichtung *f* pick-off attachment
auffinden detect
auffordern call on, prompt, request
Aufforderung *f* request
Aufforderungsbetrieb *m* normal response mode (NRM)
auffrischen recondition
Auffüllauftrag *m* replenishment order
auffüllen (re)fill, replenish, top up
auffüllen bis zur Messmarke top up to the measuring mark
Aufgabe *f* **1.** *(allg.)* (work) assignment, duty, job, task **2.** *(von Werkstücken)* loading, feeding
Aufgabefläche *f* loading tray
Aufgabenbereich *m* field of duties, scope of responsibilities, task area, range of the desired variable
Aufgabenbeschreibung *f* task description
aufgabenbezogen task-related
Aufgabengröße *f* desired variable
Aufgabenstellung *f* task

Aufgabetrichter *m* feed hopper
aufgebaut built-on
aufgeben load
Aufgeben *nt* loading
aufgekeilt feathered
aufgenommene Leistung *f* input, wattage
aufgepresste Bereifung *f* press-on tyre wheel(s)
aufgeschweißter Querstab *m* welded-on cross bar
aufgespachtelte Schicht *f* spread-on layer
aufgespritzte Schicht *f* sprayed-on layer
aufgesteckte Scheibe *f* fitted washer
aufgezogen pressed-on
aufgwandte Arbeit *f* energy expended
Aufhängeklaue *f* suspension clamp
aufhängen (an) suspend (from)
Aufhängung *f* suspension, articulation point
Aufhärtbarkeit *f* potential hardness increase
aufhärten increase the hardness, reharden
Aufhärtungsneigung *f* trend to increase hardness
Aufhärtungsriss *m* age-hardening crack
aufheben 1. *(allg.)* abolish, cancel (out), unquote **2.** *(e. Sperre)* nullify **3.** *(e. Wirkung)* eliminate
Aufhebung *f* abolishment, cancellation
aufhören cease, stop
aufkeilen key
Aufkerbdurchmesser *m* *(bei Kerbstiften)* diameter over groove edges
aufklappbar hinged
Aufklebemuffe *f* cemented socket joint
aufkleben adhere, glue on, affix, paste (on/to), stick (on/to), bond
Aufkohlung *f* carburization, cementing
Aufkohlungsmittel *nt* carburization compound, recarburizer, recarburizing agent
Aufkohlungstiefe *f* carburization depth
Aufkohlungsverhalten *nt* carburizing behaviour

aufladen 1. *(mechanisch)* load, pick up **2.** *(el.)* charge
Auflage *f* **1.** *(allg.)* loading, load support, support, condition **2.** *(e. Maschinentisches)* bearing surface **3.** *(für Werkstücke)* rest **4.** *(Grundplatte)* base **5.** *(Sitz)* seat (contact) surface
Auflagebereich *m* *(e. Dichtringes)* contact area
Auflagedruck *m* support pressure
Auflageebene *f* load bearing surface, support level, base, bearing area (or face or surface), seat area, seat engaging surface
Auflagefläche *f* *(e. Mutter)* bearing face, lower face
Auflagenvorderkante *f* front edge of the support
Auflageplättchen *nt* tip
Auflageprofil *nt* load support, load support profile member, supporting beam, support(ing) profile
Auflageprofiloberfläche *f* load support surface
Auflager *nt* **1.** *(allg.)* bearing **2.** *(Bereich zwischen Grabensohle und der durch den Auflagerwinkel gegebenen Höhe am Rohrumfang, Auflagerbett)* bedding
Auflageriegel *m* support(ing) bar, supporting beam
Auflagerrolle *f* supporting roller
Auflagerschneide *f* support knife-edge
Auflagerung *f* bedding
Auflagerwinkel *m* support angle
Auflageschiene *f* work-rest blade
Auflageseite *f* bearing side, bearing face
Auflageträger *m* support beam
Auflagewinkel *m* angle support, support angle, support bracket, angle of support
Auflast *f* stacking load
Auflastentwicklung *f* build-up of load
Auflaufstelle *f* run-on point
auflegen seat, load, install, lay on, put on
Auflegieren *nt* alloying
Auflegierungsschicht *f* alloying coating
aufliegen 1. *(allg.)* lie on/against, rest

on 2. *(Werkstück)* seat on
aufliegendes Kreuz *nt* diagonal cross
auflisten list
auflockern tease
auflösen 1. *(allg.)* dissolve, resolve, disintegrate **2.** *(Bremse)* release **3.** *(Paletten)* dismantle
Auflösung *f* **1.** *(allg.)* resolution, disintegration **2.** *(Bremse)* release, releasing **3.** *(Paletten)* dismantling, dismantlement
Auflösungsvermögen *nt* **1.** *(allg.)* resolution **2.** *(Körnung)* granularity **3.** *(Trennschärfe)* selectivity
aufmachen undo
Aufmachungseinheit *f* unit of continuous material
aufmerksam advertent, attentive
Aufmerksamkeit *f* attention, attentiveness, concentration
Aufnahme *f* **1.** *(allg.)* pick up, take-up, receiving **2.** *(als Bild)* photograph **3.** *(als Funktion e. Messgerätes)* sensing **4.** *(als Vorgang)* exposure **5.** *(Bild, Ton, Signale)* recording **6.** *(e. Meißels)* location **7.** *(für Werkstücke)* work holder **8.** *(für Werkzeuge)* fixture **9.** *(im Magazin)* reception **10.** *(Kräfte)* absorption **11.** *(von oben)* top lifting **12.** *(bewegliche ~)* movable platen **13.** *(stationäre ~)* stationary platen
Aufnahme *f* **und Orientierung des Zerspanwerkzeuges** mounting and location of the cutting tool
Aufnahmeachse *f* *(e. Zahnrades zur Bestimmung der Außermittigkeit)* mounting axis
Aufnahmebereich *m* recording range
Aufnahmebohrung *f* accommodating hole
Aufnahmedorn *m* **1.** *(allg.)* work horn **2.** *(Räummaschine)* horn, guide bar
Aufnahmeeinrichtung *f* radiography equipment
Aufnahmefähigkeit *f* capacity, efficiency
Aufnahmefeld *nt* area of exposure
Aufnahmefläche *f* seating surface
Aufnahmeflansch *m* adaptor flange
Aufnahmefolie *f* intensifying screen, exposure screen
Aufnahmefrequenz *f* radiography rate
Aufnahmegerät *nt* photographic equipment, surveying apparatus
Aufnahmemaßstab *m* scale of the survey
Aufnahmenennspannung *f* rated voltage for radiography
Aufnahmepunkt *m* location point
Aufnahmeseite *f* input side
Aufnahmestation *f* pick-up station
Aufnahmestellung *f* radiography position
Aufnahmetisch *m* **1.** *(allg.)* receiving table **2.** *(Werkstoffprüfung)* radiographic table
Aufnahmevorrichtung *f* **1.** *(allg.)* handling attachment, mounting fixture **2.** *(für Werkstücke)* workholding fixture, workholder
Aufnahmezähler *m* exposure counter
Aufnahmezapfen *m* tang
aufnehmen 1. *(allg.)* pick up, take up, accommodate, engage, retrieve, untier **2.** *(Bild, Ton, Signale)* record **3.** *(einbauen)* house **4.** *(empfangen)* receive **5.** *(Ladung)* carry **6.** *(standhalten)* withstand **7.** *(zulassen)* permit
Aufnehmer *m* **1.** *(e. Messkette)* sensor **2.** *(Tastsystem)* pick-up
aufplattieren apply in plated form
Aufprall *m* impingement, bouncing, impact, collision, crash
Aufprallboden *m* impact floor
Aufprallebene *f* plane of impact
aufprallen bounce on, impinge, collide, crash into
Aufprallfläche *f* impact face
Aufprallgeschwindigkeit *f* speed at collision
Aufprallschutz *m* collision protection, crash protection, impact protection
Aufprallstoß *m* impact
Aufprallwinkel *m* angle of impact
aufpressen press on
aufpunkten spot-weld
aufrauen rough, roughen
Aufrauung *f* grass
aufrecht upright
aufrechterhaltbare Kesselleistung *f*

boiler output just capable of being maintained
aufrechterhalten maintain
aufreiben ream
aufreißen 1. *(Oberfläche bei der Zerspanung)* tear (open) **2.** *(zeichnen)* plot **3.** *(Späne)* break up
Aufreißverpackung *f* tear-open package
Aufreißverschlussstreifen *m* tear tape
Aufreißverschlussstreifen-Appliziermaschine *f* tear tape applicator
aufrichten erect, rear up, put upright
Aufrichtmaschine *f* erecting machine
Auf-Richtung *f (e. Armatur)* direction of opening
Aufriss *m* front view (elevation)
aufrollen 1. *(allg.)* roll up, coil up **2.** *(öffnend)* unroll, uncoil
Aufruf *m* call-in, invocation
aufrufen call, invoke
aufrunden round up
aufrüsten *(EDV)* upgrade
Aufrüstung *f* upgrade
Aufsatz *m* **1.** *(e. Stufenfutters)* closer **2.** *(Zusatzeinrichtung)* rest
Aufsatzbacke *f* top jaw
Aufsatzklaue *f* top jaw, false jaw
aufsaugen absorb, soak
aufschaukeln build up
aufschäumen foam
aufschichten pile up, stack
Aufschlag *m* impact, addition, extra change
aufschlagen (auf) impact against, disintegrate, add (to)
Aufschlaggerät *nt* disintegrator
aufschlämmen disperse
Aufschlussgrad *m* degree of delignification
Aufschlussmittel *nt* decomposing agent
Aufschlussverfahren *nt* decomposition (or fusion) method
Aufschmelzgrad *m* degree of fusion
Aufschmelztiefe *f* fusion depth
Aufschmelzungsriss *m* liquation crack
aufschrauben 1. *(allg.)* bolt on, screw on **2.** *(lockern)* loosen
Aufschraubfräser *m* screw-on cutter

Aufschraubmoment *m* tightening torque
Aufschrift *f* inscription
Aufschriftwert *m* inscribed value
aufschrumpfen shrink on
aufschweißen attach by welding, weld on
Aufschwimmen *nt (e. Rohrleitung)* buoying upwards
aufsetzen hit the ground, place upon, push on, put on, deposit, mount (or place or put) on
Aufsetzrahmen *m* pallet frame
Aufsicht *f* supervision
Aufsichtstätigkeit *f* supervisory activity
Aufspachteln *nt* spreading with a float
Aufspannart *f* **in Kastenbauart** box-section type floor slab
Aufspannblock *m* planer jack
Aufspannbolzen *m* arbor, mandrel
Aufspanndorn *m* mounting arbor, mounting mandrel, tool arbor
Aufspannelement *nt* anchoring element
Aufspannen *nt* **1.** *(allg.)* chucking, fixing, clamping, mounting, loading **2.** *(Werkzeuge)* tooling
Aufspannfeld *nt* floor slab
Aufspannfläche *f* clamping area, worktable, anchoring surface
Aufspannhülse *f* anchoring sleeve
Aufspanntisch *m* boring machine table, worktable, clamping table
Aufspannung *f* **1.** *(allg.)* locating, setup **2.** *(von Meißeln)* setting **3.** *(von Werkstücken, Werkzeugen)* loading, clamping, mounting **4.** *(in einer ~)* at one setting **5.** *(auf den Hobelmaschinentisch)* planing setup **6.** *(für Senkrechtstoßarbeit)* slotting setup
Aufspannvorrichtung *f* fixture, clamping device, setup fixture, workholder
Aufspannwerkzeug *nt* clamping tool
Aufspannwinkel *m* angle plate
Aufspannzeit *f* clamping time, loading time, setting-up time, piece-handling time
Aufspannzeit *f* **der Werkzeuge** tool set-up time

aufspringen uncoil violently
Aufspritzen *nt* spraying with a float
Aufsprühmethode *f* spray-up technique
aufspulen reel up, wind up
Aufstandsfläche *f* contact surface, stability polygon, footplate
aufstapeln pile up, stack
Aufsteckarm *m* attachment arm
Aufsteckdorn *m* arbor, stub arbor
aufstecken attach, clip (or fit or slip) on, mount, fit on
Aufsteckfräsdorn *m* cutter arbor
Aufsteckfräser *m* 1. *(allg.)* arbor cutter, hole type cutter 2. *(für Aufsteckdorn)* arbor type mill
Aufsteckgetriebe *nt* mounting gear (unit), shaft-mounted gear (unit)
Aufsteckgewindebohrer *m* shell tap
Aufsteckrad *nt* pick-off gear, change gear
Aufsteckversuch *m* knife test
Aufsteckwerkzeug *nt* shell (type) tool
Aufsteckwinkelfräser *m* stub angular cutter
aufstehen get up
aufsteigen (auf) access, get (into), board, mount
aufsteigender Zahlenwert *m* ascending numerical value
aufstellen 1. *(aufrichten)* erect 2. *(installieren)* install 3. *(positionieren)* position 4. *(e. Norm)* establish
Aufstellplatz *m* location of installation
Aufstellung *f* assembly, building up, erection, installation, setting-up
Aufstellung *f* **der Maschinen** plant layout
Aufstellungsfläche *f* *(Maschine)* floor space
Aufstellungshöhe *f* height of installation
Aufstellungstemperatur *f* temperature during erection
Aufstellungszeichnung *f* installation drawing
Aufstickungstiefe *f* nitrogenizing depth
Aufstieg *m* ascent, climb
Aufstreuverfahren *nt* strewing method
Aufstrom *m* updraft
aufsuchen approach
auftanken refill, refuel, replenish
Aufteileinrichtung *f* equalizing attachment
aufteilen apportion, divide, separate, split (up)
Aufteilung *f* (sub)division, apportionment, allocation of samples, partitioning, classification
Auftrag *m* 1. *(allg.)* job, order, assignment, task 2. *(EDV)* command 3. *(Überzug)* coating 4. *(einen ~ annehmen)* accept an order, receive an order 5. *(einen ~ einlasten)* dispatch an order
Auftragfläche *f* face being built up
Auftraggeber *m* client, customer, orderer
Auftragleistung *f* weight of metal deposited in unit time, deposition rate
Auftraglöten *nt* coat soldering
Auftragnehmer *m* supplier
Auftragraupe *f* deposited run
Auftragsabwicklung *f* order clearing (or handling), order processing, order completion
Auftragsabwicklungsprozess *m* order process chain
Auftragsänderung *f* order modification
Auftragsannahme *f* acceptance of orders, receipt of orders
Auftragsart *f* type of order
Auftragsbestand *m* orders on hand
auftragschweißen deposit-weld, padweld, weld-face, weld-surface
Auftragschweißen *nt* **von Panzerungen** deposition welding of hard surfacing layers
Auftragschweißen *nt* **von Plattierungen** deposition welding of claddings
Auftragschweißen *nt* **von Pufferschichten** deposition welding of buffer layers
Auftragschweißung *f* deposition weld
Auftragsdatei *f* open order file
Auftragsdaten *pl* order(s) data
Auftragsdisposition *f* order processing

Auftragsdurchlaufzeit f order lead time
Auftragseingang m receipt of order
Auftragseinlastung f dispatch (or orders), order loading
Auftragserfüllung f fulfilment of orders, order fill rate
Auftragserstellung f order completion
Auftragsfluss m order flow
auftragsgebunden sein (z. B. von Zeichnungen, Stücklisten) be not order-tied
Auftragsgrößenrechnung f order size computation
Auftragskennzahl f order characteristic value, order indicator
Auftragskoordinaten fpl order coordinate
Auftragsleitung f project manager
Auftragsliste f order list
Auftragsnummer f order number
Auftragsposition f order item
Auftragspriorität f order priority
Auftragspritzen nt building up (flame) spraying
Auftragsprognose f order forecast
Auftragsquelle f origin of orders
Auftragsreihenfolge f sequence of orders
Auftragsreserve f order backlog
Auftragsrückmeldung f order feedback
Auftragsschweißelektrode f hard-facing electrode
Auftragsschweißung f pad-welding, surface by welding, weld-facing
Auftragsstruktur f order structure
Auftragsterminierung f order scheduling
Auftragsverarbeitung f (EDV) command processing
Auftragsverwaltung f order administration
Auftragswalze f spreader roll
Auftragszeile f line of the order
Auftragszeit f fabrication time, total machining time
Auftragung f deposition, coating, building up
Auftreffbereich m area of incidence

auftreffen contact, impact against, meet, strike
Auftreffenergie f (e. Strahlmittels) impact energy
Auftreffgeschwindigkeit f impact velocity
Auftreffpunkt m contact point, impact point
Auftreffstelle f point of impact
auftreten 1. (Schäden) crop up, occur 2. (wiederholt) recur
Auftriebmethode f buoyancy-flotation method
Auftriebsflüssigkeit f flotation liquid
Auftriebsmessung f flotation measurement
Aufwand m effort, expense, expenditure, outlay
Aufwandabschätzung f outlay estimate
Aufwand-Nutzen-Betrachtung f outlay-benefits analysis
Aufwandsermittlung f outlay calculation
Aufwärmzeit f warming up time
Aufweitdorn m taper drift
aufweiten bulge, expand, enlarge, widen
Aufweiten nt 1. (Aufweitrecken) expanding 2. (an Enden) drifting 3. (durch Drücken) expanding by spinning
Aufweitprobe f drift test specimen
Aufweit-Recken expanding
Aufweitungsoptik f drifting optics
aufwenden expend, spend
aufwickeln coil up, wind up, take up
Aufwölbung f (e. Oberfläche) bulge
aufzählen list
Aufzählung f list
aufzeichnen record
Aufzeichnung f record, recording
Aufzeichnungsgerät nt recorder
Aufzug m hoist, lift, elevator
Aufzugsfeder f power spring
Augenabstand m interocular distance
Augenhöhe f eye level
Augenschutzgerät nt eye protector
Aushärtung f rehardening
aus 1. (örtlich) from, out of 2. (abge-

schaltet) off **3.** *(wegen)* due to
aus dem Stand *m* from standstill
aus dem Vollen herausgearbeitet machined from the solid
aus einem Stück *nt* on-piece, monobloc
Ausarbeiten *nt* **der Wurzellage** working of the root run
Ausbau *m* **1.** *(Erweiterung)* addition, enlargement, expansion, extension **2.** *(Teile)* disassembly, dismantling, removal
Ausbauarbeiten *fpl* extension work
ausbaubar 1. *(dehnbar, erweiterbar)* expandable **2.** *(Teile)* detachable, removable
Ausbauchen *nt* bulging
ausbauen 1. *(abbauen)* dismantle, dismount **2.** *(erweitern)* enlarge, expand, extend
Ausbaustück *nt* sample cut from surfacings
Ausbaustufe *f* addition, extension stage
Ausbereitungseigenschaft *f* spreading property
ausbessern patch, recondition, repair
Ausbesserungsarbeiten *fpl* repair work
Ausbesserungsschweißnaht *f* repair weld
ausbeulen planish
Ausbeute *f* yield
ausbiegen bend out
ausbilden 1. *(Teil)* develop, form **2.** *(Personal)* train, instruct
Ausbilder *m* instructor, apprentice trainer
Ausbildung *f* **1.** (Personal) training **2.** (Teile) design
Ausbildungsmittel *ntpl* training aids
ausblasbare Wand *f* blowout panel
Ausblaseeinrichtung *f* blow-out facility
ausblasen blow (out), insufflate
Ausblasmaschine *f* air cleaning machine
Ausblasverschluss *m* closure for blowdown
Ausblasvorrichtung *f* blow gun
Ausbleiben *nt* non-initiation, non-appearance, failure
Ausbleichungsstufe *f* fading stage
ausblenden mask
Ausblick *m* outlook
Ausblühung *f* blistering
Ausbohr- und Stirndrehmaschine *f* boring and facing mill
ausbohren bore out, drill out, counterbore
Ausbohrstange *f* boring bar
ausbrechen 1. *(allg.)* break away, break out, tear loose **2.** *(Schneidkante)* chip
Ausbrechung *f* torn surface
Ausbreitung *f* **1.** *(e. Brandes)* spread **2.** *(el.)* propagation, expansion
Ausbreitungsform *f* thinning (or spreading) variant
Ausbreitungswiderstand *m* *(el. chem.)* propagation resistance
Ausbrennen *nt* internal ignition
ausbrennsicher proof against burnout
Ausbrennsicherheit *f* resistance to internal ignition (or burn-out)
ausbringen yield, output
Ausbringung *f* output
ausbröckeln *(Schneidkante)* crumble, spall
Ausbröckelungstemperatur *f* crumbling temperature
Ausbruch *m* **1.** *(allg.)* disruption, chipping **2.** *(bei Oberflächen)* flaking **3.** *(e. Schneide)* chipping
Ausbruchstelle *f* outbreak point
ausdehnen 1. *(allg.)* expand, extend, elongate, flare **2.** *(der Länge nach)* lengthen, stretch **3.** *(durch Wärme)* dilate
Ausdehnung *f* expansion
Ausdehnungsfuge *f* expansion joint
Ausdehnungsleistung *f* expansion pipe
Ausdehnungsverhalten *nt* expansion behaviour
Ausdehnungswasser *nt* expansion water
ausdiffundieren diffuse out
ausdrehen 1. *(allg.)* recess by turning, turn inside diameters, turn with single-point tool, bore **2.** *(innen)* bore **3.** *(spitzsenken)* sink **4.** *(zylindrisch)*

counterbore
Ausdrehmeißel *m* boring tool, trepanning tool, internal boring tool
Ausdrehung *f* 1. *(Aussparung)* recessing, borehole 2. *(Bohrungen)* turning inside diameter
Ausdruck *m* 1. *(Papier)* (hard)copy, printout 2. *(math.)* term, equation, expression
Ausdrückbuchse *f* ejection (or ejector) bush
Ausdrückbuchsenplatte *f* ejector bushing plate
ausdrucken *(Papier)* print out
ausdrücken *(mit Worten)* disengage, declutch, demesh, throw out
Ausdrückplatte *f* ejector plate
Ausdrückplattenfeder *f* ejection plate spring
auseinander nehmen disassemble, dismantle
auseinanderliegende Maße *ntpl* dimensions at different locations
Auseinanderrollen *nt* **von Rohrstangen** rolling apart
ausfahrbar telescopic
ausfahren extend, remove, retrieve, leave
Ausfahrgeschwindigkeit *f* extending speed
Ausfahrgeschwindigkeit *f* **der Ladeeinrichtung** loading device extending speed
Ausfahrt *f* exit, extension
Ausfahrweg *m* extension travel, reach
Ausfahrzeit *f* retrieval time
Ausfall *m* deficiency, failure, loss, stoppage, breakdown
ausfallen break down, fail
ausfällen settle
Ausfallkosten *pl* downtime cost(s), outage losses
Ausfallöffnung *f (Späne)* pocket
Ausfallrate *f* failure quota, failure rate, force of mortality
ausfallsicher fail-safe
Ausfallsicherung *f* protection against failure, protection against bottlenecks
Ausfallteil *nt* emerging piece
Ausfallursache *f* failure cause

Ausfallzeit *f* downtime
Ausfassbeleg *m* dislocation ticket
ausfluchten align
Ausfluchtung *f* alignment
Ausfluss *m* issue
Ausflusszeit *f* time of outflow
Ausformen *nt* demoulding
Ausformschräge *f* draw, draft
Ausformtiefe *f* demoulding depth
ausfräsen 1. *(Gesenke)* diesink, cherry 2. *(Zahnlücken)* gash
ausfugen groove
ausführen 1. *(allg.)* accomplish, carry out, perform, practice, build, construct, execute 2. *(ausüben)* exercise, carry out 3. *(e. Versuches)* conduct
ausführliche Darstellung *f* detailed representation
Ausführung *f* 1. *(allg.)* execution, construction, model, pattern, version 2. *(e. Maschine)* type 3. *(Gestaltung)* design 4. *(handwerkliche)* workmanship 5. *(Oberfläche)* finish
Ausführungsart *f* type
Ausführungsplanung *f* execution planning
Ausführungstaste *f* execution button
Ausführungszeit *f* execution time
Ausfunken *nt* spark-machining, sparking out
Ausfunkzeit *f* sparking out time
ausfüttern bush, line, pad
Ausfütterung *f* lining, padding
Ausgabe *f* output
Ausgabe Sekundärbefehl *m* start output control, SOC
Ausgabebaugruppe *f* output module
Ausgabebereich *m* output range
Ausgabeeinheit *f* output station, output unit
Ausgabegerät *nt* read out device
Ausgaberinne *f* channel, chute, unloading passage
Ausgang *m* output, exit
Ausgang *m* **mit Negation** negating output
Ausgang *m* **mit Polaritätsindikator** output with polarity indicator
Ausgangsbelastbarkeit *f* fan out
Ausgangsbereich *m* output range

Ausgangsbild *nt* output image
Ausgangsdaten *pl* basic data
Ausgangsdruck *m* output pressure
Ausgangsdurchmesser *m* rough diameter
Ausgangsformat *nt (e. Zeichnung)* starting size
Ausgangsgetriebe *nt* initial linkage
Ausgangsgröße *f* output variable, output quantity
Ausgangsimpuls *m* output pulse
Ausgangsimpulsrate *f* initial pulse rate
Ausgangsklemme *f* output terminal
Ausgangslage *f* starting position
Ausgangslastfaktor *m* fan out
Ausgangsmaterialmenge *f* initial quantity of material
Ausgangsmetall *nt* parent metal
Ausgangsmodul *nt* output module
Ausgangsnut *f* source material
Ausgangsprüfung *f* output inspection
Ausgangspunkt *m* output station
Ausgangsradionuklidlösung *f* initial radionuclide solution
Ausgangsrauheit *f* starting roughness
Ausgangsrelais *nt* output relay
Ausgangssignal *nt* output signal
Ausgangssituation *f* initial situation, starting situation, starting point
Ausgangsspannung *f* output voltage
Ausgangsstellung *f* initial position
Ausgangsstrom *m* output current
Ausgangsstufe *f* output stage
Ausgangsteil *nt* starting workpiece
Ausgangsteilbestimmung *f* starting workpiece determination
Ausgangsviskosität *f* initial viscosity
Ausgangswert *m* output value, initial value, output valve
ausgeben feed out, output
ausgebende Information *f* displayed information
Ausgeber *m (e. Messeinrichtung)* read out device
ausgeblendetes Strahlenbündel *nt* collimated ray beam
ausgebrochen torn loose
ausgebrochene Schleifkörner *ntpl* abrasive grains

ausgefahren extended
ausgefahrene Stellung *f* withdrawn position
ausgeglichen balanced
ausgehen to come to an end, run short, run out, proceed (from), start (from)
ausgehend leading out, outgoing, proceeding (from)
ausgeleuchtet fully illuminated
ausgerüstet mit fitted with
ausgeschwenkte Stellung *f* swung-out position
ausgespart recessed
ausgespart aufsetzende Elektrode *f* hollow-tipped electrode
ausgewählter Schneidenpunkt *m* selected point on the cutting edge
ausgießen 1. *(allg.)* grout 2. *(auskleiden)* line
Ausgleich *m* compensation, counterbalance, correction
Ausgleich *m* **für Verschleiß** wear take-up
ausgleichen 1. *(allg.)* compensate, correct, equalize, cancel out, counterbalance, offset 2. *(durch Spachteln)* level out
Ausgleicher *m* expansion apparatus
Ausgleichsgewicht *nt* balance weight
Ausgleichskupplung *f* compensating coupling
Ausgleichsladen *nt* equalizing charging
Ausgleichsscheibe *f* compensation washer
Ausgleichsvorrichtung *f* compensating device
Ausgleichswert *m* compensation value
Ausgleichszeit *f* compensation time
ausgleiten slip
ausglühen anneal
Aushalsen *nt* necking
Aushalsung *f* necking operation
aushalten resist, withstand
aushängen detach, disengage
Aushärten *nt* **mit anschließendem Auslagern** precipitation heat treatment
ausheben lift out, excavate
Aushebeschrägen *fpl* drew bevels
Aushub *m* lifting out, excavation

Aushubeinrichtung *f* lift-out device
auskehlen channel, fillet groove
auskleiden line
Auskleidung *f* lining material
Auskleidungsrohr *nt* lined pipe
Ausklinkeinrichtung *f* tripping mechanism
ausklinken unlock, release, disengage, trip, unlatch
Ausklinknase *f* release catch
Ausklinkvorrichtung *f* release mechanism
Ausknicken *nt* buckling, failing
Ausknickversuch *m* collapsing test
Ausknöpfbruch *m* spot weld shear failure
auskolken 1. *(allg.)* crater 2. *(Spanfläche)* pit
Auskolkung *f* 1. *(allg.)* crater, cratering 2. *(Spanfläche)* surface cratering
auskoppeln decouple
auskragen protrude, overhang, project
Auskraglänge *f* length of overhang
Auskragung *f* overhang
Auskunft *f* information
Auskunftsystem *nt* information system
auskuppeln declutch, disengage the clutch, uncouple
Ausladung *f* 1. *(allg.)* offset, overhang, projection, depth of gap 2. *(Maschinenständer)* depth of throat, reach 3. *(von Rohrleitungen)* lateral bearing zone 4. *(Werkzeug)* overhang
Auslagerauftrag *m* retrieval order
Auslagerdurchsatz *m* output rate, outfeed rate
auslagern handle out of storage, pick, output, retrieve, untier
Auslagerpunkt *m* outfeed point, output point
Auslagerreferenzsystem *nt* output reference system
Auslagerspiel *nt* retrieval cycle
Auslagerstation *f* output station, retrieval station
Auslagerstelle *f* retrieval point
Auslagerteilstrom *m* output part flow
Auslagerung *f* retrieval
Auslagervorgang *m* retrieval process
ausländisches Gewinde *nt* foreign thread
Auslass *m* discharge, outlet
Auslassdruck *m* *(e. Ventils)* outlet pressure (of a valve)
auslassen discharge, omit
auslasten charge to capacity, utilize
Auslastung *f* utilization
Auslauf *m* deceleration, discharge, exit, outlet
Auslaufarmaturen *f* drain valves
Auslaufband *nt* outfeed belt
Ausläufe *mpl* outlets
auslaufen decelerate, slow down, leak, expire, leave
Auslaufförderer *m* outfeed conveyor
Auslaufprobe *f* run-out sample
Auslaufreibung *f* stopping friction
Auslaufrutsche *f* picking trays
Auslaufstelle *f* exit point, outfeed location
Auslaufstern *m* outfeed star
auslegen 1. *(dimensionieren)* dimension (for) 2. *(Vorrichtungen)* design 3. *(Zeichnungen)* lay out
Ausleger *m* 1. *(allg.)* arm, cantilever, beam, cross arm, rail, cross-rail, boom 2. *(Kran)* jib
Ausleger(arm) *m* radial arm
Auslegerbohrmaschine *f* radial drilling machine, radial drill
Auslegerbohrmaschine *f* **mit runder Säule** round column radial drill, round column drilling machine
Auslegerfräsmaschine *f* openside planer-miller
Auslegerführungsbahn *f* arm ways
Auslegerkran *m* jib crane
Auslegerschelle *f* *(e. Radialbohrmaschine)* arm bracket
Auslegung *f* 1. *(Arbeitsvorgänge)* layout 2. *(e. Konstruktion)* design
Auslegungskriterium *nt* design criterion
Auslegungspunkt *m* design point
Ausgleichsspeicher *m* compensation memory
auslenken deflect
Auslenkung *f* deflection
Auslesepaarung *f* sorting
ausliefern deliver

Auslieferung *f* delivery
Auslieferungsauftrag *m* delivery order
Auslöseaufforderung *f* DTE clear request
Auslösebestätigung *f* clear confirmation
Auslöseeinrichtung *f* kickout
Auslösegeschwindigkeit *f* tripping speed
Auslösemechanik *f* tripping mechanism
Auslösemechanismus *m* releasing mechanism, tripping mechanism
Auslösemeldung *f* DCE clear indication
auslösen disengage, release, trip, disconnect, activate, trigger
Auslösenocken *m* trip dog
Auslöser *m* trigger, detent
Auslösesignal *nt* releasing signal
Auslösung *f* release, trip-out, kickout, disengagement, triggering, tripping, releasing
Ausmaß *nt* (e. Schadens) extent
ausmessen calliper, gauge
Ausmessgerät *nt* admeasuring apparatus
ausmittelnde Flankenlinien *fpl* averaging tooth traces
Ausmündungsstück *nt* outlet section
Ausmusterung *f* decommissioning
Ausnahmefall *m* exceptional case
Ausnehmung *f* recess
ausnutzen utilise
auspacken unpack, unwrap
Auspackmaschine *f* unpacking machine, unwrapping machine
Auspackstation *f* unpacking station
Auspuff *m* exhaust
ausrechnen compute
ausreibbar capable of being rubbed off
ausreiben ream
ausreichend sufficient
Ausreißer *m/mpl* 1. *(allg.)* outlier 2. *(bei Messwerten)* stray results
ausrichten 1. *(allg.)* line up, true (up), arrange 2. *(dynamisch)* balance 3. *(fluchtgerecht)* align 4. *(gerade)* straighten 5. *(justieren)* adjust 6. *(plan)* level (out)
ausrichten (an) align (with), arrange, unscramble
Ausrichtmaschine *f* arranging machine, unscrambler
Ausrichtmaschine *f* **für formstabile Packmittel** rigid container unscrambler
Ausrichtmaschine *f* **für Packhilfsmittel** component unscrambler
Ausrichtstation *f* alignment station
Ausrichtung *f* alignment, arrangement
ausrücken 1. *(Getriebe)* throw out of gear, disengage 2. *(Kupplung)* unclutch, disconnect 3. *(Vorschub)* trip
Ausrundung *f* fillet
ausrüsten equip, fit (out)
Ausrüster *m* outfitter
Ausrüstung *f* 1. *(Ausstattung)* attachment 2. *(e. Maschine)* equipment, accessories, attachment, outfit 3. *(Einrichtung)* equipment 4. *(Geräte)* outfit 5. *(mit Meißeln)* tooling 6. *(Zurüstung)* attachment
Aussage *f* statement, indication
aussagefähig informative, meaningful
Aussagenlogik *f* Boolean algebra
aussagenlogisch Boolean
Aussagewahrscheinlichkeit *f* statement of probability, statement confidence (or coefficient)
ausschalten 1. *(ausklinken)* release 2. *(Druckbremse)* deenergize 3. *(Getriebe)* throw out of gear 4. *(Hebel)* disengage 5. *(Kupplungen)* uncouple, unclutch 6. *(Maschine)* put out of operation, disengage 7. *(Schalter)* disconnect 8. *(Schaltgeräte)* switch off 9. *(Stromkreis)* open (or break) the circuit 10. *(Vorschub)* trip (out) 11. *(deaktivieren)* deactivate
AUS-Schalter *m* 1. *(allg.)* stop control 2. *(el.)* circuitbreaker, cutout
Ausschalthebel *m* stop lever
Ausschaltknopf *m* stop button
Ausschaltpotential *nt* cutout potential
Ausschaltstrom *m* breaking current
Ausschalttaste *f* *(bei Gefahr)* emergency knockout
Ausschalttor *nt* normally-closed gate

Ausschaltung *f* **1.** *(allg.)* switching off **2.** *(e. Maschine)* tripping, disengagement **3.** *(el.)* switching off
Ausschaltverzögerung *f* turn-off delay
Ausschaltverzögerung *f* falling delay
Ausschaltverzögerungsglied *nt* off-delay timer
Ausschaltvorgang *m* deenergizing action
Ausschaltzeit *f* break time
ausschärfen bevel
ausscheiden 1. *(absondern)* separate **2.** *(beseitigen)* remove **3.** *(Proben)* sort out
Ausscheidungsriss *m* precipitation induced crack
ausschieben extend, move, reach
ausschlachten salvage
Ausschlag *m* amplitude
ausschlagen deflect
Ausschleuselement *nt* merge element
ausschleusen discharge, feed out, merge
Ausschleuser *m* merge, outgoing merge
Ausschleusstelle *f* merge point
Ausschleustakt *m* merge cycle
Ausschleusvorgang *m* merging, method of merge
ausschließen exclude
ausschmelzen liquate, melt, fuse
Ausschmelzmodell *nt* investment pattern
Ausschmelzung *f* fused area
Ausschmelzverahren *nt* cire-perdu process, precision-casting process
ausschneiden cut (out)
Ausschneidfräsen *nt* cut-out milling
Ausschnitt *m* partial plan
ausschreiben call for tenders, invite for tenders, put out for tenders, call for bids
Ausschreibender *m* caller for tenders
Ausschreibung *f* invitation for tender, call for tender, tender, bid, call for bids
Ausschreibungsgrundlage *f* basis for the invitation for tender
Ausschub *m* extension
Ausschubmechanismus *m* reach mechanism
Ausschubweite *f* reach
Ausschuss *m* **1.** *(allg.)* rejects, scrap work, brokes *(US)* **2.** *(Abfall)* waste **3.** *(Schrott)* scrap
Ausschussflankenrachenlehre *f* "not go" effective diameter snap gauge
Ausschussgrenze *f* "Not Go" limit
Ausschussgrenzmaß *nt* "Not Go" limiting size
Ausschusskennzeichnung *f* "Not Go" identification
Ausschusskosten *pl* reject costs
Ausschusslehre *f* not-go ga(u)ge
Ausschusslehrenkörper *m* "Not Go" gauging member
Ausschusslehrring *m* "Not Go" ring gauge
Ausschussmaß *nt* "Not Go" dimension
Ausschussquote *f* reject rate, scrap percentage, scrap rate
Ausschussrachenlehre *f* "Not Go" gap gauge
Ausschussrachenlehre *f* "Not Go" calliper gauge
Ausschussseite *f* no-go end, not-go end
Ausschussteil *nt* scrap component
ausschwenken 1. *(allg.)* drop out of engagement **2.** *(e. Scheibe)* swivel
ausschwingen die down (of oscillations)
Ausschwingspiel *nt* run-down cycle
Aussehen *nt* appearance
außen outside
außen verzahntes Rad *nt* external gear
Außenabrundung *f* crest radius
Außenabstand *m* outside spread
Außenborden *nt* **durch Drücken** spinning of external flanges
aussenden emit
Außendrehen *nt* outside (or external) turning
Außendrehmeißel *m* pointed finishing tool
Außendruck *m* external pressure
Außendruckrolle *f* external pressure roll
Außendurchmesser *m* outer diameter, outside diameter, major diameter
Außenfehler *m* surface flaw
Außenfeindrehen *nt* surface finish turning

Außenflächenräumen *nt* surface broaching
Außenflächenräummaschine *f* surface broaching machine
Außenfurnier *nt* outer veneer
Außengetriebe *nt* external transmission
Außengetriebeteil *nt* external part of the transmission
Außengewinde *nt* external thread, male thread, bolt thread
Außengewindedrehen *nt* extrrnal thread turning
Außengewindeschleifmaschine *f* external thread grinder
Außenglattwalzen *nt* **von Hohlkörpern** planishing tubular bodies outside
Außenhaut *f* moulding skin
Außenkegel *m* external taper, taper shank
aussenken countersink
Außenkontur *f* plan outline, profile
Außenleiter *f* external conductor, outer conductor
Außenlinie *f* contour
Außenlötende *nt* externally soldered end
Außenluftrate *f* rate of fresh (or outside) air supply
Außenlunker *m* surface blowhole
Außenmessung *f* external measurement
Außenpassteil *nt* external fitting member
Außenplandrehen *nt* external facing
Außenplanschleifen *nt* external face grinding
Außenrad *nt* external gear wheel, externally toothed gear, external gear
Außenradpaar *nt* external gear pair
Außenräumen *nt* surface (or external) broaching
Außenräummaschine *f* external broaching machine, surface broaching machine
Außenräumwerkzeug *nt* external broach, surface broach
Außenrundläppen *nt* ring lapping, external cylindrical lapping
Außenrundläppmaschine *f* external cylindrical lapping machine
Außenrundräumen *nt* rotary surface broaching
Aussenrundschleifen *nt* external cylindrical grinding
außenschleifen surface grind
Außen-Schrägverzahnung *f* external helical gear teeth
Außensechskant *m* (e. Schraube) hexagon head
Außenspannen *nt* outside gripping
Außenspritzung *f* external spraying
außenstehender Pfeil *m* outward-positioned arrowhead
Außentaster *m* outside calliper
Außentemperatur *f* outside temperature
Außentemperaturmessung *f* outside temperature measurement
außenüberdrehen turn outside diameter
außenverzahnt externally toothed
außenverzahnte Geradstirnräder *ntpl* external straight spur gears
außenverzahntes Geradstirnrad *nt* external straight cylindrical gear
außenverzahntes Kegelrad *nt* externally toothed bevel gear
außenverzahntes Rad *nt* external gear
außenverzahntes Schrägstirnrad *nt* external helical cylindrical gear
außenverzahntes Stirnrad *nt* externally toothed spur gear
außenverzahntes Umlaufrad *nt* externally toothed planet gear
außenverzahntes Zentralrad *nt* (e. Umlaufgetriebezuges) externally toothed central gear
außenverzahntes Zwischenrad *nt* (e. Umlaufgetriebes) externally toothed intermediate gear
Außenverzahnung *f* external tooth system
Außenwand-Feuerstätte *f* jacketed type fire-place
Außenwand-Gaswasserheizer *m* jacket type gas water heater
Außenwirbeln *nt* external thread whirling
außer Betrieb out of operation

außer Betrieb setzen decommission, put out of operation, withdraw
außer Eingriff out of mesh
außerachsig eccentric
außerbetrieblich out-house
Außerbetriebnahme *f* shutdown, decommissioning
Außerbetriebsetzung *f* decommissioning
äußere Einwirkung *f* external effect
äußere/r/s external, outer, outside
außerhalb outside
außerhalb der Radbasis in a counterbalanced position
außermittig non-central, eccentric, off-centre
außermittig drehen turn off centre
außermittige Last *f* offset load
außermittiges Drehen *nt* eccentric turning
Außermittigkeit *f* centre offset, eccentricity, off-centre position, load offset
äußerste/r/s outermost
Aussetzbetrieb *m* intermittent service
aussetzen 1. *(allg.)* discontinue, fail, intermit, expose, interrupt, subject to **2.** *(e. Gefahr)* expose
aussetzender Betrieb *m* intermittent operation
Aussetzung *f* exposure
aussortieren select, sort
aussortiertes Los *nt* segregated lot
ausspannen release, dechuck, unclamp, unlock, remove, unload
Ausspannen *nt* **1.** (Werkstücke) unloading, unclamping **2.** (des Werkzeuges) tool releasing
aussparen recess
Aussparung *f* recess, notch, slot, groove, gap, clearance
aussplittern split out
Ausstapelautomatik *f* automatic destacking
ausstapeln destack, pick, retrieve
Ausstapelvorgang *m* destacking operation
ausstatten equip (with), fit (with)
Ausstattung *f* equipment, accessories
aussteifen brace, stiffen, strut
Aussteifung *f* brace, kneebrace, strut

Aussteifungsblech *nt* stiffening plate
Aussteifungskonstruktion *f* (rack) brace design, rigidity design
Aussteifungsturm *m* stiffening tower
aussteigen get off, deboard, egress, exit
AUS-Stellung *f* OFF-Position
Aussteuerungsinduktion *f* control flux density
Ausstieg *m* exit (door)
ausstopfen stuff
Ausstoß *m* output, yield
ausstoßen turn out, expel, eject
ausstrahlen emit, (e)radiate
Ausstrahlung *f* radiation
ausströmen aus issue from
Aussuchpaarung *f* selective assembly
Austausch *m* exchange, interchange, replacement
austauschbar exchangeable, interchangeable, replaceable
Austauschbarkeit *f* interchangeability, replaceability, exchangeability
Austauschbau *m* **1.** *(allg.)* interchangeable manufacture **2.** *(Fertigungstechnik)* selective assembly
austauschen exchange, interchange, replace, substitute
Austenitisierungsdauer *f* austenitizing time
Austenitisierungstemperatur *f* austenitizing temperature
austragen check out
Austreiberlappen *m* tang
Austreiblappen *m* *(e Morsekegelschaftes)* flat tang
Austreibloch *nt* drift hole
Austreibschlitz *m* drift slot
austreten 1. *(allg.)* emerge **2.** *(Gase)* emit
Austrittseingriff *m* *(Stirnradpaar mit Evolventenverzahnung)* recess contract
Austrittseingriffsstrecke *f* length of recess path
Austrittskanal *m* outlet report
Austrittspotential *nt* output potential
Austrittsstabilisator *m* outlet stabilizer
austropfen lassen allow to drain
ausüben 1. *(allg.)* execute **2.** *(Druck, Kraft)* exert (upon)
ausvulkanisieren cure

Auswaage *f* weighed-out quantity
Auswahl *f* choice, selection
Auswahl *f* **der Werkzeuge** tooling
Auswahleinheit *f* sampling unit
auswählen choose, select
Auswahlkombinations-Wäge-Füllmaschine *f* selective combination weighing machine
Auswahlsatz *m* sampling fraction
Auswälzfräseinrichtung *f* hobbing out attachment
Auswaschung *f* scouring
Auswaschverlust *m* loss of weight by washing out
auswechselbar exchangeable, removable, replaceable
auswechseln 1. *(allg.)* substitute, exchange, change **2.** *(ersetzen)* replace **3.** *(untereinander)* interchange
ausweichen turn out, deflect, give away, avoid
Ausweiskarte *f* ID card
auswerfen eject
Auswerfer *m* ejector
Auswerfersystem *nt* ejector system
Auswertdiagramm *nt* evaluation diagram
Auswerteeinheit *f* evaluation unit, interpreter unit
Auswerteelektronik *f* processing logic
Auswertelogik *f* evaluation logic
auswerten evaluate
Auswerteverfahren *nt* evaluation method
Auswertformel *f* evaluation formula
Auswertung *f* evaluation
Auswertungsbogen *m* evaluation form
Auswertungssoftware *f* evaluation software
Auswertungsverfahren *nt* evaluation procedure (or method)
auswirken auf exert, effect, result
Auswirkung *f* effect, impact
Auswuchs *m* **1.** *(Produkt)* product **2.** *(Übersteigerung)* excess
Auswuchteinrichtung *f* balancing device
auswuchten balance
Auswuchtwaage *f* balance

Auswurf *m* ejector
auszeichnen label
Auszeichnung *f* labelling
ausziehbar extensible, extractable, telescopic
ausziehbare Kühlmittel-Rückflussleitung *f* telescopic coolant return
ausziehen extract, move out, pull out
Ausziehverhältnis *nt* deposition ratio
Ausziehwerkzeug *nt* extractor
Auszubildender *m* **für Werkzeugmaschinenbedienung** trainee machine toll operator
auszulagernd outgoing
autogen schneidbar suitable for thermal cutting
autogenes Brennschneiden *nt* flame cutting gas cutting
Autogentechnik *f* autogenous technology
Autokollimationslichttaster *m* autocollimating light scanner
Automat *m* **1.** *(allg.)* automatic system, automat, machine **2.** *(Drehautomat)* automatic lathe **3.** *(Revolverautomat)* automatic turret lathe **4.** *(Schraubenautomat)* automatic screw machine
Automat *m* **mit Hilfskurvensteuerung** automatic turret lathe with auxiliary cam control
Automatendreher *m* automatic lathe operator
Automatendrehmaschine *f* automatic turret lathe
Automateneinrichter *m* automatic lathe setter
Automatenstahl *m* free-cutting steel, free-machining steel, automatic screw steel
Automatikbetrieb *m* automatic operation, automatic mode
Automatik-RBG *nt* automatic SRM
Automation *f* automation
automatisch automatic, automated
automatisch gesteuert automatically controlled
automatische Bildübertragung *f* automatic monitoring
automatischer Gasbrenner *m* automatic gas burner

automatischer *m* **Ausgleich des Totganges** automatic backlash elimination
automatischer Ölzerstäubungsbrenner *m* automatic atomizing oil burner
automatischer Tiefenvorschub *m* power down feed
automatisches Löten *nt* automatic soldering
automatisieren automate, automatize
automatisiert automated
automatisiertes Gerät *nt* automated equipment
Automatisierung *f* automation
automatisierungsgerecht suitable for automation
Automatisierungsgrad *m* degree of automation
Automatisierungsstufe *f* automation stage
Avivierechtheit *f* fastness to brightening
Avothan *nt* avothane
axial endwise, axial
axiale Tischbewegung *f* axial table feed motion
axiale Tischvorschubgeschwindigkeit *f* axial table feed speed
axialer Druck *m* end thrust
axialer Eingriff *m* axial engagement
axialer Spanwinkel *m* *(Fräser)* axial angle, axial rake
axialer Tischvorschub *m* **pro Hub** axial table feed per stroke
axiales Schleifen *nt* axial grinding
Axialgeschwindigkeit *f* axial speed
Axialität *f* alignment
Axialkraft *f* axial force
Axiallager *nt* thrust bearing
Axialmodul *nt* *(e. Verzahnung)* axial module
Axialprofil *nt* axial profile
Axialschlag *m* axial runout
Axialschnitt *m* axial plane
Axialspiel *nt* end clearance, axial backlash
Axialteilung *f* axial pitch
Axialteilungs-Abweichung *f* axial pitch variation
Axialvakuumpumpe *f* axial vacuum pump
Axialventilator *m* axial flow fan
Axialverfahren *nt* axial feed method
Axialverschiebung *f* axial displacement
axonometrische Projektion *f* axonometric projection
Azetylen *nt* acetylene
Azetylenflasche *f* acetylene cylinder
Azetylenschweißen *nt* acetylene welding

B b

B-Bild *nt* B-scope presentation
Backe *f* jaw
Backenbremse *f* block brake, shoe brake
Backengreifer *m* (pair of) gripper jaws
Backenöffnung *f* jaw opening
Backenspannung *f* vice clamping
Backentrennfläche *f* chase parting line
Bag-in-Box-Füll- und Verschließmaschine *f* **für Flüssigkeiten** liquid bag-in-box fill and seal machine
Bahn *f* **1.** *(Weg Route)* path, route **2.** *(Schienen)* track **3.** *(aquidistante ~)* equidistant path **4.** *(durchgehende ~)* continuous path (CP) **5.** *(prismatische ~)* Vee-guide, (pl.: vees)
Bahn *f* **mit Rapport** continuous length with repeating pattern
Bahnabschnitt *m* path section
Bahnabweichung *f* deviation
Bahnführung *f* track guidance
Bahnhof *m* parking station
Bahnkorrektur *f* path correction
Bahnkurve *f* trajectory
Bahnkurvenberechnung *f* trajectory calculation
Bahnneigung *f* gradient, path inclination
Bahnnormale *f* perpendicular to path
Bahnsegment *nt* route segment, section of route
Bahnspur *f* path trace
Bahnsteuerung *f* continuous path control, contouring control, path control
Bainitstufe *f* austempering region, bainit range
Bakterienwachstum *nt* growth of bacteria
Balken *m* beam, horizontal tie, mainbeam, overarm, crossrail, yoke
Balken- oder Strichcode *m* barcode
Balkendiagramm *nt* bar chart, histogram
balkenförmige Probe *f* beam-like sample
Balkenmenü *nt* **1.** *(vom oberen Bildschirmrand)* pull-down menu **2.** *(vom unteren Bildschirmrand)* pop-up menu
Balkenmethode *f* beam method
Ballast *m* ballast
Ballastbehälter *m* ballast container
Ballen *m* bale
Ballengriff *m* ball handle
Ballenklammer *f* bale clamp
ballig crowned, convex
ballig aufsetzende Elektrode *f* dome-tipped electrode
Balligdreheinrichtung *f* convex turning attachment
Balligeinrichtung *f* **1.** *(zum Schaben)* crowing attachment **2.** *(zum Schleifen balliger Formstücke)* convex grinding attachment
Balligfräseinrichtung *f* convex milling attachment
Balligkeit *f* convexity
Balligschleifmaschine *f* camber grinding machine
Balligverzahnen *nt* crowning, convex tooth cutting
Balligverzahnung *f* crowning, crowned tooth cutting, spheroid tooth form, spheroid gear cutting
Ballon *m* carboy
Band *nt* **1.** *(allg.)* band **2.** *(als Dichtmittel im Gewinde)* strip **3.** *(Förderer)* belt **4.** *(Umreifung)* tape
Band *nt* **mit wärmehärtender Klebeschicht** tape with a thermosetting layer of adhesive
Bandausschnitt *m* band gate
Bandbreite *f* bandwidth
Bandeinweglichtschranke *f* band single-way light barrier
Banderole *f* band, sleeve
banderolieren band
Banderoliermaschine *f* banding machine
Bandförderer *m* belt conveyor
Bandsäge *f* bandsaw
Bandsägeblatt *nt* bandsaw blade, saw band

Bandsägen *nt* bandsawing
Bandsägenhartlötgerät *nt* bandsawing brazing device
Bandsägenschweißgerät *nt* bandsaw blade welder
Bandschleifen *nt* abrasive belt grinding
Bandschleifer *m* (für Entrostung) belt sander
Bandschleifmaschine *f* belt grinder
Bandspan *m* fine-lace chip, ribbon chip
Bandsprühanlage *f* belt sprayer
Bandvorschubgerät *nt* belt pusher unit
Barcode *m* (Balken- oder Strichcode) barcode
Barcodefeld *nt* bar code area
Barcodestrich *m* bar code stripe
Barcodestift *m* bar code pin, bar code wand
Base *f* base
Basis *f* base, basis
Basisantriebsmodul *nt* basic drive module
Basisband *nt* base hand, base band emitter, switched thyristor, baseband
Basisfreiwinkel *m* base clearance (angle)
Basisisolation *f* basic insulation
Basissystem *nt* basic system
basisumhüllte Elektrode *f* basic covered electrode
Batterie *f* battery
Batterieantrieb *m* battery drive
Batteriebehälter *m* battery type storage tank
batteriebetrieben storage battery
Batteriedeckel *m* battery lid
Batterieeinbauraum *m* battery compartment, battery space
Batterieeinheit *f* battery unit
batterieelektrisch electric
batterieelektrisch betrieben battery powered
Batterieentladung *f* battery discharge
Batteriegewicht *nt* battery mass, service mass of battery
Batteriekasten *m* battery container
Batterieklemme *f* battery terminal
Batterieladeanschluss *m* battery charging connection
Batterieladefahrt *f* battery-charging trip
Batterieladegerät *nt* battery charger
Batterieladesystem *nt* battery charging system
Batterieladezustand *m* charging level, charging status
Batterieladung *f* battery charging
batterielos without battery
Batterie-Nennspannung *f* battery rated voltage
Batteriestandzeit *f* battery life
Batterietrog *m* battery container
Batteriewechsel *m* battery exchange
Bau *m* construction, manufacture
Bauart *f* **1.** (Design) design **2.** (Bauausführung) construction, type, style, pattern **3.** (e. Maschine) type, model, pattern
bauaufsichtliche Zulassung *f* building inspectorate approval
Bauaufwand *m* construction outlay
Bauausführung *f* construction
Baud baud
Baueinheit *f* basic construction unit
Bauelement *nt* component, member
bauen 1. (allg.) build **2.** (z. B. Gebäude konstruieren) construct
Bauform *f* design, shape
Bauglied *nt* construction member (or element), structural member
Baugröße *f* size
Baugrubenwand *f* trench wall
Baugrund *m* surface, surface foundations
Baugrundsetzungen *fpl* foundations
Baugruppe *f* assembly, sub-assembly
Baugruppenlager *nt* assembly warehouse
Bauherr *m* constructing owner
Bauhöhe *f* **1.** (allg.) overall height, headroom **2.** (e. Armatur) centreline to top height
Bauingenieur *m* civil engineer
Baujahr *nt* year of construction, year of manufacture
Baukasten *m* building block
Baukastenprinzip *nt* modular principle
Baukastenroboter *m* modular robot
Baukastenstückliste *f* modular part list

Baukastensystem *nt* unit assembly system, unit construction system, building block system, modular system
Baukastenvorrichtung *f* modular fixture
Baulänge *f* overall dimension (or length)
baulich constructional, structural
bauliche Anlagen *fpl* structural installations
baulicher Brandschutz *m* fire safety in building, structural fire protection
Baumaß *nt* structural size
Baumaße *ntpl* overall dimensions
Baumassenzahl *f* building mass factor
Baumerkmal *nt* design feature
Baumnetz *nt* tree network
Baumuster *nt* type
baumusterungsgeprüfter Kessel *m* type-tested boiler
Baumwollfeingewebe *nt* fine cotton fabric
Baumwollfeinstgewebe *nt* very fine cotton fabric
Baumwollgewebebahn *f* cotton fabric strip
Baumwollgewebeschnitzel *nt* cotton fabric shreds
Bauplaner *m* building designer
Bauprüfung *f* verification of conformity, structural examination
Baureihe *f* series, type series
bauseits gestellte Anlageteile *f* parts of the installation supplied by the employer
Baustahl *m* **1.** *(allg.)* construction steel **2.** *(allgemeiner ~)* general construction steel **3.** *(warmfester ~)* high-temperature resistant construction steel
Baustein *m* block, module
Bausteinaufruf *m* call of program module
bausteinbezogen module-related
Bausteinende *nt* end of program module
Bausteinerneuerung *f* module refreshing, module renewal
Baustelle *f* construction site
Baustellenfertigung *f* building site production

bautechnische Gründe *mpl* civil engineering reasons
Bauteil *nt* structural member, construction member, element, component, assembly
Bauteilgruppe *f* component assembly
Bauteilprüfanlage *f* component testing installation
Bautenabdichtung *f* damp proofing of buildings
Bauverantwortlicher *m* person responsible for the construction
BCD-Code *m* BCD-code (Binary Coded Decimal Code)
BCN *Abk* binary coded natural
BDE *Abk (Betriebsdatenenerfassung)* manufacturing data collection
Bedieneranzahl *f* number of operators
Be- und Entladeeinrichtung *f* loading and unloading device, loading and unloading station
Be-/Entlüftung *f* ventilation, venting
beabsichtigt intentional
beabsichtigte Schädigung *f* intentional damage
beachten note, observe, take into consideration
Beanspruchbarkeit *f* ability to withstand exposure
beanspruchen 1. *(allg.)* claim **2.** *(auf Last)* load **3.** *(elastisch belasten)* stress **4.** *(verformend)* strain **5.** *(verlangen)* demand, require
Beanspruchung *f* **1.** *(elastisch)* stress **2.** *(Belastung)* loading **3.** *(e. Maschine)* duty **4.** *(verformende)* strain, straining
Beanspruchungsablauf *m* stress pattern
Beanspruchungsart *f* type of stressing
Beanspruchungsdauer *f* duration of loading
Beanspruchungseinrichtung *f* loading device (or system)
beanspruchungsgerechte Bindung *f* bond type appropriate to the type of duty
Beanspruchungsgruppe *f* stress group
Beanspruchungsniveau *nt* level of loading

Beanspruchungsstufe f stress stage
Beanspruchungszeit f stress-time factor
beanstanden object, reject, complain about
Beanstandung f **1.** *(allg.)* objection, complaint, claim **2.** *(Annahmeverweigerung)* rejection
bearbeitbar machinable
Bearbeitbarkeit f free-machining property (or quality), ready machinability, workability
bearbeiten 1. *(allg.)* machine, work, handle, process **2.** *(Konturen)* profile, contour **3.** *(Oberflächen)* treat **4.** *(spanlos)* form, shape **5.** *(zerspanend)* machine, cut
bearbeiten mit Doppelspindelstock oder Satzfräser gang mill
Bearbeiten nt **auf rechtem Winkel** squaring
Bearbeiter m person in charge (of)
bearbeitete Fläche f machined surface
Bearbeitung f **1.** *(allg.)* processing, machining, working **2.** *(formgebende)* shaping cutting, profiling, contouring **3.** *(Nachbearbeitung)* finishing **4.** *(spanlos)* forming, shaping **5.** *(zerspanende)* machining, cutting
Bearbeitung f **einer Bohrung** hole operation
Bearbeitung f **einer Fläche** facing operation
Bearbeitung f **im ersten Arbeitsgang** first cycle machining
Bearbeitung f **mit numerischer Steuerung** numerical machining
Bearbeitung f **mit Rundvorschub** circular work
Bearbeitung f **von Innenflächen** internal work
Bearbeitungsablauf m machining (or cutting) cycle, history
Bearbeitungsaufmaß nt machining allowance
Bearbeitungsbaustein m processing module
Bearbeitungsdauer f processing duration
Bearbeitungsfläche f machining surface
Bearbeitungsfolge f sequence of operations, machining sequence
Bearbeitungsgeschwindigkeit f machining rate
Bearbeitungsgrundzeit f basic machining time
Bearbeitungshauptzeit f machine running time
Bearbeitungsmaschine f manufacturing (or processing) machine
Bearbeitungsnebenzeit f non productive time
Bearbeitungsparameter mpl machining parameters pl, handling parameters pl
Bearbeitungsreihenfolge f order of processing, processing (or operation) sequence
Bearbeitungsriefe f ridge left by the tool
Bearbeitungsschritt m job step, processing step
Bearbeitungsspur f abrasive mark, tool mark
Bearbeitungsstation f processing station
Bearbeitungsstufe f machining phase
Bearbeitungssystem nt machining system
Bearbeitungsverfahren nt machining operation
Bearbeitungsvorgang m machining operation
Bearbeitungswerkstatt f machining shop, mechanical workshop
Bearbeitungswerkzeug nt cutting tool
Bearbeitungszeichnung f operation drawing
Bearbeitungszeit f machining (or processing) time, operating time
Bearbeitungszeiten fpl machining times pl
Bearbeitungszentrum *(BAZ)* machining centre (MC)
Bearbeitungszugabe f machining (or tooling) allowance
Bearbeitungszyklus m machine cycle
beaufschlagen admit, apply (to)

Beaufschlagung *f* loading, admission
beaufsichtigen attend, supervise
Bebauungsplan *m* development scheme
Bebauungsplanung *f* development planning
Becher *m* cup
Becherfüll- und -verschließmaschine *f* cup fill and seal machine
Becken *nt* bowl
Bedampfen *nt* vapour deposition
Bedarf *m* demand, requirement(s)
Bedarfsauflösung *f* demand resolving
Bedarfsdisposition *f* demand disposal
Bedarfsermittlung *f* demand assessment
bedarfsgerecht tailored to demand, tailored to suit the needs of the market
Bedarfshochrechnung *f* requirement extrapolation
Bedarfsplanung *f* demand planning
Bedarfsverstärkung *f* demand amplification
Bedeutung *f* significance
Bedienanleitung *f* operating instructions *pl*
Bedienanweisung *f* command, operator command
Bedienbarkeit *f* (e. Maschine) functional control, operational control
Bedieneinheit *f* control panel
Bedienelement *nt* 1. (Einrichtung) actuator, control 2. (Hebel) lever
bedienen attend, control, handle, operate
Bediener *m* operator
Bedienerberührbarkeit *f* operator accessibility
Bedienerfreundlichkeit *f* operator convenience
Bedienerführung *f* (operator) prompting
Bedienerhandbuch *nt* operating manual
Bedienerplattform *f* operator's platform
Bedienerschnittstelle *f* operator interface
Bedienfeld *nt* control desk, panel
Bedienfenster *nt* operation window

Bediengerät *nt* operator panel
Bedienperson *f* operator
Bedienprotokoll *nt* operating log
Bedienrückmeldung *f* operation feedback, operator feedback
Bedienstand *m* operator's position, operator stand
Bedienstation *f* operating station
Bediensystem *nt* operating system
Bedientafel *f* operating (or control) panel
Bedienteil *nt* operating member (or element), operating component
Bedienung *f* 1. (e. Maschine) attendance, handling, operation, control 2. (Hebel) manipulation, shifting 3. (Schaltorgane) control
Bedienungs- und Wartungshandbuch *nt* operating maintenance manual
Bedienungsanleitung *f* operating instruction(s), operating manual, operating guide
Bedienungsanweisung *nt* operating instructions, operator's manual
Bedienungsart *f* mode of operation
Bedienungsbühne *f* operating platform
Bedienungseinrichtung *f* operating device, control
Bedienungselement *nt* control element, control member
Bedienungserleichterung *f* ease in operation
Bedienungsfehler *m* error in operation (or service), operating error
Bedienungsgang *m* aisle
Bedienungsgriff *m* operating handle (or lever)
Bedienungshebel *m* control lever, operating lever
Bedienungsmann *m* (e. Maschine) (UK) attendant, (US) operator
Bedienungspersonal *nt* operation personnel, operators
Bedienungsplatte *f* control panel, operation panel
Bedienungspult *nt* operating desk
Bedienungsschild *nt* instruction plate
Bedienungsseite *f* loading face

Bedienungsstand *m* control station, operator's position
Bedienungstafel *f* operating (or control) panel
Bedienungsvorschrift *f* operating (or service) instruction
Bedienungszeit *f* machine-handling time
Bedienungszentrale *f* central control panel, pendant control panel
Bedienverhalten *nt* interaction procedure
bedingen cause, condition
bedingt conditional
bedingt durch caused by
bedingt geeignet suitable to only a limited extent
bedingte Verteilung *f* conditional distribution
bedingter Erwartungswert *m* conditional expectation
bedingter Sprung *m* conditional jump
Bedingung *f* antecedent, condition
bedrucken imprint, print
Bedürfnis *nt* demand, want
beeinflussbar influenceable, subject to influence
beeinflussen affect, influence
Beeinflussung *f* influence, influencing, interference
beeinträchtigen affect adversely, impair (with), impede, inhibit
Beeinträchtigung *f* impairment, interference
beenden end, finish, terminate
Beendigung *f* ending, finishing
Betriebsisolierung *f* operating insulation
befähigen enable
Befähigungsnachweis *m*: **großer** ~ full scale proof of competence
Befähigungsnachweis *m*: **kleiner** ~ restricted proof of competence
Befehl *m* command, instruction, order
befehlen command
Befehlsart *f* instruction type
Befehlsausgabe *f* instruction output
Befehlsausgang *m* instruction output
Befehlseingang *m* instruction input
Befehlsgabe *f* initiation

Befehlsname *m* instruction name
befestigen 1. *(allg.)* attach to, apply, fasten, pin, clamp, attach, **2.** *(sichern)* secure to **3.** *(verriegeln)* lock **4.** *(verschrauben)* screw, bolt, mount, fix
Befestigung *f* fastening, locking, bolting, clamping, fitting, mounting, securing, attachment, fixing, anchorage, installation
Befestigungsabstand *m* distance of fixture
Befestigungsart *f* fastening method, type of fixture
Befestigungsbohrung *f* fixing hole
Befestigungsbolzen *m* fixing bolt
Befestigungselement *nt* fastener
Befestigungsfläche *f* mounting face, mounting surface
Befestigungsgewinde *nt* fastening screw thread
Befestigungsmaterial *nt* fixing material(s)
Befestigungsmittel *nt* fastener
Befestigungsplatte *f* mounting plate, top plate, bracket plate
Befestigungsplattenaußenmaße *ntpl* top-plate outer dimensions
Befestigungspunkt *m* fixing point, fixing position
Befestigungsschelle *f* mounting bracket
Befestigungsschicht *f* surfacing layer
Befestigungsschraube *f* clamping (or fastening) bolt
Befestigungsstift *m* securing pin, fastening pin
Befestigungsteil *nt* fixing device
Befestigungsvorrichtung *f* fixing device
befeuchten dampen, humidify
Befeuchtung *f* dampening, humidification
Befeuchtungseinrichtung *f* humidifying equipment
Befeuerung *f* heating, firing
Befinden *nt* health
befinden: als gut ~ deem to be good
Beflammung *f* impingement of the flame
beflocken *nt* flock

befördern carry, convey, transport, move, handle
Beförderung *f* conveying, conveyance, handling, transport
befriedigen satisfy
Befrostung *f* freezing
Befugnis *f* competence
befugt authorized, competent
befüllen fill
befüllt filled
Befüllung *f* filling
Befüllungsstelle *f* filling point
Befund *m* findings *pl*
begehbar accessible
begehbare Fläche *f* surface for pedestrian usage, walkway
begehen frequent, walk on
Begehen *nt:* **bei** ~ for persons walking on
Begehversuch *m* walk test
begleiten accompany
begleitend accompanying
Begleitlinie *f* tracer line
Begleitpapier *nt* accompanying document
Begleitschein *m* detailed statement
begrenzen 1. *(allg.)* border, limit, restrict, bound 2. *(z. B. Maßlinien)* terminate
Begrenzung *f* boundary, limitation
Begrenzungen *fpl* delimitations *pl*
Begrenzungslinie *f* boundary line
Begrenzungsring *m* boundary ring
Begrenzungsschalter *m* limiting (or limit) switch
Begriff *m* concept, term
begutachten appraise
behaglich cosy
Behaglichkeit *f* cosiness
Behaglichkeitsempfinden *nt* cosiness feeling
Behaglichkeitsfaktor *m* cosiness factor
behalten maintain, retain
Behälter *m* 1. *(allg.)* box, container, receiver, receptacle, through, bin, case, vessel, reservoir 2. *(Flüssigkeiten)* tank
Behälter *m* **mit Bodenentleerung** drop bottom container
Behälter *m* **mit gewölbten Boden** vessel with dished ends
Behälter *m* **mit Mantel** vessel with jacket
Behälter- und Rohrleitungsbau *m* tank and pipeline construction
Behälterauslauf *m* container outlet, tank outlet
Behälterbau *m* container construction
Behälterboden *m* container bottom, tank bottom
Behältereinlauf *m* container inlet, tank inlet
Behälterentleerungsgerät *nt* discharger
Behältergröße *f* container dimensions (pl), container size
Behälterkippgerät *nt* container tippler
Behälterregal *nt* container rack
Behälterscheitel *m* tank crown
Behältersohle *f* tank bottom
behandeln handle, treat, process
Behandlung *f* handling, processing, treatment, conditioning
Behandlungsart *f* type of treatment
beharren persist, stay
Beharrungsbeanspruchung *f* settled load
Beharrungsvermögen *nt* inertia
beheben correct, rectify, remedy
Behebung *f* correction, rectification
beheizen heat
beheizt heated
Beheizungseinrichtung *f* firing equipment
Behelfs... makeshift, temporary
Behelfskonstruktion *f* makeshift design
behelfsmäßig provisional
behindern impede, obstruct, interfere with
Behinderung *f* hindrance
Behörde *f* authority
Behördenkontakt *m* authority contact
bei at, near, for, in the case of, upon
bei Vertragsabschluss *m* upon closing of the contract
beibehalten retain, maintain
beide both
beidseitig both-way, on both sides
beigeschliffen ground
Beihalten *nt (Beihaltrecken)* corrective

stretching
Beilage *f* permanent backing strip, shim
Beilegeblech *nt* **für Annietmuttern** shim for rivet nuts
Beilegering *m* packing
Beilegescheibe *f* shim
beim Empfänger *m* at the customer's premises, at the consignee's
Beipackzettelzuführmaschine *f* leaflet feeder
Beipass *m* bypass
beischleifen grind
Beißschneiden *nt* incising
Beistellung *f* (z. B. e. Schleifscheibe) feeding, infeed
Beiwert *m* coefficient, index
Bekleben *nt* bonding
Bekleidungsmaterial *nt* clothing material
bekommen obtain, receive
Beladeeinrichtung *f* loading device
beladen load
Beladestation *f* loading station
Belag *m* coating, covering, facing, lining, plating, cover
Belagstärke *f* cover thickness
belastbar loadable
Belastbarkeit *f* load-carrying capacity, loadability, resistance to loading
belasten load, stress, increase the load of, strain
belastet loaded
Belästigung *f* nuisance
Belastung *f* *(Kraft Last)* load, loading, stressing, stress, load condition, strain
belastungsabhängig load dependent
Belastungsbegrenzer *m* **1.** *(Kraft)* force limiter **2.** *(Druck)* pressure limiter
Belastungsbild *nt* load diagram
Belastungsdauer *f* load cycle
Belastungsfaktor *m* loading factor
Belastungs-Kennwert *m* loading characteristic
Belastungskontrolle *f* loading control
Belastungsmatrix *f* load matrix
Belastungsprüfung *f* testing under load
Belastungssituation *f* load situation
Belastungsspektrum *nt* load spectrum
Belastungsstoß *m* shock load

Belastungsverlauf *m* load cycle
Belastungsvorgang *m* loading procedure
Belastungszeitspanne *f* loading time interval
Beleg *m* document
Belegcodierer *m* document encorder
belegen 1. *(allg.)* occupy **2.** *(Gerät, Speicher)* seize **3.** *(räuml.)* fill, load **4.** *(Regalfach)* load, reserve **5.** *(Schicht)* cover
Belegfluss *m* document flow
beleglos automatic, electronic, paperless
belegt loaded
Belegung *f* **1.** *(Anschlüsse)* assignment **2.** *(Regalfach)* loading, reservation
Belegungszeit *f* coating time
Belegzeit *f* action period
beleimen glue
Beleimung *f* glueing, glue system
beleuchten illuminate
Beleuchtung *f* lighting, illumination, light
Beleuchtungseinrichtung *f* light(ing) equipment, light source, illumination device
Beleuchtungsstärke *f* lighting intensity
Beleuchtungsstrahlengang *m* illumination beam path
Beleuchtungszeitspanne *f* loading time interval
Belichtungsbedingungen *fpl* exposure conditions *pl*
Belichtungsgröße *f* exposure rate
beliebiger Punkt *m* arbitrary point
beliefern supply
Belieferung *f* delivery, supply
Belieferungskette *f* supply chain
belüften aerate, air
belüftet ventilated
Belüftung *f* ventilation
Belüftungsventil *nt* vent valve
bemaßen dimension
Bemaßung *f* dimensioning
Bemaßungsgrundsatz *m* dimensioning principle
Bemaßungsregel *f* dimensioning rule
bemessen 1. *(Größe)* dimension, size

2. *(Leistungen)* rate
Bemessung *f* rating, seizing, dimensioning
Bemessungsleistung *f* rated power
Bemessungstrom *m* rated current
Bemessungswert *m* rated value
benachbart adjacent, adjoining, neighbouring
benachbarte gleichgerichtete Flanken *fpl* adjacent parallel flanks
benachbarter Betriebsbereich *m* neighbouring work area
benennen denominate, designate, term, name
Benennung *f* denomination, designation
benetzen wet, moisten
Benetzungswasser *nt* wetting water
benötigen require
benutzen use, employ, utilise
Benutzer *m* user
Benutzerführung *f* user prompting
Benutzerinformation *f* information for use
Benutzeroberfläche *f* user interface
Benutzertaskausführungszeit *f* user task execution time
Benutzerumfeld *nt* user environment
Benutzung *f* use
Benutzungsart *f* mode of action
Benzin *nt* *(US)* gasoline, *(UK)* petrol
Benzinmotor *m* gasoline engine, petrol engine
beobachten observe
Beobachter *m* observer
Beobachtung *f* **1.** *(prüfende)* observation, observance **2.** *(allg. visuelle)* viewing
Beobachtungsabstand *m* *(screen)* viewing distance
Beobachtungsgerät *nt* viewing device
Beobachtungswert *m* observed value
Beobachtungswinkel *m* viewing angle
Bequemlichkeit *f* comfort
beranden trim
beraten advise, consult
Berater *m* consultant
Beratung *f* consulting, consultancy
berechnen compute, calculate, figure
Berechnung *f* **1.** *(allg.)* calculation, computation **2.** *(überschlägige)* estimate
Berechnungsbeispiel *nt* calculation example
Berechnungsformel *f* calculation formula
Berechnungsgang *m* course of calculation
Berechnungsgrabenbreite *f* design trench width
Berechnungstabelle *f* calculation table
Berechnungsverfahren *nt* calculation method
Berechnungsvorschrift *f* calculation rule
berechtigen authorize, enable
Berechtigter *m* authorized person
Berechtigung *f* authorization
Berechtigungsstufe *f* authorization level
Beregnungsversuch *m* shower test
Bereich *m* range, zone, region, field, scope, area, section
Bereichsrechner *m* section computer
Bereichsschätzung *f* interval estimation
bereifen tyre
Bereifung *f* tyre
Bereifung *f* **aus Vollmaterial** solid tyre
Bereifung *f* **mit Lufteinschluss** semi-pneumatic tyre
bereit ready
bereitgestellt ready for use
Bereitschaft *f* readiness
Bereitschaftszeit *f* readiness time
bereitstellen make available, provide, place ready to hand, make ready for use
Bereitstellen *nt* providing
Bereitstellgenauigkeit *f* positioning accuracy
Bereitstellmenge *f* provision volume
Bereitstellplatz *m* centring location, pick-up position, pick-up location
Bereitstellsystem *nt* provision system
Bereitstelltisch *m* standby table
Bereitstellung *f* provision, presentation of items (required)
Bereitstellungsfläche *f* provision area
Bereitstellungskosten *pl* provision

cost(s)
bergab down, downhill
bergauf up, uphill
bergen recover, save, take in tow
Bergung *f* retrieval
Bergungsmöglichkeit *f* recovery facility
Bericht *m* report
berichten report
Berichterstattung *f* reporting
berichtigen adjust, correct, rectify, set right, amend
berichtigter Messwert *m* corrected measured value
Berichtigung *f* adjustment, correction, rectification
Berichtswesen *nt* reporting system
berieseln spray, sprinkle
Berieselung *f* **1.** *(allg.)* spraying, sprinkling, wetting **2.** *(Kühlmittel)* flooding
Berstdruckprüfung *f* bursting pressure test
Berstdruckversuch *m* bursting pressure test
bersten burst
Bersten *nt* bursting
Berstmembran *f* bursting diaphragm
Berstscheibe *f* bursting disc, rupture disc
Berstwiderstand *m* bursting resistance
Berücksichtigung *f* consideration
Berufsausbildung *f* vocational training
Berufsgenossenschaft *f* liability insurance association
Berufsschule *f* apprentice training school, trade school
Beruhigungsschutzeinrichtung *f* safety device against accidental contact
Beruhigungszeit *f* settling period
berührbares Teil *nt* contactable part
berühren contact, touch
berührend contacting
berührend einschließen touch and enclose within
Berührfläche *f* contact surface
Berührlinie *f* contact line
Berührpunkt *m* point of contract
Berührschirm *m* touch screen
Berührung *f* contact, tangency, touch
Berührungsbogen *m* arc of contact

berührungsempfindlich touch-sensitive
berührungsempfindliche Einrichtung *f* touch-sensitive device
berührungsempfindlicher Bildschirm *m* touch-sensitive display, touch-sensitive screen
Berührungsfläche *f* area of contact, contact area, contact surface, imprint area
berührungsfrei contactless, non-contacting, on a non-contact basis, contact-free, without contact
Berührungskorrosion *f* corrosion under deposits
Berührungslinie *f* *(e. Zahnflanke)* line of contact
berührungslos contactless, non-contacting, on a non-contact basis
berührungslose Messung *f* touchless measurement
Berührungsnormale *f* normal to the line of contact
Berührungspunkt *m* point of contact
Berührungsschutz *m* protection against accidental contact
Berührungsspannung *f* contact voltage
Berührungsthermometer *nt* contact thermometer
Berührungszone *f* *(e. Schleifscheibe)* contact zone
berußen soot
Berylliumgleichwert *m* beryllium filter equivalent
besäumen square, edge, trim
beschädigen 1. *(allg.)* damage, deteriorate **2.** *(Oberflächen)* impair, score, mar **3.** *(unbrauchbar)* spoil
Beschädigung *f* **1.** *(allg.)* damage, damaging, defect **2.** *(e. Oberfläche)* flaw, scoring **3.** *(Haarriss)* incipient crack **4.** *(Schadensausübung)* marring **5.** *(Verformung)* deformation
beschaffen acquire, procedure, purchase, resource, provide, supply
Beschaffenheit *f* **1.** *(allg.)* composition, condition **2.** *(e. Oberfläche)* finish **3.** *(Eigenschaft)* property **4.** *(Qualität)* quality **5.** *(Zustand)* condition

Beschaffung *f* acquisition, procurement, purchasing, resourcing
Beschaffungsauftrag *m* acquisition order
Beschaffungskosten *pl* acquisition cost(s)
Beschaffungslogistik *f* outbound logistics, procurement logistics
Beschaffungsmarkt *m* acquisition market
Beschaffungsprogramm *nt* acquisition program
Beschaffungsvorlaufzeit *f* procurement lead time
Beschaffungszeit *f* lead time
beschäftigen employ, occupy
beschalten wire
Beschaltung *f* wiring
Bescheinigung *f* certificate, attestation
beschichten coat, cover, face
beschichtet coated
beschichtetes Blech *nt* abrasive coating
Beschichtung *f* **1.** *(allg.)* surface coating, organic and inorganic coating, coating, facing **2.** *(chemische ~)* chemical coating **3.** *(elektrochemische ~)* electrochemical coating **4.** *(PVC ~)* polyvinyl chloride coating
Beschichtungsfolie *f* plastics surfacing film
Beschichtungsstoff *m* organic and inorganic coating material
Beschichtungsverfahren *nt* coating method
beschicken charge, feed, load
Beschickung *f* charging, feeding, loading, storage
Beschickungsart *f* feeding type
Beschickungseinrichtung *f* feeding (or feeder) attachment
Beschickungsfrequenz *f* feeding frequency
Beschickungsgang *m* charging aisle, loading aisle
Beschickungspuffer *m* charging buffer
Beschickungsroboter *m* charging robot
Beschickungsspeicher *m* charging memory
Beschickungsstelle *f* loading (or feeding) point, charging
Beschickungtrichter *m* hopper
Beschickungswagen *m* pallet carrier
Beschickungszeit *f* charging time
Beschilderung *f* marking
Beschläge *mpl* fittings, mountings *pl*
beschleunigen accelerate, speed up
beschleunigt at excessive speed
beschleunigte Rückführung *f* rapid return
beschleunigter Vorlauf *m (e. Schlittens)* rapid approach
Beschleunigung *f* acceleration, speeding up
Beschleunigungsbeanspruchung *f* acceleration load
Beschleunigungsförderer *m* acceleration conveyor
Beschleunigungskraft *f* force of acceleration
Beschleunigungsperiode *f* acceleration period
Beschleunigungsrichtung *f* direction of acceleration
Beschleunigungsweg *m* path of acceleration
beschneiden trim
Beschneiden *nt* trimming
Beschneiden *nt* **zum Entfernen eines Grates von Gußteilen oder Formwerkstücken** clipping
Beschneiden *nt* **zum Entfernen eines Schmiedegrates** flash trimming
Beschneidezugaben *f* cutting additions
beschnittene Lichtpause *f* trimmed photo print sheet
beschnittene Zeichnung *f* trimmed drawing sheet
Beschnittrand *m* trimming margin
beschränken confine, restrict, limit
beschränktes lineares Bremsvermögen *nt* restricted linear stopping power
Beschränkung *f* limitation, restriction
Beschreibbarkeit *f* suitability for writing, writing property
beschreiben describe
beschreibend descriptive

beschreibende Statistik *f* describing statistics
Beschreibung *f* description
Beschreibungsmittel *nt* description media
beschriften label, letter, mark
Beschriftung *f* labelling, lettering, marking
Beschriftungsfeld *nt* card holder
beschweren weigh
beseitigen eliminate, remove, dispose of
Beseitigung *f* disposal, elimination, removal
besenförmiger Bruch *m* brush-like fracture
besenrein in clean and tidy condition
besetzen man, occupy
Besetzung *f* occupancy of passenger spaces, manning
Besetzungsinversion *f* occupation inversion
Besetzungszahl *f* occupation number
Besichtungsöffnung *f* inspection hole
Besonderheit *f* special feature
bespritzen *(z. B. mit e. Chromatierlösung)* spray on (to)
Bessemerstahl *m* acid bessemer steel
Bestand *m* **1.** *(allg.)* inventory, stock **2.** *(z. B. bei der Inventur)* on-hand quantity
Bestandabgleich *m* stock adjustment
beständig durable resistant, stable, constant, continuous, resistant (to), immune (to), proof (against)
Beständigkeit *f* **1.** *(Bestandteil)* component **2.** *(chem.)* ingredient **3.** *(gegen)* resistance, immunity, insusceptibility
Beständigkeitsprüfung *f* withstand test
Bestandsabfrage *f* inventory enquiry
Bestandsbildung *f* increase of inventories
Bestandsführung *f* stock-keeping, inventory management
Bestandsführungskopplung *f* inventory management coupling
Bestandshaltung *f* holding of inventories
Bestandshaltungskosten *pl* inventory holding cost(s)
Bestandskontrolle *f* stock control
Bestandskosten *pl* inventory cost(s)
Bestandsminimierung *f* minimizing of inventories
Bestandsniveau *nt* stocking level
Bestandspolitik *f* stocking policy
Bestandspuffer *m* inventory buffer
Bestandsreichweite *f* inventory range, range of inventory
Bestandsübernahme *f* on-hand stock incorporation
Bestandsverringerung *f* inventory reduction
Bestandswert *m* inventory value
Bestandteil *m* component, constituent, ingredient, constituent part
bestätigen acknowledge, confirm
bestätigter Termin *m* confirmed deadline
Bestätigung *f* acknowledgement, confirmation
bestehen (aus) consist (of)
Bestellbearbeitung *f* order processing
Bestellbezeichnung *f* order designation
Bestellbezug *m* order reference
Bestelldatum *nt* order date
Bestelleingang *m* incoming orders
bestellen order
Bestellmenge *f* order quantity
Bestellmengenplanung *f* order quantity planning
Bestellnummer *f* order number
Bestellposition *f* order item
Bestellprognose *f* order forecast
Bestellprozess *m* ordering process
bestellreif ready for ordering
bestelltes Material *nt* on-order materials
Bestellung *f* order, purchase order
Bestell-Zeichnung *f* order drawing
bestimmbar determinable
bestimmen 1. *(allg.)* analyse, specify, design, define, destine **2.** *(chem.)* determine **3.** *(e. Lage)* locate **4.** *(vorschreiben)* specify, prescribe
Bestimmung *f* destination, determination
bestimmungsgemäß intended

bestimmungsgemäße Verwendung *f* proper use, specified use
bestimmungsgemäßer Betrieb *m* normal operation
Bestimmungsgröße *f* specification factor, determinant
Bestimmungsgrößen *fpl* variables *pl*
Bestimmungsmaterial *nt* defining material
Bestimmungsstück *nt* **1.** *(allg.)* element **2.** *(e. Gewindes)* thread element **3.** *(von Zahnrädern)* gear element
Bestrahlung *f* irradiation
Bestrahlungsfeld *nt* irradiated area
Bestrahlungsprotokoll *nt* irradiation record
Bestrahlungssieb *nt* irradiation sieve
Bestrahlungsuhr *f* irradiation timer
bestücken 1. *(allg.)* load, place, stock, face **2.** *(e. Werkzeugmaschine)* tool **3.** *(Werkzeug: Schneidmeißel mit Platten)* tip
Bestücken *nt* **mit Hartmetall** hard facing
Bestückung *f* loading, placement, stocking
Bestückungsautomat *m* automatic placement machine, pick-and-place machine
betätigen 1. *(allg.)* activate, actuate, operate, manipulate **2.** *(el.)* energize
Betätigung *f* actuating, actuation, operating, operation, action, manipulation, energizing
Betätigungsart *f* actuating type
Betätigungseinrichtung *f* actuator
Betätigungseinrichtung *f* **für Fahrtrichtung** travel control
Betätigungshebel *m* actuating lever
Betätigungskraft *f* actuating force
Betätigungsnocken *m* trip stop (or dog)
Betätigungsorgan *nt* actuating element, operating element
Betätigungsschlüssel *m* **für Armaturen** handling key for valves *pl*
Betauung *f* condensation, bedewing
Betaverteilung *f* beta distribution
beteiligen involve, participate (in), take part

Beteiligter *m* person involved
Beteiligung *f* involvement, participation
Beton *m* concrete
Betonauflager *nt* concrete bedding
Betondach *nt* concrete roof
Betonfußboden *m* concrete floor
Betonkonstruktion *f* concrete structure
Betonoberfläche *f* concrete surface
Betonrohr *nt* concrete pipe
Betonrohr *nt* **mit Anschlussstücken** concrete pipe with adapter fittings
Betonrohr *nt* **mit Bodenplatte** concrete pipe with bottom slab
Betonrohr *nt* **mit Eiquerschnitt** concrete pipe with egg-shaped cross-section
Betonrohr *nt* **mit Falz** concrete pipe with rebate
Betonrohr *nt* **mit Fuß** concrete pipe with base
Betonrohr *nt* **mit Gerinne** concrete pipe with channel
Betonrohr *nt* **mit Kreisquerschnitt** concrete pipe with concentric cross-section
Betonrohr *nt* **mit Muffe** concrete pipe with socket
Betonrohr *nt* **mit Scheitelzulauf** concrete pipe with top branch
Betonrohr *nt* **mit Seitenzulauf** concrete pipe with side branch
Betonrohr *nt* **mit seitlichen Ansätzen** concrete pipe with offset extensions
Betonrohr *nt* **mit Spitzende** concrete pipe with spigot end
Betonrohr *nt* **mit verstärkter Wanddicke** concrete pipe with extra wall thickness
Betonrohr *nt* **mit Zulauf** *(Abzweig)* concrete pipe with branch
Betonstahlschweißer *m* steel reinforcement welder
Betonummantelung *f* concrete surround
Beton-Vergussmasse *f* concrete joint sealing compound
Betonwand *f* concrete wall

betrachteter Schneidenpunkt *m* selected point on the cutting edge
Betrachtung *f* visual observation, analysis
Betrachtungsbereich *m* field of observation
Betrachtungsquerschnitt *m (e. Probe)* cross section under investigation
Betrachtungszeitraum *m* period of analysis
Betrag *m* amount, rate
betragen to be, amount to
betreiben operate, manage
Betreiber *m* user, owner, purchaser
betreten access, enter
Betrieb *m* **1.** *(als Gesamtheit technischer Anlagen, Werk)* plant **2.** *(Betriebsabteilung)* production department **3.** *(e. Werkzeugmaschinen, Geräte)* operation, practice, service **4.** *(Fabrik)* factory **5.** *(Fertigungsbetrieb)* manufacturing shop **6.** *(Werkstatt)* shop, workshop
Betrieb *m:* **außer ~ setzen** put out of operation (or service), shut down
Betrieb *m:* **in ~ setzen** start operation
betriebliche Nutzung *f* operational application
Betriebs- und Wartungsanleitung *f* instruction manual covering operating and regular servicing
Betriebsabrechnung *f* plant cost accounting
Betriebsabteilung *f* production department
Betriebsanforderung *f* operating requirement, service requirement
Betriebsanlage *f* plant
Betriebsanleitung *f* **1.** *(als Handbuch)* instruction handbook, instruction manual **2.** *(e. Maschine)* operating instructions
Betriebsanweisung *f* operating instruction
Betriebsart *f* **1.** *(allg.)* mode, mode (or method) of operation, operating mode **2.** *(el.)* duty cycle, duty type
Betriebsauftrag *m* production order
Betriebsaufzeichnungen *fpl* plant records

Betriebsbeanspruchung *f* service stress
betriebsbedingt determined by utilization, operation-related
betriebsbedingte Änderung *f* operation induced alteration
Betriebsbedingungen *fpl* operating conditions, service conditions
Betriebsbeginn *m* start of operation
betriebsbereit in working order, operational, ready to operate, ready for service (or use or operation)
Betriebsbereitschaft *f* readiness for operation
Betriebsbremse *f* service brake
Betriebsdaten *pl* operational data, production data, performance
Betriebsdatenerfassung (BDE) *f* manufacturing data collection, factory data acquisition, production data acquisition
Betriebsdauer *f* operating period, service life
Betriebsdruck *m* operating pressure
Betriebsdruckstufe *f* working pressure level
Betriebsebene *f* operating level
betriebseigen plant (or shop or factory or concern) own
Betriebseigenschaft *f* service property
Betriebseingriffswinkel *m* service pressure angle
Betriebseinrichtung *f* operating equipment, pl.: industrial plant
Betriebsendhalteposition *f* operating end stop position
Betriebserprobung *f* practical service test
betriebsfähig ready for operation, in good working order
Betriebsfaktor *m* application factor
betriebsfertig ready for use (or production)
Betriebsfestigkeit *f (von Pressverbänden)* service strength
Betriebsfläche *f* operating area
Betriebsflankenspiel *nt* working backlash
Betriebsfrequenz *f* operating frequency

betriebsgemäße Belastung *f* normal load occurring in operation
Betriebshalle *f* shop, workshop
Betriebshandbuch *nt* instruction handbook, instruction manual
Betriebsingenieur *m* manufacturing (or industrial or operating or production or works) engineer
betriebsintern internal
Betriebskalendertag (BKT) *m* shop calendar day (SCD)
Betriebskapazität *f* (operating) capacity
Betriebskennwert *m* characteristic value for the operation
Betriebskosten *pl* operation cost(s)
Betriebsleiter *m* plant manager
Betriebsleiterebene *f* plant manager level
Betriebsleitung *f* production control
Betriebsmasse *f* service mass
betriebsmäßig under normal service conditions, in normal operation
betriebsmäßige Bedienung *f* service condition
Betriebsmeldung *f* operating message
Betriebsmittel *nt* equipment, operational resource, plant resource, resource, industrial facilities
Betriebsmittel *ntpl* **der Schutzklasse 1** class 1 equipment
Betriebsmittelausführungszeit *f* resource run time
Betriebsmittelbau *m* tool and fixture construction, tool room
Betriebsmitteldaten *pl* equipment (or resource) data
Betriebsmittelgrundzeit *f* resource means base time
Betriebsmittelgruppe *f* production facility group
Betriebsmittelklasse *f* equipment class
Betriebsmittelkonstrukteur *m* tool and jig and fixture designer
Betriebsmittelmodell *nt* equipment model
Betriebsmittelrüstgrundzeit *f* resource means setting base time
Betriebsmittelrüstverteilzeit *f* resource means setting distribution time
Betriebsmittelrüstzeit *f* resource means setting time
Betriebsmittelzeichnung *f* production facility drawing
Betriebsmittelzeit *f* **je Einheit** available process for each unit
Betriebsnorm *f* works standard specification
Betriebsorganisation *f* factory organization
Betriebspraxis *f* manufacturing practice
Betriebsprogramm *nt* executive program
Betriebsrauheit *f* working roughness
Betriebsrauhigkeit *f* working roughness
Betriebsschraubenkraft *f* service bolt force
betriebssicher relieable in operation (or service), dependable in service, failure-safe, safe to operate, safe in operation
betriebssicherer Einsatz *m* reliability in service
Betriebssicherheit *f* operational reliability, safety of operation, operational safety
Betriebsspannung *f* operating voltage
Betriebsspannungsschwankung *f* fluctuation in operating voltage
Betriebsspindel *f* hydrometer (for technical applications)
Betriebsstätte *f* workshop
Betriebsstörung *f* breakdown, failure, stoppage, shutdown, operating trouble
Betriebsstromkreis *m* service circuit, power circuit
Betriebsstunden *fpl* operating hours
Betriebssystem *nt* operating system
Betriebstemperatur *f* operating temperature
Betriebstörung *f* operating fault
Betriebstüchtigkeit *f* operational reliability
Betriebsüberdruck *m* working overpressure, positive operating pressure
Betriebsübernahme *f* takeover
Betriebsüberwachung *f* manufacturing supervision, operation control
Betriebsumgebungstemperatur *f*

operating ambient air temperature
Betriebsunbrauchbarkeit *f* unserviceability
Betriebsunfall *m* factory accident, shop accident
Betriebsvergleich *m* factory (or manufacturing) comparison
Betriebsverhalten *nt* operating performance, performance in service, in-service behaviour
Betriebsvorschrift *f* operating instruction
Betriebswälzkegel *m* service cone of contact
Betriebswälzkreis *m* service circle of contact, working pitch circle
Betriebswälzzylinder *m* service cylinder of contact
betriebswasserseitig on the service water side
Betriebsweise *f* operating mode
Betriebswert *m* operating parameter
betriebswirtschaftlich economic
Betriebszeit *f* operating time
Betriebszustand *m* operation condition, operating (or operation) status, operating state, working condition
Bett *nt* (e. Maschine) bed, machine bed
Bettbahn *f* bedway, guideway
Bettführungsbahn *f* bedway, guideway, bed slide
Bettführungsprismen *ntpl* Vee-guideways, prismatic guideways, prismatic bedways
Bettkröpfung *f* bed gap
Bettprisma *nt* Vee-guide, Vee-way, prismatic guideway (or bedway)
Bettrevolver *m* bed turret
Bettschlitten *m* (UK) saddle, (US) carriage
Bettschlittenbahn *f* carriage track
Bettschlittenführung *f* carriage guideway(s), saddle guideway
Bettschlittenrevolverdrehmaschine *f* (US) saddle-type turret lathe, (UK) combination turret lathe
Bettschlittenwange *f* carriage wing, shear
Bettschürze *f* apron
Bettwange *f* bed shear

Beuchechtheit *f* fastness to bucking
beugen bend, bow, diffract, flex, crank
Beugung *f* diffraction
Beugungsbild *nt* diffraction figure
Beugungseigenschaft *f* diffraction property
Beugungsgitter *nt* diffraction grating
Beugungsspektrum *nt* diffraction spectrum
Beulen *nt* buckling
Beulfestigkeit *f* buckling resistance
Beulsicherheit *f* safety against buckling
Beultiefe *f* indentation depth
Beulung *f* indentation
beurteilbar assessable
beurteilen assess, judge, rate
Beurteilung *f* 1. (allg.) assessment 2. (bewertende) evaluation, rating
Beurteilungsprüfung *f* grading test
Beutel-Füll- und Verschließmaschine *f* bag fill and seal machine
Beutel-Füll- und Verschließmaschine *f* **mit Beutelzuführung von der Rolle** reel fed bag fill and seal machine
Beutel-Verschließmaschine *f* bag sealing machine
Beutel-Zuführmaschine *f* bag presenting machine
bevollmächtigen authorize
Bevollmächtigter *m* authorized representative, authorized person
bevorraten stockpile, stock up
Bevorratung *f* stockpiling
Bevorratungsbestellung *f* stock-up order
bewegen impart movement to, move, stir, agitate, travel, traverse
beweglich mobile, movable, moving, flexible
bewegliche Absperrung *f* movable guard
bewegliche Leitung *f* flexible pipe, mobile line
bewegliche Teile *ntpl* moving parts
beweglicher Meißelhalter *m* floating toolholder
beweglicher Querbalken *m* movable crossrail
beweglicher Spindelstock *m* travel-

ling head
beweglicher Tisch *m* traversing table
bewegliches Werkzeug *nt* flexible tool
bewegt in motion
bewegte Last *f* moving load
bewegte Masse *f* moving stress
bewegte Teile *ntpl* moving parts *pl*
Bewegung *f* movement, motion, traverse, travel
Bewegungsablauf *m* cyclic motion, cycle of movement (or motion), sequence of movements, travel cycle
Bewegungsamplitude *f* amplitude of movement
Bewegungsanalyse *f* movement analysis
Bewegungsart *f* motion type
Bewegungsbahn *f* movement path
Bewegungselement *nt* motion element
bewegungsempfindliche Einrichtung *f* position-sensitive device
Bewegungsenergie *f* kinetic energy
Bewegungsführung *f* motion guidance
Bewegungsfunktion *f* motion law
Bewegungsgröße *f* rate of movement
Bewegungskomponente *f* motion component
Bewegungsmelder *m* position-sensitive device, position sensor
Bewegungsmöglichkeit *f* freedom of movement
Bewegungsmuster *nt* movement example, movement pattern
Bewegungspause *f* dwell, period of dwell, time of dwell
Bewegungsphase *f* motion phase
Bewegungsraum *m* motion space
Bewegungsreibung *f* dynamic friction
Bewegungsrichtung *f* direction of motion (or travel), direction of movement
Bewegungssperre *f* motion lock-out
Bewegungsspülung *f* motion douche
Bewegungssteuerung *f* motion control
Bewegungsübertragung *f* transmission of motion
Bewegungsumkehrpunkt *m* reversing point of motion
Bewegungsverhältnis *nt* movement condition
Bewegungsvorgang *m* motion process
Bewegungswiderstand *m* resistance to motion
Bewegungszeit *f* time of movement
Bewehrungsstäbe verbinden anchor reinforcing bars
beweisen prove
bewerkstelligen accomplish
bewerten assess, evaluate, rate, weight
Bewertung *f* assessment, benchmarking, evaluation, rating
Bewertungsgröße *f* quantity for assessment, factor of evaluation
Bewertungsgruppe *f* assessment group
Bewertungsmerkmale *ntpl* assessment criteria
Bewertungssystem *nt* assessment scheme
bewirken achieve, cause, effect, generate
Bewitterung *f* **im Freien** outdoor weathering
bezahlen pay
Bezahlung *f* payment
bezeichnen 1. *(allg.)* designate, indicate, mark, specify, denote **2.** *(mit Buchstaben)* letter **3.** *(mit Zahlen)* number
Bezeichnung *f* designation, specification, marking
Bezeichnungssystematik *f* designation system
Beziehung *f* contact, relationship
Beziehungsstärke *f* intensity of contact
beziffern 1. *(allg.)* figure, calculate **2.** *(nummerieren)* number
Bezifferung *f* numbering
bezogen auf relation to
bezogene Anstiegsantwort *f* referenced ramp function response
bezogene Außermittigkeit *f* specific centre offset
bezogener Engspalt *m* specific minimum gap
bezogenes Haftmaß *nt* specific adhesion allowance
bezogenes Zerspanungsvolumen *nt*

specific volume of metal removed by grinding
Bezug *m* reference
Bezugsachse *f (z. B. bei Kreisen)* reference axis, datum axis
Bezugsbasis *f (e. Passsystems)* reference basis
Bezugsbemaßung *f* reference dimensioning
Bezugsebene *f* reference plane, reference system of plane, datum plane
Bezugseinheit *f* reference unit
Bezugselement *nt* reference element
Bezugserde *f* reference earth
Bezugsfläche *f* reference surface
Bezugsflächentastsystem *nt* reference surface contact system
Bezugsflankenlinie *f* reference tooth trace, datum tooth trace
Bezugsgröße *f* reference magnitude
Bezugshaken *m* tick
Bezugskreis *m* reference basis, reference circle
Bezugslinie *f* 1. *(allg.)* datum line, leader 2. *(e. Messschraube)* fiducial line
Bezugsmaß *nt* fixed zero dimension, absolute dimension, reference size, reference dimension
Bezugsmittelebene *f* datum median plane
Bezugsplanrad *nt* basic crown gear
Bezugsprofil *nt* 1. *(allg.)* reference profile 2. *(e. Stirnrades)* basic rack, standard basic rack tooth profile
Bezugspunkt *m* defined point, reference point
Bezugsquader *m* reference box
Bezugsschalldruck *m* reference sound pressure
Bezugssehweite *f* reference visual range
Bezugsstirnfläche *f* reference face
Bezugsstrecke *f* reference length
Bezugsstrich *m* leader
Bezugsstück *nt* master, sample, workpiece
Bezugssystem *nt* reference system
Bezugssystem *nt* **im Werkzeug-Bezugssystem** planes in the tool-in-hand system
Bezugssystem *nt* **im Wirk-Bezugssystem** planes in the tool-in-use system
Bezugstemperatur *f* basic temperature
Bezugswert *m* reference value
Bezugszahl *f* datum point, reference point
Bezugszahnstange *f* basic rack
biaxial biaxial
bidirektional bi-directional
biegbar vorglühen pre-anneal for bending
Biege- und Richtmaschine *f* bending and straightening machine
Biegebeanspruchung *f* flexural load (or loading), bending load
Biegebrechen *nt* breaking by bending
Biegedehnung *f* elongation due to bending
Biegedrillknicken *nt* torsional-flexural buckling
Biegeebene *f (bei Rohren)* plane of bending
Biege-Elastizitätsgrenze *f* limit of elasticity in bending
Biegefestigkeit *f* flexural strength at rupture, bending strength
Biegekraft *f* flexural force
Biegemoment *nt* bending moment
Biegemomentübertragung *f* transfer of bending moment
biegen bend, crank
biegen: sich ~ deflect, flex
Biegen *nt* **im Gesenk** die bending
Biegepresse *f* bending press
Biegeprüfgerät *nt* bending test apparatus
Biegeprüfpresse *f* bend test press
Biegeprüfung *f* flexing test
Biegeradius *m* bending radius
Biegerichten *nt* straightening by off-hand bending
Biegerolle *f* bending roller
Biegerücken *m* convex surface of the bend
Biegescheitel *m* crest of the bend
Biegeschwellbeanspruchung *f* pulsating flexural load
Biegeschwellversuch *m* pulsating flexural fatigue test
Biegeschwingung *f* 1. *(oszillierend)*

flexural (or bending) oscillation **2.** *(mit konstanter Frequenz)* flexural vibration
Biegeschwingungsversuch *m* flexural vibration test
Biegespannung *f* flexural stress, bending stress
Biegespannung *f* **bei 3,5% Randfaserdrehung** flexural stress at 3.5% strain of the outer fibre
biegespannungsfrei free from bending stresses
biegestarr resistant to deflection
biegesteif deflection-resistant, resistant to bending, flexurally resistant
Biegesteifigkeit *f* bending strength, resistance to deflection, flexural stiffness
Biegeträger *m* girder subject to bending, support subject to bending
Biegeumformen *nt* reforming by bending
Biegeverlappen *nt* lock forming by bending
Biegeversuch *m* flexural test
Biegeversuch *m* **mit Biegestempel** bend test jig with mandrel
Biegeversuch *m* **mit gekerbten Querbiegeproben** bend test with notched transverse bend specimens
Biegeversuch *m* **mit Längsbiegeproben** bend test with longitudinal bend specimens
Biegeversuch *m* **mit Seitenbiegeproben** bend test with lateral bend specimens
Biegevorrichtung *f* bend test jig
biegeweiches Rohr *nt* flexible pipe
Biegewelle *f* flexion wave
Biegewellengeschwindigkeit *f* flexural wave velocity
Biegewellenlänge *f* flexural wave length
Biegewerkzeug *nt* bending tool
Biegewinkel *m* **beim Bruch** angle of deflection at failure
Biegewinkel *m* **bis zum Anriss** bending angle to onset of cracking
biegezugseitige Randspannung *f* edge stress on the side subject to tensile stress in bending
Biegezylinder *m* cylindrical bending block, cylindrical former
biegsam flexible, bendable, supple
biegsame Welle *f* flexible shaft
Biegsamkeit *f* flexibility
Biegung *f* bending, flexure
Biegung *f: auf ~ beanspruchen* subject to a bending load
Bild *nt* image, picture, figure, pattern
bildabwärts page down
Bildaktualisierung *f* display update
Bildanwahl *f* display selection
bildaufwärts page up
Bildauswertung *f* image evaluation
Bilddaten *pl* image data
Bildeinstellung *f* focusing of the image
Bildelementfolgefrequenz *f* refresh rate
bilden form, shape
bilderzeugende Strahlung *f* image-forming radiation
Bildgüte *f* image quality
Bildgütenachweis *m* image quality indication (or proof analysis)
Bildgüteprüfkörper *m* image quality indicator
Bildmessgerät *nt* picture (or image) measuring apparatus
Bildmessung *f* photogrammetry
Bildpunkt *m* light point, picture element, pixel
Bildpunktmuster *nt* pixel pattern
bildregistrierendes System *nt* image recording system
Bildschirmblende *f* display (or screen) diaphragm
bildsames Einspreizen *nt* plastic spreading
Bildschärfe *f* definition of the image
Bildschicht *f* film
Bildschirm *m* display, monitor, screen, video screen
Bildschirmanzeigeeinheit *f* video display unit (VDU)
Bildschirmarbeitsplatz *m* display work station
Bildschirmmaskendatei *f* screen mask file
Bildschirmprogramm *nt* online program
Bildschirmzeile *f* VDU line

Bildsensor *m* image sensor
Bildsignal *nt* video signal
Bildspeicher *m* image storage device
Bildteil *nt* (cathode-ray-tube) module, CRT module
Bildung *f* formation, shaping, production
Bildungsvorschrift *f* encoding prescription
Bildverarbeitungsrechner *m* image processing computer
Bildvorlage *f* master illustration
Bildvorverstärkung *f* pre-image intensification
Bildwandler *m* image converter
Bildwechsel *m* display exchange
Bildwerfer *m* projector
Bildzeichen *nt* pictorial symbol
binär binary
binär codierter Dezimalcode (BCD) *m* binary-coded decimal code
Binärbildauswertung *f* binary image evaluation
Binärcode *m* binary code
binärcodiert binary-coded
binärcodierte Dezimaldarstellung *f* binary-coded decimal (BCD)
Binär-Dezimal-Code *m* binary-decimal code
binäre Schaltkette *f* binary switching chain
binärer Abschaltkreis *m* binary de-energizing circuit
binäres Schaltglied *nt* binary switching-element
binäres Speicherglied *nt* binary storage element
binäres Verknüpfungsglied *nt* binary combinational element
Binärschaltung *f* binary digital element, binary circuit element
Binärsignal *nt* binary signal
Binärstufe *f* binary stage
Binärteiler *m* binary divider
Binärzahl *f* binary number
Binärzeichen *nt* binary character
Binärziffer *f* binary digit, bit
Bindefestigkeit *f* binding strength
Bindefläche *f* bonding surface, fusion surface

Bindeglied *nt* link
Bindeharz *m* binding resin
Bindemittel *nt* **1.** *(allg.)* binding agent, bonding material **2.** *(chemische ~)* chemical binding agent **3.** *(natürliche ~)* natural binding agent
Bindemittelabwanderung *f* migration of binder
Bindemittelüberzug *m* binder coating
binden bind, bond, cement, adhere, tie
Binder *m* binder
Bindfaden *m* binding threads *pl*
Bindung *f* *(keramische)* certified bond
Bindung *f* **von Schleifkörnern** bond
Bindungsaufbau *m* bond structure
Bindungsenergie *f* bond energy
Bindungsfehler *m* bond defect
Bindungskraft *f* bonding force
Binom *m* binominal
binomial binomial
biologischer Abbaugrad *m* biodegradation
Biometriedaten *pl* biometric data
Birnenkühler *m* bulb condenser
bis 1. *(räumlich)* to **2.** *(zeitlich)* until
bis einschließlich below, up to and including
bis zu up to
Bisphenol *nt* bisphenol
Bit *nt* bit
Bitfehlerrate *f* bit error rate
Bitrate *f* bit rate
bitseriell serial by bit
bitumenbeständige PVC-weich-Bahn bitumen-resistant sheeting of non-rigid PVC
Bitumendachbahn *f* bitumen roof sheeting
Bitumen-Schweißbahn *f* bituminous waterproof sheeting for fuse welding
bituminöse Befestigung *f* bituminous surfacing
bivariat bivariate
Blankwiderstands-Durchlauferhitzer *m* bare resistance-type instantaneous heater
Blase *f* flaw, bubble
Blasebalg *m* smith's bellows
blasenfrei non-porous, without blisters, without flaws

Blasengrad *m* extent (or degree) of blistering
Blatt *nt* 1. *(allg.)* leaf 2. *(Werkzeug)* blade
Blättchen *nt* foil, lamina
Blättern *nt* browsing, paging, scrolling
Blattfederschalter *m* reed switch
Blattschraube *f* quarter-turn screw
Bläuepilz *m* blue stain
Blaugel *nt* blue gel
blauglühen open-anneal
Blauglühung *f* open-annealing
blaustichig bluish
Blech *nt* 1. *(allg.)* sheet metal, metal sheeting, plate 2. *(Erzeugnis)* steel sheet, metal sheet 3. *(Werkstoff)* sheet steel, sheet metal
Blechbearbeitung *f* sheet metal working
Blechbiegemaschine *f* plate-bending machine
Blechdicke *f* sheet thickness
Blechgehäuse *nt* sheet metal casing
Blechkantenhobelmaschine *f* plate planer, breast planer, edge planer, plate-edge planing machine
Blechkantenhobeln *nt* plate-edge planing
Blechkern *m* laminated core
Blechlager *nt* sheet storage
Blechlehre *f* sheet metal gauge
Blechpaket *nt* bundle of laminations
Blechschablone *f* sheet metal template, sheet metal stencil
Blechscheibe *f* **mit unverlierbarer Scheibe** *f* self-tapping screw with captive washer
Blechschraube *f* self-tapping screw, tapping screw, thread forming self tapping screw
Blechschraubengewinde *nt* self-tapping screw thread
Blechstreifen *m* sheet-metal strip
Blechtafel *f* sheet of metal
Blechumformung *f* sheet forming
Blechverkleidung *f* sheet metal sheathing
Blei *nt* lead
Bleiakkumulator *m* lead-acid battery
bleiben stay, remain, be permanent

bleibend permanent, residual
bleibende Bruchdehnung *f* permanent elongation at fracture
bleibende Dehnung *f* percentage permanent elongation
bleibende Dehnung *f* **kurz vor dem Reißen** permanent extension shortly before failure
bleibende Längenänderung *f* permanent linear change, permanent elongation
bleibende Sollwertabweichung *f* steady-state deviation from the desired value
Bleibronze *f* lead bronze
Bleichlauge *f* bleaching solution
Bleiglasplatte *f* lead glass panel
Bleigleichwert *m* lead equivalent value
Bleigummivorhang *m* lead rubber curtain
Bleiraster *nt* lead lined grid
Bleirohrtülle *f* lead-pipe nozzle
Blei-Säure-Batterie *f* lead-acid battery
Bleischmelze *f* fused lead bath
Bleiskizze *f* pencil sketch
Blei-Zeichnung *f* pencil drawing
Blende *f* 1. *(allg.)* slit, diaphragm, shield 2. *(Optik)* aperture
Blendensystem *nt* shielded system
Blendenventil *nt* flow-control valve with orifice
Blendschutzfilter *m* anti-dazzle filter
Blickfeld *nt* field of vision
Blickrichtung *f* facing
Blickrichtung *f* **des Fahrers** direction faced by the operator, operator facing this way
Blickrichtung *f* **entgegengesetzt zur Last** facing away from the load
Blindbestimmung *f* blank determination
Blinddeckel *m* dummy cover
Blindflansch *m* **mit Dichtleiste** blank flange with raised face
Blindflansch *m* **mit Rücksprung** blank flange with female face
Blindflansch *m* **mit Vorsprung** blank flange with male face
blindflanschen fit with blind flanges
Blindleistung *f* volt-ampere reactive

(VAR)
Blindloch *nt* blind hole, bottom hole
Blindlochscheibe *f* blind-hole plate, spectacle plate
Blindlösung *f* blank solution
Blindniet *m* blind rivet
Blindprozess *m* blind process
Blindscheibe *f* blind spade
Blind-Teil *nt* blank part
Blindverbrennung *f* blank combustion
Blindwert *m* blank value
Blindwertbestimmung *f* blank value determination
Blink-Aus-Zustand *m* blinking-off condition
Blink-Ein-Zustand *m* blinking-on condition
blinken blink, flash
Blinkfrequenz *f* blinking frequency
Blinkhub *m* blinking stroke
Blinkleuchte *f* flashing beacon
Blinklicht *nt* flashing light
Blister *m* blister
Blisterfüll- und -verschließmaschine *f* blister fill and seal machine
Blisterpackmaschine *f* blister packaging machine
Blisterverschließmaschine *f* blister sealing machine
Blitzlampe *f* flash lamp
Blitzmischer *m* instant mixer
Blitzschlag *m* lightning
Block *m* block, module
Blockabstechdrehmaschine *f* ingot slicing lathe
Blockbatterie *f* monobloc battery
Blockbild *nt* block diagram
Blockdrehbank *f* ingot turning lathe
Blockdüse *f* block nozzle
Blockfestigkeit *f* resistance to caking
Blockgreifer *m* log gripper
Blockhobelmaschine *f* ingot planer
blockierbar lockable
blockieren 1. *(allg.)* block, wedge, secure, jam 2. *(arretieren)* lock 3. *(Maschine gegeneinander)* interlock
Blockierung *f* 1. *(allg.)* jamming, locking, arresting 2. (Maschine) interlocking
Blocklager *nt* block storage, block warehouse

Blocklagerung *f* block storage
Blocklayout *nt* block layout
Blocklöten *nt* block soldering
Blockmaß *nt* slip gauge
Blockmeißelhalter *m* multiple (or combination) tool block, four-way toolblock
blockorientiert module-oriented
Blockrevolver *m* square (or four station) turret
Blockschaltbild *nt* block diagram
Blockscheibe *f* sheave
Blockscherprobekörper *m* blockshear specimen
Blockspan *m* blockboard
Blocksteuerung *f* block control
Blockstreckensteuerung *f* block section control
Blocksupport *m* block rest
blockweise by blocks
Blockzeit *f* block time
Blockzykluszeit *f* block cycle time
bloßes Auge *nt* unaided eye, naked eye
Bockkran *m* gantry crane
Bockrolle *f* fixed castor
Boden *m* ground, floor, bottom, base
Bodenabdeckung *f* floor capping
Bodenabstand *m* ground clearance
Bodenbelastung *f* ground loading
Bodenbeschaffenheit *f* floor conditions
Bodenblech *nt* bottom plate
Bodenebene *f* floor level
Bodenecho *nt* back echo
bodenfahrend floor-bound
Bodenfläche *f* floor space
Bodenfreiheit *f* ground clearance
bodengeführt floor-guided
Bodenguss *m* base casting
Bodenhöhe *f* floor height, ground level
Bodenkörper *m* sediment
Bodenlade-Abhebe-Depalettierer *m* low-level lift-off depalletizer
Bodenlade-Abhebe-Palettierer *m* low level-lift-off palletizer
Bodenlade-Depalettierer *m* low level depalletizer
Bodenlade-Palettierer *m* low level palletizer
Bodenmarkierung *f* floor marking

Bodenplatte *f* bottom plate, floor slab
Bodenrad *nt* main spindle gear
Bodenreibung *f* floor friction
Bodenrutschung *f* soil slip
Bodensatz *m* sludge
Bodenschiene *f* floor rail, rail laid on the floor
Bodensetzung *f* ground setting
Bodenstativ *nt* floor stand
Bodensteifigkeit *f* stiffness of the soil
Bodenteller *m* bottom pan
Bodentoleranz *f* ground tolerance
Bodentragfähigkeit *f* bearing capacity of the ground
Bodentraverse *f* bottom carriage
Bodenüberwachung *f* base monitoring
Bodenverankerung *f (e. Gerätes)* floor anchorage
Bodenverband *m* land community
bodenverfahrbar floor travelling (type)
Bodenverstärkung *f* shelf reinforcement
Boden-zu-Boden-Zeit *f* floor-to-floor-time
Bogen *m* arc, bow, bend, curve, curvature
Bogenanschnitt *m* first cut of curve, first cut of arc, first cut of circular arc
Bogeneinlauf *m* arc shrinkage
bogenförmig arc-shaped
Bogenlänge *f* arc length
Bogenmaß *nt* arc measure
Bogenprüfverfahren *nt* semi-circle test method
Bogenradius *m (e. Formstückes)* radius of curvature
Bogenstrich *m* curved stroke
bogenverzahnt elbowtooth
bogenverzahntes Kegelrad *nt* curved tooth bevel gear
Bogenverzahnung *f* spiral teeth
Bogenzahnkegelrad *nt* spiral bevel gear
bogiges Weiterreißen *nt* curving tear propagation
Bohr- und Drehwerk *nt* vertical boring and turning mill
Bohr- und Fräsmaschine *f* boring, drilling and milling machine
Bohr- und Fräswerk *nt* horizontal boring and milling machine
Bohr- und Plandrehmaschine *f* boring and facing lathe
Bohranbauautomat *m* automatic boring machine
Bohrausleger *m* radial drill arm
Bohrautomat *m* automatic boring machine, automatic drilling machine
Bohreinheit *f* drilling unit, boring unit
Bohreinrichtung *f* 1. *(Fräsmaschine)* boring head 2. *(Innenausdrehen)* boring attachment 3. *(Vollbohren)* drilling attachment
Bohren *nt* 1. *(aus dem Vollen)* drilling 2. *(Innenausdrehen)* boring 3. *(Gewinde)* threading
Bohrer *m* 1. *(Spiralbohrer)* drill, twist drill 2. *(Gewindebohrer)* tap 3. *(Personal)* boring machine operator
Bohrer- und Gewindebohrer-Schärfmaschine *f* drill and tap grinder
Bohreranschliff *m* drill grind
Bohrerausspitzen *nt* drill pointing
Bohrernut *f* drill flute
Bohrerspitze *f* cutting tip
Bohrerstandzeit *f* drill life
Bohrfräswerkzeug *nt* combined drill and milling cutter
Bohrfutter *nt* drill chuck
Bohrfutterkegel *m* drill socket
Bohrgewinde *nt* breast drill
Bohrglocke *f* bell-type spindle housing
Bohrknarre *f* ratchet brace
Bohrkopf *m* 1. *(e. Bohrwerkes)* boring head 2. *(e. Radialmaschine)* drillhead, drilling head 3. *(für Bohrmeißel)* boring head 4. *(für Spiralbohrer)* drilling head
Bohrlehre *f* drill jig
Bohrleistung *f* drilling capacity
Bohrloch *nt* 1. *(Vollbohrung)* drill hole, drilled hole 2. *(Innenausdrehung)* borehole 3. *(e. Schleifscheibe)* arbour hole
Bohrlochsteg *m* hole penetrameter
Bohrmaschine *f* drilling machine, drill press, boring machine, tapping machine
Bohrmaschinensäule *f* round column
Bohrmaschinenständer *m (rechteckige Bauart)* box column
Bohrmeißel *m (Innenausdrehmeißel)*

boring tool
Bohrmeißelhalter *m* boring tool holder
Bohrmitte *f* drill centre
Bohrmotor *m* spindle motor, drilling motor
Bohrpinole *f* boring sleeve, boring quill
Bohrreitstock *m* tailstock for drilling and boring
Bohrschablone *f* jig
Bohrschlichtstahl *m* (obs. für Innenausdrehmeißel) internal cutting tool, boring tool
Bohrschlitten *m* drilling slide
Bohrschneide *f* bit
Bohrspäne *mpl* drillings *pl*, borings *pl*
Bohrspindel *f* drilling spindle, drill spindle, boring spindle
Bohrspindelkopf *m* drilling spindle head, boring spindle head
Bohrspindelhülse *f* drilling spindle sleeve
Bohrstahl *m* (obs. für Bohrmeißel) boring tool
Bohrstange *f* boring bar, boring tool
Bohrstangenhalter *m* boring tool-holder
Bohrsupport *m* boring head
Bohrtechnik *f* drilling practice, boring practice
Bohrtisch *m* drilling machine table, worktable of the drilling machine
Bohrung *f* 1. (Bohrloch) drillhole, drilled hole, borehole, bore 2. (Loch) hole 3. (mittels Bohrmeißel) borehole, bore 4. (mittels Spiralbohrer) drill hole 5. (abgesetzte ~) shouldered hole 6. (durchgehende ~) throughhole 7. (geschlossene ~) blind-end hole
Bohrung *f* **mit Gewinde** threaded hole
Bohrungsdurchmesser *m* bore diameter, bore size
Bohrungsläppen *nt* internal cylindrical lapping, hole lapping
Bohrungslehre *f* internal gauge, hole gauge
Bohrungslehrung *f* gauging holes
Bohrungsmantelfläche *f* bore envelope
Bohrverfahren *nt* lancing process
Bohrvorrichtung *f* drilling fixture, boring fixture
Bohrwerk *nt* boring mill
Bohrwerkzeug *nt* drill, boring tool
Bohrzentrum *nt* boring centre
Bohrzyklen *mpl* (G80–G89) drilling cycles
Bohrzyklus *m* drilling cycle
Bolzen *m* 1. (allg.) bolt, twist lock, screw 2. (Gewindebolzen) bolt threaded pin 3. (für Bolzenschweißen) stud 4. (mit Kopf) clevis pin
Bolzen *m* **für Bolzenschweißen mit Hubzündung** stud for drawn-arc stud welding
Bolzen *m* **ohne Kopf** *m* parallel pin without head
Bolzenaufschweißen *nt* stud welding
Bolzenaufschweißpistole *f* stud welding gun
bolzenbefestigt bolted
Bolzengewinde-Lehrung *f* gauging of bolt (or male) threads
Bolzengewinde-Schneidmaschine *f* bolt thread cutting machine
Bolzenmaßmessung *f* pin dimension measurement
Bolzenschaftfräsmaschine *f* bolt milling machine
Bolzenscheibe *f* bolt washer
Bolzenschere *f* bolt cutter
Bolzenschweißen *nt* stud welding
Bolzenspannung *f* bolt clamping
Bolzenspitze *f* stud tip
Bolzenstange *f* bolt bar
Bombenverfahren *nt* bomb method
Boolesche Daten *pl* Boolean data
Boolesche Variable *f* Boolean variable
boolesche Verknüpfung *f* Boolean term
Bor *nt* boron
Borax *nt* borax
bordeigen on board
Bördel *nt* raised edge
Bördeleisen *nt* bordering tool
Bördelmaschine *f* bordering machine, clinching machine, flanging machine
börden bead, border, clinch, flange
Bördelrand *m* (e. Mutter) flanged rim
Bördelscheibe *f* (für Muttern) capstan washer

Bördelstoßkante *f* abutment of raised edge
Bördelung *f* flanging
Bördelverschließmaschine *f* can sealing machine
Bördelverschluss *m* bordering closure
Bördelwerkzeug *nt* flanging tool
Bordschwelle *f* kerb
Bordstein *m* kerb
Borfaser *f* boron fibre
Borfasergelege *nt* boron fibre
borfaserverstärkter Formstoff *m* boron fibre reinforced moulding material
Borieren *nt* boron treatment
Borkarbid *nt* boron carbide
Borstenpinsel *m* bristle brush
Böschungsstück *nt (für Betonrohre)* slope drainage fitting
Boxpalette *f* box pallet
Brachzeit *f* machine down time, idle time
Brand *m* burning, fire
Brandausbreitung *f* flame spread
Brandausbruchstelle *f* fire outbreak point
Brandbekämpfung *f* fire-fighting
Branddauer *f* fire duration
Brandfall *m* event of a fire
Brandfleck *m* burn
Brandgefährlichkeit *f* fire hazard
Brandlast *f* fire load
Brandmelder *m* smoke detector
Brandraum *m* furnace
Brandschachtverfahren *nt* fire shaft method
Brandschutz *m* fire protection
Brandsicherheit *f* resistance to fire
Brandspuren *fpl* arcing marks
Brandstadium *nt* fire stage
Brandstelle *f* fire patch
Brandverhalten *nt* fire behaviour, burning behaviour, fire performance
brauchbar applicable, serviceable, suitable
Brauchbarkeit *f* serviceability
Brauchbarkeitsdauer *f* useful life
Brauchwassererwärmer *m* industrial water heater
bräunen burnish
Braunkohle *f* brown coal, lignite

Brauseauslauf *m* rose
Brecheisen *nt* crowbar, prya
brechen crack, bevel, fracture, crush, break
Brechstange *f* jimmy, jim crow
Brechung *f* refraction
Brechungsindex *m* refractive index
Brechungskoeffizient *m* coefficient of refraction
Brechungsverhältnis *nt* refractive index
Brechungswinkel *m* angle of refraction
Brechwert *m* refractive index
Brechzahl *f* refractive index, index of refraction
breit wide
Breitband *nt* broad band
breitbandig broadband
breitbandiges Geräusch *nt* broad band noise
Breitband-Übertragung *f* broadband transmission
Breite *f* width
Breite *f* **der Eckenfase** chamfered corner length
Breite *f* **der Freiflächenfase** land width of the flank
Breite *f* **der reduzierten Spanfläche** width of reduced face
Breite *f* **der Spanflächenfase** land width of the face
Breiten *nt* spreading
breitenballige Verzahnung *f* crowned gear teeth
Breitenballigkeit *f* width crowing, crowning
Breitenmaß *nt* width dimension
Breitenschwankung *f* width variation
Breitenstauchung *f* spreading dipping
Breitenverhältnis *nt* width ratio
breiter Drehmeißel *m* wide face square nose tool
breiter Walzenfräser *m* slab mill
Breitgang *m* wide aisle
Breitkopfstift *m* clout nail
Breitmeißel *m* broad nose tool, broad cutting tool
breitmoduliertes Impulssignal *nt* width-modulated pulse signal
breitschlichten finish with broad cut,

broad cut finish, wide finish
Breitschlichtfräsen *nt* broad finish milling
Breitschlichtmeißel *m* broad finishing tool, broad nose finish tool, end-cut tool
Breitschlichtschneiden *nt* broad finish cutting
Breitschliff *m* wide wheel grinding
Breitschrift *f* wide-spaced lettering
Breitungsgrad *m* degree of flattening
Bremsanlage *f* braking system
Bremsarbeit *f* braking work
Bremsbacke *f* brake pad, braking shoe
Bremsbeginn *m:* **bei ~** when braking starts
Bremsbeginn *m:* **bis ~** until breaking starts
Bremsbelag *m* (brake) lining
Bremse *f* (dynamic) brake
Bremse *f* **anlegen** engage the brake
Bremseinrichtung *f* braking device
bremsen brake, slow down, impede
Bremsensprechverzögerung *f* brake application delay
Bremsenenergierückgewinnung *f* power reversal
Bremsenfangvorrichtung *f* brake type catching device, friction braking device
Bremsenstandzeit *f* brake life, brake service life
Bremskraft *f* braking force
Bremsmoment *m* braking torque
Bremsmotor *m* brake motor
Bremsreibpartner *m* friction part of the brake
Bremsschuh *m* brake shoe
Bremsspur *f* brake mark
Bremsstellung *f* on-position of the brake
Bremssteuerung *f* braking control
Bremssystem *nt* braking system
Bremsteil *nt* brake component
Bremstrommel *f* brake drum
Bremsverfahren *nt* braking method
Bremsverhalten *nt* braking characteristics
Bremsverlust *m* loss of braking
Bremsverzögerung *f* braking deceleration, deceleration due to braking

Bremsvorgang *m* braking procedure
Bremsweg *m* braking distance, braking path, stopping distance
Bremszeit *f* braking time
Bremszylinder *m* dashpot
Brennablauf *m* burning sequence
brennbar combustible, inflammable, flammable
brennbare Abfälle *mpl* combustible waste matter *pl*
brennbare Gase *ntpl* combustible gases
Brennbarkeitsprüfung *f* flammability test
Brennbohren *nt* flame boring
Brenndauer *f* duration per charge
brennen burn, calcine, stove
Brenner *m* cutting blowpipe, burner, torch
Brennerabschaltung *f* shutdown of the burner
Brennerarmatur *f* burner valve
Brennereinstellung *f* blowpipe setting
Brennerermüdung *f* burner nozzle
Brennerführung *f* blowpipe guidance
Brennergasfreigabe *f* release of fuel gas
Brennergeschränk *nt* burner crosspiece
Brennerkopfbohrung *f* blowpipe head port
Brennerleistung *f* burner rating
Brennerluftseite *f* primary air side
Brennerstart *m* burner start-up
Brennerstütze *f* blow-pipe support
Brennertopfwand *f* burner cup wall
Brennerwärmebelastung *f* burner heat load
Brennerwärmeleistung *f* burner thermal output
Brennflämmen *nt* flame scarfing, flame deseaming
Brennfleck *m* focal point
Brennfleckdurchmesser *m* focal point diameter
brennfleckfernste Tubusöffnung *f* applicator opening farthest from the focal point
Brennfugen *nt* flame gouging, flame grooving
Brenngasdurchfluss *m* fuel gas

throughput
Brenngasleitung *f* fuel gas line
brenngeschnittenes Teil *nt* thermal-cut (or gas-cut) part
Brenngeschwindigkeit *f* burning speed
Brennhobeln *nt* flame gouging
Brennkasten *m* burning cabinet
Brennkastenverfahren *nt* ignition cabinet method
Brennpunkt *m* focal point, focus, fire point
Brennpunktlage *f* focal point position
Brennschlacke *f* flame cutting slag
brennschneiden flame-cut, gas-cut, torch-cut
Brennschneider *m* flame cutting torch
brennschneidgeeignet suitable for thermal cutting
Brennschneidtechnik *f* thermal cutting practice, gas cutting practice
Brennschneidteil *nt* thermally cut part, gas-cut part
Brennschnitt *m* thermal cut
Brennschnittfläche *f* thermally cut surface
Brennstoff *m* fuel
Brennstoffaufgabe *f* input of fuel
Brennstoffbeschickung *f* fuel charging
Brennstoffentgaser *m* fuel degasifier
Brennstofffüllung *f* fuel charge
Brennstofflagerraum *m* fuel storage room
Brennstoffmagazin *nt* fuel hopper
Brennstoffmenge *f* fuel quantity
Brennstoffnachförderung *f* fuel feeding device
Brennstoffprobe *f* fuel sample
brennstofftechnische Ausrüstung *f* heat engineering equipment
Brennstoffvergaser *m* fuel gasifier
Brennstoffverriegelung *f* fuel feed interlock
Brennstoffwähler *m* fuel selector
Brennstrecke *f* rig
Brennweite *f* focal length
Brennwert *m* gross calorific value
Brett *nt* board
Brettaufriss *m* sheet offering maximum dimensional stability
Brewsterfenster *m* brewster window
Brille *f* steadyrest
Brille *f* **der Stopfbuchse** gland, stuffingbox gland
Brinellhärte *f* Brinell hardness
Bringplatz *nt* bring point
bröckelig crumbly, friable
bröckeln crumble
Bröckelspäne *f* crumbling chip
Bronze *f* bronze
BRT-Eingang *m* Behind Tape Reader Input (btr-input)
Bruch *m* **1.** *(allg.)* break, breakage, breaking, crack, fracture, rupture **2.** *(math.)* fraction **3.** *(Versagen)* failure
Bruchauffälligkeit *f* fracture marking
Bruchaufweitung *f* expansion at fracture
Bruchausbauchung *f* spread at fracture
Bruchbild *nt* appearance of the fracture
Bruchdehnung *f* **1.** *(allg.)* breaking elongation, elongation at failure, elongation after fracture, percentage elongation at fracture, ductile yield **2.** *(Gummi)* ultimate elongation
Bruchdurchbiegung *f* transverse rupture strength
Brucheinschnürung *f* percentage reduction of area after fracture
Bruchfallhöhe *f* fracture drop height
Bruchfestigkeit *f* residual strength
Bruchflächenbeurteilung *f* assessment of fractured surface
Bruchgefahr *f* risk of fracture
brüchig brittle, fragile
Bruchkraft *f* breaking force, tensile strength
Bruchlast *f* breaking load
Bruchlinie *f* break line
Bruchquerzuwachs *m* spread at fracture
Bruch-Schwingspielzahl *f* number of cycles to failure
bruchsicher break-proof
Bruchsicherung *f* (tube) breakage cut-out
Bruchspan *m* discontinuous chip, segmental (or fragmental) chip, tear chip

Bruchstauchung *f* compression at fracture
Bruchstelle *f* breakage point, point of rupture, breaking
Bruchstück *nt* fractured part
Bruchtemperatur *f* rupture temperature
Bruchverhalten *nt* fracture behaviour
Bruchwiderstand *m* resistance to fracture, breaking resistance
Bruchzone *f* fracture zone
Brücke *f* 1. *(allg.)* brace, saddle (carrying the table), bridge 2. *(Gerüst)* gantry
Brückengleichrichter *m* bridge rectifier
Brückenkran *m* bridge crane, gantry crane
Brückenpaternoster *nt* bridge carousel, bridge type vertical carousel
Brückenzweig *m* *(Wheatstone)* arm of a Wheatstone half-bridge
brünieren blue, bronze, burnish
Brust *f* *(Zahn)* tooth (or cutting) face
Brustbohrer *m* brace
Brustbohrmaschine *f* breast drill
Brustwinkel *m* hook angle, face angle
Bruttobedarf *m* brutto demand
Bruttogewicht *nt* gross weight
Bruttowägefüllmaschine *f* gross weighing machine
BSA Zugriff VDU access
B-Sortiment *nt* items moving at a medium place
buchen book
Buchse *f* 1. *(allg.)* bush, bushing, collar, sleeve, socket 2. *(e. Pinole)* sleeve, bush
Buchse *f* **mit Gradeinteilung** graduated collar
Buchsenplatte *f* bushing plate
Buchsenteil *nt* receptacle
Buchstabe *m* letter
Buchstabenkennung *f* *(e. Stückzahlenspalte)* letter symbol reference
Buchstabensteg *m* *(e. Schablonenschrift)* gap in a letter
Buchung *f* booking, entry
Buchungsdatum *nt* booking date
Buchungsnummer *f* booking number
Buchungsvorgang *m* entry event
buckelgeschweißtes Probestück *nt* projection welded test piece
Buckellänge *f* projection length
buckelschweißen projection-weld
Buckelschweißvorrichtung *f* projection welding dies and fixtures
bücken bend
Budgetierung *f* budgeting
Bügel *m* bar, push/pull handle, loop, rail, yoke, frame, bow
Bügelechtheit *f* fastness of the finish to ironing
Bügelgriff *m* bow, handle
Bügelmessschraube *f* micrometer calliper, micrometer, external micrometer
Bügelmitte *f* centre of push/pull bar
Bügelmutter *f* *(für Verschlüsse)* lifting nut
Bügelprobe *f* yoke test specimen
Bügelsäge *f* hack-saw, hack-saw machine
Bügelsägemaschine *f* power hacksaw
Bügelsägen *nt* hack-sawing
Bügelsicherung *f* *(e. Mutter)* screw clamp retention
Bühne *f* platform, raised storage area
Bumper *m* bumper
Bund *m* 1. *(allg.)* bundle, coil, shoulder 2. *(Absatz)* shoulder 3. *(Flansch)* flange 4. *(Hauptspindel)* collar
Bundanstauchen *nt* **im Gesenk** die collaring
Bunddurchmesser *m* collar diameter
Bündel *nt* bundle
bündeln 1. *(allg.)* concentrate, bundle 2. *(opt. Strahlen)* focus
Bundesanstalt *f* **für Materialprüfung** Federal Institute for Materials Testing
Bundesgesundheitsamt *nt* Federal Health Office
bündig flush, flush-fitting
bündig machen flush
Bundlagerung *f* bundle storage
Buntmetall *nt* non-ferrous metal
Buntpigment *nt* coloured pigment
Bürdenwiderstand *m* load impedance
Büretenhahn *m* **mit Winkelbohrung** burette stopcock with angular bore
Bürste *f* brush

bürsten brush
Bürstenbrücke *f* brush rocker, brush support
Bürstenfeuer *nt* commutator sparking
bürstenlos brushless
Bus *m* bus (business line)
busfähig bus-capable
Bussystem *nt* bus system
Butadien-Acrylintril-Vulkanisat *nt* butadiene-acrylonitrile rubber
Butan(gas) *nt* butane
Byte *nt* byte
byteweise by bytes

Cc

C-Gabel *f* C-fork
CAD (Computer unterstütze Konstruktion) *f* Computer Aided Design
Cadmium *nt* cadmium
CAE (Computer unterstütztes Ingenieurwesen) *nt* Computer Aided Engineering
CAM (Computer unterstützte Fertigung) *f* Computer Aided Manufacturing
Camlockschnellspannung *f* camlock (or cam-lock) type mounting
Camlockspindelkopf *m* cam-lock spindle nose
CAN-Bus *m* Controller Rea Network
CAP (Computer unterstützte Planung, Fertigungsvorbereitung) *f* Computer Aided Planning
CAQ (Computer unterstützte Qualitätssicherung) *f* Computer Aided Quality Assurance
Carbonatgestein *nt* carbonate rock
CAT (Computer unterstütztes Prüfen) *nt* Computer Aided Testing
CATIA Computer Aided Three-Dimensional Interactive Applications
CCD-Element *nt* CCD element
CCD-Kamera *f* **(ladungsgekoppeltes Bildwanderelement)** CCD camera
CE Concurrent engineering
Celluloseacetat-Spritzgussmasse *f* cellulose acetate injection moulding material
Celluloseacetobutyrat-Spritzgussmasse *f* cellulose aceto butyrate injection moulding material (or compound)
Cellulosebahn *f* cellulose sheeting
Cellulosefaser *f* fibrous cellulose
CE-Zeichen *nt* CE-marking
chaotische Einlagerung *f* random storage
chaotische Lagerordnung *f* random storage
Charakteristik *f* description
charakteristische Röntgenstrahlung *f* characteristic X-radiation
Charge *f* production lot, batch
Chargenbestandsführung *f* batch stock control
Chargengröße *f* bath size
Chargennummer *f* batch number
Chargenproduktion *f* batch production
Chargenprozess *m* batch prozess
Chargenzuordnung *f* batch allocation
Chargiergerät *nt* charging device
Checkliste *f* check list
Chemiezellstoff *m* chemical pulp
Chemikalienlager *nt* chemical store
chemisch chemical
chemisch beständig chemically immune
chemisch reinigen dry clean
chemische Bindemittel *ntpl* chemical binding agent
chemische Zusätze beifügen dope
chemischer Schutz *m* chemical preservation
chemisches Ablöseverfahren *nt* chemical dissolving process
chemisches Abtragen *nt* chemical abrading
chemisches Ätzen *nt* chemical etching
chemisch-thermisches Entgraten *nt* chemical-thermal burring
Chipaufnahme *f* wafer carrier
Chipsatz *m* chipset
Chipträger *m* wafer carrier
Chiquadratverteilung *f* chi squared distribution
Chlorgasdosieranlage *f* chlorinator
Chlorgasmassenstrom *m* chlorine gas mass flow
chloriertes Diphenyl *nt* chlorinated diphenyl
chloriertes VC-Homopolymerisat *nt* chlorated VC homopolymer
Chloritbleichechtheit *f* fastness to bleaching with sodium chlorite
Chlorkautschukkleber *m* chlorinated rubber adhesive

Chloroprenkautschuk m chloroprene rubber
Chlorsäure f chloric acid
Chlorwasserstoffabspaltung f splitting off of hydrogen chloride
Chrom nt chromium
chromatieren chromize
Chromatierlösung f chromating solution
Chromatierschemikalie f chromating chemical
Chromatierung f chromating, chrome diffusion
Chromatschutz m chromate protective coat
chromieren chromize
Chrommaske f chromium mask
Chromotopsäuremethode f chromotopic method
Chronologie f chronology
CIM (computerintegrierte Fertigung) CIM (Computer Integrated Manufacturing)
CL-Data (Schnittverlaufswerkzeugbahndaten) Cutter-Line Data (CLDATA)
Clip m metal clip
Clipvrschließmaschine f clip closing machine
CMP (chemisch-mechanisches Planieren)-Bearbeitung f chemical-mechanical planish processing
CNC CNC (Computerized Numerical Control)
Code m code
Codelänge f code length
Codemuster nt code pattern
Codeprüfung f code checking
Codespezifikation f code specification
Codeumsetzer m converter
Code-Umsetzer m coder converter
Codewort nt codeword
codieren code, encode

Codierer m coder, encoder
Codierleiste f coding strip
Codiermaschine f coding machine
codierte Drehgeber mpl rotary encoder, shaft encoder
Codierung f code, coding
Codierungsart f type of code
Compiler m *(Kompilierer, Übersetzer)* compiler
Compounderregung f compound excitation
Compoundmenge f compound quantity
Compoundtyp m compound type
Computer m computer
computergestützt computer-supported
Computersteuergerät nt computer control unit
Container m freight container
Containergabeltasche f container fork pocket
Containerspreader m container spreader
Containerstapler m container handler
copolymerisierbar copolymerizable
copolymerisieren copolymerize
C-Profil nt C-shaped profile
CPU CPU (Central Processing Unit)
CPU-Baugruppe f processing unit
Croningverfahren nt croning process
CRT CRT (Cathode Ray Tube)
C-Schiene f C-rail
C-Schubgabel f retractable C-fork
CSMA/CD Carrier Sense Multiple Access with Collision Detection
C-Sortiment nt slow-moving items
C-Stahl m carbon steel
Cursor m cursor
Cyanotype m cyanotype method
Cyclohexanonlösung f cyclohexanone solution

D d

Dach *nt* roof
Dachabdeckung *f* roof cover
Dachaufbau *m* turret
Dachdichtungsbahn *f* roof sealing strip
dachförmig prism-shaped
Dachlast *f* roof stress(es)
Dachprisma *nt* inverted (or prismatic) Vees, inverted V-way
Dachprismenführung *f* inverted V-guide
Dachventilator *m* roof fan
Dammarkleber *m* dammar solution adhesive
dämmen dam up, insulate
Dammleitung *f* embankment pipeline
Dämmplattenverschluss *m* insulating slab closure
Dämmstoff *m* insulating material
Dampf *m* steam, *(UK)* vapour, *(US)* vapor, fume
dampfbeheizt steam heated
Dampfdauerleistung *f* continuous steam output
Dampfdruckbegrenzer *m* steam pressure limiter
Dampfdruckregelung *f* steam pressure control
Dampfdrucküberwachung *f* monitoring of the steam pressure
Dämpfechtheit *f* fastness to steaming
Dampfeinführung *f* steam admission
Dampfeinführungsstutzen *m* steam inlet branch
dämpfen absorb, attenuate (electricity), muffle, damp, cushion
Dampfenergie *f* steam energy
Dampfentnahme *f* bleeding (or extraction) of steam, steam offtake
Dampfentwicklungskolben *m* steam generating flask
Dämpfer *m* absorber, cushion, damper, muffler
Dampferzeugeranlage *f* steam generating plant
Dampffixieren *nt* steam setting

dampfförmig vaporous
Dampfkesselbau *m* steam boiler engineering
Dampfkesselverordnung *f* steam boiler code
Dampfkesselvorschrift *f* steam boiler regulation
Dampfkühler *m* steam cooler
Dampfkühler *m* **mit Wassereinspritzung** steam boiler with water injection
Dampfnetz *nt* steam main
Dampfplissieren *nt* steam pleating
Dampfpolster *nt* steam cushion
Dampfrußbläser *m* steam soot blower
Dampfschraubverschließmaschine *f* steam capping machine
Dampfschwaden *m* vapour
Dampfstrahlen *nt* steam blasting
Dampftemperaturregelung *f* steam temperature control
Dampftemperaturregler *m* steam temperature controller
Dampfumformejektorventil *nt* steam converting ejector valve
Dämpfung *f* cushioning, damping, attenuation
Dämpfungsfähigkeit *f* damping property (or capacity or power)
Dämpfungsgröße *f* damping value
Dämpfungsverhalten *nt* damping behaviour
Dämpfungsvorgang *m* cushioning action
darstellen 1. *(allg.)* represent, plot 2. *(bildlich)* illustrate 3. *(graphisch)* represent graphically 4. *(Kennmerkmale)* feature
Darstellung *f* 1. *(allg.)* representation 2. *(ausführliche ~)* detailed representation 3. *(dimensionsbehaftete ~)* dimensionalized representation 4. *(einprägsame ~)* expressive representation 5. *(isometrische ~)* isometric projection 6. *(lagerichtige ~)* topographical representation 7. *(maßstabgetreue ~)* true-to-scale representation 8. *(mehrfarbige*

~) multi-coloured representation
Darstellung *f* **nach Ablaufsprache** sequential function chart (SFC)
Darstellungsschicht *f* presentation layer
Darstellungsweise *f* method of representation
darüber above
darüber angebracht overhead
darunter below
Datei *f* file
Dateiname *m* file name
Dateitransferprotokoll *nt* file transfer protocol (FTP)
Daten *pl* data, information
Datenarchivierung *f* data archiving
Datenaufzeichnung *f* data recording
Datenausgabe *f* data output
Datenausgang *m* data output
Datenaustausch *m* data interchange, data exchange
Datenaustauschformat *nt* data interchange format, data exchange format
Datenbank *f* data bank, data base, information base
Datenbankabfragesprache *f* structured query language
Datenbanken *fpl* data base
Datenbanksicherung *f* data bank security
Datenbestand *m* data inventory
Datenblatt *nt* data sheet
Datendokumentation *f* data documentation
Dateneingang *m* data input
Datenende *nt* end of data, EOD
Datenendeinrichtung *f* data terminal equipment (DTE)
Datenerfassung *f* data acquisition, data collection
Datenerfassungs- und Aufzeichnungssystem *nt* data logging system
Datenerhebung *f* collection of data
Datenfeld *nt* data field
Datenfernübertragung *f* remote data transmission, (data) telecommunication
Datenfluss *m* data flow
Datenflussverfolgung *f* registration of data flow
Datenflussverwaltung *f* administration of data flow
Datenfunk *m* data radio
datengesteuerte Maschine *f* numerically (or computer-) controlled machine
Datenhaltung *f* data storage
Datenkommunikation *f* data communication
Datenkonzentrator *m* data concentrator
Datenkopplung *f* data coupling
Datenlesen *nt* data acquisition
Datenmenge *f* quantity of data
Datennetz *nt* public data network (DIN 66021 T.5), interchange circuit (DIN 66020 T.2)
Datenpaar *nt* data pair
Datenquelle *f* data source
Datenschnittstelle *f* data interface
Datensicherheit *f* data security
Datensicherungsmaßnahme *f* data protection measure
Datensichtgerät *nt* video display terminal
Datenspeicher *m* data storage, data storage unit, data memory
Datenstelle *f* data position
Datenstellenzahl *f* number of data places
Datensteuerung *f* numerical control
Datenstruktur *f* data structure
Datenstrukturierung *f* data structure concept
Datentechnik *f* data systems technology
Datenträger *m* data carrier, data (storage) media/medium
Datenträgergeschwindigkeit *f* data carrier speed
Datenübertragung *f* data transfer, data transmission
Datenübertragungseinrichtung *f* data communication equipment/data circuit-terminating equipment (DCE), data transfer device
Datenübertragungsgeschwindigkeit *f* data transfer speed
Datenübertragungsmenge *f* data transmission volume
Datenübertragungsrate *f* data transfer rate, rate of data transfer

Datenübertragungsverfahren *nt* data transfer procedure
Datenverarbeitung *f* data processing
Datenverarbeitungsebene *f* data processing level
Datenvergleich *m* data comparison
Datenwort *nt* data word
Datenzugriffsmethode *f* data access method
Datenzugriffsmodul *nt* data file access module
datieren date
Datum *nt* date
Datumsprüfung *f* date verification
Daube *f* stave
Dauer ... constant, continuous, permanent, sustained
Dauer *f* duration, length (of time), period
Dauerbeanspruchbarkeit *f* long-term performance
dauerbeanspruchte Schweißung *f* weld subject to long-term stressing
Dauerbeanspruchung *f* endurance stress
Dauerbeobachtung *f* continuous observation
Dauerbelastung *f* long-term loading, constant load
Dauerbetauungsversuch *m* continuous dew test
Dauerbetrieb *m* continuous duty, continuous operation
Dauer-Biegeversuch *m* repeated flexural test
Dauerbrandeinsatz *m* slow-combustion inset
Dauerbrandfähigkeit *f* slow combustion capability
Dauerbrandherd *m* domestic slow combustion range
Dauerbruch *m* fatigue failure
dauerelastisch permanently elastic
Dauer-Faltversuch *m* permanent folding behaviour
Dauerfestigkeit *f* fatigue strength, endurance limit
Dauerfestigkeitsversuch *m* fatigue test
Dauerfestigkeitswert *m* fatigue limit strength value
Dauerform *f* permanent mould
Dauerformverfahren *nt* durable form process
Dauerfunktionsprüfung *f* long term performance test
Dauergleichstrom *m* continuous direct current
dauerhafte Form *f* durable shape
Dauerhubfestigkeit *f* stress range for fatigue limit
Dauerknickbeanspruchung *f* repeated flexural stress
Dauerknickverhalten *nt* reaction to repeated flexure
Dauerknickversuch *m* flex cracking test
Dauerkurzschluss *m* sustained short-circuit
Dauerleistung *f* continuous rating
Dauermagnet *nt* permanent magnet
Dauermodell *nt* durable model
dauern go on, last
dauernd continuous, permanent
Dauerpalette *f* returnable pallet
dauerplastisch permanently plastic
Dauerprüfung *f* endurance test
Dauerschall *m* continuous wave
Dauerschranke *f* permanent barrier
Dauerschutz *m* long-term protection
Dauerschwellversuch *m* pulsatory fatigue test
Dauerschwingbeanspruchung *f* dynamic fatigue loading
Dauerschwingsprüfmaschine *f* fatigue testing machine
Dauerschwingverhalten *nt* fatigue behaviour
Dauerschwingversuch *m* dynamic (or flexural) fatigue test
Dauerschwingversuch *m* **an einschnittig überlappten Klebungen** dynamic fatigue test on single lap joints
Dauerschwingversuch *m* **mit axialer Beanspruchung** dynamic fatigue test by axial loading, axial load fatigue testing
Dauerschwingversuch *m* **mit Eindruckschwellbereich** dynamic fatigue test by constant load pounding

Dauerstandbindefestigkeit *f* creep limit of the bond
Dauerstandfestigkeit *f* fatigue strength for infinite time, time yield, creep strength
Dauertauchversuch *m* long-term immersion test
Dauerversuch *m* endurance (or creep) test
Dauerwechselstrom *m* continuous alternating current
Dauerzustand *m* steady state
Daumen *m* cam
dazugehörig associated
D-Beiwert *m* *(Differenzierbeiwert)* derivative action factor
Deckanstrich *m* top coat
Deckblatt *nt* cover sheet, top sheet
Deckblattaufleger *m* cover sheet dispenser, top sheet dispenser
Deckbrett *nt* weather board
Decke *f* ceiling
Deckel *m* cap, lid, cover
decken cover, meet the demand
deckende Schicht *f* covering coat
Deckenfächer *m* *(Ventilator)* ceiling fan
Deckenstativ *nt* ceiling stand
Deckenvorgelege *nt* overhead countershaft
Deckfolie *f* top film
Decklagenschweißer *m* final-run welder
Decklagenüberhöhung *f* cover (or final) run reinforcement
Decklagenüberwölbung *f* cover run concavity
Decklagenunterwölbung *f* incompletely filled groove
Deckplatte *f* cover plate, top plate
Deckschicht *f* **1.** *(allg.)* plastic coating **2.** *(bei Schichtpressstoffen)* face
Deckschichtausbildung *f* surface layer formation
Deckschichtebene *f* face
Deckschichtklebung *f* face bond
Deckschichtverbindung *f* compound forming the coating layer
Deckschichtwerkstoff *m* face material
Deckschichtwiderstand *m* *(el. chem.)* surface layer resistance

Deckstreifen *m* cover strip
Deckung *f:* **zur ~ bringen** *(Flächen)* be made to coincide
Deckungsbeitrag *m* covering contribution above own costs
Deckungsbeitragskostenrechnung *f* accounting of departmental participation in covering costs
Decoder *m* decoder
decodieren decode
DEE Rückleiter *m* DTE common return
DEE umgesteuert nicht bereit *(data com.)* DTE uncontrolled not ready
defekt defective, defect
Defekt *m* defect
definierte Grenzfläche *f* defined boundary surface
Definition *f* definition
Definitionsblatt *nt* definition sheet
Deformationsmodul *m* deformation modulus
deformieren deform
Defuzziierung *f* defuzzification
Degenerierungsphase *f* decline stage
degressive Grübchenbildung *f* degressive pitting
Dehn-Stauchzyklus *m* extension and compression cycle
dehnbar elastic, flexible, ductile
dehnbares weiches Polyvinylchlorid *nt* elastomeric flexible polyvinylchloride
Dehnbarkeit *f* elasticity, ductility, flexibility
Dehnbeanspruchung *f* compressive loading, tensile loading
dehnen 1. *(ausdehnen längen)* expand **2.** *(längen Zugversuch)* elongate **3.** *(strecken)* extend **4.** *(Textilien)* stretch, strain **5.** *(elastisch)* stress **6.** *(verformend)* strain
Dehner *m* expansion fitting
Dehngeschwindigkeit *f* strain-rate
Dehngrenze *f* **1.** *(allg.)* offset yield stress, proof stress **2.** *(bleibend)* permanent elongation limit, proof stress **3.** *(0,1% ~)* offset yield strength **4.** *(0,2% ~)* creep limit, stress at 0.2% permanent strain
Dehnhülse *f* anti-fatigue sleeve

Dehnmessstreifen *m* strain gauge, strain dependent resistor
Dehnmodul *nt* modulus of elasticity
Dehnschaft *m* (e. Schraube) waisted shank
Dehnschraube *f* high-strength friction-grip bolt with waisted shank
Dehnschwingung *f* alternating strain
Dehnung *f* 1. *(bis Bruch)* elongation 2. *(bis Streckgrenze)* stress 3. *(elastische Werkstoffe)* stretch, expand 4. *(Längsdehnung z. B. Stabdehnung)* extension 5. *(bleibende ~)* percentage permanent elongation 6. *(elastische ~)* percentage elastic elongation 7. *(gesamte ~)* percentage total elongation 8. *(nichtproportionale ~)* percentage non-proportional elongation
Dehnung *f* **bei Bruch** stretch at breaking
Dehnung *f* **bei Höchstkraft** elongation at maximum load
Dehnung *f* **bei Streckspannung** elongation at yield stress
Dehnung *f* **beim Reißen** extension at break
Dehnung *f*: auf ~ beanspruchen 1. *(Druck)* load in compression 2. *(Zug)* load in tension
dehnungsabhängiger Widerstand *m* strain dependent resistor
Dehnungsbogen *m* expansion bend
Dehnungsfuge *f* expansion joint
Dehnungsmessstreifen *m* strain gauge
Dehnungsmessung *f* strain measurement, strain (force) measurement
Dehnungssensor *m* extension sensor
Dehnungstaster *m* extensometer
Dehnzunahmegeschwindigkeit *f* rate of strain increase
Deichsel *f* 1. *(allg.)* tiller, tiller handle 2. *(Anhänger)* drawbar
Deichselebene *f* tiller plane
Deichselgesenk *nt* tiller articulation point
Deichselgriff *m* tiller handle
Deichsellenkung *f* tiller steering
Deichselsteuerung *f* tiller control
Deichselwagen *m* truck with a tiller, tiller-steered truck
Dekade *f* decade
dekadische Zählröhre *f* decade counter tube
Dekaturechtheit *f* fastness to decatizing
Dekompression *f* decompression
Dekontaminierbarkeit *f* ease of decontamination
dekontaminieren decontaminate
dekorative Schichtpressstoffplatte *f* decorative laminated sheet
Dekorschicht *f* decorative layer
Dekrement *nt* **der mechanischen Dämpfung** logarithmic decrement of mechanical damping
Delaminierung *f* exfoliation
Delignifizierung *f* delignification
Delignifizierungsgrad *m* degree of delignification
Delle *f* impression, check, dent
demarkieren deselect
Demontage *f* demounting, disassembling, dismantling, dismounting
demontierbare Bereifung *f* demountable tyre wheel(s)
demontieren demount, dismount, dismantle, disassemble
Demulgierungsgrad *m* demulsion characteristic
Dengeln *nt* thinning
depalettieren depalletize
Depalettierer *m* depalletizer
Depalettierroboter *m* robot depalletizer
Dephlemmierkolonne *f* fractionating column, dephlegmator
Designlenkung *f* design control
Destillationsaufsatz *m* fractioning column
Destillationskolben *m* distillation flask
Destillattropfen *m* distillation drop
Destillatvolumen *nt* volume of distillate
Destilliervorstoß *m* receiver adaptor
Detailerkennbarkeit *f* degree of resolution of detail
Detailzeichenpapier *nt* rotogravure paper
Detailzeichnung *f* detailed drawing

Detektion *f* detection
Detektionsbereich *m* detection field
Detergent *nt* detergent
Detonation *f* detonation
Detonationssicherung *f* detonation guard
Detonationswirkung *f* detonation effect
dezentral decentralized
dezentrale Ein-/Ausgabeeinheit (-station) *f* remote I/O station (RIOS)
dezimalgeometrische Reihe *f* geometrical progression based on decimals
Dezimalpunktprogrammierung *f* decimal point programming
Dezimalsystem *nt* decimal system
Dezimalzahl *f* decimal
D-Glied *nt (differenzierendes Glied)* derivative element
D-Hülsen-Passeinsatz *m* screw-in sleeve socket for D-fuses
DHY-Fuge *f* double-bevel weld with broad root face
Diagnose *f* diagnosis
Diagnosegerät *nt* diagnosis tool
Diagnosemöglichkeit *f* diagnostics
Diagnoseverfahren *nt* diagnostics
diagnostisch diagnostic
diagonal diagonal
diagonal fahren travel diagonally, move diagonally
Diagonale *f* 1. *(allg.)* diagonal 2. *(Verstrebung)* diagonal brace
Diagonalfahrt *f* diagonal travel, diagonal motion, diagonal movement
Diagonalfahrthöhe *f* height for diagonal travel
Diagonalfräsen *nt* diagonal hobbing
Diagonalkreuz *nt* diagonal cross
Diagonalquerschaben *nt* diagonal cross scraping
Diagonalrippe *f* diagonal brace
Diagonalschaben *nt* diagonal shaving
Diagonalverband *m* diagonal brace
Diagonalverfahren *nt* diagonal technique
diagonalverrippt diagonally braced
Diagonalwalzfräseinrichtung *f* diagonal hobbing attachment
Diagramm *nt* diagram, plot

Diagrammverfahren *nt* diagram method
diakritisches Zeichen *nt* diacritical sign
Dialog *m* dialogue, dialog
Dialogauskunft *f* on-line enquiry
Dialogbefehl *m* dialogue instruction
Dialogbetrieb *m* dialog mode
Dialogmonitor *m* TP monitor
Dialogprogrammgenerator *m* dialogue program generator
Dialogstammdatenverwaltungsprogrammgenerator *m* on-line master file maintenance program generator
Dialogverarbeitung *f* on-line processing
Diamant *m* diamond
Diamantabdrehvorrichtung *f* diamond truing device
Diamantabrichten *nt* diamond truing
Diamantabrichter *m* diamond wheel dresser
Diamantabrichtgerät *nt* diamond dressing device
Diamantabrichtrolle *f* diamond roller truer
Diamantabzieheinrichtung *f* diamond dressing device
Diamantbelag *m* diamond-impregnated grinding face, diamond section
diamantbestückt diamond-tipped
Diamantbestückung *f* diamond tipping
Diamantbohren *nt* diamond boring (or drilling)
Diamantbohrkrone *f* diamond drill bit
Diamantbohrmaschine *f* diamond drilling machine
Diamanteinzelwerkzeug *nt* single-point diamond tool
diamantfrei without a diamond
Diamantgitter *nt* diamond cubic
diamanthart adamantine
Diamantkonzentration *f* diamond concentration
Diamantkorn *nt* diamond grain
Diamantkorngröße *f* diamond grain size
Diamantkornkonzentration *f* diamond grain concentration

Diamantkörnung *f* diamond grit
Diamantkristall *nt* diamond grain
diamantläppen diamond
Diamantscheibe *f* diamond-impregnated wheel
Diamantschneide *f* diamond edge
Diamantspitze *f* diamond point, diamond tip
Diamantsplitter *m* diamond particle
Diamantstandzeit *f* diamond life
Diamantstaub *m* diamond powder
Diamanttastnadel *f* diamond stylus
Diamantwerkzeug *nt* diamond tool
diametral gegenüberliegend diametrically opposed
Diametral Pitch *m* **eines Werkzeuges** cutter diametral pitch
Diametral Pitch *m* **im Normalschnitt** normal diametral pitch
Diametral Pitch *m* **im Stirnschnitt** *m* transverse diametral pitch
Diathermie-Gerät *nt* diathermic unit
Diazoverbindung *f* diazo compound
dicht compact, dense, proof, close, tight, leak-proof
Dichtband *nt* gasket strip
Dichte *f* thickness
Dichte-Aräometer *nt* density hydrometer
Dichtelement *nt* sealing element
dichten seal, make tight
Dichtewelle *f* longitudinal wave
Dichtfläche *f* 1. *(allg.)* gasket surface, sealing surface 2. *(von Rohrenden)* joint face
Dichtfunktion *f* sealing function
dichtgefaltete Probe *f* *(für Ringfaltversuche an Rohren)* close-flattened specimen
Dichtheit *f* 1. *(allg.)* leak tightness 2. *(e. Verschraubung)* pressure tightness
Dichtkante *f* *(e. Einschraubstutzens)* joint face
Dichtleiste *f* raised face
Dichtmittel *nt* jointing medium, sealing agent
Dichtring *m* packing ring, joint washer
Dichtrprüfgerät *nt* leak testing apparatus

Dichtspalt *m* jointing gap
Dichtstoff *m* 1. *(allg.)* sealing compound, sealant 2. *(kalt verarbeiteter ~)* cold processable sealant
Dichtung *f* 1. *(allg.)* sealing, seal 2. *(im Gewinde)* pressure-tight joint
Dichtung *f* **zwischen runden Flächen** gasket
Dichtungsfläche *f* seal face
Dichtungsgewinde *nt* pressure-tight sealing thread
Dichtungskitt *m* luting agent
Dichtungsring *m* packing ring, ring gasket, sealing washer
Dichtungsring *m* **für den Flansch** joint ring
Dichtungsschnur *f* packing cord
Dichtungsspalt *m* joint gap
Dichtwaage *f* balance type density meter
dick thick
Dicke *f* thickness
Dickenmaß *nt* thickness dimension
Dickenstauchung *f* thickening dipping
Dickentaster *m* thickness calliper
dickflüssig viscous
dickflüssiger machen thicken
Dicköl *nt* thick oil
Dickungsmittel *nt* thickening agent
dickwandig thick walled, heavy walled
Dielektrikum *nt* dielectric
dielektrisch dielectric
Dielektrizitätskonstante *f* dielectric constant, permittivity
dienen serve
Dienst *m* service
Dienstgüte *f* quality of service
Dienstleistung *f* service
Dienstleiter *m* service provider
Dienstprogramm *nt* utility program, service program, service routine
Dienstsignal *nt* call progress signal
Dieselaggregat *nt* diesel-driven generating set
Dieselmotor *m* diesel engine, diesel
Differentialgetriebe *nt* differential gear unit
Differentialteilgerät *nt* differential indexing head
Differenz *f* difference

Differenzdruck *m* differential pressure
Differenzdruckmanometer *nt* differential pressure manometer
Differenzdruckmesser *m* differential pressure gauge
Differenzdruckprinzip *nt* differential pressure principle
Differenzdruckschalter *m* differential pressure switch
Differenzdruckschaltpunkt *m* differential pressure switching point
Differenzialsperre *f* differential lock, differential locking
Differenzierbeiwert *m* derivative action factor
differenzierendes Verhalten *nt* derivative action
Differenzierglied *nt* derivative element
Differenzspannung *f* differential voltage, transverse mode voltage, voltage transverse mode
diffusibler Wasserstoff *m* diffusible hydrogen
Diffusion *f* diffusion
diffusionsbestimmter Prozess *m (el. chem.)* process specific to diffusion
Diffusionsschicht *f* diffusion layer
Diffusionsüberspannung *f* diffusion overvoltage
Diffusionsverschleiß *m* diffusion wear
digital digital, numeric
digital arbeitende Anlage *f* digitally operating installation
Digital/Analog-Umsetzer *m* digital-to-analogue converter (DAC)
Digital-Analog-Umsetzer *m* digital-analogue converter
Digitalausgabeeinheit *f* digital output unit
Digitaldatenspeicherung digital data storage
digitale Anzeige *f* digital readout, numeric display
digitale Bewegungssteuerung *f* digital motion control
digitale Informationsverarbeitung *f* digital data processing
digitale Steuerung *f* numerical control, digital control
Digitaleingabeeinheit *f* digital input unit
digitaler Ausgang *f* digital output
digitaler Eingang *m* digital input
digitaler Impuls *m* digital pulse
digitaler Messschritt *m* digital measuring step
digitaler Signalprozessor *m* digital signal processor
digitaler Zustand *m* digital state
digitales Eingangssignal *nt* digital input signal
digitales Messsystem *nt* digital measuring system
digitales Verknüpfungsglied *nt* logic element
digitalisieren digitizing
Digitalrechner *m* digital computer
dimensionieren proportion, determine, safe dimensions, dimension, calculate, rate for
Dimensionierung *f* dimensioning, sizing
dimensionsbehaftete Darstellung *f* dimensionalized representation
Dimensionskonstanz *f* dimensional stability
dimensionslose Darstellung *f* dimensionless representation
dimensionslose Größe *f* dimensionless quantity (or variable)
dimetrische Projektion *f* dimetric projection
DIN-gerechte Zeichnung *f* DIN-based drawing
Diode *f* diode
Diode *f* **zur Ableitung transienter Überspannung** transient absorption Z-diode
Dionat *nt* dionate
Dipolcharakter *m* dipolar character
direkt direct
direkt befeuerter Speicher *m* directly-fired storage heater
direkt proportional directly proportional to
direkt prozessgekoppelt on line
Direktanlauf *m* direct starting
Direktbeschriften *nt* direct marking
Direktbestellung *f* direct ordering, di-

rect order
direkte Adresse *f* direct address
direkte Adressierung *f* direct addressing
direkte Ausgabe *f* direct output, indication
direkte Darstellung *f* direct representation
direkte Drehmomentregelung *f* direct torque control
direkte Wegmessung *f* direct measurement
Direkteinschalter *m* direct switching starter
Direkteinschaltung *f* direct-on-line starting, direct switching
direktes Heizelementschweißen *nt* direct contact heated tool welding
direktes Teilen *nt* direct indexing
Direktheizgerät *nt* non-storage type heating appliance
Direktlagerung *f* direct storage
Direktruf *m* direct call
Direktschaltung *f* direct control
Direktversand *m* direct dispatch
Disjunktion *f* disjunction, inclusive OR
disjunktiv disjunctive
disjunktiv verknüpfte Eingänge *mpl* disjunctively combined inputs *pl*
disjunktive Verknüpfung *f* disjunctive combination
Diskette *f* floppy disk
diskontinuierlich discontinuous
diskret discrete
diskrete Zufallsvariable *f* discrete random variable
dispergieren disperse
Dispersion *f* dispersion
Dispersionsfarbe *f* plastics dispersion paint
Dispo-Bestand *m* available inventory
Disponent *m* expediter, managing clerk
disponieren make arrangements, place orders, schedule
Disponummer *f* item number
Disposition *f* **1.** *(allg.)* arrangement, disposition, provision **2.** *(Arbeitsvorbereitung)* job planning, operations planning
Dispositionsdaten *pl* disposition data
Dispositionsstelle *f* disposition centre
dispositiv organizational
Distanz *f* distance, space, spacing
Distanzbüchse *f* spacer bushing
Distanzstück *nt* distance piece, spacer, spacing piece, run spacer, spacer block
Distribution *f* distribution
Distributionslogistik *f* marketing logistics, outbound logistics
Distributionsstufe *f* distribution echelon
Divergenz *f* divergence
divergierend divergent
Diversifikation *f* diversification
diversifizieren diversify
Divisionszeichen *nt* division sign
D-Kippglied *nt* D bistable element
DNC *Abk* DNC (Direct Numerical Control)
Docht *m* wick
Dochtschmierung *f* wick-feed lubrication
Dochtwirkung *f* wicking action
Dokument *nt* document
Dokumentation *f* documentation, engineering data, reference material
dokumentieren record
Domschacht *m* manhole pit
Doppel ... twin, double, duplex
Doppelbetätigung *f* dual operating system
Doppelbuckelschweißen *nt* double projection welding
Doppeleingriff *m* *(bei Planetengetrieben)* double engagement
Doppelflip *m* double flip
Doppelfräsmaschine *f* double head milling machine, two-spindle miller, duplex milling machine
doppelgängiges Gewinde *nt* two-(or double-) start thread
Doppelgelenkanschluss *m* double articulated connection
Doppel-Gelenksteckschlüssel *m* double-ended flex head socket wrench
Doppel-Gewindestutzen *m* double male connector
Doppelgreifer *m* double gripper
Doppelhals-Siedekolben *m* double-necked distilling flask

Doppelhobelmaschine *f* duplex planer
Doppelhohlkehle *f* double round corner
Doppel-HU-Naht *f* double-I butt joint (or weld)
Doppel-HV-Fuge *f* double-bevel groove
Doppel-HV-Naht *f* double-bevel butt joint
Doppel-HY-Naht *f* double-bevel butt joint with broad root face
Doppel-HY-Naht mit Doppelkehlnaht double-bevel weld with root face welded with double fillet weld
Doppeljoch *nt* double yoke
Doppelkegelring *m (e. Rohrverschraubung)* double taper sleeve (or seal)
Doppelkegelschleifscheibe *f* double tapered grinding wheel
Doppelkopierdrehmaschine *f* dual copying lathe
Doppelkurbel *f* drag link
Doppelkurvenprinzip *nt* double cam principle
Doppellamellenkupplung *f* double multiple disc clutch
Doppellangfräsmaschine *f* double plano-milling machine, duplex plano-miller
Doppellinie *f* double rule
Doppelmeißelhalter *m* duplex toolholder
Doppelmuffenübergangsstück *nt* double socket transition piece
doppeln double, duplicate, fold
Doppelpedalsteuerung *f* double pedal drive control
Doppelplanfräsmaschine *f* double fixed-bed miller
Doppelprisma *nt* double-Vee
Doppelprismaführung *f* double Vee-guide
Doppelrad *nt* dual wheel, twin wheel
Doppelradeinbau *m* **auf Achsstummel** twin wheel stub axle mounting
Doppelregal *nt* double-sided shelving, double sided run
Doppelringschlüssel *m:* **1.** *(abgewinkelter ~)* offset double head box wrench

2. *(gerader ~)* flat double head box wrench
Doppelrolle *f* twin wheel castor
Doppelrollenmaschine *f* twin electrode wheel machine
Doppelrollenpalettenstretchwickler *m* two-reel pallet stretch-wrapper
Doppelrundhobeleinrichtung *f* duplex radial planing attachment
Doppelschaltung *f* double indexing
Doppelscheibenfenster *nt* double-glazed window
Doppelscheibenwerkzeugschleifmaschine *f* double-wheel tool grinder
Doppelschlusserregung *f* compound excitation, compound motor
Doppelschrägverzahnung *f* double helical teeth
Doppelschwinge *f* double rocker
doppelseitig bilateral, double-ended
doppelseitige Zykloidenverzahnung *f* double-sided tooth system
doppelseitiger Langlochfräser *m* double-end mill
doppelseitiges Feinstbohrwerk *nt* double-ended precision boring machine
Doppelspiel *nt* double cycle
Doppelspindelautomat *m* automatic double-head milling machine
Doppelspindelfräsmaschine *f* double column planer-miller, double housing milling machine, double-column milling machine, planer miller
Doppelspindelgesenkfräsmaschine *f* two-spindle die sinking machine
Doppelspindelmaschine *f* double-spindle machine, duplex machine
Doppelspindelplanfräsmaschine *f* duplex-head milling machine
Doppelspindelsenkrechtfräsmaschine *f* double-spindle-vertical milling attachment
Doppelständerfräsmaschine *f* double column planer-miller, double housing milling machine, double-column milling machine, planer miller
Doppelständerhobelmaschine *f* double standard planer

Doppelständerhobelmaschine *f* double-column planer
Doppelständerpresse *f* double-column press
doppelständiges Drehwerk *nt* double-column vertical turning and boring mill
Doppelsteckschlüssel *m* double-ended socket spanner
Doppelstößel-Räummaschine *f* dual ram broaching machine
Doppelstutzen *m* *(als Rohrverschraubung)* double-ended union
Doppelsupport *m* connected rest
doppelt double
doppelt wirkend double acting
Doppeltakt *m* double stroke
Doppeltaster *m* inside and outside calliper
doppelter Stromabnehmer *m* double current collector
doppeltes Abschneiden *nt* double cropping
doppeltief double-deep, double depth, twin-depth
Doppel-T-Profil *nt* H-shaped profile, I-shaped profile
Doppel-T-Träger *m* H-beam, I-beam
Doppel-V-Fuge *f* double-V groove
Doppel-V-Naht *f* double-V butt joint (or weld), X butt joint
Doppel-V-Naht *f* **mit gewölbten Oberflächen** convex double-V butt joint
Doppelwaagerechtfräsmaschine *f* double horizontal milling machine
Doppelwanddurchstrahlung *f* double-wall radiography
Doppelwaschflasche *f* double wash bottle
Doppelwort *nt* double word
Doppelwortzugriff *m* double-word addressing
Doppelzeile *f* double line
Doppelzweck *m* dual purpose
Dorn *m* 1. *(für Werkzeuge Schleifscheiben)* arbor, ram attachment 2. *(Drehdorn)* mandrel
Dornbiegeversuch *m* mandrel-bending test
Dornen *nt* off-hand piercing, indenting
Dorngabel *f* tine fork
Dornmutter *f* arbor nut
Dornpresse *f* arbor press, mandrel press
Dornrad *nt* mandrel
Dornrad-Bag-in-Box-Kartoniermaschine *f* mandrel bag-in-box machine
Dornrad-Faltschachtel-Form-, Füll- und Verschließmaschine *f* mandrel carton form fill and seal machine
Dornrad-Form-, Füll- und Verschließmaschine *f* **für flexible Packungen** mandrel flexible package form fill and seal machine
Dornrad-Form-, Füll- und Verschließmaschine *f* mandrel form fill and seal machine
Dornschlittenmaschine *f* moving mandrel machine
Dornspule *f* mandrel-mounting reel
Dornstützlager *nt* arbor supporting bracket
Dorntraglager *nt* arbor bracket
DOS *Abk* DOS (Disc Operating System)
Dose *f* can
Dosenlibelle *f* circular level
Dosieraufbaueffekt *m* dose accumulation effect
Dosiereinrichtung *f* batching equipment
dosieren batch, dose, measure out, meter out
Dosierkolben *m* dosing piston, metering piston
Dosiermaschine *f* dosing machine
Dosierpumpe *f* controlled-volume pump
Dosierung *f* proportioning, dosing
Dosiervolumen *nt* metered volume
Dosiervorrichtung *f* dosing device
Dosimetrie *f* dosimetry
Dosismessverfahren *nt* dosimetry
Dosisschwächungskoeffizient *m* dose rate reduction coefficient
Dosisüberwachungsgerät *nt* dosage monitoring device
dotieren dope
Draht *m* wire

Drahtelektrode *f* wire electrode
Drahterodieren *nt* wire eroding
Drahterodiermaschine *f* wire eroding machine
Drahtfestwiderstand *m* fixed wire-wound resistor
Drahtgeflecht *nt* wire mesh
Drahtgitter *nt* wire cage
Drahtkorn *nt* wire pellets (metallizing)
drahtlos wireless
Drahtseil *nt* wire rope, wire cable
Drahtseilklemme *f* wire drop grip
Drahtsiebboden *m* woven wire screen bottom
Drahtsteg *m* wire penetrameter
Drahtstraße *f* wire mill
Drahtwelle *f* wire wave
Drahtwendel *f* wire spiral
Drahtziehen *nt* wire drawing
Drahtziehmaschine *f* wire drawing machine
Drall *m* helix, spiral, twist
drallförmig helical
Drallfräseinrichtung *f* spiral milling attachment
Drallnut *f* helical (or spiral) flute, helical groove
Drallnuträumen *nt* helical broaching
Drallrichtung *f* hand of helix
Drallsteigerung *f* lead of helix
Drallwinkel *m* 1. *(allg.)* helix angle, spiral angle, angle of the tool helix 2. *(e. Spiralbohrers)* angle of twist
Dränabstand *m* spacing of the pipe drains
Dränfilter *m* drain filter
Dränfläche *f* drainage area
Drangkraft *f* impulse force
Drännetz *nt* drainage network
Dränpflug *m* drainage plough
Dränschacht *m* drain shaft
Dränstrang *m* line of drain pipes
Draufsicht *f* plan view, top view
D-Regeleinrichtung *f* derivative action controlling system
Dreh ... rotary, indexing
Dreh- und Bohrmaschine *f* turning and boring lathe, combination turning, drilling and boring lathe

Dreh- und Bohrwerk *nt* vertical turning and boring mill
Dreh- und Fräszentrum *nt* turning and milling centre
Dreh-, Bohr-, Abstechbank *f* turning, boring and cutting-off machine
Drehachse *f* axis of rotation (or gyration), rotation axis, fulcrum (pin), pivoting axis, spindle, centre line
Drehanodenröntgenröhre *f* rotating anode X-ray tube
Drehantrieb *m* rotating device (RBG), turning drive
Drehantrieb *m* **der Gabeln** rotating fork device
Dreharbeit *f* lathe work, turning operation (or work)
Drehausleger *m* hinged cantilever
Drehautomat *m* automatic, automatic lathe
Drehautomat *m* **ohne Revolverkopf** Swiss bush-type automatic
Drehbank *f* lathe, turning machine
drehbar 1. *(allg.)* rotatable, rotating, rotary 2. *(schwenkbar)* swivelling
drehbar gehaltenes Schneckenrad *nt* rotatably mounted wormwheel
drehbare Einspannung *f* rotatable restraint
drehbare Gabeln *fpl* rotation forks
drehbarer Schraubstock *m* swivel vice
Drehbewegung *f* 1. *(allg.)* rotation, indexing motion, turn, rotary motion 2. *(e. Tisches)* rotary feed motion 3. *(e. Werkstückes)* rotational motion
Drehbewegungsübertragung *f* transmission of rotary motion
Drehbild *nt* turned (surface) pattern
Drehbohren *nt* rotary drilling
Drehbolzen *m* pivot
Drehbormeißel *m* rotary boring tool
Drehbrechen *nt* breaking by twisting
Drehdorn *m* lathe arbor, lathe mandrel
Drehdurchmesser *m* *(UK)* turning diameter, *(US)* swing
Drehdurchmesser *m* **über Bett** swing over bed
Dreheigenfrequenz *f* natural torsional frequency

Dreheinrichtung *f* turning attachment
drehelastisch torsionally elastic
drehen 1. *(mechanisch)* rotate, revolve **2.** *(innendrehen)* bore **3.** *(plan)* face **4.** *(allg.)* swivel, swing, pivot, turn
drehen (sich ~) revolve, gyrate
drehen auf der Stelle rotate (or turn) on the spot
Drehen *nt* **zwischen Spitzen** turning between centres
drehend rotary, rotating
Dreher *m* lathe operator, metal turner
Dreherei *f* lathe room (or shop)
Drehfeld *nt* rotary field, rotating field
Drehfeldmaschine *f* induction machine
Drehfeldmotor *m* cyclic motor, synchro motor, induction motor
Drehflankenspiel *nt* circumferential backlash
Drehflankenspielschwankung *f* circumferential backlash fluctuation
Drehfräsen *nt* turn-milling
Drehfutter *nt* lathe chuck
Drehgabel *f* rotating fork
Drehgabeleinrichtung *f* rotating fork assembly
Drehgabelklammer *f* two-way fork clamper
Drehgeber *m* speed sensor
Drehgelenk *nt* pivot, revolute pair
Drehgelenkroboter *m* jointed-arm robot
Drehgenauigkeit *f* indexing accuracy
Drehgerät *nt* rotating head, rotator
Drehgeschwindigkeit *f* fork rotation speed
Drehgestell *nt* bogie
Drehhalbautomat *m* semi-automatic lathe
Drehherz *nt* dog, driving dog, driver, carrier, lathe carrier, lathe dog
Drehhöhe *f* **über Planscheibe** turning height over table
Dreh-Hub-Bewegung *f* rotational and translational movement, lift rotate movement
Dreh-Hub-Station *f* lift rotate station, lift rotate unit
Drehknopf *m* rotary button, knob, rotating head
Drehkolbenvakuumpumpe *f* rotary piston vacuum pump
Drehkolbenventil *nt* cylindrical rotary valve
Drehkorb *m* rotating cage
Drehkranz *m* slewing ring
Drehkreuz *nt* capstan (wheel), turnstile
Drehlage *f* orientation
Drehleistung *f* turning capacity
Drehling *m* insert tool, tool (holder) bit
Drehmaschine *f* lathe, turning machine
Drehmaschine *f* **für Futter- und Stangenarbeit** lathe for chucking and bar work
Drehmaschine *f* **für Futterarbeiten** lathe for chucking work, chucking lathe
Drehmaschine *f* **für Stangenarbeit** bar stock lathe
Drehmaschine *f* **in Tischausführung** bench lathe
Drehmaschine *f* **mit Drehscheibe** turnable lathe
Drehmaschine *f* **mit flachem Revolvertisch** flat turret lathe
Drehmaschine *f* **mit gekröpftem Bett** gap lathe
Drehmaschine *f* **mit Getriebespindelkasten** geared head lathe
Drehmaschine *f* **mit Hebelschaltung** lever-controlled lathe
Drehmaschine *f* **mit Räderspindelkasten** geared head lathe
Drehmaschine *f* **mit Rädervorgelege** geared lathe
Drehmaschine *f* **mit Sattelrevolver** capstan lathe, ram type turret lathe, turret lathe
Drehmaschine *f* **mit Schrägrevolverkopf** tilted turret lathe
Drehmaschine *f* **mit veränderlicher Spitzenhöhe** quick change swing lathe
Drehmaschine *f* **mit Zweibahnbett** lathe with double track bed
Drehmaschinenbett *nt* lathe bed
Drehmaschinenleitspindel *f* lathe lead-screw
Drehmaschinenreitstock *m* lathe tailstock

Drehmaschinenschlossplatte *f* lathe apron
Drehmaschinenspindel *f* work spindle, main spindle, headstock spindle
Drehmaschinensupport *m* lathe carriage, lathe rest, lathe steady
Drehmeißel *m* lathe cutting tool, lathe tool, turning tool, cutting tool for lathe work
Drehmeißelhalter *m* lathe (or turning) tool holder
Drehmeißelschaft *m* turning (or cutting) tool shank
Drehmeißelstandzeit *f* turning tool life
Drehmoment *nt* torque, engine torque
Drehmomentbegrenzung *f* torque limitation
Drehmomentenerzeugung *f* torque generation
Drehmomentenkurve *f* torque characteristic
Drehmomentenschlüssel *m* torque spanner
Drehmomentensensor *m* torque sensor
Drehmomentenstütze *f* torque (reaction) arm
Drehmomentenverlauf *m* torque characteristic
Drehmomentenwandler *m* torque converter
Drehmomentmessgerät *nt* torque measuring device
Drehmomentprüfung *f* torque testing
Drehmotor *m* torque motor
Drehplatte *f* swivel plate
Drehpol *m* centre of rotation
Drehpunkt *m* pivoting point, pivot, fulcrum
Drehregal *nt* carousel, rotary unit
Drehrichtung *f* **1.** *(allg.)* direction of rotation, sense of rotation, hand of rotation, phase sequence **2.** *(entgegengesetzte)* lefthand rotation
Drehrichtungsumkehr *f* **1.** *(mechanisch)* inversion of direction of rotation **2.** *(el.)* phase sequence change-over, phase sequence reversal, inversion
Drehriefe *f* tool mark, drag mark

Drehschablone *f* strickle tackle
Drehschalter *m* rotary switch
Drehscheibe *f* swivel
Drehschemel *m* turntable
Drehschemelachse *f* turntable axle
Drehschemelräder *ntpl* bogie wheels
Drehschubgabel *f* pivoting shuttle fork
Drehschubgelenk *nt* cylindrical joint
Drehschubglied *nt* output link
Drehschubkurbel *f* turn-slide crank
Drehschwingung *f* torsional vibration
Drehsinnwechsel *m* change in direction of rotation
Drehspäne turnings *pl*
Drehspiegel *m* rotating mirror
Drehspindel *f* lathe (or headstock or main or work) spindle
Drehspindelachse *f* lathe spindle axis
Drehspitze *f* *(UK)* lathe centre, *(US)* machine tool center, turning centre, centre
Drehstab *m* torsion bar
Drehstahl *m* lathe cutting tool, lathe tool, turning tool, cutting tool for lathe work
drehstarr torsion-proof
Drehstation *f* rotary station
Drehstellung *f* angular position
Drehstellungsabweichung *f* *(z. B. der Welle des Getriebezuges)* angular position variation
Drehstrom *m* three-phase a.c.
Drehstromanschluss *m* rotary current, three-phase current supply
Drehstromasynchronmotor *m* **mit Kurzschlussläufer** three-phase asynchronous motor with squirrel cage motor
drehstrombetätigt three-phase a.c. operated
Drehstrombetrieb *m* three-phase operation
Drehstromkurzschlussläufer *m* three-phase squirrel cage motor
Drehstromkurzschlussläufermotor *m* three-phase squirrel cage motor
Drehstrommotor *m* three-phase A. C. motor
Drehstromnetz *nt* three-phase system
Drehstromspeisung *f* three-phase cur-

Drehsupport — Dreigangschieberadgetriebe

rent feed
Drehsupport *m* swivel head
Drehteil *nt* **1.** *(allg.)* head swivel, rotating element **2.** *(e. Bettschlittens)* swivel base **3.** *(Fertigteil)* turned part, swivel **4.** *(Werkstück)* part to be turned
Drehteiluntersatz *m* swivel base
Drehteller *m* rotary plate, rotary table, turntable
Drehtellerpalettenstretchwickler *m* rotating pallet stretchwrapper
Drehtiefe *f* turning tool mark, depth of cut
Drehtisch *m* revolving table, rotary table, turntable
Drehtischfräsmaschine *f* rotary milling machine
Drehung *f* rotation, turning, revolution, gyration, twist
Drehverlappen *nt* lock forming by twisting
Drehverteiler *m* rotary distributor
Drehvollautomat *m* fully automatic lathe
Drehvorrichtung *f* turning attachment
Drehweg *m* *(e. Schlittens)* turning travel
Drehwerk *nt* face-plate lathe, rotation gear
Drehwerk *nt* **mit doppeltem Ständer** vertical turning and boring mill
Drehwerk *nt* **mit einfachem Ständer** vertical turret lathe
Drehwerkzeug *nt* lathe (or turning) tool
Drehwinkel *m* angle of tilt
Drehwinkelabweichung *f* variation in the angle of rotation
Drehzahl *f* speed, revolution, number of revolutions, revolutions per minute, rotational speed, speed of rotation
Drehzahländerung *f* **1.** *(allg.)* speed change **2.** *(stufenlose ~)* infinitely variable speed change
Drehzahlanzeiger *m* tachometer
Drehzahlbereich *m* speed range
Drehzahleinstellung *f* speed setting, speed regulation, speed adjustment
Drehzahlenreihe *f* speed range

Drehzahlkonstanz *f* speed constancy
Drehzahlregelung *f* speed control
Drehzahlstellbereich *m* range of speeds
Drehzahlsteuerung *f* speed regulation
Drehzahlstufe *f* speed increment
Drehzahltreppe *f* variation of speed range
drehzahlveränderbarer Antrieb *m* variable speed drive
Drehzahlverhältnis *nt* speed ratio
Drehzahlvorschubwähler *m* speed and feed selector
Drehzahlwächter *m* speed monitor
Drehzahlwechsel *m* speed change
Drehzahn *m* tool bit
Drehzapfen *m* pivot
Drehzentrum *nt* turning centre
drei mal vier Bit Lesespeicher read only memory
Dreibackenfutter *nt* three-jaw chuck
Dreibahnenbett *nt* multiple-track bed
Dreibein *nt* tripod
Dreibereichsverfahren *nt* tristimulus method
Drei-Birnen-Kühler *m* three-bulb condenser
Drei-C Bild *nt* C-scope presentation
dreidimensional nachformen duplicate in three dimensions
dreidimensionale Wärmeableitung *f* three-dimensional heat dissipation
dreidimensionales Fräsen *nt* pocketing
Dreidraht-Messmethode *f* three wire measurement
Dreieck *nt* triangle
dreieckig triangular
Dreieckraster *nt* triangular grid
Dreieckschaltung *f* triangle connection, delta connection
Dreiecksmessung *f* triangulation
Dreieckverfahren *nt* triangle method
dreifach triple
Dreifache, das ~ *nt* three times the...
dreifaches Teilgerät *nt* triple index centres
Dreifachhubgerüst *nt* triple mast
Dreiganggetriebe *nt* three-speed gears
Dreigangschieberadgetriebe *nt*

three-speed sliding gear drive
Dreihundert-Grad-Versprödung
300-degree-embrittlement
Dreikantfeile *f* three-cornered file, triangular file
Dreikantmutter *f* triangular nut
Dreikantschaber *m* triangular scraper
Dreikantschraube *f* triangular screw
Dreikant-Steckschlüssel *m* triangular socket key
Dreilaschenfaltschachtelverschließmaschine *f* three flap carton closing machine
Dreipunktbeanspruchung *f* three-point loading
Dreipunktsignal *nt* three-level signal
Dreirad *nt* three-wheeled, three-wheel...
Dreiradstapler *m* three-wheel truck
dreireihig three-row, triple-row
Dreischichtbetrieb *m* three-shift operation, three-shift working
Dreischichtplatte *f* three-layer slab
Dreiseitenstapelanbaugerät *nt* lateral and front attachment
Dreiseitenstapler *m* lateral and front stacking truck
dreiseitig trilateral
dreiseitiges Stapeln *nt* three-way stacking
Dreispindelfräsmaschine *f* three-spindle (or triplex) milling machine, triplex milling machine
Dreispindelplanfräsmaschine *f* three-spindle fixed-bed type milling machine, triplex manufacturing-type milling machine (or miller), *(UK)* three spindle bench-type milling machine
Dreispindeltrommelfräsmaschine *f* three-spindle drum-type milling machine
dreispindlige Vertikalfräseinheit *f* three-spindle vertical milling unit
Dreistoffhartlot *nt* ternary brazing alloy (or hard solder)
dreistufig three-stage, three-step
dreistufiges Getriebe *nt* three-stage gear transmission
Drei-Uhr-Lage *f* three-o'clock position
Dreiwegedampfumformventil *nt* thee-way steam converting valve
Dreiwegedruckminderventil *nt* three-way pressure reducing valve
Dreiwegehahn *m* three-way cock
Dreiwegeküken *nt* three-way plug
Dreizustandsausgang *m* tristate, tristate output
Drilldrahtelektrode *f* stranded wire electrode
drillen twist
Drillstab *m* stranded rod
Drillverschließmaschine *f* twist-die closing machine
Dringlichkeit *f* urgency
dritte Potenz *f* third power
Dritter/Dritte third party
drohende Gefahr *f* imminent hazard
Dröhnen *nt* drumming noise
Drop-on-demand-Tintenstrahlcodierer *m* drop on demand ink jet coder
Drossel *f* choke, reactance coil, reactor
Drosselanlage *f* restrictor system
Drosselblende *f* orifice plate
Drosseldurchgangsventil *nt* straight-way throttling valve
Drosselklappe *f* throttle valve
drosseln restrict, throttle, choke, obstruct
Drosselorgan *nt* flue damper
Drosselsystem *nt* restrictor principle of operation (centr. lubr. syst.)
Drosselung *f* slowdown, retardation, restriction
Drosselventil *nt* restrictor valve, throttling valve
Drosselverteiler *m* metering device with restrictors
Druck ausgleichen compensate pressure
Druck ausüben impart pressure
Druck ausüben auf expert pressure on
Druck *m* **1.** *(allg.)* pressure **2.** *(axialer Längsdruck)* thrust **3.** *(Betätigungsdruck)* push **4.** *(Kompressionsdruck)* compression **5.** *(Lastdruck)* load, weight
Druckabfall *m* pressure drop
Druckabfallprüfung *f* pressure drop test
Druckabfallzeit *f* pressure drop time

druckabhängig by hydraulic device
Druckabsenkung *f* pressure drop
Druckanstieg *m* rise in pressure
Druckanstiegskoeffizient *m* coefficient of pressure increase
Druckanstiegszeit *f* pressure rise time
Druckanzeige *f* pressure indication, pressure reading
Druckaufbau *m* (in d. Hauptleitung e. Zentralschmieranlage) pressure built-up
Druckausdehnungsgefäß *nt* pressurized expansion tank
Druckausfall *m* pressure loss
Druckausgabe *f* print-out
Druckausgleich *m* pressure compensation
Druckausgleichsvorgang *m* pressure compensation operation
Druckbeanspruchung *f* compensation stress
Druckbeaufschlagung *f* pressurization
Druckbegrenzer *m* pressure relief valve
Druckbegrenzung *f* pressure control
Druckbegrenzungseinrichtung *f* pressure limiting device
Druckbegrenzungsventil *nt* pressure limiting device (or valve), pressure relief valve
Druckbehälter *m* pressure tank, pressure vessel
Druckbehälterverordnung *f* statutory order on pressure vessels
druckbelastet compression-loaded
Druckbereich *m* pressure range
Druck-Beschleunigungsgrad *m* pressure acceleration impulse
druckbetätigt pressure operated
Druckbild *nt* print format
Druckbrandofen *m* through-burning stove
Druckbügel *m* compression proving ring
druckdicht pressure-tight
druckdicht (von Annietmuttern) pressure-tight
Druckdifferenz *f* pressure difference
Druckdifferenzmesseinrichtung *f* differential pressure measuring device

Druckdüse *f* pressure jet
Druckeinstellschraube *f* pressure adjusting screw
Druckeinstellung *f* pressure setting
Druckeinstellvorrichtung *f* pressure adjusting device
druckempfindlich pressure-sensitive
druckempfindliche Matte *f* pressure sensitive mat, sensor mat
drucken print
drücken 1. (allg.) press (against), push, force 2. (Fräserzahn auf Arbeitsstück) scrape (over the work) 3. (Gewinde) roll 4. (Hohlgefäße) spin 5. (nieder ~ z. B. Knopf) press, depress 6. (Puffer) compress 7. (Werkzeugschneide an der Freifläche) drag
drücken gegen press against
Drücken *nt* **eines Blechzuschnittes zu einem Hohlkörper** spinning
Drücken *nt* **von Außenborden** spinning of external flanges
Drücken *nt* **von Hohlkörpern** spinning of hallow items
Drücken *nt* **von Innenborden** spinning of inside beads
druckende Rechenmaschine *f* printing calculator
Druckentlastung *f* depressurizing
Drucker *m* printing apparatus, printer
Druckfeder *f* pressure spring
druckfest 1. (allg.) compression-proof, pressure proof 2. (Explosionsschutz) flameproof
druckfeste Kapselung *f* flameproof enclosure
Druckfestigkeit *f* **bei Raumtemperatur** cold crushing strength
Druckflüssigkeit *f* hydraulic medium
druckführende Leitung *f* pressurized pipeline
Druckgasflasche *f* pressurized gas cylinder
Druckgebläse *nt* forced draft fan
druckgeschmiert pressure-lubricated
druckgesteuert pressure-controlled, pressure-responsive
druckgießen pressure die cast
Druckgießen *nt* pressure die casting, pressure casting process

Druckgießverfahren *nt* pressure die casting process
Druckguss *m* die cast, die casting
Druckgussform *f* die cast form
Druckgusslegierung *f* die casting alloy
Druckhaltepumpe *f* pressure maintaining pump
Druckhöhe *f* pressure head
Druckkammer *f* pressure chamber
Druckkammeralterung *f* pressure chamber ageing
Druckklammer *f* squeeze clamp (attachment)
Druckknopf *m* push-button
druckknopfbetätigt push-button-actuated, push-button-operated
Druckknopfschalter *m* push-button switch
Druckknopfschaltung *f* push-button control
Druckknopfsteuerung *f* push (or press) button control
Druckknopftafel *f* push-button panel
Druckknopftaster *m* push-button station
Druckkraft *f* compression force, thrust force
Druckzone *f* **aufgebogen** compression zone bent outwards
Drucklager *nt* spigot, thrust bearing
Druckleiste *f* pressure strip
drucklos messen measure without exerting pressure
drucklose Abwasserleitung *f* pressureless drainage system
drucklose Lagerung *f* unpressurized storage
drucklose Umlaufschmierung *f* pressureless circulatory lubrication
drucklose Zeitspanne *f* pressureless interval
druckloser Behälter *m* unpressurized tank
Druckluft *f* compressed air
Druckluftanlage *f* pneumatic system (or equipment)
Druckluftbehälter *m* pressure vessel
druckluftbetätigt pneumatically actuated, pneumatically operated, air-actuated, air-operated
Druckluft-Druckminderer *m* compressed air regulator
Druckluftförderung *f* pneumatic conveying
Druckluft-Kleinbohrmaschine *f* air-power drill
Druckluftleitung *f* compressed-air line
Druckluftprinzip *nt* compressed air principle
Druckluftschaltplan *m* compressed air system plan
Druckluftspannung *f* pneumatic chucking
Druckluft-Spritzgießmaschine *f* pneumatically driven injection moulding machine
Druckluftstrahlen *nt* compressed air blasting
Druckmessgerät *nt* pressure measuring device
Druckmesskörper *m* compression proving element
Druckmessstutzen *m* pressure measurement nozzle
Druckmessverfahren *nt* measuring chamber pressure
Druckminderdurchgangsventil *nt* straight-way pressure reducing valve
Druckmindereckventil *nt* angle pressure reducing valve
Druckminderer *m* pressure reducer, pressure reducing valve
Druckmindereranschluss *m* pressure regulator connection
Druckminderung *f* depression
Druckminderventil *nt* pressure reducing valve
Druckmittel *nt* *(beim hydraulischen Lösen eines Pressverbandes)* pressurizing medium
Druckmittelspannung *f* mean compressive stress
Druckölverband *m* pressurized oil assembly
Druckreduzierer *m* pressure reducer
Druckregelventil *nt* pressure control valve
Druckregler *m* pressure regulator
Druckschalter *m* pressure switch
Druckscherversuch *m* compression

shear test
druckschmieren force-lubricate
Druckschmiergerät *nt* pressure lubricant device
Druckschmierpresse *f* grease gun
Druckschmierung *f* force-feed lubrication, forced lubrication
Druckschwelle *f* pressure threshold
Drucksignal *nt* pressure signal
Druck-Sollwertsteller *m* pressure set point setter
Druckspannung *f* compression stress
Druckspannungsbruch *m* compressive failure
Druckspannung-Stauchungs-Kurve *f* compressive stress-strain curve
Druckspannungszustand *m* state of compressive stress
Druckspeicher *m* hydraulic accumulator
Druckspülung *f* pressure douche
Druckstab *m* strut
Drucksteigerung *f* rise in pressure
Druckstelle *f* drag mark
Druckstempel *m* die
Drucksteuerung *f* pressure control
Druckstockzeichnung *f* block drawing
Druckstoß *m* shock wave effect, pressure impulse
Druckstoßarbeiten *fpl* total penetration energy
Druckstrahlläppen *nt* liquid honing
Druckstück *nt* thrust member
Drucktaste *f* press key (or button), push button
drucktragendes Armaturenteil *nt* pressure bearing valve part
Druckübertragungsmittel *nt* pressure transfer medium
Druckumformen *nt* compressive reforming
Druckumlaufschmierung *f* forced-feed circulatory lubrication
Druckventil *nt* discharge valve
Druckverfahren *nt* printing technique
Druckverformungsrest *m* residual deformation on compression, compressive set
Druckverlust *m* loss of head
Druckvermerk *m* notation

Druckvorbeanspruchung *f* compressive preloading
Druckvorlage *f* master drawing, photomaster
Druckvorwärmer *m* pressurized preheater
Druckvorwärmung *f* pressurized preheating
Druckwächter *m* pressure detector, shock wave
Drückwalzen *nt* roller spinning
Drückwalzen *nt* über kegeligen Dorn roller spinning over conical mandrel
Drückwalzen *nt* über zylindrischen Dorn roller spinning over cylindrical mandrel
Druckwasserbehälter *m* pressurized water container
Druckwasserstrahlen *nt* hydraulic blasting
Druckwelle *f* pressure wave
Druckwellenschalter *m* pressure switch
Druckzapfen *m* (e. Gewindestiftes) thrust point
D-Schraub-Passeinsatz *m* screw-in gauge ring for D-fuses
Dualsystem *nt* dual system
Dübel *m* peg, dowel, plug
dübeln peg, dowel, plug
DÜE nicht bereit DCE not ready
DÜE Rückleiter *m* DCE common return
DÜE-Information *f* DCE provided information
DU-Fuge *f* double-U butt weld
dunkel dark
Dunkelfärbung *f* darkening of colour
Dunkelfläche *f* dark field
Dunkelschaltung *f* dark switching
dünn thin
Dünnblech *nt* thin sheet metal
Dünnfilmreibung *f* thin-film friction
Dünnfilmtechnologie *f* thin-film technology
dünnschichtchromatographisches Verfahren *nt* thin-layer chromatographic method
dünnwandig thin walled
Duogerüst *nt* two-high stand

Duoreversierwalzwerk *nt* two-high reversing mill
Duowalzgerüst *nt* two-high stand
Duowalzwerk *nt* duo mill, two-high mill
Duplexausführung *f* duplex version
Duplexbetrieb *m* duplex mode
durch Fremdbezug beschaffen outsource
durch mitgehende Person *f* **gesteuert** pedestrian-controlled
durch Reibung *f* frictional
durchbiegen sag, deflect
Durchbiegen *nt* deflection
Durchbiegung *f* bending, deflection, deformation, stagging
durchbohren through-drill, pierce
durchbrechen break through, flow (fuse), burn out
durchbrennen burn out
Durchbruchspannung *f* dielectric strength breakdown voltage
Durchbruchsplan *m* penetration plan
Durchbruchspotential *nt* breakdown potential
durchdringen permeate, penetrate
Durchdringung *f* inter-penetrating feature, penetration
Durchdringungsintensität *f* penetration intensity
Durchdrücken *nt* extruding
Durchdrückknopf *m* push-through button
durchfahren im Eilgang *m* rapid-traverse
Durchfahrregal *nt* drive-through pallet racking
Durchfahrt *f* passage
durchfallen drop through, pass through
durchfedern spring
Durchfederung *f* deflection, spring
durchfließen *(Strom, Flüssigkeit)* pass, flow through
Durchfluss *m* flow
Durchflussbegrenzer *m* flow limiter
Durchflussbrauchwassererwärmer *m* instantaneous type service water heater
Durchflussmedium *nt* low medium
Durchflussmenge *f* flow quantity

Durchflussmessgerät *nt* flow measuring device
Durchflussmessquerschnitt *m* discharge measuring cross section
Durchflussmessregel *f* flow measuring rule
Durchflussmessung *f* flow measurement
Durchflussrichtung *f* direction of flow
Durchflussstoff *m* flow medium
Durchflussstoffkennzeichnung *f* flow medium marking
Durchflussvolumen *nt* flow volume
Durchflusswassererwärmer *m* instantaneous water heater
Durchflusswiderstand *m* *(im Drosselsystem e. Zentralschmieranlage)* flow restrictor
Durchflusszeit *f* flow time
Durchflutung *f* *(el.)* ampere turns, ampere windings
Durchflutungsgerät *nt* magnetic crack detection appliance
durchführbar feasible, practicable
Durchführbarkeit *f* feasibility, practicability
durchführen 1. *(allg.)* accomplish, carry out, execute, perform, practice **2.** *(Versuche)* run, conduct
Durchführung *f* **1.** *(allg.)* implementation, execution, conduct **2.** *(e. Verfahrens)* procedure **3.** *(e. Versuches)* conductance **4.** *(el.)* brushing
Durchführung *f* **gleicher Teilungen** uniform indexing
Durchführungstermin *m* execution deadline
Durchführungszeit *f* execution time
Durchgang haben pass (through)
Durchgang *m* pass, passage, throat, opening between the housing, space, sagging, deflection
durchgängige Verbindung *f* continuity
Durchgangsarmatur *f* straightway valve
Durchgangsbohrung *f* throughhole
Durchgangshöhe *f* headway
Durchgangsloch *nt* **1.** *(als Grundloch)* clearance hole **2.** *(voll durchgehendes*

Loch) throughhole
Durchgangsrückschlagventil *nt* straight check valve with shut-off feature
Durchgangsschleifen *nt* complete traverse thread grinding, through-feed grinding
Durchgangsschraube *f* bolt
durchgebrannter Schweißpunkt *m* burnt-through weld spot
durchgehen pass (through)
durchgehend continuous
durchgehende Bohrung *f* throughhole
durchgehende Hauptleitung *f* through-going mains
durchgehende Kolbenstange *f* through piston rod
durchgehende Pore *f* through-going pore
durchgehender Riss *m* through-going crack
durchgeschweißte V-Naht *f* through-welded single-V butt joint
durchgeschweißte V-Naht *f* **mit Gegenlage** through-welded single-V butt joint with backing run
durchgeschweißter Stumpfstoß *m* through-welded butt joint
durchgreifend erwärmen heat completely through
Durchhang *m* dip, sag
durchhängen sag, dip
durchkonstruiert well-designed
Durchlass *m* passage
durchlassen 1. *(techn.)* pass (through), transmit **2.** *(zulassen)* admit
durchlässig permeable
durchlässige Folie *f* transmissible film
Durchlässigkeitsgrad *m* transmittance factor
Durchlassrichtung *f* passing direction
Durchlassstrahlung *f* leakage radiation
Durchlauf *m* **1.** *(Betrieb)* pass-through **2.** *(Maschinen Prozesse)* continuous operation **3.** *(Programm)* run
Durchlaufbetrieb *m* pass-through mode
durchlaufen cross, pass (or flow or travel) through, run, traverse, to be passed through
Durchlauferhitzer *m* instantaneous water heater
Durchlauffräsmaschine *f* continuous milling machine
Durchlaufgaswassererhitzer *m* instantaneous gas water heater
Durchlauflager *nt* flow storage, dynamic storage
Durchlauflagerung *f* dynamic storage
Durchlaufmessung *f* profile check of loads in movement, checking the load whilst moving
Durchlaufregal *nt* dynamic racking, dynamic shelving, flow rack
Durchlaufregallager *nt* flow rack storage, dynamic rack storage
Durchlaufschleifen *nt* through-feed grinding
Durchlaufschmierung *f* once-through lubrication
Durchlaufstrahlanlage *f* continuous feed blasting plant
Durchlaufterminplanung *f* running schedule
Durchlaufverfahren *nt* continuous-type method
Durchlaufverzögerung *f* run deceleration
Durchlaufvorwärmer *m* continuous-type preheater
Durchlaufwärmeerzeuger *m* through heating appliance
Durchlaufwassererhitzer *m* instantaneous water heater
Durchlaufzeit *f* machining time, turnaround time, lead time, throughput time, run time
Durchleuchtungsarbeitsplatz *m* fluoroscopist's working position
Durchleuchtungsdauer *f* fluoroscopy time
Durchleuchtungseinrichtung *f* fluoroscopy equipment
Durchleuchtungsnennspannung *f* rated voltage for fluoroscopy
Durchlicht *nt* transmitted light
durchlochen punch, pierce (throughholes)

Durchlüftung *f* aeration, ventilation
Durchmesser *m* diameter
durchmesserabhängig diameter-dependent
Durchmesserausgleichsbetrag *m* sum of the diametral equivalent
durchmesserbezogene Toleranz *f* diameter-related tolerance
Durchmessermaß *nt* diameter (or diametral) dimension
Durchmesserreihe *f* diameter series
Durchmessersteigungskombination *f* diameter/pitch combination
Durchmesserzeichen *nt* diameter symbol
durchqueren cross
Durchreißarbeit *f* tear resistance
Durchreißen *nt* tearing through
Durchreißfaktor *m* tear factor
Durchreißkraft *f* tearing force
Durchreißversuch *m* tearing resistance test
Durchreißwiderstand *m* tearing resistance
Durchriss *m* crack, trough-crack
Durchrutschregal *nt* slide type racking
Durchsatz *m* throughput
Durchsatzbetrachtung *f* throughput analysis
Durchsatzermittlung *f* throughput calculation
Durchsatznachweis *m* throughput verification, proof of throughput
durchschallen scan (by sound)
durchschalten pull up
Durchschlag *m* **1.** *(allg.)* breakdown, puncture **2.** *(Flüssigkeit)* leakage **3.** *(Isolierung)* rupture
durchschlagen break down, punch, puncture
Durchschlagfeldstärke *f* dielectric strength
Durchschlagfestigkeit *f* dielectric breakdown strength
Durchschlagsicherung *f* blow-cut fuse
Durchschlagspannung *f* breakdown voltage
Durchschlagwinkel *m* overshoot angle
durchschleifen cut off (by abrasive cutting)

Durchschnitt *m* average, mean, intersection
durchschnittlich average, mean
Durchschnittsprobe *f* average sample
Durchschnittswert *m* average value
Durchschubsicherung *f* compartment end stop, back stop
durchschusshemmende Eigenschaft *f* resistance against penetration by bullets
Durchschwingen *nt* full swing
Durchsetzen *nt* *(Umformung)* partial displacement of the stock relative to adjacent parts
Durchsicht *f* *(Umformtechnik)* visibility
durchsichtig clear, transparent
durchsieben strain
durchspülen flush
durchstechen cut, hole, stab
Durchstich *m* pinhole
Durchstoß *m* through-crack, penetration
Durchstoßarbeit *f* puncturing energy
durchstoßen pierce, punch, push through, penetrate
Durchstoßkörper *m* penetrator
Durchstoßversuch *m* penetration test, puncture test
Durchstoßweg *m* penetration path
durchstrahlter Stoff *m* transirradiated material
Durchstrahlung *f* radiography, radiographing
Durchstrahlungsaufnahme *f* radiograph
Durchstrahlungsleistung *f* radiographic performance
Durchstrahlungsprüfung *f* radiographic test
Durchströmung *f* seepage
Durchtränkung *f* impregnation
Durchtritt *m* *(z. B. von Elektronen)* passage
Durchtrittsüberspannung *f* penetration overvoltage
Durchtrittswiderstand *m* penetration resistance
Durchvergütbarkeit *f* through-heat treatability
Durchwälzen *nt* generating

durchwärmen heat through
Durchwärmtemperatur *f* soaking temperature
Durchwärmzeit *f* soaking time
durchweichen soak
Durchwölbung *f* curvature through
durchziehen push through, plunge
durchziehen einer Linie draw as continuous line
Durchziehen *nt (Umformtechnik)* drawing under combined tension and compression
Durchziehrichtung *f* direction of plunging
durchzogene Maßlinie *f* continuous dimension line
Durchzug *m* rim hole
Durchzug *m* **erhöht** raised rim hole
Durchzug *m* **vertieft** recessed rim hole
Durchzughöhe *f (e. Blechdurchzuges)* rim hole height
Durchzugkraft *f* cutting force (or capacity)
Durchzugleser *m* push-through reader
Durchzugprobe *f* draw-through sample
Durchzugskraft *f* pulling power, table pull
Durchzugverhältnis *nt* rim hole height ratio
Durchzünden *nt* through ignition
Duromer *nt* duromer
Duroplastformmasse *f* thermosetting moulding material
Düse *f* nozzle, jet, tip, orifice
Düsenabstand *m* nozzle distance
Düsenanstellwinkel *m* nozzle setting angle
Düsenbrenner *m* open-flame burner
Düsendurchmesser *m* nozzle diameter
Düsenschweißen *nt* orifice welding
DVM-Flachkerbprobe *f* DVM wide notch specimen
DVM-Kleinkerbprobe *f* DVM shallow notch specimen
DV-Naht *f* double-V butt weld
DV-System *nt* computer processing system
DV-Zentrale *f* data processing centre
DXF *Abk* Data Exchange Format
DY-Naht *f* double-V butt weld with broad root face
Dynamik *f* dynamics
dynamische Belastung *f* dynamic load (or loading)
dynamische Dichtung *f* dynamic seal
dynamische Längsstabilität *f* longitudinal dynamic stability
dynamische Steifheit *f* dynamic stiffness
dynamischer Dehnmodul *nt* dynamic modulus of elasticity
dynamischer Eingang *m* dynamic input
dynamischer Kraftmesser *m* dynamometer
dynamischer Modul *nt* dynamic modulus
dynamisches Schubmodul *nt* dynamic modulus of shear
dynamisches Verhalten *nt* dynamic behaviour

E

E/A-Anschluss *m* I/O port
E/A-Kanal *m* I/O channel
E/A-Station *f* I/O station
E/A-Versorgungsanschluss *m* I/O power port
eben even, flat, plane, smooth, planar, level
Ebenbild *nt* replica
Ebene *f* plane
ebene Fläche *f* flat surface, plane surface
ebene Skale *f* plane scale
Ebenen *fpl* **im Werkzeugbezugssystem** planes (pl) in the tool-in-hand system
Ebenen *fpl* **im Wirkbezugssystem** planes (pl) in the tool-in-use system
Ebenenführung *f* plane guidance
Ebenenführungsgetriebe *nt* plane guidance mechanism
Ebenenlage *f* plane position
Ebenenparallelführung *f* parallel-plane guidance
ebener Winkel *m* plane angle
ebenes Getriebe *nt* plane gear transmission
Ebenheit *f* evenness, flatness, smoothness, planeness, levelness
Ebenheitsabweichung *f* flatness deviation
Ebenheitstoleranz *f* flatness tolerance, level tolerance
ebnen flatten, planish, smooth
Echoanzeige *f* echo indication
Echogebirge *nt* echo cluster
Echohöhe *f* echo height
Echohöhenverhältnis *nt* echo height ratio
Echoseite *f* echo side
Echtbetrieb *m* real operation, normal operation, practical operation
Echtzeit *f* real time
Echtzeitbetriebssystem *nt* real-time operating system
Echtzeitdatenbasis *f* real-time data base
Echtzeitsystem *nt* real-time system
Echtzeituhr *f* real-time clock
Echtzeitverarbeitung *f* real time processing, on-line processing
Eckbauventil *nt* angle pattern valve
Eckbohrmeißel *m* boring tool for corner work
Eckdaten *pl* key data, benchmark figures
Ecke *f* corner
ecken jam
Eckenabstumpfung *f* dulling
Eckenbohrmaschine *f* corner drilling machine
Eckenbremsen *nt* corner-deceleration
Eckenfase *f* chamfered corner (length), corner chamfer
Eckenmaß *nt* distance (or width) across corners
Eckenmeißel *m* bent finishing tool
Eckenradius *m* corner radius
Eckenrunden *nt* undershoot, corner rounding (or radiusing)
Eckenrundung *f* corner radiusing, corner roundness, rounded (or radiused) corner, corner radius
Eckenwinkel *m* (US) included cutting, (UK) edge angle, included plan angle
eckig angular, cornered
Ecknahtprüfstück *nt* corner weld test piece
Eckpunkt *m* corner point
Eckschweißung *f* angle weld
Ecksieb *nt* angle screen
Eckstahl *m:* **gebogener ~** finishing tool (or cutter)
Eckstoß *m* (Plattenverbindung) corner joint
Eckumsetzer *m* cross corner
Eckverbindung *f* corner fitting
Edelgasdruckminderer *m* shielding gas regulator
Edelgaslichtbogenschweißen *nt* inert-gas arc welding
Edelgasventil *nt* rare gas valve
Edelkorund *m* noble (or special or high-

quality) corundum
Edelmetall *nt* noble metal, precious metal
Edelpressspan *m* high-quality laminated fibre material
Edelstahl *m* high-quality steel, special steel, stainless steel
Editing *nt* program edit
EDV-System *nt* data processing system
EDV-technische Anpassung *f* data system adjusted application
effektiv effective
Effektivausbringung *f* effective output
effektiver Durchsatz *m* effective throughput
effektiver Welligkeitsgehalt *m* root mean square ripple factor
Effektivwert *m* root mean square value
Egalisiermittel *nt* levelling agent
Eichamtswaage *f* balance approved by the Official Department for Weights and Measures
Eichblock *m* calibration block
eichen (official) calibrate, measure, *(US)* gage, *(UK)* gauge
eichfähig calibratable
Eichfehlergrenze *f* verification limit of error
Eichflüssigkeit *f* calibrating solution
Eichkurve *f* calibration curve
Eichmaß *nt* gage *(US)*, gauge *(UK)*
Eichordnung *f* ordinance on weights and measures, calibration regulations
Eichstempel *m* calibration stamp, verification mark
Eichung *f* calibration block
Eigenauftrag *m* self order
Eigenfertigung *f* self production
Eigenfertigungsplanung *f* self production planning
Eigenfertigungssteuerung *f* self production control
Eigenfilter *m* self-filter
Eigenfrequenz *f* natural frequency
Eigengewicht *nt* unladen weight
Eigenheit *f* feature
Eigenkontrolle *f* self-checking
Eigenlast *f* dead load, deadweight
Eigenlastbeiwert *m* deadweight coefficient

Eigenleistung *f* internal performance
Eigenmaß *nt* own dimension
Eigenmerkmal *nt* natural characteristic
Eigenreflexionsfaktor *m* inherent reflectance factor
Eigenschaft *f* property
Eigenschaftsgrenzwert *m* property threshold value
Eigenschaftsprüfung *f* determination of properties
Eigenschwingung *f* natural frequency, pl.: self-induced vibrations
Eigenschwingzeit *f* natural oscillating period
eigensicher intrinsically safe
eigensichere Anlage *f* intrinsically safe plant
eigensicherer Stromkreis *m* intrinsically safe circuit
Eigensicherheit *f* intrinsic safety
Eigenspannung *f* inherent stress
Eigenspannungszustand *m* inherent stress condition
Eigenstabilität *f* intrinsic stability
Eigensteife *f* rigidity
Eigensteifigkeit *f* stability, rigidity
Eigenteil *nt* intrinsic piece, part of inside origin
Eigenüberwachung *f* internal (quality) control
Eigenüberwachungsprüfung *f* self-monitoring check
Eigenverbrauch *m* friction loss
Eigenzeit *f* inherent delay
eignen (sich ~) suit, be adapted for
Eignung *f* 1. *(allg.)* suitability 2. *(Personal)* qualification
eignungsgeprüfter Schweißer *m* proof tested welder
Eignungsnachweis *m* verification of suitability
Eignungsprofil *nt* qualifications profile
Eignungsprüfung *f* qualification test, suitability test
Eilauftrag *m* express order, rush order
Eilbedarf *m* urgent requirement
Eilbestellung *f* urgent order
Eilbewegung *f* rapid traverse, quick travel
Eilgang *m* 1. *(allg.)* fast traverse, quick

traverse, **2.** *(e. Tisches)* rapid traverse (or travel) **3.** *(maschinell)* rapid power traverse
Eilgangantrieb *m* rapid-traverse drive
Eilganggeschwindigkeit *f* rate of rapid motion
Eilgangnockenscheibe *f* trip dog carrier for accelerator mechanism
Eilgangsprung *m* rapid traverse jump
Eilgangsteuerung *f* rapid traverse control
Eilgangumlauf *m* quick power rotation
Eilgangvorlauf *m* power forward traverse, rapid advance (or approach)
Eilgangwelle *f* rapid power traverse shaft
eilige Arbeit *f* rush job
Eilrückgang *m* rapid return traverse
Eilrücklauf *m* rapid idle movement, quick return, quick reverse (or traverse), rapid return
Eilvorlauf *m* rapid approach, power forward traverse, rapid advance
Eilvorschub *m* rapid traverse rate of feed
Eilwälzung *f* rapid rotary motion
Eimer *m* bucket, pail
ein *(Schalterstellung)* on
ein Angebot unterbreiten tender
ein Ganzes mit integral with
Ein- und Ausfahren *nt* entering and leaving, extension and retraction
Ein- und Ausgangsgröße *f* input and output variable
Ein- und Auslagern *nt* input and output, storage and retrieval
Ein- und Auslauf *m* entry and exit
Ein- und Auslaufstelle *f* entry and exit point, infeed and outfeed location
einachsig single-axle
einachsig faserverstärkt uniaxial-fibre-reinforced
einachsige Beanspruchung auf Zug uniaxial tensile loading
einachsige Druckbeanspruchung *f* uniaxial compression load
einachsiger Spannungszustand *m* uniaxial stress condition
einachsiger faserverstärkter Kunststoff *m* uniaxial-fibre-reinforced plastics
einander anpassen fit to one another
Einatmen *nt* inhalation
EIN-AUS Funktion *f* start/stop function
Ein-Aus-Druckknopfschalter *m* On-Off push button switch
Einbahnverkehr *m* single-lane traffic, single-lane conveyance
Einbau *m* **1.** *(e. Bauteils)* installation, incorporation, **2.** *(Einpassen)* fitting, **3.** *(allg.)* assembly, mounting
Einbau *m* **auf Achsstummel** stub axle mounting
Einbau *m* **in einer Gabel** fork mounting
Einbauanlage *f* installation position
Einbauanweisung *f* installation instruction
Einbaubrenner *m* built-in burner
einbauen assemble, build, fit in(to), include, incorporate, insert, install, mount, place
Einbauhinweis *m* installation instruction
Einbaulage *f* fitting position
Einbauleser *m* pull-in reader
Einbaumaß *nt* **1.** *(allg.)* fitting dimension, mounting distance, assembly dimension, apex to back distance **2.** *(für Werkzeuge)* tool-fitting dimension
Einbaumessschraube *f* built-in micrometer
Einbauort *m* mounting location
Einbauspiel *nt* assembly clearance
Einbauvorschrift *f* mounting (or assembly) instruction
Einbauzustand *m* assembled condition
einbeschreiben inscribe
einbetonieren embed in concrete
einbetten integrate, embed, surround
Einbettung *f* surround, surround material, integration
Einbettungsüberzug *m* embedding coating (electroplating)
einbeziehen involve, integrate
Einbindung *f* *(in e. System)* integration
Ein-Birnenkühler *m* single bulb condenser
Einblasung *f* injection
einblenden collimate

einbrennen burn in
Einbrennlack *m* baking enamel
Einbrennlötung *f* fused soldering
Einbrennphosphatierverfahren *nt* phosphating by stoving processes
Einbrennrückstand *m* baking residue
einbringen apply
Einbringleistung *f* weight of electrode deposited in unit time, deposition rate
Einbruchhemmung *f* burglar resistance
einbuchen book in, check in
Einbuchung *f* entry
eindeutig clearly, definitive, unambiguous, unequivocal
eindeutige Anzeige *f* clearcut indication
eindeutige Aufschrift *f* clear inscription
Eindeutigkeit *f* unequivocality
Eindickung *f* (Öl) bodying
eindiffundieren diffuse in
eindimensional one-dimensional, univariate
eindrehen flute into, turn a neck into
Eindrehung *f* recess, neck
eindringen penetrate, ingress, enter
Eindringen *nt* **von Fremdkörpern** penetration of foreign matter (or particles)
Eindringkörper *m* penetrator
Eindringmittel *nt* penetrant
Eindringrate *f* rate of penetration
Eindringtiefe *f* depth of penetration
Eindringtiefenmesseinrichtung *f* depth measuring device
Eindrücken *nt* indenting, impressing
Eindruckfläche *f* indentation area
Eindrückhärtecharakteristik *f* indentation hardness characteristic
Eindruckmesseinrichtung *f* indentation depth measuring device
Eindruckprüfgerät *nt* indentation tester
Eindruckschwellbereich *m* indentation/pulsation range
Eindrückung *f* indentation
Eindrückversuch *m* indentation hardness test
Eindrückwiderstand *m* resistance to indentation
eine Kurve *f* **fahren** negotiate a curve, turn, corner
eine Schnittstelle *f* **bilden** interface
Einebnung *f* levelling
einengen restrict, narrow, neck down
Einengung *f* contraction narrowing, necking down, restriction
Einerdung *f* *(von Rohrleitungen)* burying
Energieausfall *m* failure of power
Einerteilung *f* unity-based division
einfach simple, single, plain
einfach wirkend single-acting
Einfachabschneiden *nt* single-cropping
Einfachabzweig *m* single branch
Einfachanschnitt *m* single gate
Einfachbelichtung *f* single exposure
Einfachbiegen *nt* single bending
einfache Aufteilung *f* **von Probeeinheiten** oneway classification
einfache Fräsmaschine *f* plain milling machine
einfache Horizontalfräsmaschine *f* plain horizontal-type knee-and-column milling machine
einfache Hypothese *f* simple hypothesis
einfache Konsolfräsmaschine *f* plain-type knee-and-column milling machine
einfache Schicht *f* simple layer
einfacher Flankendurchmesser *m* simple pitch diameter
einfacher Meißelhalter *m* plain tool post
einfacher Teilkopf *m* direct indexing head, plain dividing head
einfaches Auftragen *nt* straightforward surfacing
einfaches Teilen *nt* simple indexing
einfaches Teilgerät *nt* plain index centre
Einfachfehler *m* single fault
Einfachfräsmaschine *f* plain milling machine (with horizontal spindle)
Einfachhohlkehle *f* single round corner
Einfach-Horizontalfräsmaschine *f* plain horizontal-type knee-and-column

milling machine
Einfachlangfräsmaschine *f* plain horizontal (or open-sided) plano-miller
Einfachlastaufnahme *f* **1.** *(Vorgang)* single load capacity **2.** *(Vorrichtung)* single load-carrying device
Einfachmaschine *f* single-purpose machine
Einfachmeißelhalter *m* plain (or single) toolholder
Einfachregal *nt* single-sided run
Einfachspiel *nt* single cycle
Einfachständerfräsmaschine *f* plain knee-and-column type milling machine
Einfachstation *f* simple station
Einfachteilen *nt* plain (or simple) indexing
einfachtief single deep, single depth
Einfachwaagerechtfräsmaschine *f* plain horizontal milling machine
Einfachwechselstation *f* simple transfer station
Einfachzugriff *m* single load capacity
einfädeln infiltrate
Einfädelung *f* infiltration, junction
einfahren 1. *(allg.)* enter, engage into, drive in **2.** *(Ladungen)* insert **3.** *(Mast, Gabeln)* retract
Einfahrhilfe *f* positioning accessory
Einfahrmaß *nt* entry clearance, entry dimension, fork entry
Einfahröffnung *f* aperture, insertion opening
Einfahrregal *nt* drive-in pallet racking, drive-in racking
Einfahrt *f* entry
Einfahrtasche *f* fork entry clearance, fork entry aperture, insertion pocket
Einfahrweg *m* entry distance
Einfahrwinkel *m* entry angle
Einfahrzeit *f* storage time
Einfalldosierung *f* incident dosis rate
einfallen apply, be applied, be engaged
Einfallenschloss *nt* single latch bolt lock
Einfallschweißstelle *f* sink
Einfallstellen *f* incident places
Einfallstrahlung *f* incident radiation
Einfallswinkel *m* angle of incidence
Einfallzeit *f* **der Bremse** brake application delay, brake reaction time
Einfamilienhaus *nt* **mit Einliegerwohnung** single family house with self-contained flat
einfassen border, line, set, span
Einfassung *f* *(von Rohrdurchführungen)* apron
Einflankeneingriff *m* single flank engagement
Einflankenwälzabweichung *f* single-flank working variation
Einflankenwälzprüfung *f* single-flank working test
Einflankenwälzsprung *m* single-flank working error
Einflanschstück *nt* single flange piece
Einfließen *nt* inflow
einfluchten flush
Einfluss *m* influence
Einfluss *m* **ausüben** influence, exert an influence upon
Einfluss *m* **haben auf** have a bearing on
Einflussbereich *m* sphere of influence
Einflussfaktor *m* influence factor
Einflussgröße *f* parameter, factor of influence, influence quantity
Einflusszone *f:* **thermische** ~ thermal-affected zone
einfräsen 1. *(allg.)* mill into **2.** *(Gesenke)* sink
einfügen fit in(to), insert
Einfügung *f* insertion
Einfügungsdämpfung *f* insertion loss
Einführeinsatz *m* entry pilot
einführen feed (into), insert, let in, load, enter, launch, introduce
einführend introductory
Einführfase *f* *(bei Spannstiften)* chamfer to permit insertion
Einführkonus *m* *(bei Muffen)* entry taper
Einführung *f* introduction
Einführungsphase *f* pioneering stage
Einführungszentrierung *f* entry guidance, guidance into the aperture
Einführzapfen *m* entry pilot
einfüllen charge, feed, fill in, pour in
Einfüllstunde *f* fill-up hour
Eingabe *f* feeding, filling-in, input, entry

Eingabe Primärstatus *m* input primary status, IPS
Eingabebaugruppe *f* input module
Eingabedaten *pl* entry data, input data
Eingabefeld *nt* entry field
Eingabegerät *nt* entry unit
Eingabeglied *nt* input element
Eingabelungsverfahren *nt* up-and-down method
Eingabemöglichkeit *f* input facility
Eingabeschnittstelle *f* input interface
Eingabe-Sekundärstatus *m* input secondary status, ISS
Eingabespeicher *m* input memory, input storage
Eingabetaste *f* enter key
Eingabewert *m* input value
Eingabezeit *f* input time interval
Eingang *m* **1.** *(el.)* input **2.** *(örtlich)* entrance
Eingang *m* **mit Negation** negating input
Eingang *m* **mit Polaritätsindikator** *m* input with polarity indicator
Eingang/Ausgang (E/A) *m* input/output (I/O)
eingängiges flaches metrisches Trapezgewinde *nt* one-start stub metric trapezoidal screw thread
eingängiges Gewinde *nt* single-start screw thread, one-start (screw) thread
eingängiges metrisches Sägengewinde *nt* one-sart metric buttress thread
eingängiges Rechtsgewinde *nt* one-start right-hand screw thread
Eingangsgröße *f* input quantity
Eingangsinformation *f* input information
Eingangsklemme *f* input terminal
Eingangskontrolle *f* reception inspection
Eingangslager *nt* incoming goods warehouse, load entering storage
Eingangsprüfung *f* incoming goods inspection
Eingangspunkt *m* pick-up station
Eingangsrevision *f* inspection of incoming goods
Eingangsschaltung *f* **mit Vorbereitung** input circuit with enabling function
Eingangssignal *nt* input signal
Eingangsspannung *f* input voltage
Eingangsstrom *m* input current
Eingangsstufe *f* input stage
Eingangsverbindung *f* input connection
Eingangswert *m* input value
eingassig single-lane
eingebaut built in, embedded, incorporated, incorporating, integrated
eingebaute Treppe *f* fixed stairway
eingebautes Endmaß *nt* integrated gauge block
eingeben enter, input
eingebettet integrated, embedded
eingeengte Toleranz *f* restricted tolerance
eingefahren closed, retracted
eingefallene Lötnaht *f* brazing seam shrinking
eingeformte Fuge *f* gap formed by a mould
eingeformte Schweißstelle *f* part to be welded, surrounded by a mould
eingeformte Spanleitstufe *f* chip breaker groove
eingefrorene Spannung *f* frozen-in tension
einhärtende Wirkung *f* hardness penetration effect
eingeklebte Folie *f* film adhesively bonded between the sheets
eingelagert stored
eingelegt engaged
eingeprägt engraved
eingerastet engaged
eingerissen ragged
eingeschaltet engaged
eingeschäumter Kunststoff *m* foamed-in cellular material
eingeschlagene Lenkung *f* steering on (full) lock
eingeschliffen ground fit
eingeschliffener Spanbrecher *m* ground-in chipbreaker
eingeschlossen trapped
eingeschlossener Winkel *m* included angle

eingeschnürt brennen burn constricted
eingeschossig single-tier
eingeschränkt restricted, reduced
eingeschränkter Befehlssatz m reduced instruction set
eingespannt constrained
eingewalzte Rille f rolled-in groove
eingreifen 1. *(allg.)* act, intervene, engage **2.** *(Maschinenteile)* mesh with **3.** *(Zahnräder)* gear
Eingriff m **1.** *(allg.)* action, intervention, operator intervention, engagement **2.** *(e. Meißels)* point of cutting action **3.** *(e. Schleifscheibe)* re-entry **4.** *(e. Verzahnung)* action, mesh, engagement **5.** *(von Zahnflanken)* contact **6.** *(von Radzähnen)* engagement **7.** *(Maschinenteile)* meshing
Eingriffsebene f plane of action
Eingriffsfeld nt plane (or zone) of action
Eingriffsfläche f **1.** *(e. Radpaares)* plane of contact (or action), surface of engagement **2.** *(e. Stirnrades mit Evolventenverzahnung)* length of path of contact
Eingriffsfrequenz f tooth-meshing frequency
Eingriffsgebiet nt engagement region
Eingriffsgröße f engagement index
Eingriffslinie f path of contact, line of contact, transverse path of contact
Eingriffspunkt m point of contact, point of engagement
Eingriffsschwierigkeit f meshing difficulty
Eingriffsstelle f meshing point, point of engagement, point of gear intermesh
Eingriffsstörung f meshing interference
Eingriffsstrecke f length of path of contact
Eingriffsteilung f *(der Flanken)* normal base pitch, contact ratio
Eingriffsteilungsabweichung f normal base pitch variation
Eingriffsteilungsmessung f base pitch measurement
Eingriffstelle f action point

Eingriffsverhältnisse $ntpl$ ratio of mesh
Eingriffswinkel m transverse pressure angle, pressure angle, angle of approach
Eingriffswinkelabweichung f transverse pressure angle variation
Eingusssysteme $ntpl$ ingate systems pl
Eingussverschluss m filler cap
einhaken 1. *(allg.)* catch **2.** *(Meißel in Werkstück)* dig in
Einhalsen nt *(Verjüngen von Hohlkörpern)* bottling
Einhalsen nt **durch Drücken** contracting by spinning
einhalten fulfill maintain, meet, observe
einhalten der Toleranz hold a tolerance
Einhaltung f **1.** *(allg. Bedingungen)* fulfillment, observance **2.** *(e. Funktion)* upholding
Einhandsteuerung f hold to run control for one hand
einhängen hook in, plug in
Einhängeriegel m hook-in type beam
Einhängestift m hook-in pin
Einhängeverbindung f hook-in type fitting, clevis-type connector
Einhärtbarkeit f hardness penetrability
einhärtender Stahl m: **gering** ~ steel with only low hardness gain
Einhärtung f hardness penetration
Einhebelbedienung f single-lever control (or operation)
Einhebelsteuerung f single-lever control, mono-lever control
Einheit f **1.** *(allg.)* unit **2.** *(math.)* unit, item **3.** *(von Bauteilen)* entity
einheitlich standardized, uniform
einheitlicher Ressourcenfinder m universal resource locator (URL)
Einheitsachsenabstand m centre distance basis
Einheitsbohrung f basic-hole (system)
Einheitsdrehbank f standard lathe
Einheitsmutter f basic nut
Einheitssignal nt standard signal
Einheitsverfahren nt standard method
Einheitswelle f basic-shaft (system)
Einheitszahndicke f tooth thickness basis

Einkantensteuerung *f* one-edge tracing, one-edge control
Einkauf *m* purchasing, sourcing
einkaufen buy, purchase, source
Einkäufer *m* purchaser
Einkaufsabteilung *f* purchasing department
Einkaufsauftrag *m* purchasing order
Einkaufsdisposition *f* purchase scheduling
Einkaufsvertrag *m* purchasing contract
einkehlen channel
einkerben indent, nick, notch, score
Einkerbung *f* indentation, grooving
einkleben stick into
einklinken catch, arrest
Einknickung *f* fold
Einkomponentenkunstharzlack *m* one-component synthetic resin sealant
Einkopftechnik *f* single probe technique
einkoppeln couple
Einkopplung *f* coupling
Einkopplung *f* **von Störsignalen** coupling for interference
Einkornabrichten *nt* single-point wheel truing
Einkornabrichter *m* single-point wheel truer
Einkräuselung *f* curling
Einkristall *m* single crystal
Einkufentastsystem *nt* single-skid contact system
einkuppeln engage the clutch, throw in
Einkurvenautomat *m* single-cam operated automatic turret lathe
Einkurvensystem *nt* single-cam system
Einlagerauftrag *m* input order, storage order
Einlagerdurchsatz *m* input rate, infeed rate, storage rate
Einlagerkapazität *f* storage capacity
einlagern input, handle into storage, load, stock, store, tier
Einlagerpunkt *m* input point, infeed point, storage point
Einlagerreferenzsystem *nt* input reference system
Einlagerspiel *nt* storage cycle
Einlagerstation *f* input station

Einlagerteilstrom *m* input part-flow
Einlagerung *f* storage
Einlagerungsplatz *m* storage location
Einlagerungsquote *f* storage quota
Einlagerungsseite *f* storage side
Einlagervorgang *m* storage process
Einlagestoff *m* interlining
Einlagevliesstoff *m* non-woven interlining
einlagig single-layer, in one layer
einlagige Schweißung *f* single-run weld
Einläppen *nt* start lapping
Einlauf *m* entry, entry point, approach motion, enema
Einlaufband *nt* entry conveyor, infeed belt
Einlaufbetrieb *m* running-in period
Einlaufdruck *m* inlet pressure (valve)
Einläufe *mpl* intakes *pl*
Einlaufeinrichtung *f* infeed transfer device
einlaufen 1. *(allg.)* arrive, enter, come in **2.** *(Maschinen)* start running
einlaufend arriving, incoming
Einlaufförderer *m* infeed conveyor, input conveyor
Einlaufgrübchen *nt* initial pitting
Einlauföffnung *f* entry point, infeed slot
Einlaufphase *f* initial phase
Einlaufstelle *f* entry point, infeed location
Einlaufstern *m* infeed star, infeed star wheel
Einlaufstrecke *f* inlet path
einlegen 1. *(allg.)* apply **2.** *(Gang)* engage **3.** *(Lot)* preplace **4.** *(Teile)* insert
einleiten 1. *(allg.)* initiate, start, trigger **2.** *(Kräfte)* lead into, be absorbed
Einleitung *f* **1.** *(allg.)* initiation **2.** *(Kräfte)* absorption
Einleitungsanlage *f* single-line system (centr. lubr. system)
Einleitungssystem *nt* single-line principle of operation
Einleitungsverteiler *m* metering device with injectors
Einlinienzuführung *f* single-line feed (system)

Einlippentieflochbohrer *m* single-lipped deep-hole drill
einloggen log in
einmal jährlich once a year
einmal schreiben- oftmals lesen write once-read many
einmalige Entnahme *f* single sample
einmalige Prüfung *f* once-only test
einmaliges Abschrecken *nt* quenching once only, single quenching
Einmalproduktion *f* single production
Einmannbedienung *f* one-man control
Einmast ... single-mast
Einmauerung *f* brick setting
einmäulige Rachenlehre *f* single opening gap gauge
Einmaulschlüssel *m* single-ended open-jaw spanner, single-head engineers wrench
Einmeißelhobeln *nt* single-chisel planes
Einmeißelverfahren *nt* single chisel technique
Einmeißelwerkzeug *nt* single-point (cutting) tool
Einmeldung *f (z. B. e. Produktionsbeginns)* notification
Ein-Minuten-Dehnung *f* one minute strain
Ein-Minuten-Prüfspannung *f* one-minute test voltage
Ein-Minuten-Restdehnung *f* one minute residual strain
Ein-Minuten-Stehspannung *f* minute value of electric strength
einnehmen occupy
Einnietmutter *f* clinch nut
einordnen classify
Einordnung *f* classification
Einpack- und Auspackmaschine *f* packing and unpacking machine
einpacken wrap up, pack, pack up
Einpackmaschine *f* packing machine
einparametrisches digitales Signal *nt* single-parameter digital signal
Einpassarbeit *f* fitting at assembly
einpassen fit in(to), seat
Einpassschleifen *nt* match grinding
Einpassung *f* fitting-in

einpendeln settle
Einphasenasynchronmotor *m* single-phase asynchronous motor
Einphaseninduktionsmotor *m* single-phase induction motor
Einphasenmotor *m* start split phase motor, resistor motor
einpipettieren pipette into
Einplatinenrechner *m* monoboard computer
Einplatzlagerung *f* single-location storage
Einplatzsystem *nt* single-location system
einpolig single-pin
Einprägen *nt* stamping (characters into the surface of a workpiece)
einprägsame Darstellung *f* expressive representation
Einpressen *nt (e. Pressverbandes)* force fitting
Einpressfase *f (bei Pressverbänden)* assembly bevel
Einpresskraft *f* assembly force
Einpressmutter *f* mould insert nut, press nut
einprofilige Schleifscheibe *f* single-rib wheel
Einprofilschleifscheibe *f* single-rib (or single-edge) grinding wheel, single-rib wheel
Einprozent-Dehngrenze *f* one percent proof stress, one percent permanent limit of elongation
Einpulsbetrieb *m* single pulse operation
Einpunktmessung *f* single-point measurement
Einpunktverfahren *nt* single-point method
einrahmen frame
einrasten catch in, click in, engage, lock
einrasten: den Stift ~ insert the pin
Einrasten *nt* engaging, locking
Einrastung *f* aperture
Einraumheizung *f* single room heating
einreihig single-rowed
Einreißen *nt* tearing in
Einreißversuch *m* tearing test
einrichten 1. *(allg.)* adapt, adjust, ar-

range, position, set **2.** *(installieren)* install **3.** *(mit Zubehör)* equip **4.** *(e. Maschine mit Werkzeugen)* tool up, setup
Einrichter *m* machine setter, tool setter
Einrichtezeit *f* setup time
Einrichtung *f* **1.** *(Ausrüstung)* equipment **2.** *(Errichtung Installation)* installation **3.** *(Inbetriebnahme)* set-up **4.** *(Schalteinrichtung)* mechanism **5.** *(von Werkzeugen)* setup, tooling **6.** *(Vorrichtung)* attachment, fixture **7.** *(zum Spannen)* fixture, mechanism **8.** *(Zusatz)* accessory, attachment **9.** *(allg.)* outfit, device, facility, means, appliance
Einrichtung *f* **für den Vorschub** feeding mechanism
Einrichtung *f* **zur automatischen Späneabfuhr** automatic chip disposal unit
Einrichtungen *fpl* facilities *pl*
Einringschlüssel *m* single-ended ring spanner, single-end box wrench
Einriss *m* initial tearing
Einrolldruck *m* crusher roll pressure
Einrollen *nt* crush-dressing, curling
einrollprofilieren crush-dress
Einrollprofilieren *nt* crush dressing, crushing
Einrollvorrichtung *f* crush-dressing attachment, crush-dressing device
einrücken 1. *(allg.)* clutch, engage, slide into, start, throw in **2.** *(Hebel)* shift
Einrückung *f* engagement
Eins *f* unity
Einsatz *m* **1.** *(allg.)* application, employment, operation, use, service **2.** *(Einlage)* insert **3.** *(für Schraubendreher)* insert bit **4.** *(Passstück)* adaptor, adapter **5.** *(Werkzeug ~)* insert
Einsatzbacken *fpl* false jaws *pl*
Einsatzbedarf *m* investment demand
Einsatzbereiche *mpl* areas *pl* of application
einsatzbereit ready for operation, ready for use
einsatzbereite Reserve *f* hot standby
Einsatzbrücke *f* gap bridge
Einsatzdaten *pl* field data

einsatzgehärtet case-hardened
einsatzhärten case-harden
Einsatzkasten *m* insertable bin
Einsatzkriterium *nt* use criterion
Einsatzmaterial *nt* stock to be used
Einsatzmeißel *m* insert tool, removable tool bit, bit-type insert, bit tool, cutter bit
Einsatzmesser *nt* inserted blade
Einsatzmittelbedarf *m* resources demand
Einsatzmittelmanagement *nt* resources management
Einsatzmöglichkeit *f* application option
Einsatzprofil *nt* field profile
Einsatzstab *m* filler rod
Einsatzstahl *m* carburizing (case-hardening) steel
Einsatztag *m* operating day
Einsatzumgebung *f* operating area
Einsatzwerkzeug *nt* insertable tool, bit insert
Einsatzzeit *f* application time, operation time
Ein-Säulen-Gerät *nt* single-mast machine
einschalige Waage *f* single pan balance
einschaliger Hyperboloid *m* single-shell hyperboloid
Einschallung *f* intromission of sound
Einschallwinkel *m* intromission angle
Einschaltdauer *f* **1.** *(allg.)* operating time, working time **2.** *(el.)* duty cycle
einschalten 1. *(allg.)* start, switch on, turn on, put on **2.** *(Räderpaare)* mash **3.** *(el.)* switch on **4.** *(Getriebe)* engage **5.** *(Hebel)* switch into position **6.** *(Kupplungen, Getriebe)* engage, throw into engagement **7.** *(Motor, Maschine)* start, put into operation, engage **8.** *(Schaltgeräte)* switch in
EIN-Schalter *m* start control
Einschaltpotential *nt* cut-in potential
Einschaltsperre *f* switch-on inhibition
Einschaltstellung *f* on-position
Einschaltstrom *m* inrush current
Einschaltstrombegrenzer *m* inrush current limiter

Einschalttor *nt* normally-open gate
Einschaltverzögerung *f* start-up deceleration
Einschaltverzögerung *f* raising delay
Einschaltverzögerungsglied *nt* on-delay timer
Einschaltvorgang *m* energizing action
Einschaltzeit *f* exposure time
Einscheibe *f* single-cone pulley
Einscheibenläppmaschine *f* single-wheel lapping machine
Einschichtbetrieb *m* single-shift operation
Einschichtsicherheitsglas *nt* toughened glass
einschiebbar telescopic, extendable, retractable
einschieben 1. *(allg.)* push in, slide in **2.** *(einfügen)* insert
Einschiebmuffe *f* slip-in socket
einschlagen 1. *(allg.)* wrap in **2.** *(Lenkung)* turn, lock
einschlägig relevant
Einschlagmaschine *f* wrapping machine
Einschlagmaschine *f* **mit Winkelschweißung** L-sealing machine
einschleifen *(Sitz)* reseat
einschleusen channel, feed in, push in, inject, infiltrate
Einschleuser *m* merge, injector merge
Einschleusposition *f* input position
Einschleusstelle *f* entry, load entry
Einschleustakt *m* infeed cycle
einschließen comprise, trap
einschließlich including, inclusive
Einschluss *m* inclusion, comprisal
Einschlussthermometer *nt* enclosed scale thermometer
einschnappen catch
Einschneiden *nt* lancing
einschneidig single-edged, single-point
einschneidiger Meißel *m* single-point cutting tool
einschneidiges Werkzeug *nt* single-edged cutting tool
Einschnitt *m* indentation, recess
einschnittig überlappte Klebung *f* bonded single lap joint
einschnittig überlappter Probekörper *m* single lap jointed test specimen
Einschnürung *f* constriction
Einschnürung *f* **nach dem Bruch** percentage reduction of area after fracture
einschränken limit, reduce, restrain restrict
Einschränkung *f* restriction
Einschränkung von Toleranzfeldern *ntpl* limitation of tolerance zones
einschrauben in screw into
Einschraubgewindeloch *nt* screw-in tap hole
Einschraubgruppe *f* screw-in group
Einschraubhaken *m* screwing hook
Einschraubheizpatrone *f* screw-in heating element
Einschraubkugelkopf *m* screwed ball end
Einschraubloch *nt (für Verschlussschrauben)* screw plug hole
Einschraubmutter *f (früher Schraubdübel)* threaded (or screwed) insert
Einschraubstutzen *m* **1.** *(allg.)* screwed plug **2.** *(für Rohrverschraubungen)* double-ended union
Einschraubstutzen *m* **mit Ringsicherung** ring locked union
Einschraubzapfen *m* **1.** *(allg.)* screwed end **2.** *(e. Rohrverschraubung)* adapter end (of a union)
Einschroten *nt* partial parting by chiselling
Einschub *m* push-back cart, slide-in cart, storage cart
Einschubbahn *f* push-back lane, sliding lane, slide in, push in
Einschubeinrichtung *f* infeed transfer device
Einschubregal *nt* push-back pallet racking, push-back racking, glide-in racking, slide-in racking
Einschubstation *f* inserting platform, module station
Einschussbogen *m* slip sheet
einschwingen settle
Einschwingerscheinung *f* initial transient effect
Einschwingphase *f* transient stage
Einschwingspiel *nt* build-up cycle

Einschwingvorgang *m* transient effect
Einschwingzeit *f* settling time
einseitig one-way, one-sided, from one direction, unilateral, single-ended
einseitig durchgebrannter Schweißpunkt *m* weld spot burnt-through from one side
einseitige Flankennaht *f* one-sided lap weld
einseitige Zykloidenverzahnung *f* one-sided cycloidal tooth system
einseitiges Buckelschweißen *nt* indirect projection welding
einseitiges Erwärmen *nt* heating from one side
einseitiges Werkzeug *nt* single edged tool
Einsender *m* submitter
Einsenken *nt* die hobbing
Einsenkung *f* sinking
Einsenkung *f*: **kegelige** ~ countersinking
Einsenkung *f*: **zylindrische** ~ counterboring
einsetzen 1. *(montieren)* add, place into, insert, install, apply, use, charge, seat **2.** *(an Stelle von)* substitute
Einsortenzuführung *f* single-product feed (system)
Einspannbacke *f* chuck jaw
einspannen 1. *(allg.)* clamp, grip, mount, load, fix, locate, secure in position **2.** *(andere Werkzeuge)* retool **3.** *(in Spannfutter)* chuck **4.** *(Werkstücke)* load **5.** *(Werkzeuge)* mount, fix
Einspannschaft *m* stem
Einspannteil *nt* keyed end
Einspannung *f* **1.** *(allg.)* clamping, gripping, fixing, locating, mounting **2.** *(in ein Spannfutter)* chucking **3.** *(Meißel)* setting **4.** *(Werkstücke)* loading
Einspannung *f* **in ein Futter** chucking
Einspannvorrichtung *f* clamping fixture, jig
Einspannzapfen *m* clamping pivot
einsparen save
Einsparung *f* saving(s), reduction of costs, cutting expenses
Einsparungen *fpl* **machen** retrench, cut expenses

Einsparungsmöglichkeit *f* savings possibility
einspeisen 1. *(allg.)* feed (in), inject **2.** *(Strom)* supply
Einspeisen *nt* feeding
Einspeisung *f* power supply, supply
Einspindelautomat *m* single-spindle automatic turret lathe, *(UK)* Swiss-type automatic screw machine
Einspindelautomat *m* **ohne Revolverkopf** Swiss-type automatic screw machine, Swiss automatic
Einspindelform- und -schraubenautomat *m* single-spindle automatic screw machine
Einspindellangdrehautomat *m* Swiss bush-type automatic lathe, Swiss type screw machine
Einspindelmaschine *f* single-spindle machine
Einspindelplanfräsmaschine *f* simplex manufacturing type milling machine
Einspindelrevolverautomat *m* single-spindle automatic turret screw machine
Einspindelvielstahlautomat *m* single-spindle automatic multi-tool lathe
Einspreizen *nt* partial spreading
Einspritzdüse *f* injection nozzle
einspritzen inject
Einspritzgeschwindigkeit *f* injection speed
Einspritzphase *f* injection phase
Einspritzpumpe *f* injection pump
Einspritzstelle *f* injection point
Einspurmastgerät *nt* one-track mast device
Einstabmesskette *f* single-rod measuring cell
Einständerbauart *f* single-column construction, single column design
Einständerblechkantenhobelmaschine *f* *(US)* openside plate planer
Einständerhobelmaschine *f* openside planer
Einständerhobelmaschine *f* open-sided planer
Einständerkarusselldrehmaschine *f* single column vertical turret lathe
Einständerkonstruktion *f* open-front

design
Einständermaschine *f* single-column machine
Einstapelautomatik *f* automatic stacking
einstapeln place, stack
Einstapelvorgang *m* stacking operation
Einstechabwälzverfahren *nt* plunge-feed generating method
Einstecharbeit *f* **1.** *(allg.)* recessing, plunge cutting **2.** *(Nuten)* grooving
Einstechdrehen *nt* recess turning
einstechen 1. *(allg.)* groove, neck, plunge-cut, recess, plunge, nick, puncture, cut in, initial pierce **2.** *(aushalsen)* neck **3.** *(aussparen)* recess **4.** (Nuten) groove, slot **5.** *(Zahnlücken)* gash
Einstechfräsgerät *nt* recess milling attachment
Einstechmeißel *m* **1.** *(für Aussparungen)* recessing tool **2.** *(Nuten)* grooving tool **3.** *(zum Aushalsen)* necking tool
Einstechrundschleifmaschine *f* cylindrical plunge grinder
Einstechschleifen *nt* infeed grinding, plunge grinding, plunge-cut grinding
Einstechschleifmaschine *f* plunge-cut grinder
Einstechsupportschieber *m* recessing slide
Einstechtiefe *f* depth of recess
Einstechverfahren *nt* recessing method, grooving method, infeed method, plunge-cut method, gashing method
Einstechverfahren *nt* *(Zahnlücken)* gashing
Einstechverfahren *nt* **auf Rundschleifmaschinen** plunge-cut grinding, plunge grinding method
Einstechvorschub *m* feed-in
Einstechwälzverfahren *nt* plunge feed and rolling method
einstecken 1. *(allg.)* engage in, insert, plug in **2.** *(klammern)* tuck
Einsteckgriff *m* *(für Grenzlehrdorne)* slip-on handle
Einsteckkarte *f* insert card
Einsteckmuffe *f* slip-in socket

Einsteckschlüssel *m* face spanner
Einsteckschweißmuffenverbindung *f* slip-in weld socket joint
Einstecktiefe *f* *(bei Muffen)* depth of insertion
Einsteckverschließmaschine *f* tuck closing machine
Einsteigöffnung *f* entry opening
einstellbar adjustable
einstellbare Knaggen *fpl* adjustable dogs *pl*
einstellbare Lehre *f* adjustable gage, setting gauge
einstellbarer Anschlag *m* **zur Vorschubausrückung** *f* adjustable feed trip dog
einstellbares Drosselventil *nt* **für stufenlos veränderliche Vorschubgrößen** adjustable hydraulic flow control valve for infinitely variable feed rate
Einstellbarkeit *f* adjustability
Einstellbereich *m* range of adjustment
Einstelldaten *pl* setting data
Einstelldorn *m* setting plug (gauge)
Einstelldruck *m* pressure setting
einstellen 1. *(~ auf z. B. Tisch, Schlitten)* adjust, position **2.** *(Anschläge)* locate **3.** *(ausrichten)* align **4.** *(Hebel)* shift, move **5.** *(Maschinentisch in Arbeitsposition)* position **6.** *(Lehre Meißel)* set, position **7.** *(Messzeuge)* adjust **8.** *(verstellen)* shift **9.** *(Vorschub)* preset **10.** *(Werkzeuge)* tool, align, position
Einstellergänzungswinkel *m* approach angle, *(US)* lead angle
Einstellfehler *m* error in focusing
Einstellgenauigkeit *f* accuracy of positioning, setting accuracy
einstellig single-digit...
einstellige Ziffernskala *f* single-place digital scale
Einstellinformationen *pl* settings information
Einstelllehre *f* setting gauge (or gage)
Einstelllupe *f* focusing lens
Einstellmaß *nt* setting gauge
Einstellmessscheibe *f* **1.** *(allg.)* setting plug gauge **2.** *(über 18 mm)* setting disc

Einstellnormal *nt* setting standard
Einstellparameter *m* setting parameter
Einstellring *m* setting ring gauge
Einstellscheibe *f* levelling disc, dial
Einstellschraube *f* adjusting screw, setting screw, setscrew
Einstellskala *f* focusing scale
Einstelltoleranz *f* setting tolerance
Einstellung *f* 1. *(allg.)* adjustment, location, positioning, setup, preset 2. *(Drehautomaten)* tool layout, tooling diagram 3. *(e. Arbeitsmaschine)* setting, setup, positioning 4. *(Messsgeräte)* adjustment 5. *(Programmierung)* setting(s)
Einstellung *f* **der Arbeitsfolge** sequencing
Einstellung *f* **des Arbeitsablaufes** cycle setting
Einstellungsschalter *m* start switch
Einstellwälzfräser *m* single-position hob
Einstellwert *m* set value
Einstellwinkel *m* 1. *(Hauptschneide) (US)* entering angle, *(UK)* plan angle 2. *(Nebenschneide)* front angle, horizontal front clearance, plan relief angle, minor cutting edge angle, trail (or trailing) angle 3. *(der Stirnschneide)* cutting edge angle
Einstellzahn *m* setting tooth
Einstellzeit *f* adjusting time
Einsteuerungstermin *m* control response date
Einsteuerungsvorgang *m* control response stage
Einstich *m* 1. *(allg.)* puncture 2. *(Arbeitsergebnis)* recess, neck groove, slot, plunge cut, root clearance 3. *(Aushalsen)* necking 4. *(e. Gewindes)* clearance groove 5. *(Nuten)* grooving 6. *(schleifen)* recessing, plunge cut (grinding), infeed grinding
Einstichdurchmesser *m* root clearance diameter
Einstichmeißel *m* recessing tool
einstopfen stuff into
Einstoßen *nt* reducing (the cross-section or diameter)
Einstrahlrichtung *f* direction of incidence
Einstrahlungsgeometrie *f* geometry of radiation
Einstrahlungsrichtung *f* direction of incidence
einströmen ingress, inflow
einstufen classify, grade
Einstufenversuch *m* single level test
einstufig single-stage, single-step
einstufige Fahrsteuerung *f* single speed control
einstufiges Getriebe *nt* single-stage gear transmission
Einstufung *f* classification, grading, rating
eintauchen dip, immerse, submerge, plunge
Eintauchprisma *nt* immersion prism
Eintauchschaben *nt* immersion scraping
einteilen divide, grade, graduate, subdivide
einteilig solid, one-piece
einteilige Metallmutter *f* one-piece metal nut
einteilige Rohrschelle *f* one-piece pipe clip
einteiliger Fräser *m* solid cutter
einteiliges Räumwerkzeug *nt* solid broach
einteiliges Werkzeug *nt* forged tool, solid tool
Einteilung *f* division (into groups), grading, subdivision
eintragen enter
Eintragung *f* entry
eintreffen arrive
eintreten *(Ereignis)* occur
Eintritt *m* admission, entrance, inlet, intake
Eintritteingriffsstrecke *f* length of approach path
Eintrittseingriff *m* approach contact
Eintrittshäufigkeit *f* frequency of occurrence
Eintrittskanal *m* inlet port
Eintrittsöffnung *f* intake port
Eintrittspotential *nt* onset potential
Eintrittsspiel *nt* entry clearance
Einverfahrenwerkzeug *nt* single-pro-

cess tool
Einwaage *f* weight-in quantity, initial weight
einwählen log in
Einwahlpunkt *m* point of presence (POP)
Einwälzen *nt (Durchwälzen über alle Werkzeuge)* initial generation (generation over several cutter teeth), generating infeed
Einwalz-T-Stück *nt (Formstück für Armaturen)* expanded T-piece
Einwälzzeit *f (e. Hobelmeißels)* idle time (during the approach traverse of the cutter)
einwandern migrate
einwandfrei correct, flawless
einwandige Durchstrahlung *f* single-well radiography
einwandiger Wassererwärmer *m* single-walled water heater
Einwegbohrmaschine *f* one-way boring machine
Einwegkegelhahn *m* one-way taper stopcock
Einweglichtschraube *f* single-way light barrier
Einwegmaschine *f* one-way machine
Einwegpalette *f* disposable pallet
Einwegschräghahn *m* oblique bore one-way stopcock
Einwegstrahlmittel *nt* once through abrasive
einweisen instruct, train
Einweisung *f* instruction, training
Einwickelmaschine *f* enveloping machine
einwickeln envelop, wrap up
einwirken influence, act upon
einwirken auf act upon, affect
Einwirkung *f* effect, action, exposure
Einzahnbreitschlichtfräsen *nt* single tooth broad finish milling
Einzahnschruppen *nt* single-tooth cutting
einzeichnen plot
einzel ... individual, single
Einzelabsaugung *f* individual offtake
Einzelabweichung *f* individual variation

Einzelantrieb *m* direct motor drive, individual drive, single motor drive
Einzelbelastung *f* single load
Einzelbestand *m (im Lager)* single on-hand quantity
Einzelbewegung *f* individual movement
Einzelbuckelschweißen *nt* single-projection welding
Einzeldraht *m* single wire
Einzeldrehmeißel *m* single-point cutting tool
Einzeldruck *m* one-off print
Einzelereignisschalldruckpegel *m* single-event sound pressure level
Einzelfehler *m* single error
Einzelfehlerfläche *f* individual defective area
Einzelfehlerprüfung *f* individual error test
Einzelfertigung *f* job production, unit production, single-part production
Einzelfestlegung *f* individual stipulation
Einzel-FTF *nt* single (AGV)
Einzelgerät *nt* individual unit
Einzelgewicht *nt* individual weight
Einzelhandel *m* retail (trade)
Einzelhändler *m* retailer
Einzelheit *f* detail
Einzelimpulsbohren *nt* single impulse boring
Einzel-Istmaß *nt* individual actual size
Einzelkomponente *f* individual component
Einzelkontrolle *f* individual inspection
Einzellage *f* individual layer
Einzellagerung *f* individual storage
Einzellast *f* individual load
Einzelmaß *nt* individual size
Einzelmeldung *f* individual message
Einzelmessung *f* individual measurement
Einzelmesswert *m* individual measurement value, individual (or single) measured value
einzeln individual, single
Einzelnaht *f* individual joint (or weld)
einzelner Wert *m* individual value
einzelnes Los *nt* isolated lot

Einzelpackung f individual pack
Einzelpalettenkassette f *(für Datenspeicherung)* single disc cartridge
Einzelpalettenposition f single pallet position
Einzelpalettierung f single position palletizing
Einzelperlhärte f pellet hardness
Einzelpore f localized porosity
Einzelprobe f spot sample
Einzelpunkt-Schweißverbindung f single-spot welded joint
Einzelrad nt single wheel
Einzelrautiefe f single peak-to-valley height
Einzelreflektor m individual reflector
Einzelrille f individual groove
Einzelsatzbetrieb m single block mode
Einzelschallereignis nt single sound event
Einzelschicht f single layer
Einzelschwerpunkt m individual centre of gravity
Einzelspiel nt single cycle
Einzelstab m individual rod, single rod
Einzelstablagerung f single-rod storage
Einzelstück nt individual piece
Einzelstückfertigung f one-off production
Einzelteil nt (component) part, individual part (or component), one-off part
Einzelteilfertigung f single-piece production
Einzelteillager nt individual parts warehouse
Einzelteilung f single pitch
Einzelteilungsprüfung f individual pitch test
Einzelten nt enclosing in a tent
Einzeltoleranz f individual tolerance
Einzelton m discrete tone
Einzeluhrensystem nt single clock system
Einzeluntersuchung f individual test (or investigation)
Einzelverfügbarkeit f individual availability
Einzelverzahnung f single-cycle gear cutting, single-cycle method, individual tooth system
Einzelwerkzeug nt single-point tool
Einzelzeichen nt individual character
Einzelzeitmessung f single time measuring
Einzelziel nt individual target
einziehbar retractable
einziehen 1. *(allg.)* collect, draw in, pull in, retract **2.** *(Personen)* trap
Einzug m collection, retraction, trapping
Einzugkontur f pull-in contour
Einzugleser m pull-in reader
Einzugstelle f trapping point, pull-in point
einzukerbende Probe f specimen for incision
einzulagernd ingoing
Einzweckmaschine f single-purpose machine
Einzweckschweißer m single-purpose welder
Eiquerschnitt m egg-shaped cross-section
Eisbildung f formation of ice
Eisen nt iron
Eisenkern m iron core
eisenpulverhaltige Umhüllung f powdered iron containing covering
Eisensalzlichtpausverfahren nt ferrosalt method of reproduction
Eisenschrott m iron scrap, ferrous scrap
Eisenverlust m **1.** *(allg.)* eddy current loss, core loss, iron loss **2.** *(Magnetisierung)* magnetic loss, hysteresis loss
Eisenwerkstoff m ferrous material
E-Kanal m I-channel
elastisch flexible, elastic, resilient, springy
elastische Dehnung f percentage elastic elongation, stress, stretch
elastische Durchbiegung f deflection
Elastizität f resilience
Elastizitätseigenschaft f elasticity property
Elastizitätsgrenze f: **technische ~** technical elastic limit, 0.01% proof stress
Elastizitätsmodul nt **aus dem Biegeversuch** modulus of elasticity from the bending test

Elastizitätsmodul *nt* **aus dem Druckversuch** modulus of elasticity from the compression test
Elastizitätsmodul *nt* **aus dem Zugversuch** modulus of elasticity from the tensile test
elastoelektrisch elastoelectric
elastomechanisch elastomechanical
Elastomerbodenbelag *m* elastomer floor covering
Elastomere *ntpl* elastomers *pl*
Elastomerfertigteil *nt* finished elastomer item
Elastomerfolie *f* elastomer film
Elastomerkörper *m* elastomer component
Elastomermetallbindung *f* elastomer metal bond
Elastomerprüfung *f* testing of elastomers
Elektrik *f* electrics
elektrisch electric(al)
elektrisch angetrieben electrically driven
elektrisch leitfähig conductive
elektrisch leitfähiges Rad *nt* conductive wheel
elektrisch löschbarer programmierbarer Nur-Lese-Speicher *m* electrically erasable programmable read-only memory (EEPROM)
elektrische Anlage *f* electrical system (or installation)
elektrische Ausrüstung *f* electrical equipment
elektrische Betriebsmittel *f* electrical industrial facilities
elektrische Energie *f* electric power
elektrische Gefährdung *f* electrical hazard
elektrische Impulsfolge *f* sequence of electrical impulses
elektrische Kontaktfläche *f* electrical contact face
elektrische Ladung *f* electric charge
elektrische Längenmessung *f* electrical linear measurement
elektrische Steuerung *f* electric control system
elektrische Überlastung *f* electrical over-loading
elektrische Verbindungen *fpl* electrical junctions
elektrische Verfahren *ntpl* electrical processes
elektrische Verriegelung *f* electrical interlocking
elektrischer Kontakt *m* electrical contact
elektrischer Schlag *m* electric shock
elektrisches Aufrauen *nt* electric roughening
elektrisches Ausgangssignal *nt* electrical output (signal)
elektrisches Feld *nt* electric field
elektrisches Kaltschweißen *nt* cold welding by the arc method
elektrisches Tastschnittgerät *nt* electric stylus instrument
elektrisches Warmschweißen *nt* hot welding by the arc method
elektrisches Wechselfeld *nt* alternating electric field
elektroakustische Messung *f* electroacoustic measurement
elektroakustischer Wandler *m* electro-acoustic transducer
Elektroanstauchen *nt* upending by the electric heating method
elektrochemisch electro-chemical
elektrochemische Fertigung *f* electrochemical machining (ECM)
elektrochemische Korrosion *f* electrochemical corrosion
elektrochemischer Korrosionsschutz *m* electrochemical corrosion protection
elektrochemisches Abtragen *nt* electrochemical abrading
Elektrode *f* electrode
Elektrode *f*: **bogenförmig bewegte** ~ curved path electrode travel
Elektrode *f*: **geradlinig bewegte** ~ straight-path electrode travel
Elektrodenantrieb *m* electrode actuating mechanism
Elektrodenanzahl *f* number of electrodes
Elektrodeneindruckfehler *m* electrode indentation defect

Elektrodenführung *f* electrode guide
Elektrodenhalterung *f* electrode holder and adapter, electrode bracket assembly
Elektrodenkappe *f* electrode cap
Elektrodenoberfläche *f* electrode surface area
Elektrodenreaktion *f* electrode reaction
Elektrodenstrahlschweißnaht *f* electron beam weld
Elektrodenvorschubrolle *f* electrode feed roller
Elektrodenzündstelle *f* electrode arc strike
Elektroenergiequalität *f* power quality
Elektroerosion *f* electroerosion
Elektrofeile *f* rotary file
Elektroflurförderzeug *nt* electric truck, battery-powered truck
Elektrogewinde *nt* electric thread, Edison thread
Elektrohängebahn *f* electric monorail system (EMS), telpherage, telpher line, electric monorail conveyor
Elektrokorund *nt* fused alumina, aluminous abrasive
Elektrolufterhitzer *m* electric air heater
Elektroluftfilter *m* electrostatic air filter
Elektrolumineszenzschirm *m* electroluminescence screen
Elektrolytbehälter *m* electrolyte container
Elektrolyt *nt* electrolyte
Elektrolytdichte *f* electrolyte density
Elektrolytdurchschlag *m* breakdown in electrolyte
elektrolytisch verzinntes Weißblech *nt* electrolytically tinned tinplate
elektrolytische Korrosion *f* electrolytic corrosion
elektrolytische Oxidationsreaktion *f* electrolytic oxidation reaction
elektrolytische Reaktion *f* electrolytic reaction
elektrolytische Reduktionsreaktion *f* electrolytic reduction reaction
elektrolytischer Metallabtrag *m* electrolytic attack on the metal
Elektrolytschlamm *nt* electrolytic mud
Elektrolytumwälzung *f* electrolyte circulation
Elektrolytwiderstand *m* electrolyte resistance
Elektromagnet *m* electromagnet, solenoid
Elektromagnetbremse *f* electro-magnetic brake
Elektromagnetfilter *m* electromagnet filter
elektromagnetisch electro-magnetic
elektromagnetische Beeinflussung *f* electro-magnetic interference
elektromagnetische Lamellenbremse *f* electro-magnetic brake
elektromagnetische Verträglichkeit (EMV) *f* electro-magnetic compatibility (EMC)
Elektromagnetkopf *m* electro-magnet head, solenoid head
elektromechanisch electro-mechanical
elektromagnetische Endpunktbestimmung *f* electromagnetic dead stop method
Elektromotor *m* electric motor
elektromotorisch betriebenes Flurförderzeug *nt* **mit Verbrennungsmotor** *m* internal combustion electric truck
Elektronendurchtritt *m* passage of electrons
elektronenleitender Festkörper *m* electron-conducting solid
elektronenleitender Werkstoff *m* electro-conducting material
Elektronen-Nehmer *m* electron acceptor
Elektronenstrahl *m* electron beam
Elektronenstrahlanlage *f* electron beam plant
Elektronenstrahlbearbeitung *f* electron beam machining
Elektronenstrahler *m* electron radiator
Elektronenstrahllithographie *f* electron beam lithography
Elektronik *f* **der Ventilbasis** valve base electronics
Elektronikmotor *m* electronic motor,

d.c. motor
elektronische Beschaffung *f* e-procurement
elektronisches Handrad *nt* electronic handwheel
elektronsicher Stromwandler *m* electronic current transducer
Elektropressspan *m* electrical pressboard
Elektro-Schaltschrank *m* electric switch cabinet
Elektroschmalganghochregalstapler *m* unit narrow aisle storage and retrieval unit for highbay warehouse
elektrosensitiv electro-sensitive
Elektrospeicher *m* electrical storage heater
Elektrospritzen *nt* electric spraying
Elektrostapler *m* electric forklift truck
elektrostatisch electrostatic
elektrostatisch gefährdete Bauteile (npl) electrostatic sensitive devices
elektrostatische Aufladung *f* electrostatic charge
Elektrostauchen *nt* electric compressing
elektrotechnische Anlage *f* electrical engineering installation
elektrotechnisches Erzeugnis *nt* electrical engineering product
Elektrowärmegerät *nt* electric heating appliance
Elektrozaun *m* electric fencing
Element *nt* element
Element *nt:* **aktives ~** active element
Elemtarteilchenreaktion *f* elementary particle reaction
Elfplattenstapel *m* eleven-disc pack
Ellipsenaufnahme *f* elliptical image (or imaging)
elliptisch elliptic
Eloxalqualität *f* anodic oxidising grade
eloxieren anodize
Eluat *nt* eluate
eluieren elute
Elutionsmittel *nt* eluate
Elysierdrehen *nt* electrolytic turning
Elysieren *nt* electrolytic machining
Elysierfräsen *nt* electrolytic milling
Elysierschleifen *nt* electrolytic grinding

Emission *f* emission
Emissionsgrenzwert *m* emission limit
Emissionsschalldruckpegel *m* emission sound pressure level
Empfang *m* reception
empfangen receive
Empfänger *m* customer, consignee, receiver
Empfängerseite *f* receiver side
Empfängerwerk *nt* works of destination
Empfangsantenne *f* reception antenna
Empfangsbestätigung *f* receiving advice
Empfangspaket *nt* receive packet
Empfangsspule *f* receiver coil
empfindlich sensitive
empfindliche Geräte *npl* sensitive instruments
empfindliche Güter *ntpl* fragile goods *pl*
Empfindlichkeit *f* sensitivity
Empfindlichkeitseinstellung *f* sensitivity setting
empirische Standardabweichung *f* empirical standard deviation
empirische Verteilungsfunktion *f* empiricial distribution function
emulgatorfreies Polystyrol *nt* polystyrene not containing emulsifiers
Emulgiergerät *nt* emulsifying apparatus
emulgierbar emulsifiable
Emulgierzusatz *m* **zu Öl** *nt* emulsifier
Emulgierzylinder *m* emulsifying cylinder
Emulsion *f* **von Öl in Wasser** oil-in-water emulsion
Emulsion *f* **von Wasser in Öl** water-in-oil emulsion
Emulsionspolymerisat *nt* polymer in emulsion
Encoder *m* encoder
Endabnahme *f* final approval, final inspection
Endabschaltung *f* limiting device
Endanschlag *m* end stop, limit stop, stop
Endausschalter *m* limit switch
endbearbeiten finish

Endbearbeitung f 1. *(allg. Werkstücke)* finish machining, finishing, finish 2. *(Werkzeuge)* dressing
Endbegrenzung f end stop, limitation of travel
Endbegrenzungssystem nt end stroke device
Enddruck m final pressure
Ende nt 1. *(allg.)* end, limit 2. *(Programm)* exit 3. *(Seil)* terminal end
Endeinstellung f final position
Endempfindlichkeit f end-of-range sensitivity
enden 1. *(allg.)* end, finish 2. *(räuml.)* terminate
Endform f finishing form, final shape
Endformat nt trimmed size
Endfräsmaschine f rotary planer, end milling machine
Endgerät nt terminal, terminal station, terminal unit
Endgeschwindigkeit f final speed
Endhalteeinrichtung f end stop device, end of aisle equipment
Endhaltestelle f end stop
Endkontrolle f final inspection
Endkraterlunker m and crater cavity
Endkunde m end customer
Endlage f end position, stop position, extreme position
Endlagenabschaltung f end position disconnection
Endlagenbegrenzung f stop position limitation
Endlagenfühler m end-position sensor
Endlasche f end flap
Endlaschenfaltschachtelverschließmaschine f end flap carton closing machine
endlicher Wert m finite value
endlos continuous, infinite
Endlosguteinheit f unit of continuous material
Endmaß nt end measure, gauge block, slip gauge, end block gage
Endmontage f final assembly
Endprodukt nt final product
Endpunkt m 1. *(allg.)* node 2. *(e. Prüfbereiches)* finishing point

Endpunkttitrationsgerät nt dead stop titration apparatus
Endpunkt-Verfahren nt dead stop method
Endrücknahme f end relief
Endschalter m limit switch
Endstellung f 1. *(allg.)* extreme position, extreme of adjustment, limit 2. *(RBG)* hoist travel limit, rest position
Endstück nt rear pilot
Endstufe f output stage
Endstufenprobe f final sample
Endtaster m limit switch
Endwägung f final weighing
Endwert m final value distribution, end value
Endzapfen m journal
Endzerkleinerung f final reduction in size
Endzerkleinerungsgerät nt final reduction apparatus
Endzustand m final condition, final state
energetisch energetic
energetische Mitteilung f energy averaging
Energie f energy, power
Energie f **aufnehmend** absorbing energy, dissipating energy
Energie f **einbringen** energy input
Energie f **sparend** energy saving
Energie f **speichernd** stored energy
Energie f **speichernde Bauteile** pl stored-energy components
Energie f **wandelnd** energy converting
Energieabsorptionskoeffizient m energy transformation coefficient
Energieanlagenelektroniker m energy system electronics engineer
Energiebedarf m energy requirement
Energieeinkopplung f energy incoupling
Energieeinwirkung f energy influence, energy effect
Energiefluss m power flow, energy flow
energiefrei non-active
Energieführungskette f energy supply chain
Energieinhalt m power content
Energieniveau nt energy level

Energieprofil *nt* power profile
Energiequelle *f* source of energy, energy source
energiereich high energy
energiereiche Strahlung *f* high energy radiation
Energieschalter *m* energy switch
Energieschwächungskoeffizient *m* energy attenuation coefficient
Energiespeicher *m* energy storage mechanism
Energiesperre *f* energy lock-out
Energiesystem *nt* power supply system
energietechnische Anlage *f* power engineering plant
Energieträger *m* energy transfer medium, energy carrier
Energieumwandlungskoeffizient *m* energy conversion coefficient
Energieverbrauch *m* energy consumption, power consumption
Energieversorgung *f* energy supply, power supply
Energieversorgungseinrichtung *f* power supply system
Energiezufuhr *f* power supply, supply of energy
Entfettung *f* degreasing
Entfeuchter *m* drier, dehumidifier, demister
Entformen *nt* moulding
eng narrow, closely spaced, close
enge Auswahl *f* close limit
Engen *nt* **durch Drücken** contracting by spinning
Enghalsmesskolben *m* narrow-necked volumetric flask
engmaschig close-meshed, fine mesh gauge
Engpass *m* bottleneck
Engpassanalyse *f* bottleneck analysis
Engschrift *f* close-spaced characters (or lettering)
engtoleriert close-toleranced
Entadressierung *f* unaddress, UNA
Entaluminierung *f* dealuminification
Entbastungsechtheit *f* fastness to degumming
entdecken discover
Entdröhnungsmasse *f* anti-drumming compound
enteisen defrost
entfällt not applicable
entfernbar removable
entfernen 1. *(allg.)* remove, go away, strip **2.** *(Späne)* clear
entfernt remote
entfernt von clear of
Entfernung *f* **1.** *(allg.)* range, removal **2.** *(Strecke)* distance **3.** *(Späne)* clearing, stripping
Entfernungsmesser *m* range finder
Entfestigungsglühen *nt* annealing for removal of work-hardening
entfetten degrease, ungrease
Entfettungsmittel *nt* degreasant
entfeuchten dehumidify, demist
entflechten disentangle
Entflechtung *f* disentanglement, routing
entformen mould
Entformung *f* removal from the mould
Entformungstemperatur *f* temperature on removal from mould
Entgasung *f* degasification
Entgasungszeit *f* degassing time
entgegengesetzte Drehrichtung *f* *(e. Radpaares)* opposite direction of rotation
entgegenwirken react to, counteract
entgleisen derail, jump the rails
Entgleisung *f* derailment
entgraten 1. *(allg.)* burr, deburr **2.** *(Blech)* trim
entgruppieren degroup
enthalten contain, include, comprise
Enthitzer *m* desuperheater
Entität *f* entity
entkohlend geglühter Temperguss *m* decarburized-annealed (with heart) malleable cast iron
Entkohlungstiefe *f* decarburization depth
entkoppeln decouple, disconnect, uncouple, isolate
Entkopplung *f* decoupling, disconnection
entkuppeln unclutch, declutch
Entladebehälter *m* unloading box (or container)

Entladedauer *f* discharging duration
Entladeeinrichtung *f* unloading device
Entladeenergie *f* unloading energy
entladen unload (work), discharge, empty
Entladephase *f* discharging phase
Entladeschlussspannung *f* final discharging voltage
Entladespannung *f* discharging voltage
Entladestrom *m* discharging current
Entladetiefe *f* degree of discharging
Entladeverhalten *nt* discharging behaviour
Entladeverhältnis *nt* discharging relation
Entladezeit *f* discharging time
Entladezyklus *m* discharging cycle
Entladung *f* discharging, discharge, unloading (work)
Entladung *f* **statischer Elektrizität** electrostatic discharge
Entladungsdauer *f* discharge duration
Entladungskanal *m* discharge channel
Entladungsspalt *m* discharging gap
Entladungsvorgang *m* discharging process
entlangfahren an trace (copying)
entlasten decrease the load, relieve (of the load), unload
Entlastung *nt* unloading (work), load relieving, relief, removal of the load
Entlastungsdauer *f* unloading time
Entlastungsrohr *nt* vent pipe
Entlastungszeit *f* relief time
entleeren 1. *(allg.)* empty, exhaust **2.** *(Flüssigkeit)* drain
Entleerungsstutzen *m* discharge branch
entlüften vent, ventilate, deaerate
Entlüfter *m* air exhauster, deaerator
Entlüftung *f* venting
Entlüftungsbohrung *f* vent hole
Entlüftungseinrichtung *f* venting facility
Entlüftungshahn *m* airdrain petcock
Entlüftungsleitung *f* breather line
Entlüftungsschraube *f* venting screw, venting plug
Entlüftungsstelle *f* air bleed

Entlüftungsventil *nt* air-relieve valve, vent valve, breather
Entmischungsneigung *f* de-mixing tendency, segregation tendency
Entnahme *f* removing, removal, retrieval, pick(ing), unloading
Entnahmeeinheit *f* retrieval unit
Entnahmeeinrichtung *f* picker device
Entnahmehäufigkeit *f* retrieval frequency
Entnahmeleitung *f* **1.** *(allg.)* extraction line **2.** *(e. Ölbehälters)* take-off pipe
Entnahmerichtung *f* sampling direction
Entnahmeroboter *m* unloading robot
Entnahmerohr *nt* picker tube
Entnahmeseite *f* picking face
Entnahmestation *f* picking station
Entnahmezone *f* removal zone, access point
entnebeln demist
entnehmen retrieve, remove, take (out or from), take off, pick
entnehmen: Strom ~ draw current from
Entnetzen *nt* dewetting
Entnickelung *f* denickelification
entpaketieren depacketize, unpack
Entratungseinrichtung *f* burr-removing device
entregen de-energize
entregt de-energized
Entregung *f* de-energizing
entriegeln unlock, release, unclamp
Entriegelung *f* **1.** *(allg.)* opening, releasing, unlocking, resetting **2.** *(e. Ölbrenners)* lock-out release
Entriegelungseinrichtung *f* release device, unlocking device
Entriegelungsort *m* resetting point
entrosten derust, unrust, remove the rust from
Entroster *m* rust remover
Entrostungsverfahren *nt* derusting process
Entrostungswerkzeug *nt* rust removal tool
Entschäumer *m* anti-foaming agent, antifoam
entscheiden decide

Entscheidung *f* decision
Entscheidungsbaum *nt* decision tree
Entscheidungsfindung *f* decision making
Entscheidungsgrundlage *f* basis for decision
Entscheidungshilfe *f* decision support
Entscheidungsregel *f* decision rule
entscheidungsrelevant relevant to decision making
Entscheidungsstelle *f* decision point
Entscheidungstabelle *f* decision table
Entscheidungsunterstützungssystem (EUS) *nt* decision support system (DSS)
entschicken unload, discharge
Entschickung *f* unloading, discharging
Entschlackungseinrichtung *f* de-ashing system
entsorgen dispose, discharge, remove
Entsorgung *f* disposal, discharge, (waste) removal
Entsorgungsanlage *f* disposal unit
Entsorgungskosten *pl* disposal costs
entspannen 1. *(allg.)* de-energize, release the tension, relieve (the stress) **2.** *(Druck)* decompress **3.** *(Feder)* release the spring, slacken **4.** *(Griff)* unclamp
Entspannen *nt* decompression, de-energizing, relief
Entspannen *nt:* **thermisches ~** thermal stress relief
Entspanner *m* flash trap
entspannt stress-relieved
Entspannung *f* seasoning
Entspannungsmodul *m* relaxation modulus
Entspannungstopf *m* expansion trap
Entspannungsverhalten *nt* decomposition characteristics
Entspannungsversuch *m* relaxation test
Entsperreinrichtung *f* resetting device
entsperren unlock
entsprechen *(z. B. Norm)* correspond to, be in compliance with, comply with
entsprechend corresponding, respective, according
Entsprechung *f* correspondence, equivalent, compliance
entstapeln denest, unstack, untier, retrieve
Entstapelungsmaschine *f* denester, denesting machine, unstacker
Entstapelungsmaschine *f* **für formstabile Packmittel** rigid container denester
Entstapler *m* denester, unstacker
entstehen incur, originate
Entstehungsbrand *m* irritation stage of a fire
Entstördruckknopf *m* reset push button
entstören clear faults
Entstörung *f* elimination of fault
Entwässerungsgrube *f* drainage pit
entweichen escape, flow off
entwerfen design, plan
entwickeln develop, design
Entwickler *m* developer
Entwicklung *f* development, design
Entwicklungsanlage *f* generator unit
Entwicklungsauftrag *m* development order
Entwicklungskosten *pl* development costs
Entwicklungstendenz *f* development tendency, production trend
entwirren disentangle, untwist
Entwurf *m* design, outline, plan
Entwurfszeichnung *f* draft drawing
entzinnen detin, untin
Entzug *m* *(z. B. von Kohlenstoff)* removal
entzünden ignite
Entzundern *nt* descaling, removal of scale, scaling-off
Entzündung *f* ignition
Evolventenrad *nt* involute gear
Epizykloid *m* epicycloid
Epoxidharzformmasse *f* epoxy resin moulding material
Epoxidharzpressmasse *f* epoxy resin moulding material
Epoxidverbindung *f* epoxy compound
Epoxygruppe *f* epoxy group
Epstein-Rahmen *m* Epstein square
Erblindung *f* fogging
Erdableitungswiderstand *m* earth

leakage resistance
erdbedeckte Rohrleitung *f* soil-covered pipework, earth-covered pipeline
Erdbelastung *f* earth loading
Erdbeschleunigung *f* acceleration due to gravity
Erde *f (UK)* earth(ing), *(US)* ground
erden earth, ground
Erdgas *nt* natural gas
erdgasgefeuert natural gas-fired
Erdschluss *m* dead earth, earth connection, earth fault, ground fault
Erdung *f* earthing, grounding
Erdungsband *nt* earthing strap, grounding strap
Erdwärmdauer *f* total heating period
ereignen incur, occur
Ereignis *nt* event, occurrence
ereignisgesteuert event-driven
ereignisorientiert event-oriented
Ereignisverwaltung *f* event management
Ereigniszeitpunkt *m* moment of event
Erfahrung *f* experience, know-how
Erfahrungsbericht *m* progress report
Erfahrungshintergrund *m* experience background
erfassbar ascertainable
erfassen 1. *(techn.)* assess, collect, record, sense **2.** *(physisch)* entangle, grip, trap
Erfassung *f* **1.** *(techn.)* acquisition, assessment, collection, recording **2.** *(physisch)* entanglement, trapping
Erfassung *f* **der Wurzel** root fusion
erfinden invent
Erfolg *m* success
erfolgreich successful
erforderlich necessary, required
erfordern require
Erfordernis *f* requirement
erfüllen fulfil, meet, satisfy
Erfüllung *f* fulfilment
ergänzen complete, complement, supplement, replenish, add
ergänzend additional, supplementary
ergänzende Angaben *fpl* supplementary data *pl*
Ergänzung *f* addition, supplement
Ergänzungskegel *m* complementary cone
Ergänzungskegelspitze *f* complementary cone apex
Ergänzungskegelwinkel *m* complementary cone angle
Ergänzungsmessung *f* supplementary measurement
Ergänzungsprüfung *f* supplementary testing
Ergänzungssymbol *nt* supplementary symbol
Ergänzungszeichnung *f* supplementary drawing
Ergebnis *nt* outcome, result
Ergebnisabweichung *f* error of result
Ergebnisaufbereitung *f* organization of data, performance processing
Ergebnisdarstellung *f* representation of results
Ergebnisseite *f* result side
Ergebnisunsicherheit *f* uncertainty of measurement
Ergonomie *f* ergonomics
ergonomisch ergonomic
ergonomische Gestaltung *f* ergonomic design
ergreifen grip, make contact, trap
erhabene Schrift *f* profile letters
erhalten obtain, maintain, receive
Erhaltungsladen *m* trickle charging
erheben collect
Erhebung *f* collection (of data), data acquisition
erhitzen heat (up)
Erhitzung *f* heating-up
erhitzungsempfindlich sensitive to heating
erhöhen elevate, increase, raise
erhöht increased, raised
Erhöhung *f* increase, elevation, rise
erholen recover
Erholungsdauer *f* time of recovery
Erholungsglühen *nt* recuperative annealing
Erholungsverhalten *nt* recovery behaviour
Erholungszeit *f* recovery time, recovery period
Erholungszeitbereich *m* recovery time range

Erholungszeitspanne *f* recovery time interval
erkalten chill, cool down
erkennbar perceivable, recognizable
Erkennbarkeit *f* identification
erkennen detect, identify, recognize, sense
Erkenntnisgrenze *f* limit of detection
Erkennung *f* detection, identification, recognition
Erkennungsklasse *f* recognition class
Erkennungsmöglichkeit *f* recognition possibility
erlauben permit
erleichtern facilitate
Erleichterung *f* facilitation
ermangeln lack
ermitteln determine, detect, find out, ascertain, calculate, evaluate
Ermittlung *f* investigation, ascertainment, calculation, detection, evaluation, determination
ermöglichen allow (for), enable
ermüden fatigue, tire
Ermüdung *f* fatigue
Ermüdungsgrenze *f* fatigue strength
Ermüdungsriss *m* fatigue crack
Ermüdungsrissbildung *f* fatigue cracking
erneuern recondition, renew, renovate
Erneuerung *f* reconditioning, renewal, renewing, renovation
erneut renewed, repeated
erneut beginnen restart
Erodieranlage *f* eroding machine
erodieren erode, abrade
erodierend eroding, erosive
Erodiergeschwindigkeit *f* eroding speed
Erodierverfahren *nt* eroding process
Erodierwerkzeug *nt* eroding tool
Erosion *f* erosion
Erosionsfront *f* erosion front
Erosionsprüfung *f* erosion test
erproben test, try
Erprobung *f* trial, test(ing), pilot
erregen energize, excite
Erregerstrom *m* exciting current, energizing current
Erregerwicklung *f* exciting winding,
field coil, field winding
Erregung *f* excitation
Erregungsamplitude *f* excitation amplitude
erreichen 1. *(allg.)* reach, obtain 2. (Ergebnisse) achieve, attain
errichten build, erect, set up
Ersatz *m* replacement, substitute, substitution, spare
Ersatzgeradverzahnung *f* equivalent spur gear tooth system, equivalent spur gear teeth
Ersatzgetriebe *nt* cognate linkage
Ersatzlast *f* equivalent load
Ersatzmasse *f* equivalent mass
Ersatzmesser *nt* replacement blade
Ersatzprobe *f* substitute test specimen
Ersatz-Stirnradverzahnung *f* equivalent cylindrical gear teeth
Ersatzstromerzeuger *m* substitute power generator
Ersatzsystem *nt* equivalent system
Ersatzteil *nt* replacement part, spare part
Ersatzteilbevorratung *f* stockpiling of spare parts
Ersatzteilhaltung *f* spare parts storage
Ersatzteilkreisdurchmesser *m* equivalent reference circle diameter
Ersatzteillager *nt* replacement stock, spare part stock, spares store, spare parts store
Ersatzteilliste *f* list of spare parts
Ersatzteilzeichnung *f* spare part drawing
Ersatzverzahnung *f* equivalent tooth system
Ersatzzahndickenhalbwinkel *m* equivalent tooth thickness half angle
Ersatzzähnzahl *f* virtual number of teeth
erschüttern shake, convulse, jar, rock
Erschütterung *f* jarring, vibration, shock, percussion
erschütterungfrei vibration-free, smooth
Erschütterungsfestigkeit *f* shock resistance
erschütterungsfrei smooth, vibrationless

erschweren make (or render) difficult
Erschwernis *f* obstacle
erschwert severe
ersetzen exchange, replace, substitute
erstarren solidify
Erstarrungsfront *f* solidification front
Erstarrungsriss *m* solidification crack, crater crack
Erstarrungstemperatur *f* setting temperature
Erstarrungsverlauf *m* solidification course
Erstarrungsvorgang *m* solidification procedure
Erstauslieferung *f* first customer shipment
Erstbefüllung *f* first filling, filling for the first time
erstbelegen initialize
Erstbelegung *f* initialization
Erstbesteller *m* launch customer
Erstbestellung *f* initial order, launch order, first order
erste Freifläche *f* first flank
erste Hilfe *f* first aid
erste Spanfläche *f* first face
Ersteinstellung *f* initial setting
erstellen draw up, compile
Ersteller *m* e. Zeichnung draughtsman
Erstellung *f* compilation
Erstlieferant *m* initial supplier
Erstlot *nt* primary solder
Erstmeldung *f* first message
Erstmuster *nt* primary sample
Erstprüfung *f* original inspection, initial test
Erststufenprobe *f* primary sample
ertragen sustain
Erwärmdauer *f* heating treatment time
erwärmen warm up, heat (up)
Erwärmung *f* heating (up), generation of heat, temperature rise
Erwärmungsgut *nt* material exposed to heating
Erwärmungsprüfung *f* temperature measurement
erwarten envisage
erwartet expected, to be expected
erwartungstreue Schätzfunktion *f* unbiased estimator

Erwartungswert *m* expectation (value), expected value
Erweichen *nt* softening
Erweichen *nt* **der Schneide** loss of tool hardness
Erweichungsintervall *m* softening interval
Erweichungsverhalten *nt* softening behaviour (or characteristics)
erweisen (sich ~) prove
Erweiterbarkeit *f* capacity for expansion
erweitern 1. *(allg.)* enlarge, expand, extend, enhance, widen, diverge **2.** *(EDV)* upgrade
erweiterte Realität *f* augmented reality
erweiterte Sicherheit *f* added safety
erweitertes NAND-Glied *nt* extended NAND
erweitertes Unternehmen *nt* extended enterprise
Erweiterung *f* extension, enlargement, expansion, widening, enhancement
Erweiterungseingang *m* extension input
Erweiterungsfeld *nt* extension block
Erweiterungsfunktion *f* extender function
Erweiterungsglied *nt* extender element
Erweiterungsleitung *f* extension pipe
Erweiterungsprüfung *f* extended coverage test
Erweiterungsmöglichkeit *f* possibility to expansion
erwerben acquire, gain, obtain
Erz *nt* ore
erzeugen 1. *(Waren)* make, manufacture, produce, create, fabricate **2.** *(el.)* generate
Erzeugende *f* (e. Evolventenfläche) generator
erzeugende Gerade *f* (am Werkzeug) generating straight line
Erzeugenden-Formabweichung *f* generator form variation
Erzeugenden-Gesamtabweichung *f* total generator variation
Erzeugenden-Prüfbereich *m* genera-

tor test range
Erzeugenden-Winkelabweichung *f* generator angle variation
erzeugendes Rad *nt* generating gear
Erzeugnis *nt* make, product
Erzeugnisgruppe *f* product group
Erzeugnislager *nt* finished and unfinished products warehouse, product warehouse
Erzeugnisspektrum *nt* product spectrum
Erzeugung *f* production, manufacture, fabrication, generation, creation
Erzeugung *f* **der Verzahnung** tooth generation
Erzeugungs-Achsabstand *m* (Hohlrad) generating centre distance
Erzeugungsbedingungen *fpl* generating conditions *pl*
Erzeugungsgesetz *nt* law of generation
Erzeugungsgetriebe *nt* generating train
Erzeugungsgrenzbedingungen *fpl* limiting conditions for generating
Erzeugungskreis *m* generating circle
Erzeugungspaarungsfeld *nt* generating mating area
Erzeugungsprofilverschiebungsfaktor *m* generating addendum modification coefficient
Erzeugungsrad *nt* generating gear
Erzeugungsradpaar *nt* generating gear pair
Erzeugungswälzbahn *f* generating path of contact
Erzeugungswälzfläche *f* generating pitch surface
Erzeugungswälzkreis *m* generating circle of contact, cf. Wälzkreis
Erzeugungswinkel *m* base spiral angle
Erzeugungszahnstange *f* counterpart rack
erzielen attain, obtain
erzwungene Biegeschwingung *f* forced flexural vibrations
erzwungene Schwingung *f* forced vibrations (pl)
esterartig ester-like
Esteröl *nt* ester oil

Etagenbogen *m* offset bend
Etikett *nt* label
Etikettendruck *m* label printing
Etikettendruck- und -appliziermaschine *f* print and apply labelling machine
Etikettendrucker *m* label printer
Etiketteninspektionsmaschine *f* label inspection machine
etikettieren label
Etikettiermaschine *f* label applicator, labelling machine
Etikettiermaschine *f* **für vorgummierte Etiketten** pre-gummed label applicator
euklidisch euclidic
Euroflachpalette *f* euro flat-pallet
Europalette *f* europallet
EVA (Einkaufs-/Verkaufs-Auftrag) *m* IPO (internal purchase order)
EVA-Formular *nt* IPO form
evakuieren evacuate
Evakuierkanal *m* evacuation channel
Evakuierung *f* evacuation, pumping out
Evolventenlänge *f* involute length
Evolvente *f* involute curve, involute gear
Evolventenflanke *f* involute flank
Evolventenform *f* involute form
Evolventenfunktion *f* involute function
Evolventengeradstirnpaar *nt* involute spur gear pair
Evolventenprofil *nt* involute profile
Evolventenrad *nt* involute gear
Evolventenschrägverzahnung *f* involute helical gear teeth
Evolventenschraubfläche *f* involute helicoid
Evolventenstirnrad *nt* involute cylindrical gear
Evolventenursprungspunkt *m* involute origin
Evolventenverzahnung *f* involute gear tooth system
Evolventenwälzfräser *m* involute hob
Evolventenzahnflanke *f* involute tooth flank
evolventische Flanke *f* involute flank

EXAPT *Abk* extended APT (Automatically Programmed Tools)
Exklusiv-NOR *nt* exclusive NOR
Exklusiv-ODER *nt* exclusive OR, EX-OR
Expansionsbalg *m* expansion bellows joint
Expansionsklebfolie *f* expanding adhesive film
Expansionsspule *f* expanding coil
Expertensystem *nt* expert system, knowledge-based system
Expertenwissen *nt* (expert) knowledge
explodieren explode
Explosionsdruck *m* pressure of explosion
explosionsfähig explosive, potentially explosive
Explosionsgefahr *f* explosion hazard
explosionsgefährdet subject to the risk of explosion, potentially explosive
explosionsgefährdeter Raum *m* hazardous location
Explosionsgefährlichkeit *f* explosive risk (or hazard)
explosionsgeschützt explosion-roof
Explosionskette *f* explosion train
Explosionsklappe *f* blow-back flap
Explosionsquelle *f* incipient explosion
Explosionsschutz *m* explosion protection, explosion prevention and protection
Explosionsschutzausrüstung *f* explosion-proof equipment
Explosionsschutzbereich *m* explosion-proof area
Explosionsumformung *f* explosion-forming
Explosionsunterdrückung *f* explosion suppression
explosiv explosive

Explosivstoff *m* explosive substance
Exponent *m* exponent
Exponentialverteilung *f* exponential distribution
Expressdienst *m* express delivery
Extender-Harz *nt* extender resin
extern external
extern beschaffen outsource
externer Speicher *m* external memory
extrahierbar extractable
extrahierbare Bestandteile *f* extractable constituents
Extrem(situation) $n(f)$ extreme
Extremwert *m* extreme value, peak value
Extremwertverteilung *f* extreme value distribution
Extrudat *nt* extrudate
Extruder *m* extruder
Extruderschnecke *f* extruder screw
Extruderschneckengang *m* extruder-screw channel
Extruderzylinder *m* extruder barrel
extrudieren extrude, extrusion-mould, mould by extrusion
Extrudieren *nt* extruding, extrusion moulding
Extrusion *f* extrusion
Extrusionskolben *m* extrusion ram
Extrusionszylinder *m* extrusion cylinder
Exzenter *m* eccentric, eccentric cam
Exzenterpresse *f* eccentric press
Exzenterschneckenpumpe *f* eccentric worm pump
Exzenterwelle *f* eccentric shaft
exzentrisch eccentric, off-centre
exzentrisches Rad *nt* eccentric gear
Exzentrizität *f* amount of eccentricity, eccentricity

F f

Fabrik *f* plant, factory
Fabrikat *nt* make
Fabrikmodell *nt* factory model, plant model
Fabriknummer *f* serial number
Fabrikplanung *f* plant (or factory) planning
Fabrikrechner *m* factory computer
Fabrikschild *nt* identification plate, information plate
fabrizieren manufacture, produce
Fach *nt* **1.** *(Lehre, Spezialgebiet)* subject, field **2.** *(Feld)* bay **3.** *(Öffnung)* aperture, slot **4.** *(Regal)* (rack) compartment, (storage) bin, (storage) location
Fachabteilung *f* technical department
Fachadresse *f* racking address
Facharbeiter *m* craftsman, skilled worker, skilled labour, trained operator (or man)
Facharbeitermangel *m* shortage of skilled workers
Fachbelegtsensor *m* aperture occupied sensor
Fachbesetzfühler *m* location engaged feeler arm
Fachboden *m* shelf, shelving bottom
Fachbodenregal *nt* flat bottom shelving
Fachdetail *nt* detail of the racking compartment
Facheinfahrbreite *f* detail of the racking compartment, rack entry width
Facheinteilung *f* arrangement of the bays
fächelnd führen draw with a fanning action
Fächerscheibe *f* serrated lock washer
Fachfassungsvermögen *nt* shelving capacity
Fachfeinpositionierung *f* rack fine positioning, location fine positioning, fine positioning
Fachfreimaß *nt* rack compartment clearance
Fachgebiet *nt* subject field

fachgerecht skilful, workmanlike, experienced, skilled, specialized, correct
Fachingenieur *m* engineering specialist
Fachkompetenz *f* qualifications
Fachkoordinaten *fpl* rack compartment coordinates
Fachkräfte *fpl* skilled labour (or people)
fachkundig competent
fachliche Ausbildung *f* industrial training
Fachmonteur *m* qualified technician
Fachpersonal *nt* specialized personnel
Fachposition *f* bay position, location position
Fachpositionierung *f* location positioning
Fachraster *nt* bay grid
Fachteiler *m* divider, separating arm, shelf divider
Fachteilung *f* divider, shelf divider, division
Fachtiefe *f* depth of shelving
Fachwerkbauweise *f* lattice design
Fäden *mpl* filaments
fadenförmiger Angriff *m* filiform corrosion attack
fadengerades Weiterreißen tear propagation along a thread
Fadenkorrosion *f* filiform corrosion
Fadenkreuz *nt* graticule, cross wire
Fadenkreuzmikrometer *nt* cross wire micrometer
Fadenschutz *m* threadguard
fadenziehende Masse *f* stringy mass
fähig able, capable
Fähigkeit *f* ability, capability
Fahrantrieb *m* drive unit, travel drive (unit)
Fahrauftrag *m* driving command, drive instruction
Fahrauftragsrückmeldung *f* driving command echo
Fahrbahn *f* lane, road, runway
Fahrbahnleuchte *f* travel light
Fahrbahnteile *ntpl* road debris
fahrbar portable, mobile, movable

Fahrbefehl *m* driving command, drive instruction
Fahrbegrenzung *f* limit of travel
Fahrbeleuchtung *f* driving light
Fahrbeschleunigung *f* drive acceleration
Fahrbetrieb *m* travelling, travelling mode
Fahrbewegung *f* travel motion, travelling movement, travel
Fahrboden *m* floor
Fahrdiagramm *nt* travel diagram
fahren ride, run, traverse, (horizontal) travel, move, drive, propel
fahrende Werkbank *f* moving workbench
Fahrer *m* driver, operator
Fahrergewicht *nt* operator's weight
Fahrerkabine *f* cab, cabin, operator's cab
fahrerlos driverless
fahrerloses Flurförderzeug *nt* driverless truck
fahrerloses Transportsystem (FTS) *nt* automated guided vehicle system (AGVS), driverless transport system
Fahrerplatz *m* driver position, driving position, operator's position, operator's platform, operator's compartment
Fahrerposition *f* operating position
Fahrerschutzdach *nt* operator's overhead guard, overhead guard
Fahrersitz *m* **1.** *(allg.)* driver's seat, operator's seat **2.** *(mit ~ in Fahrtrichtung)* front-seated **3.** *(mit ~ quer zur Fahrtrichtung)* side-seated
Fahrerstand *m* control position, driving position
Fahrerstandplattform *f* operator's stand-on platform, stand-on platform
Fahrfunktion *f* driving function
Fahrgeräusche *ntpl* driving noise
Fahrgerüst *nt* mobile scaffolding
Fahrgeschwindigkeit *f* travel speed, travelling speed, horizontal travel speed, drive speed
Fahrgestell *nt* chassis
Fahrkomponente *f* travel component
Fahrkurs *m* travel path, guide path, route, course, routing, travel way, run

Fahrmotor *m* traction motor, drive motor
Fahrradgewinde *nt* bicycle screw thread, cycle thread
Fahrrahmen *m* lower carriage
Fahrregler *m* drive controller
Fahrschalter *m* controller, travel control switch
Fahrschiene *f* bottom rail, floor rail, floor-mounted rail, floor running rail, guide rail, travel rail, track rail, travelling rail
Fahrschienenkopf *m* floor rail head
Fahrspur *f* track, travel path
Fahrspurbegrenzung *f* limits of travel paths
Fahrstellung *f* travelling position
Fahrsteuerelemente *ntpl* driving controls (pl)
Fahrsteuerung *f* travelling control
Fahrstrom *m* traction current
Fahrstromunterbrechung *f* traction cut
Fahrt *f* travel, trip
Fahrtendbegrenzung *f* limit of travel
Fahrtrichtung *f* direction of travel, direction of motion
Fahrtrichtung *f* **beibehalten** maintain the path
Fahrtrichtung *f* **rückwärts** backward driving direction
Fahrtrichtung *f* **vorwärts** forward driving direction
Fahrtrichtungshebel *m* direction control lever
Fahrtrichtungsumkehr *f* **1.** *(Vorgang)* reversal of direction **2.** *(Vorrichtung)* direction change mechanism
Fahrtumkehrung *f* reversal of direction (changes)
Fahrtziel *nt* destination of travel
Fahrverhalten *nt* travelling characteristics
Fahrverkehr *m* vehicular traffic
Fahrverzögerung *f* drive braking
Fahrweg *m* **1.** *(techn. Einrichtung)* gangway, (travel) path, route **2.** *(Länge)* travel distance, travel
Fahrweg *m* **mit Führung** guide path
Fahrwegbegrenzung *f* travel limita-

tion
Fahrwegmarkierung *f* route marking(s)
Fahrweise *f* mode of operation
Fahrwerk *nt* carriage, drive mechanism, travel mechanism, travel unit, travel drive unit
Fahrwerksteile *ntpl* parts of the travel mechanism
Fahrwiderstand *m* tractive resistance, resistance to motion, rolling resistance
Fahrzeit *f* travel period
Fahrzeug *nt* vehicle, truck
Fahrzeugaußenkontur *f* truck profile
Fahrzeugbatterie *f* traction battery (unit), conveyor battery
Fahrzeuggetriebe *nt* vehicle transmission
Fahrzeugidentifizierung *f* vehicle identification
Fahrzeugklasse *f* vehicle class
Fahrzeugkonzept *nt* vehicle concept
Fahrzeuglüftungsanlage *f* vehicle ventilation system
Fahrzeugräder *ntpl* road wheels
Fahrzeugrahmen *m* chassis, chassis frame
Fahrzeugreifen *m* motor vehicle tyre
Fahrzeugrufstation *f* (vehicle) calling station
Fahrzeugschlauch *m* motor vehicle tube
Fahrzeugsteuerung *f* vehicle control system, vehicle controller
Fahrzustand *m* travel state
Faktor *m* coefficient
Faktor *m* **einer Abmessung** reduced value of a dimension
Faktortabelle *f* factor table
fakturieren invoice
Fakturierung *f* invoicing
Fall *m* fall, case
Fallbeschleunigung *f* acceleration due to free fall
fallbezogen depending on each case
Fallbodenbehälter *m* drop bottom container
Fallbolzenversuch *m* falling weight test
Falldämpfer *m* fall braking device

fallen decrease, fall, drop
fallen lassen drop
fallendes Gießen *nt* drop casting
Fallenergie *f* drop energy
Fallfolge *f* drop sequence
Fallhaken *m* **für Drehflügeltüren** door fallhook for trap doors
Fallhammer *m* drop hammer, tup, rebounding hammer
Fallhöhe *f* distance of fall
Fallhöhe *f* **beim Bruch** drop height at fracture
fällig due
Fallleitung *f* downcomer, downpipe
Fallleitungsverziehung *f* downpipe offset
Fallmasse *f* mass of additional weight
Fallpackmaschine *f* drop packing machine
Fallposition *f* vertical-downward position
Fallprüfmaschine *f* drop test machine
Fallschnecke *f* drop worm, trip worm
Fallstopp *m* fall-arrester gear
Falltisch *m* drop table
Fällungskolben *m* precipitation flask
Fallversuch *m* impact drop test
fallweise case by case
Fallwinkel *m* angle of drop, angle of fall
Fallzahl *f* number of drops
Fallzahl *f* **beim Bruch** number of drops to fracture
falsch false, improper, wrong
Falschlieferung *f* wrong delivery
Falschlufteinbruch *m* air-inleakage (at the burner barrel)
Faltbetrag *m* *(beim Ringfaltversuch von Rohren)* flatting distance
Faltbogen *m* folded bend
Faltbox *f* folding box
Falte *f* fold(ing), crimp, wrinkle
Falteinschlagmaschine *f* fold wrapping machine, overwrapping machine
falten fold, crimp
Faltenfilter *m* fluted filter
Faltkiste *f* carton, case
Faltnaht *f* fin seal
Faltprobe *f* bend specimen
Faltschachtel *f* carton, case
Faltschachtel *f* **für Beladung von**

oben top load carton
Faltschachtelaufrichtfüll- und -verschließmaschine *f* **mit Füllung von oben** top load carton erect form fill and seal machine
Faltschachtelaufrichtmaschine *f* carton (or case) erecting machine
Faltschachtel-Form-, Füll- und Verschließmaschine *f* carton fill form and seal machine
Faltschachtelmaschine *f* cartoning machine, carton closing machine
Faltschachtelverpackungsmaschine *f* **mit horizontaler Zuführung** end load case packing machine
Faltschachtelverpackungsmaschine *f* **mit Zuführung von oben/unten** top/bottom load case packing machine
Faltschachtelverschließmaschine *f* carton closing machine
Faltschachtelzuschnitt *m* carton blank, case blank
Faltschachtelzuschnittaufrichtmaschine *f* carton blank erecting machine
Faltverschließmaschine *f* fold closing machine
Faltversuch *m* technological bend test, bend-over test
Falz *m* 1. *(allg.)* crimp, fold, flange 2. *(bei Betonrohren)* rebated joint 3. *(Metallbearbeitung)* seam, welt
Falz *m* **und Nut** *f* spigot and socket
Falzen *nt* 1. *(allg.)* crimping, folding 2. *(Anlegen eines Bordes)* seaming
Falzen *nt* **durch Drücken** seaming by spinning
Falzgerät *nt* folding apparatus
Falzverbindung *f* rebated joint
Falzverschließmaschine *f* crimp closing machine
Fang *m* 1. *(allg.)* catch(ing), safety catch 2. *(Abscheider)* interceptor
Fangeinrichtung *f* arrestor
fangen catch, trap
Fangenergie *f* energy produced ba catching
Fangfall *m* event of catching, safety catch, triggering event
Fanghaken *m* safety claw
Fangklinke *f* arrestor stay
Fanglast *f* catch load, load caught
Fangmechanismus *m* catching mechanism
Fangraum *m* catching block, machine pocket
Fangrolle *f* catching roller, catching pulley
Fangschale *f* collecting tray
Fangschiene *f* catching rail
Fangschräge *f* sloping surface (in the catching block)
Fangstelle *f* catch point
Fangstift *m* catch pin
Fangverzögerung *f* deceleration during the catching operation
Fangvorgang *m* catching operation, safety gear tripping, triggering event
Fangvorrichtung *f* catching device, safety catching device, safety gear
Fangweg *m* catching path
Farbanstrich *m* painted surface
Farbaufdruck *m* colour impression
Farbausbeute *f* dye yield
Farbe *f* colour, paint
Färbebad *nt* dyebath
Farbeindringprüfung *f* dye penetrant inspection
Farbenzinkoxid *nt* lithopone
Farbfleck *m* coloured stain
farbgebender Stoff *m* colouring substance (or matter)
Farbgestaltung *f* colour arrangement
Farbindikatortitration *f* colour-indicator titration
Farblochromatierung *f* colourless chromating
farbmetrisches Verfahren *nt* colorimetric method
Farbskala *f* process colours
Farbspritzanlage *f* spray-painting unit
Farbstärke *f* tinting strength
Farbstich *m* hue
Farbstofflaser *m* dyestuff laser
Farbstofftinte *f* dye ink
Farbtiefstandard *m* depth of shade standard
Farbton *m* hue, shade

Fase *f* **1.** *(Kantenabschrägung)* bevel, chamfer, land **2.** *(Fräserzahn)* straight land **3.** *(Spiralbohrer)* margin
Fase *f* **an Stirnschneiden** face land
Fase *f* **an Umfangsschneide** top land
Fase *f* **der Spanleitstufe** *f* chip breaker land width
fasen chamfer, bevel
fasenartiger Anschliff *m* ridge
fasenartiger Anschliff *m* **auf der Spanfläche** face ride
fasenartiger Anschliff *m* **an der Schneide** primary land
Fasenbreite *f* width of land, size of land
Fasenfreiwinkel *m* *(US)* end relief angle, *(UK)* primary clearance angle, secondary clearance angle, primary clearance
Fasenhöhe *f* **des Kopfkantenbruchs** height of the tooth tip chamfer
Fasenmeißel *m* chamfering tool
Fasenspanwinkel *m* chamfer angle
Fasenwinkel *m* bevel angle
Faser *f* fibre
Faserbündel *nt* fibre bundle
faserfreies Tuch *nt* fluffless (or lintfree) cloth
Fasergut *nt* fibre material
faserig fibrous
Faserkabel *nt* fibre cable
Faserkuchen *m* pressed fibre mat
Fasermatte *f* fibre mat
Faserprüfmaschine *f* fibre testing machine
Faserseil *nt* fibre rope
Faserspanwinkel *m* land rake angle
Faserstoffbahn *f* sheet of fibrous material
Faserstoffsuspension *f* fibre stock suspension
Faserstrang *m* fibre strand
Faserstrukturelektrode *f* fibrous structure electrode
Faserstrukturplattenbatterie *f* fibrous structure-plate battery
Fass *nt* barrel, cask, drum, keg, tub
Fass- oder Kegfüll- und -verschließmaschine *f* cask or keg fill and seal machine
Fassade *f* front, face

fassadenseitig front ...
Fassauflage *f* drum chock
fassen grip, engage
Fassfüll- und -verschließmaschine *f* cask (or tub) fill and seal machine
Fassgreifer *m* drum gripper
Fasskippklammerarm *m* tippling drum clamp arm
Fassklammer *f* barrel clamp, drum clamp
Fassklammerarm *m* drum clamp arm
Fasslager *nt* gantry, drum storage stack
Fassonautomat *m* automatic forming machine
Fassondrehen *nt* form turning
Fassondrehmaschine *f* automatic forming lathe
Fassung *f* socket
Fassungsvermögen *nt* capacity
Fassverschraubung *f* screwed union on casks
fast "Null" almost zero
Fausthandschuh *m* mitt
Faustregel *f* rule of thumb
FDM *(Schmelzmodellherstellung)* Fused Deposition Modeling
Feder *f* key (in slot), spring, feather
Feder *f* **und Nut** *f* key and slot
Federaußentaster *m* outside spring calliper
Federband *nt* spring hinge
federbelastet spring-loaded
federbetätigt spring operated
Federbiegegrenze *f* elastic bending limit
Federbogen *m* resilient bend
Federcharakteristik *f* resilience characteristic
Federdruckbremse *f* spring-loaded brake
Federeigenschaft *f* springiness
Federflansch *m* tongue-faced flange
federgespannt spring-loaded
federgespannter Auslösemechanismus *m* latch- and fire mechanism
Federgreifzirkel *m* outside spring calliper
Federkeil *m* feather key
Federkennlinie *f* compression stress-strain characteristics

Federkonstante *f* spring constant
Federkraft *f* spring force
Federkraftlichtbogenschweißen *nt* arc welding with electrode fed by spring pressure
Federlochtaster *m* inside spring calliper
Federmutter *f (für Blechschrauben)* sheet spring nut
federn spring, be resilient
federnd resilient, spring-loaded
federnde gewellte Unterlegscheibe *f* wrinkle washer
federndes Druckstück *nt* spring-loaded thrust pad
federndes Sicherungselement *nt* retaining element with spring action
Federpaket *nt* spring stack
Federring *m* spring washer
Federring *m* **für Kombischrauben** spring washer for screw assemblies
Federring *m* **mit Schutzmantel** *m* spring washer with safety ring
Federring *m:* **aufgebogener** ~ positive pattern-type spring washer
Federring *m:* **gewellter** ~ crinkled spring washer
Federring *m:* **gewölbter** ~ curved spring washer, high compression load spring washer
Federring *m:* **glatter** ~ plain pattern type spring washer
Federscheibe *f* curved spring washer, spring washer
Federschraube *f* spring centre bolt
Federspanneisen *nt* compressive clamp
Federspanner *m* spring vice, spring clamp
Federspannfutter *nt* chuck spring collet, spring collet
Federspannung *f* spring tension
Federspeicher *m* spring-applied brakes, spring energy store
Federspeicherantrieb *m* stored-energy spring actuation
Federstecker *m* spring cotter
Federstift *m* spring plunger
Federstrichverfahren *nt* pen stroke method

Federung *f* spring system, resilience
Federungsvermögen *nt* flexibility, resilience
Federwaage *f* spring balance
Federweg *m* range of spring, travel of the spring system, spring excursion
Federwegbereich *m* deflection range
Federwert *m* deformation value
Federwinkel *m* deflection angle
Federzirkel *m* spring dividers
Fehlbestand *m* stock-out
fehlen be missing, be lacking (of)
fehlend absent
Fehler *m* 1. *(als Beschädigung el.)* defect, fault 2. *(Versagen)* failure 3. *(tum math. stat.)* error 4. *(versehentlicher ~)* mistake 5. *(Ungenauigkeit)* inaccuracy 6. (Makel) blemish 7. *(Mangel)* deficiency 8. *(Nachteil)* disadvantage 9. *(an Oberflächen)* imperfection 10. *(im Werkstoff)* defect, flaw 11. *(Materialfehler)* defect 12. *(SPS, EDV)* bug
Fehler *m* **beim Teilen** indexing error
Fehler *m* **erster Art** *(stat.)* error of the first kind
Fehler *m* **in der Verbindung** communication error
Fehleranalyse *f* fault analysis
fehleranfällig fault-prone
Fehleranfälligkeit *f* proneness to disorders, proneness to fault
Fehlerausbesserung *f* rectification of defects
Fehlerausschluss *m* fault exclusion
Fehlerbaum *m* fault tree
Fehlerbedingung *f* fault condition
Fehlerbehandlung *f* error treatment
Fehlerbeseitigung *f* 1. *(allg.)* fault elimination, fault repair 2. *(AESPS)* debugging
Fehlerbestimmung *f* determination of errors, localisation of faults, trouble shooting
Fehlerbild *nt* error trace
Fehlerdiagnose *f* fault diagnosis
Fehlererkennung *f* fault detection, error identification
Fehlerfall *m* event of a fault
Fehlerfläche *f:* **gesamte** ~ aggregate defective area

Fehlerfortpflanzungsgesetz *nt* error propagation law, law of propagation of errors
fehlerfrei error-free, fault-free, faultless, flawless, without error
fehlerfreie Schnittfläche *f* flawless cut surface
fehlerfreies Gewinde *nt* flawless thread
fehlerfreies Zahnrad *nt* error-free gear
Fehlergrenze *f* limit of error
Fehlergrenzenfortpflanzung *f* error limits in error limit propagation, error limit propagation
fehlerhaft defective, faulty, incorrect
fehlerhafte Einheiten *fpl* non-conforming items
fehlerhaftes Teil *nt* defective part
Fehlerkennbarkeit *f* defect discernability
Fehlerkompensation *f* error compensation
Fehlerlinie *f* *(als Wälzfehler)* error trace
fehlerlos fault-free, flawless
Fehlermeldung *f* fault indication, fault message
Fehlerprotokoll *nt* syntax and service report
Fehlerquelle *f* source of error(s)
Fehlerrate *f* error rate
Fehlerrechnung *f* calculation of errors
fehlersicher fail-safe
fehlersichere Abschaltung *f* fail-safe shutdown
Fehlersignal *nt* error signal
Fehlerstrom *m* 1. *(el.)* fault current 2. *(Differenzstrom)* residual current
Fehlerstromschutzschalter *m* residual current protective device
Fehlersuchbaum *m* fault access tree
Fehlersuche *f* fault finding
Fehlertoleranz *f* error tolerance
Fehlerumgehung *f* fault bypassing
Fehlerverfolgung *f* fault monitoring
Fehlerverlauf *m* error pattern
Fehlerwahrscheinlichkeit *f* fault probability
Fehlerzählgerät *nt* fault indicator
Fehlfunktion *f* functional disorder, malfunction
Fehlgriff *m* faulty manipulation
Fehlkonstruktion *f* faulty design
Fehlprozess *m* error process
Fehlschaltung *f* 1. *(allg.)* faulty operation (or engagement or switching) 2. *(e. Maschine)* misoperation
Fehlstelle *f* surface defect, defect, fault, flaw
Fehlsteuerung *f* faulty control
Fehlstück *nt* defective
Fehlteil *nt* missing part
Feil- und Sägemaschine *f* filing and sawing machine
Feile *f* file
feilen file
Feilenheft *nt* file handle
Feilspäne *mpl* filings
fein fine, pure, minute, precise
Feinabruf *m* precise call
Feinbearbeitung *f* fine finishing, superfinishing, precision machining, finishing, metal finishing
Feinbearbeitung *f:* **spanende ~** finish-machining
Feinbearbeitungsprozess *m* fine machining
Feinbearbeitungsverfahren *nt* fine finishing technique
Feinbewegungsschraube *f* slow motion screw
Feinblech *nt* metal sheet
Feinbohren *nt* diamond boring, fine boring, fine-hole boring, precision boring
Feinbohrmaschine *f* precision (or fine) boring machine, jig borer
Feinbohrmeißel *m* precision cutter, microbore tool
Feinbohrwerk *nt* fine boring machine, precision jig borer
Feinbohrwerkzeug *nt* fine-boring tool
Feindreheinrichtung *f* precision turning attachment
Feindrehen *nt* fine (or finish or precision) turning
Feindrehmaschine *f* precision lathe
Feindrehmeißel *m* fine turning tool
feineinstellen micro-set
Feineinstellung *f* 1. *(allg.)* fine (or micrometer) setting, micrometer (or micro

or fine) adjustment, inching, jogging
2. *(von Messzeugen)* micrometer adjustment
Feineinstellventil *nt* fine adjustment valve
Feinflächenschleifmaschine *f* surface grinder
Feinfräsen *nt* precision milling, finish milling
feinfühlige Schaltung *f* finger-tip control
Feingestalt *f* precision form
Feingewinde *nt* fine pitch thread, fine thread
Feingießen *nt* investment casting
Feingießverfahren *nt* investment casting process
Feingussmodellanschmelzverfahren *nt* precision cast iron model melting process
Feinhobelmaschine *f* **1.** *(allg.)* precision shaping machine **2.** *(Langhobelmaschine)* precision planing machine
Feinhub *m* precision hoisting gear, precision hoisting
Feinhubgeschwindigkeit *f* precision hoisting speed
feinjustierte Kante *f* carefully trued edge
feinkörnig fine-grained, close-grained
Feinlötung *f* precision soldering
Feinmaßmanometer *nt* sensitive pressure gauge
Feinmechanik *f* precision mechanics
Feinmessschieblehre *f* vernier calliper (rule), vernier calliper gauge
Feinmessschraube *f* micrometer screw
Feinmessschraublehre *f* *(Feinmessschraube)* micrometer calliper gauge, micrometer screw, micrometer
Feinmessschraublehre *f* **für Gewindemessung** screw thread micrometer (or calliper)
Feinmessschraublehre *f* **mit Ratsche** micrometer calliper with ratchet stop
Feinmesstiefenlehre *f* micrometer depth gauge
Feinmessung *f* precision measurement
Feinmesswerkzeug *nt* precision measuring tool
Feinmesswesen *nt* engineering precision measurement
Feinmesszeug *nt* precision measuring tool
Feinnachstellung *f* fine adjustment
Feinplanung *f* fine planning
Feinpositionierung *f* fine positioning
feinschichtiges Kunstharzpressholz *nt* fine-layered resin-bonded densified laminated wood
Feinschleifen *nt* finishing (or fine) grinding, precision grinding
Feinschleifverfahren *nt* precision grinding method
Feinschlichterodieren *nt* precision finish eroding
Feinschliff *m* finish grinding
Feinschneiden *nt* precision cutting, fine-edge blanking
Feinschnittwerkzeug *nt* precision cutter
Feinstaubfilter *m* fine-particle filter
feinstbearbeiten superfinish, finishmachine
Feinstbearbeitung *f* superfinishing
Feinstbearbeitungsmethode *f* microfinishing method
Feinstbearbeitungsvorgang *m* superfinishing operation
Feinstblech *nt* thin metal sheet
Feinstbohrarbeit *f* precision boring (work)
Feinstbohren *nt* precision boring, fine boring
Feinstbohrwerk *nt* precision boring machine
Feinstdreharbeit *f* superfinish turning, high precision turning
Feinstdrehmaschine *f* high precision lathe, *(US)* superfinisher
Feinsteinstellung *f* micrometer adjustment
Feinstellschraube *f* micrometer adjusting screw
feinstfräsen precision (or finish) mill
Feinsthobeln *nt* precision planing
Feinstmessung *f* measurement of maximum precision
Feinstschleifen *nt* superfine grinding

Feinstschliff *m* superfine grinding
Feinststaubfilter *m* extra-fine particle filter
feinstufig fine-step, in fine steps, sensitive
feinstufige Regelung *f* sensitive control
feinstufige Schaltbarkeit *f* sensitivity
feinstufige Schaltung *f* sensitive control
Feinstziehschleifen *nt* honing operation
Feintaster *m* sensitive tracer
Feinvorschub *m* fine feed
Feinwerktechnik *f* (light) precision engineering, fine mechanics
Feinzeiger *m* dial indicator, precision indicating gauge
Feinziehschleifen *nt* precision (or finish) honing, superfinishing
Feinzustellung *f* sensitive (or fine) adjustment
Feld *nt* **für Maßstabangaben** panel provided for scale particulars
Feld *nt* **1.** *(allg.)* field **2.** *(e. Zeichnung)* panel, block
Feldanschlussklemme *f* field wiring terminal
Feldanweisung *f* field definition
Feldbus *m* field bus
Feldbussystem *nt* field area network
Felddämpfung *f* field attenuation
Feldeinteilung *f* block subdivision
Feldindex *m* field index
Feldlinie *f* line of electric flux
Feldmessorgan *nt* field measuring device
Feldmessung *f* (land) surveying
Feldsteller *m* field regulator
Feldverdrahtung *f* field wiring
Feldversuch *m* field test
Felge *f* rim
Felgenbett *nt* base of a rim
felsiger Untergrund *m* rocky sub-base
Fenster *nt* window
Fensterheizkörper *m* window radiator
Fensterlüftung *f* window ventilation
Fensterrahmen *m* window frame
Fensterscheibe *f* window pane
Fernauflösungsvermögen *nt* far field resolution
Fernbedienung *f* remote control
Fernbedienungsgerät *nt* remote handling device
fernbetätigt remote operated
Ferndiagnose *f* remote diagnosis
ferngesteuert remote-controlled
fernhalten beware of
Fernheizanschluss *m* district heating scheme
Fernheizleitung *f* district heating line
Fernmeldetechnik *f* telecommunication
Fernmessung *f* telemetering
Fernschaltung *f* remote control
Fernschutzwirkung *f* remote protective action
Fernsteuerbefehl *m* loop signal
Fernsteuerung *f* remote control
Fernwärmeanlage *f* district heating plant
Fernzugriffsystem *nt* remote access system
Ferrit *nt* ferrite
Ferritkern *m* ferrite core
fertig finished
fertig bearbeiten finish-machine, finish-cut
fertig bearbeitetes Teil *nt* finished part
fertig drehen finish-turn
fertig fräsen finish-mill
fertig gestellt completed
fertig räumen finish broach
fertig stellen complete
Fertigbördeln *nt* final flanging
fertigen 1. *(allg. herstellen)* fabricate, manufacture, produce, turn on **2.** *(e. Verzahnung spanend ~)* cut **3.** *(zerspanend)* machine
Fertigentfettung *f* final degreasing
Fertigerzeugnisse *ntpl* finished goods
fertiges Mischgut *nt* ready mix
Fertigformat *nt* trimmed size
Fertigfräsen *nt* finish milling
Fertighonen *nt* fine honing, micro-honing
Fertigkalibrieren *nt* final sizing
Fertigkeitseigenschaft *f* mechanical (or physical) property

Fertigläppen – Fertigungsrückmeldung

Fertigläppen *nt* finish lapping
Fertigmaß *nt* finish size, finished size, finishing dimension
Fertigmaße *ntpl* finishing dimensions *pl*
Fertigprodukt *nt* finished product
Fertigschlag *m* finish draw
Fertigschleifen *nt* finish grinding
Fertigschliff *m* finish grinding, finish grind
Fertigschraube *f* bolt finished to size
Fertigstellung *f* completion
Fertigteile *f* finished parts
Fertigteillager *nt* finished parts warehouse
Fertigteillänge *f* finished part length
Fertigteilzeichnung *f* finished part drawing, prefabricated component engineering drawing
Fertigung *f* fabrication, manufacture, manufacturing, production, output
Fertigung *f* größerer Mengen bulk production
Fertigung *f* unter Einhaltung enger Toleranzen close limit production
Fertigung *f* von Einzelstücken one-off production
Fertigung *f:* elektrochemische ~ electro-chemical machining (ECM)
Fertigung *f:* flexible ~ flexible production
Fertigungsablauf *m* production process, production sequence, production run (or cycle)
Fertigungsablauforganisation *f* organization of the production process
Fertigungsaufgabe *f* production job
Fertigungsauftrag *m* production order, batch
fertigungsbedingte Schweißsicherheit *f* procedure-conditioned welding security
fertigungsbedingter Ausfall *m* manufacturing failure
fertigungsbezogene Schweißsicherheit *f* procedure-related welding security
Fertigungsfluss *m* production flow
Fertigungsgemeinkosten *pl* production general costs

fertigungsgerechte Maßeintragung *f* production-oriented dimensioning
Fertigungshilfsmittel *f* auxiliary production device
Fertigungsingenieur *m* production engineer
Fertigungsinsel *f* production island
Fertigungskapazität *f* production capacity
Fertigungskontrolle *f* fabrication quality control, industrial inspection
Fertigungskosten *pl* production cost, cost of manufacture
Fertigungslage *f* position of manufacture
Fertigungsleistung *f* output
Fertigungslohnabrechnung *f* production payroll accounting
Fertigungslos *nt* production lot, batch, charge
Fertigungsmesstechnik *f* production measuring technology
Fertigungsmesstechniker *m* production technology technologist
Fertigungsmethode *f* manufacturing method, production technique
Fertigungsmittel *ntpl* workshop facilities
Fertigungsmittelauswahl *f* workshop facilities selection
Fertigungsmittelplanung *f* workshop facilities planning
Fertigungsmittelzeichnung *f* production facility drawing
Fertigungsnummer *f* serial number
fertigungsorientiert production-oriented
Fertigungsplan *m* production plan
Fertigungsplanung *f* production planning
Fertigungsprinzip *nt* production principle
Fertigungsprogramm *nt* manufacturing programme
Fertigungsprüfung *f* process inspection
Fertigungsriss *m* full-scale marking off drawing
Fertigungsrückmeldung *f* production

acknowledgement, production feedback
Fertigungsschweißung *f* weld for fabricating purposes, production weld
Fertigungsserie *f* production run
Fertigungssicherheit *f* production (or manufacturing) security
Fertigungssortiment *nt* production range, production assortment
Fertigungsstätte *f* assembly plant, manufacturing plant, plant
Fertigungssteuerung *f* production control, operations scheduling, job routing
Fertigungsstraße *f* transfer line
Fertigungsstückliste *f* production parts list
Fertigungsstufe *f* manufacturing stage
Fertigungssystem *nt* production system
Fertigungstechnik *f* production engineering
Fertigungstechniker *m* production engineer
Fertigungstiefe *f* level of manufacturing
Fertigungsunterlagen *fpl* manufacturing documentation, manufacturing specifications
Fertigungsverfahren *nt* production method, operating procedure, manufacturing process
Fertigungszeichnung *f* production drawing
Fertigungszelle *f* production cell
Fertigwaren *fpl* finished products, finished goods
Fertigwarenlager *nt* finished goods inventory (FGI), finished good store, finished goods warehouse, finished goods stockpile
fest 1. (kraftschlüssig) tight 2. (Materialeigenschaft) solid, rigid 3. *(allg.)* strong, fixed, stationary, stable, taut, non-adjustable, permanent, firm, secure
fest angebracht permanently fixed
fest eingebaut permanently installed
fest haftend firmly adherent
fest installiert permanent, permanently installed
fest montiert fixed
Festanschlag *m* fixed stop
Festanschlagwechsel *m* variable fixed stop, change of fixed rail
Festauftrag *m* firm order
Festbettfilter *m* fixed bed filter
festbinden tie
festdrehen tighten (screw)
Festdüse *f* fixed nozzle
feste Installation *f* permanent installation
fester Anschlag *m* positive stop
fester Anschlagwinkel *m* fixed square
fester Klebstoff *m* solid adhesive
fester Tisch *m* stationary table
festes Epoxidharz *nt* solid epoxy resin
festes Gewinde *nt* solid thread
festfahren 1. *(Spindel)* stall out 2. *(Werkzeug)* stick
festfressen jam, seize, gall
festgefahren jammed, stuck (tool)
festgefahrenes Räumwerkzeug *nt* stuck broach
festgelegt predetermined, set
festgespanntes Seil *nt* taut rope
festgestellte systematische Abweichung *f* ascertained systematic deviation
festhaken hog, stall
festhalten clamp, engage, arrest, hold in place, retain, impede, secure, fasten, grip
festigen stabilise, compact, strengthen
Festigkeit *f* 1. *(Eigensteifigkeit)* rigidity 2. *(Formsteifigkeit)* stiffness 3. *(Kraftschluss)* tightness 4. *(Materialeigenschaft)* strength 5. *(Stahlkonstruktion)* stability 6. *(Zähfestigkeit)* tenacity
Festigkeitseigenschaft *f* physical property
Festigkeitsklasse *f* strength category
Festigkeitslehre *f* strength theory, theory of the strength of materials, theoretical mechanics
festigkeitsmäßig considered in strength terms
Festigkeitsprüfung *f* strength test
Festigkeits- und Härtewerte *f* strength and hardness values

festkeilen key
festklemmen jam, clamp in place, clamp (or lock) in position
Festklemmung *f* clamping, locking
festkodierter Datenträger (FDT) *m* fixed data carrier (FDC), read-only data carrier
Festkörperlaser *m* solid body laser
Festkörperlaser *m:* **kristalliner** ~ crystalline solid body laser
Festkörpervolumen *nt* volume of nonvolatile matter
festlegen determine, fix, mark
Festlegung *f* 1. *(allg.)* determination 2. *(von Maßen)* provision
Festlegung *f* **der Werkzeugwinkel** tool angle convection
Festlegung *f* **der Wirkwinkel** working angle convention
Festlünette *f* steadyrest
festmachen fix, fasten
Festmaßlehre *f* fixed gauge
Festplatte *f* hard disk
Festplatzlagerung *f* fixed location storage
Festpunkt *m* fixed point
Festscheibe *f* fixed pulley
festschrauben attach by bolts, attach by screws, bolt down
festschweißen attach by welding
festsitzen stick
Festsitzgewinde *nt* interference thread
festspannen clamp (tightly) into position, lock (in position), secure, tie, tighten, fix
feststehend fixed, stationary
feststehende Schutzeinrichtung *f* fixed guard
feststehende Spitze *f* stationary centre, dead centre
feststehender Setzstock *m* plain steadyrest
feststellbares Rückschlagdurchgangsventil *nt* screw-down straightway non-return valve
feststellbares Rückschlageckventil *nt* screw-down non-return valve
Feststellbarkeit *f* lockability
Feststellbremse *f* hand brake, immobilizing brake, parking brake
Feststelleinrichtung *f* locking device
feststellen detect, determine, state, immobilize, lock, clamp, fix
Feststellschraube *f* clamping screw, binding bolt
Feststellung *f* 1. *(Meinung)* statement 2. *(Vorrichtung)* clamping, locking 3. *(Prüfergebnisse)* finding, ascertainment
Feststellvorrichtung *f* braking device, braking and locking device
Feststoffeinschluss *m* solid inclusion
Festtintecodierer *m* solid ink coder
festverbundene Bereifung *f* bonded tyre wheel
festverdrahtet hardwired
Festwalzen *nt* solid rolling
Festwertregelung *f* fixed command control
Fett *nt* grease
Fettbehälter *m* grease reservoir
Fettbüchse *f* grease cup, greaser
Fettdurchgang *m* grease penetration
Fettdurchlässigkeit *f* grease permeability
fetten grease, lubricate
fettende Substanz *f* fat-liquoring substance
Fettfleck *m* grease spot
Fettförderung *f* pumping of grease
fettig greasy
Fettlösemittel *nt* degreasant
fettlöslich grease-soluble
Fettprüfmaschine *f* grease test rig
Fettschicht *f* grease film
Fettschmierung *f* grease lubrication
Fettverunreinigungen *fpl* grease contaminants *pl*
feucht damp, humid, moist
Feuchte *f* humidity, moisture
Feuchtebilanz *f* humidity balance
feuchtempfindlich susceptible to moisture
Feuchtemessung *f* humidity measurement, moisture measurement
feuchten moisten, wet
Feuchtentwicklung *f (von Lichtpauspapier)* semi-dry development
Feuchtigkeit *f* moisture, humidity, damp

feuchtigkeitsabweisend moisture repellent
Feuchtigkeitsdehnung *f* moisture expansion
Feuchtigkeitseinwirkung *f* effect of moisture
Feuchtigkeitskammer *f* humidity cabinet
Feuchtigkeitsschliere *f* humid stria
Feuchtklima *nt* humid atmosphere
Feuchtmasse *f* moist mass
Feuchtverfahren *nt (zur Herstellung von Lichtpausen)* semi-dry method
Feuchtwechselklima *nt* damp (or humid) alternating (or alternative) atmosphere
Feuchtzone *f* moist zone
Feuer *nt* fire
feueraluminierte Oberfläche *f* hot-dip aluminium coated surface
feuerberührte Teile *ntpl* flame-swept parts
Feuerbett *nt* firebed
feuerfest fire-resistant, refractory, fireproof
feuerfeste Ausmauerung *f* refractory lining
feuergefährdet subject to the risk of fire
Feuerlöscher *m* fire extinguisher
Feuerlufterhitzer *m* furnace-type air heater
Feuerluftheizofen *m* air heating stove
Feuerraumdruck *m* combustion space pressure
Feuerraumdruckregler *m* furnace pressure control(ler)
Feuerschutztür *f* fire protection door
feuersicher fire-proof
Feuerstätte *f* fire-place, fire box
Feuerüberspannung *f* flash-over
Feuerung *f* 1. *(allg.)* firing 2. *(Feuerungsanlage)* firing system 3. *(Feuerungsart)* firing method
Feuerungsanlage *f* firing installation (or plant)
Feuerungsautomat *m* automatic firing device
Feuerungsregler *m* firing controller
Feuerungstechnik *f* furnace engineering
Feuerungsumbau *m* conversion of the firing system
Feuerverzinkung *f* hot(-dip) galvanizing, pot galvanizing
Feuerwerksausrüstung *f* fire fighting equipment
Film *m* **mit Lichtpausschicht** *f* film with diazo coating
Filmauswertung *f* film evaluation
Filmbetrachtungsgerät *nt* illuminator
Film-Fokus-Abstand *m* focus-film distance
Filmgeräte *ntpl* film-making equipment
Filmkassette *f* film cassette
Filmschwärzung *f* density of radiograph
Filmträger *m* film base
Filmverarbeitung *f* film processing
Filter *m* filter
Filter *m:* **optischer ~** optical filter
Filterapparat *m* filtration device
Filtereinsatz *m* filter element
Filtererde *f* filtering earth
Filterhülse *f* filter cartridge
Filterleistung *f* filtration performance
Filtermethode *f* filter method
filtern filter, strain
Filterpapiermethode *f* paper filter method
Filtersieb *nt* strainer
Filtertiegel *m* filter crucible
Filtriergeschwindigkeit *f* rate of filtration
Filzdichtung *f* felt packing
Filzschrumpfung *f* felt shrinkage
Filzverhalten *nt* felting behaviour
Finanzmarkt *m* financial market
Finanzmittel *ntpl* financial resources
Finanzpolitik *f* financial policy
Finanzwirtschaft *f* financial economy
finden find
Fingerabdruckspuren *fpl* traces of fingerprints *pl*
Fingerfräseinrichtung *f* end milling attachment
Fingerfräser *m* end mill, slotting cutter, slot drill
Fingerspitze *f* finger tip
Finne *f* peen (hammer)

Firmware *f* firmware
FI-Schutz *m* fault current breaker
FI-Schutzschalter *m* residual current protective device
Fitting *f* **für Kapillarlötverbindung** fitting for soldered capillary solder fitting
Fittings *npl* **für Lötverbindungen** capillary solder fittings
fix permanent
Fixiereinrichtung *f* locating device
Fixierung *f* fixing
Fixierzapfen *m* locator pin
flach 1. *(eben)* flat, even, plain, shallow 2. *(el.)* leadless
Flachbahn *f* flat way, square way
Flachbahn- und Prismaführung *f* combined square Vee-guide
Flachbahnführung *f* square guide
Flachbau *m* low building
Flachbiegeschwingversuch *m* flat bending fatigue test
flachdichtend flat sealing
Flachdichtring *m* flat sealing ring
Flachdöpper *m* **für Senkniete** rivet set for flush head rivets
Flachdrückversuch *m* flattening test
Fläche *f* 1. *(Grundfläche)* area 2. *(am Werkstück)* surface 3. *(Stirnfläche)* face
flache Kronenmutter *f* thin castle nut
flache Rändelmutter *f* flat knurled nut
flächen spot face (bores)
Flächen *fpl* **der Gabelzinke** fork surfaces
Flächenabtrag *m* surface attack
Flächenänderung *f* surface modification
Flächenaufschüttung *f* area of fill
Flächenbeflammung *f* surface impingement of flame
Flächenbelastung *f* load per surface, load per area unit, load per square meter, load distributed over an area
Flächenberührung *f* surface touch
flächenbezogene Masse *f* area-related mass, weight per unit area
flächenbezogener Massenverlust *m* mass loss per unit area
Flächendosierprodukt *nt* area-dose product
Flächeneinheit *f* surface unit

Flächenentwässerung *f* area drainage
flächenfertig prepared, ready to use
Flächenformfräsmaschine *f* skin-miller
Flächenformtoleranz *f* tolerance of surface profile
Flächenfräsarbeit *f* surface milling operation
Flächenfräsen *nt* surface (or face) milling, facing
Flächenfräser *m* face milling cutter
Flächengebilde *nt* sheet material
Flächengewicht *nt* mass per unit area, substance, coating weight per unit area
Flächengewichtsverlust *m* weight loss per unit area
flächengleiches Rechteck *nt* rectangle of area equal to the square
flächenhaft surface ...
flächenhafter Träger *m* area-measured support
flächenhaftes Erzeugnis *nt* area-measured product
Flächenhobeln *nt* flat-surface shaping
Flächenkorrosion *f* uniform corrosion
Flächenmaß *nt* square measure
flächenmäßige Verteilung *f* area distribution, superficial distribution
Flächenmessung *f* planimetry
Flächennaht *f* surface joint, lap joint
flächennormal normal to the surface
Flächenplanung *f* area planning
Flächenportal *nt* wide gantry
Flächenschleifen *nt* surface grinding
Flächenschleifmaschine *f* 1. *(allg.)* surface grinding machine, surface grinder 2. *(senkrechte)* vertical-spindle surface grinder 3. *(waagerechte)* horizontal-spindle surface grinder
Flächenschwerpunkt *m* centre of area, bisector of area
Flächentangente *f* plane tangent
Flächenteil *nt* *(e. Schraube)* portion of the surface
Flächenträgheitsmoment *nt* axial angular impulse
Flächenunterbrechung *f* surface interruption
flächenzentriert face-centred
flaches metrisches Trapezge-

winde *nt* stub metric trapezoidal screw thread
Flachführung *f* flat way, square guideway, flat slideway
Flachgetriebe *nt* parallel shift helical gear
Flachgewinde *nt* flat thread, square thread
Flachgewindemeißel *m* square-thread tool
Flachgut *nt* flat goods
Flachgutlager *nt* flat goods warehouse
Flachgutlagersystem *nt* flat goods storage system, flat goods warehouse
Flachheizkörper *nt* panel radiator
flächig large-surface, two-dimensional
flächig aufeinanderliegen lie with surfaces one above the other
flächige Fehler *m* two-dimensional defects
flächige Formmasse *f* area-measured moulding material
flächiges Kunststofferzeugnis *nt* area-measured plastic product
flächiges Probestück *nt* test specimen in sheet form
Flachkanteinsteckschlüssel *m* **für Deckverschlüsse** flat ended key for deck screw caps *pl*
Flachkeilriemen *m* Vee-belt
Flachkopfschraube *f* **mit Schlitz** slotted pan head screw
Flachkurve *f* plate cam, disc cam
Flachlage *f* flatness
Flachlängswalzen *nt* flat longitudinal rolling
Flachlängswalzen *nt* **von Hohlkörpern** flat longitudinal rolling of hollow items
Flachlängswalzen *nt* **von Vollkörpern** flat longitudinal rolling of solid bodies
Flachläppen *nt* flat lapping
Flachläppmaschine *f* flat lapping machine
Flachlehrdorn *m* flat (type) plug gauge
Flachlehrenkörper *m* flat gauging member
Flachleiste *f* **bei Schichtpressstoffen** compressed flat rod for laminated plastics
flachliegend flat, lay-flat
Flachmeißel *m* square-nosed (or -nose) tool
Flachpalette *f* flat pallet
Flachpassung *f* flat fit
Flachprägen *nt* surfacing
Flachpressplatte *f* compressed sheet
Flachquerwalzen *nt* flat transverse rolling
Flachrevolverdrehmaschine *f* flat turret lathe
Flachrevolverkopf *m* flat turret head
Flachrundniet *m* snap head rivet, mushroom head rivet
Flachrundschraube *f* coach bolt, saucer-head screw, truss-head screw
Flachschieber *m* plain slide valve
Flachschleifen *nt* surface grinding, cylindrical grinding, face grinding
Flachschleifmaschine *f* *(Planschleifmaschine)* face grinding machine, face grinder
Flachschmiernippel *m* flat type lubricating nipple
Flachschrägwalzen *nt* flat skew rolling
Flachsenkniet *m* flat countersunk head rivet
Flachspule *f* shallow coil
Flachstauchfestigkeit *f* flat crush resistance
Flachstauchversuch *m* flat crush test
Flachstauchwiderstand *m* flat crush resistance
Flachtray *m* deep-wall tray, flat tray
Flachumpressung *f* flat laminated moulded section
Flachvollstab *m* flat rod
Flachwinkel *m* millwright steel square
Flachziehen *nt* flat drawing
Flachzugprobe *f* flat bar tension specimen
Fladepotential *nt* Flade potential
Flamme *f* flame
Flammenabheben *nt* flame lift-off
flammenatomabsorptionsspektroskopisches Verfahren *nt* flame atomic absorption, spectroscopic method
Flammenausbreitungsgeschwindigkeit *f* rate of flame propagation, flame

spread rate
Flammendurchschlag *m* flash-back
Flammendurchschlagsicherung *f* flame trap, flashback arrester
Flammenform *f* flame configuration
Flammenfühler *m* flame sensor
Flammenfühlerleitung *f* flame monitor wiring
Flammenleistung *f* flame performance
Flammenschutzkleidung *f* flameproof clothing
flammensicher flame-proof
Flammenspitze *f* tip of the flame
Flammenstrahlbrenner *m* concentric jet burner
Flammentspannen *nt* flame stress relieving
Flammenüberwachung *f* flame monitoring, flame control
Flammenüberwachungseinrichtung *f* flame monitoring device
Flammenwächter *m* flame detector
Flammenwächterrelais *nt* flame detector relay
Flammgrundieren *nt* flame priming
Flamm-Hartlöten *nt* flame brazing
flammhemmender Zusatz *m* flame-retarding additive
Flammlöten *nt* flame soldering and brazing
Flammphosphatieren *nt* flame phosphating
flammspritzen flame spray
flammspritzverzinkt galvanized by flame-spraying
Flammstockspritzen *nt* detonation spraying
Flammstrahlzündung *f* flashover
Flammwärmen *nt* flame heating
Flammwärmverfahren *nt* flame heating process
Flammweichlöten *nt* flame soldering
flammwidrig flame retardation
flammwidriges Epoxidharz *nt* flame-resistant epoxy resin
Flanke *f (e. Gewindes)* flank, side (thread), signal edge
Flankenabmaß *nt* tooth surface allowance
Flankenabweichung *f* flank variation
Flankenauswertung *f* signal edge evaluation
Flankenbeanspruchung *f* flank loading
Flankendurchmesser *m (e. Gewindes)* effective diameter, pitch, pitch diameter *(US)*
Flankendurchmesserlinie *f (e. Gewindes)* pitch line
Flankendurchmessertoleranz *f* pitch diameter tolerance
Flankenform *f* tooth surface form
Flankenfreiwinkel *m* pitch clearance angle
Flankenkehlnaht *f* side fillet weld
Flankenkorrektur *f* flank correction, modification of the flank shape
Flankenlinie *f* 1. *(allg. Zahnrad)* tooth trace 2. *(e. Schrägstirnrades)* helix
Flankenlinienabweichung *f* tooth trace variation
Flankenlinienformabweichung *f* tooth trace form variation
Flankenliniengesamtabweichung *f* tooth trace tooth variation
Flankenlinienprüfbereich *m* tooth trace test range
Flankenlinienprüfbild *nt* flank test diagram
Flankenlinienprüfung *f* trooth trace testing
Flankenlinienrücknahme *f* tooth trace relief
Flankenlinienverlauf *m* tooth trace configuration
Flankenlinienwelligkeit *f* tooth trace waviness
Flankenlinienwinkelabweichung *f* tooth trace angle variation
Flankenmaß *nt* flank measure
Flankenmikrometer *m* flank micrometer
Flankenprofil *nt* tooth surface profile
Flankenprüfbereich *m* tooth surface test range
Flankenprüfbild *nt* flank test diagram
Flankenprüfgerät *nt* flank testing machine
Flankenpunkt *m* point on the tooth surface

Flankenrichtung *f* flank direction, tooth surface direction
Flankenrichtungsfehler *m* tooth alignment error
Flankenschnitt *m* flank section
Flankenspielpasssystem *nt* (von Radpaarungen) backlash system of fits
Flankenspielschwankung *f* backlash fluctuation
Flankensteuerung *f* (bei Takteingang) flank control
Flankentaster *m* thread calliper
Flankentaster *m* **für Innengewinde** inside thread calliper
Flankenwinkel *m* (e. Gewindes) flank angle, angle of thread, thread angle, included angle
Flankenwinkelabweichung *f* included angle deviation
Flansch *m* flange
Flansch *m* **mit Anschweißbund** flange with butt welded collar
Flanschanschluss *m* flanged connection
flanschen flange
Flanschfläche *f* flange facing
Flanschmotor *m* flange-mounted motor
Flanschrad *nt* flange wheel
Flanschverbindung *f* flanged connection
Flanschverschraubung *f* screwed flanged joint
Flanschwiderstand *m* flange modulus
Flasche *f* bottle, flask
Flaschenzug *m* block and tackle, pulley block, set of pulleys
Flashspeicher *m* flash memory
flauschig fleecy
Fleck *m* blotch (oil), stain, spot
fleckenfrei stainless
Fleckenunempfindlichkeit *f* resistance to staining
Fleißwert *m* flow value
flexibel flexible
Flexibilität *f* flexibility, malleability
Flexible Fertigungsinsel *f* flexible manufacturing island
Flexible Fertigungszelle *f* flexible manufacturing cell
flexibler Packstoff *m* flexible packaging film
Flexibles Fertigungssystem (FFS) *nt* flexible manufacturing system (FMS)
Flexodruck *m* flexographic printing
Flexodruckfarbe *f* flexographic ink
Flexometerprüfung *f* flexometer test
fliegend aufgespannter Spreizdorn *m* stub expansion arbor
fliegend gelagert cantilevered, over mounted
fliegend gelagerte Räder *ntpl* cantilever wheels
Fliehkraftanlage *f* centrifugal force plant
Fließarbeit *f* flow line production
Fließband *nt* flow line
Fließbereich *m* yield range
Fließbild *nt* mimic
Fließdruck *m* flow pressure
Fließdruckbereich *m* (Gas) flow pressure range
Fließdrücken *nt* extrusion, flow turning
fließen flow, pass
fließen aus drain out
fließfähig capable of flow
Fließfertigung *f* flow production
Fließfüllungsvermögen *nt* liquid filling capacity
Fließgrenze *f* yield point
Fließkurve *f* rheogram
Fließkurven *fpl* flow curves *pl*
Fließlinienbetrieb *m* conveyor line mode
Fließmontage *f* line assembly work
fließpressen extrude
Fließpressen *nt* **mit starrem Werkzeug** impact extrusion with rigid tool
Fließpressen *nt* **mit Wirkmedien** impact extrusion with action media
Fließpressschweißen *nt* cold pressure extrusion welding
Fließprinzip *nt* flow principle
Fließspan *m* (US) continuous chip, (UK) flow chip, continuous spiral chip
Fließspannung *f* yield stress
Fließspanverfahren *nt* machining method producing continuous chips
Fließverhalten *nt* fluidity (or flow) behaviour

Fließvorgang *m* yielding phenomenon
Fließweg *m* flow path
Flimmern *nt* flickering
Flokkulator *m* flocculator
Flucht *f* 1. *(Reihe)* alignment, range, row 2. *(Entkommen)* escape
fluchten align (or be in alignment)
Fluchtgenauigkeit *f* alignment accuracy
flüchtiger Speicher *m* volatile memory
Fluchtmöglichkeit *f* escape provision
Fluchtungsfehler *m* misalignment
Fluchtweg *m* escape, escape route, escape passage
Flügel *m* vane
Flügelkreuzschlitz *m* torque-set recess
Flügelmutter *f* butterfly nut, fly nut, thumb nut, wing nut
Flügelpumpe *f* vane pump
Flügelradanemometer *nt* vane-type anemometer
Flügelschraube *f* thumb screw
Flügelzellenpumpe *f* vane cell pump, vane pump
Flugrostbildung *f* film rust formation
Flugstaubablagerung *f* fly ash deposit
Flugzeugbau *m* aircraft construction
Fluid *nt* fluid
fluidal fluidal
Fluidfilter *m* fluid filter
Fluidreibung *f* fluid friction
Fluidreibungsverlust *m* fluid friction loss
Fluor *nt* fluorine
Fluoreszenz *f* fluorescence
fluoreszenzanregend fluorescence-stimulating
Fluoreszenzanregung *f* fluorescence stimulation
Fluoreszenzlösung *f* fluorescent penetrant
Fluoreszenzprüfung *f* fluorescent inspection
Fluoreszenzverfahren *nt* fluorescent penetrant inspection method
Fluoreszenzverfahren *nt* **mit trockenem Niederschlag** dry deposit method of fluorescence inspection
Fluoreszenzverfahren *nt* **mit wässriger Lösung** wet solution method of fluorescence inspection
fluorhaltige Verbindung *f* fluorine-containing compound
Flur *m* floor, ground
Flurbereinigung *f* land clearance project
Flurförderzeug (FFZ) *nt* industrial truck, load-carrying truck, truck, automatic guided vehicle
Flurförderzeug *nt* **mit Dieselmotor** diesel truck
Flurförderzeug *nt* **mit Fahrersitz** sit-on truck, rider-controlled truck
Flurförderzeug *nt* **mit Fahrerstand** stand-on truck, rider-controlled truck
Flurförderzeug *nt* **mit Flüssiggasmotor** liquefied petroleum gas (LPG) truck
Flurförderzeug *nt* **mit Fremdstromantrieb** external source truck
Flurförderzeug *nt* **mit hebbarem Fahrerplatz** truck with elevatable operating position
Flurförderzeug *nt* **mit Hubeinrichtung** lift truck
Flurförderzeug *nt* **mit Steuerung durch gehende Personen** pedestrian-controlled truck
Flurförderzeug *nt* **mit Verbrennungsmotor** internal combustion truck
Flurförderzeug *nt* **mit Vergaserkraftstoffmotor** gasoline truck, petrol truck
flurgebunden floor-bound, path-bound
Flursteuerung *f* control from the floor
Flurstücksgrenze *f* parish bound
Fluss *m* 1. *(Stoffe)* flow 2. *(el.)* flux
Flussänderung *f* reversal of forward direction
Flussdiagramm *nt* flow diagram, flow chart
Flussdichte *f* flux density
flüssig liquid, fluid
flüssige Phase *f* liquid phase
flüssige Verunreinigung *f* **der Luft** liquid pollutants in the air
flüssiger Energieträger *m* liquid heat transfer medium
flüssiger Klebkitt *m* liquid adhesive

putty
flüssiges Lot *nt* liquid filler
Flüssiggas *nt* liquefied petroleum gas (LPG), liquefied gas
Flüssiggasauslass *m* fuel take-off
flüssiggasgesättigt saturated with liquid gas
Flüssiggasmotor *m* liquefied petroleum gas (LPG) engine
Flüssigkeit *f* liquid, fluid
Flüssigkeitsauffangtopf *m* liquid receiver
flüssigkeitsbeheizter Wärmetauscher *m* liquid-heated heat exchanger
Flüssigkeitsdruckprüfung *f* hydraulic test
flüssigkeitsempfindlich moisture-sensitive
Flüssigkeitsfilter *m* liquid filter
flüssigkeitsgelagerter Probekörper *m* test piece stored in liquids
Flüssigkeitsgetriebe *nt* hydraulic transmission drive
Flüssigkeitshonen *nt* liquid honing
Flüssigkeitskavitation *f* fluid cavitation
Flüssigkeitslaser *m* fluid laser
Flüssigkeitspumpe *f* hydraulic pump
Flüssigkeitsringvakuumpumpe *f* liquid ring vacuum pump
Flüssigkeitsringverdichter *m* liquid ring compressor
Flüssigkeitssäule *f* liquid column
Flüssigkeitsstrahl *m* fluid jet
Flüssigkeitsthermometer *nt* liquid thermometer
flüssigmetallbeheizt liquid metal-heated
Flüssigpressen *nt* fluid pressing
Flussleitstück *nt* flux-conducting component
flussmittelfreies Löten *nt* soldering without a flux
Flussmittelfüllung *f* flux filling
flussmittelgefüllter Lotstab *m* flux-filled soldering bar
Flussmittelspitzer *m* flux spatter
Flussmittelumhüllung *f* flux coating
Flussrichtung *f* forward direction

Flussstahl *m* mild steel, ingot steel, low carbon steel
fluten flood
Flutverfahren *nt* *(Phosphatierung)* flood method
Flyerkette *f* leaf chain, leaf mechanical chain, leaf type chain
Fokus *m* focus
Fokusdurchmesser *m* focus diameter
Fokus-Haut-Abstand *m* target-skin distance
Fokuslage *f* focus position
Fokusradius *m* focus radius
Fokussiereinheit *f* focussing equipment
fokussieren focus
Fokussieroptik *f* focussing optics
Fokussierung *f* focussing
Fokussierungslinse *f* focussing lens
Folge *f* sequence, series, order, progression, succession
Folge *f* **der Arbeitsgänge** machine cycle
Folge *f* **der Arbeitsvorgänge** sequence of operations
Folgeblatt *nt* continuation sheet
Folgeeinrichtung *f* follow-up servo
Folgeereignis *nt* sequential event
Folgefrequenz *f* repetition frequency
Folgekolben *m* follower piston
Folgekosten *pl* after costs, subsequent costs
folgen follow, succeed
folgend following, succeeding
Folgeprozess *m* following process
Folgeprüfung *f* sequential inspection
Folgeregelung *f* sequence automatic control
Folgeregler *m* servomechanism
folgern conclude
Folgerung *f* conclusion
Folgeschaltung *f* (automatic) sequence control
Folgeschneiden *nt* follow-die cutting
Folgeschneidwerkzeug *nt* follow-die cutter
Folgeschnitt *m* multi-angle cut, successive cut
Folgeschnitte *mpl* blank and pierce die, progressive die

Folgesteuerung *f* sequencing, sequence control
Folie *f* **1.** *(allg.)* foil, sheet, sheeting, film **2.** *(Metall)* foil **3.** *(Projektor)* transparency
Folien- und Bandeinschlagmaschine *f* film and band wrapping machine
Folienbahn *f* film web, web of film, film strip, sheet, sheeting
Foliendehnsystem *nt* film stretching device
Foliendehnung *f* film stretching
Folienende *nt* film edge
Foliengießen *nt* film casting
Folienhälfte *f* half of film
Folienkordeleinrichtung *f* film cord device
Folienkunstleder *nt* artificial leather sheeting
Foliennahtschweißen *nt* seam welding with strip
Folienprobe *f* film specimen
Folienrolle *f* film reel, reel of film
Folienschlauch *m* tubular film, tube of thermoplastic material
Folienschlauchbeutel *m* tubular bag
Folienschlauchbeutel-Form-, Füll- und -Verschließmaschine *f* tubular bag form fill and seal machine
Folienschlitten *m* film carriage
Folienschneidgerät *nt* film cutting appliance
Folienstreifen *m* film strip
Folientransport *m* film transport
Folienüberlappnahtschweißen *nt* foil lap joint welding
Folienverarbeitung *f* processing of films
Folienverpackung *f* foil packaging
Folienverschließmaschine *f* foil sealing machine
Förderanlage *f* conveyor, conveyor system, transporting plant
Förderanlagensteuerung *f* conveyor control
Förderband *nt* conveying belt, conveyor (belt), belt conveyor
Fördereinheit *f* conveying unit, handling unit

Fördereinrichtung *f* conveying unit, handling unit, handling equipment, conveyor
Förderelement *nt* conveyor
Förderer *m* conveyor
Fördergas *nt* carrier gas
Fördergeschwindigkeit *f* handling speed, transport speed
Fördergut *nt* material to be conveyed
Förderhöhe *f* delivery head
Förderkapazität *f* conveyance capacity
Förderkasten *m* tote box
Fördermenge *f* delivery rate
Fördermittel *f* sponsorship aid
fördern 1. *(allg.)* convey, furnish, displace **2.** *(Flüssigkeiten)* pump **3.** *(propagieren)* promote
Förderpumpe *f* delivery pump
Förderrichtung *f* direction of transport
Förderschnecke *f* conveyor worm, screw conveyor, feed screw
Förderseillast *f* winding rope load
Förderstrecke *f* conveyor line, conveying route, roadway
Fördertechnik *f* conveying technology, conveyor technology, conveyor system, (materials) handling technology (or engineering)
Förderung *f* conveyance, delivery, handling
Förderverhalten *nt* conveying characteristic
Fördervolumen *nt* delivery volume
Fördervorgang *m* transport
Förderzeug *nt* handling device
Förderzeuge *ntpl* handling equipment
Form *f* form, shape, contour, die, mould, configuration
Form *f* **einsetzen** mould insert
Form *f:* **verlorene** ~ lost shape
Form- und Fräseinrichtung *f* profile milling attachment
Form- und Gießverfahren *nt* form- and casting processes
form- und kraftschlüssig by form and friction grip
Form- und Lageabweichung *f* deviation in form and position
Form- und Schraubenautomat *m* automatic screw machine

Form- und Stempelhobelmaschine f punch and form shaper, form and punch shaping machine
Form- und Stempelhobler m die block shaper
Form-, Füll- und Verschließmaschine f form fill and seal machine
formabrichten form turn
Formabweichung f form deviation, shape deviation, geometrical error (or deviation or variation), irregularity of form
Formabweichungen f **(zulässige)** form errors (permissible)
Formaldehydkondensationsprodukt nt formaldehyde condensation product
Formänderung f 1. *(Größe)* strain 2. *(bleibende)* plastic deformation (remaining)
Formänderungsfestigkeit f deformation stability
Formänderungsgeschwindigkeit f deformation speed
Formänderungsgrad m degree of deformation
Formänderungsverhalten nt deformation behaviour
Formänderungsvermögen nt capability of deformation
Formänderungswiderstand m resistance to deformation
Formänderungszustände mpl deformation state
Format nt size
Formateverfahren nt (gear cutting) formate methode (or process)
Formätzen nt chemical milling
Formbarkeit f mouldability
Formbeiwert m shape coefficient
formbeständig resistant to deformation
formbeständiges Formteil nt dimensionally stable moulded part
Formbiegen nt form bending
Formblatt nt form
Formdiamant m rough diamond
Formdrängen nt form pressing
Formdreharbeiten fpl form turning jobs

Formdreheinrichtung f profile- (or form-) turning attachment
formdrehen contour-turn, form-turn, profile-turn
Formdrehmaschine f form turning lathe, contouring lathe
Formdrehmeißel m profile (or form) turning tool
Formecho nt form echo
Formel f equation, formula
Formelbestandteil m constituent of the formula, formula constituent
Formelement nt shaped element, form element
Formelement nt **des Werkstückes** element of the workpiece geometry
Formelzeichen nt sign
formen form, profile, contour, shape
Formen- und Gesenkfräsmaschine f mould and die duplicator
Formen- und Gesenknachformfräsmaschine f mould and die duplicator
Formenbau m manufacture of tools
Formenherstellung f forming production
Formfaktor m form factor
Formfehler m faux pas, form error, form fault, imperfect shape
formfehlerfrei devoid of form error
formfester Kunststoff m plastic of good dimensional stability
Formfräsen nt 1. *(allg.)* form (or profile or contour) milling, ball-end milling 2. *(Serienfräsarbeit)* duplicating
Formfräsen nt **von Schraubennuten** helical form milling
Formfräser m 1. *(allg.)* form cutter, formed milling cutter, profile cutter, form-relieved cutter 2. *(an der Spanfläche nachgeschliffen)* face-ground formed milling cutter
Formfräsmaschine f form milling machine, profiler, profile (or contour) miller
Formfräsverfahren nt form milling method
Formfront f form front
Formfüllung f shape filling, shape stopping
Formfüllungsvermögen nt shape fill-

formgebend – **Formsteifigkeit** 716

ing capacity
formgebend shaping
formgebundenes Maß *nt* mould-dependent dimension, mould related size
Formgebung *f* shaping, shape cutting, contouring, profiling, styling, forming
Formgebungszeichnung *f* form design drawing
Formgenauigkeit *f* accuracy to shape, form accuracy, geometrical precision (or accuracy), profile accuracy
formgepresstes Rundrohr *nt* moulded laminated circular tube
formgerecht true to shape
formgerecht gegossener Probekörper *m* specimen cast to the required form
formgeschäumter Kunststoff *m* cellular material formed in situ
Formgestalten *nt* shaping by design, design shaping
Formgrundstoff *m* form base material
Formhaltigkeit *f* shape stability
Formhobeln *nt* form planes
Formhobler *m* form (or contour) shaper
Formiergas *nt* shielding gas
Formiergasdruckminderer *m* inert gas regulator
Formiergasflasche *f* inert gas cylinder
Formkasten *m* shape box, box of shape
Formkohle *f* carbon mould block
Formkopier- und Profilfräsmaschine *f* form copying and profile miller
Formlängsdrehen *nt* longitudinal form turning
Formlehre *f* form tool gauge, profile gauge
Formlineal *nt* former plate
Formmaschine *f* forming machine, moulding machine
Formmaskengießverfahren *nt* shape mask casting process
Formmasseschicht *f* layer of moulding material
Formmasseteilchen *nt* particle of moulding material
Formmeißel *m* contouring tool, formed tool, sized tool, forming tool, form cutting tool

Formmethode *f* shape method
Formparameter *m* parameter of shape
Formpressen *nt* **mit Grat** closed-die press forming with flash
Formpressen *nt* **ohne Grat** closed-die press forming without flash
Formprozess *m* shape process
Formräumen *nt* form broaching
Formräumwerkzeug *nt* form broach
Formrecken *nt* stretch forming
formrichtig correctly shaped, geometrically true
Formrundkneten *nt* rotary swaging
Formrundkneten *nt* **von Außenformen** rotary swaging of external shapes
Formrundkneten *nt* **von Innenformen** rotary swaging of internal shapes
Formsand *m* form sand
Formscheibe *f* formed wheel
Formscheibenstahl *m* circular forming tool
formschleifen contour-grind, form-grind, shape-grind
Formschleifmaschine *f* form grinder
Formschleifoperation *f* form grinding operation
Formschluss *m* form closure, form-fit, form grip, positive locking, form constraint
formschlüssig form fit, having form-fit, securely fixed
formschlüssiges Verbindungselement *nt* form-locked connecting element (or fastener)
Formschnitt *m* forming cut
Formsenker *m* form counterbore
formstabil rigid
formstabiles Packmittel *nt* rigid container
formstabiles Teil *nt* part (or component) of stable shape
Formstanze *f* stamping die, stamping machine
formstanzen stamp
Formstanzen *nt* die forming by drawing
Formstauchen *nt* closed-die upsetting
Formsteifigkeit *f* stability, rigidity

Formstoff *m* moulding material
Formstoff *m* **für Modellausschmelzverfahren** investment compound
formstoßen shape with formed tool
Formstück *nt* moulded part
Formstück *nt* **aus Schaumkunststoff** pre-formed foam plastics
Formstück *nt* **mit Muffe** fitting with socket
Formstück *nt* **mit Stemmuffe** special casting with lead joint socket
Formtechnik *f* mould technology
Formteil *nt* shaped part, (pl.: shapes), machined part
Formteilung *f* parting
Formteilungsfläche *f* mould parting surface
formtreu accurate to shape
Formtreue *f* accuracy to shape
Formular *nt* blank, (printed) form
Formulardialog *m* form dialog
Formung *f* forming, shaping
Formungstemperatur *f* shaping temperature
Formverfahren *nt* form-cutting method
Formverkörperung *f* shape embodiment
Formversatz *m* mould misalignment
Formverzerrung *f* deformation, profile distortion
Formwachs *nt* forming wax
Formwerkzeuge *ntpl* forming tools *pl*
Formzahnradschleifen *nt* form-tooth grinding
Formziehen *nt* **im Gesenk** die forming by drawing
Forschung *f* research
Forschungs- und Entwicklungsabteilung *f* research and development division
fortbewegen move away, move on
fortentwickelter Brand *m* developing fire
fortlaufend continuous, progressive
fortleiten *(el.)* conduct
fortschreiten make progress, progress, take shape
fortschreitende Grübchen *nt* destructive pitting
Fortschritt *m* advance, progress
Fortschritte machen take shape, progress
Fortschrittsbericht *m* progress report
Fortschrittsüberwachung *f* progress supervision
Fortschrittszeitmessung *f* progress time measuring
fotografisch photographic
Fotozeile *f* photo line
Fotozelle *f* photocell, photoelectric cell (PEC)
Fracht *f* freight, cargo
Frachtcontainer *m* freight container
Frage-Antwort-Dialog *m* question- and answer dialog, Q and A dialog
Frame *m* frame
Franzose *m* *(Werkzeug)* monkey wrench
Fräsaggregat *nt* milling unit
Fräsapparat *m* milling attachment, milling head
Fräsarbeit *f* milling job, milling operation, milling work
Fräsarbeit *f* **an schrägen Flächen** angular milling operation
Fräsarbeitsgang *m* milling operation
Fräsautomat *m* automatic milling machine, milling automatic
Fräsbild *nt* milled surface pattern
Fräsdorn *m* cutter arbor, milling arbor
Fräsdornmutter *f* cutter arbor nut
Fräseinrichtung *f* milling attachment
fräsen 1. *(allg.)* mill, cut **2.** *(Flächen)* slab-mill **3.** *(Keilwellen)* spline **4.** *(Sechskant)* hexs **5.** *(senken)* sink **6.** *(Stirnflächen)* face **7.** *(wälzfräsen)* hob
fräsen mit breitem Walzenfräser slab-mill
fräsen mit Führersteuerung tracer mill
Fräsen *nt* **1.** *(allg.)* milling, cutting **2.** *(Gesenke)* (die-) sinking **3.** *(im Gegenlauf) (US)* conventional milling, *(UK)* ordinary milling **4.** *(Keilwellen)* splining **5.** *(plan)* face milling **6.** *(Wälzfräsen)* hobbing
Fräsen *nt* **zweier paralleler Flächen mit zwei Scheibenfräsern** straddle milling
Fräsen *nt* **einer schraubenförmigen**

Nut helical milling
Fräsen *nt* **geneigter Schlitze** angular gashing
Fräsen *nt* **gerader Nuten** straight flute milling
Fräsen *nt* **im Gegenlauf** *(US)* conventional milling, *(UK)* ordinary milling
Fräsen *nt* **in Querrichtung** cross milling
Fräsen *nt* **in Reihenfertigung** batch milling
Fräsen *nt* **keilförmiger Ausschnitte** circular recessing
Fräsen *nt* **kreisförmiger Auskehlungen** circular recessing
Fräsen *nt* **mit Fühlersteuerung** tracer milling
Fräsen *nt* **mit großem Spanwinkel** high-rake milling
Fräsen *nt* **mit großem Vorschub** high-feed milling
Fräsen *nt* **mit Hartmetallwerkzeug** carbide milling
Fräsen *nt* **mit Planetenspindelfräsmaschine** planetary milling
Fräsen *nt* **mit positiven Spanwinkel** positive rake milling
Fräsen *nt* **mit Positivschnitt des Werkzeugs** positive rake milling
Fräsen *nt* **mit Rundtischteileinrichtung** index-base milling
Fräsen *nt* **mit Satzfräsern** gang milling
Fräsen *nt* **mit Walzenfräsern** slab milling
Fräsen *nt* **mit Werkzeugsatz** gang milling
Fräsen *nt* **unterbrochener Flächen** skip milling
Fräsen *nt* **von Keilwellen** spline milling
Fräsen *nt* **von Kugel- o. Halbkugelformen** spherical milling
Fräsen *nt* **von Nuten** fluting
Fräsen *nt* **von Rundungen** radius milling
Fräsen *nt* **von Schlitzen** gashing
Fräsen *nt* **von Zahnstangen** rack milling
Fräsen *nt:* **gleichläufiges ~** climb-cut milling, climb milling, down-feed milling, up-cut milling

Fräser *m* **1.** *(allg.)* milling cutter, cutter
2. *(gefräst)* milled tooth cutter
3. *(hinterdreht)* form-relieved cutter
4. *(Wälzfräser)* hob
Fräser *m* **mit hinterdrehten Zähnen** form relieved cutter
Fräser *m* **aus Gusslegierung** cast-alloy cutter
Fräser *m* **für Halbkreisprofil** concave milling cutter, convex milling cutter
Fräser *m* **mit eingesetzten Messern** blade inserted cutter
Fräser *m* **mit eingesetzten Zähnen** built-up type cutter
Fräser *m* **mit feiner Zahnteilung** fine pitched cutter
Fräser *m* **mit Feinverzahnung** fine-tooth cutter
Fräser *m* **mit grober Zahnteilung** coarse-pitch cutter
Fräser *m* **mit Grobverzahnungen** course tooth milling cutter
Fräser *m* **mit großem Spanwinkel** high-rake cutter
Fräser *m* **mit hinterdrehten Zähnen** form relieved cutter
Fräser *m* **mit Kreuzverzahnung** staggered tooth milling cutter
Fräser *m* **mit linksgängiger Spiralverzahnung** left-hand spiral tooth milling cutter
Fräser *m* **mit negativen Spanwinkel** negative-rake cutter
Fräser *m* **mit Pfeilverzahnung** right-and-left-hand helix cutter
Fräser *m* **mit rechtsgängiger Spiralverzahnung** right-hand spiral-tooth milling cutter
Fräser *m* **mit runder Stirn** ball-end cutter, round-end cutter
Fräser *m* **mit spiralförmiger Verzahnung** helical mill
Fräser *m* **mit Spiralverzahnung** helical tooth cutter
Fräser *m* **mit versetzten Zähnen** alternate tooth milling cutter
Fräser *m* **zu einem Satz zusammengestellt** ganged cutters
Fräser *m* **zum aufstecken auf flie-**

gend angeordnetem Dorn cutter for stub-arbor mounting
Fräserabhebung *f* cutter relief, retraction of milling head, cutter lift, cutter retraction
Fräserbrust *f* face of cutter tooth
Fräserdorn *m* milling arbor, cutter arbor
Fräserdornzwischenring *m* spacing collar
Fräserdrehzahl *f* cutter speed
Fräserradiuskorrektur *f* cutter radius compensation
Fräserschleifmaschine *f* tool and cutting grinder
Fräserschneide *f* cutter edge
Fräserstandzeit *f* cutter life, milling cutter life
Fräserversatz *m* cutter misalignment
Fräserverschleiß *m* cutter wear
Fräserzahn *m* cutter tooth, cutter blade
Fräserzahnteilung *f* cutter pitch
Fräsfutter *nt* cutter chuck
Fräsgang *m* milling operation (or cycle)
Fräskopf *m* 1. *(Frässpindelkopf)* milling head, cutter head 2. *(Wälzfräsmaschine)* hobbing head 3. *(Gradefräsmaschine)* spindle carrier arm
Fräskopf *m* **mit eingesetzten Messern** cone-type face milling cutter with inserted blades
Fräskörperschlitz *m* body slot
Fräsleistung *f* milling capacity, cutting efficiency
Fräsmaschine *f* mill, milling cutter, milling machine
Fräsmaschine *f* **mit Aufspanntrommel** drum-type machine
Fräsmaschine *f* **mit außermittig schwingender Spindel** offset milling machine
Fräsmaschine *f* **mit beweglichem Spindelstock** bed-type milling machine, bench milling machine, kneeless type milling machine
Fräsmaschine *f* **mit beweglicher Doppelständerbrücke** travelling bridge miller
Fräsmaschine *f* **mit Doppelfrässpindel** double head miller (or milling machine), duplex head miller, two-spindle miller
Fräsmaschine *f* **mit drehbarem Spindelkopf** swivel head miller
Fräsmaschine *f* **mit Drehtrommel** rotary drum miller, drum-type miller
Fräsmaschine *f* **mit feststehendem Bett** bed-type milling machine
Fräsmaschine *f* **mit Fühlersteuerung** tracer-controlled milling machine (or miller)
Fräsmaschine *f* **mit hydraulischem Vorschub** hydraulic feed milling machine, fluid-feed milling machine
Fräsmaschine *f* **mit mehreren Fräsköpfen** multiple head milling machine
Fräsmaschine *f* **mit oszillierender Spindel** offset milling machine
Fräsmaschine *f* **mit Rundtisch** rotary table milling machine
Fräsmaschine *f* **mit Schalttrommel** drum-type indexing miller
Fräsmaschine *f* **mit schwenkbarem Spindelkopf** universal head milling machine
Fräsmaschine *f* **mit selbsttätigem Arbeitsablauf** auto-cycle milling machine
Fräsmaschine *f* **mit senkrecht verstellbarer Frässpindel** rise and fall miller
Fräsmaschine *f* **mit Universalspindelkopf** universal head milling machine
Fräsmaschine *f* **mit verschiebbarem Gegenhaltearm** ram-type milling machine
Fräsmaschine *f* **mit verstellbarer Spindel** traversing head miller
Fräsmaschine *f* **mit waagerechter Frässpindel** horizontal spindle milling machine
Fräsmaschine *f* **zum Ausschneiden von Umrissen aus Blechen mit Handvorschub** router
Fräsmaschinen *fpl* milling machines *pl*
Fräsmaschinenhersteller *m* milling machine column
Fräspinole *f* milling quill, milling sleeve
Frässchärfmaschine *f* tool and cutter grinder

Frässchnitt *m* milling cut
Frässpäne *f* millings
Frässpindel *f* cutter spindle, cutting spindle, milling spindle
Frässpindelhülse *f* cutting spindle quill, milling spindle quill, quill
Frässpindelkasten *m* milling headstock, milling spindle head
Frässpindelkopf *m* milling machine spindle nose, milling spindle head
Frässpindelstock *m* milling head
Frässtichel *m* single-tip cutter
Frässupport *m* milling head
Frästisch *m* milling table
Fräsvorschub *m* milling feed
Fräsweg *m* cutting path
Fräswerk *nt* horizontal boring drilling and milling machine, horizontal boring and milling machine, horizontal boring mill
Fräswerkzeug *nt* milling tool, cutter
Fräswerkzeuge *ntpl* milling tools *pl*
Fräswerkzeuge *ntpl* **mit auswechselbaren Messern** inserted blade face milling cutters
Fräszentrum *nt* milling centre
frei free
frei aufschrauben: sich ~ lassen *(z. B. Gutseite e. Gewindelehrdornes)* screw in easily
frei einführen *(e. Lehrdorn)* insert easily
frei fahrend free ranging
frei pendelnd free swinging
frei pendelnd aufgehängt freely supported
frei programmierbar freely programmable
frei stehend free standing
frei tragend cantilevered, in a cantilever position, self-contained
frei verlegte Rohrleitung *f* unburied pipeline
freiarbeiten 1. *(Flanken)* relieve, undercut **2.** *(Gewindespitzen)* clear
Freibewitterung *f* outdoor weathering
Freibewitterungsversuch *m* outdoor weathering (or exposure) test
freibeweglicher Führungsring *m* floating ring

freie Knicklänge *f* unsupported length of column
freier Abstand *m* clear entry
freier Fall *m* free fall
freier Zugang *m* open access
freies Biegen *nt* free bending
freies Fahren *nt* unrestricted travelling
freies Korrosionspotential *nt* free corrosion potential
freies Runden *nt* off-hand rounding
Freifallfangprobe *f* free-fall stop test
Freifallprobe *f* free-fall test
Freifeld *nt* *(Geräuschmessung)* free field
Freifläche *f* **1.** *(allg.)* free area, relief surface **2.** *(Hauptschneide) (US)* primary cutting edge, *(UK)* flank **3.** *(Nebenschneide)* end flank **4.** *(spanen)* surface below the cutting edge, tool flank, flank
Freiflächenfase *f* **1.** *(allg.)* tool flank chamfer, primary clearance **2.** *(Hauptschneide)* side relieve **3.** *(Nebenschneide)* end relief
Freiflächenorthogonalebene *f* tool flank orthogonal plane
Freiflächenprofil *nt* profile of the flank, flank profile
Freiflächenverschleiß *m* flank wear
Freiformen *nt* off-hand forming under compression conditions, open die forging
Freiformfläche *f* sculptured surface
Freiformschmieden *nt* hammer forging
Freigabe *f* **1.** *(Nachrichten)* release, releasing (action) **2.** *(Leitung)* enabling
Freigabemerker *m* release bit memory
Freigabeschalter *m* release switch
Freigabesignal *nt* release signal
freigeben release, allow, dispense, enable
freigeschäumter Schaumstoff *m* free-foamed cellular material
freihändig freehand
Freihandlinie *f* freehand line
Freihandschleifmaschine *f* off-hand grinder
Freiheit *f* freedom
Freiheitsgrad *m* degree of freedom
Freihub *m* free lift, free lift height

Freihubhöhe *f* free lift height
freikommen clear, come clear of
Freilager *nt* open depot, general storage area
Freilandbewitterung *f* outdoor exposure (or weathering)
Freilandversuch *m* outdoor test
Freilauf- und Überholkupplung *f* over-running clutch
freilegen *(Fehlstellen)* expose
Freileitung *f (el.)* overhead electric line
freiliegend cantilever, exposed
Freiluftklima *nt* open air climate, outdoor climate
Freimaß *nt* clearance, untoleranced dimension, free dimension (or size)
Freimaßtoleranz *f* permissible variation for sizes without tolerance indication, free size tolerance, general tolerance
Freimaßtoleranzraum *m* free size tolerance space
Freiraum *m* **1.** *(räumlich)* room, space **2.** *(Metallspritzen)* area to be left clear
freischleifen relief-grind
freischneiden cut clear
Freischneidwerkzeug *nt* clear cutter
freisetzen liberate, set free
Freispiegelleitung *f* gravity pipeline
freistehender Schornstein *m* free-standing chimney
freitragen suspend
freitragend cantilevered, unsupported, self-supporting, overhung
Freiwinkel *m* **1.** *(Drehmeißel)* clearance angle, clearance, angle of clearance, main clearance **2.** *(Räumwerkzeug)* back-off angle, back-off clearance **3.** *(Schneidwerkzeuge)*, relief, relief angle **4.** *(Seitenmeißel)* side clearance
Freiwinkel *m* **an der Fase, hinter der Schneide** angle of relief
Freiwinkel *m* **an der Freiflächenfase** primary clearance
Freiwinkel *m:* **wirksamer** ~ effective clearance angle
Freizeitgeräte *ntpl* leisure facilities, equipment for leisure
Fremdatom *nt* strange atom
fremdbezogen externally sourced
Fremdbezug *m* outsourcing
Fremdbezugsplanung *f* outsourcing planning
Fremdbezugssteuerung *f* outsourcing control
fremderregt separately excited
fremderregte Schwingung *f* forced vibrations
Fremderregung *f* separate excitation, independent excitation
fremderzeugte Schwingungen *fpl* forced vibrations *pl*
Fremdfirma *f* outside company
fremdgekühlt externally cooled
Fremdgerät *nt* third party device
Fremdgeräusch *nt* background noise
Fremdkörper *m* foreign body, foreign matter
Fremdkörperdetektionsmaschine *f* foreign body detecting machine
Fremdkühlung *f* external cooling
Fremdleistung *f* third party performance
Fremdlicht *nt* external light
Fremdlichteinfall *m* incidence of extraneous light
Fremdlichtsicherheit *f* safeguard against extraneous light, safeguard against spurious response
Fremdmetalleinschlüsse *mpl* foreign metallic inclusions *pl*
Fremdschlüssel *m* external key
Fremdstoff *m* foreign body, foreign matter
Fremdstoffe *f* impurity
Fremdstromanlage *f (electr. chem.)* external current consumption
Fremdteil *nt* part of outside origin
Fremdteilzeichnung *f* foreign part drawing
Fremdüberwachung *f* external (quality) control
Fremdvergabe *f* outsourcing
Fremdzündung *f* extraneous (or external) ignition, flash ignition
Frequenz *f* frequency
Frequenzanalysator *m* frequency analyser
Frequenzband *nt* frequency band
Frequenzbereich *m* frequency range

Frequenzbewertung *f* frequency weighting
Frequenzgenerator *m* frequency generator
frequenzgeregelt frequency-controlled, frequency-regulated
Frequenzmesser *m* frequency meter
Frequenzumrichter *m* frequency converter
Frequenzzähler *m* frequency counter
Fressbeanspruchung *f* stressing leading to scoring
fressen 1. *(fest~)* seize 2. *(Korrosion)* fret
Fressgefährdung *f* risk of scoring
Fresstragfähigkeit *f* load-carrying capacity involving heavy scoring
Fressverhalten *nt (e. Verzahnung)* scoring effect
Fressverschleiß *m* wear due to scoring
Frischbetonmischung *f* freshly mixed concrete
Frischluftbetrieb *m* fresh air operation
Frischlufteinlass *m* fresh air inlet
Frischwasserkühlung *f* open circuit water cooling
Frist *f* deadline, time limit, time target
Frittenboden *m* fritted base
Frittenwaschflasche *f* fritted wash-bottle
Front *f* front, face
Frontabschnitt *m* frontal section
Frontantrieb *m* front wheel drive
frontgetrieben front wheel drive, front wheel driven
Frontplatte *f* 1. *(allg.)* front plate 2. *(Gehäuse)* front panel
Frontseite *f* front (end), face
frontseitig front...
frontseitiges Stapeln *nt* front stacking
Frost *m* frost
Frostwechselversuch *m* frost alternating test
Frostwiderstandsfähigkeit *f* frost resistance
Frühausfall *m* early failure
Frühwarnindikator *m* early warning indicator
Frühwarnung *f* early warning
frühzeitig premature

Fuge *f* joint
Fuge *f* **mit Stegabstand** open joint
Fuge *f* **ohne Stegastand** close joint
Fügefläche *f (e. Pressverbandes)* joint surface
Fügegruppe *f* joining group
fügen join, assemble
Fügen *nt* **durch Bördeln** joining by flanging
Fügen *nt* **durch Einpressen** assembly by force fitting
Fügen *nt* **durch Schrumpfen** assembly by shrinkage
Fügen *nt* **durch Urformen** joining by creative forming
Fugendruck *m* joint pressure
Fugendurchmesser *m* interface diameter, joint diameter
Fugenfläche *f* joint surface
Fugenflanke *f* joint flank
Fugenform *f* edge form
Fugengrund *m* joint bottom
Fugenlängskante *f* longitudinal edge of groove
Fugenlöten *nt* open joint soldering (or brazing)
Fugenmasse *f* joint compound
Fugenpressung *f* interference at the joint
Fugenscherung *f* joint shear
Fugenschluss *m (bei Rohren)* jointing
Fugensicherung *f* joint safety
Fugentiefe *f* joint depth
Fügespiel *nt* clearance at the joint
Fügeteil *nt* assembly part (or component)
Fügeteilbruch *m* component failure
Fugeteilverbindung *f* displacement of bonded test piece
Fügetemperatur *f* assembly temperature
Fügevorgang *m* assembly process
Fügezeit *f* jointing time
fühlen sense, feel
Fühler *m* 1. *(e. Reglers)* sensor 2. *(Fühlersteuerung)* stylus, tracer 3. *(als Messgerät)* feeler, feeler gauge
Fühler *m* **für Nachformarbeit nach Zeichnung** line trace for profiling operations

Fühlerdruck *m* force of the stylus
fühlergesteuert tracer-controlled
fühlergesteuerte Nachformeinrichtung *f* tracer-controlled copying attachment
fühlergesteuerte Werkzeugmaschine *f* tracer-controlled machine tool
Fühlerkopf *m* sensor head, tracer head
Fühlerlehre *f* feeler gauge
Fühlerleitung *f* sensor lead
Fühler-Nachformeinrichtung *f* tracing attachment
Fühler-Nachformsteuerung *f* tracer duplicator control
Fühlersteuerung *f* contouring control, tracer control, tracing control
Fühlerstift *f* stylus
Fühlerwalze *f* roller follower, tracer roll
Fühlhebel *m* feeler pin
Fühlhebelmessgerät *nt* level gauge
Fühlhebelschraublehre *f* indicating micrometer
Fühlstift *m* tracer, feeler, stylus
führen 1. *(allg.)* pilot, guide, lead, carry, direct **2.** *(Flüssigkeit)* port **3.** *(Lastenheft)* keep **4.** *(Strom)* conduct
führen über pass across, lead across
Führerstand *m* cab, cabin, operator position
Führung *f* **1.** *(e. Schlittens)* guideway, guide(s), guidance **2.** *(Förderer)* slide, slideway **3.** *(Steuerung)* control **4.** *(Personal)* piloting, pilot
Führung *f* **am Endstück/Räumwerkzeug** back end piloting
Führung *f:* **aerostatische** ~ aerostatic guidance
Führung *f:* **hydrostatische** ~ hydrostatic guidance
Führungen *fpl* guides, ways
Führungsachse *f* axis of constraint
Führungsbahn *f* guideway, track, slideway, guidance path
Führungsbahnen *fpl* **am Ständer** column ways
Führungsbereich *m* range of the command variable
Führungsbewegung *f* guidance motion
Führungsbohrstange *f* line boring bar, piloting boring bar
Führungsbohrung *f* pilot hole, starting hole
Führungsbüchse *f* **1.** *(allg.)* guide bush **2.** *(Räumwerkzeug)* adapter
Führungseinrichtung *f* guidance means
Führungsfläche *f* guideway
Führungsfunktion *f* guide function
Führungsgestänge *nt* guide rod
Führungsgetriebe *nt* guidance mechanism
Führungsgröße *f* guide variable
Führungskegel *m* locating cone
Führungskonstruktion *f* guiding members
Führungskraft *f* stabilizing force
Führungslager *nt* *(Fräsmaschine)* arbor yoke
Führungsleiste *f* taper gib
Führungslineal *nt* guiding rule
Führungsmittel *nt* guiding member
Führungsrad *nt* guide wheel
Führungsrolle *f* contact roller, guide roller, guiding pulley
Führungssatz *m* header record
Führungssäule *f* guide column
Führungsschiene *f* guide rail, restraining rail
Führungsschiene *f:* **obere** ~ upper guide rail
Führungssignal *nt* command signal, guidance signal
Führungsspiel *nt* guide play
Führungsstange *f* guide bar
Führungsstein *m* sliding block
Führungssteuerung *f* command variable control
Führungsstift *m* former pin, guide pin
Führungsstruktur (BWL) *f* management organization
Führungsstück *nt* **1.** *(allg.)* pilot segment, rear pilot **2.** *(Räummaschinenwerkzeug)* alignment section
Führungsstück *nt* **an der Aufnahme des Räumwerkzeuges** broach front pilot
Führungssystem *nt* guide system
Führungsverhalten *nt* *(e. Regelkreises)* command variable action

Führungszähne — Funktion

Führungszähne *mpl* (Räumwerkzeug) dwell teeth *pl*
Führungszahnrad *nt* pilot gear
Führungszapfen *m* journal, spindle
Füll- und Dosiermaschine *f* filling and dosing machine
Füll- und Verschließmaschine *f* filling and sealing machine, fill and close machine
Fülldrahtelektrodenschweißen *nt* welding with cored-wire electrode
Fülldruck *m* filling pressure
Fülleinrichtung *f* filling arrangement
füllen charge, fill
Füllgrad *m* filling level
Füllgut *nt* fill goods
Füllhöhe *f* fill(ing) height, filling level
Füllhöheninspektionsmaschine *f* fill height inspection machine
Füllkasten *m* hopper
Fülllagenschweißer *m* filler-run welder
Füllleitung *f* fill pipe
Füllmaschine *f* filling machine
Füllmenge *f* fill-up quantity
Füllraum *m* 1. (e. Kessels) fuel hopper 2. (e. Ofens) charging space
Füllschacht *m* charging chute
Füllschachtaufbau *m* superimposed hopper
Füllschachtkessel *m* gravity-feed hopper type boiler
Füllschweißer *m* filler-run welder
Füllstab *m* filler rod
Füllstand *m* filling level
Füllstandsanzeige *f* maximum level indicating device, maximum liquid level device
Füllstandsanzeiger *m* liquid level indicator
Füllstandschalter *m* liquid level switch
Füllstandshöhe *f* filling level
Füllstandsmessung *f* level control, level gauging
Füllstand-Sollwertsteller *m* fill level set point setter
Füllstation *f* filling station
Füllstelle *f* filler point
füllstoffhaltig containing filler
Füllstutzen *m* fill nozzle

Fülltrichter *m* hopper
Füllung *f* filling
Füllungsgrad *m* filling degree
Füllventil *nt* filling valve
Füllvorgang *m* filling operation
Füllzeit *f* charging time
Fundament *nt* base, foundation
Fundamentplatte *f* bottom plate, base plate
Fundamentschraube *f* anchor bolt, foundation bolt
Fundamentzeichnung *f* foundation drawing
Fünferteilung *f* (e. Skala) five-based division
fünffach five times
Fünffingerhandschuh *m* wrist glove
Fünfkantrevolverkopf *m* five-station turret
Fünfspindelautomat *m* five-spindle automatic lathe
Funk *m* radio, two-way radio
Funke *m* spark
funken radio, (UK) transmit by wireless
Funken sprühen spark, emit sparks
Funkenentladung *f* spark discharge
Funkenerodieren *nt* electro discharge machining, spark eroding
Funkenerodieren *nt* spark eroding
funkenerodierend spark eroding
Funkenerodiermaschine *f* spark-erosion machine
funkenerodiert spark-eroded
Funkenerodierverfahren *nt* spark-eroding process
Funkenerosion *f* spark erosion
Funkenerosionsformen *nt* spark discharge forming
funkenerosiv spark-eroding
funkenfrei nonsparking, sparkless
Funkenschutz *m* spark guard
Funkenschweißen *nt* percussion welding
Funkenspalt *m* spark gap
Funkentstörung *f* (radio) interference suppression
Funkererosionsmaschine *f* spark erosion machine
funkferngesteuert radio-controlled
Funktion *f* function, functioning, opera-

tion
funktional functional
Funktionalparameter *m* functional parameter
funktionelle Gesamtleistung *f* performance
funktionelle Verbindung *f* logic connection
funktionieren function, operate, work
Funktionsanzeiger *m* function indicator
Funktionsart *f* type of function
Funktionsaufruf *m* function reference
Funktionsbausteinsprache (FBS) *f* function block diagram (FBD), FBD language
funktionsbedingt governed by functional requirements
funktionsbedingt dictated by functional factors
funktionsbedingte Gefahr *f* hazard due to the function involved
funktionsbedingtes Maß *nt* functionally significant dimension
Funktionsbeeinträchtigung *f* impairment of function
Funktionsbereich *m* operating sphere
Funktionsbeschreibung *f* function description, operation manual
Funktionsbestandteil *m* operating component
funktionsbezogene Maßeintragung *f* function-related dimensioning
Funktionsebene *f* functional level
Funktionseinheit *f* functional unit
Funktionselement *nt* functional element
Funktionserdanschluss *m* functional earthing point
Funktionserde *f* functional earth, functional ground
funktionsfähig functional, operational, capable of operation
Funktionsfähigkeit *f* 1. *(allg.)* functionality, proper functioning, operability 2. *(e. Aufgabengröße)* functional capability
Funktionsfläche *f* working surface
Funktionsgeber *m* resolver
funktionsgerecht meeting functional requirements
Funktionsgruppierung *f* functional grouping
Funktionskennzeichen *nt* qualifying symbol for the function
Funktionskleinspannung *f* functional extra-low voltage
Funktionsmodul *nt* function module
Funktionsmusterphase *f* prototype phase
Funktionsnachweisverfahren *nt* proper functioning verification procedure
Funktionsplan *m* functional plan
Funktionsprogramm *nt* functional program
Funktionsprototyp *m* functional prototype
Funktionsprüfung *f* function(al) test, functional verification
Funktionsschema *nt* function diagram
Funktionssicherheit *f* safe functioning, operational safety
funktionsstörender Fehler *nt* functional impairment
Funktionsstörung *f* operating fault
Funktionstabelle *f* function table
Funktionstastatur *f* function keyboard
Funktionstaste *f* function key, hot key, operation(al) control key (OCK)
funktionstechnischer Grund *m* functional reason
funktionstüchtig operative
Funktionstüchtigkeit *f* functional efficiency, functional reliability
funktionsuntüchtig non-functioning
Funktionsveränderung *f* functional change
Funktionsverlauf *m* trend of the function
funktionswichtige Bezugsebene *f* functionally important datum plane
Furanbasis *f* furan basis
Furche *f* ridge
furchen riffle
Furchen *nt* *(Anreißen)* scribing, line marking
Furnierschicht *f* veneer layer
Fuß *m* 1. *(Bauteil)* foot 2. *(Basis)* base, bottom 3. *(e. Bogens)* pedestal

4. *(Schiene)* rail foot, rail base
5. *(Zahnfuß)* root of the tooth
Fußabweiser *m* deflector
Fußausleger *m* base, pedestal footing
fußbetätigt foot-actuated, foot-controlled, foot-operated
Fußboden *m* floor
Fußbodenbelag *m* floor covering
Fußbodendurchlass *m* floor outlet
Fußbodennähe *f* near floor level
Fußbodenspeicherheizung *f* thermal storage floor heating
Fußende nt der nutzbaren Flanke lower end of effective flank
Fußfläche *f* root surface
Fußflanke *f* tooth flank, dedendum flank
Fußflankenlinie *f* root tooth trace
Fußfreiraum *m* free space for feet
Fußfreischnitt *m* relief of the tooth flank, grinding relief, undercut
Fußgänger *m* pedestrian
Fußgängerweg *m* walkway
Fußgestell *nt* basis, footing, pedestal
Fußhebel *m* foot lever, treadle
fußhebelbetätigt pedal operated
Fußhöhe *f* dedendum
Fußkegel *m* root cone
Fußkegelspitze *f* root cone apex
Fußkegelwinkel *m* root angle
Fußkehlfläche *f* root toroid
Fußklappe *f* flap operated foot valve
Fußkreis *m* dedendum circle, root circle
Fußkreisdurchmesser *m* root diameter
Fußleiste *f* base board, kickbar, plinth, toe board
Fußmantelfläche *f* root surface
Fußmotor *m* foot-mounted motor

Fußnutzkreis *m* usable root circle
Fußnutzkreisdurchmesser *m* effective root diameter, usable root diameter
Fußplatte *f* base plate, foot
Fußpresse *f* foot-operated grease gun
Fußpunkt *m* root point
Fußrücknahme *f* root relief
Fußrundung *f* root radiusing, root rounding
Fußrundungsfläche *f* fillet surface, root radiusing surface
Fußrundungsradius *m* radius of the root rounding
Fußschalter *m* floor switch, foot switch
Fußschutz *m* foot guard, foot protection
Fußwicklung *f* bottom wrap
Fußwinkel *m* dedendum angle
Futter *nt* lining, packing, chuck
Futteranlage *f* chuck register
Futterarbeit *f* chuck work
Futterautomat *m* automatic chucking machine
Futterbacken *fpl* chuck jaws *pl*
Futterbefestigung *f* chuck mounting
Futter-Halbautomat *m* semi-automatic chucking machine
Futterkessel *m* cattle feed boiler
Futterplatte *f* chuck backplate
Futterrevolverautomat *m* turret-type chucking automatic
Futterrohr-Rundgewinde *nt* knuckle thread for casing tubes
Fuzzifizierung *f* fuzzification
Fuzzy-Control *f* fuzzy control
Fuzzy-Control-Sprache *f* fuzzy control language
Fuzzy-Logik *f* fuzzy logic
Fuzzy-Operator *m* fuzzy logic operator

Gg

Gabel *f* fork, yoke
Gabelabstand *m* fork spacing
Gabelausfahrt *f* fork tension
Gabelausfahrt *f (Anweisung)* fork forwards, fork outwards
Gabelblatt *nt* (fork) blade, fork arm blade
Gabeldurchhang *m* fork sag
Gabeleinfahrtasche *f* fork entry aperture
Gabelhaken *m* hook
Gabelheben *nt* **1.** *(Bewegung)* fork lifting **2.** *(Anweisung)* fork up
Gabelhochhubwagen *m* high-lift platform truck, high-lift truck, pallet-stacking truck, pallet stacker
Gabelhöhe *f* fork height
Gabelhubfahrzeug *nt* fork-lift truck, pallet truck
Gabelhubwagen *m* fork lift truck, pallet truck
Gabelkausche *f* thimble with clevis
Gabelknick *m* heel
Gabelneiger *m* fork tippler
Gabelräder *ntpl* fork wheels
Gabelrücken *m* fork arm shank, fork shank, shank
Gabelrückfahrt *f* **1.** *(Bewegung)* fork retraction, fork withdrawal **2.** *(Anweisung)*
Gabelschaft *m* fork shank
Gabelseite *f* flank
Gabelsenken *nt* **1.** *(Bewegung)* fork lowering **2.** *(Anweisung)* fork down
Gabelspiel *nt* fork cycle
Gabelspielzeit *f* fork cycle time
Gabelspitze *f* fork tip, tip
Gabelstapler *m* fork-lift truck, fork lift, fork truck
Gabeltasche *f* fork aperture
Gabelträger *m* (fork) carriage, fork carrier, fork arm carriage, load carriage
Gabelträgerbreite *f* width of fork arm carriage
Gabelunterseite *f* lower face of the blade

Gabelverlängerung *f* fork extension, extension sleeves
Gabelversuch *m* fork test
Gabelwagen *m* fork truck, fork carriage
Gabelzinken *m* fork arm
Gabelzinkenmoment *nt* fork arm moment
Gabelzinkenspitze *f* extremity of fork arm
Galvanik *f* galvanizing
Galvanikstartschicht *f* galvanizing start layer
Galvanisation *f* electroplating, electrode positing
galvanisch galvanic
galvanisch getrennt galvanically isolated
galvanisch schlussverzinkt finally electrolytically galvanized (or tin plated)
galvanische Anode *f* galvanic anode
galvanische Stromquelle *f* galvanic current source
galvanische Trennung *f* galvanic isolation
galvanisch oberflächengeschützte Sicherungsmutter locknut with electrolytically deposited surface protection
Galvanisierautomat *m* automatic plating unit
Galvanisierbad *nt* electroplating (or electrolytic plating) bath
galvanisieren electroplate, electrodeposit
Galvanisiertrommel *f* electroplating drum
Galvanisierverfahren *nt* electroplating process
Galvanisierwanne *f* electroplating tank
Galvanisierwerkstatt *f* electroplating shop
Galvanoformung *f* electroforming
Galvanoformungsanlage *f* electroforming plant
galvanogeformter Nickel *m* electroformed nickel
Galvanometer *nt* galvanometer

Galvanoplastik *f* electrotyping, electroform
Gammabestrahlungsanlage *f* gamma-emitting system
Gammabestrahlungsanlage *f* gamma radiation plant
Gammafilmaufnahme *f* gamma-ray radiograph
Gammastrahler *m* gamma emitter
gammaverteilt gamma distributed
Gang einlegen engage the transmission
Gang *m* **1.** *(Bewegung)* motion, speed, running, gear, transmission, pass **2.** *(räuml.)* aisle, lane **3.** *(e. eingängigen Gewindes)* lead **4.** *(e. mehrgängigen Gewindes)* pitch
Gang *m:* **in ~ setzen** start, put into operation
Ganganzahl *f* number of leads
Gangbreite *f* aisle width
Gangerkennung *f* aisle detection
Gangfreimaß *nt* aisle clearance
Ganghochrichtung *f* aisle vertical direction
Ganghöhe *f* **1.** *(e. Feder)* pitch **2.** *(e. Gewindes)* lead **3.** *(e. Kegels)* taper **4.** *(e. Keils)* gradient
Ganglängsrichtung *f* aisle length direction
Gangnotbeleuchtung *f* aisle emergency lighting
Gangquerrichtung *f* aisle lateral direction
gangseitig adjacent to the aisle, along the aisle, facing the aisle, aisle side
Gangwechsel *m* change of aisle, range changing
Gantrymaschine *f* gantry machine
ganz complete, intact, integral, whole, entire
ganze Zahl *f* integer
ganzer Bildschirm *m* full screen
ganzheitliches Qualitätsmanagement *nt* total quality management
Ganzkörperschwingung *f* whole body vibration
ganzzahlig integer
ganzzahlige Potenz *f* integral power
ganzzahliger Wert *m* integer
ganzzahliges Vielfaches *nt* integral multiple
Garantie *f* guarantee, guaranty, warranty
Garantiefehlergrenze *f* guarantee limit of error
garantieren guarantee, warrant, ensure
Gartenbauglas *nt* horticultural glass
Gartenzaun *m* picket fence
Gas *nt* gas *(pl.:* gases)
gasablassendes Sicherheitsventil *nt* gas discharge safety valve
Gasabzug *m* gas issue, gas off-take
Gasabsaugung *f* gas suction, gas exhausting
Gasaufnahme *f* gas (work)
gasbefeuerter Warmlufterzeuger *m* gas-fired heater
Gasbetonbauplatte *f* gas-aerated concrete building plate
Gasbetonblockstein *m* gas-aerated concrete block
Gasbildung *f* accumulation of gases
Gasblase *f* gas flaw
Gasbrenner *m* gas torch
Gasbrenner *m* **ohne Gebläse** gas burner for use without fan
gasdicht gas-tight
Gasdruckwächter *m* gas pressure monitor
Gasdurchflussintegrator *m* gas-flow integrator
Gasdurchflusswassererwärmer *m* instantaneous gas-fired heater
Gasdurchgang *m* gas discharge, gas flow
Gasdurchlässigkeitsprüfung *f* gas permeability
Gasdurchlauferhitzer *m* instantaneous gas-fired heater
Gaseindringprüfung *f* gas penetration test
Gaseindringung *f* gas penetration
Gaseinspeisung *f* gas injection
Gaseinspeisungsrohr *nt* gas injector pipe
Gaseinstellventil *nt* gas control valve
Gasentnahme *f* withdrawal of gas
Gasentnahmehahn *m* gas draw-off valve
Gasentnahmestelle *f* gas take-off point

Gasentwicklung *f* gas formation, gassing
Gaserfassung *f* gas detection
Gaserfassungssystem *nt* gas detection system
Gaserzeugungsanlage *f* gas generating plant
gasexplosionsgefährdeter Bereich *m* explosive gas atmosphere
Gasexplosionsverfahren *nt* gas explosion process
Gasfeuerstätte *f* gas fire-place
Gasfeuerungsanlage *f* **mit Saugzugventilator** gas firing installation with induced draught fan
Gasfeuerungsautomat *m* automatic gas firing unit
Gasfeuerungsteil *nt* gas firing component
Gasflammenhärtung *f* flame hardening
Gasflaschenventil *nt* gas cylinder valve
Gasfließdruck *m* gas flow pressure
gasförmig fluid, gaseous
gasförmige Entnahme *f* vapour withdrawal
Gasfraktion *f* gas fraction
Gasfreigabe *f* gas release
Gasfühler *m* gas sensor
Gasfühlerkopf *m* gas sensor head
gasführendes Teil *nt* gas-conveying portion
Gasgerät *nt* gas appliance
Gasgruppe *f* gas group(ing)
Gaskessel *m* gas-fired boiler
Gaskonzentrationsmessung *f* gas detection, gas concentration measurement
Gaslaser *m* gas laser
Gaslaser *m:* **atomarer ~** atomic laser
Gaslöten *nt* gas brazing
Gasmangelsicherung *f* gas failure safety device
Gasmesskopf *m* gas sensor
Gasnetz *nt* gas distribution system
Gaspolster *nt* gas cushion
Gaspolsteranlage *f* gas-cushioned system
Gasporosität *f* gas porosity
Gasprüfzelle *f* gas test chamber
Gaspulverschweißen *nt* gas powder welding
Gasraum *m* vapour space
Gasrücktritt *m* gas regression
gasschweißen gas-weld
Gasschweißstab *m* gas welding filler rod
Gasse *f* aisle, lane
Gassenachse *f* aisle axis
Gassenausrüstung *f* aisle equipment
Gassenbreite *f* aisle width
gassenseitig aisle side
Gassensor *m* gas sensor
Gassenwechsel *m* change between aisles, change of aisle
gasspezifisch lane-specific
Gasspürmessgerät *nt* gas leak tester
Gasstrom *m* gas flow
gastechnische Ausrüstung *f* gas equipment
Gasumlaufwasserheizer *m* gas-fired circulatory type water heater
Gasung *f* gassing
Gasverbrauchseinrichtung *f* gas consumer installation
Gaswarnkalibriersystem *nt* forced gas test
Gaswarnsystem *nt* gas detection system
Gaszuleitung *f* gas inlet pipe
Gaszündanlage *f* gas ignition system
Gaszündbrenner *m* gas ignition burner
Gatter *nt* gate
Gauß-Verteilung *f* normal distribution
Gebäude *nt* building, facility
Gebäudeebene *f* building level
Gebäudeform *f* building form
Gebäudeschnitt *m* elevation (or sectional drawing) of the building
Gebäudestütze *f* prop, stay
Gebäudeteil *nt* building part
Gebäudeverformung *f* building deformation
Gebäudewand *f* wall
Geber *m* sensor, transmitter, encoder
Gebinde *nt* container, package
Gebläse *nt* blowing fan, blower, blow torch, fan, ventilator, booster
Gebläsebrenner *m* fan-assisted burner
gebläsegekühlt fan-cooled
gebogener Eckdrehmeißel *m* bent

cutting tool for corner work
gebogener Hobelmeißel *m* cranked planing tool
gebogener linker Meißel *m* left-bent tool
gebogener rechter Meißel *m* right-bent tool
gebogener Schlichtmeißel *m* bent finishing tool
gebogener Seitenmeißel *m* offset side tool
geboraxt boraxed
gebördeltes Rohr *nt* flanged pipe
Gebrauch *m* application, use, utilisation
gebrauchen use
gebräuchlich commonly used, usual
gebräuchlichstes Maß *nt* most commonly used measure
Gebrauchsanleitung *f* instruction for use
Gebrauchsanweisung *f* instruction for use, operation instructions
Gebrauchsbelastung *f* service load, useful life
Gebrauchsdauer *f* service life
Gebrauchsfähigkeit *f* suitability for use
Gebrauchsfähigkeitsnachweis *m* overall assessment, verification of functionality
Gebrauchslage *f (bei Zeichnungen)* position of use
Gebrauchslast *f* working load
Gebrauchstauglichkeit *f (von Normen)* practical usefulness, serviceability
Gebrauchstemperatur *f* service temperature
Gebrauchstüchtigkeit *f* service performance
Gebrauchswassertemperatur *f* service water temperature
gebraucht used, second-hand, reconditioned
gebrochene Kante *f* chamfer
gebrochene Längskante *f* corner removed from longitudinal edge of face
gebrochene Steg-Längskante *f* corner removed from longitudinal edge of root face

gebündelte Holzpakete *ntpl* packaged timber
gebündelte Lichtstrahlen *f* beams of coherent light
gebunden bound
gebundenes Schleiferkorn *nt* bonded abrasive grain
gedachte Fläche *f* notional surface
gedachtes fehlerfreies Gewinde *nt* imaginary flawless thread
gedämpft damped, gentle
gedrungen stubby
geeignet appropriate, suitable
geeignet für adapted for, suited for
geerdet earthed, grounded
gefachtes Glasseidengarn *nt* doubled glass filament
gefachtes Textilglasgarn *nt* multiple wound glass filament yarn
Gefahr *f* danger, hazard
Gefahr(en)stelle *f* dangerous spot, hazard
Gefahrbereich *m* area of hazard, danger zone, hazard zone
gefahrbringend hazardous
gefahrbringende Umgebung *f* environmental hazard
gefahrbringende Wirkung *f* dangerous effect
gefährden endanger
gefährdet hazardous
gefährdete Stelle *f* endangered point
Gefährdung *f* hazard, hazardous situation, endangering, threat
Gefährdungszeit *f* danger period
Gefahrenaussetzung *f* exposure to hazards
Gefahrenfall *m* hazardous situation
Gefahrenklasse *f* hazard category
Gefahrenquelle *f* hazard source, source of danger
Gefahrenschalter *m* emergency switch
Gefahrensicherung *f* prevention of hazards
Gefahrensymbol *nt* hazard pictorial
Gefahrenzulage *f* hazard bonus
Gefahrgut *nt* hazardous goods
Gefahrklasse *f* hazard group
gefährlich dangerous, hazardous
gefährliche Ausfallwahrscheinlich-

keit *f* probability of dangerous failure
gefährliche Bewegung *f* hazardous movement
gefährliche Güter *ntpl* hazardous materials (or goods)
gefährliche Spannung *f* hazardous voltage
gefährliches Bauteil *nt* hazardous element
gefahrlos safe
gefahrlos erreichbar reachable without any danger
Gefahrmeldung *f* danger message
Gefahrstelle *f* hazard (or danger) point
gefahrverhindernd danger inhibiting (or preventing)
Gefälle *nt* gradient
Gefällespeicher *m* gravity accumulator
Gefällstrecke *f* gradient
gefärbtes Papier *nt* stained paper
Gefäßmanometer *nt* cistern manometer
gefaste Schneide *f* chamfered cutting edge
gefedert sprung
gefederte Masse *f* flexible mass
gefederte Rolle *f* shock-absorbing castor
gefedertes Rad *nt* spring-loaded wheel
gefertigte Fläche *f* machined surface
Geflecht *nt* meshwork
gefräste Fräser *m* milled tooth cutter
Gefüge *nt* structure
Gefügeabweichung *f* deviation of structure
Gefügeaufbau *m* structural constitution
Gefügeausbildung *f* structural shape, formation of the structure
Gefügeinhomogenität *f* non-uniformity of crystalline structure
gefühlvoll sensitive
geführt guided
gefülltes Gießharz *nt* casting resin containing filler
gefurchtes Gewinde *nt* ridged thread
gegen against
gegen den Uhrzeigersinn *m* anticlockwise, counterclockwise
Gegendruckraum *m* back pressure space
Gegendruckrolle *f* reaction pressure roller
gegeneinander abwälzen roll relatively to one another
gegeneinander verriegeln interlock
gegeneinander verschieben move relative to each other
gegeneinander versetzen stagger
gegeneinander versetzte Kerbung *f* alternate nicking
gegeneinanderstoßen abut against one another
Gegenfahrbahn *f* opposite lane
Gegenflanke *f* mating tooth surface, mating flank
Gegengewicht *nt* counterweight, balance weight
Gegengewichtskontur *f* counterweight profile
Gegengewichtstapler *m* counterbalanced lift truck, counterbalanced truck
Gegenhaltekraft *f* overarm power
gegenhalten back up, hold up, dolly (riveting)
Gegenhalter *m* **1.** *(allg.)* poppet, planer poppet, steady **2.** *(Fräsmaschine)* overarm **3.** *(Räumwerkzeug)* back rest
Gegenhalterschere *f* **1.** *(allg.)* arbor brace, front brace **2.** *(Fräsmaschine)* arm brace, outboard brace
Gegenhalterstütze *f* overarm brace (or support), outer arm brace
Gegenkompoundierung *f* countercompounding, differential compounding
Gegenkraft *f* counterforce
Gegenkurve *f* opposite cam
Gegenlauffräsen *nt* conventional milling, cutting up, ordinary milling, outcut milling, upcut milling, upcutting, up-milling
Gegenlauffrässchnitt *m* conventional cut
Gegenlauffräsverfahren *nt* up-feed method of milling
gegenläufige Anzeige *f* reading in the reverse direction
gegenläufige Drehbewegung *f* opposed direction of rotation

gegenläufige Skalierung f opposed graduated scale
Gegenlaufschleifen nt up grinding, up-cut grinding
Gegenlaufwirbeln nt opposed whirling
Gegenmaßnahme f countermeasure, counteractive measure
Gegenmoment nt counter torque, lead moment
Gegenmutter f binding nut, check nut, jam nut, lock nut
Gegenplanrad nt mating crown gear
Gegenplanverzahnung f mating plane tooth system
Gegenrad nt mating gear
Gegenradumfang m mating gear circumference
Gegenrichtung f opposite direction
gegenseitig mutual, reciprocal
gegenseitige Verriegelung f interlock
Gegenspindel f screw
Gegenspitze f dead centre, tail centre
Gegenstand m object
Gegenständer m (e. Bohrwerks) end support column
Gegensteuerung f countersteering
Gegenstromapparat m counterflow exchanger
Gegenstück nt complement, companion part
Gegenstütze f counterstay
Gegentakt m differential mode, push-pull
Gegentakteinkopplung f differential mode coupling
Gegentaktendstufe f push-pull output stage
gegenüber opposite
gegenüberstellen compare with, contrast with
Gegenverkehr m two-way traffic
Gegenverzahnung f counter gear teeth
gegenwärtiger Stand m current stage
gegenwirken react, act against
Gegenzahn m mating tooth
gegliedert jointed
gegossene Lotfäden mpl cast solder filaments pl
Gehalt m content, salary
gehärteter Stahl m hardened steel
Gehäuse nt **1.** (allg.) box, case, casing, enclosure, compartment, body, frame **2.** (e. Lagers) housing **3.** (kastenförmiger Querschnitt) box section overarm
Gehäuseabdeckung f covering
Gehäuseachsabstand m housing centre distance
Gehäuseanschluss m enclosure port
Gehäuseauflagefläche f housing mounting face
Gehäuseteilfläche f housing parting face
Gehäusetemperatur f housing temperature
Gehäusewand f casing wall
geheftet stitched
gehefteter Zustand m tack-welded condition
gehemmter Ladungsdurchtritt m inhibited charge transfer
gehen walk
Gehörschädigung f hearing loss
Gehrungsschnitt m diagonal cut, mitre cut
Gehweg m walkway
geistige Überbeanspruchung f mental overload
geistige Unterbeanspruchung f mental underload
gekapselt with casing, encased, encapsulated
gekerbte Querbiegeprobe f notched transverse bend specimen
geknickte Freifläche f offset tool flank
geknickte Spanfläche f offset tool face
geknickter Linienzug m kinked line
geknotete Probe f knotted specimen
gekreuzt crossed
gekröpft cranked, swan-necked, goosenecked, offset
gekröpfter Doppelringschlüssel m off-set double-ended spanner, offset double end box wrench
gekröpfter Einringschlüssel m single-ended offset ring spanner, single end offset box wrench
gekröpfter Gewindemeißel m offset

single-point threading tool
gekröpfter Meißel *m* goose-neck tool, offset tool
gekröpfter Meißelhalter *m* knee turning toolholder
gekröpfter Ringmaulschlüssel *m* offset combination wrench
gekröpfter Schlichtmeißel *m* goose neck finishing tool, swan-necked finisher, swan-necked rougher
gekröpfter Schlichtmeißel *m* swan-necked finishing tool, *(US)* goose-necked finisher
gekrümmt curved, crooked
gekrümmte Fläche *f* curved surface
gekrümmte Skale *f* curved scale
gekupfertes Lot *nt* copper-containing solder
gekuppelter Fräsersatz *m* interlocked cutter set
geländegängig rough-terrain
geländegängiger Stapler *m* rough-terrain truck
Geländemulde *f* depression in the terrain
Geländer *nt* 1. *(allg.)* rail, guard rail, railing 2. *(Handgriff)* handrail, grabrail
Geländerfittings *mpl* railing fittings
Geländerholm *m* rail sleeper, inside or outside of handrails
Geländerrohr *nt* handrail
Geländerstütze *f* newel post, handrail post
Gelbstichigkeit *f* yellowishness
Geldfluss *m* finance flow
Gelenk *nt* articulation, joint, articulated joint, hinge, link
Gelenkarm *m* articulated arm, articulating arm
Gelenkbolzen *m* joint bolt
Gelenkgriff *m* **mit Außenvierkant** flex head nut spanner
gelenkig aufhängen *(sich um einen Zapfen drehend)* pivot
gelenkig befestigen hinge
gelenkig verbinden mit pivot on
Gelenkpunkt *m* articulation joint, pivot point
Gelenkräder *ntpl* articulated wheels
Gelenkrohr *nt* articulated pipe

Gelenkrohrverbindung *f* swivel pipe coupling
Gelenkspindelbohrmaschine *f* multiple-spindle drilling machine with universally adjustable spindle
Gelenksteckschlüssel *m* flex head socket wrench
Gelenkverbindung *f* articulation
Gelenkwelle *f* universal shaft
gelernte Arbeitskräfte *f* skilled labour
gelernter Arbeiter *m* skilled worker
gelocht pierced
gelochte Bohrung *f* pierced hole
gelten für apply for
Geltungsbereich *m (e. Toleranzsystems)* scope
Gemarkungsgrenze *f* limit of landmarks
Gemeinkosten *pl* overhead (cost)
gemeinsames Ziehen *nt* combined drawing
Gemeinschaftsversuch *m* joint test
gemeldet signalled
Gemisch *nt* mixture
gemischt composite, mixed
gemischte Logik *f* mixed logic
gemischter Betrieb *m* composite plant
gemischtzelliger Schaumstoff *m* mixed-cell foam (or expanded material)
genau accurate, correct, exact, precise
genau auf eine Toleranz *f* true within
genau bemessen closely measured
Genaubearbeitung *f* precision machining
genauere Angaben *fpl* specifications *pl*
Genauigkeit *f* accuracy, exactness, precision
Genauigkeitsanspruch *m* demand for accuracy
Genauigkeitsdrehen *nt* high-precision turning
Genauigkeitsdrehmaschine *f* precision turning machine
Genauigkeitsgrad *m* degree (or grade) of accuracy
Genauigkeitsgruppe *f* accuracy group
Genauigkeitsmesseinrichtung *f* precision measuring device
Genauigkeitsspindel *f* precision screw

spindle
Genauigkeitsteilgerät *nt* precision index centres
Genaumaß *nt* true size
Genauschneiden *nt* precision cutting
genehmigen approve
Genehmigung *f* approval
Genehmigungsprozess *m* process of approval
Genehmigungsverfahren *nt* approval procedure
geneigt inclined, skew
Generalbebauungsplan *m* general development scheme
Generalregister *nt* general purpose register
generalüberholt rebuilt
Generalüberholung *f* general overhaul
Generalunternehmer *m* general contractor
Generatornenndrehzahl *f* generator rated speed
Generatornennleistung *f* generator rated power
Generatornennspannung *f* generator rated voltage
generell general
Generieren *nt* generate
Generierung *f* generating
genormt standardized
genutet grooved
Geometrie *f* geometry
Geometrie *f* **der Schneide** *f* geometry of the cutting edge, tool geometry
geometrische Flächeneinheit *f* (*electr. chem.*) geometrical unit of area
geometrische Größe *f* geometric quantity
geometrische Reihe *f* geometric progression
geometrische Sollform *f* required geometrical design form
geometrische Zerlegung *f* geometrical resolution
geometrischer Schleifwinkel *m* geometric grinding arc
geometrischer Werkzeugspanwinkel *m* tool geometrical rake
geordnet ordered

geordnet rilliger Oberflächencharakter *m* systematically grooved surface character
gepaarte Teile *ntpl* mating parts
geperlter Ruß *m* pelletized carbon black
gepolstert padded
geprüfter Schweißer *m* approved welder
gepuffert buffered
Geraddrehen *nt* straight turning
gerade even, direct, straight
Gerade *f* straight line
gerade Flanke *f* straight flank
gerade Verschraubung *f* **mit zylindrischem Einschraubzapfen** *m* straight union with parallel adapter end
gerade verzahnt straight toothed
gerade verzahnter Scheibenfräser *m* straight tooth side and face cutter
gerade Zahl *f* even number
geradeaus straight ahead, straight forward
Geradeaus-Stellung *f* straight ahead position, straight line position, axial position
Geradeglied *nt* even element
Geradeninterpolation *f* straight line interpolation
Geradenparallelgreifer *m* straight line parallel gripper
gerader Doppelringschlüssel *m* flat double-ended ring spanner, flat double head box wrench
gerader Meißel *m* straight-cut tool
gerader Seitenmeißel *m* straight side tool
gerades Rohrstück *nt* straight length
geradflankig straight-flanked, straight-sided
geradflankiges Werkzeug *nt* straight flank tool
Geradführung *f* straight-line guidance
Geradheit *f* straightness
Geradheitsabweichung *f* error on straightness, straightness deviation
Geradheitstoleranz *f* straightness tolerance
geradlinig straight (lined), rectilinear
geradlinig verlaufen run in a straight

line
geradlinige Längsteilung *f* linear indexing
Geradlinigkeit *f* rectilinearity
Geradschneidrad *nt* straight pinion cutter
Geradschnitt *m* straight cut
Geradstirnrad *nt* spur gear
Geradstirnradpaar *nt* spur gear pair
geradverzahntes Lehrzahnrad *nt* straight-tooth master gear
Geradverzahnung *f* straight-tooth cutting, straight tooth system, straight gear cutting, spur gear teeth
geradzahlige Zähnezahlen *fpl* even numbers of teeth
Geradzahnkegelrad *nt* straight bevel gear
Geradzahnkegelradpaar *nt* straight bevel gear pair
Geradzahnkegelradverzahnung *f* straight bevel gear teeth
Geradzylinderrad *nt* spur gear
Geradzylinderradpaar *nt* spur gear pair
Gerät *nt* **1.** *(allg.)* device, equipment, instrument, implement, outfit, tool, machine **2.** *(Apparat)* apparatus, appliance, contrivance, outfit **3.** *(Kolben, Pipetten)* glassware **4.** *(Messzeug)* instrument, device
Gerät *nt* **zur Signaleingabe** device for signal input
Geräteanschlussschieber *m* appliance inlet valve
Geräteart *f* machine type
Gerätedruckregler *m* appliance pressure governor
Geräteeinstellung *f* instrument adjustment
Geräteglas *nt* laboratory glass
Gerätekategorie *f* conformity category
Gerätekonfiguration *f* hardware configuration
Gerätekonstante *f* instrument constant
Gerätekontrolle *f* apparatus check
Gerätemesslänge *f* extensometer gauge length
Gerätschaften *fpl* implements, utensils
Geräteschalter *m* equipment switch, plug switch
Geräteschild *nt* appliance rating plate
Geräte-Sicherheitsgesetz *nt* Equipment Safety Law
Gerätestatus *m* device verification
Gerätestecker *m* utensil plug, apparatus plug
Gerätetafel *f* control panel
Gerätetechnik *f* equipment engineering
gerätetechnisch device-related
geräumte Fläche *f* broached surface
Geräusch *nt* noise, sound
geräuscharm quiet, silent
geräuscharmer Lauf *m* silent running
Geräuscharmut *f* low noise level
Geräuschbildung *f* noise formation
Geräuschdämpfung *f* sound absorbing, silencing
Geräuschemission *f* noise emission
Geräuschemissionskenngröße *f* noise emission parameter
Geräuschgeber *m* noise transmitter
Geräuschgrenzwert *m* noise limit
Geräuschlautstärke *f* noise intensity
geräuschlos noiseless
Geräuschmessung *f* noise measurement
Geräuschmessverfahren *nt* noise measurement method
Geräuschpegel *m* noise level
Geräuschverhalten *nt* noise level
geräuschvoll noisy
geregelt controlled, regulated
geregeltes Abkühlen *nt* controlled cooling
gereinigtes Gas *nt* clean gas
gerichtet rectified
gerichteter Temperaturgang *m* directional thermal response
gerichtetes Glied *nt* directional element
gerieft corrugated, serrated
geriffelt serrated
gering slight, low
geringe Neigung *f* slight gradient
geringe Oberflächengüte *f* poor finish
geringe Priorität verleihen relegate to a lesser priority

geringfügig minor
geringst ... minimum
geringste Priorität *f* lowest priority
geringstmöglicher Wert *m* worst possible value
gerolltes Gewinde *nt* rolled thread
geruchlos odourless
geruchloses Schutzgas *nt* odourless shielding gas
Geruchsverschlussrohr *nt* stretch trap pipe
gerundet radiussed
gerundete Schneide *f* rounded cutting edge
gerundetes Trapezgewinde *nt* rounded trapezoidal screw thread
Gerüst *nt* **1.** *(Bau)* scaffold(ing), gantry **2.** *(Gerippe)* framework, skeleton **3.** *(Lager)* bench, horse **4.** *(Rahmen)* framing
gerüstartiges Arbeitspodest *nt* scaffold-like staging
Gerüstsubstanz *f* structural substance
Gerüstteil *nt* upright
gesamt complete, entire, overall, total, whole
Gesamtabmessungen *fpl* overall dimensions
Gesamtabnahme *f* complete acceptance
Gesamtabweichung *f* total variation
Gesamtabweichungsspanne *f* total span of error
Gesamtanlage *f* entire system
Gesamtanschlusswert *m* total connected load
Gesamtantwortzeit *f* **des Systems** total system response time (TRT)
Gesamtarbeitsleistung *f* performance
Gesamtausfall *m* total breakdown
Gesamtausgangsstrom *m* total output current
Gesamtbereich *m* whole interval
Gesamtbetrieb *m* total operation
Gesamtbetriebsfaktor *m* total application factor
Gesamtdurchsatz *m* overall throughput
gesamte Dehnung *f* percentage total elongation
gesamte Systemausgangsübertragungszeit *f* total output system transfer time
gesamte Systemeingangsübertragungszeit *f* total input system transfer time
Gesamteinbrand *m* total penetration
Gesamteinsatzkosten *pl* total cost of ownership
Gesamtempfindlichkeit *f* total sensitivity
gesamter Fräsweg *m* total table travel
Gesamtfehler *m* cumulative (or composite) error
Gesamtfertigungszeit *f* total machining time
Gesamtfläche *f* total area
Gesamtgeschossfläche *f* total floor space
Gesamtgeschossflächenbedarf *m* complete floor area demand
Gesamtgewicht *nt* total mass
Gesamtheit *f* population, totality
Gesamtheizbedarf *m* total heat requirement
Gesamthöhe *f* overall height, total head
Gesamthubhöhe *f* overall lift height
Gesamtimpulszahl *f* total pulse count
Gesamtinvestitionsvolumen *nt* total capital spending
Gesamtkonzeption *f* integrated system
Gesamtkosten *pl* total cost
Gesamtkraft *f* total force
Gesamtlänge *f* overall length
Gesamtlaufzeit *f* total operating time
Gesamtlebensdauer *f* total service life
Gesamtlösung *f* *(e. Konstruktion)* overall design
Gesamtmenge *f* overall volume
Gesamtmittelwert *m* overall mean value
Gesamtmoment *m* total torque
Gesamtmoment *m* **des Werkzeuges** total torque exerted by the tool
Gesamtnennspannungsquerschnitt *m* total cross-sectional area of the cut
Gesamtporosität *f* true porosity
gesamtresultierende Schnittkraft *f* resultant force

Gesamtschätzabweichung *f* total estimation error
Gesamtschneiden *nt* combination blanking and piercing
Gesamtschneidwerkzeug *nt* combination cutter
Gesamtspanungskraft *f* resultant cutting force
Gesamtstauchung *f* total compressive strain
Gesamtstrom *m* total current
Gesamtsystem *nt* overall system
Gesamtteilungsfehler *m* total pitch error
Gesamttoleranz *f* total tolerance
Gesamttoleranzen *fpl* overall tolerance
Gesamtüberdeckung *f* total contact ratio
Gesamtüberdeckungswälzkreisbogen *m* total arc of transmission
Gesamtüberdeckungswinkel *m* total angle of contact, total angle of transmission
Gesamtübersetzung *f* total speed increasing ratio
Gesamturteil *nt* overall assessment
Gesamtverdrehwinkel *m* overall twisting angle
Gesamtvolumenschwindung *f* total shrinkage in volume
Gesamtvorschubweg *m* total length of feed
Gesamtwärmebedarf *m* overall heat requirement
Gesamtwirkung *f* overall effectiveness
Gesamtwirkungsgrad *m* overall efficiency
Gesamtzeichnung *f* general arrangement drawing, general drawing
Gesamtzeit *f* overall time, total time
Gesamtzerspankraft des Werkzeuges total force exerted by the tool
geschaltet switched
geschalteter Reluktanzmotor *m* switched reluctance motor
geschäumte Bereifung *f* foam tyre
geschertes Öl *nt* sheared oil
geschichtet racked, stacked
geschichtete Blattfeder *f* laminated leaf spring
geschichtete Probenahme *f* stratified sampling
geschichtete Stichprobe *f* stratified sample
geschichtetes Gewebekunstleder *nt* laminated leather cloth
geschichtetes System *nt* laminated system
Geschicklichkeit *f* skill
geschirmt shielded
geschliffen ground
geschlossen 1. *(zu)* closed **2.** *(umschlossen)* enclosed, confined
geschlossene Bauweise *f* enclosed structure
geschlossene Fuge *f* continuous joint
geschlossene Heizungsanlage *f* closed-type heating system
geschlossene Kabine *f* enclosed cab, totally enclosed cab
geschlossene Maßkette *f* closed chain dimensioning
geschlossene Poren *fpl (in metallischen Überzügen)* closed (or mask) pores *pl*
geschlossene Räume *mpl* confined spaces
geschlossene Risse *mpl* closed cracks
geschlossene Zelle *f* vented cell
geschlossener Bereich *m* confined space
geschlossener Radkörper *m* complete gear body
Geschlossener Regelkreis *m* closed loop system
geschlossenes Gaspressschweißen *nt* closed square pressure gas welding
Geschlossenstellung *f (e. Armatur)* shut (or closed) position
geschlossenzelliger Schaumstoff *m* closed-cell expanded material
geschmackloses Schutzgas *nt* tasteless shielding gas
geschmeidig ductile
geschmolzen molten
geschnitzelte Pressmasse *f* chopped moulding material
Geschoss *nt* **1.** *(Etage)* storey, floor

2. *(Regal)* tier
Geschossbau *m* storey building
Geschossdecke *f* upper storey floor, ceiling
Geschossebene *f* storey level, floor level
Geschossfläche *f* floor area
Geschossfläche *f:* **nutzbare ~** usable floor area
Geschossflächenzahl *f* floor area factor
Geschosshöhe *f* floor height, storey height
geschruppt rough-machined
geschulterte Rundprobe *f* shouldered round specimen
geschürt ground and slightly roughened
geschüttet bulk
geschütteter Zustand *m* vibrated condition
geschützt protected
geschützte Schleifleitung *f* enclosed conductor system
geschützter Bereich *m* confines
geschwärzt darstellen show in black
geschweißter Bewehrungsstoß *m* welded reinforcement joint
Geschwindigkeit *f* **1.** *(e. Vorschubes)* rate **2.** *(linear Vektorgröße)* velocity **3.** *(skalare Größe)* speed
geschwindigkeitsabhängig speed-dependent
Geschwindigkeitsbegrenzer *m* overspeed governor, speed governor
Geschwindigkeitsbegrenzung *f* speed control, speed limitation
Geschwindigkeitsdruckhöhe *f* velocity head
Geschwindigkeitsfläche *f* velocity area
geschwindigkeitsgeregelt speed-controlled
Geschwindigkeitsgleichung *f* velocity equation
Geschwindigkeitskomponente *f* speed component
Geschwindigkeitskontrolle *f* speed control
Geschwindigkeitskorrektur *f* speed correction

Geschwindigkeitsquotient *m* speed quotient
Geschwindigkeitsreduziersystem *nt* speed reducing system
Geschwindigkeitsreduzierung *f* speed reducing system, speed reduction
Geschwindigkeitsregelung *f* speed operating control
Geschwindigkeitssteuerung *f* speed control
Geschwindigkeitsüberwachung *f* speed monitoring
Geschwindigkeitsvektor *m* velocity vector
Gesenk *nt* cavity block, die
Gesenk- und Formennachformfräser *m* die and mould copy miller
Gesenkarbeit *f* die-work, die-sinking
Gesenkbiegen *nt* die bending
Gesenkbördeln *nt* die flanging
Gesenkdrücken *nt* die squeezing
Gesenkfäser *m* die-sinking cutter, die mill, routing cutter, cherry
Gesenkformen *nt* die forming
Gesenkformen *nt* **mit ganz umschlossenem Werkstück** closed-die forming
Gesenkformen *nt* **mit teilwesiem Werkstück** die forming with partly enclosed work
Gesenkfräsen *nt* pocketing
Gesenkfräsmaschine *f* die-milling machine, die sinking machine, die-sinker, duplicator
Gesenkherstellung *f* die making
Gesenkherstellung *f* **durch Meisterform** die typing, die broaching
Gesenkpresse *f* die stamping press
Gesenkrichten *nt* die straightening (by press forming without flash)
Gesenkrunden *nt* radial die forming
Gesenkschmiede *f* drop forge, drop forging shop
Gesenkschmieden *nt* die forging, drop forging
Gesenkschmiedeteil *nt* die forging component (or part)
Gesenksicken *nt* die beading
Gesenkstauchen *nt* die upsetting
Gesenkziehen *nt* *(Formstanzen)* die

forming by drawing
Gesetz *nt* act, law
gesichert 1. *(geschützt)* protected **2.** *(befestigt)* secured
Gesichtsfeld *nt* field of sight
gesintertes Wolframkarbid *nt* cemented tungsten carbide
gesondert separated
gespeicherte Information *f* stored data
gesperrt blocked, interlocked
Gespräch *nt* meeting
gespreizter Bereich *m* expanded range
gespulter Schweißdraht *m* reeled filler wire
Gestalt *f* **1.** *(allg.)* shape, contour, structure, form geometry **2.** *(Konstruktion)* design **3.** *(Oberfläche)* surface configuration **4.** *(Profil)* profile
Gestaltabweichung *f* **1.** *(Oberfläche)* irregularity of surface configuration **2.** *(Form)* form deviation
gestalten design, structure, work out, shape
Gestalter *m* designer
Gestaltfestigkeit *f* shape stability
Gestaltsparameter *f* shape parameter
Gestaltung *f* construction, design, geometry
Gestaltungsebene *f* design level
Gestaltungsgrundsatz *m* principle for design
Gestaltungsmerkmal *nt* dsign feature
Gestänge *nt* **1.** *(allg.)* linkage rods *pl*, leverage **2.** *(Bahn)* track, rails and sleepers **3.** *(Maschinen)* gear, rod assembly, linkage of bars
Gestängerohrgewinde *nt* **für Brunnenbau** drill pipe thread for well sinking
Gestängerohrgewinde *nt* **für Tiefbohrtechnik** drill pipe thread for well drilling
Gestängesystem *nt* linkage system
gestanzt pierced
gestattet allowed, permitted
Gestehungskosten *pl* prime cost
gesteigert increasingly
Gestell *nt* **1.** *(allg.)* base, frame, rack, fixed link, horse, stand **2.** *(Maschinen)*

mount **3.** *(Regal)* rack, shelf
gesteuert controlled, regulated
gesteuerte Prozessoptimierung *f* feed-forward process optimization
gestopfter Zustand *m* compact condition
gestört 1. *(beeinträchtigt)* disturbed **2.** *(fehlerhaft)* defective, faulty
gestörte Kontur *f* faulty contour
gestörter Betrieb *m* faulty operation
gestreckte Länge *f* developed line
gestreckte Längen *fpl (von Rohren)* straight lengths
gestreckte Naht *f* elongated weld
gestuft stepped
gestufte Drehzahlen *fpl* variable speeds
gestürztes eiförmiges Rohr *nt* lidded oval pipe
Gesundheitsschädigung *f* damage to health
gesundheitsschädlich injurious to health
geteilt split
geteilte Felge *f* split rim
geteilte Leitspindelmutter *f* split nut, half-nuts
geteilte Radscheibe *f* split wheel centre
geteilter Walzenfräser *m* interlocking plain milling cutter
getränktes Papier *nt* impregnated paper
getrennt isolated, separated
Getriebe *nt* gear (drive or unit), gearbox, mechanism, (gear) transmission
Getriebe *nt* **mit Vorgelege** transmission with back gears
Getriebe *nt:* **stufenlos regelbares ~** infinitely variable speed gear drive
Getriebeabtriebsdrehzahl *f* gear output speed
Getriebebremsmotor *m* mechanism brake motor
Getriebebruch *m* failure of the gear
Getriebegang *m* speed range
Getriebeglied *nt* transmission element, mechanism element
Getriebegröße *f* gear size
Getriebekasten *m* gearbox

Getriebemotor *m* gear motor
getriebenes Rad *nt* driven gear
Getriebepasssystem *nt* system of fits for gear transmissions
Getriebepassung *f* gear fit
Getriebepassungsauswahl *f* gear fit selection
Getriebeplan *m* gearing layout
Getrieberad *nt* gearwheel
Getriebeschaltung *f* gear transmission control
Getriebeschmierung *f* gear lubrication
Getriebestrang *m* transmission path
Getriebestufe *f* stage of the gearing
Getriebetoleranz *f* transmission tolerance
Getriebewelle *f* gear shaft
Getriebezug *m* linkage
Getriebezug *m* **mit Übersetzung ins Langsame** speed reducing gear train
Getriebezug *m* **mit Übersetzung ins Schnelle** speed increasing gear train
Getriebestellung *f* mechanism position
gewährleisten ensure, guarantee, warrant
Gewährleistung *f* warranty
gewalzt rolled, dimpled
Gewebe *nt* tissue, woven material
Gewebe *nt* **mit Lichtpausschicht** *f* cloth with diazo coating
Gewebeband *nt* fabric based tape
Gewebebindung *f* fabric weave
Gewebeeinlage *f* woven fabric inlay
Gewebefaden *m* fabric thread
Gewebefehler *m* fault in the fabric
Gewebefinish *nt* fabric finish
Gewebeschicht *f* fabric layer
Gewehrlaufbohrer *m* rifle drill
Gewindeschneidmaschine *f* screw-threading machine
gewellt corrugated, fluted
gewellte Federscheibe *f* corrugated spring washer
Gewerbeaufsicht *f* labour inspectorate
Gewerbeaufsichtsamt *nt* trade board
Gewerbefläche *f* trade area
Gewerbegebiet *nt* commercial district
Gewerk **nt** knitted fabric, trade
Gewicht *nt* weight
gewichteter Mittelwert *m* weighted average
Gewichtsangabe *f* weight specification, weight detail
Gewichtsanteil *m* proportional by weight
Gewichtsausgleich *m* weight counterbalance, counterweight, equilibration
gewichtsbelastet weight-loaded
Gewichtsbelastung *f* weight loading
Gewichtseinstellung *f* weight adjustment
Gewichtsklassifizierungsmaschine *f* weight classifying machine
Gewichtskonstanz *f* weight constancy
Gewichtskraft *f* weight force
Gewichts-Preisauszeichnungsetikettiermaschine *f* weight price labelling machine
Gewichtsstück *nt* weight
Gewichtsveränderung *f* weight alteration
Gewichtsverteilung *f* weight distribution
Gewichtung *f* weighting
Gewichtungsfaktor *m* weighting factor
Gewinde *nt* **1.** *(allg.)* screw thread, thread **2.** *(eingängiges ~)* single start thread, single thread **3.** *(doppelgängiges ~, zweigängiges ~)* double thread, double-start thread **4.** *(dreigängiges ~)* triple thread **5.** *(viergängiges ~)* quadruple thread **6.** *(mehrgängiges ~)* multiple thread **7.** *(metrisches ~)* metric screw thread **8.** *(mit ~)* threaded **9.** *(ohne ~)* unthreaded
Gewinde *nt* **annähernd bis Kopf** threaded to head
Gewinde *nt* **für allgemeine Anwendung** general purpose screw thread, screw thread for general engineering
Gewinde *nt* **für Blechschrauben** tapping screw thread, self-tapping screw thread
Gewinde *nt* **für elektrische Glühlampenfassungen** thread for electric lamp holders
Gewinde *nt* **für die Erdölindustrie** thread used in the oil (or petroleum) industry

Gewinde *nt* **für Gefrier-Außenrohre** screw thread for external freezing pipes
Gewinde *nt* **für kleine Durchmesser** miniature screw thread
Gewinde *nt* **mit Flankenspiel** screw thread with flank clearance
Gewinde *nt* **mit großem Spiel** thread with large clearance
Gewinde *nt:* **symmetrisch geschnittenes ~** symmetrical thread
Gewinde schneiden thread
Gewinde- und Schneckenschleifmaschine *f* thread and worm grinding machine
Gewindeabmaß *nt* thread deviation
Gewindeachsenlehre *f* screw thread micrometer calliper
Gewindeanfang *m* start of the thread
Gewindeanzahl *f* number of screw threads
Gewindeart *f* thread type
Gewindeauslauf *m* thread run-out
Gewindeausschussgegenlehrdorn *m* "Not Go" mating screw gauge
Gewindeausschusslehrdorn *m* "Not Go" screw plug gauge
Gewindeausschusslehrenkörper *m* "Not Go" screw gauge member (or element)
Gewindeausschusslehrring *m* "Not Go" screw ring gauge
Gewindeauswahl *f* selected site of thread, screw thread selection
Gewindebemaßung *f* thread dimensioning
Gewindebeschädigung *f* thread damage
Gewindebezeichnung *f* screw thread designation
Gewindebohreinheit *f* tapping unit
Gewindebohren *nt* tapping, threading, thread-bore
Gewindebohrer *m* tap
Gewindebohrerhalter *m* tap holder
Gewindebohrmaschine *f* tapping machine, *(UK)* tapping, *(US)* tapper
Gewindebohrmotor *m* tapping motor
Gewindebohrung *f* threaded bore
Gewindebolzen *m* threaded pin, threaded stud

Gewindebuchse *f* closed insert nut
Gewindedarstellung *f* representation of a thread
Gewindedrehen *nt* thread turning, single point thread turning
Gewindedrehmaschine *f* screw-cutting lathe
Gewindedrehmeißel *m* threading tool
Gewindedrücken *nt* thread spinning
Gewindeeinsatz *m* threaded (or thread) insert
Gewindeeinsatz *m* **mit Ringsicherung** thread insert for serrated ring locking
Gewindeeinstechschleifen *nt* plunge-cut thread grinding
Gewindeende *nt* thread end, threaded end, screwed end
Gewindeende *nt* **mit Kegelkuppe** thread end with flat point
Gewindeende *nt* **mit Linsenkuppe** thread end with oval point
Gewindefitting *m* screwed pipe connection
Gewindeflanke *f* side of the thread, thread flank
Gewindeflankenfläche *f* flank face of the thread
Gewindeflansch *m* **mit Ansatz** screwed flange with socket
Gewindeform *f* thread profile
Gewindefräsen *nt* thread milling
Gewindefräser *m* tapping cutter, thread-milling cutter
Gewindefräser *m* **für Außendurchmesser** topping cutter
Gewindefräsmaschine *f* thread miller, thread-milling machine
gewindefreier Teil *m* unthreaded (or non-threaded) portion
Gewindefurchen *nt* thread ridging (or grooving or forming)
Gewindefurchen *nt* **von Innengewinden** international thread grooving
Gewindegang *m* thread
Gewindeganglehre *f* screw-pitch gauge
Gewindegrenzlehre *f* "Go" and "Not Go" screw limit gauge, screw limit gauge

Gewindegrenzlehrendorn *m* "Go" and "Not Go" screw plug gauge, screw limit plug gauge
Gewindegrund *m* root of a thread
Gewindegrundabmaß *nt* fundamental deviation of screw thread
Gewindegrundloch *nt* blind tapped hole
Gewinde-Gutgegenlehrdorn *m* "Go" mating screw thread gauge
Gewinde-Gutlehrdorn *m* "Go" screw thread plug gauge
Gewinde-Gutlehrenkörper *m* "Go" screw gauge member
Gewinde-Gutlehrring *m* "Go" screw ring gauge
Gewinde-Gutrachenlehre *f* "Go" screw calliper gauge
Gewindeherstellung *f* threading
Gewinde-Kenngröße *f* thread characteristics
Gewindekernbolzen *m* tap drilling
Gewindekurzzeichen *nt* thread abbreviation symbol
Gewindelänge *f* thread length
Gewindelängenmaß *nt* length of thread dimension
Gewindelängsschleifen *nt* complete traverse thread grinding
Gewindelehrdorn *m* screw plug gauge
Gewindelehre *f* screw thread gage, screw pitch gauge
Gewindelücke *f* thread groove
Gewindemeißel *m* 1. *(allg.)* threading tool (or bit) 2. *(Strehler)* thread chaser
Gewindemesseinsatz *m* threaded measuring insert
Gewindemessverfahren *nt* screw thread measuring method
Gewindenenndurchmesser *m* nominal thread diameter
Gewindenenngröße *f* nominal thread size
Gewindepassung *f* screw thread fit, thread fit
Gewindeprofil *nt* thread profile
Gewinderäderkasten *m* screw cutting gearbox
Gewinderille *f* thread groove
Gewinderohrverbindung *f* screwed pipe connection
Gewinderollen *nt* flat-die thread rolling
Gewindeschälmaschine *f* thread peeling machine
Gewindeschlagfräsen *nt* *(Wirbeln)* high-speed thread milling (roll)
Gewindeschleifen *nt* thread grinding
Gewindeschleifmaschine *f* thread-grinding machine, thread grinder
Gewindeschleifscheibe *f* thread grinding wheel
Gewindeschleifverfahren *nt* thread grinding method
Gewindeschneidanzeiger *m* screw-cutting indicator
Gewindeschneidautomatik *f* automatic thread cutting device
Gewindeschneideinrichtung *f* thread cutting attachment
Gewindeschneideisen *nt* screw threading die
Gewindeschneiden *nt* screw cutting, thread cutting
Gewindeschneidplatte *f* screw cutting plate
Gewindeschneidschraube *f* **mit Kreuzschlitz** thread cutting screw with recessed head
Gewindeschneidwerkzeug *nt* thread cutting tool
Gewindespindel *f* screw spindle
Gewindespindelkopf *m* spindle with threaded nose
Gewindespindelnase *f* threaded spindle nose
Gewindespitze *f* crest
Gewindesteigung *f* thread lead, lead, pitch
Gewindestichmaß *nt* inside thread micrometer
Gewindestift *m* grub screw
Gewindestift *m* *(als Schaftschraube mit längerem glatten Schaft)* headless screw
Gewindestift *m* **mit Innensechskant** hexagon socket set screw, Allen set screw
Gewindestift *m* **mit Innensechskant und Kegelkuppe** hexagon socket set

screw with flat point
Gewindestift *m* **mit Innensechskant und Ringschneide** hexagon socket set screw with cup point
Gewindestift *m* **mit Innensechskant und Zapfen** hexagon socket set screw with half-dog point
Gewindestift *m* **mit Schlitz** slotted headless screw
Gewindestift *m* **mit Schlitz und Kegelkuppe** slotted set screw with flat point
Gewindestift *m* **mit Schlitz und Ringschneide** slotted set screw with cup point
Gewindestift *m* **mit Schlitz und Zapfen** slotted set screw with half-dog point
Gewindestrehlen *nt* thread chasing, chasing
Gewindestutzen *m* threaded connector end
Gewindetiefe *f* depth of thread
Gewindeverbindung *f* screw point, screw fastening
Gewindewalzen *nt* round-die thread rolling, thread hobbing, thread rolling
Gewindewalzen *nt* **im Durchlaufverfahren** thread rolling by the through-feed method
Gewindewalzen *nt* **im Einstechverfahren** thread rolling by the plunge-cut method
Gewindewälzfräser *m* thread milling hob
Gewindewinkel *m* thread angle
Gewindewirbeln *nt* thread whirling
Gewindezahn *m* thread ridge, thread tooth
Gewindezapfen *m* 1. *(allg.)* threaded pin, threaded portion, thread end 2. *(e. Ballengriffes)* threaded shank
Gewinn *m* profit, prize
Gewinn *m* **abwerfen** make a profit
Gewinnanteil *m* divided
gewinnbringend profitable
Gewinneinbruch *m* collapse in profits
Gewinneinbußen *fpl* reduced income
gewogener Mittelwert *m* weighted average

gewollte Abweichung *f* intended variation
gewünscht desired
gezahnt toothed
gezielte Aufnahme *f* spotfilming
gezielte Probenahme *f* selective sampling
gezogen towed
G-Funktionen *fpl* G-functions
Gieß- und Formverfahren *nt* processes of casting
Gießansatz *m* moulding burr, moulding deposit
Gießbecken *nt* casting basin
Gießeigenschaft *f* casting characteristic
gießen 1. *(allg.)* pour, teem, cast 2. *(formen)* mould
Gießen *nt* casting
Gießen *nt:* **steigendes** ~ rising casting
Gießen *nt:* **fallendes** ~ drop casting
Gießerei *f* foundry
Gießereiform *f* foundry form
Gießereikern *m* foundry core
Gießereimodell *nt* foundry pattern
Gießereiprozess *m* foundry process
Gießereitechnologie *f* foundry technology
Gießereitiegel *m* foundry crucible
Gießform *f* mould
gießgerecht foundry-just
Gießharz *nt* watering resin
Gießharzformstoff *m* casting resin moulded material
Gießharzformstoff *m* **mit plastischem Fließen** casting resin moulded material with plastic flow
Gießharzhersteller *m* manufacturer of casting resin
Gießharzmasse *f* casting resin moulding material
Gießpfanne *f* ladle
Gießschmelzschweißen *nt* fusion welding by thermo-chemical energy
Gießtechnologie *f* foundry technology
Gießtemperatur *f* casting temperature
Gießtiegel *m* crucible
Gießtrichter *m* gate, down-gate, ingate, runner gate, sprue
Gießverfahren *nt* casting process

Gießvorgang *m* casting proceedings
giftig poisonous
Giftwert *m* toxic value
Ging-Meldung *f* went message
Gipfelfrequenz *f* peak frequency
Gips *m* plaster
Gitter *nt* grating, grid, mesh, fence
Gitteraufbau *m* grid constitution
Gitterbox *f* mesh box, skeleton container
Gitterboxpalette *f* mesh box pallet
Gittereinweglichtschranke *f* grid type single-way light barrier
Gitterfehlstelle *f* lattice vacancy defect
Gitterkonstante *f* lattice constant, grating interval
Gitterpalettenelektrode *f* grid-plate electrode
Gitterpunkt *m* grid point
Gitterreflexionslichtschranke *f* grid reflection light barrier
Gitterrost *m* grating, lattice, grid, grille
Gitterschnittprüfung *f* cross-cut test
Glänzen *nt (e. Schleifscheibe)* glazing
glänzend glossy, bright
glanzlos schwarz mat black
Glanzmetallmutter *f* all-metal nut
Glanzminderung *f* reduction of lustre
Glanznickelschicht *f* bright nickel coat
Glanzprüfung *f* gloss test
Glanzvernickelung *f* bright nickel plating
Glas *nt* 1. *(Scheibe)* glass 2. *(Gefäß)* jar
Glaselektrodeneinstabmesszelle *f* glass electrode single-rod measuring cell
Glasfaser *f* fibre glass
glasfasergefüllte Polyesterpressmasse *f* polyester compression moulding material containing glass fibre filler
glasfaserverstärkter Kunststoff *m* glass fibre reinforced plastics
glasfaserverstärkter Reaktionsharzformstoff *m* fibre-reinforced reaction resin moulding material
glasfaserverstärktes Laminat *nt* glass fibre reinforced laminate
Glasfilamentmatte *f* glass filament mat
Glasfiltertiegel *m* glass filter crucible
Glasfritte *f* sintered glass filter
Glasgewebe *nt* fibre glass fabric

Glasgewinde *nt* **für Schutzgläser** screw thread for glass guards
Glasgrieswert *m* glass grit value
glasierte Fliese *f* glazed ceramic tile
glasiger Streifen *m* glassy band
Glaskugel *f* glass bead
Glasmetallbandverschmelzung *f* glass-to-metal belt sealing
Glasmetalllötung *f* glass-metal soldering
Glasscheibe *f* glass pane
Glasseidenroving glass fibre roving
Glasseidenrovingewebe *nt* glass fibre roving fabric
Glasurrisse *mpl* crazing
Glaszustand *m* glassy state
glatt 1. *(gleichmäßig)* even, flat, plain 2. *(poliert)* polished, smooth
Glattdrücken *nt* planishing
Glätte *f* 1. *(Glattheit Strom)* smoothness, smooth 2. *(Straße)* skidding conditions
Glätte *f* **bildend** causing skidding conditions
glatte Oberfläche *f* smooth surface
glätten 1. *(allg.)* smooth, planish, flatten 2. *(e. Oberfläche)* burnish
glättende Räumnadel *f* burnishing broach
glatter Federring *m* plain pattern type spring washer
glatter Flansch *m* slip-on flange
glatter Heizkörper *m* smooth-surfaced radiator
glatter Schweißflansch *m* slip-on welding flange
glatter Spanabfluss *m* unobstructed chip disposal
glatter Teil *m (e. Stiftschraube)* plain portion
glattes Walzfell *nt* smooth surfaced sheet
glattlauffräsen climb-cut
glattlegen lay even
Glattprägen *nt* compression surface finishing
Glattschnittzone *f* plain cutting zone
glattstreichen scrape smooth
Glättung *f* smoothing
Glättung *f:* **exponentielle** ~ exponen-

tial smoothing
Glättungsfaktor *m* smoothing factor
Glättungskondensator *m* smoothing capacitor
Glättungstiefe *f* depth of surface smoothness
Glattwalzen *nt* smooth rolling
Glattwalzen *nt* **im Einstechverfahren** finish rolling by the infeed method
Glattwalzen *nt* **von Rohren im Durchlaufverfahren** reeling of tubes by the through-feed method
Glattwalzen *nt* **von Stäben im Durchlaufverfahren** finish rolling of bar stock by the through-feed method
Glättwirkung *f* polishing effect, burnishing effect
Glättzahn *m* *(Räummaschine)* burnisher
Glechstrom-Nebenschlussmotor *m* d.c. shunt motor
gleich equal (to), identical
gleich weit entfernt equidistant
gleichabständige Linien *fpl* equidistant lines
gleichachsiger Zylinder *m* coaxial cylinder
gleichberechtigt peer
gleichberechtigter Spontanbetrieb *m* asynchronous balanced mode, ABM
Gleichdick spherical triangle
gleichdicker Span *m* cut of equal depth
Gleichdickfehler *m* *(bei Wellen)* sherical triangle error
gleichfördernder Stoff *m* slippery material
gleichförmig uniform
gleichgerichtete Flanken *fpl* parallel flanks
Gleichgewicht *nt* balance
Gleichheit *f* identity, equality
Gleichlauf-Fräseinrichtung *f* anti-backlash device
Gleichlauffräsen *nt* climb cutting, climb-cut milling, cutting down, down-mill cutting
Gleichlauffräsmaschine *f* down-cut milling machine, climb-cut milling machine, down-feed milling machine
Gleichlauf-Fräsmaschine *f* climb-cut milling machine
Gleichlauf-Fräsverfahren *nt* climb-feed method
Gleichlaufschleifen *nt* down-grinding, down-cut grinding
Gleichlicht *nt* constant light
Gleichlichtbetrieb *m* constant light operation
Gleichmaßdehnung *f* percentage elongation before reduction
gleichmäßig equal, even, regular, uniform, steady, pulsation-free
gleichmäßig verteilt evently distributed
gleichmäßige Flächenkorrosion *f* uniform surface corrosion
gleichmäßiger Abstand *m* equally spaced
gleichnamige Zahnflanken *fpl* equal-handed flanks, corresponding flanks
gleichrichten rectify
Gleichrichter *m* flow straightener, rectifier
Gleichrichterdiode *f* rectifier diode
gleichschenkliges Nahtdreieck *nt* isoscele weld triangle
gleichsetzen equate
Gleichspannung *f* d.c. voltage, direct voltage
Gleichspannungsausgang *m* d.c. output
Gleichspannungsfrequenzmessverstärker *m* frequency amplifier
Gleichspannungsprüfung *f* d.c. test
Gleichspannungsversorgungsanschluss *m* d.c. power port
Gleichstrom *m* direct current
gleichstrombetätigt d.c. operated
Gleichstromgenerator *m* d.c. generator
Gleichstromimpuls *m* d.c. signal
Gleichstrommaschine *f* d.c. generator
Gleichstrommotor *m* d.c. motor
Gleichstromschütz *nt* d.c. contactor, d.c. relay
Gleichtakt *m* common mode
Gleichtakteinkopplung *f* common

mode coupling
Gleichtaktspannung f common-mode voltage, voltage common mode
Gleichung f equation
Gleichverteilung f uniform distribution, equal distribution
Gleichwert m equivalent value
gleichzeitig simultaneous, similar, at the similar time
gleichzeitig beidseitiges Schweißen nt welding on both sides simultaneously
gleichzeitiges Fräsen nt **mit zwei Fräsköpfen** l duplex milling
gleichzeitiges Fräsen nt **mit zwei Spindeln** simultaneous twin spindle milling
gleichzeitiges Räumen nt **paralleler, gegenüberliegender Flächen** straddle broaching
Gleichzeitigkeitsfaktor m diversity factor
Gleis nt track
Gleis- und fahrerloses Flurförderfahrzeug nt automatic guided vehicle (AGV)
Gleitauflage f sliding lane, sliding layer
Gleitbacke f sliding jaw
Gleitbahn f slideway
Gleitbahnöl nt slideway oil
gleiten glide, slip, slide, chute
gleitend sliding
Gleitfangvorrichtung f cushion catching device
gleitfeste Schraubenverbindung f slide-resisting screwed (or bolted) joint (or fastening)
Gleitfläche f sliding surface, slideway
Gleithemmung f prevention of slipping
Gleitindikator m sliding indicator
Gleitkomponente f sliding component
Gleitkufe f skid
Gleitlager nt plain bearing, sliding bearing, friction bearing
Gleitregal nt mobile storage system, mobile rack system
Gleitreibung f sliding friction
Gleitrichtung f sliding direction
Gleitrolle f castor
Gleitschelle f sliding bracket
Gleitschieber m adjustable block
Gleitschiene f slide, sliding rail, slide bar
Gleitschleifen nt slip grinding
Gleitschuh m skid, sliding block
Gleitschutzblech nt anti-slip plate
gleitsicher anti-slip, skid-proof
Gleitsitz m sliding fit
Gleitstielbüschelentladung f propagating brush discharge
Gleitverschleiß m wear due to sliding action
Gleitvorgang m sliding process
Gleitwerkstoff m antifriction material
Gleitziehbiegen nt form bending by a sliding-action draw
Gleitziehen nt drawing (by a sliding action)
Gleitziehen nt **über festen Stopfen (Dorn)** drawing over fixed mandrel by a sliding-action draw
Gleitziehen nt **über losen Stopfen (Dorn)** drawing over floating mandrel by a sliding-action draw
Gleitziehen nt **über mitlaufende Stange** drawing over travelling mandrel
Gleitziehen nt **von Hohlkörpern** sinking of tubular products
Gleitziehen nt **von Rohren** *(Rohrziehen)* tube drawing
Glied nt 1. *(allg.)* link, member, element, circuit 2. *(Heizkörper)* section
Glied nt **mit Zeitrasterung** element with equal interval timing
Glied nt **mit Zweipunktverhalten** element with two-level action
Gliederbauart f sectional type
Gliederheizkörper m sectional radiator
Gliedermaßstab m folding rule
gliedern divide, classify, break down
Gliederung f 1. *(allg.)* division, classification 2. *(Texte)* breakdown
Gliederverstellung f repositioning of elements (or members)
Gliedleistung f heat emission per section, output per section
Glimmerpulver nt mica powder
Glimmzeit f glow time
Globaldaten pl global data

Globoid *m* globoid
globoidisches Schneckenrad *nt* double enveloping wormwheel
Globoidschneckenrad *nt* enveloping wormwheel
Globoidschneckenradsatz *m* double enveloping worm gear set
Glockenmanometer *nt* bell type pressure gauge
Glockenschneidrad *nt* extended boss-type cutter
gelötete Liniennaht *f* brazed or soldered seam weld
glühen anneal, glow
Glühen *nt* **auf kugelige Karbide** annealing for spherical carbides
Glühen *nt* **aus der Warmformhitze** annealing from hot working heat
Glühfarben *fpl* annealing heat colours
Glühhaut *f* annealing skin
Glühkathode *f* annealing cathode
Goldfärbung *f* gold colouration
Gondel *f* gondola
Graben mit geböschten Wänden trench with sloping walls
Grabenaushub *m* excavation of trench
grabenlose Rohrdränung *f* pipe drainage without trenches
Grad *m* **1.** *(Pegel)* extent, level **2.** *(in Wortverbindung zur Kennzeichung einer Normklasse)* category
Gradeinstellung *f* graduation in degrees
Gradeinteilung *f* graduation
Gradteilung *f* angular spacing
Graduieren *nt* graduating
Grafik *f* graphic
grafisch graphical
grafische Benutzeroberfläche *f* graphical user interface
grafische Sprache *f* graphical language
Granularität *f* resolution, selectivity
Granulat *nt* granular materials, granules
granulieren granulate, shot, grain, pelletize
Granulierung *f* granulating, shotting, graining, pelletizing
graphische Darstellung *f* graphical representation, graph
Graphitierung *f* *(Spongiose)* graphite corrosion
Graphitschmiermittel *nt* graphite lubricant
graphitschwarz graphite black
Graphitskelett *nt* graphite skeleton
Grat *m* burr, flash, fin, ridge
Gratbildung *f* formation of burrs
gratig burred, overfilled
gratlos finless
graublank grey bright
Grauguss *m* cast iron
Graupastenverfahren *nt* grey paste method
gravieren engrave
Gravierfräser *m* engraving cutter
Gravierfräsmaschine *f* engraving miller
Graviermaschine *f* engraving machine
graviertes Lineal *nt* calibrated straight-edge
Graycode *m* gray code
Greifbereich *m* hand grip, hand reach
Greifeinrichtung *f* pick-off attachment, rotating pick-off device, gripping (or grabbing) device, gripping (or grapping) mechanism
greifen 1. *(einrasten)* grab, grip **2.** *(ineinander ~)* engage into, mesh in
Greifer *m* **1.** *(Klaue)* gripper, grip arm, gripping device, grabbing device, grab, tagline **2.** *(Schaufel)* scoop **3.** *(mechanischer ~)* mechanical gripper
Greiferbewegung *f* gripper motion
Greifermasse *f* gripper mass
Greifermittelachse *f* gripper's central axis
Greiferzange *f* gripping pliers, grappler, gripper tongs
Greifgenauigkeit *f* gripping exactness
Greifgeschwindigkeit *f* gripping speed
Greifkopf *m* gripper head
Greifkraft *f* gripping force
Greifkraftsicherung *f* gripping force safety
Greifobjekt *nt* handling object
Greiforgan *nt* gripper, gripping device
Greiforgan *nt* *(Roboter)* end effector
Greifrahmen *m* spreader
Greifraum *m* hand reach
Greiftaster *m* outside calliper

Greiftechnik f 1. *(Methode)* gripping method **2.** *(Vorrichtung)* grabbing device, grabbing mechanism
Greifweg *m* gripper path
Greifzange *f* gripping pliers, grappler, gripper tongs
Greifzug *m (zum Verlegen)* come-along clamp
Grenzabmaß *nt* limiting deviation
Grenzabstand *m* limit distance
Grenzbiegespannung *f* flexural stress at given deflection
Grenzdurchbiegung *f* limiting deflection
Grenzdurchmesser *m* limiting diameter
Grenzdurchsatz *m* maximum throughput
Grenze *f* border, boundary, limit
Grenze *f* **überschritten** limit exceeded
Grenzenergie *f* limiting energy
Grenzfall *m* boundary case
Grenzfläche *f* interface, boundary surface
Grenzflachlehre *f* flat limit plug gauge (or gage)
Grenzgewinderachenlehre *f* limit snap gauge
Grenzimpuls *m* limit pulse
Grenzkegel *m* limit cone
Grenzkegelwinkel *m* limit cone angle
Grenzkugelendmaß *nt* tolerance end measuring rod
Grenzkurve *f* limiting curve
Grenzlast *f* ultimate load
Grenzlastspielzahl *f* limiting number of load cycles
Grenzlehrdorn *m* cylindrical limit plug gauge, limit plug gage
Grenzlehrdorn *m* **mit Kugelbefestigung** limit plug gauge with spherical lock
Grenzlehrdorn *m* **mit Sternnutbefestigung** limit plug gauge with trilock
Grenzlehre *f* limit gauge (or gage), tolerance gauge (or gage)
Grenzlehrensystem *nt* limit (or tolerance) gauge system
Grenzlehrung *f* limit gauging
Grenzmaß *nt* **1.** *(allg. linear)* limiting size, limiting dimension **2.** *(Rundpasssystem)* limiting diameter
Grenzrachenlehre *f* limit snap gauge (or gage)
Grenzrisiko *nt* limit risk
Grenzschalter *m* limit switch
Grenzsignal *nt* limiting signal
Grenzsignalgabe *f* limiting signal transmission
Grenzstückzahl *f* limiting number of pieces
Grenztaster *m* limit switch
Grenztemperatur *f* limit of temperature
Grenzübertemperatur *f* throw-over-limit temperature
Grenzwert *m* limit, limit value, limiting value
Grenzwertgeber *m* limit value transmitter
Grenzwertverletzung *f* limit violation
Grießverfahren *nt* grain method
Griff *m* **1.** *(Bauteil)* handle, grip, handle axis, shank **2.** *(Haltegriff)* hand-hold, handle, grip
griffbereit easy-to-reach
griffig with good grip
Griffnähe *f:* **in ~** within reach
Griffstange *f* bar, handle (bar)
Griffzeit *f* machine-handling time, handling time
grob coarse, rough
grobe Spanabnahme *f* taking rough cuts
grobe Steigung *f* coarse pitch
Grobeinstellung *f* rough adjustment, rough positioning, coarse adjustment
Grobgestalt *f* rough form
Grobgewinde *nt* coarse thread
Grobkornentwickler *m* coarse grade generator
grobkörnig coarse-grained
grobkörniger Schleifkörper *m* abrasive wheel
Groblayout *nt* rough layout
Grobmessen *nt* rough measurement
Grobmessgerät *nt* low precision measuring instrument
Grobpassfehler *m* coarse form error
Grobplanung *f* rough planning

grobporige Schleifscheibe *f* open-structure wheel
grobporiger Schaumstoff *m* coarse cellular foam
Grobpositionierung *f* basic positioning
grobschleifen rough grind, *(US)* snag grind, snag
Grobschleifmaschine *f* rough grinding machine, *(US)* snagging grinder
grobschuppige Nahtoberfläche *f* large-scaled weld surface
Grobstaubfilter *m* coarse dust filter
Grobvorschubreihe *f* coarse-feed series
Grobzerspanung *f* rough machining
groß 1. *(räuml.)* large 2. *(umfangreich)* big 3. *(Werte)* high
Großarmaturen *fpl* large valves
Großdrehbank *f* heavy-duty lathe
Großdrehmaschine *f* large lathe
Größe *f* amount, rate, size, magnitude, quantity
Größe *f* 1. *(Ausmaß)* extent 2. *(Bestimmungsgröße)* element 3. *(Einflussgröße)* quantity 4. *(geom.)* size, dimension, index 5. *(math.)* quantity, factor 6. *(phys.)* magnitude, factor, value, quantity 7. *(Regelungstechnik)* variable 8. *(stat.)* quantitative characteristic 9. *(tol.)* range *(qualitative degree)* 10. *(veränderliche)* variable 11. *(von Spannungen)* magnitude 12. *(z. B. e. Kraft)* physical entity
Größe *f* **des Freiwinkels/Räummaschine** amount of back-off
Größe *f* **des Spanraumes** amount of chip space
Größe *f* **des Spanwinkels** mount of rake
Größe *f* **des Winkels** amount of angularity
Größe *f*: **kinematische** ~ kinematic quantity
große Serie *f* long-run job, long-run repetition work
Größenbezeichnung *f* dimension designation
Größengleichung *f* equation between quantities

größenspezifisch size specific
Größenstufung *f* scaling
Größenwert *m* quantitative value
Größenzusammenhang *m* relationship between variables
größer als greater than
größer gleich greater than or equal to
großer Hub *m* large lift
Großflächenproportionalzählrohr *nt* large-area proportional counter
großflächige Zwangsbenetzung *f* large-area forced wetting
Großformat *nt* large size
großformatig large sized
Großhandel *m* wholesaler(s)
Großkarusselldrehmaschine *f* double-column vertical turning and boring mill
Großladungsträger *m* large load carrier
Großlochbohrung *f* large hole boring
Großmaschinenbau *m* manufacture of heavy-duty machines
Großrad *nt* gear wheel, wheel, gear
Großrechner *m* mainframe computer
Großserienfertigung *f* long-run production, duplicate (or quantity) production, large-patch production
Großstellung *f* high setting
größt ... maximum...
größtes Flankenspiel *nt* maximum backlash
Größtmaß *nt* maximum size (or dimension or limit or value), maximum diameter, higher limit, *(US)* upper limit
Größtübermaß *nt* maximum interference
Größtwertbegrenzer *m* maximum value limiter
Grübchen bilden pit
Grübchen *nt* dimple, pit
Grübchenbildung *f* pitting
Grube *f* pit
Grubenhobelmaschine *f* pit planer, breast planer
Grudeherd *m* brown coal range
Grünanlage *f* green space
Grundabflachung *f* *(e. Gewinde)* basic truncation

Grundabmaß *nt (e. Bohrung)* fundamental deviation, standard allowance
Grundaufbau *m* basic design
Grundausrüstung *f* basic equipment
Grundbacke *f* base jaw
Grundbeschichtung *f* primer
Grund-Bestimmungsgröße *f* basic specification factor
Grundbruch *m* shear failure
Grundbruchgefahr *f* danger of shear failure
Grunddrehzahl *f* basic speed
Grunddreieck *nt* fundamental triangle
Grundeinheit *f* basic unit
Grundfärbung *f* green coloration
Grundfestigkeit *f* basic strength
Grundfläche *f* base surface, base, basis, floor area
Grundflächenbedarf *m:* **erforderlicher** required building space
Grundflächenzahl *f* base surface value
Grundflankenlinie *f* 1. *(allg.)* base tooth trace 2. *(e. Schrägstirnrades)* base helix
Grundform *f* basis shape, basic design
Grundfugenform *f* basic edge shape
Grundfunktion *f* basic function, elementary function
Grundgedanke *m* basic concept
Grundgesamtheit *f* basic population, population
Grundgestaltung *f* basic design
Grundgetriebe *nt* basic gears
Grundglut *f* basic firebed
grundieren ground, prime
grundiert primed
Grundierung *f* priming coat, primer, couch
Grundkennzahl *f* basic characteristic value
Grundklima *nt* basic climate
Grundkreisabweichung *f* base circle variation
Grundkreisbogen *m* base circle arc
Grundkreisdurchmesser *m* base circle diameter, base diameter
Grundkreisfehler *m* base-circle error
Grundkreisstreifen *nt (das Streifen an der nachlaufenden Schneidradflanke)* base circle rubbing

Grundkreisteilung *f* base circle pitch, transverse base pitch
Grundlage *f* basis
Grundleitung *f* buried sewer
Grundloch *nt* blind hole, bottom hole
Grundlochüberhang *m* blind hole extension
Grundlückenweite *f* base space width
Grundmaß *nt* basic size
Grundmetall *nt* parent metal, base metal
Grundmischung *f* basic mixture
Grundnorm *f* fundamental standard
Grundplatte *f* base, baseplate, bottom plate, floor plate, bedplate
Grundposition *f* basic position
Grundprofil *nt* basic profile
Grundprozess *m* basic process
Grundprüfung *f* basic test
Grundreihe *f (bei Toleranzfeldern)* basic range
Grundriss *m* plan view, layout
Grundschaltzeichen *nt* general symbol
Grundschrägungswinkel *m (e. Schrägstirnrades)* base helix angle
Grundschriftfeld *nt* basic title block
Grund-SPS *f* basic PLC, basic PC
Grundstellung *f* 1. *(allg.)* basic position, starting position 2. *(SPS)* home position
Grundstücksbedarf *m* property demand
Grundstücksentwässerungsanlage *f* drainage system for premises
Grundtoleranz *f* basic tolerance
Grundtoleranzreihe *f* fundamental tolerance group
Grundverknüpfung *f* logical connective
Grundwassersohle *f* ground water bed
Grundwasserwechselzone *f* ground water interchange zone
Grundwerkstoff *m* parent material, substrate, base (or basis) material
Grundzahndicke *f* base tooth thickness
Grundzahndicke *f* im **Normalschnitt** normal base thickness
Grundzahndicke *f* im **Stirnschnitt** transverse base thickness

Grundzeit *f* time base, main time
Grundzustand *m* basic status (or condition), initial condition
Grundzyklus *m* basic cycle
Grundzylinderflankenlinie *f* (e. Schrägstirnrades) base helix
Grundzylindermantel *m* base cylinder envelope
Grundzylindermantellinie *f* base cylinder director
Grundzylindernormalteilung *f* base cylinder normal pitch, normal base pitch
Grundzylinderstirnteilung *f* transverse base pitch
Grundzylindertangentialebene *f* plane tangential to the base cylinder
Grundschwingungsmessverfahren *nt* fundamental frequency method
Grundstück *nt* property
Gruppe *f* 1. *(allg.)* group, grouping 2. *(Bauteile)* assembly
Gruppenantrieb *m* group drive
Gruppeneinteilung *f* **einer Gesamtheit** population classified into groups
Gruppenfertigung *f* group production
Gruppensicherung *f* group fusing
Gruppentechnologie *f* group technology
Gruppenteilzeichnung *f* group part drawing
Gruppenzeichnung *f* group drawing
gruppieren configure, group, group together
Gruppierung *f* grouping
gültig valid
Gültigkeit *f* validity
Gummi *m* rubber
Gummibindung *f* rubber bond
Gummidichtung *f* rubber gasket
gummielastisch rubber-elastic
Gummielastizität *f* rubbery elasticity
gummieren gum
gummierte Textilien *fpl* rubberized (or rubber-coated) textiles
gummiertes Klebeband *nt* adhesive, (pre-)gummed tape
Gummifingerling *m* rubber fingerstall
Gummihärtegrad *m* degree of rubber hardness
Gummiprobe *f* rubber test specimen
gummiverdichtete Verbindung *f* rubber-gasketed joint
günstig favourable
Gurt *m* 1. *(allg.)* belt, belt band 2. *(Sicherheits~)* safety belt
Gurtbandförderer *m* belt conveyor, rubber belt conveyor
Gurtplattenstoß *m* flange plate joint
Gurtsystem *nt* belt system
Guss *m* casting, founding
Gussallgemeintoleranz *f* casting general tolerance
Gussbearbeitung *f* cast iron machining
Gusseisen *nt* cast iron
Gusseisenhalbwarmschweißen *nt* welding of locally preheated piece of cast iron
Gusseisenkaltschweißen *nt* welding of cast iron without preheat
Gusseisenwarmschweißen *nt* welding of a generally preheat piece of cast iron
Gusseisenwerkstoff *m* cast iron material
Gussfehler *m* casting flaw
Gussfreimaßtoleranz free size tolerance for castings
Gussgehäuse *nt* casting case
Gusshaut *f* skin
Gusslegierung *f* casting alloy
Gussputzerei *f* casting cleaning
Gussrohrspitzende *nt* cast iron spigot
Gussschrott *m* *(als Strahlmittel)* cast iron shot
Gussspannung *f* casting stress
Gussstück *nt* casting
Gussteil *nt* casting part, cast member, casting component
Gussteilfehler *m* cast part error
Gussteilgestaltung *f* cast part design
Gussteilmasse *f* casting stuff
Gusstoleranz *f* casting tolerance
Gusstoleranzgruppe *f* casting tolerance group
Gusstoleranzreihe *f* casting tolerance series
Gusswerkstoff *m* casting material

Gut *nt* good
Gutwerkstück *nt* "Go" workpiece
gut zerspanbar free cutting, easy machining
Gutachtenzeichnung *f* appraisal drawing
Gutarbeitslehre *f* "Go" shop gauge
Gutbefund *m* approval
Gutbereich *m* good range
Güte *f* quality
Güteanforderung *f* quality requirement
Gütebeurteilung *f* assessment of efficiency
Gütefunktion *f* power function
Gütegrad *m* quality grade, grade
Gütegradkennzeichen *nt* class identification
Gütekontrolle *f* quality control
Gütenachweis *m* quality verification
Güteprüfung *f* quality testing
Güteschutzgemeinschaft *f* quality control organization
Gütesicherung *f* quality assurance
Güteüberwachung *f* quality control
Gütevorschrift *f* quality specification
Gut-Gewindelehrring *m* "Go" ring screw gauge
Gutgrenzmaß *nt* "Go" limiting size
Gutlehre *f* "Go" gage, "Go" gauge
Gutlehrenkörper *m* "Go" gauge member
Gutmaß *nt* "Go" dimension
Gut-Messscheibe *f* "Go" gauge block
Gutmesszapfen *m* "Go" measuring plug
Gutrachenlehre *f* "Go" calliper gauge
Gut-Schlecht-Sortierung *f* good/bad sorting, good/bad sortation
Gutseite *f* go-side
Gutteil *nt* accepted part (or good)
GV-Null-Verzahnung *f* G type reference centre distance tooth system
G-V-Verzahnung *f* G type reference centre distance tooth system

H h

Haarlineal *nt* bevelled steel straight edge, knife edge, straight edge, toolmaker's knife edge, straightedge
Haarmesskante *f* knife edge
Haarnadelrohr *nt* U-tube
Haarriss *m* hairline crack, micro flaw, fissure, hair crack
Hafenklammer *f* harbour clamp
Haftbeiwert *m* coefficient of holding power
haften *(finanziell)* be liable for
haften (an) cling, stick, adhere
Haftenbleiben *nt* **von Schmutzteilen** lodgement of dirt particles
Haftetikett *nt* adhesive label, pre-glued label (pressure sensitive)
Haftfläche *f* surface for adhesion, bonding surface
Haftfolie *f* adhesive film
Haftgrundmittel *nt* wash primer
Haftklebeband *nt* pressure sensitive adhesive tape
Haftklebebandverschließmaschine *f* pressure sensitive tape sealing machine, tape sealing machine
Haftklebeetikettiermaschine *f* pressure sensitive labelling machine
Haftkraft *f* 1. *(allg.)* adhesive force 2. *(bei Passungen)* holding force
Haftmaß *nt* *(bei Pressverbänden)* effective interference
Haftmittel *nt* 1. *(allg.)* bonding agent 2. *(Kleber)* adhesive agent, sticker
haftmittelhaltige Schicht *f* adhesive retaining layer
haftnasser Boden *m* binding-wet soil
Haftpapier *nt* adhesive paper
Haftreibung *f* static friction, starting friction
Haftrelais *nt* locking relay, retentive-type relay
Haftscherfestigkeit *f* adhesive shear strength
Haftschmiere *f* adhesive grease
Haftung *f* 1. *(techn.)* adherence, adhesion, adhesive force 2. *(finanziell)* liability
Haftverhalten *nt* *(e. Kippgliedes)* memory behaviour
Haftzugfestigkeit *f* adhesive tensile strength
Hahn *m* *(Ventil)* cock
Hahnfett *nt* stopcock grease
Hahnküken *nt* taper plug
Haken *m* bracket, hook
Hakenanlage *f* hook retaining face
Hakenauflage *f* hook suspension face
hakenbefestigt hook-mounted
hakenförmig hook-on type
Hakengreifer *m* parrot beak
Hakenklemme *f* suspension catch (for door hooks)
Hakenmeißel *m* recessing tool, hook tool
Hakenschaft *m* *(e. Lasthakens)* lifting hook shank
Hakenschlüssel *m* **mit Zapfen** pin wrench
Hakenspannung *f* claw clamping
Halbautomat *m* 1. *(allg.)* semi-automatic lathe, semi-automatic machine 2. *(Drehmaschine)* semi-automatic turret lathe
halbautomatisch semi-automatic
halbautomatische Drehmaschine *f* semi-automatic lathe
halbautomatische Revolverdrehmaschine *f* semi-automatic turret lathe
halbautomatische Waagerechtfräsmaschine *f* semi-automatic horizontal milling machine
halbautomatisches Umrissfräsen *nt* semi-automatic contour milling
halbe Körnerspitze *f* semi-pointed centre
halber Flankenwinkel *m* half-angle of thread
Halbfabrikat *nt* semi-finished product
Halbhohlflachrundniet *m* semi-tubular mushroom head rivet
Halbhohlniet *m* semi-tubular rivet
Halbhohlsenkniet *m* semi-tubular

countersunk head rivet
halbieren halve
Halbkreis *m* semicircle
halbkreisförmig semicircular
halbkreisförmiger Kerb *m* semicircular groove
Halbkreisfräser *m* cutter for milling half circles
Halbkugel *f* hemisphere
Halbleiter *m* semiconductor
Halbleiterbauelemente *ntpl* semiconductor components
Halbleiterbaustein *m* semiconductor component
Halbleiterlaser *m* semiconductor laser
Halbmessermaß *nt* radial dimension
Halbmikrobürette *f* semi-micro burette
Halbmikrowaage *f* semimicro balance
Halbrundholzschraube *f* **mit Kreuzschlitz** recessed round head wood screw
Halbrundholzschraube *f* **mit Schlitz** slotted round head wood screw
Halbrundkerbnagel *m* round head grooved pin
Halbrundkopf *m* **mit Ovalansatz** round head with oval neck
Halbrundnagelschraube *f* round head self-piercing screw
Halbrundschneidschraube *f* round head thread cutting screw
Halbschattenbereich *m* penumbra region
Halbschnitt *m* half section
Halbschnittzeichnung *f* half-section drawing
Halbsilobauweise *f* semi-silo construction
halbstabil semi-rigid
Halbsteilflankennaht *f* steep-flanked single-bevel butt joint
Halbtonvorlage *f* half-tone original
Halbwaren *fpl* semi-finished goods, semi-finished products, work in progress (WIP)
Halbwarenbestand *m* Work-in-progress inventory
Halbwarmfließpressen *nt* half-temperature extrusion

Halbwarmschweißen *nt* welding of locally preheated piece
Halbzelle *f* half cell
Halbzeug *nt* pre-product
Halle *f* hall, (storage) building
Hallenbau *m* hall building
Hallendach *nt* roof of the hall
Hallengeometrie *f* hall geometry
Hallengröße *f* size of the hall
Hallenkonstruktion *f* building structure
Hallenlayout *nt* hall layout
Hallfeld *nt* reverberant sound field
Hallfreifeld *nt* free field
Hallraum *m* reverberation room
Hallraum-Verfahren *nt* reverberation room method
Hallsensor *m* Hall-effect sensor
Hallsonde *f* Hall-effect probe
halogenhaltiges Erzeugnis *nt* halogenated product
Halsansatz *m* base of the neck (of a flask)
Halsen *nt* bottling
Halslager *nt* journal bearing
Halsnaht *f* fillet weld
Halsschneidrad *nt* hub-type gear shaper cutter
Halssenker *m* counterbore
Halsstutzen *m* socket connection
Halt *m* 1. *(beenden, stoppen)* Stopp 2. *(Handgriff)* hold, holder 3. *(in einer Bewegung)* dwell 4. *(Unterstützung)* support
haltbar 1. *(Festigkeit)* durable, lasting 2. *(von Lösungen)* stable
haltbar bis best before, sell by and best before
Haltbarkeit *f* 1. *(Festigkeit)* durability 2. *(Lagerfähigkeit)* shelf life, storage stability 3. *(Lebensdauer)* life
Haltebremse *f* locking brake
Haltebremsung *f* braking to stop
Halteeingang *m* holding input
Haltegliedsteuerung *f* holding element control
Haltegriff *m* hand-hold
Haltekette *f* 1. *(allg.)* safety chain, lashings 2. *(für Vorstecker)* pin chain
Halteklemme *f* support clamp

Haltemagnet *m* no-work magnet
Haltemöglichkeit *f* 1. *(allg.)* dwelling place 2. *(Handgriff)* handhold(s)
Haltemoment *m* locking torque
halten 1. *(allg.)* carry, keep, hold, retain 2. *(anhalten)* stop, dwell 3. *(bestehen bleiben)* last 4. *(Kraft)* sustain 5. *(tragen)* support, hold
Halten *nt* **der Position** retention (of position)
Haltepunkt *m* destination, dwelling position
Halterung *f* fixture, socket, support, holder
Haltescheibe *f* holding disc (or wheel)
Halteseil *nt* 1. *(allg.)* back-up line, stay rope, tether 2. *(Greifer)* holding rope
Haltestelle *f* halt, station, stopping place
Haltestift *m* positioning pin
Haltestift *m* **der Teilscheibe** plate locking pin
Haltevorrichtung *f* work holding device
Haltezeit *f* dwell time
Haltung *f* posture
Haltungslänge *f* length of level reach
Hammer *m* hammer
hämmern hammer
Hammerplattieren *nt* hammer cladding
Hammerschneide *f* striking edge
Hammerschraube *f* **mit Nase** T-head bolt with nib
Hammerschraube *f* **mit Vierkant** T-head bolt with square neck
Hammingabstand *m* hamming distance
Hand *f* hand
Handarbeitsplatz *m* manual work station
Handauslösesignal *nt* manually operated releasing signal
Hand-Automatik-Schalter *m* manual/automatic control switch
Handbediengerät *nt* manual controller, manual control device
handbedient hand operated, manually operated
Handbedienung *f* manual control

Handbereich *m* within reach
handbetätigt hand operated, manually operated, hand-actuated, manually actuated
handbetätigte Maschine *f* hand-held machine
Handbetätigung *f* manual operation
Handbetrieb *m* manual operation, manual mode (of operation)
handbetrieben manual, pedestrian propelled
Handbremse *f* hand brake, lever brake, manual brake, parking brake
Handbremslüfteinrichtung *f* manual brake release lever
Handbuch *nt* (instruction) manual, operating manual
Handeingabesteuerung *f* manual data input control
Handeinstellung *f* hand adjustment, hand setting
Handeinstellung *f* hand positioning
Handel *m* commerce, trade, retail trade
handelsgängig commercially available
Handelslager *nt* retailer's stock
Handelsmarke ® *f* trade mark ™
Handelsware *fpl* trade goods
Handentrostung *f* rust removal by hand
Handfahrzeuge *f* hand carriage
Handfertigkeit *f* manual skill dexterity
Handfertigung *f* manual production, manual manufacture
Handformen *nt* manual form, manual shape
Handformerei *f* hand moulding shop
Handfräsmaschine *f* hand lever-operated milling machine
Handfräsvorrichtung *f* hand-operated milling attachment
Handgabelhubwagen *m* hand pallet truck
Handgasspürgerät *nt* portable gas analyzer
handgehalten hand-held
handgehalten tragbar hand-held portable
Handgerät *nt* hand unit
handgeschabt hand scraped
handgesteuert manual, manually con-

trolled
Handgriff *m* **1.** *(allg.)* handle, handhold, tiller **2.** *(e. Werkzeuges)* handle, (hand) grip
Handgussstrahlmittel *nt* chilled cast blasting agent
handhaben handle, manipulate, manage
Handhabung *f* handling, manipulation, management
Handhabungseinrichtung *f* handling device, handling equipment
Handhabungsgegenstand *m* handling object
Handhabungsgerät *nt* handling device, handling unit
Handhabungsmaschine *f* handling machine
Handhebel *m* hand lever
Handhebelbohrmaschine *f* sensitive drill press
Handhebelfräsmaschine *f* hand lever-operated milling machine
Handhebelreitstock *m* **über Zahnstange** rack-operated tailstock for hand lever control
Handheißluftgebläse *nt* hand-held hot air blower
Handhubwagen *m* (hand) pallet truck
Handknautschversuch *m* hand crumping test
Handkraft *f* manually applied force
Handkräfte *fpl* hand power forces
Handkreuz *nt* capstan wheel, star handle
Handkurbel *f* crank, winch, hand crank
Handlager *nt* area for small parts storage, stock kept at the workbench
Handläppen *nt* hand lapping
Handläppwerkzeug *nt* hand lapping tool
Handlauf *m* guard rail, hand rail, top rail
Handlösung *f* hand release
Handlung *f* action
Handlungsanweisung *f* action instruction
Handpumpe *f* hand pump (lever)
Handrad *nt* handwheel

Handrad *nt* **für Feinvorschub** fine feed handwheel
Hand-Regel-Schalter *m* manual/automatic control switch
Handregelung *f* manual control
Handreibahle *f* hand reamer
Handscanner *m* hand scanner
Handschaltung *f* manual control
Handschliff *m* offhand grinding
handschriftlich hand-written
Handschrumpfgerät *nt* shrinking gun
Handschuh *m* glove
Handschuhinnenfläche *f* palm (of gloves)
Handschüttelfrequenz *f* manual shaking rate
Handschutz *m* hand guard
Handschweiß *m* hand perspiration
Handschweißgerät *nt* hand-held welding torch
Handstampfen *nt* handstamp
Handsteuersystem *nt* manual steering system
Handsteuerung *f* manual control, manual operation
Handtuchhaken *m* towel hook
handverfahrbar pedestrian propelled
handverfahrbarer Plattformwagen *m* pedestrian propelled industrial platform truck
Handverteilung *f* hand adjustment, hand positioning
Handvorschub *m* hand feed, hand feed mechanism
Handvorwahl *f* manual preselection
Handwagen *m* hand cart, hand truck
Handwärme *f* warmth of the hand
handwerkliches Können *nt* workmanship
Handwerkzeug *nt* hand tool
Handzug *m* hand-operated mechanism
Hängeanker *m* (für Rohrleitungsaufhängung) hanger strap
Hängeanker *m* **mit Anschweißende** suspension anchor with welded bolt end
Hängedruckknopftafel *f* pendant
Hängeförderer *m* overhead conveyor
Hängekran *m* overhead crane
hängen suspend, be suspended (from)

hängen bleiben seize
hängend suspended
hängende Ausführung *f* suspended type
Hängeschalter *m* pendant
Hängeschalttafel *f* pendant control planer
hantieren handle, manipulate
Hardwareüberwacher *m* hardware monitor
harmonikaähnlicher Schutz *m* bellows type cover
harmonische Gesamtverzerrung *f* total harmonic distortion
HARMST (Hochaspektverhältnis-Mikrosystem- Technologie) *f* high aspect ratio micro system technology (HARMST)
Harnstoffbasis *f* urea resin base
Harnstoffharzleim *m* urea resin glue
Harnstoffmasse *f* aminoplast
hart aufgelötetes Plättchen *nt* brazed-on tip
hart eingelötet sandwich brazed
Hartasbestplatte *f* hard asbestos plate
härtbare Formmasse *f* thermosetting moulding material (or compound)
härtbare Pressmasse *f* thermosetting moulding material (or compound)
härtbares Formaldehydkondensationsprodukt *nt* thermosetting formaldehyde condensation product
härtbares Kunstharz *nt* thermosetting synthetic resin
Härtbarkeitsforderung *f* hardenability requirement
Härtbarkeitsstreuband *nt* hardenability response
Hartdichtungsstoff *m* hard jointing material
Härte *f* 1. *(allg.)* hardness 2. *(e. Schleifscheibe)* grade
Härte- und Festigkeitswerte *mpl* hardness and strength values
Härtebedingung *f* curing condition
Härtegrad *m* grade
härten harden
härten bei der Bearbeitung work-harden
Härteöl *nt* quenching oil

harter Schaumstoff *m* rigid cellular product (or plastics)
Härterei *f* hardening shop
Härteumwertung *f* hardness conversion
Härteverlauf *m* *(über den Querschnitt eines Bauteils)* hardness distribution
Hartgummimischung *f* hard mix from rubber
Hartguss *m* white cast iron
Hartgussstern *m* hard-iron star
Hartgussstück *nt* white-iron casting
Hartlot *nt* brazing alloy, hard solder
hartlöten braze, hard-solder
Hartlöten *nt* **mit Lotformteilen** brazing with preshaped filler
Hartmatte *f* glass-mat-base laminate
Hartmetall *nt* cemented carbide, sintered carbide, carbide metal
Hartmetallaufbohrwerkzeuge *ntpl* cement-carbide boring tool
Hartmetallauflage *f* carbide facing
hartmetallbestückt carbide-tipped
hartmetallbestückter Fräser *m* carbide-tipped cutter, hard metal tipped milling cutter
hartmetallbestückter Schaftfräser *m* **mit spiralförmiger Verzahnung** helical carbide-tipped end mill
hartmetallbestücktes Werkzeug *nt* carbide-tipped tool
Hartmetallbestückung *f* carbide facing, carbide tipping
Hartmetallbohrer *m* carbide drill
Hartmetalldrehwerkzeug *nt* carbide turning tool
Hartmetalleinsatz *m* carbide insert, cement-carbide insert, cemented insert
Hartmetallfräser *m* carbide cutter
Hartmetallmeißel *m* carbide cutting tool
Hartmetallplättchen *nt* carbide tip, cemented-carbide tip
Hartmetallschneide *f* carbide cutting edge, carbide edge, carbide tip
Hartmetallschneidenteil *nt* carbide cutting section
Hartmetallwegwerfmesser *nt* throwaway carbide insert blade
Hartmetallwerkzeug *nt* 1. *(allg.)* car-

bide tool, cemented carbide tool, sintered tool **2.** *(an der Stirn gelötet)* endbrazed carbide tool
Hartnickel *nt* solid nickel
Hartpapierstreifen *m* laminated paper strip
Hartpapiertafel *f* laminated paper panel
Hartstoffe *mpl* hard-aggregates
Hartstoffestrich *m* hard-aggregates floor screeds
Härtung *f* (durch Härten erreichter Zustand erhöhter Härte) hardened state
Härtung *nt* hardening
Härtungsfilter *m* hardening filter
Härtungsgleichwert *m* hardening equivalent value
Harz *m* resin
Harzbasis *f* resin basis (or base)
Harzfirnis *m* resin varnish
Harzlösung *f* resin solution
Harzpulver *nt* resin powder
Harzpulverschicht *f* layer of resin powder
Harzsuspension *f* resin suspension
Haspelspule *f* open-centre reel
Haube *f* hood
Haubengerät *nt* hooded apparatus
Hauen *nt* cutting (file)
häufig frequent
Häufigkeit *f* frequency
Häufigkeitsdichte *f* frequency density
Häufigkeitsdichtefunktion *f* frequency density function
Häufigkeitsstudie *f* frequency study
Häufigkeitssumme *f* cumulative sum, cumulative frequency
Häufigkeitssummenkurve *f* cumulative frequency curve
Häufigkeitssummentreppe *f* step curve of cumulative frequencies
Häufigkeitsverteilung *f* frequency distribution
häufigster Wert *m* mode
Häufung *f* accumulation
Haupt ... main, principal
Hauptabmessung *f* main dimensions, specification
Hauptabschnittfläche *f* shoulder of the cut

Hauptantrieb *m* main drive
Hauptantriebswelle *f* main shaft
Hauptbasis *f* main basis
Hauptbestandteil *m* principal component
Hauptbewegung *f* primary motion
Hauptdurchführungszeit *f* main time of processes
Haupteinschalthebel *m* main engagement lever
Hauptfahrrichtung *f* main direction of travel, priority travel
Hauptflussrichtung *f* main direction of flow
Hauptformrichtung *f* main formation direction
Hauptfrässpindel *f* main cutter spindle
Hauptfreifläche *f* major flank
Hauptgefahrenbereich *m* primary danger zone
Haupthub *m* main host, main lift
Haupthubgeschwindigkeit *f* main lift(ing) speed
Hauptkontakt *m* main contact (point)
Hauptlast *f* main load
Hauptleitung *f* mains
Hauptmaß *nt* main dimension(s)
Hauptmaßstab *m* principal scale
Hauptnutzungszeit *f* main using time
Hauptplatine *f* motherboard
Hauptpol *m* main pole
Hauptpolkern *m* main pole core
Hauptprozess *m* main process
Hauptrahmen *m* main frame structure
Hauptsammler *m* main header
Hauptsatz *m* main sentence
Hauptschalter *m* main isolator, main switch, master switch
Hauptschaltpunkt *m* central switch desk
Hauptschalttafel *f* control board, central control panel
Hauptschlitten *m* main tool slide, endworking tool slide
Hauptschluss *m* series connection
Hauptschlussmotor *m* series (wound) motor
Hauptschneide *f* **1.** *(allg.)* active cutting edge, leading cutting edge, main cutting edge, primary cutting edge, prin-

cipal cutting edge, major cutting edge, working edge 2. *(Spiralbohrer)*
Hauptschneidenwinkel *m* plan approach angle
Hauptschnittdruck *m* main tool thrust
Hauptschnittfläche *f* shoulder of the cut, work surface, primary cut surface
Hauptschnittkraft *f* main cutting force, main cutting pressure
Hauptschütz *m* main relay, main contactor
Hauptspannungsrichtung *f* main stress axis
Hauptspindel *f* 1. *(allg.)* machine spindle 2. *(Drehmaschine)* main (or work or lathe) spindle
Hauptständer *m* (Werkzeugmaschine) main column
Hauptsteuerstand *m* main control station
Hauptsteuerstelle *f* main control position
Hauptstrom *m* main current
Hauptstromleitung *f* main circuit
Hauptteil *nt* principal part
Hauptteilung *f* true scale
Haupttrennfläche *f* main parting line
Hauptverarbeitungseinheit *f* main processing unit (MPU)
Hauptversorgung *f* main supply
Hauptvorschubbewegung *f* principal feed motion
Hauptwerkzeugschlitten *m* main tool slide, end-working tool slide
Hauptzeit *f* machine time
Hauptzeiten *fpl* production time
Hausanlage *f* house installation
Hausdruckregler *m* house pressure governor
Hausflur *m* hallway
Hausgebrauch *m:* **für den** ~ for domestic use
Haushaltsbehälter *m* domestic storage tank
Haushaltsheizöl *nt* domestic heating oil
Haushaltsreinigungsmittel *nt* household cleaning agent (or detergent)
Hausnorm *f* works standard
Haustechnik *f* 1. *(techn.)* building installations 2. *(Organisation)* facility management
Hautbildung *f* skinning
Hautriss *m* skin crack
Hautsubstanz *f* hide substance
Hazen-Farbzahl *f* Hazen colour index
HD-Heißdampf *m* superheated steam
HD-Sattdampf *m* superheated steam
hebbar elevating, liftable
hebbarer Fahrerplatz *m* elevating operator position, elevating driver position
hebbarer Fahrersitz *m* liftable driver's seat
Hebebock *m* lifting jack
Hebeeinrichtung *f* lifting equipment
Hebel *m* handle, dolly, lever
Hebelarm *m* lever arm, moment arm
hebelbetätigt lever-operated
Hebelbetätigung *f* lever manipulation
Hebelfederwaage *f* lever spring balance
hebelgeschaltet lever-controlled
Hebelschaltung *f* lever control
Hebelschere *f* alligator shear, lever shear
Hebelsystem *nt* leverage
Hebelwirkung *f* lever action
Hebemagnet *m* lifting magnet
heben elevate, hoist, jack, raise
Heberleitung *f* siphon line
Heberleitungssystem *nt* siphoning system
Heberwirkung *f* siphon effect
Hebetechnik *f* lift(ing) mechanism, lifting technology
Hebevorgang *m* lifting operation
Hebevorrichtung *f* lift(ing) mechanism
Hebezeug *nt* crane, elevator, hoisting unit, lifting device (or gear or appliance), jack, pry
Heck *nt* rear
Heckantrieb *m* rear drive
Heckscheibe *f* rear window
Heft *nt* handle
heften stitch, staple
Heftklammer *f* staple
Heftklammerverschließmaschine *f* case stapling machine
Heftplan *m* tacking sequence plan
Heftrand *m* (e. Zeichnung) binding

margin
Heftstelle *f* location of tack weld
Heftverbindung *f* non-load-bearing joint
Heft-Verschließmaschine *f* staple closing machine
Heimgeräte *ntpl* domestic equipment
heiß hot
Heißdampfvulkanisierechtheit *f* fastness to vulcanizing in open steam
heißes Wechseln hot wrap
Heißfoliencodierer hot foil coder
Heißkanal-Verteilerplatte *f* hot channel distribution plate
heißlaufen get hot, heat
Heißleimsystem *nt* hot melt
Heißluft *f* hot air
Heißluftvulkanisier-Echtheit *f* fastness to vulcanizing with hot air
Heißprägen *nt* hot coining
heißschmelzen not melt
Heißschmelzklebeetikettiermaschine *f* hot melt glue labelling machine
heißschrumpfen heat shrink
Heißsiegeletikettiermaschine *f* heat seal labelling machine
heißsiegelfähig heat sealable
heißsiegeln heat seal
Heißsiegelverschließmaschine *f* heat sealing machine
Heißstart *m* hot restart
Heißwasser *nt* high temperature water, hot water
heißwasserbeheizt hot water-heated
Heißwasserbereiter *m* thermal storage water heater
Heißwasserechtheit *f* fastness to hot water
Heißwassererzeuger *m* high temperature water heating appliance
heißwasserführende Leitung *f* high temperature water conveying pipe
Heißwasserheizungsanlage *f* high temperature water (central) heating system
Heißwasserleitung *f* high temperature water pipe
Heißwasserrücklaufleitung *f* high temperature water return pipe

Heißwasserspülbad *nt* hot water rinse bath
Heißwasserstrahlen *nt* hot water blasting
Heißwasservorlauftemperatur *f* high temperature water flow temperature
Heiz- und Schneiddüse *f* preheating and cutting nozzle
Heizanlage *f* heating plant
Heizband *nt* strip heater
Heizbandträger *m* strip-heater carrier
Heizdampfventil *nt* heating system steam valve
Heizelementschwenkbiegeschweißen *nt* welding by bending using a heated tool
Heizelementwärmeimpulsschweißen *nt* impulse sealing
Heizelementnutschweißen *nt* heated tool groove welding
Heizelementrollbandschweißen *nt* band weld sealing
Heizelementschweißen *nt* heated tool welding, thermo-compression welding
Heizelementtrennnahtschweißen *nt* heated tool welding with cutting edge
Heizelementwärmekontaktschweißen *nt* heat sealing
heizen heat
Heizflächenbelastung *f* heating surface area loading
Heizgasführung *f* routing of the heating gas
Heizgaskasten *m* heating gas chamber
Heizgasweg *m* path of the heating gas
Heizgaswiderstand *m* heating gas resistance
Heizgaszufuhr *f* hot gas inlet
Heizgaszüge *mpl* heating gas flues *pl*
Heizgegendruckturbosatz *m* heating back pressure turbo-generating set
Heizgerät *nt* heater
Heizglied *nt* heating element
Heizkeil *m* heated wedge-shaped tool
Heizkeilschweißen *nt* heated wedge pressure welding
Heizkessel *m* boiler for central heating, hot water boiler, heating boiler

Heizkörper *m:* **1.** *(einreihiger ~)* single bank radiator **2.** *(glatter ~)* smooth surfaced radiator **3.** *(zweilagiger ~)* two-level radiator **4.** *(zweireihiger ~)* two-bank radiator
Heizkörperaustritt *m* radiator outlet
Heizkörpereinbau *m* radiator mounting
Heizkörpereintritt *m* radiator inlet
Heizmedium *nt* heating medium
Heizmittel *nt* heating medium
Heizöl *nt* fuel oil
Heizölbehälterrichtlinien *fpl* fuel oil storage tank code
Heizölentnahmeleitung *f* fuel oil extraction line
Heizölfilter *m* fuel oil filter
Heizölleitung *f* fuel oil piping (or line)
Heizölrücklaufleitung *f* fuel oil return line
Heizölschlauch *m* fuel oil hose
Heizölstand *m* fuel oil level
Heizölversorgung *f* fuel oil supply
Heizölvorwärmer *m* fuel oil preheater
Heizölvorwärmung *f* **1.** *(techn.)* fuel oil preheating **2.** *(Anlage)* fuel oil preheating system
Heizperiode *f* heating period
Heizraum *m* **1.** *(e. Kesselanlage)* boiler room **2.** *(e. Zentralheizung)* central heating room
Heizrohrbündel *nt* calorifier tube nest
Heizschiene *f* heated blade
Heizstrahler *m* radiant heater
Heizsystem *nt* heating system
Heiztage *f* heating days
Heiztechnik *f* heating practice (or technology)
heiztechnische Anforderung *f* heat-engineering requirement
heiztechnische Anlage *f* heating system
Heizung *f* heater, heating
Heizungsanlage *f* (central) heating system
Heizungsanlage *f* **mit periodischem Betrieb** heating plant for intermittent operation
Heizungsbedarf *m* heating demand
Heizungsherd *m* heating stove
Heizungsnetz *nt* heat distribution system
Heizungsrohr *nt* heating pipe
Heizungswasser *nt* heating circuit water
Heizwendel *nt* helical heating element, heating coil (or spiral)
Heizwendelschweißen *nt* sleeve welding with incorporated electric heating element
Heizwert *m* (net) calorific value
Helfer *m* assistant
hell bright, light
Helligkeit *f* brightness, luminosity
Helligkeitsverteilung *f* luminous distribution
Hellschaltung *f* bright switching
Helm *m* hard hat, helmet
Helmdisplay *nt* head-mounted display
hemmen arrest, block, stop, stem, impede
herab down, downwards
herabdrücken force down, press down
herabfallen drop, fall
herabfallend falling
herabgleiten skid down, disengage
herabhängend pendant
herablassen lower
herabsetzen decrease, lower, reduce, attenuate
herabsetzen auf ein Mindestmaß minimize
Herabsetzung *f* decrease, reduction, derating
Herabtropfen *nt (von Kondensat)* dripping down
heranfahren approach
heranführen advance, approach
Heranführung *f* approach
herangezogene Maßlinie *f* dimension line drawn towards the object from outside
herauffahren advance (to)
herausschrauben screw out
herausfahren disengage (from), telescope, back out
herausfallen spill out
herausführen lead through
herausheben remove, lift out
herauslösen dissolve

Herausnehmen *nt* removal
herausragen project (from), protrude (from), extend
herausragend extending, protruding, outstanding
herausreißen break out, tear out
herausrollen roll out
Herausrutschen *nt* slipping out
heraussaugen suck up
herausschieben push out
Herausschlagen *nt* spurting out, striking out
herausschleudern eject
herausspringen trip, be displaced
herausspritzen eject, spurt
herausstehen protrude
herausstehend exposed, protruding
herauszeichnen *(Einzelheiten)* draw separately (of details)
herausziehen 1. *(allg.)* back out, extract, withdraw 2. *(Linien)* draw out
Herdformen *nt* oven furnace shapes
Herdformverfahren *nt* oven furnace shape process
Herdofen *m* oven furnace
hereinziehen draw in
hergestellt made, manufactured, produced
herkömmlich conventional
Herkunft *f* origin
herleiten deduce, derive
herrichten prepare
herstellen 1. *(allg.)* fabricate, make, manufacture, produce 2. *(erstellen)* form
Hersteller *m* maker, manufacturer, producer
Herstellerangaben *fpl* manufacturer's information (or instructions)
Herstelleroriginalverpackung *f* manufacturer's original packaging
herstellerspezifisch specific to the manufacturer
Herstellgenauigkeit *f* manufacturing accuracy
Herstellkosten *f* manufacturing costs, production costs
Herstellprozess *m* production process
Herstellrisiko *nt* producer's risk
Herstelltoleranz *f* manufacturing tolerance
Herstellung *f* fabrication, manufacture, production
Herstellung *f* **von Gesenken** die making
herstellungsbedingt conditioned by the manufacturing process
Herstellungskosten *pl* manufacturing costs, production costs
Herstellungsqualität *f* manufacturing quality
Herstellungszeichnung *f* manufacturing drawing
herumfahren travel around
herumlegen wrap around
herumschalten index around
herunterfahren lower, move down
herunterfallen (auf) fall (towards)
hervorrufen cause, generate, produce
hervorstehen project (from), protrude (from)
hervorstehendes Stück *nt* boss
Herzklaue *f* plain clamp-type tool post
heterogene Mischelektrode *f* *(electr. chem.)* heterogeneous mixed electrode
heuristisch heuristic
hexadezimal hexadecimal
Hexadezimalcode *m* hexadecimal code
hexagonal hexagonal
Hexapode hexapod
HF-Generator *m* radio frequency (or r.f.) generator
H-förmig H-shaped
HF-Schweißgerät *nt* radio frequency (or r.f.) welder
Hierarchie *f* hierarchy
hierarchisches Prozessrechensystem *nt* hierarchical process computing system
Hilfs ... auxiliary
Hilfsantrieb *m* accessory drive, auxiliary drive (or actuation)
Hilfsbetriebsschalter *m* auxiliary operating switch, auxiliary duty switch
Hilfsbett *nt* **mit gehärteten Führungen** supplementary bed with hardened runways
Hilfsebene *f* auxiliary level, auxiliary plane

Hilfsebenenabstand *m* auxiliary plane distance
Hilfseinrichtung *f* auxiliary equipment
Hilfsfläche *f* auxiliary area
Hilfsfunktionen *fpl* auxiliary functions, miscellaneous functions
Hilfsgerät *nt* auxiliary device
Hilfsgröße *f* auxiliary quantity
Hilfshubeinrichtung *f* auxiliary hoist unit
Hilfshubventil *nt* auxiliary hoist valve
Hilfskontakt *m* auxiliary contact (point)
Hilfskörper *m* auxiliary body
Hilfskraftlenkung *f* power assisted steering
Hilfskreisbogen *m* auxiliary arc
Hilfslaufbahn *f* auxiliary rolling table
Hilfsmaß *nt* auxiliary dimension
Hilfsmittel *nt* auxiliary measuring device, auxiliary means, aids, technical aids
Hilfspumpe *f* booster pump
Hilfsrad *nt* auxiliary wheel
Hilfsschweißung *f* temporary weld
Hilfssitz *m* auxiliary seat
Hilfsständer *m* auxiliary upright (or column or standard)
Hilfssteuerelement *nt* servo-mechanism
Hilfssteuerwelle *f* attachment camshaft
Hilfsstoff *m* auxiliary material
Hilfsstrang *m* auxiliary winding, split phase
Hilfsstrom *m* auxiliary power
Hilfsstromschalter *m* auxiliary power switch
Hilfsstromversorgung *f* auxiliary power supply
Hilfsteilung *f* auxiliary division
Hilfsversorgungsanschluss *m* auxiliary power port
Hilfsvorrichtung *f* fit-up fixture
hin towards
hin und her to and fro
hin- und herbewegen reciprocate, shuttle (back and forth), move to and fro
Hin- und Herbewegung *f* reciprocation, reciprocating movement, to-and-fro movement
Hin- und Herbiegezahl *f* reverse bend number
hin- und herfahren move back and forth, shuttle
Hin- und Hergang *m* reciprocation
hin- und hergehen reciprocate
hin- und hergehende Bewegung *f* reciprocating motion
hin- und hergehender Hobelmeißel *m* reciprocating planing tool
hin- und hergehender Hub *m* reciprocating stroke
Hin- und Rückfahrt *f* return trip
Hin- und Rückverwindeversuch *m* reverse torsion test
hin zu towards
hinauf up, upwards
hinaus 1. *(räumlich)* out 2. *(über)* beyond
hinausfahren 1. *(allg.)* leave 2. *(über Grenzen)* overtravel
hinausgehen über overshoot
hinausgeraten über overshoot
hinausragen über extend over, overhang
hinausstehen (über) project (outside)
hindern hinder, impede, obstruct
hindern an prevent from
Hindernis *nt* impediment, obstacle, obstruction
Hinderniserkennung *f* obstacle detection
Hinderniserkennungssystem *nt* obstacle detection means
Hinderung *f* obstruction
hindurchfahren traverse
hindurchfahrend traversing
hindurchfallen pass
hindurchgehen penetrate
hindurchperlen bubble through
hinein in, inside, into
hineinfahren drive in
hineinragen project into
Hineinragen *nt* projection
hineinreichen extend into
hineinziehen draw home
Hinfahrt *f* 1. *(allg.)* journey there 2. *(Schienen)* outward journey
hinhalten hold on
hinreichender Schutz *m* proper (or ad-

equate) protection
hinsetzen *nt* set down, seat, sit down
hinten rear
hinter ... rear
Hinterachse *f* rear axle
hinterarbeiten relieve, back off
Hinterblende *f* secondary diaphragm
Hinterdreharbeit *f* relieving work
Hinterdreheinrichtung *f* relieving attachment, backing-off attachment
hinterdrehen relief-turn, relieve by turning
Hinterdrehmaschine *f* relieving lathe
hinterdreht machine relieved, relieved
hinterdrehter Formfräser *m* form-relieved cutter
hinterdrehter Fräser *m* form-relieved cutter
Hinterdrehung *f* relief, clearance
Hinterdrehvorrichtung *f* relieving attachment
Hinterdruck *m* outlet pressure, secondary pressure
Hinterdruckmanometer *nt* pressure gauge for the outlet pressure
hinterer rear
Hinterfolie *f* rear intensifying screen
hinterfräsen relief-mill
Hintergrund *m* background
Hintergrunddaten *pl* background data
Hinterkante *f* rear edge
hinterlegen 1. *(deponieren)* deposit (with) **2.** *(stützen)* back
Hinterrad *nt* rear wheel
Hinterradantrieb *m* rear drive unit
hinterschleifen relief-grind, back-off
Hinterschleifwinkel *m* rake angle, rake
Hinterschliff *m* **1.** *(allg.)* relief grinding, back-off clearance, relieving by grinding, relieving, backing off **2.** *(Spiralbohrer)* lip clearance
Hinterschliff *m* **der Fase** primary clearance, main clearance, land relief, relief
hinterschliffen relieved, relief-ground, backed off, ground to give clearance
Hinterschliffwinkel *m* relief angle, back-off angle, clearance angle
hinterstechen undercut
hinunter down, downwards
Hinweis *m* note, information

Hinweisbox *f* note box
Hinweislinie *f* reference line
Hinweisschild *nt* information plate
Hinweisüberschrift *f* *(auf Zeichnungen)* explanatory caption
hinzufügen add
Hirnholzschnittfläche *f* end grain area
Histogramm *nt* histogram
Hitze *f* heat
hitzebeständig heat-resistant, heat-resisting
Hitzeeinwirkung *f* application of heat, applying heat
Hitzestrahlung *f* radiated heat
HM-bestückt carbide-tipped
Hobel- und Fräsmaschine *f* combined planing and milling machine, planer-miller, plano-miller
Hobelantrieb *m* planer drive, shaper drive
Hobelarbeit *f* **1.** *(allg.)* planer work **2.** *(Langhobelmaschine)* planing operation **3.** *(Stößelhobelmaschine)* shaping operation
Hobelbett *nt* planer bed
Hobelbild *nt* planed surface pattern
Hobelbreite *f* planing width, shaping width
Hobeleinrichtung *f* planing attachment
Hobelgang *m* cutting stroke
Hobelkamm *m* rack-type cutter
Hobelkopfschlitten *m* tool (or arm) head slide
Hobellänge *f* planing length
Hobelmaschine *f* **1.** *(Langhobelmaschine)* planing machine, planer **2.** *(Waagerechthobler)* shaping machine, shaper **3.** *(Waagerechtstoßmaschine)* shaper
Hobelmaschine *f* **mit beweglichem Werkzeug** travelling head planer
Hobelmaschine *f* **mit Kurbelantrieb** crank planer
Hobelmaschine *f* **mit Tischantrieb** spiral drive planer
Hobelmaschine *f* **mit Tischantrieb über Stirnzahnräder** spur gear drive planer
Hobelmaschine *f* **mit Viel-**

schnittgeschwindigkeit multi-speed planer
Hobelmaschine f **mit vier Supporten** four-head planer
Hobelmaschine f **mit zwei Arbeitstischen für kontinuierliches Arbeiten** divided-table planer
Hobelmaschine f **nach dem Schablonenverfahren** form-copying planer
Hobelmaschinen fpl planing machines pl
Hobelmaschinenschraubstock m planer vice, planer vise
Hobelmaschinensupport m planer toolhead, planer head
Hobelmaschinentisch m planer platen, planer table
Hobelmeißel m **1.** (allg.) planer tool, planing tool, shaper tool **2.** (Keilnutenstoßen) key-seating tool **3.** (Stoßmeißel) slotting tool **4.** (Waagerechthobeln) shaping tool
Hobelmeißelhalter m planer toolholder, shaper toolholder
Hobelmesser nt planer tool, planing tool, shaper tool
hobeln 1. (Langhobelmaschine) plane **2.** (Waagerechtstoßmaschine) shape **3.** (Senkrechtstoßmaschine) slot **4.** (nach Wälzverfahren) generate
Hobeln nt **mit Hartmetallmeißel** carbide planing
Hobeln nt **mit mehreren Meißeln gleichzeitig** gang planing
Hobeln nt **mit Spanabnahme in beiden Richtungen** double-cut planing
Hobeln nt **nach Schablone** form planing
Hobelschläge mpl plane marks
Hobelschlitten m toolhead slide, railhead slide, cross rail slide, tool carrier slide
Hobelsupport m planing (or planer) head toolhead, rail (or slide) head
Hobeltisch m **1.** (allg.) planer table **2.** (Arbeitstisch) worktable **3.** (Aufspanntisch) platen
Hobelverfahren nt gouging process, planing method

Hobelvorrichtung f planing fixture (or attachment)
Hobler m shaping machine, shaper
hoch high
hoch gelagert at high levels
Hochaspektverhältnis-Mikrosystem-Technologie (HARMST) f high aspect ratio micro system technology (HARMST)
hochbeansprucht highly stressed
Hochdruck m high pressure
Hochdruckdüse f high pressure nozzle
Hochdruckpressen nt high pressure pressing
hochelastischer Stoff m rubber-like material
Hochenergieumformen nt high energy forming
Hochfahren nt acceleration, raising (slide)
hochfest vorgespannte Verbindung f high-strength friction grip fastening
hochfrequent radio frequency
Hochfrequenz f high frequency, radio frequency
Hochfrequenzidentifikationssystem nt radio frequency identification system
Hochfrequenzschweißen nt high-frequency welding
Hochfrequenzstromquelle f high frequency power supply
Hochfrequenztechnik f high frequency technology
Hochfrequenztrockner m dielectric drier
Hochgenauigkeitsmaschine f high-precision machine tool
Hochgeschwindigkeitsbearbeitung f high-speed machining
Hochgeschwindigkeitsschleifen nt high-speed grinding
Hochgeschwindigkeitsschneiden nt high-speed cutting (HSC)
Hochgeschwindigkeitsumformen nt high-speed forming
hochglanzpolieren finish-bright, mirror-finish
hochheben elevate, hoist, lift, raise

Hochhub *m* high lift
Hochhubwagen *m* pallet stacker, platform truck, high-lift platform truck
hochkant liegender Behälter *m* endwise horizontal tank (or container)
hochkant stehender Behälter *m* endwise vertical tank (or container)
Hochkantförderer *m* upright conveyor
hochklappbar folding (up), upward tilting
hochklappen fold up, tilt upwards
Hochlauf *m* acceleration, run-up
hochlaufen accelerate, run up
Hochlaufmoment *m* acceleration torque
hochlegiert high-alloy, high-alloyed
hochlegierter Stahl *m* high-alloy steel
Hochleistungs ~ high-speed ~, heavy-duty ~, high-duty ~
Hochleistungsautomat *m* high-duty automatic
Hochleistungsschleifen *nt* high-performance grinding
Hochleistungsdrehmaschine *f* heavy-duty lathe, high-production lathe
hochleistungsfähige Produktionsdrehmaschine *f* heavy-duty production lathe
Hochleistungsfräser *m* heavy duty milling cutter
Hochleistungsfräsmaschine *f* high-duty (or high-production) milling machine, heavy-duty miller
Hochleistungsproduktionsmaschine *f* high-duty production machine
Hochleistungsschaltanlagen *fpl* high power switchgear
Hochleistungsschneiden *nt* high-performance cutting (HPC)
Hochleistungsschnelldrehbank *f* high-speed heavy-duty lathe
Hochleistungsstarrfräsmaschine *f* high-production rigid gear hobbing machine
Hochleistungsstoßmaschine *f* heavy duty slotting machine
Hochleistungswalzenfräser *m* heavy-duty plain (or cylindrical) milling cutter
Hochleistungswalzenfräser *m* helical plain milling cutter, helical slab mill
Hochleistungswalzenfräser *m* **mit großem Drall** coarse-tooth heavy-duty plain milling cutter
Hochleistungswalzenstirnfräser *m* heavy-duty shell end mill
Hochleistungswälzfräsmaschine *f* high-duty hobber
Hochleistungszerspanung *f* high-duty metal cutting
Hochmodulfasergewebe *nt* high modulus fibre fabric
Hochofen *m* blast furnace
hochpolymerer Kunststoff *m* high-polymer plastics
hochprägen emboss
Hochpräzision *f* high precision
Hochrechnung *f* extrapolation
Hochregal *nt* high bay racking
Hochregalanlage *f* high bay warehouse
Hochregallager *nt* high bay warehouse
Hochregallagerung *f* high bay storage
Hochregalstapler *m* high-lift truck, turret truck
hochschlagzäher Kunststoff *m* high impact strength plastics
hochschleudern throw up
hochsetzen raise
Hochskala *f* vertical edgewise scale
Hochspann-Federring *m* curved spring washer, high compression load spring washer
Hochspannung *f* high voltage
Hochspannungsleitung *f* high-voltage transmisson line
Hochspannungsmotor *m* high-voltage motor
Hochspannungssteckverbindung *f* high voltage cable plug and socket
Hochsprache *f* high-level language
höchst zulässig maximum permissible
höchst zulässige Drehzahl *f* ceiling, maximum permissible speed
höchstbeanspruchte Stelle *f* most severely stressed area
Höchstbeanspruchung *f* maximum load, maximum stress
Höchstbelastung *f* maximum load
Höchstdrehzahl *f* maximum speed,

top speed
höchste Priorität *f* major priority, top priority
höchster und tiefster Punkt *m* peak and trough
Höchstgeschwindigkeit *f* maximum speed
Höchst-Kurzschlussleistung *f* maximum short circuit power
Höchstlast *f* maximum load
höchstmöglicher Wert *m* best possible value
hochstrombelastete Spule *f* coil passing a heavy current
Höchstspannung *f* maximum voltage
Höchstwert *m* maximum value
höchstwertige Binärstelle *f* most significant bit
höchstwertige Stufe *f* (e. Zählers) highest-valued stage
Höchstzugkraft *f* maximum tensile load
höchstzulässiger Zug *m* allowable maximum pull
Hochtechnologie *f* high tech (high technology)
Hochtemperaturlöten *nt* high temperature soldering
Hochtemperaturlötverbindung *f* high temperature brazed joint
hochwärmestabilisierend (bei Kunstoffen für Rohre und Formstücke) stabilized under heat
hochwertig 1. *(Qualität)* high-quality **2.** *(Werkstoffe)* high-grade
Hockdruck *m* high-pressure
Höhe *f* height, lift, level
Höhe *f* **des Profildreiecks** (e. Gewindes) basic height (or depth) of thread
Höhe *f* **über der Sehne** chordal height
Höhe *f:* **lichte** ~ inside height
hohe Form *f* **1.** *(e. Hutmutter)* domed type **2.** *(e. Mutter)* heavy type
Höhenballigkeit *f* depth crowning
Höhenbegrenzung *f* height limitation
Höhendifferenz *f* difference in height
Höheneinstellung *f* vertical adjustment
Höhenfüllmaschine *f* level filling machine

Höhenlage *f* height position, vertical position
Höhenlehre *f* height gauge
Höhenmaß *nt* height dimension
Höhenmaßstab *m* height gauge
Höhenniveau *nt* height level
Höhenpositioniermarke *f* height positioning marker
Höhenpositionierung *f* height positioning, vertical positioning
Höhenpunkt *m* height reference point
Höhenreißer *m* **mit Teilung** height gauge, surface gauge
Höhenschnitt *m* vertical section
Höhensupport *m* cross-rail head
Höhentoleranz *f* height tolerance
Höhenüberwachung *f* height monitoring
höhenverstellbar vertically adjustable
höhenverstellbares Kragarmregal *nt* cantilever racking with removable arms
Höhenverstellung *f* **1.** *(techn.)* height adjustment **2.** *(als Arbeitsvorgang)* vertical adjustment **3.** *(als Vorrichtung)* elevating mechanism
Höhenvorwahl *f* height pre-selection
hoher Vierkantansatz *m* (e. Senkschraube) long square
höhere Priorität verleihen assign a higher priority
hohl concave, female, hollow, tubular
Hohlbohr- und Ausbohrbank *f* trepanning and reboring lathe
Hohlbohrbank *f* trepanning lathe
hohlbohren hollow-bore, hollow-drill, trepan
Hohlbohrer *m* hollow-core drill, trepassing tool
Hohlbohrmaschine *f* trepanning lathe
Hohldornen *nt* hollow-punch piercing
Hohlfräser *m* hollow milling cutter
hohlgeschliffen side-relieved
Hohlgleitziehen *nt* drawing of tubular bodies, sinking
Hohlkegel *m* taper bore
Hohlkegelmeißel *m* filleting tool
Hohlkehle *f* fillet, round corner
Hohlkörper *m* hollow part, tubular part, vessel
Hohlkugel *f* hollow sphere

Hohlmeißel m hollow chisel
Hohlmeißelbohrer m mortising tool
Hohlniet m: **einteiliger ~** one-piece tubular rivet
hohlprägen emboss
Hohlprägen nt **mit Blei/Treibkitt** embossing with lead/moulding cement
Hohlprägen nt **mit Gummikissen** embossing with rubber pad
Hohlquerfließpressen nt transverse tubular impact extrusion
Hohlquerstrangpressen nt transverse tubular extrusion
Hohlrad nt **1.** (allg.) internal gear **2.** (e. Planetengetriebes) ring gear
Hohlraddurchmesser m internal gear diameter
Hohlradfuß m internal gear root
Hohlradfußkreisdurchmesser m internal gear root diameter
Hohlradkopf m internal gear tip
Hohlradkopfeckpunkt m internal gear corner point
Hohlradkopfevolvente f internal gear tip involute
Hohlradkopfhöhe f internal gear addendum
Hohlradkopfkante f internal gear tooth tip
Hohlradkopfkreisdurchmesser m internal gear tip diameter
Hohlradprofilverschiebung f internal gear addendum modification
Hohlradradius m internal gear radius
Hohlradteilungswinkel m internal gear angular pitch
Hohlradverzahnen nt internal gear cutting
Hohlradzähnezahl f number of internal gear teeth pl
Hohlradzahnfuß m internal gear tooth root
Hohlradzahnfußlückenweitengrenze f internal gear root spacewidth limit
Hohlradzahnkopf m internal gear tooth tip
Hohlradzahnkopfhöhe f internal gear addendum
Hohlradzahnprofil nt internal gear tooth profile
Hohlraum m hollow, cavity
Hohlraumgehalt m voids content
Hohlrückwärtsfließpressen nt indirect tubular impact extrusion
Hohlrückwärtsstrangpressen nt indirect tubular rod extrusion
Hohlschleifvorrichtung f concave grinding attachment
Hohlschliff m **1.** (allg.) concave grinding, hollow grinding **2.** (Schlitzsäge) side clearance
Hohlschmieden nt hollow forging
Hohlverschleiß m hollow wear
Hohlvorwärtsfließpressen nt direct tubular impact extrusion
Hohlvorwärtsstrangpressen nt straight tubular rod extrusion
Hohlwalzziehen nt roll-drawing of hollow items without central tool
Hohlwelle f hollow shaft
Hohlwellenausführung f hollow shaft gear
Hohlzahnstangenwälzfräsmaschine f concave rack hobbing machine
Hohlzylinder m hollow cylinder
holen fetch
Holmfräsmaschine f spar miller
Holplatz m fetch point
Holz nt lumber, timber, wood
Holzbearbeitungsmaschine f timber (or wood working) machine
hölzern wooden
Holzfaserplatte f moulded fibre building panel
Holzgreifer m log grapple, logging tongs
Holzkiste f wooden box, wooden case
Holzpalette f wooden pallet
Holzpellets ntpl wooden pellet
Holzplatte f wooden board, wooden plate, wooden slab
Holzschlifffaser f groundwood fibre
Holzschutz m preservation of wood
Holzstaubfeuerung f wood dust firing equipment
Holzwolleschicht f wood wool layer
homogen homogeneous
homogene Mischelektrode f homo-

geneous mixed electrode
homogene Proben *fp* homogeneous samples *pl*
Homogenisator *m* homogenizer
homogenisieren homogenize, make homogeneous
Homogenisierung *f* homogenization
Homogenität *f* homogeneity
Honahle *f* honing tool
Honelemente *npl* honing elements
honen hone
Honmaschine *f* honing machine
Honwerkzeug *nt* honing tool
horizontal horizontal, level
Horizontalausführung *f* horizontal design
Horizontalbeanspruchung *f* horizontal load, horizontal stress
Horizontalbewegung *f* horizontal motion
Horizontale *f* horizontal line, level
Horizontalfräsmaschine *f* horizontal milling machine
Horizontalhobelsupport *m* horizontal railhead
Horizontalkartoniermaschine *f* horizontal end load cartoner
Horizontalkarussell *nt* horizontal carousel
Horizontalpackmaschine *f* horizontal packing machine
Horizontalpalettenumreifungsmaschine *f* horizontal pallet strapping machine
Horizontalpositionierung *f* horizontal positioning
Horizontalsupport *m* crossrail head, railhead, toolhead, cross-slide toolbox, planing head, planer head, slide head, head
Horizontalumlauflager *nt* horizontal dynamic racking
Horizontalumreifung *f* horizontal strapping
Horizontalumschnürung *f* horizontal tying, horizontal hobbing
Horizontalverband *m* horizontal brace
Hörmelder *m* audible signal device
Horn *nt* beak
Hornanschnitt *m* first cut of horn

Horneinlauf *m* horn shrinkage
Hörschädigung *f* hearing loss
Hörtest *m* audio test
Hot-/Cold-Box-Verfahren *nt* hot-/cold-box-process
H-Profil *nt* H-shaped profile
HSC-Maschine *f* (Hochgeschwindigkeitsmaschine) high-speed-cutting-machine
Hub *m* **1.** (techn.) stroke, travel, hoist, lift, lifting **2.** (Strecke) lifting distance, lowering distance, hoist path
Hub- und Neigezylinder *m* lift and tilt cylinder
Hub- und Neigungssystem *nt* lifting and tilting system
Hub- und Senkbewegung *f* lifting and lowering movement, vertical travel
Hub(lade)bühne *f* tail board lift
Hub(werks)trommel *f* hoisting gear drum, lifting gear drum
Hubanzeiger *m* stroke indicator
Hubbauteil *nt* lifting component
Hubbegrenzung *f* hoist path limit, limitation of stroke (or travel)
Hubbeschleunigung *f* hoist acceleration, lift acceleration
Hubbewegung *f* hoisting movement, lifting movement, vertical motion
Hubbühne *f* lifting work platform
Hubeinrichtung *f* lifting accessories, lifting apparatus, lifting assembly, lifting means, lifting mechanism, lifting system, lift unit
Hubeinrichtung *f* **mit Zahnstangen** rack and pinion lifting system
Hubendlage *f* extreme point of stroke
Hubfrequenz *f* stroke frequency
Hubfrequenzbereich *m* stroke frequency range (displ. pump)
Hubgerüst *nt* lift(ing) assembly, mast (structure)
Hubgerüst *nt:* **mit ~** masted
Hubgerüstelement *nt* element of the mast structure
Hubgerüstprofil *nt* mast upright
Hubgerüstrahmen *m* mast upright
Hubgerüstschiene *f* mast upright
Hubgeschwindigkeit *f* hoisting speed, lift(ing) speed, rate of reciprocation mo-

tion
Hubhöhe *f* lift height, height of lift
Hubkette *f* lift(ing) chain
Hubklasse *f* hoisting class, lifting class, lifting category
Hubkolbenmembranverdichter *m* reciprocating diaphragm compressor
Hubkolbenpumpe *f* reciprocating pump
Hubkolbenvakuumpumpe *f* reciprocating vacuum pump
Hubkraft *f* hoisting capacity, hoisting power, lifting power, load lifting force
Hubkreis *m* lift circuit
Hubkurbeltrieb *m* stroke crank drive
Hublagenverstellung *f* adjustment for position of stroke
Hublänge *f* length of stroke
Hublast *f* lifted load, lifting load
Hublastbeiwert *m* lifted load coefficient
Hubleistung *f* hoisting capacity, lifting capacity
Hubmagnet *m* lifting magnet
Hubplattform *f* hoisting platform, lifting platform
Hubrad *nt* stroke gear
Hubsäule *f* elevating pier
Hubseil *nt* lifting cable
Hubspindel *f* jack screw
Hubstation *f* lifting station
Hubsystem *nt* lifting system
Hubtisch *m* lifting platform, lifting table, elevating platform
Hubtraverse *f* jacking beam, lifting beam
Hubverstelleinrichtung *f* stroke position mechanics
Hubvorrichtung *f* lifting device
Hubwagen *m* hand forklift truck, lifting carriage, jack, (low-)lift truck, lifting truck, powered pallet truck
Hubweg *m* lifting path, hoist path
Hubwegbegrenzer *m* hoist path limiter, stroke limitation
Hubwerk *nt* hoist mechanism, hoist unit, hoist drive unit, lifting gear, hoisting gears
Hubwerkbremse *f* hoist and brake unit
Hubzylinder *m* lift(ing) cylinder, lifting jack, lifting ram
Hubzylinderdrehzapfen *m* lift cylinder trunnion
Hüfte *f* hip
Hüfthöhe *f* hip height
Hülle *f* casing
hüllenlegierte Hochleistungselektrode *f* sheath-alloyed high performance electrode
Hüllfläche *f* enveloping surface
Hüllflächenverfahren *nt* enveloping surface method
Hülllinie *f* enveloping line
Hüllprofil *nt* boundary profile
Hüllschnitt *m* enveloping cut, profiling cut
Hülse *f* collar, adapter, quill, sleeve, socket, hull
hülsenlos skillet-free
Hülsenschliff *m* female part of ground joint
HU-Naht *f* single-I butt weld
Hupe *f* horn
Hutmanschette *f* inverted cup seal
Hutmutter *f* domed nut, acorn nut
Hutschraube *f* cap bolt
HV-Stegnaht *f* single bevel groove plus root face
HV-Verbindung *f* high strength friction grip fastening
hybrid hybrid
Hybridstation *f* combined (or balanced) station
Hydraulik *f* hydraulics, hydraulic system
Hydraulikaggregat *nt* power pack, hydraulic power pack
Hydraulikanlage *f* hydraulic system
Hydraulikfluid *m* hydraulic lifting
Hydraulikflüssigkeit *f* hydraulic oil, hydraulic fluid
Hydraulikkolben *m* hydraulic piston
Hydraulikkreis *m* hydraulic circuit
Hydraulikkupplung *f* hydraulic coupling
Hydraulikmotor *m* hydraulic motor
Hydraulikmotor *m* **mit geradliniger Bewegung** hydraulic jack
Hydrauliköl *nt* hydraulic oil
Hydrauliksystem *nt* hydraulic system

hydraulisch hydraulic
hydraulisch betätigt hydraulically operated
hydraulische Anlage *f* hydraulic equipment
hydraulische Ausrüstung *f* hydraulic equipment
hydraulische Dämpfung *f* hydraulic damping
hydraulische Kegelradhobelmaschine *f* hydraulic bevel gear generator
hydraulische Pumpe *f* hydraulic pump
hydraulische Steuermechanik *f* hydraulic control mechanism
hydraulische Steuerzentrale *f* hydraulic control centre
hydraulische Verdrängerpumpe *f* positive displacement hydraulic pump
hydraulischer Kolben *m* hydraulic piston, hydraulic ram
hydraulisches Laufrad *nt* hydraulic impeller
hydrodynamisch hydrodynamic
Hydrostat *nt* humidistat
hydrostatisch hydrostatic
hydrostatisches Hohlvorwärtsfließpressen *nt* hydrostatic direct tubular impact extrusion
hydrostatisches Vollvorwärtsfließpressen *nt* hydrostatic direct impact extrusion of rods
hydrostatisches Vorwärtsfließpressen *nt* hydrostatic direct impact extrusion
hydrostatisches Vorwärtsstrangpressen *nt* hydrostatic direct rod extrusion
hydroxidisch hydroxidic
HY-Naht *f* single-bevel weld with broad root face
HY-Naht *f* **mit Kehlnähten am Schrägstoß** single-bevel butt weld with root face, at inclined T-joint, welded with two fillets
hyperbolisches Kegelrad *nt* hyperboloid bevel gear
hyperbolisches Stirnrad *nt* hyperboloid cylindrical gear
Hyperboloid *m* hyperboloid
hyperboloidische Funktionsfläche *f* hyperboloid functional surface
Hyperboloidradpaar *nt* hyperboloid gear pair
hypergeometrische Verteilung *f* hypergeometric distribution
Hypochloritbleichechtheit *f* fastness to bleaching with hypochloride
Hypoidrad *nt* hypoid gear
Hypoidradpaar *nt* gear pair with non-parallel non-intersecting axes, hypoid gear pair
Hypothese *f* hypothesis
Hypozykloide *mpl* hypocycloid
Hysterese *f* hysteresis
Hystereseschleife *f* hysteresis loop

Ii

I-Beiwert m *(Integrierbeiwert)* integral action factor
ideal perfect
Ideallayout nt ideal layout
Idealplanung f ideal (or perfect) planning
Idealvariante f ideal variant
Ideenphase f idea phase
Identifikation f identification
Identifikationsaufgabe f identification task
Identifikationsnummer f identification number
Identifikationspunkt m identification point
Identifikationssystem nt identification system
identifizierbar possible to identify, liable to identification
identifizieren identify
Identifizierung f identification
Identifizierungsmöglichkeit f possibility to identification
identisch identical
Identität f identity
Identnummer f identification number, identity number
Identträger m identification carrier
ID-System nt identification system
I-Fuge f square butt edge
IGES Initial Graphics Exchange Specification
I-Glied nt *(integrierendes Glied)* integral element
IK-Kippglied nt mit Zweiflankensteuerung bistable element of the master-slave type
im dynamischen Zustand under dynamic conditions
im Eingriff m engaged
im entgegengesetzen Uhrzeigersinn counter-clockwise (ccw)
im Freien outdoor
im Gegenuhrzeigersinn anti-clockwise
im Gleichgewicht halten balance

im Mittel on average
im Quadrat squared
im Takt in step (with)
im Uhrzeigersinn clockwise
im Umriss fräsen contour
im Wechsel in turn
imaginärer Zylinder m imaginary cylinder
Immersionstechnik f immersion practice
impalettieren repalletize
Impedanz f impedance
Impedanzgrenzwert m impedance limit
Implementierung f implementation
implementieren implement
Implosion f implosion
Impuls m momentum, impulse, pulse
Impulsantwort f impulse response
Impulsbremsung f intermitted speed control
Impulsdauer f pulse amplitude
Impulsdiagramm nt pulse diagram
Impulsechogerät nt pulse echo equipment
Impulsechoverfahren nt pulse echo technique
Impulsenergie f pulse energy
Impulsfolge f sequence of pulses
Impulsform f pulse envelope
Impulsformer m pulse shaper, pulse former
Impulsgeber m pulse generator, impulse generator device, pulse generator, digitizer pulse transmitter
Impulsgruppe f pulse group
impulshaltiges Geräusch nt impulsive noise
Impulshaltigkeit f impulsive noise content
Impulslaufzeit f pulse transit time
Impulsleitung f impulse pipe
Impulsmagnetfeld nt pulse magnetic field
Impulsmerker m pulse bit memory
Impulsschalldruckpegel m impulse

sound pressure level
Impulsspitze *f* impulse peak
Impulssteuerung *f* pulse contact control
Impulstastverhältnis *nt* pulse duty factor
Impulsventil *nt* pulse emitting valve
Impulswandlung *f* impulse shaping
Impulswechselspannungsfrequenz *f* impulse a.c. power frequency
Impulszug *m* pulse group, pulse rain, pulse string
in Achsrichtung endwise
in Arbeit work in process (WIP), goods in process
in axialer Richtung schneidend end-cutting
in Berührung kommen make contact (with)
in Betrieb nehmen put into operation, put in to service, start up
in Bewegungsrichtung directional
in der Höhe verschiebbare Gabeln *fpl* fork height adjustable relative to cab
in die Praxis umsetzen realize
in Dreieckschaltung *f* delta-connected
in eine gerade Linie bringen align
in einer Richtung uni-directional
in Einstellung bleiben remain
in entgegengesetzter Richtung in the opposite direction
in Fußbauform foot-mounted
in Gang setzen start, initiate, put into operation
in Größe verschieden graded in size
in kaltem Zustand biegen bend cold
in Längsrichtung lengthwise
in Massen anfertigen mass-duplicate
in Ordung bringen settle
in Portalbauweise portal-type
in Prozent as a percentage
in Querrichtung lateral, transverse
in Räumen indoor
in Reichweite within reach
in Reihe in series
in Reihe schalten connect in series, connect serially
in Richtung towards
in seitlicher Richtung sidewise
in sich geschlossen self-contained
in Stand halten maintain, repair, service
in Stellung bleiben stay put
in Stellung bringen position
in Sternschaltung star-connected, Y-connected
in Streifen schneiden slice
in Waage bringen level
in zwei Richtungen bi-directional
I-Naht *f* **mit beidseitig gewölbten Oberflächen** convex square butt joint
I-Naht *f:* **einseitige ~** square butt weld, welded from one side
inaktiv non-activated, inert
Inaugenscheinnahme *f* visual examination (or inspection)
Inbetriebnahme *f* **1.** *(allg.)* commissioning (acceptance), putting into operation, setting to work, starting up **2.** *(e. Maschine)* commissioning, start-up, putting into operation (or service)
Inbetriebnahmebeschreibung *f* commissioning description, implementation description
Inbetriebnahmephase *f* starting up phase
Inbetriebnahmeprotokoll *nt* commissioning certificate
Inbetriebnahmeprozedur *f* commissioning sequence
Inbetriebsetzen *nt* starting (up)
Index *m* **1.** *(allg.)* subscript, index **2.** *(math.)* subscript **3.** *(Teilscheibe)* index
Indexfehler *m* index error
Indexklinke *f* indexing latch
Indexpaar *nt* subscript pair
Indexraststift *m* indexing latch
Indexstift *m* latch-pin, index(ing) pin
Indexteiltisch *m* indexing table
indirekt bestätigt remote operated
indirekte Kraftmessung *f* indirect force measurement
Indirekte Wegmessung *f* indirect measurement
indizieren index, indicate
Induktion *f* induction
Induktionserwärmung *f* induction heating
Induktionsglüheinrichtung *f* induct-

ance-heated annealing equipment
Induktionshärtemaschine f induction hardening machine
Induktionshärten nt induction hardening
Induktionsmesseinrichtung f flux density measuring equipment
Induktionsmotor m induction motor
Induktionsofen m induction furnace
Induktionsschweißen nt induction welding
Induktionsschweiß-Verschließmaschine f induction sealing machine
Induktionsspannung f induction voltage, induced voltage
Induktionsstrom m induction current, induced current
induktiv inductive
induktiv geführt inductively guided
induktive Schaltfahne f inductive actuating tag, inductive switching flag
induktiver Blindwiderstand m inductive reactance
induktiver Sender m inductive transmitter
induktives Hochfrequenzschweißen nt high-frequency induction welding
induktives Mittelfrequenzschweißen nt medium-frequency induction welding
induktives Widerstandspressschweißen nt induction (resistance) welding, induction pressure welding
Induktivität f inductance
Induktivsystem nt inductive system
Induktivtechnik f inductive technology
Induktor m inductor
Industrieanlage f industrial plant
Industriearmatur f industrial valve
Industrieatmosphäre f industrial atmosphere
Industriebau m industrial building construction
Industriefrequenz f industrial frequency
Industriegebiet nt industrial area
Industrielufteinwirkung f action of industrial atmosphere
Industrienetz nt industrial mains

Industrieroboter m industrial robot
Industrieschlepper m industrial tractor
induzieren induce
ineinander greifen engage, mesh, gear
ineinander passen mate, fit together
ineinander schachteln nest (into each other)
ineinander schiebbar telescopic
ineinander schieben drive together
ineinander stapeln telescopic, stack into each other
ineinander zeichnen draw in the mated condition
inertes Gas nt inert gas
Inertgasschweißung f inert arc welding
Information f information
Informationsablauf m information process
Informationsaufbereitung f data preparation
Informationsaustausch m communication, data exchange, information exchange
Informationsbedarf m information demand
Informationsdichte f information density
Informationsfluss m information flow
Informationsschild nt information plate
Informationsspeicher m information store, data memory
Informationsstelle f information point
Informationstechnik f information processing
informationstechnisches Konzept nt computerization concept
Informationsträger m data carrier
Informationsübernahme f read-in of information
informationsverarbeitendes Gerät nt information processing device
Informationsverarbeitung f data processing, information processing
Informationsverknüpfung f information link
Informationsweg m information path
Infrarot nt infrared (IR), ultrared (UR)

Infrarotbildverarbeitungssystem *nt* infrared image processing (system)
Infrarotdatenübertragung *f* infrared data transfer
Infrarotdetektor *m* infrared detector
infrarotgesteuert infrared controlled
Infrarotkappe *f* infrare hood
Infrarotleser *m* infrared reader
Infrarotlicht *nt* infrared light
Infrarotlicht-LED *f* infrared LED
Infrarotrelais *nt* infrared relay
Infrarotstrahler *m* infrared radiator
Infrarotsuchknopf *m* infrared seeker
Infrarotsystem *nt* infrared system
Infrarotübertragung *f* infrared transfer
Ingangsetzen *nt* starting, initiating
Inhalt *m* content, contents
Inhaltsverzeichnis *nt* list of contents, table of contents
Inhomogenität *f* inhomogeneity
Initialhub *m* initial lift
initialisieren initialize, initiate
Initialisierung *f* initialization
Initialschritt *m* initiating step
Initiator *m* initiator, proximitry switch
Injektor-Kammbrenner *m* injection-mixing chamber burner
Inklusives ODER *nt* inclusive OR, disjunction
Inkrement *nt* increment
inkremental incremental
Inkrementale Wegmessung *f* incremental measuring system
Inkrementalgeber *m* incremental transmitter
Inkrementalgebersystem *nt* incremental transmitter system
inkrementell incremental
innen inside
Innenabmessung *f* internal measurement (or dimension)
Innenanpassung *f* inside diameter matching
Innenarbeit *f* internal work
innenausdrehen bore, turn internally
Innenausdrehmeißel *m* internal cutting tool, inside turning tool, (Bohrmeißel) boring tool
Innenausdrehspan *m* boring chip, drilling chip
Innenausdrehzahn *m* boring bit
Innenborden *nt* **durch Drücken** spinning of inside beads
Innendreharbeit *f* inside diameter turning
Innendrehen *nt* turning inside diameters, turning internal surfaces, boring
Innendrehfutter *nt* boring chuck
Innendrehmeißel *m* boring tool, internal turning tool
Innendrehmeißelhalter *m* boring toolholder
Innendrehvorrichtung *f* **1.** *(allg.)* internal turning attachment **2.** *(Plandrehen)* internal facing attachment
Innendrehwerkzeug *nt* boring tool
Innendruck *m* internal pressure
Innendruck *m* **beim Versagen** internal pressure at failure
innendruckbeanspruchtes Teil *nt* part subjected to internal pressure
Innendruckbeanspruchung *f* internal pressure loading
Innendruckberstversuch *m* internal pressure bursting test
Innendruckrolle *f* internal pressure roll
Innendruckversuch *m* internal pressure test
Innendruckzeitstandversuch *m* internal pressure endurance test
Innendruck-Zeitstandversuch *m* internal pressure creep test
Innendurchmesser *m* inner diameter, internal diameter, inside diameter, minor diameter
Inneneckdrehmeißel *m* internal side cutting tool
Inneneinrichtung *f* interior fittings
Inneneinstechmeißel *m* inside turning tool
Innenfeindrehen *nt* inside finish turning
Innenflächenfräsen *nt* internal milling
Innenfräsapparat *m* internal milling attachment
Innenfräsen *nt* internal milling
Innengewinde *nt* internal thread, female thread, nut thread
Innengewindedrehen *nt* internal

thread turning
Innengewindefräsen *nt* internal thread milling
Innengewindefrässupport *m* internal thread milling unit
Innengewindeschneiden *nt* internal tapping, tapping, internal thread cutting
Innengewindestutzen *m* internal thread connection
Innenhobeln *nt* internal shaping
Innenkegel *m* internal taper, taper hole
Innenkeilkopfschraube *f* spline socket screw, multi-spline screw
Innenkeilnutfräsmaschine *f* internal keyseater
Innenkonturen *f* internal contours
Innenkopiereinrichtung *f* internal copying attachment
Innenlötende *nt* internally soldered end
Innenlunker *m* internal shrinkage
Innenmehrkantstoßeinrichtung *f* internal polygon slotting attachment
Innenmessgerät *nt* internal measuring instrument
Innenmessschraube *f* internal micrometer
Innenmessuhr *f* internal dial gauge
Innenmessung *f* inside measurement
Innennachformeinrichtung *f* internal copying attachment
Innenpassteil *nt* internal fitting member
Innenpinole *f* inner quill
Innenrad *nt* internally toothed gear, internal gear
Innenradfräsen *nt* internal gear milling
Innenradpaar *nt* internal gear pair
Innenraum *m* compartment
Innenräumen *nt* internal broaching
Innenräummaschine *f* internal broaching machine
Innenräumwerkzeug *nt* internal broach
Innenriss *m* internal crack, shatter crack
Innenrundläppen *nt* internal cylindrical lapping, hole-lapping
Innenrundläppmaschine *f* internal cylindrical lapping machine

Innenschleifarbeit *f* internal grinding work
Innenschleifeinrichtung *f* internal grinding attachment
Innenschleifen *nt* internal grinding
Innenschleifmaschine *f* internal grinder
Innenschleifoperation *f* internal grinding operation
Innenschleifverfahren *nt* internal grinding method
Innenschliff *m* internal grinding (or grind)
Innenschruppmeißel *m* internal roughing tool
Innenschutz *m* internal protection
Innenseite *f* inner surface
Innenseite *f* **des Gabelknickes** inside heel
Innenseitenmeißel *m* boring tool for corner work
Innenspannen *nt* inside gripping
Innenspannfutter *nt* internal chuck
Innenspindel *f* secondary spindle
Innenspritzung *f* internal (or interior) spraying
Innenstechdrehmeißel *m* right angle parting-off tool
innenstehender Pfeil *m* inward positioned arrowhead
innenstoßen slot internally
Innentaster *m* inside callipers, internal calliper gauge, inside calliper
Innentemperatur *f* inside temperature
innentragen inner contact
innenverzahnt internally toothed
innenverzahntes Geradstirnrad *nt* internal straight cylindrical gear
innenverzahntes Kegelrad *nt* internally toothed bevel gear
innenverzahntes Rad *nt* internal gear
Innenverzahnung *f* internal toothing
Innenvielzähne *mpl* **für Schrauben** serration for screws *pl*
Innenvielzahnschraube *f* screw with internal serrations
Innenvierkant *m* square hole
Innenwandung *f* inside wall
Innenwiderstand *m* internal resistance
Innenwirbeln *nt* internal thread whirl-

ing
Innenziehschleifen *nt* internal honing
innerbetrieblich in-house
Innere *nt* interior
innere Struktur *f* **eines Öls** *(Zähigkeit)* body of an oil
innerer Bereich *m* interior zone
innerhalb 1. *(räumlich)* inside **2.** *(zeitlich)* within
innerhalb einer Toleranz *f* true within
Insektenbefall *m* insect attack
Inspektion *f* inspection
Inspektionsdauer *f* inspection time
inspizieren inspect
instabil unstable
instabile Zerspanung *f* unstable metal cutting
Instabilität *f* instability
Installateur *m* fitter, plumber
Installation *f* installation
Installationsrohr *nt* tube for plumbing
Installationstechnik *f* plumbing trade
Installationsvorschrift *f* instruction for installation
installieren 1. *(allg.)* install **2.** *(Montage)* mount
Instandhaltbarkeit *f* maintainability
instandhalten maintain (in condition), service
Instandhaltung *f* maintenance, service, servicing, upkeep, repair
Instandhaltungsarbeiten *fpl* maintenance work
Instandhaltungsaufwand *m* maintenance requirements
Instandhaltungskosten *pl* maintenance cost(s)
Instandhaltungslogik *f* maintenance logistics
Instandhaltungspersonal *nt* maintenance personnel, maintenance staff, service personnel
instandsetzen recondition, repair, reservice
Instandsetzung *f* reconditioning, repair, reservicing
Instrument *nt* instrument, implement, device
Integral *nt* integral
Integralglied *nt* integral element

Integrationskonstante *f* integration constant
Integrationsmessung *f* integration measurement
Integrierbeiwert *m* integral action factor
integrieren integrate, embed
integrierendes Glied *nt* integral element
integrierendes Messgerät *nt* integrating measuring instrument
integrierendes Verhalten *nt* integral action
integriert integral, embedded
integrierte Schaltung *f* integrated circuit (IC)
integrierter Schaltkreis *m* integrated circuit (IC)
intelligent smart, intelligent
intelligentes Leistungsmodul *nt* intelligent power module
Intensität *f* intensity
intensitätsausgeglichenes Strahlenfeld *nt* intensity-equalized radiation field
Intensitätsmatrix *f* intensity matrix
Intensitätsschwankung *f* fluctuation in intensity
Intensitätsverteilung *f* intensity distribution, intensity allocation
intensivieren intensify
Intensivschleifen *nt* intensive grinding
interagieren interact (with)
Interaktion *f* interaction, transaction
Interaktionsmöglichkeit *f* possibility of interaction, possibility of transaction
interaktiv interactive
Interferenz *f* interference
Interferenzbild *nt* interference pattern
Interferenzfähigkeit *f* interference ability, interference capability
Interferenzfarben *fpl* interference colours
Interferenzfilter *m* interference filter
Interferenzfleck *m* interference spot
interferenzfrei interference-free
Interferenzgerät *nt* interference apparatus
Interferenzmaxima *ntpl* interference maxima

Interferenzmessverfahren *nt* measuring method by interferometry
Interferenzmethode *f* interference method
Interferenzmuster *nt* interference pattern
Interferenzstreifen *m* interference band, diffraction fringe
Interferometer *nt* interferometer
interlaminare Zugfestigkeit *f* interlaminar tensile strength
interlaminarer Schubbruch *m* interlaminar shear failure
intern internal
Internationales Einheitensystem *nt* international systems of units
interner Fehler *m* internal failure
Interpolation *f* interpolation
interpolieren intercalate, interpolate
Interpretation *f* interpretation
interpretieren interpret
Interpretierer *m* interpreter
Intervall *nt* interval
Intervallbewegungsspülung *f* interval motion douche
Inventar *nt* inventory, stock
Inventur *f* inventory-making
Inventurbericht *m* inventory report
Inventurbestand *m* inventory on-hand quantity, inventory stock
Inventurfunktion *f* inventory function
Inventurmeldung *f* inventory message, inventory report
Inventurverfahren *nt* inventory-making procedure
Inverkehrbringen *nt* putting into service
Inversion *f* inversion
Inverter *m* inverter
invertieren invert
invertiert inverted
Investition *f* investment
Investitionsbudget *nt* investment budget
Investitionskosten *pl* investment costs
Investitionskostenplan *m* investment (cost) plan
Investitionskostenschätzung *f* investment estimate
Investitionsplanung *f* investment planning
Investitionsrechnung *f* investment calculation
Investitionsvolumen *nt* (investment) budget, capital spending, volume of investment
Investitionsvorhaben *pl* investment frame
Ionenaustauschfilter *m* ion exchange filter
Ionenbindung *f* ion bond
Ionenlaser *m* ion laser
ionenleitendes Medium *nt* (el. chem.) ion-conducting medium
Ionenstrahl *m* ion beam
Ionenstrahlbearbeitung *f* ion beam machining
Ionisationsdosimetrie *f* ionisation dosimetry
Ionisationsmanometer *nt* ionizing manometer (pressure gauge)
Ionisieren ionize
ionisierende Strahlungsenergie *f* ionizing radiation energy
ionisiert ionized
ionisierte Strahlung *f* ionized radiation
Ionisierung *f* ionization
IPK (In-Prozess-Kontrolle) IPC (in-process control)
I-Profil *nt* i-shaped profile
I-Punkt *m* i-point
IR-drop resistance polarisation
I-Regeleinrichtung *f* integral action controlling system
Irisation *f* fogging
irregulär irregular
IR-Relais *nt* IR-relay
irreversibel non-reversible
ISO-Befestigungsgewinde *nt* ISO fastening screw thread
ISO-Einheitsbohrungssystem *nt* ISO basic-hole system
ISO-Einheitswellensystem *nt* ISO basic-shaft system
ISO-Kurzzeichen *nt* ISO symbol
Isolation *f* **1.** *(el.)* insulation **2.** *(chem.)* isolation
Isolation *f:* **thermische ~** thermal insulation

Isolationsfehler *m* current leakage
Isolationsfestigkeit *f* dielectric strength
Isolationsklasse *f* class of insulation
Isolationsprüfung *f* dielectric withstand test
Isolationsschaden *m* insulation failure
Isolationsspannung *f* dielectric withstand voltage
Isolationsüberwachung *f* insulation monitoring
Isolationsüberwachungssystem *nt* insulation monitoring device
Isolationswiderstand *m* insulation resistance, insulation strength
Isolator *m* insulator
Isolierband *nt* insulating tape
Isolierbuchse *f* insulating bush
isolieren 1. *(allg.)* insulate, isolate **2.** *(chem.)* isolate **3.** *(el.)* insulate **4.** *(trennen)* isolate
Isolierölprobe *f* insulating oil sample
Isolierplatte *f* insulation plate
Isolierschicht *f* insulation layer
Isolierstoff *m* insulating material
Isolierstoffgruppe *f* material group
Isolierstoffklasse *f* insulation class
Isolierstück *nt* insulating spacer
isoliert Insulated, isolated
Isolierung *f* insulation
Isolierung *f:* **thermische ~** thermal insulation
Isolierungsfehler *m* insulation failure
Isoliervollholz *nt* insulating solid wood
Isolierzange *f* insulating pliers
isometrische Projektion *f* isometric projection
ISO-Rundkerbprobe *f* ISO keyhole notch specimen
ISO-Spitzkerbprobe *f* ISO V-notch specimen
ISO-Toleranz- und Passsystem *nt* ISO system of fits and tolerances
ISO-Toleranzsystem *nt* ISO system of tolerances
Ist *nt* actual
Ist-Abgang *m* actual date of exit, actual output
Istabmaß *nt* actual deviation
Istabweichung *f* actual variation
Istaufnahme *f* assessment of actual inputs/outputs
Istbreitenballigkeit *f* actual crowning
Istbruchkraft *f* actual breaking load
Istdaten (pl) actual data, actual figures
Istdrehstellung *f* actual angular position
Isteingriffswinkel *m* actual pressure angle
Isterzeugende *f* actual generator
Istflankenform *f* actual tooth surface
Istflankenlinie *f* actual tooth trace
Istgröße *f* actual dimension, avtusl size
Istkegelmantellinie *f* actual cone generator
Istkegelquerschnitt *m* actual cone section
Istkegelwert *m* actual cone angle
Istkennlinie *f* actual characteristic
Istlinie *f* actual line
Istmaß *nt* actual dimension (or size)
Istmaßverteilung *f (im Toleranzfeld)* distribution of actual sizes
Istmittenabweichung *f* actual centre variation
Istprofil *nt* actual profile, effective profile
Iststeigungshöhe *f* actual lead
Istverbuchung *f* actual bookkeeping
Istwert *m* actual position, actual value, feedback signal
Istwert *m* actual figure (or value)
Istwertanzeigeskala *f* **eines Thermometers** actual temperature (indicating) scale
Istwerteingangssignal *nt* actual value input signal
Istwertgeber *m* actual value transmitter, analogue position feedback transmitter
Istzahl *f* actual figure
Istzeit *f* actual time
Istzugang *m* actual receipt
Istzustand *m* actual status, current status, as-is state
Iterationsverfahren *nt* iteration process
I-Träger *m* I-beam

J j

Jahresproduktion *f* output per annum
Jakro-Mahlverfahren *nt* Jakro beating method
jenseits beyond
Joch *nt* yoke
jodometrische Methode *f* iodometric method
Jotnaht *f* single-J butt weld
Jumper *m* jumper
justierbar adjustable
justieren 1. *(allgemein)* adjust, set, level 2. *(ausrichten)* align 3. *(e. Lage)* position, locate, level 4. *(einpassen)* fit
Justierfehler *m* maladjustment
Justierkörper *m* calibration block
Justierreflektor *m* calibration reflector
Justierreflektorecho *nt* calibration reflector echo
Justierschraube *f* levelling screw
Justierung *f* adjustment, alignment, fitting, levelling, positioning
Justierzange *f* flat nose pliers

K k

Kabel *nt* cable, wire
Kabel *nt:* **mit ~** cable-connected
Kabel verlegen install cable, lay cable, wire
Kabelanschluss *m* cable connection
Kabeleinführung *f* cable entry
Kabelmantellötung *f* cable sheath soldering
Kabelmuffe *f* sleeve
Kabelschirm *m* cable shield
Kabelverseilmaschine *f* cable stranding machine
Kabine *f* cab, cabin, operator's cab, operator compartment
Kabinendach *nt* overhead guard
Kachelgrundofen *m* tiled base stove
kadmiumhaltiges Lot *nt* cadmium-containing solder
Kadmiumlot *nt* cadmium solder
Kadmiumoxidfämpfe *mpl* cadmium oxide vapours
Käfig *m* cage
Käfigläufer *m* cage rotor, cage armature
Käfigläufermotor *m* squirrel cage motor
Kalander *m* calender
Kalanderantrieb *m* calender drive (belt)
Kalenderdatei *f* calender file
Kaliber *nt* calibre, roll opening, roll pass, groove
Kaliberdorn *m* mandrel, broach, plug (gage)
Kaliberpresse *f* sizing press
Kaliberring *m* female gauge
Kalibrierabschnitt *m* sizing section
Kalibrierarbeit *f* sizing work
Kalibriereinheit *f* calibration unit
kalibrieren calibrate, *(US)* gage, *(UK)* gauge, size (to gauge)
Kalibriergas *nt* calibration gas
Kalibriergrad *m* grade of calibration
Kalibrierkonstante *f* calibration constant
Kalibrierkorrektion *f* bore correction
Kalibrierräumwerkzeug *nt* sizing broach
Kalibrierschein *m* calibration certificate
kalibriert scaled, sized
Kalibrierung *f* calibration
Kalibrierwalze *f* sizing roll
Kalibrierzähne *mpl* sizing teeth
Kalilauge *f* caustic potash solution
Kalkulation *f* calculation
Kalkulationsschema *nt* calculation

pattern
kalkulatorisch calculatory
Kalorimetergefäß *nt* calorimeter vessel
Kalotte *f* cap, ball indentation, spherical surface
kalt cold
kalt formen mould in a cold state
kalt verformbar deformable
kalt versteiftes Schmierfett *nt* cold set grease
Kaltband *nt* cold rolled strip
kaltbearbeiten cold-form, cold-work
kaltbiegen cold-bend
Kaltbruch *m* cold shortness
Kaltdrücken *nt* spinning
Kälte *f* cold
Kältebruchtemperatur *f* cold breaking temperature
kältefest cold resisting
Kältefließfähigkeit *f* cold flow property
Kältelagerungsverhalten *nt* low temperature storage behaviour
Kältemaschinenöl *nt* refrigerator oil
Kältemittelbeständigkeit *f* refrigerant stability
Kälteschrank *m* refrigerator
Kältesprödigkeitstemperatur *f* low temperature brittleness point
kaltfließfähig cold-flowable
Kaltfließfähigkeit *f* cold flowability
kaltfließpressen cold-extrude
Kaltfließpressverfahren *nt* cold-extrusion process
Kaltfließpresswerkzeug *nt* cold-extrusion die
Kalt-Form-, Füll- und Verschließmaschine *f* cold form fill and seal machine
kaltformbar cold-formable
Kaltformbarkeit *f* cold plasticity, cold formability
kaltformen cold form, work cold
Kaltformmasse *f* cold moulding material
kaltgehärtete Gießharzmasse *f* cold setting resin moulding material
kaltgehärteter Gießharzformstoff *m* cold set casting moulded material

kaltgestaucht cold headed
kaltgewalzt cold rolled
Kalthärtbarkeit *f* strain hardenability
Kalthydratbehälter *m* hydrated lime container
Kaltkammerdruckgießmaschine *f* cold-chamber pressure die-casting machine
Kaltkammerdruckguss *m* cold-chamber pressure casting
Kaltkammermaschine *f* cold chamber machine
Kaltkammerverfahren *nt* cold-chamber process
Kaltkleben *nt* cold bonding
Kaltklebstoff *m* cold adhesive
Kaltkreissäge *f* cold circular saw
Kaltleiter *m* PTC (positive temperature coefficient) resistor
Kaltleiterfühler *m* PTC thermistor detector
Kaltlötstelle *f* cold junction
Kaltluftregelklappe *f* cold air control damper
Kaltmeißel *m* cold chisel
Kaltprofil *nt* cold rolled section
kaltrichten cold straighten
Kaltriss *m* cold crack
Kaltsäge *f* cold saw
kaltschmieden cold-forge
Kaltschweißen *nt* welding without preheat
Kaltsprödigkeit *f* cold brittleness
Kaltstart *m* cold restart, cold start
kaltstauchbar capable of being cold-headed, cold-forgeable
Kaltstauchbarkeit *f* *(von Schrauben)* cold head capability
kaltstauchen heat cold, upset cold
Kaltstauchmaschine *f* cold-heading machine, cold header
Kaltstauchmaschine *f* **mit ungeteilter Matrize** solid-die cold header
Kaltstauchmatrize *f* cold-heating die, cold heater die
Kaltumformen *nt* cold reforming, cold forming
kaltverarbeiten cold-process
kaltverfestigen work-harden
Kaltverfestigung *f* strain (or work)

hardening
kaltverformbar cold-formable, cold-workable
Kaltvulkanisierechtheit *f* fastness to cold vulcanizing
kaltwalzen cold-roll
Kaltwasserdruck *m* cold water pressure
Kaltwasserzuleitung *f* cold water inlet pipe
Kamelhaarpinsel *m* camel hair brush
Kamera *f* camera
Kameralaser *m* laser camera
Kamerasystem *nt* camera system
Kam-Meldung *f* came message
kämmen mate, mesh (gears)
kämmende Räder *ntpl* inter-meshing gears
kämmende Stellung *f* combing position
kämmendes Räderpaar *nt* intermating pair of gear wheels
Kammer *f* chamber
Kammerdurchmesser *m* chamber diameter
Kammmeißel *m* rack-shaped cutter, rack-type cutter
Kammriss *m* rack crack
Kammstapelverfahren *nt* comb staple method
Kämpferhöhe *f* springing level
Kanal *m* channel, port, conduit, duct, routing
Kanalfahrwagen *m* satellite vehicle, trolley
Kanalfeuchteregler *m* duct humidity regulator
Kanallager *nt* high bay warehouse, satellite storage
Kanallänge *f* length of bay
Kanalnetz *nt* ducting, duct system
Kanalstrecke *f* duct length
Kanalstruktur *f* channel structure
Kanaltrennung *f* 1. *(Vorgang)* bay division 2. *(Vorrichtung)* bay divider
Kanalverfahren *nt* in-duct method
Kanbanabwicklung *f* kanban processing
Kanbansystem *nt* kanban system
Kanister *m* can, canister, drum, tin (box)
Kanonenbohrer *m* cylinder bit, gun drill
Kante *f* edge
Kante *f* **e. Zahnflanke** tooth edge
kanten 1. *(allg.)* edge, cant 2. *(hochstellen)* tilt
Kanten bearbeiten edge-machine
Kantenabdeckung *f* edge covering, edge band
Kantenabschrägen *nt* bevelling of the edges
Kantenabstand *m* distance between edges
Kantenausbruch *m* edge chipping
Kantenaussprünge *f* edge cracking
Kantenbeanspruchung *f* edge stress
Kantenbeflammung *f* edge flaming
Kantenbelastung *f* edge loading
Kantenbrechen *nt* chamfering, breaking of the corners
Kanteneinreißkraft *f* edge tear load
Kanteneinzug *m* edge retraction
Kantenfestigkeit *f* edge stability
Kantenhobeln *nt* edge-planing
Kantenlineal *nt* bevelled steel straight edge, knife edge, straight edge, toolmaker's knife edge, straightedge
Kantenquellung *f* edge swelling
Kantenrundung *f* edge radiussing
Kantenschutz *m* edge protection
Kantenstauchwiderstand *m* edge crush resistance
Kantenversatz *m* linear misalignment of the edges, offset of the edges, poor in alignment
Kantenverschleiß *m* edge wear
kantig edged, angular, chiselled, polygonal, definitely edged, square edged
Kapazität *f* 1. *(allg.)* capacity 2. (el) capacitance 3. (Leistungsfähigkeit) efficiency
Kapazitätsabgleich *m* capacity adjustment
Kapazitätsabschätzung *f* capacity estimate
Kapazitätsänderung *f* capacity modification
Kapazitätsanforderung *f* capacity requirement

Kapazitätsanpassung *f* capacity adjustment
Kapazitätsausgleich *m* capacity smoothing
Kapazitätsauslastung *f* capacity utilization, plant utilization
Kapazitätshochrechnung *f* capacity extrapolation
Kapazitätsreserve *f* capacity reserve
Kapazitätsterminplanung *f* capacity schedule
kapazitive Last *f* capacitive load
kapazitiver Betrieb *m* capacitive operation
kapillaraktives Spaltlöten *nt* fusion brazing depending on capillary action
Kapillardreiwegkegelhahn *m* capillary T-bore stopcock
kapillarer Fülldruck *m* capillary filling pressure
Kapillarlötung *f* capillary soldering
Kapillarlötverbindung *f* capillary solder fitting, capillary solder joint
Kapillarviskosimeter *nt* capillary viscosimeter
Kapillarviskosimetrie *f* capillary viscosimetry
Kapitalbedarf *m* capital demand
Kapitalbedarfsplan *m* capital demand plan
Kapitalbindung *f* capital lock-up, capital tie-up
Kapitalbindungskosten *pl* capital tie-up cost(s)
Kapitaleinsatz *m* capital investment
Kappe *f* cap, bonnet, hood, cover
Kapsel *f* casing, can, capsule
kapseln encase, encapsulate, can
Kapselung *f* canning, encapsulation, casing, enclosure
Karabinerhaken *m* snap hook
Karbid *nt* carbide
Karbonisierechtheit *f* fastness to carbonizing
karburieren carburize
Kardangelenk *nt* cardan joint, Hooke's joint, universal joint
Kardanwelle *f* cardan shaft
Karosserie *f* chassis
Karren *m* truck, trolley

Kartei *f* card file, card index
Kartenleser *m* card reader
Kartenlochen *nt* card perforating, card punching
Kartenlocher *m* card perforator, card punch
Kartesische Koordinaten *fpl* Cartesian coordinates
kartesischer Roboter *m* Cartesian robot *(Hauptachsen führen die Translationsbewegung innerhalb kartesischer Raumkoordinaten aus)*
Karton *m* carton, cardboard, cartonboard
Kartonage *f* cartonboard
Kartonbox *f* cardboard box
Kartongreifer *m* cardboard grip arm
kartonieren bind in boards, carton
kartonierend binding in boards, cartoning
Kartoniermaschine *f* cartoning machine, cartoner
Kartonklammer *f* carton clamp
Kartontray *nt* cartonboard skillet, carton tray
Kartonzuschnitt *m* cartonboard blank, carton blank
Karussell *nt* carousel, circular conveyor, merry-go-round, roundabout
Karusselldrehmaschine *f* vertical turret lathe, vertical turning and boring mill
Karussellfräsmaschine *f* vertical-spindle rotary-table miller
Karuselllager *nt* carousel storage system, roundabout store
Karussellrevolverdrehmaschine *f* vertical turret lathe
Karussellsegment *nt* carousel segment
kaschieren coat, apply coatings, cover
Kassettenmagazin *nt* cartridge magazine
Kassette *f* cartridge, case, cassette
Kassettengestell *nt* cartridge frame
Kassettenlage *f* cartridge layer
Kassettenlager *nt* cartridge storage system
Kassettentunnel *m* cartridge tunnel
Kasten *m* box, case, kit, chest, bin, crate
Kastenbett *nt* box-section bed

Kastenformverfahren *nt* box section process
Kastenfuß *m* cabinet end leg, cabinet leg (lathe)
Kastenständer *m* 1. *(allg.)* box column, box-type column 2. *(e. kleineren Maschine)* cabinet floor stand
Kastenständerbauart *f* round column design, box-column design
Kastenständerbohrmaschine *f* box column drilling machine
Kastenständerradialbohrmaschine *f* box-column-type radial
Kastenstapel- und -entstapelungsmaschine *f* crate stacking/unstacking machine
Kastentisch *m* box (-type) table
Kastenwendegreifer *m* crate turnover device
Katalysator *m* catalyser
Katastrophenschutz *m* disaster control
Katawert *m* kata factor
Kathode *f* cathode
Kathodenfläche *f* cathode surface
Kathodenstrahlröhre *f* cathode ray tube (CRT)
Kathodenstrahlsystem *nt* cathode ray system
kathodischer Korrosionsschutz *m* cathodic corrosion protection
kathodischer Teilschnitt *m* cathodic partial stage
katodenseitig on the cathode side
Katze *f* trolley
Katzenkopf *m* *(US)* cathead
Katzfahrt *f* trolley travel
Katzfahrwerk *nt* trolley travelling gears
Kauf *m* purchase
kaufen buy, purchase
Kaufentscheidung *f* purchasing decision
Käufer *m* customer, purchaser, buyer
Kaustik *f* caustics, caustic curve
Kautschukkleber *m* natural rubber adhesive
Kautschukmischung *f* rubber compound
Kautschuktrockensubstanz *f* dry natural rubber substance

Kautschukvulkanisat *nt* natural rubber vulcanizate
Keg *nt* keg
Kegel *m* 1. *(math.)* cone 2. *(geom.)* taper 3. *(Werkzeug)* machine taper 4. *(schlanker ~)* slight taper
Kegelbefestigung *f* 1. *(als Fertigungsteil)* taper lock 2. *(Arbeitsvorgang)* taper lock fixing
Kegelbett *nt* conical base
Kegelbohren *nt* taper boring
Kegelbremse *f* cone brake
Kegelbuchse *f* *(Rohrverschraubung)* taper bushing
Kegeldrehautomat *m* automatic lathe for taper turning
Kegeldreheinrichtung *f* taper turning attachment
Kegeldrehen *nt* taper turning, angular turning, cone turning
Kegeldurchmessertoleranz *f* cone diameter tolerance
Kegeldurchmessertoleranzfeld *nt* zone diameter tolerance field
Kegeleinsatz *m* taper adapter
Kegelerzeugungswinkel *m* cone generating angle
Kegelfläche *f* conical surface
kegelförmig tapered, conical, cone-shaped, wedge-shaped
Kegelformtoleranz *f* cone form tolerance
Kegelfräseinrichtung *f* taper milling attachment, attachment for taper milling
Kegelfräsen *nt* taper milling
kegelig tapered, conical, bevelled
kegelig senken countersink
kegelige Fügefläche *f* conical joint surface
kegelige Stirnfläche *f* conical end surface
kegeliger Anschnitt *m* bevel, chamfer
kegeliger Einschraubzapfen *m* *(e. Rohrverschraubung)* taper adapter end
kegeliger Gesenkfräser *m* **mit runder Stirn** round-point tapering die-sinking cutter
kegeliger Gewindeprüfdorn *m* taper

check gauge
kegeliges Außengewinde *nt* tapered external thread
kegeliges Rohrgewinde *nt* tapered pipe thread
kegeliges Whitworth-Rohrgewinde *nt* tapered Whitworth pipe thread
Kegeligsenken *nt* countersinking
Kegellineal *nt* taper bar, guide rail
Kegelkerbstift *m* full length taper grooved pin
Kegelkopf *m* conical capped end
Kegelkörper *m* conical body
Kegelkuppe *f (e. Schraube e. Gewindestiftes)* flat point
Kegelkupplung *f* conical clutch
Kegellehre *f* taper gauge (or gage)
Kegelmantellinie *f* cone generator
Kegelmantelnaht *f* conical weld
Kegelpassung *f* taper fit
Kegelplanrad *nt* plane bevel gear
Kegelplanradpaar *nt* plane bevel gear pair
Kegelrad *nt* bevel gear
Kegelradbearbeitung *f* bevel gear machining
Kegelräder *ntpl* bevel gears
Kegelradformfräser *m* bevel gear formed cutter
Kegelradfräser *m* bevel gear cutter
Kegelradfräsmaschine *f* bevel gear milling machine
Kegelradgetriebe *nt* bevel gear transmission, bevel gear
Kegelradhobelmaschine *f* bevel gear generator (or planing machine)
Kegelradhobelmaschine *f* bevel gear shaper
Kegelradhobelmaschinenbau *m* design (or manufacture) of bevel gear planing machines
Kegelradhobelmeißel *m* bevel gear cutter
Kegelradhobler *m* bevel gear generator (or planer)
Kegelradpaar *nt* bevel gear pair, gear pair with intersecting axes, bevel gear pair
Kegelradstirnebene *f* transverse plane of the bevel gear
Kegelradverzahnmaschine *f* bevel gear cutting machine
Kegelradverzahnung *f* bevel gear tooth system
Kegelradvorfräsmaschine *f* bevel gear roughing machine
Kegelradwälzfräser *m* bevel gear hob
Kegelreibahle *f* taper reamer
Kegelrolle *f* tapered roller
Kegelrollenlager *nt* tapered roller bearing
Kegelschaft *m* taper shank
Kegelschleifen *nt* taper grinding
Kegelschliffhülse *f* ground taper socket
Kegelschlitten *m* former slide
Kegelschnittführung *f* guidance on conic sections
Kegelschraubenrad *nt* helical bevel gear, hypoid gear
Kegelschraubenradpaar *nt* helical bevel gear pair, hypoid gear pair
Kegelspindel *f (z. B. e. Läppmaschine)* taper spindle
Kegelstift *m* taper pin
Kegelstirnradgetriebe *nt* straight bevel gear pair
Kegeltoleranzfeld *nt* cone tolerance field
Kegeltoleranzraum *m* cone tolerance space
Kegeltoleranzsystem *nt* cone tolerance system
Kegelverhältnis *nt* taper ratio
Kegelverjüngung *f* rate of taper
Kegelverzahnung *f* taper toothing
Kegelwinkel *m* taper (or included) angle, pitch angle, vertex angle of cone
Kegelwinkeltoleranz *f* cone angle tolerance, taper angle tolerance
Kegelzapfen *m* pilot taper
Kegfüll- und -verschließmaschine *f* keg fill and seal machine
Kehle *f* groove, neck, throat
Kehlfuge *f* throat edge
Kehlhobeleinrichtung *f* die-slotting attachment
Kehlhobelmaschine *f* die block shaper, die slotter, contour shaping machine

Kehlhobeln shape curved surfaces
Kehlnaht f fillet weld, concave weld
Kehlnaht f **mit Einbrandkerbe** fillet weld with undercut
Kehlnaht f **mit hoher Oberfläche** concave fillet joint
Kehlnaht f **mit nicht erfasster Wurzel** fillet weld with no fusion at root
Kehlrad nt concave gear
Kehlschraubenlinie f base helix
Kehrgewindespindel f turnabout screw
Kehrwert m reciprocal
Keil m key, spline, wedge
Keilbahnfräsarbeit f keyway cutting operation, spline milling work
Keilbiegen nt V-form bending
keilförmig wedge-shaped
Keilleiste f tapered gib
Keilmessebene f wedge measurement plane
Keilnabe f splined groove
Keilnabenräumwerkzeug nt internal spline broach
Keilnabenstoßmeißel m keyway slotting tool
Keilnut f key groove, keyway
Keilnuten einarbeiten keyseat
Keilnuten fpl **ziehen** keygroove
Keilnuten- und Langlochfräsmaschine f keyseating and slot milling machine
Keilnutenfräsen nt keyway cutting, keyway milling, splining
Keilnutenfräser m keyway milling cutter
Keilnutenstoßen nt keyseating, keyway-cutting, keywaying
Keilnutenstoßmaschine f keyseater, keyway cutter
Keilnutenstoßmeißel m keyway tool
Keilnutenziehmaschine f draw-cut type keyseater
Keilnutmaschine f keyseater
Keilpaar nt angular parallels
Keilprofilräumnadel f spline broach
Keilriemen m fan belt, V-belt, Vee-belt
Keilriemenantrieb m V-belt drive
Keilschieber m wedge gate valve
Keilschneiden nt wedge-action cutting

Keilsitz m key seat, seat for key
Keilstab m key bar
Keilstück nt angular parallels, taper parallels
Keilverzahnung f splining
Keilverzahnungsfräser m spline milling cutter
Keilverzahnungsfräsmaschine f spline milling machine
Keilverzahnungswälzfräser m serration hob
Keilwelle f splined shaft
Keilwellenfräsmaschine f spline shaft milling machine
Keilwellenschaftfräser m spline shaft cutter
Keilwellenwälzfräser m spline hob
Keilwinkel m *(US)* lip angle, *(UK)* wedge angle, cutting angle, angle of keenness, cutting wedge angle
Keilwinkel m **des Spanbrechers** chip breaker angle
keimarme Belüftung f germ-free ventilation
Keimarmut f germ poverty
keine/r/s none
Kreisbogen m arc of circle
Keller m cellar
Kennbuchstabe m code letter
Kenndaten pl characteristic data
Kenngröße f characteristic factor, characteristic data pl
Kennlinie f characteristic curve, characteristic line, characteristic
Kennlinienfeld nt family of characteristics
Kennmerkmal nt characteristic, characteristic feature
Kennung f identifier, identification, identification signal
Kennwert m value of a statistic, parameter, characteristic value
Kennwerte mpl characteristic values, data
Kennwertmessung f measurement of characteristic value
Kennwort nt password
Kennzahl f characteristic value, indicator, rating number, rating, identification number, specifications pl

Kennzahlenmethode *f* characteristic value method
Kennzeichen *nt* characteristic mark, marker, identification
kennzeichnen mark, identify, designate
Kennzeichnung *f* designation, identification, marking
Kennziffer *f* identification figure, index figure
Keramik *f* ceramics
Keramikschneidwerkzeug *nt* ceramic cutting tool
keramisch gebundene Schleifscheibe *f* vitrified bonded grinding wheel
keramischer Dauerbrandofen *m* ceramic slow combustion stove
keramischer Einsatzmeißel *m* ceramic bit
keramischer Schneidstoff *m* ceramic cutting material
Kerbbereich *m* region of the notch
Kerbbruchdehnung *f* elongation at fracture of reduced-section specimen
Kerbe *f* chamfer, dent, kerf, notch, slot, groove, nick
Kerben *nt* grooving
kerbfreier Übergang *m* notch-free transition
Kerbmitte *f* centreline of the notch
Kerbriss *m* toe-crack
Kerbschlagarbeit *f* notched bar impact energy, impact strength
Kerbschlagbiegeversuch *m* 1. *(allg. Spitzkerb)* beam impact test 2. *(metall. Werkstoffe)* notched bar impact bending test 3. *(nach Charpy)* Charpy impact test
Kerbschlagversuch *m* notched bar impact test
Kerbverschleiß *m* notch wear
kerbverzahnen serrate
Kerbverzahnung *f* serration
Kerbwinkel *m* notch angle
Kerbzugprobe *f* notched tensile test specimen
Kern *m* centre, core, nucleus
kernbohren trepan
Kernbohrkopf *m* hollow-core drill
Kerndurchmesser *m (z. B. Gewinde)* core diameter, minor diameter
Kerndurchmesser *m* **von Zahngrund zu Zahngrund** root diameter
Kerndurchmesserlehrdorn *m* minor thread diameter plug gauge
Kerndurchmessertoleranz *f* minor diameter tolerance
Kerngebiet *nt* core region
Kernhärte *f* core hardness
Kernherstellung *f* core production
Kernhülse *f* core
Kernloch *nt* core hole
Kernmarke *f* core mark
Kernprozess *m* core process
Kernquerschnitt *m* web section, core cross-section
Kernschießverfahren *nt* core fire process
kernstablegierte Elektrode *f* electrode with alloyed core rod
Kernstabnenndurchmesser *m* nominal diameter of the core
Kernsteigerung *f* web taper
Kernstopfen *m* core plug
Kernstopfmaschine *f* core-extrusion machine
Kernstrahlungsdetektor *m* nuclear radiation detector
Kernstück *nt* core, centre
Kernstütze *f* chaplet
kerntechnische Anlage *f* nuclear plant
Kerntrockenkammer *f* core stove
Kerntrockenofen *m* core stove oven
Kerntrocknung *f* core baking drying
Kernverbund *m* sandwich
Kernverlagerung *f* core shift
Kernverschiebung *f* core shift
Kernzerschmiedung *f* forging burst, hammer pipe, split centre
Kessel *m* boiler
Kessel *m* **für feste Brennstoffe** solid fuel boiler
Kesselabgasstutzen *m* boiler flue outlet
Kesselaufstellungsraum *m* boiler room
Kesselbau *m* boiler construction
Kesselgerüst *nt* boiler framing
Kesselhaus *nt* boiler room
Kesselleistung *f* boiler output

Kesselpresse *f* autoclave press
Kesselrücklauf *m* boiler return
Kesselsohle *f* boiler base
Kesselvorlauftemperatur *f* boiler flow temperature
Kesselwärter *m* boiler attendant
Kette *f* chain
Kette *f:* **kinematische** ~ kinematic chain
Kettenantrieb *m* chain drive, motor driven chain
Kettenauslauf *m* chain discharge
Kettenendbefestigung *f* chain termination
Kettenendverbindung *f* chain termination
Kettenförderer *m* chain conveyor
Kettengetriebe *nt* chain drive
Kettenglied *nt* chain link
Kettenhub *m* chain lift
Kettenmagazin *nt* chain magazine, chain storeroom
Kettenmaße *ntpl* incremental dimensioning
Kettenrad *nt* chain wheel, pulley, sprocket, sprocket wheel
Kettenreaktion *f* chain reaction
Kettenrolle *f* chain pulley
Kettenschutz *m* chain guard
Kettenspanner *m* turnbuckle, chain adjuster, (chain) stretcher, (chain) tightener
Kettenspannung *f* chain tension
Kettensperre *f* chain barrier
Kettenstichprobenprüfung *f* chain sampling inspection
Kettenstrang *m* chain string
Kettenstruktur *f* chain structure
Kettensystem *nt* chain system
Kettenteilung *f* pitch of the chain(s)
Kettentrieb *m* chain drive
Kettenverstellgetriebe *nt* adjustable chain gear
Kettenzug *m* **1.** *(Vorrichtung)* chain hoist **2.** *(in der Kette)* pull in the chain, chain tension
K-Fuge *f* double level groove
Kieselglasschale *f* silica glass bowl
Kies-Sand-Auflager *nt* gravel-sand bedding

kindergesicherte Packung *f* child resistant package
Kinematik *f* kinematics
kinematische Größe *f* kinematic quantity
kinematische Kette *f* kinematic chain
kinematische Kornzahl *f* kinematic grain count
kinematische Schleiflänge *f* kinematic grinding length
kinematischer Schleifwinkel *m* kinematic grinding arc
kinetisch kinetic
kinetische Energie *f* kinetic energy
Kippachse *f* tilting axis
Kippantrieb *m* tilting gear
kippbar tipping, pivoting, tiltable
kippbare Kabine *f* pivoting driver compartment
Kippbewegung *f* overturning movement, tilt movement
Kippdrehzahl *f* pull-out speed
kippen tip (over), tilt, overturn, pivot, cant
Kippgabelträger *m* tippling fork arm carriage
Kippgefahr *f* danger of tipping over
Kippglied *nt* sweep element
Kippkante *f* tipping axis
Kippklammer *f* tippling clamp
Kipplinie *f* axis of unit
Kippmoment *nt* **1.** *(allg.)* overturning moment **2.** *(el.)* pull-out torque, breakdown torque
Kippschalter *m* tumbler switch, flip switch
Kippschlupf *m* pull-out slip
Kippschwingung *f* relaxation oscillation
Kippsicherheit *f* steadiness
Kippspiegel *m* tilting mirror
Kippsupport *m* swivel head
Kipptisch *m* tilting table
Kipptraverse *f* tilting cross beam
Kippung *f* tilt
Kippvorrichtung *f* tipper
Kippwert *m* slope value
Kippwinkel *m* angle of tilt
Kissen *nt* pad
Kiste *f* box, case, chest, crate

Kittflüssigkeit *f* putty liquid
Kittpulver *nt* putty powder
Klaffen *nt* gaping
Klammer *f* 1. *(Bauteil)* brace, clamp 2. *(Mathematik)* bracket
Klammer *f* **auf** left bracket
Klammer *f* **zu** right bracket
Klammerarm *m* clamp arm
Klammerdruck *m* clamp pressure
Klammergabel *f* fork clamp
klammern clamp, tuck, clip, brace
klammernd clamping, tucking
Klammerverbindung *f* clamp connection
Klammerwender *m* clamp turning device
Klapp- und Faltbox *f* flap and folding box
klappbar fold away type, folding, hinged, tilting, collapsible
Klappbox *f* cage, flap box
Klappdeckel *m* hinged lid, lift-up lid
Klappe *f* 1. *(Bauteil)* flap, trap, clapper, lid 2. *(Durchgang)* gate, trap door
Klappe *f* **mit stetigem Stellverhalten** butterfly valve with progressive adjustment characteristic
klappen flap, hinge, fold
Klappenwelle *f* butterfly valve stem
Klappgabel *f* folding fork
Klappöler *m* hinged-lid lubricator
klardurchsichtig clear transparent
Klarschrift *f* clear text, plain text, plain writing
Klarschriftcodierer *m* character encoder
Klartext *m* clear text, plain text
Klasse *f* class, cell, grade
Klassenbildung *f* classification
Klassengrenze *f* class limit
Klassenmitte *f* class midpoint
klassieren group, classify
Klassierung *f* grouping, classification
klassifizieren classify
Klassifizierung *f* classification
Klassifizierungsmöglichkeit *f* classification possibility
Klaue *f* dog, jaw, claw
Klauenfräsen *nt* dog clutch milling
Klauenkupplung *f* claw coupling

Klauenspannung *f* claw clamping
Klebanleitung *f* bonding instruction
Klebbedingung *f* bonding condition
Klebeband *nt* adhesive tape
Klebeband-Verschließmaschine *f* case taper
Klebefolie *f* adhesive film, pressure-sensitive film
Klebeigenschaft *f* adhesive property
kleben adhere (to), glue (on, to), stick (on, to)
Kleben *nt* **von Körpern mittels Klebfolie** bonding of bodies by means of bonding foil
klebend adhesive
klebender Bestandteil *m* tacky constituent
Kleber *m* **für Gummi** adhesive for vulcanised rubber
Kleber *m* **für Metall** adhesive for metal
Klebeverhalten *nt* stickiness
Klebevorgang *m* gluing operation
Klebfestigkeit *f* adhesion
Klebfläche *f* bond area
Klebflüssigkeit *f* adhesive liquid
Klebkitt *m* adhesive putty (or compound)
Klebkittmischung *f* adhesive putty mixture
Kleblöser *m* adhesive dissolver
Klebmuffe *f* cemented (or bonded) socket joint
Klebrigkeit *f* tackiness
Klebschelle *f* cementing clip
Klebschicht *f* adhesive layer
Klebschichtbruch *m* fracture in the adhesive layer
Klebschild *nt* adhesive nameplate
Klebstelle *f* bonding surface
Klebstoff *m* adhesive
Klebstoff *m* **auftragen** apply adhesive (to), glue
Klebstoff *m* **im Verarbeitungszustand** ready-for-use adhesive
Klebstoffansatz *m* adhesive formulation
Klebstoffauftrag *m* application of adhesive, gluing
Klebstoffauftragverschließmaschine *f* case gluing machine, glue

sealing machine
Klebstoffbestandteil *m* adhesive constituent
Klebstoffe *mpl* adhesives (pl)
Klebstofffilm *nt* adhesive film
Klebstoffgrundstoff *m* binder in adhesive
Klebstoffschicht *f* adhesive layer
Klebstoffverarbeitung *f* adhesive processing
Klebstutzen *m* cemented (or bonded) nozzle
Klebsuspension *f* adhesive suspension
Klebung *f* sticking, lack of fusion, bonded joint
Klebwachs *nt* adhesive wax
klein 1. *(z. B. bis ins kleinste Detail)* minute 2. *(gering)* little, slight 3. *(Objekt)* small 4. *(Zahlen)* low 5. *(kurz)* short
Kleinautomat *m* auto-lathe
Kleinbehälter *m* small container
Kleinbuchstabe *m* lower case letter
Kleindarstellung *f* small-scale representation
Kleindrehbank *f* speed lathe, hand lathe
kleine Serienarbeit *f* short-run job, small run
kleine Stückzahl *f* short-run job, small run
kleiner als *(/)* less than
kleiner gleich less than or equal to, less or equal
kleiner Hub *m* slight lift
kleiner oder gleich less or equal to
Kleingebinde *nt* small container, small package
Kleinheizkessel *m* small heating boiler
Kleinladungsträger (KLT) *m* small parts container
Kleinlochkarte *f* small punched card
Kleinmengenfertigung *f* small-quantity production
Kleinregalbediengerät *nt* miniload storage and retrieval machine
Kleinreihenfertigung *f* limited quantity production, small batch production
Kleinreihenfräsen *nt* small lot milling
Kleinschweißeinsatz *m* small welding attachment
Kleinserie *f* short run, small batch, small lot
Kleinserienfertigung *f* small batch production
kleinst... minimum
Kleinstellung *f* low setting
Kleinstflankenspiel *nt* minimum backlash
Kleinstmaß *nt* minimum limit (of size), minimum size (or limit or dimension), lower limit
Kleinstmenge *f* minimum quantity
kleinstmöglich smallest possible
Kleinstspiel *nt* allowance
Kleinstübermaß *nt* minimum interference
Kleinstückleim *m* glue in small particles
Kleinstwertbegrenzer *m* minimum value limiter
Kleinteile *ntpl* small parts
Kleinteilebehälter *m* small parts container
Kleinteilelager *nt* small parts store, small parts warehouse
Kleinwasserheizer *m* small water heater
Klemmbacke *f* clamping jaw
Klemmbelag *m* grip lining
Klemmbolzen *m* binding bolt
Klemme *f* 1. *(Bauteil)* binder, clamp, grip, clip, terminal 2. *(el.)* connector, terminal
Klemmeinrichtung *f* clamping device
klemmen 1. *(allg.)* clamp, clip, stick, jam, grip, lock 2. *(Werkstücke in Futter)* chuck
Klemmenbrett *nt* terminal board
klemmende Sicherungsmutter *f* gripping locknut
Klemmenkasten *m* conduit box, terminal box
Klemmenspannung *f* terminal voltage
Klemmhalter *m* (clamp-type) toolholder
Klemmkupplung *f* compression coupling
Klemmplatte *f* adjustable block
Klemmrolle *f* clamping roller

Klemmrollensperrfangvorrichtung *f* clamping roller catching device
Klemmschieber *m* push-pull (mechanism), puller and pusher mechanism
Klemmschraube *f* clamp, setscrew, setting screw, binder screw
Klemmschraube *f* **des Klappenträgers** apron clamping bolt
Klemmschraube *f* **für den Klappenträger** clapper clamping unit
Klemmschraube um eine Umdrehung lösen slacken the locking screw one turn
Klemmstück *nt* **1.** *(allg.)* block **2.** *(Waagrechtstoßmaschine)* adjustable block
Klemmung *f* lock, clamp
Klemmvorgang *m* clamping
Klemmvorrichtung *f* clamping device
Klempner *m* pipe fitter, plumber
Klempnerlot *nt* plumber's solder
Kletterflamme *f* climbing flame
Klima *nt* climate
Klimaanlage *f* air condition, air conditioning, air conditioner
Klimaeinflüsse *mpl* climatic effects
Klimakonstanz *f* climatic stability
Klimaraum *m* controlled atmosphere chamber, conditioning chamber
Klimatechnik *f* air conditioning technology
klimatisch climatic
Klimatisierung *f* air conditioning
Klimaverhältnisse *ntpl* climatic conditions
Klimawechsel *m* atmospheric change
Klimazelle *f* conditioning cell
Klimazentrale *f* centralized air conditioning plant
Klimazone *f* climate
Klinge *f* blade
Klinke *f* detent, latch, pawl
Klinkenrad *nt* ratchet
Klischeezeichnung *f* block drawing
Klopfeinrichtung *f* tapping device
klopfen *(Motor)* beat, knock
Klöpperboden *m* dished head, torispherical head
Klotz *m* *(Palette)* bearer
Klotzbodenbeutel *m* bag
Klotztaster *m* bearer sensing device
KLT-Greifer *m* small parts container gripper
Klumpenprobenahme *f* cluster sampling
Klumpenstichprobe *f* cluster sample
Kluppe *f* die-stock
Knabberschneiden *nt* nibbling
Knagge *f* dog, trip, cam, catch, dog stop
knallend zurückschlagen retrogress explosively
knapp scarce, short, short-run
Knappheit *f* shortage
Knarre *f* ratchet
Knebel *m* locking handle, T-handle
Knebelkerbstift *m* third length centre grooved pin
Knebelstecker *m* T-shaped locator pin
Knebelüberwurfmutter *f* wing type union nut
Kneifzange *f* pincers, pliers, nipper
kneten knead
Knick *m* **1.** *(allg.)* bend, kink, fold, buckling **2.** *(Lenkung)* articulation
Knickarm *m* buckling arm
Knickarmroboter *m* buckling arm robot
Knickbauchen *nt* acute-angle bulging
Knickbelastung *f* buckling stress
Knickbereich *m* articulation zone
Knickbiegen *nt* V-die bending, bulging
knicken fold, buckle
knickfest non-buckling
Knickfestigkeit *f* buckling strength
Knicklänge *f* buckling length
Knicklängenbeiwert *m* buckling length coefficient
Knicklenkung *f* articulated (frame) steering
Knickmechanismus *m* buckling mechanism
Knickpunkt *m* buckling point
Knickung *f* buckling
Knickversuch *m* buckling test, collapsing test
Knickzahl *f* buckling coefficient, number of flexures
Knie *nt* elbow, angle, knee
Kniegelenk *nt* hinged knee, toggle
Kniehebel *m* toggle lever

Kniehebelpresse *f* toggle press
Kniehebelziehpresse *f* toggle drawing press
Knieleiste *f* intermediate rail, knee rail
Kniestück *nt* elbow
Knittererholungswinkel *m* crease recovery angle
Knitterfaltenbildung *f* formation of creases
Knitterneigung *f* creasing tendency
Knitterstelle *f* crease, kink
Knitterwinkel *m* crease angle
Knopf *m* 1. *(Druckknopf)* button 2. *(Drehknopf)* knob
Knoten *m* node
Knotenanrisskraft *f* delamination force of the node-to-node bond
Knotenblech *nt* corner plate
Knotenebene *f* node plane
Knotenpunkt *m* 1. *(allg.)* node point, system point 2. *(Wege)* point of intersection
Knoten-Zugfestigkeit *f* knotted tensile strength
Knoten-Zugprobe *f* knotted (wire) tensile specimen
Knoten-Zugverhältnis *nt* knotted tensile ratio
Knoten-Zugversuch *m* tensile test using knotted specimens
Knüppel *m* billet (metal), tiller
Koagulatgehalt *m* coagulum content
koaxial coaxial
Koaxialitätsabweichung *f* error of coaxiality
Koaxialitätstoleranz *f* coaxiality tolerance
Koaxialkabel *nt* coaxial cable
Kobaltstahl *m* cobalt steel
Kochendwassergerät *nt* open-outlet water heater
Kochherd *m* cooking range
kodieren encode
Kodierer *m* encoder
Kodierung *f* encoding
Kodierungssystem *nt* code system
kohärent coherent
Köhärenzgrad *m* degree of coherence
Kohäsion *f* cohesion
Kohäsionsbruch *m* cohesion fracture

Kohäsionskraft *f* molecular cohesive force, intermolecular force
kohäsiv cohesive
Kohleabriebstaub *m* coal dust
Kohlebürste *f* carbon brush, graphite brush
Kohlendioxid *nt* carbon oxide
Kohlensäureester carbonic acid ester
Kohlenstaub *m* coal dust
kohlenstaubgefeuert pulverized coal fired
Kohlenstoff *m* carbon
Kohlenstoffaffinität *f* carbon affinity
kohlenstoffarmer Stahl *m* low-carbon steel
Kohlenstofffasergelege *nt* carbon fibres, CFK prepreg
Kohlenstoffgehalt *m* carbon content
Kohlenstoffstahl *m* carbon steel
Kohlenstoffverlauf *m* carbon characteristic
Kohlepapierdurchschlag *m* carbon copy (cc)
Kokille *f* chilled mould, ingot mould, die cast, moulding die
Kokillenbau *m* manufacture of chill
Kokillengießen *nt* chill casting
Kokillengießverfahren *nt* chill casting process
Kokillenguss *m* chill casting, gravity die-casting
Kolben *m* piston, plunger, ram
Kolben *m* **mit Normschliff** flask with standard ground socket
Kolbenantrieb *m* piston actuation
Kolbendampfmaschine *f* reciprocating engine
Kolbenfüllmaschine *f* volumetric piston filling machine
Kolbengaszähler *m* piston gas meter
Kolbengaszähler *m* **mit zählendem Messwerk** piston gas meter with integrating movement
Kolbenpresse *m* ram-type press
Kolbenring *m* piston ring
Kolbenstange *f* piston rod
Kolbenstangenführung *f* piston rod bearing
Kolbensteuerung *f* hydraulic tracer control

Kolbenverdichter *m* piston compressor
Kolk *m* crater
Kolkbildung *f* cratering
Kolkung *f* cratering
Kolkverschleiß *m* wear by cratering
Kollektor *m* collector, commutator
Kollektormotor *m* collector motor
kollidieren collide
Kollidurchlaufregal *nt* flow shelf, carton flow rack
Kollision *f* collision
Kollisionsschutz *m* 1. *(Eigenschaft)* collision prevention, collision protection 2. *(Vorrichtung)* collision guard
Kollisionsschutzsensorik *f* collision prevention sensors
Kollissionsschutzsensor *m* collision prevention sensor
Kollissionsverhinderung *f* collision prevention
Kollo *nt* carton, container, package
Kolonnenaufsatz *m* column attachment
Kombiblechschraube *f* tapping screw assembly
Kombidose *f* composite can
Kombination *f* combination
Kombinationsbrenner *m* combined fuel burner
Kombinationslager *nt* combined warehouse
Kombinationsmuffe *f* combination socket
Kombinationszange *f* combination pliers
Kombinierbarkeit *f* combination
kombinieren combine
kombinierte Metallmutter *f* composite metal nut
kombinierte ölhydraulische Doppelständerhobel- und -fräsmaschine hydraulic planer-miller
kombiniertes Spiel *nt* combined cycle
Kombi-Schraube *f* screw and washer assembly
Komplementwinkel *m* **des Einstellwinkels** *m* cutting edge angle, face angle, side angle
kommaförmig comma-shape, wedge-shaped

Kommando *nt* command, order
Kommandoprogramm *nt* user program procedure
Kommandotafel *f* pendant control station
Kommentar *m* comment
kommentieren comment
Kommissionierung *f* dispatch
Kommissionierungslager *nt* dispatch warehouse
Kommission *f* consignment
Kommissionierarbeitsplatz *f* commission work station, packing work station, order-picking station
Kommissioniereinheit *f* order compilation unit
kommissionieren commission, compile, pick
Kommissionierer *m* commissioner, order picker
Kommissionierfahrzeug *nt* commissioning conveyor, order picker truck
Kommissionierfaktor *m* order compilation factor
Kommissionierflurförderzeug *nt* order-picking truck
Kommissioniergang *m* pick aisle
Kommissioniergerät *nt* order picker truck, order picker
Kommissionierkopf *m* order compilation head
Kommissionierlager *nt* order-picking warehouse
Kommissionierplattform *f* order-picking platform
Kommissionierplatz *m* commissioning station, order compilation area, order-picking station
Kommissionierposition *f* order-picking position, picking face
Kommissionier-RBG *nt* SRM for order picking
Kommissionier-Roboter *m* order compilation robot
Kommissionierstapler *m* commissioning stacker, order-picking truck
Kommissionierstation *f* order-picking station
Kommissioniertisch *m* order-picking table, picking table

Kommissionierung *f* commissioning, order compilation, order picking
Kommissionierungszone *f* commissioning area, order compilation area, order-picking zone
Kommissioniervorgang *m* order compilation process, pick, picking, picking sequence, product or process
Kommissionierwagen *m* commissioning cart, order-picking cart
Kommissionierweg *m* picking sequence
Kommissionierzeit *f* pick time
Kommissionsnummer *f* 1. (Bestellung) order number 2. (Teile) steel-stamp number
Kommunikation *f* communication
Kommunikationsabstand *m* communication distance
Kommunikationsbaugruppe *f* communication module
Kommunikationsbereich *m* communication area, communication range
Kommunikationsdauer *f* communication duration
Kommunikationseigenschaften *fpl* communication characteristics
Kommunikationspartner *m* communication partner
Kommunikationsprozess *m* communication process
Kommunikationsschicht *f* session layer
Kommunikationsschluss *m* communication port
Kommunikationszeit *f* communication time
kommunizieren communicate
Kommutator *m* commutator, collector
kommutieren commute, commutate
kommutiert commuted, commutated
Kommutierung *f* commutation
kompakt dense, compact
Kompaktbauweise *f* compact design
Kompaktlager *nt* high density warehouse
kompatibel compatible
Kompatibilität *f* compatibility
Kompensation *f* compensation
Kompensationsflexometer *nt* compression flexometer
Kompensations-Gegeninduktivität compensating mutual inductance
Kompensationsschreiber *m* potentiometer recorder
Kompensationswicklung *f* compensatory coil, compensatory winding
kompensieren compensate, balance, neutralise, countervail
Kompetenz *f* competence
Kompilierer *m* compiler
komplementärer Ausgang *m* complementary output
Komplementwinkel *m* complement, complement angle
komplett complete
Komplettbearbeitung *f* complete processing
komplettieren complete
Komplettlösung *f* mass soldering
Komplettmenge *f* complete volume
komplexe Kreisverstärkung *f* complex loop gain
komplexer Modul *m* complex modulus
komplexer Regelfaktor *m* complex control factor
Komplexfett *nt* complex grease
kompliziert intricate
Komponente *f* component
Komponenten *f* **der Schnittkraft** *f* cutting force components
komponentenbasierende Automatisierung *f* component-based automation
Komponentenkraftsensor *m* **(one ... three)** components force sensor (one... three)
kompressibel compressible
Kompressibilität *f* compressibility
Kompressibilitätsfaktor *m* compressibility factor
Kompressibilitätskoeffizient *m* coefficient of compressibility
Kompression *f* compression
Kompressionsmodul *nt* bulk modulus of elasticity, modulus of cubic compressibility
Kompressionsphase *f* compression phase

Kompressionsspule *f* compression coil
Kompressionswelle *f* compressive wave
Kompressor *m* booster
komprimieren compress
Komprimierung *f* compression
Kondensatabfluss *m* condensate drain
Kondensatableiter *m* condensate trap (or drain)
Kondensatabscheider *m* condensate trap
Kondensatfeuchte *f* condensation
Kondensatkühler *m* condensate cooler
Kondensator *m* **1.** *(Kühlung)* condenser **2.** *(el.)* capacitor
Kondensator *m* **mit Luftkühlung** air-cooled condenser
Kondensator *m* **mit Wasserrückkühlung** condenser with water re-cooling
Kondensatormotor *m* capacitor motor
Kondensatrückführung *f* condensate return
Kondensatsammler *m* condensate collector
Kondenswasserbildung *f* condensation
Kondenswasserklima *nt* condensation atmosphere
Kondenswasserwechselklima *nt* condensation water alternating atmosphere
konduktives Hochfrequenzschweißen *nt* high-frequency conduction welding
konduktives Mittelfrequenzschweißen *nt* medium-frequency conduction welding
konduktives Widerstandspressschweißen *nt* conduction resistance welding
konfektionierte Erzeugnisse *f* ready-made products
Konfektionierung *f* packaging
Konfektionierungsplanung *f* packaging planning
Konfektionierungssteuerung *f* packaging control
Konfiguration *f* configuration
Konfigurationsmanagement *nt* configuration management

konfigurieren configure
konisch conical, tapered
Konjunktion *f* conjunction
Konjunktionsglied *nt* conjunction element
konjunktive Verknüpfung *f* conjunctive combination
Konkavfräser *m* concave cutter
Konklusion *f* conclusion, consequent
Konkurrent *m* competitor
konkurrieren compete
Konsignationslager *nt* consignation warehouse
konsistente Daten *pl* consistent data
Konsole *f* **1.** *(allg.)* panel **2.** *(e. Fußmotors)* pedestal **3.** *(Fräsmaschine)* knee, knee-table **4.** *(Werkzeugmaschine)* knee
Konsolenfräsmaschine *f* column-and knee-type miller, knee-and column milling machine
Konsolenfräsmaschine *f* **mit Hydrokopiereinrichtung** knee-type hydroscopic milling machine
Konsolfräsmaschine *f* **mit Sprungtischbewegung** automatic-cycle knee-type milling machine
Konsolfräsmaschine *f* **mit Universaltisch** knee- and column type milling machine with universal table, universal miller
Konsolfräsmaschine *f* **mit waagerechter Spindel** horizontal-spindle knee-and column miller
Konsolfräsmaschine *f* **mit zwei Verstellspindeln** twin-screw knee- and column type milling machine
Konsolführung *f* knee table, bracket table, knee slides *pl*
Konsolhubspindel *f* knee elevating screw
Konsolklemmung *f* knee clamping
Konsolmaschine *f* column and knee type machine
konstante Sehne *f* constant chord
konstante Zapfenlänge *f* **von Kegelstiften** constant length of threaded end
Konstanthalten *nt* ensure constancy
Konstantklima *nt* constant climate
Konstantspannung *f* constant voltage

Konstantstrom *m* constant current
konstruieren design
Konstrukteur *m* design engineer, designer
Konstruktion *f* 1. *(Entwurf, Gestaltung, Art)* design, designing 2. *(Bauwerk)* construction 3. *(Struktur)* structure
Konstruktionsabteilung *f* engineering department, design department
konstruktionsbedingte Schweißmöglichkeit *f* construction-conditioned welding feasibility
konstruktionsbezogene Schweißsicherheit *f* construction-related welding security
Konstruktionsbüro *nt* design bureau, design office
Konstruktionsfehler *m* faulty design
Konstruktionskosten *pl* design costs
Konstruktionsmerkmal *nt* design feature
Konstruktionsprüfung *f* design verification
Konstruktionsrohr *nt* structural tube
Konstruktionsstückliste *f* design parts list
Konstruktionsunterlagen *pl* design documents, documentation, design specifications
Konstruktionsvorgaben *pl* design data
Konstruktionszeichnung *f* engineering drawing, design drawing
konstruktiv begrenzt inherently limited
konstruktive Maßnahme *f* design measure
konstruktives Merkmal *nt* design feature
Kunststoffgleiter *m* plastic glider
Kontakt *m* contact, connection
Kontaktfläche *f* contact surface
Kontaktgabe *f* contact closure
Kontaktkorrosion *f* contact corrosion
Kontaktlänge *f* contact length
kontaktlos contactless, contact-free, on a non-contact basis
Kontaktplan (KOP) *m* ladder diagram (LD), relay ladder diagram

Kontaktplan *m* contact scheme (or plan)
Kontaktring *m* slip ring
Kontaktschalter *m* touch-sensitive switch
Kontaktsstrom *m* *(Logistik)* contact flow
Kontaktstärke *f* contact intensity
Kontaktsteifigkeit *f* contact stiffness
Kontaktthermometer *nt* contact thermometer
Kontaktzone *f* contact zone
Kontaminationsfleck *m* contamination spot
Kontaminationslösung *f* contamination solution
Kontaminationsmittel *nt* contamination agent
Kontenplan *m* account plan
Kontermutter *f* jam nut, lock nut
Kontierung *f* allocation of accounts
Kontingenztafel *f* contingency table
kontinuierlich continuous
kontinuierliche Zufallsvariable *f* continuous random variable (or variate)
kontinuierlicher Funktionsplan *m* continuous function chart
kontinuierlicher Tintenstrahlcodierer *m* continuous stream ink jet coder
Kontrast *m* contrast
Kontrastminderung *f* contrast reduction
kontrastreiche Wiedergabe *f* *(z. B. e. Lichtpausschicht)* high contrast reproduction
Kontrollbereich *m* monitoring area
Kontrollbuchung *f* control booking
Kontrolle *f* check(ing), control, inspection, monitoring, verification
Kontrollhilfsmittel *nt* checking aid
kontrollieren check, control, inspect, monitor
kontrollierender Anlauf *m* controlled acceleration
Kontrollkartentechnik *f* control card technique
Kontrollkörper *m* reference block
Kontrolllampe *f* control light, telltale light, indicating light

Kontrollmessung *f* control measurement
Kontrollprobe *f* control sample
Kontrollprüfung *f* control (or check) test
Kontrollpunkt *m* checking point
Kontrollrechnung *f* calculation check, verifying calculation
Kontrollschutzeinrichtung *f* control guard
Kontrollstation *f* control station
Kontrollverlust *m* loss of control
Kontrollvorgang *m* checking operation, control process
Kontrollwaage *f* checkweigher
Kontrollzeit *f* control period
Kontrollmittel *nt* inspection facility
Kontur *f* contour, plan view outline, profile, outline
Konturbohren *nt* contour boring
Konturfehler *m* profile deviation
Konturfräsen *nt* *(asymmetrisches ~)* asymmetric contour milling
Konturkontrolle *f* profile check(ing), profile gauge
konturnahe Bearbeitung *f* near-net-shape-technology
Konturzugprogrammierung *f* contour segment programming
Konus *m* cone, taper
Konuseinsatz *m* taper adapter
Konuskugellager *nt* cone bearing
Konuskupplung *f* conical clutch
Konuspenetration *f* cone penetration
Konvektion *f* convection
Konvektionsheizgerät *nt* convection type heating appliance
Konvektionsheizgerät *nt* **mit erzwungener Konvektion** convection type heater with fan
Konvektionsheizgerät *nt* **mit natürlicher Konvektion** convection type heater without fan
Konvektionsheizung *f* convection type heating
konvektive Wärmeabgabe *f* convective dissipation of heat
Konventionalstrafe *f* penalty for breach of contact
konvergent *f* converging, convergent

Konvergenz *f* convergence
Konvergenzverhältnis *nt* convergence ratio, angular magnification
Konvexfräser *m* convex cutter
Konvexlehre *f* convex profile gauge
Konzentration *f* concentration
Konzentrationsgrad *m* degree of concentration
Konzentrationsüberspannung *f* concentration overvoltage
Konzentrationswiderstand *m* concentration resistance
konzentrisch concentric
Konzept *nt* concept, design
konzipieren design
Koordinate *f* coordinate
Koordinatenachse *f* axis of coordinates
Koordinatenbemaßung *f* co-ordinate dimensioning
Koordinatenbohr- und -fräswerk *nt* jig boring mill
Koordinatenbohrmaschine *f* coordinate boring and drilling machine, coordinate jig boring machine, jig borer
Koordinateneinstellung *f* coordinate setting
Koordinatenführung *f* coordinate guidance
Koordinatengeber *m* pointing device
Koordinatenmessgerät *nt* co-ordinates measuring apparatus
Koordinatenmesstechnik *f* coordinate metrology
Koordinatenpositionierung *f* coordinate positioning
Koordinatenpunkt *m* point of coordinates
Koordinatensystem *nt* coordinate system
Koordinatentisch *m* coordinate table
Koordinatentransformation *f* coordinate transformation
Koordinatentransformation *f* coordinate transformation
Koordinatenwerte *mpl* coordinates
Koordination "Fahren" *f* driving coordinator
Koordination *f* coordination
Koordinationsbohren *nt* coordinate boring

koordinieren coordinate
Kopalkleber *m* copal solution adhesive
Kopf *m* **1.** *(allg.)* head, upper end, top layer, front **2.** *(Text)* title
Kopfanstauchen *nt* **im Gesenk** die heading
Kopfbolzen *m* shear connector
Kopfdickengrenze *f* tooth thickness limit
Kopfdrehmaschine *f* facing lathe
Kopfdrehung *f* head turn
Kopfeckpunkt *m* *(e. Ritzels)* corner point
Kopfentlade-Abhebe-Depalettierer *m* high level lift-off depalletizer
Kopfentladedepalettierer *m* high level depalletizer
Kopfevolvente *f* tip involute
Kopffläche *f* *(e. Zahnes)* tip surface, crest
Kopfflanke *f* tooth face, addendum flank
Kopfflankenlinie *f* tip tooth trace
Kopffreiheit *f* head room
Kopfguss *m* head casting
Kopfhalterung *f* head mounting
Kopfhöhe *f* addendum (gear)
Kopfhöhenänderung *f* addendum alteration
Kopfkante *f* tooth tip
Kopfkantenbruch *m* tooth tip chamfer
Kopfkegel *m* tip cone
Kopfkegelspitze *f* tip cone apex
Kopfkegelwinkel *m* tip angle
Kopfkreis *m* tip circle
Kopfkreisabmaß *nt* deviation of tip circle
Kopfkreisdurchmesser *m* tip circle diameter, tip diameter
Kopfkreisdurchmesserabmaß *nt* tip diameter deviation
Kopfkreisradius *m* tip circle radius
Kopfkürzung *f* tip easing
Kopflade-Abhebe-Palettierer *m* high level lift-off palletizer
Kopfladepalettierer *m* high level palletizer
Kopfleiste *f* column heading panel
Kopflinie *f* tip line
Kopfloch *nt* head access hole
Kopfmantelfläche *f* tip surface
Kopfmeißel *m* end-cut tool, end-cut single point tool, finishing tool (or cutter)
Kopfnutzkreis *m* usable tip circle
Kopfnutzkreis-Durchmesser *m* **am Ritzel** usable tip diameter on pinion
Kopframpe *f* front ramp
Kopfrücknahme *f* tip relief
Kopfschlagzähigkeit *f* **1.** *(allg.)* head soundness **2.** *(von Schrauben)* head impact toughness
Kopfschraube *f* cap screw
Kopfspiel *nt* *(UK)* crest clearance, *(US)* clearance, bottom clearance
Kopfspielverkleinerung *f* bottom clearance reduction
Kopfstation *f* dead-end station, stub-end station
Kopftragen tip contact
Kopfwicklung *f* top wrap
Kopfwinkel *m* addendum angle
Kopfzeile *f* title line
Kopie *f* replica
Kopier- und Gesenkfräser *m* copy and die milling cutter
Kopierwaagerechtstoßmaschine *f* copying shaper
Kopierarbeit *f* reproduction
Kopierautomat *m* automatic copier
Kopierdrehautomat *m* automatic copying lathe
Kopierdreheinrichtung *f* copy-turning attachment
kopierdrehen copy-turn, copy
Kopierdrehen *nt* contour turning, copy turning
Kopierdrehmaschine *f* *(US)* duplicating lathe, *(UK)* copying turning lathe, copying lathe, automatic copying lathe
Kopiereinrichtung *f* copying attachment, duplicating attachment, duplicator
Kopiereinrichtung *f:* **fühlergesteuerte** ~ tracer-controlled copying attachment
kopieren 1. *(allg.)* *(UK)* copy, copy-turn, *(US)* trace, reproduce **2.** *(zweidimensional)* profile, contour **3.** *(dreidimensional)* duplicate

kopierfräsen 1. *(allg.)* copy-mill **2.** *(formfräsen)* contour mill, profile mill **3.** *(mit Fühlersteuerung)* tracer mill
Kopierfräsmaschine *f* copy (or profile) milling machine, profiler, contour (or form) milling machine
Kopierfühler *m* copying tracer
Kopierhobelmaschine *f* copy-planer, contour planer
kopierhobeln copy-plane
Kopierkarte *f* copy card
Kopierlineal *nt* form plate, guide plate, master plate, template
Kopiermaschine *f* contouring machine, duplicating machine, copying mill
Kopiermeißel *m* copying tool
Kopierrolle *f* guide roller
Kopierschablone *f* template, master template, templet
Kopierschiene *f* form plate, guide plate, template
Kopierschienenhalter *m* guide bracket, form plate holder
Kopierschleifen *nt* copy grinding
Kopierschlitten *m* copying slide
Kopiersteuerung *f* tracer control
Kopierstift *m* guide pin, tracer point, tracer pin
Kopiertaster *m* copying tracer
Kopiervorrichtung *f* copying attachment (or equipment or device)
Kopiervorschubbewegung *f* copying feed motion
Kopierwerk *nt* copying attachment, copier unit
Kupolofen *m* cupola furnace
Koppel *f* coupler, connecting rod
Koppelgetriebe *nt* coupler mechanism, linkage
Koppelkurve *f* coupler curve, cam coupler
Koppelkurvengetriebe *nt* cam coupler mechanism
koppeln connect, couple, link
Koppelpunkt *m* coupler point
Koppelung *f* head mounting, coupling
Kopplung *f* coupling, linkage, linking
Kopplungsstörung *f* link fault
Kopplungssystem *nt* coupling system

Korbbandsiebmaschine *f* basket band screening machine
Korbmutter *f* bow nut
Kordel *f* cord
Kordelmutter *f* knurled nut
Kordeln *nt* diamond-shaped knurling, diamond knurling
kordiert diamond-knurled
Korn *nt* grain
Kornanteil *m* grain proportion
Kornausbruch *m* grain eruption
Körner *m* centre punch, punch mark
Körnerleim *m* granular glue
Körnermarke *f* punch mark
Körnerschraube *f* *(für Uhren)* balance screw
Körnerspitze *f* **1.** *(allg.)* *(UK)* lathe centre, *(US)* machine tool center, turning centre, centre, work centre, tailstock centre **2.** *(halbe ~)* semi-pointed centre **3.** *(umlaufende ~)* live centre
Korngefüge *nt* grain structure
Korngemenge *nt* granule mixture
korngrenzennaher Bereich *m* area near grain boundaries
Korngrenzenriss *m* intercrystalline crack
Korngröße *f* particle size, grit size
Korngrößenanalyse *f* particle size analysis
Korngrößenverteilung *f* particle size distribution
Korngruppe *f* particle size group
körnig gritty
Körnigkeit *f* granularity
Kornklasse *f* particle category
Kornlot *nt* filler metal in grain form, granular solder
Korntyp *m* type of grain
Körnung *f* grain size
Körnungsanteil *m* grading proportion
Körnungspunkt *m* punch mark
Kornverteilung *f* particle distribution
Kornzahl *f* grain count
Kornzusammensetzung *f* granulometric composition
Körper *m* body
Körperanstrengung *f* (physical) effort
Körperdrehung *f* body turn
Körperhaltung *f* posture

Körperkante *f* edge of the object
körperlich physical
Körperschall *m* structure-borne sound
Körperschallmessung *f* structure-borne sound testing
Körperschallschutz *m* protection against structure-borne noise
Körperschutz *m* bodily protection
Körperverletzung *f* bodily injury
Korrektur *f* correction
Korrekturfaktor *m* correction factor
Korrekturmeldung *f* correction message
Korrekturverantwortlicher *m* person responsible for correction
Korrekturwerte *mpl* correction values
Korrelation *f* correlation
Korrelationskoeffizient *m* coefficient of correlation
Korridor *m* corridor
korrigieren correct
korrodieren corrode
Korrosion *f* **durch unterschiedliche Belüftung** corrosion due to differential aeration
Korrosion *f* corrosion
Korrosion *f* **unter Ablagerungen** corrosion under deposits
Korrosionsbeanspruchung *f* exposure to corrosion
korrosionsbeständig corrosion resistant
Korrosionsschutzöl *nt* corrosion preventive oil
Korrosionseinfluss *m* corrosive action
Korrosionsermüdung *f* corrosion fatigue
korrosionsfest corrosion-resistant
korrosionsfördernd corrosion promoting
korrosionsgefährdet subject to the risk of corrosion
korrosionsgefährdete Lötstelle *f* soldered joint endangered by corrosion
Korrosionsgefährdung *f* corrosion hazard
Korrosionsgrad *m* corrosion category
korrosionshindernd corrosion-preventive
Korrosionsprüfung *f* corrosion test

Korrosionsschutzanlage *f* corrosion protective system
Korrosionsschutzarbeit *f* corrosion protection work
Korrosionsschutzauskleidung *f* anti-corrosion lining
Korrosionsschutzbeschichtungen *fpl* anti-corrosion coatings, protection provided by organic or inorganic coatings
Korrosionsschutzeigenschaft *f* corrosion-preventing property
korrosionsschutzgerechte Gestaltung *f* correct design for corrosion protection
Korrosionsschutzmaßnahme *f* corrosion protection measure
Korrosionsschutzmittel *nt* corrosion protection preparation
Korrosionsschutzöl *nt* corrosion inhibiting oil
Korrosionsschutzprüfung *f* anti-rust test
Korrosionsschutzsystem *nt* corrosion protection system
Korrosionsschutzüberzüge *mpl* protection provided by metallic coatings
Korrosionsschutzumhüllung *f* corrosion coating
Korrosionsschutzverhalten *nt* corrosion-preventing behaviour
Korrosionsschutzwachs *nt* corrosion inhibiting wax
Korrosionsschutzwirkung *f* corrosion protecting action
Korrosionsschutzzusatz *m* corrosion-preventing additive
Korrosionsspuren *fpl* traces of corrosion
Korrosionsstimulator *m* substance favouring corrosion
Korrosionsunempfindlichkeit *f* corrosion immunity
Korrosionsuntersuchung *f* corrosion test
korrosionsverhindernde Eigenschaft *f* corrosion preventing property
Korrosionsverschleiß *m* corrosive wear
korrosives Mittel *nt* corrosive medium

Korrosivität *f* corrosivity
Korrekturwert *m* correction value
Korund *m* corundum
Kosten *pl* cost(s)
Kosten senken reduce costs, cut expenses
Kostenart *f* kind of costs, costs type, costs sort
Kostenaufwand *m* expense
kostenbestimmte Stichprobe *f* cost-determined sample
Kostendruck *m* cost pressure, upward pressure on costs
Kostenkennzahl *f* cost indicator
Kostenmanagement *nt* cost management
Kosten-Nutzen-Analyse *f* cost-benefit analysis
Kosten-Nutzen-Verhältnis *nt* cost-benefit ratio
Kostenoptimierung *f* cost optimization
Kostenplanung *f* cost planning
Kostenrahmen *m* budget, cost framework
Kostenrechnung *f* cost accounting
kostenrelevant relevant to costs
Kostenschätzung *f* cost estimate
Kostensenkung *f* cost reduction, cutting expenses
Kostenstelle *f* cost centre
Kostenstellenbelieferung *f* cost centre delivery
Kostenvoranschlag *m* estimation, tender
Kovarianz *f* covariance
K-Punkt *m* c-point
Krackbeginn *m* start of cracking
Kraft *f* 1. *(allg.)* force, stamina, power 2. *(mechanische ~)* mechanical force
Kraft- und Arbeitsbedarf *m* strength and requires, need of power and work
Kraftabfall *m* drop in force
Kraftangriffslinie *f* load application line
Kraftangriffspunkt *m* point of application of the force, point of load incidence
Kraftangriffswinkel *m* angle of application of force
Kraftanstieg *m* increase in force

Kraftanzeige *f* load indication
Kraftanzeigebereich *m* load indication range
Kraftaufnehmer *m* load sensor
Kraftbedarf *m* need of force
Kraftbegrenzung *f* limitation of forces
Kraftberechnung *f* force calculation
kraftbetätigt power-operated
kraftbetrieben motor-driven, powered, power-driven, power-operated, self-propelled
kraftbewegtes Teil *nt* powered part
Kraft-Durchbiegungskurve *f* load-deflection curve
Kräfte *fpl* forces
Krafteinfluss *m* effect of forces
Krafteinleitung *f* transmission of force
Krafteinteilung *f* force distribution
Kräfteplan *m* force diagram
Krafterzeugungseinrichtung *f* force generating equipment
Kraftfluss *m* distribution of forces
Kraftgröße *f* force value
Kraftkomponente *f* force component
Kraftkonstanthalter *m* load stabilizer
Kraft-Längenänderungskurve *f* load-elongation curve
kraftlose Zeitspanne *f* forceless interval
Kraftmanipulator *m* power manipulator
Kraftmaschine *f* prime mover, engine
Kraftmessbereich *m* load measuring range
Kraftmessdose *f* load cell
Kraftmesseinrichtung *f* load measuring equipment
Kraftmessfehler *m* load measurement error
Kraftmessung *f* 1. *(allg.)* load measurement, force measurement 2. *(indirekte ~)* indirect force measurement
Kraftmesszelle *f* load cell
Kraftmutter *f* load-bearing nut
Kraftpfeil *m* force arrow
Kraftruhezeit *f* force off-time
Kraftsackpapier *nt* craft paper
Kraftschalter *m* energy switch
Kraftschluss *m* adhesion, friction free, friction grip, frictional connection, posi-

tive connection
Kraftschlussbeiwert *m* adhesion coefficient, friction force coefficient, friction grip coefficient
Kraftschlussgesetz *nt* law of friction forces
kraftschlüssig force-closed, having friction grip, positive, actuated by adhesion, tensionally locked
kraftschlüssig verbinden tie positively
kraftschlüssige Kräfte *fpl* frictional rubbing forces
kraftschlüssiger Antrieb *m* non-positive drive
kraftschlüssiges Sicherungselement *nt* force-locked (or friction-locked) retaining element
kraftschlüssiges Verbindungselement *nt* force-locked (or friction-locked) connecting element, force-locked fastener
Kraftspannfutter *nt* power operated chuck
Kraft-Spritzgießen *nt* power injection moulding (PIM)
Kraftstoff *m* fuel
Kraftstoffanlage *f* fuel supply system
Kraftstoffbehälter *m* fuel container, fuel tank
Kraftstoffbeständigkeit *f* resistance to fuel
Kraftstoffleckage *f* fuel leakage
Kraftstoffsystem *nt* fuel system
Kraftstoffzuleitung *f* fuel source
kraftunterstützt power-assisted, powered
Kraftverbindung *f* load-bearing connection
Kraftverbrauch *m* power consumption
Kraft-Verformungs-Diagramm *nt* load-deformation diagram
Kraft-Verformungs-Kurve *f* load-deformation curve
Kraftverschraubung *f* (als Vorgang) screwing with the aid of a power wrench
Kraftverstärkung *f* force intensification
Kraftverteilung *f* power distribution
Kraft-Weg-Diagramm *nt* load-displacement diagram

Kraftwerk *nt* power station
Kraftwirkung *f* force component (acting upon a cutting tool), dynamic effect
Kraft-Zeit-Diagramm *nt* load-time diagram
Kraftzerlegung *f* analysis of forces
Kraftzunahmegeschwindigkeit *f* rate of increase in the load
Kragarm *m* arm, cantilever, gibbet, jib
Kragarmregal *nt* cantilever shelving, cantilever rack(ing)
Kragenziehen *nt* collaring holes by drawing
Krallenspannung *f* claw clamping
Kran *m* crane
Kranarm *m* crane jib, jib type crane
Kranausleger *m* (crane) jib
Kranbahn *f* crane way
Kranbrücke *f* crane bridge
Kranfahren *nt* crane driving
Krangießpfanne *f* cradle ladle
Krankatze *f* crane trolley
Kranportal *nt* gantry
Kranzspannfutter *nt* geared scroll chuck
kraterartiger Belag *m* crater-like coating, pitted coating
kraterförmige Vertiefung *f* crater-shaped pit
kraterfreie Ausführung *f* crater-free finish
Kraterüberstand *m* crater overhang
kratzen mar, scratch, scrape
Kratzer *m* mar, scratch
Kreditkonditionen *fpl* credit terms
Kreditorenschnittstelle *f* accounts payable interface
Kreide *f* chalk
Kreidungsgrad *m* degree of chalking
Kreis *m* 1. *(geom.)* circle 2. *(Kreislauf)* loop
Kreisbahn *f* circular path
Kreisbeschleuniger *m* cyclical accelerator
Kreisbewegung *f* gyration
Kreisbild *nt* loop display
Kreisblende *f* circular aperture
Kreisbogen *m* circular arc
kreisbogenförmig arc shaped
kreisbogenförmige Teilungsgrundli-

nie *f* circular arc base line
kreisbogenförmiger Überhang *m* rounded transition
Kreisbogenverzahnung *f* circular arc gear teeth
Kreisdiagramm *nt* circle diagram, pie chart, wheel diagram
kreisen circulate
kreisend vortical
kreisende Bewegung *f* gyratory motion
kreisende Schnittbewegung *f* rotary cutting motion
Kreisevolvente *f* involute to a circle
Kreisförderer *m* 1. *(allg.)* overhead conveyor, circular conveyor, endless conveyor 2. *(an Decke)* overhead (monorail chain) conveyor 3. *(mit Gehängen)* circular conveyor with hangers
Kreisform *f* circular form
kreisförmig circular
Kreisinterpolation *f* circular interpolation
Kreiskegel *m* circular cone
Kreiskolben *m* rotary piston
Kreiskolbenpumpe *f* rotary piston pump
Kreislauf *m* cycle, circuit, loop
Kreislaufwasser *nt* circulation water
Kreiselektrode *f* circular electrode
Kreismesserkopf *m* rotary-formed milling cutter
Kreismethode *f* circle method
Kreismittelpunkt *m* centre of the circle
Kreispunktführung *f* circular point guidance
Kreisradius *m* radius of circle
Kreisringstück *nt* annular segment
kreisrund circular
Kreissäge *f* circular saw
Kreissägeblatt *nt* circular saw-blade
Kreissägeblattschärfschleifmaschine *f* circular saw grinder (grinding machine)
Kreissägemaschine *f* circular-sawing machine
Kreissägen *nt* circular sawing
Kreissägenautomat *m* automatic circular-sawing machine

Kreissägenschärfautomat *m* automatic circular saw sharpener
Kreisscheibenreflektor *m* circular disc-shaped reflector
Kreisschnitt *m* circular cut
Kreissegment *nt* arc
Kreisskala *f* circular graduation
Kreisstruktur *f* *(in e. binären Schaltsystem)* closed loop structure
Kreisteilungsabweichung *f* circular pitch variation
Kreisteilungsmessung *f* circular pitch measurement
Kreisumfang *m* circumference, perimeter, periphery of a circle
Kreiszylinderfläche *f* *(bei Stirnrädern)* surface of the pitch cylinder
kreiszylindrische Passflächen *fpl* fitting surfaces (pl) of cylindrical form
Kreuz *nt* cross
Kreuzarbeitsspur *f* cross-hatched pattern
Kreuzbetrieb *m* crossing mode
Kreuzbett *nt* cross-sliding column
Kreuzbettbauweise *f* cross-sliding-column type of construction
kreuzend übereinanderliegen lie crossing over each other
Kreuzfeuerbestrahlung *f* crossfire irradiation
Kreuzlibelle *f* cross-level
Kreuzlochlehre *f* star gauge
Kreuzlochmutter *f* round nut with set pin hole inside
Kreuzmeißel *m* cape chisel
Kreuznaht *f* cruciform joint (or weld), cross-over joint
Kreuzrollenlager *nt* cross roller bearing, cross roller way
Kreuzrollentisch *m* cross roller table, cross roller positioning table
Kreuzschieber *m* saddle
Kreuzschliff *m* cross hatch
Kreuzschliffwinkel *m* cross hatch angle
Kreuzschlitten *m* compound slide rest, compound-rest slide
Kreuzschlitzlehre *f* recess gauge
Kreuzschlitzmaß *nt* recess dimension
Kreuzschlitzschraube *f* recessed head screw

Kreuzschubkurbel *f* scotch-yoke mechanism
Kreuzspur *f* cross-hatched finish
Kreuzsteckschlüssel *m* four-way socket wrench
Kreuzsupport *m* compound slide rest
kreuzsymmetrischer Aufbau *m* symmetrical cross construction
Kreuzung *f* crossing, intersection
Kreuzungsebene *f (e. Radpaares)* midplane
Kreuzungslinie *f (e. Radpaares)* crossing line
Kreuzungspunkt *m* crossing point, point of intersection
Kreuzungsstelle *f* crossing point
Kreuzungswinkel *m* angle of intersection, crossing angle
Kreuzverbindung *f* cross construction
Kreuzverbindungsstutzen *m* cross adapter (or fitting)
kreuzverzahnter Fräser *m* alternate helical tooth cutter, alternate tooth milling cutter
kreuzverzahnter Scheibenfräser *m* staggered tooth side mill
kreuzverzahnter T-Nutenfräser *m* alternate angle staggered tooth type teeslot cutter
kreuzverzahnter Walzenfräser *m* alternate gash plain mill
Kreuzverzahnung *f* staggered arrangement (of teeth), staggered teeth, staggered tooth system
kreuzweise Schichtung *f* cross-layering
Kreuzwinkel *m* T-square
Kreuzzahn-Scheibenfräser *m* alternate angle side and face cutter
Kreuzzylinderform *f* circular-cylindrical form
kriechen crawl, creep
Kriechgang *m* creep feed, inching, jogging
Kriechgeschwindigkeit *f* creep speed, inching
Kriechmodul *nt* apparent modulus
Kriechnachgiebigkeit *f* creep yield
Kriechstrecke *f* creepage distance
Kriechstrecke *f* leakage path

kriechstromsicher resistant to leakage currents
Kriechversuch *m* creep test
Kriechweg *m* creepage distance
Kriechwegbildung *f* tracking
Kritikalitätsunfall *m* design-basis accident
kritisch critical
kritischer Bereich *m* critical region
kritischer Wert *m* critical value
kritischer Wiederholdifferenzbetrag *m* repeatability critical difference
Krone *f (e. Kronenmutter)* castellated portion
Kronenmutter *f* **1.** *(allg.)* castel nut, castle nut **2.** *(niedrige Form)* thin castle nut
Kronenrad *nt* crown wheel
Kronrevolver *m* crown turret
kröpfen double-bend, crank, offset
Kröpfung *f* offset, gap
krumm curved, crooked, bent
krümmen bend, buckle, curve, warp
Krümmung *f* bow, bend, curvature
Krümmungshalbmesser *m* radius of curvature
Krümmungskreis *m* circle of curvature
Krümmungsradius *m* radius of curvature
K-Stegnaht *f* **mit Doppelkehlnaht** double-bevel weld with root face welded with double fillet weld
Kübel *m* tub
Kubelscheibe *f* disc crank
Kubelzapfen *m* crank pin
kubisch cubic
Kubus *m* cube
Kufe *f* pallet bearer, pallet foot, foot plate, board, runner, skid
Kufenkontrolle *f* bearer check(ing), board check(ing), skid check(ing)
Kufenunterbau *m* skid mounting
Kugel *f* sphere, pellet, globule, ball
Kugelbefestigung *f* **1.** *(als Arbeitsvorgang)* spherical lock fixing **2.** *(e. Lehre)* spherical lock
Kugelbemaßung *f* dimensioning of a sphere
Kugelbuchsenverschraubung *f* ball and nipple connection

Kugeldrehen *nt* ball turning, spherical turning
Kugeldrehmaschine *f* ball turning lathe
Kugeldruckversuch *m* ball compression test
Kugeleindrückverfahren *nt* steel ball impression method
Kugelevolventenverzahnung *f* spherical involute tooth system
Kugelfallversuch *m* ball drop test, falling ball test
kugelförmig ball-shaped, spherical, globular
kugelförmiger Flächenabschnitt *m* spherical surface section
Kugelfräsen *nt* cherrying
Kugelfräser *m* cherry
Kugelgelenk *nt* ball joint
kugelgestrahlte Tellerfeder *f* shot-peened disc spring
Kugelgraphit *nt* spherical graphite
kugelig spherical
kugelig gelagert spherical seated
kugelige Fläche *f* spherical surface
kugelige Senkung *f* spherical depression
Kugellager *nt* ball bearing
Kugellagerung *f* ball bearings
Kugellenkrolle *f* inclined axle castor
Kugelmessfläche *f* spherical measurement surface
Kugelmuffe *f* cupped socket
Kugelpfanne *f* ball cup
Kugel-Schmiernippel *m* ball type lubricating nipple
Kugelschweißmuffe *f* spherical welded socket
Kugelschwimmerventil *nt* spherical float valve
Kugeltaster *m* thread calliper with ball points
Kugeltisch *m* ball bearing table, ball transfer (table)
Kugelübermaß *nt* ball oversize
Kugelumlaufspindel *f* ball screw
Kugelventil *nt* globe valve
Kugelverschluss *m* ball catch, ball fastener, ball stopper, sphere catch
Kugelziehviskosimeter *nt* ball-draw viscosimeter
Kühl-, Spül-, Schiermittel (KSSM) *nt* coolant-lubricant-detergent, washing-up liquid lubricate means
Kühleinheit *f* refrigeration unit
Kühleinrichtung *f* cooling equipment
kühlen cool, refrigerate, freeze
Kühlfalle *f* cooling trap
Kühlflüssigkeit *f* cooling liquid, coolant
Kühlhaus *nt* cold store, refrigerated warehouse, refrigerating storage house, refrigerator, freezer
Kühllast *f* cooling load
Kühlleistung *f* cooling capacity
Kühlmittel *nt* 1. *(allg.)* cutting solution, coolant, cooling liquid (or fluid or agent) 2. *(für Ölnebelkühlung)* mist coolant
Kühlmittelabführung *f* coolant removing
Kühlmittelfluss *m* coolant flow
Kühlmittelkreislauf *m* coolant circuit
Kühlmittelzuführung *f* coolant supply
Kühlraum *m* cold storage room, coolers, freezer
Kühlrohrablauf *m* delivery end of the cooling tube
Kühlrohreinlauf *m* feed end of the cooling tube
Kühlschmier-Emulsion *f* cooling lubricant emulsion
Kühlschmierstoff *m* cooling lubricant
Kühlschmierung *f* cooling lubrication
Kühlstrecke *f* cooling section
Kühlung *f* cooling, cooling system, refrigeration
Kühlungsnut *f* cooling slot
Kühlvorgang *m* cooling proceedings
Kühlzeit *f* cooling period
Kulisse *f* crank, slotted arm, quadrant, background
Kulissenantrieb *m* link drive
Kulissenstange *f* link rod
Kulissenstein *m* sliding block
Kümpeln *nt* dishing, coning
Kunde *m* client, customer
Kundenauftrag *m* customer's order placement, client order
Kundenbelieferung *f* customer supply
Kundenbeziehungsmanagement *nt* customer relationship management

(CRM)
Kundendaten *pl* client data
Kundenerwartung *f* customer expectation
kundenorientiert customer-oriented
Kundenorientierung *f* customer orientation
Kundenservice *m* customer service
kundenspezifisch customer specific
Kundenterminsteuerung *f* customer schedule control
Kundenwunsch *m* customer's need, customer's requirements
Kundenzufriedenheit *f* customer satisfaction
Kunstgummi-Leitung *f* synthetic rubber pipe
Kunstharz *nt* synthetic resin
Kunstharzasbestbodenbelag *m* resin-bonded asbestos floor covering
Kunstharzasbestpatte *f* synthetic resin-asbestos laminated wood
kunstharzausgerüstetes Gewebe *nt* fabric finished with synthetic resin
Kunstharzbindung *f* resin bond
Kunstharzpressholzerzeugnis *nt* resin-bonded densified wood lamination
Kunstharzschaum *m* expanded synthetic resin
Kunstkautschukkitt *m* synthetic rubber putty
Kunstkautschuklösung *f* synthetic rubber solution
Kunstkorund *nt* fused alumina, aluminous abrasive
künstlich artificial
künstliche Alterung *f* accelerated ageing
künstliche Intelligenz *f* artificial intelligence (AI)
Kunststoff *m* plastic(s)
Kunststoffband *nt* plastic strap, plastic tape, non-metallic strapping
Kunststoffbandage *f* plastic banding
Kunststoffbehälter *m* plastic container
kunststoffbeschichtet plastics coated, plastics faced
Kunststoffblister *m* plastic blister
Kunststoffdispersion *f* plastics dispersion

Kunststoffdispersionsfarbe *f* plastics dispersion paint
Kunststoffdränrohr *nt* plastics drain pipe
Kunststoff-Druckrohrleitung *f* plastics pressurized tubing
Kunststoffe *mpl* plastics
Kunststoffelastomerfolie *f* plastics elastomer film
Kunststofferzeugnis *nt* plastics product
Kunststofffolie *f* plastic film, foil or sheeting
Kunststofffolienverbund *m* plastics laminate
Kunststoffformmasse *f* plastics moulding material
Kunststoffformstoff *m* plastics moulded material
Kunststoffformteil *nt* plastics moulding
Kunststoffgalvanisierung *f* electroplating of plastics
Kunststoffgebiet *nt* plastics field
Kunststoffhaube *f* plastic cover
Kunststoffhilfsstoff *m* plastics auxiliary
Kunststoffisolierband *nt* plastics insulating tape
Kunststoffkasten *m* plastic box
Kunststofflatex *nt* polymer latex
Kunststofflatexfarbe *f* synthetic latex paint
Kunststoffleitung *f* plastics pipe
Kunststoffmaschine *f* plastics machine
Kunststoffpackband *nt* plastic packing
Kunststoffpalette *f* plastic pallet
Kunststoffprüfung *f* testing of plastics
Kunststoffrad *nt* solid plastic wheel, plastics gear
Kunststoffring *m* plastic ring
Kunststoffringsammelpackmaschine *f* plastic ringing machine
Kunststoffrohr *nt* plastic tube (or tubing)
Kunststoffrohrleitung *f* plastics pipeline
Kunststoffschale *f* plastic shape
Kunststoffstreifen *m* plastic strip
Kunststoffstreifen *m* plastic strip

Kunststofftafel *f* plastic sheet
Kunststofftechnik *f* plastics engineering
Kunststoffträgerfolie *f* plastic backing film
Kunststoffwanne *f* plastic tray, plastic tub
Küpenfärbung *f* vat dyeing
Kupfer *nt* copper
Kupfergleichwert *m* copper filter equivalent
Kupferguss *m* copper cast iron
Kupferhüttenschlacke *f* copper smelting slag
kupferkaschierter Schichtpressstoff *m* copper-laminated plastics
Kupferdampflaser *m* copper vapour laser
Kupferknetlegierung *f* wrought copper alloy
Kupferstreifenprüfung *f* copper strip test
Kupferverlust *m* copper loss
Kupferzink *nt* copper zinc
Kupolofenausfütterung *f* cupola lining
Kupolofengebläse *nt* cupola blower
Kupolofenschmelzen *nt* cupola melting
Kuppe *f* pinhead projection, protuberance
kuppeln couple, clutch, engage, connect
Kuppelrad *nt* clutch gear
Kuppen *nt* rounding
Kuppendrehwerkzeug *nt* ending tool
Kupplung *f* coupling, clutch
Kupplungen *fpl* coupling means
Kupplungsschaltorgan *nt* clutch operating device
Kupplungsgehäuse *nt* clutch enclosure
Kupplungsgetriebe *nt* clutch drive
Kupplungshöhe *f* coupling height
Kupplungsreibpartner *m* friction part (of the clutch)
Kupplungsscheibe *f* clutch band plate
Kurbel *f* crank, rotating handle, rotating link
Kurbelbetrieb *m* crank mechanism

kurbelbetriebene Hydraulikpumpe *f* rotating handle hydraulic pump
Kurbelgetriebe *nt* crank mechanism
kurbeln turn, wind, revolve around
Kurbelpresse *f* crank press
Kurbelschleife *f* slider-crank mechanism
Kurbelschwinge *f* crank arm, slotted arm, oscillating arm, rocker arm
Kurbelstange *f* connecting rod
Kurbelwange *f* crank cheek
Kurbelwelle *f* crankshaft
Kurbelwellendrehautomat *m* automatic crankshaft lathe
Kurbelwellendrehmaschine *f* crankshaft turning lathe
Kurbelwellenläppmaschine *f* crankshaft lapping machine
Kurbelwellenschleifmaschine *f* crankshaft grinding machine
Kurbelzapfen *m* wrist
Kurtosis *f* curtosis
Kurve *f* 1. *(allg.)* curve 2. *(Steuerung, Vorschub)* cam 3. *(Diagramm)* graph 4. *(Straße)* turn 5. *(Bogen)* bend
Kurven- und Profilfräsmaschine *f* cam and profile miller
Kurvenautomat *m* cam-controlled automatic
Kurvenbild *nt* curve display
Kurvenfahrt *f* cornering, turning
kurvenförmige Schneide *f* curved cutting edge
Kurvenfräseinrichtung *f* cam milling attachment
Kurvenfräsen *nt* cam milling
Kurvenfräsmaschine *f* cam miller
Kurvenführungsgetriebe *nt* curved guide mechanism
kurvengängig curve-going
kurvengesteuert cam-controlled
Kurvengetriebe *nt* cam trail, cam mechanism
Kurvenhebel *m* cam lever
Kurvenhobeleinrichtung *f* radius-planing attachment
Kurvenkurbelgetriebe *nt* cam-crank mechanism
Kurvenparameter *m* curve parameter
Kurvenrolle *f* cam follower roll, cam

roller
Kurvenroller *m* cam-roller
Kurvenscheibe *f* cam, cam disk
Kurvenschieber *m* sliding cam plate
Kurvenschleifeinrichtung *f* cam-grinding attachment
Kurvenschnitt *m* curved cut
Kurventrommel *f* cam drum
Kurvenwelle *f* camshaft
Kurvenzug *m* cam contour
kurz short, brief
kurzabreißende Masse *f* non-cohesive mass
Kurzausführung *f* short type
Kurzbelastung *f* short-term loading
Kurzbeschreibung *f* brief description
Kurzbezeichnung *f* abbreviated designation
Kurzbrüchigkeit *f* short brittleness
Kurzcode *m* short code
kürzen shorten
kurzer Dorn *m* stub arbour
kurzfristig for the short-term
kurzgeschlossen short circuit
Kurzgewindefräsen *nt* plunge-cut thread milling
Kurzgewindeschleifen *nt* plunge-cut thread grinding
Kurzgewindeschleifmaschine *f* plunge-cut thread grinder
Kurzhobelmaschine *f* shaping machine
Kurzhobeln *nt* 1. *(allg.)* shaping 2. *(ebener Flächen)* flat-surface-shaping 3. *(mit Hartmetallmeißel)* carbide shaping
Kurzhobler *m* shaper
Kurzhubhonen *nt* superfinishing
kurzhubig short-stroke
kurzhubige Bewegung *f* short-stroke movement
kurzhubiger Stößel *m* short strake ram
Kurzkegel *m* short taper, steep taper
Kurzkegelspindelkopf *m* short-taper spindle nose
Kurzmitteilung *f* short message
Kurzmitteilungsdienst *m* short message service

kurzschließen bypass, short-circuit
Kurzschluss *m* short circuit
kurzschlussfest short-circuit proof
kurzschlussfrei non-short-circuiting
Kurzschlussläufer *m* short-circuit rotor, squirrel-cage rotor
Kurzschlussläufermotor *m* cage motor, squirrel-cage motor
Kurzschlussläuferring *m* cage ring, short-circuit ring, end ring
Kurzschlussmotor *m* cage motor
kurzschlusssicher short-circuit proof
Kurzschlussstrom *m* short-circuit current
Kurzspan *m* brittle chip, fragmental (or segmental) chip, short chip, finely broken chip
kurzspanend shortcutting
kurzspanender Werkstoff *m* short chip material
Kurzwelle *f* short wave
kurzwellige Anteile *mpl* short-undulation components
Kurzwelligkeit *f* short-waviness
Kurzzeichen *nt* abbreviation
Kurzzeitbetrieb *m* short-time operation
kurzzeitig 1. *(allg.)* momentary, short term 2. *(el.)* transient
Kurzzeitinnendruckbeanspruchung *f* short-time internal pressure loading
Kurzzeitinnendruckversuch *m* short-term internal pressure test
Kurzzeitkorrosionsuntersuchung *f* short-term corrosion test
Kurzzeitlagerung *f* short-term storage
Kurzzeitnahbestrahlung *f* short-duration, short distance, irradiation
Kurzzeitunterbrechung *f* momentary interruption
Kurzzeitwarmfestigkeit *f* short-time thermal resistance
Kusaschaltung *f* Kusa control
Kv-Faktor *m* amplification factor
kyrillische Zeichen *ntpl* Cyrillic letter
K-Zahl *f* kappa number

L

labil instable
Labor *nt* laboratory
Laboratoriumseinrichtung *f* laboratory equipment
Laboratoriumsgeräte *ntpl* **1.** *(allg.)* laboratory outfit **2.** *(aus Glas)* laboratory glassware
Laboratoriumsmesstechnik *f* laboratory metrology
Laboratoriumsprobe *f* laboratory sample
Laboratoriumsspindel *f* laboratory hygrometer
Laboratoriumsversuch *m* laboratory test
Laborgebäude *nt* laboratory building
Laborgerät *nt* **1.** *(allg.)* laboratory apparatus (or outfit) **2.** *(aus Glas)* laboratory glassware
Labormischwalzwerk *nt* laboratory mixing mill
Laborprüfung *f* laboratory test (or examination)
Laborstativ *nt* laboratory stand
Laborversuch *m* laboratory test
Lack *m* paint
Lackgewebeband *nt* varnished fabric type
Lackglasgewebe *nt* varnished glass fabric
Lackglasgewebeband *nt* varnished glass fabric tape
lackieren paint
Lackiererei *f* paintshop
lackiert painted
Lackkratzkerbe *f* paint clearance groove
Lackleinöl *nt* refined linseed oil
Lacksoyaöl *nt* refined soya bean oil
Lackwulst *f* bead of varnish
Ladderanordnung *f* ladder arrangement
Ladeausrüstung *f* charging equipment
Ladebühne *f* charging platform
Ladeebene *f* loading surface
Ladeeingang *m* load input

Ladeeinheit *f* load unit, unit load, loading unit
Ladeeinheitensicherung *f* unit load safe-guarding
Ladeeinheitenumsetzer *m* load unit shifter
Ladeeinrichtung *f* loading attachment, loading device
Ladefaktor *m* charge coefficient
Ladefläche *f* platform
Ladegerät *nt* charger, charging test
Ladegut *nt* load
Ladehilfsmittel *nt* load accessory, load carrier, load make-up accessory, loading aid
Ladekennlinie *f* charging characteristic
Ladekran *m* loading crane
Ladelift *m* loading lift
laden **1.** *(el.)* charge **2.** *(Maschine)* load **3.** *(EDV)* download **4.** *(schaufeln)* scoop
Laden *nt* loading, charging, scooping, down-load
Ladenetz *nt* sling (or loading) net
Ladeort *m* charging station
Ladeplattform *f* screen
Laderampe *f* loading platform, load ramp
Ladespeicher *m* load memory
Ladestelle *f* charging point, loading station
Ladestrom *m* charging current
Ladetechnik *f* charging technology
Ladevorrichtung *f* magazine feeding attachment, magazine
Ladewinde *f* cargo winch
Ladezeit *f* charging time
Ladezustand *m* state of charge, battery charge
Ladezustandskontrolle *f* battery-charge monitoring
Ladezyklus *m* charging cycle
Ladung *f* **1.** *(Güter)* load, freight, cargo, loading (machine) **2.** *(el.)* charge, charging
Ladungsaustausch *m* charge exchange

Ladungsbreite *f* load width
Ladungsdurchtritt *m* (el. chem.) charge transfer
Ladungseinheit *f* loading unit
ladungsgekoppeltes Bildwandlerelement *nt* charge-coupled device, charged couple device (CCD)
ladungsgekoppeltes Speicherelement *nt* charge-coupled device, charged couple device (CCD)
Ladungshöhe *f* load height
Ladungslänge *f* load length
Ladungssicherung *f* load safeguarding, load safeguarding material
Ladungsträger *m* load carrier
Lage *f* 1. *(Position)* position 2. *(örtlich)* location 3. *(Situation)* disposition, situation 4. *(Schicht)* layer
Lage *f* der Freifläche orientation of flank
Lage *f* der Schneide orientation of cutting edge
Lage *f* der Spanfläche orientation of face
Lage *f*: eine ~ bestimmen locate
lageabhängig position-dependent
Lageabweichung *f*: **zulässige ~** admissible position deviations
Lagebestimmung *f* location
Lageerfassung *f* position sensing
Lagefehler *m* positional error
Lagefläche *f* storage area
Lagegenauigkeit *f* positional accuracy
lagegeregelt positionally controlled
Lagehinweis *m* position reference
Lagekopplung *f* position coupling
Lagenabgabestation *f* layer deposit station
Lagenbeleimung *f* layer glue system
Lagenbildung *f* assembly in layers
Lagenbindefehler *m* lack of inter-run fusion, incomplete interpass fusion
Lagenentnahme *f* layer picking, unloading of layers, retrieval of layers
Lagenmuster *nt* layer(ing) pattern
Lagensammelstation *f* layer collecting station
Lagenschema *nt* layer(ing) pattern
Lagenstapelung *f* stacking of layers
Lagenstruktur *f* layer structure

Lagenumladung *f* layer transfer
lagenunveränderlich gelagerte Radachsen *fpl* gear axes occupying non-varying positions
lagenweise layer by layer, in layers, by layers
lagenweise Anordnung *f* arrangement in layers
Lageparameter *m* location parameter
Lagepeilung *f* positioning fixing
Lageplan *m* locating plan
Lager *nt* 1. *(Kugellager)* bearing 2. *(Ersatzteile)* depot 3. *(Bestand)* stock, store, store-room, warehouse
Lagerabdichtung *f* sealing of bearings
Lagerabgang *m* warehouse exit, warehouse outgoing
Lagerabmessung *f* dimensions of the warehouse
Lageränderung *f* storage alteration
Lageranlage *f* racking installation, warehouse system
Lageranordnung *f* storage arrangement
Lagerart *f* storage type, kind of warehouse
Lagerauffüllung *f* inventory replenishment, inventory buildup, replenishment of stocks
Lagerausbuchung *f* warehouse checkout
Lagerauslastung *f* utilization of storage capacity
Lagerautomatisierung *f* automation of inventory processes
Lagerbarkeit *f* storeability
Lagerbehälter *m* storage bin, storage container
Lagerbereich *m* storage area, warehouse area, warehouse premises
Lagerbestand *m* goods on hand, goods in stock, inventory (level), stock, warehouse inventory, warehouse on-hand quantity
Lagerbestandsaufstellung *f* inventory status report
Lagerbestandsführung *f* inventory accounting, inventory control
Lagerbewegungen *fpl* inventory movements, stock movements

Lagerblock *m* storage block
Lagerbuchführung *f* inventory accounting
Lagerbüchse *f* bearing bush
Lagerbuchung *f* storage booking
Lagerbühne *f* raised storage platform, mezzanine floor
Lagerdaten *pl* inventory data
Lagerdauer *f* period of storage
Lagerebene *f* warehouse level
Lageregler *m* positional control, position control
Lagereignungsdauer *f* shelf life
Lagereinbauten *mpl* storage installations
Lagereinbuchung *f* warehouse check-in
Lagereinheit *f* storage unit
Lagereinrichtung *f* warehouse equipment
Lagerentnahme *f* stock withdrawal, withdrawal from stock
Lagerfach *nt* storage bay, storage bin, storage compartment, storage slot
Lagerfachgruppe *f* bay ground, bin group
Lagerfachkarte *f* bin card
Lagerfachöffnung *f* storage slot, bin front
Lagerfähigkeit *f* storage lift
Lagerfehlbestand *m* stock-out, stock shortage
Lagerfläche *f (z. B. e. Rades)* bearing surface
Lagerfunktion *f* storage function
Lagergasse *f* warehouse lane
Lagergebäude *nt* storage building, storehouse
Lagergröße *f* size of the warehouse
Lagergrundfläche *f* storage surface
Lagergut *nt* stored articles
Lagerhalle *f* storage building
Lagerhaltung *f* storage, stocking, stock keeping
Lagerhaltungskosten *pl* inventory holding costs
Lagerhaltungsplanung *f* inventory scheduling
Lagerhaltungsschwankungen *fpl* inventory fluctuations

Lagerhilfsmittel *nt* storage aid means
Lagerhöhe *f* store height
Lagerhüter *m* inactive inventory item
lagerichtig in correct positional arrangement
lagerichtig anbringen locate, position
lagerichtige Darstellung *f* topographical representation
Lagerichtigkeit *f* accuracy of position
Lagerist *m* stock clerk, storeman
Lagerkasten *m* storage box
Lagerkennzahlen *fpl* storage characteristic values, inventory turnover ratios
Lagerkomponente *f* warehouse component
Lagerkonfiguration *f* warehouse configuration, warehouse layout
Lagerkoordinate *f* warehouse coordinate
Lagerkörper *m* warehouse body
Lagerleitebene *f* warehouse management level
lagerlos storage-free, stockless
lagerlose Fertigung *f* stockless production
Lagermittel *ntpl* storage means
lagern stock, store, seat, house, support
Lagerort *m* storage location
Lagerortsstamm *m* warehouse master file
Lagerperiode *f* storage period
Lagerplanung *f* materials requirements planning, inventory planning
Lagerplatz *m* storage location
Lagerplatzstamm *m* warehouse locations master file
Lagerplatzvergabe *f* storage location assignment, allocation of storage locations
Lagerplatzverwaltung *f* administration of storage locations, storage location administration
Lagerposition *f* inventory item
Lagerraum *m* store-room, warehouse, storage space
Lagerräumung *f* clearance of stocks
Lagerrechner *m* warehouse computer, warehouse host computer
Lagerregelung *f* position feedback control, position(al) control

Lagerreibwert *m* bearing friction value
Lagerschale *f* bearing bush, bearing shell
Lagersitz *m* bearing seat
Lagersitzabmessungen *fpl* bearing seat dimensions
Lagerspalte *f* warehouse column
Lagerspezifikation *f* warehouse specification
Lagerstation *f* warehouse station
Lagerstrategie *f* storage strategy
Lagerstufe *f* storage level
Lagersystem *nt* storage system
Lagertechnik *f* storage technology
Lagertemperatur *f* storage temperature
Lagerturm *m* storage tower
Lagerumschlag *m* inventory sales ratio, *(US)* momentum of sales
Lagerung *f* **1.** *(Waren)* stocking, storage, immersion **2.** *(Auflager, Kugellager)* bearing
Lagerung *f* **im freien Bund** storage in free bundles
Lagerung *f* **sperriger Güter** specialized storage, specialized storage equipment
Lagerung *f* **von Langmaterial** cantilever racking storage, long goods storage
Lagerungsart *f* storage type
Lagerungsbedingungen *fpl* storage conditions
Lagerungsdauer *f* storage duration
Lagerungsdichte *f* compactness of the packing, stocking density, storage density
Lagerungsklima *nt* storage climate
Lagerverdichtung *f* storage density
Lagerverwaltung *f* warehouse administration
Lagerverwaltungsebene *f* warehouse administration level
Lagerverwaltungsrechner *m* warehouse administration computer
Lagerverwaltungssystem *nt* warehouse administration system, storage management system
Lagervorfeld *nt* access area, front area
Lagerwanne *f* storage tray
Lagerwesen *nt* warehouse control
Lagerwirtschaft *f* inventory management
Lagerzapfen *m* (bearing) journal, trunnion, bearing spigot
Lagerzapfendurchmesser *m* bearing journal diameter, bearing spigot diameter
Lagerzugang *m* warehouse entry, inventory receipt, addition to stocks
Lagesicherung *f* locating in position
lageunabhängig independent of position, position-independent
Lageunterschied *m* difference in position
Lageveränderung *f* change of position, displacement
Lagewinkel *m* orientation angle
Lagewinkel *m* **der Freiflächenorthogonalebene** tool flank orthogonal plane orientation angle
Lagewinkel *m* **der Spanflächen-Orthogonalebene** tool face orthogonal plane, orientation angle
Lagewinkel *m* **des Spanbrechers** chip breaker orientation angle
Laie *m* unskilled person, unskilled people *pl*
LAM (Lastaufnahmemittel) *nt* LHD (load handling device)
lamellar lamellar
Lamelle *f* lamina
Lamellenbremse *f* multiple disk brake, multidisk brake
lamellenförmig laminated
Lamellengraphit *m* laminated graphite
Lamellenkupplung *f* friction-disc clutch
Lamellenriss *m* lamellar tearing
Lamellenspan *m* lamellar chip
lamellieren laminate
Laminat *nt* laminate
laminieren laminate
laminiert laminated
laminiertes Glas *nt* laminated safety glass
Laminierung *f* lamination
Lampe *f* lamp, light
Lampe *f* **für optische Meldungen** telltale lamp for visual signals
Lampen *fpl* lights, lighting

Lampenschalter *m* lamp switching
LAN *Abk* Local Area Network
Landatmosphäre *f* rural atmosphere
landschaftsgebundenes Klima *nt* climate associated with the landscape
lang long, lengthy
Lang- und Senkrechtfräsmaschine *f* combined vertical and horizontal milling machine
lang andauernd long-lasting
Langbett *nt* special length bed
Langbuckel *m* elongated projection
Langdreharbeit *f* longitudinal turning work
Langdrehautomat *m* sliding head type single-spindle automatic machine, Swiss automatic, Swiss bush-type automatic, traversing-head bar machine
langdrehen slide, turn cylinder surfaces, turn longitudinal
Langdrehvorrichtung *f* longitudinal turning attachment
Länge *f* length
lange Lagerung *f* prolonged storage
längen lengthen, extend
Längenänderung *f* compressive deformation
Längenänderungsmessgerät *nt* extensometer
Längenanschlag *m* length stop, longitudinal stop
Längenausdehnung *f* extension
Längenausdehnungskoeffizient *m* longitudinal thermal expansion coefficient
Längenausgleicher *m* expansion joint
Längendehnung *f* extension, elongation
Längeneinheit *f* unit of length
Längengewicht *nt* linear weight
Längengewichtskraft *f* linear weight force
Längenkorrektur *f* tool length compensation
Längenmaß *nt* (linear) size
Längenmaßeinheit *f* linear dimension unit
Längenmesseinrichtung *f* extensometer
Längenmessgerät *nt* linear (or length) measuring instrument, deformation measuring device
Längenmessung *f* length measurement
Längenprüftechnik *f* length verification practice, length checking practice
Längenschwindmaß *nt* longitudinal shrink rule
Längenstauchung *f* lengthening of pressing
Längenteilung *f* linear indexing
Längenüberwachung *f* length monitoring
Längenverhältnis *nt* length ratio
Längenverschleiß *m* length wear
Langfeindrehen *nt* longitudinal finish turning
Langfräsmaschine *f* **1.** *(allg.)* manufacturing-type milling machine, fixed bed miller, plano-miller, plano-milling machine, planer-type milling machine **2.** *(Portalfräsmaschine)* double housing plano-miller
Langfräsmaschine *f* **in Einständerkonstruktion** open-side plano-miller
Langfräsmaschine *f* **in Einständerkonstruktion mit ausfahrbarem Seitenständer** convertible open-side planer-miller, open-side planer-miller with removable housing
Langfräsmaschine *f* **mit ausfahrbaren Seitenständern** planer-miller with removable housing
Langfräsmaschine *f* **mit verstellbarem Querbalken** adjustable-rail planer-type milling machine
Langfräsmaschine *f* **mit zwei Tischen** dual table planer type miller
Langfräsmaschine *f* **zum Flächenfräsen** slabbing machine
langfristig long-term, in the long term, for the long term
Langgewindefräsen *nt* traverse thread milling
Langgewindefräser *m* single thread milling cutter
Langgewindefräsmaschine *f* traverse thread milling machine
Langgut *nt* long goods
Langgutkassette *f* long goods carriage

Langgutlagersystem *nt* long goods storage system
Langgutpaternoster *m* long goods vertical rotary rack, long goods vertical carousel
Langhalsrundkolben *m* long necked round bottomed flask
Langhalsstehkolben *m* long-necked flat-bottomed flask
Langhobelfräsmaschine *f* planer-miller, milling planer
Langhobelmaschine *f* parallel planing machine, planer miller, planer
Langhobeln *nt* planer-milling
Langhubhonen *nt* honing
Langhubmaschine *f* long-stroke machine
Langhubräummaschine *f* long-stroke broaching machine
Langkegel *m* long taper
Langlichtbogenschweißen *nt* drawn-arc welding
Langloch *nt* oblong hole, slot, slotted hole
Langloch- und Keilnutenfräsmaschine *f* slot and keyway milling machine
langlochen slot
Langlochfräsen *nt* slotting
Langlochfräser *m* cutter mill, slotting cutter, slot drill
Langlochfräsmaschine *f* slot milling machine
Langlochnaht *f* joint with elongated plug weld
Langlochvorfräser *m* routing cutter
Langmuffe *f* long socket
Langnachformen *nt* long profiling, long copying
längs alongside, lengthwise, longitudinally
längs fahren move longitudinally, travel lengthwise
Längsabrichten *nt* traverse truing
Längsachse *f* longitudinal axis, centre line
langsam slow
langsam bewegen jog
langsam werden decelerate
Langsamdreher *m* slow-moving item

Langsameinstellung *f* inching, jogging
langsamer werden slow down
Längsanschlag *m* length feed stop, longitudinal (trip) dog, length stop, end stop
Längsballigkeit *f* (e. Zahnflanke) crowning
längsbeweglich longitudinally moveable
Längsbewegung *f* 1. (allg.) longitudinal motion, longitudinal traverse 2. (hin- und hergehende) reciprocating traverse
Längsbiegeprobe *f* longitudinal bend specimen
Längsbiegezugfestigkeit *f* longitudinal bending tensile strength
Langschlitz *m* groove
Längsdreharbeit *f* straight turning work
Längsdrehen *nt* longitudinal (or straight or plain) turning, straight turning work
Längsdruck *m* axial thrust
Längsfahren *nt* longitudinal movement
Längsfahrwagen *m* longitudinal truck
Längsfalz *m* longitudinal joint
Längsfräsen *nt* straight-milling
Längsfuge *f* longitudinal joint
Längsgang *m* longitudinal traverse
längsgesiegelt longitudinally seamed
Längsgewinde *nt* complete traverse thread
Längsgewindeschleifen *nt* complete traverse thread grinding
Längsgewindeschleifmaschine *f* reverse thread milling machine
Längshobeln *nt* longitudinal planing
Längshub *m* **zwischen den Schweißraupen** inter-run (or interpass) undercut
Längskopiereinrichtung *f* longitudinal copying attachment
Längskopieren *nt* longitudinal copying
Längskopiervorrichtung *f* longitudinal copying attachment
längskraftschlüssig longitudinally force-locked
längskraftschlüssige Verbindung *f* friction-locking joint actuated by longitudinal forces

längskraftschlüssiges einbauen install with positive locking in the longitudinal direction
Längslösekraft *f* longitudinal releasing force
Längsmittelebene *f* longitudinal centre plane, longitudinal plane of symmetry
Längsmittellinie *f* longitudinal centre line
Längsnaht *f* longitudinal seal
Längsnut *f* keyway, slot
Langspan *m* stringy chip, long lace chip
langspanend long cutting
langspanender Werkstoff *m* long-chip material
Längspresspassung *f* press fit
Längsquetscher *m* *(Rohrarmatur)* longitudinal squeezer
Längsrauheit *f* longitudinal roughness
Längsrichtung *f* perpendicular direction, lengthwise direction, machine direction
Längsriss *m* longitudinal crack, sheer draught
Längsschaben *nt* longitudinal scraping
Längsschleifen *nt* longitudinal (or traverse) grinding
Längsschleifverfahren *nt* traverse grinding method, traversing grinding method
Längsschliff *m* straight grinding
Längsschlitten *m* longitudinal slide
Längsschlupf *m* longitudinal slip
Längsschruppen *nt* straight rough turning
Längsseite *f* side wall
längsseitig at the sides, lengthwise
längsseits alongside
Längsspiel *nt* axial play
Längsstabilität *f* longitudinal stability
Längssteifigkeit *f* longitudinal stiffness
Längsträger *m* longitudinal support, main beam
Längstragseil *nt* longitudinal carrying cable
Längstraverse *f* 1. *(allg.)* longitudinal lifting beam 2. *(Verschieber)* longitudinal carriage
Längsverband *m* longitudinal member, stringer, longitudinal bracing
Längsverschiebung *f* 1. *(allg.)* longitudinal shift, longitudinal movement 2. *(von Passteilen)* longitudinal displacement
längsverstellen adjust longitudinally
Längsvorschub *m* longitudinal feed (motion), traversing feed
Längsvorschubbewegung *f* traversing feed motion
Längswalzen *nt* longitudinal rolling
Langtischflächenschleifmaschine *f* *(senkrechte)* vertical-spindle, reciprocating-table surface grinder
Langtischfräs- und Hobelmaschine *f* plano-miller, planer miller
Langtischhobelmaschine *f* planing machine, planer
Langtischmaschine *f* reciprocating-table machine
Längungsgrad *m* degree of lengthening (or elongation)
Langvorschub *m* sliding feed
langwellige Anteile *mpl* *(z. B. Rundlaufabweichung im Prüfbild)* long-undulation components
Langzeitalterung *f* long-time (or long-term) ageing test
Langzeitbelastbarkeit *f* long-term load capacity
langzeitig long-term
Langzeitinnendruckbeanspruchung *f* long-time internal pressure loading
Langzeit-Nennstrom *m* long-term rated current
langziehender Tropfen *m* drop with trailing thread
Langzug *m* longitudinal feed gear mechanism, longitudinal feed (or traverse)
Läpparbeiter *m* lapper
Läppdauer *f* lapping duration
Läppdorn *m* lapping arbor, lapping spindle, lap(ping) mandrel
Läppdruck *m* lapping pressure
Lappen 1. *(e. Sicherungsbleches)* tab 2. *(e. Sicherungsringes)* lug
läppen lap
Läppgemisch *nt* lapping mixture

Läppgemischfilm *m* lapping mixture film
Läppgemischförderung *f* lapping mixture transport
Läppgeschwindigkeit *f* lapping speed (or velocity)
Läpphülse *f* lapping sleeve, lap
Läppkäfig *m* lapping cage, spider
Läppkorn *nt* lapping abrasive
Läppmittel *nt* lapping abrasive, lapping compound
Läppmittelzuführung *f* lapping compound feed
Läppplatte *f* lapping block, lapping plate
Läppscheibe *f* lapping wheel, lap
Läppscheibenträger *m* lap carrier, lap plate holder
Läppschleifen *nt* lap-grinding
Läppschleifscheibe *f* abrasive lapping wheel
Läppspindel *f* lapping spindle
Läppverfahren *nt* lapping technique
Läppwerkzeug *nt* lapping tool
Lärm *m* noise
Lärmausbreitung *f* dissipation of noise
lärmfrei noiseless
Lärmgrenze *f* noise limit
Lärmpegel *m* noise level
lärmsensibel noise-sensitive
Lasche *f* flap, mounting link, leaf
Laschenkette *f* leaf (mechanical) chain
LASER *m* **(Licht angeregte Strahlung emittierender Resonator, Lichtverstärkung durch angeregte Strahlungsaussendung)** Light Amplification by Simulated Emission of Modification (LASER)
Laserabtragen *nt* laser eroding
Laseranwendung *f* laser use, laser application
Laserart *f* kind of laser, laser species
Laserbearbeitung *f* laser manufacturing
Laserbohrung *f* laser bore, laser hole
Lasercodierer *m* laser coder
Laserdrucker *m* laser printer
Laserfokus *m* laser focus
Lasergravur *f* laser graving
Laserhärten *nt* laser hardening

Laserlöten *nt* laser soldering
Lasermaterial *nt* laser material
Lasermaterialbearbeitungsanlage *f* laser material machining system
lasern laser
Laseroberflächenbehandlung *f* laser surface coating, laser surface finishing
Laserprinzip *nt* laser principle
Laserscanner *m* laser scanner
Laserschneidanlage *f* laser cutting equipment (or plant)
Laserschweißanlage *f* laser welding plant
Laserschweißen *nt* laser welding
Laserschweißgerät *nt* laser welder
Laserstrahl *m* laser beam, laser
Laserstrahlführung *f* laser beam guide
Laserstrahllegieren *nt* laser beam alloy
Laserstrahlpolarisationsschweißen *nt* laser beam polarization welding
Laserstrahlschneiden *nt* laser beam cutting
Laserstrahlschweißen *nt* laser beam welding
Laserstrahlung *f* laser beaming
Lasersystem *nt* laser system
Laserumschmelzen *nt* laser melting up
Laserunterstützung *f* laser support
lasierende Verfärbung *f* translucent discolouration
lasierender Anstrich *m* glazed finish
Last *f* **1.** *(allg.)* load, loading, weight **2.** *(unter ~)* **3.** *(~ aufnehmen ~ tragen)* load bearing, load carrying
Lastabmessung *f* load dimension
Lastachse *f* load axle
Lastanlage *f* front face of the shank
Lastanlagefläche *f* front face
Lastannahme *f* assumed loads, assumed load conditions, agreed load
Lastanschlagmittel *nt* load stopping aids
Lastanzeiger *m* load indicator
Lastart *f* type of load
Lastauflagefläche *f* upper face of the blade, upper face, upper surface
Lastaufnahme *f* load pick-up
Lastaufnahmeeinrichtung *f* load suspension device

Lastaufnahmemittel (LAM) *nt* load handling device (LHD), load handling accessory, load pick-up device, load handling attachment, load-carrying unit (or means or attachment), load suspension device, load bearing element, load support, load take-up, lifting unit
Lastaufnahmemittelverriegelung *f* load handling interlock
Lastaufteilung *f* load distribution
Lastbehandlung *f* load handling, load manipulation
Lastbewegung *f* load movement, movement of the load
Lastdaten *pl* on-load data
Lastdiagramm *nt* load diagram
Lastdrehzahl *f* on-load speed
Lastdrehzahlen *fpl* load rotational speed
Lastgewicht *nt* weight of the load
Lasteinwirkung *f* load effect
Lastende *nt* load end
Lastenheft *nt* (tender) specification, specification sheet, spec sheet, performance specification
Lastenschutzgitter *nt* load backrest, load restrainer
Lastfall *m* loading condition(s)
Lastführung *f* load guiding structure
Lastgabel *f* fork, load fork
Lasthaken *m* lifting hook
Lasthakenmutter *f* lifting hook nut
Lasthakenschaft *m* lifting hook shank
Last-Halbperiode *f* load half-wave
Lasthalteeinrichtung *f* load holding device
Lasthalter *m* load stabilizer
Lasthandhabung *f* load handling
Lasthandhabungssteuerung *f* load handling control
Lasthebemagnet *m* magnetic load carrying device
Lasthubeinrichtung *f* load lifting facility
Lastklasse *f* load class
Lastkollektiv *nt* load spectrum
Lastkontrolle *f* load control, loading control
Lastkontrollsystem *nt* load control system

Lastkraft *f* load force
Lastkraftwagen (Lkw) *m* lorry, *(US)* truck
Lastlageerfassung *f* load position sensing
Lastmagnet *m* lifting magnet
Lastmanipulation *f* load manipulation
Lastmoment *nt* load moment, load torque
Lastplattform *f* load carrying deck, load platform
Lastpositionsüberwachung *f* load position monitoring
Lastprofil *nt* load profile
Lastrad *nt* load wheel
Lastschub *m* load push
Lastschutzgitter *m* load backrest, load restrainer
Lastschwerpunkt *m* load centre, load centre of gravity
Lastschwerpunktabstand *m* load centre distance, load centre of gravity distance
Lastsensor *m* load sensing system, load sensor, load cell, load control
Lastsicherheitssensor *m* load safety sensor
Lastspiel *nt* stress cycle, alternative of load
Lastspielzahl *f* stress reversals, stress cycles endured
Lastspitze *f* peak load
Laststabilisierung *f* load stabilization
Laststeuerung *f* load control
Laststrom *m* load current
Lastträger *m* fork arm (carriage), load carrier, load bearing implement
Lasttraverse *f* spreader beam
Lastübergabe *f* load transfer
Lastübergabebereich *m* load transfer area
Lastübergabestelle *f* load pick-up and deposit station
lastunterfahrend load drive-under
Lastverteilung *f* load distribution, load sharing
Lastwaage *f* load weighing scales
Lastwechsel *m* transfer of the load, load transfer, load change
Lastwechselverformung *f* load trans-

fer deformation, deformation due to alternating load effects
Lastzug *m* load pull
Laubholzzellstoff *m* deciduous pulp
Lauf *m* run, working, running
Laufabweichung *f (bei Rund- und Planlauf)* run-out error
Laufachse *f* axle
Laufbahn *f* track
Laufbereich *m* running area
Laufbetrachtung *f* run analysis
Laufbreite *f* stair width
Laufeigenschaften *fpl* travel characteristics
laufen work, move, run
laufend continuous, current
laufende Aufstockung *f* continuous replenishment
laufende Nummer *f* serial number
laufende Prüfungen *fpl* routine tests *pl*
laufender Betrieb *m* current operation
Läufer *m* armature, rotor
Läufereisen *nt* rotor iron
Läuferfeld *nt* rotor field
Läuferinduktionsstrom *m* induction current of the rotor
Läuferinduktivität *f* rotor inductance
Läuferkreis *m* rotor circuit
Läufernut *f* rotor groove, armature slot
Läuferspannung *f* rotor voltage
Läuferspule *f* armature coil, rotor coil
Läuferstrom *m* rotor current
Läuferwelle *f* rotor shaft
Läuferwellenwicklung *f* rotor shaft winding
Läuferwicklung *f* armature winding, rotor winding
Läuferwiderstand *m* rotor resistance
Lauffläche *f* running surface, tread
Lauffläche *f* **der Laufräder** wheel tread, wheel running surface
Laufflächenbreite *f* tread width
Laufgenauigkeit *f* true running
Laufhemmung *f* malfunction
Laufkarte *f* **für das Werkstück** routing card
Laufkatze *f* trolley
Laufkran *m* gantry crane
Lauflinie *f* walking line

Laufpassung *f* clearance fit
Laufrad *nt* **1.** *(allg.)* drive wheel, travel wheel, track wheel **2.** *(Gebläserad)* impeller
Laufradbohrung *f* drive wheel bore
Laufraddrehsinn *m* direction of propeller rotation
Laufraddurchmesser *m* drive wheel diameter
Laufradschaufel *f* impeller blade
Laufradschaufelkante *f* impeller blade edge
Laufradumfang *m* travel wheel periphery, travel wheel perimeter
Laufraster *nt* moving grid
Laufring *m* **1.** *(allg.)* track ring **2.** *(Lager)* race
Laufrolle *f* (travel) roller, pulley
Laufruhe *f* running smoothness, smooth running, quiet running, quietness in operation, silent running
Laufschaufelverstelleinrichtung *f* impeller vane pitch adjustment device
Laufschiene *f* **1.** *(für Rollen)* runner, running rail **2.** *(Gleitschiene)* slide rail
Laufsteg *m* gangway, walkway
Lauftoleranz *f* run-out tolerance
Laufwagenzeichenmaschine *f* carriage type drafting machine
Laufwerk *nt* drive, disk drive
Laufzeit *f* **1.** *(allg.)* operating period, operating time, running time, run time **2.** *(Durchgangszeit)* in-system transfer time **3.** *(EDV)* delay time
Laufzeitklasse *f* class of operating time, operating time class
Laufzeitspeicher *m* dynamic storage, delay line storage unit
Lauge *f* leach, lye, caustic potash solution
lavendelblau lavender-blue
Layoutplanung *f* layout planning
Layoutprogramm *nt* layout program
Leasingrate *f* leasing instalment
Lebensdauer *f* durability, life, lifetime, service life, useful life
Lebensdauer *f* **der Schneidmaschine** cutting life
Lebensdauer *f* **des Messers** blade life
Lebensdauer *f* **des Werkzeuges** tool

life
Lebensmittelgesetz *nt* Food Act
Lebenszyklus *m* life cycle
Leck *nt* leak, leakage
Leckage *f* leakage
leckdicht leak-proof
lecken leak
Leckgasleitung *f* leak-off line
Leckmenge *f* leakage
Lecksicherungsgerät *nt* leak preventing device
Leckstrom *m* leakage current
LED *Abk* light emitting diode
Lederauszug *m* leather extract
Lederfettungsmittel *nt* fat liquors and greases for leather
Ledermanschettendichtung *f* leather cup
leer 1. *(allg.)* empty, void **2.** *(Fläche, Papier)* blank **3.** *(unbeladen)* unload
Leerbehälter *m* empty container
Leercontainerstapler *m* empty container handler
leeren empty
Leerfach *nt* empty compartment
Leerfahrauftrag *m* unladen trip command
Leerfahrt *f* empty trip, unladen trip, empty running
Leerfahrt durchführen move when empty, travel when empty
Leerfläche *f* blank area
Leerfluss *m* open-circuit flux
Leergebinde *nt* empty drum, empty container
Leergewicht *nt* unladen mass
Leerglas *nt* tare beaker
Leergut *nt* empties, empty containers
Leerhalbperiode *f* no-load half wave
Leerhub *m* idle return stroke, return stroke, idle stroke, back stroke
Leerlauf *m* idling, idle mode, idle time, idle running, no-load operation, no-load running
Leerlaufdrehzahl *f* idling speed torque, idling speed, idle running speed, no-load speed
leerlaufen 1. *(Maschine)* idle, run idle (engine) **2.** *(von Rohrleitungen)* drain
Leerlaufpunkt *m* idling point

Leerlaufspannung *f* no-load voltage
Leerlauftest *m* open circuit test
Leerlaufverlust *m* no-load loss
Leerlaufzeit *f* idle time
Leermessung *f* blank measurement
Leerpalette *f* empty pallet
Leerpalettenanlieferung *f* empty pallets delivery
Leerpalettenmagazin *nt* empty pallet magazine
Leersaugen *nt* emptying under suction
Leerschalthäufigkeit *f* no-load starting frequency
Leertaste *f* space bar
Leerversuch *m* dummy test
Leerweg *m* idle length
Leerzeichen *nt* space
legen lay, place, put down
Legende *f* legend
legierter Stahl *m* alloy steel
Legierung *f* alloy
Legierungsschicht *f* layer of alloy
Lehne *f* armrest, backrest
Lehrdorn *m* **mit Kegelbefestigung** plug gauge with taper lock
Lehre *f* jig, *(US)* gage, *(UK)* gauge, template
Lehre *f* **mit kugelförmigen Prüfflächen** gauge with spherical inspection faces
Lehren bohren jig-bore
Lehrenabmaß *nt* gauge deviation
Lehrenaufbau *m* gauge design
Lehrenbohr- und Fräsmaschine *f* jig boring and milling machine
Lehrenbohrarbeit *f* jig boring work
Lehrenbohren *nt* jig boring
Lehrenbohrmaschine *f* jig boring machine
Lehrenbohrwerk *nt* jig boring machine
Lehrenfräsmaschine *f* jig mill
Lehrengriff *m* gauge handle
Lehrenkörper *m* gauge member, gauge body
Lehrenmaß *nt* gauge dimension
Lehrenmaßtoleranz *f* gauge dimensional tolerance
Lehrenschleifmaschine *f* jig grinder
Lehrensegment *nt* gauge segment
Lehrensollmaß *nt* nominal gauge size

Lehrensystem *nt* gauging system
Lehrmittel *ntpl* teaching aids
Lehrring *m* ring gauge
Lehrwerkstatt *f* apprentice workshop, training workshop
Lehrzahnkörper *m* master gear blank
Lehrzahnrad *nt* precision master gear
leicht 1. *(Gewicht)* light, light in weight 2. *(Leistungen)* easy
leicht bearbeitbar easy machining
leicht entflammbar easily inflammable
leicht entflammbarer Stoff *m* readily flammable material
leicht gefärbt lightly coloured
leicht montierbar easy to mount
Leichtdachkonstruktion *f* lightweight roof structure
leichte Ausführung *f (z. B. eines Spannstiftes)* light-weight type
leichter Schnitt *m* light cut
leichtes Rohr *nt* lightweight pipe
Leichtmetall *nt* light metal
Leichtmetall-Legierung *f* light metal alloy
Leim *m* glue
Leim *m* **auftragen** apply glue (to), glue, spread glue
Leimauftrag *m* gluing, application of glue
Leimauftragwalze *f* glue spreading roll
leimen glue
Leimgerät *nt* glue reservoir
Leimspur *f* glue strip
Leimstation *f* glue deck
Leinölfirnis *m* boiled linseed oil
Leitspindelmaschine *f* lead-screw machine
Leiste *f* 1. *(Anschlagleiste)* fence 2. *(Holz)* lath, strip
leisten guide, convey, carry out, perform, effect
Leistung *f* 1. *(e. Maschine, techn. Anlage)* capacity, efficiency 2. *(e. Kraftmaschine)* power 3. *(e. Motors)* horsepower rating, power 4. *(el.)* energy power, power 5. *(e. Betriebes)* productive capacity 6. *(e. Menschen)* accomplishment 7. *(Ergebnis, Gesamtleistung)* performance, output 8. *(Nennleistung)* rating 9. *(ausbringen, abgegebene ~)* output 10. *(zugeführte ~)* input 11. *(Spitzenleistung)* achievement 12. *(Wirkungsgrad)* efficiency
Leistung *f* **einer Maschine** power of a machine
Leistungsabnahme *f* 1. *(Abfallen)* decrease of performance 2. *(Prüfung)* performance approval
Leistungsangaben *fpl* performance data
Leistungsanschluss *m (Rohre)* pipe connection
Leistungsantrieb *m* power drive system
Leistungsaufnahme *f* input, power input, power absorption, power consumption
Leistungsaufwand *m* power demand
Leistungsbedarf *m* power demand, power requirement
Leistungsbemessung *f* rating
Leistungsberechnung *f* performance calculation
Leistungsbereich *m* power range
Leistungsbereitschaft *f* performance readiness
Leistungsbilanz *f* power balance
Leistungsdaten *pl* performance data
Leistungsdichte *f* power tightness, output compactness
Leistungsdrehen *nt* high-efficiency turning
Leistungsdurchsatz *m* power throughput
Leistungseinbuße *f* emission loss
Leistungselektronik *f* power electronics
Leistungserhöhung *f* increase of output, increase of performance
leistungsfähig efficient, productive
Leistungsfähigkeit *f* performance, efficiency
Leistungsfaktor *m* power factor
Leistungsfaktorkorrektur *f* power factor correction
Leistungsgetriebe *nt* power transmission
Leistungsglied *nt* power device
Leistungsgrenze *f* limit of performance, output maximum

Leistungsindikator *m* metric, performance indicator
Leistungskennzahl *f* performance indicator
Leistungskriterium *nt* metric, performance criterion
Leistungsmerkmal *nt* user facility
Leistungsmerkmalanforderung *f* facility request
Leistungsmesser-Verhalten *nt* wattmeter method
Leistungsminderung *f* decrease of performance
Leistungsnachweis *m* performance data
Leistungs-NAND-Glied *nt* NAND buffer
Leistungsprüfung *f* performance test
Leistungsschalter *m* circuit breaker
Leistungsschild *nt* marker's name plate, output plate, rating plate
leistungsschwache Maschine *f* low capacity machine
Leistungssteller *m* power divider
Leistungstest *m* performance test
Leistungsumfang *m* scope of performance
Leistungsverlust *m* power drain, power loss, loss in performance
Leistungsvermögen *nt* performance
Leistungsverstärkung *f* power amplification
Leit- und Zugspindeldrehmaschine *f* lathe with lead screw and feed rod, regular engine lathe, engine lathe, surfacing and screw-cutting lathe
Leitblech *nt* chute
Leitdraht *m* guide wire
Leitebene *f* management level
leiten 1. *(Mitarbeiter)* guide, lead, direct **2.** *(el.)* conduct
Leiter *m* I. *m* **1.** *(el.)* conductor **2.** *(Organisator)* manager II. *f (Steig~)* ladder
Leiterplatte *f* circuit card, printed circuit board (PCB), printed wiring board
Leiterquerschnitt *m* conductor cross section
Leitfaden *m* guide
leitfähig conducting, conductive
Leitfähigkeit *f* conductivity
Leitfähigkeitsmessung *f* conductivity measurement
Leitgerät *nt* control station
Leitkanal *m* conduit
Leitlineal *nt* guide bar, lead bar, former plate, taper bar
Leitlinie *f* guide line, directrix
Leitlinienführung *f* guide line control (system), guidance (system)
leitliniengeführt guide line controlled, guided
Leitpatrone *f* leader
Leitrechner *m* master computer, guidance computer, host computer
Leitsätze *mpl* guide rules
Leitschaufelverstelleinrichtung *f* guide vane pitch adjustment device
Leitschiene *f* guide bar, guide rail
Leitsilberschicht *f* coating of conductive silver
Leitspindel *f* guide screw, lead screw
Leitspindeldrehmaschine *f* brass finisher's lathe
Leitstand *m* control station, control centre, central control room
Leitstandpersonal *nt* control centre personnel
Leitsteuerung *f* guidance control (system)
Leitsystem *nt* master system
Leittechnik *f* control system
Leittechnikmeldung *f* control system message
Leitung *f* **1.** *(allg.)* conduit, mains, line **2.** *(el.)* cable **3.** *(Strom)* supply lead **4.** *(Rohre)* pipe, piping, pipeline, conduit **5.** *(verlegte)* wiring **6.** *(Wärme)* conduction
Leitung *f* **mit Mantelrohr** pipe with jacket
Leitungen im Gebäude verlegen wire a building
Leitungsabschnitt *m* pipeline section
Leitungsbetrieb *m* line operation
Leitungsbruch *m* pipe failure
Leitungsende *nt* pipeline end
Leitungsflansch *m* pipe flange
leitungsgebunden conducted
leitungsgebundene Aussendung *f*

conducted emission
leitungsgefährdende Einwirkung *f* activities endangering the line
leitungsgeführt conducted
Leitungsnetz *nt* mains
Leitungsquerschnitt *m* conductor cross section
Leitungsschema *f* piping diagram
Leitungsschlauch *m* cable sheathing
Leitungsschwingungen *fpl* line vibrations
Leitungsteil *nt* portion of piping
Leitungstrommel *f* cable reel
Leitungsverlegung *f* pipelaying, wiring
Leitungszone *f* pipe zone
Leitungszubehör *nt* line equipment
Lenkachse *f* steer axle
Lenkantrieb *m* steering motor
Lenkdeichsel *f* tiller
Lenkeinheit *f* steering unit
lenken steer, control, direct
Lenkfläche *f* **in e. Krümmer** guide vane in an elbow
Lenkgetriebe *nt* steering gear
Lenkkraft *f* steering force
Lenkkranz *m* steering turnplate
Lenkmotor *m* steering motor
Lenkrad *nt* steer(ing) wheel
Lenkregler *m* steering control
Lenkrichtung *f* steering direction
Lenkrolle *f* (swivel) castor
Lenkstellteil *nt* steering operating control
Lenksteuerung *f* steer(ing) control
Lenksystem *nt* steering system
Lenkung *f* steering, control
Lenkungsart *f* type of control
Lenkungsrückschlag *m* steering shock, steering wheel kick-back
Lenkungssteuerung *f* steering control
Lenkungssystem *nt* steering system
Lenkvorrichtung *f* steering attachment
Lenkwinkel *m* steer angle, turning radius
Lenkwinkelgeber *m* steer angle sensor
Lenzsche Regel *f* Lenz's law
Lernmittel *ntpl* learning aids
Lernmodus *m* learning mode
lesbar readable, legible

Lesbarkeit *f* legibility
Leseabstand *m* reading distance
Lesebereich *m* reading range
Leseebene *f* reading area
Leseeinrichtung *f* reading device
Leseergebnis *nt* scanning result
Lesefeld *nt* reading field
Lesegerät *nt* reader, reading head, reading equipment, reading device
Lesekopf *m* read head
Lesemöglichkeit *f* reading option
lesen read, scan
Leseort *m* reading point
Lesepistole *f* reading run, reading pistol
Leseprinzip *nt* read principle
Leserlichkeit *f* legibility
Lesesicherheit *f* legibility
Lesestation *f* reading station
Lesestift *m* reading wand
Lesetechnik *f* reading technology
Lesevorgang *m* reading operation
Lesezyklus *m* reading cycle
Leuchtdichte *f* luminance, illuminating power
Leuchtdichteverteilung *f* luminance distribution
Leuchtdiode *f* light emitting diode (LED)
leuchten glow, shine
leuchtend bright, luminescent
Leuchtmelder *m* signal lamp, telltale lamp, indicating light
Leuchtpetroleumzündung *f* kerosene ignition
Leuchtpigment *nt* luminescent pigment
Leuchtschirm *m* fluoroscopic screen
Leuchtsignal *nt* optical signal
Leuchtwirkung *f* luminescent effect
Leuchtziffer *f* luminous digit
L-förmig L-shaped
Libelle *f* air level, spirit level
licht clear, free, unobstructed
Licht *nt* light
Lichtalterung *f* ageing under exposure to light
Lichtblitz *m* light flash (stroboscope)
Lichtbogen *m* arc
Lichtbogenbolzenschweißen *nt* **mit Ringzündung** *f* arc stud welding with

initiation by means of a collar
Lichtbogenerosion *f* arc erosion
Lichtbogenofen *m* electric arc furnace
Lichtbogen-Pressschweißen *nt* **mit magnetisch bewegtem Lichtbogen** arc pressure welding using a magnetically moved arc
Lichtbogenschmelzschweißen *nt* **mit Spitzenzündung** condenser discharge arc stud welding
Lichtbogenschweißen *nt* arc welding
Lichtbogenspritzdraht *m* arc spraying wire
Lichtbogenspritzen *nt* arc spraying
Lichtbündel *nt* light beam
Lichtbündelung *f* light beam path
Lichtdurchlass *m* light passage
lichte Abmessung *f* clearance dimension
lichte Breite *f* free width
lichte Weite *f* insider diameter, bore, bore size
Lichtempfänger *m* optoreceiver, photoreceiver, light receiver
lichtempfindlich sensitive to light
lichtempfindliche Schicht *f* (*z. B. e. Lichtpauspapiers*) light-sensitive coating
Lichtempfindlichkeit *f* light sensitivity
Lichtfarbe *f* light colour
lichtfest lightfast
Lichtfleck *m* light beam cross-section, point of light
Lichtgitter *nt* light grid
Lichtgitterrost *m* grated flooring, grating floor
Lichtgriffel *m* light pen
Lichthof *m* halo
Lichtimpuls *m* light impulse
Lichtinterferenz *f* interferometry
Lichtkante *f* feature line
Lichtnetz *nt* lighting mains
Lichtpause *f* diazocopy
Lichtpausfilm *m* diazocopy film
Lichtpausmaterial *nt* diazocopy material
Lichtpauspapier *nt* diazotype paper, photocopying paper without silver salt coating
Lichtpauspapier *nt* **auf Gewebe** mounted diazo paper
Lichtpausschicht *f* diazo coating
Lichtpausverfahren *nt* diazotype method
Lichtpunkt *m* flying spot
Lichtquant *nt* photon, light quantum
Lichtquelle *f* source of light, light source
Lichtraumprofil *nt* **1.** *(allg.)* unobstructed section profile **2.** *(des LAM)* fork clearance
Lichtrichtung *f* light direction
Lichtrissbeständigkeit *f* crack resistance on exposure
Lichtschalter *m* installation switch
Lichtschleier *m* halo, light veil
Lichtschnittverfahren *nt* light-slit method
Lichtschranke *f* light barrier, photoelectric guard, photocell
Lichtschwächung *f* attenuation of light
Lichtschwächungsfaktor *m* light attenuation factor
Lichtsendeempfänger *m* light emitter-receiver
Lichtsender *m* light emitter
Lichtsignal *nt* light signal
Lichtspalt *m* light gap
Lichtspaltverfahren *nt* light gap method
Lichtstabilisator *m* light stabilizer
Lichtstrahl *m* beam, beam of light
Lichtstrahlextrusionsschweißen *nt* light beam (or laser) welding by extrusion of filler material
Lichtstrahlungsmessung *f* luminous radiation measurement
Lichtstreukoeffizient *m* light scattering coefficient
Lichtstrom *m* light flux, luminous flux
Lichttaster *m* light scanner, light sensor
Lichttransmissionsgrad *m* luminous transmission index
lichtundurchlässig opaque
lichtunempfindlich intensive to light
Lichtunempfindlichkeit *f* light intensitivity
Lichtverhältnis *nt* light proportion
Lichtverstärker *m* light amplifier, light booster

Lichtvisierblende *f* light diaphragm, light cone
Lichtvorhang *m* light roller blind, light curtain
Lichtwelle *f* light wave
Lichtwiedergabe *f* light reproduction
Lichtzeiger *m* luminous spot
Lieferabruf *m* delivery schedule, delivery on call, delivery forecast
Lieferant *m* **1.** *(allg.)* supplier, vendor **2.** *(Subunternehmer)* sub-contractor
Lieferantenaudit *nt* supplier audit
Lieferantendaten *pl* supplier data
Lieferantennetzwerk *nt* network of suppliers
Lieferantenportfolio *nt* vendor portfolio, supplier portfolio
Lieferantenzeugnis *nt* supplier certificate
lieferbar available, deliverable
Lieferbereitschaft *f* availability of stock for delivery, readiness for delivery
Lieferform *f* as delivered form
Liefergrad *m* delivery efficiency
Lieferkette *f* supply chain
Lieferleistung *f* delivery performance
Liefermenge *f* delivery quantity
Liefermengenabweichung *f* delivery quantity deviation, deviation in delivery quantities
Liefermengeneinhaltung *f* compliance with delivery quantities
Liefermengentreue *f* delivery quantity reliability
liefern deliver, furnish, provide, supply, ship
Lieferpapiere *ntpl* shipping documents
Lieferqualität *f* delivery quality
Lieferschein *m* delivery note, bill of delivery, dispatch advice
Lieferspezifikation *f* delivery specification
Lieferstatus *m* delivery status, status of delivery
Liefertermin *m* delivery deadline, delivery date, date of delivery
Liefertermiabweichung *f* delivery date deviation
Liefertermineinhaltung *f* compliance with delivery deadlines
Liefertermintreue *f* delivery date reliability
Lieferüberwachung *f* delivery control
Lieferumfang *m* scope of delivery
Lieferung *f* delivery, shipment, supply
Lieferunterlagen *fpl* delivery documents
Lieferzeichnung *f* delivery drawing
Lieferzeit *f* **1.** *(allg.)* delivery time, period of delivery **2.** *(techn.)* (purchasing) lead time
Liefetreue *f* delivery reliability
liegen lie
liegen auf lie on, rest on
liegend in a laying position, in horizontal position
liegende Leitung *f* horizontal pipeline
liegendes Kreuz *nt* diagonal cross
Liegezeit *f* horizontal time
Lift *m* lift
Liftsystem *nt* lift system
LiGA (Lithographie, Galvanoformung, Abformung)-Verfahren *ntpl* lithographic-electroforming-forming-technology
Lineal *nt* ruler, straight edge
linealgerichtetes Rohr *nt* tube straightened against a straight edge
linear linear, straight line
Linearantrieb *m* linear drive
Linearausdehnung *f* linear expansion
lineare Skale *f* linear scale
lineare Skalenteilung *f* linear scale division
linearer Mittelwert *m* linear mean value
lineares Rollenkugellager *nt* ball and rod bearing
lineares Stoßbremsvermögen *nt* linear collision stopping power
lineares Strahlungsbremsvermögen *nt* linear radiation stopping power
Linearinterpolation *f* linear interpolation
Linear-Interpolation *f* linear interpolation
linearisiert linear
Linearisierung *f* linearization
Linearitätsabweichung *f* linearity de-

viation (or error)
Linearmotor *m* linear motor
linguistische Regel *f* linguistic rule
linguistische Variable *f* linguistic variable
linguistischer Term *m* linguistic term
Linie *f* 1. *(allg.)* mains, line 2. *(geneigte ~)* sloping line 3. *(eine ~ durchziehen)* draw as continuous line
Linien *fpl* **im gleichen Abstand** equidistant lines
Linienabstand *m* line spacing
Linienberührung *f* line contact, linear contact
Linienbreite *f* width of line
Linienemissionsstrahlung *f* line-emission radiation
linienförmige Krafteinleitung *f (Pressverband)* linear transmission of force to the assembly
Linienformtoleranz *f* profile tolerance
Liniengruppe *f* line group
linienhaft linear
Linienlagerung *f* linear storage
Liniennaht *f* line joint (or weld), seam weld
Liniennaht *f* **mit Überlappstoß** line weld on lap joint
Linienstromschnittstelle *f* current-loop interface
Linienzug *m* 1. *(allg.)* trace 2. *(geknickter ~)* kinked line
linke Seite *f* left side, left-hand side
linker Hobelmeißel *m* left-hand planing tool
linker Meißel *m* left-hand cutting tool, left-cut tool
linker Quersupport *m* left-hand rail head
linker Schruppmeißel *m* left-hand roughing tool
linker Ständer *m* left-hand column
linker Stechmeißel *m* left-hand parting tool
linkes Maximum *nt* left most maximum
links left(-hand), on the left
Linksausführung *f (Darstellung eines Teiles)* left-hand version
Linksdrall *m* left-hand twist (or spiral)

linksdrehen turn counter-clockwise
linksdrehend anti-clockwise
linksdrehender Fräser *m* top going cutter
Linksdrehung *f* anti-clockwise rotation, left-hand rotation
Linksevolvente *f* left-hand involute
Linksflanke *f* left-hand tooth surface, left flank
Linksflanken-Eingriffslinie *f* line of engagement of left-hand tooth surfaces, left-hand path of contact
Linksflankenprofil *nt* left-hand flank profile
Linksgewinde *nt* left-hand thread
Linkslauf *m* anti-clockwise rotation, left hand motion, counter-clockwise (ccw)
linksläufig left-handed rotating
linksschneidend left-hand cut(ting)
Links-Schrägverzahnung *f* left-hand helical tooth system
Linksschraubbewegung *f* left-handed helical motion
Linksschraube *f* left-hand helix
linksseitig left hand, on the left hand side
linkssteigend left-hand helical
linkssteigende Verzahnung *f* left-hand teeth
Linksteilung *f (e. Verzahnung)* left-hand pitch
Linse *f* lens
Linsenausgleicher *m* lenticular expansion joint
Linsendurchmesser *m* weld nugget diameter
linsenförmig lenticular
Linsenkuppe *f* oval point
Linsenmaßfehler *m* imperfect nugget dimension
Linsenniet *m* mushroom head rivet
Linsenschraube *f* **mit Kreuzschlitz** recessed raised cheese head screw, recessed raised fillister head screw
Linsenschraube *f* **mit Kuppe** (recessed) raised cheese head screw with point
Linsensenkblechschraube *f* raised countersunk head self-tapping screw, raised countersunk head tapping screw

Linsensenkblechschraube *f* **mit Kreuzschlitz** raised countersunk recessed head tapping screw
Linsensenkblechschraube *f* **mit Schlitz** slotted raised countersunk head tapping screw
Linsensenkholzschraube *f* raised countersunk head wood screw
Linsensenkholzschraube *f* **mit Kreuzschlitz** recessed raised countersunk head wood screw
Linsensenkschneidschraube *f* raised countersunk head tread cutting screw
Linsenstrom *m* lens current
Linsensystem *nt* lens combination, lens system
Linsenüberschneidung *f* nugget overlap
Lippe *f* lip
Liste *f* list, catalogue
Listengenerator *m* list generator
listenmäßiges Gerät *nt* catalogued device
Lithographie *f* lithography
lithographisch lithographic
Lkw *m* lorry, *(US)* truck
lokales Erweiterungsgerät *nt* local extension rack
Loch *nt* 1. *(allg.)* aperture, hole 2. *(Bohrloch)* borehole, bore
Lochabstand *m* bolt hole spacing, hole centre distance
Lochband *nt* punched tape
lochbandgesteuert punched tape controlled
Lochbandsteuerung *f* punched tape control
Lochbarkeit *f* punchability
Lochbild *nt* hole pattern
Lochblech *nt* 1. *(Metallplatte)* perforated metal plate 2. *(Boden)* grated flooring
Lochblende *f* rotating diaphragm, aperture (plate)
Lochbohren *nt* drilling
Lochbohrmaschine *f* drilling machine
Locheisen *nt* hollow punch
lochen perforate, pierce, punch
Locher *m* perforator, punch
Lochergerät *nt* tape puncher

Lochfraß *m* pitting
Lochfraßstelle *f* pied area
Lochkarte *f* perforated card, punch(ed) card
Lochkartenausgeber *m* punched card readout device
Lochkartenspeicher *m* punched card store
Lochkartentechnik *f* punched card technique
Lochkreis *m* hole circle, index circle, circle of holes
Lochmaß *nt* hole size
Lochmitte *f* hole centre
Lochmittenabstand *m* hole centre distance
Lochnaht *f* plug welded joint
Lochrandabstand *m* hole edge distance
Lochschnittwerkzeug *nt* perforator, hole cutter
Lochsiebeinsatz *m* perforated screen insert
Lochstreifen *m* perforated tape, punched tape
Lochstreifeneingabe *f* punched-tape input
lochstreifengesteuert punched tape controlled
Lochstreifenleser *m* tape reader
Lochstreifenschreibmaschine *f* automatic punch machine
Lochteilscheibe *f* index plate with holes
Lochung *f* 1. (Bohrung) aperture, perforation, (bore) hole 2. (Befestigung) fixing point
Lochversatz *m* hole mismatch
Lochzahldichte *f* density of pits
Lockenbildung *f* curling
Lockenspan *m* continuous curly chip
locker loose, slack
locker sitzender Post *m* lightly adhering rust
Lockern *nt* easing, coming loose, loosening, slacking off, releasing
Lockerung *f* loosening
Lognormalverteilung *f* log-normal distribution
logarithmische Aufzeichnung *f* loga-

rithmic plotting
logarithmisches Dekrement *nt* logarithmic decay
logarithmisches Papier *nt* log paper
Log-Datei *f* log-file
Logikelement *nt* logic element
Logikschaltung *f* logic circuitry
logische Grundverknüpfung *f* logical connective
logische Programmanpassung *f* adapting program logic
logische Verknüpfung *f* logic operation, logic linkage
logische Verknüpfungsschaltung *f* logic operation, logic linkage
Logistik *f* logistics
Logistikdienstleister *m* logistics service provider
Logistikeffizienz *f* logistic efficiency
Logistikkette *f* supply chain
Logistikkosten *pl* logistic costs, logistics costs
Logistikleistung *f* logistic performance
Logistikpartner *m* logistic partner
Logistikplanung *f* logistics planning
logistisch logistic
logistisches Grundkonzept *nt* basic logistics concept
Lohn *m* wage
Lohnhärterei *f* contract heat treatment workshop
Lohnkosten *pl* wage costs
Lohnsummen *fpl* wages
lokal local
lokale Stichprobe *f* spot sample
lokales Netzwerk *nt* local area network (LAN)
Lokalisationsgerät *nt* localizing equipment
Lokalverschleiß *m* local wear
Lokalversprödung *f* local embrittlement
LOM *f (Schichtobjektherstellung)* Laminated Object Manufacturing
longitudinal longitudinal
Longitudinalwelle *f* longitudinal wave
Los *nt* batch, charge, lot
lösbar removable, unscrewable, soluble, resolvable, solvable, detachable
lösbare Verbindung *f* detachable connection
lösbarer Schlauchanschluss *m* detachable hose connection
lösbares Teil *nt* detachable part (or member)
Losbildung *f* lot formation
losbinden untie
losbrechen break away
Losbrechmoment *m* initial breakaway torque
Löscharbeiten *fpl (Brandschutz)* firefighting operations
löschbar erasable (data storage)
löschbarer programmierbarer Nur-Lese-Speicher *m* erasable programmable read only memory (EPROM)
löschen 1. *(allg.)* cancel, delete, erase 2. (EDV) clear 3. (Feuer) extinguish 4. (Ladungen) discharge
Löschgeräte *ntpl* fire extinguishers
Löschkraft *f* releasing force
Löschvorgang *m* deletion
lose loose, slack, free
lose Backen *fpl* loose splits
Lösekraft *f (bei Pressverbänden)* separating force
lösen 1. *(allg.)* disconnect, release, unclamp, undo, unlatch, unscrew, untie, detach, disengage, solve 2. *(Pressverband)* dismantle 3. *(chem.)* solubilize, dissolve 4. *(Mutter Schraube)* loosen, slacken
loser Flansch *m* **mit Anschweißpunkt** slip-on flange with butt welded collar
loser Flansch *m* **mit Lötbund** slip-on flange with brazing collar
Lösetemperatur *f* solubility temperature
Losgröße *f* batch size, lot size
Losgrößenfertigung *f* batch production
loslassen 1. *(lösen)* release, remove contact with 2. *(abschalten)* trip
löslich soluble, dissolvable
losreißen tear off, pull off
losschrauben unbolt, unscrew, undo
Losstreuung *f* batch variation
Lösung *f* solution
Lösungsansatz *m* approach to problem

solving
lösungsgeglühter Werkstoff *m* solution annealed material
Lösungskalorimeter *nt* solution calorimeter
Lösungsmittel *nt* solvent
lösungsmittelarmer Kunststoff *m* low solvent synthetic resin
Lösungsmitteldampfentfettung *f* degreasing by solvent vapour
Lösungsmittelechtheit *f* fastness to organic solvents
lösungsmittelfreies Gießharz *nt* solvent-free casting resin
lösungsmittelhaltige Paste *f* solvent-containing paste
Lösungsmöglichkeit *f* solution
Lösungspetroleum *nt* solvent petroleum
Lösungsschema *nt* solvent scheme
Lösungsweg *m* *(e. Aufgabenstellung)* approach to solution
Lösungszustand *m* solution rate
Lot *nt* **1.** *(allg.)* plumb, solder **2.** *(als Zusatzwerkstoff)* filler metal, filler **3.** *(hochzinnlegiertes)* pewter **4.** *(mit hohem Zinkgehalt)* spelter **5.** *(über 450 °C)* brazing (filler) alloy **6.** *(unter 450 °C)* solder, soft solder **7.** *(Messgerät)* plummet, lead
Lot zuführen application of filler metal
Lotansatzstelle *f* point of application of the filler
Lotausbereitungsfehler *m* undesired wetting of base metal by filler metal
Lötbad *nt* dipping bath, solder bath, pool of solder
Lötbarkeitsprüfung *f* solderability test
lotbildendes Flussmittel *nt* solder-forming flux
Lötdepot *nt* soldering depot
Lötdraht *m* solder wire
Lotdrahtabschnitt *m* length of solder wire
löten solder
Löten *nt* **mit angelegtem Lot** soldering with preplaced filler metal
Löten *nt* **mit angesetztem Lot** soldering with hand fed filler metal
Löten *nt* **mit eingelegtem Lot** soldering with inserted filler metal
Löten *nt* **mit lotbeschichteten Teilen** soldering with components coated with filler metal
Löten *nt* **mit Lötdepot** soldering with soldering depot
Löten *nt* **unter inertem Schutzgas** brazing under an inert protective gas
Lötentwickler *m* generator for soldering duty
Lotfäden *mpl* solder filaments
Lötfahne *f* soldering tag
Lötfittings *mpl* capillary solder fittings
Lotform *f* filler shape
Lotformteil *m* preshaped filler, solder shape
Lötfugenbreite *f* close soldering joint width
Lotgift *nt* solder poison
Lötgruppe *f* soldered component, piece to be soldered
Lötkegelbuchse *f* brazed conical nipple
Lötkolben *m* copper bit for soldering, soldering bit, soldering iron
Lotkonstante *f* constant of the filler
Lötlampe *f* soldering blowlamp, blowtorch for soldering
lötlose Rohrverschraubung *f* solderless tube fitting
lötlose Schneidringrohrverschraubung *f* solderless olive type tube fitting
lötlose Verbindung *f* solderless joint
Lotmenge *f* amount of filler
Lötmittel *nt* solder, soldering flux
Lötmuffe *f* capillary socket
Lötnahtvolumen *nt* soldering seam volume
Lötöse *f* solder lug
Lötöse *f* **für Einsteckbefestigung** solder lug for slot-in fixing
Lötöse *f* **mit Drehsicherung** solder lug with no device to prevent turning
Lötöse *f* **mit Durchsteckbefestigung** solder lug with push-through fixing
Lötöse *f* **mit Nietzapfen** solder lug with rivet shank
Lötprozess *m* soldering process
Lotpunkt *m* solder point, soldering point, terminal
lotrecht vertical

Lotrechte *f* plump line
Lotschmelze *f* molten solder
Lotschweißen *nt* braze welding
Lötspalt *m* close soldering joint
Lötspaltbreite *f* close soldering joint width
Lötstelle *f* capillary joint
Lötstift *m* solder pin
Lötstift *m* **mit Bund** *m* solder pin with shoulder
Lötstift *m* **mit Flansch** *m* solder pin with flange
Lötstoppmittel *nt* soldering stopping medium
Lötstoß *m* soldering joint
Lötteil *m* soldered component, piece to be soldered
Lotüberlauf *m* filler metal overflow
Lot-Überzug *m* solder coating
Lötverbindung *f* soldered joint
Lötverhalten *nt* soldering behaviour
Lötverschließmaschine *f* solder sealing machine
Lötverschraubung *f* brazed union
Lotzusammensetzung *f* composition of the filler metal
L-Profil *nt* L-shaped profile
L-Stutzen *m* **(für Rohrverschraubungen)** L-adaptor (or fitting)
Lücke *f* gap, space
lückenbildender Förderer *m* spacing conveyor
Lückenbreite *f* gap width
Lückenfräser *m* single-angle cutter
lückenlos close, closely, without interruption, through, complete
Lückenmaß *nt* *(z. B. bei Gesenkschmiedestücken)* gap dimension
Lücken-Profiltangente *f* **am Hohlrad-Kopfkreis** space/profile tangent to the internal gear tip circle
Lückentiefe *f* *(Verzahnung)* depth of tooth, tooth height
Lückenweite *f* *(bei e. Geradstirnrad)* space-width
Lückenweite *f* **im Normalschnitt** normal space width
Lückenweite *f* **im Stirnschnitt** transverse space width
Lückenwinkel *m* gash angle, *(UK)* gashing angle
Luft *f* air
Luftabschluss *m* exclusion air
Luftabsperrklappe *f* air shut-off damper
Luftabzug *m* air vent, air escape
Luftaufbereitungsanlage *f* air preperation facility
Luftauslass *m* heater oulet
Luftbereifung *f* pneumatic tyre(s)
luftbetätigt air-actuated, air-operated
Luftbewegung *f* air motion
Luftblasen *fpl* bubbles
Luftdruck *m* 1. *(allg.)* air pressure 2. *(Reifen)* inflation pressure
Luftdruckalterung *f* compressed air ageing
Luftdurchlass *m* air passage, grille, vent
luftdurchlässig air permeable
Luftdurchlässigkeit *f* air permeability
Luftdurchsatz *m* air throughput
Luftdurchtritt *m* air passage
Luftdurchwirbelung *f* turbulent air circulation
Lufteinlass *m* air intake, air inlet
Luftemulgierung *f* air emulsification
lüften 1. *(allg.)* ventilate, aerate, air, vent 2. *(anheben, Meißel)* lift 3. *(Bremse)* release the brake, unjam
Lüfter *m* blower, fan, ventilator
Lüfterleistung *f* fan power
Lufterneuerung *f* air renewal
Lüfterraum *m* fan room
Luftfahrzeuge *ntpl* aircraft
Luftfeuchte *f* atmospheric humidity, humidity, air humidity
Luftfeuchtegefälle *nt* drop in atmospheric humidity
Luftfracht *f* air freight, air cargo
Luftführung *f* air circulation, routing of airflow
Luftgehalt *m* air void content
luftgekühlt air-cooled
Lufthärtung *f* air-hardening
Luftheizungsanlage *f* air circulation type central heating installation
Luftimpulsverfahren *nt* air impulse process
Luftkern *m* air core
Luftkernspule *f* air-core coil, air-core winding

Luftkissen *nt* cushion of air
Luftklappensteuerung *f* air damper control
Luft-Last-Verhältnissteller *m* air-load ratio setter
luftleer evacuated
Luftleistung *f* rate of airflow
Luftleiteinrichtung *f* air flow device
Luftmangelsicherung *f* air deficiency safety device
Luftnacherhitzer *m* air afterheater
Luftpostpapier *nt* **mit Lichtpausschicht** airmail paper with diazo coating
Luftreifen *m* inflatable tyre, pneumatic tyre
Luftreifenfelge *f* pneumatic tyre rim
Luftreinheit *f* air cleanness
Luftschalldämmung *f* airborne sound insulation
Luftschallemission *f* airborne sound (or noise) emission
Luftschallmessung *f* airborne noise measurement
Luftschallschutz *m* protection against air-borne noise
Luftschallübertragung *f* transmission of air-borne noise
Luftschliere *f* air stria
Luftspalt *m* air gap, interferric gap, interferric space
Luftstrecke *f* clearance (in air), air route
Luftstrom *m* air stream
Luftstromformverfahren *nt* air stream forming process
Luftstromregelung *f* air flow control
Luftstromregler *m* air flow controller
Luftströmungsfeld *nt* airflow pattern
Luftströmungsgeräusch *nt* airflow noise
Lufttechnik *f* ventilation technology
lufttechnische Anforderung *f* ventilation requirement
lufttechnische Anlage *f* ventilation system
Luftüberschusseinsteller *m* excess air adjuster
luftundurchlässig air-sealed, air-tight
Luftundurchlässigkeit *f* air-tightness

Lüftung *f* airing, ventilation, air conditioning, venting
Lüftungs- und Klimazentrale *f* centralized ventilation and air conditioning installation
Lüftungsanlage *f* **mit Befeuchtung** ventilating plant with humidifying action
Lüftungsdüse *f* outlet nozzle
Lüftungseinrichtung *f* ventilating equipment
Lüftungsgerät *nt* ventilation appliance, air conditioning appliance
Lüftungsingenieur *m* ventilation engineer
Lüftungsklappe *f* ventilation flap
Lüftungsleitung *f* ventilation line
Lüftungstechnik *f* ventilation practice (or technology)
Lüftungswärme *f* air infiltration heat requirement
Lüftungszentrale *f* central ventilating station
Luftventil *nt* breather
Luftverunreinigung *f* contamination of air
Luftvorerhitzer *m* air-pre-heater
Luftvorspülung *f* pre-ventilation, pre-purging, preliminary air scavenging
Luftvorwärmanlage *f* air preheating device
Luftwechsel *m* air change
Luftwirbeleinrichtung *f* air turbulence device
Lüftzeit *f* unjam time
Luftzusammensetzung *f* air combination
Lumineszenzdiode *f* light emitting diode (LED)
Lünette *f* steadyrest
Lünette *f:* **feststehende ~** stationary steady purpose machine
Lunker *m* cavity, void, shrinkage, pipes
Lunkerbildung *f* shrinkage forming
lunkerfrei pipeless, sound
Lunkerstelle *f* shrinkage cavity
Lupe *f* magnifying glass, loupe
Lyra-Ausgleicher *m* horseshoe expansion joint

M m

Maag-Hobelkamm *m* rack-type cutter
Maag-Zahnradhobelmaschine *f* Maag generator
Mäanderanschnitt *m* meander cuts
Mäandereinlauf *m* meander shrinkage
Machart *f* description, working
machen accomplish, make, manufacture, produce, render
Magazin *nt* 1. *(Werkstückzuführung)* magazine feeding attachment, magazine 2. *(Lager)* storeroom
Magazinautomat *m* automatic chucking machine, magazine automatic
Magazineinrichtung *f* magazine feeding (or loading) attachment
Magaziner *m (Lagerist)* stock clerk, storeman
Magazinzuführeinrichtung *f* magazine loading attachment
Magazinzuführung *f* magazine feed
Magnet *m* magnet, solenoid
Magnetband *nt* magnetic tape
Magnetbandausgeber *m* magnetic tape readout device
magnetbandgesteuerte Werkzeugmaschine *f* magnetic tape-controlled machine tool
Magnetfeld *nt* magnetic field
Magnetfeldänderung *f* alteration in magnetic fields
Magnetfeldsensor *m* magnetic field sensor
Magnetfluss *m* magnetic flux
Magnetfolie *f* magnetic foil
Magnetformverfahren *nt* magnet form process
Magnetfutter *nt* magnetic chuck
Magnetgreifer *m* magnetic gripper
Magnetimpulsschweißen *nt* magnetic pulse welding
magnetisch magnetic
magnetische Betätigung *f* solenoid operation
magnetische Durchflutung *f* magnetic penetration method
magnetische Feldlinie *f* magnetic flux line
magnetische Haftfestigkeit *f* magnetic adhesion
magnetischer Fluss *m* magnetic flux
magnetisches Streuflussverfahren *nt* magnetic leakage flux test
magnetisierbar magnetizable
magnetisieren magnetize
Magnetisierungsgerät *nt* magnetizing equipment
Magnetkarte *f* magnetic card
Magnetkupplung *f* electromagnetic clutch
Magnetrissprobe *f* magnetic crack test
Magnetrührwerk *nt* magnet stirrer
Magnetschalter *m* magnetic switch, proximity switch, solenoid switch
magnetisches Feld *nt* magnetic field
Magnetspannfutter *nt* magnetic chuck
Magnetspeicher *m* memory
Magnetspule *f* solenoid
Magnetstreifen *m* magnetic strip
Magnettafel *f* magnetic board
Magnettrommel *f* magnetic drum
Magnetventil *nt* solenoid valve
Magnetwerkstoff *m* magnetic material
Mahlbüchse *f* beater box
mahlen crush, grind, pulverise
Mahlgrad *m* freeness value brought about by beating
Mahlkörper *m* beater element
Mahlstufe *f* beating stage
Mahlzustand *m* freeness value brought about by beating
mahnen dun, remind
Mahnung *f* dunning letter, reminder
Make-or-buy-Entscheidung *f* make-or-buy decision
Makro *nt* macro
Makroelement *nt* macrocell
Makrofenster *nt* macro box
Makrofunktion *f* macro function
makrogeometrische Oberfläche *f* macrogeometrical surface pattern
Makrogestalt *f* macro form

Makroklima *nt* macro-climate
Makroriss *m* macro-crack
Makroschaltfläche *f* macro button
Makroschliff *m* macro-examination specimen, macrosection
Malerspachtel *f* spatula
Malteserkreuz *nt* Geneva cross, Geneva stop, Maltese cross
Manganphosphatschicht *f* manganese phosphate coating
Mangel *m* 1. *(Mangel)* deficiency, lack, shortage, deficit (in) 2. *(Fehler)* defect 3. *(Knappheit)* lack (of), scarcity
Mängel beseitigen remedy deficiencies
mängelbehaftet defective
Mängelbeseitigung *f* remedying of defects
mangelhaft defective, faulty, imperfect, incomplete, insufficient, deficient
Mangelladung *f* insufficient charging
Manipulation *f* manipulation
Manipulator *m* manipulator
manipulieren manipulate
Mann *m* **zur Ware** *f* man-to-part
Mann-oben-Stapler *m* man-up truck
Mann-unten-Stapler *m* man-down truck
Manöver *nt* *(UK)* manoeuvre, *(US)* maneuver
manövrieren *(UK)* manoeuvre, *(US)* maneuver
manövrierfähig *(UK)* manoeuvrable, *(US)* maneuverable
manövrierunfähig disabled
Manschette *f* sleeve, lip-type of packing, collar
Manschettenverbindung *f* sleeve joint
Mantel *m* 1. *(Jacke, Hüle, Schicht)* coat, jacket, outer casing, envelope 2. *(e. Bohrung)* boundary surface 3. *(Ummantelung)* circumferential surface
Mantelfläche *f* envelope surface, cylindrical surface, outside surface
Mantelkurvenfräseinrichtung *f* cylindrical cam milling attachment
Mantellinie *f* *(e. Grundzylinders)* director line, envelope line
Mantelschneide *f* peripheral cutting edge
Mantelstutzen *m* shell nozzle
manuell manual, by hand
manuell gesteuert manually controlled
manuell gesteuerte Tore *ntpl* manual control doors
manuelle Lastenanhebung *f* manual lifting
manuelle Programmierung *f* manual programming
manueller Antrieb *m* manual drive
manueller Wiederanlauf *m* **bei geschützten Ausgängen** manual restart of protected output
manuelles Löten *nt* hand soldering
MAP *Abk* Manufacturing Automation Protocol
Marke *f* 1. *(Hersteller)* brand, trademark 2. *(e. Skalenanzeige)* index 3. *(Reiter)* tag 4. *(Zeichen)* token, mark, marker
Marketing *nt* marketing
markieren 1. *(beschriften)* label, mark, sign, designate 2. *(EDV)* select
Markierung *f* mark, marking
Markt *m* market
Marktanalyse *f* market analysis
Markteinführungsphase *f* market introduction phase
Markterkundung *f* market reconnaissance
Marktforschung *f* market research
Marktführer *m* market leader
Marktführerschaft *f* market leadership
Marktlage *f* state of the market
marktorientiert market-oriented
marktreif ready for market, ready to market
Marktreife *f* market maturity
Marktsättigung *f* market saturation
Marktsegment *nt* market segment
Marktübersicht *f* market overall view
Marktwert *m* market value
Marktwirtschaft *f* market economy
marktwirtschaftlich free-enterprise
Martensitstufe *f* martensite region
Masche *f* mesh
Maschendraht *m* wire netting

Maschenware *f* mesh material
Maschenweite *f* mesh size
Maschine *f* **1.** *(Arbeitsmaschine)* machine **2.** *(elektrisch betätigt)* motor **3.** *(Fahrzeug, Kraftmaschine)* engine **4.** *(Verbrennungsmaschine)* engine, motor
Maschine *f* **mit verstellbarer Spindel** adjustable spindle machine
maschinell by machine
maschinelle Einrichtung *f* mechanical installation
Maschinelle Programmierung *f* Computer Aided Programming
maschineller Tiefenvorschub *m* power down feed
maschinelles Schutzgasschweißen *nt* automatic shielded-arc welding
Maschinen *f* machinery
Maschinen *f* **mit hin- und hergehender Hauptbewegung** reciprocating machinery
Maschinenachse *f* machine axis
Maschinenanbindung *f* machine link
Maschinenanlage *f* machinery plant, mechanical equipment
Maschinenanzahl *f* number of machine
Maschinenarbeiter *m* operator, machine operator
Maschinenarbeitsablauf *m* machine cycle
Maschinenausfall *m* machine breakdown
Maschinenauslastung *f* machines extent of utilization
Maschinenauswahl *f* machine selection
Maschinenbau *m* mechanical engineering, machine building, machine construction, machine building industry
Maschinenbauer *m* mechanical engineer, machine builder
Maschinenbauingenieur *m* mechanical engineer
maschinenbedingte Abweichung *f* machine-dependent deviation
Maschinenbelegung *f* machine utilization

Maschinenbelegungszeit *f* **1.** *(allg.)* machine utilization time **2.** *(benötigte ~)* required machine utilization time **3.** *(erforderliche ~)* necessary machine utilization time
Maschinenbetriebskosten *pl* machine operation costs
Maschinenbett *nt* bed, machine bed
Maschinenbett *nt* **mit Füßen** bench
Maschinenbezugsachse *f* machine reference axis
Maschinencode *m* machine code
Maschinendaten *pl* machine data
Maschinendefekt *m* machinery breakdown
Maschineneinrichtung *f* mechanical equipment
Maschinenelement *nt* machine element, component
Maschinenentwurf *m* machine design
Maschinenfläche *f* machine area
Maschinenform *f* machine shape, machine form
Maschinenformerei *f* machine moulding shop
Maschinengestell *nt* machine rack
Maschinenhalle *f* machine shop
Maschinenhauptzeiten *fpl* machine production times *pl*
Maschinenintensität *f* machine intensity
Maschinenkartei *f* catalogue of machines
Maschinenläppen *nt* machine lapping
Maschinenlaufzeit *f* machine time
Maschinenleistung *f* machine efficiency, machine capacity
Maschinenlos *nt* several machines of the same family, machine family
Maschinennullpunkt *m* machine zero point
Maschinenpark *m* machinery, machine outfit
Maschinenraum *m* machine room
Maschinenreibahle *f* machine reamer
Maschinenschild *nt* machine plate, instruction plate
Maschinenschrauberwerkzeug *nt* power socket wrench
Maschinenschraubstock *m* machine

vice
Maschinenschüttelfrequenz *f* machine shaking frequency
Maschinensicherheit *f* machinery safety
maschinenspezifische Bedingungen *fpl* conditions applicable to individual family of machines
Maschinenstamm *m* machine master file
Maschinenstammdaten *pl* machine master data
Maschinenständer *m* machine base, machine column, machine upright
Maschinenstößel *m* ram
Maschinenstundensatz *m* machine hourly rate
maschinentaktabhängig machine cycle-dependent
maschinentaktabhängiges Programmsteuergerät *nt* programmed control device dependent on machine cycle
maschinentaktgesteuert machine cycle-controlled
maschinentechnische Berechnung *f* mechanical engineering calculation
Maschinenteil *nt* machine part, machine component
Maschinentisch *m* machine table
Maschinenwärter *m* machine attendant
Maschinenwerkhalle *f* machine shop
Maschinenwerkstatt *f* machine stop
Maschinenwerkzeug *nt* industrial tool, machine shop tool
Maschinenwerkzeug *nt* **für Metall** metalcutting tool
Maschinenwesen *nt* mechanical engineering, engineering
Maschinenzeit *f* time per cut
Maschinenzubehör *nt* machine accessories
Maschinenzyklus *m* machine cycle
Maserung *f* speckles
Maske *f* **1.** *(allg.)* mask **2.** *(bewegte ~)* movable mask **3.** *(bewegte ~, Verfahren)* mask dragging **4.** *(synchronisierte ~)* synchronized mask
Maskenanordnung *f* mask layout
Maskenbit *nt* mask bit
Maskendatei *f* mask file
Maskenformverfahren *nt* mask form process
Maskengenerator *m* mask generator
maskengesteuert mask-controlled
Maskenmaterial *nt* mask material
Maskenmembranwerkstoff *m* mask membrane material
Maskenmembran *f* mask membrane
Maskenparameter *m* mask parameter
Maskenscannen *nt* **1.** *(allg.)* mask scan **2.** *(synchronisiertes ~)* synchronized mask scanning
Maskenverfahren *nt* mask method, mask process
Maskenwort *nt* mask word
Maß *nt* **1.** *(Abmessung)* dimension **2.** *(Lehre) (US)* gage, *(UK)* gauge **3.** *(Größe)* size **4.** *(Ausmaß)* extent **5.** *(Bandmaß)* tape rule **6.** *(dimensionsloses ~)* value **7.** *(Menge)* quantity **8.** *(Messergebnis)* dimension, size **9.** *(Messlineal, Werkzeug)* rule **10.** *(Messmel)* measuring instrument **11.** *(Messzeug)* measuring tool **12.** *(Metermaß)* meter rule
Maßablesung *f* dimension reading
Maßabstrich *m* scale indication yardstick
Maßabweichung *f* **1.** *(allg.)* dimensional variation, error, measure deviation **2.** *(Abmaß)* allowance **3.** *(positiv oder negativ)* deviation **4.** *(positiv und negativ)* variation **5.** *(von Fertigungsteilen)* offsize **6.** *(zulässige ~)* admissible tolerance
Maßabweichung *f* **von den Sollmaßen** deviation from the specified values
Maßänderung *f* size alteration
Maßangaben *fpl* dimension data *pl*
maßbeständig permanent to size (or dimension)
maßbeständige Tafel *f* sheet offering maximum dimensional stability
Maßbeständigkeit *f* permanence of size, dimensional stability
Maßbild *nt* block gauge, precision gauge block, combination gauge block,

slip gauge, end block, end measure, block
Maßblatt *nt* dimension sheet
Maßblock *m* block gauge, precision gauge block, combination gauge block, slip gauge, end block, end measure, block
Maßbuchstabe *m* dimension letter
Masse *f* **1.** *(phys.)* mass **2.** *(Gewicht)* weight, dead weight **3.** *(el.)* earth, grounding, ground **4.** *(Menge)* quantity
Maße *ntpl* **ohne Toleranzangaben** *fpl* untoleranced dimensions, sizes (or dimensions) without tolerance indication
Maßeingang *m* dimensional constraints
Maßeinheit *f* dimension unit
Maßeintragung *f* dimensioning
Massenanteil *m* **in Prozent** percent by weight
Massenfertigung *f* mass production, quantity production, long run production
Massenfertigungsmaschine *f* batch production machine, long run production machine
Massengehalt *m* **an Wasser** water content by mass
Massengut *nt* bulk material, bulk goods
Massenguteinheit *f* unit of bulk material
Massenherstellung *f* duplicate production
Massenkonstanz *f* mass constancy
Massenkraft *f* force of inertia
Massenphotoabsorptionskoeffizient *m* mass-photo-electric absorption coefficient
Massenschwerpunkt *m* mass centre of gravity
Massenstrom *m* mass flow rate, energy flow
Massenträgheit *f* mass inertia
Massenträgheitsmoment *m* **1.** *(allg.)* moment of mass inertia **2.** *(des Motors)* motor moment of inertia
Massenverlust *m (Gewichtsverlust)* mass loss
Massenzunahme *f (Gewichtszunahme)* mass increase
Masse-Paarbildungskoeffizient *m* mass-pair production coefficient
Massepolymerisat *nt* bulk polymer
Masseschluss *m* earth, body contract, *(US)* ground
Massetemperatur *f* mass temperature, material temperature
Masseverringerung *f* mass decrease (or reduction)
maßgenau true to size
Maßgenauigkeit *f* dimensional accuracy, accuracy of dimension, accuracy to size
maßgerecht accurate to size (or dimension), true to size, true
Maßgrenzen *f* close limits
Maßhaltigkeit *f* dimensional accuracy, dimensional stability, accuracy to size, holding of size
Maßhilfslinie *f* projection line
massiv one-piece, solid, heavy, massive
Massivbau *m* solid structure
Massivdrahtelektrode *f* solid wire electrode
massiver Fräser *m* solid cutter
massiver Fräser *m* **mit bestückter Schneide** tipped solid cutter
massiver Radkörper *m* **aus einem Werkstoff** solid wheel centre
Massivlochen *nt* indirect impact extrusion of hollow items
Massivprägen *nt* closed-die coining
Massivumformen *nt* solid forming
Maßkennzeichnung *f* identification marking of dimensions
Maßkette *f* **1.** *(allg.)* dimension chain, chain dimensioning **2.** *(geschlossene ~)* closed chain dimensioning
Maßkettentheorie *f* dimension chain theory
Maßklötzchen *nt* block gauge, precision gauge block, combination gauge block, slip gauge, end block, end measure, block
Maßkonstanz *f* constancy in size
Maßläppen *nt* forming lapping
Maßlehre *f* dimensional gauge
maßlich dimensional
maßliche Überbestimmung *f* redun-

dant dimensioning
Maßlinie *f:* **von außen herangezogene** ~ dimension line draw towards the object from outside
Maßlinien *fpl:* **übereinanderliegende** ~ dimension lines spaced one above the other
Maßlinienbegrenzung *f* dimension line termination
Maßlinienbogen *m* dimension line arc
Maßlücke *f* dimension gap
Maßnahme *f* action, measure, proceeding, provision
Maßnahmen ergreifen take measures, take action
Maßnahmenplanung *f* action plan
Maßnorm *f* dimension standard
Maßpfeil *m* dimension arrowhead
Maßprägen *nt* sizing
Maßprüfung *f* size check
Maßqualität *f* dimension quality
Maßschleifen *nt* grinding to size, size grinding
Maßschwankung *f* dimensional variation
Maßspan *m* sizing cut
Maßstab *m* **1.** *(e. Zeichnung)* scale **2.** *(e. Strichmaßstabes)* graduation **3.** *(Instrument)* measure, measuring rod, gauge, rule, yardstick **4.** *(mit Strichteilung)* rule **5.** *(ohne Strichteilung)* straight edge **6.** *(mit Nonius)* vernier scale **7.** *(in vergrößertem ~)* on a larger scale
Maßstabänderung *f* scaling
maßstabgerechte Darstellung *f* scaled drawing
maßstäblich full scale, full of scale, true to scale
maßstäblich zeichnen draw to scale
maßstäbliche Darstellung *f* representation to scale
maßstabsgetreu true to scale
Maßstelle *f* dimensioned point
Maßsystem *nt* system of measurement
maßsystematische Abweichung *f* measure systematic deviation
Maßtoleranz *f* tolerance in size, permissible variation in size, dimensional tolerance

Maßtoleranzfeld *nt* dimensional tolerance zone
Maßüberbestimmung *f* redundant dimension
Maßübertragung *f* measurement transfer
Maßverkörperung *f* material measure
Maßwalzen *nt* size rolling
Maßzahl *f* dimension figure
Maßzeichnung *f* dimensional drawing
Mast *m* mast, column
mastabgewandt facing away form the mast
Mastaufbau *m* mast structure
Mastauslenkung *f* mast deflection
Mastdurchbiegung *f* mast deflection, deflection of mast
Mastführung *f* mast guide (rail)
Mastführungstoleranz *f* mast guide rail tolerance
Mastfuß *m* mast base
Mastfußbefestigung *f* mast base mounting, mast base fastening
Mastikation *f* mastication
Mastneigung *f* mast tilting
Mastschwingung *f* mast oscillation
mastzugewandt facing the mast
metastabil metastable
Material *nt* **1.** *(allg.)* material(s), stock **2.** (abgetragenes ~) ablated material **3.** (aktives ~) active material
Materialanforderung *f* materials requisition
Materialauflösung *f* dissolution of material
Materialaufwand *m* material costs
Materialbahn *f* material path
Materialbedarf *m* material needs, material (or stock) requirements, material demand
Materialbedarfsermittlung *f* material demand assessment
materialbedingte Korrosion *f* material-dependent corrosion
materialbedingter Verlust *m* material-dependent loss
Materialbegleitschein *m* material document
Materialbereitstellung *f* materials supply

Materialbeschaffung *f* materials procurement
Materialbeschreibung *f* material description
Materialbestand *m* stock-on-hand quantity
Materialbewegung *f* stock transfer
Materialbezeichnung *f* material designation
Materialbuchung *f* material booking
Materialdicke *f* material thickness
Materialdisposition *f* material arrangements
Materialeigenschaft *f* material property
Materialentnahme *f* material withdraw
Materialentsorgung *f* material removal
Materialfarbcode *m* material colour code
Materialfehler *m* material defect
Materialfluss *m* material flow
Materialflussbereich *m* material flow part
Materialflussdarstellung *f* representation of material flow
Materialflussform *f* material flow form
Materialflusskette *f* material flow chain
Materialflusskonzept *nt* material flow concept
Materialflussmatrix *f* material flow matrix
materialflussorientiert stock-control oriented
Materialflussschema *nt* material flow diagram
Materialflusssteuerung *f* material handling controller, material handling control
Materialflusstechnik *f* materials handling engineering
Materialflussuntersuchung *f* material flow study
Materialflussvorgang *m* material flow process
Materialfreigabe *f* stock release
Materialgemeinkosten *pl* material general costs
Materialherkunftsnachweis *m* item source certificate
Materialkennzeichen *nt* material designation, material marking
Materialkosten *pl* material costs
Materiallager *nt* material warehouse, store of materials and supplies
Materialmanagement *nt* materials management
Materialplan *m* stock plan
Materialplanung *f* material (or stock) planning
Materialprüfanstalt *f* Materials Testing Institute
Materialstamm *m* material master file
Materialstammdaten *pl* material master data
Materialsteifigkeit *f* material stiffness
Materialstrom *m* material flow
Materialträger *m* material carrier
Materialverfügbarkeit *f* availability of materials
Materialverlust *m* material loss
Materialversorgung *f* materials supply
Materialversorgungsprozess *m* material supply process
Materialwahl *f* material selection
Materialwirtschaft *f* materials (or stock) management
Materialzugabe *f* stock allowance, stock left
Materialzugang *m* materials provision, materials receipt, addition to materials
Materie *f* matter
mathematisch mathematical
mathematische Statistik *f* mathematical statistics
Matrix *f* matrix
Matrixcode *m* matrix code
Matrixdrucker *m* matrix printer
Matrixkamera *f* matrix camera
Matrize *f* die, female piece
Matrizenfräsmaschine *f* die-sinking machine
Matte *f* mat
mattieren dull, frost
Mattierung *f* mat finishing, dulling, frosting
Mattscheibe *f* ground glass, focusing screen

Mattschweißstelle *f* cold lap
Mattwerden *nt* dulling
Mauerwerk *nt* stonework, masonry
Maul *nt* jaw, mouth
Maulquerschnitt *m (Betonrohre)* mole cross-section
Maulschlüssel *nt* jaw wrench, open-end wrench
Maulweite *f* wrench opening
Maustaste *f* mouse button
maximaler Arbeitsdruck *m* maximum working pressure
Maximalmenge *f* maximum quantity
maximieren maximize
Maximierung *f* maximization
Maximum *nt* maximum
Maximummaterialprofil *nt* maximum material profile
Maximumoperator *m* maximum operator
Maximumprüfdorn *m* maximum master plug gauge
Maximumprüfkörper *m* maximum check gauging member
Mechanik *f* mechanics
Mechanikerdrehmaschine *f* bench lathe
mechanisch mechanical
mechanisch betrieben mechanically operated
mechanische Bremsung *f* retarding devices
mechanische Stabilität *f* mechanical stability
mechanische Verbindungselemente *ntpl* mechanical fasteners
mechanische Verfahren *ntpl* mechanical processes
mechanische Verriegelung *f* mechanical interlock
mechanisches Beschicken *nt (e. Werkstückes)* mechanical loading
mechanisches Schaltgetriebe *nt* mechanical gear-shift system
mechanisches Verbindungselement *nt* mechanical fastener
Mechatronik *f* mechatronics
Median *m* median
Medium *nt* **1.** *(allg.)* medium **2.** *(Flüssigkeit)* fluid **3.** *(abgegebenes ~)* donor

4. *(aufnehmendes ~)* acceptor, recipient
medizinische Einrichtung *f* medical equipment
Meerwasser-Tauchprüfung *f* sea water immersion test
mehr more
mehradrig multi-core, multi-wire
mehradrig verdrillter Schweißdraht *m* multi-core stranded filler wire
Mehraufwand *m* extra expenditure, additional outlay
Mehrbahnenbett *nt* multiple-track bed
Mehrbereich-Messgerät *nt* multiple-range measuring instrument
Mehrbreitencode *m* multiple-width code
mehrdimensional multidimensional, multivariate
mehrdimensionale Verteilung *f* multinomial distribution
mehrere several
mehrfach in a series of turns, several times
mehrfach programmierbar reprogrammable
Mehrfachabbiegen *nt* multiple folding
Mehrfachabfrage *f* multiple interrogation
Mehrfachabschneiden *nt* multiple cropping
Mehrfachanschnitt *m* multiple gate
Mehrfachbedienung *f* multiple manning devices
Mehrfachbelichtung *f* multiple exposure
Mehrfachdüse *f* multiple nozzle
mehrfache Aufteilung *f (z. B. von Probeneinheiten)* multiple classification
mehrfache Radpaarung *f* gear train
mehrfacher Pressverband *m* multiple interference fit
mehrfaches Hin- und Herbiegen *nt* multiple bending in opposite directions
Mehrfachfehler *m* multiple error
Mehrfachhobeln *nt* multiple planing
Mehrfachkeilbiegen *nt* multiple V-form bending
Mehrfachlagendepallettierer *m*

multiposition depalletizer
Mehrfachlagenpalettierer multiposition palletizer
Mehrfach-LAM *nt* multiple LHD
Mehrfachlastaufnahme *f* multiple load capacity, multiple-load carrying device
Mehrfachleitung *f* multi-conductor line
Mehrfachmaske *f* multiple mask, indexed mask
Mehrfachmeißelhalter *m* combination toolholder, combination (or gang) tool block, gang toolholder
Mehrfachpackung *f* multipack
Mehrfachräder *ntpl* multiple wheels
Mehrfachrollenmaschine *f* multiple electrode wheel machine
Mehrfachrollen-Nahtschweißmaschine *f* multi-wheel seam welding machine
Mehrfachspiel *nt* multiple cycle
Mehrfachstapel *m* multiple stack
Mehrfachstapel-Umladung *f* multiple stack transfer
mehrfachtief multiple depth, multiple deep
mehrfachtiefe Lagerung *f* multiple depth storage, multiple deep storage
Mehrfachvorsatzgeräte *ntpl* multiple equipment, multiple implements
Mehrfachzelle *f* multi-cell, dynamic cell
Mehrfachzellenfunktion *f* multi-cell dynamic functioning
Mehrfachzellenschutzeinrichtung *f* dynamic cell positioning, multi-cell positioning
Mehrfachzugriff *m* multiple load capacity
Mehrfarbenlichtpauspapier *nt* multicolour light print paper
Mehrfasenstufenbohrer *m* **für Senkungen für Zylinderschrauben mit Schlitz** subland twist drill for counterbores for slotted cheese head screws
Mehrflankenschnitt *m* multi-flank cut
mehrgängiges Gewinde *nt* multiple thread
mehrgängiges Linksgewinde *nt* multi-start left-hand thread
mehrgängiges Rechtsgewinde *nt* multi-start right-hand thread
mehrgängiges, flaches metrisches Trapezgewinde *nt* multi-start stub metric trapezoidal screw thread
mehrgassig multiple-aisle, multi-lane
Mehrgeschossanlage *f* multi-tier installation
mehrgeschossig 1. *(Gebäude)* multistorey **2.** *(Regal)* multi-tier
mehrgliedriger Radiator *m* multi-section radiator
Mehrkanalmodul *nt* multi-channel module
Mehrkantbohren *nt* polygon drilling
Mehrkantdreharbeiten *fpl* polygonal turning jobs
Mehrkantdrehen *nt* polygon turning
Mehrkantensteuerung *f* multiple-edge tracing
Mehrkantprofil *nt* polygon profile, polygon
Mehrkolbenpumpenaggregat *nt* multiple plunger pumping set
Mehrkornabrichten *nt* multiple-point truing
Mehrkornabrichter *m* multiple-point truer
Mehrkreiszahnradpumpenaggregat *nt* multi-gear pumping set
Mehrkurvenautomat *m* multiple-cam operated automatic turret lathe
Mehrkurvensteuerung *f* independent cam control for each operation
Mehrkurvensystem *nt* multiple-cam system
mehrlagige Kehlnaht *f* multi-run fillet weld
mehrlagige Schweißung *f* multi-layer welding
mehrlagiger Plattenheizkörper *m* multi-level panel type radiator
Mehrleitungsanlage *f* multi-line system
Mehrleitungssystem *nt* multi-line principle operation
Mehrlinienzuführung *f* multiple line feed (system), multiline system
Mehrlochbohreinrichtung *f* multiple-

hole drilling attachment
Mehrmaschinenbelegung *f* multiple machine allocation
Mehrmeißelaufspannung *f* gang-type toolholder
Mehrpalettengabel *f* multi-pallet clamp
mehrparametrisch *(von digitalen Signalen)* multi-parameter (in character)
Mehrplatinenrechner *m* multiboard computer
mehrplatzfähig *(EDV)* multistation, capable of supporting multi-user operation
Mehrplatzlagerung *f* multi-location storage
Mehrplatzrechner *m* multi-user system, networked system
Mehrplatzsystem *nt* multi-location system
Mehrplatzsystem *nt* **(EDV)** multi-user system, network system
Mehrplatztechnik *f* multi-location system
mehrpolig multi-pin
Mehrpreis *m* extra (price), surcharge
mehrprofilige Schleifscheibe *f* multi-rib wheel
Mehrprozessorbetrieb *m* multiprocessing
mehrpunktfähig multi-point
Mehrpunktglied *nt* multi-level action element
Mehrpunkt-Regeleinrichtung *f* multi-level action controlling system
Mehrpunktschnittstelle *f* multi-point interface (MPI)
Mehrpunktverhalten *nt* **(von Gliedern)** multi-level action
Mehrradantrieb *m* multiwheel drive
Mehrrechnerbetrieb *m* multi-processing
Mehrrechnersystem *nt* multi-computer system, multi-processor system
mehrreihig in multiple rows, multi-row
mehrreihiger Plattenheizkörper *m* multi-bank panel radiator
Mehrsäulengerät *nt* multi-mast machine
Mehrscheibenbremse *f* multiple-disc brake, multi-disc brake

Mehrscheibenkupplung *f* multi-disc clutch
Mehrschichtbetrieb *m* multi-shift operation, more than one shift per day
Mehrschicht-Leichtbauplatte *f* multilayer slab
Mehrschicht-Scheibe *f* laminated pane
Mehrschichtsystem *nt* laminated system
mehrschneidig multi-blade
mehrschneidiges Werkzeug *nt* multiple-point cutting tool, multipoint tool, multi-edge cutting tool, multiple edged tool
Mehrschnittdrehmaschine *f* multi-cut lathe
Mehrschraubenverbindung *f* multiple bolted joint, multiple screw connection
mehrseitig gerichtet multi-directional
Mehrsortenzuführung *f* multi-product feed (system), multiple product feed, multiple-product system
Mehrspindelausführung *f* multiple-spindle design
Mehrspindelautomat *m* multiple-spindle automatic lathe
Mehrspindelbauart *f* multiple-spindle design
Mehrspindelbohren *nt* multiple-spindle drilling
Mehrspindelbohrkopf *m* multiple-spindle drilling head
Mehrspindelbohrmaschine *f* multiple-spindle boring machine
Mehrspindelfräsen *nt* multiple spindle milling
Mehrspindelfräsmaschine *f* multiple (or multi-head) milling machine
Mehrspindel-Fräsmaschine *f* multihead milling machine
Mehrspindelhonmaschine *f* multiple-spindle honing machine
Mehrspindelkopf *m* multiple-spindle drilling head
Mehrspindelmaschine *f* multiple-spindle machine
Mehrspindelplanfräsmaschine *f* multiple-spindle fixed-bed type milling

machine, multiple-spindle manufacturing-type milling machine, *(UK)* multi-spindle bench-type milling machine
Mehrspindelstangenautomat *m* multi-spindle bar automatic
Mehrspindler *m* multiple-spindle automatic lathe
Mehrstahlhalter *m* gang-type toolholder
mehrstellig multi-digit
mehrstellige Ziffernskala *f* multi-place digital scale
Mehrstoffmotor *m* dual-fuel engine
Mehrstromkreismodul *nt* multi-circuit module
Mehrstufen ... multi-stage, multi-step
Mehrstufenkopf *m* multiple-step push button
mehrstufig multi-echelon, multi-stage, multi-level, multistep
mehrstufige Probennahme *f* multistage sampling
mehrstufige Räderpaarung *f* multi-stage gear pairing, multi-stage gear mating
mehrstufiges Getriebe *nt* multi-stage gear transmission
Mehr-Taste *f* increase key
mehrteilig multipart
mehrteiliges Räumwerkzeug *nt* sectional broach
Mehruhrensystem *nt* multi-clock system
Mehrverbrauch *m* excess consumption
Mehrweg- *präfix* reusable, returnable
Mehrwegbehälter *m* reusable container, multi-purpose container, pay-off package
Mehrwegbohrmaschine *f* multiple-way boring machine
Mehrwegemaschine *f* multiple-way machine
Mehrwegeschalter *m* multiple-way switch
Mehrwegestapler *m* multi-directional truck
Mehrwegestapler *m* **mit Schubmast** multi-directional reach truck
Mehrwegeventil *nt* manifold valve, multiway valve

Mehrwertsteuer *f* value added tax (VAT)
Mehrzahnfräser *m* multi-point milling cutter
mehrzahnig multi-toothed
mehrzahniger Fräser *nt* multi-toothed cutter
mehrzeilig multi-line
Mehrzimmerofen *m* multi-room heating stove
Mehrzweckdrehmaschine *f* universal lathe, multi-purpose lathe
Mehrzweckfräsmaschine *f* multi-purpose milling machine
Mehrzweckmaschine *f* multiple-purpose machine
Mehrzweckschlüssel *m* **mit Innenvierkant** multi-purpose key with inner square
Meilenstein *m* milestone
Meißel *m* **1.** *(als Maschinenwerkzeug)* industrial tool, cutting tool, cutter **2.** *(Handwerkzeug)* hand tool, chisel **3.** *(einschneidiger ~)* single-point cutting tool **4.** *(gekröpfter ~)* goose-neck tool **5.** *(hartmetallbestückter ~)* carbide-tipped tool **6.** *(~ mit zwei Schneiden)* double-cutting tool **7.** *(~ mit gerader Schneidkante)* square-nosed tool
Meißelabheber *m* tool lifter
Meißelabhebung *f* tool lift (or relief), retraction of the tool
Meißelabhubsteuerung *f* tool lift control
Meißelanordnung *f* tool layout
Meißelanstellung *f* tool setting
Meißelausladung *f* overhang of the cutting tool, tool overhang
Meißeleinsatz *m* tool bit
Meißeleinsatzhalter *m* tool bit holder
Meißeleinspannung *f* tool mounting (or clamping)
Meißelhalter *m* **1.** *(allg.)* toolholder, toolbox, toolpost, toolhead **2.** *(mit Abhebung)* relieving toolholder
Meißelhalterklappe *f* toolholder clapper, tool apron, toolholder flap
Meißelhalterträger *m* toolholder carrier

Meißelhebeeinrichtung f tool-lift mechanism, tool lifter
Meißelklappe f clapper box, clapper block, tool apron, clapper
Meißellüftung f tool lift, tool relief
meißeln chisel (by hand), chip
Meißelquerschnitt m tool section
Meißelrückzug m tool relief mechanism
Meißelsatz m gang tool
Meißelschalter m master controller
Meißelschieber m saddle
Meißelschlitten m toolhead slide, head slide
Meißelschneide f cutting tool edge, cutting edge, tool chip
Meißelspitze f cutting tool nose
Meißelvorschub m tool feed
Meißelwinkel m lip angle, (UK) wedge angle
Meister m foreman
Meisterbereich m foreman area
Melaminformaldehydkondensationsharz nt melamine formaldehyde condensation resin
Melaminharzleim m melamine resin glue
Melaminharzpressmasse f melamine resin compression moulding material
Melaminphenolharz nt melamine-phenolic resin
Meldeanzeige f message display
Meldebild nt message display
Meldeeinrichtung f signalling device, alarm device
Meldeelektronik f message chronicle
Meldefolge f message sequence
Meldeleuchte f indicating lamp, indicating light
melden message, signal, state, report, indicate
Meldeort m signalling point
Meldepaar nt pair of messages
Meldeprotokoll nt message report, events log
Melder m indicator
Meldeschwall m message surge
Meldeseite f message page
Meldestatistik f message statistics
Meldesystem nt signalling system
Meldetext m message text
Meldung f 1. (allg.) message, report 2. (SPS) alarm
Meldungspriorität f message priority
Meliorationskalkung f amelioration liming
Membranarmatur f diaphragm valve
Membranausdehnungsgefäß nt diaphragm type expansion tank
Membrane f diaphragm
Membranschweißdichtung f welded diaphragm joint (or gasket)
Membransteuerung f (e. Absperrorgans) diaphragm control
Menge f amount, batch, quantity, rate, volume, tonnage
Mengenangaben fpl in volumes expressed in
Mengeneinheit f unit of volume
mengengerecht erfüllt fulfilled correctly in terms of volume (or quantity)
Mengengerüst nt quantified system parameter, quantity framework
Mengenleistung f output
mengenmäßig in terms of amount, in terms of quantity
Mengenschwankung f volume fluctuation
Mengenstrom m volume flow, material flow
Mengenstückliste f quantity list of parts, mass part list
Mengenverhalten nt quantitative behaviour
Meniskus m meniscus
menschliches Fehlverhalten nt human error(s)
Mensch-Maschine-Schnittstelle f human-machine interface (HMI), man-machine interface (MMI)
Menü nt menu
Menüdialog m menu dialog
Mercerisierechtheit f fastness to mercerizing
Merker m bit memory, memory, flag, marker
Merkmal nt 1. (Eigenschaft) characteristic 2. (Kennzeichen) feature, criterion
Merkmalsausprägung f feature presentation

Merkmalsextraktion *f* feature extraction
Merkmalsträger *m* bearer of characteristics
Merkmalstransformation *f* feature transformation
Merkmalswert *m* value of a characteristic
Mess- und Regeleinrichtungen *fpl* measurement and control devices
Messabweichung *f* error of measurement, measurement error
Messamboss *m* 1. *(e. Messschraube)* measuring anvil 2. *(e. Passimeters)* contact point
Messanlage *f* measuring installation, measuring system
Messanordnung *f* measuring arrangement, test setup
Messaufwand *m* measurement expenditure
Messausrüstung *f* (measuring) instrumentation
Messband *nt* measuring tape
Messbank *f* measuring bench
messbar measurable, determinable
Messbecher *m* volumetric cup
Messbecherfüllmaschine *f* volumetric cup filling machine
Messbereich *m* measuring range
Messbericht *m* test report on results
Messblock *m* slip gage (or gauge)
Messbolzen *m* (measuring) plunger, contact stylus
Messdaten *pl* measured data
Messdatum *nt* measured data
Messdom *m* test dome
Messdorn *m* test bar
Messdraht *m* thread measuring wire
Messdruck *m* contact pressure
Messdruckanzeiger *m* contact pressure indicator
Messdüse *f* measuring jet
Messebene *f* plane of measurement
Messeinrichtung *f* measuring equipment (or outfit or appliance), measuring system, measuring device
Messeinrichtung *f* **zum Zählen von alpha-Teilchen** measuring system for counting alpha-particles

Messeinsatz *m* contact point
Messeinteilung *f* graduation
Messelement *nt* measuring element
messen determine, check, measure, *(US)* gage, *(UK)* gauge, meter, rate, quantify
messen 1. *(mittels Lehre)* *(US)* gage, *(UK)* gauge 2. *(mittels Zähler z. B. Flüssigkeiten, Gase, Strom)* meter 3. *(masch.)* measure, take measurements 4. *(mit Stoppuhr)* time 5. *(mittels Strichmaß verstellbarer Lehre)* calliper
Messen *nt* checking, determining, measuring, *(US)* gaging, *(UK)* gauging
Messen *nt* **des Werkstücks zwischen den Bearbeitungsgängen** in-process gauging of a workpiece
Messen *nt* **mit Parallelendmaßen** gauge block measuring
Messen *nt* **nach Beendigung des Arbeitsganges** post-process gauging
Messen *nt:* **berührungslos** ~ contactless measuring, contact-free measuring, measuring without contact
Messendverstärker *m* measuring amplifier
Messer *nt* blade, cutting blade, cutter blade
Messerauswechslung *f* blade renewable
Messerblock *m* cutter holder
messerförmiges Heizelement *nt* knife-shaped heating element
Messergebnis *nt* result of measurement
Messerklemme *f* cutter clamp
Messerkopf *m* cutter head
Messerkopf *m* **mit auswechselbaren und gerieffelten Messern** serrated blade cutter
Messerlineal *nt* bevelled steel straight edge, knife edge, straight edge, toolmarker's knife edge, straightedge
Messernachschliff *m* blade grinding
Messerschneiden *nt* knife cutting
Messerstandzeit *f* cutting blade life
Messfehler *m* measuring error
Messfehlerkompensation *f* axis calibration
Messfläche *f* measurement surface,

measuring face
Messflächeninhalt *m* area of measurement surface, prescribed surface area
Messflächenmaß *nt* prescribed surface index, measurement surface ratio
Messflächenschalldruckpegel *m* surface sound pressure level
Messflügel *m* current meter
Messfühler *m* sensor, sensing probe
Messgeber *m* encoder
Messgefühl *nt* measuring touch, measure feeling
Messgegenstand *m* measuring object, object under test
Messgenauigkeit *f* accuracy of measurement, measuring precision
Messgerät *nt* **1.** *(allg.)* measuring instrument (or tool or apparatus or appliance or outfit or device), meter, gauge **2.** *(anzeigendes ~)* non-indicating measuring instrument **3.** *(registrierendes ~)* recording measuring instrument **4.** *(tragbares ~)* portable measuring device **5.** *(übertragendes ~)* transmitting measuring instrument **6.** *(zählendes ~)* counting measuring instrument
Messgerät *nt* **mit indirekter Ausgabe** measuring instrument with indirect output
Messgerät *nt* **mit Skalenanzeige** measuring instrument with analogue indication
Messgerät *nt* **mit Ziffernanzeige** *f* measuring instrument with digital indication
Messgerätehersteller *m* measuring instrument manufacturer
Messgetriebe *nt* transmission for instrumentation purposes, measuring gear
Messglocke *f* measuring bell
Messgröße *f* measured quantity, quantity to be measured, measurand, measurand value (or quantity)
Messing *nt* brass
messingfarben brass-coloured
Messinghartlot *nt* brazing spelter
Messinstrument *nt* measuring instrument
Messkapillare *f* measuring capillary

Messkegel *m* measuring cone
Messkeil *m* V head
Messkette *f* measuring system, measuring chain
Messkolben *m* volumetric flask, graduated flask
Messkopf *m* gauging head, measuring head
Messkörper *m* *(e. Lehre)* gauging member
Messkörper *m* **mit Einsteckgriff** *m* gauging member with plug-in gauge handle
Messkraft *f* measuring force
Messkraftumkehrspanne *f* measuring force reversal range, hysteresis of the measuring force
Messkraftunterschied *m* difference in measuring force
Messkreis *m* measuring circle, test circle
Messkugel *f* measuring ball
Messlänge *f* measured length, gauge length
Messlänge *f* **beim Bruch** gauge length at fracture
Messlänge *f* **nach dem Bruch** final gauge length
Messelektronik *f* electronic measuring equipment
Messlineal *nt* **1.** *(allg.)* (bevelled steel) straight-edge **2.** *(Haarlineal)* toolmarker's knife-edge straightedge **3.** *(Messerkantlineal)* knife-edge
Messlotrechte *f* vertical line for measurement
Messlupe *f* magnifying lens
Messmarke *f* mark, measuring mark, gauge mark
Messmaschine *f* measuring machine
Messmittel *nt* measuring means
Messobjekt *nt* measurement object
Messoptik *f* optical measuring system (or equipment)
Messorgan *nt* measuring element
Messposition *f* measurement position
Messprinzip *nt* measuring principle
Messprobe *f* test sample
Messprogramm *nt* measuring program
Messprotokoll *nt* measurement record,

measurement report, test chart
Messpumpe *f* metering pump
Messpunkt *m* measurement point, measuring point, data point
Messpunktanordnung *f* arrangement of measuring points
Messraumklima *nt* test room climate
Messreihe *f* series of measurement
Messrohr *nt* **mit Schwebekörper** measuring tube with floating body
Messröhre *f* measuring tube
Messrolle *f* measuring roller
Messscheibe *f* toolmaker's flat, gauge block
Messschenkel *m* measuring tube, (sliding) jaw
Messschieber *m* calliper gauge
Messschieber *m* **mit Nonius** vernier calliper
Messschieber *m* **mit Rundskala** dial calliper
Messschiene *f* beam, blade
Messschraube *f* micrometer, measuring screw
Messschwinge *f* measurement vibrator
Messsignal *nt* measurement signal
Messsonde *f* measurement probe
Messspanne *f* measuring span
Messspindel *f* measuring spindle
Messspitze *f* measuring point
Messstelle *f* measuring point, measuring station
Messstellenname *m* measurement point name
Messsteuerung *f* measuring control, measuring device
Messstift *m* feeler pin, test pin
Messstrecke *f* gauge length, gauged length
Messstreubreite *f* measuring scatterband
Messstück *nt* gauging member, measuring element
Messsystem *nt* measuring system
Messtaster *m* sensing probe
Messtechnik *f* 1. *(allg.)* metrology 2. *(als Lehrfach)* (dimensional) metrology 3. *(bei Lehren)* gauging practice 4. *(betrieblich)* measuring practice
Messtechniker *m* metrologist
messtechnisch metrological
messtechnische Gründe *mpl* technical measurement reasons
Messteilung *f* measuring line
Messtisch *m* coordinate table
Messtrommel *f* thimble
Messuhr *f* indicator, dial indicator, dial gauge (or gage), indicating calliper
Messuhrdickenmesser *m* dial thickness indicator
Messuhrenteilvorrichtung *f* dial gauge indexing attachment
Messuhrentiefenlehre *f* dial depth gauge
Messuhrtaster *m* dial indicator stylus
Messumformer *m* measuring transducer
Messumsetzer *m* measuring converter
Messung *f* 1. *(allg.)* measuring, measurement, determination, reading(s) 2. *(Eichprüfung)* calibration 3. *(mittels Festlehre) (US)* gaging, *(UK)* gauging, 4. *(mittels verstellbarer Lehre)* callipering 5. *(mittels zählender Messgeräte)* metering
Messunsicherheit *f* measurement uncertainty, uncertainty of measurement
Messventil *nt* flow control valve
Messverfahren *nt* method of measurement, gauging method, measuring method
Messverstärker *m* measuring amplifier
Messvorgang *m* gauging operation
Messvorrichtung *f* measuring device
Messvorschriften *fpl* rules (pl) of measurement
Messwandler *m* transducer
Messwaschflasche *f* graduated wash bottle
Messweite *f* capacity
Messwerk *nt* measuring mechanism
Messwerkzeug *nt* measuring tool, measuring instrument
Messwert *m* 1. *(ermittelter ~)* measured value (or quantity), measurement reading, metered value, indicated value, recorded value 2. *(Regelungstechnik)* measured variable 3. *(zu messender ~)* measuring value
Messwertabweichung *f* measurement

error
Messwertanzeige *f* measured-value indication
Messwertanzeiger *m* measured value indicator
Messwertaufnahme *f* measuring pick-up
Messwertaufnehmer *m* measured value sensor
Messwertgeber *m* measuring sensor, pick-up, transmitter, transducer, feedback device
Messwertumkehrspanne *f* measured value reversal range, measured value hysteresis
Messwertwandler *m* transducer
Messwesen *nt* metrology
Messzähnezahl *f* measured number of teeth
Messzapfen *m* anvil
Messzeigergerät *nt* indicating gauge
Messzeug *nt* measuring tool (or instrument or device or appliance)
Messzone *f* measuring zone
Messzweck *m* purpose of the measurement
Messzyklen *mpl* probing cycles
Messzylinder *m* graduated cylinder
Metall *nt* metal
Metallaktivgasschweißen *nt* active-gas-metal-arc welding
Metallbalg *m* metal bellows
Metallband *nt* metal band, metal strap
Metallbearbeitung *f* machining of metals, metalworking
Metallbehälter *m* metal container
Metalldetektionsmaschine *f* metal detecting machine
Metalldichtung *f* solid metal gasket
Metalldrücken *nt* metal spinning
Metalleffektpigment *nt* metallic effect pigment
Metallelektrodenpotential *nt* metal electrode potential
Metallfelge *f* metal rim
Metallfolie *f* metal foil
Metallgaze *f* metal ga(u)ze, wire ga(u)ze
Metallgeflecht *nt* metal braid
Metallgitter *nt* metal lattice

Metallhobelmaschine *f* metal planing machine
Metallionenreaktion *f* metal-ion reaction
metallisch metallic
metallische Verbindung *f* metal-to-metal joint
metallischer Überzug *m* metallic coating
Metallisierungsstoff *m* metallizing material
Metallklammer *f* metal staple
Metallkleben *nt* metal gluing
Metallklebstoff *m* adhesive for metal
Metallklebung *f* bonded metal joint
Metalllichtbogenschweißen *nt* **mit Fülldrahtelektrode** flux cored metal-arc welding
Metall-Metallionen-Reaktion *f* metal/metal-ion reaction
metallographisches Gefügebild *nt* metallographic micrograph
Metalloxidvaristor *m* metal oxide varistor
Metalloxyd *nt* sintered powder metal
Metallphosphatschicht *f* coat of metal phosphate
metallphysikalischer Vorgang *m* metallophysical process
Metallplatte *f* metal plate
Metallpulverbrennschneiden *nt* metal-powder flame cutting
Metallpulverschmelzschneiden *nt* metal-powder fusion cutting
Metallschablone *f* metal template
Metallschicht *f* metal coat
Metallschlauch *m* metal hose
Metallschmelze *f* metal bath
Metallschneidenelektrode *f* metal blade electrode
Metallschneidschraube *f* metallic drive screw
Metallspatel *m* metal spatula
Metallspritzarbeit *f* metal spraying work
Metallspritzbetrieb *m* metal spraying firm
Metallspritztechnik *f* metal spraying technology
Metallstempel *f* metal block

Metallstruktur *f* metallic structure
Metallteil *nt* metal part
Metallumspinnung *f* metal braiding
Metallurgie *f* metallurgy
Metallweichstoffdichtung *f* metal resilient jointing
Metallzerspanung *f* *(UK)* metal-cutting, *(US)* metalcutting
metazentrisch metacentric
Metazentrum *nt* metacentre
Metermaß *nt* meter rule
Methacrylatharz *nt* methacrylate resin
methanollöslicher Anteil *m* percentage of methanol-soluble matter
Methode *f* method
Methylenblau *nt* methylene blue
metrisches Außengewinde *nt* metric external thread
metrisches Feingewinde *nt* metric fine thread
metrisches Gewinde *nt* metric thread
metrisches Gewinde *nt* **für Festsitz** metric thread for force fit
metrisches ISO-Feingewinde *nt* ISO metric fine thread
metrisches ISO-Gewinde *nt* metric ISO thread
metrisches ISO-Trapezgewinde *nt* ISO metric trapezoidal screw thread
metrisches kegeliges Außengewinde *nt* metric tapered external screw thread
metrisches Regelgewinde *nt* standard metric thread
M-Funktion *f* M-functions
Miete *f* rent(al)
mieten hire, rent
Migration *f* migration
Mikroabformung *f* micro up-forming
Mikrobearbeitung *f* micro processing
mikrobiologisch microbiological
mikrobiologische Korrosion microbiological corrosion
Mikrocomputer *m* microcomputer
Mikroeinstellspannsystem *nt* MACS (Micro Adjusting Collect System)
Mikroerodieren *nt* micro eroding
mikrofilmgerecht suitable for microfilming
Mikrofilmtechnik *f* microfilming technique
Mikrofräsen *nt* micro milling
Mikrofurchung *f* micro riffling
Mikroklima *nt* micro-climate
Mikrokontur *f* micro contour
Mikrometer *nt* micrometer, micrometer screw (or gauge), micron
Mikrometerokular *nt* micrometer eyepiece
Mikrometerschraube *f* micrometer screw
Mikrometerspindel *f* **mit Skalentrommel** micrometer lead screw
Mikrometerokular *nt* micrometer eyepiece
Mikrophonpfad *m* microphone path
mikroporig micro-porous
Mikroprozessor *m* microcontroller, microprocessor
Mikroradiant *m* microradiant
Mikroriss *m* micro-crack
mikrorissig micro-cracked
Mikroschalter *m* micro-switch
mikroskopische Poren *fpl* microscopic (or micro-) pores
mikroskopische Risse *mpl* *(in metallischen Überzügen)* microscopic (or micro) cracks
Mikroskoptubus *m* microscope tube
Mikrospanen *nt* micro cutting
Mikrostruktur *f* 1. *(allg.)* micro structure 2. *(abgestufte ~)* graded micro structure 3. *(bewegliche ~)* movable micro structure 4. *(selbsttragende ~)* self-supporting micro structure
Mikrosuspensionspolymerisat *nt* polymer in microsuspension
Mikroumgebung *f* micro-environment
mikroverfilmen microfilm
Mikrowelle *f* microwave
Mikrowellensensor *m* microwave transmitter, micro link
Mikrowellensystem *nt* microwave system
Mikrowellentechnik *f* microwave technology
mildlegiertes Getriebeöl *nt* slightly blended gearbox oil
Millimeterbruchteil *m* fraction of a millimetre

Milliradiant *m* milliradiant
Mindergüte *f* sub-standard grade
mindern decrease, reduce
Mindestabstand *m* minimum distance
Mindestarbeitsdruck *m* minimum working pressure
Mindestauflagebreite *f* minimum support width
Mindestbestandsunterschreitung *f* stocks falling short of the minimum
Mindestbruchkraft *f* minimum breaking load
Mindestdruck *m* minimum pressure
mindestens at least
Mindestflächenpressung *f* minimum surface pressure
Mindesthärte *f* minimum hardness
Mindesthöhe *f* minimum height
Mindestkennzeichnung *f* minimum marking
Mindestluftstrecke *f* minimum clearance in air
Mindestmenge *f* minimum quantity
Mindestraumgröße *f* minimum room dimension
Mindestspandicke *f* minimum chip thickness
Mindestüberdruck *m* minimum overpressure
Mindestwenderadius *m* minimum turning radius
Mindestwert *m* minimum value, smallest value
Mindestzündtemperatur *f* minimum ignition temperature
Mineral *nt* mineral
Mineralfaser-Dämmstoff *m* mineral fibrous insulating material
mineralisch mineral
mineralisch gebundene Holzwolle *f* mineral-bound wood wool
Mineralölerzeugnis *nt* petroleum
Mineralpulverbrennschneiden *nt* mineral-powder flame cutting
Mineralstoff *m* mineral
Mineralstoffanteile *mpl* mineral substance constituents
Mineralstoffgemisch *nt* mineral aggregate
Mineralstoffprobe *f* sample of mineral substances
Mineraltrockengleitverschleiß *m* mineral-dry-friction-abrasion
Miniaturbearbeitung *f* miniature processing
Minicomputer *m* minicomputer
minimal minimum
Minimalmenge *f* minimum quantity
Minimalmengenzählung *f* minimum quantity counting
Minimeter *m* minimeter indicator (gauge)
minimieren minimize
Minimierung *f* minimization
Minimum *nt* minimum
Minimumoperator *m* minimum operator
Minimumprüfdorn *m* minimum master plug gauge
Minusabweichung *f* minus size variation
minütlich abgenommenes Spanvolumen *nt* volume removed per min
Mischanilinpunkt *m* mixed aniline point
Mischbetrieb *m* mixed mode
Mischbettfilter *m* gravel bed filter
Mischbruch *m* composite fracture
Mischdüse *f* mixer jet
Mischeinrichtung *f* mixer unit
Mischelektrode *f* mixed electrode
mischen blend, compound, mix, merge
Mischform *f* hybrid
Mischgebiet *nt* mixed region
Mischgefäß *nt* spray type exchanger
Mischguteinwaage *f* weight-in mix
Mischguthaufen *m* heap of mix
Mischgutprobe *f* mix sample
Mischkammer *f* mix chamber
Mischlösung *f* mixed solution
Mischstrecke *f* mixing section
Mischung *f* blend, mixture, mixing
Mischungsverhältnis *nt* mixture relation
Mischvorwärmer *m* mixing pre-heater
Mischvorwärmerentgaser *m* mixing pre-heater deaerator
Mischwalzwerk *nt* mixing mill
Missbrauch *m* misuse
missgriffsicher foolproof

Missverhältnis *nt* disproportion
mit Abstand von clear of
mit angeschliffenen Freiwinkel ground to give clearance
mit automatischem Arbeitsablauf auto-cycle
mit Deichsellenkung tiller-steered
mit der Stirnseite schneidend end-cutting
mit Druck beaufschlagen apply (a) pressure
mit Druckausgleich pressure-balanced
mit Eigenantrieb self-propelled
mit eigenem Antrieb self-contained drive
mit einer Leiste versehen gibbed
mit einer Schneide versehen tip (tool)
mit Fahrer driver-operated
mit Fahrersitz sit-on, sit down rider-controlled
mit Fahrerstand stand-on
mit Freiwinkel backed off
mit Fremdantrieb storage-battery
mit Frontsitz with the operator seated forward
mit Gegengewicht counterbalanced
mit Gegengewicht versehen counterbalance
mit Gewinde threaded
mit großer Teilung wide-pitched
mit Hartmetallwerkzeugen ausgerüstet carbide-tooled
mit Hilfssteuerung servo-controlled
mit Hubgerüst masted
mit Innengewinde tapped
mit Innenverrippung internally ribbed
mit Kabel cable-connected
mit Kanälen ported
mit Keilleisten nachstellbares Räumzeug *nt* gibbed surface broach assembly
mit Mitfahrer rider-controlled
mit mittlerem Hub medium-lift
mit Nut *f* grooved
mit Ölrückständen behaftet gummed with old oil
mit Ölstein abziehen oilstone
mit Pulsmodulation pulse-modulated
mit Quersitz with operated facing at right angles to the normal line of travel
mit Radius radiussed
mit Rückführung durch Feder spring returned
mit scharfer Schneide sharp-pointed
mit scharfer Spitze sharp-pointed
mit Sintermetallschneide bestückt tipped with sintered carbide
mit Steuerung durch gehende Person pedestrian-controlled
mit Stretchfolie umwickeln stretch-wrap
mit Teilstrichen versehen graduate
mit trichterförmiger Öffnung bell-mouthed
mit Verbrennungsmotor engine-powered
mit Vorsteuerung servo-controlled
mit Vorwahl preoptive
mit Zangen arbeiten tong, grasp with tongs
Mitarbeiter *m* employee
Mitarbeiterstunde *f* employee hour
miteinander kämmen gear together
miteinander kämmende Räder intermeshing gears (pl)
miteinander verriegelt interlocked with each other
mitfahren go with
Mitfahrer *m* 1. *(Fahrer)* rider 2. *(Passagier)* passenger
Mitfahrersteuerung *f* rider control
mitführen carry along, entrain
Mitgänger *m* pedestrain
Mitgängerbetrieb *m* pedestrain operation
Mitgängerflurförderzeug *nt* pedestrain-controlled (industrial) truck, hand-guided truck, pedestrain truck
mitgängergeführt pedestrain-controlled, controlled by an operator walking with the truck
mitgeführt on-board
mitgehen follow
mitgehender Rollensetzstock *m* travelling roller steady
mitgehender Setzstock *m* follow rest, follower rest
mitlaufend revolving, rotating
Mitnahme *f* entrainment, drive
Mitnahme *f* **durch Keil** key drive

Mitnahmeband *nt* conveyor belt
Mitnahmestift *m* driving pin
mitnehmbar portable
mitnehmen carry, entrain, pick up, tale along, drive
Mitnehmer *m* dog, driving carrier, carrier, driving dog, driver, work driver
Mitnehmerbolzen *m* pin of the driving plate, driver
Mitnehmerklaue *f* engaging dog
Mitnehmerlappen *m* tang
Mitnehmerloch *nt* driving hole
Mitnehmerscheibe *f* carrier plate, catch plate, driver (or driving) plate
Mitnehmerverbindung *f* drive type fastening
mitreißen drag along
Mitte *f* **1.** *(allg.)* middle **2.** *(techn.) (UK)* centre, *(US)* center
Mitte Schrifthöhe mid-height of the character
mitteilen communicate (with, to), inform (someone about something)
Mittel *nt* **1.** *(Werte)* medium **2.** *(statistisch)* average (value), mean **3.** *(chem.)* agent **4.** *(Hilfsmittel)* aid **5.** *(örtlich)* central
mittelbare Sicherheitstechnik *f* safety practice through intermediate means
Mittelebene *f* centre plane, median plane
mittelfrequenter Strom *m* medium frequency current
mittelfristig medium-term, in a medium term
mittelgroß medium-size(d)
Mittellage *f* **1.** *(Position)* central position, mean position, middle run **2.** *(Schichten)* intermediate ply
Mittellinie *f* centreline, centre line
Mittellinienkreuz *nt* centre line cross
mitteln average
Mittelpunkt *m* centre, central point, focus, hub
Mittelpunktlinie *f* centre line
Mittelpunktstrahl *m* radial line
Mittelregal *nt* centre track
Mittelschlitten *m* middle slide
Mittelschrift *f* medium-spaced lettering (or characters)

mittelschuppig medium-scaled
Mittelstand *m* medium-sized companies, small-scale business
mittelständisch medium-sized
Mittelstellung *f* mid position, mid point
Mittelteil *nt* centre portion, centrepiece
Mittelung *f* averaging
Mittelungseinrichtung *f* averaging device
Mittelungspegel *m* averaged level
Mittelverformung *f* mean strain
mittelviskose Lösung *f* solution of medium viscosity
Mittelwert *m* **1.** *(allg.)* average, mean, mean value, arithmetic mean **2.** *(gleitender ~)* gliding mean value
Mittelwertbereich *m* mean band
Mittelwertbildung *f* averaging
Mittelwertskurve *f* *(e. Schaubildes)* average-value curve
Mittelzapfen *m* central pintle, pivot
Mittelmaß *nt* **von Endmaßen** central length of gauge blocks
Mittenabstand *m* centre-to-centre distance, centre distance, dualspicing
Mittenabweichung *f* eccentricity
Mittenachse *f* centre line
Mittenbereich *m* *(e. Toleranzfeldes)* middle band, mean range
Mittenebene *f* plane of centre, central plane
Mitteninhalt *m* mean population
Mittenlinie *f* *(e. Radpaares)* central line, line of centres
Mittenspiel *nt* mean clearance
Mittentragen *nt* centre contact
Mittenübermaß *nt* mean interference
Mittenversetzung *f* centre offset
mittig central, in line with the centre
mittig aufgebrachte Kraft *f* load applied midway
Mittigkeit *f* central position, concentricity
Mittigkeitslehre *f* centre gauge
mittlere Abweichungsbetrag *m* mean deviation
mittlere Bezugslinie *f* mean reference line
mittlere Dauer *f* **bis zur Instandset-**

zung mean time to repair (MTTR)
mittlere Fehlererkennungszeit *f* mean failure detection time
mittlere Geschwindigkeit *f* average speed
mittlere Spielzeit *f* mean cycle time
mittlerer Ausfallabstand *m* mean time between failures (MTFB)
mittlerer Hub *m* medium lift
mittlerer Teil *m* central part
mittleres Schalldruckquadrant *nt* mean square sound pressure
mitverspannte Zubehörteile *f* accessories interlocked with fasteners
mitverspanntes federndes Sicherungselement *nt* co-stressed retaining element with spring action
mitwirken cooperate, collaborate
Mitwirkung *f* cooperation, collaboration
MMH (Multimomenthäufigkeit) *f* multi-moment-frequency
MMZ (Multimomentzeitmessverfahren) *nt* multi-moment time measurement
mobil mobile
mobiler Datenspeicher *m* mobile data memory
modale Funktion *f* modal function
Modalwert *m* mode
Modell *nt* model, master, pattern, type
Modellaufbau *m* model structure
Modellausschmelzverfahren *nt* investment moulding process
Modellbau *m* pattern making
Modellbildung *f* model building, model forming, modelling
Modellelement *nt* model element
Modellfräseinrichtung *f* pattern milling attachment
Modellgleichung *f* model equation
Modellholz *nt* pattern timber
modellierbares Reiblot *nt* mouldable timing solder
modellieren model
Modellierlot *nt* moulding solder
Modellierung *f* modelling
Modellierungsstufe *f* modelling level, modelling stage
Modellkonfiguration *f* model configuration
Modellmaße *ntpl* model size
Modellparameter *m* model parameter
Modellüberprüfung *f* model check, model verification
Modellversuch *m* scale model testing
Modellwerkstoff *m* model material
Modellzeichnung *f* pattern drawing
Modenstruktur *f* mode structure
Modenzahl *f* **1.** *(allg.)* mode number **2.** *(radiale ~)* radial mode number
modifizieren modify
Modul *nt* module
modulabhängiges Kopfspiel *nt* module-dependent bottom clearance
modular modular
modulares Werkzeugsystem *nt* modular tool system
Modulation *f* modulation
Modulator *m* modulator
Modulbatterie *f* modular battery
Modulbauweise *f* modular design
Modulbreite *f* module width
Modulwälzfräser *m* module hob
möglich possible
Möglichkeit *f* option, possibility
Möglichkeit *f* **der Wiederholung eines Arbeitsganges** repeatability
Mol *nt* mol, gram-molecule
Molekühlhauptkettenstück *nt* molecular main chain component
Molekül *nt* **1.** *(allg.)* molecule **2.** *(angeregtes ~)* excited dimer *(Excimer)*
Molekulargewichtsverteilung *f* distribution of molecular weight
Moleküllaser *m* molecule laser
Molmasse *f* mol mass
Molybdän *nt* molybdenum
Molybdän-Schnellstahl *m* molybdenum high speed steel
Moment *m* **der Ordnung** moment of order
Moment *m* **mehrerer Ordnungen** joint moment of several orders
Moment *mnt* **I.** *m (Augenblick)* moment **II.** *nt* **1.** *(Drehmoment)* torque **2.** *(phys.)* moment, momentum, instant
momentan immediate, instantaneous
Momentanachse *f* *(e. Wälzgetriebes)* instantaneous axis

Momentandrehung *f (e. Rades)* instantaneous rotation
momentane Übersetzung *f* instantaneous transmission ratio
Momenteinleitung *f (Pressverband)* transmission of moment to the assembly
Momentmesseinrichtung *f* device for measuring the moment
Momentsensor *m* load moment control
Monatsprogramm *nt* month's program
monoklin monoclinic
Monitor *m* monitor, screen
monochromatisch monochromatic, single-wavelength
Monogenisierungslinse *f* condenser lens
monomer monomeric
monomerer Weichmacher *m* monomeric plasticizer
monomeres Styrol *nt* monomeric styrene
Monoposition *f* single position
Monopositionsdepalettierer *m* single-position depalletizer
Monopositionspalettierer *m* single-position palletizer
monostabiles Kippglied *nt* **mit Verzögerung** delayed monostable element, delayed single shot
Montage *f* 1. *(Anbau, Einbau)* attachment 2. *(Aufspannung, Setzstock)* mounting 3. *(e. Einrichtung, Installation)* installation 4. *(e. Krans)* erection 5. *(e. Maschine)* setting up, erection 6. *(Einpassen)* fitting 7. *(Zusammenbau, Fügen)* assembly, assembling
Montageablauf *m* assembly course
Montageablaufplanung *f* assembly course planning
Montageanleitung *f* assembly instructions, mounting instructions, installation instructions, method statement
Montageanweisung *f* fitting instruction, assembly instruction, installation instruction
Montagearbeiten *fpl* assembly work, erection work
Montageauftrag *m* assembly order

Montageband *nt* assembly line
Montagebaukran *m* lower slewing crane
Montagebeschränkung *f* mounting restriction
Montageentwickler *m* general purpose portable generator
montagefertig ready to assemble, ready-to-fit, ready-to-mount
Montagegenauigkeit *f* installation accuracy, erection accuracy
montagegerechtes Gestalten *nt* design for assembly
Montagegerüst *nt* assembly scaffold, erection scaffold
Montagehilfe *f* fit-up aid
Montagehilfsschweißnaht *f* tack weld
Montagehinweis *m* mounting instruction, notes on installation *pl*
Montagekran *m* erection crane
Montagelage *f* attachment position
Montageleitrechner *m* assembly master computer
Montageleitung *f* assembly manager
Montageprogramm *nt* assembly program
Montagerechner *m* assembly computer
Montagesteuerung *f* assembly control
Montagestückliste *f* assembly parts list
Montagestufe *f* assembly stage
Montageteile *ntpl* sub-assemblies
Montagetoleranz *f* installation tolerance, erection tolerance
Montageungenauigkeit *f* inaccuracy of mounting
Montagevorrichtung *f* assembly fixture
Montagewerkstatt *f* assembly shop
Montagewerkzeug *nt* fitting and assembly tool
Monteur *m* 1. *(Mechaniker, Installateur)* fitter, assembler 2. *(Wartung)* maintenance man
montieren 1. *(installieren)* install, fit, assemble 2. *(anbringen)* attach (to) 3. *(errichten)* erect, mount, set up
Mosaikschwinger *m* crystal mosaic
Motor *m* 1. *(el.)* motor 2. *(Verbren-*

nungsmotor) engine
Motor *m* **mit regelbarer Drehzahl** adjustable speed motor
Motorachse *f* motor shaft
Motorausfall *m* dead motor
Motordrehzahl *f* motor speed
Motorenschmieröl *nt* engine lubricating oil
motorisch motorized, by motorized device, self-propelled
motorische Lastenanhebung *f* self-propelled lifting power
motorischer Antrieb *m* self-propelled driving part
Motorläufer *m* motor armature
Motorleistung *f* motor capacity, motor rating
Motormoment *nt* motor torque, engine torque
Motornennmoment *nt* rated motor torque
Motorraum *m* engine compartment
Motorsäge *f* power saw
Motorschalter *m* starter, line starter
Motorschutzschalter *m* motor-circuit switch, motor protecting switch, protective circuit breaker, protective motor switch
Motorsteuerung *f* motor control
Motorwelle *f* motor shaft, main shaft
Motorzylinder *m* engine cylinder
MSR-Technik *f* measuring and control technology
MTM *Abk* methods-time-measurement
Muffe *f* bell, bush, muff, sleeve, socket
Muffenboden *m* socket base
Muffendeckel *m* socket end cover
Muffeneingang *m* socket entry
Muffenfitting *m* sleeve fitting
Muffengewinde *nt (für Gestängerohre)* socket screw thread
Muffenkonstruktion *f* socket design
Muffenrohr *nt* socket pipe
Muffenrohrverbindung *f* spigot joint
Muffenschweißen *nt* socket welding
Muffenspaltweite *f* clearance between spigot and socket
Muffenspiel *nt* socket gap (or clearance)
Muffenstopfen *m* socket plug

Muffenverbindung *f* sleeve joint
Mühle *f* crusher, mill, pulveriser
Mulde *f* spherical depression, depression, shallow pit (corrosion), scar, pit
muldenähnliche Beschädigung *f* damage resembling a pit
Muldenbildung *f* shallow pit formation
Muldenkorrosion *f* shallow pit corrosion
müllgefeuert refuse-fired
Müllverbrennungsofen *m* refuse incinerator furnace
Multidepalettierer *m* multiposition depalletizer
Multiidentfähigkeit *f* multi-ident capability
Multiidentsystem *nt* multi-ident system
Multikapillare *f* multi-capillary
multimodale Verteilung *f* multimodal distribution
Multimomentstudie *f* multimoment study
Multinormalverteilung *f* multinormial distribution
Multipalettierer *m* multiposition palletizer
Multipliziergetriebe *nt* multiplying gear drive (or mechanism)
Multiposition *f* multiposition
Multipositionspalettierer *m* multiposition palletizer
Mundschutz *m* mask, respirator
Mundstück *nt* nozzle, tip
Mündung *f* orifice, aperture, mouthpiece
Muster *nt* **1.** *(allg.)* master, prototype, master workpiece (or component) **2.** *(e. Bauteils)* pattern **3.** *(e. Probe)* specimen, sample
Musterstück *nt* specimen, sample, sample workpiece, master
Mutter *f* nut
Mutter *f* **der Tischlängsvorschubspindel mit Spielausgleich** anti-backlash longitudinal table feed nut
Mutter *f* **mit Bügelsicherung** nut with screw clamp retention
Mutter *f* **mit Bund** collar nut

Mutter *f* **mit Fase** chamfered nut
Mutter *f* **mit Linksgewinde** left-hand nut
Mutter *f* **für T-Nuten** nut for T-slots
Mutterabkantmaschine *f* nut-bevelling machine
Mutterauflagefläche *f* nut bearing face
Muttergewinde *nt* internal thread, nut thread
Muttergewindeaußendurchmesser *m* major diameter of nut thread
Muttergewindebohren *nt* nut tapping
Muttergewindebohrer *m* nut tap
Muttergewindelänge *f* thread length of the nut
Muttergewindelehrung *f* gauging internal threads
Muttergewindeschneidautomat *m* nut-tapping automatic
Mutterkerndurchmesser *m* minor diameter of the thread
Mutternautomat *m* nut automatic
Mutternsicherung *f* nut locking feature
Mutterpalette *f* mother pallet
Mutterpause *f* master tracing
Mutterplatine *f* motherboard
Mutterschloss *nt* spline nut, lead screw nut

N n

Nabe *f* hub, boss
Nabenabstand *m* boss spacing
Nabenachse *f* boss axis
Nabendurchmesser *m* hub diameter
Nabenlänge *f* hub width
Nabenstirnfläche *f* boss (of a hub)
nach außen outwards
nach hinten back, backwards
nach Kundenwunsch bespoke, customized, made to specification, *(US)* custom made
nach links leftward, towards the left, to the left
nach oben up, upwards
nach rechts rightwards, towards the right, to the right
nach unten 1. *(allg.)* down, downwards **2.** *(Gebäude)* downstairs
nach vorn forth, forwards
nach vorn offene Konstruktion *f* open-front design
nachaltern afterage
Nachalterung *f* afteraging
Nacharbeit *f* **1.** *(allg. techn.)* remachining, rework **2.** *(spanend)* subsequent machining, re-machining, finish machining
nacharbeiten remachine, rework
nacharbeitsfrei without remachining, without reworking
Nachbarfach *nt* adjacent compartment, neighbouring compartment
Nachbargasse *f* adjacent aisle, neighbouring aisle
Nachbarraum *m* adjoining room
nachbauen reproduce, duplicate
nachbearbeiten re-machine, finish-machine
Nachbearbeitung *f* **1.** *(maschinell)* subsequent machining **2.** *(von Werkstücken)* finishing **3.** *(von Werkzeugen)* dressing
Nachbehandlung *f* additional (or subsequent) treatment, retreatment
Nachbeheizung *f* after-heating
nachbessern improve, mend, repair, overhaul, rectify
Nachbesserung *f* mend(ing), improvement, repair, overhaul, rectification, touch up
Nachbesserungsarbeiten *fpl* overhaul work, repair work, mending work
nachbestellen reorder
nachbilden copy, reproduce, simulate
Nachbildung *f* copy, replica, reproduction, simulation
nachbohren rebore
nachdrehen 1. *(allg.)* copy-turn, return, finish-turn **2.** *(Planflächen)* re-face
Nachdruck *m* post pressure
Nachdrücken *nt* resqueezing
Nachdruckhöhe *f* post pressure amount
Nachdruckphase *f* post pressure phase
Nachdruckzeit *f* post pressure period
nacheichen recalibrate
Nacheichung *f* recalibration
nacheinander one after the other, subsequently, successive
Nachentrosten *nt* subsequent derusting
Nachfahrgenauigkeit *f* follow-up accuracy, reproductive accuracy
nachfolgend consecutive, subsequent, following
nachfordern claim
Nachforderung *f* (additional) claim
Nachforderungsmanagement *nt* claim management
Nachform- und Profilfräsmaschine *f* form copying and profile miller (or milling machine)
Nachformarbeit *f* copy machining, duplicate machining, duplication, copying
nachformbar remouldable
Nachformbarkeit *f* remouldability, reformability
Nachformdreheinrichtung *f* copy-turning attachment
nachformdrehen copy, copy-turn, *(US)* duplicate, duplicate-turn
Nachformdrehmaschine *f (US)* dupli-

cating lathe, *(UK)* copy-turning lathe, copying lathe
Nachformdrehvorrichtung *f (UK)* copying attachment, *(US)* duplicating attachment
Nachformeinrichtung *f* copying attachment, duplicating attachment, duplicator
nachformen 1. *(allg.) (UK)* copy, profile, contour, *(US)* duplicate, reproduce, copy turn **2.** *(im Teilumriss)* segment copy **3.** *(zweidimensional)* profile, contour **4.** *(dreidimensional)* duplicate **5.** *(Gesenke)* die-sink **6.** *(kopieren)* reproduce (a form) **7.** *(nachformfräsen)* copy-mill **8.** *(nachformhobeln)* copy-plane, profile-plane, contour-plane
Nachformfähigkeit *f* repeatability
Nachformfeindrehen *nt* profile finish turning
Nachformfräsarbeit *f* copy milling operation
Nachformfräsautomat *m* copying miller, automatic tracer-controlled toolroom machine
nachformfräsen 1. *(allg. nachfräsen)* copy-mill **2.** *(zweidimensional)* profile, contour **3.** *(dreidimensional)* duplicate **4.** *(Gesenke)* die-sink
Nachformfräsen *nt* **1.** *(allg.)* copy milling, profile milling, pantographing **2.** *(mit Handvorschub)* routing
Nachformfräser *m* profiler
Nachformfräsmaschine *f* **1.** *(allg.)* copy-milling machine, profile miller, contour miller, duplicator, copying miller **2.** *(Formen und Gesenke)* die sinking machine, die sinker, duplicator **3.** *(Profile zweidimensional)* profiling machine, profile miller, profiler **4.** *(Präzisionsmaschine)* toolroom milling machine
Nachformfräsmaschine *f* **für zweidimensionales Fräsen** profiler
Nachformfräsmaschine *f* **mit dreidimensionaler Steuerung** duplicating machine, duplicator, machine for three-dimensional milling
Nachformfräsmaschine *f* **mit dreidimensionaler Steuerung** *(Gesenkfräsmaschine)* die sinking machine, die sinker
Nachformfräsmaschine *f* **mit Handvorschub** router
Nachformfräsmaschine *f* **mit Pantographensteuerung 1.** *(allg.)* pantograph milling machine, pantograph mold and duplicator **2.** *(für Formen und Gesenkfräsen)* pantograph die sinking machine **3.** *(für Gravierarbeiten)* pantograph engraving machine, pantograph engraver, pantograver
Nachformfräsmaschine *f* **mit Vollumrisskreisform** full-circle profiler
Nachformfühler *m* form tracer
Nachformgenauigkeit *f* copying accuracy, duplicating accuracy, accuracy of reproduction
Nachformhobeleinrichtung *f* **1.** *(Langhobelmaschine)* copy-planing attachment **2.** *(Waagerechtstoßmaschine)* copy-shaping attachment
Nachformhobelmaschine *f* copy-planer, profile-planer, contour-planer
Nachformhobeln *nt* copy planing, contour planing, copy-shaping
Nachformmaschine *f* form-duplicating machine
Nachformschleifen *nt* copy-grinding, profile grinding, contour grinding
Nachformsteuerung *f* copying system
Nachformstößelhobelmaschine *f* copying shaper
Nachformsystem *nt* electronic copying system
Nachformung *f* reproduction
Nachformverfahren *nt* copying system
Nachformwaagerechtstoßmaschine *f* copying shaper
Nachfrage *f* demand (for)
Nachfragedaten *pl* demand data
nachfragegesteuerte Produktion *f* demand-activated manufacturing
nachfragen demand (for)
Nachfrageprognose *f* demand forecast
Nachfrageschwankung *f* changes in demand, fluctuation in demand
Nachfrageüberhang *m* excess of demand, surplus demand

Nachfräsen *nt* **1.** *(Nachformfräsen)* copy milling, profiling, contouring, duplicating, die-sinking **2.** *(zweidimensional)* profile milling, profiling, contour milling, contouring **3.** *(dreidimensional)* duplicating **4.** *(Endbearbeitung)* remilling, finish milling **5.** *(Gesenke)* die-sinking
Nachfräser *m* finishing cutter
Nachführsteuerung *f* photoelectric line tracer
Nachführung *f* follow-up
Nachfüllauftrag *m* refill order, refill job, refill command, replenishment order
nachfüllen refill, replenish, top up
Nachfüllmenge *f* top up quantity
Nachfüllsystem *nt* refill system
Nachfüllwasser *nt* top-up water
nachgeben yield, sag
nachgeordnet hierarchical
nachgeschaltet downstream (of), secondary, connected in series
nachgeschaltete Stromsicherung *f* flow-operated safety device
nachgeschaltetes Bauglied *nt* (e. Messumformers) structural element next in line
nachgeschnitten recut, reground
nachgiebig resilient, soft
Nachgiebigkeit *f* resilience, yieldingness, flexibility, apparent elastic appliance
Nachglimmen *nt* afterglow
Nachhallzeitmessung *f* reverberation time measurement
nachjustieren readjust
nachladen recharge
Nachladung *f* recharge
nachlassen abate, diminish, lessen, reduce, decrease, loosen, slacken, weaken
nachlassend decreasing, reduced
nachlässig inattentive, neglectful, negligent
Nachlauf *m* **1.** *(allg.)* post-carriage, follow-up, tracking, lag **2.** *(Achsen)* axis lag **3.** *(Bearbeitung)* finishing **4.** *(Getriebe)* backlash **5.** *(Maschinen)* after-running **6.** *(Räder)* caster

Nachlaufbühne *f* finishing platform
nachlaufen lose, be slow, follow up
nachlaufende Schneidkantenflanke *f* trailing pinion cutter flank
Nachlauffehler *m* following error
Nachlaufnull *f* zero lag
Nachlaufsperre *f* divider
Nachlaufstrecke *f* tail end length
Nachlaufweg *m* **1.** *(techn.)* lollow-up path, tracking path **2.** *(Entfernung)* follow-up distance, tracking distance **3.** *(Maschinen)* slowing-down path
Nachleuchtdauer *f* persistence
nachliefern deliver in addition
Nachlieferung *f* additional delivery, additional supply, subsequent delivery
Nachmessen *nt* checking dimensions (or size or diameters)
nachplanen reface
Nachpolymerisation *f* after-polymerisation
Nachprägen *nt* resizing
Nachpresskraft *f* forge force
Nachpresszeit *f* forge time
nachprüfen check, reinspect, verify, control, recheck
Nachprüfung *f* check, verification, verification on commissioning, retest, inspection
nachrechnen check the calculation, recalculate
Nachrechnung *f* recalculation
Nachreinigung *f* subsequent cleaning
Nachricht *f* **empfangen** message received
Nachricht *f* message
nachrichten (justieren) realign, redress, restraighten
Nachrichtentechnik *f* telecommunications processing
nachrüstbar upgradable, expandable
Nachrüstsatz *m* expansion kit
Nachrüstung *f* backfitting, refitting, upgrade, retrofitting, expansion
Nachrutschen *nt* subsequent slipping
nachschärfen 1. *(techn.)* sharpen, resharpen **2.** *(schleifen)* regrind **3.** *(Werkzeuge)* dress
Nachschlagen *nt* restriking
nachschleifen sharpen, resharpen,

regrind
Nachschliff *m* regrind, resharpening, re-sharpen
Nachschliff *m* **des Werkzeugs** tool grind
Nachschmiereinleitungsverteiler *m* after-lubrication injection metering device
Nachschneiden *nt* final trimming, finish shaving, finish-cutting
Nachschub *m* supply, replenishment, feeding
Nachschubauslösung *f* supply activation
Nachschubkommissionierung *f* supply commissioning
Nachschubsteuerung *f* supply control
Nachschubstrecke *f* supply line, supply path
nachspanen reface
nachspannen reclamp, restretch
Nachspannung *f* restretching
Nachspritzen *nt* after injection
Nachspülen *nt* subsequent flushing
Nachspülung *f* *(von Rohrleitungen)* flushing
Nachspülzeit *f* post-purge period
Nachstauchlängenverlust *m* post weld upsetting length loss
Nachstauchzeit *f* post weld upsetting time
Nachstellarbeit *f* *(Bohr- und Frässpindel)* second feed
nachstellbar readjustable, adjustable
Nachstellbarkeit *f* adjustability, readjustability
Nachstellbewegung *f* compensation motion
nachstellen adjust, readjust, reset
Nachstellhülse *f* adjustment bush
Nachstellleiste *f* adjusting gib, take-up strip, taper gib
Nachstellreife *f* readjustment, time to readjustment, time between two consecutive adjustments
Nachstellung *f* adjustment, readjustment, resetting, reset
Nachstellung *f* **zum Ausgleich für Verschleiß** adjustment for wear
nachsteuern follow up

Nachteil *m* disadvantage, deficiency, impairment, drawback
nachteilig disadvantageous, unfavourable
nachträglich subsequent
Nachtrocknen *nt* subsequent trying
Nachtschicht *f* night shift
Nachverarbeitung *f* post-processing
Nachversuch *m* post-test
nachwärmen postheat
Nachweis *m* certificate, evidence, proof, verification
nachweisbar verifiable
Nachweisempfindlichkeit *f* detection sensitivity
nachweisen prove, show, verify
Nachweisstufe *f* verification stage
Nachweiswahrscheinlichkeit *f* detection probability
nachziehen *(e. Schraube)* retighten
Nachziehen *nt* *(hinter)* stretch reducing by roll drawing
Nachzündungszeit *f* post-ignition time
nackte Bitumenbahn *f* uncoated bituminous sheeting
Nadel *f* needle, broach
Nadelausreißkraft *f* needle tear-off force
Nadelausreißwiderstand *m* needle tear-off resistance
Nadeldrucker *m* dot printer, needle printer
Nadelgreifer *m* needle gripper
Nadelholzzellstoff *m* coniferous pulp
Nadelimpuls *m* needle pulse
nadelkopfartig in the manner of a nail-head
Nadellager *nt* needle bearing
Nadelpenetration *f* needle penetration
Nadelpistole *f* *(zum Entrosten)* needle scaler
nadelstichartige Vertiefung *f* *(bei Lochfraß)* pits resembling pin pricks
Nagel *m* nail
Nagelkopfschweißen *nt* nail-head welding
nageln nail, hit a nail into
Nagelverschließmaschine *f* nail closing machine

nah close, near (by), proximal
nahe close, near
Nähe *f* closeness, proximity, vicinity
nähen seam, sew, stitch
Nahe-Null-Inventur *f* near zero inventory
nähern approach
nähern *(Werte)* approximate
nähern (sich) approximate
Näherung *f* approximation
Näherungsindikator *m* proximity indicator
Näherungslösung *f* approximate solution
Näherungsschalter *m* proximity switch, proximity device
Näherungssensor *m* proximity sensor
näherungsweise approximately
nahezu virtually
Naht *f* 1. *(allg.)* fin, joint, seam, weld seam 2. *(Kunststoff)* seal 3. *(Schweißen)* weld 4. *(Stoß)* joint
Nahtabbildung *f* weld image
Nahtabstand *m* weld pitch
Nahtanhäufung *f* weld concentration
Nahtansatz *m* arc strike point
Nahtaufbau *m* weld composition
Nahtausführung *f* weld model, weld design, weld quality
Nahtbegrenzung *f* boundary of the weld
Nahtdicke *f* throat thickness
Nahtdickenunterscheidung *f* insufficient thickness
Nahtdrehwinkel *m* angle of rotation of weld
Nahtdreieck *nt* weld triangle
Nahtflanke *f* weld flank
nahtformende Backen *mpl* shoes *pl* used of form the weld
Nahtkreuzung *f* intersection of welds
nahtlos glueless, seamless, weldless, smooth
Nahtneigungswinkel *m* slope of weld
Nahtoberfläche *f* top surface of the weld
nahtschweißen seam-weld
Nahtschweißen *nt* seam welding
Nahtstelle *f* interface
Nahtübergang *m* weld transition, weld junction
Nahtunterschreitung *f* underfill
Nähverschließmaschine *f* sewing machine
NAND-Glied *nt* NAND, AND with negated output
NAND-Schaltung *f* NAND-circuit, NAND-element, NAND-gate
NAND-Verknüpfung *f* NAND logic
Nanotechnologie *f* nanotechnology
Näpfchenziehversuch *m* test using small drawn cups
Napfrückwärtsfließpressen *nt* indirect impact extrusion of cup-shaped sections
Napfvorwärtsfließpressen *nt* direct impact extrusion of cup-shaped sections
Narbe *f* scar, pit
narbig comby
narbige Oberfläche *f* scarred surface
narbiger Oberflächencharakter *m* grainy surface character
Narbigkeit *f* pitting
narrensicher fool-proof
Nase *f* 1. *(allg.)* lug 2. *(e. Keils)* gib head 3. *(e. Senkschraube)* nib 4. *(e. Sicherungsbleches)* tab
Nasenflachkeil *m* thin taper key with gib head
Nasenkeil *m* gib-head key
nass damp, moist, wet
Nassabscheider *m* wet separator
Nassberstfestigkeit *f* wet bursting strength
nassblank *(von Stahldraht)* wet bright
Nassbruchwiderstand *m* wet breaking resistance
nasschemisches Entfetten *nt* degreasing by wet chemical methods
Nassdreheinrichtung *f* wet turning attachment
Nassdruckluftstrahlen *nt* wet compressed air blasting
Nässe *f* wet, wetness
Nassfräseinrichtung *f* wet milling attachment
Nassklebebandverschließmaschine *f* gummed tape sealing machine, pre-gummed tape sealing machine

Nassklebeetikettiermaschine f wet glue labelling machine
Nasskühlturm m wet cooling tower
Nasskühlturm m **mit drückendem Lüfter** wet cooling tower with forced draught fan
Nasskühlturm m **mit saugendem Lüfter** wet cooling tower with induced draught fan
Nasspressen nt wet pressing
nassschleifen grind wet
Nassschleifmaschine f wet grinder
Nassschliff m wet cutting
Nassstrahlen nt wet blasting
Nasstintecodierer m wet ink coder
Nass-Trockenkühlturm m **mit natürlichem Zug** wet-dry cooling tower with natural draught
Nassveraschung f wet incineration
Nasszugversuch m wet tensile test
natriumgekühlt sodium-cooled
Naturgröße f *(e. Zeichnung)* full-scale representation
Naturkautschuklatex nt natural rubber latex
natürlich natural
natürliche Bindemittel ntpl natural binding agent
natürliche Einheit f natural unit
natürliche Quetschzone f natural compression yield point
Naturumlaufheißwassererzeuger m natural circulation high temperature water heating appliance
NC numerical control
NC-Achse f NC axis
NC-Programm nt NC program
NC-Programmierung f NC programming
NC-Verfahrenskette f NC-procedural chain
NC-Werkzeugmaschine f NC machine tool
Nebel m mist
neben 1. *(räumlich)* beside, next to **2.** *(außer)* apart from
Nebenantrieb m auxiliary drive
Nebendurchführungszeit f apart from execution time
Nebenecho nt subsidiary echo

nebeneinander side by side, alongside each other
nebeneinander laufend running side by side
nebeneinander liegend adjacent
Nebenerscheinung f attendant phenomenon
Nebenfehler m secondary defect
Nebenfläche f secondary area
Nebenfreifläche f minor flank
Nebengang m secondary aisle, secondary lane
Nebenleitung f secondary feed line (lubricant metering device)
Nebenlüftung f secondary ventilation
Nebennutzungszeit f apart from utilization period
Nebenprozesse mpl assisting processes
Nebenreibung f secondary friction
Nebensatz m auxiliary sentence
Nebenschluss m shunt
Nebenschlussantrieb m shunt-wound drive
Nebenschlusserregung f shunt excitation
Nebenschlussmaschine f shunt generator
Nebenschlussmotor m shunt motor
Nebenschlussmotor m **mit Stabilisierungswicklung** stabilized shunt motor
Nebenschneide f **1.** *(allg.)* *(UK)* front cutting edge, trail edge, *(US)* end-cutting edge, front edge, secondary-cutting edge **2.** *(e. Drehmeißels)* minor cutting edge
Nebenschnittfläche f secondary cut surface, machined surface
Nebenstromprobe f by-pass sample
Nebenzeit f idle time (or period), machine-handling time, non-machining time, unproductive time, dead time, *(US)* down time
negative Dehnung f negative extension
negative Überhöhung f **der Schneide** leading tool edge
Negativlichtpausfilm m film negative material
Negativschnitt m negative cut

Negativverfahren *nt* negative method
Negator *m* negator
negieren negate
negierender Verstärker *m* amplifier with negation indicator
Negierung *f* negation
neigbar tiltable, inclinable
Neigeachse *f* tilt axis, tilting axis
Neigeeinrichtung *f* tilting system
Neigegeschwindigkeit *f* tilting speed
neigen 1. *(techn.)* incline, tilt **2.** *(~ zu Entscheidung)* tend (to) **3.** *(Ebenen)* slope
Neigeplattform *f* tilting platform
Neigesystem *nt* tilting system
Neigezylinder *m* tilt cylinder
Neigezylinderbolzen *m* tilt cylinder pin
Neigung *f* **1.** *(Tendenz)* tendency **2.** *(Flächen, Ebenen, Drehmeißel)* slope, gradient, inclination **3.** *(e. Schleifkopfes)* tilt **4.** *(von Gewindegängen)* slant
Neigung *f* **zum Einhärten** tendency to take on useful hardness
Neigungsachse *f* axis of inclination
Neigungsmesseinrichtung *f* inclination measuring system
Neigungsmessgerät *nt* inclination measuring instrument
Neigungspendel *nt* inclined pendulum
Neigungstoleranz *f* angularity tolerance
Neigungswinkel *m* angle of inclination, inclination angle, angle of slope, *(US)* (positive) back-rage angle, *(UK)* (positive) front rake
Neigungswinkel *m:* **radialer** ~ radial inclination angle
Nenn ... nominal, rated
Nennabmaß *nt* nominal allowance
Nennachsenabstand *m* nominal centre distance
Nennbelastung *f* basic load, nominal load, nominal stress
Nennbeleuchtungsstärke *f* nominal brightness, nominal illuminance
Nennbetrieb *m* operation at normal rating, nominal operation
Nennbetriebsstrom *m* nominal operational current
Nennbreitenballigkeit *f* nominal crowning
Nenndaten *f* ratings
Nenndaten *ntpl* nominal data, rated data
Nenndrehzahl *f* nominal speed, rated speed
Nenndruckspannung *f* nominal compressive stress
Nenneingriffswinkel *m* nominal pressure angle
Nennergröße *f* denominator
Nennerzeugende *f* nominal generator
Nennevolvente *f* nominal involute
Nennflankenlinie *f* nominal tooth trace
Nennform *f* *(e. Flankenlinie)* nominal form
Nennfrequenz *f* rated frequency
Nenngeschwindigkeit *f* rated speed
Nenngrundkreis *m* nominal base circle
Nenngrundkreisdurchmesser *m* nominal base circle diameter
Nennheizleistung *f* rated heat output
Nennhubgeschwindigkeit *f* maximum rated lifting speed
Nennkegel *m* nominal taper
Nennkegellänge *f* basic cone length
Nennkegelwinkel *m* basic cone angle
Nennlänge *f* nominal length
Nennlast *f* rated load
Nennleistung *f* **1.** *(allg. techn.)* nominal output, nominal rating, rating, rated capacity, rated output **2.** *(el.)* nominal power **3.** *(mech.)* nominal capacity
Nennmaß *nt* nominal size (or dimension), basic size
Nennmaßbereich *m* nominal size range
Nennmoment *m* nominal torque, rated torque, nominal moment
Nennprofil *nt* nominal profile
Nennprofilverschiebung *f* nominal addendum modification
Nennschrägungswinkel *m* nominal helix angle
Nennschraubenlinie *f* nominal helix
Nennspannung *f* rated voltage

Nennspanungsdicke *f* nominal thickness of cut
Nennspanungsquerschnitt *m* nominal unit of area of cut
Nennsteigerung *f* nominal flank lead
Nennsteigungshöhe *f* nominal lead
Nennstrom *m* rated current, nominal current
Nennteilung *f* nominal flank pitch
Nenntemperatur *f* nominal temperature
Nenntragfähigkeit *f* rated capacity
Nennverjüngung *f* *(e. Kegels)* basic rate of taper
Nennweitenstufung *f* *(z. B. bei Rohren)* nominal bore progression
Nennwert *m* nominal value, rated value
Nennwinkel *m* nominal angle
Nennwinkelgeschwindigkeit *f* nominal angular frequency
Nennwirkungsgrad *m* nominal efficiency
netto net
Nettobedarf *m* net demand
Nettobedarfsermittlung *f* net demand assessment
Nettodaten *pl* net data
Nettogewicht *nt* net weight
Nettoquerschnitt *m* net cross-section
Nettowägefüllmaschine *f* net weighing machine
Netz *nt* 1. *(data)* mains, network, supply system 2. *(el.)* mains, power supply line, grid 3. *(e. graphischen Darstellung)* ruling 4. *(Konstr.)* grid
netzabhängige Rechenmaschine *f* mains powered calculator
Netzanschluss *m* electric mains, public supply, a.c. power
Netzanschluss *m* **(IT)** network termination
Netzanschlusspunkt *m* network termination point
Netzanschluss-Schalter *m* main isolator
Netzbelastung *f* system load
Netzeinspeisung *f* incoming power supply, mains power supply
netzen wet
Netzfrequenzschweißen *nt* system frequency welding
Netzgebiet *nt* ruled area
Netzkonfiguration *f* network configuration
Netzlinie *f* ruled line
Netzmanteldrahtelektrode *f* flyspun wire electrode
Netzmessung *f* system measurement
Netzmittellösung *f* solution of wetting agent
Netzplan *m* network, network plan
Netzplantechnik *f* critical path method, project network techniques
Netzplanwerk *nt* network plan works
Netzrisse *mpl* check marks, checking marks
Netzrückspeisung *f* mains regeneration
Netzrückwirkung *f* system perturbation
Netzspannung *f* supply voltage, mains voltage, system voltage
Netzspannungsausfall *m* failure of the mains voltage
Netzstrom *m* mains power
Netzstromversorgung *f* mains power supply
Netztransformator *m* mains transformer
Netztuch *nt* netting
Netzumwälzpumpe *f* mains-operated circulating pump
netzunabhängige Rechenmaschine *f* battery powered calculator
Netzunterbrechung *f* power failure
Netzwerk *nt* network
Netzwerkschicht *f* network layer
neu einrichten reset
neu rüsten retool
Neuanlage *f* new system
Neuaufspannung *f* reclamping, resetting
Neubildung *f* renewed formation
Neueinstellung *f* readjustment, resetting
Neuemulsion *f* fresh emulsion
Neuinvestition *f* net investment, new plant and equipment expenditure, investment in new plant and equipment
Neukonstruktion *f* 1. *(allg.)* redesign,

reconstruction 2. *(neuartige)* novel design
Neuliste *f* new list
Neuöl *nt* unused oil
Neuordnung *f* redesign
Neurost *m* fresh rust
neutral neutral
Neutralisationszahl *f* 1. *(alkalisch)* strong base number 2. *(sauer)* total acid number 3. *(wasserlösliche Säuren)* strong acid number
neutralisieren absorb, dissipate, neutralize
Neutralisierung *f* absorption, dissipation, neutralization
Neutralstellung *f* neutral, neutral position
Neutronendosimetrie *f* neutron dosimetry
Neuzustand *m* new condition
newtonsche Flüssigkeit *f* Newtonian fluid
n-gängiges Gewinde *nt* n-start (or multiple-start) thread
n-gliedrig n-link, n-bar
Nibbelmaschine *f* nibbling machine
nibbeln nibble
NICHT NOT
nicht artgleicher Werkstoff *m* unlike material
nicht ausgewuchtet unbalanced
nicht auswertbar avaluative
nicht beanstandet approved
nicht besitzen lack
nicht bestimmungsgemäß prohibited
nicht bildzeichnende Strahlung *f* scattered radiation
nicht brennbar non-combustible
nicht demontierbare Bereifung *f* permanently tyred wheel
nicht angetriebene Räder *ntpl* idle wheels
nicht entzündbar non-combustible
nicht fertig bearbeitet unfinished
nicht dichtende Rohrgewinde-Verbindung *f* pipe thread where pressure-tight joints are not made on the threads
nicht durchgeschweißte Doppel-I-Naht *f* non-through-welded double square butt joint
nicht durchgeschweißte Wurzel *f* incomplete penetration
nicht entkohlend geglühter Temperguss *m* non-decarburized annealed malleable cast iron
nicht fest non-permanent
nicht formstabiles Teil *nt* part (or component) of unstable shape
nicht geführt non-guided, unguided, free ranging
nicht genehmigt unauthorized
nicht geschlichtet unfinished
nicht gespeichert not stored
nicht gesplitterte Kante *f* unsplintered edge
nicht hebbar non-elevating, non-elevatable
nicht hebend non-elevating, non-lifting
nicht hinterschliffen unrelieved
nicht höhenverstellbar non-adjustable in height
nicht höhenverstellbares Kragarmregal *nt* cantilever racking with fixed arms
nicht ineinander schiebbar non-telescopic
nicht leitend insulating
nicht lösbar non-detachable, permanent
nicht löschend retentive
nicht metallisch non-metallic
nicht mittragendes Füllgut *nt* non-load bearing fill goods
nicht negierter Anschluss *m* non-negated connection
nicht pendelnd non-articulated
nicht periodisch non-periodic
nicht quittierpflichtig does/do not require acknowledgement, not requiring acknowledgement
nicht rostender Stahl *m* stainless steel
nicht sachgerecht incorrect
nicht schaltbare Kupplung *f* fast clutch
nicht selbsttragend non-self-supporting
nicht spurgebunden path independent, lane-independent
nicht stapelnd non-stacking
nicht stapelnder Hubwagen *m* non-

stacking truck, low-lift truck
nicht Strom führend idle
nicht tragbar non-portable, fixed
nicht übertragender Lichtbogen *m* non-transferred arc
nicht unterbrochene Naht *f* continuous weld
nicht unterstützt unassisted
nicht weichgemachter Kunststoff *m* unplasticized plastics
nicht zusammenhängend unconnected
nicht zwangsgesteuert non-positive, non-positively steered, unrestricted steering
nichtabschmelzende Elektrode *f* non-consumable electrode
Nichtanwendbarkeit *f (e. Norm)* non-applicability
nichtanzeigendes Messgerät *nt* non-indicating measuring instrument
nichtballiges Rad *nt* non-crowned gear
NICHT-Baugruppe *f* NOT-gate
Nichtbeachtung *f* non-observance
nichtbrennbares Gas *nt* non-combustible gas, non-flammable gas
nichtbrennbares Heizgas *nt* non-combustible heating gas
Nichtbrennbarkeit *f* non-combustibility
nichtdezimal non-decimal
nichtdichtende Verbindung *f* non-sealing connection
Nichteinhalten *nt* non-compliance
Nichteisen... non-ferrous
Nichteisenguss *m* non-ferrous casting
nichtformgebundenes Maß *nt* mould-independent dimension, mould unrelated size
nicht-ganzzahlig non-integer
NICHT-Gatter *nt* NOT-gate
nichtgeometrische Größe *f* non-geometrical quantity
Nichtgleichgewichtszustand *m* non-equilibrium state
nichthärtbare Formmasse *f* thermoplastic moulding material (or compound)
nichthärtbarer Kunststoff *m* thermoplastics
nichtig void
Nichtkernprozess *m* non-core process
nichtklebender Bestandteil *m* non-tacky constituent
Nichtleiter *m* dielectric, insulator
nichtlinear nonlinear
nichtlineare Skale *f* non-linear scale
nichtmetallisches Sicherungselement *nt* non-metalic retaining (or locking) element
Nichtmetallverbindung *f* non-metallic compound
NICHT-ODER *nt* NOT-OR, NOR
NICHT-ODER-Schaltung *f* NOR-gate
Nichtparallelität *f* non-parallelity
nichtprogrammierbare Rechenmaschine *f* calculator without programmability
nichtproportionale Dehnung *f* percentage non-proportional elongation
NICHT-Schaltelement *nt* NOT-circuit, NOT-gate, negator, negation circuit
nichtselbsttätige Regelung *f* manual control
NICHT-Stufe *f* NOT-step
nichtteilbare Zahl *f* irreducible number
nichttragende Gewindeflanke *f* non-load bearing thread flank
nichttragende Schweißverbindung *f* non-load-bearing joint
nichttragende Verbindung *f* non-load-bearing assembly
nichttragender Bewehrungsstab *m* non-load-bearing reinforcing bar
nichtüberschnittener Zahnkopf *m* non-overcut tooth tip
Nichtüberschreitung *f* non-transgression
NICHT-UND *nt* NOT AND, NAND
nichtverseifbarer Stoff *m* unsaponifiable matter
nichtzufällige Größe *f* non-random quantity
nicht-zufällige Größe *f* non-random quantity
Nichtzünden *nt* non-ignition
Nichtzusammenfallen *nt* non-coincidence

Nichtzustandekommen non-establishment
Nickel *m* nickel
Nickelstahl *m* nickel steel
Niederdruckdampfkesselanlage *f* low pressure steam raising installation
niederdrücken press down, depress, force down
Niederdruckgasanlage *f* low pressure gas system
Niederdruckgasversorgungsleitung *f* low pressure gas supply line
Niederdruckheißwassererzeuger *m* low pressure high temperature water generator
Niederdruckkokillengießverfahren *nt* low pressure chill casting process
Niederdruckkokillenguss *m* low pressure chill casting
Niederdruckpolyethylen *nt* high density polyethylene
Niederfrequenz *f* low frequency
niedergehen descend, move downward
Niederhaltedruck *m* stripper pressure
Niederhaltekraft *f* stripper force
niederhalten hold down, keep down
Niederhalter *m* blank holder, holddown, toe dog
Niederhubflurförderzeug *nt* low-lift truck
Niederhubwagen *m* pallet truck
niedermolekularer Stoff *m* low-molecular substance
Niederschlag *m* deposit
Niederschlagsmesser *m* precipitation gauge
Niederschlagsschreiber *m* precipitation recorder
Niederschlagwasserleitung *f* condensate piping
Niederschrift *f* written report
Niederspannung *f* low voltage
Niederspannungsschaltgerät *nt* low-voltage contactor, low-voltage control unit, low-voltage switching device
niederwertigste Binärstelle *f* least significant bit
niedrig low

niedrige Form *f* 1. *(e. Mutter)* thin type 2. *(e. Passfeder)* shallow pattern
niedrige Hubhöhe *f* low-lift height
niedriger Vierkantsatz *m* *(e. Senkschraube)* short square
Niedrigkommissionierer *m* low-lift order picker (truck), low-lift truck
Niedrigpräzision *f* low precision
niedrigstwertige Stufe *f* *(e. Zählers)* lowest-valued stage
Niet *m* rivet
nieten rivet
Nieter *m* riveter
Nietgruppenzeichnung *f* riveted assembly drawing
Nietkopfmacher *m* rivet header
Nietmaschine *f* riveter, riveting machine
Nietpresse *f* riveting press
Nietschergerät *nt* shear test jig
Nietstift *m* rivet pin
Nietverschließmaschine *f* rivet closing machine
Nietzunder *m* riveting scale
Nippel *m* nipple
Nitridkeramikwerkzeug *nt* nitride ceramic cutting tool
Nitrierhärtetiefe *f* nitriding hardness depth
Nitrierstahl *m* nitrided steel
Nitrocellulosekleber *m* nitrocellulose solution adhesive
Niveau *nt* level
Niveaugefäß *nt* suspended level bulb
Niveaumessung *f* level measurement
Niveauschalter *m* liquid level switch
Niveausensor *m* level sensor
Niveautoleranz *f* level tolerance
Nivellement *nt* geometrically correct levelling
nivellieren level
nochmaliges Aufspannen *nt* reclamping
Nocke *f* cam, disk cam
Nocken *fpl* cam
Nocken *m* *(Anschlagnocken)* trip dog, dog
nockenbetätigt dog actuated
Nockenfräsen *nt* cam milling
Nockenfrontdrehmaschine *f* cam

front lathe
Nockenplatte *f* cam plate
Nockenschalter *m* cam switch
Nockenscheibe *f* trip dog carrier
Nockenschleifmaschine *f* cam contour grinder
Nockenstange *f* cam stick
Nockenwelle *f* camshaft
Nockenwellenantriebsrad *nt* camshaft drive gear
Nomenklatur *f* nomenclature
nominaler Wert *m* nominal value
Nonienteilung *f* vernier scale
Nonius *m* vernier
Noniusablesung *f* vernier reading
Noniusstrich *m* vernier mark
Noniusteilstrich *m* vernier division
Noniusteilung *f* vernier division
Noniustrommel *f* vernier dial
Nordpol *m* north pole
NOR-Glied *nt* NOR, OR with negated output
NOR-Glied *nt* **mit einem negierten Eingang** NOR with one negated input
Norm *f* standard
normal normal, regular, standard
Normal *nt* standard
Normalausführung *f* standard design, standard type
Normalausrüstung *f* standard equipment
Normalbetrieb *m* regular service, normal operation
Normalbohren *nt* standard drilling (or boring)
Normaldrehen *nt* standard turning
Normale *f* normal (line)
normale Fahrerposition *f* normal operating position
Normalebene *f* normal plane
Normaleingriffsteilung *f* normal base pitch
Normaleingriffswinkel *m* normal pressure angle, normal pressure angle at a point
normalentflammbar normally inflammable
Normalflankenspiel *nt* normal backlash
Normalfräsen *nt* normal milling

Normalfreiwinkel *m* normal clearance
Normalgewindelehrdorn *m* standard plug thread gauge
Normalgewindelehrring *m* standard ring thread gauge
Normalgröße *f* standard size
Normalkeilwinkel *m* normal wedge angle
Normalklima *nt* standard temperature atmosphere, standard atmosphere, reference atmosphere, normal distribution
Normallehre *f* standard gage
Normallückenweite *f* normal space-width
Normalmodul *nt (e. Verzahnung)* normal module
Normalprofil *nt (e. Verzahnung)* normal pressure
Normalprofilwinkel *m* normal pressure angle, normal pressure angle at a point
Normalquerschnitt *m* normal section
Normalschnitt *m (e. Verzahnung)* normal section
Normalschnittfläche *f* surface of the normal section
Normalspannung *f* standard stress
Normalspanwinkel *m* normal rake
Normalstapelbehälter *m* standard stacking container
Normalstrahlung *f* normal radiation
Normalteilung *f* normal pitch
Normaltoleranz *f* standard tolerance
Normalverteilung *f (um eine Toleranzmitte)* normal distribution
Normalwinkel *m* standard square
Normalzahlenreihe *f* preferred number series
Normalzahndicke *f* normal tooth thickness
Normdruckfarbe *f* standard ink
Normenreihe *f* series of standards
Normfallbeschleunigung *f* normal acceleration of free fall
normgerecht corresponding to the standard
Normhubhöhe *f* standard lift height
normieren standardize
Normierung *f* standardization
Norm-Kleinstab *m* small standard bar

Normlichtart *f* standard illuminant
Normlot *nt* standard solder
Normprobekörper *m* standard test specimen
Normreinheitsgrad *m* standard grade of cleanliness
Normschrift *f* standardized lettering, standard lettering
Normschrift *f:* **schräge ~** sloping style standard lettering
Normschriftgröße *f* size of standard lettering
Normteil *nt* standard part
Normung *f* standardization
Normwärmeleistung *f* standard heat emission
Normzeitwert *f* standard time value
Normzeitwertkartei *f* standard time value card file
NOR-Schaltung *f* NOR-gate
Nortongetriebe *nt* quick-change gearbox
Notabschaltsystem *nt* emergency shutdown system
Notabschaltung *f* emergency shutdown, emergency disconnection
Notabsenkung *f* 1. *(techn. Funktion)* emergency lowering 2. *(Einrichtung)* emergency lowering control
Notabstieg *m* emergency egress
Not-Aus *nt* emergency stop
Not-Aus-Befehl *m* emergency stop order, emergency stop command
Not-Aus-Einrichtung *f* emergency stop equipment, emergency stop device
Notausgang *m* emergency exit
Not-Aus-Kreis *m* emergency stop circuit
Notausschalter *m (el.)* emergency cutout
Notausstieg *m* emergency exit, trapdoor
Not-Aus-Stoppbremsung *f* emergency braking to stop
Notbefehlseinrichtung *f* emergency switch off
Notbeleuchtung *f* emergency lighting
Notbetrieb *m* emergency operation
Notbetriebseinrichtung *f* emergency operating system

Notbetriebsstrategie *f* emergency operation strategy
Notbremse *f* emergency brake
Notbremssystem *nt* emergency braking system
Notbremsung *f* emergency braking
Notendschalter *m* ultimate limit switch
Notfall *m* emergency situation, (case of) emergency
Notfall *m:* **im ~** in case of emergency
Notfalleinrichtung *f* emergency device
Notfallstrategie *f* emergency strategy
Nothalt *m* emergency stop
Nothalteinrichtung *f* emergency stop, emergency stopping device
Notlaufeigenschaft *f* emergency running property
Notschalter *m* emergency stop (button), emergency switch
Notschaltung *f* emergency circuit
Notschornstein *m* emergency chimney
Notsteuerstand *m* emergency control position, emergency control stand
Notstoppeinrichtung *f* emergency stop, emergency stopping device
Notstrategie *f* emergency strategy
Notstromaggregat *nt* emergency power generation set
notwendig necessary
Notwendigkeit *f* exigence, necessity
Novolakpressmasse *f* novolak moulding material
n-stündig n-hour
Null *f* 1. *(allg.)* nil, nought 2. *(math.)* zero
Nullachsabstand *m* reference centre distance
Nullanzeige *f* zero-indication, null indication
Nullbestand *m* zero inventory
Nulldämpfung *f* zero damping
Nulleffekt *m* background
Nulleffektimpulszahl *f* background pulse count
Nulleinstellung *f* zero adjustment
Nullgetriebe *nt* null transmission
Nullhypothese *f* null hypothesis
Null-Komma-Zwei-Prozent-Grenze *f*

0,2 % proof stress
Nulllage *f* zero-position
Nulllinie *f* reference line
Nullpunkt *m* datum point
Nullpunktanzeige *f* zero indication
Nullpunktdrift *m* zero point drift
Nullpunkteinstellung *f* setting to zero point
Nullpunktkorrektur *f* zero point correction
Nullpunktverschiebung *f* zero offset
Nullrad *nt (Stirnrad in der Profilverschiebung Null)* X-zero gear
Nullradpaar *nt* X-zero gear pair
Nullspannung *f* zero potential, zero voltage
nullspannungsgesichert retentive
Nullstellung *f* neutral position
Nullung *f (el.)* earthing, earthed-natural connection
Nullverzahnung *f* uncorrected tooth system
Nullzustand *m* zero state
nummerieren number
Numerikfräsmaschine *f* numerically-controlled milling machine
numerisch numeric(al)
numerisch gesteuert numerically controlled (NC)
numerisch gesteuerte Funktion *f* numerically controlled function
numerische Berechnung *f* numerical calculation
numerische Nummer *f* numerical number
numerische Steuerung *f* numeric(al) control (NC), digital control
Nummer *f* number
Nummerkreis *m* family of numbers
Nummerndrucker *m* number printer
Nummernstelle *f* number-place
Nummerung *f* numbering
Nummerungssystematik *f* numbering systematization
Nummerungstechnik *f* numbering practice
Nur-Lese-Speicher *m* read only memory (ROM)
Nur-Minus-Abweichung *f* negative-only variation

Nur-Plus-Abweichung *f* positive-only variation
Nut *f* 1. *(allg.)* channel, flute, groove 2. *(Aufnahmenut)* T-slot 3. *(Gewinde)* groove 4. *(Keilnut)* keyway, keyseat 5. *(Kerbnut)* V-notch 6. *(Langnut, Schlitz für Planscheibe)* slot 7. *(Spanbrechernut)* chip breaker, nick 8. *(Spannut)* flute
nuten 1. *(allg.)* groove, flute, slot 2. *(Spiralbohrer)* flute 3. *(Wellen)* keyway, keyseat
Nuten ziehen draw grooves
Nutendrehen *nt* grooving, recessing, turning necks
Nutenfräsarbeit *f* 1. *(Keilnuten)* keyway cutting, keyway milling, keywaying (operation) 2. *(Spannuten)* fluting 3. *(Keilwellen)* splining
Nutenfräsautomat *m* keyway and slot milling automatic, automatic keyway and slot milling machine
Nutenfräseinrichtung *f* 1. *(Keilnaben)* splining attachment 2. *(Langnuten)* slot milling attachment
Nutenfräsen *nt* 1. *(allg.)* groove milling, slot milling, keyway milling, fluting, flute milling 2. *(Keilnuten)* keyway milling, keywaying
Nutenfräser *m* keyway cutter, slot drill, slot milling cutter, shank-type keyway cutter
Nutenfräsmaschine *f* keyway (and slot) milling machine, flute miller
Nutenhobelmeißel *m* keyway cutting tool
Nutenhobeln *nt* keyway cutting
Nutenmeißel *m* keyseating chisel
Nutenscheibe *f* **der Querschubeinrichtung** feed driving disc
Nutenschritt-, Nutentauchfräsen *nt* groove milling
Nutenstechmeißel *m* groove recessing tool
Nutensteigung *f* gash lead
Nutensteigungsfehler *m* gash lead error
Nutenstoßmaschine *f* slotter
Nutenstoßmeißel *m* slotting tool
Nutenstoßvorrichtung *f* 1. *(allg.)*

groove cutting attachment **2.** *(Keilnuten)* keyseat slotting attachment, keywaying attachment
Nutenziehmaschine *f* groove-drawing machine, pull-type keyseating machine
Nutflansch *m* groove-faced flange
nutförmig groove-shaped
Nutkurve *f* face cam
Nutmutter *f* **für Hakenschlüssel** slotted round nut for hook spanners
Nutringmanschette *f* groove-ring collar, square-base U-ring
Nutschweißen *nt* groove welding
Nutstoßen *nt* slotting
Nutüberwurfmutter *f* grooved union nut
nutzbar usable, useful, utilizable
nutzbare Breite *f* clear width
nutzbare Flanke *f* effective flank, usable flank
nutzbare Gewindelänge *f* useful thread length
nutzbarer Behälterinhalt *m* utilizable reservoir capacity
nutzbares Flankenprofil *nt* usable flank profile
Nutzbremsung *f* effective braking
nutzbringend profitable, useful
Nutzdaten *pl* user data
Nutzdatenkapazität *f* user data capacity
nutzen use, utilize
Nutzer *m* user

Nutzfläche *f* active surface
Nutzförderhöhe *f* operating head
Nutzinformation *f* useful information
Nutzkreisdurchmesser *m* usable root diameter
Nutzlast *f* payout, rated load, useful load
Nutzlastaufnahme *f* payload handling, payload pick-up
Nutzmoment *m* usable moment
Nutzprozess *m* useful process
Nutzstrahlenbereich *m* useful radiation zone
Nutzstrahlenbündel *nt* useful ray beam
Nutzstrahleneintrittsfeld *nt* useful radiation field on entering
Nutzstrahlung *f* useful radiation
Nutztiefe *f* usable depth
Nutzung *f* use, utilization
Nutzungsdauer *f* (useful) life expectancy, useful life, expected useful life, service life, period of utilization
Nutzungsfläche *f* useful area
Nutzungshäufigkeit *f* frequency of use
Nutzungszeit *f* useful life, service life, time of operation, working time, operating time
Nutzwärmeleistung *f* useful heat output
Nutzwertanalyse *f* useful value analysis

O o

oben above, at the top
oben fahrend driving above
oben geführt top-controlled
oben laufend top running
oben offen open topped
Obenhubspreader *m* top lift spreader
oben liegend overhead
Obenpalettierer *m* high-level palletizer, high infeed palletizer
Obenprobe *f* top sample
Ober ... overhead
Oberarm *m* overarm
Oberbelag *m* floor covering
Oberboden *m (e. Tanks)* tank crown, top end
obere Endstellung *f* top limit, upper rest, upper position
obere Führungsschiene *f* top guide rail
obere Grenze *f* upper limit
obere Querverbindung *f* portal tie beam
oberer Gabelhaken *m* top hook
oberer Heizwert *m* gross calorific value
oberer Seitenbereich *m (e. Toleranzfeldes)* upper side band
oberer Teil *m* upper part
oberer/oberes upper
Oberfläche *f* 1. *(allg.)* surface, top 2. *(glatte ~)* smooth surface
Oberflächenabweichung *f (zulässige)* surface deviations (admissible)
Oberflächenansprüche *mpl* surface requirements
Oberflächenausstülpung *f* surface protuberance
Oberflächenbearbeitung *f* surface machining, surface processing
Oberflächenbegrenzungstemperatur *f* surface temperature limitation, maximum surface temperature
oberflächenbehandelt surface-treated, coated
Oberflächenbehandlung *f* (surface) finish, surface treatment
Oberflächenbeschaffenheit *f* surface condition, surface texture, surface quality, surface finish
Oberflächenbeurteilung *f* surface assessment
Oberflächenbild *nt* surface appearance, surface pattern
Oberflächencharakter *m* surface character
Oberflächendurchgangswiderstand *m* surface insulation resistance
Oberflächenfehler *m* surface imperfection, surface blemish, surface flaw, surface defect, surface discontinuity
Oberflächenfeingestalt *f* surface texture
Oberflächenfeuchtigkeit *f* surface moisture
Oberflächengestalt *f* surface pattern, configuration of the surface, surface texture, surface configuration
Oberflächengestaltung *f* surface configuration
Oberflächengüte *f* finish, surface finish, surface quality
Oberflächenhärte *f* surface hardness, superficial hardness
Oberflächenhärten *nt* surface hardening
Oberflächenhärtewert *m* surface hardness value
Oberflächenisolationswiderstand *m* surface insulation resistance
Oberflächenkennzeichen *nt* surface symbol
Oberflächenkennzeichnung *f* surface indication
Oberflächenlackierung *f* surface varnishing
Oberflächenmesstechnik *f* surface metrology
Oberflächenmessung *f* surface measurement, surface quality measurement
Oberflächenmessverfahren *nt* surface measurement method
oberflächenmontierbar surface-mountable

oberflächenmontierbarer Baustein *m* surface-mountable device (SMD)
Oberflächenprobe *f* surface sample
Oberflächenprofil *nt* surface contour (or profile)
Oberflächenprüfung *f* surface examination
Oberflächenqualität *f* surface quality
Oberflächenrauheit *f* surface roughness
Oberflächensauberkeit *f* surface cleanliness
Oberflächenschnitt *m* surface section
Oberflächenschutzüberzug *m* surface protecting coating
Oberflächenstruktur *f* surface structure
Oberflächentastgerät *nt* surface profile tracer
Oberflächentemperatur *f* surface temperature
Oberflächenverfestigung *f* surface work-hardening
Oberflächenverhalten *nt* surface behaviour
Oberflächenverletzung *f* slight damage to the surface
Oberflächenvorbereitung *f* surface preparation
Oberflächenwärmeaustauscher *m* surface heat exchanger
Oberflächenwelle *f* surface undulation, surface wave
Oberflächenwiderstand *m* surface resistance
Oberflächenzersetzung *f* surface decomposition
Oberflächenzerstörung *f* surface deterioration
Oberflächenzustand *m* surface condition, surface integrity, surface finish
Oberfolie *f* upper web of film
Oberfolieneinschlagmaschine *f* fold over wrapping machine
Obergrenze *f* upper limit
oberhalb above, upside, upstream
oberirdische Lagerung *f* above-ground storage
oberirdische Rohrleitung *f* *(frei verlegte Leitung)* surface pipeline
oberirdischer Hochdruckgasbehälter *m* above-ground high pressure gasholder
Oberkante *f* top edge, upper edge
Oberkasten *m* head cast, head box
Oberlicht *nt* upper light
Oberschichtprobe *f* upper layer sample
Oberschieber *m* top slide, upper slide
Oberschlitten *m* upper slide
Oberschwingung *f* harmonic
Oberseite *f* upper face, upper surface, top
Oberspannung *f* maximum stress
oberste Stellung *f* top position
oberste/r/s uppermost, topmost
Oberteil *nt* **1.** *(allg.)* harmonic wave, upper harmonic wave, top, upper part **2.** *(e. Werkzeuges)* top force
Ober-Türschließer *m* overhead door closer
Objekt *nt* object
Objektiv *nt* objective, lens
Objektivträger *m* lens carrier
objektspezifisch object-specific
Objektträger *m* object carrier
Objektveränderung *f* change of object
ODER *nt* OR
ODER-Abhängigkeit *f* Or dependency
ODER-Glied *nt* OR-gate
ODER-Glied *nt* **mit Negation eines Einganges** OR element with one input negated
ODER-Glied *nt* **mit negiertem Ausgang** OR with negated output
ODER-Glied *nt* **mit negiertem Sperreingang** OR with negated inhibiting input
ODER-Glied *nt* **mit Sperreingang** OR with inhibiting input
ODER-NICHT *nt* nondisjunction
ODER-verknüpft OR-linked
ODER-Verknüpfung *f* disjunction
Ofen *m* **1.** *(allg.)* furnace, oven, stove **2.** *(Keramik)* kiln
Ofenalterung *f* oven ageing
Ofensockel *m* furnace base
offen open, non-closed, uncovered
offen legen disclose, externalize, pub-

lish
offen prozessgekoppelt on-line, open loop
offene CNC open-ended control
offene Flamme f unshielded (or naked) flame
offene Heizungsanlage f open type heating system
offene nicht durchgehende Pore f *(Grübchen)* open, non through going pore
offener radioaktiver Stoff m unsealed radioactive material
offener Regelkreis m open loop
offener Wirkungsweg m *(in binären Schaltsystemen)* open loop
offenes Gaspressschweißen nt open square pressure gas welding
offenes Steuerungssystem nt open control system
Offenhaltezeit f forward pressure-off time
Offenlegung f disclosure, publication
Offenstellung f *(e. Hahns)* open position
öffentliche Sicherheit f public safety
offenzelliger Schaumstoff m open-cell foam
öffnen open, release, unlock, uncover
Öffner m **1.** *(allg.)* opener **2.** *(el.)* break contact element, break contact
Öffnerwechsel m *(UK)* break-make-brake (contact), *(US)* break-make before brake (contact)
Öffnung f **1.** *(allg.)* aperture, hole opening, opening, port, orifice **2.** *(Dosen)* mouth
Öffnungsgriff m release handle
Öffnungswinkel m **1.** *(allg.)* angle of beam spread, groove angle **2.** *(Reibung)* included angle
Öffnungszeit f opening time
Offset offset compensation
Offsetdruck m offset printing
ohmsche Last f resistive load
ohmscher Widerstand m **1.** *(Bauteil)* ohmic resistor **2.** *(Größe)* linear resistance, active resistance
ohne without
ohne Berührung f **mit** clear of

ohne Freiwinkel m unrelieved
ohne Kabel nt cableless
ohne Selbsthalt m hold-to-run
ohne toten Gang m backlash-free
ökologisch ecological
Oktoide f octoid
Oktoidenverzahnung f octoid tooth system
Okular nt microscopic eye-piece, objective
Okularschraube f eyepiece (or focusing) screw
Okularschraubenmikrometer m eyepiece micrometer
Öl nt oil
Öl nt **ohne chemische Zusätze** f straight oil
Ölablasshahn m oil-drain cock
Ölabscheider m oil separator
ölanlassen oil-temper
Ölauffangeinrichtung f oil catcher
Ölbad nt oil bath
ölbefeuerte Zentralheizungsanlage f oil burning central heating system
Ölbrenner m **mit stufenloser Regelung** oil burner with stepless control
Ölbrenner m **mit Zweipunktregelung** oil burner with two-step action control
Ölbrennermotor m oil burner motor
Ölbrennerpumpe f oil burner pump
Ölbüchse f oil cup
Öldampfverlust m oil vapour loss
Ölderivat nt oil derivative
Öldichtung f oil seal
ölen oil
Öler m oiler, lubricator, oil cup
ölfest oil resistant
Ölfeuerungsanlage f oil firing plant
Ölfeuerungsautomat m automatic oil firing unit
Ölfilm m oil film
Ölfilter m oil filter
Ölfleck m oil spot
ölfrei halten keep free of oil
ölführende Leitung f oil-conveying line
Ölgebläsebrenner m atomizing oil burner

ölgehärtet oil-hardened
ölgekapselt oil-protected
ölgekühlt oil-cooled
ölhaltiger Dampf *m* oily steam
Ölheizofen *m* space heating flued oil stove
ölig greasy
ölige Späne *f* swarf
Ölkanne *f* bench oiler, oil can
Ölkapselung *f* oil immersion, oil immersion apparatus
Ölkreislauf *m* oil circuit, hydraulic circuit
Ölkühlung *f* oil cooling
Ölmengenzähler *m* oil flow meter
Ölnebel *m* oil mist
Ölnebelkühlanlage *f* spray coolant system
Ölnebelkühlung *f* spray-cooling, mist cooling
Ölnebelschmierung *f* mist-lubrication
Ölnut *f* oil groove
Ölofen *m* oil-fired furnace
Ölrückstand *m* oil residue
Ölrückstrom *m* backstreaming of oil
Öl-Speicher-Wasserheizer *m* oil storage water heater
Ölumlauf *m* oil circulation
Ölverdampfung *f* evaporation of oil
Ölverdampfungsbrenner *m* oil vaporizing burner
Ölverlust *m* failure of the hydraulic system, loss of oil
Ölverunreinigungen entfernen remove oil contaminations
Ölzahl *f* oil absorption value
Ölzerstäubungsbrenner *m* atomizing oil burner
omnidirektional omnidirectional
on-line anschließbar on-line pluggable
Operationsreihenfolge *f* operational order
Operationsverstärker *m* operational amplifier
Operationszyklus *m* operation cycle
operativ operational, functional
Opferanode *f* sacrificial anode
Optik *f* optic
Optiken *fpl:* **adaptive ~** adaptive optics
optimal optimum

Optimeter *m* optimeter, optical comparator
optimieren optimize
Optimierung *f* optimization
Optimum *nt* optimum
optisch visual, optical
optisch lesbar optically readable
optische Messeinrichtung *f* optical instrumentation
optische Messtechnik *f* interferometry
optische Polymerfaser *f* polymer optical fibre
optische Visiereinrichtung *f* optical sighting equipment
optischer Teilkopf *m* optical diding head
optisches Fühlhebelgerät *nt* optical comparator
optisches Signal *nt* optical signal
optoelektrisch optoelectric
Optoelektronik *f* optoelectronics
optoelektronisches Koppelelement *nt* optical electronic coupling element
Ordinalmerkmal *nt* ordinal characteristic
ordnen arrange, array
Ordner *m* file
Ordnung *f* arrangement, order
Ordnungsfunktion *f* order function
ordnungsgemäß orderly, proper, duly
ordnungsgemäße Fertigung *f* proper workmanship
ordnungsgemäßer Anschluss *m* correct connection
ordnungsgemäßer Arbeitsablauf *m* proper sequence of operations
Ordnungszahl *f* ordinal number, atomic number
Ordnungszustand *m* order status
Organisation *f* organization
Organisationsdaten *pl* organization data
Organisationseinheit *f* unit of organization
Organisationsmittel *ntpl* organization means
Organisationsstruktur *f* organizational structure
organisatorisch organizational

organisieren arrange, organize
orientieren align, orient, orientate
Orientierung f orientation, alignment
Orientierungseinrichtung f orientation device
Orientierungsmaschine f orienter
Orientierungsmaschine f **für formstabile Packmittel** rigid container orienter
Orientierungsspannung f orientation tension
Originalsystem nt original system
Originalvergrößerung f enlargement of the original
Originalverpackung f original packing, original package (or packaging)
Originalvorlagen fpl original documents pl
Ort m place, location
Ortbeton m job-mixed concrete, site mixed concrete
orten locate, position
orthogonale Zerspanung f orthogonal cutting
Orthogonalebene f orthogonal plane
Orthogonalfreiwinkel m orthogonal clearance
Orthogonal-Keilwinkel m orthogonal wedge angle
Orthogonalschnitt m orthogonal cut
Orthozykloide f orthocycloid, cycloid
örtlich local
örtliche Spanungsdicke f **am ausgewählten Schneidenpunkt** local thickness of cut at a selected point on the cutting edge
ortsabhängig locally defined
ortsbeweglich movable, portable
Ortschaum m in situ cellular plastics
Ortsdosierung f local dosage rate
ortsfest fixed, stationary, static
ortsfeste Einrichtung f stationary equipment
ortsfeste Lagerung f static storage
Ortstoleranz f location tolerance
ortsunabhängig independent of location
ortsveränderliche Einrichtung f portable equipment
Ortsveränderung f change of place, shifting
Ortung f location, positioning
Ortungsstab m flaw location scale
Öse f ear, eye, eyelet, loop
Oszillation f oscillation
Oszillationsbewegung f oscillating movement
oszillieren oscillate
oszillierend oscillatory, oscillating, reciprocating
Otrozellstoff m oven dry pulp
Ovalleiste f oval laminated rod
Ovalschleifmaschine f oval grinder
oxidarme Oberfläche f low oxide surface
Oxidasche f oxide ash
oxidationsempfindlich susceptible to oxidation
Oxidationsreaktion f oxidation reaction
Oxidationsstabilität f oxidation stability
Oxidationsverschleiß m oxidative wear
oxidativer Abbau m oxidative degradation
Oxidbelag m oxide coating
oxidieren oxidize
Oxidkeramik f oxide ceramic
oxidkeramischer Schneidstoff m oxide-ceramic cutting material
oxidkeramisches Schneidwerkzeug nt oxide-ceramic cutting tool
Oxidlösevermögen nt oxide-dissolving capacity
oxydationsbeständiges Öl nt antioxidant oil
Oxydhaut f oxide film
Oxydschicht f oxide layer
Ozonrissbildung f ozone cracking

P p

Paar *nt* pair
Paarbildungseffekt *m* pair formation (or production) effect
paaren pair, mate, assemble, match
Paarung *f* 1. *(allg.)* assembly 2. *(e. Rades mit dem Gegenrad)* pairing 3. *(e. Rades mit dem Werkzeug)* mating
Paarung *f* **von Toleranzfeldern** combination of tolerance zones
Paarungsabmaß *nt* mating allowance
Paarungsbedingungen *fpl* mating conditions
Paarungsfeld *nt* mating area
Paarungsflankendurchmesser *m* virtual pitch diameter
Paarungsmaß *nt* mating dimension (or size)
Paarverzahnung *f* paired tooth system
paarweise in pairs
packen pack, package
Packerei *f* packing area, shipping bay
Packgut *nt* packaged good, product for packing, packed goods
Packhilfsmittel *nt* packaging aid, packaging component
Packliste *f* packing list
Packmittel *nt* package, packaging (container), container
Packmuster *nt* packing pattern
Packstoff *m* packaging material
Packstofftransportvorrichtung *f* packaging material transport mechanism
Packstück *nt* packing unit, package, filled package
Packstückprüfung *f* testing of filled packages
Packtisch *m* packing table
Packung *f* pack, package, packing
Packungseinheit *f* packaging unit
Packungsmenge *f* packaged quantity
Packungsscheibe *f* packing shim
Paket *nt* package
Paketsortieranlage *f* package sorting system
Palette *f* pallet, stillage

Paletten ausheben lift out pallets
Paletten *fpl* **auflösen** dismantle pallets
Paletten herstellen form pallets
Palettenabsenküberwachung *f* pallet lowering protection
Palettenabsenkung *f* pallet lowering
Palettenabstand *m* pallet spacing
Palettenanzahl *f* number of pallets
Palettenauflösung *f* pallet dismantling
Palettenauflösungsmaschine *f* pallet dismantling machine
Palettenaufsetzgestell *nt* pallet converter
Palettenaufsetzrahmen *m* pallet collar
Palettenaushub *m* pallet lift-out
Palettenaushubvorrichtung *f* pallet lift-out device
Palettenauslauf *m* pallet output, pallet exit
Palettenauslaufstelle *f* pallet exit point
Palettenband *nt* pallet band
Palettenbandverriegelung *f* palletband locking
Palettenbox *f* pallet box
Palettendurchlaufregal *nt* pallet flow rack(ing)
Palettendurchschubsicherung *f* pallet back stop
Paletteneinlauf *m* pallet input, pallet entry
Paletteneinlaufstelle *f* pallet entry point
Paletteneinschubregal *nt* push-back pallet rack(ing)
Palettenerkennung *f* pallet detection
Palettengreifer *m* pallet gripper
Palettenheber *m* jack, pallet lift
Palettenherstellung *f* pallet forming
Palettenhochregallager *nt* pallet high-bay warehouse
Palettenhubwagen *m* pallet-lift truck, pallet truck
Palettenkette *f* pallet chain
Palettenkettenrolle *f* pallet chain roller

Palettenkontrolle *f* pallet check, pallet monitoring
Palettenkontrollsystem *nt* pallet monitoring system
Palettenkufe *f* pallet bearer, pallet foot, skid
Palettenladung *f* pallet load
Palettenladungssicherungsmaschine *f* pallet securing machine
Palettenladungstisch *m* lifting component, lift table
Palettenlager *nt* pallet store
palettenlos pallet-free
Palettenposition *f* pallet position
Palettenregal *nt* pallet shelving, pallet rack(ing)
Palettenregal *nt* **mit verstellbaren Balken** adjustable beam pallet racking (APR)
Palettenregallager *nt* pallet shelving store
Palettenschnellwechsel *m* rapid pallet transfer
Palettenschrumpffolienmaschine *f* pallet shrink wrapper
Palettenschrumpfhaubenüberziehmaschine *f* shrink hood applicator
Palettenschrumpfofen *m* pallet shrink oven
Palettenschrumpftunnel *m* pallet shrink tunnel
Palettenschrumpfrahmen *m* pallet shrink frame
Palettensicherungshilfsmittel *nt* pallet stabilizing accessory
Palettenstapler *m* pallet stacker
Palettenstapler/-entstapler *m* pallet stacker/unstacker
Palettenstretchfolienmaschine *f* pallet stretchwrapper
Palettentauscher *m* pallet exchanger
Palettenträger *m* pallet deck spacer
Palettentraverse *f* pallet cross beam
Palettenumgreifungsmaschine *f* pallet strapping machine
Palettenumreifungspresse *f* pallet compression strapping machine
Palettenwechsel *m* switch of pallet
Palettenwechsler *m* pallet changer
Palettenwendeklammer *f* pallet inverter, pallet turnover clamp
Palettenwender *m* pallet turnover (device)
Palettieranordnung *f* palletizing layout
palettieren palletize
palettierend palletizing
Palettierer *m* palletizer, palletizing machine
Palettierer-Depalettierer *m* palletizer-depalletizer
Palettierkapazität *f* palletizing capacity
Palettierprogramm *nt* palletizing program
Palettierroboter *m* robot palletizer, palletizer robot
palettiert palletized
Palloidspiralkegelräder *ntpl* palloid spiral bevel gear
Palloidverzahnung *f* palloid tooth system
Panne *f* failure
Pantographengesenkfräsmaschine *f* pantograph die-sinking machine
pantographengesteuerte Fräsmaschine *f* pantograph-controlled miller
Pantographengraviermaschine *f* pantographic engraving machine
Pantographennachformfräsmaschine *f* pantograph milling machine, pantograph miller
Pantographgesenkfräs- und -graviermaschine *f* pantograph die-sinking and engraving machine
Panzerplatte *f* **1.** *(hobeln)* armour plate **2.** *(Akku)* tubular plate
Panzerplattenelektrode *f* tubular-plate electrode
Panzerplattenhobelmaschine *f* armour plate planer
Panzerplattenhobelmaschine *f* **mit beweglichen Querbalken** travelling armour plate planer
Panzerplattenhobeln *nt* armour plate planing
Panzerrohrgewinde *nt* steel conduit thread

Panzerschlauch *m* armoured hose
Panzerung *f* hard surfacing layer
Papier *nt* paper
Papierfolie *f* paper film
Papierkleber *m* adhesive for paper
Papierlage *f* sheet of paper
Papierlochband *nt* punched paper type
Papierprobe *f* paper sample
Papierrolle *f* paper roll
Papierträger *m* paper carrier
Pappe *f* cardboard, cartonboard, paperboard
Pappezuschnitt *m* cartonboard blank, piece of cartonboard
Pappschachtel *f* cardboard box, cartonboard sleeve
Parabel *f* parabola
Parabelinterpolation *f* parabola interpolation
Paraffin *nt* paraffin, paraffin wax, petroleum wax
Paraffinechtheit *f* resistance to paraffin
Parallaxe *f* parallax
parallaxfreie Ablesung *f* anti-parallax reading
parallel geschaltet connected in parallel, parallelly connected
Parallel-zu-parallel-Codierer *m* parallel-to-parallel coder
Parallel-zu-seriell-Codierer *m* parallel-to-serial coder
Parallelabzweig *m* parallel branch
Parallelachsen *fpl* parallel axis
parallelachsenfreie Ablesung *f* reading free from parallax
Parallelbahn *f* parallel path
Parallelbestimmung *f* replicate
Parallelbündel *nt* parallel bunch
parallele Datenübertragung *f* parallel data transmission
Parallelendmaß *nt* block gauge, precision gauge block, combination gauge block, slip gauge, end block, end measure, block
parallelflächiges Werkstückelement *nt* parallel flat workpiece
parallel geschaltet connected in parallel
Parallelgreifer *m* parallel gripper
Parallelität *f* parallelism
Parallelitätstoleranz *f* parallelism tolerance
Parallelkurbelgetriebe *nt* parallel crank mechanism
Parallelprogrammierung *f* parallel input mode
Parallelreaktion *f* (*el. chem.*) parallel reaction
Parallelregister *nt* parallel register
Parallelreißer *m* surface gauge, scribing block, marking gauge
Parallelreißernadel *f* surface gauge scriber
Parallelschaben *nt* parallel-axes shaving
Parallelschaltung *f* parallel connection
Parallelschnittstelle *f* parallel interface
Parallelschraubzwinge *f* parallel clamp
Parallelstellung *f* parallel positioning, parallel position
Parallelstoß *m* parallel joint
Parallelstoß *m* **mit Parallelnaht** parallel joint with parallel weld
Parallelstruktur *f* parallel structure
Parallelversatz *m* offset in parallel
Parallelverschiebung *f* parallel displacement, parallel translation
Parallelverschiebung *f* (*von Fugenflanken e. Pressverbandes*) parallel displacement
Parameter *m* parameter
Parametereingabe *f* parameter input
Parametereinstellung *f* parameter setting
Parameterfehler *m* parameter error
Parameterschreiben *nt* parametric control
parametrieren parametrize, parameterize
Parametrierung *f* parameterizing
parametrisch parametric
Parametrische Programmierung *f* parametric programming
Parität *f* parity
Paritätsbit *nt* parity bit
Paritätsprüfung *f* parity check, odd-even check
Paritätszeichen *nt* parity character

Parkbremse *f* parking brake
parken park
Parkettklebstoff *m* parquet adhesive
Parkfläche *f* parking lot, parking space
partiell partial
Partikel *nt* particle, particulate
Partikeleinheit *f* particulate cleanliness
partikulär particulate
Partner *m* partner, party involved
Partnerinformation *f* party information
Passage *f* passage
Passarbeit *f* fitting work
Passdorn *m* check plug
passen fit, suit, be suitable
passend fitting, well-fitting, suitable, appropriate
Passfeder *f* **1.** *(allg.)* feather, fitting key, spline, feather key, parallel key **2.** *(niedrige ~)* thin parallel key
Passfehler *m* form error
Passfläche *f* fitting surface
Passfuge *f* fitting joint
Passgenauigkeit *f* fitting accuracy
passgerecht body-fit, dimension-fitting
passgerechte Toleranz *f* dimension-fitting tolerance
passieren pass, pass through
Passierschein *m* pass, (entry) permit
Passimeter *nt* passimeter, internal indicating gauge, indicating snap gauge
passiv passive
passive Korrosion *f* passive corrosion
passives Glied *nt* passive element
passivieren passivate
Passivkraft *f* passive force, back force
Passkerbstift *m* half length taper grooved pin, close tolerance grooved pin
Passkerbstift *m* **mit Hals** (close tolerance) grooved pin with gorge
Passkerbstift *m* **mit Nut für Sicherungsscheiben** grooved pin with slot for retaining washers
Passkerbstift *m* **mit Nut und Sicherungsringen** grooved pin with slot for retaining rings
Passlänge *f* length of fit, fitting length
Passläppen *nt* equalizing lapping
Passmaß *nt* toleranced dimension, mating dimension, fit size
Passscheibe *f* shim ring, adjustment washer
Passschraube *f* precision bolt, fitting screws, reamed bolt, fitting bolt, body-fit bolt
Passsitz *m* working fit
Passstift *m* dowel, fitting pin, alignment pin
Passstück *nt* adaptor
Passstücke *ntpl* mating members, mating parts
Passsystem *nt* system of fits
Passteil *nt* fitting member, fitting part, mating part, part to be fitted
Passtoleranz *f* fit tolerance
Passtoleranzfeld *nt* fit tolerance zone
Passung *f* fit
Passung *f* **für Einheitsbohrung** hole basis fit
Passung *f* **für Einheitswelle** shaft basis fit
Passungen *fpl* fits (pl)
Passungsauswahl *f* selection of fits
Passungscharakter *m* kind of fit
Passungsgüte *f* quality of fit
Passungslehre *f* **1.** *(Messgerät)* tolerance ga(u)ge **2.** *(Lehrfach)* theory of fits
Passungsmechanik *f* mechanics of fits
Passungsrost *m* fretting rust
Passungssitz *m* fit
Passungsspiel *nt* fitting clearance
Passungstoleranz *f* fit tolerance
Passwort *nt* password
Passwortauthentifizierung *f* password authentication
Passwortauthentifizierungsprotokoll *nt* password authentication protocol
Passwortschutz *m* password protection
Passwortsicherung *f* password protection
Paste *f* paste
Pasteneinlage *f* paste filling
Pastenverschnittharz *m* paste dilution resin
Pastenviskosität *f* paste viscosity
Patentanmeldung *f* patent application
Patentzeichnung *f* patent drawing
Paternoster *m* vertical (type) rotary

rack
Paternosterlager *nt* vertical rotary warehouse
Paternosterregal *nt* vertical carousel, vertical (type) rotary rack, paternoster rack
Patrone *f* cartridge
pausbare Zeichnung *f* reproducible drawing
Pause *f* 1. *(allg.)* break, rest-time 2. *(Maschinen)* deadtime
pausen copy, print, trace
Pausendauer *f* break (or interval) duration
pausenlos Fräsen *nt* **mit Rundschalttisch** index base milling
Pausenregelung *f* rest-time regulation
Pausenzeit *f* pause time (in the main line)
pausfähig reproducible
P-Beiwert *m* proportional action value
p-Bereich *m* proportional band
PD-Regeleinrichtung *f* proportional plus derivative action controlling system
PEARL (Abk. für Programmiersprache zur Lösung von Aufgaben im Realzeitbetrieb) Process and Equipment Automation Real Time Language
Pedal *nt* pedal, foot-operated lever, treadle
Pegel *m* level
Pegelschreiber *m* level recorder, profile recorder
Pegelverteilung *f* level distribution
peilen fix
Peilsensorik *f* fixing sensors
Peilung *f* 1. *(e. Richtung einschlagen)* bearing 2. *(Ergebnis)* fix
peinlich sauberes Prüfgerät *nt* scrupulously clean test apparatus
Pendelachse *f* articulated axle, pivoting beam-type steer axle
Pendelantrieb *m* shuttle service
Pendelausschlag *m* weaving amplitude
Pendelbewegung *f* oscillating movement
Pendeldrehpunkt *m* steer axle pivotal point, pendulum pivot

Pendeldruckknopftafel *f* pendant pushbutton station, pendant control panel
Pendelfräsarbeit *f* reciprocal milling (operation)
Pendelfräsen *nt* milling with automatic cycle table control, cycle milling, reciprocal milling, pendulum milling
Pendelfräsmaschine *f* automatic cycle milling machine
Pendelfutter *nt* floating toolholder
Pendelhärten *nt* cycle hardening
Pendel-Kraftmessung *f* pendulum load measurement
Pendelkugellager *nt* self-aligning ball bearing
Pendellager *nt* self-alignment bearing
pendeln float, shuttle, reciprocate, oscillate, swing, pivot
pendelnd articulated, swinging, oscillating, pivoting
pendelnder Lichtbogen *m* weaving arc
Pendel-Rückfall *m* pendulum fall-back
Pendelschleifen *nt* reciprocating grinding, complete traverse grinding
Pendelschleifen *nt* **mit Zustellung pro Hub** reciprocating grinding mill feed setting per stroke
Pendelschleifmaschine *f* swing frame grinder
Pendelstange *f* pendulum rod
Pendelstation *f* pendant push button panel (or station)
Pendelsystem *nt* reciprocating system
Pendeltastsystem *nt* two-skid contact system
Pendeltauchfräsen *nt* plunge-feed milling
Pendeltrennschleifmaschine *f* oscillating-type abrasive cutting machine
Pendeltrennschleifmaschine *f* oscillating-type abrasive cutting machine
Pendelung *f* articulation, articulation of the axle
Pendelverkehrfräsen *nt* milling with automatic cycle table control, cycle milling, reciprocal milling
Pendelwerkzeug *nt* floating tool
Penetration *f* penetration

Penetriermittel *nt* penetrating agent
Pentosangehalt *m* pentosan content
Perchlorsäuretitration *f* perchloric acid tiltration
perforieren perforate, punch
Pergarmentierungsmittel *nt* parchmentizing agent
Periode *f* cycle, period
Periodenanzahl *f* number of periods
Periodendauer *f* periodic duration
Periodensystem *nt* periodic system
Periodenzahl *f* number of cycles, periodicity
Periodenzeit *f* periodic time
periodisch cyclic(al), periodic(al), recurring
periodische Spitzenspannung *f* recurring peak voltage
peripher peripheral
Peripherie *f* periphery, peripheral devices (or equipment), circumference
Peripheriegerät *nt* peripheral
Peripheriegeräte *ntpl* peripheral units
Perkussion *f* percussion
Perkussionsbohren *nt* percussion boring (or drilling)
Perkussionskraft *f* ballistic power, percussive force
Perkussionszünder *m* percussion primer
Perkussionszündung *f* percussion priming
Perlit *m* pearlite
perlitisch pearlitic
perlitrandfreies Gefüge *nt (von Temperguss)* structure devoid of pearlite boundaries
Perlleim *m* pearl glue
permanent permanent
Permanentmagnet *nt* permanent magnet
permanentmagneterregter Synchronmotor *m* permanent magnet synchronous motor
Permeationskoeffizient *m* permeability coefficient
Peroxidbleichechtheit *f* fastness to bleaching with peroxide
Personal beschaffen recruit personnel
Personal *nt* personnel, staff

Personalbeschaffung *f* recruitment, personnel recruiting
Personaleinsatz *m* personnel placement, manpower assignment
Personaleinsparung *f* personnel savings
Personalkosten *pl* personnel costs
Personalkostenblock *m* personnel costs block
Personalnebenkosten *pl* ancillary personnel costs
Personalplanung *f* personnel planning
Personalqualifikation *f* qualification of personnel
Personenerkennung *f* personnel detection
Personenerkennungssystem *nt* personnel detection means, personnel detection system
persönlich personal
persönlicher digitaler Assistent *m* personal digital assistant (PDA)
Petersverrippung *f* zigzag bracing
Petrinetz *nt* Petri net
Petrinetz *nt* Petri network, Petri net
Petrinetzknoten *m* token
Petrinetzpfeil *m* arc
Petroleum *nt* kerosene
Pfahl *m* pile, post
pfeifendes Geräusch *nt* squealing sound
Pfeil *m* 1. *(allg.)* arrowhead, arrow 2. *(rund)* arc
Pfeiler *m* pillar
Pfeilfallversuch *m* falling dart test
Pfeillinie *f* arrow line
Pfeilrad *nt* herringbone gear
pfeilverzahnt with double-helical teeth, with herringbone gear teeth
Pfeilverzahnung *f* continuous double helical teeth
Pfeilzahnhobelmaschine *f* herringbone gear shaper
Pferdestärke *f* horse-power
Pfette *f* purlin
Pfettenabstand *m* purlin spacing
Pfettendach *nt* purlin roof
Pflanzensprühöl *nt* plant spray oil
Pflege *f* 1. *(Wartung)* attendance, maintenance, service, servicing, treatment,

care 2. *(Dokumentation)* updating
pflegen 1. *(warten)* attend, care for, service, maintain 2. *(dokumentieren)* update
pflegen (~ zu) tend
Pflicht *f* duty, liability
Pflichtenheft *nt* performance specification, specifications, functional specification, requirements specification
Pfosten *m* post, pillar, support, upright (post)
Pfostendruck *m* load, load per upright
Pfusch *m* bungle, slipshod work
Pfuscharbeit *f* shoddy work, slipshod work
P-Glied *nt* *(Proportionalglied)* proportional element
P-Grad *m* *(e. Regelung)* proportional degree
Phantomecho *nt* ghost echo
Phantomfallversuch *m* head form test
Phantom-ODER-Verknüpfung *f* distributed OR connection, dot OR, wired OR
Phantom-UND-Verknüpfung *f* distributed AND connection, dot AND, wired AND
Phantomverknüpfung *f* distributed connection
Phase *f* phase, stage
Phasenausfall *m* phase failure
Phasenfolge *f* phase sequence
Phasenfront *f* phase front
Phasengang *m* phase response
Phasengrenze *f* *(bei Elektroden, Elektrolyten)* phase boundary
Phasenlage *f* phase position, shaft position
Phasenlaufzeit *f* phase lag
Phasenmodulation *f* phase modulation
phasenmoduliert phase-modulated
Phasenregelkreis *m* phase-locked loop
Phasenverschiebung *f* phase displacement, phase shift
Phenolbasis *f* phenol basis
Phenolharzfolie *f* phenolic moulding material
Phenolplastharz *nt* phenolplastic resin
phenolplastisches Harz *nt* phenolplastic material (or resin)
Phenoplasthersteller *m* manufacturer of phenolic plastics
Phenoplastkitt *m* phenoplastic putty
Phenoplastleim *m* phenoplastic glue
Phenoplastschmelzklebstoff phenoplast thermal fusion adhesive
Phophatierungsprozess *m* phosphating process
Phosphatanion phosphate anion
Phosphatierungsbad *nt* phosphating bath
Phosphatschicht *f* phosphate coat
Phosphatschutzschicht *f* phosphate protective coat
photochemisch photo-chemical
Photochromie *f* **von Färbungen** photochromism of dyeings
photoelektrisch photoelectric, photoelectrically
photoelektrischer Sensor *m* photocell
Photoelektron *nt* photo electron
Photoempfänger *m* photoreceiver
Photofluoreszenz *f* photo fluorescence
Photokopierpapier *nt* photocopying paper
Photolithographie *f* photo lithography
Photon *nt* photon
Photonenenergie *f* photon energy
Photonenflussdichte *f* photon flow density
Photonenstrahl *m* photon beam
Photonenstrahlung *f* photon radiation
Photopolymer *nt* photo polymer
Phototransistor *m* phototransistor
pH-Wert *m* pH-value
physikalische Größe *f* quantity
physikalische Schicht *f* physical layer
physikalisch-metallurgisch physical-metallurgical
physikalisch-technisch physical-technical
physisch physical
Pick *m* pick
Pickel *m* pit
Picket-Fence-Anordnung *f* picket-fence arrangement
Pickleistung *f* picking capacity
PID-Regeleinrichtung *f* proportional plus integral plus derivative action con-

trolling system
Piezoaktor *m* piezo-actuator
piezoelektrisch piezo-electric
piezo-elektrischer Kraftaufnehmer *m* piezo-electric force transducer
Piezoelektrizität *f* piezo-electricity
Piezokraftmesszelle *f* piezo-electric load cell
Piezozündung *f* piezo-ignition
Pigmentextrakt *nt* pigment extract
Pilgerdorn *m* piercer, pilger mandrel
Pilgerschrittumkehrspanne *f* step-back reversal error
Pilgerschrittwalzen *nt* pilger-mill roll
Pilzbefall *m* fungal decay
Pilzkühler *m* mushroom type condenser
pilzwidrig inimical to mould
Pinole *f* **1.** *(Frässpindelpinole, Frässpindelhülse)* quill **2.** *(Säulen-, Ständer-, Radialbohrmaschine)* spindle sleeve, tailstock sleeve
Pinolenfestklemmung *f* sleeve-lock
Pinolenführung *f* centre sleeve guide, quill guide
Pinolenhub *m* stroke of quill
Pinolenverstellung *f* quill adjustment
Pipelineschieber *m* pipeline gate valve
Pipette *f* **mit Einwegspitze** pipette with disposable tip
Pipettenviskometer *nt* pipette viscosimeter
PI-Regeleinrichtung *f* proportional plus integral action controlling system
Pixel *nt* pixel, picture element
pixelweise pixel by pixel
plan flat, plane
Plan *m* blueprint, concept, layout, diagram
Plananlage *f* plain-parallel bearing
Plananschlag *m* cross stop
Planarbeit *f* facing, facing operation, transverse operation, transversal operation, surfacing (work)
planarbeiten face, surface
planbearbeiten face, surface
Planbearbeitung *f* facing, surfacing
Planbewegung *f* cross-feed motion, cross slide motion
Planbrennzeit *f* burning down time

Plandreharbeit *f* facing work, facing
Plandreharbeiten *fpl* facing operations
plandrehen face, surface, face-turn
Plandrehmaschine *f* facing machine, surfacing machine, facing (or surfacing) lathe
Plandrehmeißel *m* facing tool
Plandrehmeißelhalter *m* facing toolholder
Plandrehspan *m* facing chip
planen 1. *(flach)* face, surface, plan **2.** *(Konstruktion)* design **3.** *(zeitlich)* schedule, project
Planer *m* **1.** *(allg.)* planner **2.** *(Fertigungsplaner)* production engineer **3.** *(Systemanalytiker)* systems analyst
Planetärbewegung *f* planetary motion
Planetenbewegung *f* planetary movement
Planetengetriebe *nt* planetary gear transmission, epicyclic transmission, planetary gearing, sun (-and-planet) gear
Planetengetriebezug *m* planetary gear train, epicycloidal gear train
Planetenkurzgewindefräsmaschine *f* planetary plunge-cut thread milling machine
Planetenrad *nt* planet wheel
Planetenradträger *m* planet carrier
Planetenradwelle *f* pinion shaft
Planetenschleifmaschine *f* planetary grinder
Planetenspindel *f* planetary spindle
Planetenspindelfräsmaschine *f* planetary milling machine, planetary-type miller, planetary miller
Planetenspindelgewindefräsmaschine *f* planetary-type thread milling machine
Planetenträger *m* planet carrier, pinion cage, planet gear carrier
Planetenträger *m* *(Sonnenrad)* sun wheel
Planetenwalzen *nt* planetary rolling
Planfeindrehen *nt* facing precision (or finishing) turning
Planfläche *f* face
Planflachschleifmaschine *f* face grinder

Planfräsarbeit *f* 1. *(allg.)* face milling operation (or work), surface milling operation (or work), plain milling 2. *(Umrissfräsarbeit)* contour milling, contouring work, profiling operation
planfräsen slab-mill, plain-mill
Planfräsen *nt* **mit breitem Schnitt** slab milling
Planfräser *m* face milling cutter, face mill
Planfräsmaschine *f* fixed-bed miller, fixed-bed milling machine, solid bed type milling machine, bed-type milling machine, kneeless type milling machine, *(US)* fixed-bed type miller, manufacturing-type miller (or milling machine), *(UK)* bench milling machine
Planfräsmaschine *f* **mit drei Frässpindelköpfen** triplex fixed-bed miller, triplex-type milling machine, triplex miller, three-spindle manufacturing-type milling machine, fixed-bed (or manufacturing-bed) type milling machine with three spindle heads, *(UK)* three-spindle bench type milling machine
Planfräsmaschine *f* **mit Hebe- und Senkeinrichtung für die Spindel** rise and fall miller
Planfräsmaschine *f* **mit verstellbarem Spindelkopf** adjustable head horizontal milling machine
Plangenauigkeit *f* accuracy of flatness
plangeschliffene Klebefläche *f* surface-ground adherent
Planfräskopf *m* face milling head
Planglasplatte *f* flat glass plate
Plankopierböckchen *nt* transverse copying bracket
plankopieren copy-face, contour-face
Plankurve *f* face cam
Planläppen *nt* face lapping
Planlauf *m* 1. *(allg.)* axial running 2. *(bei Zahnrädern)* wobble
Planlaufabweichung *f* axial eccentricity
Planlauffehler *m* axial running error
Planlauftoleranz *f* *(e. Lehrzahnrades)* wobble tolerance, permissible wobble
Plannachformen *nt* face profiling, face copying

planparallel plane-parallel, coplanar
Planparallelläppen *nt* parallel face lapping
Planquadrat *nt* grid square
Planrad *nt* crown gear, crown wheel, plane gear
Planradteilebene *f* crown gear reference plane
Planradteilkreis *m* crown gear reference circle
Planradteilung *f* crown gear pitch
Planradteilungswinkel *m* crown gear angular pitch
Planradverzahnung *f* plane tooth system, rack tooth system, crown gear system
Planradzahn *m* crown gear teeth
Planradzähnezahl *f* number of crown gear teeth
Planrevolverdrehmaschine *f* cross-sliding turret lathe, fixed-centre turret lathe, turret lathe for facing operations
Planringdrehen *nt* flat-ring turning
Planscheibe *f* 1. *(allg.)* face plate, independent four-jaw chuck 2. *(Karussell)* table
Planscheibengrube *f* faceplate pit
Planschieber *m* facing slide, cross slide
Planschlag *m* axial slip
Planschleifeinrichtung *f* face grinding attachment
planschleifen face-grind, surface-grind
Planschleifmaschine *f* face-grinder, face grinding machine
planschlichten finish-face
Planschlitten *m* cross slide rest, bottom slide
plansenken spotface
Plansenker *m* spotfacer, spotfacing tool
Planspindel *f* cross-feed screw
Plansupport *m* cross-slide
Plantafel *f* plan chart
Planung *f* planning
Planungsablauf *m* planning course
Planungsabschluss *m* conclusion of planning
Planungsabschlussbericht *m* concluding planning report
Planungsaufgabe *f* planning task

Planungsdaten *pl* planning data
Planungsgrundlage *f* planning basis, planning foundation
Planungshilfsmittel *f* planning aid
Planungshorizont *m* planning horizon
Planungsmethode *f* planning method
Planungsmodell *nt* planning model
Planungsphase *f* planning phase, planning stage
Planungsregel *f* planning rule
Planungsstadium *nt* planning stage
Planungsstand *m* planning condition
Planungsteam *nt* planning team
Planungstermin *m* planning deadline
Planungsvorbereitung *f* planning preparation
Planungsvorhaben *nt* planning project
Planungszeichnung *f* planning drawing
Planverzahnung *f* plane tooth system, rack tooth system
Planvorschub *m* cross feed motion
Planwertmethode *f* planned value method
Planwiederbeschaffungszeit *f* planned replacement time
Planzahl *f* target figure
Planzeit *f* planned time
Planzug *m* transverse traverse, cross travel, cross feed
Planzugang *m* projected arrival
Plasmaauftragsschweißen *nt* plasma deposition welding
Plasmabearbeitung *f* plasma machining
Plasmabeschichtung *f* plasma deposition
Plasmabrenner *m* plasma torch
Plasmadüse *f* plasma nozzle
Plasmagasdüse *f* plasma gas nozzle
Plasmakanal *m* plasma channel
Plasmalaser *m* plasma laser
Plasmalichtbogenschweißen *nt* plasma arc welding, transferred arc welding
Plasmametallschutzgasschweißen *nt* plasma-MIG-welding
Plasmaschweißen *nt* constricted arc welding
Plasmastrahlbearbeitung *f* plasma beam machining

Plasmastrahlen *nt* plasma radiating
Plasmastrahl-Plasmalichtbogenschweißen *nt* plasma jet plasma arc welding
Plasmastrahlschweißen *nt* plasma arc welding
Plastik *f* plastics
Plastikfolie *f* plastic film
plastisch erweichen soften plastically
plastisch verformbar capable of plastic shaping
plastische Formbarkeit *f* plastic mouldability
plastische Formgebung *f* plastic shaping
plastisch-elastisches Verhalten *nt* plastic-elastic behaviour
Plastizitätsmechanik *f* mechanics of plasticity
Platin *nt* platinum
Platine *f* board, circuit board, printed circuit board (PCB), plate bar, sheet bar
Platinen *fpl* circuit boards, plates
platinieren platinize, slab
Platinnetz *nt* platinum gauze
Platinwiderstandsthermometer *nt* platinum resistance thermometer
Plättchenleim *m* flake glue
Platte *f* 1. *(allg.)* plate bar, plate, sheet 2. (Stein, Beton) slab 3. *(Unterfutterung)* packing plate 4. *(gedämpft aufliegende ~)* supported damped slab 5. *(gefedert aufliegende ~)* supported spring-mounted slab
Platte *f* **aus Hohlkasten** box-section slab
Platte *f* **mit Steg** slab with web
Platten *pl* plate (or sheet) materials
Plattenabstand *m* *(beim Ringfaltversuch von Rohren)* flatting distance
Plattenführungsscheidwerkzeug *nt* plate piloting cutter
Plattenheizkörper *m* 1. *(allg.)* panel type radiator 2. *(mehrlagiger ~)* multi-level panel type radiator 3. *(mehrreihiger ~)* multi-bank panel type radiator
Plattenlagerung *f* storage of plate or sheet materials
Plattform *f* platform, stillage
Plattformhubwagen *m* platform and

stillage truck, high-lift platform truck, fixed platform truck
Plattformstapler *m* platform stacker
Plattformwagen *m* (fixed) platform truck, high-lift platform truck, stillage truck
plattieren clad
Plattierung *f* cladding, surfacing
Plattierungsauflage *f* surface of the cladding
Platz *m* spot, space, seat, position, place, location
Platz sparend spacesaving
Platzbedarf *m* space required, space requirement
Platzcodierung *f:* **variable ~** random tool access
platzen burst, crack
Platzersparnis *f* space saving
platzieren place, locate, arrange
Platzierung *f* positioning
Platzkontrolle *f* location check
Platzleuchte *f* built-in spot light
Platzmangel *m* lack of space
platzsparend room-saving, space-saving
plausibel plausible
Plausibilität *f* plausibility
Plausibilitätskontrolle *f* plausibility check, reasonableness check, validity check
Plausibilitätstest *m* plausibility check, reasonableness check, validity check
Pleuelstange *f* piston-rod, connecting rod
Plisseefalte *f* pleat
Plissiereinschlagmaschine *f* pleat wrapping machine
plissieren pleat, crimp
Plombe *f* (lead) seal
Plombenverschluss *m* lead seal
plombieren seal (off)
Plotter *m* plotter
plötzlich sudden
plötzlicher Ausfall *m* sudden failure
Plungerkolben *m* plunger
Plusabweichung *f* plus variation, positive variation
Pneumatik *f* pneumatics
Pneumatikmotor *m* pneumatic motor

Pneumatikschlauch *m* pneumatic hose
Pneumatikventil *nt* pneumatic valve
Pneumatikzylinder *m* pneumatic cylinder, compressed air cylinder
pneumatisch pneumatic
pneumatisch betätigter Schraubstock *m* air vice
pneumatische Ausrüstung *f* pneumatic equipment
pneumatische Längenmessung *f* pneumatic length measurement, air gauging
pneumatisch-elektronischer Schalter *m* pneumatic-electronic switch
Podest *mnt* landing staying
Podest *nt* platform
Pol *m* 1. *(allg.)* pole 2. *(Stecker)* pin
Polarachse *f* polar axis
Polarisation *f* polarization
Polarisationsinterferenzfilter *m* polarization interference filter
Polarisationsstrom *m* total current
Polarisationswiderstand *m* polarization resistance
polarisierbar polarizable
Polarisierbarkeit *f* polarizability
polarisieren polarize
polarisiert polarized
Polarität *f* polarity
Polaritätsindikator *m* polarity indicator
Polaritätsumkehr *f* reversal of polarity, polarity reversal
Polarkoordinate *f* polar coordinate
Polarkoordinaten *fpl* polar coordinates
polarographisches Verfahren *nt* polarographic method
Polder *m* polder, stop
Polierbarkeit *f* polishability
polierdrücken burnish
polieren polish, burnish
polierläppen buff
Poliermaschine *f* polishing machine
Poliermittel *nt* polishing agents
Polierriefen *fpl* scoring due to polishing
Polierrollen *nt* burnishing
Poliertonerde *f* polishing alumina
Poliertrommeln *nt* barrel finishing

Polklemme *f* pole terminal
Polpaarzahl *f* number of pairs of poles
Polschichtdicke *f* effective pile thickness
Polster *nt* pad
polstern pad
Polumkehrung *f* polarity reversal, reversal of poles
polumschaltbar pole changing, pole changeable, change-pole, with reversal of poles
Polyacetaldehydkleber *m* polyacetaldehyde adhesive
Polyacrylethylenoxidkleber *m* polyacrylethylene oxide adhesive
Polyaddition *f* polyaddition, addition polymerization
Polycarbonatspritzgussmasse *f* polycarbonate injection moulding material
Polychlorbutadiankleber *m* polychlorbutadiene adhesive
Polyesterfaser *f* polyester fibre
Polyesterharz *nt* polyester resin
Polyesterharzkleber *m* polyester resin adhesive
Polyesterharzmatte *f* prepregs impregnated with polyester resin, polyester resin mat
Polyesterharzpressmasse *f* polyester resin compression moulding material
Polyesterreaktionsharz *nt* polyester reaction resin
Polyesterzwirn *m* polyester thread
Polyethylenumhüllung *f* polyethylene sheathing
Polyethylen weich low-density polyethylene
Polyethylenformmasse *f* polyethylene moulding material
Polyethylenumhüllung *f* polyethylene sheathing
Polygon *nt* polygon
Polygonkantenbildung *f* polygon edge formation
Polygonlänge *f* polygon length
Polygonrad *nt* polygonal wheel
Polygonspiegel *m* polygonal mirror
Polygonspiegelrad *nt* polygonal mirror wheel
Polygonzug *m* polygon line

Polyimid *nt* polyimide
Polyisobuthylenbahn *f* polyisobutylene sheet
Polyisopren *nt* polyisoprene
Polykondensation *f* polycondensation
Polymer *nt* polymer
Polymerisation *f* polymerization
polymerisierbares Gemisch *nt* polymerizable mixture
Polymerweichmacher *m* polymer plasticizer
Polymethanschaumstoff *m* polymethane cellular plastics
Polymethylmethacrylatspritzgussmasse *f* polymethyl-methacrylate injection moulding material (or compound)
Polystyrolflocken *fpl* polystyrene flakes
Polystyrolformmasse *f* polystyrene moulding material
Polystyrolschaumstoff *m* polystyrene cellular plastics
Polystyrolspritzgussmasse *f* polystyrene injection moulding material (or compound)
Polytropenexponent *m* polytropic exponent
Polyurethanbasis *f* polyurethane basis
Polyurethanelastomer *nt* polyurethane elastomer
Polyurethankleber *m* polyurethane solution adhesive
Polyvinylacetatkleber *m* polyvinyl acetate adhesive
Polyvinylalkoholleim *m* polyvinyl alcohol glue
Polyvinylätherkleber *m* polyvinyl ether adhesive
Polyvinylchlorid *nt* **hart** rigid polyvinyl chloride, rigid PVC
Polyvinylchlorid *nt* **weich** flexible polyvinyl chloride
Polyvinylmethyläther *m* polyvinyl methyl ether
Polzahl *f* number of poles
Poolpalette *f* pool pallet, interchangeable European pallet
Pore *f* void, pin hole, pore
porenfrei umhüllte Elektrode *f* pore-free enclosed electrode
porenhaltige Umhüllung *f* (e. Elek-

trode) porous envelope
Porenkette *f* linear porosity
Porenneigung *f* tendency to porosity
Porennest *nt* clustered porosity
Porenprüfung *f* porosity test
Porenweite *f* pore aperture
Porigkeit *f (e. Scheibe)* porosity
porös porous
Porosität *f* porosity, porousness
Porositäten *fpl* porosities
Portal *nt* 1. *(allg.)* portal, gantry 2. *(Fräsmaschine, Hobelmaschine)* bridge
Portalautomat *m* portal automatic
Portalfräsmaschine *f* planer-type milling machine, plano-miller, plano-milling machine, double column planer miller
Portalgerät *nt* portal device
Portalhubwagen *m* stacking straddle carrier, high-lift straddle carrier
Portalkran *m* gantry crane
Portallager *nt* portal warehouse
Portalroboter *m* gantry robot, portal-type robot
Portalständer *m* upright
Portalstapler *m* stacking high-lift straddle carrier
Portalwagen *m* non-stacking low-lift straddle carrier, non-stacking straddle carrier, low-lift straddle carrier
portionsweise in batches
Porzellan *nt* porcelain
Porzellanheizkörper *m* porcelain heater
Position *f* 1. *(Platz)* position 2. *(Listen)* item
Positionieranzeige *f* positioning display
Positioniereinrichtung *f* positioning device, positioning unit
positionieren position, locate
Positioniergenauigkeit *f* positioning accuracy
Positioniergeschwindigkeit *f* positioning speed
Positionierhilfe *f* positioning accessory, positioning aid
Positioniermarke *f* positioning mark, positioning marker
Positioniersensor *m* positioning sensor
Positioniersteuerung *f* positioning control
Positioniersystem *nt* positioning system
Positioniertoleranz *f* positioning tolerance
Positionierung *f* positioning
Positionierungshilfe *f* positioning accessory, positioning aid
Positionierverfahren *nt* positioning system, positioning process
Positioniervorgang *m* positioning process, positioning procedure
positionsabhängig position dependent
Positionsanzeige *f* position display
Positionsdetektor *m* detector of position
Positionsgenauigkeit *f* positional accuracy
Positionskoordinaten *fpl* positional coordinates
Positionsmarke *f* positioning mark, positioning marker
Positionsregelung *f* positioning automatic control
Positionsregler *m* positioning control system, positioning controller
Positionsschalter *m* detector of position, position switch
Positionsstreubreite *f* positioning scatterband
Positionstoleranz *f* positional tolerance
Positionstoleranz *f* **einer ebenen Fläche** positional tolerance of a flat surface
Positionsüberwachung *f* position monitoring, position sensing, positioning control system
Positionsüberwachungseinrichtung *f* positional sensor
positionsunabhängig position independent, independent of position
Positivverfahren *nt* positive method
Posten *m* lot
Postprozessor (PP) *m* postprocessor
Potentialausgleich *m* equipotential bonding, potential equalization
Potentialausgleichsanlage *f* equipotential bonding system

Potentialausgleichsschiene *f* equipotential bonding bus bar
Potentialfaktor *m* equipotential factor
potentialgebunden non-isolated
potentialgetrennt galvanically isolated
Potentialmessung *f* potential measurement
Potentialtrennung *f* potential separation
potentialunabhängig independent of the potential
Potentialveredlung *f* upgrading of the potential
potentielle Energie *f* stored energy
Potentiometer *nt* potentiometer
Potenz *f* power
Potenzial *nt* potential
potenziell potential
Pottingechtheit *f* fastness to potting
PQ (Produktquantitäts-) – Bewertung *f* product quantity (PQ) evaluation
Prägecodierer *m* emboss coder
prägen emboss
Prägen *nt* **mit Gummikissen** embossing with rubber pad
Prägerichten *nt* straightening in patterned dies
prägewalzen roller-stamp
Prägung *f* embossing
praktisch useful, handy, practical
praktische Lehrlingsprüfung *f* skill test
praktizieren practice
Prallblech *nt* baffle, baffle plate
prallen gegen knock against, bounce against, hit
Prallkern *m* baffle core
Prallwand *f* impact surface, bumper
Prämie *f* **für einen Verbesserungsvorschlag** suggestion award
Pratze *f* claw, strap
Prävention *f* prevention
präventiv preventive
Praxis *f* practice, experience
praxisnah real life, close to real life business
präzise accurate, exact, precise
Präzision *f* precision
Präzisionsarbeit *f* precision job, precision work
Präzisionsbearbeitung *f* precision machining (or finishing)
Präzisionsfräsmaschine *f* tool-room milling machine
Präzisionsgegeninduktivität *f* precision mutual inductance
Präzisionsmaßstab *m* precision scale
Präzisionsmessuhr *f* precision dial indicator
Präzisionsrefraktometer *nt* precision refractometer
Präzisionsrundschleifmaschine *f* cylindrical precision grinder
Präzisionsschallpegelmesser *m* precision sound level meter
Präzisionsschieblehre *f* vernier calliper
Präzisionsschleifen *nt* profile grinding
Präzisionsschleifverfahren *nt* precision grinding method
Präzisionsschnelldrehmaschine *f* high-speed precision lathe
Präzisionswasserwaage *f* precision spirit level
P-Regeleinrichtung *f* proportional action controlling system
Preis *m* 1. *(allg.)* price 2. *(kalkulierter ~)* calculated price
Preisauszeichnung *f* price labelling
Preisfluktuation *f* price fluctuation
Preisgestaltung *f* pricing
Preisgliederung *f* price structure
Preisliste *f* price list, sales catalogue
Prellbock *m* fixed end stop
Prellstoß *m* rebound impact
Pressauftragsschweißen *nt* pressure build-up welding
pressblank smooth as from moulding
Pressdruck *m* pressing power
Presse *f* 1. *(allg.)* press 2. *(hydraulische ~)* hydraulic press
pressen 1. *(allg.)* press, compress 2. *(formpressen)* compression mould, mould 3. *(Formmasse aus einer Druckkammer)* force out 4. *(Pressholz)* compress
Pressen *nt:* **isostatisches ~** isostatic compressing
Pressenbau *m* press building, press

manufacture
Pressform *f* die block, compression mould
pressformen compact
Pressfuge *f* press joint, interference interface
Pressfutter *nt* air chuck
Pressklemme *f* ferrule
Pressling *m* compact, pressed blank, pressing
Presslochverschraubung *f* pressed hole screw (or bolt fastening)
Pressluft *f* compressed air
Pressluftanlage *f* pneumatic equipment
Pressluftfutter *nt* air-operated chuck
Pressmasse *f* extrusion mixture
Pressmatrize *f* extrusion die
Presspassung *f* interference fit, force fit
Pressrahmen *m* moulding frame
Pressrolle *f* crusher roll, crusher wheel
Pressschweißverbindung *f* pressure-welded assembly
Presssitz *m* interference fit
Pressspantafel *f* pressboard panel
Pressstoff *m* compression moulded material, moulded material
Pressstoff *m* **aus warm härtbarer Formmasse** moulded thermosetting material
Pressstumpfschweißen *nt* **1.** *(allg.)* resistance butt welding **2.** *(von Kunststoffen)* butt press welding
presstechnische Gründe *mpl* pressing-related technical reasons
Pressteil *nt* moulding
Pressung *f* compression mould, press fit
Pressverband *m* interference fit assembly
Pressverband *m* **durch Einpressen** interference fit assembly by force fitting
Pressverband *m* **durch Schrumpfen** interference fit assembly by shrinkage
Pressverbindungsschweißen *nt* pressure joint welding
Presswerkzeugaufsatz *m* compression mould attachment
Presswerkzeugblock *m* compression mould block
Presszeit *f* compression time

primär primary
Primärbedarf *m* primary demand
Primärbefehl *m* primary command
Primärleerlaufspannung *f* primary no-load voltage
Primärleerlaufstrom *nt* primary no-load current
Primärschlüssel *m* primary key
Primarstatus *m* primary status
Primärstrahlenkegel *m* primary cone of the beam
Primärverschlemmung *f* primary sitting up
Prinzip *nt* principle
Prinzip *nt* **des sicheren Fehlverhaltens** fail-safe principle
Priorität *f* priority
Priorität erhöhen give a higher priority, assign a higher priority
Priorität geben give priority
Prioritäten setzen prioritize
Prioritätenfolge *f* order of priority
Prioritätensetzung *f* prioritization
Prioritätsstufe *f* priority
Prisma *nt* prism, solid vee
prismatisch geführte Gleitbahn *f* Vee-guide
prismatische Führung *f* prismatic bearing surface, V-way, prismatic guide ways
Prismenfräser *m* equal angle cutter, symmetrical angle cutter
Prismenführung *f* inverted Vee-guide, prismatic slideway, prismatic bearing surface, vees
Prismenführungsbahn *f* prismatic guideways, Vee-guide
Prismenmeißel *m* angle tool
Prismenstück *nt* vee block
pro per
Probe *f* **1.** *(Probekörper)* test piece, test specimen **2.** *(bei Flüssigkeiten, Gasen)* test sample **3.** *(bei Werkstoffen)* test portion **4.** *(praktischer Versuch)* trial **5.** *(Prüfkörper)* specimen **6.** *(Warenprobe)* sample
Probe *f:* **eine ~ nehmen** take a sample
Probeaufbereitung *f* sample preparation
Probebehälter *m* sampling container

Probebetrieb *m* test run, trial run, trial operation
Probebogen *m* sample sheet
Probegefäß *nt* test tube
Probekörper *m* test specimen, test piece
Probekörpergeometrie *f* specimen geometry
Probekörperhalter *m* specimen holder
Probelauf *m* trial run, running test, test run
Probenahme *f* sampling
Probenahme *f* **in festen Abständen** sampling at fixed time intervals
Probenahmegerät *nt* sampling device (or apparatus)
Probenahmeort *m* sampling site
Probenahmepumpe *f* sampling pump
Probenahmestelle *f* point of collection
Probenahmezeitpunkt *m* point in time sampling
Probenbeanspruchung *f* loading of the test specimens
Probenbehandlung *f* treatment of samples, conditioning of samples
Probenbruch *m* failure (or fracture) of the specimen
Probenehmer *m* sampler
Probeneinspannung *f* specimen clamping arrangement
Probenfluss *m* specimen flux
Probenform *f* shape for test specimens
Probenhalter *m* grip, specimen holder
Probenhaltevorrichtung *f* sample holding device
Probenkorb *m* notch in the specimen
Probenlage *f* position of specimen
Probenmasse *f* specimen mass
Probenquerschnitt *m* cross-sectional area of the test specimen
Probenquerschnitt *m:* **kleinster ~ nach dem Bruch** minimum cross-sectional area after fracture
Probenschwingung *f* sample vibration
Probenstapel *m* sample stack
Probensuspension *f* sample suspension
Probenteiler *m* sample splitter
Probenträger *m* sample carrier
Probenvorbehandlung *f* sample conditioning, preliminary treatment of test specimens
Probenvorbereitung *f* sample preparation
Probenvorratsgefäß *nt* sample storage container (or vessel)
Probenzustand *m* condition of test specimen
Probeschnitt *m* sample cut
Probestreifen *m* test strip
Probestück *nt* specimen, test specimen, sample, test piece
Probeteil *nt* subspecimen
Probeteilchen *nt* test particle
Probeteilung *f* partitioning of the sample
Probeteilungsverfahren *nt* sample splitting method
Probezeit *f* trial period
probieren try, sample, test
Probierverfahren *nt* trial and error method
Produkt *nt* product
Produktabrechnung *f* product cost accounting
Produktauslauf *m* product exit
Produktbeschreibung *f* product description
Produktbezeichnung *f* product designation
produktbezogen product-related
Produktdaten *pl* product data
Produktdatenmodell *nt* product data model
Produkteinlauf *m* product entry
Produktentwicklung *f* product development
Produktfluss *m* product flow
Produktgestaltung *f* product arrangement
Produkthaftung *f* product liability
Produktion *f* production, output, yield, manufacture
Produktionsausfall *m* production failure
Produktionsausstoß *m* production ejection
Produktionsbedarfsplanung *f* production demand planning
Produktionsbeginn *m* production start

Produktionsdaten *pl* production data
Produktionsdrehmaschine *f* production lathe
Produktionsfläche *f* production area
Produktionsfluss *m* production flow
Produktionskoordinatenbohrmaschine *f* jigless production machine
Produktionslogistik *f* production logistics
produktionslogistisch production logistics...
Produktionsmittel *nt* means of production
Produktionsmittelgestaltung *f* arrangement of means of production
Produktionsplanung *f* production planning
Produktionsplanungs- und Lenkungssystem *nt* production planning system
Produktionsplanungsübersicht *f* survey of the production plan
Produktionsprogramm *nt* production program
Produktionsprogrammplanung *f* production program planning
Produktionsschnelldrehbank *f* high-speed production lathe
Produktionsstätte *f* production facility
produktionssteigernd output-raising
Produktionssteigerung *f* production increase, output raising
Produktionssteuerung *f* production control
produktionssynchron just in time
produktionssynchrone Anlieferung *f* just in time (delivery) (JIT)
Produktivität *f* productivity
Produktivitätsreserve *f* productivity reserve
Produktivitätszielstellung *f* productivity goals
Produktkosten *pl* product costs
Produktlebensdauer *f* product life
Produktlebenszyklus *m* product life cycle
Produktmanagement *nt* product data management (PDM)
Produktmittelgruppe *f* product facility group
produktneutral product-neutral
Produktoperator *m* product operator
Produktpalette *f* product range
Produktplan *m* product plan
Produktplanung *f* product planning
Produktspektrum *nt* product range
Produktstapel *m* product stack
Produktstrukturierung *f* product structuring
Produktvergleich *m* product comparison
produzieren produce, manufacture
Profil *nt* 1. *(Formstahl)* section
 2. *(Umriss)* contour, outline, profile
Profil *nt* **der Freifläche** profile of the flank
Profil *nt* **der Spanfläche** profile of the face
Profil- und Fräserschleifmaschine *f* form and cutter machine
Profilabrichten *nt* form truing, wheel forming
Profilabtastung *f* profile tracing
Profilabweichung *f* profile variation
Profilaufzeichnung *f* profile recording
profilbezogen profile related
Profilbezugsebene *f* datum plane
Profilbezugslinie *f* profile datum line, profile reference line, datum line
Profilfehler *m* profile error
Profilflächenschleifmaschine *f* profile surface grinding machine
Profilformabweichung *f* *(e. Zahnflanke)* profile form variation
Profilfräsen *nt* profile (or form) milling, profiling
Profilfräser *m* profile milling cutter, form cutter, profile cutter
Profilfräsmaschine *f* profile milling machine
Profilgesamtabweichung *f* total profile variation
profilgeschliffener Formfräser *m* form profile cutter
Profilglattwalzen *nt* **von Hohlkörpern** smooth rolling of tubular shapes
Profilhaltigkeit *f* profile constant
profilhinterschliffener Formfräser *m* shaped profile cutter
profilhinterschliffener Fräser *m* pro-

file-relieved cutter, profile ground cutter
Profilhöhe *f* depth of fundamental triangle
profilieren profile, mould, shape, contour
profiliert moulded, ribbed
profilierte Matte *f* ribbed mat
profilierter Heizkörper *m* fluted radiator
Profilierung *f* 1. *(allg.)* fluting 2. *(feine ~)* close-pitch fluting 3. *(grobe ~)* wide-pitch fluting
Profilkontrolle *f* profile checking, profile gauge
Profilkorrekturen *f* profile corrections
Profillage *f* profile position
Profillängswalzen *nt* longitudinal rolling of shapes
Profilläppen *nt* profile lapping
Profillinienverlauf *m* *(bei Zahnflanken)* profile configuration
Profilmeißel *m* profile cutting tool
Profilmitte *f* profile centre-line
Profilmittellinie *f* profile datum line, profile reference line, datum line
Profilmodifikation *f* profile modification
Profilnormale *f* **im Berührpunkt** transverse line of action
Profilprüfbereich *m* profile test range
Profilprüfung *f* profile test
Profilquerwalzen *nt* cross rolling of shapes
Profilrautiefe *f* peak-to-valley height
Profilräumen *nt* profile broaching
Profilrolle *f* crusher roll
Profilrollenspindel *f* crusher roll spindle
Profilrücknahme *f* *(bei Verzahnungen)* profile relief
Profilscheibe *f* thread and form-grinding wheel, formed wheel
Profilschleifen *nt* contour grinding, form grinding
Profilschleifscheibe *f* thread and form grinding wheel
Profilschnitt *m* profile section
Profilschrägwalzen *nt* skew rolling of shapes
Profilschrägwalzen *nt* **von Hohlkörpern** skew rolling of tubular shapes
Profilschrägwalzen *nt* **von Vollkörpern** slew rolling of solid sections
Profiltoleranz *f* profile tolerance
Profilüberdeckung *f* transverse contact ratio
Profilüberdeckungswälzkreisbogen *m* transverse arc of transmission
Profilüberdeckungswinkel *m* ratio of the angle of contact, transverse angle of transmission
Profilverlauf *m* profile pattern
Profilverschiebung *f* **Null** zero addendum modification
Profilverschiebungsfaktor *m* addendum modification factor, profile displacement factor, addendum modification coefficient
Profilverschiebungsrichtlinien *fpl* addendum modification guidelines (pl)
Profilverschiebungssumme *f* *(bei V-Rädern)* sum of the addendum modification
profilverschobene Verzahnung *f* profile displaced tooth system
profilverschobenes Innenradpaar *nt* addendum-modified internal gear pair
Profilverzerrung *f* profile distortion
Profilwalzen *nt* profile rolling
Profilwelligkeit *f* profile waviness
Profilwinkel *m* profile angle
Profilwinkel *m* **im Normalschnitt** normal profile angle at a point
Profilwinkelabweichung *f* profile angle variation
Prognose *f* forecast
Prognosegenauigkeit *f* forecast accuracy
Prognoseverfahren *nt* forecast method
prognostizieren forecast
Programm *nt* program, programme
Programmablauf *m* program flow
Programmablaufplan *m* programming flowchart
Programmanfang *m* start of program
Programmaufbau *m* program structure
Programmausgabe *f* program output
Programmbibliothek *f* programme li-

brary
Programmdokumentation *f* software documentation
Programmeingabe *f* program input
Programmende *nt* end of program (EOP)
Programmerstellung *f* program production
Programmformat *nt* program format
Programmfräsen *nt* program milling
programmgesteuert program-controlled
programmgesteuerte Maschine *f* program-controlled machine
programmgesteuerte Revolverbohrmaschine *f* program-controlled turret-type drilling machine
Programmhorizont *m* program horizon
Programmier- und Diagnosewerkzeug *nt* programming and debugging tool (PADT)
Programmieraufgabe *f* programming task
programmierbar programmable
programmierbare Rechenmaschine *f* calculator with programmability
programmierbarer Nur-Lese-Speicher *m* programmable read only memory
Programmierbetrieb *m* programming operation
programmieren program, programme
Programmierfehler *m* programming error
Programmiergerät (PG) *nt* programming and debugging tool (PADT)
Programmierhilfsmittel *nt* programming device
Programmierkosten *pl* programming costs
Programmiersprache *f* programming language
Programmiersystem *nt* programming system
Programmierung *f* **1.** *(allg.)* programming **2.** *(manuelle ~)* manual programming **3.** *(Teach-In ~)* teach-in-programming **4.** *(werkstattorientierte~)* workshop-orientate programming
Programmierungscode *m* code of programming
Programmlaufzeit *f* program duration
Programmmakro *nt* program macro
Programmplanung *f* program planning
Programmprüfung *f* program-checking
Programmrhythmus *m* program rhythm
Programmsteuergerät *nt* programmed control device
Programmsteuerung *f* *(US)* program control, *(UK)* programming, automatic cycle (or sequence) control
Programmsteuerung *f* **mit Lochkarte** punched card programming
Programmunterbrechung *f* program interrupt
Programmverifikation *f* program verification
Programmwalze *f* program drum
Progressivanlage *f* progressive plunger system
Progressivsystem *nt* progressive plunger principle of operation
Progressivverteiler *m* progressive plunger metering device
Projektionsschirm *m* projection screen
Projekt *nt* **1.** *(allg.)* project **2.** *(e. ~ ablehnen)* turn down a project **3.** *(e. ~ durchführen)* implement a project **4.** *(e. ~ fallen lassen)* abandon a project **5.** *(~ macht Fortschritte)* project is taking shape **6.** *(e. ~ zurückstellen)* shelve a project
Projektablauf *m* course of a project
Projektabwicklung *f* project implementation, project execution
Projektbeschreibung *f* project description
Projektbeteiligter *m* stakeholder, party involved in a project
projektbezogen project-related
Projektfortschritt *m* project progress
Projektfortschrittsbericht *m* project progress report
Projektgruppe *f* project team, task force

Projekthistorie *f* project history
projektieren plan, project, design
Projektierung *f* project planning, planning phase, planning, projecting
Projektion *f* projection
Projektionsablesung *f* optical system with projection screen, projection reading
Projektionsfläche *f* projection surface
projektionsgerechte Lage *f* in the right projected position
Projektionslinse *f* projection lens
Projektionsmethode *f* projection method
Projektionsoptik *f* optical projection system
Projektkooperation *f* contractual joint venture
Projektlagebericht *m* project status report
Projektleiter *m* project manager
Projektleitung *f* project management
Projektplanung *f* project scheduling
Projektreife *f* preimplementation stage
Projektstart *m* launch
Projektstudie *f* feasibility study, preinvestment study
projektübergreifend cross-project
Projektüberwachung *f* project monitoring, project control
Projektzeichnung *f* project drawing
projizieren project
Propan *nt* propane
Propangasflasche *f* propane gas cylinder
Propanlötgerät *nt* propane-heated soldering appliance
Propanverbrauch *m* propane consumption
Proportionalbeiwert *m* proportional action factor
Proportionalglied *nt* proportional element
Proportionalprobe *f* proportional test piece
Protokoll *nt* 1. *(allg.)* journal, log, protocol, record, report 2. *(Sitzungen)* minutes
Protokolldrucker *m* logging printer
protokollieren record

Protokollierung *f* recording (of logs)
Protokollierung *f* **von Hand** manual recording
Prototyp *m* prototype
Prototypenfertigung *f* prototype manufacturing, prototype production
Prototypenmaterial *nt* prototype material
Prototypenphase *f* prototype phase
Prototypentwicklungssystem *nt* prototype development system
Prototypwerkzeug *nt* prototype die mould
Protuberanz *f (am Werkzeugzahnkopf)* protuberance
Prozent *nt* per cent
Prozentanteil *m* percentage
Prozentsatz *m* percentage
prozentual percentage, as a percentage, in per cent
Prozess *m* operation, process
Prozessabbild *nt* process image
prozessabhängig process-bound
Prozessalarm *m* process interrupt
Prozessautomatisierung *f* process automation
prozessbedingt process-related
Prozessdaten *pl* process variables, process data
Prozessdauer *f* process-duration
Prozessebene *f* process level
Prozesseigner *m* process owner
Prozessenergiequelle *f* process energy source
Prozessfeldbus *m* process field bus (PROFIBUS)
Prozessfolge *f* process succession
Prozessfolgermittlung *f* process succession assessment
Prozessführung *f* process control
Prozessführungsplatz *m* process control workstation
prozessgekoppelt process-bound
prozessgekoppelt geschlossen closed loop
Prozessgestaltung *f* process arrangement
Prozessgröße *f* process variable
Prozessidentifikation *f* process identification

Prozesskette *f* process chain
Prozesskommunikation *f* process communication
Prozesskontrollsystem *nt* process control system
Prozesskostenrechnung *f* process cost accounting
Prozessleitsystem *nt* process control system
Prozesslenkung *f* process (quality) control
Prozessmeldung *f* process message
Prozessmodell *nt* process model
Prozessoptimierung *f* process optimization
Prozessoptimierung *f:* **gesteuerte ~** feedforward process optimization
Prozessor *m* processor
prozessorientiert process-oriented
Prozessorientierung *f* process orientation
Prozessplan *m* process plan
Prozessplanerstellung *f* process plan production
Prozessplanung *f* process planning
Prozessrechner *m* process computer
prozesssicher process reliable
Prozesssicherheit *f* process reliability, process stability
Prozessstabilisierung *f* process stabilization
Prozessstabilisierung *f (unter Hauptsteuerungsprogrammen)* supervisor state
Prozesssteuerung *f* process control
Prozesssteuerungsebene *f* process control level
Prozessstufe *f* process stage
Prozessvariable *f* process variable
Prozessvariante *f* process variant
Prozessverkettung *f* process chain(ing), process chain-linking, process catenation
Prüfabmaß *nt* test dimension deviation
Prüfamt *nt* examining authorities
Prüfanlage *f* testing installation
Prüfanordnung *f* test arrangement, test setup
Prüfanweisung *f* test instruction
Prüfauftrag *m* test order

Prüfauftragsbearbeitung *f* test order processing
Prüfaufwand *m* expenditure on inspection equipment
Prüfausführung *f* inspection execution
Prüfbahn *f* test path
Prüfbarer Code *m* error detecting code
Prüfbefund *m* inspection report, test result
Prüfbeleg *m* inspection documents
Prüfbeleg *m* **erstellen** compile inspection documents
Prüfbericht *m* test report
Prüfbescheinigung *f* verification certificate, testing certificate
Prüfbild *nt* test pattern, test diagram
Prüfbildblatt *nt* test diagram chart
Prüfbildkurve *f* test diagram curve
Prüfbildlinie *f* test trace
Prüfblatt *nt* test report, inspection report, test sheet, specimen sheet, test chart
Prüfblock *m* test block
Prüfbuch *nt* logbook
Prüfbund *m (e. Lehrzahnrades)* test flange
Prüfbyte *nt* test byte
Prüfdaten *pl* test data
Prüfdatenauswertung *f* test analysis
Prüfdatenerfassung *f* test data recording
Prüfdorn *m* reference plug gauge
Prüfdrehmoment *m* proof-test torque
Prüfdruck *m* test pressure
Prüfeinrichtung *f* testing equipment (or outfit), inspection facility
Prüfeinspannvorrichtung *f* specimen clamping device
Prüfempfindlichkeit *f* test sensitivity
prüfen 1. *(chem.)* determine **2.** *(Fertigteile)* inspect **3.** *(metallographisch)* examine **4.** *(mit Lehre)* gauge **5.** *(nachprüfen)* inspect, control, check, verify **6.** *(praktisch)* try, test **7.** *(untersuchen)* investigate **8.** *(e. Messeinrichtung)* calibrate
Prüfendmaß *nt* reference gauge block
Prüfer *m* **1.** *(allg. Person)* tester, inspector **2.** *(Datenverarbeitung)* verifier **3.** *(Qualitätskontrolle)* inspector

4. *(Zeichnung)* checker
Prüfergebnis *nt* test result, test outcome
Prüferzeugnis *nt* test certificate
Prüffehler *m* test error
Prüffeld *nt* test bay
Prüffett *nt* test grease
Prüffinger *m* test finger
Prüffläche *f* **1.** *(allg.)* test face **2.** *(e. Lehre)* gauging surface
Prüfflächennormale *f* normal to the test face
Prüfflamme *f* test flame
Prüfflüssigkeit *f* test liquid
Prüffrequenz *f* test frequency
Prüfgas *nt* test gas
Prüfgasdurchfluss *m* rate of flow of the test gas
Prüfgasflasche *f* test gas bottle
Prüfgefäß *nt* test vessel, testing cup
Prüfgegenstand *m* test object
Prüfgerät *nt* test instrument
Prüfgeräte *ntpl* testing equipment
prüfgerechte Maßeintragung *f* inspection-oriented dimensioning
prüfgerechtes Gestalten *nt* design for testability
Prüfgerüst *nt* test rig
Prüfgeschwindigkeit *f* test rate
Prüfgröße *f* test statistic, measured size
Prüfgut *nt* test material
Prüfhäufigkeit *f* frequency of testing, test frequency
Prüfheizkörper *m* test heating element
Prüfinstitut *nt* test institute
Prüfklasse *f* test category
Prüfklima *nt* conditioned atmosphere, test atmosphere
Prüfkonus *m* test cone
Prüfkopf *m* probe
Prüfkopfführung *f* method of moving the probe, movement of probe
Prüfkorngröße *f* test particle size
Prüfkörper *m* test body, test piece
Prüfkosten *pl* test costs
Prüfkraft *f* test force, test load
Prüfkraftanzeige *f* test load indication, test force indication
Prüfkraftbereich *m* test load range
Prüfkraftstoff *m* test fuel

Prüfkriterium *nt* test criterion
Prüflagergehäuse *nt* test bearing housing
Prüflaminat *nt* test laminate
Prüflast *f* test load
Prüflastversuch *m* proof load test
Prüflehre *f* master ga(u)ge, check ga(u)ge
Prüfling *m* **1.** *(allg.)* equipment under test (EUT) **2.** *(bei Zahnrädern)* test gear
Prüflos *nt* test lot, inspection lot
Prüflosgröße *f* test lot size
Prüfmaschine *f* testing machine, pl.: testing machinery
Prüfmaß *nt* test dimension
Prüfmaßstab *m* reference bar
Prüfmerkmal *nt* test characteristic
Prüfmessscheibe *f* reference plug gauge
Prüfmethode *f* test method
Prüfmittel *nt* inspection equipment, inspection resource, test equipment, test medium, testing aid
Prüfmöglichkeit *f* practicability of testing
Prüfmoment *m* test moment
Prüfmuster *nt* test sample
Prüfnadelspitze *f* point of the test needle
Prüfnorm *f* testing standard
Prüfoberfläche *f* test surface
Prüfparameter test parameter
Prüfperson *f* attestor
Prüfpersonal *nt* testing staff
prüfpflichtig subject to testing
Prüfplan *m* inspection plan
Prüfplanung *f* inspection planning
Prüfplatte *f* surface plate
Prüfplattform *f* test platform
Prüfplatz *m* test location
Prüfpolynom *nt* test polynomial
Prüfpraxis *f* testing practice
Prüfprogramm *nt* test program
Prüfprotokoll *nt* inspection record, test certificate, inspection sheet, test record
Prüfpunkt *m* test point
Prüfroutine *f* check handler, check routine
Prüfschein *m* test certificate
Prüfschmirgel *m* test emery

Prüfschmirgelbogen *m* test emery paper
Prüfserie *f* series of tests
Prüfsieböffnung *f* aperture of the test sieve
Prüfstand *m* test bay, test bench, test floor
Prüfstatus *m* inspection status
Prüfstelle *f* inspection department
Prüfstempel *m* inspector's stamp, test indenter
Prüfsteuerung *f* inspection control
Prüfstift *m* test pin
Prüfstrecke *f* test path
Prüfstück *nt* test piece, test specimen
Prüfstück *nt* **für Zugfestigkeitsprüfung** tensile test specimen
Prüfstückbeanspruchung *f* loading of the test piece
Prüftechnik *f* testing technique (or practice)
prüftechnische Gesichtspunkte *mpl* test methodology
prüftechnische Gründe *mpl* test engineering reasons
prüftechnische Mängel *mpl* technical inadequacies in the testing
Prüftinte *f* test ink
Prüfumfang *m* extent of inspection, scope of testing
Prüfung *f* 1. *(chem.)* determination 2. *(Erprobung)* service test 3. *(Kontrolle)* inspection, test, check, verification 4. *(mit Festlehren)* gauging 5. *(mit Prüflehren)* callipering 6. *(mit Revisionslehre)* verification 7. *(opt. metallogr.)* examination 8. *(praktischer Versuch)* trial 9. *(Untersuchung)* investigation
Prüfung *f* **der Struktur** structural verification
Prüfungsbescheinigung *f* test certificate
Prüfungsergebnis *nt* inspection result
Prüfunterlagen *fpl* test documents
Prüfverfahren *nt* test method
Prüfvermerk *m* check note
Prüfverteilung *f* test distribution
Prüfvorrichtung *f* testing device
Prüfvorschrift *f* test specification
Prüfwert *m* test specifications, test value
Prüfwinkel *m* test angle
Prüfzeichen *nt* test symbol
Prüfzeichnung *f* test drawing, test plan
Prüfzelle *f* test chamber
Prüfziffer *f* 1. *(allg.)* check digit 2. *(EDV)* error checking number
Prüfzone *f* test zone
Prüflaboratorium *nt* test laboratory
Pseudo-absolute Wegmessung *f* pseudo-absolute measuring
PS-Formmasse *f* polystyrene moulding material
PTFE-Band *nt* PTFE strip
Puffen *nt* popping
Puffer *m* 1. *(mechanisch)* pad, dashpot, buffer 2. *(el.)* back-up
Puffer *m* **mit eingebautem Stoßdämpfer** shock-absorber buffer
Pufferbestand *m* buffer stock
Pufferbetrieb *m* buffered mode, floating operation
Pufferdauer *f* back-up duration
Pufferendkräfte *fpl* buffer end forces
Pufferfahrt *f* buffer collision
Pufferflasche *f* buffer bottle
Pufferfunktion *f* buffer function
Puffergröße *f* buffer size
Pufferhub *m* displacement of the buffer
Pufferkennlinie *f* buffer characteristic
Pufferkräfte *fpl* buffer forces
Pufferlager *nt* buffer inventory
pufferlos bufferless
Puffermedium *nt* buffer medium
puffern 1. *(mechanisch)* buffer, cushion 2. *(el.)* back up
Pufferplatte *f* buffer plate
Pufferschicht *f* buffer layer
Pufferstoß *m* buffer impact
Pufferung *f* buffering
Pufferweg *m* buffer path
Pufferzeit *f* back-up time, buffer time, float time
Pufferzone *f* buffer zone
Pulk *m:* **einem ~ bilden aus** group, bunch, form into a bunch, cluster
Pulkbildung *f* grouping, bunching, clustering
pulkfähig groupable, suitable for group-

ing
Puls *m* pulse, impulse
Pulsamplitudenmodulation *f* pulse amplitude modulation
pulsationsfrei pulsation-free
Pulsbetrieb *m* pulse operation
Pulscodemodulation *f* pulse code modulation
Pulsdauer *f* pulse duration
pulsen pulse
Pulsfolge *f* pulse train
Pulsformung *f* pulse shaping, shaping of pulses, pulse forming
Pulsfrequenz *f* pulse (repetition) frequency
Pulsfrequenzmodulation *f* pulse frequency modulation
pulsieren pulsate
pulsierend pulsatory, pulsating
Pulskennlinie *f* pulse characteristic
Pulsmodulation *f* pulse modulation
pulsmoduliert pulse-modulated
Pulsphase *f* pulse position
Pulsphasenmodulation *f* pulse position modulation
Pulsweitenmodulation *f* pulse width modulation
Pult *nt* 1. *(Tisch)* console, desk 2. *(Schaltpult)* panel
Pulver *nt* powder
Pulveraufspritzen *nt* powder spraying
pulverbeschichtet powder-coated
Pulverbeschichtung *f* powder coating
pulverförmiger Schweißzusatz *m* powdered filler metal
Pulverherstellung *f* powder production
Pulverkissen *nt* flux trough
Pulvermetall *nt* powder metal, metal powder
Pulvermetallurgie *f* powder metallurgy
pulvermetallurgisch powder-metallurgical
Pulververarbeitung *f* powder processing
Pumpbarkeit *f* pumpability
Pumpe *f* pump
Pumpe *f* **mit veränderlicher Fördermenge** variable delivery pump

pumpen pump
Pumpenaggregat *nt* pumping set
Pumpenanlagenfläche *f* pump seating face
Pumpenheizung *f* pump-assisted heating system, pumped circulation heating system
Pumplicht *nt* pump light
Pumpvorgang *m* pumping, pumping action
Pumpwiderstand *m* pumping effort
Pumpzyklus *m* pumping cycle
Punkführungsgetriebe *nt* point guidance mechanism
Punkt *m* dot, spot, point
Punkt-zu-Punkt-Bewegung *f* point-to-point (PTP) motion
Punkt-zu-Punkt-Verbindung *f* point-to-point connection
Punktanordnung *f* spot arrangement
Punktausschnitt *m* restricted gate
Punktbelastung *f* loads concentrated on a point lumped load
Punktberührung *f* point contact
Punktdurchmesser *m* spot diameter
Punktediagramm *nt* dot diagram
Punktemessung *f* spot measurement
punkten spot-weld
Punktform *f* shape of spot
punktförmig schweißen weld spot-wise
punktförmige Auflagerstelle *f* punctiform point contact
punktförmige Krafteinleitung *f* point transmission of force
punktförmiger Strahler *m* punctiform radiator
Punktierung *f* dotting
Punktlage *f* point position
Punktlast *f* lumped load, loads concentrated on a point
Punktleuchte *f* dot-lit lamp
pünktlich punctual, prompt, on-time
Pünktlichkeit *f* exactness, punctuality
Punktmustertransformation *f* point example transformation
Punktnaht *f* **am Überlappstoß** spot welded lap joint
Punktrasterverfahren *nt* dot-scanning method

Punktschätzung *f* point estimation
Punktschweißelektrode *f* **mit flach aufsetzender Elektrodenspitze** flat-tipped spot welding electrode
Punktschweißelektrode *f* **mit Zweikant** spot welding electrode with two flats
Punktschweißelektrode *f* **ohne Schlüsselflächen** spot welding electrode without spanner flats
punktschweißen spot-weld
Punktschweißung *f* spot welding
Punktsteuerung *f* point-to-point positioning control system, point-to-point control
Punktverzahnung *f* point tooth system, gear with pointed teeth
punktweises Abtasten *nt (e. Oberfläche)* point-by-point exploration
Pumpenprinzip *nt* pump principle
punzierungsfähiger Silbergehalt *m* silver content amenable to punching
PUR-Kaltschaum *m* polymethane cold foam
putzen burr, dress off, trim, clean
putzgerecht clean-just
Putzträger *m* plaster base
PVC hart-Rohr *nt* PVC rigid pipe
PVC *nt* **hart** unplasticized polyvinyl chloride, rigid PVC
PVC-Weichmacherechtheit *f* PVC plasticizer fastness
Pyramide *f* pyramid
pyramidenförmig pyramidal
Pyrolyserückstand *m* residue of pyrolysis

Qq

QS-Handbuch *nt* manual
Quader *m* **1.** *(allg.)* ashlar **2.** *(math.)* cuboid
quaderförmiger Probekörper *m* rectangular block specimen
Quadermessfläche *f* rectangular parallel-piped measurement surface
Quadermessfläche *f* **mit abgerundeten Ecken und Kanten** conformable surface
Quaderstein *m* square stone
Quadrant *m* quadrant
Quadrantskala *f* quadrant scale
Quadrat *nt* **1.** *(allg.)* quadrant, square, *(im ~)* squared **2.** *(math.)* second power
quadratisch quadratic, squared
quadratische Schließtoleranz *f* quadratic closing tolerance
quadratische Toleranzrechnung *f* quadratic tolerance calculation
quadratischer Mittelwert *m* root-mean-square
Quadratlochung *f* square perforation
Quadratmaß *nt* square dimension
Quadratwurzel *f* **aus** square root of
Quadratzeichen *nt* square symbol
quadrieren square
quadriert squared
quadrierte Abweichung *f* squared deviation
quadrierte Einzelwerte *f* sum of squares of the individual values
Quadrupel *nt* quadruple
Qualifikation *f* qualification, skills
Qualifikationsprüfung *f* qualification test
qualifizieren qualify
qualifiziert qualified, competent, skilled
Qualität *f* **1.** *(allg.)* quality **2.** *(als Klasse)* grade
Qualität *f* **prüfen** inspect the quality
qualitativ qualitative
qualitative Beschaffenheit *f* quality
Qualitätsabweichung *f* quality deviation
Qualitätsanforderung *f* quality requirement
Qualitätsarbeit *f* high-quality work
Qualitätsaudit *nt* quality audit
Qualitätsaufzeichnung *f* quality record(ing)
Qualitätsbewertung *f* quality assessment
Qualitätsdokumentation *f* quality documentation
Qualitätsforderung *f* quality demand
Qualitätsgrenzlage *f* quality level, (acceptable) quality limit
Qualitätskennung *f* quality code
Qualitätskennzahl *f* quality characteristic
Qualitätskennzeichen *nt* quality designation
Qualitätskontrolle *f* acceptance sampling, quality check, quality control, quality inspection
Qualitätskontrollplan *m* quality control plan
Qualitätslage *f* quality level
Qualitätslenkung *f* quality control, process quality control
Qualitätsmanagement *nt* quality management
Qualitätsmanagementaudit *nt* quality management audit
Qualitätsmanagementsystem *nt* quality management system
Qualitätsmerkmal *nt* quality characteristic
Qualitätsnachweis *m* verification of quality
Qualitätsplanung *f* quality planning
Qualitätspolitik *f* quality politics
Qualitätsprüfung *f* quality check (or control or inspection)
Qualitätsregelkarte *f* quality control card
Qualitätssicherung (QS) *f* quality assurance (QA), quality control
Qualitätssicherungsanforderung *f* quality assurance requirement
Qualitätssteuerung *f* quality control

Qualitätssystem *nt* quality system
Qualitätstechnik *f* quality engineering
Qualitätsüberwachung *f* quality control, quality surveillance
Qualitätsverbesserung *f* improvement of quality
Qualitätsverbindung *f* (bei Gewinden) quality connection
Qualitätsvorschrift *f* quality specification
Qualitätswerkstoff *m* high-quality material
Qualitätsziel *nt* quality target
Qualitätszirkel *m* quality circle
Qualmentwicklung *f* development of smoke
Quant *nt* quantum
Quantelung *f* quantization
Quantenabsorption *f* absorption of quanta
Quantenemission *f* emission of quanta
Quantenenergie *f* quantum energy
Quantenmechanik *f* quantum mechanics
quantenmechanisch quantum-mechanical
Quantensprung *m* quantum jump
Quantentheorie *f* quantum theory
Quantenzahl *f* quantum number
quantifizierbar quantifiable
quantifizieren quantify
Quantifizierung *f* quantification
Quantil *nt* quantile, fractile
Quantisierungseinheit *f* quantifying unit
Quantität *f* quantity
quantitativ quantitative
quantitative Größe *f* (quantitative) magnitude
quantitatives Merkmal *nt* quantitative characteristic
Quarz *nt* quartz
Quarzkristall *m* quartz crystal
quasi quasi
quasikontinuierlich quasi-continuous
Quasispanne *f* quasi range
quasistatisch quasi-static
quasisteif quasi-rigid
Quecksilber *nt* mercury
Quecksilberglasthermometer *nt* mercury in-glass thermometer
Quecksilbernitratversuch *m* mercury nitrate test
Quellcode *m* source code
Quelldatei *f* source file
Quelle/Ziel-Matrix *f* source/destination matrix
Quelle *f* source
Quellenprogramm *nt* source program
Quelle-Senke-Abstand *m* source-drain spacing
Quelle-Senke-Paar *nt* source-drain pair, source-drain couple, source drain combination
quellfest (von Beschichtungen) resistant
Quellobjekt *nt* source object
Quellschweißmittel *nt* solution welding compound
Quellung *f* (von Getriebebauteilen) swelling
Quellungsgrad *m* degree of swelling
Quellungshysterese *f* swelling hysteresis
Quellungsprodukt *nt* swelling product
Quellungszustand *m* state of swelling
Quellverhalten *nt* swelling behaviour
Quellversuch *m* swell test
quer cross, crossways, crosswise, lateral, latitudinal, transverse
quer durch across
quer einstapeln stack laterally
quer fahren move latitudinally (or transversally), travel laterally
quer gerichtet transverse
quer über across
quer verfahrbar traversing, cross-sliding, travelling laterally
quer verfahren traverse, travel laterally, move transversally
quer verlaufend cross
quer verstellen set at an angle
quer zu 1. *(allg.)* right angles to, transverse to, perpendicular to 2. *(diagonal)* diagonal to
Querachse *f* transverse axis
Queranschlag *m* cross feed stop, cross stop, facing dog
Querantrieb *m* cross drive
Querantrieb *m* der Drehgabelvor-

richtung cross drive for rotating assembly
Queranwahl *f* cross selection
Querauflage *f* lateral support, transverse carrier
Querbalken *m* 1. *(allg.)* cross arm, cross rail, cross bar, cross slide, rail, planer beam, cantilever, crossbeam, crossmember 2. *(Hobelmaschine)* horizontal rail
Querbalken *m* **mit Quervorschubgetriebekasten** crossrail with cross feed gearbox
Querbalkenführung *f* crossrail guide, rail guide
Querbalkenhöhenverstellmotor *m* crossrail elevating motor
Querbalkenklemmung *f* 1. *(allg.)* crossrail clamping 2. *(als Bauteil)* crossrail locking mechanism, crossrail clamping device, crossrail-lock clamp
Querbalkenmotor *m* crossrail motor, rail-traverse motor, rail elevating motor
Querbalkenprisma *nt* Vee-way of (the) crossrail, Vee-guide of (the) crossrail
Querbalkenschieber *m* saddle, crossrail slide
Querbalkenschlitten *m* saddle
Querbalkensupport *m* cross-rail head, rail-head, toolhead, cross-slide toolbox, planing head, planer head, slide-head, head
Querbett *nt* transverse bed, cross bed
Querbewegung *f* cross travel
Querbiegeprobe *f* transverse bend specimen
Querbiegeversuch *m* transverse bend specimen
querbohren cross-drill, cross-bore
Querdehnzahl *f* radial strain coefficient
Quereinstapelung *f* lateral stacking
Querfahren *nt* latitudinal movement
Querfahrwagen *nt* latitudinal truck
Querfließpressen *nt* transverse impact extrusion
Querförderer *m* transverse conveyor
Querfräsen *nt* cross milling, transverse milling
Querfrässupport *m* rail milling head
Querfuge *f* transverse joint

Querführung *f* cross rail, rail
Quergabelstapler *m* (single) side loading truck
Quergang *m* cross traverse
Querhaupt *nt* top rail, cross beam, cross girth, crosshead
querhobeln cross-plane. plane crosswise, transverse plane
Querhobelsupport *m* cross rail planing head, right-angle head
Querkante *f* transverse edge
Querkerben *fpl* **in der Decklage** coarse ripples (pl)
Querkraft *f* shearing force, transverse action, transverse load, transverse force, radial force, lateral force, radial stress
Querkraft *f* **senkrecht auf die Scherebene wirkend** force component acting perpendicular to shear plane
querkraftfreies Biegen *nt* bending without radial force
Querkraftübertragung *f* transmission of transverse forces
Querlochbohren *nt* cross hole drilling
Quernaht *f* transverse seal
Querneigung *f* inclination transverse to the direction of motion
Quernut *f* cross slot
Querpresspassung *f* transverse interference fit
Querpressung *f* radial interference fit
Querprüfung *f* transverse testing
Querquetscher *m* transverse squeezer
Querrauheit *f* transverse roughness
Querrichtung *f* crosswise direction, transverse direction
Querriegel *m* crossbar, traverse
Querrippe *f* cross rib
Querschaben *nt* cross scraping
Querschieber *m* cross slide, transverse slide, saddle
Querschlitten *m* 1. *(allg.)* cross slide, cross slide rest, facing slide 2. *(Drehbank)* cross slide 3. *(Messgerät)* transverse carriage 4. *(Senkrechtfräsmaschine)* shaper 5. *(Waagerechtfräsmaschine)* cross traverse slide 6. *(des Tisches)* apron slide, apron
Querschlupf *m* transverse slip
Querschneide *f* centre line between

cutting edges
Querschneidenwinkel *m* angle of point
Querschnitt *m* cross-sectional area, cross section
Querschnitt *m* **der Spannungsschicht** cross-sectional area of the pass
Querschnitt *m* **mit Rinne** *(Betonrohre)* cross-section with channel
Querschnittsbereich *m* cross sectional region
Querschnittsfläche *f* cross-sectional area
Querschnittsgeschwindigkeit *f* cross-sectional velocity
Querschnittsschwächung *f* reduction of area, contraction in area, diminished cross section
Querschnittsstauchung *f* cross section upsetting
Querschnittsverkleinerung *f* reduction in cross-sectional area
Querschubspindel *f* cross feed screw
Quersitz *m* seat perpendicular to the direction of motion, side-facing seating, *(mit ~)* with operator facing at right angles to the normal line of travel
Querskale *f* horizontal edgewise scale
Querstand *m* side-facing standing, *(mit ~)* with operator standing at right angles to the normal line of travel
Querstange *f* crossbar
Querstapler *m* side-loading truck, side-loader
Quersteifigkeit *f* transverse rigidity
Querstrangpressen *nt* transverse extrusion of rods and tubes
Quersupport *m* cross slide, rail head, tool box on cross slide
Querteiler *m* (horizontal) divider
Querträger *m* crossbeam, cross bar, cross girder, cross member, traverse
Quertraverse *f* **1.** *(allg.)* crosshead, crossbeam, traverse **2.** *(Hebezeug)* traverse lifting beam **3.** *(Verschieber)* traverse carriage, cross carriage
Querverband *m* cross-tie, traverse bracing
Querverbindung *f* portal tie beam
Querverfahrwagen *m* traverse truck
querverlaufendes Moment *nt* transverse moment
Querverschieber *m* transverse carriage, cross carriage
Querverschiebung *f* cross motion, cross feed
Querverstellung *f* cross adjustment
Querverweis *m* cross-reference
Querverweisliste *f* cross-reference list
Quervorschub *m* transverse feed, cross feed, lateral feed
Querwalzen *nt* transverse rolling, cross rolling
Querzerreißprobe *f* transverse tensile test specimen
Querzugsfestigkeit *f* transverse tensile strength
Quetschbereich *m* crushing zone
quetschen crush, trap, crimp, squeeze, compress, drag
Quetschspannung *f* compressive yield stress
Quetschstelle *f* squeezing point, squeeze point, crushing point
Quetschtube *f* collapsible tube
quietschen squeak
quittieren acknowledge, confirm
Quittierpflicht *f* obligation to acknowledgement, acknowledgement obligation
quittierpflichtig requiring acknowledgement
Quittiertaste *f* confirm key
Quittierung *f* acknowledgement, confirmation
Quittierzeitpunkt *m* acknowledgment time
Quittung *f* **1.** *(allg.)* receipt, voucher **2.** *(Rückmeldung)* acknowledgement
Quittung ausstellen give a receipt
Quittungsaustausch *m* handshake
Quittungsaustauschmitteilung *f* handshake message
Quote *f* quota, rate
Quotient *m* quotient

R r

Rachen *m* throat
Rachenlehre *f* snap gauge (or gage), gap gauge (or gage)
Rachenlehrläppmaschine *f* snap gage lapping machine
Rad *nt* 1. *(allg.)* wheel 2. *(aus einem Material)* solid wheel 3. *(aus mehreren Materialien)* composite wheel 4. *(mit Bereifung aus Vollmaterial)* solid tyred wheel 5. *(mit Bereifung mit Lufteinschluss)* semi-pneumatic tyred wheel 6. *(mit Bereifung mit veränderbarem Lufteinschluss)* pneumatic tyred wheel 7. *(mit Geradverzahnung)* gear of the spur type 8. *(mit geschäumter Bereifung)* foam tyre wheel
Radabdeckung *f* wheel hood
Radabnutzung *f* wheel wear
Radachse *f* axle (tree)
Radachsenabstand *m* distance between the axles
Radanordnung *f* arrangement of wheels
Radarm *m* outrigger
Radaufhängung *f* wheel suspension
Radbandage *f* gear ring
Radbefestigung *f* mounting of wheels
Radbohrung *f* hole through the gear
Radbreite *f* wheel width
Radbruch *m* wheel failure
Raddruck *m* wheel load, wheel pressure
Räder *ntpl* 1. *(allg.)* wheels 2. *(mit Luftbereifung)* wheels with pneumatic tyres 3. *(mit Metallfelgen)* wheels with metal rims 4. *(mit Vollgummibereifung)* wheels with solid tyres 5. *(mit Vollgummireifen für Luftreifenfelgen)* wheels with solid tyres for pneumatic rims
Räderblock *m* gear cluster
Räderfräsautomat *m* automatic gear milling machine, automatic gear cutting machine
Räderfräsautomat *m* *(Wälzfräsautomat)* automatic gear hobber (or hobbing machine)

Räderfräsmaschine *f* 1. *(allg.)* gear milling machine 2. *(Wälzverfahren)* gear hobber, gear hobbing machine
Rädergetriebe *nt* 1. *(allg.)* gear train, gear mechanism, gearbox 2. *(mit einfacher Übersetzung)* simple gear train
Räderkasten *m* gearbox
Räderkurbelgetriebe *nt* gear-crank mechanism
Räderplatte *f* apron housing
Räderspindelstock geared headstock
Rädertrieb *m* geared drive
Räderumsetzung *f* gear reduction
Räderverhältnis *nt* gearing ratio
Rädervorgelege *nt* back gears
Räderwalzfräsen *nt* gear hobbing
Räderwechselgetriebe *nt* change-gear transmission
Radfeststeller *m* wheel braking and/or locking device
radförmiges Schneidemesser *nt* pinion-type cutter
Radführungsachse *f* axis of constraint of the gear
Radhälfte *f* half of the wheel
radial radial
Radial-Axial-Verfahren *nt* radial-axial feed method
Radialbohrmaschine *f* radial drilling machine
Radialbohrmaschine *f* **mit runder Säule** round column radial drill, round column drilling machine
Radialbohrwerk *nt* radial drill
radiale Tischvorschubbewegung *f* radial table feed motion
Radialeinlauf *m* radial shrinkage
radialer Eingriff *m* radial engagement
radialer Spanwinkel *m* radial rake
radialer Tischvorschub *m* radial table feed
radiales Einkugelmaß *nt* radial single-ball measurement
radiales Einrollenmaß *nt* radial single-roll measurement
radiales Schleifen *nt* radial grinding

Radialfräsen *nt* **1.** *(allg.)* radial milling (method) **2.** *(Schneckenräder)* radial hobbing (method)
Radialkraft *f* radial force
Radialmeißel *m* radial tool, radial chisel
Radialmeißelhalter *m* radial toolholder, radial tool holder
Radialprüfung *f* radial testing
Radialschiff *m* peripheral grinding
Radialschlag *m* radial runout
Radialspiel *nt* radial backlash
Radialvakuumpumpe *f* radial vacuum pump
Radialverfahren *nt* radial-feed method
Radialvorschub *m* radial feed
Radialwelle *f* radial shaft
Radialwellendichtring *m* radial shaft sealing ring
Radialwinkel *m* hook angle, face angle, front rake angle, secondary rake
Radiant *m* radiant
Radiator *m:* **1.** *(frei aufgestellter ~)* free-mounted radiator **2.** *(mehrgliedriger ~)* multi-section radiator **3.** *(unverkleideter ~)* exposed radiator **4.** *(verkleideter ~)* covered radiator
Radiatorglied *nt* radiator section
Radien *mpl* radius
Radienfräskopf *m* radius milling head
Radienschablone *f* radius gauge
Radierfestigkeit *f* *(Papier)* resistance to erasure
Radikalbildner *m* radical former
Radius *m* **1.** *(allg.)* radius **2.** *(Wenderadius)* outside turning radius
Radius *m* **am Gewindegrund** radius at the thread root, root radius
Radius *m* **der eingeformten Spanleitstufe** chip breaker groove radius
Radius *m* **der gerundeten Schneide** rounded cutting edge radius
Radius *m* **der Spanbrechernut** chip breaker groove radius
Radiusfräser *m* corner-rounding cutter
Radiuskorrektur *f* cutter compensation
Radkappe *f* wheel boss cap, hub cap
Radkörper *m* **1.** *(allg.)* wheel body, gear body, gear blank, wheel centre **2.** *(unbearbeiteter ~)* gear blank **3.** *(aus mehreren Bestandteilen)* composite wheel centre
Radkranz *m* wheel rim, rim
Radkurve *f* cycloid
Radlager *nt* journal bearing, wheel bearing
Radlast *f* load per wheel, wheel loading
Radlaufkurve *f* cycloid
Radlinie *f* epicycloid
Radmitte *f* gear centre
Radnabe *f* wheel boss, wheel hub
Radnabengetriebe *nt* wheel hub gear
Radpaar *nt* gear pair
Radpaar *nt* **mit gekreuzten Radachsen** gear pair with non-parallel non-intersecting axes
Radpaar *nt* **mit parallelen Achsen** *(Stirnradpaar)* gear pair with parallel axes
Radpaar *nt* **mit Profilverschiebung** X-gear pair
Radpaar *nt* **mit sich schneidenden Achsen** *(Kegelradpaar)* gear pair with intersecting axes
Radpaar *nt* **mit Übersetzung ins Langsame** speed reducing gear pair
Radpaar *nt* **mit Übersetzung ins Schnelle** speed increasing gear pair
Radpaarung *f* mating gears, gear pairing
Radscheibe *f* wheel disk, wheel centre
Radschutz *m* wheel guard, wheel housing, deflector
Radstand *m* wheel base
Radstellungsanzeiger *m* wheel position indicator
Radumdrehung *f* revolution (of the wheel)
radunterstützt wheel-supported
Radverzahnung *f* gear tooth system, gear teeth
Radwechsel *m* changing of wheels
Radzahl *f* number of wheels
Radzahnabrundfräsmaschine *f* tooth chamfering machine
raffen reef, crimp, gather
Rahmen *m* frame, frame structure, framework, body, chassis
Rahmenbedingungen *fpl* general conditions
Rahmenbreite *f* frame width

Rahmenbrenner *m* frame burner
Rahmenfräsen *nt* milling of frame contours
Rahmenkante *f* frame edge
Rahmenkontur *f* chassis profile
Rahmenständer *m* housing
Rahmentiefe *f* frame depth
Rahmenvertrag *m* master agreement, outline agreement, framework contact
RAM address memory
rammen ram, collide with
Rammschutz *m* collision guard
Rampe *f* ramp, platform
Rampenfahrt *f* ramp travel
Rampenhub *m* 1. *(Bauteil)* ramp lift 2. *(Funktion)* ramp-lift function
Rampenwinkel *m* ramp angle
Rand *m* border, boundary, edge, rim, margin
Randabkohlung *f* surface decarburization
Randbedingung *f* ancillary conditions, boundary conditions, limiting conditions, boundary value
Randbiegespannung *f* bending stress on the tension side
Randeinrollen *nt* **durch Drücken** curling by spinning
Rändelfräskopf *m* knurl milling head
Rändelmeißel *m* straight knurling tool
Rändelmutter *f* knurled nut
rändeln knurl, straight-knurl
Rändeln *nt* straight-knurling, knurling
Rändelschraube *f* knurled head screw
Rändelstoßmaschine *f* knurl shaper
Rändelwerkzeug *nt* knurling tool
Randerwartungswert *m* marginal expectation
Randfaser *f* outer fibre
Randfaserdehngeschwindigkeit *f* rate of strain of the outer fibre
Randfaserdehnung *f* strain of the outer fibre, outer fibre strain
Randfaserdehnung *f* **bei Höchstkraft** strain of the outer fibre at maximum load
Randfaserdehnung *f* **beim Bruch** strain of the outer fibre at fracture
Randfeld *nt* surrounding area
Randgebiet *nt* marginal area

Randhärten *nt* superficial hardening
Randhochstellen *nt* edge raising
Randhochstellen *nt* **durch Drücken** edge raising by spinning
Randkerbe *f* lateral undercut
Randkohlenstoffgehalt *m* surface carbon content
Randoxidation *f* superficial oxidation
Randregal *nt* edge rack
Randschärfe *f* marginal definition
Randschicht *f* 1. *(allg.)* surface outer layer 2. *(nitriergehärtete ~)* nitrided case
Randschichtbehandlung *f* surface layer treatment (or processing)
Randspannung *f* boundary stress
Randvarianz *f* marginal variance
Randveränderung *f* time-edge effect
Randverteilung *f* marginal distribution
randvoll füllen fill up to the brim
Randwinkelfehler *m* wetting angle defect
Randzone *f* 1. *(allg.)* surface outer layer, edge zone 2. *(entkohlte ~)* soft skin
Randzonenbeeinflussung *f* surface outer layer influence
Rang *m* rank, ranking, grade
Rangfolge *f* sequence
Ranggröße *f* order statistic
rangieren shunt
Rangwert *m* ordered value
Rangzahl *f* rank
Raste *f* catch, detent, latch, notch, serration, retainer
rasten 1. *(ausruhen)* dwell, rest 2. *(einrasten)* catch, engage, lock, latch
Rastenabstand *m* spacing of the notches, distance between serrations
Rastenklinke *f* notch
Rastenrad *nt* notched wheel
Raster *nt* 1. *(allg.)* basic (or reference) grid, raster, screen 2. *(Zwischenraum)* spacing adjustment increment
Rasterabstand *m* grid element spacing
Rasterarretierung *f* raster locking
Rasteraufnahmetisch *m* bucky table
Rasterbodengerät *nt* bucky floor stand
Rastereinzahnumlauffräsen *nt* raster fly cutting
Rasterlinie *f* grid line

rastern screen
Rasterpunkt *m* grid point, point in the grid, picture element, scanning element
Rasterscanner *m* raster scanner
Rasterschiene *f* mounting rail
Rastersystem *nt* grid system
Rasterung *f* raster
Rasterwandgerät *nt* bucky wall stand
Rastphase *f* dwell phase
Rastscheibe *f* locking disk
Raststift *m* index plunger, latch pin, plunger pin, plunger
Raststift *m* **der Teilscheibe** locating plunger
rationalisieren rationalize
Rationalisierung *f* rationalization
Rationalisierungsansatz *m* initial rationalization stage
Rationalisierungspotential *nt* potential for rationalization
Ratschenantrieb *m* ratchet stop
ratterfrei chatter-free, chatter-proof stable
Ratterfreiheit *f* freedom from chatter
Rattermarke *f* chatter mark
Rattern *nt* chatter, chattering
Ratternarbe *f* chatter mark
Ratterschwingung *f* chatter vibration
rau coarse, rough, harsh, uneven
Rauch *m* smoke, fumes
Rauchabzug *m* smoke outlet, smoke vent
Rauchabzugsanlage *f* smoke control installation
Rauchauswurfbegrenzung *f* smoke emission limit
rauchdicht impervious to smoke
Räucheranlage *f* roasting oven
Rauchfang *m* smoke flue
Rauchfeuchteregler *m* room humidity regulator
rauchfrei free of smoke
Rauchgas *nt* flue gas, fumes *pl*
rauchgasbeheizt flue gas-heated
Rauchgaspyrometer *nt* flue-gas pyrometer
Rauchgasregelklappe *f* flue gas control flap
Rauchgassäule *f* column of flue gas
Rauchgastemperatur *f* burnt gas temperature
Rauchgasumgehung *f* flue gas by-pass
Rauchkanal *m* smoke duct
Rauchmeldeanlage *f* smoke alarm system
Rauchrohr *nt* smoke pipe
Rauchschornstein *m* smoke chimney
Rauchschutz *m* protection from smoke
Rauchschutztür *f* smoke protection door
Raudrehen *nt* rough turning
Rauheitsspitze *f* roughness peak
Raugewinde *nt* **mit gerissenen Flanken** rough thread with fissured flanks
Rauheit *f* roughness
Rauheitsmessgröße *f* roughness parameter, surface roughness value
Rauhigkeit *f* roughness, unevenness
Raunormal *nt* roughness standard
Rautiefe *f* peak-to-valley height, roughness height
Rautiefenbemessung *f* roughness height rating
Raum *m* space, room, cavity
Räum- und Glättwerkzeug *nt* combination broach-burnisher tool
Räum- und Zentriermaschine *f* broach and centre machine
Räumarbeit *f* broaching job, broaching operation, broaching work
Räumaufspannung *f* broaching setup
Raumausnutzung *f* cube utilization, space utilization
Raumbedarfsmaß *nt* *(bei Armaturen)* space requirement dimension
Raumbedarfsmaße *ntpl* details of space requirements
Raumbeleuchtung *f* room (or space) lighting
Räumdorn *m* push broach
Räumdurchgang *m* broaching pass
Räumen *nt* 1. *(allg.)* broaching, clearing 2. *(ebene Flächen)* straight broaching 3. *(runde Durchbrüche)* round-hole broaching 4. *(von Drallnuten)* helical broaching
Raumersparnis *f* room saving(s)
Raumformfräsen *nt* three-dimensional tracer milling, cavity milling

Raumformfräsung *f* three-dimensional milling operation
Raumgetriebe *nt* spatial mechanism
Raumheizgerät *nt* room heating appliance
Raumheizkörper *m* space heater
Raumhöhe *f* room height
Raumklimagerät *nt* room air conditioner
Raumkosten *pl* space costs
räumlich spatial, geometrical, three-dimensional, cubic
räumlich gekrümmt curved three-dimensionally
räumliche Anordnung *f* spatial arrangement
Räumlichkeitsgrad *m* **der Spannungen** spatial factor of stresses
Raumluftfeuchte *f* interior (or inside), air humidity
Raumluftfeuchtewert *m* inside air humidity value
Raumlufttechnik *f* air conditioning technology
Raumlufttemperatur *f* room air temperature
Raumluftzustand *m* interior air condition
Räummaschine *f* broaching machine, broach, broacher
raumnachformen duplicate in three dimensions
Räumnadel *f* pull broach, internal broach, broach
Räumnadelanhebezylinder *m* broach lifter cylinder
Räumnadelhalter *m* broach holder
Räumnadelziehmaschine *f* pull-type broaching machine
Raumnutzungsgrad *m* space utilization factor
Raumplan *m* room plan
Räumschlitten *m* broach slide, broach ram
Räumspäne *mpl* broachings *pl*
Raumsparregallager *nt* space saving rack store
Räumstößel *m* broaching roam, broach ram
Raumtemperatur *f* ambient temperature
Raumtemperaturregler *m* thermostat
Raumumschließungsflächen *fpl* boundary surfaces of the space, surface enclosing the space
Raumvolumen *nt* room (or space) volume
Räumvorrichtung *f* broaching fixture
Räumwerkzeug *nt* broach, broach tool, broaching tool
Räumwerkzeug *nt* **für drallförmige Nuten** helical broach, helical spline broach
Räumwerkzeug *nt* **für Keilnuten** keyway broach
Räumwerkzeug *nt* **für Sonderformen** form broach
Räumwerkzeug *nt* **mit eingesetzten Zähnen** inserted teeth broach
Räumwerkzeug *nt* **mit kreisförmigen Querschnitt** circular broach
Räumwerkzeug *nt* **mit Tiefenstaffelung der Zähne** depth cutting type of broach
Räumwerkzeuge broaching tools
Räumwerkzeugträger *m* broach carrier
Räumwerkzeugzubringerschlitten *m* broach-handling slide
raumzentriert space-centred, body-centred
Raupenzeichnung *f* run formation
Rauschanzeige *f* noise trace (or indication)
Rauschen *nt* noise
Rauschunterdrückung *f* noise suppression
Raute *f* rhomb, rhombus, lozenge
rautenförmig lozenged, rhomb shaped, rhombic, rhoboidal, diamond shaped
rautenförmig angeordnet diamond pattern
Rayleigh-Länge Rayleigh-length
RC-Glättung *f* RC-smoothing
RC-Verfahrenskette *f* RC-procedural chain
reagieren react (to), respond
Reaktion *f* reaction, response
Reaktionsbeschleuniger *m* reaction accelerator

reaktionsbestimmter Prozess *m (el. chem.)* process specific to reaction
Reaktionsharz *nt* reaction resin
Reaktionsharzbeton *m* reaction resin concrete
Reaktionsharzformstoff *m* reaction resin moulded material
Reaktionsharz-Härter *m* reacting resin hardener
Reaktionsharzmasse *f* reaction resin moulding material
Reaktionshemmung *f* inhibition of the reaction
Reaktionskraft *f* reaction force
Reaktionslot *nt* solder-forming flux
Reaktionsmessung *f* reaction measurement
Reaktionspartner *m* reaction partner
Reaktionsprodukt *nt* reaction product
Reaktionsschicht *f* adherent surface layer (due to corrosion)
Reaktionsüberspannung *f* reaction overvoltage
Reaktionswiderstand *m* reaction resistance
Reaktionszeit *f* response time, reaction time
Reaktiv-Kleber *m* reactive adhesive
Reaktorschweißung *f* reactor weld
realisierbar feasible, realizable
Realisierbarkeit *f* feasibility
realisieren implement, carry out, realize
Realisierung *f* implementation, realization
Realisierungsphase *f* implementation stage
Realisierungsvariante *f* version to be realized
Reallayout *nt* real layout
Realplanung *f* real planning
Realvariante *f* real variant
Realzeitbetrieb *m* real time processing
Realzeitprogramm *nt* real-time program
Realzeitsprache *f* real time language
Rechen *m* 1. *(Harke)* rake 2. *(Getriebe)* rack
Rechenfehler *m* miscalculation, computational mistake, calculation error
Rechenglied *nt* computing element
Rechengröße *f* calculation factor (or quantity), operand
Rechenmaschine *f* **für Dauereinsatz** calculator for extensive use
Rechenmaschine *f* **für gelegentlichen Gebrauch** calculator for occasional use
Rechenmaschine *f* **für netzabhängigen und netzunabhängigen Betrieb** main/battery powered calculator
Rechenmaschine *f* **mit aufladbarer Batterie** calculator powered by rechargeable battery
Rechenmaschine *f* **mit programmgesteuertem Speicher zum Akkumulieren** calculator with programme-controlled adressable storage
Rechenmaschine *f* **mit tastengesteuertem Speicher zum Akkumulieren** calculator with keyboard-controlled addressable storage
Rechenmaschine *f* **mit Einwegbatterie** calculator powered by disposable battery
Rechenmaschine *f* **ohne Speicher zum Akkumulieren** calculator without addressable storage
Rechenprogramm *nt* calculation program, computer program
Rechenschaubild *nt* nomogram
Rechenschieber *m* slide rule
rechentechnisch in terms of calculation
Rechenwert *m* design value
Rechenzeit *f* computing time
rechnen calculate, compute
Rechner *m* calculator, computer
Rechnerbetriebssystem *nt* disk operating system
rechnergesteuert computer-controlled
rechnergestützt computer-aided
rechnergestützte Betriebsdatenerfassung *f* production data acquisition
rechnergestützte Betriebsleitung *f* production control
rechnergestützte Prozess- und Anlagenüberwachung *f* process monitoring
rechnergestützte Prozessleitung *f*

process control
rechnergestütztes Messen *nt* computer-assisted measurement
rechnergezeichnet computer-drawn
Rechnergrobkonzept *nt* calculator coarse draft
rechnerisch calculated
rechnerische Beanspruchung *f* design stress
rechnerische Nutzungsdauer *f* calculated useful life
rechnerische Toleranzfindung *f* finding the tolerances by calculation
Rechnerlast *f* computer load
Rechnersimulation *f* computer simulation
Rechnersystem *nt* computer system
Rechnerwerk *nt* computer processor
Rechnung *f* invoice
Rechnungslegung *f* rendering of accounts
rechte Seite *f* right side, right-hand side
Rechteck *nt* rectangle
rechteckig rectangular
rechteckige Form *f* box section
Rechteckkanal *m* rectangular duct
Rechteckspule *f* rectangular coil
rechter Drehmeißel *m* right-hand turning (or cutting) tool
rechter Meißel *m* right-hand cutting tool, *(US)* right-cut tool, *(UK)* right-hand tool
rechter Schruppmeißel *m* right-hand roughing tool
rechter Seitenmeißel *m* right-hand side-cutting tool, right-hand side tool
rechter Ständer *m* right-hand column
rechter Stechmeißel *m* right-hand cut-off tool, right-hand parting tool
rechter Winkel *m* right angle
rechtes Maximum *nt* right most maximum
rechts right, on the right
Rechtsausführung *f (Darstellung eines Teiles)* right-hand version
Rechtsdrall *m* right-hand helix, right-hand spiral
rechtsdrehend clockwise
rechtsdrehender Fräser *m* top coming cutter

Rechtsdrehung *f* clockwise rotation, right-hand rotation
Rechtsevolvente *f* right-hand involute
Rechtsflanke *f* right-hand tooth surface, right flank
Rechtsflankeneingriffslinie *f* line of engagement of right-hand tooth surfaces, right hand path of contact
Rechtsflankenprofil *nt* right-hand flank profile
Rechtsgewinde *nt* right-hand thread
Rechtslauf *m* clockwise rotation, right-hand motion
Rechtsmeißel *m* right-hand cutting tool, *(US)* right-cut tool, *(UK)* right-hand tool
rechtsschneidend right-cut, right-hand cutting
rechtsschneidender Drehmeißel *m* right-hand turning tool
rechtsschneidender Fräser *m* right-cut milling cutter, right-hand milling cutter
Rechtsschrägverzahnung *f* right-hand helical tooth system
Rechtsschraubbewegung *f* right-handed helical motion
Rechtsschraube *f* right-hand helix
rechtsseitig right hand, on the right-hand side
rechtssteigend *(e. Schraubenlinie)* right-handed, right hand
rechtssteigende Verzahnung *f* right-hand teeth
Rechtsteilung *f* right-hand pitch
Rechtsverordnung *f* statutory order
Rechtwinkel *m* stretch angle
rechtwinklig orthogonal, perpendicular, right-angled, square, rectangular, quadratic
rechtwinklig aufeinanderstoßen meet each other at right angles
rechtwinklig zu at right angles to, perpendicular to
rechtwinklig zueinander square with each other
rechtwinklig zueinander liegen lie at right angles to each other
Rechtwinkligkeit *f* squareness, rectangularity, right angularity

Rechtwinkligkeitstoleranz f perpendicularity tolerance, squareness tolerance
Reckalterung f strain ag(e)ing
Reckdrücken nt *(Drückwalzen)* roller spinning
Reckeinrichtung f stretching unit
recken 1. *(allg.)* stretch form, strain, draw out, elongate, lengthen 2. *(Maschinen)* inch forward
Recken nt **von Flachstäben in der Halbzeugfertigung** straightening (flat bars) by stretching
Recken nt **von Hohlkörpern** hollow forging
Reckgeschwindigkeit f rate of strain
Reckgrad m degree of stretching
Reckstauchen nt gathering by die stretching
Reckung f 1. *(allg.)* stretching, stretch forming 2. *(Maschinen)* forward inching
Reckwalzen nt *(Schmiedewalzen)* forge rolling, strain rolling
Recycling nt recycling
Redoxpotential nt redox potential
Redoxreaktion f redox reaction
Reduktion f reduction
Reduktionsreaktion f *(el. chem.)* reduction reaction
redundant redundant
redundante Ansteuerung f dual-channel triggering
redundante Steuerung f redundant control system
Redundanz f redundancy
Reduziereinsatz m collet
reduzieren reduce, decrease
reduzierendes Schutzgas nt reducing protective gas
Reduziermuffe f reducing socket
Reduzierstück nt reducer
Reduzierstutzen m *(für Rohrverschraubungen)* reducing union
reduzierte Spanfläche f reduced face
reduzierte Zufallsgröße f reduced random quantity
Reduzierung f reduction (of), decrease (of)
Reedkontakt m reed contact
reelle Zahl f real number
Referenzauslagerplatz m reference output location
Referenzebene f reference plane
Referenzeinlagerplatz m reference input location
Referenzgerade f reference datum
referenzieren reference
Referenzierung f referencing
Referenzlagerplatz m reference storage location
Referenzmarke f reference mark(er)
Referenzpunkt m reference point
Reff nt reef
Reffeinrichtung f reefing unit, reefing device, crimping unit
Reflektogramm nt reflectogram
reflektierend reflecting, reflective
reflektierend machen reflectorize
reflektiert werden reverberate
Reflektor m reflector
Reflexfolie f reflecting foil, reflective tape
Reflexion f reflection
Reflexionseigenschaft f reflective characteristic
Reflexionsfilter m reflection filter
Reflexionsgrad m degree of reflection
Reflexionslichtschranke f reflection light barrier
Reflexionslichttaster m reflection light scanner
Reflexionsmarke f reflection tag
Reflexionsoptik f reflection optics
Reflexionsphotometer nt reflection photometer
Reflexionsspiegel m reflecting mirror
Reflexionszeilenlichttaster m reflection line-scanning light scanner
Refraktionsinterzept nt refraction intercept
Regal nt racking, shelf, shelving
Regal nt **bedienen** service a rack
Regal nt **mit festen Fachböden** non-adjustable racking
Regal nt **mit Rück- und Seitenwänden** closed shelf, closed shelving
Regal nt **mit verstellbaren Fachböden** adjustable racking
regalabhängig rackbound
Regalanlage f rack system, racking

Regalauslenkung *f* rack deflection
Regalbediengerät (RGB) *nt* storage and retrieval machine (SRM), S/R-machine
Regalbediensystem *nt* shelf operating system
Regalbedienung *f* rack servicing
Regalbereich *m* rack area
Regalbreite *f* rack width
Regalbühne *f* rack-supported mezzanine, mezzanine deck
Regalfach *nt* rack aperture, rack compartment
Regalfläche *f* shelf space
Regalförderzeug (RFZ) *nt* storage and retrieval machine (SRM)
Regalgang *m* aisle, rack aisle, shelving aisle
Regalgasse *f* rack aisle
Regalhöhe *f* rack height
Regalkonstruktion *f* rack structure, integrated structure
Regalkopf *m* head of the rack, rack head
Regalkopftraverse *f* rack head carriage
Regallager *nt* rack store
Regallagerung *f* rack storage, shelving
Regallänge *f* rack length
Regallängsriegel *m* the rack's longitudinal bar
Regalmodul *nt* rack module
Regalpflege *f* rack jobbing
Regalraster *nt* shelf grid
Regalreihe *f* rack bay
Regalrücken *m* (rack) spine, back of the rack, spine of the rack
Regalschwingung *f* rack vibration
Regalseite *f* face (of the rack)
Regalstahlbau *m* racking steelwork
Regalständer *m* rack support, rack upright
Regalstandort *m* rack location
Regalstapler *m* rack stacker, high-level stacker
Regalsteher *m* rack upright
Regalstütze *f* rack strut, rack support, rack upright
Regalsystem *nt* rack system, shelving system
Regalsystemebene *f* rack system level, rack system plane
Regaltiefe *f* rack depth, shelving depth
Regaltyp *m* rack type
regalunabhängig non-rackbound
Regalverband *m* rack bracing
regalverfahrend for travel on the rack structure, travelling on the rack structure
Regalvorfeld *nt* access area, front area
Regalzeile *f* rack run, row of shelves
Regel *f* rule, norm
Regelabschaltung *f* normal shut-down
Regelabweichung *f* off-set
regelbar *(verstellbar)* adjustable, controllable
Regelbereich *m* range of control
Regelbetrieb *m* normal operation
Regelbetriebsbedingungen *fpl* normal operating conditions, normal operation
Regeldifferenz *f* negative deviation (of the variable)
Regeldurchgangsventil *nt* straightway control valve
Regeleinrichtung *f* control system, control device, control gear, closed loop controlling system
Regelgerät *nt* controller, governor
Regelgewinde *nt* coarse-pitch thread, regular type screw thread
Regelglied *nt* control element
Regelgröße *f* controlled variable, feedback quantity
Regelkennlinie *f* control characteristic
Regelklappe *f* control butterfly valve
Regelkreis *m* closed loop control, control circuit, control loop
Regelkupplung *f* speed control coupling
Regellastgetriebe *nt* variable-load drive
Regelleistung *f* economic output
regelmäßig regular, routine
regeln control, regulate, govern, vary
Regeln *fpl (Vorschriften)* rules
Regelnadelventil *nt* needle regulating valve
Regelorgan *nt* für Fördermenge delivery control member
Regelprobestück *nt* standard test piece

Regelprüfung *f* regular test
Regelrolle *f* regulating roll
Regelschaltung *f* normal shut down
Regelscheibe *f* *(Vorschubscheibe)* control wheel, regulating wheel
Regelschieber *m* control gate valve
Regelschleife *f* loop, servo loop
Regelspanne *f* control range
Regelstrecke *f* closed loop controlled system, control loop
Regelteil *nt* control part
Regelung *f* **1.** *(allg.)* control, automatic control **2.** *(als Gesamtanlage, in der die Regelung stattfindet)* closed loop control plant **3.** *(als Vorgang)* closed loop control (process) **4.** *(SPS)* feedback control **5.** *(mit geschlossenem Ein- und Ausgang)* closed-loop control **6.** *(selbsttätige ~)* automatic control
Regelungs- und Steuerungstechnik *f* automatic control technology
Regelungsobjekt *nt* equipment under control, control technology
Regelungstechnik *f* automatic control, control technology
regelungstechnische Lösung *f* solution from the control system view-point
Regelventil *nt* control valve
Regelvorrichtung *f* control unit
Regelwerk *nt* **1.** *(allg.)* guidelines, body of rules and regulations **2.** *(techn.)* regulator, control equipment
Regelwiderstand *m* rheostat
Regenerierbehälter *m* regenerating tank
Regenfallrohr *nt* downpipe
Regenrinne *f* gutter
Regenrohr *nt* rain water pipe
Regenspende *f* rain yield factor
Regenwasserabflussspende *f* storm water discharge yield factor
Regionallager *nt* regional stock
Register *nt* record, index, register
Registrierempfindlichkeit *f* recording sensitivity
registrieren record, register
registrierendes Messgerät *nt* recording measuring instrument
Registrierung *f* recording, registration
Regler *m* control unit, control system, controller, controlling means, automatic controller
Reglerseil *nt* overspeed governor rope
Regression *f* regression
Regressionsfläche *f* regression surface
Regressionsfunktion *f* regression equation
Regressionsgerade *f* regression line
Regressionskurve *f* regression curve
Regressionsrechnung *f* regression calculation
Regulator *m* governor
Regulierbarkeit *f* **1.** *(Messgeräte)* adjustability **2.** *(Regelbarkeit)* controllability
regulieren regulate
rechtsläufig right-handed rotating
Reibahle *f* reamer
Reibahlennutfräser *m* reamer fluting cutter
Reibarbeit *f* reaming operation
Reibbelag *m* friction lining
Reibberührung *f* contact to friction
Reibbewegung *f* frictional motion
Reibbolzenschweißen *nt* friction stud welding
Reibbremse *f* friction brake
Reibechtheit *f* fastness to rubbing
Reibeigenschaft *f* friction property
Reibelement *nt* friction element
Reibelot *nt* tinning solder
reiben *vi/* **1.** *(allg.)* abrade, rub, produce friction, slide with friction, gall, ream **2.** *(stirnschneidendes)* counter-sink
reibend abrasive, frictional
Reibfläche *f* friction area, friction surface
Reibkoeffizient *m* friction coefficient
Reibkupplung *f* friction clutch
Reiboberfläche *f* friction surface
Reibpaarung *f* frictional pairing
Reibpartner *m* friction partner
Reibradantrieb *m* wheel and disk drive
Reibrad *nt* frictional wheel
Reibradgetriebe *nt* frictional wheel gear, friction gear, friction transmission
Reibrolle *f* friction roller
Reibsäge *f* friction saw
Reibschweißen *nt* friction welding, spin welding

Reibstelle *f* wear point
Reibung *f* abrasion, friction
Reibungsarbeit *f* friction energy
reibungsfrei frictionless, smooth, unobstructed, troublefree
Reibungsgeschehen *nt* friction process
Reibungskraft *f* frictional force
Reibungskupplung *f* friction clutch, sliding clutch
Reibungsschluss *m* *(bei Sicherungsmuttern)* friction grip (or locking)
Reibungsverlust *m* friction(al) loss, friction and winding losses
Reibungsvorschub *m* movement by friction surface
Reibungswärme *f* frictional heat
Reibungswiderstand *m* frictional resistance
Reibverschleiß *m* rubbing wear
Reibwerkzeug *nt* reamer
Reibwert *m* coefficient of friction
reichen extend, reach for
Reichweite *f* 1. *(Gegenstände)* reach 2. *(Strahlung)* range
Reife *f* maturity
reifen mature, ripen
Reifen *m* tyre, *(US)* tire
Reifenballast *m* tyre ballast
Reifenbreite *f* tyre width
Reifendruck *m* tyre inflation pressure
Reifenphase *f* maturity stage
Reifenregal *nt* tyre racking
Reihe *f* 1. *(allg.)* succession, sequence, set, row, batch, series, run 2. *(Anordnung)* alignment 3. *(Regal)* bay 4. *(Schicht)* tier
Reihenabstand *m* *(bei Nieten)* distance between rows
Reihenaufnahme *f* mass radiograph
Reihenaufspannung *f* line setup
Reihenbildung *f* assembly in rows
Reihenbildungstisch *m* row preparation table
Reihenbohrmaschine *f* gang drilling machine
Reihenfertigung *f* batch production
Reihenfertigungsmaschine *f* batch production machine, long run production machine

Reihenfolge *f* 1. *(allg.)* sequence, order 2. *(Stellung in der Serie)* seriation
Reihenklemme *f* terminal block
reihenmäßige Herstellung *f* batch production, duplicate production
Reihensammlung *f* collection of rows
Reihenschaltung *f* series connection, serial connection
Reihenschieber *m* row pusher
Reihenschlusserregung *f* series excitation
Reihenschlussmaschine *f* series wound dynamo
Reihenschlussmotor *m* inverse speed-motor, series characteristic motor
rein clean, pure
Reindichte *f* true density
reine Schweißzeit *f* productive welding time
reiner Bereich *m* clean zone
Reinhaltung *f* housekeeping, purification
Reinheit *f* cleanliness, purity
Reinheitsgrad *m* 1. *(allg.)* degree of purity 2. *(e. Oberfläche)* level (or degree) of cleanliness 3. *(zur Analyse)* purity grade (reagent grade)
reinigen clean, purge, purify (from)
Reinigerzusatz *m* detergent additive
Reinigung *f* cleaning, purgation, purification
Reinigungsmaschine *f* cleaner, cleaning machine
Reinigungsmöglichkeit *f* cleanability
Reinigungsprüfung *f* purging test
Reinigungsrohr *nt* cleaning pipe
Reinigungsschritt *m* cleaning stage
Reinradgetriebe *nt* friction gearing
Reinraum *m* cleanroom
Reinraumbedingungen *fpl* cleanroom conditions
Reinraumproduktion *f* cleanroom manufacture
Reinraumsystem *nt* cleanroom system
Reinraumtechnik *f* cleanroom technology
Reißdehnung *f* elongation at break (or failure), elongation due to tearing
reißen crack, break, disrupt, rip, split, tear, sever, part, drag, jerk, rupture,

burst, fracture
reißen von Spänen break up into segments
Reißkraft *f* breaking load
Reißlänge *f* breaking length
Reißnadel *f* scriber
Reißrichtung *f* direction ot tearing
Reißscheibe *f* bursting disc
Reißspan *m (US)* discontinuous chip, segmental (or fragmental) chip, *(UK)* tear chip, chip broken up into segments, fractured chip
Reißstock *m* surface gauge, scribing block, marking gauge
Reißstrecke *f* tear length
Reißzeug *nt* drawing instrument
Reitnagel *m* centre sleeve, dead centre
Reitstock *m* footstock, tailstock
Reitstockkörner *m* tailstock centre
Reitstockoberteil *nt* tailstock barrel
Reitstockpinole *f* tailstock sleeve
Reitstockplanscheibe *f* tailstock faceplate
Reitstockspindel *f* footstock sleeve, tailstock spindle sleeve
Reitstockspitze *f* tailstock centre, tail centre
Reitstockunterteil *nt* tailstock base
Reitstockverstellung *f* tailstock setover, offsetting of the tailstock
reizerzeugendes Gas *nt* irritant gas
Reklamation *f* complaint
Reklamation *f* **bearbeiten** handle complaints, settle complaints, process complaints
Reklamationsabwicklung *f* handling of complaints
Reklamationsbearbeitung *f* complaints processing, settling of complaints
reklamieren query, make a complaint, complain about
Rekristallisation *f* recrystallization
Rekristallisationsgeschwindigkeit *f* rate of recrystallization
Rekristallisationsglühen *nt* recrystallization annealing
Rekristallisationsgrenze *f* limit of recrystallization
Rekristallisationstemperatur *f* temperature of recrystallization, recrystallization temperature
Rekristallisationstextur *f* recrystallization texture
rekristallisieren recrystallize
Relais *nt* relay
Relaiskasten *m* relay box
Relaiskontaktplan *m* relay ladder diagram
Relaisschalter *m* relay-actuated switch
Relaisschaltung *f* relay connection
Relaisschiene *f* relay rail
Relaisschrank *m* relay rack
Relaissystem *nt* relay control system
Relation *f* relation, relationship
relativ relative
relativ zu in relation to
Relativbewegung *f* relative motion (or movement)
Relativdrehung *f* relative rotation
relative Einschaltdauer *f* duty cycle factor
relative Häufigkeitssumme *f* cumulative relative frequency
relative Kerbschlagzähigkeit *f* relative notched impact strength
relative Luftfeuchtigkeit *f* relative humidity
relative Querschnittsänderung *f* percentage reduction of area
relative Spannungsrissbeständigkeit *f* relative resistance to environmental stress cracking
relative Standardabweichung *f* variation coefficient
relative Winkelgeschwindigkeit *f* normalized angular velocity, relative angular velocity
Relativmaß *nt* relative dimension
Relativmaßprogrammierung *f* relative dimension programming
Relaxationsmodul *m* relaxation modulus
Relaxationsspektrum *nt* relaxation spectrum
Relaxationsverhalten *nt* relaxation behaviour
Reluktanzmotor *m* reluctance motor
remanent remanent, retentive
remanente Induktion *f* residual magnetic flux density

Remanenz *f* remanence, retentivity
Remanenzflussdichte *f* residual induction
Remotedrucker *m* remote printer
Rentabilität *f* profitability, profitableness
Reparatur *f* repair, overhaul, reserving, repairwork
Reparaturarbeitsplatz *m* repair workstation
Reparaturarbeitsplatz-Rechner *m* repair workstation computer
Reparaturdauer *f* repair time
Reparaturmuffe *f* repair socket
reparieren recondition, repair, overhaul, salvage
Repetition *f* re-start, repetition
Reproduktion *f* replica, reproduction, repetition
Reproduktionsgenauigkeit *f* repetitive accuracy
Reproduktionsverfahren *nt* reproduction process
Reproduzierbarkeit *f* reproducibility, repeatability, capability of being duplicated
Reproduzierbarkeit *f* **der Ergebnisse** repeatability (or reproducibility) of the results
reproduzieren reproduce, repeat, duplicate, copy
Reserve *f* reserve, back-up
Reservebedarf *m* reserve demand
Reservefläche *f* reserve area
Reservepalette *f* reserve pallet
reservieren reserve
Reversierstetigförderer *m* reversing continuous conveyer
Reservierung *f* reservation
Reservierungsmenge *f* reservation quantity
Resistenz *f* resistance
Resistenzschicht *f* 1. *(allg.)* resist layer 2. *(entfernbare ~)* removable resist
Resonanzlängenverfahren *nt* length of natural frequency method
Resonanzschärfe *f* quality factor
Resonator *m* resonator, resonant cavity
Ressourcenmanagement management of resources

Rest *m* 1. *(allg.)* rest, remainder, residual, balance 2. *(Rückstand)* residue 3. *(Überschuss)* remain, residue
Restdehnung *f* residual strain
Restdruck *m* residual pressure
Restdurchlaufzeit *f* residue lead time
Resteindruck *m* residual indentation
Restfahrstrecke *f* remaining range, remaining travel
Restfestigkeit *f* residual strength
Restgaspartialdruck *m* residual gas partial pressure
Restgefahr *f* residual hazard
Restimpulsrate *f* residual pulse rate
Restkapazität *f* residual capacity
restlich residual, remaining
Restmenge *f* remaining quantity
Restquerschnitt *m* residual cross-section
Restrisiko *nt* residual risk
Restschwingungsamplitude *f* residual oscillation amplitude
Reststandzeit *f* residual tool (cutting) life
Reststreifen *nt* stripping
Reststrom *m* residual current
Reststück *nt* offcut
Reststückzuschlag *m* offcut factor
Resttragfähigkeit *f* residual load capacity
Restvarianz *f* residual variance
Restwelligkeit *f* remaining ripple, residual ripple
Restwertanzeige *f* residual value indication
Resultat *nt* result, outcome
resultieren result (in/from)
resultierend resultant
Resultierende *f* resultant
Retardationsprozess *m* retardation process
retardierter Ausgang *m* postponed output
Rettung *f* rescue
Rettungsweg *m* rescue passage, escape route
reversibel reversible, reversing
reversible Wärmedehnung *f* reversible thermal expansion
reversierbar reversible, reversing

reversierbare Bewegung *f* shuttle-type movement
reversierbarer Gurtbandförderer *m* shuttle belt conveyor
Reversierbetrieb *m* reversing mode
reversieren reverse, oscillate
Reversiermotor *m* reversing motor, reversible motor
Reversierverfahren *nt* reversion process
Reversierwalzgerüst *nt* reversing mill stand
Reversierwalzwerk *nt* reversing mill
Revision *f* inspection department, inspection
Revolver *m* *(Werkzeugmaschine)* turret
Revolverachse *f* turret spindle
Revolverautomat *m* automatic turret screw machine, turret automatic, automatic turret lathe
Revolverbank *f* hexagon turret lathe
Revolverbohrmaschine *f* vertical turret machine for boring, drilling, facing and tapping
Revolverdreharbeit *f* turret lathe work
Revolverdrehen *nt* turning-in turret lathe, turret turning
Revolverdrehmaschine *f* 1. *(allg.)* turret lathe, turret screw machine 2. *(selbsttätige ~)* automatic turret lathe 3. *(für Futterarbeiten)* chucking lathe (or machine)
Revolverdrehmaschine *f* **für Stangenarbeiten** turret lathe for bar work
Revolverdrehmaschine *f* **mit Querschlitten auf dem Bettschlitten** cross-sliding hexagon turret lathe, *(UK)* combination turret lathe
Revolverdrehmaschine *f* **mit Sattelrevolver** *(US)* ram type turret lathe, *(UK)* capstan lathe
Revolverkopf *m* turret head, turret
Revolverkopfschalten *m* turret indexing
Revolverkopfstellung *f* turret position
Revolverkopfsteuerung *f* turret control
Revolverkopierdrehmaschine *f* copying turret lathe
Revolverkopiermaschine *f* copying turret lathe
Revolverkurve *f* turret cam
Revolverschlitten *m* turret slide
Revolversegmenthebel *m* turret segment lever
Revolverspeicher *m* turret storage
Rezeptor *m* receptor
Rezeptur *f* recipe
RFZ-Regal *nt* crane racking
RGB (Regelbediengerät) *nt* SRM (storage and retrieval machine), S/R machine
rheologischer Zustand *m* rheological condition
rhythmisch unterschiedliche Krafteinwirkung *f* rhythmically varying force, rhythmical force variations
Rhythmus *m* rhythm, frequency, cycle
Richtanalyse *f* reference analysis
Richtcharakteristik *f* directional characteristic, directivity
richten (auf) adjust (to), aim (at), centre (on/at), direct (to/towards/at), point (at), level (at), align, planish, straighten, project
richtig correct, proper, true, right
richtiger Wert *m* conventional true value
Richtigkeit *f* correctness, exactness, accuracy, trueness
Richtlinien *fpl* guidance, guidelines, regulations, directives
Richtmittel *nt* laying-out tool
Richtung *f* direction, way, sense, hand
richtungs ... directional
richtungsabhängig directionally dependent, directional
richtungsabhängiger Vergleicher *m* directional comparator
Richtungsfeststeller *m* directional locking device
Richtungskonstante *f* slope
Richtungstaste *f* arrow key
Richtungstoleranz *f* orientation tolerance
Richtungsumkehr *f* inversion of the direction, reversal of the direction
richtungsunabhängig directionally independent
Richtwert *m* recommended value, ref-

erence value
Richtwirkung *f* directional efficiency
Richtwirkungsmaß *nt* directivity index
Riechrohr *nt* telltale pipe
Riefe *f* 1. *(allg.)* groove, nick, grain marks *pl*, wheel marks, channel, chute, flute, ridge 2. *(in Fügeflächen)* score mark, score
riefen groove, flute, channel, ridge
Riefenbildung *f* scoring
riefenfrei without tooling marks
riefenlos ridgeless
Riefenwinkel *m* drag angle
Riegel *m* 1. *(allg.)* bolt, latch, lock bar, locking, beam 2. *(Gebäude)* bar
Riegelbolzen *m* twist lock
Riemen *m* belt
Riemengetriebe *nt* belt gear
Riemenniet *m* flat countersunk head rivet
Riemenrad *nt* belt pulley
Riemenscheibe *f* belt pulley
Riemenspannrolle *f* idler pulley
Riemenvorgelege *nt* countershaft
Riemenzug *m* belt pull
Rieselentgasung *f* trickling deaerator
Riffellochung *f* corrugated perforation
riffeln riffle, serrate
Riffelscheibe *f* fluting roll
Rille *f* 1. *(allg.)* ridge, scratch, groove, nick 2. *(Schlitz)* slot
rillen groove
Rillenabstand *m* roughness width
rillenartige Vertiefung *f* groove-like depression
Rillendrehen *nt* grooving
Rillengrund *m* bottom of the groove
Rillenkugellager *nt* grooved ball bearing
Rillennute *f* groove
Rillenprofil *nt* groove profile
Rillenrichtung *f* groove direction
Rillenschar *f* groove complex, family of grooves
Rillenscheibe *f* pulley, disk wheel, sheave
Rillenschraube *f* screw with undercut
Rillenstrehler *m* groove chaser
Rillentiefe *f* scratch depth

Rillenverlauf *m* groove track
rillig undulatory
Rilligkeit *f* grooveness
Rundheitstoleranz *f* circularity tolerance
Ring *m* 1. *(allg.)* annulus, ferrule, ring 2. *(Dichtungen)* washer 3. *(el.)* coil
Ringanalyse *f* ring analysis
Ringanschnitt *m* ring gate
Ringbiegezugfestigkeit *f* ring bending tensile strength
Ringbund *m* coiled bundle, bundled coil
Ringfaltprobe *f* flattening test specimen
Ringfeder *f* annular spring
ringförmig annular, ring-shaped, toroidal
ringförmige Auskehlung *f* annular groove
Ringführung *f* ring guidance, ring guide
Ringmagnet *m* annular magnet
Ring-Maulschlüssel *m* ring spanner, combination wrench
Ringösenverfahren *nt* ring eye method
Ringplatte *f* annular plate
Ringprobe *f* ring test piece
Ringscheibe *f* annular ring
Ringspalt *m* annular clearance
Ringspule *f* toroidal coil, toroid
Ringstauchwiderstand *m* ring crush resistance
ringsum verlaufende Naht *f* circumferential joint
Ringverkehr *m* ring traffic, ring conveyance
Ringversuch *m* inter-laboratory test, robin test, cooperative test
Ring-Versuch *m* round-robin test
Ringwalzen *nt* ring rolling
Ringzugprobe *f* ring tensile test specimen
Ringzugversuch *m* ring tensile test
Rinne *f* channel, chute, groove, spout
Rippe *f* rib, web, fin (tube)
Rippe *f* **zum Versteifen** bracing rip
rippen fin
Rippenrohr *nt* gilled tube

Risiko *nt* risk
Risikoabschätzung *f* risk estimation
Risikobestand *m* safety stock
Risikobewertung *f* risk assessment
Risikoeinschätzung *f* risk estimation
Risikomanagement *nt* risk management
Risikoverringerung *f* risk reduction
riskieren risk, put at risk
Riss *m* **1.** *(allg.)* fracture, crack, fissure **2.** *(durch Zerreißen)* break, disruption rip, tear(ing) **3.** *(Sprung)* fissure **4.** *(Zeichnung)* sectional drawing
rissanfällig susceptible to cracking
Rissanfälligkeit *f* susceptibility to cracking
Rissbeginn *m* commencement of crack
Rissbildung *f* cracking, crack formation
Rissbildungsgrenze *f* crack initiation limit
rissempfindlicher Werkstoff *m* material prone to cracking
Rissfreiheit *f* freedom from cracks
Riss-Lehre *f* template based on drawings
Rissprüfung *f* test for cracks
Rissverlauf *m* crack configuration, run of the crack
Risswachstum *nt* crack growth
Ritzel *nt* pinion
Ritzel und Rad pinion and wheel
Ritzelantrieb *m* pinion drive
Ritzelbezugsprofil *nt* standard basic rack tooth profile of pinion
Ritzelflanke *f* pinion flank
Ritzelfuß *m* pinion root
Ritzelgrundkreis *m* pinion base circle
Ritzelkopfeckpunkt *m* pinion corner point
Ritzelkopfhöhe *f* pinion addendum
Ritzelkopfkreisdurchmesser *m* pinion tip diameter
Ritzelkopfnutzkreisdurchmesser *m* usable pinion tip diameter
Ritzelprofilverschiebungsfaktor *m* pinion addendum modification coefficient
Ritzelverzahnung *f* pinion tooth system
Ritzelwelle *f* pinion shaft

Ritzelzahn *m* pinion tooth
Ritzelzahnfuß *m* pinion tooth root
Ritzelzahnkopf *m* pinion tooth tip
Ritzelzahnkopfdicke *f* pinion tooth tip thickness
ritzen scratch, score
Ritzlinie *f* score
RMPD (Schnellmikroproduktentwicklung) Rapid Micro Product Development
Robertsscher Satz *m* Roberts' theorem
Roboter *m* robot, industrial robot
Roboterbedienung *f* robot operation
Robotereinsatz *m* robotics, use of robots
Roboterentnahme *f* withdrawal by robots
Robotersteuerung *f* robot control
Robotertechnik *f* robotics
Roboterwirkglied *nt* effector
Robotpalettenstretchwickler *m* robot pallet stretch wrapper
robust rugged, robust
Robustheit *f* ruggedness, robustness
roh 1. *(allg.)* rough, crude, underdressed, coarse **2.** *(unverarbeitet)* raw **3.** *(Werkstück)* blank
Rohblatt *nt* basic sheet
Roheisen *nt* pig iron
Roherzeugnis *nt* raw product
Rohgussmaß *nt* rough casting dimension
Rohkautschuk *m* raw (natural) rubber
Rohkautschukballen *m* raw rubber bale
Rohling *m* blank, work blank
Rohmaß *nt* rough dimension
Rohmaterial *nt* raw material
Rohmateriallager *nt* raw materials warehouse
Rohprodukt *nt* raw product
Rohproduktelager *nt* raw products inventory (RPI)
Rohr ... tubular
Rohr *nt* **1.** *(allg.)* conduit, duct **2.** *(Gussrohre)* pipe **3.** *(Stahlrohre)* tube
Rohr *nt* **mit angegossenen Flanschen** pipe with integrally cast flanges
Rohr *nt* **mit aufgeschraubten Flanschen** pipe with screwed-on flanges

Rohr *nt* **mit beidseitiger Steckmuffe** pipe with sliding socket at both ends
Rohr *nt* **mit einseitiger Steckmuffe** pipe with sliding joint at one end
Rohr *nt* **mit glatten Enden** pipe with smooth ends
Rohr *nt* **mit Schweißfase** pipe with welding bevel
Rohrabschnitt *m* tube segment
Rohranordnung *f* tube system, piping layout
Rohranschluss *m* pipe connection, pipe joint, pipe fitting, *(US)* hook-up (to)
Rohrauflager *nt* pipe support
Rohrauflagerung *f* pipe bedding
Rohrbefestigung *f* piping anchorage
Rohrbiegemaschine *f* pipe bending machine
Rohrbogen *m* pipe bend
Rohrbogen *m* **von 90°** quarter bend
Rohrbruch *m* pipe break, pipe failure, pipe fracture, pipe fracturing
Rohrbündel *nt* tube bundle
Röhrchenfeder *f* stencil pen
Röhre *f* tube, duct
Rohre *ntpl* tubing
Rohreinbau *m* pipe installation
Röhrenbrennfleck *m* focal spot of tube
Rohrendschnitt *m* cut made on pipe ends
Rohrendverschluss *m* pipe end closure cap
Röhrengehäuse *nt* tube casing (or housing)
Röhrenlibelle *f* cylindrical spirit level vial
Röhrenlot *nt* **mit Flussmittelseele** tubular solder with flux core
Röhrenschutzgehäuse *nt* tube shield casing, protective tube housing
Röhrenspannung *f* tube voltage
Röhrenstromstärke *f* tube current intensity
Rohrfläche *f* pipe surface
rohrförmig tubular
Rohrgeruchverschluss *m* pipe stench trap
Rohrgewinde *nt* pipe thread
Rohrgewinde *nt* **für nicht selbstdichtende Gewindeverbindungen** pipe thread for non-pressure tight screw joints
Rohrgleitlager *nt* sliding pipe support
Rohrgrabensohle *f* bottom of the pipe trench
Rohrheizkörper *m* tubular radiator
Rohrkragarm *m* tubular cantilever, tubular arm
Rohrkupplung *f* pressure union, pipe coupling
Rohrlängsnaht *f* longitudinal weld on a pipe
Rohrlegearbeit *f* pipe-laying operation
Rohrleitung *f* **1.** *(allg.)* conduit, pipeline, rigid line, tubing, tube pitch, mains, line **2.** *(erdbedeckte ~)* earth-covered pipeline **3.** *(frei verlegte ~)* unburied pipeline **4.** *(oberirdische ~)* surface pipeline **5.** *(tragfähige ~)* pipeline capable of bearing load
Rohrleitungen *fpl* **aus glasfaserverstärktem Kunststoff** pipeline of glass fibre reinforced plastics
Rohrleitungsabschnitt *m* pipeline section
Rohrleitungsanlage *f* pipeline system
Rohrleitungsanschluss *m* pipeline connection
Rohrleitungsaufhängung *f* pipe hanging
Rohrleitungsbau *m* pipeline construction
Rohrleitungsbauarbeit *f* pipe construction work
Rohrleitungsbauunternehmen *nt* pipe-laying contractors
Rohrleitungsplan *m* piping plan, *(US)* hook-up, pipe-work drawing
Rohrleitungsteil *nt* pipeline component, part of the pipeline, pipeline fitting
rohrlose Dränage/Dränung *f* open-ditch drainage
rohrloser Drän *m* open ditch
Rohrmuffe *f* connecting sleeve, pipe bell
Rohrnetzplan *m* pipe system diagram
Rohrrippe *f* gill
Rohrscheitel *m* crown of the pipe, pipe crest
Rohrschelle *f* pipe clamp

Rohrschelle *f* **für Wandbefestigungen** wall mounted pipe clip
Rohrschema *nt* pipework diagram
Rohrschlüssel *m* pipe wrench
Rohrsohle *f* pipe bottom
Rohrsonde *f* tubular probe
Rohrstapel *m* stack of pipes
Rohrsteifigkeit *f* stiffness of the pipe
Rohrstrecke *f* length of pipe, pipework
Rohrstreifenprobe *f* tube strip test specimen
Rohrstutzenmitte *f* spigot centre line
Rohrsystem *nt* system comprising piping components, piping system, pipework
Rohrteil *nt* piping components
Rohrteil *nt* **mit zylindrischem Gewinde** piping component with parallel thread
Rohrüberschneidung *f* pipe intersection
Rohrumhüllung *f* pipe coating (or covering)
Rohrverbindungsteil *nt* pipe jointing component
Rohrverformung *f* deformation of the pipe
Rohrverlegungsrichtlinien *fpl* pipe-laying rules
Rohrverschluss *m* pipe end plug
Rohrverschraubung *f* **mit Bunddichtung** pipe union with flat seat
Rohrverschraubung *f* **mit Kegeldichtung** pipe union with taper seat
Rohrverschraubung *f* **mit Klebung mit Flachdichtung** screwed pipe joint for bonding with flat sealing ring
Rohrverschraubungsabschluss *m* screwed pipe connection
Rohrwand *f* wall of pipe
Rohrzange *f* pipe wrench
Rohrziehen *nt* tube drawing
Rohstange *f* bar stock
Rohstoff *m* raw material, raw piece
Rohstoffrecycling *nt* raw material recycling
Rohteil *nt* unfinished part, blank
Rohteilauswahl *f* unfinished part selection
Rohteildicke *f* **1.** *(allg.)* unmachined part calliper **2.** *(Fließdrücken)* blank thickness
Rohteilformgebung *f* unfinished part design
Rohteillänge *f* unfinished part length
Rohteilsachnummer *f* unfinished part serial number
Rohteilzeichnung *f* blank component drawing, basic part drawing
Rollladenklappe *f* roller blind type flap valve
Rollbandschweißen *nt* band weld sealing
Rollbiegen *nt* curling
Röllchen *nt* skatewheel
Röllchenbahn *f* inclined track with skatewheels, skatewheel conveyor
Röllchenleiste *f* wheel channel
Röllchenschiene *f* wheel track
Röllchenteppich *m* skatewheel conveyor bed
Rolle *f* **1.** *(allg.)* roll, roller, caster, castor, coil **2.** *(ohne Hülse)* roll **3.** *(Träger mit Hülse)* reel **4.** *(Antrieb, Seilzug)* pulley
Rolle *f* **mit Pendelachse** twin-wheel castor with a pivoting axle
rollen roll, curl
Rollen *nt* **1.** *(allg.)* rolling **2.** *(Reckstauchen)* gathering
Rollenantrieb *m* roller drive
Rollenauslauf *m* roller discharge
Rollenbahn *f* **1.** *(allg.)* (gravity) roller conveyor, inclined track with rollers **2.** *(Einständerhobelmaschine)* auxiliary rolling table
Rollenbahn *f* **mit Reibantrieb** *m* friction-driven live roller conveyor
Rollenbahnspirale *f* spiral roller conveyor
Rollenbahnstrecke *f* gravity roller lane
Rolleneinschlagmaschine *f* roll wrapping machine
Rollenendschalter *m* roller limit switch, limit stop roller switch
Rollenförderer *m* roller conveyor
Rollengang *m* rolling mill table, roller conveyor
Rollengestell *nt* roller conveyor frame
Rollenhubwagen *m* roll lifting cart, transport cart

Rollenkette *f* roller chain, roller mechanical chain, roller type chain
Rollenkettenförderer *m* chain driven roller conveyor, roller chain conveyor, roller-flight conveyor
Rollenkippklammer *f* roll upender
Rollenklammer *f* roll clamp
Rollenkörper *m* rolling member
Rollenkranz *m* roller ring
Rollenkranzlagerung *f* roller ring bearing
Rollenkugellager *nt* cylindrical roller bearing
Rollenlager *nt* roller bearing
Rollenlagerung *f* electrode wheel bearing assembly
Rollenleiste *f* roller channel
Rollennahtschweißen *nt* roll seam welding
Rollennahtschweißung *f* seam weld
Rollenschälversuch *m* floating roller peel test
Rollenschelle *f* roller bracket
Rollenschiene *f* roller track, roller rail
Rollenspiel *nt* roller clearance
Rollenteilung *f* pitch of the rollers
Rollenteppich *m* roll bed, powered roll bed, roll bed conveyor
Rollentisch *m* roller table
Rollenumlaufführung *f* roller circulating guidance
Rollenverzahnung *f* roller toothed gear system
Rollenwagen *m* roll cart
Rollenzählwerk *nt* roller counter
Rollenzellenpumpenaggregat *nt* roller vane pumping set
Rollkraft *f* rolling force
Rollkreis *m* (bei Zykloiden) rolling circle
Rollkugel *f* trackball
Rollpalette *f* roll pallet
Rollprofileinrichtung *f* wheel crushing attachment, roller crushing attachment
Rollprofiliereinrichtung *f* wheel crushing attachment, roller crushing attachment
Rollreibung *f* roller friction, rolling friction, wheel friction
Rollringdichtung *f* O-ring gasket
Rollringgetriebe *nt* rolling ring drive, rolling ring mechanism
Rolltransformatorschweißen *nt* resistance welding using rotating transformer
Rollwiderstand *m* rolling resistance, rolling drag
Ronden *fpl* circular blanks, circles
Rondendurchmesser *m* circular blank diameter
Röntgenstrahl *m* X-ray
röntgen X-ray
Röntgenaufnahmegerät *nt* X-ray equipment for radiography
Röntgenbild *nt* X-ray image
Röntgendurchleuchtungsgerät *nt* X-ray fluoroscopic (or radioscopic) equipment
Röntgeneinrichtung *f* X-ray equipment
Röntgenfilmaufnahme *f* X-ray radiograph
Röntgenfluoreszenzstrahlung *f* fluorescent X-radiation
Röntgengenerator *m* **mit Netzangleich** X-ray generator with mains current correction
Röntgengerät *nt* X-ray equipment
Röntgenprüfung *f* X-ray examination (inspection)
Röntgenprüfverfahren *nt* X-ray test method
Röntgenraumbildungsgerät *nt* X-ray stereo equipment
Röntgenröhre *f* X-ray tube
Röntgenröhrenspannung *f* X-ray tube voltage
Röntgenröhrenstromstärke *f* X-ray current intensity
Röntgenschattenbild *nt* X-ray pattern
Röntgenschutzkanzel *f* mobile X-ray protective seat
Röntgenschutzkleidung *f* X-ray protective clothing
Röntgenserienaufnahme *f* series radiogram
röntgenstrahlenempfindlich X-ray sensitive (of pick-up tubes)
Röntgenstrahler *m* X-radiator
Röntgenstrahlung *f* X-radiation

Röntgentiefenlithographie *f* X-ray depth lithography
Röntgenverfahren *nt* X-ray technique
Rosshaarbürste *f* horsehair bristle
Rost *m* 1. *(allg.)* grid, grated flooring 2. *(durch Oxidation)* rust
rostbeständig stainless, rustless, rustproof, rust-resisting
Rostbildung *f* rust formation, rusting
rosten rust
Rostentfetter *m* rust remover
rostfrei stainless
rostgefährdet liable to rust
Rostgrad *m* rustiness
rostig rusty
Rostklopfhammer *m* rust removing impact hammer
Rostlöser *m* rust remover
Rostnarbe *f* corrosion pit
Rostschutz *m* rust prevention, rust-proofing
Rostschutzdauer *f* life of rust protection
Rostschutzmittel *nt* rust preventive
Rostschutzöl *nt* anti-corrosion oil
Rostschutzüberzug *m* rust-proofing coating
Rostschutzverfahren *nt* rust protection method
Rostschutzvorschriften *fpl* rust protection regulations *pl*
Rostsschutzgrundierung *f* rust-proof priming
Roststabilisator *m* rust stabilizer
Rostträgheit *f* resistance to rusting
Rostumwandler *m* rust converter
Rostumwandlungsverfahren *nt* rust conversion process
Rotation *f* rotation
Rotationsabnehmer *m* rotation picker
Rotationsabscheider *m* rotating separator
Rotationsachse *f* axis of rotation
Rotationsbewegung *f* rotational motion, rotary movement
Rotationsflexometer *nt* rotation flexometer
Rotationsformen *fpl* rotational moulding
Rotationsgeschwindigkeit *f* rotation speed
Rotationskammer *f* rotating chamber
Rotationskammerfüllmaschine *f* rotating chamber filling machine
Rotationsnachformfräsen *nt* rotational copy milling
rotationssymmetrisch rotationally symmetrical, axially symmetrical
Rotationsverdampfer *m* rotary evaporator
rotatorisch rotational
rotatorisch variabler Differenzial-Transformator *m* rotational variable differential transformer
Rotfärbung *f* reddish colouration
rotieren 1. *(allg.)* rotate, revolve, turn around 2. *(schnell, wirbeln)* spin
rotierend rotating, revolving, rotary
rotierende Klammer *f* rotating clamp
rotierende Läppscheibe *f* rotary lapping wheel
rotierende Schnittbewegung *f* rotary cutting motion
Rotlicht-LED *f* red light LED
Rotor *m* rotor, armature
Rotorfräswerk *nt* milling machine
rotorintegriertes Getriebe *nt* rotor-integrated gear
Rotornutenfräsmaschine *f* rotor slot milling machine
Routineprüfung *f* routine inspection
Rovinggewebe *nt* roving fabric
RPD (Schnellproduktentwicklung) Rapid Product Development, Rapid Prototyping
RS-Kippglied mit Zweizustandssteuerung *f* RS master-slave bistable element
RS-Kippglied *nt* RS bistable element
Ruck *m* 1. *(allg.)* hitch, jerk, jolt 2. *(Kabel, Seil)* surge
ruckartig jerky
Rückbiegen *nt* reverse bending
Rückbiegeversuch *m* rebend test
Rückdrehen *nt* reversing
Rückebene *f* back plane
Rücken-an-Rücken back-to-back
Rücken *m* back, spine
Rucken *nt* inching, jogging
rucken *vi* jerk, jiggle, move

ruckend jerking
Rückenkegel *m* back cone
Rückenkegelwinkel *m* back cone angle
Rückenloch *nt* single bolt hole
Rückenlochbefestigung *f* single bolt fixing
Rückenstütze *f* back rest
rückenverstrebt spine-braced
Rückenverstrebung *f* bay cross bracing, spine bracing
Rückenwinkel *m (e. Fräsmessers)* axial rake angle
Rückenwinkel *m (US)* end clearance angle, *(UK)* secondary front cutting edge clearance angle, clearance, angle of clearance, clearance angle, main clearance, land relief, relief, relief angle, back-off clearance
Rückfahrscheinwerfer *m* reversing light
Rückfahrt *f* return journey
Rückfederung return spring
Rückfederungswinkel *m* return spring angle
Rückflanke *f (e. Radzahnes)* non-working flank
Rückfluss *m* backflow, reflux, drain
Rückflussleitung *f* exhaust line, return line
Rückflussverhinderer *m* return flow inhibitor
ruckfrei smooth, without jolt(ing)
Rückfreiwinkel *m* back clearance angle
rückführen recycle
rückführen in den Umlauf recirculate
Rückführgröße *f* return variable
Rückführung *f* recirculation, return, feedback, recycling, returning
Rückgang *m* **1.** *(Funktion)* return stroke, backstroke **2.** *(Bewegung)* return motion, return traverse, return travel
rückgewinnen salvage
Rückgewinnungsgrad *m* reclamation index
Rückgut *nt* recycling material
Rückhalteseil *nt* stay rope
Rückhaltesicherung *f* operator restraining device, operator restraint system, restraint system

Rückholfeder *f* retraining spring, recuperating spring, recuperator, restoring spring
Rückholvorrichtung *f* return motion device
Rückhub *m* **1.** *(allg.)* return stroke, return travel, backstroke **2.** *(Stößel)* upstroke
Rückhubstörung *f* return-stroke interference
Rückkehr *f* **1.** *(Funktion)* final return motion, return **2.** *(Bewegung)* reverse motion
Rückkeilwinkel *m* back wedge angle
rückkoppeln couple, feed back
Rückkopplung *f* feedback, reaction
Rückkopplungsschleife *f* feedback loop
Rückkraft *f* thrust force
Rücklauf *m* **1.** *(allg.)* backward movement, non-cutting stroke, relieving stroke, reverse motion (or movement), reverse stroke, return stroke, retraction, back-run, reflux, return travel **2.** *(leerer ~)* idle return
Rücklaufanschluss *m* return connection
Rücklaufbegrenzung *f* return speed limitation
rücklaufen return, reverse, retract
Rücklaufgeschwindigkeit *f (Hobelmaschine)* return speed
Rücklaufmaterial *nt* return material, reclaimed material
Rücklaufspan *m* drawcut
Rücklaufsperre *f* return stop, back-run safety device
Rücklauftemperatur *f* return temperature
Rücklaufwasser *nt* return-circuit water
Rücklaufweg *m* return stroke
Rücklieferung *f* return
Rückmeldeentscheidung *f* feedback decision
rückmelden acknowledge, echo, give feedback
Rückmeldung *f* acknowledgement, acknowledgement message, echo, feedback
Rücknahme *f* **1.** *(allg.)* taking back,

cancelling **2.** *(Maschinenteile)* retraction **3.** *(Waren)* repurchase
Rückprall *m* rebound, bouncing, recoil
Rückprall-Elastizität *f* rebound resilience
Rückprallhöhe *f* height of rebound
Rucksacknaht *f* knapsack weld
Rückschaltdifferenz *f* switch back difference (pressure switch)
Rückschaltwerk *nt* intermediate feed mechanism
Rückschlag *m* **1.** *(allg.)* recoil, backfiring, flashback, reaction **2.** *(Lenkung)* kick-back, steering shock
Rückschlagarmatur *f* non-return valve
Rückschlagdurchgangsventil *nt* straight-way non-return valve
Rückschlageckventil *nt* angle non-return valve
rückschlagfreie Lenkung *f* non-reactive steering
Rückschlagfunktion *f* non-return function
Rückschlagklappe *f* swing check valve
Rückschlagsicherung *f* backlash eliminator
Rückschlagventil *nt* check valve, non-return valve
Rückschlagventil *nt* **bei Hydraulikantrieben** hydraulic lowering control valve
Rückseite *f* back(ing), rear side, reverse, heel
rückseitig rear, in the rear
rückseitiges Anfasen *nt* chamfering from the rear
rückseitiges Plandrehen *nt* backface
rücksetzbar *(von Kippgliedern)* resettable
Rücksetzeingang *m* reset input
rücksetzen reset
Rücksetzen *nt* reset, RES
Rücksetzzustand *m (bei Speichergliedern)* reset condition
Rückspanwinkel *m* back rake
Rückspiegel *m* reverse mirror, rear-view mirror
Rückspiegel *m* (äußerer ~) exterior rear-view mirror
Rückspiegelverstellung *f* rear-view mirror adjustment
Rücksprungflansch *m* female-faced flange
Rückstand *m* **1.** *(allg., im direkten Vergleich)* remainder, residual matter, residue **2.** *(Aufträge)* backlog
Rückstandsbildung *f* residue formation
rückstandsfrei residue-free
rückstandslos verbrennen burn without leaving any residue
rückstellen reset
Rückstellkraft *f* restoring force
Rückstellung *f* **1.** *(Bewegung)* return motion, return, reset device **2.** *(Bilanz)* (transfer to) reserve **3.** *(pneum., in Ausgangslage)* reset, adjustment **4.** *(QM)* replacement **5.** *(Reduzierung)* reduction, setback
Rückstellungsschalter *m* reset switch, readjustment switch
rückstrahlende Wärme *f* back-radiated heat
Ruckstromkanal *m* return channel
Rücktasteinrichtung *f* rear touch device
Rücktitration *f* back titration
Rücktransport *m* return transport
rückverfolgbar traceable
Rückverfolgbarkeit *f* traceability
rückverfolgen trace back
Rückverfolgung *f* tracing back
Rückverformungskurve *f* spring-back curve
Rückvergrößerung *f* re-enlargement
Rückvergrößerungsverfahren *nt* re-enlarging process
Ruckvorschub *m* intermitted feed
rückwägen reweighing
Rückwälzung *f* reverse roll motion, backward rolling motion, return rolling action
Rückwand *f* **1.** *(allg.)* back wall, rear wall **2.** *(Gehäuse)* back panel, rear panel
Rückwandbus *m* backplane bus
Rückwandecho *nt* back echo
Rückwandechofolge *f* back wall echo train
Rückwandplatine *f* backplane

rückwärtig back, backward, rear, reverse, at the rear
rückwärtiger Raststift *m (Teilscheibe)* back pin
rückwärtiges Ende *nt* rear end
rückwärts backward, reverse, aback
rückwärts fahren reverse, drive backwards
rückwärts hobeln shape on the return stroke, shape on the backstroke
rückwärts laufen lassen reverse
rückwärts neigen tilt backwards
Rückwärtsbewegung *f* return motion
Rückwärtsfahren *nt* backward drive, reverse direction
Rückwärtsfließpressen *nt* indirect impact extrusion
Rückwärtsgang *m* 1. reverse 2. *(in ~ schalten)* go into reverse
Rückwärtsneigung *f* backward tilt
Rückwärtsstrangpressen *nt* indirect extrusion of rods and tubes
Rückwärtsterminplanung *f* backward schedule
Rückwärtsverstellung *f* aft adjustment
Rückwärtszählen *nt* count down
Rückweg *m* 1. *(allg.)* return path, way back 2. *(Regeln)* backward path, backward channel 3. *(den ~ einschlagen)* head back
ruckweise jerky
ruckweise bewegen jerk
Rückweisung *f (e. Lieferung)* rejection
Rückwinkel *m (US)* back-rake angle, *(UK)* back rake
Rückwirkung *f* 1. *(allg.)* reaction 2. *(Getriebe, Bewegungen)* backlash
rückwirkungsfrei non-interacting
rückziehbar 1. *(entnehmbar, zurückziehbar)* withdrawable 2. *(von Schneidwerkzeugen)* retractable
Rückzugfeder *f* release spring
rückzündsicher immune from sustained backfire
Rückzündung *f* sustained backfire
Ruhe *f* quietness, silence, rest, dwell
Ruheenergie *f* rest energy
Ruhegleitreibung *f* static sliding friction
Ruhelage *f* position of rest, stopped position, rest position
ruhend stationary, at rest
ruhende Beanspruchung *f* steady stress, dead load
ruhende Luft *f* still air
ruhende Zugbeanspruchung *f* motionless (or constant) tensile stress
Ruhepause *f* rest
Ruhepotential *nt* open-circuit potential
Ruhereibung *f* static friction
Ruherollreibung *f* static rolling friction
Ruhespannung *f* rest potential
Ruhestellung *f* 1. *(allg.)* rest position, home position, neutral position, position of rest 2. *(Ausgangsstellung)* reset position
Ruhestrom *m* quiescent current
Ruhezone *f* rest zone
Ruhezustand *m* 1. *(allg.)* non-operated condition 2. *(e. Getriebes)* idle condition
ruhig quiet, silent, smooth
ruhiger Lauf *m* silent running
rühren agitate, stir
rund circular, cylindrical, spherical, round, rounded
Rundbiegen *nt* circular bending
Runddichtring *m* round sealing ring
Runddrehen *nt* cylindrical turning
Runddrehmeißel *m* round nose turning tool
runde Aufnahme *f* an quadratischem Räumwerkzeug round-pilot at a square broach
Rundeisen *nt* round bar
runden 1. *(e. Gewindegrund)* radius 2. *(math.)* round off
Runden *nt* circular form bending
runder Schraubenkopf *m* fillister head
rundes Werkstück *nt* circular work
Rundformmeißel *m* circular turning tool, circular forming tool
Rundformmeißelhalter *m* circular form toolpost
Rundfräsarbeit *f* circular milling operation
Rundfräseinrichtung *f* circular milling attachment, rotary milling attachment
Rundfräsen *nt* 1. *(allg.)* circular milling, rotary milling, rotary-table milling

2. *(Rundfräsverfahren)* circular (or rotary) milling operation, circular (or rotary) milling
Rundfräsmaschine *f* **1.** *(einfache ~)* plain milling machine **2.** *(Rundtischfräsmaschine)* rotary table miller (or milling machine)
Rundfräspindel *f* planetary milling quill
Rundfrästisch *m* circular milling table
Rundführung *f (Fräsmaschine)* clamp bed
Rundfunk *m* radio, wireless
Rundfunkwellensystem *nt* radio wave system
Rundgewinde *npl* **für Atemschutzgeräte** knuckle thread for breathing apparatus
Rundgewinde *nt (zur Kennzeichnung des Gewindeprofils)* round thread
Rundgewinde *nt* **als Fertigungsmittel** knuckle thread
Rundgewinde *nt* **für Teile aus Blech** knuckle thread for sheet metal components
Rundgewinde *nt* **mit flacher Flanke** round thread with flat flank
Rundgewinde *nt* **mit großer Tragtiefe** round thread with increased bearing depth
Rundgewinde *nt* **mit Spiel** round thread with clearance
Rundgewinde *nt* **mit steiler Flanke** round thread with steep flank
Rundgreifer *m* round grip arm
Rundheit *f* circularity, roundness
Rundheitsabweichung *f* concentricity deviation, deviation on roundness
Rundheitsprüfung *f* concentricity test
Rundhobelapparat *m* radial planing attachment, radius planing attachment, circular planing attachment, attachment for shaping cylindrical work
Rundhobeleinrichtung *f* radial planing attachment, radius planing attachment, circular planing (or motion) attachment, attachment for shaping cylindrical work
Rundhobeleinrichtung *f* **für konkave Flächen** radius planing attachment for machining external curves
Rundhobeln *nt* radial planing (operation)
Rundkneten *nt* rotary swaging (for reducing bars or tubes)
Rundkneten *nt* **im Vorschubverfahren** rotary swaging by the high-feed method
Rundkneten *nt* **von Einstechverfahren** rotary swaging by the infeed method
Rundkopfschraube *f* cheese-head screw
Rundkopiereinrichtung *f* circular copying attachment
Rundkopieren *nt* circular profiling, cylindrical contouring
Rundkopierfräsapparat *m* circular milling attachment
Rundkörper *m* round component
Rundläppen *nt* cylindrical lapping
Rundlauf *m* **1.** *(radialer ~)* concentricity, true running **2.** *(e. Tisches)* rotation
Rundlaufabweichung *f* concentricity variation
Rundlaufbohrmaschine *f* rotary piston drill
rundlaufen run true
rundlaufend circular, true
Rundlauffehler *m* concentricity error, error in concentricity, radial run-out, true-running error
Rundlauffräsen *nt* rotary-table milling, rotary milling
Rundlauffräsmaschine *f* **1.** *(allg.)* rotary milling machine, rotary miller **2.** *(Rundtischfräsmaschine)* rotary-table miller (or milling machine)
Rundlaufgenauigkeit *f* true-running accuracy, concentricity
Rundlaufsenkrechtfräsmaschine *f* **1.** *(allg.)* vertical spindle rotary-table miller **2.** *(Rundtischfräsautomat)* vertical-spindle rotary continuous miller, vertical continuous rotary miller **3.** *(Rundtischfräsmaschine)* vertical-spindle rotary-table miller (or milling machine), rotary-table miller with vertical spindle
Rundlauftoleranz *f* concentricity tolerance

Rundlauftolerierung *f* concentricity tolerancing
Rundloch *nt* round hole
Rundlochblech *nt* perforated plate with round holes
Rundlochperforation *f* round hole perforation
Rundmagnet *m* round magnet
Rundmaterial *nt* round stock, round bars, rounds
Rundmeißel *m* round boring tool, round-nose tool, radius tool
Rundnutenfräsen *nt* circular slot milling
Rundpassung *f* cylindrical fit
Rundräumen *nt* rotary broaching
Rundsäule *f* round column
Rundsäulenbohrmaschine *f* round column drilling machine, round column drill, round-column-type radial
Rundschaft *m* shaft
rundschaftbefestigt shaft-mounted
Rundschaltmaschine *f* rotary indexing machine
Rundschalttisch *m* indexing rotary table
Rundscherprobekörper *m* round-shaped shear specimen
Rundscheuerversuch *m* rotary abrasion test
Rundschleifarbeit *f* cylindrical grinding operation
Rundschleifen *nt* cylindrical grinding, plain grinding, cylindrical surface grinding
Rundschleifen *nt* **zwischen Spitzen** centre-type grinding
Rundschleifmaschine *f* centreless grinder, plain grinding machine, cylindrical (or plain) grinder
Rundschleifmaschine *f* **mit Messsteuerung** match-grinding machine
Rundschweißstab *m* round welding rod
Rundskala *f* 1. *(allg.)* graduated dial scale 2. *(e. Nonius)* dial division
Rundstab *m* 1. *(allg.)* round bar, round rod 2. *(nur Motoren)* round hole
Rundstabläufer *m* round (pole) rotor
Rundstahlbügel *m* *(für Rohrleitungen)* U-bolt pipe hanger
Rundstange *f* round bar, round rod
rundstangenförmig roll-shaped
rundstirnige Passfeder round-ended feather key
Rundstoßen *nt* circular slotting
Rundstrahlröhre *f* panoramic tube
Rundstrehler *m* circular chaser
Rundteilen *nt* circular spacing
Rundteilen *nt* **des Werkstücks** circular division of work
Rundtisch *m* 1. *(Bezug auf Arbeitsweise)* rotary table, rotating table, rotary worktable, circular revolving table 2. *(Bezug auf Formgebung)* circular table, round worktable, round table
Rundtisch *m* **mit Teileinrichtung** circular diving table, indexing rotary table
Rundtischflächenschleifmaschine *f* *(waagerechte)* horizontal-spindle rotary-table surface grinder
Rundtischfräsautomat *m* 1. *(allg.)* continuous rotary miller (or milling machine), rotary continuous miller 2. *(Rundlaufsenkrechtfräsmaschine)* vertical-spindle rotary continuous miller, vertical continuous rotary miller, vertical-spindle rotary-table miller
Rundtischfräsmaschine *f* 1. *(allg.)* rotary-table miller (or milling machine) 2. *(Rundtischfräsautomat)* vertical-spindle continuous rotary miller (or milling machine), vertical continuous rotary miller 3. *(Rundtischprofilfräsmaschine)* rotary profile miller (or milling machine) 4. *(Rundtischsenkrechtfräsmaschine)* vertical-spindle rotary-table miller
Rundtischkopierfräsmaschine *f* **mit Fühlersteuerung** tracer controlled profiler with rotary table
Rundtischkurven- und -profilfräsmaschine *f* rotary cam and profile milling machine
Rundtischkurvenfräsmaschine *f* rotary cam miller, rotary cam milling machine
Rundtischmaschine *f* rotary table machine
Rundtischprofilfräsmaschine *f* rotary profile miller, rotary profile milling ma-

chine, rotary-table milling machine, rotary-type miller, rotary milling machine
Rundtischschaltautomat *m* round table indexing automatic
Rundtrockner *m* round dryer
Rundumleuchte *f* rotating flasher, warning beacon
Rundumpressung *f* round laminated moulded section
Rundumsicht *f* allround visibility
Rundung *f (von Zahlen)* rounding (off)
Rundung *f* **am Zahnfuß** gullet
rundungsbedingte Erhöhung *f (von Kosten)* rounding increase brought about rounding
Rundungsradius *m* rounding radius
Rundungsregel *f* rounding rule
Rundungswert *m* rounding value
Rundversuch *m* co-operative test
Rundvibrator *m* rounding vibrator
Rundvorschub *m* circular feed, rotary feed
Rundwalzen round roll
Runge *f* **1.** *(allg.)* stake, upright **2.** *(Palette)* post of a pallet
Rungenpalette *f* post pallet, *(US)* stacking pallet
Rungenregal *nt* rack for vertical storage of sheet materials
Rungenteilung *f* separating bar
Rungenverbindung *f* rail
rußfrei free of soot
Rußzahl *f* smoke spot number
rüsten set up
Rüsterholungszeit prepare-recovering time
Rüstgrundzeit preparation time base
Rüstkosten *pl* preproduction cost, cost of change-over, set-up costs, start-up costs

Rüstverteilzeit preparation allowance time
Rüstvorgang *m* **1.** *(allg.)* change-over **2.** *(Arbeitsbeginn)* set-up, setting-up, start-up **3.** *(Arbeitsende)* shut-down, take-down **4.** *(gesamt)* set-up and shutdown
Rüstzeit *f* **1.** *(allg.)* set-up time, start-up time, setting-up time, setting time, tooling time, preparation time **2.** *(Arbeitsende)* shut down time **3.** *(gesamte Rüstzeit)* set-up and shut-down time
rutilbasischumhüllte Stabelektrode *f* rutile basic covered rod electrode
rutilsauerumhüllte Elektrode *f* rutile acid covered electrode
rutilumhüllte Elektrode *f* rutile covered electrode
rutilzelluloseumhüllte Elektrode *f* rutile cellulose covered electrode
Rutsche *f* chute, slide
rutschen glide, slide, slip, skid, float, chute
Rutschgefahr *f* slip hazard, danger of slipping
rutschgefährdetes Gelände *nt* terrain liable to slips
rutschhemmend anti-skid, non-slip, slip resistant
Rutschkupplung *f* friction clutch, slip clutch
Rutschmoment *nt* slipping moment
Rutschnabe *f* sliding hub
Rutschzeit *f* slip time
Rüttelgerät *nt* vibrator
rütteln vibrate, jar, jolt, rock, shake, jerk
Rüttelschiene *f* vibratory feeder, vibratory rail, vibratory in-line, vibratory track

S s

Säbel *m* strip sabre
Säbeln *nt* camber
Sachbuchhaltung *f* general bookkeeping department
sachgerecht 1. *(allg.)* correct, appropriate, proper 2. *(nicht ~)* incorrect
Sachkontenschnittstelle *f* inventory accounts interface
sachkundig skilled, expert, specialized, competent
Sachkundiger *m* specialist, expert
Sachlage *f* situation
sachlich essential
sachlicher Gesichtspunkt *m* objective criterion
Sachmerkmal *nt* article characteristic
Sachmittel *ntpl* physical resources, material and equipment
Sachmittelkosten *pl* material and equipment costs
Sachschutz *m* property protection
Sachverständiger *m* expert
Sack *m* bag, sack
Sackloch *nt* blind hole, bottom hole
Sackverschließmaschine *f* sack sealing machine
Sackzuführmaschine *f* sack presenting machine
Säge *f* saw
Sägeblatt *nt* saw blade
Sägegewinde *nt* buttress, saw-tooth thread
sägen saw
Sägengewinde *nt* buttress thread
Sägespäne *mpl* saw waste
Sägezahn *m* saw tooth
saisonal seasonal
salbenartig konsistent paste-like consistent
Saldenliste *f* balance ledger
Salzschmelze *f* fused salt bath
Salzsprühnebel *m* atomised salt spray
Sammelbehälter *m* reservoir
Sammelfehler *m* cumulative error, composite error
Sammelfehlerprüfung *f* composite error testing
Sammelheizung *f* collective heating system
Sammelhubwagen *m* order picker truck
Sammelleitung *f* main sewer
Sammellinse *f* field lens
Sammelmagnet *nt* collecting magnet
Sammelmeldung *f* group message
sammeln accumulate, assemble, collect, group
Sammeln *nt* *(Reckstauchen)* gathering
Sammelpack *nt* group package
Sammelpackbehälter *m* group container
Sammelpackbehälteraufrichtmaschine *f* group container erecting machine
Sammelpackbehälterbe- und -entlademaschine *f* group container loading and unloading machine
Sammelpackbehälterverschließmaschine *f* group container sealing machine
Sammelpackmaschine *f* group packaging machine, transit packaging machine
Sammelpackung *f* group package
Sammelprobe *f* bulk (or gross) sample, composite sample
Sammelprobenentnahme *f* bulk sampling
Sammelrohr *nt* header
Sammelstelle *f* accumulation point, collection point, merge point
Sammelzeichnung *f* collection drawing
Sammelzustandsanzeige *f* group status indication
Sand *m* sand
Sandanbackung *f* sand remains
Sandaufbereitung *f* sand dressing
Sandbunker *m* sand bunker
Sandeinschluss *m* sand inclusion
Sandguss *m* sand casting, sand founding

Sandkapselung *f* powder filling
Sandrieselverfahren *nt* sand trickling method
Sandscheibe *f* sand washer
sandstrahlen sand-blast
Sandteil *nt* sand particle
Sandverdichtung *f* compression of sand
sanft soft, smooth, gentle
Sanftanlauf *m* low-load start, soft start
sanieren refurbish, renew, improve
Sanierung *f* refurbishment, renewal
Sanitäranlage *f* sanitation facilities
Sankey-Diagramm *nt* Sankey diagram, energy flow diagram
Saphir *m* sapphire
Satellitenfahrwagen *m* satellite vehicle, trolley
Satellitensystem *nt* satellite system
satt aufliegen *(von Unterlegscheiben)* seat solidly
Sattdampfzylinderöl *nt* saturated steam cylinder oil
satte Auflage *f (e. Mutter)* full bearing
Sattel *m* saddle
Sattelfräsen *nt* saddle milling, gang milling, ganging
Sattelmoment *m* pull-up torque
Sattelrevolverdrehmaschine *f (US)* ram-type turret lathe, *(UK)* capstan lathe
Sattelrevolverdrehmaschine *f* **mit waagerecht angeordnetem Revolver** fixed-centre turret machine, sliding hexagon turret lathe
Sattelstück *nt* saddle fitting
sättigen saturate
Sättigung *f* saturation
Sättigungsphase *f* saturation stage
Sättigungspunkt *m* saturation point
Sättigungsverhalten *nt* saturation behaviour
Satz *m* set, batch
Satzendezeichen *nt* end of block character
Satzfräsen *nt* gang milling
Satzfräser *m* gang-cutter, gang-mill, gang milling cutter
Satzfreiheit *f* freedom from sediment
Satzlänge *f (variable ~)* variable block format

Satznummer *f* block number
Satzräderverzahnung *f* X-zero tooth system
Satzsuchen *nt* block/sequence search
Satzüberlesen *nt* block delete
Satzzeichnung *f* set drawing
Satzzykluszeit *f* block cycle time
sauber clean, tidy, neat
sauberer Schliff *m* clean cut
Sauberkeit *f* cleanliness, tidiness, neatness
Sauberkeitsschicht *f (in der Grabensohle)* granular sub-grade course
Sauerstoff *m* oxygen
Sauerstoffabsperrventil *nt* oxygen shut-off valve
Sauerstoffacetylenschweiß- und -schneidbrenner *m* oxy-acetylene welding and cutting blowpipe
Sauerstoffdruckalterung *f* oxygen pressure ageing
Sauerstoffdruckkammer *f* oxygen pressure chamber
Sauerstoffdruckminderer *m* oxygen pressure regulator
Sauerstoffdurchfluss *m* oxygen throughput
sauerumhüllte Elektrode *f* acid covered electrode
Saugball *m* suction bulb
Saugeinrichtung *f* suction device
saugen 1. *(allg.)* absorb, suck 2. *(Flüssigkeiten, Gase)* draw
Sauger *m* sucker
Saugfähigkeit *f* pulling power
Saugfilter *m* strainer, suction filter
Sauggreifer *m* sucking gripper
Saughöhe *f* capillary rise, suction lift
Saugkammer *f* suction port
Saugkopf *m* suction cup, vacuum cup
Saugkopfstrahlen *nt* suction-head blasting
Saugkorb *m* suction strainer
Saugluftspannfutter *nt* vacuum chuck
Saugrahmen *m* suction frame
Saugseite *f* suction side
Saugspülung *f* sucking douche
Saugvorstoß *m* suction adaptor
Saugwirkung *f* suction

Saugzugbrenner *m* induced draught burner
Saugzuggebläse *nt* induced draught fan, induced draft fan
Säule *f* column, round column mast
Säulenbohrmaschine *f* circular drilling machine, round column drill
Säulendepalletierer *m* column depalletizer
Säulenführungsschneidwerkzeug *nt* column piloting cutter
Säulengerät *nt* column instrument
Säulenpalettierer *m* column palletizer
Säulenplatte *f* dowel pin plate
Säulenstapelung *f* column stacking
Säulenstreckenlast *f* distributed load of the mast
Säure *f* acid
Säureechtheit *f* fastness to acid spotting
Säurespuren *fpl* acid traces
säureunlöslich acid insoluble
Scanfrequenz *f* scan frequency
Scanlinie *f* scan line
scannen scan
Scanner *m* scanner
Scannersystem *nt* scanner system
Scanverfahren *nt* scan process, scan method
Schabefestigkeit *f* resistance to abrasion
schaben shave, scrape
Schabennut *f* self-clearing groove
Schaber *m* scraper, scraping tool
Schabeschnitt *m* shaving cut
Schabeverfahren *nt* shaving method
Schabewerkzeug *nt* shaving tool
Schabfräser *m* shaving tool
Schablone *f* stencil, templet, template, master plate, pattern, former
Schablonenformhobeln *nt* form planing
Schablonenfräsmaschine *f* profile milling machine, profiler
Schablonenhobelmaschine *f* form planing machine
Schablonenhobeln planing by generating template planes
Schablonenschwenkeinrichtung *f* template swivelling device
Schablonenträger *m* template carrier
Schablonenverfahren *nt* form-copy planing
Schabrad *nt* rotary shave cutter
Schacht *m* shaft
Schachtautomat *m* shaft dispensing system
Schachtel *f* box, carton, case
Schachtelkörper *m* carton body, body part
Schachtelmodell *nt* hierarchical classification
schachteln nest
Schachtelung *f* nesting
Schachtelungstiefe *f* nesting depth
Schachtelzuschnitt *m* carton blank
Schachtfutter *nt* shaft lining
Schachtkommissionierer *m* shaft commissioning system, shaft order compilation system
Schachtofen *m* pit furnace
Schachtsystem *nt* shaft system
Schachtunterteil *nt* manhole bottom section
schaden damage, harm
Schaden *m* 1. *(allg.)* damage 2. *(Nachteil)* disadvantage
Schadenersatz *m* recovery of damages, indemnity
Schadenlokalisierung *f* fault localization
Schadensanalyse *f* failure analysis
Schadensart *f* failure mode
Schadensbaum *m* fault tree
Schadensersatzanspruch *m* claim for indemnity
Schadensfall *m* (case of) loss, event of loss, event of damage
schadensicher restricted breathing
schadhaft damaged, defective, faulty
schädigende Wirkung *f* damaging effect, harmful effect
schädigendes Ereignis *nt* event causing damage
Schädigungsarbeit *f* damaging energy
Schädigungskraft *f* damaging force
Schädigungsmerkmal *nt* criterion of damage
Schädigungspunkt *m* damage level

Schädigungsverformung *f* damaging deformation
schädlich injurious, harmful
schädliche Bestandteile *mpl* harmful constituents
Schädlichkeit *f* harmfulness
Schadstoff *m* harmful substance, pollutant, toxic
Schadstoffatmosphäre *f* pollutant atmosphere
Schaft *m* 1. *(allg.)* shaft 2. *(e. Werkzeuges)* shank 3. *(e. Schraube)* body 4. *(e. Ritzels, Kegelrades)* stem
Schaftfräsen *nt* end milling
Schaftfräser *m* 1. *(allg.)* end mill cutter, shank cutter, solid-type end mill, end mill, end millers, shank-type milling cutter 2. *(für T-Nuten)* T-slot cutter 3. *(mit kegeligem Schaft)* taper shank end mill 4. *(mit Kugelstirn)* spherical end mill 5. *(mit runder Stirn)* ball-end mill, ball-nose end mill 6. *(mit Spiralverzahnung)* spiral end mill 7. *(mit ungerader Nutenzahl)* odd-fluted end mill 8. *(mit Zylinderschaft)* straight-shank end mill
Schaftkegel *m* taper shank
Schaftmeißel *m* shank-type cutting tool
Schaftmeißelhalter *m* shank tool holder
Schaftquerschnitt *m* shank cross-section
Schaftschneidrad *nt* shank type gear shaper cutter
Schäkel *m* clevis
Schäldiagramm *nt* peel diagram
Schale *f* 1. *(Gefäß)* tray 2. *(Hülle)* shell 3. *(Napf)* cup, bowl 4. *(Waagschale, Pfanne)* pan 5. *(Trog)* trough
Schälen *nt* pre-turning, skin-turning
schälender Schnitt *m* slabbing cut
Schalenfuß *m* *(e. Werkzeugmaschine)* pan base
Schalenkupplung *f* compression coupling, clamp coupling
Schälfräsen *nt* slab milling
Schälfräser *m* slab milling cutter
Schälfräsmaschine *f* slab milling machine
Schlagbiegebeanspruchung *f* impact bending load

Schall *m* 1. *(allg.)* sound 2. *(störend, Lärm)* noise
schallabsorbierend sound-absorbing
Schallabstrahlung *f* sound radiation
Schallausbreitung *f* sound propagation
Schalldämmmaßnahme *f* sound insulation measure
Schalldämmung *f* sound attenuation
Schalldämpfung *f* sound-damping
schalldicht sound-proof
Schalldiffusor *m* sound diffuser
Schalldissipation *f* sound dissipation
Schalldruckamplitude *f* sound pressure amplitude
Schalldruckpegel *m* sound pressure level
Schalldruckpegelmessung *f* sound pressure level measurement
Schalldruckspektrum *nt* sound pressure spectrum
Schalldruckspitze *f* sound pressure peak
Schalleinfallsrichtung *f* direction of sound incidence
Schallenergie *f* sound energy
Schallfeld *nt* sound field
Schallfrequenz *f* sound frequency
schallfreier Raum *m* sound-free region
Schallkernimpedanz *f* characteristic acoustic impedance
Schallleistung *f* sound power
Schallleistungspegel *m* sound power level
Schallleistungsspektrum *nt* sound power spectrum
Schallminderung *f* silencing
Schallpegel *m* sound level, noise level
Schallpegelmesser *m* sound level meter
Schallplatteneffekt *m* record effect
Schallquelle *f* noise source
Schallschluckstoff *m* sound absorbing medium
Schallschluckstrecke *f* sound-absorbing section
Schallschutz *m* sound proofing
Schallsendeimpuls *m* transmitted sound pulse
Schallspektrum *nt* noise spectrum
Schallstreuung *f* sound dispersion

Schallunsicherheit *f* contact uncertainty
Schallwellenlänge *f* wavelength of the sound
Schallwellenwiderstand *m* characteristic impedance
Schälrad *nt* skiving wheel
Schälradfreiwinkel *m* clearance angle of the circular skiving cutter
Schälschnitt *m* **1.** *(auf Span bezogen)* curling cut **2.** *(drehen)* skin turning cut **3.** *(fräsen)* slabbing cut
Schaltalgebra *f* switching algebra, circuit algebra
Schaltanlage *f* switching installation
schaltbar 1. *(allg.)* switchable **2.** *(Kupplung)* engaging and disengaging
schaltbare Kupplung *f* engaging and disengaging clutch, loose coupling
schaltbare und formschlüssige Kupplung *f* mechanical clutch
Schaltbefehl *m* on/off command, alter statement
Schaltbetrieb *m* switched mode
Schaltbetriebsdruck *m* operating pressure of the pneumatic switch
Schaltbewegung *f* switching movement, feed motion
Schaltbrett *nt* switchboard
Schaltdifferenz *f* switch difference
Schaltdruck *m* switching pressure
Schalteingang *m* gate input
Schaltelement *nt* logic element, circuitry element, gate, circuit
Schaltelemente *ntpl* controls *pl*
schalten 1. *(Drehzahlen)* change **2.** *(el.)* switch **3.** *(Flurförderung)* change gears, shift gear **4.** *(Getriebe)* shift **5.** *(Hebel)* shift, move, manipulate, operate **6.** *(Maschine)* operate, start, engage, control
Schalter *m* switch, selector, switching device, contactor, connector, interruptor, control lever
Schalterstellung *f* switch position
Schaltfahne *f* actuating tag
Schaltfeld *nt* control panel
Schaltfläche *f* button
Schaltfolge *f* switching sequence
Schaltfunktion *f* on/off command, AND/OR operation
Schaltgabel *f* selector fork
Schaltgabelreibmoment *nt* selector fork friction moment
Schaltgenauigkeit *f* switching accuracy
Schaltgerät *nt* switchgear
Schalthäufigkeit *f* cycle frequency, shift frequency, number of switching actuations, operating frequency, switching frequency
Schalthebel *m* control lever, switch lever, operating lever
Schalthysterese *f* switching hysteresis
Schaltimpuls *m* switching pulse
Schaltinformation *f* switching information
Schaltkasten *m* switchgear box, control panel
Schaltkasten *m* **mit Schnellverstellung für die Supportbewegung** feed box with rapid traverse motor for traversing the railhead
Schaltkette *f* switching chain
Schaltklinke *f* catch, pawl, jumper, ratchet
Schaltkraft *f* shifting force
Schaltkreis *m* control circuit
Schaltkupplung *f* clutch
Schaltleiste *f* connecting block
Schaltmatte *f* safety shutdown mat, sensor mat
Schaltnetzteil *nt* switched mode power supply
Schaltnocke *f* control cam, switching cam
Schaltorgan *nt* control element, control member
Schaltplan *m* circuit diagram, wiring diagram
Schaltpult *nt* control console, control desk, control station
Schaltpunkt *m* switching point
Schaltrad *nt* feed ratchet wheel
Schaltradwälzfräser *m* index gear hob
Schaltraum *m* switch room
Schaltschlüssel *m* key-operated switch
Schaltschnecke *f* control worm
Schaltschrank *m* control board, control cubicle, control cabinet, switch cabinet,

switch cupboard, switchgear cabinet, electronic control box
Schaltschritt *m* switching step
Schaltsignal *nt* switching signal
Schaltsignalausgabe *f* switching signal output
Schaltstange *f* gear lever
Schaltstelle *f* control point
Schaltsteuerung *f* control mechanism
Schaltstift *m* trip dog
Schaltstrom *m* current on contact
Schaltstück *nt* switch piece
Schaltstufe *f* switch stage
Schaltsystem *nt* switching system (or circuitry)
Schalttafel *f* (control) panel, switch panel, control station, switchboard
Schalttisch *m* indexing table
Schalttischautomat *m* indexing table automatic
Schalttischfräsen *nt* index milling
Schalttischfräsmaschine *f* index milling machine
Schalttor *nt* switching gate
Schaltüberdruck *m* switching overpressure
Schaltung *f* 1. *(e. Getriebe)* control 2. *(e. Hebels)* manipulation 3. *(e. Kupplung, Maschine)* engagement 4. *(e. Motors)* starting, cycle 5. *(e. Schlittenbewegung)* tripping 6. *(el.)* circuit, control element, switching, layout, wiring 7. *(von Hand)* hand control 8. *(kombinatorische ~)* combinatory switching 9. *(selbsttätige ~)* automatic control
Schaltvorgang *m* switching actuation, switching operation, switching process
Schaltvorrichtung *f* control device
Schaltwarte *f* control room
Schaltwerk *nt* indexing mechanism, control gear
Schaltzahl *f* number of cycles, operation number
Schaltzeichen *nt* graphical symbol
Schaltzeit *f* control time
Schaltzeiten bestimmen time
Schälversuch *m* peel test
Schälwiderstand *m* resistance to peeling (or stripping), peel resistance

scharf 1. *(allg. scharfkantig)* sharp, keen, sharp-edged **2.** *(abgegrenzt)* crisp, determined **3.** *(opt.)* clean, clear, distinct
Schärfe *f* **1.** *(allg.)* sharpness, power **2.** *(e. Werkzeuges)* sharpness **3.** *(opt.)* focus
scharfe Kontrolle *f* strict control
scharfe Menge *f* crisp set
Scharfeinstellung *f* focusing
schärfen scarf, sharpen, regrind
Schärfen *nt* *(von Werkzeugen)* sharpening
Schärfentiefe *f* depth of focus
scharfkantig sharp-edged
scharfkantig biegen give a sharp bend
scharfkantige Öffnung *f* sharp-edged orifice
scharfkantige Schneide *f* sharp-cornered cutting edge (or tool nose)
Scharfkantigkeit *f* edge sharpness
Scharfschleifen *nt* sharpening
Scharnier *nt* hinge, turning pair, turning joint
Scharnierstift *m* hinged pin
Scharparameter *m* family parameter
schartig ragged
schartige Scheibenkante *f* ragged wheel edge
Schatten *m* shade
Schattenwirkung *f* shade effect
Schätzbereich *m* estimation interval, confidence interval
schätzen estimate, rate
Schätzfähigkeit *f* ability to estimate
Schätzfehler *m* estimation error
Schätzfunktion *f* estimate, estimator
Schätzung *f* estimation, estimate
Schätzungenauigkeit *f* accuracy of estimating
Schätzungsintervall *m* estimation interval
Schätzvermögen *nt* estimating ability
Schätzwert *m* value of a statistic, estimate value
Schaubild *nt* graph, diagram
Schaufel *f* blade
schaufeln shovel, scoop
Schauloch *nt* window
Schaum *m* foam

schäumen foam
Schaumglas *nt* cellular glass
Schaumgummi *m* cellular rubber
Schaumkunststoff *m* cellular plastics, foam plastics
Schaumkunststoffschicht *f* foam plastics layer
Schäumprüfung *f* foaming test
Schaumstoff *m* cellular plastics, cellular material
Schaumstoffgefüge *nt* cellular plastics (or foam) structure
Schaumstoffprobe *f* cellular test specimen
Schäumungseigenschaft *f* foaming characteristic
Schäumvermögen *nt* foaming power
Scheckenfüllmaschine *f* auger filling machine
Scheibe *f* **1.** *(allg. techn. Bauteil) (UK)* disk, *(US)* disc, plate, **2.** *(Fenster)* pane, glass, window aperture **3.** *(Radkörper)* web **4.** *(Riemenscheibe)* pulley **5.** *(Schleifscheibe)* wheel **6.** *(Unterlegscheibe)* washer **7.** *(Wählscheibe)* dial
Scheibe *f* **aus Sichtblech** washer of laminated shim material
Scheibe *f* **für HV-Verbindungen** washer for high strength friction grip fastenings
Scheibe *f* **für Kombi-Blechschrauben** washer for tapping screw assemblies
Scheibe *f* **für Neigungsausgleich** self-aligning washer
Scheibenabrichter *m* wheel dresser
Scheibenbreite *f* width of wheel face
Scheibenbremse *f* disk brace
Scheibenebenheit *f* disc flatness
Scheibenfeder *f* **1.** *(Keil)* Woodruff key **2.** *(Spannscheibe)* curved washer
Scheibenfräsen *nt* side milling
Scheibenfräser *m* side mill, side milling cutter, side and face milling cutter, straddle mill, disc miller
Scheibenfräser *m* **mit einseitiger Verzahnung** half-side milling cutter
Scheibenkurve *f* disc cam, plate cam
Scheibenleistung *f* cutting wheel efficiency

Scheibenrad *nt* (centre) web disk wheel, solid wheel
Scheibenrevolver *m* disc turret
Scheibenschneidrad *nt* disc-type shaper cutter
Scheibenstirnfläche *f* wheel face
Scheibenverschleiß *m* disc wear
Scheibenwalzen *nt* type rolling, rolling circular shapes
Scheibenwischer *m* windscreen wiper
Scheiberegister *nt* shift register
scheiden sort, part, part off
Scheinleistung *f* apparent power
Scheinleistungsaufnahme *f* apparent power input
Scheinwiderstand *m* impedance
Scheitel *m* apex
Scheiteldruckkraft *f* crushing load
Scheitellinie *f* crown line
Scheitelpunkt *m* apex
Scheitelüberdeckung *f* depth of cover material over the crown of the pipe
Scheitelwertabweichung *f* peak value deviation
Scheitelzulauf *m* *(als Formstück)* top branch
Schellack *m* shellac
Schellackkleber *m* shellac adhesive
Schelle *f* bracket, clip, clamp
Schelle *f* **in Schlaufenform** loop type clamp (or clip)
schematische Darstellung *f* diagrammatic representation
Schemazeichnung *f* schematic drawing
Schenkel *m* **1.** *(allg.)* arm, leg, side, angle, beam, stock, flap **2.** *(Rahmen)* yoke ear
Schenkellänge *f* leg length
Schenkelweite *f* **1.** *(Gabeln)* fork width **2.** *(Rahmen)* ear width
Schenkelweiterreißversuch *m* flap tear propagation
Scherbeanspruchung *f* shear load (or loading)
scherbeständig scour-proof
Scherbruch *m* shear failure
Schere *f* **1.** *(allg.)* shear, brace, overarm braces, (pair of) scissors **2.** *(Maschinen)* shear, shearing machine, shears

Scherebene *f* shear plane
scheren clip, shear, cut
scherender Schnitt *m* shear cut
Scherengabelhubwagen *m* scissor lift pallet truck
Scherengreifer *m* scissor grab, scissor gripper
Scherenhebebühne *f* scissor lift
Scherenhub *m* scissor lifting
Scherenhubtisch *m* articulated lifting platform
Scherenkonstruktion *f* scissor design
Scherenpfanne *f* shear pan
Scherenreach *m* shear reach
Scherfestigkeit *f* shear strength
Scherfläche *f (e. Gewindeganges)* shearing area
Schergeschwindigkeit *f* shear speed
Scherkraft *f* shear plane tangential force, shearing force
Schermeißel *m* shear tool
Schernormalkraft *f* shear plane perpendicular force
Scherprobe *f* shear specimen
Scherquerschnitt *m* shear cross-section
Scherscheibenviskosimeter *nt* shearing disc viscosimeter
Scherschneiden *nt* shear-action cutting, shearing
Scherschneidenwerkzeug *nt* shear-action cutting tool
Scherspan *m* continuous chip, shear chip
Scherspanablauf *m* flow of shear chips
Scherstabilität *f* shear stability
Scherstelle *f* shearing point
Scherung *f (auf ~ beanspruchen)* load in shear
Scherviskosität *f* shear viscosity
Schervorgang *m* shear process
Scherwelle *f* shear wave
Scherwinkel *m* shear plane angle, shear angle
Scherwinkelbeziehung *f* shear plane angle relationship
Scherwinkelverhältnis *nt* shear plane angle proportion
Scherzone *f* shear zone
Scherzugkraft *f* tensile shearing load

Scherzugkraftabfall *m* reduction in the tensile shearing load
Scherzugversuch *m* tensile shear test
Scheuerfestigkeit *f* abrasion resistance
scheuern chafe, gall
Scheuerprüfung *f* abrasion test
Schicht *f* **1.** *(allg.)* film, lamina, lamination, layer, coat(ing) **2.** *(Arbeit)* shift **3.** *(dielektrische ~)* dielectric layer **4.** *(einfache ~)* single layer **5.** *(gebundene ~)* bundled layer **6.** *(gekreuzte ~)* interlocked layer **7.** *(überlappende ~)* overlapping layer
Schichtanordnung *f* layer layout, layer pattern
Schichtaufnahmegerät *nt* tomographic equipment
Schichtbetrieb *m* shift operation
Schichtdicke *f* thickness of layer
Schichtebene *f* plane of lamination
Schichtenbildungstisch *m* layer preparation table
Schichtfestigkeit *f* layer strength
schichtförmige Korrosion *f* layer-wise corrosion
Schichtführer *m* shift leader
Schichtleiter *m* shift supervisor
Schichtplan *m* shift schedule
Schichtpressstoff *m* laminate, laminated plastics
Schichtpressstofferzeugnis *nt* laminated plastics product
Schichtpressstofftafel *f* laminated plastics panel
Schichtstoff *m* laminate, laminated plastics
Schichtstoffverbund *m* laminate
Schichtung *f* layering
schichtweise aufgebaut built up in layers
Schiebeanker *m* displacement type armature
Schiebeeingang *m* shift input, shifting input, shift
Schiebeeinrichtung *f* pushing device, pushing mechanism
Schiebekeil *m* feather key
schieben push, slide, shift, thrust
schiebende Drahtförderung *f* wire fed forward by a pushing action

Schieber *m* **1.** *(Bauteil)* face slide, head slide, valve, gate valve, slider, toolholder, tool head slide (support), translating part **2.** *(e. Messschiebers)* sliding member, slider **3.** *(e. Parallelreißers)* sliding clamp
Schieber *m* **mit stetigem Stellverhalten** gate valve with progressive adjustment characteristic
Schieberad *nt* shifting gear, sliding gear
Schieberadgetriebe *nt* sliding gear drive
Schieberanschlussstück *nt* valve collar
Schieberraste *f* slide lock
Schieberspindel *f* gate valve stem
Schiebertrieb *m* follower drive
Schieberwerkzeug *nt* **mit Backentrennfläche** slide mould with split parting line
Schiebestutzen *m* sliding type fitting
Schiebetisch *m* sliding table
Schiebevorgang *m* shift operation, pushing
Schiebezahnräder *ntpl* sliding gears *pl*
Schieblehre *f* slide calliper rule
Schiebung *f* translation, translational motion
Schiebungsbruch *m* shear fracture
Schiedsfall *m* arbitration case
Schiedsprobe *f* arbitration test specimen
Schiedsversuch *m* arbitration test
schief bevelled, tilted, inclined, sloping, (a)skew, aslope, oblique
Schiefe *f* skewness
Schiefstellung *f* inclination (from the vertical), deflection
Schiene *f* **1.** *(allg.)* rail, railway track, beam **2.** *(Leiste)* bar
Schienendurchbiegung *f* rail deflection, rail deformation
Schienenfuß *m* rail foot, rail base, lower flange of rail
schienengebunden railborne, rail-dependent, rail-mounted, restricted to the rails
schienengebundener Kran *m* track-bound crane
schienengeführt rail-guided, rail-mounted
Schienenhängebahn *f* overhead track conveyor
Schienenklammer *f* **1.** *(allg.)* safety claw **2.** *(Nagel)* rail spike
Schienenklemme *f* rail anchor, rail anchoring device, rail clamp
Schienenkopf *m* head of the rail, rail head
Schienenkopfbreite *f* rail had width
Schienenräumer *m* rail guard, rail sweep, sweeper, *(US)* fender, cow-catcher
Schienenstoß *m* rail joint
Schienenstrang *m* (rail) track, trackage
Schienenvergussmasse *f* rail joint sealing compound
Schienenweiche *f* **1.** *(allg.)* shunt, switch, points **2.** *(obere Schiene)* rail junction
Schießen *nt* shooting, firing
Schiffsrohrleitungsbau *m* piping system in shipbuilding
Schild *nt* **1.** *(allg.)* sign **2.** *(Etikett)* label **3.** *(Schutz)* shield
Schilderpfahl *m* *(an Rohrgräben)* signpost
Schimmelwachstum *nt* mould growth
Schirm *m* **1.** *(el.)* sheath, shielding **2.** *(Projektion, Schutz)* screen
Schirmbildaufnahmegerät *nt* miniature photofluorographic equipment
Schirmbildkamera *f* photofluorographic camera
Schirmdämpfung *f* shielding effectiveness
Schirmdämpfungsfaktor *m* shielding effectiveness
Schlacke *f* slag
Schlackenaustrag *m* de-clinkering facility
Schlackeneinschluss *m* slag inclusion
Schlackenschutz *m* slag protection
Schlackenschütze *m* slag marksman
Schlackensieb *nt* slag strainer, slag sieve
Schlackenstrahlmittel *nt* slag basting
schlaff loose, slack
schlaffarmierter Stahlbeton *m* reinforced concrete with untensioned re-

inforcement
Schlaffheit *f* looseness, slackness
Schlaffkette *f* slack chain
Schlaffkettenschalter *m* clack chain protection, clack chain switch
Schlaffkettensicherung *f* slack chain detection device
Schlaffseil *nt* slack rope, slack wire rope
Schlaffseilschalter *m* slack rope protection, slack rope switch
Schlaffseilsicherung *f* slack (wire) rope detection device
Schlag *m* **1.** *(allg. mechan.)* blow, impact, stroke, percussion, chatter, runout **2.** *(el.)* electric shock
Schlagart *f* lay
schlagartig impulsive, jerky
schlagartige Beanspruchung *f (von Bauteilen)* impact loading (of components)
schlagartige Zündung *f* spontaneous ignition
Schlagberührung *f* contact to impact
Schlagbeständigkeit *f* resistance to impact
Schlagbiegeversuch *m* impact flexural test, impact bending test
Schlagbiegeversuch *m* **nach Charpy** Charpy impact flexural test
Schlagbohren *nt* percussion drilling
Schlagebene *f* plane of impact
Schlageinrichtung *f* hammer arrangement
Schlagempfindlichkeit *f* impact sensitivity
schlagen 1. *(allg.)* beat, blow, strike, hit **2.** *(Seil)* lay
schlagfest impact resistant
Schlagfestigkeit *f* impact strength
Schlagfräsen *nt* fly-cutting
Schlagfräser *m* fly cutter
Schlagfräser *m* **mit eingesetztem Meißel** inserted tooth fly mill
Schlagfräserdorn *m* fly-cutter arbor
Schlagkolbengerät *nt (zum Entrosten)* impact piston device
Schlaglänge *f* length of lay
Schlagloch *nt* pothole, *(US)* pitch-hole
Schlagmaulschlüssel *m* open-ended slugging spanner (or wrench)

Schlagprüfgerät *nt* impact testing apparatus
Schlagprüfung *f* impact test, impact withstand test
Schlagringschlüssel *m* slugging ring spanner, slugging box wrench
Schlagschraubendreher *m* hand impact screw driver
Schlagverhalten *nt* impact behaviour
Schlagversuch *m* tensile impact test
schlagzäh impact strength
schlagzäh modifiziert *(von Kunststoffen für Rohre und Formstücke)* modified to impact strength
Schlagzahn *m* fly cutter
Schlagzahnfräsarbeit *f* fly-cutting operation
Schlagzahnfräsen *nt* fly-cutting
Schlagzugfestigkeit *f* tensile impact strength
Schlagzugverhalten *nt* tensile impact behaviour
Schlagzugversuch *m* tensile impact test
Schlagzugzähigkeit *f* tensile impact strength
schlämmen *(Betonrohre)* give a slurry type seal coating
Schlammgehalt *m* sludge content
Schlammuntersuchung *f* examination of sludge
Schlangeneinlauf *m* snake shrinkage
Schlangenpaternoster *nt* vertical carousel in serpentine form
schlank slender
schlanker Kegel *m* slender taper, long taper
Schlankheit *f* slenderness
Schlankheitsgrad *m* slenderness ratio
Schlauch *m* hose, pressure flexible hose, tube
Schlauchanschluss *m* joint
Schlaucharmatur *f* pipe assembly
Schlauchbruch *m* hose bursting, hose failure
Schlauchkupplung *f* joint
Schlaucholive *f* tube clip
Schlauchprobe *f* wormhole
schlecht bad, poor
schlecht gespannt poorly clamped

schleichen creep, crawl
Schleichfahrt *f* creep speed (travel)
Schleichfahrzeit *f* creep speed running time
Schleichgang *m* creep speed, creep feed
Schleierschwärzung *f* fog density
Schleifahle *f* honing tool (fixtured)
Schleifband *nt* earthing strap, abrasive belt
Schleifbeanspruchung *f* abrasion stress
Schleifbezugspunkt *m* grinding principal point
Schleifbock *m* wheelhead
Schleifbürste *f* contact brush
Schleifdruck *m* grinding pressure, wheel pressure
Schleife *f* loop
Schleifeingriffswinkel *m* grinding pressure angle
schleifen 1. *(allg.)* drag, grind, sharpen 2. *(abschleifen)* grind, abrade 3. *(ziehen)* drag, trail, slide 4. *(~ auf)* rub along 5. *(ins Volle)* center grind 6. *(spitzenlos ~)* grind centreless
Schleifer *m* grinding machine operator
Schleiffläche *f* 1. *(Arbeitsfläche e. Schleifwerkzeuges)* grinding face 2. *(bearbeitete Fläche am Werkstück)* ground surface 3. *(e. Schleifscheibe)* wheel face
Schleifgang *m* pass
Schleifgrat *m* burr, feather-edge
Schleifkontakt *m* sliding contact
Schleifkontaktfläche *f* grinding contact surface
Schleifkontaktschweißen *nt* resistance welding using sliding contacts
Schleifkopf *m* wheelhead
Schleifkorn *nt* abrasive (or cutting) grain, grinding abrasive, abrasive grit
Schleifkörper *m* abrasive body, abrasive member, abrasive stick, honing stick, abrasive wheel
Schleifkörperabmessung *f* abrasive body dimension
Schleifkörperbetriebsgemisch *nt* abrasive body operation mixture
Schleifkörpereinzelgewicht *nt* one abrasive body weight
Schleifkörperform *f* abrasive body shape
Schleifkörperschutzhaube *f* protective cowl on grinders
Schleifkörperüberlauf *m* abrasive body overrunning
Schleifkörperverschleiß *m* abrasive body wear
Schleifkraft *f* grinding force
Schleifkurve *f* grinding cam
Schleifleistung *f* grinding efficiency, grinding performance
Schleifleitung *f* contact line, collector line
Schleifmarke *f* grit mark
Schleifmaschine *f* grinding machine, *(US)* grinder
Schleifmaschine *f* **zum Schleifen planer Flächen** face grinder *(UK)*
Schleifmaterial *nt* abrasive
Schleifmittel *nt* abrasives, cutting agent
Schleifmittelart *f* cutting agent type
Schleifmittelkörnung *f* cutting agent grain
Schleiföl *nt* cutting oil
Schleifpulver *nt* abrasive powder
Schleifring *m* ring wheel
Schleifringläufer *m* slip ring rotor
Schleifringläufermotor *m* slip ring motor
Schleifriss *m* grinding crack, grinding checks *pl*
Schleifrisse *mpl* check marks, checking marks
Schleifroboter *m* grinding robot
Schleifscheibe *f* 1. *(allg.)* grinding wheel 2. *(einprofilige)* single-rib wheel 3. *(keramisch gebundene)* vertified wheel 4. *(mehrprofilige)* multi-rib wheel
Schleifscheibeabrichtdiamant *m* grinding wheel dressing diamond
Schleifscheibenabrichter *m* grinding wheel dresser
Schleifscheibenbindung *f* wheel bond
Schleifscheibenbreite *f* grinding wheel width, width of wheel face
Schleifscheibendrehzahl *f* grinding

wheel rotational frequency
Schleifscheibendurchmesser *m* grinding wheel diameter
Schleifscheibeneingriffswinkel *m* wheel pressure angle
Schleifscheibenfläche *f* grinding wheel surface
Schleifscheibenhärte *f* wheel grade
Schleifscheibenprofil *nt* grinding wheel profile, contour of wheel face
Schleifscheibenradius *m* grinding wheel radius
Schleifscheibenumfangsgeschwindigkeit *f* grinding wheel peripheral speed
Schleifscheibenverschleißvolumen *nt* volumetric grinding wheel wear, volume of wheel grain wear
Schleifschiebenumfangslänge *f* peripheral length of grinding wheel
Schleifschlitten *m* wheel slide, wheelhead slide
Schleifsegment *nt* wheel segment
Schleifspäne *mpl* swarf
Schleifspindel *f* wheel spindle
Schleifspuren *fpl* grinding (or wheel) marks
Schleifstaub *m* abrasive grit, abrasive dust
Schleifstein *m* grindstore
Schleifstellung *f* grinding position
Schleifstoff *m* *(verbrauchter)* grit
Schleifsupport *m* grinding head
Schleiftisch *m* grinding table
Schleifverhältnis G *nt* grinding relation
Schleifvorrichtung *f* grinding attachment
Schleifwerkzeug *nt* grinding cutter (or tool), abrasive tool
Schleifwinkel *m* grinding arc
Schleifwirkung *f* abrasive effect
Schleifzeit *f* grinding time
Schleifzugabe *f* grinding allowance
Schleifzüge *mpl* feed lines, wavy traverse lines
schleppen tow, drag, haul, trail
Schlepper *m* tow tractor, towing tractor, tractor
Schleppförderer *m* drag chain conveyor
Schleppkabel *nt* trailing cable
Schleppkabelzug *m* pull of trailing cable
Schleppkabelzustromführung *f* trailing cable supply
Schleppkette *f* drag chain
Schleppkettenförderer *m* drag (chain) conveyor, chain-pulled conveyor
Schlepptisch *m* drag table
Schleppzeigergerät *nt* drag-indicator tester
Schleuderdrehzahl *f* overspeed
Schleudergießen *nt* sling casting
Schleudergießverfahren *nt* sling casting process
Schleuderguss *m* sling casting
schleudern 1. *(allg.)* throw, catapult, sling, spin **2.** *(Fahrzeug)* skid
Schleuderradprinzip *nt* centrifugal wheel principle
Schleuderstrahlen *nt* *(Entrostung)* centrifugal blasting
Schleuse *f* lock
schleusen pass through, lock
Schlichtarbeit *f* finish-machining operation
Schlichtbearbeitbarkeit *f* finish-machinability
schlichtdrehen finish-turn
Schlichte *f* facing material, slur, wash moulding
schlichten 1. *(allg.)* finish-machine, finish **2.** *(fräsen)* finish-mill **3.** *(drehen)* finish-turn **4.** *(e. Aussenkung mit einstellbarem Hohlfräser)* finish-trepan
Schlichterodieren *nt* finish eroding
Schlichteteilchen *nt* finishing particle
schlichtfräsen finish-mill
Schlichtfräser *m* **1.** *(allg.)* finishing cutter **2.** *(Wälzfräser)* finishing hob
Schlichtfrässpindel *f* finishing-milling spindle
Schlichthobelmeißel *m* end-cutting finishing tool
Schlichthobeln *nt* finish-planing
Schlichtmeißel *m* **1.** *(allg.)* finishing tool (or cutter) **2.** *(gekröpfter ~) (US)* goose-necked finishing tool, *(UK)* swan-necked finishing tool, swan-necked finisher

Schlichtmesser *nt* finish cutting blade
schlichträumen finish broach
Schlichträumwerkzeug *nt* finishing broach
Schlichtschleifen *nt* finsih grinding
Schlichtschliff *m* finish grind
Schlichtschneideinsatz *m* **aus Hartmetall zum Aufstecken auf Räumwerkzeug-Tragkörper** solid-carbide finishing shell
Schlichtschnitt *m* finishing cut
Schlichtstahl *m* finishing tool (or cutter)
Schlickergießen *nt* slip casting
Schlieren *fpl* cords
Schließbewegung *f* closing motion
Schließeinheit *f* closing unit
schließen 1. *(allg.)* close **2.** *(Leitung)* cut off **3.** *(Programm)* close down
Schließen *nt* **der Enden hohler Werkstücke im Gesenk** closing (ends of hollow items) in dies
Schließer *m* **1.** *(el.)* make contact **2.** *(Vorrichtung)* closer
Schließerwechsel *m* make-make-break contact
Schließkommando *nt* closure demand
Schließkraft *f* closing force, forward force
Schließmaß *nt* closing dimension
Schließring *m* **1.** *(allg.)* self-locking collar **2.** *(für Neigungsausgleich)* self-aligning (self-locking) collar **3.** *(mit Gewinde für Passbolzen)* threaded self-locking collar
Schließsignal *nt* closure signal
Schließtoleranz *f* closing tolerance
Schließzeit *f* forward time
Schließzeiteinstellung *f* closing time adjustment
Schliff *m* **1.** *(allg.)* grinding cut, grind **2.** *(Oberflächenzustand)* surface condition **3.** *(Schleifarbeit)* grinding operation **4.** *(Schleiffläche)* grinding face
Schliffbild *nt* ground surface pattern
Schliffflasche *f* ground flask
Schliffgenauigkeit *f* grinding accuracy
Schliffgüte *f* grinding finish
Schliffhülse *f* ground socket

Schliffkern *m* ground stopper
Schliffprobe *f* polished specimen
Schliffthermometer *nt* ground thermometer
Schlitten *m* **1.** *(allg.)* *(US)* slide, *(UK)* ram, carriage, saddle **2.** *(mit Kugelführung)* ball slide **3.** *(mit Rollenführung)* roller slide
Schlittenführung *f* carriage guideways, carriage slideways, ramways, saddle slideways
Schlittenhub *m* ram stroke
Schlittenklemmung *f* saddle clamp, saddle clamping
Schlittenrevolver *m* saddle-type turret
Schlittenrevolverdrehmaschine *f* *(mit aufgebautem, in Längsrichtung verschiebbarem Revolverkopf)* *(UK)* combination turret lathe, *(US)* saddle-type turret lathe
Schlittenschieber *m* **1.** *(allg.)* slide, slide rest, tool slide **2.** *(Kurvenhobeln)* slide member
Schlittenweg *m* traverse of the slide
Schlitz *m* slot, groove, nick
Schlitzbolzen *m* slotted bolt
Schlitzdruckprüfung *f* slotted disc water pressure test
Schlitzdüse *f* slot type nozzle
Schlitzeinrichtung *f* slotting device
schlitzen 1. *(allg.)* slot, slot-mill, split **2.** *(aussparen)* recess **3.** *(Nuten)* groove **4.** *(Schraubenköpfe)* slot
Schlitzen *nt* **von Kronenmuttern** castellating
Schlitzfräsarbeit *f* slot milling operation
Schlitzfräsen *nt* slot milling, slot milling gashing
Schlitzfräser *m* **1.** *(allg.)* splitting cutter **2.** *(für Keilnuten)* keyway cutter **3.** *(für Schrauben)* slotting saw
Schlitzgrund *m* base of slot
Schlitzhohlleiter *m* slotted microwave guide
Schlitzmutterndreher *m* slotted screw driver
Schlitzstopfen *m* slotted screwed sealing plug
Schloss *nt* split unit, half-nuts

Schlossfalle f lock latch
Schlosskasten m apron housing, apron
Schlosskasten m **für Revolverkopf** apron for saddle-type turret
Schlosskastengehäuse nt (UK) apron box, apron housing
Schlosskastengetriebe nt feedbox
Schlossmutter f split nut, half-nut, leadscrew nut
Schlossplatte f apron wall, apron front, apron housing, lathe apron
Schluckvolumen nt (e. Druckschalters) swallowing capacity
Schlummerbetrieb m dozing mode, slumber mode
Schlupf m slip, slippage, slipping, slack
schlupffrei non-slip
Schlupfverlust m slip loss, loss due to slippage
Schlupfwiderstand m slipping resistance
Schlüssel m 1. (für Schloss) key 2. (für Schraubenköpfe) spanner, wrench
Schlüsselabhängigkeit f key dependence
Schlüsselabhängigkeitssystem nt key dependence system
Schlüsselfläche f spanner flat
Schlüsselfräser m wrench cutter
Schlüsselführung f (bei Zylindernschrauben mit Innensechskant) pilot recess
Schlüsselloch nt keyhole
schlüsselloses Futter nt wrenchless check
Schlüsselmaß nt spanner size
Schlüsselprozess m key process
Schlüsselsatz m 1. (allg.) set of keys 2. (für Schraubenwerkzeuge) set of spanners (or wrenches)
Schlüsselschalter m key-operated switch, key switch
Schlüsseltransfersystem nt key interlocking device
Schlüsselweite f wrench opening width across fits
Schlussglühen nt last stage of annealing
schlussverzinkt finally galvanized
schlussverzinkter Draht m wire galvanized after drawing
schlussverzinnter Draht m wire tinned after drawing
schmal narrow
Schmalbandspektralanalyse f narrow band spectral analysis
Schmalgang m narrow aisle
Schmalgangstapler m narrow aisle truck
schmalzartige Masse f greasy mass
Schmelzauftragschweißen nt fusion built-up welding
Schmelzbadverhalten nt behaviour of the molten pool
Schmelzbetrieb m smelting factory
Schmelze f melt, molten material, fused material
schmelzen melt, fuse, smelt, liquefy
Schmelzerei f smelting facility
Schmelzfluss m pool of molten metal
schmelzgeschweißte Punktnaht f fusion-welded spaced spot weld
Schmelzgießen nt melt casting
Schmelzindex m melt flow index
Schmelzintervall nt melting interval
Schmelzkammerkessel m slag tap fired boiler
Schmelzkante f fusion edge, top edge
Schmelzklebstoff m thermal fusion adhesive
Schmelzkörper m ceramic pyrometer
Schmelzlegierung f fusible alloy
Schmelzlöten nt fusion soldering
Schmelzofen m smelter, melting furnace
Schmelzofenbeschickung f smelter charging
Schmelzperlenkette f train of fused beads
Schmelzpunkt m melting point
Schmelzschneiden nt melt cutting
Schmelzschweißen nt fusion welding
Schmelzschweißen nt **mit magnetisch bewegten Lichtbogen** arc welding using a magnetically moved arc
Schmelzschweißverschließmaschine f fusion sealing machine
Schmelzsicherung f melting fuse
Schmelztauchüberzug m hot dip coating

Schmelztauchverfahren *nt* hot dip method
Schmelztauchverzinnung *f* hot dip tinning
Schmelztemperatur *f* melting temperature
Schmelztiegel *m* melting crucible, melting basin
Schmelzung *f* melting, smelting, fusion
Schmelzverbindungsschweißen *nt* fusion joint welding
Schmelzverlust *m* melting loss
Schmelzwärme *f* melting heat, heat of fusion
Schmelzzone *f* melting zone, zone of fusion
Schmiedebetrieb *m* forging plant, forge, forging shop
Schmiedegesenk *nt* forging die, drop forging die
schmieden forge
Schmieden *nt* **im Gesenk** die forging, drop forging
Schmiedestück *nt* forging
Schmiedestückzeichnung *f* forging drawing
Schmiedewalzen *nt* forge rolling
Schmiedezeit *f* post-weld time
Schmiegungsebene *f* osculating plane
Schmierbüchse *f* oil cup
schmieren lubricate, oil, grease
Schmierfett *nt* grease
Schmierfettkneter *m* grease-worker
Schmierflüssigkeit *f* lubrication fluid
Schmiergerät *nt* lubricating equipment
Schmiermittel *nt* lubricant
Schmiermittelrückführung *f* lubricant return
Schmiernippel *m* lubricating nipple, greasing nipple
Schmiernut *f* oil groove
Schmieröl *nt* lubricating oil, lubrication oil
Schmierölvorlauf *m* first-run lubrication oil
Schmierstelle *f* lubricating point, oiling point
Schmierstoff *m* lubricant
Schmierstoffaufbereitung *f* lubricant reconditioning
Schmierstoffbehälter *m* lubricant reservoir
Schmierstoffe *mpl* lubricants
Schmierstofffüllstelle *f* lubricant filter point
Schmierstoffrückstände *mpl* lubricant residues
Schmierstoffsollbedarf *m* theoretical lubricant demand
Schmierstoffstrom *m* stream of lubricant
Schmierstoffverteiler *m* lubricant metering device
Schmierstoffvolumen *nt* volume of lubricant
Schmiertakt *m* lubrication cycle
Schmiertaktzähler *m* lubricating cycle counter
Schmiertaktzeit *f* lubrication cycle time
Schmiertechnik *f* lubrication engineering
Schmierung *f* lubricating, lubrication, greasing
Schmirgel *m* emery
Schmirgelbogen *m* sheet of emery paper
Schmirgelkorn *nt* abrasive grain
Schmirgeln *nt* sanding
Schmitt-Trigger *m* threshold detector, Schmitt trigger
Schmorkontakt *m* fusing contact
Schmorstelle *f* arcing spot
Schmutz *m* dirt
schmutzig dirty
schmutzintensiv extremely dirty
Schmutznute *fpl* dirt groove
schnappen catch
Schnapper *m* latch
Schnappriegel *m* support leg, locking bar
Schnappriegel-/Schaltradanlage *f* pivoting support peg system
Schnappriegelanlage *f* support peg system
Schnecke *f* auger, worm, (endless) screw
Schneckendrehzahl *f* worm rotational speed
Schneckenfräsautomat *m* automatic

worm hobbing machine
Schneckenfräsen *nt* worm milling, worm cutting
Schneckenfräsmaschine *f* worm miller, worm milling machine, worm cutting machine
Schneckenfräsvorrichtung *f* worm milling attachment
Schneckengetriebe *nt* worm gear, worm gear pair (or drive)
Schneckengewindefräsen *nt* worm thread milling
Schneckengewindefräsmaschine *f* worm thread milling machine
Schneckenrad *nt* worm gear, worm wheel
Schneckenräderwälzfräsmaschine *f* worm wheel generating machine
Schneckenradfräsen *nt* worm gear (or wheel) cutting, worm wheel hobbing
Schneckenradfräser *m* 1. *(allg.)* worm gear milling cutter 2. *(Wälzfräsen)* worm gear hob, worm wheel hob
Schneckenradsatz *m* worm gear set, worm gear pair
Schneckenradschaftfräser *m* shank-type worm gear (or wheel) hob
Schneckenradschlichtfräser *m* worm gear (or wheel) finishing hob
Schneckenradwälzfräser *m* worm-wheel hob
Schneckenschraubrad *nt* crossed helical worm gear
Schneckentriebe worm gears
Schneckenwälzfräsmaschine *f* worm hobbing machine
Schneckenwelle *f* worm shaft
Schneidarbeit *f* cutting action, cutting operation
Schneidbacke *f* die, cutting die
Schneidbearbeitbarkeit *f* cutting machinability
Schneidbewegung *f* cutting motion
Schneidbohrer *m* tap
Schneidbohrung *f* cutting orifice
Schneidbreite *f* cutting width
schneidbrennen flame-cut
Schneidbrenner *m* cutting torch, flame cutter
Schneiddiamant *m* cutting diamond

Schneiddüsenbohrung *f* cutting nozzle part
Schneide *f* 1. *(allg.)* edge, bit, lip, cutting edge, striking edge 2. *(Blatt-, Draht-, Band-, Scheibe)* cutting edge (leaf, wire, band, disc) 3. *(mit Rechtsdrall)* right-hand helical cutting edge 4. *(mit Linksdrall)* left-hand helical cutting edge 5. *(aktive ~)* active cutting edge 6. *(unterbrochene ~)* interrupted cutting edge
Schneidebene *f* cutting plane
Schneidegrat *m* flash
Schneideinsatz *m* 1. *(allg.)* insert 2. *(für das Räumwerkzeug)* broach insert
Schneideisen *nt* threading die, die
Schneiden *nt* 1. *(allg.)* blanking, trimming, cutting 2. *(Halbzeug)* cropping 3. *(Scherschneiden)* shearing 4. *(aus dem Vollen)* cutting from the solid 5. *(gegen elastische Kissen)* shearing against elastic pad 6. *(in einem Durchgang)* one-pass cutting 7. *(funkenerosives ~)* spark erode cutting 8. (*Abschneiden)* cutting off 9. *(Scheren)* shearing 10. *(Kreuzung, math. Schnittpunkt)* intersection
Schneidenansatz *m* built-up cutting edge
Schneidenanzeiger *m* knife edge type pointer
Schneidenaufbau *m* building up of the (cutting) edge
Schneidenausbildung *f* shape of cutting edge
Schneidenausbruch *m* chipping of the cutting edge, edge chipping
Schneidenbelastung *f* tool thrust
Schneidenbezugpunkt *m* cutting edge principal point
Schneidenebene *f* plane of cutting edge, cutting edge plane
Schneidenecke *f* corner, tool nose, tool point
Schneideneingriff *m* point of cutting action, tool engagement point of cutting action
Schneideneinsatz *m* **für das Räumwerkzeug** surface broach bar
Schneidenende *nt* end of cutting

Schneidengeometrie *f* cutting tool geometry, cutting edge geometry
Schneidenhalter *m (Räumwerkzeug)* holder
Schneidenkopf *m* tool point
Schneidennormalebene *f* tool edge normal plane
Schneidenprofil *nt* cutting edge profile
Schneidenpunkt *m* cutting point
Schneidenradiuskorrektur *f* tool nose compensation
Schneidenrücken *m (Kante zwischen Fase und Zahnrücken)* heel of the tooth
Schneidenspitze *f* tool point
Schneidenteil *m* cutting section
Schneidenteil *m* **des Räumwerkzeuges** broach cutting section, active portion of a broach
Schneidenträger *m* cutting edge support
Schneidenwinkel *m (US)* side-cutting edge angle, *(UK)* face angle, plan angle, cutting edge angle, true cutting angle
Schneidenzähne *mpl (Räumwerkzeug)* cutting teeth
Schneideschablone *f* cutting template
Schneidfähigkeit *f* cutting property (or quality or capacity), *(US)* cuttability
Schneidfläche *f* cutting face
Schneidflüssigkeit *f* cutting fluid
Schneidhaltigkeit *f* ability to maintain cutting power (or to retrain cutting edge), edge-holding property (or quality), cutting ability, cuttability
Schneidkante *f* cutting edge
Schneidkantenfase *f* straight land
Schneidkantengestaltung *f* cutting edge design
Schneidkantenrundung cutting edge roundness
Schneidkantenversatz *m* cutting edge misalignment
Schneidkantenversetzung *f* offset of the cutting edges
Schneidkeil *m* cutting wedge, wedge
Schneidkeramik *f* cutting ceramics
Schneidkluppe *f* hand die stock, stock and die
Schneidkopf *m* die hand
Schneidkraft *f* cutting force

Schneidlegierung *f* alloy for cutting tools
Schneidleistung *f* cut performance
Schneidlippe *f* cutting edge
Schneidmeißel *nt* cutting tool
Schneidmetall *nt* cutting alloy
Schneidmühle *f* rotary cutter
Schneidplättchen *nt* carbide tip
Schneidplatte *f* insert, tool bit, cutting tip, cutting tool tip, cutting insert, (carbide) tip
Schneidrad *nt* gear cutting tool, gear shaping cutter, shaper cutter, pinion type cutter
Schneidradabhebung *f* pinion cutter lift
Schneidradfeld *nt* pinion cutter zone
Schneidradflanke *f* pinion cutter flank
Schneidradprofilverschiebung *f* pinion cutter addendum modification
Schneidradprofilverschiebungsfaktor *m* pinion cutter addendum modification coefficient
Schneidradzähnezahl *f* number of teeth of the pinion type cutter
Schneidradzahnfuß *m* pinion cutter tooth root
Schneidrate *f* cutting instalment
Schneidrichtung *f* hand of cut
Schneidring *m* olive, cutting ring
Schneidrücken *m* land
Schneidschraube *f* thread cutting screw
Schneidspalt *m* cutting gap, blade clearance
Schneidspäne *mpl* chips, cuttings
Schneidspitze *f* abrasive cutting point
Schneidstahl *m* cutting tool
Schneidstempel *m* punch
Schneidstoff *m* cutting material
Schneidstoffarten *fpl* types of cutting material
Schneidstoffauswahl *f* cutting material selection
Schneidstoffe *mpl* cutting materials
Schneidstoffzusammensetzung *f* cutting material composition
Schneidteil *nt* cutting part
Schneidverfahren *nt* cutting process, cutting method

Schneidvorgang *m* cutting process
Schneidweg *m* cutting distance
Schneidwerkstoff *m* cutting medium, tool material
Schneidwerkzeug *nt* cutter, cutting tool
Schneidwerkzeugplättchen *nt* cutting tool tip
Schneidwinkel *m* cutting angle
Schneidzahn *m* cutting tooth
schnell fast, high-speed, quick, rapid, speedy
Schnellarbeitsstahl *m* high-speed steel
Schnellläufer *m* fast-moving item
Schnellaufschlussverfahren *nt* high-speed fusion method
Schnellauftrag *m* rush order
Schnellautomat *m* high-speed automatic
Schnellbewitterung *f* accelerated weathering
Schnellbohrvorrichtung *f* high-speed drilling attachment
Schnelldampferzeuger *m* high speed steam raising unit
Schnelldrehen *nt* high-velocity turning
Schnelldrehmaschine *f* high-speed lathe
Schnelldrehstahl *m* high-speed steel
Schnelldrucker *m* high-speed printer
schneller laufen lassen speed up
Schnellfahrt *f* rapid travel
Schnellfräseinrichtung *f* high-speed milling attachment
Schnellfräsmaschine *f* high-speed milling machine
Schnellfräsvorrichtung *f* high-speed milling attachment
Schnellgang *m* 1. *(allg.)* rapid power traverse 2. *(Eilgang e. Schlittens, Tisches)* rapid (or quick) traverse 3. *(maschineller ~)* rapid power traverse, power rapid (or quick) traverse, quick power traverse movement (or motion) 4. *(Planscheibe, Rundtisch)* quick rotation
Schnellhobler *m* high-speed shaper
Schnellkorrosionsuntersuchung *f* accelerant corrosion test
Schnelllaufspindel *f* high-speed spindle
Schnellprüfverfahren *nt* accelerated test procedure
Schnellreinigungsbehälter *m* rapid cleaning tank
Schnellrücklauf *m* rapid return (traverse), rapid return motion
Schnellrückzug *m (e. Meißels)* quick withdrawal
Schnellschaltkupplung *f* quick-action clutch
Schnellschaltung *f* high-speed gear change
Schnellschlussantrieb *m* quick closing actuator
Schnellschnittdrehmaschine *f* high-speed lathe
Schnellschraubenschlitzmaschine *f* high-speed screw slotter
Schnellschweißdüse *f* speed welding nozzle
Schnellschweißgerät *nt* high speed welding equipment
Schnellschweißpulver *nt* high speed flux
Schnellserienaufnahme *f* rapid series exposure
Schnellspannfutter *nt* quick-action chuck
Schnellstahl *m* high speed steel
Schnellstahlplättchen *nt* high speed steel tip
Schnelltrieb *nt* fast drive
Schnellverstellung *f* rapid power traverse
Schnellwaage *f* high-speed weigher
Schnellwechsel *m* rapid transfer, quick change
Schnellwechseleinrichtung *f* chick-change device
Schnellwechselfräsdorn *m* quick-change cutter arbor
Schnellwechselfutter *nt* quick-change chuck
Schnellwechselgetriebe *nt* quick-change mechanism
Schnellwechselhalterung *f* quick change mounting
Schnellwechselkopf *m* quick-change toolholder

Schnellwechselmeißelhalter *m* quick-change toolholder
Schnellwechselstation *f* rapid transfer station
Schnellwechselsystem *nt* quick change system
Schnellwert-Glied *nt* logic threshold
Schnellzerspanung *f* high-speed stock removal
Schnellzerspanung *f* **mit Hartmetallwerkzeugen** high-speed carbide tool machining
Schnellzugriff *m* immediate access
Schnitt *m* 1. *(allg.)* section, crop, cut (ting), intersection, incision 2. *(als Vorgang)* sectioning 3. *(Arbeitsfläche)* machined surface cut 4. *(Bewegung)* cutting movement 5. *(Schnittbahn)* cutting path 6. *(Schnittbewegung)* cutting movement 7. *(Schnittfläche)* real surface 8. *(Schnittweg)* cutting distance 9. *(Span)* chip 10. *(Verzahnung)* intersection 11. *(Zeichnung im Querschnitt)* sectional drawing 12. *(Zeichnung)* section 13. *(im ~ darstellen)* represent in section
Schnitt *m* **mit geringer Spantiefe** light cut
Schnittarbeit *f* cutting work
Schnittbahn *f* cutting path
Schnittbau *m* punch and die making
Schnittbearbeitbarkeit *f* machinability, free-cutting property, free machining quality
Schnittbewegung *f* cutting motion (or movement), primary motion
Schnittbildverfahren *nt* section diagram method
Schnittbreite *f* width of cut, cut width
Schnittdarstellung *f* sectional representation
Schnittdruck *m* tool load, tool thrust
Schnittebene *f* plane of section
Schnittenergie *f* cutting energy
Schnittfähigkeit *f* 1. *(allg.)* cuttability, cutting power 2. *(Zerspanbarkeit)* machinability
Schnittfläche *f* 1. *(allg.)* area of cut, shoulder of (the) cut, sectional area, work surface 2. *(z. B. e. Zahnflanke)* surface of intersection
Schnittflächen-Gütemuster *nt* quality sample of cut surfaces
Schnittflächenprofil *nt* profile of the cut surface
Schnittflanke *f* cut surface, face of the cut, kerf wall
Schnittflankenwinkel *m* angle of cut flank
Schnittfolge *f* cutting sequence
Schnittfront *f* cut front
Schnittfrontneigung *f* cut front inclination
Schnittfuge *f* cut joint
Schnittfugenbreite cut joint width
Schnittgeschwindigkeit *f* rate of cutting, cutting speed (or rate), surface speed
Schnittgeschwindigkeiten verwenden employ cutting speeds
Schnittgeschwindigkeitsregelung *f* automatic control of cutting speeds
Schnittgrat *m* burr
Schnittgröße *f* internal force variable, stress resultant, cutting (or machining) variable
Schnittgrößen *fpl* cutting sizes
Schnitthaltigkeit *f* cuttability, ability to hold the cutting power
Schnitthub *m* cutting stroke, forward stroke
Schnittiefe *f* **je Zahn** cut per tooth
Schnittkante *f* cut edge
Schnittkennzeichnung *f* indication of sections
Schnittkraft *f* 1. *(allg.)* cutting force, force of the cut, cutting load, cutting pressure 2. *(Hobeltisch)* table pull 3. *(Maschine)* cutting power, cutting force, cutting load, cutting thrust, force component in the direction of cutting 4. *(senkrechte)* tool thrust 5. *(spezifische ~)* specific cutting force
Schnittkraftanstieg *m* cutting force rising
Schnittkraftbeziehung *f* cutting force relationship
Schnittkraftkomponente *f* component of force in cutting
Schnittlänge *f* length of cut

Schnittlast *f* cutting load
Schnittleistung *f* cutting capacity, cutting power
Schnittlinie *f* cutting line, intersection line, line of intersection, section boundary
Schnittmatrize *f* cutting die
Schnittmoment *m* cutting torque
Schnittnormalkraft *f* cutting perpendicular force
Schnittpunkt *m* point of intersection, intersection
Schnittrichtung *f* direction of cutting, direction of the cut, hand of (the) cut, (direction of) primary motion
Schnittstelle *f* cutting point, point of cut, interface, port
Schnittstellendefinition *f* interface definition
Schnittstellenfunktionalität *f* interface functions
Schnittstellenpartner *m* interface partner
Schnittteil *nt* cut part
Schnitttiefe *f* 1. *(allg.)* cutting depth, depth of cut, working engagement 2. *(e. Schleifscheibe)* depth of grain cut 3. *(e. Schneide)* back engagement, depth of cut
Schnittverlaufs-, Werkzeugbahndaten *pl* cutter location data (CLDATA)
Schnittvolumen *nt* cut
Schnittvorschub *m* cutting feed
Schnittweg *m* *(Weg, den der Schneidenpunkt auf dem Werkstück in Schnittrichtung schneidend zurücklegt)* cutting path, cutting distance
Schnittwerkzeug *nt* blanking and cutting die
Schnittwinkel *m* 1. *(Schneidenwinkel)* cutting angle, *(UK)* wedge (or lip) angle, cutting tool angle, true cutting angle 2. *(Keilwinkel)* wedge angle
Schnittzeit *f* cutting time
Schnitzel *nt* cutting
Schnüffelventil *nt* breather
Schnur *f* cord, string, lace
Schock *m* shock, jolt
schocken shock

Schockschweißen *nt* shock welding
schonen prevent damage
Schonung *f* saving
Schornsteinanlage *f* chimney (or smokestack) installation
Schornsteinleistung *f* chimney performance
Schornsteinmündung *f* chimney outlet
Schornsteinwange *f* chimney flank
schraffieren hatch
schraffierte Linie *f* shaded line
schraffierter Bereich *m* hatched area
Schraffur *f* hatch, hatching, section lines, section lining
schräg angled, diagonal, bevel, canted, inclined, sloped, oblique, skew
schräg gegeneinander stoßen meet the other at an angle
schräg laufen skew
schräg legen cant
schräg stellen incline, pitch
Schräg- und Kurvenhobeleinrichtung *f* planing attachment for machining radius and contours
Schrägabzweig *m* *(e. Rohrleitung)* Y-branch
Schrägbelastung *f* wedge loading
Schrägbohrung *f* diagonal hole
Schrägdurchschallung *f* oblique transmission
Schräge *f* chamfer, bevel, obliquity
schräge Fläche *f* inclined surface
schräge Normschrift *f* sloping style standard lettering
Schrägeinfall *m* oblique incidence
Schrägeinschallung *f* oblique intromission
Schrägeinstechschleifen *nt* angular plunge grinding
Schrägeinstellung *f* angular setting
schräger Schnitt *m* angular cut
schräger Spanwinkel *m* oblique rake
schräger Tiefenvorschub *m* angular downfeed
schräges Fräsen *nt* **in axialer Richtung des Schaftfräsers** angular end milling
schrägfräsen mill at an angle, angular milling

Schrägführung *f* inclined run
schräghalten hold at an oblique angle
Schräghobeleinrichtung *f* attachment for planing inclined flat surfaces
Schräghobeln *nt* angular planing, planing inclined (flat) surfaces, plane at an angle
Schrägkante *f* bevelled edge
Schrägkippen *nt* angular tilt
Schräglage *f* tilt, declination
Schräglagenkorrektur *f* tilt correction
Schräglager *nt* inclined roller bearing
Schräglauf *m* skew, running askew
Schräglaufkraft *f* force due to running askew
schräg liegende Ebene *f* inclined plane
Schrägrohrmanometer *nt* inclined tube manometer
Schrägrolle *f* skew roller
Schrägrollenbahn *f* skew roller conveyor
Schrägschleifen *nt* oblique grinding, angular grinding
Schrägschlitzklemme *f* oblique slotted clamp
Schrägschneiden *nt* angle cutting
Schrägschneidrad *nt* helical pinion cutter
Schrägschnitt *m* 1. *(Vorgang)* oblique section, diagonal (or bevel) cut(ting) 2. *(Arbeitsergebnis)* diagonal (or angle) cut
Schrägsitzventil *nt* Y-valve, inclined seat valve
schräg stehender Brenner *m* angled position of the burner
schrägstellbar inclinable
schrägstellen set at an angle, tilt
Schrägstellung *f* angular adjustment, angular positioning, angular tilt, amount of angularity, inclination, tilt, skewed position, tilting, slope, sloping, pitch
Schrägstirnrad *nt* helical spur gear
Schrägstirnradpaar *nt* helical gear pair, parallel helical gear pair
Schrägstoß *m* inclined tee joint
Schrägstrich *m* oblique stroke
Schrägtragen inclined contact
Schrägungswinkel *m* 1. *(allg.)* helix angle, lead angle 2. *(bei bogenverzahnten Kegelrädern)* spiral angle
Schrägungswinkelabweichung *f* helix angle variation
Schrägungswinkelbereich *m* helix angle range
schrägverstellbar 1. *(allg.)* adjustable to an angular position, angular adjustable 2. *(neigbar)* inclinable
Schrägverstellung *f* angular adjustment
schräg verzahnt helically toothed
schräg verzahnte Zahnstange *f* helical rack
schräg verzahntes Lehrzahnrad *nt* helical master gear
schräg verzahntes Rad *nt* helical gear, gear of the single helical type
schräg verzahntes Stirnrad *nt* helical spur gear
schräg verzahntes Zahnrad *nt* spiral gear
Schrägverzahnung *f* angular teeth, helical teeth, helical tooth system, spiral-tooth system, helical gearing
Schrägverzahnungs-Bezugsfläche *f* reference surface of the helical teeth
Schrägwalzen *nt* 1. *(allg.)* skew rolling. 2. *(von Formteilen)* skew rolling of shapes 3. *(von Hohlkörpern)* skew rolling of tubular products 4. *(von Hohlkörpern über eine Stange mit Schulterwalzen)* skew rolling of tubular products over a piercer rod using stepped rolls 5. *(zum Aufweiten über Stopfen mit scheibenförmigen Walzen)* skew rolling for expanding over a piercer rod using disc-shaped rolls 6. *(zum Lochen)* skew rolling for piercing holes 7. *(zum Lochen mit kegelförmigen Walzen)* cone-roll piercing 8. *(zum Lochen mit tonnenförmigen Walzen)* barrel-type rool piercing
Schrägzahnkegelrad *nt* helical bevel gear
Schrägzahnkegelradpaar *nt* helical bevel gear pair
Schrägzahnradstoßmaschine *f* helical (or spiral) gear shaper
Schrägzahnschieber *m* slide for helical

cutting
Schrägzahnstirnrad *nt* helical tooth spur gear
Schrägzugversuch *m* wedge tensile test, angular tensile test
Schrägzylinderrad *nt* helical gear
Schrägzylinderradpaar *nt* helical gear pair
Schrank *m* cupboard, cabinet, case
Schranke *f* 1. *(allg.)* barrier 2. *(sich öffnende ~)* opening barrier
Schränken *nt* tooth setting
Schränkmaschine *f* saw-setting machine
Schränkung *f* tooth set
Schraubachse *f* helix axis
Schraube *f* 1. *(allg.)* bolt, screw 2. *(mit Dehnschaft)* screw (or bolt) with waisted shank 3. *(mit dünnem Schaft)* screw (or bolt) with reduced shank 4. *(mit eben aufliegendem Kopf)* screw with flat-sealing head 5. *(mit gewindefreier Schaftlänge)* bolt with plain shaft length 6. *(mit Kreuzschlitz)* recessed head screw 7. *(mit Schlitz)* slotted head screw 8. *(mit unverlierbarem Unterlegteil)* screw with captive washer
schrauben screw
Schrauben-, Mutter-, Rohrgewindeschneidmaschine *f* bolt, nut and tube threading machine
Schraubenanziehmaschine *f* nut runner
Schraubenautomat *m* automatic screw machine
Schraubenbolzen *m* 1. *(allg.)* stud-bolt 2. *(mit Dehnschaft)* stud-bolt with waisted shank
Schraubenbruchspan *m* coil chip
Schraubendreher *m* 1. *(für Gewindestifte mit Schlitz)* screwdriver for slotted grub screws 2. *(für Kopfschrauben mit Schlitz)* screwdriver for slotted head screws 3. *(für Kreuzschlitzschrauben)* screwdriver for recessed head screws 4. *(für Schlitzschrauben)* screwdriver for slotted head screws 5. *(für Innenvielzahnschrauben)* screwdriver bit for screws with internal serrations
Schraubendrehereinsatz *m* **für Innenkeilprofilschrauben** screwdriver bit for multispline screws
Schraubendruckfeder *f* helical compression spring
Schraubenfeder *f* coil spring, helical spring
schraubenförmig helical
schraubenförmige Nut *f* helical groove
Schraubenführungs-Steigungshöhe *f* helical guidance lead
Schraubenfutter *f* cat-head, screw chuck
Schraubengang *m* helix
Schraubengewinde *nt* screw thread
Schraubenkopfsenkung *f (als Arbeitsvorgang)* screw head counterbore
Schraubenkraft *f* bolt force
Schraubenkurve *f* helical curve
Schraubenlinie *f* helical line, spiral line, helical curve, helix, helices *pl*
Schraubenlinienbogen *m* helix arc, helical arc
Schraubenlinienform *f* helical form
Schraubenlinieninterpolation *f* helix interpolation
Schraubenliniennahtschweißung *f* welding yielded a helical seam
schraubenlinig helical
Schrauben-Muttern-Verbindung *f* bolt/nut fastening
Schraubenrad *nt* helical gear
Schraubenschlitzen *nt* screw slotting
Schraubenschlitzfräser *m* screw-slotting cutter, slotting saw
Schraubenschlitzmaschine *f* screw slotter
Schraubenschlitzsäge *f* screw slotting saw
Schraubenschlitzvorrichtung *f* screw-head slotting attachment
Schraubenschlüssel *m* spanner, wrench
schraubensichernder Gewindeeinsatz *m* screw-locking (or screw-retaining) thread insert
Schraubensicherung *f* screw (or bolt) retaining device
Schraubenspan *m* screw chip
Schraubenspindelpumpenaggre-

gat *nt* screw pumping aggregate
Schraubenüberstand *m* length of projection of thread (or bolt) end
Schraubenverbindung *f* 1. *(allg.)* screwed connection, screw joint, bolt joint 2. *(mit Dehnschaft)* bolted fastening with waisted shank
Schraubenzieher *m* screw driver
Schraubfitting *m* screwed fitting
Schraubfläche *f* helix surface
Schraubfräsen *nt* (*Wälzfräsen*) screwing milling hobs
Schraubgetriebe *nt* helical type gear transmission, screw-motion transmission
schraubige Flankenlinie *f* helical tooth trace
Schraubklemme *f* srew rail clip, screw rail anchor
Schraubklemmung *f* U-bolt grip
Schraublinie *f* (*als geometrischer Begriff*) helix, helices *pl*
Schraubmuffenverbindung *f* screwed and socketed joint
Schraubnagel *m* screw nail
Schraubpunkt *m* helix point
Schraubrad *nt* crossed helical gear
Schraubradpaar *nt* crossed helical gear pair, gear pair with non-parallel non-intersecting axes
Schraubstock *m* 1. *(allg.)* vice 2. *(für rundes Stangenmaterial)* round bar vice
Schraubstockbacken *fpl* vice jaws
Schraubstockspannung *f* vice clamping
Schraubventil *nt* screw type valve
Schraubverbindung *f* screwed (or bolted) fastening, screwed joint, bolted joint, screwed connection
Schraubverschließmaschine *f* screw capping machine
Schraubverschluss *m* screw plug, twisted cap
Schraubwälzfläche *f* helical pitch surface
Schraubwälzgetriebe *nt* helical rolling type gear transmission
Schraubwälzschleifen screw-generating grinding
Schraubwälzschleifen *nt* helical roll grinding
Schraubwerkzeug *nt* assembly tools for screws and nuts
Schreib-/Leseabstand *m* read/write distance
Schreib-/Lesegerät *nt* read/write device
Schreib-/Lesekopf *m* read/write head
Schreib-/Leseverhalten *nt* read/write behaviour
schreiben write, record
Schreiben *nt* (*ständiges, nicht unterbrochenes ~*) serial scribing
Schreiber *m* recording apparatus, recorder
Schreibfehler *m* device write fault
Schreibgerät *nt* writing implement, recording implement, logger
Schreibkopf *m* write head
Schreib-Lese-Speicher *m* address memory
Schreibmaschinenzeilenhöhe *f* typewriter spacing
Schreibrichtung *f* (*z. B. von Maßen*) direction of writing
Schreibspitzenauslenkung *f* pen tip deflection
Schreibzyklus *m* write cycle, writing cycle
Schrift *f* text, writing
Schriftart *f* typeface, script
Schriftfeld *nt* title block
Schriftgröße *f* size of lettering
Schriftgutverfilmung *f* filing of textual material
Schriftgutvorlagen *fpl* original written documents
Schriftschablone *f* lettering stencil
Schriftzeichen *nt* character
Schriftzeile *f* line
schriftzeilenweise *f* line by line
Schritt *m* step, pitch, increment, stage
Schrittgeschwindigkeit *f* 1. *(allg.)* transmission speed, signalling speed, modulation rate 2. *(Flurförderung)* walking speed
Schrittmotor *m* step motor, stepping motor
Schrittschaltgetriebe *nt* stepping mechanism

Schrittschaltung *f* jogging control, inching control
Schrittschaltwerk *nt* step-by-step switch
Schrittteilmethode *f* block method of spacing
Schrittteilung *f* block indexing
Schrittvorschub *m* incremental jog
schrittweise step by step, incremental, progressive
Schrittweite *f* increment
Schritt- und Wiederholverfahren *nt* step-and-repeat-technology
schroff wirkendes Abschreckmittel *nt* intensively acting quenchant
Schrott *m* **1.** *(allg.)* scrap, scrap metals **2.** *(Ausschuss)* waste
Schrottgreifer *m* scrap grapple
Schrotthaufen *m* scrap heap, scrap pile
Schrumpf *m* shrinkage
Schrumpf-Anlage *f* installation for shrinkage
Schrumpfeinrichtung *f* shrinking equipment, shrinking unit
Schrumpfeinschlagen *nt* shrinkwrapping
Schrumpfen *nt* shrinking, reduction
Schrumpffolie *f* shrinking film, thermoplastic film, thermoplastic material
Schrumpffolieneinschlagmaschine *f* shrink wrapping machine, shrinkwrapping machine, wrapping machine for shrink films
Schrumpffolieneinwickelmaschine *f* sleeve wrapping machine
Schrumpffolienumhüllung *f* shrink wrap, shrinkwrap
Schrumpfhaube *f* shrink hood
Schrumpfhaubenüberziehmaschine *f* shrink hood applicator
Schrumpfhülse *f* shrink sleeve
Schrumpfhülsenüberziehmaschine *f* shrink sleeving machine
Schrumpfkraft *f* shrink force
Schrumpfofen *m* shrink oven, shrinking furnace
Schrumpfpackung *f* shrinkwrap pack
Schrumpfpistole *f* shrinking gun, shrinking pistol
Schrumpfrahmen *m* shrink frame
Schrumpfschlauch *m* shrinkable tubing
Schrumpftank *m* dip tank
Schrumpftunnel *m* shrink tunnel
Schrumpfung *f* shrinking, shrinkage
Schrumpfungseigenschaft *f* shrinkage property
Schrumpfungsmessung *f* shrinkage measurement
Schrumpfverband *m* shrinkage assembly
Schrumpfverhalten *nt* shrinkage behaviour
schrumpfverpacken shrink wrap, shrinkwrap
Schrumpfverpackung *f* shrink wrap
Schrupparbeit *f* roughing operation, roughing work, roughing
Schruppautomat *m* automatic roughing lathe
Schruppbearbeitbarkeit *f* rough machinability
Schruppbearbeitung *f* rough machining
Schruppbohren *nt* rough-boring
Schruppdrehen *nt* rough turning
Schruppdurchgang *m* roughing pass
schruppen rough, take a roughing cut, roughing work, rough-machine
Schrupperodieren *nt* rough eroding
Schruppfräsen *nt* **1.** *(allg.)* rough milling **2.** *(dreidiemsionales ~ von Gesenken)* rough-routing
Schruppfräser *m* **1.** *(allg.)* roughing cutter, stocking cutter **2.** *(Schruppwälzfräser)* roughing hob
Schruppfrässpindel *f* rough milling spindle
Schruppgeschwindigkeit *f* roughing speed, rate of roughing feed
Schrupphobeln *nt* rough planing
Schruppmeißel *m* roughing tool, roughing cutter
Schruppräumwerkzeug *nt* rougher, roughing broach
Schruppschleifen *nt* rough grinding
Schruppschliff *m* roughing grind
Schruppschnitt *m* roughing cut, roughing operation
Schruppspan *m* roughing cut

Schruppstahl *m* roughing tool, roughing cutter
Schruppwälzfräser *m* roughing hob
Schruppwerkzeug *nt* roughing tool
Schruppzahn *m* roughing tooth
Schub *m* push, thrust
Schubachse *f* axis of translation
Schubbeanspruchung *f* shear loading
Schubbewegung *f* translatory motion
Schubbruch *m* shear failure
Schubeinrichtung *f* push mechanism
Schubflanke *f* thrust flank
Schubgabel *f* fork extender, retractable fork (arm carriage)
Schubgabelstapler *m* reach truck
Schubgabelträger *m* reach fork carrier
Schubgelenk *nt* prismatic pair
Schubgerade *f* slider straight
Schubkraft *f* thrust, shearing force
Schubkurbel *f* slider crank
Schublade *f* drawer
Schubladenunterteilung *f* drawer divider
Schublehre *f* calliper rule, vernier calliper, slide calliper
Schubmast *m* reach mechanism, reach mast, retractable mast
Schubmaststapler *m* reach mast truck
Schubmittelbeanspruchung *f* mean shear stress
Schubmittelspannung *f* mean shear stress
Schubrahmen *m* C-push frame
Schubrahmenstapler *m* straddle fork lift truck, straddle reach truck
Schubriss *m* push crack
Schubschlepper *m* pushing tractor
Schubschwinge *f* slider-and-rocker
Schubspannung shear stress
Schubspannungsbruch *m* interlaminar failure, shear failure
Schubstangenförderer *m* push-rod conveyor
Schubstapler *m* reach truck
Schubsteifigkeit *f* shear rigidity, shear stiffness
Schubsystem *nt* reach system
Schubstange *f* push rod
Schubumformen *nt* reforming by shear
Schubverformung *f* shear deformation
Schubversuch *m* shear test in flatwise plane
Schubvorrichtung *f* pushing device, shifting device
Schuh *m* **mit Stahlkappen** steel-toed shoe
Schuhbesohlungsmaterial *nt* shoe soling material
schulen train
Schülpe *f* scab
Schülpenbildung *f* scab formation
Schulter *f* shoulder
Schulterstab *m* bar with wider gripping ends, shouldered test bar
Schulung *f* training
Schulungsmaßnahme *f* training activity
Schuppe *f* flake
Schüreinrichtung *f* riddling arrangement
schüren riddle
Schürze *f* apron housing, apron
Schüttelfrequenz *f* shaking rate
Schüttelkolben *m* shaking flask
schütteln shake, vibrate
Schüttelzylinder *m* shaking cylinder
schütten empty, throw, pour
Schüttentleerung *f* bulk emptying
Schüttgut *nt* bulk, bulk good(s), bulk material
Schüttgutschaufel *f* scoop
Schüttguttransport *m* bulk transport
Schüttvolumen *nt* bulk volume
Schutz *m* cover, guard, safeguard, protection, preservation
Schutzanzugstoff *m* material for protective clothing
Schutzart *f* 1. *(allg.)* type of protection, protective system 2. *(Maschinen)* degree of protection
Schutzauftragung *f* protective coating
Schutzausrüstung *f* protective equipment
Schutzbeschichtung *f* protective coating
Schutzbinde *f* protective band
Schutzblech *nt* guard plate
Schutzbrille *f* protective goggles, goggles *pl*, safety glasses

Schutzdach *nt* overhead guard, overhead protection, protection roof
Schutzdauer *f* period of protection
Schutzeinrichtung *f* guard, protective equipment, protective device, safeguard, safety feature, guarding, shield
Schutzeinrichtung *f* **mit Annäherungsreaktion** sensing device
Schutzelement *nt* protection element
schützen shield, protect (from/against), guard (from)
Schutzerde *f* protective earth, protective ground
Schutzerdung *f* protective earthing, protective grounding
Schutzfase *f* protective chamfer
Schutzfenster *nt* protective window
Schutzfolie *f* protective film
Schutzgas *nt* protective atmosphere, protective gas
Schutzgasengspaltschweißen *nt* narrow-gap gas-shielded welding
Schutzgaslöten *nt* soldering under protective atmospheres
Schutzgasschweißdraht *m* shielded-arc filler wire
Schutzgefäß *nt* protective vessel
Schutzgehäuse *nt* protective casing
Schutzgeländer *nt* guard rail(s)
Schutzgitter *nt* protective grating, load back rest, protective gloves
Schutzhaube *f* protective hood, safety guard, wheel guard
Schutzhelm *m* safety helmet
Schutzimpedanz *f* protective impedance
Schutzisolation *f* *(von Schraubendrehern)* protective insulation
Schutzisolierung *f* protective insulation
Schutzkabine *f* protective cabin
Schutzkanzel *f* mobile protective seat
Schutzkappe *f* protective cap
Schutzklasse *f* protective class
Schutzkleidung *f* protective clothing
Schutzkleinspannung *f* protective extra-low voltage (PELV)
Schutzkorb *m* protective cage
Schutzlage *f* protective stratum
Schutzleiter *m* protective earthing (conductor), earth conductor
Schutzleiteranschluss *m* protective earthing port
Schutzleitungssystem *nt* protective conductor system
Schutzmaßnahme *f* safety means, protective arrangement, protective measure, precaution
Schutzpotential *nt* *(el. chem.)* protection potential
Schutzpotenzialausgleichsanlage *f* protective equipotential bonding system
Schutzschalter *m* circuit protector, protective switch
Schutzschicht *f* 1. *(allg.)* protective layer, insulating layer 2. *(Bau)* wear-resisting layer
Schutzschichtbildung *f* formation of a protective layer
Schutzschild *nt* shield
Schutzschirm *m* shield, protective screen
Schutzschuhe *mpl* safety footwear
Schutzschürze *f* protective apron
Schutzsenkung *f* *(e. Gewindeloches)* protective sinking
Schutzspule *f* safety coil
Schutzstrom *m* protective current
Schutzstromgerät *nt* protection current device
Schutzsystem *nt* protection system
Schutzüberzug *m* protective coating
Schutzverpackung *f* protective packaging
Schutzvorrichtung *f* protection device, safety guard
Schutzwand *f* shielding wall
Schutzwirkung *f* protective effect
Schutzziel *nt* protection, protection target
Schutzzone *f* restricted area
schwach weak, slight, flimsy
schwächen weaken
Schwachstelle *f* critical point, potential trouble spot, weak point, weak spot
Schwachstellenanalyse *f* weak-point analysis, examination of weakest points
Schwächung *f* *(der Zahndicke)* weakening
Schwächungsgleichwert *m* attenua-

tion equivalent value
Schwade *f* damp, vapour
Schwalbenschwanz *m* dovetail
Schwalbenschwanzführung *f* dovetail
Schwalbenschwanznuten ausarbeiten dovetail
Schwalllöten *nt* flood soldering
Schwammgefüge *nt* sponge structure
schwanken oscillate, vibrate, sway, undulate, swing, fluctuate, vary, pulsate, rock
schwanken zwischen vary from, range between
schwankend unsteady, swaying, swinging, fluctuating, varying
Schwankung *f* fluctuation, variability, variableness, oscillation, undulation, swinging, sway, variation, pulsation
Schwankungsbreite *f* fluctuation range
Schwarzgrundverfahren *nt* blackground method
Schwärzung *f* density
Schwärzungsbedingung *f* density condition
Schwärzungsbereich *m* density range
Schwärzungsdifferenz *f* difference in density
schwarz-weiß black-and-white
Schwebekörper *m* floating body
Schwebekörperprinzip *nt* float principle
schwebend pendant
Schwebeverfahren *nt* suspension method
Schwebstofffilter *m* filter for suspended matter
Schwefel *m* sulphur
Schwefelkohlenstoff *m* carbon disulfide
Schwefelschmelzklebstoff *m* sulphur thermal fusion adhesive
Schweifen *nt* off-hand curving by stretching
Schweiß- und Lötnähte *fpl* welded brazed and soldered joints
Schweißausführung *f* execution of the weld
Schweißbereich *m* weld zone

Schweißbügel *m* C-type spot welding head
Schweißechtheit *f* resistance to sweat
Schweißen *nt* **1.** *(allg.)* welding **2.** *(in Lage und Gegenlage)* welding from both sides in one pass **3.** *(mit umschließendem Induktor)* welding using a surrounding inductor **4.** *(mit Dauergleichstrom)* welding using continuous direct current **5.** *(mit Dauerstrom)* welding using continuous current **6.** *(mit Dauerwechselstrom)* welding using continuous alternating current **7.** *(mit Druckprogramm)* welding with programme pressure control **8.** *(mit gestreckter Naht)* welding with elongated weld **9.** *(mit Hochfrequenz)* high-frequency welding **10.** *(mit Hubzündung)* welding with drawn arc **11.** *(mit impulsförmigem Gleichstrom)* welding using pulsed direct current **12.** *(mit Mittelfrequenz)* medium frequency welding **13.** *(mit Netzfrequenz)* system frequency welding **14.** *(mit stabförmigen Induktoren)* welding using rod inductors **15.** *(mit Strom- und/oder Kraftprogramm)* welding using multi-current cycle and/or multiforce cycle **16.** *(mit Stromabfall)* pulsation welding **17.** *(mit Stromanstieg)* welding with slope control **18.** *(mit unterbrochenem Gleichstrom)* welding with intermittent direct current **19.** *(mit unterbrochenem Wechselstrom)* welding with intermittent alternating current **20.** *(mit Wechselstrom und Phasenanschnitt)* welding using alternating current and phase shift **21.** *(gleichzeitig beidseitiges ~)* welding on both sides simultaneously **22.** *(pendelndes ~)* welding with weaving **23.** *(schleppendes ~)* welding with torch directed towards the finished part of the weld **24.** *(stechendes ~)* welding with torch directed towards the part of the weld still to be made
Schweißende *nt* weld-on end
Schweißenergiequelle *f* welding power supply
Schweißer *m* welder, welding operator
Schweißfaltversuch *m* weld bend test

Schweißfläche *f* interface of the weld nugget
Schweißfugenfläche *f* welding joint face
Schweißgeschwindigkeit *f* weld speed
Schweißgruppenzeichnung *f* welded assembly drawing
Schweißgutfestigkeit *f* strength of the weld metal
Schweißgutmasse *f* amount of deposited metal
Schweißgutüberlauf *m* **1.** *(allg.)* excessive roll-over (or pass) **2.** *(Decklage)* tool overlap **3.** *(Wurzelseite)* root overlap
Schweißhauptzeit *f* productive welding time
Schweißhilfsstoff *m* welding auxiliary material
Schweißkegelbuchse *f (e. Rohres)* welded conical nipple
Schweißkraft *f* welding load (liquid lubricant), welding force
Schweißlöten *nt* brazing, hard soldering
Schweißmaschinensteuerung *f* welding machine control
Schweißmöglichkeit *f* welding feasibility
Schweißnaht *f* weld (seam), welding, weldment joint
Schweißnahtbereich *m* weld zone
Schweißnahtflächenschwerachse *f* gravity axis of the weld area
Schweißnahtform *f* weld shape
Schweißnahtlänge *f* weld length
Schweißnahtprüfung *f* weld inspection
Schweißnahtreste *mpl* remains (pl) of the weld
Schweißnahtwertigkeit *f* weld efficiency rating
Schweißnahtzwischenprüfung *f* intermediate testing of welds
Schweißnebenzeit *f* time for ancillary work
Schweißpanzern *nt* hardfacing
Schweißplattierung *f* cladding by welding
Schweißplatz *m* welding station
Schweißpresskraft *f* weld compression force
Schweißpresszeit *f* weld compression time
Schweißpunkt *m* spaced spot weld, spot weld
Schweißschnur *f* filler filament
Schweißsicherheit *f* weld reliability
Schweißsinnbild *nt* weld symbol
Schweißstoßart *f* form of welding joint
Schweißstoßfläche *f* weld face
Schweißstrahlnaht *f* weldable steel wire
Schweißstreifen *m* filler strip
SchweißStromstärkebereich *m* welding current range
schweißtechnische Einrichtung *f* welding equipment
schweißtechnische Fertigung *f* fabrication by welding
schweißtechnische Gestaltung *f* welding design
schweißtechnische Vorrichtung *f* welding fixture
schweißtechnisches Personal *nt* welding personnel
Schweißtiefe *f* weld depth
Schweißung *f* weld, welding, weldment
Schweißverbindung *f* welded assembly, welded joint
Schweißverfahren *nt* welding procedure
Schweißverschließmaschine *f* weld sealing machine
Schweißzeit *f (reine ~)* productive welding time
Schweißzugversuch *m* welding tensile test
Schweißzusatz *m* consumable, welding addition, welding filler (metal), filler material
Schweißzusatzvorschubgeschwindigkeit *f* wire feed speed
Schweißzusatzwerkstoff *m* consumable welding material, filler material, welding filler
Schwelgas *nt* low-temperature gas
Schwellbereich *m* pulsation range

Schwelle *f* threshold
Schwellenwert *m* threshold value
Schwellwert *m* first break
Schwenkachse *f* swivel axis, pivot
Schwenkarbeitsbühne *f* swivelling work platform
Schwenkarm *m* selective compliance assembly robot arm (SCARA), swivelling arm
Schwenkarmroboter *m* SCARA-robot
schwenkbar 1. *(allg.)* articulated, pivoting, swivelling, rotating, swivel-mounted **2.** *(Bohr-, Fräskopf)* tiltable **3.** *(Scharnierdeckel)* hinged **4.** *(Ständer)* slewable
schwenkbare Bedienungstafel *f* swivelling control pendant
schwenkbare Deichsel *f* articulated tiller handle
schwenkbare Halterung *f* swivelling holder
schwenkbare Schalttafel *f* pendant switchboard
schwenkbarer Fahrerplatz *m* rotating operator seat
schwenkbarer Spindelkopf *m* swivel head
Schwenkbarkeit *f* swivelling feature
Schwenkbereich *m* swept volume
Schwenkbewegung *f* **1.** *(allg.)* swivelling movement, oscillating rotation, slewing motion **2.** *(Kran)* rotating motion **3.** *(Roboter)* swivel
Schwenkbiegen *nt* swing-folding, hemming, bending about the line of the notch
Schwenkbiegeschweißen *nt* welding by bending using a heated tool
Schwenkbohrmaschine *f* radial drilling machine *(UK)*, radial drill *(US)*
Schwenkbohrmaschine *f* **mit runder Säule** round column radial drill
Schwenkbrenner *m* swing burner
Schwenkbrennerverfahren *nt* swivelling burner method
Schwenkeinrichtung *f* slewing mechanism, rotating mechanism, swivelling mechanism
Schwenkelement *nt* swivel element
schwenken 1. *(allg.)* pivot, swivel, slew, *(US)* slue, turn swing, hinge **2.** *(Fräskopf)* tilt, swing to an angular position **3.** *(Hebel)* shift **4.** *(weg-, aufwärts, abwärts, seitwärts, rundschwenken)* swing out of the way (upward, downward, sideways, round)
Schwenkgabelstapler *m* articulated fork truck
Schwenkhebel *m* pivoted lever
Schwenkkonstruktion *f* slewing mast structure, swivelling structure
Schwenkkopf *m* swivel head
Schwenkkörper *m* tumbler yoke
Schwenkkugellager *nt* rose bearing
Schwenklager *nt* swivel bearing
Schwenkmast *m* rotating mast, slewing mast
Schwenkmastdreiseitenstapler *m* rotating mast sideloading lift truck, rotating mast lateral and front stacking truck
Schwenkmeißel *m* swing cutting tool
Schwenkposition *f (e. Schwenkscheibe)* swivelled position
Schwenkrad *nt* tumbler gear
Schwenkrädergetriebe *nt* quick-change mechanism
Schwenkradius *m* swept radius
Schwenkschablone *f* swivelling template (or templet)
Schwenkscheibe *f* captive C washer
Schwenkschubeinrichtung *f* articulated retractable device
Schwenkschubgabel *f* articulated retractable fork, L-head fork
Schwenktisch *m* swivelling worktable, swivel table, swivelling knee, swivel knee, swivelling angle plate table
Schwenktischfräsen *nt* milling with dual setups, swivelling knee milling
Schwenktor *nt* hinged door
schwer 1. *(gewichtig)* heavy **2.** *(schwerwiegend)* severe **3.** *(schwierig)* difficult
schwer bearbeitbar difficult to machine
schwer entflammbar difficult to ignite, fire-resistant, flame retardant
schwer entzündlicher Fußbodenbelag *m* difficulty flammable floor covering
Schweranlauf *m* full-load start, start un-

der load, heavy start
schwere Arbeit *f* slog
Schwere *f* severity
Schwerelinienverfahren *nt* lines of gravity method
schwerentflammbarer Kunststoff *m* low-flammability plastics
Schwerentflammbarkeit *f* low flammability
schwerer Lüfter *m* flywheel fan
schwerflüchtige Flüssigkeit *f* low volatile liquid
Schwergut *nt* heavy parts
Schwergutlagerung *f* heavy parts storage
Schwerkraft *f* gravity, gravitational force
Schwerkraftauslauf *m* gravity discharge
schwerkraftbetrieben gravity-driven, gravity-powered
Schwerkraftentleerung *f* unloading by gravity
Schwerkraftfüllmaschine *f* gravity filling machine
Schwerkraftgegenstromsichter *m* gravitation-counterflow sizer
Schwerkraftgießen *nt* gravity force casting, force of gravity casting
Schwerkraftheizung *f* gravity-circulated heating system
Schwerkraftkokillenguss *m* gravity chill casting, gravity die-casting
Schwerkraftlichtbogenschweißen *nt* gravity arc welding with covered electrode
Schwerkraftluftheizungsanlage *f* gravity type air heating system
Schwerkraftprinzip *nt* gravity, law of gravitation
Schwerkraftrollenbahn *f* gravity roller conveyor, gravity roller system
Schwerlastförderer *m* heavy load conveyor
Schwerlasttraverse *f* heavy load spreader, heavy (load) lifting beam
Schwerlastregal *nt* heavy load shelving, heavy load rack
Schwerlastrolle *f* heavy (load) roller
Schwerpunkt *m* **1.** *(allg.)* centre of gravity, centre of mass, centroid (or area) **2.** *(el.)* node
Schwerpunktbestimmung *f* determination of (the centre) gravity
Schwerpunktbewegung *f* centre-of-mass motion
Schwerpunktkoordinate *f* node coordinate
Schwerpunktlage *f* point of gravity
Schwerpunktmitte *f* centroid
Schwerpunktveränderung *f* change in centre of gravity position
Schwerpunktverfahren *nt* node method
Schwerstwerkzeugmaschine *f* elephant machine tool
Schwesterwerkzeug *nt* alternate tool
schwierig difficult, intricate
schwimmende Gasglocke *f* floating bell gasholder
schwimmende Geräte *ntpl* floating plant, buoyancy units
Schwimmer *m* float
Schwimmermanometer *nt* float pressure gauge
Schwimmerschalter *m* float switch
Schwimmersteuerung *f (e. Absperrorgans)* stop valve with float control
Schwimmhautbildung *f* float layer formation
Schwimmschalter *f* liquid level switch
Schwindmaß *nt* reduction measure, shrinkage dimension
Schwindung *f* reduction, shrinkage
Schwindungseigenschaft *f* shrinkage property
Schwindvorrichtung *f* shrinkage block
Schwingantrieb *m* crank drive
Schwingarm *m* rocker arm, oscillating arm
Schwingbeanspruchung *f* fluctuating (or fluctuation) stress, vibrational loading
Schwingbeiwert *m* oscillation coefficient, vibration coefficient
Schwingbewegung *f* vibratory motion
Schwingdurchmesser *m (UK)* turning diameter, *(US)* swing
Schwinge *f* rocker, oscillating crank
Schwingebene *f* plane of swing

schwingen 1. *(allg.)* vibrate, oscillate, rock **2.** *(langsam)* swing
schwingende Beanspruchung *f* **1.** *(Dauerschwingversuch)* cyclic loading **2.** *(Aufspannfelder)* subject to alternating loads **3.** *(e. Tellerfeder)* dynamic loading
schwingende Biegebeanspruchung *f* alternating flexural loading
schwingende Kurbelschleife *f* swinging arm
schwingende Zunge *f* vibrating reed
schwingendes Werkzeug *nt* vibrating tool
Schwinger *m* oscillator
Schwingfrequenz *f* oscillating frequency
Schwinggehäuse *nt* swivel spindle carrier
Schwinghub *m* cycle stroke
Schwingisolierung *f* insulation against vibrations
Schwingklemme *f* vibration clamp
Schwingkreis *m* oscillating circuit, resonant circuit
Schwingläppen swing lapping
Schwingprüfmaschine *f* fatigue testing machine
Schwingschleifen *nt* **1.** *(allg.)* superfinish grinding **2.** *(Kurzhubhonen)* superfinishing
Schwingspannung *f* *(sinusförmige ~)* sinusoidal alternating stress
Schwingspiegel *m* oscillatory mirror, oscillating mirror, swing mirror
Schwingspiegelsystem *nt* oscillating mirror system
Schwingspiegelvorsatz *m* oscillating mirror add-on
Schwingspiel *nt* fatigue cycle, cycle
Schwingspieldrehzahl *f* number of cycles
Schwingspielfrequenz *f* cycle frequency
Schwingspielzahl *f* number of fatigue cycles
Schwingstrom *m* vibrator current
Schwingung *f* **1.** *(freie)* swing, oscillation **2.** *(konstante Frequenz)* vibration **3.** *(Resonanz)* vibration **4.** *(Wellen)* oscillation, oscillatory wave **5.** *(fremderregte ~)* forced vibration
Schwingungen *fpl* **höherer Ordnung** higher harmonics
Schwingungsamplitude *f* oscillation amplitude
Schwingungsarm *m* rocking arm, pawl arm
schwingungsarmer Lauf *m* low-vibration running
Schwingungsaufnehmer *m* vibration pick-up
Schwingungsausschlag *m* amplitude of oscillation, degree of oscillation, oscillation amplitude
Schwingungsband *nt* vibration antinode
Schwingungsbeanspruchung *f* cyclic stress, stress due to oscillation, vibration loading
schwingungsdämpfend vibration damping
Schwingungsdämpfung *f* vibration damping, suppression
Schwingungsdynamik *f* oscillation dynamics
Schwingungsebene *f* oscillation level
Schwingungseigenschaft *f* vibration property
Schwingungserreger *m* oscillation generator, vibration generator
Schwingungserregung *f* excitation of vibrations
Schwingungsfestigkeit *f* resistance to vibration
schwingungsfrei free from vibrations, vibration-free, vibrationless, non-vibrating, pulsation-free
schwingungsgedämpftes geschichtetes System *nt* damped laminated system
Schwingungsisolierung *f* vibration insulation
Schwingungssteifigkeit *f* resistance to dynamic stresses
schwingungsunempfindlich not susceptible to vibrations, insensitive to vibrations
Schwingungsverfahren *nt* vibration method (with constant frequency, vari-

able vibration, longitude and constant tensile load), vibration behaviour
Schwingungsverhalten *nt* vibrational characteristics
Schwingungsverlauf *m* wave form
Schwingziehschleifen swing pull grinding
Schwitzeffekt *m* condensation effect
Schwitzwassergerät *nt* damp heat apparatus
Schwitzwasserklima *nt* condensation climate
Schwitzwasserklima *nt* damp heat atmosphere
Schwitzwasserkonstantklima *nt* standard damp heat atmosphere
Schwitzwasserwechselklima *nt* alternating damp heat atmosphere
Schwund *m* contraction, shrinkage
Schwungmasse *f* gyrating mass
Schwungrad *nt* flywheel
Schwungzahnkranz *m* flywheel ring gear
scrollen scroll
Scrollen *nt* scrolling
Sechseck *nt* hexagon
sechseckig hexagonal
Sechsfachmeißelhalter *m* six-way tool block
Sechsfachpresswerkzeug *nt* six-fold compression mould
Sechskant *m* hex(agon)
Sechskantblechschraube *f* hexagon head (sheet metal) tapping screw
Sechskantbolzen *m* hexagon bolt
Sechskantbund *m* hexagonal bundle
Sechskantdehnschraube *f* hexagon head bolt with waisted shank
Sechskantfläche *f* *(e. Mutter)* hexagon flat
Sechskantgrund *m* hexagon bottom
Sechskantholzschraube *f* hexagon head wood screw
Sechskanthutmutter *f* hexagon cap nut
sechskantig hexagonal
Sechskantmutter *f* hexagon(al) nut
Sechskantmutter *f* **mit großer Schlüsselweite** hexagon nut with large width across flats
Sechskantrevolverkopf *m* hexagon turret
Sechskantrohr *nt* hexagon tube
Sechskantschlüssel *m* hex(agonal) wrench
Sechskantschneidschraube *f* hexagon head thread cutting screw
Sechskantschraube *f* **1.** *(allg.)* hexagon bolt, hexagon head screw **2.** *(für Fertigungsmittel in der Luftfahrt)* hexagon bolt for aircraft workshop facilities **3.** *(mit Ansatzspitze)* hexagon set screw with coned half dog point **4.** *(mit großer Schlüsselweite für HV-Verbindungen)* hexagon bolt with large width across flats for high strength friction grip fastenings **5.** *(mit kleinem Sechskant und Ansatzspitze)* hexagon set screw with half dog point **6.** *(mit kleinem Sechskant und Zapfen)* hexagon set screw with full dog point **7.** *(mit Zapfen)* hexagon head screw with full dog point
Sechskantschraubendreher *m* hexagon screwdriver, hexagon wrench key
Sechskantschraubendrehereinsatz *m* hexagon wrench key insert
Sechskantschweißmutter *f* hexagon weld nut
Sechskantstiftschlüssel *m* **mit Zapfen** hexagon wrench key with pilot
Sechskanttiefe *f* *(z. B. e. Verschlussschraube)* hexagon socket depth
Sechskantumpressung *f* hexagonal laminated moulded section
Sechskantvollstab *m* hexagon rod
Sechsspindelautomat *m* six-spindle automatic bar machine
Sechsspindelhalbautomat *m* six-spindle automatic screw machine
sechsspindelige Bohrmaschine *f* six spindle drilling machine
Sechsspindler *m* six-spindle automatic lathe
sechsstufiger Räderkasten *m* six speed gearbox
Sedimentationsanalyse *f* sedimentation analysis
Sedimentationsschichten *fpl* sedimentary strata

Segment *nt* segment
Segmentscheibe *f* segmented wheel
Sehne *f* chord
Sehnenbiegung *f* chord deflection, chord inflection
Sehnenmaß *nt* chordal dimension
Sehnenmessung *f* chordal measurement
sehr gering minute
Sehschärfe *f* visual acuity
Sehwinkel *m* angle of vision
Seigerung *f* segregation, liquation process
Seigerungsverhalten *nt* segregation behaviour
Seil *nt* 1. *(allg.)* rope, cable 2. *(Drahtseil)* wire rope
Seilantrieb *m* rope drive
Seilendbefestigung *f* rope termination
Seilförderer *m* cable conveyor
Seilgrund *m* bottom of the groove
Seilhub *m* rope lift
Seilkürzer *m* fall arrestor (for safety equipment), retractor
Seilrad *nt* grooved wheel
Seilrille *f* groove
Seilrolle *f* pulley, rope pulley, wire rope guide pulley
Seiltrieb *m* rope drive
Seiltrommel *f* rope drum
Seiltrumm *nt* end of rope
Seilwinde *f* winch, cable winch, hoisting winch, rope winch
Seilwindung *f* turn (of rope)
Seilzug *m* 1. *(allg.)* wire rope 2. *(Betätigungsseil)* tackle line, draw wire 3. *(Spannung)* cable pull, tension in the cable 4. *(Winde)* tackle, winch
Seilzugbremse *f* cable brake
Seilzugsicherung *f* tackle locking device, rope locking device, rope lock, locking device
Seite *f* 1. *(z. B. Bauteil)* face, side, edge, hand, end 2. *(Text)* page
Seiten ... lateral
Seitenansicht *f* side view, side elevation
Seitenausladung *f* lateral clearance
Seitenbereich *m (e. Toleranzfeldes)* side band

Seitenbiegeprobe *f* lateral bend specimen
Seitendrehmeißel *m* side-turning tool
Seiteneinstellung *f* lateral adjustment
seitenfahrend driving along the side
Seitenfaltbeutel *m* satchel bag
Seitenfalte *f* gusset, side gusset
Seitenfläche *f* side face
Seitenfräsen *nt* side milling
Seitenfreiwinkel *m* side clearance, chamfer relief angle
Seitenführung *f* lateral guide(s), side guide
Seitenführungsrolle *f* side guide roller
Seitengenauigkeit *f* alignment accuracy, side accuracy
Seitenguss *m* side casting
Seitenhubspreader *m* side lift spreader
Seiteninhalt *m* side content
Seitenkeilwinkel *m* side wedge angle
Seitenkippgerät *nt* side tippler
Seitenklappe *f* side flap
Seitenklemme *f* side clamp
Seitenkraft *f* lateral force, side thrust
Seitenlage *f* lateral position
Seitenlager *nt* side bearing
Seitenmeißel *m* 1. *(allg.)* side tool, side cutting tool, shoulder tool 2. *(abgesetzter ~)* offset side-cutting tool 3. *(abgesetzter linker ~)* left-offset cutting tool 4. *(abgesetzter rechter ~)* right-offset cutting tool
Seitennaht *f* side seam seal
Seitenquittierung *f* page acknowledgement
Seitenrampe *f* side ramp
Seitenschieber *m* lateral slide, side loader, sidehandling, sideload handling, sideload handling device, lateral handling device, side shift
Seitenschlag *m (e. Lagers)* radial runout
Seitenschleifen *nt* lateral grinding
Seitenschruppmeißel *m* side rougher
Seitenschub *m* side thrust, sidehandling, sideload handling, lateral handling, lateral handling facilities
Seitenschutz *m* guards at the sides, side guards, side protection
Seitenschwenkgabel *f* trilateral re-

tractable fork, trilateral head
Seitenshuttle *nt* sideways moving shuttle
Seitenspanwinkel *m* 1. *(allg.)* side rake angle, *(UK)* side top rake angle, shank side rake, *(US)* side rake, side housing 2. *(an der Spanflächenfase)* primary side rake angle 3. *(hinter Fase)* secondary side rake angle
Seitenstabilität *f* lateral stability
Seitenständer *m* side column
Seitenstapelanbaugerät *nt* lateral attachment
Seitenstapler *m* lateral stacking truck, lateral truck, side-loading fork truck
Seitensupport *m* horizontal head, side box, side head, side tool-head, side toolbox
Seitenteil *nt* side member
Seitenüberwachung *f* width monitoring
Seitenverschleiß *m* side wear
Seitenverschließmaschine *f* edge sealing machine
seitenverschlossen side-seamed
Seitenverstellung *f* lateral adjustment
Seitenverstrebung *f* frame cross bracing
Seitenwand *f* sidewall, sidesheet
seitenwandloser Spulenkörper *m* reel without cheeks
Seitenwange *f* cheek
seitenweise by page
Seitenwinkel *m* 1. *(Drehmeißel) (US)* side rake angle, *(UK)* shank side rake 2. *(Fräser)* secondary rake 3. *(Radialwinkel)* radial rake angle
Seitenzulauf *m* side branch
seitlich side, sideways, sidewise, lateral
seitlich ausfahrendes LAM *Abk.* lateral handling device
seitlich ausweichen deflect sideways
seitlich hinterschliffen side-relieved
seitlich verklebt side seam glued
seitlicher Freiwinkel *m* side clearance
seitlicher Vorschub *m* lateral feed
Sektorskala *f* sector scale
Sekundärverschlämmung *f* secondary silting up
sekundär secondary

Sekundärbefehl *m* secondary command, SC
Sekundär-Dauerstrom *m* continuous secondary current
sekundärer Freiwinkel *m* secondary clearance
Sekundärimpedanz *f* secondary impedance
Sekundärkurzschlussstrom *m* secondary short circuit current
Sekundärleerlaufspannung *f* secondary no-load voltage
Sekundärspannungsbereich *m* secondary voltage range
selbsterregt self-starting
selbstabbindender Kautschukkleber *m* self-setting natural rubber adhesive
Selbstähnlichkeit *f* self-similarity
selbstansaugend self-priming
Selbstausgleich *m* self-compensation
Selbstauslösung *f* automatic release
Selbstausschalter *m* automatic circuit-breaker
Selbstbau *m* self-construction
Selbstbauprofil *nt* slotted section
Selbstbremsung *f* self-braking
selbstdichtende Gewindeverbindung *f* pressure-tight screw joint (or screw fastening)
Selbstentlader *m* tilting cart, tipper
selbsterregte Schwingung *f* self-induced vibrations
Selbsterregung *f* auto-excitation, self-excitation, differential excitation
selbstfahrend self-propelled
Selbstgang *m* automatic traverse, power traverse
Selbstglättungsverhalten *nt* self-smoothing behaviour
selbsthaftende Schicht *f* self-adhesive layer
selbsthaltend 1. *(allg.)* sealing, locking 2. *(Taste)* holding
Selbsthaltung *f* lock, catch, positive location
selbsthärtender Zweikomponentenstoff *m* self-curing two-component material
selbsthemmend non-reversible, self-

locking, self-sustaining
Selbsthemmung *f* self-locking, self-locking device, automatic lock
Selbstklebeband *nt* pressure-sensitive tape, self-adhesive tape
selbstklebend pressure-sensitive, self-adhesive
selbstklebendes Isolierband *nt* pressure-sensitive adhesive insulating tape
selbstklebendes Schmirgelpapier *nt* self-adhesive emery paper
Selbstkosten *pl* prime costs
Selbstlockerung *f* spontaneous slackening
Selbstprüfung *f* auto-test, self-test
Selbstreinigungsvermögen *nt* self-cleaning property
selbstschaltend self-indexing
selbstschärfend self-sharpening
Selbstschärfung *f* self-sharpening (action)
selbstschließend self-closing
selbstschneidende Elektrode *f* self-cutting electrode
selbstsichernde Mutter *f* self-locking nut, prevailing torque type locknut
selbstsichernde Sechskantmutter *f* prevailing torque type hexagon locknut
selbstsichernder Gewindeteil *m* (e. Mutter) prevailing torque part (of the nut)
selbstsicherndes Bauteil *nt* self-locking building element
selbstständig autonomous, independent
Selbststellglied *nt* automatic actuator
selbststeuernd autonomous
selbsttätig self-acting, automatic
selbsttätig absperrende Sicherung *f* automatic-acting shut-off feature
selbsttätig wirkend automatically acting
selbsttätig wirkende Bremse *f* automatically acting brake
selbsttätige Nachformfräsmaschine *f* 1. (allg.) automatic tracer-controlled miller 2. (für Gesenke, Pressformen usw.) duplicator, die-sinker, profile miller, profiler
selbsttätige Regelung *f* automatic closed loop control
selbsttätige Überwachung *f* automatic monitoring
selbsttätiger Schnellgang *m* rapid power traverse
selbsttätiger Vorschub *m* power feed
selbsttätiges Lösen *nt* (e. Mutter) self-loosening
Selbsttest *m* auto-test, self-test
selbsttragend 1. (allg.) self-supporting, self-contained 2. (nicht ~) non-self-supporting
selbstüberwachend automatically monitored, self-regulating
Selbstüberwachung *f* autosupervision, self-monitoring
selbstvulkanisierender Kautschukkleber *m* self-vulcanizing natural rubber adhesive
selbstzentrierend self-centring, autocentring
Selbstzentrierung *f* self-centring, autocentring
Selektionsgitter *nt* selective grating
selektiver Angriff *m* selective attack
selten rare
Semantik *f* semantics
Sende-/Empfangseinheit *f* send/receive unit
Sende-/Empfangseinrichtung *f* send/receive device
Sendeberechtigung *f* permission to transmit, authorization token, token
Sendeberechtigung *f* "Weiterreichen" token passing
Sendeberechtigungsmarke *f* token
Sendebereich *m* transmission range
Sendefrequenz *f* transmitter frequency
senden 1. (allg.) send 2. (Signale) transmit 3. (Strahlen) emit
Sendepaket *nt* send packet
Sender *m* 1. (allg.) sender 2. (Signale) transmitter 3. (Strahlen) emitter
Sender/Empfänger *m* transmitter/receiver, transceiver
Sender-Empfänger-Lichttaster *m* emitter receiver light scanner
Sendespule *f* transmission coil
Sendimpulsstärke *f* intensity of transmitted pulse

Sendung *f* **1.** *(Daten)* mission, sending **2.** *(Waren)* consignment
Sendungsanzahl *f* number of consignments
Sendungsgröße *f* consignment size
Sendzimir-Verzinkung *f* Sendzimir galvanizing (coating)
Senkbewegung *f* lowering motion, lowering movement, descent, downward motion
Senkblechschraube *f* countersunk (flat) head tapping screw
Senkblechschraube *f* **mit Kreuzschlitz** recessed countersunk (flat) head wood screw
Senkblechschraube *f* **mit Schlitz** slotted countersunk (flat) head tapping screw
Senkbolzen *m* countersunk bolt
Senke *f* drain, sink
senken *(sich ~)* settle
senken 1. *(allg.)* lower **2.** *(kegelig, bohren, gravieren)* countersink **3.** *(zylindrisch)* counterbore **4.** *(reduzieren)* reduce **5.** *(hinablassen)* descend
Senker *m* counterbore, countersinking cutter
Senkerodieren *nt* lower eroding
Senkerodiermaschine *f* lower eroding machine
Senkgeschwindigkeit *f* lowering speed, rate of descent
Senkholzschraube *f* **mit Vierkantansatz** countersunk square neck bolt for woodwork
Senknietverbindung *f* countersunk rivet joint
Senkpassschraube *f* **mit Flügelkreuzschlitz** countersunk head fitting screw with torque-set recess
senkrecht 1. *(lotrecht)* perpendicular **2.** *(vertikal)* vertical (to)
senkrecht zur Arbeitsebene *f* perpendicular to the working plane
senkrecht zur Werkstückoberfläche schneidendes Räumwerkzeug *nt* depth cutting type of broach
Senkrechtabhebung *f* vertical lift
Senkrechtbewegung *f* vertical feed motion
Senkrechtbohrmaschine *f* vertical boring machine, vertical drilling machine, upright drilling machine
Senkrechtbohrwerk *nt* vertical boring mill
Senkrechtdrehautomat *m* vertical automatic production lathe
Senkrechtdurchschallung *f* vertical transmission
Senkrechte *f* perpendicular, vertical, plumb line, normal line
senkrechte Normschrift *f* vertical style standard lettering
Senkrechteinfall *m* normal incidence
Senkrechteinschallung *f* vertical intromission
Senkrechtförderer *m* elevator, vertical conveyor
Senkrechtfräs- und -lehrenbohrmaschine *f* vertical miller and jig borer
Senkrechtfräsapparat *m* vertical milling head
Senkrechtfräsarbeit *f* vertical milling, vertical milling job
Senkrechtfräsautomat *m* **1.** *(allg.)* vertical-spindle continuous milling machine **2.** *(mit Rundtisch)* vertical-spindle rotary continuous milling machine
Senkrechtfräseinrichtung *f* rise- and fall milling attachment
Senkrechtfräsen *nt* vertical milling
Senkrechtfräskopf *m* vertical milling head, vertical cutting head, vertical cutter head, vertical spindle head
Senkrechtfräsmaschine *f* **1.** *(allg.)* vertical-spindle miller (or milling machine), vertical milling machine **2.** *(mit längs- und querbeweglichem Spindelkasten)* vertical (fixed-bed) miller with longitudinally and cross traversing headstock **3.** *(mit Rundtisch)* vertical-spindle rotary-type milling machine **4.** *(mit Rundtisch für durchlaufendes Fräsen)* vertical continuous rotary miller (or milling machine), continuous rotary milling machine, rotary milling machine **5.** *(mit Selbstgang)* vertical milling machine with automatic table traverse and fall miller **6.** *(mit senkrecht beweglicher Frässpindel)* rise- and fall fixed-

bed milling machine, rise- and fall miller
Senkrechtfrässpindelkopf *m* vertical milling spindle head
Senkrechtfrässpindelstock *m* vertical milling spindle head
Senkrechtfräsvorrichtung *f* **1.** *(allg.)* vertical milling attachment, vertical-spindle attachment **2.** *(mit Kreuzschlitten)* compound vertical milling attachment, compound vertical-spindle attachment
Senkrechthobelmaschine *f (US)* slotter, *(UK)* slotting machine
Senkrechthobeln *nt* strike, knock, push, jog, shape
Senkrechtkonsolfräsmaschine *f* vertical type knee- and column miller (or milling machine), vertical-spindle column- and knee miller, vertical knee- and column type milling machine, column- and knee type vertical-spindle milling machine
Senkrechtkopierfräsmaschine *f* vertical profiling machine, vertical copy-milling machine
Senkrechtlangfräsmaschine *f* vertical planer-miller, vertical plano-milling machine
Senkrechtnachformfräsmaschine *f* **1.** *(für dreidimensionale Gesenkarbeit)* vertical duplicator, vertical die-sinker **2.** *(für zweidimensionales Fräsen)* vertical profiler with two-dimensional control
Senkrechtnutenfräsmaschine *f* vertical slot milling machine
Senkrechtplanfräsmaschine *f* vertical-spindle fixed-bed type milling machine, vertical-spindle manufacturing-type milling machine, kneeless-type vertical milling machine
Senkrechtproduktionsfräsmaschine *f* manufacturing-type milling machine with vertical spindle, vertical-spindle fixed-bed type milling machine
Senkrechtprüfkopf *m* vertical probe
Senkrechtrundtischfräsautomat *m* **mit zwei Spannstellen und vier Doppelfräsköpfen** double station vertical-spindle rotary continuous milling machine with four double-unit milling heads
Senkrechtrundtischfräsmaschine *f* vertical-spindle rotary-table milling machine, vertical-spindle miller with rotary table
Senkrechtschlitten *m* toolhead slide, crossrail slide, head slide
Senkrechtschnitt *m* normal section, square cut
Senkrechtschnittkraft *f* vertical tool thrust
Senkrechtschraube *f* countersink bolt
Senkrechtstoßeinrichtung *f* slotting attachment
Senkrechtstößelhobelmaschine *f* **1.** *(allg.)* vertical shaper **2.** *(mit schrägstellbarer Stößelführung)* vertical shaper with adjustable inclination of the ram, vertical shaper with swivel toolhead
Senkrechtstoßen *nt* slotting
Senkrechtstoßmaschine *f* **1.** *(allg.)* *(US)* slotter, *(UK)* slotting machine, (rarely) vertical slotting and shaping machine **2.** *(Senkrechtstößelhobelmaschine)* vertical shaper (or shaping machine) **3.** *(mit Kurbelscheibenantrieb)* crank slotter (or slotting machine) **4.** *(mit Zahnräderantrieb)* geared slotting machine **5.** *(zur Bearbeitung von Matrizen)* die slotter
Senkrechtstoßräummaschine *f (mit Abwärtsbewegung des Räumschlittens)* vertical push-down broaching machine
Senkrechtverstellung *f* vertical adjustment
Senkrechtvierspindelbohr- und -gewindebohreinheit *f* vertical multiple-spindle drilling and tapping unit
Senkrechtvorschub *m* **1.** *(allg.)* vertical downfeed, downfeed, depth feed **2.** *(schräger ~)* angular downfeed
Senkrechtzahnradstoßmaschine *f* vertical gear generator
Senkschneidschraube *f* countersunk head thread cutting screw
Senkschraube *f* **1.** *(allg.)* countersink bolt **2.** *(mit Gewinde und Kopf)* countersunk head screw threaded to head

3. *(mit Innensechskant)* hexagon socket countersunk (flat) head screw **4.** *(mit Kreuzschlitz)* recessed countersunk (flat) head screw **5.** *(mit Schlitz)* slotted countersunk (flat) head screw **6.** *(mit zwei Nasen)* countersunk double-nib bolt
Senkung *f* **1.** *(als Arbeitsvorgang)* sinking **2.** *(Arbeitsergebnis)* counterbore, countersink **3.** *(kegelige)* countersinking **4.** *(zylindrische)* counterboring **5.** *(für Zylinderschrauben)* counterbore for cheese head screws
Senkvorgang *m* descent
Senkwerkzeug *nt* countersinking tool, counterboring tool
Sensitivitätsbetrachtung *f* sensitivity analysis
Sensor *m* **in der Gabelspitze** fork tip sensor
Sensor *m* sensor
Sensordaten *pl* sensor data
Sensordatenaufbeitung *f* sensor data conditioning
Sensorebene *f* sensor level
Sensoren *mpl* sensor
Sensorensauswahl *f* sensor selection
Sensorik *f* sensors
sensorisches Untersuchungsgerät *nt* apparatus for sensory analysis
sensorlos sensorless
Sensortechnik *f* **1.** *(Technik)* sensor technology **2.** *(Wissenschaft)* sensor engineering
separat separate
Separator *m* separator
Separierfähigkeit *f* ability to separate
Separierzone *f* separation zone
sequentiell sequential
sequentieller Funktionsplan *m* sequential function chart
sequentielles Programm *nt* sequential program
Sequenz *f* sequence
Serie *f* lot, series, batch
seriell serial
Seriell-zu-parallel-Codierer serial-to-parallel coder
serielle Datenübertragung *f* serial data transmission

Serienarbeit *f* repetition job
Serienbrenner *m* series-manufactured burner
Serienfertigung *f* series production (work), duplicate production, batch production, repetition work, long run production
Serienfräsen *nt* repetition milling
Seriengießverfahren *nt* batch casting process
Serienhubwerk *nt* serial hoist unit
serienmäßig in series, serial
serienmäßige Herstellung *f* large batch production, series production
Seriennummer *f* serial number
Serienstücke *ntpl* repetitive parts
Serienteil *nt* duplicate part
Serienübergabe *f* serial transmission
Serviceeinsatzgrenze *f* on-site service guarantee
Servicegrad *m* service level, degree of service, service ratio
Servoabtastrate *f* servo cycle time
Servolenkung *f* power(-assisted) steering
Servomotor *m* servo (motor), servo drive
Servosteuerung *f* servo control
SE-Senkrechtprüfkopf *m* vertical transmitter-receiver probe
SE-Technik *f* transmitter-receiver technique
Setzblock *m* steady
Setzeingang *m* set input
Setzeinpack-/-auspackmaschine *f* place packing/unpacking machine
setzen 1. *(allg., IT)* set **2.** *(Objekte)* place, lay **3.** *(senken, sich ~)* settle
Setzen *nt* *(von Rohteilen für das Fließpressen)* pancaking (of the sheared slug for extrusion)
Setzstock *m* steadyrest
Setzstockbacke *f* shoe
Setzstufe *f* riser
Setzung *f* settlement, settling
Setzungsmulde *f* settlement (of the foundations), settling
SE-Winkelprüfkopf *m* angle transmitter-receiver probe
S-Förderer *m* S-conveyor

SGC *Abk. (Körperaushärteverfahren)* Solid Ground Curing
Shaper *m* horizontal-type shaper, shaping machine, shaper
Shapingmaschine *f* horizontal-type shaper, shaping machine, shaper
sicher reliable, dependable, secure safe
sichere Betriebsperiode *f* safe work period (SWP)
sichere Feststellung *f* secure locking
sicherer Arbeitsbereich *m* safe operating area
Sicherheit *f* 1. *(allg.)* safety, safeguard, guard 2. *(e. Toleranz)* confidence coefficient
Sicherheitsabblaseeinrichtung *f* safety blow-off device
Sicherheitsabschaltung *f* safety shutdown
Sicherheitsabsperrvorrichtung *f* safety shut-off device
Sicherheitsabstand *m* safety clearance, safety distance, distance of reach
Sicherheitsanforderung *f* safety requirement
Sicherheitsanlage *f* safety system
Sicherheitsanschlagnocke *f* safety stop dog
Sicherheitsauflage *f* safety regulation
Sicherheitsausdehnungsleitung *f* safety expansion pipe
Sicherheitsausschalter *m* cutout
Sicherheitsbauteile *ntpl* safety-related parts
Sicherheitsbefehl *m* safety instruction
Sicherheitsbeiwert *m* safety coefficient
Sicherheitsbestand *m* safety stock
Sicherheitsbestimmung *f* safety requirement, safety regulation
sicherheitsbezogen safety related
Sicherheitsblockierung *f* interlocking safety control
Sicherheitsbremse *f* emergency brake
Sicherheitsbrille *f* goggles, safety glasses
Sicherheitsdatenblatt *nt* safety datasheet
Sicherheitsdurchgangsventil *nt* straight safety valve
Sicherheitseckventil *nt* angle safety valve
Sicherheitseinrichtung *f* safety device, safety equipment, safety gear
Sicherheitsfahrschaltung *f* dead man's device
Sicherheitsfaktor *m* safety factor
Sicherheitsfangritzel *nt* pinion which operates the safety gear, pinion which operates the catching device
Sicherheitsfarbe *f* safety colour
Sicherheitsfläche *f* safety area
Sicherheitsgasschlauch *m* gas safety tubing
sicherheitsgefährdend hazardous
sicherheitsgerechtes Gestalten *nt* designing conform to safety principles
Sicherheitsglas *nt* safety glass
Sicherheitsgrenztaster *m* safety limit switch
Sicherheitsgründe *mpl* safety considerations
Sicherheitsgrundsätze *mpl* safety principles
Sicherheitsgurt *m* safety belt
Sicherheitshandschuhe *f* safety gloves
Sicherheitskleinspannung *f* safety extra-low voltage (SELV)
Sicherheitsklinke *f* safety latch
Sicherheitskontakt *m* safety contact
Sicherheitskupplung *f* safety clutch
Sicherheitsmaßnahme *f* safety measure
Sicherheitsmaßnahmen einleiten *(z. B. bei Gefahr einer Gasrohrleitung)* initiate emergency safety measures
Sicherheitsmerkmal *nt* safety feature
Sicherheitsmutter *f* safety nut
Sicherheitsniveau *nt* level of safety
Sicherheitsnorm *f* safety standard
Sicherheitsproblem *nt* safety problem
Sicherheitsregel *f* safety rule
Sicherheitsrisiko *nt* safety risk
Sicherheitsrücklaufleitung *f* safety return pipe
Sicherheitsrutschkupplung *f* friction safety clutch
Sicherheitsschalter *m* safety switch, safety device
Sicherheitsschiene *f* safety rail
Sicherheitsschloss *nt* safety lock

Sicherheitsschuhe *mpl* safety shoes
Sicherheitssichtebene *f* safety viewing glass
Sicherheitssperre *f* backlocking
Sicherheitssperrklinke *f* keeper, safety pawl
Sicherheitsstift *m* safety pin
Sicherheitsstromkreis *m* safety circuit
Sicherheitstechnik *f* safety technology, safety practice
sicherheitstechnisch from a safety point of view
sicherheitstechnische Anforderung *f* safety requirement
sicherheitstechnische Festlegung *f* safety practice stipulations
sicherheitstechnische Maßnahmen *fpl* safety practice measures
sicherheitstechnisches Mittel *nt* safety practice aid
Sicherheitstemperaturbegrenzer *m* safety temperature limiter
Sicherheitsumkehrschalter *m* safety reverser
Sicherheitsventil *nt* relief valve, blow-off valve, safety valve, safety pressure relief valve
Sicherheitsvorkehrung *f* safety provision
Sicherheitsvorlaufleitung *f* safety flow pipe
Sicherheitsvorrichtung *f* safety device, safeguard
Sicherheitswechselventil *nt* safety change-over valve
Sicherheitszeichen *f* safety sign
Sicherheitszeit *f* "Anlauf" "start-up" safety time, opening time
Sicherheitszeit *f* "Betriebszustand" "operating" safety time, closing time
Sicherheitszuschlag *m* safety factor
sichern 1. *(allg.)* restrain, secure, safeguard, guard ensure **2.** *(befestigen)* fasten secure **3.** *(durch Verriegelung)* lock secure **4.** *(gegen Gefahr)* render safe, safeguard, guard **5.** *(schützen)* protect (against)
Sichern *nt* **von Palettenladungen** pallet securing
sicherstellen assure, ensure, make sure, secure, safeguard
Sicherstellung *f* safety assurance
Sicherung *f* **1.** *(allg.)* safety device, safety feature, safeguard, fuse **2.** *(Oberbegriff techn. Einrichtung)* locking feature **3.** *(el.)* cut-out, fuse **4.** *(Sicherungselement)* locking device, retaining element, prevailing torque type element **5.** *(der Güte)* maintenance of quality **6.** *(gegen Abstürzen)* anti-falling device **7.** *(gegen Entgleisen)* anti-derailment device **8.** *(gegen Umkippen/Umstürzen)* anti-derailment device
Sicherungsblech *nt* lock washer, retaining washer
Sicherungsblech *nt* **mit Innenmasse** internal tab washer
Sicherungsblock *m* safety block
Sicherungselement *nt* locking element, retaining element, safety bar, fuse element
Sicherungskasten *m* switchbox
Sicherungskette *f* safety chain
Sicherungskopie *f* back-up copy
Sicherungsmaschine *f* securing machine
Sicherungsmutter *f* prevailing torque-type locknut, retaining nut, locknut
Sicherungsnadel *f* **1.** *(allg.)* retaining pin **2.** *(für versenkte Zylinderschrauben)* safety cup
Sicherungsprogramm *nt* assurance program
Sicherungsring *m* locking ring, lockwasher, retaining ring
Sicherungsring *m* **mit Lappen** retaining ring with lug
Sicherungsschraube *f* lock bolt
Sicherungsseil *nt* safety cable
Sicherungsstift *m* cotter
Sicherungsstütze *f* safety support
Sicherungsteil *nt* *(e. Mutter)* locking element, prevailing torque element
Sicherungsteil *nt* **aus Nichtmetall** *(bei kombinierten Metallmuttern)* non-metallic prevailing torque element
Sicherungsvorrichtung *f* safeguard
Sicherungswirkung *f* locking (or retaining) effect
Sicht *f* visibility

Sichtanzeige f readout, visual display, visual indication
Sichtausgeber m visual read out device
sichtbar machen nt (e. Röntgenbildes) display (an X-ray pattern)
Sichtbarwerden nt becoming visible
Sichtbild nt multi-section pattern
Sichtertemperaturregler m sifter temperature controller
Sichtfeld nt field of view
Sichtkontrolle f visual control
Sichtmelder m visual signal device
Sichtmessung f visibility test
Sichtprüfung f visual inspection (or examination)
Sichtschlitz m viewing slot
Sichtverbindung f view, visual contact
Sichtvermerk m endorsement
Sicke f crease, reinforcing fin
Sicken nt beading, creasing
Sickerleitung f seepage water drain pipe
Sickerpackung f seepage water drain packing
Sickung f swaging
Sieb nt screen, sieve, strainer
Siebdruckfarbe f screen printing ink
Siebeinsatz m screen insert, strainer
sieben screen, sieve
Siebhalterung f sieve holder
Sieblehre f screen gauge
Siebrahmen m sieve frame
Siebrückstandsbestimmung f test sieving
Siedebeginn m initial boiling point
Siedeendpunkt m end point distillation
siedende Anteile mpl boiling fractions
Siedestab m immersion heater
siegeln seal
Siegelrandbeutel m sachet
Siegelrandbeutelform-, -füll- und -verschließmaschine f sachet form fill and seal machine
Siegelwerkzeug nt sealing bar
Signal nt signal
Signalabgabe f signal emission
Signalanschluss m signal interface, signal port
Signalaufbereitung f signal processing
Signalbegrenzer m volume limiter

Signaleingang m signal input (device)
Signaleinsteller m signal adjuster
Signalflanke f signal edge
Signalfluss m information flow, signal flow
Signalflussweg m signal flow path
Signalfolge f signal sequence
Signalgeber m sensor element, signal encoder, signal transmitter, transducer
Signalhupe f horn
signalisieren signal
Signallampe f signal lamp, control lamp, warning lamp, pilot lamp
Signallaufbahn f signal diagram
Signalleitung f signal cable
Signalleuchte f signal light
Signalpegelumsetzer m signal level converter
Signalpolarität f signal polarity
Signal-Rausch-Abstand m signal-to-noise ratio
Signalschaltung f signal switching
Signalspannung f signal potential
Signalstruktur f signal structure
Signalumformer m signal converter
Signalumsetzer m signal transducer, signal converter
Signalveränderung f signal alteration, signal modification
Signalverarbeitung f signal processing
Signalverlängerung f signal prolongation
Signalverlust m signal loss
Signalverstärker m signal amplifier
Signalverwertung f signal exploitation
Signalverzögerung f signal delay
Signalwandler m signal converter
Signalweiche f change-over gate
Signalzustand "Eins" m mark
Signalzustand "Null" m space
signifikantes Testergebnis nt significant test result
Signifikanzniveau nt significance level
Silberauflage f silver plating
Silberfärbung f silver colouration
Silberhalogenid m silver halide
silberhaltiges Hartlot nt silver-bearing brazing filler alloy
Silberlot nt silver solder
Silbersalzpapier nt silver sensitized pa-

per
Silberschliere *f* silver stria
Silberstreifenprüfung *f* silver strip test
Silberwarenlot *nt* silverware solder
Silikatbildung *f* silicate bond
Silikatplastikmasse *f* silicate plastics material
Silikon *nt* silicone
silikone Strahlmittel *mpl* siliconic blasting agent
Silikonfettfilm *m* film of silicone grease
Silikonharz *nt* silicone resin
Silikonkatschukknetmasse *f* silicone rubber mastic
Silikonkautschukgießmasse *f* silicone rubber casting compound
Silikonkautschukmasse *f* silicone rubber compound
Silikosegefahr *f* silicosis
Silizium *nt* silicon
Siliziumkarbid *nt* silicon carbide
Silo *nt* silo
Silobauweise *f* silo design, silo rack type, silo rack construction
Silothoerie *f* silo theory
Simlatorkern *m* simulator core
simplex simplex, half-duplex
Simplexbetrieb *m* simplex operation
Simplexbremse *f* simplex brake
Simplexübertragung *f* simplex transmission
Simulation *f* simulation
Simulationsbetrieb *m* simulation operation
Simulationsexperiment *nt* simulation experiment, simulation trial
simulationsgestützt simulation-based
Simulationslauf *m* simulation run
Simulationsmodell *nt* simulation model
Simulationsprozessverknüpfung *f* simulation process coupling
Simulationsrückmeldung *f* simulation feedback
Simulationssprache *f* simulation language
Simulationsstudie *f* simulation study
Simulationsuntersuchung *f* simulation study
Simulator *m* simulator

Simulatorprogrammierung *f* simulator programming
simulieren simulate
Simulierer *m* simulation program
simultan simultaneous
Simultanschichtaufnahme *f* simultaneous tomograph
Singleman-RBG *nt* single-man S/R machine
Singleton *nt* singleton
Sinkbewegung *f* descent
sinken descend, fall, drop, decrease
Sinneswahrnehmung *f* sensory perception
sinnvoll appropriate
Sinter *m* scale
Sinterformteile sinter shaped parts
Sinterkarbid *nt* cemented carbide, sintered carbide
Sintermetall *nt* sintered metal, sintered carbide metal, cemented carbide
sintern cement, cake, sinter
Sinterpunkt *m* sintering point
Sinterstoff *m* sintering substance
Sintervorgang *m* sintering process
Sinterwerkstoff *m* sintering material
sinusförmig sinousoidal
sinusförmiger Verlauf *m* sinusoidal characteristics
Sinusfunktion *f* sine function
Sinusgenerator *m* sine wave generator
Sinushalbwelle *f* half sine (wave)
Sinuskurve *f* sine curve, sinusoidal curve
Sinuslineal *nt* sine bar
Sinuswelle *f* sine wave
Siphonbogen *m* siphon bend
Sirene *f* siren
Sitz *m* seat, seating, fit
Sitz neu schleifen reseat
sitzen sit, seated
Sitzende *nt* spigot end (or mouldings)
Sitzfläche *f* seat, seating
Sitzflurförderzeug *nt* sit-on truck
Sitzgabelstapler *m* fork truck with seated driver, driver-controlled fork truck
Sitzhalterung *f* seat mounting
Sitzindexpunkt *m* seat index point
Sitzposition *f* seating

Sitzverstellung *f* adjustment of the operator's seat
Skala *f* scale, dial
Skale *f* **mit gerader Teilungsgrundlinie** scale with straight base line
Skale *f* **mit kreisbogenförmiger Teilungsgrundlinie** scale with circular line
Skalenanzeige *f* **1.** *(allg.)* analog reading scale indication **2.** *(e. Messschraube)* vernier reading
Skalenbezifferung *f* scale numbering
Skalenendwert *m* maximum scale value
Skalenhülse *f* *(Messschraube)* barrel
Skalenkonstante *f* scale factor, scale constant
Skalenring *m* dial, collar, graduated collar
Skalenscheibe *f* dial, graduated disk
Skalenschraube *f* scale screw
Skalenteil *nt* scale division
Skalenteil *nt* **mit Ziffernschritt** scale division with digital increment
Skalenteilungswert *m* scale interval
Skalenträger *m* scale carrier
Skalentrommel *f* **1.** *(allg.)* graduated collar, thimble **2.** *(Fräsmaschine)* collar
Skalenwert *m* scale interval
Skalenwinkel *m* scale angle
skalieren scale
Skidförderanlage *f* skid conveyor system
Skidförderer *m* skid conveyor
Skineinschlagmaschine *f* skin packing machine
Skinverpackungsmaschine *f* skin packing machine
Skinverpackung *f* skin package
Skizze *f* **1.** *(Entwurf)* sketch, draft **2.** *(Plan)* design, drawing
skizzieren sketch, draw, draft
Sleevemaschine *f* sleeve machine
Slingerverfahren *nt* slinger process
SLS *Abk.* *(Pulverlasersintern)* Selective Laser Sintering
Sockel *m* **1.** *(Maschine)* base **2.** *(Motor)* pedestal **3.** *(Ständer)* knee **4.** plinth
Sockelplatte *f* base plate
Sodakochechtheit *f* fastness to soda boiling
sofort immediately
Sofortmaßnahme *f* immediate measure, urgent measure
Software *f* software
Softwareagent *m* software agent
Softwareanpassung *f* software adaptation
Softwarebaustein *m* software element
Softwareendschalter *m* software limit switch
Softwareerstellung *f* software development
Softwarefehler *m* software fault
softwaregesteuert software-controlled
Softwarestruktur *f* software structure
Softwaretaster *m* softkey
Sog *m* suction, wake
Sohle *f* **1.** *(allg.)* base **2.** *(e. Maschine)* underside **3.** *(e. Maschinenbettes)* bottom
solange Vorrat reicht until stocks are exhausted
Solidustemperatur *f* solidus temperature
Soll *nt* target
Sollanzeige *f* desired indication
Solldrehstellung *f* theoretical angular position
Sollgrundzylinder *m* design base cylinder
Soll-Ist-Vergleich *m* set-actual comparison, target-performance comparison
Soll-Istwert-Vergleicher *m* desired value/actual value comparator
Solllage *f* reference position, nominal location, theoretical position
Sollmaß *nt* specified dimension, theoretical size, specified size, nominal dimension
Sollmenge *f* target quantity
Sollmodell *nt* to-be model
Solloberfläche *f* design surface
Sollposition *f* command position
Sollqualität *f* specified quality
Sollrichtung *f* design direction
Sollverbrauch *m* target consumption
Sollwert *m* reference value, desired value, nominal value, rated value required value, set point, set value, target value,

theoretical figure
Sollwert *m* command position
Sollwert-(Einstell-)Skala *f* desired temperature (set point) scale
Sollwertabweichung *f* deviation from the desired value
Sollwertgeber *m* set-point transmitter, reference value transmitter
Sollzeit *f* target time, nominal time
Sollzusammensetzung *f* nominal composition
Sollzustand *m* desired status, required status
Sommerwarmwasserbereitung *f* summer hot water service
Sonde *f* probe
Sondefunktion *f* special function
Sonderanbaugerät *nt* special attachment
Sonderausführung *f* special design, auxiliary equipment
Sonderausstattung *f* extra equipment, special equipment
Sonderbaufläche *f* special building area
Sonderbauform *f* special construction
Sondereinrichtung *f* special attachment
Sonderfall *m* special case
Sonderfräsmaschine *f* special milling machine
Sondergusseisen *nt* special cast iron
Sonderkonstruktion *f* special design
Sonderlast *f* special load
Sonderlastfall *m* special case of loading
Sonderlehre *f* special gauge
Sondermaschine *f* special-purpose machine
Sonderpaternoster *m* special vertical carousel
Sonderprofil *nt* special profile
Sonderstahl *m* alloy steel
Sondervermerk *m* special note
Sonderwunsch *m* **1.** *(allg.)* extra, variation, potion **2.** *(auf ~)* optional
Sonderzeichen *nt* special character, special symbol
Sonderzubehör *nt* extra equipment
Sonneneinstrahlung *f* solar radiation
Sonnenheizungsanlage *f* solar heating plant
Sonnenrad *nt* central pinion, sun gear, sun wheel
Sonnenwärmeeinstrahlung *f* solar radiation
Sonotrodenstirnfläche *f* sonotrode end face
Sorte *f* kind (of), type, grade, brand
Sortenkennzeichnung *f* identification of grades
sortenrein single-product, mono-product, single-grade, mono-grade
Sortenzeichnung *f* variant drawing
Sortieranlage *f* **1.** *(allg.)* sorting plant, grading plant **2.** *(Sichtanlage)* picking plant
sortieren grade, sort, separate, size-grade, classify, pick
Sortierer *m* sorter, sorting machine
Sortierfunktion *f* sorting function
Sortiermaschine *f* sorting machine
Sortiermerkmal *nt* sort key, sort criterion
Sortierprogramm *nt* sorter, sort program
Sortierstelle *f* sorting point
Sortierwaage *f* weight grading machine
Sortimentslager *nt* retail warehouse
Sortiment *nt* assortment (of goods), product line, product range
Sortimentstiefe *f* product assortment depth
Spachtelbelag *m* coating spread with a float
Spalt *m* aperture, clearance, gap, clearance space, crack, split
Spaltbedingungen *fpl* gap conditions
Spaltbreite *f* gap width
Spalte *f* **1.** *(allg.)* cleft, fissure, interstice, rift, gap **2.** *(Tabelle)* column
spalten split, cleave, rive
Spaltfilter *m* gap-type filter
Spaltkraft *f* splitting force, delamination load
Spaltlötverbindung *f* close soldering joint
Spaltmotor *m* shade-pole motor, split-pole motor
Spaltoszillation *f* gap oscillation

Spaltzugprüfung *f (von Betonrohren)* splitting tensile test
Span *m* 1. *(allg.)* chip, cut 2. *(Abreißspan)* segmental chip, fragmental chip, discontinuous chip 3. *(Bohrspäne)* borings 4. *(Drehspäne)* turnings 5. *(Frässpäne)* millings 6. *(Hobelspäne von Holz)* shavings 7. *(Hobelspäne)* facings 8. *(Kurzspan)* fragmental chip, segmental chip, chip fragment 9. *(Schneidspäne)* cuttings 10. *(einen feinen ~ nehmen)* take a light cut 11. *(kurzgebrochener ~)* short-brittle chip, chip broken up into small fragments
Spanabfluss *m* escape of chips, chip flow, flow of a chips
Spanabfuhr *f* chisel disposal
spanabhebende Bearbeitung *f* machining, cutting, cutting operation
spanabhebendes Bearbeiten *nt* machining
spanabhebendes Verfahren *nt* cutting technique
spanabhebendes Werkzeug *nt* cutting tool
Spanablauf *m* chip flow
Spanablaufwinkel *m* chip flow angle
Spanabnahme *f* 1. *(allg.)* chip removal, metal removal, amount of metal removed, stock removal, removal of chips 2. *(Zerspanvorgang)* taking down a cut, taking cuts
Spanabstreifer *m* scraper for removing swarf, swarf scraper
Spananhäufung *f* accumulation of chips (or chip fragments)
Spanart *f* type of chip
Spanarten *fpl* chip categories
Spanausbildung *f* process of chip formation
spanbar machinable, cuttable
Spanbarkeit *f* cuttability
Spanbildung *f* chip formation
Spanbrecher *m* chip breaker
Spanbrecherabstand *m* chip breaker distance
Spanbrecherbezugspunkt *m* defined point on the chip breaker
Spanbrecherhöhe *f* chip breaker height
Spanbrecherkeilwinkel *m* chip breaker wedge angle
Spanbrechernut *f* nick, chip-breaking groove
Spanbreite *f* width of chip
Spanbreitung *f* chip flattening
Spanbruchstück *nt* part of discontinuous chip
Spanbrust *f* rake
Spandickenstauchung *f* chip thickness compression ratio
Spandickung *f* chip thicknessing
Spandurchgang *m* chip clearance
Späneabfall *m* swarf
Späneabfluss *m* chip flow
Späneabfuhr *f* disposal of chips, chip removal, discharge of chips, swarf removal
Späneauffangraum *m* chip compartment
Späneauffangrinne *f* chip trough
Spänebeseitigung *f* chip removal, chip disposal
Spänefall *m* flow of chips
Spänefang *m* chip collector, chip chute
Spänefangraum *m* chip compartment
Spänefangschale *f* chip pan, chip tray
Spänefluss *m* chip flow
Spänemulde *f* swarf tray
spanen cut, machine, remove chips
spanende Bearbeitung *f* cutting machining, chip-forming machining, *(UK)* metal cutting, *(US)* metalcutting
spanende Fertigung *f* cutting manufacturing
spanende Formgebung *f* metal cutting
spanende Vorbearbeitung *f* roughing operation
spanendes Fertigungsverfahren *nt* metal-cutting production procedure
spanendes Werkzeug *nt* cutting tool
Spanentstehung *f* chip formation
Späneraum *m* chip clearance, chip compartment
Spänerinne *f* chip trough
Spänerutsche *f* chip chute, swarf chute
Späneschale *f* chip pan, chip tray
Spänestau *m* chip clogging, chip congestion

Späneteilchen *nt* chip fragment (or particle)
Spänetrog *m* trough
Späneverstopfung *f* chip clogging
Spänewanne *f* swarf pan, chip pan
Spanfänger *m* chip collector
Spanfangschale *f* chip collector, chip tray, chip pan, swarf tray
Spanfläche *f* 1. *(allg.)* chip bearing surface, rake, rake face 2. *(Werkzeug)* face, tool (or cutting) face 3. *(e. Drehmeißels)* top face 4. *(e. Fräserzahnes)* face of tooth
Spanflächenbreite *f* **an der Spanbrechernut** chip breaker land width
Spanflächenfase *f* 1. *(allg.)* face land, land of the face, primary rake relief, tool face relief, chip groove 2. *(mit negativem Spanwinkel)* primary rake 3. *(erste ~)* first face 4. *(reduzierte ~)* reduced face 5. *(zweite ~)* second face
Spanflächenlagefehler *m* positional error in the front rake, rake position error
Spanflächennormalkraft *f* tool force tangential force
Spanflächenorthogonalebene *f* tool face orthogonal plane
Spanflächentangentialkraft *f* tool face tangential force
Spanflächenverschleiß *m* wear of cutting face
Spanflächenwinkel *m* true rake angle
Spanfluss *m* chip flow, flow of the chip
Spanflussrichtung *f* chip flow direction
Spanförderer *m* chip conveyor
Spanform *f* form of chip, chip forms *pl*
Spanformer *m* chip breaker
Spanformung *f* chip formation
Spange *f* 1. *(Haken)* cramp, hook 2. *(Schnalle)* buckle, clasp
spangebende Bearbeitung *f* machining, cutting operation
spangebende Formung *f* shape cutting
spangebendes Formverfahren *nt* non-generating cutting method
Spangeschwindigkeit *f* chip speed
Spangröße *f* chip variable

Spankürzung *f* chip shortening
Spanleistung *f* stock removal, cutting capacity
Spanleitblech *nt* chip chute
Spanleitrille *f* **mit Fase** land and groove type of chipbreaker
Spanleitstufe *f* ground-in step type chipbreaker, ground-in chip breaker, chip breaker groove (or nick)
Spanlenkung *f* chip control
Spanlocke *f* chip curl
spanlose Formgebung *f* metal forming
spanloses Verfahren *nt* chipless process
Spanlücke *f* gash
Spanmenge *f* amount of metal removed, metal removal rate
Spannbacke *f* clamping jaw, gripping jaw, grip, jaw
Spannbock *m* poppet, planer poppet
Spannbolzen *m* clamp bolt, clamping bolt
Spannbrücke *f* clamping jaw
Spannbüchse *f* work-holding bushing, spring collet
Spanndorn *m* mounting arbor, tool arbor, draw-in arbor, cutter arbor, arbor, mandrel
Spanne *f* 1. *(allg.)* interval, range, spread 2. *(am Radumfang)* span 3. *(metr.)* span 4. *(Preise)* margin
Spanneinrichtung *f* chucking fixture, workholding device, gripping mechanism
Spanneisen *nt* clamp, strap, holding strap
Spanneisen *nt* **mit Stift** finger clamp
Spannelement *nt* clamping member (or element)
spannen 1. *(allg.)* chuck, hold, secure (to), set up, fix, stretch, tense 2. (e. Feder) tension 3. (e. Spannzange) close 4. (einspannen) clamp, grip 5. (in e. Futter) secure in position 6. (Schrauben) tighten 7. (Werkstücke) clamp, mount, load
Spannenabweichung *f* span variation
Spannenmitte *f* mid-range
Spanner *m* clamping fixture, chucking

fixture, holding device, gripping fixture
Spannfinger *m* toe dog
Spannflansch *m* mounting flange
Spannfutter *nt* **1.** *(allg.)* chuck, cutter chuck **2.** *(Zangenspannfutter)* collet chuck
Spannfutter *nt* **mit Dauermagnet** permanent magnetic chuck
Spannglocke *f* clamping bell
Spannhülse *f* turret bushing, tool hole bush
Spannklaue *f* **1.** *(allg.)* plain toolpost, jaw, clamping claw **2.** *(Drehherz)* lathe dog
Spannklauengreifer *m* clamping claw gripper
Spannkolben *m* clamp dog
Spannkopf *m* puller, chuck
Spannkraft *f* holding power, clamping force
Spannkurve *f* chucking cam
Spannlage *f* clamping position
Spannlagebestimmung *f* clamping position setting
Spannleiste *f* clamping gib
Spannmittel *nt* clamping fixture
Spannmutter *f* locknut
Spannnut *f* T-slot
Spannpalette *f* stretch pallet
Spannpatrone *f* draw-in collet
Spannpratze *f* plain clamp-type toolpost, clamping jaw
Spannriegel *m* swing latch
Spannrolle *f* guiding pulley
Spannscheibe *f* **1.** *(für Schraubenverbindung)* conical spring washer **2.** *(für Kombischrauben)* conical spring washer for screw assemblies
Spannschlitz *m* clamping slot
Spannschraube *f* clamp, drawbolt, poppet
Spannspindel *f* chucking spindle, lead screw
Spannstation *f* tensioning station
Spannstelle *f* tensioning point
Spannstift *m* spring pin, spring dowel pin, brace
Spannung *f* **1.** (e. Riemens) tension **2.** (el.) voltage **3.** (phys.) stress, strain **4.** (verformende) strain **5.** (mit

bestimmter bleibender Verlängerung) permanent set stress **6.** (unter el. ~ stehende Teile) parts carrying voltage
Spannungformer *m* voltage shaper
Spannungsabbau *m* stress relief, reduction in tension
Spannungsabfall *m* voltage drop, line drop, fall of voltage, *(US)* brownout
spannungsabhängiger Widerstand *m* variable resistor, varistor
Spannungsabweichung *f* voltage variation
Spannungsamplitude *f* stress amplitude
Spannungsangleichung *f* voltage adjustment
Spannungsanlassrissigkeit *f* strainage cracking
Spannungsausgleich *m* stress equalization
Spannungsbeiwert *m* stress coefficient
Spannungserholung *f* stress relaxation
Spannungserzeugung *f* current generation, current production
Spannungsfenster *nt* voltage window
Spannungsfestigkeit *f* electric strength, minute value
Spannungsformänderungsverhalten *nt* stress deformation behaviour
spannungsfreier Zustand *m* tensionless state
Spannungs-Frequenz-Umsetzer *m* voltage-to-frequency converter
spannungsführend live
Spannungskalibrator *m* voltage calibration
Spannungskollektiv *nt* stress spectrum
Spannungslaufkurve *f* curve of stress versus number of cycles
spannungslos idle
Spannungsmessung *f* **1.** *(phys. mechan.)* tension gauge **2.** *(el.)* voltage metering
Spannungspegel *m* voltage level
Spannungsprüfer *m* voltage detector
Spannungsquerschnitt *m* stress area
Spannungsrissbeständigkeit *f* resist-

ance to environmental stress cracking, resistance to stress crazing
Spannungsrisspotential *nt* stress corrosion cracking potential
Spannungsschwankung *f* voltage fluctuation
Spannungsspitze *f* voltage peak, peak voltage, voltage surge, stress peak
Spannungsteiler *m* voltage divider
Spannungsverbindung *f* **mit Anzug** stressed-type fastening with taper action
Spannungs-Verformungs-Diagramm *nt* stress-strain diagram
Spannungsverhältnis *nt* stress ratio
Spannungswandler *m* voltage transformer
Spannungswelligkeit *f* voltage ripple
Spannungswert *m* stress value
Spannungs-Zeit-Diagramm *nt* stress-time curve
Spannungszunahmegeschwindigkeit *f* rate of stress increase
Spannut *f* **1.** *(allg.)* chip groove, chip pocket, flute, T-slot **2.** *(e. Fräsers)* gash
Spannutenfräsen *nt* flute milling
Spannvorrichtung *f* chucking device, workholding device (or fixture), clamping fixture (or device), chuck, spanner, gripping appliance
Spannweite *f* **1.** *(Einspannung, Maschine)* span, width, range, chucking capacity **2.** *(Zug)* tension width **3.** *(der Schraubstockbacken)* capacity of vice jaws, opening capacity
Spannwerkzeug *nt* clamping fixture (or device), chucking fixture, holding device, gripping fixture, clamping tool, fixture
Spannzange *f* **1.** *(allg.)* draw-in collet chuck, grip, collet **2.** *(Werkstücke)* workholding fixture
Spannzeug *nt* clamping fixture (or device), chucking fixture, holding device, gripping fixture, clamping tool, fixture
Spannzeugzeichnung *f* fixture drawing
Spanplatte *f* **1.** *(allg.)* chip collector, chip tray **2.** *(Holz)* chip board, flake board
Spanprüfung *f* chip test

Spanquerschnitt *m* cross-sectional area of chip, chip cross-sectional area
Spanquerschnittsstauchung *f* chip cross-section upsetting
Spanraum *m* chip clearance, flute
Spanstärke *f* depth of cut
Spanstärke *f* **am Anfang des Schnittes** commencement chip thickness
Spanstauung *f* clogging of chips
Spanstufe *f* chip breaker
Spantiefe *f* cutting depth, depth of cut, rate of cut, stock removal
Spantiefe *f* **je Zahn/Fräsen** chip load per tooth
Spantiefenvorwähler *m* depth of cut preselector
Spanumfangswinkel *m* *(Fräser)* angle of approach
Spanung *f* **1.** *(spangebende Bearbeitung)* machining operation, cutting operation **2.** *(Zerspanung)* metal cutting, shape cutting, cutting action, cutting process (or operation)
Spanungsbreite *f* cutting width, width of cut
Spanungsdicke *f* cutting thickness, thickness of cut
Spanungsdynamometer *nt* *(rotierendes ~)* rotary cutting dynamometer (RCD)
Spanungsgröße *f* machinability rating, machining variable, metal-cutting quantity
Spanungshauptgruppe *f* cutting main group
Spanungskraft *f* *(resultierende ~)* (resultant) cutting force
Spanungskraftmesser *m* *(rotierender ~)* rotary cutting dynamometer (RCD)
Spanungsleistung *f* cutting performance, cutting power
Spanungsmessebene *f* cut dimension plane
Spanungsoptimierung *f* machining optimization
Spanungsquerschnitt *m* cross sectional area of cut, sectional area of chip *pl*
Spanungsschicht *f* pass
Spanungsverhältnis *nt* cutting rela-

tion
Spanungsvolumen *nt* cutting volume
Spanungswerkzeuge *ntpl* cutting tool
Spanverstopfung *f* chip entanglement
Spanvolumen *nt (Fräser)* basic rating
Spanwinkel *m* **1.** *(allg.)* cutting rake, rake angle, tool rake angle, rake, undercut angle **2.** *(als Arbeitswinkel)* working angle, true angle **3.** *(senkrecht zur Nebenschneide) (UK)* cutting edge back rake, *(US)* normal back rake **4.** *(senkrecht zur Schneide)* normal rake **5.** *(Werkzeugwinkel) (UK)* cutting edge side rake, *(US)* rake angle
sparen economize, save
Sparflamme *f* pilot flame
Sparmaßnahme *f* economy measure
sparsam economical
Sparsamkeit *f* economy
Spartransformator *m* auto-transformer, one-coil transformer
Spatverfahren *nt* spatula rub-out method
Spediteur *m* forwarding agent, (freight) forwarder
Spedition *f* **1.** *(Überbegriff)* forwarding trade, forwarding company **2.** *(Unternehmen)* forwarding agent
Speditionskosten *pl* forwarding expenses, forwarding charges
Speichelechtheit *f* resistance to spittle
Speicher *m* memory, rack (tools), store, reservoir, store-room
Speicherausnutzung *f* memory utilization
Speicherauswahlsteuerung *f* memory selection control
Speicherbehälter *m* storage tank
Speicherbereich *m* memory area
Speicherblock *m* block of memory
Speicherbrauchwassererwärmer *m* storage type service water heater
Speicherdichte *f* storage density
Speicherebene *f* storage level
Speicherfunktion *f* memory function
Speicherglied *nt* memory device
Speicherheizgerät *nt* thermal storage heater
Speicherinhalt *m* memory content, stored content

Speicherkapazität *f* storage capacity
Speicherkarte *f* memory card
Speicher-Kohle-Wasserheizer *m* coal-fired water heater with storage cylinder
Speichermedium *nt* storage medium
Speichermenge *f* amount of storage
Speichermodul *nt* dynamic (or accumulative) modulus, storage modulus
speichern **1.** *(allg.)* memorize, record, store **2.** *(Software)* save
speichernde Elemente *ntpl* stored components
Speicherplatz *m* storage place
Speicherprogrammierbare Steuerung (SPS) *f* programmable controller (PC), programmable logic controller (PLC)
speicherprogrammierbares Steuersystem *nt* programmable control system, PC system
speicherprogrammiert programmable
Speicherpufferung *f* memory back-up
Speichertyp *m* type of memory
Speicherung *f* storage
Speicherverhalten *nt* storage property
Speicherwassererwärmer *m* storage water heater
Speicherzelle *f* memory location, memory cell, memory unit, register
Speisedruck *m* feed pressure
Speisefettechtheit *f* resistance to fats
Speiseleitung *f* feed line, supply line
Speiser *m* feeder
Speisespannung *f* supply voltage, terminal pressure
Speisesystem *nt* feed system
Speisewasserentgaser *m* feed water de-aerator
Speisewasserregelung *f* feed water control
Speisewasservorerwärmer *m* feed water preheater
Spektralbandfilter *m* spectral band filter
spektraler Strahldichtefaktor *m* spectral gloss factor
spektraler Transmissionsgrad *m* light transmittance
spektralphotometrisch spectrophotometrical

Sperrdampf *m* sealing steam
Sperre *f* **1.** *(allg.)* lock, stop, barrier **2.** *(als Schaltelement)* lock-out **3.** *(Hängebahn)* stop station **4.** *(Vorrichtung)* catch, safety catch
sperren arrest, guard, hold, interlock, lock, retain, shut, bolt, block, stop
Sperrfangvorrichtung *f* catching device, dead stop gripping device
Sperrflüssigkeit *f* sealing liquid
Sperrgetriebe *nt* pawl and ratchet mechanism, ratchet and pawl mechanism
Sperrgut *nt* bulky good(s)
Sperrhaken *m* catch
sperrig bulky, unwieldy, awkward shaped
Sperrklinke *f* catch, detent, pawl, detent pawl
Sperrklinkeneinrichtung *f* click-and pawl, click-and dog arrangement
Sperrlager *nt* blocked storage
Sperrrad *nt* ratchet
Sperrriegel *m* locking bolt
Sperrschichtmantel *m* barrier layer
Sperrspannung *f* reverse voltage
Sperrstellung *f* locking position, blocking position
Sperrteil *nt* closure (or closing) element
Sperrung *f* blocking, blocking action, sealing
Sperrvermerk *m* hold tag, lock flag, notice of non-negotiability
Sperrwasser *nt* sealing water
Sperrwerk *nt* pawl-and ratchet mechanism, ratchet and pawl mechanism
Sperrzahn *m* ratchet
Sperrzahnrad *nt* **mit Sperrklinke** ratchet and pawl
Sperrzapfen *m* indexing bolt, indexing pin
Spezialvorrichtung *f* special fixture
speziell special
spezifische Heizleistung *f* specific heat output
spezifische Schnittkraft specific cutting force
spezifischer Durchgangswiderstand *m* volume resistivity
spezifischer Klebstoffauftrag *m* specific adhesive spread
spezifisches Spanvolumen *nt* metal-removal rate
sphärische Evolvente *f* spherical involute
sphärische Evolventenschraubenfläche *f* spherical involute helicoid
sphärisches Getriebe *nt* spherical gear transmission
Spiegel *m* mirror
Spiegelbildbearbeitung *f* mirror image operation
Spiegelbildkopiereinrichtung *f* reverse image attachment
spiegelbildkopieren produce mirror-image parts
spiegelbildlich mirror images of each other
spiegelbildlich gleiche Evolventenzahnflanken *fpl* mirror-imaged identical involute tooth flanks
spiegelbildliches Kopieren *nt* mirror-copying
spiegelbildliches Nachformen *nt* reverse mirror duplicating
Spiegeldrehzahl *f* mirror speed, mirror revolutions per minute
Spiegelfeinmessgerät *nt* martens mirror
spiegelfreier Zahneingriff *m* zero-play tooth engagement
spiegeln mirror, reflect
Spiegelrad *nt* mirror wheel
Spiel *nt* **1.** *(techn. Spielraum haben)* play, backlash, clearance, looseness **2.** *(Arbeitsspiel)* cycle **3.** *(bei Lehrdornen)* shake **4.** *(e. Lagers)* slackness **5. an der Zahnwurzel** root clearance **6.** *(Toleranz)* allowance
Spieländerung *f* *(bei Zahnflanken)* backlash modification
Spielausgleich *m* backlash compensation, backlash eliminator
Spielausgleicheinrichtung *f* anti-backlash device
spielbehaftet loose, playing
Spielbestimmung *f* backlash determination
Spielflanke *f* clearance flank
spielfrei backlash-free, no-backlash, free

of play, without any play
spielfrei abwälzen *(Zahnräder)* mesh with zero backlash
spielfreie Paarung *f* zero-backlash mating
spielfreier Achsabstand *m* zero-backlash centre distance
spielfreier Eingriff *m* zero-backlash engagement
spielfreier Zustand *m* zero-play condition
Spielpassung *f* clearance fit
Spielraum *m* **1.** *(allg.)* clearance, play, backlash **2.** *(Toleranz)* tolerance
spielverändernder Einfluss *m* backlash-modifying effect
Spielvergrößerung *f* backlash increase
spielverkleinernde Einflüsse *mpl* backlash-reducing factors
Spielverminderung *f* reduction of backlash
Spielzahl *f* number of cycles
Spielzahlanforderung *f* cycle requirement
Spielzeit *f* cycle time
Spielzeitüberprüfung *f* cycle time verification
Spindel *f* **1.** *(allg.)* screw, spindle **2.** *(für Supportbewegung)* feed screw for traversing railheads **3.** *(Gewinde)* lead screw **4.** *(Hubwerk, Masch.)* screw jack **5.** *(mit Flachgewinde)* square-threaded screw **6.** *(mit Schraubenpumpe)* scroll **7.** *(zur Verstellung des Ständerschlittens)* side-headscrew
Spindelantrieb *m* leadscrew drive, leadscrew mechanism, spindle drive
Spindelaxialspiel *nt* spindle end clearance play
Spindelbund *m* spindle collar
Spindeldrehzahl *f* spindle speed
Spindelende *nt* spindle nose
Spindelfeststelleinrichtung *f* spindle clamp
Spindelfräsautomat *m* spindle hobber
Spindelhubsystem *nt* screw lifting system
Spindelhülse *f* **1.** *(allg.)* spindle quill, quill **2.** *(außermittige)* eccentric quill **3.** *(ausziehbare ~)* sliding spindle quill

Spindelkasten *m* headstock
Spindelkastensenkrechtbewegung *f* headstock rise-and fall motion
Spindelkastenverstellung *f* spindle head movement
Spindelkegel *m* spindle taper, spindle nose, nose
Spindelkopf *m* **1.** *(allg.)* spindle nose, spindle head **2.** *(beweglicher ~)* travelling spindle head
Spindelkopfsenkrechtverstellung *f* adjustment of the spindle head
Spindelkopfträger *m* spindle head carrier
Spindellagerung *f* spindle bearing
Spindellaufwendeschalter *m* spindle reverse switch
Spindelnase *f* spindle nose, nose
Spindelorientierung *f* spindle orientation
Spindelpinole *f* spindle quill
Spindelplanlauf *m* spindle thrust
Spindelpresse *f* **1.** *(allg.)* screw press **2.** *(mechanische ~)* power screw press
Spindelquerweg *m* spindle transverse travel
Spindelrundlauf *m* spindle true running
Spindelstillsetzeinrichtung *f* spindle stopping attachment
Spindelstock *m* head, headstock, spindle head, spindle stock, work spindle, main spindle
Spindelstockmotor *m* headstock-motor
Spindelsturz spindle fall
Spindeltrommel *f* spindle drum
Spindelvorschub *m* spindle feed
Spindelvorschubkurve *f* spindle feed cam
spinnnetzartige Oberflächenrisse *mpl* cobweb-like surface cracks
Spiralbohrer *m* twist drill
Spiralbruchspan *m* spiral discontinuous chip
Spiraldichtung *f* *(für Flanschverbindungen)* spiral wound gasket
Spirale *f* spiral, helix (helices *pl*), coil
Spiralfeder *f* spiral spring
spiralförmig in a spiral pattern, helical,

spiral
Spiralfräsarbeit *f* spiral milling, screw milling
Spiralfräseinrichtung *f* spiral milling attachment
Spiralfräsen *nt* helical milling, spiral milling
Spiralfräskopf *m* spiral milling head
spiralgenuteter Fräser *m* spiral-tooth milling cutter, helical milling cutter
Spiralkegelrad *nt* spiral bevel gear
Spiralkegelräderwälzfräsmaschine *f* spiral bevel gear hobbing machine
Spiralkegeltellerrad *nt* spiral bevel crown gear
Spiralnut *f* spiral flute, spiral groove
Spiralnuten *nt* flute cutting
Spiralnutenfräsen *nt* helical milling
Spiralspan *m* spiral chip, coil chip, curly chip
Spiralspannstift *m* spiral spring pin
Spiralspanstück *nt* spiral chip part
Spiralstretch *m* spiral stretch wrap
Spiralstretchmaschine *f* spiral stretch wrapper
Spiralteilkopf *m* spiral dividing head
spiralverzahnter Fräser *m* 1. *(allg.)* helix tooth cutter, spiral mill 2. *(mit Führungszapfen)* helical mill with pilot
Spiralverzahnung *f* helical teeth
Spiralwicklung *f* spiral wrapping
Spiralwinkel *m* spiral lead angle, spiral angle
Spiralzahnkegelrad *nt* spiral bevel gear
spitz 1. *(allg.)* pointed, sharp-pointed 2. *(mit Spitzen)* peaked 3. *(Winkel)* acute
spitz zulaufen taper
Spitze *f* 1. *(allg.)* crest, top, end 2. *(e. Gerätes)* tip 3. *(e. Meißels)* nose, tip, point 4. *(e. Spindel bei Drehmaschinen)* nose, lathe centre 5. *(geom.)* apex 6. *(Gewindestift, Schraube)* cone point 7. *(Körnerspitze) (UK)* lathe centre, *(US)* center 8. *(Wert)* peak
spitzen sharpen, point
Spitzenabstand *m* tip distance
Spitzendreharbeit *f* between-centres turning operation
Spitzendrehmaschine *f* 1. *(allg.)* centre lathe 2. *(mit Leitspindel)* engine lathe
spitzengezahnter Formfräser *m* shaped profile cutter
Spitzengrenzlinie *f* tip limit line
Spitzenhöhe *f* height of centres
Spitzenlast *f* load peak, peak load
spitzenlos centereless
spitzenlose Innenschleifmaschine *f* centreless-type internal grinding machine
spitzenlose Schleifmaschine *f* centreless cylindrical grinder
spitzenloses Rundschleifen *nt* centreless cylindrical grinding
spitzenloses Schleifen *nt* centreless grinding
spitzenloses Schleifverfahren *nt* centreless grinding method
Spitzenmoment *nt* peak torque
Spitzenspannung *f* peak voltage
Spitzenspanwinkel *m* back slope, back rake angle, front rake angle, front top rake angle, shank back rake
Spitzenspiel *nt* crest clearance, root clearance
Spitzenwinkel *m* 1. *(e. Meißels) (UK)* included plan angle, *(US)* nose angle 2. *(e. Spiralbohrers)* angle of point, point angle
Spitzenzündung *f* tip ignition
spitzer Winkel *m* acute angle
Spitzflamme *f* pointed flame
Spitzgewinde *nt* V-thread
spitzgezahnter Fräser *m* saw-tooth cutter
Spitzsenken *nt* countersinking
Spitzsenker *m* countersink
Spitzwerden *nt* pointing
Spitzwinkel *m* pointing tool
Spitzzirkel *m* toolmarker's dividers
Spline *m* spline
Splinefunktion *f* spline function
Splineinterpolation *f* spline interpolation
Splint *m* split pin
Splitterschutzbeton *m* missile shielding concrete

Splittstreuer *m* chipper
spontan spontaneous
Spontanbetrieb *m* asynchronous response mode, ARM
Spontanfreigabe *f* offhand release
Sportgeräte *ntpl* sports equipment
Sprache *f* **1.** *(Land)* language **2.** *(gesprochen)* voice
Spracheingabe *f* voice entry, voice input
sprachlich linguistic
Sprachumfang *m* language extent
Sprachverbindung *f* voice
Sprachverständigung *f* speech
Spreizbüchse *f* split bushing
Spreizdorn *m* stub expansion arbor, expansion arbor
spreizen spread, straddle, expand
Spreizen *nt* spreading, straddling
Spreizenstapler *m* straddle truck
Spreizmagnet *m* separation magnet
Spreizmesserkopf *m* spread cutter head
Spreizringkupplung *f* radially expanding clutch
Sprengbolzen *m* explosive stud
Sprengkammer *f* explosion chamber
Sprengladung *f* explosive charge
Sprengringnute snap ring groove
Sprengstoff *m* explosive
springen 1. *(zerspringen)* burst, **2.** *(zuschnappen)* spring **3.** *(zurück)* bounce **4.** *(überspringen)* spring, override **5.** *(reißen)* crack **6.** *(hüpfen, überspringen)* leap, jump, bound
Sprinkler *m* sprinkler
Sprinkleranlage *f* sprinkler installation
Sprinklerdüse *f* sprinkler head, sprinkler nozzle
spritzbar einstellen *(z. B. Spachtel)* adjust to spraying consistency
Spritzbereich *m* splash zone
Spritzbetrieb *m* spraying firm
Spritzdüse *f* lubricant spattering nozzle
Spritzeinheit *f* injection unit
Spritzeinrichtung *f* transfer device
spritzgegossenes Zahnrad *nt* injection moulded gear
spritzgießbar injection-mouldable
Spritzgießbarkeit *f* injection mouldability
Spritzgießeinheit *f* injection moulding unit
Spritzgießen *nt* injection moulding
Spritzgießmasse *f* injection moulding material
Spritzgießvorgang *m* injection moulding operation
Spritzgussformstück *nt* injection-moulded fitting
Spritzgussklebfitting *m* injection-moulded adhesive fitting
Spritzgussmasse *f* injection mixture
Spritzgut *nt* sprayed metal
Spritzhaube *f* splash guard
spritziger Span *m* short and brittle chip
Spritzkugelgrube *f* injection spherical hole
Spritzpressen *nt* plunger moulding
Spritzpressvorgang *m* plunger (or transfer) moulding operation
Spritzpresswerkzeug *nt* transfer mould
Spritzschicht *f* sprayed-on coating
Spritzschutz *m* splash guard
Spritzteilabmessung *f* injection-moulded part dimension
Spritzung *f* spraying
Spritzverdeck *nt* splash guard
Spritzverfahren *nt* spray process
Spritzverhalten *nt* spatter behaviour
spritzwassergeschützt splash-proof
Spritzwasserzone *f* splash water zone
Sprödbruchneigung *f* liability to brittle fracture
spröde brittle, gritty
spröd-harter Schaumstoff *m* brittle-rigid cellular plastics
Sprödriss *m* ductility-dip crack, brittle crack
Sprühbereich *m* spray zone
Sprühdüse *f* lubricant spray valve
sprühen sputter
Sprühentgasung *f* spray de-aerator
Sprühgut *nt* sprayed material
Sprühkühlung *f* mist cooling
Sprühnebel *m* atomized spray
Sprühöl *nt* spray oil
Sprühschmierung *f* lubricant spraying
Sprühverfahren *nt* spray coat method

Sprung m 1. *(e. Schrägstirnrades)* overlap length 2. *(el.)* bounce 3. *(Riss)* crack 4. *(Stufe)* increment 5. *(Sprung, Satz)* jump, leap, bound, spring 6. *(Bruchstelle)* break 7. *(Spalte, Kluft)* fissure
Sprungabstand m skip distance
sprungartige Änderung f step-wise change
Sprungausfall m sudden failure
Sprunghöhe f *(e. Eingangssignals)* step height
Sprungrohr nt offset
Sprungschaltung f intermitted feed, jump feed
Sprungstichprobenprüfung f skip lot sampling
Sprungteilung f block indexing
Sprungtischfräsen nt intermitted feed milling
Sprungtischschaltung f intermitted table feed
Sprungtischvorschub m jump feed
Sprungüberdeckung f overlap ratio
Sprungüberdeckungswälzkreisbogen m overlap arc
Sprungvorschub m intermitted feed, skip-feeding, automatic cycle table control
Sprungvorschub m **für Leerwege im Eilgang** skip-feeding for rapid traverse between gaps
SPS-Grundsystem nt basic PC-system
SPS-Programm nt PC-program
SPS-System nt PC-system, programmable controller system
Spüldüse f washing nozzle
Spule f coil, reel
Spüleffekt m purging effect
spulen *(um, auf)* coil (round, up), wind (round, up)
spülen cleanse, flush, rinse, wash, scavenge, purge
Spulenerregung f coil excitation
Spulenkörper m reel
Spülflüssigkeit f washing (or rinsing) liquid, flushing liquid
Spülmittel nt rinsing medium
Spültrichter m flushing funnel
Spülung f 1. *(allg.)* rinsing, washing, purging 2. *(kombinierte ~)* combined douche 3. *(offene ~)* open douche
Spülzeit f purge period, scavenging time
Spund m bung, plug
Spundfass nt barrel with screw cap
Spur f gage *(US)*, gauge *(UK)*, trace, channel (tape), track, lane, path
Spurführung f 1. *(allg.)* guidance 2. *(Spurhalten)* tracking
spurgebunden path-dependent
Spurkranz m wheel flange
Spurkranzrad nt single flanged rail wheel
Spurkranzreibung f friction of flanges
Spurrolle f track roller, guide roll
Spurspiel nt clearance
Spurweite f gauge, track (width)
Staatliches Materialprüfungsamt nt State Materials Testing Office
Stab m 1. *(allg.)* bar, rod, lath 2. *(el.)* bar rotor 3. *(Stahl)* rod
Stabachse f bar axis
Stabdiagramm nt bar diagram
Stabelektrode f stick electrode
Stabelektrode f **mit legiertem Kernstab** rod electrode with alloy core rod
Stabelektroden-Kerndraht m rod electrode core wire
Stabelektrodenpaket nt pack of rod electrodes
Stabelektrodenzündstelle f rod electrode arc strike
stabförmig bar-shaped, rod-shaped
stabförmiges Erzeugnis nt rod-shaped product
stabil stable, rigid, strong, sturdy, robust, rugged
Stabilisator m stabilizer
stabilisieren stabilize
Stabilisierungsrippe f reinforcing rib, reinforcing fin
Stabilisierungswicklung f stabilizing winding
Stabilität f stability, ruggedness, rigidity
Stabilitätsgrenze f critical buckling stress
Stabläufer m bar armature, cage rotor
Stabmagnet nt bar magnet
Stabmaterial nt material, rod material
Stabprobe f dumb-bell test piece
Stabwelle f bar wave

Stabwerk *nt* girder with rigid and movable bearings
Stabziehen *nt* bar drawing
Stadium *nt* stage
Stadtatmosphäre *f* urban atmosphere
Stahl *m* **1.** *(allg.)* steel **2.** *(beruhigt vergossener ~)* killed steel **3.** *(halbberuhigter ~)* balanced steel **4.** *(hochgekohlter ~)* high-carbon steel **5.** *(hochlegierter ~)* high-alloy steel **6.** *(hochzugfester ~)* high-tensile steel **7.** *(kohlenstoffarmer ~)* mild (low carbon) steel **8.** *(legierter ~)* alloy steel **9.** *(lufthärtender ~)* air-hardening steel **10.** *(ölhärtender ~)* oil-hardening steel **11.** *(rostfreier ~)* stainless steel **12.** *(sonderberuhigter ~)* aluminium-killed steel, abnormal steel **13.** *(unberuhigter ~)* unkilled steel **14.** *(unlegierter ~)* unalloyed (plain) steel **15.** *(vergüteter ~)* hardened and tempered steel **16.** *(wasserhärtender ~)* water-hardening steel
Stahlband *nt* steel band, steel strapping, steel strip
Stahlbau *m* **1.** *(Gebäude)* steel construction, structural steel work **2.** *(Technik)* structural steel engineering
Stahlbeton *m* reinforced concrete
Stahlbetondruckrohrleitung *f* reinforced concrete pressure pipeline
Stahlblech *nt* steel plate, steel sheet
Stahlfachboden *m* steel shelf
Stahlfräserrohling *m* steel cutter blank
Stahlguss *m* cast steel
Stahlgussflansch *m* cast steel flange
Stahlhalter *m* toolholder
Stahlhalterklappe *f* clapper box, toolholder clapper, tool apron, apron, clapper block, clapper
Stahlhalterkopf *m* tool block
Stahlkorn *nt* steel grit
Stahllaufrad *nt* steel rim travel wheel
Stahlleichtbau *m* light-gauge steel construction
Stahlleiter *m* ray conductor
Stahlmessband *nt* steel measuring tape
Stahlparameter jet parameter
Stahlplatte *f* steel plate
Stahlrohrtülle *f* steel tube nozzle
Stahlrolle *f* steel coil
Stahlsand *m* steel shot
Stahlschiene *f* steel rail
Stahlschmelze *f* heat
Stahlschrott *m* steel scrap
Stahlschweißer *m* welder for welding steel
Stahlseil *nt* steel cable
Stahlspritzdraht *m* steel spraying wire
Stahl-Stahl-Paarung *f* steel-on-steel pairs
Stahluntergrund *m* steel base
Stahlwerksschlacke *f* steelworks slag
Stahlwolle *f* steel wool
Stammdaten *pl* master data
Stammdatenabgleich *m* master data adjustment
Stammdatenerfassung *f* master data collection
Stammdatensatz *m* master data set
Stammdatenübernahme *f* master file incorporation
Stammdatenverwaltung *f* master data administration
Stammlösung *f* stock solution
Stammzeichnung *f* master drawing
stampfbar rammable
Stampfbarkeit *f* rammability
Stampfdichte *f* compacted apparent bulk density
stampfen ram, pun, tamp
Stampfer *m* rammer, punner, tamper
Stampflehm *m* rammed clay
Stampfmasse *f* ramming mixture, tamping compound, tamped clay
Stampfvolumen *nt* tamped volume
Stampfwerkzeug *nt* ramming tool
Stand *m* **1.** *(Anzeige)* reading **2.** *(Bedienungsstand)* (operator's) stand **3.** *(Flüssigkeiten)* level **4.** *(Lage)* state **5.** *(Standort)* position, location **6.** *(Stehen)* upright position **7.** *(der Technik)* stage of technical knowledge **8.** *(neuester ~ der Technik)* state of the art
Standard *m* standard
Standardabweichung *f* standard deviation
Standardausführung *f* standard design
Standardeinstellung *f* default

Standardfall *m* standard case
Standardfarbtiefe *f* standard depth of shade
Standardgerät *nt* standard machine
standardisieren standardize
standardisierte Verteilung *f* standardized distribution
Standardkosten *fpl* unit costs *pl*
Standardleistung *f* standard performance, standard rating
Standardpotential *nt* standard state potential
Standardpräzision *f* standard precision
Standardpreis *m* standard price
Standardtestmischung *f* standard test mix
Standardvorrichtung *f* standard fixture
Standardwasserstoffelektrode *f* standard hydrogen electrode
Standardwasserstoffpotential *nt* standard hydrogen potential
Standardwert *m* default value
Ständer *m* **1.** *(e. Drehautomaten)* machine base **2.** *(e. leichten Maschine)* stand, floor stand **3.** *(e. Maschine)* stand, pedestal, post, base **4.** *(el.)* stator **5.** *(Säule)* column, upright (standard) **6.** *(schwere Bauart)* (upright) housing
Ständer *m* **mit Prismenführung** column with V-ways
Ständerachse *f* upright axis
Ständeranlasser *m* stator starter
Ständeranlassverfahren *nt* stator starting technique, stator starting method
Ständeranschluss *m* stator lead
Ständerausführung *f* column way
Ständerblech *nt* stator lamination, stator plate
Ständerblechpaket *nt* bundle of stator laminations, bundle of stator plates
Ständerbohrmaschine *f* upright drilling machine, vertical drilling machine, box-column drilling machine
Ständerdrehfeld *nt* stator rotary field
Ständerdurchgang *m* throat, opening between uprights
Ständereisen *nt* stator iron
Ständerfräsmaschine *f* knee- and column-type milling machine
Ständerfrequenz *f* stator frequency
Ständerführung *f* column ways
Ständerführungsbahn *f* knee-ways, knee-slides, ways for (supporting and) guiding the knee
Ständerfuss *m* column base
Ständerklemmung *f* column clamp mechanism
Ständermaschine *f* column-type machine
Ständernut *f* stator groove, stator slot
Ständerpaar *nt* pair of uprights
Ständerprisma *nt* column Vees
Ständerrahmen *m* upright frame
Ständerregal *nt* **1.** *(allg.)* upright rack **2.** *(Stabmaterial)* vertical bar rack
Ständerschieber *m* hob slide, crossrail head
Ständerspeisung *f* stator feed
Ständerstrom *m* stator current
Ständerverstellung *f* column travel, column traverse, column movement
Ständervorschub *m* column traversing feed
Ständerwange *f* column face
Ständerwicklung *f* stator winding, stator coil
Standfestigkeit *f* stability, rigidity
Standfläche *f* standing position, platform, floor space
Standgabelstapler *m* fork truck with standing driver
Standgetriebe *nt* fixed-axle gear transmission
Standgrößen status sizes
standhalten resist, withstand
Standhöhe *f* standing level
ständiger Arbeitsplatz *m* permanent work station
Standkriterien status criteria
Standmoment *nt* stabilizing moment
Standort *m* location, position, site
Standortbestimmung *f* **1.** *(allg.)* siting, fixing of the location **2.** *(el.)* determination of bearing
Standortentscheidung *f* locational decision
Standortfaktor *m* factor of location

standortgefertigter Behälter *m* locally manufactured tank assembled together on site
Standortidentifizierung *f* identification of position (I/P)
Standortvariante *f* location variant
Standortwahl *f* choice of location
Standplattform *f* stand-on platform
Standplatz *m* standing position, standing space
Standroboter *m* standing robot
Standschraublehre *f* bench micrometer
standsicher stable
Standsicherheit *f* stability
Standsicherheitsnachweis *m* stability analysis
Standsicherheitsprüfung *f* stability test
Standsicherheitsrechnung *f* stability calculation
Standvermögen *nt* non-sag property, endurance
Standzahl *f* tool life index figure
Standzeit *f* wear life, tool life, tool cutting life, between-grind life, service life, useful life, life, endurance
Standzeit *f* **der Schneide** life of the cutting edge, cutting life
Standzeit *f* **des Räumwerkzeuges zwischen zwei Nachschliffen** between-grind broach life
Standzeit *f* **eines Messers** blade life
Standzeit *f* **zwischen zwei Anschliffen** grinding life
Standzeitabfall *m* drop in tool life
Standzeitbeziehung *f* tool cutting life relationship
Standzeitgewinn *m* gain in tool life
Standzeitkriterium *nt* tool life criterion
Standzeitschaubild *nt* tool life diagram
Standzeitschnittgeschwindigkeit *f* tool life cutting speed
Standzeitschnittgeschwindigkeiten service life cutting velocities
Standzeitüberwachung *f* tool monitoring
Standzeitverhalten *nt* tool life characteristics
Stange *f* bar, rod
Stangenanschlag *m* bar stop
stangenarbeit *f* bar work
Stangenautomat *m* bar automatic, automatic bar machine
Stangenführung *f* stock reel
Stangenfutterdrehmaschine *f* stock chucking turning machine
Stangenmaterial *nt* bar material(s), bar stock
Stangenspannung *f* bar chucking
Stangenvorschub *m* stock feed
Stangenvorschubeinrichtung *f* bar feeding attachment
Stangenwerkstoff *m* bar material
Stangenzirkel *m* beam trammels, trammel point
Stampfdichte *f* tamped apparent density
Stanzbarkeit *f* punching property
Stanze *f* blanking machine, punching machine, stamping press
stanzen 1. *(allg.)* blank, punch **2.** *(pressen)* stamp
Stanzerei *f* *(Werkstatt)* pressworking shop
Stanzteil *nt* blanking, punching, tampered part
Stanzvorrichtung *f* stamping device
Stapel *m* **1.** *(allg.)* stack, pile **2.** *(IT)* batch
Stapelautomatik *f* automatic stacking (system)
stapelbar stackable
Stapelbarkeit *f* stackability
Stapelbehälter *m* **1.** *(allg.)* stacking box, stacking container **2.** *(ineinander gestapelt)* nesting container
Stapelbildung *f* preparation of stacks, stack formation
Stapelbügel *m* drop-on lid, stacking rail
Stapeleinheit *f* stacking unit
Stapelfähigkeit *f* stackability
Stapelfaktor *m* *(bei Blechen)* stacking factor
Stapelförderer *m* stack conveyor
Stapelgang *m* stacking aisle
Stapelhilfsmittel *nt* stacking aid, stacking accessory

Stapelhöhe f **1.** *(allg.)* stacking height **2.** *(bei Rohren)* stack height
Stapelhöhenanpassung f stacking height adjustment
Stapeljoch nt stacking frame
Stapelkasten m stacking box, stacking crate
Stapelkran m stacker crane
stapeln 1. *(allg.)* stack, pile **2.** *(schichten)* tier
stapelnd 1. stacking **2.** *(nicht ~)* non-stacking
Stapelpalette f **1.** *(allg.)* stacking pallet, post pallet **2.** *(ineinander gestapelt)* nesting pallet, stackable pallet
Stapelplatte f stillage
Stapelprogramm nt stacking program
Stapelrand m stacking edge
Stapelschema nt stacking pattern
Stapelspitze f top of rack
Stapelsystem nt stacking system
Stapelumladung f stack transfer
Stapelung f stacking, batching
Stapelverarbeitung f batch processing
Stapelverarbeitungsmaterial nt batch terminal
Stapelverfahren nt stacking method
Stapelwanne f stacking tray
Stapelware f staple, staple goods
stapelweise by stack, by batch
stapelweise verarbeiten batch
Stapelzeiger m stack pointer
Stapler m **1.** *(allg.)* stacker, stacker truck, stacking high-lift truck, storage and retrieval unit **2.** *(mit veränderlicher Reichweite)* variable reach truck
Staplertasche f fork entry aperture
Staplerumrisse mpl truck configurations
stark 1. *(allg.)* strong, powerful **2.** *(stabil)* sturdy **3.** *(Strom)* high-power **4.** *(intensiv)* intense
Stärke f **1.** *(allg.)* power, strength, stamina **2.** *(Dicke)* thickness, size
starke Neigung f steep gradient
stark lösender Klebstoff m adhesive with rapid solvent action
Starkstrom m high-voltage current, power current
Starkstromanlage f power plant, power installation
starr fixed, rigid
starre Einspannung f rigid restraint
starre Gabeln fpl fixed forks
Starrfräsmaschine f rigid milling machine
Starrheit f rigidity
Starrwälzfräsmaschine f rigid gear hobbing machine
Start m start, start up
Start- und Stoppeinrichtung f starting and stopping device, start-stop base
Startbefehl m start instruction
Startbereitschaft f readiness for action
Startbohrung f starting hole
Startdatenausgabe f start output data, SOD
Startdateneingabe f start input data, SID
starten start, start running, actuate
Starter m starter
Starterbatterie f starter battery
Startflamme f starting flame
Startflammenüberwachung f monitoring of the starting flame
Startimpuls m starting pulse
Startleistung f starting output
Startmerker m start bit memory
Startpunktkoordinaten fpl start point coordinates
Startreibung f static friction, starting friction
Statik f statics, structural analysis
Statikzeichnung f static drawing
Station f station
stationär fixed, stationary, steady
stationäre Biegeschwingung f steady state flexural vibration
stationäre Strömung f steady flow
Stationsdrucker m local pointer
Stationsniveau nt station level
Stationstyp m station type
statisch 1. *(allg.)* static, structural **2.** *(bewegungslos)* stationary
statische Bauteile $ntpl$ structural components
statische Belastung f static load (or loading)
statische Förderhöhe f static discharge head

statische Höhe *f* static head
statische Kornzahl *f* static grain count
statische Längsstabilität *f* longitudinal static stability
statische Saughöhe *f* static suction lift
statische Seitenstabilität *f* lateral static stability
statische Stabilität *f* static stability, structural stability, structural support
statische Verifizierung *f* structural test, structural verification
statischer Blindleistungskompensator *m* static VAR (volt-amperes reactive) compensator
statischer Elastizitätsmodul *m* static modulus of elasticity, Young's modulus of elasticity
statischer Nachweis *m* (e. Bauausführung) structural analysis
Statistik *f* 1. (allg.) statistic 2. (Wissenschaft) statistics
statistisch statistical
statistische Auswertung *f* statistical evaluation
statistische Einzeltoleranz *f* statistical individual tolerance
statistische Prozesslenkung *f* statistical process control
statistische Schließtoleranz *f* statistic closing tolerance
statistische Sicherheit *f* confidence level
statistische Toleranz *f* statistical tolerance
statistische Tolerierung *f* statistic tolerancing
statistischer Anteilsbereich *m* statistical tolerance interval
statistischer Test *m* significance test
Stativ *nt* tripod
Stativmuffe *f* tripod sleeve
Stativring *m* stand ring
Stator *m* stator
Status *m* status
Statusmeldung *f* status message
Stau *m* congestion, (traffic) jam, pile-up
Staub *m* dust
Staubablagerung *f* duct deposit
Staubabsauger *m* suction dust remover

Staubauswurfbegrenzung *f* dust emission control
staubbelastet dusty
Staubbildung *f* formation of dust
Staubdeckel *m* port cover
staubdicht dust-proof, dust-tight
Staubentwickler *m* dust carbide generator
Staubforschungsinstitut *nt* dust research institute
staubfreies Strahlen *nt* dust-free blasting
staubgefährdet subject to the risk of dust
staubgeschützt dust-protected
staubig dusty
staubintensiv extremely dusty
Staubklappenanemometer *nt* stagnation anemometer
Staub-Luft-Gemisch *nt* air/dust mixture
Staubpartikel *nt* dust particle
Staubschutz *m* 1. (allg.) dust guards *pl* 2. (el.) dust-proof protection, protection from conductible dust
Staucharbeit *f* compress work
stauchen compress, upset
Stauchfehler *m* compression error
Stauchhärte *f* compression stress value
Stauchkraft *f* upsetting force
Stauchlängenverlust *m* upset length loss
Stauchprüfung *f* compression test
Stauchschlittenhub *m* upsetting slide stroke
Stauchschlittenvorwärtsbewegung *f* forward motion of the upsetting slide
Stauchspannung *f* 1. (allg.) compression offset yield stress, compression yield 2. (2% ~) offset compressive yield stress
Stauchung *f* upsetting, (upsetting) deformation, compression, crowding
Stauchungsgrad *m* degree of upsetting
Stauchungswerte *mpl* deformation data
Stauchverhältnis *nt* compression relationship
Stauchweg *m* compression travel

Stauchwiderstand *m* compression resistance, crush resistance
Stauchwiderstandsprüfung *f* compression resistance test
Stauchwulst *f* *(bei Rohren)* upset ridge
Staudruck *m* stagnation (dynamic) head (pressure)
stauen pile up, accumulate, dam, retain, clog, stagnate, choke, jam
Staukettenförderer *m* accumulating chain conveyor, free-flow (chain) conveyor
Staurollenförderer *m* accumulating roller conveyor, free-flow (roller) conveyor
Stauscheibe *f* baffle plate
Stauung *f* blockage, clogging
Stauzone *f* stagnation zone
Stechdrehmeißel *m* parting tool
stechen 1. *(allg.)* prick, lance **2.** *(mit Stab)* stab
stechendes Schweißen *nt* welding with torch directed towards the part of the weld still to be made
Stechmeißel *m* cut-off tool, cutting-off tool, parting tool, parting-off tool, recessing tool
Stechschleifen *nt* pricking grinding
steckbar pluggable, insertable
Steckdose *f* plug socket, wall socket
stecken 1. *(allg.)* plug, insert, stick **2.** *(ineinander stecken)* nest **3.** *(stecken bleiben)* stall, get stuck, stick
Stecker *m* *(el.)* male (connector), plug
Stecker *m* **ziehen** unplug, withdraw the plug
Steckerbuchse *f* female (connector), receptacle
Steckerfeld *nt* plug panel
Steckergehäuse *nt* connector shell, plug cover
Steckgeländer *nt* slot-in guard rail
Steckkerbstift *m* half length reverse grooved pin
Stecklasche *f* flap
Stecklascheninspektionsmaschine *f* open flap detector
Steckmuffe *f* plug-in socket
Steckmuffenverbindung *f* spigot and socket joint
Steckschlüssel *m* **1.** *(allg.)* box spanner, socket wrench (or spanner) **2.** *(mit Griff)* pin type socket wrench
Steckschlüsseleinsatz *m* *(für Sechskantschrauben)* hexagon socket wrench
Steckverbindung *f* connector, plug connection, plug and socket device
Steckvorrichtung *f* plug device, coupler connector
Steg *m* **1.** *(allg.)* division, partition wall **2.** *(bei Radgetrieben)* arm **3.** *(in e. Schablone)* ligament **4.** *(Profil)* web
Stegabstand *m* root gap
Stegblech *nt* web plate
Stegblechlängsstoß *m* longitudinal joint of web plate
Stegblechquerstoß *m* transverse joint of web plate
Stegbreiten *nt* gate width
Stegeinsetzmaschine *f* division inserting machine
Stehanodenröhre *f* stationary anode tube
Stehbolzen *m* staybolt
Stehbolzenbohrmaschine *f* staybolt drilling machine
stehen 1. stand **2.** *(stehen bleiben)* stop, stall
stehend standing, in a standing position, in vertical position, in a upright position
Steher *m* (rack) upright, support, stand
Steherachse *f* upright axis
Steherfuß *m* upright foot
Steherkopf *m* top of the rack upright, upright head
Stehsicherheit *f* safety when standing
steif rigid, stiff
Steife *f* stiffness, brace
Steifigkeit *f* **1.** *(Stabilität)* stability **2.** *(Formsteifigkeit)* stiffness **3.** *(statische)* rigidity
Steifigkeitsprüfgerät *nt* stiffness testing apparatus
steigen 1. *(allg.)* ascend, rise, increase, mount **2.** *(klettern)* climb, go up
steigende Bemaßung *f* rising dimensioning sequence
steigendes Gießen *nt* rising casting
Steiger *m* riser, rising gate, outgate,

open riser, sprue, rising hole vent
Steigerholz *nt* riser stick
Steigermodell *nt* riser pattern
steigern increase, raise
Steigerung *f* increase
Steigfähigkeit *f* negotiable gradient
Steigförderer *m* continuous handling equipment, continuous conveyor
Steigschutz *m* guarding of ladder access
Steigschutzeinrichtung *f* self-locking safety anchorage
Steigtrichter *m* outgate
Steigtrichteransatz *m* sprue
Steigung *f* **1.** *(örtl.)* upgrade, uphill **2.** (e. eingängigen Gewindes) lead **3.** *(e. Gewindes)* (flank) lead, pitch **4.** *(e. Kegels)* taper **5.** *(e. mehrgängigen Gewindes)* pitch **6.** *(Ganghöhe)* lead **7.** *(Temperaturen)* rise **8.** *(der Schraubenlinie)* lead of helix **9.** *(der Tischvorschubspindel)* lead of feed screw **10.** *(Größe)* (ascending) gradient
Steigungsabweichung *f* pitch variation
Steigungsfahrt *f* uphill travel, uphill motion
Steigungsfehlerkorrektur *f* lead error compensation
Steigungsgenauigkeit *f (e. Gewindes)* accuracy of load
Steigungshöhe *f (e. Zahnflanke)* lead
Steigungshöhenabweichung *f* lead variation
Steigungsrichtung *f* direction of hand
Steigungswinkel *m* pitch
Steigungswinkel *m* **von Gewinden** helix angle of threads
Steigwinkel *m* angle of rise
steil steep
Steilabfall *m* steep front, steep fall-off
steiler Kegel *m* steep taper, short taper
Steilflankennaht *f* steep-flanked single-V butt joint
steilgängiges Trapezgewinde *nt* coarse pitch trapezoidal screw thread
Steilheit *f* slope of the operating characteristic
Steilkegel *m* steep angle taper, steep taper, short taper
Steilstrecke *f* steeply sloping section

Steinablagerung *f* scale deposit
Steinfang *m* solids trap
steiniger Untergrund *m* stone sub-base
Steinklammer *f* brick clamp
Steinschleuse *f* solids interceptor
Steinzeugrohrmuffe *f* stoneware pipe socket
Stellantrieb *m* actuating drive
Stellbereich *m* regulating range
Stelldurchgangsventil *nt* straight-way adjusting valve
Stelle *f* **1.** *(allg.örtl.)* place, location, station, position, point, spot, area **2.** *(freie Stelle)* vacancy **3.** *(Personal)* post, job, position
Stelleinrichtung *f* controlling equipment
Stelleisen *nt* quadrant
stellen 1. *(allg.)* place, position, put **2.** *(einstellen)* set **3.** *(regeln)* adjust, regulate **4.** *(steuern)* control
Stellenbesetzung *f* filling of vacancies
Stellenplanung *f* staffing schedule, job index
Steller *m (aktives Glied)* manipulator
Stellgerät *nt* positioning element, final control element, manipulating unit
Stellgeschwindigkeit *f* manipulating speed
Stellgetriebe *nt* actuator transmission
Stellglied *nt* **1.** *(allg.)* actuator, final control(ling) element, control element **2.** *(Steuerorgan)* positioning element, final control element
Stellgrößensprung *m* step-wise change of the manipulated variable
Stellkeil *m* adjusting key
Stellklappe *f* adjusting butterfly valve
Stellklaue *f* adjusting dog
Stellleiste *f* (adjustment) gib
Stellmotor *m* servo motor
Stellort *m* regulating point, point of control
Stellplatz *m* space, storage location, storage position
Stellplatzkoordinaten *fpl* position coordinates
Stellplatzteilung *f* bay division
Stellring *m* adjusting ring

Stellschieber *m* adjusting gate valve
Stellschraube *f* setscrew, setting screw, expansion screw
Stellspindel *f* adjusting screw
Stellteil *nt* control device, control, control mechanism, control lever, operating control, adjusting member (or part), actuator component
Stellteil *nt* **für Beschleunigung** accelerator control lever
Stellung *f* position, setting
Stellungsanzeige *f* positional indication
Stellverhalten *nt* adjustment characteristic
Stellweg *m* *(e. Stellschraube)* adjustment travel
Stellwirkung *f* regulating action
Stempel *m* **1.** *(allg.)* male die, puncheon, stamp, seal **2.** *(Presse)* plunger **3.** *(Ramme, Stößel)* ram **4.** *(Stanzen)* punch, chop
Stempelbefestigung *f* stamp attachment
Stempeldruck *m* ram pressure
Stempeldurchdrückversuch *m* perforation test
Stempelform *f* punch form
Stempelfräseinrichtung *f* punch milling attachments
Stempelfräsen *nt* punch milling
Stempelhobler *m* punch shaper
Stempelkraft *f* ram force
stempeln seal, stamp, punch, chop
Stempelung *f* mark, stamp
Stereolithographie (SL) *f* stereo lithography
Stern *m* star
Stern-Dreieck-Anlauf *m* star-delta start(ing)
Stern-Dreiecks-Anlassverfahren *nt* star-delta starting
sternförmig radial, star-shaped
sternförmige Schichtung *f* star-shaped layering
sternförmiger Riss *m* star-shaped crack, radiating crack
Sterngetriebe *nt* star gear
Sterngriff *m* star handle, star knob
Sternnutbefestigung *f* **1.** *(als Arbeitsvorgang)* trilock fixing **2.** *(z. B. e. Grenzlehrdornes)* trilock
Sternpunkt *m* star point, neutral, zero conductor
Sternpunktanlasswiderstand *m* Y-starting resistor
Sternrad *nt* star wheel
Sternrevolver *m* conventional hexagon turret
Sternrevolverdrehmaschine *f* hexagon turret lathe
Sternrevolverspeicher *m* conventional hexagon turret storage
Sternschaltung *f* star connection, star-connected three-phase system, Y-connection
Sternspannung *f* star voltage, phase voltage, voltage to neutral
Stretchhülsenüberziehmaschine *f* stretch sleeving machine
stetig constant, continuous, steady
stetig geregelter Brenner *m* continuously controlled burner
stetig wirkende Regeleinrichtung *f* continuous controlling system
stetig wirkendes Glied continuous acting element
stetige Regeleinrichtung *f* continuous controlling system
stetige Zufallsvariable *f* continuous random variable
stetiger Übergang *m* continuous transition
Stetigförderanlage *f* continuous hauling plant
Steuer- und Regelbarkeit *f* controllability
Steuer- und Schutzschaltgerät *nt* control and protective switching device
Steuer-/Regelgerät *nt* control circuit device
Steuerabhängigkeit *f* control dependency
Steueranlage *f* control system
Steueranweisung *f* control instruction
steuerbar controllable, steerable
steuerbarer Halbleitergleichrichter *m* silicon controlled rectifier
Steuerdaten *pl* control data
Steuerdeichsel *f* tiller

Steuerdruck *m* pilot pressure
Steuereingang *m* control input
Steuereinheit *f* control unit
Steuereinrichtung *f* control device, control equipment, control system, open loop controlling system, regulating device, control
Steuerelement *nt* control element
Steuergasleitung *f* pilot gas pipe
Steuergerät *nt* control unit, controller device, controller, regulating device
Steuergriff *m* control lever
Steuerhebel *m* control lever
Steuerimpuls *m* control impulse
Steuerkabine *f* control cab
Steuerkette *f* open loop control
Steuerknüppel *m* control stick, joystick
Steuerknüppel *m* **fixiert** stick fixed
Steuerknüppel *m* **frei** stick free
Steuerkommando *nt* control command
Steuerkopf *m* control box
Steuerkreis *m* control circuit
Steuerkurve *f* cam
Steuerleitung *f* **1.** *(allg.)* control circuit, control line **2.** *(el.)* trip line
Steuerlogik *f* control logic
Steuerluft *f* control air, compressed air
steuern 1. *(überwachen)* control **2.** *(lenken)* direct, steer
Steuern *nt* control, open loop control
steuernder Ausgang *m* controlling output
Steuerorgan *nt* positioning element, final control element, controller
Steuerpendant *nt* control pendant
Steuerprogramm *nt* control program, controller, executive control program, supervisor
Steuerprogrammspeicher *m* control memory circuit
Steuerpult *nt* control desk, control console, control panel
Steuerschalter *m* control switch, master switch, master controller, main control switch
Steuerscheibe *f* control disc
Steuerschieber *m* control slide valve, shifter
Steuerschrank *m* control box

Steuerspannung *f* control voltage
Steuerstand *m* control position, control stand (or console), operating position, operating stand
Steuerstelle *f* control point, control station
Steuerstrecke *f* open loop controlled system, controlled system
Steuerstrom *m* **1.** *(el.)* control current **2.** *(Regeln)* pilot current, signal current
Steuerstromkreis *m* control circuit, *(US)* pilot circuit
Steuersystem *nt* control system
Steuertafel *f* control panel
Steuertrommel *f* control barrel
Steuerüberdruck *m* control overpressure (displacement body)
Steuerung *f* **1.** *(allg.)* controller, machine control unit, control, control system, (automatic) control mechanism, functional operation **2.** *(SPS)* open-loop control **3.** *(durch gehende Person)* pedestrian control **4.** *(mit Lochkartenleser)* punched card control **5.** *(mit Verbundschalter)* joystick control **6.** *(von Hand)* manual control, hand control **7.** *(von Werkzeugmaschinen)* machine tool control **8.** *(speicherprogrammierbare)* programmable controller (PC), programmable logic controller (PLC)
Steuerungen *fpl* control devices
Steuerungs- und Informationsprotokoll *nt* control and information protocol
Steuerungsart *f* control system, control mode
Steuerungsbereich *m* control area
Steuerungsebene *f* control level
Steuerungseinrichtung *f* control equipment
Steuerungselement *nt* control element
Steuerungshierarchie *f* control hierarchy
Steuerungskomponente *f* control element
Steuerungskonzept *nt* control concept
Steuerungsmittel *nt* control means
Steuerungsobjekt *nt* equipment under control

Steuerungsprogramm *nt* control program
Steuerungsregel *f* control rule
Steuerungssoftware *f* control(ler) software, control(ler) program, executive program
Steuerungsstrategie *f* control strategy
Steuerungssystem *nt* **mit Rückmeldung** feedback
Steuerungstechnik *f* open loop control
Steuerungsverfahren *nt* control technique
Steuerventil *nt* control valve, pulse emitting valve
Steuervorgang *m* control operation
Steuerwelle *f* camshaft
Steuerzeichen *nt* control character
Steuerzentrale *f* control centre
Stich *m* 1. *(allg.)* puncture, stab 2. *(Nadeln)* stitch
Stichausreißkraft *f* stitch tear resistance
Stichelhaus *nt (Spannklaue)* plain toolpost
Stichelklaue *f* plain toolpost
Stichgang *m* stub aisle
Stichgangstrategie *f* stub aisle strategy
Stichgleis *nt* spur, track, stub track
Stichmarke *f* internal calliper gauge
Stichmaß *nt* inside micrometer
Stichmaßprüfer *m* centre distance tester
Stichprobe *f* 1. *(allg.)* off-hand sample, spot check, random sample, random test 2. *(bei Verpackungen)* spot sample
Stichprobenabweichung *f* sample error
Stichprobenaufbau *m* sample composition
Stichprobeneinheit sample unit
Stichprobenkenngröße *f* statistic
Stichprobenkontrolle *f* random sampling, random testing
Stichprobenprüfplan *m* sampling plan
Stichprobenprüfung *f* sampling inspection
Stichprobentheorie *f* theory of sampling
Stichprobenumfang *m* sampling size
Stichprobenvorschrift *f* spot check specification
stichprobenweise on a spot check basis
stichprobenweise prüfen spot-check
Stichstelle *f* piercing point
Stichtag *m* closing date
Stichtagsinventur *f* closing date inventory, closing date inventory-making
Stickoxidechtheit *f* fastness to nitrogen oxides
Stickstoff abgebendes Mittel *nt* medium yielding nitrogen
Stickstoff *m* nitrogen
Stickstoffdruckminderer *m* nitrogen regulator
Stickstoffflasche *f* nitrogen cylinder
Stiel *m* post, support, stay, handle, stick, stem, shank
Stielstrahlung *f* stem radiation
Stift *m* pin, pintle, stud, plug, peg, stem
Stiftauszugskraft *f* stem retention force, stem pull-out force
Stiftbolzen *m* stud
Stiftdurchmesser *m* stem diameter
Stiftheber *m* pin lifter
Stiftlänge *f* stem length
Stiftschlüssel *m* pin-type wrench
Stiftschraube *f* stud
Stiftschraube *f* **für T-Nutensteine** stud for tongues for T-slots
Stiftschraube *f* **mit Ringsicherung** stud with serrated ring lock
stilllegen decommission, shut down
Stilllegung *f* decommissioning, shutdown
Stillsetzeinrichtung *f* stopping attachment
stillsetzen 1. *(allg.)* stop, bring to rest, shut down, trip, park 2. *(Maschine)* put out of operation (or service) 3. *(Ventilator)* shutdown 4. *(Vorschubbewegung)* trip, arrest
Stillsetzung *f* shutdown, stop, tripping
Stillsetzweg *m* stopping distance
Stillstand *m* 1. *(allg.)* deadlock, downtime, halt, standstill, rest, stoppage, stillstand, dwell 2. *(zum ~ kommen)* come to a standstill, come to a halt
Stillstandsdauer *f* idle time, dwell
Stillstandsmoment *nt* standstill torque

Stillstandszeit f **1.** *(allg.)* stop period, rest period, stoppage time, time of dwell **2.** *(IT)* downtime
stillstehen be out of action, stop
stillstehend stationary, stagnant
Stippen fpl fibre clots, spots
Stirn f face, front, end
Stirnabstand m end distance
Stirnabstand-Härte-Kurve f end-distance hardness curve
Stirneingriffsteilung f transverse normal base pitch
Stirneingriffswinkel m transverse pressure angle
Stirnen nt face milling
Stirnfläche f front end, end face, fusion face, face
Stirnfläche f **des Gabelrückens** shank top
Stirnflächen nt *(als Arbeitsvorgang)* squaring
Stirnflächenabstand m distance between fusion (or abutting) faces
Stirnflächenverschleiß m front end wear
Stirnfräsen nt end milling, face milling
Stirnfräser m face mill, face milling cutter, facing cutter, end mill, facing-type milling cutter
Stirnfräskopf m face milling cutter
Stirnfreiwinkel m end clearance angle, angle vertical to the cutter axis
Stirnfugennaht f end groove weld
Stirnhinterschliffwinkel m end relief angle
Stirnkeilwinkel m end-lip angle
Stirnlängskante f side of gap face
Stirnlaufgenauigkeit f true running of end faces
Stirnmodul nt transverse module
Stirnplanradpaar nt contrate gear pair
Stirnprofilwinkel m transverse pressure angle, transverse pressure angle at a point
Stirnrad nt **1.** *(allg.)* spur gear **2.** *(Geradzahnstirnrad)* spur gear **3.** *(Schrägzylinderrad)* helical gear **4.** *(Zylinderrad)* cylindrical gear **5.** *(mit Doppelschrägverzahnung)* double helical gear **6.** *(mit Evolventenverzahnung)* cylindrical gear with involute teeth
Stirnradgeradverzahnung f spur gear teeth
Stirnradgetriebe nt cylindrical gear transmission, (reduction) helical gear
Stirnradherstellung f cylindrical gear production
Stirnradpaar nt **1.** *(allg.)* cylindrical gear pair, gear pair with parallel axes **2.** *(mit Doppelschrägverzahnung)* double helical gear pair
Stirnradverzahnung f cylindrical gear tooth system, cylindrical gear teeth, spur gear tooth system
Stirnradwälzfräser m spur gear hob
Stirnradwälzfräsmaschine f spur gear generating machine
Stirnschleifkörper m face grinding wheel
Stirnschliff m face grinding
Stirnschneide f face cutting edge, face cutter edge, front cutting edge, front edge, peripheral cutting edge
Stirnschnitt m transverse section
Stirnschnittebene f plane of transverse section
Stirnschraubrad nt cylindrical crossed helical gear
Stirnschraubradpaar nt cylindrical crossed helical gear pair
Stirnseite f front end, front face, face, front wall, front side
Stirnseitenabstand m distance between end faces
Stirnseitenkante f side of fusion face
stirnseitig at the front, at the ends, in front-side position
Stirnteilung f **1.** *(allg.)* transverse pitch, pitch **2.** *(Teilkreisteilung)* reference circle pitch
Stirnteilungswinkel m transverse pitch angle
Stirnzahn m radial tooth, end tooth
Stirnzahndicke f *(bei e. Geradstirnrad)* transverse tooth thickness
Stirnzähne mpl teeth on the end
Stirnzapfen m end journal
stochastischer Zusammenhang m stochastic relation
Stockpunkt m pour point

Stockwerk *nt* floor, storey, *(US)* story
Stockwerkkessel *m* single-floor boiler
Stockwerklager *nt* multi-storey warehouse, multi-floor warehouse
Stockwerksflur *m* landing
Stoff *m* 1. *(Substanz)* matter 2. *(e. Werkstückes)* material
Stoffdichte *f* stock concentration
Stoffeigenschaft *f* material characteristic
Stoffeigenschaftsänderung *f* alteration in material characteristic
Stofffluss *m* material flow
Stoffhaftung *f* material adhesion
Stoffkreislauf *m* material circulation
Stoffkuchen *m* stock cake
Stoffprobe *f* stock sample
Stoffschluss *m* metallic continuity
stoffschlüssiges Fügen *nt* positive substance jointing
Stoffuntersuchung *f* testing of materials
Stoffverbinden *nt* welding
Stollenfräser *m* milling cutter with parallel rows of teeth
Stolpergefahr *f* danger of stumbling, risk of stumbling
stolpern stumble, trip
Stolperstelle *f* place liable to cause stumbling, tripping point
Stopfbuchsausgleichslager *nt* sliding expansion joint
Stopfbuchse *f* stuffing box
Stopfbuchsendichtung *f* stuffing box packing
Stopfbuchsenmuffe *f* gland type socket
Stopfdichte *f* powder density
Stopfen *m* plug
Stopfenpfanne *f* bottom-pour
Stopfenwalzen *nt* **von Rohren** plug rolling of tubes (over stationary mandrel)
Stopfenwalzwerk *nt* plug mill
Stopp *m* stop
Stoppbremsung *f* braking to stop
stoppen stop, arrest, check, halt
Stopper *m* stopper
Stoppfunktion *f* stop function
Stoppmodus *m* stop mode

Störabschalter *m* flame fault shutdown
Störabschaltung *f* fault shut-down
störanfällig 1. *(allg.)* fault-prone, susceptible to disorders 2. *(el.)* interference-prone
Störanfälligkeit *f* fault liability, proneness to disorders, susceptibility to failure, susceptibility to faults, susceptibility to failure, interference liability
Störaussendung *f* emission, emitted interference
Störbereich *m* range of the disturbance variable
Störeinfluss *m* interfering factor
Störempfindlichkeit *f* interference susceptibility
stören disturb, interfere with
Störfall *m* accident, breakdown, event of fault, failure, incident, case of malfunction, upset
Störfallmagnet *nt* accident management, incident management
Störfeld *nt* interference field
Störfestigkeit *f* immunity
Störfestigkeitsgrad *m* immunity level
Störfestigkeitszone *f* immunity zone
Störfreiheit *f* freedom from interference
Störgröße *f* disturbance variable
Störgrößenaufschaltung *f* disturbance variable feedforward
Störimpuls *m* 1. *(allg.)* interference pulse 2. *(von kurzer Dauer)* glitch
Störimpulsunterdrückung *f* interference pulse suppression
Störkante *f* obstruction, obstructing edge, outer edge
Störlichtblende *f* shield
stornieren cancel
Stornierfeld *nt* cancel button
Stornierung *f* 1. *(allg.)* cancellation 2. *(Rechnungswesen)* reversal
Stornobuchung *f* negative booking, reversal, reversing entry
Störort *m* point of disturbance
Störpegel *m* noise level, interference level
Störplan *m* fault plan
Störschutzbeschaltung *f* transient suppression device

Störschwingungen *fpl* disturbing vibrations
Störsignal *nt* 1. *(allg.)* interference, junk 2. *(zusätzliches)* dropin
Störstrahlenschutzvorrichtung *f* device affording protection against scattered radiation
Störstrahlung *f* disturbance radiation, stray radiation
Störung *f* 1. *(allg.)* disorder, disturbance, perturbation, trouble, failure, fault, malfunction, interruption, operational fault, breakdown 2. *(el.)* interference, fault
Störungsauswirkung *f* effect of faults
störungsbehaftet faulty
Störungsbeseitigung *f* fault elimination, fault repair, troubleshooting, emergency maintenance, repair of fault
Störungsbuch *nt* fault log, logbook
Störungsdauer *f* downtime, fault duration
störungsfrei trouble-free, error-free
Störungsmelder *m* fault indicator
Störungsmeldung *f* disturbance message, fault message, fault report
Störungsprotokollierung *f* fault recording, failure logging
Störungsspeicher *m* failure memory
Störungsursache *f* cause of the fault, source of disturbance
Störungszustand *m* fault status
Stoß *m* 1. *(allg.)* stroke, push, impulse, percussion, shock, jolt 2. *(el.)* surge 3. (Schlag) impact 4. *(Verbindung, Fuge)* joint
Stoßanfang *m* start of the groove
stoßartig intermittent, impulsive, periodic, shocklike
stoßartige Beanspruchung *f* impact loading
Stoßaufnahme *f* resiliency
Stoßbeanspruchung *f* shock loading
Stoßbeiwert *m* impact coefficient
Stoßbelastung *f* impact load, shock load
Stoßbereich *m* joint area
Stoßbremsvermögen *nt* collision stopping power
stoßdämpfend shock (or impact) absorbing
Stoßdämpfer *m* cushioning cylinder, shock absorber, dashpot
Stoßdämpferanschlag *m* stop damper
Stoßdämpfung *f* shock absorption
Stoßeinrichtung *f* slotting attachment
Stößel *m* ram, ram tool, tappet
Stößelabstützung *f* ram support
Stößelflachbahnführung *f* flat ramways, square ramways
Stößelführung *f* ram bearing, ram guide
Stößelführungsbahn *f* ram guideway, ramways
Stößelhobelmaschine *f* shaper, shaping machine
Stößelhub *m* ram stroke, stroke of the ram
Stößelkopf *m* 1. *(allg.)* ram head, toolhead (or tool head) 2. *(Waagerechtstoßmaschine)* head
Stößelkopfschlitten *m* ram head slide, toolhead slide
Stößelschlitten *m* tool carrier slide
Stößelsupport *m* ram head
Stößelverlauf *m* forward (or cutting) stroke of the ram
Stößelweg *m* 1. *(allg.)* travel of the ram, ram travel 2. *(Hub)* ram stroke
stoßen 1. *(allg.)* knock, jog 2. *(auf ein Hindernis)* abut, contract 3. *(Schlitten gegen Anschlag)* strike (against) 4. *(Keilnuten)* keyseat, keyway, push 5. *(Senkrechtstoßmaschine)* slot 6. *(Waagerechtstoßmaschine)* shape 7. *(Wälzverfahren)* shape by the generating method 8. *(Zahnräder)* shape
Stoßenergie *f* impact energy
Stoßfaktor *m* dynamic factor, impact coefficient, shock coefficient
stoßfest shock-proof, rough-service
Stoßfestigkeit *f* 1. *(allg.)* shock resistance 2. *(Schweißen)* joint efficiency
Stoßfläche *f* abutting end
Stoßflanke *f* face of butt weld
stoßfrei 1. *(allg.)* pulsation-free, smooth, shockless, shock-free 2. *(Verbindungen)* without joints
Stoßfuge *f* butt joint, gash
Stoßgrad *m* impact factor

Stoßkörper *m* tup
Stoßläppen *nt* joint lapping
Stößläppmaschine *f* joint lapping machine
Stoßmaschine *f* **1.** *(allg.) (US)* slotter, *(UK)* slotting machine **2.** *(waagerecht)* horizontal pushcut shaper **3.** *(mit schwenkbarem Stößelkopf)* vertical (push-cut) shaper, vertical shaper
Stoßmaschinenstößel *m* slotter ram
Stoßmeißel *m* slotting tool, slotter, pinion-type cutter
Stoßmesser *nt* shaper cutter
Stoßnaht *f* bead seal, butt seam, butt weld, butt joint
stoßräumen push-broach
Stoßräummaschine *f* press type broaching machine
stoßartige Wechselbeanspruchung *f* alternating shock load
Stoßspannung *f* energy surge, surge voltage, impulse voltage
Stoßstange *f* *(Senkrechtstoßmaschine)* slotting bar
Stoßstelle *f* location of the joints, thrusting point, intersection
stoßunempfindlich not susceptible to shocks
Stoßversuch *m* impact test
Stoßwerkzeug *nt* slotting tool, shaper cutter
stottern *(ruckweise gleiten)* stick-slip
straff 1. *(allg.)* tight, taut, tensioned, firm **2.** *(straff einspannen)* clamp taut
Strahl *m* **1.** *(allg.)* jet, ray **2.** *(Licht)* beam **3.** *(Strömung)* stream
Strahlachse *f* stream axis
Strahlaustrittsgeschwindigkeit *f* jet velocity
Strahlbildung *f* beam shaping
Strahlbündel *nt* ray bunch
Strahleinwirkung *f* ray effect
strahlen beam, emit rays, ray, radiate
strählen chase
Strahlen *nt* **1.** *(allg.)* blasting **2.** *(im Freien)* sandblasting carried out in the open **3.** *(mit Stahlkies)* shot-blasting
Strahlenausbreitung *f* propagation of radiation
Strahlenaustrittsfenster *nt* ray exit window
Strahlenbelastung *f* radiation exposure
strahlend radiant, radiating
Strahleneintrittsseite *f* ray entry side
Strahlenergie *f* radiation energy
strahlenexponiert exposed to radiation
strahleninduziert induced by radiation
Strahlenquelle *f* radiation source
Strahlenschliff *m* **1.** *(mit Bezug auf den Arbeitsvorgang)* arc grinding, radiating cut **2.** *(zur Kennzeichnung des Schleifbildes)* ray ground finish
Strahlenschutzbeton *m* radiation shielding concrete
Strahlenschutzdosimeter *nt* radiation protection dosimeter
Strahlenschutzmittel *nt* anti-radiation stabilizer
Strahlenschutzprüfung *f* radiation protection test
Strahlenschutzregel *f* radiation protection rule
Strahlenschutzstoff *m* radiation shielding material
Strahlenschutzzubehör *nt* radiation protection accessories
Strahlenschwächung *f* radiation attenuation
Strahlenumkehr *f* radiation reversal
Strahlenverfahrenstechnik *f* technology of blasting
Strahlenvernetzung *f* radiation cross-linking
Strahlenwarngerät *nt* X-ray warning device
Strahler *m* emitter, ray emitter, radiator
Strahlflüssigkeitspumpe *f* liquid jet pump
Strahlformung *f* ray forming, ray formation, beam shaping
Strahlführung *f* ray directing, ray manipulation
Strahlgestaltung *f* beam shaping
Strahlgut *nt* material to be sandblasted
Strahlhalle *f* blasting hall
Strahlintegral *m* ray integral
Strahlkabine *f* blasting cubicle
Strahlkennzahl *f* ray index

Strahlkontraktion *f* flow contraction
Strahlläppanlage *f* liquid honing equipment
Strahlläppen *nt* liquid honing *(US)*, vapour blast liquid honing *(UK)*
Strahlmittel *nt* blasting abrasive, blasting agent
Strahlmittel-Durchsatz *m* rate of delivery of the blasting abrasive
Strahlmittelumlauf *m* recirculation of blasting abrasives
Strahlqualität jet quality on performance
Strahlqualitätszahl (K) *f* beam quality performance number
Strahlquerschnitt *m* ray cross section
Strahlschweißen *nt* beam welding
Strahlspanen *nt* shoulder milling
Strahlumlenkung *f* beam direction change, beam reversing
Strahlung *f* **1.** *(allg.)* radiation **2.** *(synchrone ~)* synchronous radiation
Strahlungsaussendung *f* radiation sending out
Strahlungs-Bremsvermögen *nt* radiation stopping power
Strahlungsdetektor *m* radiation detector
strahlungsempfindliches Papier *nt* radiation-sensitive paper
Strahlungsenergie *f* radiation energy
Strahlungsfeld *nt* radiation field
Strahlungsfeldgröße *f* radiation field variable (or quantity)
Strahlungsheizelement *nt* radiant heating element
Strahlungsheizgerät *nt* radiation type heating appliance
Strahlungsheizung *f* radiant heating
Strahlungshitze *f* radiant heat
Strahlungsimpuls *m* radiation impulse
Strahlungsintensität *f* radiation intensity
Strahlungsleistung *f* emissive power, radiant intensity, energy radiated
Strahlungsmessgerät *nt* radiation meter
Strahlungspyrometer *nt* radiation pyrometer
Strahlungsquelle *f* radiation source

Strahlungsschutz *m* radiation protection, shielding
Strahlungsspektrum *nt* radiation spectrum
Strahlungstechnik *f* radiation technology
Strahlungsunterbrechung *f* beam interruption
Strahlungswärmeabgabe *f* output of radiant heat
Strahlverdichter *m* jet compressor
Strahlverfahren *nt* **1.** *(allg.)* jet method **2.** *(Ionen, Laser)* beam processes
Strahlverfahrenstechnik *f* blasting technology
Strahlwinkel *m* angle of blasting
Strang *m* **1.** *(allg.)* cable, line, rope, strand **2.** *(Aufreihung)* string
Strangadresse *f* line destination
Stranggießen *nt* continuous casting
Stranggießverfahren *nt* continuous casting process
Strangguss *m* continuous casting
Strangpressen *nt* **1.** *(allg.)* extrusion of rods and tubes, extrusion **2.** *(mit starrem Werkzeug)* rod extrusion with rigid tool **3.** *(mit Wirkmedien)* rod extrusion with action media **4.** *(von Strängen mit hohlem Querschnitt)* straight tubular extrusion **5.** *(von Strängen mit vollem Querschnitt)* rod extrusion
Strangspannung *f* phase voltage, voltage to neutral
Strangziehen *nt* slab drawing
Straßenablauf *m* road drain
Straßenkanal *m* public highway sewer
Straßenkappe *f* *(für Gasrohrleitungen)* street cap
Straßenteerausflussgerät *nt* road tar discharge apparatus
Straßenverkehr *m* road traffic
Straßenverkehrsbelastung *f* loads imposed by road traffic
Strategie *f* strategy
strategisch strategic
Strebe *f* strut, brace, bracing, truss
Strecke *f* **1.** *(allg.)* distance, way, road, route, section **2.** *(Schienen)* track **3.** *(Steuerstrecke, Regelstrecke)* controlled system

strecken stretch, extend, lengthen, rack, elongate
Streckenbegehung f section patrol
Streckenenergie f energy input per unit length
Streckengrenze f elastic limit, limit of elasticity, yield point
Streckenlänge f trackage
Streckenmessung f telemetry
Streckensteuerung f straight cut control, straight line control
Streckgrenze f yield point
Streckmetall nt expanded metal
Streckprozess m stretching process
Streckreduzierwalzen nt reducing by roll stretching
Streckrichten nt (von Flachstäben) straightening (flat bars) by stretching
Streckziehen nt stretch drawing to shape
Strehleinrichtung f chasing attachment
strehlen chase
Strehler m chaser
Strehlerbacken m chasing die
Strehlgang m chasing stroke
streichbar of brushing consistency
Streifen m 1. (eines Materials) strip, strap, tape 2. (gedacht, gezeichnet) stripe
Streifenabtastung f rectilinear scanning
Streifenauslenkung m band deviation
Streifenbild nt fringe pattern
Streifenblech nt strip sheet
Streifenbreite f stripe width
Streifendiagramm nt strip chart
Streifenfehler m tape error
Streifenform-, -füll- und -verschließmaschine f strip packaging machine
Streifenformat nt strip size
streifenförmiges Prüfbild nt strip type test diagram
Streifenführungen touching guides
streifengesteuert tape-controlled
Streifenlesegeschwindigkeit f tape-reading speed
Streifenlesekopf m tape reader
Streifenleser m tape reader
Streifenlocher m tape puncher, tape punch
Streifenlochung f tape punching
Streifenmaterial nt strip stock
Streifenpresse f slitting press
Streifenprobe f strip specimen
Streifenschere f rotary slitting press
Streifenschreiber m strip-chart recorder
Streifentor nt strip door
Streifenvorschub m tape feed
streifig striated
Streifigkeit f streaking
Stretcheinschlagmaschine f stretch film wrapping machine
Stretchfolie f stretch film
Stretchfolienband nt band of thermoplastic film
Stretchfolieneinschlagmaschine f stretch film wrapping machine, stretch wrapping machine
Stretchfolieneinwickelmaschine f stretch banding machine
Stretchfolienhülse f tube of plastic material, tube of thermoplastic film
Stretchfolienrolle f stretch film roll
Stretchfolienrollenträger m stretch film roll carrier
Stretchfolienspiraleinwickelmaschine f spiral stretch wrapper, stretch film bundling machine
Stretchhaube f stretch hood
Stretchhaubenüberziehmaschine f stretch hood applicator
Stretchhülse f stretch sleeve
Stretchverpackung f stretch wrap (pack)
Stretchwickelmaschine f stretch wrapping machine
stretchwickeln stretch wrap, stretch-wrap
Stretchwickler m stretch wrapper, stretchwrapper, stretch wrapping machine
Stretchwicklung f stretch wrap
Streuband nt scatter band
streuen scatter, stray
Streufeld nt scatter field, stray field
Streufilter m scattering filter
Streugrenze f 1. (allg.) scattering limit 2. (QM) limit of variation

Streukoeffizient *m* dispersion coefficient
Streulichtstrom *m* stream of scattered light
Streustrahlenraster *nt* scattered radiation grid
Streustrahlenschutz *m* protection against scattered radiation
Streustrom *m* stray electric current
Streustromableitung *f* derivation of stray current
Streustromabsaugung *f* absorption of stray current
Streustromgefährdung *f* hazard from stray currents
Streustromkreis *m* stray current circuit
Streuung *f* 1. *(allg.)* dispersion, variation, scattering 2. *(e. Emission)* dispersion 3. *(von Messwerten)* variability
Streuungsmaß *nt* measure of variability
Strich *m* 1. *(Linie)* line 2. *(Balken)* bar 3. *(Querstrich)* dash 4. *(Streifenmarkierung)* strip, stripe 5. *(Zeichnen, Bewegung)* stroke
Strichbreite *f* strip width, stroke width, thickness of stripes
Strichcode *m* bar code
Strichcodelesestift *m* bar code scanner
Strichcodesystem *nt* bar code system
Strichcodierung *f* bar coding
Strichdicke *f* stroke thickness
Strichendmaß *nt* hairline gauge, line gauge block
Strichlinie *f* dash line
Strichmaß *nt* rule
strichpunktierter Kreis *m* chain-line circle
Strichpunktlinie *f* chain line
Strichrasterverfahren *nt* line-scanning method
Strichskala *f* line scale (graduation)
Strick *m* rope
Strickleiter *f* rope ladder
Strohzellstoff *m* strawpulp
Strom *m* 1. *(Material)* stream 2. *(el.)* (electric) current, (electric) power 3. *(Energieversorger)* deliver current 4. *(Fließen)* flow 5. *(~ einspeisen)* feed (in) current, supply with current 6. *(~ entnehmen von)* draw current (from) 7. *(~ führend)* live, current-carrying energized 8. *(~ liefern)* source current, supply with current, current sourcing 9. *(~ liefernder Ausgang)* source mode output 10. *(~ ziehend)* current sinking 11. *(~ ziehender Ausgang)* sink mode output 12. *(nicht ~ führend)* idle
Stromabnehmer *m* collector brush
stromabwärts downstream
Stromangleichung *f* current adjustment
Stromaufnahme *f* current absorption
stromaufwärts upstream
Stromausfall *m* loss of power, power failure, blackout
Strombahn *f* current path
Strombegrenzer *m* current limiter
Strombegrenzung *f* current limitation
Stromdichte-Potential-Kurve *f* current density-potential curve
Stromeinspeisung *f* power supply
strömen flow, pass through
Stromentnahme *f* current consumption, current drain, drawing of current
Stromerzeuger *m* generator
stromführend abgeschmolzener Schweißdraht *m* filler wire consumed with carrying current
stromführendes Teil *nt* current carrying part
Stromgenerator *m* power generator
Stromkontakt *m* electrical contact
Stromkontaktrohr *nt* current contact tube
Stromkreis *m* power circuit, (electric) circuit
Stromkreiswert *m* circuit value
Stromleitung *f* current conduction, current line
Stromlieferung *f* current delivery, power supply
Stromlinie *f* streamline
stromlos de-energized
stromlose Zeitspanne *f* zero current interval
stromloser Zeitabschnitt *m* zero-current period
Stromnetz *nt* current network

Strompfad *m* path of the current, rung
Stromprogramm *nt* current control programme
Stromquelle *f* source of current, power source
Stromregelung *f* current control
Stromregelventil *nt* pressure-compensated flow-control valve
Stromrichter *m* **1.** *(allg.)* current converter, power converter **2.** *(netzseitig)* current source inverter
Stromrichtung *f* current direction
Stromschiene *f* **1.** *(allg.)* bus bar **2.** *(SPS)* power rail
Stromstärke *f* intensity
Strömung *f* stream, flow, fluid flow
Strömung *f* **in einer Richtung** one-way flow
Strömungsfeld *nt* **der Lüftungsanlage** airflow of the ventilating system
Strömungsgeschwindigkeit *f* rate of flow
Strömungsgetriebe *nt* hydraulic transmission, fluid transmission
Strömungskupplung *f* fluid coupling
Strömungslinie *f* streamline
Strömungsmenge *f* rate of flow
Strömungsschalter *m* flow switch
Strömungssicherung *f* flow safety device
Stromventil *nt* flow-control valve
Stromverbraucher *m* electric device
Stromverdrängungseigenschaft *f* current displacement (quality), skin effect
Stromverdrängungsmotor *m* eddy current motor
Stromversorgungsnetz *nt* supply network
Stromwandler *m* **1.** *(allg.)* current transformer, transformer **2.** *(Messwertumformer)* transducer
Stromwender *m* commutator, reversing switch
Stromzufuhr *f* current supply, supply current
Struktogramm *nt* (program) structure chart, structogram
Struktogrammsinnbild *nt* structure chart symbol
Struktur *f* structure, texture
Strukturbaum *m* structure tree
strukturell structural, textural
strukturieren structure
strukturierte Abfragesprache *f* structured query language
strukturierte Oberfläche *f* textured surface
strukturierte Steuerungssprache *f* structured control language
strukturierter Text *m* structured text (ST)
Strukturierungsmittel *nt* means of structuring
Strukturkennzahl *f* structural indicator
Strukturplan *m* structure plan
Strukturstückliste *f* structural bill of materials
Stub-Acme-Gewinde *nt* stub Acme thread
Stück *nt* **1.** *(allg.)* component, part, piece, workpiece, unit **2.** *(aus einem ~)* one-piece, single-piece
Stückbearbeitung *f* piece production machining
Stückgut *nt* unit load
Stückgutandrücker *m* unit load pusher, unit load press
Stückgutprozess *m* unit load process
Stückgutsammelstation *f* unit load merge point
Stückgutstrom *m* unit load flow
stückiges Gut *nt* solid
Stückkosten *pl* unit cost per piece, piece-production cost, operation cost per piece
Stückliste *f* list of parts, parts list, (US) bill of materials (BOM)
Stücklistenauflösung *f* bill (of materials) explosion, parts explosion
Stücklistenverarbeitung *f* parts list processing, processing the list of parts
Stückpreis *m* unit price
Stückprüfung *f* routine testing, standard routine test
Stückteil *nt* component
Stückverzinken *nt* piecework zinc coating
Stückzahl *f* **1.** *(allg.)* count, quantity, number of units **2.** *(klein)* batch

3. (*beim Räumen*) broaching rate **4.** (*die das Werkzeug während seiner Lebensdauer fertigen kann*) life capacity of a tool **5.** (*je Stunde*) pieces per hour
Stückzähler *m* piece counter
Stückzeichnung *f* detail drawing, component drawing
Stückzeit *f* machining time per piece
Stückzeitverkürzung *f* reduction in machining time per piece
Studienversuch *m* test for study purposes
Stufe *f* **1.** (*allg.*) stage, shoulder, step, increment, class, level **2.** (*e. Drehzahl*) range **3.** (*e. Leiter*) step, tread **4.** (*e. Motors*) speed **5.** (*Kolben e. Spannfutters*) step
stufen graduate
Stufenblock *m* guide block
Stufenbreite *f* (*e. Treppe*) step depth
Stufenbruch *m* stepped break
Stufendorn *m* progressive plug gauge (or gage)
Stufendrehstift *m* sliding tee bar with reduced diameters
Stufenfräsen *nt* shoulder milling, step milling
Stufenfutter *nt* step chuck
Stufengetriebe *nt* speed change transmission, variable speed drive
Stufengraben *m* stepped trench
Stufenhobelmeißel *m* corrugated tool
Stufenhobeln *nt* stepped planing
Stufenhöhe *f* instep clearance
Stufenkeil *m* stepped wedge
stufenlos continuous, smooth, infinitely variable, stepless
stufenlos auf Null herab regeln reduce steplessly to zero
stufenlos geregelt continuously controlled, infinitely variable
stufenlos regelbar continuously adjustable, infinitely variable, steplessly variable
stufenlos regelbare Vorschübe *mpl* infinitely variable feeds (pl)
stufenlos schaltbar continuously switchable
stufenlos veränderlich steplessly variable

stufenlos veränderliche Drehzahl *f* steplessly variable speed
stufenlos verstellbar progressively adjustable
stufenlos verstellbares Getriebe *nt* infinitely variable speed gear transmission
stufenlos verstellen vary infinitely
stufenlose Drehzahländerung *f* infinitely variable speed changes, stepless speed changing
stufenlose Drehzahlregelung *f* infinitely variable speed regulation (or control), infinitely variable adjustment
stufenlose Verstellung *f* infinitely variable speed drive
stufenloser Antrieb *m* infinitely variable speed transmission
stufenloses Getriebe *nt* infinitely variable change-speed gear
Stufenlötung *f* step soldering
Stufenofen *m* zone type furnace
Stufenrad *nt* cluster gear
Stufenräderblock *m* gear cone
Stufenrädergetriebe *nt* variable speed gear drive, speed change gear drive
Stufenschaltung *f* variable-speed control
Stufenscheibe *f* (*US*) cone pulley, (*UK*) stepped pulley, step cone, stepped cone pulley
Stufenscheibenantrieb *m* cone drive
Stufenscheibengetriebe *nt* cone pulley drive
Stufenschritt *m* progression
Stufensprung *m* **1.** (*allg.*) progression **2.** (*von Drehzahlen*) progressive ratio, progressive grading of speeds, geometric progression, progression factor **3.** (*von Zahlenwerten*) gradation
Stufentiefe *f* toe clearance
stufenweise step by step
Stufenweite *f* step width
stufig stepwise
stufig gesteuert step-controlled
Stufung *f* graduation, phase approach, increment, progression, grading
Stuhlrollenversuch *m* chair castor test
Stulpe *f* cuff
stülpen (*über*) place over, put over

Stülpziehen *nt* reverse redrawing
stumpf blunt, dull
stumpf aneinanderfügen butt
Stumpf *m* stub, stump, end
stumpfes Aussehen *nt* dull appearance
stumpfschweißen butt-weld
Stumpfstoß *m* **mit Gratnaht** butt joint with flash
Stumpfstoß *m* **mit X-Naht** butt joint with double-V weld
stumpfwinklig obtuse-angled
Stundenleistung *f* pieces per hour
Sturz *m* **1.** *(allg.)* fall, overturning **2.** *(Bau)* lintel
Sturzberechnung *f* spindle fall calculation
stürzen 1. *(fallen)* fall **2.** *(umdrehen)* overturn **3.** *(kippen)* tip
Sturzguss *m* slush casting
Sturzzug *m* down-swept flue
Stützarm *m* arbor support
Stützblock *m* backing block, supporting block, jack
Stütze *f* **1.** *(allg.)* column, support, stanchion, upright, bracket, brace **2.** *(Bau)* pier
stützen support, back
Stutzen *m* socket
Stützenabstand *m* support spacing
Stutzenanschlussmaß *nt* nozzle connection dimension
Stützenfuß *m* support foot
Stutzennaht *f* stub weld
Stützenprofil *nt* column profile, stanchion profile
Stützenstoß *m* column splice, stanchion splice
Stützenversatz *m* support displacement
Stützenvorderkante *f* front edge of the support
Stützkörperwerkstoff *m* backing material
Stützkraft *f* supporting force
Stützlast *f* supporting force
Stützprozess *m* supporting process
Stützpunkt *m* **1.** *(Basis)* base **2.** *(Drehpunkt)* fulcrum **3.** *(Ruhepunkt)* supporting point
Stützrad *nt* stabilizer wheel, stabilizing wheel

Stützring *m* back-up ring, back-up washer
Stützrolle *f* support roll
Stützscheibe *f* back-up washer
Stütztraverse *f* overarm brace
Stützweite *f* **1.** *(allg.)* distance between supports, bearing, span **2.** *(freie ~)* clear span
Styrol-Butadien-Kautschuk *m* styrene butadiene rubber
Styrolcopolymer *nt* styrene copolymer
Styrolcopolymerisat *nt* styrene copolymer
Styrolhomopolymerisat *nt* styrene homopolymer
Sublimation *f* sublimation
Sublimationskurve *f* sublimation curve, hoar-frost line
Sublimationspunkt *m* sublimation point temperature
Sublimationswärme *f* heat of sublimation
Submikrometerbereich *m* submicrometre range
Substanzverlust *m* loss in substance
Substrat *nt* **1.** *(allg.)* substrate **2.** *(el. leitendes ~)* electric conductive substrate
Subsystem *nt* subsystem
Subtrahierer *m* subtractor, subtraction unit
Subunternehmer *m* subcontractor
Subunternehmervertrag *m* subcontact
Suche *f* search (for)
suchen search (for), locate, localize, look (for)
Suchsystem *nt* search system
Südpol *m* south pole
Sulfitzellstoff *m* sulphite pulp
Summand *m* summand
summarische Wirkungsgrößen *fpl* summary indices of action
Summe *f* amount, sum, total
Summenabweichung *f* cumulative variation
Summenfehler *m* cumulative error
Summenlinie *f* cumulative frequency polygon
Summenstrom *m* total current
Summenstromdichte-Potential-

kurve *f* total current density-potential curve
Summenteilfehler *m* accumulated tooth spacing error
Summenteilungsprüfung *f* cumulative pitch test
Summentoleranz *f* aggregate tolerance
Summenzeile *f* total line
summieren sum, total, accumulate
Summiergetriebe *nt* summing mechanism
Summierglied *nt* summing element, comparing element
Summierung *f* summation
Sumpftemperatur *f* temperature of the liquid in distillation flask
Sumpfthermometer *nt* flask thermometer
Support *m* **1.** *(allg.)* cross-rail head, railhead, toolhead, cross-slide toolbox, planing head, planer head, slide head, head, carriage, slide rest, tool box, tool slide **2.** *(Abwälz ~)* hobbing unit **3.** *(Doppel ~)* duplex tool rest, connected slide rests, duplex head, double head **4.** *(Fräs ~)* milling head, milling head slide **5.** *(Hobelmaschinen ~)* planer toolhead, planer head **6.** *(Meißelhalter ~)* planing head **7.** *(Rund ~)* rotary table **8.** *(Schwenk ~)* swivelling slide rest, swivelling tool rest, swing rest **9.** *(Ständer ~)* sidehead, side toolbox **10.** *(Werkzeug ~)* toolbox
Supportbewegung *f* toolside movement
Supportführung *f* carriage track (or way)
Supportquerbalken *m* cross-beam, crossrail (or cross rail)
Supportsattel *m* toolhead saddle
Supportschieber *m* toolhead slide, crossrail slide
Supportschlossplatte *f* *(Drehmaschine)* apron
Supportspindel *f* crossrail feed screw
Supportträger *m* **1.** *(allg.)* cantilever **2.** *(Ausleger)* rail, beam **3.** *(Querbalken)* crossrail
Supportverstellung *f* set-over of the compound rest

Suppressordiode *f* voltage regulative diode
Suspension *f* suspension
Suspensionspolymerisat *nt* polymer in suspension
Symbol *nt* symbol
Symbolisierung *f* symbolization
Symmetrie *f* symmetry
Symmetrieachse *f* axis of symmetry
Symmetrietoleranz *f* symmetry tolerance
synchron synchronous
Synchronantrieb *m* synchronous drive
Synchronbereich *m* synchronous range
Synchronbewegung *f* synchronous motion
Synchrondrehzahl *f* synchronous speed
synchrone Datenübertragung *f* synchronous data transmission
synchrone Datenübetragungsprozedur *f* synchronous data link control
synchrones Zeitmultiplexverfahren *nt* synchronous time division multiplexing
Synchronfahrweise *f* synchronous operation
Synchrongetriebe *nt* synchromesh
Synchronisation *f* synchronization
Synchronisationsmoment *nt* synchronizing torque
synchronisieren synchronize
synchronisiertes Steuern *nt* interlocked control
Synchronisierung *f* synchronization, synchronization unit
Synchronlauf *m* synchronous operation
Synchronmotor *m* synchronous motor
Synchronpaternoster *nt* synchronous vertical carousel
Synchronring *m* synchronizer ring
Syntax *m* syntax
Syntaxstruktogramm *nt* syntax structogram
synthetisch synthetic
System der Einheitsmutter *f* basic nut system, nut-basis system
System *nt* system

Systemabfragetaste *f* system request key
Systemabsturz *m* system crash
Systemachse *f* system axis, datum axis
Systemadministrator *m* administrator (ADMIN)
Systemanalyse *f* system analysis
Systemarchitektur *f* system architecture
systematische Abweichung *f* systematic error
systematische Ergebnisabweichung *f* error (or bias) of result
systematische Probennahme *f* systematic sampling
systematischer Fehler *m* systematic error
Systemausfall *m* system breakdown, system crash
Systemausführung *f* system output
Systemausgang *m* system output
Systemausgangsgröße *f* system output variable
Systemauslastung *f* system utilization
Systembauweise *f* system design
Systembediener *m* system operator (SYSOP)
Systembedienungsbefehl *m* system command
systembedingt system dependent
Systembetreuer *m* system attendant
Systembetreuung *f* system support
Systemdurchsatz *m* system throughput
Systeme *f* **vorbestimmter Zeiten** systems of preset times
Systemebene *f* datum, datum plane, system level
systemeigen native
systemeigener Code *m* native code
Systemeigentest *m* system self-test
Systemeinführung *f* system implementation
Systemeingang *m* system input
Systemeingangsgröße *f* system input variable
Systemeinstellung *f* system setting
Systemerdebezugspunkt *m* system earth reference point
Systemerweiterung *f* system expansion
systemextern external
Systemfehler *m* system error, system fault spark
Systemfehlerbehebung *f* system recovery
systemfrei open
systemfreie Kommunikation *f* open systems interconnection (OSI)
Systemgrenze *f* border of system, system border, system limit, system boundary
Systemintegrator *m* system integrator
systemintern system-internal, intrasystem
Systeminterndaten *pl* system internal data *pl*
Systemkernmodul *m* system core module
Systemkernprogramm *nt* system core program
systemkompatibel system-compatible, compatible with the system
Systemkomponente *f* system component
Systemkontrolleinheit *f* system control unit (SCU)
Systemlast *f* system load
Systemlastdaten *pl* system load data
Systemlieferant *m* system supplier
systemnaher Modul *m* system related module
Systempartner *m* partner in the system
Systemplaner *m* system planner
Systemprotokoll *nt* system log
Systemprüfung *f* system check
Systemschulung *f* system training
Systemsoftware *f* system software
Systemspeicher *m* system memory
systemspezifisch system-specific
Systemsprache *f* system language
Systemsteuerung *f* system control
Systemsteuerungssprache *f* system control language
Systemstörung *f* system failure
Systemtakt *m* system clock (pulse)
Systemtechnik *f* system technology
systemtechnische Lösung *f* system solution
systemübergreifend cross-system

Systemüberwachung f system monitoring
Systemuhr f system clock
Systemumwelt f system environment
systemunabhängig system-independent
Systemvariable f system variable
Systemverantwortliche/r f, m (person) responsible for systems
Systemverhalten nt system behaviour
Systemverzeichnis nt system directory, system folder
Systemvorschlag m system proposal
Systemzeit f system time
Systemzeituhr f system timer
Systemzustand m control mode, system status, system state
Systemzuverlässigkeit f system reliability

T t

Tabakrauch *m* tobacco smoke
Tabelle *f* **1.** *(allg.)* chart, table, worksheet, spreadsheet **2.** *(Aufstellung)* list
Tabellenkalkulationsprogramm *nt* spreadsheet program
Tabellenmaß *nt* tabular dimension
Tabellenzeichnung *f* tabular drawing
Tablar *nt* shelf, tray
Tablarfördertechnik *f* tray handling system, tray handling technology
Tablarlager *nt* miniload system, miniload storage system, tray storage system
Tablett *nt* tray
tablettieren tablet, pellet
Tablettiermaschine *f* tabletting machine, pelleter
Tablettierung *f* tabletting, pelleting
Tafel *f* panel, plate
Tag *m* day
tageslichtähnlich akin to daylight
Tageslichtquote *f* daylight quota (or proportion)
Tagesraum *m* dayroom
täglich daily, day to day
Taillenform *f* waste form
Takt *m* **1.** *(e. Arbeitsmaschine)* cycle **2.** *(el.)* clock pulse **3.** *(Verbrennungsmotoren)* stroke
Taktbetrieb *m* cycled operation
takten clock, synchronize
Taktgeber *m* clock generator, clock unit, master clock
taktgetrieben cycle-driven
Taktmerker *m* clock memory
Taktschaltventil *nt* two-way valve dependent on lubrication cycle
Taktschaltwerk *nt* timing gear
Taktzahl *f* number of cycles
Taktzeit *f* cycle time
Talfahrt *f* downward run, downhill travel, downhill motion
Tallharz *nt* liquid resin
Tandemräder *ntpl* tandem wheels
Tangentenberührungspunkt *m* tangent contact point
Tangente *f* tangent

Tangentenabschnitt *m* tangent portion
Tangentenebene *f* tangential plane
Tangentenfühlersteuerung *f* copying attachment with tangential tracer control
Tangentialanschnitt *m* tangential starting cut
Tangentialdrehmeißel *m* tangential turning tool
tangentiale Tischvorschubbewegung *f* tangential table feed motion
tangentiale Tischvorschubgeschwindigkeit *f* tangential table feed speed
Tangentialebene *f* tangential plane
Tangentialeinlauf *m* tangential shrinkage
Tangentialeinrichtung *f* tangential attachment
Tangentialfräsen *nt* tangential hobbing
Tangentialgeschwindigkeit *f* tangential speed
Tangentialmeißel *m* tangential cutter
Tangentialprofil *nt* tangential profile
Tangentialschnitt *m* tangential section
Tangentialschnittlinie *f* line of tangential section
Tangentialspindelstock *m* tangential-feed headstock, tangential spindle head
Tangentialstreckziehen *nt* tangential stretch drawing to shape
Tangentialverfahren *nt* tangential feed method
Tangentialwälzfräsen *nt* tangential hobbing
Tangentialwälzverfahren *nt* tangential hobbing
Tangentkeilbefestigung *f* tangential keying
tangieren touch, be tangent
Tank *m* **1.** *(Treibstoff)* tank, fuel tank **2.** *(allg. Aufnahme von Flüssigkeiten)* receiver, reservoir, container
Tankwagenkupplung *f* tanker vehicle coupling

Tankwagenpumpe *f* tanker vehicle pump
Tannenbaumprofil *nt* fir tree profile
Tasche *f* pocket
Taschenfräsen *nt* pocket milling
Taschenmessschieber *m* **mit Rundskala** pocket dial calliper
Taschenplattenbatterie *f* pocket-type plate battery
Taschenrechner *m* hand-held calculator
Täschnermaterial *nt* wallet-making material
Tastatur *f* keyboard
Tastatureingabe *f* keyboard entry, keyboard input
Taste *f* key, push-button
Tastebene *f* scanning plane
Tasteinrichtung *f* tracing fixture
tasten touch, sense, scan, trace, feel
Tastendruck *m* keypress, keystroke, tracer contact pressure
Tastendruck *m:* **durch ~** activating a key, pressing a key
Tastenfeld *nt* key field, key panel, keyboard section
Tastenleiste *f* key row, row of keys
Tastenordnung *f* keyboard layout
Tastensteuerung *f* push-button control
Taster *m* **1.** *(allg.)* form tracer, feeler, feeler pin, stylus, tracer, callipers (pl), scanner, sensing device, sensor, calliper **2.** *(Druckschalter)* push-button, key button, jog key **3.** *(Tasthebel)* touching lever
Tastermessuhr *f* dial gauge calliper
Tasterschneide *f* tracer tip
Tastersteuerung *f* tracer control
Tastfinger *m* tracer, stylus
Tastfläche *f* scanning area
Tastgefühl *nt* touch
Tastgerät *nt* tracer (or tracing) device
Tastkopf *m* feeler head
Tastrolle *f* follower roll
Tastschalter *m* push-button, switch, momentary switch
Tastscheibe *f* tracer disc
Tastschlitten *m* tracer slide
Tastschnittgerät *nt* contact (stylus) instrument

Tastspitze *f* scanning tip, tracer point, stylus
Tastspitzenauslenkung *f* stylus deflection
Tastspitzenwinkel *m* contact tip angle
Taststift *m* feeler, tracer finger, tracer pin, feeler pin, stylus
Taststrahl *m* sensor beam
Taststrecke *f* contact distance
Tastsystem *nt* contact system
Tastvergleich *m* tactile comparison
Tastvergleiche *mpl* tactile comparison
Tastverhältnis *nt* pulse duty factor
Tastvorschub *m* tracer feed
Tastweite *f* scanning range
Tastzirkel *m* **1.** *(allg.)* hermaphrodite calliper, morphy calliper, jenny **2.** *(Werkstattausdruck)* odd leg
Tätigkeit *f* action
Tätigkeitsart *f* action type
Tätigkeitsdauer *f* action length
Tätigkeitsgrad *m* degree of action
Tätigkeitszeit *f* action time
tatsächlich actual
tatsächliche Schnittrichtung *f* actual (or effective) direction of cut
tatsächlicher Wert *m* real value, actual value
Tauchbad *nt* immersion bath
Tauchemaillieren *nt* dip enamelling
tauchen immerse, dip
tauchfräsen lunge-cut mill, plunge mill
Tauchfräsmaschine *f* plunge milling machine
Tauchkolben *m* plunger
Tauchlängsfräsen *nt* plunge-feed hobbing
Tauchmesszelle *f* immersion measuring cell
Tauchnetzvermögen *nt* dip-wetting ability, dip-wettability
Tauchschlitz *m (e. Senkschraube)* socket head slot
Tauchtechnik *f* immersion practice
tauchverbronzt bronze plated by immersion
Tauchverfahren *nt* plunge-feed method
tauchverkupfert copper plated by immersion

Tauchverzinnen *nt* dip tinning
Tauchwägeverfahren *nt* dipping and weighing method
Tauchwasch- und Konservieranlage *f* dip washing and preservation equipment
Tauchzahl *f (galv.)* number of dips
Taumel *m (e. Verzahnung)* wobble
taumeln nutate, wobble
Taumelscheibe *f* socket ring, swashplate, wobbling disc, wobble plate
Taupunktkorrosion *f* dew point corrosion
Tausch *m* exchange, pooling
tauschen exchange, pool
Tauschfähigkeit *f* 1. *(allg.)* exchangeability 2. *(z. B. Paletten)* reusability
Tauschpalette *f* exchange pallet, pool pallet
Tauwasserableitung *f* discharge of condensate
Taxi-Betrieb *m* taxi mode
Taylorscher Grundsatz *m* Taylor principle
Teach-in-Oberfläche *f* teach-in surface
Teach-in-Verfahren *nt* teach-in process, teach-in mode
Technik *f* 1. *(Wissenschaft)* engineering science, engineering 2. *(angewandte)* technology, technology engineering, practice, technique
Technikbewertung *f* technology assessment
technisch festgelegt specified
technische Anlage *f* plant
technische Belüftung *f* artificial ventilation
technische Daten *pl* technical data, technical specifications
technische Elastizitätsgrenze *f* technical elastic limit, 0.01% proof stress
technische Regeln *fpl* technical code of practice
technische Verordnung *f* statutory technical order
technische Zeichnung *f* engineering drawing, technical drawing
technischer Dienst *m* engineering service *m*
technischer Überwachungsverein *m* technical control board, Test Code Association
technisches Erzeugnis *nt* technical product
Technologie *f* technology
technologische Daten *pl* technological data
technologischer Biegeversuch *m* technological bend test, bend-over test
Teerasphaltbeton *m* tar bitumen concrete
Teerbinder *m* tar binder
Teer-Bitumendachbahn *f* tar-bitumen roof sheeting
Teerdachbahn *f* tar roof sheeting
teergetränkt tar impregnated
Teerverfestigung *f* tar stabilization
Teflon-Gefäß *nt* teflon container
Teil *m, nt* I. *m* 1. *(allg.)* section, portion, segment 2. *(Bruchteil)* fraction II. *nt* part, piece, element, component, member
Teil(ungs)genauigkeit *f* accuracy of spacing, spacing accuracy
Teilabnahme *f* partial acceptance, partial inspection
Teilanlagenbild *nt* plant segment display
Teilanzeigebereich *m* subrange
Teilapparat *m* 1. *(allg.)* index device (or unit), indexing attachment (or fixture or device), dividing apparatus 2. *(einfacher ~)* plain index centre
Teilarbeit *f* index head operation
Teilarbeiten *fpl* indexing work
Teilaufgabe *f* subtask, job step
Teilauftrag *m* part order
Teilausfall *m* partial failure
Teilausschnitt *m* partial cut-out
teilautomatisch semi-automatic, partially automatic
teilautomatischer Gasbrenner *m* semi-automatic gas burner
teilautomatischer Ölbrenner *m* semi-automatic oil burner
Teilbebauungsplan *m* part development scheme
Teilbedingung *f* subcondition
Teilbereich *m* subsection, subdomain, subrange

Teilbewegung *f* indexing movement
Teilbildschirm *m* screen segment
Teilbrenner *m* component burner
Teilchen *nt* particle, fragment
Teilchenenergie *f* particle energy
Teilchenfluenz *f* particle fluence
Teilchenflussdichte *f* particle flow density
Teilchengröße *f* particle size
Teilchenschema *nt* particle scheme
Teilchenstrahlung *f* particle radiation
Teilchenverschiebung *f* particle displacement
teildurchlässig semipermeable, semitransparent
Teildurchsatz *m* part throughput
Teile *ntpl* parts
Teileabmessung *f* section dimension, part dimension, element dimension
Teileaufmaße *ntpl* overmeasure, oversize
Teilebene *f* reference plane
Teilefamilien *fpl* group technology
Teilefertigung *f* parts production
Teilefertigungsprogramm *nt* parts production program
Teileform *f* element form
Teileformgebung *f* piece design, part surface formation, workpiece fabrication
Teilefunktionsfläche *f* parts working surface
Teileinrichtung *f* index base, dividing attachment, indexing attachment
Teileinschlagmaschine *f* wrapping machine which partially wraps products
Teilekommissionierung *f* parts commissioning
Teilelager *nt* parts warehouse
Teilelagerung *f* parts storage
Teileliste *f* bill of materials (BOM), parts list
Teilelogistik *f* materials handling system
teilen 1. *(math.)* divide 2. *(räuml.)* space 3. *(splitten)* split 4. *(trennen)* separate 5. *(katalogisieren)* index
Teilen *nt* **eines Kreisumfanges** circumferential indexing
Teilen *nt* **nach Winkelmaß** angular indexing
Teileprogramm *nt* piece program
Teilequalität *f* part quality
Teiler *m* 1. *(math.)* divisor, factor 2. *(einer Einheit)* submultiple
Teilerandschicht *f* part surface layer
Teilerwärmung *f* partial heating
Teilestamm *m* master parts record, parts history, parts master data
Teilestammdatei *f* master parts record
Teilestammsatz *m* master parts record unit
Teilestammdaten *pl* data of the master parts record
Teilevielfalt *f* variety of parts
Teilfehler *m* indexing error
Teilfläche *f* 1. *(allg.)* reference surface 2. *(e. Außenzylinders)* partial surface
Teilflamme *f* component flame
Teilflammenüberwachung *f* monitoring of the component flame
Teilflankenlinie *f* reference tooth trace
Teilflankenwinkel *m* 1. *(allg.)* half angle of thread, flank angle 2. *(e. Verzahnung)* reference tooth trace
Teilfunktion *f* subfunction
teilgeformt partly formed
Teilgerät *nt* indexing device, index centre
Teilgerät *nt* **mit drei Arbeitsspindeln** triple index centre
Teilgerät *nt* **mit einer Teilspindel** single-spindle index centre
Teilgerät *nt* **mit einer Teilspindel, einfaches** ~ plain index centre, index centre
Teilgesamtheit *f* subpopulation
Teilgetriebe *nt* sub-train of a gear transmission, sub-mechanism
Teilgewicht *nt* partial load, partial mass
Teilkegel *m* reference cone
Teilkegelfläche *f* reference surface
Teilkegellänge *f* cone distance
Teilkegelmantel *m* reference cone envelope
Teilkegelmantelfläche *f* pitch cone surface
Teilkegelmantellinie *f* reference cone envelope line
Teilkegelspitze *f* reference cone apex

Teilkegelwinkel *m* pitch cone angle, pitch angle, reference cone angle
Teilkopf *m* indexing-head, dividing-head
Teilkopf *m* **für weite Bereiche** wide-range divider
Teilkopfgerät *nt* index centre
Teilkopfspindel *f* indexing head spindle
Teilkreis *m* pitch circle, reference circle, graduated circle
Teilkreisabstand *m* centre distance modification
Teilkreisabstandsfaktor *m* centre distance modification coefficient
Teilkreisbogen *m* pitch circle arc, reference circle arc
Teilkreisdurchmesser *m (e. Stirnrades)* reference diameter
Teilkreisebene *f* reference circle plane
Teilkreisnähe *f* vicinity of the pitch circle
Teilkreisteilung *f* transverse pitch, pitch, reference circle pitch
teilkristallin semicrystalline
Teilkurbel *f* index crank
Teilladezyklus *m* intermediate charge cycle
Teilladung *f* intermediate charge/charging, partial charge/charging
Teillast *f* partial load, underload
Teillastbereich *m* underload range
Teillieferung *f* partial shipment, part delivery
Teilluftstrom *m* partial air stream
teilmechanisches Metall-Aktivgas-Schweißen *nt* part-mechanized metal active gas welding
teilmechanisiertes Löten *nt* part-mechanized soldering
Teilmenge *f* **1.** *(math.)* subset **2.** *(Waren)* part volume
Teilmessspanne *f* local measuring span
Teilmontage *f* sub-assembly
teilnehmen an participate in
Teilnehmer *m* **1.** *(allg.)* participant **2.** *(Netzwerk)* subscriber
Teilnehmeranschlussleitung *f* subscriber line
Teilprobe *f* divided sample, subspecimen

Teilprogramm *nt* part program
Teilprozess *m* subprocess
Teilprüfung *f* component testing
Teilschallleistungspegel *m* partial sound power level
Teilscheibe *f* dividing-head plate, index disc (or: disk), index plate
Teilscheibe *f* **für weiten Teilbereich** high-division index plate
Teilschnitt *m* part section
Teilschnittzeichnung *f* part sectional drawing
Teilschritt *m (el. chem.)* partial stage
Teilschrumpffolienumhüllung *f* part shrink wrap, partial shrink wrap
teilselbsttätige Stumpfschweißmaschine *f* semi-automatic butt welding machine
Teilstrecke *f* (partial) section, partial distance, partial journey, length, path section
Teilstreckennetz *nt* store-and forward network
Teilstrich *m* scale mark, graduation
Teilstrichabstand *m* scale spacing
Teilstrom *m* partial current, component current
Teilstromdichte-Potential-Kurve *f* partial current density-potential curve
Teilsystem *nt* subsystem
Teilsystemausfall *m* breakdown in parts of the system
Teiltrommel *f* graduated indexing dial
Teilübergabe *f* part transfer
Teilummantelung *f* partial surround
Teilumrissnachformen *nt* segment copying
Teilung *f* **1.** *(e. Nonius)* division **2.** *(e. Planverzahnung)* linear pitch **3.** *(e. Skala)* graduation **4.** *(Gewinde, Ketten, Zahnrad)* pitch **5.** *(Maßstäbe)* graduation **6.** *(Zahnflanken)* spacing **7.** *(Separieren)* separation
Teilung *f* **des Werkstücks nach Winkelmaß** angular division of work(piece)
Teilungsabweichung *f* pitch variation
Teilungsebene *f* parting plane, plane of division
Teilungseinheit *f* division unit
Teilungseinzelabweichung *f* individ-

ual pitch variation
Teilungsfehler *m* error of the division, spacing error, dividing error, pitch error
teilungsfehlerfreies Gewinde *nt* screw thread without flaws in flank pitch
Teilungsfläche *f* parting surface, joint surface
Teilungsgenauigkeit *f* spacing accuracy, pitch accuracy
Teilungsgesamtabweichung *f* total pitch variation
Teilungshülse *f* sleeve, barrel
Teilungslinie *f* dividing line
Teilungsmessung *f* pitch measurement
Teilungsprüfung *f* pitch test
Teilungspunkt *m* division point
Teilungsräderkasten *m* indexing gearbox
Teilungsrest *m* remainder
Teilungsschaltung *f* indexing
Teilungsschwankung *f* pitch fluctuation
Teilungsspannenabweichung *f* pitch-span variation
Teilungsspannenkurve *f* pitch-span curve
Teilungsspanntoleranz *f (bei der Zahnweitenmessung)* pitch-span tolerance
Teilungssprung *m* pitch error
Teilungssteg *m* division
Teilungssumme *f* pitch span
Teilungssummenabweichung *f* cumulative pitch-span variation
Teilungswert *m* scale interval
Teilungswinkel *m* angular pitch
Teilungszeichen *nt* scale mark
Teilverfahren *nt* indexing (or dividing) method
Teilwälzschleifen *nt* partial generate grinding
teilweise partial, by parts
teilweise Füllung *f* part filling
Teilzahnrad *nt* index gear
Teilzeichnung *f* detail drawing, component drawing
Teilziel *nt* subgoal, subobjective
Teilzuführungseinrichtung *f* hopper
Teilzylinder *m* reference cylinder

Teilzylinderflankenlinie *f* **1.** *(allg.)* reference cylinder tooth trace **2.** *(e. Schrägstirnrades)* reference helix
Teilzylindermantellinie *f* pitch cylinder director, reference cylinder envelope line
T-Einschraubstutzen *m* **in Stoßausführung** *(für Rohrverschraubungen)* double-ended union used as an adaptor for butt joints
Teleskop *nt* telescope
Teleskoparm *m* telescopic arm
Teleskopförderer *m* telescopic conveyor
Teleskopgabel *f* telescopic fork, telescopic load fork
Teleskopgabelzinken *m* telescopic fork arm
Teleskophubgerüst *nt* telescopic mast
Teleskophubzylinder *m* compound lifting jack
teleskopierbar telescopic
teleskopieren telescope
teleskopisch telescopic(al)
Teleskopmast *m* telescoping mast, extension mast, free-lift mast
Teleskopspindel *f* screw within a telescopic cover
Teleskopsystem *nt* telescopic system
Teleskoptisch *m* telescopic table
Tellerbeschicker *m* disc feeder
Tellerfeder *f* disc spring
Tellermagazin *nt* disc magazine, disc storeroom
Tellerrad *nt* face gear, crown gear
Temperatur *f* temperature
temperaturabhängig temperature-dependent
temperaturabhängiger Widerstand *m* temperature sensitive resistor
Temperaturabnahme *f* surface decrease
Temperaturanstieg *m* temperature rise
Temperaturbeanspruchbarkeit *f* permissible temperature stress
Temperaturbegrenzer *m* temperature limiter
Temperaturbereich *m* temperature range

temperaturbeständig temperature resistant
Temperaturbeständigkeit f temperature resistance, temperature stability
Temperaturdifferenz f temperature difference
Temperaturegelspiegel m temperature control cycle
Temperatur-Farbstift m temperature indicating crayon
Temperaturfühler m thermosensor, temperature probe
Temperaturfühler m temperature sensor
Temperaturführung f temperature control, temperature management
Temperaturgrenze f temperature limit, thermal limit
Temperaturklasse f temperature class
Temperaturkontrolle f temperature control
Temperaturlaufkurve f temperature versus number of cycles
Temperaturleitzahl f coefficient of thermal conductivity
Temperaturmessung f measurement of temperature, thermometry
Temperaturmesswert m temperature (reading)
Temperaturregeleinrichtung f temperature-regulating appliance
Temperaturregler m temperature control
Temperaturschritt m temperature step
Temperaturschwankung f fluctuation of temperature, thermal cycling effect
Temperatur-Sollwertsteller m temperature set point setter
Temperaturspreizung f temperature spread
Temperaturstufe f temperature level
Temperaturverträglichkeit f temperature tolerance
Temperaturwächter m thermostat, temperature monitor
Temperaturwechsel m 1. *(allg.)* change of temperature 2. *(plötzlicher)* thermal shock
Temperaturwechselfestigkeit f thermal shock stability
Temperaturwechselprüfung f thermal cycling test, alternating temperature test
Temperatur-Zeit-Folge f temperature-time sequence
Temperatur-Zeit-Grenze f temperature-time-limit
Temperguss m 1. *(allg.)* malleable cast iron 2. *(schwarzer ~)* blackheart malleable cast iron 3. *(weißer ~)* whiteheart malleable cast iron
Temperiereinrichtung f temperature conditioning device
Temperieren nt temperature conditioning, temper
Temperierflüssigkeit f temperature-control liquid
Temperiermittel nt temperature conditioning medium
Temperierplan m temperature control plan
Temperiersystem nt temperature system
temperiertes Glas nt toughened glass
Temperierung f temperature control
Temperkohle f temper carbon
tempern malleabilize, anneal
Temperofen m malleabilizing furnace
Temperroheisen nt malleable pig
Tempertopf m annealing pot
Temperverfahren nt 1. *(allg.)* malleabilizing process, annealing process 2. *(amerikanisches ~)* black-heart malleabilizing process 3. *(deutsches ~)* white-heart malleabilizing process
Tendenz f tendency
Tensidlösung f tenside solution
Termin m 1. *(allg. zeitl.)* date, deadline, target date, time target 2. *(Vereinbarung)* appointment
Terminablaufplanung f schedule course planning
Terminabweichung f schedule variance
Terminal nt terminal
Termindisposition f schedule disposal
Termindringlichkeit f schedule urgency
Termineinhaltung f faithfulness to deadlines, schedule effectiveness

Terminfeinplanung *f* fine time schedule
termingerecht on schedule, on time
termingerecht erfüllt fulfilled correctly in terms of deadlines
terminieren schedule
Terminierung *f* timing
Terminlogik *f* schedule logic
Terminplan *m* time schedule, schedule
Terminplanung *f* schedule
Terminverschiebung *f* time shifting
Terminverzug *m* schedule delay, scheduling delay
Terminverzugskosten *pl* cost by delayed performance
Terminwirtschaft *f* time planning
Terminziel *nt* target date
Test *m* test
Test *m* **zum Halten der Last** hydraulic leakage test
Testablauf *m* test sequence
Testbarkeit *f* testability
Testeinrichtung *f* test equipment
testen test, check, try (out)
Testgröße *f* test statistic, measured size
Testlauf *m* test run
Testprogramm *nt* **1.** *(allg.)* test program, check program **2.** *(Prüfprogramm)* check routine
Testpunkt *m* test point
Testspiel *nt* test cycle
Teststück *nt* test piece
Testverfahren *nt* test method
Testwert *m* test value
Testzeit *f* test duration
Text *m* text
Textangaben *fpl (z. B. auf e. Zeichnung)* textual information
Textdateidaten *pl* text file data *pl*
textiles Flächengebilde *nt* textile fabric area-measured material
Textilglasgarn *nt* textile glass roving, glass filament yarn
Textilglasroving *nt* textile glass roving
Textilprüfung *f* test on textiles
Textilschnitzel-Pressmasse *f* fabric-filled moulding material
Textilumflechtung *f* textile braiding
Textkommunikation *f* text communication

Textsprache *f* textual language
Textur *f* texture
T-Glied *nt (Totzeitglied)* lag element
thermisch thermal
thermische Einflusszone *f* thermal-affected zone
thermische Entrostung *f* thermal rust removal
thermische Isolierung *f* thermal insulation
thermische Schneidtechnik *f* thermal cutting practice
thermische Zersetzung *f* thermal decomposition
thermischer Längenausdehnungskoeffizient *m* coefficient of linear thermal expansion
thermischer Wirkungsgrad *m* **des Lichtbogens** thermal efficiency of the arc
thermisches Abtragen *nt* thermal gouging
thermisches Entspannen *nt* thermal stress relief
thermisches Schneidverfahren *nt* thermal cutting process
thermisches Schweißen *nt* thermal cutting
thermisches Spitzen *nt* thermal spraying
thermisches Verfahren *nt* thermal process
thermoakustisch thermal acoustical
Thermoaräometer *nt* thermo-hydrometer
Thermodrucker *m* thermoprinter, thermal printer
Thermoelement *nt* thermocouple
Thermoelementanemometer *nt* thermocouple anemometer
Thermokopierverfahren *nt* thermo-copying process
Thermolumineszensdosimetrie *f* thermoluminescence dosimetry
Thermometergefäß *nt* thermometer vessel
Thermometerhalterung *f* thermometer holder
Thermometerkapillare *f* capillary tubes of the thermometer

Thermometerstopfen *m* thermometer plug
Thermometerstutzen *m* thermometer socket
thermoplastisch thermoplastic, thermoformable
thermoplastische Pressmasse *f* thermoplastic moulding material (or compound)
thermoplastische Spritzgussmasse *f* thermoplastic injection moulding material (or compound)
thermoplastischer Kunststoff *m* thermoplast
Thermoplastpolymer *nt* thermoplastic polymer
thermostatische Absicherung *f* thermostatic safety device
Thermotransferdrucker *m* thermotransfer printer
Thorin-Indikator-Lösung *f* thorin indicator solution
Thyristor *m* silicon controlled rectifier (SCR), thryristor
thyristorgesteuerte Drossel *f* thyristor-controlled reactor
Thyristorstellung *f* thyristor regulator, actuator control
tief deep, low
tief gekröpfter Doppelringschlüssel *m* deep offset double-ended ring spanner, deep offset double-end box wrench
Tiefbohrmaschine *f* bench drilling machine
Tiefdruck *m* intaglio printing
Tiefe *f* depth
Tiefe *f* **der Spanbrechernut** chip breaker groove depth
Tiefen mit formlos festen Stoffen mit kraftgebundener Wirkung cupping with amorphous solid materials having an effect associated with force
Tiefen *nt* **1.** *(allg.)* impressing **2.** *(gewölbter Werkstücke)* cupping
Tiefen *nt* **durch Detonation eines Sprengstoffes** cupping by detonation with an explosive
Tiefen *nt* **durch Explosion eines Gasgemisches** cupping by explosion of a gas mixture
Tiefen *nt* **durch Funkenentladung** *f* cupping by spark discharge
Tiefen *nt* **durch kurzzeitige Entspannung hochkomprimierter Gase** cupping by temporary expansion of highly compressed gases
Tiefen *nt* **mit Druckluft** cupping with compressed air
Tiefen *nt* **mit Flüssigkeiten mit energiegebundener Wirkung** cupping with fluids having an effect associated with energy
Tiefen *nt* **mit Flüssigkeiten mit kraftgebundener Wirkung** cupping with fluids having an effect associated with force
Tiefen *nt* **mit formlos festen Stoffen mit energiegebundener Wirkung** cupping with amorphous solid materials having an effect associated with energy
Tiefen *nt* **mit Gasen kraftgebundener Wirkung** cupping with gases having an effect associated with force
Tiefen *nt* **mit Gasen mit energiegebundener Wirkung** cupping with gases having an effect associated with energy
Tiefen *nt* **mit Magnetfeldern** cupping with magnetic fields
Tiefen *nt* **mit nachgiebigem Werkzeug** cupping with compliant tool
Tiefen *nt* **mit starrem Werkzeug** cupping with rigid tool
Tiefen *nt* **mit Werkzeugen** *ntpl* cupping with tools
Tiefen *nt* **mit Wirkenergie** cupping with active energy
Tiefen *nt* **mit Wirkmedien mit energiegebundener Wirkung** cupping with action media with effect associated with energy
Tiefen *nt* **mit Wirkmedien mit kraftgebundener Wirkung** cupping with action media with effected associated with force
Tiefen *nt* **mit Wirkmedien** *ntpl* cupping with action media
Tiefenanschlag *m* back stop, depth stop

Tiefenauflage *f* skid channel support
Tiefenauflösungsvermögen *nt* depth resolving power
Tiefenausladung *f* throat depth
Tiefenbalken *m* cross bar (support)
Tiefeneinstellnormal *nt* depth-setting standard
Tiefenfaktor *m* depth factor
Tiefenfräsen *nt* depth milling
Tiefenlehre *f* slide calliper (rule), sliding calliper, calliper square
Tiefenmessschieber *m* depth gauge
Tiefenmessstange *f* depth measuring blade
Tiefenmessung *f* depth measurement
Tiefenmikrometer *nt* depth micrometer
Tiefenrichtung *f* (in) depth
Tiefenschieblehre *f* rule depth gauge
Tiefentladung *f* deep discharge
Tiefenverband *m* cross brace
Tiefenvorschub *m* downfeed, depth feed, infeed
Tiefenzustellspindel *f* down-feed screw
Tiefenzustellung *f* depth feed adjustment
Tiefersetzen *nt* setting deeper
Tiefkühlanlage *f* refrigeration plant
tiefkühlen refrigerate, deep-freeze, quick-freeze
Tiefkühllager *nt* low-temperature warehouse
tiefliegende Bohrung *f* deep-level borehole
Tieflochbohrbohrwerkzeug *nt* deep-hole tool
Tieflochbohren *nt* deep-hole drilling, deep-hole boring
Tieflochbohrer *m* deep-hole boring tool
Tieflochbohrmaschine *f* deep-hole boring machine, deep-hole drilling machine
Tieflochfräsen *nt* deep-hole milling
Tieflockern *nt* (e. Boden) deep tilling
Tiefpassfilterung *f* low-pass filtering
tiefprägen deboss
Tiefschleifen *nt* creep feed grinding, infeed grinding
Tiefschweißen *nt* deep welding
Tiefstwert *m* minimum value
Tiefungsprüfwerkzeug *nt* cupping test tool
Tiefungsverhalten *nt* cupping behaviour
Tiefzieharbeit *f* deep draw work
tiefziehbar vorglühen (z. B. Draht) pre-anneal for deep drawing
tiefziehen deep-draw
Tiefziehen *nt* **durch Einwirkung eines Magnetfeldes** deep drawing by the effect of a magnetic field
Tiefziehen *nt* **durch elektrische Entladung** deep drawing by electric discharge
Tiefziehen *nt* **durch Sprengstoffdetonation** deep drawing by detonation of an explosive
Tiefziehen *nt* **im Erstzug** deep drawing in first draw
Tiefziehen *nt* **mit einseitigem Flüssigkeitsdruck** deep drawing with fluid pressure on one side
Tiefziehen *nt* **mit Flüssigkeiten mit energiegebundener Wirkung** deep drawing with fluids with effect associated with energy
Tiefziehen *nt* **mit Flüssigkeiten mit kraftgebundener Wirkung** deep drawing with fluids with effect associated with force
Tiefziehen *nt* **mit formlos festen Stoffen mit energiegebundener Wirkung** deep drawing with amorphous solids with effect associated with energy
Tiefziehen *nt* **mit formlos festen Stoffen mit kraftgebundener Wirkung** deep drawing with amorphous solids with effect associated with force
Tiefziehen *nt* **mit Gasdruck durch einseitigen Überdruck** deep drawing with gas pressure with positive pressure on one side, deep drawing with gas pressure with evacuation of the matrix
Tiefziehen *nt* **mit Gasen mit energiegebundener Wirkung** deep drawing with gases with effect associated with energy

Tiefziehen *nt* **mit Gasen mit kraftgebundener Wirkung** deep drawing with gases with effect associated with force
Tiefziehen *nt* **mit Gummikissen** *nt* deep drawing with rubber pad
Tiefziehen *nt* **mit Gummistempel** *m* deep drawing with rubber punch
Tiefziehen *nt* **mit Membran** *f* deep drawing with membrane
Tiefziehen *nt* **mit nachgiebigen Kissen** *nt* deep drawing with compliant pad
Tiefziehen *nt* **mit nachgiebigen Stempel** deep drawing with compliant punch
Tiefziehen *nt* **mit nachgiebigen Werkzeug** *nt* deep drawing with compliant tool
Tiefziehen *nt* **mit Sand/Stahlkugeln** *fpl* deep drawing with sand/steel balls
Tiefziehen *nt* **mit starrem Werkzeug** *nt* deep drawing with rigid tool
Tiefziehen *nt* **mit Wasserbeutel** *m* deep drawing with water bag
Tiefziehen *nt* **mit Werkzeugen** *ntpl* deep drawing with tools
Tiefziehen *nt* **mit Wirkenergie** *f* deep drawing with active energy
Tiefziehen *nt* **mit Wirkmedien mit energiegebundener Wirkung** deep drawing with action media with effect associated with energy
Tiefziehen *nt* **mit Wirkmedien mit kraftgebundener Wirkung** deep drawing with action media with effect associated with force
Tiefziehen *nt* **mit Wirkmedien** *ntpl* deep drawing with action media
Tiefziehen *nt* **mit zweiseitigem Flüssigkeitsdruck** deep drawing with fluid pressure on both sides
Tiefziehform-, -füll-und -verschließmaschine *f* deep draw form, fill and seal machine
Tiefziehpackung *f* deep drawn pack
Tiegel *m* crucible, tie
Tiegel-Kalk-Verfahren *nt* crucible-lime process
Tiegelkippgerät *nt* crucible tippler
Tiegelofen *m* crucible furnace
Timesharing *nt* time sharing
Tinte *f* ink
Tintenstrahlcodierer *m* ink jet coder
Tintenstrahldrucker *m* ink jet printer
tippen 1. *(Hebel)* tip **2.** *(Schalter)* jog **3.** *(Schlitten)* inch
tippschalten jog, inch
Tippschalter *m* inching switch (or button), jogging switch
Tippschaltung *f* inching control, finger tip control, jogging control
Tisch *m* **1.** *(allg.)* table, platform **2.** *(allseitig neigbar)* universally tilting table **3.** *(ausschwenkbarer ~)* swivelling table **4.** *(drehbar)* swivel table **5.** *(fester ~)* stationary table **6.** *(geteilter ~)* divided table **7.** *(hin- und hergehender)* shuttle-type table **8.** *(mit der Maschine fest verbunden)* bed, saddle **9.** *(neigbarer ~)* tilting table, inclinable table **10.** *(schrägverstellbarer)* inclinable table, tiltable table, tilting table **11.** *(zum Spannen der Werkstücke)* worktable, table, platen
Tischabsenkung *f* table lowering
Tischanschlag *m* **1.** *(allg.)* table stop dog, table trip dog **2.** *(für Sprungvorschub)* table skip-feed stop
Tischantrieb *m* table drive
Tischantrieb *m* **über Schrägzahnräder** helical drive
Tischantriebskasten *m* gearbox for table drive
Tischauflagefläche *f* table bearing surface
Tischauslöseschalter *m* table trip switch
Tischbohr- und -fräswerk *nt* table-type boring drilling and milling machine
Tischbohrmaschine *f* bench drilling machine
Tischdrehmaschine *f* bench lathe
Tischeilgang *m* rapid table traverse
Tischeinschaltung *f* table engagement, table start
Tischeinstellung *f* table setting
Tischendstellung *f* extreme table position
Tischentlastung *f* table relief

Tischfeststellung *f* table locking (or clamping)
Tischfräseilgang *m* rapid traverse of milling table
Tischfräsvorschub *m* milling feed of table
Tischführung *f* table guide-way
Tischhandantrieb *m* manual table drive
Tischhobelmaschine *f* planing machine, planer
Tischhöhenverstellung *f* vertical adjustment of table
Tischhub *m* table stroke, table traverse
Tischklemmung *f* 1. *(Funktion)* table locking 2. *(Bauteil)* table lock, table locking mechanism
Tischknagge *f* table dog
Tischlängsbewegung *f* longitudinal table traverse, rectilinear table feed motion
Tischquervorschub *m* transverse table feed
Tischrechner *m* desk-top calculator
Tischrevolverdrehmaschine *f* bench turret lathe
Tischrücklauf *m* table return
Tischrundbewegung *f* 1. *(allg.)* rotary table feed 2. *(selbsttätige)* self-acting rotary indexing motion (of the table)
Tischsattel *m* saddle
Tischschrägverstellung *f* angular table setting
Tischselbstgang *m* table power traverse
Tischsenkrechtbewegung *f* vertical table movement
Tischspindel *f* table feed-screw
Tischspindelmutter *f* table-screw nut
Tischstütze *f* supporting bracket
Tischumkehr *f* table reversal
Tischumsteuerung *f* table reversal
Tischventilator *m* table fan
Tischverriegelung *f* table lock
Tischverstellkurbel *f* table hand crank
Tischvorlauf *m* table forward stroke
Tischvorschub *m* 1. *(axial)* table feed 2. *(radial)* table infeed
Tischvorschub *m* **durch Spindel und Mutter** screw and nut table feeding

Tischvorschubbewegung *f* table feed motion
Tischvorschubgetriebe *nt* table feedbox
Tischvorschubspindel *f* table feed screw
Tischweg *m* table traverse (or travel or motion), table stroke
Titan *nt* titanium
Titanlegierung *f* titanium alloy
Titrationsendpunkt *m* titration end point
Titrierbürette *f* titrating burette
Titrierflüssigkeit *f* titrating liquid
Titriergefäß *nt* titration vessel
Titrierlösungsmittel *nt* titration solvent
T-Nut *f* T-slot
T-Nutenschraube *f* T-slot bolt
Token *m* token
Tokenring *m* token loop, token ring
Tokenverfahren *nt* token passing
Toleranz *f* allowance, limit, tolerance
Toleranz *f* **des größten Durchmessers** *(Hüllkörperdurchmesser bei Gesenkschmiedestücken)* enveloping body diameter
Toleranz *f* **des Schließmaßes** *(e. Maßkette)* arithmetic closing tolerance
toleranzabhängig depending on tolerance
Toleranzangabe *f* tolerance indication, tolerance data *pl*
Toleranzauffassung *f* tolerance conception
Toleranzband *nt* tolerance band
Toleranzberechnung *f* tolerance calculation
Toleranzbereich *m* range of tolerance
Toleranzbestimmung *f* tolerance provision
Toleranzen *fpl* **und Passungen** *fpl* tolerances and fits
Toleranzfamilie *f* tolerance family
Toleranzfeld *nt* 1. *(allg.)* tolerance field, tolerance zone 2. *(Zwischenraum)* clearance space
Toleranzfeldauswahl *f* tolerance zone selection

Toleranzfeldmitte *f* centre of the tolerance zone
Toleranzfestlegung *f* tolerance provision, tolerance specification
toleranzfrei tolerance-free
Toleranzgleichung *f* tolerance equation
Toleranzgrenze *f* tolerance limit
Toleranzgröße *f* tolerance size
Toleranzgruppe *f* tolerance group
toleranzhaltig be within tolerances
Toleranzkette *f* tolerance chain
Toleranzklasse *f* tolerance class
Toleranzkopplung *f* tolerance coupling
Toleranzkurzzeichen *nt* tolerance symbol
Toleranzmitte *f* tolerance centre
Toleranznorm *f* tolerance standard
Toleranzproblem *nt* tolerance problem
Toleranzqualität *f* tolerance grade (or quality)
Toleranzrechnung *f* tolerance calculation
Toleranzreihe *f* tolerance group
Toleranzrelation *f* tolerance relationship
Toleranzstufe *f* degree of accuracy, tolerance step
Toleranzunterschied *m* tolerance difference
Toleranzuntersuchung *f* tolerance investigation
Toleranzveränderung *f* tolerance modification
Toleranzwert *m* tolerance value
Toleranzzone *f* tolerance zone
Toleranzzone *f* **für die Geradheit der Mantelfläche** tolerance zone for the straightness of the generator
Toleranzzone *f* **für die Rundheit des Querschnittes** tolerance zone for the roundness of the section
tolerieren 1. *(allg.)* tolerate 2. *(Toleranzen angeben)* draw the tolerances into a design
toleriertes Maß *nt* toleranced dimension
Tolerierung *f* tolerancing
Tolerierungsmaßnahme *f* tolerancing measure
Tolerierungsproblem *nt* tolerancing problem
Ton *m* clay
Toner *m* toner
Tonhaltigkeit *f (Geräusch)* tonal contact
Tonnenform *f* barrel shape
Tönung *f* colouration
TOP *Abk* Technical and Office Protocol
Topffräser *m* cup-shaped cutter
Topfscheibe *f* cup wheel
Tor *nt* door, gate
Torflügel *m* wing of a door/of a gate
Tornister *m* manpack, knapsack, satchel
Toroide *f* toroid
Toroidgetriebe *nt* toroidal drive
Toroidspule *f* toroidal coil, toroid
Torsion *f* torsion
Torsionsbeanspruchung *f* torsional strain
Torsionsschwingung *f* torsional oscillation
Torsionsschwingungsversuch *m* torsional vibration test
Torsionssteifigkeit *f* stiffness in torsion
Torsionsstütze *f* torsion support
Torsionssteifheit *f* stiffness in torsion
Totalausfall *m* total breakdown, complete failure
Totalfeststeller *m* total breaking and/or locking device
tote Spitze *f* dead centre
tote Zone *f* dead zone
toter Gang *m* lost motion (play), dead travel, (threading) backlash
toter Rücklauf *m* idle return stroke, idle backstroke
Totgewicht *nt* dead weight
Totmanneinrichtung *f* dead man device, dead man's handle, dead man's button, hold-to-run handle
Totmannprinzip *nt* hold-to-run principle
Totmannschaltung *f* dead man's control, hold-to-run control
Totpunkt *m* dead centre
Totweg *m* idle path
Totzeit *f* idle time, dead time, *(US)* downtime, delay time

Totzeitglied *nt* lag element
Touchreader *m* touch reader
toxisch toxic
TPD *Abk (Dreidimensionaldrucken)* Three Dimensional Printing
Trafoeinstellung *f* transformer setting
Trag-/Zugmittel *nt* lifting/traction unit, transmission element
Traganteil *m* 1. *(allg.)* percentage ratio of contact area 2. *(z. B. der Flankenfläche)* load-carrying portion
Tragbalken *m* girder
tragbar portable
tragbare Schalteinrichtung *f* portable control unit
Tragbildprüfung *f* contact pattern test
Tragdorn *m* carrying ram, boom
träge inert, inactive
träge-elastische Dehnung *f* sluggish-elastic extension
Tragelement *nt* supporting member
tragen 1. *(allg.)* bear, carry 2. *(stützen)* support 3. *(transportieren)* tote 4. *(unterstützen)* back
tragend load-bearing, supporting
tragende Gewindeflanke *f* pressure flank, load flank, load bearing flank
tragende Gewindelänge *f* load-bearing (or effective) thread length, length of engagement
tragende Schweißverbindung *f* load-bearing welded joint
tragende Verbindung *f* load-bearing assembly
tragendes Armaturenteil *nt* load-bearing valve part
tragendes Konstruktionsteil *nt* load-bearing structural member
Trageplatte *f* bearing plate
Träger *m* carrier, crossrail
Träger *m* 1. *(Auflage)* bracket, sustainer 2. *(Balken)* beam, girder 3. *(Bewehrung)* truss 4. *(Kragarm)* cantilever 5. *(Stütze)* support 6. *(Trägermaterial)* substrate 7. *(beweglicher ~)* movable platen 8. *(stationärer ~)* stationary platen
Trägerfahrzeug *nt* load bearing vehicle, tractor
Trägerfolie *f* backing film
Trägerfrequenzverfahren *nt* carrier frequency method
Trägergas *nt* carrier gas
Trägergewebe *nt* supporting fabric
Trägerleitplatte *f* motherboard
trägerlos unsupported
Trägermaterial *nt* substrate material
Trägermittel *nt* carrier preparation
Trägerpappe *f* backing card
Trägerplattform *f* carrier platform
Trägerwelle *f* carrier wave
Trägerwerkstoff *m* base material, substrate material
Tragetasche *f* tote bag
tragfähig 1. *(allg.)* capable of bearing, portative 2. *(Bau)* stable, good bearing 3. *(Hub)* capable of lifting
tragfähige Rohrleitung *f* pipeline capable of bearing load
tragfähiges Gewinde *nt* load-bearing screw thread
Tragfähigkeit *f* 1. *(allg.)* capacity, lifting capacity, carrying capacity, load (-carrying) capacity, safe working load 2. *(Bauwesen)* bearing capacity
Tragfähigkeitsberechnung *f* calculation of load-carrying capacity
Tragfähigkeitsschild *nt* (load) capacity plate
Tragflüssigkeit *f* liquid vehicle
Trägheit *f* inertia
trägheitsbedingter Fehler *m* error due to inertia forces
Trägheitskraft *f* inertia force
Trägheitsmoment *nt* moment of inertia
Trägheitsradius *m* radius of gyraion, radius of inertia
Traghülse *f* spindle sleeve
Tragkegel *m* bearing cone
Tragkette *f* carrying chain, drag bar
Tragkettenförderer *m* carrying chain conveyor, drag bar feeder
Tragkonstruktion *f* supporting structure, supporting framework
Tragkraft *f* 1. *(allg.)* carrying force, carrying power 2. *(der Achse)* load capacity 3. *(Ladeleistung)* loading capacity
Traglager *nt* 1. *(Last, z. B. Bauwesen)* journal bearing, bearing support 2. *(Fräsdorn)* yoke, arbor yoke 3. *(Fräs-*

maschine) arbor support
Traglast *f* **1.** *(allg.)* ultimate load **2.** *(Auflast)* load, burden
Traglastbereich *m* load range
Tragluftflussregler *m* carrier air flow controller
Tragluftshalle *f* airhouse, air-inflated structure, air-inflated tent
Tragmittel *nt* load lifting means, load supporting means, load carrying means, suspension element, suspension equipment, lifting element, means of suspension, means of support
Tragmittelpaar *nt* pair of suspension elements
Tragmutter *f* load bearing nut
Tragrolle *f* **1.** *(allg.)* support roller, idler, load bearing roller **2.** *(Hängebahn)* carrying roller **3.** *(gerade ~)* straight idler **4.** *(muldenförmige ~)* trough-shaped idler, trough roller
Tragrollensatz *m* idler assembly
Tragsatz *m* carrier assembly
Tragseil *nt* (load) carrying rope
Tragtiefe *f* **1.** *(allg.)* depth of engagement **2.** *(e. Gewindes)* load-bearing depth
Tragwerk *nt* supporting works
Trajektorie *f* trajectory
Trajektoriengenerierung *f* trajectory generator
Tränkbarkeit *f* suitability for impregnation
Tränkharzmasse *f* impregnating resin material
Tränkharzformstoff *m* impregnating resin moulded material
Tränkungswert *m* coefficient of impregnation
Transaktion *f* transaction
Transaktionsdauer *f* duration of transaction
transaktionsgetrieben transaction-driven
Transfer *m* transfer
Transferantrieb *m* transfer drive
transferieren transfer
transferpressen transfer mould, plunger mould
Transferpressvorgang *m* transfer moulding operation
Transferstraße *f* transfer line
Transferticket *nt* transfer ticket
Transformator *m* transformer
Transformatorprinzip *nt* transformer principle
transformierte Zufallsgröße *f* transformed random quantity
transient transient
Transistor *m* transistor
Translation *f* **1.** *(parallel)* translation **2.** *(Roboter)* side travel
Translationsbewegung *f* translational motion, movement of translation
translatorisch translational
translatorisch bewegtes Teil *nt* part moving backwards and forwards
Transmission *f* transmission
Transmissionsantrieb *m* line shaft transmission
Transmissionsfunktion *f* transmission function
Transmissionslichttaster *m* transmission light scanner
Transmissionsoptik *f* transmission optics
Transmissionswelle *f* transmission shaft, line shaft
Transmissionszeilenlichttaster *m* transmission line-scanning light scanner
transparent transparent
Transparentfolie *f* **1.** *(allg.)* transparent film **2.** *(metallisch)* transparent foil
Transparentkontrast *m* translucent contrast
Transparentkontrastpause *f* translucent contrast copy
Transparentpapier *nt* translucent paper, tracing paper
Transparentpapier *nt* **mit Lichtpausschicht** translucent paper with diazo coating
Transparentvordruck *m* **für Zeichnungen** preprint for the photo-reproduction of drawings (pl)
Transparentzeichenpapier *nt* rotogravure paper
Transparenz *f* transparency, transparence
transpassive Korrosion *f* transpassive

corrosion
transpassiver Zustand *m* transpassive condition
Transport *m* **1.** *(allg.)* transport, handling, conveyance **2.** *(Überführung)* transfer, transit
Transport *m* **des Werkstücks** work handling
transportabel transportable, movable, portable
Transportabschnitt *m* stage of transport
Transportanforderung *f* transport request
Transportanweisung *f* transport instruction
Transportaufgabe *f* transport task
Transportauftrag *m* transport assignment, transport command
Transportauftragsverwaltung *f* transport command administration, transport command processor
Transportband *nt* belt conveyor, conveying belt, feed wheel
Transportbeauftragter *m* (person) responsible for transportation
Transportbefehl *m* transfer instruction
Transportbehälter *m* transport receptacle, transport container
Transportbehälterart *f* transport container type
Transportbelastung *f* transport load
Transportbereich *m* transport range
Transportbeton *m* ready-mixed concrete
Transporteinheit *f* transport unit
Transporteinrichtung *f* materials handling equipment, handling equipment
Transporteur *m* protractor
Transportfläche *f* transport area
transportgerecht designed for transport
Transportgeschwindigkeit *f* travel speed, transport speed
Transportgröße *f* transport value
Transportgüter *ntpl* transport goods
Transportintensität *f* transport intensity
Transportintensitätsmatrix *f* transport intensity matrix

Transportkasten *m* tote box
Transportkette *f* **1.** *(Bauteil)* conveyor chain **2.** *(Förderer)* chain conveyor **3.** *(Serie)* chain of transportation means
Transportkommissionierkasten *m* tote box
Transportkosten *pl* cost of conveyance, transport costs, handling costs
Transportkreislauf *m* circuit of transportation, circuit of conveyance
Transportleistung *f* **1.** *(allg.)* conveying capacity, transport capacity **2.** *(e. einzelnen Förderers)* hauling capacity
Transportleistungsziffer *f* transport coefficient
Transportmatrix *f* transport matrix
Transportmittel *nt* means of transport(ation), handling means
Transportorganisation *f* transport organization
Transportplanung *f* transport planning
Transportrichtung *f* direction of travel
Transportrolle *f* conveyor roller, feed roll, transport roller, sprocket wheel
Transportschaden *m* damage sustained during transport (or in transit)
Transportschicht *f* transport layer, transport service
Transportschnecke *f* screw conveyor
Transportsicherung *f* securing device, transportation lock
Transportstellung *f* transporting position
Transportsystem *nt* conveying system
Transportvorgang *m* handling operation
Transportwagen *m* transport cart, transport trolley, transfer car, haulage car
Transportweg *m* conveying distance, transport route
Transportzeit *f* transport time
transversal transverse
Transversalwelle *f* transverse wave
Trapez *nt* trapezium, *(US)* trapezoid
Trapezanschnitt *m* trapezium starting cut
Trapezblech *nt* sheet with trapezoidal corrugations, trapezoidal sheeting
Trapezblockfelder *f* trapezoid block

spring
Trapezeinlauf *m* trapezoid shrinkage
trapezförmig trapezoidal
Trapezgewinde *nt* Acme thread
Trapezgewinde *nt* **allgemeiner Anwendung** general purpose trapezoidal screw thread
Trapezgewinde *nt*, **eingängig mit Spiel** one-(or single-)start trapezoidal screw thread with clearance
Trapezgewinde *nt*, **zweigängig mit Spiel** two-(or double-)start trapezoidal screw thread with clearance
Traverse *f* cross beam, cross girth, crosshead, top beam, top rail
Traverse *f* **mit eingebautem Getriebe** crossbeam accommodating gear mechanism
traversieren traverse
traversierende Stößelhobelmaschine *f* traverse shaper, travelling-head shaper
traversierende Waagerechtstoßmaschine *f* traverse shaper
Tray *nt* tray, skillet
Trayaufricht-, -füll- und -verschließmaschine *f* tray erect load and seal machine
Trayaufrichtmaschine *f* skillet erecting machine, tray erecting machine
Trayentstapelungsmaschine *f* tray denesting machine
Traystapler *m* tray stacker
Trayzuschnitt *m* tray blank
treffen meet, hit
treiben drive, push
Treiben *nt* **von Flach- oder Hohlkörpern am Blech** driving
treibendes Rad *nt* driving gear
Treiber *m* driver
Treiberprogramm *nt* drive program
Treibkraft *f* motive power
Treibmittel *nt* propellant
Treibmittelenergie *f* propellant energy
Treibmittelvakuumpumpe *f* fluid entrainment vacuum pump
Treibriemen *m* drive belt
Treibscheibe *f* driving disk, driving wheel
Treibstoff *m* fuel

Treibstofftank *m* fuel tank
trennbruchsicher rupture-proof
trennen 1. *(allg.)* part (off), separate, disconnect (from), cut off (by abrasive cutting), disengage **2.** *(trennschleifen)* severing, cut-off grinding
trennend disjoining, separative
trennende Schutzeinrichtung *f* electrosensitive protection device
Trennfläche *f* interface
Trennfolie *f* separating film
Trennklemme *f* disconnect terminal
Trennkraft *f* adhesion strength
Trennmaschine *f* cutting-off machine
Trennnahtschweißen *nt* heated tool welding with cutting edge
Trennsäge *f* cut-off saw
Trennschalter *m* isolator, circuit breaker, disconnecting switch, separating contactor
Trennscheibe *f* abrasive wheel
Trennschleifen *nt* cut-off grinding
Trennschleifmaschine *f* abrasive wheel cutting-off machine, abrasive cutting machine, abrasive cut-off machine
Trennschnitt *m* *(als Arbeitsvorgang)* cut-off operation
Trenntechnik *f* separating technology, cutting technology
Trennung *f* disengagement, separation, isolation
Trennungsblech *nt* baffle plate
Trennungsebene *f* plane of separation
Trennvermögen *nt* resolution
Trennvorgang *m* separating process
Trennwand *f* dividing wall, partition (wall), partition panel
Trennwerkzeug *nt* parting tool
Treppe *f* stair, stairs
Treppenbau *m* stair construction
Treppeneinlauf *m* stair shrinkage
Treppengeländer *nt* staircase railing
Treppenhaus *nt* stairway
Treppenlaufhöhe *f* height of flight
Treppenpodest *nt* staircase landing
Treppenstufe *f* stair step, stair tread
treten 1. *(allg.)* tread **2.** *(zwischen)* step between **3.** *(Pedale)* pedal
Triangulation *f* triangulation
Trichter *m* funnel

Trichter *m* **mit kurzem Stiel** short-stem funnel
trichterförmige Zuführungseinrichtung *f* feed hopper
Trichtermodell *nt* funnel model
Trichterschmiernippel *m* cup head lubricating nipple
Trieb *m* 1. *(allg.)* pinion 2. *(Antrieb)* drive, transmission 3. *(kraftschlüssiger ~)* non-positive drive 4. *(stufenloser ~)* infinitely variable speed transmission 5. *(zwangsläufiger ~)* positive drive
Triebkraft *f* motive power
Triebkranz *m* scroll gear
Triebstock *m* driving pin
Triebstockbolzen *m* pinion stud
Triebstockkette *f* pinion chain
Triebstockrad *nt* cylindrical lantern gear
Triebstockradpaar *nt* cylindrical lantern pinion and wheel
Triebstockverzahnung *f* cylindrical lantern tooth system, pin tooth gearing
Triebstockzahnstange *f* lantern (pin) rack
Triebwerk *nt* (driving) mechanism
Triebwerksgruppe *f* driving mechanism class, operating classification
Trinkgeschirr *nt* drinking utensils
Trinkwasserleitungsanlage *f* pipe installation for drinking water
trinkwasserseitig on the drinking water side
Tritt *m* step, footstep, tread, treadle
Trittleiste *f* kicking plate
Trittleiter *f* rung ladder
Trittschall *m* footstep sound
Trittschallpegel *m* structure-borne sound level
Trittsicherheit *f* safety when walking
Trittstufe *f* step, stair
trocken dry
Trockenabrichten *nt* dry truing
Trockenbiegefestigkeit *f* dry bending strength
trockenblank *(von Draht)* dry bright
Trockenfräsen *nt* dry milling
Trockengaszähler *m* dry gas meter
Trockenhitzefixierechtheit *f* fastness to dry-heat setting
Trockenhitzeplissierechtheit *f* fastness to dry-heat pleating
Trockenkanal *m* drying channel
Trockenmasse *f* dry weight
Trockenmittel *nt* desiccant
Trockenpressen *nt* dry pressing
Trockenreinigungsechtheit *f* fastness to dry cleaning
Trockenrückstand *m* residue on evaporation
Trockenschleifen *nt* dry grinding, dry cutting
Trockenschliff *m* dry cutting
Trockenschwindung *f* shrinkage during drying
Trockensubstanz *f* solids content
Trockentinte *f* dry ink
trockenwarmes Klima *nt* hot-dry climate
Trockenzone *f* dry zone
trocknen dry
Trocknungsmaschine *f* drying machine
Trocknungszustand *m* state of drying
Trog *m* pan, trough, tray
Trogvibrator *m* pan vibrator
Trommel *f* 1. *(allg.)* round turret head, spindle drum, drum, reel, barrel 2. *(Kabeltrommel)* cable drum
Trommelbehandlung *f* drum treatment
Trommelbremse *f* drum brake
Trommeldrehautomat *m* automatic drum-type turret lathe
Trommelfräsmaschine *f* drum-type milling machine, drum-type miller, drum miller, rotary drum milling machine
Trommelfräsmaschine *f* **für durchlaufendes Fräsen** drum-type continuous milling machine
Trommelfräsmaschine *f* **mit Indexschaltung** drum-type indexing miller (or milling machine)
Trommelgalvanisierapparat *m* barrel plating
Trommelgleitschleifen *nt* barrel slide grinding
Trommelgreifer *m* drum gripper
Trommelkörper *m* barrel body

Trommelkurve *f* cylinder cam, barrel cam, drum cam
Trommelmagazin *nt* drum magazine
Trommelmotor *m* drum motor
Trommelpfanne *f* drum pan
Trommelpolieren *nt* tumbling
Trommelpolierverfahren *nt* barrel tunbling process
Trommelregal *nt* drum racking
Trommelreitstock *m* turret tailstock
Trommelrevolver *m* drum-type turret
Trommelrevolverdrehmaschine *f* drum-type turret lathe, turret lathe for facing operations
Trommelschalten *nt* drum indexing
Trommelschaltung *f* spindle drum indexing
Trommelschälversuch *m* climbing drum peel test
Trommeltrockner *m* barrel dryer
Trommelverriegelung *f* spindle drum interlocking
Trompetenrohr *nt* coiled tube, siphon
tropfen drop, drip
Tropfpunktgerät *nt* dropping point apparatus
Tropfverlust *m* drip loss
Trübungsmessung *f* measurement of turbidity
Trübungspunkt *m* cloud point
Trübungstitration *f* turbidimetric titration
Trübungstitrationszahl *f* turbidity titration number
Trübungszahl *f* turbidity number
Trumm *nt* 1. *(allg.)* end of rope 2. *(Band)* belt 3. *(gezogenes Trumm)* taut span
T-Schottstutzen *m* T-bulkhead union
T-Stift *m* T-stud
T-Stoß *m* single-T joint
T-Stück *nt* tee-piece
T-Stutzen *m* 1. *(allg.)* T-adaptor (or fitting) 2. *(für Rohrverschraubungen)* T-union
TUL *Abk* transport-traffic (volume)-storage
Tümpelform *f* basin form
Tunnel *m* 1. *(allg.)* channel, tunnel 2. *(Unterführung)* underground passage
Tunnelanguss *m* **mit Punktanschnitt** tunnel sprue with restricted gate
Tüpfelprüfung *f* drop test
Tür *f* door
Tür *f* **mit elektrischer Sicherheitssperre** electrically interlocked door
Türbewegung *f* door motion
Turbine *f* turbine
Turboaxialverdichter *m* axial flow turbo compressor
Turbokupplung *f* fluid turbo coupling
Turbulator *m* turbulator
Turboradialverdichter *m* centrifugal turbo-compressor
Turbovakuumpumpe *f* turbo-vacuum pump
Turbulenz *f* eddy
Türflügel *m* leaf
Türfüllung *f* door panel
Türhaken *m* door hook
Türklemme *f* spring type holder (for trap doors)
Türschließer *m* door closer
Türschließer *m* **mit hydraulischer Dämpfung** door closer with hydraulic damping
Türschließmittel *ntpl* door closing means
Türschlüssel *m* door key
Türzarge *f* frame of the door
Tusche *f* drawing ink
Tuscheschreibgerät *nt* ink writing instrument
Tuscheschreibgerät *nt* **mit Röhrchenfeder** *f* ink writing instrument with stencil pen
Tuscheskizze *f* ink sketch
Tuschezeichengerät *nt* ink drawing instrument
Tuschierplatte *f* standard surface plate, surface plate
Typ *m* 1. *(allg.)* model, type 2. *(Ausführung)* design, type
Typenblatt *nt* type data sheet
typgeprüfte Ausführung *f* type-tested model (or pattern)
typische Ausführung *f* basic design
typisierte Formmasse *f* type-assigned moulding material
Typnachprüfung *f* type re-testing
Typprüfung *f* type test

U u

über 1. *(ein Thema)* about, concerning **2.** *(el., über zwei Punkte)* across **3.** *(räumlich, Niveau, Werte)* above, over **4.** *(Strecken)* via **5.** *(zeitlich, größer als, hinweg über)* over
über dem Erdboden above ground level
über Draht wirebound
über ein Rohr verbinden pipe with
über ein Sensor via a sensor
über Zahnräder verbunden mit geared to
Überbau *m* superstructure, projection, overhang
überbeanspruchen overstrain, overstress, overload
Überbeanspruchung *f* excessive strain, excessive stress, overstress, overload
überbelasten overload
Überbestimmung *f (doppelte Maßangabe)* redundant dimensioning
überbetrieblich interplant, supra-plant
überbrücken 1. *(örtlich)* bridge **2.** *(umleiten)* bypass **3.** *(stummschalten)* mute
Überbrückung *f* **1.** *(örtlich)* bridgeover **2.** *(Umleitung)* bypass **3.** *(stummschalten)* muting configure
Überbrückungsfunktion *f* muting function
Überbrückungssignal *nt* mute signal
Überbrückungsstrahl *m* muting beam
überdachen 1. *(allg.)* roof in, roof over, span by a roof **2.** *(Förderer)* cover, enclose
überdacht roofed, under roof, covered, enclosed
Überdachung *f* **1.** *(allg.)* roofing **2.** *(Förderer)* conveyor belt housing, cover, enclosure
Überdeckung *f* **1.** *(überlappen)* overlap **2.** *(Zahnradpaare mit parallelen Achsen)* contact ratio
Überdeckungsanzeiger *m* overlap indicator
Überdeckungsgrad *m* **1.** *(allg.)* engagement factor **2.** *(e. Profils)* overlap factor (or degree)
Überdeckungshöhe *f (von Rohrleitungen)* depth of cover
überdimensionieren overdimension, oversize
Überdrehungsgrad *m* overturning degree
Überdrehzahl *f* overspeed
Überdruck *m* **1.** *(allg.)* excess pressure, overpressure, positive pressure **2.** *(in Reifen)* overinflation **3.** *(kurzfristig)* pressure shock
Überdruckanlage *f* positive pressure attachment
Überdruckbereich *m* positive pressure region
Überdruckbetrieb *m* pressurized operation
Überdruckbrenner *m* positive pressure burner
Überdruckfüllmaschine *f* pressure filling machine
überdruckgekapselt pressurized
Überdruckkapselung *f* pressurized apparatus, pressurizing
Überdruckprüfung *f* overpressure test
Überdruckventil *nt* pressure control valve, (safety) pressure relief valve
Überdruckvorrichtung *f* pressurizing device
übereinander on top of each other
übereinander lagern superimpose
übereinander liegend 1. *(allg.)* adjacent, superimposed, lying upon another **2.** *(geschichtet)* sandwiched **3.** *(gestapelt)* stacked
übereinander setzen stack
übereinander laufend running one above another
Übereinandersetzen *nt* stacking
übereinstimmen mit 1. *(allg.)* correspond (to), coincide, comply (with) **2.** *(Meinungen)* agree, accord **3.** *(passen)* match, suit **4.** *(Systeme, Regeln)*

comply (with)
übereinstimmend 1. *(allg.)* consistent, compatible (with) **2.** *(Formen)* congruent **3.** *(Meinungen)* unaminous, concordant
Übereinstimmung *f* **1.** *(allg.)* conformance, agreement, accordance, consistency, correspondence **2.** *(Formen)* congruence, match **3.** *(Systeme, Regeln)* conformity, compliance
überfahren 1. *(allg.)* cross **2.** *(Fußgänger)* run down, knock down **3.** *(hinausschießen)* overshoot **4.** *(Kabel)* entangle with **5.** *(Lasten)* straddle **6.** *(Signale)* overtravel, overrun, override
Überfahrlager *nt* gantry robot system
Überfahrplatte *f* dockboard
Überfärbungsechtheit *f* fastness to cross-dyeing
überfluten flood
Überformat *nt* oversize format
Übergabe *f* delivery, handling over, putting into service, deposit, transfer, transferral
Übergabeförderer *m* transfer conveyor
Übergabeplatz *m* transfer point, discharge point, deposit point
Übergabeposition *f* transfer location, transfer point, transfer position, transfer station
Übergabestation *f* transfer station
Übergabestelle *f* P & D station, pick-up and delivery station, pick-up and deposit station
Übergabevorrichtung *f* transfer device
Übergang *m* **1.** *(Position)* transfer, crossover **2.** *(Netze)* gateway **3.** *(Wege)* passage, passing **4.** *(Zustände)* transition, changeover, conversion
Übergang *m* **zu neuer Serie** job change over
Übergangsabstand *m* transfer distance
Übergangsfrist *f* transitional period
Übergangshülse *f* adapter
Übergangspassung *f* transition fit
Übergangsradius *m* transition radius

Übergangsstück *nt* transition piece
Übergangsverhalten *nt* transient behaviour
Übergangswinkel *m* transition angle
Übergangszeit *f* transitional period
Übergasen *nt* over-gassing
übergeben consign, deliver, give over, hand over, turn over, pass (on to), transfer
übergehen 1. *(allg.)* pass over (to), switch over (to), turn (to), grade (into), change gradually into **2.** *(auslassen)* omit, override
übergehen in blend into, merge into
übergeordnet primary, superordinate, master, higher order
übergeordnete Steuerung *f* master control system
Übergeschwindigkeit *f* overspeed
übergreifen 1. *(allg.)* lap over, overlap **2.** *(mit Händen)* reach over, access from above
Übergreifungsstoß *m* lap joint
Übergröße *f* oversize
Überhang *m* overhang, projection
überhängen jut out, stand out, project, overhang, hang over, protrude
überhängend (überstehend) projecting, protruding, overhanging **2.** *(vorkragend)* cantilever
überhängende Ladung *f* **1.** *(hinten ~)* load projecting behind the vehicle **2.** *(seitlich ~)* wide load
Überhangwinkel *m* overhang angle
überhöht stepped
überhöhte Schweißraupe *f* raised welding bead
Überhöhung *f* **1.** *(allg.)* stepping, elevation **2.** *(von Zahn zu Zahn / Räumen)* rise per tooth
überholen 1. *(allg.)* recondition **2.** *(Drehzahlen)* overtake **3.** *(Maschine)* overhaul
Überholung *f* **1.** *(allg.)* reconditioning **2.** *(Drehzahlen)* overtaking, overtaking principle **3.** *(e. Maschine)* overhauling
Überkragung *f* overhang
Überladebrücke *f* bridge plate, loading bridge, transfer bridge
überladen 1. *(allg.)* overload **2.** *(Akku)*

overcharge 3. *(in anderes Fzg.)* transfer, transship
Überladung *f* overcharge, overloading
Überladungserkennungssystem *nt* overload sensing device
Überladungswarnleuchte *f* overload telltale lamp, overload signal lamp
überlagern 1. *(allg.)* super(im)pose 2. *(Signale)* interfere, overlay 3. *(Waren)* overstore
Überlagerung *f* superimposition
Überlagerungsbewegung *f* superimposed motion
Überlänge *f* overlength, excessive length
Überlappbreite *f* lap width
überlappen overlap, lap
überlappend overlapping
Überlappfläche *f* lapped area
Überlappnaht *f* over(lap) seal
Überlappnahtwiderstandsschweißung *f* resistance lap seam welding
Überlapp-Prüfstück *nt* lap test piece
Überlappschweißung *f* lap seam, lap weld
Überlappstoß *m* **mit Quetschnaht** lap joint with compression weld
Überlappstoß *m* **mit Überlappnaht** lap joint with lap weld
überlappt schweißen lap-weld
Überlappung *f* overlap, overlapping
Überlaschung *f* fish joint, fishing
Überlast *f* 1. *(allg.)* overcharge, overload 2. *(Kran)* stalling load 3. *(Mehrgewicht)* excess load, excess weight, overweight 4. *(zus. Belastung)* surcharge
Überlastabschaltung *f* overload cutoff
Überlastabschaltvorrichtung *f* overload cutout device
Überlastanzeige *f* overload indicator, safe load indicator
Überlastauslösung *f* overload release
Überlastbarkeit *f* overload capacity, *(US)* peak load allowance
Überlastdrehzahl *f* overload speed
überlasten 1. *(allg.)* overload, overcharge, overburden 2. *(beanspruchen)*
Überlastfahrt *f* overloaded run, overloaded travel
überlastfest overload-proof

Überlastkupplung *f* overload clutch
Überlastprüfung *f* overload test
Überlastschalter *m* circuit breaker, overload switch, overload release, overcurrent release, excess-current switch
Überlastschnellabschaltung *f* overload scram, *(US)* overload trip
Überlastschutz *m* overload protection
Überlastsicherung *f* overload protection, overload safety device
Überlaststrom *m* excess current, overload current
Überlastung *f* 1. *(allg.)* overload(ing), overcharging 2. *(Überbeanspruchung)* overstress, excessive force
Überlastungskupplung *f* overload clutch
Überlastungsschutz *m* overload protection
Überlastungsstromstoß *m* overload surge current
Überlastversuch *m* proof test, overload test
Überlauf *m* oversize
Überlaufanschlag *m* overrun limit
Überlaufspeicher *m* overflow storage heater
Überlauftrichter *m* overflow funnel
Überlaufwasser *nt* overflow water
Überlaufweg *m* overrun path, overrunning distance
Überlebenswahrscheinlichkeit *f* survival probability
überlegen superior (to)
Übermaß *nt* oversize, interference, allowance
Übermaß *nt* **als Bearbeitungszugabe für...** amount of stock left for
übermäßig excess, excessive
Übermaßrichtwert *m* interference guide value
Übermaßzeichnung *f* drawing dealing with oversize parts
Übermenge *f* excess quantity
übermitteln convey, transmit
Übermittlung *f* 1. *(materiell)* transmission 2. *(nur Daten)* communication
Übernahme *f* 1. *(allg.)* take over, taking over, transfer, acceptance 2. *(e. Information)* read-in

Übernahmeposition *f* acceptance position, pick-up location
übernehmen 1. *(akzeptieren)* accept **2.** *(angleichen)* take over **3.** *(Stückgut)* pick up
überprüfen 1. *(Masch.)* check, inspect, look over, test **2.** *(vergleichen)* check, verify **3.** *(prüfen, kontrollieren)* examine, control, verify
Überprüfung *f* **1.** *(Masch.)* check, inspection, test **2.** *(vergleichend)* verification, check **3.** *(Prüfung, Kontrolle)* control, examination
Überpunktmethode *f* over-point method
Überrollbügel *m* roll bar
überrollen 1. *(Gegenstände)* roll over, roll on **2.** *(drehen)* contort
Überrollschutz *m* roll over protective structure
Überschallprüfung *f* ultrasonic testing
Überschichtung *f* *(e. Oberfläche)* surface lamination
überschieben push onto, put over
Überschiebmuffe *f* sliding type socket, shrunk-on sleeve
Überschlagspannung *f* over-voltage
überschleifen finish by grinding
überschneiden cut, intersect, overlap, overcut, top
Überschneidung *f* cutting (across), overcutting, intersection, overlapping
überschnittenes Stirnrad *nt* topped spur gear
überschnittenes Zahnrad *nt* overcut gear
überschreiten cross, traverse, pass over, exceed, overshoot, transgress
Überschreiten *nt* **der Strecke** overstraining beyond the elastic limit
Überschreitung *f* exceedance, exceeding, transgression
Überschreitung *f* **von Richtwerten** overstepping
Überschreitung *f* **von Toleranzen** transgression
Überschreitungswahrscheinlichkeit *f* transgression probability
Überschrift *f* heading, headline, title
überschritten overshot

Überschuss *m* excess, surplus
überschüssig excess
überschüssiges Metall *nt* surplus metal
überschütten cover
Überschüttung *f* covering, cover material
Überschüttungshöhe *f* depth of cover
überschwingen overshoot, ring
Überschwingen *nt* overshooting, ringing
Überschwingerfrequenz *f* ringing frequency
überschwingungsfrei free of harmonics
Überschwingweite *f* overshoot
übersehen 1. *(schauen)* overlook, overview **2.** *(vernachlässigen)* ignore, overlook, neglect
übersetzen 1. *(Zahnräder)* gear **2.** *(Kräfte)* transmit **3.** *(Programm)* compile, interpret **4.** *(Sprache)* translate
übersetzen und starten compile and go
Übersetzer *m* compiler, interpreter
Übersetzung *f* **1.** *(e. Hebels)* leverage **2.** *(Getriebe)* gear (ratio), transmission (ratio), speed transformation **3.** *(Programm)* compilation, interpretation **4.** *(Sprache)* translation
Übersetzung *f* **ins Langsame** speed reducing ratio
Übersetzung *f* **ins Schnelle** speed increasing ratio
Übersetzungsabweichung *f* transmission deviation
Übersetzungskonstanz *f* transmission constancy
Übersetzungslauf *m* compilation run
Übersetzungssystem *nt* source system
Übersetzungsverhältnis *nt* transmission ratio, speed ratio
Übersetzungszeit *f* compilation time, compile time
Übersicht *f* **1.** *(sehen)* overview **2.** *(Zeichnung)* general plan
übersichtlich clear, clearly arranged
Übersichtsbild *nt* overview display
Übersichtsfeld *nt* overview field
Übersichtszeichnung *f* general ar-

rangement drawing, general drawing, general plan
überspannen overstrain, overstretch, straddle
Überspannung *f* 1. *(allg. el.)* excess voltage, overvoltage, surge voltage 2. *(Halbleiter)* transient (voltage)
Überspannungsableiter *m* surge voltage protector, high rupture fuse, overvoltage suppressor
Überspannungsbegrenzer *m* overvoltage limiter
Überspannungsbegrenzungseinrichtung *f* transient suppression means
Überspannungsimpuls *m* transient
Überspannungskategorie *f* overvoltage category
Überspannungsschutz *m* 1. *(allg. el.)* overvoltage protection, voltage surge protection 2. *(Halbleiter)* transient voltage suppression
Überspannungsschutzdiode *f* transient voltage suppression diode
Überspannungsschutzeinrichtung *f* overvoltage protective device, surge protective device, surge voltage protector
überspreizen overspread, straddle
überspringen skip
überstehen project, protrude, overhang
überstehend projecting, overhanging, cantilever
überstehender Kopf *m* protruding head
übersteigen exceed
übersteuern 1. *(allg.)* overcontrol 2. *(el.)* overdrive, overmodulate 3. *(Fzg., Automatisierung)* oversteer 4. *(überspringen)* override
Übersteuerung *f* overcontrol, overdrive, overmodulation, oversteer
überstreichen scan
Überstrom *m* overcurrent
überströmen flood
Überstromschutz *m* overcurrent protection
Überstromschutzeinrichtung *f* overcurrent protective device
übersynchron oversynchronous, supersynchronous, hypersynchronous

übersynchrone Bremsung *f* hypersynchronous braking
Übertemperatur *f* overtemperature, excess temperature
Übertemperaturschutz *m* overtemperature protection
Übertemperatursicherung *f* overtemperature safety device
Übertrag *m* carry over, amount carried, forward, add carry
übertragbar transferable, transmissible
übertragbare Kraft *f* transmittable force
übertragbares Moment *nt* transmissible moment
übertragen 1. *(Antrieb, Kräfte)* transmit 2. *(ausweiten)* spread 3. *(Daten)* move 4. *(e. Profil auf das Werkstück)* impart (to) 5. *(el.)* transduce 6. *(Gewindegänge)* transpose 7. *(Maße, Methoden)* transfer 8. *(Übertrag)* carry forward, carry over
übertragendes Messgerät *nt* transmitting measuring instrument
Übertrager *m* 1. *(allg.)* transducer, transformer 2. *(Geber)* transmitter 3. *(Netzwerke)* repeater
Übertragsbit *nt* carry bit
Übertragseingang *m* carry input
Übertragung *f* 1. *(allg.)* transfer, transposition 2. *(Getriebe, Daten)* transmission
Übertragungsabschnitt *m* transmission link
Übertragungsabstand *m* transfer distance
Übertragungsabweichung *f* transmission deviation, transmission variation
Übertragungsausgang *m* carry output
Übertragungsbedingung *f* transfer condition
Übertragungsbefehl *m* transfer statement
Übertragungsbeiwert *m* **der Regelstrecke** *f* steady-state transfer factor
Übertragungselement *nt* power transmission member
Übertragungsende *nt* end of transmis-

sion
Übertragungsendezeichen *nt* end-of transmission label
Übertragungsfehler *m* transmission error
Übertragungsfunktion *f* transmission function
Übertragungsgeschwindigkeit *f* transmission speed
Übertragungsglied *nt* transmission member, transfer element
Übertragungskanal *m* transmission channel
Übertragungskennlinie *f* transmission characteristic
Übertragungsleitung *f* transmission line
Übertragungsmenge *f* transmission rate
Übertragungsmittel *nt* transmission agent
Übertragungsmoment *nt* transmitted torque
Übertragungsprinzip *nt* transfer principle
Übertragungsprotokoll *nt* transmission protocol
Übertragungsstrecke *f* transmission circuit, transmission distance, transmission link, transmission path
Übertragungssystem *nt* transmission system
Übertragungsverfahren *nt* transmission method
Übertragungszeit *f* transfer time, transmission time
Übervorschub *m* excess feed, surplus feed
überwachen 1. *(kontrollieren)* inspect, control, monitor **2.** *(beaobachten)* observe **3.** *(beaufsichtigen)* supervise
Überwacherprogramm *nt* tracer, trace program
Überwachung *f* **1.** *(allg.)* supervision, inspection, control, monitoring **2.** *(Überprüfung von primären und abgeleiteten Prozess- und Anlagedaten)* process monitoring
Überwachungseinrichtung *f* monitoring equipment

Überwachungsfunktion *f* monitoring function
Überwachungsgerät *nt* monitoring device
Überwachungssystem *nt* control system
Überwachungsvertrag *m* supervision contract
Überwalzung *f* seam
Überwalzzahl *f* seam number
Überwärmung *f* over-heating
überwiegender Anteil *m* preponderant proportion
Überwurfmutter *f* box nut, cap nut, spigot nut, union nut
Überwurfmutter *f* **mit Druckring und Schneidring** union nut with compression ring and olive
Überwurfschraube *f* *(für Rohrverschraubungen)* socket union
Überzeit *f* overtiming
überziehen 1. *(allg.)* cover **2.** *(anstreichen)* coat **3.** *(Materialien, Folien)* stretch over
überzogen coated
Überzug *m* **1.** *(allg.)* coat(ing), cover **2.** *(Folien)* wrap **3.** *(Schicht)* layer
Überzugsoberfläche *f* surface of the coating
Überzugsschichtdicke *f* coating thickness
Überzugsspritzen *nt* coating by (flame) spraying
Überzugswerkstoff *m* coating material
Überzünden *nt* over-igniting
Übertragungeinrichtung *f* transmission unit
üblich common, standard, ordinary, usual, generally accepted
üblicherweise usually, ordinarily
U-Bogenausgleicher *m* U-bend expansion joint
U-förmig U-shaped
U-Fuge *f* single-U joint
Uhr *f* clock
Uhrglasschale *f* watch glass dish
Uhrmacherdrehmaschine *f* watch and instrument maker's lathe
Uhrzeigersinn *m* **1.** *(allg.)* clockwise direction **2.** *(im Uhrzeigersinn)* clockwise

3. *(gegen Uhrzeigersinn)* anti-clockwise, counterclockwise
Uhrzeit *f* time, time of day
Ulltraschallbohren *nt* ultrasonic drilling
Ultraschall *m* ultrasonic
Ultraschallanzeige *f* ultrasonic indication
Ultraschallbohrer *m* ultrasonic drill
Ultraschallbohrmaschine *f* ultrasonic drilling machine
Ultraschallimpuls *m* ultrasonic pulse
Ultraschallimpulsechogerät *nt* ultrasonic pulse-echo instrument
Ultraschallprüfgerät *nt* ultrasonic testing instrument
Ultraschallschwingläppen (USM) *nt* ultrasonic swing lapping
Ultraschallstoßläppen *nt* ultrasonic joint lapping
Ultraschallwarmschweißen *nt* ultrasonic hot welding
Ultraschallzerspanung *f* ultrasonic machining
Ultraviolettstrahler *m* ultra-violet radiation source
Ultraviolettstreulicht *nt* ultra-violet scattered light
um ... Grad *m* by ... degrees
um den Faktor *m* by the factor
Umarbeiten *nt* modify, rework
Umbau *m* 1. *(allg.)* conversion, modification, redesign, reconstruction 2. *(Modernisierung)* rebuilding
Umbauarbeiten *fpl* conversion work
umbauen 1. *(allg.)* convert, modify, reconstruct 2. *(modernisieren)* rebuild
Umbauungsgrad *m* degree of rebuilding, degree od changing
umbördeln bead, flange, border, crimp, roll
Umbördelung *f* bead
umdrehen make a U-turn, turn (over), upturn, flip, reverse
Umdrehung *f* revolution, turn, rotation
Umdrehung *f* **pro Minute** *f* revolutions per minute (rpm)
Umdrehungszahl *f* number of revolutions, speed, number of revolutions per minute (rpm)

Umdrehungszähler *m* revolution counter
Umfang *m* periphery
Umfang *m* 1. *(Ausmaß)* dimension, size, extent 2. *(Fassungsvermögen)* capacity 3. *(Kontur)* contour, outline 4. *(Kreis)* circumference 5. *(Lieferung)* scope 6. *(Maße)* perimeter 7. *(Menge)* volume 8. *(Stichproben)* size
Umfangeinstechschleifen *nt* peripheral plunge grinding
umfangreich ample, voluminous
Umfangschleifen *nt* peripheral grinding, circumferential grinding
Umfangschneide *f* peripheral cutting edge
Umfangschneidenwinkel *m* peripheral cutting edge angle
Umfangsfläche *f* circumferential surface
Umfangsfräsen *nt* peripheral milling
Umfangsgeschwindigkeit *f* circumferential speed, peripheral velocity (or speed)
Umfangskraft *f* peripheral force
Umfangslänge *f* peripheral length
Umfangslinie *f* circumferential line
Umfangsrichtung *f* circumferential direction
Umfangsschleifrad *nt* straight grinding wheel
Umfangsschliff *m* peripheral grinding
Umfangsschneiden *nt* peripheral cutting edges
Umfangswälzfräsen *nt* peripheral milling
Umfangszähne *f* teeth on the periphery
umfassen 1. *(allg.)* comprehend, include, comprise 2. *(einschließen)* encircle 3. *(umklammern)* embrace
Umfassungswinkel *m* contact angle
Umfeld *nt* environment
Umfeldbedingungen *fpl* environmental conditions
umflochtener Schlauch *m* braided hose
Umformarbeit *f* forming work
Umformatierung *f* re-formatting
umformen 1. *(el.)* convert, transform

2. *(maschinell)* form **3.** *(wiederformen)* reshape
Umformer *m* *(Signale)* transformer
Umformgeschwindigkeit *f* forming speed
Umformgrade *mpl* natural strains
Umformkräfte *fpl* forming forces
Umformleistung *f* forming power
Umformmaschine *f* forming machine
Umformtechnik *f* forming technology
Umformung *f* conversion, transformation, metal-forming
Umformvorgang *m* forming process
Umformwiderstand *m* forming resistance
umgeben encircle, environ, surround
Umgebung *f* **1.** *(allg.)* environment **2.** *(Gegend)* surrounding **3.** *(Nähe)* vicinity **4.** *(Raum)* neighbourhood, ambiance
Umgebungsbedingung *f* environmental condition, ambient condition
Umgebungsdruck *m* atmosphere pressure
Umgebungseinfluss *m* environmental influence
Umgebungsmedium *nt* surrounding medium
Umgebungsklima *nt* ambient atmosphere
Umgebungskorrektur *f* environmental correction
Umgebungsluft *f* surrounding air
Umgebungstemperatur *f* ambient temperature
umgehbar capable of being bypassed
umgehen 1. *(el.)* bypass **2.** *(überspringen)* override **3.** *(vermeiden)* avoid
Umgehung *f* bypass
Umgehungsleitung *f* bypass (feeder), bypass line
Umgehungsschalter *m* shunt switch, override switch
umgekehrt inverse, contrary, reverse, vice versa
umgekehrt proportional inversely proportional
umgekehrtes Vorzeichen *nt* opposite sign

umgestalten modify
Umgestaltung *f* redesign
umgreifen 1. *(allg.)* encompass **2.** *(mit den Händen)* access from behind, reach around
umgrenzen 1. *(allg.)* circumscribe, limit, define **2.** *(umgeben)* surround
umgrenzend surrounding
Umgrenzung *f* boundary
Umgrenzung *f* **des lichten Raumes** clearance gauge
Umgrenzungsprofil *nt* loading gauge
umhüllen 1. *(allg.)* envelop, cover, jacket **2.** *(Kabel)* sheath **3.** *(Überzug)* coat **4.** *(Verpackung)* wrap, sleeve
umhüllt wrapped, coated
umhüllter Schweißdraht *m* covered filler wire
Umhüllung *f* **1.** *(allg.)* coating, cover **2.** *(Kabel)* sheathing **3.** *(Schutz)* guard **4.** *(Verkleidung)* shell, case **5.** *(Verpackung)* sleeve, wrapping
Umhüllungsfolie *f* wrapping film, wrapping foil
Umhüllungsmaschine *f* sleeving machine, wrapping machine
Umhüllungsmasse *f* covering material (or compound)
Umhüllungsvariante *f* wrapping pattern
Umhüllungswiderstand *m* *(e. Elektrode)* envelope resistance
Umkehr *f* reverse, reversal, return
umkehrbar reversible
umkehren return, reverse
umkehren reverse, invert
Umkehrspanne *f* hysteresis
Umkehrspiel *nt* backlash
Umkehrung *f* reversion, reversing, reversal
Umkehrwalzgerüst *nt* reversing mill stand
umkippen overturn, turn over, tip over, tip, topple over, upset, tilt, cant
Umkippfestigkeit *f* resistance to overturning
umklammern clip, clasp, clutch, embrace
umkonstruieren redesign
Umkreis *m* perimeter

Umladeelement *nt* transfer element
umladen transfer, transship, unload and reload
Umladestelle *f* transfer station
Umladevorrichtung *f* transshipping device
Umladung *f* 1. *(Material)* transfer, transshipment, reload 2. *(el.)* charge reversal
Umladungseinheit *f* transfer unit
Umlage *f* apportionment of costs, proportionate costs, contribution, allocation, charge
umlagern redeposit, redeposition
Umlagerung *f* redepositing, repositioning
Umlauf *m* cycle, gyration
Umlaufbestand *m* work in progress (WIP), work in progress inventory, WIP inventory
Umlaufbewegung *f* rotary movement, rotation
Umlaufbiegen *nt* rotary straightening
Umlaufdurchmesser *m* swing
umlaufen rotate, spin, revolve, circulate, gyrate, turn (around)
umlaufen (~ lassen) circulate
umlaufend circulating, circulatory, continuous, rotating, rotary, revolving
umlaufende Kehlnaht *f* circumferential fillet joint
umlaufende Körnerspitze *f* live centre
umlaufende Spitze *f* live centre
umlauffähig with complete rotatability, completely rotatable
Umlaufförderer *m* fixed tray conveyor, circulating conveyor
Umlauffräsen *nt* profile milling, profiling
Umlaufgaswasserheizer *m* circulatory type gas water heater
Umlaufgeschwindigkeit *f* rotational speed, circulation speed
Umlaufgetriebezug *m* epicycloidal gear train, planetary gear train
Umlaufhärten *nt* spin hardening
Umlauflager *nt* circulation storage system
Umlaufleitung *f* bypass pipe

Umlaufpalettenstretchwickler *m* fixed pallet stretch wrapper (or stretch-wrapper)
Umlaufrad *nt* epicyclic gear, planet gear
Umlaufregal *nt* horizontal carousel
Umlaufregallager *nt* 1. *(allg.)* horizontal carousel store 2. *(vertikales ~)* vertical horizontal carousel store
Umlaufschmieranlage *f* circulating lubricating system
Umlaufstation *f* rotary station
Umlaufthermostat *nt* circulation thermostat
Umlaufvorschubhärten *nt* spin-progressive hardening
Umlaufwasserheizer *m* circulating type water heater
Umlaufzeit *f* cycle time, turnaround time
umlegen apportion, allocate, distribute
Umlegung *f* apportionment, allocation, distribution
umleiten 1. *(Daten)* reroute 2. *(Verkehr)* bypass, divert 3. *(Warensendung)* reconsign, redirect
Umleitung *f* 1. *(Verkehr)* diversion 2. *(Warensendung)* reconsignment
Umlenkantenne *f* repeater antenna
Umlenkblech *nt* 1. *(allg.)* deflector, baffle plate 2. *(Leitblech)* guide plate
umlenken deflect, deviate
Umlenkrad *nt* deflection pulley, deflection sheave, return sheave, reversing wheel
Umlenkspiegel *m* deflection mirror, tilted mirror
Umlenkung *f* direction change
Umlenkung *f* **der Handelsströme** deflection of trade
Umlenkungsmechanismus *m* deflection mechanism
Umlenkzunge *f* deflector blade
Umluftbetrieb *m* recirculating air operation
Umlüftung *f* recirculation ventilation
ummanteln 1. *(allg.)* sheath, encase, cover, jacket 2. *(Kabel)* coat, sheath 3. *(Maschine)* (en)case
ummantelt sheathed
ummantelter Schlauch *m* sheathed

hose
Ummantelung *f* encasement, encasing, jacket, sheathing, case, housing, surround
Ummantelungsbeton *m* concrete for a surround
umnummerieren renumber
umordnen rearrange, reorder
umpacken repack
Umpalettieren *nt* repalletizing
umplanen re-schedule
umpolen change poles, commutate, reverse the polarity of
Umpolung *f* (pole) reversal, pole-changing
umprogrammierbar reprogrammable
umprogrammieren reprogram
Umprogrammierung *f* reprogramming
Umrechnung *f* conversion
Umrechnungsformel *f* conversion formula
umreifen 1. *(allg.)* strap **2.** *(Fässer)* hoop
Umreifung *f* **1.** *(allg.)* strapping **2.** *(Fässer)* hoop-casing
Umreifungsanlage *f* strapping plant
Umreifungsband *nt* **1.** *(allg.)* (tightening) strap, tensional strapping **2.** *(Fässer)* hoop
Umreifungskopf *m* strapping head
Umreifungsverschließmaschine *f* **1.** *(allg.)* strapping machine **2.** *(Fässer)* hoop-casing machine
umrichten reset
Umrichter *m* **1.** *(allg. el.)* (frequency) converter **2.** *(Gleichrichter)* d.c. voltage changer **3.** *(Maschine)* static frequency changer
Umrichtezeit *f* resetting time, setting time, set-up time
Umriss *m* contour, outline, configurations, shape
Umrissbohren *nt* contour boring
Umrissdrehen *nt* contour turning
umrissfräsen contour-mill
Umrissfräsen *nt* contour milling, contouring profile milling
Umrissfräsmaschine *f* contour milling machine

Umrissfräsverfahren *nt* contour milling method
Umrissfühler *m* counter tracer
Umrissfühlersteuerung *f* contouring tracer control
Umrisshobeln *nt* contour planing
Umrisskopieren *nt* contouring, contour copying profiling
Umrisskopiervorrichtung *f* profile tracer attachment
Umrissnachformfräsmaschine *f* profile milling machine (with two-dimensional control), profile miller, profiler, contour milling machine
Umrissnachformfräsmaschine *f* **mit Fühlersteuerung** tracer-controlled profile milling machine (with two-dimensional control), tracer-controlled profiler
Umrissnachformhobelmaschine *f* contour shaper
Umrissnachformhobeln *nt* contour planing
umrüsten convert, retool, reset, retrofit, tool change over
Umrüstsatz *m* conversion kit, conversion set
Umrüstung *f* **1.** *(allg.)* changeover, change of attachment, conversion, reset(ting) **2.** *(für andere Seite)* changeover and resetting
Umrüstzeit *f* reset time, changeover time
Umsatz *m* sales volume, turnover
umschalten 1. *(el.)* switch over **2.** *(Getriebe)* change gears **3.** *(Hebel)* change over **4.** *(Revolverkopf)* revolve, index **5.** *(Riemen, Gang)* shift **6.** *(Schalter, Hebel)* change over, switching **7.** *(Signalflusswege)* re-direct (a signal flow path) **8.** *(Tisch, Spindel)* reverse **9.** *(umkehren)* reverse **10.** *(Revolverkopf)* index
Umschalter *m* **1.** *(allg.)* change-over switch, commutator, reversing switch, alternation switch **2.** *(Regelschalter)* switchgroup
Umschaltfrequenz *f* switching frequency, switching rate, commutating frequency

Umschaltgenauigkeit f indexing accuracy
Umschalthebel m reversing lever
Umschalttor nt change-over gate
Umschaltverzögerung f deceleration by pole-changing
Umschaltvolumen nt changing volume
Umschaltweg m distance travelled during speed change
Umschaltzeit f transit time
Umschaltzeit f **von schneller zu langsamer Geschwindigkeit** fast/slow speed switching time, switching time from fast to slow speed
Umschlag m **1.** *(Betriebswirtschaft)* turnover **2.** *(Material)* handling, transshipment, amount of goods handled
Umschlag m **und Lagerung** rehandling and storage
Umschlag m **und Spedition** rehandling and forwarding
Umschlagbohren nt shift drilling
umschlagen 1. *(allg.)* handle, rehandle, transship **2.** *(Betriebswirtschaft)* transact **3.** *(Gegenbewegung gehen)* go into reverse
Umschlaggreifer m rehandling grab
Umschlaglager nt transshipment warehouse
Umschlagplatz m place of transshipment
Umschlagpunkt m transshipment point
Umschlagshäufigkeit f
1. *(Betriebswirtschaft)* rate of turnover
2. *(Eigenkapital)* rate of equity turnover
3. *(Warenbestand)* rate of inventory turnover, inventory sales ratio
Umschlagskennzahlen fpl turnover ratios
Umschlagsleistung f turnover performance, turnover capacity, handling rate, throughput
Umschlagslogistik f transshipment logistics
Umschlagverfahren nt shift (milling) method
Umschlagverkehr m transshipment traffic

Umschlagzeit f **1.** *(Waren)* replacement period **2.** *(Relais)* change-over time, transit time
Umschleifen nt planetary grinding
umschließen enclose
umschlingen 1. *(allg.)* enlace, enfold, entangle, loop, twine, wrap (around) **2.** *(Schrumpffolie)* shrink-wrap **3.** *(verdrehen, verflechten)* twist
Umschlingung f enlacement
Umschlingungswinkel m **1.** *(allg.)* circumferential angle, angle of wrap **2.** *(Maschine)* angle of (belt) contact, *(US)* belt wrap
umschmelzen melt up
umschnüren tie up, hoop, lace
Umschnürung f tying, hooping, lacing
Umsetzbrücke f transfer car
Umsetzbrückenverriegelung f transfer car interlock
Umsetzeinrichtung f transfer device, transfer facility, transfer unit
umsetzen 1. *(Waren, Material)* transfer, shift, transform **2.** *(Betriebswirtschaft)* sell **3.** *(el.)* convert
Umsetzen nt transfer, aisle-to-aisle transfer
Umsetzer m **1.** *(Waren, Material)* transfer element, shifter, director **2.** *(el.)* converter
Umsetzgang m transfer aisle
Umsetzprogramm nt conversion program
Umsetzregal nt transfer system
Umsetzstation f **1.** *(allg.)* transfer station **2.** *(Maschine)* reversing station
Umsetzung f **1.** *(allg.)* transfer, shift(ing) **2.** *(el.)* conversion
Umsetzvorgang m shifting process, transfer move
Umsetzzeit f transfer time
umspannen 1. *(Werkzeuge)* reset, rechuck, relocate, span **2.** *(el.)* transform
Umspannung f **1.** *(allg.)* resetting, relocation **2.** *(e. Arbeitsstückes)* rechucking, re-loading, reclamping, resetting
Umspannvorrichtung f rechucking appliance
umstapeln 1. *(allg.)* restack

2. *(Paletten)* depalletize
Umstapelvorgang *m* **1.** *(allg.)* restacking move **2.** *(Paletten)* depalletizing process
Umstapelzeit *f* **1.** *(allg.)* restacking time **2.** *(Paletten)* cycle time
Umsteckrad *nt* loose change gear, pick-off gear
Umstellbrandkessel *m* convertible-fuel boiler
umstellen (auf) 1. *(allg.)* adapt, change over, convert (to) **2.** *(räuml.)* relocate **3.** *(schalten)* switch (to) **4.** *(Werkzeug)* retool
Umstellung *f* **1.** *(allg.)* adaptation, changeover, conversion **2.** *(räuml.)* relocation
Umstellzeit *f* changeover time, adaptation time
umstempeln restamp
Umstempelung *f* restamping
umsteuerbar reversible
Umsteuerhebel *m* reversing lever
Umsteuerknagge *f* reverse dog
umsteuern reverse
Umsteuern *nt* **der Vorschubrichtung** feed reverse control
Umsteuerschalter *m* **für den Spindelmotor** spindle motor reversing switch
Umsteuerung *f* reversal, reversing traverse
Umsteuerung *f* **im Eilrücklauf** rapid reverse
Umsteuerventil *nt* change-over valve
umstürzen 1. *(allg.)* overturn, tip over, tip, turn over, upset **2.** *(Verpackung)* roll
umwälzen circulate (in closed circuit)
Umwälzpumpe *f* circulation pump
Umwälzzahl *f* circulation index
umwandeln convert (into), transform (into), commute (into)
Umwandeln *nt* **in der Bainitstufe** transforming in the austempering region
Umwandler *m* **1.** *(Energie, Signale)* transducer **2.** *(Frequenzen, Strom)* converter
Umwandlung *f* conversion
Umwandlungsgetriebe *nt* translating gears

Umwandlungsneigung *f* tendency to transformation
Umwandlungsverhalten *nt* transformation behaviour
umwehren enclose, guard, protect
Umwehrung *f* (perimeter) enclosure, guards, protection device, protector, screening, guarding
Umwelt *f* environment
Umweltbedingungen *fpl* environmental conditions (or circumstances)
Umweltbelastung *f* environmental stresses (pl)
Umwelteinflüsse *f* environmental influences
Umwelteinflussgröße *f* environmental parameter
Umweltprüfverfahren *nt* environmental test procedure
Umweltschutz *m* environmental protection
Umwertungsbeziehung *f* conversion relationship
Umwertungstreuband *nt* conversion scatter band
Umwickelmaschine *f* wrapping machine
umwickeln (stretch) wrap (around)
Umwindungsgarn *nt* core spun yarn
umzäunen enclose, guard, fence (in)
Umzäunung *f* (perimeter) enclosure, (perimeter) guards, fence, fencing
umzeichnen redraw
unabhängig independent, self-contained, irrespective (of)
unabsperrbares Ausdehnungsgefäß *nt* expansion tank without shut-off facility
unangemessen undue
unangepasst maladjusted, unadjusted, inadequate
unauffälliger Fehler *m* unobtrusive defect
unauffälliger Kratzer *m* unobtrusive scratch
unaufgefordert unrequested, unsolicited
unausgeglichen unbalanced
unbeabsichtigt inadvertent, unintended, unintentional

unbearbeitet unmachined, unfinished
unbearbeitete Tafel *f* **aus Kunstharzpressholz** untreated sheet of resin-bonded densified laminated wood
unbearbeitetes Werkstück *nt* unmachined work, rough work
unbeaufsichtigt unattended, supervised
unbedingt unconditional
unbedingter Sprung *m* unconditional jump
unbefestigt unfortified, unsecured, unimproved
unbefestigter Boden *m* unimproved natural terrain
unbefugt unauthorized
unbefugtes Benutzen *nt* unauthorized use
unbefugtes Betreten *nt* unauthorized access
unbegrenzt unlimited
unbehandelt untreated
unbeladen empty, unladen
unbelastet 1. (Kraft) unloaded, not under load 2. (entspannt) unstressed 3. (Motoren) on no-load, off-load
unbelasteter Zustand *m* no-load condition, unloaded state
unbelastetes Getriebe *nt* unloaded gear transmission
unbelichtet unexposed
unbemaßt undimensioned
unberücksichtigt unconsidered, ignored
unberücksichtigt lassen discount, ignore, neglect
unbeschaltet blank, unwired
unbeschichtet uncoated
unbeschichtete Oberfläche *f* uncoated surface
unbeschnittenes Blatt *nt* untrimmed sheet
unbeständig unstable
unbeweglich immovable
unbewegliche Annietmutter *f* non-floating rivet nut
unbewertet unweighted
Unbrauchbarwerden *nt* **des Werkzeugs** tool failure
UND *Abk* AND

UND-Abhängigkeit *f* AND dependency
undeutlich machen *(e. Darstellung)* detract from the clarity
UND-Gatter *nt* AND-gate
UND-Glied *nt* **mit einem dynamischen Eingang** AND element with one dynamic input
UND-Glied *nt* **mit Negation eines Eingangs** AND with one input negated
UND-Glied *nt* **mit negiertem Ausgang** AND with negated output
undicht leaking, leaky, untight
undicht sein leak
Undichtheit *f* leakage, leakiness, escape
Undichtwerden *nt* leaking
UND-Schaltkreis *m* AND circuit
UND-Schaltung *f* AND element, AND gate
undurchführbar impracticable, unfeasible
UND-Verknüpfung *f* AND relation, AND gating
uneben 1. *(Oberfläche allg.)* unequal, uneven, unlevel 2. *(höckrig, wellig)* rough 3. *(löchrig)* pitted
Unebenheit *f* 1. *(allg.)* out-of-flatness, unevenness, inequality 2. *(einzelne)* dent, depression, pit
uneingeschränkt unrestricted, without restrictions
unempfindlich insensitive, indifferent, immune
Unempfindlichkeit *f* insensitivity, immunity
Unempfindlichkeit *f* **gegen Störungen** interference immunity
Unempfindlichkeitsbereich *m* dead zone
Unempfindlichkeitsprüfung *f* immunity test
unendlicher Wert *m* infinite value
unerwartet unexpected
unerwünscht undesirable
unfachgemäß inexpert
Unfall *m* accident
Unfallforschung *f* accident research
Unfallgefahr *f* risk of accident
Unfallgefährdung *f* accident hazard
Unfallschutz *m* accident protection

Unfallverhütung *f* accident prevention, prevention of accidents
Unfallverhütungsvorschriften *fpl* accident prevention regulations, regulations for the prevention of industrial accidents
ungealtert unaged
ungealterte Probe *f* unaged test specimen
ungebändigte Wärme *f* unrestrained heat
ungedehnter Zustand *m* unstretched condition
ungeeignet unsuitable, unfit, improper, inappropriate, inadequate
ungefährlich harmless
ungefährlich machen render safe
Ungefährmaß *nt* approximate size, approximate dimension
ungefedert non-sprung, unsprung
ungefederte Massen *fpl* unsprung weight
ungeformter Kunststoff *m* unmoulded plastics
ungehindert unhampered, unimpeded, unobstructed, unobstructedly
ungehinderter Durchtritt *m* free passage
ungekapselt without casing
ungekerbte Flachprobe *f* non-reduced section flat specimen
ungeknotete Probe *f* unknotted specimen
ungekürzte Zahnköpfe *mpl* unrelieved (or non-relieved) tooth tips
ungeleimte Cellulosefasern *fpl* unsized cellulose fibres
ungelernt unskilled
ungelöstes Material *nt* undissolved material
ungemahlener Rohstoff *m* unbeaten raw material
ungenau inaccurate, untrue
Ungenauigkeit *f* inaccuracy
ungenügend insufficient, deficient
ungenügende Fugenfüllung *f* underfill
ungeordnet unordered, inordinate, random
ungeordnet rilliger Oberflächencharakter *m* non-systematically grooved surface character
ungeordnete Fasern *fpl* unarranged fibres (pl)
ungepaart unpaired
ungepackt unpacked
ungepuffert unbuffered
ungerade odd, uneven, unlevel, out of truth
ungerade Zahl *f* odd number
Ungeradeglied *nt* odd
ungeregelt uncontrolled, unregulated, open-loop
ungerichtet non-directional, omnidirectional, undirected
ungesättigte Verbindung *f* unsaturate
ungesättigtes Polyesterharz *nt* unsaturated polyester resin
ungeschertes Öl *nt* unsheared oil
ungeschichtete Probenahme *f* simple random sampling
ungeschult untrained
ungeschützt exposed, unguarded, unprotected
ungeschwächte Strahlung *f* unattenuated radiation
ungesichert unsecured
ungesicherte Stoßfuge *f* unsecured butt joint
ungespannt loose, slack
ungespanntes Trumm *nt* slack side of a belt, slack span
ungestrecktes Harnstoffharz *nt* unextended urea resin
ungesund unhealthy
ungewellte Federscheibe *f* uncorrugated spring washer
ungewölbte Federscheibe *f* undished spring washer
unglasierte Fliese *f* unglazed ceramic tile
ungleich different, unequal
ungleiche Teilung *f* increment cut, irregular spacing
ungleiche Zeit *f* unequal period
ungleiches Teilen *nt* unequal spacing
Ungleichheit *f* irregularity, inequality
ungleichmäßig 1. *(ungleichförmig)* irregular, non-uniform **2.** *(uneben)* un-

even
Ungleichmäßigkeit *f* inconsistency
Ungleichmäßigkeitskoeffizient *m* irregularity coefficient
ungleichnamige Zahnflanken *fpl* opposite flanks
Ungleichschenkligkeit *f* unequal leg length
Ungleichwandigkeit *f* non-uniformity of wall thickness
Ungleichwinkligkeit *f* variation from equiangularity, unequal angularity
ungültig invalid, not applicable (n.a.)
ungültig werden be invalidated
Ungültigkeit *f* invalidity
ungünstig 1. *(allg.)* unfavourable *(Steigerung: least favourable)* **2.** *(Wetter)* contrary
ungehüllte Stabelektrode *f* covered rod electrode, covered cast-core electrode
Unhüllungsrückstände *mpl* covering residues
unidirektional unidirectional
unimodal unimodal
unimodale Verteilung *f* unimodal distribution
universal universal, all-purpose
Universalbohr- und Fräsmaschine *f* universal boring and milling machine
Universalbohr- und Fräsmaschine *f* **mit schwenkbarem Spindelkasten und drehbarem Ständer** universal boring drilling and milling machine with swivelling spindle head and rotary column
Universalbohrmeißel *m* universal boring tool
Universaldrehmaschine *f* universal lathe, general-purpose lathe
Universalfeinbohrwerk *nt* universal precision boring machine
Universalfräskopf *m* universal milling head, universal cutter head, universal hobbing head
Universalfräsmaschine *f* universal milling machine, universal miller, universal knee-and-column type milling machine
Universalfräsmaschine *f* **mit zwei Paaren einander gegenüberstehender Frässpindelköpfe** universal double-duplex milling machine
Universalfrässupport *m* universal milling attachment, universal-type spindle head
Universalfräsvorrichtung *f* universal head-milling attachment
Universalfräsvorrichtung *f* *(für Spiralfräsarbeiten)* universal spiral indexing attachment
Universalfutter *nt* concentric chuck, universal gear scroll chuck, self-centring chuck, universal chuck
Universalgewindefräsmaschine *f* universal thread milling attachment
Universalgravier- und Nachformfräsmaschine *f* universal engraving and duplicating machine
Universalhobelmaschine *f* *(Vor- und Rücklaufschlitten)* universal planer for two-way cutting
Universalkonsolfräsmaschine *f* universal-type knee-and-column milling machine, universal knee- and column (type) milling machine, universal milling machine, universal miller
Universalläppmaschine *f* universal lapping machine
Universalmaschine *f* universal machine, general-purpose machine
Universalmotor *m* series motor, universal motor
Universalnachformfräsmaschine *f* universal pantograph die-sinking machine
Universalnietverbindung *f* universal rivet joint
Universalpantographgesenkfräsmaschine *f* universal pantograph die-sinking machine, universal pantograph die-sinker, universal pantograph machine
Universalrundschleifmaschine *f* universal cylindrical grinder
Universalsattelrevolverdrehmaschine *f* universal ram-type turret lathe
Universalschnellfräsapparat *m* high-speed universal milling attachment
Universalschnellfräsmaschine *f* uni-

versal high speed milling machine
Universalschriftengravierfräsmaschine *f* universal letter engraving machine
Universalspindelkopf *m* swivelling attachment
Universal-Spitzendrehmaschine *f* universal centre lathe, universal centre lathe
Universalständerfräsmaschine *f* universal knee-and-column type milling machine
Universalteilgerät *nt* universal index centre
Universalteilkopf *m* universal dividing head
Universalwerkzeug *nt* general utility tool
Universalwerkzeug- und Gesenkfräsmaschine *f* universal tool milling machine and die-sinker
Universalwerkzeugfräs- und Bohrmaschine *f* universal tool milling and boring machine
Universalwerkzeugfräsmaschine *f* universal tool milling machine
Universalwerkzeugschleifmaschine *f* universal cutter and tool grinding machine
Universalwinkelfräskopf universal angular milling attachment
universeller asynchroner Send-/Empfangsbaustein *m* universal asynchronous receiver/transmitter (UART)
universeller serieller Bus *m* universal serial bus (USB)
unkaschierte Kunststofffolie *f* unlaminated plastics foil
unkontrolliert uncontrolled
unkritisch uncritical
unlegierter Kohlenstoffstahl *m* plain carbon steel
unlösbar verbinden *(Teile zu einer Gruppe)* connect together non-demountably
unlösbare Verbindung *f* permanent joint
unmagnetisch non-magnetic
unmittelbare Sicherheitstechnik *f* safety practice through intrinsic design

unmittelbare Wirkung *f* direct effect
unnötig unnecessary
Unparallelität *f* non-parallelism (or parallelity), out-of-parallelism
unparteiische Probenahme *f* impartial sampling
unperiodische Schwingbeanspruchung *f* aperiodic fluctuating stress
unpolarisiert non-polarized
unquittiert unacknowledged
Unregelmäßigkeit *f* irregularity
unreine Luft *f* polluted air
unrichtig incorrect
unrund untrue, out of truth, out of round
unrundes Rad *nt* non-round gear
Unrundheit *f* lack of roundness, out-of-roundness, non-circularity
Unrundlauf *m* runout, untrue running
unrund laufend untrue-running
unsachgemäße Behandlung *f* mishandling
unsachgemäßer Gebrauch *m* misuse
unsachgemäßes Verhalten *nt* incorrect behaviour
unsauberer Schliff *m* poor grinding cut
Unsauberkeit *f (e. Oberfläche)* surface fuzz
unschädlich unharmful
unschädlich machen render harmless
unscharf 1. *(undeutlich, verschwommen)* indistinct **2.** *(opt.)* blurred, fuzzy **3.** *(stumpf)* blunt, dull, edgeless
Unschärfe *f* blur, fuzziness, lack of focus, lack of definition
unscharfe Menge *f* fuzzy set
unsicher uncertain, unstable
Unsicherheit *f* uncertainty
Unsicherheitsfaktor *m* uncertainty factor
Unsicherheitsspanne *f* uncertainty margin
unsichtbare Kante *f* hidden edge
unsortierte Zellstoffe *f* unscreened pulp
unstabil instable, unstable
Unstarrheit *f* instability
unstetig discontinuous, non-continuous
unstetig wirkendes Glied *nt* discon-

tinuous acting element
unstetiger Übergang *m* discontinuous transition
Unstetigförderer *m* non-continuous conveyor
Unstetigkeitsgebiet *nt* nonsteady region
unsulfonierbar unsulphonated
Unsymmetriegröße *f* non-symmetrical quantity
unsymmetrische Nahtvorbereitung *f* asymmetric edge preparation
unteilbar indivisible
unten 1. *(allg.)* below, under(neath) **2.** *(Gebäude)* downstairs **3.** *(Gefäße)* at the bottom
unten fahrend driving below
unten laufend floor running
Untenpalettierer *m* low infeed palletizer
unter 1. *(unterhalb)* below **2.** *(räuml.)* under **3.** *(Werte)* less than
unter Beibehaltung von whilst maintaining
unter Druck pressurized
unter Druck setzen impart pressure
unter Druck setzen pressurize
unter Eigenlast in the unladen state
Unter... bottom
Unterbau *m* base frame, substructure
unterbauen bolster, brace, jack, pack, shim
Unterbauung *f* packing
Unterbodeneinrichtung *f* underfloor service
Unterbodenmelioration *f* B-horizon
Unterbrandofen *m* under-burning stove
unterbrechen 1. *(allg.)* intermit, interrupt, cut off, discontinue **2.** *(e. Stromkreis)* break, disconnect
Unterbrechung *f* interruption, break
unterbrechungsfrei uninterruptible
unterbrechungsfreie Stromversorgung *f* uninterruptible lower supply
unterbringen accommodate, house, place, store
Unterbringung *f* storage, accommodation
unterbrochen gezeichnetes Teil *nt* part (or component) shown with break lines
unterbrochene Fuge *f* discontinuous joint
unterbrochene Kehlnaht *f* interrupted fillet weld
unterbrochene Kehlnaht *f* **mit Vormaß** intermittent fillet joint with end distance
unterbrochene Schneide *f* interrupted cutting edge
unterbrochene Zustellung *f* incremental infeed
unterbrochener radialer Tischvorschub *m* incremental radial infeed
unterbrochener Schnitt *m* intermitted (or interrupted) cut
unterbrochenes Härten *nt* interrupted hardening
Unterdruckförderer *m* vacuum conveyor
Unterdruck *m* depression, low pressure, negative pressure, suction, underpressure, (partial) vacuum
Unterdruckabfall *m* negative pressure drop
Unterdruckanlage *f* negative pressure attachment
Unterdruckanzeige *f* underpressure indicator
Unterdruckbereich *m* negative pressure region
unterdrücken suppress
Unterdruckerzeugung *f* generation of underpressure
Unterdruckfüllmaschine *f* vacuum filling machine
Unterdruckmesser *m* vacuum pressure gauge
Unterdrucksetzung *f* pressurization
Unterdrückung *f* suppression
Unterdrückungsbereich *m* suppressed range
Unterdruckventil *nt* suction relief valve
untere Endstellung *f* bottom limit
untere Explosionsgrenze (UEG) *f* lower explosion limit (LEL)
untere und obere Anschrägung *f* blade taper

untere/r/s lower
Unterelement *nt* subelement
unterer Gabelhaken *m* bottom hook
unterer Seitenbereich *m (e. Toleranzfeldes)* lower side band
unterer Teil *m* lower part
unteres Ende *nt* bottom
unterfahrbare Palette *f* general purpose pallet
unterfahren drive under, underpin
Unterfahrhöhe *f* underclearance
Unterfahrtechnik *f* underclearance method
Unterfahrwagen *m* drive-under truck
Unterflansch *m* bottom flange
Unterflur ... floor-mounted, underfloor
Unterflurschleppkettenförderer *m* single-strand floor-mounted truck conveyor, underfloor chain-pulled conveyor
Unterflurförderanlage *f* floor-mounted conveying system, underfloor conveying system
Unterflurförderer *m* floor-mounted truck conveyor
Unterflurkettenförderer *m* underfloor chain conveyor
Unterflurschleppförderer *m* underfloor drag conveyor
Unterfolienform-, -füll- und -verschließmaschine *f* lower reel low wrapping machine
Untergesenk *nt* bottom die
Untergestell *nt* base
untergliedern partition
Untergliederung *f* subdivision, partition
untergreifen reach under, access from beneath
Untergriff *m* undercut
Untergrund *m* **1.** *(allg.)* subsoil, subgrade, surface, underground, underlay **2.** *(e. Werkstoffes)* base material, basis, substrate (material) **3.** *(Farben)* ground
Untergrundbehandlung *f* treatment of base material
Untergrundfarbe *f* ground colour
Untergruppe *f* subgroup, subordinate group, subassembly
unterhalb below, underneath, downstream

Unterhaltungskosten *pl* maintenance costs
unterirdischer Röhrengasbehälter *m* underground tubular gasholder
Unterkante *f* bottom edge, lower edge, bottom surface, lower surface
Unterkasten *m* under cast, under box
Unterkonstruktion *f* substructure
unterkühlt cooled to extremely low temperatures
Unterlage *f* **1.** *(Bauteil)* base, bed, pad, support, plate, bedding layer, backing, back-up **2.** *(Dokumentation)* document **3.** *(Verstärkung)* backing **4.** *(Zwischenlage)* spacer
Unterlager *nt* stock-sub-location, lower bed
unterlagert 1. *(allg.)* supported **2.** *(el.)* secondary **3.** *(Regeln)* subsidiary
Unterlagsschaumstoff *m* foam lining material
Unterlagsstoff *m* backing material
Unterlagsblech *nt* spacer, backing plate
Unterlegeblock *m* packing block
Unterlegeklotz *m* block
unterlegen pack (with), put under, underlay, lay underneath, bolster, shim
Unterlegplatte *f* spacer, shim
Unterlegscheibe *f* (plain) washer, packing shim, grommet
Unterlegscheibe *f* **für die Mutter** bolt washer
Unterlegstreifen *m* backing strip, liner
Unterlegstück *nt* shim
Unterlegteil *nt* washer component
unterliegen subject
Untermaß *nt* undersize
Untermenge *f* subset
Untermischverfahren *nt* preliminary mixing process
Unternehmen *nt* enterprise, company
Unternehmensleitebene *f* management level
Unternehmensorganisation *f* corporate organization
Unternehmenspolitik *f* company policy
unternehmenspolitisch company policy
unternehmensspezifisch company-

specific
unternehmensübergreifend multiplant, supra-plant, inter-plant
Unterprogramm *nt* subroutine, subprogram, macro
Unterpulververbindungsschweißen *nt* submerged arc joint welding
unterrichten instruct
Unterrostung *f* under-rusting
untersagen forbid, prohibit
untersagt forbidden, prohibit
unterscheiden discriminate (between), distinguish, differentiate (between), differ (from), vary
Unterscheidung *f* nosing depth
Unterschicht *f* backing
Unterschichtprobe *f* lower layer sample
Unterschieber *m* bottom slide
Unterschied *m* difference
unterschiedlich varying
Unterschiedsmessung *f* differential measurement
Unterschleifung *f* undergrinding
Unterschlitten *m* cross slide, saddle, base slide
unterschneiden undercut
Unterschneidung *f* 1. *(konstr.)* drip mould, drip nose 2. *(Schnitt)* undercut 3. *(Stufe)* projection of tread
Unterschnitt *m* cutter interference, undercut
unterschnittfrei free of undercut
unterschreiten fall below, under-run
Unterschreiten *nt* **des Taupunktes** passage below the dew point
Unterseite *f* underside, lower side, bottom side
untersetzen *(Getriebe)* reduce
Untersetzungsgetriebe *nt* step-down gear, reducing gear, speed reducing gears (or unit)
Untersicht *f* inverted plan
Unterspannung *f* 1. *(allg.)* undervoltage 2. *(Versorgungsnetz)* brownout
Unterspülung *f* under-cutting
Unterstand *m* shelter
Unterstopfung *f* packing beneath (or under)

unterstützen 1. *(Last)* carry, support 2. *(einseitig)* suspend 3. *(persönlich)* assist
Unterstützung *f* 1. *(Last)* support 2. *(persönl.)* assistance 3. *(Verstärkung)* backing
untersuchen investigate, inspect, examine, test, study, analyse
Untersuchung *f* inspection, examination, investigation, testing, test, study
Untersuchungsbericht *m* examination report
Untersuchungspraxis *f* testing practice
Untersuchungsstelle *f* examination centre
Untersuchungszeichnung *f* study drawing
Untersuchungsziel *nt* study objective
Untersupport *m* bottom slide
Unterteil *nt* base, bottom (force or part), side, lower part
unterteilbar dividable
unterteilen divide into sections, subdivide, split up, partition, classify (into groups)
Unterteilung *f* subdivision, partition, classification
Untertischdurchleuchtung *f* below-table fluoroscopy
Untertrumm *nt* return belt
Unterwanderung *f* sub-surface migration
unterweisen instruct
Unterweisung *f* instruction
unterwerfen subject (to)
untoleriertes Maß *nt* untoleranced dimension (or size)
ununterbrechbar uninterruptible
ununterbrochen permanent, uninterrupted
ununterbrochener Dauerbetrieb *m* sustained continuous operation
ununterbrochenes Räumen *nt* continuous broaching
unveränderbar invariable, unchangeable
unveränderlich invariable
unverändert unaltered, unchanged, unvaried

unverarbeitetes Ausgangsmaterial *nt* unprocessed starting material
unverbrannt non-burned, unburned
unverbranntes Gas *nt* unburnt gas
unverbraucht unused
unverdichteter Boden *m* uncompacted soil
unvergällt undenaturated
unverhältnismäßig disproportionate, unreasonable
unverkleideter Heizkörper *m* exposed radiator
unverlierbare Scheibe *f* captive washer
unverlierbare Schraube *f* captive screw
unverlierbares Unterlegteil *nt* captive washer component
Unverlierbarkeit *f* captivity
unvermeidbare Gefahr *f* unavoidable (or inevitable) danger
unverpackt unpacked, loose
unverputzt unrendered
unverschleißbar unwearable
unversehrt integer
Unversehrtheit *f* integrity
unverträglich (mit) incompatible (with)
Unverträglichkeit *f* incompatibility
unverwischbar indelible
unverzinkt ungalvanized
unverzüglich immediate, forthwith
Unvollkommenheit *f* imperfection
unvollständig incomplete
unvollständig geformtes Gewinde *nt* incompletely formed thread
unwirksam ineffective
Unwucht *f* imbalance, unbalance, out-of balance
Unwuchtmotor *m* imbalance motor
unzerspanbar non-machinable, unmachinable
unzugänglich inaccessible
unzulänglich deficient, inadequate
unzulässig forbidden, unacceptable, impermissible, inadmissible, undue
unzutreffend inapplicable
unzweckmäßig impracticable, unsuitable, inappropriate
U-Profil *nt* U-shaped profile
Urethankautschuk *m* urethane rubber
Urformen *nt* creative forming
Urformtechnik *f* casting technology
Urformwerkzeug *nt* casting tool
Urmeter *m* standard meter
Ursache *f* cause, reason
Urschablone *f* template master, master template
Ursprung *m* origin
ursprünglich original, initial
Ursprungsland *nt* country of origin
Ursprungspunkt *m* zero point, point of origin
Ursprungszeichnung *f* original drawing
Ursprungszustand *m* original condition
Urzeichnung *f* original
USM *Abk (Ultraschallschwingläppen)* ultrasonic swing lapping
UST-Gewinde *nt* unified screw thread
UV-Strahlung *f* ultra-violet radiation

V v

Vakuum *nt* **1.** *(allg.)* vacuum **2. ein ~ erzeugen** apply a vacuum, evacuate
Vakuumformverfahren *nt* vacuum form process
Vakuumheber *m* vacuum lifter, vacuum load carrying device
Vakuumkammer *f* vacuum chamber
Vakuumpumpe *f* vacuum pump
Vakuumsauger *m (Saugschale)* suction pad (or cup), vacuum pad (or cup)
Vakuumtraverse *f* vacuum (lifting) beam, vacuum lifting frame
Vakuumvorverdichten *nt* vacuum precompressing
Valenzband *nt* valence band
Valenzelektron *nt* valence-electron
Valenzelektronenkonzentration *f* valence-electron concentration
validieren validate
Validierung *f* validation
variabel variable, variant
Variabilität *f* variableness, variability
Variable *f* variable
variable Fahrsteuerung *f* variable speed control
variable Platzcodierung *f* random tool access
variable Satzlänge *f* variable block format
Variablenprüfung *f* inspection by variables, variables test
variabler Widerstand *m* variable resistor, varistor
Variante *f* **1.** *(allg.)* alternative, variant, option, version **2.** *(Abänderung)* modification, variation
Variantenvergleich *m* variant comparison
Variantenvielfalt *f* variety of variant
Varianz *f* variance
varianzbestimmte Stichprobe *f* variance-determined sample
Variationskoeffizient *m* coefficient of variation, variation coefficient
variieren vary, diversify
Varistor *m* varistor

V-Bahn *f* V-way, Vee, vees *pl*
VC-Monomer *nt* VC monomer
VC-Polymerisat *nt* VC polymer
Vektorregelung *f* vector control
Vektor *m* vector
Vektorgrafik *f* **1.** *(Einzelbild)* vector graphic **2.** *(Technik)* vector graphics
Vektorvorschub *m* vector feed rate
Ventil *nt* valve
Ventilator *m* ventilator, blower, fan
Ventilatorenlaufrad *nt* fan impeller
Ventilgewinde *nt* valve thread
Ventilkörper *m* control block
Ventilschleifmaschine *f* valve seat grinder
Ventilsitzfräseinrichtung *f* seat dresser
Ventilsteuerung *f* valve control
verallgemeinern generalize
veränderbar alterable, changeable
veränderlich changing, variable, variant
veränderliche Empfindlichkeit *f* variable sensitivity
veränderliche Größe *f (in e. graphischen Darstellung)* variable quantity
Veränderlichkeit *f* variability
verändern 1. *(allg.)* alter **2.** *(modifizieren)* modify **3.** *(variieren)* vary **4.** *(wechseln)* change
Veränderung *f* alteration, change, variation, modification
Veränderung *f* **der Stellung** relocation
verankern 1. *(allg.)* anchor, fix, guy **2.** *(verstreben)* brace
Verankerung *f* **1.** *(allg.)* anchoring, fixing, guy **2.** *(Bau)* anchor, anchorage **3.** *(Verstrebung)* bracing
Verankerungsmethode *f* anchoring method, method of fixing
Verankerungsmöglichkeit *f* bonding characteristic
veranschlagen rate
verantwortlich responsible
Verantwortlicher *m* responsible person
Verantwortlichkeit *f* responsibleness

Verantwortung *f* responsibility
verarbeitbar processable
verarbeitbare Werkstoffe *f* possible materials
verarbeiten 1. *(allg.)* work, process **2.** *(bearbeiten)* machine **3.** *(behandeln)* treat
Verarbeitung *f* **1.** *(allg.)* processing **2.** *(Bearbeitung)* machining **3.** *(Behandlung)* treatment
Verarbeitungsbedingung *f* processing condition
Verarbeitungseigenschaft *f* processing property
Verarbeitungseinheit *f* processing unit
verarbeitungsfertig angesetzte Mischung *f* ready-for-use prepared mixture
verarbeitungsfertiger Zustand *m* ready-for-use condition
Verarbeitungshilfsmittel *nt* processing aid, processing auxiliaries *pl*
Verarbeitungsmaschine *f* machine for processing materials, processing machine
Verarbeitungsmerkmal *nt* processing feature
Verarbeitungsmodul *nt* processing module
Verarbeitungsrichtlinien *fpl* processing guidelines
Verarbeitungsschwindung *f* moulding shrinkage
Verarbeitungsstabilisator *m* processing stabilizer
Verarbeitungstechnik *f* processing technique
Verarbeitungszustand *m* ready-for-use state, condition for use
Veraschungsrückstand *m* ash residue
Veraschungstiegel *m* incineration (or ashing) crucible
verästelter Riss *m* branching crack
Verband *m* **1.** *(techn.)* brace, bracing **2.** *(Montage)* assembly **3.** *(Bau)* bond
verbessern 1. *(allg.)* improve, optimize **2.** *(korrigieren)* correct
Verbesserung *f* **1.** *(allg.)* improvement, optimization **2.** *(Korrektur)* correction
Verbesserungsprozess *m* process of improvement
Verbesserungsvorschlag *m* suggestion for improvement
verbiegen buckle
Verbiegung *f* deflection
verbieten forbid, prohibit, interdict
verbinden 1. *(allg.)* couple, tie, unite, splice, combine **2.** *(aneinanderbefestigen)* join, link **3.** *(chem.)* mix **4.** *(el.)* connect (to) **5.** *(fügen)* join, joint **6.** *(kleben, löten, verfugen)* bond **7.** *(verriegeln)* lock together **8.** *(verschrauben)* bolt (together) **9.** *(durch Zahnräder)* gear
Verbinder *m* connector
verbindlich binding
Verbindung *f* **1.** *(allg.)* bonding, connection, *(UK)* connexion, interconnection **2.** *(bei Rohren)* joint **3.** *(chem.)* compound **4.** *(el.)* junction, connection **5.** *(IT)* linkage, communication **6.** *(mittels Schrauben)* screwed (or bolted) fastening **7.** *(durch Zahnräder)* gearing
Verbindung *f* **herstellen** connect
Verbindung *f* **trennen** disconnect
Verbindungsbogen *m* connecting bend
Verbindungselement *nt* *(mechanisches ~)* fastening element, fastener, fitting
Verbindungselement *nt* **mit Gewinde** threaded fastener
Verbindungsglied *m* link
Verbindungsimpedanz *f* bonding impedance
Verbindungskabel *nt* connecting cable, connector cable
Verbindungslasche *f* connecting cable
Verbindungsleitung *f* **1.** *(allg.)* connecting piping, connecting conduit **2.** *(el.)* connecting line, junction line **3.** *(Schaltung)* link circuit
Verbindungslinie *f* connecting line
verbindungslos connectionless
Verbindungslöten *nt* joint soldering
Verbindungsmuffe *f* connection sleeve, union socket
Verbindungsrundnaht *f* circumferen-

tial joint weld
Verbindungsschicht *f* data link layer, session layer
Verbindungsschichtdicke *f* compound layer thickness
Verbindungssechskant *nt (für Maschinenschrauber)* hexagon drive extension
Verbindungsstange *f* connecting rod
Verbindungsstelle *f* joint
Verbindungsstift *m* connecting pin
Verbindungstechnik *f* technique for joining parts
Verbindungsteil *nt* 1. *(allg.)* adaptor, connecting (or fastening) element, link, connector 2. *(als Schraubwerkzeug)* extension insert bit 3. *(Steckschlüssel)* extension, insert
Verbindungsvierkant *m* 1. *(als Maschinenschrauber)* square drive adaptor, driving square 2. *(abgesetzter ~)* square coupler
Verbindungsvierkant *m* **für Maschinenschrauberwerkzeuge** driving square for pocket socket wrenches
verbleiben remain, stay
verblitzen flash
verblocken interlock
Verblockung *f* 1. *(allg.)* interlock 2. *(Abschaltung einer Ölfeuerungsanlage)* tripping device (a cut-off system of an oil burning system)
Verbördeln *nt* pre-flanging
Verbot *nt* interdiction, prohibition
verboten forbidden, prohibit
Verbotszeichen *nt* prohibiting sign
Verbrauch *m* 1. *(allg.)* consumption 2. *(Energie)* dissipation
verbrauchen 1. *(allg.)* consume 2. *(aufbrauchen)* use up 3. *(Energie)* dissipate, consume 4. *(Platz)* take up
Verbraucher *m* 1. *(allg.)* consumer 2. *(el.)* load
Verbraucherort *m* consumer site
Verbrauchsartikel *f* commodities, commodity goods
verbrauchsbesteuertes Material *nt* consumption-controlled stock
Verbrauchsdaten *pl* consumption data
Verbrauchsgüter *ntpl* consumer goods
Verbrauchsleitung *f* supply pipeline
Verbrauchsmaterial *nt* consumables
Verbrauchsmenge *f* consumption rate
Verbrauchsschmieranlage *f* total loss lubrication system
verbrauchte Schlagarbeit *f* absorbed impact energy
verbrennen burn, combust
Verbrennung *f* 1. *(allg.)* burning 2. *(medizinische Verletzung)* burn 3. *(techn.)* combustion
Verbrennungsablauf *m* combustion process
Verbrennungsluft *f* combustion air
Verbrennungsluftbegrenzer *m* combustion air limiter
Verbrennungsluftklappe *f* combustion air throttle valve
Verbrennungsmotor *m* 1. *(allg.)* internal combustion engine, IC engine, engine 2. *(mit ~)* combustion process
verbrennungsmotorisch combustion-engined
Verbrennungsschale *f* combustion dish
verbrennungstechnische Prüfung *f* combustion performance test(ing)
Verbrennungstiegel *m* combustion crucible (or cup)
verbronzen bronze-plate
verbrühen scald
Verbrühung *f* scald
Verbund *m* 1. *(allg.)* combination, laminate, network 2. *(Beton)* bond 3. *(Schichten)* sandwich 4. *(Stapel)* bundle 5. *(im ~ stapeln)* bundle
Verbund(sicherheits)glas (VSG) *nt* laminated glass, multilayer glass
Verbundarbeit *f* combined-operation work
Verbundausführung *f* composite design (or type or pattern)
Verbundfolie *f* laminate, foil laminate, compound foil, sandwich foil
Verbundfolie *f* composite film
Verbundfoliendeckel *m* foil laminate lid
Verbundgruppenzeichnung *f* composite assembly drawing
Verbundpapier *nt* paper laminate

Verbundprobe *f* bonded specimen
Verbundschleifen *nt* combination plunge traverse grinding
Verbundspan *m* combined pressboard
Verbundspannstift *m* compound spring type straight pin
Verbundspantafel *f* combined pressboard sheet
Verbundstapel *m* bundle, stack of bundle
Verbundstapelung *f* bundling
Verbundsystem *nt* composite specimen
Verbundteilen *nt* compound indexing
Verbundwerkzeug *nt* compound tool
Verdampfung *f* evaporation
Verdampfungsbrenner *m* vaporizing burner
Verdampfungsgut *nt* evaporating material
Verdampfungstiegel *m* evaporation crucible
Verdeckung *f* screening, guarding, hood
verderben spoil
verdichten 1. *(allg.)* compress, compact **2.** *(veflüssigen)* condense
Verdichter *m* **1.** *(Gase)* compressor **2.** *(Verflüssiger)* condenser
Verdichterdüse *f* restrictor (lubricant metering device)
verdichtungsfähiger Boden *m* compactable soil
verdoppeln double, duplicate
Verdoppler *m* doubler, doubling circuit
Verdopplung *f* doubling, duplication
verdrahten wire (up)
Verdrahtung *f* wiring
Verdrahtungsfehler *m* wiring error
verdrängen displace
Verdränger *m* displacement body (pump), displacement device
Verdrängerbauart *f* positive displacement design
Verdrängerfüllmaschine *f* displacement filling machine
Verdrängerphase *f* displacement phase (pump)
Verdrängerpumpe *f* positive displacement pump

Verdrängungstiegel *m* displacement cylinder
verdrehen distort, twist warp
Verdrehmoment *nt* moment of torsion, twisting moment
Verdrehschiebungsbruch *m* torsional shear fracture
Verdrehspiel *nt* circumferential backlash, torsional play, twisting play
Verdrehung *f* twist(ing), distortion, horizontal twisting, torsion
Verdrehungsbeanspruchung *f* torsional strain, twisting strain
Verdrehungsfestigkeit *f* torsional strength
Verdrehungskraft *f* twisting force
Verdrehungsmoment *nt* torque
Verdrehungssteifigkeit *f* resistance to twisting
Verdrehungswinkel *m* torsion angle, twisting angle
Verdrehwinkel *m* angle of twist
verdrillen twist
verdrillte Doppelleitung *f* twisted pair
verdrillter Schweißdraht *m* stranded filler wire
Verdrillung *f* **1.** *(allg.)* twisting **2.** *(el.)* transposition of lines
verdübeln peg
Verdünnbarkeit *f* dilutability
verdunsten evaporate, vaporize, volatilize
Verdunstung *f* evaporation
Verdunstungsbeanspruchung *f* evaporate ageing (procedure)
Verdunstungsmesser *m* evaporation meter
veredeln finish, refine
vereinbaren 1. *(allg.)* agree, agree upon, specify **2.** *(IT)* declare, define
vereinbartes Steuerzeichen *nt* specified control character
Vereinbarung *f* **1.** *(allg.)* agreement, convention **2.** *(IT)* declaration
Vereinbarungsanweisung *f* declarative statement
Vereinbarungsteil *nt* declaratives, declaration part
Vereinbarungszeichen *nt* declarator,

declarative character
vereinfachen 1. *(allg.)* simplify
2. *(Arbeit)* deskill **3.** *(math.)* reduce, cancel out
vereinfacht simplified
vereinfachte Ansicht *f* simplified view
Vereinfachung *f* simplification
vereinheitlichen 1. *(allg.)* unify, unitize **2.** *(Standards)* harmonize
vereinheitlicht unified, unitized, harmonized
Vereinheitlichung *f* **1.** *(allg.)* unification **2.** *(Standards)* harmonization
vereinigen unite
vereinzeln separate, marshal into singles, single (out)
vereinzelte Einschlüsse *mpl* isolated inclusions
Vereinzelung *f* separation, singling
Vereinzelungsgerät *nt* singling unit
Vereinzelungsmaschine *f* single liner
Vereinzelungsmaschine *f* **für formstabile Packmittel** rigid container single liner
Vereinzelungsprozess *m* singling process
Vereisung *f* freezing
verengen contract, narrow, restrict, neck
Verengung *f* restriction, constriction
verfahrbar mobile, travelling
verfahrbares Regal *nt* mobile shelving, mobile racking
Verfahren *nt* **1.** *(Arbeitsweise)* procedure, method **2.** *(Bewegung)* movement, moving, travelling, propelling **3.** *(Prozess)* process, technique **4.** *(elektrische ~)* electrical processes **5.** *(mechanische ~)* mechanical processes
Verfahren *nt* **des Gleichlauffräsens** in-cut method
Verfahrensablauf *m* procedure, method
Verfahrensabläufe *f* operational sequences
Verfahrensanweisung *f* process instruction
verfahrensbedingt by the nature of the process
Verfahrensbeschreibung *f* description of procedures
Verfahrensbesonderheiten *f* procedure special features
Verfahrensfehler *m* methodological error
Verfahrensgang *m* procedure, method
Verfahrensgrundsatz *m* process principle
Verfahrenshauptgruppe *f* technique main group, process principal
Verfahrenskennzeichnung *f* processes characterization
Verfahrenskette *f* process chain
Verfahrenskinematik *f* process kinematics
Verfahrensschema *nt* operative system
verfahrenstechnische Anlage *f* process plant
verfahrenstechnische Einrichtungen *fpl* process engineering equipment
Verfahrensübersicht *f* summary of processes
Verfahrensvarianten *f* process variants
Verfahrschlitten *m* (mobile) carriage
Verfahrwagen *m* (mobile) carriage
Verfahrweg *m* travel (path), traverse path
verfälschen falsify
Verfärbungsbereich *m* discolouration range
Verfärbungsverfahren *nt* discoloration method
verfestigen strengthen
Verfestigung *f* solidification
Verfilzungsstoff *m* felting material
verflüssigbar liquifiable
verfolgen track, trace, follow
Verfolgung *f* tracking, tracing
verformbar 1. *(allg.)* ductile, plastic, workable **2.** *(deformierbar)* deformable
verformen 1. *(allg.)* reform, form, shape **2.** *(biegen)* deflect **3.** *(deformieren)* deform **4.** *(verdrehen)* contort
Verformung *f* **1.** *(allg.)* change in shape, forming, strain **2.** *(Biegen)* deflection **3.** *(Deformation)* deformation **4.** *(Verdrehen)* contortion, distortion
Verformungsbehinderung *f* deformation impediment
Verformungsdifferenz *f* deformation

difference
Verformungsgrenze *f* deformation limit
Verformungskenngröße *f* deformation characteristic
Verformungskörper *m* deformation element
Verformungsrest *m* permanent set
Verformungsspiel *nt* deformation cycle
Verformungsverhalten *nt* deformation behaviour
Verformungsvorgang *m* deformation process
Verformungswechsel *m* alternating strain
Verformungswinkel *m* angle of deformation, deformation angle
Verformungs-Zeit-Diagramm *nt* strain-time-curve
Verformungszone *f* deformation zone
verfügbar available
Verfügbarkeit *f* availability
Verfügbarkeitsermittlung *f* availability calculation
Verfügbarkeitsgrad *m* rated availability, availability ratio
Verfügbarkeitskenngröße *f* availability characteristic
Verfügbarkeitskontrolle *f* on-hand-status check
Verfügbarkeitsnachweis *m* availability verification
Verfügbarkeitstest *m* availability test
Verfüllmaterial *nt* back-fill material
Vergabe *f* award of contract, allocation
Vergabeentscheidung *f* decision to place the order
Vergabeunterlagen *fpl* tender documents
Vergaser *m* carburettor
Vergaserkraftstoff *m* petrol, gasoline, carburettor fuel
Vergasungsraum *m* gasification space
Vergasungstechnik *f* gasification engineering
vergeben allocate, award a contact, place an order
Vergießeinrichtung *f* potting equipment

vergießen 1. *(allg.)* teem **2.** *(mit Harz)* pot
Vergilbung *f* yellowing
verglasen glaze
Verglasung *f* glazing
Vergleich *m* comparison
vergleichbar comparable
Vergleichbarkeit *f* reproducibility, precision, comparability
vergleichen compare (to/with)
vergleichend comparative
Vergleicher *m* comparator, discriminator
Vergleichgrenze *f* reproducibility limit
Vergleichsanstrich *m* reference coating
Vergleichsbedingung *f* reproducibility condition
Vergleichsbrandmenge *f* reference combustion quantity
Vergleichselement *nt* reference element
Vergleichsgetriebe *nt* reference gear unit
Vergleichskennzahl *f* comparative characteristic value
Vergleichskörper *m* calibration (or reference) block
Vergleichslösung *f* reference solution
Vergleichsmaß *nt* reference gauge
Vergleichsmesseinrichtung *f* reference measuring system
Vergleichsmuster *nt* reference sample
Vergleichsnormal *nt* standard of comparison
Vergleichsoperation *f* comparing operation
Vergleichsoperator *m* relation operator
Vergleichspräzision *f* reproducibility
Vergleichspunkt *m* benchmark
Vergleichsreflektor *m* reference reflector
Vergleichsschaltquelle *f* reference sound source
Vergleichsskala *f* reference scale
Vergleichsspannung *f* comparison stress
Vergleichsstandardabweichung *f* reproducibility standard deviation

Vergleichsstelle *f* comparing point
Vergleichsstoff *m* reference material
Vergleichsstrecke *f* comparison section
Vergleichsstreifen *m* reference strip
Vergleichstandardabweichung *f* reproducibility standard deviation, precision
Vergleichstreubereich *m* comparison-tolerance
Vergleichstreukörper *m* comparative scattering body
Vergleichsuntersuchung *f* comparative test
Vergleichsversuch *m* comparison test
Vergleichszahl *f* comparative index
Vergleichszahl *f* **der Kriechwegbildung** *f* comparative tracking index (CTI)
vergossene Fuge *f* grouted joint
vergrößern 1. *(allg.)* increase, magnify **2.** *(Fördermenge)* augment **3.** *(Werte)* increase
vergrößert zeichnen draw to a larger scale
Vergrößerung *f* increase, magnification
vergussgekapselt encapsulated
Vergusskapselung *f* encapsulation
Vergussmasse *f* **1.** *(allg.)* sealing compound **2.** *(Mörtel)* grouting compound, grout
Vergussmassenschicht *f* layer of joint sealing compound
Vergussmittel *nt* sealing material
Vergütungsstahl *m* heat-treated steel, heat treatable steel
Verhalten *nt* *(UK)* behaviour, *(US)* behavior, response
Verhalten *nt* **bei tiefen Temperaturen** low temperature behaviour
Verhältnis *nt* **1.** *(allg.)* relation, proportion **2.** *(math.)* ratio **3.** *(kinematisches ~)* kinematic ratio
Verhältniszahl *f* ratio
verhindern impede, prevent
Verhinderung(smaßnahme) *f* prevention
verhüten prevent
Verhütung *f* prevention
verifizieren verify
Verifizierung *f* verification

Verjüngen *nt* reducing (the cross-section or diameter)
Verjüngen *nt* **von Hohlkörpern** open pointing
Verjüngen *nt* **von Vollkörpern** rotary pointing, reducing the ends of solid bodies
Verjüngung *f* constriction, taper, degree of taper
verkabeln cable, wire
Verkabelung *f* cabling, wiring
Verkabelungsplan *m* cable layout
Verkauf *m:* **einen ~ abschließen** conclude a sale, effect a sale
verkaufen sell
Verkäufer *m* seller, vendor
Verkaufsbericht *m* sales data report
Verkaufsdaten *pl* sales data
Verkaufslager *nt* sales warehouse
Verkaufsplanung *f* **1.** *(allg.)* sales planning **2.** *(Zahlenaufstellung)* sales forecast report
Verkaufsprognose *f* sales forecast, retail forecast
Verkaufszahlen *fpl* sales figures
Verkehr *m* traffic, movement
Verkehrsbereich *m* traffic area
Verkehrsfehlergrenze *f* in-service limit of error
Verkehrsfläche *f* traffic area
Verkehrslast *f* live load
Verkehrsregelung *f* flow regulation, traffic management, traffic regulation
Verkehrsstau *m* **1.** *(allg.)* congestion, bottleneck **2.** *(Straßenverkehr)* traffic jam
Verkehrsweg *m* traffic route, transportation route, traffic way, passageway
verkeilen wedge, fasten by wedges, key
verketten 1. *(allg.)* concatenate **2.** *(Bauteil)* chain **3.** *(Datei)* interlink **4.** *(Arbeitsabläufe)* link
Verkettung *f* chaining, (con)catenation, linage, interlinkage, interlinking
Verkettungssystem *nt* interlinkage system, interlinking system
Verkieselung *f* *(e. Untergrundes)* silification
verkleben 1. *(allg.)* glue together, gum, paste together, conglutinate **2.** *(befes-*

tigen) adhere, bond **3.** *(dichten)* lute
Verklebung *f* adhesion, bonding, conglutination, gluing
Verklebungsschwierigkeit *f* difficulty in bonding
verkleiden cover, case, jacket, sheath
verkleideter Heizkörper *m* covered radiator
Verkleidung *f* **1.** *(allg.)* sheathing, panelling, cover, housing, lining **2.** *(Bau)* facing, siding **3.** *(e. Gefahrenstelle)* cladding, enclosing guard **4.** *(e. Motors)* casing **5.** *(Maschinen)* case, cover, guard
verkleinerter Maßstab *m* reduced scale
Verkleinerung *f* reduction
Verkleinerungsfaktor *m* reducing ratio
verklemmen seize, brace, jam, get jammed
Verklemmung *f* jamming, deadlock
Verknäuelung *f* interlacing
verknüpfen connect, link, chain
verknüpfte Eingänge *mpl* combined inputs *pl*
Verknüpfung *f* **1.** *(allg.)* connection **2.** *(IT)* link, linkage, chaining **3.** *(log. Schaltung)* linkage wiring, logic operation, connective, switching operation
Verknüpfungsadresse *f* link address
Verknüpfungsergebnis *nt* logic operation
Verknüpfungsfunktion *f* link function
Verknüpfungsnetzwerk *nt* connective network
Verknüpfungssteuerung *f* logic control system
verkörpern embody
verkrümmen warp
Verkrümmung *f* warpage
verkupfern copper
verkürzen shorten, reduce
Verkürzung *f* shortening, reduction
Verladeanlage *f* loading plant
Verladeband *nt* loading belt
Verlademasse *f* shipping mass
verladen 1. *(allg.)* load, ship **2.** *(Handel)* deflect
Verladerampe *f* loading platform
Verladung *f* loading, shipment

verlagern 1. *(allg.)* displace, relocate, transfer **2.** *(Lasten)* shift
Verlagerung *f* **1.** *(allg.)* displacement, relocation, transfer **2.** *(Handel)* deflection **3.** *(Lasten)* shift
verlängern lengthen, elongate, extend, prolong(ate)
Verlängerung *f* **1.** *(allg.)* elongation, extension, lengthening, prolongation **2.** *(Fortsatz)* projection
Verlängerungsmessgerät *nt* extensometer
Verlängerungsstück *nt* elongation piece, lengthening piece, extension piece
verlangsamen 1. *(allg.)* slow down, decelerate **2.** *(bremsen)* retard
Verlangsamung *f* slowing-down, deceleration
verlassen 1. *(allg.)* leave **2.** *(aussteigen)* egress
Verlauf *m* **1.** *(allg.)* course, process, run, characteristic **2.** *(der Härte über einen Querschnitt des Bauteils)* distribution
verlaufen go, run, run untrue
Verlegbarkeit *f* laying compatibility
Verlegeanleitung *f* pipe-laying instruction
verlegefertiges Stahlrohr *nt* steel pipe ready for laying
Verlegegenauigkeit *f* laying accuracy
Verlegehaken *m* pipe hook
Verlegekorrektur *f* correction of the alignment
verlegen 1. *(örtlich)* place, position **2.** *(Kabel)* install, lay
Verlegen in Anschüttmasse *f* laying in made ground
verlegetechnische Maßnahme *f* technical laying disposition
Verlegetoleranz *f* positioning tolerance
Verleimbarkeit *f* gluing ability
verletzen injure, hurt, violate
Verletzung *f* injury, hurt, violation
Verletzungsgefahr *f* risk of injury
Verletzungsgrenze *f* limit for preventing injuries
verlieren 1. *(allg.)* lose **2.** *(Energie)* dissipate
verlorene Form *f* lost shape

Verlust *m* loss, dissipation
Verlust *m* **der Maßgenauigkeit** size loss
Verlustanteil *m* part of loss
Verlustbremsung *f* dissipative braking
Verluste *mpl* losses *pl*
Verlusthöhe *f* loss of head
Verlustleistung *f* power dissipation, power loss
Verlustmenge *f* **je Zeiteinheit** *f* waste quantity per unit time
Verlustmodul *nt* loss modulus, modulus of loss
Verlustschicht *f* sacrificial layer
Verlustschmierung *f* loss lubrication
Verlustwärme *f* lost heat
Verlustzeit *f* idle time (or period), machine-handling time, non-machining time, unproductive time, dead time, *(US)* down time
vermaßen dimension
vermaßt dimensioned
Vermaßung *f* dimensioning
vermeiden 1. *(allg.)* avoid, prevent **2.** *(umgehen)* bypass
Vermeidung *f* avoidance, prevention
vermengen blend
vermessen *(US)* gage, *(UK)* gauge
Vermessung *f* measuring, surveying
Vermessungsriss *m* survey plan
Vermessungstechnik *f* surveying practice
vermieten let, lease, rent
Vermietung *f* leasing, rental, renting
vermindern decrease, diminish, reduce, lessen
Verminderung *f* diminution, decrease, reduction
Vermögen *nt* **1.** *(Kapital)* asset(s) **2.** *(Leistung)* power **3.** *(Fähigkeit)* ability
Vermutung *f* assumption
vernachlässigbar negligible
vernachlässigen neglect, ignore
Vernachlässigung *f* neglect, ignoring
vernetzen net, network
vernetzt networked
Vernetzung *f* networking, connectivity
Vernetzungsisotherm *nt* interlacing isotherm
Vernetzungsreaktion *f* cross-linking reaction
vernieten rivet
Vernietung *f* riveted joint
Verockerung *f* sedimentation of iron ochre
verordnen prescribe, regulate
Verordnung *f* ordinance, prescription, regulation
verpacken 1. *(allg.)* pack **2.** *(abpacken)* package
Verpackung *f* box, case, packing, packaging, packaging material
Verpackungsart *f* type of packaging
Verpackungsautomat *m* (automatic) packaging machine
Verpackungsband *nt* packaging strap, strapping
Verpackungseinheit *f* packaging unit
Verpackungskonzept *nt* packaging concept
Verpackungsmaschine *f* packaging machine
Verpackungsmaterial *nt* packaging material
Verpackungsmittel *nt* packing material
Verpackungsoberfläche *f* packaging surface
Verpackungsprüfung *f* packaging test
Verpackungsverordnung *f* packaging ordinance
Verpackungsverschluss *m* pack seal
Verpackungswesen *nt* packaging practice
Verpackungszeichnung *f* packing drawing
Verpackungszyklus *m* packaging cycle
verplomben seal, tag
Verplombung *f* lead sealing, security tagging
Verpolschutz *m* polarity reversal protection
Verpolung *f* polarity reversal, reverse polarity
verpolungssicher protected against reverse polarity
verpressen 1. *(allg.)* (com)press, compact **2.** *(z. B. Cellulosebahnen)* compress (or laminate) under heat

3. *(einspritzen)* inject
Verpuffungsklappe *f* blowback flap
verriegeln interlock, bar, block, secure, trap, lock
Verriegelung *f* **1.** *(allg.)* interlock, locking, lock, twist lock, lockout **2.** *(als Bauelement)* interlocking device **3.** *(Arbeitsvorgang)* interlocking **4.** *(von Vorrichtungen)* interlocking arrangement
Verriegelungseinrichtung *f* locking device
Verriegelungselement *nt* interlocking element
Verriegelungsstift *m* locking pin
verringern decrease, reduce, minimize
Verringerung *f* decrease, reduction
Verringerung *f* **der Größe** size loss
verrippt ribbed
verrippter Boden *m* ribbed base
Verrippung *f* finning, ribbing
verrottungsbeständig rot-proof, resistance to rotting
verrutschen shift, displace, slip
Verrutschen *nt* shift
versagen break down, fail, malfunction
Versagensart *f* type of failure
versagenssicher fail-safe
Versammlungsraum *m* assembly room
Versand *m* dispatch, shipment
Versandauftrag *m* dispatch order, shipping order
Versandlager *nt* dispatch warehouse
Versandpackung *f* transport package
Versandzeichnung *f* despatch drawing
Versatz *m* **1.** *(allg.)* offset, misalignment, displacement, mismatch, packing **2.** *(z. B. von Linien)* parallel offset
verschärfte Prüfung *f* tightened inspection
verschiebbar 1. *(allg.)* shiftable, movable **2.** *(gleitend)* sliding
verschiebbarer Anschlagwinkel *m* adjustable square
Verschiebbarkeit *f* travel
Verschiebebewegung *f* shifting movement
verschieben 1. *(allg.)* shift, move (about), displace, traverse, advance **2.** *(rangieren)* shunt **3.** *(sich ~)* travel

Verschieber *m* shifter
Verschieberädergetriebe *nt* sliding gear mechanism
Verschieberegal *nt* mobile shelving
Verschieberegallager *nt* mobile shelving rack store
Verschiebewagen *m* transfer carriage, transfer car, switching carriage, slide truck
Verschiebeweg *m* traverse distance, length of traverse
verschieblicher Maßstab *m* movable scale
Verschiebung *f* **1.** *(allg.)* displacement, shift **2.** *(e. Schlitten, Ständer,...)* traverse, travel, traversing **3.** *(in falsche Lage)* dislocation, misalignment **4.** *(Schieberäder, Fräser)* shift (milling) method
Verschlammungsgefahr *f* risk of silting up
verschlechtern degrade, worsen, deteriorate, disimprove
Verschlechterung *f* degradation, worsening, deterioration, disimprovement
verschleiert cloudy
Verschleiß *m* wear, abrasion, tear
Verschleiß *m* **an der Werkzeugschneide** edge wear
Verschleiß *m* **ausgleichen** compensate for wear
Verschleißarten *f* wear types
Verschleißausfall *m* failure caused by wear, wear-out failure
Verschleißausgleich *m* adjustment for wear
Verschleißbeständigkeit *f* anti-wear properties *pl*
Verschleißbetrag *m* amount of wear (or abrasion)
Verschleißcharakteristik *f* abrasion characteristic
Verschleißdurchsatzmenge *f* wear throughput quantity
verschleißen wear (out), abrade
Verschleißerscheinung *f* (sign of) wear
Verschleißfase *f* wear land
verschleißfest resistant to wear, wear resistant, abrasion-proof, wear proof

Verschleißfestigkeit f anti-wear properties, resistance to wear, wear resistance
Verschleißform f type of wear, wear factor
Verschleißformen f wear forms
Verschleißfortschritt m **beim Werkzeug** rate tool of wear
verschleißfrei free from wear, non-wearing, wearless, wear-free
Verschleißgebiet nt abrasion field
Verschleißgröße f amount of wear, wear factor
Verschleißlebensdauer f wear lifespan
Verschleißmarke f wear mark
Verschleißmarkenbreite f width of wear mark, wear land value, land wear
Verschleißmessung f wear measurement
Verschleißmulde f crater
Verschleißrate f wear instalment
Verschleißstandzeit f tool life between resharpening
Verschleißstrecke f wear distance
Verschleißteil nt 1. *(allg.)* wear part, wearing part 2. *(Wegwerfteil)* expendable part
Verschleißteilchen nt abraded particle
Verschleißteilzeichnung f drawing dealing with wearing parts
Verschleißverhalten nt wear behaviour
Verschleißvolumen nt volume of metal worn away
Verschleißwiderstand m wear (or abrasion) resistance
Verschleißwirkung f abrasive (or wearing) action
Verschleißursache f wear reason
verschleißen 1. *(zu machen)* close 2. *(abdichten, verschweißen)* seal 3. *(Schlüssel)* lock
Verschließhilfsmittel nt closing material
Verschließmaschine f closing machine, sealing machine
Verschließmaschine f **für formstabile Packmittel** rigid container sealing machine
Verschließmittel nt closing material, closure
verschlossene Zelle f sealed cell
Verschluss m 1. *(allg.)* lock, seal 2. *(Schloss)* closure 3. *(unter ~ halten)* keep under lock
Verschlussdeckel m **zum Eindrücken** sealing push-in cap
verschlüsseln code, encode
Verschlüsselung f coding, encoding
Verschlusshahn m stopcock
Verschlusskappe f breech cover
Verschlussorgan nt shut-off device (or member)
Verschlussscheibe f sealing washer
Verschlussschraube f screwed sealing plug, screw plug, sealing plug
Verschlussschraube f **für Ölablass** screwed drain plug
Verschlussschraube f **mit Innensechskant** hexagon socket screw sealing plug
Verschlussschraube f **über gesamte Gewindelänge** full-length engagement of the screw (or bolt) thread
Verschlussstift m locking pin
Verschlussstopfen m sealing plug
verschmelzen blend
Verschmelzung f glass-to-glass sealing
Verschmelzungsfrequenz f fusion frequency
Verschmutzbarkeit f soilability
verschmutzen 1. *(allg.)* dirty, soil, pollute 2. *(Wasser, Baustoffe)* contaminate
verschmutzte Substanz f contaminant, pollutant
Verschmutzung f contamination, dirt, pollution
Verschmutzungsgrad m degree of pollution
verschneiden cut badly
Verschnitt m cuttings, waste, refuse
Verschnittbitumensplit m cut-back bitumen chippings
verschrauben 1. *(allg.)* bolt together 2. *(zuschrauben)* screw down
Verschraubung f bolting, screwing
verschrotten scrap, dispose
Verschrottung f scrapping, disposal
verschütten spill

verschweißen weld together
verschwenden waste
Verschwendung *f* waste
versehen mit equip (with), provide (with), fit (with)
versehentlich accidental
versehentliche Einschaltung *f* faulty engagement
versehentliches Schalten *nt* unintentional switching
versenden dispatch, ship
versenken 1. *(zylindrisch)* counterbore **2.** *(kegelig)* countersink
Versetzband *nt* transfer belt
versetzen 1. *(allg.)* displace, shift, offset **2.** *(absetzen)* offset **3.** *(abwechselnd)* stagger **4.** *(verlegen)* move, transfer
versetzt um turned through
versetzt zeichnen *(z. B. Schraffurlinien)* draw staggered
versetzte Doppelkehlnaht *f* staggered double-fillet joint
versetzte Schweißkante *f* edge misalignment
Versetzung *f* **1.** *(allg.)* displacement, shift(ing) **2.** *(Masch.)* offset, misalignment **3.** *(Verlegung)* transfer
verseucht polluted
versichern insure
Versicherung *f* insurance
Versickerung *f* seepage
versiegeln seal
Versiegelung *f* sealing
versinken sink
versorgen supply, provide
Versorger *m* supplier
Versorgung *f* supply
Versorgungsanlage *f* supply unit
Versorgungsanschluss *m* power interface, power port
Versorgungsdruck *m* supply pressure
Versorgungsengpass *m* supply bottleneck
Versorgungskette *f* supply chain
Versorgungskettenmanagement *nt* supply chain management
Versorgungskreis *m* supply circle
Versorgungsleitung *f* supply line
Versorgungsnetz *nt* supply network
Versorgungssicherheit *f* security of supply, supply guarantee
Versorgungsspannung *f* supply voltage
verspannen 1. *(allg.)* twist, warp **2.** *(abspannen)* brace
Verspannung *f* **1.** *(allg.)* twisting, warping **2.** *(Abspannung)* bracing
verspiegelte Seite *f* reflecting (or mirrored) side
verspleißen splice, twist together
Verspleißung *f* spliced joint
Verstampfung *f* ramming
verstärken 1. *(allg.)* strengthen, reinforce, boost, increase **2.** *(el.)* amplify
Verstärker *m* amplifier
Verstärkerhinterfolie *f* rear intensifier screen
Verstärkerhülse *f* reinforcing sleeve
Verstärkermesskette *f* amplifier chain
Verstärkung *f* reinforcement, strengthening, increase, amplification
Verstärkung *f* **der Ansaugmenge** suction boost
Verstaubung *f* depositing of dust
versteifen 1. *(verstärken)* reinforce, stiffen, strengthen **2.** *(verstreben)* brace, strut
Versteifung *f* bracing, strutting, stiffening, reinforcement, strut
Versteifungselement *nt* bracing member, stiffening member, reinforcing member
Versteinungsgefahr *f* danger of scaling
verstellbar adjustable, variable, movable, tiltable, tilting
verstellbare Gegenhalterscheren *f* *(Fräsmaschine)* adjustable overarm braces
verstellbarer Anschlag *m* adjustable dog
verstellbares Spanneisen *nt* offset clamp
verstellbares Zeigerpaar *nt* **für Teilscheibe** adjustable index sector
Verstellbarkeit *f* adjustability
Verstellbereich *m* adjustable range, range of adjustment, regulating range
verstellen 1. *(allg.)* adjust, regulate, vary **2.** (bewegen) move, shift **3.** *(e. Hebel)* shift, move, reposition

4. *(einstellen)* set, adjust **5.** *(nachstellen)* readjust, reset **6.** *(Wege)* obstruct
Verstellen *nt* **1.** *(allg.)* adjustment, regulation **2.** *(Bewegung)* displacement, moving, shifting **3.** *(Wege)* obstruction **4.** *(z. B. e. Stellglied)* positioning
Verstellführung *f* moving guidance
Verstellhebel *m* adjusting lever
Verstellkraft *f* power for acting levers
Verstellspindel *f* lead screw, jack screw
Verstelltraverse *f* adjustable crossbeam
Verstellung *f* **1.** *(Regulierung)* adjustment, regulation **2.** *(Bewegung)* motion **3.** *(maschinell)* power traverse **4.** *(von Hand)* shifting
verstopfen choke
verstopftes Abzugsrohr *nt* blocked telltale pipe
Verstopfung *f* *(durch Späne)* clogging
verstreben brace, strut
Verstrebung *f* **1.** *(allg.)* brace, bracing **2.** *(Querstrebe)* cross-struts, diagonal members
verstreckbarer Kunststoff *m* stretchable plastics material
verstreichen elapse
verstreuen dissipate
Verstricken *nt* yarning
Versuch *m* **1.** *(allg.)* test, testing **2.** *(Abnahmeversuch)* inspection test **3.** *(Anlauf)* attempt **4.** *(Erprobung)* trial, shop test **5.** *(Experiment)* experiment **6.** *(Kontrollversuch)* check **7.** *(praktischer ~)* field test
versuchen 1. *(allg.)* test, try, probe **2.** *(Anlauf machen)* attempt **3.** *(experimentieren)* experiment
Versuchsanlage *f* test installation, pilot plant
Versuchsanordnung *f* test arrangement, test set-up
Versuchsdurchführung *f* test procedure, procedure for conducting tests, conduct of test
Versuchsprobe *f* test specimen
Versuchsreihe *f* series of tests, test series
Versuchsstadium *nt* experimental stage

Versuchsteil *m* test item
Versuchsvorbereitung *f* test preparation
vertauschen swap, exchange, interchange
Vertauschen *nt* swapping
Verteilanlage *f* **1.** *(allg.)* distribution system **2.** *(Förderer)* distributing conveyor
verteilen 1. *(allg.)* distribute, spread, dissipate, allocate **2.** *(aufteilen)* dispense, apportion, proportion **3.** *(verbreiten)* spread
Verteiler *m* **1.** *(allg.)* distributor **2.** *(ein Eingang und viele Ausgänge)* connector
Verteilerdüse *f* manifold (lubricant metering device)
Verteilergetriebe *nt* transfer gear box
Verteilernut *f* distribution groove
Verteillager *nt* distribution warehouse
Verteilmaschine *f* dispensing machine
Verteilrechen *m* distribution rake
Verteilregel *f* distribution rule
Verteilstation *f* distributing station
Verteilung *f* **1.** *(allg.)* allocation, distribution **2.** *(Aufteilung)* dispension, apportionment **3.** *(Verbreitung)* spreading
Verteilung *f* **der Belastung** spreading of the load
Verteilungsanlage *f* distribution installation
verteilungsfreier Test *m* distribution-free test
Verteilungsfunktion *f* distribution function, cumulative probability function
verteilungsgebundener Test *m* parametric test
Verteilungsleitung *f* manifold
Verteilwagen *m* distribution trolley
Verteilzeit *f* distribution time, allowance
Vertiefung *f* **1.** *(allg.)* recess **2.** *(Delle)* dent **3.** *(e. Fläche)* depression
vertikal vertical
vertikal umreifen strap vertically
vertikale Diagonalaussteifung *f* bay cross bracing
Vertikale *f* vertical datum, vertical (line), perpendicular

Vertikalförderer *m* vertical conveyor
Vertikalformfüll- und -verschließmaschine *f* vertical form, fill and seal machine
Vertikalfräsapparat *m* vertical milling attachment
Vertikalfräsarbeit *f* vertical milling operation
Vertikalfräseinheit *f* vertical milling unit
Vertikalfräsen *nt* vertical milling
Vertikalfräskopf *m* vertical milling head (or attachment)
Vertikalfräsmaschine *f* vertical milling machine, vertical-spindle milling machine
Vertikalfrässchlitten *m* vertical milling head
Vertikalhub *m* lift
Vertikalhub *m* **der Ladeeinrichtung** lift of loading device
Vertikalkartoniermaschine *f* vertical cartoner
Vertikalkettenstrang *m* vertical chain (string)
Vertikalkombikommissionierer *m* vertical sideloader/order picker
Vertikalkommissionierer *m* vertical order picker
Vertikalnutenfräsmaschine *f* vertical slot milling machine
Vertikalnutenlangfräsmaschine *f* vertical keyway milling machine
Vertikalpalettenumreifungsmaschine *f* vertical pallet strapping machine
Vertikalpaternoster *nt* vertical carousel
Vertikalprofil *nt* vertical extrusion
Vertikalsenkung *f* vertical lowering
Vertikalumlauflager *nt* vertical circulation storage system
Vertikalumreifung *f* vertical strapping, vertical lacing
Vertikalumreifungsmaschine *f* vertical strapping machine
Vertikalverformung *f* vertical deformation
Vertikalvergrößerung *f* vertical magnification

Vertikalweg *m* vertical path
Vertrag *m* contract
vertraglich compatible
vertraglich festgelegt contractually stipulated
Verträglichkeit *f* compatibility
Verträglichkeitspegel *m* compatibility level
Vertragsabschluss *m* conclusion of a contract
Vertragsänderung *f* alteration/modification (of a contract)
Vertragspartei *f* contract party, contracting party
Vertragsprüfung *f* contract examination
Vertrauensbereich *m* confidence interval
Vertrauensgrenze *f* confidence limit
Vertrauensniveau *nt* confidence level
Vertrieb *m* 1. *(allg.)* distribution, marketing, sales 2. *(Abteilung)* marketing department, sales department
Vertriebskosten *pl* marketing costs
Vertriebslager *nt* sales depot
Vertriebsprogramm *nt* distribution system
Vertriebssystem *nt* distribution system
verunreinigen contaminate, pollute, render impure
verunreinigte Atmosphäre *f* polluted atmosphere
Verunreinigung *f* 1. *(allg.)* contamination, pollution 2. *(Fremdkörper)* impurity
verursachen cause, bring about, generate, originate, produce, result
Verursacher *m* causer, originator
Verursacher *m* **von Umweltverschmutzung** polluter
Vervielfachungsgetriebe *nt* multiplying gear drive
Vervielfältigung *f* reproduction
vervielfältigungsgerechte Ausführung *f* preparation in a form suitable for reproduction
Vervielfältigungsversuch *m* *(bei Schriften)* duplicating trial
verwahren 1. *(lagern)* keep, store 2. *(mit Blech)* flash, protect

Verwahrung f 1. *(lagern)* (safe)keeping, storage 2. *(Bau, mit Blech)* flashing, protection
verwalten administer, manage
Verwaltung f 1. *(allg.)* administration, management 2. *(Buchführung)* accountancy
Verwaltungsfläche f administration area
Verwaltungsgebäude nt administration building
Verwaltungskosten pl administration costs
Verwaltungssystem nt administration system
Verwaltungsvorschrift f administrative regulation
verwechseln confuse, mix, mistake
Verwechslung f confusion
Verweildauer f dwell time, retention period, storage period, stay
verweilen dwell
Verweilzeit f dwell
verwendbar usable
verwenden (als) use, utilize, employ (for)
Verwender m user
Verwendung f function, use, usage, application, employment
Verwendungsart f location of utilization
Verwendungsbereich m range of application, field of use
verwendungsfertig ready for use
verwerfen *(sich verziehen)* warp, reject
verwickeln entangle, get entangled (in/with)
verwickelt intricate
Verwilderung f *(z. B. auf dem Gebiet der Rundgewinde)* proliferation (e. g. of knuckle threads)
Verwindachse f torsion axis
Verwindebruch m torsional fracture
verwinden twist, warp
Verwinden nt *(Schränken)* tooth setting
Verwindeprüfgerät nt torsion testing appliance
Verwindeversuch m torsion test (or testing)

Verwindezahl f number of twists
Verwindung f torsion, twist, warping, distortion, twisting
verwindungsfähig twistable
verwindungssteif resistant to warping, torsion-stiff, torsion-resistant
Verwitterungsbeständigkeit f weathering resistance
verzahnen 1. *(eingreifen)* mesh, interlock, gear 2. *(Zähne formen)* tooth, indent, cut teeth, tooth, cut gears 3. *(Wälzverfahren)* generate teeth, hob teeth
Verzahnen nt **in Paketen** gear cutting in clusters
Verzahnen nt **von Stirnrädern** cutting cylindrical gears
Verzahnmaschine f gear cutting machine, gear hobbing machine, gear generating machine, gear generator
verzahntes Zylinderrad nt toothed cylindrical gear
Verzahntoleranz f gear tooth tolerance
Verzahnung f 1. *(allg.)* gear cutting, tooth production, gear production, gear design, cutting of teeth, indentation, gear tooth system, gearing, toothing 2. *(Ausstatten mit Zähnen)* tooth forming, gear cutting, indenting 3. *(Verzahnungsart)* tooth system 4. *(Wälzverfahren)* gear hobbing, generation of teeth
Verzahnungsabwälzfräser m gear hob
Verzahnungsabweichung f tooth system deviation
Verzahnungsachse f gear teeth axis, gear-cutting axis
Verzahnungscharakteristik f teeth characteristics
Verzahnungseinzelabweichung f gear tooth individual variation
Verzahnungsfehler m gear cutting error
Verzahnungsfräser m gear milling cutter, gear tooth cutter, tooth milling cutter
Verzahnungsgeometrie f tooth geometry
Verzahnungshonen nt tooth honing

Verzahnungsmaschine f 1. *(allg.)* gear cutting machine 2. *(Wälzverfahren)* generating machine, generator, hobbing machine
Verzahnungspassung f gear tooth fit
Verzahnungsprofil nt tooth profile, gear tooth profile
Verzahnungsqualität f gear tooth quality
Verzahnungstechnik f gear cutting technique, gear engineering
Verzahnungsteil nt gear element
Verzahnungstoleranzsystem nt gear tooth tolerance system
Verzahnungsverfahren nt gear-cutting process
Verzahnungswälzfräser m gear hob
Verzahnungswerkzeug nt gear-cutting tool, gear cutter
verzapfen mortise
Verzeichnis nt directory
verzerren distort, deform
Verzerrung f distortion, deformation
verzerrungsfrei free from distortion, distortionless
verziehen buckle, warp, distort
Verziehung f offset
verzinken 1. *(allg.)* zinc, galvanize 2. *(verschwalben)* dovetail
verzinkt zinc coating, galvanized
Verzinsung f pay interest
verzogen crooked, distorted, warped
verzogene Fallleitung f offset downcomer pipe
verzögern 1. *(bremsen)* brake 2. *(verlangsamen)* decelerate, slow down, retard, lag 3. *(zeitlich)* delay, lag
Verzögerung f 1. *(allg.)* delay, lag, retardation, braking, deceleration 2. *(zeitlich)* delay time lag
Verzögerungs- und Anhaltenocke f deceleration and stopping cam
verzögerungsarme Regelstrecke f low-lag plant
Verzögerungsbremse f retarding device
Verzögerungsdauer f period of deceleration, time of dwell
verzögerungsfrei durchzünden ignite completely without any time-lag

Verzögerungsfreiheit f *(e. Reglers)* absence of lag
Verzögerungsglied nt timer
Verzögerungsglied nt **mit Abgriffen** tapped delay element
Verzögerungskraft f forc due to rolling friction
Verzögerungsnocke f deceleration cam
Verzögerungsperiode f deceleration period
Verzögerungsschaltung f delay circuit
Verzögerungszeit f delay period, delay time
Verzug m distortion, warpage
verzugsfrei non-warping
Verzunderung f high temperature oxidation
verzurren secure
verzweigen 1. *(allg.)* branch, go to, ramify 2. *(gabelförmig)* bifurcate
Verzweigung f 1. *(allg.)* branching, ramification 2. *(gabelförmig)* bifurcation
Verzweigungsadresse f branch address
Verzweigungsbefehl m branch instruction
Verzweigungselemente npl branch-off units
Verzweigungsgrad m branching factor
Verzweigungsstelle f branch(ing) point, decision point
V-Grundfugennorm f basic single V-butt weld
Vibration f vibration
vibrationsfest vibration resistant
Vibrationsförderer m vibration conveyor
Vibrator m vibration generator, vibrator
vibrieren vibrate, oscillate
Vicatstift m Vicat indenting tip
Vielbuckelschweißen nt multiple projection welding
vieldeutig ambiguous
vieleckig polygonal
vielfach multiple, many times, in many cases
vielfach einstellbar multipurpose

Vielfachläppvorrichtung *f* multiple lapping attachment
vielfarbig multi-coloured
Vielgestaltigkeit *f* **1.** *(allg.)* versatility **2.** *(e. Werkstückes)* complex shape
Vielkant *m* polygon
Vielkeilverzahnung *f* multiple splining
Vielkeilwelle *f* spline shaft
Vielkristall *m* polycrystal
Vielmeißelautomat *m* multi-cut lathe, multi-tool lathe, single spindle automatic lathe
Vielmeißelhalter *m* multiple toolholder
vielparametrisch multi-parameter
Vielpunktsteuerung *f* multi point control (MPC)
vielschneidig multi-edged
Vielschnittautomat *m* automatic multicut lathe
Vielschnittdrehmaschine *f* multi-tool production lathe, multi-cut lathe, multiple tool lathe
Vielschnittkopierdrehmaschine *f* multi-cut copying lathe
Vielschnittrevolverdrehmaschine *f* multicut turret lathe
Vielschnittwerkzeug *nt* multiple cutting tool
vielseitig flexible, versatile
Vielseitigkeit *f* versatility
Vielspindelbohrmaschine *f* multiple-spindle drilling machine
Vielstahlautomat *m* automatic multi-tool lathe, automatic multicut lathe
Vielstahldrehmaschine *f* multi-cut lathe, multi-tool lathe
Vielstahlhalter *m* multiple toolholder, multiple tool block
Vielstahlschnelldrehbank *f* high-speed multi-tool lathe
Vielstationenbohr- und -fräsmaschine *f* multi-station boring and milling machine
Vielwegbohrmaschine *f* multiple-way boring machine
Vielzweckrevolverdrehmaschine *f* multipurpose turret lathe
Vierbackenfutter *nt* four-jaw chuck
Viereckraster *nt* square grid
Viereckverfahren *nt* square-grid method
vierfach 1. *(allg.)* fourfold, quadruple **2.** *(el.)* quadruplex
Vierfachhubgerüst *nt* quadruple mast
Vierfachmeißelhalter *m* four-way tool block
Vierkant ... square(d)
Vierkant *m* square
Vierkantansatz *m* square neck
Vierkantdrehmeißel *m* square cutting tool
Vierkanteisen *nt* square
Vierkantformmeißel *m* square forming tool
vierkantig four-edged, square
Vierkantmeißel *m* square cutting tool
Vierkantringschlüssel *m* square ring spanner, square box wrench
Vierkantscheibe *f* **für HV-Verbindungen** square washer for high strength friction grip fastenings
Vierkantschraube *f* **mit Ansatzkuppe** square head bolt with half dog point
Vierkantschraube *f* **mit Kernansatz** square head bolt with half dog point
Vierkantschweißmutter *f* square weld nut
Vierkantschweißmutter *f* square weld nut
Vierkantvollstab *m* square rod
Vierkantwerkzeug *m* square toolhead
Vierkugelapparat *m* four ball tester
Vierpunktbelastung *f* four-point loading
Vierradantrieb *m* four wheel drive
Vierradbremse *f* four wheel brake
Vierradlenkung *f* four wheel steering
Vierradstapler *m* four wheel truck
vierseitige Fläche *f* four-sided area
Vierspindelautomat *m* four spindle automatic lathe
Vierspindelfutterautomat *m* four-spindle automatic chucking machine, four-spindle chucking automatic
vierspindelige fühlergesteuerte Fräsmaschine *f* four-spindle tracer milling machine
Vierspindelnachformfräs-

maschine *f* für zweidimensionales Fräsen four-spindle profiler with two-dimensional control
Vierspindelnachformfräsmaschine *f* mit Fühlersteuerung four-spindle tracer milling machine
Vierspindelstangenautomat *m* four-spindle automatic bar machine
Vierspindler *m* four spindle automatic lathe
vierspindlige Bohrmaschine *f* four spindle drilling machine
Vierstoffhartlot *nt* quaternary brazing filler alloy
Viertelkonuspenetration *f* quarter-scale cone penetration
Viertelkonus *m* one-quarter cone
Vierwegebohrmaschine *f* four-way-drilling (or boring) machine, four-way boring machine
Vierwegeflachpalette *f* four-way flat pallet
Vierwegemischer *m* four way mixer valve
Vierwegepalette *f* single-face four-way entry pallet, four-way pallet
Vierwegestapler *m* four-directional (lift) truck
Vinylasbestplatte *f* vinyl-asbestos tile
Vinylchloridcopolymerisat *nt* vinyl chloride copolymer
Vinylchloridhomopolymerisat *nt* vinyl chloride homopolymer
Vinylchloridmischpolymerisat *nt* vinyl chloride copolymer
Vinylchloridpolymerisat *nt* vinyl chloride pure polymer
Vinylchloridreinpolymerisat *nt* vinyl chloride pure polymer
virtuell virtual
virtueller Eingang *m* virtual input
Visiereinrichtung *f* sighting device
viskoelastischer Stoff *m* visco-elastic material
viskoelastisches Verhalten *nt* visco-elastic behaviour
viskos viscous
Viskose *f* viscose
Viskosereibung *f* viscous friction
Viskosität *f* viscosity

Viskositätsabfall *m* viscosity loss
Viskositätsaufbau *m* viscosity build-up
Viskositäts-Dichte-Konstante *f* viscosity-density constant
Viskositäts-Dichte-Verhältnis *m* viscosity-density ratio
visualisieren visualize
Visualisierung *f* visualization
visuell optical, visual
V-Kreis *m* X-circle
V-Kreis-Bogen *m* *(zwischen den beiden Zahnflanken)* X-circle arc
V-Kreis-Durchmesser *m* *(e. Stirnrades)* X-circle diameter
V-Kreis-Teilung *f* *(bei Geradstirnrad)* X-circle pitch
Vlieskunstleder *nt* artificial leather on a bonded fabric basis
V-minus-Radpaar *nt* gear pair at reduced centres
V-Naht *f* am Eckstoß single-Vee groove for corner joint
V-Naht *f* mit ebener Oberfläche flat single-V butt joint
V-Naht *f* mit Gegenlage single-V butt joint with backing run, single-Vee groove with sealing run
V-Naht *f* mit Gegenlage und ebener Oberfläche flat single-V butt joint with flat backing run
V-Naht *f* mit verschiedenen Anschlussquerschnitten single-V butt joint with different abutting cross-sections
V-Nahtüberhöhung *f* reinforcement of single-Vee groove
V-Null Getriebe *nt* V-zero transmission, V-null transmission
V-Null Radpaar *nt* gear pair with reference centre distance
V-Null-Innenradpaar *nt* internal gear pair at reference centre distance
V-Null-Verzahnung *f* reference centre distance tooth system
voll full, fully-loaded, complete, maximum
Voll ... solid
vollaustenitisches Schweißgut *nt* fully austenitic weld metal
Vollautomat *m* 1. *(allg.)* fully automatic

machine **2.** *(Drehbank)* fully automatic lathe
vollautomatisch automatic
Vollbohrarbeit *f* drilling operation
vollbohren drill
Vollbohrspan *m* drilling chip, boring chip
Vollbohrung *f* **1.** *(mittels Bohrmeißel)* boring **2.** *(mittels Spiralbohrer)* drilling
volle Drehzahl *f* maximum speed
volle Flanke *f* full flank
volle Leistung *f* full power
Voll-Einschlagmaschine *f* wrapping machine forming a complete wrap
vollelektrisch all-electric
vollenden complete
vollentsalztes Wasser *nt* demineralized water
Vollentsalzung *f* complete demineralization
voller Querschnitt *m* solid section
volles Drehmoment *nt* full load torque
vollflächig all-over, fully flat
Vollformgießverfahren *nt* full form casting process
Vollformgutlehre *f* full form "Go" gauge
Vollfräser *m* solid milling cutter
vollfugig jointed flush
vollgekapselt 1. *(allg.)* totally enclosed **2.** *(el.)* metal-clad
vollgraphisch fully graphic
Vollgummirad *nt* bonded tyre wheel
Vollgummireifen *m* solid tyre
vollkantig full squared, full-edged, flatted
vollkantig angular edged
Vollkausche *f* solid thimble
Vollkegel *m* taper shank
vollkraftbetrieben full power
Vollkreis *m* full circle
Vollladezyklus *m* full-charge cycle
Vollladung *f* full charging
Volllast *f* full load
Volllastanlauf *m* full-load start
Volllastdrehzahl *f* full-load speed
Volllastlebensdauer *f* load life, life under full load
Vollautomat *m* fully automatic machine

Volllehrdorn *m* solid plug gauge
Volllinie *f* **1.** *(allg.)* continuous line **2.** *(schmale ~)* narrow continuous line
vollmechanisches Plasmaschweißen *nt* fully mechanized plasma welding
vollmechanisiertes Löten *nt* fully mechanized soldering
Vollmeißel *m* solid cutting tool, solid tool, forged tool
Vollpalettenrollenbahn *f* full pallet roller conveyor
Vollpappe *f* cardboard
Vollpipette *f* transfer pipette
vollplastischer Zustand *m* fully plastic condition
Vollprägen *nt* closed-die coining
Vollprüfung *f* full test
Vollquerfließpressen *nt* transverse rod impact extrusion
Vollquerstrangpressen *nt* transverse rod extrusion
Vollrückwärtsfließpressen *nt* indirect rod impact extrusion
Vollrückwärtsfließpressen *nt* indirect rod impact extrusion
Vollrückwärtsstrangpressen *nt* indirect extrusion of rods
Vollschaftschraube *f* full-shank bolt
Vollschnitt *m* full section
Vollschrumpffolienumhüllung *f* complete shrink wrap
vollschwarzer Pfeil *m* solid black arrow
vollselbsttätige Maschine *f* fully automatic machine
vollständig complete, entire, full
vollständige vertikale Integration *f* complete vertical integration
Vollständigkeit *f* completeness, entireness
volltragend gedachte Flankenlinie *f* tooth trace thought of as fully bearing
Vollumrissnachformfräsmaschine *f* full-circle profiling machine, full-circle profiler
Vollvorwärtsfließpressen *nt* direct impact extrusion of rods
Vollvorwärtsfließpressen *nt* direct impact extrusion of rods

Vollvorwärtsstrangpressen *nt* direct extrusion of rods
Vollwälzfräser *m* solid hob
Vollwand *f* solid wall
vollwandig massive, solid, solid-walled
Vollwelle *f* solid shaft
Vollwellengleichrichtung *f* full wave rectification
vollzylindrischer Lehrdorn *m* fully cylindrical plug gauge
Volumen *nt* volume
Volumenabnahme *f* decrease of volume
Volumenberechnung *f* volumetric calculation
Volumendurchfluss *m* volumetric flow
Volumenfehlbetrag *m* volumetric deficiency
volumenhafte Fehler *mpl* three dimensional defects
Volumenkonstanz *f* volume constancy
Volumenmessgerät *nt* volume measuring instrument, volumeter
Volumenmessung *f* volume measurement
Volumennachschwindung *f* aftershrinkage in volume
Volumenschwindung *f* shrinkage in volume
Volumenstrom *m* volume flow (rate)
Volumenstromfüllmaschine *f* flow meter filling machine
Volumenstrommessgerät *nt* floe meter
Volumenstromsteuerung *f* volume flow control
Volumentrübung *f* volume turbidity
Volumenzunahme *f* increase in volume
volumetrischer Wirkungsgrad *m* volumetric efficiency
von (Ort) from
von ... bis ... from ... to ...
von der Rolle zugeführt reel-fed
von einem Ende aus gesteuert end-controlled
von Hand betätigt hand-operated, manually operated
von Hand by hand, manual(ly)
von Hand beistellen feed by hand
von oben from above
von oben nach unten top down, in a vertical downward direction
von unten from below
von unten nach oben bottom-up, from the bottom up, in a vertical upward direction
vor 1. *(räumlich)* in front of **2.** *(zeitlich)* before, prior to
vor Ort on site
Vor- und Rücklaufhobeln *nt* two-way planning
Vorabnahme *f* preliminary inspection, pre-inspection, preliminary acceptance
Voranstrichmittel *nt* primer
Vorarbeit *f* preceding operation
vorarbeiten pre-machine, rough finish
voraus ahead
vorauseilen 1. *(allg.)* hurry ahead, precede **2.** *(el.)* lead
vorauseinstellen pre-adjust
vorausgehend previous, preceding
Vorausplanung *f* preliminary planning
vorausschauend anticipatory, preventive
vorausschauende Bahnbetrachtung *f* look ahead function
voraussehbar foreseeable
voraussetzen assume, presuppose, premise
Voraussetzung *f* assumption, condition, premise, prerequisite
Vorbasis *f* pre-basis
Vorbau *m* front part
Vorbaumaß *nt* lost load centre
Vorbauten *pl* protruding units
Vorbeanspruchung *f* pre-stressing
vorbearbeiten pre-machine, rough-machine
Vorbearbeitung *f* preliminary machine, rough machining, pre-machining, roughing, prior machining operations *pl*
Vorbearbeitungszeichnung *f* preoperation drawing
Vorbehaltung *f* preconditioning, conditioning
Vorbehaltungsklima *nt* conditioning atmosphere
vorbehandeln pretreat, preprocess
Vorbehandlung *f* pretreatment, pre-

paratory treatment, preprocessing, preparation, preconditioning
vorbeifahren (an) overtake
vorbeiführen pass by, direct along
vorbeiströmen by-pass *vi*
vorbeiziehen draw along
Vorbelastung *f* preliminary load
vorbelegen 1. *(allg.)* preallocate **2.** *(IT)* preempt, initialize (with)
Vorbelegung *f* **1.** *(allg.)* preallocation, preempting **2.** *(Information eines Feldsatzes)* default
vorbereiten prepare
vorbereitender Eingang *m* enabling input
Vorbereitung *f* preparation
Vorbereitungsarbeit *f* preparatory work
Vorbereitungsphase *f* lead-up
vorbeschichten precoat
Vorbeschichtung *f* precoat
vorbesetzen preallocate, preset
vorbestimmt predetermined, preset
Vorbeugemaßnahme *f* (measure of) precaution, preventive measure
vorbeugen avoid, prevent, parry, obviate
vorbeugender Brandschutz *m* fire prevention
Vorbohrdurchmesser *m* rough drilling diameter
vorbohren predrill, rough-bore
Vorbohrung *f* starting hole, pilot hole
vorbringen advance
vordehnen prestretch, elongate
Vordehnung *f* prestretch, prestretching, elongation
Vorder- und Hinterradantrieb *m* front and rear drive unit
vorder/e/er/es front
Vorderachse *f* front axle
Vorderansicht *f* front elevation
Vorderblende *f* anterior diaphragm
Vorderendfutter *nt* front extension chuck
vorderer Ständer *m* front standard
vorderes Ende *nt* front end
vorderes Spindelende *nt* front spindle end
Vorderfläche *f* face, front face

Vorderfolie *f* front intensifying screen
Vorderkante *f* front edge, leading edge
Vorderkanteneinstellung *f* (e. Hobelmaschine) setting of the front cutting edge, forward edge adjustment
Vorderrad *nt* front wheel
Vorderschlitten *m* front slide
Vorderschutz *m* guards at the outside edge
Vorderseite *f* front, front end, front face, face
Vorderseite *f* **der Gabel** inside of a fork
Vorderständer *m* front upright
Vorderwand *f* front wall, front
Vorderwandklappe *f* front flap
Vordesinfektion *f* pre-sterilization
vordrehen pre-turn, pre-machine, rough-turn
Vordruck *m* inlet pressure, primary pressure, form, blank
Vordruckzeichnung *f* preprinted drawing
Vordüse *f* pilot jet
voreilend advance, leading, anticipating, preceding
voreilende Drehstellungsabweichung *f* leading angular position variation
Voreilung *f* advance, lead
voreingestellt preset
voreinstellbar presettable
Voreinstell-Eingang *m* preset input, preset
voreinstellen preset, preadjust
Voreinstellglied *nt* presetting element
Voreinstellung *f* **1.** *(allg.)* presetting, preadjustment, preset, preadjusting **2.** *(IT)* default value
Vorendschalter *m* preliminary switch
Vorentrosten *nt* preliminary derusting
Vorentwässerung *f* initial drainage
Vorentwicklungsphase *f* pre-development phase
Vorentwurfszeichnung *f* preliminary draft drawing
Vorfahrt *f* right of way
Vorfahrt *f* **beachten** watch the right of way
Vorfahrt *f* **missachten** fail to observe

give-way right
Vorfahrtsregel *f* give-way right
Vorfeld *nt* access area, front area
vorfertigen prefabricate
Vorfertigung *f* **1.** *(allg.)* prefabrication, preproduction **2.** *(Material)* prefabricated materials
Vorfilterung *f* pre-filtration
vorformatieren preformat
Vorformung *f* preforming
Vorfräseinrichtung *f* rough milling attachment
vorfräsen 1. *(allg.)* rough-cut, rough-mill, pre-mill **2.** *(Zahnlücken) (US)* stock, *(UK)* gash
Vorfräsen *nt* **runder Gesenkformen** roughing cherrying operation
Vorfräsen *nt* **von Zahnlücken** gashing, stocking
Vorfräser *m* **1.** *(allg.)* rough cutter, roughing cutter **2.** *(Zahnräder) (US)* stocking cutter, *(UK)* gash milling cutter
Vorfrässpindel *f* rough-milling spindle
Vorführzapfen *m* *(e. Gewindebohrers)* pilot (on tap)
Vorgabe *f* specification, allowed time, requirements
Vorgabezahndicke *f* specified tooth thickness
Vorgabezeit *f* allowed time
Vorgabezeitermittlung *f* allowed time establishment
Vorgang *m* action, operation, process, procedure, transaction
Vorgangszuordnung *f* process allocation
vorgeben specify, require, allow
vorgebohrtes Loch *nt* predrilled hole
vorgefertigt pre-made, prefabricated
vorgeformte Masse *f* preformed moulding material
vorgegeben given, predetermined, specified, preset
vorgegebene Ebene *f* specified (or predetermined or defined) plane
vorgegebene Messzeit *f* specified measuring time
vorgegebene Stellung *f* pre-set position
vorgegebener Sollwert *m* predetermined desired value
vorgegebener Wert *m* given value, specified value
vorgegebenes Maß *nt* prescribed deviation (or size)
vorgegossenes Loch *nt* cored hole
vorgehen proceed
Vorgehensweise *f* procedure
vorgeklebt pre-glued
vorgelagert upstream (of)
Vorgelege *nt* countershaft
Vorgelegewelle *f* countershaft
vorgeneigt tilted forwards
vorgeschaltet upstream (of)
vorgeschäumte Teilchen *npl* pre-foamed particles
Vorgeschichte *f* extended
vorgesehen provided
vorgesehene Schweißung *f* envisaged weld
vorgesehener Verwendungszweck *m* intended use
vorgesehenes Feld *nt* *(in e. Zeichnung)* panel provided for the purpose
Vorgesetzter *m* superior
vorgespannt preloaded
vorgestaltet *(vorformatiert)* preformatted
vorgestanzt precut
vorgewählt preselected
vorgewählte automatische Lenkung *f* automated steering acquisition
vorgummieren pregum
Vorhaben *nt* project, proposal
vorhanden available, existing
Vorhandensein *nt* availability, existence
Vorhang *m* curtain
Vorhangeinweglichtschranke *f* roller blind single-way light barrier, light roller blind
Vorhängeschloss *nt* padlock
Vorhanghaken *m* curtain hook
Vorhärtung *f* precuring
vorher eingestellt preadjusted
vorher einstellen preset
vorhergehend preceding
vorhersehbar foreseeable
vorhersehen anticipate, forecast, foresee

vorhobeln rough-plane
Vorhonen *nt* rough honing
Vorkalkulation *f* cost scheduling
Vorkammerbuchse *f* advance chamber bushing
Vorkehrung *f* provision, arrangement, precaution
Vorkehrungen treffen make arrangements, make provisions
vorkleben pre-glue
Vorkraft *f* pre-load
vorkragen project, protrude
vorkrümmen pre-bend
Vorkrümmung *f* pre-bending
Vorlage *f* pattern, model, template, original
Vorlagenbehälter *m* seal housing
Vorläppen *nt* rough lapping
Vorlauf *m* **1.** *(Bewegung)* forward motion, forward rotation **2.** *(Band, Film)* leader **3.** *(Programme)* beginning routine **4.** *(Transport)* pre-carriage, on-carriage **5.** *(Stoffe)* flow
Vorlaufanschluss *m* flow connection
vorlaufende Flamme *f* leading flame
vorlaufende Schneidradflanke *f* leading pinion cutter flank
Vorlaufgeschwindigkeit *f* speed of forward stroke, speed of cutting stroke, rate of cutting speed
Vorlaufkugel *f (e. Ubbelohde-Viskosimeter)* subsidiary bulb (of Ubbelohde suspended-level viscosimeter)
Vorlauföl *nt* feed oil
Vorlaufschnittgeschwindigkeit *f* cutting speed during the forward stroke
Vorlaufstrecke *f* advance length
Vorlauftemperatur *f* flow temperature
Vorlaufzeit *f* lead time
Vorlegekeil *m* chock, block
Vorlegeleiste *f* chock, block
vorlegen 1. *(örtlich)* place **2.** *(zur Genehmigung)* submit
Vorlegewelle *f* countershaft
Vorlochdurchmesser *m (bei Blechdurchzügen)* prepunched hole diameter
Vormaß *nt* end distance
Vormaterial *nt* primary material
Vormontage *f* **1.** *(allg.)* preassembly, subassembly **2.** *(Probe)* trial erection **3.** *(Untergruppe)* subassembly
vormontieren preassemble, subassemble
vorn ahead, in front
vorneigen tilt forwards
Vorortpuffer *m* on-site buffer
vorplanen plan in advance
Vorplanung *f* concept planning, preliminary planning, pilot project
Vorplanungsphase *f* concept phase
Vorpresskraft *f* squeeze force
Vorpresswerkzeug *nt* pre-forming mould
Vorpresszeit *f* squeeze time
Vorprojekt *nt* preliminary project
vorprojektieren project conceptually
vorprojektiert preconfigured, conceptually projected
Vorprojektierung *f* preliminary projection
Vorprüfung *f* design check, design verification, preliminary test (or testing), preliminary scrutiny
Vorpumpe *f* booster pump
vorquetschen crowd
Vorrang *m* priority
vorrangig priority, overriding
vorrangiges Rücksetzen *nt* overriding reset
Vorrangschaltung *f* priority control
Vorrat *m* stock, stockpile, inventory, goods on hand, stock-in-trade
vorrätig available, in stock
Vorratsaufstockung *f* inventory build-up
Vorratsbehälter *m* **1.** *(allg.)* bin, storage container **2.** *(Tank)* store tank, reservoir
Vorratsgaswasserheizer *m* gas storage water heater
Vorratsmenge *f* feedstock
Vorratsschmierung *f* pack lubrication
Vorratssystem *nt* stock system
Vorratswasserheizer *m* storage water heater
vorreinigen clean before hand
Vorreservierung *f* pre-reservation
Vorrichtung *f* **1.** *(allg.)* device, equipment, fixture, attachment, facility, appliance, arrangement, mechanism

2. *(e. Bohrmaschine)* jig **3.** *(Spannzeug)* fixture **4.** *(Test ~)* test (jig) **5.** *(Zurüstung)* attachment
Vorrichtungen *fpl (für Werkzeugmaschinen)* jigs and fixtures
Vorrichtungsauswahl *f* mechanism selection
Vorrichtungsbau *m* design of jigs and fixtures
vorrücken 1. *(Meißel, Schlitten, Tisch,...)* advance, move forward, jog **2.** *(schrittweise mit kleinster Drehzahl)* inch
Vorsätze *mpl* resolutions
Vorsatzgerät *nt* attachment, implement
vorschalten connect upstream, connect in series
Vorschaltgetriebe *nt* primary mechanism, transfer case
Vorschau *f* **1.** *(allg.)* forecast **2.** *(Programme)* preview
Vorschauauftrag *m* forecast order
Vorscherebene *f* pre-shear plane
Vorschieben *nt* **1.** *(Meißel)* advance **2.** *(Werkstücke)* feeding (forward), moving (forward) **3.** *(ausfahren)* extension
Vorschlag *m* suggestion
Vorschleifen *nt (US)* snag grinding, snagging
Vorschmiereinleitungsverteiler *m* prelubrication injector metering device
Vorschneider *m* rough cutter
Vorschneidmeißel *m* roughing tool
Vorschneidzahn *m* roughing tooth
vorschreiben specify, prescribe
Vorschrift *f* **1.** *(allg.)* regulation, prescription **2.** *(Anweisung)* instruction
vorschruppen rough
Vorschruppen *nt (Wälzverfahren)* roughing by generation
Vorschub *m* **1.** *(allg.)* amount of feed, feed, feed rate **2.** *(als Bewegung)* feeding path, feed motion **3.** *(als Größe)* feed motion **4.** *(je Zahn / Räumwerkzeug)* degree of taper **5.** *(Schleifscheibe)* in-feed
Vorschubantrieb *m* feed gear mechanism
Vorschubapparat *m* feeder

Vorschubausrückung *f* feed trip
Vorschubbereich *m* range of feeds
Vorschubbewegung *f* feed motion
Vorschubeingriff *m* feed engagement
Vorschubeinrichtung *f* automatic advance
Vorschubeinstellscheibe *f* feed dial
Vorschubeinstellung *f* feed setting
Vorschubenergie *f* feed energy
Vorschubfeinzustellung *f* fine feed setting
Vorschubgabelträger *m* load extender
Vorschubgerät *nt* feed device
Vorschubgeschwindigkeit *f* advance speed, rate of feed, feed rate, feed speed
Vorschubgetriebe *nt* feed gear mechanism, feeding mechanism, feed gear train, feed gearbox, feedbox
Vorschubgewindespindel *f* feed screw
Vorschubgröße *f* feed rate, rate of feed, amount of feed
Vorschubkette *f* feed chain
Vorschubklinkenrad *nt* feed ratchet wheel
Vorschubknagge *f* feed dog
Vorschubkopf *m* feed-control knob
Vorschubkraft *f* longitudinal force, feed force, feed thrust
Vorschubleistung *f* feed power
Vorschubmarke *f* feed mark
Vorschubnormalkraft *f* feed perpendicular force
Vorschuborgan *nt* feed transmission agent
Vorschubrad *nt* feed sprocket wheel
Vorschubräderkasten *m* feed gearbox, feedbox
Vorschubregelung *f* feed control
Vorschubregler *m* feed regulator
Vorschubreihe *f (Regelscheibe)* regulation wheel, control wheel
Vorschubreihen *fpl* feed rows
Vorschubrichtung *f* direction of the feed motion
Vorschubrichtungswinkel *m* feed motion angle
Vorschubschalter *m* feed switch
Vorschubschalthebel *m* feed control lever

Vorschub-Schaltkasten *m* feedbox
Vorschubschleifverfahren *nt* *(Längsschleifverfahren)* traverse grinding method
Vorschubschlitten *m* stock feed slide
Vorschubsteuerung *f* feed control
Vorschubstufungen *fpl* feed steppings
Vorschubtrommel *f* feed drum
Vorschubumsteuerung *f* feed reverse, feed reversal
Vorschubvorwähler *m* feed pre-selector
Vorschubwähler *m* feed selector
Vorschubwahlschalter *m* feed selection switch, feed selector
Vorschubweg *m* feed travel
Vorschubweglängen *fpl* lengthen of feed
Vorschubwelle *f* feed rod, feed shaft
Vorschubwert *m* feed rate, rate of feed
Vorschweißbördel unturned welding flange
Vorschweißflansch *m* welding neck flange
vorsehen provide
vorsenken *(Gewindelöcher)* pre-counterbore
Vorserie *f* pilot lot, pilot production
Vorserienlogistik *f* preproduction logistics
Vorserienphase *f* pilot production phase
Vorsicht *f* care, caution
Vorsichtsmaßnahme *f* (measure of) precaution, safety measure
Vorsichtsmaßregel *f* precaution
vorsortieren presort
Vorspalte *f* precolumn
Vorspannbolzen *m* preloading bolt
vorspannen prestress, pretension, bias, preload
Vorspannfederweg *m* preload deflection
Vorspannkraft *f* *(e. Sicherungsmutter)* preload
Vorspannmöglichkeit *f* facility for prestressing
Vorspannung *f* **1.** *(mechanisch)* initial stress, prestress(ing), pretensioning, preload(ing), mean stress **2.** *(el.)* bias voltage
Vorsprungflansch *m* male-faced flange
Vorspülung *f* preliminary scavenging
Vorspülzeit *f* prepurge period, pre-scavenging time
vorstanzen precut
Vorstauzone *f* pre-stagnation zone
Vorsteuerelement *nt* servo-mechanism
Vorsteuerung *f* feed forward
Vorstreichverfahren *nt* previous application method
Vortäuschen *nt* simulation
Vortäuschung *f* simulation
Vorteil *m* advantage
vorteilhaft advantageous
Vortrocknung *f* pre-desiccation
Vortyp *m* pre-assigned type
vortypisierte Formmasse *f* pre-assigned moulding material
vorübergehend temporary, transient
vorübergehende Sollwertabweichung *f* transient deviation from the desired value
Voruntersuchung *f* preliminary examination, preliminary investigation
vorverarbeiten preprocess
Vorverarbeitung *f* preprocessing
Vorverstärkung *f* pre-intensification
Vorverzahnwerkzeug *nt* roughing cutter
Vorwahl *f* preselection
vorwählbar preselectable, presettable, preselective
Vorwähleinrichtung *f* preselection mechanism
vorwählen preselect, preset
Vorwähler *m* preselector
Vorwählschaltung *f* **1.** *(Funktion)* preselection control, preselector mechanism **2.** *(Bauelement)* preselector
Vorwählscheibe *f* preselector dial
Vorwälzfräser *m* roughing hob
Vorwärmung *f* preheating
vorwarnen forewarn, prewarn
Vorwarngrenze *f* prewarning limit
Vorwarnmeldung *f* prewarning message
Vorwarnung *f* forewarning, prewarning

vorwärts forward, ahead
vorwärts fahren drive forwards, move forwards, travel forwards
Vorwärtsbewegung *f* forward movement
Vorwärtsfahrtrichtung *f* forward travel direction
Vorwärtsfließpressen *nt* direct impact extrusion
Vorwärtsgang *m* forward gear, forward speed
Vorwärtsneigung *f* forward tilt
Vorwärtsrichtung *f* forward direction
Vorwärts-Rückwärts-Schieberegister *nt* bidirectional shift register
Vorwärts-Strangpressen *nt* direct extrusion of rods and tubes
Vorwärtsterminplanung *f* forward schedule
Vorwärtsverstellung *f* fore adjustment
Vorwärtszählen *nt* count up
Vorwaschen *nt* (*Entrosten*) pre-washing
Vorweite *f* (*als Schleiffehler*) bellmouthing
Vorwerkstoff *m* primary material
Vorwiderstand *m* preresistor
vorwinkeln pre-angle
Vorzeichen *nt* sign
Vorzeichenbit *nt* sign bit
Vorzeichenregel *f* sign rule
Vorzeichenumkehr *f* sign inversion
vorzeitig premature
Vorzerkleinerung *f* pre-disintegration
Vorzerkleinerungsgerät *nt* pre-reduction apparatus
Vorzone *f* access area, forecourt, front area
Vorzonenbestand *m* buffer area onhand quantity
Vorzugsfarbe *f* preferred colour
Vorzugsmaß *nt* preferred dimension
Vorzugsrichtung *f* preferential direction
Vorzugssteigung *f* preferred lead
Vorzugstoleranz *f* preferred tolerance field
Vorzündungszeit *f* pre-ignition time
vorzunehmende Arbeit *f* work in hand
Vorzustand *m* prior state
V-Plus-Radpaar *nt* gear pair at extended centres
V-Prisma *nt* **1.** (*allg.*) V-way, Vee **2.** (*umgekehrtes ~*) inverted Vee-way
V-Probe *f* V-notch specimen
V-Rad *nt* X-gear
V-Radpaar *nt* X-gear pair, gear pair with modified centre distance
Vulkametrie *f* curemetry, measurement of plasticity
V-U-Naht *f* V-U butt joint
V-Verzahnung *f* X-tooth system
V-Wurzel *f* V root
V-Zylinder *m* (*e. Stirnrades*) X-cylinder
V-Zylinder-Normalteilung *f* X-cylinder normal pitch

WA *(Warenausgang)* outgoing goods department, dispatch
Waage *f* **1.** *(Gerät)* scale(s), weighing machine, weighing scales, weigher **2.** *(Gegengewicht)* balance
waagerecht level, horizontal
Waagerechtbohr- und -fräsmaschine *f* horizontal boring drilling and milling machine, horizontal boring and milling machine, horizontal boring mill
Waagerechtbohr- und -fräsmaschine *f* **mit axialverschiebbarem Tisch** planer-type horizontal boring and milling machine
Waagerechtbohr- und -fräsmaschine *f* **mit drehbarem Aufspanntisch** horizontal boring drilling and milling machine with rotary worktable
Waagerechtbohr- und -fräsmaschine *f* **mit feststehenden Ständer, längs, quer und rund verstellbarem Tisch und Lünette** horizontal boring drilling and milling machine with non-traversing column, traversing rotary worktable and boring stay
Waagerechtbohr- und -fräsmaschine *f* **mit kreuzbeweglichem Aufspanntisch** horizontal boring drilling and milling machine with compound table
Waagerechtbohr-, -fräs- und -gewindebohrmaschine *f* horizontal boring milling drilling and tapping machine
Waagerechtbohren *nt* **1.** *(Innenausdrehen)* horizontal boring **2.** *(Vollbohren)* horizontal drilling
Waagerechtbohrmaschine *f* horizontal boring machine
Waagerechtbohrmaschine *f* **zum Innenausdrehen** horizontal boring machine
Waagerechtbohrwerk *nt* horizontal boring mill

Waagerechte *f* **1.** *(allg.)* horizontal (line) **2.** *(Ebene)* level, horizontal plane
Waagerechtfeinstbohrwerk *nt* horizontal precision boring machine
Waagerechtflächenschleifmaschine *f* horizontal surface grinder
Waagerechtfräs- und -bohrmaschine *f* horizontal milling and boring machine
Waagerechtfräsmaschine *f* **1.** *(allg.)* horizontal milling machine, horizontal miller **2.** *(Doppelständer ~)* double-column horizontal milling machine (or miller) **3.** *(Einfach ~)* plain horizontal milling machine
Waagerechtfrässpindelkopf *m* horizontal milling spindle head
Waagerechthandhebelfeinstfräsmaschine *f* horizontal precision hand lever milling machine
Waagerechthobeln *nt* horizontal planning
Waagerechtinnenräummaschine *f* horizontal internal broaching machine
Waagerechtkonsolfräsmaschine *f* horizontal knee- and column type miller (or milling machine)
Waagerechtnachformfräsmaschine *f* **für zweidimensionales Fräsen** horizontal profiler with two dimensional control
Waagerechtproduktionsfräsmaschine *f* horizontal manufacturing-type milling machine, horizontal fixed-bed milling machine (or miller), fixed-bed milling machine with horizontal spindle
Waagerechtprofilfräsmaschine *f* *(für horizontale Gesenkarbeit)* horizontal duplicator, die-sinker
Waagerechtstarrfräsmaschine *f* horizontal rigid milling machine
Waagerechtstoßmaschine *f* **1.** *(allg.)* horizontal-type shaper, shaping machine, shaper **2.** *(Schnellhobler)* shaping machine, shaper **3.** *(Waagerecht-*

zahnradfräsmaschine) horizontal gear hobber
Waagerechtstoßmaschine *f* **mit Kurbelschleifantrieb** crank shaper
Waagerechtstoßmaschine *f* **mit Stößelantrieb durch Zahnstange** geared shaper
Waagerechtstoßmaschine *f* **mit traversierendem Stößel** traverse-bed shaper
Waagerechtstoßmaschine *f* **mit waagerecht verlaufendem Stößel** horizontal shaper
Waagerechtstoßmaschine *f* **mit ziehendem (schiebendem) Schnitt** draw-cut (push-cut) shaper
Wabe *f* honeycomb
wabenartiges Gitter *nt* honeycomb
Wabenkern *m* honey-comb core
Wabenkernverbund *m* honeycomb sandwich
Wabenlager *nt* honeycomb warehouse, pigeon-hole warehouse
Wabenlagerung *f* honeycomb storage, pigeon-hole storage
Wabenregal *nt* honeycomb shelving, honeycomb racking, pigeon-hole racking
Wabenregalanlage *f* honeycomb shelving system, honeycomb racking system, pigeon-hole racking system
Wabenregalzeile *f* honeycomb shelving row
Wachflamme *f* pilot flame
Wachflammenleitung *f* pilot flame line
Wachsauftrag *m* wax coating
Wachsechtheit *f* resistance to wax
wachsen grow, increase
wachskaschierter Packstoff *m* wax-backed packaging material
Wachstum *nt* growth, increase
Wachstumsphase *f* growth stage
Wächter *m* detector, monitor
wackeln totter
Wägeeinrichtung *f* weighing unit
Wägefüllmaschine *f* gravimetric filling machine
Wägeglas *nt* weighing glass
wägen weigh, scale

Wagen *m* **1.** *(Fahrzeug)* vehicle, carriage, truck **2.** *(Transportbehälter)* cart, trolley
Wagen *m* **mit Drehschemel** turntable truck
Wagen *m* **mit fester Plattform** fixed height platform truck, fixed height load carrying truck
Wagenvorschub *m* carriage
Wägepipette *f* weighing pipette
Waggon *m* wagon
Waggonbau *m* wagon construction
Wägung *f* weighing
Wahl *f* **1.** *(Möglichkeiten)* alternative, choice, option **2.** *(Entscheidung, EDV)* selection
Wahl *f*: **nach ~ des Verwenders** at the direction of the user
wählen choose, select, dial
wählergesteuerte Fräsmaschine *f* dial-type milling machine
wahllos random
Wahlschalter *m* mode switch, selector switch
Wahlscheibe *f* dial
wahlweise optional
Wählzeichenfolge *f* selection signals
während during
wahrer Wert *m* true value
Wahrheitstabelle *f* operation table, truth table
Wahrheitstafel *f* truth table
wahrnehmbar perceptible
Wahrnehmung *f* perception
wahrscheinlich probable
Wahrscheinlichkeit *f* probability
Wahrscheinlichkeitsaussage *f* probability statement
Wahrscheinlichkeitsdichte *f* probability density
Wahrscheinlichkeitsfunktion *f* probability function
Wahrscheinlichkeitsrechnung *f* probability calculus, probability theory
Wahrscheinlichkeitstheorie *f* theory of probability, probability theory
Wahrscheinlichkeitsverteilung *f* probability distribution
Walkechtheit *f* fastness to fulling (or milling)

Walkfläche *f* milling surface
Walkpenetration *f* worked penetration
Wälzabweichung *f* working variation
Wälzachse *f* rolling axis
Wälzarbeit *f* hobbing (operation), generating, roll work
Walzaufschrift *f* rolling inscription, engraved text
Wälzautomat *m* automatic hobber
Wälzbahn *f* path of contact
Wälzbewegung *f* generating motion, rolling motion
Walzbiegen *nt* roll bending
Walzbördeln *nt* roll flanging
Walzdrehmoment roll torque
Walzdruck *m* roll pressure
Walze *f* cylinder, drum, roll(er)
Wälzebene *f* pitch plane
Wälzeinzelabweichung *f* individual working variation
Wälzen *nt* 1. *(rollen, drehen)* rolling action, rolling 2. *(wälzfräsen)* generating, hobbing, slab milling, plane milling 3. *(als Arbeitsverfahren)* generating (or hobbing) method
Walzen *nt* **von Band/Blech** rolling of strip/sheet
Walzen *nt* **von Profilstäben** rolling of sectional bars
Walzen *nt* **von Rohren ohne Innenwerkzeug** rolling of tubes without internal tool
Walzen *nt* **von Rohren über Stange** rotary piercing of tubes over a plug
Walzen *nt* **von Stäben/Draht** rolling of bars/wire
Walzen *nt* **von Vielnutwellen** rolling of multiple-spline shafts
Walzen *nt* **von Vierkantrollen** rolling of square tubes
Walzenauftragsverfahren *nt* reverse roll coat method
Walzendrehmaschine *f* roll turning lathe
Walzenfräser *m* 1. *(allg.)* plain milling cutter, plain cutter, cylindrical milling cutter, plain (or cylindrical) milling machine, cylindrical slab miller, light-duty plain milling cutter 2. *(mit Steigungswinkel über 45°)* helical mill 3. *(breiter als sein Durchmesser)* slabbing cutter
Walzenlager *nt* roller bearing
Walzenschleifen *nt* roll grinding
Walzenstirnfräsen *nt* face milling (operation), plain milling, side milling
Walzenstirnfräser *m* shell end mill, end face mill
Walzenvorschubapparat *m* roll feed device
Walzenzapfenfräsmaschine *f* roll neck milling machine
Wälzfehler *m* total error range, pitch error
Wälzfläche *f* pitch surface
Wälzfräseinrichtung *f* hobbing attachment
walzfräsen slab-mill, plane- (or peripheral)mill, hob, generate
Wälzfräser *m* hob, hobbing cutter, slab milling cutter
Wälzfräser *m* **zum Abrunden** topping hob
Wälzfräsmaschine *f* gear hobbing machine, hobber, hobbing machine
Wälzfräsverfahren *nt* generating method, hobbing method (or process)
Wälzführung *f* roll-motion guidance
Wälzgerade *f* rack pitch line
Walzgeschwindigkeit rolling speed
Wälzgetriebe *nt* roll-motion transmission, rolling gear transmission
Wälzgetrieberadpaar *nt* rolling type gear pair
Walzhauptzeit roll main time
Wälzhebel *m* cradle link
Wälzhobelmaschine *f* generating gear planing machine, gear generator, gear shaper
Wälzhobeln *nt* generating planing (method), generating shaping, chisel planing
Wälzhobelverfahren *nt* reciprocating-cutter generating method
Wälzkegel *m* (gear cutting) rolling cone, pitch cone
Wälzkegelradhobelmaschine *f* bevel gear generator
Wälzkolbenvakuumpumpe *f* Roots vacuum booster
Wälzkörper *m* rolling element, roll

body, cradle, generating cradle
Walzkraft roll(ing) force
Wälzkreisbogen *m* pitch circle arc
Wälzkreisdurchmesser *m* (*e. Stirnrades*) pitch diameter
Wälzlager *nt* rolling bearing, rolling contact bearing, antifriction bearing
Wälzlagerfettprüfmaschine *f* rolling bearing grease test rig
Wälzlagerreibung *f* roller bearing friction
Wälzlänge *f* working length
Walzloch *nt* rolling hole
Wälzmaschine *f* generating machine, generator
Wälzmöglichkeit *f* (*e. Schraubengetriebe*) rolling capacity
Wälzprägen *nt* roller marking
Walzprinzip *nt* roll principle
Walzprofilieren *nt* roll forming to shape
Wälzprüfung *f* working test
Wälzpunkt *m* point of contact, imaginary pitch point
Walzrichten *nt* roll straightening
Walzrichten *nt* **mit mehreren Walzen** mangling
Wälzrollen *nt* generating rolling
Walzrunden *nt* **zu kegeligen Werkstücken** crimping
Walzrunden *nt* **zu zylindrischen Werkstücken** roll rounding
Wälzrundlaufabweichung *f* working concentricity variation
Wälzschälen *nt* generating skiving, skiving
Wälzschleifen *nt* generating grinding
Wälzschleifmaschine *f* generating grinder
Walzschnecke *f* rolling worm
Walzsicken *nt* roll beading
Wälzstellung *f* position in the joint rolling motion
Walzstirnfräsen *nt* face milling
Wälzstoßen *nt* 1. (*allg.*) shaping by the generating method, generating shaping, generation shaping 2. (*geradverzahnter Stirnräder*) generation by shaping of straight spur gears 3. (*mit Kammmeißel*) generation by planing with rack shaped cutter
Wälzstoßmaschine *f* gear shaper
Wälzstoßwerkzeug *nt* generating shaping tool
Wälzsummenteilungsabweichung *f* cumulative working pitch variation
Wälzsupport *m* hobbing unit, hobbing slide
Wälzung *f* rolling motion, rolling action, roll motion, generating motion
Wälzverfahren *nt* generating method, generating process
Wälzvorgang *m* roll-motion, working action, generating action
Wälzwerkzeug *nt* generating cutter, generating tool, hobbing tool
wälzzahnen cut gears by the generating method, generate (gears)
Wälzzahnrad *nt* generated gear
Walzzeichen *nt* rolling mark
Walzziehbiegen *nt* roll draw bending to shape in a multiple-roll unit
Walzziehen *nt* 1. (*allg.*) roll drawing 2. (*über festen Stopfen/Dorn*) roll drawing over stationary mandrel/plug 3. (*über losen Stopfen/Dorn*) roll drawing over floating mandrel/plug 4. (*über mitlaufende Stange*) roll drawing over travelling (live) rod 5. (*von Bändern/Blechen*) roll drawing of strip/sheet 6. (*von Draht*) roll drawing of wire 7. (*von Hohlkörpern*) roll drawing of hollow items 8. (*von Stäben*) roll drawing of bars 9. (*von Vollkörpern*) roll drawing of solid items
Wälzzylinderflankenlinie *f* (*e. Schrägstirnrades*) pitch helix
Wand *f* wall
Wandabsorption *f* absorption through the wall
wandbefestigt wall-mounted
Wandbefestigung *f* wall fastening, wall mounting
Wandbelag *m* wall covering
Wanddicke *f* wall thickness
Wanddicken *fpl* wall thicknesses
Wanddickensprung *m* wall thickness discrepancy
wandeln change, convert, transform
Wanderecho *nt* migrant echo

wandern creep, loose, travel
wandernde Einzellast *f* single live load
wanderungsfähiger Stoff *m* substance capable of migration
Wanderungssinn *m (e. Ladungsträgers)* direction of transport
Wandler *m* **1.** *(in andere Stromart)* converter **2.** *(Messwertgeber)* transducer **3.** *(Umspanner)* transformer
Wandventilator *m* wall-mounted fan
Wandverkleidung *f* wall covering
Wange *f* **1.** *(Flanke)* flank **2.** *(e. Kurbelwelle)* cheek **3.** *(e. Maschinenbettes)* shear **4.** *(e. Ständers)* face (of a column), front wall of the machine base
Wanne *f* pan, tray
WA-Prüfung *f* inspection of outgoing goods
Ware *f* **abgeben** handle over goods
Ware *f* **einlagern** store goods
Ware *f* **entladen** unload goods
Ware *f* **identifizieren** identify goods
Ware *f* **in Arbeit** work in process
Ware *f* **ins Lager einbuchen** check in goods into the warehouse
Ware *f* **transportieren** transport goods
Ware *f* **zum Mann** goods-to-man, parts-to-man
Waren *fpl* good(s), merchandise, products, material
Waren *fpl* **vereinnahmen** receive goods
Warenabgabe *f* handling over goods
Warenanhänger *m* hanging label
Warenanlieferung *f* goods delivery
Warenannahme *f* **1.** *(Vorgang)* acceptance of goods, receipt of goods **2.** *(Abteilung)* incoming goods department, goods receiving department
Warenausgang *m* **1.** *(Abteilung)* outgoing goods department, dispatch **2.** *(Vorgang)* goods issue, sale of withdrawal of goods, outgoing merchandise
Warenausgangslager *nt* finished goods warehouse, outgoing merchandise inventory, load leaving storage
warenbegleitend accompanying the goods
Warenbegleitschein *m* document accompanying goods, accompanying document, transshipment note
Warenbereitstellung *f* provision of goods
Warenbestand *m* stock on hand, stock in trade
Warendisposition *f* material planning, provision of goods
Wareneingang *m* **1.** *(Abteilung)* acceptance, goods-in, incoming goods point, goods arrival, incoming goods department, incoming goods entry, receipt of goods **2.** *(Vorgang)* acceptance of goods, receipt of goods
Wareneingang *m* **buchen** book incoming goods
Wareneingangsbescheinigung *f* delivery receipt
Wareneingangsbuchung *f* incoming goods booking
Wareneingangsdatum *nt* goods received date, date of receipt
Wareneingangsfunktion *f* incoming goods function
Wareneingangskontrolle *f* incoming (goods) inspection, inspection of incoming shipments
Wareneingangslager *nt* incoming goods warehouse, load entering storage
Wareneingangsliste *f* incoming goods list
Wareneingangsnummer *f* incoming goods number
Wareneingangsposition *f* incoming goods item
Wareneingangsprüfung *f* quality conformance inspection, inspection of incoming goods
Wareneingangsschein *m* receiving slip, receiving ticket, incoming goods note
Warenfluss *m* flow of goods, product flow, merchandise flow
Warenflussverfolgung *f* product flow monitoring, merchandise flow registration
Warengruppe *f* class of products
Warenidentifikation *f* identification of goods, goods identification, product identification
Warenkennzeichnung *f* goods mark-

ing, goods labelling
Warenlager *nt* warehouse stock, merchandise inventory
Warenmuster *nt* commercial sample
Warenpuffer *m* inventory buffer, product buffer
Warensendung *f* consignment of goods
Warensortiment *nt* assortment of goods, product range
Warenübergabe *f* goods transfer
Warenumschlag *m* handling of goods
Warenvereinnahmung *f* receipt of goods
Warenverteilsystem *nt* goods distribution system, product distribution system
Warenwirtschaftssystem (WWS) *nt* merchandise information system (MIS)
warm hot
warm formbar mouldable under heat
warm formbare Pressmasse *f* thermo-setting (or thermoforming) compression moulding material
warm formen mould under heat
warm härtbar capable of being cured in the hot condition
warm härtbare Formmasse *f* thermo-setting moulding material
warm härtbare Pressmasse *f* thermo-setting compression moulding material
warmabbindender Klebstoff *m* thermo-setting adhesive
Wärmausgleichszeit *f* heat equalization time
Warmauslagern *nt* elevated temperature age hardening
Warmbearbeiten *nt* hot working
Warmbetrieb *m* plant with a hot atmosphere
Warmbildsamkeit *f* thermoplasticity
Warmdehngrenze *f* proof stress at elevated temperature
Warmdruckversuch *m* hot compression test
Wärme *f* heat
Wärmeabfuhr *f* heat removal, heat dissipation
Wärmeabstrahlung *f* radiation of heat
Wärmeabzug *m* heat vent
Wärmealterung *f* thermal ageing
Wärmeauftrieb *m* thermal upthrust
Wärmeausdehnung *f* thermal expansion
Wärmeaustausch *m* heat exchange
Wärmebeanspruchung *f* thermal stress
Wärmebedarf *m* 1. *(allg.)* heat requirement 2. *(spezifischer ~)* specific heat requirement
Wärmebedarfsrechnung *f* heat requirement calculation
wärmebeeinflusste Zone *f* heat-affected zone
wärmebehandeln heat treat
Wärmebehandlung *f* heat treatment
Wärmebehandlungsanweisung *f* heat treatment instruction
Wärmebehandlungsplan *m* heat treatment schedule
Wärmebehandlungstechnik *f* heat treatment technology
Wärmebelastung *f* thermal loading
wärmebeständig heat resistant
Wärmebeständigkeit *f* heat-proof quality
Wärmebilanz *f* heat balance
Wärmedämmschicht *f* thermal insulating layer
Wärmedämmung *f* thermal insulation
Wärmedehnung *f* thermal expansion, dilatation
Wärmedurchgangfaktor *m* thermal transmittance factor
Wärmedurchgangswert *m* thermal transmittance value
Wärmedurchgangszahl *f* thermal transmittance
Wärmedurchlassgrad *m* degree of thermal transparency
Wärmeeinwirkung *f* application of heat, action of heat
Wärmeentzug *m* heat extraction
Wärmeerzeuger *m* **mit Feuerung für Heizöl** heat generator burning fuel oil
wärmefest heat resistant, high temperature
Wärmefestigkeit *f* resistance to heat, high temperature stability
Wärmefluss *m* heat flow
Wärmeführung *f* heat control

wärmegedämmte Wand *f* thermally insulated wall
Wärmegefälle *nt* temperature gradient
Wärmegrundschaltplan *m* fundamental heat circuit diagram
Wärmehärte *f* red hardness
wärmehärtende Klebschicht *f* thermosetting adhesive layer
Wärmeimpulsschweißen *nt* impulse sealing
Warmeindrücken *nt* hot indentation, impression (or indentation) under heat
Wärmeisolation *f* heat insulation, thermal insulation
wärmeisoliert heat-insulated, with heat insulation
Wärmeklasse *f* insulation class, thermal class
Wärmekontaktschweißen *nt* thermal contact welding
Wärmekraftanlage *f* thermal power plant
Wärmekräfte *fpl* thermal forces
Wärmekurve *f* heating curve
Wärmeleistung *f* heat emission, heat yield
Wärmeleitdüse *f* heat guide nozzle
wärmeleitend heat conducting
Wärmeleitfähigkeit *f* thermal conductivity
Wärmeleitung *f* heat dissipation
Wärmeleitungsschweißen *nt* heat dissipation welding
Wärmelieferung *f* heat supply
Wärmemenge *f* quantity of heat
Wärmemengenbedarf *m* demand of heat quantity
Wärmemengenverlust *m* loss of heat quantity
Wärmequelle *f* heat source, source of heat
Wärmerissigkeit *f* heat checking
Wärmerissneigung *f* tendency to hot cracking
Wärmeröhre *f* hot cupboard
Wärmeschild *nt* heat sink
Wärmeschrumpfung *f* heat shrinking
Wärmeschutzarbeit *f* heat conservation work
Wärmeschutzisolierung *f* heat insulation
Wärmeschutzmantel *m* thermal insulation jacket
Wärmespeicherwirkung *f* heat storage effect
Wärmestabilisator *m* thermal stabilizer
Wärmestrahler *m* radiant heater
Wärmestrahlung *f* thermal radiation
wärmestrahlungsarm with a low level of heat radiation
Wärmestromdichte *f* heat flow density
wärmetechnischer Kennwert *m* thermal characteristic
Wärmeträger *m* heat carrier
Wärmeträgeröl *nt* heat transfer oil
wärmetrocknend thermo-drying
Wärmeübergang *m* heat transition
Wärmeüberträger *m* heat transfer medium
Wärmeübertragung *f* heat transfer
Wärmeübertragungsfläche *f* heat transfer surface
Wärmeübertragungs-Flüssigkeit *f* heat-transfer liquid
Wärmeübertragungsmittel *nt* heat-transfer medium
Wärmeverbrauch *m* heat consumption
Wärmeverbraucher *m* heat consumer, heat consuming appliance
Wärmeverhalten *nt* thermal behaviour
Wärmewechselfestigkeit *f* high-temperature alternating stress resistance
Wärmewirkung *f* thermal effect
Wärmezufuhr *f* heat supply
warmfest heat resistant
Warmfestigkeit *f* high-temperature strength
warmfeuchtes Klima *nt* hot humid climate
Warm-Form-, Füll- und Verschließmaschine *f* thermoform fill and seal machine
warmformen hot form, thermoform
Warmformen *nt* hot forming, thermoforming
Warmformgebung *f* hot forming, thermoforming
Warmgasextrusionsschweißen *nt* hot gas welding by extrusion of filler

material
Warmgasfächelschweißen *nt* hot gas welding with torch separate from filler rod
Warmgashandschweißen *nt* manual hot gas welding
Warmgasschnellschweißverfahren *nt* hot gas welding process
Warmgasüberlappschweißen *nt* hot gas overlap welding
Warmgasziehschweißen *nt* hot gas string bead welding
warmgeformt thermoformed
warmgehärteter Gießharzformstoff *m* thermoset casting resin moulding material
warmgehärteter Pressstoff *m* themoset moulded material
warmgewalzt hot-rolled
warmgezogen hot-drawn
warmhärtende Gießharzmasse *f* thermosetting casting resin moulding material
Warmkaltverfestigen *nt* hot/cold work hardening
Warmkammerverfahren *nt* hot-chamber process
Warmkleben *nt* heat-bonding
Warmkleber *m* heat-setting adhesive
Warmlagerung *f* storage under heat, heat storage
Warmlagerungstemperatur *f* heat-storage temperature
Warmlagerungsversuch *m* heat storage energy
Warmlufterzeuger *m* fan-assisted air heater
Warmluftheizung *f* ducted warm air system
Warmluftschleier *m* curtain of warm air
Warmphosphatieren *nt* hot phosphating
warmpressen hot-mould, hot compression mould
Warmriss *m* thermal crack, hot crack
Warmrissneigung *f* hot crack tendency
Warmstart *m* warm restart
Warmtrennen *nt* parting under heat

warmverformbar thermoformable
Warmverformung *f* thermoforming
warmwalzen hot roll
Warmwassergebrauchsleitung *f* hot water service pipe
Warmwasserheizung *f* hot water (central heating) system
Warmwasserheizung *f* **mit Vorlauftemperatur** hot water heating system with flow temperature
Warmwasserkessel *m* hot water boiler
Warmwasserversorgungsanlage *f* hot water supply installation
Warmzerspanung *f* metal cutting at elevated temperatures
warmziehen hot draw
Warnanlage *f* warning device, warning system
Warnblinker *m* hazard flasher
Warnblinklampe *f* warning beacon
Warnbox *f* *(EDV)* alert box
Warneinrichtung *f* warning device, warning means, warning system
warnen warn
Warngrenze *f* warning limit
Warnlampe *f* tell-tale light, warning light
Warnlicht *nt* optical warning device
Warnmeldung *f* warning message
Warnschild *nt* danger sign, warning label
Warnsignal *nt* danger signal, alarm, alert
Warnsymbol *nt* warning symbol
Warnsystem *nt* warning system
Warnung *f* warning, caution
Warnungsvorschrift *f* warning prescription
Warnzeichen *nt* warning sign
Wartbarkeit *f* ease of maintenance, ease of servicing, maintainability
Warte *f* control room
Wartebefehl *m* wait command, wait instruction, suspend command
Warten *nt* **1.** *(Pflege)* maintenance, service **2.** *(auf jemanden ~)* waiting, staying
Warteschlange *f* queue, waiting line, waiting list
Warteschlange bilden queue

Warteschlange *f:* aus einer ~ entnehmen dequeue
Warteschlange *f:* in eine ~ einreihen queue
Warteschlangenbildung *f* queuing
Warteschlangenspeicher *m* pushup storage
Warteschleife *f* waiting loop
Wartezeit *f* 1. *(allg.)* waiting time, waiting period delay, dead time, *(US)* downtime 2. *(Arbeitsabläufe)* attendance time
Wartezustand *m* wait state
Wartung *f* 1. *(e. Maschine, Pflege)* maintenance 2. *(Bedienung)* attendance 3. *(Kundendienst)* service, servicing, upkeep-servicing
Wartungsabstand *m* maintenance interval
Wartungsanleitung *f* maintenance instruction, maintenance manual, service manual, workmanship manual
Wartungsarbeit *f* maintenance work, servicing operation
wartungsarm low- maintenance
Wartungsaufwand *m* maintenance costs
Wartungsbereich *m* maintenance area
Wartungsbühne *f* maintenance platform
Wartungseinheit *f* maintenance unit, service unit
wartungsfrei maintenance free, without operator attention
Wartungshandbuch *nt* maintenance manual, service manual
Wartungsheft *nt* maintenance log, owner protection plan booklet, user's logbook
Wartungsintervall *nt* maintenance interval, maintenance rate
Wartungsplan *m* maintenance schedule
Wartungsposition *f* maintenance position
Wartungsstand *m* maintenance position
Wartungsvertrag *m* maintenance contract
waschen wash

Waschmittellösung *f* detergent solution
Waschprüfung *f* washing test
Washprimer *m* wash primer, self-etch primer
Wasser *nt* water
wasserablassendes Ventil *nt* water drain valve
Wasserabscheidevermögen *nt* demulsibility
Wasserabschreckverfahren *nt* water quenching method
wasserabstoßend water repellent
wasserabweisend water repellent
Wasseraufbereitung *f* water treatment, water conditioning
wasserberührte Teile *npl* water-swept parts
wasserbeständig water resistant
wasserdampfflüchtig water vapour volatile
Wasserdampfsättigungsdruck *m* saturation water vapour pressure
Wasserdampfspaltung *f* dissociation of steam
Wasserdampfumformer *m* steam converter
wasserdicht watertight
Wasserdurchfluss *m* water flow, water throughput
Wassereindringtiefe *f* depth of water penetration
Wassereindringversuch *m* water penetration test
Wassereinfülltemperatur *f* water fill temperature
Wassereinspritzventil *nt* water injection valve
Wassereinwirkung *f* action of water
Wassererwärmer *m* water heater, calorifier
Wassererwärmungsanlage *f* water heating installation
Wassererwärmungsanlagenbau *m* construction of water heating installations
Wasserfleck *m* water stain
Wasserglas *nt* water glass, liquid glass
Wasserglasverfahren *nt* water glass process

Wasserhaushaltsgesetz *nt* water balance law
Wasserhaushaltswert *m* water balance coefficient
Wasserheizkörper *m* water radiator
Wasserheizung *f* water-heating system
Wasserheizungskessel *m* water heating boiler
wässerige Chlorlösung *f* aqueous chlorine solution
Wassermangelsicherung *f* low-water safety device (or cut-out)
Wassermenge *f* water volume
Wassermengenregler *m* water volume controller
Wasserprobe *f* water sample
Wasserrohrnetz *nt* water mains system
Wasserrückkühlanlage *f* water recirculation cooling plant
Wasserrückkühlung *f* water re-cooling
Wasserschlag *m* water hammer
Wasserschleife *f* water loop
Wasserschneidanlage *f* water cutting plant
wasserschutzrechtliche Verordnung *f* water protection law regulation
wasserseitiger Widerstand *m* water-side flow resistance
Wasserspeicher *m* water storage tank
Wasserstandshöhenanzeiger *m* water level indicator
Wasserstandsmarke *f* water level mark
Wasserstandsüberwachung *f* monitoring of the water level
Wasserstoff *m* hydrogen
Wasserstoffaufnahme *f* take-up of hydrogen
Wasserstoffdruckminderer *m* hydrogen regulator
Wasserstoffriss *m* hydrogen induced crack, delayed crack
Wasserstrahl *m* water jet
Wasserstrahlbearbeitung water jet machining
Wasserströmungswächter *m* water flow monitor
Wassertopf *m* condensate trap
Wasserstandbegrenzer *m* water level limiter

Wasserumwälzung *f* water circulation
Wasserversorgungsnetz *nt* water supply mains
Wasserverunreinigung *f* contamination of water
Wasserwaage *f* spirit level, water trap, interceptor
Wasserwechselzone *f* zone of fluctuating water level
Wasserzähler *m* **mit Messkammern** water meter with measuring chambers
Wasserzuflussventil *nt* water inlet valve
wässrige Lösung *f* aqueous solution
Wattestopfen *m* plug of cotton wool
Wattetupfer *m* cotton wool wad
Wattsche Kette *f* Watt's chain
web-basierter Datenaustausch *m* web-based data exchange
Webmaschinenschraube *f* bolt for looms
Wechselbeanspruchung *f* cyclic stress
Wechsel *m* 1. *(Austausch)* change, exchange, swap 2. *(Umstellung)* change-over, alternation 3. *(Veränderung)* change
Wechselbatterie *f* exchange battery
Wechselbehälter *m* exchangeable container, swap body
Wechselbetrieb *m* alternate operation, alternate communication, half duplex transmission
Wechselbiegemaschine *f* reversed (or alternating) bending testing machine
Wechselbrandkessel *m* dual fuel boiler, multifuel boiler
Wechselfeld *nt* alternating field
Wechselinduktion *f* mutual inductance
Wechselklima *nt* **mit feuchter Wärme** alternating climate of the hot humid type
Wechsellagerung *f* alternating storage
Wechsellichtbetrieb *m* alternating light operation
wechseln 1. *(allg.)* change, reverse 2. *(umstellen)* alternate 3. (verändern) vary 4. *(wechseln zu)* switch 5. *(austauschen)* exchange, replace,

swap **6.** *(Gang ~)* shift gear
Wechselrad *nt* change gear, loose gear
Wechselräder *npl* **für den Vorschub** feed change gear
Wechselräderberechnung *f* change gear calculation
Wechselrädergetriebe *nt* change gear drive, change gear mechanism
Wechselrädergetriebekasten *m* change gear box
Wechselräderkasten *m* change gear box
Wechselrädersatz *m* set of change gears
Wechselräderschere *f* quadrant
Wechselrichter *m* inverter, inverse rectifier, d.c.-a.c. converter
wechselseitig bi-directional, alternate, mutual, reciprocal, from either direction
wechselsinnig back and forth
Wechselspannung *f* AC voltage, a.c. voltage
Wechselspannungsausgang *m* AC output
Wechselspannungsversorgungsanschluss *m* AC power port
Wechselstrom *m* alternating current, AC, a.c.
wechselstrombetätigt AC-operated
Wechselstromgenerator *m* AC generator
Wechselstrommaschine *f* alternator, AC machine
Wechselstromnetz *nt* AC system, AC network, AC mains
Wechselstromversorgung *f* AC mains power supply
Wechselventil *nt* shuttle valve
wechselweise schalten control independently
Wechselwirkung *f* **1.** *(allg.)* interaction, reciprocal action, reciprocal effect **2.** *(Regeln)* dialog
Wechselwirkungsglied *nt* interaction term
Wechselwirkungswahrscheinlichkeit *f* probability of interaction
Wechsler *m* change-over contact
Wechslerschließer *m* make-brake-make (contact), make before change-over

Weg *m* **1.** *(allg.)* way, route **2.** *(Gehweg, Steg)* walkway **3.** *(Meißel)* path **4.** *(Schlitten, Werkzeug)* traverse, travel, movement, motion **5.** *(Stößel)* stroke
Wegbedingung *f* route condition
Wege *mpl* ways
Wege und Zeiten *pl* ways and times
Wegebohrmaschine *f* way-boring machine
Wegeventil *nt* direction control valve
Wegezeit *f* path time, journey time, travel time, travel period
wegfliegen eject
Wegfühler *m* position sensor
Weggeber *m* position encoder
weggebunden path bound
Wegimpulsgeber *m* path pulse generator
Weginformation *f* route information
Weg-Istwert *m* actual position
Weglänge *f* path length, distance
wegleiten carry off
Wegmarke *f* path marker, route marker
Wegmesseinrichtung *f* position measuring equipment
Wegmesssysteme *npl* position measuring system
wegnehmen 1. *(allg.)* remove, take away, eliminate **2.** *(Gas ~)* cut off the engine
Wegplansteuerung *f* position scheduled control
wegrosten rust away
wegrutschen slide (away)
wegspülen flush away, wash away
Wegstrecke *f* path, distance, travel path
Wegwerfwerkzeuge *npl* throw-aways
wegziehen draw off, pull off, pull away, remove
Weichdichtung *f* resilient jointing, soft packing
Weichdichtungsstoff *m* soft jointing material
Weiche *f* **1.** *(allg.)* switch, shunt, point **2.** *(el.)* separating filter
weiche Zündung *f* smoothly running ignition
weichelastischer Schaumstoff *m* flexible cellular material

weichelastischer Zustand *m* soft-elastic state
Weichenzungenhobelmaschine *f* frog and switch planer, switch rail planer
weiches Polyvinylchlorid *nt* flexible polyvinyl chloride
weichgummiartig like soft rubber
Weichgummimischung *f* soft mix from rubber
Weichlotbad *nt* soft solder bath
Weichlotlegierung *f* soft solder alloy
Weichlötstelle *f* soft soldered joint
Weichlöttemperatur *f* soft soldering temperature
weichmacherabgebender Kunststoff *m* plastics releasing plasticiser
weichmacherabgebende Folie *f* film (or foil or sheeting) releasing plasticiser
Weichmacheraufnahme *f* plasticiser absorption
weichmacheraufnehmende Folie *f* plasticiser-absorbing film (or foil or sheeting)
weichmacheraufnehmender Kunststoff *m* plasticiser-absorbing plastic
Weichmacherdampfkonzentration *f* concentration of plasticiser vapour
Weichmacherextraktion *f* extraction of plasticiser
weichmacherfreie Folie *f* unplasticized film
weichmacherfreie Formmasse *f* unplasticized moulding material
weichmacherfreie PVC-Formmasse *f* unplasticized PVC moulding material
weichmacherfreier Kunststoff *m* unplasticized plastics
weichmacherfreies Polyvinylchlorid *nt* unplasticized polyvinyl chloride
weichmacherhaltige Folie *f* plasticised film (or foil or sheeting)
weichmacherhaltige Formmasse *f* plasticised moulding material
weichmacherhaltige Kunststofffolie *f* plasticised plastics film
weichmacherhaltiger Kunststoff *m* plasticised plastics
Weichpackung *f* soft packing

Weifverfahren *nt* reel method
weinrote Verfärbung *f* claret red discoloration
Weißblech *nt* tinplate
weißglühend white-hot
Weißöl *nt* white oil
Weißrostbildung *f* white rust formation
Weißstrick *m* white yarn
weit 1. *(Distanz)* wide, broad **2.** *(geräumig)* large, spacious
Weite *f* **1.** *(Distanz)* width, breadth **2.** *(Geräumigkeit)* capacity, largeness
weiten widen, expand, flare
Weiten *nt* **durch Drücken** expanding by spinning
Weiten *nt* **durch Einwirkung eines Magnetfeldes** expanding by effect of a magnetic field
Weiten *nt* **durch elektrische Entladung** expanding by electric discharge
Weiten *nt* **durch Funkenentladung** expanding by spark discharge
Weiten *nt* **durch kurzzeitige Entspannung hoch komprimierter Gase** expanding by temporary expansion of highly compressed gases
Weiten *nt* **durch Sprengstoffdetonation** expanding by detonation of explosives
Weiten *nt* **mit Dorn** expanding with mandrel
Weiten *nt* **mit Flüssigkeiten mit energiegebundener Wirkung** expanding with liquids with effect associated with energy
Weiten *nt* **mit Flüssigkeiten mit kraftgebundener Wirkung** expanding with liquids with effect associated with force
Weiten *nt* **mit formlos festen Stoffen mit energiegebundener Wirkung** expanding with amorphous solids with effect associated with energy
Weiten *nt* **mit formlos festen Stoffen mit kraftgebundener Wirkung** expanding with amorphous solids with effect associated with force
Weiten *nt* **mit Gasdruck** expanding with gas pressure

Weiten *nt* **mit Gasen** expanding with gases
Weiten *nt* **mit Gasen mit energiegebundener Wirkung** expanding with gases with effect associated with energy
Weiten *nt* **mit Gasen mit kraftgebundener Wirkung** expanding with gases with effect associated with force
Weiten *nt* **mit Gummistempel** expanding with rubber punch
Weiten *nt* **mit nachgiebigem Werkzeug** expanding with compliant tool
Weiten *nt* **mit Sand/Stahlkugeln** expanding with sand/steel balls
Weiten *nt* **mit Spreizwerkzeug** expanding with spreading tool
Weiten *nt* **mit starrem Werkzeug** expanding with rigid tool
Weiten *nt* **mit Wasserbeutel** expanding with water bag
Weiten *nt* **mit Werkzeugen** expanding with tools
Weiten *nt* **mit Wirkenergie** expanding with active energy
Weiten *nt* **mit Wirkmedien** expanding with action media
Weiten *nt* **mit Wirkmedien mit energiegebundener Wirkung** expanding with action media with effect associated with energy
Weiten *nt* **mit Wirkmedien mit kraftgebundener Wirkung** expanding with action media with effect associated with force
Weiterbetrieb *m* recommissioning
Weiterführung *f* onward transmission
Weitergabe *f* 1. *(allg.)* onward transmission, transfer 2. *(IT)* relaying 3. *(Signale)* transduction
weitergeben pass on, transfer, impart, relay
weiterglimmen continue to glow
weiterleiten 1. *(allg.)* pass on, transfer 2. *(Signale)* send up, transmit 3. *(weiterschicken)* forward
Weiterleitung *f* 1. *(allg.)* forwarding, transfer 2. *(el.)* transmission
Weiterreißbarkeit *f* tear growth work
weiterreißen propagate the tear
Weiterreißen *nt* tongue-tearing, tearing, tear propagation
Weiterreißgeschwindigkeit *f* tear growth rate
Weiterreißprüfgerät *nt* tear growth tester
Weiterreißprüfung *f* tear growth test
Weiterreißwiderstand *m* tongue-tear resistance, tear growth resistance
Weiterschaltbedingung *f* 1. *(allg.)* step enabling condition 2. *(Signale)* transfer condition
weiterschalten *(vt)* 1. *(allg.)* switch, index, override 2. *(Signale)* transfer
Weiterschaltung *f* 1. *(allg.)* switching 2. *(Maschinen)* indexing, overriding 3. *(Signale)* transfer
Weiterschlag *m* additional (second) draw
Weiterübertragung *f* *(e. Signals)* onward transmission
weiterverarbeiten process, manufacture
weiterverarbeitend manufacturing, processing
Weiterverarbeitung *f* (further) processing, downstream operations, manufacturing operation, finishing
Weiterverarbeitungsbetrieb *m* finishing plant
weiterverkaufen retail
Weiterverkehrsnetz *nt* wide area network (WAN)
Weithalsflasche *f* wide-necked flask
Weithalsmesskolben *m* wide-necked graduated flask
Weithalsschliffflasche *f* wide-necked glass flask with a ground neck
Wellbiegen *nt* corrugating
Welle *f* 1. *(Maschinenbauteil)* shaft 2. *(el.)* wave 3. *(im Draht)* convolution 4. *(Spindel)* spindle
wellen flute
Wellen *fpl* convolutions
Wellenabstand *m* waviness width
Wellenbildner *m* fluter
Wellendichtring *m* rotary shaft seal, radial packing ring
Wellendrehmaschine *f* shaft turning lathe
Wellendurchführung *f* rotating joint

Wellenende *nt* shaft end
Wellenform *f* waveform
Wellenkamm *m* (e. *Oberfläche*) wave peak
Wellenkupplung *f* shaft coupling
Wellenlager *nt* journal (bearing)
Wellenlänge *f* wavelength
Wellenlängennormal *nt* wavelength standard
wellenlängenstabilisiertes Laser *nt* wavelength stabilized laser
Wellenlehre *f* shaft gauge
Wellenn-Naben-Verbindung *f* shaft hub joint
Wellenspalte *f* rotating joint
Wellenstumpf *m* shaft end, stub shaft
Wellentheorie *f* wave theory
Wellentiefe *f* depth of waviness
Wellenverbindung *f* shaft connection
Wellenverlagerung *f* shaft dislocation
Wellenzapfen *m* journal
wellig corrugated, wavy
Welligkeit *f* ripple, waviness
Welligkeitsmessstrecke *f* measuring length for the waviness
Welligkeitsprofil *nt* profile of waviness
Welligkeitstaststrecke *f* traversing length for a waviness
Wellpappe *f* corrugated board, corrugated cardboard, fibreboard
Wellpappefaltschachtel *f* corrugated (board) case
Wellpappezuschnitt *m* corrugated board blank
Weltkoordinatensystem *nt* world coordinate system
Wende *f* turn, U-turn, reversal
Wendebetrieb *m* shuttle service, rotating mode
Wendedurchlass *m* turning passage
Wendeeinrichtung *f* manipulator
Wendegetriebe *nt* reverse gear
Wendeherzgetriebe *nt* reversing mechanism
Wendekreis *m* turning radius, vehicle clearance
Wendel *m* (continuous) spiral, coil
Wendelspan *m* spiral chip, coil chip, coiled-up chip, curly chip, continuous curly chip
Wendemaschine *f* turnover unit
Wendemechanik *f* flipping mechanism
wenden (*vi/vt*) **1.** (*allg.*) turn (back), make a U-turn, manoeuvre **2.** (*Strom*) commutate, invert **3.** (*umwenden*) turn over, reverse, flip **4.** (*auf der Stelle*) turn on the spot, rotate on the spot
Wenden *nt* **von Schneidplatten** indexing of inserts
Wendeplattenverfahren *nt* rollover board process, flip plate method
Wendepol *m* commutating pole, reciprocating pole, compole, interpole
Wender *m* **1.** (*allg.*) turnover device, reversing device **2.** (el.) reversing switch
Wendeschneidplatte *f* replaceable insert
Wendestation *f* roll-over station
Wendevorgang *m* turnover, turning procedure
Wendevorrichtung *f* turnover device, roll-over fixture
Wendezugeinrichtung *f* push-pull device
Wendigkeit *f* manoeuvrability
Wendung *f* turn
Weniger-Taste *f* decrease key
werfen cast, throw
Werk *nt* works, (production) plant, factory
Werkbank *f* workbench, bench
Werkbankfräsmaschine *f* bench milling machine
Werkereinsatz *m* labour
Werkerselbstprüfung *f* worker self testing
werkgerechte Ausführung *f* workmanship
Werkhalle *f* shop
Werknorm *f* works standard, company standard, in-house standard
Werkprüfdruck *m* works test pressure
werkseitig hergestellt factory-made
Werksgelände *nt* factory premises
werksintern (*Vorschriften*) on an internal works basis
werksinterne Kontrolle *f* internal quality control
Werksprüfung *f* inspection test
Werkstatt *f* workshop, shop, machine

shop
Werkstattauftrag *m* workshop order
Werkstattausdruck *m* shop term
Werkstattentwickler *m* workshop generator
Werkstattfertigung *f* workshop production
werkstattorientierte Programmierung (WOP) *f* shop floor programming
Werkstattprüfung *f* inspection test
Werkstattschieblehre *f* common calliper rule (or square)
Werkstattschraublehre *f* micrometer gauge
Werkstatttechnik *f* workshop practice
werkstattübliche Abweichung *f* variation within the usual scale of workshop practice
Werkstattwinkel *m* workshop T-square
Werkstattzeichnung *f* workshop drawing
Werkstoff *m* 1. *(allg.)* material, stock 2. *(abgetragener ~)* abraded material
Werkstoffabnahme *f* stock removal
Werkstoffabtrag *m* material erosion
Werkstoffabtragung *f* stock removal
Werkstoffabweichung *f* material deviation
Werkstoffausnutzung *f* material utilization
Werkstoffauspressung *f* material expulsion
Werkstoffauswahl *f* material selection
werkstoffbedingt material-conditioned, conditioned by the material, material related
Werkstoffeigenschaft *f* material property
Werkstoffeinsparung *f* saving in material
werkstofferfüllter Teil *m* **eines Gewindes** portion of screw thread filled with material
Werkstofffehler *m* material defect
Werkstofffestigkeit *f* strength of materials
werkstofffreier Teil *m* **eines Gewindes** portion of screw thread devoid of material

Werkstoffführung *f* bar stock guide, bar guide
Werkstoffinhomogenität *f* non-uniformity of the material
Werkstoffnummer *f* material number
Werkstoffprobe *f* material sample
Werkstoffprüfmaschine *f* material testing machine
Werkstoffprüfung *f* material testing, testing of materials
Werkstoffreduzierung material reduction
Werkstoffspannung *f* work gripping
Werkstoffstange *f* bar stock
Werkstoffvergleichstabelle material comparative table
Werkstoffverhalten *nt* material behaviour
Werkstoffvolumen *nt* 1. *(allg.)* material volume 2. *(abgenommenes ~)* amount of material removed 3. *(je Nachschliff abgenommenes ~)* volume removed per regrind
Werkstoffzufuhr *f* stock feed, work feed
Werkstoffzugabe *f* stock allowance, stock left for
Werkstück *nt* 1. *(allg.)* workpiece, work part, component, part, piece, piece of work 2. *(als Fertigungsteil)* production part, work 3. *(bewegtes ~ Verfahren)* workpiece dragging
Werkstück *nt* **in Bearbeitung** work in hand
Werkstückachse *f* axis of work
Werkstückauflage *f* work rest
Werkstückaufspannung *f* work setting
Werkstückaufspannvorrichtung *f* workholding fixture, work locating fixture, work fixture
Werkstückauswerfeinrichtung *f* part-ejection device
Werkstückauswerfer *m* work ejector
Werkstückbasiskoordinatensystem *nt* work part coordinate system
Werkstückbearbeitung *f* workpiece machining, workpiece cutting, workpiece processing, workpiece handling
Werkstückbewegungseinrichtung *f*

work-moving attachment
Werkstückbolzengewinde *nt* workpiece bolt thread
Werkstückdaten *pl* workpiece data
Werkstückeigenschaft *f* workpiece property
Werkstückflankenwinkel *m* flank angle of workpiece
Werkstückfluss *m* work parts flow
Werkstückflusssystem *nt* work parts flow system
Werkstückgegenfläche *f* workpiece reverse side
Werkstückgeometrie *f* workpiece geometry
Werkstückgeschwindigkeit *f* rate of travel of workpiece
Werkstückgewinde *nt* workpiece screw thread
Werkstückgrenzmaß *nt* limiting size of workpiece
Werkstückgrößtmaß *nt* workpiece maximum dimension
Werkstückhalter *m* work carrier
Werkstückhalterung *f* workpiece mount
Werkstückkasten *m* work tray
Werkstückkegelrad *nt* bevel gear blank
Werkstückkleinstmaß *nt* workpiece minimum dimension
Werkstückkosten *pl* workpiece costs
Werkstücklehrung *f* workpiece gauging
Werkstückmuttergewinde *nt* workpiece nut thread
Werkstücknullpunkt *m* part program zero
Werkstückqualität *f* quality of workpieces, workpiece quality
Werkstückschnittfläche *f* work surface
Werkstückseitenkante *f* side edge of workpiece
Werkstückspanneinrichtung *f* workholding fixture, work locating fixture, work fixture
Werkstückspanner *m* workholding fixture, work locating fixture, work fixture
Werkstückspannung *f* work chucking
Werkstückspindel *f* work spindle
Werkstückspindeltrommel *f* workspindle drum
Werkstücktangentialgeschwindigkeit *f* workpiece tangential velocity
Werkstücktoleranz *f* work tolerance, workpiece tolerance
Werkstückträger *m* workpiece carrier
Werkstückumspannung *f* relocating work
Werkstückverzahnung *f* gear teeth on the workpiece
Werkstückvorschub *m* work feed
Werkstückwechsel *m* workpiece changer
Werkstückzubringung *f* part feeding, work feeding
Werkstückzuführung *f* workpiece feed
Werkszeugnis *nt* work test report, works certificate
Werktisch *m* work bench
Werkzeug *nt* tool, implement
Werkzeug *nt* **mit Einfachanschnitt** mould with single gate
Werkzeug *nt* **mit hart aufgelöteten Hartmetallplättchen** brazed-tip carbide tool
Werkzeug *nt* **mit hart aufgelöteter Schneide** brazed-tip tool
Werkzeug *nt* **mit Mehrfachanschnitt** mould with multiple gate
Werkzeug- und Gesenkfräsmaschine *f* tool and die miller
Werkzeugabhebung *f* tool lift
Werkzeuganordnung *f* **1.** *(allg.)* tooling layout, tooling setup, tooling arrangement **2.** *(Zeichnung)* tooling diagram
Werkzeugantriebsseite *f* mould driving side
Werkzeugauflage *f* tool rest
Werkzeugaufruf *m* tool function
Werkzeugaufspanndorn *m* tool mandrel, tool arbo(u)r
Werkzeugauswahl *f* tool selection
Werkzeugauswerfer *m* tool ejector
Werkzeugbahn *f* tool path
Werkzeugbestückung *f* tooling layout
Werkzeugbezugsebene *f* tool refer-

ence plane
Werkzeugbezugsprofil *nt* standard tool profile, cutter standard basic rack tooth profile
Werkzeugbezugssystem tool reference system
Werkzeugbohr- und -fräsmaschine *f* tool drilling and milling machine
Werkzeugcodierung *f* tool coding
Werkzeugdaten *pl* tool data
Werkzeugdurchgang *m* passage of a tool
Werkzeugeingriffswinkel *m* nominal pressure angle
Werkzeugfräs- und -bohrmaschine *f* tool milling and boring machine
Werkzeugfräsmaschine *f* cutter milling machine, toolroom milling machine, tool milling machine
werkzeuggebundenes Maß *nt* mould-dependent dimension
Werkzeuggestaltung *f* tool design, construction of tools
Werkzeughalter *m* toolholder
Werkzeughalter *m* **des Zugorgans der Räummaschine** broach pull head
Werkzeughaltung *f* tool storage
Werkzeugkeilmessebene *f* tool wedge measure plane
Werkzeugkoordinaten *fpl* tool coordinate
Werkzeugkoordinatensystem *nt* tool coordinate system
Werkzeugkopfhöhe *f* tool addendum
Werkzeugkorrektur *f* tool compensation
Werkzeugkosten *pl* tool costs
Werkzeuglänge *f* tool length
Werkzeugmacherdrehmaschine *f* toolroom lathe, precision lathe
Werkzeugmacherei *f* toolmaking, toolroom
Werkzeugmacherfräsmaschine *f* toolroom milling machine
Werkzeugmanagementsystem *nt* tool management system
Werkzeugmaschine (WZM) *f* machine tool, tool machine
Werkzeugmaschine *f* **nach Baukastenweise** building brick machine tool

Werkzeugmaschinenabteilung *f* machine tool division
Werkzeugmaschinenbau *m* machine tool manufacture, machine tool building, machine tool industry
Werkzeugmaschinenfabrik *f* machine tool plant
Werkzeugmaschinenfachmann *m* machine tool expert
Werkzeugmaschinensteuerung *f* machine tool control system
Werkzeugmodul *nt* cutter module
Werkzeugrückenfreiwinkel *m* tool back clearance
Werkzeugrückkeilwinkel *m* tool back wedge angle
Werkzeugrückspanwinkel *m* tool back rake
Werkzeugsatz *m* gang tool
Werkzeugschaft *m* tool shank
Werkzeugschleifen *nt* tool grinding
Werkzeugschleifmaschine *f* tool and cutter grinder
Werkzeugschlitten *m* saddle, carriage, tool slide
Werkzeugschneide *f* cutting edge of the tool, cutting tool edge, cutting tool tip
Werkzeugschneidenebene *f* tool cutting edge plane, cutting plane
Werkzeugschneidennormalebene *f* cutting edge normal plane
Werkzeugseitenfreiwinkel *m* tool side clearance
Werkzeugseitenkeilwinkel *m* tool side wedge angle
Werkzeugseitenspanwinkel *m* tool side rake
Werkzeugspanner *m* toolholder
Werkzeugspanwinkel *m* tool rake
Werkzeugspeicher *m* tool storage
Werkzeugspitze *f* nose
Werkzeugstahl *m* 1. *(allg.)* tool steel 2. *(unlegierter ~)* plain tool steel
werkzeugsteuernde Vorrichtung *f* jig
Werkzeugsupport *m* tool box, (vertical boring mill) toolhead, head
Werkzeugsystem *nt* tool system
Werkzeugteil *nt* tool element

Werkzeugteilung *f* nominal pitch of the cutter
Werkzeugträger *m* **1.** *(allg.)* toolholder, toolhead, tool head, tool carrier, toolbox, planer head **2.** *(Auslegersupport)* rail head **3.** *(Seitensupport)* sidehead
Werkzeugumstellung *f* retooling
Werkzeugverschleiß *m* tool wear
Werkzeugverwaltung *f* tool management
Werkzeugvoreinstellung *f* tool presetting
Werkzeugwechsel *m* tool interchange
Werkzeugwechsler *m* tool changer
Werkzeugwinkel *m* **1.** *(allg.)* tool angle, nominal rake angle **2.** *(senkrecht zur Hauptschneide)* side rake angle **3.** *(Wirkwinkel)* working angle
Werkzeugzahn *m* cutting tooth
Werkzeugzahnkopf *m* tip of the cutter tooth
Werkzeugzahnkopfhöhe *f* tool addendum factor
Werkzeugzeichnung *f* tool drawing
Werkstückelement *nt* workpiece element
Wert *m* rate, value, data *pl*
Werteänderung *f* value-change
Wertebereich *m* range of values
Wertetabelle *f* **1.** *(allg.)* data table **2.** *(IT)* truth table
Wertetripel *nt* triad
Werteverlauf *m* value pattern (or band)
Wertigkeit *f* quality rating
Wertigkeitsverhältnis *nt* quality index
Wertschöpfung *f* value added, real net output
Wertschöpfungsaktivitäten *fpl* value-added activities
Wertschöpfungskette *f* value-added chain
Wettbewerb *m* competition
Wettbewerbsdruck *m* competitive pressures
Wettbewerbsvorteil *m* competitive advantage
Wetterechtheit *f* fastness to weathering
wetterfest weatherproof
wettergeschützt weatherproof
Whithworth-Feingewinde *nt* Whitworth fine pitch thread
Wichte *f* force per volume
wichtig important
Wichtigkeit *f* importance
Wichtung *f* weighting
Wichtungsfaktor *m* weighing factor
Wickelarm *m* rotating arm
Wickelband *nt* wrapping tape
Wickelfalzrohr *nt* folded spiral- seam pipe
Wickelkopf *m* **1.** *(allg.)* strapping head, wrapping head **2.** *(el.)* end windings, end connections
Wickelmasse *f* wrapping compound
wickeln wind (around), wrap around, strap, coil
Wickelprogramm *nt* wrapping program
Wickelring *m* wrapping ring
Wickelschicht *f* wrapped coating
Wickelstretch *m* stretch wrap
Wickelstretchverpackung *f* stretch wrap pack(ing)
Wickelzahl *f* wrapping number
Wickelzuschlag *m* wrap allowance
Wickler *m* **1.** *(Aufnahme)* coiler, take-up **2.** *(Verpackungsmaschine)* wrapping machine
Wicklung *f* winding, wrap
Wicklungsstrang *m* phase winding
Wicklungswiderstand *m* winding resistance, coil resistance
Widerlager *nt* support, anvil, abutment
widersprechend inconsistent, contradictory, contrary
Widerspruch *m* contradiction
widerspruchsfrei consistent
Widerspruchsfreiheit *f* consistency
Widerstand *m* **1.** *(Größe)* resistance **2.** *(Bauteil)* resistor
Widerstandsbuckelschweißung *f* (resistance) projection welding
Widerstandsbuckelschweißverbindung *f* projection joint by resistant welding
Widerstandserwärmung *f* resistant heating
widerstandsfähig resistant

widerstandsgeschweißte Liniennaht f resistance-welded seam weld
widerstandsgeschweißte Punktnaht f resistance-welded spaced spot weld
Widerstandskennlinie f resistor characteristic
Widerstandskraft f resisting force
Widerstandsmembran f resistance membrane
Widerstandsmoment nt section modulus, moment of resistance
Widerstandsnormal nt standard resistance
Widerstandspolarisation f (el. chem.) resistance polarisation
Widerstandspunkt m resistance spot, point of resistance
Widerstandsrollnahtschweißung f resistance (roller) seam welding, seam weld
Widerstandstemperaturfühler m resistance temperature detector
Widerstandswärme f resistance heat
widerstehen withstand, offer resistance, resist
wieder zusammensetzen reassemble
Wiederanlauf m restart, restarting, repetition
wiederanlaufen restart
wiederanlaufen lassen restart
wiederauffüllen replenish, refill
wiederaufladen recharge
wiederauftragen resurface
wiederbefüllen refill, replenish
Wiederbeschaffungszeit f replacement time
wiedereinlagern reshelf
Wiedereinlagerung f restorage, reshelving
wiedereinschalten 1. (allg.) restart, restore power, reset **2.** (Relais) reclose
Wiedereinschaltschutz m reset contractor
Wiedereinschaltsperre f reclosure preventing device
Wiedereintrittszyklus m re-entry cycle
Wiederersatz m replacement
Wiedergabe f **1.** (allg.) reproduction, playback **2.** (Daten) retrieval

wiedergeben 1. (allg.) reproduce, playback, render **2.** (Bilder) picture **3.** (Daten) retrieve
wiedergewinnen recover
Wiedergewinnungsgrad m recovery index
wiederhergestellt werden recover
wiederherstellen restore, reconstitute
Wiederherstellung f restoration, recovery, renewal
Wiederherstellung f **der Betriebsbereitschaft** machine recovery, machine recovery procedure
wiederholbar 1. (allg.) repeatable **2.** (reproduzierbar) reproducible **3.** (wiederkehrend) recursive, recurring
Wiederholbarkeit f repeatability, reproducibility
Wiederholbedingungen fpl repetition conditions
wiederholen 1. (allg.) repeat, reiterate, recur, reproduce **2.** (Abläufe) rerun
Wiederholgenauigkeit f precision, repeatability, repeatable accuracy, repeating accuracy
Wiederholgrenze f repeatability limit
Wiederholmessreihe f repeatability measurement series
Wiederholpräzision f repeatability
Wiederholstandardabweichung f repeatability standard deviation
Wiederholstreubereich m repetition tolerance
wiederholt repeated, reiterated, recurring
Wiederholteil nt repetition part
Wiederholung f repetition, reiteration, recurrence, replication
Wiederholungsanforderung f (automatic) request for repetition
Wiederholungsbedingungen fpl repeatability conditions
Wiederholungsbefehl m repetition instruction
Wiederholungslauf m (EDV) rerun
Wiederholungszeichen nt repeating label
Wiederinbetriebnahme f restarting
Wiederinstandsetzung f reserving
wiederkehren recur

wiederkehrend periodic, recurring, recurrent, repeated
wiederprogrammierbarer Festspeicher *m* reprogrammable read-only memory (REPROM)
wiederprogrammieren reprogrammable
Wiederverkauf *m* resale
wiederverkaufen resell, retail
Wiederverkäufer *m* reseller, retailer
Wiederverkäuferpreis *m* wholesale price
Wiederverkaufspreis *m* resale price, retail price, retailer's price
wiederverschließbar reclosable
wiederverschließen reclose, relock
wiederverwenden reuse, reemploy, reutilize
Wiederverwendung *f* reuse, reutilization, reemployment
wiederzuführen recirculate (lubricant)
Wiederzündversuch *m* re-ignition (or relighting) attempt
Wiegeeinrichtung *f* weighing device
wiegen weigh, scale
wildgewickelte Ringspule *f* roughly wound annular coil
wildgewickelte Spule *f* roughly wound coil
willkürlich arbitrary
willkürliche Einheiten *fpl* arbitrary units
Wind *m* **1.** *(allg.)* wind **2.** *(Gebläseluft)* blast (air)
Winddruck *m* wind pressure
Winde *f* winch, whim, hoist
Windeinwirkung *f* effect of wind
winden 1. *(allg.)* wind, reel **2.** *(aufwinden, heben)* lift, hoist, raise
Windgeschwindigkeit *f* **1.** *(allg.)* wind speed **2.** *(skalar)* wind velocity
Windhubsystem *nt* winch lifting system
Windkraft *f* wind force
Windlast *f* wind load (stressing), load due to wind pressure, wind stress, wind load
Windmesser *m* wind velocity indicator, wind gauge
windschief warped, skew, (wind-) inclined
Windschutzscheibe *f* front window, front (wind)shield, windscreen, *(US)* windshield
Windstärke *f* wind force, wind intensity
Windung *f* **1.** *(allg.)* winding, turn **2.** *(Verpackung)* wrap
winkel ... angular
Winkel *m* **1.** *(allg.)* angle, elbow **2.** *(Werkzeug)* engineer's square
Winkel *m* **am Schneidteil** angle on the cutting part
Winkelangaben *fpl* angle data
Winkelantrieb *m* angular drive
Winkelbereich *m* angular range
Winkelbeschleunigung *f* angular acceleration
Winkelbewegung *f* angular movement
Winkelcodierer *m* angle encoder, shaft encoder
Winkeldurchmesser *m* diameter of turns
Winkeleinheit *f* angular unit
Winkeleinstellung *f* angular setting
Winkeleisen *nt* angle plate
Winkelendmaß *nt* angle gauge, angle block
Winkelfehler *m* angular error, angle error
Winkelfräseinrichtung *f* angle milling fixture, angle milling attachment
Winkelfräsen *nt* angular milling
Winkelfräser *m* angle milling cutter, angular cutter
Winkelfräser *m* **für Werzeuge mit gefrästen Zähnen für Spannuten mit Drall** double-angle cutter, odd angle cutter
Winkelfräser *m* **mit Zylinderschaft** angle end mill
Winkelfräskopf *m* angular milling head, angular milling attachment
Winkelfrässpindel *f* angle milling spindle
Winkelfrequenz *f* angular frequency
Winkelführung *f* angular guide
Winkelgang *m* intersecting aisle
Winkelgangbreite *f* width of intersecting aisle

Winkelgeber *m* angle transmitter
winkelgetreue Übersetzung *f* true angle ratio
winkelgetreue Übertragung *f* true-angle transmission
Winkelgreifer *m* angular gripper
Winkelgrenzmaß *nt* angular limit of size
Winkelgriff *m* offset handle
Winkeligdrehen *nt* angular turning
Winkeligkeit *f* angularity
Winkelistmaß *nt* actual angular size
Winkel-Lichttaster *m* angle light scanner
Winkelmaß *nt* angular size, angle measure, angular dimension
Winkelmesser *m* protractor
Winkelmessgerät *nt* angle measuring instrument, angle measuring device
Winkelmessung *f* angle measurement, angular position measurement
Winkelmesswandler *m* angle transducer
Winkelnennmaß *nt* nominal angular size
Winkelnormale *f* angle standard
Winkelprobe *f* bent-over test specimen, angled test specimen, angled specimen
Winkelprobe *f* **mit Einschnitt** angled specimen with incision
Winkelprüfkopf *m* angle probe
Winkelschälversuch *m* T-peel test, hundred and eighty degree peel test
Winkelschottstutzen in Stoßausführung *f* **für Rohrverschraubungen** elbow bulkhead fitting for butt joints
Winkelschottverschraubung *f* bulkhead union elbow
Winkelschraubendreher *m* cranked wrench key, offset screwdriver
Winkelschraubendreher *m* **für Innenkeilprofilschrauben** key for spline socket screws
Winkelschraubendreher *m* **für Innensechskantschrauben** key for hexagon socket screws
Winkelschraubendreher *m* **mit Zapfen für Innensechskantschrauben** hexagon socket screw key with pilot
Winkelschrittgeber *m* angular encoder
Winkelsollmaß *nt* desired angular size
Winkelstecker *m* bent locator pin
Winkelstirnfräser *m* angle milling cutter, single angle cutter, angular half side mill
Winkelteilung *f* angular spacing
Winkeltisch *m* knee-table, console, knee
Winkeltoleranz *f* angular tolerance
Winkeltrieb *m* bell-crank drive
Winkelverbindungsstutzen *m* *(für Rohrverschraubungen)* pipe union elbow
Winkelverformung *f* angular strain, angular deformation
Winkelversatz *m* angular misalignment
Winkelverschiebung *f* angular displacement
Winkelvorschub *m* angular feed
Winkelwasserwaage *f* square spirit level
Winklelabweichung *f* deviation of the angle(s), angular deviation
winklig angular, square, at an angle
Winterheizung *f* winter space heating
Wippanschlag *m* swinging stop
Wippe *f* **1.** *(allg.)* hinged plate, hinged slide rails, compensator **2.** *(Fußlenkung)* oscillating platform **3.** *(Schüttgut)* tilting chute **4.** *(Schwinge)* rocker
wippen 1. *(allg.)* seesaw, swing **2.** *(schwingen)* rock **3.** *(kippen)* tip
Wippen *nt* *(Bordkran)* luffing
Wipper *m* tipper, tippler
Wippkran *m* level luffing crane, derrick crane
Wipptisch *m* tilting table, rising table
Wirbel *m* eddy
wirbelig vortical
Wirbelmeißel *m* whirling tool
Wirbeln *nt* whirling, roll, eddy
Wirbelspanung *f* cutting by the whirling method
Wirbelstrom *m* eddy current
Wirbelstromverfahren *nt* eddy current method
Wirbelzerspanung *f* cutting by whirl-

ing process
Wirkbereich *m* effective range, operating range
Wirkbewegung *f* active cutting motion
Wirkbezugsebene *f* working reference plane
Wirkbezugssystem *nt* tool-in-use-system, effect reference system
Wirkeinstellergänzungswinkel *m* working approach angle, *(US)* working lead angle
Wirkeinstellwinkel *m* working cutting edge angle
Wirkeinstellwinkel *m* **der Nebenschneide** working minor cutting edge angle
wirken act (as/upon), effect, function (as), operate, work
Wirkenergie *f* working energy
Wirkfläche *f* effective area
Wirkfreiwinkel *m* working clearance
Wirkfuge *f* acting groove
Wirkgeschwindigkeit *f* resultant cutting speed
Wirkhauptschneide *f* working major cutting edge
Wirkimpuls *m* active pulse
Wirkkeilmessebene *f* active wedge measured plane
Wirkkeilwinkel *m* working wedge angle
Wirkkraft *f* working force
Wirklagewinkel *m* working orientation angle
Wirkleistung *f* working power
Wirkleitung *f* differential pressure pipe
wirklich actual, effective, real
Wirkmedium *nt* active medium
Wirknebenschneide *f* working minor cutting edge
Wirkneigungswinkel *m* working cutting edge inclination
Wirknormalfreiwinkel *m* working normal clearance
Wirknormalkeilwinkel *m* normal wedge angle
Wirknormalkraft *f* working perpendicular force
Wirknormalspanwinkel *m* working normal rake
Wirkorthogonalebene *f* working orthogonal plane
Wirkorthogonalfreiwinkel *m* working orthogonal clearance
Wirkorthogonalkeilwinkel *m* working orthogonal wedge angle
Wirkorthogonalspanwinkel *m* working orthogonal rake
Wirkpaar *nt* working pair
Wirkradius *m* effective radius
Wirkrichtung *f* resultant cutting direction
Wirkrichtungswinkel *m* resultant cutting speed angle
Wirkrückebene *f* working back plane
Wirkrückfreiwinkel *m* working back clearance
Wirkrückkeilwinkel *m* working back wedge angle
Wirkrückspanwinkel *m* working back rake
wirksam effective, efficient, efficacious, active, acting
wirksamer Spanwinkel *m* true rake angle
wirksames Übermaß *nt* effective interference
Wirksamkeit *f* effectiveness, efficacy
Wirksamwerden *nt* engagement
Wirkschneidenebene *f* working cutting edge plane
Wirkschneidennormalebene *f* cutting edge normal plane
Wirkseitenfreiwinkel *m* working side clearance
Wirkseitenkeilwinkel *m* working side wedge angle
Wirkseitenspanwinkel *m* working side rake
Wirkspanwinkel *m* true-rake angle, working rake
Wirkstelle *f* action place
Wirkung *f* action, effect
Wirkungsablauf *m* sequence of action
Wirkungsbereich *m* range of effectiveness
Wirkungsgrad *m* effect, efficiency
Wirkungsgrad *m* **bei der Zerspanung** cutting efficiency
Wirkungsgröße *f* parameter

Wirkungsleistung *f* effective power
Wirkungslinie *f* line of action
wirkungsmäßige Abhängigkeit *f* **von Signalen** action-related dependence of signals
wirkungsmäßige Betrachtung *f* *(e. Regelung oder Steuerung)* action-related consideration
wirkungsmäßiges Verhalten *nt (von Gliedern)* action-related behaviour
Wirkungsrichtung *f* direction of action
Wirkungsweg *m* path of action, signal flow path
Wirkungsweise *f* working principle
Wirkungszusammenhang *m* action-related connection
Wirkvorschub *m* effective feed
Wirkweg *m* effective travel
Wirkweise *f* mode of action
Wirkwiderstand *m* actual resistance, effective resistance
Wirkwinkel *m* working angle, *(US)* true rake angle, true rake, top rake angle, *(UK)* maximum rake
Wirkzeit *f* effective time
wirkliche Tragfläche *f* actual capacity
Wirrspan *m* snarling chip, snarly chip, entangled chip, chip tangle
wirtschaftlich economical, profitable, cost-effective
Wirtschaftlichkeit *f* economic efficiency, operational efficiency, profitability, economy
Wirtschaftlichkeitsanalyse *f* economic feasibility study
Wirtschaftlichkeitsprüfung *f* economic efficiency checking
Wirtschaftlichkeitsrechnung *f* economy calculation, efficiency calculation, estimate of operating economy, feasibility study
Wischbeständigkeit *f* wipe resistance
wischen wipe
Wischer *m* **1.** *(allg.)* windscreen wiper, *(US)* windshield wiper **2.** *(el.)* line transient
Wischkontakt *m* wiping contact
Wismut *nt* bismuth
Wissen *nt* knowledge
wissensbasierend knowledge-based

Wissensbasis *f* knowledge basis
Wissensmanagement *nt* knowledge management
Witterung *f* weather
witterungsunempfindlich weatherproof
Wobbelfrequenz *f* wobble frequency
wobbeln *(vi/vt)* wobble, sweep
Woche *f* week
Wochendurchschnitt *m* average rate per week
Wochenprogramm *nt* week's programme
wöchentlich weekly
WO-Emulsion *f* water-in-oil emulsion
wölben 1. *(allg.)* arch, bend, curve, deflect **2.** *(Flächen)* warp
Wölbhöhle *f* bulge height
Wölbmoment *nt* **1.** *(allg.)* bending moment **2.** *(Flächen)* warping moment
Wölbspannung *f* bending stress, warping stress
Wölbung *f* **an der Riemenscheibe** pulley crown
Wölbung *f* **1.** *(allg.)* arch, bending, curvature, deflection, convexity **2.** *(Flächen)* warpage
Wölbversuch *m* vaulting test
Wölbwiderstand *m* resistance to warping, warping resistance
Wolframkarbid bestücktes Messer *nt* tungsten-carbide tipped blade
Wolframkarbid *nt* tungsten carbide
Wolframkarbideinsatz *m* tungsten-carbide insert
Wolframkarbidmesserkopf *m* tungsten-carbide face milling cutter
Wolframplasmaschweißen *nt* plasma arc welding
Wolframschnellstahl *m* tungsten high-speed steel
Wolframspritzer *m* tungsten spatter
WOP (Werkstattorientierte Programmierung) *f* shop floor progamming
Work-Factory-System *nt* work-factory-system
Wort *nt* program word, word
Wort *nt* **verarbeitend** word processing
Wortangaben *fpl (auf e. Zeichnung)*

verbal notes
Wortverarbeitung *f* word processing
Wraparoundfaltschachtelverpackungsmaschine *f* wraparound case packing machine
Wraparoundkartoniermaschine *f* wraparound cartoner
Wraparoundtrayverpackungsmaschine *f* wraparound tray packing machine
Wraparoundumhüllungsmaschine *f* wraparound sleeving machine
Wraparoundverdeckelungsmaschine *f* wraparound lidding machine
wuchten balance
Wuchtgüte *f* balance quality
Wuchtvorrichtung *f* balancing fixture
Wulstnaht *f* upset weld
Wulstrand *m* meniscus
Würfel *m* cube

Würfeldruckprüfung *f* cube test
würfelförmig cubical
Würfelleim *m* cube glue
Wurzel *f* **1.** *(math.)* square root, root **2.** *(Quadratwurzel von)* (square) root (of)
Wurzel *f* **aus dem Mittelwert der Quadrate** root-mean square average (rms)
Wurzel *f* **ziehen aus** extract a root, take a root
wurzelabweisender Stoff *m* root-rejecting substance
Wurzelkerbe *f* root concavity (or notch), shrinkage groove
Wurzelpunkt *m* root point
Wurzelrückfall *m* concavity on root side, root concavity
Wurzelschweißer *m* root-run welder
wurzelseitiges Nachscheißen *nt* re-welding on the root side

X$_x$

x% Stauchspannung f x% compressive offset yield, x% compression yield
X-Achse f X-axis, abscissa
Xenonbogenstrahlung f xenon arc radiation
X-Fuge f double-V groove

X-Koordinate f X-coordinate
x-mm Stauchwiderstand m x mm compression resistance
X-Quarz nt X-cut crystal
Xylolverfahren nt xylene method

Y$_y$

Y-Achse f Y-axis, ordinate
Y-Kreis-Teilung f Y-circle pitch

Y-Zylinder-Normteilung f Y-cylinder normal pitch

Z$_z$

zackig ragged
zäh tough, sluggish
Zähbruch m ductile fracture
Zähfestigkeit f tenacity
zähflüssig viscous
zähflüssiges Fett nt high viscosity grease
zäh-harter Schaumstoff m viscous-hard cellular plastics
Zähigkeit f toughness
Zähigkeitseigenschaft f toughness property
Zähigkeitsverhalten nt toughness (or tenacity) behaviour
Zahl f 1. *(math.)* number, figure, numeral 2. *(einstellige)* digit 3. *(Ziffer)* cipher 4. *(ganze~)* integer 5. *(ungerade)* odd number
zählbar countable
Zählcode m counting code
Zähleingang m counting input
Zähleinheit f unit for counting
zahlen pay, remit, count, figure
zählen count, number, score, meter

Zahlenabgaben fpl numerical data, figures
Zahlencode m (numerical) code
zählendes Messgerät nt counting measuring instrument
Zahlenebene f number plane
Zahlenfaktor m numerical factor
zahlenmäßige Darstellung f numerical representation
Zahlenmaterial nt figures
Zahlenscheibe f dial
Zahlenstelle f digit
Zahlenwert m numerical value
Zahlenwertgleichung f numerical equation
Zähler m 1. *(allg.)* counter, meter, numerator 2. *(el.)* integrating meter
Zähler m **ablesen** read the counter, read the meter
Zählerableser m meter man
Zählerablesung f meter reading
Zählerbaugruppe f counter module
Zählerstand m counter reading, meter reading, count of the counter, count

Zählerstellung f counter position
Zählfüllmaschine f count filling machine
Zählnummer f code number
Zählröhre f counter tube
zählstatistischer Fehler m count-statistical error
Zählstufe f counting stage
Zählung f counting, metering, payment, remittance
Zahlungsfreigabe f remittance advice
Zahlungsplan m payment plan, payment schedule, instalment plan
Zählwerk nt integrator
Zahn m 1. *(Zahnrad)* (gear) tooth 2. *(Kettenrad)* sprocket 3. *(Maschine, Nocken)* lifting cog
Zahnauslauf m tooth exit
Zahnbreite f 1. *(allg.)* tooth width 2. *(Zahnrad)* width of tooth face
Zahnbrust f 1. *(e. Fräsers)* tooth face 2. *(e. Spanfläche)* face, cutting face
Zahnbrustwinkel m tooth face angle
Zahndicke f **auf dem Grundzylinder im Normalschnitt** normal base thickness
Zahndicke f **auf dem Grundzylinder im Stirnschnitt** transverse base thickness
Zahndicke f **im Normalschnitt** normal tooth thickness
Zahndicke f **im Stirnschnitt** transverse tooth thickness
Zahndickenabmaß nt tooth thickness deviation
Zahndickenänderung f tooth thickness alteration
Zahndickenänderungsfaktor m tooth thickness alteration factor
Zahndickenfehler m tooth thickness error
Zahndickengrenzmaß nt tooth thickness limiting size
Zahndickengröße f tooth thickness quantity
Zahndickenhalbwinkel m tooth thickness half angle
Zahndickenmessung f chordal measurement
Zahndickenpasssystem nt tooth thickness system of fits
Zahndickenschwankung f tooth thickness fluctuation
Zahndickensehne f normal chordal tooth thickness
Zahndickensehnenschwankung f normal chordal tooth thickness fluctuation
Zahneingriff m 1. *(allg.)* meshing (of the teeth), tooth engagement 2. *(e. Fräsers in das Werkstück)* tooth entrance
zahnen serrate, cut teeth, tooth
Zähnezahl f number of teeth
Zähnezahl f **des Zahnrades** gear-tooth number
Zähnezahlfaktor m gear-tooth number factor
Zähnezahlsumme f total number of teeth
Zähnezahlverhältnis nt gear ratio
Zahnflanke f 1. *(allg.)* face of the tooth, tooth profile, flank of tooth 2. *(obere Hälfte)* addendum flank 3. *(untere Hälfte)* tooth flank
Zahnflankenabstand m flank spacing
Zahnflankenfräser m gear tooth face cutter
Zahnflankenschaben nt tooth flank scraping
Zahnflankenschleifen nt tooth generation grinding, gear teeth grinding
Zahnflankenschleifmaschine f gear tooth grinder, gear grinder
Zahnflankenspiel nt face play, flank play
Zahnflankentragfähigkeit f flank bearing
Zahnflankenveränderung f flank modification
Zahnform f profile shape of the tooth
Zahnformfehler m tooth profile error
Zahnformfräsen nt gear milling
Zahnformvorfräser m stocking cutter, gear roughing cutter, *(UK)* gashing cutter, gear stocking cutter, stocking gear milling cutter
Zahnformvorfräser m **für Fräszahnlücken** gashing cutter
Zahnfreiwinkel m tooth clearance an-

gle
Zahnfuß *m* tooth dedendum, dedendum (pl.: dedenda), root, base of gear tooth, root of a gear tooth
Zahnfußausrundung *f* fillet
Zahnfußfestigkeit *f* strength at the root
Zahnfußfläche *f* tooth root surface
Zahnfußhöhe *f* dedendum
Zahnfußlückenweite *f* root space width
Zahnfußspannung *f* tooth root stress
Zahnfußtragfähigkeit *f* root bearing
Zahngetriebe *nt* gear drive
Zahngrund *m* 1. *(Zahnlücke)* root of the tooth, root, tooth gullet, gullet 2. *(e. Wälzhobelmeißels)* bottom of the tooth space
Zahngrundabrundung *f* root radius, radius at bottom of tooth
Zahnhöhe *f* depth of tooth, tooth height, whole depth of tooth space, tooth depth
Zahnhöhenänderung *f* tooth depth variation
Zahnkante *f* tooth edge
Zahnkantenabrundfräser *m* tooth chamfering cutter
Zahnkantenfräsmaschine *f* tooth-end rounding machine
Zahnkette *f* sprocket chain, toothed chain, silent chain
Zahnkopf *m* tooth crest, tip, addendum
Zahnkopfabrundung *f* tip relief, top radius
Zahnkopfecke *f* tooth face tip
Zahnkopfhöhe *f* addendum
Zahnkopfhöhenfaktor *m* whole depth factor
Zahnkopfkante *f* tooth face at the tip
Zahnkopfkürzung *f* tip relief
Zahnkranz *m* gear ring, toothed ring, sprocket, chain wheel
Zahnlücke *f* 1. *(allg.)* tooth space, gash, gullet, pocket 2. *(e. Fräsers)* tooth gap 3. *(e. Säge)* tooth gullet
Zahnlückenfehler *m* gear tooth spacing error
Zahnlückenfräsen *nt* gashing
Zahnlückengrund *m* bottom of the tooth space
Zahnlückengrundfläche *f* surface at the bottom of the tooth space
Zahnlückenhalbwinkel *m* tooth space half angle
Zahnluftmessgerät *nt* tooth clearance tester
Zahnmessschieblehre *f* gear-tooth calliper
Zahnmitte *f* tooth centre
Zahnmittenlinie *f* tooth centre line
Zahnplatte *f* rack
Zahnprofil *nt* profile shape of the tooth, tooth design, tooth shape, gear tooth profile
Zahnrad *nt* gear, toothed gear
Zahnrad *nt* **mit Außenverzahnung** external gear
Zahnrad *nt* **mit Bogenverzahnung** spiral gear
Zahnradbezugsprofil *nt* gear standard basic rack tooth profile
Zahnradbreite *f* gear width
Zahnräder *ntpl* gear wheels
Zahnradfertigung *f* gear wheel manufacturing
Zahnradfräseinrichtung *f* gear cutting attachment
Zahnradfräsen *nt* 1. *(allg.)* gear cutting, gear milling 2. *(Wälzverfahren)* gear hobbing
Zahnradfräser *m* gear cutter
Zahnradfräsmaschine *f* gear cutting machine, gear milling machine
Zahnradgetriebe *nt* toothed gearing, pinion, gear drive
Zahnradhobelmaschine *f* 1. *(allg.)* gear planer (or planing machine) 2. *(Stoßverfahren)* gear shaper 3. *(Wälzverfahren)* gear generator
Zahnradkettensteuerung *f* sprocket and chain steering
Zahnradkörper *m* gear blank
Zahnradläppmaschine *f* gear lapping machine
Zahnradnabe *f* gear hub
Zahnradpaar *nt* gear pair
Zahnradpaar *nt* **mit Bogenverzahnung** spiral gear pair
Zahnradpaar *nt* **mit parallelen**

Achsen gear pair with parallel axes
Zahnradpaarung *f* gear pairing
Zahnradprüfgerät *nt* gear tester
Zahnradpumpenaggregat *nt* gear type pumping set
Zahnradrohling *m* gear blank
Zahnradschaben *nt* gear shaving
Zahnradschleifen *nt* gear grinding
Zahnradstoßmaschine *f* **1.** *(allg.)* gear slotting machine **2.** *(Waagerechtstoßmaschine)* gear shaper **3.** *(Wälzstoßmaschine)* gear generator
Zahnradteilungsfehler *m* gear tooth pitch error
Zahnradübersetzung *f* gearing ratio, gear ratio, gear train
Zahnraduntersetzung *f* gear reduction
Zahnradvorgelege *nt* back gearing, back gears
Zahnradwälzfräsautomat *m* automatic gear hobbing machine
Zahnradwälzfräser *m* gear hob
Zahnradwälzfräsmaschine *f* gear hobber (or hobbing machine)
Zahnradwälzfräsmaschine *f* gear hobbing machine, gear generation machine
Zahnradwälzfräsverfahren *nt* gear hobbing technique
Zahnradwälzschleifmaschine *f* gear-generating grinder
Zahnradwälzstoßmaschine *f* gear generator
Zahnriemen *m* profile belt, toothed belt, synchronous belt, sprocket belt
Zahnriementrieb *m* synchronous belt drive
Zahnritzel *nt* pinion
Zahnrücken *m* **1.** *(allg.)* tooth back **2.** *(e. Reibahle)* land
Zahnrückendicke *f* size of land
Zahnrückenfase *f* straight land
Zahnscheibe *f* **für Kombischrauben** serrated lock washer for screw assemblies
Zahnschräge *f* slope of the tooth
Zahnschrägewinkel *m* helix angle
Zahnsegment *nt* segment gear
Zahnspitze *f* tooth tip

Zahnstange *f* gear rack, (toothed) rack
Zahnstangenantrieb *m* rack and pinion drive
Zahnstangenbezugsebene *f* rack datum plane
Zahnstangenflanke *f* rack flank
zahnstangenförmig rack-shaped
zahnstangenförmiges Wälzwerkzeug *nt* rack type generating cutter
Zahnstangenfräsvorrichtung *f* rack-milling attachment
Zahnstangenheber *m* rack and pinion jack
Zahnstangenradpaar *nt* rack and pinion pair
Zahnteilung *f* **1.** *(allg.)* spacing of teeth, tooth pitch, tooth spacing, pitch **2.** *(Sehne)* chordal pitch **3.** *(Teilkreis)* circular pitch
Zahntrieb *m* pinion (gear)
Zahnungseinsätze *mpl* *(Räummaschine)* built-up teeth
Zahnverformung *f* tooth deformation
Zahnverstellung *f* tooth setting
Zahnweite *f* base tangent length
Zahnweitenabmaß *nt* base tangent length deviation
Zahnweitenmessschraube *f* base tangent length callipers
Zahnweitenschieblehre *f* base tangent length micrometer
Zahnweitenschwankung *f* base tangent length fluctuation
Zahnweitentoleranz *f* base tangent length tolerance
Zahnwelle *f* toothed shaft, gear shaft
Zahnwellenwälzfräser *m* spline hob
Zange *f* **1.** *(Beißzange)* pincers *pl*, pliers *pl* **2.** *(Greifzange)* tongs
Zangen *fpl:* **mit ~ arbeiten** tong, grasp with tongs
Zangenaufnahme *f* collet gripping (or clamping), collet mounting
Zangengreifer *m* tong gripper, gripper finger
Zangengriff *m* handle, tong
Zangenlötmaschine *f* resistance (or gun) soldering machine
Zangenspannfutter *nt* spring-collet chuck

Zangenspannung *f* collet gripping mechanism, collet chucking
Zangenvorschubapparat *m* pliers feed device
Zapfen *m* 1. *(bei Gestängerohren)* spigot 2. *(Einführzapfen)* entry pilot 3. *(Einstechbolzen)* pivot 4. *(Gewindestift)* half-dog point 5. *(Maschine)* cog 6. *(mech.)* journal, trunnion 7. *(Schaft)* stem 8. *(Schraube)* full dog point 9. *(Schraubendreher)* pilot 10. *(Splint)* point 11. *(Verschraubung)* adaptor end 12. *(allg.)* pintle, pin, stud, peg, finger
Zapfendurchmesser *m* stem diameter
Zapfengewinde *nt (für Gestängerohre)* spigot screw thread
Zapfenlager *nt* 1. *(allg.)* pivot bearing, trunnion bearing 2. *(Achse)* journal bearing
Zapfenlänge *f* stem length
Zapfenmantelfläche *f* journal envelope
Zapfenmitte *f* centre of the journal
Zapfenreibung *f* journal friction
Zapfenschlüssel *m* pin wrench
Zapfenschraube *f* **mit Schlitz** slotted screw with full dog point
Zapfensenker *m* piloted counterbore, counterbore with guide (pilot)
Zaun *m* fence, fencing
Zehnerblocktastatur *f* ten key block-keyboard
Zehnkugelrohr *nt* Meyer's tube
Zeichen *nt* 1. *(Schild, Symptom)* sign 2. *(alphanumerisch)* character 3. *(optisch)* signal 4. *(Programmierung)* symbol 5. *(Verpackung)* mark
Zeichenarbeit *f* drawing (office) work
Zeichenbrett *nt* drawing board
Zeichenbrett *nt* **mit Zusatzfläche** drawing board with free margin
Zeichendreieck *nt* set square
Zeichenebene *f* plane of the drawing
Zeichenfeld *nt* character area
Zeichenfläche *f* drawing area
Zeichenfolge *f* sequence of characters, character string, string
Zeichenkette *f* (character) string
Zeichenkontrast *m* contrast character to background

Zeichenmaschine *f* drafting machine
Zeichenmittel *nt* drawing instrument
Zeichenmittelabstand *m* character centreline spacing
Zeichenschiene *f* tee square, T-square
Zeichentakt *m* byte timing
Zeichenvorrat *m* character set
zeichenweiser Betrieb *m* character mode
zeichnen 1. *(allg.)* draw, draft 2. *(IT)* plot
zeichnen: gekürzt ~ draw in shortened form
Zeichner/in *m/f* 1. *(allg.)* draughtsman/draughtswoman, draftsman, draftswoman, draughtsperson, draftsperson 2. *(Entwerfer)* designer
zeichnerisch graphical, drawing
zeichnerisches Verfahren *nt* graphical method
Zeichnung *f* drawing, design, engineering drawing
Zeichnungen anfertigen produce drawings
Zeichnungen *fpl* **mit vorgedruckten Darstellungen** drawing containing preprinted representations
Zeichnungsänderung *f* amendment of drawing
Zeichnungsänderungsdienst *m* drawing amendment service
Zeichnungsaustausch *m* exchange of drawings
Zeichnungsblatt *nt* drawing sheet
Zeichnungseintragung *f* entry in a drawing
Zeichnungsersteller *m* drawing producer
Zeichnungserstellung *f* preparation of drawings
Zeichnungsfeld *nt* drawing area, drawing panel
Zeichnungsformat *nt* size of drawing
zeichnungsgeprüft checked by drawing scrutiny
Zeichnungshauptlage *f* longest edge of the drawing
Zeichnungsmaßstab *m* scale of the drawing
Zeichnungsnorm *f* drawing practice

standard
Zeichnungsoriginal *nt* original drawing
Zeichnungsprüfung *f* drawing scrutiny
Zeichnungsrichtlinien *fpl* principles for the preparation of drawings
Zeichnungssatz *m* set of drawings
Zeichnungsschriftfeld *nt* title block
Zeichnungssystematik *f* systematic arrangement of drawings
Zeichnungsträger *m* drawing board
Zeichnungsunterlagen *fpl* graphical documents
Zeichnungsverfilmung *f* filming of drawings
Zeichnungsvordruck *m* preprinted drawing sheet
Zeichnungswesen *nt* drawing practice
zeigen 1. *(allg.)* show, indicate **2.** *(darstellen)* display **3.** *(demonstrieren)* demonstrate
zeigen auf point to
Zeiger *m* pointer, indicator
Zeigerablesung *f* pointer reading, indicator reading
Zeigeranschlag *m* pointer deflection
Zeigerausschlag *m* deflection of the pointer, pointer deflection
Zeigerlehre *f* dial indicator
Zeigerspitze *f* pointer tip, tip of the pointer
Zeigervariable *f* pointer variable
Zeile *f* **1.** *(allg.)* line **2.** *(Reihe, Lager)* row
Zeilenabtastfrequenz *f* scanning frequency
Zeilenabtastung *f* horizontal scanning, line scanning
Zeilenanzeige *f* line display
zeilenförmige Korrosion *f* linear corrosion
Zeilenfräsarbeit *f* line-by-line milling (operation), parallel stroke milling operation
Zeilenfräsen *nt* parallel stroke milling, straight milling, line-by-line milling
Zeilenfräsverfahren *nt* line-by-line milling method, parallel stroke milling method

Zeilenkamera *f* (multi-) row camera
Zeilenlagerung *f* row stacking, row storage
Zeilenlichttaster *m* line-scanning light scanner
Zeilennachformfräsen *nt* line copy milling
Zeilensprung *m* line-spacing
Zeilenvorschub *m* straight feed
zeilenweise line by line, rowwise
zeilenweise Eingabe *f* line input
Zeit bis zur Marktreife *f* time to market
Zeit *f* time
Zeit *f* **einrichten** time
Zeit *f* **ermitteln** measure time
Zeit *f* **je Einheit** *f* time each unit
Zeit *f* **messen** measure time, time
Zeit *f* **sparend** time saving
zeitabhängig time dependent, time controlled
zeitabhängige Spannung *f* time-dependent stress
zeitabhängiges Programmsteuergerät *nt* program controlled timing device
Zeitabschnitt *m* time segment, time slot, period
Zeitachse *f* time axis
Zeitaufnahme *f* time recording
Zeitausgleich *m* compensatory time off, time offset, time smoothing
Zeitberechnung *f* time calculation
Zeitbewertung *f* time weighting
zeitbezogen time-related
zeitbezogene Temperaturzunahme *f* time-referenced temperature increase
Zeitbruchfestigkeit *f* creep rupture strength
Zeit-Bruch-Linie *f* fracture versus time curve
Zeitdauer *f* period (of time)
Zeitdehnspannung *f* creep strength
Zeitdiagramm *nt* time-dependency diagram
Zeiteinheit *f* **1.** *(allg.)* unit of time, time unit, unit time **2.** *(IT)* clock unit **3.** *(je ~)* per unit time
Zeiten *fpl* times
Zeitermittlung *f* time measurement
Zeitersparnis *f* saving of time

Zeitfenster *nt* time frame, time window
Zeitfläche *f* *(Zeitintegral der Funktion)* time integral
Zeitfüllmaschine *f* timed flow filling machine
Zeitfunktion *f* time function
Zeitgeber *m* timing unit, timer
Zeitgeberregister *nt* time register
Zeitgeberschaltung *f* timing circuit
zeitgebunden time dependent
Zeitgebung *f* timing
zeitgleich isochronous, simultaneous, at the same time
Zeitglied *nt* time relay, timer
Zeitintegral *nt* time integral
Zeitkalkulation *f* time calculation
Zeitkonstante *f* time constant
zeitlich temporal
zeitlich begrenzt temporary, time-limited, limited in time, limited duration
zeitliche Ableitung *f* *(e. Eingangssignals)* time derivative
zeitliche Begrenzung *f* time limit, time limitation, temporal limitation
Zeitmengenabstand *m* inventory level as function of time
Zeitmengendefizit *nt* inventory stickout as function of time
Zeitmessung *f* time measurement, timing
Zeitmultiplex *nt* time-division multiplex (TDM)
Zeitmultiplexbetrieb *m* time division multiplexing (TDM)
zeitnah prompt, real-time, on schedule
Zeitnutzung *f* time using
Zeitnutzungsgrad *m* degree of time using
Zeitplan *m* time schedule, schedule
Zeitplanregelung *f* time schedule closed loop control
Zeitplansteuerung *f* time schedule open loop control
Zeitplanung *f* time scheduling
Zeitprogrammsteuerung *f* time-controlled system
zeitproportionale Probenahme *f* time-dependent sampling
Zeitpunkt *m* date, time, point in time, moment

Zeitpunktglied *nt* two-level action element
Zeitraffer *m* 1. *(Funktion)* fast motion, quick motion 2. *(Einrichtung)* quick-motion apparatus
Zeitraffung *f* quick motion effect, time compression, acceleration
Zeitraffungsfaktor *m* acceleration factor
Zeitrasterung *f* equal-interval timing
Zeitraum *m* period
Zeitrelais *nt* time relay
Zeitschalter *m* time switch, timer
Zeitschaltwerk *nt* timing gear mechanism
Zeitschätzung *f* time estimate
Zeitschreiber *m* time recorder
Zeitschwellfestigkeit *f* fatigue stress under fluctuating stress
Zeitspanndehnung *f* time-stress-strain
Zeitspanne *f* duration, time span, period (of time)
Zeitspanungsvolumen *nt* material removal rate
Zeitstandbiegeverhalten *nt* creep behaviour in bending
Zeitstandbiegeversuch *m* cree bending test
Zeitstandbindfestigkeit *f* creep rupture strength of the bond
Zeitstanddruckversuch *m* time-dependent creep compression test, creep compressive test
Zeitstandinnendruckversuch *m* internal pressure creep rupture test, internal pressure endurance test
Zeitstandprobe *f* stress-rupture test specimen
Zeitstandschaubild *nt* creep diagram
Zeitstandscherversuch *m* creep-shear test
Zeitstandzugfestigkeit *f* tensile creep rupture strength
Zeitstandzugverhalten *nt* creep behaviour in tension, tensile creep test
Zeitstempel *m* 1. *(allg.)* time stamp 2. *(Datum)* date stamp 3. *(Stunden)* hour stamp
Zeittakt *m* clock pulse
zeittaktgesteuert time-cycle controlled

zeittaktgleich isochronous
zeittaktungsgleich anisochronous
Zeitüberwachung *f* timer supervision, time out
Zeitüberwachungseinrichtung *f* watchdog (timer)
zeitunabhängiger Elastizitätsmodul *m* time-independent elastic modulus
Zeit-Verformungs-Grenze *f* time-deformation limit
Zeit-Verformungs-Linie *f* curve-of deformation against time
Zeit-Verformungs-Linie *f* curve of deformation versus time
zeitversetzt asynchronous, delayed, time-displaced
zeitverzögert time-delayed, time lagged
Zeitverzögerung *f* backoff, time delay, lag time
Zeit-Weg-Diagramm *nt* time travel diagram
zeitweilig temporary
Zeitzählwerk *nt* timer
Zelle *f* **1.** *(allg.)* cell, manufacturing cell, chamber **2.** *(Kabine)* box, cabin
Zelleneinbau *m* cell mounting
Zellengefäß *nt* **1.** *(allg.)* cell container **2.** *(Akku)* cell box
Zellenofen *m* cell-type oven, cell oven
Zellenrechner *m* cell computer, cell controller
Zellenspeicher *m* cellular storage heater
Zellensteuerung *f* cell control
Zellgefüge *nt* cellular structure
Zellstoffballen *m* pulp bale, baled pulp
Zellstoffchlorierung *f* pulp chlorination
Zellstoffprobe *f* pulp sample
zelluloseumhüllte Elektrode *f* cellulose covered electrode
Zelt *nt* tent
Zement *m* cement
Zementsandformverfahren *nt* cement sand forming process
Zementsandverfahren *nt* cement sand process
Zenerdiode *f* Zener diode, breakdown diode

zentral central
Zentrale *f* **1.** *(räuml.)* central office, headquarters **2.** *(IT)* main frame
zentrale Versorgung *f* centralized supply (of oil-fired furnaces)
zentrale Warmwasserbereitungsanlage *f* centralized hot water installation
Zentraleinheit *f* central processing unit (CPU)
zentrales Moment *nt* central moment
zentrales Ritzel *nt* sun gear
Zentralfeststeller *m* central braking and/or locking device
Zentralrechner *m* host system, host computer, mainframe computer
Zentralsteuerhebel *m* central control lever
Zentralsteuerung *f* central control
Zentralstrahl *m* central ray
Zentralwert *m* median
Zentralwertbereich *m* median band
Zentrierbohren *nt* centre drilling
Zentrierbohrung *f* centre hole (or bore)
zentrieren *(UK)* centre, *(US)* centre, position, true
Zentrierfehler *m* centring error
Zentrierfutter *nt* self-centring chuck
Zentriergenauigkeit *f* accuracy of positioning
Zentrierhilfe *f* centring accessory
Zentrierhülse *f* centring sleeve
Zentrierkante *f* centring edge
Zentrierlager *nt* locating bearing
Zentriermeißel *m* centring tool
Zentrierplatz *m* centring position, centring location
Zentrierpunkt *m* centring point
Zentrierring *m* centring collar
Zentrierstation *f* centring station
Zentrierung *f* *(UK)* centring, *(US)* centring
Zentriervorrichtung *f* centring device
zentrifugal centrifugal
Zentrifugalkraft *f* centrifugal force
Zentrifugenbecher *m* centrifuge beaker
zentrigierte Zufallsgröße *f* centred random quantity
zentripetal centripetal

zentrisch centrical, centred
zentrisch drehen turn true
zentrisch laufen run true
zentrische Bezugsfläche *f* concentric datum surface
Zentriwinkel *m* subtending angle, centre angle
Zentrum *nt* centre, *(US)* centre, centre point
zerbrechen break, crack, fracture
zerbrechlich fragile, frail
Zerbrechlichkeit *f* fragility
zerfressen corrode, erode, cauterise, pit
zergliedern dissect, dismember, analyze
Zergliederung *f* analysis, dissection
Zerkleinerungsgut *nt* material to be reduced in size
zerlegbar 1. *(allg.)* dismountable **2.** *(Elemente)* decomposable **3.** *(Warensendung)* separable
zerlegen 1. *(allg.)* dismantle, dismount, separate **2.** *(auseinander nehmen)* disassemble, detach **3.** *(Datenpaket)* depacketize **4.** *(Elemente)* decompose, dissect **5.** *(klassifizieren)* classify, itemize **6.** *(math.)* divide up **7.** *(phys.)* decompose, resolve **8.** *(Warensendung)* break down (into) **9.** *(zergliedern)* dismember
Zerlegung *f* **1.** *(allg.)* disassembly, dismantling, separation, dissection, resolution **2.** *(chem.)* dissolution **3.** *(Elemente)* decomposition **4.** *(Klassifizierung)* classification
Zerreißbeanspruchung *f* stressing in tension
zerreißen break, burst, disrupt, rip, rupture, tear
Zerreißmaschine *f* tensile testing machine
Zerreißversuch *m* stress-rupture test, tensile test
Zerschneideblattsystem *nt* sheet dissection system
Zerschneideblattzeichnung *f* dissection-sheet drawing
Zerschneiden *nt* cutting up
zersetzbar decomposable
zersetzen 1. *(allg.)* decompose **2.** *(auflösen)* disintegrate, dissolve **3.** *(zerbröckeln)* crumble

Zersetzung *f* **1.** *(allg.)* decomposition **2.** *(Auflösung)* disintegration, solution **3.** *(Zerbröckeln)* crumbling
Zersetzungserscheinung *f* decomposition phenomenon
Zersetzungskolben *m* decomposing flask
Zersetzungsprodukt *nt* decomposition product
Zersetzungstemperatur *f* decomposition temperature
Zerspanarbeit *f* cutting operation
zerspanbar machinable, free-cutting
Zerspanbarkeit *f* machinability, machining (or cutting) property, cuttability, ease of machining (or cutting), free machining (or cutting) property, metal removing capacity
Zerspanbarkeitsgröße *f* machining variable, machinability rating (or variable)
Zerspanbewegung *f* cutting movement
zerspanen machine, take cuts, cut, remove metal (by cutting)
Zerspanen *nt* **mit scherenden Schnitt** shear cutting
Zerspanen *nt* **ohne Überhöhung der Schneide** orthogonal cutting
zerspanende Bearbeitung *f* **auf Taktstraße** in-line transfer machining
zerspanendes Werkzeug *nt* cutting tool
Zerspangröße *f* **1.** *(allg.)* (metal) cutting element **2.** *(Fertigungstechnik)* machining (or cutting) variable **3.** *(geometrische)* metal cutting quantity, geometrical component of metal-cutting
Zerspankraft *f* force exerted by the tool, (total) cutting force, total force
Zerspankraftkomponente *f* component of the cutting force
Zerspanleistung *f* metal removing capacity, cutting efficiency
Zerspanmethode *f* cutting technique
Zerspantechnik *f* metal-cutting technology, metal-cutting technique, metal cutting practice
zerspantes Volumen *nt* volume of

metal removed
Zerspanung *f* **1.** *(allg.)* metal cutting, shape cutting, cutting action, cutting process, cutting, stock removal **2.** *(spanabhebende Bearbeitung)* machining, cutting operation
Zerspanungsarbeit *f* cutting operation, machining operation, machining job, metal cutting work
Zerspanungseigenschaft *f* cutting (or machining) property, machining quality
Zerspanungsforschung *f* metal-cutting research
Zerspanungsgeometrie *f* geometry of metal cutting
Zerspanungsgröße *f* machining (or cutting) variable
Zerspanungskinematik *f* kinematics of metal cutting
Zerspanungsleistung *f* cutting efficiency, cutting capacity, metal-cutting capacity, machining output
Zerspanungsmenge *f* volume of metal removed
Zerspanungsmittel *nt* cutting medium
Zerspanungsprobe *f* test cutting
Zerspanungstechnik *f* metal-cutting technology, metal-cutting technique, metal cutting practice
Zerspanungsverfahren *nt* metal-cutting process
Zerspanungsvolumen *nt* material removal, volume of the metal removed by cutting
Zerspanungsvorgang *m* cutting operation, cutting cycle
Zerspanungswerkzeug *nt* metal-cutting tool
Zerspanvorgang *f* machining operation, cutting operation, chip removing process
Zerspanwerkzeug *nt* metal-cutting tool
zersprengen burst
Zerspringen *nt* *(des Strahlmittels)* splitting
zerstäuben atomize, spray, break up into a fine mist, pulverize, reduce the dust, sputter
Zerstäuben *nt* atomizing, spraying, pulverization, reduction the dust, sputtering
Zerstäubungsdüse *f* atomizing nozzle
zerstörbar destructible
zerstören destroy, demolish, destruct, bust, ruin, spoil
zerstörende Schweißnahtprüfung *f* destructive testing of welds
Zerstörfestigkeit *f* surge immunity
Zerstörung *f* destruction, demolition, deterioration
zerstörungsfrei nondestructive, indestructible
zerstörungsfreie Werkstoffprüfung *f* nondestructive testing
zerstreuen diverge
Zerteilen *nt* severing, dividing
Zerteilerelement *nt* dispersion element
zertrümmern *(Strahlmittel)* break down
zickzackförmige Leitungsführung *f* zigzag configuration of the pipeline
ziehbar einstellen *(einen Spachtel)* adjust to ductile consistency
Ziehbiegewerkzeug *nt* stretch bending tool
ziehen 1. *(allg.)* pull, draw **2.** *(dehnen)* stretch **3.** *(Gerätestecker)* unplug, withdraw, extract **4.** *(Linien, Material)* draw **5.** *(schleppen)* haul, tow
Ziehen *nt* **1.** *(allg.)* drawing, pull(ing) **2.** *(Dehnen)* stretching **3.** *(inneres)* tension **4.** *(mech.)* traction **5.** *(Schleppen)* haulage, towing **6.** *(Stecker)* withdrawal, extraction **7.** *(Verbau)* withdrawal
Ziehkeilgetriebe *nt* diving key transmission
Ziehkopf *m* draw head, pull head, puller
Ziehkopf *m* **mit Backenspannung** jaw-type pull head
Ziehräumen *nt* pull broaching
Ziehräummaschine *f* **mit nach unten gehendem Arbeitsgang** broach pull down machine
Ziehräumnadel *f* **mit kreisförmigen Querschnitt** round broach pull type
Ziehring *m* draw ring
ziehschleifen *(honen)* hone

Ziehschleifmaschine *f* honing machine
Ziehspalt *m* punch and die clearance
Ziehtechnik *f* 1. *(Funktion)* pulling technique 2. *(Vorrichtung)* pulling mechanism
Ziehverhältnis *nt* blank-draw ratio
Ziehverhältnisse *ntpl* draw conditions
Ziehvorgang *m* pulling
Ziehvorrichtung *f* pulling device, pulling mechanism, insertion
Ziehwerk *nt* **an der Räummaschine** broach puller
Ziel *nt* 1. *(allg.)* goal, objective, aim 2. *(örtl., Bestimmung)* destination 3. *(zahlenmäßig)* target
Ziel *nt* **setzen** set a goal, set an objective, set a target
Zieladresse *f* destination address
Zielaufnahmegerät *nt* spot film device
Zielbestand *m* target inventory
Zieldefinition *f* setting of goals, statement of objectives
zielen auf aim at, target at, drive at
Zielerreichungsgrad *m* degree of goal accomplishment
Zielerreichung *f* achievement of objectives, goal accomplishment
Zielformulierung *f* statement of objectives, policy formulation
Zielfunktion *f* functional target, objective function
zielgesteuert goal-driven
Zielgrößen *fpl* target value, target figures
Zielhierarchie *f* hierarchy of objectives, hierarchy of goals
Zielkennzeichen *nt* destination mark
Zielort *m* destination, final destination
Zielsetzung *f (Vorgang)* setting of objectives, setting of goals
Zielsteuerung *f* control system
Zielsystem *nt* system of objectives
Ziffer *f* cipher, figure, digit
Zifferblatt *nt* dial
Ziffernanzeige *f* digital reading, numerical indication
Ziffernfeld *nt* numeric keypad
Ziffernfolge *f* digital sequence, sequence of digits, sequence of figures
Ziffernschritt *m* digital increment, digital division
Ziffernschrittwert *m* digital interval
Ziffernskala *f* digital scale
Zifferntastatur *f* numeric key
Ziffernträger *m* numeral carrier
zigarettenglutbeständig resistant to glowing cigarettes
Zink *nt* zinc
Zinken *m* fork, prong (of a fork), tine
Zinkenabstand *m (äußerer)* width across forks
Zinkenbreite *f* width of prong
Zinkenverstellgerät *nt* fork positioner, fork adjusting device
Zinkhaftung *f* zinc adhesion
Zinkspritzschicht *f* zinc sprayed coating
Zinkstaubbeschichtung *f* zinc dust coating
Zinküberzug *m* zinc coating, tin coating
Zins *m* interest
Zinssatz *m* interest rate
Zipfelprüfung *f* earing test
Zirkel *m* 1. *(allg.)* compasses *pl*, dividers *pl* 2. *(Tasterzirkel)* toolmaker's calliper
Zirkon *nt* zircon
Zirkonium *nt* zirconium
Zirkularfräsen *nt* circular milling
Zirkularinterpolation *f* circular interpolation
Zirkularpolarisation *f* circular polarization
Zirkulation *f* circulation
zirkulieren circulate
Zoll *m* I. *m* 1. *(Einrichtung)* customs duty, tariff, tax 2. *(Verwaltung)* customs II. *nt (Maß)* inch
Zolldatenkontrolle *f* tax control
Zollgewinde *nt* English thread
Zollpapiere *ntpl* customs documents, clearing documents
Zollsatz *m* tariff rate
Zolltarif *m* customs tariff
Zolltarifnummer *f* customs tariff number (CTN)
Zone *f* zone, area
Zonenanzeige *f* zone indicator
Zoneneinteilung *f* classification of

zones, classification of areas, zoning
Zonung *f* zoning
zoomen zoom
Zoom-Funktion *f* zooming
Z-Profil *nt* Z-shaped profile
zu *(geschlossen)* closed
zu fest anziehen overtighten
zu locker anziehen undertighten
zu niedrig auslegen underrate
Zubehör *nt* accessory, accessory product, accessories, appurtenance(s), fittings, supplies, attachment
Zubehörteil *nt* accessory part, supply item, supply part
Zubringeinrichtung *f* **an der Räummaschine** broach handling unit
zubringen feed, handle, load
Zubringer *m* feeder loader, feeding device, feeder
Zubringerband *nt* feeder
Zubringerkopf *m* *(Räumen)* retriever head
Zubringung *f* handling
Zubringung *f* **des Räumwerkzeuges** broach handling
Zudosierung *f* metered addition
Zufall *m* accident, coincidence, random event, chance
zufällig accidental, (co)incidental, random, in a random manner
zufällige Ergebnisabweichung *f* random error of result
zufällige Zuordnung *f* randomization
zufälliger Fehler *m* random error
Zufallsausfall *m* chance failure, random failure, random malfunction
Zufallsauswahl *f* random sample
zufallsbedingt random
Zufallseinfluss *m* random influence
Zufallsfehler *m* random error
Zufallsgröße *f* random variable, variate
Zufallskomponente *f* random component
Zufallsprobenahme *f* random sampling
Zufallsstichprobe *f* random sample
Zufallsstreuung *f* random variability
Zufallsursache *f* random cause
Zufallsvariable *f* random variable, variate

Zufallsvektor *m* random vector
Zufallsverfahren *nt* random process, random procedure
Zufallszugriff *m* random access
Zuflussstrom *m* delivery flow
zufördern feed in
zufördernd feed-in
Zuförderung *f* feed, infeed
Zufuhr *f* conveyance, transport, supply feed, feed, supply
Zuführdruck *m* feeding pressure
Zuführeinrichtung *f* feeder equipment, feeder
zuführen 1. *(allg.)* feed, supply, approach 2. *(beschicken)* load
Zuführschnecke *f* feeding screw
Zuführstrecke *f* feed line, incoming line
Zuführsystem *nt* feed system
Zuführung *f* feed, feeding, loading
Zuführung *f* **von** supply of
Zuführung *f* **von Werkstücken über Leitblech** chute feed
Zuführungsleitung *f* feeder
Zug *m* 1. *(ziehen)* pull, pulling, draw, traction 2. *(Spannung)* tension
Zug- und Leitspindeldrehmaschine *f* engine lathe
Zug- und Leitspindeldrehmaschine *f* engine lathe
Zugabe *f* allowance, addition
Zugabe *f* **für...** amount of stock left for
Zugabestufungen drawing staggerings
Zugang *m* 1. *(allg.)* access, entrance 2. *(Personen)* man-way 3. *(Rechner)* admission 4. *(Waren)* entry, arrivals, receipt
Zugang *m* **zum Gefahrenbereich** access to danger zone
Zugänge *mpl* access ways
zugänglich accessible
Zugänglichkeit *f* accessibility
Zugangsbeanspruchung *f* tensile load
Zugangsberechtigung *f* access authorization, right of access, right to admission
Zugangsebene *f* access level
Zugangskontrolle *f* access supervision, admission supervision
Zugangsmenge *f* received quantity

Zugangsmöglichkeit *f* access, possibility of access
Zugangsplattform *f* access platform
Zugangssicherung *f* control of access
Zugangstermin *m* incoming date
Zugangstür *f* access door
zugbeanspruchte Seite *f* side stressed in tension
Zugbedarf *m* draught requirement
Zugbegrenzer *m* draught limiter
zugbelastet tensile-loaded
Zugbelastung *f* pulling load
zugblankes Rohr *nt* bright drawn tube
Zugbügel *m* tensile proving ring
Zug-Druck-Prüfzylinder *m* tension-compression testing cylinder
Zugdruckumformen *nt* tenso-compressive reforming
Zug-Druck-Versuch *m* push-pull test
zugeben add
zugehörig belonging (to), related, allied, associated (to), linked
zugehörige Zahl *f* associated number
zugehöriges Ritzel *nt* mating pinion
Zugehörigkeit *f* affiliation, membership
Zugehörigkeitsfunktion *f* membership function
Zugehörigkeitsgrad *m* degree of membership
Zugeinrichtung *f* pull mechanism
zugelassen 1. *(allg.)* approved, permitted **2.** *(behördlich)* registered
zugelastisch tenso-elastic
zugeschärfte Kante *f* feather edge
Zugfeder *f* tension spring
Zugfederung *f* tension spring
Zug-Federwaage *f* tension spring balance
Zugfestigkeit *f* tensile strength
Zugflanke *f* traction flank
zugfreie Lüftung *f* draught-free ventilation
Zughaken *m* tow hook
zügig ziehen run continuously
zügig wirkende Kräfte *f* steadily increasing loads
zügiger Lauf *m* steady running
Zugkette *f* **1.** *(allg.)* pull chain **2.** *(zugübertragend)* tension chain
Zugkettenförderer *m* pull chain conveyor
Zugkraft *f* **1.** *(Spannung)* pull, pulling force, tensile force **2.** *(Arbeit)* tractive effort **3.** *(Raupen)* traction, traction force **4.** *(Schlepper)* drawbar pull, tractive force
Zuglufttempfindlichkeit *f* sensitivity to draught
Zugmaschine *f* industrial tractor, towing vehicle
Zugmittel *nt* traction mechanism, traction transmission element
Zugmittelgetriebe *nt* pulley mechanism
Zugmittelspannung *f* mean tensile stress
Zugprobe *f* tensile test piece (or specimen)
Zugprüfmaschine *f* **mit Neigungspendel** tensile testing machine with pendulum weighing mechanism
Zugregeleinrichtung *f* draught regulating device
zugreifen (auf) access
Zugriff *m* access
Zugriffsberechtigung *f* authorization, token, access authorization
Zugriffshäufigkeit *f* access frequency
Zugriffshöhe *f* access height
Zugriffsöffnung *f* aperture, access opening
Zugriffspfad *m* access path
Zugriffsrecht *nt* access entitlement, access authority, right to access
Zugriffsrichtung *f* access direction
Zugriffsschlüssel *m* key for access
Zugriffszeit *f* access time
Zugscherfestigkeit *f* tensile transverse resistance
Zugscherversuch *m* tensile shear test, shear test by tensile loading
Zugschraube *f* draw-in bolt
Zugschubvorrichtung *f* push-pull mechanism, insertion/extraction
Zugschwellbeanspruchung *f* pulsating tensile stress
Zugspannungsbruch *m* tensile failure
Zugspindel *f* feed rod, feed shaft
Zugspindeldrehmaschine *f* ordinary-

type engine lathe
Zugstab *m* **1.** *(allg.)* tensional member, tensional bar **2.** *(Streckensicherung)* single-line token **3.** *(Zerreißstab)* tensile test bar
Zugstange *f* drawbar, pull bar, towing bar, draw rod
Zugumformen *nt* tensile reforming
Zugverformungsrest *m* tension set
Zugversuch *m* tension test, tensile test
Zugvorrichtung *f* pulling device, pulling mechanism
Zugvorspannung *f* tensile pre-loading
Zugwelle *f* feed rod
Zugzone *f* tension zone
Zugzone *f*: **aufgebogene ~** tension zone bent outwards
Zuhaltekraft *f* locking pressure
Zuhaltung *f* guard locking, bolt
Zuhaltungsschloss *nt* dead lock
Zukauf *m* complementary purchase
zukaufen buy externally, purchase externally, source externally
Zukaufteile *ntpl* bought parts, purchased parts
zukünftig future
zulassen 1. *(allg.)* allow, permit **2.** *(Fahrzeug)* register **3.** *(genehmigen)* approve **4.** *(Personen)* authorize
zulässig admissible, permissible, allowable
zulässige Abweichung *f* **für Maße ohne Toleranzangaben** permissible variation for sizes without tolerance indication, cf. Allgemeintoleranz und Freimaßtoleranz
zulässige Beanspruchung *f* safety load, safety stress
zulässige Belastung *f* safe load
zulässige Biegebeanspruchung *f* permissible bending stress
zulässige Formabweichung *f* permissible geometrical variation
zulässige Last *f* safe load
zulässige Laufabweichung *f* permissible running error
zulässige Maßabweichung *f* permissible dimensional variation
zulässige Toleranz *f* permissible variation

zulässiger Betriebsdruck *m* permissible working pressure
Zulassung *f* **1.** *(allg.)* allowance, permit **2.** *(Fahrzeug)* vehicle registration **3.** *(Genehmigung)* approval **4.** *(Personen)* authorization
Zulauf *m* **1.** *(Stofffluss)* feed, supply, intake **2.** *(Abzweig)* branch **3.** *(Öffnung)* inlet
Zulaufleitung *f* charging line, feed line, intake line
Zulaufquerschnitt *m* intake cross-section
Zulaufrichtung *f* feed direction
Zulaufrollengang *m* charging roller, conveyor
zulaufseitiger Boden *m* inflow side bend
zuleiten feed, supply
Zuleitung *f* feed line, feeder, incoming supply, supply (line), source
Zuleitungsanlasswiderstand *m* supply resistor, starting resistor
Zuleitungsstrang *m* incoming supply line
Zulieferer *m* (component) supplier, outside supplier
Zulieferindustrie *f* (component) supplying industry
zuliefern supply
Zulieferteile *ntpl* supplied parts
Zulieferung *f* supply
Zuliefervertrag *m* subcontract
Zuluft *f* incoming air
Zuluftfilter *m* air input filter, intake filter
Zuluftöffnung *f* inlet opening
Zuluftquerschnitt *m* inlet cross-section
Zuluftrate *f* inlet instalment
Zulufttemperatur *f* inlet temperature
zum Leuchten bringen light
zum Stehen bringen stall
zum Stehen kommen stall
zum Stillstand bringen stop, stall, bring a standstill
zumessen meter
Zunahme *f* accretion, augmentation, growth, increase, increment, raise
Zunahme *f* **der Lagerbestände** inventory buildup

Zünddraht *m* firing (or ignition) wire
Zünddurchschlag *m* flame transmission
Zündeinrichtung *f* ignition device
zünden ignite, catch fire
Zunder *m* *(Walzzunder)* scale
Zunderarmglühen *nt* low scale annealing
Zunderbildung *f* scale formation
Zunderschutz *m* protection against scaling
Zunderung *f* high temperature oxidation
zündfähig (in)flammable
Zündflamme *f* pilot flame
Zündflammenbildung *f* formation of the ignition flame
Zündflammenbrenner *m* ignition flame burner
Zündflammenüberwachung *f* monitoring of the ignition flame
Zündflammenzündung *f* pilot-flame ignition
Zündgasfilter *m* ignition gas filter
Zündgasflamme *f* pilot gas flame
Zündgasventil *nt* ignition gas valve
Zündhilfe *f* strikting aid
Zündhilfsmitel *nt* ignition aid
Zündlampe *f* ignition lamp
Zündphase *f* ignition phase
Zündpunkt *m* kindling temperature, ignition point
Zündquelle *f* ignition source, source of ignition
Zündring *m* ignition ring
Zündschalter *m* ignition switch
Zündschutz *m* protection against explosion, explosion protection
Zündschutzart *f* type of protection
Zündschutzgas *nt* protective gas
Zündsicherung *f* ignition safety device
Zündspannung *f* ignition voltage
Zündspur *f* multiple arc strikes
Zündstelle *f* striking point, arc strike, arc burn
Zündstromkreis *m* ignition circuit
Zündstromleitung *f* ignition lead
Zündtemperatur *f* ignition temperature
Zündtransformator *m* ignition transformer
Zündung *f* **1.** *(Vorgang)* ignition **2.** *(Vorrichtung)* ignition system
Zündungsentladung *f* ignition stage-discharge
Zündungszeit *f* ignition time
Zündverzögerung *f* ignition delay
zunehmen accrue, accumulate, grow, increase, rise
zunehmend growing, increasing
Zunge *f* flue wall
Zungenweiterreißversuch *m* tongue tear growth test
zuordnen 1. *(allg.)* assign, coordinate, allocate **2.** *(Merkmale)* attribute
Zuordnung *f* **1.** *(allg.)* allocation, assignment, reference, association **2.** *(Merkmale)* attribution **3.** *(von Genauigkeitsgraden)* allocation
Zuordnungsliste *f* allocation list, allocation table, reference list
Zuordnungssystem *nt* correlation system
Zuordnungstabelle *f* allocation table
zur Analyse *f* reagent grade
zur Kenntnis nehmen note
zur Seite *f* the side, sidewards, aside
Zu-Richtung *f* direction of closing
zurren lash, tie down
Zurrgurt *m* lashing strap
Zurrmittel *nt* lashing(s)
Zurrring *m* lashing ring
zurückhalten *(hindern)* restrain
zurück back, backward(s)
zurückbleibende Drehstellungsabweichung *f* lagging angular position
zurückfließen lassen drain
zurückgerutscht slid back
zurückgesandt returned
zurückgeschoben pushed back, back
zurückhalten keep back, arrest, retain
zurücklagern push back into storage, reshelf
zurücklegen 1. *(an seinen Platz)* put back **2.** *(Strecke)* travel **3.** *(Waren)* put aside
zurückmischen mix back
zurücknehmen retract, take back, withdraw, cancel, undo
zurückrutschen slide back

zurückschieben push back
zurückschlagen retrogress
zurücksenden send back, return
zurücksetzen back up, reset
zurückstehend stored to the back
zurückstellen 1. *(neu stellen)* reset, restore 2. *(Geld)* shelve, put aside, put off 3. *(Uhr)* put back 4. *(zeitl. verschieben)* defer, postpone, shelve
zurückstoßen back up
zurücktreten regress
zurückverfolgen trace back
Zurückverfolgen *nt* tracing back
zurückweisen reject
zurückziehbar retractable
zurückziehen retract, withdraw
Zurüsten *nt* setting up
Zurüstung *f* attachment, equipment
zusammen mit together with
Zusammenarbeit *f* cooperation, team work
zusammenarbeiten work together, cooperate
Zusammenbau *m* assembly (fitting), mounting, erection, assemblage
zusammenbauen assemble, mount, fit together, erect
Zusammenbauzeichnung *f* assembling drawing
zusammenbrechen collapse, break down, fail
zusammendrücken compress, press, crush, squeeze
Zusammendrückung *f* compression, pressing rate
zusammenfallen 1. *(zerstörend)* collapse 2. *(zeitl.)* coincide
zusammenfassen 1. *(gruppieren)* group (together) 2. *(Inhalte)* resume, summarize
Zusammenfassung *f* summary, grouping, resume
zusammenfügen 1. *(allg.)* assemble, connect, join 2. *(Daten)* packetize 3. *(vereinen)* combine
Zusammenfügung *f* assembly, connection, joining, junction, combination, packetizing
zusammenführen join, merge
Zusammenführung *f* mergence, junction, converging section
Zusammenführungselement *nt* merging unit
zusammengebaut gezeichnete Teile *ntpl* parts drawn in the assembled condition
zusammengedrückt compressed
zusammengefaltete Probe *f* flattened specimen
zusammengehörende Teile *ntpl* objects assembled to one another
zusammengesetzt aus composed of
zusammengesetzte Gegenstände *mpl* objects assembled together
zusammengesetzte Hypothese *f* composite hypothesis
zusammengesetzte Nähte *fpl* compound joints (
zusammengesetztes Räumwerkzeug *nt* broach assembly
zusammengesetztes Werkzeug *nt* composite tool
zusammenhalten hold together, keep together
Zusammenhang *m* cohesion, context, correlation, interaction, (inter) relationship, connection
zusammenhängen adhere, stick together, cohere, connect, relate
zusammenhängend connected, coherent, adherent, associated, related
zusammenhängend: nicht ~ unconnected
zusammenhängender Metallüberzug *m* cohesive metal coat
zusammenheften stitch together
zusammenklammern staple
zusammenklappbar collapsible, folding
zusammenklappen collapse, fold
zusammenlaufen converge, join, merge
zusammenlegbar collapsible, folding
zusammenlegen collapse, fold
Zusammenprall *m* collision
zusammenprallen collide, a collision occurs, collisions occur
zusammenpressen compress, press together
zusammenschrumpfen shrink

zusammensetzen assemble, compose, put together, be composed (of), be made up (of), fit
Zusammensetzung *f* composition, structure
Zusammenspiel *nt* **1.** *(allg.)* interaction, interrelation **2.** *(Personen)* cooperation, team work
zusammenstellen 1. *(allg.)* assemble, compile, list, group **2.** *(Systeme)* configure
Zusammenstellung *f* assembly, compilation, composition, grouping, merging
Zusammenstellungszeichnung *f* assembly drawing
Zusammenstoß *m* collision, crash
zusammenstoßen collide, crash
Zusammenstoßsicherung *f* anti-collision protection
Zusammensturz *m* break(ing)-down, collapse
zusammenstürzen break down, collapse
zusammentreffen meet, merge, join
zusammenwirken 1. *(Personen)* work together, cooperate **2.** *(masch.)* interact
Zusatz ... auxiliary, addition
Zusatz *m* addition, additive, appendix, supplement
Zusatzausrüstung *f* accessory, ancillary equipment, extra equipment, auxiliary equipment
Zusatzballastgewicht *nt* auxiliary ballast weight
Zusatzbeanspruchung *f* additional stress
Zusatzbelastung *f* additional load(ing)
Zusatzbelüftung *f* additional ventilation
Zusätze *mpl* additive, addition
Zusatzeinrichtung *f* extra equipment, additional equipment, attachment, special attachment, extra attachment, ancillary device
Zusatzfläche *f* *(z. B. e. Zeichenbretts)* free margin, extra space
Zusatzfunktion *f* additional function
Zusatzgerät *nt* **1.** *(allg.)* accessory, attachment, ancillary equipment **2.** *(IT)* add-on

Zusatzgewicht *nt* ballast
Zusatzhub *m* additional lift, supplementary lift
Zusatzlast *f* additional load
zusätzlich additional, in addition to, supplementary, auxiliary
Zusatzmittel *nt* additive
Zusatzprogramm *nt* supplementary programme
Zusatzprüfung *f* additional test
Zusatzpumpe *f* supplementary pump
Zusatzsymbol *nt* additional symbol
Zusatztoleranz *f* additional tolerance
Zusatztriebwerk *nt* booster
Zusatzverstärker *m* booster
Zusatzvorschub *m* auxiliary feed
Zusatzwerkstoff *m* **1.** *(allg.)* added filler material **2.** *(artfremder ~)* filler material of different composition **3.** *(artgleicher ~)* filler material of the same composition
Zusatzzeit *f* addition time
zuschalten interconnect, hook up, cut in
Zuschlag *m* **1.** *(zusätzlich)* addition, additional factor **2.** *(Geld)* additional charge, surcharge
Zuschlagsfaktor *m* additional factor
zuschneiden cut (to size)
Zuschnitt *m* blank, cutting
Zuschnittauftrag *m* cutting order
Zuschnitte *mpl* cuts, blanks
Zuschnittlänge *f* cut length
Zuschub *m* feed
Zuschubbewegung *f* infeed motion
Zustand *m* condition, state, status
zuständig authorized, competent, responsible
Zuständigkeit *f* competence, responsibility
Zustandsabfrage *f* status enquiry
Zustandsänderung *f* change of state
Zustandsanzeige *f* status indication, status indicator
Zustandsdaten *pl* status data
Zustandsgröße *f* status variable
Zustandsinformation *f* status information
Zustandskennung *f* status identification

Zustandsmeldung *f* status message
Zustandsschaubild *nt* status scheme
Zustandssteuerung *f* state control
zusteigen mount, get on
Zustellbewegung *f* infeed motion
Zustellbewegung *f* plunge-feed movement
zustellen 1. *(allg.)* advance, set **2.** *(Werkzeug)* infeed
Zustellhandrad *nt* infeed handwheel
Zustelltiefe *f* feed setting depth
Zustellung *f* **1.** *(Werkzeug)* setting, feed, feed setting **2.** *(Justierung)* adjustment
Zustellzyklus *m* infeed cycle
Zustieg *m* access, entrance
Zuströmdruck *m* inlet pressure
zuteilen allocate, apportion, dose, distribute, assign
Zuteilung *f* **1.** *(allg.)* allocation, apportionment, distribution **2.** *(Ausgleich)* arbitration **3.** *(Zuweisung)* assignment
Zuteilungsquerschnitt *m* arbitration cross-section
Zutritt *m* access, entrance
Zutritt *m* **verboten!** No admittance!, Keep off!
Zutrittsverbot *nt* access prohibition
zuverlässig reliable
Zuverlässigkeit *f* reliability
Zuverlässigkeitsanalyse *f* reliability analysis
Zuverlässigkeitskenngröße *f* reliability attribute, reliability characteristic
Zuverlässigkeitsrate *f* reliability level
Zuverlässigkeitssicherung *f* reliability assurance
Zuverlässigkeitswachstum *nt* reliability growth
Zuwachs *m* increase, increment
Zuwachsbemaßung *f* *(von unterbrochenen Nähten)* progressive dimensioning
zuweisen allocate, assign
Zuweisung *f* allocation, assignment
Zwang *m* constraint, force, restraint
Zwangabschaltung *f* automatic controlled stop
zwängen force
Zwanglauf *m* positive movement, constrained motion
Zwanglaufheißwassererzeuger *m* forced circulation high temperature water heating appliance
Zwanglaufprinzip *nt* forced circulation principle
Zwanglaufsicherung *f* constrained contact
Zwanglaufwärmeerzeuger *m* forced circulation heat generator
zwangsangetrieben positively mechanized
Zwangsbelüftung *f* forced air circulation, forced external cooling
Zwangsführung *f* positive guidance, restricted guidance
zwangsgeführt positively guided
zwangsgelenkt positively steered, restricted steering
zwangsgesteuerte Absperrung *f* positively controlled shut-off device
zwangsgesteuerte Einrichtung *f* positively controlled device
Zwangskräfte *fpl* action of forces, reactive forces
zwangsläufig automatic, positive, controlled, compulsory
zwangsläufig wirkend positively acting
zwangsläufige Mitnahme *f* positive drive
zwangsläufiger Antrieb *m* positive drive
Zwangslenkung *f* positive steering, restricted steering
Zwangslüftung *f* forced ventilation
zwangsöffnend automatically opening, positively opening
zwangspositionieren position automatically, position positively
Zwangspositionierung *f* automatic positioning, positive positioning
Zwangstrennung *f* automatic disconnection
zwangsweise positive, compulsory
zwangsweise gesichert gegen positively prevented from
zweiachsig four-wheeled, two-axle, biaxial
zweiachsiger Spannungszustand *m*

biaxial stress condition
zweiadrig two-core
zweiarmig double-armed
Zweibackenfutter *nt* two-jaw chuck
Zweibehälterprinzip *nt* two-bin principle
Zweibreitencode *m* two-width code
zweidimensional two-dimensional, bivariate
zweidimensionale Normalverteilung *f* two-dimensional (or bivariate) normal distribution
zweidimensionale Wärmeableitung *f* two-dimensional heat dissipation
Zweidrahtleitung *f* twisted pair
Zweierteilung *f* dual-based division
zweifach double, twofold, twice, twin
zweifache Aufteilung *f* cross classification
Zweifache *nt:* **das ~** double
zweifache Varianzanalyse *f* cross classification
Zweifachhubgerüst *nt* double mast
Zweiflankeneingriff *m* two-flank engagement
Zweiflankenmessung *f* dual flank measurement
Zweiflankensteigung *f* dual flank lead
Zweiflankenteilung *f* dual flank pitch
Zweiflankenwälzabstand *m* two-flank working distance
Zweiflankenwälzabstandsabmaß *nt* deviation of dual flank roll test centre distance
Zweiflankenwälzabweichung *f* two-flank working variation
Zweiflankenwälzfehler *m* dual flank composite error
Zweiflankenwälzprüfgerät *nt* dual flank roll tester
Zweiflankenwälzprüfung *f* two-flank total composite error test, two-flank working test
Zweiflankenwälzsprung *m* two-flank working error
zweiflügelige Tür *f* double-leaf door
Zweig *m* **1.** *(Branche)* branch **2.** *(IT)* leg, path
Zweiganggetriebe *nt* two-speed gear drive
zweigängiges Bolzengewinde *nt* two-start (or double-start) bolt thread
Zweigangschieberadgetriebe *nt* two-speed sliding gear drive
zweigassig two-lane
zweigipflige Verteilung *f* bimodal distribution
Zweihandauslösung *f* two-hand release
Zweihandbedienung *f* two-hand control, two-hand operation
Zweihandschaltung *f* two-hand control device
Zweihandschaltung *f* **1.** *(als Vorrichtung)* two-hand control unit **2.** *(Arbeitsvorgang)* two-hand control
Zweihandsteuergerät *nt* two-hand control device
Zweihandsteuerung *f* hold-to-run control for two hands, two-hand safety control
Zweikegelweite *f* dual cone width
Zweikegelweitenabmaß *nt* deviation of dual cone width
Zweikegelweitenabmessung *f* dual cone width measurement
Zweikomponentenbeschichtung *f* two-component coating
Zweikomponentenkunstharzlack *m* two-component synthetic resin sealant
Zweikugelmaß *nt* two-ball measurement
zweilagiger Heizkörper *m* two-level radiator
Zweileitungssystem *nt* two-line principle of operation
Zweilochmutterndreher *m* pin type face wrench
Zweilot *nt* secondary solder
zweimaliges Härten *nt* hardening twice over
Zweimeißelwälzhobeln *nt* two chisel roll planing
Zweimeißelhobelmaschine *f* two-tool planer, twin-tool planer
Zweimeißelkegelradhobelmaschine *f* twin tool generating bevel gear planer, twin cutter bevel gear generator

Zweimeißelverfahren *nt* two chisel technique
Zweimeißelwälzhobeln *nt* tooth generation by twin reciprocating tools
zweiphasenverriegelt two-state interlocking
Zweiphasenverriegelung *f* two-state interlocking
zweiphasig two-phase, two-state
Zweipol *m* two-pole
zweipolig 1. *(allg.)* bipolar, two-pole, double-pole **2.** *(Stecker)* two-pin
Zwei-Prozent- (2%-)Stauchspannung *f* offset compressive yield stress
Zweipunktaufhängung *f* two-point suspension
Zweipunktausschusslehre *f* two-point "Not Go" gauge
Zweipunktberührung *f* two-point contact
Zweipunktmessung *f* two-point measurement
Zweipunktregeleinrichtung *f* two-level action controlling system
Zweipunktregelung *f* two-level action control
Zweipunktregler *m* two-step action controller
Zweipunktsignal *nt* two-level signal
Zweipunktverhalten *nt* two-level action
zweireihig double-row(ed), two-row
zweireihige Punktnaht *f* double row spaced spot weld
zweireihiger Heizkörper *m* two-bank radiator
Zweirollenmaß *nt* two-roller measurement
Zweisäulengerät *nt* twin-mast machine, two-mast machine
zweischalige Waage *f* double pan balance
Zweischeibenläppmaschine *f* two-wheel lapping machine
Zweischicht *f* double layer, two-layer
Zweischichtbetrieb *m* two-shift operation
Zweischichtensicherheitsglas *nt* laminated safety glass
Zweischichtplatte *f* two-layer slab

Zweischlag *m* double link
zweischneidig double-edged
Zweiseitenstapler *m* lateral stacking truck
zweiseitig two-sided, bilateral
zweiseitig schneidendes Räumwerkzeug *nt* double-cut broach
zweiseitiger Schaftfräser *m* double-end mill
zweiseitiges Buckelschweißen *nt* direct projection welding
Zweispeziesrechenmaschine *f* two-operation calculating machine (or calculator)
Zweispindelabflächmaschine *f* zum gleichzeitigen Fräsen der Stirnflächen von Wellen double-end milling machine
Zweispindelfräsmaschine *f* two-spindle milling machine
Zweispindelfräsmaschine *f* mit einander gegenüberliegenden Spindeln zur Bearbeitung von Werkstücken double-end miller, double-end milling machine
zweispindelige Trommelfräsmaschine *f* two-spindle drum milling machine
Zweispindelkopf *m* two-spindle attachment
Zweispindellangnutenkopierfräsmaschine *f* two-spindle keyway copying miller
Zweispindelplanfräsmaschine *f* (US) two-spindle fixed-bed type milling machine, two-spindle manufacturing-type milling machine, duplex fixed-bed miller, duplex-type milling machine, duplex miller, fixed-bed (or manufacturing-bed) type milling machine with double horizontal spindle, (UK) two-spindle bench-type milling machine
Zweispindelprofilfräsmaschine *f* two-spindle profile miller (or milling machine)
Zweispindelrundtischfräsautomat *m* automatic two-spindle (or double-spindle) rotary type miller
Zweispindeltrommelfräsmaschine *f* two-spindle rotary drum miller

Zweispurbrückengerät *nt* two-track bridge device
zweispurig two-track, double-tracked
Zweiständerfräsmaschine *f* double-column milling machine
Zweiständerfräsmaschine *f* *(Portalfräswerk)* planer-miller
Zweiständerhobel- und -fräsmaschine *f* double-column planing and milling machine, *(US)* planer-miller
Zweiständerhobelmaschine *f* double-housing planer (or planing machine), double-column planer, standard-type planer
Zweiständerkarusselldrehmaschine *f* double-column vertical turning and boring mill
Zweiständermaschine *f* standard planer, double-housing planer
Zweiständerplanfräsmaschine *f* double column planer-miller, double housing milling machine, double-column milling machine, planer miller
Zweiständersenkrechträummaschine *f* two-column vertical broaching machine
Zweiständerstarrhobelmaschine *f* rigid double-column planing machine
Zweistrahlkompensationsverfahren *nt* two-beam compensation method
zweistufiges Getriebe *nt* two-stage gear transmission (or drive)
zweite Freifläche *f* second flank
zweite Spanfläche *f* second face
zweiteilige Rohrschelle *f* **für Wandbefestigung** wall mounted two-piece pipe clip
zweiter Arbeitsgang *m* second cycle operation
Zweiwegebohrmaschine *f* two-way boring machine, two-way drilling machine
Zweiwegehobelvorrichtung *f* double-cutting tool assembly
Zweiwegemaschine *f* two-way machine
Zweiwegepalette *f* two-way pallet
Zweiweghobeln *nt* double-stroke planing

Zweiwegtafel *f* two-way table
zweiwöchig two-week
Zweizungenziehfeder *f* bow-type drawing pen
Zwickel *m* spaces either side of the bottom half of the pipe
Zwickelverdichtung *f* compacting in the space between pipe and trench wall, compaction on either side of the bottom half of the pipe
Zwillings ... twin
Zwillingsfräsmaschine *f* twin-head gear cutting machine
Zwillingsrad *nt* twin wheel
Zwillingsräummaschine *f* dual ram broaching machine
Zwillingsreifen *mpl* twin tyres
Zwillingszahnradfräsmaschine *f* twin-head gear cutting machine
Zwinge *f* ferrule
zwingen force, compel, constrain
Zwingenspannung *f* vice clamping
zwischen 1. *(in d. Me)* between 2. *(zwischenliegend)* intermediate
Zwischenabnahme *f* intermediate inspection, in-process inspection
Zwischenankunftszeit *f* interarrival time
Zwischenantrieb *m* intermediate drive
Zwischenbereich *m* *(z. B. e. Toleranzlage)* intermediate range
Zwischenbericht *m* progress report
Zwischenbescheid *m* intermediate message, in-process message
Zwischenbeurteilung *f* intermediate assessment
Zwischenbewegung *f* intermediate movement
Zwischenbogen *m* layer pad, layer sheet
Zwischenbogeneinlage *f* layer pad insertion
Zwischenbühne *f* mezzanine floor, raised storage platform
Zwischenergebnis *nt* intermediate result, preliminary result
Zwischenfraktion *f* intermediate fraction
zwischengeschaltet intermediate, interconnected, serially connected

Zwischengeschoss *nt* mezzanine floor, suspended ceiling
Zwischenglied *nt* (connecting) link, interlink, motion link, interconnection
Zwischengröße *f* intermediate size
Zwischenkopierpapier *nt* intermediate copying paper
Zwischenladung *f* **1.** *(Material)* intermediate charge, partial charge **2.** *(Vorgang)* intermediate charging, partial charging
Zwischenlage *f* intermediate layer, layer pad, layer sheet spacer
Zwischenlagenaufleger/-abheber *m* layer pad inserter/remover
Zwischenlageneinleger *m* layer sheet dispenser
Zwischenlagenhubplattform *f* layer transfer lift platform
Zwischenlagenkleber *m* bonding agent, interlayer adhesive
Zwischenlagentemperatur *f* interpass temperature
Zwischenlager *nt* in-process inventory, in-process stock, intermediate storage facility, intermediate bearing
Zwischenlagerfläche *f* intermediate storage facility area
zwischenlagern store intermediately
Zwischenlagerung *f* intermediate storage, in-process storage
Zwischenlegblech *nt* shim
Zwischenmaske *f* intermediate mask
Zwischenplatte *f* baffle plate
Zwischenpodest *nt* mezzanine floor, raised storage platform
Zwischenprodukt *nt* intermediate product
Zwischenprüfung *f* intermediate inspection
Zwischenpuffer *m* intermediate buffer, intermediate storage location
zwischenpuffern store intermediately
Zwischenrad *nt* intermediate gear
Zwischenraum *m* **1.** *(allg.)* space, distance, clearance, **2.** *(Lücke)* gap **3.** *(bei Linien)* intervening space
Zwischenresultat *nt* intermediate result
Zwischenring *m* collar

zwischenschalten interconnect, insert, connect in series
Zwischenschicht *f* intermediate coating
Zwischenschieber *m* **1.** *(allg.)* intermediate slide **2.** *(Kurzhobeln)* saddle
Zwischenschneide *f* drag
Zwischensiebung *f* intermediate screening
Zwischenspeicher *m* buffer memory, buffer storage, intermediate memory, intermediate storage
zwischenspeichern buffer, store temporarily
Zwischenspeicherung *f* temporary storage
Zwischenstab *m* intermediate rail
Zwischenstellung *f* intermediate position
Zwischenstück *nt* adapter, sleeve
Zwischenstück *nt* **für Schaftfräser** end mill adapter
Zwischenstufe *f* intermediate stage
Zwischensumme *f* subtotal
Zwischentraglager *nt* **für den Dorn** intermediate arbor support
Zwischenverbindung *f* connector
Zwischenwand *f* partition (wall)
Zwischenwerte *mpl* intermediate half steps, intermediate points
Zwischenzeit *f* meantime
Zwischenziel *nt* intermediate target
Zwölfkantdehnschraube *f* double hexagon head (or twelve-point) bolt with waisted shank
Zwölfkantmutter *f* double hexagon head (or twelve-point) nut
Zwölfkantmutter *m* **mit Bund** double hexagon head (or twelve-point) nut with collar
Zwölfkantpassschraube *f* double hexagon head fitting bolt
Zwölfkantschraube *f* double hexagon bolt, twelve-point bolt
Zwölfplattenstapel *m* twelve disk pack
Zwölf-Uhr-Lage *f* twelve o'clock position
zyklisch cyclic
zyklische Blockprüfung *f* cyclic re-

dundancy check (CRC)
Zykloide *f* cycloid
Zykloidenabschnitt *m* cycloid
Zykloidengetriebe *nt* cycloidal gear
Zykloidenradpaar *nt* cycloidal gear pair
Zykloidenradpaar *nt* cycloidal gear pair
Zykloidenverzahnung *f* cycloidal tooth system, cycloidal gear teeth, cycloidal gear
Zykloidenzahnrad *nt* cycloidal gear
Zykloidverzahnung *f* cycloidal tooth system
Zyklokautschuk *m* cyclised natural rubber
Zyklokautschukkleber *m* cyclised natural rubber adhesive
Zyklus *m* cycle
Zykluszeit *f* cycle time
Zylinder *m* cylinder, jack
Zylinder *m* **mit dämpfendem Endanschlag** cushion cylinder
Zylinderblechschraube *f* slotted pan head tapping screw
Zylinderbohr- und -fräswerk *nt* cylinder boring and milling machine
Zylinderbohrmaschine *f* cylinder boring machine
Zylinderdurchmesser *m* diameter of the cylinder
Zylinderfläche *f* cylindrical surface, circumferential surface
Zylinderformtoleranz *f* cylindricity tolerance
Zylinderlehrdorn *m* cylindrical plug gauge
Zylindermutter *f* barrel nut
Zylindernutkurve *f* cylindrical cam groove
Zylinderrad *nt (Stirnrad)* cylindrical gear
Zylinderrad *nt* **mit Doppelschrägverzahnung** crossed helical gear pair
Zylinderradpaar *nt (Stirnradpaar)* cylindrical gear pair
Zylinderradpaar *nt* **mit Doppelschrägverzahnung** double helical gear pair
Zylinderradverzahnung *f* cylindrical tooth system
Zylinderraum *m* loading bush (or chamber)
Zylinderrollenlager *nt* cylindrical roller bearing, parallel roller journal bearing
Zylinderschaft *m* straight shank
Zylinderschnecke *f* cylindrical worm
Zylinderschneckenradsatz *m* cylindrical worm gear set
Zylinderschneidschraube *f* cheese head thread cutting screw
Zylinderschraube *f* **mit Innensechskant** hexagon socket head cap screws
Zylinderschraube *f* **mit Schlitz** slotted cheese (or fillister) head screw
Zylinderschraubradpaar *nt* crossed helical gear pair
Zylinderspule *f* cylindrical coil
Zylinderstift *m* full length parallel grooved pin, parallel pin, unthreaded stud
Zylinderstift *m* **mit Einführende** *nt* full length parallel grooved pin with pilot
Zylinderstift *m* **ohne Kuppe** parallel pin with flat end
Zylindertemperatur *f* cylinder temperature
Zylinderverfahren *nt* cylinder method
zylindrisch cylindrical
zylindrisch senken counterbore, countersink
Zylindrischdrehen *nt* cylindrical turning
zylindrische Bohrung *f* straight bore
zylindrische Gewindeverbindung *f* straight screw tread connection (or fastening)
zylindrische Presspassung *f* cylindrical interference fit
zylindrischer Gewindegrenzlehrring *m* parallel Go/Not Go screw ring gauge
zylindrisches Außengewinde *nt* parallel external screw thread
zylindrisches Innengewinde *nt* parallel internal screw thread
Zylindrizität *f* cylindricity, parallelity, straightness